LANGENSCHEIDT'S SHORTER GERMAN DICTIONARY

GERMAN-ENGLISH
ENGLISH-GERMAN

New edition 1987

Edited by
THE LANGENSCHEIDT
EDITORIAL STAFF

Hodder & Stoughton

*Published in the British Commonwealth
by Hodder & Stoughton Limited*

Preface

For over 130 years Langenscheidt's bilingual dictionaries have been essential tools for the student of languages. For several decades Langenscheidt's German-English dictionaries have been used not only for academic work, but in all walks of life.

However, languages are in a constant process of change. To keep you abreast of these changes, Langenscheidt has compiled this new Dictionary. Many words which have entered the German and English languages in the last few years have been included in the vocabulary.

The Dictionary has been considerably <u>enlarged</u>, not only to accommodate the new words, but also to make space for a number of <u>user-friendly innovations.</u> The demands for more detailed notes for the user have now been met. The somewhat abstract short notes have been replaced by a more detailed and graphic explanation of the peculiarities of the Dictionary.

The Dictionary also provides clear answers to questions of declension and conjugation in more than 15,000 German noun and verb entries.

The phonetic transcription of the German and English headwords follows the principles laid down by the International Phonetic Association (IPA).

In addition to the vocabulary, this Dictionary contains <u>special quick-reference sections</u> of proper names, abbreviations, weights and measures, and an <u>alphabetical list of German and English irregular verbs.</u>

Designed for the widest possible variety of uses, this Dictionary, with its <u>more than 48,000 entries and phrases,</u> will be of great value to students, teachers and tourists, and will find a place in home and office libraries alike.

Contents

How do you use the Dictionary?

Don't be afraid of words you don't know!

This Dictionary does all that it can to make it as easy as possible for you to look up and become familiar with a word.

How and where do you find a word?

Strict alphabetical order has been maintained throughout the Dictionary. The principle parts (infinitive, preterite, and past participle) of the irregular German and English verbs as well as the irregular plural forms of English nouns have also been given in their proper alphabetical order, e.g.:

>**gebissen** *p.p. of beißen*
>**bitten** *p.p. von bite*
>**men** *pl. von man*

In the German-English section we have treated the umlauts *ä ö ü* as *a o u*, rather than as *ae oe ue*.

When trying to locate a particular German or English word, you can use the boldface **catchwords** at the top corner of each page as a guide. These catchwords show you (on the left-hand side) the *first* boldface word on the left-hand page and (on the right-hand side) the *last* boldface word on the right-hand page, e.g. **Konflikt – köstlich** on page 188 and 189.

How do you spell the word?

As in a monolingual dictionary you can check the spelling of any word in this Dictionary. In the German-English section the American spelling has been given in the following ways:

>*theat|re, Am. -er, defen|ce, Am. -se*
>*council(l)or, hono(u)r*
>*plough, Am. plow*

and in the English-German section as follows:

>*centre, Am. -ter – theatre, Am. -ter*
>*dialogue, Am. -log – programme, Am. -gram*
>*colo(u)r – hono(u)r – travel(l)er*

In a very few cases a letter in round brackets indicates that a particular word can be spelled in two different ways: *judg(e)ment = judgment or judgement.*

In the English-German section the dots within a headword indicate syllabification breaks.

What do the various typefaces mean?

All German and English headwords are printed **in bold face**, as are the Arabic numerals used to distinguish the various parts of speech and grammatical forms of a word:

> **klopfen 1.** *v/i. heart, pulse:* beat; ... **2.** *v/t.* knock, drive (*nail, etc.*)
> **feed** ... **1.** Futter *n*; ... **2.** (*fed*) *v/t.* füttern; **~·back** ...

Italics are used a) for grammatical and subject label abbreviations: *adj., adv., v/i., v/t., econ., pol., zo.,* etc.; b) to indicate the gender of a German word: *m, f, n*; c) for any details added to give more precise information about a word or a particular meaning of a word, e.g.:

> **mild** ... *weather, punishment, etc.*: mild
> **schälen** ... pare, peel (*fruit, potatoes, etc.*)
> **file¹** ... *Computer*: Datei *f*
> **page** ... Seite *f* (*e-s Buches, e-r Zeitung etc.*)

Lightface type is used for all idiomatic phrases:

> **gut** ... ganz ~ not bad
> **Lage** ... in der ~ sein zu inf. be able to inf.
> **depend** ... it ~s F es kommt (ganz) darauf an
> **line** ... hold the ~ teleph. am Apparat bleiben

All translations are printed in normal type.

How do you pronounce the word?

The phonetic transcription of a word indicates how you should pronounce it. So that *everyone* could know precisely which signs represent which sounds, an international phonetic alphabet was established. As the signs used by the International **P**honetic **A**ssociation are considered standard, we now talk of the **IPA phonetic alphabet**.

The phonetic symbols in square brackets – [ ] – are used in the Dictionary to describe how you should pronounce the German or English headword, e.g.:

> **fest** [fɛst] – **Hilfe** ['hɪlfə]
> **coat** [kəʊt] – **message** ['mesɪdʒ]

Guide to Pronunciation
for the German-English Section

The length of vowels is indicated by [:] following the vowel symbol, the stress by ['] preceding the stressed syllable. The glottal stop [ʔ] is the forced stop between one word or syllable and a following one beginning with a vowel, as in *unentbehr-lich* [un'ʔɛnt'beːrliç]. No transcription of compounds is given if the parts appear as separate headwords.

A. Vowels

[a] as in French *carte*: *Mann* [man].

[ɑː] as in *father*: *Wagen* ['vɑːgən].

[e] as in *bed*: *Edikt* [e'dikt].

[eː] resembles the sound in *day*: *Weg* [veːk].

[ə] unstressed e as in *ago*: *Bitte* ['bitə].

[ɛ] as in *fair*: *männlich* ['mɛnliç], *Geld* [gɛlt].

[ɛː] same sound but long: *zählen* ['tsɛːlən].

[i] as in *it*: *Wind* [vint].

[iː] as in *meet*: *hier* [hiːr].

[ɔ] as in *long*: *Ort* [ɔrt].

[ɔː] same sound but long as in *draw*: *Komfort* [kɔm'fɔːr].

[o] as in *molest*: *Moral* [mo'rɑːl].

[oː] resembles the English sound in *go* [gəʊ] but without the [ʊ]: *Boot* [boːt].

[øː] as in French *feu*. The sound may be acquired by saying [e] through closely rounded lips: *schön* [ʃøːn].

[ø] same sound but short: *Ökonomie* [økono'miː].

[œ] as in French *neuf*. The sound resembles the English vowel in *her*. Lips, however, must be well rounded as for [ɒ]: *öffnen* ['œfnən].

[u] as in *book*: *Mutter* ['mutər].

[uː] as in *boot*: *Uhr* [uːr].

[y] almost like the French u as in *sur*. It may be acquired by saying [ɪ] through fairly closely rounded lips: *Glück* [glyk].

[yː] same sound but long: *führen* ['fyːrən].

B. Diphthongs

[aɪ] as in *like*: *Mai* [maɪ].

[aʊ] as in *mouse*: *Maus* [maʊs].

[ɔY] as in *boy*: *Beute* ['bɔytə], *Läufer* ['lɔyfər].

C. Consonants

[b] as in *better*: *besser* ['bɛsər].

[d] as in *dance*: *du* [duː].

[f] as in *find*: *finden* ['findən], *Vater* ['fɑːtər], *Philosoph* [filo'zoːf].

[g] as in *gold*: *Gold* [gɔlt], *Geld* [gɛlt].

[ʒ] as in *measure*: *Genie* [ʒe'niː], *Journalist* [ʒurna'list].

[h] as in *house* but not aspirated: *Haus* [haʊs].

[ç] an approximation to this sound may be acquired by assuming the mouth-configuration for [ɪ] and emitting a strong current of breath: *Licht* [liçt], *Mönch* [mœnç], *lustig* ['lustiç].

[x] as in Scottish *loch*. Whereas [ç] is pronounced at the front of the mouth, [x] is pronounced in the throat: *Loch* [lɔx].

[j] as in *year*: *ja* [jɑː].

[k] as in *kick*: *keck* [kɛk], *Tag* [tɑːk], *Chronist* [kro'nist], *Café* [ka'feː].

[l] as in *lump*. Pronounced like English initial "clear l": *lassen* ['lasən].

[m] as in *mouse*: *Maus* [maʊs].

[n] as in *not*: *nein* [naɪn].

[ŋ] as in *sing*, *drink*: *singen* ['ziŋən], *trinken* ['triŋkən].

[p] as in *pass*: *Paß* [pas], *Trieb* [triːp], *obgleich* [ɔp'glaɪç].

8

[r] as in *rot*. There are two pronun-
ciations: the frontal or lingual r
and the uvular r (the latter unknown in England): *rot* [roːt].

[s] as in *miss*. Unvoiced when final,
doubled, or next a voiceless consonant: *Glas* [glɑːs], *Masse*
['masə], *Mast* [mast], *naß* [nas].

[z] as in *zero*. S voiced when initial
in a word or syllable: *Sohn*
[zoːn], *Rose* ['roːzə].

[ʃ] as in *ship*: *Schiff* [ʃif], *Charme*
[ʃarm], *Spiel* [ʃpiːl], *Stein*
[ʃtaɪn].

[t] as in *tea*: *Tee* [teː], *Thron* [troːn],
Stadt [ʃtat], *Bad* [bɑːt], *Findling*
['fintliŋ], *Wind* [vint].

[v] as in *vast*: *Vase* ['vɑːzə], *Winter*
['vintər].

[ã, ɛ̃, õ] are nasalized vowels. Exam-
ples: *Ensemble* [ãˈsãːbəl], *Terrain* [tɛˈrɛ̃ː], *Bonbon* [bõˈbõː].

List of Suffixes

The German suffixes are not transcribed unless they are
parts of headwords.

-bar	[-baːr]	-ist	[-ist]
-chen	[-çən]	-keit	[-kaɪt]
-d	[-t]	-lich	[-liç]
-de	[-də]	-ling	[-liŋ]
-ei	[-aɪ]	-losigkeit	[-loːziçkaɪt]
-en	[-ən]	-nis	[-nis]
-end	[-ənt]	-sal	[-zaːl]
-er	[-ər]	-sam	[-zaːm]
-haft	[-haft]	-schaft	[-ʃaft]
-heit	[-haɪt]	-sieren	[-ziːrən]
-ie	[-iː]	-ste	[-stə]
-ieren	[-iːrən]	-tät	[-tɛːt]
-ig	[-iç]	-tum	[-tuːm]
-ik	[-ik]	-ung	[-uŋ]
-in	[-in]	-ungs-	[-uŋs-]
-isch	[-iʃ]		

Guide to the Phonetic Transcriptions in the English-German Section

A. Vowels and Diphthongs

[iː]	see	[siː]		[ə]	consist	[kənˈsist]
[ɪ]	it	[ɪt]		[ɜː]	bird	[bɜːd]
[e]	get	[get]		[eɪ]	day	[deɪ]
[æ]	cat	[kæt]		[əʊ]	go	[gəʊ]
[ɑː]	father	[ˈfɑːðə]		[aɪ]	fly	[flaɪ]
[ɒ]	not	[nɒt]		[aʊ]	how	[haʊ]
[ɔː]	saw	[sɔː]		[ɔɪ]	boy	[bɔɪ]
[ʊ]	put	[pʊt]		[ɪə]	sheer	[ʃɪə]
[uː]	too	[tuː]		[ʊə]	tour	[tʊə]
[ʌ]	up	[ʌp]		[eə]	vary	[ˈveərɪ]

The length of a vowel is indicated by the symbol [ː], e.g. *ask*
[ɑːsk], *astir* [əˈstɜː].

The following French nasal sounds are used occasionally: [ã] as in French *blanc*, [ɔ̃] as in French *bonbon* and [ɛ̃] as in French *vin*.

B. Consonants

[r]	bright	[braɪt]	[z]	zone	[zəʊn]
[ŋ]	ring	[rɪŋ]	[ʃ]	ship	[ʃɪp]
[ŋk]	ink	[ɪŋk]	[ʒ]	measure	['meʒə]
[j]	yes	[jes]	[tʃ]	chicken	['tʃɪkɪn]
[f]	fat	[fæt]	[dʒ]	judge	[dʒʌdʒ]
[v]	very	['verɪ]	[θ]	thin	[θɪn]
[w]	well	[wel]	[ð]	then	[ðen]
[s]	soul	[səʊl]			

To save space in the individual entries, we shall limit ourselves to a short note here on the ending -ed* and the plural -s** of the English headwords. These endings will then appear in the vocabulary without phonetics, unless they are exceptions to the rules.

* [-d] after vowels and voiced consonants; [-t] after unvoiced consonants; [-ɪd] after final d and t.

** [-z] after vowels and voiced consonants; [-s] after unvoiced consonants.

Stress

In the German and English headwords the sign ' (the stress accent) preceding a syllable indicates that this syllable is stressed.

> **durchschlagen** ['durçʃlɑːgən] – **durchschlagen** [durç'ʃlɑːgən]
> **'nachsehen** – '~senden
> **record** [rɪ'kɔːd] – **record** ['rekɔːd]
> **gamekeeper** ['geɪmkiːpə]

If in an English entry the headword is followed by a word which has the same stress, no stress accent is given for the second word – it is always stressed in exactly the same way as the word preceding it, e.g.:

> **helper** ['helpə] – **helpful** [~fl = 'helpfl]

What do the abbreviations and symbols tell you?

Wherever possible, we have used pictorial symbols and/or abbreviations to indicate the subject area from which a headword and/or some of its meanings are taken. A pictorial symbol or an abbreviation placed immediately after a headword applies to all translations given in the entry. Any symbol or abbreviation preceding an individual translation refers to this translation only. If the abbreviation is followed by a colon, it applies to all the following translations. Thus in the German-English section an F placed before the German or English part of an example sentence indicates that only that part of the sentence is used familiarly. On the other hand, an F: placed before the German part indicates that the example and translation belong to the same linguistic usage level.

Labels denoting figurative usage have been placed between the example phrases or sentences and their translations. This is also sometimes the case with other labels.

F	*familiar*, umgangssprachlich.	🚂	*railway, railroad*, Eisenbahn.
V	*vulgar*, vulgär.	✈	*aviation*, Flugwesen.
†	*archaic*, veraltet.	✉	*postal affairs*, Postwesen.
✎	*rare, little used*, selten.	♪	*musical term*, Musik.
⊞	*scientific term*, wissenschaftlich.	△	*architecture*, Architektur.
⚘	*botany*, Botanik, Pflanzenkunde.	⚡	*electrical engineering*, Elektrotechnik.
⊕	*engineering*, Technik; *handicraft*, Handwerk.	⚖	*legal term*, Rechtswissenschaft.
⚒	*mining*, Bergbau.	A̷	*mathematics*, Mathematik.
✕	*military term*, militärisch.	✓	*farming*, Landwirtschaft.
⚓	*nautical term*, Schiffahrt.	⚗	*chemistry*, Chemie.
✝	*commercial term*, Handelswesen.	✻	*medicine*, Medizin.

In addition, the English-German section contains the sign ⚠, which is intended as a warning against typical mistakes:

actual ... ⚠ *nicht aktuell*

A further symbol is the box: □. When placed after an English adjective, this box means that the corresponding adverb is formed regularly by adding *-ly* to the adjective or by transforming *-le* to *-ly* or *-y* to *-ily*, e.g.:

beautiful □ = *beautifully*
acceptable □ = *acceptably*
happy □ = *happily*

Adverbs can also be formed by adding *-ally* to the adjective form. Such cases have been treated as follows:

authentic ... (~*ally*) = *authentically*

What does the **tilde (~)** mean?

One symbol which you will meet constantly in the entries is a sign indicating repetition, the tilde (~ ², ~ ²). The boldface tilde (~) replaces either the whole headword or the part of the headword preceding the vertical bar (|). The lightface tilde (~) represents the entry immediately preceding it, which itself might have been formed with the help of a boldface tilde:

> **Ski** ... **~fahrer** (= Skifahrer), **~läufer** (= Skiläufer)
> **ab|blasen** ... **~bringen:** j-n ~ (= abbringen) von ...
> **foot** ... **~ball** (= football)
> **happi|ly** ... **~ness** (= happiness)

When the initial letter of an entry changes in a run-on entry from small to capital or vice versa, the simple tilde (~) is replaced by the following symbol ⍉:

> **dick** ... **⍉kopf** (= Dickkopf)
> **Geschicht|e** ... **⍉lich** (= geschichtlich)
> **representative** ... House of ⍉s
> (= House of Representatives)

The same procedure has been used in the phonetics. The simple tilde is used for the whole word or for the part of the word which is repeated unchanged. Only the syllables or letters which change are added:

> **bewegen¹** [bə've:gən] – **bewegen²** [~]
> **Beweis** [bə'vais] ... **⍉en** [~zən]
> **chap¹** [tʃæp] – **chap²** [~] – **chap³** [~]
> **per|suade** [pə'sweid] ... **~suasion** [~ʒn]
> **destruc|tion** [dɪ'strʌkʃn] ... **~tive** [~tɪv]

In addition to the symbols, you will find the following **abbreviations** for grammatical terms and special subject areas:

a.	also, auch.	*b.s.*	bad sense, in schlechtem Sinne.
abbr.	abbreviation, Abkürzung.		
acc.	accusative (case), Akkusativ.	*bsd.*	especially, besonders.
adj.	adjective, Adjektiv.		
adv.	adverb, Adverb.	*cj.*	conjunction, Konjunktion.
allg.	commonly, allgemein.	*co.*	comic(al), scherzhaft.
Am.	American English, amerikanisches Englisch.	*coll.*	collectively, als Sammelwort.
		comp.	comparative, Komparativ.
anat.	anatomy, Anatomie.	*contp.*	contemptuously, verächtlich.
appr.	approximately, etwa.		
arch.	architecture, Architektur.	*dat.*	dative (case), Dativ.
art.	article, Artikel.	*dem.*	demonstrative, hinweisend.
ast.	astronomy, Astronomie.		
attr.	attributively, attributiv.	*ea.*	one another, each other, einander.
biol.	biology, Biologie.	*eccl.*	ecclesiastical, kirchlich.
Brit.	British, britisch.	*econ.*	economics, Wirtschaft.
Brt.	British English, britisches Englisch.	*e-e, e-e, e-e a(n),* eine.	
		e.g.	for example, zum Beispiel.

12

e-m, *e-m*, *e-m to a(n)*, einem.

e-n, *e-n*, *e-n a(n)*, einen.

eng S. *in narrower sense*, in engerem Sinne.

e-r, *e-r*, *e-r of a(n)*, *to a(n)*, einer.

e-s, *e-s*, *e-s of a(n)*, eines.

esp. *especially*, besonders.

et., *et.*, *et.* *something*, etwas.

etc., *etc. and so on*, und so weiter.

f *feminine*, weiblich.

fig. *figuratively*, bildlich.

frz. *French*, französisch.

gen. *genitive (case)*, Genitiv.

geogr. *geography*, Geographie.

geol. *geology*, Geologie.

geom. *geometry*, Geometrie.

ger. *gerund*, Gerundium.

Ggs. *antonym*, Gegensatz.

gr. *grammar*, Grammatik.

h *have*, haben.

hist. *history*, Geschichte.

hunt. *hunting*, Jagdwesen.

ichth. *ichthyology*, Ichthyologie.

impers. *impersonal*, unpersönlich.

indef. *indefinite*, unbestimmt.

inf. *infinitive (mood)*, Infinitiv.

int. *interjection*, Interjektion.

interr. *interrogative*, fragend.

iro. *ironically*, ironisch.

irr. *irregular*, unregelmäßig.

j., *j.*, *j.* *someone*, jemand.

j-m, *j-m*, *j-m to s.o.*, jemandem.

j-n, *j-n*, *j-n someone*, jemanden.

j-s, *j-s*, *j-s someone's*, jemandes.

konkr. *concretely*, konkret.

ling. *linguistics*, Sprachwissenschaft.

lit. *literary*, nur in der Schriftsprache vorkommend.

m *masculine*, männlich.

m-e, *m-e*, *m-e my*, meine.

m-r *of my*, *to my*, meiner.

metall. *metallurgy*, Metallurgie.

meteor. *meteorology*, Meteorologie.

min. *mineralogy*, Mineralogie.

mot. *motoring*, Kraftfahrwesen.

mount. *mountaineering*, Bergsteigen.

mst *mostly*, *usually*, meistens.

myth. *mythology*, Mythologie.

n *neuter*, sächlich.

nom. *nominative (case)*, Nominativ.

npr. *proper name*, Eigenname.

od. *or*, oder.

opt. *optics*, Optik.

orn. *ornithology*, Ornithologie.

o.s. *oneself*, sich.

P. *person*, Person.

p. *person*, Person.

paint. *painting*, Malerei.

parl. *parliamentary term*, parlamentarischer Ausdruck.

pass. *passive voice*, Passiv.

pers. *personal*, persönlich.

pharm. *pharmacy*, Pharmazie.

phls. *philosophy*, Philosophie.

phot. *photography*, Photographie.

phys. *physics*, Physik.

physiol. *physiology*, Physiologie.

pl. *plural*, Plural.

poet. *poetry*, Dichtung.

pol. *politics*, Politik.

poss. *possessive*, besitzanzeigend.

p.p. *past participle*, Partizip Perfekt.

p.pr. *present participle*, Partizip Präsens.

pred. *predicative*, prädikativ.

pres. *present*, Präsens.

pret. *preterit(e)*, Präteritum.

print. *printing*, Buchdruck.

pron. *pronoun*, Pronomen.

prov. *provincialism*, Provinzialismus.

prp. *preposition*, Präposition.

psych. *psychology*, Psychologie.

refl. *reflexive*, reflexiv.

rel. *relative*, Relativ...

rhet. *rhetoric*, Rhetorik.

S., S. *thing*, Sache.

s. *see*, *refer to*, siehe.

schott. *Scottish*, schottisch.

s-e, *s-e*, *s-e his*, *one's*, seine.

sep. *separable*, abtrennbar.

sg. *singular*, Singular.

sl. *slang*, Slang.

s-m, *s-m*, *s-m to his*, *to one's*, seinem.

s-n, *s-n*, *s-n his*, *one's*, seinen.

s.o., *s.o.*, *s.o. someone*, jemand(en).

s-r, *s-r*, *s-r of his*, *of one's*, *to his*, *to one's*, seiner.

s-s, *s-s*, *s-s of his*, *of one's*, seines.

s.th., *s.th.*, *s.th. something*, etwas.

subj.	*subjunctive (mood)*, Konjunktiv.	*vet.*	*veterinary medicine*, Tiermedizin.
sup.	*superlative*, Superlativ.	*vgl.*	*compare*, vergleiche.
surv.	*surveying*, Landvermessung.	*v/i.*	*intransitive verb*, intransitives Verb.
tel.	*telegraphy*, Telegraphie.	*v/refl.*	*reflexive verb*, reflexives Verb.
teleph.	*telephony*, Fernsprechwesen.	*v/t.*	*transitive verb*, transitives Verb.
thea.	*theatre*, Theater.		
TM	*trademark*, Warenzeichen.		
TV	*television*, Fernsehen.	*weitS.*	*in a wider sense*, in weiterem
typ.	*typography*, Typographie.		Sinne.
u., u.	*and*, und.		
univ.	*university*, Hochschulwesen, Studentensprache.	*z.B.*	*for example*, zum Beispiel.
		zo.	*zoology*, Zoologie.
		zs., zs.,	*zs. together*, zusammen.
v/aux.	*auxiliary verb*, Hilfsverb.	*Zssg(n)*	*compound word(s)*, Zusammensetzung(en).
vb.	*verb*, Verb.		

A few words on the translations

You will no doubt have already noticed that it is very rare for there to be only one translation after any headword. In most cases the headword has several translations which are related in meaning and are separated from one another by a comma. However, the headword itself can also have several very different meanings, depending on the context in which it is used.

When a word has several meanings, a semicolon is used to separate them from one another. But the various meanings of a word are often so far apart from one another that it is not enough simply to separate them by a semicolon. In such cases we use several different methods to separate the translations:

a) the headword is repeated and given a superior number:

leben[1] ... live
Leben[2] *n* ... life
Tor[1] *n* ... gate
Tor[2] *m* ... fool

chap[1] ... Riß *m*
chap[2] ... Kerl *m*
chap[3] ... Kinnbacke *f*

b) When a headword can be several different parts of speech (a noun, verb, adjective, etc.) the various translations are distinguished by boldface Arabic numerals:

böse ... **1.** bad (*adjective*)
        2. ♀ *n* evil (*noun*)
work ... **1.** Arbeit *f* (*noun*)
        2. *v/i.* arbeiten (*verb*)
green ... **1.** grün (*adjective*)
        2. Grün *n* (*noun*)

In the German-English section boldface Arabic numerals are also used to distinguish transitive, intransitive and reflexive verbs (if this affects their translation) and to indicate the different meanings of nouns which can occur in more than one gender:

> **bohren** ... **1.** *v/t.* bore
> **2.** *v/i.* drill
> **Bund** ... **1.** *m* ...; **2.** *n* ...

Boldface Arabic numerals are also used to show that where there is a change of meaning a noun or verb may be differently inflected or conjugated:

> **Bau** ... *m* **1.** (-[e]s/*no pl.*) ...; **2.** (-[e]s/-ten) ...; **3.** (-[e]s/-e) ...
> **schwimmen** *v/i.* (*irr.*, *ge-*) **1.** (*sein*) ...; **2.** (*h*) ...

If grammatical indications come before the subdivision they refer to all translations following:

> **Alte** (-*n*/-*n*) **1.** *m* ...; **2.** *f* ...
> **humpeln** ... *v/i.* (*ge-*) **1.** (*sein*) ...; **2.** (*h*) ...

As you know, British and American English sometimes use different terms to denote the same thing. The American *sidewalk* and the British *pavement* are both "Bürgersteig" in German, whereas only in American English does *fall* have the meaning "Herbst". In this Dictionary words which are chiefly used in British English are marked *Brt.* and those which are more typically American *Am.*

Grammar in the Dictionary, too?

It is often possible for you to arrive at the correct grammatical use of a word from the "additional information" which belongs to it. If, for instance, a headword (a verb, adjective or noun) is governed by certain prepositions, these are given together with the English or German translations and placed next to the appropriate translation. If the German or English preposition is the same for all or several translations, it is given only once before or after the first translation and then also applies to the translations which follow it.

The following methods are used to relate the prepositions to their appropriate headwords:

> **abrücken** ... **1.** *v/t.* move away (*von* from) ...
> **befestigen** ... *v/t.* fasten (*an dat.* to), fix (to), attach (to) ...

dissent ... anderer Meinung sein (*from* als) ...
dissimilar ... (*to*) unähnlich (*dat.*); verschieden (von) ...

With German prepositions which can take the dative or the accusative, the case is given in brackets:

enter ... (ein)treten in (*acc.*) ...

Notes on special grammatical conventions used in the German-English section:

a) **nouns**

The inflectional forms (*genitive singular / nominative plural*) follow immediately after the indication of gender. No forms are given for compounds if the parts appear as separate headwords.

The horizontal stroke replaces the part of the word which remains unchanged in the inflexion:

Affe *m* (-*n*/-*n*) – **Affäre** *f* (-/-*n*)

The sign ⁼ indicates that an umlaut appears in the inflected form in question:

Blatt *n* (-[*e*]*s*/⁼*er*).

b) **verbs** (see also the list of irregular German verbs on page 744)

Verbs have been treated in the following ways:

1. bändigen *v/t.* (*ge-, h*)

The past participle of this verb is formed by means of the prefix *ge-* and the auxiliary verb *haben*: *er hat gebändigt*.

2. abfassen *v/t.* (*sep., -ge-, h*)

In conjugation the prefix *ab* must be separated from the primary verb *fassen*: *er faßt ab*; *er hat abgefaßt*.

3. verderben *v/i.* (*irr., no -ge-, sein*)

irr. following the verb refers the reader to the list of irregular German verbs in the appendix (page 744) for the principal parts of this particular verb: *es verdarb*; *es ist verdorben*.

4. abfallen *v/i.* (*irr. fallen, sep., -ge-, sein*)

A reference such as *irr. fallen* indicates that the compound verb *abfallen* is conjugated in exactly the same way as the primary verb *fallen* as given in the list of irregular verbs: *er fiel ab; er ist abgefallen.*

5. sieden *v/t. and v/i.* ([*irr.*,] *ge-, h*)

The square brackets indicate that *sieden* can be treated as a regular or irregular verb: *er siedete or er sott; er hat gesiedet or er hat gesotten.*

In the English-German section of the Dictionary, round brackets can be found in some entries after the square brackets for the phonetics. These round brackets indicate that the headword has a grammatical peculiarity in one of the following points:

a) **irregular plural**

   child ... (*pl. children*) – **to·ma·to** ... (*pl. -toes*)
   a·nal·y·sis ... (*pl. -ses* [-si:z])

b) **irregular verbs** (see also the list of irregular English verbs on page 746)

   go ... (*went, gone*) – **shut** ... (*shut*)
   learn ... (*learned or learnt*)
   out·grow ... (*-grew, -grown*)

c) **doubling of the final consonant**

   hit ... (*-tt-*) – **trav·el** ... (*esp. Brt. -ll-, Am. a. -l-*)

c and b)

shut ... (*-tt-; shut*) – **out·bid** ... (*-dd-; -bid*)

d) **final –c becomes –ck–**

   frol·ic ... (*-ck-*) = *frolicking*

e) **comparative and superlative forms**

   good ... (*better, best*)
   an·gry ... (*-ier, -iest*) – **sore** ... (∼*r*, ∼*st*)

You will have seen from these notes that this Dictionary offers more than simply word-for-word equivalents as are to be found in the vocabulary sections of textbooks.

PART I

GERMAN-ENGLISH
DICTIONARY

A

Aal *ichth.* [a:l] *m* (-[e]s/-e) eel; '2-
glatt *adj.* (as) slippery as an eel.
Aas [a:s] *n* **1.** (-es/≈-e) carrion,
carcass; **2.** *fig.* (-es/Äser) beast;
'⁓geier *orn. m* vulture.
ab [ap] **1.** *prp.* (*dat.*): ⁓ Brüssel from
Brussels onwards; ⁓ Fabrik, Lager
etc. ✝ ex works, warehouse, *etc.*;
2. *prp.* (*dat.*, F *acc.*): ⁓ erstem *or*
ersten März from March 1st, on
and after March 1st; **3.** ✝ *prp.* (*gen.*)
less; ⁓ Unkosten less charges; **4.** *adv.
time: von jetzt* ⁓ from now on, in
future; ⁓ *und zu* from time to time,
now and then; *von da* ⁓ from that
time forward; *space: thea.* exit, *pl.*
exeunt; *von da* ⁓ from there
(on).
abänder|n ['ap⁹-] *v/t.* (*sep.*, -ge-, h)
alter, modify; *parl.* amend; '2ung
f alteration, modification; *parl.*
amendment (*to bill, etc.*); '2ungs-
antrag *parl. m* amendment.
abarbeiten ['ap⁹-] *v/t.* (*sep.*, -ge-, h)
work off (*debt*); *sich* ⁓ drudge, toil.
Abart ['ap⁹-] *f* variety.
'**Abbau** *m* **1.** (-[e]s/*no pl.*) pulling
down, demolition (*of structure*);
dismantling (*of machine, etc.*); dismissal, discharge (*of personnel*);
reduction (*of staff, prices, etc.*);
cut (*of prices, etc.*); **2.** ⚒ (-[e]s/-e)
working, exploitation; '2en *v/t.*
(*sep.*, -ge-, h) pull *or* take down,
demolish (*structure*); dismantle
(*machine, etc.*); dismiss, discharge
(*personnel*); reduce (*staff, prices,
etc.*); cut (*prices, etc.*); ⚒ work,
exploit.
'**ab|beißen** *v/t.* (*irr.* beißen, *sep.*,
-ge-, h) bite off; '⁓bekommen *v/t.*
(*irr.* kommen, *sep.*, -ge-, h) get
off; *s-n Teil or et.* ⁓ get one's share;
et. ⁓ be hurt, get hurt.
abberuf|en *v/t.* (*irr.* rufen, *sep.*, *no*
-ge-, h) recall; '2ung *f* recall.
'**ab|bestellen** *v/t.* (*sep.*, *no* -ge-, h)
countermand, cancel one's order
for (*goods, etc.*); cancel one's subscription to, discontinue (*news-

paper, etc.*); '⁓biegen *v/i.* (*irr.* biegen, *sep.*, -ge-, *sein*) *p.* turn off;
road: turn off, bend; *nach rechts
(links)* ⁓ turn right (left); *von e-r
Straße* ⁓ turn off a road.
'**Abbild** *n* likeness; image; 2en
['⁓dən] *v/t.* (*sep.*, -ge-, h) figure,
represent; *sie ist auf der ersten
Seite abgebildet* her picture is on
the front page; ⁓ung ['⁓duŋ] *f*
picture, illustration.
'**abbinden** *v/t.* (*irr.* binden, *sep.*,
-ge-, h) untie, unbind, remove; ✃
ligate, tie up.
'**Abbitte** *f* apology; ⁓ *leisten or tun*
make one's apology (*bei j-m wegen
et.* to s.o. for s.th.); '2n *v/t.* (*irr.*
bitten, *sep.*, -ge-, h): *j-m et.* ⁓
apologize to s.o. for s.th.
'**ab|blasen** *v/t.* (*irr.* blasen, *sep.*,
-ge-, h) blow off (*dust, etc.*); call
off (*strike, etc.*), cancel; ⚔ break
off (*attack*); '⁓blättern *v/i.* (*sep.*,
-ge-, *sein*) *paint, etc.:* scale, peel
(off); ✃ *skin:* desquamate; ⚘ shed
the leaves; '⁓blenden (*sep.*, -ge-, h)
1. *v/t.* screen (*light*); *mot.* dim, dip
(*headlights*); **2.** *v/i. mot.* dim *or* dip
the headlights; *phot.* stop down;
'⁓blitzen F *v/i.* (*sep.*, -ge-, *sein*)
meet with a rebuff; ⁓ *lassen* snub;
'⁓brausen (*sep.*, -ge-) **1.** *v/i./refl.* (h)
have a shower(-bath), douche; **2.** F
v/i. (*sein*) rush off; '⁓brechen (*irr.*
brechen, *sep.*, -ge-) **1.** *v/t.* (h) break
off (*a. fig.*); pull down, demolish
(*building, etc.*); strike (*tent*); *fig.*
stop; *das Lager* ⁓ break up camp,
strike tents; **2.** *v/i.* (*sein*) break off;
3. *fig.* *v/i.* (h) stop; '⁓bremsen *v/t.*
and v/i. (*sep.*, -ge-, h) slow down;
brake; '⁓brennen (*irr.* brennen,
sep., -ge-) **1.** *v/t.* (h) burn down
(*building, etc.*); let *or* set off (*firework*); **2.** *v/i.* (*sein*) burn away *or*
down; *s. abgebrannt*; '⁓bringen
v/t. (*irr.* bringen, *sep.*, -ge-, h) get
off; *j-n* ⁓ *von* argue s.o. out of;
dissuade s.o. from; '⁓bröckeln *v/i.*
(*sep.*, -ge-, *sein*) crumble (*a. ✝*).

'**Abbruch** m pulling down, demolition (of building, etc.); rupture (of relations); breaking off (of negotiations, etc.); fig. damage, injury; j-m ~ tun damage s.o.

'**ab|brühen** v/t. (sep., -ge-, h) scald; s. abgebrüht; '**~bürsten** v/t. (sep., -ge-, h) brush off (dirt, etc.); brush (coat, etc.); '**~büßen** v/t. (sep., -ge-, h) expiate, atone for (sin, etc.); serve (sentence). [bet.\

Abc [a:be:'tse:] n (-/-) ABC, alpha-\

'**abdank|en** v/i. (sep., -ge-, h) resign; ruler: abdicate; '**2ung** f (-/-en) resignation; abdication.

'**ab|decken** v/t. (sep., -ge-, h) uncover; untile (roof); unroof (building); clear (table); cover; '**~dichten** v/t. (sep., -ge-, h) make tight; seal up (window, etc.); ⊕ pack (gland, etc.); '**~dienen** v/t. (sep., -ge-, h): s-e Zeit ~ ✕ serve one's time; '**~drängen** v/t. (sep., -ge-, h) push aside; '**~drehen** (sep., -ge-, h) **1.** v/t. twist off (wire); turn off (water, gas, etc.); ⚡ switch off (light); **2.** ⊕, ✈ v/i. change one's course; '**~drosseln** mot. v/t. (sep., -ge-, h) throttle.

'**Abdruck** m (-[e]s/⁼e) impression, print, mark; cast; '**2en** v/t. (sep., -ge-, h) print; publish (article).

'**abdrücken** (sep., -ge-, h) **1.** v/t. fire (gun, etc.); F hug or squeeze affectionately; sich ~ leave an impression or a mark; **2.** v/i. pull the trigger.

Abend ['a:bənt] m (-s/-e) evening; am ~ in the evening, at night; heute abend tonight; morgen (gestern) abend tomorrow (last) night; s. essen; '**~anzug** m evening dress; '**~blatt** n evening paper; '**~brot** n supper, dinner; '**~dämmerung** f (evening) twilight, dusk; '**~essen** n s. Abendbrot; '**~gesellschaft** f evening party; '**~kasse** thea. f box-office; '**~kleid** n evening dress or gown; '**~land** n (-[e]s/no pl.) the Occident; **2ländisch** adj. ['~lendiʃ] western, occidental; '**~mahl** eccl. n (-[e]s/-e) the (Holy) Communion, the Lord's Supper; '**~rot** n evening or sunset glow.

abends adv. ['a:bənts] in the evening.

'**Abend|schule** f evening school, night-school; '**~sonne** f setting

sun; '**~toilette** f evening dress; '**~wind** m evening breeze; '**~zeitung** f evening paper.

Abenteu|er ['a:bəntɔyər] n (-s/-) adventure; '**2erlich** adj. adventurous; fig.: strange; wild, fantastic; **~rer** ['~rɔyrər] m (-s/-) adventurer.

aber ['a:bər] **1.** adv. again; Tausende und ~ Tausende thousands upon thousands; **2.** cj. but; oder ~ otherwise, (or) else; **3.** int.: ~! now then!; ~, ~! come, come!; ~ nein! no!, on the contrary!; **4.** ♀ n (-s/-) but.

'**Aber|glaube** m superstition; **2-gläubisch** adj. ['~glɔybiʃ] superstitious.

aberkenn|en ['ap⁹-] v/t. (irr. kennen, sep., no -ge-, h): j-m et. ~ deprive s.o. of s.th. (a. ♯⁄♯); dispossess s.o. of s.th.; '**2ung** f (-/-en) deprivation (a. ♯⁄♯); dispossession.

aber|malig adj. ['a:bərma:liç] repeated; **~mals** adv. ['~s] again, once more.

ab|ernten ['ap⁹-] v/t. (sep., -ge-, h) reap, harvest; **~essen** ['ap⁹-] (irr. essen, sep., -ge-, h) **1.** v/t. clear (plate); **2.** v/i. finish eating; '**~fahren** (irr. fahren, sep., -ge-) **1.** v/i. (sein) leave (nach for), depart (for), start (for); set out or off (for); **2.** v/t. (h) carry or cart away (load).

'**Abfahrt** f departure (nach for), start (for); setting out or off (for); skiing: downhill run; '**~sbahnsteig** m departure platform; '**~slauf** m skiing: downhill race; '**~ssignal** n starting-signal; '**~szeit** f time of departure; ⊕ a. time of sailing.

'**Abfall** m defection (von from), falling away (from); esp. pol. secession (from); eccl. apostasy (from); Abfälle pl. waste, refuse, rubbish, Am. a. garbage; ⊕ clippings pl., shavings pl.; at butcher's: offal; '**~eimer** m dust-bin, Am. ash can; '**2en** v/i. (irr. fallen, sep., -ge-, sein) leaves, etc.: fall (off); ground, etc.: slope (down); fig. fall away (von from); esp. pol. secede (from); eccl. apostatize (from); ~ gegen come off badly by comparison with, be inferior to; '**~erzeugnis** n waste product; by-product.

'**abfällig** adj. judgement, etc.: adverse, unfavo(u)rable; remark: disparaging, depreciatory.

'Abfallprodukt n by-product; waste product.

'ab|fangen v/t. (irr. fangen, sep., -ge-, h) catch; snatch (ball, etc.); intercept (letter, etc.); △, ✗ prop; ✗ check (attack); ✈ flatten out; mot., ✈ right; '**.färben** v/i. (sep., -ge-, h): der Pullover färbt ab die colo(u)r of the pull-over runs (auf acc. on); ~ auf (acc.) influence, affect.

'abfass|en v/t. (sep., -ge-, h) compose, write, pen; catch (thief, etc.); '**2ung** f composition; wording.

'ab|faulen v/i. (sep., -ge-, sein) rot off; '**.fegen** v/t. (sep., -ge-, h) sweep off; '**.feilen** v/t. (sep., -ge-, h) file off.

abfertig|en ['apfertigən] v/t. (sep., -ge-, h) dispatch (a. 🕮); customs: clear; serve, attend to (customer); j-n kurz ~ snub s.o.; '**2ung** f (-/-en) dispatch; customs: clearance; schroffe ~ snub.

'abfeuern v/t. (sep., -ge-, h) fire (off), discharge.

'abfind|en v/t. (irr. finden, sep., -ge-, h) satisfy, pay off (creditor); compensate; sich mit et. ~ resign o.s. to s.th.; put up with s.th.; '**2ung** f (-/-en) settlement; satisfaction; compensation; '**2ung(summe)** f indemnity; compensation.

'ab|flachen v/t. and v/refl. (sep., -ge-, h) flatten; '**.flauen** v/i. (sep., -ge-, sein) wind, etc.: abate; interest, etc.: flag; ♥ business: slacken; '**~fliegen** v/i. (irr. fliegen, sep., -ge-, sein) leave by plane; ✈ take off, start; '**.fließen** v/i. (irr. fließen, sep., -ge-, sein) drain or flow off or away. [parture.]

'Abflug ✈ m take-off, start, de-

'Abfluß m flowing or draining off or away; discharge (a. 🕮); drain (a. fig.); sink; outlet (of lake, etc.).

'abfordern v/t. (sep., -ge-, h): j-m et. ~ demand s.th. of or from s.o.

Abfuhr ['apfu:r] f (-/-en) removal; fig. rebuff.

'abführ|en (sep., -ge-, h) **1.** v/t. lead off or away; march (prisoner) off; pay over (money) (an acc. to); **2.** ✗ v/i. purge (the bowels), loosen the bowels; '**.end** ✗ adj. purgative, aperient, laxative; '**2mittel** ✗ n purgative, aperient, laxative.

'abfüllen v/t. (sep., -ge-, h) decant;

in Flaschen ~ bottle; Bier in Fässer ~ rack casks with beer.

'Abgabe f sports: pass; casting (of one's vote); sale (of shares, etc.); mst ~n pl. taxes pl.; rates pl., Am. local taxes pl.; duties pl.; '**2frei** adj. tax-free; duty-free; '**2npflichtig** adj. taxable; dutiable; liable to tax or duty.

'Abgang m departure; start; thea. exit (a. fig.); retirement (from a job); loss, wastage; deficiency (in weight, etc.); ✗ discharge; ✗ miscarriage; nach ~ von der Schule after leaving school.

'abgängig adj. missing.

'Abgangszeugnis n (school-)leaving certificate, Am. a. diploma.

'Abgas n waste gas; esp. mot. exhaust gas. [toil-worn, worn-out.]

abgearbeitet adj. ['apgə²arbaɪtət]]

'abgeben v/t. (irr. geben, sep., -ge-, h) leave (bei, an dat. at); hand in (paper, etc.); deposit, leave (luggage); cast (one's vote); sports: pass (ball, etc.); sell, dispose of (goods); give off (heat, etc.); e-e Erklärung ~ make a statement; s-e Meinung ~ express one's opinion (über acc. on); j-m et. ~ von et. give s.o. some of s.th.; e-n guten Gelehrten ~ make a good scholar; sich ~ mit occupy o.s. with s.th.; sie gibt sich gern mit Kindern ab she loves to be among children.

'abge|brannt adj. burnt down; F fig. hard up, sl. broke; '**.brüht** fig. adj. ['.bry:t] hardened, callous; '**.droschen** adj. trite, hackneyed; '**.feimt** adj. ['.faɪmt] cunning, crafty; '**.griffen** adj. worn; book: well-thumbed; '**.härtet** adj. ['.hertət] hardened (gegen to), inured (to); '**.härmt** adj. ['.hermt] care-worn.

'abgehen (irr. gehen, sep., -ge-) **1.** v/i. (sein) go off or away; leave, start, depart; letter, etc.: be dispatched; post: go; thea. make one's exit; side-road: branch off; goods: sell; button, etc.: come off; stain, etc.: come out; ✗ be discharged; (von e-m Amt) ~ give up a post; retire; von der Schule ~ leave school; ~ von digress from (main subject); deviate from (rule); alter, change (one's opinion); relinquish (plan, etc.); diese Eigenschaft geht ihm ab he lacks this quality; gut ~ end well, pass off well; *hiervon geht or gehen ... ab* ✝ less, minus; **2.** *v/t.* (h) measure by steps; patrol.

abge|hetzt *adj.* ['apgəhɛtst] harassed; exhausted; run down; breathless; **~kartet** F *adj.* ['ˌkartət]: *~e Sache* prearranged affair, put-up job; **'~legen** *adj.* remote, distant; secluded; out-of-the-way; **~macht** *adj.* ['ˌmaxt]: *~!* it's a bargain *or* deal!; **~magert** *adj.* ['ˌmaːgərt] emaciated; **~neigt** *adj.* ['ˌnaɪkt] disinclined (*dat.* for *s.th.*; *zu tun* to do), averse (to; from doing), unwilling (*zu tun* to do); **~nutzt** *adj.* ['ˌnʊtst] worn-out.

Abgeordnete ['apgəˀɔrdnətə] *m, f* (-n/-n) deputy, delegate; *in Germany*: member of the Bundestag *or* Landtag; *Brt.* Member of Parliament, *Am.* Representative.

'abgerissen *fig. adj.* ragged; shabby; *style, speech*: abrupt, broken.

'Abgesandte *m, f* (-n/-n) envoy; emissary; ambassador.

'abgeschieden *fig. adj.* isolated; secluded; retired; **'Qheit** *f* (-/-en) seclusion; retirement.

'abgeschlossen *adj.* flat: self-contained; *training, etc.*: complete.

abgeschmackt *adj.* ['apgəʃmakt] tasteless; tactless; **'Qheit** *f* (-/-en) tastelessness; tactlessness.

'abgesehen *adj.*: *~ von* apart from, *Am. a.* aside from.

abge|spannt *fig. adj.* ['apgəʃpant] exhausted, tired, run down; **'~standen** *adj.* stale, flat; **'~storben** *adj.* numb; dead; **~stumpft** *adj.* ['ˌʃtʊmpft] blunt(ed); *fig.* indifferent (*gegen* to); **'~tragen** *adj.* worn-out; threadbare, shabby.

'abgewöhnen *v/t.* (sep., -ge-, h): *j-m et.* ~ break *or* cure s.o. of s.th.; *sich das Rauchen* ~ give up smoking.

abgezehrt *adj.* ['apgətseːrt] emaciated, wasted.

'abgießen *v/t.* (irr. *gießen*, sep., -ge-, h) pour off; 🜄 decant; ⊕ cast.

'Abglanz *m* reflection (*a. fig.*).

'abgleiten *v/i.* (irr. *gleiten*, sep., -ge-, sein) slip off; slide off; glide

'Abgott *m* idol. [off.|

abgöttisch *adv.* ['apgœtiʃ]: *j-n ~ lieben* idolize *or* worship s.o.; dote (up)on s.o.

'ab|grasen *v/t.* (sep., -ge-, h) graze; *fig.* scour; **'~grenzen** *v/t.* (sep.,

-ge-, h) mark off, delimit; demarcate (*a. fig.*); *fig.* define.

'Abgrund *m* abyss; precipice; chasm, gulf; *am Rande des ~s* on the brink of disaster.

'Abguß *m* cast.

'ab|hacken *v/t.* (sep., -ge-, h) chop *or* cut off; **'~haken** *fig. v/t.* (sep., -ge-, h) tick *or* check off; **'~halten** *v/t.* (irr. *halten*, sep., -ge-, h) hold (*meeting, examination, etc.*); keep out (*rain*); *j-n von der Arbeit ~* keep s.o. from his work; *j-n davon ~ et. zu tun* keep *or* restrain s.o. from doing s.th.; *et. von j-m ~* keep s.th. away from s.o.; **'~handeln** *v/t.* (sep., -ge-, h) discuss, treat; *j-m et. ~* bargain s.th. out of s.o.

abhanden *adv.* [ap'handən]: *~ kommen* get lost.

'Abhandlung *f* treatise (*über acc.* [up]on), dissertation ([up]on, concerning); essay. [clivity.|

'Abhang *m* slope, incline; de-|

'abhängen 1. *v/t.* (sep., -ge-, h) take down (*picture, etc.*); 🚂 uncouple; **2.** *v/i.* (irr. *hängen*, sep., -ge-, h): *~ von* depend (up)on.

abhängig *adj.* ['apheŋiç]: *~ von* dependent (up)on; **'Qkeit** *f* (-/*no pl.*) dependence (*von* [up]on).

ab|härmen ['aphɛrmən] *v/refl.* (sep., -ge-, h) pine away (*über acc.* at); **'~härten** *v/t.* (sep., -ge-, h) harden (*gegen* to), inure (to); *sich ~ harden o.s.* (*gegen* to), inure o.s. (to); **'~hauen** (irr. *hauen*, sep., -ge-, h) **1.** *v/t.* (h) cut *or* chop off; **2.** F *v/i.* (sein) be off; *hau ab! sl.* beat it!, scram!; **'~häuten** *v/t.* (sep., -ge-, h) skin, flay; **'~heben** (irr. *heben*, sep., -ge-, h) **1.** *v/t.* lift *or* take off; *teleph.* lift (*receiver*); (with)draw (*money*); *sich ~ von* stand out against; *fig. a.* contrast with; **2.** *v/i.* cut (the cards); *teleph.* lift the receiver; **'~heilen** *v/i.* (sep., -ge-, sein) heal (up); **'~helfen** *v/i.* (irr. *helfen*, sep., -ge-, h): *e-m Übel ~* cure *or* redress an evil; *dem ist nicht abzuhelfen* there is nothing to be done about it; **'~hetzen** *v/refl.* (sep., -ge-, h) tire o.s. out; rush, hurry.

'Abhilfe *f* remedy, redress, relief; *~ schaffen* take remedial measures.

'abhobeln *v/t.* (sep., -ge-, h) plane (away, down).

abhold adj. ['aphɔlt] averse (dat. to s.th.); ill-disposed (towards s.o.).

'**ab|holen** v/t. (sep., -ge-, h) fetch; call for, come for; j-n von der Bahn ~ go to meet s.o. at the station; '**holzen** v/t. (sep., -ge-, h) fell, cut down (trees); deforest; '**horchen** ⚔ v/t. (sep., -ge-, h) auscultate, sound; '**hören** v/t. (sep., -ge-, h) listen in to, intercept (telephone conversation); e-n Schüler ~ hear a pupil's lesson.

Abitur [abi'tuːr] n (-s/⚔-e) school-leaving examination (qualifying for university entrance).

'**ab|jagen** v/t. (sep., -ge-, h): j-m et. ~ recover s.th. from s.o.; '**kanzeln** F v/t. (sep., -ge-, h) reprimand, F tell s.o. off; '**kaufen** v/t. (sep., -ge-, h): j-m et. ~ buy or purchase s.th. from s.o.

Abkehr fig. ['apkeːr] f (-/no pl.) estrangement (von from); withdrawal (from); '**2en** v/t. (sep., -ge-, h) sweep off; sich ~ von turn away from; fig.: take no further interest in; become estranged from; withdraw from.

'**ab|klingen** v/i. (irr. klingen, sep., -ge-, sein) fade away; pain, etc.: die down; pain, illness: ease off; '**klopfen** (sep., -ge-, h) 1. v/t. knock (dust, etc.) off; dust (coat, etc.); ⚔ sound, percuss; 2. v/i. conductor: stop the orchestra; '**knicken** v/t. (sep., -ge-, h) snap or break off; bend off; '**knöpfen** v/t. (sep., -ge-, h) unbutton; F j-m Geld ~ get money out of s.o.; '**kochen** (sep., -ge-, h) 1. v/t. boil; scald (milk); 2. v/i. cook in the open air (a. ⚒); '**kommandieren** ⚔ v/t. (sep., no -ge-, h) detach, detail; second (officer).

Abkomme ['apkɔmə] m (-n/-n) descendant.

'**abkommen** 1. v/i. (irr. kommen, sep., -ge-, sein) come away, get away or off; von e-r Ansicht ~ change one's opinion; von e-m Thema ~ digress from a topic; vom Wege ~ lose one's way; 2. 2 n (-s/-) agreement.

abkömm|lich adj. ['apkœmliç] dispensable; available; er ist nicht ~ he cannot be spared; '**2ling** ['~liŋ] m (-s/-e) descendant.

'**ab|koppeln** v/t. (sep., -ge-, h) uncouple; '**kratzen** (sep., -ge-) 1. v/t. (h) scrape off; 2. sl. v/i. (sein) kick the bucket; '**kühlen** v/t. (sep., -ge-, h) cool; refrigerate; sich ~ cool down (a. fig.).

Abkunft ['apkunft] f (-/⚔-e) descent; origin, extraction; birth.

'**abkürz|en** v/t. (sep., -ge-, h) shorten; abbreviate (word, story, etc.); den Weg ~ take a short cut; '**2ung** f (-/-en) abridgement; abbreviation; short cut.

'**abladen** v/t. (irr. laden, sep., -ge-, h) unload; dump (rubbish, etc.).

'**Ablage** f place of deposit; filing tray; files pl.; cloak-room.

'**ab|lagern** (sep., -ge-) 1. v/t. (h) season (wood, wine); age (wine); sich ~ settle; be deposited; 2. v/i. (sein) wood, wine: season; wine: age; '**lassen** (irr. lassen, sep., -ge-, h) 1. v/t. let (liquid) run off; let off (steam); drain (pond, etc.); 2. v/i. leave off (von et. [doing] s.th.).

'**Ablauf** m running off; outlet, drain; sports: start; fig. expiration, end; nach ~ von at the end of; '**2en** (irr. laufen, sep., -ge-) 1. v/i. (sein) run off; drain off; period of time: expire; ✝ bill of exchange: fall due; clock, etc.: run down; thread, film: unwind; spool: run out; gut ~ end well; 2. v/t. (h) wear out (shoes); scour (region, etc.); sich die Beine ~ run one's legs off; s. Rang.

'**Ableben** n (-s/ no pl.) death, decease (esp. ⚖), ⚖ demise.

'**ab|lecken** v/t. (sep., -ge-, h) lick (off); '**legen** (sep., -ge-, h) 1. v/t. take off (garments); leave off (garments); give up, break o.s. of (habit); file (documents, letters, etc.); make (confession, vow); take (oath, examination); Zeugnis ~ bear witness (für to; von of); s. Rechenschaft; 2. v/i. take off one's (hat and) coat.

'**Ableger** ♀ m (-s/-) layer, shoot.

'**ablehn|en** (sep., -ge-, h) 1. v/t. decline; refuse; reject (doctrine, candidate, etc.); turn down (proposal, etc.); 2. v/i. decline; dankend ~ decline with thanks; '**end** adj. negative; '**2ung** f (-/-en) refusal; rejection.

'**ableit|en** v/t. (sep., -ge-, h) divert (river, etc.); drain off or away (water, etc.); gr., ♔, fig. derive (aus, von from); *fig.* infer (from); '2ung *f* diversion; drainage; *gr.*, ⅍ derivation (*a. fig.*).

'ab|lenken *v/t.* (*sep.*, -ge-, *h*) turn aside; divert (*suspicion, etc.*) (von from); *phys., etc.*: deflect (*rays, etc.*); *j-n von der Arbeit* ~ distract s.o. from his work; '~lesen *v/t.* (*irr. lesen, sep.*, -ge-, *h*) read (*speech, etc.*); read (off) (*values from instruments*); '~leugnen *v/t.* (*sep.*, -ge-, *h*) deny, disavow, disown.

'abliefer|n *v/t.* (*sep.*, -ge-, *h*) deliver; hand over; surrender; '2ung *f* delivery.

'ablöschen *v/t.* (*sep.*, -ge-, *h*) blot (up) (*ink*); ⊕ temper (*steel*).

'ablös|en *v/t.* (*sep.*, -ge-, *h*) detach; take off; ⚔, *etc.*: relieve; supersede (*predecessor in office*); discharge (*debt*); redeem (*obligation*); *sich* ~ come off; *fig.* alternate, take turns; '2ung *f* detachment; ⚔, *etc.*: relief; *fig.* supersession; discharge; redemption.

'abmach|en *v/t.* (*sep.*, -ge-, *h*) remove, detach; *fig.* settle, arrange (*business, etc.*); agree (up)on (*price, etc.*); '2ung *f* (-/-en) arrangement, settlement; agreement.

'abmager|n *v/i.* (*sep.*, -ge-, *sein*) lose flesh; grow lean *or* thin; '2ung *f* (-/-en) emaciation.

'ab|mähen *v/t.* (*sep.*, -ge-, *h*) mow (off); '~malen *v/t.* (*sep.*, -ge-, *h*) copy.

'Abmarsch *m* start; ⚔ marching off; '2ieren *v/i.* (*sep.*, *no* -ge-, *sein*) start; ⚔ march off.

'abmeld|en *v/t.* (*sep.*, -ge-, *h*): *j-n von der Schule* ~ give notice of the withdrawal of a pupil (from school); *sich polizeilich* ~ give notice to the police of one's departure (from town, *etc.*); '2ung *f* notice of withdrawal; notice of departure.

'abmess|en *v/t.* (*irr. messen, sep.*, -ge-, *h*) measure; '2ung *f* (-/-en) measurement.

'ab|montieren *v/t.* (*sep.*, *no* -ge-, *h*) disassemble; dismantle, strip (*machinery*); remove (*tyre, etc.*); '~mühen *v/refl.* (*sep.*, -ge-, *h*) drudge, toil; '~nagen *v/t.* (*sep.*, -ge-, *h*) gnaw off; pick (*bone*).

Abnahme ['apna:mə] *f* (-/⚔-n) taking off; removal; ⚔ amputation; ✝ taking delivery; ✝ purchase; ✝

sale; ⊕ acceptance (*of machine, etc.*); administering (*of oath*); decrease, diminution; loss (*of weight*).

'abnehm|en (*irr. nehmen, sep.*, -ge-, *h*) **1.** *v/t.* take off; remove; *teleph.* lift (*receiver*); ⚔ amputate; gather (*fruit*); ⊕ accept (*machine, etc.*); *j-m et.* ~ take s.th. from s.o.; ✝ *a.* buy *or* purchase s.th. from s.o.; *j-m zuviel* ~ overcharge s.o.; **2.** *v/i.* decrease, diminish; decline; lose weight; *moon*: wane; *storm*: abate; *days*: grow shorter; '2er ✝ *m* (-s/-) buyer; customer; consumer.

'Abneigung *f* aversion (*gegen* to); disinclination (to); dislike (to, of, for); antipathy (against, to).

abnorm *adj.* [ap'nɔrm] abnormal; anomalous; exceptional; 2i'tät *f* (-/-en) abnormality; anomaly.

'abnötigen *v/t.* (*sep.*, -ge-, *h*): *j-m et.* ~ extort s.th. from s.o.

'ab|nutzen *v/t. and v/refl.* (*sep.*, -ge-, *h*), '~nützen *v/t. and v/refl.* (*sep.*,-ge-,*h*)wear out; '2nutzung *f,* '2nützung *f* (-/-en) wear (and tear).

Abonn|ement [abɔn(ə)'mã:] *n* (-s/ -s) subscription (*auf acc.* to); '~ent [~'nɛnt] *m* (-en/-en) subscriber; 2ieren [~'ni:rən] *v/t.* (*no* -ge-, *h*) subscribe to (*newspaper*); 2iert *adj.* [~'ni:rt]: ~ sein auf (*acc.*) take in (*newspaper, etc.*).

abordn|en ['ap⁹-] *v/t.* (*sep.*, -ge-, *h*) depute, delegate, *Am. a.* deputize; '2ung *f* delegation, deputation.

Abort [a'bɔrt] *m* (-[e]s/-e) lavatory, toilet.

'ab|passen *v/t.* (*sep.*, -ge-, *h*) fit, adjust; watch for, wait for (*s.o., opportunity*); waylay *s.o.*; '~pflük-ken *v/t.* (*sep.*, -ge-, *h*) pick, pluck (off), gather; '~plagen *v/refl.* (*sep.*, -ge-, *h*) toil; '~platzen *v/i.* (*sep.*, -ge-, *sein*) burst off; fly off; '~prallen *v/i.* (*sep.*, -ge-, *sein*) rebound, bounce (off); ricochet; '~putzen *v/t.* (*sep.*, -ge-, *h*) clean (off, up); wipe off; polish; '~raten *v/i.* (*irr. raten, sep.*, -ge-, *h*): *j-m von* dissuade s.o. from, advise s.o. against; '~räumen *v/t.* (*sep.*, -ge-, *h*) clear (away); '~reagieren *v/t.* (*sep.*, *no* -ge-, *h*) work off (*one's anger, etc.*); *sich* ~ ✝ *a.* let off steam.

'abrechn|en (*sep.*, -ge-, *h*) **1.** *v/t.* deduct; settle (*account*); **2.** *v/i.*: *mit j-m* ~ settle with s.o.; *fig.* settle (ac-

counts) with s.o., F get even with s.o.; **ⁱ2ung** f settlement (of accounts); deduction, discount.

ⁱAbrede f: in ⁓ stellen deny or question s.th.

ⁱabreib|en v/t. (irr. reiben, sep., -ge-, h) rub off; rub down (body); polish; **ⁱ2ung** f rub-down; F fig. beating.

ⁱAbreise f departure (nach for); **ⁱ2n** v/i. (sep., -ge-, sein) depart (nach for), leave (for); start (for), set out (for).

ⁱabreiß|en (irr. reißen, sep., -ge-) **1.** v/t. (h) tear or pull off; pull down (building); s. abgerissen; **2.** v/i. (sein) break off; button, etc.: come off; **ⁱ2kalender** m tear-off calendar.

ⁱab|richten v/t. (sep., -ge-, h) train (animal), break (horse) (in); **⁓rie-geln** v/t. (sep., -ge-, h) bolt, bar (door); block (road).

ⁱAbriß m draft; summary; abstract; (brief) outlines pl.; brief survey.

ⁱab|rollen (sep., -ge-) v/t. (h) and v/i. (sein) unroll; uncoil; unwind, unreel; roll off; **⁓rücken** (sep., -ge-) **1.** v/t. (h) move off or away (von from), remove; **2.** ✕ v/i. (sein) march off, withdraw.

ⁱAbruf m call; recall; auf ⁓ ✝ on call; **ⁱ2en** v/t. (irr. rufen, sep., -ge-, h) call off (a. ✝); call away; recall; 🕮 call out.

ⁱab|runden v/t. (sep., -ge-, h) round (off); **⁓rupfen** v/t. (sep., -ge-, h) pluck off.

abrupt adj. [ap'rupt] abrupt.

ⁱabrüst|en ✕ v/i. (sep., -ge-, h) disarm; **ⁱ2ung** ✕ f disarmament.

ⁱabrutschen v/i. (sep., -ge-, sein) slip off, glide down; ✈ skid.

ⁱAbsage f cancellation; refusal; **ⁱ2n** (sep., -ge-, h) **1.** v/t. cancel, call off; refuse; recall (invitation); **2.** v/i. guest: decline; j-m ⁓ cancel one's appointment with s.o.

ⁱabsägen v/t. (sep., -ge-, h) saw off; F fig. sack s.o.

ⁱAbsatz m stop, pause; typ. paragraph; ✝ sale; heel (of shoe); landing (of stairs); **ⁱ2fähig** ✝ adj. saleable, marketable; **⁓markt** ✝ m market, outlet; **⁓möglichkeit** ✝ f opening, outlet.

ⁱabschaben v/t. (sep., -ge-, h) scrape off.

ⁱabschaff|en v/t. (sep., -ge-, h)

abolish; abrogate (law); dismiss (servants); **ⁱ2ung** f (-/-en) abolition; abrogation; dismissal.

ⁱab|schälen v/t. (sep., -ge-, h) peel (off), pare; bark (tree); **⁓schalten** v/t. (sep., -ge-, h) switch off, turn off or out; ⚡ disconnect.

ⁱabschätz|en v/t. (sep., -ge-, h) estimate; value; assess; **ⁱ2ung** f valuation; estimate; assessment.

ⁱAbschaum m (-[e]s/no pl.) scum; fig. a. dregs pl.

ⁱAbscheu m (-[e]s/no pl.) horror (vor dat. of), abhorrence (of); loathing (of); disgust (for).

ⁱabscheuern v/t. (sep., -ge-, h) scour (off); wear out; chafe, abrade.

abscheulich adj. [ap'ʃɔyliç] abominable, detestable, horrid; **2keit** f (-/-en) detestableness; atrocity.

ⁱab|schicken v/t. (sep., -ge-, h) send off, dispatch; ✉ post, esp. Am. mail; **⁓schieben** v/t. (irr. schieben, sep., -ge-, h) push or shove off.

Abschied ['apʃiːt] m (-[e]s/⁑-e) departure; parting; leave-taking; farewell; dismissal; ✕ discharge; ⁓ nehmen take leave (von of), bid farewell (to); j-m den ⁓ geben dismiss s.o., ✕ discharge s.o.; s-n ⁓ nehmen resign, retire; **⁓s-feier** f farewell party; **⁓sgesuch** n resignation.

ⁱab|schießen v/t. (irr. schießen, sep., -ge-, h) shoot off; shoot, discharge, fire (off) (fire-arm); launch (rocket); kill, shoot; (shoot or bring) down (aircraft); s. Vogel; **⁓schin-den** v/refl. (irr. schinden, sep., -ge-, h) toil and moil, slave, drudge; **⁓schirmen** v/t. (sep., -ge-, h) shield (gegen from); screen (from), screen off (from); **⁓schlachten** v/t. (sep., -ge-, h) slaughter, butcher.

ⁱAbschlag ✝ m reduction (in price); auf ⁓ on account; **ⁱ2en** ['⁓gən] v/t. (irr. schlagen, sep., -ge-, h) knock off, beat off; strike off; cut off (head); refuse (request); repel (attack).

abschlägig adj. ['apʃlɛːgiç] negative; **⁓e** Antwort refusal, denial.

ⁱAbschlagszahlung f payment on account; instal(l)ment.

ⁱabschleifen v/t. (irr. schleifen, sep., -ge-, h) grind off; fig. refine, polish.

ⁱAbschlepp|dienst mot. m towing service, Am. a. wrecking service;

'Qen v/t. (sep., -ge-, h) drag off; mot. tow off.

'abschließen (irr. schließen, sep., -ge-, h) 1. v/t. lock (up); ⊕ seal (up); conclude (letter, etc.); settle (account); balance (the books); effect (insurance); contract (loan); fig. seclude, isolate; e-n Handel ~ strike a bargain; sich ~ seclude o.s.; 2. v/i. conclude; '~d 1. adj. concluding; final; 2. adv. in conclusion.

'Abschluß m settlement; conclusion; ⊕ seal; '~prüfung f final examination, finals pl., Am. a. graduation; '~zeugnis n leaving certificate; diploma.

'ab|schmeicheln v/t. (sep., -ge-, h): j-m et. ~ coax s.th. out of s.o.; '~schmelzen (irr. schmelzen, sep., -ge-) v/t. (h) and v/i. (sein) melt (off); ⊕ fuse; '~schmieren ⊕ v/t. (sep., -ge-, h) lubricate, grease; '~schnallen v/t. (sep., -ge-, h) unbuckle; take off (ski, etc.); '~schneiden (irr. schneiden, sep., -ge-, h) 1. v/t. cut (off); slice off; den Weg ~ take a short cut; j-m das Wort ~ cut s.o. short; 2. v/i.: gut ~ come out or off well.

'Abschnitt m ⚕ coupon; typ. section, paragraph; counterfoil, Am. a. stub (of cheque, etc.); stage (of journey); phase (of development); period (of time).

'ab|schöpfen v/t. (sep., -ge-, h) skim (off); '~schrauben v/t. (sep., -ge-, h) unscrew, screw off.

'abschrecken v/t. (sep., -ge-, h) deter (von from); scare away; '~d adj. deterrent; repulsive, forbidding.

'abschreib|en (irr. schreiben, sep., -ge-, h) 1. v/t. copy; write off (debt, etc.); plagiarize; in school: crib; 2. v/i. send a refusal; 'Qer m copyist; plagiarist; 'Qung ⚕ f (-/-en) depreciation.

'abschreiten v/t. (irr. schreiten, sep., -ge-, h) pace (off); e-e Ehrenwache ~ inspect a guard of hono(u)r.

'Abschrift f copy, duplicate.

'abschürf|en v/t. (sep., -ge-, h) graze, abrade (skin); 'Qung f (-/-en) abrasion.

'Abschuß m discharge (of fire-arm); launching (of rocket); hunt. shooting; shooting down, downing (of aircraft); '~rampe f launching platform.

abschüssig adj. ['apfysiç] sloping; steep.

'ab|schütteln v/t. (sep., -ge-, h) shake off (a. fig.); fig. get rid of; '~schwächen v/t. (sep., -ge-, h) weaken, lessen, diminish; '~schweifen v/i. (sep., -ge-, sein) deviate; fig. digress; '~schwenken v/i. (sep., -ge-, sein) swerve; ⚔ wheel; '~schwören v/i. (irr. schwören, sep., -ge-, h) abjure; forswear; '~segeln v/i. (sep., -ge-, sein) set sail, sail away.

abseh|bar adj. ['apze:ba:r]: in ~er Zeit in the not-too-distant future; '~en (irr. sehen, sep., -ge-, h) 1. v/t. (fore)see; j-m et. ~ learn s.th. by observing s.o.; es abgesehen haben auf (acc.) have an eye on, be aiming at; 2. v/i.: ~ von refrain from; disregard.

abseits ['apzaits] 1. adv. aside, apart; football, etc.: off side; 2. prp. (gen.) aside from; off (the road).

'absend|en v/t. ([irr. senden] sep., -ge-, h) send off, dispatch; ⚒ post, esp. Am. mail; 'Qer ⚒ m sender.

absengen v/t. (sep., -ge-, h) singe off.

'Absenker ⚘ m (-s/-) layer, shoot.

'absetz|en (sep., -ge-, h) 1. v/t. set or put down, deposit; deduct (sum); take off (hat); remove, dismiss (official); depose, dethrone (king); drop, put down (passenger); ⚕ sell (goods); typ. set up (in type); thea.: ein Stück ~ take off a play; 2. v/i. break off, stop, pause; 'Qung f (-/-en) deposition; removal, dismissal.

'Absicht f (-/-en) intention, purpose, design; 'Qlich 1. adj. intentional; 2. adv. on purpose.

'absitzen (irr. sitzen, sep., -ge-) 1. v/i. (sein) rider: dismount; 2. v/t. (h) serve (sentence), F do (time).

absolut adj. [apzo'lu:t] absolute.

absolvieren [apzɔl'vi:rən] v/t. (no -ge-, h) absolve; complete (studies); get through, graduate from (school).

'absonder|n v/t. (sep., -ge-, h) separate; ⚗ secrete; sich ~ withdraw; 'Qung f (-/-en) separation; ⚗ secretion.

ab|sorbieren [apzɔr'bi:rən] v/t. (no -ge-, h) absorb; '~speisen fig. v/t. (sep., -ge-, h) put s.o. off.

abspenstig adj. ['apfpɛnstiç]: ~

machen entice away (*von* from).

'absperr|en *v/t.* (*sep.,* -ge-, *h*) lock; shut off; bar (*way*); block (*road*); turn off (*gas, etc.*); **'2hahn** *m* stopcock.

'ab|spielen *v/t.* (*sep.,* -ge-, *h*) play (*record, etc.*); play back (*tape recording*); *sich* ~ happen, take place; **'~sprechen** *v/t.* (*irr. sprechen, sep.,* -ge-, *h*) deny; arrange, agree; **'~springen** *v/i.* (*irr. springen, sep.,* -ge-, *sein*) jump down *or* off; ✈ jump, bale out, (*Am. only*) bail out; rebound.   [off.↲

'Absprung *m* jump; *sports:* take-↲

'abspülen *v/t.* (*sep.,* -ge-, *h*) wash up; rinse.

'abstamm|en *v/i.* (*sep.,* -ge-, *sein*) be descended; *gr.* be derived (*both: von* from); **'2ung** *f* (-/-en) descent; *gr.* derivation.

'Abstand *m* distance; interval; ✝ compensation, indemnification; ~ *nehmen von* desist from.

'ab|statten ['apʃtatən] *v/t.* (*sep.,* -ge-, *h*): *e-n Besuch* ~ pay a visit; *Dank* ~ return *or* render thanks; **'~stauben** *v/t.* (*sep.,* -ge-, *h*) dust.

'abstech|en (*irr. stechen, sep.,* -ge-, *h*) **1.** *v/t.* cut (*sods*); stick (*pig, sheep, etc.*); stab (*animal*); **2.** *v/i.* contrast (*von* with); **'2er** *m* (-s/-) excursion, trip; detour.

'ab|stecken *v/t.* (*sep.,* -ge-, *h*) unpin, undo; fit, pin (*dress*); *surv.* mark out; **'~stehen** *v/i.* (*irr. stehen, sep.,* -ge-, *h*) stand off; stick out, protrude; *s. abgestanden*; **'~steigen** *v/i.* (*irr. steigen, sep.,* -ge-, *sein*) descend; alight (*von* from) (*carriage*); get off, dismount (*from*) (*horse*); put up (*in dat.* at) (*hotel*); **'~stellen** *v/t.* (*sep.,* -ge-, *h*) put down; stop, turn off (*gas, etc.*); park (*car*); *fig.* put an end to *s.th.*; **'~stempeln** *v/t.* (*sep.,* -ge-, *h*) stamp; **'~sterben** *v/i.* (*irr. sterben, sep.,* -ge-, *sein*) die off; *limb:* mortify.

Abstieg ['apʃtiːk] *m* (-[e]s/-e) descent; *fig.* decline.

'abstimm|en (*sep.,* -ge-, *h*) **1.** *v/i.* vote; **2.** *v/t.* tune in (*radio*); *fig.:* harmonize; time; ✝ balance (*books*); **'2ung** *f* voting; tuning.

Abstinenzler [apsti'nɛntslər] *m* (-s/-) teetotal(l)er.

'abstoppen (*sep.,* -ge-, *h*) **1.** *v/t.*

stop; slow down; *sports:* clock, time; **2.** *v/i.* stop.

'abstoßen *v/t.* (*irr. stoßen, sep.,* -ge-, *h*) knock off; push off; clear off (*goods*); *fig.* repel; *sich die Hörner* ~ sow one's wild oats; **'~d** *fig. adj.* repulsive.

abstrakt *adj.* [ap'strakt] abstract.

'ab|streichen *v/t.* (*irr. streichen, sep.,* -ge-, *h*) take *or* wipe off; **'~streifen** *v/t.* (*sep.,* -ge-, *h*) strip off; take *or* pull off (*glove, etc.*); slip off (*dress*); wipe (*shoes*); **'~streiten** *v/t.* (*irr. streiten, sep.,* -ge-, *h*) contest, dispute; deny.

'Abstrich *m* deduction, cut; 🎗 swab.

'ab|stufen *v/t.* (*sep.,* -ge-, *h*) graduate; gradate; **'~stumpfen** (*sep.,* -ge-) **1.** *v/t.* (*h*) blunt; *fig.* dull (*mind*); **2.** *fig. v/i.* (*sein*) become dull.

'Absturz *m* fall; ✈ crash.

'ab|stürzen *v/i.* (*sep.,* -ge-, *sein*) fall down; ✈ crash; **'~suchen** *v/t.* (*sep.,* -ge-, *h*) search (*nach* for); scour *or* comb (*area*) (for).

absurd *adj.* [ap'zurt] absurd, preposterous.

Abszeß 🎗 [aps'tsɛs] *m* (Abszesses/ Abszesse) abscess.

Abt [apt] *m* (-[e]s/⁼e) abbot.

'abtakeln ⚓ *v/t.* (*sep.,* -ge-, *h*) unrig, dismantle, strip.

Abtei [ap'taɪ] *f* (-/-en) abbey.

Ab|'teil 🚆 *n* compartment; **'2teilen** *v/t.* (*sep.,* -ge-, *h*) divide; △ partition off; **'~teilung** *f* division; **~'teilung** *f* department; ward (*of hospital*); compartment; ✕ detachment; **~'teilungsleiter** *m* head of a department.

'abtelegraphieren *v/i.* (*sep., no -ge-, h*) cancel a visit, *etc.* by telegram.

Äbtissin [ɛp'tɪsɪn] *f* (-/-nen) abbess.

'ab|töten *v/t.* (*sep.,* -ge-, *h*) destroy, kill (*bacteria, etc.*); **'~tragen** *v/t.* (*irr. tragen, sep.,* -ge-, *h*) carry off; pull down (*building*); wear out (*garment*); pay (*debt*).

abträglich *adj.* ['aptrɛːklɪç] injurious, detrimental.

'abtreib|en (*irr. treiben, sep.,* -ge-) **1.** *v/t.* (*h*) drive away *or* off; *ein Kind* ~ procure abortion; **2.** ⚓, ✈ *v/i.* (*sein*) drift off; **'2ung** *f* (-/-en) abortion.

'abtrennen *v/t.* (*sep.,* -ge-, *h*) detach; separate; sever (*limbs, etc.*); take (*trimmings*) off (*dress*).

'**abtret|en** (*irr. treten, sep., -ge-*)
1. *v/t.* (h) wear down (*heels*); wear
out (*steps, etc.*); *fig.* cede, transfer;
2. *v/i.* (*sein*) retire, withdraw,
resign; *thea.* make one's exit; '**2er**
m (*-s/-*) doormat; '**2ung** *f* (*-/-en*)
cession, transfer.

'**ab|trocknen** (*sep., -ge-*) **1.** *v/t.* (h)
dry (up); wipe (dry); *sich ~* dry
oneself, rub oneself down; **2.** *v/i.*
(*sein*) dry up, become dry; '**~trop-
fen** *v/i.* (*sep., -ge-, sein*) liquid: drip;
dishes, vegetables: drain.

abtrünnig *adj.* ['aptrynɪç] unfaithful, disloyal; *eccl.* apostate; 2e ['∼ɡə]
m (*-n/-n*) deserter; *eccl.* apostate.

'**ab|tun** *v/t.* (*irr. tun, sep., -ge-, h*)
take off; settle (*matter*); *fig.*: dispose
of; dismiss; *~urteilen* ['apʔ-] *v/t.*
(*sep., -ge-, h*) pass sentence on *s.o.*;
'**~wägen** *v/t.* ([*irr. wägen,*] *sep., -ge-,
h*) weigh (out) (*goods*); *fig.* consider care-
fully; '**~wälzen** *v/t.* (*sep., -ge-, h*)
roll away; *fig.* shift; '**~wandeln**
v/t. (*sep., -ge-, h*) vary, modify;
'**~wandern** *v/i.* (*sep., -ge-, sein*)
wander away; migrate (*von from*).

'**Abwandlung** *f* modification, variation.

'**abwarten** (*sep., -ge-*) **1.** *v/t.* wait
for, await; *s-e Zeit ~* bide one's
time; **2.** *v/i.* wait.

abwärts *adv.* ['apvɛrts] down, down-
ward(s).

'**abwaschen** *v/t.* (*irr. waschen, sep.,
-ge-, h*) wash (off, away); bathe;
sponge off; wash up (*dishes, etc.*).

'**abwechseln** (*sep., -ge-, h*) **1.** *v/t.*
vary, alternate; **2.** *v/i.* vary; alternate; *mit j-m ~* take turns; '**~d** *adj.*
alternate.

'**Abwechs(e)lung** *f* (*-/-en*) change;
alternation; variation; diversion;
zur ~ for a change.

'**Abweg** *m*: *auf ~e geraten* go astray;
2**ig** *adj.* ['∼ɡɪç] erroneous, wrong.

'**Abwehr** *f* defen|ce, *Am. -se*; ward-
ing off (*of thrust, etc.*); '**~dienst** ✗
m counter-espionage service; '2**en**
v/t. (*sep., -ge-, h*) ward off; avert;
repulse, repel; ward off (*attack,
enemy*).

'**abweich|en** *v/i.* (*irr. weichen, sep.,
-ge-, sein*) deviate (*von from*),
swerve (from); differ (from);
compass-needle: deviate; '2**ung** *f* (*-/-en*)
deviation; difference; deflexion,
(*Am. only*) deflection.

'**abweiden** *v/t.* (*sep., -ge-, h*) graze.

'**abweis|en** *v/t.* (*irr. weisen, sep.,
-ge-, h*) refuse, reject; repel (*a.* ✗);
rebuff; '**~end** *adj.* unfriendly, cool;
'2**ung** *f* refusal, rejection; repulse
(*a.* ✗); rebuff.

'**ab|wenden** *v/t.* ([*irr. wenden,*] *sep.,
-ge-, h*) turn away; avert (*disaster,
etc.*); parry (*thrust*); *sich ~* turn
away (*von from*); '**~werfen** *v/t.* (*irr.
werfen, sep., -ge-, h*) throw off; ✈
drop (*bombs*); shed, cast (*skin, etc.*),
shed (*leaves*); yield (*profit*).

'**abwert|en** *v/t.* (*sep., -ge-, h*) deval-
uate; '2**ung** *f* devaluation.

abwesen|d *adj.* ['apveːzənt] absent;
'2**heit** *f* (*-/✗ -en*) absence.

'**ab|wickeln** *v/t.* (*sep., -ge-, h*) un-
wind, unreel; wind off; transact
(*business*); '**~wiegen** *v/t.* (*irr. wiegen,
sep., -ge-, h*) weigh (out) (*goods*);
'**~wischen** *v/t.* (*sep., -ge-, h*) wipe
(off); '**~würgen** *v/t.* (*sep., -ge-, h*)
strangle, throttle, choke; *mot.* stall;
'**~zahlen** *v/t.* (*sep., -ge-, h*) pay off;
pay by instal(l)ments; '**~zählen**
v/t. (*sep., -ge-, h*) count (out, over).

'**Abzahlung** *f* instal(l)ment, payment on account; '**~sgeschäft** *n*
hire-purchase.

'**abzapfen** *v/t.* (*sep., -ge-, h*) tap,
draw off.

'**Abzehrung** *f* (*-/-en*) wasting away,
emaciation; ✗ consumption.

'**Abzeichen** *n* badge; ✈ marking.

'**ab|zeichnen** *v/t.* (*sep., -ge-, h*)
copy, draw; mark off; initial; tick
off; *sich ~ gegen* stand out against;
'**~ziehen** (*irr. ziehen, sep., -ge-*)
1. *v/t.* (h) take off, remove; A
subtract; strip (*bed*); bottle (*wine*);
phot. print (*film*); *typ.* pull (*proof*);
take out (*key*); *das Fell ~* skin
(*animal*); **2.** *v/i.* (*sein*) go away; ✗
march off; *smoke*: escape; *thunderstorm, clouds*: move on.

'**Abzug** *m* departure; ✗ withdrawal,
retreat; ⊕ drain; outlet; deduction
(*of sum*); *phot.* print; *typ.* proof
(*-sheet*).

abzüglich *prp.* (*gen.*) ['aptsyːklɪç]
less, minus, deducting.

'**Abzugsrohr** *n* waste-pipe.

abzweig|en ['aptsvaɪɡən] (*sep., -ge-*)
1. *v/t.* (h) branch; divert (*money*);
sich ~ branch off; **2.** *v/i.* (*sein*)
branch off; '2**ung** *f* (*-/-en*) branch;
road-junction.

ach int. [ax] oh!, ah!, alas!; ~ **so!** oh, I see!

Achse ['aksə] f (-/-n) axis; ⊕: axle; shaft; axle(-tree) (*of carriage*); *auf der* ~ on the move.

Achsel ['aksəl] f (-/-n) shoulder; *die* ~*n zucken* shrug one's shoulders; '**~höhle** f armpit.

acht[1] [axt] **1.** *adj.* eight; *in* ~ *Tagen* today week, this day week; *vor* ~ *Tagen* a week ago; **2.** 2̃ f (-/-en) (figure) eight.

Acht[2] [~] f (*/no pl.*) ban, outlawry; attention; *außer acht lassen* disregard; *sich in acht nehmen* be careful; be on one's guard (*vor j-m or et.* against s.o. *or* s.th.); look out (*for* s.o. *or* s.th.).

'**achtbar** *adj.* respectable.

'**achte** *adj.* eighth; 2̃l ['~əl] n (-s/-) eighth (part).

'**achten** (ge-, h) **1.** *v/t.* respect, esteem; regard; **2.** *v/i.:* ~ *auf* (*acc.*) pay attention to; *achte auf meine Worte* mark or mind my words; *darauf* ~, *daß* see to it that, take care that.

ächten ['ɛçtən] *v/t.* (ge-, h) outlaw, proscribe; ban.

'**Achter** m (-s/-) *rowing:* eight.

'**achtfach** *adj.* ['axtfax] eightfold.

'**achtgeben** *v/i.* (*irr. geben, sep.,* -ge-, h) be careful; pay attention (*auf acc.* to); take care (of); *gib acht!* look or watch out!, be careful!

'**achtlos** *adj.* inattentive, careless, heedless.

Acht'**stundentag** m eight-hour day.

'**Achtung** f (-/*no pl.*) attention; respect, esteem, regard; ~! look out!; ✗ attention!; ~ *Stufe!* mind the step!; 2̃svoll *adj.* respectful.

'**achtzehn** *adj.* eighteen; ~**te** *adj.* ['~tə] eighteenth.

'**achtzig** *adj.* ['axtsiç] eighty; '~**ste** *adj.* eightieth.

ächzen ['ɛçtsən] *v/i.* (ge-, h) groan, moan.

Acker ['akər] m (-s/̈) field; '~**bau** m agriculture; farming; 2̃**bautreibend** *adj.* agricultural, farming; '~**geräte** n/pl. farm implements pl.; '~**land** n arable land; '2̃**n** *v/t. and v/i.* (ge-, h) plough, till, *Am.* plow.

addi|eren [a'di:rən] *v/t.* (*no* -ge-, h) add (up); 2̃**tion** [adi'tsjo:n] f (-/-en) addition, adding up.

Adel ['a:dəl] m (-s/*no pl.*) nobility, aristocracy; '2̃**ig** *adj.* noble; '2̃**n** *v/t.* (ge-, h) ennoble (*a. fig.*); *Brt.* knight, raise to the peerage; '~**s-stand** m nobility; aristocracy; *Brt.* peerage.

Ader ['a:dər] f (-/-n) ✗, *wood, etc.*: vein; *anat.:* vein; artery; *zur* ~ *lassen* bleed.

adieu int. [a'djø:] good-bye, farewell, adieu, F cheerio.

Adjektiv gr. ['atjekti:f] n (-s/-e) adjective.

Adler orn. ['a:dlər] m (-s/-) eagle; '~**nase** f aquiline nose.

adlig *adj.* ['a:dliç] noble; 2̃**e** ['~gə] m (-n/-n) nobleman, peer.

Admiral ⚓ [atmi'ra:l] m (-s/-e, ⸰e) admiral.

adopt|ieren [adɔp'ti:rən] *v/t.* (*no* -ge-, h) adopt; 2̃**ivkind** [~'ti:f-] n adopted child.

Adressat [adrɛ'sa:t] m (-en/-en) addressee, consignee (*of goods*).

Adreßbuch ['adrɛs-] n directory.

Adress|e [a'drɛsə] f (-/-n) address; direction; *per* ~ care of (*abbr.* c/o); 2̃**ieren** [~'si:rən] *v/t.* (*no* -ge-, h) address, direct; ✝ consign; *falsch* ~ misdirect.

adrett *adj.* [a'drɛt] smart, neat.

Adverb gr. [at'vɛrp] n (-s/-ien) adverb.

Affäre [a'fɛ:rə] f (-/-n) (love) affair; matter, business, incident. [key.]

Affe zo. ['afə] m (-n/-n) ape; mon-]

Affekt [a'fɛkt] m (-[e]s/-e) emotion; passion; 2̃**iert** *adj.* [~'ti:rt] affected.

'**affig** F *adj.* foppish; affected; silly.

Afrikan|er [afri'ka:nər] m (-s/-) African; 2̃**isch** *adj.* African.

After anat. ['aftər] m (-s/-) anus.

Agent [a'gɛnt] m (-en/-en) agent; broker; *pol.* (secret) agent; ~**ur** [~'tu:r] f (-/-en) agency.

aggressiv *adj.* [agrɛ'si:f] aggressive.

Agio ✝ ['a:ʒio] n (-s/*no pl.*) agio, premium.

Agitator [agi'ta:tɔr] m (-s/-en) agitator. [(brooch.)]

Agraffe [a'grafə] f (-/-n) clasp;]

agrarisch *adj.* [a'gra:riʃ] agrarian.

Ägypt|er [ɛ'gyptər] m (-s/-) Egyptian; 2̃**isch** *adj.* Egyptian.

ah int. [a:] ah!

aha int. [a'ha] aha!, I see!

Ahle ['a:lə] f (-/-n) awl, pricker; punch.

Ahn [ɑ:n] *m* (-[e]s, -en/-en) ancestor, ~en *pl. a.* forefathers *pl.*

ähneln ['ɛ:nəln] *v/i.* (ge-, h) be like, resemble.

ahnen ['ɑ:nən] *v/t.* (ge-, h) have a presentiment *or* that; suspect; divine.

ähnlich *adj.* ['ɛ:nliç] like, resembling; similar (*dat.* to); *iro.: das sieht ihm ~* that's just like him; **2keit** *f* (-/-en) likeness, resemblance; similarity.

Ahnung ['ɑ:nuŋ] *f* (-/-en) presentiment; foreboding; notion, idea; **2slos** *adj.* unsuspecting; **2svoll** *adj.* full of misgivings.

Ahorn ♀ ['ɑ:hɔrn] *m* (-s/-e) maple (-tree).

Ähre ♀ ['ɛ:rə] *f* (-/-n) ear, head; spike; ~n *lesen* glean.

Akademie [akade'mi:] *f* (-/-n) academy, society; ~**ker** [~'de:mikər] *m* (-s/-) university man, *esp. Am.* university graduate; **2sch** *adj.* [~'de:miʃ] academic.

Akazie ♀ [a'kɑ:tsjə] *f* (-/-n) acacia.

akklimatisieren [aklimati'zi:rən] *v/t. and v/refl.* (no -ge-, h) acclimatize, *Am.* acclimate.

Akkord [a'kɔrt] *m* (-[e]s/-e) ♪ chord; ♱: contract; agreement; composition; *im ~* ♱ by the piece *or* job; ~**arbeit** *f* piece-work; ~**arbeiter** *m* piece-worker; ~**lohn** *m* piece-wages *f.*

akkreditieren [akredi'ti:rən] *v/t.* (no -ge-, h) accredit (*bei* to); **2iv** [~'ti:f] *n* (-s/-e) credentials *pl.*; ♱ letter of credit.

Akku F ⊕ ['aku] *m* (-s/-s), ~**mulator** ⊕ [~mu'lɑ:tɔr] *m* (-s/-en) accumulator, (storage-)battery.

Akkusativ *gr.* ['akuzati:f] *m* (-s/-e) accusative (case).   [acrobat.]

Akrobat [akro'bɑ:t] *m* (-en/-en)⟨

Akt [akt] *m* (-[e]s/-e) act(ion), deed; *thea.* act; *paint.* nude.

Akte ['aktə] *f* (-/-n) document, deed; file; ~n *pl.* records *pl.*, papers *pl.*; deeds *pl.*, documents *pl.*; *zu den ~n* to be filed; *zu den ~n legen* file; ~**ndeckel** *m* folder; ~**nmappe** *f*, ~**ntasche** *f* portfolio; briefcase; **'~nzeichen** *n* reference *or* file number.

Aktie ♱ ['aktsjə] *f* (-/-n) share, *Am.* stock; ~n *besitzen* hold shares, *Am.* hold stock; **'~nbesitz** *m* share-

holdings *pl.*, *Am.* stockholdings *pl.*; **'~ngesellschaft** *f appr.* joint-stock company, *Am.* (stock) corporation; **'~nkapital** *n* share-capital, *Am.* capital stock.

Aktion [ak'tsjo:n] *f* (-/-en) action; activity; *pol., etc.*: campaign, drive; ⚔ operation; **~är** [~'nɛ:r] *m* (-s/-e) shareholder, *Am.* stockholder.

aktiv *adj.* [ak'ti:f] active.

Aktiva ♱ [ak'ti:va] *n/pl.* assets *pl.*; ~**posten** [~'ti:f-] *m* asset (*a. fig.*).

aktuell *adj.* [aktu'ɛl] current, present-day, up-to-date, topical.

Akustik [a'kustik] *f* (-/no *pl.*) acoustics *sg., pl.*; **2isch** *adj.* acoustic.

akut *adj.* [a'ku:t] acute.

Akzent [ak'tsɛnt] *m* (-[e]s/-e) accent; stress; **2uieren** [~u'i:rən] *v/t.* (no -ge-, h) accent(uate).

Akzept ♱ [ak'tsɛpt] *n* (-[e]s/-e) acceptance; ~**ant** [~'tant] *m* (-en/-en) acceptor; **2ieren** [~'ti:rən] *v/t.* (no -ge-, h) accept.

Alarm [a'larm] *m* (-[e]s/-e) alarm; *~ blasen or schlagen* ⚔ sound *or* give the alarm; ~**bereitschaft** *f: in ~ sein* stand by; **2ieren** [~'mi:rən] *v/t.* (no -ge-, h) alarm.

Alaun 🜍 [a'laun] *m* (-[e]s/-e) alum.

albern *adj.* ['albərn] silly, foolish.

Album ['album] *n* (-s/Alben) album.

Alge ♀ ['algə] *f* (-/-n) alga, seaweed.

Algebra 🜨 ['algebra] *f* (-/no *pl.*) algebra.

Alibi 🝆 ['alibi] *n* (-s/-s) alibi.

Alimente [ali'mɛntə] *pl.* alimony.

Alkohol ['alkohol] *m* (-s/-e) alcohol; **2frei** *adj.* non-alcoholic, *esp. Am.* soft; ~**es** *Restaurant* temperance restaurant; ~**iker** [~'ho:likər] *m* (-s/-) alcoholic; **2isch** *adj.* [~'ho:liʃ] alcoholic; **'~schmuggler** *m* liquor-smuggler, *Am.* bootlegger; **'~verbot** *n* prohibition; **'~vergiftung** *f* alcoholic poisoning.

all¹ [al] **1.** *pron.* all; ~*e* everybody; ~*es im* ~*em* on the whole; *vor* ~*em* first of all; **2.** *adj.* all; every, each; any; ~*e beide* both of them; *auf* ~*e Fälle* in any case, at all events; ~*e Tage* every day; ~*e zwei Minuten* every two minutes.

All² [~] *n* (-s/no *pl.*) *the* universe.

alle F *adj.* all gone; ~ *werden* come to an end; *supplies, etc.*: run out.

Allee [a'le:] *f* (-/-n) avenue; (tree-lined) walk.

allein [a'laɪn] **1.** *adj.* alone; single; unassisted; **2.** *adv.* alone; only; **3.** *cj.* yet, only, but, however; 2**berechtigung** *f* exclusive right; 2**besitz** *m* exclusive possession; 2**herrscher** *m* absolute monarch, autocrat; dictator; **~ig** *adj.* only, exclusive, sole; 2**sein** *n* loneliness, solitariness, solitude; **~stehend** *adj. p.*: alone in the world; single; *building, etc.*: isolated, detached; 2**verkauf** *m* exclusive sale; monopoly; 2**vertreter** *m* sole representative *or* agent; 2**vertrieb** *m* sole distributors *pl.*

allemal *adv.* ['alə'mɑːl] always; *ein für ~* once (and) for all.

'**allen'falls** *adv.* if need be; possibly, perhaps; at best.

allenthalben † *adv.* ['alənt'halbən] everywhere.

'**aller**|'**best** *adj.* best ... of all, very best; **~dings** *adv.* ['~'dɪŋs] indeed; to be sure; **~!** certainly!, *Am.* F sure!; '**~erst 1.** *adj.* first ... of all, very first; foremost; **2.** *adv.*: *zu ~* first of all.

Allergie ⚕ [aler'giː] *f* (-/-n) allergy. '**aller**|'**hand** *adj.* of all kinds *or* sorts; F *das ist ja ~!* F I say!; *sl.* that's the limit!; '2**heiligen** *n* (-/*no pl.*) All Saints' Day; **~lei** *adj.* ['~'laɪ] of all kinds *or* sorts; '2**lei** *n* (-/-s) medley; '**~letzt 1.** *adj.* last of all, very last; latest (*news, fashion, etc.*); **2.** *adv.*: *zu ~* last of all; '**~liebst 1.** *adj.* dearest of all; (most) lovely; **2.** *adv.*: *am ~en* best of all; '**~meist 1.** *adj.* most; **2.** *adv.*: *am ~en* mostly; chiefly; '**~nächst** *adj.* very next; '**~neu(e)st** *adj.* the very latest; '2**seelen** *n* (-/*no pl.*) All Souls' Day; '**~seits** *adv.* on all sides; universally; '**~wenigst** *adv.*: *am ~en* least of all.

'**alle**|'**samt** *adv.* one and all, all together; '**~zeit** *adv.* always, at all times, for ever.

'**all**|'**gegenwärtig** *adj.* omnipresent, ubiquitous; '**~ge'mein 1.** *adj.* general; common; universal; **2.** *adv.*: *im ~en* in general, generally; 2**ge-'meinheit** *f* (-/-en) generality; universality; general public; 2**heilmittel** *n* panacea, cure-all (*both a. fig.*).

Allianz [ali'ants] *f* (-/-en) alliance. **alli'ier**|**en** *v/refl.* (*no -ge-, h*) ally

o.s. (*mit* to, with); 2**te** *m* (-n/-n) ally.

'**all**|'**jährlich 1.** *adj.* annual; **2.** *adv.* annually, every year; '2**macht** *f* (-/*no pl.*) omnipotence; **~'mächtig** *adj.* omnipotent, almighty; **~mählich** [~'mɛːlɪç] **1.** *adj.* gradual; **2.** *adv.* gradually, by degrees.

Allopathie ⚕ [alopa'tiː] allopathy. **all**|'**seitig** *adj.* ['alzaɪtɪç] universal; all-round; '2**strom** ⚡ *m* (-[e]s/*no pl.*) alternating current/direct current (*abbr.* A.C./D.C.); '2**tag** *m* workday; week-day; *fig.* everyday life, daily routine; '**~täglich** *adj.* daily; *fig.* common, trivial; '2**tagsleben** *n* (-s/*no pl.*) everyday life; '**~wissend** *adj.* omniscient; '2**'wissenheit** *f* (-/*no pl.*) omniscience; '**~'wöchentlich** *adj.* weekly; '**~zu** *adv.* (much) too; '**~zu'viel** *adv.* too much. [alp.]

Alm [alm] *f* (-/-en) Alpine pasture.]

Almosen ['almoːzən] *n* (-s/-) alms; ~ *pl.* alms *pl.*, charity.

Alp|**druck** ['alp-] *m* (-[e]s/~e), '**~drücken** *n* (-s/*no pl.*) nightmare.

Alpen ['alpən] *pl.* Alps *pl.*

Alphabet [alfa'beːt] *n* (-[e]s/-e) alphabet; 2**isch** *adj.* alphabetic(al).

'**Alptraum** *m* nightmare.

als *cj.* [als] than; as, like; (in one's capacity) as; but, except; *temporal*: after, when; as; *~ ob* as if, as though; *so viel ~* as much as; *er ist zu dumm, ~ daß er es verstehen könnte* he is too stupid to understand it; **~'bald** *adv.* immediately; '**~'dann** *adv.* then.

also ['alzoː] **1.** *adv.* thus, so; **2.** *cj.* therefore, so, consequently; *na ~!* there you are!

alt[1] *adj.* [alt] old; aged; ancient, antique; stale; second-hand.

Alt[2] ♪ [~] *m* (-s/-e) alto, contralto. **Altar** [al'taːr] *m* (-[e]s/~e) altar. **Alteisen** ['alt?-] *n* scrap-iron.

'**Alte** (-n/-n) **1.** *m* old man; F: *der ~* the governor; *hist.*: *die ~n pl.* the ancients *pl.*; **2.** *f* old woman.

'**Alter** *n* (-s/-) age; old age; seniority; *er ist in meinem ~* he is my age; *von mittlerem ~* middle-aged.

älter *adj.* ['ɛltər] older; senior; *der ~e Bruder* the elder brother.

altern ['altərn] *v/i.* (ge-, *h, sein*) grow old, age.

Alternative [alternaˈtiːvə] f (-/-n) alternative; *keine ~ haben* have no choice.

'**Alters**|**grenze** f age-limit; retirement age; '**~heim** n old people's home; '**~rente** f old-age pension; '**2schwach** adj. decrepit; senile; '**~schwäche** f decrepitude; '**~versorgung** f old-age pension.

Altertum ['altɐtuːm] n **1.** (-s/no pl.) antiquity; **2.** (-s/ˈ-ˈer) mst *Altertümer pl.* antiquities pl.

altertümlich adj. ['altɐtyːmlɪç] ancient, antique, archaic.

'**Altertums**|**forscher** m arch(a)eologist; '**~kunde** f arch(a)eology.

ältest adj. ['ɛltəst] oldest; eldest (*sister, etc.*); earliest (*recollections*); **2e** m (-n/-n) elder; senior; *mein ~r* my eldest (son).

Altistin ♪ [alˈtɪstin] f (-/-nen) alto-singer, contralto-singer.

'**altklug** adj. precocious, forward.

ältlich adj. ['ɛltlɪç] elderly, oldish.

'**Alt**|**material** n junk, scrap; salvage; '**~meister** m doyen, dean, F Grand Old Man (*a. sports*); *sports:* ex-champion; **2modisch** adj. old-fashioned; '**~papier** n waste paper; '**~philologe** m classical philologist *or* scholar; '**~stadt** f old town *or* city; '**~warenhändler** m second-hand dealer; ~'**weibersommer** m Indian summer; gossamer.

Aluminium ⚗ [aluˈmiːnjum] n (-s/no pl.) aluminium, *Am.* aluminum.

am prp. [am] = *an dem.*

Amateur [amaˈtøːr] m (-s/-e) amateur. [*bosse*] anvil.|

Amboß ['ambɔs] m (Ambosses/Am-|

ambulan|**t** ✚ adj. [ambuˈlant]: ~ *Behandelter* out-patient; **2z** [~ts] f (-/-en) ambulance.

Ameise zo. ['aːmaɪzə] f (-/-n) ant; '**~nhaufen** m ant-hill.

Amerikan|**er** [ameriˈkaːnɐr] m (-s/-), ~**erin** f (-/-nen) American; **2isch** adj. American.

Amme ['amə] f (-/-n) (wet-)nurse.

Amnestie [amnɛsˈtiː] f (-/-n) amnesty, general pardon.

Amor ['aːmɔr] m (-s/no pl.) Cupid.

Amortis|**ation** [amɔrtizaˈtsjoːn] f (-/-en) amortization, redemption; **2ieren** [~ˈziːrən] v/t. (no -ge-, h) amortize, redeem; pay off.

Ampel ['ampəl] f (-/-n) hanging lamp; traffic light.

Amphibie zo. [amˈfiːbjə] f (-/-n) amphibian.

Ampulle [amˈpulə] f (-/-n) ampoule.

Amput|**ation** ✚ [amputaˈtsjoːn] f (-/-en) amputation; **2ieren** ✚ [~ˈtiːrən] v/t. (no -ge-, h) amputate; ~**ierte** m (-n/-n) amputee. [*bird.*]

Amsel orn. ['amzəl] f (-/-n) black-|

Amt [amt] n (-[e]s/ˈ-ˈer) office; post; charge; office, board; official duty, function; (telephone) exchange; **2ieren** [~ˈtiːrən] v/i. (no -ge-, h) hold office; officiate; **2lich** adj. official; '**~mann** m district administrator; *hist.* bailiff.

'**Amts**|**arzt** m medical officer of health; '**~befugnis** f competence, authority; '**~bereich** m, '**~bezirk** m jurisdiction; '**~blatt** n gazette; '**~eid** m oath of office; '**~einführung** f inauguration; '**~führung** f administration; '**~geheimnis** n official secret; '**~gericht** n appr. district court; '**~geschäfte** n/pl. official duties pl.; '**~gewalt** f (official) authority; '**~handlung** f official act; '**~niederlegung** f (-/⚒-en) resignation; '**~richter** m appr. district court judge; '**~siegel** n official seal; '**~vorsteher** m head official.

Amulett [amuˈlɛt] n (-[e]s/-e) amulet, charm.

amüs|**ant** adj. [amyˈzant] amusing, entertaining; ~**ieren** [~ˈziːrən] v/t. (no -ge-, h) amuse, entertain; *sich ~* amuse *or* enjoy o.s., have a good time.

an prp. **1.** prp. (dat.): at; on, upon; in; against; to; by, near, close to; ~ *der Themse* on the Thames; ~ *der Wand* on *or* against the wall; *es ist ~ dir zu inf.* it is up to you to *inf.*; *am Leben alive*; *am 1. März* on March 1st; *am Morgen* in the morning; **2.** prp. (acc.): to; on; on to; at; against; about; *bis ~* as far as, up to; **3.** adv. on; *von heute ~* from this day forth, from today; *von nun or jetzt ~* from now on.

analog adj. [anaˈloːk] analogous (*dat. or zu* to, with).

Analphabet [anˈ(ʔ)alfabeːt] m (-en/-en) illiterate (person).

Analys|**e** [anaˈlyːzə] f (-/-n) analysis; **2ieren** [~ˈziːrən] v/t. (no -ge-, h) analy|se, *Am.* -ze.

Anämie 🧬 [anɛˈmiː] f (-/-n) an(a)e-mia.

Ananas [ˈananas] f (-/-, -se) pine-apple.

Anarchie [anarˈçiː] f (-/-n) anarchy.

Anatom|ie [anatoˈmiː] f (-/no pl.) anatomy; **⁀isch** adj. [~ˈtoːmiʃ] anatomical.

'**anbahnen** v/t. (sep., -ge-, h) pave the way for, initiate; open up; *sich* ~ be opening up.

'**Anbau** m 1. 🌱 (-[e]s/no pl.) cultiva-tion; 2. 🔺 (-[e]s/-ten) outbuilding, annex, extension, addition; '**⁀en** v/t. (sep., -ge-, h) 🌱 cultivate, grow; 🔺 add (an acc. to); '**⁀fläche** 🌱 f arable land.

'**anbehalten** v/t. (irr. halten, sep., no -ge-, h) keep (garment, etc.) on.

an'**bei** † adv. enclosed.

'**an|beißen** (irr. beißen, sep., -ge-, h) 1. v/t. bite into; 2. v/i. fish: bite; '**⁀bellen** v/t. (sep., -ge-, h) bark at; **⁀beraumen** [ˈ⁀bəraumən] v/t. (sep., no -ge-, h) appoint, fix; '**⁀be-ten** v/t. (sep., -ge-, h) adore, wor-ship.

'**Anbetracht** m: in ~ considering, in consideration of.

'**anbetteln** v/t. (sep., -ge-, h) beg from, solicit alms of.

'**Anbetung** f (-/⁀-en) worship, adoration; '**⁀swürdig** adj. adorable.

'**an|bieten** v/t. (irr. bieten, sep., -ge-, h) offer; '**⁀binden** v/t. (irr. binden, sep., -ge-, h) bind, tie (up) ~ an (dat., acc.) tie to; s. angebun-den; '**⁀blasen** v/t. (irr. blasen, sep., -ge-, h) blow at or (up)on.

'**Anblick** m look; view; sight, as-pect; '**⁀en** v/t. (sep., -ge-, h) look at; glance at; view; eye.

'**an|blinzeln** v/t. (sep., -ge-, h) wink at; '**⁀brechen** (irr. brechen, sep., -ge-) 1. v/t. (h) break into (provi-sions, etc.); open (bottle, etc.); 2. v/i. (sein) begin; day: break, dawn; '**⁀brennen** (irr. brennen, sep., -ge-) 1. v/t. (h) set on fire; light (cigar, etc.); 2. v/i. (sein) catch fire; burn; '**⁀bringen** v/t. (irr. bringen, sep., -ge-, h) bring; fix (an dat. to), at-tach (to); place; † dispose of (goods); lodge (complaint); s. ange-bracht.

'**Anbruch** m (-[e]s/no pl.) begin-ning; break (of day).

'**anbrüllen** v/t. (sep., -ge-, h) roar at.

Andacht [ˈandaxt] f (-/-en) devo-tion(s pl.); prayers pl.

andächtig adj. [ˈandɛçtiç] devout.

'**andauern** v/i. (sep., -ge-, h) last, continue, go on.

'**Andenken** n (-s/-) memory, re-membrance; keepsake, souvenir; *zum* ~ *an* (acc.) in memory of.

ander adj. [ˈandər] other; differ-ent; next; opposite; *am* ~*en* Tag (on) the next day; e-n Tag um den ~en every other day; ein ~er Freund another friend; nichts ~es nothing else.

andererseits adv. [ˈandərərˈzaits] on the other hand.

ändern [ˈɛndərn] v/t. (ge-, h) alter, change; ich kann es nicht ~ I can't help it; sich ~ alter; change.

'**andern|falls** adv. otherwise, else.

anders adv. [ˈandərs] otherwise; differently (als from); else; j-~ somebody else; ich kann nicht ~, ich muß weinen I cannot help cry-ing; ~ werden change.

'**ander|seits** adv. s. andererseits. '**⁀wo** adv. elsewhere.

anderthalb adj. [ˈandərtˈhalp] one and a half. [tion.]

Änderung f (-/-en) change, altera-⌐

ander|wärts adv. [ˈandərˈverts] elsewhere; '**⁀weitig 1.** adj. other; 2. adv. otherwise.

'**andeuten** v/t. (sep., -ge-, h) indi-cate; hint; intimate; imply; sug-gest; '**⁀ung** f intimation; hint; suggestion.

'**Andrang** m rush; 🧬 congestion.

andre adj. [ˈandrə] s. andere.

'**andrehen** v/t. (sep., -ge-, h) turn on (gas, etc.); ⚡ switch on (light).

'**androh|en** v/t. (sep., -ge-, h): j-m et. ~ threaten s.o. with s.th.; '**⁀ung** f threat.

aneignen [ˈanˀ-] v/refl. (sep., -ge-, h) appropriate; acquire; adopt; seize; usurp.

aneinander adv. [anˀaiˈnandər] to-gether; **⁀geraten** v/i. (irr. raten, sep., no -ge-, sein) clash (mit with).

anekeln [ˈanˀ-] v/t. (sep., -ge-, h) disgust, sicken.

Anerbieten [ˈanˀ-] n (-s/-) offer.

anerkannt adj. [ˈanˀ-] acknowl-edged, recognized.

anerkenn|en [ˈanˀ-] v/t. (irr. ken-nen, sep., no -ge-, h) acknowledge (als as), recognize; appreciate; own (*child*); hono(u)r (*bill*); '2ung f (-/-en) acknowledgement; recognition; appreciation.

'anfahr|en (*irr. fahren, sep., -ge-*) **1.** *v/i.* (sein) start; ℀ descend; *angefahren kommen* drive up; **2.** *v/t.* (h) run into; carry, convey; *j-n* ~ let fly at s.o.; '2t f approach; drive.

'Anfall ⚕ m fit, attack; '2en (*irr. fallen, sep., -ge-*) **1.** *v/t.* (h) attack; assail; **2.** *v/i.* (sein) accumulate; *money:* accrue.

anfällig *adj.* ['anfɛliç] susceptible (*für* to); prone to (*diseases, etc.*).

'Anfang m beginning, start, commencement; ~ *Mai* at the beginning of May, early in May; '2en *v/t. and v/i.* (*irr. fangen, sep., -ge-*, h) begin, start, commence.

Anfäng|er ['anfɛŋər] m (-s/-) beginner; '2lich **1.** *adj.* initial; **2.** *adv.* in the beginning.

anfangs *adv.* ['anfaŋs] in the beginning; '2buchstabe m initial (letter); *großer* ~ capital letter; 2gründe ['~grʏndə] m/pl. elements pl.

'anfassen (*sep., -ge-*, h) **1.** *v/t.* seize; touch; handle; **2.** *v/i.* lend a hand.

anfecht|bar ⚖ ['anfɛçtbaːr] contestable; '~en *v/t.* (*irr. fechten, sep., -ge-*, h) contest, dispute; ⚖ avoid (*contract*); '2ung f (-/-en) contestation; ⚖ avoidance; *fig.* temptation.

an|fertigen ['anfɛrtigən] *v/t.* (*sep., -ge-*, h) make, manufacture; '~feuchten *v/t.* (*sep., -ge-*, h) moisten, wet, damp; '~feuern *v/t.* (*sep., -ge-*, h) fire, heat; *sports:* cheer; *fig.* encourage; '~flehen *v/t.* (*sep., -ge-*, h) implore; '~fliegen ✈ *v/t.* (*irr. fliegen, sep., -ge-*, h) approach, head for (*airport, etc.*); '2flug m ✈ approach (flight); *fig.* touch, tinge.

'anforder|n *v/t.* (*sep., -ge-*, h) demand; request; claim; '2ung f demand; request; claim.

'Anfrage f inquiry; '2n *v/i.* (*sep., -ge-*, h) ask (*bei j-m* s.o.); inquire (*bei j-m nach et.* of s.o. about s.th.).

an|freunden ['anfrɔʏndən] *v/refl.* (*sep., -ge-*, h): *sich* ~ *mit* make friends with; '~frieren *v/i.* (*irr. frieren, sep., -ge-*, sein) freeze on (*an dat. or acc.* to); '~fügen *v/t.* (*sep., -ge-*, h) join, attach (*an acc.* to); '~fühlen *v/t.* (*sep., -ge-*, h) feel, touch; *sich* ~ feel.

Anfuhr ['anfuːr] f (-/-en) conveyance, carriage.

'anführ|en *v/t.* (*sep., -ge-*, h) lead; allege; ✕ command; quote, cite (*authority, passage, etc.*); dupe, fool, trick; '2er m (ring)leader; '2ungszeichen *n/pl.* quotation marks pl., inverted commas pl.

'Angabe f declaration; statement; instruction; F *fig.* bragging, showing off.

'angeb|en (*irr. geben, sep., -ge-*, h) **1.** *v/t.* declare; state; specify; allege; give (*name, reason*); ✝ quote (*prices*); denounce, inform against; **2.** *v/i. cards:* deal first; F *fig.* brag, show off, *Am.* blow; '2er m (-s/-) informer; F braggart, *Am.* blowhard; '~lich *adj.* ['~pliç] supposed; pretended, alleged.

angeboren *adj.* innate, inborn; ⚕ congenital.

'Angebot n offer (*a.* ✝); *at auction sale:* bid; ✝ supply.

'ange|bracht *adj.* appropriate, suitable; well-timed; '~bunden *adj.*: *kurz* ~ *sein* be short (*gegen* with).

'angehen (*irr. gehen, sep., -ge-*) **1.** *v/i.* (sein) begin; *meat, etc.:* go bad, go off; *es geht an* it will do; **2.** *v/t.* (h): *j-n* ~ concern s.o.; *das geht dich nichts an* that is no business of yours.

'angehör|en *v/i.* (*sep., no -ge-*, h) belong to; 2ige ['~igə] m, f (-n/-n): *seine* ~n pl. his relations pl.; *die nächsten* ~n pl. the next of kin.

Angeklagte ⚖ ['angəklaːktə] m, f (-n/-n) *the* accused; prisoner (at the bar); defendant.

Angel ['aŋəl] f (-/-n) hinge; fishing-tackle, fishing-rod.

'angelegen *adj.*: *sich et.* ~ *sein lassen* make s.th. one's business; '2heit f business, concern, affair, matter.

'Angel|gerät n fishing-tackle; '2n (*ge-*, h) **1.** *v/i.* fish (*nach* for), angle (for) (*both a. fig.*); ~ *in* fish (*river, etc.*); **2.** *v/t.* fish (*trout*); '~punkt *fig.* m pivot.

'Angel|sachse m Anglo-Saxon; '2sächsisch *adj.* Anglo-Saxon.

'Angelschnur f fishing-line.

'ange|messen *adj.* suitable, appropriate; reasonable; adequate; '~nehm *adj.* pleasant, agreeable, pleasing; *sehr* ~! glad *or* pleased to meet you; **~regt** adj. ['~re:kt] stimulated; *discussion*: animated, lively; '**~sehen** adj. respected, esteemed.

Angesicht n (-[e]s/-er, -e) face, countenance; von ~ zu ~ face to face; '**2s** prp. (gen.) in view of.

ngestammt adj. ['angə∫tamt] hereditary, innate.

Angestellte ['angə∫teltə] m, f (-n/-n) employee; die ~n pl. the staff.

ange|trunken adj. tipsy; **~wandt** adj. ['~vant] applied; '**~wiesen** adj.: ~ sein auf (acc.) be dependent or thrown (up)on.

angewöhnen v/t. (sep., -ge-, h): j-m et. ~ accustom s.o. to s.th.; sich et. ~ get into the habit of s.th.; take to (smoking).

Angewohnheit f custom, habit.

Angina 🜊 [aŋ'gi:na] f (-/Anginen) angina; tonsillitis.

angleichen v/t. (irr. gleichen, sep., -ge-, h) assimilate (an acc. to, with), adjust (to); sich ~ an (acc.) assimilate to or with, adjust or adapt o.s. to.

Angler ['aŋlər] m (-s/-) angler.

angliedern v/t. (sep., -ge-, h) join; annex; affiliate.

Anglist [aŋ'glist] m (-en/-en) professor or student of English, Angli(ci)st.

angreif|en v/t. (irr. greifen, sep., -ge-, h) touch; draw upon (capital, provisions); attack; affect (health, material); 🜊 corrode; exhaust; '**2er** m (-s/-) aggressor, assailant.

angrenzend adj. adjacent; adjoining.

Angriff m attack, assault; in ~ nehmen set about; '**~skrieg** m offensive war; '**2slustig** adj. aggressive.

Angst [aŋst] f (-/⸚e) fear; anxiety; anguish; ich habe ~ I am afraid (vor dat. of); '**~hase** m coward.

ängstigen ['eŋstigən] v/t. (ge-, h) frighten, alarm; sich ~ be afraid (vor dat. of); be alarmed (um about).

ängstlich adj. ['eŋstliç] uneasy, nervous; anxious; afraid; scrupulous; timid; '**2keit** f (-/no pl.) anxiety; scrupulousness; timidity.

an|haben v/t. (irr. haben, sep., -ge-, h) have (garment) on; das kann mir nichts ~ that can't do me any harm; '**~haften** v/i. (sep., -ge-, h) stick, adhere (dat. to); '**~haken** v/t. (sep., -ge-, h) hook on; tick (off), Am. check (off) (name, item).

'anhalten (irr. halten, sep., -ge-, h) **1.** v/t. stop; j-n ~ zu et. keep s.o. to s.th.; den Atem ~ hold one's breath; **2.** v/i. continue, last; stop; um ein Mädchen ~ propose to a girl; '**~d** adj. continuous; persevering.

'Anhaltspunkt m clue.

'Anhang m appendix, supplement (to book, etc.); followers pl., adherents pl.

'anhäng|en (sep., -ge-, h) **1.** v/t. hang on; affix, attach, join; add; couple (on) (coach, vehicle); **2.** v/i. (irr. hängen) adhere to; '**2er** m (-s/-) adherent, follower; pendant (of necklace, etc.); label, tag; trailer (behind car, etc.).

anhänglich adj. ['anheŋliç] devoted, attached; '**2keit** f (-/no pl.) devotion, attachment.

Anhängsel ['anheŋzəl] n (-s/-) appendage.

'anhauchen v/t. (sep., -ge-, h) breathe on; blow (fingers).

'anhäuf|en v/t. and v/refl. (sep., -ge-, h) pile up, accumulate; '**2ung** f accumulation.

'an|heben v/t. (irr. heben, sep., -ge-, h) lift, raise; '**~heften** v/t. (sep., -ge-, h) fasten (an acc. to); stitch (to).

an'heim|fallen v/i. (irr. fallen, sep., -ge-, sein): j-m ~ fall to s.o.; **~stellen** v/t. (sep., -ge-, h): j-m et. ~ leave s.th. to s.o.

'Anhieb m: auf ~ at the first go.

'Anhöhe f rise, elevation, hill.

'anhören v/t. (sep., -ge-, h) listen to; sich ~ sound.

Anilin 🜊 [ani'li:n] n (-s/no pl.) anilin(e).

'ankämpfen v/i. (sep., -ge-, h): ~ gegen struggle against.

'Ankauf m purchase.

Anker ⚓ ['aŋkər] m (-s/-) anchor; vor ~ gehen cast anchor; '**~kette** ⚓ f cable; '**2n** ⚓ v/i. (ge-, h) anchor; '**~uhr** f lever watch.

'anketten v/t. (sep., -ge-, h) chain (an dat. or acc. to).

'Anklage f accusation, charge; ⚖ a. indictment; '**2n** v/t. (sep., -ge-, h) accuse (gen. or wegen of), charge (with); ⚖ a. indict (for).

'Ankläger m accuser; öffentlicher ~ ⚖ public prosecutor, Am. district attorney.

'anklammern v/t. (sep., -ge-, h)

clip *s.th.* on; *sich* ~ cling (*an dat. or acc.* to).

'Anklang m: ~ *an* (acc.) suggestion of; ~ *finden* meet with approval.

'an|kleben *v/t.* (*sep.*, *-ge-*, *h*) F stick on (*an dat. or acc.* to); glue on (to); paste on (to); gum on (to); **'~kleiden** *v/t.* (*sep.*, *-ge-*, *h*) dress; *sich* ~ dress (o.s.); **'~klopfen** *v/i.* (*sep.*, *-ge-*, *h*) knock (*an acc.* at); **'~knipsen** ⚡ *v/t.* (*sep.*, *-ge-*, *h*) turn *or* switch on; **'~knüpfen** (*sep.*, *-ge-*, *h*) **1.** *v/t.* tie (*an dat. or acc.* to); *fig.* begin; *Verbindungen* ~ form connexions *or* (*Am. only*) connections; **2.** *v/i.* refer (*an acc.* to); **'~kommen** *v/i.* (*irr. kommen*, *sep.*, *-ge-*, *sein*) arrive; ~ *auf* (acc.) depend (up)on; *es darauf* ~ *lassen* run the risk, risk it; *darauf kommt es an* that is the point; *es kommt nicht darauf an* it does not matter.

Ankömmling ['ankœmliŋ] *m* (*-s/-e*) new-comer, new arrival.

'ankündig|en *v/t.* (*sep.*, *-ge-*, *h*) announce; advertise; **'2ung** *f* announcement; advertisement.

Ankunft ['ankunft] *f* (*-/no pl.*) arrival.

'an|kurbeln *v/t.* (*sep.*, *-ge-*, *h*) mot. crank up; *die Wirtschaft* ~ F boost the economy; **'~lächeln** *v/t.* (*sep.*, *-ge-*, *h*), **'~lachen** *v/t.* (*sep.*, *-ge-*, *h*) smile at.

'Anlage *f* construction; installation; ⊕ plant; grounds *pl.*, park; plan, arrangement, layout; enclosure (*to letter*); ✝ investment; talent; predisposition, tendency; *öffentliche* ~*n pl.* public gardens *pl.*; **'~kapital** ✝ *n* invested capital.

'anlangen (*sep.*, *-ge-*) **1.** *v/i.* (*sein*) arrive at; **2.** *v/t.* (*h*) F touch; concern; *was mich anlangt* as far as I am concerned, (speaking) for myself.

Anlaß ['anlas] *m* (*Anlasses/Anlässe*) occasion; *ohne allen* ~ without any reason.

'anlass|en *v/t.* (*irr. lassen*, *sep.*, *-ge-*, *h*) F leave *or* keep (*garment, etc.*) on; leave (*light, etc.*) on; ⊕ start; set going; *sich gut* ~ promise well; **'2er** *mot. m* (*-s/-*) starter.

anläßlich *prp.* (*gen.*) ['anlesliç] on the occasion of.

'Anlauf *m* start, run; **'2en** (*irr. laufen*, *sep.*, *-ge-*) **1.** *v/i.* (*sein*) run up;

start; tarnish, (grow) dim; ~ *gegen* run against; **2.** ⚓ *v/t.* (*h*) call *or* touch at (*port*).

'an|legen (*sep.*, *-ge-*, *h*) **1.** *v/t.* put (*an acc.* to, against); lay out (*garden*); invest (*money*); level (*gun*); put on (*garment*); found (*town*); ✱ apply (*dressing*); lay in (*provisions*); *Feuer* ~ *an* (acc.) set fire to; **2.** *v/i.* ⚓: land; moor; ~ *auf* (acc.) aim at; **'~lehnen** *v/t.* (*sep.*, *-ge-*, *h*) lean (*an acc.* against); leave *or* set (*door*) ajar; *sich* ~ *an* (acc.) lean against *or* on.

Anleihe ['anlaɪə] *f* (*-/-n*) loan.

'anleit|en *v/t.* (*sep.*, *-ge-*, *h*) guide (*zu* to); instruct (*in dat.* in); **'2ung** *f* guidance, instruction; guide.

'Anliegen *n* (*-s/-*) desire, request.

'an|locken *v/t.* (*sep.*, *-ge-*, *h*) allure, entice; decoy; **'~machen** *v/t.* (*sep.*, *-ge-*, *h*) fasten (*an acc.* to), fix (to); make, light (*fire*); ⚡ switch on (*light*); dress (*salad*); **'~malen** *v/t.* (*sep.*, *-ge-*, *h*) paint.

'Anmarsch *m* approach.

anmaß|en ['anma:sən] *v/refl.* (*sep.*, *-ge-*, *h*) arrogate *s.th.* to o.s.; assume (*right*); presume; **'~end** *adj.* arrogant; **'2ung** *f* (*-/-en*) arrogance, presumption.

'anmeld|en *v/t.* (*sep.*, *-ge-*, *h*) announce, notify; *sich* ~ *bei* make an appointment with; **'2ung** *f* announcement, notification.

'anmerk|en *v/t.* (*sep.*, *-ge-*, *h*) mark; note down; *j-m et.* ~ observe *or* perceive *s.th.* in *s.o.*; **'2ung** *f* (*-/-en*) remark; note; annotation; comment.

'anmessen *v/t.* (*irr. messen*, *sep.*, *-ge-*, *h*): *j-m e-n Anzug* ~ measure *s.o.* for a suit; *s. angemessen.*

'Anmut *f* (*-/no pl.*) grace, charm, loveliness; **'2ig** *adj.* charming, graceful, lovely.

'an|nageln *v/t.* (*sep.*, *-ge-*, *h*) nail on (*an acc.* to); **'~nähen** *v/t.* (*sep.*, *-ge-*, *h*) sew on (*an acc.* to).

annäher|nd *adj.* ['annɛ:ərnt] approximate; **'2ung** *f* (*-/-en*) approach.

Annahme ['anna:mə] *f* (*-/-n*) acceptance; receiving-office; *fig.* assumption, supposition.

'annehm|bar *adj.* acceptable; *price*: reasonable; **'~en** (*irr. nehmen*, *sep.*, *-ge-*, *h*) **1.** *v/t.* accept, take; *fig.*:

suppose, take it, *Am.* guess; assume; contract (*habit*); adopt
(*child*); *parl.* pass (*bill*); *sich*
(*gen.*) ~ attend to s.th.; befriend
s.o.; **2.** *v/i.* accept; **˚lichkeit** *f*
(-/-en) amenity, agreeableness.

Annexion [anɛkˈsjoːn] *f* (-/-en) an-
nexation.

Annonce [aˈnõːsə] *f* (-/-en) advertisement.   [mous.⟩

anonym *adj.* [anoˈnyːm] anony-⟩

anordn|en [ˈanʔ-] *v/t.* (sep., -ge-, h)
order; arrange; direct; **˚ung** *f*
arrangement; direction; order.

anpacken *v/t.* (sep., -ge-, h) seize,
grasp; *fig.* tackle.

anpass|en *v/t.* (sep., -ge-, h) fit,
adapt, suit; adjust; try *or* fit (*garment*) on; *sich* ~ adapt o.s. (*dat.* to);
˚ung *f* (-/-en) adaptation; **˚ungs-
fähig** *adj.* adaptable.

anpflanz|en *v/t.* (sep., -ge-, h) cul-
tivate, plant; **˚ung** *f* cultivation;
plantation.

Anprall [ˈanpral] *m* (-[e]s/⁊-e)
impact; *fig.* *v/i.* (sep., -ge-, sein)
strike (*an acc.* against).

anpreisen *v/t.* (*irr.* preisen, sep.,
-ge-, h) commend, praise; boost,
push.

Anprobe *f* try-on, fitting.

an|probieren *v/t.* (sep., no -ge-, h)
try *or* fit on; **˚raten** *v/t.* (*irr.* raten,
sep., -ge-, h) advise; **˚rechnen** *v/t.*
(sep., -ge-, h) charge; hoch ~ value
highly.

Anrecht *n* right, title, claim (*auf
acc.* to).

Anrede *f* address; **˚n** *v/t.* (sep.,
-ge-, h) address, speak to.

anreg|en *v/t.* (sep., -ge-, h) stimu-
late; suggest; **˚end** *adj.* stimula-
tive, stimulating; suggestive; **˚ung**
f stimulation; suggestion.

Anreiz *m* incentive; **˚en** *v/t.* (sep.,
-ge-, h) stimulate; incite.

an|rennen *v/i.* (*irr.* rennen, sep.,
-ge-, sein): ~ gegen run against;
angerannt kommen come running;
˚richten *v/t.* (sep., -ge-, h) prepare, dress (*food, salad*); cause, do
(*damage*).

anrüchig *adj.* [ˈanrʏçiç] disrepu-
table.

anrücken *v/i.* (sep., -ge-, sein)
approach.

Anruf *m* call (*a.* teleph.); **˚en** *v/t.*
(*irr.* rufen, sep., -ge-, h) call (*zum

Zeugen* to witness); *teleph.* ring up,
F phone, *Am.* call up; hail (*ship*);
invoke (*God, etc.*); appeal to (*s.o.'s
help*).

anrühren *v/t.* (sep., -ge-, h) touch;
mix.

Ansage *f* announcement; **˚n** *v/t.*
(sep., -ge-, h) announce; **˚r** *m* (-s/-)
announcer; compère, *Am.* master
of ceremonies.

ansammeln *v/t.* (sep., -ge-, h) collect, gather; accumulate, amass;
sich ~ collect, gather; accumulate.

ansässig *adj.* [ˈanzɛsiç] resident.

Ansatz *m* start.

an|schaffen *v/t.* (sep., -ge-, h) pro-
cure, provide; purchase; *sich et.* ~
provide *or* supply o.s. with s.th.;
˚schalten *⚡ v/t.* (sep., -ge-, h)
connect; switch on (*light*).

anschau|en *v/t.* (sep., -ge-, h) look
at, view; **˚lich** *adj.* clear, vivid;
graphic.

Anschauung *f* (-/-en) view; perception; conception; intuition;
contemplation; **˚smaterial** [-ʔ-] visual or illus-
trative material; **˚sunterricht** [ˈan-
ʃauʊŋʔ-] *m* visual instruction, ob-
ject-lessons *pl.*; **˚svermögen** *n*
intuitive faculty.

Anschein *m* (-[e]s/*no pl.*) appearance; **˚end** *adj.* apparent, seeming.

an|schicken *v/refl.* (sep., -ge-, h):
sich ~, et. zu tun get ready for s.th.;
prepare for s.th.; set about doing
s.th.; **˚schirren** [ˈʃirən] *v/t.* (sep.,
-ge-, h) harness.

Anschlag *m* ⊕ stop, catch; ♪
touch; notice; placard, poster, bill;
estimate; calculation; plot; e-n ~
auf j-n verüben make an attempt on
s.o.'s life; **˚brett** [ˈ-k-] *n* notice-
board, *Am.* bulletin board; **˚en**
[ˈ-ɡən] (*irr.* schlagen, sep., -ge-, h)
1. *v/t.* strike (*an dat. or acc.* against),
knock (against); post up (*bill*); ♪
touch; level (*gun*); estimate, rate;
2. *v/i.* strike (*an acc.* against), knock
(against); *dog*: bark; ⚔ take (effect);
food: agree (*bei* with); **˚säule**
[ˈ-k-] *f* advertising pillar; **˚zettel**
[ˈ-k-] *m* notice; placard, poster, bill.

anschließen *v/t.* (*irr.* schließen,
sep., -ge-, h) fix with a lock; join,
attach, annex; ⊕, ⚡ connect; *sich
j-m* ~ join s.o.; *sich e-r Meinung* ~
follow an opinion; **˚d** *adj.* adjacent
(*an acc.* to); subsequent (to).

Anschluß m joining; ⚙, ⚡, teleph., gas, etc.: connexion, (Am. only) connection; ~ haben an (acc.) 🚂, boat: connect with; ~ run in connexion with; ~ finden make friends (an acc. with), F pal up (with); teleph.: ~ bekommen get through; '~dose ⚡ f (wall) socket; '~zug 🚂 m connecting train, connexion.

an|schmiegen v/refl. (sep., -ge-, h): sich ~ an (acc.) nestle to; '~schmieren v/t. (sep., -ge-, h) (be)smear, grease; F fig. cheat; '~schnallen v/t. (sep., -ge-, h) buckle on; bitte ~! ✈ fasten seat-belts, please!; '~schnauzen F v/t. (sep., -ge-, h) snap at, blow s.o. up, Am. a. bawl s.o. out; '~schneiden v/t. (irr. schneiden, sep., -ge-, h) cut; broach (subject).

Anschnitt m first cut or slice.

an|schrauben v/t. (sep., -ge-, h) screw on (an dat. or acc. to); '~schreiben v/t. (irr. schreiben, sep., -ge-, h) write down; sports, games: score; et. ~ lassen have s.th. charged to one's account; buy s.th. on credit; '~schreien v/t. (irr. schreien, sep., -ge-, h) shout at.

Anschrift f address.

an|schuldigen ['anʃuldıgən] v/t. (sep., -ge-, h) accuse, incriminate; '~schwärzen v/t. (sep., -ge-, h) blacken; fig. a. defame.

anschwell|en (irr. schwellen, sep., -ge-) **1.** v/i. (sein) swell; increase, rise; **2.** v/t. (h) swell; '2ung f swelling.

anschwemm|en ['anʃvɛmən] v/t. (sep., -ge-, h) wash ashore; geol. deposit (alluvium); '2ung f (-/-en) wash; geol. alluvial deposits pl., alluvium.

ansehen 1. v/t. (irr. sehen, sep., -ge-, h) (take a) look at; view; regard, consider (als as); et. mit ~ witness s.th.; ~ für take for; man sieht ihm sein Alter nicht an he does not look his age; **2.** 2 n (-s/no pl.) authority, prestige; respect; F appearance, aspect.

ansehnlich adj. ['anze:nlıç] considerable; good-looking.

an|seilen mount. v/t. and v/refl. (sep., -ge-, h) rope; '~sengen v/t. (sep., -ge-, h) singe; '~setzen (sep., -ge-, h) **1.** v/t. put (an acc. to); add (to); fix, appoint (date); rate; fix,

quote (prices); charge; put forth (leaves, etc.); put on (flesh); put (food) on (to boil); Rost ~ rust; **2.** v/i. try; start; get ready.

Ansicht f (-/-en) sight, view; fig. view, opinion; meiner ~ nach in my opinion; zur ~ ✝ on approval; '~s-(post)karte f picture postcard; '~ssache f matter of opinion.

ansied|eln v/t. and v/refl. (sep., -ge-, h) settle; '2ler m settler; '2lung f settlement.

Ansinnen n (-s/-) request, demand.

anspann|en v/t. (sep., -ge-, h) stretch; put or harness (horses, etc.) to the carriage, etc.; fig. strain, exert; '2ung fig. f strain, exertion.

anspeien v/t. (irr. speien, sep., -ge-, h) spit (up)on or at.

anspiel|en v/i. (sep., -ge-, h) cards: lead; sports: lead off; football: kick off; ~ auf (acc.) allude to, hint at; '2ung f (-/-en) allusion, hint.

anspitzen v/t. (sep., -ge-, h) point, sharpen.

Ansporn m (-[e]s/⚡ -e) spur; '2en v/t. (sep., -ge-, h) spur s.o. on.

Ansprache f address, speech; e-e ~ halten deliver an address.

ansprechen v/t. (irr. sprechen, sep., -ge-, h) speak to, address; appeal to; '~d adj. appealing.

an|springen (irr. springen, sep., -ge-) **1.** v/i. (sein) engine: start; **2.** v/t. (h) jump (up)on, leap at; '~spritzen v/t. (sep., -ge-, h) splash (j-n mit et. s.th. on s.o.); (be-) sprinkle.

Anspruch m claim (a. 🏛) (auf acc. to), pretension (to); 🏛 title (to); ~ haben auf (acc.) be entitled to; in ~ nehmen claim s.th.; Zeit in ~ nehmen take up time; '2slos adj. unpretentious; unassuming; '2svoll adj. pretentious.

an|spülen v/t. (sep., -ge-, h) s. anschwemmen; '~stacheln v/t. (sep., -ge-, h) goad (on).

Anstalt ['anʃtalt] f (-/-en) establishment, institution; ~en treffen zu make arrangements for.

Anstand m **1.** (-[e]s/⚡ -e) hunt. stand; objection; **2.** (-[e]s/⚡ -e) good manners pl.; decency, propriety.

anständig adj. ['anʃtɛndıç] decent; respectable; price: fair, handsome; '2keit f (-/⚡) decency.

Anstands|gefühl n sense of propri-

'**anstarren** v/t. (sep., -ge-, h) stare or gaze at.

anstatt prp. (gen.) and cj. [an'ʃtat] instead of.

'**anstaunen** v/t. (sep., -ge-, h) gaze at s.o. or s.th. in wonder.

'**ansteck|en** v/t. (sep., -ge-, h) pin on; put on (ring); 🟥 infect; set on fire; kindle (fire); light (candle, etc.); '~**end** adj. infectious; contagious; fig. a. catching; '2**ung** 🟥 f (-/-en) infection; contagion.

'**an|stehen** v/i. (irr. stehen, sep., -ge-, h) queue up (nach for), Am. stand in line (for); '~**steigen** v/i. (irr. steigen, sep., -ge-, sein) ground: rise, ascend; fig. increase.

'**anstell|en** v/t. (sep., -ge-, h) engage, employ, hire; make (experiments); draw (comparison); turn on (light, etc.); manage; sich ~ queue up (nach for), Am. line up (for); sich dumm ~ set about s.th. stupidly; '~**ig** adj. handy, skil(l)ful; '2**ung** f place, position, job; employment.

Anstieg ['anʃtiːk] m (-[e]s/-e) ascent.

'**anstift|en** v/t. (sep., -ge-, h) instigate; '2**er** m instigator; '2**ung** f instigation.

'**anstimmen** v/t. (sep., -ge-, h) strike up (tune).

'**Anstoß** m football: kick-off; fig. impulse; offen|ce, Am. -se; ~ erregen give offence (bei to); ~ nehmen an (dat.) take offence at; ~ geben zu et. start s.th., initiate s.th.; '2**en** (irr. stoßen, sep., -ge-) **1.** v/t. (h) push, knock (acc. or an against); nudge; **2.** v/i. (sein) knock (an acc. against); border (on, upon); adjoin; **3.** v/i. (h): mit der Zunge ~ lisp; auf j-s Gesundheit ~ drink (to) s.o.'s health; '~**end** adj. adjoining.

anstößig adj. ['anʃtøːsiç] shocking.

'**an|strahlen** v/t. (sep., -ge-, h) illuminate; floodlight (building, etc.); fig. beam at s.o.; '~**streben** v/t. (sep., -ge-, h) aim at, aspire to, strive for.

'**anstreich|en** v/t. (irr. streichen, sep., -ge-, h) paint; whitewash; mark; underline (mistake); '2**er** m (-s/-) house-painter; decorator.

anstreng|en ['anʃtrɛŋən] v/t. (sep., -ge-, h) exert; try (eyes); fatigue; Prozeß ~ bring an action (gegen j-n against s.o.); sich ~ exert o.s.; '~**end** adj. strenuous; trying (für to); '2**ung** f (-/-en) exertion, strain, effort.

'**Anstrich** m paint, colo(u)r; coat (-ing); fig.: tinge; air.

'**Ansturm** m assault; onset; ~ auf (acc.) rush for; ✝ run on (bank).

'**anstürmen** v/i. (sep., -ge-, sein) storm, rush.

'**Anteil** m share, portion; ~ nehmen an (dat.) take an interest in; sympathize with; '~**nahme** ['~naːmə] f (-/no pl.) sympathy; interest; '~**schein** ✝ m share-certificate.

Antenne [an'tɛnə] f (-/-n) aerial!.

Antialkoholiker [anti'alko'hoːlikər, '~] m (-s/-) teetotaller.

antik adj. [an'tiːk] antique.

Antilope zo. [anti'loːpə] f (-/-n) antelope.

Antipathie [antipa'tiː] f (-/-n) antipathy.

'**antippen** F v/t. (sep., -ge-, h) tap.

Antiquar [anti'kvaːr] m (-s/-e) second-hand bookseller; ~**iat** [~'jaːt] n (-[e]s/-e) second-hand bookshop; 2**isch** adj. and adv. [~'kvaːriʃ] second-hand.

Antiquitäten [antikvi'tɛːtən] f/pl. antiques pl.

'**Anti-Rakete** f anti-ballistic missile.

antiseptisch 🟥 adj. [anti'zɛptiʃ] antiseptic.

Antlitz ['antlits] n (-es/🟥 -e) face, countenance.

Antrag ['antraːk] m (-[e]s/🟥e) offer, proposal; application, request; parl. motion; ~ stellen auf (acc.) make an application for; parl. put a motion for; '~**steller** m (-s/-) applicant; parl. mover; 🟥🟥 petitioner.

'**an|treffen** v/t. (irr. treffen, sep., -ge-, h) meet with, find; '~**treiben** (irr. treiben, sep., -ge-) **1.** v/i. (sein) drift ashore; **2.** v/t. (h) drive (on); fig. impel; '~**treten** (irr. treten, sep., -ge-) **1.** v/t. (h) enter upon (office); take up (position); set out on (journey); enter upon take possession of (inheritance); **2.** v/i. (sein) take one's place; ✕ fall in.

'**Antrieb** m motive, impulse; ⊕ drive, propulsion.

'**Antritt** m (-[e]s/🟥 -e) entrance (into office); taking up (of position); setting out (on journey); entering into possession (of inheritance).

'**antun** v/t. (irr. tun, sep., -ge-, h): j-m et. ~ do s.th. to s.o.; sich et. ~ lay hands on o.s.

'**Antwort** f (-/-en) answer, reply (auf acc. to); '**2en** (ge-) **1.** v/i. answer (j-m s.o.), reply (j-m to s.o.; both: auf acc. to); **2.** v/t. answer (auf acc. to), reply (to); '**~schein** m (international) reply coupon.

'**an|vertrauen** v/t. (sep., no -ge-, h): j-m et. ~ (en)trust s.th. with s.th., entrust s.th. to s.o.; confide s.th. to s.o.; '**~wachsen** v/i. (irr. wachsen, sep., -ge-, sein) take root; fig. increase; ~ an (acc.) grow on to.

Anwalt ['anvalt] m (-[e]s/⸚e) lawyer; solicitor, Am. attorney; counsel; barrister, Am. counsel(l)or; fig. advocate.

'**Anwandlung** f fit; impulse.

'**Anwärter** m candidate, aspirant; expectant.

Anwartschaft ['anvartʃaft] f (-/-en) expectancy; candidacy; prospect (auf acc. of).

'**anweis|en** v/t. (irr. weisen, sep., -ge-, h) assign; instruct; direct; s. angewiesen; '**2ung** f assignment; instruction; direction; ✝: cheque, Am. check; draft; s. Postanweisung.

'**anwend|en** v/t. ([irr. wenden] sep., -ge-, h) employ, use; apply (auf acc. to); s. angewandt; '**2ung** f application.

'**anwerben** v/t. (irr. werben, sep., -ge-, h) ✕ enlist, enrol(l); engage.

'**Anwesen** n estate; property.

'**anwesen|d** adj. present; '**2heit** f (-/no pl.) presence.

'**Anzahl** f (-/no pl.) number; quantity.

'**anzahl|en** v/t. (sep., -ge-, h) pay on account; pay a deposit; '**2ung** f (first) instal(l)ment; deposit.

'**anzapfen** v/t. (sep., -ge-, h) tap.

'**Anzeichen** n symptom; sign.

Anzeige ['antsaigə] f (-/-n) notice, announcement; ✝ advice; advertisement; ⚖ information; '**2n** v/t. (sep., -ge-, h) announce, notify; ✝ advise; advertise; indicate; ⊕ instrument: indicate, show; thermometer: read (degrees); j-n ~ denounce s.o., inform against s.o.

'**anziehen** (irr. ziehen, sep., -ge-, h) **1.** v/t. draw, pull; draw (rein); tighten (screw); put on (garment);

dress; fig. attract; **2.** v/i. draw; prices: rise; '**~d** adj. attractive, interesting.

'**Anziehung** f attraction; '**~skraft** f attractive power; attraction.

'**Anzug** m **1.** -[e]s/⸚e) dress; suit; **2.** (-[e]s/no pl.): im ~ sein storm: be gathering; danger: be impending.

anzüglich adj. ['antsy:kliç] personal; '**2keit** f (-/-en) personality.

'**anzünden** v/t. (sep., -ge-, h) light, kindle; strike (match); set (building) on fire.

apathisch adj. [a'pa:tiʃ] apathetic.

Apfel ['apfəl] m (-s/⸚) apple; '**~mus** n apple-sauce; **~sine** [⸚'zi:nə] f (-/-n) orange; '**~wein** m cider.

Apostel [a'pɔstəl] m (-s/-) apostle.

Apostroph [apɔ'stro:f] m (-s/-e) apostrophe.

Apotheke [apo'te:kɔ] f (-/-n) chemist's shop, pharmacy, Am. drugstore; **~r** m (-s/-) chemist, Am. druggist, pharmacist.

Apparat [apa'ra:t] m (-[e]s/-e) apparatus; device; teleph.: am ~! speaking!; teleph.: am ~ bleiben hold the line.

Appell [a'pɛl] m (-s/-e) ✕: roll-call; inspection; parade; fig. appeal (an acc. to); **2ieren** [⸚'li:rən] v/i. (no -ge-, h) appeal (an acc. to).

Appetit [ape'ti:t] m (-[e]s/-e) appetite; **2lich** adj. appetizing, savo(u)ry, dainty.

Applaus [a'plaus] m (-es/⸚ -e) applause.

Aprikose [apri'ko:zə] f (-/-n) apricot.

April [a'pril] m (-[s]/-e) April.

Aquarell [akva'rɛl] n (-s/-e) watercolo(u)r (painting), aquarelle.

Aquarium [a'kva:rium] n (-s/ Aquarien) aquarium.

Äquator [ɛ'kva:tɔr] m (-s/⸚ -en) equator.

Ära ['ɛ:ra] f (-/⸚ Ären) era.

Arab|er ['arabɔr] m (-s/-) Arab; **2isch** adj. [a'ra:biʃ] Arabian, Arab(ic).

Arbeit ['arbart] f (-/-en) work; labo(u)r, toil; employment, job; task; paper; workmanship; bei der ~ at work; sich an die ~ machen, an die ~ gehen set to work; (keine) ~ haben be in (out of) work; die ~ niederlegen stop work, down tools;

'²en (ge-, h) **1.** *v/i.* work; labo(u)r,
toil; **2.** *v/t.* work; make.

'**Arbeiter** *m* (-s/-) worker; work-
man, labo(u)rer, hand; '**⸗in** *f*
(-/-nen) female worker; working
woman, workwoman; '**⸗klasse** *f*
working class(es *pl.*); '**⸗partei** *f*
Labo(u)r Party; '**⸗schaft** *f* (-/-en),
'**⸗stand** *m* working class(es *pl.*),
labo(u)r.

'**Arbeit|geber** *m* (-s/-), '**⸗geberin** *f*
(-/-nen) employer; '**⸗nehmer** *m*
(-s/-), '**⸗nehmerin** *f* (-/-nen)
employee.

'**arbeitsam** *adj.* industrious.

'**Arbeits|amt** *n* labo(u)r exchange;
'**⸗anzug** *m* overall; '**⸗beschaffung**
f (-/-en) provision of work; '**⸗be-
scheinigung** *f* certificate of employment; '**⸗einkommen** *n* earned
income; '**²fähig** *adj.* able to work;
'**⸗gericht** *n* labo(u)r *or* industrial
court; '**⸗kleidung** *f* working
clothes *pl.*; '**⸗kraft** *f* working
power; worker, hand; *Arbeitskräfte
pl.* a. labo(u)r; '**⸗leistung** *f* efficiency; power (*of engine*); output
(*of factory*); '**⸗lohn** *m* wages *pl.*,
pay; '**²los** *adj.* out of work, unemployed; '**⸗lose** *m* (-n/-n): *die* ~n
pl. the unemployed *pl.*; '**⸗losen-
unterstützung** *f* unemployment
benefit; ~ *beziehen* F be on the dole;
'**⸗losigkeit** *f* (-/*no pl.*) unemployment; '**⸗markt** *m* labo(u)r market;
'**⸗minister** *m* Minister of Labour,
Am. Secretary of Labor; '**⸗nach-
weis(stelle** *f*) *m* employment
registry office, *Am.* labor registry
office; '**⸗niederlegung** *f* (-/-en)
strike, *Am.* F a. walkout; '**⸗pause** *f*
break, intermission; '**⸗platz** *m* place
of work; job; '**⸗raum** *m* workroom; '**²scheu** *adj.* work-shy;
'**⸗scheu** *f* aversion to work; '**⸗
schutzgesetz** *n* protective labo(u)r
law; '**⸗tag** *m* working day, workday; '**²unfähig** *adj.* incapable of
working; disabled; '**⸗weise** *f* practice, method of working; '**⸗willige**
m (-n/-n) non-striker; '**⸗zeit** *f*
working time; working hours *pl.*;
'**⸗zeug** *n* tools *pl.*; '**⸗zimmer** *n*
workroom; study.

Archäo|loge [arçeo'lo:gə] *m* (-n/-n)
arch(a)eologist; **⸗logie** [₋o'gi:] *f*
(-/*no pl.*) arch(a)eology.

Arche ['arçə] *f* (-/-n) ark.

Architekt [arçi'tɛkt] *m* (-en/-en)
architect; **⸗ur** [₋'tu:r] *f* (-/-en)
architecture.

Archiv [ar'çi:f] *n* (-s/-e) archives *pl.*;
record office.

Areal [are'a:l] *n* (-s/-e) area.

Arena [a're:na] *f* (-/*Arenen*) arena;
bullring; (circus-)ring.

arg *adj.* [ark] bad; wicked; gross.

Ärger ['ɛrgər] *m* (-s/*no pl.*) vexation,
annoyance; anger; '**²lich** *adj.*
vexed, F mad, angry (*auf, über acc.*
at *s.th.*, with *s.o.*); annoying, vex-
atious; '**²n** *v/t.* (ge-, *h*) annoy, vex,
irritate, fret; bother; *sich* ~ feel
angry *or* vexed (*über acc.* at, about
s.th.; with *s.o.*); '**⸗nis** *n* (-ses/-se)
scandal, offen|ce, *Am.* -se.

'**Arg|list** *f* (-/*no pl.*) cunning, craft
(-iness); '**²listig** *adj.* crafty, cunning; '**²los** *adj.* guileless; artless,
unsuspecting; **⸗wohn** ['~vo:n] *m*
(-[e]s/*no pl.*) suspicion; '**²wöhnen**
['~vø:nən] *v/t.* (ge-, *h*) suspect;
'**²wöhnisch** *adj.* suspicious.

Arie ♪ ['a:rjə] *f* (-/-n) aria.

Aristokrat [aristo'kra:t] *m* (-en/-en),
⸗in *f* (-/-nen) aristocrat; **⸗ie** [₋kra-
'ti:] *f* (-/-n) aristocracy.

Arkade [ar'ka:də] *f* (-/-n) arcade.

arm[1] *adj.* [arm] poor.

Arm[2] [~] *m* (-[e]s/-e) arm; branch
(*of river, etc.*); F: *j-n auf den* ~
nehmen pull s.o.'s leg.

Armaturenbrett [arma'tu:rənbrɛt]
n instrument board, dash-board.

'**Arm|band** *n* bracelet; **⸗banduhr**
['armbant⁹-] *f* wrist watch; '**⸗
bruch** *m* fracture of the arm.

Armee [ar'me:] *f* (-/-n) army.

Ärmel ['ɛrməl] *m* (-s/-) sleeve;
'**⸗kanal** *m the* (English) Channel.

'**Armen|haus** *n* alms-house, *Brt.*
a. workhouse; '**⸗pflege** *f* poor
relief; '**⸗pfleger** *m* guardian of the
poor; welfare officer; '**⸗unter-
stützung** *f* poor relief.

ärmlich *adj.* ['ɛrmliç] *s.* armselig.

'**armselig** *adj.* poor; wretched;
miserable; shabby; paltry.

Armut ['armu:t] *f* (-/*no pl.*) poverty.

Aroma [a'ro:ma] *n* (-s/*Aromen,
Aromata, -s*) aroma, flavo(u)r;
fragrance.

Arrest [a'rɛst] *m* (-es/-e) arrest;
confinement; seizure (*of goods*);
detention (*of pupil, etc.*); ~ *bekommen* be kept in.

Art [ɑːrt] f (-/-en) kind, sort; ♀, zo. species; manner, way; nature; manners pl.; breed, race (of animals); auf die(se) ~ in this way; '℃en v/i. (ge-, sein): ~ nach take after. [artery.\

Arterie anat. [ar'teːrjə] f (-/-n)\

artig adj. ['ɑːrtiç] good, well-behaved; civil, polite; '℃keit f (-/-en) good behavio(u)r; politeness; civility, a. civilities pl.

Artikel [ar'tiːkəl] m (-s/-) article; commodity.

Artillerie [artilə'riː] f (-/-n) artillery.

Artist [ar'tist] m (-en/-en), **~in** f (-/-nen) circus performer.

Arznei [arts'naɪ] f (-/-en) medicine, F physic; **~kunde** f (-/no pl.) pharmaceutics; **~mittel** n medicine, drug.

Arzt [ɑːrtst] m (-es/ᵘe) doctor, medical man; physician.

Ärztin ['ɛːrtstin] f (-/-nen) woman or lady doctor.

ärztlich adj. ['ɛːrtstliç] medical.

As [as] n (-ses/-se) ace.

Asche ['aʃə] f (-/-n) ash(es pl.); '**~nbahn** f sports: cinder-track, mot. dirt-track; '**~nbecher** m ash-tray; **~nbrödel** ['~nbrøːdəl] n (-s/no pl.), **~nputtel** ['~nputəl] n 1. (-s/no pl.) Cinderella; 2. (-s/-) drudge.

Ascher'mittwoch m Ash Wednesday.

'**asch'grau** adj. ash-grey, ashy, Am. ash-gray.

äsen hunt. ['ɛːzən] v/i. (ge-, h) graze, browse.

Asiat [az'jɑːt] m (-en/-en), **~in** f (-/-nen) Asiatic, Asian; ℃isch adj. Asiatic, Asian.

Asket [as'keːt] m (-en/-en) ascetic.

Asphalt [as'falt] m (-[e]s/-e) asphalt; ℃ieren [~'tiːrən] v/t. (no -ge-, h) asphalt.

aß [ɑːs] pret. of essen.

Assistent [asis'tent] m (-en/-en), **~in** f (-/-nen) assistant.

Ast [ast] m (-es/ᵘe) branch, bough; knot (in timber); '**~loch** n knot-hole.

Astro'naut [astro'naʊt] m (-en/-en) astronaut; **~nom** [~'noːm] m (-en/-en) astronomer.

Asyl [a'zyːl] n (-s/-e) asylum; fig. sanctuary.

Atelier [atə'lje:] n (-s/-s) studio.

Atem ['ɑːtəm] m (-s/no pl.) breath;

außer ~ out of breath; '℃los adj. breathless; '**~not** f difficulty in breathing; '**~pause** f breathing-space; '**~zug** m breath, respiration.

Äther ['ɛːtər] m 1. (-s/no pl.) the ether; 2. ♣ (-s/-) ether; ℃isch adj. [ε'teːriʃ] ethereal, etheric.

Athlet [at'leːt] m (-en/-en), **~in** f (-/-nen) athlete; **~ik** f (-/no pl.) athletics mst sg.; ℃isch adj. athletic.

atlantisch adj. [at'lantiʃ] Atlantic.

Atlas ['atlas] m 1. geogr. (-/no pl.) Atlas; 2. (-, -ses/-se, Atlanten) maps: atlas; 3. (-, -ses/-se) textiles: satin.

atmen ['ɑːtmən] v/i. and v/t. (ge-, h) breathe.

Atmosphär|e [atmo'sfɛːrə] f (-/-n) atmosphere; ℃isch adj. atmospheric.

'**Atmung** f (-/-en) breathing, respiration.

Atom [a'toːm] n (-s/-e) atom; ℃ar adj. [ato'mɑːr] atomic; **~bombe** f atomic bomb, atom-bomb, A-bomb; **~energie** f atomic or nuclear energy; **~forschung** f atomic or nuclear research; **~kern** m atomic nucleus; **~kraftwerk** n nuclear power station; **~meiler** m atomic pile, nuclear reactor; **~physiker** m atomic physicist; **~reaktor** m nuclear reactor, atomic pile; **~versuch** m atomic test; **~waffe** f atomic or nuclear weapon; **~wissenschaftler** m atomic scientist; **~zeitalter** n atomic age.

Attent|at [aten'tɑːt] n (-[e]s/-e) (attempted) assassination; fig. outrage; **~äter** [~eːtər] m (-s/-) assailant, assassin.

Attest [a'test] n (-es/-e) certificate; ℃ieren [~'tiːrən] v/t. (no -ge-, h) attest, certify.

Attraktion [atrak'tsjoːn] f (-/-en) attraction.

Attrappe [a'trapə] f (-/-n) dummy.

Attribut [atri'buːt] n (-[e]s/-e) attribute; gr. attributive.

ätz|en ['etsən] v/t. (ge-, h) corrode; ♣ cauterize; etch (metal plate); '**~end** adj. corrosive; caustic (a. fig.); '℃ung f (-/-en) corrosion; ♣ cauterization; etching.

au int. [aʊ] oh!; ouch!

auch cj. [aʊx] also, too, likewise; even; ~ nicht neither, nor; wo ~ (immer) wher(eso)ever; ist es ~ wahr? is it really true?

Audienz [audi'ɛnts] *f* (-/-en) audience, hearing.

auf [auf] **1.** *prp.* (*dat.*) (up)on; in; at; of; by; ~ *dem Tisch* (up)on the table; ~ *dem Markt* in the market; ~ *der Universität* at the university; ~ *e-m Ball* at a ball; **2.** *prp.* (*acc.*) on; in; at; to; towards (*a.* ~ ... *zu*); up; ~ *deutsch* in German; ~ *e-e Entfernung von* at a range of; ~ *die Post etc.* gehen go to the post-office, *etc.*; ~ *ein Pfund gehen 20 Schilling* 20 shillings go to a pound; *es geht* ~ *neun* it is getting on to nine; ~ ... *hin* on the strength of; **3.** *adv.* up(wards); ~ *und ab gehen* walk up and down *or* to and fro; **4.** *cj.*: ~ *daß* (in order) that; ~ *daß nicht* that not, lest; **5.** *int.*: ~! up!

auf|arbeiten ['auf⁹-] *v/t.* (*sep.*, -ge-, h) work off (*arrears of work*); furbish up; F do up (*garments*); **~atmen** fig. ['auf⁹-] *v/i.* (*sep.*, -ge-, h) breathe again.

Aufbau *m* (-[e]s/no pl.) building up; construction (*of play, etc.*); F *esp. Am.* setup (*of organization*); *mot.* body (of car, etc.); **2en** *v/t.* (*sep.*, -ge-, h) erect, build up; construct.

auf|bauschen *v/t.* (*sep.*, -ge-, h) puff out; *fig.* exaggerate; **~beißen** *v/t.* (*irr.* beißen, sep., -ge-, h) crack; **~bekommen** *v/t.* (*irr.* kommen, sep., no -ge-, h) get open (*door*); be given (*a task*); **~bessern** *v/t.* (*sep.*, -ge-, h) raise (*salary*); **~bewahren** *v/t.* (*sep.*, no -ge-, h) keep; preserve; **~bieten** *v/t.* (*irr.* bieten, sep., -ge-, h) summon; exert; ✕ raise; **~binden** *v/t.* (*irr.* binden, sep., -ge-, h) untie; **~bleiben** *v/i.* (*irr.* bleiben, sep., -ge-, sein) sit up *or* door, *etc.*: remain open; **~blenden** (*sep.*, -ge-, h) **1.** *v/t.* turn up the headlights; **2.** *v/t.* fade in (*scene*); **~blicken** *v/i.* (*sep.*, -ge-, h) look up; raise one's eyes; **~blitzen** *v/i.* (*sep.*, -ge-, h, sein) flash (up); **~blühen** *v/i.* (*sep.*, -ge-, sein) bloom; flourish.

aufbrausen *fig. v/i.* (*sep.*, -ge-, sein) fly into a passion; **~d** *adj.* hot-tempered.

auf|brechen (*irr.* brechen, sep., -ge-) **1.** *v/t.* (h) break open; force open; **2.** *v/i.* (sein) burst open; set out (*nach* for); **~bringen** *v/t.* (*irr.* bringen, sep., -ge-, h) raise (*money, troops*); capture (*ship*); rouse *or* irritate *s.o.*

Aufbruch *m* departure, start.

auf|bügeln *v/t.* (*sep.*, -ge-, h) iron; **~bürden** *v/t.* (*sep.*, -ge-, h): *j-m et.* ~ impose s.th. on s.o.; **~decken** *v/t.* (*sep.*, -ge-, h) uncover; spread (*cloth*); *fig.* disclose; **~drängen** *v/t.* (*sep.*, -ge-, h) force, obtrude (*j-m* [up]on s.o.); **~drehen** *v/t.* (*sep.*, -ge-, h) turn on (gas, etc.).

aufdringlich *adj.* obtrusive.

Aufdruck *m* (-[e]s/-e) imprint; surcharge.

aufdrücken *v/t.* (*sep.*, -ge-, h) impress.

aufeinander *adv.* [auf⁹aɪ'nandər] one after *or* upon another; **2folge** *f* succession; **~folgend** *adj.* successive.

Aufenthalt ['aufɛnthalt] *m* (-[e]s/-e) stay; residence; delay; 🚉 stop; **~sgenehmigung** *f* residence permit.

auferlegen ['auf⁹ɛrleːɡən] *v/t.* (*sep.*, no -ge-, h) impose (*j-m* on s.o.).

aufersteh|en ['auf⁹ɛrˌʃteːən] *v/i.* (*irr.* stehen, sep., no -ge-, sein) rise (from the dead); **2ung** *f* (-/-en) resurrection.

auf|essen ['auf⁹-] *v/t.* (*irr.* essen, sep., -ge-, h) eat up; **~fahren** *v/i.* (*irr.* fahren, sep., -ge-, sein) ascend; start up; *fig.* fly out; ⚓ run aground; *mot.* drive *or* run (*auf acc.* against, into).

Auffahrt *f* ascent; driving up; approach; drive, *Am.* driveway; **~srampe** *f* ramp.

auf|fallen *v/i.* (*irr.* fallen, sep., -ge-, sein) be conspicuous; *j-m* ~ strike *s.o.*; **~fallend** *adj.*, **~fällig** *adj.* striking; conspicuous; flashy.

auffangen *v/t.* (*irr.* fangen, sep., -ge-, h) catch (up); parry (*thrust*).

auffass|en *v/t.* (*sep.*, -ge-, h) conceive; comprehend; interpret; **2ung** *f* conception; interpretation; grasp.

auffinden *v/t.* (*irr.* finden, sep., -ge-, h) find, trace, discover, locate.

aufforder|n *v/t.* (*sep.*, -ge-, h) ask, invite; call (up)on; *esp.* ⚖ summon; **2ung** *f* invitation; *esp.* ⚖ summons.

auffrischen (*sep.*, -ge-) **1.** *v/t.* (h) freshen up, touch up; brush up (*knowledge*); revive; **2.** v/i. (*sein*) *wind*: freshen.

'**aufführ|en** v/t. (*sep.*, -ge-, *h*) *thea.* represent, perform, act; enumerate; enter (*in list*); einzeln ~ specify, *Am.* itemize; sich ~ behave; '2**ung** f *thea.* performance; enumeration; entry; specification; conduct.

'**Aufgabe** f task; problem; *school*: homework; posting, *Am.* mailing (*of letter*); booking (*of luggage*), *Am.* checking (*of baggage*); resignation (*from office*); abandonment; giving up (*business*); es sich zur ~ machen make it one's business.

'**Aufgang** m ascent; *ast.* rising; staircase.

'**aufgeb|en** (*irr. geben*, *sep.*, -ge-, *h*) **1.** v/t. give up, abandon; resign from (*office*); insert (*advertisement*); post, *Am.* mail (*letter*); book (*luggage*), *Am.* check (*baggage*); hand in, send (*telegram*); ✝ give (*order*); set, *Am.* assign (*homework*); set (*riddle*); **2.** v/i. give up *or* in.

'**Aufgebot** n public notice; ✕ levy; *fig.* array; banns *pl.* (*of marriage*).

'**aufgehen** v/i. (*irr. gehen*, *sep.*, -ge-, *sein*) open; ⚖ leave no remainder; *sewing*: come apart; *paste*, *star*, *curtain*: rise; *seed*: come up; ~ *in* (*dat.*) be merged in; *fig.* be devoted to (*work*); *in Flammen* ~ go up in flames.

aufgeklärt adj. ['aufgəklɛːrt] enlightened; '2**heit** f (-/no pl.) enlightenment.

'**Aufgeld** ✝ n agio, premium.

aufge|legt adj. ['aufgəleːkt] disposed (zu for); in the mood (zu inf. for ger., to inf.); gut (schlecht) ~ in a good (bad) humo(u)r; '~**schlossen** fig. adj. open-minded; ~**weckt** fig. adj. ['~vɛkt] bright.

'**auf|gießen** v/t. (*irr. gießen*, *sep.*, -ge-, *h*) pour (on); make (*tea*); '~**greifen** v/t. (*irr. greifen*, *sep.*, -ge-, *h*) snatch up, *fig.* take up; seize.

'**Aufguß** m infusion.

'**auf|haben** (*irr. haben*, *sep.*, -ge-, *h*) **1.** v/t. have on (*hat*); have open (*door*); have to do (*task*); **2.** F v/i.: das Geschäft hat ~ the shop is open; '~**haken** v/t. (*sep.*, -ge-, *h*) unhook; '~**halten** v/t. (*irr. halten*, *sep.*, -ge-, *h*) keep open; stop, detain, delay; hold up (*traffic*); sich ~ stay;

sich ~ *bei* dwell on; sich ~ *mit* spend one's time on; '~**hängen** v/t. (*irr. hängen*, *sep.*, -ge-, *h*) hang (up); ⊕ suspend.

'**aufheb|en** v/t. (*irr. heben*, *sep.*, -ge-, *h*) lift (up), raise; pick up; raise (*siege*); keep, preserve; cancel, annul, abolish; break off (*engagement*); break up (*meeting*); sich ~ neutralize; die Tafel ~ rise from the table; gut aufgehoben sein be well looked after; viel Aufhebens machen make a fuss (von about); '2**ung** f (-/-en) raising; abolition; annulment; breaking up.

'**auf|heitern** v/t. (*sep.*, -ge-, *h*) cheer up; sich ~ *weather*: clear up; *face*: brighten; '~**hellen** v/t. and v/refl. (*sep.*, -ge-, *h*) brighten.

'**aufhetz|en** v/t. (*sep.*, -ge-, *h*) incite, instigate s.o.; '2**ung** f (-/-en) instigation, incitement.

'**auf|holen** (*sep.*, -ge-, *h*) **1.** v/t. make up (for); ⚓ haul up; **2.** v/i. gain (gegen on); pull up (to); '~**hören** v/i. (*sep.*, -ge-, *h*) cease, stop; *Am.* quit (*all*: zu tun doing); F: da hört (sich) doch alles auf! that's the limit!, *Am.* that beats everything!; '~**kaufen** v/t. (*sep.*, -ge-, *h*) buy up.

'**aufklär|en** v/t. (*sep.*, -ge-, *h*) clear up; enlighten (über acc. on); ✕ reconnoit|re, *Am.* -er; sich ~ clear up; '2**ung** f enlightenment; ✕ reconnaissance.

'**auf|kleben** v/t. (*sep.*, -ge-, *h*) paste on, stick on, affix on; '~**klinken** v/t. (*sep.*, -ge-, *h*) unlatch; '~**knöpfen** v/t. (*sep.*, -ge-, *h*) unbutton.

'**aufkommen 1.** v/i. (*irr. kommen*, *sep.*, -ge-, *sein*) rise; recover (*from illness*); come up; come into fashion or use; *thought*: arise; ~ für et. answer for s.th.; ~ gegen prevail against s.o.; **2.** ⚥ n (-s/no pl.) rise; recovery.

auf|krempeln ['aufkrɛmpəln] v/t. (*sep.*, -ge-, *h*) turn up, roll up; tuck up; '~**lachen** v/i. (*sep.*, -ge-, *h*) burst out laughing; '~**laden** v/t. (*irr. laden*, *sep.*, -ge-, *h*) load; ⚡ charge.

'**Auflage** f edition (*of book*); circulation (*of newspaper*); ⊕ support.

'**auf|lassen** v/t. (*irr. lassen*, *sep.*, -ge-, *h*) F leave open (*door, etc.*); F

keep on (*hat*); ⚹⚹ cede; '**~lauern**
v/i. (*sep.*, -ge-, *h*): j-m ~ lie in wait
for s.o.

'**Auflauf** *m* concourse; riot; *dish*:
soufflé; '**2en** *v/i.* (*irr. laufen, sep.*,
-ge-, *sein*) *interest*: accrue; ⚓ run
aground.

'**auflegen** (*sep.*, -ge-, *h*) **1.** *v/t.* put
on, lay on; apply (*auf acc.* to);
print, publish (*book*); *teleph.* hang
up; **2.** *teleph. v/i.* ring off.

'**auflehn|en** *v/t.* (*sep.*, -ge-, *h*) lean
(on); *sich* ~ lean (on); *fig.* rebel,
revolt (*gegen* against); '**2ung** *f*
(-/-en) rebellion.

'**auf|lesen** *v/t.* (*irr. lesen, sep.*, -ge-,
h) gather, pick up; '**~leuchten** *v/i.*
(*sep.*, -ge-, *h*) flash (up); '**~liegen**
v/i. (*irr. liegen, sep.*, -ge-, *h*) lie
(*auf dat.* on).

'**auflös|bar** *adj.* (dis)soluble; '**~en**
v/t. (*sep.*, -ge-, *h*) undo (*knot*);
break up (*meeting*); dissolve (*salt,*
etc.; *marriage, business, Parliament,*
etc.); solve (⚹, *riddle*); disintegrate;
fig. aufgelöst upset; '**2ung** *f* (dis-)
solution; disintegration.

'**aufmach|en** *v/t.* (*sep.*, -ge-, *h*)
open; undo (*dress, parcel*); put up
(*umbrella*); make up, get up; *sich* ~
wind: rise; set out (*nach acc.* for);
make for; *die Tür* ~ answer the
door; '**2ung** *f* (-/-en) make-up,
get-up.

aufmarschieren *v/i.* (*sep.*, *no* -ge-,
sein) form into line; ~ *lassen* ✕
deploy.

aufmerksam *adj.* attentive (*gegen*
to); j-n ~ *machen auf* (*acc.*) call
s.o.'s attention to; '**2keit** *f* (-/-en)
attention; token.

aufmuntern *v/t.* (*sep.*, -ge-, *h*)
rouse; encourage; cheer up.

Aufnahme ['aufnɑ:mə] *f* (-/-n) taking up (*of work*); reception; admission; *phot.*: taking; photograph,
shot; shooting (*of a film*); '**2fähig**
adj. capable of absorbing; *mind*:
receptive (*für* of); '**~gebühr** *f* admission fee; '**~gerät** *n phot.* camera; recorder; '**~prüfung** *f* entrance examination.

aufnehmen *v/t.* (*irr. nehmen, sep.*,
-ge-, *h*) take up; pick up; take s.o.
in; take down (*dictation, etc.*); take
s.th. in (*mentally*); receive (*guests*);
admit; raise, borrow (*money*); draw
up, record; shoot (*film*); *phot.* take

(*picture*); *gut* (*übel*) ~ take well (ill);
es ~ *mit* be a match for.

aufopfer|n ['auf?-] *v/t.* (*sep.*, -ge-,
h) sacrifice; '**2ung** *f* sacrifice.

'**auf|passen** *v/i.* (*sep.*, -ge-, *h*) attend
(*auf acc.* to); watch; *at school*: be
attentive; look out; ~ *auf* (*acc.*) take
care of; '**~platzen** *v/i.* (*sep.*, -ge-,
sein) burst (open); '**~polieren** *v/t.*
(*sep.*, *no* -ge-, *h*) polish up; '**~pral-**
len *v/i.* (*sep.*, -ge-, *sein*): *auf den*
Boden ~ strike the ground; '**~pum-**
pen *v/t.* (*sep.*, -ge-, *h*) blow up (*tyre,*
etc.); '**~raffen** *v/t.* (*sep.*, -ge-, *h*)
snatch up; *sich* ~ rouse o.s. (*zu* for);
muster up one's energy; '**~räumen**
(*sep.*, -ge-, *h*) **1.** *v/t.* put in order;
tidy (up), *Am.* straighten up; clear
away; **2.** *v/i.* tidy up; ~ *mit* do
away with.

'**aufrecht** *adj. and adv.* upright (*a.*
fig.), erect; '**~erhalten** *v/t.* (*irr.*
halten, sep., *no* -ge-, *h*) maintain,
uphold; '**2erhaltung** *f* (-/*no pl.*)
maintenance.

'**aufreg|en** *v/t.* (*sep.*, -ge-, *h*) stir up,
excite; *sich* ~ get excited or upset
(*über acc.* about); *aufgeregt* excited; upset; '**2ung** *f* excitement,
agitation.

'**auf|reiben** *v/t.* (*irr. reiben, sep.*,
-ge-, *h*) chafe (*skin, etc.*); *fig.*: destroy; exhaust, wear s.o. out; '**~**
reißen (*irr. reißen, sep.*, -ge-, *h*) **1.** *v/t.*
(*h*) rip or tear up *or* open; fling
open (*door*); open (*eyes*) wide;
2. *v/i.* (*sein*) split open, burst.

'**aufreiz|en** *v/t.* (*sep.*, -ge-, *h*) incite,
stir up; '**~end** *adj.* provocative;
'**2ung** *f* instigation.

'**aufrichten** *v/t.* (*sep.*, -ge-, *h*) set
up, erect; *sich* ~ stand up; straight-
en; sit up (*in bed*).

'**aufrichtig** *adj.* sincere, candid;
'**2keit** *f* sincerity, cando(u)r.

'**aufriegeln** *v/t.* (*sep.*, -ge-, *h*) un-
bolt.

'**Aufriß** △ *m* elevation.

'**aufrollen** *v/t. and v/refl.* (*sep.*,
-ge-, *h*) roll up; unroll.

'**Aufruf** *m* call, summons; '**2en** *v/t.*
(*irr. rufen, sep.*, -ge-, *h*) call up;
call on s.o.

Aufruhr ['aufru:r] *m* (-[e]s/-e) uproar, tumult; riot, rebellion.

'**aufrühr|en** *v/t.* (*sep.*, -ge-, *h*) stir
up; revive; *fig.* rake up; '**2er** *m*
(-s/-) rebel; '**~erisch** *adj.* rebellious.

'**Aufrüstung** ⚔ f (re)armament.
'**auf|rütteln** v/t. (sep., -ge-, h) shake up; rouse; '**~sagen** v/t. (sep., -ge-, h) say, repeat; recite.
aufsässig adj. ['aufzɛsiç] rebellious.
'**Aufsatz** m essay; composition; ⊕ top.
'**auf|saugen** v/t. (sep., -ge-, h) suck up; 🜄 absorb; '**~scheuchen** v/t. (sep., -ge-, h) scare (away); disturb; rouse; '**~scheuern** v/t. (sep., -ge-, h) scour; ♂ chafe; '**~schichten** v/t. (sep., -ge-, h) pile up; '**~schieben** v/t. (irr. schieben, sep., -ge-, h) slide open; fig.: put off; defer; postpone; adjourn.
'**Aufschlag** m striking; impact; additional or extra charge; facing (on coat), lapel (of coat); cuff (on sleeve); turn-up (on trousers); tennis: service; **2en** ['~gən] (irr. schlagen, sep., -ge-) **1.** v/t. (h) open; turn up (sleeve, etc.); take up (abode); pitch (tent); raise (prices); cut (one's knee) open; **2.** v/i. (sein) strike, hit; ✝ rise, go up (in price); tennis: serve.
'**auf|schließen** v/t. (irr. schließen, sep., -ge-, h) unlock; open; '**~schlitzen** v/t. (sep., -ge-, h) slit or rip open.
'**Aufschluß** fig. m information.
'**auf|schnallen** v/t. (sep., -ge-, h) unbuckle; '**~schnappen** (sep., -ge-) **1.** v/t. (h) snatch; fig. pick up; **2.** v/i. (sein) snap open; '**~schneiden** (irr. schneiden, sep., -ge-, h) **1.** v/t. cut open; cut up (meat); **2.** fig. v/i. brag, boast.
'**Aufschnitt** m (slices pl. of) cold meat, Am. cold cuts pl.
'**auf|schnüren** v/t. (sep., -ge-, h) untie; unlace; '**~schrauben** v/t. (sep., -ge-, h) screw (auf acc. on); unscrew; '**~schrecken** (sep., -ge-) **1.** v/t. (h) startle; **2.** v/i. (irr. schrecken, sein) start (up).
'**Aufschrei** m shriek, scream; fig. outcry.
'**auf|schreiben** v/t. (irr. schreiben, sep., -ge-, h) write down; '**~schreien** v/i. (irr. schreien, sep., -ge-, h) cry out, scream.
'**Aufschrift** f inscription; address, direction (on letter); label.
'**Aufschub** m deferment; delay; adjournment; respite.
'**auf|schürfen** v/t. (sep., -ge-, h)

graze (skin); '**~schwingen** v/refl. (irr. schwingen, sep., -ge-, h) soar, rise; sich zu et. ~ bring o.s. to do s.th.
'**Aufschwung** m fig. rise, Am. upswing; ✝ boom.
'**aufsehen 1.** v/i. (irr. sehen, sep., -ge-, h) look up; **2.** 💈 n (-s/no pl.) sensation; ~ erregen cause a sensation; '**~erregend** adj. sensational.
'**Aufseher** m overseer; inspector.
'**aufsetzen** (sep., -ge-, h) **1.** v/t. set up; put on (hat, countenance); draw up (document); sich ~ sit up; **2.** 🜄 v/i. touch down.
'**Aufsicht** f (-/-en) inspection, supervision; store: shopwalker, Am. floorwalker; '**~sbehörde** f board of control; '**~srat** m board of directors.
'**auf|sitzen** v/i. (irr. sitzen, sep., -ge-, h) rider: mount; '**~spannen** v/t. (sep., -ge-, h) stretch; put up (umbrella); spread (sails); '**~sparen** v/t. (sep., -ge-, h) save; fig. reserve; store up; '**~sperren** v/t. (sep., -ge-, h) open wide; '**~spielen** (sep., -ge-, h) **1.** v/t. and v/i. strike up; **2.** v/refl. show off; sich ~ als set up for s.th.; '**~spießen** v/t. (sep., -ge-, h) pierce; with horns: gore; run through, spear; '**~springen** v/i. (irr. springen, sep., -ge-, sein) jump up; door: fly open; crack; skin: chap; '**~spüren** v/t. (sep., -ge-, h) hunt up; track down; '**~stacheln** fig. v/t. (sep., -ge-, h) goad; incite, instigate; '**~stampfen** v/i. (sep., -ge-, h) stamp (one's foot).
'**Aufstand** m insurrection; rebellion; uprising, revolt.
aufständisch adj. ['aufʃtɛndiʃ] rebellious; '**2e** m (-n/-n) insurgent, rebel.
'**auf|stapeln** v/t. (sep., -ge-, h) pile up; ✝ store (up); '**~stechen** v/t. (irr. stechen, sep., -ge-, h) puncture, prick open; ♂ lance; '**~stecken** v/t. (sep., -ge-, h) pin up; put up (hair); '**~stehen** v/i. (irr. stehen, sep., -ge-) **1.** (sein) stand up; rise, get up; revolt; **2.** F (h) stand open; '**~steigen** v/i. (irr. steigen, sep., -ge-, sein) rise, ascend; 🜄 take off; rider: mount.
'**aufstell|en** v/t. (sep., -ge-, h) set up, put up; ⚔ draw up; post (sentries); make (assertion); set (example); erect (column); set (trap);

nominate (*candidate*); draw up (*bill*); lay down (*rule*); make out (*list*); set up, establish (*record*); '**℣ung** f putting up; drawing up; erection; nomination; ✝ statement; list.

Aufstieg ['aʊfʃtiːk] m (-[e]s/-e) ascent, *Am. a.* ascension; *fig.* rise.

'**auf|stöbern** *fig. v/t.* (*sep.*, -*ge*-, h) hunt up; '**℣stoßen** (*irr. stoßen*, *sep.*, -*ge*-) **1.** *v/t.* (h) push open; ~ *auf* (*acc.*) knock against; **2.** *v/i.* (h, sein) *of food:* rise, repeat; belch; '**℣streichen** *v/t.* (*irr. streichen*, *sep.*, -*ge*-, h) spread (*butter*).

'**Aufstrich** m spread (*for bread*).

'**auf|stützen** *v/t.* (*sep.*, -*ge*-, h) prop up, support *s.th.*; *sich* ~ *auf* (*acc.*) lean on; '**℣suchen** *v/t.* (*sep.*, -*ge*-, h) visit (*places*); go to see *s.o.*, look *s.o.* up.

'**Auftakt** m ♩ upbeat; *fig.* prelude, preliminaries *pl.*

'**auf|tauchen** *v/i.* (*sep.*, -*ge*-, sein) emerge, appear, turn up; '**℣tauen** (*sep.*, -*ge*-) **1.** *v/t.* (h) thaw; **2.** *v/i.* (sein) thaw (*a. fig.*); '**℣teilen** *v/t.* (*sep.*, -*ge*-, h) divide (up), share.

Auftrag ['aʊftraːk] m (-[e]s/℣e) commission; instruction; mission; ⚖ mandate; ✝ order; **℣en** ['℣ɡən] *v/t.* (*irr. tragen*, *sep.*, -*ge*-, h) serve (up) (*meal*); lay on (*paint*); wear out (*dress*); *j-m et.* ~ charge *s.o.* with *s.th.*; '**℣geber** ['℣k-] m (-s/-) employer; customer; principal; '**℣erteilung** ['℣ks ℣ɛrtaɪluŋ] f (-/-en) placing of an order.

'**auf|treffen** *v/i.* (*irr. treffen*, *sep.*, -*ge*-, sein) strike, hit; '**℣treiben** *v/t.* (*irr. treiben*, *sep.*, -*ge*-, h) hunt up; raise (*money*); '**℣trennen** *v/t.* (*sep.*, -*ge*-, h) rip; unstitch (*seam*).

'**auftreten 1.** *v/i.* (*irr. treten*, *sep.*, -*ge*-, sein) tread; *thea.*, *witness*, *etc.:* appear (*als* as); behave, act; *difficulties:* arise; **2.** **℣** n (-s/no pl.) appearance; occurrence (*of events*); behavio(u)r.

'**Auftrieb** m *phys. and fig.* buoyancy; ⚓ lift; *fig.* impetus.

'**Auftritt** m *thea.* scene (*a. fig.*); appearance (*of actor*).

'**auf|trumpfen** *fig. v/i.* (*sep.*, -*ge*-, h) put one's foot down; '**℣tun** *v/t.* (*irr. tun*, *sep.*, -*ge*-, h) open; *sich* ~ open; *chasm:* yawn; *society:* form; '**℣türmen** *v/t.* (*sep.*, -*ge*-, h) pile or heap

up; *sich* ~ tower up; pile up; *difficulties:* accumulate; '**℣wachen** *v/i.* (*sep.*, -*ge*-, sein) awake, wake up; '**℣wachsen** *v/i.* (*irr. wachsen*, *sep.*, -*ge*-, sein) grow up.

'**Aufwallung** f ebullition, surge.

Aufwand ['aʊfvant] m (-[e]s/no pl.) expense, expenditure (*an dat.* of); pomp; splendid or great display (*of words*, *etc.*).

'**aufwärmen** *v/t.* (*sep.*, -*ge*-, h) warm up.

'**Aufwarte|frau** f charwoman, *Am. a.* cleaning woman; '**℣n** *v/i.* (*sep.*, -*ge*-, h) wait (up)on *s.o.*, attend on *s.o.*; wait (at table).

aufwärts *adv.* ['aʊfvɛrts] upward(s).

'**Aufwartung** f attendance; visit; *j-m s-e* ~ *machen* pay one's respects to *s.o.*, call on *s.o.*

'**aufwasch|en** *v/t.* (*irr. waschen*, *sep.*, -*ge*-, h) wash up; '**℣wasser** n dish-water.

'**auf|wecken** *v/t.* (*sep.*, -*ge*-, h) awake(n), wake (up); '**℣weichen** (*sep.*, -*ge*-) **1.** *v/t.* (h) soften; soak; **2.** *v/i.* (sein) soften, become soft; '**℣weisen** *v/t.* (*irr. weisen*, *sep.*, -*ge*-, h) show, exhibit; produce; '**℣wenden** *v/t.* ([*irr. wenden*,] *sep.*, -*ge*-, h) spend; *Mühe* ~ take pains; '**℣werfen** *v/t.* (*irr. werfen*, *sep.*, -*ge*-, h) raise (*a. question*).

'**aufwert|en** *v/t.* (*sep.*, -*ge*-, h) revalorize; revalue; '**℣ung** f revalorization; revaluation.

'**aufwickeln** *v/t. and v/refl.* (*sep.*, -*ge*-, h) wind up, roll up.

aufwiegel|n ['aʊfviːɡəln] *v/t.* (*sep.*, -*ge*-, h) stir up, incite, instigate; '**℣ung** f (-/-en) instigation.

'**aufwiegen** *fig. v/t.* (*irr. wiegen*, *sep.*, -*ge*-, h) make up for.

Aufwiegler ['aʊfviːɡlər] m (-s/-) agitator; instigator.

'**aufwirbeln** (*sep.*, -*ge*-) **1.** *v/t.* (h) whirl up; raise (*dust*); *fig. viel Staub* ~ create a sensation; **2.** *v/i.* (sein) whirl up.

'**aufwisch|en** *v/t.* (*sep.*, -*ge*-, h) wipe up; '**℣lappen** m floor-cloth.

'**aufwühlen** *v/t.* (*sep.*, -*ge*-, h) turn up; *fig.* stir.

'**aufzähl|en** *v/t.* (*sep.*, -*ge*-, h) count up; *fig.* enumerate, *Am. a.* call off; specify, *Am.* itemize; '**℣ung** f (-/-en) enumeration; specification.

'**auf|zäumen** *v/t.* (*sep.*, -*ge*-, h)

bridle; **'zehren** v/t. (sep., -ge-, h) consume.

'aufzeichn|en v/t. (sep., -ge-, h) draw; note down; record; **'2ung** f note; record.

'auf|zeigen v/t. (sep., -ge-, h) show; demonstrate; point out (mistakes, etc.); disclose; **'zziehen** (irr. ziehen, sep., -ge-) **1.** v/t. (h) draw or pull up; (pull) open; hoist (flag); bring up (child); mount (picture); wind (up) (clock, etc.); j-n ~ tease s.o., pull s.o.'s leg; Saiten auf e-e Violine ~ string a violin; **2.** v/i. (sein) × draw up; storm: approach.

'Aufzucht f rearing, breeding.

'Aufzug m ⊕ hoist; lift, Am. elevator; thea. act; attire; show.

'aufzwingen v/t. (irr. zwingen, sep., -ge-, h): j-m et. ~ force s.th.upon

'Augapfel ['auk?-] m eyeball. [s.o.]

Auge ['augə] n (-s/-n) eye; sight; ✿ bud; in meinen ~ in my view; im ~ behalten keep an eye on; keep in mind; aus den ~n verlieren lose sight of; ein ~ zudrücken turn a blind eye (bei to); ins ~ fallen strike the eye; große ~n machen open one's eyes wide; unter vier ~n face to face, privately; kein ~ zutun not to get a wink of sleep.

'Augen|arzt m oculist, eye-doctor; **'zblick** m moment, instant; **'2-blicklich 1.** adj. instantaneous; momentary; present; **2.** adv. instant(aneous)ly; at present; **'zbraue** f eyebrow; **zentzündung** ✳ f inflammation of the eye; **'zheilkunde** f ophthalmology; **'zklinik** f ophthalmic hospital; **'zleiden** ✳ n eye-complaint; **'zlicht** n eyesight; **'zlid** n eyelid; **'zmaß** n: ein gutes ~ a sure eye; nach dem ~ by eye; **'zmerk** ['zmerk] n (-[e]s/no pl.): sein ~ richten auf (acc.) turn one's attention to; have s.th. in view; **'zschein** m appearance; in ~ nehmen examine, view, inspect; **'2-scheinlich** adj. evident; **'zwasser** n eyewash, eye-lotion; **'zwimper** f eyelash; **'zzeuge** m eyewitness.

August [au'gust] m (-[e]s, - /-e) August.

Auktion [auk'tsjoːn] f (-/-en) auction; **zator** [zo'naːtɔr] m (-s/-en) auctioneer.

Aula ['aula] f (-/Aulen, -s) (assembly) hall, Am. auditorium.

aus [aus] **1.** prp. (dat.) out of; from; of; by; for; in; ~ Achtung out of respect; ~ London kommen come from London; ~ diesem Grunde for this reason; ~ Ihrem Brief ersehe ich I see from your letter; **2.** adv. out; over; die Schule ist ~ school is over; F: von mir ~ for all I care; auf et. ~ sein be keen on s.th.; es ist ~ mit ihm it is all over with him; das Spiel ist ~! the game is up!; per weiß weder ein noch ~ he is at his wit's end; on instruments, etc.: an — — on — off.

ausarbeit|en ['aus?-] v/t. (sep., -ge-, h) work out; elaborate; **'2ung** f (-/-en) working-out; elaboration; composition.

aus|arten ['aus?-] v/i. (sep., -ge-, sein) degenerate; get out of hand; **'zatmen** ['aus?-] (sep., -ge-, h) **1.** v/i. breathe out; **2.** v/t. breathe out; exhale (vapour, etc.); **'zbaggern** v/t. (sep., -ge-, h) dredge (river, etc.); excavate (ground).

'Ausbau m (-[e]s/-ten) extension; completion; development; **'2en** v/t. (sep., -ge-, h) develop; extend; finish, complete; ⊕ dismantle (engine). [sep., no -ge-, h)stipulate.]

'ausbedingen v/t. (irr. bedingen,)

'ausbesser|n v/t. (sep., -ge-, h) mend, repair, Am. F a. fix; **'2ung** f repair, mending.

'Ausbeut|e f (-/~-n) gain, profit; yield; × output; **'2en** v/t. (sep., -ge-, h) exploit; sweat (workers); **'zung** f (-/-en) exploitation.

'ausbild|en v/t. (sep., -ge-, h) form, develop; train; instruct; educate; × drill; **'2ung** f development; training; instruction; education; × drill.

'ausbitten v/t. (irr. bitten, sep., -ge-, h): sich et. ~ request s.th.; insist on s.th.

'ausbleiben 1. v/i. (irr. bleiben, sep., -ge-, sein) stay away, fail to appear; **2.** 2 n (-s/no pl.) non-arrival, non-appearance; absence.

'Ausblick m outlook (auf acc. over, on), view (of), prospect (of); fig. outlook (on).

'aus|bohren v/t. (sep., -ge-, h) bore, drill; **'zbrechen** (irr. brechen, sep., -ge-) **1.** v/t. (h) break out; vomit; **2.** v/i. (sein) break out; fig. burst out (laughing, etc.).

'ausbreit|en v/t. (sep., -ge-, h) spread (out); stretch (out) (arms, wings); display; sich ~ spread; **'2ung** f (-/<-en) spreading.

'ausbrennen (irr. brennen, sep., -ge-) **1.** v/t. (h) burn out; ♂ cauterize; **2.** v/i. (sein) burn out.

'Ausbruch m outbreak; eruption (of volcano); escape (from prison); outburst (of emotion).

'aus|brüten v/t. (sep., -ge-, h) hatch (a. fig.); **'~bürgern** v/t. (sep., -ge-, h) denationalize, expatriate.

'Ausdauer f perseverance; **'2nd** adj. persevering; ♀ perennial.

'ausdehn|en v/t. and v/refl. (sep., -ge-, h) extend (auf acc. to); expand; stretch; **'2ung** f expansion; extension; extent.

'aus|denken v/t. (irr. denken, sep., -ge-, h) think s.th. out, Am. a. think s.th. up, contrive, devise, invent; imagine; **'~dörren** v/t. (sep., -ge-, h) dry up; parch; **'~drehen** v/t. (sep., -ge-, h) turn off (radio, gas); ♂ turn off, switch off (light).

'Ausdruck m **1.** (-[e]s/no pl.) expression; **2.** (-[e]s/=e) expression; term.

'ausdrück|en v/t. (sep., -ge-, h) press, squeeze (out); stub out (cigarette); fig. express; **'~lich** adj. express, explicit.

'ausdrucks|los adj. inexpressive, expressionless; blank; **'~voll** adj. expressive; **'2weise** f mode of expression; style.

'Ausdünstung f (-/-en) exhalation; perspiration; odo(u)r, smell.

auseinander adv. ['aus⁹a'nandər] asunder, apart; separate(d); **~bringen** v/t. (irr. bringen, sep., -ge-, h) separate, sever; **~gehen** v/i. (irr. gehen, sep., -ge-, h) meeting, crowd: break up; opinions: differ; friends: part; crowd: disperse; roads: diverge; **~nehmen** v/t. (irr. nehmen, sep., -ge-, h) take apart or to pieces; ⊕ disassemble, dismantle; **~setzen** fig. v/t. (sep., -ge-, h) explain; sich mit j-m ~ ✝ compound with s.o.; argue with s.o.; have it out with s.o.; sich mit e-m Problem ~ get down to a problem; come to grips with a problem; **2setzung** f (-/-en) explanation; discussion; settlement (with creditors, etc.); kriegerische ~ armed conflict.

auserlesen adj. ['aus⁹-] exquisite, choice; select(ed).

auserwählen ['aus⁹-] v/t. (sep., no -ge-, h) select, choose.

'ausfahr|en (irr. fahren, sep., -ge-) **1.** v/i. (sein) drive out, go for a drive; ⚓ leave (port); **2.** v/t. (h) take (baby) out (in pram); take s.o. for a drive; rut (road); ✈ lower (undercarriage); **'2t** f drive; excursion; way out, exit (of garage, etc.); gateway; departure.

'Ausfall m falling out; ✝: loss; deficit; **'2en** v/i. (irr. fallen, sep., -ge-, sein) fall out; not to take place; turn out, prove; ~ lassen drop; cancel; die Schule fällt aus there is no school; **'2end** adj. offensive, insulting.

'aus|fasern v/i. (sep., -ge-, sein) ravel out, fray; **'~fegen** v/t. (sep., -ge- h) sweep (out).

ausfertig|en ['ausfertigən] v/t. (sep., -ge-, h) draw up (document); make out (bill, etc.); issue (passport); **'2ung** f (-/-en) drawing up; issue; draft; copy; in doppelter ~ in duplicate. [chen find me; discover.]

ausfindig adj. ['ausfindiç]: ~ ma-)

'Ausflucht f (-/=e) excuse, evasion, shift, subterfuge.

'Ausflug m trip, excursion, outing.

Ausflügler ['ausfly:klər] m (-s/-) excursionist, tripper, tourist.

'Ausfluß m flowing out; discharge (a. ♂); outlet, outfall.

'aus|fragen v/t. (sep., -ge-, h) interrogate, Am. a. quiz; sound; **'~fransen** v/i. (sep., -ge-, sein) fray.

Ausfuhr ✝ ['ausfu:r] f (-/-en) export(ation); **'~artikel** ✝ m export (article).

'ausführ|bar adj. practicable; ✝ exportable; **'~en** v/t. (sep., -ge-, h) execute, carry out, perform, Am. a. fill; ✝ export; explain; j-n ~ take s.o. out.

'Ausfuhr|genehmigung f export permit; **'~handel** m export trade.

'ausführlich 1. adj. detailed; comprehensive; circumstantial; **2.** adv. in detail, at (some) length; **'2keit** f (-/no pl.) minuteness of detail; particularity; comprehensiveness; copiousness.

'Ausführung f execution, performance; workmanship; type, make;

explanation; '**~sbestimmungen** ✝ f/pl. export regulations pl.

'**Ausfuhr|verbot** n embargo on exports; '**~waren** f/pl. exports pl.; '**~zoll** m export duty.

'**ausfüllen** v/t. (sep., -ge-, h) fill out or up; fill in, complete (form); Am. fill out (blank).

'**Ausgabe** f distribution; edition (of book); expense, expenditure; issue (of shares, etc.); issuing office.

'**Ausgang** m going out; exit; way out; outlet; end; result; '**~skapital** ✝ n original capital; '**~spunkt** m starting-point; '**~sstellung** f starting-position.

'**ausgeben** v/t. (irr. geben, sep., -ge-, h) give out; spend (money); issue (shares, etc.); sich ~ für pass o.s. off for, pretend to be.

ausge|beult adj. ['ausgəbɔylt] baggy; **~bombt** adj. ['~bɔmpt] bombed out; **~dehnt** adj. ['~de:nt] expansive, vast, extensive; **~dient** adj. ['~di:nt] worn out; superannuated; retired, pensioned off; **~er Soldat** ex-serviceman, veteran; '**~fallen** fig. adj. odd, queer, unusual.

'**ausgehen** v/i. (irr. gehen, sep., -ge-, sein) go out; take a walk; end; colour: fade; hair: fall out; money, provisions: run out; **uns gehen die Vorräte aus** we run out of provisions; **darauf ~** aim at; **gut etc. ~** turn out well, etc.; **leer ~** come away empty-handed; **von et. ~** start from s.th.

'**ausge|lassen** fig. adj. frolicsome, boisterous; '**~nommen** prp. **1.** (acc.) except (for); **2.** (nom.): **Anwesende ~** present company excepted; **~prägt** adj. ['~prɛ:kt] marked, pronounced; **~rechnet** fig. adv. ['~rɛçnət] just; **~ er** he of all people; **~ heute** today of all days; '**~schlossen** fig. adj. impossible.

'**ausgestalten** v/t. (sep., no -ge-, h) arrange (celebration); **et. zu et. ~** develop or turn s.th. into s.th.

ausge|sucht fig. adj. ['ausgəzuːxt] exquisite, choice; '**~wachsen** adj. full-grown; **~zeichnet** fig. adj. ['~tsaiçnət] excellent.

ausgiebig adj. ['ausgiːbiç] abundant, plentiful; meal: substantial.

'**ausgießen** v/t. (irr. gießen, sep., -ge-, h) pour out.

Ausgleich ['ausglaiç] m (-[e]s/-e)

compromise; compensation; ✝ settlement; sports: equalization (of score); tennis: deuce (score of 40 all); '**2en** v/t. (irr. gleichen, sep., -ge-, h) equalize; compensate (loss); ✝ balance.

'**aus|gleiten** v/i. (irr. gleiten, sep., -ge-, sein) slip, slide; '**~graben** v/t. (irr. graben, sep., -ge-, h) dig out or up (a. fig.); excavate; exhume (body).

Ausguck ⚓ ['ausguk] m (-[e]s/-e) look-out.

'**Ausguß** m sink; '**~eimer** m slop-pail.

'**aus|haken** v/t. (sep., -ge-, h) unhook; '**~halten** (irr. halten, sep., -ge-, h) **1.** v/t. endure, bear, stand; ♩ sustain (note); **2.** v/i. hold out; last; '**~händigen** ['~hɛndigən] v/t. (sep., -ge-, h) deliver up, hand over, surrender.

'**Aushang** m notice, placard, poster.

'**aushänge|n 1.** v/t. (sep., -ge-, h) hang or put out; unhinge (door); **2.** v/i. (irr. hängen, sep., -ge-, h) have been hung or put out; '**2~schild** n signboard.

aus|harren ['ausharən] v/i. (sep., -ge-, h) persevere; hold out; '**~hauchen** v/t. (sep., -ge-, h) breathe out, exhale; '**~heben** v/t. (irr. heben, sep., -ge-, h) dig (trench); unhinge (door); recruit, levy (soldiers); excavate (earth); rob (nest); clean out, raid (nest of criminals); '**~helfen** v/i. (irr. helfen, sep., -ge-, h) help out.

'**Aushilf|e** f (temporary) help or assistance; **sie hat e-e ~** she has s.o. to help out; '**2~sweise** adv. as a makeshift; temporarily.

'**aushöhl|en** v/t. (sep., -ge-, h) hollow out; '**2~ung** f hollow.

'**aus|holen** v/t. (sep., -ge-, h) **1.** v/i. raise one's hand (as if to strike); **weit ~** go far back (in narrating s.th.); **2.** v/t. sound, pump s.o.; '**~horchen** v/t. (sep., -ge-, h) sound, pump s.o.; '**~hungern** v/t. (sep., -ge-, h) starve (out); '**~husten** v/t. (sep., -ge-, h) cough up; '**~kennen** v/refl. (irr. kennen, sep., -ge-, h) know one's way (about place); be well versed, be at home (in subject); **er kennt sich aus** he knows what's what; '**~kleiden** v/t. (sep., -ge-, h) undress; ⊕ line, coat; **sich ~** undress; '**~klopfen** v/t. (sep., -ge-, h) beat (out); dust (*garment*); knock out (*pipe*); **klügeln** ['ˌkly:gəln] v/t. (*sep.*, -ge-, *h*) work s.th. out; contrive; puzzle s.th. out.

'**auskommen 1.** v/i. (*irr.* kommen, *sep.*, -ge-, *sein*) get out; escape; ~ *mit* manage with s.th.; get on with s.o.; ~ *ohne* do without; *mit dem Geld* ~ make both ends meet; **2.** 2 *n* (-s/*no pl.*) competence, competency.

'**auskundschaften** v/t. (*sep.*, -ge-, *h*) explore; ✕ reconnoit|re, *Am.* -er, scout.

Auskunft ['auskunft] *f* (-/ᵉe) information; inquiry office, inquiries *pl.*, *Am.* information desk; '**stelle** *f* inquiry office, inquiries *pl.*, *Am.* information bureau.

'**aus|lachen** v/t. (*sep.*, -ge-, *h*) laugh at, deride; '**laden** v/t. (*irr.* laden, *sep.*, -ge-, *h*) unload; discharge (*cargo from ship*); cancel s.o.'s invitation, put off (*guest*).

'**Auslage** *f* display, show (*of goods*); *in der* ~ in the (shop) window; ~*n pl.* expenses *pl.*

'**Ausland** *n* (-[e]s/*no pl.*): *das* ~ foreign countries *pl.*; *ins* ~, *im* ~ abroad.

Ausländ|er ['auslɛndər] *m* (-s/-), '**erin** *f* (-/-nen) foreigner; alien; '**2isch** *adj.* foreign; ⚥, *zo.* exotic.

'**Auslandskorrespondent** *m* foreign correspondent.

'**auslass|en** v/t. (*irr.* lassen, *sep.*, -ge-, *h*) let out (*water*); melt (down) (*butter*); render down (*fat*); let out (*garment*); let down (*hem*); leave out, omit (*word*); cut s.th. out; miss or cut out (*meal*); miss (*dance*); s-n *Zorn an j-m* ~ vent one's anger on s.o.; *sich* ~ *über* (*acc.*) say s.th. about; express one's opinion about; '**2ung** *f* (-/-en) omission; remark, utterance; '**2ungszeichen** *gr. n* apostrophe.

'**aus|laufen** v/i. (*irr.* laufen, *sep.*, -ge-, *sein*) run *or* leak out (*aus et.* of s.th.); leak; end (*in* s.th.); *machine*: run down; ⚓ (set) sail; '**leeren** v/t. (*sep.*, -ge-, *h*) empty; ✕ evacuate (*bowels*).

'**ausleg|en** v/t. (*sep.*, -ge-, *h*) lay out; display (*goods*); explain, interpret; advance (*money*); '**2ung** *f* (-/-en) explanation, interpretation.

'**aus|leihen** v/t. (*irr.* leihen, *sep.*, -ge-, *h*) lend (out), *esp. Am.* loan;

'**lernen** v/i. (*sep.*, -ge-, *h*) finish one's apprenticeship; *man lernt nie aus* we live and learn.

'**Auslese** *f* choice, selection; *fig.* pick; '**2n** v/t. (*irr.* lesen, *sep.*, -ge-, *h*) pick out, select; finish reading (*book*).

'**ausliefer|n** v/t. (*sep.*, -ge-, *h*) hand or turn over, deliver (up); extradite (*criminal*); *ausgeliefert sein* (*dat.*) be at the mercy of; '**2ung** *f* delivery; extradition.

'**aus|liegen** v/i. (*irr.* liegen, *sep.*, -ge-, *h*) be displayed, be on show; '**löschen** v/t. (*sep.*, -ge-, *h*) put out, switch off (*light*); extinguish (*fire*; *a. fig.*); efface (*word*); wipe out, erase; '**losen** v/t. (*sep.*, -ge-, *h*) draw (lots) for.

'**auslös|en** v/t. (*sep.*, -ge-, *h*) ⊕ release; redeem, ransom (*prisoner*); redeem (*from pawn*); *fig.* cause, start; arouse (*applause*); '**2er** *m* (-s/-) ⊕ release, *esp. phot.* trigger.

'**aus|lüften** v/t. (*sep.*, -ge-, *h*) air, ventilate; '**machen** v/t. (*sep.*, -ge-, *h*) make out, sight, spot; *sum:* amount to; constitute, make up; put out (*fire*); ⚡ turn out, switch off (*light*); agree on, arrange; settle; *es macht nichts aus* it does not matter; *würde es Ihnen et.* ~, *wenn ...?* would you mind (*ger.*) ...?; '**malen** v/t. (*sep.*, -ge-, *h*) paint; *sich et.* ~ picture s.th. to o.s.; imagine s.th.

'**Ausmaß** *n* dimension(s *pl.*), measurement(s *pl.*); *fig.* extent.

aus|mergeln ['ausmɛrgəln] v/t. (*sep.*, -ge-, *h*) emaciate; exhaust; '**merzen** ['ˌmɛrtsən] v/t. (*sep.*, -ge-, *h*) eliminate; eradicate; '**messen** v/t. (*irr.* messen, *sep.*, -ge-, *h*) measure.

Ausnahm|e ['ausnɑːmə] *f* (-/-n) exception; '**2sweise** *adv.* by way of exception; exceptionally.

'**ausnehmen** v/t. (*irr.* nehmen, *sep.*, -ge-, *h*) take out; draw (*fowl*); F fleece s.o.; *fig.* except, exempt; '**d 1.** *adj.* exceptional; **2.** *adv.* exceedingly.

'**aus|nutzen** v/t. (*sep.*, -ge-, *h*) utilize; take advantage of; *esp.* ✶, ✕ exploit; '**packen** v/t. (*sep.*, -ge-, *h*) **1.** v/t. unpack; **2.** F *fig.* v/i. speak one's mind; '**pfeifen** *thea.* v/t. (*irr.* pfeifen, *sep.*, -ge-, *h*) hiss; '**plaudern** v/t. (*sep.*, -ge-, *h*) blab *or* let out; '~polstern *v/t.* (*sep.*, -ge-, *h*) stuff, pad; wad; '~probie-ren *v/t.* (*sep.*, *no* -ge-, *h*) try, test.

'Auspuff *mot.* ['auspuf] *m* (-[e]s/-e) exhaust; '~gas *mot. n* exhaust gas; '~rohr *mot. n* exhaust-pipe; '~topf *mot. m* silencer, *Am.* muffler.

'aus|putzen *v/t.* (*sep.*, -ge-, *h*) clean; '~quartieren *v/t.* (*sep.*, *no* -ge-, *h*) dislodge; ✕ billet out; '~radieren *v/t.* (*sep.*, *no* -ge-, *h*) erase; '~rangieren *v/t.* (*sep.*, *no* -ge-, *h*) discard; '~rauben *v/t.* (*sep.*, -ge-, *h*) rob; ransack; '~räu-men *v/t.* (*sep.*, -ge-, *h*) empty, clear (out); remove (*furniture*); '~rech-nen *v/t.* (*sep.*, -ge-, *h*) calculate, compute; reckon (out), *Am.* figure out *or* up (*all a.* fig.).

'Ausrede *f* excuse, evasion, subter-fuge; '2n (*sep.*, -ge-, *h*) **1.** *v/i.* finish speaking; ~ *lassen* hear *s.o.* out; **2.** *v/t.:* j-m et. ~ dissuade s.o. from s.th.

'ausreichen *v/i.* (*sep.*, -ge-, *h*) suf-fice; '~d *adj.* sufficient.

'Ausreise *f* departure; 🛥 voyage out.

'ausreiß|en (*irr.* reißen, *sep.*, -ge-) **1.** *v/t.* (*h*) pull *or* tear out; **2.** *v/i.* (*sein*) run away; '2er *m* runaway.

'aus|renken *v/t.* ['ausrɛŋkən] (*sep.*, -ge-, *h*) dislocate; '~richten *v/t.* (*sep.*, -ge-, *h*) straighten; ✕ dress; adjust; deliver (*message*) do, effect; accomplish; obtain; arrange (*feast*); *richte ihr e-n Gruß von mir aus!* remember me to her!; '~rotten ['~rɔtən] *v/t.* (*sep.*, -ge-, *h*) root out; *fig.* extirpate, exterminate.

'Ausruf *m* cry; exclamation; '2en (*irr.* rufen, *sep.*, -ge-,*h*) **1.** *v/i.* cry out, exclaim; **2.** *v/t.* proclaim; '~e-zeichen *n* exclamation mark, *Am. a.* exclamation point; '~ung *f* (-/-en) proclamation; '~ungszeichen *n s.* Ausrufezeichen. [-ge-, *h*) rest.]

'ausruhen *v/i.*, *v/t.* and *v/refl.* (*sep.*,)

'ausrüst|en *v/t.* (*sep.*, -ge-, *h*) fit out; equip; '2ung *f* outfit, equip-ment, fittings *pl.* [disseminate.]

'aussäen *v/t.* (*sep.*, -ge-, *h*) sow; *fig.*)

'Aussage *f* statement; declaration; ⚖ evidence; *gr.* predicate; '2n (*sep.*, -ge-, *h*) **1.** *v/t.* state, declare; ⚖ depose; **2.** ⚖ *v/i.* give evidence.

'Aussatz ⚕ *m* (-es/*no pl.*) leprosy.

'aus|saugen *v/t.* (*sep.*, -ge-, *h*) suck

(out); *fig.* exhaust (*land*); '~schal-ten *v/t.* (*sep.*, -ge-, *h*) eliminate; ⚡ cut out, switch off, turn off *or* out (*light*).

'Ausschank ['ausʃaŋk] *m* (-[e]s/⁓e) retail (*of alcoholic drinks*); public house, F pub.

'Ausschau *f* (-/*no pl.*): ~ *halten nach* be on the look-out for, watch for.

'ausscheid|en (*irr.* scheiden, *sep.*, -ge-) **1.** *v/t.* (*h*) separate; ⚕, ⚗, *physiol.* eliminate; ⚗ secrete; **2.** *v/i.* (*sein*) retire; withdraw; *sports:* drop out; '2ung *f* separa-tion; elimination (*a. sports*); ⚗ secretion.

'aus|schiffen *v/t. and v/refl.* (*sep.*, -ge-, *h*) disembark; '~schimpfen *v/t.* (*sep.*, -ge-, *h*) scold, tell *s.o.* off, berate; '~schirren *v/t.* ['~ʃirən] (*sep.*,-ge-, *h*) unharness; '~schlach-ten *v/t.* (*sep.*, -ge-, *h*) cut up; can-nibalize (*car, etc.*); *fig.* exploit, make the most of; '~schlafen (*irr.* schlafen, *sep.*, -ge-, *h*) **1.** *v/i.* sleep one's fill; **2.** *v/t.* sleep off (*effects of drink, etc.*).

'Ausschlag *m* ⚕ eruption, rash; deflexion (*of pointer*); *den* ~ *geben* settle it; '2en ['~ʃlaɡən] (*irr.* schlagen, *sep.*, -ge-) **1.** *v/t.* (*h*) knock *or* beat out; line; refuse, decline; **2.** *v/i.* (*h*) *horse:* kick; *pointer:* deflect; **3.** *v/i.* (*h, sein*) bud; '2gebend *adj.* ['~k-] decisive.

'ausschließ|en (*irr.* schließen, *sep.*, -ge-, *h*) shut *or* lock out; *fig.:* exclude; expel; *sports:* disqualify; '~lich *adj.* exclusive.

'Ausschluß *m* exclusion; expulsion; *sports:* disqualification.

'ausschmücken *v/t.* (*sep.*, -ge-, *h*) adorn, decorate; *fig.* embellish.

'Ausschnitt *m* cut; décolleté, (low) neck (*of dress*); cutting, *Am.* clip-ping (*from newspaper*); *fig.* part, section.

'ausschreib|en *v/t.* (*irr.* schreiben, *sep.*, -ge-, *h*) write out; copy; write out (*word*) in full; make out (*in-voice*); announce; advertise; '2ung *f* (-/-en) announcement; advertise-ment.

'ausschreit|en (*irr.* schreiten, *sep.*, -ge-) **1.** *v/i.* (*sein*) step out, take long strides; **2.** *v/t.* (*h*) pace (*room*), measure by steps; '2ung *f* (-/-en) excess; ~en *pl.* riots *pl.*

'Ausschuß m refuse, waste, rubbish; committee, board.

'aus|schütteln v/t. (sep., -ge-, h) shake out; **'~schütten** v/t. (sep., -ge-, h) pour out; spill; † distribute (dividend); j-m sein Herz ~ pour out one's heart to s.o.; **'~schwärmen** v/i. (sep., -ge-, sein) swarm out; ~ (lassen) ✕ extend, deploy.

'ausschweif|end adj. dissolute; **'℧ung** f (-/-en) debauchery, excess.

'ausschwitzen v/t. (sep., -ge-, h) exude.

'aussehen 1. v/i. (irr. sehen, sep., -ge-, h) look; wie sieht er aus? what does he look like?; es sieht nach Regen aus it looks like rain; **2.** ℧ n (-s/ no pl.) look(s pl.), appearance.

außen adv. ['ausən] (on the) outside; von ~ her from (the) outside; nach ~ (hin) outward(s); **'℧aufnahme** f film: outdoor shot; **'℧bordmotor** m outboard motor.

'aussenden v/t. ([irr. senden,] sep., -ge-, h) send out.

'Außen|hafen m outport; **'~handel** m foreign trade; **'~minister** m foreign minister; Foreign Secretary, Am. Secretary of State; **'~ministerium** n foreign ministry; Foreign Office, Am. State Department; **'~politik** f foreign policy; **'℧politisch** adj. of or referring to foreign affairs; **'~seite** f outside; surface; **'~seiter** m (-s/-) outsider; **'~stände** ✝ ['~ʃtɛndə] pl. outstanding debts pl., Am. accounts pl. receivable; **'~welt** f outer or outside world.

außer ['ausər] **1.** prp. (dat.) out of; beside(s), Am. aside from; except; ~ sich sein be beside o.s. (vor Freude with joy); **2.** cj.: ~ daß except that; ~ wenn unless; **'~dem** cj. besides, moreover.

äußere ['ɔysərə] **1.** adj. exterior, outer, external, outward; **2.** ℧ n (Äußer[e]n/no pl.) exterior, outside, outward appearance.

'außer|gewöhnlich adj. extraordinary; exceptional; **'~halb 1.** prp. (gen.) outside, out of; beyond; **2.** adv. on the outside.

äußerlich adj. ['ɔysərliç] external, outward; **'℧keit** f (-/-en) superficiality; formality.

äußern ['ɔysərn] v/t. (ge-, h) utter, express; advance; sich ~ matter:

manifest itself; p. express o.s.

'außer'ordentlich adj. extraordinary.

äußerst ['ɔysərst] **1.** adj. outermost; fig. utmost, extreme; **2.** adv. extremely, highly.

außerstande adj. [ausər'ʃtandə] unable, not in-a position.

'Äußerung f (-/-en) utterance, remark.

'aussetz|en (sep., -ge-, h) **1.** v/t. set or put out; lower (boat); promise (reward); settle (pension); bequeath; expose (child); expose (dat. to); et. ~ an (dat.) find fault with; **2.** v/i. intermit; fail; activity: stop; suspend; mot. misfire; **'℧ung** f (-/-en) exposure (of child, to weather, etc.) (a. ✝).

'Aussicht f (-/-en) view (auf acc. of); fig. prospect (of), chance (of); in ~ haben have in prospect; **'℧slos** adj. hopeless, desperate; **'℧sreich** adj. promising, full of promise.

'aussöhn|en ['ausˌzøːnən] v/t. (sep., -ge-, h) reconcile s.o. (mit to s.th., with s.o.); sich ~ reconcile o.s. (to s.th., with s.o.); **'℧ung** f (-/-en) reconciliation.

'aussondern v/t. (sep., -ge-, h) single out; separate.

'aus|spannen (sep., -ge-, h) **1.** v/t. stretch, extend; F fig. steal (s.o.'s girl friend); unharness (draught animal); **2.** fig. v/i. (take a) rest, relax; **'~speien** v/t. and v/i. (irr. speien, sep., -ge-, h) spit out.

'aussperr|en v/t. (sep., -ge-, h) shut out; lock out (workmen); **'℧ung** f (-/-en) lock-out.

'aus|spielen (sep., -ge-, h) **1.** v/t. play (card); **2.** v/i. at cards: lead; er hat ausgespielt he is done for; **'~spionieren** v/t. (sep., no -ge-, h) spy out.

'Aussprache f pronunciation, accent; discussion.

'aussprechen (irr. sprechen, sep., -ge-, h) **1.** v/t. pronounce, express; sich ~ für (gegen) declare o.s. for (against); **2.** v/i. finish speaking.

'Ausspruch m utterance; saying; remark.

'aus|spucken v/i. and v/t. (sep., -ge-, h) spit out; **'~spülen** v/t. (sep., -ge-, h) rinse.

'Ausstand m strike, Am. F a. walkout; in den ~ treten go on strike, Am. F a. walk out.

ausstatt|en ['ausʃtatən] v/t. (sep.,
-ge-, h) fit out, equip; furnish;
supply (mit with); give a dowry to
(daughter); get up (book); 'ung f
(-/-en) outfit, equipment; furniture; supply; dowry; get-up (of
book).

'**aus|stechen** v/t. (irr. stechen, sep.,
-ge-, h) cut out (a. fig.); put out
(eye); 'stehen (irr. stehen, sep.,
-ge-, h) **1.** v/i. payments: be outstanding; **2.** v/t. endure, bear;
'steigen v/i. (irr. steigen, sep.,
-ge-, sein) get out or off, alight.

'**ausstell|en** v/t. (sep., -ge-, h) ex-
hibit; make out (invoice); issue
(document); draw (bill); '2er m (-s/-)
exhibitor; drawer; 'ung f exhibition, show; 'ungsraum m
show-room.

'**aussterben** v/i. (irr. sterben, sep.,
-ge-, sein) die out; become extinct.
'**Aussteuer** f trousseau, dowry.
'**ausstopfen** v/t. (sep., -ge-, h) stuff;
wad, pad.

'**ausstoß|en** v/t. (irr. stoßen, sep.,
-ge-, h) thrust out, eject; expel;
utter (cry); heave (sigh); ✕ cashier;
'ung f (-/-en) expulsion.

'**aus|strahlen** v/t. and v/i. (sep.,
-ge-, h) radiate; 'strecken v/t.
(sep., -ge-, h) stretch (out); 'streichen v/t. (irr. streichen, sep., -ge-, h)
strike out; smooth (down); '-
streuen v/t. (sep., -ge-, h) scatter;
spread (rumours); 'strömen v/i. (sep.,
-ge-) **1.** v/i. (sein) stream out; gas,
light: emanate; gas, steam: escape;
2. v/t. (h) pour (out); 'suchen v/t.
(sep., -ge-, h) choose, select.

'**Austausch** m exchange; '2bar adj.
exchangeable; '2en v/t. (sep., -ge-,
h) exchange.

'**austeil|en** v/t. (sep., -ge-, h) dis-
tribute; deal out (blows); '2ung f
distribution.

Auster zo. ['austər] f (-/-n) oyster.
'**austragen** v/t. (irr. tragen, sep.,
-ge-, h) deliver (letters, etc.); hold
(contest).

Austral|ier [au'stra:liər] m (-s/-)
Australian; 2isch adj. Australian.
'**austreib|en** v/t. (irr. treiben, sep.,
-ge-, h) drive out; expel; '2ung f
(-/-en) expulsion.

'**aus|treten** (irr. treten, sep., -ge-)
1. v/t. (h) tread or stamp out; wear
out (shoes); wear down (steps);

2. v/i. (sein) emerge, come out;
river: overflow its banks; retire
(aus from); F ease o.s.; aus
leave (society, etc.); 'trinken (irr.
trinken, sep., -ge-, h) **1.** v/t. drink
up; empty, drain; **2.** v/i. finish
drinking; '2tritt m leaving; retirement; 'trocknen (sep., -ge-) **1.** v/t.
(h) dry up; drain (land); parch
(throat, earth); **2.** v/i. (sein) dry up.
ausüb|en ['aus?-] v/t. (sep., -ge-, h)
exercise; practi|se, Am. -ce (profes-
sion); exert (influence); '2ung f
practice; exercise.

'**Ausverkauf** ✝ m selling off or out
(of stock); sale; '2t ✝, thea. adj.
sold out; theatre notice: 'full house'.
'**Auswahl** f choice; selection; ✝
assortment.   [choose, select.]
'**auswählen** v/t. (sep., -ge-, h)]
'**Auswander|er** m emigrant; '2n
v/i. (sep., -ge-, sein) emigrate; 'ung
f emigration.

auswärt|ig adj. ['ausvɛrtiç] out-of-
town; non-resident; foreign; das
Auswärtige Amt s. Außenministerium; 's adv. ['s] outward(s); out
of doors; out of town; abroad;
essen dine out.

'**auswechseln 1.** v/t. (sep., -ge-, h)
exchange; change; replace; **2.** 2 n
(-s/no pl.) exchange; replacement.
'**Ausweg** m way out (a. fig.); outlet;
fig. expedient.

'**ausweichen** v/i. (irr. weichen, sep.,
-ge-, sein) make way (for); fig.
evade, avoid; 'd adj. evasive.
Ausweis ['ausvais] m (-es/-e) (bank)
return; identity card, Am. identi-
fication (card); 2en ['zən] v/t. (irr.
weisen, sep., -ge-, h) turn out; expel;
evict; deport; show, prove; sich
prove one's identity; 'papiere
n/pl. identity papers pl.; 'ung
['zuŋ] f expulsion; 'ungsbefehl
m expulsion order.

'**ausweiten** v/t. and v/refl. (sep.,
-ge-, h) widen, stretch, expand.
'**auswendig 1.** adj. outward, outside; **2.** adv. outwardly, outside;
fig. by heart.

'**aus|werfen** v/t. (irr. werfen, sep.,
-ge-, h) throw out, cast; eject; ⚗
expectorate; allow (sum of money);
'werten v/t. (sep., -ge-, h) evalu-
ate; analyze, interpret; utilize, exploit; 'wickeln v/t. (sep., -ge-, h)
unwrap; 'wiegen v/t. (irr. wiegen,

sep., -ge-, h) weigh out; '**~wirken**
v/refl. (sep., -ge-, h) take effect,
operate; sich ~ auf (acc.) affect;
'**⁢wirkung** f effect; '**~wischen** v/t.
(sep., -ge-, h) wipe out, efface;
'**~wringen** v/t. (irr. wringen, sep.,
-ge-, h) wring out.

'**Auswuchs** m excrescence, out-
growth (a. fig.), protuberance.

'**Auswurf** m 🜊 expectoration; fig.
refuse, dregs pl.

'**aus|zahlen** v/t. (sep., -ge-, h) pay
out; pay s.o. off; '**~zählen** v/t.
(sep., -ge-, h) count out.

'**Auszahlung** f payment.

'**Auszehrung** f (-/-en) consumption.

'**auszeichn|en** v/t. (sep., -ge-, h)
mark (out); fig. distinguish (sich
o.s.); '**~ung** f marking; distinction;
hono(u)r; decoration.

'**auszieh|en** (irr. ziehen, sep., -ge-)
1. v/t. (h) draw out, extract; take
off (garment); sich ~ undress; **2.** v/i.
(sein) set out; move (out), remove,
move house; '**⁢platte** f leaf (of table).

'**Auszug** m departure; 🛠 marching
out; removal; extract, excerpt
(from book); summary; 🕆 statement (of account). [tic, genuine.\

authentisch adj. [au'tɛntiʃ] authen-\

Auto ['auto] n (-s/-s) (motor-)car,
Am. a. automobile; ~ fahren drive,
motor; '**~bahn** f motorway, autobahn; **~biogra'phie** f autobiog-
raphy; '**~bus** ['~bus] m (-ses/-se)
(motor-)bus; (motor) coach; '**~bus-**

haltestelle f bus stop; **~didakt**
[~di'dakt] m (-en/-en) autodidact,
self-taught person; '**~droschke** f
taxi(-cab), Am. cab; '**~fahrer** m
motorist; **~'gramm** n autograph;
~'grammjäger m autograph hunter; '**~händler** m car dealer; '**~kino**
n drive-in cinema; **~krat** [~'kra:t]
m (-en/-en) autocrat; **~kratie** [~a-
ti:] f (-/-n) autocracy; **~mat**
[~'ma:t] m (-en/-en) automaton;
slot-machine, vending machine;
~'matenrestaurant n self-service
restaurant, Am. automat; **~mation**
⊕ [~ma'tsjo:n] f (-/no pl.) automation; 2'**matisch** adj. automatic;
'**~mechaniker** m car mechanic;
~mobil [~mo'bi:l] n (-s/-e) s. Auto;
2**nom** adj. [~'no:m] autonomous;
~nomie [~o'mi:] f (-/-n) autonomy.

Autor ['autor] m (-s/-en) author.

'**Autoreparaturwerkstatt** f car
repair shop, garage. [thor(ess).\

Autorin [au'to:rin] f (-/-nen) au-\

autori|sieren [autori'zi:rən] v/t. (no
-ge-, h) authorize; **~tär** adj. [~'tɛ:r]
authoritarian; 2'**tät** f (-/-en) authority.

'**Auto|straße** f motor-road; '**~ver-**
mietung f (-/-en) car hire service.

avisieren [avi'zi:rən] v/t. (no
-ge-, h) advise.

Axt [akst] f (-/⁼e) ax(e).

Azetylen 🜔 [atsety'le:n] n (-s/no
pl.) acetylene. [2n adj. azure.\

Azur [a'tsu:r] m (-s/no pl.) azure;\

B

Bach [bax] m (-[e]s/⁼e) brook, Am.
a. run. [port.\

Backbord ⚓ ['bak-] n (-[e]s/-e)\

Backe ['bakə] f (-/-n) cheek.

backen ['bakən] (irr., -ge-, h) **1.**
v/t. bake; fry; dry (fruit); **2.** v/i.
bake; fry.

'**Backen|bart** m (side-)whiskers pl.,
Am. a. sideburns pl.; '**~zahn** m
molar (tooth), grinder.

Bäcker ['bɛkər] m (-s/-) baker; **~ei**
[~'rai] f (-/-en) baker's (shop),
bakery.

'**Back|fisch** m fried fish; fig. girl in
her teens, teenager, Am. a. bobby
soxer; '**~obst** n dried fruit; '**~ofen**

m oven; '**~pflaume** f prune; '**~pul-**
ver n baking-powder; '**~stein** m
brick; '**~ware** f baker's ware.

Bad [ba:t] n (-[e]s/⁼er) bath; in river,
etc.: a. bathe; s. Badeort; ein ~ nehmen take or have a bath.

Bade|anstalt f ['ba:də⁹-] f (public
swimming) baths pl.; '**~anzug** m
bathing-costume, bathing-suit; '**~-**
hose f bathing-drawers pl., (bath-
ing) trunks pl.; '**~kappe** f bathing-
cap; '**~kur** f spa treatment; '**~man-**
tel m bathing-gown, Am. bathrobe;
'**~meister** m bath attendant; swimming-instructor; 2**n** (ge-, h) **1.** v/t.
bath (baby, etc.); bathe (eyes, etc.);

B

2. v/i. bath, tub; have or take a bath; in river, etc.: bathe; ~ gehen go swimming; '~ofen m geyser, boiler, Am. a. water heater; '~ort m watering-place; spa; seaside resort; '~salz n bath-salt; '~strand m bathing-beach; '~tuch n bath-towel; '~wanne f bath-tub; '~zimmer n bathroom.

Bagatell|e [baga'tɛlə] f (-/-n) trifle, trifling matter, bagatelle; 2i'sieren v/t. (no -ge-, h) minimize (the importance of), Am. a. play down.

Bagger ['bagər] m (-s/-) excavator; dredge(r); '2n v/i. and v/t. (ge-, h) excavate; dredge.

Bahn [ba:n] f (-/-en) course; path; 🚂 railway, Am. railroad; mot. lane; trajectory (of bullet, etc.); ast. orbit; sports: track, course, lane; skating: rink; bowling: alley; '2brechend adj. pioneer(ing), epoch-making; art: avant-gardist; '~damm m railway embankment, Am. railroad embankment; '2en v/t. (ge-, h) clear, open (up) (way); den Weg ~ prepare or pave the way (dat. for); sich e-n Weg ~ force or work or elbow one's way; '~hof m (railway-)station, Am. (railroad-)station; '~linie f railway-line, Am. railroad line; '~steig m platform; '~steig-karte f platform ticket; '~über-gang m level crossing, Am. grade crossing.

Bahre ['ba:rə] f (-/-n) stretcher, litter; bier.

Bai [baɪ] f (-/-en) bay; creek.

Baisse ✝ ['bɛ:s(ə)] f (-/-n) depression (on the market); fall (in prices); auf ~ spekulieren ✝ bear, speculate for a fall, Am. sell short; '~spekulant m bear.

Bajonett ✗ [bajo'nɛt] n (-[e]s/-e) bayonet; das ~ aufpflanzen fix the bayonet.

Bake ['ba:kə] f (-/-n) ⚓ beacon; 🚂 warning-sign.

Bakterie [bak'te:rjə] f (-/-n) bacterium, microbe, germ.

bald adv. [balt] soon; shortly; before long; F almost, nearly; early; so ~ als möglich as soon as possible; ~ hier, ~ dort now here, now there; '~ig adj. ['~dɪç] speedy; ~e Antwort ✝ early reply; [valerian.]

Baldrian ['baldria:n] m (-s/-e)

Balg [balk] **1.** m (-[e]s/⁺e) skin; body (of doll); bellows pl.; **2.** F m, n (-[e]s/⁺er) brat, urchin; 2en ['bal-gən] v/refl. (ge-, h) scuffle (um for), wrestle (for).

Balken ['balkən] m (-s/-) beam; rafter.

Balkon [bal'kõ:; ~'ko:n] m (-s/-s, -s/-e) balcony; thea. dress circle, Am. balcony; ~tür f French window.

Ball [bal] m (-[e]s/⁺e) ball; geogr., ast. a. globe; ball, dance; auf dem ~ at the ball. [lad.]

Ballade [ba'la:də] f (-/-n) bal-

Ballast ['balast] m (-es/⁺-e) ballast; fig. burden, impediment; dead weight.

'ballen¹ v/t. (ge-, h) (form into a) ball; clench (fist); sich ~ (form into a) ball; cluster.

'Ballen² m (-s/-) bale; anat. ball; ~ Papier ten reams pl.

Ballett [ba'lɛt] n (-[e]s/-e) ballet; ~änzer [ba'lɛttɛntsər] m (-s/-) ballet-dancer.

ball|förmig adj. ['balfœrmɪç] ball-shaped, globular; '2kleid n ball-dress.

Ballon [ba'lõ:; ~'o:n] m (-s/-s; -s/-s, -e) balloon.

'Ball|saal m ball-room; '~spiel n ball-game, game of ball.

Balsam ['balza:m] m (-s/-e) balsam, balm (a. fig.); 2ieren [~a'mi:rən] v/t. (no -ge-, h) embalm.

Balz [balts] f (-/-en) mating season; display (by cock-bird).

Bambus ['bambus] m (-ses/-se) bamboo; '~rohr n bamboo, cane.

banal adj. [ba'na:l] commonplace, banal, trite; trivial; 2ität [~ali'tɛ:t] f (-/-en) banality; commonplace; triviality.

Banane [ba'na:nə] f (-/-n) banana; ~nstecker ⚡ m banana plug.

Band [bant] **1.** m (-[e]s/⁺e) volume; **2.** n (-[e]s/⁺er) band; ribbon; tape; anat. ligament; **3.** fig. n (-[e]s/-e) bond, tie; **4.** 2 pret. of binden.

Bandag|e [ban'da:ʒə] f (-/-n) bandage; 2ieren [~a'ʒi:rən] v/t. (no -ge-, h) (apply a) bandage.

Bande ['bandə] f (-/-n) billiards: cushion; fig. gang, band.

bändigen ['bɛndigən] v/t. (ge-, h) tame; break in (horse); subdue (a. fig.); fig. restrain, master.

B

Bandit [ban'di:t] *m* (-en/-en) bandit.
'**Band**|**maß** *n* tape measure; '~**säge**
f band-saw; '~**scheibe** *anat.* *f*
intervertebral disc; '~**wurm** *zo.* *m*
tapeworm.

bang *adj.* [baŋ], ~**e** *adj.* ['~ə] anxious
(*um* about), uneasy (about), con-
cerned (for); *mir ist* ~ I am afraid
(*vor dat.* of); *j-m bange machen*
frighten *or* scare s.o.; '~**en** *v/i.*
(*ge-*, *h*) be anxious *or* worried (*um*
about).

Bank [baŋk] *f* **1.** (-/~e) bench;
school: desk; F *durch die* ~ without
exception, all through; *auf die*
lange ~ *schieben* put off, postpone;
shelve; **2.** † (-/-en) bank; *Geld auf*
der ~ money in the bank; '~**anwei-**
sung *f* cheque, *Am.* check; '~**aus-**
weis *m* bank return *or* statement;
'~**beamte** *m* bank clerk *or* official;
'~**einlage** *f* deposit.

Bankett [baŋ'kɛt] *n* (-[e]s/-e) banquet.

'**Bank**|**geheimnis** *n* banker's duty
of secrecy; '~**geschäft** † *n* bank
(-ing) transaction, banking operation; '~**haus** *n* bank(ing-house).

Bankier [baŋk'je:] *m* (-s/-s) banker.

'**Bank**|**konto** *n* bank(ing) account;
'~**note** *f* (bank) note, *Am.* (bank)
bill.

bankrott [baŋ'krɔt] **1.** *adj.* bankrupt; **2.** ♀ *m* (-[e]s/-e) bankruptcy,
insolvency, failure; ~ *machen* fail,
go *or* become bankrupt.

'**Bankwesen** *n* banking.

Bann [ban] *m* (-[e]s/-e) ban; *fig.*
spell; *eccl.* excommunication; '~**en**
v/t. (*ge-*, *h*) banish (*a. fig.*); exorcize
(*devil*); avert (*danger*); *eccl.* ex-
communicate; spellbind.

Banner ['banər] *n* (-s/-) banner (*a.*
fig.); standard; '~**träger** *m* stand-
ard-bearer.

'**Bann**|**fluch** *m* anathema; '~**meile**
f precincts *pl.*; ⚖ *area around*
government buildings within which
processions and meetings are prohib-
ited.

bar[1] [ba:r] **1.** *adj.*: *e-r Sache* ~
destitute *or* devoid of s.th.; ~*es*
Geld ready money, cash; ~*er Unsinn*
sheer nonsense; **2.** *adv.*: ~ *bezahlen*
pay in cash, pay money down.

Bar[2] [~] *f* (-/-s) bar; night-club.

Bär [bɛ:r] *m* (-en/-en) bear; *j-m e-n*
~*en aufbinden* hoax s.o.

Baracke [ba'rakə] *f* (-/-n) barrack;
~**lager** *n* hutment.

Barbar [bar'ba:r] *m* (-en/-en) barbarian; ~**ei** [~a'raɪ] *f* (-/-en) bar-
barism; barbarity; ♀**isch** [~'ba:rɪʃ]
adj. barbarian; barbarous; *art,*
taste: barbaric.

'**Bar**|**bestand** *m* cash in hand; '~**be-**
trag *m* amount in cash.

'**Bärenzwinger** *m* bear-pit.

barfuß *adj. and adv.* ['ba:r-], ~**füßig**
adj. and adv. ['~fy:sıç] barefoot.

barg [bark] *pret. of bergen.*

'**Bar**|**geld** *n* cash, ready money;
'♀**geldlos** *adj.* cashless; ~**er** *Zah-*
lungsverkehr cashless money trans-
fers *pl.*; ♀**häuptig** *adj. and adv.*
['~hɔʏptɪç] bare-headed, uncovered.

Bariton ♪ ['ba:ritɔn] *m* (-s/-e)
baritone.   [launch.)

Barkasse ⚓ [bar'kasə] *f* (-/-n))

barmherzig *adj.* [barm'hɛrtsɪç]
merciful, charitable; *der* ~*e Sama-*
riter the good Samaritan; ♀**e**
Schwester Sister of Mercy *or* Charity; ♀**keit** *f* (-/-en) mercy, charity.

Barometer [baro'-] *n* barometer.

Baron [ba'ro:n] *m* (-s/-e) baron; ~**in**
f (-/-nen) baroness.

Barre ['barə] *f* (-/-n) bar.

Barren ['barən] *m* (-s/-) *metall.* bar,
ingot, bullion; *gymnastics:* parallel
bars *pl.*

Barriere [bar'jɛ:rə] *f* (-/-n) barrier.

Barrikade [bari'ka:də] *f* (-/-n)
barricade; ~*n errichten* raise barri-
cades.

barsch *adj.* [barʃ] rude, gruff, rough.

'**Bar**|**schaft** *f* (-/-en) ready money,
cash; '~**scheck** † *m* open cheque,
Am. open check.

barst [barst] *pret. of bersten.*

Bart [ba:rt] *m* (-[e]s/~e) beard; bit
(*of key*); *sich e-n* ~ *wachsen lassen*
grow a beard.

bärtig *adj.* ['bɛ:rtıç] bearded.

'**bartlos** *adj.* beardless.

'**Barzahlung** *f* cash payment; *nur*
gegen ~ † terms strictly cash.

Basis ['ba:zıs] *f* (-/Basen) base; *fig.*
basis.

Baß ♪ [bas] *m* (Basses/Bässe) bass;
'~**geige** *f* bass-viol.

Bassist [ba'sıst] *m* (-en/-en) bass
(singer).

Bast [bast] *m* (-es/-e) bast; velvet
(*on antlers*).

Bastard ['bastart] *m* (-[e]s/-e) bas-

B

tard; half-breed; *zo.*, ⚥ hybrid.

bast|eln ['bastəln] (ge-, h) 1. *v/t.*
build, ⚡ rig up; 2. *v/i.* build; '2ler
m (-s/-) amateur craftsman, do-it-
yourself man.

bat [ba:t] *pret. of* bitten.

Bataillon [batal'jo:n] *n* (-s/-e)
battalion.

Batist [ba'tist] *m* (-[e]s/-e) cambric.

Batterie ✗, ⚡ [batə'ri:] *f* (-/-n)
battery.

Bau [bau] *m* 1. (-[e]s/*no pl.*) building, construction; build, frame;
2. (-[e]s/-ten) building, edifice;
3. (-[e]s/-e) burrow, den (*a. fig.*),
earth.

'Bau|arbeiter *m* workman in the
building trade; '**~art** *f* architecture,
style; method of construction;
mot. type, model.

Bauch [baux] *m* (-[e]s/⸚e) *anat.*
abdomen, belly; paunch; *ship:*
bottom; '2**ig** *adj.* big-bellied; bulgy;
'**~landung** *f* belly landing; '**~red-**
ner *m* ventriloquist; '**~schmerzen**
m/pl., '**~weh** *n* (-s/*no pl.*) belly-ache,
stomach-ache.

bauen ['bauən] (ge-, h) 1. *v/t.* build,
construct; erect; raise; build, make
(*nest*); make (*violin, etc.*); 2. *v/i.*
build; ~ *auf* (*acc.*) trust (in); rely
or count *or* depend on.

Bauer ['bauər] 1. *m* (-n, -s/-n)
farmer; peasant, countryman; *chess:*
pawn; 2. *n*, *m* (-s/-) (bird-)cage.

Bäuerin ['bɔyərin] *f* (-/-nen) farmer's wife; peasant woman.

Bauerlaubnis ['bauʔ-] *f* building
permit.

bäuerlich *adj.* ['bɔyərliç] rural,
rustic.

Bauern|fänger *contp.* ['bauərn-
fɛŋər] *m* (-s/-) trickster, confidence
man; '**~haus** *n* farm-house; '**~hof**
m farm.

'bau|fällig *adj.* out of repair,
dilapidated; '2**gerüst** *n* scaffold
(-ing); '2**handwerker** *m* craftsman
in the building trade; '2**herr** *m*
owner; '2**holz** *n* timber, *Am.* lumber; '2**jahr** *n* year of construction;
~ *1969* 1969 model *or* make; '2**ka-**
sten *m* box of bricks; '2**kunst** *f*
architecture.

'baulich *adj.* architectural; struc-
tural; *in gutem ~en Zustand* in good
repair.

Baum [baum] *m* (-[e]s/⸚e) tree.

'Baumeister *m* architect.

baumeln ['bauməln] *v/i.* (ge-, h)
dangle, swing; *mit den Beinen* ~
dangle *or* swing one's legs.

'Baum|schere *f* (*eine a pair of*)
pruning-shears *pl.*; '**~schule** *f*
nursery (*of young trees*); '**~stamm**
m trunk; '**~wolle** *f* cotton; '2**wol-**
len *adj.* (made of) cotton.

'Bau|plan *m* architect's *or* building
plan; '**~platz** *m* building plot *or* site,
Am. location; '**~polizei** *f* Board of
Surveyors.

Bausch [bauʃ] *m* (-es/-e, ⸚e) pad;
bolster; wad; *in ~ und Bogen* alto-
gether, wholesale, in the lump;
'2**en** *v/t.* (ge-, h) swell; *sich* ~ bulge,
swell out, billow (out).

'Bau|stein *m* brick, building stone;
building block; *fig.* element; '**~**
stelle *f* building site; '**~stil** *m* (architectural) style; '**~stoff** *m* building material; '**~unternehmer** *m*
building contractor; '**~zaun** *m*
hoarding.

Bay|er ['baiər] *m* (-n/-n) Bavarian;
'2(e)**risch** *adj.* Bavarian.

Bazill|enträger 🔬 [ba'tsilən-] *m*
(germ-)carrier; **~us** [~us] *m* (-/*Ba-*
zillen) bacillus, germ.

beabsichtigen [bə'apziçtigən] *v/t.*
(*no* -ge-, h) intend, mean, propose
(*zu tun* to do, doing).

be'acht|en *v/t.* (*no* -ge-, h) pay at-
tention to; notice; observe; **~ens-**
wert *adj.* noteworthy, remarkable;
~lich *adj.* remarkable; considerable; 2**ung** *f* attention; consideration; notice; observance.

Beamte [bə'amtə] *m* (-n/-n) official,
officer, *Am. a.* officeholder; functionary; Civil Servant. [quieting.)

be'ängstigend *adj.* alarming, dis-)

beanspruch|en [bə'anʃpruxən] *v/t.*
(*no* -ge-, h) claim, demand; require
(*efforts, time, space, etc.*); ⊕ stress;
2**ung** *f* (-/-en) claim; demand (*gen.*
on); ⊕ stress, strain.

beanstand|en [bə'anʃtandən] *v/t.*
(*no* -ge-, h) object to; 2**ung** *f* (-/-en)
objection (*gen.* to).

beantragen [bə'antra:gən] *v/t.* (*no*
-ge-, h) apply for; 🏛, *parl.* move,
make a motion; propose.

be'antwort|en *v/t.* (*no* -ge-, h) an-
swer (*a. fig.*), reply to; 2**ung** *f*
(-/-en) answer, reply; *in ~* (*gen.*) in
answer *or* reply to.

be'arbeit|en v/t. (no -ge-, h) work; ✗ till; dress (leather); hew (stone); process; ♫ treat; ⚖ be in charge of (case); edit, revise (book); adapt (nach from); esp. ♪ arrange; j-n ~ work on s.o.; batter s.o.; **2ung** f (-/-en) working; revision (of book); thea. adaptation; esp. ♪ arrangement; processing; ♫ treatment.

be'argwöhnen v/t. (no -ge-, h) suspect, be suspicious of.

beaufsichtig|en [bə'aufziçtigən] v/t. (no -ge-, h) inspect, superintend, supervise, control; look after (child); **2ung** f (-/-en) inspection, supervision, control.

be'auftrag|en v/t. (no -ge-, h) commission (zu inf. to inf.), charge (mit with); **2te** [~ktə] m (-n/-n) commissioner; representative; deputy; proxy.

be'bauen v/t. (no -ge-, h) ⚒ build on; ✗ cultivate.

beben ['be:bən] v/i. (ge-, h) shake (vor dat. with), tremble (with); shiver (with); earth: quake.

Becher ['bɛçər] m (-s/-) cup (a. fig.).

Becken ['bɛkən] n (-s/-) basin, Am. a. bowl; ♪ cymbal(s pl.); anat. pelvis.

bedacht adj. [bə'daxt]: ~ sein auf (acc.) look after, be concerned about, be careful or mindful of; darauf ~ sein zu inf. be anxious to inf.

be'dächtig adj. [bə'dɛçtiç] deliberate.

bedang [bə'daŋ] pret. of bedingen.

be'danken v/refl. (no -ge-, h): sich bei j-m für et. ~ thank s.o. for s.th.

Bedarf [bə'darf] m (-[e]s/no pl.) need (an dat. of), want (of); ✝ demand (for); **~sartikel** [bə'darfs?-] m/pl. necessaries pl., requisites pl.

bedauerlich adj. [bə'dauərliç] regrettable, deplorable.

be'dauern 1. v/t. (no -ge-, h) feel or be sorry for s.o.; pity s.o.; regret, deplore s.th.; **2.** **2** n (-s/no pl.) regret; pity; **~swert** adj. pitiable, deplorable.

be'deck|en v/t. (no -ge-, h) cover; ✗ escort; ⚓ convoy; **~t** adj. sky: overcast; **2ung** f cover(ing); ✗ escort; ⚓ convoy.

be'denken v/t. (irr. denken, no -ge-, h) consider; think s.th. over;

j-n in s-m Testament ~ remember s.o. in one's will; **2.** **2** n (-s/-) consideration; objection; hesitation; scruple; **~los** adj. unscrupulous.

be'denklich adj. doubtful; character: a. dubious; situation, etc.: dangerous, critical; delicate; risky.

Be'denkzeit f time for reflection; ich gebe dir e-e Stunde ~ I give you one hour to think it over.

be'deut|en v/t. (no -ge-, h) mean, signify; stand for; **~end** adj. important, prominent; sum, etc. considerable; **~sam** adj. significant.

Be'deutung f meaning, significance; importance; 2los adj. insignificant; meaningless; 2svoll adj. significant; **~swandel** ling. m semantic change.

be'dien|en (no -ge-, h) **1.** v/t. serve; wait on; ⊕ operate, work (machine); ✗ serve (gun); answer (telephone); sich ~ at table: help o.s.; **2.** v/i. serve; wait (at table); cards: follow suit; **2ung** f (-/-en) service, esp. ✝ attendance; in restaurant, etc.: service; waiter, waitress; shop assistant(s pl.).

beding|en [bə'diŋən] v/t. ([irr.] no -ge-, h) condition; stipulate; require; cause; imply; **~t** adj. conditional (durch on); restricted; ~ sein durch be conditioned by; **2ung** f (-/-en) condition; stipulation; ~en pl. ✝ terms pl.; **~ungslos** adj. unconditional.

be'dräng|en v/t. (no -ge-, h) press hard, beset; **2nis** f (-/-se) distress.

be'droh|en v/t. (no -ge-, h) threaten; menace; **~lich** adj. threatening; **2ung** f threat, menace (gen. to).

be'drück|en v/t. (no -ge-, h) oppress; depress; deject; **2ung** f (-/-en) oppression; depression; dejection.

bedungen [bə'duŋən] p.p. of bedingen.

be'dürf|en v/i. (irr. dürfen, no -ge-, h): e-r Sache ~ need or want or require s.th.; **2nis** n (-ses/-se) need, want, requirement; sein ~ verrichten relieve o.s. or nature; **2nisanstalt** [bə'dyrfnis?-] f public convenience, Am. comfort station; **~tig** adj. needy, poor, indigent.

be'ehren v/t. (no -ge-, h) hono(u)r, favo(u)r; ich beehre mich zu inf. I have the hono(u)r to inf.

B

be'eilen *v/refl.* (*no* -ge-, *h*) hasten, hurry, make haste, *Am.* F *a.* hustle.
beeindrucken [bə'aındrukən] *v/t.* (*no* -ge-, *h*) impress, make an impression on.
beeinfluss|en [bə'aınflussən] *v/t.* (*no* -ge-, *h*) influence; affect; *parl.* lobby; 2**ung** *f* (-/-en) influence; *parl.* lobbying.
beeinträchtig|en [bə'aıntrɛçtigən] *v/t.* (*no* -ge-, *h*) impair, injure, affect (adversely); 2**ung** *f* (-/-en) impairment (*gen.* of); injury (to).
be'end|en *v/t.* (*no* -ge-, *h*), **~igen** [~igən] *v/t.* (*no* -ge-, *h*) (bring to an) end, finish, terminate; 2**igung** [~iguŋ] *f* (-/-en) ending, termination.
beengt *adj.* [bə'ɛŋkt] *space*: narrow, confined, cramped; *sich ~ fühlen* feel cramped (for room); feel oppressed *or* uneasy.
be'erben *v/t.* (*no* -ge-, *h*): *j-n ~* be s.o.'s heir.
beerdig|en [bə'e:rdigən] *v/t.* (*no* -ge-, *h*) bury; 2**ung** *f* (-/-en) burial, funeral.
Beere ['be:rə] *f* (-/-n) berry.
Beet ⚘ [be:t] *n* (-[e]s/-e) bed.
befähig|en [bə'fɛ:igən] *v/t.* (*no* -ge-, *h*) enable (*zu inf.* to *inf.*); qualify (*für, zu* for); **~t** *adj.* [~çt] (cap)able; 2**ung** *f* (-/-en) qualification; capacity.
befahl [bə'fɑ:l] *pret. of befehlen.*
befahr|bar *adj.* [bə'fɑ:rbɑ:r] passable, practicable, trafficable; ⚓ navigable; **~en** *v/t.* (*irr. fahren, no* -ge-, *h*) drive *or* travel on; ⚓ navigate (*river*).
be'fallen *v/t.* (*irr. fallen, no* -ge-, *h*) attack; befall; *disease*: *a.* strike; *fear*: seize.
be'fangen *adj.* embarrassed; self-conscious; prejudiced (*a.* ⚖); ⚖ bias(s)ed; 2**heit** *f* (-/-en) embarrassment; self-consciousness; ⚖ bias, prejudice.
be'fassen *v/refl.* (*no* -ge-, *h*): *sich ~ mit* occupy o.s. with; engage in; attend to; deal with.
Befehl [bə'fe:l] *m* (-[e]s/-e) command (*über acc.* of); order; 2**en** (*irr., no* -ge-, *h*) **1.** *v/t.* command; order; **2.** *v/i.* command; 2**igen** ⚔ [~igən] *v/t.* (*no* -ge-, *h*) command.
Be'fehlshaber *m* (-s/-) commander(-in-chief); 2**isch** *adj.* imperious.
be'festig|en *v/t.* (*no* -ge-, *h*) fasten (*an dat.* to), fix (to), attach (to); ⚔ fortify; *fig.* strengthen; 2**ung** *f* (-/-en) fixing, fastening; ⚔ fortification; *fig.* strengthening.
be'feuchten *v/t.* (*no* -ge-, *h*) moisten, damp; wet.
be'finden 1. *v/refl.* (*irr. finden, no* -ge-, *h*) be; **2.** 2 *n* (-s/*no pl.*) (state of) health.
be'flaggen *v/t.* (*no* -ge-, *h*) flag.
be'flecken *v/t.* (*no* -ge-, *h*) spot, stain (*a. fig.*); *fig.* sully.
beflissen *adj.* [bə'flisən] studious; 2**heit** *f* (-/*no pl.*) studiousness, assiduity.
befohlen [bə'fo:lən] *p.p. of befehlen.*
be'folg|en *v/t.* (*no* -ge-, *h*) follow, take (*advice*); obey (*rule*); adhere to (*principle*); 2**ung** *f* (-/⚒-en) observance (of); adherence (to).
be'förder|n *v/t.* (*no* -ge-, *h*) convey, carry; haul (*goods*), transport; forward; ✝ ship (*a.* ⚓); promote (to be) (*a.* ⚔); 2**ung** *f* conveyance, transport(ation), forwarding; promotion; 2**ungsmittel** *n* (means of) transport, *Am.* (means of) transportation.
be'fragen *v/t.* (*no* -ge-, *h*) question, interview; interrogate.
be'frei|en *v/t.* (*no* -ge-, *h*) (set) free (*von* from); liberate (*nation, mind, etc.*) (from); rescue (*captive*) (from); exempt *s.o.* (from); deliver *s.o.* (*aus, von* from); 2**er** *m* liberator; 2**ung** *f* (-/-en) liberation, deliverance; exemption.
Befremden [bə'frɛmdən] *n* (-s/ *no pl.*) surprise.
befreund|en [bə'frɔʏndən] *v/refl.* (*no* -ge-, *h*): *sich mit j-m ~* make friends with s.o.; *sich mit et. ~* get used to s.th., reconcile o.s. to s.th.; **~et** *adj.* friendly; on friendly terms; *~ sein* be friends.
befriedig|en [bə'fri:digən] *v/t.* (*no* -ge-, *h*) satisfy; appease (*hunger*); meet (*expectations, demand*); pay off (*creditor*); **~end** *adj.* satisfactory; 2**ung** *f* (-/-en) satisfaction.
be'fristen *v/t.* (*no* -ge-, *h*) set a time-limit.
be'frucht|en *v/t.* (*no* -ge-, *h*) fertilize; fructify; fecundate; impregnate; 2**ung** *f* (-/-en) fertilization; fructification; fecundation; impregnation.

Befug|nis [bə'fuːknɪs] f (-/-se) authority, warrant; *esp.* ⚖ competence; 2t *adj.* authorized; competent.

be'fühlen v/t. (no -ge-, h) feel; touch, handle, finger.

Be'fund m (-[e]s/-e) result; finding(s pl.); ⚕ diagnosis.

be'fürcht|en v/t. (no -ge-, h) fear, apprehend; suspect; 2ung f (-/-en) fear, apprehension, suspicion.

befürworten [bə'fyːrvɔrtən] v/t. (no -ge-, h) plead for, advocate.

begab|t *adj.* [bə'gaːpt] gifted, talented; 2ung f [⸚buŋ] f (-/-en) gift, talent(s pl.).

begann [bə'gan] *pret.* of beginnen.

be'geben v/t. (irr. geben, no -ge-, h) † negotiate (bill of exchange); sich ~ happen; sich ~ nach go to, make for; sich in Gefahr ~ expose o.s. to danger.

begegn|en [bə'geːgnən] v/i. (no -ge-, sein) meet s.o. or s.th., meet with; *incident*: happen to; anticipate, prevent; 2ung f (-/-en) meeting.

be'gehen v/t. (irr. gehen, no -ge-, h) walk (on); inspect; celebrate (*birthday, etc.*); commit (*crime*); make (*mistake*); ein Unrecht ~ do wrong.

begehr|en [bə'geːrən] v/t. (no -ge-, h) demand, require; desire, crave (for); long for; ~lich *adj.* desirous, covetous.

begeister|n [bə'gaɪstərn] v/t. (no -ge-, h) inspire, fill with enthusiasm; sich ~ für feel enthusiastic about; 2ung f (-/no pl.) enthusiasm, inspiration.

Be'gier f, ~de [⸚də] f (-/-n) desire (*nach* for), appetite (for); concupiscence; 2ig *adj.* eager (*nach* for, *auf acc.* for; zu *inf.* to *inf.*), desirous (*nach* of; zu *inf.* to *inf.*), anxious (zu *inf.* to *inf.*).

be'gießen v/t. (irr. gießen, no -ge-, h) water; baste (*roasting meat*); F wet (*bargain*).

Beginn [bə'gɪn] m (-[e]s/no pl.) beginning, start, commencement, origin; 2en v/t. and v/i. (irr. no -ge-, h) begin, start, commence.

beglaubig|en [bə'glaubɪgən] v/t. (no -ge-, h) attest, certify; legalize, authenticate; 2ung f (-/-en) attestation, certification; legalization; 2ungsschreiben n credentials pl.

be'gleichen † v/t. (irr. gleichen, no -ge-, h) pay, settle (*bill, debt*).

be'gleit|en v/t. (no -ge-, h) accompany (a. ♪ auf dat. on), escort; attend (a. fig.); see (s.o. home, etc.); 2er m (-s/-) companion, attendant; escort; ♪ accompanist; 2erscheinung f attendant symptom; 2schreiben n covering letter; 2ung f (-/-en) company; attendants pl.; retinue (of sovereign, etc.); esp. ✕ escort; ⚓, ✕ convoy; ♪ accompaniment.

be'glückwünschen v/t. (no -ge-, h) congratulate (zu on).

begnadig|en [bə'gnaːdɪgən] v/t. (no -ge-, h) pardon; pol. amnesty; 2ung f (-/-en) pardon; pol. amnesty.

begnügen [bə'gnyːgən] v/refl. (no -ge-, h): sich ~ mit content o.s. with, be satisfied with.

begonnen [bə'gɔnən] p.p. of beginnen.

be'graben v/t. (irr. graben, no -ge-, h) bury (a. fig.); inter.

Begräbnis [bə'grɛːpnɪs] n (-ses/-se) burial; funeral, obsequies pl.

begradigen [bə'graːdɪgən] v/t. (no -ge-, h) straighten (*road, frontier, etc.*).

be'greif|en v/t. (irr. greifen, no -ge-, h) comprehend, understand; ~lich *adj.* comprehensible.

be'grenz|en v/t. (no -ge-, h) bound, border; fig. limit; 2theit f (-/-en) limitation (of knowledge); narrowness (of mind); 2ung f (-/-en) boundary; bound, limit; limitation.

Be'griff m idea, notion, conception; comprehension; im ~ sein zu inf. be about or going to inf.

be'gründ|en v/t. (no -ge-, h) establish, found; give reasons for, substantiate (*claim, charge*); 2ung f establishment, foundation; fig. substantiation (of claim or charge); reason.

be'grüß|en v/t. (no -ge-, h) greet, welcome; salute; 2ung f (-/-en) greeting, welcome; salutation.

begünstig|en [bə'gynstɪgən] v/t. (no -ge-, h) favo(u)r; encourage; patronize; 2ung (-/-en) f favo(u)r; encouragement; patronage.

begutachten [bə'guːtʔ-] v/t. (no -ge-, h) give an opinion on; examine; ~ lassen obtain expert opinion on, submit s.th. to an expert.

B

begütert *adj.* [bə'gy:tərt] wealthy, well-to-do.

be'haart *adj.* hairy.

behäbig *adj.* [bə'hɛ:biç] phlegmatic, comfort-loving; *figure:* portly.

be'haftet *adj.* afflicted (*with disease, etc.*).

behag|en [bə'ha:gən] **1.** *v/i.* (*no -ge-, h*) please *or* suit *s.o.*; **2.** ♀ *n* (*-s/no pl.*) comfort, ease; **⁓lich** *adj.* [⁓k-] comfortable; cosy, snug.

be'halten *v/t.* (*irr. halten, no -ge-, h*) retain; keep (*für sich* to o.s.); remember.

Behälter [bə'hɛltər] *m* (*-s/-*) container, receptacle; box; *for liquid:* reservoir; *for oil, etc.:* tank.

be'hand|eln *v/t.* (*no -ge-, h*) treat; deal with (*a. subject*); ⊕ process; ⚕ treat; dress (*wound*); **♀lung** *f* treatment; handling; ⊕ processing.

be'hängen *v/t.* (*no -ge-, h*) hang, drape (*mit with*); *sich ⁓ mit* cover *or* load o.s. with (*jewellery*).

beharr|en [bə'harən] *v/i.* (*no -ge-, h*) persist (*auf dat.* in); **⁓lich** *adj.* persistent; **♀lichkeit** *f* (*-/no pl.*) persistence.

be'hauen *v/t.* (*no -ge-, h*) hew, trim (*wood*).

behaupt|en [bə'hauptən] *v/t.* (*no -ge-, h*) assert; maintain; **♀ung** *f* (*-/-en*) assertion; statement.

Behausung [bə'hauzuŋ] *f* (*-/-en*) habitation; lodging.

Be'helf *m* (*-[e]s/-e*) expedient, (make)shift; *s. Notbehelf;* **♀en** *v/refl.* (*irr. helfen, no -ge-, h*): *sich ⁓ mit* make shift with; *sich ⁓ ohne* do without; **⁓sheim** *n* temporary home.

behend *adj.* [bə'hɛnt], **⁓e** *adj.* [⁓də] nimble, agile; smart; **♀igkeit** [⁓d-] *f* (*-/no pl.*) nimbleness, agility; smartness. [lodge, shelter.]

be'herbergen *v/t.* (*no -ge-, h*)|

be'herrsch|en *v/t.* (*no -ge-, h*) rule (over), govern; command (*situation, etc.*), have command of (*language*); *sich ⁓* control o.s.; **♀er** *m* ruler (*gen.* over, of); **♀ung** *f* (*-/-en*) command, control.

beherzigen [bə'hɛrtsigən] *v/t.* (*no -ge-, h*) take to heart, (bear in) mind.

be'hexen *v/t.* (*no -ge-, h*) bewitch.

be'hilflich *adj.*: *j-m ⁓ sein* help s.o. (*bei* in).

be'hindern *v/t.* (*no -ge-, h*) hinder, hamper, impede; handicap; obstruct (*a. traffic, etc.*).

Behörde [bə'hø:rdə] *f* (*-/-n*) authority, *mst* authorities *pl.*; board; council.

be'hüten *v/t.* (*no -ge-, h*) guard, preserve (*vor dat.* from).

behutsam *adj.* [bə'hu:tza:m] cautious, careful; **♀keit** *f* (*-/no pl.*) caution.

bei *prp.* (*dat.*) [baɪ] *address:* ⁓ *Schmidt* care of (*abbr.* c/o) Schmidt; ⁓*m Buchhändler* at the bookseller's; ⁓ *uns* with us; ⁓ *der Hand nehmen* take by the hand; *ich habe kein Geld ⁓ mir* I have no money about or on me; ⁓ *der Kirche* near the church; ⁓ *guter Gesundheit* in good health; *wie es ⁓ Schiller heißt* as Schiller says; *die Schlacht ⁓ Waterloo* the Battle of Waterloo; ⁓ *e-m Glase Wein* over a glass of wine; ⁓ *alledem* for all that; *Stunden nehmen ⁓* take lessons from *or* with; ⁓ *günstigem Wetter* weather permitting.

'beibehalten *v/t.* (*irr. halten, sep., no -ge-, h*) keep up, retain.

'Beiblatt *n* supplement (*zu* to).

'beibringen *v/t.* (*irr. bringen, sep., -ge-, h*) bring forward; produce (*witness, etc.*); *j-m et. ⁓* impart (*news, etc.*) to s.o.; teach s.o. *s.th.*; inflict (*defeat, wound, etc.*) on s.o.

Beichte ['baɪçtə] *f* (*-/-n*) confession; **♀n** *v/t. and v/i.* (*ge-, h*) confess.

beide *adj.* ['baɪdə] both; *nur wir ⁓* just the two of us; *in ⁓n Fällen* in either case.

beider|lei *adj.* ['baɪdərlaɪ] of both kinds; ⁓ *Geschlechts* of either sex; **'⁓seitig 1.** *adj.* on both sides; mutual; **2.** *adv.* mutually; **'⁓seits 1.** *prp.* on both sides (*gen.* of); **2.** *adv.* mutually.

'Beifahrer *m* (*-s/-*) (front-seat) passenger; assistant driver; *motor racing:* co-driver.

'Beifall *m* (*-[e]s/no pl.*) approbation; applause; cheers *pl.*

'beifällig *adj.* approving; favo(u)rable.

'Beifallsruf *m* acclaim; ⁓*e pl.* cheers *pl.*

'beifügen *v/t.* (*sep., -ge-, h*) add; enclose.

'Beigeschmack *m* (*-[e]s/no pl.*)

'**Beihilfe** f aid; allowance; for study: grant; for project: subsidy; $\frac{t}{t}$ aiding and abetting; j-m ~ leisten $\frac{t}{t}$ aid and abet s.o.

'**beikommen** v/i. (irr. kommen, sep., -ge-, sein) get at.

Beil [baɪl] n (-[e]s/-e) hatchet; chopper; cleaver; ax(e).

'**Beilage** f supplement (to newspaper); F trimmings pl. (of meal); vegetables pl.

beiläufig adj. ['baɪləfɪç] casual; incidental.

'**beileg|en** v/t. (sep., -ge-, h) add (dat. to); enclose; settle (dispute); '**Qung** f (-/-en) settlement.

Beileid ['baɪlaɪt] n condolence; j-m sein ~ bezeigen condole with s.o. (zu on, upon).

'**beiliegen** v/i. (irr. liegen, sep., -ge-, h) be enclosed (dat. with).

'**beimessen** v/t. (irr. messen, sep., -ge-, h) attribute (dat. to), ascribe (to); attach (importance) (to).

'**beimisch|en** v/t. (sep., -ge-, h): e-r Sache et. ~ mix s.th. with s.th.; '**Qung** f admixture.

Bein [baɪn] n (-[e]s/-e) leg; bone.

'**beinah(e)** adv. almost, nearly.

'**Beiname** m appellation; nickname.

'**Beinbruch** m fracture of the leg.

beiordnen ['baɪ'?-] v/t. (sep., -ge-, h) adjoin; co-ordinate (a. gr.).

'**beipflichten** v/i. (sep., -ge-, h) agree with s.o.; assent to s.th.

'**Beirat** m (-[e]s/=e) adviser, counsel(l)or; advisory board.

be'irren v/t. (no -ge-, h) confuse.

beisammen adv. [baɪ'zamən] together.

'**Beisein** n presence; im ~ (gen.) or von in the presence of s.o., in s.o.'s presence.

bei'seite adv. aside, apart; Spaß ~! joking apart!

'**beisetz|en** v/t. (sep., -ge-, h) bury, inter; '**Qung** f (-/-en) burial, funeral.

'**Beisitzer** $\frac{t}{t}$ m (-s/-) assessor; associate judge; member of committee).

'**Beispiel** n example, instance; zum ~ for example or instance; '**Qhaft** adj. exemplary; '**Qlos** adj. unprecedented, unparalleled; unheard of.

beißen ['baɪsən] (irr., ge-, h) **1.** v/t. bite; fleas, etc.: bite, sting; **2.** v/i. bite (auf acc. on; in acc. into);

fleas, etc.: bite, sting; smoke: bite, burn (in dat. in); pepper, etc.: bite, burn (auf dat. on); '**d** adj. biting, pungent (both a. fig.); pepper, etc.: hot.

'**Beistand** m assistance.

'**beistehen** v/i. (irr. stehen, sep., -ge-, h): j-m ~ stand by or assist or help s.o.

'**beisteuern** v/t. and v/i. (sep., -ge-, h) contribute (zu to).

Beitrag ['baɪtraːk] m (-[e]s/=e) contribution; share; subscription, Am. dues pl.; article (in newspaper, etc.).

'**bei|treten** v/i. (irr. treten, sep., -ge-, sein) join (political party, etc.); '**Qtritt** m joining.

'**Beiwagen** m side-car (of motorcycle); trailer (of tram).

'**Beiwerk** n accessories pl.

'**beiwohnen** v/i. (sep., -ge-, h) assist or be present at, attend.

bei'zeiten adv. early; in good time.

beizen ['baɪtsən] v/t. (ge-, h) corrode; metall. pickle; bate (hides); stain (wood); ✿ cauterize; hunt. hawk.

bejahen [bə'jaːən] v/t. (no -ge-, h) answer in the affirmative, affirm; '**d** adj. affirmative.

be'jahrt adj. aged.

Bejahung f (-/-en) affirmation, affirmative answer; fig. acceptance.

be'jammern s. beklagen.

be'kämpfen v/t. (no -ge-, h) fight (against), combat; fig. oppose.

bekannt adj. [bə'kant] known (dat. to); j-n mit j-m ~ machen introduce s.o. to s.o.; **Qe** m, f (-n/-n) acquaintance, mst friend; '**lich** adv. as you know; ~**machen** v/t. (sep., -ge-, h) make known; **Qmachung** f (-/-en) publication; public notice; **Qschaft** f (-/-en) acquaintance.

be'kehr|en v/t. (no -ge-, h) convert; **Qte** m, f (-n/-n) convert; **Qung** f (-/-en) conversion (zu to).

be'kenn|en v/t. (irr. kennen, no -ge-, h) admit; confess; sich schuldig ~ $\frac{t}{t}$ plead guilty; sich ~ zu declare o.s. for; profess s.th.; **Qtnis** n (-ses/-se) confession; creed.

be'klagen v/t. (no -ge-, h) lament, deplore; sich ~ complain (über acc. of, about); ~**swert** adj. deplorable, pitiable.

Beklagte [bə'klaːktə] m, f (-n/-n) civil case: defendant, the accused.

be'klatschen v/t. (no -ge-, h) applaud, clap.

be'kleben v/t. (no -ge-, h) glue or stick s.th. on s.th.; mit Etiketten ~ label s.th.; mit Papier ~ paste s.th. up with paper; e-e Mauer mit Plakaten ~ paste (up) posters on a wall.

bekleckern F [bə'klɛkərn] v/t. (no -ge-, h) stain (garment); sich ~ soil one's clothes. [daub; blot.)

be'klecksen v/t. (no -ge-, h) stain,)

be'kleid|en v/t. (no -ge-, h) clothe, dress; hold; fill (office, etc.); ~ mit invest with; **2ung** f clothing, clothes pl.

be'klemm|en v/t. (no -ge-, h) oppress; **2ung** f (-/-en) oppression; anguish, anxiety.

be'kommen (irr. kommen, no -ge-) **1.** v/t. (h) get, receive; obtain; get, catch (illness); have (baby); catch (train, etc.); Zähne ~ teethe, cut one's teeth; **2.** v/i. (sein): j-m (gut) ~ agree with s.o.; j-m nicht or schlecht ~ disagree with s.o.

bekömmlich adj. [bə'kœmliç] wholesome (dat. to).

beköstig|en [bə'kœstigən] v/t. (no -ge-, h) board, feed; **2ung** f (-/ɐ̃ -en) board(ing).

be'kräftig|en v/t. (no -ge-, h) confirm; **2ung** f (-/-en) confirmation.

be'kränzen v/t. (no -ge-, h) wreathe, festoon. [criticize.)

be'kritteln v/t. (no -ge-, h) carp at,)

be'kümmern v/t. (no -ge-, h) afflict, grieve; trouble; s. kümmern.

be'laden v/t. (irr. laden, no -ge-, h) load; fig. burden.

Belag [bə'laːk] m (-[e]s/ɐ̃e) covering; ⊕ coat(ing); surface (of road); foil (of mirror); 𝒮ʳ fur (on tongue); (slices of) ham, etc. (on bread); filling (of roll).

Belager|er [bə'laːgərər] m (-s/-) besieger; **2n** v/t. (no -ge-, h) besiege, beleaguer; **~ung** f siege.

Belang [bə'laŋ] m (-[e]s/-e) importance; ~e pl. interests pl.; **2en** v/t. (no -ge-, h) concern; 𝒮ʳ sue; **2los** adj. unimportant; **~losigkeit** f (-/-en) insignificance.

be'lasten v/t. (no -ge-, h) load; fig. burden; 𝒮ʳ incriminate; mortgage (estate, etc.); j-s Konto (mit e-r Summe) ~ † charge or debit s.o.'s account (with a sum).

belästig|en [bə'lɛstigən] v/t. (no -ge-, h) molest; trouble; bother; **2ung** f molestation; trouble.

Be'lastung f (-/-en) load (a. 𝒮, ⊕); fig. burden; † debit; encumbrance; 𝒮ʳ incrimination; erbliche ~ hereditary taint; **~szeuge** 𝒮ʳ m witness for the prosecution.

be'laufen v/refl. (irr. laufen, no -ge-, h): sich ~ auf (acc.) amount to.

be'lauschen v/t. (no -ge-, h) overhear, eavesdrop on s.o.

be'leb|en fig. v/t. (no -ge-, h) enliven, animate; stimulate; **~t** adj. street: busy, crowded; stock exchange: brisk; conversation: lively, animated.

Beleg [bə'leːk] m (-[e]s/-e) proof; 𝒮ʳ (supporting) evidence; document; voucher; **2en** [~gən] v/t. (no -ge-, h) cover; reserve (seat, etc.); prove, verify; univ. enrol(l) or register for, Am. a. sign up for (course of lectures, term); ein Brötchen mit et. ~ put s.th. on a roll, fill a roll with s.th.; **~schaft** f (-/-en) personnel, staff; labo(u)r force; **~stelle** f reference; **2t** adj. engaged, occupied; hotel, etc.: full; voice: thick, husky; tongue: coated, furred; **~es Brot** (open) sandwich.

be'lehr|en v/t. (no -ge-, h) instruct, inform; sich ~ lassen take advice; **~end** adj. instructive; **2ung** f (-/-en) instruction; information; advice.

beleibt adj. [bə'laɪpt] corpulent, stout, bulky, portly.

beleidig|en [bə'laɪdigən] v/t. (no -ge-, h) offend (s.o.; ear, eye, etc.); insult; **~end** adj. offensive; insulting; **2ung** f (-/-en) offen|ce, Am. -se; insult.

be'lesen adj. well-read.

be'leucht|en v/t. (no -ge-, h) light (up), illuminate (a. fig.); fig. shed or throw light on; **2ung** f (-/-en) light(ing); illumination; **2ungskörper** m lighting appliance.

be'licht|en phot. v/t. (no -ge-, h) expose; **2ung** phot. f exposure.

Be'lieb|en n (-s/no pl.) will, choice; nach ~ at will; es steht in Ihrem ~ I leave it to you; **2ig 1.** adj. any; jeder ~e anyone; **2.** adv. at pleasure; ~ viele as many as you like; **2t** adj. [~pt] popular (bei with); **~theit** f (-/no pl.) popularity.

be'liefer|n v/t. (no -ge-, h) supply,

furnish (*mit* with); 2ung *f* (-/*no pl.*) supply.

bellen ['bɛlən] *v/i.* (ge-, h) bark.

belobigen [bə'lo:bigən] *v/t.* (*no* -ge-, h) commend, praise.

be'lohn|en *v/t.* (*no* -ge-, h) reward; recompense; 2ung *f* (-/-en) reward; recompense;   [*j-n ~* lie to s.o.]

be'lügen *v/t.* (*irr.* lügen, *no* -ge-, h):

belustig|en [bə'lustigən] *v/t.* (*no* -ge-, h) amuse, entertain; *sich ~* amuse o.s.; 2ung *f* (-/-en) amusement, entertainment.

bemächtigen [bə'mɛçtigən] *v/refl.* (*no* -ge-, h): *sich e-r Sache ~* take hold of s.th., seize s.th.; *sich e-r Person ~* lay hands on s.o., seize s.o.

be'malen *v/t.* (*no* -ge-, h) cover with paint; paint; daub.

bemängeln [bə'mɛŋəln] *v/t.* (*no* -ge-, h) find fault with, cavil at.

be'mannen *v/t.* (*no* -ge-, h) man.

be'merk|bar *adj.* perceptible; ~en *v/t.* (*no* -ge-, h) notice, perceive; remark, mention; ~enswert *adj.* remarkable (*wegen* for); 2ung *f* (-/-en) remark.

bemitleiden [bə'mitlaidən] *v/t.* (*no* -ge-, h) pity, commiserate (with); ~swert *adj.* pitiable.

be'müh|en *v/t.* (*no* -ge-, h) trouble (*j-n in* or *wegen* et. s.o. about s.th.); *sich ~* trouble o.s.; endeavo(u)r; *sich um e-e Stelle ~* apply for a position; 2ung *f* (-/-en) trouble; endeavo(u)r; effort.

be'nachbart *adj.* neighbo(u)ring; adjoining, adjacent (to).

benachrichtig|en [bə'naːxriçtigən] *v/t.* (*no* -ge-, h) inform, notify; ✝ advise; 2ung *f* (-/-en) information; notification; ✝ advice.

benachteilig|en [bə'naːxtailigən] *v/t.* (*no* -ge-, h) place *s.o.* at a disadvantage, discriminate against *s.o.*; handicap; *sich benachteiligt fühlen* feel handicapped *or* at a disadvantage; 2ung *f* (-/-en) disadvantage; discrimination; handicap.

be'nehmen 1. *v/refl.* (*irr.* nehmen, *no* -ge-, h) behave (o.s.); **2.** 2 *n* (-s/*no pl.*) behavio(u)r, conduct.

be'neiden *v/t.* (*no* -ge-, h) envy (*j-n um* et. s.o. s.th.); ~swert *adj.* enviable.

be'nennen *v/t.* (*irr.* nennen, *no* -ge-, h) name.   [rascal; urchin.]

Bengel ['bɛŋəl] *m* (-s/-) (little)

benommen *adj.* [bə'nɔmən] bemused, dazed, stunned; *~ sein* in a daze.   [require, want.]

be'nötigen *v/t.* (*no* -ge-, h) need,)

be'nutz|en *v/t.* (*no* -ge-, h) use (*a. patent, etc.*); make use of; avail o.s. of (*opportunity*); take (*tram, etc.*); 2ung *f* use.

Benzin [bɛn'tsiːn] *n* (-s/-e) 🚗 benzine; *mot.* petrol, F juice, *Am.* gasoline, F gas; ~motor *m* petrol engine, *Am.* gasoline engine; *s.* Tank.

beobacht|en [bə'o:baxtən] *v/t.* (*no* -ge-, h) observe; watch; *police:* shadow; 2er *m* (-s/-) observer; 2ung *f* (-/-en) observation.

beordern [bə'ɔrdərn] *v/t.* (*no* -ge-, h) order, command.

be'packen *v/t.* (*no* -ge-, h) load (*mit* with).   [(*mit* with).]

be'pflanzen *v/t.* (*no* -ge-, h) plant)

bequem *adj.* [bə'kveːm] convenient; comfortable; *p.:* easy-going; lazy; ~en *v/refl.* (*no* -ge-, h): *sich ~* zu condescend to; consent to; 2lichkeit *f* (-/-en) convenience; comfort, ease; indolence.

be'rat|en (*irr.* raten, *no* -ge-, h) **1.** *v/t.* advise *s.o.*; consider, debate, discuss *s.th.*; *sich ~* confer (*mit j-m* with s.o.; *über* et. on *or* about s.th.); **2.** *v/i.* confer; *über* et. ~ consider, debate, discuss s.th., confer on *or* about s.th.; 2er *m* (-s/-) adviser, counsel(l)or; consultant; ~schlagen (*no* -ge-, h) **1.** *v/i. s.* beraten 2; **2.** *v/refl.* confer (*mit j-m* with s.o.; *über* et. on *or* about s.th.); 2ung *f* (-/-en) advice; debate; consultation; conference; 2ungsstelle *f* advisory bureau.

be'raub|en *v/t.* (*no* -ge-, h) rob, deprive (*gen.* of); 2ung *f* (-/-en) robbery, deprivation.

be'rauschen *v/t.* (*no* -ge-, h) intoxicate (*a. fig.*).

be'rechn|en *v/t.* (*no* -ge-, h) calculate; ✝ charge (*zu* at); ~end *adj.* calculating, selfish; 2ung *f* calculation.

berechtig|en [bə'rɛçtigən] *v/t.* (*no* -ge-, h): *j-n ~ zu* entitle s.o. to; authorize s.o. to; ~t *adj.* [~çt] entitled (*zu* to); qualified (to); *claim:* legitimate; 2ung *f* (-/-en) title (*zu* to); authorization.

be'red|en *v/t.* (*no* -ge-, h) talk *s.th.*

over; persuade *s.o.*; gossip about *s.o.*; **2samkeit** [⁓tza:mkaɪt] *f* (-/no *pl.*) eloquence; **⁓t** *adj.* [⁓t] eloquent (*a. fig.*).

Be'reich *m, n* (-[e]s/-e) area; reach; *fig.* scope, sphere; *science, etc.*: field, province; **2ern** *v/t.* (no -ge-,h) enrich; *sich* ⁓ enrich o.s.; **⁓erung** *f* (-/-en) enrichment.

be'reif|en *v/t.* (no -ge-, h) hoop (*barrel*); tyre, (*Am. only*) tire (*wheel*); **2ung** *f* (-/-en) (set of) tyres *pl.*, (*Am. only*) (set of) tires *pl.*

be'reisen *v/t.* (no -ge-, h) tour (in), travel (over); *commercial traveller*: cover (*district*).

bereit *adj.* [bə'raɪt] ready, prepared; **⁓en** *v/t.* (no -ge-, h) prepare; give (*joy, trouble, etc.*); **⁓s** *adv.* already; **2schaft** *f* (-/-en) readiness; *police*: squad; **⁓stellen** *v/t.* (*sep.*, -ge-, h) place *s.th.* ready; provide; **2ung** *f* (-/-en) preparation; **⁓willig** *adj.* ready, willing; **2willigkeit** *f* (-/no *pl.*) readiness, willingness.

be'reuen *v/t.* (no -ge-, h) repent (of); regret, rue.

Berg [bɛrk] *m* (-[e]s/-e) mountain; hill; ⁓ *pl.* von ⁓ heaps *pl.* of, piles *pl.* of; über den ⁓ sein be out of the wood, *Am.* be out of the woods; über alle ⁓e off and away; die Haare standen ihm zu ⁓e his hair stood on end; **2'an** *adv.* s. bergauf; **⁓arbeiter** *m* miner; **2'auf** *adv.* uphill (*a. fig.*); **⁓bahn** 🚞 *f* mountain railway; **⁓bau** *m* (-[e]s/*pl.*) mining.

bergen ['bɛrgən] *v/t.* (*irr.*, -ge-, h) save; rescue *s.o.*; ⚓ salvage, salve.   [hilly.\]

bergig *adj.* ['bɛrgɪç] mountainous,\
'Berg|kette *f* mountain chain or range; **'⁓mann** ⚒ *m* (-[e]s/Bergleute) miner; **'⁓predigt** *f* (-/no *pl.*) *the* Sermon on the Mount; **'⁓recht** *n* mining laws *pl.*; **'⁓rennen** *mot. n* mountain race; **'⁓rücken** *m* ridge; **'⁓rutsch** *m* landslide, landslip; **'⁓spitze** *f* mountain peak; **'⁓steiger** *m* (-s/-) mountaineer; **'⁓sturz** *m* s. Bergrutsch.

'Bergung *f* (-/-en) ⚓ salvage; rescue; **⁓sarbeiten** ['bɛrguŋs⁓-] *f/pl.* salvage operations *pl.*; rescue work.

'Bergwerk *n* mine; **⁓saktien** ['bɛrkvɛrks⁹-] *f/pl.* mining shares *pl.*

Bericht [bə'rɪçt] *m* (-[e]s/-e) report

(*über acc.* on); account (of); **2en** (no -ge-, h) **1.** *v/t.* report; *j-m et.* ⁓ inform s.o. of s.th.; tell s.o. about s.th.; **2.** *v/i.* report (*über acc.* on); *journalist: a.* cover (*über et. s.th.*); **⁓erstatter** *m* (-s/-) reporter; correspondent; **⁓erstattung** *f* reporting; report(s *pl.*).

berichtig|en [bə'rɪçtɪgən] *v/t.* (no -ge-, h) correct (*s.o.; error, mistake, etc.*); put right (*mistake*); emend (*corrupt text*); ♱ settle (*claim, debt, etc.*); **2ung** *f* (-/-en) correction; emendation; settlement.

be'riechen *v/t.* (*irr.* riechen, no -ge-, h) smell *or* sniff at.

Berliner [bɛr'li:nər] **1.** *m* (-s/-) Berliner; **2.** *adj.* (of) Berlin.

Bernstein ['bɛrnʃtaɪn] *m* amber; *schwarzer* ⁓ jet.

bersten ['bɛrstən] *v/i.* (*irr.*, -ge-, sein) burst (*fig. vor dat.* with).

berüchtigt *adj.* [bə'rʏçtɪçt] notorious (*wegen* for), ill-famed.

berücksichtig|en [bə'rʏkzɪçtɪgən] *v/t.* (no -ge-, h) take *s.th.* into consideration, pay regard to *s.th.*; consider *s.o.*; **2ung** *f* (-/-en) consideration; regard.

Beruf [bə'ru:f] *m* (-[e]s/-e) calling; profession; vocation; trade; occupation; **2en 1.** *v/t.* (*irr.* rufen, no -ge-, h): *j-n* zu *e-m* Amt ⁓ appoint s.o. to an office; sich auf *j-n* ⁓ refer to s.o.; **2.** *adj.* competent; qualified; **2lich** *adj.* professional; vocational.

Be'rufs|ausbildung *f* vocational *or* professional training; **⁓beratung** *f* vocational guidance; **⁓kleidung** *f* work clothes *pl.*; **⁓krankheit** *f* occupational disease; **⁓schule** *f* vocational school; **⁓spieler** *m* *sports*: professional (player); **2tätig** *adj.* working; **⁓tätige** [⁓gə] *pl.* working people *pl.*

Be'rufung *f* (-/-en) appointment (*zu* to); ⚖ appeal (*bei dat.* to); reference (*auf acc.* to); **⁓sgericht** *n* court of appeal.

be'ruhen *v/i.* (no -ge-, h): ⁓ *auf* (*dat.*) rest *or* be based on; *et. auf sich* ⁓ *lassen* let a matter rest.

beruhig|en [bə'ru:ɪgən] *v/t.* (no -ge-, h) quiet, calm; soothe; *sich* ⁓ calm down; **2ung** *f* (-/-en) calming (down); soothing; comfort; **2ungsmittel** 💊 *n* sedative.

berühmt adj. [bə'ry:mt] famous (wegen for); celebrated; **2heit** f (-/-en) fame, renown; famous or celebrated person, celebrity; person of note.

be'rühr|en v/t. (no -ge-, h) touch (a. fig.); touch (up)on (subject); **2ung** f (-/-en) contact; touch; in ~ kommen mit come into contact with.

be'sag|en v/t. (no -ge-, h) say; mean, signify; **~t** adj. [~kt] (afore-)said; above(-mentioned).

besänftigen [bə'zɛnftigən] v/t. (no -ge-, h) appease, calm, soothe.

Be'satz m (-es/~e) trimming; braid.

Be'satzung f ✕ occupation troops pl.; ✕ garrison; ⚓, ✈ crew; **~s-macht** ✕ f occupying power.

be'schädig|en v/t. (no -ge-, h) damage, injure; **2ung** f damage, injury (gen. to).

be'schaffen 1. v/t. (no -ge-, h) procure; provide; raise (money); **2.** adj.: gut (schlecht) ~ sein be in good (bad) condition or state; **2heit** f(-/-en)state,condition;properties pl.

beschäftig|en [bə'ʃɛftigən] v/t. (no -ge-, h) employ, occupy; keep busy; sich ~ occupy or busy o.s.; **2ung** f (-/-en) employment; occupation.

be'schäm|en v/t. (no -ge-, h) (put to) shame, make s.o. feel ashamed; **~end** adj. shameful, humiliating; **~t** adj. ashamed (über acc. of); **2ung** f (-/-en) shame; humiliation.

beschatten [bə'ʃatən] v/t. (no -ge-, h) shade; fig. shadow s.o., Am. sl. tail s.o.

be'schau|en v/t. (no -ge-, h) look at, view; examine, inspect (goods, etc.); **~lich** adj. contemplative, meditative.

Bescheid [bə'ʃaɪt] m (-[e]s/-e) answer; 🕀 decision; information (über acc. on, about); ~ geben let s.o. know; ~ bekommen be informed or notified; ~ hinterlassen leave word (bei with, at); ~ wissen be informed, know, F be in the know.

bescheiden adj. [bə'ʃaɪdən] modest, unassuming; **2heit** f (-/no pl.) modesty.

bescheinig|en [bə'ʃaɪnigən] v/i. (no -ge-, h) certify, attest; den Empfang ~ acknowledge receipt; es wird hiermit bescheinigt, daß this is to certify that; **2ung** f (-/-en) certification; attestation; certificate; receipt; acknowledgement.

be'schenken v/t. (no -ge-, h): j-n ~ make s.o. a present; j-n mit et. ~ present s.o. with s.th.; j-n reichlich ~ shower s.o. with gifts.

be'scher|en v/t. (no -ge-, h): j-n ~ give s.o. presents (esp. for Christmas); **2ung** f (-/-en) presentation of gifts; F fig. mess.

be'schieß|en v/t. (irr. schießen, no -ge-, h) fire or shoot at or on; bombard (a. phys.), shell; **2ung** f (-/-en) bombardment.

be'schimpf|en v/t. (no -ge-, h) abuse, insult; call s.o. names; **2ung** f (-/-en) abuse; insult, affront.

be'schirmen v/t. (no -ge-, h) shelter, shield, guard, protect (vor dat. from); defend (against).

be'schlafen v/t. (irr. schlafen, no -ge-, h): et. ~ sleep on a matter, take counsel of one's pillow.

Be'schlag m 🕀 metal fitting(s pl.); furnishing(s pl.) (of door, etc.); shoe (of wheel, etc.); (horse)shoe; 🕀🕀 seizure, confiscation; in ~ nehmen, mit ~ belegen seize; 🕀🕀 seize, attach (real estate, salary, etc.); confiscate (goods, etc.); monopolize s.o.'s attention.

be'schlagen 1. v/t. (irr. schlagen, no -ge-, h) cover (mit with); 🕀 fit, mount; shoe (horse); hobnail (shoe); **2.** v/i. (irr. schlagen, no -ge-, h) window, wall, etc.: steam up; mirror, etc.: cloud or film over; **3.** adj. windows, etc.: steamed-up; fig. well versed (auf, in dat. in).

Beschlagnahme [bə'ʃla:kna:mə] f (-/-n) seizure; confiscation (of contraband goods, etc.); 🕀🕀 sequestration, distraint (of property); ✕ requisition (of houses, etc.); embargo, detention (of ship); **2n** v/t. (no -ge-, h) seize; attach (real estate); confiscate; 🕀🕀 sequestrate, distrain upon (property); ✕ requisition; ⚓ embargo.

beschleunig|en [bə'ʃlɔynigən] v/t. (no -ge-, h) mot. accelerate; hasten; speed up; s-e Schritte ~ quicken one's steps; **2ung** f (-/-en) acceleration.

be'schließen v/t. (irr. schließen, no -ge-, h) end, close, wind up; resolve, decide.

Be'schluß m decision, resolution, Am. a. resolve; 🕀🕀 decree; **2fähig** adj.: ~ sein form or have a quorum;

B

~**fassung** f (passing of a) resolution.

be'**schmieren** v/t. (no -ge-, h) (be)smear (with grease, etc.).

be'**schmutzen** v/t. (no -ge-, h) soil (a. fig.), dirty; bespatter.

be'**schneiden** v/t. (irr. schneiden, no -ge-, h) clip, cut; lop (tree); trim, clip (hair, hedge, etc.); dress (vinestock, etc.); fig. cut down, curtail, F slash.

beschönig|en [bə'ʃø:nigən] v/t. (no -ge-, h) gloss over, palliate; 2ung f (-/-en) gloss, palliation.

beschränk|en [bə'frɛŋkən] v/t. (no -ge-, h) confine, limit, restrict, Am. a. curb; sich ~ auf (acc.) confine o.s. to; ~t fig. adj. of limited intelligence; 2ung f (-/-en) limitation, restriction.

be'**schreib**|en v/t. (irr. schreiben, no -ge-, h) write on (piece of paper, etc.), cover with writing; describe, give a description of; 2ung f (-/-en) description; account.

be'**schrift**|en v/t. (no -ge-, h) inscribe; letter; 2ung f (-/-en) inscription; lettering.

beschuldig|en [bə'ʃuldigən] v/t. (no -ge-, h) accuse (gen. of [doing] s.th.), esp. ⅛ charge (with); 2te [~ktə] m, f (-n/-n) the accused; 2ung f (-/-en) accusation, charge.

Be'**schuß** m (Beschusses/no pl.) bombardment.

be'**schütz**|en v/t. (no -ge-, h) protect, shelter, guard (vor dat. from); 2er m (-s/-) protector; 2ung f (-/-en) protection.

be'**schwatzen** v/t. (no -ge-, h) talk s.o. into (doing) s.th., coax s.o. into (doing s.th.).

Beschwerde [bə'ʃve:rdə] f (-/-n) trouble; ⅍ complaint; complaint (über acc. about); ⅛ objection (gegen to); ~**buch** n complaints book.

beschwer|en [bə'ʃve:rən] v/t. (no -ge-, h) burden (a. fig.); weight (loose sheets, etc.); lie heavy on (stomach); weigh on (mind, etc.); sich ~ complain (über acc. about, of; bei to); ~**lich** adj. troublesome.

beschwichtigen [bə'ʃviçtigən] v/t. (no -ge-, h) appease, calm (down), soothe.

be'**schwindeln** v/t. (no -ge-, h) tell

a fib or lie; cheat, F diddle (um out of).

be'**schwipst** F adj. tipsy.

be'**schwör**|en v/t. (irr. schwören, no -ge-, h) take an oath on s.th.; implore or entreat s.o.; conjure (up), invoke (spirit); 2ung f (-/-en) conjuration.

be'**seelen** v/t. (no -ge-, h) animate, inspire.

be'**sehen** v/t. (irr. sehen, no -ge-, h) look at; inspect; sich et. ~ look at s.th.; inspect s.th.

beseitig|en [bə'zaitigən] v/t. (no -ge-, h) remove, do away with; 2ung f (-/-en) removal.

Besen ['be:zən] m (-s/-) broom; '~**stiel** m broomstick.

besessen adj. [bə'zɛsən] obsessed, possessed (von by, with); wie ~ like mad; 2e m, f (-n/-n) demoniac.

be'**setz**|en v/t. (no -ge-, h) occupy (seat, table, etc.); fill (post, etc.); man (orchestra); thea. cast (play); ✕ occupy; trim (dress, etc.); set (crown with jewels, etc.); ~t adj. engaged, occupied; seat: taken; F bus, etc.: full up; hotel: full; teleph. engaged, Am. busy; 2ung f (-/-en) thea. cast; ✕ occupation.

besichtig|en [bə'ziçtigən] v/t. (no -ge-, h) view, look over; inspect (a. ✕); visit; 2ung f (-/-en) sightseeing; visit (gen. to); inspection (a. ✕).

be'**sied**|eln v/t. (no -ge-, h) colonize, settle; populate; 2lung f (-/-en) colonization, settlement.

be'**siegeln** v/t. (no -ge-, h) seal (a. fig.).

be'**siegen** v/t. (no -ge-, h) conquer; defeat, beat (a. sports).

be'**sinn**|en v/refl. (irr. sinnen, no -ge-, h) reflect, consider; sich ~ auf (acc.) remember, think of; ~**lich** adj. reflective, contemplative.

Be'**sinnung** f (-/no pl.) reflection; consideration; consciousness; (wieder) zur ~ kommen recover consciousness; fig. come to one's senses; 2**los** adj. unconscious.

Be'**sitz** m possession; in ~ nehmen, ~ ergreifen von take possession of; 2**anzeigend** gr. adj. possessive; 2**en** v/t. (irr. sitzen, no -ge-, h) possess; ~**er** m (-s/-) possessor, owner, proprietor; den ~ wechseln change hands; ~**ergreifung** f taking possession (*von* of), occupation; **~tum** *n* (-s/=er), **~ung** *f* (-/-en) possession; property; estate.

be'sohlen [bə'zo:lən] *v/t.* (*no* -ge-, *h*) sole.

besold|en [bə'zɔldən] *v/t.* (*no* -ge-, *h*) pay a salary to (*civil servant, etc.*); pay (*soldier*); **2ung** *f* (-/-en) pay; salary.

besonder *adj.* [bə'zɔndər] particular, special; peculiar; separate; **2-heit** *f* (-/-en) particularity; peculiarity; **~s** *adv.* especially, particularly; chiefly, mainly; separately.

besonnen *adj.* [bə'zɔnən] sensible, considerate, level-headed; prudent; discreet; **2heit** *f* (-/*no pl.*) considerateness; prudence; discretion; presence of mind.

be'sorg|en *v/t.* (*no* -ge-, *h*) get (*j-m et. s.o. s.th.*), procure (*s.th. for s.o.*); do, manage; **2nis** [~knis] *f* (-/-se) apprehension, fear, anxiety, concern (*über acc.* about, at); **~nis-erregend** *adj.* alarming; **~t** *adj.* [~kt] uneasy (*um* about); worried (about); concerned (about); anxious (*um* for, about); **2ung** *f* (-/-en) procurement; management; errand; **~en machen** go shopping.

be'sprech|en *v/t.* (*irr.* sprechen, *no* -ge-, *h*) discuss, talk *s.th.* over; arrange; review (*book, etc.*); **sich ~ mit** confer with (*über acc.* about); **2ung** *f* (-/-en) discussion; review; conference.

be'spritzen *v/t.* (*no* -ge-, *h*) splash, (be)spatter.

besser ['bɛsər] **1.** *adj.* better; superior; **2.** *adv.* better; '**~n** *v/t.* (ge-, *h*) (make) better, improve; reform; **sich ~** get *or* become better, improve, change for the better; mend one's ways; '**2ung** *f* (-/-en) improvement; change for the better; reform (*of character*); **s** improvement, recovery; **gute ~!** I wish you a speedy recovery!

best [bɛst] **1.** *adj.* best; *der erste* **~e** (just) anybody; **~en Dank** thank you very much; *sich von s-r* **~en** *Seite zeigen* be on one's best behavio(u)r; **2.** *adv.* best; *am* **~en** best; *aufs* **~e,** **~ens** in the best way possible; *zum* **~en geben** recite (*poem*), tell (*story*), oblige with (*song*); *j-n zum* **~en haben** *or* *halten* make fun of s.o., F pull s.o.'s leg; *ich danke* **~ens!** thank you very much!

Be'stand *m* (continued) existence; continuance; stock; † stock-in-trade; † cash in hand; **~ haben** be lasting, last.

be'ständig *adj.* constant, steady; lasting; continual; *weather:* settled; **2keit** *f* (-/-en) constancy, steadiness; continuance.

Bestand|saufnahme † [bə-'ʃtants?-] *f* stock-taking, *Am.* inventory; **~teil** *m* component, constituent; element, ingredient; part.

be'stärken *v/t.* (*no* -ge-, *h*) confirm, strengthen, encourage (*in dat.* in).

bestätig|en [bə'ʃtɛ:tigən] *v/t.* confirm (*a.* ‡‡ *verdict,* † *order*); attest; verify (*statement, etc.*); ratify (*law, treaty*); † acknowledge (*receipt*); **2ung** *f* (-/-en) confirmation; attestation; verification; ratification; acknowledgement.

bestatt|en [bə'ʃtatən] *v/t.* (*no* -ge-, *h*) bury, inter; **2ung** *f* (-/-en) burial, interment; funeral; **2ungsinstitut** [bə'ʃtatuŋs?-] *n* undertakers *pl.*

'Beste **1.** *n* (-n/*no pl.*) the best (thing); *zu deinem* **~n** in your interest; *zum* **~n der Armen** for the benefit of the poor; *das* **~ daraus machen** make the best of it; **2.** *m, f* (-n/-n): *er ist der* **~ in s-r Klasse** he is the best in his class.

Besteck [bə'ʃtɛk] *n* (-[e]s/-e) ‡‡ (*case or set of*) surgical instruments *pl.*; (*single set of*) knife, fork and spoon; (*complete set of*) cutlery, *Am.* a. flatware.

be'stehen **1.** *v/t.* (*irr.* stehen, *no* -ge-, *h*) come off victorious in (*combat, etc.*); have (*adventure*); stand, undergo (well) (*test, trial*); pass (*test, examination*); **2.** *v/i.* (*irr.* stehen, *no* -ge-, *h*) be, exist; continue, last; **~ auf** (*dat.*) insist (up)on; **~ aus** consist of (*dat.*); **~ in** (-s/*no pl.*) existence; continuance; passing.

be'stehlen *v/t.* (*irr.* stehlen, *no* -ge-, *h*) steal from, rob.

be'steig|en *v/t.* (*irr.* steigen, *no* -ge-, *h*) climb (up) (*mountain, tree, etc.*); mount (*horse, bicycle, etc.*); ascend (*throne*); get into *or* on, board (*bus, train, plane*); **2ung** *f* ascent; accession (*to throne*).

be'stell|en *v/t.* (*no* -ge-, *h*) order; † *a.* place an order for; subscribe to (*newspaper, etc.*); book, reserve (*room, seat, etc.*); make an appointment with *s.o.*; send for (*taxi, etc.*); cultivate, till (*soil, etc.*); give (*message, greetings*); j-n zu sich ~ send for *s.o.*; 2ung *f* order; subscription (to); booking, *esp. Am.* reservation; ✒ cultivation; message.

'besten'falls *adv.* at (the) best.

be'steuer|n *v/t.* (*no* -ge-, *h*) tax; 2ung *f* taxation.

besti|alisch *adj.* [bɛst'jɑːliʃ] bestial; brutal; inhuman; *weather, etc.*: beastly; 2e [ˈ~jə] *f* (-/-en) beast; *fig.* brute, beast, inhuman person.

be'stimmen (*no* -ge-, *h*) **1.** *v/t.* determine, decide; fix (*date, place, price, etc.*); appoint (*date, time, place, etc.*); prescribe; define (*species, word, etc.*); j-n für *or* zu et. ~ designate *or* intend s.o. for s.th.; **2.** *v/i.*: ~ über (*acc.*) dispose of.

be'stimmt 1. *adj.* voice, manner, *etc.*: decided, determined, firm; time, *etc.*: appointed, fixed; point, number, *etc.*: certain; answer, *etc.*: positive; tone, answer, intention, idea: definite (*a. gr.*); ~ nach ⚓, ✈ bound for; **2.** *adv.* certainly, surely; 2heit *f* (-/-en) determination, firmness; certainty.

Be'stimmung *f* determination; destination (*of s.o. for the church, etc.*); designation, appointment (*of s.o. as successor, etc.*); definition; ⚖ provision (*in document*); (*amtliche*) ~en *pl.* (official) regulations *pl.*; ~sort [bə'ʃtimuŋs?-] *m* destination.

be'straf|en *v/t.* (*no* -ge-, *h*) punish (*wegen, für* for; *mit* with); 2ung *f* (-/-en) punishment.

be'strahl|en *v/t.* (*no* -ge-, *h*) irradiate (*a.* ✵); 2ung *f* irradiation; ✵ ray treatment, radiotherapy.

Be'streb|en *n* (-s/*no pl.*), ~ung *f* (-/-en) effort, endeavo(u)r.

be'streichen *v/t.* (*irr.* streichen, *no* -ge-, *h*) coat, cover; spread; *mit Butter* ~ butter.

be'streiten *v/t.* (*irr.* streiten, *no* -ge-, *h*) contest, dispute, challenge (*point, right, etc.*); deny (*facts, guilt, etc.*); defray (*expenses, etc.*); fill (*programme*).

be'streuen *v/t.* (*no* -ge-, *h*) strew, sprinkle (*mit* with); *mit Mehl* ~ flour; *mit Zucker* ~ sugar.

be'stürmen *v/t.* (*no* -ge-, *h*) storm, assail (*a. fig.*); pester, plague (*s.o. with questions, etc.*).

be'stürz|t *adj.* dismayed, struck with consternation (*über acc.* at); 2ung *f*(-/-en) consternation, dismay.

Besuch [bə'zuːx] *m* (-[e]s/-e) visit (*gen., bei, in dat.* to); call (*bei* on; *in dat.* at); attendance (*gen.* at) (*lecture, church, etc.*); visitor(s *pl.*), company; 2en *v/t.* (*no* -ge-, *h*) visit; call on, go to see; attend (*school, etc.*); frequent; ~er *m* visitor, caller; ~szeit *f* visiting hours *pl.*

be'tasten *v/t.* (*no* -ge-, *h*) touch, feel, finger; ✵ palpate.

betätigen [bə'tɛːtigən] *v/t.* (*no* -ge-, *h*) ⊕ operate (*machine, etc.*); put on, apply (*brake*); sich ~ als act *or* work as; sich politisch ~ dabble in politics.

betäub|en [bə'tɔʏbən] *v/t.* (*no* -ge-, *h*) stun (*a. fig.*), daze (*by blow, noise, etc.*); deafen (*by noise, etc.*); slaughtering: stun (*animal*); ✵ an(a)esthetize; 2ung *f* (-/-en) ✵ an(a)esthetization; ✵ an(a)esthesia; *fig.* stupefaction; 2ungsmittel ✵ *n* narcotic, an(a)esthetic.

beteilig|en [bə'tailigən] *v/t.* (*no* -ge-, *h*): j-n ~ give s.o. a share (*an dat.* in); sich ~ take part (*an dat., bei* in), participate (*a.* ⚖) (*in*); 2te [~çtə] *m, f* (-n/-n) person *or* party concerned; 2ung *f* (-/-en) participation (*a.* ⚖, ✝), partnership; share, interest (*a.* ✝).

beten ['beːtən] *v/i.* (*ge*-, *h*) pray (*um* for), say one's prayers; *at table:* say grace.

be'teuer|n *v/t.* (*no* -ge-, *h*) protest (*one's innocence*); swear (*to s.th.*; *that*); 2ung *f* protestation; solemn declaration.

be'titeln *v/t.* (*no* -ge-, *h*) entitle (*book, etc.*); style (*s.o. 'baron', etc.*).

Beton ⊕ [be'tõː; be'tɔːn] *m* (-s/-s; -s/-e) concrete.

be'tonen *v/t.* (*no* -ge-, *h*) stress; *fig. a.* emphasize.

betonieren [beto'niːrən] *v/t.* (*no* -ge-, *h*) concrete.

Be'tonung *f* (-/-en) stress; emphasis.

betör|en [bə'tøːrən] *v/t.* (*no* -ge-, *h*) dazzle; infatuate; bewitch; 2ung *f* (-/-en) infatuation.

Betracht [bə'traxt] *m* (-[e]s/*no pl.*): *in* ~ ziehen take into consideration; (*nicht*) *in* ~ kommen (not) to come into question; 2en *v/t.* (*no* -ge-, *h*) view; contemplate; *fig. a.* consider.

beträchtlich *adj.* [bə'trɛçtliç] considerable.

Be'trachtung *f* (-/-en) view; contemplation; consideration.

Betrag [bə'tra:k] *m* (-[e]s/ӿe) amount, sum; **2en** [‿gən] **1.** *v/t.* (*irr.* tragen, *no* -ge-, h) amount to; **2.** *v/refl.* (*irr.* tragen, *no* -ge-, h) behave (o.s.); **3.** **2** *n* (-s/*no pl.*) behavio(u)r, conduct.

be'trauen *v/t.* (*no* -ge-, h): j-n mit et. ‿ entrust *or* charge s.o. with s.th.

be'trauern *v/t.* (*no* -ge-, h) mourn (for, over).

Betreff [bə'trɛf] *m* (-[e]s/-e) *at head of letter:* reference; **2en** *v/t.* (*irr.* treffen, *no* -ge-, h) befall; refer to; concern; *was ... betrifft* as for, as to; **2end** *adj.* concerning; *das ‿e Geschäft* the business referred to *or* in question; **2s** *prp.* (*gen.*) concerning; as to.

be'treiben 1. *v/t.* (*irr.* treiben, *no* -ge-, h) carry on (*business, etc.*); pursue (*one's studies*); operate (*railway line, etc.*); **2.** **2** *n* (-s/*no pl.*): auf ‿ von at *or* by s.o.'s instigation.

be'treten 1. *v/t.* (*irr.* treten, *no* -ge-, h) step on; enter (*room, etc.*); **2.** *adj.* embarrassed, abashed.

betreu|en [bə'trɔyən] *v/t.* (*no* -ge-, h) look after; attend to; care for; **2ung** *f* (-/*no pl.*) care (gen. of, for).

Betrieb [bə'tri:p] *m* (-[e]s/-e) working, running, *esp. Am.* operation; business, firm, enterprise; plant, works *sg.*; workshop, *Am. a.* shop; *fig.* bustle; *in ‿* working; **2sam** *adj.* active; industrious.

Be'triebs|anleitung *f* operating instructions *pl.*; **‿ausflug** *m* firm's outing; **‿ferien** *pl.* (firm's, works) holiday; **‿führer** *m s.* Betriebsleiter; **‿kapital** *n* working capital; **‿kosten** *pl.* working expenses *pl.*, *Am.* operating costs *pl.*; **‿leiter** *m* (works) manager, superintendent; **‿leitung** *f* management; **‿material** *n* working materials *pl.*; **⚙** rolling stock; **‿rat** *m* works council; **2sicher** *adj.* safe to operate; foolproof; **‿störung** *f* breakdown; **‿unfall** *m* industrial accident, accident while at work.

be'trinken *v/refl.* (*irr.* trinken, *no* -ge-, h) get drunk.

betroffen *adj.* [bə'trɔfən] afflicted (*von* by), stricken (with); *fig.* disconcerted.

be'trüben *v/t.* (*no* -ge-, h) grieve, afflict.

Be'trug *m* cheat(ing); fraud (*a.* ⚖); deceit.

be'trüg|en *v/t.* (*irr.* trügen, *no* -ge-, h) deceive; cheat (*a. at games*); defraud; F skin; **2er** *m* (-s/-) cheat, deceiver, impostor, confidence man, swindler, trickster; **‿erisch** *adj.* deceitful, fraudulent.

be'trunken *adj.* drunken; *pred.* drunk; **2e** *m* (-n/-n) drunk(en man).

Bett [bɛt] *n* (-[e]s/-en) bed; **‿bezug** *m* plumeau case; **‿decke** *f* blanket; bedspread, coverlet.

Bettel|brief ['bɛtəl-] *m* begging letter; **‿ei** [‿'lai] *f* (-/-en) begging, mendicancy; **2n** *v/i.* (ge-, h) beg (*um* for); ‿ gehen go begging; **‿stab** *m*: an den ‿ bringen reduce to beggary.

'Bett|gestell *n* bedstead; **2lägerig** *adj.* ['‿lɛ:gəriç] bedridden, confined to bed, *Am. a.* bedfast; **‿laken** *n* sheet.

Bettler ['bɛtlər] *m* (-s/-) beggar, *Am. sl.* panhandler.

'Bett|überzug *m* plumeau case; **‿uch** ['bɛttu:x] *n* sheet; **‿vorleger** *m* bedside rug; **‿wäsche** *f* bedlinen; **‿zeug** *n* bedding.

be'tupfen *v/t.* (*no* -ge-, h) dab.

beug|en ['bɔygən] *v/t.* (*no* -ge-, h) bend, bow; *fig.* humble, break (*pride*); *gr.* inflect (*word*), decline (*noun, adjective*); *sich ‿* bend (*vor dat.* to), bow (to); **'2ung** *f* (-/-en) bending; *gr.* inflection, declension.

Beule ['bɔylə] *f* (-/-n) bump, swelling; boil; *on metal, etc.:* dent.

beunruhig|en [bə'unru:igən] *v/t.* (*no* -ge-, h) disturb, trouble, disquiet, alarm; *sich ‿ über* (*acc.*) be uneasy about, worry about; **2ung** *f* (-/*no pl.*) disturbance; alarm; uneasiness.

beurkund|en [bə'u:rkundən] *v/t.* (*no* -ge-, h) attest, certify, authenticate; **2ung** *f* (-/-en) attestation, certification, authentication.

beurlaub|en [bə'u:rlaubən] *v/t.* (*no* -ge-, h) give *or* grant s.o. leave (of absence); give s.o. time off; suspend (*civil servant, etc.*); **2ung** *f* (-/-en) leave (of absence); suspension.

beurteil|en [bə'urtaɪlən] v/t. (no -ge-, h) judge (nach by); **Qung** f (-/-en) judg(e)ment.

Beute ['bɔytə] f (-/no pl.) booty, spoil(s pl.); loot; prey; hunt. bag; fig. prey, victim (gen. to).

Beutel ['bɔytəl] m (-s/-) bag; purse; pouch.

'Beutezug m plundering expedition.

bevölker|n [bə'fœlkərn] v/t. (no -ge-, h) people, populate; **Qung** f (-/-en) population.

bevollmächtig|en [bə'fɔlmɛçtɪgən] v/t. (no -ge-, h) authorize, empower; **Qte** [‿çtə] m, f (-n/-n) authorized person or agent, deputy; pol. plenipotentiary; **Qung** f (-/-en) authorization.

be'vor cj. before.

bevormund|en fig. [bə'fo:rmʊndən] v/t. (no -ge-, h) patronize, keep in tutelage; **Qung** f (-/-en) patronizing, tutelage.

be'vorstehen v/i. (irr. stehen, sep., -ge-, h) be approaching, be near; crisis, etc.: be imminent; j-m ‿ be in store for s.o., await s.o.; **‿d** adj. approaching, imminent.

bevorzug|en [bə'fo:rtsu:gən] v/t. (no -ge-, h) prefer; favo(u)r; ᵗᵗᵏ privilege; **Qung** f (-/-en) preference.

be'wach|en v/t. (no -ge-, h) guard, watch; **Qung** f (-/-en) guard; escort.

bewaffn|en [bə'vafnən] v/t. (no -ge-, h) arm; **Qung** f (-/-en) armament; arms pl.

be'wahren v/t. (no -ge-, h) keep, preserve (mst fig.: secret, silence, etc.).

be'währen v/refl. (no -ge-, h) stand the test, prove a success; sich ‿ als prove o.s. (as) (a good teacher, etc.); sich ‿ in prove o.s. efficient in (one's profession, etc.); sich nicht ‿ prove a failure.

be'wahrheiten v/refl. (no -ge-, h) prove (to be) true; prophecy, etc.: come true.

be'währt adj. friend, etc.: tried; solicitor, etc.: experienced; friendship, etc.: long-standing; remedy, etc.: proved, proven.

Be'währung f ᵗᵗᵏ probation; in Zeiten der ‿ in times of trial; s. bewähren; **‿sfrist** ᵗᵗᵏ f probation.

bewaldet [bə'valdət] wooded, woody, Am. a. timbered.

bewältigen [bə'vɛltɪgən] v/t. (no -ge-, h) overcome (obstacle); master (difficulty); accomplish (task).

be'wandert adj. (well) versed (in dat. in), proficient (in); in e-m Fach gut ‿ sein have a thorough knowledge of a subject.

be'wässer|n v/t. (no -ge-, h) water (garden, lawn, etc.); irrigate (land, etc.); **Qung** f (-/-en) watering; irrigation.

bewegen¹ [bə've:gən] v/t. (irr., no -ge-, h): j-n ‿ zu induce or get s.o. to.

beweg|en² [‿] v/t. and v/refl. (no -ge-, h) move, stir; **Qgrund** [‿k-] m motive (gen., für for); **‿lich** adj. [‿k-] movable; p., mind, etc.: agile, versatile; active; **Qlichkeit** [‿k-] f (-/no pl.) mobility; agility, versatility; **‿t** adj. [‿kt] sea: rough, heavy; fig. moved, touched; voice: choked, trembling; life: eventful; times, etc.: stirring, stormy; **Qung** f (-/-en) movement; motion (a. phys.); fig. emotion; in ‿ setzen set going or in motion; **‿ungslos** adj. motionless, immobile.

be'weinen v/t. (no -ge-, h) weep or cry over; lament (for, over).

Beweis [bə'vaɪs] m (-es/-e) proof (für of); ‿e (pl.) evidence (esp. ᵗᵗᵏ); **Qen** [‿zən] v/t. (irr. weisen, no -ge-, h) prove; show (interest, etc.); **‿führung** f argumentation; **‿grund** m argument; **‿material** n evidence; **‿stück** n (piece of) evidence; ᵗᵗᵏ exhibit. [take it at that.]

be'wenden vb.: es dabei ‿ lassen|

be'werb|en v/refl. (irr. werben, no -ge-, h): sich ‿ um apply for, Am. run for; stand for; compete for (prize); court (woman); **Qer** m (-s/-) applicant (um for); candidate; competitor; suitor; **Qung** f application; candidature; competition; courtship; **Qungsschreiben** n (letter of) application.

bewerkstelligen [bə'vɛrkʃtɛlɪgən] v/t. (no -ge-, h) manage, effect, bring about.

be'wert|en v/t. (no -ge-, h) value (auf acc. at; nach by); **Qung** f valuation.

bewillig|en [bə'vɪlɪgən] v/t. (no -ge-, h) grant, allow; **Qung** f (-/-en) grant, allowance.

be'wirken v/t. (no -ge-, h) cause; bring about, effect.

be'wirt|en v/t. (no -ge-, h) entertain; **~schaften** v/t. (no -ge-, h) farm (land); ✗ cultivate (field); manage (farm, etc.); ration (food, etc.); control (foreign exchange, etc.); **Ⴝung** f (-/-en) entertainment; hospitality.

bewog [bə'voːk] pret. of bewegen¹; **~en** [bə'voːgən] p.p. of bewegen¹.

be'wohn|en v/t. (no -ge-, h) inhabit, live in; occupy; **Ⴝer** m (-s/-) inhabitant; occupant.

bewölk|en [bə'vœlkən] v/refl. (no -ge-, h) sky: cloud up or over; brow: cloud over, darken; **~t** adj. sky: clouded, cloudy, overcast; brow: clouded, darkened; **Ⴝung** f (-/no pl.) clouds pl.

be'wunder|n v/t. (no -ge-, h) admire (wegen for); **~nswert** adj. admirable; **Ⴝung** f (-/-en) admiration.

bewußt adj. [bə'vust] deliberate, intentional; sich e-r Sache ~ sein be conscious or aware of s.th.; die ~e Sache the matter in question; **~los** adj. unconscious; **Ⴝsein** n (-s/no pl.) consciousness.

be'zahl|en (no -ge-, h) 1. v/t. pay; pay for (s.th. purchased); pay off, settle (debt); 2. v/i. pay (für for); **Ⴝung** f payment; settlement.

be'zähmen v/t. (no -ge-, h) tame (animal); restrain (one's anger, etc.); sich ~ control or restrain o.s.

be'zauber|n v/t. (no -ge-, h) bewitch, enchant (a. fig.); fig. charm, fascinate; **Ⴝung** f (-/-en) enchantment, spell; fascination.

be'zeichn|en v/t. (no -ge-, h) mark; describe (als as), call; **~end** adj. characteristic, typical (für of); **Ⴝung** f indication (of direction, etc.); mark, sign, symbol; name, designation, denomination.

be'zeugen v/t. (no -ge-, h) ⚖ testify to, bear witness to (both a. fig.); attest.

be'zieh|en v/t. (irr. ziehen, no -ge-, h) cover (upholstered furniture, etc.); put cover on (cushion, etc.); move into (flat, etc.); enter (university); draw (salary, pension, etc.); get, be supplied with (goods); take in (newspaper, etc.); sich ~ sky: cloud over; sich ~ auf (acc.) refer to; **Ⴝer** m (-s/-) subscriber (gen. to).

Be'ziehung f relation (zu et. to s.th.; zu j-m with s.o.); connexion, (Am. only) connection (zu with); in die-

ser ~ in this respect; **Ⴝsweise** adv. respectively; or rather.

Bezirk [bə'tsirk] m (-[e]s/-e) district, Am. a. precinct; s. Wahlbezirk.

Bezogene † [bə'tsoːgənə] m (-n/-n) drawee.

Bezug [bə'tsuːk] m cover(ing), case; purchase (of goods); subscription (to newspaper); in ~ auf (acc.) with regard or reference to, as to; ~ nehmen auf (acc.) refer to, make reference to.

bezüglich [bə'tsyːkliç] 1. adj. relative, relating (both: auf acc. to); 2. prp. (gen.) regarding, concerning.

Be'zugsbedingungen † f/pl. terms pl. of delivery.

be'zwecken v/t. (no -ge-, h) aim at; ~ mit intend by.

be'zweifeln v/t. (no -ge-, h) doubt, question.

be'zwing|en v/t. (irr. zwingen, no -ge-, h) conquer (fortress, mountain, etc.); overcome, master (feeling, difficulty, etc.); sich ~ keep o.s. under control, restrain o.s.; **Ⴝung** f (-/-en) conquest; mastering.

Bibel ['biːbəl] f (-/-n) Bible.

Biber zo. ['biːbər] m (-s/-) beaver.

Bibliothek [biblio'teːk] f (-/-en) library; **~ar** [~e'kaːr] m (-s/-e) librarian.

biblisch adj. ['biːbliʃ] biblical, scriptural; **~e Geschichte** Scripture.

bieder adj. ['biːdər] honest, upright, worthy (a. iro.); simple-minded; **Ⴝkeit** f (-/no pl.) honesty, uprightness; simple-mindedness.

bieg|en ['biːgən] (irr., ge-) 1. v/t. (h) bend; 2. v/refl. (h) bend; sich vor Lachen ~ double up with laughter; 3. v/i. (sein): um e-e Ecke ~ turn (round) a corner; **~sam** adj. ['biːkzaːm] wire, etc.: flexible; body: lithe, supple; pliant (a. fig.); **Ⴝsamkeit** f (-/no pl.) flexibility; suppleness; pliability; **Ⴝung** f (-/-en) bend, wind (of road, river); curve (of road, arch).

Biene zo. ['biːnə] f (-/-n) bee; '~nkönigin** f queen bee; '~nkorb** m (bee)hive; '~nschwarm** m swarm of bees; '~nstock** m (bee)hive; '~nzucht** f bee-keeping; '~nzüchter** m bee-keeper.

Bier [biːr] n (-[e]s/-e) beer; helles ~ pale beer, ale; dunkles ~ dark beer;

B

stout, porter; ~ *vom Faß* beer on draught; '~**brauer** *m* brewer; '~**brauerei** *f* brewery; '~**garten** *m* beer-garden; '~**krug** *m* beer-mug, *Am.* stein.

Biest [bi:st] *n* (-es/-er) beast, brute.

bieten ['bi:tən] (*irr.*, ge-, h) **1.** *v/t.* offer; † *at auction sale:* bid; *sich ~ opportunity, etc.:* offer itself, arise, occur; **2.** † *v/i. at auction sale:* bid.

Bigamie [biga'mi:] *f* (-/-n) bigamy.

Bilanz [bi'lants] *f* (-/-en) balance; balance-sheet, *Am. ~* statement; *fig.* result, outcome; *die ~ ziehen* strike a balance; *fig.* take stock (*of one's life, etc.*).

Bild [bilt] *n* (-[e]s/-er) picture; image; illustration; portrait; *fig.* idea, notion; '~**bericht** *m press:* picture story.

bilden ['bildən] *v/t.* (ge-, h) form; shape; *fig.:* educate, train (*s.o., mind, etc.*); develop (*mind, etc.*); form, be, constitute (*obstacle, etc.*); *sich ~* form; *fig.* educate o.s., improve one's mind; *sich e-e Meinung ~* form an opinion.

Bilder|buch ['bildər-] *n* picture-book; '~**galerie** *f* picture-gallery; '~**rätsel** *n* rebus.

'**Bild|fläche** *f:* F *auf der ~ erscheinen* appear on the scene; F *von der ~ verschwinden* disappear (from the scene); '~**funk** *m* radio picture transmission; television; '~**hauer** *m* (-s/-) sculptor; **~hauerei** [~'rai] *f* (-/-en) sculpture; '2**lich** *adj.* pictorial; *word, etc.:* figurative; '~**nis** *n* (-ses/-se) portrait; '~**röhre** *f* picture *or* television tube; '~**säule** *f* statue; '~**schirm** *m* (television) screen; '2**schön** *adj.* most beautiful; '~**seite** *f* face, head (*of coin*); '~**streifen** *m* picture *or* film strip; '~**telegraphie** *f* (-/no *pl.*) phototelegraphy.

'**Bildung** *f* (-/-en) forming, formation (*both a. gr.:* of plural, etc.); constitution (*of committee, etc.*); education; culture; (good) breeding. [*sg.*; billiard-table.]

Billard ['biljart] *n* (-s/-e) billiards

billig *adj.* ['bilç] just, equitable; fair; *price:* reasonable, moderate; *goods:* cheap, inexpensive; *recht und ~* right and proper; **~en** ['~gən] *v/t.* (ge-, h) approve of, *Am. a.* approbate; '2**keit** *f* (-/no *pl.*) justness,

equity; fairness; reasonableness, moderateness; 2**ung** ['~guŋ] *f* (-/-⸮-en) approval, sanction.

Binde ['bində] *f* (-/-n) band; tie; ⚕ bandage; (arm-)sling; *s. Damenbinde*; '~**gewebe** *anat. n* connective tissue; '~**glied** *n* connecting link; '~**haut** *anat. f* conjunctiva; '~**hautzündung** ⚕ *f* conjunctivitis; '2**n** (*irr.*, ge-, h) **1.** *v/t.* bind, tie (*an acc.* to); bind (*book, etc.*); make (*broom, wreath, etc.*); knot (*tie*); *sich ~ bind or commit or engage o.s.; **2.** *v/i.* bind; unite; ⊕ cement, *etc.:* set, harden; '~**strich** *m* hyphen; '~**wort** *gr. n* (-[e]s/⸗er) conjunction.

Bindfaden ['bint-] *m* string; packthread.

'**Bindung** *f* (-/-en) binding (*a. of ski*); ♪ slur, tie, ligature; *fig.* commitment (*a. pol.*); engagement; **~en** *pl.* bonds *pl.*, ties *pl.*

binnen *prp.* (*dat., a. gen.*) ['binən] within; ~ *kurzem* before long.

'**Binnen|gewässer** *n* inland water; '~**hafen** *m* close port; '~**handel** *m* domestic *or* home trade, *Am.* domestic commerce; '~**land** *n* inland, interior; '~**verkehr** *m* inland traffic *or* transport.

Binse ♀ ['binzə] *f* (-/-n) rush; F: *in die ~n gehen go to pot;* '~**nwahrheit** *f,* '~**nweisheit** *f* truism.

Biochemie [bioçe'mi:] *f* (-/no *pl.*) biochemistry.

Biograph|ie [biogra'fi:] *f* (-/-n) biography; 2**isch** *adj.* [~'gra:fiʃ] biographic(al).

Biolog|ie [biolo'gi:] *f* (-/no *pl.*) biology; 2**isch** *adj.* [~'lo:giʃ] biological.

Birke ♀ ['birkə] *f* (-/-n) birch(-tree).

Birne ['birnə] *f* (-/-n) ∉ pear; ∉ (electric) bulb; *fig. sl.* nob, *Am.* bean.

bis [bis] **1.** *prp.* (*acc.*) *space:* to, as far as; *time:* till, until, by; *zwei ~ drei* two *or* three, two to three; ~ *auf weiteres* until further orders, for the meantime; ~ *vier zählen* count up to four; *alle ~ auf drei* all but *or* except three; **2.** *cj.* till, until.

Bisamratte *zo.* ['bi:zam-] *f* muskrat.

Bischof ['biʃɔf] *m* (-s/⸗e) bishop.

bischöflich *adj.* ['biʃøfliç] episcopal.

bisher adv. [bis'he:r] hitherto, up to now, so far; **~ig** adj. until now; hitherto existing; former.

Biß [bis] 1. m (Bisses/Bisse) bite; 2. ♀ pret. of **beißen**.

bißchen ['bisçən] 1. adj.: ein ~ a little, a (little) bit of; 2. adv.: ein ~ a little (bit).

Bissen ['bisən] m (-s/-) mouthful; morsel; bite.

'bissig adj. biting (a. fig.); remark: cutting; Achtung, ~er Hund! beware of the dog!

Bistum ['bistu:m] n (-s/ɤer) bishopric, diocese.

bisweilen adv. [bis'vaɪlən] sometimes, at times, now and then.

Bitte ['bitə] f (-/-n) request (um for); entreaty; auf j-s ~ (hin) at s.o.'s request.

'bitten (irr., ge-, h) 1. v/t.: j-n um et. ~ ask or beg s.o. for s.th.; j-n um Entschuldigung ~ beg s.o.'s pardon; dürfte ich Sie um Feuer ~? may I trouble you for a light?; bitte please; (wie) bitte? (I beg your) pardon?; bitte! offering s.th.: (please,) help yourself, (please,) do take some or one; danke (schön) — bitte (sehr)! thank you — not at all, you're welcome, don't mention it, F that's all right; 2. v/i.: um et. ~ ask or beg for s.th.

'bitter adj. ['bitər] bitter (a. fig.); frost: sharp; **2keit** f (-/-en) bitterness; fig. a. acrimony; **'~lich** adv. bitterly.

'Bitt|gang ♣♣ eccl. m procession; **'~schrift** f petition; **'~steller** m (-s/-) petitioner.

bläh|en ['blɛ:ən] (ge-, h) 1. v/t. inflate, distend, swell out; belly (out), swell out (sails); sich ~ sails: belly (out), swell out; skirt: balloon out; 2. ♣♣ v/i. cause flatulence; **'~end** ♣♣ adj. flatulent; **'2ung** ♣♣ f (-/-en) flatulence; F wind.

Blam|age [bla'ma:ʒə] f (-/-n) disgrace, shame; **2ieren** [~'mi:rən] v/t. (no -ge-, h) make a fool of s.o. disgrace; sich ~ make a fool of o.s.

blank adj. [blaŋk] shining, shiny, bright; polished; F fig. broke.

blanko ♥ ['blaŋko] 1. adj. form, etc.: blank, not filled in; in blank; 2. adv.: ~ verkaufen stock exchange: sell short; **'2scheck** m blank cheque, Am. blank check; **'2unterschrift** f

blank signature; **'2vollmacht** f full power of attorney, carte blanche.

Bläschen ♣♣ ['blɛ:sçən] n (-s/-) vesicle, small blister.

Blase ['bla:zə] f (-/-n) bubble; blister (a. ♣♣); anat. bladder; bleb (in glass); ⊕ flaw; **'~balg** m (ein a pair of) bellows pl.; **'2n** (irr., ge-, h) 1. v/t. blow; blow, sound; play (wind-instrument); 2. v/i. blow.

Blas|instrument ♪ ['bla:s-] n wind-instrument; **'~kapelle** f brass band.

blaß adj. [blas] pale (vor dat. with); ~ werden turn pale; keine blasse Ahnung not the faintest idea.

Blässe ['blɛsə] f (-/no pl.) paleness.

Blatt [blat] n (-[e]s/ɤer) leaf (of book, ♀); petal (of flower); leaf, sheet (of paper); blade (of oar, saw, airscrew, etc.); sheet (of metal); cards: hand; (news)paper.

Blattern ♣♣ ['blatərn] pl. smallpox.

blättern ['blɛtərn] v/i. (ge-, h): in e-m Buch ~ leaf through a book, thumb a book.

'Blatternarb|e f pock-mark; **'2ig** adj. pock-marked.

'Blätterteig m puff paste.

'Blatt|gold n gold-leaf, gold-foil; **'~laus** zo. f plant-louse; **'~pflanze** f foliage plant.

blau [blau] 1. adj. blue; F fig. drunk, tight, boozy; ~er Fleck bruise; ~es Auge black eye; mit e-m ~en Auge davonkommen get off cheaply; 2. ♀ n (-s/no pl.) blue (colo[u]r); Fahrt ins ~e mystery tour. [blue.]

bläuen ['blɔyən] v/t. (ge-, h) (dye))

'blau|grau adj. bluish grey; **'2-jacke** ♣ f bluejacket, sailor.

'bläulich adj. bluish.

'Blausäure ♣♣ f (-/no pl.) hydrocyanic or prussic acid.

Blech [blɛç] n (-[e]s/-e) sheet metal; metal sheet, plate; F fig. balderdash, rubbish, Am. sl. ~ baloney; **'~büchse** f tin, Am. can; **'2ern** adj. (of) tin; sound: brassy; sound, voice: tinny; **'~musik** f brass-band music; **'~waren** f/pl. tinware.

Blei [blaɪ] (-[e]s/-e) 1. n lead; 2. F n, m (lead) pencil.

bleiben ['blaɪbən] v/i. (irr., ge-, sein) remain, stay, be left; ruhig ~ keep calm; ~ bei keep to s.th., stick to s.th.; bitte bleiben Sie am Apparat teleph. hold the line, please; **'~d**

adj. lasting, permanent; '**‿lassen** *v/t.* (irr. *lassen*, *sep.*, *no* -ge-, *h*) leave *s.th.* alone; *laß das bleiben!* don't do it!; leave it alone!; stop that (*noise, etc.*)!

bleich *adj.* [blaɪç] pale (*vor dat.* with); '**‿en** (ge-) **1.** *v/t.* (*h*) make pale; bleach; blanch; **2.** *v/i.* (irr., *sein*) bleach; lose colo(u)r, fade; '**‿süchtig** *# adj.* chlorotic, green-sick.

bleiern *adj.* (of) lead, leaden (*a. fig.*). '**Blei│rohr** *n* lead pipe; '**‿soldat** *m* tin soldier; '**‿stift** *m* (lead) pencil; '**‿stifthülse** *f* pencil cap; '**‿stift-spitzer** *m* (-s/-) pencil-sharpener; '**‿vergiftung** *# f* lead-poisoning.

Blend│e ['blɛndə] *f* (-/-n) *phot.* diaphragm, stop; △ blind *or* sham window; '**2en** (ge-, *h*) **1.** *v/t.* (*h*) dazzle (*both a. fig.*); **2.** *v/i. light:* dazzle the eyes; **‿laterne** ['blɛnt-] *f* dark lantern.

blich [blɪç] *pret.* of bleichen 2.

Blick [blɪk] *m* (-[e]s/-e) glance, look; view (*auf acc.* of); *auf den ersten* ‿ at first sight; *ein böser* ‿ an evil *or* angry look; '**2en** *v/i.* (ge-, *h*) look, glance (*auf acc.*, *nach* at); '**‿fang** *m* eye-catcher.

blieb [bli:p] *pret.* of bleiben.

blies [bli:s] *pret.* of blasen.

blind *adj.* [blɪnt] blind (*a. fig.*: gegen, für to; vor *dat.* with); *metal:* dull, tarnished; *window:* opaque (*with age, dirt*); *mirror:* clouded, dull; *cartridge:* blank; **‿er Alarm** false alarm; **‿er Passagier** stow-away; *auf e-m Auge* ‿ blind in one eye.

'**Blinddarm** *anat.* *m* blind gut; appendix; '**‿entzündung** *# f* appendicitis.

Blinde ['blɪndə] (-n/-n) **1.** *m* blind man; **2.** *f* blind woman; **‿nanstalt** ['blɪndən⁹-] *f* institute for the blind; '**‿nheim** *n* home for the blind; '**‿nhund** *m* guide dog, *Am. a.* seeing-eye dog; '**‿nschrift** *f* braille.

'**blind│fliegen** *✈* (irr. *fliegen*, *sep.*, -ge-) *v/t.* (*h*) *and v/i.* (*sein*) fly blind *or* on instruments; '**2flug** *✈ m* blind flying *or* flight; '**2gänger** *m* ✕ blind shell, dud; *F fig.* washout; '**2heit** *f* (-/*no pl.*) blindness; '**‿lings** *adv.* ['‿lɪŋs] blindly; at random; '**2schleiche** *zo. f* (-/-n) slow-worm,

blind-worm; '**‿schreiben** *v/t. and v/i.* (irr. *schreiben*, *sep.*, -ge-, *h*) touch-type.

blink│en ['blɪŋkən] *v/i.* (ge-, *h*) star, light: twinkle; *metal, leather, glass, etc.:* shine; signal (with lamps), flash; *mot. m* (-s/-) flashing indicator; '**2feuer** *n* flashing light.

blinzeln ['blɪntsəln] *v/i.* (ge-, *h*) blink (*at light, etc.*); wink.

Blitz [blɪts] *m* (-es/-e) lightning; '**‿ableiter** *m* (-s/-) lightning-conductor; '**2en** *v/i.* (ge-, *h*) flash; *es blitzt* it is lightening; '**‿gespräch** *teleph.* *n* special priority call; '**‿licht** *phot. n* flash-light; '**2schnell** *adv.* with lightning speed; '**‿strahl** *m* flash of lightning.

Block [blɔk] *m* **1.** (-[e]s/⁼e) block; slab (*of cooking chocolate*); block, log (*of wood*); ingot (*of metal*); *parl., pol.,* ✝ bloc; **2.** (-[e]s/⁼e, -s) block (*of houses*); pad, block (*of paper*); **‿ade** ✕, ⊕ ['‿ka:də] *f* (-/-n) blockade; **‿adebrecher** *m* (-s/-) blockade-runner; **‿haus** *n* log cabin; **2ieren** ['‿ki:rən] (*no* -ge-, *h*) **1.** *v/t.* block (up); lock (*wheel*); **2.** *v/i.* brakes, *etc.*: jam.

blöd *adj.* [blø:t], **‿e** *adj.* ['‿də] imbecile; stupid, dull; silly; '**2heit** *f* (-/-en) imbecility; stupidity, dullness; silliness; '**2sinn** *m* imbecility; rubbish, nonsense; '**‿sinnig** *adj.* imbecile; idiotic, stupid, foolish.

blöken ['blø:kən] *v/i.* (ge-, *h*) *sheep, calf:* bleat.

blond *adj.* [blɔnt] blond, fair (-haired).

bloß [blo:s] **1.** *adj.* bare, naked; mere; **‿e Worte** mere words; *mit dem* **‿en Auge** *wahrnehmbar* visible to the naked eye; **2.** *adv.* only, merely, simply, just.

Blöße ['blø:sə] *f* (-/-n) bareness, nakedness; *fig.* weak point *or* spot; *sich e-e* ‿ *geben* give o.s. away; lay o.s. open to attack; *keine* ‿ *bieten* be invulnerable.

'**bloß│legen** *v/t.* (*sep.*, -ge-, *h*) lay bare, expose; '**‿stellen** *v/t.* (*sep.*, -ge-, *h*) expose, compromise, unmask; *sich* ‿ compromise o.s.

blühen ['bly:ən] *v/i.* (ge-, *h*) blossom, flower, bloom; *fig.* flourish, thrive, prosper; ✝ boom.

Blume ['blu:mə] *f* (-/-n) flower; *wine:* bouquet; *beer:* froth.

'**Blumen|beet** n flower-bed; '**~blatt** n petal; '**~händler** m florist; '**~strauß** m bouquet or bunch of flowers; '**~topf** m flowerpot; '**~zucht** f floriculture.

Bluse ['blu:zə] f (-/-n) blouse.

Blut [blu:t] n (-[e]s/no pl.) blood; ~ vergießen shed blood; böses ~ machen breed bad blood; '**~andrang** ⚕ m congestion; '**~arm** adj. bloodless; ~ an(a)emic; '**~armut** ⚕ f an(a)emia; '**~bad** n carnage, massacre; '**~bank** ⚕ f blood bank; '**~blase** f blood blister; '**~druck** m blood pressure; '**~dürstig** adj. ['~dyrstiç] bloodthirsty.

Blüte ['bly:tə] f (-/-n) blossom, bloom, flower; esp. fig. flower; prime, heyday (of life).

Blutegel ['blu:t⁹e:gəl] m⚕ leech.

'**bluten** v/i. (ge-, h) bleed (aus from); aus der Nase ~ bleed at the nose.

Bluterguß ⚕ ['blu:t⁹-] m effusion of blood.

'**Blütezeit** f flowering period or time; fig. a. prime, heyday.

'**Blut|gefäß** anat. n blood-vessel; '**~gerinnsel** ⚕ [~gərinzəl] n (-s/-) clot of blood; '**~gruppe** f blood group; '**~hund** zo. m bloodhound; '**blutig** adj. bloody, blood-stained; es ist mein ~er Ernst I am dead serious; ~er Anfänger mere beginner, F greenhorn.

'**Blut|körperchen** ['blu:tkœrpərçən] n (-s/-) blood corpuscle; '**~kreislauf** m (blood) circulation; '**~lache** f pool of blood; '**2leer** adj., '**2los** adj. bloodless; '**~probe** f blood test; '**~rache** f blood feud or revenge or vengeance, vendetta; '**2rot** adj. blood-red; crimson; '**2rünstig** adj. ['~rynstiç] bloodthirsty; bloody; '**~schande** f incest; '**~spender** m blood-donor; '**2stillend** adj. blood-sta(u)nching; '**~sturz** m h(a)emorrhage; '**~sverwandt** adj. related by blood (mit to); '**~sverwandtschaft** f blood-relationship, consanguinity; '**~übertragung** f blood-transfusion; '**~ung** f (-/-en) bleeding, h(a)emorrhage; '**2unterlaufen** adj. eye: blood-shot; '**~vergießen** n bloodshed; '**~vergiftung** f blood-poisoning.

Bö [bø] f (-/-en) gust, squall.

Bock [bɔk] m (-[e]s/ᵘe) deer, hare,

rabbit: buck; he-goat, F billy-goat; sheep: ram; gymnastics: buck; e-n ~ schießen commit a blunder, sl. commit a bloomer; den ~ zum Gärtner machen set the fox to keep the geese; '**2en** v/i. (ge-, h) horse: buck; child: sulk; p. be obstinate or refractory; mot. move jerkily, Am. F a. buck; '**2ig** adj. stubborn, obstinate, pigheaded; '**~sprung** m leap-frog; gymnastics: vault over the buck; Bocksprünge machen caper, cut capers.

Boden ['bo:dən] m (-s/ᵘ) ground; ✍ soil; bottom; floor; loft; '**~kammer** f garret, attic; '**2los** adj. bottomless; fig. enormous; unheard-of; '**~personal** ✈ n ground personnel or staff, Am. ground crew; '**~reform** f land reform; '**~satz** m grounds pl.; sediment; '**~schätze** ['~ʃɛtsə] m/pl. mineral resources pl.; '**2ständig** adj. native, indigenous.

bog [bo:k] pret. of biegen.

Bogen ['bo:gən] m (-s/-, ᵘ) bow, bend, curve; Å arc; ∆ arch; skiing: turn; skating: curve; sheet (of paper); '**2förmig** adj. arched; '**~gang** ∆ m arcade; '**~lampe** ƒ ⚡ arc-lamp; '**~schütze** m archer, bowman.

Bohle ['bo:lə] f (-/-n) thick plank, board.

Bohne ['bo:nə] f (-/-n) bean; grüne ~n pl. French beans pl., Am. string beans pl.; weiße ~n pl. haricot beans pl.; F blaue ~n pl. bullets pl.; '**~nstange** f beanpole (a. F fig.).

bohnern ['bo:nərn] v/t. (ge-, h) polish (floor, etc.), (bees)wax (floor).

bohr|en ['bo:rən] (ge-, h) 1. v/t. bore, drill (hole); sink, bore (well, shaft); bore, cut, drive (tunnel, etc.); 2. v/i. drill (a. dentistry); bore; '**2er** ⊕ m (-s/-) borer, drill.

'**böig** adj. squally, gusty; ✈ bumpy.

Boje ['bo:jə] f (-/-n) buoy.

Bollwerk ✕ ['bɔlvɛrk] n bastion, bulwark (a. fig.).

Bolzen ⊕ ['bɔltsən] m (-s/-) bolt.

Bombard|ement [bɔmbardə'mã:] n (-s/-s) bombardment; bombing; shelling; **2ieren** [~'di:rən] v/t. (no -ge-, h) bomb; shell; bombard (a. fig.).

Bombe ['bɔmbə] f (-/-n) bomb; fig. bomb-shell; '**2nsicher** adj. bomb-

B

proof; F *fig.* dead sure; '**~nschaden** *m* bomb damage; '**~r** ✠ ✖ *m* (-s/-) bomber. [er; credit note.]

Bon ✝ [bõː] *m* (-s/-s) coupon; vouch-]

Bonbon [bõˈbõː] *m, n* (-s/-s) sweet (-meat), bon-bon, F goody, *Am.* candy. [*Am. a.* big shot.]

Bonze F [ˈbɔntsə] *m* (-n/-n) bigwig,]

Boot [boːt] *n* (-[e]s/-e) boat; '**~shaus** *n* boat-house; '**~smann** *m* (-[e]s/*Bootsleute*) boatswain.

Bord [bɔrt] 1. *n* (-[e]s/-e) shelf; 2. ⚓, ✈ *m*: an ~ on board, aboard (*ship, aircraft, etc.*); über ~ overboard; von ~ gehen go ashore; '**~funker** ⚓, ✈ *m* wireless *or* radio operator; '**~stein** *m* kerb, *Am.* curb.

borgen [ˈbɔrɡən] *v/t.* (ge-, h) borrow (*von, bei* from, of); lend, *Am. a.* loan (*j-m et.* s.th. to s.o.).

Borke [ˈbɔrkə] *f* (-/-n) bark (*of tree*).

borniert *adj.* [bɔrˈniːrt] narrow-minded, *of* restricted intelligence.

Borsalbe [ˈboːr-] *f* boracic ointment.

Börse [ˈbœrzə] *f* (-/-n) purse; ✝ stock exchange; stock-market; money-market; '**~nbericht** *m* market report; '**2nfähig** *adj.* stock: negotiable on the stock exchange; '**~nkurs** *m* quotation; '**~nmakler** *m* stock-broker; '**~nnotierung** *f* (official, stock exchange) quotation; '**~npapiere** *n/pl.* listed securities *pl.*; '**~nspekulant** *m* stock-jobber; '**~nzeitung** *f* financial newspaper.

Borste [ˈbɔrstə] *f* (-/-n) bristle (*of hog or brush, etc.*); '**2ig** *adj.* bristly.

Borte [ˈbɔrtə] *f* (-/-n) border (*of carpet, etc.*); braid, lace.

'**bösartig** *adj.* malicious, vicious; 🦠 malignant; '**2keit** *f* (-/-en) viciousness; 🦠 malignity.

Böschung [ˈbœʃuŋ] *f* (-/-en) slope; embankment (*of railway*); bank (*of river*).

böse [ˈbøːzə] 1. *adj.* bad, evil, wicked; malevolent, spiteful; angry (*über acc.* at, about; *auf j-n* with s.o.); *er meint es nicht* ~ he means no harm; 2. 2 *n* (-n/*no pl.*) evil; 2**wicht** [ˈ~viçt] *m* (-[e]s/-er, -e) villain, rascal.

bos|haft *adj.* [ˈbɔshaft] wicked; spiteful; malicious; '**2heit** *f* (-/-en) wickedness; malice; spite.

'**böswillig** *adj.* malevolent; ~e Ab-

sicht 🏛 malice prepense; ~es Verlassen 🏛 wilful desertion; '**2keit** *f* (-/-en) malevolence.

bot [boːt] *pret. of* bieten.

Botan|ik [boˈtaːnik] *f* (-/*no pl.*) botany; '**~iker** *m* (-s/-) botanist; **2isch** *adj.* botanical.

Bote [ˈboːtə] *m* (-n/-n) messenger; '**~ngang** *m.* errand; *Botengänge machen* run errands.

'**Botschaft** *f* (-/-en) message; *pol.* embassy; '**~er** *m* (-s/-) ambassador; *in British Commonwealth countries*: High Commissioner.

Bottich [ˈbɔtiç] *m* (-[e]s/-e) tub; wash-tub; *brewing*: tun. vat.

Bouillon [buˈljõː] *f* (-/-s) beef tea.

Bowle [ˈboːlə] *f* (-/-n) *vessel*: bowl; *cold drink consisting of fruit, hock and champagne or soda-water*: *appr.* punch.

box|en [ˈbɔksən] 1. *v/i.* (ge-, h) box; 2. *v/t.* (ge-, h) punch *s.o.*; 3. 2 *n* (-s/*no pl.*) boxing; pugilism; '**2er** *m* (-s/-) boxer; pugilist; '**2handschuh** *m* boxing-glove; '**2kampf** *m* boxing-match, bout, fight; '**2sport** *m* boxing.

Boykott [bɔyˈkɔt] (-[e]s/-e) boycott; **2ieren** [~ˈtiːrən] *v/t.* (no -ge-, h) boycott.

brach [braːx] 1. *pret. of* brechen; 2. **~** *adv.* fallow; uncultivated (*both a. fig.*).

brachte [ˈbraxtə] *pret. of* bringen.

Branche ✝ [ˈbrãˈʃə] *f* (-/-n) line (*of business*), trade; branch.

Brand [brant] *m* (-[e]s/"e) burning, fire, blaze; 🦠 gangrene; ♣, 🌾 blight, smut, mildew; '**~blase** *f* blister; '**~bombe** *f* incendiary bomb; 2**en** [ˈ~dən] *v/i.* (ge-, h) surge (*a. fig.*), break (*an acc.*, *gegen* against); '**~fleck** *m* burn; 2**ig** *adj.* [ˈ~diç] ♣, 🌾 blighted, smutted; 🦠 gangrenous; '**~mal** *n* brand; *fig.* stigma, blemish; '**2marken** *v/t.* (ge-, h) brand (*animal*); *fig.* brand *or* stigmatize *s.o.*; '**~mauer** *f* fire (-proof) wall; '**~schaden** *m* damage caused by *or* loss suffered by fire; '**2schatzen** *v/t.* (ge-, h) lay (*town*) under contribution; sack, pillage; '**~stätte** *f*, '**~stelle** *f* scene of fire; '**~stifter** *m* incendiary, *Am.* F *a.* firebug; '**~stiftung** *f* arson; **~ung** [ˈ~duŋ] *f* (-/-en) surf, surge, breakers *pl.*; '**~wache** *f* fire-watch;

'**✲wunde** f burn; scald; '**✲zeichen** n brand.

brannte ['brantə] pret. of brennen.

Branntwein ['brantvaɪn] m brandy, spirits pl.; whisk(e)y; gin; '**✲brennerei** f distillery.

braten ['braːtən] **1.** v/t. (irr., ge-, h) in oven: roast; grill; in frying-pan: fry; bake (apple); am Spieß ✲ roast on a spit, barbecue; **2.** v/i. (irr., ge-, h) roast; grill; fry; in der Sonne ✲ p. roast or grill in the sun; **2** m (-s/-) roast (meat); joint; '**2fett** m dripping; '**2soße** f gravy.

'**Brat|fisch** m fried fish; '**✲hering** m grilled herring; '**✲huhn** n roast chicken; '**✲kartoffeln** pl. fried potatoes pl.; '**✲ofen** m (kitchen) oven; '**✲pfanne** f frying-pan, Am. a. skillet; '**✲röhre** f s. Bratofen.

Brauch [braux] m (-[e]s/ue) custom, usage; use, habit; practice; '**2bar** adj. p., thing: useful; p. capable, able; thing: serviceable; '**2en** (h) **1.** v/t. (ge-) need, want; require; take (time); use; **2.** v/aux. (no ge-): du brauchst es nur zu sagen you only have to say so; er hätte nicht zu kommen ✲ he need not have come; '**✲tum** n (-[e]s/uer) custom; tradition; folklore.

Braue ['brauə] f (-/-n) eyebrow.

brau|en ['brauən] v/t. (ge-, h) brew; '**2er** m (-s/-) brewer; **2erei** [✲'raɪ] f (-/-en) brewery; '**2haus** n brewery.

braun adj. [braun] brown; horse: bay; ✲ werden get a tan (on one's skin).

Bräune ['brɔɪnə] f (-/no pl.) brown colo(u)r; (sun) tan; '**2n** (ge-, h) **1.** v/t. make or dye brown; sun: tan; **2.** v/i. tan.

'**Braunkohle** f brown coal, lignite.

'**bräunlich** adj. brownish.

Brause ['brauzə] f (-/-n) rose, sprinkling-nozzle (of watering can); s. Brausebad; s. Brauselimonade; '**✲bad** n shower(-bath); '**✲limonade** f fizzy lemonade; '**2n** v/i. (ge-, h) wind water etc.: roar; rush; have a shower(-bath); '**✲pulver** n effervescent powder.

Braut [braut] f (-/ue) fiancée; on wedding-day: bride; '**✲führer** m best man.

Bräutigam ['brɔɪtigam] m (-s/-e) fiancé; on wedding-day: bridegroom, Am. a. groom.

'**Braut|jungfer** f bridesmaid; '**✲kleid** n wedding-dress; '**✲kranz** m bridal wreath; '**✲leute** pl., '**✲paar** n engaged couple; on wedding-day: bride and bridegroom; '**✲schleier** m bridal veil.

brav adj. [braːf] honest, upright; good, well-behaved; brave.

bravo int. ['braːvo] bravo!, well done!

Bravour [bra'vuːr] f (-/no pl.) bravery, courage; brilliance.

Brecheisen ['brɛç²-] n crowbar; (burglar's) jemmy, Am. a. jimmy.

'**brechen** ['brɛçən] (irr., ge-) **1.** v/t. (h) break; pluck (flower); refract (ray, etc.); fold (sheet of paper); quarry (stone); vomit; die Ehe ✲ commit adultery; sich ✲ break (one's leg, etc.); opt. be refracted; **2.** v/i. (h) break; vomit; mit j-m ✲ break with s.o.; **3.** v/i. (sein) break, get broken; bones: break, fracture.

'**Brech|mittel** ✲ n emetic; F fig. sickener; '**✲reiz** m nausea; '**✲stange** f crowbar, Am. a. pry; '**✲ung** opt. f (-/-en) refraction.

Brei [braɪ] m (-[e]s/-e) paste; pulp; mash; pap (for babies); made of oatmeal: porridge; (rice, etc.) pudding; '**2ig** adj. pasty; pulpy; pappy.

breit adj. [braɪt] broad, wide; zehn Meter ✲ ten metres wide; ✲e Schichten der Bevölkerung large sections of or the bulk of the population; '**✲beinig 1.** adj. with legs wide apart; **2.** adv.: ✲ gehen straddle.

Breite ['braɪtə] f (-/-n) breadth, width; ast., geogr. latitude; '**2n** v/t. (ge-, h) spread; '**✲ngrad** m degree of latitude; '**✲nkreis** m parallel (of latitude).

'**breit|machen** v/refl. (sep., -ge-, h) spread o.s.; take up room; '**✲schlagen** v/t. (irr. schlagen, sep., -ge-, h): F j-n ✲ persuade s.o.; F j-n zu et. ✲ talk s.o. into (doing) s.th.; '**2seite** ✚ f broadside.

Bremse ['brɛmzə] f (-/-n) zo. gadfly; horse-fly; ⊕ brake; '**2n** (ge-, h) v/i. brake, put on the brakes; slow down; **2.** v/t. brake, put on the brakes to; slow down; fig. curb.

'**Brems|klotz** m brake-block; ✚ wheel chock; '**✲pedal** n brake pedal; '**✲vorrichtung** f brake-mechanism; '**✲weg** m braking distance.

brennbar

brenn|bar *adj.* ['brɛnbaːr] combustible, burnable; **~dauer** *f* burning time; **~en** (*irr.*, ge-, h) **1.** *v/t.* burn; distil(l) (*brandy*); roast (*coffee*); bake (*brick, etc.*); **2.** *v/i.* burn; be ablaze, be on fire; *wound, eye*: smart, burn; *nettle*: sting; *vor Ungeduld* ~ burn with impatience; *F darauf* ~ *zu inf.* be burning to *inf.*; es brennt! fire!

'Brenn|er *m* (-s/-) *p.* distiller; *fixture*: burner; **~essel** *f* ['brɛnnɛsəl] *f* stinging nettle; **~glas** *n* burning glass; **~holz** *n* firewood; **~material** *n* fuel; **~öl** *n* lamp-oil; fuel-oil; **~punkt** *m* focus, focal point; *in den* ~ *rücken* bring into focus (*a. fig.*); *im* ~ *des Interesses stehen* be the focus of interest; **~schere** *f* curling-tongs *pl.*; **~spiritus** *m* methylated spirit; **~stoff** *m* combustible; *mot.* fuel.

brenzlig ['brɛntsliç] **1.** *adj.* burnt; *matter*: dangerous; *situation*: precarious; **~er** *Geruch* burnt smell, smell of burning; **2.** *adv.*: *es riecht* ~ it smells of burning.

Bresche ['brɛʃə] *f* (-/-n) breach (*a. fig.*), gap; *in die* ~ *springen* help *s.o.* out of a dilemma.

Brett [brɛt] *n* (-[e]s/-er) board; plank; shelf; spring-board; **~spiel** *n* game played on a board.

Brezel ['breːtsəl] *f* (-/-n) pretzel.

Brief [briːf] *m* (-[e]s/-e) letter; **~aufschrift** *f* address (on a letter); **~beschwerer** *m* (-s/-) paperweight; **~bogen** *m* sheet of notepaper; **~geheimnis** *n* secrecy of correspondence; **~karte** *f* correspondence card (*with envelope*); **~kasten** *m* letter-box; pillar-box; *Am.* mailbox; **Qlich** *adj. and adv.* by letter, in writing; **~marke** *f* (postage) stamp; **~markensammlung** *f* stamp-collection; **~öffner** *m* letter-opener; **~ordner** *m* letter-file; **~papier** *n* notepaper; **~porto** *n* postage; **~post** *f* mail, post; **~tasche** *f* wallet, *Am. a.* billfold; **~taube** *f* carrier pigeon, homing pigeon, homer; **~träger** *m* postman, *Am.* mailman; **~umschlag** *m* envelope; **~waage** *f* letter-balance; **~wechsel** *m* correspondence; **~zensur** *f* postal censorship.

brief [briːt] *pret. of braten.*

Brikett [bri'kɛt] *n* (-[e]s/-s) briquet (-te).

Brillant [bril'jant] **1.** *m* (-en/-en) brilliant, cut diamond; **2.** **2** *adj.* brilliant; **~ring** *m* diamond ring.

Brille ['brilə] *f* (-/-n) (*eine a pair of*) glasses *pl.* or spectacles *pl.*, goggles *pl.*; lavatory seat; **~nfutteral** *n* spectacle-case; **~nträger** *m* person who wears glasses.

bringen ['briŋən] *v/t.* (*irr.*, ge-, h) bring; take; see (*s.o. home, etc.*); put (*in order*); make (*sacrifice*); yield (*interest*); *an den Mann* ~ dispose of, get rid of; *j-n dazu* ~ *et. zu tun* make *or* get s.o. to do s.th.; *et. mit sich* ~ involve s.th.; *j-n um et.* ~ deprive s.o. of s.th.; *j-n zum Lachen* ~ make s.o. laugh.

Brise ['briːzə] *f* (-/-n) breeze.

Brit|e ['britə] *m* (-n/-n) Briton, *Am. a.* Britisher; *die* ~*n pl.* the British *pl.*; **Qisch** *adj.* British.

bröckeln ['brœkəln] *v/i.* (ge-, h) crumble; become brittle.

Brocken ['brɔkən] **1.** *m* (-s/-) piece; lump (*of earth or stone, etc.*); morsel (*of food*); *F ein harter* ~ *a* hard nut; **2.** **2** *v/t.* (ge-, h): *Brot in die Suppe* ~ break bread into soup.

brodeln ['broːdəln] *v/i.* (ge-, h) bubble, simmer.

Brombeer|e ['brɔm-] *f* blackberry; **~strauch** *m* blackberry bush.

Bronchialkatarrh [brɔnçi'aːl-katar] *m* bronchial catarrh; **~ien** *anat. f/pl.* bronchi(a) *pl.*; **~itis** [~'çiːtis] *f* (-/Bronchitiden) bronchitis.

Bronze ['brõːsə] *f* (-/-n) bronze; **~medaille** *f* bronze medal.

Brosche ['brɔʃə] *f* (-/-n) brooch.

broschier|en [brɔ'ʃiːrən] *v/t.* (*no* -ge-, h) sew, stitch (*book*); **~t** *adj.* *book*: paper-backed, paper-bound; *fabric*: figured.

Broschüre [brɔ'ʃyːrə] *f* (-/-n) booklet; brochure; pamphlet.

Brot [broːt] *n* (-[e]s/-e) bread; loaf; *sein* ~ *verdienen* earn one's living; **~aufstrich** *m* spread.

Brötchen ['brøːtçən] *n* (-s/-) roll.

'Brot|korb *m*: *j-m den* ~ *höher hängen* put s.o. on short allowance; **Qlos** *fig. adj.* unemployed; unprofitable; **~rinde** *f* crust; **~schneidemaschine** *f* bread-cutter; **~schnitte** *f* slice of bread;

ˎstudium *n* utilitarian study; **ˎteig** *m* bread dough.
Bruch [brux] (-[e]s/ˀe) break(ing); breach; *ℱ* fracture (*of bones*); *ℱ* hernia; crack; fold (*in paper*); crease (*in cloth*); split (*in silk*); *♃* fraction; breach (*of promise*); violation (*of oath, etc.*); violation, infringement (*of law, etc.*); **ˎband** *ℱ n* truss.
brüchig *adj.* ['bryçiç] fragile; brittle, *voice:* cracked.
'**Bruch|landung** *≴ f* crash-landing; **ˎrechnung** *f* fractional arithmetic, F fractions *pl.*; **ˎstrich** *♃ m* fraction bar; **ˎstück** *n* fragment (*a. fig.*); **ˎteil** *m* fraction; *im* ˴ *e-r Sekunde* in a split second; **ˎzahl** *f* fraction(al) number.
Brücke ['brykə] *f* (-/-n) bridge; *carpet:* rug; *sports:* bridge; e-e ˴ *schlagen über* (*acc.*) build *or* throw a bridge across, bridge (*river*); **ˎn-kopf** *⚔ m* bridge-head; **ˎnpfeiler** *m* pier (*of bridge*).
Bruder ['bru:dər] *m* (-s/ˀ) brother; *eccl.* (lay) brother, friar; **ˎkrieg** *m* fratricidal *or* civil war; **ˎkuß** *m* fraternal kiss.
brüderlich ['bry:dərliç] **1.** *adj.* brotherly, fraternal; **2.** *adv.:* ˴ *teilen* share and share alike; **ˀkeit** *f* (-/*no pl.*) brotherliness, fraternity.
Brühe ['bry:ə] *f* (-/-n) broth; stock; beef tea; F dirty water; *drink:* F dishwater; **ˀheiß** *adj.* scalding hot; **ˎwürfel** *m* beef cube.
brüllen ['brylən] *v/i.* (ge-, h) roar; bellow; *cattle:* low; *bull:* bellow; *vor Lachen* ˴ roar with laughter; **ˎdes Gelächter** roar of laughter.
brumm|en ['brumən] *v/i.* (ge-, h) *p.* speak in a deep voice, mumble; growl (*a. fig.*); *insect:* buzz; *engine:* buzz, boom; *fig.* grumble, *Am.* F grouch; *mir brummt der Schädel* my head is buzzing; **ˀbär** *fig. m* grumbler, growler, *Am.* F grouch; **ˀer** *m* (-s/-) bluebottle; dung-beetle; **ˎig** *adj.* grumbling, *Am.* F grouchy. [brunette.]
brünett *adj.* [bry'nɛt] *woman:*]
Brunft *hunt.* [brunft] *f* (-/ˀe) rut; **ˎzeit** *f* rutting season.
Brunnen ['brunən] *m* (-s/-) well; spring; fountain (*a. fig.*); e-n ˴ *graben* sink a well; **ˎwasser** *n* pump-water, well-water.

Brunst [brunst] *f* (-/ˀe) *zo.* rut (*of male animal*), heat (*of female animal*); lust, sexual desire.
brünstig *adj.* ['brynstiç] *zo.* rutting, in heat; lustful.
Brust [brust] *f* (-/ˀe) chest, *anat.* thorax; breast; (woman's) breast(s *pl.*), bosom; *aus voller* ˴ at the top of one's voice, lustily; **ˎbild** *n* half-length portrait.
brüsten ['brystən] *v/refl.* (ge-, h) boast, brag.
'**Brust|fell** *anat. n* pleura; **ˎfell-entzündung** *ℱ f* pleurisy; **ˎka-sten** *m,* **ˎkorb** *m* chest, *anat.* thorax; **ˎschwimmen** *n* (-s/*no pl.*) breast-stroke.
Brüstung ['brystuŋ] *f* (-/-en) balustrade, parapet.
'**Brustwarze** *anat. f* nipple.
Brut [bru:t] *f* (-/-en) brooding, sitting; brood; hatch; fry, spawn (*of fish*); *fig.* F brood, (bad) lot.
brutal *adj.* [bru'ta:l] brutal; **ˀität** [ˌali'tɛːt] *f* (-/-en) brutality.
Brutapparat *zo.* [bru:tˀ-] *m* incubator.
brüten ['bry:tən] *v/i.* (ge-, h) brood, sit (*on egg*); incubate; ˴ *über* (*dat.*) brood over.
'**Brutkasten** *ℱ m* incubator.
brutto *✝ adv.* ['bruto] gross; **ˀge-wicht** *n* gross weight; **ˀregister-tonne** *f* gross register ton; **ˀver-dienst** *m* gross earnings *pl.*
Bube ['bu:bə] *m* (-n/-n) boy, lad; knave, rogue; *cards:* knave, jack; **ˎnstreich** *m,* **ˎnstück** *n* boyish prank; knavish trick.
Buch [bu:x] *n* (-[e]s/ˀer) book; volume; **ˎbinder** *m* (book-)binder; **ˎdrucker** *m* printer; **ˎdruckerei** [ˌˈraɪ] *f* printing; printing-office, *Am.* print shop.
Buche ♀ ['bu:xə] *f* (-/-n) beech.
buchen ['bu:xən] *v/t.* (ge-, h) book, reserve (*passage, flight, etc.*); *book-keeping:* book (*item, sum*), enter (*transaction*) in the books; *et. als Erfolg* ˴ count s.th. as a success.
Bücher|abschluß *✝* ['by:çər-] *m* closing of *or* balancing of books; **ˎbrett** *n* bookshelf; **ˎei** [ˌˈraɪ] *f* (-/-en) library; **ˎfreund** *m* book-lover, bibliophil(e); **ˎrevisor** *✝ m* (-s/-en) auditor; accountant; **ˎschrank** *m* bookcase; **ˎwurm** *m* bookworm.

'Buch|fink orn. m chaffinch; **'~hal-ter** m (-s/-) book-keeper; **'~hal-tung** f book-keeping; **'~handel** m book-trade; **'~händler** m book-seller; **'~handlung** f bookshop, Am. bookstore.

Büchse ['byksə] f (-/-n) box, case; tin, Am. can; rifle; **'~nfleisch** n tinned meat, Am. canned meat; **'~nöffner** ['byksən°-] m tin-opener, Am. can opener.

Buchstab|e ['bu:xʃta:bə] m (-n/-n) letter, character; typ. type; **ℒieren** [~'bi:rən] v/t. (no -ge-, h) spell.

buchstäblich ['bu:xʃtɛːpliç] **1.** adj. literal; **2.** adv. literally; word for word.

Bucht [buxt] f (-/-en) bay; bight; creek, inlet.

'Buchung f (-/-en) booking, reservation; book-keeping: entry.

Buckel ['bukəl] **1.** m (-s/-) hump, hunch; humpback, hunchback; boss, stud, knob; **2.** f (-/-n) boss, stud, knob.

'buckelig adj. s. bucklig.

bücken ['bykən] v/refl. (ge-, h) bend (down), stoop.

bucklig adj. ['bukliç] humpbacked, hunchbacked.

Bückling ['byklin] m (-s/-e) bloater, red herring; fig. bow.

Dude ['bu:də] f (-/-n) stall, booth; hut, cabin, Am. shack; F: place; den; (student's, etc.) digs pl.

Budget [by'dʒe:] n (-s/-s) budget.

Büfett [by'fe:; by'fɛt] n (-[e]s/-s, -[e]s/-e) sideboard, buffet; buffet, bar, Am. a. counter; kaltes ~ buffet supper or lunch.

Büffel ['byfəl] m (-s/-) zo. buffalo; F fig. lout, blockhead.

Bug [bu:k] m (-[e]s/-e) ⚓ bow; ✈ nose; fold; (sharp) crease.

Bügel ['by:gəl] m (-s/-) bow (of spectacles, etc.); handle (of handbag, etc.); coat-hanger; stirrup; **'~brett** n ironing-board; **'~eisen** n (flat-)iron; **'~falte** f crease; **'ℒn** v/t. (ge-, h) iron (shirt, etc.), press (suit, skirt, etc.).

Bühne ['by:nə] f (-/-n) platform (a. ⊕); scaffold; thea. stage; fig.: a. the stage; die politische ~ the political scene; **~nanweisungen** ['by:-nən°-] f/pl. stage directions pl.; **'~nbild** n scene(ry); décor; stage design; **'~ndichter** m playwright,

dramatist; **'~nlaufbahn** f stage career; **'~nstück** n stage play.

buk [bu:k] pret. of backen.

Bull|auge ⚓ ['bul-] n porthole, bull's eye; **'~dogge** zo. f bulldog.

Bulle ['bulə] **1.** zo. m (-n/-n) bull; **2.** eccl. f (-/-n) bull.

Bummel F ['buməl] m (-s/-) stroll; spree, pub-crawl, sl. binge; **~ei** [~'lai] f (-/-en) dawdling; negligence; **'ℒn** v/i. (ge-) **1.** (sein) stroll, saunter; pub-crawl; **2.** (h) dawdle (on way, at work), waste time; **'~streik** m go-slow (strike), Am. slowdown; **'~zug** m slow train, Am. way train.

Bummler ['bumlər] m (-s/-) saunterer, stroller; loafer, Am. F a. bum; dawdler.

Bund [bunt] **1.** m (-[e]s/⁺e) pol. union, federation, confederacy; (waist-, neck-, wrist)band; **2.** n (-[e]s/-e) bundle (of faggots); bundle, truss (of hay or straw); bunch (of radishes, etc.).

Bündel ['byndəl] n (-s/-) bundle, bunch; **'ℒn** v/t. (ge-, h) make into a bundle, bundle up.

Bundes|bahn ['bundəs-] f Federal Railway(s pl.); **'~bank** f Federal Bank; **'~genosse** m ally; **'~gerichtshof** m Federal Supreme Court; **'~kanzler** m Federal Chancellor; **'~ministerium** n Federal Ministry; **'~post** f Federal Postal Administration; **'~präsident** m President of the Federal Republic; **~rat** m Bundesrat, Upper House of German Parliament; **'~republik** f Federal Republic; **'~staat** m federal state; confederation; **'~tag** m Bundestag, Lower House of German Parliament.

bündig adj. ['byndiç] style, speech: concise, to the point, terse.

Bündnis ['byntnis] n (-ses/-se) alliance; agreement.

Bunker ['bunkər] m (-s/-) ✕, coal, fuel, etc.: bunker; bin; air-raid shelter; ✕ bunker, pill-box; ⚓ (submarine) pen.

bunt adj. [bunt] (multi-)colo(u)red, colo(u)rful; motley; bird, flower, etc.: variegated; bright, gay; fig. mixed, motley; full of variety; **'ℒdruck** m colo(u)r-print(ing); **'ℒstift** m colo(u)red pencil, crayon.

Bürde ['byrdə] *f* (-/-n) burden (*a. fig.*: für j-n to s.o.), load.

Burg [burk] *f* (-/-en) castle; fortress, citadel (*a. fig.*).

Bürge ⚥ ['byrgə] *m* (-n/-n) guarantor, security, surety, bailsman; sponsor; '⚥n *v/i.* (ge-, h): für j-n ⁓ stand guarantee *or* surety *or* security for s.o., *Am. a.* bond s.o.; stand bail for s.o.; vouch *or* answer for s.o.; sponsor s.o.; für et. ⁓ stand security for s.th., guarantee s.th.; vouch *or* answer for s.th.

Bürger ['byrgər] *m* (-s/-) citizen; townsman; '⚥krieg *m* civil war.

'**bürgerlich** *adj.* civic, civil; ⁓e Küche plain cooking; Verlust der ⁓en Ehrenrechte loss of civil rights; Bürgerliches Gesetzbuch German Civil Code; '⚥e *m* (-n/-n) commoner.

'**Bürger|meister** *m* mayor; in Germany: *a.* burgomaster; in Scotland: provost; '⚥recht *n* civic rights *pl.*; citizenship; '⚥schaft *f* (-/-en) citizens *pl.*; '⚥steig *m* pavement, *Am.* sidewalk; '⚥wehr *f* militia.

Bürgschaft ['byrkʃaft] *f* (-/-en) security; bail; guarantee.

Büro [by'roː] *n* (-s/-s) office; ⚥angestellte *m*, *f* (-n/-n) clerk; ⚥arbeit *f* office-work; ⚥klammer *f* paper-clip; ⚥krat [⁓o'kraːt] *m* (-en/-en) bureaucrat; ⚥kratie [⁓o-kra'tiː] *f* (-/-n) bureaucracy; red tape; ⚥kratisch *adj.* [⁓o'kraːtiʃ] bureaucratic; ⚥stunden *f/pl.* office hours *pl.*; ⚥vorsteher *m* head *or* senior clerk.

Bursch [burʃ] *m* (-en/-en), ⁓e ['⁓ə] *m* (-n/-n) boy, lad, youth; F chap, *Am. a.* guy; ein übler ⁓ a bad lot, F a bad egg.

burschikos *adj.* [burʃi'koːs] free and easy; *esp. girl*: boyish, unaffected, hearty.

Bürste ['byrstə] *f* (-/-n) brush; '⚥n *v/t.* (ge-, h) brush. [shrub.\

Busch [buʃ] *m* (-es/⁓e) bush,\

Büschel ['byʃəl] *n* (-s/-) bunch; tuft, handful (*of hair*); wisp (*of straw or hair*).

'**Busch|holz** *n* brushwood, underwood; '⚥ig *adj.* hair, eyebrows, *etc.*: bushy, shaggy; covered with bushes *or* scrub, bushy; '⚥messer *n* bushknife; machete; '⚥neger *m* maroon; '⚥werk *n* bushes *pl.*, shrubbery, *Am. a.* brush.

Busen ['buːzən] *m* (-s/-) bosom, breast (*esp. of woman*); *fig.* bosom, heart; *geog.* bay, gulf; '⚥freund *m* bosom friend.

Bussard *orn.* ['busart] *m* (-[e]s/-e) buzzard.

Buße ['buːsə] *f* (-/-n) atonement (*for sins*), penance; repentance; satisfaction; fine; ⁓ tun do penance.

büßen ['byːsən] (ge-, h) **1.** *v/t.* expiate, atone for (*sin, crime*); er mußte es mit s-m Leben ⁓ he paid for it with his life; das sollst du mir ⁓! you'll pay for that!; **2.** *v/i.* atone, pay (für for).

'**Büßer** *m* (-s/-) penitent.

'**buß|fertig** *adj.* penitent, repentant, contrite; '⚥fertigkeit *f* (-/no pl.) repentance, contrition; '⚥tag *m* day of repentance; Buß- und Bettag day of prayer and repentance.

Büste ['bystə] *f* (-/-n) bust; '⚥n-halter *m* (-s/-) brassière, F bra.

Büttenpapier ['bytən-] *n* handmade paper.

Butter ['butər] *f* (-/no pl.) butter; '⚥blume ♀ *f* buttercup; '⚥brot *n* (slice *or* piece of) bread and butter; F: für ein ⁓ for a song; '⚥brotpapier *n* greaseproof paper; '⚥dose *f* butter-dish; '⚥faß *n* butter-churn; '⚥milch *f* buttermilk; '⚥n *v/i.* (ge-, h) churn.

C

Café [ka'feː] *n* (-s/-s) café, coffeehouse.

Cape [keːp] *n* (-s/-s) cape.

Cell|ist ♪ [tʃe'list] *m* (-en/-en) violoncellist, (')cellist; ⁓o ♪ ['⁓o] *n* (-s/-s, Celli) violoncello, (')cello.

Celsius ['tsɛlzius]: 5 Grad ⁓ (*abbr.* 5° C) five degrees centigrade.

Chaiselongue [ʃɛz(ə)'lõ:] *f* (-/-n, -s) chaise longue, lounge, couch.

Champagner [ʃam'panjər] *m* (-s/-) champagne.

Champignon ♀ ['ʃampinjõ] m (-s/-s) champignon, (common) mushroom.

Chance ['ʃã:s(ə)] f (-/-n) chance; keine ~ haben not to stand a chance; sich eine ~ entgehen lassen miss a chance or an opportunity; die ~n sind gleich the chances or odds are even.

Chaos ['ka:ɔs] n (-/no pl.) chaos.

Charakter [ka'raktər] m (-s/-e) character; nature; **~bild** a character (sketch); **~darsteller** thea. m character actor; **~fehler** m fault in s.o.'s character; 2**fest** adj. of firm or strong character; 2**i'sieren** v/t. (no -ge-, h) characterize, describe (als acc. as); **~i'sierung** f (-/-en), **~istik** [~'ristik] f (-/-en) characterization; 2**istisch** adj. [~'ristiʃ] characteristic or typical (für of); 2**los** adj. characterless, without (strength of) character, spineless; **~rolle** thea. f character role; **~zug** m characteristic, feature, trait.

charm|ant adj. [ʃar'mant] charming, winning, 2**e** [~ʃarm] m (-s/no pl.) charm, grace.

Chassis [ʃa'si:] n (-/-) mot., radio: frame, chassis.

Chauffeur [ʃɔ'fø:r] m (-s/-e) chauffeur, driver.

Chaussee [ʃo'se:] f (-/-n) highway, (high) road.

Chauvinismus [ʃovi'nismus] m (-/no pl.) jingoism; chauvinism.

Chef [ʃef] m (-s/-s) head, chief; ✝ principal, F boss; senior partner.

Chem|ie [çe'mi:] f (-/no pl.) chemistry; **~iefaser** f chemical fib|re, Am. -er; **~ikalien** [~çi'ka:ljən] f/pl. chemicals pl.; **~iker** ['çe:mikər] m (-s/-) (analytical) chemist; 2**isch** adj. ['çe:miʃ] chemical.

Chiffr|e ['ʃifər] f (-/-n) number; cipher; in advertisement: box number; 2**ieren** [ʃi'fri:rən] v/t. (no -ge-, h) cipher, code (message, etc.); write in code or cipher.

Chines|e [çi'ne:zə] m (-n/-n) Chinese, contp. Chinaman; 2**isch** adj. Chinese.

Chinin ♀ [çi'ni:n] n (-s/no pl.) quinine.

Chirurg [çi'rurk] m (-en/-en) surgeon; **~ie** [~'gi:] f (-/-en) surgery; 2**isch** adj. [~'giʃ] surgical.

Chlor ♀ [klo:r] n (-s/no pl.) chlo-

rine; 2**en** v/t. (ge-, h) chlorinate (water); **~kalk** ♀ m chloride of lime.

Chloroform ♀ [kloro'fɔrm] n (-/no pl.) chloroform; 2**ieren** ♀ [~'mi:-rən] v/t. (no -ge-, h) chloroform.

Cholera ♀ ['ko:ləra] f (-/no pl.) cholera.

cholerisch adj. [ko'le:riʃ] choleric, irascible.

Chor [ko:r] m 1. △ a. n (-[e]s/-e, ⁿe) chancel, choir; (organ-)loft; 2. (-[e]s/ⁿe) in drama: chorus; singers: choir, chorus; piece of music: chorus; **~al** [ko'ra:l] m (-s/ⁿe) choral(e); hymn; **~gesang** m choral singing, chorus; **~sänger** m member of a choir; chorister.

Christ [krist] m (-en/-en) Christian; **~baum** m Christmas-tree; **~enheit** f (-/no pl.): die ~ Christendom; **~entum** n (-s/no pl.) Christianity; **~kind** n (-[e]s/no pl.) Christ-child, Infant Jesus; 2**lich** adj. Christian.

Chrom [kro:m] n (-s/no pl.) metal: chromium; pigment: chrome.

chromatisch ♪, opt. adj. [kro'ma:-tiʃ] chromatic; (icle.)

Chronik ['kro:nik] f (-/-en) chron-)

chronisch adj. ['kro:niʃ] disease: chronic (a. fig.).

Chronist [kro'nist] m (-en/-en) chronicler.

chronologisch adj. [krono'lo:giʃ] chronological. (mately.)

circa adv. ['tsirka] about, approxi-)

Clique ['klikə] f (-/-n) clique, set, group, coterie; **~nwirtschaft** f (-/no pl.) cliquism.

Conférencier [kõferã'sje:] m (-s/-s) compère, Am. master of ceremonies.

Couch [kautʃ] f (-/-s) couch.

Coupé [ku'pe:] n (-s/-s) mot. coupé; ✎ 🚃 compartment.

Couplet [ku'ple:] n (-s/-s) comic or music-hall song.

Coupon [ku'põ] m (-s/-s) coupon; dividend-warrant; counterfoil.

Courtage ✝ [kur'ta:ʒə] f (-/-n) brokerage.

Cousin [ku'zɛ̃] m (-s/-s), **~e** [~i:nə] f (-/-n) cousin.

Creme [krɛ:m, kre:m] f (-/-s) cream (a. fig.: only sg.).

Cut [kœt, kat] m (-s/-s), **~away** ['kœtəve:, 'katəve:] m (-s/-s) cutaway (coat), morning coat.

D

da [dɑ:] **1.** *adv. space:* there; ~ *wo* where; *hier und* ~ here and there; ~ *bin ich* here I am; ~ *haben wir's!* there we are!; *von* ~ *an* from there; *time:* ~ *erst* only then, not till then; *von* ~ *an* from that time (on), since then; *hier und* ~ now and then *or* again; **2.** *cj. time:* as, when, while; *nun,* ~ *du es einmal gesagt hast* now (that) you have mentioned it; *causal:* as, since, because; ~ *ich krank war, konnte ich nicht kommen* as *or* since I was ill I couldn't come.

dabei *adv.* [dɑ'baɪ, *when emphatic:* 'dɑ:baɪ] near (at hand), by; about, going (*zu inf.* to inf.), on the point (of *ger.*); besides; nevertheless, yet, for all that; *was ist schon* ~? what does it matter?; *lassen wir es* ~ let's leave it at that; ~ *bleiben* stick to one's point, persist in it.

da'bei|bleiben *v/i.* (*irr.* bleiben, *sep.,* -ge-, sein) stay with it *or* them; **~sein** *v/i.* (*irr.* sein, *sep.,* -ge-, sein) be present *or* there; **~stehen** *v/i.* (*irr.* stehen, *sep.,* -ge-, h) stand by *or* near.

'dableiben *v/i.* (*irr.* bleiben, *sep.,* -ge-, sein) stay, remain.

da capo *adv.* [dɑ'kɑ:po] *at opera, etc.:* encore.

Dach [dax] *n* (-[e]s/⸚er) roof; *fig.* shelter; **'~antenne** *f* roof aerial; **'~decker** *m* (-s/-) roofer; tiler; slater; **'~fenster** *n* skylight; dormer window; **'~garten** *m* roofgarden; **'~gesellschaft** † *f* holding company; **'~kammer** *f* attic, garret; **'~pappe** *f* roofing felt; **'~rinne** *f* gutter, eaves *pl.*

dachte ['daxtə] *pret. of* denken.

Dachs *zo.* [daks] *m* (-es/-e) badger; **'~bau** *m* (-[e]s/-e) badger's earth.

'Dach|sparren *m* rafter; **'~stube** *f* attic, garret; **'~stuhl** *m* roof framework; **'~ziegel** *m* (roofing) tile.

dadurch [dɑ'durç, *when emphatic:* 'dɑ:durç] **1.** *adv.* for this reason, in this manner *or* way, thus; by it *or* that; **2.** *cj.:* ~, *daß* owing to (the fact that), because; by *ger.*

dafür *adv.* [dɑ'fy:r, *when emphatic:* 'dɑ:fy:r] for it *or* that; instead (of it); in return (for it), in exchange; ~ *sein* be in favo(u)r of it; ~ *sein zu*

inf. be for *ger.*, be in favo(u)r of *ger.*; *er kann nichts* ~ it is not his fault; ~ *sorgen, daß* see to it that.

Da'fürhalten *n* (-s/*no pl.*): *nach meinem* ~ in my opinion.

dagegen [dɑ'ge:gən, *when emphatic:* 'dɑ:ge:gən] **1.** *adv.* against it *or* that; in comparison with it, compared to it; ~ *sein* be against it, be opposed to it; *ich habe nichts* ~ I have no objection (to it); **2.** *cj.* on the other hand, however.

daheim *adv.* [dɑ'haɪm] at home.

daher [dɑ'he:r, *when emphatic:* 'dɑ:-he:r] **1.** *adv.* from there; *prefixed to verbs of motion:* along; *fig.* from this, hence; ~ *kam es, daß* thus it happened; *that is:* ~ *es, daß* thus it happened that; **2.** *cj.* therefore; that is (the reason) why.

dahin *adv.* [dɑ'hin, *when emphatic:* 'dɑ:hin] there, to that place; gone, past; *prefixed to verbs of motion:* along; *j-n* ~ *bringen, daß* induce s.o. to *inf.*; *m-e Meinung geht* ~, *daß* my opinion is that.

da'hingestellt *adj.:* es ~ *sein lassen* (,ob) leave it undecided (whether).

dahinter *adv.* [dɑ'hintər, *when emphatic:* 'dɑ:hintər] behind it *or* that, at the back of it; es *steckt nichts* ~ there is nothing in it.

da'hinterkommen *v/i.* (*irr.* kommen, *sep.,* -ge-, sein) find out about it.

damalig *adj.* ['dɑ:mɑ:liç] then, of that time; *der* ~*e Besitzer* the then owner; '~*s adv.* then, at that time.

Damast [dɑ'mast] *m* (-es/-e) damask.

Dame ['dɑ:mə] *f* (-/-n) lady; *dancing, etc.:* partner; *cards, chess:* queen; *s.* Damespiel; **'~brett** *n* draught-board, *Am.* checkerboard.

'Damen|binde *f* (woman's) sanitary towel, *Am.* sanitary napkin; **'~doppel** *n* *tennis:* women's doubles *pl.*; **'~einzel** *n* *tennis:* women's singles *pl.*; **'~haft** *adj.* ladylike; **'~konfektion** *f* ladies' ready-made clothes *pl.*; **'~mannschaft** *f* *sports:* women's team; **'~schneider** *m* ladies' tailor, dressmaker.

'Damespiel *n* (game of) draughts *pl.*, *Am.* (game of) checkers *pl.*

damit 1. *adv.* [dɑ'mit, *when emphatic:* 'dɑ:mit] with it *or* that, therewith, herewith; by it *or* that; *was will er ~ sagen?* what does he mean by it?; *wie steht es ~?* how about it?; *~ einverstanden sein* agree to it?; **2.** *cj.* (in order) that, in order to *inf.*; so (that); *~ nicht lest,* (so as) to avoid that; for fear that (*all with subjunctive*). [asinine.]

dämlich F *adj.* ['dɛːmlɪç] silly,]

Damm [dam] *m* (-[e]s/=e) dam; dike, dyke; 🚢 embankment; embankment, *Am.* levee (*of river*); roadway; *fig.* barrier; '**~bruch** *m* bursting of a dam *or* dike.

dämmer|ig *adj.* ['dɛmərɪç] dusky; '**2licht** *n* twilight; '**~n** *v/i.* (ge-, h) dawn (*a. fig.*: F *j-m* on s.o.); grow dark *or* dusky; '**2ung** *f* (-/-en) twilight, dusk; *in the morning:* dawn.

Dämon ['dɛːmɔn] *m* (-s/-en) demon; **2isch** *adj.* [dɛ'moːnɪʃ] demoniac(al).

Dampf [dampf] *m* (-[e]s/=e) steam; vapo(u)r; '**~bad** *n* vapo(u)r-bath; '**~boot** *n* steamboat; '**2en** *v/i.* (ge-, h) steam.

dämpfen ['dɛmpfən] *v/t.* (ge-, h) deaden (*pain, noise, force of blow*); muffle (*bell, drum, oar*); damp (*sound, oscillation, fig. enthusiasm*); ♪ mute (*stringed instrument*); soften (*colour, light*); attenuate (*wave*); steam (*cloth, food*); stew (*meat, fruit*); *fig.* suppress, curb (*emotion*).

Dampfer *m* (-s/-) steamer, steam-ship.

Dämpfer *m* (-s/-) damper (*a.* ♪ *of piano*); ♪ mute (*for violin, etc.*).

Dampf|heizung *f* steam-heating; '**~kessel** *m* (steam-)boiler; '**~maschine** *f* steam-engine; '**~schiff** *n* steamer, steamship; '**~walze** *f* steam-roller.

danach *adv.* [da'naːx, *when emphatic:* 'daːnaːx] after it *or* that; afterwards; subsequently; accordingly; *ich fragte ihn ~* I asked him about it; *iro. er sieht ganz ~ aus* he looks very much like it.

Däne ['dɛːnə] *m* (-n/-n) Dane.

daneben *adv.* [da'neːbən, *when emphatic:* 'daːneːbən] next to it *or* that, beside it *or* that; besides, moreover; beside the mark.

da'nebengehen F *v/i.* (*irr. gehen, sep., -ge-, sein*) *bullet, etc.:* miss the target *or* mark; *remark, etc.:* miss one's effect, F misfire.

daniederliegen [da'niːdər-] *v/i.* (*irr. liegen, sep., -ge-, h*) be laid up (*an dat.* with); *trade:* be depressed.

dänisch *adj.* ['dɛːnɪʃ] Danish.

Dank [daŋk] *m* (-[e]s/*no pl.*) thanks *pl.*, gratitude; reward; *j-m ~ sagen* thank s.o.; *Gott sei ~!* thank God!; **2.** ♀ *prp.* (*dat.*) owing *or* thanks to; '**2bar** *adj.* thankful, grateful (*j-m* to s.o.; *für* for); profitable; '**~barkeit** *f* (-/*no pl.*) gratitude; '**2en** *v/i.* (ge-, h) thank (*j-m für et.* s.o. for s.th.); *danke* (*schön*)! thank you (very much)!; *danke* thank you; *nein, danke* no, thank you; *nichts zu ~* don't mention it; '**2enswert** *adj. thing:* one can be grateful for; *efforts, etc.:* kind; *task, etc.:* rewarding, worth-while; '**~gebet** *n* thanksgiving (*prayer*); '**~schreiben** *n* letter of thanks.

dann *adv.* [dan] then; *~ und wann* (every) now and then.

daran *adv.* [da'ran, *when emphatic:* 'daːran] at (*or* by, in, on, to) it *or* that; *sich ~ festhalten* hold on tight to it; *~ festhalten* stick to it; *nahe ~ sein zu inf.* be on the point *or* verge of *ger.*

da'rangehen *v/i.* (*irr. gehen, sep., -ge-, sein*) set to work; set about *ger.*

darauf *adv.* [da'rauf, *when emphatic:* 'daːrauf] *space:* on (top of) it *or* that; *time:* thereupon, after it *or* that; *am Tage ~* the day after, the next *or* following day; *zwei Jahre ~* two years later; *~ kommt es an* that's what matters; *~hin adv.* [darau'hɪn, *when emphatic:* 'daːraufhɪn] thereupon.

daraus *adv.* [da'raus, *when emphatic:* 'daːraus] out of it *or* that, from it *or* that; *~ folgt* hence it follows; *was ist ~ geworden?* what has become of it?; *ich mache mir nichts ~* I don't care *or* mind (about it).

darben ['darbən] *v/i.* (ge-, h) suffer want; starve.

darbiet|en ['daːr-] *v/t.* (*irr. bieten, sep., -ge-, h*) offer, present; perform; '**2ung** *f* (-/-en) *thea., etc.:* performance.

'darbringen *v/t.* (*irr. bringen, sep., -ge-, h*) offer; make (*sacrifice*).

darein *adv.* [da'raɪn, *when em-*

phatic: ['dɑːrain] into it *or* that, therein.

da'rein|finden *v/refl. (irr. finden, sep., -ge-, h)* put up with it; **~mischen** *v/refl. (sep., -ge-, h)* interfere (with it); **~reden** *v/i. (sep., -ge-, h)* interrupt; *fig.* interfere.

darin *adv.* ['dɑːrin, *when emphatic:* 'dɑːrin] in it *or* that; therein; es war nichts ~ there was nothing in it *or* them.

darleg|en ['dɑːr-] *v/t. (sep., -ge-, h)* lay open, expose, disclose; show; explain; demonstrate; point out; **'2ung** *f (-/-en)* exposition; explanation; statement.

Darlehen ['dɑːrleːən] *n (-s/-)* loan.

Darm [darm] *m (-[e]s/ːe)* gut, *anat.* intestine; (sausage-)skin; *Därme pl.* intestines *pl.,* bowels *pl.*

'darstell|en *v/t. (sep., -ge-, h)* represent; show, depict; delineate; describe; *actor:* interpret (*character, part*), represent (*character*); *graphic arts:* graph, plot (*curve, etc.*); **'2er** *thea. m (-s/-)* interpreter (*of a part*); actor; **'2ung** *f* representation; *thea.* performance.

'dartun *v/t. (irr. tun, sep., -ge-, h)* prove; demonstrate; set forth.

darüber *adv.* [da'ryːbər, *when emphatic:* 'dɑːryːbər] over it *or* that; across it; in the meantime; ~ werden Jahre vergehen it will take years; wir sind ~ hinweg we got over it; ein Buch ~ schreiben write a book about it.

darum ['dɑːrum, *when emphatic:* 'dɑːrum] **1.** *adv.* around it *or* that; er kümmert sich nicht ~ he does not care; es handelt sich ~ zu *inf.* the point is to *inf.;* **2.** *cj.* therefore, for that reason; ~ ist er nicht gekommen that's (the reason) why he hasn't come.

darunter *adv.* [da'runtər, *when emphatic:* 'dɑːruntər] under it *or* that; beneath it; among them; less; zwei Jahre und ~ two years and under; *was verstehst du ~!* what do you understand by it?

das [das] *s. der.*

dasein ['dɑː-] **1.** *v/i. (irr. sein, sep., -ge-, sein)* be there *or* present; exist; **2.** ♀ *n (-s/no pl.)* existence; life; being.

daß *cj.* [das] that; ~ nicht less; es sei denn, ~ unless; ohne ~ with-

'dastehen *v/i. (irr. stehen, sep., -ge-, h)* stand (there).

Daten ['dɑːtən] *pl.* data *pl. (a. ⊕),* facts *pl.;* particulars *pl.;* **'~verarbeitung** *f (-/-en)* data processing.

datieren [da'tiːrən] *v/t. and v/i. (no -ge-, h)* date.　　　　　[(case).]

Dativ *gr.* ['dɑːtiːf] *m (-s/-e) dative]*

Dattel ['datəl] *f (-/-n)* date.

Datum ['dɑːtum] *n (-s/Daten)* date.

Dauer ['dauər] *f (-/no pl.),* duration; continuance; auf die ~ in the long run; für die ~ von for a period *or* term of; von ~ sein last well; **'2haft** *adj.* peace, *etc.:* lasting; *material, etc.:* durable; *colour, dye:* fast; **'~karte** *f* season ticket, *Am.* commutation ticket; **'~lauf** *m* jog-trot; endurance-run; **'2n** *v/i. (ge-, h)* continue, last; take (*time*); **'~welle** *f* permanent wave, F perm.

Daumen ['daumən] *m (-s/-)* thumb; j-m den ~ halten keep one's fingers crossed (for s.o.); **'~abdruck** *m (-[e]s/ːe)* thumb-print.

Daune ['daunə] *f (-/-n):* ~(n *pl.)* down; **'~ndecke** *f* eiderdown (quilt).

davon *adv.* [da'fɔn, *when emphatic:* 'dɑːfɔn] of it *or* that; thereof; from it *or* that; off, away; was habe ich ~? what do I get from it?; das kommt ~! it serves you right!

da'von|kommen *v/i. (irr. kommen, sep., -ge-, sein)* escape, get off; **~laufen** *v/i. (irr. laufen, sep., -ge-, sein)* run away.

davor *adv.* [da'foːr, *when emphatic:* 'dɑːfoːr] *space:* before it *or* that, in front of it *or* that; er fürchtet sich ~ he is afraid of it.

dazu *adv.* [da'tsuː, *when emphatic:* 'dɑːtsuː] to it *or* that; for it *or* that; for that purpose; in addition to that; noch ~ at that; ~ gehört Zeit it requires time.

da'zu|gehörig *adj.* belonging to it; **~kommen** *v/i. (irr. kommen, sep., -ge-, sein)* appear (on the scene); find time.

dazwischen *adv.* [da'tsviʃən] between (them), in between; **~kommen** *v/i. (irr. kommen, sep., -ge-, sein)* intervene, happen.

Debatt|e [de'batə] *f (-/-n)* debate; **2ieren** [~'tiːrən] *(no -ge-, h)* **1.** *v/t.*

discuss; debate; **2.** *v/i.* debate (*über acc.* on).

Debüt [de'by:] *n* (-s/-s) first appearance, début.

dechiffrieren [deʃi'fri:rən] *v/t.* (*no -ge-*, *h*) decipher, decode.

Deck ⚓ [dɛk] *n* (-[e]s/-s, ⚓-e) deck; **'˷adresse** *f* cover (address); **'˷bett** *n* feather bed.

Decke ['dɛkə] *f* (-/-n) cover(ing); blanket; (travel[l]ing) rug; ceiling; **'˷l** *m* (-s/-) lid, cover (*of box or pot*, *etc.*); lid (*of piano*); (book-)cover; **'˷n** (ge-, *h*) **1.** *v/t.* cover; *den Tisch ˷* lay the table; **2.** *v/i. paint:* cover.

'Deck|mantel *m* cloak, mask, disguise; **'˷name** *m* assumed name, pseudonym; **'˷ung** *f* (-/-en) cover; security.

defekt [de'fɛkt] **1.** *adj.* defective, faulty; **2.** ♀ *m* (-[e]s/-e) defect, fault.

definieren [defi'ni:rən] *v/t.* (*no -ge-*, *h*) define; **♀ition** [˷i'tsjo:n] *f* (-/-en) definition; **˷itiv** *adj.* [˷i'ti:f] definite; definitive.

Defizit ✝ ['de:fitsit] *n* (-s/-e) deficit, deficiency.

Degen ['de:gən] *m* (-s/-) sword; *fencing:* épée.

degradieren [degra'di:rən] *v/t.* (*no -ge-*, *h*) degrade, *Am. a.* demote.

dehn|bar *adj.* [de:nba:r] extensible; elastic; *metal:* ductile; *notion*, *etc.:* vague; **'˷en** *v/t.* (ge-, *h*) extend; stretch; **'♀ung** *f* (-/-en) extension; stretch(ing).

Deich [daɪç] *m* (-[e]s/-e) dike, dyke.

Deichsel ['daɪksəl] *f* (-/-n) pole, shaft.

dein *poss. pron.* [daɪn] your; *der* (*die*, *das*) *˷e* yours; *ich bin ˷ I* am yours; *die Deinen pl.* your family; **˷er-seits** *adv.* ['˷ər'zaɪts] for *or* on your part; **'˷es'gleichen** *pron.* your like, your (own) kind, F the like(s) of you.

Dekan *eccl. and univ.* [de'ka:n] *m* (-s/-e) dean.

Deklam|ation [deklama'tsjo:n] *f* (-/-en) declamation; reciting; **♀ieren** [˷'mi:rən] *v/t. and v/i.* (*no -ge-*, *h*) recite; declaim.

Deklin|ation *gr.* [deklina'tsjo:n] *f* (-/-en) declension; **♀ieren** *gr.* [˷-'ni:rən] *v/t.* (*no -ge-*, *h*) decline.

Dekor|ateur [dekora'tø:r] *m* (-s/-e) decorator; window-dresser; *thea.*

scene-painter; **˷ation** [˷'tsjo:n] *f* (-/-en) decoration; (window-)dressing; *thea.* scenery; **♀ieren** [˷'ri:rən] *v/t.* (*no -ge-*, *h*) decorate; dress (*window*).

Dekret [de'kre:t] *n* (-[e]s/-e) decree.

delikat *adj.* [deli'ka:t] delicate (*a. fig.*); delicious; *fig.* ticklish; **♀esse** [˷a'tɛsə] *f* (-/-n) delicacy; dainty.

Delphin *zo.* [dɛl'fi:n] *m* (-s/-e) dolphin.

Dement|i [de'mɛnti] *n* (-s/-s) (formal) denial; **♀ieren** [˷'ti:rən] *v/t.* (*no -ge-*, *h*) deny, give a (formal) denial of.

'dem|entsprechend *adv.*, **'˷gemäß** *adv.* correspondingly, accordingly; **'˷nach** *adv.* therefore, hence; accordingly; **'˷'nächst** *adv.* soon, shortly, before long.

demobilisier|en (*no -ge-*, *h*) **1.** *v/t.* demobilize; disarm; **2.** *v/i.* disarm; **♀ung** *f* (-/-en) demobilization.

Demokrat [demo'kra:t] *m* (-en/-en) democrat; **˷ie** [˷a'ti:] *f* (-/-n) democracy; **♀isch** *adj.* [˷'kra:tiʃ] democratic.

demolieren [demo'li:rən] *v/t.* (*no -ge-*, *h*) demolish.

Demonstr|ation [demɔnstra'tsjo:n] *f* (-/-en) demonstration; **♀ieren** [˷'stri:rən] *v/t. and v/i.* (*no -ge-*, *h*) demonstrate.

Demont|age [demɔn'ta:ʒə] *f* (-/-n) disassembly; dismantling; **♀ieren** [˷'ti:rən] *v/t.* (*no -ge-*, *h*) disassemble; dismantle.

Demut ['de:mu:t] *f* (-/*no pl.*) humility, humbleness.

demütig *adj.* ['de:my:tiç] humble; **˷en** ['˷gən] *v/t.* (ge-, *h*) humble, humiliate.

denk|bar ['dɛŋkba:r] **1.** *adj.* conceivable; thinkable, imaginable; **2.** *adv.:* *˷ einfach* most simple; **'˷en** (*irr.*, ge-, *h*) **1.** *v/i.* think; *˷ an* (*acc.*) think of; remember; *˷ über* (*acc.*) think about; *j-m zu ˷ geben* set s.o. thinking; **2.** *v/t.* think; *sich et. ˷* imagine *or* fancy s.th.; *das habe ich mir gedacht* I thought as much; **'♀mal** *n* monument; memorial; **'♀schrift** *f* memorandum; memoir; **'♀stein** *m* memorial stone; **'˷würdig** *adj.* memorable; **♀zettel** *fig. m* lesson.

denn [dɛn] **1.** *cj.* for; *mehr ˷ je* more than ever; **2.** *adv.* then; *es sei ˷,* *daß* unless, except; *wieso* ~? how so.

dennoch *cj.* ['dɛnnɔx] yet, still, nevertheless; though.

Denunzi|ant [denun'tsjant] *m* (-en/-en) informer; **~iation** [~'tsjo:n] *f* (-/-en) denunciation; **2ieren** [~'tsi:rən] *v/t.* (no -ge-, h) inform against, denounce.

Depesche [de'pɛʃə] *f* (-/-n) dispatch; telegram, F wire; wireless.

deponieren [depo'ni:rən] *v/t.* (no -ge-, h) deposit.

Depositen ✝ [depo'zi:tən] *pl.* deposits *pl.*; **~bank** *f* deposit bank.

der [de:r], **die** [di:], **das** [das] **1.** *art.* the; **2.** *dem. pron.* that, this; he, she, it; *die pl.* these, those, they, them; **3.** *rel. pron.* who, which, that.

'der'artig *adj.* such, of such a kind, of this *or* that kind.

derb *adj.* [dɛrp] *cloth:* coarse, rough; *shoes, etc.:* stout, strong; *ore, etc.:* massive; *p.:* sturdy; rough; *food:* coarse; *p., manners:* rough, coarse; *way of speaking:* blunt, unrefined; *joke:* crude; *humour:* broad.

der'gleichen *adj.* such, of that kind; *used as a noun:* the like, such a thing; *und* ~ and the like; *nichts* ~ nothing of the kind.

der- ['de:rje:nigə], **'die-**, **'dasjenige** *dem. pron.* he who, she who, that which; diejenigen *pl.* those who, those which.

der- [de:r'zɛlbə], **die-**, **das'selbe** *dem. pron.* the same; he, she, it.

Desert|eur [dezɛr'tø:r] *m* (-s/-e) deserter; **2ieren** [~'ti:rən] *v/i.* (no -ge-, sein) desert.

desgleichen [dɛs'glaiçən] **1.** *dem. pron.* such a thing; **2.** *cj.* likewise.

deshalb ['dɛshalp] **1.** *cj.* for this *or* that reason; therefore; **2.** *adv.:* *ich tat es nur* ~, *weil* I did it only because. [(no -ge-, h) disinfect.)

desinfizieren [dɛs⁹infi'tsi:rən] *v/t.*

Despot [dɛs'po:t] *m* (-en/-en) despot; **2isch** *adj.* despotic.

destillieren [dɛsti'li:rən] *v/t.* (no -ge-, h) distil.

desto *adv.* ['dɛsto] (all, so much) the; ~ *besser* all the better; ~ *erstaunter* (all) the more astonished.

deswegen *cj. and adv.* ['dɛs've:gən] *s.* deshalb.

Detail [de'tai] *n* (-s/-s) detail.

Detektiv [detɛk'ti:f] *m* (-s/-e) detective.

deuten ['dɔytən] (ge-, h) **1.** *v/t.* interpret; read (*stars, dream, etc.*). **2.** *v/i.:* ~ *auf* (acc.) point at.

'deutlich *adj.* clear, distinct, plain.

deutsch *adj.* [dɔytʃ] German; **2e** *m, f* (-n/-n) German.

'Deutung *f* (-/-en) interpretation, explanation.

Devise [de'vi:zə] *f* (-/-n) motto; ~n *pl.* ✝ foreign exchange *or* currency.

Dezember [de'tsɛmbər] *m* (-[s]/-) December.

dezent *adj.* [de'tsɛnt] *attire, etc.:* decent, modest; *literature, etc.:* decent; *behaviour:* decent, proper; *music, colour:* soft, restrained; *lighting, etc.:* subdued.

Dezernat [detsɛr'nɑ:t] *n* (-[e]s/-e) (administrative) department.

dezimal *adj.* [detsi'mɑ:l] decimal; **2bruch** *m* decimal fraction; **2stelle** *f* decimal place.

dezi'mieren *v/t.* (no -ge-, h) decimate; *fig. a.* reduce (drastically).

Diadem [dia'de:m] *n* (-s/-e) diadem.

Diagnose [dia'gno:zə] *f* (-/-n) diagnosis.

diagonal *adj.* [diago'nɑ:l] diagonal; **2e** *f* (-/-n) diagonal.

Dialekt [dia'lɛkt] *m* (-[e]s/-e) dialect; **2isch** *adj.* dialectal.

Dialog [dia'lo:k] *m* (-[e]s/-e) dialogue, Am. a. dialog.

Diamant [dia'mant] *m* (-en/-en) diamond.

Diät [di'ɛ:t] *f* (-/no pl.) diet; *diät leben* live on a diet.

dich *pers. pron.* [diç] you; ~ (selbst) yourself.

dicht [diçt] **1.** *adj.* fog, rain, etc.: dense; *fog, forest, hair:* thick; *eyebrows:* bushy, thick; *crowd:* thick, dense; *shoe, etc.:* (water)tight; **2.** *adv.:* ~ *an* (dat.) *or* *bei* close to.

'dichten¹ *v/t.* (ge-, h) make tight.

'dichten² (ge-, h) **1.** *v/t.* compose, write; **2.** *v/i.* compose *or* write poetry; **2er** *m* (-s/-) poet; author; **2erisch** *adj.* poetic(al); **2erin** *f* poetry.

'Dichtung¹ ⊕ *f* (-/-en) seal(ing).

'Dichtung² *f* (-/-en) poetry; fiction; poem, poetic work.

dick *adj.* [dik] *wall, material, etc.:* thick; *book:* thick, bulky; *p.* fat, stout; **2e** *f* (-/-en) thickness; bulkiness; *p.* fatness, stoutness; **~fellig** *adj. p.* thick-skinned; **~flüssig** *adj.*

thick; viscid, viscous, syrupy; 2**icht** [′‿ɪçt] n (-[e]s/-e) thicket; '2**kopf** m stubborn person, F pig-headed person; '‿**leibig** adj. [′‿laɪbɪç] corpulent; fig. bulky.

die [diː] s. der.

Dieb [diːp] m (-[e]s/-e) thief, Am. F a. crook; ‿**erei** [diːbə′raɪ] f (-/-en) thieving, thievery.

Diebes|bande [′diːbəs-] f band of thieves; '‿**gut** n stolen goods pl.

dieb|isch adj. [′diːbɪʃ] thievish; fig. malicious; 2**stahl** [′diːp-] m (-[e]s/ ⁼e) theft, ʒɪ̃ mst larceny.

Diele [′diːlə] f (-/-n) board, plank; hall, Am. a. hallway.

dienen [′diːnən] v/i. (ge-, h) serve (j-m s.o.; als as; zu for; dazu, zu inf. to inf.); womit kann ich ‿? what can I do for you?

'**Diener** m (-s/-) (man-, domestic) servant; fig. bow (vor dat. to); '‿**in** f (-/-nen) (woman-)servant, maid; '‿**schaft** f (-/-en) servants pl.

'**dienlich** adj. useful, convenient; expedient; suitable.

Dienst [diːnst] m (-es/-e) service; duty; employment; ‿ haben be on duty; im (außer) ‿ on (off) duty.

Dienstag [′diːnstaːk] m (-[e]s/-e) Tuesday.

'**Dienst|alter** n seniority, length of service; '2**bar** adj. subject (j-m to s.o.); subservient (to); '‿**bote** m domestic (servant), Am. help; '2**eifrig** adj. (over-)eager (in one's duty); '2**frei** adj. off duty; ‿er Tag day off; '‿**herr** m master; employer; '‿**leistung** f service; '2**lich** adj. official; '‿**mädchen** n maid, Am. help; '‿**mann** m (street-)porter; '‿**stunden** f/pl. office hours pl.; '2**tauglich** adj. fit for service or duty; 2**tuend** adj. [′‿tuːənt] on duty; 2**untauglich** adj. unfit for service or duty; '‿**weg** m official channels pl.; '‿**wohnung** f official residence.

dies [diːs], ‿**er** [′diːzər], ‿**e** [′diːzə], ‿**es** [′diːzəs] adj. and dem. pron. this; diese pl. these; dieser Tage one of these days; used as a noun: this one; he, she, it; diese pl. they.

Dieselmotor [′diːzəl-] m Diesel engine.

dies|jährig adj. [′diːsjɛːrɪç] of this year, this year's; '‿**mal** adv. this time; for (this) once; '‿**seits** [′‿zaɪts]

1. adv. on this side; 2. prp. (gen.) on this side of.

Dietrich [′diːtrɪç] m (-s/-e) skeleton key; picklock.

Differenz [dɪfə′rɛnts] f (-/-en) difference; disagreement.

Diktat [dɪk′taːt] n (-[e]s/-e) dictation; nach ‿ at or from dictation; ‿**or** [‿ɔr] m (-s/-en) dictator; 2**o-risch** adj. [‿a′toːrɪʃ] dictatorial; ‿**ur** [‿a′tuːr] f (-/-en) dictatorship.

dik′tieren v/t. and v/i. (no -ge-, h) dictate.

Dilettant [dilɛ′tant] m (-en/-en) dilettante, dabbler; amateur.

Ding [dɪŋ] n (-[e]s/-e) thing; guter ‿e in good spirits; vor allen ‿en first of all, above all.

Diphtherie 🜸 [dɪfte′riː] f (-/-n) diphtheria.

Diplom [di′ploːm] n (-[e]s/-e) diploma, certificate.

Diplomat [diplo′maːt] m (-en/-en) diplomat; diplomatist; ‿**ie** [‿a′tiː] f (-/no pl.) diplomacy; 2**isch** adj. [‿′maːtɪʃ] diplomatic (a. fig.).

dir pers. pron. [diːr] (to) you.

direkt [di′rɛkt] 1. adj. direct; ‿er Wagen 🚃 through carriage, Am. through car; 2. adv. direct(ly). 2**ion** [‿′tsjoːn] f (-/-en) direction; management; board of directors; 2**or** [di′rɛktɔr] m (-s/-en) director; manager; headmaster, Am. principal; 2**orin** [‿′toːrin] f (-/-nen) headmistress, Am. principal; 2**rice** [‿′triːs(ə)] f (-/-n) directress; manageress.

Dirig|ent 🎵 [diri′gɛnt] m (-en/-en) conductor; 2**ieren** 🎵 [‿′giːrən] v/t. and v/i. (no -ge-, h) conduct.

Dirne [′dɪrnə] f (-/-n) prostitute.

Disharmon|ie 🎵 [disharmo′niː] f (-/-n) disharmony, dissonance (both a. fig.); 2**isch** adj. [‿′moːnɪʃ] discordant, dissonant.

Diskont 🟊 [dis′kɔnt] m (-s/-e) discount; 2**ieren** [‿′tiːrən] v/t. (no -ge-, h) discount.

diskret adj. [dis′kreːt] discreet; 2**ion** [‿e′tsjoːn] f (-/no pl.) discretion.

Disku|ssion [disku′sjoːn] f (-/-en) discussion, debate; 2′**tieren** (no -ge-, h) 1. v/t. discuss, debate; 2. v/i.: ‿ über (acc.) have a discussion about, debate (up)on.

dispo|nieren [dispo′niːrən] v/i. (no

-ge-, h) make arrangements; plan ahead; dispose (über acc. of); **Qsition** [⸝zi'tsjo:n] f (-/-en) disposition; arrangement; disposal.

Distanz [di'stants] f (-/-en) distance (a. fig.); **Qieren** [⸝'tsi:rən] v/refl. (no -ge-, h): sich ～ von dis(as)sociate o.s. from.

Distel ♀ ['distəl] f (-/-n) thistle.

Distrikt [di'strikt] m (-[e]s/-e) district; region; area.

Disziplin [distsi'pli:n] f (-/-en) discipline.

Divid|ende ♱ [divi'dɛndə] f (-/-n) dividend; **Qieren** [⸝'di:rən] v/t. (no -ge-, h) divide (durch by).

Diwan ['di:va:n] m (-s/-e) divan.

doch [dɔx] **1.** cj. but, though; however, yet; **2.** adv. in answer to negative question: yes; bist du noch nicht fertig? — ～! aren't you ready yet? — yes, I am; also ～! I knew it!, I was right after all!; komm ～ herein! do come in!; nicht ～! don't!

Docht [dɔxt] m (-[e]s/-e) wick.

Dock ⚓ [dɔk] n (-[e]s/-s) dock.

Dogge zo. ['dɔgə] f (-/-n) Great Dane.

Dohle orn. ['do:lə] f (-/-n) (jack)daw.

Doktor ['dɔktɔr] m (-s/-en) doctor.

Dokument [doku'mɛnt] n (-[e]s/-e) document; ⚖ instrument; **～arfilm** [⸝'ta:r-] m documentary (film).

Dolch [dɔlç] m (-[e]s/-e) dagger; poniard; **～stoß** m dagger-thrust.

Dollar ['dɔlar] m (-s/-s) dollar.

dolmetsch|en ['dɔlmɛtʃən] v/i. and v/t. (ge-, h) interpret; **Qer** m (-s/-) interpreter.

Dom [do:m] m (-[e]s/-e) cathedral.

Domäne [do'mɛ:nə] f (-/-n) domain (a. fig.); province.

Domino [do'mi:no] (-s/-s) **1.** m domino; **2.** n (game of) dominoes pl.

Donner ['dɔnər] m (-s/-) thunder; **Qn** v/i. (ge-, h) thunder (a. fig.); **～schlag** m thunderclap (a. fig.); **～wetter** n: F ～! my word!, by Jove!; F zum ～! F confound it!, sl. damn it.

Doppel ['dɔpəl] n (-s/-) duplicate; tennis, etc.: double, **Qn** doubles pl.; **～bett** n double bed; **～decker** m (-s/-) ✈ biplane; double-decker (bus); **～ehe** f bigamy; **～gänger** ['～gɛŋər] m (-s/-) double; **～punkt**

m colon; **'～sinn** m double meaning, ambiguity; **Qsinnig** adj. ambiguous, equivocal; **'～stecker** ⚡ m two-way adapter; **Qt 1.** adj. double; **2.** adv. doubly; twice; **'～zentner** m quintal; **Qzüngig** adj. ['～tsyŋiç] two-faced.

Dorf [dɔrf] n (-[e]s/⸚er) village; **'～bewohner** m villager.

Dorn [dɔrn] m **1.** (-[e]s/-en) thorn (a. fig.), prickle, spine; j-m ein ～ im Auge sein be a thorn in s.o.'s flesh or side; **2.** (-[e]s/-e) tongue (of buckle); spike (of running-shoe, etc.); ⊕ punch; **Qig** adj. thorny (a. fig.).

dörr|en ['dœrən] v/t. (ge-, h) dry; **Qfleisch** n dried meat; **Qgemüse** n dried vegetables pl.; **Qobst** n dried fruit.

Dorsch ichth. [dɔrʃ] m (-es/-e) cod(fish).

dort adv. [dɔrt] there; over there; **'～her** adv. from there; **'～hin** adv. there, to that place; **'～ig** adj. there, in or of that place.

Dose ['do:zə] f (-/-n) box; tin, Am. can; **～nöffner** ['do:zən?-] m (-s/-) tin-opener, Am. can opener.

Dosis ['do:zis] f (-/Dosen) dose (a. fig.).

dotieren [do'ti:rən] v/t. (no -ge-, h) endow.

Dotter ['dɔtər] m, n (-s/-) yolk.

Dozent [do'tsɛnt] m (-en/-en) (university) lecturer, Am. assistant professor.

Drache ['draxə] m (-n/-n) dragon; **'～n** m (-s/-) kite; fig. termagant, shrew, battle-axe.

Dragoner [dra'go:nər] m (-s/-) ⚔ dragoon (a. fig.).

Draht [dra:t] m (-[e]s/⸚e) wire; **Qen** v/t. (ge-, h) telegraph, wire; **～geflecht** n (-[e]s/-e) wire netting; **～hindernis** ⚔ n wire entanglement; **Qig** adj. p. wiry; **Qlos** adj. wireless; **～seilbahn** f funicular (railway); **～stift** m wire tack; **'～zieher** F fig. m (-s/-) wire-puller.

drall adj. [dral] girl, legs, etc.: plump; woman: buxom.

Drama ['dra:ma] n (-s/Dramen) drama; **～tiker** [dra'ma:tikər] m (-s/-) dramatist; **Qtisch** adj. [dra-'ma:tiʃ] dramatic.

dran F adv. [dran] s. daran; er ist gut (übel) ～ he's well (badly) off; ich bin ～ it's my turn.

Drang [draŋ] **1.** *m* (-[e]s/⁀⁀e) pressure, rush; *fig.* urge; **2.** ⁀ *pret. of dringen.*

drängen ['drɛŋən] (ge-, h) **1.** *v/t.* press (*a. fig.*), push; *fig.* urge; *creditor:* dun; *sich ~* crowd, throng; **2.** *v/i.* press, be pressing *or* urgent.

drangsalieren [draŋza'li:rən] *v/t.* (*no -ge-, h*) harass, vex, plague.

drastisch *adj.* ['drastiʃ] drastic.

drauf F *adv.* [drauf] s. *darauf; ~ und dran sein zu inf.* be on the point of *ger.;* **⁀gänger** ['⁀gɛŋər] *m* (-s/-) dare-devil; Am. *sl.* a. go-getter.

draus F *adv.* [draus] s. *daraus.*

draußen *adv.* ['drausən] outside; out of doors; abroad; out at sea.

drechs|eln ['drɛksəln] *v/t.* (ge-, h) turn (*wood, etc.*); **⁀ler** ['⁀slər] *m* (-s/-) turner.

Dreck F [drɛk] *m* (-[e]s/*no pl.*) dirt; mud; filth (*a. fig.*); *fig.* trash; F *~ am Stecken haben* not to have a clean slate; F *das geht dich einen ~ an* that's none of your business; **⁀ig** *adj.* dirty; filthy.

Dreh|bank ['dre:-] *f* (-/⁀⁀e) (turning-)lathe; **⁀bar** *adj.* revolving, rotating; **⁀bleistift** *m* propelling pencil; **⁀buch** *n* scenario; script; **⁀bühne** *thea. f* revolving stage; **⁀en** *v/t.* (ge-, h) turn; twist (*film*); roll (*cigarette*); *es dreht sich darum zu inf.* it is a matter of *ger.; sich ~* turn; **⁀kreuz** *n* turnstile; **⁀orgel** *f* barrel-organ; **⁀punkt** *m* ⊕ centre of rotation, Am. center of rotation, pivot (*a. fig.*); **⁀strom** ⁀ *m* three-phase current; **⁀stuhl** *m* swivel-chair; **⁀tür** *f* revolving door; **⁀ung** *f* (-/-en) turn; rotation.

drei *adj.* [drai] three; **⁀beinig** *adj.* three-legged; **⁀eck** *n* triangle; **⁀eckig** *adj.* triangular; **⁀erlei** ['⁀ər'lai] of three kinds *or* sorts; **⁀fach** *adj.* ['⁀fax] threefold, treble, triple; **⁀farbig** *adj.* three-colo(u)r(ed); **⁀fuß** *m* tripod; **⁀jährig** *adj.* ['⁀jɛːriç] three-year-old; triennial; **⁀mal** *adv.* three times; **⁀malig** *adj.* done *or* repeated three times; three; **⁀meilenzone** ⊕, ⁀ *f* three-mile limit; **⁀rad** *n* tricycle; **⁀seitig** *adj.* three-sided; trilateral; **⁀silbig** *adj.* trisyllabic.

dreißig *adj.* ['draisiç] thirty; **⁀ste** *adj.* thirtieth.

dreist *adj.* [draist] bold, audacious;

cheeky, saucy; **⁀igkeit** *f* (-/-en) boldness, audacity; cheek, sauciness.

'drei|stimmig ♪ *adj.* for *or* in three voices; **⁀tägig** *adj.* ['⁀tɛːgiç] three-day; **⁀teilig** *adj.* in three parts, tripartite; **⁀zehn(te)** *adj.* thirteen(th).

dresch|en ['drɛʃən] *v/t. and v/i.* (*irr.*, ge-, h) thresh; thrash; **⁀flegel** *m* flail; **⁀maschine** *f* threshing-machine.

dressieren [drɛ'si:rən] *v/t.* (*no -ge-, h*) train; break in (*horse*).

drillen ⁀ , ⁀ ['drilən] *v/t.* (ge-, h) drill.

Drillinge ['drilinə] *m/pl.* triplets *pl.*

drin F *adv.* [drin] s. *darin.*

dringen ['driŋən] *v/i.* (*irr.*, ge-) **1.** (sein): *~ durch* force one's way through *s.th.*, penetrate *or* pierce *s.th.; ~ aus* break forth from *s.th.; noise:* come from; *~ in* (*acc.*) penetrate into; *in j-n ~* urge *or* press *s.o.; an die Öffentlichkeit ~* get abroad; **2.** (h): *~ auf* (*acc.*) insist on, press for; **⁀d** *adj.* urgent, pressing; *suspicion:* strong.

'dringlich *adj.* urgent, pressing; **⁀keit** *f* (-/*no pl.*) urgency.

drinnen *adv.* ['drinən] inside; indoors.

dritt|e *adj.* ['dritə] third; **⁀el** *n* (-s/-) third; **⁀ens** *adv.* thirdly; **⁀letzt** *adj.* last but two.

Drog|e ['dro:gə] *f* (-/-n) drug; **⁀erie** [droga'ri:] *f* (-/-n) chemist's (shop), Am. drugstore; **⁀ist** [dro-'gist] *m* (-en/-en) (retail pharmaceutical) chemist.

drohen ['dro:ən] *v/i.* (ge-, h) threaten, menace.

Drohne ['dro:nə] *f* (-/-n) zo. drone (*a. fig.*).

dröhnen ['drø:nən] *v/i.* (ge-, h) *voice, etc.:* resound; *cannon, drum, etc.:* roar; *voice, cannon:* boom.

Drohung ['dro:uŋ] *f* (-/-en) threat, menace.

drollig *adj.* ['drɔliç] amusing, quaint, comical.

Dromedar zo. [drɔme'daːr] *n* (-s/-e) dromedary.

drosch [drɔʃ] *pret. of dreschen.*

Droschke ['drɔʃkə] *f* (-/-n) taxi (-cab), Am. a. cab, hack; **⁀nkutscher** *m* cabman, driver, Am. a. hackman.

Drossel orn. ['drɔsəl] f (-/-n) thrush; '2n ⊕ v/t. (ge-, h) throttle.

drüben adv. ['dry:bən] over there, yonder.

drüber F adv. ['dry:bər] s. darüber.

Druck [druk] m 1. (-[e]s/⁼e) pressure; squeeze (of hand, etc.); 2. typ. (-[e]s/-e) print(ing); '**bogen** m printed sheet; '**buchstabe** m block letter.

drucken ['drukən] v/t. (ge-, h) print; ~ lassen have s.th. printed, publish.

drücken ['drykən] (ge-, h) 1. v/t. press; squeeze (hand, etc.); force down (prices, wages, etc.); lower (record); press, push (button, etc.); F sich ~ vor (dat.) or von shirk (work, etc.); 2. v/i. shoe: pinch.

'**Drucker** m (-s/-) printer.

'**Drücker** m (-s/-) door-handle; trigger.

Drucker|ei [drukə'raɪ] f (-/-en) printing office, Am. printery, print shop; '**schwärze** f printer's or printing-ink.

'**Druck|fehler** m misprint; '**fehlerverzeichnis** n errata pl.; '**fertig** adj. ready for press; '**kammer** f pressurized cabin; '**knopf** m patent fastener, snap-fastener; ≠ push-button; '**luft** f compressed air; '**pumpe** f pressure pump; '**sache** (n pl.) ⅋ f printed matter, Am. a. second-class or third-class matter; '**schrift** f block letters; publication; '**taste** f press key.

drum F adv., cj. [drum] s. darum.

drunter F adv. ['druntər] s. darunter.

Drüse anat. ['dry:zə] f (-/-n) gland.

du pers. pron. [du:] you.

Dublette [du'blɛtə] f (-/-n) duplicate.

ducken ['dukən] v/refl. (ge-, h) duck, crouch; fig. cringe (vor dat. to, before).

Dudelsack ♪ ['du:dəl-] m bagpipes pl.

Duell [du'ɛl] n (-s/-e) duel; 2**ieren** [due'li:rən] v/refl. (no -ge-, h) (fight a) duel (mit with).

Duett ♪ [du'ɛt] n (-[e]s/-e) duet.

Duft [duft] m (-[e]s/⁼e) scent, fragrance, perfume; 2**en** v/i. (ge-, h) smell, have a scent, be fragrant; '2**end** adj. fragrant; '2**ig** adj. dainty, fragrant.

duld|en ['duldən] (ge-, h) 1. v/t.

bear, stand, endure, suffer (pain, grief, etc.); tolerate, put up with; 2. v/i. suffer; ~**sam** adj. ['-t-] tolerant; '2**samkeit** f (-/no pl.) tolerance; **ung** ['⌣duŋ] f (-/⌣-en) toleration; sufferance.

dumm adj. [dum] stupid, dull, Am. F dumb; '2**heit** f (-/-en) stupidity, dullness; stupid or foolish action; '2**kopf** m fool, blockhead, Am. sl. a. dumbbell.

dumpf adj. [dumpf] smell, air, etc.: musty, fusty; atmosphere: stuffy, heavy; sound, sensation, etc.: dull; '**ig** adj. cellar, etc.: damp, musty.

Düne ['dy:nə] f (-/-n) dune, sandhill. [manure.\

Dung [duŋ] m (-[e]s/no pl.) dung,\

dünge|n ['dyŋən] v/t. (ge-, h) dung, manure; fertilize; '2**r** m (-s/-) s. Dung; fertilizer.

dunkel ['duŋkəl] 1. adj. dark; dim; fig. obscure; idea, etc.: dim, faint, vague; 2. 2 n (-s/no pl.) s. Dunkelheit.

Dünkel ['dyŋkəl] m (-s/no pl.) conceit, arrogance; 2**haft** adj. conceited, arrogant.

'**Dunkel|heit** f (-/no pl.) darkness (a. fig.); fig. obscurity; '**kammer** phot. f dark-room; '2**n** v/i. (ge-, h) grow dark, darken.

dünn adj. [dyn] paper, material, voice, etc.: thin; hair, population, etc.: thin, sparse; liquid: thin, watery; air: rare(fied).

Dunst [dunst] m (-es/⁼e) vapo(u)r; haze, mist; fume.

dünsten ['dynstən] (ge-, h) 1. v/t. steam (fish, etc.); stew (fruit, etc.); 2. v/i. steam.

'**dunstig** adj. vaporous; hazy.

Duplikat [dupli'ka:t] n (-[e]s/-e) duplicate.

Dur ♪ [du:r] n (-/-) major.

durch [durç] 1. prp. (acc.) through; 2. adv.: die ganze Nacht ~ all night long; ~ und ~ through and through; thoroughly.

durcharbeiten ['durç⁼-] (sep., -ge-, h) 1. v/t. study thoroughly; sich ~ durch work through (book, etc.); 2. v/i. work without a break.

durch'aus adv. through and through; thoroughly; by all means; absolutely, quite; ~ nicht not at all, by no means.

'**durch|biegen** v/t. (irr. biegen, sep.,

-ge-, h) bend; deflect (*beam, etc.*); sich ~ *beam, etc.*: deflect, sag; '~**blättern** v/t. (*sep., -ge-, h*) glance or skim through (*book, etc.*), Am. thumb through, skim; '2**blick** m: ~ auf (*acc.*) view through to, vista over, view of; '~**blicken** v/i. (*sep., -ge-, h*) look through; ~ lassen, daß give to understand that.

durch|'**bluten** v/t. (*no -ge-, h*) supply with blood; ~'**bohren** v/t. (*no -ge-, h*) pierce; perforate; mit Blicken ~ look daggers at s.o.

'**durch**|**braten** v/t. (*irr. braten, sep., -ge-, h*) roast thoroughly; ~**brechen** (*irr. brechen*) 1. ['~breçən] v/i. (*sep., -ge-, sein*) break through or apart; 2. ['~] v/t. (*sep., -ge-, h*) break apart or in two; 3. [~'breçən] v/t. (*no -ge-, h*) break through, breach; run (*blockade*); crash (*sound barrier*); '~**brennen** v/i. (*irr. brennen, sep., -ge-, sein*) & *fuse*: blow; F *fig.* run away; *woman*: elope; '~**bringen** v/t. (*irr. bringen, sep., -ge-, h*) bring or get through; dissipate, squander (*money*); '2**bruch** m ✕ breakthrough; rupture; breach; *fig.* ultimate success.

durch'**denken** v/t. (*irr. denken, no -ge-, h*) think s.th. over thoroughly.

'**durch**|**drängen** v/refl. (*sep., -ge-, h*) force or push one's way through; ~**dringen** (*irr. dringen*) 1. ['~driŋən] v/i. (*sep., -ge-, sein*) penetrate (through); win acceptance (mit for) (*proposal*); 2. [~'driŋən] v/t. (*no -ge-, h*) penetrate, pierce; *water, smell, etc.*: permeate.

durcheinander [durç°ar'nandər] 1. *adv.* in confusion or disorder; pell-mell; 2. 2 n (*-s/-*) muddle, mess, confusion; ~**bringen** v/t. (*irr. bringen, sep., -ge-, h*) confuse s.o.; fig. mix (*things*) up; ~**werfen** v/t. (*irr. werfen, sep., -ge-, h*) throw into disorder; *fig.* mix up.

durchfahr|**en** (*irr. fahren*) 1. ['~fa:-rən] v/i. (*sep., -ge-, sein*) go or pass or drive through; 2. [~'fa:rən] v/t. (*no -ge-, h*) go or pass or travel or drive through; traverse (*tract of country, etc.*); '2t f passage (through); gate(way); ~ verboten! no thoroughfare!

'**Durchfall** m ✂ diarrh(o)ea; F *fig.* failure, Am. a. flunk; 2**en** (*irr. fallen*) 1. ['~falən] v/i. (*sep., -ge-, sein*)

fall through; fail, F get ploughed (*in examination*); *thea.* be a failure, *sl.* be a flop; ~ lassen reject, F plough; 2. [~'falən] v/t. (*no -ge-, h*) fall or drop through (*space*).

'**durch**|**fechten** v/t. (*irr. fechten, sep., -ge-, h*) fight or see s.th. through; '~**finden** v/refl. (*irr. finden, sep., -ge-, h*) find one's way (through).

durch|'**flechten** v/t. (*irr. flechten, no -ge-, h*) interweave, intertwine; ~'**forschen** v/t. (*no -ge-, h*) search through, investigate; explore (*region, etc.*).

'**Durchfuhr** ✝ f (*-/-en*) transit.

durchführ|**bar** adj. ['durçfy:rbɑːr] practicable, feasible, workable; '~**en** v/t. (*sep., -ge-, h*) lead or take through or across; *fig.* carry out or through; realize; '2**ungsbestimmung** f (implementing) regulation.

'**Durchgang** m passage; ✝ transit; *sports*: run; '~**sverkehr** m through traffic; ✝ transit traffic; '~**szoll** m transit duty.

'**durchgebraten** adj. well done.

'**durchgehen** (*irr. gehen, sep., -ge-*) 1. v/i. (*sein*) go or walk through; *bill*: pass, be carried; run away or off; abscond; *woman*: elope; *horse*: bolt; 2. v/t. (*sein*) go through (*street, etc.*); 3. v/t. (*h, sein*) go or look or read through (*work, book, etc.*); '~d 1. adj. continuous; ~er Zug through train; 2. adv. generally; throughout.

durch'**geistigt** adj. spiritual.

'**durch**|**greifen** v/i. (*irr. greifen, sep., -ge-, h*) put one's hand through; *fig.* take drastic measures or steps; '~**greifend** adj. drastic; radical, sweeping; '2**halten** (*irr. halten, sep., -ge-, h*) 1. v/t. keep up (*pace, etc.*); 2. v/i. hold out; '~**hauen** v/t. (*irr. hauen, sep., -ge-, h*) cut or chop through; *fig.* give s.o. a good hiding; '~**helfen** v/i. (*irr. helfen, sep., -ge-, h*) help through (a. *fig.*); '~**kämpfen** v/t. (*sep., -ge-, h*) fight out; sich ~ fight one's way through; '~**kneten** v/t. (*sep., -ge-, h*) knead or work thoroughly; '~**kommen** v/i. (*irr. kommen, sep., -ge-, sein*) come or get or pass through; *sick person*: pull through; *in examination*: pass.

durch'**kreuzen** v/t. (*no -ge-, h*) cross, foil, thwart (*plan, etc.*).

Durch|laß ['durçlas] *m* (*Durchlasses/Durchlässe*) passage; '**2lassen** *v/t.* (*irr. lassen, sep., -ge-, h*) let pass, allow to pass, let through; *Wasser* ~ leak; '**2lässig** *adj.* pervious (to), permeable (to); leaky.

durchlaufen (*irr. laufen*) **1.** ['durləufən] *v/i.* (*sep., -ge-, sein*) run or pass through; **2.** ['~] *v/t.* (*sep., -ge-, h*) wear out (*shoes, etc.*); **3.** [~'laufən] *v/t.* (*no -ge-, h*) pass through (*stages, departments, etc.*); *sports:* cover (*distance*). [live through.]

durch'leben *v/t.* (*no -ge-, h*) go or [read through.]

durchlesen *v/t.* (*irr. lesen, sep., -ge-, h*) read through.

durchleuchten (*h*) **1.** ['~lɔyçtən] *v/i.* (*sep., -ge-*) shine through; **2.** [~'lɔyçtən] *v/t.* (*no -ge-*) ☢ X-ray; *fig.* investigate.

durchlöchern [durç'lœçərn] *v/t.* (*no -ge-, h*) perforate, make holes into *s.th.*

durchmachen *v/t.* (*sep., -ge-, h*) go through (*difficult times, etc.*); undergo (*suffering*). [through.]

Durchmarsch *m* march(ing)

Durchmesser *m* (*-s/-*) diameter.

durch'nässen *v/t.* (*no -ge-, h*) wet through, soak, drench.

durch|nehmen *v/t.* (*irr. nehmen, sep., -ge-, h*) go through or over (*subject*); '~**pausen** *v/t.* (*sep., -ge-, h*) trace, calk (*design, etc.*).

durchqueren [durç'kve:rən] *v/t.* (*no -ge-, h*) cross, traverse.

durch|rechnen *v/t.* (*sep., -ge-, h*) (re)calculate, check; '**2reise** *f* journey or way through; ~**reisen 1.** ['~raizən] *v/i.* (*sep., -ge-, sein*) travel or pass through; **2.** [~'raizən] *v/t.* (*no -ge-, h*) travel over or through or across; '**2reisende** *m, f* (*-n/-n*) person travel(l)ing through, *Am. a.* transient; 🚆 through passenger; '~**reißen** (*irr. reißen, sep., -ge-*) **1.** *v/i.* (*sein*) tear, break; **2.** *v/t.* (*h*) tear asunder, tear in two; ~**schauen** **1.** ['~ʃauən] *v/i. and v/t.* (*sep., -ge-*) look through; **2.** *fig.* [~'ʃauən] *v/t.* (*no -ge-*) see through.

durchscheinen *v/i.* (*irr. scheinen, sep., -ge-, h*) shine through; '~**d** *adj.* translucent; transparent.

durchscheuern *v/t.* (*sep., -ge-, h*) rub through; ~**schießen** (*irr. schießen*) **1.** [~'ʃi:sən] *v/i.* (*sep., -ge-, h*) shoot through; **2.** [~] *v/i.* (*sep.,*

-*ge-, sein*) *water:* shoot or race through; **3.** [~'ʃi:sən] *v/t.* (*no -ge-, h*) shoot *s.th.* through; *typ.:* space out (*lines*); interleave (*book*).

Durchschlag *m* colander, strainer; carbon copy; **2en** (*irr. schlagen*) **1.** ['~ʃla:gən] *v/t.* (*sep., -ge-, h*) break or pass through; strain (*peas, etc.*); *sich* ~ get along, make one's way; **2.** ['~] *v/i.* (*sep., -ge-, h*) *typ.* come through; take or have effect; **3.** [~'ʃla:gən] *v/t.* (*no -ge-, h*) pierce; *bullet:* penetrate; '**2end** *adj.* effective, telling; ~**papier** ['~k-] *n* copying paper.

durchschneiden *v/t./i. schneiden, h*) **1.** ['~ʃnaidən] (*sep., -ge-*) cut through; **2.** [~'ʃnaidən] (*no -ge-*) cut through, cut in two.

Durchschnitt *m* cutting through; ⊕ section, profile; ⚕ intersection; *fig.* average; *im* ~ on an average; '**2lich 1.** *adj.* average; normal; **2.** *adv.* on an average; normally; '~**swert** *m* average value.

durch|sehen (*irr. sehen, sep., -ge-, h*) **1.** *v/i.* see or look through; **2.** *v/t.* see or look through *s.th.*; look *s.th.* over, go over *s.th.*; '~**seihen** *v/t.* (*sep., -ge-, h*) filter, strain; ~**setzen** *v/t.* (*h*) **1.** ['~zetsən] (*sep., -ge-*) put (*plan, etc.*) through; force through; *seinen Kopf* ~ have one's way; *sich* ~ *opinion, etc.*: gain acceptance; **2.** [~'zetsən] (*no -ge-*) intersperse.

Durchsicht *f* looking through or over; examination; correction; *typ.* reading; '**2ig** *adj.* glass, water, etc.: transparent; *fig.* clear, lucid; '~**igkeit** *f* (*-/no pl.*) transparency; *fig.* clarity, lucidity.

durch|sickern *v/i.* (*sep., -ge-, sein*) seep or ooze through; *news, etc.*: leak out; ~**sieben** *v/t.* (*h*) **1.** ['~zi:bən] (*sep., -ge-*) sieve, sift; bolt (*flour*); **2.** [~'zi:bən] (*no -ge-*) riddle (*with bullets*); ~**sprechen** *v/t.* (*irr. sprechen, sep., -ge-, h*) discuss, talk over; ~**stechen** *v/t.* (*irr. stechen, h*) **1.** ['~ʃteçən] (*sep., -ge-*) stick (*needle, etc.*) through *s.th.*; stick through *s.th.*; **2.** [~'ʃteçən] (*no -ge-*) pierce; cut through (*dike, etc.*); ~**stecken** *v/t.* (*sep., -ge-, h*) pass or stick through.

Durchstich *m* cut(ting).

durch'stöbern *v/t.* (*no -ge-, h*) ransack (*room, pockets, etc.*); rummage through (*drawers*, *papers*, *etc.*).

'durchstreichen v/t. (*irr. streichen*, *sep.*, *-ge-*, *h*) strike *or* cross out, cancel.

durch'streifen v/t. (*no -ge-*, *h*) roam *or* wander through *or* over *or* across.

durch'such|en v/t. (*no -ge-*, *h*) search (*a.* 🏴); **2ung** *f* (*-/-en*) search.

durchtrieben *adj.* ['durç'tri:bən] cunning, artful; **2heit** *f* (*-/no pl.*) cunning, artfulness.

durch'wachen v/t. (*no -ge-*, *h*) pass (*the night*) waking.

durch'wachsen *adj. bacon:* streaky.

durchwandern 1. ['⏜vandərn] v/i. (*sep.*, *-ge-*, *sein*) walk *or* pass through; **2.** [⏜'vandərn] v/t. (*no -ge-*, *h*) walk *or* pass through (*place*, *area*, *etc.*).

durch'weben v/t. (*no -ge-*, *h*) interweave; *fig. a.* intersperse.

durchweg *adv.* ['durçvek] throughout, without exception.

durch'weichen 1. [⏜'vaiçən] v/i. (*sep.*, *-ge-*, *sein*) soak; **2.** [⏜'vaiçən] v/t. (*no -ge-*, *h*) soak, drench; **'⏜winden** v/refl. (*irr. winden*, *sep.*, *-ge-*, *h*) worm *or* thread one's way through; **⏜wühlen** (*h*) **1.** *fig.* ['⏜vy:lən] v/refl. (*sep.*, *-ge-*) work one's way through; **2.** [⏜'vy:lən] v/t. (*no -ge-*) rummage; **⏜zählen** v/t. (*sep.*, *-ge-*, *h*) count; **⏜ziehen** (*irr. ziehen*) **1.** ['⏜tsi:ən] v/i. (*sep.*, *-ge-*, *sein*) pass *or* go *or* come *or* march through; **2.** ['⏜] v/t. (*sep.*, *-ge-*, *h*) pull (*thread*, *etc.*) through; **3.** [⏜'tsi:ən] v/t. (*no -ge-*, *h*) go *or* travel through; *scent*, *etc.*: fill, pervade (*room*, *etc.*).

durch'zucken v/t. (*no -ge-*, *h*) flash through.

'Durchzug *m* passage through; draught, *Am.* draft.

dürfen ['dyrfən] (*irr.*, *h*) **1.** v/i. (*ge-*): *ich darf* (*nicht*) I am (not) allowed to; **2.** v/aux. (*no -ge-*): *ich darf inf.* I am permitted *or* allowed to *inf.*; I may *inf.*; *du darfst nicht inf.* you must not *inf.*; *iro.*: *wenn ich bitten darf* if you please.

durfte ['durftə] *pret. of* dürfen.

dürftig *adj.* ['dyrftiç] poor; scanty.

dürr *adj.* [dyr] *wood*, *leaves*, *etc.*: dry; *land:* barren, arid; *p.* gaunt, lean, skinny; **2e** *f* (*-/-n*) dryness; barrenness; leanness.

Durst [durst] *m* (*-es/no pl.*) thirst (*nach* for); **⏜ haben** be thirsty.

dürsten ['dyrstən] v/i. (*ge-*, *h*): **⏜** *nach* thirst for.

'durstig *adj.* thirsty (*nach* for).

Dusche ['duʃə] *f* (*-/-n*) shower (*-bath*); **'2n** v/refl. *and* v/i. (*ge-*, *h*) have a shower(-bath).

Düse ['dy:zə] *f* (*-/-n*) ⊕ nozzle; 🛬 jet; **⏜nantrieb** ['⏜n⏞-] *m* jet propulsion; *mit* **⏜** jet-propelled; **'⏜nflugzeug** *n* jet(-propelled) aircraft, F jet; **'⏜njäger** 🛬 *m* jet fighter.

düster *adj.* ['dy:stər] dark, gloomy (*both a. fig.*); *light:* dim; *fig.:* sad; depressing; **'2heit** *f* (*-/no pl.*), **'2keit** *f* (*-/no pl.*) gloom(iness).

Dutzend ['dutsənt] *n* (*-s/-e*) dozen; *ein* **⏜** *Eier* a dozen eggs; **⏜e von Leuten** dozens of people; **'2weise** *adv.* by the dozen, in dozens.

Dynam|ik [dy'na:mik] *f* (*-/no pl.*) dynamics; **2isch** *adj.* dynamic(al).

Dynamit [dyna'mi:t] *n* (*-s/no pl.*) dynamite.

Dynamo [dy'ha:mò] *m* (*-s/-s*), **⏜maschine** *f* dynamo, generator.

D-Zug ['de:tsu:k] *m* express train.

E

Ebbe ['ebə] *f* (*-/-n*) ebb(-tide); low tide; **'2n** v/i. (*ge-*, *sein*) ebb.

eben ['e:bən] **1.** *adj.* even; plain; level; ⚓ plane; *zu* **⏜er Erde** on the ground floor, *Am.* on the first floor; **2.** *adv.* exactly; just; **⏜**

erst just now; **'2bild** *n* image, likeness; **⏜bürtig** *adj.* ['⏜byrtiç] of equal birth; *j-m* **⏜ sein** be a match for s.o., be s.o.'s equal; **'⏜'da** *adv.*, **'⏜'da'selbst** *adv.* at the very (same) place, just there; *quoting books:*

ibidem (*abbr.* ib., ibid.); '~**der**, '~**die**, '~**das** *dem. pron.* = '~**der**'**selbe**, '~**die**'**selbe**, '~**das**'**selbe** *dem. pron.* the very (same); '~**des**'**wegen** *adv.* for that very reason.

Ebene ['e:bənə] *f* (-/-n) plain; A plane; *fig.* level.

'**eben|erdig** *adj. and adv.* at street level; on the ground floor, *Am.* on the first floor; '~**falls** *adv.* likewise; '2**holz** *n* ebony; '~**maß** *n* symmetry; harmony; regularity (*of features*); '~**mäßig** *adj.* symmetrical; harmonious; regular; '~**so** *adv.* just so; just as ...; likewise; '~**sosehr** *adv.*, '~**soviel** *adv.* just as much; '~**sowenig** *adv.* just as little *or* few (*pl.*), no more.

Eber *zo.* ['e:bər] *m* (-s/-) boar; '~**esche** ♀ *f* mountain-ash.

ebnen ['e:bnən] *v/t.* (ge-, h) level; *fig.* smooth.

Echo ['ɛço] *n* (-s/-s) echo.

echt *adj.* [ɛçt] genuine; true; pure; real; *colour*: fast; *document*: authentic; '2**heit** *f* (-/*no pl.*) genuineness; purity; reality; fastness; authenticity.

Eck [ɛk] *n* (-[e]s/-e) *s.* **Ecke**; '~**ball** *m sports*: corner-kick; '~**e** *f* (-/-n) corner; edge; '2**ig** *adj.* angular; *fig.* awkward; '~**platz** *m* corner-seat; '~**stein** *m* corner-stone; '~**zahn** *m* canine tooth.

edel *adj.* ['e:dəl] noble; *min.* precious; *organs of the body*: vital; '~**denkend** *adj.* noble-minded; '~**mann** *m* nobleman; '2**mut** *m* generosity; '~**mütig** *adj.* ['~my:tiç] noble-minded, generous; '2**stein** *m* precious stone; gem.

Edikt [e'dikt] *n* (-[e]s/-e) edict.

Efeu ♀ ['e:fɔy] *m* (-s/*no pl.*) ivy.

Effekt [ɛ'fɛkt] *m* (-[e]s/-e) effect; ~**en** *pl.* effects *pl.*; ♦: securities *pl.*; stocks *pl.*; ~**enhandel** *m* dealing in stocks; ~**hascherei** [~haʃə'raɪ] *f* (-/-en) claptrap; 2**iv** *adj.* [~'ti:v] effective; 2**uieren** [~u'i:rən] *v/t.* (*no* -ge-, h) effect; execute, *Am. a.* fill; 2**voll** *adj.* effective, striking.

egal *adj.* [e'ga:l] equal; F all the same.

Egge ['ɛgə] *f* (-/-n) harrow; '2**n** *v/t.* (ge-, h) harrow.

Egois|mus [ego'ismus] *m* (-/*Egois*-

men) ego(t)ism; ~**t** *m* (-en/-en) ego-(t)ist; 2**tisch** *adj.* selfish, ego(t)is-tic(al).

ehe[1] *cj.* ['e:ə] before.

Ehe[2][~] *f* (-/-n) marriage; matrimony; '~**anbahnung** *f* (-/-en) matrimonial agency; '~**brecher** *m* (-s/-) adulterer; '~**brecherin** *f* (-/-nen) adulteress; '2**brecherisch** *adj.* adulterous; '~**bruch** *m* adultery; '~**frau** *f* wife; '~**gatte** *m*, '~**gattin** *f* spouse; '~**leute** *pl.* married people *pl.*; '2**lich** *adj.* conjugal; *child*: legitimate; '~**losigkeit** *f* (-/*no pl.*) celibacy; single life.

ehemal|ig *adj.* ['e:əma:liç] former, ex-...; old; '~**s** *adv.* formerly.

'**Ehe|mann** *m* husband; '~**paar** *n* married couple.

'**eher** *adv.* sooner; rather; more likely; je ~, desto besser the sooner the better.

'**Ehering** *m* wedding ring.

ehern *adj.* ['e:ərn] brazen, of brass.

'**Ehe|scheidung** *f* divorce; '~**schlie**-**ßung** *f* (-/-en) (contraction of) marriage; '~**stand** *m* (-[e]s/*no pl.*) married state, matrimony; '~**stifter** *m*, '~**stifterin** *f* (-/-nen) matchmaker; '~**vermittlung** *f s.* Eheanbahnung; '~**versprechen** *n* promise of marriage; '~**vertrag** *m* marriage contract.

Ehrabschneider ['e:r⁹apʃnaɪdər] *m* (-s/-) slanderer.

'**ehrbar** *adj.* hono(u)rable, respectable; modest; '2**keit** *f* (-/*no pl.*) respectability; modesty.

Ehre ['e:rə] *f* (-/-n) hono(u)r; zu ~n (*gen.*) in hono(u)r of; '2**n** *v/t.* (ge-, h) hono(u)r; esteem.

'**ehren|amtlich** *adj.* honorary; '2**bürger** *m* honorary citizen; '2**dok-tor** *m* honorary doctor; '2**erklä-rung** *f* (full) apology; '2**gast** *m* guest of hono(u)r; '2**gericht** *n* court of hono(u)r; '~**haft** *adj.* hon-o(u)rable; '2**kodex** *m* code of hon-o(u)r; '2**legion** ['~legio:n] *f* (-/*no pl.*) Legion of Hono(u)r; '2**mann** *m* man of hono(u)r; '2**mitglied** *n* honorary member; '2**platz** *m* place of hono(u)r; '2**recht** *n*: *bürgerliche* ~**e** *pl.* civil rights *pl.*; '2**rettung** *f* rehabilitation; '~**rührig** *adj.* defamatory; '2**sache** *f* affair of hono(u)r; point of hono(u)r; '~**voll** *adj.* hon-o(u)rable; '~**wert** *adj.* hono(u)rable;

'⎓wort *n* (-[e]s/-e) word of hono(u)r.

ehr|erbietig *adj.* ['e:r⁹ɛrbi:tiç] respectful; '⎓erbietung *f* (-/-en) reverence; '⎓furcht *f* (-/⎓-en) respect; awe; '⎓furchtgebietend *adj.* awe-inspiring, awesome; '⎓fürchtig *adj.* ['⎓fyrçtiç] respectful; '⎓gefühl *n* (-[e]s/*no pl.*) sense of hono(u)r; '⎓geiz *m* ambition; '⎓geizig *adj.* ambitious.

'ehrlich *adj.* honest; *commerce, game*: fair; *opinion*: candid; ⎓ *währt am längsten* honesty is the best policy; '⎓keit *f* (-/*no pl.*) honesty; fairness.

'ehrlos *adj.* dishono(u)rable, infamous; '⎓igkeit *f* (-/-en) dishonesty, infamy.

'ehr|sam *adj. s.* ehrbar; '⎓ung *f* (-/-en) hono(u)r (conferred on *s.o.*); '⎓vergessen *adj.* dishono(u)rable, infamous; '⎓verlust ⚖ *m* (-es/*no pl.*) loss of civil rights; '⎓würdig *adj.* venerable, reverend.

ei¹ *int.* ah! ah!, indeed!

Ei² [⎓] *n* (-[e]s/-er) egg; *physiol.* ovum.

Eibe ♀ ['aɪbə] *f* (-/-n) yew(-tree).

Eiche ♀ ['aɪçə] *f* (-/-n) oak(-tree).

⎓l ['⎓l] *f* (-/-n) ♀ acorn; *cards*: club; ⎓lhäher *orn.* ['⎓hɛːər] *m* (-s/-) jay.

eichen¹ ['aɪçən] *v/t.* (ge-, h) ga(u)ge.

eichen² *adj.* (-) oaken, of oak.

Eich|hörnchen *zo.* ['aɪçhœrnçən] *n* (-s/-) squirrel; '⎓maß *n* standard.

Eid [att] *m* (-es/-e) oath; '⎓brüchig *adj.*: ⎓ *werden* break one's oath.

Eidechse *zo.* ['aɪdɛksə] *f* (-/-n) lizard.

eidesstattlich ⚖ *adj.* ['aɪdəs-] in lieu of (an) oath; ⎓e *Erklärung* statutory declaration.

'eidlich 1. *adj.* sworn; 2. *adv.* on oath.

'Eidotter *m, n* yolk.

'Eier|kuchen *m* omelet(te), pancake; '⎓schale *f* egg-shell; '⎓stock *anat. m* ovary; '⎓uhr *f* egg-timer.

Eifer ['aɪfər] *m* (-s/*no pl.*) zeal; eagerness; ardo(u)r; '⎓er *m* (-s/-) zealot; '⎓sucht *f* (-/*no pl.*) jealousy; '⎓süchtig *adj.* jealous (*auf acc.* of).

eifrig *adj.* ['aɪfriç] zealous, eager; ardent.

eigen *adj.* ['aɪgən] own; particular; strange, odd; *in compounds*: ...-owned; peculiar (*dat.* to); '⎓art *f* peculiarity; '⎓artig *adj.* peculiar;

singular; ⎓brötler ['⎓brø:tlər] *m* (-s/-) odd *or* eccentric person, crank; '⎓gewicht *n* dead weight; ⎓händig *adj. and adv.* ['⎓hɛndiç] with one's own hands; '⎓heim *n* house of one's own; homestead; '⎓heit *f* (-/-en) peculiarity; oddity; *of language*: idiom; '⎓liebe *f* self-love; '⎓lob *n* self-praise; '⎓mächtig *adj.* arbitrary; '⎓name *m* proper name; ⎓nützig *adj.* ['⎓nytsiç] self-interested, selfish; '⎓s *adv.* expressly, specially; on purpose.

'Eigenschaft *f* (-/-en) quality (*of s.o.*); property (*of s.th.*); *in s-r ⎓ als* in his capacity as; '⎓swort *gr. n* (-[e]s/⎓er) adjective.

'Eigensinn *m* (-[e]s/*no pl.*) obstinacy; '⎓ig *adj.* wil(l)ful, obstinate.

'eigentlich 1. *adj.* proper; actual; true, real; 2. *adv.* properly (speaking).

'Eigentum *n* (-s/⎓er) property.

Eigentüm|er ['aɪgənty:mər] *m* (-s/-) owner, proprietor; '⎓lich *adj.* peculiar; odd; '⎓lichkeit *f* (-/-en) peculiarity.

'Eigentums|recht *n* ownership; copyright; ⎓wohnung *f* freehold flat. [dividual.]

'eigenwillig *adj.* self-willed, *fig.* in-⎓

eign|en ['aɪgnən] *v/refl.* (ge-, h): *sich ⎓ für* be suited for; '⎓ung *f* (-/-en) aptitude, suitability.

'Eil|bote *m* express messenger; *durch ⎓n* by special delivery; '⎓brief ✉ *m* express letter, *Am.* special delivery letter.

Eile ['aɪlə] *f* (-/*no pl.*) haste, speed; hurry; '⎓n *v/i.* (ge-, sein) hasten, make haste; hurry; *letter, affair*: be urgent; '⎓nds *adv.* ['⎓ts] quickly, speedily.

'Eil|fracht *f*, '⎓gut *n* express goods *pl.*, *Am.* fast freight; '⎓ig *adj.* hasty, speedy; urgent; *es ⎓ haben* be in a hurry.

Eimer ['aɪmər] *m* (-s/-) bucket, pail.

ein [aɪn] 1. *adj.* one; 2. *indef. art.* a, an.

einander *adv.* [aɪ'nandər] one another; each other.

ein|arbeiten ['aɪn⁹-] *v/t.* (sep., -ge-, h): *j-n ⎓ in* (*acc.*) make s.o. acquainted with; ⎓armig ['aɪn⁹-] one-armed; ⎓äschern ['aɪn⁹ɛʃərn] *v/t.* (sep., -ge-, h) burn to ashes; cremate (*dead body*); '⎓äscherung *f* (-/-en) cremation; **~atmen** ['aɪnɂ-] *v/t.* (*sep.*, -ge-, *h*) breathe, inhale; **~äugig** *adj.* ['aɪnɂɔɣɪç] one-eyed.

'**Einbahnstraße** *f* one-way street.

'**einbalsamieren** *v/t.* (*sep.*, *no* -ge-, *h*) embalm.

'**Einband** *m* (-[e]s/ːe) binding; cover.

'**ein|bauen** *v/t.* (*sep.*, -ge-, *h*) build in; install (*engine, etc.*); '**~behalten** *v/t.* (*irr.* halten, *sep.*, *no* -ge-, *h*) detain; '**~berufen** *v/t.* (*irr.* rufen, *sep.*, *no* -ge-, *h*) convene; ⚔ call up, *Am.* induct.

'**einbett|en** *v/t.* (*sep.*, -ge-, *h*) embed; '**2zimmer** *n* single(-bedded) room.

'**einbild|en** *v/refl.* (*sep.*, -ge-, *h*) fancy, imagine; '**2ung** *f* imagination, fancy; conceit.

'**einbinden** *v/t.* (*irr.* binden, *sep.*, -ge-, *h*) bind (*books*).

'**Einblick** *m* insight (in *acc.* into).

'**einbrechen** (*irr.* brechen, *sep.*, -ge-) **1.** *v/t.* (*h*) break open; **2.** *v/i.* (*sein*) break in; *of night, etc.*: set in; **~ in** (*acc.*) break into (*house*).

'**Einbrecher** *m* at night: burglar; by day: housebreaker.

'**Einbruch** *m* ⚔ invasion; housebreaking, burglary; *bei* ~ *der Nacht* at nightfall; '**~(s)diebstahl** *m* house-breaking, burglary.

'**einbürger|n** ['aɪnbʏɡərn] *v/t.* (*sep.*, -ge-, *h*) naturalize; '**2ung** *f* (-/-en) naturalization.

'**Ein|buße** *f* loss; '**2büßen** *v/t.* (*sep.*, -ge-, *h*) lose, forfeit.

'**ein|dämmen** ['aɪndɛmən] *v/t.* (*sep.*, -ge-, *h*) dam (up); embank (*river*); *fig.* check; '**~deutig** *adj.* unequivocal; clear, plain.

'**eindring|en** *v/i.* (*irr.* dringen, *sep.*, -ge-, *sein*) enter; penetrate; intrude; ~ *in* (*acc.*) penetrate (into); force one's way into; invade (*country*); '**~lich** *adj.* urgent; **2ling** ['~lɪŋ] *m* (-s/-e) intruder; invader.

'**Eindruck** *m* (-[e]s/ːe) impression.

'**ein|drücken** *v/t.* (*sep.*, -ge-, *h*) press in; crush (in) (*hat*); break (*pane*); '**~drucksvoll** *adj.* impressive; **~engen** ['aɪnɂ-] *v/t.* (*sep.*, -ge-, *h*) narrow; *fig.* restrain.

ein|er ['aɪnər], '**~e**, '**~(e)s** *indef. pron.* one.

Einer² [~] *m* (-s/-) ♫ unit, digit; *rowing*: single sculler, skiff.

einerlei ['aɪnər'laɪ] **1.** *adj.* of the same kind; immaterial; *es ist mir* ~ it is all the same to me; **2.** 2 *n* (-s/*no pl.*) sameness; monotony; humdrum (*of one's existence*).

einerseits *adv.* ['aɪnər'zaɪts] on the one hand.

einfach *adj.* ['aɪnfax] simple; single; plain; *meal:* frugal; *ticket:* single, *Am.* one-way; '**2heit** *f* (-/*no pl.*) simplicity.

'**einfädeln** ['aɪnfɛːdəln] *v/t.* (*sep.*, -ge-, *h*) thread; *fig.* start, set on foot; contrive.

'**Einfahrt** *f* entrance, entry.

'**Einfall** *m* ⚔ invasion; idea, inspiration; '**2en** *v/i.* (*irr.* fallen, *sep.*, -ge-, *sein*) fall in, collapse; break in (*on a conversation*), interrupt, cut short; chime in; ♪ join in; invade; *j-m* ~ occur to s.o.

Ein|falt ['aɪnfalt] *f* (-/*no pl.*) simplicity; silliness; '**2fältig** *adj.* ['~fɛltɪç] simple; silly; '**~faltspinsel** *m* simpleton, *Am.* F sucker.

'**ein|farbig** *adj.* one-colo(u)red, uni-colo(u)red; plain; '**~fassen** *v/t.* (*sep.*, -ge-, *h*) border; set (*precious stone*); '**2fassung** *f* border; setting; '**~fetten** *v/t.* (*sep.*, -ge-, *h*) grease; oil; '**~finden** *v/refl.* (*irr.* finden, *sep.*, -ge-, *h*) appear; arrive; '**~flechten** *fig. v/t.* (*irr.* flechten, *sep.*, -ge-, *h*) put in, insert; '**~fließen** *v/i.* (*irr.* fließen, *sep.*, -ge-, *sein*) flow in; ~ *in* (*acc.*) flow into; ~ *lassen* mention in passing; '**~flößen** *v/t.* (*sep.*, -ge-, *h*) infuse.

'**Einfluß** *m* influx; *fig.* influence; '**2reich** *adj.* influential.

ein|förmig *adj.* ['aɪnfœrmɪç] uniform; monotonous; **~frieden** ['~friːdən] *v/t.* (*sep.*, -ge-, *h*) fence, enclose; '**2friedung** *f* (-/-en) enclosure; '**~frieren** (*irr.* frieren, *sep.*, -ge-) **1.** *v/i.* (*sein*) freeze (in); **2.** *v/t.* (*h*) freeze (*food*); '**~fügen** *v/t.* (*sep.*, -ge-, *h*) put in; *fig.* insert; *sich* ~ fit in.

Einfuhr ♱ ['aɪnfuːr] *f* (-/-en) import(ation); '**~bestimmungen** *f/pl.* import regulations *pl.*

'**einführen** *v/t.* (*sep.*, -ge-, *h*) ♱ import; introduce (*s.o., custom*); insert; initiate; install (*s.o. in an office*).

'**Einfuhrwaren** ♱ *f/pl.* imports *pl.*

Eingabe f petition; application.

Eingang m entrance; entry; arrival (of goods); nach ~ on receipt; **'~s-buch ✝** n book of entries.

'eingeben v/t. (irr. geben, sep., -ge-, h) give, administer (medicine) (dat. to); prompt, suggest (to).

'einge|bildet adj. imaginary; conceited (auf acc. of); **'~boren** adj. native; **'2borene** m, f (-n/-n) native.

Eingebung ['aɪngəbuŋ] f (-/-en) suggestion; inspiration.

einge|denk adj. ['aɪŋɡədɛŋk] mindful (gen. of); **'~fallen** adj. eyes, cheeks: sunken, hollow; emaciated; **~fleischt** fig. adj. ['~gəflaɪʃt] inveterate; confirmed; **~er Junggeselle** confirmed bachelor.

'eingehen (irr. gehen, sep., -ge-) **1.** v/i. (sein) mail, goods: come in, arrive, **♀**, animal: die; cease (to exist); material: shrink; ~ auf (acc.) agree to; enter into; **2.** v/t. (h, sein) enter into (relationship); contract (marriage); **ein Risiko ~** run a risk, esp. Am. take a chance; **e-n Vergleich ~** come to terms; **Verbindlichkeiten ~** incur liabilities; **e-e Wette ~** make a bet; **eingegangene Gelder** n/pl. receipts pl.; **'~d** adj. detailed; thorough; examination: close.

Eingemachte ['aɪngəmaxtə] n (-n/ no pl.) preserves pl.; pickles pl.

'eingemeinden v/t. (sep., no -ge-, h) incorporate (dat. into).

'einge|nommen adj. partial (für to); prejudiced (gegen against); **von sich ~ conceited**; **'2sandt ↖** n (-s/-s) letter to the editor; **~schnappt** F fig. adj. ['~gəʃnapt] offended, touchy; **~sessen** adj. long-established; **'2ständnis** n confession, avowal; **'~stehen** v/t. (irr. stehen, sep., no -ge-, h) confess, avow.

Eingeweide anat. ['aɪngəvaɪdə] pl. viscera pl.; intestines pl.; bowels pl.; esp. of animals: entrails pl.

'einge|wöhnen v/refl. (sep., no -ge-, h) accustom o.s. (in acc. to); acclimatize o.s., Am. acclimate o.s. (to); get used (to).

eingewurzelt adj. ['~gəvurtsəlt] deep-rooted, inveterate.

'eingießen v/t. (irr. gießen, sep., -ge-, h) pour in or out.

eingleisig adj. ['aɪnglaɪzɪç] single-track.

'ein|graben v/t. (irr. graben, sep.,**

-ge-, h) dig in; bury; engrave; **sich ~ ⚔** dig o.s. in, entrench o.s.; fig. engrave itself (on one's memory); **'~gravieren** v/t. (sep., no -ge-, h) engrave.

'eingreifen 1. v/i. (irr. greifen, sep., -ge-, h) intervene; ~ in (acc.) interfere with; encroach on (s.o.'s rights); in die Debatte ~ join in the debate; **2.** ⊝ n (-s/no pl.) intervention.

'Eingriff m fig. encroachment; **⚕** operation.

einhaken v/t. (sep., -ge-, h) fasten; **sich bei j-m ~** take s.o.'s arm.

'Einhalt m (-[e]s/no pl.): ~ **gebieten** (dat.) put a stop to; **'2en** fig. (irr. halten, sep., -ge-, h) **1.** v/t. observe, keep; **2.** v/i. stop, leave off (zu tun doing).

'ein|hängen ([irr. hängen,] sep., -ge-, h) **1.** v/t. hang in; hang up, replace (receiver); **sich bei j-m ~** take s.o.'s arm, link arms with s.o.; **2.** teleph. v/i. hang up; **'~heften** v/t. (sep., -ge-, h) sew or stitch in.

'einheimisch adj. native (in dat. to), indigenous (to) (a. **♀**); **⚕** endemic; product: home-grown; **'2e** m, f (-n/-n) native; resident.

Einheit f (-/-en) unity; oneness; **⚛**, phys., ⚔ unit; **'2lich** adj. uniform; **'~spreis** m standard price.

'einheizen (sep., -ge-, h) **1.** v/i. make a fire; **2.** v/t. heat (stove).

einhellig adj. ['aɪnhɛlɪç] unanimous.

'einholen (sep., -ge-, h) **1.** v/t. catch up with, overtake; make up for (lost time); make (inquiries); take (order); seek (advice); ask for (permission); buy; **2.** v/i.: ~ **gehen** go shopping.

'Einhorn zo. n unicorn.

'einhüllen v/t. (sep., -ge-, h) wrap (up or in); envelop.

einig adj. ['aɪnɪç] united; ~ **sein** agree; **nicht ~ sein** differ (über acc. about); **~e** indef. pron. ['~gə] several; some; **~en** ['~ɪgən] v/t. (ge-, h) unite; **sich ~** come to terms; **~ermaßen** adv. ['~gər'maːsən] in some measure; somewhat; **~es** indef. pron. ['~gəs] some(thing); **'2keit** f (-/no pl.) unity; concord; **2ung** ['~g-] f (-/-en) union; agreement.

ein|impfen ['aɪn?-] v/t. (sep., -ge-, h) **⚕** inoculate (a. fig.); **'~jagen** v/t.**

(sep., -ge-, h): j-m Furcht ~ scare s.o.

einjährig adj. ['aɪnjɛːriç] one-year-old; esp. ♀ annual; animal: yearling.

'**ein|kalkulieren** v/t. (sep., no -ge-, h) take into account, allow for; '**~kassieren** v/t. (sep., no -ge-, h) cash; collect.

'**Einkauf** m purchase; Einkäufe machen s. einkaufen 2; '2**en** (sep., -ge-, h) **1.** v/t. buy, purchase; **2.** v/i. make purchases, go shopping.

'**Einkäufer** m buyer.

'**Einkaufs|netz** n string bag; '**~preis** ✝ m purchase price; '**~tasche** f shopping-bag.

'**ein|kehren** v/i. (sep., -ge-, sein) put up or stop (at an inn); '**~kerben** v/t. (sep., -ge-, h) notch; '**~kerkern** v/t. (sep., -ge-, h) imprison; '**~klagen** v/t. (sep., -ge-, h) sue for; '**~klammern** v/t. (sep., -ge-, h) typ. bracket; put in brackets.

'**Einklang** m unison; harmony.

'**ein|kleiden** v/t. (sep., -ge-, h) clothe; fit out; '**~klemmen** v/t. (sep., -ge-, h) squeeze (in); jam; '**~klinken** (sep., -ge-) **1.** v/t. latch; **2.** v/i. (sein) latch; engage; '**~knicken** (sep., -ge-) v/t. (h) and v/i. (sein) bend in, break; '**~kochen** (sep., -ge-) **1.** v/t. (h) preserve; **2.** v/i. (sein) boil down or away.

'**Einkommen** n (-s/-) income, revenue; '**~steuer** f income-tax.

'**einkreisen** v/t. (sep., -ge-, h) encircle.

Einkünfte ['aɪnkʏnftə] pl. income, revenue.

'**einlad|en** v/t. (irr. laden, sep., -ge-, h) load (in) (goods); fig. invite; '2**ung** f invitation.

'**Einlage** f enclosure (in letter); ✝ investment; deposit (of money); gambling: stake; inserted piece; ♪ arch-support; temporary filling (of tooth); '2**rn** ✝ v/t. (sep., -ge-, h) store (up).

Einlaß ['aɪnlas] m (Einlasses/Einlässe) admission, admittance.

'**einlassen** v/t. (irr. lassen, sep., -ge-, h) let in, admit; ~ in (acc.) ⊕ imbed in; sich ~ in or auf (both acc.) engage in, enter into.

'**ein|laufen** v/i. (irr. laufen, sep., -ge-, sein) come in, arrive; ship: enter; material: shrink; '**~leben**

v/refl. (sep., -ge-, h) accustom o.s. (in acc. to).

'**einlege|n** v/t. (sep., -ge-, h) lay or put in; insert; ⊕ inlay; deposit (money); pickle; preserve (fruit); Berufung ~ lodge an appeal (bei to); Ehre ~ mit gain hono(u)r or credit by; '2**sohle** f insole, sock.

'**einleit|en** v/t. (sep., -ge-, h) start; introduce; '**~end** adj. introductory; '2**ung** f introduction.

'**ein|lenken** fig. v/i. (sep., -ge-, h) come round; '**~leuchten** v/i. (sep., -ge-, h) be evident or obvious; '**~liefern** v/t. (sep., -ge-, h) deliver (up); in ein Krankenhaus ~ take to a hospital, Am. hospitalize; '**~lösen** v/t. (sep., -ge-, h) ransom (prisoner); redeem (pledge); ✝ hono(u)r (bill); cash (cheque); ✝ meet (bill); '**~machen** v/t. (sep., -ge-, h) preserve (fruit); tin, Am. can.

'**einmal** adv. once; one day; auf ~ all at once; es war ~ once (upon a time) there was; nicht ~ not even; 2**eins** n (-/-) multiplication table; '**~ig** adj. single; unique.

'**Einmarsch** m marching in, entry; 2**ieren** v/i. (sep., no -ge-, sein) march in, enter.

'**ein|mengen** v/refl. (sep., -ge-, h), '**~mischen** v/refl. (sep., -ge-, h) meddle, interfere (in acc. with), esp. Am. sl. butt in.

'**Einmündung** f junction (of roads); mouth (of river).

einmütig adj. ['aɪnmyːtiç] unanimous; '2**keit** f (-/no pl.) unanimity.

Einnahme ['aɪnnaːmə] f (-/-n) ⚔ taking, capture; mst ~n pl. takings pl., receipts pl.

'**einnehmen** v/t. (irr. nehmen, sep., -ge-, h) take (meal, position, ⚔); ✝ take (money); ✝ earn, make (money); take up, occupy (room); fig. captivate; '**~d** adj. taking, engaging, captivating.

'**einnicken** v/i. (sep., -ge-, sein) doze or drop off.

Einöde ['aɪnʔ-] f desert, solitude.

'**ein|ordnen** ['aɪnʔ-] v/t. (sep., -ge-, h) arrange in proper order; classify; file (letters, etc.); '**~packen** v/t. (sep., -ge-, h) pack up; wrap up; '**~pferchen** v/t. (sep., -ge-, h) pen in; fig. crowd, cram; '**~pflanzen** v/t. (sep., -ge-, h) plant; fig. implant; '**~pökeln** v/t. (sep., -ge-, h) pickle, salt; '**_prägen** v/t. (sep., -ge-, h) imprint; impress; sich ~ commit itself; commit s.th. to one's memory; '**_quartieren** v/t. (sep., no -ge-, h) quarter, billet; '**_rahmen** v/t. (sep., -ge-, h) frame; '**_räumen** fig. v/t. (sep., -ge-, h) grant, concede; '**_rechnen** v/t. (sep., -ge-, h) comprise, include; '**_reden** (sep., -ge-, h) **1.** v/t.: j-m ~ persuade or talk s.o. into (doing) s.th.; **2.** v/i.: auf j-n ~ talk insistently to s.o.; '**_reichen** v/t. (sep., -ge-, h) hand in, send in, present; '**_reihen** (sep., -ge-, h) insert (unter acc. in); class (with); place (among); sich ~ take one's place.

einreihig adj. ['aɪnraɪç] jacket: single-breasted.

'**Einreise** f entry; '**_erlaubnis** f, '**_genehmigung** f entry permit.

'**ein|reißen** (irr. reißen, sep., -ge-) **1.** v/t. tear; pull down (building); **2.** v/i. (sein) tear; abuse, etc.: spread; **_renken** ['_rɛŋkən] v/t. (sep., -ge-, h) ♔ set; fig. set right.

'**einricht|en** v/t. (sep. -ge-, h) establish; equip; arrange; set up (shop); furnish (flat); es ~ manage; sich ~ establish o.s., settle down; economize; sich ~ auf (acc.) prepare for; '**_ung** f establishment; arrangement, esp. Am. setup; equipment; furniture; fittings pl. (of shop); institution.

'**ein|rollen** v/t. (sep., -ge-, h) roll up or in; sich ~ roll up; curl up; '**_rosten** v/i. (sep., -ge-, sein) rust; screw, etc.: rust in; '**_rücken** (sep., -ge-) **1.** v/i. (sein) enter, march in; ⚔ join the army; **2.** v/t. (h) insert (advertisement in a paper); typ. indent (line, word, etc.); '**_rühren** v/t. (sep., -ge-, h) stir (in).

eins adj. [aɪns] one.

einsam adj. lonely, solitary; '**_keit** f (-/_-en) loneliness, solitude.

'**einsammeln** v/t. (sep., -ge-, h) gather; collect.

'**Einsatz** m inset; insertion (of piece of material); gambling: stake, pool; ♪ striking in, entry; employment; engagement (a. ⚔); ⚔ action, operation; unter ~ s-s Lebens at the risk of one's life.

'**ein|saugen** v/t. (sep., -ge-, h) suck in; fig. imbibe; '**_schalten** v/t. (sep., -ge-, h) insert; ⚡ switch or turn on; den ersten Gang ~ mot. go into first or bottom gear; sich ~ intervene; '**_schärfen** v/t. (sep., -ge-, h) inculcate (dat. upon); '**_schätzen** v/t. (sep., -ge-, h) assess, appraise, estimate (auf acc. at); value (a. fig.); '**_schenken** v/t. (sep., -ge-, h) pour in or out; '**_schicken** v/t. (sep., -ge-, h) send in; '**_schieben** v/t. (irr. schieben, sep., -ge-, h) insert; '**_schiffen** v/t. and v/refl. (sep., -ge-, h) embark; '**_schiffung** f (-/-en) embarkation; '**_schlafen** v/i. (irr. schlafen, sep., -ge-, sein) fall asleep; **_schläfern** ['_ʃlɛːfərn] v/t. (sep., -ge-, h) lull to sleep; ♔ narcotize.

'**Einschlag** m striking (of lightning); impact (of missile); fig. touch; '**⁀en** (irr. schlagen, sep., -ge-, h) **1.** v/t. drive in (nail); break (in); smash (in); wrap up; take (road); tuck in (hem, etc.); enter upon (career); **2.** v/i. shake hands; lightning, missile: strike; fig. be a success; nicht ~ fail; (wie e-e Bombe) ~ cause a sensation; auf j-n ~ belabour s.o.

einschlägig adj. ['aɪnʃlɛːgɪç] relevant, pertinent.

'**Einschlagpapier** n wrapping-paper.

'**ein|schleichen** v/refl. (irr. schleichen, sep., -ge-, h) creep or sneak in; '**_schleppen** v/t. (sep., -ge-, h) ⚓ tow in; import (disease); '**_schleusen** fig. v/t. (sep., -ge-, h) channel or let in; '**_schließen** v/t. (irr. schließen, sep., -ge-, h) lock in or up; enclose; ⚔ surround, encircle; fig. include; '**_schließlich** prp. (gen.) inclusive of; including, comprising; '**_schmeicheln** v/refl. (sep., -ge-, h) ingratiate o.s. (bei with); '**_schmeichelnd** adj. insinuating; '**_schmuggeln** v/t. (sep., -ge-, h) smuggle in; '**_schnappen** v/i. (sep., -ge-, sein) catch; fig. s. eingeschnappt; '**_schneidend** fig. adj. incisive, drastic.

'**Einschnitt** m cut, incision; notch.

'**ein|schnüren** v/t. (sep., -ge-, h) lace (up); '**_schränken** ['_ʃrɛŋkən] v/t. (sep., -ge-, h) restrict, confine; reduce (expenses); sich ~ economize; '**⁀schränkung** f (-/-en) restriction; reduction.

'**Einschreibe|brief** m registered letter; '**⁀n** v/t. (irr. schreiben, sep., '**ein**|**schreiten 1.** *fig. v/i. (irr. schreiten, sep., -ge-, sein)* step in, interpose, intervene; take action *(gegen against)*; **2.** ⚄ *n (-s/no pl.)* intervention.

'**ein**|**schrumpfen** *v/i. (sep., -ge-, sein)* shrink; '**~schüchtern** *v/t. (sep., -ge-, h)* intimidate; bully; '**⚄schüchterung** *f (-/-en)* intimidation; '**~schulen** *v/t. (sep., -ge-, h)* put to school.

'**Einschuß** *m* bullet-hole; † invested capital.

'**ein**|**segnen** *v/t. (sep., -ge-, h)* consecrate; confirm *(children)*; '**⚄segnung** *f* consecration; confirmation.

'**einsehen 1.** *v/t. (irr. sehen, sep., -ge-, h)* look into; *fig.*: see, comprehend; realize; **2.** ⚄ *n (-s/no pl.)*: ein ~ haben show consideration.

'**einseifen** *v/t. (sep., -ge-, h)* soap; lather *(beard)*; F *fig.* humbug *(s.o.)*.

einseitig *adj.* ['aɪnzaɪtɪç] one-sided; ⚕, *pol.*, ⚖ unilateral.

'**einsend**|**en** *v/t. (irr. senden, sep., -ge-, h)* send in; '**⚄er** *m (-s/-)* sender; contributor *(to a paper)*.

'**einsetz**|**en** *(sep., -ge-, h)* **1.** *v/t.* set or put in; stake *(money)*; insert; institute, instal(l), appoint *(s.o.)* *fig.* use, employ; risk *(one's life)*; *sich ~ für* stand up for *(s.o.)*; **2.** *v/i. fever, flood, weather*: set in; ♪ strike in; '**⚄ung** *f (-/-en)* insertion; appointment, installation.

'**Einsicht** *f (-/-en)* inspection; *fig.* insight, understanding; judiciousness; '**⚄ig** *adj.* judicious; sensible.

'**einsickern** *v/i. (sep., -ge-, sein)* soak in; infiltrate.

'**Einsiedler** *m* hermit.

einsilbig *adj.* ['aɪnzɪlbɪç] monosyllabic; *fig.* taciturn; '**⚄keit** *f (-/no pl.)* taciturnity.

'**einsinken** *v/i. (irr. sinken, sep., -ge-, sein)* sink (in).

Einspänn|**er** *m (-s/-)* ['aɪnʃpɛnər] one-horse carriage; '**⚄ig** *adj.* one-horse.

'**ein**|**sparen** *v/t. (sep., -ge-, h)* save, economize; '**~sperren** *v/t. (sep., -ge-, h)* imprison; lock up, confine; '**~springen** *v/i. (irr. springen, sep., -ge-, sein)* ⊕ catch; *fig.* step in,

help out; *für j-n ~* substitute for *s.o.*; '**~spritzen** *v/t. (sep., -ge-, h)* inject; '**⚄spritzung** *f (-/-en)* injection.

'**Einspruch** *m* objection, protest, veto; appeal; **~srecht** *n* veto.

'**einspurig** *adj.* single-track.

einst *adv.* [aɪnst] once; one *or* some day.

'**Einstand** *m* entry; *tennis*: deuce.

'**ein**|**stecken** *v/t. (sep., -ge-, h)* put in; pocket; plug in; '**~steigen** *v/i. (irr. steigen, sep., -ge-, sein)* get in; ~! 🚋 take your seats!, *Am.* all aboard!

'**einstell**|**en** *v/t. (sep., -ge-, h)* put in; ⚕ enrol(l), enlist, *Am.* muster in; engage, employ, *Am. a.* hire; give up; stop, cease, *Am. a.* quit *(payment, etc.)*; adjust *(mechanism)* *(auf acc.* to); opt., focus (on) *(a. fig.)*; *die Arbeit ~* cease working; strike, *Am. a.* walk out; *sich ~* appear; *sich ~ auf (acc.)* be prepared for; adapt o.s. to; '**⚄ung** *f* ⚕ enlistment; engagement; adjustment; focus; (mental) attitude, mentality.

'**einstimm**|**en** *v/i. (sep., -ge-, h)* join in; '**~ig** *adj.* unanimous; **⚄igkeit** *f (-/no pl.)* unanimity.

einstöckig *adj.* ['aɪnʃtœkɪç] one-storied.

'**ein**|**streuen** *fig. v/t. (sep., -ge-, h)* intersperse; '**~studieren** *v/t. (sep., no -ge-, h)* study; *thea.* rehearse; '**~stürmen** *v/i. (sep., -ge-, sein)*: *auf j-n ~* rush at *s.o.*; '**⚄sturz** *m* falling in, collapse; '**~stürzen** *v/i. (sep., -ge-, sein)* fall in, collapse.

einst|**weilen** *adv.* ['aɪnst'vaɪlən] for the present; in the meantime; '**~weilig** *adj.* temporary.

'**ein**|**tauschen** *v/t. (sep., -ge-, h)* exchange *(gegen* for); '**~teilen** *v/t. (sep., -ge-, h)* divide *(in acc.* into); classify; '**~teilig** *adj.* one-piece; '**⚄teilung** *f* division; classification.

eintönig *adj.* ['aɪntøːnɪç] monotonous; '**⚄keit** *f (-/✎)* monotony.

'**Eintopf(gericht** *n) m* hot-pot; stew.

'**Eintracht** *f (-/no pl.)* harmony, concord.

einträchtig *adj.* ['aɪntrɛçtɪç] harmonious.

'**eintragen** *v/t. (irr. tragen, sep., -ge-, h)* enter; register; bring in,

yield (*profit*); sich ~ in (*acc.*) sign.
einträglich adj. ['aɪntrɛːkliç] profitable.

'**Eintragung** f (-/-en) entry; registration.

'**ein|treffen** v/i. (irr. treffen, sep., -ge-, sein) arrive; happen; come true; '~treiben v/t. (irr. treiben, sep., -ge-, h) drive in or home; collect (*debts, taxes*); '~treten (irr. treten, sep., -ge-) **1.** v/i. (sein) enter; occur, happen, take place; ~ für stand up for; ~ in (*acc.*) enter into (*rights*); enter upon (*possession*); enter (*room*); join (*the army, etc.*); **2.** v/t. (h) kick in (*door*); sich et. ~ run s.th. into one's foot.

'**Eintritt** m entry, entrance; admittance; beginning, setting-in (*of winter, etc.*); ~ frei! admission free!; ~ verboten! no admittance!; '~geld n entrance or admission fee; sports: gate money; '~skarte f admission ticket.

'**ein|trocknen** v/i. (sep., -ge-, sein) dry (up); '~trüben v/refl. (sep., -ge-, h) become cloudy or overcast; ~üben ['aɪnˀ-] v/t. (sep., -ge-, h) practi|se, Am. -ce s.th.; train s.o.

einver|leiben ['aɪnfɛrlaɪbən] v/t. ([sep.,] no -ge-, h) incorporate (dat. in); annex (to); F sich et. ~ eat or drink s.th.; '2nehmen n (-s/no pl.) agreement, understanding; in gutem ~ on friendly terms; '~standen adj.: ~ sein agree; '2ständnis n agreement.

'**Einwand** m (-[e]s/=e) objection (gegen to).

'**Einwander|er** m immigrant; '2n v/i. (sep., -ge-, sein) immigrate; '~ung f immigration.

'**einwandfrei** adj. unobjectionable; perfect; faultless; alibi: sound.

einwärts adv. ['aɪnvɛrts] inward(s).

'**Einwegflasche** f one-way bottle, non-return bottle.

'**einweih|en** v/t. (sep., -ge-, h) eccl. consecrate; inaugurate; ~ in (acc.) initiate s.o. into; '~ung f (-/-en) consecration; inauguration; initiation.

'**einwend|en** v/t. ([irr. wenden,] sep., -ge-, h) object; '2ung f objection.

'**einwerfen** (irr. werfen, sep., -ge-, h) **1.** v/t. throw in (a. fig.); smash, break (window-pane); post, Am.

mail (*letter*); interject (*remark*); **2.** v/i. football: throw in.

'**einwickel|n** v/t. (sep., -ge-, h) wrap (up), envelop; '2papier n wrapping-paper.

einwillig|en ['aɪnvɪlɪgən] v/i. (sep., -ge-, h) consent, agree (in acc. to); '2ung f (-/-en) consent, agreement.

'**einwirk|en** v/i. (sep., -ge-, h): ~ auf (acc.) act up[on]; influence; effect; '2ung f influence; effect.

Einwohner ['aɪnvoːnər] m (-s/-), '~in f (-/-nen) inhabitant, resident.

'**Einwurf** m throwing in; football: throw-in; fig. objection; slit (for letters, etc.); slot (for coins).

'**Einzahl** gr. f (-/⚹-en) singular (number); '2en v/t. (sep., -ge-, h) pay in; '~ung f payment; deposit (at bank).

einzäunen ['aɪntsɔʏnən] v/t. (sep., -ge-, h) fence in.

Einzel ['aɪntsəl] n (-s/-) tennis: single, Am. singles pl.; ~gänger ['-gɛŋər] m (-s/-) outsider; F lone wolf; '~handel ⚕ m retail trade; '~händler ⚕ m retailer, retail dealer; '~heit f (-/-en) detail, item; ~en pl. particulars pl., details pl.; '2n **1.** adj. single; particular; individual; separate; of shoes, etc.: odd; im ~en in detail; **2.** adv.: ~ angeben or aufführen specify, esp. Am. itemize; '~ne m (-n/-n) the individual; '~verkauf m retail sale; '~wesen n individual.

'**einziehen** (irr. ziehen, sep., -ge-) **1.** v/t. (h) draw in; post ⊕ retract; ✗ call up, Am. draft, induct; ⚹⚹ seize, confiscate; make (inquiries) (über acc. on, about); **2.** v/i. (sein) enter; move in; liquid: soak in; ~ in (acc.) move into (flat, etc.).

einzig adj. ['aɪntsɪç] only; single; sole; unique; '~artig adj. unique, singular.

'**Einzug** m entry, entrance; moving in.

'**einzwängen** v/t. (sep., -ge-, h) squeeze, jam.

Eis [aɪs] n (-es/no pl.) ice; ice-cream; '~bahn f skating-rink; '~bär zo. m polar bear; '~bein n pickled pork shank; '~berg m iceberg; '~decke f sheet of ice; '~diele f ice-cream parlo(u)r.

Eisen ['aɪzən] n (-s/⚹) iron.

'**Eisenbahn** f railway, Am. railroad;

mit der ~ by rail, by train; '~er m (-s/-) railwayman; '~fahrt f railway journey; '~knotenpunkt m (railway) junction; '~unglück n railway accident; '~wagen m railway carriage, Am. railroad car; coach.

'Eisen|blech n sheet-iron; '~erz n iron-ore; '~gießerei f iron-foundry; '⌀haltig adj. ferruginous; '~hütte f ironworks sg., pl.; '~waren f/pl. ironmongery, esp. Am. hardware; '~warenhändler m ironmonger, esp. Am. hardware dealer.

eisern adj. ['aɪzərn] iron, of iron.

'Eis|gang n breaking up of the ice; ice-drift; '⌀gekühlt adj. ['⌀gəky:lt] iced; '⌀grau adj. hoary; '~hockey n ice-hockey; ⌀ig adj. ['aɪzɪç] icy; '⌀kalt adj. icy (cold); '~kunstlauf m figure-skating; '~lauf m, '~laufen n (-s/no pl.) skating; skate; '~läufer m skater; '~meer n polar sea; '~schnellauf m speed-skating; '~scholle f ice-floe; '~schrank m s. Kühlschrank; '~vogel orn. m kingfisher; '~zapfen m icicle; '~zeit geol. f ice-age.

eitel adj. ['aɪtəl] vain (auf acc. of); conceited; mere; '⌀keit f (-/-en) vanity.

Eiter ✳ ['aɪtər] m (-s/no pl.) matter, pus; '~beule ✳ f abscess; '⌀ig ✳ adj. purulent; '⌀n ✳ v/i. (ge-, h) fester, suppurate; '~ung ✳ f (-/-en) suppuration.

eitrig ✳ adj. ['aɪtrɪç] purulent.

'Eiweiß n (-es/-e) white of egg; ⌀ albumen; '⌀haltig ⌀ adj. albuminous.

'Eizelle f egg-cell, ovum.

Ekel ['e:kəl] 1. m (-s/no pl.) disgust (vor dat. at), loathing; aversion; ✳ nausea; 2. F n (-s/-) nasty person; '⌀erregend adj. nauseating, sickening; '⌀haft adj., '⌀ig adj. revolting; fig. disgusting; '⌀n v/refl. (ge-, h): sich ~ be nauseated (vor dat. at); fig. be or feel disgusted (at).

eklig adj. ['e:klɪç] s. ekelhaft.

elasti|sch adj. [e'lastɪʃ] elastic; ⌀zität [~tsi'tɛ:t] f (-/no pl.) elasticity.

Elch zo. [ɛlç] m (-[e]s/-e) elk, moose.

Elefant zo. [ele'fant] m (-en/-en) elephant.

elegan|t adj. [ele'gant] elegant;

smart; ⌀z [~ts] f (-/no pl.) elegance.

elektrifizier|en [elektrifi'tsi:rən] v/t. (no -ge-, h) electrify; ⌀ung f (-/-en) electrification.

Elektri|ker [e'lektrikər] m (-s/-) electrician; ⌀sch adj. electric(al); ⌀sieren [~'zi:rən] v/t. (no -ge-, h) electrify.

Elektrizität [elektritsi'tɛ:t] f (-/no pl.) electricity; ~sgesellschaft f electricity supply company; ~s-werk n (electric) power station, power-house, Am. power plant.

Elektrode [elek'tro:də] f (-/-n) electrode.

Elektro|gerät [e'lektro-] n electric appliance; ~lyse [~'ly:zə] f (-/-n) electrolysis.

Elektron ⚡ [e'lektron] n (-s/-en) electron; ~engehirn [~'tro:nən-] n electronic brain; ~ik [~'tro:nik] f (-/no pl.) electronics sg.

Elektro'technik f electrical engineering; ~er m electrical engineer.

Element [ele'ment] n (-[e]s/-e) element.

elementar adj. [elemen'ta:r] elementary; ⌀schule elementary or primary school, Am. grade school.

Elend ['e:lɛnt] 1. n (-[e]s/no pl.) misery; need, distress; 2. ⌀ adj. miserable, wretched; needy, distressed; '~sviertel n slums pl.

elf [ɛlf] 1. adj. eleven; 2. ⌀ f (-/-en) eleven (a. sports).

Elf² [~] m (-en/-en), ~e ['ɛlfə] f (-/-n) elf, fairy.

'Elfenbein n (-[e]s/🟦-e) ivory; '⌀ern adj. ivory.

Elf'meter m football: penalty kick; ~marke f penalty spot.

'elfte adj. eleventh.

'Ellbogen anat. m (-s/-) elbow.

Elle ['ɛlə] f (-/-n) yard; anat. ulna.

Elster orn. ['ɛlstər] f (-/-n) magpie.

elter|lich adj. ['ɛltərlɪç] parental; '⌀n pl. parents pl.; '~nlos adj. parentless, orphaned; '⌀nteil m parent.   [(-/-n) enamel.\

Email [e'ma:j] n (-s/-s), ~le [~] f\

Emanzipation [emantsipa'tsjo:n] f (-/-en) emancipation.

Embargo [ɛm'bargo] n (-s/-s) embargo.   [bolism.\

Embolie ✳ [ɛmbo'li:] f (-/-n) em-\

Embryo biol. ['ɛmbryo] m (-s/-s, -nen) embryo.

Emigrant [emi'grant] *m* (-en/-en) emigrant.

empfahl [ɛm'pfaːl] *pret. of* empfehlen.

Empfang [ɛm'pfaŋ] *m* (-[e]s/ᴗe) reception (*a. radio*); receipt (*of s.th.*); *nach or bei* ᴗ on receipt; **'2en** *v/t.* (*irr. fangen, no* -ge-, *h*) receive; welcome; conceive (*child*).

Empfänger [ɛm'pfɛŋər] *m* (-s/-) receiver, recipient; payee (*of money*); addressee (*of letter*); † consignee (*of goods*).

em'pfänglich *adj.* susceptible (*für* to); **2keit** *f* (-/no pl.) susceptibility. **Em'pfangs|dame** *f* receptionist; **ᴗgerät** *n* receiver, receiving set; **ᴗschein** *m* receipt; **ᴗzimmer** *n* reception-room.

empfehl|en [ɛm'pfeːlən] *v/t.* (*irr., no* -ge-, *h*) recommend; commend; ᴗ *Sie mich* (*dat.*) please remember me to; **ᴗenswert** *adj.* (re)commendable; **2ung** *f* (-/-en) recommendation; compliments *pl.*

empfinden [ɛm'pfindən] *v/t.* (*irr. finden, no* -ge-, *h*) feel; perceive.

empfindlich *adj.* [ɛm'pfintliç] sensitive (*a. phot.*, 🔍) (*für, gegen* to); *pred. a.* susceptible (*gegen* to); delicate; tender; *p.:* touchy, sensitive; *cold:* severe; *pain, loss, etc.:* grievous; *pain:* acute; **2keit** *f* (-/-en) sensitivity; sensibility; touchiness; delicacy.

empfindsam *adj.* [ɛm'pfintzaːm] sensitive; sentimental; **2keit** *f* (-/-en) sensitiveness; sentimentality.

Empfindung [ɛm'pfinduŋ] *f* (-/-en) perception; sensation; sentiment; **2slos** *adj.* insensible; *esp. fig.* unfeeling; **ᴗsvermögen** *n* faculty of perception.

empfohlen [ɛm'pfoːlən] *p.p. of* empfehlen. [wards.⟩

empor *adv.* [ɛm'poːr] up, up-⟩

em'pören [ɛm'pøːrən] *v/t.* (*no* -ge-, *h*) incense; shock; *sich* ᴗ revolt (*a. fig.*), rebel; grow furious (*über acc.* at); empört indignant, shocked (*both: über acc.* at).

em'por|kommen *v/i.* (*irr. kommen, sep.,* -ge-, *sein*) rise (in the world); **2kömmling** [ᴗkœmliŋ] *m* (-s/-e) upstart; **ᴗragen** *v/i.* (*sep.,* -ge-, *h*) tower, rise; **ᴗsteigen** *v/i.* (*irr. steigen, sep.,* -ge-, *sein*) rise, ascend.

Em'pörung *f* (-/-en) rebellion, revolt; indignation.

emsig *adj.* [ɛm'zɪç] busy, industrious, diligent; **2keit** *f* (-/no pl.) busyness, industry, diligence.

Ende ['ɛndə] *n* (-s/-n) end; *am* ᴗ at *or* in the end; after all; eventually; *zu* ᴗ *gehen* end; expire; run short; **'2n** *v/i.* (*ge-, h*) end; cease, finish.

end|gültig *adj.* ['ɛntgyltiç] final, definitive; **'ᴗlich** *adv.* finally, at last; **ᴗlos** *adj.* ['ᴗloːs] endless; **'2punkt** *m* final point; **'2runde** *f sports:* final; **'2station** *f* terminus, *Am.* terminal; **'2summe** *f* (sum) total.

Endung *ling.* ['ɛnduŋ] *f* (-/-en) ending, termination.

Endzweck ['ɛnt-] *m* ultimate object.

Energie [enɛr'giː] *f* (-/-n) energy; **2los** *adj.* lacking in energy.

e'nergisch *adj.* vigorous; energetic.

eng *adj.* [ɛŋ] narrow; *clothes:* tight; close; intimate; *im* ᴗeren *Sinne* strictly speaking.

engagieren [āga'ʒiːrən] *v/t.* (*no* -ge-, *h*) engage, *Am. a.* hire.

Enge ['ɛŋə] *f* (-/-n) narrowness; *fig.* straits *pl.*

Engel ['ɛŋəl] *m* (-s/-) angel.

'engherzig *adj.* ungenerous, petty.

Engländer ['ɛŋlɛndər] *m* (-s/-) Englishman; *die* ᴗ *pl.* the English *pl.*; **'ᴗin** *f* (-/-nen) Englishwoman.

englisch *adj.* ['ɛŋliʃ] English; British.

'Engpaß *m* defile, narrow pass, *Am. a.* notch; *fig.* bottle-neck.

en gros † *adv.* [ā'groː] wholesale.

En'groshandel † *m* wholesale trade.

'engstirnig *adj.* narrow-minded.

Enkel ['ɛŋkəl] *m* (-s/-) grandchild; grandson; **ᴗin** *f* (-/-nen) granddaughter.

enorm *adj.* [e'nɔrm] enormous; F *fig.* tremendous.

Ensemble *thea.*, ♪ [ā'sā:bəl] *n* (-s/-s) ensemble; company.

entart|en [ɛnt'aːrtən] *v/i.* (*no* -ge-, *sein*) degenerate; **2ung** *f* (-/-en) degeneration.

entbehr|en [ɛnt'beːrən] *v/t.* (*no* -ge-, *h*) lack; miss; want; do without; **ᴗlich** *adj.* dispensable; superfluous; **2ung** *f* (-/-en) want, privation.

ent'bind|en (*irr. binden, no* -ge-,

1. *v/t.* dispense, release (*von* from); deliver (*of a child*); **2.** *v/i.* be confined; **2ung** *f* dispensation, release; delivery; **2ungsheim** *n* maternity hospital.

ent'blöß|en *v/t.* (*no* -ge-, h) bare, strip; uncover (*head*); **~t** *adj.* bare.

ent'deck|en *v/t.* (*no* -ge-, h) discover; detect; disclose; **~er** *m* (-s/-) discoverer; **2ung** *f* discovery.

Ente ['ɛntə] *f* (-/-n) *orn.* duck; *false report:* F canard, hoax.

ent'ehr|en *v/t.* (*no* -ge-, h) dishono(u)r; **2ung** *f* degradation; rape.

ent'eign|en *v/t.* (*no* -ge-, h) expropriate; dispossess; **2ung** *f* expropriation; dispossession.

ent'erben *v/t.* (*no* -ge-, h) disinherit.

entern ['ɛntərn] *v/t.* (ge-, h) board, grapple (*ship*).

ent'|fachen *v/t.* (*no* -ge-, h) kindle; *fig. a.* rouse (*passions*); **~fallen** *v/i.* (*irr.* fallen, *no* -ge-, sein): j-m ~ escape s.o.'s memory; *auf* j-n ~ fall to s.o.'s share; *s.* weg-fallen; **~falten** *v/t.* (*no* -ge-, h) unfold; *fig.:* develop; display; *sich* ~ unfold; *fig.* develop (*zu* into).

ent'fern|en *v/t.* (*no* -ge-, h) remove; *sich* ~ withdraw; **~t** *adj.* distant, remote (*both a. fig.*); **2ung** *f* (-/-en) removal; distance; range; **2ungs-messer** *phot. m* (-s/-) range-finder.

ent'|flammen (*no* -ge-) *v/t.* (h) *and* *v/i.* (sein) inflame; **~'fliehen** *v/i.* (*irr.* fliehen, *no* -ge-, sein) flee, escape (*aus or dat.* from); **~'frem-den** *v/t.* (*no* -ge-, h) estrange; alienate (*j-m* from s.o.).

ent'führ|en *v/t.* (*no* -ge-, h) abduct, kidnap; run away with; **2er** *m* abductor, kidnap(p)er; **2ung** *f* abduction, kidnap(p)ing.

ent'gegen 1. *prp.* (*dat.*) in opposition to, contrary to; against; **2.** *adv.* towards; **~gehen** *v/i.* (*irr.* gehen, *sep.*, -ge-, sein) go to meet; **~ge-setzt** *adj.* opposite; *fig.* contrary; **~halten** *v/t.* (*irr.* halten, *sep.*, -ge-, h) hold out; *fig.* object; **~kommen** *v/i.* (*irr.* kommen, *sep.*, -ge-, sein) come to meet; *fig.* meet s.o.('s wishes) halfway; **2kommen** *n* (-s/*no pl.*) obligingness; **~kommend** *adj.* obliging; **~nehmen** *v/t.* (*irr.* nehmen, *sep.*, -ge-, h) accept, receive; **~sehen** *v/i.* (*dat.*) (*irr.* sehen, *sep.*, -ge-, h) await; look for-

ward to; **~setzen** *v/t.* (*sep.*, -ge-, h) oppose; **~stehen** *v/i.* (*irr.* stehen, *sep.*, -ge-, h) be opposed (*dat.* to); **~strecken** *v/t.* (*sep.*, -ge-, h) hold or stretch out (*dat.* to); **~treten** *v/i.* (*dat.*) (*irr.* treten, *sep.*, -ge-, sein) step up to *s.o.*; oppose; face (*danger*).

entgegn|en [ɛnt'ge:gnən] *v/i.* (*no* -ge-, h) reply; return; retort; **2ung** *f* (-/-en) reply; retort.

ent'gehen *v/i.* (*irr.* gehen, *no* -ge-, sein) escape.

entgeistert *adj.* [ɛnt'gaɪstərt] a-ghast, thunderstruck, flabbergasted.

Entgelt [ɛnt'gɛlt] *n* (-[e]s/*no pl.*) recompense; **2en** *v/t.* (*irr.* gelten, *no* -ge-, h) atone or suffer or pay for.

entgleis|en [ɛnt'glaɪzən] *v/i.* (*no* -ge-, sein) run off the rails, be derailed; *fig.* (make a) slip; **2ung** *f* (-/-en) derailment; *fig.* slip.

ent'gleiten *v/i.* (*irr.* gleiten, *no* -ge-, sein) slip (*dat.* from).

ent'halt|en *v/t.* (*irr.* halten, *no* -ge-, h) contain, hold, include; *sich* ~ (*gen.*) abstain or refrain from; **~sam** *adj.* abstinent; **2samkeit** *f* (-/*no pl.*) abstinence; **2ung** *f* abstention. [decapitate.]

ent'haupten *v/t.* (*no* -ge-, h) behead.

ent'hüll|en *v/t.* (*no* -ge-, h) uncover; unveil; *fig.* reveal, disclose; **2ung** *f* (-/-en) uncovering; unveiling; *fig.* revelation, disclosure.

Enthusias|mus [ɛntuzi'asmus] *m* (-/*no pl.*) enthusiasm; **~t** *m* (-en/-en) enthusiast; *film, sports:* F fan; **2tisch** *adj.* enthusiastic.

ent'kleiden *v/t. and v/refl.* (*no* -ge-, h) undress.

ent'kommen 1. *v/i.* (*irr.* kommen, *no* -ge-, sein) escape (*j-m* s.o.; *aus* from), get away or off; **2.** ~ *n* (-s/*no pl.*) escape.

entkräft|en [ɛnt'krɛftən] *v/t.* (*no* -ge-, h) weaken, debilitate; *fig.* refute; **2ung** *f* (-/-en) weakening; debility; *fig.* refutation.

ent'lad|en *v/t.* (*irr.* laden, *no* -ge-, h) unload; *esp.* ⚡ discharge; explode; *sich* ~ *esp.* ⚡ discharge; *gun:* go off; *anger:* vent itself; **2ung** *f* unloading; *esp.* ⚡ discharge; explosion.

ent'lang 1. *prp.* (*dat.*; *acc.*) along; **2.** *adv.* along; *er geht die Straße* ~ he goes along the street.

ent'larven *v/t.* (*no* -ge-, h) unmask; *fig. a.* expose.

ent'lass|en v/t. (irr. lassen, no -ge-, h) dismiss, discharge; F give s.o. the sack, Am. a. fire; 2ung f (-/-en) dismissal, discharge; 2ungsgesuch n resignation.

ent'lasten v/t. (no -ge-, h) unburden; ⚖ exonerate, clear (from suspicion).

Ent'lastung f (-/-en) relief; discharge; exoneration; ~straße f by-pass (road); ~zeuge m witness for the defen[c]e, Am. -se.

ent'laufen v/i. (irr. laufen, no -ge-, sein) run away (dat. from); ~ledigen [~'le:digən] v/refl. (gen.) (no -ge-, h): rid o.s. of s.th., get rid of s.th.; acquit o.s. of (duty); execute (orders); ~leeren v/t. (no -ge-, h) empty. [of-the-way.)

ent'legen adj. remote, distant, out-⌐

ent'|lehnen v/t. (no -ge-, h) borrow (dat. or aus from); ~'locken v/t. (no -ge-, h) draw, elicit (dat. from); ~'lohnen v/t. (no -ge-, h) pay (off); ~'lüften v/t. (no -ge-, h) ventilate; ~militarisieren [~militari'zi:rən] v/t. (no -ge-, h) demilitarize; ~mutigen [~'mu:tigən] v/t. (no -ge-, h) discourage; ~'nehmen v/t. (irr. nehmen, no -ge-, h) take (dat. from); ~ aus (with)draw from; fig. gather or learn from; ~'rätseln v/t. (no -ge-, h) unriddle; ~'reißen v/t. (irr. reißen, no -ge-, h) snatch away (dat. from); ~'richten v/t. (no -ge-, h) pay; ~'rinnen v/i. (irr. rinnen, no -ge-, sein) escape (dat. from); ~'rollen v/t. (no -ge-, h) unroll; ~'rücken v/t. (no -ge-, h) remove (dat. from), carry off or away; ~'rückt adj. entranced; lost in thought.

ent'rüst|en v/t. (no -ge-, h) fill with indignation; sich ~ become angry or indignant (über acc. at s.th., with s.o.); ~et adj. indignant (über acc. at s.th., with s.o.); 2ung f indignation.

ent'sag|en v/i. (no -ge-, h) renounce, resign; 2ung f (-/-en) renunciation, resignation.

ent'schädig|en v/t. (no -ge-, h) indemnify, compensate; 2ung f indemnification, indemnity; compensation.

ent'scheid|en (irr. scheiden, no -ge-, h) 1. v/t. decide; sich ~ question, etc.: be decided; p.: decide (für for; gegen

against; über acc. on); come to a decision; 2. v/i. decide; ~end adj. decisive; crucial; 2ung f decision.

entschieden adj. [ɛnt'ʃi:dən] decided; determined, resolute; 2heit f (-/no pl.) determination.

ent'schließen v/refl. (irr. schließen, no -ge-, h) resolve, decide, determine (zu on s.th.; zu inf. to inf.), make up one's mind (zu inf. to inf.).

ent'schlossen adj. resolute, determined; 2heit f (-/no pl.) resoluteness.

ent'schlüpfen v/i. (no -ge-, sein) escape, slip (dat. from).

Ent'schluß m resolution, resolve, decision, determination.

entschuldig|en [ɛnt'ʃuldigən] v/t. (no -ge-, h) excuse; sich ~ apologize (bei to; für for); sich ~ lassen beg to be excused; 2ung f (-/-en) excuse; apology; ich bitte (Sie) um ~ I beg your pardon.

ent'senden v/t. (irr. senden, no -ge-, h) send off, dispatch; delegate, depute.

ent'setz|en 1. v/t. (no -ge-, h) dismiss (from a position); ⚔ relieve; frighten; sich ~ be terrified or shocked (über acc. at); 2. 2 n (-/no pl.) horror, fright; ~lich adj. horrible, dreadful, terrible, shocking.

ent'sinnen v/refl. (gen.) (irr. sinnen, no -ge-, h) remember or recall s.o., s.th.

ent'spann|en v/t. (no -ge-, h) relax; unbend; sich ~ relax; political situation: ease; 2ung f relaxation; pol. détente.

ent'sprech|en v/i. (irr. sprechen, no -ge-, h) answer (description, etc.); correspond; meet (demand); ~end adj. corresponding; appropriate; 2ung f (-/-en) equivalent.

ent'springen v/i. (irr. springen, no -ge-, sein) escape (dat. from); river: rise, Am. head; s. entstehen.

ent'stammen v/i. (no -ge-, sein) be descended from; come from or of, originate from.

ent'steh|en v/i. (irr. stehen, no -ge-, sein) arise, develop (both: aus from); 2ung f (-/-en) origin.

ent'stell|en v/t. (no -ge-, h) disfigure; deface, deform; distort; 2ung f disfigurement; distortion, misrepresentation.

ent'täusch|en v/t. (no -ge-, h) dis-

appoint; ⚥**ung** f disappointment.
ent'thronen v/t. (no -ge-, h) dethrone.
entvölker|n [ɛnt'fœlkərn] v/t. (no -ge-, h) depopulate; ⚥**ung** f (-/-en) depopulation.
ent'wachsen v/i. (irr. wachsen, no -ge-, sein) outgrow.
entwaffn|en [ɛnt'vafnən] v/t. (no -ge-, h) disarm; ⚥**ung** f (-/-en) disarmament.
ent'warnen v/i. (no -ge-, h) civil defence: sound the all-clear (signal).
ent'wässer|n v/t. (no -ge-, h) drain; ⚥**ung** f (-/-en) drainage; ⚓ dehydration.
ent'weder cj.: ~ ... oder either ... or.
ent|'weichen v/i. (irr. weichen, no -ge-, sein) escape (aus from); ~'**weihen** v/t. (no -ge-, h) desecrate, profane; ~'**wenden** v/t. (no -ge-, h) pilfer, purloin (j-m et. s.th. from s.o.); ~'**werfen** v/t. (irr. werfen, no -ge-, h) draft, draw up (document); design; sketch, trace out, outline; plan.
ent'wert|en v/t. (no -ge-, h) depreciate, devaluate; cancel (stamp); ⚥**ung** f depreciation, devaluation; cancellation.
ent'wickeln v/t. (no -ge-, h) develop (a. phot.); evolve; sich ~ develop.
Entwicklung [ɛnt'viklʊŋ] f (-/-en) development; evolution; ~**shilfe** f development aid.
ent|'wirren v/t. (no -ge-, h) disentangle, unravel; ~'**wischen** v/i. (no -ge-, sein) slip away, escape (j-m [from] s.o.; aus from); j-m ~ give s.o. the slip; ~**wöhnen** [~'vøːnən] v/t. (no -ge-, h) wean.
Ent'wurf m sketch; design; plan; draft.
ent|'wurzeln v/t. (no -ge-, h) uproot; ~'**ziehen** v/t. (irr. ziehen, no -ge-, h) deprive (j-m et. s.o. of s.th.); withdraw (dat. from); sich ~ avoid, elude; evade (responsibility); ~'**ziffern** v/t. (no -ge-, h) decipher, make out; tel. decode.
ent'zücken 1. v/t. (no -ge-, h) charm, delight; 2. ⚥ n (-s/no pl.) delight, rapture(s pl.), transport(s pl.). [ing.]
ent'zückend adj. delightful; charm-⌐
Ent'zug m (-[e]s/no pl.) withdrawal; cancellation (of licence); deprivation.

entzünd|bar adj. [ɛnt'tsʏntbaːr] (in)flammable; ~**en** v/t. (no -ge-, h) inflame (a. 🎗), kindle; sich ~ catch fire; 🎗 become inflamed; ⚥**ung** 🎗 f inflammation.
ent'zwei adv. asunder, in two, to pieces; ~**en** v/t. (no -ge-, h) disunite, set at variance; sich ~ quarrel, fall out (both: mit with); ~**gehen** v/i. (irr. gehen, sep., -ge-, sein) break, go to pieces; ⚥**ung** f (-/-en) disunion.
Enzian ⚘ ['ɛntsjaːn] m (-s/-e) gentian.
Enzyklopädie [ɛntsyklopɛ'diː] f (-/-n) (en)cyclop(a)edia.
Epidemie 🎗 [epide'miː] f (-/-n) epidemic (disease).
Epilog [epi'loːk] m (-s/-e) epilog(ue).
episch adj. ['eːpiʃ] epic.
Episode [epi'zoːdə] f (-/-n) episode.
Epoche [e'pɔxə] f (-/-n) epoch.
Epos ['eːpɔs] n (-/Epen) epic (poem).
er pers. pron. [eːr] he.
erachten [ɛr'-] 1. v/t. (no -ge-, h) consider, think, deem; 2. ⚥ n (-s/no pl.) opinion; m-s ~s in my opinion.
erbarmen [ɛr'barmən] 1. v/refl. (gen.) (no -ge-, h) pity or commiserate s.o.; 2. ⚥ n (-s/no pl.) pity, compassion, commiseration; mercy; ~**swert** adj. pitiable.
erbärmlich adj. [ɛr'bɛrmliç] pitiful, pitiable; miserable; behaviour: mean.
er'barmungslos adj. pitiless, merciless, relentless.
er'bau|en v/t. (no -ge-, h) build (up), construct; raise; fig. edify; ⚥**er** m (-s/-) builder; constructor; ~**lich** adj. edifying; ⚥**ung** fig. f (-/-en) edification, Am. uplift.
Erbe ['ɛrbə] 1. m (-n/-n) heir; 2. n (-s/no pl.) inheritance, heritage.
er'beben v/i. (no -ge-, sein) tremble, shake, quake.
'erben v/t. (ge-, h) inherit.
er'beuten v/t. (no -ge-, h) capture.
er'bieten v/refl. (irr. bieten, no -ge-, h) offer, volunteer.
'Erbin f (-/-nen) heiress.
er'bitten v/t. (irr. bitten, no -ge-, h) beg or ask for, request, solicit.
er'bitter|n v/t. (no -ge-, h) embitter, exasperate; ⚥**ung** f (-/🔾 -en) bitterness, exasperation.
Erbkrankheit 🎗 ['ɛrp-] f hereditary disease.

erblassen [ɛr'blasən] v/i. (no -ge-, sein) grow or turn pale, lose colo(u)r.

Erblasser ♂ ['ɛrblasər] m (-s/-) testator; **~in** f (-/-nen) testatrix.

er'bleichen v/i. (no -ge-, sein) s. erblassen.

erblich adj. ['ɛrpliç] hereditary; **Ωkeit** physiol. f (-/no pl.) heredity.

er'blicken v/t. (no -ge-, h) perceive, see; catch sight of.

erblinden [ɛr'blindən] v/i. (no -ge-, sein) grow blind; **Ωung** f (-/-en) loss of sight.

er'brechen 1. v/t. (irr. brechen, no -ge-, h) break or force open; vomit; sich ~ ♂ vomit; **2.** ♀ n (-s/no pl.) vomiting.

Erbschaft ['ɛrpʃaft] f (-/-en) inheritance, heritage.

Erbse ♀ ['ɛrpsə] f (-/-n) pea; **~n-brei** m pease-pudding, Am. pea purée; **~nsuppe** f pea-soup.

Erb|stück ['ɛrp-] n heirloom; **~sünde** f original sin; **~teil** n (portion of an) inheritance.

Erd|arbeiter ['ɛrt-] m digger, navvy; **~ball** m globe; **~beben** n (-s/-) earthquake; **~beere** ♀ f strawberry; **~boden** m earth; ground, soil; **~e** ['ɛːrdə] f (-/♂ -n) earth; ground; soil; world; **Ωen** ♂ v/t. (ge-, h) earth, ground.

er'denklich adj. imaginable.

Erdgeschoß [ɛːrt-] n ground-floor, Am. first floor.

er'dichten v/t. (no -ge-, h) invent, feign; **~et** adj. fictitious.

erdig adj. ['ɛːrdiç] earthy.

Erd|karte ['ɛːrt-] f map of the earth; **~kreis** m earth, world; **~kugel** f globe; **~kunde** f geography; **~leitung** f earth-connexion, earth-wire, Am. ground wire; **~nuß** f peanut; **~öl** n mineral oil, petroleum.

er'dolchen v/t. (no -ge-, h) stab (with a dagger).

Erdreich ['ɛːrt-] n ground, earth.

er'dreisten v/refl. (no -ge-, h) dare, presume.

er'drosseln v/t. (no -ge-, h) strangle, throttle.

er'drücken v/t. (no -ge-, h) squeeze or crush to death; **~d** fig. adj. overwhelming.

Erd|rutsch ['ɛːrt-] m landslip; landslide (a. pol.); **~schicht** f layer of earth, stratum; **~teil** m

part of the world; geogr. continent.

er'dulden v/t. (no -ge-, h) suffer, endure.

er'eifern v/refl. (no -ge-, h) get excited, fly into a passion.

er'eignen v/refl. (no -ge-, h) happen, come to pass, occur.

Ereignis [ɛr'aiknis] n (-ses/-se) event, occurrence; **Ωreich** adj. eventful.

Eremit [ere'miːt] m (-en/-en) hermit, anchorite.

ererbt adj. [ɛr'ɛrpt] inherited.

er'fahr|en 1. v/t. (irr. fahren, no -ge-, h) learn; hear; experience; **2.** adj. experienced, expert, skil(l)-ful; **Ωung** f (-/-en) experience; practice; skill.

er'fassen v/t. (no -ge-, h) grasp (a. fig.), seize, catch; cover; register; record.

er'find|en v/t. (irr. finden, no -ge-, h) invent; **Ωer** m inventor; **~erisch** adj. inventive; **Ωung** f (-/-en) invention.

Erfolg [ɛr'fɔlk] m (-[e]s/-e) success; result; **Ωen** [~gən] v/i. (no -ge-, sein) ensue, follow; happen; **Ωlos** adj. [~k-] unsuccessful; vain; **Ωreich** adj. [~k-] successful.

er'forder|lich adj. necessary, required; **~n** v/t. (no -ge-, h) require, demand; **Ωnis** n (-ses/-se) requirement, demand, exigence, exigency.

er'forsch|en v/t. (no -ge-, h) inquire into, investigate; explore (country); **Ωer** m investigator; explorer; **Ωung** f investigation; exploration.

er'freu|en v/t. (no -ge-, h) please; delight; gratify; rejoice; sich e-r Sache ~ enjoy s.th.; **~lich** adj. delightful, pleasing, pleasant, gratifying.

er'frier|en v/i. (irr. frieren, no -ge-, sein) freeze to death; **Ωung** f (-/-en) frost-bite.

er'frisch|en v/t. (no -ge-, h) refresh; **Ωung** f (-/-en) refreshment.

er'froren adj. limb: frost-bitten.

er'füll|en v/t. (no -ge-, h) fill; fig. fulfil(l); perform (mission); comply with (s.o.'s wishes); meet (requirements); **Ωung** f fulfil(l)ment; performance; compliance; **Ωungsort** ♱, ♫ [ɛr'fyluŋs²-] m place of performance (of contract).

ergänz|en [ɛr'gɛntsən] v/t. (no -ge-,

h) complete, complement; supplement; replenish (*stores, etc.*); **~end** *adj.* complementary, supplementary; **2ung** *f* (-/-*en*) completion; supplement; replenishment; *gr.* complement; **2ungsband** *m* (-[*e*]*s*/*⁔e*) supplementary volume.

er'geben 1. *v/t.* (*irr.* geben, *no* -ge-, *h*) yield, give; prove; *sich* ~ surrender; difficulties: arise; devote o.s. to *s.th.*; *sich* ~ *aus* result from; *sich* ~ *in* (*acc.*) resign o.s. to; **2.** *adj.* devoted (*dat.* to); **~st** *adv.* respectfully; **2heit** *f* (-/*no pl.*) devotion.

Ergeb|nis [ɛr'ge:pnis] *n* (-ses/-se) result, outcome; *sports:* score; **~ung** [~bʊŋ] *f* (-/-*en*) resignation; ✕ surrender.

er'gehen *v/i.* (*irr.* gehen, *no* -ge-, *sein*) be issued; ~ *lassen* issue, publish; *über sich* ~ *lassen* suffer, submit to; *wie ist es ihm ergangen?* how did he come off?; *sich* ~ *in* (*dat.*) indulge in. [rich.]

ergiebig *adj.* [ɛr'gi:biç] productive.⟩

er'gießen *v/refl.* (*irr.* gießen, *no* -ge-, *h*) flow (*in acc.* into; *über acc.* over).

er'götz|en 1. *v/t.* (*no* -ge-, *h*) delight; *sich* ~ *an* (*dat.*) delight in; **2.** **2** *n* (-s/*no pl.*) delight; **~lich** *adj.* delightful.

er'greif|en *v/t.* (*irr.* greifen, *no* -ge-, *h*) seize; grasp; take (*possession, s.o.'s part, measures, etc.*); take to (*flight*); take up (*profession, pen, arms*); *fig.* move, affect, touch; **2ung** *f* (-/✕ -*en*) seizure.

Er'griffenheit *f* (-/*no pl.*) emotion.

er'gründen *v/t.* (*no* -ge-, *h*) fathom; *fig.* penetrate, get to the bottom of.

Er'guß *m* outpouring; effusion.

er'haben *adj.* elevated; *fig.* exalted, sublime; ~ *sein über* (*acc.*) be above; **2heit** *f* (-/✕ -*en*) elevation; *fig.* sublimity.

er'halt|en 1. *v/t.* (*irr.* halten, *no* -ge-, *h*) get; obtain; receive; preserve, keep; support, maintain; *sich* ~ *von* subsist on; **2.** *adj.:* gut ~ in good repair *or* condition; **2ung** *f* preservation; maintenance. [able.]

erhältlich *adj.* [ɛr'hɛltliç] obtain-⟩

er'hängen *v/t.* (*no* -ge-, *h*) hang; **~härten** *v/t.* (*no* -ge-, *h*) harden; *fig.* confirm; **~haschen** *v/t.* (*no* -ge-, *h*) snatch, catch.

er'heben *v/t.* (*irr.* heben, *no* -ge-, *h*)

lift, raise; elevate; exalt; levy, raise, collect (*taxes, etc.*); *Klage* ~ bring an action; *sich* ~ rise; *question, etc.:* arise; **~end** *fig. adj.* elevating; **~lich** *adj.* [~p-] considerable; **2ung** [~bʊŋ] *f* (-/-*en*) elevation; levy (*of taxes*); revolt; rising ground.

er'heiter|n *v/t.* (*no* -ge-, *h*) cheer up, amuse; **~'hellen** *v/t.* (*no* -ge-, *h*) light up; *fig.* clear up; **~'hitzen** *v/t.* (*no* -ge-, *h*) heat; *sich* ~ get *or* grow hot; **~'hoffen** *v/t.* (*no* -ge-, *h*) hope for.

er'höh|en *v/t.* (*no* -ge-, *h*) raise; increase; **2ung** *f* (-/-*en*) elevation; rise (*in prices, wages*); advance (*in prices*); increase.

er'hol|en *v/refl.* (*no* -ge-, *h*) recover; (take *a*) rest, relax; **2ung** *f* (-/-*en*) recovery; recreation; relaxation; **2ungsurlaub** [ɛr'ho:lʊŋs⁹-] *m* holiday, *Am.* vacation; recreation leave; ✗ convalescent leave, sick-leave.   [(*request*).]

er'hören *v/t.* (*no* -ge-, *h*) hear; grant⟩

erinner|n [ɛr'inərn] *v/t.* (*no* -ge-, *h*): *j-n* ~ *an* (*acc.*) remind s.o. of; *sich* ~ (*gen.*), *sich* ~ *an* (*acc.*) remember s.o. *or* s.th., recollect *s.th.*; **2ung** *f* (-/-*en*) remembrance; recollection; reminder; **~en** *pl.* reminiscences *pl.*

er'kalten *v/i.* (*no* -ge-, *sein*) cool down (*a. fig.*), get cold.

er'kält|en *v/refl.* (*no* -ge-, *h*): *sich* (*sehr*) ~ catch (a bad) cold; **2ung** *f* (-/-*en*) cold.

er'kennen *v/t.* (*irr.* kennen, *no* -ge-, *h*) recognize (*an dat.* by); perceive, discern; realize.

er'kenntlich *adj.* perceptible; *sich* ~ *zeigen* show one's appreciation; **2keit** *f* (-/-*en*) gratitude; appreciation.

Er'kenntnis 1. *f* perception; realization. **2.** ⚖ *n* (-ses/-se) decision, sentence, finding.

Erker ['ɛrkər] *m* (-s/-) bay; '**~fenster** *n* bay-window.

er'klär|en *v/t.* (*no* -ge-, *h*) explain; account for; declare, state; *sich* ~ declare (*für* for; *gegen* against); **~lich** *adj.* explainable, explicable; **~t** *adj.* professed, declared; **2ung** *f* explanation; declaration.

er'klingen *v/i.* (*irr.* klingen, *no* -ge-, *sein*) (re)sound, ring (out).

erkoren *adj.* [ɛr'ko:rən] (s)elect, chosen.

E

er'krank|en v/i. (no -ge-, sein) fall ill, be taken ill (an dat. of, with); become affected; 2ung f (-/-en) illness, sickness, falling ill.

er|'kühnen v/refl. (no -ge-, h) venture, presume, make bold (zu inf. to inf.); ~'kunden v/t. (no -ge-, h) explore; ⚔ reconnoit|re, Am. -er.

erkundig|en [ɛr'kundigən] v/refl. (no -ge-, h) inquire (über acc. after; nach after or for s.o.; about s.th.); 2ung f (-/-en) inquiry.

er|'lahmen fig. v/i. (no -ge-, sein) grow weary, tire; slacken; interest: wane, flag; ~'langen v/t. (no -ge-, h) obtain, get.

Er|laß [ɛr'las] m (Erlasses/Erlasse) dispensation, exemption; remission (of debt, penalty, etc.); edict, decree; 2'lassen v/t. (irr. lassen, no -ge-, h) remit (debt, penalty, etc.); dispense (j-m et. s.o. from s.th.); issue (decree); enact (law).

erlauben [ɛr'laubən] v/t. (no -ge-, h) allow, permit; sich et. ~ indulge in s.th.; sich ~ zu inf. ~ beg to inf. Erlaubnis [ɛr'laupnis] f (-/no pl.) permission; authority; ~schein m permit.

er|'läuter|n v/t. (no -ge-, h) explain, illustrate; comment (up)on; 2ung f explanation, illustration; comment. Erle ⚘ ['ɛrlə] f (-/-n) alder.

er'leb|en v/t. (no -ge-, h) (live to) see; experience; go through; 2nis [~pnis] n (-ses/-se) experience; adventure.

erledig|en [ɛr'le:digən] v/t. (no -ge-, h) dispatch; execute; settle (matter); ~t adj. [~çt] finished, settled; fig.: played out; F done for; F: du bist für mich ~ I am through with you; 2ung [~gun] f (-/~ -en) dispatch; settlement.

er|'leichter|n v/t. (no -ge-, h) lighten (burden); fig.: make easy, facilitate; relieve; 2ung f (-/-en) ease; relief; facilitation; ~en pl. facilities pl.

er|'leiden v/t. (irr. leiden, no -ge-, h) suffer, endure; sustain (damage, loss); ~'lernen v/t. (no -ge-, h) learn, acquire.

er'leucht|en v/t. (no -ge-, h) illuminate; fig. enlighten; 2ung f (-/-en) illumination; fig. enlightenment.

er'liegen v/i. (irr. liegen, no -ge-, sein) succumb (dat. to).   [true.]

erlogen adj. [ɛr'lo:gən] false, un-

Erlös [ɛr'lø:s] m (-es/-e) proceeds pl. erlosch [ɛr'lɔʃ] pret. of erlöschen; ~en 1. p.p. of erlöschen; 2. adj. extinct.

er'löschen v/i. (irr., no -ge-, sein) go out; fig. become extinct; contract: expire.

er'lös|en v/t. (no -ge-, h) redeem; deliver; 2er m (-s/-) redeemer, deliverer; eccl. Redeemer, Saviour; 2ung f redemption; deliverance.

ermächtig|en [ɛr'mɛçtigən] v/t. (no -ge-, h) authorize; 2ung f (-/-en) authorization; authority; warrant.

er'mahn|en v/t. (no -ge-, h) admonish; 2ung f admonition.

er'mangel|n v/i. (no -ge-, h) be wanting (gen. in); 2ung f (-/no pl.): in ~ (gen.) in default of, for want of, failing.

er'mäßig|en v/t. (no -ge-, h) abate, reduce, cut (down); 2ung f (-/-en) abatement, reduction.

er'matt|en 1. v/t. (no -ge-, h) fatigue, tire, exhaust; 2. v/i. (sein) tire, grow weary; fig. slacken; 2ung f (-/~ -en) fatigue, exhaustion.

er'messen 1. v/t. (irr. messen, no -ge-, h) judge; 2. 2 n (-s/no pl.) judg(e)ment; discretion.

er'mitt|eln v/t. (no -ge-, h) ascertain, find out; ⚖ investigate; 2(e)lung [~(ə)lun] f (-/-en) ascertainment; inquiry; ⚖ investigation.

er'möglichen v/t. (no -ge-, h) render or make possible.

er'mord|en v/t. (no -ge-, h) murder; assassinate; 2ung f (-/-en) murder; assassination.

er'müd|en (no -ge-) 1. v/t. (h) tire, fatigue; 2. v/i. (sein) tire, get tired or fatigued; 2ung f (-/~ -en) fatigue, tiredness.

er'munter|n v/t. (no -ge-, h) rouse, encourage; animate; 2ung f (-/-en) encouragement, animation.

ermutig|en [ɛr'mu:tigən] v/t. (no -ge-, h) encourage; 2ung f (-/-en) encouragement.

er'nähr|en v/t. (no -ge-, h) nourish, feed; support; 2er m (-s/-) breadwinner, supporter; 2ung f (-/~ -en) nourishment; support; physiol. nutrition.

er'nenn|en v/t. (irr. nennen, no -ge-, h) nominate, appoint; 2ung f nomination, appointment.

er'neu|ern v/t. (no -ge-, h) renew,

renovate; revive; **2erung** f renewal, renovation; revival; **~t** adv. once more.

erniedrig|en [ɛr'niːdrigən] v/t. (no -ge-, h) degrade; humiliate, humble; **2ung** f (-/-en) degradation; humiliation.

Ernst [ɛrnst] **1.** m (-es/no pl.) seriousness; earnest(ness); gravity; im ~ in earnest; **2. 2** adj. = **'2haft** adj., **'2lich** adj. serious, earnest; grave.

Ernte ['ɛrntə] f (-/-n) harvest; crop; **~'dankfest** n harvest festival; **'2n** v/t. (ge-, h) harvest, gather (in), reap (a. fig.).

er'nüchter|n v/t. (no -ge-, h) (make) sober; fig. disillusion; **2ung** f (-/-en) sobering; fig. disillusionment.

Er'ober|er m (-s/-) conqueror; **2n** v/t. (no -ge-, h) conquer; **~ung** f (-/-en) conquest.

er'öffn|en v/t. (no -ge-, h) open; inaugurate; disclose (j-m et. s.th. to s.o.); notify; **2ung** f opening; inauguration; disclosure.

erörter|n [ɛr'œrtərn] v/t. (no -ge-, h) discuss; **2ung** f (-/-en) discussion.

Erpel orn. ['ɛrpəl] m (-s/-) drake.

erpicht adj. [ɛr'piçt]: ~ auf (acc.) bent or intent or set or keen on.

er'press|en v/t. (no -ge-, h) extort (von from); blackmail; **2er** m (-s/-), **2erin** f (-/-nen) extort(ion)er; blackmailer; **2ung** f (-/-en) extortion; blackmail.

er'proben v/t. (no -ge-, h) try, test.

erquick|en [ɛr'kvikən] v/t. (no -ge-, h) refresh; **2ung** f (-/-en) refreshment.

er|'raten v/t. (irr. raten, no -ge-, h) guess, find out; **~'rechnen** v/t. (no -ge-, h) calculate, compute, work out.

erreg|bar adj. [ɛr'reːkbaːr] excitable; **~en** [~gən] v/t. (no -ge-, h) excite; cause; **2er** m (-s/-) exciter (a. *♪*); *♪* germ, virus; **2ung** [~guŋ] f excitation; excitement.

er'reich|bar adj. attainable; within reach or call; **~en** v/t. (no -ge-, h) reach; fig. achieve, attain; catch (train); come up to (certain standard).

er'rett|en v/t. (no -ge-, h) rescue; **2ung** f rescue.

er'richt|en v/t. (no -ge-, h) set up, erect; establish; **2ung** f erection; establishment.

er|'ringen v/t. (irr. ringen, no -ge-, h) gain, obtain; achieve (success); **~'röten** v/i. (no -ge-, sein) blush.

Errungenschaft [ɛr'ruŋənʃaft] f (-/-en) acquisition; achievement.

Er'satz m (-es/no pl.) replacement; substitute; compensation, amends sg., damages pl.; indemnification; s. Ersatzmann, Ersatzmittel; ~ leisten make amends; **~mann** m substitute; **~mine** f refill (for pencil); **~mittel** n substitute, surrogate; **~reifen** mot. m spare tyre, (Am. only) spare tire; **~teil** ⊕ n, m spare (part).

er|'schaffen v/t. (irr. schaffen, no -ge-, h) create; **2ung** f (-/no pl.) creation.

er|'schallen v/i. ([irr. schallen,] no -ge-, sein) (re)sound; ring.

er|'scheinen 1. v/i. (irr. scheinen, no -ge-, sein) appear; **2. 2** n (-s/no pl.) appearance; **2ung** f (-/-en) appearance; apparition; vision.

er|'schießen v/t. (irr. schießen, no -ge-, h) shoot (dead); **~'schlaffen** v/i. (no -ge-, sein) tire; relax; fig. languish, slacken; **~'schlagen** v/t. (irr. schlagen, no -ge-, h) kill, slay; **~'schließen** v/t. (irr. schließen, no -ge-, h) open; open up (new market); develop (district).

er'schöpf|en v/t. (no -ge-, h) exhaust; **2ung** f exhaustion.

erschrak [ɛr'ʃraːk] prét. of erschrecken 2.

er'schreck|en 1. v/t. (no -ge-, h) frighten, scare; **2.** v/i. (irr., no -ge-, sein) be frightened (über acc. at); **~d** adj. alarming, startling.

erschrocken [ɛr'ʃrɔkən] **1.** p.p. of erschrecken 2; **2.** adj. frightened, terrified.

er'schütter|n [ɛr'ʃytərn] v/t. (no -ge-, h) shake; fig. shock, move; **2ung** f (-/-en) shock; fig. emotion; *♪* concussion; ⊕ percussion.

er'schweren v/t. (no -ge-, h) make more difficult; aggravate.

er'schwing|en v/t. (irr. schwingen, no -ge-, h) afford; **~lich** adj. within s.o.'s means; prices: reasonable.

er|'sehen v/t. (irr. sehen, no -ge-, h) see, learn, gather (all: aus from); **~'sehnen** v/t. (no -ge-, h) long for; **~'setzen** v/t. (no -ge-, h) repair; make up for, compensate (for); replace; refund.

er'sichtlich adj. evident, obvious.

er'sinnen v/t. (irr. sinnen, no -ge-, h) contrive, devise.

er'spar|en v/t. (no -ge-, h) save; j-m et. ~ spare s.o. s.th.; **2nis** f (-/-se) saving.

er'sprießlich adj. useful, beneficial.

erst [e:rst] **1.** adj.: der (die, das) ~e the first; **2.** adv. first; at first; only; not ... till or until.

er'starr|en v/i. (no -ge-, sein) stiffen; solidify; congeal; set; grow numb; fig. blood: run cold; ~t adj. benumbed; **2ung** f (-/-en) numbness; solidification; congealment; setting.

erstatt|en [ɛr'ʃtatən] v/t. (no -ge-, h) restore; s. ersetzen; Bericht ~ (make a) report; **2ung** f (-/-en) restitution.

'Erstaufführung f thea. first night or performance, premiere; film: a. first run.

er'staun|en 1. v/i. (no -ge-, sein) be astonished (über acc. at); **2.** v/t. (no -ge-, h) astonish; **3.** 2 n astonishment; in ~ setzen astonish; ~lich adj. astonishing, amazing.

er'stechen v/t. (irr. stechen, no -ge-, h) stab.

er'steig|en v/t. (irr. steigen, no -ge-, h) ascend, climb; **2ung** f ascent.

erstens adv. ['e:rstəns] first, firstly.

er'stick|en (no -ge-) v/t. (h) and v/i. (sein) choke, suffocate; stifle; **2ung** f (-/-en) suffocation. [rate, F A 1.]

'erstklassig adj. first-class, first-}

er'streben v/t. (no -ge-, h) strive after or for; ~swert adj. desirable.

er'strecken v/refl. (no -ge-, h) extend; sich ~ über (acc.) cover.

er'suchen 1. v/t. (no -ge-, h) request; **2.** 2 n (-s/-) request.

er'|tappen v/t. (no -ge-, h) catch, surprise; s. frisch; ~'tönen v/i. (no -ge-, sein) (re)sound.

Ertrag [ɛr'tra:k] m (-[e]s/¨e) produce, yield; proceeds pl., returns pl.; ✗ output; **2en** [~gən] v/t. (irr. tragen, no -ge-, h) bear, endure; suffer; stand. [able.]

erträglich adj. [ɛr'trɛ:klɪç] toler-}

er'|tränken v/t. (no -ge-, h) drown; ~'trinken v/i. (irr. trinken, no -ge-, sein) be drowned, drown; ~'übrigen [ɛr'ʔy:brɪgən] v/t. (no -ge-, h) save; spare (time); sich ~ be unnecessary; ~'wachen v/i. (no -ge-, sein) awake, wake up.

er'wachsen 1. v/i. (irr. wachsen, no -ge-, sein) arise (aus from); **2.** adj. grown-up, adult; **2e** m, f (-n/-n) grown-up, adult.

er'wäg|en v/t. (irr. wägen, no -ge-, h) consider, think s.th. over; **2ung** f (-/-en) consideration.

er'wähl|en v/t. (no -ge-, h) choose, elect.

er'wähn|en v/t. (no -ge-, h) mention; **2ung** f (-/-en) mention.

er'wärmen v/t. (no -ge-, h) warm, heat; sich ~ warm (up).

er'wart|en v/t. (no -ge-, h) await, wait for; fig. expect; **2ung** f expectation.

er'|wecken v/t. (no -ge-, h) wake, rouse; fig. awake; cause (fear); arouse (suspicion); ~'wehren v/refl. (gen.) (no -ge-, h) keep or ward off; ~'weichen v/t. (no -ge-, h) soften; fig. move; ~'weisen v/t. (irr. weisen, no -ge-, h) prove; show (respect); render (service); do, pay (honour); do (favour).

er'weiter|n v/t. and v/refl. (no -ge-, h) expand, enlarge, extend, widen; **2ung** f (-/-en) expansion, enlargement, extension.

Erwerb [ɛr'vɛrp] m (-[e]s/-e) acquisition; living; earnings pl.; business; **2en** [~bən] v/t. (irr. werben, no -ge-, h) acquire; gain; earn.

erwerbs|los adj. [ɛr'vɛrpslo:s] unemployed; ~tätig adj. (gainfully) employed; ~unfähig adj. [ɛr-'vɛrps'ʔ-] incapable of earning one's living; **2zweig** m line of business.

Erwerbung [ɛr'vɛrbuŋ] f acquisition.

er'wider|n [ɛr'vi:dərn] v/t. (no -ge-, h) return; answer, reply; retort; **2ung** f (-/-en) return; answer, reply.

er'wischen v/t. (no -ge-, h) catch, trap, get hold of.

er'wünscht adj. desired; desirable; welcome.

er'würgen v/t. (no -ge-, h) strangle, throttle. [brass.]

Erz ✗ [e:rts] n (-es/-e) ore; poet.}

er'zähl|en v/t. (no -ge-, h) tell; relate; narrate; **2er** m, **2erin** f (-/-nen) narrator; writer; **2ung** f narration; (short) story, narrative.

'Erz|bischof eccl. m archbishop; ~bistum eccl. n archbishopric; ~engel eccl. m archangel.

er'zeug|en v/t. (no -ge-, h) beget; produce; make, manufacture; **2er** m (-s/-) father (of child); ✝ producer; **2nis** n produce; production; ⊕ product; **2ung** f production.

'Erz|feind m arch-enemy; **'~herzog** m archduke; **'~herzogin** f archduchess; **'~herzogtum** n archduchy.

er'ziehe|n v/t. (irr. ziehen, no -ge-, h) bring up, rear, raise; educate; **2r** m (-s/-) educator; teacher, tutor; **2rin** f (-/-nen) teacher; governess; **~risch** adj. educational, pedagogic (-al).

Er'ziehung f (-/✎ -en) upbringing; breeding; education; **~sanstalt** [ɛr'tsiː:ʊŋs⁹-] f reformatory, approved school; **~swesen** n (-s/no pl.) educational matters pl. or system.

er|'zielen v/t. (no -ge-, h) obtain; realize (price); achieve (success); sports: score (points, goal); **~'zürnen** v/t. (no -ge-, h) make angry, irritate, enrage; **~'zwingen** v/t. (irr. zwingen, no -ge-, h) (en)force; compel; extort (von from).

es pers. pron. [ɛs] **1.** pers.: it, he, she; wo ist das Buch? — ~ ist auf dem Tisch where is the book? — it is on the table; das Mädchen blieb stehen, als ~ seine Mutter sah the girl stopped when she saw her mother; **2.** impers.: it; ~ gibt there is, there are; ~ ist kalt it is cold; ~ klopft there is a knock at the door.

Esche ♀ ['ɛʃə] f (-/-n) ash(-tree).

Esel zo. ['eːzəl] m (-s/-) donkey; esp. fig. ass; **~ei** [~'laı] f (-/-en) stupidity, stupid thing, folly; **'~s-brücke** f at school: crib, Am. pony; **~sohr** ['eːzəls⁹-] n dog's ear (of book).

Eskorte [ɛs'kɔrtə] f (-/-n) ✕ escort; ♣ convoy.

Espe ♀ ['ɛspə] f (-/-n) asp(en). **'eßbar** adj. eatable, edible.

Esse ['ɛsə] f (-/-n) chimney.

essen ['ɛsən] **1.** v/i. (irr. essen, ge-, h) eat; zu Mittag ~ (have) lunch; dine, have dinner; zu Abend ~ dine, have dinner; esp. late at night: sup, have supper; auswärts ~ eat or dine out; **2.** v/t. (irr. essen, ge-, h) eat; et. zu Mittag etc. ~ have s.th. for lunch, etc.; **3.** 2 n (-s/-) eating; food; meal; dish; midday meal: lunch, dinner; evening meal: dinner; last meal of the day:

supper; **'2zeit** f lunch-time; dinner-time; supper-time.

Essenz [ɛ'sɛnts] f (-/-en) essence.

Essig ['ɛsɪç] m (-s/-e) vinegar; **'~gurke** f pickled cucumber, gherkin.

'Eß|löffel m soup-spoon; **'~nische** f dining alcove, Am. dinette; **'~tisch** m dining-table; **'~waren** f/pl. eatables pl., victuals pl., food; **'~zim-mer** n dining-room.

etablieren [eta'bliː:rən] v/t. (no -ge-, h) establish, set up.

Etage [e'taː:ʒə] f (-/-n) floor, stor(e)y; **~nwohnung** f flat, Am. a. apartment.

Etappe [e'tapə] f (-/-n) ✕ base; fig. stage, leg.

Etat [e'taː:] m (-s/-s) budget, parl. the Estimates pl.; **~sjahr** n fiscal year. [or sg.]

Ethik ['eː:tik] f (-/✎ -en) ethics pl.]

Etikett [eti'kɛt] n (-[e]s/-e, -s) label, ticket; tag; gummed: Am. a. sticker; **~e** f (-/-n) etiquette; **2ieren** [~'tiː:rən] v/t. (no -ge-, h) label.

etliche indef. pron. ['ɛtlɪçə] some, several.

Etui [e'tviː] n (-s/-s) case.

etwa adv. ['ɛtva] perhaps, by chance; about, Am. a. around; **~ig** adj. ['~⁹ɪç] possible, eventual.

etwas ['ɛtvas] **1.** indef. pron. something; anything; **2.** adj. some; any; **3.** adv. somewhat; **4.** 2 n (-/-): das gewisse ~ that certain something.

euch pers. pron. [ɔʏç] you; ~ (selbst) yourselves.

euer poss. pron. ['ɔʏər] your; der (die, das) eu(e)re yours.

Eule orn. ['ɔʏlə] f (-/-n) owl; **~n nach Athen tragen** carry coals to Newcastle.

euresgleichen pron. ['ɔʏrəs'glaıçən] people like you, F the likes of you.

Europä|er [ɔʏro'pɛː:ər] m (-s/-) European; **2isch** adj. European.

Euter ['ɔʏtər] n (-s/-) udder.

evakuieren [evaku'iː:rən] v/t. (no -ge-, h) evacuate.

evangeli|sch adj. [evaŋ'geːlɪʃ] evangelic(al); Protestant; Lutheran; **2um** ['~jum] n (-s/Evangelien) gospel.

eventuell [eventu'ɛl] **1.** adj. possible; **2.** adv. possibly, perhaps.

ewig adj. ['eː:vɪç] eternal; everlasting; perpetual; auf ~ for ever;

'2**keit** f (-/-en) eternity; F: *seit e-r* ~ for ages.

exakt adj. [ε'ksakt] exact; '2**heit** f (-/-en) exactitude, exactness; accuracy.

Exam|en [ε'ksɑːmən] n (-s/-, Examina) examination, F exam; 2**inieren** [ˌami'niːrən] v/t. (no -ge-, h) examine.

Exekutive [εksəkuˈtiːvə] f (-/no pl.) executive power.

Exempel [ε'ksεmpəl] n (-s/-) example, instance.

Exemplar [εksεmˈplɑːr] n (-s/-e) specimen; copy (of book).

exerzier|en ✕ [εksεr'tsiːrən] v/i. and v/t. (no -ge-, h) drill; 2**platz** ✕ m drill-ground, parade-ground.

Exil [ε'ksiːl] n (-s/-e) exile.

Existenz [εksis'tεnts] f (-/-en) existence; living, livelihood; ~**minimum** n subsistence minimum.

exis'tieren v/i. (no -ge-, h) exist; subsist.

exotisch adj. [ε'ksoːtiʃ] exotic.

exped|ieren [εkspeˈdiːrən] v/t. (no -ge-, h) dispatch; 2**ition** [ˌiˈtsjoːn] f (-/-en) dispatch, forwarding; expedition; ✝ dispatch or forwarding office.

Experiment [εksperiˈmεnt] n (-[e]s/-e) experiment; 2**ieren** [ˌˈtiːrən] v/i. (no -ge-, h) experiment.

explo|dieren [εksploˈdiːrən] v/i. (no -ge-, sein) explode, burst; 2**sion** [ˌˈzjoːn] f (-/-en) explosion; ~**siv** adj. [ˌˈziːf] explosive.

Export [εks'pɔrt] m (-[e]s/-e) export(ation); 2**ieren** [ˌˈtiːrən] v/t. (no -ge-, h) export.

extra adj. ['εkstra] extra; special; '2**blatt** n extra edition (of newspaper), Am. extra. [tract.]

Extrakt [εks'trakt] m (-[e]s/-e) ex-]

Extrem [εks'treːm] **1.** n (-s/-e) extreme; **2.** 2 adj. extreme.

Exzellenz [εkstsε'lεnts] f (-/-en) Excellency.

exzentrisch adj. [εks'tsεntriʃ] eccentric.

Exzeß [εks'tsεs] m (Exzesses/Exzesse) excess.

F

Fabel ['fɑːbəl] f (-/-n) fable (a. fig.); plot (of story, book, etc.); '2**haft** adj. fabulous; marvellous; '2**n** v/i. (ge-, h) tell (tall) stories.

Fabrik [fa'briːk] f (-/-en) factory, works sg., pl., mill; ~**ant** [ˌi'kant] m (-en/-en) factory-owner, mill-owner; manufacturer; ~**arbeit** f factory work; s. Fabrikware; ~**arbeiter** m factory worker or hand; ~**at** [ˌi'kaːt] n (-[e]s/-e) make; product; ~**ationsfehler** [ˌa'tsjoːns-] m flaw; ~**besitzer** m factory-owner; ~**marke** f trade mark; ~**stadt** f factory or industrial town; ~**ware** f manufactured article; ~**zeichen** n s. Fabrikmarke.

Fach [fax] n (-[e]s/ⁿer) section, compartment, shelf (of bookcase, cupboard, etc.); pigeon-hole (in desk); drawer; fig. subject; s. Fachgebiet; '~**arbeiter** m skilled worker; '~**arzt** m specialist (für in); '~**ausbildung** f professional training; '~**ausdruck** m technical term.

fächeln ['fεçəln] v/t. (ge-, h) fan s.o.

Fächer ['fεçər] m (-s/-) fan; 2**förmig** adj. ['ˌfœrmiç] fan-shaped.

'**Fach|gebiet** n branch, field, province; '~**kenntnisse** f/pl. specialized knowledge; '~**kreis** m: in ~en among experts; '2**kundig** adj. competent, expert; '~**literatur** f specialized literature; '~**mann** m expert; 2**männisch** adj. ['ˌmεniʃ] expert; '~**schule** f technical school; '~**werk** △ n framework.

Fackel ['fakəl] f (-/-n) torch; '2**n** F v/i. (ge-, h) hesitate, F shilly-shally; '~**zug** m torchlight procession.

fad adj. [faːt], ~**e** adj. ['fɑːdə] food: insipid, tasteless; stale; p. dull, boring.

Faden ['fɑːdən] m (-s/ⁿ) thread (a. fig.); fig.: an e-m ~ hängen hang by a thread; '~**nudeln** f/pl. vermicelli pl.; 2**scheinig** adj. ['ˌʃaɪnɪç] threadbare; excuse, etc.: flimsy, thin.

fähig adj. ['fεːiç] capable (zu inf. of ger.; gen. of); able (to inf.); '2**keit** f (-/-en) (cap)ability; talent, faculty.

fahl *adj.* [fɑːl] pale, pallid; *colour*: faded; *complexion*: leaden, livid.

fahnd|en ['fɑːndən] *v/i.* (ge-, h): **nach j-m ~** search for s.o.; '**~ung** *f* (-/-en) search.

Fahne ['fɑːnə] *f* (-/-n) flag; standard; banner; ⚓, ✕, *fig.* colo(u)rs *pl.*; *typ.* galley-proof.

'**Fahnen|eid** *m* oath of allegiance; '**~flucht** *f* desertion; '**2flüchtig** *adj.*: **~ werden** desert (the colo[u]rs); '**~stange** *f* flagstaff, *Am.* a. flagpole.

'**Fahr|bahn** *f*, '**~damm** *m* roadway.

Fähre ['fɛːrə] *f* (-/-n) ferry(-boat).

fahren ['fɑːrən] (*irr.*, ge-) **1.** *v/i.* (sein) *driver, vehicle, etc.*: drive, go, travel; *cyclist*: ride, cycle; ⚓ sail; *mot.* motor; **mit der Eisenbahn ~** go by train *or* rail; **spazieren~** go *for* or take a drive; **mit der Hand ~ über** (*acc.*) pass one's hand over; **~ lassen** let go or slip; **gut** (*schlecht*) **~ bei** do *or* fare well (badly) at or with; **er ist gut dabei gefahren** he did very well out of it; **2.** *v/t.* (h) carry, convey; drive (*car, train, etc.*); ride (*bicycle, etc.*).

'**Fahrer** *m* (-s/-) driver; '**~flucht** *f* (-/*no pl.*) hit-and-run offence; *Am.* hit-and-run offense.

'**Fahr|gast** *m* passenger; *in taxi*: fare; '**~geld** *n* fare; '**~gelegenheit** *f* transport facilities *pl.*; '**~gestell** *n mot.* chassis; ✈ undercarriage, landing gear; '**~karte** *f* ticket; '**~kartenschalter** *m* booking-office, *Am.* ticket office; '**2lässig** *adj.* careless, negligent; '**~lässigkeit** *f* (-/-en) carelessness, negligence; '**~lehrer** *mot. m* driving instructor; '**~plan** *m* timetable, *Am.* a. schedule; '**2planmäßig 1.** *adj.* regular, *Am.* scheduled; **2.** *adv.* on time, *Am.* a. on schedule; '**~preis** *m* fare; '**~rad** *n* bicycle, F bike; '**~schein** *m* ticket; '**~schule** *mot. f* driving school, school of motoring; '**~stuhl** *m* lift, *Am.* elevator; '**~stuhlführer** *m* lift-boy, lift-man, *Am.* elevator operator; '**~stunde** *mot. f* driving lesson.

Fahrt [fɑːrt] *f* (-/-en) ride, drive, journey; voyage, passage; trip; **~ ins Blaue** mystery tour; **in voller ~** (at) full speed.

Fährte ['fɛːrtə] *f* (-/-n) track (*a. fig.*); **auf der falschen ~ sein** be on the wrong track.

'**Fahr|vorschrift** *f* rule of the road; '**~wasser** *n* ⚓ navigable water; *fig.* track; '**~weg** *m* roadway; '**~zeug** *n* vehicle; ⚓ vessel.

Fakt|or ['faktɔr] *m* (-s/-en) factor; **~otum** [~'toːtʊm] *n* (-s/-s, Faktoten) factotum; **~ur** † [~'tuːr] *f* (-/-en), **~ura** † [~'tuːra] *f* (-/Fakturen) invoice.

Fakultät *univ.* [fakul'tɛːt] *f* (-/-en) faculty.

Falke *orn.* ['falkə] *m* (-n/-n) hawk, falcon.

Fall [fal] *m* (-[e]s/⁻e) fall (*of body, stronghold, city, etc.*); gr., ﬔ, ✞ case; *gesetzt den ~* suppose; *auf alle Fälle* at all events; *auf jeden ~* in any case, at any rate; *auf keinen ~* on no account, in no case.

Falle ['falə] *f* (-/-n) trap (*a. fig.*); pitfall (*a. fig.*); **e-e ~ stellen** set a trap (*j-m* for s.o.).

fallen ['falən] **1.** *v/i.* (*irr.*, ge-, sein) fall, drop; ✕ be killed in action; *shot*: be heard; *flood water*: subside; **auf j-n ~** suspicion, *etc.*: fall on s.o.; **~ lassen** drop (*plate, etc.*); **2.** ⚹ *n* (-s/*no pl.*) fall(ing).

fällen ['fɛlən] *v/t.* (ge-, h) fell, cut down (*tree*); ✕ lower (*bayonet*); ﬔ pass (*judgement*), give (*decision*).

'fallenlassen *v/t.* irr. lassen, sep., no -ge-, h) drop (*plan, claim, etc.*).

fällig ['fɛlɪç] *adj.* † due; payable; '**2keit** *f* (-/⁻-en) maturity; '**2keitstermin** *m* date of maturity.

'**Fall|obst** *n* windfall; '**~reep** ⚓ ['~reːp] *n* (-[e]s/-e) gangway.

falls *cj.* [fals] if; in the event of *ger.*; in case.

'**Fall|schirm** *m* parachute; '**~schirmspringer** *m* parachutist; '**~strick** *m* snare; '**~tür** *f* trap door.

falsch [falʃ] **1.** *adj.* false; wrong; *bank-note, etc.*: counterfeit; *money*: base; *bill of exchange, etc.*: forged; *p.* deceitful; **2.** *adv.*: **~ gehen** *watch*: go wrong; **~ verbunden!** *teleph.* sorry, wrong number.

fälsch|en ['fɛlʃən] *v/t.* (ge-, h) falsify; forge, fake (*document, etc.*); counterfeit (*bank-note, coin, etc.*); fake (*calculations, etc.*); tamper with (*financial account*); adulterate (*food, wine*); '**2er** *m* (-s/-) forger, faker; adulterator.

'**Falsch|geld** *n* counterfeit or bad or base money; '**~heit** *f* (-/-en) falseness, falsity; duplicity, deceitfulness; **'~meldung** f false report; **'~münzer** m (-s/-) coiner; **'~münzerwerkstatt** f coiner's den; **'2spielen** v/i. (sep., -ge-, h) cheat (at cards); **'~spieler** m card-sharper.

'Fälschung f (-/-en) forgery; falsification; fake; adulteration.

Falt|boot ['falt-] n folding canoe, Am. foldboat, faltboat; **~e** ['~ə] f (-/-n) fold; pleat (in skirt, etc.); crease (in trousers); wrinkle (on face); **'2en** v/t. (-ge-, h) fold; clasp or join (one's hands); **'2ig** adj. folded; pleated; wrinkled.

Falz [falts] m (-es/-e) fold; rabbet (for woodworking, etc.); bookbinding: guard; **'2en** v/t. (-ge-, h) fold; rabbet. [informal.\]

familiär adj. [famil'jɛːr] familiar;\]

Familie [fa'miːljə] f (-/-n) family (a. zo., ♀).

Fa'milien|angelegenheit f family affair; **~anschluß** m: **~** haben live as one of the family; **~nachrichten** f/pl. in newspaper: birth, marriage and death announcements pl.; **~name** m family name, surname, Am. a. last name; **~stand** m marital status.

Fanati|ker [fa'naːtikər] m (-s/-) fanatic; **2sch** adj. fanatic(al).

Fanatismus [fana'tismus] m (-/no pl.) fanaticism.

fand [fant] pret. of finden.

Fanfare ['fanˈfaːrə] f (-/-n) fanfare, flourish (of trumpets).

Fang [faŋ] m (-[e]s/⸗e) capture, catch(ing); hunt. bag; **'2en** v/t. (irr. ge-, h) catch (animal, ball, thief, etc.); **'~zahn** m fang (of dog, wolf, etc.); tusk (of boar).

Farb|band ['farp-] n (typewriter) ribbon; **~e** ['~bə] f (-/-n) colo(u)r; paint; dye; complexion; cards: suit; **2echt** adj. ['farp?-] colo(u)r-fast.

färben ['fɛrbən] v/t. (ge-, h) colo(u)r (glass, food, etc.); dye (material, hair, Easter eggs, etc.); tint (hair, paper, glass); stain (wood, fabrics, glass, etc.); sich **~** take on or assume a colo(u)r; sich rot **~** turn or go red.

'farben|blind adj. colo(u)r-blind; **'2druck** m (-[e]s/-e) colo(u)r print; **'~prächtig** adj. splendidly colo(u)rful.

Färber ['fɛrbər] m (-s/-) dyer.

Farb|fernsehen ['farp-] n colo(u)r television; **'~film** m colo(u)r film; **2ig** adj. ['~biç] colo(u)red; glass: tinted, stained; fig. colo(u)rful; **2los** adj. ['~p-] colo(u)rless; **'~photographie** f colo(u)r photography; **'~stift** m colo(u)red pencil; **'~stoff** m colo(u)ring matter; **'~ton** m tone; shade, tint.

Färbung ['fɛrbuŋ] f (-/-en) colo(u)ring (a. fig.); shade (a. fig.).

Farnkraut ♀ ['farnkraut] n fern.

Fasan orn. [fa'zaːn] m (-[e]s/-e[n]) pheasant. [val.\]

Fasching ['faʃiŋ] m (-s/-e, -s) carni-\]

Fasel|ei [faːzə'lai] f (-/-en) drivelling, waffling; twaddle; **'2n** v/i. (ge-, h) blather; F waffle.

Faser ['faːzər] f (-/-n) anat., ♀, fig. fib|re, Am. -er; cotton, wool, etc.: staple; **'2ig** adj. fibrous; **'2n** v/i. (ge-, h) wool: shed fine hairs.

Faß [fas] n (Fasses/Fässer) cask, barrel; tub; vat; **'~bier** n draught beer.

Fassade △ [fa'saːdə] f (-/-n) façade, front (a. fig.); **~nkletterer** m (-s/-) cat burglar.

fassen ['fasən] (ge-, h) **1.** v/t. seize, take hold of; catch, apprehend (criminal); hold; s. einfassen; fig. grasp, understand, believe; pluck up (courage); form (plan); make (decision); sich **~** compose o.s.; sich kurz **~** be brief; **2.** v/i.: **~** nach reach for. [ceivable.\]

'faßlich adj. comprehensible, con-\]

'Fassung f (-/-en) setting (of jewels); ⚡ socket; fig.: composure; draft (-ing); wording, version; die **~** verlieren lose one's self-control; aus der **~** bringen disconcert; **'~kraft** f (powers of) comprehension, mental capacity; **'~svermögen** n (holding) capacity; fig. s. Fassungskraft.

fast adv. [fast] almost, nearly; **~** nichts next to nothing; **~** nie hardly ever.

fasten ['fastən] v/i. (ge-, h) fast; abstain from food and drink; **'2zeit** f Lent.

'Fast|nacht f (-/no pl.) Shrovetide; carnival; **'~tag** m fast-day.

fatal adj. [fa'taːl] situation, etc.: awkward; business, etc.: unfortunate; mistake, etc.: fatal.

fauchen ['fauxən] v/i. (ge-, h) cat, etc.: spit; F p. spit (with anger); locomotive, etc.: hiss.

faul adj. [faul] fruit, etc.: rotten, bad; fish, meat: putrid, bad; fig. lazy, indolent, idle; fishy; ~e Ausrede lame excuse; '~en v/i. (ge-, h) rot, go bad, putrefy.

faulenze|n ['faulɛntsən] v/i. (ge-, h) idle; laze, loaf; '2r m (-s/-) idler, sluggard, F lazy-bones.

'Faul|heit f (-/no pl.) idleness, laziness; '2ig adj. putrid.

Fäulnis ['fɔylnɪs] f (-/no pl.) rottenness; putrefaction; decay.

'Faul|pelz m s. Faulenzer; '~tier n zo. sloth (a. fig.).

Faust [faust] f (-/=e) fist; auf eigene ~ on one's own initiative; '~handschuh m mitt(en); '~schlag m blow with the fist, punch, Am. F a. slug.

Favorit [favo'riːt] m (-en/-en) favo(u)rite.

Faxe ['faksə] f (-/-n): ~n machen (play the) fool; ~n schneiden pull or make faces.

Fazit ['faːtsɪt] n (-s/-e, -s) result, upshot; total; das ~ ziehen sum or total up.

Februar ['feːbruaːr] m (-[s]/-e) February.

fecht|en ['fɛçtən] v/i. (irr., ge-, h) fight; fenc. fence; '2er m (-s/-) fencer.

Feder ['feːdər] f (-/-n) feather; (ornamental) plume; pen; ⊕ spring; '~bett n feather bed; '~busch m tuft of feathers; plume; '~gewicht n boxing, etc.: featherweight; '~halter m (-s/-) penholder; '~kiel m quill; '~kraft f elasticity, resilience; '~krieg m paper war; literary controversy; '2leicht adj. (as) light as a feather; '~lesen n (-s/no pl.): nicht viel ~s machen mit make short work of; '~messer n penknife; '2n v/i. (ge-, h) be elastic; '2nd adj. springy, elastic; '~strich m stroke of the pen; '~vieh n poultry; '~zeichnung f pen-and-ink drawing.

Fee [feː] f (-/-n) fairy.

Fegefeuer ['feːgəfɔyər] n purgatory.

fegen ['feːgən] v/t. (ge-, h) sweep; clean.

Fehde ['feːdə] f (-/-n) feud; private war; in ~ liegen be at feud; F be at daggers drawn.

Fehl [feːl] m: ohne ~ without fault or blemish; '~betrag m deficit, deficiency.

fehlen ['feːlən] v/i. (ge-, h) be absent; be missing or lacking; do wrong; es fehlt ihm an (dat.) he lacks; was fehlt Ihnen? what is the matter with you?; weit gefehlt! far off the mark!

Fehler ['feːlər] m (-s/-) mistake, error, F slip; fault; ⊕ defect, flaw; '2frei adj., '2los adj. faultless, perfect; ⊕ flawless; '2haft adj. faulty; defective; incorrect.

'Fehl|geburt f miscarriage, abortion; '2gehen v/i. (irr. gehen, sep., -ge-, sein) go wrong; '~griff fig. m mistake, blunder; '~schlag fig. m failure; '2schlagen fig. v/i. (irr. schlagen, sep., -ge-, sein) fail, miscarry; '~schuß m miss; '2treten v/i. (irr. treten, sep., -ge-, sein) make a false step; '~tritt m false step; slip; fig. slip, fault; '~urteil ҭ҂ n error of judg(e)ment; '~zündung mot. f misfire, backfire.

Feier ['faɪər] f (-/-n) ceremony; celebration; festival; festivity; '~abend m finishing or closing time; ~ machen finish, F knock off; '2lich adj. promise; oath, etc.: solemn; act: ceremonial; '~lichkeit f (-/-en) solemnity; ceremony; '2n (ge-, h) 1. v/t. hold (celebration); celebrate, observe (feast, etc.); 2. v/i. make holiday; '~tag m holiday; festive day.

feig adj. [faɪk] cowardly.

feige[1] adj. ['faɪgə] cowardly.

Feige[2] [~] f (-/-n) fig; '~nbaum ♀ m fig-tree; '~nblatt n fig-leaf.

Feig|heit ['faɪkhaɪt] f (-/no pl.) cowardice, cowardliness; '~ling ['~lɪŋ] m (-s/-e) coward.

feil adj. [faɪl] for sale, to be sold; fig. venal; '~bieten v/t. (irr. bieten, sep., -ge-, h) offer for sale.

Feile ['faɪlə] f (-/-n) file; '2n (ge-, h) 1. v/t. file (a. fig.); fig. polish; 2. v/i.: ~ an (dat.) file (at); fig. polish (up).

feilschen ['faɪlʃən] v/i. (ge-, h) bargain (um for), haggle (for, about), Am. a. dicker (about).

fein adj. [faɪn] fine; material, etc.: high-grade; wine, etc.: choice; fabric, etc.: delicate, dainty; manners: polished; p. polite; distinction: subtle.

Feind [faɪnt] m (-[e]s/-e) enemy (a. ✕); **ℒlich** adj. hostile, inimical; **ℒschaft** f (-/-en) enmity; animosity, hostility; **ℒselig** adj. hostile (gegen to); **ℒseligkeit** f (-/-en) hostility; malevolence.

'fein|fühlend adj., **'ℒfühlig** adj. sensitive; **ℒgefühl** n sensitiveness; delicacy; **ℒgehalt** m (monetary) standard; **ℒheit** f (-/-en) fineness; delicacy, daintiness; politeness; elegance; **ℒkost** f high-class groceries pl., Am. delicatessen; **ℒmechanik** f precision mechanics; **ℒschmecker** m (-s/-) gourmet, epicure; **ℒsinnig** adj. subtle.

feist adj. [faɪst] fat, stout.

Feld [fɛlt] n (-[e]s/-er) field (a. ✕, ✕, sports); ground, soil; plain; chess: square; △, ⊕ panel, compartment; ins ~ ziehen take the field; **ℒarbeit** f agricultural work; **ℒbett** n camp-bed; **ℒblume** f wild flower; **ℒdienst** ✕ m field service; **ℒflasche** f water-bottle; **ℒfrucht** f fruit of the field; **ℒgeschrei** n war-cry, battle-cry; **ℒherr** m general; **ℒkessel** m camp-kettle; **ℒlazarett** ✕ n field-hospital; **ℒlerche** orn. f skylark; **ℒmarschall** m Field Marshal; **ℒmarschmäßig** ✕ adj. in full marching order; **ℒmaus** zo. f field-mouse; **ℒmesser** m (land) surveyor; **ℒpost** ✕ f army postal service; **ℒschlacht** ✕ f battle; **ℒstecher** m (-s/-) (ein a pair of) field-glasses pl.; **ℒstuhl** m camp-stool; **ℒwebel** ['ℒve:bəl] m (-s/-) sergeant; **ℒweg** m (field) path; **ℒzeichen** ✕ n standard; **ℒzug** m ✕ campaign (a. fig.), (military) expedition; Am. fig. a. drive.

Felge ['fɛlgə] f (-/-n) felloe (of cart-wheel); rim (of car wheel, etc.).

Fell [fɛl] n (-[e]s/-e) skin, pelt, fur (of dead animal); coat (of cat, etc.); fleece (of sheep).

Fels [fɛls] m (-en/-en), **ℒen** ['ℒzən] m (-s/-) rock; **ℒblock** ['fɛls-] m rock; boulder; **ℒig** adj. ['ℒzɪç] rocky.

Fenchel ♀ ['fɛnçəl] m (-s/no pl.) fennel.

Fenster ['fɛnstər] n (-s/-) window; **ℒbrett** n window-sill; **ℒflügel** m casement (of casement window); sash (of sash window); **ℒkreuz** n cross-bar(s pl.); **ℒladen** m shutter;

ℒrahmen m window-frame; **ℒriegel** m window-fastener; **ℒscheibe** f (window-)pane; **ℒsims** m, n window-sill.

Ferien ['fe:rjən] pl. holiday(s pl.), esp. Am. vacation; leave, Am. a. furlough; parl. recess; ✝✝ vacation, recess; **ℒkolonie** f children's holiday camp.

Ferkel ['fɛrkəl] n (-s/-) young pig; contp. p. pig.

fern [fɛrn] 1. adj. far (off), distant; remote; 2. adv. far (away); von ~ from a distance.

'Fernamt teleph. n trunk exchange, Am. long-distance exchange.

'fernbleiben 1. v/i. (irr. bleiben, sep., -ge-; sein) remain or stay away (dat. from); 2. ♀ n (-s/no pl.) absence (from school, etc.); absenteeism (from work).

Fern|e ['fɛrnə] f (-/-n) distance; remoteness; aus der ~ from or at a distance; **ℒer** 1. adj. farther; fig.: further; future; 2. adv. further (-more), in addition, also; ~ liefen ... also ran ...; **ℒflug** ✕ m long-distance flight; **ℒgelenkt** adj. ['ℒgə-lɛŋkt] missile: guided; aircraft, etc.: remote-control(l)ed; **'ℒgespräch** teleph. n trunk call, Am. long-distance call; **ℒgesteuert** adj. s. ferngelenkt; **ℒglas** n binoculars pl.; **'ℒhalten** v/t. and v/refl. (irr. halten, sep., -ge-, h) keep away (von from); **'ℒheizung** f district heating; **'ℒlaster** F mot. m long-distance lorry, Am. long haul truck; **'ℒlenkung** f (-/-en) remote control; **ℒliegen** v/i. (irr. liegen, sep., -ge-, h): es liegt mir fern zu inf. I am far from ger.; **ℒrohr** n telescope; **ℒschreiber** m teleprinter, Am. teletypewriter; **'ℒsehen** 1. n (-s/no pl.) television; 2. ♀ v/i. (irr. sehen, sep., -ge-, h) watch television; **'ℒseher** m television set; p. television viewer, televiewer; **'ℒsehsendung** f television broadcast, telecast; **ℒsicht** f visual range.

'Fernsprech|amt n telephone exchange, Am. a. central; **'ℒanschluß** m telephone connection; **'ℒer** m telephone; **'ℒleitung** f telephone line; **'ℒzelle** f telephone box.

'fern|stehen v/i. (irr. stehen, sep., -ge-, h) have no real (point of) contact (dat. with); **ℒsteuerung** f

s. *Fernlenkung*; '2**unterricht** *m* correspondence course *or* tuition; '2**verkehr** *m* long-distance traffic.

Ferse ['fɛrzə] *f* (-/-n) heel.

fertig *adj.* ['fɛrtiç] ready; *article, etc.*: finished; *clothing*: ready-made; *mit et.* ~ **werden** get s.th. finished; *mit et.* ~ **sein** have finished s.th.; '~**bringen** *v/t.* (*irr.* bringen, *sep.,* -ge-, h) bring about; manage; '2**keit** *f* (-/-en) dexterity; skill; fluency (*in the spoken language*); '~**machen** *v/t.* (*sep.,* -ge-, h) finish, complete; get *s.th.* ready; *fig.* finish, settle *s.o.'s* hash; *sich* ~ **machen** get ready; '2**stellung** *f* completion; '2**waren** *f/pl.* finished goods *pl. or* products *pl.*

fesch F *adj.* [fɛʃ] *hat, dress, etc.*: smart, stylish, chic; dashing.

Fessel ['fɛsəl] *f* (-/-n) chain, fetter, shackle; *vet.* fetlock; *fig.* bond, fetter, tie; '~**ballon** *m* captive balloon; '2**n** *v/t.* (ge-, h) chain, fetter, shackle; *j-n* ~ **hold** *or* arrest *s.o.'s* attention; fascinate s.o.

fest [fɛst] 1. *adj.* firm; solid; fixed; fast; *principle*: firm, strong; *sleep*: sound; *fabric*: close; 2. 2 *n* (-es/-e) festival, celebration; holiday, *eccl.* feast; '~**binden** *v/t.* (*irr.* binden, *sep.,* -ge-, h) fasten, tie (*an dat.* to); '2**essen** *n* banquet, feast; '~**fahren** *v/refl.* (*irr.* fahren, *sep.,* -ge-, h) get stuck; *fig.* reach a deadlock; '2**halle** *f* (festival) hall; '~**halten** (*irr.* halten, *sep.,* -ge-, h) 1. *v/i.* hold fast *or* tight; ~ **an** (*dat.*) adhere *or* keep to; 2. *v/t.* hold on to; hold tight; *sich* ~ **an** (*dat.*) hold on to; '~**igen** ['~igən] *v/t.* (ge-, h) consolidate (*one's* position, *etc.*); strengthen (*friendship, etc.*); stabilize (*currency*); 2**igkeit** ['~ç-] *f* (-/no pl.) firmness; solidity; '2**land** *n* mainland, continent; '~**legen** *v/t.* (*sep.,* -ge-, h) fix, set; *sich auf et.* ~ **commit** o.s. to s.th.; '~**lich** *adj.* *meal, day, etc.*: festive; *reception, etc.*: ceremonial; '2**lichkeit** *f* (-/-en) festivity; festive character; '~**machen** (*sep.,* -ge-, h) 1. *v/t.* fix, fasten, attach (*an dat.* to); ⚓ moor; 2. ⚓ *v/i.* moor; put ashore; '2**mahl** *n* banquet, feast; 2**nahme** ['~naːmə] *f* (-/-n) arrest; '~**nehmen** *v/t.* (*irr.* nehmen, *sep.,* -ge-, h) arrest, take into custody; '2**rede** *f* speech

of the day; '~**setzen** *v/t.* (*sep.,* -ge-, h) fix, set; *sich* ~ **dust,** *etc.*: become ingrained; *p.* settle (down); '2**spiel** *n* festival; '~**stehen** *v/i.* (*irr.* stehen, *sep.,* -ge-, h) stand firm; *fact:* be certain; '~**stehend** *adj.* fixed, stationary; *fact:* established; '~**stellen** *v/t.* (*sep.,* -ge-, h) establish (*fact, identity, etc.*); ascertain, find out (*fact, s.o.'s whereabouts, etc.*); state; see, perceive (*fact, etc.*); '2**stellung** *f* establishment; ascertainment; statement; '2**tag** *m* festive day; festival, holiday, *eccl.* feast; '2**ung** ✕ *f* (-/-en) fortress; '2**zug** *m* festive procession.

fett [fɛt] 1. *adj.* fat; fleshy; *voice:* oily; *land, etc.:* rich; 2. 2 *n* (-[e]s/-e) fat; grease (*a.* ⊕); '2**druck** *typ.* *m* bold type; '2**fleck** *m* grease-spot; '~**ig** *adj.* hair, skin, *etc.:* greasy, oily; *fingers, etc.:* greasy; *substance:* fatty.

Fetzen ['fɛtsən] *m* (-s/-) shred, rag, *Am. a.* frazzle; scrap (*of paper*); *in* ~ in rags.

feucht *adj.* [fɔyçt] *climate, air, etc.:* damp, moist; *air, zone, etc.:* humid; '2**igkeit** *f* (-/no pl.) moisture (*of substance*); dampness (*of place, etc.*); humidity (*of atmosphere, etc.*).

Feuer ['fɔyər] *n* (-s/-) fire; light; *fig.* ardo(u)r; ~ **fangen** catch fire; *fig.* fall for (*girl*); '~**alarm** *m* fire alarm; '2**beständig** *adj.* fire-proof, fire-resistant; '~**bestattung** *f* cremation; '~**eifer** *m* ardo(u)r; '2**fest** *adj.* s. feuerbeständig; '2**gefährlich** *adj.* inflammable; '~**haken** *m* poker; '~**löscher** *m* (-s/-) fire extinguisher; '~**melder** *m* (-s/-) fire-alarm; '2**n** (ge-, h) 1. ✕ *v/i.* shoot, fire (*auf acc.* at, on); 2. F *fig. v/t.* hurl; '~**probe** *fig. f* crucial test; '2**rot** *adj.* fiery (red), (as) red as fire; '~**schiff** ⚓ *n* lightship; '~**schutz** *m* fire prevention; ✕ covering fire; '~**sgefahr** *f* danger *or* risk of fire; '2**speiend** *adj.:* ~**er Berg** volcano; '~**spritze** *f* fire engine; '~**stein** *m* flint; '~**versicherung** *f* fire insurance (company); '~**wache** *f* fire station, *Am. a.* firehouse; '~**wehr** *f* fire-brigade, *Am. a.* fire department; '~**wehrmann** *m* fireman; '~**werk** *n* (display of) fireworks *pl.*; '~**werkskörper** *m* firework; '~-

zange f (e-e a pair of) firetongs pl.; '**zeug** n lighter.

feurig adj. ['fɔyriç] fiery (a. fig.); fig. ardent.

Fiasko [fi'asko] n (-s/-s) (complete) failure, fiasco; sl. flop. [primer.

Fibel ['fi:bəl] f (-/-n) spelling-book,

Fichte ♀ ['fiçtə] f (-/-n) spruce; '**nnadel** f pine-needle.

fidel adj. [fi'de:l] cheerful, merry, jolly, Am. F a. chipper.

Fieber ['fi:bər] n (-s/-) temperature, fever; ~ haben have or run a temperature; '**anfall** m attack or bout of fever; '2**haft** adj. feverish (a. fig.); febrile; '2**krank** adj. ill with fever; '**mittel** n febrifuge; '2**n** v/i. (ge-, h) have or run a temperature; ~ nach crave or long for; '**schauer** m chill, shivers pl.; '**tabelle** f temperature-chart; '**thermometer** n clinical thermometer.

fiel [fi:l] pret. of fallen.

Figur [fi'gu:r] f (-/-en) figure; chess: chessman, piece.

figürlich adj. [fi'gy:rliç] meaning, etc.: figurative. [pork, etc.).

Filet [fi'le:] n (-s/-s)fillet (of beef,

Filiale [fi'ljɑ:lə] f (-/-n) branch.

Filigran|arbeit f) [fili'grɑ:n(⁹-)] n (-s/-e) filigree.

Film [film] m (-[e]s/-e) film, thin coating (of oil, wax, etc.); phot. film; film, (moving) picture, Am. a. motion picture, F movie; e-n ~ ein!egen phot. load a camera; '**atelier** n film studio; '**aufnahme** f filming, shooting (of a film); film (of sporting event, etc.); '2**en** (ge-, h) 1. v/t. film, shoot (scene, etc.); 2. v/i. film; make a film; '**gesellschaft** f film company, Am. motion-picture company; '**kamera** f film camera, Am. motion-picture camera; '**regisseur** m film director; '**reklame** f screen advertising; '**schauspieler** m film or screen actor, Am. F movie actor; '**spule** f (film) reel; '**streifen** m film strip; '**theater** n cinema, Am. motion-picture or F movie theater; '**verleih** m (-[e]s/-e) film distributors pl.; '**vorführer** m projectionist; '**vorstellung** f cinema performance, Am. F movie performance.

Filter ['filtər] (-s/-) 1. m (coffee-, etc.) filter; 2. ⊕ n filter; '2**n** v/t. (ge-, h) filter (water, air, etc.); fil-

trate (water, impurities, etc.); strain (liquid); '**zigarette** f filter-tipped cigarette.

Filz [filts] m (-es/-e) felt; fig. F skinflint; '2**ig** adj. felt-like; of felt; fig. F niggardly, stingy; '**laus** f crab louse.

Finanz|amt [fi'nants⁹amt] n (inland) revenue office, office of the Inspector of Taxes; ~**en** f/pl. finances pl.; 2**iell** adj. [~'tsjɛl] financial; 2**ieren** [~'tsi:rən] v/t. (no -ge-, h) finance (scheme, etc.), sponsor (radio programme, etc.); '**lage** f financial position; '**mann** m financier; '**minister** m minister of finance; Chancellor of the Exchequer, Am. Secretary of the Treasury; '**ministerium** n ministry of finance; Exchequer, Am. Treasury Department; '**wesen** n (-s/no pl.) finances pl.; financial matters pl.

Findelkind ['fɪndəl-] n foundling.

finden ['fɪndən] (irr., ge-, h) 1. v/t. find; discover, come across; find, think, consider; wie ~ Sie ...? how do you like ...?; sich ~ thing: be found (again); 2. v/i.: ~ zu find one's way to. [finder's reward.)

'**Finder** m (-s/-) finder; '**lohn** m

'**findig** adj. resourceful, ingenious.

Findling ['fɪntlɪŋ] m (-s/-e) foundling; geol. erratic block, boulder.

fing [fɪŋ] pret. of fangen.

Finger ['fɪŋər] m (-s/-) finger; sich die ~ verbrennen burn one's fingers; er rührte keinen ~ he lifted no finger; '**abdruck** m fingerprint; '**fertigkeit** f manual skill; '**hut** m thimble; ♀ foxglove; '2**n** v/i. (ge-, h): ~ nach fumble for; '**spitze** f finger-tip; '**spitzengefühl** fig. n sure instinct; '**übung** ♪ f finger exercise; **zeig** ['~tsaik] m (-[e]s/-e) hint, F pointer.

Fink orn. [fɪŋk] m (-en/-en) finch.

finster adj. ['fɪnstər] night, etc.: dark; shadows, wood, etc.: sombre; night, room, etc.: gloomy, murky; person, nature: sullen; thought, etc.: sinister, sombre, gloomy; '2**nis** f (-/no pl.) darkness, gloom.

Finte ['fɪntə] f (-/-n) feint; fig. a. ruse, trick.

Firma † ['fɪrma] f (-/Firmen) firm, business, company.

firmen eccl. ['fɪrmən] v/t. (ge-, h) confirm.

'**Firmen|inhaber** *m* owner of a firm; '**~wert** *m* goodwill.

Firn [firn] *m* (-[e]s/-e) firn, névé.

First △ [first] *m* (-es/-e) ridge; '**~ziegel** *m* ridge tile.

Fisch [fiʃ] *m* (-es/-e) fish; '**~dampfer** *m* trawler; '**○en** *v/t. and v/i.* (ge-, h) fish; '**~er** *m* (-s/-) fisherman; '**~erboot** *n* fishing-boat; '**~erdorf** *n* fishing-village; **~erei** [~'rai] *f* (-/-en) fishery; fishing; '**~fang** *m* fishing; '**~geruch** *m* fishy smell; '**~gräte** *f* fish-bone; '**~grätenmuster** *n* herring-bone pattern; '**~händler** *m* fishmonger, *Am.* fish dealer; '**○ig** *adj.* fishy; '**~laich** *m* spawn; '**~leim** *m* fish-glue; '**~mehl** *n* fish-meal; '**~schuppe** *f* scale; '**~tran** *m* train-oil; '**~vergiftung** *f* fish-poisoning; '**~zucht** *f* pisciculture, fish-hatching; '**~zug** *m* catch, haul, draught (of fish).

fiskalisch *adj.* [fis'ka:liʃ] fiscal, governmental.

Fiskus ['fiskus] *m* (-/△ -se, Fisken) Exchequer, *esp. Am.* Treasury; government.

Fistel ['fistəl] *f* (-/-n) fistula; '**~stimme** ♪ *f* falsetto.

Fittich ['fitiç] *m* (-[e]s/-e) *poet.* wing; *j-n unter s-e ~e nehmen* take s.o. under one's wing.

fix *adj.* [fiks] *salary, price, etc.*: fixed; *quick, clever, smart; e-e ~ Idee an obsession; ein ~er Junge* a smart fellow; **○ierbad** *phot.* [fi-'ksi:rba:t] *n* fixing bath; **~ieren** [fi'ksi:rən] *v/t. (no -ge-, h)* fix (*a. phot.*); fix one's eyes (up)on, stare at *s.o.*; '**○stern** *ast. m* fixed star; '**○um** *n* (-s/Fixa) fixed *or* basic salary.

flach *adj.* [flax] *roof, etc.*: flat; *ground, etc.*: flat, level, even; *water, plate, fig.*: shallow; *A* plane.

Fläche ['flɛçə] *f* (-/-n) surface, *A* a. plane; sheet (*of water, snow, etc.*); *geom.* area; tract, expanse (*of land, etc.*); '**~ninhalt** *A* ['flɛçən?-] *m* (surface) area; '**~nmaß** *n* square *or* surface measure.

'**Flach|land** *n* plain, flat country; '**~rennen** *n turf*: flat race.

Flachs ♀ [flaks] *m* (-es/no pl.) flax.

flackern ['flakərn] *v/i.* (ge-, h) light, flame, eyes, etc.: flicker, wave; *voice*: quaver, shake.

Flagge ✕ ['flagə] *f* (-/-n) flag,

---

colo(u)rs *pl.*; '**○n** *v/i.* (ge-, h) fly *or* hoist a flag; signal (with flags).

Flak ✕ [flak] *f* (-/-, -s) anti-aircraft gun; anti-aircraft artillery.

Flamme ['flamə] *f* (-/-n) flame; blaze; '**~nmeer** *n* sea of flames; '**~nwerfer** ✕ *m* (-s/-) flame-thrower.

Flanell [fla'nɛl] *m* (-s/-e) flannel; **~anzug** *m* flannel suit; **~hose** *f* flannel trousers *pl.*, flannels *pl.*

Flank|e ['flaŋkə] *f* (-/-n) flank (*a. △, ⊕, ✕, mount.*); side; **○ieren** [~'ki:rən] *v/t.* (no -ge-, h) flank.

Flasche ['flaʃə] *f* (-/-n) bottle; flask.

'**Flaschen|bier** *n* bottled beer; '**~hals** *m* neck of a bottle; '**~öffner** *m* (-s/-) bottle-opener; '**~zug** ⊕ *m* block and tackle.

flatter|haft *adj.* ['flatərhaft] *girl, etc.*: fickle, flighty; *mind*: fickle, volatile; '**~n** *v/i.* (ge-) **1.** (h, sein) *bird, butterfly, etc.*: flutter (about); *bird, bat, etc.*: flit (about). **2.** (h) *hair, flag, garment, etc.*: stream; fly; *mot. wheel*: shimmy, wobble; *car steering*: judder; **3.** (sein): *auf den Boden ~* flutter to the ground.

flau *adj.* [flau] weak, feeble, faint; *sentiment, reaction, etc.*: lukewarm; *drink*: stale; *colour*: pale, dull; ✝ *market, business, etc.*: dull, slack; *~e Zeit* slack period.

Flaum [flaum] *m* (-[e]s/no pl.) down, fluff; fuzz.

Flau|s [flaus] *m* (-es/-e), **~sch** [~ʃ] *m* (-es/-e) tuft (*of wool, etc.*); napped coating.

Flausen F ['flauzən] *f/pl.* whims *pl.*, fancies *pl.*, (funny) ideas *pl.*; F fibs *pl.*; *j-m ~ in den Kopf setzen* put funny ideas into s.o.'s head; *j-m ~ vormachen* tell s.o.'s fibs.

Flaute ['flautə] *f* (-/-n) ♧ dead calm; *esp.* ✝ dullness, slack period.

Flecht|e ['flɛçtə] *f* (-/-n) braid, plait (*of hair*); ♀ lichen; ♂ herpes; '**○en** *v/t.* (irr., ge-, h) braid, plait (*hair, ribbon, etc.*); weave (*basket, wreath, etc.*); wreath (*flowers*); twist (*rope, etc.*); '**~werk** *n* wickerwork.

Fleck [flɛk] *m* (-[e]s/-e, -en) **1.** mark (*of dirt, grease, etc.*; *zo.*); spot (*of grease, paint, etc.*); smear (*of oil, blood, etc.*); stain (*of wine, coffee, etc.*); blot (*of ink*); place, spot; *fig.* blemish, spot, stain; **2.** patch (*of material*); *bootmaking*: heel-piece;

'**~en** *m* (-s/-) s. *Fleck 1*; small
(market-)town, townlet; '**~enwas-**
ser *n* spot or stain remover; '**~fie-**
ber ύ *n* (epidemic) typhus; '**☿ig**
adj. spotted; stained.
Fledermaus *zo.* ['fle:dər-] *f* bat.
Flegel ['fle:gəl] *m* (-s/-) flail; *fig.*
lout, boor; **~ei** [~'laɪ] *f* (-/-en) rudeness; loutishness; '**☿haft** *adj.* rude-
ill-mannered; loutish; '**~jahre** *pl.*
awkward age.
flehen ['fle:ən] **1.** *v/i.* (ge-, h) en-
treat, implore (*zu j-m* s.o.; *um et.*
s.th.); **2.** ☿ *n* (-s/*no pl.*) supplication,
imploration, entreaty.
Fleisch [flaɪʃ] *n* (-es/*no pl.*) flesh;
meat; ☿ pulp; '**~brühe** *f* meat-
broth; beef tea; '**~er** *m* (-s/-)
butcher; **~erei** [~'raɪ] *f* (-/-en)
butcher's (shop), *Am.* butcher
shop; '**~extrakt** *m* meat extract;
'**☿fressend** *adj.* carnivorous; '**~**
hackmaschine *f* mincing machine,
mincer, *Am.* meat grinder; '**☿ig** *adj.*
fleshy; ☿ pulpy; '**~konserven** *f/pl.*
tinned or potted meat, *Am.* canned
meat; '**~kost** *f* meat (food); '**☿lich**
adj. desires, *etc.*: carnal, fleshly;
'**☿los** *adj.* meatless; '**~pastete** *f*
meat pie, *Am. a.* potpie; '**~speise** *f*
meat dish; '**~vergiftung** *f* meat or
ptomaine poisoning; '**~ware** *f* meat
(product); '**~wolf** *m* s. *Fleischhack-*
maschine.
Fleiß [flaɪs] *m* (-es/*no pl.*) diligence,
industry; '**☿ig** *adj.* diligent, industrious, hard-working.
fletschen ['fletʃən] *v/t.* (ge-, h): *die*
Zähne ~ animal: bare its teeth; *j.:*
bare one's teeth.
Flicken ['flɪkən] **1.** *m* (-s/-) patch;
2. ☿ *v/t.* (ge-, h) patch (*dress, tyre,*
etc.); repair (*shoe, roof, etc.*); cobble
(*shoe*).
'**Flick|schneider** *m* jobbing tailor;
'**~schuster** *m* cobbler; '**~werk** *n*
(-[e]s/*no pl.*) patchwork.
Flieder ☿ ['fli:dər] *m* (-s/-) lilac.
Fliege ['fli:gə] *f* (-/-n) *zo.* fly;
bow-tie.
'**fliegen 1.** *v/i.* (*irr.*, ge-, sein) fly;
go by air; **2.** *v/t.* (*irr.*, ge-, sein) fly,
pilot (*aircraft, etc.*); convey (*goods,*
etc.) by air; **3.** ☿ *n* (-s/*no pl.*) flying;
✈ *a.* aviation.
Fliegen|fänger ['fli:gənfɛŋər] *m*
(-s/-) fly-paper; '**~fenster** *n* fly-
screen; '**~gewicht** *n* boxing, *etc.*:

flyweight; '**~klappe** *f* fly-flap, *Am.*
fly swatter; '**~pilz** ☿ *m* fly agaric.
'**Flieger** *m* (-s/-) flyer; ✈ airman,
aviator; pilot; F plane, bomber;
cycling: sprinter; '**~abwehr** ✈ *f*
anti-aircraft defen|ce, *Am.* -se; '**~**
alarm ✈ *m* air-raid alarm or warning; '**~bombe** ✈ *f* aircraft bomb;
'**~offizier** ✈ *m* air-force officer.
flieh|en ['fli:ən] (*irr.*, ge-) **1.** *v/i.*
(sein) flee (*vor dat.* from); run away;
2. *v/t.* (h) flee, avoid, keep away
from; '**☿kraft** *phys.* ☿ centrifugal
force. [(floor-)tile.\
Fliese ['fli:zə] *f* (-/-n) (wall-)tile;\
Fließ|band ['fli:s-] *n* (-[e]s/*~er*) con-
veyor-belt; assembly-line; '**☿en** *v/i.*
(*irr.*, ge-, *sein*) *river, traffic, etc.:*
flow; *tap-water, etc.:* run; '**☿end 1.**
adj. water: running; *traffic:* moving;
speech, etc.: fluent; **2.** *adv.: ~ lesen*
(*sprechen*) read (speak) fluently;
'**~papier** *n* blotting-paper.
Flimmer ['flɪmər] *m* (-s/-) glimmer,
glitter; '**☿n** *v/i.* (ge-, h) glimmer,
glitter; *television, film:* flicker; *es*
flimmert mir vor den Augen everything is dancing in front of my eyes.
flink *adj.* [flɪŋk] quick, nimble,
brisk.
Flinte ['flɪntə] *f* (-/-n) shotgun; *die*
~ ins Korn werfen throw up the
sponge.
Flirt [flœrt] *m* (-es/-s) flirtation;
'**☿en** *v/i.* (ge-, h) flirt (*mit* with).
Flitter ['flɪtər] *m* (-s/-) tinsel (*a.fig.*),
spangle; '**~kram** *m* cheap finery;
'**~wochen** *pl.* honeymoon.
flitzen F ['flɪtsən] *v/i.* (ge-, sein)
whisk, scamper; dash (off, *etc.*).
flocht [flɔxt] *pret. of* **flechten.**
Flock|e ['flɔkə] *f* (-/-n) flake (*of*
snow, soap, etc.); flock (*of wool*);
'**☿ig** *adj.* fluffy, flaky.
flog [flo:k] *pret. of* **fliegen.**
floh¹ [flo:] *pret. of* **fliehen.**
Floh² *zo.* [~] *m* (-[e]s/*~e*) flea.
Flor [flo:r] *m* (-s/-e) bloom, blossom; *fig.* bloom, prime; gauze;
crêpe, crape.
Florett *fenc.* [flo'rɛt] *n* (-[e]s/-e) foil.
florieren [flo'ri:rən] *v/i.* (*no* -ge-, h)
business, etc.: flourish, prosper,
thrive.
Floskel ['flɔskəl] *f* (-/-n) flourish;
empty phrase.
floß¹ [flɔs] *pret. of* **fließen.**
Floß² [flo:s] *n* (-es/*~e*) raft, float.

Flosse ['flɔsə] f (-/-n) fin; flipper (of penguin, etc.).

flöß|en ['flø:sən] v/t. (ge-, h) raft, float (timber, etc.); '2er m (-s/-) rafter, raftsman.

Flöte ♪ ['flø:tə] f (-/-n) flute; '2n (ge-, h) 1. v/i. (play the) flute; 2. v/t. play on the flute.

flott adj. [flɔt] ⚓ floating, afloat; pace, etc.: quick, brisk; music, etc.: gay, lively; dress, etc.: smart, stylish; car, etc.: sporty, racy; dancer, etc.: excellent.

Flotte ['flɔtə] f (-/-n) ⚓ fleet; ⚔ navy; '**_nstützpunkt** ⚔ m naval base.

Flotille ⚓ [flɔ'tiljə] f (-/-n) flotilla.

Flöz geol., ⚒ [flø:ts] n (-es/-e) seam; layer, stratum.

Fluch [flu:x] m (-[e]s/⸚e) curse, malediction; eccl. anathema; curse, swear-word; '2en v/i. (ge-, h) swear, curse.

Flucht [fluxt] f (-/-en) flight (vor dat. from); escape (aus dat. from); line (of windows, etc.); suite (of rooms); flight (of stairs).

flücht|en ['flyçtən] (ge-) v/i. (sein) and v/refl. (h) flee (nach, zu to); run away; escape; '**_ig** adj. fugitive (a. fig.); thought, etc.: fleeting; fame, etc.: transient; p. careless, superficial; 🜂 volatile; 2**ling** ['_lɪŋ] m (-s/-e) fugitive; pol. refugee; '2**lingslager** n refugee camp.

Flug [flu:k] m (-[e]s/⸚e) flight; im _(e) rapidly; quickly; '**_abwehrrakete** f anti-aircraft missile; '**_bahn** f trajectory (of rocket, etc.); ≽ flight path; '**_ball** m tennis, etc.: volley; '**_blatt** n handbill, leaflet, Am. a. flier; '**_boot** ≽ n flying-boat; '**_dienst** ≽ m air service.

Flügel ['fly:gəl] m (-s/-) wing (a. △, ≽, ⚔); blade, vane (of propeller, etc.); s. Fensterflügel, Türflügel, Lungenflügel; sail (of windmill, etc.); ♪ grand piano; '**_fenster** △ n casement-window; '2**lahm** adj. broken-winged; '**_mann** ⚔ m marker; flank man; '**_tür** △ f folding door.

Fluggast ['flu:k-] m (air) passenger.

flügge adj. ['flygə] fledged; _ werden fledge; fig. begin to stand on one's own feet.

'**Flug|hafen** m airport; '**_linie** f ≽ air route; airline; '**_platz** m airfield, aerodrome, Am. a. airdrome;

airport; '**_sand** geol. m wind-blown sand; '**_schrift** f pamphlet; '**_sicherung** f air traffic control; '**_sport** m sporting aviation; '**_wesen** n aviation, aeronautics.

'**Flugzeug** n aircraft, aeroplane, F plane, Am. a. airplane; '**_bau** m aircraft construction; '**_führer** m pilot; '**_halle** f hangar; '**_rumpf** m fuselage, body; '**_träger** m aircraft carrier, Am. sl. flattop; '**_unglück** n air crash or disaster.

Flunder ichth. ['flundər] f (-/-n) flounder.

Flunker|ei F [fluŋkə'raɪ] f (-/-en) petty lying, F fib(bing); '2n v/i. (ge-, h) F fib, tell fibs.

fluoreszieren [fluɔrɛs'tsi:rən] v/i. (no -ge-, h) fluoresce.

Flur [flu:r] 1. f (-/-en) field, meadow; poet. lea; 2. m (-[e]s/-e) (entrance-)hall.

Fluß [flus] m (Flusses/Flüsse) river, stream; flow(ing); fig. fluency, flux; 2'**abwärts** adv. downriver, downstream; 2'**aufwärts** adv. upriver, upstream; '**_bett** n river bed.

flüssig adj. ['flysiç] fluid, liquid; metal: molten, melted; 🕈 money, capital, etc.: available, in hand; style: fluent, flowing; '2**keit** f (-/-en) fluid, liquid; fluidity; liquidity; availability; fluency.

'**Fluß|lauf** m course of a river; '**_mündung** f mouth of a river; '**_pferd** zo. n hippopotamus; '**_schiffahrt** f river navigation or traffic.

flüstern ['flystərn] v/i. and v/t. (ge-, h) whisper.

Flut [flu:t] f (-/-en) flood; high tide, (flood-)tide; fig. flood, torrent, deluge; '2**en** (ge-) 1. v/i. (sein) water, crowd, etc.: flood, surge (über acc. over); 2. v/t. (h) flood (dock, etc.); '**_welle** f tidal wave.

focht [fɔxt] pret. of fechten.

Fohlen zo. ['fo:lən] 1. n (-s/-) foal; male: colt; female: filly; 2. ♀ v/i. (ge-, h) foal.

Folge ['fɔlgə] f (-/-n) sequence, succession (of events); instalment, part (of radio series, etc.); consequence, result; series; set, suit; future; _n pl. aftermath.

'**folgen** v/i. (dat.) (ge-, sein) follow; succeed (j-m s.o.; auf acc. to); follow, ensue (aus from); obey (j-m s.o.); **~dermaßen** *adv.* ['~dərmaː-sən] as follows; '**~schwer** *adj.* of grave consequence, grave.

'**folgerichtig** *adj.* logical; consistent.

folger|n ['fɔlgərn] *v/t.* (ge-, h) infer, conclude, deduce (*aus* from); '**Qung** *f* (-/-en) inference, conclusion, deduction.

'**folgewidrig** *adj.* illogical; inconsistent.

folglich *cj.* ['fɔlklɪç] therefore, consequently.

folgsam *adj.* ['fɔlkzaːm] obedient; '**Qkeit** *f* (-/*no pl.*) obedience.

Folie ['foːljə] *f* (-/-n) foil.

Folter ['fɔltər] *f* (-/-n) torture; *auf die ~ spannen* put to the rack; *fig.* F *a.* keep on tenterhooks; '**Qn** *v/t.* (ge-, h) torture, torment; '**~qual** *f* torture, *fig. a.* torment.

Fonds ✝ [fõ] *m* (-/-) fund (*a. fig.*); funds *pl.*

Fontäne [fɔn'tɛːnə] *f* (-/-n) fountain.

foppen ['fɔpən] *v/t.* (ge-, h) tease, F pull s.o.'s leg; hoax, fool.

forcieren [fɔr'siːrən] *v/t.* (*no* -ge-, h) force (up).

'**Förder|band** *n* (-[e]s/⸚er) conveyor-belt; '**Qlich** *adj.* conducive (*dat.* to); promotive (*of*); '**~korb** ⚒ *m* cage.

fordern ['fɔrdərn] *v/t.* (ge-, h) demand; claim (*compensation, etc.*); ask (*price, etc.*); challenge (*to duel*).

fördern ['fœrdərn] *v/t.* (ge-, h) further, advance, promote; ⚒ haul, raise (*coal, etc.*); *zutage ~* reveal, bring to light.

'**Forderung** *f* (-/-en) demand; claim; charge; challenge.

'**Förderung** *f* (-/-en) furtherance, advancement, promotion; ⚒ haulage; output. [trout.]

Forelle *ichth.* [fo'rɛlə] *f* (-/-n)

Form [fɔrm] *f* (-/-en) form; figure, shape; model; ⊕ mo(u)ld; *sports:* form, condition; **Qal** *adj.* [~'maːl] formal; **~alität** [~ali'tɛːt] *f* (-/-en) formality; **~at** [~'maːt] *n* (-[e]s/-e) size; *von* ~ of distinction; **~el** ['~əl] *f* (-/-n) formula; **Qell** *adj.* [~'mɛl] formal; '**Qen** *v/t.* (ge-, h) form (*object, character, etc.*); shape, fashion (*wood, metal, etc.*); mo(u)ld (*clay, character, etc.*); '**~enlehre** *gr.* *f* accidence; '**~fehler** *m* informality.

flaw; **Qieren** [~'miːrən] *v/t.* (*no* -ge-, h) form; draw up, line up; *sich ~* line up.

förmlich *adj.* ['fœrmlɪç] formal; ceremonious; **Qkeit** *f* (-/-en) formality; ceremoniousness.

'**formlos** *adj.* formless, shapeless; *fig.* informal.

Formular [fɔrmu'laːr] *n* (-s/-e) form, *Am. a.* blank.

formu'lieren *v/t.* (*no* -ge-, h) formulate (*question, etc.*); word, phrase (*question, contract, etc.*).

forsch *adj.* [fɔrʃ] vigorous, energetic; smart, dashing.

forsch|en ['fɔrʃən] *v/i.* (ge-, h): *~ nach* (*dat.*) search for *or* after; *~ in* (*dat.*) search (through); '**Qer** *m* (-s/-) researcher, research worker.

'**Forschung** *f* (-/-en) research (work); '**~sreise** *f* (exploring) expedition; '**~sreisende** *m* explorer.

Forst [fɔrst] *m* (-es/-e[n]) forest; '**~aufseher** *m* (forest-)keeper, gamekeeper. [ranger.]

Förster ['fœrstər] *m* (-s/-) forester;]

'**Forst|haus** *n* forester's house; '**~revier** *n* forest district; '**~wesen** *n*, '**~wirtschaft** *f* forestry.

Fort[1] ⚔ [foːr] *n* (-s/-s) fort.

fort[2] *adv.* [fɔrt] away, gone; on; gone, lost; *in e-m ~* continuously; *und so ~* and so on *or* forth; *s. a.* weg.

'**fort|bestehen** *v/i.* (*irr.* stehen, *sep.*, *no* -ge-, h) continue, persist; '**~bewegen** *v/t.* (*sep.*, *no* -ge-, h) move (on, away); *sich ~* move, walk; '**Qdauer** *f* continuance; '**~dauern** *v/i.* (*sep.*, -ge-, h) continue, last; '**~fahren** *v/i.* (*irr.* fahren, *sep.*, -ge-) **1.** (*sein*) depart, leave; drive off; **2.** (*h*) continue, keep on (*et. zu tun* doing s.th.); '**~führen** *v/t.* (*sep.*, -ge-, h) continue, carry on; '**Qgang** *m* departure, leaving; continuance; '**~gehen** *v/i.* (*irr.* gehen, *sep.*, -ge-, *sein*) go (away), leave; '**~geschritten** *adj.* advanced; '**Qkommen** *n* (-s/*no pl.*) progress; '**~laufend** *adj.* consecutive, continuous; '**~pflanzen** *v/t.* (*sep.*, -ge-, h) propagate; *sich ~ biol.* propagate, reproduce; *phys.*, *disease*, *rumour:* be propagated; '**Qpflanzung** *f* propagation; reproduction; '**~reißen** *v/t.* (*irr.* reißen, *sep.*, -ge-, h) avalanche, *etc.:* sweep *or* carry away; '**~schaffen** *v/t.* (sep., -ge-, h) get or take away, remove; '**~schreiten** *v/i.* (irr. schreiten, sep., -ge-, sein) advance, proceed, progress; '**~schreitend** adj. progressive; '**²schritt** m progress; '**~schrittlich** adj. progressive; '**~setzen** *v/t.* (sep., -ge-, h) continue, pursue; '**~setzung** f (-/-en) continuation, pursuit; ~ folgt to be continued; '**~während 1.** adj. continual, continuous; perpetual; **2.** adv. constantly, always.

Forum ['fo:rum] n (-s/Foren, Fora and -s) forum.

Foto... ['fo:to-] s. Photo...

Foyer [foa'je:] n (-s/-s) thea. foyer, Am. and parl. lobby; hotel: foyer, lounge.

Fracht [fraxt] f (-/-en) goods pl.; 🚃 carriage, freight; ♓, ✈ freight (-age), cargo; '**~brief** m ♓ consignment note, Am., ✈ bill of lading; '**~dampfer** m cargo steamer, freighter; '**~er** m (-s/-) freighter; '**²frei** adj. carriage or freight paid; '**~führer** m carrier, Am. a. teamster; '**~geld** n carriage charges pl., ✈, ♓, Am. freight; '**~gut** n goods pl., freight; '**~stück** n package.

Frack [frak] m (-[e]s/⸚e, -s) dress coat, tail-coat, F tails; '**~anzug** m dress-suit.

Frag|e ['fra:gə] f (-/-n) question; gr., reth. interrogation; problem, point; e-e ~ stellen ask a question; in ~ stellen question; '**~ebogen** m questionnaire; form; '**²en** (ge-, h) **1.** *v/t.* ask; question; es fragt sich, ob it is doubtful whether; **2.** *v/i.* ask; '**~er** m (-s/-) questioner; '**~ewort** n (-[e]s/⸚er) interrogative; '**~ezeichen** n question-mark, point of interrogation, Am. mst interrogation point; **²lich** adj. ['fra:k-] doubtful, uncertain; in question; **²los** adv. ['fra:k-] undoubtedly, unquestionably.   [fragment.]

Fragment [frag'mɛnt] n (-[e]s/-e)] **fragwürdig** adj. ['fra:k-] doubtful, dubious, questionable.

Fraktion parl. [frak'tsjo:n] f (-/-en) (parliamentary) group.

frank|ieren [fraŋ'ki:rən] *v/t.* (no -ge-, h) prepay, stamp; '**~o** adv. ['⸚o] free; post(age) paid; parcel: carriage paid.

Franse ['franzə] f (-/-n) fringe.

Franz|ose [fran'tso:zə] m (-n/-n)

Frenchman; die ~n pl. the French pl.; **~ösin** [⸚'ø:zin] f (-/-nen) Frenchwoman; **²ösisch** adj. [⸚'ø:ziʃ] French.

fräs|en ⊕ ['frɛ:zən] *v/t.* (ge-, h) mill; **²maschine** ['frɛ:s-] f milling-machine.

Fraß [fra:s] **1.** F m (-es/-e) sl. grub; **2.** ² pret. of fressen.

Fratze ['fratsə] f (-/-n) grimace, F face; ~n schneiden make grimaces.

Frau [frau] f (-/-en) woman; lady; wife; ~ X Mrs X.

'**Frauen|arzt** m gyn(a)ecologist; '**~klinik** f hospital for women; '**~rechte** n/pl. women's rights pl.; '**~stimmrecht** pol. n women's suffrage; '**~zimmer** mst contp. n female, woman.

Fräulein ['frɔylain] n (-s/-, F -s) young lady; teacher; shop-assistant; waitress; ~ X Miss X.

'**fraulich** adj. womanly.

frech adj. [frɛç] impudent, insolent, F saucy, cheeky, Am. F a. sassy, sl. fresh; lie, etc.: brazen; thief, etc.: bold, daring; '**²heit** f (-/-en) impudence, insolence; F sauciness, cheek; boldness.

frei adj. [frai] free (von from, of); position: vacant; field: open; parcel: carriage-paid; journalist, etc.: free-lance; liberal; candid, frank; licentious; ~ Haus franco domicile; ~er Tag day off; im Freien in the open air.

'**Frei|bad** n open-air bath; '**~beuter** ['⸚bɔytər] m (-s/-) freebooter; '**²bleibend** ✝ adj. price, etc.: subject to alteration; offer: conditional; '**~brief** m charter; fig. warrant; '**~denker** m (-s/-) freethinker.

Freier ['fraiər] m (-s/-) suitor.

'**Frei|exemplar** n free or presentation copy; '**~frau** f baroness; '**~gabe** f release; '**²geben** (irr. geben, sep., -ge-, h) **1.** *v/t.* release; give (s.o. an hour, etc.) off; **2.** *v/i.*: j-m ~ give s.o. time off; '**²gebig** adj. generous, liberal; '**~gebigkeit** f (-/-en) generosity, liberality; '**~gepäck** n free luggage; '**²haben** *v/i.* (irr. haben, sep., -ge-, h) have a holiday; have a day off; '**~hafen** m free port; '**²halten** *v/t.* (irr. halten, sep., -ge-, h) keep free or clear; in restaurant: treat; '**~handel** m free trade.

'Freiheit f (-/-en) liberty; freedom; *dichterische* ~ poetic licence, *Am.* poetic license.

'Frei|herr m baron; **'~karte** f free (*thea. a.* complimentary) ticket; **'2lassen** v/t. (*irr.* lassen, *sep.*, *-ge-*, h) release, set free *or* at liberty; *gegen Kaution* ~ 🏛 release on bail; **'~lassung** f (-/-en) release; **'~lauf** m free-wheel.

'freilich adv. indeed, certainly, of course; admittedly.

'Frei|lichtbühne f open-air stage *or* theat|re, *Am.* -er; **'2machen** v/t. (*sep.*, *-ge-*, h) & prepay, stamp (*letter, etc.*); *sich* ~ undress, take one's clothes off; **'~marke** f stamp; **'~maurer** m freemason; **~maurerei** [_'raɪ] f (-/no pl.) freemasonry; **'~mut** m frankness, **2mütig** adj. ['_myːtɪç] frank; **'2schaffend** adj.: **~er** *Künstler* free-lance artist; **~schärler** 🗡 ['_ʃɛːrlɔr] m (-s/-) volunteer, irregular; **'~schein** m licen|ce, *Am.* -se; **'2sinnig** adj. liberal; **'2sprechen** v/t. (*irr.* sprechen, *sep.*, *-ge-*, h) *esp. eccl.* absolve (*von* from); 🏛 acquit (of); release (*apprentice*) from his articles; **'~sprechung** f (-/-en) *esp. eccl.* absolution; release from articles; = **'~spruch** 🏛 m acquittal; **'~staat** pol. m free state; **'2stehen** v/i. (*irr.* stehen, *sep.*, *-ge-*, h) house, *etc.*: stand empty; *es steht Ihnen frei zu inf.* you are free *or* at liberty to *inf.*; **'2stellen** v/t. (*sep.*, *-ge-*, h): *j-n* ~ exempt s.o. (*von* from) (*a.* 🗡); *j-m et.* ~ leave s.th. open to s.o.; **'~stoß** m football: free kick; **'~tag** m Friday; **'~tod** m suicide; **'2tragend** △ adj. cantilever; **'~treppe** f outdoor staircase; **'2willig** 1. adj. voluntary; 2. adv. a. of one's own free will; **~willige** ['_vɪlɪgə] m (-n/-n) volunteer; **'~zeit** f free *or* spare *or* leisure time; **'2zügig** adj. ['_tsyːgɪç] free to move; **'~zügigkeit** f (-/no pl.) freedom of movement.

fremd adj. [frɛmt] strange; foreign; alien; extraneous; **'~artig** adj. strange; exotic.

Fremde ['frɛmdə] 1. f (-/no pl.) distant *or* foreign parts; *in der* ~ far away from home, abroad; 2. m, f (-n/-n) stranger; foreigner; **'~buch** n visitors' book; **'~nführer** m guide, cicerone; **'~nheim** n

boarding house; **~nindustrie** ['frɛmdənʔ-] f tourist industry; **'~nlegion** 🗡 f Foreign Legion; **'~nverkehr** m tourism, tourist traffic; **'~nzimmer** n spare (bed-)room; *tourism:* room.

'Fremd|herrschaft f fofeign rule; **'~körper** ♂ m foreign body; **2ländisch** adj. ['_lɛndɪʃ] foreign, exotic; **'~sprache** f foreign language; **'2sprachig** adj., **'2sprachlich** adj. foreign-language; **'~wort** n (-[e]s/ʉer) foreign word.

Frequenz phys. [fre'kvɛnts] f (-/-en) frequency.

fressen ['frɛsən] 1. v/t. (*irr.*, ge-, h) eat; *beast of prey:* devour; F p. devour, gorge; 2. v/i. (*irr.*, ge-, h) eat; F p. gorge; 3. 2 n (-s/no pl.) feed, food.

'Freß|gier f voracity, gluttony; **'~napf** m feeding dish.

Freude ['frɔydə] f (-/-n) joy, gladness; delight; pleasure; ~ *haben an* (*dat.*) find *or* take pleasure in.

'Freuden|botschaft f glad tidings pl.; **'~fest** n happy occasion; **'~feuer** n bonfire; **'~geschrei** n shouts pl. of joy; **'~tag** m day of rejoicing, red-letter day; **'~taumel** m transports pl. of joy.

'freud|estrahlend adj. radiant with joy; **'~ig** adj. joyful; happy; ~es *Ereignis* happy event; **'~los** adj. ['frɔytloːs] joyless, cheerless.

freuen ['frɔyən] v/t. (ge-, h): *es freut mich, daß* I am glad *or* pleased (that); *sich* ~ *über* (*acc.*) be pleased about *or* with, be glad about; *sich* ~ *auf* (*acc.*) look forward to.

Freund [frɔynt] m (-es/-e) (boy-)friend; **'~in** ['_dɪn] f (-/-nen) (girl-)friend; **'2lich** adj. friendly, kind, nice; cheerful, bright; *climate:* mild; **'~lichkeit** f (-/-en) friendliness, kindness; **'~schaft** f (-/-en) friendship; ~ *schließen* make friends (*mit* with); **'2schaftlich** adj. friendly.

Frevel ['freːfəl] m (-s/-) outrage (*an dat.*, *gegen* on), crime (against); **'2haft** adj. wicked, outrageous; impious; **'2n** v/i. (ge-, h) commit a crime *or* outrage (*gegen* against).

Frevler ['freːflɔr] m (-s/-) evil-doer, offender; blasphemer.

Friede(n) ['friːdə(n)] m (*Friedens/Frieden*) peace; *im Frieden* in peacetime; *laß mich in Frieden!* leave me alone!

'**Friedens|bruch** *m* violation of (the) peace; '**~stifter** *m* peacemaker; '**~störer** *m* (-s/-) disturber of the peace; '**~verhandlungen** *f/pl.* peace negotiations *pl.*; '**~vertrag** *m* peace treaty.

fried|fertig *adj.* ['fri:t-] peaceable, peace-loving; '**♀hof** *m* cemetery, graveyard; churchyard; *s. friedfertig;* '**~liebend** *adj.* peace-loving.

frieren ['fri:rən] *v/i.* (*irr.*, ge-) **1.** (*sein*) *liquid:* freeze, become frozen; *river, etc.:* freeze (up); *window-pane, etc.:* freeze over; **2.** (*h*) be or feel cold; *mich friert* or *ich friere an den Füßen* my feet are cold.

Fries △ [fri:s] *m* (-es/-e) frieze.

frisch [friʃ] **1.** *adj. food, flowers, etc.:* fresh; *egg:* new-laid; *linen, etc.:* clean; *auf* **~***er Tat ertappen* catch red-handed; **2.** *adv.:* **~** *gestrichen!* wet paint!; **♀e** Am. fresh paint!; **♀e** ['~ə] *f* (-/*no pl.*) freshness.

Friseu|r [fri'zøːr] *m* (-s/-e) hairdresser; (*men's*) barber; '**~se** [~zə] *f* (-/-n) (woman) hairdresser.

fri'sier|en *v/t.* (*no* -ge-, *h*): *j-n* **~** do or dress s.o.'s hair; *F: einen Wagen* **~** *mot.* tune up or soup up or hot up a car; *sich* **~** do one's hair; **♀kommode** *f* dressing-table; **♀salon** *m* hairdressing saloon; **♀tisch** *m s. Frisierkommode.*

Frist [frist] *f* (-/-en) (fixed or limited) period of time; time allowed; term; ⅌ prescribed time; ⅌, ✝ respite, grace; '**♀en** *v/t.* (ge-, *h*): *sein Dasein* **~** scrape along, scrape a living.

Frisur [fri'zuːr] *f* (-/-en) hair-style, hair-do, coiffure.

frivol [fri'voːl] *adj.* frivolous, flippant; **♀ität** [~oli'tɛːt] *f* (-/-en) frivolity, flippancy.

froh [fro:] *adj.* joyful, glad; cheerful; happy; gay (*a. colour*).

fröhlich *adj.* ['frøːliç] gay, merry, cheerful, happy, Am. F *a.* chipper; '**♀keit** *f* (-/~ -en) gaiety, cheerfulness; merriment.

froh'locken *v/i.* (*no* -ge-, *h*) shout for joy, be jubilant; exult (*über acc.* at, in); gloat (over); '**♀sinn** *m* (-[e]s/*no pl.*) gaiety, cheerfulness.

fromm *adj.* [frɔm] *p.* pious, religious; *life, etc.:* godly; *prayer, etc.:* devout; *horse, etc.:* docile; **~e** *Lüge* white lie; **~er** *Wunsch* wishful thinking, idle wish.

Frömmelei [frœmə'laɪ] *f* (-/-en) affected piety, bigotry.

'**Frömmigkeit** *f* (-/-en) piety, religiousness; godliness; devoutness.

Fron [fro:n] *f* (-/-en), '**~arbeit** *f*, '**~dienst** *hist. m* forced or compulsory labo(u)r or service; *fig.* drudgery.

frönen ['frøːnən] *v/i.* (*dat.*) (ge-, *h*) indulge in; be a slave to.

Front [frɔnt] *f* (-/-en) △ front, façade, face; ✕ front (line), line; *pol.*, ✝, *etc.:* front.

fror [froːr] *pret. of* frieren.

Frosch *zo.* [frɔʃ] *m* (-es/ue) frog; '**~perspektive** *f* worm's-eye view.

Frost [frɔst] *m* (-es/ue) frost; chill; '**~beule** *f* chilblain.

frösteln ['frœstəln] *v/i.* (ge-, *h*) feel chilly, shiver (with cold).

'**frostig** *adj.* frosty (*a. fig.*); *fig.* cold, frigid, icy.

'**Frost|salbe** ♂ *f* chilblain ointment; '**~schaden** *m* frost damage; '**~schutzmittel** *mot. n* anti-freezing mixture; '**~wetter** *n* frosty weather.

frottier|en [frɔ'tiːrən] *v/t.* (*no* -ge-, *h*) rub; **♀(hand)tuch** *n* Turkish towel.

Frucht [fruxt] *f* (-/ue) ♀ fruit (*a. fig.*); *corn:* crop; *fig.* reward, result; '**♀bar** *adj.* fruitful (*esp. fig.*); fertile (*a. biol.*); '**~barkeit** *f* (-/*no pl.*) fruitfulness; fertility; **♀br-ingend** *adj.* fruit-bearing; *fig.* fruitful; '**♀en** *fig. v/i.* (ge-, *h*) be of use; '**~knoten** ♀ *m* ovary; '**♀los** *adj.* fruitless; *fig. a.* ineffective.

früh [fry:] **1.** *adj.* early; *am* **~***en Morgen* in the early morning; **~***es Aufstehen* early rising; **~***e Anzeichen* early symptoms; **~***er former;* **2.** *adv.* in the morning; **~** *aufstehen* rise early; *heute* **~** this morning; *morgen* **~** tomorrow morning; **~***er* earlier; formerly, in former times; **~***estens* at the earliest; '**♀aufsteher** *m* (-s/-) early riser, F early bird; '**♀e** *f* (-/*no pl.*): *in aller* **~** very early in the morning; '**♀geburt** *f* premature birth; premature baby or animal; '**♀gottesdienst** *m* early service;

'2**jahr** n, '2**ling** ['ˈ‿liŋ] m (-s/-e) spring; ~**morgens** adv. early in the morning; '‿**reif** fig. adj. precocious; '2**sport** m early morning exercises; '2**stück** n breakfast; '‿**stücken** (ge-, h) **1.** v/i. (have) breakfast; **2.** v/t. have s.th. for breakfast; '2**zug** 🚂 m early train.

Fuchs [fuks] m (-es/‿e) zo. fox (a. fig.); horse: sorrel.

Füchsin zo. ['fyksin] f (-/-nen) shefox, vixen.

'**Fuchs**|**jagd** f fox-hunt(ing); '‿**pelz** m fox-fur; '2'**rot** adj. foxy-red, sorrel; '‿**schwanz** m foxtail; ⊕ pad-saw; ♣ amarant(h); '2'**teufels**-**wild** F adj. mad with rage, F hopping mad.

fuchteln ['fuxtəln] v/i. (ge-, h): ~ **mit** (dat.) wave (one's hands) wildly.

Fuder ['fuːdər] n (-s/-) cart-load; tun (of wine). [♩ fugue.]

Fuge ['fuːgə] f (-/-n) ⊕ joint; seam; ♩

füg|**en** ['fyːgən] v/refl. (ge-, h) submit, give in, yield (dat., in acc. to); comply (with); ~**sam** adj. ['fyːk‿] (com)pliant; manageable.

'**fühl**|**bar** adj. ['fyːlbɑːr] tangible, palpable; fig. sensible, noticeable; '‿**en** (ge-, h) **1.** v/t. feel; be aware of; sich glücklich ~ feel happy; **2.** v/i.: mit j-m ~ feel for or sympathize with s.o.; '2**er** m (-s/-) feeler (a. fig.); '2**ung** f (-/-en) touch, contact (a. ⚔); ~ haben be in touch (mit with); ~ verlieren lose touch.

fuhr [fuːr] pret. of fahren.

Fuhre ['fuːrə] f (-/-n) cart-load.

führen ['fyːrən] (ge-, h) **1.** v/t. lead, guide (blind person, etc.); show (zu dat. to); wield (paint-brush, etc.); ⚔ command (regiment, etc.); have, bear (title, etc.); carry on (conversation, etc.); conduct (campaign, etc.); ✝ run (shop, etc.); deal in (goods); lead (life); keep (diary, etc.); ⚖ try (case); wage (war) (mit, gegen against); ~ durch show round; sich ~ conduct o.s., behave (o.s.); **2.** v/i. path, etc.: lead, run, go (nach, zu to); sports, etc.: (hold the) lead, be ahead; ~ zu lead to, result in; '‿**d** adj. leading, prominent, Am. a. banner.

'**Führer** m (-s/-) leader (a. pol., sports); guide(-book); '‿**raum** 🚀 m cockpit; '‿**schein** mot. m driving licence, Am. driver's license; '‿**sitz**

m mot. driver's seat, ⚔ pilot's seat; '‿**stand** 🚂 m (driver's) cab.

'**Fuhr**|**geld** n, '‿**lohn** m cartage, carriage; '‿**mann** m (-[e]s/‿er, Fuhrleute) carter, carrier, wag(g)oner; driver; '‿**park** m fleet (of lorries), Am. fleet (of trucks).

'**Führung** f (-/-en) leadership; conduct, management; guidance; conduct, behavio(u)r; sports, etc.: lead; '‿**szeugnis** n certificate of good conduct.

'**Fuhr**|**unternehmer** m carrier, haulage contractor, Am. a. trucker, teamster; '‿**werk** n (horse-drawn) vehicle; cart, wag(g)on.

Fülle ['fylə] f (-/no pl.) fullness (a. fig.); corpulence, plumpness, stoutness; fig. wealth, abundance, profusion.

füllen[1] ['fylən] v/t. (ge-, h) fill (a. tooth); stuff (cushion, poultry, etc.).

Füllen[2] zo. [‿] n (-s/-) foal; male: colt; female: filly.

'**Füll**|**er** F m (-s/-), '‿**feder**(**halter** m) f fountain-pen; '‿**horn** n horn of plenty; '‿**ung** f (-/-en) filling; panel (of door, etc.).

Fund [funt] m (-[e]s/-e) finding, discovery; find.

Fundament[funda'ment]n(-[e]s/-e) 🏛 foundation; fig. basis.

'**Fund**|**büro** n lost-property office; '‿**gegenstand** m object found; '‿**grube** fig. f rich source, mine.

fünf [fynf] five; '2**eck** n pentagon; '‿**fach** adj. ['‿fax] fivefold, quintuple; '2**kampf** m sports: pentathlon; '2**linge** ['‿liŋə] m/pl. quintuplets pl.; '‿**te** adj. fifth; '2**tel** n (-s/-) fifth; '‿**tens** adv. fifthly, in the fifth place; '‿**zehn**(**te**) adj. fifteen(th); '‿**zig** adj. ['‿tsiç] fifty; '‿**zigste** adj. fiftieth.

fungieren [fuŋ'giːrən] v/i. (no -ge-, h): ~ als officiate or act as.

Funk [funk] m (-s/no pl.) radio, wireless; '‿**anlage** f radio or wireless installation or equipment; '‿**bastler** m do-it-yourself radio ham; '‿**bild** n photo-radiogram.

Funke ['funkə] m (-ns/-n) spark; fig. a. glimmer.

'**funkeln** v/i. (ge-, h) sparkle, glitter; star: twinkle, sparkle.

'**Funken**[1] esp. fig. m (-s/-) s. Funke.

'**funken**[2] v/t. (ge-, h) radio, wireless, broadcast.

'**Funk|er** m (-s/-) radio or wireless operator; '**∼gerät** n radio (communication) set; '**∼spruch** m radio or wireless message; '**∼station** f radio or wireless station; '**∼stille** f radio or wireless silence; '**∼streifenwagen** m radio patrol car.

Funktion [fuŋk'tsjo:n] f (-/-en) function; **∼är** [∼tsjo'nɛ:r] m (-s/-e) functionary, official; **2ieren** [∼o-'ni:rən] v/i. (no -ge-, h) function, work.

'**Funk|turm** m radio or wireless tower; '**∼verkehr** m radio or wireless communication; '**∼wagen** m radio car; '**∼wesen** n (-s/no pl.) radio communication.

für prp. (acc.) [fy:r] for; in exchange or return for; in favo(u)r of; in s.o.'s place; Schritt ∼ Schritt step by step; Tag ∼ Tag day after day; ich ∼ meine Person ... as for me, I ...; das Für und Wider the pros and cons pl.

'**Fürbitte** f intercession.

Furche ['furçə] f (-/-n) furrow (a. in face); rut; ⊕ groove; '**2n** v/t. (ge-, h) furrow (a. face); ⊕ groove.

Furcht [furçt] f (-/no pl.) fear, dread; aus ∼ vor for fear of; '**2bar** adj. awful, terrible, dreadful.

fürchten ['fyrçtən] (ge-, h) **1.** v/t. fear, dread; sich ∼ vor (dat.) be afraid or scared of; **2.** v/i.: ∼ um fear for.

'**fürchterlich** adj. s. furchtbar.

'**furcht|los** adj. fearless; '**2losigkeit** f (-/no pl.) fearlessness; '**∼sam** adj. timid, timorous; '**2samkeit** f (-/no pl.) timidity.

Furie fig. ['fu:rjə] f (-/-n) fury.

Furnier ⊕ [fur'ni:r] n (-s/-e) veneer; **2en** v/t. (no -ge-, h) veneer.

'**Für|sorge** f care; öffentliche ∼ public welfare work; '**∼sorgeamt** n welfare department; '**∼sorgeerziehung** f corrective training for juvenile delinquents; '**∼sorger** m (-s/-) social or welfare worker; '**2sorglich** adj. considerate, thoughtful, solicitous; '**∼sprache** f intercession (für for, bei with); '**∼sprecher** m intercessor.

Fürst [fyrst] m (-en/-en) prince; sovereign; '**∼enhaus** n dynasty; '**∼enstand** m prince's rank; '**∼en-**

tum n (-s/∼er) principality; '**2lich 1.** adj. princely (a. fig.), royal; fig. magnificent, sumptuous; **2.** adv.: ∼ leben live like a lord or king; '**∼lichkeiten** f/pl. royalties pl.

Furt [furt] f (-/-en) ford.

Furunkel ✠ [fu'ruŋkəl] m (-s/-) boil, furuncle.

'**Fürwort** gr. n (-[e]s/∼er) pronoun.

Fusel F ['fu:zəl] m (-s/-) low-quality spirits, F rotgut.

Fusion ✝ [fu'zjo:n] f (-/-en) merger, amalgamation.

Fuß [fu:s] m (-es/∼e) foot; ∼ fassen find a foothold; fig. become established; auf gutem (schlechtem) ∼ stehen mit be on good (bad) terms with; zu ∼ on foot; zu ∼ gehen walk; gut zu ∼ sein be a good walker; '**∼abstreifer** m (-s/-) door-scraper, door-mat; '**∼angel** f mantrap; '**∼ball** m (association) football, F and Am. soccer; '**∼ballspieler** m football player, footballer; '**∼bank** f footstool; '**∼bekleidung** f footwear, footgear; '**∼boden** m floor (-ing); '**∼bodenbelag** m floor covering; '**∼bremse** mot. f foot-brake; '**2en** v/i. (ge-, h): ∼ auf (dat.) be based or founded on; **∼gänger** ['∼gɛŋər] m (-s/-) pedestrian; '**∼gelenk** anat. n ankle joint; '**∼note** f footnote; '**∼pfad** m footpath; '**∼sack** m foot-muff; '**∼sohle** anat. f sole of the foot; '**∼soldat** ✗ m footsoldier, infantryman; '**∼spur** f footprint; track; '**∼stapfe** ['∼ʃtapfə] f (-/-n) footprint, fig. a. footstep; '**∼steig** m footpath; '**∼tritt** m kick; '**∼wanderung** f walking tour, hike; '**∼weg** m footpath.

Futter ['futər] n **1.** (-s/no pl.) food, sl. grub, Am. F a. chow; feed, fodder; **2.** (-s/-) lining; △ casing.

Futteral [futə'ra:l] n (-s/-e) case (for spectacles, etc.); cover (of umbrella); sheath (of knife).

'**Futtermittel** n feeding stuff.

füttern ['fytərn] v/t. (ge-, h) feed; line (dress, etc.); △ case.

'**Futter|napf** m feeding bowl or dish; '**∼neid** fig. m (professional) jealousy; '**∼stoff** m lining (material).

'**Fütterung** f (-/-en) feeding; lining; △ casing. [(tense).}

Futur gr. [fu'tu:r] n (-s/-e) future}

G

gab [gɑːp] *pret. of* geben.
Gabe ['gɑːbə] *f* (-/-n) gift, present; alms; donation; *&* dose; talent.
Gabel ['gɑːbəl] *f* (-/-n) fork; '**_n** *v/refl.* (ge-, h) fork, bifurcate; '**_ung** *f* (-/-en) bifurcation.
gackern ['gakərn] *v/i.* (ge-, h) cackle.
gaffen ['gafən] *v/i.* (ge-, h) gape; stare.
Gage ['gɑːʒə] *f* (-/-n) salary, pay.
gähnen ['gɛːnən] **1.** *v/i.* (ge-, h) yawn; **2.** *2n m* (-s/*no pl.*) yawning.
Gala ['gala] *f* (-/*no pl.*) gala; in ~ in full dress.
galant *adj.* [ga'lant] gallant; courteous; *2erie* [~ə'riː] *f* (-/-n) gallantry, courtesy.
Galeere ⚓ [ga'leːrə] *f* (-/-n) galley.
Galerie [galə'riː] *f* gallery.
Galgen ['galgən] *m* (-s/-) gallows, gibbet; '**_frist** *f* respite; '**_gesicht** *n* gallows-look, hangdog look; '**_humor** *m* grim humo(u)r; '**_strick** *m*, '**_vogel** *m* gallows-bird, hangdog.
Galle *anat.* ['galə] *f* (-/-n) bile (*of person*); gall (*of animal*) (*a. fig.*); '**_nblase** *anat.* *f* gall-bladder; '**_nleiden** *&* *n* bilious complaint; '**_nstein** *&* *m* gall-stone, bile-stone.
Gallert ['galərt] *n* (-[e]s/-e), **_e** [ga'lɛrtə] *f* (-/-n) gelatine, jelly.
gallig *fig. adj.* bilious.
Galopp [ga'lɔp] *m* (-s/-s, -e) gallop; canter; *2ieren* [~'piːrən] *v/i.* (*no -ge-, sein*) gallop; canter.
galt [galt] *pret. of* gelten.
galvani|sch *adj.* [gal'vɑːniʃ] galvanic; **_sieren** [~ani'-] *v/t.* (*no -ge-, h*) galvanize.
Gang[1] [gaŋ] *m* (-[e]s/⁼e) walk; *s. Gangart; fig.* motion; running, working (*of machine*); errand; way; course (*of a meal, etc.*); passage(-way); alley; corridor, gallery; *in vehicle, between seats:* gangway, *esp. Am.* aisle; 🚇 corridor, *Am.* aisle; *fencing:* pass; *anat.* duct; *mot.* gear; erster (zweiter, dritter, vierter) ~ low *or* bottom (second, third, top) gear; *in* ~ *bringen or setzen* set going *or* in motion, *Am.* operate; *in* ~ *kommen* get going, get started; *im* ~ *sein* be in motion; ⊕ be working *or* running; *fig.* be

in progress; *in vollem* ~ in full swing.
gang[2] *adj.* [~]: ~ *und gäbe* customary, traditional.
'**Gang|art** *f* gait, walk (*of person*); pace (*of horse*); '2**bar** *adj.* road: practicable, passable; *money:* current; *✝ goods:* marketable; *s. gängig.*
Gängelband ['gɛŋəl-] *n* leading-strings *pl.*; *am* ~ *führen* keep in leading-strings, lead by the nose.
gängig *adj.* ['gɛŋiç] *money:* current; *✝ goods:* marketable; *_er Ausdruck* current word *or* phrase.
Gans *orn.* [gans] *f* (-/⁼e) goose.
Gänse|blümchen ♣ ['gɛnzəblyːmçən] *n* (-s/-) daisy; '**_braten** *m* roast goose; '**_feder** *f* goose-quill; '**_füßchen** ['~fyːsçən] *n/pl.* quotation marks *pl.*, inverted commas *pl.*; '**_haut** *f* goose-skin; *fig. a.* goose-flesh, *Am. a.* goose pimples *pl.*; '**_klein** *n* (-s/*no pl.*) (goose-)giblets *pl.*; '**_marsch** *m* single *or* Indian file; **_rich** *orn.* ['~riç] *m* (-s/-e) gander; '**_schmalz** *n* goose-grease.
ganz [gants] **1.** *adj.* all; entire, whole; complete, total, full; *den _en Tag* all day (long); **2.** *adv.* quite; entirely, *etc.* (*s. 1.*); very; *_ Auge (Ohr)* all eyes (ears); ~ *und gar* wholly, totally; ~ *und gar nicht* not at all; *im _en* on the whole, generally; in all; *✝ in the lump;* 2**e** *n* (-n/*no pl.*) whole; totality; *aufs* ~ *gehen* go all out, *esp. Am. sl.* go the whole hog.
gänzlich *adj.* ['gɛntsliç] complete, total, entire.
'**Ganztagsbeschäftigung** *f* full-time job *or* employment.
gar [gɑːr] **1.** *adj. food:* done; **2.** *adv.* quite, very; even; ~ *nicht* not at all.
Garage [ga'rɑːʒə] *f* (-/-n) garage.
Garantie [garan'tiː] *f* (-/-n) guarantee, warranty, 🕮 guaranty; 2**ren** *v/t.* (*no -ge-, h*) guarantee, warrant.
Garbe ['garbə] *f* (-/-n) sheaf.
Garde ['gardə] *f* (-/-n) guard.
Garderobe [gardə'roːbə] *f* (-/-n) wardrobe; cloakroom, *Am.* check-room; *thea.* dressing-room; **_nfrau** *f* cloak-room attendant, *Am.* hat-check girl; **_nmarke** *f* check; **_nschrank** *m* wardrobe; **_nständer**

m coat-stand, hat-stand, hall-stand.

Garderobiere [gardərɔ'bjɛ:rə] *f* (-/-n) *s.* Garderobenfrau; *thea.* wardrobe mistress.

Gardine [gar'di:nə] *f* (-/-n) curtain.

gär|en ['gɛ:rən] *v/i.* (*irr.*, ge-, *h*, *sein*) ferment; '**⁀mittel** *n* ferment.

Garn [garn] *n* (-[e]s/-e) yarn; thread; cotton; net; *j-m ins* ⁀ *gehen* fall into s.o.'s snare.

Garnele *zo.* [gar'ne:lə] *f* (-/-n) shrimp.

garnieren [gar'ni:rən] *v/t.* (*no -ge-*, *h*) trim; garnish (*esp. a dish*).

Garnison ✕ [garni'zo:n] *f* (-/-en) garrison, post.

Garnitur [garni'tu:r] *f* (-/-en) trimming; ⊕ fittings *pl.*; set.

garstig ['garstiç] nasty, bad; ugly.

'**Gärstoff** *m* ferment.

Garten ['gartən] *m* (-s/⁀) garden; '**⁀anlage** *f* gardens *pl.*, park; '**⁀arbeit** *f* gardening; '**⁀bau** *m* horticulture; '**⁀erde** *f* (garden-)mo(u)ld; '**⁀fest** *n* garden-party, *Am. a.* lawn party; '**⁀geräte** *n/pl.* gardening-tools *pl.*; '**⁀stadt** *f* garden city.

Gärtner ['gɛrtnər] *m* (-s/-) gardener; **⁀ei** [⁀'rai] *f* (-/-en) gardening, horticulture; nursery; '**⁀in** *f* (-/-nen) gardener. [tation.)

Gärung ['gɛ:ruŋ] *f* (-/-en) fermen-)

Gas [ga:s] *n* (-es/-e) gas; ⁀ *geben mot.* open the throttle, *Am.* step on the gas; '**⁀anstalt** *f* gas-works, *Am. a.* gas plant; '**⁀behälter** *m* gasometer, *Am.* gas tank *or* container; '**⁀beleuchtung** *f* gaslight; '**⁀brenner** *m* gas-burner; **⁀förmig** *adj.* ['⁀fœrmiç] gaseous; '**⁀hahn** *m* gas-tap; '**⁀herd** *m* gas-stove, *Am.* gas range; '**⁀leitung** *f* gas-mains *pl.*; '**⁀messer** *m* (-s/-) gas-meter; '**⁀ofen** *m* gas-oven; '**⁀pedal** *mot. n* accelerator (pedal), *Am.* gas pedal.

Gasse ['gasə] *f* (-/-n) lane, by-street, alley(-way); '**⁀nhauer** *m* (-s/-) street ballad, popular song; '**⁀njunge** *m* street arab.

Gast [gast] *m* (-es/⁀e) guest; visitor; customer (*of public house, etc.*); *thea.*: guest (artist); guest star; '**⁀arbeiter** *m* foreign worker; '**⁀bett** *n* spare bed.

Gäste|buch ['gɛstə-] *n* visitors' book; '**⁀zimmer** *n* guest-room; spare (bed)room; *s.* Gaststube.

'**gast|freundlich** *adj.* hospitable; '**⁀freundschaft** *f* hospitality; '**⁀geber** *m* (-s/-) host; '**⁀geberin** *f* (-/-nen) hostess; '**⁀haus** *n*, '**⁀hof** *m* restaurant; inn; hotel; '**⁀hörer** *univ. m* guest student, *Am. a.* auditor.

gastieren *thea.* [gas'ti:rən] *v/i.* (*no -ge-*, *h*) appear as a guest.

'**gast|lich** *adj.* hospitable; '**⁀mahl** *n* feast, banquet; '**⁀recht** *n* right of *or* to hospitality; '**⁀rolle** *thea. f* guest part; starring part *or* role; '**⁀spiel** *thea. n* guest appearance *or* performance; starring (performance); '**⁀stätte** *f* restaurant; '**⁀stube** *f* taproom; restaurant; '**⁀wirt** *m* innkeeper, landlord; '**⁀wirtin** *f* innkeeper, landlady; '**⁀wirtschaft** *f* inn, public house, restaurant; '**⁀zimmer** *n s.* Gästezimmer.

'**Gas|uhr** *f* gas-meter; '**⁀werk** *n s.* Gasanstalt.

Gatte ['gatə] *m* (-n/-n) husband; spouse, consort.

Gatter ['gatər] *n* (-s/-) lattice; railing, grating.

'**Gattin** *f* (-/-nen) wife; spouse, consort.

Gattung ['gatuŋ] *f* (-/-en) kind; sort; type; species; genus.

gaukeln ['gaukəln] *v/i.* (ge-, *h*) juggle; birds, *etc.*: flutter.)

Gaul [gaul] *m* (-[e]s/⁀e) (old) nag.

Gaumen *anat.* ['gaumən] *m* (-s/-) palate.

Gauner ['gaunər] *m* (-s/-) scoundrel, swindler, sharper, *sl.* crook; **⁀ei** [⁀'rai] *f* (-/-en) swindling, cheating, trickery.

Gaze ['ga:zə] *f* (-/-n) gauze.

Gazelle *zo.* [ga'tsɛlə] *f* (-/-n) gazelle.

Geächtete [gə'ɛçtətə] *m, f* (-n/-n) outlaw.

Gebäck [gə'bɛk] *n* (-[e]s/-e) baker's goods *pl.*; pastry; fancy cakes *pl.*

ge'backen *p.p. of* backen.

Gebälk [gə'bɛlk] *n* (-[e]s/*no pl.*) framework, timber-work; beams *pl.*

gebar [gə'ba:r] *pret. of* gebären.

Gebärde [gə'bɛ:rdə] *f* (-/-n) gesture; **⁀n** *v/refl.* (*no -ge-*, *h*) conduct o.s., behave; '**⁀nspiel** *n* (-[e]s/*no pl.*) gesticulation; dumb show, pantomime; '**⁀nsprache** *f* language of gestures.

Gebaren [gə'ba:rən] *n* (-s/*no pl.*) conduct, deportment, behavio(u)r.

gebären [gə'bɛ:rən] v/t. (irr., no -ge-, h) bear, bring forth (a. fig.); give birth to.

Ge|bäude [gə'bɔydə] n (-s/-) building, edifice, structure; **~bell** [~'bɛl] n (-[e]s/no pl.) barking.

geben ['ge:bən] v/t. (irr., ge-, h) give (j-m et. s.o. s.th.); present (s.o. with s.th.); put; yield s.th.; deal (cards); pledge (one's word); von sich ~ emit; utter (words); bring up, vomit (food); et. (nichts) ~ auf (acc.) set (no) great store by; sich geschlagen ~ give in; sich zufrieden ~ content o.s. (mit with); sich zu erkennen ~ make o.s. known; es gibt there is, there are; was gibt es? what is the matter?; thea.: gegeben werden be on.

Gebet [gə'be:t] n (-[e]s/-e) prayer.

ge'beten p.p. of bitten.

Gebiet [gə'bi:t] n (-[e]s/-e) territory; district; region; area; fig.: field; province; sphere.

ge'biet|en (irr. bieten, no -ge-, h) **1.** v/t. order, command; **2.** v/i. rule; **2er** m (-s/-) master, lord, governor; **2erin** f (-/-nen) mistress; **~erisch** adj. imperious; commanding.

Gebilde [gə'bildə] n (-s/-) form, shape; structure; **2t** adj. educated; cultured, cultivated.

Gebirg|e [gə'birgə] n (-s/-) mountains pl.; mountain chain or range; **2ig** adj. mountainous; **~sbewohner** m mountaineer; **~szug** m mountain range.

Ge'biß n (Gebisses/Gebisse) (set of) teeth; (set of) artificial or false teeth, denture; harness: bit.

ge|'bissen p.p. of beißen; **~'blasen** p.p. of blasen; **~'blichen** p.p. of bleichen 2; **~'blieben** [~'bli:bən] p.p. of bleiben; **~'blümt** adj. [~'bly:mt] pattern, design: flowered; material: sprigged; **~'bogen 1.** p.p. of biegen; **2.** adj. bent, curved; **~boren** [~'bo:rən] **1.** p.p. of gebären; **2.** adj. born; ein ~er Deutscher German by birth; ~e Schmidt née Smith.

ge'borgen 1. p.p. of bergen; **2.** adj. safe, sheltered; **2heit** f (-/no pl.) safety, security.

geborsten [gə'bɔrstən] p.p. of bersten.

Ge'bot n (-[e]s/-e) order; command; bid(ding), offer; eccl.: die Zehn ~e pl. the Ten Commandments pl.; **2en** p.p. of bieten.

ge|bracht [gə'braxt] p.p. of bringen; **~brannt** [~'brant] p.p. of brennen; **~'braten** p.p. of braten.

Ge'brauch m **1.** (-[e]s/no pl.) use; **⚕** application; **2.** (-[e]s/⁼e) usage, practice; custom; **2en** v/t. (no -ge-, h) use, employ; **2t** adj. clothes, etc.: second-hand.

gebräuchlich adj. [gə'brɔyçliç] in use; usual, customary.

Ge'brauchs|anweisung f directions pl. or instructions pl. for use; **~artikel** m commodity, necessary, requisite; personal article; **2fertig** adj. ready for use; coffee, etc.: instant; **~muster** ⚮ n sample; registered design.

Ge'braucht|wagen mot. m used car; **~waren** f/pl. second-hand articles pl.

Ge'brechen n (-s/-) defect, infirmity; affliction.

ge'brechlich adj. fragile; p.: frail, weak; infirm; **2keit** f (-/-en) fragility; infirmity. [chen.\]

gebrochen [gə'brɔxən] p.p. of bre-\]

Ge|brüder [gə'bry:dər] pl. brothers pl.; **~brüll** [~'bryl] n (-[e]s/no pl.) roaring; lowing (of cattle).

Gebühr [gə'by:r] f (-/-en) due; duty; charge; rate; fee; **~en** pl. fee(s pl.), dues pl.; **2en** v/i. (no -ge-, h) be due (dat. to); sich ~ be proper or fitting; **2end** adj. due; becoming; proper; **2enfrei** adj. free of charge; **2enpflichtig** adj. liable to charges, chargeable.

gebunden [gə'bundən] **1.** p.p. of binden; **2.** adj. bound.

Geburt [gə'bu:rt] f (-/-en) birth; **~enkontrolle** f, **~enregelung** f birth-control; **~enziffer** f birth-rate.

gebürtig adj. [gə'byrtiç]: ~ aus a native of.

Ge'burts|anzeige f announcement of birth; **~fehler** m congenital defect; **~helfer** m obstetrician; **~hilfe** f obstetrics, midwifery; **~jahr** n year of birth; **~land** n native country; **~ort** m birth-place; **~schein** m birth certificate; **~tag** m birthday; **~urkunde** f birth certificate.

Gebüsch [gə'byʃ] n (-es/-e) bushes pl., undergrowth, thicket.

gedacht [gə'daxt] *p.p.* of denken.

Gedächtnis [gə'dɛçtnis] *n* (-ses/-se) memory; remembrance, recollection; *im* ∼ *behalten* keep in mind; *zum* ∼ (*gen.*) in memory of; ∼**feier** *f* commemoration.

Gedanke [gə'daŋkə] *m* (-ns/-n) thought; idea; *in* ∼*n* (*versunken or verloren*) absorbed in thought; *sich* ∼*n machen über* (*acc.*) worry about.

Ge'danken|**gang** *m* train of thought; ∼**leser** *m*, ∼**leserin** *f* (-/-nen) thought-reader; **2los** *adj.* thoughtless; ∼**strich** *m* dash; **2voll** *adj.* thoughtful, pensive.

Ge|**därm** [gə'dɛrm] *n* (-[e]s/-e) *mst pl.* entrails *pl.*, bowels *pl.*, intestines *pl.*; ∼**deck** [∼'dɛk] *n* (-[e]s/-e) cover; menu; *ein* ∼ *auflegen* lay a place.

gedeihen [gə'daɪən] **1.** *v/i.* (*irr.*, *no* -ge-, *sein*) thrive, prosper; **2.** **2** *n* (-s/*no pl.*) thriving, prosperity.

ge'denken 1. *v/i.* (*gen.*) (*irr.* denken, *no* -ge-, *h*) think of; remember, recollect; commemorate; mention; ∼ *zu inf.* intend to *inf.*; **2.** **2** *n* (-s/*no pl.*) memory, remembrance (*an acc.* of).

Ge'denk|**feier** *f* commemoration; ∼**stein** *m* memorial stone; ∼**tafel** *f* commemorative *or* memorial tablet.

Ge'dicht *n* (-[e]s/-e) poem.

gediegen [gə'di:gən] *adj.* solid; pure; **2heit** *f* (-/*no pl.*) solidity; purity.

gedieh [gə'di:] *pret.* of gedeihen; ∼**en** *p.p.* of gedeihen.

Gedräng|**e** [gə'drɛŋə] *n* (-s/*no pl.*) crowd, throng; **2t** *adj.* crowded, packed, crammed; *style:* concise.

ge|**droschen** [gə'drɔʃən] *p.p.* of dreschen; ∼**drückt** *fig. adj.* depressed; ∼**drungen** [∼'druŋən] **1.** *p.p.* of dringen; **2.** *adj.* compact; squat, stocky, thickset.

Geduld [gə'dult] *f* (-/*no pl.*) patience; **2en** [∼.dən] *v/refl.* (*no* -ge-, *h*) have patience; **2ig** [∼.dɪç] *adj.* patient.

ge|**dunsen** *adj.* [gə'dunzən] bloated; ∼**durft** [∼'durft] *p.p.* of dürfen **1.**; ∼**ehrt** *adj.* [∼.'e:rt] hono(u)red; *correspondence*: *Sehr* ∼*er Herr N.!* Dear Sir, Dear Mr N.; ∼**eignet** *adj.* [∼'aɪgnət] fit (*für, zu, als* for *s.th.*); suitable (to, for); qualified (for).

Gefahr [gə'fa:r] *f* (-/-en) danger, peril; risk; *auf eigene* ∼ at one's own risk; ∼ *laufen zu inf.* run the risk of *ger.*

gefährden [gə'fɛ:rdən] *v/t.* (*no* -ge-, *h*) endanger; risk.

ge'fahren *p.p.* of fahren.

gefährlich *adj.* [gə'fɛ:rlɪç] dangerous.

ge'fahrlos *adj.* without risk, safe.

Gefährt|**e** [gə'fɛ:rtə] *m* (-en/-en), ∼**in** *f* (-/-nen) companion, fellow.

Gefälle [gə'fɛlə] *n* (-s/-) fall, slope, incline, descent, gradient, *esp. Am. a.* grade; fall (*of river, etc.*).

Ge'fallen 1. *m* (-s/-) favo(u)r; **2.** *n* (-s/*no pl.*): ∼ *finden an* (*dat.*) take (a) pleasure in, take a fancy to *or* for; **3.** **2** *v/i.* (*irr.* fallen, *no* -ge-, *h*) please (*j-m s.o.*); *er gefällt mir* I like him; *sich et.* ∼ *lassen* put up with s.th.; **4.** **2** *p.p.* of fallen.

gefällig *adj.* [gə'fɛlɪç] pleasing, agreeable; *p.:* complaisant, obliging; kind; **2keit** *f* (-/-en) complaisance, kindness; favo(u)r; ∼**st** *adv.* (if you) please.

ge'fangen 1. *p.p.* of fangen; **2.** *adj.* captive, imprisoned; **2e** *m* (-n/-n), *f* (-n/-n) prisoner, captive; **2en-lager** *n* prison(ers') camp; **2-nahme** *f* (-/*no pl.*) capture; seizure, arrest; ∼**nehmen** *v/t.* (*irr.* nehmen, *sep.-*, -ge-, *h*) take prisoner; *fig.* captivate; **2schaft** *f* (-/*no pl.*) captivity, imprisonment; ∼**setzen** *v/t.* (*sep.-*, -ge-, *h*) put in prison.

Gefängnis [gə'fɛŋnɪs] *n* (-ses/-se) prison, jail, gaol, *Am. a.* penitentiary; ∼**direktor** *m* governor, warden; ∼**strafe** *f* (sentence *or* term of) imprisonment; ∼**wärter** *m* warder, gaoler, jailer, (prison) guard.

Gefäß [gə'fɛ:s] *n* (-es/-e) vessel.

gefaßt *adj.* [gə'fast] composed; ∼ *auf* (*acc.*) prepared for.

Ge'fecht [gə'fɛçt] *n* (-[e]s/-e) engagement; combat, fight; action; ∼**fieder** [∼'fi:dər] *n* (-s/-) plumage, feathers *pl.*

ge|'**fleckt** *adj.* spotted; ∼**flochten** [∼'flɔxtən] *p.p.* of flechten; ∼**flogen** [∼'flo:gən] *p.p.* of fliegen; ∼**flohen** [∼'flo:ən] *p.p.* of fliehen; ∼**flossen** [∼'flɔsən] *p.p.* of fließen.

Ge|'**flügel** *n* (-s/*no pl.*) fowl; poultry; ∼**flüster** [∼'flystər] *n* (-s/*no pl.*) whisper(ing). [ten.]

gefochten [gə'fɔxtən] *p.p.* of fech-]

Ge'folg|e n (-s/no pl.) retinue, train, followers pl.; attendants pl.; **~schaft** [~kʃaft] f (-/-en) followers pl.

gefräßig adj. [gə'frɛːsiç] greedy, voracious; **2keit** f (-/no pl.) greediness, gluttony, voracity.

ge'fressen p.p. of fressen.

ge'frier|en v/i. (irr. frieren, no -ge-, sein) congeal, freeze; **2fleisch** n frozen meat; **2punkt** m freezing-point; **2schutz(mittel** n) m anti-freeze.

gefroren [gə'froːrən] p.p. of frieren; **2e** [~ə] n (-n/no pl.) ice-cream.

Gefüge [gə'fyːgə] n (-s/-) structure, texture.

ge'fügig adj. pliant; **2keit** f (-/no pl.) pliancy.

Gefühl [gə'fyːl] n (-[e]s/-e) feeling, touch; sense (für of); sensation; **~los** adj. unfeeling, insensible (gegen to); **2sbetont** adj. emotional; **2voll** adj. (full of) feeling; tender, sentimental.

ge'funden p.p. of finden; **~gangen** [~'gaŋən] p.p. of gehen.

ge'geben p.p. of geben; **~enfalls** adv. in that case; if necessary.

gegen prp. (acc.) ['geːgən] space, time: towards; against; ⚥ versus; about, Am. around; by; compared with; (in exchange) for; remedy: for; freundlich sein **~** be kind to (-wards); **~** bar for cash.

'Gegen|angriff m counter-attack; **'~antrag** m counter-motion; **'~antwort** f rejoinder; **'~befehl** m counter-order; **'~beschuldigung** f countercharge; **'~besuch** m return visit; **'~bewegung** f counter-movement; **'~beweis** m counter-evidence.

Gegend ['geːgənt] f (-/-en) region, area.

'Gegen|dienst m return service, service in return; **'~druck** m counter-pressure; fig. reaction; **2ei'nander** adv. against one another or each other; **'~erklärung** f counter-statement; **'~forderung** f counter-claim; **'~frage** f counter-question; **'~geschenk** n return present; **'~gewicht** n counterbalance, counterpoise; **'~gift** ✠ n antidote; **'~kandidat** m rival candidate; **'~klage** f countercharge; **'~leistung**

f return (service), equivalent; **~lichtaufnahme** phot. ['gəːgən-liçt?-] f back-lighted shot; **'~liebe** f requited love; keine **~** finden meet with no sympathy or enthusiasm; **'~maßnahme** f counter-measure; **'~mittel** n remedy (gegen for), antidote (against, for); **'~partei** f opposite party; **'~probe** f check-test; **'~satz** m contrast; opposition; im **~** zu in contrast to or with, in opposition to; **2sätzlich** adj. ['~zetsliç] contrary, opposite; **'~seite** f opposite side; **'2seitig** adj. mutual, reciprocal; **'~seitigkeit** f (-/no pl.) auf **~** assurance: mutual; auf **~** be-ruhen be mutual; **'~spieler** m games, sports: opponent; antago-nist; **'~spionage** f counter-espio-nage; **'~stand** m object; subject, topic; **'~strömung** f counter-cur-rent; **'~stück** n counterpart; match; **'~teil** n contrary, reverse; im **~** on the contrary; **'2teilig** adj. contrary, opposite; **2'über 1.** adv. opposite; **2.** prp. (dat.) opposite (to); to (-wards); as against; face to face with; **~über** n (-s/-) vis-à-vis; **2'überstehen** v/i. (irr. stehen, sep., -ge-, h) (dat.) be faced with; face; **~überstellung** esp. ⚥ f confron-tation; **'~vorschlag** m counter-proposal; **~wart** ['~vart] f (-/no pl.) presence; present time; gr. present tense; **2wärtig** ['~vertiç] **1.** adj. present; actual; **2.** adv. at present; now; **'~wehr** f defen|ce, Am. -se; resist-ance; **'~wert** m equivalent; **'~wind** m contrary wind, head wind; **'~wirkung** f counter-effect, reaction; **'2zeichnen** v/t. (sep., -ge-, h) countersign; **'~zug** m counter-move (a. fig.); ⚥ corresponding train.

ge'gessen [gə'gɛsən] p.p. of essen; **~glichen** [~'gliçən] p.p. of glei-chen; **~gliedert** adj. articulate, jointed; **~glitten** [~'glitən] p.p. of gleiten; **~glommen** [~'glɔmən] p.p. of glimmen.

Gegner ['geːgnər] m (-s/-) adver-sary, opponent; **~schaft** f (-/-en) opposition.

ge'golten [gə'gɔltən] p.p. of gelten; **~goren** [~'goːrən] p.p. of gären; **~gossen** [~'gɔsən] p.p. of gießen; **~graben** p.p. of graben; **~griffen** [~'grifən] p.p. of greifen; **~habt** [~'haːpt] p.p. of haben.

Gehalt [gə'halt] **1.** *m* (-[e]s/-e) contents *pl.*; capacity; merit; **2.** *n* (-[e]s/-er) salary; **2en** *p.p. of* halten; **2los** [.lo:s] *adj.* empty; **~sempfänger** [gə'halts9-] *m* salaried employee *or* worker; **~serhöhung** [gə'halts9-] *f* rise (in salary), *Am.* raise; **2voll** *adj.* rich; substantial; *wine:* racy.

gehangen [gə'haŋən] *p.p. of* hängen **1.**

gehässig *adj.* [gə'hɛsiç] malicious, spiteful; **2keit** *f* (-/-en) malice, spitefulness.

ge'hauen *p.p. of* hauen.

Ge|häuse [gə'hɔyzə] *n* (-s/-) case, box; cabinet; shell; core (*of apple*, *etc.*); **~hege** [.'he:gə] *n* (-s/-) enclosure.

geheim *adj.* [gə'haɪm] secret; **2-dienst** *m* secret service.

Ge'heimnis *n* (-ses/-se) secret; mystery; **~krämer** *m* mysterymonger; **2voll** *adj.* mysterious.

Ge'heim|polizei *f* secret police; **~polizist** *m* detective; plain-clothes man; **~schrift** *f* cipher; *tel.* code.

ge'heißen *p.p. of* heißen.

gehen ['ge:ən] *v/i.* (*irr.*, *ge-*, *sein*) go; walk; leave; *machine:* go, work; *clock, watch:* go; *merchandise:* sell; *wind:* blow; *paste:* rise; *wie geht es Ihnen?* how are you (getting on)?; *das geht nicht* that won't do; *in sich ~* repent; *wieviel Pfennige ~ auf e-e Mark?* how many pfennigs go to a mark?; *das Fenster geht nach Norden* the window faces *or* looks north; *es geht nichts über* (*acc.*) there is nothing like; *wenn es nach mir ginge* if I had my way.

Geheul [gə'hɔyl] *n* (-[e]s/*no pl.*) howling.

Ge'hilf|e *m* (-n/-n), **~in** *f* (-/-nen) assistant; *fig.* helpmate.

Ge'hirn *n* (-[e]s/-e) brain(s *pl.*); **~erschütterung** *f* concussion (of the brain); **~schlag** *m* cerebral apoplexy.

gehoben [gə'ho:bən] **1.** *p.p. of* heben; **2.** *adj.* *speech, style:* elevated; **~e Stimmung** elated mood.

Gehöft [gə'hø:ft] *n* (-[e]s/-e) farm (-stead).

geholfen [gə'hɔlfən] *p.p. of* helfen.

Gehölz [gə'hœlts] *n* (-es/-e) wood, coppice, copse.

Gehör [gə'hø:r] *n* (-[e]s/*no pl.*)

hearing; ear; *nach dem ~* by ear; *j-m ~ schenken* lend an ear to s.o.; *sich ~ verschaffen* make o.s. heard.

ge'horchen *v/i.* (*no -ge-*, *h*) obey (*j-m* s.o.).

ge'hör|en *v/i.* (*no -ge-*, *h*) belong (*dat. or zu* to); *es gehört sich* it is proper *or* fit *or* right *or* suitable; *das gehört nicht hierher* that's not to the point; **~ig 1.** *adj.* belonging (*dat. or zu* to); fit, proper, right; due; F good; **2.** *adv.* duly; F thoroughly.

gehorsam [gə'ho:rza:m] **1.** *adj.* obedient; **2.** **2** *m* (-s/*no pl.*) obedience.

'Geh|steig *m*, **'~weg** *m* pavement, *Am.* sidewalk; **'~werk** ⊕ *n* clockwork, works *pl.*

Geier *orn.* ['gaɪər] *m* (-s/-) vulture.

Geige ♪ ['gaɪgə] *f* (-/-n) violin, F fiddle; (*auf der*) *~ spielen* play (on) the violin; **'~nbogen** ♪ *m* (violin-) bow; **'~nkasten** ♪ *m* violin-case; **'~r** ♪ *m* (-s/-), **'~rin** ♪ *f* (-/-nen) violinist.

'Geigerzähler *phys.* *m* Geiger counter.

geil *adj.* [gaɪl] lascivious, wanton; luxuriant.

Geisel ['gaɪzəl] *f* (-/-n) hostage.

Geiß *zo.* [gaɪs] *f* (-/-en) (she-, nanny-)goat; **'~blatt** ♀ *n* (-[e]s/*no pl.*) honeysuckle, woodbine; **'~bock** *zo.* *m* he-goat, billy-goat.

Geißel ['gaɪsəl] *f* (-/-n) whip, lash; *fig.* scourge; **'2n** *v/t.* (*ge-*, *h*) whip, lash; *fig.* castigate.

Geist [gaɪst] *m* (-es/-er) spirit; mind, intellect; wit; ghost; sprite.

'Geister|erscheinung *f* apparition; **'2haft** *adj.* ghostly.

'geistes|abwesend *adj.* absentminded; **'2arbeiter** *m* brainworker, white-collar worker; **'2-blitz** *m* brain-wave, flash of genius; **'2gabe** *f* talent; **'2gegenwart** *f* presence of mind; **'~gegenwärtig** *adj.* alert; quick-witted; **'~gestört** *adj.* mentally disturbed; **'~krank** *adj.* insane, mentally ill; **'2krankheit** *f* insanity, mental illness; **'~-schwach** *adj.* feeble-minded, imbecile; **'~verwandt** *adj.* congenial; **'2wissenschaften** *f/pl.* the Arts *pl.*, the Humanities *pl.*; **'2zustand** *m* state of mind.

'geistig *adj.* intellectual, mental;

spiritual; ~e Getränke n/pl. spirits pl.

'geistlich adj. spiritual; clerical; sacred; 'Qe m (-n/-n) clergyman; minister; 'Qkeit f (-/no pl.) clergy.

'geist|los adj. spiritless; dull; stupid; '~reich adj., '~voll adj. ingenious, spirited.

Geiz [gaɪts] m (-es/no pl.) avarice; '~hals m miser, niggard; 'Qig adj. avaricious, stingy, mean.

Gejammer [gə'jamər] n (-s/no pl.) lamentation(s pl.), wailing.

gekannt [gə'kant] p.p. of kennen.

Geklapper [gə'klapər] n (-s/no pl.) rattling.

Geklirr [gə'klir] n (-[e]s/no pl.), ~e [~ə] n (-s/no pl.) clashing, clanking.

ge|klungen [~'kluŋən] p.p. of klingen; ~'kniffen [~'knifən] p.p. of kneifen; ~'kommen p.p. of kommen; ~konnt [~'kɔnt] p.p. of können 1, 2.

Ge|kreisch [gə'kraɪʃ] n (-es/no pl.) screaming, screams pl.; shrieking; ~kritzel ['kritsəl] n (-s/no pl.) scrawl(ing), scribbling, scribble.

ge|krochen [gə'krɔxən] p.p. of kriechen; ~künstelt adj. [~'kynstəlt] affected.

Gelächter [gə'lɛçtər] n (-s/-) laughter.

ge'laden p.p. of laden.

Ge'lage n (-s/-) feast; drinking-bout.

Gelände [gə'lɛndə] n (-s/-) ground; terrain; country; area; Qgängig mot. adj. cross-country; ~lauf m sports: cross-country race or run.

Geländer [gə'lɛndər] n (-s/-) railing, balustrade; banisters pl.

ge'lang pret. of gelingen.

ge'langen v/i. (no -ge-, sein): ~ an (acc.) or in (acc.) arrive at, get or come to; ~ zu attain (to), gain.

ge'lassen 1. p.p. of lassen; **2.** adj. calm, composed.

Gelatine [ʒela'ti:nə] f (-/no pl.) gelatin(e).

ge'laufen p.p. of laufen; ~läufig adj. [~'lɔʏfiç] current; fluent, easy; tongue: voluble; familiar; '~launt adj. [~'launt] in a (good, etc.) humo(u)r or Am. mood.

Geläut [gə'lɔʏt] n (-[e]s/-e), ~e [~ə] n (-s/-) ringing (of bells); chimes pl. (of church bells).

gelb adj. [gɛlp] yellow; '~lich adj.

yellowish; '**Qsucht** ⚕ f (-/no pl.) jaundice.

Geld [gɛlt] n (-[e]s/-er) money; im ~ schwimmen be rolling in money; zu ~ machen turn into cash; '~angelegenheit f money-matter; '~anlage f investment; '~ausgabe f expense; '~beutel m purse; '~entwertung f devaluation of the currency; '~erwerb m money-making; '~geber m (-s/-) financial backer, investor; '~geschäfte n/pl. money transactions pl.; 'Qgierig adj. greedy for money, avaricious; '~mittel n/pl. funds pl., resources pl.; '~schein m bank-note, bill; '~schrank m strong-box, safe; '~sendung f remittance; '~strafe f fine; '~stück n coin; '~tasche f money-bag; notecase, Am. billfold; '~überhang m surplus money; '~umlauf m circulation of money; '~umsatz m turnover (of money); '~verlegenheit f pecuniary embarrassment; '~wechsel m exchange of money; '~wert m (-[e]s/no pl.) value of money, money value.

Gelee [ʒə'le:] n, m (-s/-s) jelly.

ge'legen 1. p.p. of liegen; **2.** adj. situated, Am. a. located; convenient, opportune; Qheit f (-/-en) occasion; opportunity; chance; facility; bei ~ on occasion.

Ge'legenheits|arbeit f casual or odd job, Am. a. chore; ~arbeiter m casual labo(u)rer, odd-job man; ~kauf m bargain.

ge'legentlich 1. adj. occasional; **2.** prp. (gen.) on the occasion of.

ge'lehr|ig adj. docile; Qigkeit f (-/no pl.) docility; Qsamkeit f (-/no pl.) learning; ~t adj. [~t] learned; Qte [~ə] m (-n/-n) learned man, scholar.

Geleise [gə'laɪzə] n (-s/-) rut, track; 🚆 rails pl., line, esp. Am. tracks pl.

Geleit [gə'laɪt] n (-[e]s/-e) escort; attendance; j-m das ~ geben accompany s.o.; Qen v/t. (no -ge-, h) accompany, conduct; escort; '~zug ⚓ m convoy.

Gelenk anat., ⊕, ⚘ [gə'lɛŋk] n (-[e]s/-e) joint; Qig adj. pliable, supple.

ge'lernt adj. worker: skilled; trained; ~lesen p.p. of lesen.

Geliebte [gə'li:ptə] (-n/-n) **1.** m lover; **2.** f mistress, sweetheart.

geliehen [gə'li:ən] *p.p. of* leihen.

ge'linde 1. *adj.* soft, smooth; gentle; 2. *adv.: gelinde gesagt* to put it mildly, to say the least.

gelingen [gə'liŋən] 1. *v/i. (irr., no -ge-, sein)* succeed; *es gelingt mir zu inf.* I succeed in *ger.*; 2. ♀ *n (-s/no pl.)* success.

ge'litten *p.p. of* leiden.

gellen ['gɛlən] *(ge-, h)* 1. *v/i.* shrill; yell; *of ears:* ring, tingle; 2. *v/t.* shrill; yell; '**⸝d** *adj.* shrill, piercing.

ge'loben *v/t. (no -ge-, h)* vow, promise.

Gelöbnis [gə'lø:pnɪs] *n (-ses/-se)* promise, pledge; vow.

ge'logen *p.p. of* lügen.

gelt|en ['gɛltən] *(irr., ge-, h)* 1. *v/t.* be worth; 2. *v/i.* be of value; be valid; go; count; *money:* be current; *maxim, etc.:* hold *(good or* true); et. ⸝ have credit *or* influence; *j-m* ⸝ concern s.o.; ⸝ *für or als* pass for, be reputed *or* thought *or* supposed to be; ⸝ *für* apply to; ⸝ *lassen* let pass, allow; ⸝*d machen* maintain, assert; *s-n Einfluß bei j-m* ⸝*d machen* bring one's influence to bear on s.o.; *das gilt nicht* that is not fair; that does not count; *es galt unser Leben* our life was at stake; '♀**ung** *f (-/⸝ -en)* validity; value; currency; authority *(of person);* ♀**ung** ⸝ *kommen* tell; take effect; show; '♀**ungsbedürfnis** *n* desire to show off.   [ise; vow.]

Gelübde [gə'lypdə] *n (-s/-)* prom-

gelungen [gə'luŋən] 1. *p.p. of* gelingen; 2. *adj.* successful; amusing, funny; F: *das ist ja* ⸝! that beats everything!

gemächlich *adj.* [gə'mɛ:çlɪç] comfortable, easy; ♀**keit** *f (-/no pl.)* ease, comfort.

Gemahl [gə'ma:l] *m (-[e]s/-e)* consort; husband.

ge'mahlen *p.p. of* mahlen.

Gemälde [gə'mɛ:ldə] *n (-s/-)* painting, picture; ⸝**galerie** *f* picture-gallery.

gemäß *prp. (dat.)* [gə'mɛ:s] according to; ⸝**igt** *adj.* moderate; temperate *(a. geogr.).*

gemein *adj.* [gə'maɪn] common; general; low, vulgar, mean, coarse; et. ⸝ *haben mit* have s.th. in common with.

Gemeinde [gə'maɪndə] *f (-/-n)* community; parish; municipality; *eccl.* congregation; ⸝**bezirk** *m* district; municipality; ⸝**rat** *m* municipal council; ⸝**steuer** *f* rate, *Am.* local tax; ⸝**vorstand** *m* district council.

ge'mein|gefährlich *adj.* dangerous to the public; ⸝**er Mensch** public danger, *Am.* public enemy; ♀**heit** *f (-/-en)* vulgarity; meanness; mean trick; ⸝**nützig** *adj.* of public utility; ♀**platz** *m* commonplace; ⸝**sam** *adj.* common; joint; mutual; ♀**schaft** *f (-/-en)* community; intercourse; ⸝**schaftlich** *adj. s.* gemeinsam; ♀**schaftsarbeit** *f* team-work; ♀**sinn** *m (-[e]s/no pl.)* public spirit; ⸝**verständlich** *adj.* popular; ♀**wesen** *n* community; ♀**wohl** *n* public welfare.

Ge'menge *n (-s/-)* mixture.

ge'messen 1. *p.p. of* messen; 2. *adj.* measured; formal; grave.

Gemetzel [gə'mɛtsəl] *n (-s/-)* slaughter, massacre.

ge'mieden [gə'mi:dən] *p.p. of* meiden.

Gemisch [gə'mɪʃ] *n (-es/-e)* mixture; ⸝ compound, composition.

ge'mocht [gə'mɔxt] *p.p. of* mögen; ⸝**molken** [gə'mɔlkən] *p.p. of* melken.

Gemse *zo.* ['gɛmzə] *f (-/-n)* chamois.

Gemurmel [gə'murməl] *n (-s/no pl.)* murmur(ing).

Gemüse [gə'my:zə] *n (-s/-)* vegetable(s *pl.);* greens *pl.;* ⸝**anbau** *m* vegetable gardening, *Am.* truck farming; ⸝**garten** *m* kitchen garden; ⸝**händler** *m* greengrocer.

gemußt [gə'must] *p.p. of* müssen 1.

Gemüt [gə'my:t] *n (-[e]s/-er)* mind; feeling; soul; heart; disposition; temper; ♀**lich** *adj.* good-natured; genial; comfortable, snug, cosy, cozy; ⸝**lichkeit** *f (-/no pl.)* snugness, cosiness; easy-going; genial temper.

Ge'müts|art *f* disposition, nature, temper, character; ⸝**bewegung** *f* emotion; ♀**krank** *adj.* emotionally disturbed; melancholic; depressed; ⸝**krankheit** *f* mental disorder; melancholy; ⸝**ruhe** *f* composure; ⸝**verfassung** *f,* ⸝**zustand** *m* state of mind, humo(u)r.

ge'mütvoll *adj.* emotional; full of feeling.

genannt [gə'nant] *p.p. of* nennen.

genas [gə'nɑːs] *pret. of* genesen.

genau *adj.* [gə'nau] exact, accurate; precise; strict; *es ~ nehmen (mit)* be particular (about); **2eres** full particulars *pl.*; **2igkeit** *f* (-/-en) accuracy, exactness; precision; strictness.

genehm *adj.* [gə'neːm] agreeable, convenient; **~igen** [~igən] *v/t.* (no -ge-, h) grant; approve (of); **2igung** *f* (-/-en) grant; approval; licen|ce, *Am.* -se; permit; permission; consent.

geneigt *adj.* [gə'naikt] well disposed (*j-m* towards s.o.); inclined (*zu* to).

General ✕ [genə'rɑːl] *m* (-s/-e, ⸗e) general; **~bevollmächtigte** *m* chief representative *or* agent; **~direktor** *m* general manager, managing director; **~'feldmarschall** ✕ *m* field-marshal; **~intendant** *thea. m* (artistic) director; **~konsul** *m* consul-general; **~konsulat** *n* consulate-general; **~leutnant** ✕ *m* lieutenant-general; **~major** ✕ *m* major-general; **~probe** *thea. f* dress rehearsal; **~stab** ✕ *m* general staff; **~stabskarte** ✕ *f* ordnance (survey) map, *Am.* strategic map; **~streik** *m* general strike; **~versammlung** *f* general meeting; **~vertreter** *m* general agent; **~vollmacht** *f* full power of attorney.

Generation [genəra'tsjoːn] *f* (-/-en) generation.

generell *adj.* [genə'rɛl] general.

genes|en [gə'neːzən] **1.** *v/i.* (*irr.*, *no* -ge-, *sein*) recover (von from); **2.** *p.p. of* **1**; **2ende** *m*, *f* (-n/-n) convalescent; **2ung** *f* (-/⸗, -en) recovery.

genial *adj.* [gen'jɑːl] highly gifted, ingenious; **2ität** [~ali'tɛːt] *f* (-/no *pl.*) genius.

Genick [gə'nik] *n* (-[e]s/-e) nape (of the neck), (back of the) neck.

Genie [ʒe'niː] *n* (-s/-s) genius.

ge'nieren *v/t.* (no -ge-, h) trouble, bother; *sich ~* feel *or* be embarrassed *or* shy; be self-conscious.

genießen [gə'niːsən] *v/t.* (*irr.*, *no* -ge-, h) enjoy; eat; drink; *et. ~* take some food *or* refreshments; *j-s Vertrauen ~* be in s.o.'s confidence.

Genitiv *gr.* ['geːnitiːf] *m* (-s/-e) genitive (case); possessive (case).

ge|nommen [gə'nɔmən] *p.p. of* nehmen; **~'normt** *adj.* standardized; **~noß** [~'nɔs] *pret. of* genießen.

Genoss|e [gə'nɔsə] *m* (-n/-n) companion, mate; comrade (*a. pol.*); **2en** *p.p. of* genießen; **~enschaft** *f* (-/-en) company, association; co(-)operative (society); **~in** *f* (-/-nen) (female) companion; comrade (*a. pol.*). [cient.]

genug *adj.* [gə'nuːk] enough, suffi-]

Genüg|e [gə'nyːgə] *f* (-/no *pl.*): *zur ~* enough, sufficiently; **2en** *v/i.* (no -ge-, h) be enough, suffice; *das genügt* that will do; *j-m ~* satisfy s.o.; **2end** *adj.* sufficient; **2sam** *adj.* [~k-] easily satisfied; frugal; **~samkeit** [~k-] *f* (-/no *pl.*) modesty; frugality.

Genugtuung [gə'nuːktuːuŋ] *f* (-/-en) satisfaction. [gender.]

Genus *gr.* ['geːnus] *n* (-/Genera)]

Genuß [gə'nus] *m* (Genusses/Genüsse) enjoyment; pleasure; use; consumption; taking (*of food*); *fig.* treat; **~mittel** *n* semi-luxury; **~sucht** *f* (-/no *pl.*) thirst for pleasure; **2süchtig** *adj.* pleasure-seeking.

Geo|graph [geo'grɑːf] *m* (-en/-en) geographer; **~graphie** [~a'fiː] *f* (-/no *pl.*) geography; **2graphisch** *adj.* [~'grɑːfiʃ] geographic(al); **~loge** [~'loːgə] *m* (-n/-n) geologist; **~logie** [~lo'giː] *f* (-/no *pl.*) geology; **2logisch** *adj.* [~'loːgiʃ] geologic(al); **~metrie** [~me'triː] *f* (-/-n) geometry; **2metrisch** *adj.* [~'meːtriʃ] geometric(al).

Gepäck [gə'pɛk] *n* (-[e]s/no *pl.*) luggage, ✕ *or Am.* baggage; **~annahme** *f* luggage (registration) counter, *Am.* baggage (registration) counter; **~aufbewahrung** *f* (-/-en) left-luggage office, *Am.* checkroom; **~ausgabe** *f* luggage delivery office, *Am.* baggage room; **~netz** *n* luggage-rack, *Am.* baggage rack; **~schein** *m* luggage-ticket, *Am.* baggage check; **~träger** *m* porter, *Am. a.* redcap; *on bicycle*: carrier; **~wagen** *m* luggage van, *Am.* baggage car.

ge|pfiffen [gə'pfifən] *p.p. of* pfeifen; **~pflegt** *adj.* [~'pfleːkt] *appearance*: well-groomed; *hands*, *garden*, *etc.*: well cared-for; *garden*, *etc.*: well-kept.

Gepflogenheit [gə'pfloːgənhait] *f* (-/-en) habit; custom; usage.

Ge|plapper [gə'plapər] *n* (-s/*no pl.*) babbling, chattering; **~plauder** [~-'plaudər] *n* (-s/*no pl.*) chatting, small talk; **~polter** [~'pɔltər] *n* (-s/*no pl.*) rumble; **~präge** [~'prɛː-gə] *n* (-s/-) impression; stamp (*a. fig.*).

ge|priesen [gə'priːzən] *p.p. of* preisen; **~quollen** [~'kvɔlən] *p.p. of* quellen.

gerade [gə'rɑːdə] **1.** *adj.* straight (*a. fig.*); *number, etc.*: even; direct; *bearing*: upright, erect; **2.** *adv.* just; *er schrieb ~* he was (just) writing; *nun ~* now more than ever; *~ an dem Tage* on that very day; **3.** ♀ *f* (-*n*/-*n*) Ⓐ straight line; straight(*of race-course*); *linke*(*rechte*) *~ boxing:* straight left (right); **~'aus** *adv.* straight on *or* ahead; **~he'raus** *adv.* frankly; **~wegs** *adv.* [~nvɛːks] directly; **~stehen** *v/i.* (*irr.* stehen, *sep.*, -ge-, *h*) stand erect; *~ für* answer for *s.th.*; **~wegs** *adv.* [~vɛːks] straight, directly; **~'zu** *adv.* straight; almost; downright.

ge'rannt *p.p. of* rennen.

Gerassel [gə'rasəl] *n* (-s/*no pl.*) clanking; rattling.

Gerät [gə'rɛːt] *n* (-[e]s/-e) tool, implement, utensil; ⊕ gear; *teleph.*, *radio:* set; apparatus; equipment; *elektrisches ~* electric(al) appliance.

ge'raten 1. *v/i.* (*irr.* raten, *no* -ge-, *sein*) come *or* fall *or* get (*an acc.* by, upon; *auf acc.* on, upon; *in acc.* in, into); (*gut*) *~* succeed, turn out well; *in Brand ~* catch fire; *ins Stocken ~* come to a standstill; *in Vergessenheit ~* fall *or* sink into oblivion; *in Zorn ~* fly into a passion; **2.** *p.p. of* raten.

Gerate'wohl *n: aufs ~* at random.

geräumig *adj.* [gə'rɔymiç] spacious.

Geräusch [gə'rɔyʃ] *n* (-es/-e) noise; ♀**los** *adj.* noiseless; ♀**voll** *adj.* noisy.

gerb|en ['gɛrbən] *v/t.* (ge-, *h*) tan; ♀**er** *m* (-s/-) tanner; ♀**erei** [~'raɪ] *f* (-/-en) tannery.

ge'recht *adj.* just, righteous, *~ werden* (*dat.*) do justice to; be fair to; meet; please *s.o.*; fulfil (*requirements*); ♀**igkeit** *f* (-/*no pl.*) justice; righteousness; *j-m ~ widerfahren lassen* do s.o. justice. [rumo(u)r.]

Ge'rede *n* (-s/*no pl.*) talk; gossip;)

ge'reizt *adj.* irritable, irritated; ♀**heit** *f* (-/*no pl.*) irritation.

ge'reuen *v/t.* (*no* -ge-, *h*): *es gereut mich* I repent (of) it, I am sorry for it.

Gericht [gə'riçt] *n* (-[e]s/-e) dish, course; *s. Gerichtshof; mst rhet. and fig.* tribunal; ♀**lich** *adj.* judicial, legal.

Ge'richts|barkeit *f* (-/-en) jurisdiction; **~bezirk** *m* jurisdiction; **~diener** *m* (court) usher; **~gebäude** *n* court-house; **~hof** *m* lawcourt, court of justice; **~kosten** *pl.* (law-)costs *pl.*; **~saal** *m* courtroom; **~schreiber** *m* clerk (of the court); **~stand** *m* (legal) domicile; venue; **~tag** *m* court-day; **~verfahren** *n* legal proceedings *pl.*, lawsuit; **~verhandlung** *f* (court) hearing; trial; **~vollzieher** *m* (-s/-) (court-)bailiff.

gerieben [gə'riːbən] *p.p. of* reiben.

gering *adj.* [gə'rɪŋ] little, small; trifling, slight; mean, low; poor; inferior; **~achten** *v/t.* (*sep.*, -ge-, *h*) think little of; disregard; **~er** *adj.* inferior, less, minor; **~fügig** *adj.* insignificant, trifling, slight; **~schätzen** *v/t.* (*sep.*, -ge-, *h*) *s. geringachten*; **~schätzig** *adj.* disdainful, contemptuous, slighting; ♀**schätzung** *f* (-/*no pl.*) disdain; disregard; **~st** *adj.* least; *nicht im ~en* not in the least.

ge'rinnen *v/i.* (*irr.* rinnen, *no* -ge-, *sein*) curdle (*a. fig.*); congeal; coagulate, clot.

Ge'rippe *n* (-s/-) skeleton (*a. fig.*); ⊕ framework.

ge|rissen [gə'rɪsən] **1.** *p.p. of* reißen; **2.** *fig. adj.* cunning, crafty, smart; **~ritten** [~'rɪtən] *p.p. of* reiten.

germanis|ch *adj.* [gɛr'mɑːnɪʃ] Germanic, Teutonic; ♀**t** [~a'nɪst] *m* (-en/-en) Germanist, German scholar; student of German.

gern(e) *adv.* ['gɛrn(ə)] willingly, gladly; *~ haben or mögen* be fond of, like; *er singt ~* he is fond of singing, he likes to sing.

ge'rochen *p.p. of* riechen.

Geröll [gə'rœl] *n* (-[e]s/-e) boulders *pl.*

geronnen [gə'rɔnən] *p.p. of* rinnen.

Gerste ♀ ['gɛrstə] *f* (-/-n) barley; **~nkorn** *n* barleycorn; ♫ sty(e).

Gerte ['gɛrtə] *f* (-/-n) switch, twig.

Geruch [gə'rux] *m* (-[e]s/-e) smell, odo(u)r; scent; *fig.* reputation; ♀**los**

G

adj. odo(u)rless, scentless; **~ssinn** *m* (-[e]s/ *no pl.*) sense of smell.

Gerücht [gə'ryçt] *n* (-[e]s/-e) rumo(u)r.

ge'ruchtilgend *adj.*: **~es Mittel** deodorant.

ge'rufen *p.p.* of rufen.

ge'ruhen *v/i.* (*no* -ge-, h) deign, condescend, be pleased.

Gerümpel [gə'rympəl] *n* (-s/ *no pl.*) lumber, junk.

Gerundium *gr.* [gə'rundjum] *n* (-s/ *Gerundien*) gerund.

gerungen [gə'ruŋən] *p.p.* of ringen.

Gerüst [gə'ryst] *n* (-[e]s/-e) scaffold(ing); stage; trestle.

ge'salzen *p.p.* of salzen.

gesamt *adj.* [gə'zamt] whole, entire, total, all; **~ausgabe** *f* complete edition; **~betrag** *m* sum total; **~deutsch** *adj.* all-German.

gesandt [gə'zant] *p.p.* of senden; **~e** [**~ə**] *m* (-n/-n) envoy; **~schaft** *f* (-/-en) legation.

Ge'sang *m* (-[e]s/‖e) singing; song; **~buch** *eccl. n* hymn-book; **~slehrer** *m* singing-teacher; **~verein** *m* choral society, *Am.* glee club.

Gesäß *anat.* [gə'zɛ:s] *n* (-es/-e) seat, buttocks *pl.*, posterior, F bottom, behind.

ge'schaffen *p.p.* of schaffen 1.

Geschäft [gə'ʃɛft] *n* (-[e]s/-e) business; transaction; affair; occupation; shop, *Am.* store; **~ig** *adj.* busy, active; **~igkeit** *f* (-/ *no pl.*) activity; **~lich** 1. *adj.* business ...; commercial; 2. *adv.* on business.

Ge'schäfts|bericht *m* business report; **~brief** *m* business letter; **~frau** *f* business woman; **~freund** *m* business friend, correspondent; **~führer** *m* manager; **~haus** *n* business firm; office building; **~inhaber** *m* owner *or* holder of a business; shopkeeper; **~jahr** *n* financial *or* business year, *Am.* fiscal year; **~lage** *f* business situation; **~leute** *pl.* businessmen *pl.*; **~mann** *m* businessman; **~mäßig** *adj.* business-like; **~ordnung** *f* standing orders *pl.*; rules *pl.* (of procedure); **~papiere** *n/pl.* commercial papers *pl.*; **~partner** *m* (business) partner; **~räume** *m/pl.* business premises *pl.*; **~reise** *f* business trip; **~reisende** *m* commercial travel(l)er, *Am.* travel(l)ing salesman; **~schluß** *m*

closing-time; *nach* **~** a. after business hours; **~stelle** *f* office; **~träger** *m pol.* chargé d'affaires; ✝ agent, representative; **~tüchtig** *adj.* efficient; smart; **~unternehmen** *n* business enterprise; **~verbindung** *f* business connexion *or* connection; **~viertel** *n* business cent|re, *Am.* -er; *Am.* downtown; shopping cent|re, *Am.* -er; **~zeit** *f* office hours *pl.*, business hours *pl.*; **~zimmer** *n* office, bureau; **~zweig** *m* branch (of business), line (of business).

geschah [gə'ʃa:] *pret.* of geschehen.

geschehen [gə'ʃe:ən] 1. *v/i.* (*irr.*, *no* -ge-, sein) happen, occur, take place; be done; *es geschieht ihm recht* it serves him right; 2. *p.p.* of 1; 3. **2** *n* (-s/-) events *pl.*, happenings *pl.*

gescheit *adj.* [gə'ʃaɪt] clever, intelligent, bright.

Geschenk [gə'ʃɛŋk] *n* (-[e]s/-e) present, gift; **~packung** *f* gift-box.

Geschicht|e [gə'ʃiçtə] *f* 1. (-/-) story; tale; *fig.* affair; 2. (-/ *no pl.*) history; **~lich** *adj.* historical; **~sforscher** *m*, **~sschreiber** *m* historian.

Ge'schick *n* 1. (-[e]s/-e) fate; destiny; 2. (-[e]s/ *no pl.*) = **~lichkeit** *f* (-/-en) skill; dexterity; aptitude; **~t** *adj.* skil(l)ful; dexterous; apt; clever.

ge'schieden [gə'ʃi:dən] *p.p.* of scheiden; **~schienen** [**~**'ʃi:nən] *p.p.* of scheinen.

Geschirr [gə'ʃir] *n* (-[e]s/-e) vessel; dishes *pl.*; china; earthenware, crockery; service; *horse*: harness.

ge'schlafen *p.p.* of schlafen; **~'schlagen** *p.p.* of schlagen.

Ge'schlecht *n* (-[e]s/-er) sex; kind; species; race; family; generation; *gr.* gender; **2lich** *adj.* sexual.

Ge'schlechts|krankheit ✱ *f* venereal disease; **~reife** *f* puberty; **~teile** *anat. n/pl.* genitals *pl.*; **~trieb** *m* sexual instinct *or* urge; **~verkehr** *m* (-[e]s/ *no pl.*) sexual intercourse; **~wort** *gr. n* (-[e]s/‖er) article.

ge'schlichen [gə'ʃliçən] *p.p.* of schleichen; **~schliffen** [**~**'ʃlifən] 1. *p.p.* of schleifen 2; 2. *adj. jewel:* cut; *fig.* polished; **~schlossen**

[~'ʃlɔsən] **1.** *p.p. of* schließen; **2.** *adj. formation*: close; collective; ~e *Gesellschaft* private party; ~**schlungen** [~'ʃluŋən] *p.p. of* schlingen.

Geschmack [gə'ʃmak] *m* (-[e]s/~e, *co.* ᵘer) taste (*a. fig.*); flavo(u)r; ~ *finden an* (*dat.*) take a fancy to; **2los** *adj.* tasteless; *pred. fig.* in bad taste; ~(s)**sache** *f* matter of taste; **2voll** *adj.* tasteful; *pred. fig.* in good taste.

ge|schmeidig *adj.* [gə'ʃmaidiç] supple, pliant; ~**schmissen** [~'ʃmisən] *p.p. of* schmeißen; ~**schmolzen** [~'ʃmɔltsən] *p.p. of* schmelzen.

Geschnatter [gə'ʃnatər] *n* (-s/*no pl.*) cackling (*of geese*); chatter(ing) (*of girls, etc.*).

ge|schnitten [gə'ʃnitən] *p.p. of* schneiden; ~**schoben** [~'ʃo:bən] *p.p. of* schieben; ~**scholten** [~'ʃɔltən] *p.p. of* schelten.

Geschöpf [gə'ʃœpf] *n* (-[e]s/-e) creature.

ge'schoren *p.p. of* scheren.

Geschoß [gə'ʃɔs] *n* (Geschosses/ Geschosse) projectile; missile; stor(e)y, floor. [Ben.\

geschossen [gə'ʃɔsən] *p.p. of* schie-\

Ge'schrei *n* (-[e]s/*no pl.*) cries *pl.*; shouting; *fig.* noise, fuss.

ge|schrieben [gə'ʃri:bən] *p.p. of* schreiben; ~**schrie(e)n** [~'ʃri:(ə)n] *p.p. of* schreien; ~**schritten** [~'ʃritən] *p.p. of* schreiten; ~**schunden** [~'ʃundən] *p.p. of* schinden.

Geschütz ⚔ [gə'ʃyts] *n* (-es/-e) gun, cannon; ordnance.

Geschwader ⚔ [gə'ʃva:dər] *n* (-s/-) ⚓ squadron; ✈ wing, *Am.* group.

Geschwätz [gə'ʃvɛts] *n* (-es/*no pl.*) idle talk; gossip; **2ig** *adj.* talkative.

geschweige *cj.* [gə'ʃvaigə]: ~ (*denn*) not to mention; let alone, much less.

geschwiegen [gə'ʃvi:gən] *p.p. of* schweigen.

geschwind *adj.* [gə'ʃvint] fast, quick, swift; **2igkeit** [~diçkait] *f* (-/-en) quickness; speed, pace; *phys.* velocity; rate; *mit e-r* ~ *von* ... at the rate of ...; **2igkeitsbegren-zung** *f* speed limit.

Geschwister [gə'ʃvistər] *n* (-s/-): ~ *pl.* brother(s *pl.*) and sister(s *pl.*).

ge|schwollen [gə'ʃvɔlən] **1.** *p.p. of* schwellen; **2.** *adj. language*: bom-

bastic, pompous; ~**schwommen** [~'ʃvɔmən] *p.p. of* schwimmen.

geschworen [gə'ʃvo:rən] *p.p. of* schwören; **2e** [~ə] *m, f* (-n/-n) juror; *die* ~ *pl.* the jury; **2engericht** *n* jury.

Geschwulst ⚕ [gə'ʃvulst] *f* (-/ᵘe) swelling; tumo(u)r.

ge|schwunden [gə'ʃvundən] *p.p. of* schwinden; ~**schwungen** [~'ʃvuŋən] *p.p. of* schwingen.

Geschwür ⚕ [gə'ʃvy:r] *n* (-[e]s/-e) abscess, ulcer.

ge'sehen *p.p. of* sehen.

Gesell ⚒ [gə'zɛl] *m* (-en/-en), ~**e** [~ə] *m* (-n/-n) companion, fellow; ⊕ journeyman; **2en** *v/refl.* (*no -ge-, h*) associate, come together; *sich zu j-m* ~ join s.o.; **2ig** *adj.* social; sociable.

Ge'sellschaft *f* (-/-en) society; company (*a.* ✝); party; *j-m* ~ *leisten* keep s.o. company; ~**er** *m* (-s/-) companion; ✝ partner; ~**erin** *f* (-/-nen) (lady) companion; ✝ partner; **2lich** *adj.* social.

Ge'sellschafts|dame *f* (lady) companion; ~**reise** *f* party tour; ~**spiel** *n* party *or* round game; ~**tanz** *m* ball-room dance.

gesessen [gə'zɛsən] *p.p. of* sitzen.

Gesetz [gə'zɛts] *n* (-es/-e) law; statute; ~**buch** *n* code; statute-book; ~**entwurf** *m* bill; ~**eskraft** *f* legal force; ~**essammlung** *f* code; **2gebend** *adj.* legislative; ~**geber** *m* (-s/-) legislator; ~**gebung** *f* (-/-en) legislation; **2lich 1.** *adj.* lawful, legal; **2.** *adv.*: ~ *geschützt* patented, registered; **2los** *adj.* lawless; **2mä-ßig** *adj.* legal; lawful.

ge'setzt 1. *adj.* sedate, staid; sober; mature; **2.** *cj.*: ~ *den Fall,* (*daß*) ... suppose *or* supposing (that) ...

ge'setzwidrig *adj.* unlawful, illegal.

Ge'sicht *n* (-[e]s/-er) face; countenance; *fig.* character; *zu* ~ *bekommen* catch sight *or* a glimpse of; set eyes on.

Ge'sichts|ausdruck *m* (facial) expression; ~**farbe** *f* complexion; ~**kreis** *m* horizon; ~**punkt** *m* point of view, viewpoint, aspect, *esp. Am.* angle; ~**zug** *m mst Gesichtszüge pl.* feature(s *pl.*), lineament(s *pl.*).

Ge'sims *n* ledge.

Gesinde [gə'zində] *n* (-s/-) (domestic) servants *pl.*; ~**l** [~l] *n* (-s/*no pl.*) rabble, mob.

ge'sinn|t *adj. in compounds*: ...-minded; *wohl* ~ well disposed (*j-m towards* s.o.); **2ung** *f* (*-/-en*) mind; conviction; sentiment(s *pl.*); opinions *pl.*

gesinnungs|los *adj.* [gə'zinuŋslo:s] unprincipled; **~treu** *adj.* loyal; **2wechsel** *m* change of opinion; *esp. pol.* volte-face.

ge'sittet *adj.* [gə'zitət] civilized; well-bred, well-mannered; **~'soffen** *p.p. of* saufen; **~sogen** [~'zo:gən] *p.p. of* saugen; **~sonnen** [~'zɔnən] **1.** *p.p. of* sinnen; **2.** *adj.* minded, disposed; **~sotten** [~'zɔtən] *p.p. of* sieden; **~'spalten** *p.p. of* spalten.

Ge'spann *n* (*-[e]s/-e*) team, *Am. a.* span; *oxen:* yoke; *fig.* pair, couple.

ge'spannt *adj.* tense (*a. fig.*); *rope:* tight, taut; *fig.* intent; *attention:* close; *relations:* strained; ~ *sein auf (acc.)* be anxious for; *auf ~em Fuß* on bad terms; **2heit** *f* (*-/no pl.*) tenseness, tension.

Gespenst [gə'ʃpɛnst] *n* (*-es/-er*) ghost, spect|re, *Am. -er;* **2isch** *adj.* ghostly.

Ge'spiel|e *m* (*-n/-n*), **~in** *f* (*-/-nen*) playmate.

gespien [gə'ʃpi:n] *p.p. of* speien.

Gespinst [gə'ʃpinst] *n* (*-es/-e*) web, tissue (*both a. fig.*); spun yarn.

gesponnen [gə'ʃpɔnən] *p.p. of* spinnen.

Gespött [gə'ʃpœt] *n* (*-[e]s/no pl.*) mockery, derision, ridicule; *zum ~ der Leute werden* become a laughing-stock.

Gespräch [gə'ʃprɛ:ç] *n* (*-[e]s/-e*) talk; conversation; *teleph.* call; dialogue; **2ig** *adj.* talkative.

ge'sprochen [gə'ʃrɔxən] *p.p. of* sprechen; **~'sprossen** *p.p. of* sprießen; **~sprungen** [~'ʃpruŋən] *p.p. of* springen.

Gestalt [gə'ʃtalt] *f* (*-/-en*) form, figure, shape; stature; **2en** *v/t. and v/refl.* (*no -ge-, h*) form, shape; **~ung** *f* (*-/-en*) formation; arrangement, organization.

gestanden [gə'ʃtandən] *p.p. of* stehen.

ge'ständ|ig *adj.*: ~ *sein* confess; **2nis** [~t-] *n* (*-ses/-se*) confession.

Ge'stank *m* (*-[e]s/no pl.*) stench.

gestatten [gə'ʃtatən] *v/t.* (*no -ge-, h*) allow, permit.

Geste ['gɛstə] *f* (*-/-n*) gesture.

ge'stehen (*irr. stehen, no -ge-, h*) **1.** *v/t.* confess, avow; **2.** *v/i.* confess.

Ge|'stein *n* (*-[e]s/-e*) rock, stone; **~stell** [~'ʃtɛl] *n* (*-[e]s/-e*) stand, rack, shelf; frame; trestle, horse.

gestern *adv.* ['gɛstərn] yesterday; ~ *abend* last night.

gestiegen [gə'ʃti:gən] *p.p. of* steigen.

Ge'stirn *n* (*-[e]s/-e*) star; *astr.* constellation; **2t** *adj.* starry.

ge|stoben [gə'ʃto:bən] *p.p. of* stieben; **~stochen** [~'ʃtɔxən] *p.p. of* stechen; **~stohlen** [~'ʃto:lən] *p.p. of* stehlen; **~storben** [~'ʃtɔrbən] *p.p. of* sterben; **~'stoßen** *p.p. of* stoßen; **~strichen** [~'ʃtriçən] *p.p. of* streichen.

gestrig *adj.* ['gɛstriç] of yesterday, yesterday's ...

ge'stritten *p.p. of* streiten.

Gestrüpp [gə'ʃtryp] *n* (*-[e]s/-e*) brushwood; undergrowth.

gestunken [gə'ʃtuŋkən] *p.p. of* stinken.

Gestüt [gə'ʃty:t] *n* (*-[e]s/-e*) stud farm; *horses kept for breeding, etc.:* stud.

Gesuch [gə'zu:x] *n* (*-[e]s/-e*) application, request; petition; **2t** *adj.* wanted; sought-after; *politeness:* studied.

gesund *adj.* [gə'zunt] sound, health-y; salubrious; wholesome (*a. fig.*); **~er Menschenverstand** common sense; **~en** [~dən] *v/i.* (*no -ge-, sein*) recover.

Ge'sundheit *f* (*-/no pl.*) health (-iness); wholesomeness (*a. fig.*); *auf j-s ~ trinken* drink (to) s.o.'s health; **2lich** *adj.* sanitary; ~ *geht es ihm gut* he is in good health.

Ge'sundheits|amt *n* Public Health Department; **~pflege** *f* hygiene; public health service; **2schädlich** *adj.* injurious to health, unhealthy, unwholesome; **~wesen** *n* Public Health; **~zustand** *m* state of health, physical condition.

ge|sungen [gə'zuŋən] *p.p. of* singen; **~sunken** [~'zuŋkən] *p.p. of* sinken; **~tan** [~'ta:n] *p.p. of* tun.

Getöse [gə'tø:zə] *n* (*-s/no pl.*) din, noise.

ge'tragen 1. *p.p. of* tragen; **2.** *adj.* solemn.

Getränk [gə'trɛŋk] *n* (*-[e]s/-e*) drink, beverage. [venture.]

ge'trauen *v/refl.* (*no -ge-, h*) dare,⌐

Getreide [gə'traɪdə] n (-s/-) corn, esp. Am. grain; cereals pl.; ~(**an**)**bau** m corn-growing, esp. Am. grain growing; ~**pflanze** f cereal plant; ~**speicher** m granary, grain silo, Am. elevator.

ge'treten p.p. of treten.

ge'treu(lich) adj. faithful, loyal; true.

Getriebe [gə'tri:bə] n (-s/-) bustle; ⊕ gear(ing); ⊕ drive.

ge|**trieben** [gə'tri:bən] p.p. of treiben; ~**troffen** [~'trɔfən] p.p. of treffen; ~**trogen** [~'tro:gən] p.p. of trügen.

ge'trost adv. confidently.

ge'trunken p.p. of trinken.

Ge|**tue** [gə'tu:ə] n (-s/no pl.) fuss; ~**tümmel** [~'tyməl] n (-s/-) turmoil; ~**viert** [~'fi:rt] n (-[e]s/-e) square.

Gewächs [gə'vɛks] n (-es/-e) growth (a. ⚕); plant; vintage; ~**haus** n greenhouse, hothouse, conservatory.

ge|**wachsen 1.** p.p. of wachsen; **2.** adj.: j-m ~ sein be a match for s.o.; e-r Sache ~ sein be equal to s.th.; sich der Lage ~ zeigen rise to the occasion; ~**wagt** adj. [~'va:kt] risky; bold; ~**wählt** adj. [~'vɛ:lt] style: refined; ~'**wahr** adj.: ~ werden (acc. or gen.) perceive s.th.; become aware of s.th.; ~ werden, daß become aware that.

Gewähr [gə've:r] f (-/no pl.) guarantee, warrant, security; **2en** v/t. (no -ge-, h) grant, allow; give, yield, afford; j-n ~ lassen let s.o. have his way; leave s.o. alone; **2leisten** v/t. (no -ge-, h) guarantee.

Ge'wahrsam m (-s/-e) custody, safe keeping.

Ge'währsmann m informant, source.

Gewalt [gə'valt] f (-/-en) power; authority; control; force, violence; höhere ~ act of God; mit ~ by force; ~**herrschaft** f despotism, tyranny; **2ig** adj. powerful, mighty; vehement; vast; ~**maßnahme** f violent measure; **2sam 1.** adj. violent; **2.** adv. a. forcibly; ~ öffnen force open; open by force; ~**tat** f act of violence; **2tätig** adj. violent.

Gewand [gə'vant] n (-[e]s/⁻er) garment, robe; esp. eccl. vestment.

ge'wandt 1. p.p. of wenden 2; **2.** adj. agile, nimble, dexterous, adroit; clever; **2heit** f (-/no pl.) agility, nimbleness; adroitness, dexterity; cleverness.

ge'wann pret. of gewinnen.

Gewäsch F [gə'vɛʃ] n (-es/no pl.) twaddle, nonsense.

ge'waschen p.p. of waschen.

Gewässer [gə'vɛsər] n (-s/-) water(s pl.).

Gewebe [gə've:bə] n (-s/-) tissue (a. anat. and fig.); fabric, web; texture.

Ge'wehr n gun; rifle; ~**kolben** m (rifle-)butt; ~**lauf** m (rifle-, gun-) barrel.

Geweih [gə'vaɪ] n (-[e]s/-e) horns pl., head, antlers pl.

Gewerbe [gə'vɛrbə] n (-s/-) trade, business; industry; ~**freiheit** f freedom of trade; ~**schein** m trade licen|ce, Am. -se; ~**schule** f technical school; ~**steuer** f trade tax; **2treibend** adj. carrying on a business, engaged in trade; ~**treibende** m (-n/-n) tradesman.

gewerb|**lich** adj. [gə'vɛrplɪç] commercial, industrial; ~**smäßig** adj. professional.

Ge'werkschaft f (-/-en) trade(s) union, Am. labor union; ~**ler** m (-s/-) trade(s)-unionist; **2lich** adj. trade-union; ~**sbund** m Trade Union Congress, Am. Federation of Labor.

ge|**wesen** [gə've:zən] p.p. of sein; ~**wichen** [~'vɪçən] p.p. of weichen.

Gewicht [gə'vɪçt] n (-[e]s/-e) weight, Am. F a. heft; e-r Sache ~ beimessen attach importance to s.th.; ~ haben carry weight (bei dat. with); ~ legen auf et. lay stress on s.th.; ins ~ fallen be of great weight, count, matter; **2ig** adj. weighty (a. fig.).

ge|**wiesen** [gə'vi:zən] p.p. of weisen; ~**willt** adj. [~'vɪlt] willing.

Ge|**wimmel** [gə'vɪməl] n (-s/no pl.) swarm; throng; ~**winde** ⊕ [~'vɪndə] n (-s/-) thread.

Gewinn [gə'vɪn] m (-[e]s/-e) gain; † gains pl.; profit; lottery ticket: prize; game: winnings pl.; ~**anteil** m dividend; ~**beteiligung** f profit-sharing; **2bringend** adj. profitable; **2en** (irr., no -ge-, h) **1.** v/t. win; gain; get; **2.** v/i. win; gain; fig. improve; **2end** adj. manner, smile: winning, engaging; ~**er** m (-s/-) winner.

Ge'wirr n (-[e]s/-e) tangle, entanglement; *streets*: maze; *voices*: confusion.

gewiß [gə'vis] **1.** adj. certain; *ein gewisser Herr N.* a certain Mr. N., one Mr. N.; **2.** adv.: ~! certainly!, to be sure!, *Am.* sure!

Ge'wissen n (-s/-) conscience; **2haft** adj. conscientious; **2los** adj. unscrupulous; **~sbisse** m/pl. remorse, pangs pl. of conscience; **~sfrage** f question of conscience.

gewissermaßen adv. [gəvisər'ma:sən] to a certain extent.

Ge'wißheit f (-/-en) certainty; certitude.

Gewitter [gə'vitər] n (-s/-) (thunder)storm; **2n** v/i. (no -ge-, h): es gewittert there is a thunderstorm; **~regen** m thunder-shower; **~wolke** f thundercloud.

ge|woben [gə'vo:bən] p.p. of weben; **~wogen 1.** p.p. of wägen and wiegen[1]; **2.** adj. (dat.) well or kindly disposed towards, favo(u)rably inclined towards.

gewöhnen [gə'vø:nən] v/t. (no -ge-, h) accustom, get used (an acc. to).

Gewohnheit [gə'vo:nhait] f (-/-en) habit; custom; **2smäßig** adj. habitual.

ge'wöhnlich adj. common; ordinary; usual, customary; habitual; common, vulgar.

ge'wohnt adj. customary, habitual; (es) ~ sein zu inf. be accustomed or used to inf.

Gewölbe [gə'vœlbə] n (-s/-) vault.

ge|wonnen [gə'vɔnən] p.p. of gewinnen; **~worben** [~'vɔrbən] p.p. of werben; **~worden** [~'vɔrdən] p.p. of werden; **~worfen** [~'vɔrfən] p.p. of werfen; **~wrungen** [~'vruŋən] p.p.p. of wringen.

Gewühl [gə'vy:l] n (-[e]s/no pl.) bustle; milling crowd.

gewunden [gə'wundən] **1.** p.p. of winden; **2.** adj. twisted; winding.

Gewürz [gə'vyrts] n (-es/-e) spice; condiment; **~nelke** ♀ f clove.

ge'wußt p.p. of wissen.

Ge|'zeit f: mst ~en pl. tide(s pl.); **~'zeter** n (-s/no pl.) (shrill) clamo(u)r.

ge|'ziert adj. affected; **~zogen** [~'tso:gən] p.p. of ziehen.

Gezwitscher [gə'tsvitʃər] n (-s/no pl.) chirping, twitter(ing).

gezwungen [gə'tsvuŋən] **1.** p.p. of zwingen; **2.** adj. forced, constrained.

Gicht ☞ [giçt] f (-/no pl.) gout; **2isch** ☞ adj. gouty; **~knoten** ☞ m gouty knot.

Giebel ['gi:bəl] m (-s/-) gable(-end).

Gier [gi:r] f (-/no pl.) greed(iness) (nach for); **2ig** adj. greedy (nach for, of).

'Gießbach m torrent.

gieß|en ['gi:sən] (irr., ge-, h) **1.** v/t. pour; ⊕ cast, found; water (flowers); **2.** v/i.: es gießt it is pouring (with rain); **2er** m (-s/-) founder; **2erei** [~'rai] f (-/-en) foundry; **2kanne** f watering-can or -pot.

Gift [gift] n (-[e]s/-e) poison; venom (esp. of snakes) (a. fig.); malice, spite; **2ig** adj. poisonous; venomous; malicious, spiteful; **~schlange** f venomous or poisonous snake; **~zahn** m poison-fang.

Gigant [gi'gant] m (-en/-en) giant.

Gimpel orn. ['gimpəl] m (-s/-) bullfinch.

ging [giŋ] pret. of gehen.

Gipfel ['gipfəl] m (-s/-) summit; top; peak; **~konferenz** pol. f summit meeting or conference; **2n** v/i. (ge-, h) culminate.

Gips [gips] m (-es/-e) min. gypsum; ⊕ plaster (of Paris); **~abdruck** m, **~abguß** m plaster cast; **2en** v/t. (ge-, h) plaster; **~verband** m plaster (of Paris) dressing.

Giraffe zo. [gi'rafə] f (-/-n) giraffe.

girieren ✝ [ʒi'ri:rən] v/t. (no -ge-, h) endorse, indorse (bill of exchange).

Girlande [gir'landə] f (-/-n) garland.

Giro ✝ ['ʒi:ro] n (-s/-s) endorsement, indorsement; **~bank** f clearing-bank; **~konto** n current account.

girren ['girən] v/i. (ge-, h) coo.

Gischt [gift] m (-es/☞ -e) and f (-/☞ -en) foam, froth; spray; spindrift.

Gitarre ♪ [gi'tarə] f (-/-n) guitar.

Gitter ['gitər] n (-s/-) grating; lattice; trellis; railing; **~bett** n crib; **~fenster** n lattice-window.

Glacéhandschuh [gla'se:-] m kid glove.

Glanz [glants] m (-es/no pl.) brightness; lust|re, Am. -er; brilliancy; splendo(u)r.

glänzen ['glɛntsən] v/i. (ge-, h) glitter, shine; '**~d** adj. bright, brilliant; fig. splendid.

'**Glanz|leistung** f brilliant achievement or performance; '**~papier** n glazed paper; '**~punkt** m highlight; '**~zeit** f golden age, heyday.

Glas [glɑːs] n (-es/⸚er) glass; '**~er** ['⸚zər] m (-s/-) glazier.

gläsern adj. ['glɛːzərn] of glass; fig. glassy.

'**Glas|glocke** f (glass) shade or cover; globe; bell-glass; '**~hütte** f glassworks sg., pl.

glasieren [glaˈziːrən] v/t. (no -ge-, h) glaze; ice, frost (cake).

glasig adj. ['glɑːziç] glassy, vitreous.

'**Glasscheibe** f pane of glass.

Glasur [glaˈzuːr] f (-/-en) glaze, glazing; enamel; icing, frosting (on cakes).

glatt [glat] **1.** adj. smooth (a. fig.); even; lie, etc.: flat, downright; road, etc.: slippery; **2.** adv. smoothly, evenly; ~ anliegen fit closely or tightly; ~ rasiert clean-shaven; et. ~ ableugnen deny s.th. flatly.

Glätte ['glɛtə] f (-/-n) smoothness; road, etc.: slipperiness.

'**Glatteis** n glazed frost, icy glaze, Am. glaze; F: j-n aufs ~ führen lead s.o. up the garden path.

'**glätten** v/t. (ge-, h) smooth.

Glatze ['glatsə] f (-/-n) bald head.

Glaube ['glaubə] m (-ns/⸚-n) faith, belief (an acc. in); '**2n** (ge-, h) **1.** v/t. believe; think, suppose, Am. a. guess; **2.** v/i. believe (j-m s.o.; an acc. in).

'**Glaubens|bekenntnis** n creed, profession or confession of faith; '**~lehre** f, '**~satz** m dogma, doctrine.

glaubhaft adj. ['glaup-] credible, plausible; authentic.

gläubig adj. ['glɔʏbiç] believing, faithful; '**2e** ['⸚gə] m, f (-n/-n) believer; '**2er** † ['⸚gər] m (-s/-) creditor.

glaubwürdig adj. ['glaup-] credible.

gleich [glaɪç] **1.** adj. equal (an dat. in); the same; like; even, level; in ~er Weise likewise; zur ~en Zeit at the same time; es ist mir ~ it's all the same to me; das ~e the same; as much; er ist nicht (mehr) der ~e

he is not the same man; **2.** adv. alike, equally; immediately, presently, directly, at once; just; es ist ~ acht (Uhr) it is close on or nearly eight (o'clock); **~altrig** adj. ['⸚altriç] (of) the same age; '**~artig** adj. homogeneous; similar; uniform; '**~bedeutend** adj. synonymous; equivalent (to); tantamount (mit to); '**~berechtigt** adj. having equal rights; '**~bleibend** adj. constant, steady; '**~en** v/i. (irr., ge-, h) equal; resemble.

'**gleich|falls** adv. also, likewise; '**~förmig** adj. ['⸚fœrmiç] uniform; '**~gesinnt** adj. like-minded; '**2gewicht** n balance (a. fig.); equilibrium, equipoise; pol.: ~ der Kräfte balance of power; '**~gültig** adj. indifferent (gegen to); es ist mir ~ I don't care; ~, was du tust no matter what you do; '2**gültigkeit** f indifference; '2**heit** f (-/-en) equality; likeness; '2**klang** m unison; consonance, harmony; '**~kommen** v/i. (irr. kommen, sep., -ge-, sein): e-r Sache ~ amount to s.th.; j-m ~ equal s.o.; '**~laufend** adj. parallel; '**~lautend** adj. consonant; identical; '**~machen** v/t. (sep., -ge-, h) make equal (dat. to), equalize (to or with); '2**maß** n regularity; evenness; fig. equilibrium; '**~mäßig** adj. equal; regular; constant; even; '2**mut** m equanimity; '**~mütig** adj. even-tempered; calm; **~namig** adj. ['⸚nɑːmiç] of the same name; '2**nis** n (-ses/-se) parable; rhet. simile; '**~sam** adv. as it were, so to speak; '**~schalten** v/t. (sep., -ge-, h) ⊕ synchronize; pol. co-ordinate, unify; '**~seitig** adj. equilateral; '**~setzen** v/t. (sep., -ge-, h) equate (dat. or mit with); '**~stehen** v/i. (irr. stehen, sep., -ge-, h) be equal; '**~stellen** v/t. (sep., -ge-, h) equalize, equate (dat. with); put s.o. on an equal footing (with); '2**stellung** f equalization, equation; '2**strom** ⨎ m direct current; '2**ung** ⅍ f (-/-en) equation; '**~wertig** adj. equivalent, of the same value, of equal value; '**~zeitig** adj. simultaneous; synchronous; contemporary.

Gleis [glaɪs] n (-es/-e) s. Geleise.

gleiten ['glaɪtən] v/i. (irr., ge-, sein) glide, slide.

'**Gleit|flug** m gliding flight, glide,

⚓ volplane; '**∼schutzreifen** *m* non-skid tyre, (*Am. only*) non-skid tire; '**∼schutz(vorrichtung** *f) m* anti-skid device.

Gletscher ['glɛtʃər] *m* (-s/-) glacier; '**∼spalte** *f* crevasse.

glich [gliç] *pret. of* gleichen.

Glied [gli:t] *n* (-[e]s/-er) *anat.* limb; member (*a. anat.*); link; ⚓ rank, file; **2ern** ['∼dərn] *v/t.* (ge-, h) joint, articulate; arrange; divide (*in acc.* into); '**∼erung** *f* (-/-) articulation; arrangement; division; formation; **∼maßen** ['∼tma:sən] *pl.* limbs *pl.*, extremities *pl.*

glimmen ['glimən] *v/i.* ([*irr.*,] ge-, h) *fire:* smo(u)lder (*a. fig.*); glimmer; glow.

glimpflich ['glimpfliç] **1.** *adj.* lenient, mild; **2.** *adv.:* ∼ *davonkommen* get off lightly.

glitschig *adj.* ['glitʃiç] slippery.

glitt [glit] *pret. of* gleiten.

glitzern ['glitsərn] *v/i.* (ge-, h) glitter, glisten.

Globus ['glo:bus] *m* (-, -ses/Globen, Globusse) globe.

Glocke ['glɔkə] *f* (-/-n) bell; shade; (glass) cover.

'**Glocken∣schlag** *m* stroke of the clock; '**∼spiel** *n* chime(s *pl.*); '**∼stuhl** *m* bell-cage; '**∼turm** *m* bell tower, belfry.

Glöckner ['glœknər] *m* (-s/-) bell-ringer.

glomm [glɔm] *pret. of* glimmen.

Glorie ['glo:rjə] *f* (-/-n) glory; '**∼n-schein** *fig. m* halo, aureola.

glorreich *adj.* ['glo:r-] glorious.

glotzen F ['glɔtsən] *v/i.* (ge-, h) stare.

Glück [glyk] *n* (-[e]s/*no pl.*) fortune; good luck; happiness, bliss, felicity; prosperity; *auf gut* ∼ on the off chance; ∼ *haben* be lucky, succeed; *das* ∼ *haben zu inf.* have the good fortune to *inf.*; *j-m* ∼ *wünschen* congratulate s.o. (*zu* on); *viel* ∼*!* good luck!; *zum* ∼ fortunately; **2bringend** *adj.* lucky.

Glucke *orn.* ['glukə] *f* (-/-n) sitting hen. [*gen.*\
'**glücken** *v/i.* (ge-, sein) *s.* gelin-|

gluckern ['glukərn] *v/i.* (ge-, h) *water, etc.:* gurgle.

'**glücklich** *adj.* fortunate; happy; lucky; '**∼er∣weise** *adv.* fortunately.

'**Glücksbringer** *m* (-s/-) mascot.

glück'selig *adj.* blissful, blessed, happy. [gurgle.\
glucksen ['gluksən] *v/i.* (ge-, h)|

'**Glücks∣fall** *m* lucky chance, stroke of (good) luck; '**∼göttin** *f* Fortune; '**∼kind** *n* lucky person; '**∼pfennig** *m* lucky penny; '**∼pilz** *m* lucky person; '**∼spiel** *n* game of chance; *fig.* gamble; '**∼stern** *m* lucky star; '**∼tag** *m* happy *or* lucky day, red-letter day.

'**glück∣strahlend** *adj.* radiant(ly happy); **2wunsch** *m* congratulation, good wishes *pl.*; compliments *pl.*; ∼ *zum Geburtstag* many happy returns (of the day).

Glüh∣birne ⚡ ['gly:-] *f* (electric-light) bulb; '**2en** *v/i.* (ge-, h) glow; *iron:* red-hot; *coal:* live; *fig.* ardent, fervid; '**2(end)heiß** *adj.* burning hot; '**∼lampe** *f* incandescent lamp; '**∼wein** *m* mulled wine; **∼würmchen** *zo.* ['∼vyrmçən] *n* (-s/-) glow-worm.

Glut [glu:t] *f* (-/-en) heat, glow (*a. fig.*); glowing fire, embers *pl.*; *fig.* ardo(u)r.

Gnade ['gna:də] *f* (-/-n) grace; favo(u)r; mercy; clemency; pardon; ⚓ quarter.

'**Gnaden∣akt** *m* act of grace; '**∼brot** *n* (-[e]s/*no pl.*) bread of charity; '**∼frist** *f* reprieve; '**∼gesuch** *n* petition for mercy.

gnädig *adj.* ['gnɛ:diç] gracious; merciful; *address:* 2e *Frau* Madam.

Gnom [gno:m] *m* (-en/-en) gnome, goblin.

Gobelin [gobə'lɛ̃:] *m* (-s/-s) Gobelin tapestry.

Gold [gɔlt] *n* (-[e]s/*no pl.*) gold; '**∼barren** *m* gold bar, gold ingot, bullion; '**∼borte** *f* gold lace; 2**en** *adj.* ['∼dən] gold; *fig.* golden; '**∼feder** *f* gold nib; '**∼fisch** *m* goldfish; '2**gelb** *adj.* golden(-yellow); **∼gräber** ['∼grɛ:bər] *m* (-s/-) gold-digger; '**∼grube** *f* gold-mine; '2**haltig** *adj.* gold-bearing, containing gold; 2**ig** *fig. adj.* ['∼diç] sweet, lovely, *Am.* F *a.* cute; '**∼mine** *f* gold-mine; '**∼münze** *f* gold coin; '**∼schmied** *m* goldsmith; '**∼schnitt** *m* gilt edge; *mit* ∼ gilt-edged; '**∼stück** *n* gold coin; '**∼waage** *f* gold-balance; '**∼währung** *f* gold standard.

Golf[1] geogr. [gɔlf] m (-[e]s/-e) gulf.
Golf[2] [~] n (-s/no pl.) golf; '~**platz** m golf-course, (golf-)links pl.; '~**schläger** m golf-club; '~**spiel** n golf; '~**spieler** m golfer.
Gondel ['gɔndəl] f (-/-n) gondola; ⚡ mst car.
gönnen ['gœnən] v/t. (ge-, h): j-m et. ~ allow or grant or not to grudge s.o. s.th.
'**Gönner** m (-s/-) patron; Am. a. sponsor; '2**haft** adj. patronizing.
gor [goːr] pret. of gären.
Gorilla zo. [go'rila] m (-s/-s) gorilla.
goß [gɔs] pret. of gießen.
Gosse ['gɔsə] f (-/-n) gutter (a. fig.).
Gott [gɔt] m (-es, ⚡ -s/⸚er) God; god, deity; '2**ergeben** adj. resigned (to the will of God).
'**Gottes|dienst** eccl. m (divine) service; '2**fürchtig** adj. godfearing; '~**haus** n church, chapel; '~**läste-rer** m (-s/-) blasphemer; '~**läste-rung** f blasphemy.
'**Gottheit** f (-/-en) deity, divinity.
Göttin ['gœtin] f (-/-nen) goddess.
göttlich adj. ['gœtliç] divine.
gott|lob int. thank God or goodness!; '~**los** adj. godless; impious; F fig. deed: unholy, wicked; '2**ver-trauen** n trust in God.
Götze ['gœtsə] m (-n/-n) idol; '~**nbild** n idol; '~**ndienst** m idolatry.
Gouvern|ante [guvɛr'nantə] f (-/-n) governess; ~**eur** [~'nøːr] m (-s/-e) governor.
Grab [graːp] n (-[e]s/⸚er) grave, tomb, sepulch|re, Am. -er.
Graben ['graːbən] **1.** m (-s/⸚) ditch; ✕ trench; **2.** ⚻ v/t. (irr., ge-, h) dig; animal: burrow.
Grab|gewölbe ['graːp-] n vault, tomb; '~**mal** n monument; tomb, sepulch|re, Am. -er; '~**rede** f funeral sermon; funeral oration or address; '~**schrift** f epitaph; '~**stätte** f burial-place; grave, tomb; '~**stein** m tombstone; gravestone.
Grad [graːt] m (-[e]s/-e) degree; grade, rank; 15 ~ Kälte 15 degrees below zero; '~**einteilung** f gradua-tion; '~**messer** m (-s/-) graduated scale, graduator; fig. criterion; '~**netz** n map: grid.
Graf [graːf] m (-en/-en) in Britain: earl; count.
Gräfin ['grɛːfin] f (-/-nen) countess.
'**Grafschaft** f (-/-en) county.

Gram [graːm] **1.** m (-[e]s/no pl.) grief, sorrow; **2.** ⚻ adj.: j-m ~ sein bear s.o. ill will or a grudge.
grämen ['grɛːmən] v/t. (ge-, h) grieve; sich ~ grieve (über acc. at, for, over).
Gramm [gram] n (-s/-e) gramme, Am. gram.
Grammati|k [gra'matik] f (-/-en) grammar; 2**sch** adj. grammatical.
Granat min. [gra'naːt] m (-[e]s/-e) garnet; ~**e** ✕ f (-/-n) shell; grenade; ~**splitter** ✕ m shell-splinter; ~**trichter** ✕ m shell-crater; ~**wer-fer** ✕ m (-s/-) mortar.
Granit min. [gra'niːt] m (-s/-e) granite.
Granne ⚘ ['granə] f (-/-n) awn, beard.
Graphi|k ['graːfik] f (-/-en) graphic arts pl.; 2**sch** adj. graphic(al).
Graphit min. [gra'fiːt] m (-s/-e) graphite.
Gras ⚘ [graːs] n (-es/⸚er) grass; 2**bewachsen** adj. ['~bəvaksən] grass-grown, grassy; 2**en** ['~zən] v/i. (ge-, h) graze; '~**halm** m blade of grass; '~**narbe** f turf, sod; '~**platz** m grass-plot, green.
grassieren [gra'siːrən] v/i. (no -ge-, h) rage, prevail.
gräßlich adj. ['grɛsliç] horrible; hideous, atrocious.
Grassteppe ['graːs-] f prairie, savanna(h).
Grat [graːt] m (-[e]s/-e) edge, ridge.
Gräte ['grɛːtə] f (-/-n) (fish-)bone.
Gratifikation [gratifika'tsjoːn] f (-/-en) gratuity, bonus.
gratis adv. ['graːtis] gratis, free of charge.
Gratul|ant [gratu'lant] m (-en/-en) congratulator; ~**ation** [~'tsjoːn] f (-/-en) congratulation; 2**ieren** [~-'liːrən] v/i. (no -ge-, h) congratulate (j-m zu et. s.o. on s.th.); j-m zum Geburtstag ~ wish s.o. many happy returns (of the day).
grau adj. [grau] grey, esp. Am. gray.
'**grauen**[1] v/i. (ge-, h) day: dawn.
'**grauen**[2] **1.** v/i. (ge-, h): mir graut vor (dat.) I shudder at, I dread; **2.** 2 n (-s/no pl.) horror (vor dat. of); '~**erregend** adj., '~**haft** adj., '~**voll** adj. horrible, dreadful.
gräulich adj. ['grɔyliç] greyish, esp. Am. grayish.
Graupe ['graupə] f (-/-n) (peeled)

barley, pot-barley; '**∼ln** 1. *f/pl.* sleet; 2. ♀ *v/i.* (ge-, h) sleet.

'**grausam** *adj.* cruel; '**♀keit** *f* (-/-en) cruelty.

'**grausen** ['grauzən] 1. *v/i.* (ge-, h) *s. grauen²* 1; 2. ♀ *n* (-s/*no pl.*) horror (*vor dat.* of).

'**grausig** *adj.* horrible. [graver.]

Graveur [gra'vøːr] *m* (-s/-e) en-]

gravieren [gra'viːrən] *v/t.* (*no* -ge-, h) engrave; '**∼d** *fig. adj.* aggravating.

gravitätisch *adj.* [gravi'tɛːtiʃ] grave; dignified; solemn; stately.

Grazie ['graːtsjə] *f* (-/-n) grace(fulness).

graziös *adj.* [gra'tsjøːs] graceful.

greifen ['graifən] (*irr.*, ge-, h) 1. *v/t.* seize, grasp, catch hold of; ♪ touch (*string*); 2. *v/i.*: an den Hut ∼ touch one's hat; ∼ nach grasp *or* snatch at; um sich ∼ spread; *j-m unter die Arme* ∼ give s.o. a helping hand; *zu strengen Mitteln* ∼ resort to severe measures; *zu den Waffen* ∼ take up arms.

Greis [grais] *m* (-es/-e) old man; **♀enhaft** *adj.* ['∼zən-] senile (*a.* ♣); **∼in** ['∼zin] *f* (-/-nen) old woman.

grell *adj.* [grɛl] *light*: glaring; *colour*: loud; *sound*: shrill.

Grenze ['grɛntsə] *f* (-/-n) limit; *territory*: boundary; *state*: frontier, borders *pl.*; e-e ∼ *ziehen* draw the line; '**♀n** *v/i.* (ge-, h); ∼ *an* (*acc.*) border on (*a. fig.*); *fig.* verge on; '**♀nlos** *adj.* boundless.

'**Grenz|fall** *m* border-line case; '**∼land** *n* borderland; '**∼linie** *f* boundary *or* border line; '**∼schutz** *m* frontier *or* border protection; frontier *or* border guard; '**∼stein** *m* boundary stone; '**∼übergang** *m* frontier *or* border crossing(-point).

Greuel ['grɔyəl] *m* (-s/-) horror; abomination; atrocity; '**∼tat** *f* atrocity.

Griech|e ['griːçə] *m* (-n/-n) Greek; '**♀isch** *adj.* Greek; △, *features*: Grecian.

griesgrämig *adj.* ['griːsgrɛːmiç] morose, sullen.

Grieß [griːs] *m* (-es/-e) gravel (*a.* ♣), grit; semolina; '**∼brei** *m* semolina pudding.

Griff [grif] 1. *m* (-[e]s/-e) grip, grasp, hold; ♪ touch; handle (*of knife, etc.*); hilt (*of sword*); 2. ♀ *pret. of greifen.*

Grille ['grilə] *f* (-/-n) *zo.* cricket; *fig.* whim, fancy; '**♀nhaft** *adj.* whimsical.

Grimasse [gri'masə] *f* (-/-n) grimace; ∼*n schneiden* pull faces.

Grimm [grim] *m* (-[e]s/*no pl.*) fury, rage; '**♀ig** *adj.* furious, fierce, grim.

Grind [grint] *m* (-[e]s/-e) scab, scurf.

grinsen ['grinzən] 1. *v/i.* (ge-, h) grin (*über acc.* at); sneer (at); 2. ♀ *n* (-s/*no pl.*) grin; sneer.

Grippe ♣ ['gripə] *f* (-/-n) influenza, F flu(e), grippe.

grob *adj.* [grɔp] coarse; gross; rude; *work, skin*: rough; '**♀heit** *f* (-/-en) coarseness; grossness; rudeness; ∼*en pl.* rude things *pl.*

grölen F ['grøːlən] *v/t. and v/i.* (ge-, h) bawl.

Groll [grɔl] *m* (-[e]s/*no pl.*) grudge, ill will; '**♀en** *v/i.* (ge-, h) *thunder*: rumble; *j-m* ∼ bear s.o. ill will *or* a grudge.

Gros¹ † [grɔs] *n* (-ses/-se) gross.

Gros² [groː] *n* (-/-) main body.

Groschen ['grɔʃən] *m* (-s/-) penny.

groß *adj.* [groːs] great; large; big; *figure*: tall; huge; *fig.* great; grand; *heat*: intense; *cold*: severe; *loss*: heavy; *die* ♀*en pl.* the grown-ups *pl.*; *im* ∼*en* wholesale, on a large scale; *im* ∼*en* (*und*) *ganzen* on the whole; ∼*er Buchstabe* capital (letter); *das* ∼*e Los* the first prize; *ich bin kein* ∼*er Tänzer* I am not much of a dancer; '**∼artig** *adj.* great, grand, sublime; first-rate; '**♀aufnahme** *f film*: close-up.

Größe ['grøːsə] *f* (-/-n) size; largeness; height, tallness; quantity (*esp.* ♠); *importance*: greatness; *p.* celebrity; *thea.* star.

'**Großeltern** *pl.* grandparents *pl.*

'**großenteils** *adv.* to a large *or* great extent, largely.

'**Größenwahn** *m* megalomania.

'**Groß|grundbesitz** *m* large landed property; '**∼handel** † *m* wholesale trade; '**∼handelspreis** † *m* wholesale price; '**∼händler** † *m* wholesale dealer, wholesaler; '**∼handlung** † *f* wholesale business; '**∼herzog** *m* grand duke; '**∼industrielle** *m* big industrialist.

Grossist [grɔ'sist] *m* (-en/-en) † Großhändler.

groß|jährig *adj.* ['groːsjɛːriç] of age;

~ *werden* come of age; '**2jährigkeit** *f* (-/no *pl.*) majority, full (legal) age; '**2kaufmann** *m* wholesale merchant; '**2kraftwerk** ⚡ *n* superpower station; '**2macht** *f* great power; '**2maul** *n* braggart; '**2mut** *f* (-/no *pl.*) generosity; **~mütig** *adj.* ['~my:tiç] magnanimous, generous; '**2mutter** *f* grandmother; '**2neffe** *m* great-nephew, grandnephew; '**2nichte** *f* great-niece, grand-niece; '**2onkel** *m* greatuncle, grand-uncle; '**2schreibung** *f* (-/-en) use of capital letters; capitalization; '**~sprecherisch** *adj.* boastful; '**~spurig** *adj.* arrogant; '**2stadt** *f* large town or city; '**~städtisch** *adj.* of or in a large town or city; '**2tante** *f* great-aunt, grandaunt.

größtenteils *adv.* ['grø:stəntaɪls] mostly, chiefly, mainly.

'**groß|tun** *v/i.* (*irr.* tun, *sep.*, *-ge-*, h) swagger, boast; *sich mit et.* **~** boast or brag of or about s.th.; '**2vater** *m* grandfather; '**2verdiener** *m* (-s/-) big earner; '**2wild** *n* big game; '**~ziehen** *v/t.* (*irr.* ziehen, *sep.*, *-ge-*, h) bring up (*child*); rear, raise (*child*, *animal*); **~zügig** *adj.* ['~tsy:giç] liberal; generous; broad-minded; *planning:* a. on a large scale.

grotesk *adj.* [gro'tɛsk] grotesque.

Grotte ['grɔtə] *f* (-/-n) grotto.

grub [gru:p] *pret.* of graben.

Grübchen ['gry:pçən] *n* (-s/-) dimple.

Grube ['gru:bə] *f* (-/-n) pit; ⚒ mine, pit.

Grübel|ei [gry:bə'laɪ] *f* (-/-en) brooding, musing, meditation; **2n** ['~ln] *v/i.* (ge-, h) muse, meditate, ponder (*all:* über *acc.* on, over), *Am.* F a. mull (over).

'**Gruben|arbeiter** ⚒ *m* miner; '**~gas** ⚒ *n* fire-damp; '**~lampe** ⚒ *f* miner's lamp.

Gruft [gruft] *f* (-/⸚e) tomb, vault.

grün [gry:n] **1.** *adj.* green; **~er** *Hering* fresh herring; **~er** *Junge* greenhorn; **~** *und blau schlagen* beat *s.o.* black and blue; *vom* **~en** *Tisch aus* armchair (*strategy, etc.*); **2.** **2** *n* (-s/no *pl.*) green; verdure.

Grund [grunt] *m* (-[e]s/⸚e) ground; soil; bottom (*a. fig.*); land, estate; foundation; *fig.:* motive; reason; argument; *von* **~** *auf* thoroughly,

fundamentally; '**~ausbildung** *f* basic instruction; ⚔ basic (military) training; '**~bedeutung** *f* basic or original meaning; '**~bedingung** *f* basic or fundamental condition; '**~begriff** *m* fundamental or basic idea; **~e** *pl.* principles *pl.*; rudiments *pl.*; '**~besitz** *m* land or property; '**~besitzer** *m* landowner; '**~buch** *n* land register.

gründ|en ['gryndən] *v/t.* (ge-, h) establish; ✝ promote; *sich* **~** *auf* (*acc.*) be based or founded on; '**2er** *m* (-s/-) founder; ✝ promoter.

'**grund|falsch** *adj.* fundamentally wrong; '**2farbe** *f* ground-colo(u)r; *opt.* primary colo(u)r; '**2fläche** *f* base; area (*of room, etc.*); '**2gebühr** *f* basic rate or fee; flat rate; '**2gedanke** *m* basic or fundamental idea; '**2gesetz** *n* fundamental law; 🏛 *appr.* constitution; '**2kapital** ✝ *n* capital (fund); '**2lage** *f* foundation, basis; '**~legend** *adj.* fundamental, basic.

gründlich *adj.* ['gryntliç] thorough; *knowledge:* profound.

'**Grund|linie** *f* base-line; '**2los** *adj.* bottomless; *fig.:* groundless; unfounded; '**~mauer** *f* foundationwall.   [Thursday.\

Grün'donnerstag *eccl. m* Maundy

'**Grund|regel** *f* fundamental rule; '**~riß** *m* △ ground-plan; outline; compendium; '**~satz** *m* principle; '**2sätzlich 1.** *adj.* fundamental; **2.** *adv.* in principle; on principle; '**~schule** *f* elementary or primary school; '**2stein** *m* △ foundation-stone; *fig.* corner-stone; '**~steuer** *f* land-tax; '**~stock** *m* basis, foundation; '**~stoff** *m* element; '**~strich** *m* down-stroke; '**~stück** *n* plot (of land); 🏛 (real) estate; premises *pl.*; '**~stücksmakler** *m* real estate agent, *Am.* realtor; '**~ton** *m* ♪ keynote; ground shade.

'**Gründung** *f* (-/-en) foundation, establishment.

'**grund|ver'schieden** *adj.* entirely different; '**2wasser** *geol. n* (under-)ground water; '**2zahl** *gr. f* cardinal number; '**2zug** *m* main feature, characteristic.

'**grünlich** *adj.* greenish.

'**Grün|schnabel** *fig. m* greenhorn; whipper-snapper; '**~span** *m* (-[e]s/no *pl.*) verdigris.

grunzen ['gruntsən] v/i. and v/t. (ge-, h) grunt.

Grupp|e ['grupə] f (-/-n) group; ✕ section, Am. squad; **⁓ieren** [⁓'pi:rən] v/t. (no -ge-, h) group, arrange in groups; **sich ⁓** form groups.

Gruselgeschichte ['gru:zəl-] f tale of horror, spine-chilling story or tale, F creepy story or tale.

Gruß [gru:s] m (-es/⁓e) salutation; greeting; esp. ✕, ♣ salute; mst **Grüße** pl. regards pl.; respects pl., compliments pl.

grüßen ['gry:sən] v/t. (ge-, h) greet, esp. ✕ salute; hail; **⁓ Sie ihn von mir** remember me to him; **j-n ⁓ lassen** send one's compliments or regards to s.o.

Grütze ['grytsə] f (-/-n) grits pl., groats pl.

guck|en ['gukən] v/i. (ge-, h) look; peep, peer; **⁓loch** n peep- or spyhole.

Guerilla ✕ [ge'ril(j)a] f (-/-s) guer(r)illa war.

gültig adj. ['gyltiç] valid; effective, in force; legal; coin: current; ticket: available; **⁓keit** f (-/no pl.) validity; currency (of money); availability (of ticket).

Gummi ['gumi] n, m (-s/-s) gum; (india-)rubber; **⁓ball** m rubber ball; **⁓band** n elastic (band), rubber band; **⁓baum** ♣ m gum-tree; (india-)rubber tree.

gum'mieren v/t. (no -ge-, h) gum.

Gummi|handschuh m rubber glove; **⁓knüppel** m truncheon, Am. club; **⁓schuhe** m/pl. rubber shoes pl., Am. rubbers pl.; **⁓sohle** f rubber sole; **⁓stiefel** m wellington (boot), Am. rubber boot; **⁓zug** m elastic; elastic webbing.

Gunst [gunst] f (-/no pl.) favo(u)r, goodwill; **zu ⁓en** (gen.) in favo(u)r of.

günst|ig adj. ['gynstiç] favo(u)rable; omen: propitious; **im ⁓sten Fall** at best; **zu ⁓en Bedingungen** ♣ on easy terms; **⁓ling** ['⁓liŋ] m (-s/-e) favo(u)rite.

Gurgel ['gurgəl] f (-/-n): **j-m an die ⁓ springen** leap or fly at s.o.'s throat; **⁓n** v/i. (ge-, h) ♣ gargle; gurgle.

Gurke ['gurkə] f (-/-n) cucumber; pickled: gherkin.

gurren ['gurən] v/i. (ge-, h) coo.

Gurt [gurt] m (-[e]s/-e) girdle; harness: girth; strap; belt.

Gürtel ['gyrtəl] m (-s/-) belt; girdle; geogr. zone.

Guß [gus] m (Gusses/Güsse) ⊕ founding, casting; typ. fount, Am. font; rain: downpour, shower; **⁓eisen** n cast iron; **⁓eisern** adj. cast-iron; **⁓stahl** m cast steel.

gut[1] [gu:t] **1.** adj. good; **⁓e Worte** fair words; **⁓es Wetter** fine weather; **⁓er Dinge** or **⁓en Mutes sein** be of good cheer; **⁓e Miene zum bösen Spiel machen** grin and bear it; **⁓ so!** good!, well done!; **⁓ werden** get well, heal; fig. turn out well; **ganz ⁓** not bad; **schon ⁓!** never mind!, all right!; **sei so ⁓** (will you) be so kind as to inf.; **auf ⁓ deutsch** in plain German; **j-m ⁓ sein** love or like s.o.; **2.** adv. well; **ein ⁓ gehendes Geschäft** a flourishing business; **du hast ⁓ lachen** it's easy or very well for you to laugh; **es ⁓ haben** be lucky; be well off.

Gut[2] [⁓] n (-[e]s/⁓er) possession, property; (landed) estate; † goods pl.

Gut|achten n (-s/-) (expert) opinion; **⁓achter** m (-s/-) expert; consultant; **⁓artig** adj. good-natured; ♣ benign; **⁓dünken** ['⁓dynkən] n (-s/no pl.): **nach ⁓** at discretion or pleasure.

Gute 1. n (-n/no pl.) the good; **⁓s tun** do good; **2.** m, f (-n/-n): **die ⁓n** pl. the good pl.

Güte ['gy:tə] f (-/no pl.) goodness, kindness; † class, quality; **in ⁓** amicably; F: **meine ⁓!** good gracious!; **haben Sie die ⁓ zu** inf. be so kind as to inf.

Güter|abfertigung f dispatch of goods; = **⁓annahme** f goods office, Am. freight office; **⁓bahnhof** m goods station, Am. freight depot or yard; **⁓gemeinschaft** ⚖ f community of property; **⁓trennung** ⚖ f separation of property; **⁓verkehr** m goods traffic, Am. freight traffic; **⁓wagen** m (goods) wag(g)on, Am. freight car; offener **⁓** (goods) truck; geschlossener **⁓** (goods) van, Am. boxcar; **⁓zug** m goods train, Am. freight train.

gut|gelaunt adj. good-humo(u)red;

'**_gläubig** adj. acting or done in good faith; s. leichtgläubig; '**_haben** v/t. (irr. haben, sep., -ge-, h) have credit for (sum of money); '**_haben** † n credit (balance); '**_heißen** v/t. (irr. heißen, sep., -ge-, h) approve (of); '**_herzig** adj. good-natured, kind-hearted.

'**gütig** adj. good, kind(ly).

'**gütlich** adv.: sich _ einigen settle s.th. amicably; sich _ tun an (dat.) regale o.s. on.

'**gut|machen** v/t. (sep., -ge-, h) make up for, compensate, repair; **_mütig** adj. ['_my:tiç] good-natured; '**2mütigkeit** f (-/\~ -en) good nature.   [of an estate.]

'**Gutsbesitzer** m landowner; owner]

'**Gut|schein** m credit note, coupon,

voucher; '**2schreiben** v/t. (irr. schreiben, sep., -ge-, h): j-m e-n Betrag _ put a sum to s.o.'s credit; '**_schrift** † f credit(ing).

'**Guts|haus** n farm-house; manor house; '**_herr** m lord of the manor; landowner; '**_hof** m farmyard; estate, farm; '**_verwalter** m (land-lord's) manager or steward.

'**gutwillig** adj. willing; obliging.

Gymnasi|albildung [gymna'zja:l-] f classical education; '**_ast** [_ast] m (-en/-en) appr. grammar-school boy; **_um** [_'na:zjum] n (-s/Gymnasien) appr. grammar-school.

Gymnasti|k [gym'nastik] f (-/no pl.) gymnastics pl.; **2sch** adj. gymnastic.   [(-n/-n) gyn(a)ecologist.]

Gynäkologe ♂ [gynɛ:ko'lo:gə] m]

H

Haar [haːr] n (-[e]s/-e) hair; sich die _e kämmen comb one's hair; sich die _e schneiden lassen have one's hair cut; aufs _ to a hair; um ein _ by a hair's breadth; '**_ausfall** m loss of hair; '**_bürste** f hairbrush; '**2en** v/i. and v/refl. (ge-, h) lose or shed one's hairs; '**_esbreite** f: um _ by a hair's breadth; '**2fein** adj. (as) fine as a hair; fig. subtle; '**_gefäß** anat. n capillary (vessel); '**2ge'nau** adj. exact to a hair; '**2ig** adj. hairy; in compounds: ...-haired; '**2'klein** adv. to the last detail; '**_klemme** f hair grip, Am. bobby pin; '**_nadel** f hairpin; '**_nadelkurve** f hairpin bend; '**_netz** n hair-net; '**_öl** n hair-oil; '**2scharf 1.** adj. very sharp; fig. very precise; 2. adv. by a hair's breadth; '**_schneidemaschine** f (e-e a pair of) (hair) clippers pl.; '**_schneider** m barber, (men's) hairdresser; '**_schnitt** m haircut; '**_schwund** m loss of hair; '**_spalte'rei** f (-/-en) hair-splitting; '**2sträubend** adj. hair-raising, horrifying; '**_tracht** f hair-style, coiffure; '**_wäsche** f hair-wash, shampoo; '**_wasser** n hair-lotion; '**_wuchs** m growth of the hair; '**_wuchsmittel** n hair-restorer.

Habe ['ha:bə] f (-/no pl.) property; belongings pl.

haben ['ha:bən] **1.** v/t. (irr., ge-, h) have; F fig.: sich _ (make a) fuss; etwas (nichts) auf sich _ be of (no) consequence; unter sich _ be in control of, command; zu _ † goods: obtainable, to be had; da _ wir's! there we are!; **2.** ♀ † n (-s/-) credit (side).

Habgier ['ha:p-] f avarice, covetousness; '**2ig** adj. avaricious, covetous.

habhaft adj. ['ha:phaft]: _ werden (gen.) get hold of; catch, apprehend.

Habicht orn. ['ha:biçt] m (-[e]s/-e) (gos)hawk.

Hab|seligkeiten ['ha:p-] f/pl. property, belongings pl.; '**_sucht** f s. Habgier; '**2süchtig** adj. s. habgierig.

Hacke ['hakə] f (-/-n) ♂ hoe, mattock; (pick)axe; heel.

Hacken ['hakən] **1.** m (-s/-) heel; die _ zusammenschlagen ⚔ click one's heels; **2.** ♀ v/t. (ge-, h) ♂ hack (soil); mince (meat); chop (wood).

'**Hackfleisch** n minced meat, Am. ground meat.

Häcksel ['hɛksəl] n, m (-s/no pl.) chaff, chopped straw.

Hader ['ha:dər] m (-s/no pl.) dispute, quarrel; discord; '**2n** v/i. (ge-, h) quarrel (mit with).

Hafen ['ha:fən] m (-s/\") harbo(u)r;

port; '**~anlagen** f/pl. docks pl.; '**~arbeiter** m docker, Am. a. longshoreman; '**~damm** m jetty; pier; '**~stadt** f seaport.

Hafer ['haːfər] m (-s/-) oats pl.; '**~brei** m (oatmeal) porridge; '**~flocken** f/pl. porridge oats pl.; '**~grütze** f groats pl., grits pl.; '**~schleim** m gruel.

Haft ⚖ [haft] f (-/no pl.) custody; detention, confinement; '**2bar** adj. responsible, ⚖ liable (für for); '**~befehl** m warrant of arrest; '**2en** v/i. (ge-, h) stick, adhere (an dat. to); ~ für ⚖ answer for, be liable for. **Häftling** ['hɛftliŋ] m (-s/-e) prisoner. '**Haftpflicht** ⚖ f liability; '**2ig** adj. liable (für for); '**~versicherung** f third-party insurance.

'**Haftung** f (-/-en) responsibility, ⚖ liability; mit beschränkter ~ limited.

Hagel ['haːgəl] m (-s/-) hail; fig. a. shower, volley; '**~korn** n hailstone; '**2n** v/i. (ge-, h) hail (a. fig.); '**~schauer** m shower of hail, (brief) hailstorm.

hager adj. ['haːgər] lean, gaunt; scraggy, lank.

Hahn [haːn] m 1. orn. (-[e]s/⁔e) cock; rooster; 2. ⊕ (-[e]s/⁔e, -en) (stop)cock, tap, Am. a. faucet; '**~enkampf** m cock-fight; '**~enschrei** m cock-crow.

Hai ichth. [hai] m (-[e]s/-e), '**~fisch** m shark.

Hain poet. [hain] m (-[e]s/-e) grove; wood.

häkel|n ['hɛːkəln] v/t. and v/i. (ge-, h) crochet; '**2nadel** f crochet needle or hook.

Haken ['haːkən] 1. m (-s⌐) hook (a. boxing); peg; fig. snag, catch; 2. ♀ v/i. (ge-, h) get stuck, jam. '**hakig** adj. hooked.

halb [halp] 1. adj. half; eine ~e Stunde half an hour, a half-hour; eine ~e Flasche Wein a half-bottle of wine; ein ~es Jahr half a year; ~e Note ♩ minim, Am. a. half note; ~er Ton ♩ semitone, Am. a. half tone; 2. adv. half; ~ voll half full; ~ soviel half as much; es schlug ~ it struck the half-hour.
'**halb|amtlich** adj. semi-official; '**2bruder** m half-brother; '**2dunkel** n semi-darkness; dusk, twilight; '**~er** prp. (gen.) ['halbər] on

account of; for the sake of; '**2fabrikat** ⊕ n semi-finished product; '**~gar** adj. underdone, Am. a. rare; '**2gott** m demigod; '**2heit** f (-/-en) half-measure.

halbieren [hal'biːrən] v/t. (no -ge-, h) halve, divide in half; A bisect. '**Halb|insel** f peninsula; '**2jahr** n half-year, six months pl.; '**2jährig** adj. ['~jɛːriç] half-year, six months; of six months; '**2jährlich** 1. adj. half-yearly; 2. adv. a. twice a year; '**~kreis** m semicircle; '**~kugel** f hemisphere; '**2laut** 1. adj. low, subdued; 2. adv. in an undertone; '**2mast** adv. (at) half-mast, Am. a. (at) half-staff; '**~messer** A m (-s/-) radius; '**~mond** m half-moon, crescent; '**2part** adv.: ~ machen go halves, F go fifty-fifty; '**~schuh** m (low) shoe; '**~schwester** f half-sister; '**~tagsbeschäftigung** f part-time job or employment; '**2tot** adj. half-dead; **2wegs** adv. ['~'veːks] half-way; fig. to some extent, tolerably; '**~welt** f demi-monde; **2wüchsig** adj. ['~vyːksiç] adolescent, Am. a. teen-age; '**~zeit** f sports: half(-time). [dump.]

Halde ['haldə] f (-/-n) slope; ☓ **half** [half] pret. of helfen.

Hälfte ['hɛlftə] f (-/-n) half, ⚖ moiety; die ~ von half of.

Halfter ['halftər] m, n (-s/-) halter.

Halle ['halə] f (-/-n) hall; hotel: lounge; tennis: covered court; ✈ hangar.

hallen ['halən] v/i. (ge-, h) (re)sound, ring, (re-)echo.

'**Hallen|bad** n indoor swimming-bath, Am. a. natatorium; '**~sport** m indoor sports pl.

hallo [ha'loː] 1. int. hallo!, hello!, hullo!; 2. ♀ fig. n (-s/-s) hullabaloo.

Halm ♀ [halm] m (-[e]s/-e) blade; stem, stalk; straw.

Hals [hals] m (-es/⁔e) neck; throat; ~ über Kopf head over heels; auf dem ~e haben have on one's back, be saddled with; sich den ~ verrenken crane one's neck; '**~abschneider** fig. m extortioner, F shark; '**~band** n necklace; collar (for dog, etc.); '**~entzündung** ⚕ f sore throat; '**~kette** f necklace; string; chain; '**~kragen** m collar; '**~schmerzen** m/pl.: ~ haben have a sore throat; '**2starrig** adj. stub-

Handelsvertrag

born, obstinate; '**⁓tuch** n neckerchief; scarf; '**⁓weite** f neck size.

Halt [halt] m -(e)s/-e) hold; foothold, handhold; support (a. fig.); fig.: stability; security, mainstay.

halt 1. int. stop!; ⚔ halt!; **2.** F adv. just; das ist ⁓ so that's the way it is.

'**haltbar** adj. material, etc.: durable, lasting; colour: fast; fig. theory, etc.: tenable.

'**halten** (irr., ge-, h) **1.** v/t. hold (fort, position, water, etc.); maintain (position, level, etc.); keep (promise, order, animal, etc.); make, deliver (speech); give, deliver (lecture); take in (newspaper); ⁓ für regard as, take to be; take for; es ⁓ mit side with; be fond of; kurz⁓ keep ⁓ short; viel (wenig) ⁓ von think highly (little) of; sich ⁓ hold out; last; food: keep; sich gerade ⁓ hold o.s. straight; sich gut ⁓ in examination, etc.: do well; p. be well preserved; sich ⁓ an (acc.) adhere or keep to; **2.** v/i. stop, halt; ice: bear; rope, etc.: stand the strain; ⁓ zu stick to or by; ⁓ auf (acc.) set store by, value; auf sich ⁓ pay attention to one's appearance; have self-respect.

'**Halte|punkt** m 🚉, etc.: wayside stop, halt; shooting: point of aim; phys. critical point; '**⁓r** m -s/-) keeper; a. owner; devices: ... holder; '**⁓stelle** f stop; 🚉 station, stop; '**⁓signal** 🚉 n stop signal.

halt|los adj. ['haltlo:s] p. unsteady, unstable; theory, etc.: baseless, without foundation; '**⁓machen** v/i. (sep., -ge-, h) stop, halt; vor nichts ⁓ stick or stop; at nothing; '**2ung** f (-/-en) deportment, carriage; pose; fig. attitude (gegenüber towards); self-control; stock exchange: tone.

hämisch adj. ['hɛ:miʃ] spiteful, malicious.

Hammel ['hamǝl] m -s/-, ⁼) wether; '**⁓fleisch** n mutton; '**⁓keule** f leg of mutton; '**⁓rippchen** n (-s/-) mutton chop.

Hammer ['hamǝr] m (-s/⁼) hammer; (auctioneer's) gavel; unter den ⁓ kommen come under the hammer.

hämmern ['hɛmǝrn] (ge-, h) **1.** v/t. hammer; **2.** v/i. hammer (a. an dat. at door, etc.); hammer away (auf dat. at piano); heart, etc.: throb (violently), pound.

Hämorrhoiden 🦠 [hɛ:mɔro'i:dǝn]

f/pl. h(a)emorrhoids pl., piles pl.

Hampelmann ['hampǝlman] m jumping-jack; fig. (mere) puppet.

Hamster zo. ['hamstǝr] m (-s/-) hamster; '**2n** v/t. and v/i. (ge-, h) hoard.

Hand [hant] f (-/⁼e) hand; j-m die ⁓ geben shake hands with s.o.; an ⁓ (gen.) or von with the help or aid of; aus erster ⁓ first-hand, at first hand; bei der ⁓, zur ⁓ at hand; ⁓ und Fuß haben be sound, hold water; seine ⁓ im Spiele haben have a finger in the pie; '**⁓arbeit** f manual labo(u)r or work; (handi)craft; needlework; '**⁓arbeiter** m manual labo(u)rer; '**⁓bibliothek** f reference library; '**⁓breit** f (-/-) hand's breadth; **2.** ♀ adj. a hand's breadth across; '**⁓bremse** mot. f hand-brake; '**⁓buch** n manual, handbook.

Hände|druck ['hɛndǝ-] m (-[e]s/⁼e) handshake; '**⁓klatschen** n (-s/no pl.) (hand-)clapping; applause.

Handel ['handǝl] m **1.** (-s/no pl.) commerce; trade; business; market; traffic; transaction, deal, bargain; **2.** (-s/⁼) Händel pl. quarrels pl., contention; '**2n** v/i. (ge-, h) act, take action; ✝ trade (mit with s.o., in goods), deal (in goods); bargain (um for), haggle (over); ⁓ von treat of, deal with; es handelt sich um it concerns, it is a matter of.

'**Handels|abkommen** n trade agreement; '**⁓bank** f commercial bank; '**2einig** adj.: ⁓ werden come to terms; '**⁓genossenschaft** f traders' co-operative association; '**⁓gericht** n commercial court; '**⁓gesellschaft** f (trading) company; '**⁓haus** n business house, firm; '**⁓kammer** f Chamber of Commerce; '**⁓marine** f mercantile marine; '**⁓minister** m minister of commerce; President of the Board of Trade, Am. Secretary of Commerce; '**⁓ministerium** n ministry of commerce; Board of Trade, Am. Department of Commerce; '**⁓reisende** m commercial traveller, Am. traveling salesman, F drummer; '**⁓schiff** n merchantman; '**⁓schiffahrt** f merchant shipping; '**⁓schule** f commercial school; '**⁓stadt** f commercial town; '**2üblich** adj. customary in trade; '**⁓vertrag** m commercial treaty, trade agreement.

H

'handeltreibend adj. trading.
'Hand|feger m (-s/-) hand-brush; **'~fertigkeit** f manual skill; **'2fest** adj. sturdy, strong; fig. well-founded, sound; **'~feuerwaffen** f/pl. small arms pl.; **'~fläche** f flat of the hand, palm; **'2gearbeitet** adj. hand-made; **'~geld** n earnest money; ✗ bounty; **'~gelenk** anat. n wrist; **'~gemenge** n scuffle, mêlée; **'~gepäck** n hand luggage, Am. hand baggage; **'~granate** ✗ f hand-grenade; **'2greiflich** adj. violent; fig. tangible, palpable; ~ werden turn violent, Am. a. get tough; **'~griff** m grasp; handle, grip; fig. manipulation; **'~habe** fig. f handle; **'2haben** v/t. (ge-, h) handle, manage; operate (machine, etc.); administer (law); **'~karren** m hand-cart; **'~koffer** m suitcase, Am. a. valise; **'~kuß** m kiss on the hand; **'~langer** m (-s/-) hodman, handy man; fig. dog's-body, henchman. [trader.\
Händler ['hɛndlər] m (-s/-) dealer,\
'handlich adj. handy; manageable.
Handlung ['handluŋ] f (-/-en) act, action; deed; thea. action, plot; † shop, Am. store.
'Handlungs|bevollmächtigte m proxy; **'~gehilfe** m clerk; shop-assistant, Am. salesclerk; **'~reisende** m s. Handelsreisende; **'~weise** f conduct; way of acting.
'Hand|rücken m back of the hand; **'~schelle** f handcuff, manacle; **'~schlag** m handshake; **'~schreiben** n autograph letter; **'~schrift** f handwriting; manuscript; **'2-schriftlich** 1. adj. hand-written; 2. adv. in one's own handwriting; **'~schuh** m glove; **'~streich** ✗ m surprise attack, coup de main; im ~ nehmen take by surprise; **'~tasche** f handbag, Am. a. purse; **'~tuch** n towel; **'~voll** f (-/-) handful; **'~wagen** m hand-cart; **'~werk** n (handi)craft, trade; **'~werker** m (-s/-) (handi)craftsman, artisan; workman; **'~werkzeug** n (kit of) tools pl.; **'~wurzel** anat. f wrist; **'~zeichnung** f drawing.
Hanf ♀ [hanf] m (-[e]s/no pl.) hemp.
Hang [haŋ] m (-[e]s/⸚e) slope, incline, declivity; hillside; fig. inclination, propensity (zu for; zu inf. to inf.); tendency (to).

Hänge|boden ['hɛŋə-] m hanging-loft; **'~brücke** ⌂ f suspension bridge; **'~lampe** f hanging lamp; **'~matte** f hammock.
hängen ['hɛŋən] 1. v/i. (irr., ge-, h) hang, be suspended; adhere, stick, cling (an dat. to); ~ an (dat.) be attached or devoted to; 2. v/t. (ge-, h) hang, suspend; **'~bleiben** v/i. (irr. bleiben, sep., -ge-, sein) get caught (up) (an dat. on, in); fig. stick (in the memory).
hänseln ['hɛnzəln] v/t. (ge-, h) tease (wegen about), F rag.
Hansestadt ['hanzə-] f Hanseatic town.
Hanswurst [hans'-] m (-es/-e, F ⸚e) merry andrew; Punch; fig. contp. clown, buffoon.
Hantel ['hantəl] f (-/-n) dumb-bell.
hantieren [han'ti:rən] v/i. (no -ge-, h) be busy (mit with); work (an dat. on).
Happen ['hapən] m (-s/-) morsel, mouthful, bite; snack.
Harfe ♪ ['harfə] f (-/-n) harp.
Harke ⚊ ['harkə] f (-/-n) rake; **'2n** v/t. and v/i. (ge-, h) rake.
harmlos adj. ['harmlo:s] harmless, innocuous; inoffensive.
Harmon|ie [harmo'ni:] f (-/-n) harmony (a. ♪); **2ieren** v/i. (no -ge-, h) harmonize (mit with); fig. a. be/be in keeping (with); **~ika** ♪ [~'mo:-nika] f (-/-s, Harmoniken) accordion; mouth-organ; **2isch** adj. [~'mo:niʃ] harmonious.
Harn [harn] m (-[e]s/-e) urine; **'~blase** anat. f (urinary) bladder; **'2en** v/i. (ge-, h) pass water, urinate.
Harnisch ['harniʃ] m (-es/-e) armo(u)r; in ~ geraten be up in arms (über acc. about).
'Harnröhre anat. f urethra.
Harpun|e [har'pu:nə] f (-/-n) harpoon; **2ieren** [~u'ni:rən] v/t. (no -ge-, h) harpoon.
hart [hart] 1. adj. hard; fig. a. harsh; heavy, severe; 2. adv. hard; ~ arbeiten work hard.
Härte ['hɛrtə] f (-/-n) hardness; fig. a. hardship; severity; **2n** (ge-, h) 1. v/t. harden (metal); temper (steel); case-harden (iron, steel); 2. v/i. and v/refl. harden, become or grow hard; steel: temper.
'Hart|geld n coin(s pl.), specie; **'~gummi** m hard rubber; † ebon-

ite, vulcanite; '2**herzig** *adj.* hard-hearted; 2**köpfig** *adj.* [ˈkœpfiç] stubborn, headstrong; 2**näckig** *adj.* [ˈ.nɛkiç] *p.* obstinate, obdurate; *effort:* dogged, tenacious; ⚓ *ailment:* refractory.

Harz [haːrts] *n* (-es/-e) resin; ♪ rosin; *mot.* gum; '2**ig** *adj.* resinous.

Hasardspiel [haˈzart-] *n* game of chance; *fig.* gamble.

haschen [ˈhaʃən] (ge-, h) **1.** *v/t.* catch (hold of), snatch; *sich ~ children:* play tag; **2.** *v/i.:* ~ *nach* snatch at; *fig.* strain after (*effect*), fish for (*compliments*).

Hase [ˈhaːzə] *m* (-n/-n) *zo.* hare; *ein alter ~* an old hand, an old-timer.

Haselnuß ♀ [ˈhaːzəlnus] *f* hazelnut.

'**Hasen|braten** *m* roast hare; '~**fuß** F *fig. m* coward, F funk; '~**panier** F *n: das ~ ergreifen* take to one's heels; '~**scharte** ♀ *f* hare-lip.

Haß [has] *m* (Hasses/*no pl.*) hatred.

'**hassen** *v/t.* (ge-, h) hate.

häßlich *adj.* [ˈhɛsliç] ugly; *fig. a.:* nasty, unpleasant.

Hast [hast] *f* (-/*no pl.*) hurry, haste; rush; *in wilder ~* in frantic haste; '2**en** *v/i.* (ge-, sein) hurry, hasten; rush; '2**ig** *adj.* hasty, hurried.

hätscheln [ˈhɛːtʃəln] *v/t.* (ge-, h) caress, fondle, pet; pamper, coddle.

hatte [ˈhatə] *pret. of haben.*

Haube [ˈhaubə] *f* (-/-n) bonnet (*a.* ⊕, *mot.*); cap; *orn.* crest, tuft; *mot. Am. a.* hood. [howitzer.]

Haubitze ⚔ [hauˈbitsə] *f* (-/-n)/

Hauch [haux] *m* (-[e]s/⚓ -e) breath; *fig.:* waft, whiff (*of perfume, etc.*); touch, tinge (*of irony, etc.*); '2**en** (ge-, h) **1.** *v/i.* breathe; **2.** *v/t.* breathe, whisper; *gr.* aspirate.

Haue [ˈhauə] *f* (-/-n) 🪓 hoe, mattock; pick; F hiding, spanking; '2**n** (*irr.*,) ge-, h) **1.** *v/t.* hew (*coal, stone*); cut up (*meat*); chop (*wood*); cut (*hole, steps, etc.*); beat (*child*); *sich ~* (have a) fight; **2.** *v/i.:* ~ *nach* cut at, strike out at.

Haufen [ˈhaufən] *m* (-s/-) heap, pile (*both* F *a. fig.*); *fig.* crowd.

häufen [ˈhɔʏfən] *v/t.* (ge-, h) heap (up), pile (up); accumulate; *sich ~* pile up, accumulate; *fig.* become more frequent, increase.

'**häufig** *adj.* frequent; '2**keit** *f* (-/*no pl.*) frequency.

'**Häufung** *fig. f* (-/-en) increase, *fig.* accumulation.

Haupt [haupt] *n* (-[e]s/⚓er) head; *fig.* chief, head, leader; '~**altar** *m* high altar; '~**anschluß** *teleph. m* subscriber's main station; '~**bahnhof** 🚂 *m* main *or* central station; '~**beruf** *m* full-time occupation; '~**buch** ♱ *n* ledger; '~**darsteller** *thea. m* leading actor; '~**fach** *univ. n* main *or* principal subject, *Am. a.* major; '~**film** *m* feature (film); '~**geschäft** *n* main transaction; '~**geschäftsstelle** *f* head *or* central office; '~**gewinn** *m* first prize; '2**grund** *m* main reason; '~**handelsartikel** ♱ *f* [ˈhaupthandəlsʔ-] *m* staple. [chief(tain).)

Häuptling [ˈhɔʏptliŋ] *m* (-s/-e)/

'**Haupt|linie** 🚂 *f* main *or* trunk line; '~**mann** ⚔ *m* (-[e]s/*Hauptleute*) captain; '~**merkmal** *n* characteristic feature; '~**postamt** *n* general post office, *Am.* main post office; '~**punkt** *m* main *or* cardinal point; '~**quartier** *n* headquarters *sg. or pl.*; '~**rolle** *thea. f* lead(ing part); '~**sache** *f* main thing *or* point; '2**sächlich** *adj.* main, chief, principal; '~**satz** *gr. m* main clause; '~**stadt** *f* capital; '2**städtisch** *adj.* metropolitan; '~**straße** *f* main street; major road; '~**treffer** *m* first prize; jackpot; '~**verkehrsstraße** *f* main road; arterial road; '~**verkehrsstunden** *f/pl.*, '~**verkehrszeit** *f* rush hour(s *pl.*), peak hour(s *pl.*); '~**versammlung** *f* general meeting; '~**wort** *gr. n* (-[e]s/⚓er) substantive, noun.

Haus [haus] *n* (-es/⚓er) house; building; home, family, household; dynasty; ♱ (business) house, firm; *parl.* House; *nach ~e* home; *zu ~e* at home, F in; '~**angestellte** *f* (-n/-n) (house-)maid; '~**apotheke** *f* (household) medicine-chest; '~**arbeit** *f* housework; '~**arrest** *m* house arrest; '~**arzt** *m* family doctor; '~**aufgaben** *f/pl.* homework, F prep; '2**backen** *fig. adj.* homely; '~**bar** *f* cocktail cabinet; '~**bedarf** *m* household requirements *pl.*; '~**besitzer** *m* house-owner; '~**diener** *m* (man-)servant; *hotel:* porter, boots *sg.*

hausen [ˈhauzən] *v/i.* (ge-, h) live; play *or* work·havoc (*in a place*).

'Haus|flur m (entrance-)hall, esp. Am. hallway; **'∼frau** f housewife; **'∼halt** m household; **'∾halten** v/i. (irr. halten, sep., -ge-, h) be economical (mit with), economize(on); **∼hälterin** ['∼hɛltərin] f (-/-nen) housekeeper; **'∼halt(s)plan** parl. m budget; **'∼haltung** f housekeeping; household, family; **'∼haltwaren** f/pl. household articles pl.; **'∼herr** m master of the family; landlord.

hausier|en [hau'ziːrən] v/i. (no -ge-, h) hawk, peddle (mit et. s.th.); ∼ gehen be a hawker or pedlar; **2er** m (-s/-) hawker, pedlar.

'Haus|kleid n house dress; **'∼knecht** m boots; **'∼lehrer** m private tutor.

häuslich adj. ['hɔyslıç] domestic; domesticated; **'2keit** f (-/no pl.) domesticity; family life; home.

'Haus|mädchen n (house-)maid; **'∼mannskost** f plain fare; **'∼meister** m caretaker; janitor; **'∼mittel** n popular medicine; **'∼ordnung** f rules pl. of the house; **'∼rat** m household effects pl.; **'∼recht** n domestic authority; **'∼sammlung** f house-to-house collection; **'∼schlüssel** m latchkey; front-door key; **'∼schuh** m slipper.

'Hauss|e ♣ ['hoːs(ə)] f (-/-n) rise, boom; **'∼ier** m [hos'jeː] m (-s/-s) speculator for a rise, bull.

'Haus|stand m household; e-n ∼ gründen set up house; **'∼suchung** ♣ f house search, domiciliary visit, Am. a. house check; **'∼tier** n domestic animal; **'∼tür** f front door; **'∼verwalter** m steward; **'∼wirt** m landlord; **'∼wirtin** f (-/-nen) landlady.

Haut [haut] f (-/∾e) skin; hide; film; bis auf die ∼ to the skin; aus der ∼ fahren jump out of one's skin; F e-e ehrliche ∼ an honest soul; **'∼abschürfung ✵** f skin abrasion; **'∼arzt ✵** m dermatologist; **'∼ausschlag ✵** m rash; **'∼eng** adj. garment: skin-tight; **'∼farbe** f complexion.

Hautgout [o'gu] m (-s/no pl.) high taste.

häutig adj. ['hɔytıç] membranous; covered with skin.

'Haut|krankheit f skin disease; **'∼pflege** f care of the skin; **'∼**

schere f (e-e pair of) cuticle scissors pl. [age.]

Havarie ♣ [hava'riː] f (-/-n) aver-|

H-Bombe ✗ ['haː-] f H-bomb.

he int. [heː] hi!, hi there!; I say!

Hebamme ['heːp°amə] f midwife.

Hebe|baum ['heːbə-] m lever (for raising heavy objects); **'∼bühne** mot. f lifting ramp; **'∼eisen** n crowbar; **'∼kran** m lifting crane.

Hebel ⊕ ['heːbəl] m (-s/-) lever; **'∼arm** m lever arm.

heben ['heːbən] v/t. (irr., ge-, h) lift (a. sports), raise (a. fig.); heave (heavy load); hoist; recover (treasure); raise (sunken ship); fig. promote, improve, increase; sich ∼ rise, go up.

Hecht ichth. [hɛçt] m (-[e]s/-e) pike.

Heck [hɛk] n (-[e]s/-e, -s) ♣ stern; mot. rear; ✈ tail.

Hecke ['hɛkə] f (-/-n) ✿ hedge; zo. brood, hatch; **'2n** v/t. and v/i. (ge-, h) breed, hatch; **'∼nrose ✿** f dog-rose. [hallo!]

heda int. ['heːdaː] hi (there)!,|

Heer [heːr] n (-[e]s/-e) ✗ army; fig. a. host; **'∼esdienst** m military service; **'∼esmacht** f military force(s pl.); **'∼eszug** m military expedition; **'∼führer** m general; **'∼lager** n (army) camp; **'∼schar** f army, host; **'∼straße** f military road; highway; **'∼zug** m s. Heereszug.

Hefe ['heːfə] f (-/-n) yeast; barm.

Heft [hɛft] n (-[e]s/-e) dagger, etc.: haft; knife: handle; fig. reins pl.; exercise book; periodical, etc.: issue, number.

'heft|en v/t. (ge-, h) fasten, fix (an acc. on to); affix, attach (to); pin on (to); tack, baste (seam, etc.); stitch, sew (book); **'2faden** m basting thread.

'heftig adj. storm, anger, quarrel, etc.: violent, fierce; rain, etc.: heavy; pain, etc.: severe; speech, desire, etc.: vehement, passionate; p. irascible; **'2keit** f (-/∾, -en) violence, fierceness; severity; vehemence; irascibility.

'Heft|klammer f paper-clip; **'∼pflaster** n sticking plaster.

hegen ['heːgən] v/t. (ge-, h) preserve (game); nurse, tend (plants); have, entertain (feelings); harbo(u)r (fears, suspicions, etc.).

Hehler ɪ̣ʒ ['he:lər] *m* (-s/-) receiver (of stolen goods); '**ei** [⁓'raɪ] *f* (/-en) receiving (of stolen goods).

Heide ['haɪdə] **1.** *m* (-n/-n) heathen; **2.** *f* (/-/-n) heath(-land); = '**kraut** ⚥ *n* heather; '**land** *n* heath(-land).

'**Heiden|geld** F *n* pots *pl.* of money; '**lärm** F *m* hullabaloo; '**spaß** F *m* capital fun; '**tum** *n* (-s/*no pl.*) heathenism.   [(-ish).]

heidnisch *adj.* ['haɪdnɪʃ] heathen]

heikel *adj.* ['haɪkəl] *p.* fastidious, particular; *problem, etc.*: delicate, awkward.

heil [haɪl] **1.** *adj. p.* safe, unhurt; whole, sound; **2.** ♀ *n* (-[e]s/*no pl.*) welfare, benefit; *eccl.* salvation; **3.** *int.* hail!

Heiland *eccl.* ['haɪlant] *m* (-[e]s/-e) Saviour, Redeemer.

'**Heil|anstalt** *f* sanatorium, *Am. a.* sanitarium; '**bad** *n* medicinal bath; spa; '♀**bar** *adj.* curable; '♀**en** (ge-) **1.** *v/t.* (h) cure, heal; ⁓ *von* cure *s.o.* of; **2.** *v/i.* (sein) heal (up); '**gehilfe** *m* male nurse.

heilig *adj.* ['haɪlɪç] holy; sacred; solemn; ♀**er** *Abend* Christmas Eve; ♀**e** ['⁓gə] *m, f* (-n/-n) saint; ⁓**en** ['⁓gən] *v/t.* (ge-, h) sanctify (*a. fig.*), hallow; '♀**keit** *f* (-/*no pl.*) holiness; sacredness, sanctity; '**sprechen** *v/t.* (*irr. sprechen, sep.,* -ge-, h) canonize; '♀**sprechung** *f* (-/-en) canonization; '♀**tum** *n* (-[e]s/*⁓*er) sanctuary; sacred relic; ♀**ung** ['⁓guŋ] *f* (-/-en) sanctification (*a. fig.*), hallowing.

'**Heil|kraft** *f* healing *or* curative power; '♀**kräftig** *adj.* healing, curative; '**kunde** *f* medical science; '♀**los** *fig. adj.* confusion: utter, great; '**mittel** *n* remedy, medicament; '**praktiker** *m* non-medical practitioner; '**quelle** *f* medicinal spring; '♀**sam** *adj.* curative; *fig.* salutary.   [Army.]

Heilsarmee ['haɪlsˀ-] *f* Salvation]

'**Heil|ung** *f* (-/-en) cure, healing, successful treatment; '**verfahren** *n* therapy.

heim [haɪm] **1.** *adv.* home; **2.** ♀ *n* (-[e]s/-e) home; hostel; '♀**arbeit** *f* homework, outwork.

Heimat ['haɪma:t] *f* (-/-⚥-en) home; own country; native land; '**land** *n* own country, native land; '**lich** *adj.* native; '♀**los** *adj.* homeless;

'**ort** *m* home town *or* village; '**vertriebene** *m* expellee.

Heimchen *zo.* ['haɪmçən] *n* (-s/-) cricket.

'**heimisch** *adj. trade, industry, etc.*: home, local, domestic; ⚥, *zo., etc.*: native, indigenous; ⁓ *werden* settle down; become established; *sich* ⁓ *fühlen* feel at home.

Heim|kehr ['haɪmke:r] *f* (-/*no pl.*) return (home), homecoming; '♀**kehren** *v/i.* (*sep.,* -ge-, sein); '♀**kommen** *v/i.* (*irr. kommen, sep.,* -ge-, sein) return home.

'**heimlich** *adj. plan, feeling, etc.*: secret; *meeting, organization, etc.*: clandestine; *glance, movement, etc.*: stealthy, furtive.

'**Heim|reise** *f* homeward journey; '♀**suchen** *v/t.* (*sep.,* -ge-, h) *disaster, etc.*: afflict, strike; *ghost:* haunt; *God:* visit, punish; '**tücke** *f* underhand malice, treachery; '**tückisch** *adj.* malicious, treacherous, insidious; '♀**wärts** *adv.* ['⁓verts] homeward(s); '**weg** *m* way home; '**weh** *n* homesickness, nostalgia; ⁓ *haben* be homesick.

Heirat ['haɪra:t] *f* (-/-en) marriage; '♀**en** (ge-, h) **1.** *v/t.* marry; **2.** *v/i.* marry, get married.

'**Heirats|antrag** *m* offer *or* proposal of marriage; '♀**fähig** *adj.* marriageable; '**kandidat** *m* possible marriage partner; '**schwindler** *m* marriage impostor; '**vermittler** *m* matrimonial agent.

heiser *adj.* ['haɪzər] hoarse; husky; '♀**keit** *f* (-/*no pl.*) hoarseness; huskiness.

heiß *adj.* [haɪs] hot; *fig. a.* passionate, ardent; *mir ist* ⁓ I am *or* feel hot.

heißen ['haɪsən] (*irr.,* ge-, h) **1.** *v/t.*: *e-n Lügner* ⁓ call *s.o.* a liar; *willkommen* ⁓ welcome; **2.** *v/i.* be called; mean; *wie* ⁓ *Sie?* what is your name?; *was heißt das auf englisch?* what's that in English?

heiter *adj.* ['haɪtər] *day, weather:* bright; *sky:* bright, clear; *p., etc.:* cheerful, gay; serene; '♀**keit** *f* (-/*no pl.*) brightness; cheerfulness, gaiety; serenity.

heiz|en ['haɪtsən] (ge-, h) **1.** *v/t.* heat (*room, etc.*); light (*stove*); fire (*boiler*); **2.** *v/i.* stove, *etc.*: give out heat; turn on the heating; *mit*

H

Kohlen ~ burn coal; '2er *m* (-s/-) stoker, fireman; '2kissen *n* electric heating pad; '2körper *m* central *heating*: radiator; *≠* heating element; '2material *n* fuel; '2ung *f* (-/-en) heating.

Held [hɛlt] *m* (-en/-en) hero.

'Helden|gedicht *n* epic (poem); '2haft *adj.* heroic, valiant; '~mut *m* heroism, valo(u)r; 2mütig *adj.* ['~my:tiç] heroic; '~tat *f* heroic *or* valiant deed; '~tod *m* hero's death; '~tum *n* (-[e]s/*no pl.*) heroism.

helfen ['hɛlfən] *v/i.* (*dat.*) (*irr.*, ge-, h) help, assist, aid; ~ *gegen* be good for; *sich nicht zu ~ wissen* be helpless.

'Helfer *m* (-s/-) helper, assistant; '~shelfer *m* accomplice.

hell *adj.* [hɛl] *sound, voice, light, etc.*: clear; *light, flame, etc.*: bright; *hair*: fair; *colour*: light; *ale*: pale; '~blau *adj.* light-blue; '~blond *adj.* very fair; '~hörig *adj. p.* quick of hearing; *fig.* perceptive; *△* poorly sound-proofed; '2seher *m* clairvoyant.

Helm [hɛlm] *m* ([-e]s/-e) ⚔ helmet; *△* dome, cupola; ⚓ helm; '~busch *m* plume.

Hemd [hɛmt] *n* (-[e]s/-en) shirt; vest; '~bluse *f* shirt-blouse, *Am.* shirtwaist. [hemisphere.]

Hemisphäre [he:mi'sfɛ:rə] *f* (-/-n)

hemm|en ['hɛmən] *v/t.* (ge-, h) check, stop (*movement, etc.*); stem (*stream, flow of liquid*); hamper (*free movement, activity*); be a hindrance to; *psych.*: *gehemmt sein* be inhibited; '2nis *n* (-ses/-se) hindrance, impediment; '2schuh *m* slipper; *fig.* hindrance, F drag (*für acc.* on); '2ung *f* (-/-en) stoppage, check; *psych.*: inhibition.

Hengst *zo.* [hɛŋst] *m* (-es/-e) stallion.

Henkel ['hɛŋkəl] *m* (-s/-) handle, ear.

Henker ['hɛŋkər] *m* (-s/-) hangman, executioner; F: *zum ~!* hang it (all)!

Henne *zo.* ['hɛnə] *f* (-/-n) hen.

her *adv.* [he:r] here; hither; *es ist schon ein Jahr ~, daß ... or seit ...* it is a year since ...; *wie lange ist es ~, seit ...* how long is it since ...; *hinter* (*dat.*) ~ *sein* be after; ~ *damit!* out with it!

herab *adv.* [hɛ'rap] down, downward; **~lassen** *v/t.* (*irr. lassen*, *no* -ge-, h) let down, lower; *fig. sich ~* condescend; **~lassend** *adj.* condescending; **~setzen** *v/t.* (*sep.*, -ge-, h) take down; *fig.* belittle, disparage *s.o.*; ♠ reduce, lower, cut (*price, etc.*); **2setzung** *fig. f* (-/-en) reduction; disparagement; **~steigen** *v/i.* (*irr. steigen*, *sep.*, -ge-, *sein*) climb down, descend; **~würdigen** *v/t.* (*sep.*, -ge-, h) degrade, belittle, abase.

heran *adv.* [hɛ'ran] close, near; up; *nur ~!* come on!; **~bilden** *v/t.* (*sep.*, -ge-, h) train, educate (*zu* as *s.th.*, to be *s.th.*); **~kommen** *v/i.* (*irr. kommen, sep.*, -ge-, *sein*) come or draw near; approach; ~ *an* (*acc.*) come up to *s.o.*; measure up to; **~wachsen** *v/i.* (*irr. wachsen, sep.*, -ge-, *sein*) grow (up) (*zu* into).

herauf *adv.* [hɛ'rauf] up(wards), up here; upstairs; **~beschwören** *v/t.* (*irr. schwören*, *no* -ge-, h) evoke, call up, conjure up (*spirit, etc.*); *fig. a.* bring about, provoke, give rise to (*war, etc.*); **~steigen** *v/i.* (*irr. steigen, sep.*, -ge-, *sein*) climb up (here), ascend; **~ziehen** *v/t.* (*irr. ziehen, sep.*, -ge-) 1. *v/t.* (h) pull or hitch up (*trousers, etc.*); 2. *v/i.* (*sein*) cloud, *fig.*: come up.

heraus *adv.* [hɛ'raus] out, out here; *zum Fenster ~* out of the window; ~ *mit der Sprache!* speak out!; **~bekommen** *v/t.* (*irr. kommen, sep., no* -ge-, h) get out; get (*money*) back; *fig.* find out; **~bringen** *v/t.* (*irr. bringen, sep.*, -ge-, h) bring or get out; *thea.* stage; **~finden** *v/t.* (*irr. finden, sep.*, -ge-, h) find out; *fig. a.* discover; **2forderer** *m* (-s/-) challenger; **~fordern** *v/t.* (*sep.*, -ge-, h) challenge (*to a fight*); provoke; **2forderung** *f* (-/-en) challenge; provocation; **~geben** (*irr. geben, sep.*, -ge-, h) 1. *v/t.* surrender; hand over; restore; edit (*periodical, etc.*); publish (*book, etc.*); issue (*regulations, etc.*); 2. *v/i.* give change (*auf acc.* for); **2geber** *m* (-s/-) editor; publisher; **~kommen** *v/i.* (*irr. kommen, sep.*, -ge-, *sein*) come out; *fig. a.* appear, be published; **~nehmen** *v/t.* (*irr. nehmen, sep.*, -ge-, h) take out; *sich viel ~* take liberties; **~putzen** *v/t.* (*sep.*,

-ge-, h) dress up; sich ~ dress (o.s.) up; ~reden v/refl. (sep., -ge-, h) talk one's way out; ~stellen v/t. (sep., -ge-, h) put out; fig. emphasize, set forth; sich ~ emerge, turn out; ~strecken v/t. (sep., -ge-, h) stretch out; put out; fig. ~streichen v/t. (irr. streichen, sep., -ge-, h) cross out, delete (word, etc.); fig. extol, praise; ~winden fig. v/refl. (irr. winden, sep., -ge-, h) extricate o.s. (aus from).

herb adj. [hɛrp] fruit, flavour, etc.: tart; wine, etc.: dry; features, etc.: austere; criticism, etc.: harsh; disappointment, etc.: bitter.

herbei adv. [hɛr'baɪ] here; ~! come here!; ~eilen [hɛr'baɪ?-] v/i. (sep., -ge-, sein) come hurrying; ~führen fig. v/t. (sep., -ge-, h) cause, bring about, give rise to; ~schaffen v/t. (sep., -ge-, h) bring along; procure.

Herberge ['hɛrbɛrgə] f (-/-n) shelter, lodging; inn.

'Herbheit f (-/no pl.) tartness; dryness; fig.: austerity; harshness, bitterness.

Herbst [hɛrpst] m (-[e]s/-e) autumn, Am. a. fall.

Herd [he:rt] m (-[e]s/-e) hearth, fireplace; stove; fig. seat, focus.

Herde ['he:rdə] f (-/-n) herd (of cattle, pigs, etc.) (contp. a. fig.); flock (of sheep, geese, etc.).

herein adv. [hɛ'raɪn] in (here); ~! come in!; ~brechen fig. v/i. (irr. brechen, sep., -ge-, sein) night: fall; ~ über (acc.) misfortune, etc.: befall; ~fallen v/i. (irr. fallen, sep., -ge-, sein) be taken in.

'her|fallen v/i. (irr. fallen, sep., -ge-, sein): ~ über (acc.) attack (a. fig.), fall upon; ℰ fig. pull to pieces; '℈gang m course of events, details pl.; '~geben v/t. (irr. geben, sep., -ge-, h) give up, part with, return; yield; sich ~ zu lend o.s. to; '~gebracht fig. adj. traditional; customary; '~halten (irr. halten, sep., -ge-, h) 1. v/t. hold out; 2. v/i.: ~ müssen be the one to pay or suffer (für for).

Hering ichth. ['he:rɪŋ] m (-s/-e) herring.

'her|kommen v/i. (irr. kommen, sep., -ge-, sein) come or get here; come or draw near; ~ von come from; fig. a. be due to, be caused by; ~kömmlich adj. ['~kœmlɪç]

traditional; customary; ℒkunft ['~-kunft] f (-/no pl.) origin; birth, descent; '~leiten v/t. (sep., -ge-, h) lead here; fig. derive (von from); '~leitung fig. f derivation.

Herold ['he:rɔlt] m (-[e]s/-e) herald.

Herr [hɛr] m (-n, ⚔-en/-en) lord, master; eccl. the Lord; gentleman; ~ Maier Mr Maier; mein ~ Sir; m-e ~en gentlemen; ~ der Situation master of the situation.

'Herren|bekleidung f men's clothing; '~einzel n tennis: men's singles pl.; '~haus n manor-house; ℒlos adj. ['~lo:s] ownerless; '~reiter m sports: gentleman-jockey; '~-schneider m men's tailor; '~zimmer n study; smoking-room.

herrichten ['he:r-] v/t. (sep., -ge-, h) arrange, prepare.

'herrisch adj. imperious, overbearing; voice, etc.: commanding, peremptory.

'herrlich adj. excellent, glorious, magnificent, splendid; 'ℒkeit f (-/-en) glory, splendo(u)r.

'Herrschaft f (-/-en) rule, dominion (über acc. of); fig. mastery; master and mistress; m-e ~en! ladies and gentlemen!; 'ℒlich adj. belonging to a master or landlord; fig. high-class, elegant.

herrsch|en ['hɛrʃən] v/i. (ge-, h) rule (über acc. over); monarch: reign (over); govern; fig. prevail, be; 'ℒer m (-s/-) ruler; sovereign, monarch; 'ℒsucht f thirst for power; '~süchtig adj. thirsting for power; imperious.

'her|rühren v/i. (sep., -ge-, h): ~ von come from, originate with; '~sagen v/t. (sep., -ge-, h) recite; say (prayer); '~stammen v/i. (sep., -ge-, h): ~ von or aus be descended from; come from; be derived from; '~stellen v/t. (sep., -ge-, h) place here; ✝ make, manufacture, produce; 'ℒstellung f (-/-en) manufacture, production.

herüber adv. [hɛ'ry:bər] over (here), across.

herum adv. [hɛ'rum] (a)round; about; ~führen v/t. (sep., -ge-, h) show (a)round; ~ in (dat.) show over; ~lungern v/i. (sep., -ge-, h) loaf or loiter or hang about; ~reichen v/t. (sep., -ge-, h) pass or hand round; ~sprechen v/refl. (irr.

sprechen, *sep.*, -ge-, *h*) get about, spread; **~treiben** *v/refl.* (*irr.* treiben, *sep.*, -ge-, *h*) F gad *or* knock about.

herunter *adv.* [he'rʊntər] down (here); downstairs; *von oben* ~ down from above; **~bringen** *v/t.* (*irr.* bringen, *sep.*, -ge-, *h*) bring down; *fig. a.* lower, reduce; **~kommen** *v/i.* (*irr.* kommen, *sep.*, -ge-, *sein*) come down(stairs); *fig.*: come down in the world; deteriorate; **~machen** *v/t.* (*sep.*, -ge-, *h*) take down; turn (*collar, etc.*) down; *fig.* give *s.o.* a dressing-down; pull to pieces; **~reißen** *v/t.* (*irr.* reißen, *sep.*, -ge-, *h*) pull *or* tear down; *fig.* pull to pieces; **~sein** F *fig. v/i.* (*irr.* sein, *sep.*, -ge-, *sein*) be low in health; **~wirtschaften** *v/t.* (*sep.*, -ge-, *h*) run down.

hervor *adv.* [hɛr'foːr] forth, out; **~bringen** *v/t.* (*irr.* bringen, *sep.*, -ge-, *h*) bring out, produce (*a. fig.*); yield (*fruit*); utter (*word*); **~gehen** *v/i.* (*irr.* gehen, *sep.*, -ge-, *sein*) *p.* come (*aus* from); come off (*victorious*) (from); *fact, etc.*: emerge (from); be clear *or* apparent (from); **~heben** *v/t.* (*irr.* heben, *sep.*, -ge-, *h*) stress, emphasize; give prominence to; **~holen** *v/t.* (*sep.*, -ge-, *h*) produce; **~ragen** *v/i.* (*sep.*, -ge-, *h*) project (*über acc.* over); *fig.* tower (above); **~ragend** *adj.* projecting, prominent; *fig.* outstanding, excellent; **~rufen** *v/t.* (*irr.* rufen, *sep.*, -ge-, *h*) *thea.* call for; *fig.* arouse, evoke; **~stechend** *fig. adj.* outstanding; striking; conspicuous.

Herz [hɛrts] *n* (-ens/-en) *anat.* heart (*a. fig.*); *cards:* hearts *pl.*; *fig.* courage, spirit; *sich ein* ~ *fassen* take heart; *mit ganzem* ~*en* whole-heartedly; *sich et. zu* ~*en nehmen* take s.th. to heart; *es nicht übers* ~ *bringen zu inf.* not to have the heart to *inf.*; **~anfall** *m* heart attack.

'**Herzens**|**brecher** *m* (-s/-) lady-killer; '**~lust** *f*: *nach* ~ to one's heart's content; '**~wunsch** *m* heart's desire.

'**herz**|**ergreifend** *fig. adj.* heart-moving; '**2fehler** ♣ *m* cardiac defect; '**2gegend** *anat. f* cardiac region; '**~haft** *adj.* hearty, good; '**~ig** *adj.* lovely, *Am. a.* cute; **2infarkt** ♣ ['~ʔinfarkt] *m* (-[e]s/-e) cardiac

infarction; '**2klopfen** ♣ *n* (-s/*no pl.*) palpitation; '**~krank** *adj.* having heart trouble; '**~lich 1.** *adj.* heartfelt; cordial, hearty; ~*es Beileid* sincere sympathy; **2.** *adv.*: ~ *gern* with pleasure; '**~los** *adj.* heartless; unfeeling.

Herzog ['hɛrtsoːk] *m* (-[e]s/⸚e, -e) duke; '**~in** *f* (-/-nen) duchess; '**~tum** *n* (-[e]s/⸚er) dukedom; duchy.

'**Herz**|**schlag** *m* heartbeat; ♣ heart failure; '**~schwäche** ♣ *f* cardiac insufficiency; '**~verpflanzung** ♣ *f* heart transplant; '**2zerreißend** *adj.* heart-rending.

Hetz|**e** ['hɛtsə] *f* (-/-n) hurry, rush; instigation (*gegen acc.* against); baiting (of); '**2en** (ge-) **1.** *v/t.* (*h*) course (*hare*); bait (*bear, etc.*); hound: hunt, chase (*animal*); *fig.* hurry, rush; *sich* ~ hurry, rush; *e-n Hund auf j-n* ~ set a dog at s.o.; **2.** *v/i.* (*h*) *fig.*: cause discord; agitate (*gegen* against); **3.** *fig. v/i.* (*sein*) hurry, rush; '**~er** *fig. m* (-s/-) instigator; agitator; '**2erisch** *adj.* virulent, inflammatory; '**~jagd** *f* hunt(ing); *fig.*: virulent campaign; rush, hurry; '**~presse** *f* yellow press.

Heu [hɔy] *n* (-[e]s/*no pl.*) hay; '**~boden** *m* hayloft.

Heuchel|**ei** [hɔyçə'lai] *f* (-/-en) hypocrisy; '**2n** (ge-, *h*) **1.** *v/t.* simulate, feign, affect; **2.** *v/i.* feign, dissemble; play the hypocrite.

'**Heuchler** *m* (-s/-) hypocrite; '**2isch** *adj.* hypocritical.

heuer ['hɔyər] **1.** *adv.* this year; **2.** ♀ ♧ *f* (-/-n) pay, wages *pl.*; '**~n** *v/t.* (ge-, *h*) hire; ♧ engage, sign on (*crew*), charter (*ship*).

heulen ['hɔylən] *v/i.* (ge-, *h*) wind, *etc.*: howl; *storm, wind, etc.*: roar; *siren:* wail; F *p.* howl, cry.

'**Heu**|**schnupfen** ♣ *m* hay-fever; '**~schrecke** *zo.* ['~ʃrɛkə] *f* (-/-n) grasshopper, locust.

heut|**e** *adv.* ['hɔytə] today; ~ *abend* this evening, tonight; ~ *früh*, ~ *morgen* this morning; ~ *in acht Tagen* today *or* this day week; *vor acht Tagen* a week ago today; '**~ig** *adj.* this day's, today's; present; **~zutage** *adv.* ['hɔyttsutaːgə] nowadays, these days.

Hexe ['hɛksə] *f* (-/-n) witch, sorceress; *fig.*: hell-cat; hag; '**2n** *v/i.* (ge-, *h*) practice witchcraft; F *fig.* work miracles; '~nkessel *fig. m* inferno; '~nmeister *m* wizard, sorcerer; '~nschuß ✱ *m* lumbago; ~rei [~- 'raɪ] *f* (-/-en) witchcraft, sorcery, magic.

Hieb [hiːp] **1.** *m* (-[e]s/-e) blow, stroke; lash, cut (*of whip, etc.*); *a.* punch (*with fist*); *fenc.* cut; ~e *pl.* hiding, thrashing; **2.** ⚥ *pret.* of hauen.

hielt [hiːlt] *pret.* of halten.

hier *adv.* [hiːr] here; in this place; ~! present!; ~ entlang! this way!

hier|an *adv.* ['hiːran, *when emphatic* 'hiːran] at *or* by *or* in *or* on *or* to it *or* this; ~auf *adv.* ['hiːrauf, *when emphatic* 'hiːrauf] on it *or* this; after this *or* that, then; ~aus *adv.* ['hiːraus, *when emphatic* 'hiːraus] from *or* out of it *or* this; ~bei *adv.* ['hiːrbaɪ, *when emphatic* 'hiːrbaɪ] here; in this case, in connection with this; ~durch *adv.* ['hiːrdurç, *when emphatic* 'hiːrdurç] through here; by this, hereby; ~für *adv.* ['hiːrfyːr, *when emphatic* 'hiːrfyːr] for it *or* this; ~her *adv.* ['hiːrheːr, *when emphatic* 'hiːrheːr] here, hither; *bis* ~ as far as here; ~in *adv.* ['hiːrin, *when emphatic* 'hiːrin] in it *or* this; in here; ~mit *adv.* ['hiːrmit, *when emphatic* 'hiːrmit] with it *or* this, herewith; ~nach *adv.* ['hiːrnaːx, *when emphatic* 'hiːrnaːx] after it *or* this; according to this; ~über *adv.* ['hiːryːbər, *when emphatic* 'hiːryːbər] over it *or* this; over here; on this (subject); ~unter *adv.* ['hiːruntər, *when emphatic* 'hiːruntər] under it *or* this; among these; by this *or* that; ~von *adv.* ['hiːrfɔn, *when emphatic* 'hiːrfɔn] of *or* from it *or* this; ~zu *adv.* ['hiːrtsuː, *when emphatic* 'hiːrtsuː] with it *or* this; (in addition) to this.

hiesig *adj.* ['hiːziç] of *or* in this place *or* town, local.

hieß [hiːs] *pret.* of heißen.

Hilfe ['hilfə] *f* (-/-n) help; aid, assistance; succour; relief (*für* to); ~! help!; *mit* ~ *von* with the help *or* aid of; '~ruf *m* shout *or* cry for help.

'hilf|los *adj.* helpless; '~reich *adj.* helpful.

'Hilfs|aktion *f* relief measures *pl.*;

'~arbeiter *m* unskilled worker *or* labo(u)rer; '2bedürftig *adj.* needy, indigent; '~lehrer *m* assistant teacher; '~mittel *n* aid; device; remedy; expedient; '~motor *m*: *Fahrrad mit* ~ motor-assisted bicycle; '~quelle *f* resource; '~schule *f* elementary school for backward children; '~werk *n* relief organization.

Himbeere ♀ ['himbeːrə] *f* rasp- [berry.]

Himmel ['himəl] *m* (-s/-) sky, heavens *pl.*; *eccl., fig.* heaven; '~bett *n* tester-bed; '2blau *adj.* sky-blue; '~fahrt *eccl. f* ascension (of Christ); Ascension-day; '2schreiend *adj.* crying.

'Himmels|gegend *f* region of the sky; cardinal point; '~körper *m* celestial body; '~richtung *f* point of the compass, cardinal point; direction; '~strich *m* region, climate zone.

'himmlisch *adj.* celestial, heavenly.

hin *adv.* [hin] there; gone, lost; ~ *und her* to and fro, *Am.* back and forth; ~ *und wieder* now and again *or* then; ~ *und zurück* there and back.

hinab *adv.* [hi'nap] down; ~steigen *v/i.* (*irr.* steigen, *sep.,* -ge-, *sein*) climb down, descend.

hinarbeiten ['hin⁹-] *v/i.* (*sep.,* -ge-, *h*): ~ *auf* (*acc.*) work for *or* towards.

hinauf *adv.* [hi'nauf] up (there); upstairs; ~gehen *v/i.* (*irr.* gehen, *sep.,* -ge-, *sein*) go up (stairs); *prices, wages, etc.*: go up, rise; ~steigen *v/i.* (*irr.* steigen, *sep.,* -ge-, *sein*) climb up, ascend.

hinaus *adv.* [hi'naus] out; ~ *mit euch!* out with you!; *auf* (*viele*) *Jahre* ~ for (many) years (to come); ~gehen *v/i.* (*irr.* gehen, *sep.,* -ge-, *sein*) go *or* walk out; ~ *über* (*acc.*) go beyond, exceed; ~ *auf* (*acc.*) *window, etc.*: look out on, overlook; *intention, etc.*: drive *or* aim at; ~laufen *v/i.* (*irr.* laufen, *sep.,* -ge-, *sein*) run *or* rush out; ~ *auf* (*acc.*) come *or* amount to; ~schieben *fig. v/t.* (*irr.* schieben, *sep.,* -ge-, *h*) put off, postpone, defer; ~werfen *v/t.* (*irr.* werfen, *sep.,* -ge-, *h*) throw out (*aus* of); turn *or* throw *or* F chuck *s.o.* out.

'Hin|blick *m*: *im* ~ *auf* (*acc.*) in view of, with regard to; '2bringen *v/t.*

(*irr.* bringen, *sep.,* -ge-, *h*) take there; while away, pass (*time*).

hinder|lich adj. ['hındərlıç] hindering, impeding; *j-m* ~ *sein* be in s.o.'s way; **'~n** *v/t.* (*ge-, h*) hinder, hamper (*bei, in dat.* in); ~ *an* (*dat.*) prevent from; *sports:* obstacle; *turf,* *etc.:* fence; **2nis** *n* (-ses/-se) hindrance; obstacle; turf, *etc.:* fence; **2nisrennen** *n* obstacle-race.

hin'durch adv. through; all through; throughout; across.

hinein adv. [hı'naın] in; ~ *mit dir!* in you go!; **~gehen** *v/i.* (*irr.* gehen, *sep.,* -ge-, *sein*) go in; ~ *in* (*acc.*) go into; *in den Topf gehen ... hinein* the pot holds *or* takes ...

'Hin|fahrt *f* journey *or* way there; **2fallen** *v/i.* (*irr.* fallen, *sep.,* -ge-, *sein*) fall (down); **2fällig** adj. *p.* frail; *regulation, etc.:* invalid; ~ *machen* invalidate, render invalid.

hing [hıŋ] *pret. of* hängen 1.

'Hin|gabe *f* devotion (*an acc.* to); **2geben** *v/t.* (*irr.* geben, *sep.,* -ge-, *h*) give up *or* away; *sich* ~ (*dat.*) give o.s. to; devote o.s. to; **~gebung** *f* (-/-en) devotion; **2gehen** *v/i.* (*irr.* gehen, *sep.,* -ge-, *sein*) go *or* walk there; go (*zu* to); *path, etc.:* lead there; lead (*zu to a place*); **2halten** *v/t.* (*irr.* halten, *sep.,* -ge-, *h*) hold out (*object, etc.*); put s.o. off.

hinken ['hıŋkən] *v/i.* (*ge-*) **1.** (*h*) limp (*auf dem rechten Fuß* with one's right leg), have a limp; **2.** (*sein*) limp (along).

'hin|länglich adj. sufficient, adequate; **'~legen** *v/t.* (*sep.,* -ge-, *h*) lay *or* put down; *sich* ~ lie down; **'~nehmen** *v/t.* (*irr.* nehmen, *sep.,* -ge-, *h*) accept, take; put up with; **'~raffen** *v/t.* (*sep.,* -ge-, *h*) *death, etc.:* snatch *s.o.* away, carry *s.o.* off; **'~reichen** *v/t.* (*sep.,* -ge-, *h*) **1.** *v/t.* reach *or* stretch *or* hold out (*dat.* to); **2.** *v/i.* suffice; **'~reißen** *fig. v/t.* (*irr.* reißen, *sep.,* -ge-, *h*) carry away; enrapture, ravish; **'~reißend** adj. ravishing, captivating; **'~richten** *v/t.* (*sep.,* -ge-, *h*) execute, put to death; **2richtung** *f* execution; **'~setzen** *v/t.* (*sep.,* -ge-, *h*) set *or* put down; *sich* ~ sit down; **2sicht** *f* regard, respect; *in* ~ *auf* (*acc.*) = **'~sichtlich** *prp.* (*gen.*) with regard to, as to, concerning; **'~stellen** *v/t.*

(*sep.,* -ge-, *h*) place; put; put down; et. ~ *als* represent s.th. as; make s.th. appear (as).

hintan|setzen [hınt'an-] *v/t.* (*sep.,* -ge-, *h*) set aside; **2setzung** *f* (-/-en) setting aside; **~stellen** *v/t.* (*sep.,* -ge-, *h*) set aside; **2stellung** *f* (-/-en) setting aside.

hinten adv. ['hıntən] behind, at the back; in the background; in the rear.

hinter *prp.* ['hıntər] **1.** (*dat.*) behind, *Am. a.* back of; ~ *sich lassen* outdistance; **2.** (*acc.*) behind; **2bein** *n* hind leg; **2bliebenen** *pl.* [~'bli:bənən] the bereaved *pl.*; surviving dependants *pl.*; **~'bringen** *v/t.* (*irr.* bringen, *no* -ge-, *h*): *j-m et.* ~ inform s.o. of s.th. (secretly); **~ei'nander** adv. one after the other; in succession; **2gedanke** *m* ulterior motive; **~'gehen** *v/t.* (*irr.* gehen, *no* -ge-, *h*) deceive, F double-cross; **2'gehung** *f* (-/-en) deception; **2grund** *m* background (*a. fig.*); **2halt** *m* ambush; **~hältig** adj. ['~hɛltıç] insidious; underhand; **2haus** *n* back *or* rear building; **~'her** adv. behind; afterwards; **2hof** *m* backyard; **2kopf** *m* back of the head; **~'lassen** *v/t.* (*irr.* lassen, *no* -ge-, *h*) leave (behind); **2'lassenschaft** *f* (-/-en) property (left), estate; **~legen** *v/t.* (*no* -ge-, *h*) deposit, lodge (*bei* with); **2'legung** *f* (-/-en) deposit(ion); **2'list** *f* deceit; craftiness; insidiousness; **~'listig** adj. deceitful; crafty; insidious; **2mann** *m* ⚔ rear-rank man; *fig.:* † subsequent endorser; *pol.:* backer; wire-puller; instigator; **2n** F *m* (-s/-) backside, behind, bottom; **2rad** *n* rear wheel; **~rücks** adv. ['~ryks] from behind; *fig.* behind his, *etc.* back; **2seite** *f* back; **2teil** *n* back (part); rear (part); F *s.* Hintern; **~'treiben** *v/t.* (*irr.* treiben, *no* -ge-, *h*) thwart, frustrate; **2treppe** *f* backstairs *pl.*; **2tür** *f* back door; **~'ziehen** 🕀 *v/t.* (*irr.* ziehen, *no* -ge-, *h*) evade (*tax, duty, etc.*); **2'ziehung** *f* evasion.

hinüber adv. [hı'ny:bər] over (there); across.

Hin- und 'Rückfahrt *f* journey there and back, *Am.* round trip.

hinunter adv. [hı'nʊntər] down (there); downstairs; **~schlucken**

v/t. (*sep.*, -ge-, *h*) swallow (down);
fig. swallow.

'Hinweg¹ *m* way there *or* out.

hinweg² *adv.* ['hin'vek] away, off;
~**gehen** *v/i.* (*irr. gehen*, *sep.*, -ge-
sein): ~ *über* (*acc.*) go *or* walk over
or across; *fig.* pass over, ignore;
~**kommen** *v/i.* (*irr. kommen*, *sep.*,
-ge-, *sein*): ~ *über* (*acc.*) get over
(*a. fig.*); ~**sehen** *v/i.* (*irr. sehen*,
sep., -ge-, *h*): ~ *über* (*acc.*) see *or*
look over; *fig.* overlook, shut one's
eyes to; ~**setzen** *v/refl.* (*sep.*, -ge-,
h): sich ~ *über* (*acc.*) ignore, disregard, make light of.

Hin|weis ['hinvais] *m* (-es/-e) refer-
ence (*auf acc.* to); hint (at); indication (of); '**2weisen** (*irr. weisen*, *sep.*,
-ge-, *h*) **1.** *v/t.*: j-n ~ *auf* (*acc.*) draw
or call s.o.'s attention to; **2.** *v/i.*: ~
auf (*acc.*) point at *or* to, indicate (*a.
fig.*); *fig.*: point out; hint at; '**2wer-
fen** *v/t.* (*irr. werfen*, *sep.*, -ge-, *h*)
throw down; *fig.*: dash off (*sketch,
etc.*); say *s.th.* casually; '**2wirken**
v/i. (*sep.*, -ge-, *h*): ~ *auf* (*acc.*)
work towards; use one's influence
to; '**2ziehen** (*irr. ziehen*, *sep.*,
-ge-) **1.** *fig. v/t.* (*h*) attract *or* draw
there; sich ~ *space*: extend (*bis zu*
to), stretch (to); *time*: drag on;
2. *v/i.* (*sein*) go *or* move there;
'**2zielen** *fig. v/i.* (*sep.*, -ge-, *h*): ~
auf (*acc.*) aim *or* drive at.

hin'zu *adv.* there; near; in addition;
~**fügen** *v/t.* (*sep.*, -ge-, *h*) add (*zu*
to) (*a. fig.*); **2fügung** *f* (-/-en) addition; ~**kommen** *v/i.* (*irr. kommen*, *sep.*, -ge-, *sein*) come up (*zu*
to); supervene; be added; es kommt
(*noch*) *hinzu*, daß add to this that,
(and) moreover; ~**rechnen** *v/t.*
(*sep.*, -ge-, *h*) add (*zu* to), include
(in, among); ~**setzen** *v/t.* (*sep.*,
-ge-, *h*) s. *hinzufügen*; ~**treten** *v/i.*
(*irr. treten*, *sep.*, -ge-, *sein*) s. *hinzukommen*; join; ~**ziehen** *v/t.* (*irr.
ziehen*, *sep.*, -ge-, *h*) call in
(*doctor, etc.*).

Hirn [hirn] *n* (-[e]s/-e) *anat.* brain;
fig. brains *pl.*, mind; '~**gespinst** *n*
figment of the mind, chimera; '**2los**
fig. adj. brainless, senseless; '~-
schale *anat.* *f* brain-pan, cranium;
'~**schlag** ⚕ *m* apoplexy; '**2ver-
brannt** *adj.* crazy, F crack-brained,
cracky.

Hirsch *zo.* [hirʃ] *m* (-es/-e) *species*:

deer; stag, hart; '~**geweih** *n*
(stag's) antlers *pl.*; '~**kuh** *f* hind;
'~**leder** *n* buckskin, deerskin.

Hirse ⚘ ['hirzə] *f* (-/-n) millet.

Hirt [hirt] *m* (-en/-en), ~**e** ['~ə] *m*
(-n/-n) herdsman; shepherd.

hissen ['hisən] *v/t.* (*ge-*, *h*) hoist,
raise (*flag*); ⚓ *a.* trice up (*sail*).

Histori|ker [hi'sto:rikər] *m* (-s/-)
historian; **2sch** *adj.* historic(al).

Hitz|e ['hitsə] *f* (-/-no *pl.*) heat;
'**2ebeständig** *adj.* heat-resistant,
heat-proof; '~**ewelle** *f* heat-wave,
hot spell; '**2ig** *adj. p.* hot-tempered,
hot-headed; *discussion*: heated;
'~**kopf** *m* hothead; '~**schlag** ⚕ *m*
heat-stroke.

hob [ho:p] *pret. of heben*.

Hobel ⊕ ['ho:bəl] *m* (-s/-) plane;
'~**bank** *f* carpenter's bench; '**2n**
v/t. (*ge-*, *h*) plane.

hoch [ho:x] **1.** *adj.* high; *church
spire, tree, etc.*: tall; *position, etc.*:
high, important; *guest, etc.*: distinguished; *punishment, etc.*: heavy,
severe; *age*: great, old; hohe See
open sea, high seas *pl.*; **2.** *adv.*:
~ lebe ...! long live ...! **3.** **2** *n* (-s/-s)
cheer; toast; *meteorology*: high
(-pressure area).

'hoch|achten *v/t.* (*sep.*, -ge-, *h*)
esteem highly; '**2achtung** *f* high
esteem *or* respect; '~**achtungsvoll**
1. *adj.* (most) respectful; **2.** *adv.
correspondence*: yours faithfully *or*
sincerely, *esp. Am.* yours truly;
'**2adel** *m* greater *or* higher nobility;
'**2amt** *eccl. n* high mass; '**2antenne**
f overhead aerial; '**2bahn** *f* elevated
or overhead railway, *Am.* elevated
railroad; '**2betrieb** *m* intense activity, rush; '**2burg** *fig. f* stronghold; '~**deutsch** *adj.* High *or* standard German; '**2druck** *m* high pressure (*a. fig.*); mit ~ arbeiten work at
high pressure; '**2ebene** *f* plateau,
tableland; '~**fahrend** *adj.* high-
handed, arrogant; '~**fein** *adj.*
superfine; **2form** *f*: in ~ in top
form; '**2frequenz** ⚡ *f* high frequency; '**2gebirge** *n* high mountains *pl.*; '**2genuß** *m* great enjoyment; '**2glanz** *m* high polish;
'**2haus** *n* multi-stor(e)y building,
skyscraper; '~**herzig** *adj.* noble-
minded; generous; '**2herzigkeit** *f*
(-/-en) noble-mindedness; generosity; '**2konjunktur** ⚕ *f* boom,

business prosperity; '**2land** n upland(s pl.), highlands pl.; '**2mut** m arrogance, haughtiness; **mütig** adj. [ˈmyːtiç] arrogant, haughty; **näsig** F adj. [ˈnɛːziç] stuck-up; '**2ofen** ⊕ m blast-furnace; '**rot** adj. bright red; '**2saison** f peak season, height of the season; '**schätzen** v/t. (sep., -ge-, h) esteem highly; '**2schule** f university; academy; '**2seefischerei** f deep-sea fishing; '**2sommer** m midsummer; '**2spannung** ⚡ f high tension or voltage; '**2sprung** m sports: high jump.

höchst [høːçst] 1. adj. highest; fig. a.: supreme; extreme; 2. adv. highly, most, extremely.

Hochstap|elei [hoːxʃtaːpəˈlaɪ] f (-/-en) swindling; '**ler** m (-s/-) confidence man, swindler.

höchstens adv. [ˈhøːçstəns] at (the) most, at best.

'**Höchst|form** f sports: top form; '**geschwindigkeit** f maximum speed; speed limit; '**leistung** f sports: record (performance); ⊕ maximum output (of machine, etc.); '**lohn** m maximum wages pl.; '**maß** n maximum; '**preis** m maximum price.

'**hoch|trabend** fig. adj. high-flown; pompous; '**2verrat** m high treason; '**2wald** m high forest; '**2wasser** n high tide or water; flood; '**wertig** adj. high-grade, high-class; '**2wild** n big game; '**2wohlgeboren** m (-s/-) Right Hono(u)rable.

Hochzeit [ˈhɔxtsaɪt] f (-/-en) wedding; marriage; '**2lich** adj. bridal, nuptial; '**geschenk** n wedding present; '**sreise** f honeymoon (trip).

Hocke [ˈhɔkə] f (-/-n) gymnastics: squat-vault; skiing: crouch; '**2n** v/i. (ge-, h) squat, crouch; '**r** m (-s/-) stool.

Höcker [ˈhœkər] m (-s/-) surface, etc.: bump; camel, etc.: hump; p. hump, hunch; '**2ig** adj. animal: humped; p. humpbacked, hunchbacked; surface, etc.: bumpy, rough, uneven.

Hode anat. [ˈhoːdə] m (-n/-n), f (-/-n), '**n** anat. m (-s/-) testicle.

Hof [hoːf] m (-[e]s/ᵘe) court(yard); farm; king, etc.: court; ast. halo; j-m den ~ machen court s.o.; '**da-**

me f lady-in-waiting; '**2fähig** adj. presentable at court.

Hoffart [ˈhɔfart] f (-/no pl.) arrogance, haughtiness; pride.

hoffen [ˈhɔfən] (ge-, h) 1. v/i. hope (auf acc. for); trust (in); 2. v/t.: das Beste ~ hope for the best; '**t-lich** adv. it is to be hoped that, I hope, let's hope.

Hoffnung [ˈhɔfnuŋ] f (-/-en) hope (auf acc. for, of); in der ~ zu inf. in the hope of ger., hoping to inf.; s-e ~ setzen auf (acc.) pin one's hopes on; '**2slos** adj. hopeless; '**2svoll** adj. hopeful; promising.

'**Hofhund** m watch-dog.

höfisch adj. [ˈhøːfiʃ] courtly.

höflich adj. [ˈhøːfliç] polite, civil, courteous (gegen to); '**2keit** f (-/-en) politeness, civility, courtesy.

'**Hofstaat** m royal or princely household; suite, retinue.

Höhe [ˈhøːə] f (-/-n) height; ⚡, ast., geogr. altitude; hill; peak; amount (of bill, etc.); size (of sum, fine, etc.); level (of price, etc.); severity (of punishment, etc.); ♪ pitch; in gleicher ~ mit on a level with; auf der ~ sein be up to the mark; in die ~ up(wards).

Hoheit [ˈhoːhaɪt] f (-/-en) pol. sovereignty; title: Highness; '**s-gebiet** n (sovereign) territory); '**s-gewässer** n/pl. territorial waters pl.; '**szeichen** n national emblem.

'**Höhen|kurort** m high-altitude health resort; '**luft** f mountain air; '**sonne** f mountain sun; ⚡ ultra-violet lamp; '**steuer** f ⚡ elevator; '**zug** m mountain range.

'**Höhepunkt** m highest point; ast., fig. culmination, zenith; fig. a.: climax; summit, peak.

hohl adj. [hoːl] hollow (a. fig.); cheeks, etc.: sunken; hand: cupped; sound: hollow, dull.

Höhle [ˈhøːlə] f (-/-n) cave, cavern; den, lair (of bear, lion, etc.) (both a. fig.); hole, burrow (of fox, rabbit, etc.); hollow; cavity.

'**Hohl|maß** n dry measure; '**raum** m hollow, cavity; '**spiegel** m concave mirror.

Höhlung [ˈhøːluŋ] f (-/-en) excavation; hollow, cavity.

'**Hohlweg** m defile.

Hohn [hoːn] m (-[e]s/no pl.) scorn, disdain; derision.

höhnen ['hø:nən] *v/i.* (ge-, h) sneer, jeer, mock, scoff (*über acc.* at).

'**Hohngelächter** *n* scornful *or* derisive laughter.

'**höhnisch** *adj.* scornful; sneering, derisive.

Höker ['hø:kər] *m* (-s/-) hawker, huckster; '**2n** *v/i.* (ge-, h) huckster, hawk about.

holen ['ho:lən] *v/t.* (ge-, h) fetch; go for; *a.* ∼ *lassen* send for; draw (*breath*); *sich e-e Krankheit* ∼ catch a disease; *sich bei j-m Rat* ∼ seek s.o.'s advice.

Holländer ['hɔlɛndər] *m* (-s/-) Dutchman.

Hölle ['hœlə] *f* (-/⚹-n) hell.

'**Höllen|angst** *fig. f:* *e-e* ∼ *haben* be in a mortal fright *or* F blue funk; '∼**lärm** F *fig. m* infernal noise; '∼**maschine** *f* infernal machine, time bomb; '∼**pein** F *fig. f* torment of hell. [*a. fig.*).\

'**höllisch** *adj.* hellish, infernal (*both*)

holper|ig *adj.* ['hɔlpəriç] surface, road, *etc.*: bumpy, rough, uneven; *vehicle, etc.*: jolty, jerky; *verse, style, etc.*: rough, jerky; '∼**n** (ge-) **1.** *v/i.* (sein) *vehicle*: jolt, bump; **2.** *v/i.* (h) *vehicle*: jolt, bump; be jolty *or* bumpy.

Holunder ⚹ [ho'lundər] *m* (-s/-) elder.

Holz [hɔlts] *n* (-es/⸗er) wood; timber, *Am.* lumber; '∼**bau** △ *m* wooden structure; '∼**bildhauer** *m* wood-carver; '∼**blasinstrument** ♪ *n* woodwind instrument; '∼**boden** *m* wood(en) floor; wood-loft.

'**hölzern** *adj.* ['hœltsərn] wooden; *fig. a.* clumsy, awkward.

'**Holz|fäller** *m* (-s/-) woodcutter, woodman, *Am. a.* lumberjack, logger; '∼**hacker** *m* (-s/-) wood-chopper, woodcutter, *Am.* lumberjack; '∼**händler** *m* wood *or* timber merchant, *Am.* lumberman; '∼**haus** *n* wooden house, *Am.* frame house; '**2ig** *adj.* woody; '∼**kohle** *f* charcoal; '∼**platz** *m* wood *or* timber yard, *Am.* lumberyard; '∼**schnitt** *m* woodcut, wood-engraving; '∼**schnitzer** *m* wood-carver; '∼**schuh** *m* wooden shoe, clog; '∼**stoß** *m* pile *or* stack of wood; stake; '∼**weg** *fig. m: auf dem* ∼ *sein* be on the wrong track; '∼**wolle** *f* wood-wool; fine wood shavings *pl., Am. a.* excelsior.

Homöopath ⚹ [homøo'pa:t] *m* (-en/-en) hom(o)eopath(ist); ∼**ie** [∼a'ti:] *f* (-/*no pl.*) hom(o)eopathy; **2isch** *adj.* [∼'pa:tiʃ] hom(o)eopathic.

Honig ['ho:niç] *m* (-s/-e) honey; '∼**kuchen** *m* honey-cake; ginger-bread; '**2süß** *adj.* honey-sweet, honeyed (*a. fig.*); '∼**wabe** *f* honey-comb.

Honor|ar [hono'ra:r] *n* (-s/-e) fee; royalties *pl.*; salary; ∼**atioren** [∼a-'tsjo:rən] *pl.* notabilities *pl.*; **2ieren** [∼'ri:rən] *v/t.* (*no* ge-, h) fee, pay a fee to; ✝ hono(u)r, meet (*bill of exchange*).

Hopfen ['hɔpfən] *m* (-s/-) ♀ hop; *brewing:* hops *pl.*

hops|a *int.* ['hɔpsa] (wh)oops!; up-sadaisy!; '∼**en** *v/i.* (ge-, sein) hop, jump.

hörbar *adj.* ['hø:rba:r] audible.

horch|en ['hɔrçən] *v/i.* (ge-, h) listen (*auf acc.* to); eavesdrop; '**2er** *m* (-s/-) eavesdropper.

Horde ['hɔrdə] *f* (-/-n) horde, gang.

hör|en ['hø:rən] (ge-, h) **1.** *v/t.* hear; listen (in) to (*radio*); attend (*lecture, etc.*); hear, learn; **2.** *v/i.* hear (*von dat.* from); listen; ∼ *auf* (*acc.*) listen to; *schwer* ∼ be hard of hearing; ∼ *Sie mal!* look here!; I say!; '**2er** *m* (-s/-) hearer; *radio:* listener(-in); *univ.* student; *teleph.* receiver; '**2erschaft** *f* (-/-en) audience; '**2gerät** *n* hearing aid; '∼**ig** *adj.: j-m* ∼ *sein* be enslaved to s.o.; '**2igkeit** *f* (-/*no pl.*) subjection.

Horizont [hori'tsɔnt] *m* (-[e]s/-e) horizon; skyline; *s-n* ∼ *erweitern* broaden one's mind; *das geht über meinen* ∼ that's beyond me; **2al** *adj.* [∼'ta:l] horizontal.

Hormon [hɔr'mo:n] *n* (-s/-e) hormone.

Horn [hɔrn] *n* **1.** (-[e]s/⸗er) horn (*of bull*); ♪, *mot., etc.*: horn; ✗ bugle; peak; **2.** (-[e]s/-e) horn, horny matter; '∼**haut** *f* horny skin; *anat.* cornea (*of eye*).

Hornisse *zo.* [hɔr'nisə] *f* (-/-n) hornet.

Hornist ♪ [hɔr'nist] *m* (-en/-en) horn-player; ✗ bugler.

Horoskop [horo'sko:p] *n* (-s/-e) horoscope; *j-m das* ∼ *stellen* cast s.o.'s horoscope.

'**Hör|rohr** *n* ear-trumpet; ⚹ stethoscope; '∼**saal** *m* lecture-hall;

'**~spiel** n radio play; '**~weite** f: in ~ within earshot.

Hose ['ho:zə] f (-/-n) (e-e a pair of) trousers pl. or Am. pants pl.; slacks pl.

'**Hosen|klappe** f flap; '**~latz** ['~lats] m (-es/~e) flap; fly; '**~tasche** f trouser-pocket; '**~träger** m: (ein Paar) ~ pl. (a pair of) braces pl. or Am. suspenders pl.

Hospital [hɔspi'ta:l] n (-s/-e, ~er) hospital.

Hostie eccl. ['hɔstjə] f (-/-n) host, consecrated or holy wafer.

Hotel [ho'tɛl] n (-s/-s) hotel; **~besitzer** m hotel owner or proprietor; **~gewerbe** n hotel industry; **~ier** [~'je:] m (-s/-s) hotel-keeper.

Hub ⊕ [hu:p] m (-[e]s/~e) mot. stroke (of piston); lift (of valve, etc.); '**~raum** mot. m capacity.

hübsch adj. [hypʃ] pretty, nice; good-looking, handsome; attractive.

'**Hubschrauber** ⚞ m (-s/-) helicopter.

Huf [hu:f] m (-[e]s/-e) hoof; '**~eisen** n horseshoe; '**~schlag** m hoof-beat; (horse's) kick; '**~schmied** m farrier.

Hüft|e anat. ['hyftə] f (-/-n) hip; esp. zo. haunch; '**~gelenk** n hip-joint; '**~gürtel** m girdle; suspender belt, Am. garter belt.

Hügel ['hy:gəl] m (-s/-) hill(ock); '**2ig** adj. hilly.

Huhn orn. [hu:n] n (-[e]s/~er) fowl, chicken; hen; junges ~ chicken.

Hühnchen ['hy:nçən] n (-s/-) chicken; ein ~ zu rupfen haben have a bone to pick (mit with).

Hühner|auge ⚘ ['hy:nər-] n corn; '**~ei** n hen's egg; '**~hof** m poultry-yard, Am. chicken yard; '**~hund** zo. m pointer, setter; '**~leiter** f chicken-ladder.

Huld [hult] f (-/no pl.) grace, favo(u)r; **2igen** ['~digən] v/i. (dat.) (ge-, h) pay homage to (sovereign, lady, etc.); indulge in (vice, etc.); '**~igung** f (-/-en) homage; '**2reich** adj., '**2voll** adj. gracious.

Hülle ['hylə] f (-/-n) cover(ing), wrapper; letter, balloon, etc.: envelope; book, etc.: jacket; umbrella, etc.: sheath; '**2n** v/t. (ge-, h) wrap, cover, envelope (a. fig.); sich in Schweigen ~ wrap o.s. in silence.

Hülse ['hylzə] f (-/-n) legume, pod (of leguminous plant); husk, hull (of rice, etc.); skin (of pea, etc.); ✗ case; '**~nfrucht** f legume(n); leguminous plant; '**~nfrüchte** f/pl. pulse.

human adj. [hu'ma:n] humane; **2ität** [~ani'tɛ:t] f (-/no pl.) humanity.

Hummel zo. ['huməl] f (-/-) bumble-bee.

Hummer zo. ['humər] m (-s/-) lobster.

Humor [hu'mo:r] m (-s/⚘-e) humo(u)r; **~ist** [~o'rist] m (-en/-en) humorist; **2istisch** adj. [~o'ristiʃ] humorous.

humpeln ['humpəln] v/i. (ge-) 1. (sein) hobble (along), limp (along); 2. (h) have a limp, walk with a limp.

Hund [hunt] m (-[e]s/-e) zo. dog; ✗ tub; ast. dog, canis; auf den ~ kommen go to the dogs.

'**Hunde|hütte** f dog-kennel, Am. a. doghouse; '**~kuchen** m dog-biscuit; '**~leine** f (dog-)lead or leash; '**~peitsche** f dog-whip.

hundert ['hundərt] 1. adj. a or one hundred; 2. ⚥ n (-s/-e) hundred; fünf vom ~ five per cent; zu ~en by hundreds; '**~fach** adj., '**~fältig** adj. hundredfold; '**2'jahrfeier** f centenary, Am. a. centennial; '**~jährig** adj. ['~jɛ:riç] centenary, a hundred years old; '**~st** adj. hundredth.

'**Hunde|sperre** f muzzling-order; '**~steuer** f dog tax.

Hündin zo. ['hyndin] f (-/-nen) bitch, she-dog; '**2sch** adj. doggish; fig. servile, cringing.

'**hunds|gemein** F adj. dirty, mean, scurvy; '**~mise'rabel** F adj. rotten, wretched, lousy; '**2tage** m/pl. dog-days pl.

Hüne ['hy:nə] m (-n/-n) giant.

Hunger ['huŋər] m (-s/no pl.) hunger (fig. nach for); ~ bekommen get hungry; ~ haben be or feel hungry; '**~kur** f starvation cure; '**~leider** F m (-s/-) starveling, poor devil; '**~lohn** m starvation wages pl.; '**2n** v/i. (ge-, h) hunger (fig. nach after, for); go without food; ~ lassen starve ɀ.o.; '**~snot** f famine; '**~streik** m hunger-strike; '**~tod** m death from starvation; '**~tuch** fig. n: am ~ nagen have nothing to bite.

'**hungrig** adj. hungry (fig. nach for).

Hupe mot. ['hu:pə] f (-/-n) horn,

hooter; klaxon; **'⊙n** v/i. (ge-, h) sound one's horn, hoot.

hüpfen ['hypfən] v/i. (ge-, sein) hip, skip; gambol, frisk (about).

Hürde ['hyrdə] f (-/-n) hurdle; fold, pen; '**⸤rennen** hurdle-race.

Hure ['hu:rə] f (-/-n) whore, prostitute. [agile, nimble.\]

hurtig adj. ['hurtiç] quick, swift;\]

Husar ✕ [hu'za:r] m (-en/-en) hussar.

husch int. [huʃ] in or like a flash; shoo!; '**⸤en** v/i. (ge-, sein) slip, dart; small animal: scurry, scamper; bat, etc.: flit.

hüsteln ['hy:stəln] **1.** v/i. (ge-, h) cough slightly; **2.** ⸤ n (-s/no pl.) slight cough.

husten ['hu:stən] **1.** v/i. (ge-, h) cough; **2.** ⸤ m (-s/⸜-) cough.

Hut [hu:t] **1.** m (-[e]s/ᵘe) hat; den ⸤ abnehmen take off one's hat; ⸤ ab vor (dat.)! hats off to ...!; **2.** f (-/no pl.) care, charge; guard; auf der ⸤ sein be on one's guard (vor dat. against).

hüte|n ['hy:tən] v/t. (ge-, h) guard, protect, keep watch over; keep (secret); tend (sheep, etc.); das Bett ⸤ be confined to (one's) bed; sich ⸤ vor (dat.) beware of; '**⸤r** m (-s/-) keeper, guardian; herdsman.

'**Hut|futter** n hat-lining; '**⸤krempe**

---

f hat-brim; '**⸤macher** m (-s/-) hatter; '**⸤nadel** f hat-pin.

Hütte ['hytə] f (-/-n) hut; cottage, cabin; ⊕ metallurgical plant; mount. refuge; '**⸤nwesen** ⊕ n metallurgy, metallurgical engineering.

Hyäne zo. [hy'ɛ:nə] f (-/-n) hy(a)ena.

Hyazinthe ♀ [hya'tsintə] f (-/-n) hyacinth. [hydrant.\]

Hydrant [hy'drant] m (-en/-en)\]

Hydrauli|k phys. [hy'draulik] f (-/no pl.) hydraulics pl.; ⸤sch adj. hydraulic.

Hygien|e [hy'gje:nə] f (-/no pl.) hygiene; ⸤isch adj. hygienic(al).

Hymne ['hymnə] f (-/-n) hymn.

Hypno|se [hyp'no:zə] f (-/-n) hypnosis; ⸤tisieren [⸜oti'zi:rən] v/t. and v/i. (no -ge-, h) hypnotize.

Hypochond|er [hypo'xɔndər] m (-s/-) hypochondriac; ⸤risch adj. hypochondriac.

Hypotenuse ♙ [hypote'nu:zə] f (-/-n) hypotenuse.

Hypothek [hypo'te:k] f (-/-en) mortgage; e-e ⸤ aufnehmen raise a mortgage; ⸤arisch adj. [⸜e'ka:riʃ]: ⸤e Belastung mortgage.

Hypothe|se [hypo'te:zə] f (-/-n) hypothesis; ⸤tisch adj. hypothetical.

Hyster|ie psych. [hyste'ri:] f (-/-n) hysteria; ⸤isch psych. adj. [⸜'te:riʃ] hysterical.

I

ich [iç] **1.** pers. pron. I; **2.** ⸤ n (-[s]/-[s]) self; psych. the ego.

Ideal [ide'a:l] **1.** n (-s/-e) ideal; **2.** ⸤ adj. ideal; ⸤isieren [⸜ali'zi:rən] v/t. (no -ge-, h) idealize; ⸤ismus [⸜a'lismus] m (-/Idealismen) idealism; ⸤ist [⸜a'list] m (-en/-en) idealist.

Idee [i'de:] f (-/-n) idea, notion.

identi|fizieren [identifi'tsi:rən] v/t. (no -ge-, h) identify; sich ⸤ identify o.s.; ⸤sch adj. [i'dentiʃ] identical; ⸤tät [⸜'tɛ:t] f (-/no pl.) identity.

Ideolog|ie [ideolo'gi:] f (-/-n) ideology; ⸤isch adj. [⸜'lo:giʃ] ideological.

Idiot [idi'o:t] m (-en/-en) idiot; ⸤ie [⸜o'ti:] f (-/-n) idiocy; ⸤isch adj. [⸜'o:tiʃ] idiotic.

Idol [i'do:l] n (-s/-e) idol.

Igel zo. ['i:gəl] m (-s/-) hedgehog.

Ignor|ant [igno'rant] m (-en/-en) ignorant person, ignoramus; ⸤anz [⸜ts] f (-/no pl.) ignorance; ⸤ieren v/t. (no -ge-, h) ignore, take no notice of.

ihm pers. pron. [i:m] p. (to) him; thing: (to) it.

ihn pers. pron. [i:n] p. him; thing: it.

'ihnen pers. pron. (to) them; **Ihnen** sg. and pl. (to) you.

ihr [i:r] **1.** pers. pron.: (2nd pl. nom.) you; (3rd sg. dat.) (to) her; **2.** poss. pron.: her; their; Ihr sg. and pl. your; der (die, das) ⸤e hers; der (die, das) Ihre sg. and pl. yours; ⸤erseits ['⸜ɔr'zaɪts] adv. on her part; on their part; Ihrerseits sg. and pl. on your part; '**⸤es'gleichen** pron. (of)

her *or* their kind, her *or* their equal;
Ihresgleichen sg. (of) your kind,
your equal; *pl.* (of) your kind,
your equals; '**.et'wegen** *adv.* for
her *or* their sake, on her *or* their
account; *Ihretwegen* sg. *or* pl. for
your sake, on your account; '**.et-**
'**willen** *adv.: um ~ s. ihretwegen;*
.ige *poss. pron.* ['.igə]: der (die,
das) ~ hers; theirs; der (die, das)
Ihrige yours.

illegitim *adj.* [ilegi'ti:m] illegitimate.

illusorisch *adj.* [ilu'zo:riʃ] illusory,
deceptive.

illustrieren [ilu'stri:rən] *v/t.* (no
-ge-, h) illustrate.

Iltis *zo.* ['iltis] *m* (-ses/-se) fitchew,
polecat.

im *prp.* [im] = *in dem.* [inary.]
imaginär *adj.* [imagi'nɛ:r] imag-
'**Imbiß** *m* light meal, snack; '**.stube**
f snack bar.

Imker ['imkər] *m* (-s/-) bee-master,
bee-keeper.

immatrikulieren [imatriku'li:rən]
v/t. (no-ge-, h) matriculate, enrol(l);
sich ~ lassen matriculate, enrol(l).

immer *adv.* ['imər] always; ~ *mehr*
more and more; ~ *wieder* again *or*
time and again; *für ~* for ever, for
good; '**²grün** ♀ *n* (-s/-e) evergreen;
'**.'hin** *adv.* still, yet; '**.'zu** *adv.*
always, continually.

Immobilien [imo'bi:ljən] *pl.* im-
movables *pl.*, real estate; **.händler**
m s. Grundstücksmakler.

immun *adj.* [i'mu:n] immune (gegen against, from); **²ität** [.uni'tɛ:t]
f (-/no pl.) immunity.

Imperativ *gr.* ['imperati:f] *m* (-s/-e)
imperative (mood).

Imperfekt *gr.* ['imperfɛkt] *n* (-s/-e)
imperfect (tense), past tense.

Imperialis|mus [imperia'lismus] *m*
(-/no pl.) imperialism; **.t** *m* (-en/-en)
imperialist; **²tisch** *adj.* imperial-
istic.

impertinent *adj.* [imperti'nɛnt]
impertinent, insolent.

impf|en ♀ ['impfən] *v/t.* (ge-, h)
vaccinate, inoculate; '**²schein** *m*
certificate of vaccination *or* inoculation; '**²stoff** ♀ *m* vaccine,
serum; '**²ung** *f* (-/-en) vaccination,
inoculation.

imponieren [impo'ni:rən] *v/i.* (no
-ge-, h): *j-m ~* impress s.o.

Import ♀ [im'pɔrt] *m* (-[e]s/-e)
import(ation); **.eur** ♀ [..'tø:r] *m*
(-s/-e) importer; **²ieren** [..'ti:rən]
v/t. (no -ge-, h) import.

imposant *adj.* [impo'zant] imposing,
impressive.

imprägnieren [imprɛ'gni:rən] *v/t.*
(no -ge-, h) impregnate; (water-)
proof (*raincoat, etc.*).

improvisieren [improvi'zi:rən] *v/t.*
and v/i. (no -ge-, h) improvise.

Im'puls *m* (-es/-e) impuls; **²iv** *adj.*
[..'zi:f] impulsive. [be able.\]
imstande *adj.* [im'ʃtandə]: ~ *sein*\
in *prp.* (*dat.; acc.*) [in] **1.** *place:* in,
at; within; into, in; *with names*
of important towns: in, ⚐ at, of;
with names of villages and less im-
portant towns: at; *im Hause* in the
house, indoors; *im ersten Stock*
on the first floor; ~ *der Schule*
(*im Theater*) at school (the thea-
t|re, *Am.* -er); ~ *die Schule* (~*s*
Theater) to school (the theat|re,
Am. -er); ~ *England* in England;
waren Sie schon einmal in England?
have you ever been to England?;
2. *time:* in, at, during; within; ~
drei Tagen (with)in three days;
heute ~ vierzehn Tagen today fortnight; *im Jahre 1960* in 1960; *im*
Februar in February; *im Frühling* in
(the) spring; ~ *der Nacht* at night;
~ *letzter Zeit* lately, of late, recently;
3. *mode:* ~ *großer Eile* in great haste;
~ *Frieden leben* live at peace; ~
Reichweite within reach; **4.** *condi-*
tion, state: *im Alter von fünfzehn*
Jahren at (the age of) fifteen; ~ *Be-*
handlung under treatment.

'**Inbegriff** *m* (quint)essence; em-
bodiment, incarnation; paragon;
'**²en** *adj.* included, inclusive (of).
'**Inbrunst** *f* (-/no pl.) ardo(u)r,
fervo(u)r.

'**inbrünstig** *adj.* ardent, fervent.

in'dem *cj.* whilst, while; by (*ger.*);
~ *er mich ansah, sagte er* looking at
me he said.

Inder ['indər] *m* (-s/-) Indian.

in'des(sen) 1. *adv.* meanwhile; **2.**
cj. while; however.

Indianer [in'dja:nər] *m* (-s/-)
(American *or* Red) Indian.

Indikativ *gr.* ['indikati:f] *m* (-s/-e)
indicative (mood).

'**indirekt** *adj.* indirect.

indisch *adj.* ['indiʃ] Indian.

J

indiskret *adj.* indiscreet; **⊇ion** [‿e'tsjo:n] *f* (-/-en) indiscretion.

indiskutabel *adj.* ['indiskuta:bəl] out of the question.

individu|ell *adj.* [individu'el] individual; **⊇um** [‿'vi:duum] *n* (-s/ Individuen) individual.

Indizienbeweis ⚥ [in'di:tsjən-] *m* circumstantial evidence.

Indoss|ament ✝ [indɔsa'mɛnt] *n* (-s/-e) endorsement, indorsement; **⊇ieren** ✝ [‿'si:rən] *v/t.* (no -ge-, h) indorse, endorse.

Industrialisierung [industriali'zi:-ruɳ] *f* (-/-en) industrialization.

Industrie [indus'tri:] *f* (-/-n) industry; **‿anlage** *f* industrial plant; **‿arbeiter** *m* industrial worker; **‿ausstellung** *f* industrial exhibition; **‿erzeugnis** *n* industrial product; **‿gebiet** *n* industrial district or area; **⊇ll** *adj.* [‿i'el] industrial; **‿lle** [‿i'elə] *m* (-n/-n) industrialist; **‿staat** *m* industrial country.

ineinander *adv.* [in°ar'nandər] into one another; **‿greifen** ⊕ *v/i.* (irr. greifen, sep., -ge-, h) gear into one another, interlock.

infam *adj.* [in'fɑ:m] infamous.

Infanter|ie ⚔ [infantə'ri:] *f* (-/-n) infantry; **‿ist** ⚔ *m* (-en/-en) infantryman.

Infektion ⚕ [infek'tsjo:n] *f* (-/-en) infection; **‿skrankheit** ⚕ *f* infectious disease.

Infinitiv *gr.* ['infiniti:f] *m* (-s/-e) infinitive (mood).

infizieren [infi'tsi:rən] *v/t.* (no -ge-, h) infect. [flation.]

Inflation [infla'tsjo:n] *f* (-/-en) in-]

in'folge *prp.* (gen.) in consequence of, owing or due to; **‿dessen** *adv.* consequently.

Inform|ation [infɔrma'tsjo:n] *f* (-/-en) information; **⊇ieren** [‿mi'ran] *v/t.* (no -ge-, h) inform; falsch ‿ misinform.

Ingenieur [inʒe'njø:r] *m* (-s/-e) engineer.

Ingwer ['invər] *m* (-s/no pl.) ginger.

Inhaber ['inha:bər] *m* (-s/-) owner, proprietor (of business or shop); occupant (of flat); keeper (of shop); holder (of power, share, etc.); bearer (of cheque, etc.).

Inhalt *m* (-[e]s/-e) contents *pl.* (of bottle, book, etc.); tenor (of speech); geom. volume; capacity (of vessel).

Inhalts|angabe *f* summary; **⊇los** *adj.* empty, devoid of substance; **⊇reich** *adj.* full of meaning; life: rich, full; **‿verzeichnis** *n* on parcel: list of contents; in book: table of contents.

Initiative [initsja'ti:və] *f* (-/no pl.) initiative; die ‿ ergreifen take the initiative.

Inkasso ✝ [in'kaso] *n* (-s/-s, Inkassi) collection.

inkonsequen|t *adj.* inconsistent; **⊇z** ['‿ts] *f* (-/-en) inconsistency.

In'krafttreten *n* (-s/no pl.) coming into force, taking effect (of new law, etc.).

Inland *n* (-[e]s/no pl.) home (country); inland.

inländisch *adj.* ['inlendiʃ] native; inland; home; domestic; product: home-made.

Inlett ['inlet] *n* (-[e]s/-e) bedtick.

in'mitten *prp.* (gen.) in the midst of, amid(st).

'inne|haben *v/t.* (irr. haben, sep., -ge-, h) possess, hold (office, record, etc.); occupy (flat); **‿halten** *v/i.* (irr. halten, sep., -ge-, h) stop, pause.

innen *adv.* ['inən] inside, within; indoors; nach ‿ inwards.

'Innen|architekt *m* interior decorator; **‿ausstattung** *f* interior decoration, fittings *pl.*, furnishing; **‿minister** *m* minister of the interior; Home Secretary, Am. Secretary of the Interior; **‿ministerium** *n* ministry of the interior; Home Office, Am. Department of the Interior; **‿politik** *f* domestic policy; **‿seite** *f* inner side, inside; **‿stadt** *f* city, Am. downtown.

inner *adj.* ['inər] interior; inner; ⚕, pol. internal; **⊇e** *n* (-n/no pl.) interior; Minister(ium) des Innern s. Innenminister(ium); **⊇eien** [‿'raiən] *f/pl.* offal(s pl.); **‿halb 1.** *prp.* (gen.) within; **2.** *adv.* within, inside; **‿lich** *adv.* inwardly; esp. ⚕ internally.

innig *adj.* ['iniç] intimate, close; affectionate.

Innung ['inuɳ] *f* (-/-en) guild, corporation.

inoffiziell *adj.* ['in°-] unofficial.

ins *prp.* [ins] = in das.

Insasse ['inzasə] *m* (-n/-n) inmate; occupant, passenger (of car).

'**Inschrift** f inscription; legend (on coin, etc.).

Insekt zo. [in'zɛkt] n (-[e]s/-en) insect.

Insel ['inzəl] f (-/-n) island; '**~bewohner** m islander.

Inser|at [inzə'rɑːt] n (-[e]s/-e) advertisement, F ad; **2ieren** [~'riːrən] v/t. and v/i. (no ge-, h) advertise.

insge|'heim adv. secretly; **~'samt** adv. altogether.

in'sofern cj. so far; **~** als in so far as.

insolvent ✝ adj. ['inzɔlvɛnt] insolvent.

Inspekt|ion [inspɛk'tsjoːn] f (-/-en) inspection; **~or** [in'spɛktɔr] m (-s/-en) inspector; surveyor; overseer.

inspirieren [inspi'riːrən] v/t. (no -ge-, h) inspire.

inspizieren [inspi'tsiːrən] v/t. (no -ge-, h) inspect (troops, etc.); examine (goods); survey (buildings).

Install|ateur [instala'tøːr] m (-s/-e) plumber; (gas- or electrical) fitter; **2ieren** [~'liːrən] v/t. (no -ge-, h) install.

instand adv. [in'ʃtant]: **~** halten keep in good order; keep up; ⊕ maintain; **~** setzen repair; **2haltung** f maintenance; upkeep.

'**inständig** adv.: j-n **~** bitten implore or beseech s.o.

Instanz [in'stants] f (-/-en) authority; ⁂ instance; **~enweg** ⁂ m stages of appeal; auf dem **~** through the prescribed channels.

Instinkt [in'stiŋkt] m (-[e]s/-e) instinct; **2iv** [~'tiːf] instinctively.

Institut [insti'tuːt] n (-[e]s/-e) institute.

Instrument [instru'mɛnt] n (-[e]s/-e) instrument.

inszenier|en esp. thea. [instse'niːrən] v/t. (no -ge-, h) (put on the) stage; **2ung** thea. f (-/-en) staging, production.

Integr|ation [integra'tsjoːn] f (-/-en) integration; **2ieren** [~'griːrən] v/t. (no -ge-, h) integrate.

intellektuell adj. [intelɛktu'ɛl] intellectual, highbrow; **2e** m (-n/-n) intellectual, highbrow.

intelligen|t adj. [inteli'gɛnt] intelligent; **2z** [~ts] f (-/-en) intelligence.

Intendant thea. [inten'dant] m (-en/-en) director. [intense.]

intensiv adj. [inten'ziːf] intensive;

interess|ant adj. [intere'sant] interesting; **2e** [~'rɛsə] n (-s/-n) interest (an dat., für in); **2engebiet** [~'rɛsən-] n field of interest; **2engemeinschaft** [~'rɛsən-] f community of interests; combine, pool, trust; **2ent** [~'sɛnt] m (-en/-en) interested person or party; ✝ prospective buyer, esp. Am. prospect; **~ieren** [~'siːrən] v/t. (no -ge-, h) interest (für in); sich **~** für take an interest in.

intern adj. [in'tɛrn] internal; **2at** [~'nɑːt] n (-[e]s/-e) boarding-school.

international adj. [internatsjo'nɑːl] international.

inter|'nieren v/t. (no -ge-, h) intern; **2'nierung** f (-/-en) internment; **2'nist** ⚕ m (-en/-en) internal specialist, Am. internist.

inter|pretieren [interpre'tiːrən] v/t. (no -ge-, h) interpret; **2punktion** [~puŋk'tsjoːn] f (-/-en) punctuation; **2vall** [~'val] n (-s/-e) interval; **~venieren** [~ve'niːrən] v/i. (no -ge-, h) intervene; **2'zonenhandel** m interzonal trade; **2'zonenverkehr** m interzonal traffic.

intim adj. [in'tiːm] intimate (mit with); **2ität** [~imi'tɛːt] f (-/-en) intimacy.

'**intoleran|t** adj. intolerant; **2z** ['~ts] f (-/-en) intolerance.

intransitiv gr. adj. ['intranziti:f] intransitive.

Intrig|e [in'triːgə] f (-/-n) intrigue, scheme, plot; **2ieren** [~i'giːrən] v/i. (no -ge-, h) intrigue, scheme, plot.

Invalid|e [inva'liːdə] m (-n/-n) invalid; disabled person; **~enrente** f disability pension; **~ität** [~idi'tɛːt] f (-/no pl.) disablement, disability. [ventory, stock.]

Inventar [invɛn'tɑːr] n (-s/-e) in-

Inventur ✝ [invɛn'tuːr] f (-/-en) stock-taking; **~** machen take stock.

invest|ieren ✝ [invɛs'tiːrən] v/t. (no -ge-, h) invest; **2ition** ✝ [~i'tsjoːn] f (-/-en) investment.

inwie|'fern cj. to what extent; in what way or respect; **~'weit** cj. how far, to what extent.

in'zwischen adv. in the meantime, meanwhile.

Ion phys. [i'oːn] n (-s/-en) ion.

ird|en adj. ['irdən] earthen; '**~isch** adj. earthly; worldly; mortal.

Ire ['iːrə] *m* (-n/-n) Irishman; *die* ~*n pl.* the Irish *pl.*

irgend *adv.* ['irgənt] *in compounds:* some; any (*a. negative and in questions*); *wenn ich* ~ *kann* if I possibly can; '~**'ein(e)** *indef. pron. and adj.* some(one); any(one); '~**'einer** *indef. pron. s. irgend jemand*; '~**'ein(e)s** *indef. pron.* some; any; ~ **etwas** *indef. pron.* something; anything; ~ **jemand** *indef. pron.* someone; anyone; '~**'wann** *adv.* some time (or other); '~**'wie** *adv.* somehow; anyhow; '~**'wo** *adv.* somewhere; anywhere; '~**'wo'her** *adv.* from somewhere; from anywhere; '~**'wo'hin** *adv.* somewhere; anywhere.

'irisch *adj.* Irish.

Iron|ie [iro'niː] *f* (-/-n) irony; **2isch** *adj.* [i'roːniʃ] ironic(al).

irre ['irə] **1.** *adj.* confused; *꒿* insane; mad; **2.** ꒷ *f* (-/no *pl.*): *in die* ~ *gehen* go astray; **3.** ꒷ *m, f* (-n/-n) lunatic; mental patient; *wie ein* ~*r* like a madman; '~**führen** *v/t.* (*sep.*, -ge-, h) lead astray; *fig.* mislead; '~**gehen** *v/i.* (*irr. gehen, sep.*, -ge-, *sein*) go astray, stray; lose one's way; '~**machen** *v/t.* (*sep.*, -ge-, h) puzzle, bewilder; perplex; confuse; '~**n 1.** *v/i.* (ge-, h) err; wander; **2.** *v/refl.* (ge-, h) be mistaken (*in dat. in s.o., about s.th.*); be wrong.

'Irren|anstalt *꒿ f* lunatic asylum, mental home *or* hospital; '~**arzt** *m* alienist, mental specialist; '~**haus** *꒿ n s.* Irrenanstalt.

'irrereden *v/i.* (*sep.*, -ge-, h) rave.

'Irr|fahrt *f* wandering; Odyssey; '~**garten** *m* labyrinth, maze; '~**glaube** *m* erroneous belief; false doctrine, heterodoxy; heresy; '2**gläubig** *adj.* heterodox; heretical; '2**ig** *adj.* erroneous, mistaken, false, wrong.

irritieren [iri'tiːrən] *v/t.* (*no* -ge-, h) irritate, annoy; confuse.

'Irr|lehre *f* false doctrine, heterodoxy; heresy; '~**licht** *n* will-o'-the-wisp, jack-o'-lantern; '2**sinn** *m* insanity; madness; '2**sinnig** *adj.* insane; mad; *fig.*: fantastic; terrible; '~**sinnige** *m, f* (-n/-n) *s. irre* 3; '~**tum** *m* (-s/⸚er) error, mistake; *im* ~ *sein* be mistaken; '2**tümlich** ['~tyːmliç] **1.** *adj.* erroneous; **2.** *adv.* = '2**tümlicherweise** *adv.* by mistake; mistakenly, erroneously; '~**wisch** *m s.* Irrlicht; *p.* flibbertigibbet.

Ischias ['iʃias] *f*, F *a.: n, m* (-/no *pl.*) sciatica.

Islam ['islam, is'laːm] *m* (-s/no *pl.*) Islam.

Isländ|er ['iːslɛndər] *m* (-s/-) Icelander; '2**isch** *adj.* Icelandic.

Isolator *꒿* [izo'laːtɔr] *m* (-s/-en) insulator.

Isolier|band *꒿* [izo'liːr-] *n* insulating tape; **2en** *v/t.* (*no* -ge-, h) isolate; ~**masse** *꒿ f* insulating compound; ~**schicht** *꒿ f* insulating layer; ~**ung** *f* (-/-en) isolation (*a. ꒿*); quarantine; *꒿* insulation.

Isotop ꒷, *phys.* [izo'toːp] *n* (-s/-e) isotope.

Israeli [isra'eːli] *m* (-s/-s) Israeli.

Italien|er [ital'jeːnər] *m* (-s/-) Italian; **2isch** *adj.* Italian.

I-Tüpfelchen *fig.* ['iːtʏpfəlçən] *n* (-s/-): *bis aufs* ~ to a T.

J

ja [jaː] **1.** *adv.* yes; ꬰ, *parl.* aye, *Am. parl. a.* yea; ~ *doch*, ~ *freilich* yes, indeed; to be sure; *da ist er* ~! well, there he is!; *ich sagte es Ihnen* ~ I told you so; *tut es* ~ *nicht!* don't you dare do it!; *vergessen Sie es* ~ *nicht!* be sure not to forget it!; **2.** *cj.:* ~ *sogar*, ~ *selbst* nay (even); *wenn* ~ if so; *er ist* ~ *mein Freund* why, he is my friend; **3.** *int.:* ~, *weißt du*

denn nicht, daß why, don't you know that.

Jacht ꬰ [jaxt] *f* (-/-en) yacht; '~**klub** *m* yacht-club.

Jacke ['jakə] *f* (-/-n) jacket.

Jackett [ʒa'kɛt] *n* (-s/-e, -s) jacket.

Jagd [jaːkt] *f* (-/-en) hunt(ing); *with a gun:* shoot(ing); chase; *s. Jagdrevier; auf (die)* ~ *gehen* go hunting *or* shooting, *Am. a.* gunning; ~ *machen auf (acc.)* hunt after *or* for;

'**~aufseher** m gamekeeper, Am. game warden; '**~bomber** ✕ m (-s/-) fighter-bomber; '**~büchse** f sporting rifle; '**~flinte** f sporting gun; fowling-piece; '**~flugzeug** ✕ n fighter (aircraft); '**~geschwader** ✕ n fighter wing, Am. fighter group; '**~gesellschaft** f hunting or shooting party; '**~haus** n shooting-box or -lodge, hunting-box or -lodge; '**~hund** m hound; '**~hütte** f shooting-box, hunting-box; '**~pächter** m game-tenant; '**~rennen** n steeplechase; '**~revier** n hunting-ground, shoot; '**~schein** m shooting licen|ce, Am. -se; '**~schloß** n hunting seat; '**~tasche** f game-bag.

jagen ['jaːgən] (ge-, h) **1.** v/i. go hunting or shooting, hunt; shoot; rush, dash; **2.** v/t. hunt; chase; aus dem Hause ~ turn s.o. out (of doors).

Jäger ['jeːgər] m (-s/-) hunter, huntsman, sportsman; ✕ rifleman; '**~latein** F fig. n huntsmen's yarn, tall stories pl.

Jaguar zo. ['jaːguaːr] m (-s/-e) jaguar.

jäh adj. [jeː] sudden, abrupt; precipitous, steep.

Jahr [jaːr] n (-[e]s/-e) year; ein halbes ~ half a year, six months pl.; einmal im ~ once a year; im ~e 1900 in 1900; mit 18 ~en, im Alter von 18 ~en at (the age of) eighteen; letztes ~ last year; das ganze ~ hindurch or über all the year round; ♀'**aus** adv.: ~, jahrein year in, year out; year after year; '**~buch** n year-book, annual; ~'**ein** adv. s. jahraus.

'**jahrelang 1.** adv. for years; **2.** adj.: ~e Erfahrung (many) years of experience.

jähren ['jeːrən] v/refl. (ge-, h): es jährt sich heute, daß ... it is a year ago today that ..., it is a year today since ...

'**Jahres|abonnement** n annual subscription (to magazine, etc.); thea. yearly season ticket; '**~abschluß** m annual statement of accounts; '**~anfang** m beginning of the year; zum ~ die besten Wünsche! best wishes for the New Year; '**~bericht** m annual report; '**~einkommen** n annual or yearly income; '**~ende** n end of the year; '**~gehalt** n annual salary; '**~tag** m anniversary; '**~wechsel** m turn of the year; '**~zahl**

f date, year; '**~zeit** f season, time of the year.

'**Jahrgang** m volume, year (of periodical, etc.); p. age-group; univ., school: year, class; wine: vintage.

Jahr'hundert n (-s/-e) century; ~**feier** f centenary, Am. centennial; ~**wende** f turn of the century.

jährig adj. ['jeːriç] one-year-old.

jährlich ['jeːrliç] **1.** adj. annual, yearly; **2.** adv. every year; yearly, once a year.

'**Jahr|markt** m fair; ~**tausend** n (-s/-e) millennium; ~'**tausendfeier** f millenary; ~'**zehnt** n (-[e]s/-e) decade.

'**Jähzorn** m violent (fit of) temper; irascibility; ♀**ig** adj. hot-tempered; irascible.

Jalousie [ʒaluˈziː] f (-/-n) (Venetian) blind, Am. a. window shade.

Jammer ['jamər] m (-s/no pl.) lamentation; misery; es ist ein ~ it is a pity.

jämmerlich adj. ['jemərliç] miserable, wretched; piteous; pitiable (esp. contp.).

jammer|n ['jamərn] v/i. (ge-, h) lament (nach, um for; über acc. over); moan; wail; whine; '**~schade** adj.: es ist ~ it is a thousand pities, it is a great shame.

Januar ['januaːr] m (-[s]/-e) January.

Japan|er [jaˈpaːnər] m (-s/-) Japanese; die ~ pl. the Japanese pl.; ♀**isch** adj. Japanese.

Jargon [ʒarˈgõ] m (-s/-s) jargon, cant, slang.

Jasmin ♀ [jasˈmiːn] m (-s/-e) jasmin(e), jessamin(e).

'**Jastimme** parl. f aye, Am. a. yea.

jäten ['jeːtən] v/t. (ge-, h) weed.

Jauche ['jauxə] f (-/-n) ✗ liquid manure; sewage.

jauchzen ['jauxtsən] v/i. (ge-, h) exult, rejoice, cheer; vor Freude ~ shout for joy.

jawohl adv. [jaˈvoːl] yes; yes, indeed; yes, certainly; that's right; ✕, etc.: yes, Sir!

'**Jawort** n consent; j-m das ~ geben accept s.o.'s proposal (of marriage).

je [jeː] **1.** adv. ever, at any time; always; ohne ihn ~ gesehen zu haben without ever having seen him; seit eh und ~ since time immemorial, always; distributive with numerals:

~ **zwei** two at a time, two each, two by two, by or in twos; *sie bekamen* ~ *zwei Äpfel* they received two apples each; *für* ~ *zehn Wörter* for every ten words; *in Schachteln mit or zu* ~ *zehn Stück verpackt* packed in boxes of ten; **2.** *cj.:* ~ *nach Größe* according to or depending on size; ~ *nachdem* it depends; ~ *nachdem, was er für richtig hält* according as he thinks fit; ~ *nachdem, wie er sich fühlt* depending on how he feels; ~ *mehr, desto besser* the more the better; ~ *länger,* ~ *lieber* the longer the better; **3.** *prp.:* *die Birnen kosten e-e Mark* ~ *Pfund* the pears cost one mark a pound; *s. pro.*

jede|(r, -s) *indef. pron.* ['je:də(r, -s)] every; any; *of a group:* each; *of two persons:* either; jeder, der whoever; jeden zweiten Tag every other day; '**~n'falls** *adv.* at all events, in any case; '**~r'mann** *indef. pron.* everyone, everybody; '**~r'zeit** *adv.* always, at any time; '**~s'mal** *adv.* each or every time; ~ wenn whenever.

jedoch *cj.* [je'dɔx] however, yet, nevertheless.

'**jeher** *adv.:* von or seit ~ at all times, always, from time immemorial.

jemals *adv.* ['je:ma:ls] ever, at any time.

jemand *indef. pron.* ['je:mant] someone, somebody; *with questions and negations:* anyone, anybody.

jene|(r, -s) *dem. pron.* ['je:nə(r, -s)] that (one); jene pl. those pl.

jenseitig *adj.* ['jenzaitiç] opposite.

'**jenseits 1.** *prp.* (gen.) on the other side of, beyond, across; **2.** *adv.* on the other side, beyond; **3.** ♀ *n* (-/no pl.) the other or next world, the world to come, the beyond.

jetzig *adj.* ['jetsiç] present, existing; *prices, etc.:* current.

jetzt *adv.* [jetst] now, at present; bis ~ until now; so far; eben ~ just now; erst ~ only now; für ~ for the present; gleich ~ at once, right away; noch ~ even now; von ~ an from now on.

jeweil|ig *adj.* ['je:'vailiç] respective; **~s** *adv.* ['.s] respectively, at a time; from time to time (*esp.* ⚖).

Joch [jɔx] *n* (-[e]s/-e) yoke; *in mountains:* col, pass, saddle; ⚠

bay; '**~bein** *anat. n* cheek-bone.

Jockei ['dʒɔki] *m* (-s/-s) jockey.

Jod ♣ [jo:t] *n* (-[e]s/no pl.) iodine.

jodeln ['jo:dəln] *v/i.* (ge-, h) yodel.

Johanni [jo'hani] *n* (-/no pl.), **~s** ['.s] *n* (-/no pl.) Midsummer day; **~s-beere** *f* currant; rote ~ red currant; **~stag** *m eccl.* St John's day; Midsummer day.

johlen ['jo:lən] *v/i.* (ge-, h) bawl, yell, howl.

Jolle ⚓ ['jɔlə] *f* (-/-n) jolly-boat, yawl, dinghy.

Jongl|eur [ʒõ'glø:r] *m* (-s/-e) juggler; ♀**ieren** *v/t. and v/i.* (no -ge-, h) juggle.

Journal [ʒur'na:l] *n* (-s/-e) journal; newspaper; magazine; diary; ♣ log-book; **~ist** ['.a'list] *m* (-en/-en) journalist, *Am. a.* newspaperman.

Jubel ['ju:bəl] *m* (-s/no pl.) jubilation, exultation, rejoicing; cheering; '**~n** *v/i.* (ge-, h) jubilate; exult, rejoice (*über acc.* at).

Jubil|ar [jubi'la:r] *m* (-s/-e) person celebrating his jubilee, *etc.*; **~äum** ['.eːum] *n* (-s/ Jubiläen) jubilee.

Juchten ['juxtən] *m, n* (-s/no pl.), '**~leder** *n* Russia (leather).

jucken ['jukən] (ge-, h) **1.** *v/i.* itch; **2.** *v/t.* irritate, (make) itch; F *sich* ~ scratch (o.s.).

Jude ['ju:də] *m* (-n/-n) Jew; ♀**n-feindlich** *adj.* anti-Semitic; '**~n-tum** *n* (-s/no pl.) Judaism; '**~n-ver-folgung** *f* persecution of Jews, Jew-baiting; pogrom.

Jüd|in ['jy:din] *f* (-/-nen) Jewess; ♀**isch** *adj.* Jewish.

Jugend ['ju:gənt] *f* (-/no pl.) youth; '**~amt** *n* youth welfare department; '**~buch** *n* book for the young; '**~-freund** *m* friend of one's youth; school-friend; '**~fürsorge** *f* youth welfare; '**~gericht** *n* juvenile court; '**~herberge** *f* youth hostel; '**~jahre** *n/pl.* early years, youth; '**~krimi-nalität** *f* juvenile delinquency; '♀**-lich** *adj.* youthful, juvenile, young; '**~liche** *m, f* (-n/-n) young person; juvenile; young man, youth; young girl; teen-ager; '**~liebe** *f* early or first love, calf-love, *Am. a.* puppy love; old sweetheart or flame; '**~-schriften** *f/pl.* books for the young; '**~schutz** *m* protection of children and young people; '**~streich** *m* youthful prank; '**~werk** *n* early work

(of author); ~e pl. a. juvenilia pl.;
'~zeit f (time or days of) youth.

Jugoslav|e [ju:go'sla:və] m (-en/-en)
Jugoslav, Yugoslav; **2isch** adj.
Jugoslav, Yugoslav.

Juli ['ju:li] m (-[s]/-s) July.

jung adj. [juŋ] young; youthful;
peas: green; beer, wine: new; ~es
Gemüse young or early vegetables
pl.; F fig. young people, small fry.

'**Junge 1.** m (-n/-n) boy, youngster;
lad; fellow, chap, Am. guy; cards:
knave, jack; **2.** n (-n/-n) young;
puppy (of dog); kitten (of cat); calf
(of cow, elephant, etc.); cub (of beast
of prey); ~ werfen bring forth
young; ein ~s a young one; **2nhaft**
adj. boyish; '~nstreich m boyish
prank or trick.

jünger ['jyŋər] **1.** adj. younger, junior; er ist drei Jahre ~ als ich he is
my junior by three years, he is
three years younger than I; **2.** 2 m
(-s/-) disciple.

Jungfer ['juŋfər] f (-/-n): alte ~
old maid or spinster.

'**Jungfern|fahrt** ♣ f maiden voyage
or trip; '~flug ✈ m maiden flight;
'~rede f maiden speech.

'**Jung|frau** f maid(en), virgin; 2-
fräulich adj. ['~frɔʏlɪç] virginal;
fig. virgin; '~fräulichkeit f (-/no
pl.) virginity, maidenhood; '~ge-
selle m bachelor; '~gesellenstand
m bachelorhood; '~gesellin f
(-/-nen) bachelor girl.

Jüngling ['jyŋlɪŋ] m (-s/-e) youth,
young man.

jüngst [jyŋst] **1.** adj. youngest; time:
(most) recent, latest; das 2e Gericht, der 2e Tag Last Judg(e)ment,
Day of Judg(e)ment; **2.** adv. recently, lately.

'**jungverheiratet** adj. newly married; '2en pl. the newlyweds pl.

Juni ['ju:ni] m (-[s]/-s) June; '~kä-
fer zo. m cockchafer, June-bug.

junior ['ju:njɔr] **1.** adj. junior;
2. 2 m (-s/-en) junior (a. sports).

Jura ['ju:ra] n/pl.: ~ studieren read
or study law.

Jurist [ju'rɪst] m (-en/-en) lawyer;
law-student; **2isch** adj. legal.

Jury [ʒy'ri:] f (-/-s) jury.

justier|en ⊕ [jus'ti:rən] v/t. (no
-ge-, h) adjust; **2ung** ⊕ f (-/-en)
adjustment.

Justiz [ju'sti:ts] f (-/no pl.) (administration of) justice; **~beamte** m
judicial officer; **~gebäude** n court-
house; **~inspektor** m judicial officer; **~irrtum** m judicial error; **~**
minister m minister of justice;
Lord Chancellor, Am. Attorney
General; **~ministerium** n ministry of justice; Am. Department of
Justice; **~mord** m judicial murder.

Juwel [ju've:l] m, n (-s/-en) jewel,
gem; **~en** pl. jewel(le)ry; **~ier** [~e-
'li:r] m (-s/-e) jewel(l)er.

Jux F [juks] m (-es/-e) (practical)
joke, fun, spree, lark; prank.

K

(Compare also C and Z)

Kabel ['ka:bəl] n (-s/-) cable.

Kabeljau ichth. ['ka:bəljau] m
(-s/-e, -s) cod(fish).

'**kabeln** v/t. and v/i. (ge-, h) cable.

Kabine [ka'bi:nə] f (-/-n) cabin; at
hairdresser's, etc.: cubicle; cage
(of lift).

Kabinett pol. [kabi'nɛt] n (-s/-e)
cabinet, government.

Kabriolett [kabrio'lɛt] n (-s/-e)
cabriolet, convertible.

Kachel ['kaxəl] f (-/-n) (Dutch or
glazed) tile; '~ofen m tiled stove.

Kadaver [ka'da:vər] m (-s/-) carcass.

Kadett [ka'dɛt] m (-en/-en) cadet.

Käfer zo. ['kɛ:fər] m (-s/-) beetle,
chafer.

Kaffee ['kafe, ka'fe:] m (-s/-s) coffee; (')~bohne ♀ f coffee-bean;
(')~kanne f coffee-pot; (')~mühle
f coffee-mill or -grinder; (')~satz
m coffee-grounds pl.; (')~tasse f
coffee-cup.

Käfig ['kɛ:fiç] m (-s/-e) cage (a. fig.).

kahl adj. [ka:l] p. bald; tree, etc.:
bare; landscape, etc.: barren, bleak;
rock, etc.: naked; '2kopf m bald-
head, baldpate; **~köpfig** adj. ['~-
kœpfiç] bald(-headed).

Kahn [kɑːn] *m* (-[e]s/⸚e) boat; river-barge; ~ *fahren* go boating; '**~fahren** *n* (-s/*no pl.*) boating.

Kai [kaɪ] *m* (-s/-e, -s) quay, wharf.

Kaiser ['kaɪzər] *m* (-s/-) emperor; '**~krone** *f* imperial crown; '²*lich adj.* imperial; '**~reich** *n*, '**~tum** *n* (-[e]s/⸚er) empire; '**~würde** *f* imperial status.

Kajüte ⚓ [ka'jyːtə] *f* (-/-n) cabin.

Kakao [ka'kɑːo] *m* (-s/-s) cocoa; ♥ *a.* cacao.

Kakt|ee ♥ [kak'teː(ə)] *f* (-/-n), **~us** ♥ ['~us] *m* (-/*Kakteen*, F *Kaktusse*) cactus.

Kalauer ['kɑːlaʊər] *m* (-s/-) stale joke; pun.

Kalb *zo.* [kalp] *n* (-[e]s/⸚er) calf; ²**en** ['~bən] *v/i.* (ge-, h) calve; '**~fell** *n* calfskin; '**~fleisch** *n* veal; '**~leder** *n* calf(-leather).

'**Kalbs|braten** *m* roast veal; '**~keule** *f* leg of veal; '**~leder** *n s. Kalbleder*; '**~nierenbraten** *m* loin of veal.

Kalender [ka'lɛndər] *m* (-s/-) calendar; almanac; '**~block** *m* date-block; '**~jahr** *n* calendar year; **~uhr** *f* calendar watch or clock.

Kali ♀ ['kɑːli] *n* (-s/-s) potash.

Kaliber [ka'liːbər] *n* (-s/-) calib|re, *Am.* -er (*a. fig.*), bore (*of firearm*).

Kalk [kalk] *m* (-[e]s/-e) lime; *geol.* limestone; lime-burner; '²**en** *v/t.* (ge-, h) whitewash (*wall, etc.*); 𝄞 lime (*field*); '²**ig** *adj.* limy; '**~ofen** *m* limekiln; '**~stein** *m* limestone; '**~steinbruch** *m* limestone quarry.

Kalorie [kalo'riː] *f* (-/-n) calorie.

kalt *adj.* [kalt] *climate, meal, sweat, etc.*: cold; *p., manner, etc.*: cold, chilly, frigid; *mir ist* ~ I am cold; **~e** *Küche* cold dishes *pl. or* meat, *etc.*; *j-m die* **~e** *Schulter zeigen* give s.o. the cold shoulder; **~blütig** *adj.* ['~bly:tiç] cold-blooded (*a. fig.*).

Kälte ['kɛltə] *f* (-/*no pl.*) cold; chill; coldness, chilliness (*both a. fig.*); *vor* ~ *zittern* shiver with cold; *fünf Grad* ~ five degrees below zero; '**~grad** *m* degree below zero; '**~welle** *f* cold spell.

'**kalt|stellen** *fig. v/t.* (*sep.*, -ge-, h) shelve, reduce to impotence; '²**welle** *f* cold wave.

kam [kɑːm] *pret. of* **kommen.**

Kamel *zo.* [ka'meːl] *n* (-[e]s/-e) camel; **~haar** *n textiles*: camel hair.

Kamera *phot.* ['kaməra] *f* (-/-s) camera.

Kamerad [kamə'rɑːt] *m* (-en/-en) comrade; companion; mate, F pal, chum; **~schaft** *f* (-/-en) comradeship, companionship; ²**schaftlich** *adj.* comradely, companionable.

Kamille ♥ [ka'milə] *f* (-/-n) camomile; **~ntee** *m* camomile tea.

Kamin [ka'miːn] *m* (-s/-e) chimney (*a. mount.*); fireplace, fireside; **~sims** *m*, *n* mantelpiece; **~vorleger** *m* hearth-rug; **~vorsetzer** *m* (-s/-) fender.

Kamm [kam] *m* (-[e]s/⸚e) comb; crest (*of bird or wave*); crest, ridge (*of mountain*).

kämmen ['kɛmən] *v/t.* (ge-, h) comb; *sich* (*die Haare*) ~ comb one's hair.

Kammer ['kamər] *f* (-/-n) (small) room; closet; *pol.* chamber; board; 𝕫𝕥 division (*of court*); '**~diener** *m* valet; '**~frau** *f* lady's maid; '**~gericht** 𝕫𝕥 *n* supreme court; '**~herr** *m* chamberlain; '**~jäger** *m* vermin exterminator; '**~musik** *f* chamber music; '**~zofe** *f* chambermaid.

'**Kamm|garn** *n* worsted (yarn); '**~rad** ⊕ *n* cogwheel.

Kampagne [kam'panjə] *f* (-/-n) campaign.

Kampf [kampf] *m* (-[e]s/⸚e) combat, fight (*a. fig.*); struggle (*a. fig.*); battle (*a. fig.*); *fig.* conflict; *sports*: contest, match; *boxing*: fight, bout; '**~bahn** *f sports*: stadium, arena; ²**bereit** *adj.* ready for battle.

kämpfen ['kɛmpfən] *v/i.* (ge-, h) fight (*gegen* against; *mit* with; *um* for) (*a. fig.*); struggle (*a. fig.*); *fig.* contend, wrestle (*mit* with).

Kampfer ['kampfər] *m* (-s/*no pl.*) camphor.

Kämpfer ['kɛmpfər] *m* (-s/-) fighter (*a. fig.*); ✕ combatant, warrior.

'**Kampf|flugzeug** *n* tactical air-craft; '**~geist** *m* fighting spirit; '**~platz** *m* battlefield; *fig.*, *sports*: arena; '**~preis** *m sports*: prize; ✝ cut-throat price; '**~richter** *m* referee, judge, umpire; ²**unfähig** *adj.* disabled.

kampieren [kam'piːrən] *v/i.* (*no -ge-*, h) camp.

Kanal [ka'nɑːl] *m* (-s/⸚e) canal; channel (*a.* ⊕, *fig.*); *geogr. the* Channel; sewer, drain; **~isation**

K

[⸝aliza'tsjoːn] f (-/-en) *river:* canalization; *town, etc.:* sewerage; drainage; **⸝isieren** [⸝ali'ziːrən] v/t. (no -ge-, h) canalize; sewer.

Kanarienvogel *orn.* [ka'naːrjən-] m canary(-bird).

Kandare [kan'daːrə] f (-/-n) curb (-bit).

Kandid|at [kandi'daːt] m (-en/-en) candidate; applicant; **⸝atur** [⸝a'tuːr] f (-/-en) candidature, candidacy; **⸝ieren** [⸝'diːrən] v/i. (no -ge-, h) be a candidate (*für* for); ~ *für* apply for, stand for, *Am.* run for (*office, etc.*).

Känguruh *zo.* ['kɛŋguru:] n (-s/-s) kangaroo.

Kaninchen *zo.* [ka'niːnçən] n (-s/-) rabbit; **⸝bau** m rabbit-burrow.

Kanister [ka'nistər] m (-s/-) can.

Kanne ['kanə] f (-/-n) *milk, etc.:* jug; *coffee, tea:* pot; *oil, milk:* can; **⸝gießer** f *fig.* m political wiseacre.

Kannibal|e [kani'baːlə] m (-n/-n) cannibal; **⸝isch** *adj.* cannibal.

kannte ['kantə] *pret.* of kennen.

Kanon ♩ ['kaːnɔn] m (-s/-s) canon.

Kanon|ade [kanoˈnaːdə] f (-/-n) cannonade; **⸝e** [⸝'noːnə] f (-/-n) × cannon, gun; F *fig.:* big shot; *esp. sports:* ace, crack.

Ka'nonen|boot × n gunboat; **⸝donner** m boom of cannon; **⸝futter** *fig.* n cannon-fodder; **⸝kugel** × cannon-ball; **⸝rohr** n gun barrel.

Kanonier [kano'niːr] m (-s/-e) gunner.

Kant|e ['kantə] f (-/-n) edge; brim; **'⸝en** m (-s/-) end of loaf; **'⸝en** v/t. (ge-, h) square (*stone, etc.*); set on edge; tilt; edge (*skis*); **'⸝ig** *adj.* angular, edged; square(d).

Kantine [kan'tiːnə] f (-/-n) canteen.

Kanu ['kaːnu] n (-s/-s) canoe.

Kanüle ⚕ [ka'nyːlə] f (-/-n) tubule, cannula.

Kanzel ['kantsəl] f (-/-n) *eccl.* pulpit; ⚔ cockpit; × (gun-)turret.; **'⸝redner** m preacher.

Kanzlei [kants'laɪ] f (-/-en) office.

'Kanzler m (-s/-) chancellor.

Kap *geogr.* [kap] n (-s/-s) headland.

Kapazität [kapatsi'tɛːt] f (-/-en) capacity; *fig.* authority.

Kapell|e [ka'pɛlə] f (-/-n) *eccl.* chapel; ♩ band; **⸝meister** m bandleader, conductor.

kaper|n ⚓ ['kaːpərn] v/t. (ge-, h)

capture, seize; **'⸝schiff** n privateer.

kapieren F [ka'piːrən] v/t. (no -ge-, h) grasp, get.

Kapital [kapi'taːl] **1.** n (-s/-e, -ien) capital, stock, funds *pl.*; ~ *und Zinsen* principal and interest; **2.** ♀ *adj.* capital; **⸝anlage** f investment; **⸝flucht** f flight of capital; **⸝gesellschaft** f joint-stock company; **⸝isieren** [⸝ali'ziːrən] v/t. (no -ge-, h) capitalize; **⸝ismus** [⸝a'lismus] m (-/no pl.) capitalism; **⸝ist** [⸝a'list] m (-en/-en) capitalist; **⸝markt** [⸝'tɔːl-] m capital market; **⸝verbrechen** n capital crime.

Kapitän [kapi'tɛːn] m (-s/-e) captain; ~ *zur See* naval captain; **⸝leutnant** m (senior) lieutenant.

Kapitel [ka'pitəl] n (-s/-) chapter (*a. fig.*).

Kapitul|ation × [kapitula'tsjoːn] f (-/-en) capitulation, surrender; **⸝ieren** [⸝'liːrən] v/i. (no -ge-, h) capitulate, surrender.

Kaplan *eccl.* [ka'plaːn] m (-s/≈e) chaplain.

Kappe ['kapə] f (-/-n) cap; hood (*a.* ⊕); bonnet; '**⸝n** v/t. (ge-, h) cut (*cable*); lop, top (*tree*).

Kapriole [kapri'oːlə] f (-/-n) *equitation:* capriole; *fig.:* caper; prank.

Kapsel ['kapsəl] f (-/-n) case, box; ♀, ⚕, *anat., etc.:* capsule.

kaputt *adj.* [ka'put] broken; *elevator, etc.:* out of order; *fruit, etc.:* spoilt; *p.:* ruined; tired out, F fagged out; **⸝gehen** v/i. (*irr.* gehen, *sep.,* -ge-, sein) break, go to pieces; spoil.

Kapuze [ka'puːtsə] f (-/-n) hood; *eccl.* cowl.

Karabiner [kara'biːnər] m (-s/-) carbine.

Karaffe [ka'rafə] f (-/-n) carafe (*for wine or water*); decanter (*for liqueur, etc.*).

Karambol|age [karambo'laːʒə] f (-/-en) collision, crash; *billiards:* cannon, *Am. a.* carom; **⸝ieren** v/i. (no -ge-, sein) cannon, *Am. a.* carom; F *fig.* collide.

Karat [ka'raːt] n (-[e]s/-e) carat.

Karawane [kara'vaːnə] f (-/-n) caravan.

Karbid [kar'biːt] n (-[e]s/-e) carbide.

Kardinal *eccl.* [kardi'naːl] m (-s/≈e) cardinal. [Friday.]

Karfreitag *eccl.* [kaːr'-] m Good

karg adj. [kark] soil: meagre; vegetation: scant, sparse; meal: scanty, meagre, frugal; **~en** ['~gən] v/i. (ge-, h): ~ mit be sparing of.

kärglich adj. ['kɛrkliç] scanty, meagre; poor.

kariert adj. [ka'riːrt] check(ed), chequered, Am. checkered.

Karik|atur [karika'tuːr] f (-/-en) caricature, cartoon; **~ieren** [~'kiːrən] v/t. (no -ge-, h) caricature, cartoon.

karmesin adj. [karme'ziːn] crimson.

Karneval ['karnəval] m (-s/-e, -s) Shrovetide, carnival.

Karo ['kaːro] n (-s/-s) square, check; cards: diamonds pl.

Karosserie mot. [karɔsə'riː] f (-/-n) body.

Karotte ♀ [ka'rɔtə] f (-/-n) carrot.

Karpfen ichth. ['karpfən] m (-s/-) carp.

Karre ['karə] f (-/-n) cart; wheelbarrow.

Karriere [kar'jɛːrə] f (-/-n) (successful) career.

Karte ['kartə] f (-/-n) card; postcard; map; chart; ticket; menu, bill of fare; list.

Kartei [kar'taɪ] f (-/-en) card-index; **~karte** f index-card, filing-card; **~schrank** m filing cabinet.

Kartell ✝ [kar'tɛl] n (-s/-e) cartel.

'Karten|brief m letter-card; **'~haus** n ⚓ chart-house; fig. house of cards; **'~legerin** f (-/-nen) fortune-teller from the cards; **'~spiel** n card-playing; card-game.

Kartoffel [kar'tɔfəl] f (-/-n) potato, F spud; **~brei** m mashed potatoes pl.; **~käfer** m Colorado or potato beetle, Am. a. potato bug; **~schalen** f/pl. potato peelings pl.

Karton [kar'tõː, kar'tɔːn] m (-s/-s, -e) cardboard, pasteboard; cardboard box, carton. [Kartei.\]

Kartothek [karto'teːk] f (-/-en) s.\]

Karussell [karu'sɛl] n (-s/-s, -e) roundabout, merry-go-round, Am. a. car(r)ousel.

Karwoche eccl. ['kaːr-] f Holy or Passion Week.

Käse ['kɛːzə] m (-s/-) cheese.

Kasern|e ⚔ [ka'zɛrnə] f (-/-n) barracks pl.; **~enhof** m barrack-yard or -square; **2ieren** [~'niːrən] v/t. (no -ge-, h) quarter in barracks, barrack.

'käsig adj. cheesy; complexion: pale, pasty.

Kasino [ka'ziːno] n (-s/-s) casino, club(-house); (officers') mess.

Kasperle ['kasperlə] n, m (-s/-) Punch; **'~theater** n Punch and Judy show.

Kasse ['kasə] f (-/-n) cash-box; till (in shop, etc.); cash-desk, pay-desk (in bank, etc.); pay-office (in firm); thea., etc.: box-office, booking-office; cash; bei ~ in cash.

'Kassen|abschluß ✝ m balancing of the cash (accounts); **'~anweisung** f disbursement voucher; **'~bestand** m cash in hand; **'~bote** m bank messenger; **'~buch** n cash book; **'~erfolg** m thea., etc.: box-office success; **'~patient** ✚ m panel patient; **'~schalter** m bank, etc.: teller's counter.

Kasserolle [kasə'rɔlə] f (-/-n) stewpan, casserole.

Kassette [ka'sɛtə] f (-/-n) box (for money, etc.); casket (for jewels, etc.); slip-case (for books); phot. plateholder.

kassiere|n [ka'siːrən] (no -ge-, h) 1. v/i. waiter, etc.: take the money (für for); 2. v/t. take (sum of money); collect (contributions, etc.); annul; ⚖ quash (verdict); **2r** m (-s/-) cashier; bank: a. teller; collector.

Kastanie ♀ [ka'staːnjə] f (-/-n) chestnut.

Kasten ['kastən] m (-s/⁐, ⚒ -) box; chest (for tools, etc.); case (for violin, etc.); bin (for bread, etc.).

Kasus gr. ['kaːsus] m (-/-) case.

Katalog [kata'loːk] m (-[e]s/-e) catalogue, Am. a. catalog; **2isieren** [~ogi'ziːrən] v/t. (no -ge-, h) catalogue, Am. a. catalog.

Katarrh ✚ [ka'tar] m (-s/-e) (common) cold, catarrh.

katastroph|al adj. [katastro'faːl] catastrophic, disastrous; **2e** [~'stroːfə] f (-/-n) catastrophe, disaster.

Katechismus eccl. [kate'çismus] m (-/Katechismen) catechism.

Katego|rie [katego'riː] f (-/-n) category; **2risch** adj. [~'goːriʃ] categorical.

Kater ['kaːtər] m (-s/-) zo. male cat, tom-cat; fig. s. Katzenjammer.

Katheder [ka'teːdər] n, m (-s/-) lecturing-desk.   [cathedral.\]

Kathedrale [kate'draːlə] f (-/-n)

Katholi|k [kato'li:k] *m* (-en/-en) (Roman) Catholic; **≗sch** *adj.* [ˌ'~'to:liʃ] (Roman) Catholic.

Kattun [ka'tu:n] *m* (-s/-e) calico; cotton cloth *or* fabric; chintz.

Katze *zo.* ['katsə] *f* (-/-n) cat; '**~n-jammer** F *fig. m* hangover, morning-after feeling.

Kauderwelsch ['kaudərvɛlʃ] *n* (-[s]/ *no pl.*) gibberish, F double Dutch; **'≗en** *v/i.* (ge-, h) gibber, F talk double Dutch. [chew.]

kauen ['kauən] *v/t. and v/i.* (ge-, h)

kauern ['kauərn] (ge-, h) **1.** *v/i.* crouch; squat; **2.** *v/refl.* crouch (down); squat (down); duck (down).

Kauf [kauf] *m* (-[e]s/⸚e) purchase; bargain, F good buy; acquisition; purchasing, buying; '**~brief** *m* deed of purchase; '**≗en** *v/t.* (ge-, h) buy, purchase; acquire (*or* purchase); *sich et.* ~ buy o.s. s.th., buy s.th. for o.s. [purchaser; customer.]

Käufer ['kɔyfər] *m* (-s/-) buyer,

Kauf|haus *n* department store; '**~laden** *m* shop, *Am. a.* store.

käuflich ['kɔyflɪç] **1.** *adj.* for sale; purchasable; *fig.* open to bribery, bribable; venal; **2.** *adv.*: ~ *erwerben* (acquire by) purchase; ~ *überlassen* transfer by way of sale.

'Kauf|mann *m* (-[e]s/*Kaufleute*) businessman; merchant; trader, dealer, shopkeeper; *Am. a.* storekeeper; **≗männisch** *adj.* ['~mɛnɪʃ] commercial, mercantile; '**~vertrag** *m* contract of sale.

'Kaugummi *m* chewing-gum.

kaum *adv.* [kaum] hardly, scarcely, barely; ~ *glaublich* hard to believe.

'Kautabak *m* chewing-tobacco.

Kaution [kau'tsjo:n] *f* (-/-en) security, surety; ⚖ *mst* bail.

Kautschuk ['kautʃuk] *m* (-s/-e) caoutchouc, pure rubber.

Kavalier [kava'li:r] *m* (-s/-e) gentleman; beau, admirer.

Kavallerie ⚔ [kavələ'ri:] *f* (-/-n) cavalry, horse.

Kaviar ['ka:viar] *m* (-s/-e) caviar(e).

keck *adj.* [kɛk] bold; impudent, saucy, cheeky; **≗heit** *f* (-/-en) boldness; impudence, sauciness, cheekiness.

Kegel ['ke:gəl] *m* (-s/-) *games*: skittle, pin; *esp.* ♟, ⊕ cone; ~ *schieben s. kegeln*; '**~bahn** *f* skittle, alley, *Am.* bowling alley; **≗förmig**

adj. ['~fœrmɪç] conic(al), coniform; tapering; **≗n** *v/i.* (ge-, h) play (at) skittles *or* ninepins, *Am.* bowl.

Kegler ['ke:glər] *m* (-s/-) skittleplayer, *Am.* bowler.

Kehl|e ['ke:lə] *f* (-/-n) throat; '**~kopf** *anat. m* larynx.

Kehre ['ke:rə] *f* (-/-n) (sharp) bend; turn; **'≗n** *v/t.* (ge-, h) sweep, brush; turn (*nach oben* upwards); *j-m den Rücken ~* turn one's back on s.o.

Kehricht ['ke:rɪçt] *m*, *n* (-[e]s/ *no pl.*) sweepings *pl.*, rubbish.

'Kehrseite *f* wrong side, reverse; *esp. fig.* seamy side.

'kehrtmachen *v/i.* (sep., -ge-, h) turn on one's heel; ⚔ turn *or* face about. [chide.]

keifen ['kaifən] *v/i.* (ge-, h) scold,)

Keil [kail] *m* (-[e]s/-e) wedge; gore, gusset; '**~e** F *f* (-/ *no pl.*) thrashing, hiding; '**~er** *zo. m* (-s/-) wild-boar; **~erei** F [ˌ'~'rai] *f* (-/-en) row, scrap; **≗förmig** *adj.* ['~fœrmɪç] wedgeshaped, cuneiform; '**~kissen** *n* wedge-shaped bolster; '**~schrift** *f* cuneiform characters *pl.*

Keim [kaim] *m* (-[e]s/-e) ♟, *biol.* germ; ♟: seed-plant; shoot; sprout; *fig.* seeds *pl.*, germ, bud; **'≗en** *v/i.* (ge-, h) germinate; seeds, plants, potatoes, *etc.*: sprout; *fig.* b(o)urgeon; **≗frei** *adj.* sterilized, sterile; '**~träger** ⚕ *m* (germ-)carrier; '**~zelle** *f* germ-cell.

kein *indef. pron.* [kain] *as adj.*: ~(*e*) no, not any; ~ *anderer als* none other but; *as noun*: ~*er*, ~*e*, ~(*e*)*s* none, no one, nobody; ~*er von beiden* neither (of the two); ~*er von uns* none of us; '**~es'falls** *adv.*, **~es-wegs** *adv.* ['~'ve:ks] by no means, not at all; '**~mal** *adv.* not once, not a single time.

Keks [ke:ks] *m*, *n* (-, -es/-, -e) biscuit, *Am.* cookie; cracker.

Kelch [kɛlç] *m* (-[e]s/-e) cup, goblet; *eccl.* chalice, communion-cup; ♟ calyx.

Kelle ['kɛlə] *f* (-/-n) scoop; ladle; *tool*: trowel.

Keller ['kɛlər] *m* (-s/-) cellar; basement; **~ei** [ˌ'~'rai] *f* (-/-en) wine-vault; '**~geschoß** *n* basement; '**~meister** *m* cellarman.

Kellner ['kɛlnər] *m* (-s/-) waiter; '**~in** *f* (-/-nen) waitress.

Kelter ['kɛltər] *f* (-/-n) winepress; **'2n** *v/t.* (ge-, h) press.

kenn|en ['kɛnən] *v/t.* (irr., ge-, h) know, be acquainted with; have knowledge of *s.th.*; **'~enlernen** *v/t.* (sep., -ge-, h) get *or* come to know; make *s.o.'s* acquaintance, meet *s.o.*; **'2er** *m* (-s/-) expert; connoisseur; **'~tlich** *adj.* recognizable (*an dat.* by); **~** *machen* mark; label; **'2t** (-/-se) knowledge; **~** *nehmen von* take not(ic)e of; **'2zeichen** *n* mark, sign; *mot.* registration (number), *Am.* license number; *fig.* hallmark, criterion; **'~zeichnen** *v/t.* (ge-, h) mark, characterize.

kentern ⚓ ['kɛntərn] *v/i.* (ge-, sein) capsize, keel over, turn turtle.

Kerbe ['kɛrbə] *f* (-/-n) notch, nick; slot; **'2n** *v/t.* (ge-, h) notch, nick, indent.

Kerker ['kɛrkər] *m* (-s/-) gaol, jail, prison; **'~meister** *m* gaoler, jailer.

Kerl F [kɛrl] *m* (-s, ⚘ -es/-e, F -s) man; fellow, F chap, bloke, *esp. Am.* guy.

Kern [kɛrn] *m* (-[e]s/-e) kernel (*of nut, etc.*); stone, *Am.* pit (*of cherry, etc.*); pip (*of orange, apple, etc.*); core (*of the earth*); *phys.* nucleus; *fig.* core, heart, crux; *Kern... s. a. Atom...*; **'~energie** *f* nuclear energy; **'~forschung** *f* nuclear research; **'~gehäuse** *n* core; **'2ge'sund** *adj.* thoroughly healthy, F as sound as a bell; **'2ig** *adj.* full of pips; *fig.*: pithy; solid; **'~punkt** *m* central *or* crucial point; **'~spaltung** *f* nuclear fission.

Kerze ['kɛrtsə] *f* (-/-n) candle; **'~nlicht** *n* candle-light; **'~nstärke** *f* candle-power.

keß F *adj.* [kɛs] pert, jaunty; smart.

Kessel ['kɛsəl] *m* (-s/-) kettle; cauldron; boiler; hollow.

Kette ['kɛtə] *f* (-/-n) chain; range (*of mountains, etc.*); necklace; **'2n** *v/t.* (ge-, h) chain (*an acc.* to).

Ketten|hund *m* watch-dog; **'~raucher** *m* chain-smoker; **'~reaktion** *f* chain reaction.

Ketzer ['kɛtsər] *m* (-s/-) heretic; **~ei** [~'raɪ] *f* (-/-en) heresy; **'2isch** *adj.* heretical.

keuch|en ['kɔʏçən] *v/i.* (ge-, h) pant, gasp; **'2husten** ⚘ *m* (w)hooping cough.   [(*of mutton, pork, etc.*).]

Keule ['kɔʏlə] *f* (-/-n) club; leg⟩

keusch *adj.* [kɔʏʃ] chaste, pure; **'2heit** *f* (-/*no pl.*) chastity, purity.

kichern ['kɪçərn] *v/i.* (ge-, h) giggle, titter.

Kiebitz ['ki:bɪts] *m* (-es/-e) *orn.* pe(e)wit; F *fig.* kibitzer; **'2en** F *fig. v/i.* (ge-, h) kibitz.

Kiefer ['ki:fər] **1.** *anat. m* (-s/-) jaw(-bone); **2.** ⚘ *f* (-/-n) pine.

Kiel [ki:l] *m* (-[e]s/-e) ⚓ keel; quill; **'~raum** *m* bilge, hold; **'~wasser** *n* wake (*a. fig.*).

Kieme *zo.* ['ki:mə] *f* (-/-n) gill.

Kies [ki:s] *m* (-es/-e) gravel; *sl. fig.* dough; **'2el** ['~zəl] *m* (-s/-) pebble, flint; **'~weg** *m* gravel-walk.

Kilo ['ki:lo] *n* (-s/-[s]), **~gramm** [kilo'gram] *n* kilogram(me); **~hertz** [~'hɛrts] *n* (-/*no pl.*) kilocycle per second; **~meter** *m* kilomet|re, *Am.* -er; **~watt** *n* kilowatt.

Kimme ['kɪmə] *f* (-/-n) notch.

Kind [kɪnt] *n* (-[e]s/-er) child; baby. **'Kinder|arzt** *m* p(a)ediatrician; **~ei** [~'raɪ] *f* (-/-en) childishness; childish trick; trifle; **'~frau** *f* nurse; **'~fräulein** *n* governess; **'~funk** *m* children's program(me); **'~garten** *m* kindergarten, nursery school; **'~lähmung** ⚘ *f* infantile paralysis, polio(myelitis); **'2leicht** *adj.* very easy *or* simple, F as easy as winking *or* as ABC; **'~lied** *n* children's song; **'2los** *adj.* childless; **'~mädchen** *n* nurse(maid); **'~spiel** *n* children's game; *ein ~ s. kinderleicht*; **'~stube** *f* nursery; *fig.* manners *pl.*, upbringing; **'~wagen** *m* perambulator, F pram, *Am.* baby carriage; **'~zeit** *f* childhood; **'~zimmer** *n* children's room.

'Kindes|alter *n* childhood, infancy; **'~beine** *n/pl.*: *von ~ an* from childhood, from a very early age; **'~kind** *n* grandchild.

'Kind|heit *f* (-/*no pl.*) childhood; **'2isch** *adj.* ['~dɪʃ] childish; **'2lich** *adj.* childlike.

Kinn *anat.* [kɪn] *n* (-[e]s/-e) chin; **'~backe** *f*, **'~backen** *m* (-s/-) jaw(-bone); **'~haken** *m* *boxing:* hook to the chin; uppercut; **'~lade** *f* jaw(-bone).

Kino ['ki:no] *n* (-s/-s) cinema, F *the pictures pl.*, *Am.* motion-picture theater, F *the movies pl.*; *ins ~ gehen* go to the cinema *or* F pictures, *Am.* F go to the movies; **'~besu-**

cher *m* cinema-goer, *Am.* F moviegoer; **~vorstellung** *f* cinema-show, *Am.* motion-picture show.

Kippe F [ˈkipə] *f* (-/-n) stub, fag-end, *Am. a.* butt; *auf der ~ stehen or sein* hang in the balance; '**~n** (*ge-*) **1.** *v/i.* (*sein*) tip (over), topple (over), tilt (over); **2.** *v/t.* (*h*) tilt, tip over *or* up.

Kirche [ˈkirçə] *f* (-/-n) church.

'**Kirchen|älteste** *m* (-n/-n) churchwarden, elder; '**~buch** *n* parochial register; '**~diener** *m* sacristan, sexton; '**~gemeinde** *f* parish; '**~jahr** *n* ecclesiastical year; '**~lied** *n* hymn; '**~musik** *f* sacred music; '**~schiff** △ *n* nave; '**~steuer** *f* church-rate; '**~stuhl** *m* pew; '**~vorsteher** *m* churchwarden.

'**Kirch|gang** *m* church-going; **~gänger** [ˈ~gɛŋər] *m* (-s/-) church-goer; '**~hof** *m* churchyard; '**2lich** *adj.* ecclesiastical; '**~spiel** *n* parish; '**~turm** *m* steeple; **~weih** [ˈ~vaɪ] *f* (-/-en) parish fair.

Kirsche [ˈkirʃə] *f* (-/-n) cherry.

Kissen [ˈkisən] *n* (-s/-) cushion; pillow; bolster, pad.

Kiste [ˈkistə] *f* (-/-n) box, chest, crate.

Kitsch [kitʃ] *m* (-es/*no pl.*) trash, rubbish; '**2ig** *adj.* shoddy, trashy.

Kitt [kit] *m* (-[e]s/-e) cement; putty.

Kittel [ˈkitəl] *m* (-s/-) overall; smock, frock.

'**kitten** *v/t.* (*ge-*, *h*) cement; putt.

kitz|eln [ˈkitsəln] (*ge-*) **1.** *v/t.* tickle; **2.** *v/i.*: *meine Nase kitzelt* my nose is tickling; '**~lig** *adj.* ticklish (*a. fig.*).

Kladde [ˈkladə] *f* (-/-n) rough notebook, waste-book.

klaffen [ˈklafən] *v/i.* (*ge-*, *h*) gape, yawn.

kläffen [ˈklɛfən] *v/i.* (*ge-*, *h*) yap, yelp.

klagbar ɪ̯t̯ *adj.* [ˈklaːkbaːr] *matter, etc.*: actionable; *debt, etc.*: suable.

Klage [ˈklaːgə] *f* (-/-n) complaint; lament; ɪ̯t̯ action, suit; '**2n** (*ge-*, *h*) **1.** *v/i.* complain (*über acc.* of, about; *bei* to); lament; ɪ̯t̯ take legal action (*gegen* against); **2.** *v/t.*: *j-m et. ~* complain to s.o. of *or* about s.th.

Kläger ɪ̯t̯ [ˈklɛːgər] *m* (-s/-) plaintiff; complainant.

kläglich *adj.* [ˈklɛːkliç] pitiful, piteous, pitiable; *cries, etc.*: plaintive; *condition*: wretched, lamentable; *performance, result, etc.*: miserable, poor; *failure, etc.*: lamentable, miserable.

klamm [klam] **1.** *adj.* *hands, etc.*: numb *or* stiff with cold, clammy; **2.** **2** *f* (-/-en) ravine, gorge, canyon.

Klammer [ˈklamər] *f* (-/-n) ⊕ clamp, cramp; (*paper-*)*clip*; *gr., typ.*, Ⓐ bracket, parenthesis; '**2n** (*ge-*, *h*) **1.** *v/t.* clip together; ⚕ close (*wound*) with clips; *sich ~ an* (*acc.*) cling to (*a. fig.*); **2.** *v/i.* boxing: clinch.

Klang [klaŋ] **1.** *m* (-[e]s/ⷎe) sound, tone (*of voice, instrument, etc.*); tone (*of radio, etc.*); clink (*of glasses, etc.*); ringing (*of bells, etc.*); timbre; **2.** ♀ *pret.* of *klingen*; '**2los** *adj.* toneless; '**2voll** *adj.* sonorous.

Klappe [ˈklapə] *f* (-/-n) flap, flap, drop leaf (*of table, etc.*); shoulder strap (*of uniform, etc.*); tailboard (*of lorry, etc.*); ⊕, ♀, *anat.* valve; ♪ key; F *fig.*: bed; trap; '**2n** (*ge-*, *h*) **1.** *v/t.*: *nach oben ~* tip up; *nach unten ~* lower, put down; **2.** *v/i.* clap, flap; *fig.* come off well, work out fine, *Am. sl. a.* click.

Klapper [ˈklapər] *f* (-/-n) rattle; '**2ig** *adj.* *vehicle, etc.*: rattly, ramshackle; *furniture*: rickety; *person, horse, etc.*: decrepit; '**~kasten** F *m* wretched piano; rattletrap; '**2n** *v/i.* (*ge-*, *h*) clatter, rattle (*mit et. s.th.*); *er klapperte vor Kälte mit den Zähnen* his teeth were chattering with cold; '**~schlange** *zo.* *f* rattlesnake, *Am. a.* rattler.

'**Klapp|kamera** *phot.* *f* folding camera; '**~messer** *n* clasp-knife, jack-knife; '**~sitz** *m* tip-up *or* flap seat; '**~stuhl** *m* folding chair; '**~tisch** *m* folding table, *Am. a.* gate-leg(ged) table; **~ult** *f* [ˈklap-pult] *n* folding desk.

Klaps [klaps] *m* (-es/-e) smack, slap; '**2en** *v/t.* (*ge-*, *h*) smack, slap.

klar *adj.* [klaːr] clear; bright; transparent, limpid; pure; *fig.*: clear, distinct; plain; evident, obvious; *sich ~ sein über* (*acc.*) be clear about; *~en Kopf bewahren* keep a clear head.

klären [ˈklɛːrən] *v/t.* (*ge-*, *h*) clarify; *fig.* clarify, clear up, elucidate.

'**klar|legen** v/t. (sep., -ge-, h),
'**~stellen** v/t. (sep., -ge-, h) clear up.
'**Klärung** f (-/-en) clarification; fig. a. elucidation.

Klasse ['klasə] f (-/-n) class, category; school: class, form, Am. a. grade; (social) class.

'**Klassen|arbeit** f (test) paper; '2bewußt adj. class-conscious; '~bewußtsein n class-consciousness; '~buch n class-book; '~haß m class-hatred; '~kamerad m classmate; '~kampf m class-war(fare); '~zimmer n classroom, schoolroom.

klassifizier|en [klasifi'tsi:rən] v/t. (no -ge-, h) classify; 2ung f (-/-en) classification.

Klass|iker ['klasikər] m (-s/-) classic; '2isch adj. classic(al).

klatsch [klatʃ] 1. int. smack!, slap!; 2. 2 m (-es/-e) smack, slap; F fig.: gossip; scandal; 2base ['~ba:zə] f (-/-n) gossip; '2e ['~e (-/-n) fly-flap; '~en (ge-, h) 1. v/t. fling, hurl; Beifall ~ clap, applaud (j-m s.o.) 2. v/i. splash; applaud, clap; F fig. gossip; '~haft adj. gossiping, gossipy; '2maul F n s. Klatschbase; '~naß F adj. soaking wet.

Klaue ['klauə] f (-/-n) claw; paw; fig. clutch.   [cell.]

Klause ['klauzə] f (-/-n) hermitage;

Klausel ['klauzəl] f (-/-n) clause; proviso; stipulation.

Klaviatur ♪ [klavja'tu:r] f (-/-en) keyboard, keys pl.

Klavier ♪ [kla'vi:r] n (-s/-e) piano (-forte); ~konzert n piano concert or recital; ~lehrer m piano teacher; ~sessel m music-stool; ~stimmer m (-s/-) piano-tuner; ~stunde f piano-lesson.

kleb|en ['kle:bən] (ge-, h) 1. v/t. glue, paste, stick; 2. v/i. stick, adhere (an dat. to); '~end adj. adhesive; '2epflaster n adhesive or sticking plaster; '~rig adj. adhesive, sticky; '2stoff m adhesive; glue.

Klecks [kleks] m (-es/-e) blot (of ink); mark (of dirt, grease, paint, etc.); spot (of grease, paint, etc.); stain (of wine, coffee, etc.); '2en (ge-) 1. v/i. (h) make a mark or spot or stain; 2. v/i. (sein) ink, etc.: drip (down); 3. v/t. (h): et. auf et. ~ splash or spill s.th. on s.th.

Klee ♧ [kle:] m (-s/no pl.) clover, trefoil.

Kleid [klaɪt] n (-[e]s/-er) garment; dress, frock; gown; ~er pl. clothes pl.; 2en ['~dən] v/t. (ge-, h) dress, clothe; sich ~ dress (o.s.); j-n gut ~ suit or become s.o.

Kleider|ablage ['klaɪdər-] f cloakroom, Am. a. checkroom; '~bügel m coat-hanger; '~bürste f clothes-brush; '~haken m clothes-peg; '~schrank m wardrobe; '~ständer m hat and coat stand; '~stoff m dress material.

'**kleidsam** adj. becoming.

Kleidung ['klaɪduŋ] f (-/-en) clothes pl., clothing; dress; '~sstück n piece or article of clothing; garment.

Kleie ['klaɪə] f (-/-n) bran.

klein [klaɪn] 1. adj. little (only attr.), small; fig. a. trifling, petty; 2. adv.: ~ schreiben write with a small (initial) letter; ~ anfangen start in a small or modest way; 3. noun: von ~ auf from an early age; '2auto n baby or small car; '2bahn f narrow-ga(u)ge railway; '2bildkamera f miniature camera; '2geld n (small) change; '~gläubig adj. of little faith; '2handel ✝ m retail trade; '2händler m retailer; '2heit f (-/no pl.) smallness, small size; '2holz n firewood, matchwood, kindling.

Kleinigkeit f (-/-en) trifle, triviality; '~skrämer m pettifogger.

'**Klein|kind** n infant; '2laut adj. subdued; '2lich adj. paltry; pedantic, fussy; '~mut m pusillanimity; despondency; '2mütig adj. ['~my:tiç] pusillanimous; despondent; '2schneiden v/t. (irr. schneiden, sep., -ge-, h) cut into small pieces; '~staat m small or minor state; '~stadt f small town; '~städter m small-town dweller, Am. a. small-towner; '2städtisch adj. small-town, provincial; '~vieh n small livestock.

Kleister ['klaɪstər] m (-s/-) paste; '2n v/t. (ge-, h) paste.

Klemm|e ['klɛmə] f (-/-n) ⊕ clamp; ⚡ terminal; F in der ~ sitzen be in a cleft stick, F be in a jam; '2en v/t. (ge-, h) jam, squeeze, pinch; '~er m (-s/-) pince-nez; '~schraube ⊕ f set screw.

Klempner ['klɛmpnər] m (-s/-) tin-man, tin-smith, Am. a. tinner; plumber.

Klerus ['kle:rus] *m* (-/*no pl.*) clergy.

Klette ['klɛtə] *f* (-/-n) ♀ bur(r); *fig. a.* leech.

Kletter|er ['klɛtərər] *m* (-s/-) climber; '**⹂n** *v/i.* (ge-, sein) climb, clamber (*auf e-n Baum* [up] a tree); '**⹂pflanze** *f* climber, creeper.

Klient [kli'ɛnt] *m* (-en/-en) client.

Klima ['kli:ma] *n* (-s/-s, -te) climate; *fig. a.* atmosphere; '**⹂anlage** *f* air-conditioning plant; **⹂tisch** *adj.* [⹂'ma:tiʃ] climatic.

klimpern ['klimpərn] *v/i.* (ge-, h) jingle, chink (*mit et. s.th.*); F strum *or* tinkle away (*auf acc.* on, at *piano, guitar*).

Klinge ['kliŋə] *f* (-/-n) blade.

Klingel ['kliŋəl] *f* (-/-n) bell, hand-bell; '**⹂knopf** *m* bell-push; '**⹂n** *v/i.* (ge-, h) ring (the bell); *doorbell, etc.:* ring; *es klingelt* the doorbell is ringing; '**⹂zug** *m* bell-pull.

klingen ['kliŋən] *v/i.* (irr., ge-, h) sound; *bell, metal, etc.:* ring; *glasses, etc.:* clink; *musical instrument:* speak.

Klini|k ['kli:nik] *f* (-/-en) nursing home; private hospital; clinic(al hospital); '**⹂sch** *adj.* clinical.

Klinke ['kliŋkə] *f* (-/-n) latch; (door-) handle.

Klippe ['klipə] *f* (-/-n) cliff; reef; crag; rock; *fig.* rock, boulder.

klirren ['kliɾən] *v/i.* (ge-, h) *window-pane, chain, etc.:* rattle; *chain, swords, etc.:* clank, jangle; *keys, spurs, etc.:* jingle; *glasses, etc.:* clink, chink; *pots, etc.:* clatter; *~ mit* rattle; jingle.

Klistier ⚕ [kli'sti:r] *n* (-s/-e) enema.

Kloake [klo'a:kə] *f* (-/-n) sewer, cesspool (*a. fig.*).

Klob|en ['klo:bən] *m* (-s/-) ⊕ pulley, block; log; '**⹂ig** *adj.* clumsy (*a. fig.*).

klopfen ['klɔpfən] (ge-, h) **1.** *v/i. heart, pulse:* beat, throb; knock (*at door, etc.*); tap (*on shoulder*); pat (*on cheek*); *es klopft* there's a knock at the door; **2.** *v/t.* knock, drive (*nail, etc.*).

Klöppel ['klœpəl] *m* (-s/-) clapper (*of bell*); *lacemaking:* bobbin; beetle; '**⹂spitze** *f* pillow-lace, bone-lace.

Klops [klɔps] *m* (-es/-e) meat ball.

Klosett [klo'zɛt] *n* (-s/-e, -s) lavatory, (water-)closet, W.C., toilet, **⹂papier** *n* toilet-paper.

Kloß [klo:s] *m* (-es/⸚e) earth, clay, *etc.:* clod, lump; *cookery:* dumpling.

Kloster ['klo:stər] *n* (-s/⸚) cloister; monastery; convent, nunnery; '**⹂bruder** *m* friar; '**⹂frau** *f* nun; '**⹂ge-lübde** *n* monastic vow.

Klotz [klɔts] *m* (-es/⸚e) block, log (*a. fig.*).

Klub [klup] *m* (-s/-s) club; '**⹂kame-rad** *m* clubmate; '**⹂sessel** *m* lounge-chair.

Kluft [kluft] *f* **1.** (-/⸚e) gap (*a. fig.*), crack; cleft; gulf, chasm (*both a. fig.*); **2.** F (-/-en) outfit, F togs *pl.;* uniform.

klug *adj.* [klu:k] clever; wise, intelligent, sensible; prudent; shrewd; cunning; '**2heit** *f* (-/*no pl.*) clever-ness; intelligence; prudence; shrewdness; good sense.

Klump|en ['klumpən] *m* (-s/-) lump (*of earth, dough, etc.*); clod (*of earth, etc.*); nugget (*of gold, etc.*); heap; '**⹂fuß** *m* club-foot; '**2ig** *adj.* lumpy; cloddish.

knabbern ['knabərn] (ge-, h) **1.** *v/t.* nibble, gnaw; **2.** *v/i.* nibble, gnaw (*an dat.* at).

Knabe ['kna:bə] *m* (-n/-n) boy; lad; F *älter.~* F old chap.

'**Knaben|alter** *n* boyhood; '**⹂chor** *m* boys' choir; '**2haft** *adj.* boyish.

Knack [knak] *m* (-[e]s/-e) crack, snap, click; '**2en** (ge-, h) **1.** *v/t. wood:* crack; *fire:* crackle; click; **2.** *v/t.* crack (*nut, etc.*); F crack open (*safe*); *e-e harte Nuß zu ~ haben* have a hard nut to crack; '**⹂s** [⹂s] *m* (-es/-e) *s* Knack; F *fig.* defect; '**2en** *v/i. clapper, etc.:* s. *knacken* 1.

Knall [knal] *m* (-[e]s/-e) crack, bang (*of shot*); bang (*of explosion*); crack (*of rifle or whip*); report (*of gun*); detonation, explosion, report; '**⹂bonbon** *m, n* cracker; '**⹂effekt** *fig. m* sensation; '**2en** *v/i.* (ge-, h) *rifle, whip:* crack; *fireworks, door, etc.:* bang; *gun:* fire; *cork, etc.:* pop; *explosive, etc.:* detonate.

knapp *adj.* [knap] *clothes:* tight, close-fitting; *rations, etc.:* scanty, scarce; *style, etc.:* concise; *lead, victory, etc.:* narrow; *majority, etc.:* bare; *mit ⹂er Not* entrinnen have a narrow escape; *~ werden* run short; '**2e** ⚒ *m* (-n/-n) miner; '**2halten** *v/t.* (irr. halten, sep., -ge-, h) keep *s.o.* short; '**2heit** *f* (-/*no pl.*) scarcity, shortage; conciseness; '~schaft ⚒ f (-/-en) miners' society.

Knarre ['knarə] f (-/-n) rattle; F rifle, gun; '2n v/i. (ge-, h) creak; *voice*: grate.

knattern ['knatərn] v/i. (ge-, h) crackle; *machine-gun, etc.*: rattle; *mot.* roar.

Knäuel ['knɔʏəl] m, n (-s/-) clew, ball; *fig.* bunch, cluster.

Knauf [knauf] m (-[e]s/¨e) knob, pommel (*of sword*).

Knauser ['knauzər] m (-s/-) niggard, miser, skinflint; ~ei [~'raɪ] f (-/-en) niggardliness, miserliness; '2ig adj. niggardly, stingy; '2n v/i. (ge-, h) be stingy.

Knebel ['kne:bəl] m (-s/-) gag; '2n v/t. (ge-, h) gag; *fig.* muzzle (*press*).

Knecht [knɛçt] m (-[e]s/-e) servant; farm-labo(u)rer, farm-hand; slave; '2en v/t. (ge-, h) enslave; tyrannize; subjugate; '~schaft f (-/no pl.) servitude, slavery.

kneif|en ['knaɪfən] (*irr.*, ge-, h) **1.** v/t. pinch, nip; **2.** v/i. pinch; F *fig.* back out, *Am.* F *a.* crawfish; '2er m (-s/-) pince-nez; '2zange f (e-e a pair of) pincers pl. or nippers pl.

Kneipe ['knaɪpə] f (-/-n) public house, tavern, F pub, *Am. a.* saloon; '2n v/i. (ge-, h) carouse, tipple, F booze; ~rei f (-/-en) drinking-bout, carousal.

kneten ['kne:tən] v/t. (ge-, h) knead (*dough, etc.*); 🩺 *a.* massage (*limb, etc.*).

Knick [knik] m (-[e]s/-e) *wall, etc.*: crack; *paper, etc.*: fold, crease; *path, etc.*: bend; '2en v/t. (ge-, h) fold, crease; bend; break.   [Knauser.\

Knicker F ['knikər] m (-s/-) s.J

Knicks [kniks] m (-es/-e) curts(e)y; e-n ~ machen = '2en v/i. (ge-, h) (drop a) curts(e)y (*vor dat.* to).

Knie [kni:] n (-s/-) knee; '2fällig adv. on one's knees; '~kehle anat. f hollow of the knee; '2n v/i. (ge-, h) kneel, be on one's knees; '~scheibe anat. f knee-cap, knee-pan; '~strumpf m knee-length sock.

Kniff [knif] m **1.** (-[e]s/-e) crease, fold; *fig.* trick, knack; **2.** 2 *pret. of* kneifen; 2(e)lig adj. ['~(ə)liç] tricky; intricate.

knipsen ['knipsən] (ge-, h) **1.** v/t.

clip, punch (*ticket, etc.*); F *phot.* take a snapshot of, snap; **2.** F *phot.* v/i. take snapshots.

Knirps [knirps] m (-es/-e) little man; little chap, F nipper; '2ig adj. very small.

knirschen ['knirʃən] v/i. (ge-, h) *gravel, snow, etc.*: crunch, grind; *teeth, etc.*: grate; mit den Zähnen ~ grind or gnash one's teeth.

knistern ['knistərn] v/i. (ge-, h) *woodfire, etc.*: crackle; *dry leaves, silk, etc.*: rustle.

knitter|frei adj. ['knitər-] crease-resistant; '2n v/t. and v/i. (ge-, h) crease, wrinkle.

Knoblauch ♣ ['kno:plaux] m (-[e]s/no pl.) garlic.

Knöchel anat. ['knœçəl] m (-s/-) knuckle; ankle.

Knoch|en anat. ['knɔxən] m (-s/-) bone; '~enbruch m fracture (of a bone); '2ig adj. bony.

Knödel ['knø:dəl] m (-s/-) dumpling.

Knolle ♣ ['knɔlə] f (-/-n) tuber; bulb.

Knopf [knɔpf] m (-[e]s/¨e) button.

knöpfen ['knœpfən] v/t. (ge-, h) button.

'**Knopfloch** n buttonhole.

Knorpel ['knɔrpəl] m (-s/-) cartilage, gristle.

Knorr|en ['knɔrən] m (-s/-) knot, knag, gnarl; '2ig adj. gnarled, knotty.

Knospe ♣ ['knɔspə] f (-/-n) bud; '2n v/i. (ge-, h) (be in) bud.

Knot|en ['kno:tən] **1.** m (-s/-) knot (*a. fig.,* ⚓); **2.** 2 v/t. (ge-, h) knot; '~enpunkt m ⊕ junction; intersection; '2ig adj. knotty.

Knuff F [knuf] m (-[e]s/¨e) poke, cuff, nudge; '2en F v/t. (ge-, h) poke, cuff, nudge.

knülle|n ['knʏlən] v/t. and v/i. (ge-, h) crease, crumple; '2r F m (-s/-) hit.

knüpfen ['knʏpfən] v/t. (ge-, h) make, tie (*knot, etc.*); make (*net*); knot (*carpet, etc.*); tie (*shoe-lace, etc.*); strike up (*friendship, etc.*); attach (*condition, etc.*) (*an acc.* to).

Knüppel ['knʏpəl] m (-s/-) cudgel.

knurren ['knurən] v/i. (ge-, h) growl, snarl; *fig.* grumble (*über acc.* at, over, about); *stomach*: rumble.

knusp(e)rig adj. ['knusp(ə)riç] crisp, crunchy.

Knute ['knuːtə] f (-/-n) knout.

Knüttel ['knʏtəl] m (-s/-) cudgel.

Kobold ['koːbɔlt] m (-[e]s/-e) (hob-)goblin, imp.

Koch [kɔx] m (-[e]s/⸚e) cook; '~buch n cookery-book, Am. cookbook; '2en (ge-) 1. v/t. boil (water, egg, fish, etc.); cook (meat, vegetables, etc.) (by boiling); make (coffee, tea, etc.); 2. v/i. water, etc.: boil (a. fig.); do the cooking; be a (good, etc.) cook; '~er m (-s/-) cooker.

Köcher ['kœçər] m (-s/-) quiver.

Koch|kiste f haybox; '~löffel m wooden spoon; '~nische f kitchenette; '~salz n common salt; '~topf m pot, saucepan.

Köder ['køːdər] m (-s/-) bait (a. fig.); lure (a. fig.); '2n v/t. (ge-, h) bait; lure; fig. a. decoy.

Kodex ['koːdɛks] m (-es, -/-e, Kodizes) code.

Koffer ['kɔfər] m (-s/-) (suit)case; trunk; '~radio n portable radio (set).

Kognak ['kɔnjak] m (-s/-s, ⚡ -e) French brandy, cognac.

Kohl ⚘ [koːl] m (-[e]s/-e) cabbage.

Kohle ['koːlə] f (-/-n) coal; charcoal; ⚡ carbon; wie auf (glühenden) ~n sitzen be on tenterhooks.

Kohlen|bergwerk n coal-mine, coal-pit, colliery; '~eimer m coalscuttle; '~händler m coal-merchant; '~kasten m coal-box; '~revier ⚒ n coal-district; '~säure ⚗ f carbonic acid; '~stoff ⚛ m carbon.

Kohle|papier n carbon paper; '~zeichnung f charcoal-drawing.

Kohl|kopf ⚘ m (head of) cabbage; '~rübe ⚘ f Swedish turnip.

Koje ⚓ ['koːjə] f (-/-n) berth, bunk.

Kokain [koka'iːn] n (-s/no pl.) cocaine, sl. coke, snow.

kokett adj. [ko'kɛt] coquettish; 2erie [~ə'riː] f (-/-n) coquetry, coquettishness; ~ieren [~'tiːrən] v/i. (no -ge-, h) coquet, flirt (mit with; a. fig.).

Kokosnuß ⚘ ['koːkɔs-] f coconut.

Koks [koːks] m (-es/-e) coke.

Kolben ['kɔlbən] m (-s/-) butt (of rifle); ⊕ piston; '~stange f piston-rod.

Kolchose [kɔl'çoːzə] f (-/-n) collective farm, kolkhoz.

Kolleg univ. [kɔ'leːk] n (-s/-s, -ien) course of lectures; '~e [~gə] m (-n/-n) colleague; '~ium [~gjum] n (-s/Kollegien) council, board; teaching staff.

Kollekt|e eccl. [kɔ'lɛktə] f (-/-n) collection; ~ion [~'tsjoːn] f (-/-en) collection, range.

Koller ['kɔlər] m (-s/-) vet. staggers pl.; F fig. rage, tantrum; '2n v/i. 1. (h) turkey-cock: gobble; pigeon: coo; bowels: rumble; vet. have the staggers; 2. (sein) ball, tears, etc.: roll.

kolli|dieren [kɔli'diːrən] v/i. (no -ge-, sein) collide; fig. clash; 2sion [~'zjoːn] f (-/-en) collision; fig. clash, conflict.

Kölnischwasser ['kœlniʃ-] n eau-de-Cologne.

Kolonialwaren [koloʹnjaː-] f/pl. groceries pl.; '~händler m grocer; '~handlung f grocer's (shop), Am. grocery.

Kolon|ie [koloʹniː] f (-/-n) colony; 2isieren [~i'ziːrən] v/t. (no -ge-, h) colonize.

Kolonne [koʹlɔnə] f (-/-n) column; convoy; gang (of workers, etc.).

kolorieren [koloʹriːrən] v/t. (no -ge-, h) colo(u)r.

Kolo|ß [koʹlɔs] m (Kolosses/Kolosse) colossus; 2ssal adj. [~'saːl] colossal, huge (both a. fig.).

Kombin|ation [kɔmbinaʹtsjoːn] f (-/-en) combination; overall; ⚡ flying-suit; football, etc.: combined attack; 2ieren [~'niːrən] (no -ge-, h) 1. v/t. combine; 2. v/i. reason, deduce; football, etc.: combine, move.

Kombüse ⚓ [kɔmʹbyːzə] f (-/-n) galley, caboose. [comet.]

Komet ast. [koʹmeːt] m (-en/-en)]

Komfort [kɔmʹfoːr] m (-s/no pl.) comfort; 2abel adj. [~ɔrʹtaːbəl] comfortable.

Komik ['koːmik] f (-/no pl.) humo(u)r, fun(niness); '~er m (-s/-) comic actor, comedian.

komisch adj. ['koːmiʃ] comic(al), funny; fig. funny, odd, queer.

Komitee [komiʹteː] n (-s/-s) committee.

Kommand|ant ⚔ [kɔmanʹdant] m (-en/-en), ~eur ⚔ [~ʹdøːr] m (-s/-e) commander, commanding officer; 2ieren [~ʹdiːrən] (no -ge-, h) 1. v/i.

order, command, be in command; **2.** *v/t.* ✗ command, be in command of; order; **~itgesellschaft** ✝ [~'dɪːt-] *f* limited partnership; **~o** [~'mando] *n* (-s/-s) ✗ command, order; order(s *pl.*), directive(s *pl.*); ✗ detachment; **~obrücke** ⚓ *f* navigating bridge.

kommen ['kɔmən] *v/i.* (*irr.*, ge-, sein) come; arrive; ~ *lassen* send for *s.o.*, order *s.th.*; *et.* ~ *sehen* foresee; *an die Reihe* ~ it is one's turn; ~ *auf* (*acc.*) think of, hit upon; remember; *zu dem Schluß* ~, *daß* decide that; *hinter et.* ~ find *s.th.* out; *um et.* ~ lose *s.th.*; *zu et.* ~ come by *s.th.*; *wieder zu sich* ~ come round or to; *wie* ~ *Sie dazu!* how dare you!

Komment|ar [kɔmɛn'taːr] *m* (-s/-e) commentary, comment; **~ator** [~tɔr] *m* (-s/-en) commentator; **~ieren** [~'tiːrən] *v/t.* (no -ge-, h) comment on.

Kommissar [kɔmi'saːr] *m* (-s/-e) commissioner; superintendent; *pol.* commissar.

Kommißbrot F [kɔ'mis-] *n* army or ration bread, *Am. a.* G.I. bread.

Kommission [kɔmi'sjoːn] *f* (-/-en) commission (*a.* ✝); committee; **~är** ✝ [~o'nɛːr] *m* (-s/-e) commission agent.

Kommode [kɔ'moːdə] *f* (-/-n) chest of drawers, *Am.* bureau.

Kommunis|mus *pol.* [kɔmu'nismus] *m* (-/no *pl.*) communism; *et.* ~**t** *m* (-en/-en) communist; **2tisch** *adj.* communist(ic).

Komöd|iant [kɔmø'djant] *m* (-en/ -en) comedian; *fig.* play-actor; **~ie** [~'møːdjə] *f* (-/-n) comedy; ~ *spielen* play-act.

Kompagnon ✝ [kɔmpan'jõː] *m* (-s/-s) (business-)partner, associate.

Kompanie ✗ [kɔmpa'niː] *f* (-/-n) company.

Kompaß ['kɔmpas] *m* (*Kompasses/ Kompasse*) compass. [petent.\

kompetent *adj.* [kɔmpe'tɛnt] com-\

komplett *adj.* [kɔm'plɛt] complete.

Komplex [kɔm'plɛks] *m* (-es/-e) complex (*a. psych.*); block (*of houses*).

Kompliment [kɔmpli'mɛnt] *n* (-[e]s/-e) compliment.

Komplize [kɔm'pliːtsə] *m* (-n/-n) accomplice.

komplizier|en [kɔmpli'tsiːrən] *v/t.*

(no -ge-, h) complicate; **~t** *adj. machine, etc.*: complicated; *argument, situation, etc.*: complex; **~er Bruch** ✚ compound fracture.

Komplott [kɔm'plɔt] *n* (-[e]s/-e) plot, conspiracy.

kompo|nieren ♩ [kɔmpo'niːrən] *v/t. and v/i.* (no -ge-, h) compose; **2nist** *m* (-en/-en) composer; **2sition** [~zi'tsjoːn] *f* (-/-en) composition.

Kompott [kɔm'pɔt] *n* (-[e]s/-e) compote, stewed fruit, *Am. a.* sauce.

komprimieren [kɔmpri'miːrən] *v/t.* (no -ge-, h) compress.

Kompromi|ß [kɔmpro'mis] *m* (*Kompromisses/Kompromisse*) compromise; **2los** *adj.* uncompromising; **2ttieren** [~'tiːrən] *v/t.* (no -ge-, h) compromise.

Kondens|ator [kɔndɛn'zaːtɔr] *m* (-s/-en) ⚡ capacitor, condenser (*a.* ⚛); **2ieren** [~'ziːrən] *v/t.* (no -ge-, h) condense.

Kondens|milch [kɔn'dɛns-] *f* evaporated milk; **~streifen** ✈ *m* condensation *or* vapo(u)r trail; **~wasser** *n* water of condensation.

Konditor [kɔn'diːtɔr] *m* (-s/-en) confectioner, pastry-cook; **~ei** [~ito'raɪ] *f* (-/-en) confectionery, confectioner's (shop); **~eiwaren** *f/pl.* confectionery.

Konfekt [kɔn'fɛkt] *n* (-[e]s/-e) sweets *pl.*, sweetmeat, *Am. a.* soft candy; chocolates *pl.*

Konfektion [kɔnfɛk'tsjoːn] *f* (-/-en) (manufacture of) ready-made clothing; **~sanzug** [kɔnfɛk'sjoːns-] *m* ready-made suit; **~sgeschäft** *n* ready-made clothes shop.

Konfer|enz [kɔnfe'rɛnts] *f* (-/-en) conference; **2ieren** [~'riːrən] *v/i.* (no -ge-, h) confer (*über acc.* on).

Konfession [kɔnfe'sjoːn] *f* (-/-en) confession, creed; denomination; **2ell** *adj.* [~o'nɛl] confessional, denominational; **~sschule** [~'sjoːns-] *f* denominational school.

Konfirm|and *eccl.* [kɔnfir'mant] *m* (-en/-en) candidate for confirmation, confirmee; **~ation** [~'tsjoːn] *f* (-/-en) confirmation; **2ieren** [~'miːrən] *v/t.* (no -ge-, h) confirm.

konfiszieren ⚖ [kɔnfis'tsiːrən] *v/t.* (no -ge-, h) confiscate, seize.

Konfitüre [kɔnfi'tyːrə] *f* (-/-n) preserve(s *pl.*), (whole-fruit) jam.

K

Konflikt

Konflikt [kɔn'flikt] *m* (-[e]s/-e) conflict. [*mit* agree *or* concur with.\
konform *adv.* [kɔn'fɔrm]: ~ *gehen*]\
konfrontieren [kɔnfrɔn'tiːrən] *v/t.* (*no* -ge-, h) confront (*mit* with).\
konfus *adj.* [kɔn'fuːs] *p.*, *a. ideas*: muddled; *p.* muddle-headed.\
Kongreß [kɔn'grɛs] *m* (*Kongresses*/*Kongresse*) congress; *Am. parl.* Congress; **~halle** *f* congress hall.\
König ['køːnɪç] *m* (-s/-e) king; **2lich** *adj.* [' køː-] royal; regal; **~reich** [' køː-] *n* kingdom; **~swürde** [' køː-] *f* royal dignity, kingship; '**~tum** *n* (-s/-er) monarchy; kingship.\
Konjugation *gr.* [kɔnjuga'tsjoːn] *f* (-/-en); **2ieren** [ʲ'giːrən] *v/t.* (*no* -ge-, h) conjugate.\
Konjunktiv *gr.* ['kɔnjuŋktiːf] *m* (-s/-e) subjunctive (mood); **~ur** [ʲ'tuːr] *f* (-/-en) trade *or* business cycle; economic *or* business situation.\
konkret *adj.* [kɔn'kreːt] concrete.\
Konkurrent [kɔnku'rɛnt] *m* (-en/-en) competitor, rival.\
Konkurrenz [kɔnku'rɛnts] *f* (-/-en) competition; competitors *pl.*, rivals *pl.*; *sports*: race; **2fähig** *adj.* able to compete; competitive; **~geschäft** *n* rival business *or* firm; **~kampf** *m* competition.\
konkurrieren [kɔnku'riːrən] *v/i.* (*no* -ge-, h) compete (*mit* with; *um* for).\
Konkurs [kɔn'kurs] *m* (-es/-e) bankruptcy, insolvency; failure; ~ *anmelden* file a petition in bankruptcy; *in* ~ *gehen or geraten* become insolvent, go bankrupt; **~erklärung** *f* declaration of insolvency; **~masse** *f* bankrupt's estate; **~verfahren** *n* bankruptcy proceedings *pl.*; **~verwalter** *m* trustee in bankruptcy; liquidator.\
können ['kœnən] **1.** *v/i.* (*irr.*, ge-, h): *ich kann nicht* I can't, I am not able to; **2.** *v/t.* (*irr.*, ge-, h) know, understand; *e-e Sprache* ~ know a language, have command of a language; **3.** *v/aux.* (*irr.*, *no* -ge-, h) be able to *inf.*, be capable of *ger.*; be allowed *or* permitted to *inf.*; *es kann sein* it may be; *du kannst hingehen* you may go there; *er kann schwimmen* he can swim, he knows how to swim; **4.** **2** *n* (-s/*no pl.*) ability; skill; proficiency.

Konnossement [kɔnɔsə'mɛnt] *n* (-[e]s/-e) bill of lading.\
konnte ['kɔntə] *pret. of* können.\
konsequent *adj.* [kɔnze'kvɛnt] consistent; **2z** [ʲ-ts] *f* (-/-en) consistency; consequence; *die ~en ziehen do the only thing one can.*\
konservativ *adj.* [kɔnzerva'tiːf] conservative.\
Konserven [kɔn'zɛrvən] *f/pl.* tinned *or Am.* canned foods *pl.*; **~büchse** *f*, **~dose** *f* tin, *Am.* can; **~fabrik** *f* tinning factory, *esp. Am.* cannery.\
konservieren [kɔnzer'viːrən] *v/t.* (*no* -ge-, h) preserve.\
Konsonant *gr.* [kɔnzo'nant] *m* (-en/-en) consonant.\
Konsortium [kɔn'zɔrtsjum] *n* (-s/*Konsortien*) syndicate.\
konstruieren [kɔnstru'iːrən] *v/t.* (*no* -ge-, h) *gr.* construe; ⊕: construct; design.\
Konstrukteur ⊕ [kɔnstruk'tøːr] *m* (-s/-e) designer; **~tion** ⊕ [ʲ'tsjoːn] *f* (-/-en) construction; **~tionsfehler** ⊕ *m* constructional defect.\
Konsul *pol.* ['kɔnzul] *m* (-s/-n) consul; **~at** *pol.* [ʲ'laːt] *n* (-[e]s/-e) consulate; **2tieren** *v/t.* (*no* -ge-, h) consult, seek *s.o.*'s advice.\
Konsum [kɔn'zuːm] *m* **1.** (-s/*no pl.*) consumption; **2.** (-s/-s) co-operative shop, *Am.* co-operative store, F co-op; **3.** (-s/*no pl.*) consumers' co-operative society, F co-op; **~ent** [ʲ'mɛnt] *m* (-en/-en) consumer; **2ieren** [ʲ'miːrən] *v/t.* (*no* -ge-, h) consume; **~verein** *m* s. Konsum 3.\
Kontakt [kɔn'takt] *m* (-[e]s/-e) contact (*a. ⚡*); *in* ~ *stehen mit* be in contact *or* touch with.\
Kontinent ['kɔntinɛnt] *m* (-[e]s/-e) continent.\
Kontingent [kɔntiŋ'gɛnt] *n* (-[e]s/-e) ⚔ contingent, quota (*a. ✝*).\
Konto ✝ ['kɔnto] *n* (-s/*Konten*, *Kontos*, *Konti*) account; **~auszug** ✝ *m* statement of account; **~korrentkonto** ✝ [ʲkɔ'rɛnt-] *n* current account.\
Kontor [kɔn'toːr] *n* (-s/-e) office; **~ist** [ʲ'rɪst] *m* (-en/-en) clerk.\
Kontrast [kɔn'trast] *m* (-es/-e) contrast.\
Kontrolle [kɔn'trɔlə] *f* (-/-n) control; supervision; check; **2ieren** [ʲ'liːrən] *v/t.* (*no* -ge-, h) control; supervise; check.

Kontroverse [kɔntro'vɛrzə] f (-/-n) controversy.

konventionell adj. [kɔnvɛntsjo'nɛl] conventional.

Konversation [kɔnvɛrza'tsjo:n] f (-/-en) conversation; **∼slexikon** n encyclop(a)edia.

Konzentr|ation [kɔntsɛntra'tsjo:n] f (-/-en) concentration; **2ieren** [∼'tri:rən] v/t. (no -ge-, h) concentrate, focus (attention, etc.) (auf acc. on); sich ∼ concentrate (auf acc. on).

Konzern ✝ [kɔn'tsɛrn] m (-s/-e) combine, group.

Konzert ♪ [kɔn'tsɛrt] n (-[e]s/-e) concert; recital; concerto; **∼saal** ♪ m concert-hall.

Konzession [kɔntsɛ'sjo:n] f (-/-en) concession; licen|ce, Am. -se; **2ieren** [∼o'ni:rən] v/t. (no -ge-, h) license.

Kopf [kɔpf] m (-[e]s/⸚e) head; top; brains pl.; pipe: bowl; ein fähiger ∼ a clever fellow; ∼ hoch! chin up!; j-m über den ∼ wachsen outgrow s.o.; fig. get beyond s.o.; **'∼arbeit** f brain-work; **'∼bahnhof** 🚂 m terminus, Am. terminal; **'∼bedeckung** f headgear, headwear.

köpfen ['kœpfən] v/t. (ge-, h) behead, decapitate; football: head (ball).

'Kopf|ende n head; **'∼hörer** m headphone, headset; **'∼kissen** n pillow; **2los** adj. headless; fig. confused; **'∼nicken** n (-s/no pl.) nod; **'∼rechnen** n (-s/no pl.) mental arithmetic; **'∼salat** m cabbage-lettuce; **'∼schmerzen** m/pl. headache; **'∼sprung** m header; **'∼tuch** n scarf; **2über** adv. head first, headlong; **'∼weh** n (-[e]s/-e) s. Kopfschmerzen; **'∼zerbrechen** n (-s/no pl.): j-m ∼ machen puzzle s.o.

Kopie [ko'pi:] f(-/-n) copy; duplicate; phot., film: print; **∼rstift** m indelible pencil.

Koppel ['kɔpəl] 1. f (-/-n) hounds: couple; horses: string; paddock; 2. ✗ n (-s/-) belt; **2n** v/t. (ge-, h) couple (a. ⊕, ✈).

Koralle [ko'ralə] f (-/-n) coral; **∼n-fischer** m coral-fisher.

Korb [kɔrp] m (-[e]s/⸚e) basket; fig. refusal; Hahn im ∼ cock of the walk; **'∼möbel** n/pl. wicker furniture.

Kordel ['kɔrdəl] f (-/-n) string,

Korinthe [ko'rintə] f (-/-n) currant.

Kork [kɔrk] m (-[e]s/-e), **'∼en** m (-s/-) cork; **'∼(en)zieher** m (-s/-) corkscrew.

Korn [kɔrn] 1. n (-[e]s/⸚er) seed; grain; 2. n (-[e]s/-e) corn, cereals pl.; 3. n (-[e]s/🔩-e) front sight; 4. F m (-[e]s/-) (German) corn whisky.

körnig adj. ['kœrniç] granular; in compounds: ...-grained.

Körper ['kœrpər] m (-s/-) body (a. phys., ⚗); 🜂 solid; **'∼bau** m build, physique; **2behindert** adj. ['∼bə-hindərt] (physically) disabled, handicapped; **'∼beschaffenheit** f constitution, physique; **'∼fülle** f corpulence; **'∼geruch** m body-odo(u)r; **'∼größe** f stature; **'∼kraft** f physical strength; **2lich** adj. physical; corporal; bodily; **'∼pflege** f care of the body, hygiene; **'∼schaft** f (-/-en) body; 🏛 corporation; **'∼verletzung** 🏛 f bodily harm, physical injury.

korrekt adj. [ko'rɛkt] correct; **2or** [∼ɔr] m (-s/-en) (proof-)reader; **2ur** [∼'tu:r] f (-/-en) correction; **2ur-bogen** m proof-sheet.

Korrespond|ent [kɔrɛspɔn'dɛnt] m (-en/-en) correspondent; **∼enz** [∼ts] f (-/-en) correspondence; **2ieren** [∼'di:rən] v/i. (no -ge-, h) correspond (mit with).

korrigieren [kɔri'gi:rən] v/t. (no -ge-, h) correct.

Korsett [kɔr'zɛt] n (-[e]s/-e, -s) corset, stays pl.

Kosename ['ko:zə-] m pet name.

Kosmetik [kɔs'me:tik] f (-/no pl.) beauty culture; **∼erin** f (-/-nen) beautician, cosmetician.

Kost [kɔst] f (-/no pl.) food, fare; board; diet; **2bar** adj. present, etc.: costly, expensive; health, time, etc.: valuable; mineral, etc.: precious.

'kosten¹ v/t. (ge-, h) taste, try, sample.

'Kosten² 1. pl. cost(s pl.); expense(s pl.), charges pl.; auf ∼ (gen.) at the expense of; 2. 2 v/t. (ge-, h) cost; take, require (time, etc.); **'∼anschlag** m estimate, tender; **2frei** 1. adj. free; 2. adv. free of charge; **2los** s. kostenfrei.

Kost|gänger ['kɔstgɛŋər] m (-s/-) boarder; **'∼geld** n board-wages pl.

köstlich adj. ['kœstliç] delicious.

'Kost|probe f taste, sample (a. fig.); 'Sspielig adj. ['~ʃpiːliç] expensive, costly.

Kostüm [kɔsˈtyːm] n (-s/-e) costume, dress; suit; ~fest n fancy-dress ball.

Kot [koːt] m (-[e]s/no pl.) mud, mire; excrement.

Kotelett [kotˈ(ə)ˈlet] n (-[e]s/-s, ⚓ -e) pork, veal, lamb: cutlet; pork, veal, mutton: chop; ~en pl. sidewhiskers pl., Am. a. sideburns pl.

'Kot|flügel mot. m mudguard, Am. a. fender; 'Sig adj. muddy, miry.

Krabbe zo. ['krabə] f (-/-n) shrimp; crab.

krabbeln ['krabəln] v/i. (ge-, sein) crawl.

Krach [krax] m (-[e]s/-e, -s) crack, crash (a. ✝); quarrel, sl. bust-up; F row; ~ machen kick up a row; 'Sen v/i. (ge-) 1. (h) thunder: crash; cannon: roar, thunder; 2. (sein) crash (a. ✝), smash.

krächzen ['kreçtsən] v/t. and v/i. (ge-, h) croak.

Kraft [kraft] 1. f (-/⁔e) strength; force (a. ⚔); power (a. ⚡, ⊕); energy; vigo(u)r; efficacy; in ~ sein (setzen, treten) be in (put into, come into) operation or force; außer ~ setzen repeal, abolish (law); 2. ⚗ prp. (gen.) by virtue of; '~anlage ⚡ f power plant; '~brühe f beef tea; '~fahrer m driver, motorist; '~fahrzeug n motor vehicle.

kräftig adj. ['kreftiç] strong (a. fig.), powerful; fig. nutritious, rich; ~en ['~gən] (ge-, h) 1. v/t. strengthen; 2. v/i. give strength.

'kraft|los adj. powerless; feeble; weak; 'Sprobe f trial of strength; 'Srad n motor cycle; 'Sstoff mot. m fuel; '~voll adj. powerful (a. fig.); 'Swagen m motor vehicle; 'Swerk ⚡ n power station.

Kragen ['kraːgən] m (-s/-) collar; '~knopf m collar-stud, Am. collar button.

Krähe orn. ['kreːə] f (-/-n) crow; 'Sn v/i. (ge-, h) crow.

Kralle ['kralə] f (-/-n) claw (a. fig.); talon, clutch.

Kram [kraːm] m (-[e]s/no pl.) stuff, odds and ends pl.; fig. affairs pl., business.

Krämer ['kreːmər] m (-s/-) shop-keeper.

Krampf ⚕ [krampf] m (-[e]s/⁔e) cramp; spasm, convulsion; '~ader ⚕ f varicose vein; 'Shaft adj. ⚕ spasmodic, convulsive; laugh: forced.

Kran ⊕ [kraːn] m (-[e]s/⁔e, -e) crane.

krank adj. [kraŋk] sick; organ, etc.: diseased; ~ sein p. be ill, esp. Am. be sick; animal: be sick or ill; ~ werden p. fall ill or esp. Am. sick; animal: fall sick; 'Se m, f (-n/-n) sick person, patient, invalid.

kränkeln ['kreŋkəln] v/i. (ge-, h) be sickly, be in poor health.

kranken fig. v/i. (ge-, h) suffer (an dat. from).

kränken ['kreŋkən] v/t. (ge-, h) offend, injure; wound or hurt s.o.'s feelings; sich ~ feel hurt (über acc. at, about).

'Kranken|bett n sick-bed; '~geld n sick-benefit; '~haus n hospital; '~kasse f health insurance (fund); '~kost f invalid diet; '~lager n s. Krankenbett; '~pflege f nursing; '~pfleger m male nurse; '~schein m medical certificate; '~schwester f (sick-)nurse; '~versicherung f health or sickness insurance; '~wagen m ambulance; '~zimmer n sick-room.

'krank|haft adj. morbid, pathological; 'Sheit f (-/-en) illness, sickness; disease.

'Krankheits|erreger ⚕ m pathogenic agent; '~erscheinung f symptom (a. fig.).

'kränklich adj. sickly, ailing.

'Kränkung f (-/-en) insult, offen|ce, Am. -se.

Kranz [krants] m (-es/⁔e) wreath; garland.

Kränzchen fig. ['krentsçən] n (-s/-) tea-party, F hen-party.

kraß adj. [kras] crass, gross.

kratzen ['kratsən] (ge-, h) 1. v/i. scratch; 2. v/t. scratch; sich ~ scratch (o.s.).

kraulen ['kraulən] (ge-, h) 1. v/t. (h) scratch gently; 2. v/i. (sein) sports: crawl.

kraus adj. [kraus] curly, curled; crisp; frizzy; die Stirn ~ ziehen knit one's brow; 'Se f (-/-n) ruff(le), frill.

kräuseln ['krɔyzəln] v/t. (ge-, h) curl, crimp (hair, etc.); pucker *(lips)*; *sich ~ hair*: curl; *waves, etc.*: ruffle; *smoke*: curl *or* wreath up.

Kraut ♀ [kraʊt] *n* **1.** (-[e]s/⸗er) plant; herb; **2.** (-[e]s/*no pl.*) tops *pl.*; cabbage; weed.

Krawall [kra'val] *m* -[e]s/-e riot; shindy, F row, s. rumpus.

Krawatte [kra'vatə] *f* (-/-n) (neck-)tie.

Kreatur [krea'tuːr] *f* (-/-en) creature.

Krebs [kreːps] *m* (-es/-e) *zo.* crayfish, *Am. a.* crawfish; *ast.* Cancer, Crab; *✠* cancer; *~e pl.* ✝ returns *pl.*

Kredit ✝ [kre'diːt] *m* (-[e]s/-e) credit; *auf ~* on credit; **2fähig** ✝ *adj.* credit-worthy.

Kreide ['kraɪdə] *f* (-/-n) chalk; *paint.* crayon.

Kreis [kraɪs] *m* (-es/-e) circle *(a.fig.)*; *ast.* orbit; *⚡* circuit; district, *Am.* county; *fig.*: sphere, field; range.

kreischen ['kraɪʃən] (ge-, h) **1.** *v/i.* screech, scream; squeal, shriek; *circular saw, etc.*: grate (on the ear); **2.** *v/t.* shriek, screech *(insult, etc.)*.

Kreisel ['kraɪzəl] *m* (-s/-) (whipping-)top; **'~kompaß** *m* gyro-compass.

kreisen ['kraɪzən] *v/i.* (ge-, h) (move in a) circle; revolve, rotate; *✈*, *bird*: circle; *bird*: wheel; *blood, money*: circulate.

kreis|förmig *adj.* ['kraɪsfœrmiç] circular; **'2lauf** *m physiol., money, etc.*: circulation; *business, trade*: cycle; **'2laufstörungen** *✠ f/pl.* circulatory trouble; **'~rund** *adj.* circular; **'2säge** ⊕ *f* circular saw, *Am. a.* buzz saw; **'2verkehr** *m* roundabout (traffic).

Krempe ['krɛmpə] *f* (-/-n) brim *(of hat)*.

Krempel F ['krɛmpəl] *m* (-s/*no pl.*) rubbish, stuff, lumber.

krepieren [kre'piːrən] *v/i.* (*no -ge-, sein*) *shell*: burst, explode; *sl.* kick the bucket, peg *or* snuff out; *animal*: die, perish.

Krepp [krɛp] *m* (-s/-s, -e) crêpe; crape; **~apier** ['krɛppapiːr] *n* crêpe paper; **'~sohle** *f* crêpe(-rubber) sole.

Kreuz [krɔʏts] **1.** *n* (-es/-e) cross *(a. fig.)*; crucifix; *anat.* small of the back; *cards*: club(s *pl.*); ♪ sharp; *zu ~(e) kriechen eat*

humble pie; **2.** ♀ *adv.*: *~ und quer* in all directions; criss-cross.

'kreuzen (ge-, h) **1.** *v/t.* cross, fold *(arms, etc.)*; ♀, *zo.* cross(-breed), hybridize; *sich ~ roads*: cross, intersect; *plans, etc.*: clash; **2.** *⚓ v/i.* cruise.

'Kreuzer *⚓ m* (-s/-) cruiser.

'Kreuz|fahrer *hist. m* crusader; **'~fahrt** *f hist.* crusade; *⚓* cruise; **'~feuer** *n* ✕ cross-fire *(a. fig.)*; **2igen** ['krɔʏigən] *v/t.* (ge-, h) crucify; **'~igung** *f* (-/-en) crucifixion; **'~otter** *zo. f* common viper; **'~ritter** *hist. m* knight of the Cross; **'~schmerzen** *m/pl.* back ache; **'~spinne** *zo. f* garden- *or* cross-spider; **'~ung** *f* (-/-en) 🚗, roads, etc.: crossing, intersection; *roads*: crossroads; ♀, *zo.* cross-breeding, hybridization; **'~verhör** *🏛 n* cross-examination; *ins ~ nehmen* cross-examine; **'2weise** *adv.* crosswise, crossways; **'~worträtsel** *n* cross-word (puzzle); **'~zug** *hist. m* crusade.

kriech|en ['kriːçən] *v/i.* (*irr.*, ge-, *sein*) creep, crawl; *fig.* cringe *(vor dat.* to, before); **'2er** *contp. m* (-s/-) toady; **2erei** *contp.* [.~'raɪ] *f* (-/-en) toadyism.

Krieg [kriːk] *m* (-[e]s/-e) war; *im ~* at war; *s. führen.*

kriegen F ['kriːgən] *v/t.* (ge-, h) catch, seize; get.

Krieg|er ['kriːgər] *m* (-s/-) warrior; **'~erdenkmal** *n* war memorial; **'2erisch** *adj.* warlike; militant; **'2führend** *adj.* belligerent; **'~führung** *f* warfare.

'Kriegs|beil *fig. n: das ~ begraben* bury the hatchet; **2beschädigt** *adj.* ['.~bəʃeːdiçt] war-disabled; **'~beschädigte** *m* (-n/-n) disabled ex-serviceman; **'~dienst** ✕ *m* war service; **'~dienstverweigerer** *m* (-s/-) conscientious objector; **'~erklärung** *f* declaration of war; **'~flotte** *f* naval force; **'~gefangene** *m* prisoner of war; **'~gefangenschaft** *f* captivity; **'~gericht** *🏛 n* court martial; **'~gewinnler** ['.~gəvinlər] *m* (-s/-) war profiteer; **'~hafen** *m* naval port; **'~kamerad** *m* wartime comrade; **'~list** *f* stratagem; **'~macht** *f* military forces *pl.*; **'~minister** *hist. m* minister of war; Secretary of State for War,

Am. Secretary of War; '**~ministerium** *hist. n* ministry of war; War Office, *Am.* War Department; '**~rat** *m* council of war; '**~schauplatz** ✕ *m* theat|re *or Am.* -er of war; '**~schiff** *n* warship; '**~schule** *f* military academy; '**~teilnehmer** *m* combatant; ex-serviceman, *Am.* veteran; '**~treiber** *m* (-s/-) warmonger; '**~verbrecher** *m* war criminal; '**~zug** *m* (military) expedition, campaign.

Kriminal|beamte [krimi'nɑːl-] *m* criminal investigator, *Am.* plainclothes man; '**~film** *m* crime film; thriller; **~polizei** *f* criminal investigation department; **~roman** *m* detective *or* crime novel, thriller, *sl.* whodun(n)it.

kriminell *adj.* [krimi'nel] criminal; ℒe *m* (-n/-n) criminal.

Krippe ['krɪpə] *f* (-/-n) crib, manger; crèche.

Krise ['kriːzə] *f* (-/-n) crisis.

Kristall [kris'tal] **1.** *m* (-s/-e) crystal; **2.** *n* (-s/*no pl.*) crystal(-glass); ℒ**isieren** [ˌi'zi:rən] *v/i.* and *v/refl.* (no -ge-, *h*) crystallize.

Kriti|k [kri'tiːk] *f* (-/-en) criticism; ♪, *thea.*, etc.: review, criticism; F *unter aller* ~ beneath contempt; ~ *üben an* (*dat.*) *s.* kritisieren; '**~ker** ['kriːtikər] *m* (-s/-) critic; *books:* reviewer; ℒ**sch** *adj.* ['kriːtiʃ] critical (*gegenüber* of); ℒ**sieren** [kriti'ziːrən] *v/t.* (no -ge-, *h*) criticize; review (*book*).

kritt|eln ['kritəln] *v/t.* (ge-, *h*) find fault (*an dat.* with), cavil (at); ℒ**ler** ['~lər] *m* (-s/-) fault-finder, caviller.

Kritzel|ei [kritsə'laɪ] *f* (-/-en) scrawl(ing), scribble, scribbling; '**ℒn** *v/t.* and *v/i.* (ge-, *h*) scrawl, scribble.

kroch [krɔx] *pret. of* kriechen.

Krokodil *zo.* [kroko'diːl] *n* (-s/-e) crocodile.

Krone ['kroːnə] *f* (-/-n) crown; coronet (*of duke, earl, etc.*).

krönen ['krøːnən] *v/t.* (ge-, *h*) crown (*zum König* king) (*a. fig.*).

'**Kron|leuchter** *m* chandelier; lust|re, *Am.* -er; electrolier; '**~prinz** *m* crown prince; '**~prinzessin** *f* crown princess.

'**Krönung** *f* (-/-en) coronation, crowning; *fig.* climax, culmination.

'**Kronzeuge** ⚖ *m* chief witness;

King's evidence, *Am.* State's evidence.

Kropf ⚕ [krɔpf] goit|re, *Am.* -er.

Kröte *zo.* ['krøːtə] *f* (-/-n) toad.

Krücke ['krykə] *f* (-/-n) crutch.

Krug [kruːk] *m* (-[e]s/⁏e) jug, pitcher; jar; mug; tankard.

Krume ['kruːmə] *f* (-/-n) crumb; ✓ topsoil.

Krümel ['kryːməl] *m* (-s/-) small crumb; '**ℒn** *v/t.* and *v/i.* (ge-, *h*) crumble.

krumm *adj.* [krum] *p.* bent, stooping; *limb, nose, etc.:* crooked; *spine:* curved; *deal, business, etc.:* crooked; '**~beinig** *adj.* bandy- *or* bow-legged.

krümmen ['krymən] *v/t.* (ge-, *h*) bend (*arm, back, etc.*); crook (*finger, etc.*); curve (*metal sheet, etc.*); *sich* ~ *person, snake, etc.:* writhe; *worm, etc.:* wriggle; *sich vor Schmerzen* ~ writhe with pain; *sich vor Lachen* ~ be convulsed with laughter.

'**Krümmung** *f* (-/-en) road, etc.: bend; *arch, road, etc.:* curve; *river, path, etc.:* turn, wind, meander; *earth's surface, spine, etc.:* curvature.

Krüppel ['krypəl] *m* (-s/-) cripple.

Kruste ['krustə] *f* (-/-n) crust.

Kübel ['kyːbəl] *m* (-s/-) tub; pail, bucket.

Kubik|meter [ku'biːk-] *n, m* cubic met|re, *Am.* -er; **~wurzel** & *f* cube root.

Küche ['kyçə] *f* (-/-n) kitchen; cuisine, cookery; *s. kalt.*

Kuchen ['kuːxən] *m* (-s/-) cake, flan; pastry.

'**Küchen|gerät** *n*, '**~geschirr** *n* kitchen utensils *pl.*; '**~herd** *m* (kitchen-)range; cooker, stove; '**~schrank** *m* kitchen cupboard *or* cabinet; '**~zettel** *m* bill of·fare, menu.

Kuckuck *orn.* ['kukuk] *m* (-s/-e) cuckoo.

Kufe ['kuːfə] *f* (-/-n) ⚙ skid; *sleigh, etc.:* runner.

Küfer ['kyːfər] *m* (-s/-) cooper; cellarman.

Kugel ['kuːgəl] *f* (-/-n) ball; ✕ bullet; &, *geogr.* sphere; *sports:* shot, weight; ℒ**förmig** *adj.* ['~fœrmiç] spherical, ball-shaped, globular; '**~gelenk** ⊕, *anat.* *n* ball-and-socket joint; '**~lager** ⊕ *n* ball-bearing; '**2n** (ge-) **1.** v/i. (sein) ball, etc.: roll; **2.** v/t. (h) roll (ball, etc.); sich ~ children, etc.: roll about; F double up (vor with laughter); '~schreiber m ball-(point)-pen; '~stoßen n (-s/no pl.) sports: putting the shot or weight.

Kuh zo. [ku:] f (-/-e) cow.

kühl adj. [ky:l] cool (a. fig.); '**2anlage** f cold-storage plant; '**2e** f (-/no pl.) cool(ness); '~en v/t. (ge-, h) cool (wine, wound, etc.); chill (wine, etc.); '**2er** m mot. m (-s/-) radiator; '**2raum** m cold-storage chamber; '**2schrank** m refrigerator, F fridge.

kühn adj. [ky:n] bold (a. fig.), daring, audacious.   [a. cow barn.]

'**Kuhstall** m cow-house, byre, Am.

Küken orn. ['ky:kən] n (-s/-) chick.

kulant ✝ adj. [ku'lant] firm, etc.: accommodating, obliging; price, terms, etc.: fair, easy.

Kulisse [ku'lisə] f (-/-n) thea. wing, side-scene; fig. front; ~n pl. a. scenery; hinter den ~n behind the scenes.

Kult [kult] m (-[e]s/-e) cult, worship.

kultivieren [kulti'vi:rən] v/t. (no -ge-, h) cultivate (a. fig.).

Kultur [kul'tu:r] f (-/-en) ♪ cultivation; fig.: culture; civilization; **2ell** adj. [~u'rel] cultural; ~**film** [~u'~] m educational film; ~**geschichte** f history of civilization; ~**volk** n civilized people.

Kultus ['kultus] m (-/Kulte) s. Kult; '~**minister** m minister of education and cultural affairs; '~**ministerium** n ministry of education and cultural affairs.

Kummer ['kumər] m (-s/no pl.) grief, sorrow; trouble, worry.

kümmer|lich adj. ['kymərliç] life, etc.: miserable, wretched; conditions, etc.: pitiful, pitiable; result, etc.: poor; resources: scanty; '~**n** v/t. (ge-, h) es kümmert mich I bother, I worry; sich ~ um look after, take care of; see to; meddle with.

'**kummervoll** adj. sorrowful.

Kump|an F [kum'pa:n] m (-s/-e) companion; F mate, chum, Am. f a. buddy; ~**el** ['~pəl] m (-s/-, F -s) ✗ pitman, collier; F work-mate; F s. Kumpan.

Kunde ['kundə] **1.** m (-n/-n) cus-

tomer, client; **2.** f (-/-n) knowledge.

Kundgebung ['kunt-] f (-/-en) manifestation; pol. rally.

kündig|en ['kyndigən] (ge-, h) **1.** v/i.: j-m ~ give s.o. notice; **2.** v/t. ✝ call in (capital); ✝✝ cancel (contract); pol. denounce (treaty); '**2ung** f (-/-en) notice; ✝ calling in; ✝✝ cancellation; pol. denunciation.

'**Kundschaft** f (-/-en) customers pl., clients pl.; custom, clientele; '~**er** ✗ m (-s/-) scout; spy.

künftig ['kynftiç] **1.** adj. event, years, etc.: future; event, programme, etc.: coming; life, world, etc.: next; **2.** adv. in future, from now on.

Kunst [kunst] f (-/-e) art; skill; '~**akademie** f academy of arts; '~**ausstellung** f art exhibition; '~**druck** m art print(ing); '~**dünger** m artificial manure, fertilizer; '**2fertig** adj. skilful, skilled; '**2fertigkeit** f artistic skill; '~**gegenstand** m objet d'art; **2gerecht** adj. skilful; professional; expert; '~**geschichte** f history of art; '~**gewerbe** n arts and crafts pl.; applied arts pl.; '~**glied** n artificial limb; '~**griff** m trick, dodge; artifice; knack; '~**händler** m art-dealer; '~**kenner** m connoisseur of or in art; '~**leder** n imitation or artificial leather.

Künstler ['kynstlər] m (-s/-) artist; ♪, thea. performer; '**2isch** adj. artistic.

künstlich adj. ['kynstliç] eye, flower, light, etc.: artificial; teeth, hair, etc.: false; fibres, dyes, etc.: synthetic.

'**Kunst|liebhaber** m art-lover; '~**maler** m artist, painter; '~**reiter** m equestrian; circus-rider; ~**schätze** ['~ʃetsə] m/pl. art treasures pl.; '~**seide** f artificial silk, rayon; '~**stück** n feat, trick, F stunt; '~**tischler** m cabinet-maker; '~**verlag** m art publishers pl.; **2voll** adj. artistic, elaborate; '~**werk** n work of art.

kunterbunt F fig. adj. ['kuntər-] higgledy-piggledy.

Kupfer ['kupfər] n (-s/no pl.) copper; '~**geld** n copper coins pl., F coppers pl.; '**2n** adj. (of) copper; '**2rot** adj. copper-colo(u)red; '~**stich** m copper-plate engraving.

Kupon [ku'põ:] m (-s/-s) s. Coupon.

Kuppe ['kupə] f (-/-n) rounded hilltop; nail: head.

Kuppel △ [ˈkupəl] f (-/-n) dome, cupola; **~ei** ɕɪ̯ [ˈ~lai] f (-/-en) procuring; **2n** (ge-, h) **1.** v/t. s. koppeln; **2.** mot. v/i. declutch.

Kuppl|er [ˈkuplər] m (-s/-) pimp, procurer; **~ung** f (-/-en) ⊕ coupling (a. 🚗); mot. clutch.

Kur [kuːr] f (-/-en) course of treatment, cure.

Kür [kyːr] f (-/-en) sports: s. Kürlauf; voluntary exercise.

Kuratorium [kuraˈtoːrium] n (-s/ Kuratorien) board of trustees.

Kurbel ⊕ [ˈkurbəl] f (-/-n) crank, winch, handle; **2n** (ge-, h) **1.** v/t. shoot (film); in die Höhe ~ winch up (load, etc.); wind up (car window, etc.); **2.** v/i. crank. [pumpkin.)

Kürbis ♀ [ˈkyrbis] m (-ses/-se))

'Kur|gast m visitor to or patient at a health resort or spa; **~haus** n spa hotel.

Kurier [kuˈriːr] m (-s/-e) courier, express (messenger).

kurieren ⚕ [kuˈriːrən] v/t. (no -ge-, h) cure.

kurios adj. [kurˈjoːs] curious, odd, strange, queer. [skating.)

'Kürlauf m sports: free (roller))

'Kur|ort m health resort; spa; **~pfuscher** m quack (doctor); **~pfusche'rei** f (-/-en) quackery.

Kurs [kurs] m (-es/-e) ✝ currency; ✝ rate, price; ⚓ and fig. course; course, class; **~bericht** ✝ m market-report; **~buch** 🚂 n railway guide, Am. railroad guide.

Kürschner [ˈkyrʃnər] m (-s/-) furrier.

kursieren [kurˈziːrən] v/i. (no -ge-, h) money, etc.: circulate, be in circulation; rumour, etc.: circulate, be afloat, go about.

Kursivschrift typ. [kurˈziːf-] f (-/-en) italics pl. [class.)

'Kursus [ˈkurzus] m (-/Kurse) course,)

'Kurs|verlust ✝ m loss on the stock exchange; **~wert** ✝ m market value; **~zettel** ✝ m stock exchange list.

Kurve [ˈkurvə] f (-/-n) curve; road, etc.: a. bend, turn.

kurz [kurts] **1.** adj. space: short; time, etc.: short, brief; ~ und bündig brief, concise; ~e Hose shorts pl.; mit ~en Worten with a few words; den kürzeren ziehen get the worst of it; **2.** adv. in short; ~ angebunden

sein be curt or sharp; ~ und gut in short, in a word; ~ vor London short of London; sich ~ fassen be brief or concise; in ~em before long, shortly; vor ~em a short time ago; zu ~ kommen come off badly, get a raw deal; um es ~ zu sagen to cut a long story short; '2arbeit ✝ f short-time work; '2arbeiter ✝ m short-time worker; **~atmig** adj. [ˈ~ʔaːtmiç] short-winded.

Kürze [ˈkyrtsə] f (-/no pl.) shortness; brevity; in ~ shortly, before long; '2n v/t. (ge-, h) shorten (dress, etc.) (um by); abridge, condense (book, etc.); cut, reduce (expenses, etc.).

'kurz|er'hand adv. without hesitation; on the spot; '2film m short (film); '2form f shortened form; **~fristig** adj. short-term; ✝ bill, etc.: short-dated; '2geschichte f (short) short story; **~lebig** adj. [ˈ~leːbiç] short-lived; '2nachrichten f/pl. news summary.

kürzlich adv. [ˈkyrtsliç] lately, recently, not long ago.

'Kurz|schluß ⚡ m short circuit, F short; '**~schrift** f shorthand, stenography; '2sichtig adj. short-sighted, near-sighted; 2'um adv. in short, in a word.

'Kürzung f (-/-en) shortening (of dress, etc.), abridg(e)ment, condensation (of book, etc.); cut, reduction (of expenses, etc.).

'Kurz|waren f/pl. haberdashery, Am. dry goods pl., notions pl.; '**~weil** f (-/no pl.) amusement, entertainment; '2weilig adj. amusing, entertaining; **~welle** ⚡ f short wave; radio: short-wave band.

Kusine [kuˈziːnə] f (-/-n) s. Cousine.

Kuß [kus] m (Kusses/Küsse) kiss; '2echt adj. kiss-proof. [kiss.)

küssen [ˈkysən] v/t. and v/i.(ge-, h))

'kußfest adj. s. kußecht.

Küste [ˈkystə] f (-/-n) coast; shore.

'Küsten|bewohner m inhabitant of a coastal region; '**~fischerei** f inshore fishery or fishing; '**~gebiet** n coastal area or region; '**~schiffahrt** f coastal shipping.

Küster eccl. [ˈkystər] m (-s/-) verger, sexton, sacristan.

Kutsch|bock [ˈkutʃ-] m coach-box; '**~e** f (-/-n) carriage, coach; '**~enschlag** m carriage-door, coach-door; '**~er** m (-s/-) coachman; 2ie-

ren [ˌ~'tʃiːrən] (*no* -ge-) **1.** *v/t.* (*h*) drive *s.o.* in a coach; **2.** *v/i.* (*h*) (drive *a*) coach; **3.** *v/i.* (*sein*) (drive *or* ride in a) coach.

Kutte ['kutə] *f* (-/-n) cowl.

Kutter ⚓ ['kutər] *m* (-s/-) cutter.

Kuvert [ku'vert; ku'veːr] *n* (-[e]s/-e; -s/-s) envelope; *at table*: cover.

Kux ⚒ [kuks] *m* (-es/-e) mining share.

L

Lab *zo.* [laːp] *n* (-[e]s/-e) rennet.
labil *adj.* [la'biːl] unstable (*a.* ⊕, ✱); *phys.*, ♛ labile.
Labor [la'boːr] *n* (-s/-s, -e) *s. Laboratorium;* ~**ant** [labo'rant] *m* (-en/-en) laboratory assistant; ~**atorium** [labora'toːrjum] *n* (-s/ Laboratorien) laboratory; **2ieren** [ˌ~o'riːrən] *v/i.* (*no* -ge-, *h*): ~ *an* (*dat.*) labo(u)r under, suffer from.
Labyrinth [laby'rint] *n* (-[e]s/-e) labyrinth, maze.
Lache ['laxə] *f* (-/-n) pool, puddle.
lächeln ['leçəln] **1.** *v/i.* (ge-, *h*) smile (*über acc.* at); *höhnisch* ~ sneer (*über acc.* at); **2.** 2 *n* (-s/*no pl.*) smile; *höhnisches* ~ sneer.
lachen ['laxən] **1.** *v/i.* (ge-, *h*) laugh (*über acc.* at); **2.** 2 *n* (-s/*no pl.*) laugh(ter).
lächerlich *adj.* ['leçərliç] ridiculous, laughable, ludicrous; *absurd; derisory,* scoffing; ~ *machen* ridicule; *sich* ~ *machen* make a fool of o.s.
Lachs *ichth.* [laks] *m* (-es/-e) salmon.
Lack [lak] *m* (-[e]s/-e) (gum-)lac; varnish; lacquer, enamel; **2ieren** [la'kiːrən] *v/t.* (*no* -ge-, *h*) lacquer, varnish, enamel; ~**leder** *n* patent leather; ~**schuhe** *m/pl.* patent leather shoes *pl.*, F patents *pl.*
Lade|**fähigkeit** ['laːdə-] *f* loading capacity; ~**fläche** *f* loading area; ~**hemmung** ✕ *f* jam, stoppage; ~**linie** ⚓ *f* load-line.
laden[1] ['laːdən] *v/t.* (*irr.*, ge-, *h*) load; load (*gun*), charge (*a.* ⚡); freight, ship; ⚖ cite, summon; invite, ask (*guest*).
Laden[2] [ˌ~] *m* (-s/⁀) shop, *Am.* store; shutter; ~**besitzer** *m s. Ladeninhaber;* ~**dieb** *m* shop-lifter; ~**diebstahl** *m* shop-lifting; ~**hüter** *m* drug on the market; ~**inhaber** *m* shopkeeper, *Am.* store-

keeper; ~**kasse** *f* till; ~**preis** *m* selling-price, retail price; ~**schild** *n* shopsign; ~**schluß** *m* closing time; *nach* ~ after hours; ~**tisch** *m* counter.
Lade|**platz** *m* loading-place; ~**rampe** *f* loading platform *or* ramp; ~**raum** *m* loading space; ⚓ hold; ~**schein** ⚓ *m* bill of lading.
Ladung *f* (-/-en) loading, load, freight; ⚓ cargo; ⚡ charge (*a. of gun*); ⚖ summons.
lag [laːk] *pret. of liegen.*
Lage ['laːgə] *f* (-/-en) situation, position; site, location (*of building*); state, condition; attitude; *geol.* layer, stratum; round (*of beer, etc.*); *in der* ~ *sein zu inf.* be able to *inf.*, be in a position to *inf.*; *versetzen Sie sich in meine* ~ put yourself in my place.
Lager ['laːgər] *n* (-s/-) couch, bed; den, lair (*of wild animals*); *geol.* deposit; ⊕ bearing; warehouse, storehouse, depot; store, stock (✝ *pl. a. Läger*); ✕, *etc.*: camp, encampment; *auf* ~ ✝ on hand, in stock; ~**buch** *n* stock-book; ~**feuer** *n* camp-fire; ~**geld** *n* storage; ~**haus** *n* warehouse; **2n** (ge-, *h*) **1.** *v/i.* lie down, rest; ✕ (en)camp; ✝ be stored; **2.** *v/t.* lay down; ✕ (en)camp; ✝ store, warehouse; *sich* ~ lie down, rest; ~**platz** *m* ✝ depot; resting-place; ✕, *etc.*: camp-site; ~**raum** *m* store-room; ~**ung** *f* (-/-en) storage (*of goods*).
Lagune [la'guːnə] *f* (-/-n) lagoon.
lahm *adj.* [laːm] lame; ~**en** *v/i.* (ge-, *h*) be lame.
lähmen ['leːmən] *v/t.* (ge-, *h*) (make) lame; paraly|se, *Am.* -ze (*a. fig.*).
lahmlegen *v/t.* (*sep.*, -ge-, *h*) paraly|se, *Am.* -ze; obstruct.
Lähmung ✱ *f* (-/-en) paralysis.
Laib [laip] *m* (-[e]s/-e) loaf.

L

Laich [laɪç] *m* (-[e]s/-e) spawn;
'2en *v/i.* (ge-, h) spawn.
Laie ['laɪə] *m* (-n/-n) layman;
amateur; '_nbühne *f* amateur
theat|re, *Am.* -er.
Lakai [la'kaɪ] *m* (-en/-en) lackey
(*a. fig.*), footman.
Lake ['lɑːkə] *f* (-/-n) brine, pickle.
Laken ['lɑːkən] *n* (-s/-) sheet.
lallen ['lalən] *v/i. and v/t.* (ge-, h)
stammer; babble.
Lamelle [la'mɛlə] *f* (-/-n) lamella,
lamina; ♀ gill (*of mushrooms*).
lamentieren [lamen'tiːrən] *v/i.* (no
-ge-, h) lament (*um* for; *über acc.*
over).
Lamm *zo.* [lam] *n* (-[e]s/ᵘer) lamb;
'_fell *n* lambskin; '2fromm *adj.*
(as) gentle *or* (as) meek as a lamb.
Lampe ['lampə] *f* (-/-n) lamp.
'**Lampen|fieber** *n* stage fright;
'_licht *n* lamplight; '_schirm *m*
lamp-shade.
Lampion [lã'pjõː] *m, n* (-s/-s) Chinese lantern.
Land [lant] *n* (-[e]s/ᵘer, *poet.* -e)
land; country; territory; ground,
soil; *an* ᵥ *gehen go ashore; auf dem*
ᵥ*e in the country; aufs* ᵥ *gehen go
into the country; außer* ᵥ*es gehen
go abroad; zu* ᵥ*e by land*; '_arbei-
ter *m* farm-hand; '_besitz *m*
landed property; '2 real estate;
'_besitzer *m* landowner, landed
proprietor; '_bevölkerung *f* rural
population.
Lande|bahn ✈ ['landə-] *f* runway;
'_deck ⚓ *n* flight-deck. [land.]
land|einwärts *adv.* upcountry, in-
landen ['landən] (ge-) **1.** *v/i.* (sein)
land; **2.** *v/t.* (h) ⚓ disembark
(*troups*); ✈ land, set down (*troups*).
'**Landenge** *f* neck of land, isthmus.
Landeplatz ✈ ['landə-] *m* landing-
field.
Ländereien [lɛndə'raɪən] *pl.* landed
property, lands *pl.*, estates *pl.*
Länderspiel ['lɛndər-] *n* sports:
international match.
Landes|grenze ['landəs-] *f* frontier,
boundary; '_innere *n* interior, inland, upcountry; '_kirche *f* national church; *Brt.* Established Church;'
'_regierung *f* government; *in
Germany:* Land government; '_
sprache *f* native language, vernacular; '2üblich *adj.* customary;
'_verrat *m* treason; '_verräter *m*

traitor to his country; '_verteidi-
gung *f* national defen|ce, *Am.* -se.
'**Land|flucht** *f* rural exodus; '_frie-
densbruch ⚖ *m* breach of the
public peace; '_gericht *n* appr.
district court; '_gewinnung *f*
(-/-en) reclamation of land; '_gut *n*
country-seat, estate; '_haus *n*
country-house, cottage; '_karte *f*
map; '_kreis *m* rural district;
2läufig *adj.* ['_lɔʏfiç] customary,
current, common.
ländlich *adj.* ['lɛntliç] rural, rustic.
'**Land|maschinen** *f/pl.* agricultural
or farm equipment; '_partie *f*
picnic, outing, excursion into the
country; '_plage *iro. f* nuisance;
'_rat *m* (-[e]s/ᵘe) appr. district
president; '_ratte ⚓ *f* landlubber;
'_recht *n* common law; '_regen *m*
persistent rain.
'**Landschaft** *f* (-/-en) province,
district, region; countryside, scenery; *esp. paint.* landscape; '2lich
adj. provincial; scenic (*beauty, etc.*).
'**Landsmann** *m* (-[e]s/*Landsleute*)
(fellow-)countryman, compatriot;
was sind Sie für ein ᵥ? what's your
native country?
'**Land|straße** *f* highway, high road;
'_streicher *m* (-s/-) vagabond,
tramp, *Am. sl.* hobo; '_streit-
kräfte *f/pl.* land forces *pl.,* the
Army; ground forces *pl.*; '_strich
m tract of land, region; '_tag *m*
Landtag, Land parliament.
Landung ['landuŋ] *f* (-/-en) ⚓, ✈
landing; disembarkation; arrival;
'_sbrücke ⚓ *f* floating: landing-
stage; pier; '_ssteg ⚓ *m* gangway,
gang-plank.
'**Land|vermesser** *m* (-s/-) surveyor;
'_vermessung *f* land-surveying;
2wärts *adv.* ['_vɛrts] landward(s);
'_weg *m*: *auf dem* ᵥ*e* by land;
'_wirt *m* farmer, agriculturist;
'_wirtschaft *f* agriculture, farming; '2wirtschaftlich *adj.* agricultural; *s. Maschinen f/pl. s.
Landmaschinen*; '_zunge *f* spit.
lang [laŋ] **1.** *adj.* long; *p.* tall; *er
machte ein* ᵥ*es Gesicht* his face fell;
2. *adv.* long; *e-e Woche* ᵥ for a
week; *über kurz oder* ᵥ sooner or
later; ᵥ(e) *anhaltend* continuous;
ᵥ(e) *entbehrt* long-missed; ᵥ(e) *er-
sehnt* long-wished-for; *das ist
schon* ᵥ(e) *her* that was a long time

ago; ~ und breit at (full or great) length; noch ~(e) nicht not for a long time yet; far from ger.; wie ~e lernen Sie schon Englisch? how long have you been learning English?; **∙atmig** adj. ['∙a:tmiç] long-winded; '∙e adv. s. lang 2.

Länge ['lɛŋə] f (-/-n) length; tallness; geogr., ast. longitude; der ~ nach (at) full length, lengthwise.

langen ['laŋən] v/i. (ge-, h) suffice, be enough; ~ nach reach for.

'**Längen|grad** m degree of longitude; '**∙maß** n linear measure.

'**länger 1.** adj. longer; ~e Zeit (for) some time, 2. adv. longer; ich kann es nicht ~ ertragen I cannot bear it any longer; je ~, je lieber the longer the better.

Langeweile f (-, Langenweile/no pl.) boredom, tediousness, ennui.

'**lang|fristig** adj. long-term; '**∙jährig** adj. of long standing; ~e Erfahrung (many) years of experience; '**2lauf** m skiing: cross-country run or race.

'**länglich** adj. longish, oblong.

'**Langmut** f (-/no pl.) patience, forbearance.

längs [lɛŋs] **1.** prp. (gen., dat.) along(side of) sg.; ~ der Küste fahren ♎ (sail along the) coast; **2.** adv. lengthwise; '**2achse** f longitudinal axis.

'**lang|sam** adj. slow; **2schläfer** ['∙ʃlɛ:fər] m (-s/-) late riser, lie-abed; '**2spielplatte** f long-playing record.

längst adv. [lɛŋst] long ago or since; ich weiß es ~ I have known it for a long time; '**∙ens** adv. at the longest; at the latest; at the most.

'**lang|stielig** adj. long-handled; ♀ long-stemmed, long-stalked; '**2-streckenlauf** m long-distance run or race; '**2weile** f (-, Langenweile/no pl.) s. Langeweile; '**∙weilen** v/t. (ge-, h) bore; sich ~ be bored; '**∙weilig** adj. tedious, boring, dull; ~e Person bore; '**2welle** f ∮ long wave; radio: long wave band; **∙wierig** adj. ['∙vi:riç] protracted, lengthy; ♣ lingering.

Lanze ['lantsə] f (-/-n) spear, lance.

Lappalie [la'pɑ:liə] f (-/-n) trifle.

Lapp|en ['lapən] m (-s/-) patch; rag; duster; (dish- or floor-)cloth; anat., ♀ lobe; '**∙ig** adj. flabby.

läppisch adj. ['lɛpiʃ] foolish, silly.

Lärche ♀ ['lɛrçə] f (-/-n) larch.

Lärm [lɛrm] m (-[e]s/no pl.) noise; din; ~ schlagen give the alarm; '**2en** v/i. (ge-, h) make a noise; '**2end** adj. noisy.

Larve ['larfə] f (-/-n) mask; face (often iro.); zo. larva, grub.

las [lɑ:s] pret. of lesen.

lasch F adj. [laʃ] limp, lax.

Lasche ['laʃə] f (-/-n) strap; tongue (of shoe).

lassen ['lasən] (irr., h) **1.** v/t. let; leave; laß das! don't!; laß das Weinen! stop crying!; ich kann es nicht ~ I cannot help (doing) it; sein Leben ~ für sacrifice one's life for; **2.** v/i. (ge-): von et. ~ desist from s.th., renounce s.th.; do without s.th.; **3.** v/aux. (no -ge-) allow, permit, let; make, cause; drucken ~ have s.th. printed; gehen ~ let s.o. go; ich habe ihn dieses Buch lesen ~ I have made him read this book; von sich hören ~ send word; er läßt sich nichts sagen he won't take advice; es läßt sich nicht leugnen there is no denying (the fact).

lässig adj. ['lɛsiç] indolent, idle; sluggish; careless.

Last [last] f (-/-en) load; burden; weight; cargo, freight; fig. weight, charge, trouble; zu ~en von ✝ to the debit of; j-m zur ~ fallen be a burden to s.o.; j-m et. zur ~ legen lay s.th. at s.o.'s door or to s.o.'s charge; '**∙auto** n s. Lastkraftwagen.

'**lasten** v/i. (ge-, h): ~ auf (dat.) weigh or press (up)on; '**2aufzug** m goods lift, Am. freight elevator.

Laster ['lastər] n (-s/-) vice.

Lästerer ['lɛstərər] m (-s/-) slanderer, backbiter.

'**lasterhaft** adj. vicious; corrupt.

Läster|maul ['lɛstər-] n s. Lästerer; '**2n** v/i. (ge-, h) slander, calumniate, defame; abuse; '**∙ung** f (-/-en) slander, calumny.

lästig adj. ['lɛstiç] troublesome, annoying; uncomfortable, inconvenient.

'**Last|kahn** m barge, lighter; '**∙-kraftwagen** m lorry, Am. truck; '**∙schrift** ✝ f debit; '**∙tier** n pack animal; '**∙wagen** m s. Lastkraftwagen.

Latein [la'taın] n (-s/no pl.) Latin; **2isch** adj. Latin.

Laterne [laˈtɛrnə] f (-/-n) lantern; street-lamp; **˷npfahl** m lamp-post.

latschen F [ˈlɑːtʃən] v/i. (ge-, sein) shuffle (along).

Latte [ˈlatə] f (-/-n) pale; lath; sports: bar; **˷nkiste** f crate; **˷verschlag** m latticed partition; **˷nzaun** m paling, Am. picket fence.

Lätzchen [ˈlɛtsçən] n (-s/-) bib, feeder.

lau adj. [lau] tepid, lukewarm (a. fig.).

Laub [laup] n (-[e]s/no pl.) foliage, leaves pl.; **˷baum** m deciduous tree.

Laube [ˈlaubə] f (-/-n) arbo(u)r, bower; **˷ngang** m arcade.

Laub|frosch zo. m tree-frog; **˷säge** f fret-saw.

Lauch ♀ [laux] m (-[e]s/-e) leek.

Lauer [ˈlauər] f (-/no pl.): auf der ˷ liegen or sein lie in wait or ambush, be on the look-out; **˷2n** v/i. (ge-, h) lurk (auf acc. for); ˷ auf (acc.) watch for; **˷2nd** adj. louring, lowering.

Lauf [lauf] m (-[e]s/⸚e) run(ning); sports: a. run, heat; race; current (of water); course; barrel (of gun); ♪ run; im ˷e der Zeit in (the) course of time; **˷bahn** f career; **˷bursche** m errand-boy, office-boy; **˷disziplin** f sports: running event.

laufen (irr., ge-) 1. v/i. (sein) run; walk; flow; time: pass, go by, elapse; leak; die Dinge ˷ lassen let things slide; j-n ˷ lassen let s.o. go; 2. v/t. (sein, h) run; walk; **˷d** adj. running; current; regular; **˷en** Monats ✝ instant; auf dem ˷en sein be up to date, be fully informed.

Läufer [ˈlɔyfər] m (-s/-) runner (a. carpet); chess: bishop; football: half-back.

Lauf|masche f ladder, Am. a. run; **˷paß** F m sack, sl. walking papers pl.; **˷planke** ♣ f gang-board, gang-plank; **˷schritt** m: im ˷ running; **˷steg** m footbridge; ♣ gangway.

Lauge [ˈlaugə] f (-/-n) lye.

Laun|e [ˈlaunə] f (-/-n) humo(u)r; mood; temper; caprice, fancy, whim; guter ˷ in (high) spirits; **˷2enhaft** adj. capricious; **˷2isch** adj. moody; wayward.

Laus zo. [laus] f (-/⸚e) louse; **˷bub**

[ˈbuːp] m (-en/-en) young scamp, F young devil, rascal.

lausch|en [ˈlauʃən] v/i. (ge-, h) listen; eavesdrop; **˷ig** adj. snug, cosy; peaceful.

laut [laut] 1. adj. loud (a. fig.); noisy; 2. adv. aloud, loud(ly); (sprechen Sie) ˷er! speak up!, Am. louder!; 3. prp. (gen., dat.) according to; ✝ as per; 4. **2** m (-[e]s/-e) sound; **˷2e** ♪ f (-/-n) lute; **˷en** v/i. (ge-, h) sound; words, etc.: run; read; ˷ auf (acc.) passport, etc.: be issued to.

läuten [ˈlɔytən] (ge-, h) 1. v/i. ring; toll; es läutet the bell is ringing; 2. v/t. ring; toll.

lauter adj. pure; clear; genuine; sincere; mere, nothing but, only.

läuter|n [ˈlɔytərn] v/t. (ge-, h) purify; ⊕ cleanse; refine; **˷2ung** f (-/-en) purification; refining.

laut|los adj. noiseless; mute; silent; silence: hushed; **˷2schrift** f phonetic transcription; **˷2sprecher** m loud-speaker; **˷2stärke** f sound intensity; radio: (sound-)volume; **2˷stärkeregler** [ˈre:glər] m (-s/-) volume control.

lauwarm adj. tepid, lukewarm.

Lava geol. [ˈlaːva] f (-/-Laven) lava.

Lavendel ♀ [laˈvɛndəl] m (-s/-) lavender.

lavieren [laˈviːrən] v/i. (no -ge-, h, sein) ♣ tack (a. fig.).

Lawine [laˈviːnə] f (-/-n) avalanche.

lax adj. [laks] lax, loose; morals: a. easy.

Lazarett [latsaˈrɛt] n (-[e]s/-e) (military) hospital.

leben[1] [ˈleːbən] (ge-, h) 1. v/i. live; be alive; ˷ Sie wohl! good-bye!, farewell!; j-n hochleben lassen cheer s.o.; at table: drink s.o.'s health; von et. ˷ live on s.th.; hier lebt es sich gut it is pleasant living here; 2. v/t. live (one's life).

Leben[2] [˷] n (-s/-) life; stir, animation, bustle; am ˷ bleiben remain alive, survive; am ˷ erhalten keep alive; ins neues ˷ beginnen turn over a new leaf; ins ˷ rufen call into being; sein ˷ aufs Spiel setzen risk one's life; sein ˷ lang all one's life; ums ˷ kommen lose one's life; perish.

lebendig adj. [leˈbɛndiç] living; pred.: alive; quick; lively.

Lebens|alter n age; **˷anschau-**

ung f outlook on life; '**~art** f manners pl., behavio(u)r; '**~auffassung** f philosophy of life; '**~bedingungen** f/pl. living conditions pl.; '**~beschreibung** f life, biography; '**~dauer** f span of life; ⊕ durability; '**2echt** adj. true to life; '**~erfahrung** f experience of life; '**2fähig** adj. ⚕ and fig. viable; '**~gefahr** f danger of life; ~! danger (of death)!; unter ~ at the risk of one's life; '**2gefährlich** adj. dangerous (to life), perilous; '**~gefährte** m life's companion; '**~größe** f life-size; in ~ at full length; '**~kraft** f vital power, vigo(u)r, vitality; '**2länglich** adj. for life, lifelong; '**~lauf** m course of life; personal record, curriculum vitae; '**2lustig** adj. gay, merry; '**~mittel** pl. food (-stuffs pl.), provisions pl., groceries pl.; '**2müde** adj. weary or tired of life; '**2notwendig** adj. vital, essential; '**~retter** m life-saver, rescuer; '**~standard** m standard of living; '**~unterhalt** m livelihood; s-n ~ verdienen earn one's living; '**~versicherung** f life-insurance; '**~wandel** m life, (moral) conduct; '**~weise** f mode of living, habits pl.; gesunde ~ regimen; '**~weisheit** f worldly wisdom; '**2wichtig** adj. vital, essential; ~e Organe pl. vitals pl.; '**~zeichen** n sign of life; '**~zeit** f lifetime; auf ~ for life.

lechzen ['lɛçtsən] v/i. (ge-, h): ~ nach languish or yearn or pant for.

Leck [lɛk] **1.** n (-[e]s/-s) leak; **2.** 2 adj. leaky; ~ werden ⚓ spring a leak.

lecken ['lɛkən] (ge-, h) **1.** v/t. lick; **2.** v/i. lick, leak.

lecker adj. ['lɛkər] dainty; delicious; '**2bissen** m dainty, delicacy.

Leder ['le:dər] n (-s/-) leather; in

~ gebunden leather-bound; '**2n** adj. leathern, of leather.

ledig ['le:diç] single, unmarried; child: illegitimate; '**~lich** adv. ['~k-] solely, merely.

Lee ⚓ [le:] f (-/no pl.) lee (side).

leer [le:r] **1.** adj. empty; vacant; void; vain; blank; **2.** adv.: ~ laufen idle; '**2e** f (-/no pl.) emptiness, void (a. fig.); phys. vacuum; '**~en** v/t. (ge-, h) empty; clear (out); pour out; '**2gut** ✝ n empties pl.; '**2lauf** m ⊕ idling; mot. neutral gear; fig. waste of energy; '**~stehend** adj. flat; empty, unoccupied, vacant.

legal adj. [le'ga:l] legal, lawful.

Legat [le'ga:t] **1.** m (-en/-en) legate; **2.** ⚖ n (-[e]s/-e) legacy.

legen ['le:gən] (ge-, h) **1.** v/t. lay; place, put; sich ~ wind, etc.: calm down, abate; cease; Wert ~ auf (acc.) attach importance to; **2.** v/i. hen: lay.

Legende [le'gɛndə] f (-/-n) legend.

legieren [le'gi:rən] v/t. (no -ge-, h) ⊕ alloy; cookery: thicken (mit with).

Legislative [legisla'ti:və] f (-/-n) legislative body or power.

legitim adj. [legi'ti:m] legitimate; **~ieren** [~i'mi:rən] v/t. (no -ge-, h) legitimate; authorize; sich ~ prove one's identity.

Lehm [le:m] m (-[e]s/-e) loam; mud; '**2ig** adj. loamy.

Lehne ['le:nə] f (-/-n) support; arm, back (of chair); '**~en** (ge-, h) **1.** v/i. lean (an dat. against); **2.** v/t. lean, rest (an acc., gegen against); sich ~ an (acc.) lean against; sich ~ auf (acc.) rest or support s.o. (up-) on; sich aus dem Fenster ~ lean out of the window; '**~sessel** m, '**~stuhl** m armchair, easy chair.

Lehrbuch ['le:r-] n textbook.

Lehre ['le:rə] f (-/-n) rule, precept; doctrine; system; science; theory; lesson, warning; moral (of fable); instruction, tuition; ⊕ ga(u)ge; ⊕ pattern; in der ~ sein be apprenticed (bei to); in die ~ geben apprentice, article (both: bei, zu to); '**2n** v/t. (ge-, h) teach, instruct; show.

'**Lehrer** m (-s/-) teacher; master, instructor; '**~in** f (-/-nen) (lady) teacher; (school)mistress; '**~kollegium** n staff (of teachers).

'**Lehr|fach** n subject; '**~film** m instructional film; '**~gang** *m* course (of instruction); '**~geld** *n* premium; '**~herr** *m* master, *sl.* boss; '**~jahre** *n/pl.* (years *pl.* of) apprenticeship; '**~junge** *m s.* Lehrling; '**~körper** *m* teaching staff; *univ.* professoriate, faculty; '**~kraft** *f* teacher; professor; '**~ling** *m* (-s/-e) apprentice; '**~mädchen** *n* girl apprentice; '**~meister** *m* master; '**~methode** *f* method of teaching; '**~plan** *m* curriculum, syllabus; '**2reich** *adj.* instructive; '**~satz** *m* ⅍ theorem; doctrine; *eccl.* dogma; '**~stoff** *m* subject-matter, subject(s *pl.*); '**~stuhl** *m* professorship; '**~vertrag** *m* articles *pl.* of apprenticeship, indenture(s *pl.*); '**~zeit** *f* apprenticeship.

Leib [laip] *m* (-[e]s/-er) body; belly, *anat.* abdomen; womb; *bei lebendigem ~e* alive; *mit ~ und Seele* body and soul; *sich j-n vom ~e halten* keep s.o. at arm's length; '**~arzt** *m* physician in ordinary, personal physician; '**~chen** *n* (-s/-) bodice.

Leibeigen|e ['laip²aigənə] *m* (-n/-n) bond(s)man, serf; '**~schaft** *f* (-/*no pl.*) bondage, serfdom.

Leibes|erziehung ['laibəs-] *f* physical training; '**~frucht** *f* f(o)etus; '**~kraft** *f*: *aus Leibeskräften pl.* with all one's might; '**~übung** *f* bodily *or* physical exercise.

Leib|garde *f* body-guard; '**~gericht** *n* favo(u)rite dish; **2haftig** *adj.* [~'haftiç]: *der ~e Teufel* the devil incarnate; '**2lich** *adj.* bodily, corpor(e)al; '**~rente** *f* life-annuity; '**~schmerzen** *m/pl.* stomach-ache, belly-ache, ⅍ colic; '**~wache** *f* body-guard; '**~wäsche** *f* underwear.

Leiche ['laiçə] *f* (-/-n) (dead) body, corpse.

Leichen|beschauer ⅍⅍ ['laiçənbə-ʃauər] *m* (-s/-) *appr.* coroner; '**~bestatter** *m* (-s/-) undertaker, *Am. a.* mortician; '**~bittermiene** F *f* woebegone look *or* countenance; '**2blaß** *adj.* deadly pale; '**~halle** *f* mortuary; '**~schau** ⅍⅍ *f appr.* (coroner's) inquest; '**~schauhaus** *n* morgue; '**~tuch** *n* (-[e]s/≠er) shroud; '**~verbrennung** *f* cremation; '**~wagen** *m* hearse. [Leiche.\]

Leichnam ['laiçna:m] *m* (-[e]s/-e) *s.*\
leicht [laiçt] **1.** *adj.* light; easy; slight; *tobacco:* mild; **2.** *adv.:* es ~

nehmen take it easy; '**2athlet** *m* athlete; '**2athletik** *f* athletics *pl.*, *Am.* track and field events *pl.*; '**~fertig** *adj.* light(-minded); careless; frivolous, flippant; '**2fertigkeit** *f* levity; carelessness; frivolity, flippancy; '**2gewicht** *n boxing:* lightweight; '**~gläubig** *adj.* credulous; '**~hin** *adv.* lightly, casually; **2igkeit** ['~iç-] *f* (-/-en) lightness; ease, facility; '**~lebig** *adj.* easy-going; '**2metall** *n* light metal; '**2sinn** *m* (-[e]s/*no pl.*) frivolity, levity, carelessness; '**~sinnig** *adj.* light-minded, frivolous; careless; '**~verdaulich** *adj.* easy to digest; '**~verständlich** *adj.* easy to understand.

leid [lait] **1.** *adv.:* es tut mir ~ I am sorry (*um* for), I regret; **2.** 2 *n* (-[e]s/*no pl.*) injury, harm; wrong; grief, sorrow; **~en** ['~dən] *v/i.* (*irr.*, ge-, *h*) **1.** *v/i.* suffer (*an dat.* from); **2.** *v/t.:* (*nicht*) ~ *können* (dis)like; **2en** ['~dən] *n* (-s/-) suffering; ⅍ complaint; **~end** ⅍ *adj.* ['~dənt] ailing.

'**Leidenschaft** *f* (-/-en) passion; '**2lich** *adj.* passionate; ardent; vehement; '**2slos** *adj.* dispassionate.

'**Leidens|gefährte** *m*, '**~gefährtin** *f* fellow-sufferer.

leid|er *adv.* ['laidər] unfortunately; *int.* alas!; ~ *muß ich fort.* I'm (so) sorry to *inf.*; *ich muß ~ gehen* I am afraid I have to go; '**~ig** *adj.* disagreeable; '**~lich** *adj.* ['lait-] tolerable; fairly well; **2tragende** ['lait-] *m, f* (-n/-n) mourner; *er ist der ~ dabei* he is the one who suffers for it; **2wesen** ['lait-] *n* (-s/*no pl.*): *zu meinem ~ to my regret.

Leier ♪ ['laiər] *f* (-/-n) lyre; '**~kasten** *m* barrel-organ; '**~kastenmann** *m* organ-grinder.

Leih|bibliothek ['lai-] *f*, '**~bücherei** *f* lending *or* circulating library, *Am. a.* rental library; **2en** *v/t.* (*irr.*, ge-, *h*) lend; borrow (*von* from); '**~gebühr** *f* lending fee(s *pl.*); '**~haus** *n* pawnshop, *Am. a.* loan office; '**2weise** *adv.* as a loan.

Leim [laim] *m* (-[e]s/-e) glue; F *aus dem ~ gehen* get out of joint; F: *auf den ~ gehen* fall for it, fall into the trap; **2en** *v/t.* (ge-, *h*) glue; size.

Lein ♀ [lain] *m* (-[e]s/-e) flax.

Leine ['lainə] *f* (-/-n) line, cord; (dog-)lead, leash.

'**leinen** ['laɪnən] **1.** *adj.* (of) linen; **2.** ⅌ *n* (-s/-) linen; *in* ~ *gebunden* cloth-bound; '⅌**schuh** *m* canvas shoe.

'**Lein|öl** *n* linseed-oil; '~**samen** *m* linseed; '~**wand** *f* (-/no *pl.*) linen (cloth); *paint.* canvas; *film:* screen.

leise *adj.* ['laɪzə] low, soft; gentle; slight, faint; ~*r stellen* turn down (*radio*).

Leiste ['laɪstə] *f* (-/-n) border, ledge; △ fillet; *anat.* groin.

'**leisten** ['laɪstən] **1.** *v/t.* (ge-, *h*) do; perform; fulfil(l); take (*oath*); render (*service*); *ich kann mir das* ~ I can afford it; **2.** ⅌ ⊕ *m* (-s/-) last; boot-tree, *Am.* ⅌ shoetree; '⅌**bruch** ⚕ *m* inguinal hernia.

'**Leistung** *f* (-/-en) performance; achievement; work(manship); result(s *pl.*); ⊕ capacity; output (*of factory*); benefit (*of insurance company*); '⅌**fähig** *adj.* productive, efficient, ⊕ *a.* powerful; '~**sfähigkeit** *f* efficiency; ⊕ productivity; ⊕ capacity, producing-power.

Leit|artikel ['laɪt-] *m* leading article, leader, editorial; '~**bild** *n* image; example.

'**leiten** ['laɪtən] *v/t.* (ge-, *h*) lead, guide; conduct (*a. phys., ♪*); *fig.* direct, run, manage, operate; preside over (*meeting*); '~**d** *adj.* leading; *phys.* conductive; ~*e Stellung* key position.

'**Leiter 1.** *m* (-s/-) leader; conductor (*a. phys., ♪*); guide; manager; **2.** *f* (-/-n) ladder; '~**in** *f* (-/-nen) leader; conductress, guide; manageress; '~**wagen** *m* rack-wag(g)on.

'**Leit|faden** *m* manual, textbook, guide; '~**motiv** ♪ *n* leit-motiv; '~**spruch** *m* motto; '~**tier** *n* leader; '~**ung** *f* (-/-en) lead(ing), conducting, guidance; management, direction, administration, *Am.* operation; *phys.* conduction; ⚡ lead; circuit; *tel.* line; mains *pl.* (*for gas, water, etc.*); pipeline; *die* ~ *ist besetzt teleph.* the line is engaged *or Am.* busy.

'**Leitungs|draht** *m* conducting wire, conductor; '~**rohr** *n* conduit(-pipe); main (*for gas, water, etc.*); '~**wasser** *n* (-s/⁛) tap water.

'**Leitwerk** ≼ *n* tail unit *or* group, empennage.

Lekt|ion [lɛk'tsjoːn] *f* (-/-en) lesson;

~**or** ['lɛktər] *m* (-s/-en) lecturer; reader; '~**üre** [~'tyːrə] *f* **1.** (-/no *pl.*) reading; **2.** (-/-en) books *pl.*

Lende *anat.* ['lɛndə] *f* (-/-n) loin(s *pl.*).

lenk|bar *adj.* ['lɛŋkbaːr] guidable, manageable, tractable; ⊕ steerable, dirigible; '~**en** *v/t.* (ge-, *h*) direct, guide; turn; rule; govern; drive (*car*); ⚓ steer; *Aufmerksamkeit* ~ *auf* (*acc.*) draw attention to; '⅌**rad** *mot.* *n* steering wheel; '⅌**säule** *mot.* *f* steering column; '⅌**stange** *f* handle-bar (*of bicycle*); '⅌**ung** *mot.* *f* (-/-en) steering-gear.

Lenz [lɛnts] *m* (-es/-e) spring.

Leopard *zo.* [leo'part] *m* (-en/-en) leopard.

Lepra ⚕ ['leːpra] *f* (-/no *pl.*) leprosy.

Lerche *orn.* ['lɛrçə] *f* (-/-n) lark.

lern|begierig *adj.* [' ~-] eager to learn, studious; '~**en** *v/t. and v/i.* (ge-, *h*) learn; study.

Lese ['leːzə] *f* (-/-n) gathering; *s. Weinlese*; '~**buch** *n* reader; '~**lampe** *f* reading-lamp.

lesen ['leːzən] (*irr.*, ge-, *h*) **1.** *v/t.* read; ♪ gather; *Messe* ~ *eccl.* say mass; **2.** *v/i.* read; *univ.* (give a) lecture (*über acc.* on); '~**swert** *adj.* worth reading.

'**Leser** *m* (-s/-), '~**in** *f* (-/-nen) reader; ♪ gatherer; vintager; '⅌**lich** *adj.* legible; '~**zuschrift** *f* letter to the editor. **.**

'**Lesezeichen** *n* book-mark.

'**Lesung** *parl.* *f* (-/-en) reading.

letzt *adj.* [lɛtst] last; final; ultimate; ~*e Nachrichten pl.* latest news *pl.*; ~*e Hand anlegen* put the finishing touches (*an acc.* to); *das* ~*e* the last thing; *der* ~*ere* the latter; *der* (*die, das*) *Letzte* the last (one); *zu guter Letzt* last but not least; finally; '~**ens** *adv.*, '~**hin** *adv.* lately, of late; '~**lich** *adv. s. letztens*; finally; ultimately.

Leucht|e ['lɔʏçtə] *f* (-/-n) (*fig.* shining) light, lamp (*a. fig.*), luminary (*a. fig., esp. p.*); '⅌**en** *v/i.* (ge-, *h*) (give) light, shine (forth); beam, gleam; '~**en** *n* (-s/no *pl.*) shining, light, luminosity; '⅌**end** *adj.* shining, bright; luminous; brilliant (*a. fig.*); '~**er** *m* (-s/-) candlestick; *s. Kronleuchter*; '⅌**feuer** *n* ⚓, ≼, *etc.*: beacon(-light), flare (light); '~**käfer** *zo.* *m* glow-worm; '~**kugel** ⚔ *f*

Very light; flare; '**~turm** m lighthouse; '**~ziffer** f luminous figure.

leugnen ['lɔʏɡnən] v/t. (ge-, h) deny; disavow; contest.

Leukämie ⚕ [lɔʏkɛ'miː] f (-/-n) leuk(a)emia.

Leumund ['lɔʏmunt] m (-[e]s/no pl.) reputation, repute; character; '**~szeugnis** 🖋 n character reference.

Leute ['lɔʏtə] pl. people pl.; persons pl.; ✗, pol. men pl.; workers: hands pl.; F folks pl.; domestics pl., servants pl.

Leutnant ✗ ['lɔʏtnant] m (-s/-s, ⚓ -e) second lieutenant.

leutselig adj. ['lɔʏtze:liç] affable.

Lexikon ['lɛksikɔn] n (-s/Lexika, Lexiken) dictionary; encyclop(a)edia.

Libelle zo. [li'bɛlə] f (-/-n) dragonfly.

liberal adj. [libe'raːl] liberal.

Licht [liçt] **1.** n (-[e]s/-er) light; brightness; lamp; candle; hunt. eye; ~ machen ⚡ switch or turn on the light(s pl.); das ~ der Welt erblicken see the light, be born; **2.** ⚡ adj. light, bright; clear; ~er Augenblick 🖋 lucid interval; '**~anlage** f lighting plant; '**~bild** n photo (-graph); '**~bildervortrag** m slide lecture; '**~blick** fig. m bright spot; '**~bogen** ⚡ m arc; '⚡**durchlässig** adj. translucent; '⚡**echt** adj. fast (to light), unfading; '⚡**empfindlich** adj. sensitive to light, phot. sensitive; ~ machen sensitize.

'**lichten** v/t. (ge-, h) clear (forest); den Anker ~ ⚓ weigh anchor; sich ~ hair, crowd: thin.

lichterloh adv. ['liçtər'loː] blazing, in full blaze.

'**Licht|geschwindigkeit** f speed of light; '**~hof** m glass-roofed court; patio; halo (a. phot.); '**~leitung** f lighting mains pl.; '**~maschine** mot. f dynamo, generator; '**~pause** f blueprint; '**~quelle** f light source, source of light; '**~reklame** f neon sign; '**~schacht** m well; '**~schalter** m (light) switch; '**~schein** m gleam of light; '⚡**scheu** adj. shunning the light; '**~signal** n light or luminous signal; '**~spieltheater** n s. Filmtheater, Kino; '**~strahl** m ray or beam of light (a. fig.); '⚡**undurchlässig** adj. opaque; [ing, glade.]

'**Lichtung** f (-/-en) clearing, open-[

'**Lichtzelle** f s. Photozelle.

Lid [liːt] n (-[e]s/-er) eyelid.

lieb adj. [liːp] dear; nice, kind; child: good; in letters: ~er Herr N.; dear Mr N.; ~er Himmel! good Heavens!, dear me!; es ist mir ~, daß I am glad that; '⚡**chen** n (-s/-) sweetheart.

Liebe ['liːbə] f (-/no pl.) love (zu a, for); aus ~ for love; aus ~ zu for the love of; '⚡**n** (ge-, h) **1.** v/t. love; be in love with; be fond of, like; **2.** v/i. (be in) love; '**~nde** m, f (-rₙ/-n): die ~n pl. the lovers pl.

'**liebens|wert** adj. lovable; charming; '**~würdig** adj. lovable, amiable; das ist sehr ~ von Ihnen that is very kind of you; '⚡**würdigkeit** f (-/-en) amiability, kindness.

'**lieber 1.** adj. dearer; **2.** adv. rather, sooner; ~ haben prefer, like better.

'**Liebes|brief** m love-letter; '**~dienst** m favo(u)r, kindness; good turn; '**~erklärung** f: e-e ~ machen declare one's love; '**~heirat** f love-match; '**~kummer** m lover's grief; '**~paar** n (courting) couple, lovers pl.; '**~verhältnis** n love-affair.

'**liebevoll** adj. loving, affectionate.

lieb|gewinnen ['liːp-] v/t. (irr. gewinnen, sep., no -ge-, h) get or grow fond of; '**~haben** v/t. (irr. haben, sep., -ge-, h) love, be fond of; '⚡**haber** m (-s/-) lover; beau; fig. amateur; ⚡**haberei** fig. [~'rai] f (-/-en) hobby; '⚡**haberpreis** m fancy price; '⚡**haberwert** m sentimental value; '**~kosen** v/t. (no -ge-, h) caress, fondle; '⚡**kosung** f (-/-en) caress; '**~lich** adj. lovely, charming, delightful.

Liebling ['liːpliŋ] m (-s/-e) darling; favo(u)rite; esp. animals: pet; esp. form of address: darling, esp. Am. honey; '**~sbeschäftigung** f favo(u)rite occupation, hobby.

lieb|los adj. ['liːp-] unkind; careless; '⚡**schaft** f (-/-en) (love-)affair; '⚡**ste** m, f (-n/-n) sweetheart; darling.

Lied [liːt] n (-[e]s/-er) song; tune.

liederlich adj. ['liːdərliç] slovenly, disorderly; careless; loose, dissolute.

lief [liːf] pret. of laufen.

Lieferant [liːfə'rant] m (-en/-en) supplier, purveyor; caterer.

Liefer|auto ['liːfar-] n s. Liefer-[

wagen; '2bar *adj.* to be delivered; available; '~bedingungen *f/pl.* terms *pl.* of delivery; '2frist *f* term of delivery; '2n *v/t.* (ge-, h) deliver; j-m et. ~ furnish *or* supply s.o. with s.th.; '~schein *m* delivery note; '~ung *f* (-/-en) delivery; supply; consignment; instal(l)ment (*of book*); '~ungsbedingungen *f/pl.* s. Liefer-bedingungen; '~wagen *m* delivery-van, *Am.* delivery wagon.

Liege ['li:gə] *f* (-/-n) couch; bed-chair.

liegen ['li:gən] *v/i.* (*irr.*, ge-, h) lie; *house, etc.*: be (situated); *room*: face; an wem liegt es? whose fault is it? es liegt an *or* bei ihm zu *inf.* it is for him to *inf.*; es liegt daran, daß the reason for it is that; es liegt mir daran zu *inf.* I am anxious to *inf.*; es liegt mir nichts daran it does not matter *or* it is of no consequence to me; '~bleiben *v/i.* (*irr.* bleiben, sep., -ge-, sein) stay in bed; break down (*on the road, a. mot., etc.*); *work, etc.*: stand over; fall behind; ✝ *goods*: remain on hand; '~lassen *v/t.* (*irr.* lassen, sep., [-ge-,] h) leave; leave behind; leave alone; leave off (*work*); j-n links ~ ignore s.o., give s.o. the cold shoulder; '2schaften *f/pl.* real estate.

'**Liege|stuhl** *m* deck-chair; '~wagen 🚃 *m* couchette coach.

lieh [li:] *pret.* of leihen.

ließ [li:s] *pret.* of lassen.

Lift [lift] *m* (-[e]s/-e, -s) lift, *Am.* elevator.

Liga ['li:ga] *f* (-/Ligen) league.

Likör [li'kø:r] *m* (-s/-e) liqueur, cordial.

lila *adj.* ['li:la] lilac.

Lilie 🌼 ['li:ljə] *f* (-/-n) lily.

Limonade [limo'na:də] *f* (-/-n) soft drink, fruit-juice; lemonade.

Limousine *mot.* [limu'zi:nə] *f* (-/-n) limousine, saloon car, *Am.* sedan.

lind *adj.* [lint] soft, gentle; mild.

Linde 🌼 ['lində] *f* (-/-n) lime(-tree), linden(-tree).

linder|n ['lindərn] *v/t.* (ge-, h) soften; mitigate; alleviate; soothe; allay, ease (*pain*); '2ung *f* (-/~ -en) softening; mitigation; alleviation; easing.

Lineal [line'a:l] *n* (-s/-e) ruler.

Linie ['li:njə] *f* (-/-n) line; '~npa-pier *n* ruled paper; '~nrichter *m*

sports: linesman; '2ntreu *pol. adj.*: ~ sein follow the party line.

lin(i)ieren [li'ni:rən; lini'i:rən] *v/t.* (*no* -ge-, h) rule, line.

link *adj.* [liŋk] left; ~e Seite left (-hand) side, left; *of cloth*: wrong side; '2e *f* (-n/-n) *the* left (hand); *pol.* the Left (Wing); *boxing*: the left; '~isch *adj.* awkward, clumsy.

links *adv.* on *or* to the left; 2händer ['~hendər] *m* (-s/-) left-hander, *Am. a.* southpaw.

Linse ['linzə] *f* (-/-n) 🌼 lentil; *opt.* lens.

Lippe ['lipə] *f* (-/-n) lip; '~nstift *m* lipstick.

liquidieren [likvi'di:rən] *v/t.* (*no* -ge-, h) liquidate (*a. pol.*); wind up (*business company*); charge (*fee*).

lispeln ['lispəln] *v/i.* and *v/t.* (ge-, h) lisp; whisper.

List [list] *f* (-/-en) cunning, craft; artifice, ruse, trick; stratagem.

Liste ['listə] *f* (-/-n) list, roll.

'**listig** *adj.* cunning, crafty, sly.

Liter ['li:tər] *n, m* (-s/-) lit|re, *Am.* -er.

literarisch *adj.* [lite'rɑ:riʃ] literary.

Literatur [litera'tu:r] *f* (-/-en) literature; ~beilage *f* literary supplement (*in newspaper*); ~ge-schichte *f* history of literature; ~verzeichnis *n* bibliography.

litt [lit] *pret.* of leiden.

Litze ['litsə] *f* (-/-n) lace, cord, braid; ⚡ strand(ed wire).

Livree [li'vre:] *f* (-/-n) livery.

Lizenz [li'tsɛnts] *f* (-/-en) licen|ce, *Am.* -se; ~inhaber *m* licensee.

Lob [lo:p] *n* (-[e]s/*no pl.*) praise; commendation; 2en ['lo:bən] *v/t.* (ge-, h) praise; 2enswert *adj.* ['lo:bəns-] praise-worthy, laudable; ~gesang ['lo:p-] *m* hymn, song of praise; ~hudelei [lo:bphu:də'lai] *f* (-/-en) adulation, base flattery.

löblich *adj.* ['lø:pliç] s. lobenswert.

Lobrede ['lo:p-] *f* eulogy, panegyric.

Loch [lɔx] *n* (-[e]s/"er) hole; '2en *v/t.* (ge-, h) perforate, pierce; punch (*ticket, etc.*); '~er *m* (-s/-) punch, perforator; '~karte *f* punch(ed) card.

Locke ['lɔkə] *f* (-/-n) curl, ringlet.

'**locken**[1] *v/t.* and *v/refl.* (ge-, h) curl.

'**locken**[2] *v/t.* (ge-, h) *hunt.*: bait; decoy (*a. fig.*); *fig.* allure, entice.

'**Locken|kopf** m curly head; **.wickler** ['~vɪklər] m (-s/-) curler, roller.

locker adj. ['lɔkər] loose; slack; '**.n** v/t. (ge-, h) loosen; slacken; relax (*grip*); break up (*soil*); sich ~ loosen, (be)come loose; give way; fig. relax.

'**lockig** adj. curly.

'**Lock|mittel** n s. Köder; '**.vogel** m decoy (a. fig.); Am. a. stool pigeon (a. fig.).

lodern ['lo:dərn] v/i. (ge-, h) flare, blaze.

Löffel ['lœfəl] m (-s/-) spoon; ladle; '**.n** v/t. (ge-, h) spoon up; ladle out; '**.voll** m (-/-) spoonful.

log [lo:k] pret. of lügen.

Loge ['lo:ʒə] f (-/-n) thea. box; *free-masonry:* lodge; '**.nschließer** thea. m (-s/-) box-keeper.

logieren [lo'ʒi:rən] v/i. (no -ge-, h) lodge, stay, Am. a. room (all: bei with; in dat. at).

logisch adj. ['lo:giʃ] logical; '**.er-'weise** adv. logically.

Lohn [lo:n] m (-[e]s/**.**e) wages pl., pay(ment); hire; fig. reward; '**.büro** n pay-office; '**.empfänger** m wage-earner; '**.en** v/t. (ge-, h) compensate, reward; sich ~ pay; es lohnt sich zu inf. it is worth while ger., it pays to inf.; '**.end** adj. paying; advantageous; fig. rewarding; '**.erhöhung** f increase in wages, rise, Am. raise; '**.forderung** f demand for higher wages; '**.steuer** f tax on wages or salary; '**.stopp** m (-s/no pl.) wage freeze; '**.tarif** m wage rate; '**.tüte** f pay envelope.

lokal [lo'ka:l] **1.** adj. local; **2.** ♀ n (-[e]s/-e) locality, place; restaurant; public house, F pub, F local, Am. saloon.

Lokomotiv|e [lokomo'ti:və] f (-/-n) (railway) engine, locomotive; **.führer** [~'ti:f-] m engine-driver, Am. engineer.

Lorbeer ♀ ['lɔrbe:r] m (-s/-en) laurel, bay.

Lore ['lo:rə] f (-/-n) lorry, truck.

Los[1] [lo:s] n (-es/-e) lot; lottery ticket; fig. fate, destiny, lot; das Große ~ ziehen win the first prize, Am. sl. hit the jackpot; durchs ~ entscheiden decide by lot.

los[2] [~] **1.** pred. adj. loose; free; was ist ~? what is the matter?, F what's up?, Am. F what's cooking?; ~ sein

be rid of; **2.** int.: ~! go (on or ahead)!

losarbeiten ['lo:s?-] v/i. (sep., -ge-, h) start work(ing).

lösbar adj. ['lø:sba:r] soluble, ♀ a. solvable.

'**los|binden** v/t. (irr. binden, sep., -ge-, h) untie, loosen; '**.brechen** (irr. brechen, sep., -ge-) **1.** v/t. (h) break off; **2.** v/i. (sein) break or burst out.

Lösch|blatt ['lœʃ-] n blotting-paper; '**.en** v/t. (ge-, h) extinguish, put out (*fire, light*); blot out (*writing*); erase (*tape recording*); cancel (*debt*); quench (*thirst*); slake (*lime*); ♣ unload; '**.er** m (-s/-) blotter; '**.papier** n blotting-paper.

lose adj. ['lo:zə] loose.

'**Lösegeld** n ransom.

losen ['lo:zən] v/i. (ge-, h) cast or draw lots (um for).

lösen ['lø:zən] v/t. (ge-, h) loosen, untie; buy, book (*ticket*); solve (*task, doubt, etc.*); break off (*engagement*); annul (*agreement, etc.*); ♋ dissolve; ein Schuß löste sich the gun went off.

'**los|fahren** v/i. (irr. fahren, sep., -ge-, sein) depart, drive off; '**.gehen** v/i. (irr. gehen, sep., -ge-, sein) go or be off; come off, get loose; gun: go off; begin, start; F auf j-n ~ fly at s.o.; '**.haken** v/t. (sep., -ge-, h) unhook; '**.kaufen** v/t. (sep., -ge-, h) ransom, redeem; '**.ketten** v/t. (sep., -ge-, h) unchain; '**.kommen** v/i. (irr. kommen, sep., -ge-, sein) get loose or free; '**.lachen** v/i. (sep., -ge-, h) laugh out; '**.lassen** v/t. (irr. lassen, sep., -ge-, h) let go; release.

löslich ♋ adj. ['lø:sliç] soluble.

'**los|lösen** v/t. (sep., -ge-, h) loosen, detach; sever; '**.machen** v/t. (sep., -ge-, h) unfasten, loosen; sich ~ disengange (o.s.) (von from); '**.reißen** v/t. (irr. reißen, sep., -ge-, h) tear off; sich ~ break away, esp. fig. tear o.s. away (both: von from); '**.sagen** v/refl. (sep., -ge-, h): sich ~ von renounce; '**.schlagen** (irr. schlagen, sep., -ge-, h) **1.** v/t. knock off; **2.** v/i. open the attack; auf j-n ~ attack s.o.; '**.schnallen** v/t. (sep., -ge-, h) unbuckle; '**.schrauben** v/t. (sep., -ge-, h) unscrew, screw off; '**.sprechen** v/t. (irr. sprechen, *sep.*, -ge-, *h*) absolve (*von* of, from); acquit (of); free (from, of); '~**stürzen** *v/i.* (*sep.*, -ge-, *sein*) ~ *auf* (*acc.*) rush at.

Losung ['lo:zuŋ] *f* **1.** (-/-en) ✕ password, watchword; *fig.* slogan; **2.** *hunt.* (-/*no pl.*) droppings *pl.*, dung.

Lösung ['lø:zuŋ] *f* (-/-en) solution; '~**smittel** *n* solvent.

los|**werden** *v/t.* (*irr.* werden, *sep.*, -ge-, *sein*) get rid of, dispose of; '~**ziehen** *v/i.* (*irr.* ziehen, *sep.*, -ge-, *sein*) set out, take off, march away.

Lot [lo:t] *n* (-[e]s/-e) plumb(-line), plummet.

löten ['lø:tən] *v/t.* (ge-, *h*) solder.

Lotse ⚓ ['lo:tsə] *m* (-n/-n) pilot; '**2n** *v/t.* (ge-, *h*) ⚓ pilot (*a. fig.*).

Lotterie [lɔtə'ri:] *f* (-/-n) lottery; ~**gewinn** *m* prize; ~**los** *n* lottery ticket.

Lotto ['lɔto] *n* (-s/-s) numbers pool, lotto.

Löwe zo. ['lø:və] *m* (-n/-n) lion. **Löwen**|**anteil** F *m* lion's share; '~**maul** ⚘ *n* (-[e]s/*no pl.*) snapdragon; '~**zahn** ⚘ *m* (-[e]s/*no pl.*) dandelion. **Löwin** zo. *f* (-/-nen) lioness.

loyal *adj.* [loa'ja:l] loyal.

Luchs zo. [luks] *m* (-es/-e) lynx.

Lücke ['lykə] *f* (-/-n) gap; blank, void (*a. fig.*); '~**nbüßer** *m* stopgap; '**2nhaft** *adj.* full of gaps; *fig.* defective, incomplete; '**2nlos** *adj.* without a gap; *fig.*: unbroken; complete; ~**er Beweis** close argument.

lud [lu:t] *pret.* of **laden**.

Luft [luft] *f* (-/ː-e) air; breeze; breath; *frische* ~ *schöpfen* take the air; *an die* ~ *gehen* go for an airing; *aus der* ~ *gegriffen* (totally) unfounded, fantastic; *es liegt et. in der* ~ there is s.th. in the wind; *in die* ~ *fliegen* be blown up, explode; *in die* ~ *gehen* explode, *sl.* blow one's top; *in die* ~ *sprengen* blow up; F *j-n an die* ~ *setzen* turn s.o. out, *Am.* *sl.* give s.o. the air; *sich or s-n Gefühlen* ~ *machen* give vent to one's feelings.

'**Luft**|**alarm** *m* air-raid alarm; '~**angriff** *m* air raid; '~**aufnahme** *f* aerial photograph; '~**ballon** *m* (air-)balloon; '~**bild** *n* aerial photograph, airview; '~**blase** *f* air-bubble; '~**brücke** *f* air-bridge; *for supplies, etc.*: air-lift.

Lüftchen ['lyftçən] *n* (-s/-) gentle breeze.

'**luft**|**dicht** *adj.* air-tight; '**2druck** *phys. m* (-[e]s/*no pl.*) atmospheric *or* air pressure; '**2druckbremse** ⊕ *f* air-brake; '~**durchlässig** *adj.* permeable to air.

lüften ['lyftən] (ge-, *h*) **1.** *v/i.* air; **2.** *v/t.* air; raise (*hat*); lift (*veil*); disclose (*secret*).

'**Luft**|**fahrt** *f* aviation, aeronautics; '~**feuchtigkeit** *f* atmospheric humidity; '**2gekühlt** ⊕ *adj.* air-cooled; '~**hoheit** *f* air sovereignty; '**2ig** *adj.* airy; breezy; flimsy; '~**kissen** *n* air-cushion; '~**klappe** *f* air-valve; '~**korridor** *m* air corridor; '~**krankheit** *f* airsickness; '~**krieg** *m* aerial warfare; '~**kurort** *m* climatic health resort; '~**landetruppen** *f/pl.* airborne troops *pl.*; '**2leer** *adj.* void of air, evacuated; ~**er Raum** vacuum; '~**linie** *f* air line, bee-line; '~**loch** *n* ✕ air-pocket; vent(-hole); '~**post** *f* air mail; '~**pumpe** *f* air-pump; '~**raum** *m* airspace; '~**röhre** *anat. f* windpipe, trachea; '~**schacht** *m* air-shaft; '~**schaukel** *f* swing-boat; '~**schiff** *n* airship; '~**schloß** *n* castle in the air *or* in Spain; '~**schutz** *m* air-raid protection; '~**schutzkeller** *m* air-raid shelter; '~**sprünge** ['⸺ʃpryŋə] *m/pl.*: ~ *machen* cut capers *pl.*; gambol; '~**stützpunkt** ✕ *m* air base.   [tion.] '**Lüftung** *f* (-/-en) airing; ventila-

'**Luft**|**veränderung** *f* change of air; '~**verkehr** *m* air-traffic; '~**verkehrsgesellschaft** *f* air transport company, airway, *Am.* airline; '~**verteidigung** ✕ *f* air defen|ce, *Am.* -se; '~**waffe** ✕ *f* air force; '~**weg** *m* airway; *auf dem* ~ by air; '~**zug** *m* draught, *Am.* draft.

Lüge ['ly:gə] *f* (-/-n) lie, falsehood; *j-n* ~ *strafen* give the lie to s.o.

'**lügen** *v/i.* (*irr.*, ge-, *h*) (tell a) lie; '~**haft** *adj.* lying, mendacious; untrue, false.

Lügner ['ly:gnər] *m* (-s/-), '~**in** *f* (-/-nen) liar; '**2isch** *adj.* s. lügenhaft.

Luke ['lu:kə] *f* (-/-n) dormer- *or* garret-window; hatch.

Lümmel ['lyməl] *m* (-s/-) lout, boor; saucy fellow; '**2n** *v/refl.* (ge-, *h*) loll, lounge, sprawl.

L

Lump [lump] m (-en/-en) ragamuffin, beggar; cad, *Am. sl.* rat, heel; scoundrel.

'**Lumpen 1.** m (-s/-) rag; **2.** ⚥ *vb.*: *sich nicht ~ lassen* come down handsomely; '**~pack** n rabble, riffraff; '**~sammler** m rag-picker.

'**lumpig** adj. ragged; *fig.*: shabby, paltry; mean.

Lunge ['luŋə] f (-/-n) anat. lungs pl.; *of animals:* a. lights pl.

'**Lungen|entzündung** ♨ f pneumonia; '**~flügel** anat. m lung; '**⚥krank** ♨ adj. suffering from consumption, consumptive; '**~kranke** ♨ m, f consumptive (patient); '**~krankheit** ♨ f lung-disease; '**~schwindsucht** ♨ f (pulmonary) consumption.

lungern ['luŋərn] v/i. (ge-, h) s. *herumlungern.*

Lupe ['lu:pə] f (-/-n) magnifying-glass; *unter die ~ nehmen* scrutinize, take a good look at.

Lust [lust] f (-/ᵉe) pleasure, delight; desire; lust; *~ haben zu inf.* have a mind to *inf.*, feel like *ger.*; *haben Sie ~ auszugehen?* would you like to go out?

lüstern adj. ['lystərn] desirous (*nach*

of), greedy (of, for); lewd, lascivious, lecherous.

'**lustig** adj. merry, gay; jolly, cheerful; amusing, funny; *sich ~ machen über* (acc.) make fun of; '**⚥keit** f (-/no pl.) gaiety, mirth; jollity, cheerfulness; fun.

Lüstling ['lystliŋ] m (-s/-e) voluptuary, libertine.

'**lust|los** adj. dull, spiritless; ♰ flat; '**⚥mord** m rape and murder; '**~spiel** n comedy.

lutschen ['lutʃən] v/i. and v/t. (ge-, h) suck. [ward.]

Luv ⚓ [lu:f] f (-/no pl.) luff, wind-]

luxuriös adj. [luksu'rjø:s] luxurious.

Luxus ['luksus] m (-/no pl.) luxury (a. fig.); '**~artikel** m luxury; '**~ausgabe** f de luxe edition (of books); '**~ware** f luxury (article); fancy goods pl.

Lymph|drüse anat. ['lymf-] f lymphatic gland; '**~e** f (-/-n) lymph; ♨ vaccine; '**~gefäß** anat. n lymphatic vessel.

lynchen ['lynçən] v/t. (ge-, h) lynch.

Lyrik ['ly:rik] f (-/no pl.) lyric verses pl., lyrics pl.; '**~er** m (-s/-) lyric poet.

'**lyrisch** adj. lyric; lyrical (a. fig.).

M

Maat ⚓ [ma:t] m (-[e]s/-e[n]) (ship's) mate.

Mache F ['maxə] f (-/no pl.) make-believe, window-dressing, *sl.* eyewash; *et. in der ~ haben* have s.th. in hand.

machen ['maxən] (ge-, h) **1.** v/t. make; do; produce, manufacture; give (*appetite, etc.*); sit for, undergo (*examination*); come or amount to; make (*happy, etc.*); *was macht das (aus)?* what does that matter?; *das macht nichts!* never mind!, that's (quite) all right!; *da(gegen) kann man nichts ~* that cannot be helped; *ich mache mir nichts daraus* I don't care about it; *mach, daß du fortkommst!* off with you!; *j-n ~ lassen, was er will* let s.o. do as he pleases; *sich ~ an* (acc.) go or set about; *sich et. ~ lassen* have s.th. made; **2.** F v/i.: *na, mach schon!*

hurry up!; '⚥**schaften** f/pl. machinations pl.

Macht [maxt] f (-/ᵉe) power; might; authority; control (*über* acc. of); *an der ~ pol.* in power; '**~befugnis** f authority, power; '**~haber** pol. m (-s/-) ruler.

mächtig adj. ['mɛçtiç] powerful (a. fig.); mighty; immense, huge; *~ sein* (gen.) be master of s.th.; have command of (*language*).

'**Macht|kampf** m struggle for power; '**~los** adj. powerless; '**~politik** f power politics sg., pl.; policy of the strong hand; '**~spruch** m authoritative decision; '**~voll** adj. powerful (a. fig.); '**~vollkommenheit** f authority; '**~wort** n (-[e]s/-e) word of command; *ein ~ sprechen* put one's foot down.

'**Machwerk** n concoction, F put-up job; *elendes ~* bungling work.

Mädchen ['mɛːtçən] n (-s/-) girl; maid(-servant); ~ für alles maid of all work; fig. a. jack of all trades; **'2haft** adj. girlish; '**~name** m girl's name; maiden name; '**~schule** f girls' school.

Made zo. ['maːdə] f (-/-n) maggot, mite; fruit: worm.

Mädel ['mɛːdəl] n (-s/-, F -s) girl, lass(ie).

madig adj. ['maːdiç] maggoty, full of mites; fruit: wormeaten.

Magazin [maga'tsiːn] n (-s/-e) store, warehouse; ✕, in rifle, periodical: magazine.

Magd [maːkt] f (-/⁼e) maid(-servant).

Magen ['maːgən] m (-s/⁼, a. -) stomach, F tummy; animals: maw; '**~beschwerden** f/pl. stomach or gastric trouble, indigestion; '**~bitter** m (-s/-) bitters pl.; '**~geschwür** 𝔰 n gastric ulcer; '**~krampf** 𝔰 m stomach cramp; '**~krebs** 𝔰 m stomach cancer; '**~leiden** n gastric complaint; '**~säure** f gastric acid.

mager adj. ['maːgər] meag|re, Am. -er (a. fig.); p., animal, meat: lean, Am. a. scrawny; '**2milch** f skim milk.

Magie [ma'giː] f (-/no pl.) magic; **~r** ['maːgjər] m (-s/-) magician.

magisch adj. ['maːgiʃ] magic(al).

Magistrat [magis'traːt] m (-[e]s/-e) municipal or town council.

Magnet [ma'gneːt] m (-[e]s, -en/ -e[n]) magnet (a. fig.); lodestone; **2isch** adj. magnetic; **2isieren** [~eti'ziːrən] v/t. (no -ge-, h) magnetize; '**~nadel** [~'gneːt-] f magnetic needle.

Mahagoni [maha'goːni] n (-s/no pl.) mahogany (wood).

mähen ['mɛːən] v/t. (ge-, h) cut, mow, reap.

Mahl [maːl] n (-[e]s/⁼er, -e) meal, repast.

'**mahlen** (irr., ge-, h) **1.** v/t. grind, mill; **2.** v/i. tyres: spin.

'**Mahlzeit** f s. Mahl; F feed.

Mähne ['mɛːnə] f (-/-n) mane.

mahn|en ['maːnən] v/t. (ge-, h) remind, admonish (both: an acc. of); j-n wegen e-r Schuld ~ press s.o. for payment, dun s.o.; '**2mal** n (-[e]s/-e) memorial; '**2ung** f (-/-en) admonition; ✝ reminder, dunning; '**2zettel** m reminder.

Mai [mai] m (-[e]s, -/-e) May; '**~baum** m maypole; **~glöckchen** ✿ ['~glœkçən] n (-s/-) lily of the valley; '**~käfer** zo. m cockchafer, may-beetle, may-bug.

Mais ✿ [mais] m (-es/-e) maize, Indian corn, Am. corn.

Majestät [majɛs'tɛːt] f (-/-en) majesty; **2isch** adj. majestic; **~s-beleidigung** f lèse-majesty.

Major ✕ [ma'joːr] m (-s/-e) major.

Makel ['maːkəl] m (-s/-) stain, spot; fig. a. blemish, fault; '**2los** adj. stainless, spotless; fig. a. unblemished, faultless, immaculate.

mäkeln F ['mɛːkəln] v/i. (ge-, h) find fault (an dat. with), carp (at), F pick (at).

Makler ✝ ['maːklər] m (-s/-) broker; '**~gebühr** ✝ f brokerage.

Makulatur ⊕ [makula'tuːr] f (-/-en) waste paper.

Mal¹ [maːl] n (-[e]s/-e, ⁼er) mark, sign; sports: start(ing-point), goal; spot, stain; mole.

Mal² [~] **1.** n (-[e]s/-e, -e) time; für dieses ~ this time; zum ersten ~e for the first time; mit e-m ~ all at once, all of a sudden; **2.** 2 adv. times, multiplied by; drei ~ fünf ist fünfzehn three times five is or are fifteen; F s. einmal.

'**malen** v/t. (ge-, h) paint; portray.

'**Maler** m (-s/-) painter; artist; **~ei** [~'rai] f (-/-en) painting; '**2isch** adj. pictorial, painting; fig. picturesque.

'**Malkasten** m paint-box.

'**malnehmen** 𝒜 v/t. (irr. nehmen, sep., -ge-, h) multiply (mit by).

Malz [malts] n (-es/no pl.) malt; '**~bier** n malt beer.

Mama [ma'maː, F 'mama] f (-/-s) mamma, mammy, F ma, Am. F a. mummy, mom.

man indef. pron. [man] one, you, we; they, people; ~ sagte mir I was told.   [manager.]

Manager ['menidʒər] m (-s/-)}

manch [manç], '**~er**, '**~e**, '**~es** adj. and indef. pron. many a; ~e pl. some, several; **~erlei** adj. ['~ər'lai] diverse, different; all sorts of, ... of several sorts; auf ~ Art in various ways; used as a noun: many or various things; '**~mal** adv. sometimes, at times.

Mandant 𝔰𝔱 [man'dant] m (-en/-en) client.

Mandarine ♀ [manda'riːnə] f (-/-n) tangerine.

Mandat [man'daːt] n (-[e]s/-e) authorization; ⚖ brief; pol. mandate; parl. seat.

Mandel ['mandəl] f (-/-n) ♀ almond; anat. tonsil; '~baum ♀ m almond-tree; '~entzündung ⚕ f tonsillitis. [ring, manège.]

Manege [ma'neːʒə] f (-/-n) (circus-)

Mangel¹ ['maŋəl] m **1.** (-s/no pl.) want, lack, deficiency; shortage; penury; aus ~ an for want of; ~ leiden an (dat.) be in want of; **2.** (-s/=) defect, shortcoming.

Mangel² [~] f (-/-n) mangle; calender.

'**mangelhaft** adj. defective; deficient; unsatisfactory; '2igkeit f (-/no pl.) defectiveness; deficiency.

'**mangeln¹** v/i. (ge-, h): es mangelt an Brot there is a lack or shortage of bread, bread is lacking or wanting; es mangelt ihm an (dat.) he is in need of or short of or wanting in, he wants or lacks.

'**mangeln²** v/t. (ge-, h) mangle (clothes, etc.); ⊕ calender (cloth, paper).

'**mangels** prp. (gen.) for lack or want of; esp. ⚖ in default of.

'**Mangelware** † f scarce commodity; goods pl. in short supply.

Manie [ma'niː] f (-/-n) mania.

Manier [ma'niːr] f (-/-en) manner; 2**lich** adj. well-behaved; polite, mannerly. [manifesto.]

Manifest [mani'fɛst] n (-es/-e)

Mann [man] m (-[e]s/=er) man; husband.

'**mannbar** adj. marriageable; '2-keit f (-/no pl.) puberty, manhood.

Männchen ['mɛnçən] n (-s/-) little man; zo. male; birds: cock.

'**Mannes|alter** n virile age, manhood; '~kraft f virility.

mannig|fach adj. ['manıç-], '~faltig adj. manifold, various, diverse; '2faltigkeit f (-/no pl.) manifoldness, variety, diversity.

männlich adj. ['mɛnlıç] male; gr. masculine; fig. manly; '2keit f (-/no pl.) manhood, virility.

'**Mannschaft** f (-/-en) (body of) men; ⚓ crew; sports: team, side; '~führer m sports: captain; '~sgeist m (-es/no pl.) sports: team spirit.

Manöv|er [ma'nøːvər] n (-s/-) manœuvre, Am. maneuver; 2**rieren** [~'vriːrən] v/i. (no -ge-, h) manœuvre, Am. maneuver.

Mansarde [man'zardə] f (-/-n) attic, garret; '~nfenster n dormer-window.

mansche|n F ['manʃən] (ge-, h) **1.** v/t. mix, work; **2.** v/i. dabble (in dat. in); 2**rei** F f (-/-en) mixing, F mess; dabbling.

Manschette [man'ʃɛtə] f (-/-n) cuff; '~nknopf m cuff-link.

Mantel ['mantəl] m (-s/=) coat; overcoat, greatcoat; cloak, mantle (both a. fig.); ⊕ case, jacket; (outer) cover (of tyre).

Manuskript [manu'skrıpt] n (-[e]s/-e) manuscript; typ. copy.

Mappe ['mapə] f (-/-n) portfolio, brief-case; folder; s. a. Schreibmappe, Schulmappe.

Märchen ['mɛːrçən] n (-s/-) fairytale; fig. (cock-and-bull) story, fib; '~buch n book of fairy-tales; '2haft adj. fabulous (a. fig.). [ten.]

Marder zo. ['mardər] m (-s/-) mar-

Marine [ma'riːnə] f (-/-n) marine; ✕ navy, naval forces pl.; ~**minister** m minister of naval affairs; First Lord of the Admiralty, Am. Secretary of the Navy; ~**ministerium** n ministry of naval affairs; the Admiralty, Am. Department of the Navy.

marinieren [mari'niːrən] v/t. (no -ge-, h) pickle, marinade.

Marionette [mario'nɛtə] f (-/-n) puppet, marionette; ~**ntheater** n puppet-show.

Mark [mark] **1.** f (-/-) coin: mark; **2.** n (-[e]s/no pl.) anat. marrow; ♀ pith; fig. core.

markant adj. [mar'kant] characteristic; striking; (well-)marked.

Marke ['markə] f (-/-n) mark, sign, token; ⚙, etc.: stamp; † brand, trade-mark; coupon; '~nartikel † m branded or proprietary article.

mar·kier|en (no -ge-, h) **1.** v/t. mark (a. sports); † brand (cattle, goods, etc.); **2.** F fig. v/i. put it on; 2**ung** f (-/-en) mark(ing).

'**markig** adj. marrowy; fig. pithy.

Markise [mar'kiːzə] f (-/-n) blind, (window-)awning.

'**Markstein** m boundary-stone, landmark (a. fig.).

Markt [markt] *m* (-[e]s/⸚e) ✝ market; *s.* Marktplatz; fair; *auf den* ~ *bringen* ✝ put on the market; '~flecken *m* small market-town; '~platz *m* market-place; '~schreier *m* (-s/-) quack; puffer.

Marmelade [marmə'laːdə] *f* (-/-n) jam; marmalade *(made of oranges)*.

Marmor ['marmɔr] *m* (-s/-e) marble; **2ieren** [~o'riːrən] *v/t.* (no -ge-, h) marble, vein, grain; **2n** *adj.* ['~ɔrn] (of) marble.   [whim, caprice.)

Marotte [ma'rɔtə] *f* (-/-n) fancy,)

Marsch [marʃ] **1.** *m* (-es/⸚e) march (*a.* ♪); **2.** *f* (-/-en) marsh, fen.

Marschall ['marʃal] *m* (-s/⸚e) marshal.

'**Marsch|befehl** ✕ *m* marching orders *pl.*; **2ieren** [~'ʃiːrən] *v/i.* (no -ge-, sein) march; '~land *n* marshy land.

Marter ['martər] *f* (-/-n) torment, torture; '**2n** *v/t.* (ge-, h) torment, torture; '~pfahl *m* stake.

Märtyrer ['mɛrtyrər] *m* (-s/-) martyr; '~tod *m* martyr's death; '~tum *n* (-s/no *pl.*) martyrdom.

Marxis|mus [mar'ksismus] *m* (-/no *pl.*) Marxism; '~t *pol. m* (-en/-en) Marxian, Marxist; **2tisch** *pol. adj.* Marxian, Marxist.

März [mɛrts] *m* (-[e]s/-e) March.

Marzipan [martsi'paːn] *n*, ✕ *m* (-s/-e) marzipan, marchpane.

Masche ['maʃə] *f* (-/-n) mesh; *knitting:* stitch; F *fig.* trick, line; '2n-fest *adj.* ladder-proof, *Am.* run-proof.

Maschine [ma'ʃiːnə] *f* (-/-n) machine; engine.

maschinell *adj.* [maʃi'nɛl] mechanical; ~e *Bearbeitung* machining.

Ma'schinen|bau ⊕ *m* (-[e]s/no *pl.*) mechanical engineering; ~**gewehr** ✕ *n* machine-gun; **2mäßig** *adj.* mechanical; automatic; ~**pistole** ✕ *f* sub-machine-gun; ~**schaden** *m* engine trouble; ~**schlosser** *m* (engine) fitter; ~**schreiberin** *f* (-/-nen) typist; ~**schrift** *f* typescript.

Maschin|erie [maʃinə'riː] *f* (-/-n) machinery; ~**ist** [~'nist] *m* (-en/-en) machinist.

Masern ['maːzərn] *pl.* measles *pl.*

Mask|e ['maskə] *f* (-/-n) mask (*a. fig.*); '~enball *m* fancy-dress *or* masked ball; ~**erade** [~'raːdə] *f* (-/-n) masquerade; **2ieren** [~'kiː-

rən] *v/t.* (no -ge-, h) mask; *sich* ~ put on a mask; dress o.s. up (*als* as).

Maß [maːs] **1.** *n* (-es/-e) measure; proportion; *fig.* moderation; ~e *pl. und Gewichte pl.* weights and measures *pl.*; ~e *pl.* room, *etc.*: measurements *pl.*; **2.** *f* (-/-[e]) *appr.* quart (*of beer*); **3.** **2** *pret. of* messen.

Massage [ma'saːʒə] *f* (-/-n) massage.

'**Maßanzug** *m* tailor-made *or* bespoke suit, *Am. a.* custom(-made) suit.

Masse ['masə] *f* (-/-n) mass; bulk; substance; multitude; crowd; ⚖ assets *pl.*, estate; *die breite* ~ the rank and file; F e-e ~ a lot of, F lots *pl. or* heaps *pl.* of.

'**Maßeinheit** *f* measuring unit.

'**Massen|flucht** *f* stampede; '~grab *n* common grave; '~güter ✝ [~'gy:-tər] *n/pl.* bulk goods *pl.*; '**2haft** *adj.* abundant; '~produktion ✝ *f* mass production; '~versammlung *f* mass meeting, *Am. a.* rally; '2weise *adv.* in masses, in large numbers.

Masseu|r [ma'søːr] *m* (-s/-e) masseur; ~**se** [~zə] *f* (-/-n) masseuse.

'**maß|gebend** *adj.* standard; authoritative, decisive; *board:* competent; *circles:* influential, leading; '**2halten** *v/i.* (*irr.* halten, *sep.*, -ge-, h) keep within limits, be moderate.

mas'sieren *v/t.* (no -ge-, h) massage, knead.

'**massig** *adj.* massy, bulky, solid.

mäßig *adj.* ['mɛːsiç] moderate; *food, etc.*: frugal; ✝ *price:* moderate, reasonable; *result, etc.*: poor; ~**en** ['~-gən] *v/t.* (ge-, h) moderate; *sich* ~ moderate *or* restrain o.s.; '**2ung** *f* (-/-en) moderation; restraint.

massiv [ma'siːf] **1.** *adj.* massive, solid; **2.** **2** *geol. n* (-s/-e) massif.

'**Maß|krug** *m* beer-mug, *Am. a.* stein; '**2los** *adj.* immoderate; boundless; exorbitant, excessive; extravagant; ~**nahme** ['~naːmə] *f* (-/-n) measure, step, action; '**2regeln** *v/t.* (ge-, h) reprimand; inflict disciplinary punishment on; '~schneider *m* bespoke *or Am.* custom tailor; '~stab *m* measure, rule(r); *maps, etc.*: scale; *fig.* yardstick, standard; '**2voll** *adj.* moderate.

Mast¹ ⚓ [mast] *m* (-es/-e[n]) mast.

Mast² 🖋 [~] *f* (-/-en) fattening; mast, food; **~darm** *anat. m* rectum.

mästen ['mɛstən] *v/t.* (ge-, h) fatten, feed; stuff (*geese, etc.*).

'**Mastkorb** ⚓ *m* mast-head, crows-nest.

Material [mater'ja:l] *n* (-s/-ien) material; substance; stock, stores *pl.*; *fig.*: material, information; evidence; **~ismus** *phls.* [~a'lismus] *m* (-/*no pl.*) materialism; **~ist** [~a'list] *m* (-en/-en) materialist; **2istisch** *adj.* [~a'listiʃ] materialistic.

Materie [ma'te:rjə] *f* (-/-n) matter (*a. fig.*), stuff; *fig.* subject; **2ll** *adj.* [~er'jɛl] material.

Mathemati|k [matema'ti:k] *f* (-/*no pl.*) mathematics *sg.*; **~ker** [~'ma:-tikər] *m* (-s/-) mathematician; **2sch** *adj.* [~'ma:tiʃ] mathematical.

Matinee *thea.* [mati'ne:] *f* (-/-n) morning performance.

Matratze [ma'tratsə] *f* (-/-n) mattress.

Matrone [ma'tro:nə] *f* (-/-n) matron; **2nhaft** *adj.* matronly.

Matrose ⚓ [ma'tro:zə] *m* (-n/-n) sailor, seaman.

Matsch [matʃ] *m* (-es/*no pl.*), **~e** [~ə] *f* (-/*no pl.*) pulp, squash; mud, slush; **2ig** *adj.* pulpy, squashy; muddy, slushy.

matt *adj.* [mat] faint, feeble; *voice, etc.*: faint; *eye, colour, etc.*: dim; *colour, light,* 🕈 *stock exchange, style, etc.*: dull; *metal*: tarnished; *gold, etc.*: dead, dull; *chess*: mated; 💡 *bulb*: non-glare; ~ *geschliffen glass*: ground, frosted, matted; ~ *setzen at chess*: (check)mate *s.o.*

Matte ['matə] *f* (-/-n) mat.

'**Mattigkeit** *f* (-/*no pl.*) exhaustion, feebleness; faintness.

'**Mattscheibe** *f* *phot.* focus(s)ing screen; *television*: screen.

Mauer ['mauər] *f* (-/-n) wall; **~blümchen** *fig.* ['~bly:mçən] *n* (-s/-) wall-flower; **2n** [~n] (ge-, h) **1.** *v/i.* make a wall, lay bricks; **2.** *v/t.* build (in stone *or* brick); **~stein** *m* brick; **~werk** *n* masonry, brickwork.

Maul [maul] *n* (-[e]s/⁼er) mouth; *sl.*: halt's ~! shut up!; **2en** F *v/i.* (ge-, h) sulk, pout; **~esel** *zo. m* mule, hinny; **~held** F *m* braggart;

~korb *m* muzzle; **~schelle** F *f* box on the ear; **~tier** *zo. n* mule; **~wurf** *zo. m* mole; **~wurfshügel** *m* molehill.

Maurer ['maurər] *m* (-s/-) bricklayer, mason; **~meister** *m* master mason; **~polier** *m* bricklayers' foreman.

Maus *zo.* [maus] *f* (-/⁼e) mouse; **~efalle** ['~zə-] *f* mousetrap; **2en** ['~zən] (ge-, h) **1.** *v/i.* catch mice; **2.** F *v/t.* pinch, pilfer, F swipe.

Mauser ['mauzər] *f* (-/*no pl.*) mo(u)lt(ing); *in der* ~ *sein* be mo(u)lting; '**2n** *v/refl.* (ge-, h) mo(u)lt.

Maximum ['maksimum] *n* (-s/*Maxima*) maximum.

Mayonnaise [majo'nɛ:zə] *f* (-/-n) mayonnaise.

Mechani|k [me'ça:nik] *f* **1.** (-/*no pl.*) mechanics *mst sg.*; **2.** ⊕ (-/-en) mechanism; **~ker** *m* (-s/-) mechanic; **2sch** *adj.* mechanical; **2sieren** [~ani'zi:rən] *v/t.* (*no* ge-, h) mechanize; **~sm̵us** ⊕ [~a'nismus] *m* (-/*Mechanismen*) mechanism; *clock, watch, etc.*: works *pl.*

meckern ['mɛkərn] *v/i.* (ge-, h) bleat; *fig.* grumble (*über acc.* over, at, about), carp (at); nag (at); *sl.* grouse, *Am. sl.* gripe.

Medaill|e [me'daljə] *f* (-/-n) medal; **~on** [~'jõ:] *n* (-s/-s) medallion; locket.

Medikament [medika'mɛnt] *n* (-[e]s/-e) medicament, medicine.

Medizin [medi'tsi:n] *f* **1.** (-/*no pl.*) (science of) medicine; **2.** (-/-en) medicine, F physic; **~er** *m* (-s/-) medical man; medical student; **2isch** *adj.* medical; medicinal.

Meer [me:r] *n* (-[e]s/-e) sea (*a. fig.*), ocean; **~busen** *m* gulf, bay; **~enge** *f* strait(s *pl.*); **~esspiegel** *m* sea level; **~rettich** ⚘ *m* horse-radish; **~schweinchen** *zo. n* guinea-pig.

Mehl [me:l] *n* (-[e]s/-e) flour; meal; **~brei** *m* pap; **2ig** *adj.* floury, mealy; farinaceous; **~speise** *f* sweet dish, pudding; **~suppe** *f* gruel.

mehr [me:r] **1.** *adj.* more; *er hat* ~ *Geld als ich* he has (got) more money than I; **2.** *adv.* more; *nicht* ~ no more, no longer, not any longer; *ich habe nichts* ~ I have nothing left; **2arbeit** *f* additional work; overtime; '²**ausgaben** f/pl. additional expenditure; '²**betrag** m surplus; '²**deutig** adj. ambiguous; '²**einnahme(n** pl.) f additional receipts pl.; '**en** v/t. (ge-, h) augment, increase; sich ~ multiply, grow; '**ere** adj. and indef. pron. several, some; '**fach 1.** adj. manifold, repeated; **2.** adv. repeatedly, several times; '²**gebot** n higher bid; '²**heit** f (-/-en) majority, plurality; '²**kosten** pl. additional expense; '**malig** adj. repeated, reiterated; **mals** adv. ['ma:ls] several times, repeatedly; '**sprachig** adj. polyglot; '**stimmig** ♪ adj. **er** Gesang part-song; '²**verbrauch** m excess consumption; '²**wertsteuer** ✝ f (-/no pl.) value-added tax; '²**zahl** f majority; gr. plural (form); die ~ (gen.) most of.

meiden ['maɪdən] v/t. (irr., ge-, h) avoid, shun, keep away from.

Meile ['maɪlə] f (-/-n) mile; '**nstein** m milestone.

mein poss. pron. [maɪn] my; der (die, das) ~e my; die ²**en** pl. my family, F my people or folks pl.; ich habe das ~e getan I have done all I can; ~e Damen und Herren! Ladies and Gentlemen!

Meineid ɟɦ ['maɪn?-] m perjury; '²**ig** adj. perjured.

meinen ['maɪnən] v/t. (ge-, h) think, believe, be of (the) opinion, Am. a. reckon, guess; say; mean; wie ~ Sie das? what do you mean by that?; ~ Sie das ernst? do you (really) mean it?; es gut ~ mean well.

meinetwegen adv. ['maɪnət'-] for my sake; on my behalf; because of me, on my account; for all I care; I don't mind or care.

'**Meinung** f (-/-en) opinion (über acc., von about, of); die öffentliche ~ (the) public opinion; meiner ~ nach in my opinion, to my mind; j-m (gehörig) die ~ sagen give s.o. a piece of one's mind; '**saustausch** ['maɪnuŋs?-] m exchange of views (über acc. on); '**sverschiedenheit** f difference of opinion (über acc. on); disagreement.

Meise orn. ['maɪzə] f (-/-n) titmouse.

Meißel ['maɪsəl] m (-s/-) chisel; ²**n** v/t. and v/i. (ge-, h) chisel; carve.

meist [maɪst] **1.** adj. most; die ~en

Leute most people; die ~e Zeit most of one's time; **2.** adv.: s. meistens; am ~en most (of all); ²**bietende** ['-'bi:təndə] m (-n/-n) highest bidder; **ens** adv. ['-ɔns], '**enteils** adv. mostly, in most cases; usually.

Meister ['maɪstər] m (-s/-) master, sl. boss; sports: champion; ²**haft 1.** adj. masterly; **2.** adv. in a masterly manner or way; '²**n** v/t. (ge-, h) master; '**schaft** f **1.** (/no pl.) mastery; **2.** (-/-en) sports: championship, title; '**stück** n, '**werk** n masterpiece.

'**Meistgebot** n highest bid, best offer.

Melanchol|ie [melaŋko'li:] f (-/-n) melancholy; ²**isch** adj. [.'lo:liʃ] melancholy; ~ sein F have the blues.

Melde|amt ['mɛldə-] n registration office; '**liste** f sports: list of entries; '²**n** v/t. (ge-, h) announce; j-m et. ~ inform s.o. of s.th.; officially: notify s.th. to s.o.; j-n ~ enter s.o.'s name (für, zu for); sich ~ report o.s. (bei to); school, etc.: put up one's hand; answer the telephone; enter (one's name) (für, zu for examination, etc.); sich ~ zu apply for; sich auf ein Inserat ~ answer an advertisement.

'**Meldung** f (-/-en) information, advice; announcement; report; registration; application; sports: entry.

melke|n ['mɛlkən] v/t. ([irr.,] ge-, h) milk; '²**r** m (-s/-) milker.

Melod|ie [melo'di:] f (-/-n) melody; tune, air; ²**isch** adj. [.'lo:diʃ] melodious, tuneful.

Melone [me'lo:nə] f (-/-n) ♀ melon; F bowler(-hat), Am. derby.

Membran [mɛm'bra:n] f (-/-en), **e** f (-/-n) membrane; teleph. a. diaphragm.

Memme F ['mɛmə] f (-/-n) coward; poltroon.

Memoiren [memo'a:rən] pl. memoirs pl.

Menagerie [menaʒə'ri:] f (-/-n) menagerie.

Menge ['mɛŋə] f (-/-n) quantity; amount; multitude; crowd; in großer ~ in abundance; persons, animals: in crowds; e-e ~ Geld plenty of money, F lots pl. of money; e-e ~ Bücher a great many books; '²**n** v/t. (ge-, h) mix, blend; sich ~ mix (unter acc. with), mingle (with); *sich ~ in* (acc.) meddle *or* interfere with.

Mensch [mɛnʃ] *m* (-en/-en) human being; man; person, individual; *die ~en pl.* people *pl.*, the world, mankind; *kein ~* nobody.

'**Menschen|affe** *zo. m* anthropoid ape; '**~alter** *n* generation, age; '**~feind** *m* misanthropist; '²**feindlich** *adj.* misanthropic; '**~fresser** *m* (-s/-) cannibal, man-eater; '**~freund** *m* philanthropist; '²**~freundlich** *adj.* philanthropic; '**~gedenken** *n* (-s/*no pl.*): *seit ~* from time immemorial, within the memory of man; '**~geschlecht** *n* human race, mankind; '**~haß** *m* misanthropy; '**~kenner** *m* judge of men *or* human nature; '**~kenntnis** *f* knowledge of human nature; '**~leben** *n* human life; '²**leer** *adj.* deserted; '**~liebe** *f* philanthropy; '**~menge** *f* crowd (of people), throng; '²**möglich** *adj.* humanly possible; '**~raub** *m* kidnap(p)ing; '**~rechte** *n/pl.* human rights *pl.*; '²**scheu** *adj.* unsociable, shy; '**~seele** *f*: *keine ~* not a living soul; '**~verstand** *m* human understanding; *gesunder ~* common sense, F horse sense; '**~würde** *f* dignity of man. race, mankind.|

'**Menschheit** *f* (-/*no pl.*) human 'menschlich *adj.* human; *fig.* humane; '²**keit** *f* (-/*no pl.*) human nature; humanity, humaneness.

Mentalität [mɛntali'tɛːt] *f* (-/-en) mentality.

merk|bar *adj.* ['mɛrkbaːr] *s.* merklich; '²**buch** *n* notebook; '**~en** (ge-, h) **1.** *v/i.: ~ auf* (acc.) pay attention to, listen to; **2.** *v/t.* notice, perceive; find out, discover; *sich et. ~* remember s.th.; bear s.th. in mind; '**~lich** *adj.* noticeable, perceptible; '²**mal** *n* (-[e]s/-e) mark, sign; characteristic, feature.

'**merkwürdig** *adj.* noteworthy, remarkable; strange, odd, curious; '**~erweise** *adv.* ['~gər'-] strange to say, strangely enough; '²**keit** *f* (-/-en) remarkableness; curiosity; peculiarity.

meßbar *adj.* ['mɛsbaːr] measurable.

Messe ['mɛsə] *f* (-/-n) ✝ fair; *eccl.* mass; ✗, ⚓ mess.

messen ['mɛsən] *v/t.* (*irr.*, ge-, h)

measure; ⚓ sound; *sich mit j-m ~* compete with s.o.; *sich nicht mit j-m ~ können* be no match for s.o.; *gemessen an* (dat.) measured against, compared with.

Messer ['mɛsər] *n* (-s/-) knife; ⚕ scalpel; *bis aufs ~* to the knife; *auf des ~s Schneide* on a razor-edge *or* razor's edge; '**~griff** *m* knifehandle; '**~held** *m* stabber; '**~klinge** *f* knife-blade; '**~schmied** *m* cutler; '**~schneide** *f* knife-edge; '**~stecher** *m* (-s/-) stabber; **~stecherei** [~ʃtɛçə'raɪ] *f* (-/-en) knifing, knifebattle; '**~stich** *m* stab with a knife.

Messing ['mɛsɪŋ] *n* (-s/*no pl.*) brass; '**~blech** *n* sheet-brass.

'**Meß|instrument** *n* measuring instrument; '**~latte** *f* surveyor's rod; '**~tisch** *m* surveyor's *or* plane table.

Metall [me'tal] *n* (-s/-e) metal; **~arbeiter** *m* metal worker; ²**en** *adj.* (of) metal, metallic; **~geld** *n* coin(s *pl.*), specie; **~glanz** *m* metallic lust|re, *Am.* -er; ²**haltig** *adj.* metalliferous; **~industrie** *f* metallurgical industry; **~waren** *f/pl.* hardware.

Meteor *ast.* [mete'oːr] *m* (-s/-e) meteor; **~ologe** [~oro'loːgə] *m* (-n/-n) meteorologist; **~ologie** [~orolo'giː] *f* (-/*no pl.*) meteorology.

Meter ['meːtər] *n, m* (-s/-) met|re, *Am.* -er; '**~maß** *n* tape-measure.

Method|e [me'toːdə] *f* (-/-n) method; ⊕ *a.* technique; ²**isch** *adj.* methodical. [metropolis.]

Metropole [metro'poːlə] *f* (-/-n)|

Metzel|ei [mɛtsə'laɪ] *f* (-/-en) slaughter, massacre; '²**n** *v/t.* (ge-, h) butcher, slaughter, massacre.

Metzger ['mɛtsgər] *m* (-s/-) butcher; **~ei** [~'raɪ] *f* (-/-en) butcher's (shop).

Meuchel|mord ['mɔʏçəl-] *m* assassination; '**~mörder** *m* assassin.

Meute ['mɔʏtə] *f* (-/-n) pack of hounds; *fig.* gang; **~rei** [~'raɪ] *f* (-/-en) mutiny; '**~rer** *m* (-s/-) mutineer; '²**risch** *adj.* mutinous; '²**rn** *v/i.* (ge-, h) mutiny (gegen against).

mich *pers. pron.* [mɪç] me; *~ (selbst)* myself.

mied [miːt] *pret. of* meiden.

Mieder ['miːdər] *n* (-s/-) bodice, corset; '**~waren** *f/pl.* corsetry.

Miene ['miːnə] *f* (-/-n) countenance, air; feature; *gute ~ zum bösen Spiel machen* grin and bear it; **~ machen zu** *inf.* offer *or* threaten to *inf.*

mies F *adj.* [mi:s] miserable, poor; out of sorts, seedy.

Miet|e ['mi:tə] *f* (-/-n) rent; hire; **zur ~ wohnen** live in lodgings, be a tenant; 'Qen *v/t.* (ge-, h) rent (*land, building, etc.*); hire (*horse, etc.*); (take on) lease (*land, etc.*); ♣, ✈ charter; '**~er** *m* (-s/-) tenant; lodger, *Am. a.* roomer; ☆ lessee; 'Qfrei *adj.* rent-free; '**~shaus** *n* block of flats, *Am.* apartment house; '**~vertrag** *m* tenancy agreement; lease; '**~wohnung** *f* lodgings *pl.*, flat, *Am.* apartment.

Migräne ✸ [mi'grɛ:nə] *f* (-/-n) migraine, megrim; sick headache.

Mikrophon [mikro'fo:n] *n* (-s/-e) microphone, F mike.

Mikroskop [mikro'sko:p] *n* (-s/-e) microscope, Qisch *adj.* microscopic(al).

Milbe *zo.* ['milbə] *f* (-/-n) mite.

Milch [milç] *f* (-/no *pl.*) milk; milt, soft roe (*of fish*); '**~bar** *f* milk-bar; '**~bart** *fig. m* stripling; '**~brötchen** *n* (French) roll; '**~gesicht** *n* baby face; '**~glas** *n* frosted glass; 'Qig *adj.* milky; '**~kanne** *f* milk-can; '**~kuh** *f* milk cow (*a. fig.*); '**~mäd-chen** F *n* milkmaid, dairymaid; '**~mann** F *m* milkman, dairyman; '**~pulver** *n* milk-powder; '**~reis** *m* rice-milk; '**~straße** *ast. f* Milky Way, Galaxy; '**~wirtschaft** *f* dairy-farm(ing); '**~zahn** *m* milk-tooth.

mild [milt] 1. *adj.* weather, punishment, *etc.*: mild; air, weather, light, *etc.*: soft; wine, *etc.*: mellow, smooth; reprimand, *etc.*: gentle; 2. *adv.*: et. **~ beurteilen** take a lenient view of s. th.

milde ['mildə] 1. *adj. s.* mild 1; 2. *adv.*: **~ gesagt** to put it mildly; 3. Q *f* (-/no *pl.*) mildness; softness; smoothness; gentleness.

milder|n ['mildərn] *v/t.* (ge-, h) soften, mitigate; soothe, alleviate (*pain, etc.*); **~de Umstände** ☆ extenuating circumstances; 'Qung *f* (-/-en) softening, mitigation; alleviation.

'**mild|herzig** *adj.* charitable; 'Qherzigkeit *f* (-/no *pl.*) charitableness; '**~tätig** *adj.* charitable; 'Qtätigkeit *f* charity.

Milieu [mil'jø:] *n* (-s/-s) surroundings *pl.*, environment; class, circles *pl.*; local colo(u)r.

Militär [mili'tɛ:r] 1. *n* (-s/no *pl.*) military, armed forces *pl.*; army; 2. *m* (-s/-s) military man, soldier; **~attaché** [~ataʃe:] *m* (-s/-s) military attaché; **~dienst** *m* military service; Qisch *adj.* military; **~musik** *f* military music; **~regierung** *f* military government; **~zeit** *f* (-/no *pl.*) term of military service.

Miliz ✕ [mi'li:ts] *f* (-/-en) militia; **~soldat** ✕ *m* militiaman.

Milliarde [mil'jardə] *f* (-/-n) thousand millions, milliard, *Am.* billion.

Millimeter [mili'-] *n, m* millimet|re, *Am.* -er.

Million [mil'jo:n] *f* (-/-en) million; **~är** [~o'nɛ:r] *m* (-s/-e) millionaire.

Milz *anat.* [milts] *f* (-/-en) spleen, milt.

minder ['mindər] 1. *adv.* less; nicht **~** no less, likewise; 2. *adj.* less(er); smaller; minor; inferior; '**~begabt** *adj.* less gifted; **~bemittelt** *adj.* ['~bəmitəlt] of moderate means; 'Qbetrag *m* deficit, shortage; 'Qeinnahme *f* shortfall in receipts; 'Qgewicht *n* short weight; 'Qheit *f* (-/-en) minority; '**~jährig** *adj.* ['~jɛ:riç] under age, minor; 'Qjährigkeit *f* (-/no *pl.*) minority; '**~n** *v/t. and v/refl.* (ge-, h) diminish, lessen, decrease; 'Qung *f* (-/-en) decrease, diminution; '**~wertig** *adj.* inferior, of inferior quality; 'Qwertigkeit *f* (-/no *pl.*) inferiority; † inferior quality; 'Qwertigkeitskomplex *m* inferiority complex.

mindest *adj.* ['mindəst] least; slightest; minimum; nicht die **~e** Aussicht not the slightest chance; nicht im **~en** not in the least, by no means; zum **~en** at least; 'Qalter *n* minimum age; 'Qanforderungen *f/pl.* minumum requirements *pl.*; 'Qbetrag *m* lowest amount; 'Qeinkommen *n* minimum income; '**~ens** *adv.* at least; 'Qgebot *n* lowest bid; 'Qlohn *m* minimum wage; 'Qmaß *n* minimum; auf ein **~** herabsetzen minimize; 'Qpreis *m* minimum price.

Mine ['mi:nə] *f* (-/-n) ☈, ✕, ♣ mine; pencil: lead; ball-point-pen: refill.

Mineral [minə'rɑːl] n (-s/-e, -ien) mineral; **Șisch** adj. mineral; **~ogie** [ˌɑloʹgiː] f (-/no pl.) mineralogy; **~wasser** n (-s/=) mineral water.

Miniatur [minia'tuːr] f (-/-en) miniature; **~gemälde** n miniature.

Minirock ['mini-] m miniskirt.

Minister [mi'nistər] m (-s/-) minister; Secretary (of State), Am. Secretary; **~ium** [ˌ'teːrjum] n (-s/Ministerien) ministry; Office, Am. Department; **~präsident** m prime minister, premier; in Germany, etc.: minister president; **~rat** m (-[e]s/=e) cabinet council.

minus adv. ['miːnus] minus, less, deducting.

Minute [mi'nuːtə] f (-/-n) minute; **~nzeiger** m minute-hand.

mir pers. pron. [miːr] (to) me.

Mischehe ['miʃ?-] f mixed marriage; intermarriage; **Șen** v/t. (ge-, h) mix, mingle; blend (coffee, tobacco, etc.); alloy (metal); shuffle (cards); sich ~ in (acc.) interfere in; join in (conversation); sich ~ unter (acc.) mix or mingle with (the crowd); **Șling** ['ˌlin] m (-s/-e) half-breed, half-caste; ⚥, zo. hybrid; **~masch** F ['ˌmaʃ] m (-es/-e) hotch-potch, jumble; **'~ung** f (-/-en) mixture; blend; alloy.

mißachten [mis'-] v/t. (no -ge-, h) disregard, ignore, neglect; slight, despise; **Șachtung** f disregard, neglect; **'~behagen** n v/i. (no -ge-, h) displease; **2.** ⚥ n discomfort, uneasiness; **Șbildung** f malformation, deformity; **~'billigen** v/t. (no -ge-, h) disapprove (of); **Șbilligung** f disapproval; **Șbrauch** m abuse; misuse; **~'brauchen** v/t. (no -ge-, h) abuse; misuse; **~bräuchlich** adj. ['ˌbrɔʏçliç] abusive; improper; **~'deuten** v/t. (no -ge-, h) misinterpret; **Șdeutung** f misinterpretation.

missen ['misən] v/t. (ge-, h) miss; do without, dispense with.

'Mißerfolg m failure; fiasco; **'~ernte** f bad harvest, crop failure.

Missetat ['misə-] f misdeed; crime; **'~täter** m evil-doer, offender; criminal.

miß'fallen v/i. (irr. fallen, no -ge-, h): j-m ~ displease s.o.; **Șfallen** n (-s/no pl.) displeasure, dislike; **'~fällig 1.** adj. displeasing, shock-

ing; disparaging; **2.** adv.: sich ~ äußern über (acc.) speak ill of; **Șgeburt** f monster, freak (of nature), deformity; **'Șgeschick** n bad luck, misfortune; mishap; **~gestimmt** fig. adj. ['ˌgəʃtimt] s. mißmutig; **~'glücken** v/i. (no -ge-, sein) fail; **~'gönnen** v/t. (no -ge-, h): j-m et. ~ envy or grudge s.o. s.th.; **Șgriff** m mistake, blunder; **Șgunst** f envy, jealousy; **'~günstig** adj. envious, jealous; **~'handeln** v/t. (no -ge-, h) ill-treat; maul, sl. manhandle; **Ș'handlung** f ill-treatment; mauling, sl. manhandling; ⚖ assault and battery; **Șheirat** f misalliance; **'~hellig** adj. dissonant, dissentient; **Șhelligkeit** f (-/-en) dissonance, dissension, discord.

Mission [mis'joːn] f (-/-en) mission (a. pol. and fig.); **~ar** [ˌo'naːr] m (-s/-e) missionary.

'Mißklang m dissonance, discord (both a. fig.); **'~kredit** fig. m (-[e]s/no pl.) discredit; in ~ bringen bring discredit upon s.o.

miß'lang pret. of mißlingen; **'~lich** adj. awkward; unpleasant; **~liebig** adj. ['ˌliːbiç] unpopular; **~lingen** [ˌ'linən] v/i. (irr., no -ge-, sein) fail; **Șlingen** n (-s/no pl.) failure; **Șmut** m ill humo(u)r; discontent; **'~mutig** adj. ill-humo(u)red; discontented; **~'raten 1.** v/i. (irr. raten, no -ge-, sein) fail; turn out badly; **2.** adj. wayward; ill-bred; **Șstand** m nuisance; grievance; **Șstimmung** f ill humo(u)r; **Șton** m (-[e]s/=e) dissonance, discord (both a. fig.); **~'trauen** v/i. (no -ge-, h): j-m ~ distrust or mistrust s.o.; **Ștrauen** n (-s/no pl.) distrust, mistrust; **'~trauisch** adj. distrustful; suspicious; **Șvergnügen** n (-s/no pl.) displeasure; **'~vergnügt** adj. displeased; discontented; **Șverhältnis** n disproportion; incongruity; **Șverständnis** n misunderstanding; dissension; **'~verstehen** v/t. (irr. stehen, no -ge-, h) misunderstand, mistake (intention, etc.); **Șwirtschaft** f maladministration, mismanagement.

Mist [mist] m (-es/-e) dung; manure; dirt; F fig. trash, rubbish; **'~beet** n hotbed.

Mistel ⚘ ['mistəl] f (-/-n) mistletoe.

'**Mist|gabel** f dung-fork; '**~haufen**
m dung-hill.

mit [mit] **1.** prp. (dat.) with; ~ 20
Jahren at (the age of) twenty; ~ e-m
Schlage at a blow; ~ Gewalt by
force; ~ der Bahn by train; **2.** adv.
also, too; ~ dabeisein be there too,
be (one) of the party.

Mit|arbeiter ['mit⁹-] m co-worker;
writing, art, etc.: collaborator;
colleague; newspaper, etc.: contrib-
utor (an dat. to); **2benutzen** v/t.
(sep., no -ge-, h) use jointly or in
common; '**~besitzer** m joint owner;
'**~bestimmungsrecht** n right of
co-determination; '**~bewerber** m
competitor; '**~bewohner** m co-
inhabitant, fellow-lodger; **2brin-
gen** v/t. (irr. bringen, sep., -ge-, h)
bring along (with one); **~bringsel**
['~briŋzəl] n (-s/-) little present;
'**~bürger** m fellow-citizen; **2ein-
ander** adv. [mit⁹ai'nandər] together, jointly; with each other,
with one another; **~empfinden**
['mit⁹-] n (-s/no pl.) sympathy;
'**~erbe** ['mit⁹-] m co-heir; '**~esser** ⚥
['mit⁹-] m (-s/-) blackhead; **2fah-
ren** v/i. (irr. fahren, sep., -ge-, sein):
mit j-m ~ drive or go with s.o.; j-n
~ lassen give s.o. a lift; **2fühlen**
v/i. (sep., -ge-, h) sympathize (mit
with); **2geben** v/t. (irr. geben, sep.,
-ge-, h) give along (dat. with); '**~ge-
fühl** n sympathy; **2gehen** v/i.
(irr. gehen, sep., -ge-, sein): mit j-m
~ go with s.o.; '**~gift** f (-/-en)
dowry, marriage portion.

'**Mitglied** n member; '**~erver-
sammlung** f general meeting;
'**~erzahl** f membership; '**~sbeitrag**
m subscription; '**~schaft** f (-/no pl.)
membership.

mit|hin adv. consequently, there-
fore; **2inhaber** ['mit⁹-] m co-
partner; '**2kämpfer** m fellow-
combatant; '**~kommen** v/i. (irr.
kommen, sep., -ge-, sein) come along
(mit with); fig. be able to follow;
'**2läufer** pol. m nominal member;
contp. trimmer.

'**Mitleid** n (-[e]s/no pl.) compassion,
pity; sympathy; aus ~ out of pity;
~ haben mit have or take pity on;
'**~enschaft** f (-/no pl.): in ~ ziehen
affect; implicate, involve; damage;
'**2ig** adj. compassionate, pitiful;
2(s)los adj. ['~t-] pitiless, merciless;

2(s)voll adj. ['~t-] pitiful, compassionate.

'**mit|machen** (sep., -ge-, h) **1.** v/i.
make one of the party; **2.** v/t. take
part in, participate in; follow, go
with (fashion); go through (hard-
ships); '**2mensch** m fellow creature; '**~nehmen** v/t. (irr. nehmen,
sep., -ge-, h) take along (with one);
fig. exhaust, wear out; j-n (im Auto)
~ give s.o. a lift; '**~nichten** adv.
['~'niçtən] by no means, not at all;
'**~rechnen** v/t. (sep., -ge-, h) include (in the account); nicht ~
leave out of account; nicht mitge-
rechnet not counting; '**~reden**
(sep., -ge-, h) **1.** v/i. join in the
conversation; **2.** v/t.: ein Wort or
Wörtchen mitzureden haben have a
say (bei in); '**~reißen** v/t. (irr.
reißen, sep., -ge-, h) tear or drag
along; fig. sweep along.

'**Mitschuld** f complicity (an dat.
in); **2ig** adj. accessary (an dat. to
crime); '**~ige** m accessary, accomplice.

'**Mitschüler** m schoolfellow.

'**mitspiel|en** (sep., -ge-, h) **1.** v/i.
play (bei with); sports: be on the
team; thea. appear, star (in a play);
join in a game; matter: be in-
volved; j-m arg or übel ~ play s.o.
a nasty trick; **2.** fig. v/t. join in
(game); '**2er** m partner.

'**Mittag** m midday, noon; heute **2** at
noon today; zu ~ essen lunch, dine;
'**~essen** n lunch(eon), dinner; **2s**
adv. at noon.

'**Mittags|pause** f lunch hour; '**~
ruhe** f midday rest; '**~schlaf** m,
'**~schläfchen** n after-dinner nap,
siesta; '**~stunde** f noon; '**~tisch**
fig. m lunch, dinner; '**~zeit** f noon-
tide; lunch-time, dinner-time.

Mitte ['mitə] f (-/-n) middle;
cent|re, Am. -er; die goldene ~ the
golden or happy mean; aus unserer
~ from among us; ~ Juli in the
middle of July; ~ Dreißig in the
middle of one's thirties.

'**mitteil|en** v/t. (sep., -ge-, h): j-m
et. ~ communicate s.th. to s.o.;
impart s.th. to s.o.; inform s.o. of
s.th.; make s.th. known to s.o.;
'**~sam** adj. communicative; **2ung**
f (-/-en) communication; information; communiqué.

Mittel ['mitəl] n (-s/-) means sg.,

way; remedy (*gegen* for); average; A mean; *phys.* medium; ~ *pl. a.* means *pl.*, funds *pl.*, money; ~ *pl. und Wege* ways and means *pl.*; '~**alter** *n* Middle Ages *pl.*; '2**alterlich** *adj.* medi(a)eval; 2**bar** *adj.* mediate, indirect; '~**ding** *n:* *ein ~ zwischen ... und ...* something between ... and ...; '~**finger** *m* middle finger; '~**gebirge** *n* highlands *pl.*; 2**groß** *adj.* of medium height; medium-sized; '~**läufer** *m sports:* centre half back, *Am.* center half back; '2**los** *adj.* without means, destitute; 2**mäßig** *adj.* middling; mediocre; '~**mäßigkeit** *f* (-/*no pl.*) mediocrity; '~**punkt** *m* cent|re, *Am.* -er; *fig. a.* focus; '2**s** *prp.* (*gen.*) by (means of), through; '~**schule** *f* intermediate school, *Am.* high school; '~**smann** *m* (-[e]s/*~er, Mittelsleute*) mediator, go-between; '~**stand** *m* middle classes *pl.*; '~**stürmer** *m sports:* centre forward, *Am.* center forward; '~**weg** *fig. m* middle course; '~**wort** *gr. n* (-[e]s/*~er*) participle.

mitten *adv.* ['mitən]: ~ *in* or *an* or *auf* or *unter* (*acc.*) *or* (*dat.*) in the midst or middle of; ~ *entzwei* right in two; ~ *im Winter* in the depth of winter; ~ *in der Nacht* in the middle or dead of night; ~ *ins Herz* right into the heart; ~'**drin** F *adv.* right in the middle; ~'**durch** F *adv.* right through or across.

Mitter|nacht f ['mitər-] f midnight; *um* ~ at midnight; 2**nächtig** *adj.* ['~nɛçtiç], 2**nächtlich** *adj.* midnight.

Mittler ['mitlər] **1.** *m* (-s/-) mediator, intercessor; **2.** 2 *adj.* middle, central; average, medium; '2'**weile** *adv.* meanwhile, (in the) meantime.

Mittwoch ['mitvɔx] *m* (-[e]s/-e) Wednesday; '2**s** *adv.* on Wednesday(s), every Wednesday.

mit|'unter *adv.* now and then, sometimes; '~**verantwortlich** *adj.* jointly responsible; 2**welt** f (-/*no pl.*): *die* ~ our, *etc.* contemporaries *pl.*

'**mitwirk|en** *v/i.* (*sep.*, -ge-, h) co-operate (*bei* in), contribute (*to*), take part (in); 2**ende** *m* (-n/-n) *thea.* performer, actor, player (*a. ♪*); *die* ~*n pl.* the cast; '2**ung** *f* (-/*no pl.*) co(-)operation, contribution.

'**Mitwisser** *m* (-s/-) confidant; ♂♂ accessary. [rechnen.]

'**mitzählen** *v/t.* (*sep.*, -ge-, h) *s. mit-*]
Mix|becher ['miks-] *m* (cocktail-) shaker; '2**en** *v/t.* (ge-, h) mix; '~**tur** [~'tu:r] *f* (-/-en) mixture.

Möbel ['mø:bəl] *n* (-s/-) piece of furniture; ~ *pl.* furniture; '~**händler** *m* furniture-dealer; '~**spediteur** *m* furniture-remover; '~**stück** *n* piece of furniture; '~**tischler** *m* cabinet-maker; '~**wagen** *m* pantechnicon, *Am.* furniture truck.

mobil *adj.* [mo'bi:l] mobile; F active, nimble; ~ *machen* ⚔ mobilize; 2**iar** [~i̯l'ja:r] *n* (-s/-e) furniture; movables *pl.*; ~**isieren** [~ili-'zi:rən] *v/t.* (*no* -ge-, h) ⚔ mobilize; ✝ realize (*property, etc.*); 2**machung** ⚔ [mo'bi:lmaxuŋ] *f* (-/-en) mobilization.

möblieren [mø'bli:rən] *v/t.* (*no* -ge-, h) furnish; *möbliertes Zimmer* furnished room, F bed-sitter.

mochte ['mɔxtə] *pret.* of *mögen.*

Mode ['mo:də] *f* (-/-n) fashion, vogue; use, custom; *die neueste* ~ the latest fashion; *in* ~ in fashion or vogue; *aus der* ~ *kommen* grow or go out of fashion; *die* ~ *bestimmen* set the fashion; '~**artikel** *m/pl.* fancy goods *pl.*, novelties *pl.*; '~**farbe** *f* fashionable colo(u)r.

Modell [mo'dɛl] *n* (-s/-e) ⊕, *fashion, paint.*: model; pattern, design; ⊕ *mo(u)ld; j-m ~ stehen paint.* pose for s.o.; ~**eisenbahn** *f* model railway; 2**ieren** [~'li:rən] *v/t.* (*no* -ge-, h) model, mo(u)ld, fashion.

'**Moden|schau** *f* dress parade, fashion-show; '~**zeitung** *f* fashion magazine.

Moder ['mo:dər] *m* (-s/*no pl.*) must, putrefaction; '~**geruch** *m* musty smell; '2**ig** *adj.* musty, putrid.

modern[1] ['mo:dərn] *v/i.* (ge-, h) putrefy, rot, decay.

modern[2] *adj.* [mo'dɛrn] modern; progressive; up-to-date; fashionable; ~**isieren** [~i'zi:rən] *v/t.* (*no* -ge-, h) modernize, bring up to date.

'**Mode|salon** *m* fashion house; '~**schmuck** *m* costume jewel(le)ry; '~**waren** *f/pl.* fancy goods *pl.*; '~**zeichner** *m* fashion-designer.

modifizieren [modifi'tsi:rən] *v/t.* (*no* -ge-, h) modify.

modisch adj. ['mo:diʃ] fashionable, stylish. [liner.)

Modistin [mo'distin] f (-/-nen) mil-)

Mogel|ei F [mo:gə'laɪ] f (-/-en) cheat; **'⚥n** F v/i. (ge-, h) cheat.

mögen ['mø:gən] (irr., h) **1.** v/i. (ge-) be willing; _ich mag nicht_ I don't like to; **2.** v/t. (ge-) want, wish; like, be fond of; _nicht ~_ dislike; not to be keen on (_food, etc._); _lieber ~_ like better, prefer; **3.** v/aux. (no -ge-) may, might; _ich möchte wissen_ I should like to know; _ich möchte lieber gehen_ I would rather go; _das mag (wohl) sein_ that's (well) possible; _wo er auch sein mag_ wherever he may be; _mag er sagen, was er will_ let him say what he likes.

möglich ['mø:klɪç] **1.** adj. possible, practicable, feasible; _market, criminal, etc._: potential; _alle ~en_ all sorts of; _alles ~e_ all sorts of things; _sein ~stes tun_ do one's utmost _or_ level best; _nicht ~!_ you don't say (so)!; _so bald etc. wie ~ =_ **2.** adv.: _~st bald etc._ as soon, etc., as possible; **'~er|weise** adv. possibly, if possible; perhaps; **'⚥keit** f (-/-en) possibility; chance; _nach ~_ if possible.

Mohammedan|er [mohame'da:-nər] m (-s/-) Muslim, Moslem, Mohammedan; **⚥isch** adj. Muslim, Moslem, Mohammedan.

Mohn ⚥ [mo:n] m (-[e]s/-e) poppy.

Möhre ⚥ ['mø:rə] f (-/-n) carrot.

Mohrrübe ⚥ ['mo:r-] f carrot.

Molch zo. [mɔlç] m (-[e]s/-e) salamander; newt.

Mole ⚓ ['mo:lə] f (-/-n) mole, jetty.

molk [mɔlk] pret. of melken.

Molkerei [mɔlkə'raɪ] f (-/-en) dairy; **~produkte** n/pl. dairy products pl.

Moll ♩ [mɔl] n (-/-) minor (key).

mollig F adj. ['mɔlɪç] snug, cosy; plump, rounded.

Moment [mo'mɛnt] (-[e]s/-e) **1.** m moment, instant; _im ~_ at the moment; **2.** n motive; fact(or); ⊕ momentum; ⊕ impulse (a. fig.); **⚥an** [~'ta:n] **1.** adj. momentary; **2.** adv. at the moment, for the time being; **~aufnahme** phot. f snapshot, instantaneous photograph.

Monarch [mo'narç] m (-en/-en) monarch; **~ie** [~'çi:] f (-/-n) monarchy.

Monat ['mo:nat] m (-[e]s/-e) month; **'⚥elang 1.** adj. lasting for months;

2. adv. for months; **'⚥lich 1.** adj. monthly; **2.** adv. monthly, a month.

Mönch [mœnç] m (-[e]s/-e) monk, friar.

'Mönchs|kloster n monastery; **'~-kutte** f (monk's) frock; **'~leben** n monastic life; **'~orden** m monastic order; **'~zelle** f monk's cell.

Mond [mo:nt] m (-[e]s/-e) moon; _hinter dem ~ leben_ be behind the times; **'~fähre** f lunar module; **'~finsternis** f lunar eclipse; **'⚥hell** adj. moonlit; **'~schein** m (-[e]s/no pl.) moonlight; **'~sichel** f crescent; **'⚥süchtig** adj. moonstruck.

Mono|log [mono'lo:k] m (-s/-e) monologue, _Am. a._ monolog; soliloquy; **'~pol** ✝ n (-s/-e) monopoly; **⚥polisieren** [~oli'zi:rən] v/t. (no -ge-, h) monopolize; **⚥ton** adj. monotonous; **~tonie** [~to'ni:] f (-/-n) monotony.

Monstrum ['mɔnstrum] n (-s/Monstren, Monstra) monster.

Montag ['mo:nta:k] m Monday; **'⚥s** adv. on Monday(s), every Monday.

Montage ⊕ [mɔn'ta:ʒə] f (-/-n) mounting, fitting; setting up; assemblage, assembly.

Montan|industrie [mɔn'ta:n-] f coal and steel industries pl.; **~union** f European Coal and Steel Community.

Mont|eur [mɔn'tø:r] m (-s/-e) ⊕ fitter, assembler; _esp. mot._, ✈ mechanic; **~euranzug** m overall; **⚥ieren** [~'ti:rən] v/t. (no -ge-, h) mount, fit; set up; assemble; **~ur** ✕ [~'tu:r] f (-/-en) regimentals pl.

Moor [mo:r] n (-[e]s/-e) bog; swamp; **'~bad** n mud-bath; **'⚥ig** adj. boggy, marshy.

Moos ⚥ [mo:s] n (-es/-e) moss; **'⚥ig** adj. mossy.

Moped mot. ['mo:pɛt] n (-s/-s) moped.

Mops zo. [mɔps] m (-es/⚥e) pug; **'⚥en** (ge-, h) F pilfer, pinch; sl.: _sich ~_ be bored stiff.

Moral [mo'ra:l] f (-/~ -en) morality; morals pl.; moral; ✕, etc.: morale; **⚥isch** adj. moral; **⚥isieren** [~ali'zi:rən] v/i. (no -ge-, h) moralize.

Morast [mo'rast] m (-es/⚥e) slough, morass; s. Moor; mire, mud; **⚥ig** adj. marshy; muddy, miry.

Mord [mɔrt] m (-[e]s/-e) murder

(an dat. of); e-n ~ begehen commit murder; '**~anschlag** m murderous assault; **2en** ['~dən] v/i. (ge-, h) commit murder(s).

Mörder ['mœrdər] m (-s/-) murderer; **2isch** adj. murderous; climate, etc.: deadly; † competition: cut-throat.

'**Mord|gier** f lust of murder, blood-thirstiness; **2gierig** adj. blood-thirsty; '**~kommission** f homicide squad; '**~prozeß** ʦ̑ʦ̑ m murder trial.

'**Mords|angst** F f blue funk, sl. mortal fear; '**~glück** F n stupendous luck; '**~kerl** F m devil of a fellow; '**~spektakel** F m hullabaloo.

Morgen ['mɔrgən] **1.** m (-s/-) morning; measure: acre; am ~ s. morgens; **2.** 2 adv. tomorrow; ~ früh (abend) tomorrow morning (evening or night); ~ in acht Tagen tomorrow week; '**~ausgabe** f morning edition; '**~blatt** n morning paper; '**~dämmerung** f dawn, daybreak; '**~gebet** n morning prayer; '**~gymnastik** f morning exercises pl.; '**~land** n (-[e]s/no pl.) Orient, East; '**~rock** m peignoir, dressing-gown, wrapper (for woman); '**~röte** f dawn; '2s adv. in the morning; '**~zeitung** f morning paper.

'**morgig** adj. of tomorrow.

Morphium pharm. ['mɔrfium] n (-s/no pl.) morphia, morphine.

morsch adj. [mɔrʃ] rotten, decayed; brittle.

Mörser ['mœrzər] m (-s/-) mortar (a. ⚔).

Mörtel ['mœrtəl] m (-s/-) mortar.

Mosaik [moza'i:k] n (-s/-en) mosaic; '**~fußboden** m mosaic or tessellated pavement.

Moschee [mɔ'ʃe:] f (-/-n) mosque.

Moschus ['mɔʃus] m (-/no pl.) musk.

Moskito zo. [mɔs'ki:to] m (-s/-s) mosquito; '**~netz** n mosquito-net.

Moslem ['mɔslem] m (-s/-s) Muslim, Moslem.

Most [mɔst] m (-es/-e) must, grape-juice; of apples: cider; of pears: perry. [mustard.]

Mostrich ['mɔstriç] m(-[e]s/no pl.)⟩

Motiv [mo'ti:f] n (-s/-e) motive, reason; paint., ♪ motif; **2ieren** [~i'vi:rən] v/t. (no -ge-, h) motivate.

Motor [mo'to:r] m (-s/-en) engine, esp. ⚡ motor; '**~boot** n motor boat; '**~defekt** m engine or ⚡ motor

trouble; '**~haube** f bonnet, Am. hood; **2isieren** [motori'zi:rən] v/t. (no -ge-, h) motorize; **~isierung** [motori'zi:ruŋ] f (-/no pl.) motor-ization; '**~rad** n motor (bi)cycle; '**~radfahrer** m motor cyclist; '**~roller** m (motor) scooter; '**~sport** m motoring.

Motte zo. ['mɔtə] f (-/-n) moth.

'**Motten|kugel** f moth-ball; '2sicher adj. mothproof; '2zerfressen adj. moth-eaten.

Motto ['mɔto] n (-s/-s) motto.

Möwe orn. ['mø:və] f (-/-n) sea-gull, (sea-)mew.

Mücke zo. ['mykə] f (-/-n) midge, gnat, mosquito; aus e-r ~ e-n Elefanten machen make a mountain out of a molehill; '**~nstich** m gnat-bite. [hypocrite.⟩

Mucker ['mukər] m (-s/-) bigot,⟩

müd|e adj. ['my:də] tired, weary; e-r Sache ~ sein be weary or tired of s.th.; **2igkeit** f (-/no pl.) tired-ness, weariness.

Muff [muf] m **1.** (-[e]s/-e) muff; **2.** (-[e]s/no pl.) mo(u)ldy or musty smell; '**~e** ⊕ f (-/-n) sleeve, socket; '**2eln** F v/i. (ge-, h) munch; mumble; **2ig** adj. smell, etc.: musty, fusty; air: close; fig. sulky, sullen.

Mühe ['my:ə] f (-/-n) trouble, pains pl.; (nicht) der ~ wert (not) worth while; j-m ~ machen give s.o. trouble; sich ~ geben take pains (mit over, with s.th.); **2los** adj. effortless, easy; '**2n** v/refl. (ge-, h) take pains, work hard; '**2voll** adj. troublesome, hard; laborious.

Mühle ['my:lə] f (-/-n) mill.

'**Müh|sal** f (-/-e) toil, trouble; hardship; '**2sam**, '**2selig 1.** adj. toilsome, troublesome; difficult; **2.** adv. laboriously; with difficulty.

Mulatte [mu'latə] m (-n/-n) mulatto.

Mulde ['muldə] f (-/-n) trough; depression, hollow.

Mull [mul] m (-[e]s/-e) mull.

Müll [myl] m (-[e]s/no pl.) dust, rubbish, refuse, Am. a. garbage; '**~abfuhr** f removal of refuse; '**~eimer** m dust-bin, Am. garbage can.

Müller ['mylər] m (-s/-) miller.

'**Müll|fahrer** m dust-man, Am. garbage collector; '**~haufen** m dust-heap; '**~kasten** m s. Mülleimer; '**~kutscher** m s. Müllfahrer; '**~wa-**

müssen

gen *m* dust-cart, *Am.* garbage cart.

Multipli|kation Ⱥ [multiplika-'tsjo:n] *f* (-/-en) multiplication; **≈zieren** Ⱥ [~'tsi:rən] *v/t.* (*no -ge-, h*) multiply (*mit* by).

Mumie ['mu:mjə] *f* (-/-n) mummy.

Mumps ✻ [mumps] *m*, F *f* (-/*no pl.*) mumps.

Mund [munt] *m* (-[e]s/⸗er) mouth; **den ~ halten** hold one's tongue; **den ~ voll nehmen** talk big; **sich den ~ verbrennen** put one's foot in it; **nicht auf den ~ gefallen sein** have a ready *or* glib tongue; *j-m* **über den ~ fahren** cut s.o. short; '**~art** *f* dialect; '**≈artlich** *adj.* dialectal.

Mündel ['myndəl] *m, n* (-s/-), *girl:* *a.* *f* (-/-n) ward, pupil; '**≈sicher** *adj.*: **~e Papiere** *n/pl.* ✝ gilt-edged securities *pl.*

münden ['myndən] *v/i.* (ge-, h): **~ in** (*acc.*) river, *etc.*: fall *or* flow into; *street, etc.*: run into.

'**mund|faul** *adj.* too lazy to speak; '**~gerecht** *adj.* palatable (*a. fig.*); '**≈harmonika** ♪ *f* mouth-organ; '**≈höhle** *anat.* *f* oral cavity.

mündig ⅀⅄ *adj.* ['myndiç] of age; **~ werden** come of age; '**≈keit** *f* (-/*no pl.*) majority.

mündlich ['myntliç] **1.** *adj.* oral, verbal; **2.** *adv.* *a.* by word of mouth.

'**Mund|pflege** *f* oral hygiene; '**~raub** ⅀⅄ *m* theft of comestibles; '**~stück** *n* mouthpiece (*of musical instrument, etc.*); tip (*of cigarette*); '**≈tot** *adj.*: **~ machen** silence *or* gag s.o.

'**Mündung** *f* (-/-en) mouth; *a.* estuary (*of river*); muzzle (*of fire-arms*).

'**Mund|vorrat** *m* provisions *pl.*, victuals *pl.*; '**~wasser** *n* (-s/⸗) mouth-wash, gargle; '**~werk** F *fig. n:* **ein gutes ~ haben** have the gift of the gab.

Munition [muni'tsjo:n] *f* (-/-en) ammunition.

munkeln F ['muŋkəln] (ge-, h) **1.** *v/i.* whisper; **2.** *v/t.* whisper, rumo(u)r; **man munkelt** there is a rumo(u)r [lively; merry.]

munter *adj.* ['muntər] awake; *fig.*]

Münz|e ['myntsə] *f* (-/-n) coin; (small) change; medal; mint; **für bare ~ nehmen** take at face value; *j-m* **et. mit gleicher ~ heimzahlen** pay s.o. back in his own coin; '**~einheit** *f* (monetary) unit, standard of currency; '**≈en** *v/t.* (ge-, h) coin, mint; **gemünzt sein auf** (*acc.*) be meant for, be aimed at; '**~fernsprecher** *teleph.* *m* coin-box telephone; '**~fuß** *m* standard (*of coinage*); '**~wesen** *n* monetary system.

mürbe *adj.* ['myrbə] tender; *pastry, etc.*: crisp, short; *meat:* well-cooked; *material:* brittle; F *fig.* worn-out, demoralized; F *j-n ~ machen* break s.o.'s resistance; F **~ werden** give in.

Murmel ['murməl] *f* (-/-n) marble; '**≈n** *v/t. and v/i.* (ge-, h) mumble, murmur; '**~tier** *zo.* *n* marmot.

murren ['murən] *v/i.* (ge-, h) grumble, F grouch (*both: über acc.* at, over, about).

mürrisch *adj.* ['myriʃ] surly, sullen.

Mus [mu:s] *n* (-es/-e) pap; stewed fruit.

Muschel ['muʃəl] *f* (-/-n) *zo.*: mussel; shell, conch; *teleph.* ear-piece.

Museum [mu'ze:um] *n* (-s/Museen) museum.

Musik [mu'zi:k] *f* (-/*no pl.*) music; **~alienhandlung** [~i'ka:ljən-] *f* music-shop; **≈alisch** [~i'ka:liʃ] musical; **~ant** [~i'kant] *m* (-en/-en) musician; **~automat** *m* juke-box; **~er** ['mu:zikər] *m* (-s/-) musician; bandsman; **~instrument** *n* musical instrument; **~lehrer** *m* music-master; **~stunde** *f* music-lesson; **~truhe** *f* radio-gram(ophone), *Am.* radio-phonograph.

musizieren [muzi'tsi:rən] *v/i.* (*no -ge-, h*) make *or* have music.

Muskat ✿ [mus'ka:t] *m* (-[e]s/-e) nutmeg; **~nuß** ✿ *f* nutmeg.

Muskel ['muskəl] *m* (-s/-n) muscle; '**~kater** F *m* stiffness and soreness, *Am.* *a.* charley horse; '**~kraft** *f* muscular strength; '**~zerrung** ✻ *f* pulled muscle.

Muskul|atur [muskula'tu:r] *f* (-/-en) muscular system, muscles *pl.*; **≈ös** *adj.* [~'lø:s] muscular, brawny.

Muß [mus] *n* (-/*no pl.*) necessity; **es ist ein ~** it is a must.

Muße ['mu:sə] *f* (-/*no pl.*) leisure; spare time; **mit ~** at one's leisure.

Musselin [musə'li:n] *m* (-s/-e) muslin.

müssen ['mysən] (*irr., h*) **1.** *v/i.* (ge-): **ich muß** I must; **2.** *v/aux.* (*no -ge-*): **ich muß** I must, I have to;

M

I am obliged *or* compelled *or* forced to; I am bound to; *ich habe gehen* ~ I had to go; *ich müßte (eigentlich) wissen* I ought to know.

müßig *adj.* ['myːsiç] idle; superfluous; useless; '²**gang** *m* idleness, laziness; **²gänger** ['ˌgɛŋər] *m* (-s/-) idler, loafer; lazy-bones.

mußte ['mustə] *pret. of* müssen.

Muster ['mustər] *n* (-s/-) model; example, paragon; design, pattern; specimen; sample; '~**betrieb** *m* model factory *or* ~ farm; '~**gatte** *m* model husband; '²**gültig**, ²**haft** **1.** *adj.* model, exemplary, perfect; **2.** *adv.*: *sich* ~ *benehmen* be on one's best behavio(u)r; '~**kollektion** ✝ *f* range of samples; '~**n** *v/t.* (ge-, *h*) examine; eye; ✕ inspect, review; figure, pattern (*fabric, etc.*); '~**schutz** *m* protection of patterns and designs; '~**ung** *f* (-/-en) examination; ✕ review; pattern (*of fabric, etc.*); '~**werk** *n* standard work.

Mut [muːt] *m* (-[e]s/*no pl.*) courage; spirit; pluck; ~ *fassen* pluck up courage, summon one's courage; *den* ~ *sinken lassen* lose courage *or* heart; *guten* ~*(e)s sein* be of good cheer; '²**ig** *adj.* courageous, plucky; '²**los** *adj.* discouraged; despondent; '~**losigkeit** *f* (-/*no pl.*) discouragement; despondency; ²**maßen** ['~maːsən] *v/t.* (ge-, *h*) suppose, guess, surmise; '²**maßlich** *adj.* presumable; supposed; *heir:* presumptive; '~**maßung** *f* (-/-en) supposition, surmise; *bloße* ~*en pl.* guesswork.

Mutter ['mutər] *f* **1.** (-/ⁿ) mother; **2.** ⊕ (-/-n) nut; '~**brust** *f* mother's breast; '~**leib** *m* womb.

mütterlich *adj.* ['mytərliç] motherly; maternal; ~**erseits** *adv.* ['~ər'zaits] on *or* from one's mother's side; *uncle, etc.*: maternal.

'**Mutter**|**liebe** *f* motherly love; '²**los** *adj.* motherless; '~**mal** *n* birth-mark, mole; '~**milch** *f* mother's milk; '~**schaft** *f* (-/*no pl.*) maternity, motherhood; ²'**seelen**-al'**lein** *adj.* all *or* utterly alone; ~**söhnchen** ['~zøːnçən] *n* (-s/-) milksop, *sl.* sissy; '~**sprache** *f* mother tongue; '~**witz** *m* (-es/*no pl.*) mother wit.

Mutwill|**e** *m* wantonness; mischievousness; '²**ig** *adj.* wanton; mischievous; wilful.

Mütze ['mytsə] *f* (-/-n) cap.

Myrrhe ['myrə] *f* (-/-n) myrrh.

Myrte ♀ ['myrtə] *f* (-/-n) myrtle.

mysteri|**ös** *adj.* [myster'jøːs] mysterious; ²**um** [~'teːrjum] *n* (-s/*Mysterien*) mystery.

Mystifi|**kation** [mystifika'tsjoːn] *f* (-/-en) mystification; ²**zieren** [~'tsiːrən] *v/t.* (*no* -ge-, *h*) mystify.

Mysti|**k** ['mystik] *f* (-/*no pl.*) mysticism; ²**sch** *adj.* mystic(al).

Myth|**e** ['myːtə] *f* (-/-n) myth; '²**isch** *adj.* mythic; *esp. fig.* mythical; ~**ologie** [mytolo'giː] *f* (-/-n) mythology; ²**ologisch** *adj.* [myto-'loːgiʃ] mythological; ~**os** ['~os] *m* (-/*Mythen*), ~**us** ['~us] *m* (-/*Mythen*) myth.

N

na *int.* [na] now!, then!, well!, *Am. a.* hey!

Nabe ['naːbə] *f* (-/-n) hub.

Nabel *anat.* ['naːbəl] *m* (-s/-) navel.

nach [naːx] **1.** *prp.* (*dat.*) *direction, striving:* after; to(wards), for (*a.* ~ ... *hin or zu*); *succession:* after; *time:* after, past; *manner, measure, example:* according to; ~ *Gewicht* by weight; ~ *deutschem Geld* in German money; ~ *e-r* ~ *andern* one by one; *fünf Minuten* ~ *eins* five minutes past one; **2.** *adv.* after;

~ *und* ~ little by little, gradually; ~ *wie vor* now as before, still.

nachahm|**en** ['naːxʔaːmən] *v/t.* (*sep.,* -ge-, *h*) imitate, copy; counterfeit; '~**ens**'**wert** *adj.* worthy of imitation, exemplary; '²**er** *m* (-s/-) imitator; '²**ung** *f* (-/-en) imitation; copy; counterfeit, fake.

Nachbar ['naxbaːr] *m* (-n, -s/-n), '~**in** *f* (-/-nen) neighbo(u)r; '~**schaft** *f* (-/-en) neighbo(u)rhood, vicinity. [ment.]

'**Nachbehandlung** ✁ *f* after-treat-

'**nachbestell|en** v/t. (sep., no -ge-, h) repeat one's order for s.th.; '**2ung** f repeat (order).

'**nachbeten** v/t. (sep., -ge-, h) echo.

'**Nachbildung** f copy, imitation; replica; dummy.

'**nachblicken** v/i. (sep., -ge-, h) look after.

nachdem cj. [naːx'deːm] after, when; je ~ according as.

'**nachdenk|en** v/i. (irr. denken, sep., -ge-, h) think (über acc. over, about); reflect, meditate (über acc. on); '**2en** n (-s/no pl.) reflection, meditation; musing; '**~lich** adj. meditative, reflecting; pensive.

'**Nachdichtung** f free version.

'**Nachdruck** m **1.** (-[e]s/no pl.) stress, emphasis; **2.** typ. (-[e]s/-e) reprint; unlawfully: piracy, pirated edition; '**2en** v/t. (sep., -ge-, h) reprint; unlawfully: pirate.

nachdrücklich ['naːxdryklɪç] **1.** adj. emphatic, energetic; forcible; positive; **2.** adv.: ~ betonen emphasize.

nacheifern ['naːx[?]-] v/i. (sep., -ge-, h) emulate s.o.

nacheinander adv. [naːx[?]aɪ'nandər] one after another, successively; by or in turns.

nachempfinden ['naːx[?]-] v/t. (irr. empfinden, sep., no -ge-, h) s. nachfühlen.

nacherzähl|en ['naːx[?]-] v/t. (sep., no -ge-, h) repeat; retell; dem Englischen nacherzählt adapted from the English; '**2ung** ['naːx[?]-] f repetition; story retold, reproduction.

'**Nachfolge** f succession; '**2n** v/i. (sep., -ge-, sein) follow s.o.; j-m im Amt ~ succeed s.o. in his office; '**~r** m (-s/-) follower; successor.

'**nachforsch|en** v/i. (sep., -ge-, h) investigate; search for; '**2ung** f investigation, inquiry, search.

'**Nachfrage** f inquiry; † demand; '**2n** v/i. (sep., -ge-, h) inquire (nach after).

'**nach|fühlen** v/t. (sep., -ge-, h): es j-m ~ feel or sympathize with s.o.; '**~füllen** v/t. (sep., -ge-, h) fill up, refill; '**~geben** v/i. (irr. geben, sep., -ge-, h) give way (dat. to); yield, give in, yield (to); '**2gebühr** ☞ f surcharge; '**~gehen** v/i. (irr. gehen, sep., -ge-, sein) follow (s.o., business, trade, etc.); pursue (pleasure); attend to (business); investigate

s.th.; watch: be slow; '**2geschmack** m (-[e]s/no pl.) after-taste.

nachgiebig adj. ['naːxgiːbɪç] elastic, flexible; fig. a. yielding, compliant; '**2keit** f (-/-en) flexibility; compliance.

'**nachgrübeln** v/i. (sep., -ge-, h) ponder, brood (both: über acc. over), muse (on).

nachhaltig adj. ['naːxhaltɪç] lasting, enduring.

nach'her adv. afterwards; then; bis ~! see you later!, so long!

'**Nachhilfe** f help, assistance; '**~lehrer** m coach, private tutor; '**~unterricht** m private lesson(s pl.), coaching.

'**nach|holen** v/t. (sep., -ge-, h) make up for, make good; '**2hut** ⚔ f (-/-en) rear(-guard); die ~ bilden bring up the rear (a. fig.); '**~jagen** v/i. (sep., -ge-, sein) chase or pursue s.o.; '**~klingen** v/i. (irr. klingen, sep., -ge-, h) resound, echo.

'**Nachkomme** m (-n/-n) descendant; ~n pl. esp. ⚖ issue; '**2n** v/i. (irr. kommen, sep., -ge-, sein) follow; come later; obey (order); meet (liabilities); '**~nschaft** f (-/-en) descendants pl., esp. ⚖ issue.

'**Nachkriegs...** post-war.

Nachlaß ['naːxlas] m (Nachlasses/ Nachlasse, Nachlässe) ☞ reduction, discount; assets pl., estate, inheritance (of deceased).

'**nachlassen** (irr. lassen, sep., -ge-, h) **1.** v/t. reduce (price); **2.** v/i. deteriorate; slacken, relax; diminish; pain, rain, cold.: abate; storm: calm down; strength: wane; interest: flag.

'**nachlässig** adj. careless, negligent.

'**nach|laufen** v/i. (irr. laufen, sep., -ge-, sein) run (dat. after); '**~lesen** v/t. (irr. lesen, sep., -ge-, h) in book: look up; ⚘ glean; '**~liefern** ☞ v/t. (sep., -ge-, h) deliver subsequently; repeat delivery of; '**~lösen** v/t. (sep., -ge-, h): e-e Fahrkarte ~ take a supplementary ticket; buy a ticket en route; '**~machen** v/t. (sep., -ge-, h) imitate (j-m etw. s.o. in s.th.); copy; counterfeit, forge; '**~messen** v/t. (irr. messen, sep., -ge-, h) measure again.

'**Nachmittag** m afternoon; '**2s** adv. in the afternoon; '**~svorstellung** thea. f matinée.

Nach|nahme ['naːxnaːmə] f (-/-n)

cash on delivery, *Am.* collect on delivery; *per* ~ **schicken** send C.O.D.; '**~name** *m* surname, last name; '**~porto** 🅱 *n* surcharge.

'**nach|prüfen** *v/t.* (*sep.*, -ge-, *h*) verify; check; '**~rechnen** *v/t.* (*sep.*, -ge-, *h*) reckon over again; check (*bill*).

'**Nachrede** *f:* üble ~ 🆉🆉 defamation (of character); *oral:* slander, *written:* libel; '🅱n *v/t.* (*sep.*, -ge-, *h*): *j-m Übles* ~ slander s.o.

Nachricht ['naːxrɪçt] *f* (-/-en) news; message; report; information, notice; ~ **geben** s. **benachrichtigen**; '**~enagentur** *f* news agency; '**~endienst** *m* news service; ✖ intelligence service; '**~ensprecher** *m* newscaster; '**~enwesen** *n* (-s/*no pl.*) communications *pl.*

'**nachrücken** *v/i.* (*sep.*, -ge-, *sein*) move along.

'**Nach|ruf** *m* obituary (notice); '**~ruhm** *m* posthumous fame.

'**nachsagen** *v/t.* (*sep.*, -ge-, *h*) repeat; *man sagt ihm nach, daß* he is said to *inf.*

'**Nachsaison** *f* dead *or* off season.

'**nachschicken** *v/t.* (*sep.*, -ge-, *h*) s. **nachsenden**.

'**nachschlage|n** *v/t.* (*irr.* **schlagen**, *sep.*, -ge-, *h*) consult (*book*); look up (*word*); '🅱**werk** *n* reference-book.

'**Nach|schlüssel** *m* skeleton key; '**~schrift** *f* *in letter:* postscript; '**~schub** *esp.* ✖ *m* supplies *pl.*; '**~schubweg** ✖ *m* supply line.

'**nach|sehen** (*irr.* **sehen**, *sep.*, -ge-, *h*) **1.** *v/i.* look after; ~, *ob* (go and) see whether; **2.** *v/t.* look after; examine, inspect; check; overhaul (*machine*); s. **nachschlagen**; *j-m et.* ~ indulge s.o. in s.th.; '**~senden** *v/t.* ([*irr.* **senden**] *sep.*, -ge-, *h*) send after; send on, forward (*letter*) (*j-m* to s.o.).

'**Nachsicht** *f* indulgence; '🅱**ig** *adj.*, 🅱**svoll** *adj.* indulgent, forbearing.

'**Nachsilbe** *gr* *f* suffix.

'**nach|sinnen** *v/i.* (*irr.* **sinnen**, *sep.*, -ge-, *h*) muse, meditate (*über acc.* [up]on); '**~sitzen** *v/i.* (*irr.* **sitzen**, *sep.*, -ge-, *h*) *pupil:* be kept in.

'**Nach|sommer** *m* St. Martin's summer, *esp. Am.* Indian summer; '**~speise** *f* dessert. '**~spiel** *fig.* *n* sequel.

'**nach|spionieren** *v/i.* (*sep.*, *no* -ge-, *h*) spy (*dat.* on); '**~sprechen** *v/i.* *and v/t.* (*irr.* **sprechen**, *sep.*, -ge-, *h*) repeat; '**~spülen** *v/t.* (*sep.*, -ge-, *h*) rinse; '**~spüren** *v/i.* (*sep.*, -ge-, *h*) (*dat.*) track, trace.

nächst [nɛːçst] **1.** *adj.* succession, *time:* next; *distance, relation:* nearest; **2.** *prp.* (*dat.*) next to, next after; '🅱**beste** *m, f, n* (-*n*/-*n*-): *der* (*die*) ~ anyone; *das* ~ anything; *er fragte den* ~*n* he asked the next person he met.

'**nachstehen** *v/i.* (*irr.* **stehen**, *sep.*, -ge-, *h*): *j-m in nichts* ~ be in no way inferior to s.o.

'**nachstell|en** (*sep.*, -ge-, *h*) **1.** *v/t.* place behind; put back (*watch*); ⊕ adjust (*screw, etc.*); **2.** *v/i.*: *j-m* ~ be after s.o.; '🅱**ung** *fig.* *f* persecution.

'**Nächstenliebe** *f* charity.

'**nächstens** *adv.* shortly, (very) soon, before long.

'**nach|streben** *v/i.* (*sep.*, -ge-, *h*) s. **nacheifern**; '**~suchen** *v/i.* (*sep.*, -ge-, *h*): ~ *um* apply for, seek.

Nacht [naxt] *f* (-/*e*e) night; *bei* ~, *des* ~*s* s. *nachts*; '**~arbeit** *f* nightwork; '**~asyl** *n* night-shelter; '**~ausgabe** *f* night edition (*of newspaper*); '**~dienst** *m* night-duty.

'**Nachteil** *m* disadvantage, drawback; *im* ~ *sein* be at a disadvantage; '🅱**ig** *adj.* disadvantageous.

'**Nacht|essen** *n* supper; '**~falter** *zo.* *m* (-*s*/-) moth; '**~gebet** *n* evening prayer; '**~geschirr** *n* chamberpot; '**~hemd** *n* night-gown, *Am. a.* night robe; *for men:* nightshirt.

Nachtigall *orn.* ['naxtɪgal] *f* (-/-en) nightingale.

'**Nachtisch** *m* (-es/*no pl.*) sweet, dessert.

'**Nachtlager** *n* (*a*) lodging for the night; bed.

nächtlich *adj.* ['nɛçtlɪç] nightly, nocturnal.

'**Nacht|lokal** *n* night-club; '**~mahl** *n* supper; '**~portier** *m* night-porter; '**~quartier** *n* night-quarters *pl.*

Nachtrag ['naːxtraːk] *m* (-[*e*]s/*e*e) supplement; '🅱**en** *v/t.* (*irr.* **tragen**, *sep.*, -ge-, *h*) carry (*j-m et.* s.th. after s.o.); add; † post up (*ledger*); *j-m et.* ~ bear s.o. a grudge; '**~end** *adj.* unforgiving, resentful.

namenlos

nachträglich adj. ['naːxtrɛːkliç] additional; subsequent.

nachts adv. [naxts] at or by night.

'Nacht|schicht f night-shift; '**Ջ-schlafend** adj.: zu ∼er Zeit in the middle of the night; '**∼schwärmer** fig. m night-reveller; '**∼tisch** m bedside table; '**∼topf** m chamberpot; '**∼vorstellung** thea. f night performance; '**∼wache** f nightwatch; '**∼wächter** m (night-)watchman; **∼wandler** ['∼vandlər] m (-s/-) sleep-walker; '**∼zeug** n night-things pl.

'nachwachsen v/i. (irr. wachsen, sep., -ge-, sein) grow again.

'Nachwahl parl. f by-election.

Nachweis ['naːxvaɪs] m (-es/-e) proof, evidence; '**Ջbar** adj. demonstrable; traceable; **Ջen** ['∼zən] v/t. (irr. weisen, sep., -ge-, h) point out, show; trace; prove; '**Ջlich** adj. s. nachweisbar.

'Nach|welt f posterity; '**∼wirkung** f after-effect; consequences pl.; aftermath; '**∼wort** n (-[e]s/-e) epilog(ue); '**∼wuchs** m (-[e]s/no pl.) rising generation.

'nach|zahlen v/t. (sep., -ge-, h) pay in addition; '**∼zählen** v/t. (sep., -ge-, h) count over (again), check; '**Ջzahlung** f additional payment.

Nachzügler ['naːxtsyːklər] m (-s/-) straggler, late-comer.

Nacken ['nakən] m (-s/-) nape (of the neck), neck.

nackt adj. [nakt] naked, nude; bare (a. fig.); young birds: unfledged; truth: plain.

Nadel ['naːdəl] f (-/-n) needle; pin; brooch; '**∼arbeit** f needlework; '**∼baum** ♀ m conifer(ous tree); '**∼stich** m prick; stitch; fig. pinprick.

Nagel ['naːgəl] m (-s/-) anat., ⊕ nail; of wood: peg; spike; stud; die Arbeit brennt mir auf den Nägeln it's a rush job; '**∼haut** f cuticle; '**∼lack** m nail varnish; 'Ջn v/t. (ge-, h) nail (an or auf acc. to); **∼necessaire** ['∼nesesɛːr] n (-s/-s) manicure-case; 'Ջneu F adj. bran(d)-new; '**∼pflege** f manicure.

nage|n ['naːgən] (ge-, h) **1.** v/i. gnaw; ∼ an (dat.) gnaw at; pick (bone); **2.** v/t. gnaw; 'Ջtier zo. n rodent, gnawer.

nah adj. [naː] near, close (bei to); nearby; danger: imminent.

Näharbeit ['nɛː?-] f needlework, sewing.

'Nahaufnahme f film: close-up.

nahe adj. ['naːə] s. nah.

Nähe ['nɛːə] f (-/no pl.) nearness, proximity; vicinity; in der ∼ close by.

'nahe|gehen v/i. (irr. gehen, sep., -ge-, sein) (dat.) affect, grieve; '**∼kommen** v/i. (irr. kommen, sep., -ge-, sein) (dat.) approach; get at (truth); '**∼legen** v/t. (sep., -ge-, h) suggest; '**∼liegen** v/i. (irr. liegen, sep., -ge-, h) suggest itself, be obvious.

nahen ['naːən] **1.** v/i. (ge-, sein) approach; **2.** v/refl. (ge-, h) approach (j-m s.o.).

nähen ['nɛːən] v/t. and v/i. (ge-, h) sew, stitch.

näher adj. ['nɛːər] nearer, closer; road: shorter; das Nähere (further) particulars pl. or details pl.

'Näherin f (-/-nen) seamstress.

'nähern v/t. (ge-, h) approach (dat. to); sich ∼ approach (j-m s.o.).

'nahe zu adv. nearly, almost.

'Nähgarn n (-[e]s/-e) sewing-cotton.

Nahkampf ⚔ m close combat.

nahm [naːm] pret. of nehmen.

'Näh|maschine f sewing-machine; '**∼nadel** f (sewing-)needle.

nähren ['nɛːrən] v/t. (ge-, h) nourish (a. fig.), feed; nurse (child); sich ∼ von live or feed on.

nahrhaft adj. ['naːrhaft] nutritious, nourishing.

'Nahrung f (-/no pl.) food, nourishment, nutriment.

'Nahrungs|aufnahme f intake of food; '**∼mittel** n/pl. food(-stuff), victuals pl.

'Nährwert m nutritive value.

Naht [naːt] f (-/ⁱe) seam; ⚕ suture.

'Nahverkehr m local traffic.

'Nähzeug n sewing-kit.

naiv adj. [na'iːf] naïve, naive, simple; Ջität [naivi'tɛːt] f (-/no pl.) naïveté, naivety, simplicity.

Name ['naːmə] m (-ns/-n) name; im ∼n (gen.) on behalf of; dem ∼n nach nominal(ly), in name only; dem ∼n nach kennen know by name; die Dinge beim rechten ∼n nennen call a spade a spade; darf ich um Ihren ∼n bitten? may I ask your name?

'namen|los adj. nameless, anony-

N
O

mous; *fig.* unutterable; '~s **1.** *adv.* named, by the name of, called; **2.** *prp.* (*gen.*) in the name of.

'**Namens|tag** *m* name-day; '~**vetter** *m* namesake; '~**zug** *m* signature.

namentlich ['nɑːməntliç] **1.** *adj.* nominal; **2.** *adv.* by name; especially, in particular.

'**namhaft** *adj.* notable; considerable; ~ *machen* name.

nämlich ['nɛːmliç] **1.** *adj.* the same; **2.** *adv.* namely, that is (to say).

nannte ['nantə] *pret.* of *nennen*.

Napf [napf] *m* (-[e]s/⁼e) bowl, basin.

Narb|e ['narbə] *f* (-/-n) scar; '**2ig** *adj.* scarred; *leather:* grained.

Narko|se [nar'koːzə] *f* (-/-n) narcosis; **2tisieren** [ˌoti'ziːrən] *v/t.* (*no* -ge-, *h*) narcotize.

Narr [nar] *m* (-en/-en) fool; jester; *zum ~en halten* = **2en** *v/t.* (ge-, *h*) make a fool of, fool.

'**Narren|haus** F *n* madhouse; '~**kappe** *f* fool's-cap; '2**sicher** *adj.* foolproof.

'**Narrheit** *f* (-/-en) folly.

Närrin ['nerin] *f* (-/-nen) fool, foolish woman.

'**närrisch** *adj.* foolish, silly; odd.

Narzisse ♀ [nar'tsisə] *f* (-/-n) narcissus; *gelbe* ~ daffodil.

nasal *adj.* [na'zɑːl] nasal; ~*e Sprechweise* twang.

nasch|en ['naʃən] (ge-, *h*) **1.** *v/i.* nibble (*an dat.* at); *gern* ~ have a sweet tooth; **2.** *v/t.* nibble; eat *s.th.* on the sly; **2erei** [ˌʃaiˌrən] *f/pl.* dainties *pl.*, sweets *pl.*; '~**haft** *adj.* fond of dainties or sweets.

Nase ['nɑːzə] *f* (-/-n) nose; *die* ~ *rümpfen* turn up one's nose (*über acc.* at).

näseln ['nɛːzəln] *v/i.* (ge-, *h*) speak through the nose, nasalize; snuffle.

'**Nasen|bluten** *n* (-s/*no pl.*) nosebleeding; '~**loch** *n* nostril; '~**spitze** *f* tip of the nose.

naseweis *adj.* ['nɑːzəvais] pert, saucy.

nasführen ['nɑːs-] *v/t.* (ge-, *h*) fool, dupe.

Nashorn *zo.* ['nɑːs-] *n* rhinoceros.

naß *adj.* [nas] wet; damp, moist.

Nässe ['nɛsə] *f* (-/*no pl.*) wet(ness); moisture; ♫ humidity; '2**n** (ge-, *h*) **1.** *v/t.* wet; moisten; **2.** ♫ *v/i.* discharge.

'**naßkalt** *adj.* damp and cold, raw.

Nation [na'tsjoːn] *f* (-/-en) nation.

national *adj.* [natsjo'nɑːl] national; **2hymne** *f* national anthem; **2ismus** [ˌa'lismus] *m* (-/*Nationalismen*) nationalism; **2ität** [ˌali'tɛːt] *f* (-/-en) nationality; **2mannschaft** *f* national team.

Natter ['natər] *f* (-/-n) *zo.* adder, viper; *fig.* serpent.

Natur [na'tuːr] *f* **1.** (-/*no pl.*) nature; **2.** (-/-en) constitution; temper(ament), disposition, nature; *von* ~ by nature.

Naturalien [natu'rɑːljən] *pl.* natural produce *sg.*; *in* ~ in kind.

naturalisieren [naturali'ziːrən] *v/t.* (*no* -ge-, *h*) naturalize.

Naturalismus [natura'lismus] *m* (-/*no pl.*) naturalism.

Naturanlage [na'tuːr-] *f* (natural) disposition.

Naturell [natu'rɛl] *n* (-s/-e) natural disposition, nature, temper.

Na'tur|ereignis *n*, ~**erscheinung** *f* phenomenon; ~**forscher** *m* naturalist, scientist; **2gemäß** *adj.* natural; ~**geschichte** *f* natural history; ~**gesetz** *n* law of nature, natural law; **2getreu** *adj.* true to nature; life-like; ~**kunde** *f* (natural) science.

natürlich [na'tyːrliç] **1.** *adj.* natural; genuine; innate; unaffected; **2.** *adv.* naturally, of course.

Na'tur|produkte *n/pl.* natural products *pl.* or produce *sg.*; ~**schutz** *m* wild-life conservation; ~**schutzgebiet** *n*, ~**schutzpark** *m* national park, wild-life (p)reserve; ~**trieb** *m* instinct; ~**wissenschaft** *f* (natural) science; ~**wissenschaftler** *m* (natural) scientist.

Nebel ['neːbəl] *m* (-s/-) fog; mist; haze; smoke; '2**haft** *fig. adj.* nebulous, hazy, dim; '~**horn** *n* fog-horn.

neben *prp.* (*dat.*; *acc.*) ['neːbən] beside, by (the side of); near to; against, compared with; apart *or Am. a.* aside from, besides.

neben|an *adv.* next door; close by; **2anschluß** *teleph.* ['neːbənʔ-] *m* extension (line); **2arbeit** ['neːbənʔ-] *f* extra work; **2ausgaben** ['neːbənʔ-] *f/pl.* incidental expenses *pl.*, extras *pl.*; **2ausgang** ['neːbənʔ-] *m* side-exit, side-door; '2**bedeutung** *f* secondary meaning, connotation;

~'**bei** adv. by the way; besides; 2**beruf** m side-line; ~**beruflich** adv. as a side-line; in one's spare time; 2**beschäftigung** f s. Nebenberuf; 2**buhler** ['~bu:lər] m (-s/-) rival; ~**ei'nander** adv. side by side; ~ bestehen co-exist; 2**eingang** ['ne:bən?-] m side-entrance; 2**einkünfte** ['ne:bən?-] pl., 2**einnahmen** ['ne:bən?-] f/pl. casual emoluments pl., extra income; 2**erscheinung** ['ne:bən?-] f accompaniment; 2**fach** n subsidiary subject, Am. minor (subject); 2**fluß** m tributary (river); 2**gebäude** n annex(e); outhouse; 2**geräusch** n radio: atmospherics pl., interference, jamming; 2**gleis** 🚂 n siding, side-track; 2**handlung** thea. f underplot; 2**haus** n adjoining house; ~'**her** adv., ~'**hin** adv. by his or her side; s. nebenbei; 2**kläger** 🏛 m co-plaintiff; 2**kosten** pl. extras pl.; 2**mann** m person next to one; 2**produkt** n by-product; 2**rolle** f minor part (a. thea.); 2**sache** f minor matter, side issue; ~**sächlich** adj. subordinate, incidental; unimportant; 2**satz** gr. m subordinate clause; 2**stehend** adj. in the margin; 2**stelle** f branch; agency; teleph. extension; 2**straße** f bystreet, by-road; 2**strecke** 🚂 f branch line; 2**tisch** m next table; 2**tür** f side-door; 2**verdienst** m incidental or extra earnings pl.; 2**zimmer** n adjoining room.

'**neblig** adj. foggy, misty, hazy.

nebst prp. (dat.) [ne:pst] together with, besides; including.

neck|en ['nɛkən] v/t. (ge-, h) tease, banter, sl. kid; 2**erei** [~'raɪ] f (-/-en) teasing, banter; '~**isch** adj. playful; droll, funny.

Neffe ['nɛfə] m (-n/-n) nephew.

negativ ['nega'ti:f] 1. adj. negative; 2. 2 n (-s/-e) negative.

Neger ['ne:gər] m (-s/-) negro; '~**in** f (-/-nen) negress.

nehmen ['ne:mən] v/t. (irr., ge-, h) take; receive; charge (money); zu sich ~ take, have (meal); j-m et. ~ take s.th. from s.o.; ein Ende ~ come to an end; es sich nicht ~ lassen zu inf. insist upon ger.; streng genommen strictly speaking.

Neid [naɪt] m (-[e]s/no pl.) envy; 2**en** ['naɪdən] v/t. (ge-, h): j-m et.

~ envy s.o. s.th.; ~**er** ['~dər] m (-s/-) envious person; ~**hammel** ['naɪt-] m dog in the manger; 2**isch** ['~dɪʃ] envious (auf acc. of); 2**los** adj. ['naɪt-] ungrudging.

Neige ['naɪgə] f (-/-n) decline; barrel: dregs pl.; glass: heeltap; zur ~ gehen (be on the) decline; esp. 🏛 run short; 2**n** (ge-, h) 1. v/t. and v/refl. bend, incline; 2. v/i.: er neigt zu Übertreibungen he is given to exaggeration.

'**Neigung** f (-/-en) inclination (a. fig.); slope, incline.

nein adv. [naɪn] no. [tar.)

Nektar ['nɛkta:r] m (-s/no pl.) nec-)

Nelke 🌱 ['nɛlkə] f (-/-n) carnation, pink; spice: clove.

nennen ['nɛnən] v/t. (irr., ge-, h) name; call; term; mention; nominate (candidate); sports: enter (für for); sich ... ~ be called ...; '~**swert** adj. worth mentioning.

'**Nenn|er** A m (-s/-) denominator; '~**ung** f (-/-en) naming; mentioning; nomination (of candidates); sports: entry; '~**wert** m nominal or face value; zum ~ 🏛 at par.

Neon 🔬 ['ne:ɔn] n (-s/no pl.) neon; '~**röhre** f neon tube.

Nerv [nɛrf] m (-s/-en) nerve; j-m auf die ~en fallen or gehen get on s.o.'s nerves.

'**Nerven|arzt** m neurologist; '2**aufreibend** adj. trying; '~**heilanstalt** f mental hospital; '~**kitzel** m (-s/no pl.) thrill, sensation; '2**krank** adj. neurotic; 2**leidend** adj. neuropathic, neurotic; '~**schwäche** f nervous debility; '2**stärkend** adj. tonic; '~**system** n nervous system; '~**zusammenbruch** m nervous breakdown.

nerv|ig adj. ['nɛrvɪç] sinewy; ~**ös** adj. [~'vø:s] nervous; 2**osität** [~ozi'tɛ:t] f (-/no pl.) nervousness.

Nerz zo. [nɛrts] m (-es/-e) mink.

Nessel 🌿 ['nɛsəl] f (-/-n) nettle.

Nest [nɛst] n (-es/-er) nest; F fig. bed; F fig. hick or one-horse town.

nett adj. [nɛt] nice, neat, pretty, Am. a. cute; pleasant; kind.

netto 🏛 adv. ['nɛto] net, clear.

Netz [nɛts] n (-es/-e) net; fig. network; '~**anschluß** ⚡ m mains connection, power supply; '~**haut** anat. f retina; '~**spannung** ⚡ f mains voltage.

neu adj. [nɔy] new; fresh; recent; modern; ~ere Sprachen modern languages; ~este Nachrichten latest news; von ~em anew, afresh; ein ~es Leben beginnen turn over a new leaf; was gibt es Neues? what is the news?, Am. what is new?

'**Neu|anschaffung** f (-/-en) recent acquisition; **2artig** adj. novel; '~auflage typ. f, '~ausgabe typ. f new edition; reprint; '~bau m (-[e]s/-ten) new building; '~bearbeitet adj. revised; '~e m (-n/-n) new man; new-comer; novice; **2entdeckt** adj. recently discovered.

neuer|dings ['nɔyərdiŋs] adv. of late, recently; '2er m (-s/-) innovator.

Neuerscheinung ['nɔyʔ-] f new book or publication.

'**Neuerung** f (-/-en) innovation.

'**neu|geboren** adj. new-born; '~gestalten v/t. (sep., -ge-, h) reorganize; '2gestaltung f reorganization; '2gier f, 2gierde ['~də] f (-/no pl.) curiosity, inquisitiveness; '~gierig adj. curious (auf acc. about, of), inquisitive, sl. nos(e)y; ich bin ~, ob I wonder whether or if; '2heit f (-/-en) newness, freshness; novelty.

'**Neuigkeit** f (-/-en) (e-e a piece of) news.

'**Neu|jahr** n New Year('s Day); '~land n (-[e]s/no pl.): ~ erschließen break fresh ground (a. fig.); '2lich adv. the other day, recently; '~ling m (-s/-e) novice; contp. greenhorn; '2modisch adj. fashionable; '~mond m (-[e]s/no pl.) new moon.

neun adj. [nɔyn] nine; '~te ninth; '2tel n (-s/-) ninth part; '~tens adv. ninthly; '~zehn adj. nineteen; '~zehnte adj. nineteenth; ~zig adj. ['~tsiç] ninety; '~zigste adj. ninetieth.

'**Neu|philologe** m student or teacher of modern languages; '~regelung f reorganization, rearrangement.

neutr|al adj. [nɔy'tra:l] neutral; 2alität [~ali'tɛ:t] f (-/no pl.) neutrality; 2um gr. ['nɔytrum] 2 (-s/Neutra, Neutren) neuter.

'**neu|vermählt** adj. newly married; die 2en pl. the newly-weds pl.; '2wahl f new election; '~wertig adj. as good as new; '2zeit f (-/no pl.) modern times pl.

nicht adv. [niçt] not; auch ~ nor; ~ anziehend unattractive; ~ besser no better; ~ bevollmächtigt non-commissioned; ~ einlösbar † inconvertible; ~ erscheinen fail to attend.

'**Nicht|achtung** f disregard; '2amtlich adj. unofficial; '~angriffspakt pol. m non-aggression pact; '~annahme f non-acceptance; '~befolgung f non-observance.

Nichte ['niçtə] f (-/-n) niece.

'**nichtig** adj. null, void; invalid; vain, futile; für ~ erklären declare null and void, annul; '2keit f (-/-en) nullity; vanity, futility.

'**Nichtraucher** m non-smoker.

nichts [niçts] **1.** indef. pron. nothing, naught, not anything; **2.** 2 n (-/no pl.) nothing(ness); fig.: nonentity; void; '~ahnend adj. unsuspecting; ~desto'weniger adv. nevertheless; '~nutzig adj. ['~nutsiç] good-for-nothing, worthless; '~sagend adj. insignificant; 2tuer ['~tu:ər] m (-s/-) idler; '~würdig adj. vile, base, infamous.

'**Nicht|vorhandensein** n absence; lack; '~wissen n ignorance.

nick|en ['nikən] v/i. (ge-, h) nod; bow; '2erchen F n (-s/-): ein ~ machen take a nap, have one's forty winks.

nie adv. [ni:] never, at no time.

nieder ['ni:dər] **1.** adj. low; base, mean, vulgar; value, rank: inferior; **2.** adv. down.

'**Nieder|gang** m decline; '2gedrückt adj. dejected, downcast; '2gehen v/i. (irr. gehen, sep., -ge-, sein) go down; ✈ descend; storm: break; '2geschlagen adj. dejected, downcast; '2hauen v/t. (irr. hauen, sep., -ge-, h) cut down; '2kommen v/i. (irr. kommen, sep., -ge-, sein) be confined; be delivered (mit of); '~kunft ['~kunft] f (-/⸚e) confinement, delivery; '~lage f defeat; † warehouse; branch; '2lassen v/t. (irr. lassen, sep., -ge-, h) let down; sich ~ settle (down); bird: alight; sit down; establish o.s.; settle (in dat. at); '~lassung f (-/-en) establishment; settlement; branch, agency; '2legen v/t. (sep., -ge-, h) lay or put down; resign (position); retire from (business); abdicate; die Arbeit ~ (go on) strike, down tools,

Am. F *a.* walk out; *sich ~* lie down, go to bed; '2**machen** *v/t.* (*sep.*, -ge-, *h*) cut down; massacre; '~**schlag** *m* 🜍 precipitate; sediment; precipitation (*of rain, etc.*); *radioactive:* fall-out; *boxing:* knock-down, knock-out; '2**schlagen** *v/t.* (*irr. schlagen, sep.,* -ge-, *h*) knock down; *boxing:* a. floor; cast down (*eyes*); suppress; put down, crush (*rebellion*); 🜨 quash; *sich ~* 🜍 precipitate; '2**schmettern** *fig.* *v/t.* (*sep.,* -ge-, *h*) crush; '2**setzen** *v/t.* (*sep.,* -ge-, *h*) set *or* put down; *sich ~* sit down; *birds:* perch, alight; '2**strecken** *v/t.* (*sep.,* -ge-, *h*) lay low, strike to the ground, floor; '2**trächtig** *adj.* base, mean; F beastly; '~**ung** *f* (-/-en) lowlands *pl.*

niedlich *adj.* ['ni:tliç] neat, nice, pretty, *Am. a.* cute. [nail.]

Niednagel ['ni:t-] *m* agnail, hangnail.

niedrig *adj.* ['ni:driç] low (*a. fig.*); moderate; *fig.* mean, base.

niemals *adv.* ['ni:ma:ls] never, at no time.

niemand *indef. pron.* ['ni:mant] nobody, no one, none; '2**sland** *n* (-[e]s/*no pl.*) no man's land.

Niere ['ni:rə] *f* (-/-n) kidney; '~**nbraten** *m* loin of veal.

nieseln F ['ni:zəln] *v/i.* (ge-, *h*) drizzle; '2**regen** F *m* drizzle.

niesen ['ni:zən] *v/i.* (ge-, *h*) sneeze.

Niet ⊕ [ni:t] *m* (-[e]s/-e) rivet; '~**e** *f* (-/-n) *lottery:* blank; F *fig.* washout; '2**en** ⊕ *v/t.* (ge-, *h*) rivet.

Nilpferd *zo.* ['ni:l-] *n* hippopotamus.

Nimbus ['nimbus] *m* (-/-se) halo (*a. fig.*), nimbus.

nimmer *adv.* ['nimər] never; '~**mehr** *adv.* nevermore; '2**satt** *m* (-, -[e]s/-e) glutton; '2**wiedersehen** F *n: auf ~* never to meet again; *er verschwand auf ~* he left for good. [*dat. at*).]

nippen ['nipən] *v/i.* (ge-, *h*) sip (*an*)

Nipp|es ['nipəs] *pl.*, '~**sachen** *pl.* (k)nick-(k)nacks *pl.*

nirgend|s *adv.* ['nirgənts], '~**(s)wo** *adv.* nowhere.

Nische ['ni:ʃə] *f* (-/-n) niche, recess.

nisten ['nistən] *v/i.* (ge-, *h*) nest.

Niveau [ni'vo:] *n* (-s/-s) level; *fig. a.* standard.

nivellieren [nive'li:rən] *v/t.* (*no* -ge-, *h*) level, grade.

Nixe ['niksə] *f* (-/-n) water-nymph, mermaid.

noch [nɔx] **1.** *adv.* still; yet; *~ ein* another, one more; *~ einmal* once more *or* again; *~ etwas* something more; *~ etwas?* anything else?; *~ heute* this very day; *~ immer* still; *~ nicht* not yet; *~ nie* never before; *~ so* ever so; *~ im 19. Jahrhundert* as late as the 19th century; *es wird ~ 2 Jahre dauern* it will take two more *or* another two years; **2.** *cj.:* *s. weder*; **~malig** *adj.* ['~ma:liç] repeated; **~mals** *adv.* ['~ma:ls] once more *or* again.

Nomad|e [no'ma:də] *m* (-n/-n) nomad; 2**isch** *adj.* nomadic.

Nominativ *gr.* ['no:minati:f] *m* (-s/-e) nominative (case).

nominieren [nomi'ni:rən] *v/t.* (*no* -ge-, *h*) nominate.

Nonne ['nɔnə] *f* (-/-n) nun; '~**nkloster** *n* nunnery, convent.

Nord *geogr.* [nɔrt], **~en** *m* ['~dən] *m* (-s/*no pl.*) north; 2**isch** *adj.* ['~diʃ] northern.

nördlich *adj.* ['nœrtliç] northern, northerly.

'**Nord|licht** *n* northern lights *pl.*; **~ost(en** *m*) north-east; '~**pol** *m* North Pole; 2**wärts** *adv.* ['~vɛrts] northward(s), north; **~'west(en** *m*) north-west.

nörg|eln ['nœrgəln] *v/i.* (ge-, *h*) nag, carp (*an dat.* at); grumble; 2**ler** *m* ['~lər] *m* (-s/-) faultfinder, grumbler.

Norm [nɔrm] *f* (-/-en) standard; rule; norm.

normal *adj.* [nɔr'ma:l] normal; regular; *measure, weight, time:* standard; **~isieren** [~ali'zi:rən] *v/t./refl.* (*no* -ge-, *h*) return to normal.

'**norm|en** *v/t.* (ge-, *h*), **~ieren** [~'mi:rən] *v/t.* (*no* -ge-, *h*) standardize.

Not [no:t] *f* (-/-e) need, want; necessity; difficulty, trouble; misery; danger, emergency, distress (*a.* ⚓); *~ leiden* suffer privations; *in ~ geraten* become destitute, get into trouble; *in ~ sein* to be in trouble; *zur ~* at a pinch; *es tut not, daß* it is necessary that. [notary.]

Notar [no'ta:r] *m* (-s/-e) (public)

'**Not|ausgang** *m* emergency exit; '~**behelf** *m* makeshift, expedient, stopgap; '~**bremse** *f* emergency brake; **'⸦brücke** f temporary bridge; **⸦durft** ['⸦durft] f (-/no pl.): s-e ⸦ verrichten relieve o.s.; **²dürftig** adj. scanty, poor; temporary.

Note ['no:tə] f (-/-n) note (a. ♪); pol. note, memorandum; school: mark.

'Noten|bank ✝ f bank of issue; **'⸦schlüssel** ♪ m clef; **'⸦system** ♪ n staff.

'Not|fall m case of need, emergency; **'²falls** adv. if necessary; **²gedrungen** adv. of necessity, needs.

notier|en [no'ti:rən] v/t. (no -ge-, h) make a note of, note (down); ✝ quote; **²ung** ✝ f (-/-en) quotation.

nötig adj. ['nø:tiç] necessary; ⸦ haben need; **⸦en** ['⸦gən] v/t. (ge-, h) force, oblige, compel; press, urge (guest); **'⸦en'falls** adv. if necessary; **²ung** f (-/-en) compulsion; pressing; 🕱🕱 intimidation.

Notiz [no'ti:ts] f (-/-en) notice, memorandum; ⸦ nehmen von take notice of; pay attention to; keine ⸦ nehmen von ignore; sich ⸦en machen take notes; **⸦block** m pad, Am. a. scratch pad; **⸦buch** n notebook.

'Not|lage f distress; emergency; **'²landen** ⯰ v/i. (-ge-, sein) make a forced or emergency landing; **'⸦landung** ⯰ f forced or emergency landing; **²leidend** adj. needy, destitute; distressed; **'⸦lösung** f expedient; **'⸦lüge** f white lie.

notorisch adj. [no'to:riʃ] notorious.

'Not|ruf teleph. m emergency call; **'⸦signal** n emergency or distress signal; **'⸦sitz** mot. m dick(e)y(-seat), Am. a. rumble seat; **'⸦stand** m emergency; **'⸦standsarbeiten** f/pl. relief works pl.; **'⸦standsgebiet** n distressed area; **'⸦standsgesetze** n/pl. emergency laws pl.; **'⸦verband** m first-aid dressing; **'⸦verordnung** f emergency decree; **'⸦wehr** f self-defen|ce, Am. -se; **²wendig** adj. necessary; **'⸦wendigkeit** f (-/-en) necessity; **'⸦zucht** f (-/no pl.) rape.

Novelle [no'vɛlə] f (-/-n) short story, novella; parl. amendment.

November [no'vɛmbər] m (-[s]/-) November. [time.]

Nu [nu:] m (-/no pl.): im ⸦ in no

Nuance [ny'ã:sə] f (-/-n) shade.

nüchtern adj. ['nyçtərn] empty, fasting; sober (a. fig.); matter-of-fact; writings: jejune; prosaic; cool; plain; **²heit** f (-/no pl.) sobriety; fig. soberness.

Nudel ['nu:dəl] f (-/-n) noodle.

null [nul] **1.** adj. null; nil; tennis: love; ⸦ und nichtig null and void; **2.** ♀ f (-/-en) nought, cipher (a. fig.); zero; **²punkt** m zero.

numerieren [numə'ri:rən] v/t. (no -ge-, h) number; numerierter Platz reserved seat.

Nummer ['numər] f (-/-n) number (a. newspaper, thea.); size (of shoes, etc.); thea. turn; sports: event; **'⸦nschild** mot. n number-plate.

nun [nu:n] **1.** adv. now, at present; then; ⸦? well?; ⸦ also well then; **2.** int. now then!; **'⸦mehr** adv. now.

nur adv. [nu:r] only; (nothing) but; merely; ⸦ noch only.

Nuß [nus] f (-/Nüsse) nut; **'⸦kern** m kernel; **'⸦knacker** m (-s/-) nutcracker; **'⸦schale** f nutshell.

Nüstern ['ny:stərn] f/pl. nostrils pl.

nutz adj. [nuts] s. nütze; **²anwendung** f practical application; **'⸦bar** adj. useful; **'⸦bringend** adj. profitable.

nütze adj. ['nytsə] useful; zu nichts ⸦ sein be of no use, be good for nothing.

Nutzen ['nutsən] **1.** m (-s/-) use; profit, gain; advantage; utility; **2.** ♀ v/i. and v/t. (ge-, h) s. nützen.

nützen ['nytsən] (ge-, h) **1.** v/i.: zu et. ⸦ be of use or useful for s.th.; j-m ⸦ serve s.o.; es nützt nichts zu inf. it is no use ger.; **2.** v/t. use, make use of; put to account; avail o.s. of, seize (opportunity).

'Nutz|holz n timber; **'⸦leistung** f capacity.

nützlich adj. ['nytsliç] useful, of use; advantageous.

'nutz|los adj. useless; **²nießer** ['⸦ni:sər] m (-s/-) usufructuary; **²nießung** f (-/-en) usufruct.

'Nutzung f (-/-en) using; utilization.

Nylon ['nailɔn] n (-s/no pl.) nylon; **⸦strümpfe** ['⸦ʃtrympfə] m/pl. nylons pl., nylon stockings pl.

Nymphe ['nymfə] f (-/-n) nymph.

O

o *int.* [o:] oh!, ah!; ~ *weh!* alas!, oh dear (me)!

Oase [o'ɑ:zə] *f* (-/-n) oasis.

ob *cj.* [ɔp] whether, if; *als* ~ as if, as though.

Obacht ['o:baxt] *f* (-/*no pl.*): ~ *geben auf* (*acc.*) pay attention to, take care of, heed.

Obdach ['ɔpdax] *n* (-[e]s/*no pl.*) shelter, lodging; **2los** *adj.* unsheltered, homeless; **'~lose** *m, f* (-n/-n) homeless person; **'~losenasyl** *n* casual ward.

Obdu|ktion [ɔpduk'tsjo:n] *f* (-/-en) post-mortem (examination), autopsy; **2zieren** [~'tsi:rən] *v/t.* (*no* -ge-, *h*) perform an autopsy on.

oben *adv.* ['o:bən] above; *mountain*: at the top; *house*: upstairs; on the surface; *von* ~ from above; *von* ~ *bis unten* from top to bottom; *von* ~ *herab behandeln* treat haughtily; '~**an** *adv.* at the top; '~**auf** *adv.* on the top; on the surface; **~drein** *adv.* ['~'draɪn] into the bargain, at that; **~erwähnt** *adj.* ['o:bən?ɛrvɛ:nt], '~**genannt** *adj.* above-mentioned, aforesaid; '~**hin** *adv.* superficially, perfunctorily.

ober ['o:bər] **1.** *adj.* upper, higher; *fig. a.* superior; **2.** ≈ *m* (-s/-) (head) waiter; *German cards*: queen.

Ober|arm ['o:bɑr?-] *m* upper arm; **~arzt** ['o:bɑr?-] *m* head physician; **~aufseher** ['o:bɑr?-] *m* superintendent; **~aufsicht** ['o:bɑr?-] *f* superintendence; **~befehl** ≈ *m* supreme command; **'~befehlshaber** ≈ *m* commander-in-chief; '~**bekleidung** *f* outer garments *pl.*, outer wear; '~**bürgermeister** *m* chief burgomaster; Lord Mayor; '~**deck** ⚓ *n* upper deck; '~**fläche** *f* surface; **2flächlich** *adj.* ['~flɛçlɪç] superficial; *fig. a.* shallow; '2**halb** *prp.* (*gen.*) above; '~**hand** *fig. f*: *die* ~ *gewinnen über* (*acc.*) get the upper hand of; '~**haupt** *n* head, chief; '~**haus** *Brt. parl. n* House of Lords; '~**hemd** *n* shirt; '~**herrschaft** *f* supremacy.

'Oberin *f* (-/-nen) *eccl.* Mother Superior; *at hospital*: matron.

ober|irdisch *adj.* ['o:bɑr?-] over-ground, above ground; ⚡ overhead; '2**kellner** *m* head waiter; '2**kiefer** *anat. m* upper jaw; '2**körper** *m* upper part of the body; '2**land** *n* upland; '2**lauf** *m* upper course (*of river*); '2**leder** *n* upper; '2**leitung** *f* chief management; ⚡ overhead wires *pl.*; '2**leutnant** ≈ *m* (*Am.* first) lieutenant; '2**licht** *n* skylight; '2**lippe** *f* upper lip; '2**schenkel** *m* thigh; '2**schule** *f* secondary school, *Am. a.* high school.

oberst 1. *adj.* uppermost, topmost, top; highest (*a. fig.*); *fig.* chief, principal; *rank, etc.*: supreme; **2.** ≈ *m* (-en, -s/-en, -e) colonel. **'Ober|staatsanwalt** ⚖ *m* chief public prosecutor; '~**stimme** ♪ *f* treble, soprano.

'Oberst|leutnant ≈ *m* lieutenant-colonel.

'Ober|tasse *f* cup; '~**wasser** *fig. n*: ~ *bekommen* get the upper hand.

obgleich *cj.* [ɔp'glaɪç] *(al)*though.

'Obhut *f* (-/*no pl.*) care, guard; protection; custody; *in* (*seine*) ~ *nehmen* take care *or* charge of.

obig *adj.* ['o:bɪç] above(-mentioned), aforesaid.

Objekt [ɔp'jɛkt] *n* (-[e]s/-e) object (*a. gr.*); project; ✝ a. transaction. **objektiv** [ɔpjɛk'ti:f] **1.** *adj.* objective; impartial, detached; actual, practical; **2.** ≈ *n* (-s/-e) object-glass, objective; *phot.* lens; **2ität** [~ivi-'tɛ:t] *f* (-/*no pl.*) objectivity; impartiality.

obligat *adj.* [obli'gɑ:t] obligatory; indispensable; inevitable; **2ion** ✝ [~a'tsjo:n] *f* (-/-en) bond, debenture; **~orisch** *adj.* [~a'to:rɪʃ] obligatory (*für on*), compulsory, mandatory.

'Obmann *m* chairman; ✝ foreman (*of jury*); umpire; ✝ shop-steward, spokesman.

Oboe ♪ [o'bo:ə] *f* (-/-n) oboe, hautboy.

Obrigkeit ['o:brɪçkaɪt] *f* (-/-en) *the* authorities *pl.*; government; **2lich** *adj.* magisterial, official; '~**sstaat** *m* authoritarian state.

ob'schon *cj.* *(al)*though.

Observatorium *ast.* [ɔpzɛrva'to:rjum] *n* (-s/Observatorien) observatory.

Obst [o:pst] *n* (-es/*no pl.*) fruit; '~bau *m* fruit-culture, fruit-growing; '~baum *m* fruit-tree; '~ernte *f* fruit-gathering; fruit-crop; '~garten *m* orchard; '~händler *m* fruiterer, *Am.* fruitseller; '~züchter *m* fruiter, fruit-grower.

obszön *adj.* [ɔps'tsø:n] obscene, filthy.

ob'wohl *cj.* (al)though.

Ochse *zo.* ['ɔksə] *m* (-n/-n) ox; bullock; '~nfleisch *n* beef.

öde ['ø:də] **1.** *adj.* deserted, desolate; waste; *fig.* dull, tedious; **2.** *☌ f* (-/-n) desert, solitude; *fig.* dullness, tedium.

oder *cj.* ['o:dər] or.

Ofen ['o:fən] *m* (-s/⁓) stove; oven; kiln; furnace; '~heizung *f* heating by stove; '~rohr *n* stove-pipe.

offen *adj.* ['ɔfən] open (*a. fig.*); *position:* vacant; *hostility:* overt; *fig.* frank, outspoken.

'offen'bar *adj.* **1.** obvious, evident; apparent; **2.** *adv. a.* it seems that; ~en [ɔfən'-] *v/t.* (*no -ge-, h*) reveal, disclose; manifest; *sich j-m* ~ open one's heart to s.o.; **☌ung** [ɔfən'-] *f* (-/-en) manifestation; revelation; **☌ungseid** *☌* [ɔfən'ba:ruŋs⁹-] *m* oath of manifestation.

'Offenheit *fig. f* (-/*no pl.*) openness, frankness.

'offen|herzig *adj.* open-hearted, sincere; frank; '~kundig *adj.* public; notorious; '~sichtlich *adj.* manifest, evident, obvious.

offensiv *adj.* [ɔfɛn'zi:f] offensive; **☌e** [~və] *f* (-/-n) offensive.

'offenstehen *v/i.* (*irr.* stehen, sep., -ge-, h*) stand open; *† bill:* be outstanding; *fig.* be open (*j-m* to s.o.); *es steht ihm offen zu inf.* he is free *or* at liberty to *inf.*

öffentlich ['œfəntliç] **1.** *adj.* public; ~es Ärgernis public nuisance; ~er Dienst Civil Service; **2.** *adv.* publicly, in public; ~ auftreten make a public appearance; '**☌keit** *f* (-/*no pl.*) publicity; *the* public; *in aller* ~ in public.

offerieren [ɔfə'ri:rən] *v/t.* (*no -ge-, h*) offer. [tender.\
Offerte [ɔ'fɛrtə] *f* (-/-n) offer;\
offiziell *adj.* [ɔfi'tsjɛl] official.

Offizier *☌* [ɔfi'tsi:r] *m* (-s/-e) (com-

missioned) officer; ~skorps *☌* [~sko:r] *n* (-/-) body of officers, *the* officers *pl.*; ~smesse *f* *☌* officers' mess; *⚓ a.* wardroom.

offiziös *adj.* [ɔfi'tsjø:s] officious, semi-official.

öffn|en ['œfnən] *v/t.* (ge-, h) open; *a.* uncork (*bottle*); *☌* dissect (*body*); *sich* ~ open; '**☌er** *m* (-s/-) opener; '**☌ung** *f* (-/-en) opening, aperture; '**☌ungszeiten** *f/pl.* hours *pl.* of opening, business hours *pl.*

oft *adv.* [ɔft] often, frequently.

öfters *adv.* ['œftərs] *s.* oft.

oftmal|ig *adj.* frequent, repeated; '~s *adv. s.* oft.

oh *int.* [o:] o(h)!

ohne ['o:nə] **1.** *prp.* (*acc.*) without; **2.** *cj.:* ~ daß, ~ zu *inf.* without *ger.*; ~'dies *adv.* anyhow, anyway; ~'gleichen *adv.* unequal(l)ed, matchless; ~'hin *adv. s.* ohnedies.

'Ohn|macht *f* (-/-en) powerlessness, impotence; *☌* faint, unconsciousness; *in* ~ *fallen* faint, swoon; ~machtsanfall *☌* ['o:nmaxts⁹-] *m* fainting fit, swoon; '**☌mächtig** *adj.* powerless; impotent; *☌* unconscious; ~ *werden* faint, swoon.

Ohr [o:r] *n* (-[e]s/-en) ear; *fig. a.* hearing; *ein* ~ *haben für* have an ear for; *ganz* ~ *sein* be all ears; *j-n übers* ~ *hauen* cheat s.o., *sl.* do s.o. (in the eye); *bis über die* ~en up to the ears *or* eyes.

Öhr [ø:r] *n* (-[e]s/-e) eye (*of needle*).

Ohren|arzt *m* aurist, ear specialist; '**☌betäubend** *adj.* deafening; '~leiden *n* ear-complaint; '~schmalz *n* ear-wax; '~schmaus *m* treat for the ears; '~schmerzen *m/pl.* earache; '~zeuge *m* ear-witness.

Ohr|feige *f* box on the ear(s), slap in the face (*a. fig.*); '**☌feigen** *v/t.* (ge-, h): *j-n* ~ box s.o.'s ear(s), slap s.o.'s face; '~läppchen ['~lɛpçən] *n* (-s/-) lobe of ear; '~ring *m* ear-ring.

Ökonom|ie [økono'mi:] *f* (-/-n) economy; **☌isch** *adj.* [~'no:miʃ] economical.

Oktav [ɔk'ta:f] *n* (-s/-e) octavo; ~e *♪* [~və] *f* (-/-n) octave.

Oktober [ɔk'to:bər] *m* (-[s]/-) October.

Okul|ar *opt.* [oku'la:r] *n* (-s/-e) eye-piece, ocular; **☌ieren** *♪* *v/t.* (*no -ge-, h*) inoculate, graft.

Öl [øːl] n (-[e]s/-e) oil; ~ ins Feuer gießen add fuel to the flames; ~ auf die Wogen gießen pour on oil on the (troubled) waters; **'~baum** ♀ m olive-tree; **'~berg** eccl. m (-[e]s/no pl.) Mount of Olives; **2en** v/t. (ge-, h) oil; **a.** lubricate; **'~farbe** f oil-colo(u)r, oil-paint; **'~gemälde** n oil-painting; **'~heizung** f oil heating; **2ig** adj. oily (a. fig.).

Oliv|e ♀ [oˈliːvə] f (-/-n) olive; **~enbaum** ♀ m olive-tree; **2grün** adj. olive(-green).

Öl|male'rei f oil-painting; **'~quelle** f oil-spring, gusher; oil-well; **'~ung** f (-/-en) oiling; ⊕ a. lubrication; Letzte ~ eccl. extreme unction.

Olympi|ade [olympˈjaːdə] f (-/-n) Olympiad; a. Olympic Games pl.; **2sch** adj. [oˈlympiʃ] Olympic; Olympische Spiele pl. Olympic Games pl.

'Ölzweig m olive-branch.

Omelett [ɔm(ə)ˈlɛt] n (-[e]s/-e, -s), **~e** [~ˈlɛt] f (-/-n) omelet(te).

Om|en [ˈoːmɛn] n (-s/-, Omina) omen, augury; **2inös** adj. [omiˈnøːs] ominous.

Omnibus [ˈɔmnibus] m (-ses/-se) (omni)bus; (motor-)coach; **'~haltestelle** f bus-stop.

Onkel [ˈɔŋkəl] m (-s/-, F -s) uncle.

Oper [ˈoːpər] f (-/-n) ♪ opera; opera-house.

Operat|eur [opəraˈtøːr] m (-s/-e) operator; ♀ surgeon; ✕ [~ˈtsjoːn] f (-/-en) operation; **~ionssaal** ✕ m operating room, Am. surgery; **2iv** ✕ adj. [~ˈtiːf] operative.

Operette ♪ [opəˈrɛtə] f (-/-n) operetta.

operieren [opəˈriːrən] (no -ge-, h) **1.** v/t.: j-n ~ ✕ operate (up)on s.o. (wegen for); **2.** ✕, ✕ v/i. operate; sich ~ lassen ✕ undergo an operation.

'Opern|glas n, **~gucker** F [ˈ~gukər] m (-s/-) opera-glass(es pl.); **'~haus** n opera-house; **'~sänger** m opera-singer, operatic singer; **'~text** m libretto, book (of an opera).

Opfer [ˈɔpfər] n (-s/-) sacrifice; offering; victim (a. fig.); ein ~ bringen make a sacrifice; j-m zum ~ fallen be victimized by s.o.; **'~gabe** f offering; **2n** (ge-, h) **1.** v/t. sacrifice; immolate; sich für et. ~ sacrifice o.s. for s.th.; **2.** v/i. (make a)

sacrifice (dat. to); **'~stätte** f place of sacrifice; **'~tod** m sacrifice of one's life; **'~ung** f (-/-en) sacrificing, sacrifice; immolation.

Opium [ˈoːpjum] n (-s/no pl.) opium.

opponieren [ɔpoˈniːrən] v/i. (no -ge-, h) be opposed (gegen to), resist.

Opposition [ɔpoziˈtsjoːn] f (-/-en) opposition (a. parl.); **~sführer** parl. m opposition leader; **~spartei** parl. f opposition party.

Optik [ˈɔptik] f (-/♀-en) optics; phot. lens system; fig. aspect; **'~er** m (-s/-) optician.

Optim|ismus [ɔptiˈmismus] m (-/no pl.) optimism; **~ist** m (-en/-en) optimist; **2istisch** adj. optimistic.

'optisch adj. optic(al); ~e Täuschung optical illusion.

Orakel [oˈraːkəl] n (-s/-) oracle; **2haft** adj. oracular; **2n** v/i. (no -ge-, h) speak oracularly; **~spruch** m oracle.

Orange [oˈrãːʒə] f (-/-n) orange; **2farben** adj. orange-colo(u)red; **~nbaum** ♀ m orange-tree.

Oratorium ♪ [oraˈtoːrjum] n (-s/Oratorien) oratorio.

Orchester ♪ [ɔrˈkɛstər] n (-s/-) orchestra. [orchid.)

Orchidee ♀ [ɔrçiˈdeːə] f (-/-n)

Orden [ˈɔrdən] m (-s/-) order (a. eccl.); order, medal, decoration.

'Ordens|band n ribbon (of an order); **'~bruder** eccl. m brother, friar; **'~gelübde** eccl. n monastic vow; **'~schwester** eccl. f sister, nun; **'~verleihung** f conferring (of) an order.

ordentlich adj. [ˈɔrdentliç] tidy; orderly; proper; regular; respectable; good, sound; ~er Professor univ. professor in ordinary.

ordinär adj. [ɔrdiˈnɛːr] common, vulgar, low.

ordn|en [ˈɔrdnən] v/t. (ge-, h) put in order; arrange, fix (up); settle (a. † liabilities); **2er** m (-s/-) at festival, etc.: steward; for papers, etc.: file.

'Ordnung f (-/-en) order; arrangement; system; rules pl., regulations pl.; class; in ~ bringen put in order.

ˈordnungs|gemäß, **ˈ‿mäßig 1.** *adj.*
orderly, regular; **2.** *adv.* duly; **ˈ2ruf**
parl. m call to order; **ˈ2strafe** *f*
disciplinary penalty; fine; **ˈ‿widrig**
adj. contrary to order, irregular;
ˈ2zahl *f* ordinal number.

Ordonnanz ⚔ [ɔrdoˈnants] *f* (-/-en)
orderly.

Organ [ɔrˈɡaːn] *n* (-s/-e) organ.

Organisat|ion [ɔrɡaniˈtsjoːn] *f*
(-/-en) organization; **‿ionstalent** *n*
organizing ability; **‿or** [‿ˈzaːtɔr] *m*
(-s/-en) organizer; **2orisch** *adj.*
[‿aˈtoːriʃ] organizational, organizing.

orˈganisch *adj.* organic.

organiˈsieren *v/t.* (no -ge-, h)
organize; *sl.* scrounge; *(nicht) orga-
nisiert(er Arbeiter)* (non-)unionist.

Organismus [ɔrɡaˈnismus] *m* (-/Or-
ganismen) organism; 🐟 *a.* system.

Organist ♪ [ɔrɡaˈnist] *m* (-en/-en)
organist.

Orgel ♪ [ˈɔrɡəl] *f* (-/-n) organ, *Am.
a.* pipe organ; **ˈ‿bauer** *m* organ-
builder; **ˈ‿pfeife** *f* organ-pipe;
ˈ‿spieler ♪ *m* organist.

Orgie [ˈɔrɡjə] *f* (-/-n) orgy.

Oriental|e [orienˈtaːlə] *m* (-n/-n)
oriental; **2isch** *adj.* oriental.

orientier|en [orienˈtiːrən] *v/t.* (no
-ge-, h) inform, instruct; *sich ‿*
orient(ate) o.s. *(a. fig.)*; inform o.s.
(über acc. of); *gut orientiert sein
über (acc.)* be well informed about,
be familiar with; **2ung** *f* (-/-en)
orientation; *fig. a.* information; *die
‿ verlieren* lose one's bearings.

Origin|al [origiˈnaːl] **1.** *n* (-s/-e)
original; **2.** 2 *adj.* original; **‿alität**
[‿aliˈtɛːt] *f* (-/-en) originality; **2ell**
adj. [‿ˈnɛl] original; *design, etc.:*
ingenious.

Orkan [ɔrˈkaːn] *m* (-[e]s/-e) hur-
ricane; typhoon; **2artig** *adj. storm:*
violent; *applause:* thunderous,
frenzied.

Ornat [ɔrˈnaːt] *m* (-[e]s/-e) robe(s
pl.), vestment.

Ort [ɔrt] *m* (-[e]s/-e) place; site;
spot, point; locality; place, village,
town; *‿ der Handlung thea.* scene
(of action); *an ‿ und Stelle* on the
spot; *höher(e)n ‿(e)s* at higher
quarters; **ˈ2en** *v/t.* (ge-, h) locate.

ortho|dox *adj.* [ɔrtoˈdɔks] orthodox;
2graphie [‿ɡraˈfiː] *f* (-/-n) orthog-
raphy; **‿graphisch** *adj.* [‿ˈɡra-
fiʃ] orthographic(al); **2päde** 🩺
[‿ˈpɛːdə] *m* (-n/-n) orthop(a)edist;
2pädie [‿pɛˈdiː] *f* (-/*no pl.*) ortho-
p(a)edics, orthop(a)edy; **‿pädisch**
adj. [‿ˈpɛːdiʃ] orthop(a)edic.

örtlich *adj.* [ˈœrtliç] local; 🩺 *a.*
topical; **ˈ2keit** *f* (-/-en) locality.

ˈOrts|angabe *f* statement of place;
ˈ2ansässig *adj.* resident, local;
‿ansässige [ˈ‿ɡə] *m* (-n/-n) resident; **ˈ‿beschreibung** *f* topogra-
phy; **ˈ‿besichtigung** *f* local inspection.

ˈOrtschaft *f* (-/-en) place, village.

ˈOrts|gespräch *teleph. n* local call;
ˈ‿kenntnis *f* knowledge of a place;
ˈ2kundig *adj.* familiar with the
locality; **ˈ‿name** *m* place-name;
ˈ‿verkehr *m* local traffic; **ˈ‿zeit** *f*
local time.

Öse [ˈøːzə] *f* (-/-n) eye, loop; eyelet
(*of shoe*).

Ost *geogr.* [ɔst] east; **ˈ‿en** *m* (-s/*no
pl.*) east; *the East; der Ferne (Nahe)
‿* the Far (Near) East.

ostentativ *adj.* [ɔstentaˈtiːf] ostentatious.

Oster|ei [ˈoːstɐ‿ʔ-] *n* Easter egg;
ˈ‿fest *n* Easter; **ˈ‿hase** *m* Easter
bunny *or* rabbit; **ˈ‿lamm** *n* paschal
lamb; **ˈ‿n** *n* (-/-) Easter.

Österreich|er [ˈøːstəraiçɐ] *m* (-s/-)
Austrian; **2isch** *adj.* Austrian.

östlich [ˈœstliç] **1.** *adj.* eastern;
wind, etc.: easterly; **2.** *adv.:* ‿ *von*
east of.

ost|wärts *adv.* [ˈɔstverts] east-
ward(s); **ˈ2wind** *m* east(erly)
wind.

Otter *zo.* [ˈɔtɐ] **1.** *m* (-s/-) otter;
2. *f* (-/-n) adder, viper.

Ouvertüre ♪ [uverˈtyːrə] *f* (-/-n)
overture.

oval [oˈvaːl] **1.** *adj.* oval; **2.** 2 *n*
(-s/-e) oval.

Ovation [ovaˈtsjoːn] *f* (-/-en) ovation; *j-m ‿en bereiten* give s.o.
ovations.

Oxyd 🧪 [ɔˈksyːt] *n* (-[e]s/-e) oxide;
2ieren [‿yˈdiːrən] (no -ge-) **1.** *v/t.*
(h) oxidize; **2.** *v/i.* (sein) oxidize.

Ozean [ˈoːtseaːn] *m* (-s/-e) ocean.

P

Paar [paːr] **1.** *n* (-[e]s/-e) pair; couple; **2.** ♀ *adj.*: ein ~ a few, some; j-m ein ~ Zeilen schreiben drop s.o. a few lines; '♀en *v/t.* (ge-, h) pair, couple, mate (animals); sich ~ (form a) pair; animals: mate; fig. join, unite; '♣lauf m sports: pair-skating; '♣läufer m sports: pair-skater; '♀mal *adv.*: ein ~ several or a few times; '♣ung f (-/-en) coupling; mating, copulation; fig. union; '♀weise *adv.* in pairs or couples, by twos.

Pacht [paxt] f (-/-en) lease, tenure, tenancy; money payment: rent; '♀en *v/t.* (ge-, h) (take on) lease; rent.

Pächter ['pɛçtər] m (-s/-), '♣in f (-/-nen) lessee, lease-holder; tenant.

'**Pacht|ertrag** m rental; '♣geld n rent; '♣gut n farm; '♣vertrag m lease; '♀weise *adv.* on lease.

Pack [pak] **1.** m (-[e]s/-e, -e) s. Packen²; **2.** n (-[e]s/no pl.) rabble.

Päckchen ['pɛkçən] n (-s/-) small parcel, Am. a. package; ein ~ Zigaretten a pack(et) of cigarettes.

packen¹ ['pakən] (ge-, h) **1.** *v/t.* pack (up); seize, grip, grasp, clutch; collar; fig. grip, thrill; F pack dich! F clear out!, sl. beat it!; **2.** *v/i.* pack (up); **3.** ♀ n (-s/no pl.) packing.

Packen² [~] m (-s/-) pack(et), parcel; bale.

'**Packer** m (-s/-) packer; '♣ei [~'raɪ] f **1.** (-/-en) packing-room; **2.** (-/no pl.) packing.

'**Pack|esel** fig. m drudge; '♣material n packing materials pl.; '♣papier n packing-paper, brown paper; '♣pferd n pack-horse; '♣ung f (-/-en) pack(age), packet; ♣ pack; e-e ~ Zigaretten a pack(et) of cigarettes; '♣wagen m s. Gepäckwagen.

Pädagog|e [peda'goːgə] m (-n/-n) pedagog(ue), education(al)ist; '♣ik f (-/no pl.) pedagogics, pedagogy; ♀isch *adj.* pedagogic(al).

Paddel ['padəl] n (-s/-) paddle; '♣boot n canoe; '♀n *v/i.* (ge-, h, sein) paddle, canoe.

Page ['paːʒə] m (-n/-n) page.

pah *int.* [paː] pah!, pooh!, pshaw!

Paket [pa'keːt] n (-[e]s/-e) parcel, packet, package; '♣annahme ♣ f parcel counter; '♣karte ♣ f dispatch-note; '♣post f parcel post; '♣zustellung ♣ f parcel delivery.

Pakt [pakt] m (-[e]s/-e) pact; agreement; treaty.

Palast [pa'last] m (-es/-e) palace.

Palm|e ♀ ['palmə] f (-/-n) palm (-tree); '♣öl n palm-oil; ~'sonntag *eccl.* m Palm Sunday.

panieren [pa'niːrən] *v/t.* (no -ge-, h) crumb.

Pani|k ['paːnik] f (-/-en) panic; stampede; '♀sch *adj.* panic; von ~em Schrecken erfaßt panic-stricken.

Panne ['panə] f (-/-n) breakdown, mot. a. engine trouble; tyres: puncture; fig. blunder.

panschen ['panʃən] (ge-, h) **1.** *v/i.* splash (about); **2.** *v/t.* adulterate (wine, etc.).

Panther zo. ['pantər] m (-s/-) panther.

Pantine [pan'tiːnə] f (-/-n) clog.

Pantoffel [pan'tɔfəl] m (-s/-n, F -) slipper; unter dem ~ stehen be henpecked; '♣held F m henpecked husband.

pantschen ['pantʃən] *v/i.* and *v/t.* (ge-, h) s. panschen.

Panzer ['pantsər] m (-s/-) armo(u)r; ✗ tank; zo. shell; '♣abwehr ✗ f anti-tank defen|ce, Am. -se; '♣glas n bullet-proof glass; '♣hemd n coat of mail; '♣kreuzer ✗ m armo(u)red cruiser; '♀n *v/t.* (ge-, h) armo(u)r; '♣platte f armo(u)r-plate; '♣schiff ✗ n ironclad; '♣schrank m safe; '♣ung f (-/-en) armo(u)r-plating; '♣wagen m armo(u)red car; ✗ tank.

Papa [pa'paː, F 'papa] m (-s/-s) papa, F pa, dad(dy), Am. a. pop.

Papagei orn. [papa'gaɪ] m (-[e]s, -en/-e[n]) parrot.

Papier [pa'piːr] n (-s/-e) paper; ~e pl. papers pl., documents pl.; papers pl., identity card; ein Bogen ~ a sheet of paper; ♀en *adj.* (of) paper; fig. dull; '♣fabrik f paper-mill; '♣geld n (-[e]s/no pl.) paper-money; banknotes pl., Am. bills pl.; '♣korb m waste-paper-basket; '♣schnitzel F n *or m/pl.* scraps *pl.* of paper; **~tüte** *f* paper-bag; **~waren** *f/pl.* stationery.

'**Papp|band** *m* (-[e]s/-̈e) paperback; '**~deckel** *m* pasteboard, cardboard.

Pappe ['papə] *f* (-/-n) pasteboard, cardboard.

Pappel ⚘ ['papəl] *f* (-/-n) poplar.

päppeln F ['pɛpəln] *v/t.* (ge-, h) feed (with pap).

papp|en F ['papən] (ge-, h) **1.** *v/t.* paste; **2.** *v/i.* stick; '**~ig** *adj.* sticky; '**2karton** *m*, '**2schachtel** *f* cardboard box, carton.

Papst [pɑːpst] *m* (-es/-̈e) pope.

päpstlich *adj.* ['pɛːpstliç] papal.

'**Papsttum** *n* (-s/*no pl.*) papacy.

Parade [pa'rɑːdə] *f* (-/-n) parade; ⚔ review; *fencing:* parry.

Paradies [para'diːs] *n* (-es/-e) paradise; **2isch** *adj. fig.* [~'diːziʃ] heavenly, delightful. [ical.]

paradox *adj.* [para'dɔks] paradox-]

Paragraph [para'grɑːf] *m* (-en, -s/-en) article, section; paragraph; section-mark.

parallel *adj.* [para'leːl] parallel; **2e** *f* (-/-n) parallel.

Paralys|e ⚕ [para'lyːzə] *f* (-/-n) paralysis; **2ieren** ⚕ [~y'ziːrən] *v/t.* (*no* -ge-, h) paralyse.

Parasit [para'ziːt] *m* (-en/-en) parasite.

Parenthese [parɛn'teːzə] *f* (-/-n) parenthesis.

Parforcejagd [par'fɔrs-] *f* hunt(-ing) on horseback (with hounds), *after hares:* coursing.

Parfüm [par'fyːm] *n* (-s/-e, -s) perfume, scent; **~erie** [~ymə'riː] *f* (-/-n) perfumery; **2ieren** [~y'miːrən] *v/t.* (*no* -ge-, h) perfume, scent.

pari † *adv.* ['pɑːri] par; *al* ~ at par.

parieren [pa'riːrən] (*no* -ge-, h) **1.** *v/t. fencing:* parry (*a. fig.*); pull up (*horse*); **2.** *v/i.* obey (*j-m s.o.*).

Park [park] *m* (-s/-s, -e) park; '**~anlage** *f* park; '**~aufseher** *m* parkkeeper; '**2en** (ge-, h) **1.** *v/i.* park; ~ *verboten!* no parking!; **2.** *v/t.* park.

Parkett [par'kɛt] *n* (-[e]s/-e) parquet; *thea.* (orchestra) stalls *pl.*, *esp. Am.* orchestra *or* parquet.

'**Park|gebühr** *f* parking-fee; '**~licht** *n* parking light; '**~platz** *m* (car-)park, parking lot; '**~uhr** *mot. f* parking meter.

Parlament [parla'mɛnt] *n* (-[e]s/-e) parliament; **2arisch** *adj.* [~'tɑːriʃ] parliamentary.

Parodie [paro'diː] *f* (-/-n) parody; **2ren** *v/t.* (*no* -ge-, h) parody.

Parole [pa'roːlə] *f* (-/-n) ⚔ password, watchword; *fig.* slogan.

Partei [par'taɪ] *f* (-/-en) party (*a. pol.*); *j-s* ~ *ergreifen* take s.o.'s part, side with s.o.; **~apparat** *pol. m* party machinery; **~gänger** [~gɛŋər] *m* (-s/-) partisan; **2isch** *adj.*, **2lich** *adj.* partial (*für* to); prejudiced (*gegen* against); **2los** *pol. adj.* independent; **~mitglied** *pol. n* party member; **~programm** *n* platform; **~tag** *pol. m* convention; **~zugehörigkeit** *pol. f* party membership.

Parterre [par'tɛr] *n* (-s/-s) ground floor, *Am.* first floor; *thea.:* pit, *Am.* parterre, *Am.* parquet circle.

Partie [par'tiː] *f* (-/-n) ⚓ parcel, lot; outing, excursion; *cards, etc.:* game; ♪ part; *marriage:* match.

Partitur ♪ [parti'tuːr] *f* (-/-en) score.

Partizip *gr.* [parti'tsiːp] *n* (-s/-ien) participle.

Partner ['partnər] *m* (-s/-), '**~in** *f* (-/-nen) partner; *film: a.* co-star; '**~schaft** *f* (-/-en) partnership.

Parzelle [par'tsɛlə] *f* (-/-n) plot, lot, allotment.

Paß [pas] *m* (Passes/Pässe) pass; passage; *football, etc.:* pass; passport.

Passage [pa'sɑːʒə] *f* (-/-n) passage; arcade.

Passagier [pasa'ʒiːr] *m* (-s/-e) passenger, *in taxis: a.* fare; **~flugzeug** *n* air liner.

Passah ['pasa] *n* (-s/*no pl.*), '**~fest** *n* Passover.

Passant [pa'sant] *m* (-en/-en), **~in** *f* (-/-nen) passer-by.

'**Paßbild** *n* passport photo(graph).

passen ['pasən] (ge-, h) **1.** *v/i.* fit (*j-m s.o.*); *auf acc. or für or zu* et. s.th.); suit (*j-m s.o.*), be convenient; *cards, football:* pass; ~ *zu* go with, match (with); **2.** *v/refl.* be fit or proper; '**~d** *adj.* fit, suitable; convenient (*für* for).

passier|bar *adj.* [pa'siːrbɑːr] passable, practicable; **~en** (*no* -ge-) **1.** *v/i.* (sein) happen; **2.** *v/t.* (h) pass (over *or* through); **2schein** *m* pass, permit.

Passion [pa'sjo:n] *f* (-/-en) passion; hobby; *eccl.* Passion.

passiv ['pasi:f] **1.** *adj.* passive; **2.** ♀ *gr. n* (-s/♀-e) passive (voice); **♀a** ✝ [pa'si:va] *pl.* liabilities *pl.*

Paste ['pastə] *f* (-/-n) paste.

Pastell [pa'stɛl] *n* (-[e]s/-e) pastel.

Pastete [pa'ste:tə] *f* (-/-n) pie; **~n-bäcker** *m* pastry-cook.

Pate ['pa:tə] **1.** *m* (-n/-n) godfather; godchild; **2.** *f* (-/-n) godmother; **~nkind** *n* godchild; **~nschaft** *f* (-/-en) sponsorship.

Patent [pa'tɛnt] *n* (-[e]s/-e) patent; ✗ commission; *ein ~ anmelden* apply for a patent; **~amt** *n* Patent Office; **~anwalt** *m* patent agent; **♀ieren** [~'ti:rən] *v/t.* (*no* -ge-, h) patent; *et. ~ lassen* take out a patent for s.th.; **~inhaber** *m* patentee; **~urkunde** *f* letters patent.

Patient [pa'tsjɛnt] *m* (-en/-en), **~in** *f* (-/-nen) patient.

Patin ['pa:tin] *f* (-/-nen) godmother.

Patriot [patri'o:t] *m* (-en/-en), **~in** *f* (-/-nen) patriot.

Patron [pa'tro:n] *m* (-s/-e) patron, protector; *contp.* fellow, bloke, customer; **~at** [~o'na:t] *n* (-[e]s/-e) patronage; **~e** [pa'tro:nə] *f* (-/-n) cartridge, *Am. a.* shell.

Patrouille [pa'truljə] *f* (-/-n) patrol; **♀ieren** ✗ [~'ji:rən] *v/i.* (*no* -ge-, h) patrol.

Patsch|e F *fig.* ['patʃə] *f* (-/*no pl.*): *in der ~ sitzen* be in a fix *or* scrape; **♀en** F *v/t.* (h) slap; **♀naß** *adj.* dripping wet, drenched.

patzig F *adj.* ['patsiç] snappish.

Pauke ♪ ['paukə] *f* (-/-n) kettle-drum; **♀n** F *v/i. and v/t.* (ge-, h) *school:* cram.

Pauschal|e [pau'ʃa:lə] *f* (-/-n), **~summe** *f* lump sum.

Pause ['pauzə] *f* (-/-n) pause, stop, interval; *school:* break, *Am.* recess; *thea.* interval, *Am.* intermission; ♪ rest; *drawing:* tracing; **♀n** *v/t.* (ge-, h) trace; **♀nlos** *adj.* uninterrupted, incessant; **~nzeichen** *n* *wireless:* interval signal.

pau'sieren *v/i.* (*no* -ge-, h) pause.

Pavian *zo.* ['pa:via:n] *m* (-s/-e) baboon.

Pavillon ['paviljõ] *m* (-s/-s) pavilion.

Pazifist [patsi'fist] *m* (-en/-en) pacif(ic)ist.

Pech [pɛç] *n* **1.** (-[e]s /-e) pitch; **2.** F *fig.* (-[e]s/*no pl.*) bad luck; **~strähne** F *f* run of bad luck; **~vogel** F *m* unlucky fellow.

pedantisch *adj.* [pe'dantiʃ] pedantic; punctilious, meticulous.

Pegel ['pe:gəl] *m* (-s/-) water-ga(u)ge.

peilen ['pailən] *v/t.* (ge-, h) sound (*depth*); take the bearings of (*coast*).

Pein [pain] *f* (-/*no pl.*) torment, torture, anguish; **♀igen** ['~igən] *v/t.* (ge-, h) torment; **~iger** ['~igər] *m* (-s/-) tormentor.

'**peinlich** *adj.* painful, embarrassing; particular, scrupulous, meticulous.

Peitsche ['paitʃə] *f* (-/-n) whip; **♀n** *v/t.* (ge-, h) whip; **~nhieb** *m* lash.

Pelikan *orn.* ['pe:lika:n] *m* (-s/-e) pelican.

Pell|e ['pɛlə] *f* (-/-n) skin, peel; **♀en** *v/t.* (ge-, h) skin, peel; **~kartoffeln** *f/pl.* potatoes *pl.* (boiled) in their jackets *or* skins.

Pelz [pɛlts] *m* (-es/-e) fur; *garment: mst* furs *pl.*; **♀gefüttert** *adj.* fur-lined; **~händler** *m* furrier; **~handschuh** *m* furred glove; '**♀ig** *adj.* furry; *tongue:* furred; **~mantel** *m* fur coat; '**~stiefel** *m* fur-lined boot; '**~tiere** *n/pl.* fur-covered animals *pl.*

Pendel ['pɛndəl] *n* (-s/-) pendulum; '**♀n** *v/i.* (ge-, h) oscillate, swing; 🚌 shuttle, *Am.* commute; '**~tür** *f* swing-door; '**~verkehr** 🚌 *m* shuttle service.

Pension [pã'sjõ:, pɛn'zjo:n] *f* (-/-en) (old-age) pension, retired pay; board; boarding-house; **~är** [~o-'nɛ:r] *m* (-s/-e) (old-age) pensioner; boarder; **~at** [~o'na:t] *n* (-[e]s/-e) boarding-school; **♀ieren** [~o'ni:rən] *v/t.* (*no* -ge-, h) pension (off); *sich ~ lassen* retire; **~sgast** *m* boarder.

Pensum ['pɛnzum] *n* (-s/*Pensen*, *Pensa*) task, lesson.

perfekt 1. *adj.* [pɛr'fɛkt] perfect; *agreement:* settled; **2.** ♀ *gr. n* (-[e]s/-e) perfect (tense).

Pergament [pɛrga'mɛnt] *n* (-[e]s/-e) parchment.

Period|e [per'jo:də] *f* (-/-n) period; ⚕ periods *pl.*; **♀isch** *adj.* periodic (-al).

Peripherie [perife'ri:] *f* (-/-n) circumference; outskirts *pl.* (*of town*).

Perle ['pɛrlə] f (-/-n) pearl; *of glass*: bead; '2n v/i. (ge-, h) sparkle; '~kette f pearl necklace; '~nschnur f string of pearls *or* beads.

'**Perl|muschel** *zo.* f pearl-oyster; ~mutt ['~mut] n (-s/no pl.), ~mutter f (-/no pl.) mother-of-pearl.

Person [pɛr'zoːn] f (-/-en) person; *thea.* character.

Personal [pɛrzo'naːl] n (-s/no pl.) staff, personnel; '~abteilung f personnel office; '~angaben f/pl. personal data pl.; '~ausweis m identity card; '~chef m personnel officer *or* manager *or* director; '~ien [~jən] pl. particulars pl., personal data pl.; '~pronomen gr. n personal pronoun.

Per'sonen|verzeichnis n list of persons; *thea.* dramatis personae pl.; '~wagen m 🚂 (passenger-)carriage *or* Am. car, coach; *mot.* (motor-)car; '~zug 🚂 m passenger train.

personifizieren [pɛrzonifi'tsiːrən] v/t. (no -ge-, h) personify.

persönlich adj. [pɛr'zøːnlɪç] personal; *opinion, letter*: a. private; **2keit** f (-/-en) personality; personage.

Perücke [pɛ'rykə] f (-/-n) wig.

Pest 🐀 [pɛst] f (-/no pl.) plague.

Petersilie 🌿 [petər'ziːljə] f (-/-n) parsley.

Petroleum [pe'troːleum] n (-s/no pl.) petroleum; *for lighting, etc.*: paraffin, *esp. Am.* kerosene.

Pfad [pfaːt] m (-[e]s/-e) path, track; '~finder m boy scout; '~finderin f (-/-nen) girl guide, Am. girl scout.

Pfahl [pfaːl] m (-[e]s/⁀e) stake, pale, pile.

Pfand [pfant] n (-[e]s/⁀er) pledge; 🕇 deposit, security; *real estate*: mortgage; *game*: forfeit; '~brief 🕇 m debenture (bond).

pfänden 🕇🕇 ['pfɛndən] v/t. (ge-, h) seize *s.th.*; distrain upon *s.o. or s.th.*

'**Pfand|haus** n s. *Leihhaus*; '~leiher m (-s/-) pawnbroker; '~schein m pawn-ticket. [distraint.]

'**Pfändung** 🕇🕇 f (-/-en) seizure;]

Pfann|e ['pfanə] f (-/-n) pan; '~kuchen m pancake.

Pfarr|bezirk ['pfar-] m parish; '~er m (-s/-) parson; *Church of England*: rector, vicar; *dissenters*: minister; '~gemeinde f parish; '~haus n

parsonage; *Church of England*: rectory, vicarage; *Church of England*: rectory, vicarage; '~kirche f parish church; '~stelle f (church) living.

Pfau orn. [pfau] m (-[e]s/-en) peacock.

Pfeffer ['pfɛfər] m (-s/-) pepper; '~gurke f gherkin; '2ig adj. peppery; '~kuchen m gingerbread; '~minze 🌿 ['~mintsə] f (-/no pl.) peppermint; '~minzplätzchen n peppermint; '2n v/t. (ge-, h) pepper; '~streuer m (-s/-) pepperbox, pepper-castor.

Pfeife ['pfaifə] f (-/-n) whistle; ✕ fife; pipe (*of organ, etc.*); (tobacco-)pipe; '2n (irr., ge-, h) **1.** v/i. whistle (*dat.* to, for); *radio*: howl; pipe; **2.** v/t. whistle; pipe; '~nkopf m pipe-bowl.

Pfeil [pfail] m (-[e]s/-e) arrow.

Pfeiler ['pfailər] m (-s/-) pillar (a. *fig.*); pier (*of bridge, etc.*).

'**pfeil**|'**schnell** adj. (as) swift as an arrow; '2spitze f arrow-head.

Pfennig ['pfɛniç] m (-[e]s/-e) coin: pfennig; *fig.* penny, farthing.

Pferch [pfɛrç] m (-[e]s/-e) fold, pen; '2en v/t. (ge-, h) fold, pen; *fig.* cram.

Pferd zo. [pfeːrt] n (-[e]s/-e) horse; *zu* ~e on horseback.

Pferde|geschirr ['pfeːrdə-] n harness; '~koppel f (-/-n) paddock, Am. a. corral; '~rennen n horserace; '~schwanz m horse's tail; *hair-style*: pony-tail; '~stall m stable; '~stärke ⊕ f horsepower.

pfiff[1] [pfif] pret. of *pfeifen*.

Pfiff[2] m (-[e]s/-e) whistle; *fig.* trick; '2ig adj. cunning, artful.

Pfingst|en eccl. ['pfiŋstən] n (-/-), '~fest eccl. n Whitsun(tide); '~montag eccl. m Whit Monday; '~rose 🌿 f peony; '~sonntag eccl. m Whit Sunday.

Pfirsich ['pfirziç] m (-[e]s/-e) peach.

Pflanz|e ['pflantsə] f (-/-n) plant; '2en v/t. (ge-, h) plant, set; pot; '~enfaser f vegetable fib|re, Am. -er; '~enfett n vegetable fat; '2enfressend adj. herbivorous; '~er m (-s/-) planter; '~ung f (-/-en) plantation.

Pflaster ['pflastər] n (-s/-) 🩹 plaster; *road*: pavement; '~er m (-s/-) paver, pavio(u)r; '2n v/t. (ge-, h) 🩹 plaster; pave (*road*); '~stein m paving-stone; cobble.

Pflaume ['pflaumə] f (-/-n) plum; dried: prune.

Pflege ['pfle:gə] f (-/-n) care; nursing; cultivation (of art, garden, etc.); ⊕ maintenance; in ~ geben put out (child) to nurse; in ~ nehmen take charge of; '2bedürftig adj. needing care; ~befohlene ['~bəfo:lənə] m, f (n/-n) charge; '~eltern pl. foster-parents pl.; '~heim ⚔ n nursing home; '~kind n foster-child; '2n (ge-, h) v/t. take care of; attend (to); foster (child); ⚔ nurse; maintain; cultivate (art, garden); 2. v/i.: ~ zu inf. be accustomed or used or wont to inf., be in the habit of ger.; sie pflegte zu sagen she used to say; '~r m (-s/-) fosterer; ⚔ male nurse, trustee; 🕸 guardian, curator; '~rin f (-/-nen) nurse.

Pflicht [pfliçt] f (-/-en) duty (gegen to); obligation; '2bewußt adj. conscious of one's duty; '2eifrig adj. zealous; '~erfüllung f performance of one's duty; '~fach n school, univ.: compulsory subject; '~gefühl n sense of duty; '2gemäß adj. dutiful; '2getreu adj. dutiful, loyal; '2schuldig adj. in duty bound; '2vergessen adj. undutiful, disloyal; '~verteidiger 🕸 m assigned counsel.

Pflock [pflɔk] m (-[e]s/⁼e) plug, peg.

pflücken ['pflykən] v/t. (ge-, h) pick, gather, pluck. [Am. plow.]

Pflug [pflu:k] m (-[e]s/⁼e) plough,

pflügen ['pfly:gən] v/t. and v/i. (ge-, h) plough, Am. plow.

Pforte ['pfɔrtə] f (-/-n) gate, door.

Pförtner ['pfœrtnər] m (-s/-) gatekeeper, door-keeper, porter, janitor.

Pfosten ['pfɔstən] m (-s/-) post.

Pfote ['pfo:tə] f (-/-n) paw.

Pfropf [pfrɔpf] m (-[e]s/-e) s. Pfropfen.

'**Pfropfen** 1. m (-s/-) stopper, cork; plug; ❤ clot (of blood); 2. ♀ v/t. (ge-, h) stopper; cork; fig. cram; ⚔ graft.

Pfründe eccl. ['pfryndə] f (-/-n) prebend; benefice, (church) living.

Pfuhl [pfu:l] m (-[e]s/-e) pool, puddle; fig. sink, slough.

pfui int. [pfui] fie!, for shame!

Pfund [pfunt] n (-[e]s/-e) pound; 2ig F adj. ['~diç] great, Am. swell; '2weise adv. by the pound.

pfusch|en F ['pfuʃən] (ge-, h) 1. v/i. bungle, botch. 2. v/t. bungle, botch; 2erei F [~'rai] f (-/-en) bungle, botch.

Pfütze ['pfytsə] f (-/-n) puddle, pool.

Phänomen [fɛno'me:n] n (-s/-e) phenomenon; 2al adj. [~e'na:l] phenomenal.

Phantasie [fanta'zi:] f (-/-n) imagination, fancy; vision; ♪ fantasia; 2ren (no -ge-, h) 1. v/i. dream; ramble; ⚔ be delirious or raving; ♪ improvise; 2. v/t. dream; ♪ improvise.

Phantast [fan'tast] m (-en/-en) visionary, dreamer; 2isch adj. fantastic; F grand, terrific.

Phase ['fa:zə] f (-/-n) phase (a. ⚡), stage.

Philanthrop [filan'tro:p] m (-en/-en) philanthropist.

Philolog|e [filo'lo:gə] m (-n/-n), ~in f (-/-nen) philologist; ~ie [~o-'gi:] f (-/-n) philology.

Philosoph [filo'zo:f] m (-en/-en) philosopher; ~ie [~o'fi:] f (-/-n) philosophy; 2ieren [~o'fi:rən] v/i. (no -ge-, h) philosophize (über acc. on); 2isch adj. [~'zo:fiʃ] philosophical.

Phlegma ['flɛgma] n (-s/no pl.) phlegm; 2tisch adj. [~'ma:tiʃ] phlegmatic.

phonetisch adj. [fo'ne:tiʃ] phonetic.

Phosphor 🜍 ['fɔsfɔr] m (-s/no pl.) phosphorus.

Photo F ['fo:to] 1. n (-s/-s) photo; 2. m (-s/-s) = '~apparat m camera.

Photograph [foto'gra:f] m (-en/-en) photographer; ~ie [~a'fi:] f 1. (-/no pl.) no art.: photography; 2. (-/no pl.) an art.: photograph, F: photo, picture; 2ieren [~a'fi:rən] (no -ge-, h) 1. v/t. photograph; take a picture of; sich ~ lassen have one's photo(graph) taken; 2. v/i. photograph; 2isch adj. [~'gra:fiʃ] photographic.

Photo|kopie f photostat; ~kopiergerät** n photostat; '~zelle f photoelectric cell.

Phrase ['fra:zə] f (-/-n) phrase.

Physik [fy'zi:k] f (-/no pl.) physics sg.; 2alisch adj. [~i'ka:liʃ] physical; ~er ['fy:zikər] m (-s/-) physicist.

physisch adj. ['fy:ziʃ] physical.

Pian|ist [pia'nist] m (-en/-en) pianist; ~o [pi'a:no] n (-s/-s) piano.

Picke ⊕ ['pikə] f (-/-n) pick(axe).

Pickel ['pikəl] m (-s/-) pimple; ⊕

pick(axe); ice-pick; '**_ig** *adj.*
pimpled, pimply.

picken ['pɪkən] *v/i. and v/t.* (ge-, h)
pick, peck.

picklig *adj.* ['pɪklɪç] *s.* pickelig.

Picknick ['pɪknɪk] *n* (-s/-e, -s) picnic.

piekfein F *adj.* ['piːk'-] smart, tip-
top, slap-up.

piep(s)en ['piːp(s)ən] *v/i.* (ge-, h)
cheep, chirp, peep; squeak.

Pietät [pie'tɛːt] *f* (-/*no pl.*) reverence;
piety; **_los** *adj.* irreverent; **_voll**
adj. reverent.

Pik [piːk] **1.** *m* (-s/-e, -s) peak; **2.** F
m (-s/-e): e-n ~ auf j-n haben bear
s.o. a grudge; **3.** *n* (-s/-s) *cards:*
spade(s *pl.*).

pikant *adj.* [pi'kant] piquant, spicy
(*both a. fig.*); *das Pikante* the
piquancy.

Pike ['piːkə] *f* (-/-n) pike; *von der ~
auf dienen* rise from the ranks.

Pilger ['pɪlgər] *m* (-s/-) pilgrim;
'**_fahrt** *f* pilgrimage; **_n** *v/i.* (ge-,
sein) go on *or* make a pilgrimage;
wander.

Pille ['pɪlə] *f* (-/-n) pill.

Pilot [pi'loːt] *m* (-en/-en) pilot.

Pilz ♀ [pɪlts] *m* (-es/-e) fungus,
edible: mushroom, *inedible:* toad-
stool.

pimp(e)lig F *adj.* ['pɪmp(ə)lɪç]
sickly; effeminate.

Pinguin *orn.* ['pɪŋguiːn] *m* (-s/-e)
penguin.

Pinsel ['pɪnzəl] *m* (-s/-) brush; F *fig.*
simpleton; '**_n** *v/t. and v/i.* (ge-, h)
paint; daub; '**_strich** *m* stroke of
the brush.

Pinzette [pɪn'tsɛtə] *f* (-/-n) (e-e *a.*
pair of) tweezers *pl.*

Pionier [pio'niːr] *m* (-s/-e) pioneer,
Am. a. trail blazer; ✕ engineer.

Pirat [pi'rɑːt] *m* (-en/-en) pirate.

Pirsch *hunt.* [pɪrʃ] *f* (-/*no pl.*) deer-
stalking, *Am. a.* still hunt.

Piste ['pɪstə] *f* (-/-n) *skiing, etc.:*
course; ✕ runway.

Pistole [pɪs'toːlə] *f* (-/-n) pistol, *Am.*
F *a.* gun, rod; **_ntasche** *f* holster.

placieren [pla'siːrən] *v/t.* (*no* -ge-,
h) place; *sich ~ sports:* be placed
(*second, etc.*).

Plackerei F [plakə'raɪ] *f* (-/-en)
drudgery.

plädieren [plɛ'diːrən] *v/i.* (*no* -ge-,
h) plead (*für* for).

Plädoyer ṭ̣ [plɛdoa'jeː] *n* (-s/-s)
pleading.

Plage ['plɑːgə] *f* (-/-n) trouble,
nuisance, F plague; torment; '**_n**
v/t. (ge-, h) torment; trouble,
bother; F plague; *sich ~* toil, drudge.

Plagiat [plag'jɑːt] *n* (-[e]s/-e)
plagiarism; *ein ~ begehen* plagia-
rize.

Plakat [pla'kɑːt] *n* (-[e]s/-e) poster,
placard, bill; **_säule** *f* advertisement
pillar.

Plakette [pla'kɛtə] *f* (-/-n) plaque.

Plan [plɑːn] *m* (-[e]s/-e) plan;
design, intention; scheme.

Plane ['plɑːnə] *f* (-/-n) awning, tilt.

'**planen** *v/t.* (ge-, h) plan; scheme.

Planet [pla'neːt] *m* (-en/-en) planet.

planieren ⊕ [pla'niːrən] *v/t.* (*no*
-ge-, h) level.

Planke ['plaŋkə] *f* (-/-n) plank,
board.

plänkeln ['plɛŋkəln] *v/i.* (ge-, h)
skirmish (*a. fig.*).

'**plan|los 1.** *adj.* planless, aimless,
desultory; **2.** *adv.* at random;
'**_mäßig 1.** *adj.* systematic, planned; **2.** *adv.* as planned.

planschen ['planʃən] *v/i.* (ge-, h)
splash, paddle.

Plantage [plan'tɑːʒə] *f* (-/-n) plantation.

Plapper|maul F ['plapər-] *n* chat-
terbox; '**_n** F *v/i.* (ge-, h) chatter,
prattle, babble.

plärren F ['plɛrən] *v/i. and v/t.* (ge-,
h) blubber; bawl.

Plasti|k [plastɪk] **1.** *f* (-/*no pl.*)
plastic art; **2.** *f* (-/-en) sculpture; ✄
plastic; **3.** ⊕ *n* (-s/-s) plastic;
'**_sch** *adj.* plastic; three-dimen-
sional.

Platin [pla'tiːn] *n* (-s/*no pl.*) plati-
num.

plätschern ['plɛtʃərn] *v/i.* (ge-, h)
dabble, splash; *water:* ripple, murmur.

platt *adj.* [plat] flat, level, even; *fig.*
trivial, commonplace, trite; F *fig.*
flabbergasted.

Plättbrett ['plɛt-] *n* ironing-board.

Platte ['platə] *f* (-/-n) plate; dish;
sheet (*of metal, etc.*); flag, slab (*of
stone*); *mountain:* ledge; top (*of
table*); tray, salver; disc, record;
F *fig.* bald pate; *kalte ~* cold meat.

plätten ['plɛtən] *v/t.* (ge-, h)
iron.

'Platten|spieler m record-player; **'~teller** m turn-table.

'Platt|form f platform; **'~fuß** m flat-foot; F mot. flat; **'~heit** fig. f (-/-en) triviality; commonplace, platitude, Am. sl. a. bromide.

Platz [plats] m (-es/⁔e) place; spot, Am. a. point; room, space; site; seat; square; round: circus; sports: ground; tennis: court; ~ behalten remain seated; ~ machen make way or room (dat. for); ~ nehmen take a seat, sit down, Am. a. have a seat; ist hier noch ~? is this seat taken or engaged or occupied?; den dritten ~ belegen sports: be placed third, come in third; **'~anweiserin** f (-/-nen) usherette.

Plätzchen ['plɛtsçən] n (-s/-) snug place; spot; biscuit, Am. cookie. **'platzen** v/i. (ge-, sein) burst; explode; crack, split.

'Platz|patrone f blank cartridge; **'~regen** m downpour.

Plauder|ei [plaudə'raɪ] f (-/-en) chat; talk; small talk; **'2n** v/i. (ge-, h) (have a) chat (mit with), talk (to); chatter.

plauz int. [plauts] bang!

Pleite F ['plaɪtə] **1.** f (-/-n) smash; fig. failure; **2.** 2 F adj. (dead) broke, Am. sl. bust.

Plissee [pli'se:] n (-s/-s) pleating; **~rock** m pleated skirt.

Plomb|e ['plɔmbə] f (-/-n) (lead) seal; stopping, filling (of tooth); **2ieren** [⌐'bi:rən] v/t. (no -ge-, h) seal; stop, fill (tooth).

plötzlich adj. ['plœtslɪç] sudden.

plump adj. [plump] clumsy; **~** int. plump, plop; **'~sen** v/i. (ge-, sein) plump, plop, flop.

Plunder F ['plundər] m (-s/no pl.) lumber, rubbish, junk.

plündern ['plyndərn] (ge-, h) **1.** v/t. plunder, pillage, loot, sack; **2.** v/i. plunder, loot. [(number).]

Plural gr. ['plu:ra:l] m (-s/-e) plural

plus adv. [plus] plus.

Plusquamperfekt gr. ['pluskvamperfɛkt] n (-s/-e) pluperfect (tense), past perfect.

Pöbel ['pø:bəl] m (-s/no pl.) mob, rabble; **'2haft** adj. low, vulgar.

pochen ['pɔxən] v/i. (ge-, h) knock, rap, tap; heart: beat, throb, thump; auf sein Recht ~ stand on one's rights.

Pocke ⚕ ['pɔkə] f (-/-n) pock; **'~n** ⚕ pl. smallpox; **'2narbig** adj. pock-marked.

Podest [po'dɛst] n, m (-es/-e) pedestal (a. fig.).

Podium ['po:dium] n (-s/Podien) podium, platform, stage.

Poesie [poe'zi:] f (-/-n) poetry.

Poet [po'e:t] m (-en/-en) poet; **2isch** adj. poetic(al).

Pointe [po'ɛ̃:tə] f (-/-n) point.

Pokal [po'ka:l] m (-s/-e) goblet; sports: cup; **~endspiel** n sports: cup final; **~spiel** n football: cup-tie.

Pökel|fleisch ['pø:kəl-] n salted meat; **'2n** v/t. (ge-, h) pickle, salt.

Pol [po:l] m (-s/-e) pole; ⚡ a. terminal; **2ar** adj. [po'la:r] polar (a. ⚡).

Pole [po:lə] m (-n/-n) Pole.

Polemi|k [po'le:mik] f (-/-en) polemic(s pl.); **2sch** adj. polemic (-al); **2sieren** [⌐mi'zi:rən] v/i. (no -ge-, h) polemize.

Police [po'li:s(ə)] f (-/-n) policy.

Polier ⊕ [po'li:r] m (-s/-e) foreman; **2en** v/t. (no -ge-, h) polish, burnish; furbish.

Politi|k [poli'ti:k] f (-/⁔-en) policy; politics sg., pl.; **~ker** [po'li:tikər] m (-s/-) politician; statesman; **2sch** adj. [po'li:tiʃ] political; **2sieren** [⌐iti'zi:rən] v/i. (no -ge-, h) talk politics.

Politur [poli'tu:r] f (-/-en) polish; lust|re, Am. -er, finish.

Polizei [poli'tsaɪ] f (-/⁔-en) police; **~beamte** m police officer; **~knüppel** m truncheon, Am. club; **~kommissar** m inspector; **2lich** adj. (of or by the) police; **~präsident** m president of police; Brt. Chief Constable, Am. Chief of Police; **~präsidium** n police headquarters pl.; **~revier** n police-station; police precinct; **~schutz** m: unter ~ under police guard; **~streife** f police patrol; police squad; **~stunde** f (-/no pl.) closing-time; **~verordnung** f police regulation(s pl.); **~wache** f police-station.

Polizist [poli'tsɪst] m (-en/-en) policeman, constable, sl. bobby, cop; **~in** f (-/-nen) policewoman.

polnisch adj. ['pɔlnɪʃ] Polish.

Polster ['pɔlstər] n (-s/-) pad; cushion; bolster; s. Polsterung; **'~möbel** n/pl. upholstered furniture; upholstery; **'2n** v/t. (ge-, h) upholster, stuff; pad, wad; '**~sessel** *m*, '**~stuhl** *m* upholstered chair; '**~ung** *f* (-/-en) padding, stuffing; upholstery.

poltern ['pɔltərn] *v/i.* (ge-, h) make a row; rumble; *p.* bluster.

Polytechnikum [poly'tɛçnikum] *n* (-s/Polytechnika, Polytechniken) polytechnic (school).

Pommes frites [pɔm'frit] *pl.* chips *pl.*, *Am.* French fried potatoes *pl.*

Pomp [pɔmp] *m* (-[e]s/*no pl.*) pomp, splendo(u)r; '**2haft** *adj.*, **2ös** *adj.* [~'pø:s] pompous, splendid.

Pony ['pɔni] **1.** *zo.* *n* (-s/-s) pony; **2.** *m* (-s/-s) *hairstyle*: bang, fringe.

popul|är *adj.* [popu'lɛ:r] popular; **2arität** [~ari'tɛ:t] *f* (-/*no pl.*) popularity.

Por|e ['po:rə] *f* (-/-n) pore; **2ös** *adj.* [po'rø:s] porous; permeable.

Portemonnaie [pɔrtmɔ'nɛ:] *n* (-s/-s) purse.

Portier [pɔr'tje:] *m* (-s/-s) *s. Pförtner.*

Portion [pɔr'tsjo:n] *f* (-/-en) portion, share; ⚔ ration; helping, serving; *zwei ~en Kaffee* coffee for two.

Porto ['pɔrto] *n* (-s/-s, Porti) postage; '**2frei** *adj.* post-free; prepaid, *esp. Am.* postpaid; '**2pflichtig** *adj.* subject to postage.

Porträt [pɔr'trɛ:; ~t] *n* (-s/-s; -[e]s/-e) portrait, likeness; **2ieren** [~ɛ'ti:rən] *v/t.* (*no* -ge-, h) portray.

Portugies|e [pɔrtu'gi:zə] *m* (-n/-n) Portuguese; *die ~n pl.* the Portuguese *pl.*; **2isch** *adj.* Portuguese.

Porzellan [pɔrtsɛ'lɑ:n] *n* (-s/-e) porcelain, china.

P

Posaune [po'zaʊnə] *f* (-/-n) ♪ trombone; *fig.* trumpet.

Pose ['po:zə] *f* (-/-n) pose, attitude; *fig. a.* air.

Position [pozi'tsjo:n] *f* (-/-en) position; social standing; ⚓ station.

positiv *adj.* ['po:ziti:f] positive.

Positur [pozi'tu:r] *f* (-/-en) posture; *sich in ~ setzen* strike an attitude.

Posse *thea.* ['pɔsə] *f* (-/-n) farce.

'**Possen** *m* (-s/-) trick, prank; '**2haft** *adj.* farcical, comical; '**~reißer** *m* (-s/-) buffoon, clown.

possessiv *gr. adj.* ['pɔsɛsi:f] possessive.

pos'sierlich *adj.* droll, funny.

Post [pɔst] *f* (-/-en) post, *Am.* mail; mail, letters *pl.*; post office; *mit der ersten ~* by the first delivery; '**~amt** *n* post office; '**~anschrift** *f* mailing address; '**~anweisung** *f* postal order; '**~beamte** *m* post-office clerk; '**~bote** *m* postman, *Am.* mailman; '**~dampfer** *m* packet-boat.

Posten ['pɔstən] *m* (-s/-) post, place, station; job; ⚔ sentry, sentinel; item; entry; *goods*: lot, parcel.

'**Postfach** *n* post-office box.

pos'tieren *v/t.* (*no* -ge-, h) post, station, place; *sich ~* station o.s.

'**Post|karte** *f* postcard, *with printed postage stamp*: *Am. a.* postal card; '**~kutsche** *f* stage-coach; '**2lagernd** *adj.* to be (kept until) called for, poste restante, *Am.* (in care of) general delivery; '**~leitzahl** *f* post-code; '**~minister** *m* minister of post; *Brt.* and *Am.* Postmaster General; '**~paket** *n* postal parcel; '**~schalter** *m* (post-office) window; '**~scheck** *m* postal cheque, *Am.* postal check; '**~schließfach** *n* post-office box; '**~sparbuch** *n* post-office savings-book; '**~stempel** *m* postmark; '**2wendend** *adv.* by return of post; '**~wertzeichen** *n* (postage) stamp; '**~zug** 🚂 *m* mail-train.

Pracht [praxt] *f* (-/⚒ -en, ¨e) splendo(u)r, magnificence; luxury.

prächtig *adj.* ['prɛçtiç] splendid, magnificent; gorgeous; grand.

'**prachtvoll** *adj. s. prächtig.*

Prädikat [prɛdi'kɑ:t] *n* (-[e]s/-e) *gr.* predicate; *school, etc.*: mark.

prägen ['prɛ:gən] *v/t.* (ge-, h) stamp; coin (*word, coin*).

prahlen ['prɑ:lən] *v/i.* (ge-, h) brag, boast (*mit* of); *~ mit* show off *s.th.*

'**Prahler** *m* (-s/-) boaster, braggart; **~ei** [~'raɪ] *f* (-/-en) boasting, bragging; '**2isch** *adj.* boastful; ostentatious.

Prakti|kant [prakti'kant] *m* (-en/-en) probationer; '**~ker** *m* (-s/-) practical man; expert; **~kum** ['~kum] *n* (-s/Praktika, Praktiken) practical course; '**2sch** *adj.* practical; useful, handy; *~er Arzt* general practitioner; **2zieren** ⚕, ⚖ [~'tsi:rən] *v/i.* (*no* -ge-, h) practi|se, *Am.* -ce medicine *or* the law.

Prälat *eccl.* [prɛ'lɑ:t] *m* (-en/-en) prelate.

Praline [pra'li:nə] *f* (-/-n): *~n pl.* chocolates *pl.*

prall adj. [pral] tight; plump; sun: blazing; '.en v/i. (ge-, sein) bounce or bound (auf acc.; gegen against).

Prämi|e ['prɛːmjə] f (-/-n) ⚕ premium; prize; bonus; �²(i)eren [prɛ'miːrən, premiːiːrən] v/t. (no -ge-, h) award a prize to.

prang|en ['praŋən] v/i. (ge-, h) shine, make a show; '²er m (-s/-) pillory.

Pranke ['praŋkə] f (-/-n) paw.

pränumerando adv. [prɛːnumə'rando] beforehand, in advance.

Präpa|rat [prɛpa'raːt] n (-[e]s/-e) preparation; microscopy: slide; ²'rieren v/t. (no -ge-, h) prepare.

Präposition gr. [prepozi'tsjoːn] f (-/-en) preposition.

Prärie [prɛ'riː] f (-/-n) prairie.

Präsens gr. ['prɛːzɛns] n (-/Präsentia, Präsenzien) present (tense).

Präsi|dent [prɛziˈdɛnt] m (-en/-en) president; chairman; ²'dieren v/i. (no -ge-, h) preside (über acc. over); be in the chair; ~dium n (-s/Präsidien) presidency, chair.

prasseln ['prasəln] v/i. (ge-, h) fire: crackle; rain: patter.

prassen ['prasən] v/i. (ge-, h) feast, carouse.

Präteritum gr. [prɛ'teːritum] n (-s/Präterita) preterite (tense); past tense.

Praxis ['praksis] f 1. (-/no pl.) practice; 2. (-/Praxen) practice (of doctor or lawyer).

Präzedenzfall [prɛtse'dɛnts-] m precedent; ⚖ a. case-law.

präzis adj. [prɛ'tsiːs], ~e adj. [~zə] precise.

predig|en ['preːdigən] v/i. and v/t. (ge-, h) preach; '²er m (-s/-) preacher; clergyman; ²t ['~dɪçt] f (-/-en) sermon (a. fig.); fig. lecture.

Preis [prais] m (-es/-e) price; cost; competition: prize; award; reward; praise; um jeden ~ at any price or cost; '~ausschreiben n (-s/-) competition.   [praise.]

preisen ['praizən] v/t. (irr., ge-, h)
'**Preis|erhöhung** f rise or increase in price(s); '~gabe f abandonment; revelation (of secret); '²geben v/t. (irr. geben, sep., -ge-, h) abandon; reveal, give away (secret); disclose, expose; '²gekrönt adj. prizewinning, prize (novel, etc.); '~gericht n jury; '~lage f range of

prices; '~liste f price-list; '~nachlaß m price cut; discount; '~richter m judge, umpire; '~schießen n (-s/-) shooting competition; '~stopp m (-s/no pl.) price freeze; '~träger m prize-winner; '²wert adj.: ~ sein be a bargain.

prell|en ['prɛlən] v/t. (ge-, h) fig. cheat, defraud (um of); sich et. ~ ⚕ contuse or bruise s.th.; '²ung ⚕ f (-/-en) contusion.

Premier|e thea. [prəm'jɛːrə] f (-/-n) première, first night; ~minister [~'je:-] m prime minister.

Presse ['prɛsə] f 1. (-/-n) ⊕, typ. press; squeezer; 2. (-/no pl.) newspapers generally: the press; '~amt n public relations office; '~freiheit f freedom of the press; '~meldung f news item; '²n v/t. (ge-, h) press; squeeze; '~photograph m press-photographer; '~vertreter m reporter; public relations officer.

Preßluft ['prɛs-] f (-/no pl.) compressed air.

Prestige [prɛs'tiːʒə] n (-s/no pl.) prestige; ~ verlieren a. lose face.

Preuß|e ['prɔysə] m (-n/-n) Prussian; '²isch adj. Prussian.

prickeln ['prikəln] v/i. (ge-, h) prick(le), tickle; itch; fingers: tingle.

Priem [priːm] m (-[e]s/-e) quid.

pries [priːs] pret. of preisen.

Priester ['priːstər] m (-s/-) priest; '~in f (-/-nen) priestess; '²lich adj. priestly; sacerdotal; '~rock m cassock.

prim|a F adj. ['priːma] first-rate, F A 1; ⚕ a. prime; F swell; ~är adj. [priˈmɛːr] primary.

Primel ⚘ ['priːməl] f (-/-n) primrose.

Prinz [prints] m (-en/-en) prince; ~essin [~'tsɛsin] f (-/-nen) princess; '~gemahl m prince consort.

Prinzip [prin'tsiːp] n (-s/-ien) principle; aus ~ on principle; im ~ in principle, basically.

Priorität [prioriˈtɛːt] f 1. (-/-en) priority; 2. (-/no pl.) time: priority.

Prise ['priːzə] f (-/-n) ⚓ prize; e-e ~ a pinch of (salt, snuff).

Prisma ['prisma] n (-s/Prismen) prism.   [bed.]

Pritsche ['pritʃə] f (-/-n) bat; plank-

privat adj. [pri'vaːt] private; ²adresse f home address; ²mann m (-[e]s/Privatmänner, Privatleute)

P

private person *or* gentleman; **~patient** *m* paying patient; **~person** *f* private person; **~schule** *f* private school.

Privileg [privi'le:k] *n* (-[e]s/-ien, -e) privilege.

pro *prp.* [pro:] per; ~ *Jahr* per annum; ~ *Kopf* per head; ~ *Stück* a piece.

Probe ['pro:bə] *f* (-/-n) experiment; trial, test; *metall.* assay; sample; specimen; proof; probation; check; *thea.* rehearsal; audition; *auf* ~ on probation, on trial; *auf die* ~ *stellen* (put to the) test; **'~abzug** *typ.*, *phot. m* proof; **'~exemplar** *n* specimen copy; **'~fahrt** *f* ⚓ trial trip; *mot.* trial run; **'~flug** *m* test *or* trial flight; **'~n** *v/t.* (ge-, h) exercise; *thea.* rehearse; **'~nummer** *f* specimen copy *or* number; **'~seite** *typ. f* specimen page; **'~sendung** *f* goods on approval; **'~weise** *adv.* on trial; *p. a.* on probation; **'~zeit** *f* time of probation.

probieren [pro'bi:rən] *v/t.* (no -ge-, h) try, test; taste (*food*.)

Problem [pro'ble:m] *n* (-s/-e) problem; **~atisch** [~e'ma:tiʃ] *adj.* problematic(al).

Produkt [pro'dukt] *n* (-[e]s/-e) product (*a. Å*); *↗* produce; result; **~ion** [~'tsjo:n] *f* (-/-en) production; output; **~iv** [~'ti:f] *adj.* productive.

Produz|ent [produ'tsent] *m* (-en/-en) producer; **~ieren** [~'tsi:rən] *v/t.* (no -ge-, h) produce; *sich* ~ perform; *contp.* show off.

professionell *adj.* [profesio'nɛl] professional, by trade.

Profess|or [pro'fesɔr] *m* (-s/-en) professor; **~ur** [~'su:r] *f* (-/-en) professorship, chair.

Profi ['pro:fi] *m* (-s/-s) *sports:* professional, F pro. [*on tyre:* tread.)

Profil [pro'fi:l] *n* (-s/-e) profile;)

Profit [pro'fi:t] *m* (-[e]s/-e) profit; **~ieren** [~i'ti:rən] *v/i.* (no -ge-, h) profit (*von* by).

Prognose [pro'gno:zə] *f* (-/-n) *ℱ* prognosis; *meteor.* forecast.

Programm [pro'gram] *n* (-s/-e) program(me); *politisches* ~ political program(me), *Am.* platform.

Projektion [projɛk'tsjo:n] *f* (-/-en) projection; **~sapparat** [projɛk-'tsjo:ns?-] *m* projector.

proklamieren [prokla'mi:rən] *v/t.* (no -ge-, h) proclaim.

Prokur|a ✝ [pro'ku:ra] *f* (-/*Prokuren*) procuration; **~ist** [~ku'rist] *m* (-en/-en) confidential clerk.

Proletari|er [prole'ta:rjər] *m* (-s/-) proletarian; **~sch** *adj.* proletarian.

Prolog [pro'lo:k] *m* (-[e]s/-e) prolog(ue).

prominen|t *adj.* [promi'nent] prominent; **~z** [~ts] *f* (-/*no pl.*) notables *pl.*, celebrities *pl.*; high society.

Promo|tion *univ.* [promo'tsjo:n] *f* (-/-en) graduation; **~vieren** [~'vi:-rən] *v/i.* (no -ge-, h) graduate (*an dat.* from), take one's degree.

Pronomen *gr.* [pro'no:men] *n* (-s/-, *Pronomina*) pronoun.

Propeller [pro'pɛlər] *m* (-s/-) ⚓, ✈ (screw-)propeller, screw; ✈ airscrew.

Prophe|t [pro'fe:t] *m* (-en/-en) prophet; **~tisch** *adj.* prophetic; **~zeien** [~e'tsaiən] *v/t.* (no -ge-, h) prophesy; predict, foretell; **~zeiung** *f* (-/-en) prophecy; prediction.

Proportion [propɔr'tsjo:n] *f* (-/-en) proportion.

Prosa ['pro:za] *f* (-/*no pl.*) prose.

prosit *int.* ['pro:zit] your health!, here's to you!, cheers!

Prospekt [pro'spekt] *m* (-[e]s/-e) prospectus; brochure, leaflet, folder.

prost *int.* [pro:st] *s.* prosit.

Prostituierte [prostitu'i:rtə] *f* (-n/-n) prostitute.

Protest [pro'test] *m* (-es/-e) protest; ~ *einlegen* *or* *erheben gegen* (enter a) protest against.

Protestant *eccl.* [protes'tant] *m* (-en/-en) Protestant; **~isch** *adj.* Protestant.

protes|tieren *v/i.* (no -ge-, h): *gegen et.* ~ protest against s.th., object to s.th.

Prothese *ℱ* [pro'te:zə] *f* (-/-n) pro(s)thesis; *dentistry:* a. denture; artificial limb.

Protokoll [proto'kɔl] *n* (-s/-e) record, minutes *pl.* (*of meeting*); *diplomacy:* protocol; *das* ~ *aufnehmen* take down the minutes; *das* ~ *führen* keep the minutes; *zu* ~ *geben* ₮ℒ depose, state in evidence; *zu* ~ *nehmen* take down, record; **~ieren** [~'li:rən] (no -ge-, h) **1.** *v/t.* record, take down (on record); **2.** *v/i.* keep the minutes.

Protz *contp.* [prɔts] *m* (-en, -es/

-e[n]) braggart, F show-off; '2en *v/i.* (ge-, h) show off (*mit dat.* with); '2ig *adj.* ostentatious, showy.

Proviant [pro'vjant] *m* (-s/⚓-e) provisions *pl.*, victuals *pl.*

Provinz [pro'vints] *f* (-/-en) province; *fig. the* provinces *pl.*; 2ial *adj.* [~'tsja:l], 2iell *adj.* [~'tsjɛl] provincial.

Provis|ion ✝ [provi'zjo:n] *f* (-/-en) commission; 2orisch *adj.* [~'zo:riʃ] provisional, temporary.

provozieren [provo'tsi:rən] *v/t.* (*no* -ge-, h) provoke.

Prozent [pro'tsɛnt] *n* (-[e]s/-e) per cent; ⚓satz *m* percentage; proportion; 2ual *adj.* [~u'a:l] percental; ⚓er Anteil percentage.

Prozeß [pro'tsɛs] *m* (Prozesses/Prozesse) process; 🜋: action, lawsuit; trial; (legal) proceedings *pl.*; e-n ⚓ gewinnen win one's case; e-n ⚓ gegen j-n anstrengen bring an action against s.o., sue s.o.; j-m den ⚓ machen try s.o., put s.o. on trial; kurzen ⚓ machen mit make short work of.

prozessieren [protse'si:rən] *v/i.* (*no* -ge-, h): mit j-m ⚓ go to law against s.o., have the law of s.o.

Prozession [protse'sjo:n] *f* (-/-en) procession.

prüde *adj.* ['pry:də] prudish.

prüf|en ['pry:fən] *v/t.* (ge-, h) examine; try, test; quiz; check, verify; '⚓end *adj. look:* searching, scrutinizing; '2er *m* (-s/-) examiner; '2ling *m* (-s/-e) examinee; '2stein *fig. m* touchstone; '2ung *f* (-/-en) examination; *school, etc.: a.* F exam; test; quiz; verification, checking, check-up; e-e ⚓ machen go in for *or* sit for *or* take an examination.

'**Prüfungs|arbeit** *f*, '⚓aufgabe *f* examination-paper; '⚓ausschuß *m*, '⚓kommission *f* board of examiners.

Prügel ['pry:gəl] 1. *m* (-s/-) cudgel, club, stick; 2. F *fig. pl.* beating, thrashing; ⚓ei *f* [~'laı] *f* (-/-en) fight, row; '⚓knabe *m* scapegoat; '2n F *v/t.* (ge-, h) cudgel, flog; beat (up), thrash; sich ⚓ (have a) fight.

Prunk [pruŋk] *m* (-[e]s/*no pl.*) splendo(u)r; pomp, show; '2en *v/i.* (ge-, h) make a show (*mit* of), show off (*mit et. s.th.*); '2voll *adj.* splendid, gorgeous.

Psalm *eccl.* [psalm] *m* (-s/-en) psalm.

Pseudonym [psɔrdo'ny:m] *n* (-s/-e) pseudonym.

pst *int.* [pst] hush!

Psychi|ater [psyçi'a:tər] *m* (-s/-) psychiatrist, alienist; 2sch *adj.* ['psy:çiʃ] psychic(al).

Psycho|analyse [psyço?ana'ly:zə] *f* (-/*no pl.*) psychoanalysis; ⚓analytiker [~tikər] *m* (-s/-) psychoanalist; ⚓loge [~'lo:gə] *m* (-n/-n) psychologist; ⚓se [~'ço:zə] *f* (-/-n) psychosis; panic.

Pubertät [puber'tɛ:t] *f* (-/*no pl.*) puberty.

Publikum ['pu:blikum] *n* (-s/*no pl.*) *the* public; audience; spectators *pl.*, crowd; readers *pl.*

publiz|ieren [publi'tsi:rən] *v/t.* (*no* -ge-, h) publish; 2ist *m* (-en/-en) publicist; journalist.

Pudding ['pudiŋ] *m* (-s/-e, -s) cream.

Pudel *zo.* ['pu:dəl] *m* (-s/-) poodle; '2'naß F *adj.* dripping wet, drenched.

Puder ['pu:dər] *m* (-s/-) powder; '⚓dose *f* powder-box; compact; '2n *v/t.* (ge-, h) powder; sich ⚓ powder o.s. *or* one's face; '⚓quaste *f* powder-puff; '⚓zucker *m* powdered sugar.

Puff F [puf] *m* (-[e]s/⚓e, -e) poke, nudge; '2en (ge-, h) 1. F *v/t.* nudge; 2. *v/i.* pop; '⚓er 🚃 *m* (-s/-) buffer.

Pullover [pu'lo:vər] *m* (-s/-) pullover, sweater.

Puls 🎵 [puls] *m* (-es/-e) pulse; '⚓ader *anat.* *f* artery; 2ieren [~'zi:rən] *v/i.* (*no* -ge-, h) pulsate, throb; '⚓schlag 🎵 *m* (-s/-) pulsation.

Pult [pult] *n* (-[e]s/-e) desk.

Pulver ['pulfər] *n* (-s/-) powder; gunpowder; F *fig.* cash, *sl.* brass, dough; '2erig *adj.* powdery; 2erisieren [~vəri'zi:rən] *v/t.* (*no* -ge-, h) pulverize; '2rig *adj.* ['~friç] powdery.

Pump F [pump] *m* (-[e]s/-e): auf ⚓ on tick; '⚓e *f* (-/-n) pump; '2en (ge-, h) 1. *v/i.* pump; 2. *v/t.* pump; F *fig.:* give s.th. on tick; borrow (et. von j-m s.th. from s.o.).

Punkt [puŋkt] *m* (-[e]s/-e) point (*a. fig.*); dot; *typ., gr.* full stop, period; spot, place; *fig.* item; article, clause (*of agreement*); der springende ⚓ the

P

point; *toter* ~ deadlock, dead end;
wunder ~ tender subject, sore point;
~ *zehn Uhr* on the stroke of ten, at
10 (o'clock) sharp; *in vielen ~en* on
many points, in many respects;
nach ~en siegen sports: win on
points; **2ieren** [~'tiːrən] *v/t. (no
-ge-, h)* dot, point; ✺ puncture,
tap; *drawing, painting:* stipple.
pünktlich *adj.* ['pʏŋktliç] punctual;
~ *sein* be on time; **2keit** *f (-/no pl.)*
punctuality.

Punsch [punʃ] *m (-es/-e)* punch.
Pupille [pu'pilə] *f (-/-n)* pupil.
Puppe ['pupə] *f (-/-n)* doll *(a. fig.)*;
puppet *(a. fig.)*; *tailoring:* dummy;
zo. chrysalis, pupa; **'~nspiel** *n*
puppet-show; **'~nstube** *f* doll's
room; **'~nwagen** *m* doll's pram,
Am. doll carriage *or* buggy.
pur *adj.* [puːr] pure, sheer.
Püree [py'reː] *n (-s/-s)* purée, mash.
Purpur ['purpur] *m (-s/no pl.)*
purple; **2farben** *adj.*, **2n** *adj.*,
2rot *adj.* purple.
Purzel|baum ['purtsəl-] *m* somer-
sault; *e-n* ~ *schlagen* turn a somersault; **2n** *v/i. (ge-, sein)* tumble.
Puste F ['puːstə] *f (-/no pl.)* breath;
ihm ging die ~ *aus* he got out of
breath.

Pustel ✻ ['pustəl] *f (-/-n)* pustule,
pimple.
pusten ['puːstən] *v/i. (ge-, h)* puff,
pant; blow.
Pute *orn.* ['puːtə] *f (-/-n)* turkey
(-hen); **'~r** *orn.* *m (-s/-)* turkey
(-cock); **'2r'rot** *adj.* (as) red as a
turkey-cock.
Putsch [putʃ] *m (-es/-e)* putsch,
insurrection; riot; **'2en** *v/i. (ge-, h)*
revolt, riot.
Putz [puts] *m (-es/-e) on garments:*
finery; ornaments *pl.*; trimming;
△ roughcast, plaster; **'2en** *v/t.
(ge-, h)* clean, cleanse; polish,
wipe; adorn; snuff *(candle)*; polish,
Am. shine *(shoes)*; *sich* ~ smarten *or*
dress o.s. up; *sich die Nase* ~ blow
or wipe one's nose; *sich die Zähne* ~
brush one's teeth; **'~frau** *f* char-
woman, *Am. a.* scrubwoman; **'2ig**
adj. droll, funny; **'~lappen** *m*
cleaning rag; **'~zeug** *n* cleaning
utensils *pl.*
Pyjama [pi'dʒaːma] *m (-s/-s)* (*ein
a suit of*) pyjamas *pl.* or *Am. a.*
pajamas *pl.*
Pyramide [pyra'miːdə] *f (-/-n)*
pyramid *(a. ♈)*; ✗ stack *(of rifles)*;
2nförmig *adj.* [~nfœrmiç] pyram-
idal.

Q

Quacksalber ['kvakzalbər] *m (-s/-)*
quack (doctor); **~ei** F [~'raɪ] *f
(-/-en)* quackery; **'2n** *v/i. (ge-, h)*
(play the) quack.
Quadrat [kva'draːt] *n (-[e]s/-e)*
square; *2 Fuß im* ~ *2* feet square;
ins ~ *erheben* square; **2isch** *adj.*
square; ♈ *equation:* quadratic;
~meile *f* square mile; **~meter** *n, m*
square met|re, *Am. -er;* **~wurzel**
♈ *f* square root; **~zahl** ♈ *f* square
number.
quaken ['kvaːkən] *v/i. (ge-, h)* duck:
quack; *frog:* croak.   [squeak.]
quäken ['kvɛːkən] *v/i. (ge-, h)*
Quäker ['kvɛːkər] *m (-s/-)* Quaker,
member of the Society of Friends.
Qual [kvaːl] *f (-/-en)* pain; torment;
agony.
quälen ['kvɛːlən] *v/t. (ge-, h)* torment *(a. fig.)*; torture; ago-

nize; *fig.* bother, pester; *sich* ~ toil,
drudge.
Qualifikation [kvalifika'tsjoːn] *f
(-/-en)* qualification.
qualifizieren [kvalifi'tsiːrən] *v/t.
and v/refl. (no -ge-, h)* qualify (*zu
for*).
Qualit|ät [kvali'tɛːt] *f (-/-en)*
quality; **2ativ** [~a'tiːf] **1.** *adj.*
qualitative; **2.** *adv.* as to quality.
Quali'täts|arbeit *f* work of high
quality; **~stahl** *m* high-grade steel;
~ware *f* high-grade *or* quality
goods *pl.*
Qualm [kvalm] *m (-[e]s/no pl.)*
dense smoke; fumes *pl.*; vapo(u)r,
steam; **'2en** *(ge-, h)* **1.** *v/i.* smoke,
give out vapo(u)r *or* fumes; F *p.*
smoke heavily; **2.** F *v/t.* puff (away)
at *(cigar, pipe, etc.)*; **'2ig** *adj.*
smoky.

'**qualvoll** adj. very painful; pain: excruciating; fig. agonizing, harrowing.

Quantit|ät [kvantiˈtɛːt] f (-/-en) quantity; **Ջativ** [ˌʌˈtiːf] **1.** adj. quantitative; **2.** adv. as to quantity.

Quantum [ˈkvantum] n (-s/Quanten) quantity, amount; quantum (a. phys.).

Quarantäne [karanˈtɛːnə] f (-/-n) quarantine; in ~ legen (put in) quarantine;   [curd(s pl.).\

Quark [kvark] m (-[e]s/no pl.)\

Quartal [kvarˈtaːl] n (-s/-e) quarter (of a year); univ. term.

Quartett [kvarˈtɛt] n (-[e]s/-e) ♪ quartet(te); cards: four.

Quartier [kvarˈtiːr] n (-s/-e) accommodation;   ✕ quarters pl., billet.   [(powder-)puff.\

Quaste [ˈkvastə] f (-/-n) tassel;\

Quatsch F [kvatʃ] m (-es/no pl.) nonsense, fudge, sl. bosh, rot, Am. sl. a. baloney; **Ջen** F v/i. (ge-, h) twaddle, blether, sl. talk rot; (have a) chat; '**ᵥkopf** F m twaddler.

Quecksilber [ˈkvɛk-] n mercury, quicksilver.

Quelle [ˈkvɛlə] f (-/-n) spring, source (a. fig.); oil: well; fig. fountain, origin; **Ջn** v/i. (irr., ge-, sein) gush, well; **ᵥnangabe** [ˈkvɛlənʔ-] f mention of sources used; '**ᵥnforschung** f original research.

Quengel|ei F [kvɛŋəˈlaɪ] f (-/-en) grumbling, whining; nagging; '**Ջn** F v/i. (ge-, h) grumble, whine; nag.

quer adv. [kveːr] crossways, crosswise; F fig. wrong; F ~ gehen go wrong; ~ über (acc.) across.

'**Quer|e** f (-/no pl.): der ~ nach crossways, crosswise; F j-m in die ~

kommen cross s.o.'s path; fig. thwart s.o.'s plans; '**ᵥfrage** f cross-question; '**ᵥkopf** fig. m wrong-headed fellow; '**Ջschießen** F v/i. (irr. schießen, sep., -ge-, h) try to foil s.o.'s plans; '**ᵥschiff** △ n transept; '**ᵥschläger** ✕ m ricochet; '**ᵥschnitt** m cross-section (a. fig.); '**ᵥstraße** f cross-road; zweite ~ rechts second turning to the right; '**ᵥtreiber** m (-s/-) schemer; '**ᵥtreibe'rei** f (-/-en) intriguing, machination.

Querulant [kveruˈlant] m (-en/-en) querulous person, grumbler, Am. sl. a. griper.

quetsch|en [ˈkvɛtʃən] v/t. (ge-, h) squeeze, sⁱ bruise, contuse; sich den Finger ~ jam one's finger; '**Ջung** sⁱ f (-/-en), '**Ջwunde** sⁱ f bruise, contusion.

quick adj. [kvik] lively, brisk.

quieken [ˈkviːkən] v/i. (ge-, h) squeak, squeal.

quietsch|en [ˈkviːtʃən] v/i. (ge-, h) squeak, squeal; door-hinge, etc.: creak, squeak; brakes, etc.: screech; '**ᵥver'gnügt** F adj. (as) jolly as a sandboy.

Quirl [kvirl] m (-[e]s/-e) twirling-stick; '**Ջen** v/t. (ge-, h) twirl.

quitt adj. [kvit]: ~ sein mit j-m be quits or even with s.o.; jetzt sind wir ~ that leaves us even; **ᵥieren** [ˌˈtiːrən] v/t. (no -ge-, h) receipt (bill, etc.); quit, abandon (post, etc.); '**Ջung** f (-/-en) receipt; fig. answer; gegen ~ against receipt.

quoll [kvɔl] pret. of quellen.

Quot|e [ˈkvoːtə] f (-/-n) quota, share, portion; '**ᵥient** Ⱥ [kvoˈtsjɛnt] m (-en/-en) quotient.

R

Rabatt ✝ [raˈbat] m (-[e]s/-e) discount, rebate.

Rabe orn. [ˈraːbə] m (-n/-n) raven; '**Ջnschwarz** F adj. raven, jet-black.

rabiat adj. [raˈbjaːt] rabid, violent.

Rache [ˈraxə] f (-/no pl.) revenge, vengeance; retaliation.

Rachen anat. [ˈraxən] m (-s/-) throat, pharynx; jaws pl.

rächen [ˈrɛçən] v/t. (ge-, h) avenge,

revenge; sich ~ an (dat.) revenge o.s. or be revenged on.

'**Rachen|höhle** anat. f pharynx; '**ᵥkatarrh** sⁱ m cold in the throat.

'**rach|gierig** adj., '**ᵥsüchtig** adj. revengeful, vindictive.

Rad [raːt] n (-[e]s/ᵘer) wheel; (bi)cycle, F bike; (ein) ~ schlagen peacock: spread its tail; sports: turn cart-wheels; unter die Räder kommen go to the dogs; '**∼achse** f axle(-tree).

Radar ['rɑːdɑːr, rɑ'dɑːr] m, n (-s/-s) radar.

Radau F [ra'dau] m (-s/no pl.) row, racket, hubbub.

radebrechen ['rɑːdə-] v/t. (ge-, h) speak (language) badly, murder (language).

radeln ['rɑːdəln] v/i. (ge-, sein) cycle, pedal, F bike.

Rädelsführer ['rɛːdəls-] m ringleader.

Räderwerk ⊕ ['rɛːdər-] n gearing.

'**rad|fahren** v/i. (irr. fahren, sep., -ge-, sein) cycle, (ride a) bicycle, pedal, F bike; '**⁀fahrer** m cyclist, Am. a. cycler or wheelman.

radier|en [ra'diːrən] v/t. (no -ge-, h) rub out, erase; art: etch; **⁀gummi** m (india-)rubber, esp. Am. eraser; **⁀messer** n eraser; **⁀ung** f (-/-en) etching.

Radieschen ♀ [ra'diːsçən] n (-s/-) (red) radish.

radikal adj. [radi'kɑːl] radical.

Radio ['rɑːdjo] n (-s/-s) radio, wireless; im ∼ on the radio, on the air; **⁀aktiv** phys. adj. [radjoak'tiːf] radio(-)active; **⁀er** Niederschlag fall-out; '**⁀apparat** m radio or wireless (set).

Radium ⚗ ['rɑːdjum] n (-s/no pl.) radium.

Radius ⚕ ['rɑːdjus] m (-/Radien) radius.

'**Rad|kappe** f hub cap; '**⁀kranz** m rim; '**⁀rennbahn** f cycling track; '**⁀rennen** n cycle race; '**⁀sport** m cycling; '**⁀spur** f rut, track.

raffen ['rafən] v/t. (ge-, h) snatch up; gather (dress).

raffiniert adj. [rafi'niːrt] refined; fig. clever, cunning.

ragen ['rɑːgən] v/i. (ge-, h) tower, loom.

Ragout [ra'guː] n (-s/-s) ragout, stew, hash.

Rahe ⚓ ['rɑːə] f (-/-n) yard.

Rahm [rɑːm] m (-s/no pl.) cream.

Rahmen ['rɑːmən] 1. m (-s/-) frame; fig.: frame, background, setting; scope; aus dem ∼ fallen be out of place; 2. ♀ v/t. (ge-, h) frame.

Rakete [ra'keːtə] f (-/-n) rocket; e-e ∼ abfeuern or starten launch a rocket; dreistufige ∼ three-stage rocket; **∼nantrieb** [ra'keːtənˀ-] m

rocket propulsion; mit ∼ rocketpropelled; **∼nflugzeug** n rocket (-propelled) plane; **∼ntriebwerk** n propulsion unit.

Ramm|bär ⊕ ['ram-] m, '**∼bock** m, '**∼e** f (-/-n) ram(mer); '**⁀en** v/t. (ge-, h) ram.

Rampe ['rampə] f (-/-n) ramp, ascent; '**∼nlicht** n footlights pl.; fig. limelight.

Ramsch [ramʃ] m (-es/✎-e) junk, trash; im ∼ kaufen buy in the lump; '**∼verkauf** m jumble-sale; '**∼ware** f job lot.

Rand [rant] m (-[e]s/✍er) edge, brink (a. fig.); fig.: verge; border; brim (of hat, cup, etc.); rim (of plate, etc.); margin (of book, etc.); lip (of wound); Ränder pl. under the eyes: rings pl., circles pl.; vor Freude außer ∼ und Band geraten be beside o.s. with joy; er kommt damit nicht zu ∼e he can't manage it; '**∼bemerkung** f marginal note; fig. comment.

rang[1] [raŋ] pret. of ringen.

Rang[2] [..] m (-[e]s/✍e) rank, order; ✕ rank; position; thea. tier; erster ∼ thea. dress-circle, Am. first balcony; zweiter ∼ thea. upper circle, Am. second balcony; ersten ∼es firstclass, first-rate; j-m den ∼ ablaufen get the start or better of s.o.

Range ['raŋə] m (-n/-n), f (-/-n) rascal; romp.

rangieren [rɑ̃'ʒiːrən] (no -ge-, h) 1. ✎ v/t. shunt, Am. a. switch; 2. fig. v/i. rank.

'**Rang|liste** f sports, etc.: ranking list; ✕ army-list, navy or air-force list; '**∼ordnung** f order of precedence.

Ranke ♀ ['raŋkə] f (-/-n) tendril; runner.

Ränke ['rɛŋkə] m/pl. intrigues pl.

'**ranken** v/refl. (ge-, h) creep, climb.

rann [ran] pret. of rinnen.

rannte ['rantə] pret. of rennen.

Ranzen ['rantsən] m (-s/-) knapsack; satchel.

ranzig adj. ['rantsiç] rancid, rank.

Rappe zo. ['rapə] m (-n/-n) black horse.

rar adj. [rɑːr] rare, scarce.

Rarität [rari'tɛːt] f (-/-en) rarity; curiosity, curio.

rasch adj. [raʃ] quick, swift, brisk; hasty; prompt.

rascheln ['raʃəln] v/i. (ge-, h) rustle.
rasen¹ ['ra:zən] v/i. (ge-) **1.** (h) rage, storm; rave; **2.** (sein) race, speed; '**.d** adj. raving; frenzied; speed: tearing; pains: agonizing; headache: splitting; j-n ~ machen drive s.o. mad.
Rasen² [~] m (-s/-) grass; lawn; turf; '**.platz** m lawn, grass-plot.
Raserei F [ra:zə'raɪ] f (-/-en) rage, fury; frenzy, madness; F mot. scorching; j-n zur ~ bringen drive s.o. mad.

Rasier|apparat [ra'zi:r-] m (safety) razor; '**2en** v/t. (no -ge-, h) shave; sich ~ (lassen get a) shave; '**.klinge** f razor-blade; '**.messer** n razor; '**.pinsel** m shaving-brush; '**.seife** f shaving-soap; '**.wasser** n after-shave lotion; '**.zeug** n shaving kit.
Rasse ['rasə] f (-/-n) race; zo. breed.
rasseln ['rasəln] v/i. (ge-, h) rattle.
Rassen|frage f (-/no pl.) racial issue; '**.kampf** m race conflict; '**.problem** n racial issue; '**.schranke** f colo(u)r bar; '**.trennung** f (-/no pl.) racial segregation; '**.unruhen** f/pl. race riots pl.
'rasserein adj. thoroughbred, pure-bred.
'rassig adj. thoroughbred; fig. racy.
Rast [rast] f (-/-en) rest, repose; break, pause; '**2en** v/i. (ge-, h) rest, repose; '**2los** adj. restless; '**.platz** m resting-place; mot. picnic area.
Rat [ra:t] m **1.** (-[e]s/no pl.) advice, counsel; suggestion; fig. way out; zu ~e ziehen consult; j-n um ~ fragen ask s.o.'s advice; **2.** (-[e]s/~e) council, board; council(l)or, alderman.
Rate ['ra:tə] f (-/-n) instal(l)ment (a. †); auf ~n † on hire-purchase.
'raten (irr., ge-, h) **1.** v/i. advise, counsel (j-m zu inf. s.o. to inf.); **2.** v/t. guess, divine.
'raten|weise adv. by instal(l)ments; '**2zahlung** † f payment by instal(l)ments.
'Rat|geber m (-s/-) adviser, counsel(l)or; '**.haus** n town hall, Am. a. city hall.
ratifizieren [ratifi'tsi:rən] v/t. (no -ge-, h) ratify.
Ration [ra'tsjo:n] f (-/-en) ration, allowance; '**2ell** adj. [~o'nɛl] rational; efficient; economical; **2ieren** [~o'ni:rən] v/t. (no -ge-, h) ration.

'rat|los adj. puzzled, perplexed, at a loss; '**.sam** adj. advisable; expedient; '**2schlag** m (piece of) advice, counsel.
Rätsel ['rɛ:tsəl] n (-s/-) riddle, puzzle; enigma, mystery; '**2haft** adj. puzzling; enigmatic(al), mysterious.
Ratte ['ratə] f (-/-n) rat.
rattern ['ratərn] v/i. (ge-, h, sein) rattle, clatter.
Raub [raup] m (-[e]s/no pl.) robbery; kidnap(p)ing; piracy (of intellectual property); booty, spoils pl.; '**.bau** m (-[e]s/no pl.): ~ treiben ✗ exhaust the land; ✗ rob a mine; ~ treiben mit undermine (one's health); '**2en** ['~bən] v/t. (ge-, h) rob, take by force, steal; kidnap; j-m et. ~ rob or deprive s.o. of s.th.
Räuber ['rɔʏbər] m (-s/-) robber; '**.bande** f gang of robbers; '**2isch** adj. rapacious, predatory.
'Raub|fisch ichth. m fish of prey; '**.gier** f rapacity; '**2gierig** adj. rapacious; '**.mord** m murder with robbery; '**.mörder** m murderer and robber; '**.tier** zo. n beast of prey; '**.überfall** m hold-up, armed robbery; '**.vogel** orn. m bird of prey; '**.zug** m raid.
Rauch [raux] m (-[e]s/no pl.) smoke; fume; '**2en** (ge-, h) **1.** v/i. smoke; fume; p. (have a) smoke; **2.** v/t. smoke (cigarette); '**.er** m (-s/-) smoker; s. Raucherabteil.   [eel.\
Räucheraal ['rɔʏçər²-] m smoked]
Raucherabteil   ['rauxər²-] n smoking-car(riage), smoking-compartment, smoker.
'Räucher|hering m red or smoked herring, kipper; '**2n** (ge-, h) **1.** v/t. smoke, cure (meat, fish); **2.** v/i. burn incense.
'Rauch|fahne f trail of smoke; '**.fang** m chimney, flue; '**.fleisch** n smoked meat; '**2ig** adj. smoky; '**.tabak** m tobacco; '**.waren** f/pl. tobacco products pl.; furs pl.; '**.zimmer** n smoking-room.
Räude ['rɔʏdə] f (-/-n) mange, scab; '**2ig** adj. mangy, scabby.
Rauf|bold contp. ['raufbɔlt] m (-[e]s/-e) brawler, rowdy, Am. sl. tough; '**2en** (ge-, h) **1.** v/t. pluck, pull; sich die Haare ~ tear one's hair; **2.** v/i. fight, scuffle; '**.erei** [~'raɪ] f (-/-en) fight, scuffle.

rauh *adj.* [rau] rough; rugged; *weather*: inclement, raw; *voice*: hoarse; *fig.*: harsh; coarse, rude; F: in ~en Mengen galore; **'2reif** *m* (-[e]s/*no pl.*) hoar-frost, *poet.* rime.

Raum [raum] *m* (-[e]s/=e) room, space; expanse; area; room; premises *pl.*; **'~anzug** *m* space suit.

räumen ['rɔymən] *v/t.* (ge-, h) remove, clear (away); leave, give up, *esp.* ✗ evacuate; vacate (*flat*).

'Raum|fahrt *f* astronautics; **'~flug** *m* space flight; **'~inhalt** *m* volume, capacity; **'~kapsel** *f* capsule.

räumlich *adj.* ['rɔymliç] relating to space, of space, spatial.

'Raum|meter *n*, *m* cubic met|re, *Am.* -er; **'~schiff** *n* space craft or ship; **'~sonde** *f* space probe; **'~station** *f* space station.

'Räumung *f* (-/-en) clearing, removal; *esp.* ✝ clearance; vacating (*of flat*), *by force*: eviction; ✗ evacuation (*of town*); **'~sverkauf** ✝ *m* clearance sale.

raunen ['raunən] (ge-, h) **1.** *v/i.* whisper, murmur; **2.** *v/t.* whisper, murmur; *man raunt* rumo(u)r has it.

Raupe *zo.* ['raupə] *f* (-/-n) caterpillar; **'~nschlepper** ⊕ *m* caterpillar tractor. [scram!]

raus *int.* [raus] get out!, *sl.*beat it!,⟩

Rausch [rauʃ] *m* (-es/=e) intoxication, drunkenness; *fig.* frenzy, transport(s *pl.*); e-n ~ haben be drunk; **'2en** *v/i.* (ge-) **1.** (h) leaves, rain, silk: rustle; water, wind: rush; surf: roar; applause: thunder; **2.** (sein) movement: sweep; **'~gift** *n* narcotic (drug), F dope.

räuspern ['rɔyspərn] *v/refl.* (ge-, h) clear one's throat.

Razzia ['ratsja] *f* (-/Razzien) raid, round-up.

reagieren [rea'giːrən] *v/i.* (*no* -ge-, h) react (auf acc. [up]on; to); *fig. and* ⊕ *a.* respond (to).

Reaktion [reak'tsjoːn] *f* (-/-en) reaction (a. pol.); *fig. a.* response (auf acc. to); **'~är** [~o'nɛːr] **1.** *m* (-s/-e) reactionary; **2.** ⚢ *adj.* reactionary.

Reaktor *phys.* [re'aktɔr] *m* (-s/-en) (nuclear) reactor, atomic pile.

real *adj.* [re'aːl] real; concrete; **~isieren** [reali'ziːrən] *v/t.* (*no* -ge-,

h) realize; **2ismus** [rea'lismus] *m* (-/*no pl.*) realism; **~istisch** *adj.* [rea'listif] realistic; **2ität** [reali'tɛːt] *f* (-/-en) reality; **2schule** *f* nonclassical secondary school.

Rebe ⚘ ['reːbə] *f* (-/-n) vine.

Rebell [re'bɛl] *m* (-en/-en) rebel; **2ieren** [~'liːrən] *v/i.* (*no* -ge-, h) rebel, revolt, rise; **2isch** *adj.* rebellious.

Reb|huhn *orn.* ['rep-] *n* partridge; **~laus** *zo.* ['reːp-] *f* vine-fretter, phylloxera; **~stock** ⚘ ['reːp-] *m* vine.

Rechen ['reçən] *m* (-s/-) rake; grid.

Rechen|aufgabe *f* (arithmetical) problem; **'~fehler** *m* arithmetical error, miscalculation; **'~maschine** *f* calculating-machine; **'~schaft** *f* (-/*no pl.*): ~ ablegen give or render an account (über acc. of), account or answer (for); zur ~ ziehen call to account (wegen for); **'~schieber** Ⓐ *m* slide-rule.

rechne|n ['reçnən] (ge-, h) **1.** *v/t.* reckon, calculate; estimate, value; charge; ~ zu rank with or among(st); **2.** *v/i.* count; ~ auf (acc.) or mit count or reckon or rely (up)on; **'~risch** *adj.* arithmetical.

'Rechnung *f* (-/-en) calculation, sum, reckoning; account, bill; invoice (of goods); in restaurant: bill, *Am.* check; score; auf ~ on account; ~ legen render an account (über acc. of); e-r Sache ~ tragen make allowance for s.th.; es geht auf meine ~ in restaurants: it is my treat, *Am.* F this is on me; **'~sprüfer** *m* auditor.

recht¹ [reçt] **1.** *adj.* right; real; legitimate; right, correct; zur ~en Zeit in due time, at the right moment; ein ~er Narr a regular fool; *mir ist es* ~ I don't mind; ~ haben be right; j-m ~ geben agree with s.o.; **2.** *adv.* right(ly), well; very; rather; really; correctly; ganz ~! quite (so)!; es geschieht ihm ~ it serves him right; ~ gern gladly, with pleasure; ~ gut quite good or well; ich weiß nicht ~ I wonder.

Recht² [~] *n* (-[e]s/-e) right (auf acc. to), title (to), claim (on), interest (in); privilege; power, authority; ⚖ law; justice; ~ sprechen administer justice; mit ~ justly;

'**Rechte** f (-n/-n) right hand; *boxing*: right; *pol. the* Right.

Rechteck ['rɛçtʔ-] n (-[e]s/-e) rectangle; '**₂ig** adj. rectangular.

recht|fertigen ['rɛçtfɛrtɪgən] v/t. (ge-, h) justify; defend, vindicate; '**₂fertigung** f (-/-en) justification; vindication, defen|ce, *Am.* -se; '**₂gläubig** adj. orthodox; **₂habe-risch** adj. [ˈ.haːbərɪʃ] dogmatic; '**₂lich** adj. legal, lawful, legitimate; honest, righteous; '**₂los** adj. without rights; outlawed; '**₂losigkeit** f (-/no pl.) outlawry; '**₂mäßig** adj. legal, lawful, legitimate; '**₂mäßigkeit** f (-/no pl.) legality, legitimacy.

rechts adv. [rɛçts] on or to the right (hand).

'**Rechts|anspruch** m legal right or claim (auf acc. on, to); title (to); '**₂anwalt** m lawyer, solicitor; barrister, *Am.* attorney (at law); '**₂außen** m (-/-) *football*: outside right; '**₂beistand** m legal adviser, counsel.

'**recht|schaffen 1.** adj. honest, righteous; **2.** adv. thoroughly, downright, F awfully; '**₂schreibung** f (-/-en) orthography, spelling.

'**Rechts|fall** m case, cause; '**₂frage** f question of law; issue of law; '**₂gelehrte** m jurist, lawyer; '**₂gültig** adj. s. rechtskräftig; '**₂kraft** f (-/no pl.) legal force or validity; '**₂kräftig** adj. valid, legal; judgement: final; '**₂kurve** f right-hand bend; '**₂lage** f legal position or status; '**₂mittel** n legal remedy; '**₂nachfolger** m assign, assignee; '**₂person** f legal personality; '**₂pflege** f administration of justice, judicature.

'**Rechtsprechung** f (-/-en) jurisdiction.

'**Rechts|schutz** m legal protection; '**₂spruch** m legal decision; judg(e)-ment; sentence; verdict (of jury); '**₂steuerung** mot. f (-/-en) right-hand drive; '**₂streit** m action, lawsuit; '**₂verfahren** n (legal) proceedings pl.; '**₂verkehr** mot. m right-hand traffic; '**₂verletzung** f infringement; '**₂vertreter** m s. Rechtsbeistand; '**₂weg** m: den ~ beschreiten take legal action, go to law; unter Ausschluß des ~es eliminating legal proceedings; '**₂widrig**

adj. illegal, unlawful; '**₂wissenschaft** f jurisprudence.

'**recht|wink(e)lig** adj. right-angled; '**₂zeitig 1.** adj. punctual; opportune; **2.** adv. in (due) time, punctually, *Am.* on time.

Reck [rɛk] n (-[e]s/-e) *sports*: horizontal bar.

recken ['rɛkən] v/t. (ge-, h) stretch; sich ~ stretch o.s.

Redakt|eur [redak'tøːr] m (-s/-e) editor; **₂ion** [ˈ.tsjoːn] f (-/-en) editorship; editing, wording; editorial staff, editors pl.; editor's or editorial office; **₂ionell** adj. [.tsjoˈnɛl] editorial.

Rede ['reːdə] f (-/-n) speech; oration; language; talk, conversation; discourse; direkte ~ gr. direct speech; indirekte ~ gr. reported or indirect speech; e-e ~ halten make or deliver a speech; zur ~ stellen call to account (wegen for); davon ist nicht die ~ that is not the point; davon kann keine ~ sein that's out of the question; es ist nicht der ~ wert it is not worth speaking of; '**₂gewandt** adj. eloquent; '**₂kunst** f rhetoric; '**₂n** (ge-, h) **1.** v/t. speak; talk; **2.** v/t. speak (mit to); talk (to), chat (with); discuss (über et. s.th.); sie läßt nicht mit sich ~ she won't listen to reason.

Redensart ['reːdəns?-] f phrase, expression; idiom; proverb, saying.

redigieren [redi'giːrən] v/t. (no -ge-, h) edit; revise.

redlich ['reːtlɪç] **1.** adj. honest, upright; sincere; **2.** adv.: sich ~ bemühen take great pains.

Redner ['reːdnər] m (-s/-e) speaker; orator; '**₂bühne** f platform; '**₂isch** adj. oratorical, rhetorical; '**₂pult** n speaker's desk.

redselig adj. ['reːtzeːlɪç] talkative.

reduzieren [redu'tsiːrən] v/t. (no -ge-, h) reduce (auf acc. to).

Reede ⚓ ['reːdə] f (-/-n) roads pl., roadstead; '**₂r** m (-s/-) shipowner; '**₂rei** f (-/-en) shipping company or firm.

reell [re'ɛl] **1.** adj. respectable, honest; business firm: solid; goods: good; offer: real; **2.** adv.: ~ bedient werden get good value for one's money.

Refer|at [refe'raːt] n (-[e]s/-e) report; lecture; paper; ein ~ halten *esp. univ.* read a paper; **~endar** [~ɛnˈdaːr] *m* (-s/-e) 🏛 junior lawyer; *at school:* junior teacher; **~ent** [~ˈrɛnt] *m* (-en/-en) reporter, speaker; **~enz** [~ˈrɛnts] *f* (-/-en) reference; **2ieren** [~ˈriːrən] *v/i.* (no -ge-, h) report (*über acc.* [up]on); (give a) lecture (on); *esp. univ.* read a paper (on).

reflektieren [reflɛkˈtiːrən] (no -ge-, h) **1.** *phys. v/t.* reflect; **2.** *v/i.* reflect (*über acc.* [up]on); ~ *auf (acc.)* 🕇 think of buying; be interested in.

Reflex [reˈflɛks] *m* (-es/-e) *phys.* reflection or reflexion; 🟂 reflex (action); **2iv** *gr. adj.* [~ˈksiːf] reflexive.

Reform [reˈfɔrm] *f* (-/-en) reform; **~er** *m* (-s/-) reformer; **2ieren** [~ˈmiːrən] *v/t.* (no -ge-, h) reform.

Refrain [rəˈfrɛ̃ː] *m* (-s/-s) refrain, chorus, burden.

Regal [reˈɡaːl] *n* (-s/-e) shelf.

rege *adj.* [ˈreːɡə] active, brisk, lively; busy.

Regel [ˈreːɡəl] *f* (-/-n) rule; regulation; standard; *physiol.* menstruation, menses *pl.*; *in der* ~ as a rule; **2los** *adj.* irregular; disorderly; **2mäßig** *adj.* regular; **2n** *v/t.* (ge-, h) regulate, control; arrange, settle; put in order; **2recht** *adj.* regular; **~ung** *f* (-/-en) regulation, control; arrangement, settlement; **2widrig** *adj.* contrary to the rules, irregular; abnormal; *sports:* foul.

regen[1] [ˈreːɡən] *v/t. and v/refl.* (ge-, h) move, stir.

Regen[2] [~] *m* (-s/-) rain; *vom* ~ *in die Traufe kommen* jump out of the frying-pan into the fire, get from bad to worse; **2arm** *adj.* dry; **~bogen** *m* rainbow; **~bogenhaut** *anat. f* iris; **2dicht** *adj.* rain-proof; **~guß** *m* downpour; **~mantel** *m* waterproof, raincoat, mac(k)intosh, F mac; **2reich** *adj.* rainy; **~schauer** *m* shower (of rain); **~schirm** *m* umbrella; **~tag** *m* rainy day; **~tropfen** *m* raindrop; **~wasser** *n* rain-water; **~wetter** *n* rainy weather; **~wolke** *f* rain-cloud; **~wurm** *zo. m* earthworm, *Am. a.* angleworm; **~zeit** *f* rainy season.

Regie [reˈʒiː] *f* (-/-n) management; *thea., film:* direction; *unter der* ~ *von* directed by.

regier|en [reˈɡiːrən] (no -ge-, h)

1. *v/i.* reign; **2.** *v/t.* govern (*a. gr.*), rule; **2ung** *f* (-/-en) government, *Am.* administration; reign.

Re'gierungs|antritt *m* accession (to the throne); **~beamte** *m* government official; *Brt.* Civil Servant; **~bezirk** *m* administrative district; **~gebäude** *n* government offices *pl.*

Regiment [regiˈmɛnt] *n* **1.** (-[e]s-e) government, rule; **2.** 🟂 (-[e]s-er) regiment.

Regisseur [reʒiˈsøːr] *m* (-s/-e) *thea.* stage manager, director; *film:* director.

Regist|er [reˈɡistər] *n* (-s/-) register (*a. ♪*), record; index; **~ratur** [~raˈtuːr] *f* (-/-en) registry; registration.

registrier|en [regisˈtriːrən] *v/t.* (no -ge-, h) register, record; **2kasse** *f* cash register.

reglos *adj.* [ˈreːkloːs] motionless.

regne|n [ˈreːɡnən] *v/i.* (ge-, h) rain; *es regnet in Strömen* it is pouring with rain; **~risch** *adj.* rainy.

Regreß 🏛 🕇 [reˈɡrɛs] *m* (Regresses/Regresse) recourse; **2pflichtig** 🏛, 🕇 *adj.* liable to recourse.

regulär *adj.* [reguˈlɛːr] regular.

regulier|bar *adj.* [reguˈliːrbaːr] adjustable, controllable; **~en** *v/t.* (no -ge-, h) regulate, adjust; control.

Regung [ˈreːɡuŋ] *f* (-/-en) movement, motion; emotion; impulse; **2slos** *adj.* motionless.

Reh *zo.* [reː] *n* (-[e]s/-e) deer, roe; *female:* doe.

rehabilitieren [rehabiliˈtiːrən] *v/t.* (no -ge-, h) rehabilitate.

'Reh|bock *zo. m* roebuck; **2braun** *adj.*, **2farben** *adj.* fawn-colo(u)red; **~geiß** *zo. f* doe; **~kalb** *zo. n*, **~kitz** *zo. n* [ˈ~kits] *n* (-es/-e) fawn.

Reib|e [ˈraɪbə] *f* (-/-n), **~eisen** [ˈraɪpʔ-] *n* grater.

reib|en [ˈraɪbən] (*irr.*, ge-, h) **1.** *v/i.* rub (*an dat.* [up]on); **2.** *v/t.* rub, grate; pulverize; *wund* ~ chafe, gall; **2erei** F *fig.* [~ˈraɪ] *f* (-/-en) (constant) friction; **2ung** *f.* (-/-en) friction; **~ungslos** *adj.* frictionless; *fig.* smooth.

reich[1] *adj.* [raɪç] rich (*an dat.* in); wealthy; ample, abundant, copious.

Reich[2] [~] *n* (-es/-e) empire; kingdom (*of animals, vegetables, minerals*); *poet., rhet., fig.* realm.

reichen [ˈraɪçən] (ge-, h) **1.** *v/t.* offer; serve (*food*); *j-m et.* ~ hand *or* pass s.th. to s.o.; *sich die Hände* ~ join hands; **2.** *v/i.* reach; extend; suffice; *das reicht!* that will do!

reich|haltig *adj.* ['raɪçhaltɪç] rich; abundant, copious; '**~lich 1.** *adj.* ample, abundant, copious, plentiful; ~ *Zeit* plenty of time; **2.** F *adv.* rather, fairly, F pretty, plenty; '**2tum** *m* (*-s/⸚er*) riches *pl.*; wealth (*an dat.* of).

'**Reichweite** *f* reach; ⚔ range; *in* ~ within reach, near at hand.

reif[1] *adj.* [raɪf] ripe, mature.

Reif[2] [~] *m* (*-[e]s/no pl.*) white *or* hoar-frost, *poet.* rime.

'**Reife** *f* (*-/no pl.*) ripeness, maturity.

'**reifen**[1] *v/i.* (ge-) **1.** (*sein*) ripen, mature; **2.** (*h*): *es hat gereift* there is a white or hoar-frost.

'**Reifen**[2] *m* (*-s/-*) hoop; ring; tyre, (*Am. only*) tire; *as ornament:* circlet; ~ *wechseln mot.* change tyres; '**~panne** *mot. f* puncture, *Am. a.* blowout.

'**Reife|prüfung** *f s. Abitur;* '**~zeugnis** *n s. Abschlußzeugnis.*

'**reiflich** *adj.* mature, careful.

Reihe ['raɪə] *f* (*-/-n*) row; line; rank; series; number; *thea.* row, tier; *der* ~ *nach* by turns; *ich bin an der* ~ *it is my turn.*

'**Reihen|folge** *f* succession, sequence; *alphabetische* ~ alphabetical order; '**~haus** *n* terrace-house, *Am.* row house; '**2weise** *adv.* in rows.

Reiher *orn.* ['raɪər] *m* (*-s/-*) heron.

Reim [raɪm] *m* (*-[e]s/-e*) rhyme; '**2en** (ge-, h) **1.** *v/i.* rhyme; **2.** *v/t. and v/refl.* rhyme (*auf acc.* with).

rein *adj.* [raɪn] pure; clean; clear; ~*e Wahrheit* plain truth; '**2ertrag** *m* net proceeds *pl.*; '**2fall** F *m* letdown; '**2gewicht** *n* net weight; '**2gewinn** *m* net profit; '**2heit** *f* (*-/no pl.*) purity; cleanness.

'**reinig|en** *v/t.* (ge-, h) clean(se); *fig.* purify; '**2ung** *f* (*-/-en*) clean(s)ing; *fig.* purification; cleaners *pl.*; *chemische* ~ dry cleaning; '**2ungsmittel** *n* detergent, cleanser.

'**rein|lich** *adj.* clean; cleanly; neat, tidy; '**2machefrau** *f* charwoman; '**~rassig** *adj.* pedigree, thoroughbred, *esp. Am.* purebred; '**2schrift** *f* fair copy.

Reis[1] ♀ [raɪs] *m* (*-es/-e*) rice.

Reis[2] ♀ [~] *n* (*-es/-er*) twig, sprig.

Reise ['raɪzə] *f* (*-/-n*) journey; ⚓,

♐ voyage; travel; tour; trip; passage; '**~büro** *n* travel agency *or* bureau; '**~decke** *f* travel(l)ing-rug; '**2fertig** *adj.* ready to start; '**~führer** *m* guide(-book); '**~gepäck** *n* luggage, *Am.* baggage; '**~gesellschaft** *f* tourist party; '**~kosten** *pl.* travel(l)ing-expenses *pl.*; '**~leiter** *m* courier; '**2n** *v/i.* (ge-, *sein*) travel, journey; ~ *nach* go to; *ins Ausland* ~ go abroad; '**~nde** *m, f* (*-n/-n*) (♐ commercial) travel(l)er; *in trains:* passenger; *for pleasure:* tourist; **~necessaire** ['~nesɛːr] *n* (*-s/-s*) dressing-case; '**~paß** *m* passport; '**~scheck** *m* traveller's cheque, *Am.* traveler's check; '**~schreibmaschine** *f* portable typewriter; '**~tasche** *f* travel(l)ing-bag, grip(sack).

Reisig ['raɪzɪç] *n* (*-s/no pl.*) brushwood.

Reißbrett ['raɪs-] *n* drawing-board.

reißen ['raɪsən] **1.** *v/t.* tear; pull; *an sich* ~ seize; *sich* ~ scratch o.s. (*an dat.* with); *sich* ~ *um* scramble for; **2.** *v/i.* (*irr.*, ge-, *sein*) break; burst; split; tear; *mir riß die Geduld* I lost (all) patience; **3.** ♀ F ⚚ *n* (*-s/no pl.*) rheumatism; '**~d** *adj.* rapid; *animal:* rapacious; *pain:* acute; ~*en Absatz finden* sell like hot cakes.

'**Reiß|er** F *m* (*-s/-*) draw, box-office success; thriller; '**~feder** *f* drawing-pen; '**~leine** ⚚ *f* rip-cord; '**~nagel** *m s. Reißzwecke;* '**~schiene** *f* (T-)square; '**~verschluß** *m* zipfastener, zipper, *Am. a.* slide fastener; '**~zeug** *n* drawing instruments *pl.*; '**~zwecke** *f* drawing-pin, *Am.* thumbtack.

Reit|anzug ['raɪt-] *m* riding-dress; '**~bahn** *f* riding-school, manège; riding-track; '**2en** (*irr.*, ge-) **1.** *v/i.* (*sein*) ride, go on horseback; **2.** *v/t.* (*h*) ride; '**~er** *m* (*-s/-*) rider, horseman; ⚔, *police:* trooper; *filing:* tab; ~*e'rei* *f* (*-/-en*) cavalry; '**~erin** *f* (*-/-nen*) horsewoman; '**~gerte** *f* riding-whip; '**~hose** *f* (riding-) breeches *pl.*; '**~knecht** *m* groom; '**~kunst** *f* horsemanship; '**~lehrer** *m* riding master; '**~peitsche** *f* riding-whip; '**~pferd** *zo.* *n* ridinghorse, saddle-horse; '**~schule** *f* riding-school; '**~stiefel** *m/pl.* riding-boots *pl.*; '**~weg** *m* bridle-path.

Reiz [raɪts] m (-es/-e) irritation; charm, attraction; allurement; **'2bar** adj. sensitive; irritable, excitable, Am. sore; **'2en** (ge-, h) **1.** v/t. irritate (a. 𝔰); excite; provoke; nettle; stimulate, rouse; entice, (al)lure, tempt, charm, attract; **2.** v/i. cards: bid; **'2end** adj. charming, attractive; Am. cute; lovely; **'2los** adj. unattractive; **'∼mittel** n stimulus; 𝔰 stimulant; **'∼ung** f (-/-en) irritation; provocation; **'2voll** adj. charming, attractive.

rekeln F ['reːkəln] v/refl. (ge-, h) loll, lounge, sprawl.

Reklamation [reklama'tsjoːn] f (-/-en) claim; complaint, protest.

Reklame [re'klaːmə] f (-/-n) advertising; advertisement, F ad; publicity; ∼ machen advertise; ∼ machen für et. advertise s.th.

rekla'mieren (no -ge-, h) **1.** v/t. (re)claim; **2.** v/i. complain (wegen about).

Rekonvaleszen|t [rekɔnvales'tsɛnt] m (-en/-en), **∼tin** f (-/-nen) convalescent; **∼z** [∼ts] f (-/no pl.) convalescence.

Rekord [re'kɔrt] m (-[e]s/-e) sports, etc.: record.

Rekrut ✕ [re'kruːt] m (-en/-en) recruit; **2ieren** ✕ [∼u'tiːrən] v/t. (no -ge-, h) recruit.

Rektor ['rɛktɔr] m (-s/-en) headmaster, rector, Am. principal; univ. chancellor, rector, Am. president.

relativ adj. [rela'tiːf] relative.

Relief [rel'jɛf] n (-s/-s, -e) relief.

Religi|on [reli'gjoːn] f (-/-en) religion; **2ös** adj. [∼ø:s] religious; pious, devout; **∼osität** [∼ozi'tɛːt] f (-/no pl.) religiousness; piety.

Reling ⚓ ['reːlɪŋ] f (-/-s, -e) rail.

Reliquie [re'liːkvjə] f (-/-n) relic.

Ren zo. [rɛn; reːn] n (-s/-s; -s/-e) reindeer.

Renn|bahn ['rɛn-] f racecourse, Am. race track, horse-racing: a. the turf; mot. speedway; **'∼boot** n racing boat, racer.

rennen ['rɛnən] **1.** v/i. (irr., ge-, sein) run; race; **2.** v/t. (irr., ge-, h): j-n zu Boden ∼ run s.o. down; **3.** 2 n (-s/-) run(ning); race; heat.

'Renn|fahrer m mot. racing driver, racer; racing cyclist; **'∼läufer** m ski racer; **'∼mannschaft** f racecrew; **'∼pferd** zo. n racehorse, racer;

'∼rad n racing bicycle; racer; **'∼sport** m racing; horse-racing: a. the turf; **'∼stall** m racing stable; **'∼strecke** f racecourse, Am. race track; mot. speedway; distance (to be run); **'∼wagen** m racing car, racer.

renommiert adj. [reno'miːrt] famous, noted (wegen for).

renovieren [reno'viːrən] v/t. (no -ge-, h) renovate, repair; redecorate (interior of house).

rent|abel adj. [rɛn'taːbəl] profitable, paying; **'2e** f (-/-n) income, revenue; annuity; (old-age) pension; rent; **2enempfänger** ['rɛntənˀ-] m s. Rentner; rentier.

Rentier zo. ['rɛn-] n s. Ren.

rentieren [rɛn'tiːrən] v/refl. (no -ge-, h) pay.

Rentner ['rɛntnər] m (-s/-) (old-age) pensioner.

Reparatur [repara'tuːr] f (-/-en) repair; **∼werkstatt** f repair-shop; mot. a. garage, service station.

repa'rieren v/t. (no -ge-, h) repair, Am. F fix.

Report|age [repɔr'taːʒə] f (-/-en) reporting, commentary, coverage; **∼er** [re'pɔrtər] m (-s/-) reporter.

Repräsent|ant [reprɛzɛn'tant] m (-en/-en) representative; **∼antenhaus** Am. parl. n House of Representatives; **2ieren** (no -ge-, h) **1.** v/t. represent; **2.** v/i. cut a fine figure.

Repressalie [reprɛ'saːljə] f (-/-n) reprisal.

reproduzieren [reprodu'tsiːrən] v/t. (no -ge-, h) reproduce.

Reptil zo. [rɛp'tiːl] n (-s/-ien, ✍ -e) reptile.

Republik [repu'bliːk] f (-/-en) republic; **∼aner** pol. [∼i'kaːnər] m (-s/-) republican; **2anisch** adj. [∼i'kaːnɪʃ] republican.

Reserve [re'zɛrvə] f (-/-n) reserve; **∼rad** mot. n spare wheel.

reser'vier|en v/t. (no -ge-, h) reserve; ∼ lassen book (seat, etc.), **∼t** adj. reserved (a. fig.).

Resid|enz [rezi'dɛnts] f (-/-en) residence; **2ieren** v/i. (no -ge-, h) reside.

resignieren [rezi'gniːrən] v/i. (no -ge-, h) resign.

Respekt [re'spɛkt] m (-[e]s/no pl.) respect; **2ieren** [∼'tiːrən] v/t. (no

-ge-, h) respect; 2los adj. irreverent, disrespectful; 2voll adj. respectful.

Ressort [rɛ'soːr] n (-s/-s) department; province.

Rest [rɛst] m (-es/-e, ✝ -er) rest, remainder; residue (a. 🔧); esp. ✝ remnant (of cloth); leftover (of food); das gab ihm den ~ that finished him (off).

Restaurant [rɛsto'rãː] n (-s/-s) restaurant.

'**Rest|bestand** m remnant; '~betrag m remainder, balance; 2lich adj. remaining; '2los adv. completely; entirely; '~zahlung f payment of balance; final payment.

Resultat [rezul'taːt] n (-[e]s/-e) result, outcome; sports: score.

retten ['rɛtən] v/t. (ge-, h) save; deliver, rescue.

Rettich 🌿 ['rɛtiç] m (-s/-e) radish.

'**Rettung** f (-/-en) rescue; deliverance; escape.

'**Rettungs|boot** n lifeboat; '~gürtel m lifebelt; 2los adj. irretrievable, past help or hope, beyond recovery; '~mannschaft f rescue party; '~ring m life-buoy.

Reue ['rɔyə] f (-/no pl.) repentance (über acc. of), remorse (at); '2en v/t. (ge-, h): et. reut mich I repent (of) s.th.; '2voll adj. repentant; 2(müt)ig adj. ['~(myːt)iç] repentant.

Revanche [re'vãːʃ(ə)] f (-/-n) revenge; ~spiel n return match.

revan'chieren v/refl. (no -ge-, h) take or have one's revenge (an dat. on); return (für et. s.th.).

Revers 1. [re'vɛːr] n, m (-/-) lapel (of coat); 2. [re'vɛrs] m (-es/-e) declaration; 🔧 bond.

revidieren [revi'diːrən] v/t. (no -ge-, h) revise; check; ✝ audit.

Revier [re'viːr] n (-s/-e) district, quarter; s. Jagdrevier.

Revision [revi'zjoːn] f (-/-en) revision (a. typ.); ✝ audit; 🔧 appeal; ~ einlegen 🔧 lodge an appeal.

Revolt|e [re'vɔltə] f (-/-n) revolt, uprising; 2ieren [~'tiːrən] v/i. (no -ge-, h) revolt, rise (in revolt).

Revolution [revolu'tsjoːn] f (-/-en) revolution; ~är [~o'nɛːr] 1. m (-s/-e) revolutionary; 2. ♀ adj. revolutionary.

Revolver [re'vɔlvər] m (-s/-) revolver, Am. F a. gun.

Revue [rə'vyː] f (-/-n) review; thea. revue, (musical) show; ~ passieren lassen pass in review.

Rezens|ent [retsen'zɛnt] m (-en/-en) critic, reviewer; 2ieren v/t. (no -ge-, h) review, criticize; ~ion [~'zjoːn] f (-/-en) review, criticism.

Rezept [re'tsɛpt] n (-[e]s/-e) 🏥 prescription; cooking: recipe (a. fig.).

Rhabarber 🌿 [ra'barbər] m (-s/no pl.) rhubarb.

rhetorisch adj. [re'toːriʃ] rhetorical.

rheumati|sch ♀ adj. [rɔy'maːtiʃ] rheumatic; 2smus ♀ [~'tismus] m (-/Rheumatismen) rheumatism.

rhythm|isch adj. ['rytmiʃ] rhythmic(al); 2us ['~us] m (-/Rhythmen) rhythm.

richten ['riçtən] v/t. (ge-, h) set right, arrange, adjust; level, point (gun) (auf acc. at); direct (gegen at); 🔧 judge; execute; zugrunde ~ ruin, destroy; in die Höhe ~ raise, lift up; sich ~ nach conform to, act according to; take one's bearings from; gr. agree with; depend on; price: be determined by; ich richte mich nach Ihnen I leave it to you.

'**Richter** m (-s/-) judge; '2lich adj. judicial; '~spruch m judg(e)ment, sentence.

'**richtig 1.** adj. right, correct, accurate; proper; true; just; ein ~er Londoner a regular cockney; 2. adv.: ~ gehen clock: go right; '2keit f (-/no pl.) correctness; accuracy; justness; '~stellen v/t. (sep., -ge-, h) put or set right, rectify.

'**Richt|linien** f/pl. (general) directions pl., rules pl.; '~preis ✝ m standard price; '~schnur f ⊕ plumb-line; fig. rule (of conduct), guiding principle.

'**Richtung** f (-/-en) direction; course, way; fig. line; ~anzeiger mot. ['riçtuŋs-] m (-s/-) flashing indicator, trafficator; '2weisend adj. directive, leading, guiding.

'**Richtwaage** ⊕ f level.

rieb [riːp] pret. of reiben.

riechen ['riːçən] (irr., ge-, h) 1. v/i. smell (nach of; an dat. at); sniff (an dat. at); 2. v/t. smell; sniff.

rief [riːf] pret. of rufen.

riefeln ⊕ ['riːfəln] v/t. (ge-, h) flute, groove.

Riegel ['riːgəl] m (-s/-) bar, bolt; bar, cake (of soap); bar (of chocolate).

Riemen ['riːmən] m (-s/-) strap, thong; belt; ⚓ oar.

Ries [riːs] n (-es/-e) ream.

Riese ['riːzə] m (-n/-n) giant.

rieseln ['riːzəln] v/i. (ge-) **1.** (sein) small stream: purl, ripple; trickle; **2.** (h): es rieselt it drizzles.

ries|engroß adj. ['riːzən'-], '**~enhaft** adj., '**~ig** adj. gigantic, huge; '2**in** f (-/-nen) giantess.

riet [riːt] pret. of raten.

Riff [rif] n (-[e]s/-e) reef.

Rille ['rilə] f (-/-n) groove; ⊕ a. flute. [tance.]

Rimesse † [ri'mɛsə] f (-/-n) remit-

Rind zo. [rint] n (-[e]s/-er) ox; cow; neat; ~er pl. (horned) cattle pl.; zwanzig ~er twenty head of cattle.

Rinde ['rində] f (-/-n) ♀ bark; rind (of fruit, bacon, cheese); crust (of bread).

'**Rinder|braten** m roast beef; '**~herde** f herd of cattle; '**~hirt** m cowherd, Am. cowboy.

'**Rind|fleisch** n beef; '**~(s)leder** n neat's-leather, cow-hide; '**~vieh** n (horned) cattle pl., neat pl.

Ring [riŋ] m (-[e]s/-e) ring; circle; link (of chain); † ring, pool, trust, Am. ⸿ combine; '**~bahn** f circular railway.

ringel|n ['riŋəln] v/refl. (ge-, h) curl, coil; '2**natter** zo. f ringsnake.

ring|en ['riŋən] (irr., ge-, h) **1.** v/i. wrestle; struggle (um for); nach Atem ~ gasp (for breath); **2.** v/t. wring (hands, washing); '2**er** m (-s/-) wrestler.

ring|förmig adj. ['riŋfœrmiç] annular, ring-like; '2**kampf** m sports: wrestling(-match); '2**richter** m boxing: referee.

rings adv. [riŋs] around; '**~he'rum** adv., '**~'um** adv., '**~um'her** adv. round about, all (a)round.

Rinne ['rinə] f (-/-n) groove, channel; gutter (of roof or street); gully; '2**en** v/i. (irr., ge-, ge-, sein) run, flow; drip; leak; '**~sal** ['~zaːl] n (-[e]s/-e) watercourse, streamlet; '**~stein** m gutter; sink (of kitchen unit).

Rippe ['ripə] f (-/-n) rib; ⚕ groin; bar (of chocolate); '2**n** v/t. (ge-, h) rib; '**~nfell** anat. n pleura; '**~nfellentzündung** ⚕ f pleurisy; '**~nstoß** m dig in the ribs; nudge.

Risiko ['riːziko] n (-s/-s, Risiken)

risk; ein ~ eingehen take a risk.

risk|ant adj. [ris'kant] risky; '**~ieren** v/t. (no -ge-, h) risk.

Riß [ris] **1.** m (Risses/Risse) rent, tear; split (a. fig.); crack; in skin: chap; scratch; ⊕ draft, plan; fig. rupture; **2.** 2 pret. of reißen.

rissig adj. ['risiç] full of rents; skin, etc.: chappy; ~ werden crack.

Rist [rist] m (-es/-e) instep; back of the hand; wrist.

Ritt [rit] **1.** m (-[e]s/-e) ride; **2.** 2 pret. of reiten.

'**Ritter** m (-s/-) knight; zum ~ schlagen knight; '**~gut** n manor; '2**lich** adj. knightly, chivalrous; '2**lichkeit** f (-/-en) gallantry, chivalry.

rittlings adv. ['ritliŋs] astride (auf e-m Pferd a horse).

Ritz [rits] m (-es/-e) crack, chink; scratch; '**~e** f (-/-n) crack, chink; fissure; '2**en** v/t. (ge-, h) scratch; cut.

Rival|e [ri'vaːlə] m (-n/-n) rival; '**~in** f (-/-nen) rival; 2**isieren** [~ali'ziːrən] v/i. (no -ge-, h) rival (mit j-m s.o.); '**~ität** [~ali'tɛːt] f (-/-en) rivalry.

Rizinusöl ['riːtsinus?-] n (-[e]s/no pl.) castor oil.

Robbe zo. ['rɔbə] f (-/-n) seal.

Robe ['roːbə] f (-/-n) gown; robe.

Roboter ['rɔbɔtər] m (-s/-) robot.

robust adj. [ro'bust] robust, sturdy, vigorous.

roch [rɔx] pret. of riechen.

röcheln ['rœçəln] (ge-, h) **1.** v/i. rattle; **2.** v/t. gasp out (words).

Rock [rɔk] m (-[e]s/⸚e) skirt; coat, jacket; '**~schoß** m coat-tail.

Rodel|bahn ['roːdəl-] f toboggan-run; '2**n** v/i. (ge-, h, sein) toboggan, Am. a. coast; '**~schlitten** m sled(ge), toboggan.

roden ['roːdən] v/t. (ge-, h) clear (land); root up, stub (roots).

Rogen ichth. ['roːgən] m (-s/-) roe, spawn.

Roggen ♀ ['rɔgən] m (-s/-) rye.

roh adj. [roː] raw; fig.: rough, rude; cruel, brutal; oil, metal: crude; '2**bau** m (-[e]s/-ten) rough brickwork; '2**eisen** n pig-iron.

Roheit ['roːhaɪt] f (-/-en) rawness; roughness (a. fig.); fig.: rudeness; brutality.

'**Roh|ling** m (-[e]s/-e) brute, ruffian; '**~material** n raw material; '**~produkt** n raw product.

Rohr [ro:r] *n* (-[e]s/-e) tube, pipe; duct; ♀: reed; cane.

Röhre ['rø:rə] *f* (-/-n) tube, pipe; duct; *radio*: valve, *Am.* (electron) tube.

'**Rohr**|**leger** *m* (-s/-) pipe fitter, plumber; '**~leitung** *f* plumbing; pipeline; '**~post** *f* pneumatic dispatch *or* tube; '**~stock** *m* cane; '**~zucker** *m* cane-sugar.

'**Rohstoff** *m* raw material.

Rolladen ['rɔlla:dən] *m* (-s/ᵘ, -) rolling shutter.

'**Rollbahn** ✈ *f* taxiway, taxi-strip.

Rolle ['rɔlə] *f* (-/-n) roll; roller; coil (*of rope, etc.*); pulley; *beneath furniture*: cast[or, -er]; mangle; *thea.* part, role; *fig.* figure; **~** *Garn* reel of cotton, *Am.* spool of thread; *das spielt keine* **~** that doesn't matter, it makes no difference; *Geld spielt keine* **~** money (is) no object; *aus der* **~** *fallen* forget o.s.

'**rollen** (ge-) **1.** *v/i.* (sein) roll; ✈ taxi; **2.** *v/t.* (h) roll; wheel; mangle (*laundry*).

'**Rollenbesetzung** *thea.* *f* cast.

'**Roller** *m* (-s/-) *children's toy*: scooter; *mot.* (motor) scooter.

'**Roll**|**feld** ✈ *n* manœuvring area, *Am.* maneuvering area; '**~film** *phot.* *m* roll film; '**~kragen** *m* turtle neck; '**~schrank** *m* roll-fronted cabinet; '**~schuh** *m* roller-skate; '**~schuhbahn** *f* roller-skating rink; '**~stuhl** *m* wheel chair; '**~treppe** *f* escalator; '**~wagen** *m* lorry, truck.

Roman [ro'ma:n] *m* (-s/-e) novel, (work of) fiction; *novel of adventure and fig.*: romance; **~ist** [~a'nist] *m* (-en/-en) Romance scholar *or* student; **~schriftsteller** *m* novelist.

Romanti|**k** [ro'mantik] *f* (-/no pl.) romanticism; **2sch** *adj.* romantic.

Röm|**er** ['rø:mər] *m* (-s/-) Roman; **2isch** *adj.* Roman.

röntgen ['rœntgən] *v/t.* (ge-, h) X-ray; '**2aufnahme** *f*, '**2bild** *n* X-ray; '**2strahlen** *m/pl.* X-rays *pl.*

rosa *adj.* ['ro:za] pink.

Rose ['ro:zə] *f* (-/-n) ♀ rose; ⚕ erysipelas.

'**Rosen**|**kohl** ♀ *m* Brussels sprouts *pl.*; '**~kranz** *eccl.* *m* rosary; '**2rot** *adj.* rose-colo(u)red, rosy; '**~stock** ♀ *m* (-[e]s/ᵘe) rose-bush.

'**rosig** *adj.* rosy (*a. fig.*), rose-colo(u)red, roseate.

Rosine [ro'zi:nə] *f* (-/-n) raisin.

Roß *zo.* [rɔs] *n* (Rosses/Rosse, F Rösser) horse, *poet.* steed; '**~haar** *n* horsehair.

Rost [rɔst] *m* **1.** (-es/no pl.) rust; **2.** (-es/-e) grate; gridiron; grill; '**~braten** *m* roast joint.

'**rosten** *v/i.* (ge-, h, sein) rust.

rösten ['rø:stən] *v/t.* (ge-, h) roast, grill; toast (*bread*); fry (*potatoes*).

'**Rost**|**fleck** *m* rust-stain; *in cloth*: iron-mo(u)ld; '**2frei** *adj.* rustless, rustproof; *esp. steel*: stainless; '**2ig** *adj.* rusty, corroded.

rot [ro:t] **1.** *adj.* red; **2.** ⚥ *n* (-s/-, F -s) red.

Rotationsmaschine *typ.* [rota-'tsjo:ns-] *f* rotary printing machine.

'**rot**|**backig** *adj.* ruddy; '**~blond** *adj.* sandy.

Röte ['rø:tə] *f* (-/no pl.) redness, red (colo[u]r); blush; '**2n** *v/t.* (ge-, h) redden; paint *or* dye red; *sich* **~** redden; flush, blush.

'**rot**|**gelb** *adj.* reddish yellow; '**~glühend** *adj.* red-hot; '**2haut** *f* redskin.

rotieren [ro'ti:rən] *v/i.* (no -ge-, h) rotate, revolve.

Rot|**käppchen** ['ro:tkɛpçən] *n* (-s/-) Little Red Riding Hood; '**~kehlchen** *orn.* *n* (-s/-) robin (redbreast).

rötlich *adj.* ['rø:tliç] reddish.

'**Rot**|**stift** *m* red crayon *or* pencil; '**~tanne** ♀ *f* spruce (fir).

Rotte ['rɔtə] *f* (-/-n) band, gang.

'**Rot**|**wein** *m* red wine; claret; '**~wild** *zo.* *n* red deer.

Rouleau [ru'lo:] *n* (-s/-s) *s.* Rollladen; blind, *Am.* (window) shade.

Route ['ru:tə] *f* (-/-n) route.

Routine [ru'ti:nə] *f* (-/no pl.) routine, practice.

Rübe ♀ ['ry:bə] *f* (-/-n) beet; *weiße* **~** (Swedish) turnip, *Am. a.* rutabaga; *rote* **~** red beet, beet(root); *gelbe* **~** carrot.

Rubin [ru'bi:n] *m* (-s/-e) ruby.

ruch|**bar** *adj.* ['ru:xba:r]: **~** *werden* become known, get about *or* abroad; '**~los** *adj.* wicked, profligate.

Ruck [ruk] *m* (-[e]s/-e) jerk, *Am.* F yank; jolt (*of vehicle*).

Rück|**antwort** ['ryk'-] *f* reply; *Postkarte mit* **~** reply postcard; *mit bezahlter* **~** *telegram*: reply paid;

Q R

'**2bezüglich** *gr. adj.* reflexive; '**.blick** *m* retrospect(ive view) (*auf acc.* at); reminiscences *pl.*

rücken[1] ['rykən] (ge-) **1.** *v/t.* (h) move, shift; **2.** *v/i.* (*sein*) move; *näher* ~ near, approach.

Rücken[2] [~] *m* (-s/-) back; ridge (*of mountain*); '**.deckung** *fig. f* backing, support; '**.lehne** *f* back (*of chair, etc.*); '**.mark** *anat. n* spinal cord; '**.schmerzen** *m/pl.* pain in the back, back ache; '**.schwimmen** *n* (-s/*no pl.*) back-stroke swimming; '**.wind** *m* following *or* tail wind; '**.wirbel** *anat. m* dorsal vertebra.

Rück|erstattung ['ryk?-] *f* restitution; refund (*of money*), reimbursement (*of expenses*); '**.fahrkarte** *f* return (ticket), *Am. a.* round-trip ticket; '**.fahrt** *f* return journey *or* voyage; *auf der* ~ on the way back; '**.fall** *m* relapse; '**2fällig** *adj.*: ~ *werden* relapse; '**.flug** *m* return flight; '**.frage** *f* further inquiry; '**.gabe** *f* return, restitution; '**.gang** *fig. m* retrogression; † recession, decline; '**2gängig** *adj.* retrograde; ~ *machen* cancel; '**.grat** *anat. n* (-[e]s/-e) spine, backbone (*both a. fig.*); '**.halt** *m* support; '**2haltlos** *adj.* unreserved, frank; '**.hand** *f* (-/*no pl.*) *tennis:* backhand (stroke); '**.kauf** *m* repurchase; '**.kehr** ['~ke:r] *f* (-/*no pl.*) return; '**.kopp(e)lung** ⚡ *f* (-/-en) feedback; '**.lage** *f* reserve (*pl.*); savings *pl.*; '**2läufig** *fig. adj.* ['~lɔyfiç] retrograde; '**.licht** *mot. n* tail-light, tail-lamp, rear-light; '**2lings** *adv.* backwards; from behind; '**.marsch** *m* march back *or* home; retreat; '**.porto** ✆ *n* return postage; '**.reise** *f* return journey, journey back *or* home.

'**Rucksack** *m* knapsack, ruck-sack.

'**Rück|schlag** *m* backstroke; *fig.* setback; '**.schluß** *m* conclusion, inference; '**.schritt** *fig. m* retrogression, set-back; *pol.* reaction; '**.seite** *f* back, reverse; *a.* tail (*of coin*); '**.sendung** *f* return; '**.sicht** *f* respect, regard, consideration (*auf j-n* for s.o.); '**2sichtslos** *adj.* inconsiderate (*gegen of*), regardless (*of*); ruthless; reckless; ~*es Fahren mot.* reckless driving; '**2sichtsvoll**

adj. regardful (*gegen of*); considerate, thoughtful; '**.sitz** *mot. m* back-seat; '**.spiegel** *mot. m* rear-view mirror; '**.spiel** *n sports:* return match; '**.sprache** *f* consultation; ~ *nehmen mit* consult (*lawyer*), consult with (*fellow workers*); *nach* ~ *mit* on consultation with; '**.stand** *m* arrears *pl.*; backlog; ♬ residue; *im* ~ *sein mit* be in arrears *or* behind with; '**2ständig** *fig. adj.* old-fashioned, backward; ~*e Miete* arrears of rent; '**.stoß** *m* recoil; kick (*of gun*); '**.strahler** *m* (-s/-) rear reflector, cat's eye; '**.tritt** *m* with-drawal, retreat; resignation; '**.tritt-bremse** *f* back-pedal brake, *Am.* coaster brake; '**.versicherung** *f* reinsurance; **2wärts** *adv.* ['~verts] back, backward(s); '**.wärtsgang** *mot. m* reverse (gear); '**.weg** *m* way back, return.

'**ruckweise** *adv.* by jerks.

'**rück|wirkend** *adj.* reacting; ⚖, *etc.*: retroactive, retrospective; '**2wirkung** *f* reaction; '**2zahlung** *f* repayment; '**2zug** *m* retreat.

Rüde ['ry:də] **1.** *zo. m* (-n/-n) male dog *or* fox *or* wolf; large hound; **2.** ♀ *adj.* rude, coarse, brutal.

Rudel ['ru:dəl] *n* (-s/-) troop; pack (*of wolves*); herd (*of deer*).

Ruder ['ru:dər] *n* (-s/-) oar; rudder (*a.* ✈); helm; '**.boot** *n* row(ing)-boat; '**.er** *m* (-s/-) rower, oarsman; '**.fahrt** *f* row; '**2n** (ge-) **1.** *v/i.* (h, *sein*) row; **2.** *v/t.* (h) row; '**.regatta** ['~regata] *f* (-/*Ruderregatten*) boat race, regatta; '**.sport** *m* rowing.

Ruf [ru:f] *m* (-[e]s/-e) call; cry, shout; summons; *univ.* call; reputation, repute; fame; standing, credit; '**2en** (*irr.*, ge-, h) **1.** *v/i.* call; cry, shout; **2.** *v/t.* call; ~ *lassen* send for. '**Ruf|name** *m* Christian *or* first name; '**.nummer** *f* telephone number; '**.weite** *f* (-/*no pl.*): *in* ~ within call *or* earshot.

Rüge ['ry:gə] *f* (-/-n) rebuke, censure, reprimand; '**2n** *v/t.* (ge-, h) rebuke, censure, blame.

Ruhe ['ru:ə] *f* (-/*no pl.*) rest, repose; sleep; quiet, calm; tranquillity; silence; peace; composure; *sich zur* ~ *setzen* retire; ~! quiet!, silence!; *immer mit der* ~! take it easy!; *lassen Sie mich in* ~! let me alone!; '**2bedürftig** *adj.*: ~ *sein* want *or* need rest; '**~gehalt** n pension; '2**los** adj. restless; '2**n** v/i. (ge-, h) rest, repose; sleep; laß die Vergangenheit ~! let bygones be bygones!; '**~pause** f pause; lull; '**~platz** m resting-place; '**~stand** m (-[e]s/no pl.) retirement; im ~ retired; in den ~ treten retire; in den ~ versetzen superannuate, pension off, retire; '**~stätte** f: letzte ~ last resting-place; '**~störer** m (-s/-) disturber of the peace, peacebreaker; '**~störung** f disturbance (of the peace), disorderly behavio(u)r, riot.

'**ruhig** adj. quiet; mind, water: tranquil, calm; silent; ⊕ smooth.

Ruhm [ruːm] m (-[e]s/no pl.) glory, fame, renown.

rühm|en ['ryːmən] v/t. (ge-, h) praise, glorify; sich e-r Sache ~ boast of s.th.; '**~lich** adj. glorious, laudable.

'**ruhm|los** adj. inglorious; '**~reich** adj. glorious.

Ruhr 𝒔 [ruːr] f (-/no pl.) dysentery.

Rühr|ei ['ryːr?-] n scrambled egg; '2**en** (ge-, h) **1.** v/t. stir, move; fig. touch, move, affect; sich ~ stir, move, bustle; **2.** v/i.: an et. ~ touch s.th.; wir wollen nicht daran ~ let sleeping dogs lie; '2**end** adj. touching, moving; '2**ig** adj. active, busy; enterprising; nimble; '2**selig** adj. sentimental; '**~ung** f (-/no pl.) emotion, feeling.

Ruin [ruˈiːn] m (-s/no pl.) ruin; decay; **~e** f (-/-) ruin(s pl.); fig. ruin, wreck; 2**ieren** [ruiˈniːrən] v/t. (no -ge-, h) ruin; destroy, wreck; spoil; sich ~ ruin o.s.

rülpsen ['rylpsən] v/i. (ge-, h) belch.

Rumän|e [ruˈmɛːnə] m (-n/-n) Ro(u)manian; 2**isch** adj. Ro(u)manian.

Rummel F ['ruməl] m (-s/no pl.) hurly-burly, row; bustle; revel; in publicity: F ballyhoo; '**~platz** m fun fair, amusement park.

rumoren [ruˈmoːrən] v/i. (no -ge-, h) make a noise or row; bowels: rumble.

Rumpel|kammer F ['rumpəl-] f lumber-room; '2**n** F v/i. (ge-, h, sein) rumble.

Rumpf [rumpf] m (-[e]s/✒e) anat. trunk, body; torso (of statue); ⊕ hull, frame, body; ✈ fuselage, body.

rümpfen ['rympfən] v/t. (ge-, h): die Nase ~ turn up one's nose, sniff (über acc.! at).

rund [runt] **1.** adj. round (a. fig.); circular; **2.** adv. about; '2**blick** m panorama, view all (a)round; 2**e** ['rundə] f (-/-n) round; sports: lap; boxing: round; round, patrol; beat (of policeman); in der or die ~ (a)round; **~en** ['~dən] v/refl. (ge-, h) (grow) round; '2**fahrt** f drive round (town, etc.); s. Rundreise; '2**flug** m circuit (über of); '2**frage** f inquiry, poll.

'**Rundfunk** m broadcast(ing); broadcasting service; broadcasting company; radio, wireless; im ~ over the wireless, on the radio or air; '**~anstalt** f broadcasting company; '**~ansager** m (radio) announcer; '**~gerät** n radio or wireless set; '**~gesellschaft** f broadcasting company; '**~hörer** m listener(-in); ~ pl. a. (radio) audience; '**~programm** n broadcast or radio program(me); '**~sender** m broadcast transmitter; broadcasting or radio station; '**~sendung** f broadcast; '**~sprecher** m broadcaster, broadcast speaker, (radio) announcer; '**~station** f broadcasting or radio station; '**~übertragung** f radio transmission, broadcast(ing); broadcast (of programme).

'**Rund|gang** m tour, round, circuit; '**~gesang** m glee, catch; '2**he'raus** adv. in plain words, frankly, plainly; 2**he'rum** adv. round about, all (a)round; '2**lich** adj. round(ish); rotund, plump; '**~reise** f circular tour or trip, sight-seeing trip, Am. a. round trip; '**~schau** f panorama; newspaper: review; '**~schreiben** n circular (letter); '2**weg** adv. flatly, plainly.

Runz|el ['runtsəl] f (-/-n) wrinkle; '2**elig** adj. wrinkled; '2**eln** v/t. (ge-, h) wrinkle; die Stirn ~ knit one's brows, frown; '2**lig** adj. wrinkled.

Rüpel ['ryːpəl] m (-s/-) boor, lout; '2**haft** adj. coarse, boorish, rude.

rupfen ['rupfən] v/t. (ge-, h) pull up or out, pick; pluck (fowl) (a. fig.). [fig. rude.]

ruppig adj. ['rupiç] ragged, shabby;

Rüsche ['ryːʃə] f (-/-n) ruffle, frill.

Ruß [ruːs] m (-es/no pl.) soot.

Russe ['rusə] *m* (-n/-n) Russian.
Rüssel ['rysəl] *m* (-s/-) trunk (*of elefant*); snout (*of pig*). [*adj.* sooty.]
'**ruß|en** *v/i.* (ge-, h) smoke; '**~ig**)
'**russisch** *adj.* Russian.
rüsten ['rystən] (ge-, h) **1.** *v/t.* and *v/refl.* prepare, get ready (zu for); **2.** *esp.* ✕ *v/i.* arm.
rüstig *adj.* ['rystiç] vigorous, strong;
'**2keit** *f* (-/*no pl.*) vigo(u)r.
'**Rüstung** *f* (-/-en) preparations *pl.*; ✕ arming, armament, armo(u)r;
~sindustrie ['rystuŋ?-] *f* armament industry.

'**Rüstzeug** *n* (set of) tools *pl.*, implements *pl.*; *fig.* equipment.
Rute ['ruːtə] *f* (-/-n) rod; switch; *fox's tail:* brush.
Rutsch [rutʃ] *m* (-es/-e) (land)slide; F short trip; '**~bahn** *f*, '**~e** *f* (-/-n) slide, chute; '**2en** *v/i.* (ge-, sein) glide, slide; slip; *vehicle:* skid; '**2ig** *adj.* slippery.
rütteln ['rytəln] (ge-, h) **1.** *v/t.* shake, jog; jolt; **2.** *v/i.* shake, jog; *car:* jolt; *an der Tür* ~ rattle at the door; *daran ist nichts zu* ~ that's a fact.

S

Saal [zaːl] *m* (-[e]s/*Säle*) hall.
Saat ✕ [zaːt] *f* (-/-en) sowing; standing *or* growing crops *pl.*; seed (*a. fig.*); '**~feld** ✕ *n* cornfield; '**~gut** ✕ *n* (-[e]s/*no pl.*) seeds *pl.*; '**~kartoffel** ✕ *f* seed-potato.
Sabbat ['zabat] *m* (-s/-e) Sabbath.
sabbern F ['zabərn] *v/i.* (ge-, h) slaver, slobber, *Am. a.* drool; twaddle, *Am. sl. a.* drool.
Säbel ['zɛːbəl] *m* (-s/-) sab|re, *Am.* -er; *mit dem* ~ *rasseln pol.* rattle the sabre; '**~beine** *n/pl.* bandy legs *pl.*; '**2beinig** *adj.* bandy-legged; '**~hieb** *m* sabre-cut; '**2n** F *fig. v/t.* (ge-, h) hack.
Sabot|age [zabo'taːʒə] *f* (-/-n) sabotage; **~eur** [~ø:r] *m* (-s/-e) saboteur; **2ieren** *v/t.* (no -ge-, h) sabotage.
Sach|bearbeiter ['zax-] *m* (-s/-) official in charge; *social work:* case worker; '**~beschädigung** *f* damage to property; '**2dienlich** *adj.* relevant, pertinent; useful, helpful.
'**Sache** *f* (-/-n) thing; affair, matter, concern; ⅌ case; point; issue; ~n *pl.* things *pl.*; *beschlossene* ~ foregone conclusion; e-e ~ *für sich* a matter apart; (*nicht*) *zur* ~ *gehörig* (ir)relevant, *pred. a.* to (off) the point; *bei der* ~ *bleiben* stick to the point; *gemeinsame* ~ *machen mit* make common cause with.
'**sach|gemäß** *adj.* appropriate, proper; '**2kenntnis** *f* expert knowledge; '**~kundig** *adj. s. sachverständig*; '**2lage** *f* state of affairs,

situation; '**~lich 1.** *adj.* relevant, pertinent, *pred. a.* to the point; matter-of-fact, business-like; unbias(s)ed; objective; **2.** *adv.:* ~ *einwandfrei od. richtig* factually correct.
sächlich *gr. adj.* ['zɛçliç] neuter.
'**Sachlichkeit** *f* (-/*no pl.*) objectivity; impartiality; matter-of-factness.
'**Sach|register** *n* (subject) index; '**~schaden** *m* damage to property.
Sachse ['zaksə] *m* (-n/-n) Saxon.
sächsisch *adj.* ['zɛksiʃ] Saxon.
sacht *adj.* [zaxt] soft, gentle; slow.
Sach|verhalt ['zaxfɛrhalt] *m* (-[e]s/-e) facts *pl.* (of the case); '**2verständig** *adj.* expert; '**~verständige** *m* (-n/-n) expert, authority; ⅌ expert witness; '**~wert** *m* real value.
Sack [zak] *m* (-[e]s/⁎e) sack; bag; *mit* ~ *und Pack* with bag and baggage; '**~gasse** *f* blind alley, cul-de-sac, impasse (*a. fig.*), *Am. a.* dead end (*a. fig.*); *fig.* deadlock; '**~leinwand** *f* sackcloth.
Sadis|mus [za'dismus] *m* (-/*no pl.*) sadism; **~t** *m* (-en/-en) sadist; **2tisch** *adj.* sadistic.
säen ['zɛːən] *v/t.* and *v/i.* (ge-, h) sow (*a. fig.*).
Saffian ['zafjaːn] *m* (-s/*no pl.*) morocco.
Saft [zaft] *m* (-[e]s/⁎e) juice (*of vegetables or fruits*); sap (*of plants*) (*a. fig.*); '**2ig** *adj.* fruits, *etc.*: juicy; *meadow, etc.:* lush; *plants:* sappy (*a. fig.*); *joke, etc.:* spicy, coarse; '**2los** *adj.* juiceless; sapless (*a. fig.*).

Sage ['zɑːgə] f (-/-n) legend, myth; *die ~ geht* the story goes.

Säge ['zɛːgə] f (-/-n) saw; '**~blatt** n saw-blade; '**~bock** m saw-horse, *Am. a.* sawbuck; '**~fisch** *ichth.* m sawfish; '**~mehl** n sawdust.

sagen ['zɑːgən] (ge-, h) **1.** v/t. say; *j-m et.* ~ tell s.o. s.th., say s.th. to s.o.; *j-m ~ lassen,* daß send s.o. word that; *er läßt sich nichts* ~ he will not listen to reason; *das hat nichts zu* ~ that doesn't matter; *j-m gute Nacht* ~ bid s.o. good night; **2.** v/i. say; *es ist nicht zu* ~ it is incredible *or* fantastic; *wenn ich so* ~ *darf* if I may express myself in these terms; *sage und schreibe* believe it or not; no less than, as much as.

'**sägen** v/t. and v/i. (ge-, h) saw.

'**sagenhaft** adj. legendary, mythical; F *fig.* fabulous, incredible.

Säge|späne ['zɛːgəʃpɛːnə] m/pl. sawdust; '**~werk** n sawmill.

sah [zɑː] pret. of sehen.

Sahne ['zɑːnə] f (-/no pl.) cream.

Saison [zɛ'zõː] f (-/-s) season; **2be-dingt** adj. seasonal.

Saite ['zaɪtə] f (-/-n) string, chord (a. fig.); **~ninstrument** ['zaɪtən⁹-] n stringed instrument.

Sakko ['zako] m, n (-s/-s) lounge coat; '**~anzug** m lounge suit.

Sakristei [zakrɪs'taɪ] f (-/-en) sacristy, vestry.

Salat [za'lɑːt] m (-[e]s/-e) salad; ⚘ lettuce.

Salbe ['zalbə] f (-/-n) ointment; **2en** v/t. (ge-, h) rub with ointment; anoint; '**~ung** f (-/-en) anointing, unction (a. fig.); **2ungsvoll** fig. adj. unctuous.

saldieren † [zal'diːrən] v/t. (no -ge-, h) balance, settle.

Saldo † ['zaldo] m (-s/Salden, Saldos, Saldi) balance; *den ~ ziehen* strike the balance; '**~vortrag** † m balance carried down.

Saline [za'liːnə] f (-/-n) salt-pit, salt-works.

Salmiak ['salmjak] m, n (-s/no pl.) sal-ammoniac, ammonium chloride; **~geist** m (-es/no pl.) liquid ammonia.

Salon [za'lõː] m (-s/-s) drawing-room, *Am. a.* parlor; ⚓ saloon; **2fähig** adj. presentable; '**~löwe** fig. m lady's man, carpet-knight;

~wagen 🚃 m saloon-car, saloon carriage, *Am.* parlor car.

Salpeter 🜋 [zal'peːtər] m (-s/no pl.) saltpet|re *Am.* -er; nit|re, *Am.* -er.

Salto ['zalto] m (-s/-s, Salti) somersault; *~ mortale* break-neck leap; *e-n ~ schlagen* turn a somersault.

Salut [za'luːt] m (-[e]s/-e) salute; *~ schießen* fire a salute; **2ieren** [~u'tiːrən] v/i. (no -ge-, h) (stand at the) salute.

Salve ['zalvə] f (-/-n) volley; ⚓ broadside; salute.

Salz [zalts] n (-es/-e) salt; '**~berg-werk** n salt-mine; '**2en** v/t. ([irr.,] ge-, h) salt; '**~faß** n, '**~fäßchen** ['~fɛsçən] n (-s/-) salt-cellar; '**~gurke** f pickled cucumber; '**~hal-tig** adj. saline, saliferous; '**~hering** m pickled herring; '**2ig** adj. salt(y); s. salzhaltig; '**~säure** 🜋 f hydro-chloric *or* muriatic acid; '**~wasser** n (-s/⁼) salt water, brine; '**~werk** n salt-works, saltern.

Same ['zɑːmə] m (-ns/-n), '**~n** m (-s/-) ⚘ seed (a. fig.); biol. sperm, semen; '**~nkorn** ⚘ n grain of seed.

Sammel|büchse ['zaməl-] f collecting-box; '**~lager** n collecting point; *refugees, etc.:* assembly camp; '**2n** (ge-, h) **1.** adj. gather; collect (stamps, etc.); *sich ~* gather; fig.: concentrate; compose o.s.; **2.** v/i. collect money (für for) '**~platz** m meeting-place, place of appointment; ✕, ⚓ rendezvous.

Sammler ['zamlər] m (-s/-) collector; '**~ung** f **1.** (-/-en) collection; **2.** fig. (-/no pl.) composure; concentration.

Samstag ['zams-] m Saturday.

samt¹ [zamt] **1.** adv.: *~ und sonders* one and all; **2.** prp. (dat.) together *or* along with.

Samt² [~] m (-[e]s/-e) velvet.

sämtlich ['zɛmtlıç] **1.** adj. all (to-gether); complete; **2.** adv. all (to-gether *or* all of them).

Sanatorium [zana'toːrjum] n (-s/Sanatorien) sanatorium, *Am. a.* sanitarium.

Sand [zant] m (-[e]s/-e) sand; *j-m ~ in die Augen streuen* throw dust into s.o.'s eyes; *im ~e verlaufen* end in smoke, come to nothing.

Sandale [zan'dɑːlə] f (-/-n) sandal.

'**Sand|bahn** f sports: dirt-track; '**~bank** f sandbank; '**~boden** m

S

sandy soil; '~grube f sand-pit; 2ig adj. ['~diç] sandy; '~korn n grain of sand; '~mann fig. m (-[e]s/no pl.) sandman, dustman; '~papier n sandpaper; '~sack m sand-bag; '~stein m sandstone.

sandte ['zantə] pret. of senden.

'Sand|torte f Madeira cake; '~uhr f sand-glass; '~wüste f sandy desert.

sanft adj. [zanft] soft; gentle, mild; smooth; slope, death, etc.: easy; ~er Zwang non-violent coercion; mit ~er Stimme softly, gently; ~mütig adj. ['~my:tiç] gentle, mild; meek.

sang [zaŋ] pret. of singen.

Sänger ['zɛŋər] m (-s/-) singer.

Sanguini|ker [zaŋgu'i:nikər] m (-s/-) sanguine person; 2sch adj. sanguine.

sanier|en [za'ni:rən] v/t. (no -ge-, h) improve the sanitary conditions of; esp. ✝: reorganize; readjust; 2ung f (-/-en) sanitation; esp. ✝: reorganization; readjustment.

sanitär adj. [zani'tɛ:r] sanitary.

Sanität|er [zani'tɛ:tər] m (-s/-) ambulance man; ✕ medical orderly.

sank [zaŋk] pret. of sinken.

Sankt [zaŋkt] Saint, St.

sann [zan] pret. of sinnen.

Sard|elle ichth. [zar'dɛlə] f (-/-n) anchovy; ~ine ichth. [~i:nə] f (-/-n) sardine.

Sarg [zark] m (-[e]s/ⁿe) coffin, Am. a. casket; '~deckel m coffin-lid.

Sarkas|mus [zar'kasmus] m (-/⁀ Sarkasmen) sarcasm; 2tisch adj. [~tiʃ] sarcastic.

saß [za:s] pret. of sitzen.

Satan ['za:tan] m (-s/-e) Satan; fig. devil; 2isch fig. adj. [za'tɑ:niʃ] satanic.

Satellit ast.,pol. [zatɛ'li:t] m (-en/-en) satellite; ~enstaat pol. m satellite state.

Satin [sa'tɛ̃:] m (-s/-s) satin; sateen.

Satir|e [za'ti:rə] f (-/-n) satire; ~iker [~ikər] m (-s/-) satirist; 2isch adj. satiric(al).

satt adj. [zat] satisfied, satiated, full; colour: deep, rich; sich ~ essen eat one's fill; ich bin ~ I have had enough; F et. ~ haben be tired or sick of s.th., sl. be fed up with s.th.

Sattel ['zatəl] m (-s/ⁿ) saddle; '~gurt m girth; '2n v/t. (ge-, h) saddle.

'Sattheit f (-/no pl.) satiety, fullness; richness, intensity (of colours).

sättig|en ['zɛtigən] (ge-, h) 1. v/t. satisfy, satiate; 2. v/i. food: be substantial; 2ung f (-/-en) satiation; fig. saturation.

Sattler ['zatlər] m (-s/-) saddler; ~ei [~'raɪ] f (-/-en) saddlery.

'sattsam adv. sufficiently.

Satz [zats] m (-es/ⁿe) gr. sentence; clause; phls. maxim; ♫, phys. saturate; 2. v/i. food: be substantial; 2ung f (-/-en) saturation; ♫ fig. saturation.

Satz [zats] m (-es/ⁿe) gr. sentence; clause; phls. maxim; ♭ proposition, theorem; ♩ movement; tennis, etc.: set; typ. setting, composition; sediment, dregs pl., grounds pl.; rate (of prices, etc.); set (of stamps, tools, etc.); leap, bound.

'Satzung f (-/-en) statute, by-law; '2sgemäß adj. statutory.

'Satzzeichen gr. n punctuation mark.

Sau [zau] f 1. (-/ⁿe) zo. sow; fig. contp. filthy swine; 2. hunt. (-/-en) wild sow.

sauber adj. ['zaubər] clean; neat (a. fig.), tidy; attitude: decent; iro. fine, nice; '2keit f (-/no pl.) clean(li)ness; tidiness, neatness; decency (of attitude).

säuber|n ['zɔybərn] v/t. (ge-, h) clean(se); tidy, clean up (room, etc.); clear (von of); purge (of, from) (a. fig., pol.); 2ungsaktion pol. f purge.

sauer ['zauər] 1. adj. sour (a. fig.), acid (a. ♫); cucumber: pickled; task, etc.: hard, painful; fig. morose, surly; 2. adv.: ~ reagieren auf et. take s.th. in bad part.

säuer|lich ['zɔyərliç] sourish, acidulous; '~n v/t. (ge-, h) (make) sour, acidify (a. ♫); leaven (dough).

'Sauer|stoff ♫ m (-[e]s/no pl.) oxygen; '~teig m leaven.

saufen ['zaufən] v/t. and v/i. (irr., ge-, h) animals: drink; F p. sl. soak, lush.

Säufer F ['zɔyfər] m (-s/-) sot, sl. soak.

saugen ['zaugən] (irr., ge-, h) 1. v/i. suck (an et. s.th.); 2. v/t. suck.

säuge|n ['zɔygən] v/t. (ge-, h) suckle, nurse; '2tier n mammal.

Säugling ['zɔyklɪŋ] m (-s/-e) baby, suckling; '~sheim n baby-farm, baby-nursery.

'Saug|papier n absorbent paper; '~pumpe f suction-pump; '~wirkung f suction-effect.

Säule ['zɔʏlə] *f* (-/-n) △, *anat.* column (*a.* of smoke, mercury, etc.); pillar, support (*both a. fig.*); '**~ngang** *m* colonnade; '**~nhalle** *f* pillared hall; portico.

Saum [zaum] *m* (-[e]s/ᴇe) seam, hem; border, edge.

säum|en ['zɔʏmən] *v/t.* (ge-, h) hem; border, edge; *die Straßen ~* line the streets; '**~ig** *adj.* payer: dilatory.

'**Saum|pfad** *m* mule-track; '**~tier** *n* sumpter-mule.

Säure ['zɔʏrə] *f* (-/-n) sourness; acidity (*a. ⚗ of stomach*); '**~** acid.

Saure'gurkenzeit *f* silly *or* slack season.

säuseln ['zɔʏzəln] (ge-, h) **1.** *v/i.* leaves, wind: rustle, whisper; **2.** *v/t. p.* say airily, purr.

sausen ['zauzən] *v/i.* (ge-) **1.** (sein) F rush, dash; *bullet, etc.*: whiz(z), whistle; **2.** (h) *wind*: whistle, sough.

'**Saustall** *m* pigsty; F *fig. a.* horrid mess.

Saxophon ♪ [zakso'fo:n] *n* (-s/-e) saxophone.

Schab|e ['ʃa:bə] *f* (-/-n) *zo.* cockroach; ⊕ *s.* Schabeisen; '**~efleisch** *n* scraped meat; '**~eisen** ⊕ *n* scraper, shaving-tool; '**~emesser** ⊕ *n* scraping-knife; '**~en** *v/t.* (ge-, h) scrape (*a.* ⊕); grate, rasp; scratch; '**~er** ⊕ *m* (-s/-) scraper.

Schabernack ['ʃa:bərnak] *m* (-[e]s/-e) practical joke, hoax, prank.

schäbig *adj.* ['ʃɛ:biç] shabby (*a. fig.*), F seedy, *Am.* F *a.* dowdy, tacky; *fig.* mean.

Schablone [ʃa'blo:nə] *f* (-/-n) model, pattern; stencil; *fig.*: routine; cliché; **2haft** *adj.*, **2nmäßig** *adj.* according to pattern; *fig.*: mechanical; *attr. a.* routine.

Schach [ʃax] *n* (-s/-s) chess; ~*! check!; ~ und matt!* checkmate!; *in* *or im* ~ *halten* keep *s.o.* in check; '**~brett** *n* chessboard.

schachern ['ʃaxərn] *v/i.* (ge-, h) haggle (*um* about, over), chaffer (about, over), *Am. a.* dicker; ~ *mit* barter (away).

'**Schach|feld** *n* square; '**~figur** *f* chess-man, piece; *fig.* pawn; '**2-'matt** *adj.* (check)mated; *fig.* tired out, worn out; '**~spiel** *n* game of chess.   [a. pit.]

Schacht [ʃaxt] *m* (-[e]s/ᴇe) shaft; ⚒

Schachtel ['ʃaxtəl] *f* (-/-n) box; F *alte ~* old frump.

'**Schachzug** *m* move (at chess); *geschickter ~* clever move (*a. fig.*).

schade *pred. adj.* ['ʃa:də]: *es ist ~* it is a pity; *wie ~!* what a pity!; *zu ~ für* too good for.

Schädel ['ʃɛ:dəl] *m* (-s/-) skull; cranium; '**~bruch** ⚕ *m* fracture of the skull.

schaden ['ʃa:dən] **1.** *v/i.* (ge-, h) damage, injure, harm; hurt (*j-m* s.o.); be detrimental (*to s.o.*); *das schadet nichts* it does not matter, never mind; **2.** ⌀ *m* (-s/ᴇ) damage (*an dat.* to); injury, harm; infirmity; hurt; loss; '**2ersatz** *m* indemnification, compensation; *damages pl.*; ~ *verlangen* claim damages; ~ *leisten* pay damages; *auf ~ (ver)klagen* ⚖ sue for damages; '**2freude** *f* malicious enjoyment of others' misfortunes, schadenfreude; '**~froh** *adj.* rejoicing over others' misfortunes.

schadhaft *adj.* ['ʃa:thaft] damaged, defective, faulty; *building, etc.*: dilapidated; *pipe, etc.*: leaking; *tooth, etc.*: decayed.

schädig|en ['ʃɛ:digən] *v/t.* (ge-, h) damage, impair; wrong, harm; '**2ung** *f* (-/-en) damage (*gen.* to), impairment (of); prejudice (to).

schädli|ch *adj.* ['ʃɛ:tliç] harmful, injurious; ,noxious; detrimental, prejudicial; '**2ng** ['~ŋ] *m* (-s/-e) *zo.* pest; ⚘ destructive weed; noxious person; ~*e pl.* ✗ *a.* vermin.

schadlos *adj.* ['ʃa:tlo:s]: *sich ~ halten* recoup *or* idemnify o.s. (*für* for).

Schaf [ʃa:f] *n* (-[e]s/-e) *zo.* sheep; *fig.* simpleton; '**~bock** *zo. m* ram.

Schäfer ['ʃɛ:fər] *m* (-s/-) shepherd; '**~hund** *m* sheep-dog; Alsatian (wolf-hound).

Schaffell ['ʃa:fɛl] *n* sheepskin.

schaffen ['ʃafən] **1.** *v/t.* (irr., ge-, h) create, produce; **2.** *v/t.* (ge-, h) convey, carry, move; take, bring; cope with, manage; **3.** *v/i.* (ge-, h) be busy, work.

Schaffner ['ʃafnər] *m* (-s/-) 🚋 guard, *Am.* conductor; *tram, bus*: conductor.

'**Schafhirt** *m* shepherd.   [fold.]

Schafott [ʃa'fɔt] *n* (-[e]s/-e) scaffold.

'**Schaf|pelz** *m* sheepskin coat; '**~stall** *m* fold.

Schaft [ʃaft] *m* (-[e]s/⸚e) shaft (*of lance, column, etc.*); stick (*of flag*); stock (*of rifle*); shank (*of tool, key, etc.*); leg (*of boot*); '⸜**stiefel** *m* high boot; ~ *pl. a.* Wellingtons *pl.*

'**Schaf**|**wolle** *f* sheep's wool; '⸜**zucht** *f* sheep-breeding, sheep-farming.

schäkern ['ʃɛːkərn] *v/i.* (ge-, h) jest, joke; flirt.

schal[1] *adj.* [ʃaːl] insipid; stale; *fig. a.* flat.

Schal[2] *m* (-s/-e, -s) scarf, muffler; comforter.

Schale ['ʃaːlə] *f* (-/-n) bowl; ⊕ scale (*of scales*); shell (*of eggs, nuts, etc.*); peel, skin (*of fruit*); shell, crust (*of tortoise*); paring, peeling; F: *sich in* ~ *werfen* doll o.s. up.

schälen ['ʃɛːlən] *v/t.* (ge-, h) remove the peel *or* skin from; pare, peel (*fruit, potatoes, etc.*); *sich* ~ *skin*: peel *or* come off.

Schalk [ʃalk] *m* (-[e]s/-e, ⸚e) rogue, wag; '**⸚haft** *adj.* roguish, waggish.

Schall [ʃal] *m* (-[e]s/⸜-e, ⸚e) sound; '⸜**dämpfer** *m* sound absorber; *mot.* silencer, *Am.* muffler; silencer (*on fire-arms*); '**⸚dicht** *adj.* sound-proof; '**⸚en** *v/i.* ([*irr.*,] ge-, h) sound; ring, peal; '**⸚end** *adj.:* ~*es Gelächter* roars *pl. or* a peal of laughter; '⸜**mauer** *f* sound barrier; '⸜**platte** *f* record, disc, disk; '⸜**welle** *f* sound-wave.

schalt [ʃalt] *pret. of* **schelten.**

'**Schaltbrett** ⚡ *n* switchboard.

schalten ['ʃaltən] (ge-, h) **1.** *v/i.* ⚡ switch; *mot.* change *or* shift gears; direct, rule; **2.** *v/t.* ⊕ actuate; operate, control.

'**Schalter** *m* (-s/-) 🎫, *theatre, etc.:* booking-office; 🏦, *bank, etc.:* counter; ⚡ switch; ⊕, *mot.* controller.

'**Schalt**|**hebel** *m mot.* gear lever; ⊕, 🚂 control lever; ⚡ switch lever; '⸜**jahr** *n* leap-year; '⸜**tafel** ⚡ *f* switchboard, control panel; '⸜**tag** *m* intercalary day.

Scham [ʃaːm] *f* (-/*no pl.*) shame; bashfulness, modesty; *anat.* privy parts *pl.*, genitals *pl.*

schämen ['ʃɛːmən] *v/refl.* (ge-, h) be *or* feel ashamed (*gen. or wegen* of).

'**Scham**|**gefühl** *n* sense of shame; '**⸚haft** *adj.* bashful, modest; '⸜**haftigkeit** *f* (-/*no pl.*) bashfulness,

modesty; '**⸚los** *adj.* shameless; impudent; '⸜**losigkeit** *f* (-/-en) shamelessness; impudence; '**⸚rot** *adj.* blushing; ~ *werden* blush; '⸜**röte** *f* blush; '⸜**teile** *anat. m/pl.* privy parts *pl.*, genitals *pl.*

Schande ['ʃandə] *f* (-/⸜-n) shame, disgrace.

schänden ['ʃɛndən] *v/t.* (ge-, h) dishono(u)r, disgrace; desecrate, profane; rape, violate; disfigure.

Schandfleck *fig.* ['ʃant-] *m* blot, stain; eyesore.

schändlich ['ʃɛntliç] *adj.* shameful, disgraceful, infamous; '**⸚keit** *f* (-/-en) infamy.

'**Schandtat** *f* infamous act(ion).

'**Schändung** *f* (-/-en) dishono(u)r-ing; profanation, desecration; rape, violation; disfigurement.

Schanze ['ʃantsə] *f* (-/-n) ✕ entrenchment; ⚓ quarter-deck; *sports:* ski-jump; '**⸚n** *v/i.* (ge-, h) throw up entrenchments, entrench.

Schar [ʃaːr] *f* (-/-en) troop, band; *geese, etc.:* flock; ✎ ploughshare, *Am.* plowshare; '**⸚en** *v/t.* (ge-, h) assemble, collect; *sich* ~ *a.* flock (*um round*).

scharf [ʃarf] **1.** *adj.* sharp; *edge:* keen; *voice, sound:* piercing, shrill; *smell, taste:* pungent; *pepper, etc.:* hot; *sight, hearing, intelligence, etc.:* keen; *answer, etc.:* cutting; ✕ *ammunition:* live; ~ *sein auf* (*acc.*) be very keen on; **2.** *adv.:* ~ *ansehen* look sharply at; ~ *reiten* ride hard; '**⸚blick** *fig. m* (-[e]s/*no pl.*) clearsightedness.

Schärfe ['ʃɛrfə] *f* (-/-n) sharpness; keenness; pungency; '**⸚n** *v/t.* (ge-, h) put an edge on, sharpen; strengthen (*memory*); sharpen (*sight, hearing, etc.*).

'**Scharf**|**macher** *fig. m* (-s/-) firebrand, agitator; '⸜**richter** *m* executioner; '⸜**schütze** ✕ *m* sharpshooter, sniper; '**⸚sichtig** *adj.* sharp-sighted; *fig.* clear-sighted; '⸜**sinn** *m* (-[e]s/*no pl.*) sagacity; acumen; '**⸚sinnig** *adj.* sharp-witted, shrewd; sagacious.

Scharlach ['ʃarlax] *m* **1.** (-s/-e) scarlet; **2.** ☞ (-s/*no pl.*) scarlet fever; '**⸚rot** *adj.* scarlet.

Scharlatan ['ʃarlatan] *m* (-s/-e) charlatan, quack (doctor); mountebank.

scheiden

Scharmützel [ʃarˈmʏtsəl] n (-s/-) skirmish.

Scharnier ⊕ [ʃarˈniːr] n (-s/-e) hinge, joint.

Schärpe [ˈʃɛrpə] f (-/-n) sash.

scharren [ˈʃarən] (ge-, h) **1.** v/i. scrape (*mit den Füßen* one's feet); *hen, etc.*: scratch; *horse*: paw; **2.** v/t. *horse*: paw (ground).

Schart|e [ˈʃartə] f (-/-n) notch, nick; *mountains*: gap, *Am.* notch; *e-e ~ auswetzen* repair a fault; wipe out a disgrace; **2ig** adj. jagged, notchy.

Schatten [ˈʃatən] m (-s/-) shadow (*a. fig.*); shade (*a. paint.*); **~bild** n silhouette; **2haft** adj. shadowy; **~kabinett** pol. n shadow cabinet; **~riß** m silhouette; **~seite** f shady side; *fig.* seamy side.

schattier|en [ʃaˈtiːrən] v/t. (no -ge-, h) shade, tint; **2ung** f (-/-en) shading; shade (*a. fig.*), tint.

schattig adj. shady.

Schatz [ʃats] m (-es/⁼e) treasure; *fig.* sweetheart, darling; **~amt** † n Exchequer, *Am.* Treasury (Department); **~anweisung** † f Treasury Bond, *Am. a.* Treasury Note.

schätzen [ˈʃɛtsən] v/t. (ge-, h) estimate; value (*auf acc.* at); price (at); rate; appreciate; esteem; *sich glücklich ~ zu inf.* be delighted to *inf.*; **~swert** adj. estimable.

Schatz|kammer f treasury; **~meister** m treasurer.

Schätzung f **1.** (-/-en) estimate, valuation; rating; **2.** (-/no pl.) appreciation, estimation; esteem.

Schatzwechsel † m Treasury Bill.

Schau [ʃau] f (-/-en) inspection, show, exhibition; *zur ~ stellen* exhibit, display.

Schauder [ˈʃaudər] m (-s/-) shudder(ing), shiver, tremor; *fig.* horror, terror; **2haft** adj. horrible, dreadful; F *fig. a.* awful; **2n** v/i. (ge-, h) shudder (*both: vor dat. at*).

schauen [ˈʃauən] v/i. (ge-, h) look (*auf acc.* at).

Schauer [ˈʃauər] m (-s/-) rain, *etc.*: shower (*a. fig.*); shudder(ing), shiver; attack, fit; thrill; **2lich** adj. dreadful, horrible; **2n** v/i. (ge-, h) *s. schaudern*; **~roman** m penny dreadful, thriller.

Schaufel [ˈʃaufəl] f (-/-n) shovel,

dust-pan; **2n** v/t. and v/i. (ge-, h) shovel.

Schaufenster n shop window, *Am. a.* show-window; **~bummel** m: *e-n ~ machen* go window-shopping; **~dekoration** f window-dressing; **~einbruch** m smash-and-grab raid.

Schaukel [ˈʃaukəl] f (-/-n) swing; **2n** (ge-, h) **1.** v/i. swing; *ship, etc.*: rock; **2.** v/t. rock (*baby, etc.*); **~pferd** n rocking-horse; **~stuhl** m rocking-chair, *Am. a.* rocker.

Schaum [ʃaum] m (-[e]s/⁼e) foam; *beer, etc.*: froth, head; *soap*: lather; **~bad** n bubble bath.

schäumen [ˈʃɔymən] v/i. (ge-, h) foam, froth; lather; *wine, etc.*: sparkle.

Schaum|gummi n, m foam rubber; **2ig** adj. foamy, frothy; **~wein** m sparkling wine.

Schau|platz m scene (of action), theat|re, *Am.* -er; **~prozeß** ⚖ m show trial.

schaurig adj. [ˈʃauriç] horrible, horrid.

Schau|spiel n spectacle; *thea.* play; **~spieler** m actor, player; **~spielhaus** n playhouse, theat|re, *Am.* -er; **~spielkunst** f (-/no pl.) dramatic art, *the* drama); **~steller** m (-s/-) showman.

Scheck † [ʃɛk] m (-s/-s) cheque, *Am.* check; **~buch** n, **~heft** n chequebook, *Am.* checkbook.

scheckig adj. spotted; *horse*: piebald.

scheel [ʃeːl] **1.** adj. squint-eyed, cross-eyed; *fig.* jealous, envious; **2.** adv.: *j-n ~ ansehen* look askance at s.o.

Scheffel [ˈʃɛfəl] m (-s/-) bushel; **2n** v/t. (ge-, h) amass (*money, etc.*).

Scheibe [ˈʃaibə] f (-/-n) disk, disc (*a. of sun, moon*); *esp. ast.* orb; slice (*of bread, etc.*); pane (*of window*); *shooting*: target; **~nhonig** m honey in combs; **~nwischer** mot. m (-s/-) wind-screen wiper, *Am.* windshield wiper.

Scheide [ˈʃaidə] f (-/-n) sword, *etc.*: sheath, scabbard; border, boundary; **~münze** f small coin; **2n** (*irr.*, ge-) **1.** v/t. (h) separate; ⚗ analyse; ⚖ divorce; *sich ~ lassen von j-m* divorce (*one's husband or wife*); **2.** v/i. (sein) depart; part (*von* with); *aus dem Dienst* ~ retire from service; *aus dem Leben* ~ depart from this life; '~wand *f* partition; '~weg *fig. m* cross-roads *sg.*

'**Scheidung** *f* (-/-en) separation; ⚖ divorce; '~sgrund ⚖ *m* ground for divorce; '~sklage ⚖ *f* divorce-suit; *die* ~ *einreichen* file a petition for divorce.

Schein [ʃaɪn] *m* **1.** (-[e]s/*no pl.*) shine; *sun, lamp, etc.*: light; *fire*: blaze; *fig.* appearance; **2.** (-[e]s/-e) certificate; receipt; bill; (bank-) note; '2**bar** *adj.* seeming, apparent; '2**en** *v/i.* (*irr., ge-, h*) shine; *fig.* seem, appear; look; '~**grund** *m* pretext, preten|ce, *Am.* -se; 2**heilig** *adj.* sanctimonious, hypocritical; '~**tod** 𝆕 *m* suspended animation; '2**tot** *adj.* in a state of suspended animation; '~**werfer** *m* (-s/-) reflector, projector; ✕, ⚓, 🔫 searchlight; *mot.* headlight; *thea.* spotlight.

Scheit [ʃaɪt] *n* (-[e]s/-e) log, billet.

Scheitel [ˈʃaɪtəl] *m* (-s/-) crown or top of the head; *hair*: parting; summit, peak; *esp.* 𝐀 vertex; '2**n** *v/t.* (ge-, h) part (*hair*).

Scheiterhaufen [ˈʃaɪtər-] *m* (funeral) pile; stake.

'**scheitern** *v/i.* (ge-, sein) ⚓ run aground, be wrecked; *fig.* fail, miscarry. [box on the ear.)

Schelle [ˈʃɛlə] *f* (-/-n) (little) bell;)

'**Schellfisch** *ichth. m* haddock.

Schelm [ʃɛlm] *m* (-[e]s/-e) rogue; '~**enstreich** *m* roguish trick; 2**isch** *adj.* roguish, arch.

Schelte [ˈʃɛltə] *f* (-/-n) scolding; '2**n** (*irr., ge-, h*) **1.** *v/t.* scold, rebuke; **2.** *v/i.* scold.

Schema [ˈʃeːma] *n* (-s/-s, -ta, *Schemen*) scheme; model, pattern; arrangement; 2**tisch** *adj.* [ʃeˈmaːtɪʃ] schematic.

Schemel [ˈʃeːməl] *m* (-s/-) stool.

Schemen [ˈʃeːmən] *m* (-s/-) phantom, shadow; '2**haft** *adj.* shadowy.

Schenke [ˈʃɛŋkə] *f* (-/-n) public house, F pub; tavern, inn.

Schenkel [ˈʃɛŋkəl] *m* (-s/-) *anat.* thigh; *anat.* shank; *triangle, etc.*: leg; 𝐀 *angle*: side.

schenken [ˈʃɛŋkən] *v/t.* (ge-, h) give; remit (*penalty, etc.*); *j-m et.* ~ give s.o. s.th., present s.o. with s.th., make s.o. a present of s.th.

'**Schenkung** ⚖ *f* (-/-en) donation; ~**surkunde** ⚖ [ˈʃɛŋkuŋs?-] *f* deed of gift.

Scherbe [ˈʃɛrbə] *f* (-/-n), '~**n** *m* (-s/-) (broken) piece, fragment.

Schere [ˈʃeːrə] *f* (-/-n) (e-e a pair of) scissors *pl.*; *zo.* crab, *etc.*: claw; '2**n** *v/t.* **1.** (*irr., ge-, h*) shear (*a. sheep*), clip; shave (*beard*); cut (*hair*), clip, prune (*hedge*); **2.** (ge-, h): *sich um et.* ~ trouble about s.th.; '~**nschleifer** *m* (-s/-) knife-grinder; ~**rei** [~ˈraɪ] *f* (-/-en) trouble, bother.

Scherz [ʃɛrts] *m* (-es/-e) jest, joke; ~ *beiseite* joking apart; *im* ~, *zum* ~ in jest *or* joke; ~ *treiben mit* make fun of; '2**en** *v/i.* (ge-, h) jest, joke; '2**haft** *adj.* joking, sportive.

scheu [ʃɔʏ] **1.** *adj.* shy, bashful, timid; *horse*: skittish; ~ *machen* frighten; **2.** ♀ *f* (-/*no pl.*) shyness; timidity; aversion (*vor dat.* to).

scheuchen [ˈʃɔʏçən] *v/t.* (ge-, h) scare, frighten (away).

scheuen (ge-, h) **1.** *v/i.* shy (*vor dat.* at), take fright (at); **2.** *v/t.* shun, avoid; fear; *sich* ~ *vor* (*dat.*) shy at, be afraid of.

Scheuer|**lappen** [ˈʃɔʏər-] *m* scouring-cloth, floor-cloth; '~**leiste** *f* skirting-board; '2**n** (ge-, h) **1.** *v/t.* scour, scrub; chafe; **2.** *v/i.* chafe.

'**Scheuklappe** *f* blinker, *Am. a.* blinder.

Scheune [ˈʃɔʏnə] *f* (-/-n) barn.

Scheusal [ˈʃɔʏzaːl] *n* (-[e]s/-e) monster.

scheußlich *adj.* [ˈʃɔʏslɪç] hideous, atrocious (F *a. fig.*), abominable (F *a. fig.*); 2**keit** *f* **1.** (-/*no pl.*) hideousness; **2.** (-/-en) abomination; atrocity.

Schi [ʃiː] *m* (-s/-er) *etc. s.* **Ski**, *etc.*

Schicht [ʃɪçt] *f* (-/-en) layer; *geol.* stratum (*a. fig.*); *at work*: shift; (social) class, rank, walk of life; '2**en** *v/t.* (ge-, h) arrange *or* put in layers, pile up; classify; '2**weise** *adv.* in layers; *work*: in shifts.

Schick [ʃik] **1.** *m* (-[e]s/*no pl.*) chic, elegance, style; **2.** ♀ *adj.* chic, stylish, fashionable.

schicken [ˈʃikən] *v/t.* (ge-, h) send (*nach, zu* to); remit (*money*); *nach j-m* ~ send for s.o.; *sich* ~ *für* become, suit, befit *s.o.*; *sich* ~ *in* put up with, resign o.s. to *s.th.*

'**schicklich** *adj.* becoming, proper,

seemly; '⁀**keit** f (-/no pl.) propriety, seemliness.

'**Schicksal** n (-[e]s/-e) fate, destiny.

'**Schiebe|dach** mot. ['ʃiːbə-] n sliding roof; '⁀**fenster** n sash-window; '⁀**n** (irr., ge-, h) 1. v/t. push, shove; shift (blame) (auf acc. on to); F fig. sell on the black market; 2. F fig. v/i. profiteer; '⁀**r** m (-s/-) bolt (of door); ⊕ slide; fig. profiteer, black marketeer, sl. spiv; '⁀**tür** f sliding door.

'**Schiebung** fig. f (-/-en) black marketeering, profiteering; put-up job.

schied [ʃiːt] pret. of scheiden.

Schieds|gericht ['ʃiːts-] n court of arbitration, arbitration committee; '⁀**richter** m arbitrator; tennis, etc.: umpire; football, etc.: referee; '⁀**richterlich** adj. arbitral; '⁀**spruch** m award, arbitration.

schief [ʃiːf] 1. adj. sloping, slanting, oblique; face, mouth: wry; fig. false, wrong; ⁀e Ebene ⚔ inclined plane; 2. adv.: j-n ⁀ ansehen look askance at s.o.

Schiefer ['ʃiːfər] m (-s/-) slate; splinter; '⁀**stift** m slate-pencil; '⁀**tafel** f slate.

'**schiefgehen** v/i. (irr. gehen, sep., -ge-, sein) go wrong or awry.

schielen ['ʃiːlən] v/i. (ge-, h) squint, be cross-eyed; ⁀ auf (acc.) squint at; leer at.

schien [ʃiːn] pret. of scheinen.

Schienbein ['ʃiːn-] n shin(-bone), tibia.

Schiene ['ʃiːnə] f (-/-n) 🚋, etc.: rail; ⚕ splint; '⁀**n** ⚕ v/t. (ge-, h) splint.

schießen ['ʃiːsən] (irr., ge-) 1. v/t. (h) shoot; tot ⁀ shoot dead; ein Tor ⁀ score (a goal); Salut ⁀ fire a salute; 2. v/i. (h): auf j-n ⁀ shoot or fire at; gut ⁀ be a good shot; 3. v/i. (sein) shoot, dart, rush.

'**Schieß|pulver** n gunpowder; '⁀**scharte** ⚔ f loop-hole, embrasure; '⁀**scheibe** f target; '⁀**stand** m shooting-gallery or -range.

Schiff [ʃif] n (-[e]s/-e) ⚓ ship, vessel; △ church: nave.

Schiffahrt ['ʃifaːrt] f (-/-en) navigation.

'**schiff|bar** adj. navigable; '⁀**bau** m shipbuilding; '⁀**bauer** m (-s/-) ship-

builder; '⁀**bruch** m shipwreck (a. fig.); ⁀ erleiden be shipwrecked; fig. make or suffer shipwreck; '⁀**brüchig** adj. shipwrecked; '⁀**brücke** f pontoon-bridge; '⁀**en** v/i. (ge-, sein) navigate, sail; '⁀**er** m (-s/-) sailor; boatman; navigator; skipper.

'**Schiffs|junge** m cabin-boy; '⁀**kapitän** m (sea-)captain; '⁀**ladung** f shipload; cargo; '⁀**makler** m shipbroker; '⁀**mannschaft** f crew; '⁀**raum** m hold; tonnage; '⁀**werft** f shipyard, esp. ⚔ dockyard, Am. a. navy yard.

Schikan|e [ʃiˈkaːnə] f (-/-n) vexation, nasty trick; ⁀**ieren** [⁀kaˈniːrən] v/t. (no -ge-, h) vex, ride.

Schild [ʃilt] 1. ⚔ m (-[e]s/-e) shield, buckler; 2. n (-[e]s/-er) shop, etc.: sign(board), facia; name-plate; traffic: signpost; label; cap: peak; '⁀**drüse** anat. f thyroid gland.

'**Schilder|haus** ⚔ n sentry-box; '⁀**maler** m sign-painter; '⁀**n** v/t. (ge-, h) describe, delineate; '⁀**ung** f (-/-en) description, delineation.

'**Schild|kröte** zo. f tortoise; turtle; '⁀**wache** f sentinel, sentry.

Schilf ⚘ [ʃilf] n (-[e]s/-e) reed; '⁀**ig** adj. reedy; '⁀**rohr** n reed.

schillern ['ʃilərn] v/i. (ge-, h) show changing colo(u)rs; be iridescent.

Schimmel ['ʃiməl] m 1. zo. (-s/-) white horse; 2. ⚘ (-s/no pl.) mo(u)ld, mildew; '⁀**ig** adj. mo(u)ldy, musty; '⁀**n** v/i. (ge-, h) become mo(u)ldy, Am. a. mo(u)ld.

Schimmer ['ʃimər] m (-s/no pl.) glimmer, gleam (a. fig.); '⁀**n** v/i. (ge-, h) glimmer, gleam.

Schimpanse zo. [ʃimˈpanzə] m (-n/-n) chimpanzee.

Schimpf [ʃimpf] m (-[e]s/-e) insult; disgrace; mit ⁀ und Schande ignominiously; '⁀**en** (ge-, h) 1. v/i. rail (über acc., auf acc. at, against); 2. v/t. scold; j-n e-n Lügner ⁀ call s.o. a liar; '⁀**lich** adj. disgraceful (für to), ignominious (to); '⁀**name** m abusive name; '⁀**wort** n term of abuse; ⁀e pl. a. invectives pl.

Schindel ['ʃindəl] f (-/-n) shingle.

schinden ['ʃindən] v/t. (irr., ge-, h) flay, skin (rabbit, etc.); sweat (worker); sich ⁀ drudge, slave, sweat.

'**Schinder** m (-s/-) knacker; fig. sweater, slave-driver; ⁀**ei** fig. [⁀ˈraɪ]

f (-/-en) sweating; drudgery, grind.
Schinken ['ʃiŋkən] *m* (-s/-) ham.
Schippe ['ʃipə] *f* (-/-n) shovel; '**~n**
v/t. (ge-, h) shovel.
Schirm [ʃirm] *m* (-[e]s/-e) umbrella;
parasol, sunshade; (*wind, television,
etc.*): screen; *lamp*: shade; *cap*: peak,
visor; '**~futteral** *n* umbrella-case;
'**~herr** *m* protector; patron; '**~herr-
schaft** *f* protectorate; patronage;
unter der ~ von event: under the
auspices of; '**~mütze** *f* peaked cap;
'**~ständer** *m* umbrella-stand.
Schlacht ⚔ [ʃlaxt] *f* (-/-en) battle
(*bei of*); '**~bank** *f* shambles; '2**en**
v/t. (ge-, h) slaughter, butcher.
Schlächter ['ʃlɛçtər] *m* (-s/-) butcher.
'**Schlacht|feld** ⚔ *n* battle-field;
'**~haus** *n*, '**~hof** *m* slaughter-house,
abattoir; '**~kreuzer** ⚓ *m* battle-
cruiser; '**~plan** *m* ⚔ plan of action
(*a. fig.*); '**~schiff** ⚓ *n* battleship;
'**~vieh** *n* slaughter cattle.
Schlack|e ['ʃlakə] *f* (-/-n) *wood,
coal*: cinder; *metall.* dross (*a. fig.*),
slag; *geol.* scoria; '2**ig** *adj.* drossy,
slaggy; F *weather*: slushy.
Schlaf [ʃlaːf] *m* (-[e]s/*no pl.*) sleep;
im ~(e) in one's sleep; *e-n leichten
(festen) ~ haben* be a light (sound)
sleeper; *in tiefem ~e liegen* be fast
asleep; '**~abteil** ⚙ *n* sleeping-
compartment; '**~anzug** *m* (*ein a pair
of*) pyjamas *pl. or Am.* pajamas *pl.*
Schläfchen ['ʃlɛːfçən] *n* (-s/-) doze,
nap, F forty winks *pl.*; *ein ~ machen*
take a nap, F have one's forty winks.
'**Schlafdecke** *f* blanket.
Schläfe ['ʃlɛːfə] *f* (-/-n) temple.
'**schlafen** *v/i.* (*irr.*, ge-, h) sleep; *~
gehen, sich ~ legen* go to bed.
schlaff *adj.* [ʃlaf] slack, loose;
muscles, etc.: flabby, flaccid; *plant,
etc.*: limp; *discipline, morals, etc.*:
lax; '2**heit** *f* (-/*no pl.*) slackness;
flabbiness; limpness; *fig.* laxity.
'**Schlaf|gelegenheit** *f* sleeping ac-
commodation; '**~kammer** *f* bedroom; '**~krankheit** ⚕ *f* sleeping-
sickness; '**~lied** *n* lullaby; '2**los**
adj. sleepless; '**~losigkeit** *f* (-/*no
pl.*) sleeplessness, ⚕ insomnia;
'**~mittel** ⚗ *n* soporific; '**~mütze** *f*
nightcap; *fig.* sleepyhead.
schläfrig *adj.* ['ʃlɛːfriç] sleepy,
drowsy; '2**keit** *f* (-/*no pl.*) sleep-
iness, drowsiness.

'**Schlaf|rock** *m* dressing-gown, *Am.
a.* robe; '**~saal** *m* dormitory; '**~sack**
m sleeping-bag; '**~stelle** *f* sleeping-
place; night's lodging; '**~tablette**
⚗ *f* sleeping-tablet; '2**trunken** *adj.*
very drowsy; '**~wagen** ⚙ *m* sleep-
ing-car(riage), *Am. a.* sleeper;
'**~wandler** ['~vandlər] *m* (-s/-)
sleep-walker, somnambulist; '**~
zimmer** *n* bedroom.
Schlag [ʃlaːk] *m* (-[e]s/⁔e) blow (*a.
fig.*); stroke (*of clock, piston*) (*a.
tennis, etc.*); slap (*with palm of hand*);
punch (*with fist*); kick (*of horse's
hoof*); ⚡ shock; beat (*of heart or
pulse*); clap (*of thunder*); warbling
(*of bird*); door (*of carriage*); ⚕
apoplexy; *fig.* race, kind, sort; breed
(*esp. of animals*); *Schläge bekommen* get a beating; *~ sechs Uhr* on
the stroke of six; '**~ader** *anat. f*
artery; '**~anfall** ⚕ *m* (stroke of)
apoplexy, stroke; '2**artig** 1. *adj.*
sudden, abrupt; 2. *adv.* all of a
sudden; '**~baum** *m* turnpike.
schlagen ['ʃlaːgən] (*irr.*, ge-, h)
1. *v/t.* strike, beat, hit; punch; slap;
beat, defeat; fell (*trees*); fight
(*battle*); *Alarm ~* sound the alarm;
zu Boden ~ knock down; *in den
Wind ~* cast *or* fling to the winds;
sich ~ (have a) fight; *sich et. aus
dem Kopf or Sinn ~* put s.th. out of
one's mind, dismiss s.th. from one's
mind; 2. *v/i.* beat, strike; *heart,
pulse*: beat, throb; *clock*: strike;
bird: warble; *das schlägt nicht in
mein Fach* that is not in my line;
um sich ~ lay about one; '**~d** *fig. adj.*
striking.
Schlager ['ʃlaːgər] *m* (-s/-) ♪ song
hit; *thea.* hit, draw, box-office
success; *book*: best seller.
Schläger ['ʃlɛːgər] *m* (-s/-) rowdy,
hooligan; *cricket, etc.*: batsman;
horse: kicker; *cricket, etc.*: bat;
golf: club; *tennis, etc.*: racket;
hockey, etc.: stick; '**~ei** ['~raɪ] *f*
(-/-en) tussle, fight.
'**schlagfertig** *fig. adj.* quick at
repartee; *~e Antwort* repartee;
'2**fertigkeit** *fig. f* (-/*no pl.*) quickness at repartee; '2**instrument** ♪ *n*
percussion instrument; '2**kraft** *f*
(-/*no pl.*) striking power (*a.* ⚔);
'2**loch** *n* pot-hole; '2**mann** *m* rowing: stroke; '2**ring** *m* knuckle-
duster, *Am. a.* brass knuckles *pl.*;

'²sahne f whipped cream; '²schatten m cast shadow; '²seite ⚓ f list; ~ haben ⚓ list; F fig. be half-seas-over; '²uhr f striking clock; '²werk n clock: striking mechanism; '²wort n catchword, slogan; '²zeile f headline; banner headline, Am. banner; '²zeug ♪ n in orchestra: percussion instruments pl.; in band: drums pl., percussion; '²zeuger ♪ m (-s/-) in orchestra: percussionist; in band: drummer.

schlaksig adj. ['ʃlaːksɪç] gawky.

Schlamm [ʃlam] m (-[e]s/⚓-e, ⚓e) mud, mire; '~bad n mud-bath; '²ig adj. muddy, miry.

Schlämmkreide ['ʃlɛm-] f (-/no pl.) whit(en)ing.

Schlamp|e ['ʃlampə] f (-/-n) slut, slattern; '²ig adj. slovenly, slipshod.

schlang [ʃlan] pret. of schlingen.

Schlange ['ʃlaŋə] f (-/-n) zo. snake, rhet. serpent (a. fig.); fig.: snake in the grass; queue, Am. a. line; ~ stehen queue up (um for), Am. line up (for).

schlängeln ['ʃlɛŋəln] v/refl. (ge-, h): sich ~ durch person: worm one's way or o.s. through; path, river, etc.: wind (one's way) through, meander through.

'Schlangenlinie f serpentine line.

schlank adj. [ʃlaŋk] slender, slim; '²heit f (-/no pl.) slenderness, slimness; '²heitskur f: e-e ~ machen slim.

schlapp F adj. [ʃlap] tired, exhausted, worn out; '²e F f (-/-n) reverse, setback; defeat; '~machen F v/i. (sep., -ge-, h) break down, faint.

schlau adj. [ʃlau] sly, cunning, crafty, clever, F cute.

Schlauch [ʃlaux] m (-[e]s/⚓e) tube; hose; car, etc.: inner tube; '~boot n rubber dinghy, pneumatic boat.

Schlaufe ['ʃlaufə] f (-/-n) loop.

schlecht [ʃlɛçt] 1. adj. bad; wicked; poor; temper: ill; quality: inferior; ~e Laune haben be in a bad temper; ~e Aussichten poor prospects; ~e Zeiten hard times; mir ist ~ I feel sick; 2. adv. badly, ill; ~erdings adv. ['ʃəːrdɪŋs] absolutely, downright, utterly; ~gelaunt adj. ['~gəlaunt] ill-humo(u)red, in a bad temper; '~hin adv. plainly, simply; '²igkeit f (-/-en) badness, wicked-

ness; ~en pl. base acts pl., mean tricks pl.; '~machen v/t. (sep., -ge-, h) run down, backbite; ~weg adv. ['~vek] plainly, simply.

schleich|en ['ʃlaiçən] v/i. (irr., ge-, sein) creep (a. fig.); sneak, steal; '²er m (-s/-) creeper; fig. sneak; '²handel m illicit trade; smuggling, contraband; '²händler m smuggler, contrabandist; '²weg m secret path.

Schleier ['ʃlaiər] m (-s/-) veil (a. fig.); mist: a. haze; den ~ nehmen take the veil; '²haft fig. adj. mysterious, inexplicable.

Schleife ['ʃlaifə] f (-/-n) loop (a. ✈); slip-knot; bow; wreath: streamer; loop, horse-shoe bend.

'schleif|en 1. v/t. (irr., ge-, h) whet (knife, etc.); cut (glass, precious stones); polish (a. fig.); 2. v/t. (ge-, h) ♪ slur; drag, trail; ✗ raze (fortress, etc.); 3. v/i. (ge-, h) drag, trail; '²stein m grindstone, whetstone.

Schleim [ʃlaim] m (-[e]s/-e) slime; ⚕ mucus, phlegm; '~haut anat. f mucous membrane; '²ig adj. slimy (a. fig.); mucous.

schlemm|en ['ʃlɛmən] v/i. (ge-, h) feast, gormandize; '²er m (-s/-) glutton, gormandizer; ²erei [~'rai] f (-/-en) feasting; gluttony.

schlen|dern ['ʃlɛndərn] v/i. (ge-, sein) stroll, saunter; ²drian ['~driːan] m (-[e]s/no pl.) jogtrot; beaten track.

schlenkern ['ʃlɛŋkərn] (ge-, h) 1. v/t. dangle, swing; 2. v/i.: mit den Armen ~ swing one's arms.

Schlepp|dampfer ['ʃlɛp-] m steam tug, tug(boat); '~e f (-/-n) train (of woman's dress); '²en (ge-, h) 1. v/t. carry with difficulty, haul, Am. F a. tote; ⚓, ✈, mot. tow, haul; ⚓ tug; ✝ tout (customers); sich ~ drag o.s., 2. v/i. dress: drag, trail; '²end adj. speech: drawling; gait: shuffling; style: heavy; conversation, etc.: tedious; '~er ⚓ m (-s/-) steam tug, tug(boat); '~tau n tow(ing)-rope; ins ~ nehmen take in or on tow (a. fig.).

Schleuder ['ʃlɔydər] f (-/-n) sling, catapult (a. ✈), Am. a. slingshot; spin drier; '²n (ge-, h) 1. v/t. fling, hurl (a. fig.); sling, catapult (a. ✈); spin-dry (washing); 2. mot. v/i.

S

skid; '**~preis** † *m* ruinous or give-away price; *zu* **~en** dirt-cheap.

schleunig *adj.* ['ʃlɔʏnɪç] prompt, speedy, quick.

Schleuse ['ʃlɔʏzə] *f* (-/-n) lock, sluice; '**2n** *v/t.* (ge-, h) lock (*boat*) (up *or* down); *fig.* manœuvre, *Am.* maneuver.

schlich [ʃlɪç] *pret. of* schleichen.

schlicht *adj.* [ʃlɪçt] plain, simple; modest, unpretentious; *hair:* smooth, sleek; '**~en** *fig. v/t.* (ge-, h) settle, adjust; settle by arbitration; '**2er** *fig. m* (-s/-) mediator; arbitrator.

schlief [ʃliːf] *pret. of* schlafen.

schließ|en ['ʃliːsən] (*irr.*, ge-, h) **1.** *v/t.* shut, close; shut down (*factory, etc.*); shut up (*shop*); contract (*marriage*); conclude (*treaty, speech, etc.*); *parl.* close (*debate*); *in die Arme* **~** clasp in one's arms; *in sich* **~** comprise, include; *Freundschaft* **~** make friends (*mit* with); **2.** *v/i.* shut, close; *school:* break up; *aus et.* **~** *auf* (*acc.*) infer *or* conclude *s.th.* from *s.th.*; '**2fach** ⓝ *n* post-office box; '**~lich** *adv.* finally, eventually; at last; after all.

Schliff [ʃlɪf] **1.** *m* (-[e]s/-e) polish (*a. fig.*); precious stones, glass: cut; **2.** ⓠ *pret. of* schleifen 1.

schlimm [ʃlɪm] **1.** *adj.* bad; evil, wicked, nasty; serious; F bad, sore; **~er** worse; *am* **~sten**, *das* 2ste the worst; *es wird immer* **~er** things are going from bad to worse; **2.** *adv.:* **~** *daran sein* be badly off; '**~sten'falls** *adv.* at (the) worst.

Schling|e ['ʃlɪŋə] *f* (-/-n) loop, sling (*a. ⚕*); noose; coil (*of wire or rope*); *hunt.* snare (*a. fig.*); *den Kopf in die* **~** *stecken* put one's head in the noose; '**~el** *m* (-s/-) rascal, naughty boy; '**2en** *v/t.* (*irr.*, ge-, h) wind, twist; plait; *die Arme* **~** *um* (*acc.*) fling one's arms round; *sich um et.* **~** wind round; '**~pflanze** ⚘ *f* creeper, climber.

Schlips [ʃlɪps] *m* (-es/-e) (neck)tie.

Schlitten ['ʃlɪtən] *m* (-s/-) sled(ge); sleigh; *sports:* toboggan.

'**Schlittschuh** *m* skate; **~** *laufen* skate; '**~läufer** *m* skater.

Schlitz [ʃlɪts] *m* (-es/-e) slit, slash; slot; '**2en** *v/t.* (ge-, h) slit, slash.

Schloß [ʃlɔs] **1.** *n* (Schlosses/Schlös-

ser) lock (*of door, gun, etc.*); castle; palace; *ins* **~** *fallen door:* snap to; *hinter* **~** *und Riegel* behind prison bars; **2.** ⚢ *pret. of* schließen.

Schlosser ['ʃlɔsər] *m* (-s/-) locksmith; mechanic, fitter.

Schlot [ʃloːt] *m* (-[e]s/-e, **~**e) chimney; flue; ⚓, ⚙ funnel; '**~feger** *m* (-s/-) chimney-sweep(er).

schlotter|ig *adj.* ['ʃlɔtərɪç] shaky, tottery; loose; '**~n** *v/i.* (ge-, h) *garment:* hang loosely; *p.* shake, tremble (*both: vor dat.* with).

Schlucht [ʃluxt] *f* (-/-en) gorge, mountain cleft; ravine, *Am.* gulch.

schluchzen ['ʃluxtsən] *v/i.* (ge-, h) sob.

Schluck [ʃluk] *m* (-[e]s/-e, **~**e) draught, swallow; mouthful, sip; '**~auf** *m* (-s/no pl.) hiccup(s *pl.*).

'**schlucken 1.** *v/t. and v/i.* (ge-, h) swallow (*a. fig.*); **2.** ⚢ *m* (-s/no pl.) hiccup *pl.*).

schlug [ʃluːk] *pret. of* schlagen.

Schlummer ['ʃlumər] *m* (-s/no pl.) slumber; '**2n** *v/i.* (ge-, h) slumber.

Schlund [ʃlunt] *m* (-[e]s/**~**e) *anat.* pharynx; *fig.* abyss, chasm, gulf.

schlüpf|en ['ʃlʏpfən] *v/i.* (ge-, h) slip, slide; *in die Kleider* **~** slip on one's clothes; *aus den Kleidern* **~** slip out of *or* slip off one's clothes; '**2er** *m* (-s/-) (*ein a pair of*) knickers *pl. or* drawers *pl. or* F panties *pl.*; briefs *pl.*

Schlupfloch ['ʃlupf-] *n* loop-hole.

'**schlüpfrig** *adj.* slippery; *fig.* lascivious.

'**Schlupfwinkel** *m* hiding-place.

schlurfen ['ʃlurfən] *v/i.* (ge-, sein) shuffle, drag one's feet.

schlürfen ['ʃlʏrfən] *v/t. and v/i.* (ge-, h) drink *or* eat noisily; sip.

Schluß [ʃlus] *m* (Schlusses/Schlüsse) close, end; conclusion; *parl.* closing (*of debate*).

Schlüssel ['ʃlʏsəl] *m* (-s/-) key (*zu* of; *fig.* to); ♪ clef; *fig.:* code; quota; '**~bart** *m* key-bit; '**~bein** *anat. n* collar-bone, clavicle; '**~bund** *m, n* (-[e]s/-e) bunch of keys; '**~industrie** *fig. f* key industry; '**~loch** *n* keyhole; '**~ring** *m* key-ring.

'**Schluß|folgerung** *f* conclusion, inference; '**~formel** *f in letter:* complimentary close.

schlüssig *adj.* ['ʃlʏsɪç] *evidence:*

conclusive; *sich ~ werden* make up one's mind (*über acc.* about).

'Schluß|licht n 🚗, *mot.*, *etc.*: taillight; *sports*: last runner; bottom club; **'~runde** f *sports*: final; **'~schein** † m contract-note.

Schmach [ʃmaːx] f (-/*no pl.*) disgrace; insult; humiliation.

schmachten ['ʃmaxtən] v/i. (ge-, h) languish (*nach* for), pine (for).

schmächtig adj. ['ʃmɛçtiç] slender, slim; *ein ~er Junge* a (mere) slip of a boy. [miliating.]

'schmachvoll adj. disgraceful; hu-]

schmackhaft adj. ['ʃmakhaft] palatable, savo(u)ry.

schmäh|en ['ʃmɛːən] v/t. (ge-, h) abuse, revile; decry, disparage; slander, defame; **'~lich** adj. ignominious, disgraceful; **'Sschrift** f libel, lampoon; **'Sung** f (-/-en) abuse; slander, defamation.

schmal adj. [ʃmaːl] narrow; *figure*: slender, slim; *face*: thin; *fig.* poor, scanty.

schmäler|n ['ʃmɛːlərn] v/t. (ge-, h) curtail; impair; belittle; **'Sung** f (-/-en) curtailment; impairment; detraction.

'Schmal|film *phot.* m substandard film; **'~spur** 🚗 f narrow ga(u)ge; **'~spurbahn** 🚗 f narrow-ga(u)ge railway; **'Sspurig** 🚗 adj. narrow-ga(u)ge.

Schmalz [ʃmalts] n (-es/-e) grease; lard; **'Sig** adj. greasy; lardy; F *fig.* soppy, sentimental.

schmarotz|en [ʃmaˈrɔtsən] v/i. (no -ge-, h) sponge (*bei* on); **Ser** m (-s/-) 🌱, *zo.* parasite; *fig. a.* sponge.

Schmarre F ['ʃmarə] f (-/-n) slash, cut; scar.

Schmatz [ʃmats] m (-es/-e) smack, loud kiss; **'Sen** v/i. (ge-, h) smack (*mit den Lippen* one's lips); eat noisily.

Schmaus [ʃmaus] m (-es/¨e) feast, banquet; *fig.* treat; **Sen** v/i. ['~zən] (ge-, h) feast, banquet.

schmecken ['ʃmɛkən] (ge-, h) **1.** v/t. taste, sample; **2.** v/i.: ~ *nach* taste or smack of (*both a. fig.*); *dieser Wein schmeckt mir* I like or enjoy this wine.

Schmeichel|ei [ʃmaɪçəˈlaɪ] f (-/-en) flattery; cajolery; **'Shaft** adj. flattering; **'Sn** v/i. (ge-, h): *j-m ~* flatter s.o.; cajole s.o.

Schmeichler ['ʃmaɪçlər] m (-s/-) flatterer; **'Sisch** adj. flattering; cajoling.

schmeiß|en F ['ʃmaɪsən] (*irr.*, ge-, h) **1.** v/t.: throw, fling, hurl; slam, bang (*door*); **2.** v/i.: *mit Geld um sich ~* squander one's money; **'Sfliege** zo. f blowfly, bluebottle.

Schmelz [ʃmɛlts] m **1.** (-es/-e) enamel; *fig.* (-es/*no pl.*) bloom; ♪ sweetness, mellowness; **'Sen** (*irr.*, ge-) **1.** v/i. (*sein*) melt (*a. fig.*); liquefy; *fig.* melt away, dwindle; **2.** v/t. (*h*) melt; smelt, fuse (*ore*, *etc.*); liquefy; **~erei** [~ˈraɪ] f (-/-en), **'~hütte** f foundry; **'~ofen** m smelting furnace; **'~tiegel** m melting-pot, crucible.

Schmerbauch ['ʃmeːr-] m paunch, pot-belly, F corporation, *Am. sl. a.* bay window.

Schmerz [ʃmɛrts] m (-es/-en) pain (*a. fig.*); ache; *fig.* grief, sorrow; **'Sen** (ge-, h) **1.** v/i. pain (*a. fig.*), hurt; ache; **2.** v/t. pain (*a. fig.*); hurt; *fig.* grieve, afflict; **'Shaft** adj. painful; **'Slich** adj. painful, grievous; **'Slindernd** adj. soothing; **'Slos** adj. painless.

Schmetter|ling zo. ['ʃmɛtərliŋ] m (-s/-e) butterfly; **'Sn** (ge-, h) **1.** v/t. dash (*zu Boden* to the ground); *in Stücke* to pieces); **2.** v/i. crash; *trumpet*, *etc.*: bray, blare; *bird*: warble.

Schmied [ʃmiːt] m (-[e]s/-e) (black-)smith; **~e** ['~də] f (-/-n) forge, smithy; **~eeisen** ['~də⁹-] n wrought iron; **~ehammer** m sledge(-hammer); **Sen** ['~dən] v/t. (ge-, h) forge; make, devise, hatch (*plans*).

schmiegen ['ʃmiːɡən] v/refl. (ge-, h) nestle (*an acc.* to).

schmiegsam adj. ['ʃmiːkzaːm] pliant, flexible; supple (*a. fig.*); **'Skeit** f (-/*no pl.*) pliancy, flexibility; suppleness (*a. fig.*).

Schmier|e ['ʃmiːrə] f (-/-n) grease; *thea. contp.* troop of strolling players, *sl.* penny gaff; **'Sen** v/t. (ge-, h) smear; ⊕ grease, oil, lubricate; butter (*bread*); spread (*butter*, *etc.*); scrawl, scribble; *painter*: daub; **~enkomödiant** ['~kɔmøˈdjant] m (-en/-en) strolling actor, barnstormer, *sl.* ham (actor); **~erei** [~ˈraɪ] f (-/-en) scrawl; *paint.* daub; **'Sig** adj. greasy; dirty; *fig.*: filthy;

F smarmy; '~mittel ⊕ n lubricant.
Schminke ['ʃmiŋkə] f (-/-n) make-up (a. thea.), paint; rouge; thea. grease-paint; '2n v/t. and v/refl. (ge-, h) paint, make up; rouge (o.s.); put on lipstick.
Schmirgel ['ʃmirgəl] m (-s/no pl.) emery; '2n v/t. (ge-, h) (rub with) emery; '~papier n emery-paper.
Schmiß [ʃmis] 1. m (Schmisses/Schmisse) gash, cut; (duelling-) scar; 2. F m (Schmisses/no pl.) verve, go, Am. sl. a. pep; 3. ♀ pret. of schmeißen.
schmoll|en ['ʃmɔlən] v/i. (ge-, h) sulk, pout; '2winkel m sulking-corner.
schmolz [ʃmɔlts] pret. of schmelzen.
Schmor|braten ['ʃmoːr-] m stewed meat; '2en v/t. and v/i. (ge-, h) stew (a. fig.).
Schmuck [ʃmuk] 1. m (-[e]s/⁎-e) ornament; decoration; jewel(le)ry, jewels pl.; 2. ♀ adj. neat, smart, spruce, trim.
schmücken ['ʃmykən] v/t. (ge-, h) adorn, trim; decorate.
'**schmuck|los** adj. unadorned; plain; '2sachen f/pl. jewel(le)ry, jewels pl.
Schmuggel ['ʃmugəl] m (-s/no pl.), ~ei [~'laɪ] f (-/-en) smuggling; '2n v/t. and v/i. (ge-, h) smuggle; '~ware f contraband, smuggled goods pl. [smuggler.]
Schmuggler ['ʃmuglər] m (-s/-)]
schmunzeln ['ʃmuntsəln] v/i. (ge-, h) smile amusedly.
Schmutz [ʃmuts] m (-es/no pl.) dirt; filth; fig. a. smut; '2en v/i. (ge-, h) soil, get dirty; '~fink fig. m mudlark; '~fleck m smudge, stain; fig. blemish; '2ig adj. dirty; filthy; fig. a. mean, shabby.
Schnabel ['ʃnɑːbəl] m (-s/⁎) bill, esp. bird of prey: beak.
Schnalle ['ʃnalə] f (-/-n) buckle; '2n v/t. (ge-, h) buckle; strap.
schnalzen ['ʃnaltsən] v/i. (ge-, h): mit den Fingern ~ snap one's fingers; mit der Zunge ~ click one's tongue.
schnappen ['ʃnapən] (ge-, h) 1. v/i. lid, spring, etc.: snap; lock: catch; nach et. ~ snap or snatch at; nach Luft ~ gasp for breath; 2. F v/t. catch, sl. nab (criminal).
'**Schnapp|messer** n flick-knife; '~schloß n spring-lock; '~schuß phot. m snapshot.

Schnaps [ʃnaps] m (-es/⁎e) strong liquor, Am. hard liquor; brandy; ein (Glas) ~ a dram.
schnarch|en ['ʃnarçən] v/i. (ge-, h) snore; '2er m (-s/-) snorer.
schnarren ['ʃnarən] v/i. (ge-, h) rattle; jar.
schnattern ['ʃnatərn] v/i. (ge-, h) cackle; fig. a. chatter, gabble.
schnauben ['ʃnaubən] (ge-, h) 1. v/i. snort; vor Wut ~ foam with rage; 2. v/t.: sich die Nase ~ blow one's nose. [pant, puff, blow; wheeze.]
schnaufen ['ʃnaufən] v/i. (ge-, h)]
Schnauz|bart ['ʃnauts-] m m(o)ustache; '~e f (-/-n) snout, muzzle; nozzle; teapot, etc.: spout; sl. slap; potato-trap; '2en F v/i. (ge-, h) jaw.
Schnecke zo. ['ʃnɛkə] f (-/-n) snail; slug; '~nhaus n snail's shell; '~ntempo n: im ~ at a snail's pace.
Schnee [ʃneː] m (-s/no pl.) snow; '~ball m snowball; '~ballschlacht f pelting-match with snowballs; 2bedeckt adj. ['~bədɛkt] snow-covered, mountain-top: snow-capped; '2blind adj. snow-blind; '~blindheit f snow-blindness; '~brille f (e-e a pair of) snow-goggles pl.; '~fall m snow-fall; '~flocke f snow-flake; '~gestöber n (-s/-) snow-storm; ~glöckchen ♀ ['~glœkçən] n (-s/-) snowdrop; '~grenze f snow-line; '~mann m snow man; '~pflug m snow-plough, Am. snowplow; '~schuh m snow-shoe; '~sturm m snow-storm, blizzard; '~wehe f (-/-n) snow-drift; '2'weiß adj. snow-white.
Schneid F [ʃnaɪt] m (-[e]s/no pl.) pluck, dash, sl. guts pl.
Schneide ['ʃnaɪdə] f (-/-n) edge; '~mühle f sawmill; '2n (irr., ge-, h) 1. v/t. cut; carve (meat); pare, clip (finger-nails, etc.); 2. v/i. cut.
'**Schneider** m (-s/-) tailor; ~ei [~'raɪ] f 1. (-/no pl.) tailoring; dress-making; 2. (-/-en) tailor's shop; dressmaker's shop; '~in f (-/-nen) dressmaker; '~meister m master tailor; '2n (ge-, h) 1. v/i. tailor; do tailoring; do dressmaking; 2. v/t. make, tailor.
'**Schneidezahn** m incisor.
'**schneidig** fig. adj. plucky, dashing, keen; smart, Am. sl. a. nifty.
schneien ['ʃnaɪən] v/i. (ge-, h) snow.

schnell [ʃnɛl] **1.** *adj.* quick, fast; rapid; swift, speedy; *reply, etc.*: prompt; sudden; **2.** *adv.*: ~ *fahren* drive fast; ~ *handeln* act promptly *or* without delay; *(mach)* ~! be quick!, hurry up!

Schnelläufer ['ʃnɛlɔyfər] *m* sprinter; speed skater.

'**schnell|en** (ge-) *v/t.* (h) *and v/i.* (sein) jerk; '**≗feuer** ✕ *n* rapid fire; '**≗hefter** *m* (-s/-) folder.

'**Schnelligkeit** *f* (-/*no pl.*) quickness, fastness; rapidity; swiftness; promptness; speed, velocity.

'**Schnell|imbiß** *m* snack (bar); '**≁imbißstube** *f* snack bar; '**≁kraft** *f* (-/*no pl.*) elasticity; '**≁verfahren** *n* 🏛 summary proceeding; ⊕ high-speed process; '**≁zug** 🚂 *m* fast train, express (train).

schneuzen ['ʃnɔytsən] *v/refl.* (ge-, h) blow one's nose.

schniegeln ['ʃniːgəln] *v/refl.* (ge-, h) dress *or* smarten *or* spruce (o.s.) up.

Schnipp|chen ['ʃnɪpçən] *n*: F *j-m ein* ~ *schlagen* outwit *or* overreach s.o.; '**≗isch** *adj.* pert, snappish, *Am.* F *a.* snippy.

Schnitt [ʃnɪt] **1.** *m* (-[e]s/-e) cut; dress, *etc.*: cut, make, style; pattern; *book*: edge; Ⓐ (inter)section; *fig.*: average; F profit; **2.** ♀ *pret. of* schneiden; '**≁blumen** *f/pl.* cut flowers *pl.*; '**≁e** *f* (-/-n) slice; '**≁er** *m* (-s/-) reaper, mower; '**≁fläche** Ⓐ *f* section(al plane); '**≗ig** *adj.* streamline(d); '**≁muster** *n* pattern; '**≁punkt** *m* (point of) intersection; '**≁wunde** *f* cut, gash.

schnitzen ['ʃnɪtsən] *v/t.* (ge-, h) carve, cut (in wood).

'**Schnitzer** *m* (-s/-) carver; F *fig.* blunder, *Am. sl. a.* boner; **≁ei** [~'raɪ] *f* **1.** (-/-en) carving, carved work; **2.** (-/*no pl.*) carving.

schnöde *adj.* ['ʃnøːdə] contemptuous; disgraceful; base, vile; ~*r* Mammon filthy lucre.

Schnörkel ['ʃnœrkəl] *m* (-s/-) flourish (*a. fig.*), scroll (*a.* △).

schnorr|en F ['ʃnɔrən] *v/t. and v/i.* (ge-, h) cadge; '**≗er** *m* (-s/-) cadger.

schnüff|eln ['ʃnyfəln] *v/i.* (ge-, h) sniff, nose (*both: an dat.* at); *fig.* nose about, *Am.* F *a.* snoop around; '**≗ler** *fig.* *m* (-s/-) spy, *Am.* F *a.* snoop; F sleuth(-hound).

Schnuller ['ʃnʊlər] *m* (-s/-) dummy, comforter.

Schnulze F ['ʃnʊltsə] *f* (-/-n) sentimental song *or* film *or* play, F tear-jerker.

Schnupf|en ['ʃnʊpfən] **1.** *m* (-s/-) cold, catarrh; **2.** ♀ *v/i.* (ge-, h) take snuff; '**≁er** *m* (-s/-) snuff-taker; '**≁tabak** *m* snuff.

schnuppe F *adj.* ['ʃnʊpə]: *das ist mir* ~ I don't care (F a damn); '**≁rn** *v/i.* (ge-, h) sniff, nose (*both: an dat.* at).

Schnur [ʃnuːr] *f* (-/⁼e, ✎ -en) cord; string, twine; *tape*; ⚡ flex.

Schnür|band ['ʃnyːr-] *n* lace; **≁chen** ['~çən] *n* (-s/-): *wie am* ~ like clockwork; '**≗en** (ge-, h) lace (up); (bind) with cord, tie up.

'**schnurgerade** *adj.* dead straight.

Schnurr|bart ['ʃnur-] *m* m(o)ustache; '**≗en** (ge-, h) **1.** *v/i.* wheel, *etc.*: whir(r); *cat*: purr (*a. fig.*); F *fig.* cadge; **2.** F *fig. v/t.* cadge.

Schnür|senkel ['ʃnyːzɛŋkəl] *m* (-s/-) shoe-lace, shoe-string; '**≁stiefel** *m* lace-boot.

schnurstracks *adv.* ['ʃnuːr'ʃtraks] direct, straight; on the spot; at once, *sl.* straight away.

schob [ʃoːp] *pret. of* schieben.

Schober ['ʃoːbər] *m* (-s/-) rick, stack.

Schock [ʃɔk] **1.** *n* (-[e]s/-e) three-score; **2.** 🞧 *m* (-[e]s/-s, ✎ -e) shock; **≗ieren** [~'kiːrən] *v/t.* (*no* ge-) shock, scandalize.

Schokolade [ʃokoˈlaːdə] *f* (-/-n) chocolate.

scholl [ʃɔl] *pret. of* schallen.

Scholle ['ʃɔlə] *f* (-/-n) clod (of earth), *poet.* glebe; floe (*of ice*); *ichth.* plaice.

schon *adv.* [ʃoːn] already; ~ *lange* for a long time; ~ *gut!* all right!; ~ *der Gedanke* the very idea; ~ *der Name* the bare name; *hast du* ~ *einmal* ...? have you ever ...?; *mußt du* ~ *gehen?* need you go yet?; ~ *um 8 Uhr* as early as 8 o'clock.

schön [ʃøːn] **1.** *adj.* beautiful; *man*: handsome (*a. fig.*); *weather*: fair, fine (*a. iro.*); *das* ~*e Geschlecht* the

S

fair sex; *die* ∼*en Künste* the fine arts; ∼*e Literatur* belles-lettres *pl.*; **2.** *adv.*: ∼ *warm* nice and warm; *du hast mich* ∼ *erschreckt* you gave me quite a start.

schonen ['ʃoːnən] *v/t.* (ge-, h) spare (*j-n s.o.*; *j-s Leben s.o.*'s life); take care of; husband (*strength, etc.*); *sich* ∼ take care of o.s., look after o.s.

'**Schönheit** *f* **1.** (-/*no pl.*) beauty; *of woman*: *a.* pulchritude; **2.** (-/-*en*) beauty; beautiful woman, belle; '∼**spflege** *f* beauty treatment.

'**schöntun** *v/i.* (*irr.* tun, sep., -ge-, h) flatter (*j-m s.o.*); flirt (*dat.* with).

'**Schonung** *f* **1.** (-/*no pl.*) mercy; sparing, forbearance; careful treatment; **2.** (-/-*en*) tree-nursery; '**2slos** *adj.* unsparing, merciless, relentless. [*a.* crest.]

Schopf [ʃɔpf] *m* (-[e]s/ᵚe) tuft; *orn.*)

schöpfen ['ʃœpfən] *v/t.* (ge-, h) scoop, ladle; draw (*water at well*); draw, take (*breath*); take (*courage*); *neue Hoffnung* ∼ gather fresh hope; *Verdacht* ∼ become suspicious.

'**Schöpf|er** *m* (-s/-) creator; '**2erisch** *adj.* creative; '∼**ung** *f* (-/-*en*) creation.

schor [ʃoːr] *pret. of* scheren.

Schorf ⚕ [ʃɔrf] *m* (-[e]s/-e) scurf, scab, crust; '**2ig** *adj.* scurfy; scabby.

Schornstein ['ʃɔrn-] *m* chimney, ⊕, ⚓ funnel; '∼**feger** *m* (-s/-) chimney-sweep(er).

Schoß 1. [ʃoːs] *m* (-es/ᵚe) lap; womb; *coat*: tail; **2.** [ʃɔs] *pret. of* schießen.

Schote ⚘ ['ʃoːtə] *f* (-/-*n*) pod, husk.

Schott|e ['ʃɔtə] *m* (-n/-n) Scot, Scotchman, Scotsman; *die* ∼*n pl.* the Scotch *pl.*; '∼**er** *m* (-s/-) gravel; (road-)metal; '**2isch** *adj.* Scotch, Scottish.

schräg [ʃrɛːk] **1.** *adj.* oblique, slanting; sloping; **2.** *adv.*: ∼ *gegenüber* diagonally across (*von* from).

schrak [ʃraːk] *pret. of* schrecken 2.

Schramme ['ʃramə] *f* (-/-*en*) scratch; *skin*: *a.* abrasion; '**2n** *v/t.* (ge-, h) scratch; graze, abrade (*skin*).

Schrank [ʃraŋk] *m* (-[e]s/ᵚe) cupboard, *esp. Am.* closet; wardrobe.

'**Schranke** *f* (-/-*n*) barrier (*a. fig.*); 🚊 *a.* (railway-)gate; ⚖ bar; ∼*n pl. fig.* bounds *pl.*, limits *pl.*; '**2nlos** *fig. adj.* boundless; unbridled; '∼**nwärter** 🚊 *m* gate-keeper.

'**Schrankkoffer** *m* wardrobe trunk.

Schraube ['ʃraubə] *f* (-/-*n*) ⊕ screw; ⚓ screw(-propeller); '**2n** *v/t.* (ge-, h) screw.

'**Schrauben|dampfer** ⚓ *m* screw (steamer); '∼**mutter** ⊕ *f* nut; '∼**schlüssel** ⊕ *m* spanner, wrench; '∼**zieher** ⊕ *m* screwdriver.

Schraubstock ⊕ ['ʃraup-] *m* vice, *Am.* vise.

Schrebergarten ['ʃreːbər-] *m* allotment garden.

Schreck [ʃrɛk] *m* (-[e]s/-e) fright, terror; consternation; '∼**bild** *n* bugbear; '∼**en** *m* (-s/-) fright, terror; consternation; '**2en** (ge-) **1.** (*h*) frighten, scare; **2.** *v/i.* (*irr.*, sein): *only in compounds*; '∼**ensbotschaft** *f* alarming *or* terrible news; '∼**ensherrschaft** *f* reign of terror; '**2haft** *adj.* fearful, timid; '**2lich** *adj.* terrible, dreadful (*both a.* F *fig.*); '∼**schuß** *m* scare shot; *fig.* warning shot.

Schrei [ʃrai] *m* (-[e]s/-e) cry; shout; scream.

schreiben ['ʃraibən] **1.** *v/t. and v/i.* (*irr.*, ge-, h) write (*j-m* to s.o.; *über acc.* on); *mit der Maschine* ∼ type(write); **2.** *v/t.* (*irr.*, ge-, h) spell; **3.** **2** *n* (-s/-) letter.

'**Schreiber** *m* (-s/-) writer; secretary, clerk.

schreib|faul *adj.* ['ʃraip-] lazy in writing; '**2feder** *f* pen; '**2fehler** *m* mistake in writing *or* spelling, slip of the pen; '**2heft** *n* exercise-book; '**2mappe** *f* writing-case; '**2maschine** *f* typewriter; (*mit der*) ∼ *schreiben* type(write); '**2material** *n* writing-materials *pl.*, stationery; '**2papier** *n* writing-paper; '**2schrift** *typ. f* script; '**2tisch** *m* (writing-)desk; '**2ung** *f* (-/-*en*) spelling; '**2unterlage** *f* desk pad; '**2waren** *f*/*pl.* writing-materials *pl.*, stationery; '**2warenhändler** *m* stationer; '**2zeug** *n* writing-materials *pl.*

'**schreien** (*irr.*, ge-, h) **1.** *v/t.* shout; scream; **2.** *v/i.* cry (out) (*vor dat.* with *pain, etc.*); *nach* for *bread, etc.*); shout (*vor* with); scream (*with*); '∼**d** *adj. colour*: loud; *injustice*: flagrant.

schreiten ['ʃraitən] *v/i.* (*irr.*, ge-, sein) step, stride (*über acc.* across); *fig.* proceed (*zu* to).

schrie [ʃriː] *pret. of* schreien.
schrieb [ʃriːp] *pret. of* schreiben.
Schrift [ʃrift] *f* (-/-en) (hand-)writing, hand; *typ.* type; character, letter; writing; publication; *die Heilige* ~ the (Holy) Scriptures *pl.*; '~art *f* type; '2deutsch *adj.* literary German; '~führer *m* secretary; '~leiter *m* editor; '2lich 1. *adj.* written, in writing; 2. *adv.* in writing; '~satz *m* ɪɪ pleadings *pl.*; *typ.* composition, type-setting; '~setzer *m* compositor, type-setter; '~sprache *f* literary language; '~steller *m* (-s/-) author, writer; '~stück *n* piece of writing, paper, document; '~tum *n* (-s/*no pl.*) literature; '~wechsel *m* exchange of letters, correspondence; '~zeichen *n* character, letter.
schrill [ʃril] shrill, piercing.
Schritt [ʃrit] 1. *m* (-[e]s/-e) step (*a. fig.*); pace (*a. fig.*); ~e unternehmen take steps; 2. 2 *pret. of* schreiten; '~macher *m* (-s/-) *sports*: pace-maker; '2weise 1. *adj.* gradual; 2. *adv.* a. step by step.
schroff *adj.* [ʃrɔf] rugged, jagged; steep, precipitous; *fig.* harsh, gruff; ~er *Widerspruch* glaring contradiction.
schröpfen ['ʃrœpfən] *v/t.* (ge-, h) ๕ cup; *fig.* milk, fleece.
Schrot [ʃroːt] *m*, *n* (-[e]s/-e) crushed grain; small shot; '~brot *n* wholemeal bread; '~flinte *f* shotgun.
Schrott [ʃrɔt] *m* (-[e]s/-e) scrap (-iron *or* -metal).
schrubben ['ʃrubən] *v/t.* (ge-, h) scrub.
Schrulle ['ʃrulə] *f* (-/-n) whim, fad.
schrumpf|en ['ʃrumpfən] *v/i.* (ge-, sein) shrink (*a.* ⊕, ๕, *fig.*); '2ung *f* (-/-en) shrinking; shrinkage.
Schub [ʃuːp] *m* (-[e]s/⁼e) push, shove; *phys.*, ⊕ thrust; *bread, people, etc.*: batch; '~fach *n* drawer; '~karren *m* wheelbarrow; '~kasten *m* drawer; '~kraft *phys.*, ⊕ *f* thrust; '~lade *f* (-/-n) drawer.
Schubs F [ʃups] *m* (-es/-e) push; '2en F *v/t.* (ge-, h) push.
schüchtern *adj.* ['ʃʏçtərn] shy, bashful, timid; *girl*: coy; '2heit *f* (-/*no pl.*) shyness, bashfulness, timidity; coyness (*of girl*).
schuf [ʃuːf] *pret. of* schaffen 1.
Schuft [ʃuft] *m* (-[e]s/-e) scoundrel,

rascal; cad; '2en F *v/i.* (ge-, h) drudge, slave, plod; '2ig *adj.* scoundrelly, rascally; caddish.
Schuh [ʃuː] *m* (-[e]s/-e) shoe; *j-m et. in die* ~e schieben put the blame for s.th. on s.o.; *wissen, wo der* ~ *drückt* know where the shoe pinches; '~anzieher *m* (-s/-) shoehorn; '~band *n* shoe-lace *or* -string; '~creme *f* shoe-cream, shoe-polish; '~geschäft *n* shoe-shop; '~löffel *m* shoehorn; '~macher *m* (-s/-) shoemaker; '~putzer *m* (-s/-) shoeblack, *Am. a.* shoeshine; '~sohle *f* sole; '~spanner *m* (-s/-) shoetree; '~werk *n*, '~zeug F *n* foot-wear, boots and shoes *pl.*
'Schul|amt *n* school-board; '~arbeit *f* homework; '~bank *f* (school-)desk; '~beispiel *n* test-case, typical example; '~besuch *m* (-[e]s/*no pl.*) attendance at school; '~bildung *f* education; *höhere* ~ secondary education; '~buch *n* school-book.
Schuld [ʃult] *f* 1. (-/*no pl.*) guilt; fault, blame; *es ist s-e* ~ it is his fault, he is to blame for it; 2. (-/-en) debt; ~en machen contract *or* incur debts; '2bewußt *adj.* conscious of one's guilt; '2en ['~dən] *v/t.* (ge-, h): *j-m et.* ~ owe s.o. s.th.; *j-m Dank* ~ be indebted to s.o. (*für* for); '2haft *adj.* ['~haft] culpable.
'Schuldiener *m* school attendant *or* porter.
schuldig *adj.* ['ʃuldiç] guilty (*e-r Sache* of s.th.); *respect, etc.*: due; *j-m et.* ~ sein owe s.o. s.th.; *Dank* ~ sein be indebted to s.o. (*für* for); *für* ~ *befinden* ɪɪ find guilty; '2e ['~gə] *m*, *f* (-n/-n) guilty person; culprit; '2keit *f* (-/*no pl.*) duty, obligation.
'Schuldirektor *m* headmaster, *Am. a.* principal.
'schuld|los *adj.* guiltless, innocent; '2losigkeit *f* (-/*no pl.*) guiltlessness, innocence; '2ner *m* (-s/-) debtor; '2schein *m* evidence of debt, certificate of indebtedness, IOU (= I owe you); '2verschreibung *f* bond, debt certificate.
Schule ['ʃuːlə] *f* (-/-n) school; *höhere* ~ secondary school, *Am. a.* high school; *auf or in der* ~ at school; *in die* ~ *gehen* go to school; '2n *v/t.* (ge-, h) train, school; *pol.* indoctrinate.

Schüler [ˈʃyːlər] *m* (-s/-) schoolboy, pupil; *phls.*, *etc.*: disciple; '**~austausch** *m* exchange of pupils; '**~in** *f* (-/-nen) schoolgirl.

'**Schul|ferien** *pl.* holidays *pl.*, vacation; '**~fernsehen** *n* educational TV; '**~funk** *m* educational broadcast; '**~gebäude** *n* school(house); '**~geld** *n* school fee(s *pl.*), tuition; '**~hof** *m* playground, *Am. a.* schoolyard; '**~kamerad** *m* schoolfellow; '**~lehrer** *m* schoolmaster, teacher; '**~mappe** *f* satchel; '**⁀meistern** *v/t.* (ge-, h) censure pedantically; '**~ordnung** *f* school regulations *pl.*; '**⁀pflichtig** *adj.* schoolable; '**⁀rat** *m* supervisor of schools, school inspector; '**~schiff** *n* training-ship; '**~schluß** *m* end of school; end of term; '**~schwänzer** *m* (-s/-) truant; '**~stunde** *f* lesson.

Schulter [ˈʃʊltər] *f* (-/-n) shoulder; '**~blatt** *anat. n* shoulder-blade; '⁀n *v/t.* (ge-, h) shoulder.

'**Schul|unterricht** *m* school, lessons *pl.*; school instruction; '**~versäumnis** *f* (-/no pl.) absence from school; '**~wesen** *n* educational system; '**~zeugnis** *n* report.

schummeln F [ˈʃʊməln] *v/i.* (ge-, h) cheat, *Am.* F *a.* chisel.

Schund [ʃʊnt] **1.** *m* (-[e]s/no pl.) trash, rubbish (*both a. fig.*); **2.** ⁀ *pret. of* schinden; '**~literatur** *f* trashy literature; '**~roman** *m* trashy novel, *Am. a.* dime novel.

Schuppe [ˈʃʊpə] *f* (-/-n) scale; *~n pl. on head:* dandruff; '**⁀en 1.** *m* (-s/-) shed; *mot.* garage; ✈ hangar; **2.** ⁀ *v/t.* (ge-, h) scale (*fish*); *sich ~ skin:* scale off; '⁀ig *adj.* scaly.

Schür|eisen [ˈʃyːrʔ-] *n* poker; '⁀en *v/t.* (ge-, h) poke; stoke; *fig.* fan, foment.

schürfen [ˈʃʏrfən] (ge-, h) **1.** ⛏ *v/i.* prospect (*nach* for); ⛏ *v/t.* prospect for; *sich den Arm ~* graze one's arm.

Schurk|e [ˈʃʊrkə] *m* (-n/-n) scoundrel, knave; **~erei** [~ˈraɪ] *f* (-/-en) rascality, knavish trick; '⁀isch *adj.* scoundrelly, knavish.

Schürze [ˈʃʏrtsə] *f* (-/-n) apron; *children:* pinafore; '⁀n *v/t.* (ge-, h) tuck up (*skirt*); tie (*knot*); purse (*lips*); '**~njäger** *m* skirt-chaser, *Am. sl.* wolf.

Schuß [ʃʊs] *m* (Schusses/Schüsse)

shot (*a. sports*); ammunition: round; *sound:* report; charge; *wine, etc.:* dash (*a. fig.*); *in ~ sein* be in full swing, be in full working order.

Schüssel [ˈʃʏsəl] *f* (-/-n) basin (*for water, etc.*); bowl, dish, tureen (*for soup, vegetables, etc.*).

'**Schuß|waffe** *f* fire-arm; '**~weite** *f* range; '**~wunde** *f* gunshot wound.

Schuster [ˈʃuːstər] *m* (-s/-) shoemaker; '⁀n *fig. v/i.* (ge-, h) s. pfuschen.

Schutt [ʃʊt] *m* (-[e]s/no pl.) rubbish, refuse; rubble, debris.

Schüttel|frost ⚕ [ˈʃʏtəl-] *m* shivering-fit; '⁀n *v/t.* (ge-, h) shake; *den Kopf ~* shake one's head; *j-m die Hand ~* shake hands with s.o.

schütten [ˈʃʏtən] (ge-, h) **1.** *v/t.* pour; spill (*auf acc.* on); **2.** *v/i.*: *es schüttet* it is pouring with rain.

Schutz [ʃʊts] *m* (-es/no pl.) protection (*gegen, vor dat.* against), defen|ce, *Am.* -se (against, from); shelter (from); safeguard; cover; '**~brille** *f* (e-e *a pair of*) goggles *pl.*

Schütze [ˈʃʏtsə] *m* (-n/-n) marksman, shot; ✗ rifleman; '⁀n *v/t.* (ge-, h) protect (*gegen, vor dat.* against, from), defend (against, from), guard (against, from); shelter (from); safeguard (*rights, etc.*).

Schutzengel [ˈʃʊtsʔ-] *m* guardian angel.

'**Schützen|graben** ✗ *m* trench; '**~könig** *m* champion shot.

'**Schutz|haft** 🏛 *f* protective custody; '**~heilige** *m* patron saint; '**~herr** *m* patron, protector; '**~impfung** ⚕ *f* protective inoculation; *smallpox:* vaccination.

Schützling [ˈʃʏtslɪŋ] *m* (-s/-e) protégé, *female:* protégée.

'**schutz|los** *adj.* unprotected; defen|celess, *Am.* -seless; '⁀mann *m* (-[e]s/⁀er, Schutzleute) policeman, (*police*) constable, *sl.* bobby, *sl.* cop; '⁀marke *f* trade mark, brand; '⁀mittel *n* preservative; ⚕ prophylactic; '⁀patron *m* patron saint; '⁀umschlag *m* (dust-)jacket, wrapper; '⁀zoll *m* protective duty.

Schwabe [ˈʃvaːbə] *m* (-n/-n) Swabian.

schwäbisch *adj.* [ˈʃvɛːbɪʃ] Swabian.

schwach *adj.* [ʃvax] *resistance, team, knees (a. fig.), eyes, heart, voice, character, tea, gr. verb,* ✝ *demand,* etc.: weak; *person, etc.*: infirm; *person, recollection, etc.*: feeble; *sound, light, hope, idea, etc.*: faint; *consolation, attendance, etc.*: poor; *light, recollection, etc.*: dim; *resemblance*: remote; *das ~e Geschlecht* the weaker sex; *~e Seite* weak point or side.

Schwäche ['ʃvɛçə] f (-/-n) weakness (a. *fig.*); infirmity; *fig.* foible; *e-e ~ haben für* have a weakness for; '**2n** v/t. (ge-, h) weaken (a. *fig.*); impair (health).

'**Schwach|heit** f (-/-en) weakness; *fig. a.* frailty; '**~kopf** m simpleton, soft(y), *Am.* F a. sap(head); '**2köpfig** adj. ['~kœpfiç] weak-headed, soft, *Am. sl. a.* sappy.

schwäch|lich adj. ['ʃvɛçliç] weakly, feeble; delicate, frail; '**2ling** m (-s/-e) weakling (a. *fig.*).

'**schwach|sinnig** adj. weak-or feeble-minded; '**2strom** ∮ m (-[e]s/*no pl.*) weak current.

Schwadron ⚔ [ʃva'droːn] f (-/-en) squadron; **2ieren** [~o'niːrən] v/i. (*no* -ge-, h) swagger, vapo(u)r.

Schwager ['ʃvaːgər] m (-s/⁼) brother-in-law.

Schwägerin ['ʃvɛːgərin] f (-/-nen) sister-in-law. [swallow.]

Schwalbe orn. ['ʃvalbə] f (-/-n)

Schwall [ʃval] m (-[e]s/-e) swell, flood; *words*: torrent.

Schwamm [ʃvam] **1.** m (-[e]s/⁼e) sponge; ⚕ fungus; ⚕ dry-rot; **2.** ⚕ pret. of schwimmen; '**2ig** adj. spongy; *face, etc.*: bloated.

Schwan orn. [ʃvaːn] m (-[e]s/⁼e) swan.

schwand [ʃvant] pret. of schwinden.

schwang [ʃvaŋ] pret. of schwingen.

schwanger adj. ['ʃvaŋər] pregnant, with child, in the family way.

schwängern ['ʃvɛŋərn] v/t. (ge-, h) get with child, impregnate (a. *fig.*).

'**Schwangerschaft** f (-/-en) pregnancy.

schwanken ['ʃvaŋkən] v/i. (ge-, h) **1.** (h) *earth, etc.*: shake, rock; ✝ *prices*: fluctuate; *branches, etc.*: sway; *fig.* waver, oscillate, vacillate; **2.** (sein) stagger, totter.

Schwanz [ʃvants] m (-es/⁼e) tail (a. ⚔, *ast.*); *fig.* train.

schwänz|eln ['ʃvɛntsəln] v/i. (ge-, h) wag one's tail; *fig.* fawn (um [up]on); '**~en** v/t. (ge-, h) cut (lecture, etc.);

die Schule ~ play truant, *Am. a.* play hooky.

Schwarm [ʃvarm] m (-[e]s/⁼e) bees, *etc.*: swarm; *birds*: a. flight, flock; *fish*: school, schoal; *birds, girls, etc.*: bevy; F *fig.* fancy, craze; *p.*: idol, hero; flame.

schwärmen ['ʃvɛrmən] v/i. (ge-, h) bees, *etc.*: swarm; *fig.*: revel; rave (von about, of), gush (over); ~ *für* be wild about, adore s.o.

'**Schwärmer** m (-s/-) enthusiast; *esp. eccl.* fanatic; visionary; *fireworks*: cracker, squib; *zo.* hawkmoth; **~ei** [~'raɪ] f (-/-en) enthusiasm (für for); idolization; ecstasy; *esp. eccl.* fanaticism; '**2isch** adj. enthusiastic; gushing; raving; adoring; *esp. eccl.* fanatic(al).

Schwarte ['ʃvartə] f (-/-n) bacon: rind; F *fig.* old book.

schwarz adj. [ʃvarts] black (a. *fig.*); dark; dirty; ~es Brett notice-board, *Am.* bulletin board; ~es Brot brown bread; ~er Mann bog(e)y; ~er Markt black market; ~ auf weiß in black and white; *auf die* ~e *Liste setzen* blacklist; '**2arbeit** f illicit work; '**2brot** n brown bread; '**2e** m, f (-n/-n) black.

Schwärze ['ʃvɛrtsə] f (-/*no pl.*) blackness (a. *fig.*); darkness; '**2n** v/t. (ge-, h) blacken.

'**schwarz|fahren** F v/i. (*irr.* fahren, sep., -ge-, sein) travel without a ticket; *mot.* drive without a licence; '**2fahrer** m fare-dodger; *mot.* person driving without a licence; '**2fahrt** f ride without a ticket; *mot.* drive without a licence; '**2handel** m illicit trade, black marketeering; '**2händler** m black marketeer; '**2hörer** m listener without a licence.

'**schwärzlich** adj. blackish.

'**Schwarz|markt** m black market; '**~seher** m pessimist; *TV*: viewer without a licence; '**~sender** m pirate broadcasting station; '**~weißfilm** m black-and-white film.

schwatzen ['ʃvatsən] v/i. (ge-, h) chat; chatter, tattle.

schwätz|en ['ʃvɛtsən] v/i. (ge-, h) s. schwatzen; '**2er** m (-s/-) chatterbox; tattler, prattler; gossip.

'**schwatzhaft** adj. talkative, garrulous.

Schwebe *fig.* ['ʃveːbə] f (-/*no pl.*): *in der* ~ *sein* be in suspense; *law,* *rule, etc.:* be in abeyance; '**_bahn** *f* aerial railway *or* ropeway; '**2n** *v/i.* (ge-, *h)* be suspended; *bird:* hover *(a. fig.);* glide; *fig.* be pending *(a. ⁂); in Gefahr ~ be* in danger.

Schwed|e ['ʃveːdə] *m* (-n/-n) Swede; '**2isch** *adj.* Swedish.

Schwefel 🜍 ['ʃveːfəl] *m* (-s/no pl.) sulphur, *Am. a.* sulfur; '**_säure** 🜍 *f (-/no pl.)* sulphuric acid, *Am. a.* sulfuric acid.

Schweif [ʃvaɪf] *m* (-[e]s/-e) tail *(a. ast.); fig.* train; '**2en** (ge-) **1.** *v/i.* (sein) rove, ramble; **2.** ⊕ *v/t.* (h) curve; scallop.

schweigen ['ʃvaɪgən] **1.** *v/i. (irr.,* ge-, *h)* be silent; **2.** 2 *n* (-s/no pl.) silence; '**_d** *adj.* silent.

schweigsam *adj.* ['ʃvaɪkzaːm] taciturn; '**2keit** *f* (-/no pl.) taciturnity.

Schwein [ʃvaɪn] *n* **1.** (-[e]s/-e) *zo.* pig, hog, swine *(all a. contp. fig.);* **2.** F (-[e]s/no pl.): *~ haben* be lucky.

'**Schweine|braten** *m* roast pork; '**_fleisch** *n* pork; '**_hund** F *contp.* *m* swine; **_rei** [~ˈraɪ] *f (-/-en)* mess; dirty trick; smut(ty story); '**_stall** *m* pigsty *(a. fig.).*

'**schweinisch** *fig. adj.* swinish; smutty.

'**Schweinsleder** *n* pigskin.

Schweiß [ʃvaɪs] *m* (-es/-e) sweat, perspiration; '**2en** ⊕ *v/t.* (ge-, *h)* weld; '**_er** ⊕ *m* (-s/-) welder; '**_fuß** *m* perspiring foot; '**2ig** *adj.* sweaty, damp with sweat.

Schweizer ['ʃvaɪtsər] *m* (-s/-) Swiss; *on farm:* dairyman.

schwelen ['ʃveːlən] *v/i.* (ge-, *h)* smo(u)lder *(a. fig.).*

schwelg|en ['ʃvɛlgən] *v/i.* (ge-, *h)* lead a luxurious life; revel; *fig.* revel *(in dat.* in); '**2er** *m* (-s/-) revel(l)er; epicure; 2**erei** [~ˈraɪ] *f (-/-en)* revel(ry), feasting; '**_erisch** *adj.* luxurious; revel(l)ing.

Schwell|e ['ʃvɛlə] *f*(-/-n) sill, threshold *(a. fig.);* 🚉 sleeper, *Am.* tie; '**2en 1.** *v/i. (irr.,* ge-, *sein)* swell (out); **2.** *v/t.* (ge-, *h)* swell; '**_ung** *f* (-/-en) swelling.

Schwemme ['ʃvɛmə] *f (-/-n)* watering-place; horse-pond; *at tavern, etc.:* taproom; 🖫 glut *(of fruit, etc.).*

Schwengel ['ʃvɛŋəl] *m* (-s/-) clapper *(of bell);* handle *(of pump).*

schwenk|en ['ʃvɛŋkən] (ge-) **1.** *v/t.* (h) swing; wave *(hat, etc.);* brandish *(stick, etc.);* rinse *(washing);* **2.** *v/i.* (sein) turn, wheel; '**2ung** *f (-/-en)* turn; *fig.* change of mind.

schwer [ʃveːr] **1.** *adj.* heavy; *problem, etc.:* hard, difficult; *illness, mistake, etc.:* serious; *punishment, etc.:* severe; *fault, etc.:* grave; *wine, cigar, etc.:* strong; *~e Zeiten* hard times; *2 Pfund ~ sein* weigh two pounds; **2.** *adv.:* *~ arbeiten* work hard; *~ hören* be hard of hearing; '**2e** *f (-/no pl.)* heaviness; *phys.* gravity *(a. fig.);* severity; '**_fällig** *adj.* heavy, slow; clumsy; '**2gewicht** *n sports:* heavy-weight; *fig.* main emphasis; '**2gewichtler** *m* (-s/-) *sports:* heavy-weight; '**_hörig** *adj.* hard of hearing; '**2industrie** *f* heavy industry; '**2kraft** *phys. f (-/no pl.)* gravity; '**_lich** *adv.* hardly, scarcely; '**2mut** *f (-/no pl.)* melancholy; **_mütig** *adj.* ['~myːtɪç] melancholy; '**2punkt** *m* centre of gravity, *Am.* center of gravity; *fig.:* crucial point; emphasis.

Schwert [ʃveːrt] *n* (-[e]s/-er) sword.

'**Schwer|verbrecher** *m* felon; '**2verdaulich** *adj.* indigestible, heavy; '**2verständlich** *adj.* difficult *or* hard to understand; '**2verwundet** *adj.* seriously wounded; '**2wiegend** *fig. adj.* weighty, momentous. [nurse.]

Schwester ['ʃvɛstər] *f (-/-n)* sister.)

schwieg [ʃviːk] *pret. of schweigen.*

Schwieger|eltern ['ʃviːgər-] *pl.* parents-in-law *pl.;* '**_mutter** *f* mother-in-law; '**_sohn** *m* son-in-law; '**_tochter** *f* daughter-in-law; '**_vater** *m* father-in-law.

Schwiel|e ['ʃviːlə] *f (-/-n)* callosity; '**2ig** *adj.* callous.

schwierig *adj.* ['ʃviːrɪç] difficult, hard; '**2keit** *f (-/-en)* difficulty, trouble.

Schwimm|bad ['ʃvɪm-] *n* swimming-bath, *Am.* swimming pool; '**2en** *v/i. (irr.,* ge-, *h)* **1.** (sein) swim; *thing:* float; *ich bin über den Fluß geschwommen* I swam across the river; *in Geld ~* be rolling in money; **2.** (h) swim; *ich habe lange unter Wasser geschwommen* I swam under water for a long time; '**_gür-**

tel m swimming-belt; lifebelt; '~haut f web; '~lehrer m swimming-instructor; '~weste f life-jacket.

Schwindel ['ʃvindəl] m (-s/no pl.) vertigo, giddiness, dizziness; F fig.: swindle, humbug, sl. eyewash; cheat, fraud; '~anfall ♣ m fit of dizziness; '♀erregend adj. dizzy (a. fig.); '~firma ♣ f long firm, Am. wildcat firm; '♀n v/i. (ge-, h) cheat, humbug, swindle.

schwinden ['ʃvindən] v/i. (irr., ge-, sein) dwindle, grow less; strength, colour, etc.: fade.

'**Schwindl|er** m (-s/-) swindler, cheat, humbug; liar; '♀ig ♣ adj. giddy, dizzy.

Schwind|sucht ♣ ['ʃvint-] f (-/no pl.) consumption; '♀süchtig ♣ adj. consumptive.

Schwing|e ['ʃviŋə] f (-/-n) wing, poet. pinion; swingle; '♀en (irr., ge-, h) **1.** v/t. swing; brandish (weapon); swingle (flax); **2.** v/i. swing; ⊕ oscillate; sound, etc.: vibrate; '~ung f (-/-en) oscillation; vibration.

Schwips F [ʃvips] m (-es/-e): e-n ~ haben be tipsy, have had a drop too much.

schwirren ['ʃvirən] v/i. (ge-) **1.** (sein) whir(r); arrow, etc.: whiz(z); insects: buzz; rumours, etc.: buzz, circulate; **2.** (h): mir schwirrt der Kopf my head is buzzing.

'**Schwitz|bad** n sweating-bath, hot-air bath, vapo(u)r bath; '♀en (ge-, h) **1.** v/i. sweat, perspire; **2.** F fig. v/t.: Blut und Wasser ~ be in great anxiety.

schwoll [ʃvɔl] pret. of schwellen.

schwor [ʃvoːr] pret. of schwören.

schwören ['ʃvøːrən] (irr., ge-, h) **1.** v/t. swear; e-n Meineid ~ commit perjury; j-m Rache ~ vow vengeance against s.o.; **2.** v/i. swear (bei by); ~ auf (acc.) have great belief in, F swear by.

schwül adj. [ʃvyːl] sultry, oppressively hot; '♀e f (-/no pl.) sultriness. [bast.]

Schwulst [ʃvulst] m (-es/♯e) bom-

schwülstig adj. ['ʃvylstiç] bombastic, turgid.

Schwund [ʃvunt] m (-[e]s/no pl.) dwindling; wireless, etc.: fading; ♣ atrophy.

Schwung [ʃvuŋ] m (-[e]s/♯e) swing;

fig. verve, go; flight (of imagination); buoyancy; '♀haft ♣ adj. flourishing, brisk; '~rad ⊕ n flywheel; watch, clock: balance-wheel; '♀voll adj. full of energy or verve; attack, translation, etc.: spirited; style, etc.: racy.

Schwur [ʃvuːr] m (-[e]s/♯e) oath; '~gericht ♣ n England, Wales: appr. court of assize.

sechs [zeks] **1.** adj. six; **2.** ♀ f (-/-en) six; '♀eck n (-[e]s/-e) hexagon; '~eckig adj. hexagonal; '~fach adj. sixfold, sextuple; '~mal adv. six times; '~monatig adj. lasting or of six months, six-months ...; '~monatlich **1.** adj. six-monthly; **2.** adv. every six months; **~stündig** adj. ['~ʃtyndiç] lasting or of six hours, six-hour ...; ♀'tagerennen n cycling: six-day race; '~tägig adj. ['~tɛːgiç] lasting or of six days.

sechs|te ['zekstə] adj. sixth; ♀'tel n (-s/-) sixth (part); '~tens adv. sixthly, in the sixth place.

sech|zehn(te) adj.['zɛç-] sixteen(th); '~zig adj. ['~tsiç] sixty; '~zigste adj. sixtieth.

See [zeː] **1.** m (-s/-n) lake; **2.** f (-/no pl.) sea; an die ~ gehen go to the seaside; in ~ gehen or stechen put to sea; auf ~ at sea; auf hoher ~ on the high seas; zur ~ gehen go to sea; **3.** f (-/-n) sea, billow; '~bad n seaside resort; '~fahrer m sailor, navigator; '~fahrt f navigation; voyage; '♀fest adj. seaworthy; ~ sein be a good sailor; '~gang m (motion of the) sea; '~hafen m seaport; '~handel ♣ m maritime trade; '~herrschaft f naval supremacy; '~hund zo. m seal; '♀krank adj. seasick; '~krankheit f (-/no pl.) seasickness; '~krieg m naval war(fare).

Seele ['zeːlə] f (-/-n) soul (a. fig.); mit or von ganzer ~ with all one's heart.

'**Seelen|größe** f (-/no pl.) greatness of soul or mind; '~heil n salvation, spiritual welfare; '♀los adj. soulless; '~qual f anguish of mind, (mental) agony; '~ruhe f peace of mind; coolness.

'**seelisch** adj. psychic(al), mental.

'**Seelsorge** f (-/no pl.) cure of souls; ministerial work; '~r m (-s/-) pastor, minister.

S

'**See**|**macht** f naval power; '**mann** m (-[e]s/Seeleute) seaman, sailor; '**meile** f nautical mile; '**not** f (-/no pl.) distress (at sea); '**räuber** m pirate; **räuberei** [~'raɪ] f (-/-en) piracy; '**recht** n maritime law; '**reise** f voyage; '**schiff** n seagoing ship; '**schlacht** f naval battle; '**schlange** f sea serpent; '**sieg** m naval victory; '**stadt** f seaside town; '**streitkräfte** f/pl. naval forces pl.; **²tüchtig** adj. seaworthy; '**warte** f naval observatory; '**weg** m sea-route; auf dem ~ by sea; '**wesen** n (-s/no pl.) maritime or naval affairs pl.

Segel ['ze:gəl] n (-s/-) sail; unter ~ gehen set sail '**boot** n sailing-boat, Am. sailboat; sports: yacht; '**flie-gen** n (-s/no pl.) gliding, soaring; '**flug** m gliding flight, glide; '**flugzeug** n glider; '²n (ge-) 1. v/i. (h, sein) sail; sports: yacht; 2. v/t. (h) sail; '**schiff** n sailing-ship, sailing-vessel; '**sport** m yachting; '**tuch** n (-[e]s/-e) sailcloth, canvas.

Segen ['ze:gən] m (-s/-) blessing (a. fig.), esp. eccl. benediction; '²s-reich adj. blessed.

Segler ['ze:glər] m (-s/-) sailing-vessel, sailing-ship; fast, good, etc. sailer; yachtsman.

segn|**en** ['ze:gnən] v/t. (ge-, h) bless; '²ung f (-/-en) s. Segen.

sehen ['ze:ən] (irr., ge-, h) 1. v/i. see; gut ~ have good eyes; ~ auf (acc.) look at; be particular about; ~ nach look for; look after; 2. v/t. see; notice; watch; observe; '**swert** adj. worth seeing; '²**swürdigkeit** f (-/-en) object of interest, curiosity; ~en pl. sights pl. (of a place).

Seher ['ze:ər] m (-s/-) seer, prophet; '**blick** m (-[e]s/no pl.) prophetic vision; '**gabe** f (-/no pl.) gift of prophecy.

'**Seh**|**fehler** m visual defect; '**kraft** f vision, eyesight.

Sehne ['ze:nə] f (-/-n) anat. sinew, tendon; string (of bow); Å chord.

'**sehnen** v/refl. (ge-, h) long (nach for), yearn (for, after); sich danach ~ zu inf. be longing to inf. [nerve.|

'**Sehnerv** anat. m visual or optic]

'**sehnig** adj. sinewy (a. fig.), stringy.

'**sehn**|**lich** adj. longing; ardent;

passionate; '²**sucht** f longing, yearning; '**süchtig** adj., '**suchts-voll** adj. longing, yearning; eyes, etc.: a. wistful.

sehr adv. [ze:r] before adj. and adv.: very, most; with vb.: (very) much, greatly.

'**Seh**|**rohr** ⚓ n periscope; '**weite** f range of sight, visual range; in ~ within eyeshot or sight.

seicht adj. [zaɪçt] shallow (fig. a. superficial.

Seide ['zaɪdə] f (-/-n) silk.

'**seiden** adj. silk, silken (a. fig.); '²**flor** m silk gauze; '²**glanz** m silky lust|re, Am. -er; '²**händler** m mercer; '²**papier** n tissue(-paper); '²**raupe** zo. f silkworm; '²**spin-nerei** f silk-spinning mill; '²**stoff** m silk cloth or fabric.

'**seidig** adj. silky.

Seife ['zaɪfə] f (-/-n) soap.

'**Seifen**|**blase** f soap-bubble; '**ki-stenrennen** n soap-box derby; '**lauge** f (soap-)suds pl.; '**pulver** n soap-powder; '**schale** f soap-dish; '**schaum** m lather.

'**seifig** adj. soapy.

seih|**en** ['zaɪən] v/t. (ge-, h) strain, filter; '²**er** m (-s/-) strainer, colander.

Seil [zaɪl] n (-[e]s/-e) rope; '**bahn** f funicular or cable railway; '**er** m (-s/-) rope-maker; '**tänzer** m rope-dancer.

sein¹ [zaɪn] 1. v/i. (irr., ge-, sein) be; exist; 2. ² n (-s/no pl.) being; existence.

sein² poss. pron. [~] his, her, its (in accordance with gender of possessor); der (die, das) ~e his, hers, its; ~ Glück machen make one's fortune; die Seinen pl. his family or people.

'**seiner**|'**seits** adv. for his part; '**zeit** adv. then, at that time; in those days.

'**seines**|**gleichen** pron. his equal(s pl.); j-n wie ~ behandeln treat s.o. as one's equal; er hat nicht ~ he has no equal; there is no one like him.

seit [zaɪt] 1. prp. (dat.): ~ 1945 since 1945; ~ drei Wochen for three weeks; 2. cj. since; es ist ein Jahr her, ~ ... it is a year now since ...; '**dem** [~'de:m] 1. adv. since or from that time, ever since; 2. cj. since.

Seite ['zaɪtə] f (-/-n) side (a. fig.); flank (a. ✕, △); page (of book).

'**Seiten|ansicht** f profile, side-view; '~**blick** m side-glance; '~**flügel** △ m wing; '~**hieb** fig. m innuendo, sarcastic remark; '2**s** prp. (gen.) on the part of; by; '~**schiff** △ n church: aisle; '~**sprung** fig. m extra-marital adventure; '~**straße** f bystreet; '~**stück** fig. n counterpart (zu of); '~**weg** m by-way.

seit'her adv. since (then, that time).

'**seit|lich** adj. lateral; ~**wärts** adv. ['~vɛrts] sideways; aside.

Sekret|är [zekre'tɛːr] m (-s/-e) secretary; bureau; ~**ariat** [~ari'aːt] n (-[e]s/-e) secretary's office; secretariat(e); ~**ärin** f (-/-nen) secretary.

Sekt [zɛkt] m (-[e]s/-e) champagne.

Sekt|e ['zɛktə] f (-/-n) sect; ~**ierer** [~'tiːrər] m (-s/-) sectarian.

Sektor ['zɛktɔr] m (-s/-en) ⚔, ✕, pol. sector; fig. field, branch.

Sekunde [ze'kundə] f (-/-n) second; ~**nbruchteil** m split second; ~**nzeiger** m second-hand.

selb adj. [zɛlp] same; ~**er** F pron. ['~bər] s. selbst 1.

selbst [zɛlpst] 1. pron. self; personally; ich ~ I myself; von ~ p. of one's own accord; thing: by itself, automatically; 2. adv. even; 3. 2 n (-/no pl.) (one's own) self; ego.

selbständig adj. ['zɛlpʃtɛndiç] independent; sich ~ machen set up for o.s.; 2**keit** f (-/no pl.) independence.

'**Selbst|anlasser** mot. m self-starter; '~**anschluß** teleph. m automatic connection; '~**bedienungsladen** m self-service shop; '~**beherrschung** f self-command, self-control; '~**bestimmung** f self-determination; '~**betrug** m self-deception; 2**bewußt** adj. self-confident, self-reliant; '~**bewußtsein** n self-confidence, self-reliance; '~**binder** m (-s/-) tie; '~**erhaltung** f self-preservation; '~**erkenntnis** f self-knowledge; '~**erniedrigung** f self-abasement; 2**gefällig** adj. (self-)complacent; '~**gefälligkeit** f (-/no pl.) (self-)complacency; '~**gefühl** n (-[e]s/no pl.) self-reliance; 2**gemacht** adj. ['~gəmaxt] home-made; '2**gerecht** adj. self-right-

eous; '~**gespräch** n soliloquy, monolog(ue); '2**herrlich** 1. adj. high-handed, autocratic(al); 2. adj. with a high hand; '~**hilfe** f self-help; '~**kostenpreis** ✝ m cost price; '~**laut** gr. m vowel; '2**los** adj. unselfish, disinterested; '~**mord** m suicide; '~**mörder** m suicide; '2**mörderisch** adj. suicidal; '2**sicher** adj. self-confident, self-assured; '~**sucht** f (-/no pl.) selfishness, ego(t)ism; '2**süchtig** adj. selfish, ego(t)istic(al); '2**tätig** ⊕ adj. self-acting, automatic; '~**täuschung** f self-deception; '~**überwindung** f (-/no pl.) self-conquest; '~**unterricht** m self-instruction; '~**verleugnung** f self-denial; '~**versorger** m (-s/-) self-supporter; '2**verständlich** 1. adj. self-evident, obvious; 2. adv. of course, naturally; ~! a. by all means!; '~**verständlichkeit** f 1. (-/-en) matter of course; 2. (-/no pl.) matter-of-factness; '~**verteidigung** f self-defen|ce, Am. -se; '~**vertrauen** n self-confidence, self-reliance; '~**verwaltung** f self-government, autonomy; 2**zufrieden** adj. self-satisfied; '~**zufriedenheit** f self-satisfaction; '~**zweck** m (-[e]s/no pl.) end in itself.

selig adj. ['zeːliç] eccl. blessed; late, deceased; fig. blissful, overjoyed; '2**keit** fig. f (-/-en) bliss, very great joy.

Sellerie ⚘ ['zɛləriː] m (-s/-[s]), f (-/-) celery.

selten ['zɛltən] 1. adj. rare; scarce; 2. adv. rarely, seldom; 2**heit** f (-/-en) rarity, scarcity; rarity, curio(sity); '2**heitswert** m (-[e]s/no pl.) scarcity value.

Selterswasser ['zɛltərs-] n (-s/ᵘ) seltzer (water), soda-water.

seltsam adj. ['zɛltzaːm] strange, odd.

Semester univ. [ze'mɛstər] n (-s/-) term.

Semikolon gr. [zemi'koːlɔn] n (-s/-s, Semikola) semicolon.

Seminar [zemi'naːr] n (-s/-e) univ. seminar; seminary (for priests).

Senat [ze'naːt] m (-[e]s/-e) senate; parl. Senate.

send|en ['zɛndən] v/t. 1. (lirr.,) ge-, h) send; forward; 2. (ge-, h) transmit; broadcast, Am. a. radio(broadcast); telecast; '2er m (-s/-) transmitter; broadcasting station.

'Sende|raum m (broadcasting) studio; '~zeichen n interval signal.

'Sendung f (-/-en) ✝ consignment, shipment; broadcast; fig. mission. [♀).]

Senf [zɛnf] m (-[e]s/-e) mustard (a.)

sengen ['zɛŋən] v/t. (ge-, h) singe, scorch; '~d adj. heat: parching.

senil adj. [ze'ni:l] senile; 2ität [~ili'tɛ:t] f (-/no pl.) senility.

senior adj. ['ze:niɔr] senior.

Senk|blei ['zɛŋk-] n △ plumb, plummet; ♣ a. sounding-lead; '2e geogr. f (-/-en) depression, hollow; '2en v/t. (ge-, h) lower; sink (a. voice); let down; bow (head); cut (prices, etc.); sich ~ land, buildings, etc.: sink, subside; ceiling, etc.: sag; '~fuß ℱ m flat-foot; '~fußeinlage f arch support; '~grube f cesspool; '2recht adj. vertical, esp. ♣ perpendicular; '~ung f (-/-en) geogr. depression, hollow; lowering, reduction (of prices); ℱ sedimentation.

Sensation [zɛnza'tsjo:n] f (-/-en) sensation; 2ell [~o'nɛl] sensational; ~slust f (-/no pl.) sensationalism; ~spresse f yellow press.

Sense ['zɛnzə] f (-/-n) scythe.

sensi|bel adj. [zɛn'zi:bəl] sensitive; 2bilität [~ibili'tɛ:t] f (-/no pl.) sensitiveness.

sentimental adj. [zɛntimɛn'ta:l] sentimental; 2ität [~ali'tɛ:t] f (-/-en) sentimentality.

September [zɛp'tɛmbər] m (-[s]/-) September.

Serenade ♩ [zere'na:də] f (-/-n) serenade.

Serie ['ze:rjə] f (-/-n) series; set; billiards: break; '2nmäßig 1. adj. standard; 2. adv.: ~ herstellen produce in mass; '~nproduktion f mass production.

seriös adj. [ze'rjø:s] serious; trustworthy, reliable.

Serum ['ze:rum] n (-s/Seren, Sera) serum.

Service¹ [zɛr'vi:s] n (-s/-) service, set.

Service² ['zø:rvis] m, n (-/-s) service.

servier|en [zɛr'vi:rən] v/t. (no -ge-, h) serve; 2wagen m trolley(-table).

Serviette [zɛr'vjɛtə] f (-/-n) (table-)napkin.

Sessel ['zɛsəl] m (-s/-) armchair, easy chair; '~lift m chair-lift.

seßhaft adj. ['zɛshaft] settled, established; resident.

Setzei ['zɛts²-] n fried egg.

'setzen (ge-) 1. v/t. (h) set, place, put; typ. compose; ☞ plant; erect, raise (monument); stake (money) (auf acc. on); sich ~ sit down, take a seat; bird: perch; foundations of house, sediment, etc.: settle; 2. v/i. (h): ~ auf (acc.) back (horse, etc.); 3. v/i. (sein): ~ über (acc.) leap (wall, etc.); clear (hurdle, etc.); jump (ditch, etc.).

'Setzer typ. m (-s/-) compositor, type-setter; ~ei typ. [~'raɪ] f (-/-en) composing-room.

Seuche ['zɔʏçə] f (-/-n) epidemic (disease).

seufz|en ['zɔʏftsən] v/i. (ge-, h) sigh; 2er m (-s/-) sigh.

sexuell adj. [zɛksu'ɛl] sexual.

sezieren [ze'tsi:rən] v/t. (no -ge-, h) dissect (a. fig.).

sich refl. pron. [ziç] oneself; sg. himself, herself, itself; pl. themselves; sg. yourself, pl. yourselves; each other, one another; sie blickte ~ um she looked about her.

Sichel ['ziçəl] f (-/-n) sickle; s. Mondsichel.

sicher ['ziçər] 1. adj. secure (vor dat. from), safe (from); proof (against); hand: steady; certain, sure; positive; aus ~er Quelle from a reliable source; e-r Sache ~ sein be sure of s.th.; 2. adv. s. sicherlich; um ~ zu gehen to be on the safe side, to make sure.

'Sicherheit f (-/-en) security; safety; surety, certainty; positiveness; assurance (of manner); in ~ bringen place in safety; '~snadel f safety-pin; '~sschloß n safety-lock.

'sicher|lich adv. surely, certainly; undoubtedly; er wird ~ kommen he is sure to come; '~n v/t. (ge-, h) secure (a. ✕, ⊕); guarantee (a. ✝); protect, safeguard; sich et. ~ secure (prize, seat, etc.); '~stellen v/t. (sep., -ge-, h) secure; '2ung f (-/-en) securing; safeguard(ing); ✝ security, guaranty; ⊕ safety device; ✦ fuse.

Sicht [ziçt] f (-/no pl.) visibility;

view; *in ~ kommen* come in(to) view or sight; *auf lange ~* in the long run; *auf or bei ~* ✝ at sight; '**2bar** *adj.* visible; '**2en** *v/t.* (ge-, h) ⚓ sight; *fig.* sift; '**2lich** *adv.* visibly; '**~vermerk** *m* visé, visa (*on passport*).

sickern ['zikərn] *v/i.* (ge-, sein) trickle, ooze, seep.

sie *pers. pron.* [zi:] *nom.:* sg. she, *pl.* they; *acc.:* sg. her, *pl.* them; *Sie nom. and acc.:* sg. and pl. you.

Sieb [zi:p] *n* (-[e]s/-e) sieve; riddle (*for soil, gravel, etc.*).

sieben¹ ['zi:bən] *v/t.* (ge-, h) sieve, sift; riddle.

sieben² [~] **1.** *adj.* seven; **2.** 2 *f* (-/-) (number) seven; *böse ~* shrew, vixen; '**~fach** *adj.* sevenfold; '**~mal** *adj.* seven times; '**2sachen** F *f/pl.* belongings *pl.*, F traps *pl.*; '**~te** *adj.* seventh; '**2tel** *n* (-s/-) seventh (part); '**~tens** *adv.* seventhly, in the seventh place.

sieb|zehn(te) *adj.* ['zi:p-] seventeen(th); **~zig** *adj.* ['~tsiç] seventy; '**~zigste** *adj.* seventieth.

siech *adj.* [zi:ç] sickly; '**2tum** *n* (-s/*no pl.*) sickliness, lingering illness.

Siedehitze ['zi:də-] *f* boiling-heat.

siedeln ['zi:dəln] *v/i.* (ge-, h) settle; *Am. a.* homestead.

siede|n ['zi:dən] *v/t. and v/i.* ([irr.,] ge-, h) boil, simmer; '**2punkt** *m* boiling-point (*a. fig.*).

Siedler ['zi:dlər] *m* (-s/-) settler; *Am. a.* homesteader; '**~stelle** *f* settler's holding; *Am. a.* homestead. [ing estate.]

'**Siedlung** *f* (-/-en) settlement; hous-[

Sieg [zi:k] *m* (-[e]s/-e) victory (*über acc.* over); *sports:* a. win; *den ~ davontragen* win the day, be victorious.

Siegel ['zi:gəl] *n* (-s/-) seal (*a. fig.*); signet; '**~lack** *m* sealing-wax; '**2n** *v/t.* (ge-, h) seal; '**~ring** *m* signet-ring.

sieg|en ['zi:gən] *v/i.* (ge-, h) be victorious (*über acc.* over), conquer *s.o.*; *sports:* win; '**2er** *m* (-s/-) conqueror, *rhet.* victor; *sports:* winner.

Siegeszeichen ['zi:gəs-] *n* trophy.

'**siegreich** *adj.* victorious, triumphant.

Signal [zi'gna:l] *n* (-s/-e) signal; **2isieren** [~ali'zi:rən] *v/t.* (*no* -ge-, h) signal.

Silbe ['zilbə] *f* (-/-n) syllable; '**~n-trennung** *f* syllabi(fi)cation.

Silber ['zilbər] *n* (-s/*no pl.*) silver; *s. Tafelsilber*; '**2n** *adj.* (of) silver; '**~zeug** F *n* silver plate, *Am. a.* silverware.

Silhouette [zilu'etə] *f* (-/-n) silhouette; skyline.

Silvester [zil'vestər] *n* (-s/-), **~abend** *m* new-year's eve.

simpel ['zimpəl] **1.** *adj.* plain, simple; stupid, silly; **2.** 2 *m* (-s/-) simpleton.

Sims [zims] *m*, *n* (-es/-e) ledge; sill (*of window*); mantelshelf (*of fireplace*); shelf; △ cornice.

Simul|ant [zimu'lant] *m* (-en/-en) *esp.* ⚔, ⚓ malingerer; **2ieren** (*no* -ge-, h) **1.** *v/t.* sham, feign, simulate (*illness, etc.*); **2.** *v/i.* sham, feign; *esp.* ⚔, ⚓ malinger.

Sinfonie ♪ [zinfo'ni:] *f* (-/-n) symphony.

sing|en ['ziŋən] *v/t. and v/i.* (irr., ge-, h) sing; *vom Blatt ~* sing at sight; *nach Noten ~* sing from music; '**2sang** F *m* (-[e]s/*no pl.*) singsong; '**2spiel** *n* musical comedy; '**2stimme** ♪ *f* vocal part.

Singular *gr.* ['ziŋgula:r] *m* (-s/-e) singular (number).

'**Singvogel** *m* song-bird, songster.

sinken ['ziŋkən] *v/i.* (irr., ge-, sein) sink; *ship:* a. founder, go down; ✝ *prices:* fall, drop, go down; *den Mut ~ lassen* lose courage.

Sinn [zin] *m* (-[e]s/-e) sense; taste (*für* for); tendency; sense, meaning; *von ~en sein* be out of one's senses; *im ~ haben* have in mind; *in gewissem ~e* in a sense; '**~bild** *n* symbol, emblem; '**2bildlich** *adj.* symbolic(al), emblematic; '**2en** *v/i.* (irr., ge-, h): *auf Rache ~* meditate revenge.

'**Sinnen|lust** *f* sensuality; '**~mensch** *m* sensualist; '**~rausch** *m* intoxication of the senses.

sinnentstellend *adj.* ['zin?-] garbling, distorting. [world.]

'**Sinnenwelt** *f* (-/*no pl.*) material[

'**Sinnes|änderung** *f* change of mind; '**~art** *f* disposition, mentality; '**~organ** *n* sense-organ; '**~täuschung** *f* illusion, hallucination.

'**sinn|lich** *adj.* sensual; material; '**2lichkeit** *f* (-/*no pl.*) sensuality; '**~los** *adj.* senseless; futile, useless;

S

Sinnlosigkeit

'⍀losigkeit f (-/-en) senselessness; futility, uselessness; '⍀reich adj. ingenious; '⍀verwandt adj. synonymous.

Sipp|e ['zipə] f (-/-n) tribe; (blood-)relations pl.; family; '⍀schaft contp. f (-/-en) relations pl.; fig. clan, clique; die ganze ~ the whole lot.

Sirene [zi're:nə] f (-/-n) siren.

Sirup ['zi:rup] m (-s/-e) syrup, Am. sirup; treacle, molasses sg.

Sitte ['zitə] f (-/-n) custom; habit; usage; ~n pl. morals pl.; manners pl.

'Sitten|bild n, '⍀gemälde n genre (-painting); fig. picture of manners and morals; '⍀gesetz n moral law; '⍀lehre f ethics pl.; '⍀los adj. immoral; '⍀losigkeit f (-/-en) immorality; '⍀polizei f vice squad; '⍀prediger m moralizer; '⍀richter fig. m censor, moralizer; '⍀streng adj. puritanic(al).

'sittlich adj. moral; '⍀keit f (-/no pl.) morality; '⍀keitsverbrechen n sexual crime.

'sittsam adj. modest; '⍀keit f (-/no pl.) modesty.

Situation [zitua'tsjo:n] f (-/-en) situation.

Sitz [zits] m (-es/-e) seat (a. fig.); fit (of dress, etc.); 'sitzen v/i. (irr., ge-, h) sit, be seated; dress, etc.: fit; blow, etc.: tell; F fig. do time; ~ bleiben remain seated, keep one's seat; '⍀bleiben v/i. (irr. bleiben, sep., -ge-, sein) girl at dance: F be a wallflower; girl: be left on the shelf; at school: not to get one's remove; ~ auf (dat.) be left with (goods) on one's hands; '⍀d adj.: ~e Tätigkeit sedentary work; '⍀lassen v/t. (irr. lassen, sep., [no] -ge-, h) leave s.o. in the lurch, let s.o. down; girl: jilt (lover); leave (girl) high and dry; auf sich ~ pocket (insult, etc.).

'Sitz|gelegenheit f seating accommodation, seat(s pl.); ~ bieten für seat; '⍀platz m seat; '⍀streik m sit-down or stay-in strike.

'Sitzung f (-/-en) sitting (a. parl., paint.); meeting, conference; '⍀speriode f session.

Skala ['ska:la] f (-/Skalen, Skalas) scale (a. ♪); dial (of radio set); fig. gamut; gleitende ~ sliding scale.

Skandal [skan'da:l] m (-s/-e) scandal; row, riot; ♀ös adj. [~a'lo:s] scandalous.

Skelett [ske'lɛt] n (-[e]s/-e) skeleton.

Skep|sis ['skepsis] f (-/no pl.) scepticism, Am. a. skepticism; ~tiker ['~tikər] m (-s/-) sceptic, Am. a. skeptic; '♀tisch adj. sceptical, Am. a. skeptical.

Ski [ʃi:] m (-s/-er, ~) ski; ~ laufen or fahren ski; '⍀fahrer m, '⍀läufer m skier; '⍀lift m ski-lift; '⍀sport m (-[e]s/no pl.) skiing.

Skizz|e ['skitsə] f (-/-n) sketch (a. fig.); ♀ieren [~'tsi:rən] v/t. (no -ge-, h) sketch, outline (both a. fig.).

Sklav|e ['skla:və] m (-n/-n) slave (a. fig.); '⍀enhandel m slave-trade; '⍀enhändler m slave-trader; ~e'rei f (-/-en) slavery; '♀isch adj. slavish.

Skonto ✝ ['skɔnto] m, n (-s/-s, ✎ Skonti) discount.

Skrupel ['skru:pəl] m (-s/-) scruple; '⍀los adj. unscrupulous.

Skulptur [skulp'tu:r] f (-/-en) sculpture.

Slalom ['sla:lɔm] m (-s/-s) skiing, etc.: slalom.

Slaw|e ['sla:və] m (-n/-n) Slav; '♀isch adj. Slav(onic).

Smaragd [sma'rakt] m (-[e]s/-e) emerald; ♀grün adj. emerald.

Smoking ['smo:kiŋ] m (-s/-s) dinner-jacket, Am. a. tuxedo, F tux.

so [zo:] 1. adv. so, thus; like this or that; as; ~ ein such a; ~ ... wie as ... as; nicht ~ ... wie not so ... as; ~ oder ~ by hook or by crook; 2. cj. so, therefore, consequently; ~ daß so that; ~bald cj. [zo:'-]: ~ (als) as soon as.

Socke ['zɔkə] f (-/-n) sock; '⍀l m (-s/-) ∆ pedestal, socle; socket (of lamp); '⍀n m (-s/-) sock; '⍀nhalter m/pl. suspenders pl., Am. garters pl.

Sodawasser ['zo:da-] n (-s/⍀) soda(-water).

Sodbrennen ⚕ ['zo:t-] n (-s/no pl.) heartburn.

soeben adv. [zo:'-] just (now).

Sofa ['zo:fa] n (-s/-s) sofa.

sofern cj. [zo:'-] if, provided that; ~ nicht unless.

soff [zɔf] pret. of saufen.

sofort adv. [zo:'-] at once, immediately, directly, right or straight away; ~ig adj. immediate, prompt.

Sog [zo:k] 1. m (-[e]s/-e) suction; ⚓

wake (a. fig.), undertow; **2.** ♀ pret. of saugen.

so|gar adv. [zo'-] even; **~genannt** adj. ['zo:-] so-called; **~gleich** adv. [zo'-] s. sofort.

Sohle ['zo:lə] f (-/-n) sole; bottom (of valley, etc.); ⚒ floor.

Sohn [zo:n] m (-[e]s/ᴇe) son.

solange cj. [zo'-]: ~ (als) so or as long as. [such.]

solch pron. [zɔlç] such; als ~e(r) as]

Sold ⚔ [zɔlt] m (-[e]s/-e) pay.

Soldat [zɔl'da:t] m (-en/-en) soldier; der unbekannte ~ the Unknown Warrior or Soldier. [cenary.]

Söldner ['zœldnər] m (-s/-) mer-]

Sole ['zo:lə] f (-/-n) brine, salt water.

solid adj. [zo'li:t] solid (a. fig.); basis, etc.: sound; ✝ firm, etc.: sound, solvent; prices: reasonable, fair; p. steady, staid, respectable.

solidarisch adj. [zoli'da:riʃ]: sich ~ erklären mit declare one's solidarity with.

solide adj. [zo'li:də] s. solid.

Solist [zo'list] m (-en/-en) soloist.

Soll ✝ [zɔl] n (-[s]/-[s]) debit; (output) target.

'**sollen** (h) **1.** v/i. (ge-): ich sollte (eigentlich) I ought to; **2.** v/aux. (irr., no -ge-): er soll he shall; he is to; he is said to; ich sollte I should; er sollte (eigentlich) zu Hause sein he ought to be at home; er sollte seinen Vater niemals wiedersehen he was never to see his father again.

Solo ['zo:lo] n (-s/-s, Soli) solo.

somit cj. [zo'-] thus; consequently.

Sommer ['zɔmər] m (-s/-) summer; **~frische** f (-/-n) summer-holidays pl.; summer-resort; '2**lich** adj. summer-like, summer(l)y; '**~sprosse** f freckle; '2**sprossig** adj. freckled; '**~wohnung** f summer residence, Am. cottage, summer house; '**~zeit** f **1.** (-/-en) season: summertime; **2.** (-/no pl.) summer time, Am. daylight-saving time.

Sonate ♩ [zo'na:tə] f (-/-n) sonata.

Sonde ['zɔndə] f (-/-n) probe.

Sonder|angebot ['zɔndər-] n special offer; '2**ausgabe** f special (edition); '2**bar** adj. strange, odd; '**~beilage** f inset, supplement (of newspaper); '**~berichterstatter** m special correspondent; '2**lich 1.** adj. special, peculiar; **2.** adv.: nicht ~

not particularly; '**~ling** m (-s/-e) crank, odd person; '2**n 1.** cj. but; nicht nur, ~ auch not only, but (also); **2.** v/t. (ge-, h): die Spreu vom Weizen ~ sift the chaff from the wheat; '**~recht** n privilege; '**~zug** 🚂 m special (train).

sondieren [zɔn'di:rən] (no -ge-, h) **1.** v/t. 𝒮 probe (a. fig.); **2.** fig. v/i. make tentative inquiries.

Sonn|abend ['zɔn²-] m (-s/-e) Saturday; '**~e** f (-/-n) sun; '2**en** v/t. (ge-, h) (expose to the) sun; sich ~ sun o.s. (a. fig. in dat. in); bask in the sun.

'**Sonnen|aufgang** m sunrise; '**~bad** n sun-bath; '**~brand** m sunburn; '**~bräune** f sunburn, tan, Am. (sun) tan; '**~brille** f (e-e a pair of) sunglasses pl.; '**~finsternis** f solar eclipse; '**~fleck** m sun-spot; '2**klar** fig. adj. (as) clear as daylight; '**~licht** n (-[e]s/no pl.) sunlight; '**~schein** m (-[e]s/no pl.) sunshine; '**~schirm** m sunshade, parasol; '**~segel** n awning; '**~seite** f sunny side (a. fig.); '**~stich** 𝒮 m sunstroke; '**~strahl** m sunbeam; '**~uhr** f sun-dial; '2**untergang** m sunset, sundown; '2**verbrannt** adj. sunburnt, tanned; '**~wende** f solstice.

'**sonnig** adj. sunny (a. fig.).

'**Sonntag** m Sunday.

'**Sonntags|anzug** m Sunday suit or best; '**~fahrer** mot. contp. m Sunday driver; '**~kind** n person born on a Sunday; fig. person born under a lucky star; '**~rückfahrkarte** 🚂 f week-end ticket; '**~ruhe** f Sunday rest; '**~staat** F co. m (-[e]s/no pl.) Sunday go-to-meeting clothes pl.

sonor adj. [zo'no:r] sonorous.

sonst [zɔnst] **1.** adv. otherwise, with pron. else; usually, normally; wer ~? who else?; wie ~ as usual; ~ nichts nothing else; **2.** cj. otherwise, or else; '**~ig** adj. other; '**~wie** adv. in some other way; '**~wo** adv. elsewhere, somewhere else.

Sopran ♩ [zo'pra:n] m (-s/-e) soprano; sopranist; **~istin** ♩ [~a'nistin] f (-/-nen) soprano, sopranist.

Sorge ['zɔrgə] f (-/-n) care; sorrow; uneasiness, anxiety; ~ tragen für take care of; sich ~n machen um be anxious or worried about; mach dir keine ~n don't worry.

'sorgen (ge-, h) **1.** v/i.: ~ für care for, provide for; take care of, attend to; dafür ~, daß take care that; **2.** v/refl.: sich ~ um be anxious or worried about; '~frei adj., '~los adj. carefree, free from care; '~voll adj. full of cares; face: worried, troubled.

Sorg|falt ['zɔrkfalt] f (-/no pl.) care(fulness); 2**fältig** adj. ['~feltiç] careful; 2**lich** adj. careful, anxious; 2**los** adj. carefree; thoughtless; negligent, careless; 2**sam** adj. careful.

Sort|e ['zɔrtə] f (-/-n) sort, kind, species, Am. a. stripe; 2**ieren** [~'ti:rən] v/t. (no -ge-, h) (as)sort; arrange; ~**iment** [~i'ment] n (-[e]s/-e) assortment.

Soße ['zo:sə] f (-/-n) sauce; gravy.

sott [zɔt] pret. of sieden.

Souffl|eurkasten thea. [su'flø:r-] m prompt-box; prompter's box; ~**euse** thea. [~zə] f (-/-n) prompter; 2**ieren** thea. (no -ge-, h) **1.** v/i. prompt (j-m s.o.); **2.** v/t. prompt.

Souverän [suvə're:n] **1.** m (-s/-e) sovereign; **2.** 2 adj. sovereign; fig. superior; ~**ität** [~eni'te:t] f (-/no pl.) sovereignty.

so|viel [zo-] **1.** cj. so or as far as; ~ ich weiß so far as I know; **2.** adv.: doppelt ~ twice as much; ~**weit 1.** cj.: ~ es mich betrifft in so far as it concerns me, so far as I am concerned; **2.** adv.: ~ ganz gut not bad (for a start); ~**wieso** adv. [zovi'zo:] in any case, anyhow, anyway.

Sowjet [zɔ'vjet] m (-s/-s) Soviet; 2**isch** adj. Soviet.

sowohl cj. [zo'-]: ~ ... als (auch) ~ both ... and ..., ... as well as ...

sozial [zo'tsja:l] social; 2**demokrat** m social democrat, ~**isieren** [~ali'zi:rən] v/t. (no -ge-, h) socialize; 2**isierung** [~ali'zi:ruŋ] f (-/-en) socialization; 2**ist** m [~a'list] m (-en/-en) socialist; ~**istisch** adj. [~a'listiʃ] socialist.

Sozius ['zo:tsjus] m (-/-se) ♱ partner; mot. pillion-rider; '~**sitz** mot. m pillion.

sozusagen adv. [zotsu'za:gən] so to speak, as it were.

Spachtel ['ʃpaxtəl] m (-s/-), f (-/-n) spatula.

spähe|n ['ʃpɛ:ən] v/i. (ge-, h) look

out (nach for); peer; '2**r** m (-s/-) look-out; ✕ scout.

Spalier [ʃpa'li:r] n (-s/-e) trellis, espalier; fig. lane; ~ **bilden** form a lane.

Spalt [ʃpalt] m (-[e]s/-e) crack, split, rift, crevice, fissure; '~**e** f (-/-n) s. Spalt; typ. column; 2**en** v/t. ([irr.,] ge-, h) split (a. fig. hairs); cleave (block of wood, etc.); sich ~ split (up); '~**ung** f (-/-en) splitting, cleavage; fig. split; eccl. schism.

Span [ʃpa:n] m (-[e]s/ᵘe) chip, shaving, splinter.

Spange ['ʃpaŋə] f (-/-n) clasp; buckle; clip; slide (in hair); strap (of shoes); bracelet.

Span|ier ['ʃpa:njər] m (-s/-) Spaniard; 2**isch** adj. Spanish.

Spann [ʃpan] **1.** m (-[e]s/-e) instep; **2.** 2 pret. of spinnen; '~**e** f (-/-n) span; ✂, orn. spread (of wings); ♱ margin; 2**en** (ge-, h) **1.** v/t. stretch (rope, muscles, etc.); cock (rifle); bend (bow, etc.); tighten (spring, etc.); vor den Wagen ~ harness to the carriage; s. gespannt; **2.** v/i. be (too) tight; 2**end** adj. exciting, thrilling; gripping; '~**kraft** f (-/no pl.) elasticity; fig. energy; '~**ung** f (-/-en) tension (a. fig.); ⚡ voltage; ⊕ strain, stress; ♼ span; fig. close attention.

Spar|büchse ['ʃpa:r-] f money-box; 2**en** (ge-, h) **1.** v/t. save (money, strength, etc.); put by; **2.** v/i. save; economize, cut down expenses; ~ mit be chary of (praise, etc.); '~**er** m (-s/-) saver.

Spargel ❦ ['ʃpargəl] m (-s/-) asparagus.

'Spar|kasse f savings-bank; '~**konto** n savings-account.

spärlich adj. ['ʃpe:rliç] crop, dress, etc.: scanty; population, etc.: sparse; hair: thin.

Sparren ['ʃparən] m (-s/-) rafter, spar.

'sparsam 1. adj. saving, economical (mit of); **2.** adv.: ~ leben lead a frugal life, economize; ~ umgehen mit use sparingly, be frugal of; 2**keit** f (-/no pl.) economy, frugality.

Spaß [ʃpa:s] m (-es/ᵘe) joke, jest; fun, lark; amusement; aus or zum ~ in fun; ~ beiseite joking apart; er hat nur ~ gemacht he was only joking; '**en** v/i. (ge-, h) joke, jest, make fun; *damit ist nicht zu ~* that is no joking matter; '**haft** adj., '**ig** adj. facetious, waggish; '**macher** m (-s/-), '**vogel** m wag, joker.

spät [ʃpɛːt] **1.** adj. late; advanced; *zu ~* too late; *am ~en Nachmittag* late in the afternoon; *wie ~ ist es?* what time is it?; *er kommt 5 Minuten zu ~* he is five minutes late (*zu for*); *~ in der Nacht* late at night.

Spaten ['ʃpaːtən] m (-s/-) spade.

'**spät**|**er 1.** adj. later; **2.** adv. later on; afterward(s); *früher oder ~* sooner or later; **~stens** adv. ['~stəns] at the latest.

Spatz orn. [ʃpats] m (-en, -es/-en) sparrow.

spazieren [ʃpaˈtsiːrən] v/i. (no -ge-, sein) walk, stroll; **~fahren** (*irr. fahren, sep., -ge-*) **1.** v/i. (sein) go for a drive; **2.** v/t. (h) take for a drive; take (*baby*) out (in pram); **~gehen** v/i. (*irr. gehen, sep., -ge-, sein*) go for a walk.

Spa|**zier**|**fahrt** f drive, ride; **~gang** m walk, stroll; *e-n ~ machen* go for a walk; **~gänger** [~gɛŋər] m (-s/-) walker, stroller; **~weg** m walk.

Speck [ʃpɛk] m (-[e]s/-e) bacon.

Spedi|**teur** [ʃpediˈtøːr] m (-s/-e) forwarding agent; (furniture) remover; **~tion** [~ˈtsjoːn] f (-/-en) forwarding agent *or* agency.

Speer [ʃpeːr] m (-[e]s/-e) spear; *sports:* javelin; '**werfen** v/i (*sep/no pl.*) javelin-throw(ing); '**werfer** m (-s/-) javelin-thrower.

Speiche ['ʃpaɪçə] f (-/-n) spoke.

Speichel ['ʃpaɪçəl] m (-s/no pl.) spit(tle), saliva; '**lecker** fig. m (-s/-) lickspittle, toady.

Speicher ['ʃpaɪçər] m (-s/-) granary; warehouse; garret, attic.

speien ['ʃpaɪən] (*irr., ge-, h*) **1.** v/t. spit out (*blood, etc.*); *volcano, etc.:* belch (*fire, etc.*); **2.** v/i. spit; vomit, be sick.

Speise ['ʃpaɪzə] f (-/-n) food, nourishment; meal; dish; '**eis** n ice-cream; '**kammer** f larder, pantry; '**karte** f bill of fare, menu; '**n** (ge-, h) **1.** v/i. s. *essen 1*; *at restaurants:* take one's meals; **2.** v/t. feed; ⊕, ⚡ a. supply (*mit with*); '**nfolge** f menu; '**röhre** anat. f

gullet, (o)esophagus; '**saal** m dining-hall; '**schrank** m (meat-) safe; '**wagen** 🚃 m dining-car, diner; '**zimmer** n dining-room.

Spektakel F [ʃpɛkˈtaːkəl] m (-s/-) noise, din.

Spekul|**ant** [ʃpekuˈlant] m (-en/-en) speculator; **~ation** [~aˈtsjoːn] f (-/-en) speculation; ✝ a. venture; **2ieren** [~ˈliːrən] v/i. (no -ge-, h) speculate (*auf acc. on*).

Spelunke [ʃpeˈluŋkə] f (-/-n) den; drinking-den, Am. F a. dive.

Spende ['ʃpɛndə] f (-/-n) gift; alms pl.; contribution; '**2n** v/t. (ge-, h) give; donate (*money to charity, blood, etc.*); *eccl.* administer (*sacraments*); bestow (*praise*) (*dat. on*); '**r** m (-s/-) giver; donor.

spen|**dieren** v/t. (no -ge-, h): *j-m et. ~* treat s.o. to s.th., stand s.o. s.th.

Sperling orn. ['ʃpɛrliŋ] m (-s/-e) sparrow.

Sperr|**e** ['ʃpɛrə] f (-/-n) barrier; 🚃 barrier, Am. gate; toll-bar; ⊕ lock(ing device), detent; barricade; ✝, ⚓ embargo; ⚓ blockade; *sports:* suspension; '**2en** (ge-, h) **1.** v/t. close; ✝, ⚓ embargo; cut off (*gas supply, electricity, etc.*); stop (*cheque, etc.*); *sports:* suspend; **2.** v/i. jam, be stuck; '**holz** n plywood; '**konto** n blocked account; '**kreis** ⚡ m wave-trap; '**sitz** *thea.* m stalls pl., Am. orchestra; '**ung** f (-/-en) closing; stoppage (*of cheque, etc.*); ✝, ⚓ embargo; ⚓ blockade; '**zone** f prohibited area.

Spesen ['ʃpeːzən] pl. expenses pl., charges pl.

Spezial|**ausbildung** [ʃpeˈtsjaːl?-] f special training; **~fach** n special(i)ty; **~geschäft** ✝ n one-line shop, Am. specialty store; **2isieren** [~ali'ziːrən] v/refl. (no -ge-, h) specialize (*auf acc. in*); **~ist** [~a'list] m (-en/-en) specialist; **~ität** [~ali'tɛːt] f (-/-en) special(i)ty.

speziell adj. [ʃpeˈtsjɛl] specific, special, particular.

spezifisch adj. [ʃpeˈtsiːfiʃ]: *~es Gewicht* specific gravity.

Sphäre ['sfɛːrə] f (-/-n) sphere (a. fig.).

Spick|**aal** ['ʃpik-] m smoked eel; '**2en** (ge-, h) **1.** v/t. lard; *fig.* (inter-)

lard (*mit* with); F: *j-n* ~ grease s.o.'s palm; **2.** F *fig. v/i.* crib.

spie [ʃpi:] *pret. of speien.*

Spiegel [ˈʃpi:gəl] *m* (-s/-) mirror (*a. fig.*), looking-glass; ˈ**~bild** *n* reflected image; ˈ**2**ˈ**blank** *adj.* mirror-like; **~ei** [ˈʃpi:gəlʔ-] *n* fried egg; ˈ**2**ˈ**glatt** *adj. water*: glassy, unrippled; *road, etc.*: very slippery; ˈ**2n** (ge-, *h*) **1.** *v/i.* shine; **2.** *v/refl.* be reflected; ˈ**~schrift** *f* mirror-writing.

Spieg(e)lung [ˈʃpi:g(ə)luŋ] *f* (-/-en) reflection, reflexion; mirage.

Spiel [ʃpi:l] *n* (-[e]s/-e) play (*a. fig.*); game (*a. fig.*); match; ♪ playing; *ein ~ Karten* a pack of playing-cards, *Am. a.* a deck; *auf dem ~ stehen* be at stake; *aufs ~ setzen* jeopardize, stake; ˈ**~art** ♀, *zo. f* variety; ˈ**~ball** *m tennis*: game ball; *billiards*: red ball; *fig.* plaything, sport; ˈ**~bank** *f* (-/-en) gaming-house; ˈ**2en** (ge-, *h*) **1.** *v/i.* play; gamble; *~ mit* play with; *fig. a.* toy with; **2.** *v/t.* play (*tennis, violin, etc.*); *thea.* act, play (*part*); *mit j-m Schach ~* play s.o. at chess; *den Höflichen ~* do the polite; ˈ**2end** *fig. adv.* easily; ˈ**~er** *m* (-s/-) player; gambler; **~e**ˈ**rei** *f* (-/-en) pastime; child's amusement; ˈ**~ergebnis** *n sports*: result, score; ˈ**~feld** *n sports*: (playing-)field; pitch; ˈ**~film** *m* feature film *or* picture; ˈ**~gefährte** *m* playfellow, playmate; ˈ**~karte** *f* playing-card; ˈ**~leiter** *m thea.* stage manager; *cinematography*: director; *sports*: referee; ˈ**~marke** *f* counter, *sl.* chip; ˈ**~plan** *m thea., etc.*: program(me); repertory; ˈ**~platz** *m* playground; ˈ**~raum** *fig. m* play, scope; ˈ**~regel** *f* rule (of the game); ˈ**~sachen** *f/pl.* playthings *pl.*, toys *pl.*; ˈ**~schuld** *f* gambling-debt; ˈ**~schule** *f* infant-school, kindergarten; ˈ**~tisch** *m* card-table; gambling-table; ˈ**~uhr** *f* musical box, *Am.* music box; ˈ**~verderber** *m* (-s/-) spoil-sport, killjoy, wet blanket; ˈ**~waren** *f/pl.* playthings *pl.*, toys *pl.*; ˈ**~zeit** *f thea.* season; *sports*: time of play; ˈ**~zeug** *n* toy(s *pl.*), plaything(s *pl.*).

Spieß [ʃpi:s] *m* (-es/-e) spear, pike; spit; *den ~ umdrehen* turn the tables; ˈ**~bürger** *m* bourgeois, Philistine, *Am. a.* Babbit; ˈ**2bürgerlich** *adj.* bourgeois, Philistine; ˈ**~er** *m* (-s/-) *s. Spießbürger*; ˈ**~geselle** *m* accomplice; ˈ**~ruten** *f/pl.*: *~ laufen* run the gauntlet (*a. fig.*).

spinal *adj.* [ʃpiˈnɑ:l]: *~e Kinderlähmung* ⚕ infantile paralysis, poliomyelitis, F polio.

Spinat ♀ [ʃpiˈnɑ:t] *m* (-[e]s/-e) spinach.

Spind [ʃpint] *n, m* (-[e]s/-e) wardrobe, cupboard; ⚔, *sports, etc.*: locker.

Spindel [ˈʃpindəl] *f* (-/-n) spindle; ˈ**2**ˈ**dürr** *adj.* (as) thin as a lath.

Spinn|e *zo.* [ˈʃpinə] *f* (-/-n) spider; ˈ**2en** (*irr.*, ge-, *h*) **1.** *v/t.* spin (*a. fig.*); hatch (*plot, etc.*); **2.** *v/i. cat*: purr; F *fig.* be crazy, *sl.* be nuts; ˈ**~engewebe** *n* cobweb; ˈ**~er** *m* (-s/-) spinner; F *fig.* silly; **~e**ˈ**rei** *f* (-/-en) spinning; spinning-mill; ˈ**~maschine** *f* spinning-machine; ˈ**~webe** *f* (-/-n) cobweb.

Spion [ʃpiˈo:n] *m* (-s/-e) spy, intelligencer; *fig.* judas; **~age** [~oˈnɑ:ʒə] *f* (-/*no pl.*) espionage; **2ieren** [~oˈni:rən] *v/i.* (*no* -ge-, *h*) (play the) spy.

Spiral|e [ʃpiˈrɑ:lə] *f* (-/-n) spiral (*a.* ✈), helix; **2förmig** *adj.* [~fœrmiç] spiral, helical.

Spirituosen [ʃpirituˈo:zən] *pl.* spirits *pl.*

Spiritus [ˈʃpi:ritus] *m* (-/-se) spirit, alcohol; ˈ**~kocher** *m* (-s/-) spirit stove.

Spital [ʃpiˈtɑ:l] *n* (-s/⸚er) hospital; alms-house; home for the aged.

spitz [ʃpits] **1.** *adj.* pointed (*a. fig.*); ⩓ *angle*: acute; *fig.* poignant; *~e Zunge* sharp tongue; **2.** *adv.*: *~ zulaufen* taper (off); ˈ**2bube** *m* thief; rogue, rascal (*both a. co.*); **2büberei** [~by:bəˈraı] *f* (-/-en) roguery, rascality (*both a. co.*); **~bübisch** *adj.* [ˈ~by:biʃ] *eyes, smile, etc.*: roguish.

ˈ**Spitz|e** *f* (-/-n) point (*of pencil, weapon, jaw, etc.*); tip (*of nose, finger, etc.*); nib (*of tool, etc.*); spire; head (*of enterprise, etc.*); lace; *an der ~ liegen sports*: be in the lead; *j-m die ~ bieten* make head against s.o.; *auf die ~ treiben* carry to an extreme; ˈ**~el** *m* (-s/-) (common) informer; ˈ**2en** *v/t.* (ge-, *h*) point, sharpen; *den Mund ~* purse (up) one's lips; *die Ohren ~* prick up one's ears (*a. fig.*).

ˈ**Spitzen|leistung** *f* top perform-

S

ance; ⊕ maximum capacity; '⸜**lohn** m top wages pl.

'**spitz**|'**findig** adj. subtle, captious; '⸜**findigkeit** f (-/-en) subtlety, captiousness; '⸜**hacke** f pickax(e), pick; '⸜**ig** adj. pointed; fig. a. poignant; '⸜**marke** typ. f head(ing); '⸜**name** m nickname.

Splitter ['ʃplitər] m (-s/-) splinter, shiver; chip; '⸜**frei** adj. glass: shatterproof; '⸜**ig** adj. splintery; '⸜**n** v/i. (ge-, h, sein) splinter, shiver; '⸜**nackt** F adj. stark naked, Am. a. mother-naked; '⸜**partei** pol. f splinter party.

spontan adj. [ʃpɔn'taːn] spontaneous.

sporadisch adj. [ʃpo'raːdiʃ] sporadic.

Sporn [ʃpɔrn] m (-[e]s/Sporen) spur; die Sporen geben put or set spurs to (horse); sich die Sporen verdienen win one's spurs; '⸜**en** v/t. (ge-, h) spur.

Sport [ʃpɔrt] m (-[e]s/⸜-e) sport; fig. hobby; ⸜ treiben go in for sports; '⸜**ausrüstung** f sports equipment; '⸜**geschäft** n sporting-goods shop; '⸜**kleidung** f sport clothes pl., sportswear; '⸜**lehrer** m games-master; '⸜**lich** adj. sporting, sportsmanlike; figure: athletic; '⸜**nachrichten** f/pl. sports news sg., pl.; '⸜**platz** m sports field; stadium.

Spott [ʃpɔt] m (-[e]s/no pl.) mockery; derision; scorn; ⸜(s-n) ⸜ treiben mit make sport of; '⸜'**billig** F adj. dirt-cheap.

Spötte|**lei** [ʃpœtə'lai] f (-/-en) raillery, sneer, jeer; '⸜**ln** v/i. (ge-, h) sneer (über acc. at), jeer (at).

'**spotten** v/i. (ge-, h) mock (über acc. at); jeer (at); jeder Beschreibung ⸜ beggar description.

Spötter ['ʃpœtər] m (-s/-) mocker, scoffer; ⸜**ei** [⸜'rai] f (-/-en) mockery.

'**spöttisch** adj. mocking; sneering; ironical.

'**Spott**|**name** m nickname; '⸜**preis** m ridiculous price; für e-n ⸜ for a mere song; '⸜**schrift** f lampoon, satire.

sprach [ʃpraːx] pret. of sprechen.

'**Sprache** f (-/-en) speech; language (a. fig.); diction; zur ⸜ bringen bring up, broach; zur ⸜ kommen come up (for discussion).

'**Sprach**|**eigentümlichkeit** f idiom;

'⸜**fehler** ☞ m impediment (in one's speech); '⸜**führer** m language guide; '⸜**gebrauch** m usage; '⸜**gefühl** n (-[e]s/no pl.) linguistic instinct; ⸜**kundig** adj. ['⸜kundiç] versed in languages; '⸜**lehre** f grammar; '⸜**lehrer** m teacher of languages; '⸜**lich** adj. linguistic; grammatical; '⸜**los** adj. speechless; '⸜**rohr** n speaking-trumpet, megaphone; fig.: mouthpiece; organ; '⸜**schatz** m vocabulary; '⸜**störung** ☞ f impediment (in one's speech); '⸜**wissenschaft** f philology, science of language; linguistics pl.; '⸜**wissenschaftler** m philologist; linguist; ⸜**wissenschaftlich** adj. philological; linguistic.

sprang [ʃpraŋ] pret. of springen.

'**Sprech**|**chor** ['ʃpreç-] m speaking chorus; '⸜**en** (irr., ge-, h) **1.** v/i. speak (language, truth, etc.); ꜩ pronounce (judgement); say (prayer); j-n zu ⸜ wünschen wish to see s.o.; j-n schuldig ⸜ ꜩ pronounce s.o. guilty; F Bände ⸜ speak volumes (für for); **2.** v/t. speak; talk (both: mit to, with; über acc., von of, about); er ist nicht zu ⸜ you cannot see him; '⸜**er** m (-s/-) speaker; radio: announcer; spokesman; '⸜**fehler** m slip of the tongue; '⸜**stunde** f consulting-hours pl.; '⸜**übung** f exercise in speaking; '⸜**zimmer** n consulting-room, surgery.

spreizen ['ʃpraitsən] v/t. (ge-, h) spread (out); a. straddle (legs); sich ⸜ pretend to be unwilling.

Spreng|**bombe** ⚔ ['ʃpreŋ-] f high-explosive bomb, demolition bomb; '⸜**el** eccl. m (-s/-) diocese, see; parish; '⸜**en** (ge-) **1.** v/t. (h) sprinkle, water (road, lawn, etc.); blow up, blast (bridge, rocks, etc.); burst open (door, etc.); spring (mine, etc.); gambling: break (bank); break up (meeting, etc.); **2.** v/i. (sein) gallop; '⸜**stoff** m explosive; '⸜**ung** f (-/-en) blowing-up, blasting; explosion; '⸜**wagen** m water(ing)-cart.

Sprenkel ['ʃpreŋkəl] m (-s/-) speckle, spot; '⸜**n** v/t. (ge-, h) speckle, spot.

Spreu [ʃprɔy] f (-/no pl.) chaff; s. sondern 2.

Sprich|**wort** ['ʃpriç-] n (-[e]s/⸜er) proverb, adage; ⸜**wörtlich** adj. proverbial (a. fig.).

S

sprießen [ˈʃpriːsən] v/i. (irr., ge-, sein) sprout; germinate.

Spring|brunnen [ˈʃpriŋ-] m fountain; '2en v/i. (irr., ge-, sein) jump, leap; ball, etc.: bounce; swimming: dive; burst, crack, break; in die Augen ~ strike the eye; ~ über (acc.) jump (over), leap, clear; '~er m (-s/-) jumper; swimming: diver; chess: knight; '~flut f spring tide.

Sprit [ʃprit] m (-[e]s/-e) spirit, alcohol; F mot. fuel, petrol, sl. juice; Am. gasoline, F gas.

Spritz|e [ˈʃpritsə] f (-/-n) syringe (a. ⚕); squirt; ⊕ fire-engine; j-m e-e ~ geben ⚕ give s.o. an injection; '2en (ge-) 1. v/t. (h) sprinkle, water (road, lawn, etc.); splash (water, etc.) (über acc. on, over); 2. v/i. (h) splash; pen: splutter; 3. v/i. (sein) F fig. dash, flit; ~ aus (wound, etc.): spurt or spout from (wound, etc.); '~er m (-s/-) splash; '~tour F f: e-e ~ machen go for a spin.

spröde adj. [ˈʃprøːdə] glass, etc.: brittle; skin: chapped, chappy; esp. girl: prudish, prim, coy.

Sproß [ʃprɔs] 1. m (Sprosses/Sprosse) ♀ shoot, sprout, scion (a. fig.); fig. offspring; 2. ♀ pret. of sprießen.

Sprosse [ˈʃprɔsə] f (-/-n) rung, round, step. [Sproß 1.; co. son.]

Sprößling [ˈʃprœslɪŋ] m (-s/-e) ♀ s.]

Spruch [ʃprux] m (-[e]s/-e) saying; dictum; ⅋ sentence; ⅋ verdict; '~band n banner; '2reif adj. ripe for decision.

Sprudel [ˈʃpruːdəl] m (-s/-) mineral water; '2n v/i. (ge-) 1. v/t. (h) bubble, effervesce; 2. (sein): ~ aus or von gush from.

sprüh|en [ˈʃpryːən] (ge-) 1. v/t. (h) spray, sprinkle (liquid); throw off (sparks); Feuer ~ eyes: flash fire; 2. v/i. (h): ~ vor sparkle with (wit, etc.); es sprüht it is drizzling; 3. v/i. (sein) sparks: fly; '2regen m drizzle.

Sprung [ʃpruŋ] m (-[e]s/-e) jump, leap, bound; swimming: dive; crack, fissure; '~brett n sports: springboard; fig. stepping-stone; '~feder f spiral spring.

Spuck|e F [ˈʃpukə] f (-/no pl.) spit(tle); '2en v/i. (ge-) h) 1. v/t. spit (out) (blood, etc.); 2. v/i. spit; engine: splutter; '~napf m spittoon, Am. a. cuspidor.

Spuk [ʃpuːk] m (-[e]s/-e) apparition, ghost, co. spook; F fig. noise; '2en v/i. (ge-, h): ~ in (dat.) haunt (a place); hier spukt es this place is haunted.

Spule [ˈʃpuːlə] f (-/-n) spool, reel; bobbin; ⚡ coil; '2n v/t. (ge-, h) spool, reel.

spülen [ˈʃpyːlən] (ge-, h) 1. v/t. rinse (clothes, mouth, cup, etc.); wash up (dishes, etc.); an Land ~ wash ashore; 2. v/i. flush the toilet.

Spund [ʃpunt] m (-[e]s/-e) bung; plug; '~loch n bunghole.

Spur [ʃpuːr] f (-/-en) trace (a. fig.); track (a. fig.); print (a. fig.); rut (of wheels); j-m auf der ~ sein be on s.o.'s track.

spür|en [ˈʃpyːrən] v/t. (ge-, h) feel; sense; perceive; '2sinn m (-[e]s/no pl.) scent; fig. a. flair (für for).

Spurweite 🚂 f ga(u)ge.

sputen [ˈʃpuːtən] v/refl. (ge-, h) make haste, hurry up.

Staat [ʃtaːt] m 1. F (-[e]s/no pl.) pomp, state; finery; ~ machen mit make a parade of; 2. (-[e]s/-en) state; government; '~enbund m (-[e]s/-e) confederacy, confederation; '2enlos adj. stateless; '2lich adj. state; national; political; public.

Staats|angehörige m, f (-n/-n) national, citizen, esp. Brt. subject; '~angehörigkeit f (-/no pl.) nationality, citizenship; '~anwalt ⅋ m public prosecutor, Am. prosecuting attorney; '~beamte m Civil Servant, Am. a. public servant; '~begräbnis n state or national funeral; '~besuch m official or state visit; '~bürger m citizen; '~bürgerkunde f (-/no pl.) civics sg.; '~bürgerschaft f (-/-en) citizenship; '~dienst m Civil Service; '2eigen adj. state-owned; '~feind m public enemy; '2feindlich adj. subversive; '~gewalt f (-/no pl.) supreme power; '~haushalt m budget; '~hoheit f (-/no pl.) sovereignty; '~kasse f treasury, Brt. exchequer; '~klugheit f political wisdom; '~kunst f (-/no pl.) statesmanship; '~mann m statesman, 2männisch adj. [ˈ~mɛnɪʃ] statesmanlike; '~oberhaupt n head of (the) state; '~papiere n/pl. Government securities pl.; '~rat m Privy Council; '~recht n public law; '~schatz m s. Staatskasse;

'**~schulden** f/pl. national debt; '**~sekretär** m under-secretary of state; '**~streich** m coup d'état; '**~trauer** f national mourning; '**~vertrag** m treaty; '**~wesen** n polity; '**~wirtschaft** f public sector of the economy; '**~wissenschaft** f political science; '**~wohl** n public weal.

Stab [ʃtaːp] m (-[e]s/⸗e) staff (a. fig.); bar (of metal, wood); crosier, staff (of bishop); wand (of magician); relay-race, ♪ conducting: baton; pole-vaulting: pole.

stabil adj. [ʃtaˈbiːl] stable (a. ✝); health: robust.

stabilisier|en [ʃtabiliˈziːrən] v/t. (no -ge-, h) stabilize (a. ✝); **2ung** f (-/-en) stabilization (a. ✝).

stach [ʃtaːx] pret. of stechen.

Stachel [ˈʃtaxəl] m (-s/-n) prickle (of plant, hedgehog, etc.); sting (of bee, etc.); tongue (of buckle); spike (of sports shoe); fig.: sting; goad; '**~beere** ♀ f gooseberry; '**~draht** m barbed wire; '**2ig** adj. prickly, **stachlig** adj. s. stachelig. [thorny.]

Stadi|on [ˈʃtaːdjɔn] n (-s/Stadien) stadium; **~um** [ˈ~um] n (-s/Stadien) stage, phase.

Stadt [ʃtat] f (⸗e) town; city.

Städt|chen [ˈʃtɛːtçən] n (-s/-) small town; '**~ebau** m (-[e]s/no pl.) town-planning; '**~er** m (-s/-) townsman; ~ pl. townspeople pl.

'**Stadt|gebiet** n urban area; '**~gespräch** n teleph. local call; fig. town talk, talk of the town; '**~haus** n town house.

städtisch adj. [ˈʃtɛːtiʃ] municipal.

'**Stadt|plan** m city map; plan (of a town); '**~planung** f town-planning; '**~rand** m outskirts pl. (of a town); '**~rat** m (-[e]s/⸗e) town council; town council(l)or; '**~teil** m, '**~viertel** n quarter.

Staffel [ˈʃtafəl] f (-/-n) relay; relay-race. '**~ei** paint. f (-/-en) easel; '**~lauf** m relay-race; '**2n** v/t. (ge-, h) graduate (taxes, etc.); stagger (hours of work, etc.).

Stahl¹ [ʃtaːl] m (-[e]s/⸗e, -e) steel. **stahl²** [~] pret. of stehlen.

stählen [ˈʃtɛːlən] v/t. (ge-, h) ⊕ harden (a. fig.), temper.

'**Stahl|feder** f steel pen; steel spring; '**~kammer** f strong-room; '**~stich** m steel engraving.

stak [ʃtaːk] pret. of stecken 2.

Stall [ʃtal] m (-[e]s/⸗e) stable (a. fig.); cow-house, cowshed; pigsty, Am. a. pigpen; shed; '**~knecht** m stableman; '**~ung** f (-/-en) stabling; **~en** pl. stables pl.

Stamm [ʃtam] m (-[e]s/⸗e) ♀ stem (a. gr.), trunk; fig.: race; stock; family; tribe; '**~aktie** ✝ f ordinary share, Am. common stock; '**~baum** m family or genealogical tree, pedigree (a. zo.); '**~buch** n album; book that contains the births, deaths, and marriages in a family; zo. stud-book; '**2eln** (ge-, h) **1.** v/t. stammer (out); **2.** v/i. stammer; '**~eltern** pl. ancestors pl., first parents pl.; '**2en** v/i. (ge-, sein): ~ von or aus come from (town, etc.), Am. a. hail from; date from (certain time); gr. be derived from; aus gutem Haus ~ be of good family; '**~gast** m regular customer or guest, F regular.

stämmig adj. [ˈʃtɛmiç] stocky; thickset, squat(ty).

'**Stamm|kapital** ✝ n share capital, Am. capital stock; '**~kneipe** F f one's favo(u)rite pub, local; '**~kunde** m regular customer, patron; '**~tisch** m table reserved for regular guests; **~utter** [ˈʃtammʊtər] f (-/⸗) ancestress; '**~vater** m ancestor; '**2verwandt** adj. cognate, kindred; pred. of the same race.

stampfen [ˈʃtampfən] (ge-) **1.** v/t. (h) mash (potatoes, etc.); aus dem Boden ~ conjure up; **2.** v/i. (h) stamp (one's foot); horse: paw; **3.** v/i. (sein): ~ durch plod through; ♨ pitch through.

Stand [ʃtant] **1.** m (-[e]s/⸗e) stand (-ing), standing or upright position; footing, foothold; s. Standplatz; stall; fig.: level; state; station, rank, status; class; profession; reading (of thermometer, etc.); ast. position; sports: score; auf den neuesten ~ bringen bring up to date; e-n schweren ~ haben have a hard time (of it); **2.** ♀ pret. of stehen.

Standarte [ʃtanˈdartə] f (-/-n) standard, banner.

'**Standbild** n statue.

Ständchen [ˈʃtɛntçən] n (-s/-) serenade; j-m ein ~ bringen serenade s.o.

Ständer [ˈʃtɛndər] m (-s/-) stand; post, pillar, standard.

S

'Standes|amt n registry (office), register office; **'2amtlich** adj.: ~e Trauung civil marriage; **'~beamte** m registrar; **'~dünkel** m pride of place; **'2gemäß** adj., **'2mäßig** adj. in accordance with one's rank; **'~person** f person of rank or position; **'~unterschied** m social difference.

'standhaft adj. steadfast; firm; constant; ~ bleiben stand pat; resist temptation; **'2igkeit** f (-/no pl.) steadfastness; firmness.

'standhalten v/i. (irr. halten, sep., -ge-, h) hold one's ground; j-m or e-r Sache ~ resist s.o. or s.th.

ständig adj. ['ʃtɛndiç] permanent; constant; income, etc.: fixed.

'Stand|ort m position (of ship, etc.); ✕ garrison, post; **'~platz** m stand; **'~punkt** fig. m point of view, standpoint, angle, Am. a. slant; **'~quartier** ✕ n fixed quarters pl.; **'~recht** ✕ n martial law; **'~uhr** f grandfather's clock.

Stange ['ʃtaŋə] f (-/-n) pole; rod, bar (of iron, etc.); staff (of flag); Anzug or Kleid von der ~ sl. reach-me-down, Am. F hand-me-down.

stank [ʃtaŋk] pret. of stinken.

Stänker|(er) contp. ['ʃtɛŋkər(ər)] m (-s/-) mischief-maker, quarrel(l)er; **'2n** F v/i. (ge-, h) make mischief.

Stanniol [ʃta'njoːl] n (-s/-e) tin foil.

Stanze ['ʃtantsə] f (-/-n) stanza; ⊕ punch, stamp, die; **'2n** ⊕ v/t. (ge-, h) punch, stamp.

Stapel ['ʃtaːpəl] m (-s/-) pile, stack; ⚓ stocks pl.; vom or von ~ lassen ⚓ launch; vom or von ~ laufen ⚓ be launched; **'~lauf** ⚓ m launch; **'2n** v/t. (ge-, h) pile (up), stack; **'~platz** m dump; emporium.

stapfen ['ʃtapfən] v/i. (ge-, sein) plod (durch through).

Star 1. [ʃtaːr] m (-[e]s/-e) orn. starling; ✻ cataract; j-m den ~ stechen open s.o.'s eyes; 2. [staːr] m (-s/-s) thea., etc.: star.

starb [ʃtarp] pret. of sterben.

stark [ʃtark] 1. adj. strong (a. fig.); stout, corpulent; fig.: intense; large; ~e Erkältung bad cold; ~er Raucher heavy smoker; ~e Seite strong point, forte; 2. adv. very much; ~ erkältet sein have a bad cold; ~ übertrieben grossly exaggerated.

Stärke ['ʃtɛrkə] f (-/-n) strength (a. fig.); stoutness, corpulence; fig.: intensity; largeness; strong point, forte; ⚗ starch; **'2n** v/t. (ge-, h) strengthen (a. fig.); starch (linen, etc.); sich ~ take some refreshment(s).

'Starkstrom ⚡ m heavy current.

'Stärkung f (-/-en) strengthening; fig. a. refreshment; **'~smittel** n restorative; ✻ tonic.

starr [ʃtar] 1. adj. rigid (a. fig.), stiff; gaze: fixed; ~ vor (dat.) numb with (cold, etc.); transfixed with (horror, etc.); dumbfounded with (amazement, etc.); 2. adv.: j-n ~ ansehen stare at s.o.; **'~en** v/i. (ge-, h) stare (auf acc. at); vor Schmutz ~ be covered with dirt; **'2heit** f (-/no pl.) rigidity (a. fig.), stiffness; **'2kopf** m stubborn or obstinate fellow; **'~köpfig** adj. ['~kœpfiç] stubborn; obstinate; **'2krampf** ✻ m (-[e]s/no pl.) tetanus; **'2sinn** m (-[e]s/no pl.) stubbornness, obstinacy; **'~sinnig** adj. stubborn, obstinate.

Start [ʃtart] m (-[e]s/-s, ✈ -e) start (a. fig.); ✈ take-off; **'~bahn** ✈ f runway; **'2bereit** adj. ready to start; ✈ ready to take off; **'2en** (ge-) 1. v/i. (sein) start; ✈ take off; 2. v/t. (h) start; fig. a. launch; **'~er** m (-s/-) sports: starter; **'~platz** m starting-place.

Station [ʃta'tsjoːn] f (-/-en) station; ward (of hospital); (gegen) freie ~ board and lodging (found); ~ machen break one's journey; **'~svorsteher** 🚉 m station-master, Am. a. station agent.

Statist [ʃta'tist] m (-en/-en) thea. supernumerary (actor), F super; film: extra; **~ik** f (-/-en) statistics pl., sg.; **~iker** m (-s/-) statistician; **2isch** adj. statistic(al).

Stativ [ʃta'tiːf] n (-s/-e) tripod.

Statt [ʃtat] 1. f (-/no pl.): an Eides ~ in lieu of an oath; an Kindes ~ annehmen adopt; 2. ♀ prp. (gen.) instead of; ~ zu inf. instead of ger.; ~ meiner in my place.

Stätte ['ʃtɛtə] f (-/-n) place, spot; scene (of events).

'statt|finden v/i. (irr. finden, sep., -ge-, h) take place, happen; **'~haft** adj. admissible, allowable; legal.

'Statthalter m (-s/-) governor.

'stattlich adj. stately; impressive; sum of money, etc.: considerable.

S

Statue [ˈʃtaːtuə] *f* (-/-n) statue.
statuieren [ʃtatuˈiːrən] *v/t.* (*no* -ge-, *h*): *ein Exempel* ~ make an example (*an dat.* of).
Statur [ʃtaˈtuːr] *f* (-/-en) stature, size.
Statut [ʃtaˈtuːt] *n* (-[e]s/-en) statute; ~*en pl.* regulations *pl.*; ✝ articles *pl.* of association.
Staub [ʃtaʊp] *m* (-[e]s/⊕ -e, ⸚e) dust; powder.
Staubecken [ˈʃtaʊʔ-] *n* reservoir.
stauben [ˈʃtaʊbən] *v/i.* (ge-, *h*) give off dust, make *or* raise a dust.
stäuben [ˈʃtɔʏbən] (ge-, *h*) **1.** *v/t.* dust; **2.** *v/i.* spray.
ˈ**Staub|faden** ⚘ *m* filament; **2ig** *adj.* [ˈ~biç] dusty; **~sauger** [ˈ~p-] *m* (-s/-) vacuum cleaner; **~tuch** [ˈ~p-] *n* (-[e]s/⸚er) duster.
stauchen ⊕ [ˈʃtaʊxən] *v/t.* (ge-, *h*) upset, jolt.
ˈ**Staudamm** *m* dam.
Staude ⚘ [ˈʃtaʊdə] *f* (-/-n) perennial (plant); head (of lettuce).
stau|en [ˈʃtaʊən] *v/t.* (ge-, *h*) dam (up) (*river, etc.*); ⚓ stow; *sich* ~ *waters, etc.*: be dammed (up); *vehicles*: be jammed; ˈ**2er** ⚓ *m* (-s/-) stevedore.
staunen [ˈʃtaʊnən] **1.** *v/i.* (ge-, *h*) be astonished (*über acc.* at); **2.** 2 *n* (-s/*no pl.*) astonishment; ˈ**~swert** *adj.* astonishing.
Staupe *vet.* [ˈʃtaʊpə] *f* (-/-n) distemper.
ˈ**Stau|see** *m* reservoir; ˈ**~ung** *f* (-/-en) damming (up) (*of water*); stoppage; ⚕ congestion (*a. of traffic*); jam; ⚓ stowage.
stechen [ˈʃtɛçən] (*irr.*, ge-, *h*) **1.** *v/t.* prick; *insect, etc.*: sting; *flea, mosquito, etc.*: bite; *card*: take, trump (*other card*); ⊕ engrave (*in or auf acc.* on); cut (*lawn, etc.*); *sich in den Finger* ~ prick one's finger; **2.** *v/i.* prick; stab (*nach* at); *insect, etc.*: sting; *flea, mosquito, etc.*: bite; *sun*: burn; *j-m in die Augen* ~ strike s.o.'s eye; ˈ**~d** *adj. pain, look, etc.*: piercing; *pain*: stabbing.
Steck|brief ⚖ [ˈʃtɛk-] *m* warrant of apprehension; ˈ**2brieflich** ⚖ *adv.*: *er wird* ~ *gesucht* a warrant is out against him; ˈ**~dose** ⚡ *f* (wall) socket; ˈ**2en** **1.** *v/t.* (ge-, *h*) put; *esp.* ⊕ insert (*in acc.* into); F stick; pin (*an acc.* to, on); ⚘ set, plant; **2.** *v/i.* ([*irr.*,] ge-, *h*) be; stick, be stuck; *tief in Schulden* ~ be deeply in debt; ˈ**~en** *m* (-s/-) stick; ˈ**2enbleiben** *v/i.* (*irr. bleiben, sep.*, -ge-, *sein*) get stuck; *speaker, etc.*: break down; ˈ**~enpferd** *n* hobby-horse; *fig.* hobby; ˈ**~er** ⚡ *m* (-s/-) plug; ˈ**~kontakt** ⚡ *m s. Steckdose*; ˈ**~nadel** *f* pin.
Steg [ʃteːk] *m* (-[e]s/-e) foot-bridge; ⚓ landing-stage; ˈ**~reif** *m* (-[e]s/-e): *aus dem* ~ extempore, offhand (*both a. attr.*); *aus dem* ~ *sprechen* extemporize, F ad-lib.
stehen [ˈʃteːən] *v/i.* (*irr.*, ge-, *h*) stand; be; be written; *dress*: suit, become (*j-m* s.o.); ~ *vor* be faced with; *gut* ~ *mit* be on good terms with; *es kam ihm or ihn teuer zu* ~ it cost him dearly; *wie steht's mit ...?* what about ...?; *wie steht das Spiel?* what's the score?; ~ *bleiben* remain standing; ˈ**~bleiben** *v/i.* (*irr. bleiben, sep.*, -ge-, *sein*) stand (still), stop; leave off reading, *etc.*; ˈ**~lassen** *v/t.* (*irr. lassen, sep.*, [*no*] -ge-, *h*) turn one's back (up)on; leave (*meal*) untouched; leave (behind), forget; leave alone.
ˈ**Steher** *m* (-s/-) *sports*: stayer.
ˈ**Steh|kragen** *m* stand-up collar; ˈ**~lampe** *f* standard lamp; ˈ**~leiter** *f* (e-e a pair of) steps *pl.*, step-ladder.
stehlen [ˈʃteːlən] (*irr.*, ge-, *h*) **1.** *v/t.* steal; *j-m Geld* ~ steal s.o.'s money; **2.** *v/i.* steal.
ˈ**Stehplatz** *m* standing-room; ˈ**~inhaber** *m Am.* F standee; *in bus, etc.*: straphanger.
steif *adj.* [ʃtaɪf] stiff (*a. fig.*); numb (*vor Kälte* with cold); ˈ**~halten** *v/t.* (*irr. halten, sep.* -ge-, *h*): F *die Ohren* ~ keep a stiff upper lip.
Steig [ʃtaɪk] *m* (-[e]s/-e) steep path; ˈ**~bügel** *m* stirrup.
steigen [ˈʃtaɪgən] **1.** *v/i.* (*irr.*, ge-, *sein*) *flood, barometer, spirits, prices, etc.*: rise; *mists, etc.*: ascend; *blood, tension, etc.*: mount; *prices, etc.*: increase; *auf e-n Baum* ~ climb a tree; **2.** 2 *n* (-s/*no pl.*) rise; *fig. a.* increase.
steigern [ˈʃtaɪgərn] *v/t.* (ge-, *h*) raise; increase; enhance; *gr.* compare.
ˈ**Steigerung** *f* (-/-en) raising; increase; enhancement; *gr.* comparison; ˈ**~sstufe** *gr. f* degree of comparison.

S

Steigung ['ʃtaɪɡuŋ] f (-/-en) rise, gradient, ascent, grade.

steil adj. [ʃtaɪl] steep; precipitous.

Stein [ʃtaɪn] m (-[e]s/-e) stone (a. ⚕, ♟), Am. F a. rock; s. Edel♫; '**⌂alt** F adj. (as) old as the hills; '**⌂bruch** m quarry; '**⌂druck** m 1. (-[e]s/no pl.) lithography; **2.** (-[e]s/-e) lithograph; '**⌂drucker** m lithographer; ♫**ern** adj. stone-..., of stone; fig. stony; '**⌂gut** n (-[e]s/-e) crockery, stoneware, earthenware; ♫**ig** adj. stony; '**⌂igen** ['⌂ɡən] v/t. (ge-, h) stone; '**⌂igung** ['⌂ɡuŋ] f (-/-en) stoning; '**⌂kohle** f mineral coal; pit-coal; **⌂metz** m ['⌂mɛts] m (-en/-en) stonemason; '**⌂obst** n stone-fruit; '♫**reich** F adj. immensely rich; '**⌂salz** n (-es/no pl.) rock-salt; '**⌂setzer** m (-s/-) pavio(u)r; '**⌂wurf** m throwing of a stone; fig. stone's throw; '**⌂zeit** f (-/no pl.) stone age.

Steiß [ʃtaɪs] m (-es/-e) buttocks pl., rump; '**⌂bein** anat. n coccyx.

Stelldichein co. ['ʃtɛldɪçʔaɪn] n (-[s]/-[s]) meeting, appointment, rendezvous, Am. F a. date.

Stelle ['ʃtɛlə] f (-/-n) place; spot; point; employment, situation, post, place, F job; agency, authority; passage (of book, etc.); freie ⌂ vacancy; an deiner ⌂ in your place, if I were you; auf der ⌂ on the spot; zur ⌂ sein be present.

'**stellen** v/t. (ge-, h) put, place, set, stand; regulate (watch, etc.); set (watch, trap, task, etc.); stop (thief, etc.); hunt down (criminal); furnish, supply, provide; Bedingungen ⌂ make conditions; e-e Falle ⌂ a. lay a snare; sich ⌂ give o.s. up (to the police); stand, place o.s. (somewhere); sich krank ⌂ feign or pretend to be ill.

'**Stellen**|**angebot** n position offered, vacancy; '**⌂gesuch** n application for a post; ♫**weise** adv. here and there, sporadically.

'**Stellung** f (-/-en) position, posture; position, situation, (place of) employment; position, rank, status; arrangement (a. gr.); ✕ position; ⌂ nehmen give one's opinion (zu on), comment (upon); **⌂nahme** ['⌂naːmə] f (-/-n) attitude (zu to[wards]); opinion (on); comment (on); '♫**slos** adj. unemployed.

'**stellvertret**|**end** adj. vicarious,

representative; acting, deputy; **⌂er Vorsitzender** vice-chairman, deputy chairman; '♫**er** m representative; deputy; proxy; '♫**ung** f representation; substitution; proxy.

Stelz|**bein** contp. ['ʃtɛlts-] n wooden leg; '**⌂e** f (-/-n) stilt; '♫**en** mst iro. v/i. (ge-, sein) stalk.

stemmen ['ʃtɛmən] v/t. (ge-, h) lift (weight); sich ⌂ press (gegen against); fig. resist or oppose s.th.

Stempel ['ʃtɛmpəl] m (-s/-) stamp; ⊕ piston; ♀ pistil; '**⌂geld** F n the dole; '**⌂kissen** F ink-pad; '♫**n** (ge-, h) **1.** v/t. stamp; hallmark (gold, silver); **2.** v/i. F: ⌂ gehen be on the dole.

Stengel ♀ ['ʃtɛŋəl] m (-s/-) stalk, stem.

Steno F ['ʃteno] f (-/no pl.) s. Stenographie; '**⌂gramm** n (-s/-e) stenograph; **⌂graph** [⌂'ɡraːf] m (-en/-en) stenographer; **⌂graphie** [⌂a'fiː] f (-/-n) stenography, shorthand; ♫**graphieren** [⌂a'fiːrən] (no -ge-, h) **1.** v/t. take down in shorthand; **2.** v/i. know shorthand; ♫**graphisch** [⌂'ɡraːfiʃ] **1.** adj. shorthand, stenographic; **2.** adv. in shorthand; **⌂typistin** [⌂ty'pistin] f (-/-nen) shorthand-typist.

Stepp|**decke** ['ʃtɛp-] f quilt, Am. a. comforter; '♫**en** (ge-, h) **1.** v/t. quilt; stitch; **2.** v/i. tap-dance.

Sterbe|**bett** ['ʃtɛrbə-] n deathbed; '**⌂fall** m (case of) death; '**⌂kasse** f burial-fund.

'**sterben 1.** v/i. (irr., ge-, sein) die (a. fig.) (an dat. of); esp. ♫ decease; **2.** ♫ n (-s/no pl.): im ⌂ liegen be dying.

sterblich ['ʃtɛrplɪç] **1.** adj. mortal; **2.** adv.: ⌂ verliebt sein be desperately in love (in acc. with); ♫**keit** f (-/no pl.) mortality; '♫**keitsziffer** f death-rate, mortality.

stereotyp adj. [stereo'tyːp] typ. stereotyped (a. fig.); **⌂ieren** typ. [⌂y'piːrən] v/t. (no -ge-, h) stereotype.

steril adj. [ʃteˈriːl] sterile; **⌂isieren** [⌂ili'ziːrən] v/t. (no -ge-, h) sterilize.

Stern [ʃtɛrn] m (-[e]s/-e) star (a. fig.); '**⌂bild** ast. n constellation; '**⌂deuter** m (-s/-) astrologer; '**⌂deutung** f astrology; '**⌂enbanner** n Star-Spangled Banner, Stars and Stripes pl., Old Glory; '**⌂fahrt**

mot. f motor rally; '**~gucker** F *m* (-s/-) star-gazer; '2**hell** *adj.* starry, starlit; '**~himmel** *m* (-s/no *pl.*) starry sky; '**~kunde** *f* (-/no *pl.*) astronomy; '**~schnuppe** *f* (-/-n) shooting star; '**~warte** *f* observatory.

stet *adj.* [∫te:t], '**~ig** *adj.* continual, constant; steady; '2**igkeit** *f* (-/no *pl.*) constancy, continuity; steadiness; **~s** *adv.* always; constantly.

Steuer ['∫tɔʏər] **1.** *n* (-s/-) ⚓ helm, rudder; steering-wheel; **2.** *f* (-/-n) tax; duty; rate, local tax; '**~amt** *n s. Finanzamt;* '**~beamte** *m* revenue officer; '**~berater** *m* (-s/-) tax adviser; '**~bord** ⚓ *n* (-[e]s/-e) starboard; '**~erhebung** *f* levy of taxes; '**~erklärung** *f* tax-return; '**~ermäßigung** *f* tax allowance; '2**frei** *adj.* tax-free; *goods:* duty-free; '**~freiheit** *f* (-/no *pl.*) exemption from taxes; '**~hinterziehung** *f* tax-evasion; '**~jahr** *n* fiscal year; '**~klasse** *f* tax-bracket; '**~knüppel** ✈ *m* control lever or stick; '**~mann** *m* (-[e]s/**~er**, *Steuerleute*) ⚓ helmsman, steersman, *Am. a.* wheelsman; coxwain (*a. rowing*); '2**n** (ge-) **1.** *v/t.* (*h*) ⚓, ✈ steer, navigate, pilot; ⊕ control; *fig.* direct, control; **2.** *v/i.* (*h*) check *s.th.*; **3.** *v/i.* (sein): **~** in (*acc.*) ⚓ enter (*harbour, etc.*); **~** nach ⚓ be bound for; '2**pflichtig** *adj.* taxable; *goods:* dutiable; '**~rad** *n* steering-wheel; '**~ruder** ⚓ *n* helm, rudder; '**~satz** *m* rate of assessment; '**~ung** *f* (-/-en) ⚓, ✈ steering; ⊕, ⚡ control (*a. fig.*); ✈ controls *pl.*; '**~veranlagung** *f* tax assessment; '**~zahler** *m* (-s/-) taxpayer; ratepayer.

Steven ⚓ ['∫te:vən] *m* (-s/-) stem; stern-post.

Stich [∫tıç] *m* (-[e]s/-e) prick (*of needle, etc.*); sting (*of insect, etc.*); stab (*of knife, etc.*); *sewing:* stitch; *cards:* trick; ⊕ engraving; ♗ stab; **~** halten hold water; *im* **~** *lassen* abandon, desert, forsake.

Stichel|ei *fig.* [∫tıçə'laı] *f* (-/-en) gibe, jeer; '2**n** *fig. v/i.* (ge-, *h*) gibe (*gegen* at), jeer (at).

'**Stich|flamme** *f* flash; '2**haltig** *adj.* valid, sound; **~** *sein* hold water; '**~probe** *f* random test or sample, *Am. a.* spot check; '**~tag** *m* fixed day; '**~wahl** *f* second ballot; '**~**

wort *n* **1.** *typ.* (-[e]s/**~er**) headword; **2.** *thea.* (-[e]s/-e) cue; '**~wunde** *f* stab.

sticken ['∫tıkən] *v/t. and v/i.* (ge-, *h*) embroider.

'**Stick|garn** *n* embroidery floss; '**~husten** ♬ *m* (w)hooping cough; '2**ig** *adj.* stuffy; close; '**~stoff** ♬ *m* (-[e]s/no *pl.*) nitrogen.

stieben ['∫ti:bən] *v/i.* (*irr.,*) ge-, *h*, sein) sparks, *etc.*: fly about.

Stief... ['∫ti:f-] step...

Stiefel ['∫ti:fəl] *m* (-s/-) boot; '**~knecht** *m* bootjack; '**~schaft** *m* leg of a boot.

'**Stief|mutter** *f* (-/**~**) stepmother; '**~mütterchen** ♣ ['**~**mʏtərçən] *n* (-s/-) pansy; '**~vater** *m* stepfather.

stieg [∫ti:k] *pret. of* **steigen**.

Stiel [∫ti:l] *m* (-[e]s/-e) handle; helve (*of weapon, tool*); haft (*of axe*); stick (*of broom*); ♣ stalk.

Stier [∫ti:r] **1.** *zo. m* (-[e]s/-e) bull; **2.** ♀ *adj.* staring; '2**en** *v/i.* (ge-, *h*) stare (*auf acc.* at); '**~kampf** *m* bull-fight.

stieß [∫ti:s] *pret. of* **stoßen**.

Stift [∫tıft] **1.** *m* (-[e]s/-e) pin; peg; tack; pencil, crayon; F *fig.:* youngster; apprentice; **2.** *n* (-[e]s/-e, -er) charitable institution; '2**en** *v/t.* (ge-, *h*) endow, give, *Am. a.* donate; found; *fig.* cause; make (*mischief, peace*); '**~er** *m* (-s/-) donor; founder; *fig.* author; '**~ung** *f* (-/-en) (charitable) endowment, donation; foundation.

Stil [∫ti:l] *m* (-[e]s/-e) style (*a. fig.*); 2**gerecht** *adj.* stylish; 2**isieren** [∫tili'zi:rən] *v/t.* (no -ge-, *h*) stylize; 2**istisch** *adj.* [∫ti'lıstıç] stylistic.

still *adj.* [∫tıl] still, quiet, silent; ✝ dull, slack; secret; **~!** silence!; *im* **~**en secretly; *der* **~**e *Gesellschafter* ✝ sleeping or silent partner; *der* 2e Ozean the Pacific (Ocean); '2**e** *f* (-/no *pl.*) stillness, quiet(ness); silence; *in aller* **~** quietly, silently; privately; 2**eben** *paint.* ['∫tılle:bən] *n* (-s/-) still life; '**~egen** ['∫tıle:gən] *v/t.* (sep., -ge-, *h*) shut down (*factory, etc.*); stop (*traffic, etc.*); '**~en** *v/t.* (ge-, *h*) soothe (*pain*); appease (*appetite*); quench (*thirst*); sta(u)nch (*blood*); nurse (*baby*); '**~halten** *v/i.* (*irr.* halten, sep., -ge-, *h*) keep still; '**~iegen** ['∫tılli:gən] *v/i.* (*irr.* liegen, sep., -ge-, *h*) factory,

etc.: be shut down; *traffic:* be suspended; *machines, etc.:* be idle.
stillos *adj.* ['ʃti:llo:s] without style.
'**stillschweigen 1.** *v/i.* (*irr. schweigen, sep.,* -ge-, *h*) be silent; ~ *zu et.* ignore s.th.; **2.** ♀ *n* (-s/*no pl.*) silence; secrecy; ~ *bewahren* observe secrecy; *et. mit* ~ *übergehen* pass s.th. over in silence; '~d *adj.* silent; *agreement, etc.:* tacit.
'**Still|stand** *m* (-[e]s/*no pl.*) standstill; *fig.:* stagnation (*a.* ✝); deadlock; '♀**stehen** *v/i.* (*irr. stehen, sep.,* -ge-, *h*) stop; be at a standstill; *stillgestanden!* ✕ attention!
'**Stil|möbel** *n/pl.* period furniture; '♀**voll** *adj.* stylish.
Stimm|band *anat.* ['ʃtim-] *n* (-[e]s/⁼er) vocal c(h)ord; '♀**berechtigt** *adj.* entitled to vote; '~**e** *f* (-/-n) voice (*a. ♪, fig.*); vote; comment; *♪* part; '♀**en** (ge-, *h*) **1.** *v/t.* tune (*piano, etc.*); *j-n fröhlich* ~ put s.o. in a merry mood; **2.** *v/i.* be true *or* right; *sum, etc.:* be correct; ~ *für* vote for; '~**enmehrheit** *f* majority *or* plurality of votes; '~**enthaltung** *f* abstention; '~**enzählung** *f* counting of votes; '~**gabel** *♪ f* tuning-fork; '~**recht** *n* right to vote; *pol.* franchise; '~**ung** *f* (-/-en) *♪* tune; *fig.* mood, humo(u)r; '♀**ungsvoll** *adj.* impressive; '~**zettel** *m* ballot, voting-paper.
stinken ['ʃtiŋkən] *v/i.* (*irr.,* ge-, *h*) stink (*nach of*); *F fig.* be fishy.
Stipendium *univ.* ['ʃti'pɛndjum] *n* (-s/*Stipendien*) scholarship; exhibition.
stipp|en ['ʃtipən] *v/t.* (ge-, *h*) dip, steep; '♀**visite** *f F* flying visit.
Stirn [ʃtirn] *f* (-/-en) forehead, brow; *fig.* face, cheek; *j-m die* ~ *bieten* make head against s.o.; *s. runzeln;* '~**runzeln** *n* (-s/*no pl.*) frown(ing).
stob [ʃto:p] *pret. of* stieben.
stöbern *F* ['ʃtø:bərn] *v/i.* (ge-, *h*) rummage (*about*) (*in dat. in*).
stochern ['ʃtɔxərn] *v/i.* (ge-, *h*): ~ *in* (*dat.*) poke (*fire*); pick (*teeth*).
Stock [ʃtɔk] *m* **1.** (-[e]s/⁼e) stick; cane; *♪* baton; beehive; *♀* stock; **2.** (-[e]s/-) stor(e)y, floor; *im ersten* ~ on the first floor, *Am.* on the second floor; '♀**be'trunken** *F adj.* dead drunk; '♀'**blind** *F adj.* stone-blind; '♀'**dunkel** *F adj.* pitch-dark.

Stöckelschuh ['ʃtœkəl-] *m* high-heeled shoe.
stocken *v/i.* (ge-, *h*) stop; *liquid:* stagnate (*a. fig.*); *speaker:* break down; *voice:* falter; *traffic:* be blocked; *ihm stockte das Blut* his blood curdled.
'**Stock|engländer** *F m* thorough *or* true-born Englishman; '♀'**finster** *F adj.* pitch-dark; '~**fleck** *m* spot of mildew; '♀**(fleck)ig** *adj.* foxy, mildewy; '♀'**nüchtern** *F adj.* (as) sober as a judge; '~**schnupfen** *♂ m* chronic rhinitis; '♀**taub** *F adj.* stone-deaf; '~**ung** *f* (-/-en) stop (-page); stagnation (*of liquid*) (*a. fig.*); block (*of traffic*); '~**werk** *n* stor(e)y, floor.
Stoff [ʃtɔf] *m* -[e]s/-e) matter, substance; material, fabric, textile; material, stuff; *fig.:* subject(-matter); food; '♀**lich** *adj.* material.
stöhnen ['ʃtø:nən] *v/i.* (ge-, *h*) groan, moan.
Stolle ['ʃtɔlə] *f* (-/-n) loaf-shaped Christmas cake; '~**n** *m* (-s/-) *s.* Stolle; ✕ tunnel, gallery (*a.* ✕).
stolpern ['ʃtɔlpərn] *v/i.* (ge-, *sein*) stumble (*über acc. over*), trip (over) (*both a. fig.*).
stolz [ʃtɔlts] **1.** *adj.* proud (*auf acc. of*) (*a. fig.*); haughty; **2.** ♀ *m* (-es/*no pl.*) pride (*auf acc. in*); haughtiness; **~ieren** [~'tsi:rən] *v/i.* (*no* -ge-, *sein*) strut, flaunt.
stopfen ['ʃtɔpfən] (ge-, *h*) **1.** *v/t.* stuff; fill (*pipe*); cram (*poultry, etc.*); darn (*sock, etc.*); *j-m den Mund* ~ stop s.o.'s mouth; **2.** *♂ v/i.* cause constipation.
'**Stopf|garn** *n* darning-yarn; '~**nadel** *f* darning-needle.
Stoppel ['ʃtɔpəl] *f* (-/-n) stubble; '~**bart** *F m* stubbly beard; '♀**ig** *adj.* stubbly.
stopp|en ['ʃtɔpən] (ge-, *h*) **1.** *v/t.* stop; time, *F* clock; **2.** *v/i.* stop; '♀**licht** *mot. n* stop-light; '♀**uhr** *f* stop-watch.
Stöpsel ['ʃtœpsəl] *m* (-s/-) stopper, cork; plug (*a. ∮*); *F fig.* whipper-snapper; '♀**n** *v/t.* (ge-, *h*) stopper, cork; plug (up).
Storch *orn.* [ʃtɔrç] *m* (-[e]s/⁼e) stork.
stören ['ʃtø:rən] (ge-, *h*) **1.** *v/t.* disturb; trouble; *radio:* jam (*reception*); *lassen Sie sich nicht* ~! don't let me disturb you!; *darf ich Sie*

kurz ~? may I trouble you for a minute?; **2.** *v/i.* be intruding; be in the way; **2fried** ['~fri:t] *m* (-[e]s/-e) troublemaker; intruder.

störr|ig *adj.* ['ʃtœriç], **'~isch** *adj.* stubborn, obstinate; *a. horse:* restive.

'Störung *f* (-/-en) disturbance; trouble (*a.* ⊕); breakdown; *radio:* jamming, interference.

Stoß [ʃtoːs] *m* (-es/⁔e) push, shove; thrust (*a. fencing*); kick; butt; shock; knock, strike; blow; *swimming, billiards:* stroke; jolt (*of car, etc.*); pile, stock, heap; **'~dämpfer** *mot. m* shock-absorber; **2en** (*irr.*, ge-) **1.** *v/t.* (*h*) push, shove; thrust (*weapon, etc.*); kick; butt; knock, strike; pound (*pepper, etc.*); *sich* ~ *an* (*dat.*) strike *or* knock against; *fig.* take offence at; **2.** *v/i.* (*h*) thrust (*nach an.*); kick (at); butt (at); *goat, etc.:* butt; *car:* jolt; ~ *an* (*acc.*) adjoin, border on; **3.** *v/i.* (*sein*): F ~ *auf* (*acc.*) come across; meet with (*opposition, etc.*); ~ *gegen an* (*acc.*) knock *or* strike against.

'Stoß|seufzer *m* ejaculation; **'~stange** *mot. f* bumper; **'2weise** *adv.* by jerks; by fits and starts; **'~zahn** *m* tusk.

stottern ['ʃtɔtərn] (ge-, *h*) **1.** *v/t.* stutter (out) *or* stammer; **2.** *v/i.* stutter; stammer; F *mot.* conk (out).

Straf|anstalt ['ʃtraːf²-] *f* penal institution; prison; *Am.* penitentiary; **'~arbeit** *f* imposition, F impo(t); **'2bar** *adj.* punishable, penal; **'~e** *f* (-/-en) punishment; ⚖, ✝, *sports, fig.* penalty; fine; *bei* ~ *von* on *or* under pain of; *zur* ~ as a punishment; **'2en** *v/t.* (ge-, *h*) punish.

straff *adj.* [ʃtraf] tight; *rope:* a. taut; *fig.* strict, rigid.

'straf|fällig *adj.* liable to prosecution; **'2gesetz** *n* penal law; **'2gesetzbuch** *n* penal code.

sträf|lich *adj.* ['ʃtrɛːfliç] culpable; reprehensible; inexcusable; **2ling** ['~lɪŋ] *m* (-s/-e) convict, *Am. sl. a.* lag.

'straf|los *adj.* unpunished; **'2losigkeit** *f* (-/*no pl.*) impunity; **'2porto** *n* surcharge; **'2predigt** *f* severe lecture; *j-m e-e* ~ *halten* lecture s.o. severely; **'2prozeß** *m* criminal action; **'2raum** *m football:* penalty

area; **'2stoß** *m football:* penalty kick; **'2verfahren** *n* criminal proceedings *pl.*

Strahl [ʃtraːl] *m* (-[e]s/-en) ray (*a. fig.*); beam; flash (*of lightning, etc.*); jet (*of water, etc.*); **2en** *v/i.* (ge-, *h*) radiate; shine (*vor dat.* with); *fig.* beam (*vor dat.* with), shine (with); **'~ung** *f* (-/-en) radiation, rays *pl.*

Strähne ['ʃtrɛːnə] *f* (-/-n) lock, strand (*of hair*); skein, hank (*of yarn*); *fig.* stretch.

stramm *adj.* [ʃtram] tight; *rope:* a. taut; stalwart; *soldier:* smart.

strampeln ['ʃtrampəln] *v/i.* (ge-, *h*) kick.

Strand [ʃtrant] *m* (-[e]s/⁔-e, ⁔e) beach; **'~anzug** *m* beach-suit; **2en** ['~dən] *v/i.* (ge-, *sein*) ⚓ strand, run ashore; *fig.* fail, founder; **'~gut** *n* stranded goods *pl.*; *fig.* wreckage; **'~korb** *m roofed wicker chair for use on the beach*; **~promenade** ['~proməna:də] *f* (-/-n) promenade, *Am.* boardwalk.

Strang [ʃtraŋ] *m* (-[e]s/⁔e) cord (*a. anat.*); rope; halter (*for hanging s.o.*); trace (*of harness*); 🚂 track; *über die Stränge schlagen* kick over the traces.

Strapaz|e [ʃtraˈpaːtsə] *f* (-/-n) fatigue; toil; **2ieren** [~aˈtsiːrən] *v/t.* (*no* ge-, *h*) fatigue, strain (*a. fig.*); wear out (*fabric, etc.*); **2ierfähig** *adj.* [~aˈtsiːr-] long-lasting; **2iös** *adj.* [~aˈtsjøːs] fatiguing.

Straße ['ʃtraːsə] *f* (-/-n) road, highway; street (*of town, etc.*); strait; *auf der* ~ on the road; in the street.

'Straßen|anzug *m* lounge-suit, *Am.* business suit; **'~bahn** *f* tram(way), tram-line, *Am.* street railway, streetcar line; *s. Straßenbahnwagen*; **'~bahnhaltestelle** *f* tram stop, *Am.* streetcar stop; **'~bahnwagen** *m* tram(-car), *Am.* streetcar; **'~beleuchtung** *f* street lighting; **'~damm** *m* roadway; **'~händler** *m* hawker; **'~junge** *m* street arab, *Am.* street Arab; **'~kehrer** *m* (-s/-) scavenger, street orderly; **'~kreuzung** *f* crossing, cross roads; **'~reinigung** *f* street-cleaning, scavenging; **'~rennen** *n* road-race.

strategisch *adj.* [ʃtraˈteːgiʃ] strategic(al).

sträuben ['ʃtrɔybən] *v/t.* (ge-, *h*) ruffle up (*its feathers, etc.*); *sich* ~

hair: stand on end; *sich ~ gegen* kick against *or* at.

Strauch [ˈʃtraux] *m* (-[e]s/ᵘer) shrub; bush.

straucheln [ˈʃtrauxəln] *v/i.* (ge-, *sein*) stumble (*über acc.* over, at), trip (over) (*both a. fig.*).

Strauß [ʃtraus] *m* **1.** *orn.* (-es/-e) ostrich; **2.** (-es/ᵘe) bunch (*of flowers*), bouquet; strife, combat.

Strebe [ˈʃtreːbə] *f* (-/-n) strut, support, brace.

streben 1. *v/i.* (ge-, h): ~ *nach* strive for *or* after, aspire to *or* after; **2.** ⒉ *n* (-s/*no pl.*) striving (*nach* for, after), aspiration (for, after); effort, endeavo(u)r.

Streber *m* (-s/-) pusher, careerist; *at school*: *sl.* swot.

strebsam *adj.* [ˈʃtreːpzaːm] assiduous; ambitious; ⒉**keit** *f* (-/*no pl.*) assiduity; ambition.

Strecke [ˈʃtrɛkə] *f* (-/-n) stretch; route; tract, extent; distance (*a. sports*); course; 🚂, *etc.*: section, line; *hunt.* bag; *zur* ~ *bringen hunt.* bag, hunt down (*a. fig.*); ⒉**n** *v/t.* (ge-, h) stretch, extend; dilute (*fluid*); *sich* ~ stretch (o.s.); *die Waffen* ~ lay down one's arms; *fig. a.* give in.

Streich [ʃtraiç] *m* (-[e]s/-e) stroke; blow; *fig.* trick, prank; *j-m e-n* ~ *spielen* play a trick on s.o.; ⒉**eln** [ˈ~əln] *v/t.* (ge-, h) stroke, caress; pat; ⒉**en** (*irr.*, ge-) **1.** *v/t.* (h) rub; spread (*butter, etc.*); paint; strike out, delete, cancel (*a. fig.*); strike, lower (*flag, sail*); **2.** *v/i.* (*sein*) prowl (*um round*); **3.** *v/i.*(h): *mit der Hand über et.* ~ pass one's hand over s.th.; '~**holz** *n* match; '~**instrument** ♩ *n* stringed instrument; '~**orchester** *n* string band; '~**riemen** *m* strop.

Streif [ʃtraif] *m* (-[e]s/-e) *s.* Streifen; '~**band** *n* (-[e]s/ᵘer) wrapper; '~**e** *f* (-/-n) patrol; patrolman; raid.

'streifen (ge-) **1.** *v/t.* (h) stripe, streak; graze, touch lightly in passing, brush; touch (up)on (*subject*); **2.** *v/i.* (*sein*): ~ *durch* rove, wander through; **3.** *v/i.* (h): ~ *an* (*acc.*) graze, brush; *fig.* border *or* verge on; **4.** ⒉ *m* (-s/-) strip; stripe; streak.

'streif|ig *adj.* striped; ⒉**licht** *n* sidelight; ⒉**schuß** ✕ *m* grazing shot; ⒉**zug** *m* ramble; ✕ raid.

Streik [ʃtraik] *m* (-[e]s/-s) strike, *Am.* F *a.* walkout; *in den* ~ *treten* go on strike, *Am.* F *a.* walk out; '~**brecher** *m* (-s/-) strike-breaker, blackleg, scab; ⒉**en** *v/i.* (ge-, h) (be on) strike; go on strike, *Am.* F *a.* walk out; '~**ende** [ˈ~əndə] *m, f* (-n/-n) striker; '~**posten** *m* picket.

Streit [ʃtrait] *m* (-[e]s/-e) quarrel; dispute; conflict; 🏛 litigation; ⒉**bar** *adj.* pugnacious; ⒉**en** *v/i. and v/refl.* (*irr.*, ge-, h) quarrel (*mit* with; *wegen* for; *über acc.* about); '~**frage** *f* controversy, (point of) issue; ⒉**ig** *adj.* debatable, controversial; *j-m et.* ~ *machen* dispute s.o.'s right to s.th.; '~**igkeiten** *f/pl.* quarrels *pl.*; disputes *pl.*; ~**kräfte** ✕ [ˈ~krɛftə] *f/pl.* (military *or* armed) forces *pl.*; ⒉**lustig** *adj.* pugnacious, aggressive; ⒉**süchtig** *adj.* quarrelsome; pugnacious.

streng [ʃtrɛŋ] **1.** *adj.* severe; stern; strict; austere; *discipline, etc.*: rigorous; *weather, climate*: inclement; *examination*: stiff; **2.** *adv.*: ~ *vertraulich* in strict confidence; ⒉**e** *f* (-/*no pl.*) *s.* streng 1: severity; sternness; strictness; austerity; rigo(u)r; inclemency; stiffness; '~**genommen** *adv.* strictly speaking; '~**gläubig** *adj.* orthodox.

Streu [ʃtrɔy] *f* (-/-en) litter; ⒉**en** *v/t.* (ge-, h) strew, scatter; '~**zucker** *m* castor sugar.

Strich [ʃtriç] *m* (-[e]s/-e) stroke; line; dash; tract (*of land*); *j-m e-n* ~ *durch die Rechnung machen* queer s.o.'s pitch; **2.** ⒉ *pret. of* streichen; '~**regen** *m* local shower; ⒉**weise** *adv.* here and there.

Strick [ʃtrik] *m* (-[e]s/-e) cord; rope; halter, rope (*for hanging s.o.*); F *fig.* (young) rascal; ⒉**en** *v/t. and v/i.* (ge-, h) knit; '~**garn** *n* knitting-yarn; '~**jacke** *f* cardigan, jersey; '~**leiter** *f* rope-ladder; '~**nadel** *f* knitting-needle; '~**waren** *f/pl.* knitwear; '~**zeug** *n* knitting(-things *pl.*).

Striemen [ˈʃtriːmən] *m* (-s/-) weal, wale.

Strippe F [ˈʃtripə] *f* (-/-n) band; string; shoe-lace; *an der* ~ *hängen* be on the phone.

stritt [ʃtrit] *pret. of* streiten; '~**ig** *adj.* debatable, controversial; ~*er Punkt* (point of) issue.

Stroh [ʃtroː] *n* (-[e]s/*no pl.*) straw;

thatch; **'⁓dach** n thatch(ed roof); **'⁓halm** m straw; *nach e-m ⁓ greifen* catch at a straw; **'⁓hut** m straw hat; **'⁓mann** m man of straw; scarecrow; *fig.* dummy; **'⁓sack** m straw mattress; **'⁓witwe** F f grass widow.

Strolch [ʃtrɔlç] m (-[e]s/-e) scamp, F vagabond; **⁷en** v/i. (ge-, sein): ⁓ *durch* rove.

Strom [ʃtroːm] m (-[e]s/⁓e) stream (a. *fig.*); (large) river; ⁄ current (a. *fig.*); *es regnet in Strömen* it is pouring with rain; **⁷ab(wärts)** adv. down-stream; **⁷auf(wärts)** adv. up-stream.

strömen ['ʃtrøːmən] v/i. (ge-, sein) stream; flow, run; *rain*: pour; *people*: stream, pour (*aus* out of; *in* acc. into).

'Strom|kreis ⁄ m circuit; **'⁓linienform** f (-/no pl.) streamline shape; **⁷linienförmig** adj. streamline(d); **'⁓schnelle** f (-/-n) rapid, Am. a. riffle; **'⁓sperre** ⁄ f stoppage of current. [trend, tendency.]

'Strömung f (-/-en) current; *fig. a.*]

'Stromzähler ⁄ m electric meter.

Strophe ['ʃtroːfə] f (-/-n) stanza, verse.

strotzen ['ʃtrɔtsən] v/i. (ge-, h): ⁓ *von* abound in; teem with (*blunders, etc.*); burst with (*health, etc.*).

Strudel ['ʃtruːdəl] m (-s/-) eddy, whirlpool; *fig.* whirl; **⁷n** v/i. (ge-, h) swirl, whirl. [ture.]

Struktur [ʃtrʊkˈtuːr] f (-/-en) struc-]

Strumpf [ʃtrʊmpf] m (-[e]s/⁓e) stocking; **'⁓band** n (-[e]s/⁓er) garter; **'⁓halter** m (-s/-) suspender, Am. garter; **'⁓waren** f/pl. hosiery.

struppig adj. ['ʃtrʊpɪç] *hair*: rough, shaggy; *dog, etc.*: shaggy.

Stube ['ʃtuːbə] f (-/-n) room.

'Stuben|hocker *fig.* m (-s/-) stay-at-home; **'⁓mädchen** n chambermaid; **⁷rein** adj. house-trained.

Stück [ʃtyk] n (-[e]s/-e) piece (a. ♩); fragment; head (*of cattle*); lump (*of sugar*); *thea.* play; *aus freien ⁓en* of one's own accord; *in ⁓e gehen* or *schlagen* break to pieces; **'⁓arbeit** f piece-work; **⁷weise** adv. piece by piece; (by) piecemeal; † by the piece; **'⁓werk** *fig.* n patchwork.

Student [ʃtuˈdɛnt] m (-en/-en), **⁓in** f (-/-nen) student, undergraduate.

Studie ['ʃtuːdjə] f (-/-n) study (*über*

---

acc., zu of, in) (a. *art, literature*); *paint, etc.*: sketch; **'⁓nrat** m (-[e]s/⁓e) *appr.* secondary-school teacher; **'⁓nreise** f study trip.

studier|en [ʃtuˈdiːrən] (*no* -ge-, h) **1.** v/t. study, read (*law, etc.*); **2.** v/i. study; be a student; **⁷zimmer** n study.

Studium ['ʃtuːdjʊm] n (-s/Studien) study (a. *fig.*); studies *pl.*

Stufe ['ʃtuːfə] f (-/-n) step; *fig.*: degree; grade; stage.

'Stufen|folge *fig.* f gradation; **'⁓leiter** f step-ladder; *fig.* scale; **⁷weise 1.** adj. gradual; **2.** adv. gradually, by degrees.

Stuhl [ʃtuːl] m (-[e]s/⁓e) chair, seat; *in a church*: pew; *weaving*: loom; **⁄ s. Stuhlgang;** **'⁓bein** n leg of a chair; **'⁓gang** ♂ m (-[e]s/no pl.) stool; motion; **'⁓lehne** f back of a chair.

stülpen ['ʃtylpən] v/t. (ge-, h) put (*über* acc. over); clap (*hat*) (*auf* acc. on).

stumm adj. [ʃtʊm] dumb, mute; *fig. a.* silent; ⁄r. silent, mute.

Stummel ['ʃtʊməl] m (-s/-) stump;]

'Stummfilm m silent film. [stub.]

Stümper F ['ʃtʏmpər] m (-s/-) bungler; **⁓ei** F [⁓ˈraɪ] f (-/-en) bungling; bungle; **⁷haft** adj. bungling; **⁷n** F v/i. (ge-, h) bungle, botch.

stumpf [ʃtʊmpf] **1.** adj. blunt; A angle: obtuse; *senses*: dull, obtuse; apathetic; **2.** ⁓ m (-[e]s/⁓e) stump, stub; *mit ⁓ und Stiel* root and branch; **⁷sinn** m (-[e]s/no pl.) stupidity, dul(l)ness; **'⁓sinnig** adj. stupid, dull.

Stunde ['ʃtʊndə] f (-/-n) hour; lesson, Am. a. period; **⁷n** v/t. (ge-, h) grant respite for.

'Stunden|kilometer m kilometre per hour, Am. kilometer per hour; **⁷lang 1.** adj.: *nach ⁓em Warten* after hours of waiting; **2.** adv. for hours (and hours); **'⁓lohn** m hourly wage; **'⁓plan** m time-table, Am. schedule; **⁷weise 1.** adj.: ⁓ *Beschäftigung* part-time employment; **2.** adv. by the hour; **'⁓zeiger** m hour-hand.

stündlich ['ʃtʏntlɪç] **1.** adj. hourly; **2.** adv. hourly, every hour; at any hour.

'Stundung f (-/-en) respite.

stur F *adj.* [ʃtuːr] *gaze:* fixed, staring; *p.* pigheaded, mulish.

Sturm [ʃturm] *m* (-[e]s/ᵘe) storm (*a. fig.*); ⚓ gale.

stürm|en [ˈʃtyrmən] (ge-) 1. *v/t.* (h) ✗ storm (*a. fig.*); 2. *v/i.* (h) *wind:* storm, rage; *es stürmt* it is stormy weather; 3. *v/i.* (sein) rush; 'Ler *m* (-s/-) *football, etc.:* forward; 'Lisch *adj.* stormy; *fig.:* impetuous; tumultuous.

'Sturm|schritt ✗ *m* double-quick step; 'Ltrupp ✗ *m* storming-party; 'Lwind *m* storm-wind.

Sturz [ʃturts] *m* (-es/ᵘe) fall, tumble; overthrow (*of government, etc.*); *fig.* ruin; ✝ slump; 'Lbach *m* torrent.

stürzen [ˈʃtyrtsən] (ge-) 1. *v/i.* (sein) (have a) fall, tumble; *fig.* rush, plunge (*in acc.* into); 2. *v/t.* (h) throw; overthrow (*government, etc.*); *fig.* plunge (*in acc.* into); precipitate (into); *j-n ins Unglück* ∼ ruin s.o.; *sich in Schulden* ∼ plunge into debt.

'Sturz|flug ✈ *m* (nose)dive; 'Lhelm *m* crash-helmet.

Stute *zo.* [ˈʃtuːtə] *f* (-/-n) mare.

Stütze [ˈʃtytsə] *f* (-/-n) support, prop, stay (*all a. fig.*).

stutzen [ˈʃtutsən] (ge-, h) 1. *v/t.* cut (*hedge*); crop (*ears, tail, hair*); clip (*hedge, wing*); trim (*hair, beard, hedge*); dock (*tail*); lop (*tree*); 2. *v/i.* start (*bei at*); stop dead *or* short.

'stützen *v/t.* (ge-, h) support, prop, stay (*all a. fig.*); ∼ *auf* (*acc.*) base *or* found on; *sich* ∼ *auf* (*acc.*) lean on; *fig.* rely (up)on; *argument, etc.:* be based on.

'Stutz|er *m* (-s/-) dandy, fop, *Am. a.* dude; 'Lig *adj.* suspicious; ∼ *machen* make suspicious.

'Stütz|pfeiler △ *m* abutment; 'Lpunkt *m phys.* fulcrum; ✗ base.

Subjekt [zupˈjɛkt] *n* (-[e]s/-e) *gr.* subject; *contp.* individual; 2iv *adj.* [Lˈtiːf] subjective; Livität [Liviˈtɛːt] *f* (-/*no pl.*) subjectivity.

Substantiv *gr.* [ˈzupstantiːf] *n* (-s/-e) noun, substantive; 2isch *gr. adj.* [ˈLviʃ] substantival.

Substanz [zupˈstants] *f* (-/-en) substance (*a. fig.*).

subtra|hieren 𝔄 [zuptraˈhiːrən] *v/t.* (*no* -ge-, h) subtract; 2ktion 𝔄

[Lkˈtsjoːn] *f* (-/-en) subtraction.

Such|dienst [ˈzuːx-] *m* tracing service; 'Le *f* (-/*no pl.*) search (*nach* for); *auf der* ∼ *nach* in search of; '2en (ge-, h) 1. *v/t.* seek (*advice, etc.*); search for; look for; *Sie haben hier nichts zu* ∼ you have no business to be here; 2. *v/i.:* ∼ *nach* seek for *or* after; search for; look for; 'Ler *phot. m* (-s/-) view-finder.

Sucht [zuxt] *f* (-/ᵘe) mania (*nach* for), rage (for), addiction (to).

süchtig *adj.* [ˈzyçtɪç] having a mania (*nach* for); ∼ *sein* be a drug addict; 2e [ˈLɡə] *m, f* (-n/-n) drug addict *or* fiend.

Süd *geogr.* [zyːt], ∼en [ˈLdən] *m* (-s/*no pl.*) south; 2früchte [ˈzyːt-fryçtə] *f/pl.* fruits from the south; '2lich 1. *adj.* south(ern); southerly; 2. *adv.:* ∼ *von* (to the) south of; ∼'ost *geogr.*, ∼'osten *m* (-s/*no pl.*) south-east; 2'östlich *adj.* south-east(ern); 'Lpol *geogr. m* (-s/*no pl.*) South Pole; 2wärts *adv.* [ˈLvɛrts] southward(s); ∼'west *geogr.*, ∼'westen *m* (-s/*no pl.*) south-west; 2'westlich *adj.* south-west(ern); 'Lwind *m* south wind.

süffig F *adj.* [ˈzyfɪç] palatable, tasty.

suggerieren [zugeˈriːrən] *v/t.* (*no* -ge-, h) suggest.

suggestiv *adj.* [zugɛsˈtiːf] suggestive.

Sühne [ˈzyːnə] *f* (-/-n) expiation, atonement; '2n *v/t.* (ge-, h) expiate, atone for.

Sülze [ˈzyltsə] *f* (-/-n) jellied meat.

summ|arisch *adj.* [zuˈmaːrɪʃ] summary (*a. ⚖*); '2e *f* (-/-n) sum (*a. fig.*); (sum) total; amount.

'summen (ge-, h) 1. *v/i.* bees, etc.: buzz, hum; 2. *v/t.* hum (*song, etc.*).

sum'mieren *v/t.* (*no* -ge-, h) sum *or* add up; *sich* ∼ run up.

Sumpf [zumpf] *m* (-[e]s/ᵘe) swamp, bog, marsh; '2ig *adj.* swampy, boggy, marshy.

Sünd|e [ˈzyndə] *f* (-/-n) sin (*a. fig.*); 'Lenbock F *m* scapegoat; 'Ler *m* (-s/-) sinner; 2haft [ˈLt-] 1. *adj.* sinful; 2. *adv.:* F ∼ *teuer* awfully expensive; 2ig [ˈLdɪç] *adj.* sinful; 2igen [ˈLdɪɡən] *v/i.* (ge-, h) (commit a) sin.

Superlativ [ˈzuːperlatiːf] *m* (-s/-e) *gr.* superlative degree; *in* ∼*en sprechen* speak in superlatives.

Suppe ['zupə] *f* (-/-n) soup; broth.
'Suppen|löffel *m* soup-spoon; '**~schöpfer** *m* soup ladle; '**~schüssel** *f* tureen; '**~teller** *m* soup-plate.

surren ['zurən] *v/i.* (ge-, h) whir(r); *insects:* buzz.

Surrogat [zuro'gɑːt] *n* (-[e]s/-e) substitute.

suspendieren [zuspɛn'diːrən] *v/t.* (*no* -ge-, h) suspend.

süß *adj.* [zyːs] sweet (*a. fig.*); '²**e** *f* (-/*no pl.*) sweetness; '**~en** *v/t.* (ge-, h) sweeten; '²**igkeiten** *pl.* sweets *pl.*, sweetmeats *pl.*, *Am. a.* candy; '**~lich** *adj.* sweetish; mawkish (*a. fig.*); '²**stoff** *m* saccharin(e); '²**wasser** *n* (-s/-) fresh water.

Symbol [zym'boːl] *n* (-s/-e) symbol; **~ik** *f* (-/*no pl.*) symbolism; ²**isch** *adj.* symbolic(al).

Symmetr|ie [zyme'triː] *f* (-/-n) symmetry; ²**isch** *adj.* [~'meːtriʃ] symmetric(al).

Sympath|ie [zympa'tiː] *f* (-/-n) liking; ²**isch** *adj.* [~'pɑːtiʃ] likable; *er ist mir ~* I like him;

~isieren [~i'ziːrən] *v/i.* (*no* -ge-, h) sympathize (*mit* with).

Symphonie ♪ [zymfo'niː] *f* (-/-n) symphony; **~orchester** *n* symphony orchestra.

Symptom [zymp'toːm] *n* (-s/-e) symptom; ²**atisch** *adj.* [~o'mɑːtiʃ] symptomatic (*für* of). [synagogue.\
Synagoge [zyna'goːgə] *f* (-/-n)\
synchronisieren [zynkroni'ziːrən] *v/t.* (*no* -ge-, h) synchronize; dub.

Syndik|at [zyndi'kɑːt] *n* (-[e]s/-e) syndicate; **~us** ['zyndikus] *m* (-/-se, *Syndizi*) syndic.   [syncope.\
Synkope ♪ [zyn'koːpə] *f* (-/-n)\
synonym [zyno'nyːm] **1.** *adj.* synonymous; **2.** ²**n** (-s/-e) synonym.

Syntax *gr.* ['zyntaks] *f* (-/-en) syntax.

synthetisch *adj.* [zyn'teːtiʃ] synthetic.

System [zys'teːm] *n* (-s/-e) system; scheme; ²**atisch** *adj.* [~e'mɑːtiʃ] systematic(al), methodic(al).

Szene ['stseːnə] *f* (-/-n) scene (*a. fig.*); *in ~ setzen* stage; **~rie** [stsenə'riː] *f* (-/-n) scenery.

T

Tabak ['tɑːbak, 'tabak, ta'bak] *m* (-s/-e) tobacco; (')**~händler** *m* tobacconist; (')**~sbeutel** *m* tobacco-pouch; (')**~sdose** *f* snuff-box; (')**~waren** *pl.* tobacco products *pl.*, F smokes *pl.*

tabellarisch [tabɛ'lɑːriʃ] **1.** *adj.* tabular; **2.** *adv.* in tabular form.

Tabelle [ta'bɛlə] *f* (-/-n) table; schedule.

Tablett [ta'blɛt] *n* (-[e]s/-e, -s) tray; *of metal:* salver; **~e** *pharm.* *f* (-/-n) tablet; lozenge.

Tachometer [taxo'-] *n, m* (-s/-) ⊕ tachometer; *mot. a.* speedometer.

Tadel ['tɑːdəl] *m* (-s/-) blame; censure; reprimand, rebuke, reproof; reproach; *at school:* bad mark; '²**los** *adj.* faultless, blameless; excellent, splendid; '²**n** *v/t.* (ge-, h) blame (*wegen* for); censure; reprimand, rebuke, reprove; scold; find fault with.

Tafel ['tɑːfəl] *f* (-/-n) table; plate (*a. book illustration*); slab; *on houses, etc.:* tablet, plaque; slate; black-

board; signboard, notice-board, *Am.* billboard; cake, bar (*of chocolate, etc.*); dinner-table; dinner; ²**förmig** *adj.* ['~fœrmiç] tabular; '**~geschirr** *n* dinner-service, dinner-set; '**~land** *n* tableland, plateau; '²**n** *v/i.* (ge-, h) dine; feast, banquet; '**~service** *n s. Tafelgeschirr;* '**~silber** *n* silver plate, *Am.* silverware.

Täf(e)lung ['tɛːf(ə)luŋ] *f* (-/-en) wainscot, panelling.

Taft [taft] *m* (-[e]s/-e) taffeta.

Tag [tɑːk] *m* (-[e]s/-e) day; *officially:* a. date; *am or bei ~e* by day; *e-s ~es* one day; *den ganzen ~* all day long; *~ für ~* day by day; *über ~e* ⚒ aboveground; *unter ~e* ⚒ underground; *heute vor acht ~en* a week ago; *heute in acht (vierzehn) ~en* today *or* this day week (fortnight), a week (fortnight) today; *denkwürdiger or freudiger ~* red-letter day; *freier ~* day off; *guten ~!* how do you do?; good morning!; good afternoon!; F hallo!, hullo!, *Am.*

hello!; *am hellichten* ~*e* in broad daylight; *es wird* ~ it dawns; *an den* ~ *bringen* (*kommen*) bring (come) to light; *bis auf den heutigen* ~ to this day; 2'**aus** *adv.*: ~, *tagein* day in, day out.

Tage|blatt ['tɑːgə-] *n* daily (paper); '~**buch** *n* journal, diary.

tagein *adv.* [tɑːk'aɪn] *s.* tagaus.

tage|lang *adv.* ['tɑːgə-] day after day, for days together; 2**lohn** *m* day's *or* daily wages *pl.*; 2**löhner** ['~løːnər] *m* (*-s/-*) day-labo(u)rer; '~**n** *v/i.* (ge-, h) dawn; hold a meeting, meet, sit; ʒʒ be in session; 2**reise** *f* day's journey.

Tages|anbruch ['tɑːgəsʔ-] *m* daybreak, dawn; *bei* ~ at daybreak *or* dawn; '~**befehl** ✕ *m* order of the day; '~**bericht** *m* daily report, bulletin; '~**einnahme** † *f* receipts *pl. or* takings *pl.* of the day; '~**gespräch** *n* topic of the day; '~**kasse** *f thea.* box-office, booking-office; *s.* Tageseinnahme; '~**kurs** † *m* current rate; *stock exchange:* quotation of the day; '~**licht** *n* daylight; '~**ordnung** *f* order of the day, agenda; *das ist an der* ~ that is the order of the day, that is quite common; '~**presse** *f* daily press; '~**zeit** *f* time of day; daytime; *zu jeder* ~ at any hour, at any time of the day; '~**zeitung** *f* daily (paper).

tage|weise *adv.* ['tɑːgə-] by the day; 2**werk** *n* day's work; man-day.

täglich *adj.* ['tɛːklɪç] daily.

tags *adv.* [tɑːks]: ~ *darauf* the following day, the day after; ~ *zuvor* (on) the previous day, the day before.

'**Tagschicht** *f* day shift.

tagsüber *adv.* ['tɑːksʔ-] during the day, in the day-time.

Tagung ['tɑːguŋ] *f* (*-/-en*) meeting.

Taille ['taljə] *f* (*-/-n*) waist; bodice (*of dress*).

Takel ⚓ ['tɑːkəl] *n* (*-s/-*) tackle; '~**age** ⚓ [takə'lɑːʒə] *f* (*-/-n*) rigging, tackle; 2**n** ⚓ *v/t.* (ge-, h) rig (*ship*); '~**werk** ⚓ *n s.* Takelage.

Takt [takt] *m* **1.** (*-[e]s/-e*) ♩ time, measure; bar; *mot.* stroke; *den* ~ *halten* ♩ keep time; *den* ~ *schlagen* ♩ beat time; **2.** (*-[e]s/no pl.*) tact; 2**fest** *adj.* steady in keeping time; *fig.* firm; '~**ik** ✕ *f* (*-/-en*) tactics *pl. and sg.* (*a. fig.*); '~**iker** *m* (*-s/-*)

tactician; 2**isch** *adj.* tactical; 2**los** *adj.* tactless; '~**stock** *m* baton; '~**strich** ♩ *m* bar; 2**voll** *adj.* tactful.

Tal [tɑːl] *n* (*-[e]s/=er*) valley, *poet. a.* dale; *enges* ~ glen.

Talar [tɑ'lɑːr] *m* (*-s/-e*) ʒʒ, *eccl.*, *univ.* gown; ʒʒ robe.

Talent [ta'lɛnt] *n* (*-[e]s/-e*) talent, gift, aptitude, ability; 2**iert** *adj.* [~'tiːrt] talented, gifted.

'**Talfahrt** *f* downhill journey; ⚓ passage downstream.

Talg [talk] *m* (*-[e]s/-e*) suet; *melted:* tallow; '~**drüse** *anat. f* sebaceous gland; 2**ig** *adj.* ['~giç] suety; tallowish, tallowy; '~**licht** *n* tallow candle.

Talisman ['tɑːlisman] *m* (*-s/-e*) talisman, (good-luck) charm.

'**Talsperre** *f* barrage, dam.

Tampon ♂ [tɑ̃'põ:, 'tampɔn] *m* (*-s/-s*) tampon, plug.

Tang ♣ [taŋ] *m* (*-[e]s/-e*) seaweed.

Tank [taŋk] *m* (*-[e]s/-s, -e*) tank; 2**en** *v/i.* (ge-, h) get (some) petrol, *Am.* get (some) gasoline; '~**er** ⚓ *m* (*-s/-*) tanker; '~**stelle** *f* petrol station, *Am.* gas *or* filling station; '~**wagen** *m mot.* tank truck, *Am. a.* gasoline truck, tank trailer; ʒʒ tank-car; ~**wart** ['~vart] *m* (*-[e]s/-e*) pump attendant.

Tanne ♣ ['tanə] *f* (*-/-n*) fir(-tree).

'**Tannen|baum** *m* fir-tree; '~**nadel** *f* fir-needle; '~**zapfen** *m* fir-cone.

Tante ['tantə] *f* (*-/-n*) aunt.

Tantieme [tɑ̃'tjɛːmə] *f* (*-/-n*) royalty, percentage, share in profits.

Tanz [tants] *m* (*-es/=e*) dance.

tänzeln ['tɛntsəln] *v/i.* (ge-, h, sein) dance, trip, frisk. [(h) dance.)

'**tanzen** (ge-) *v/i.* (h, sein) *and v/t.*)

Tänzer ['tɛntsər] *m* (*-s/-*), '~**in** *f* (*-/-nen*) dancer; *thea.* ballet-dancer; partner.

'**Tanz|lehrer** *m* dancing-master; '~**musik** *f* dance-music; '~**saal** *m* dancing-room, ball-room, dance-hall; '~**schule** *f* dancing-school; '~**stunde** *f* dancing-lesson.

Tapete [ta'peːtə] *f* (*-/-n*) wallpaper, paper-hangings *pl.*

tapezier|en [tape'tsiːrən] *v/t.* (*no -ge-, h*) paper; 2**er** *m* (*-s/-*) paperhanger; upholsterer.

tapfer *adj.* ['tapfər] brave; valiant, heroic; courageous; 2**keit** *f* (*-/no* *pl.*) bravery, valo(u)r; heroism; courage.

tappen ['tapən] *v/i.* (ge-, *sein*) grope (about), fumble. [awkward.\

täppisch *adj.* ['tɛpiʃ] clumsy,\

tapsen F ['tapsən] *v/i.* (ge-, *sein*) walk clumsily.

Tara † ['ta:ra] *f* (-/*Taren*) tare.

Tarif [ta'ri:f] *m* (-s/-e) tariff, (table of) rates *pl.*, price-list; **2lich** *adv.* according to tariff; **lohn** *m* standard wage(s *pl.*); **vertrag** *m* collective *or* wage agreement.

tarn|en ['tarnən] *v/t.* (ge-, *h*) camouflage; *esp. fig.* disguise; **2ung** *f* (-/-en) camouflage.

Tasche ['taʃə] *f* (-/-n) pocket (*of garment*); (hand)bag; pouch; *s. Aktentasche, Schultasche.*

Taschen|buch *n* pocket-book; **dieb** *m* pickpocket, *Am. sl.* dip; **geld** *n* pocket-money; *monthly:* allowance; **lampe** *f* (electric) torch, *esp. Am.* flashlight; **messer** *n* pocket-knife; **spielerei** *f* juggle(ry); **tuch** *n* (pocket) handkerchief; **uhr** *f* (pocket-)watch; **wörterbuch** *n* pocket dictionary.

Tasse ['tasə] *f* (-/-n) cup.

Tastatur [tasta'tu:r] *f* (-/-en) keyboard, keys *pl.*

Tast|e ['tastə] *f* (-/-n) key; **2en** (ge-, *h*) **1.** *v/i.* touch; grope (*nach* for, after), fumble (for); **2.** *v/t.* touch, feel; *sich ~* feel *or* grope one's way; **sinn** *m* (-[e]s/*no pl.*) sense of touch.

Tat [ta:t] **1.** *f* (-/-en) action, act, deed; offen|ce, *Am.* -se, crime; *in der ~* indeed, in fact, as a matter of fact, really; *auf frischer ~ ertappen* catch *s.o.* red-handed; *zur ~ schreiten* proceed to action; *in die ~ umsetzen* implement, carry into effect; **2.** 2 *pret.* of *tun*; **bestand** th *m* facts *pl.* of the case; **2enlos** *adj.* inactive, idle.

Täter ['tɛ:tər] *m* (-s/-) perpetrator, offender, author.

tätig *adj.* ['tɛ:tiç] active; busy; *~ sein bei* work at; be employed with; **en** † ['~gən] *v/t.* (ge-, *h*) effect, transact; conclude; **2keit** *f* (-/-en) activity; occupation, business, job; profession.

Tat|kraft *f* (-/*no pl.*) energy; enterprise; **2kräftig** *adj.* energetic, active.

tätlich *adj.* ['tɛ:tliç] violent; *~ werden gegen* assault; **2keiten** *f/pl.* (acts *pl.* of) violence; th assault (and battery).

Tatort th ['ta:tʔ-] *m* (-[e]s/-e) place *or* scene of a crime.

tätowieren [tɛto'vi:rən] *v/t.* (no -ge-, *h*) tattoo.

Tat|sache *f* (matter of) fact; **sachenbericht** *m* factual *or* documentary report, matter-of-fact account; **2sächlich** *adj.* actual, real. [pat.\

tätscheln ['tɛtʃəln] *v/t.* (ge-, *h*) pet,\

Tatze ['tatsə] *f* (-/-n) paw, claw.

Tau¹ [tau] *n* (-[e]s/-e) rope, cable.

Tau² [~] *m* (-[e]s/*no pl.*) dew.

taub *adj.* [taup] deaf (*fig.: gegen* to); *fingers, etc.:* benumbed, numb; *nut:* deaf, empty; *rock:* dead; **es Ei** addle egg; *auf e-m Ohr ~ sein* be deaf of *or* in one ear.

Taube *orn.* ['taubə] *f* (-/-n) pigeon; **nschlag** *m* pigeon-house.

Taub|heit *f* (-/*no pl.*) deafness; numbness; **2stumm** *adj.* deaf and dumb; **stumme** *m, f* (-n/-n) deaf mute.

tauch|en ['tauxən] (ge-) **1.** *v/t.* (*h*) dip, plunge; **2.** *v/i.* (*h, sein*) dive, plunge; dip; *submarine:* submerge; **2er** *m* (-s/-) diver; **2sieder** *m* (-s/-) immersion heater.

tauen ['tauən] *v/i.* (ge-) **1.** (*h, sein*): *der Schnee qr es taut* the snow *or* it is thawing; *der Schnee ist von den Dächern getaut* the snow has melted off the roofs; **2.** (*h*): *es taut* dew is falling.

Taufe ['taufə] *f* (-/-n) baptism, christening; **2n** *v/t.* (ge-, *h*) baptize, christen.

Täufling ['tɔyfliŋ] *m* (-s/-e) child *or* person to be baptized.

Tauf|name *m* Christian name, *Am. a.* given name; **pate 1.** *m* godfather; **2.** *f* godmother; **patin** *f* godmother; **schein** *m* certificate of baptism.

taug|en ['taugən] *v/i.* (ge-, *h*) be good, be fit, be of use (*all:* zu for); (*zu*) *nichts ~* be good for nothing, be no good, be of no use; **2enichts** *m* (-, -es/-e) good-for-nothing, *Am. sl.* dead beat; **lich** *adj.* ['tauk-] good, fit, useful (*all:* für, zu for, to *inf.*); able; ✕, ♣ able-bodied.

Taumel ['tauməl] *m* (-s/*no pl.*)

giddiness; rapture, ecstasy; '**2ig** *adj.* reeling; giddy; '**2n** *v/i.* (ge-, sein) reel, stagger; be giddy.

Tausch [tauʃ] *m* (-es/-e) exchange; barter; '**2en** *v/t.* (ge-, h) exchange; barter (*gegen* for).

täuschen ['tɔʏʃən] *v/t.* (ge-, h) deceive, delude, mislead (on purpose); cheat; *sich* ~ deceive o.s.; be mistaken; *sich* ~ *lassen* let o.s. be deceived; '**~d** *adj.* deceptive, delusive; *resemblance:* striking.

'**Tauschhandel** *m* barter.

'**Täuschung** *f* (-/-en) deception, delusion.

tausend *adj.* ['tauzənt] a thousand; '**~fach** *adj.* thousandfold; '**2fuß** *zo.* *m*, '**2füß(l)er** *zo.* ['~fy:s(l)ər] *m* (-s/-) millepede, milliped(e), *Am. a.* wireworm; '**~st** *adj.* thousandth; '**2stel** *n* (-s/-) thousandth (part).

'**Tau|tropfen** *m* dew-drop; '**~wetter** *n* thaw.

Taxameter [taksa'-] *m* taximeter.

Taxe ['taksə] *f* (-/-n) rate; fee; estimate; *s. Taxi.*

Taxi ['taksi] *n* (-[s]/-[s]) taxi(-cab), cab, *Am. a.* hack.

ta'xieren *v/t.* (*no* -ge-, h) rate, estimate; *officially:* value, appraise.

'**Taxistand** *m* cabstand.

Technik ['tɛçnik] *f* **1.** (-/*no* pl.) technology; engineering; **2.** (-/-en) skill, workmanship; technique, practice; ♪ execution; '**~er** *m* (-s/-) (technical) engineer; technician; **~um** ['~um] *n* (-s/*Technika, Techniken*) technical school.

'**technisch** *adj.* technical; **~e** *Hochschule* school of technology.

Tee [te:] *m* (-s/-s) tea; '**~büchse** *f* tea-caddy; '**~gebäck** *n* scones *pl.*, biscuits *pl.*, *Am. a.* cookies *pl.*; '**~kanne** *f* teapot; '**~kessel** *m* tea-kettle; '**~löffel** *m* tea-spoon.

Teer [te:r] *m* (-[e]s/-e) tar; '**2en** *v/t.* (ge-, h) tar.

'**Tee|rose** ♀ *f* tea-rose; '**~sieb** *n* tea-strainer; '**~tasse** *f* teacup; '**~wärmer** *m* (-s/-) tea-cosy.

Teich [taiç] *m* (-[e]s/-e) pool, pond.

Teig [taik] *m* (-[e]s/-e) dough, paste; **2ig** *adj.* ['~giç] doughy, pasty; '**~waren** *f/pl.* farinaceous food; noodles *pl.*

Teil [tail] *m, n* (-[e]s/-e) part; portion, share; component; ⚖ party;

zum ~ partly, in part; *ich für mein* ~ ... for my part I ...; **2bar** *adj.* divisible; '**~chen** *n* (-s/-) particle; '**2en** *v/t.* (ge-, h) divide; *fig.* share; **2haben** *v/i.* (*irr.* haben, sep., -ge-, h) participate, (have a) share (*both:* an *dat.* in); '**~haber** † *m* (-s/-) partner; **~nahme** ['~na:mə] *f* (-/no *pl.*) participation (*an dat.* in); *fig.:* interest (in); sympathy (with); **2nahmslos** ['~na:mslo:s] *adj.* indifferent, unconcerned; passive; apathetic; '**~nahmslosigkeit** *f* (-/no *pl.*) indifference; passiveness; apathy; '**2nehmen** *v/i.* (*irr.* nehmen, sep., -ge-, h): ~ *an* (*dat.*) take part or participate in; join in; be present at, attend at; *fig.* sympathize with; '**~nehmer** *m* (-s/-) participant; member; *univ., etc.:* student; contestant; *sports:* competitor; *teleph.* subscriber; **2s** *adv.* [~s] partly; '**~strecke** *f* section; stage, leg; 🚌 fare stage; '**~ung** *f* (-/-en) division; '**2weise** *adv.* partly, partially, in part; '**~zahlung** *f* (payment by) instal(l)ments.

Teint [tɛ̃:] *m* (-s/-s) complexion.

Tele|fon [tele'fo:n] *n* (-s/-e) *etc. s. Telephon, etc.*; **~graf** [~'gra:f] *m* (-en/-en) *etc. s. Telegraph, etc.*; **~gramm** [~'gram] *n* (-s/-e) telegram, wire; *overseas:* cable(gram).

Telegraph [tele'gra:f] *m* (-en/-en) telegraph; '**~enamt** [~'gra:fn-] *n* telegraph office; **2ieren** [~a'fi:rən] *v/t. and v/i.* (*no* -ge-, h) telegraph, wire; *overseas:* cable; **2isch** [~'gra:fiʃ] **1.** *adj.* telegraphic; **2.** *adv.* by telegram, by wire; by cable; '**~ist** [~a'fist] *m* (-en/-en), '**~istin** *f* (-/-nen) telegraph operator, telegrapher, telegraphist.

Teleobjektiv *phot.* ['te:le-] *n* telephoto lens.

Telephon [tele'fo:n] *n* (-s/-e) telephone, F phone; *am* ~ on the (tele)phone; *ans* ~ *gehen* answer the (tele)phone; *am* ~ *haben* be on the (tele)phone; **~anschluß** *m* telephone connexion *or* connection; **~buch** *n* telephone directory; **~gespräch** *n* (tele)phone call; conversation *or* chat over the (tele)phone; **~hörer** *m* (telephone) receiver, handset; **2ieren** [~o'ni:rən] *v/i.* (*no* -ge-, h) telephone, F phone; *mit j-m* ~ ring s.o. up, *Am.* call s.o. up; **2isch** *adv.* [~'fo:niʃ] by (tele)phone, over the (tele)phone; **~ist** [~ɔ'nist] *m* (-en/-en), **~istin** *f* (-/-nen) (telephone) operator, telephonist; **~vermittlung** *f* s. *Telephonzentrale;* **~zelle** *f* telephone kiosk *or* box, call-box, *Am.* telephone booth; **~zentrale** *f* (telephone) exchange.

Teleskop *opt.* [tele'sko:p] *n* (-s/-e) telescope.

Teller ['tɛlər] *m* (-s/-) plate.

Tempel ['tɛmpəl] *m* (-s/-) temple.

Temperament [tɛmpəra'mɛnt] *n* (-[e]s/-e) temper(ament); *fig.* spirit(s *pl.*); **2los** *adj.* spiritless; **2voll** *adj.* (high-)spirited.

Temperatur [tɛmpəra'tu:r] *f* (-/-en) temperature; *j-s ~ messen* take s.o.'s temperature.

Tempo ['tɛmpo] *n* (-s/-s, *Tempi*) time; pace; speed; rate.

Tendenz [tɛn'dɛnts] *f* (-/-en) tendency; trend; **2iös** *adj.* [~'tsjø:s] tendentious.

Tennis ['tɛnis] *n* (-/*no pl.*) (lawn) tennis; **~ball** *m* tennis-ball; **~platz** *m* tennis-court; **~schläger** *m* (tennis-)racket; **~spieler** *m* tennis player; **~turnier** *n* tennis tournament.

Tenor ♪ [te'no:r] *m* (-s/⁒e) tenor.

Teppich ['tɛpiç] *m* (-s/-e) carpet; **~kehrmaschine** *f* carpet-sweeper.

Termin [tɛr'mi:n] *m* (-s/-e) appointed time *or* day; ⁒⁒, ✝ date, term; *sports:* fixture; *äußerster ~* final date, dead(-)line; **~geschäfte** ✝ *n*/*pl.* futures *pl.*; **~kalender** appointment book *or* pad; ⁒⁒ causelist, *Am.* calendar; **~liste** ⁒⁒ *f* causelist, *Am.* calendar.

Terpentin [tɛrpən'ti:n] *n* (-s/-e) turpentine.

Terrain [tɛ'rɛ̃:] *n* (-s/-s) ground; plot; building site.

Terrasse [tɛ'rasə] *f* (-/-en) terrace; **2förmig** *adj.* [~nfœrmiç] terraced, in terraces.

Terrine [tɛ'ri:nə] *f* (-/-en) tureen.

Territorium [tɛri'to:rjum] *n* (-s/ *Territorien*) territory.

Terror ['tɛrɔr] *m* (-s/*no pl.*) terror; **2isieren** [~ɔri'zi:rən] *v/t.* (*no -ge-*, *h*) terrorize.

Terz ♪ [tɛrts] *f* (-/-en) third; **~ett** ♪ [~'tsɛt] *n* (-[e]s/-e) trio.

Testament [tɛsta'mɛnt] *n* (-[e]s/-e) (last) will, (*often:* last will and) testament; *eccl.* Testament; **2arisch** [~'ta:riʃ] **1.** *adj.* testamentary; **2.** *adv.* by will; **~svollstrecker** *m* (-s/-) executor; *officially:* administrator.

testen ['tɛstən] *v/t.* (*ge-*, *h*) test.

teuer *adj.* ['tɔyər] dear (*a. fig.*), expensive; *wie ~ ist es?* how much is it?

Teufel ['tɔyfəl] *m* (-s/-) devil; *der ~* the Devil, Satan; *zum ~!* F dickens!, hang it!; *wer zum ~?* F who the devil *or* deuce?; *der ~ ist los* the fat's in the fire; *scher dich zum ~!* F go to hell!, go to blazes!; **~ei** [~'lai] *f* (-/-en) devilment, mischief, devilry, *Am.* deviltry; **~skerl** F *m* devil of a fellow.

teuflisch *adj.* devilish, diabolic(al).

Text [tɛkst] *m* (-es/-e) text; words *pl.* (*of song*); book, libretto (*of opera*); **~buch** *n* book; libretto.

Textil|ien [tɛks'ti:ljən] *pl.*, **~waren** *pl.* textile fabrics *pl.*, textiles *pl.*

textlich *adv.* concerning the text.

Theater [te'a:tər] *n* **1.** (-s/-) theat|re, *Am.* -er; stage; **2.** F (-s/*no pl.*) playacting; **~besucher** *m* playgoer; **~karte** *f* theatre ticket; **~kasse** *f* box-office; **~stück** *n* play; **~vorstellung** *f* theatrical performance; **~zettel** *m* playbill.

theatralisch *adj.* [tea'tra:liʃ] theatrical, stagy.

Theke ['te:kə] *f* (-/-n) *at inn:* bar, *Am. a.* counter; *at shop:* counter.

Thema ['te:ma] *n* (-s/*Themen, Themata*) theme, subject; topic (*of discussion*).

Theolog|e [teo'lo:gə] *m* (-n/-n) theologian, divine; **~ie** [~o'gi:] *f* (-/-n) theology.

Theoret|iker [teo're:tikər] *m* (-s/-) theorist; **2isch** *adj.* theoretic(al).

Theorie [teo'ri:] *f* (-/-n) theory.

Therapie ⚕ [tera'pi:] *f* (-/-n) therapy. 　　　　　　　　　　　　[spa.]

Thermalbad [tɛr'ma:l-] *n* thermal

Thermometer [tɛrmo'-] *n* (-s/-) thermometer; **~stand** *m* (thermometer) reading.

Thermosflasche ['tɛrmɔs-] *f* vacuum bottle *or* flask, thermos (flask).

These [te:zə] *f* (-/-n) thesis.

Thrombose ⚕ [trɔm'bo:zə] *f* (-/-n) thrombosis.

Thron [tro:n] *m* (-[e]s/-e) throne; **~besteigung** *f* accession to the throne; '∼erbe *m* heir to the throne, heir apparent; '∼folge *f* succession to the throne; '∼folger *m* (-s/-) successor to the throne; '∼rede *parl. f* Queen's *or* King's Speech.

Thunfisch *ichth.* ['tu:n-] *m* tunny, tuna.

Tick F [tik] *m* (-[e]s/-s, -e) crotchet, fancy, kink; e-n ∼ haben have a bee in one's bonnet.

ticken ['tikən] *v/i.* (ge-, h) tick.

tief [ti:f] **1.** *adj.* deep (*a. fig.*); *fig.*: profound; low; *im* ∼sten Winter in the dead *or* depth of winter; **2.** *adv.*: bis ∼ in die Nacht far into the night; *das läßt* ∼ *blicken* that speaks volumes; *zu* ∼ *singen* sing flat; **3.** ♀ *meteor.* *n* (-[e]s/-s) depression, low(-pressure area); '♀bau *m* civil *or* underground engineering; '♀druckgebiet *meteor.* *n* s. *Tief*; '♀e *f* (-/-n) depth (*a. fig.*); *fig.* profundity; '♀ebene *f* low plain, lowland; '♀enschärfe *phot. f* depth of focus; '♀flug *m* low-level flight; '♀gang ⚓ *m* draught, *Am.* draft; ∼gebeugt *fig. adj.* ['∼gəbɔykt] deeply afflicted, bowed down; '∼gekühlt *adj.* deep-frozen; '∼greifend *adj.* fundamental, radical; '♀land *n* lowland(s *pl.*); '∼liegend *adj. eyes*: sunken; *fig.* deep-seated; '♀schlag *m boxing:* low hit; '∼schürfend *fig. adj.* profound; thorough; '♀see *f* deep sea; '∼sinnig *adj.* thoughtful, pensive; F melancholy; '♀stand *m* (-[e]s/*no pl.*) low level.

Tiegel ['ti:gəl] *m* (-s/-) saucepan, stew-pan; ⊕ crucible.

Tier [ti:r] *n* (-[e]s/-e) animal; beast; brute; *großes* ∼ *fig. sl.* bigwig, big bug, *Am.* big shot; '∼arzt *m* veterinary (surgeon), F vet, *Am. a.* veterinarian; '∼garten *m* zoological gardens *pl.*, zoo; '∼heilkunde *f* veterinary medicine; '♀isch *adj.* animal; *fig.* bestial, brutish, savage; '∼kreis *ast. m* zodiac; ∼quälerei [∼kvɛ:lə'raɪ] *f* (-/-en) cruelty to animals; '∼reich *n* (-[e]s/*no pl.*) animal kingdom; '∼schutzverein *m* Society for the Prevention of Cruelty to Animals.

Tiger *zo.* ['ti:gər] *m* (-s/-) tiger; '∼in *zo. f* (-/-nen) tigress.

tilg|en ['tilgən] *v/t.* (ge-, h) extinguish; efface; wipe *or* blot out, erase; *fig.* obliterate; annul, cancel;

discharge, pay (*debt*); redeem (*mortgage*, etc.); '♀ung *f* (-/-en) extinction; extermination; cancel(l)ing; discharge, payment; redemption.

Tinktur [tiŋk'tu:r] *f* (-/-en) tincture. [*sitzen* F be in a scrape.]

Tinte ['tintə] *f* (-/-n) ink; *in der* ∼ '**Tinten|faß** *n* (-ink-pot, desk: inkwell; '∼fisch *ichth. m* cuttle-fish; '∼fleck *m*, '∼klecks *m* (ink-)blot; '∼stift *m* indelible pencil.

Tip [tip] *m* (-s/-s) hint, tip; '♀pen (ge-, h) **1.** *v/i.* F type; *fig.* guess; *j-m auf die Schulter* ∼ tap s.o. on his shoulder; **2.** *v/t.* tip; foretell, predict; F type.

Tiroler [ti'ro:lər] **1.** *m* (-s/-) Tyrolese; **2.** *adj.* Tyrolese.

Tisch [tiʃ] *m* (-es/-e) table; *bei* ∼ at table; *den* ∼ *decken* lay the table *or* cloth, set the table; *reinen* ∼ *machen* make a clean sweep (*damit* of it); *zu* ∼ *bitten* invite *or* ask to dinner *or* supper; *bitte zu* ∼! dinner is ready!; '∼decke *f* tablecloth; '♀fertig *adj. food:* readyprepared; '∼gast *m* guest; '∼gebet *n: das* ∼ *sprechen* say grace; '∼gesellschaft *f* dinner-party; '∼gespräch *n* table-talk; '∼lampe *f* table-lamp; desk lamp.

Tischler ['tiʃlər] *m* (-s/-) joiner; carpenter; cabinet-maker; ∼ei [∼'raɪ] *f* (-/-en) joinery; joiner's workshop.

'**Tisch|platte** *f* top (of a table), table top; leaf (*of extending table*); '∼rede *f* toast, after-dinner speech; '∼tennis *n* table tennis, ping-pong; '∼tuch *n* table-cloth; '∼zeit *f* dinner-time.

Titan [ti'ta:n] *m* (-en/-en) Titan; '♀isch *adj.* titanic.

Titel ['ti:təl] *m* (-s/-) title; e-n ∼ (*inne*)*haben sports:* hold a title; '∼bild *n* frontispiece; cover picture (*of magazine*, etc.); '∼blatt *n* titlepage; cover (*of magazine*); '∼halter *m* (-s/-) *sports:* title-holder; '∼kampf *m boxing:* title fight; '∼rolle *thea. f* title-role.

titulieren [titu'li:rən] *v/t.* (*no* -ge-, h) style, call, address as.

Toast [to:st] *m* (-es/-e, -s) toast (*a. fig.*).

tob|en ['to:bən] *v/i.* (ge-, h) rage, rave, storm, bluster; *children:* romp; ♀sucht ♂ ['to:p-] *f* (-/*no pl.*)

raving madness, frenzy; **~süchtig** adj. ['to:p-] raving mad, frantic.

Tochter ['tɔxtər] f (-/⸚) daughter; **'~gesellschaft** † f subsidiary company.

Tod [to:t] m (-[e]s/⸚ -e) death; 🕇 decease.

Todes|angst ['to:dəs?-] f mortal agony; fig. mortal fear; **Todesängste ausstehen** be scared to death, be frightened out of one's wits; **'~anzeige** f obituary (notice); **'~fall** m (case of) death; **Todesfälle** pl. deaths pl., ✕ casualties pl.; **'~kampf** m death throes pl., mortal agony; **'~strafe** f capital punishment, death penalty; **bei ~ verboten** forbidden on or under pain or penalty of death; **'~ursache** f cause of death; **'~urteil** n death or capital sentence, death-warrant.

Tod|feind m deadly or mortal enemy; **'2krank** adj. dangerously ill.

tödlich adj. ['tø:tliç] deadly; fatal; wound: a. mortal.

'tod|'müde adj. dead tired; **'~schick** F adj. dashing, gorgeous; **'~sicher** F adj. cock-sure; **'2sünde** f deadly or mortal sin.

Toilette [toa'lɛtə] f (-/-n) dress(ing): toilet; lavatory; gentlemen's or ladies' room, esp. Am. toilet.

Toi|letten|artikel m/pl. toilet articles pl., Am. a. toiletry; **~papier** n toilet-paper; **~tisch** m toilet (-table), dressing-table, Am. a. dresser.

toleran|t adj. [tole'rant] tolerant (gegen of); **2z** [~ts] f 1. (-/no pl.) tolerance, toleration (esp. eccl.); 2. ⊕ (-/-en) tolerance, allowance.

toll [tɔl] 1. adj. (raving) mad, frantic; mad, crazy, wild (all a. fig.); fantastic; noise, etc.: frightful, F awful; das ist ja ~ F that's (just) great; 2. adv.: es ~ treiben carry on like mad; es zu ~ treiben go too far; **'~en** v/i. (ge-, h, sein) children: romp; **'2haus** fig. n bedlam; **'2heit** f (-/-en) madness; mad trick; **'~kühn** adj. foolhardy; rash; **'2wut** vet. f rabies.

Tolpatsch F ['tɔlpatʃ] m (-es/-e) awkward or clumsy fellow; **'2ig** F adj. awkward, clumsy.

Tölpel F ['tœlpəl] m (-s/-) awkward or clumsy fellow; boob(y).

Tomate 🎵 [to'ma:tə] f (-/-n) tomato.

Ton¹ [to:n] m (-[e]s/-e) clay.

Ton² [~] m (-[e]s/⸚e) sound; ♪ tone (a. of language); ♪ single: note; accent, stress; fig. tone; paint. tone, tint, shade; guter ~ good form; den ~ angeben set the fashion; zum guten ~ gehören be the fashion; große Töne reden or F spucken F talk big, boast; **'~abnehmer** m pick-up; **'2angebend** adj. setting the fashion, leading; **'~arm** m pick-up arm (of record-player); **'~art** ♪ f key; **'~band** n recording tape; **'~bandgerät** n tape recorder.

tönen ['tø:nən] (ge-, h) 1. v/i. sound, ring; 2. v/t. tint, tone, shade.

tönern adj. ['tø:nərn] (of) clay, earthen.

'Ton|fall m in speaking: intonation, accent; **'~film** m sound film; **'~lage** f pitch; **'~leiter** ♪ f scale, gamut; **'2los** adj. soundless; fig. toneless; **'~meister** m sound engineer.

Tonne ['tɔnə] f (-/-n) large: tun; smaller: barrel, cask; ⚓ measure of weight: ton.

Tonsilbe gr. f accented syllable.

Tonsur [tɔn'zu:r] f (-/-en) tonsure.

'Tönung paint. f (-/-en) tint, tinge, shade.

'Tonwaren f/pl. s. Töpferware.

Topf [tɔpf] m (-[e]s/⸚e) pot.

Töpfer ['tœpfər] m (-s/-) potter; stove-fitter; **~ei** [~'raɪ] f (-/-en) pottery; **'~ware** f pottery, earthenware, crockery.

topp¹ int. [tɔp] done!, agreed!

Topp² ⚓ [~] m (-s/-e, -s) top; masthead.

Tor¹ [to:r] n (-[e]s/-e) gate; gateway (a. fig.); football: goal; skiing: gate.

Tor² [~] m (-en/-en) fool.

Torf [tɔrf] m (-[e]s/no pl.) peat.

Torheit ['to:rhaɪt] f (-/-en) folly.

'Torhüter m gate-keeper; sports: goalkeeper.

töricht adj. ['tø:riçt] foolish, silly.

Törin ['tø:rin] f (-/-nen) fool(ish woman).

torkeln ['tɔrkəln] v/i. (ge-, h, sein) reel, stagger, totter.

'Tor|latte f sports: cross-bar; **'~lauf** m skiing: slalom; **'~linie** f sports: goal-line.

Tornister [tɔr'nistər] m (-s/-) knapsack; satchel.

torpedieren [tɔrpe'di:rən] *v/t.* (*no -ge-, h*) torpedo (*a. fig.*).
Torpedo [tɔr'pe:do] *m* (*-s/-s*) torpedo; **~boot** *n* torpedo-boat.
'**Tor|pfosten** *m* gate-post; *sports:* goal-post; '**~schuß** *m* shot at the goal; '**~schütze** *m* *sports:* scorer.
Torte ['tɔrtə] *f* (*-/-n*) fancy cake, *Am.* layer cake; tart, *Am.* pie.
Tortur [tɔr'tu:r] *f* (*-/-en*) torture; *fig.* ordeal.
Tor|wart ['to:rvart] *m* (*-[e]s/-e*) *sports:* goalkeeper; '**~weg** *m* gateway.
tosen ['to:zən] *v/i.* (*ge-, h/sein*) roar, rage; '**~d** *adj. applause:* thunderous.
tot *adj.* [to:t] dead (*a. fig.*); deceased; **~er Punkt** ⊕ dead cent|re, *Am.* -er; *fig.:* deadlock; fatigue; **~es Rennen** *sports:* dead heat.
total *adj.* [to'ta:l] total, complete.
'**tot|arbeiten** *v/refl.* (*sep., -ge-, h*) work o.s. to death; '**2e** (*-n/-n*) **1.** *m* dead man; (dead) body, corpse; *die ~n pl.* the dead *pl.,* the deceased *pl.* or departed *pl.;* ✕ casualties *pl.;* **2.** *f* dead woman.
töten ['tø:tən] *v/t.* (*ge-, h*) kill; destroy; murder; deaden (*nerve, etc.*).
'**Toten|bett** *n* deathbed; '**2blaß** *adj.* deadly *or* deathly pale; '**~blässe** *f* deadly paleness *or* pallor; '**2bleich** *adj. s.* totenblaß; '**~gräber** ['~grɛ:bər] *m* (*-s/-*) grave-digger (*a. zo.*); '**~hemd** *n* shroud; '**~kopf** *m* death's-head (*a. zo.*); emblem of death: a. skull and cross-bones; '**~liste** *f* death-roll (*a.* ✕), *esp.* ✕ casualty list; '**~maske** *f* death-mask; '**~messe** *eccl. f* mass for the dead, requiem; '**~schädel** *m* death's-head, skull; '**~schein** *m* death certificate; '**2still** *adj.* (as) still as the grave; '**~stille** *f* dead(ly) silence, deathly stillness.
'**tot|geboren** *adj.* still-born; '**2geburt** *f* still birth; '**~lachen** *v/refl.* (*sep., -ge-, h*) die of laughing.
Toto ['to:to] *m, F a. n* (*-s/-s*) football pools *pl.*
'**tot|schießen** *v/t.* (*irr. schießen, sep., -ge-, h*) shoot dead, kill; '**2schlag** *m* manslaughter, homicide; '**~schlagen** *v/t.* (*irr. schlagen, sep., -ge-, h*) kill (*a. time*), slay; '**~schweigen** *v/t.* (*irr. schweigen, sep., -ge-, h*) hush up; '**~ste-**

chen *v/t.* (*irr. stechen, sep., -ge-, h*) stab to death; '**~stellen** *v/refl.* (*sep., -ge-, h*) feign death.
'**Tötung** *f* (*-/-en*) killing, slaying; ‡‡ homicide; *fahrlässige ~* ‡‡ manslaughter.
Tour [tu:r] *f* (*-/-en*) tour; excursion, trip; ⊕ turn, revolution; *auf ~en kommen mot.* pick up speed; '**~en-wagen** *mot. m* touring car.
Tourist [tu'rist] *m* (*-en/-en*), '**~in** *f* (*-/-nen*) tourist.
Tournee [tur'ne:] *f* (*-/-s, -n*) tour.
Trab [tra:p] *m* (*-[e]s/no pl.*) trot.
Trabant [tra'bant] *m* (*-en/-en*) satellite.
trab|en ['tra:bən] *v/i.* (*ge-, h, sein*) trot; **2rennen** ['tra:p-] *n* trotting race.
Tracht [traxt] *f* (*-/-en*) dress, costume; uniform; fashion; load; *e-e (gehörige) ~ Prügel* a (sound) thrashing; *~en v/i.* (*ge-, h*): *~ nach* et. strive for; *j-m nach dem Leben ~* seek s.o.'s life.
trächtig *adj.* ['trɛçtiç] (big) with young, pregnant. [tradition.\
Tradition [tradi'tsjo:n] *f* (*-/-en*)\
traf [tra:f] *pret. of* treffen.
Trag|bahre ['tra:k-] *f* stretcher, litter; '**2bar** *adj.* portable; *dress:* wearable; *fig.:* bearable; reasonable; **~e** ['~gə] *f* (*-/-n*) hand-barrow; *s. Tragbahre.*
träge *adj.* ['trɛ:gə] lazy, indolent; *phys.* inert (*a. fig.*).
tragen ['tra:gən] (*irr., ge-, h*) **1.** *v/t.* carry; bear (*costs, name, responsibility, etc.*); bear, endure; support; bear, yield (*fruit,* ✝ *interest, etc.*); wear (*dress, etc.*); bei sich ~ have about one; *sich gut ~ material:* wear well; *zur Schau ~* show off; **2.** *v/i. tree:* bear, yield; *gun, voice:* carry; *ice:* bear.
Träger ['trɛ:gər] *m* (*-s/-*) carrier; porter (*of luggage*); holder, bearer (*of name, licence, etc.*); wearer (*of dress*); (shoulder-)strap (*of slip, etc.*); ⊕ support; △ girder.
Trag|fähigkeit ['tra:k-] *f* carrying *or* load capacity; ⚓ tonnage; '**~fläche** ✈ *f,* '**~flügel** ✈ *m* wing, plane.
Trägheit ['trɛ:khaɪt] *f* (*-/no pl.*) laziness, indolence; *phys.* inertia (*a. fig.*).
tragisch *adj.* ['tra:gɪʃ] tragic (*a. fig.*); *fig.* tragical.

T

Tragödie [traˈgøːdjə] f (-/-n) tragedy.

Trag|riemen ['traːk-] m (carrying) strap; sling (of gun); '**~tier** n pack animal; '**~tüte** f carrier-bag; '**~weite** f range; fig. import(ance), consequences pl.; von großer ~ of great moment.

Train|er ['trɛːnər] m (-s/-) trainer; coach; 2**ieren** [~ˈniːrən] (no -ge-, h) 1. v/t. train; coach; 2. v/i. train; '**~ing** [~ɪŋ] n (-s/-s) training; '**~ingsanzug** m sports: track suit.

traktieren [trakˈtiːrən] v/t. (no -ge-, h) treat (badly).

Traktor ⊕ ['traktɔr] m (-s/-en) tractor.

trällern ['trɛlərn] v/t. and v/i. (ge-, h) troll.

trampel|n ['trampəln] v/i. (ge-, h) trample, stamp; '2**pfad** m beaten track.

Tran [traːn] m (-[e]s/-e) train-oil, whale-oil.

Träne ['trɛːnə] f (-/-n) tear; in ~n ausbrechen burst into tears; '2**n** v/i. (ge-, h) water; '**~ngas** n teargas.

Trank [traŋk] 1. m (-[e]s/⁼e) drink, beverage; ⚕ potion; 2. 2 pret. of trinken.

Tränke ['trɛŋkə] f (-/-n) wateringplace; '2**n** v/t. (ge-, h) water (animals); soak, impregnate (material).

Trans|formator ⚡ [transfɔrˈmaːtɔr] m (-s/-en) transformer; ~**fusion** ⚕ [~uˈzjoːn] f (-/-en) transfusion.

Transistorradio [tranˈzistɔr-] n transistor radio or set.

transitiv gr. adj. ['tranzitiːf] transitive.

transparent [transpaˈrɛnt] 1. adj. transparent; 2. 2 n (-[e]s/-e) transparency; in political processions, etc.: banner.

transpirieren [transpiˈriːrən] v/i. (no -ge-, h) perspire.

Transplantation ⚕ [transplantaˈtsjoːn] f transplant (operation).

Transport [transˈpɔrt] m (-[e]s/-e) transport(ation), conveyance, carriage; 2**abel** adj. [~ˈtaːbəl] portable; ~**er** m (-s/-) ⚓, ✈ (troop-)transport; ✈ transport (aircraft or plane); 2**fähig** adj. transportable; sick person: a. transferable; 2**ieren** [~ˈtiːrən] v/t. (no -ge-, h) transport, convey, carry; ~**unternehmen** n carrier.

Trapez [traˈpeːts] n (-es/-e) ⬨ trapezium, Am. trapezoid; gymnastics: trapeze.

trappeln ['trapəln] v/i. (ge-, sein) horse: clatter; children, etc.: patter.

Trass|ant ✝ [traˈsant] m (-en/-en) drawer; ~**at** ✝ [~ˈsaːt] m (-en/-en) drawee; ~**e** ⊕ f (-/-n) line; 2**ieren** [~ˈsiːrən] v/t. (no -ge-, h) ⊕ lay or trace out; ~ auf (acc.) ✝ draw on.

trat [traːt] pret. of treten.

Tratte ✝ ['tratə] f (-/-n) draft.

Traube ['traubə] f (-/-n) bunch of grapes; grape; cluster; '**~nsaft** m grape-juice; '**~nzucker** m grape-sugar, glucose.

trauen ['trauən] (ge-, h) 1. v/t. marry; sich ~ lassen get married; 2. v/i. trust (j-m s.o.), confide (dat. in); ich traute meinen Ohren nicht I could not believe my ears.

Trauer ['trauər] f (-/no pl.) sorrow, affliction; for dead person: mourning; '**~botschaft** f sad news; '**~fall** m death; '**~feier** f funeral ceremonies pl., obsequies pl.; '**~flor** m mourning-crape; '**~geleit** n funeral procession; '**~gottesdienst** m funeral service; '**~kleid** n mourning (-dress); '**~marsch** m funeral march; '2**n** v/i. (ge-, h) mourn (um for); be in mourning; '**~spiel** n tragedy; '**~weide** ♀ f weeping willow; '**~zug** m funeral procession.

Traufe ['traufə] f (-/-n) eaves pl.; gutter; s. Regen².

träufeln ['trɔyfəln] v/t. (ge-, h) drop, drip, trickle. [cosy, snug.)

traulich adj. ['traulɪç] intimate;)

Traum [traum] m (-[e]s/⁼e) dream (a. fig.); reverie; das fällt mir nicht im ~ ein! I would not dream of (doing) it!; '**~bild** n vision; '**~deuter** m (-s/-) dream-reader.

träum|en ['trɔymən] v/i. and v/t. (ge-, h) dream; '2**en** f (-[e]s/-) dreamer (a. fig.); 2**erei** [~ˈrai] f (-/-en) dreaming; fig. a. reverie (a. ♪), day-dream, musing; '**~erisch** adj. dreamy; musing.

traurig adj. ['traurɪç] sad (über acc. at), Am. F blue; wretched.

'**Trau|ring** m wedding-ring; '**~schein** m marriage certificate or lines pl.; '**~ung** f (-/-n) marriage, wedding; '~zeuge *m* witness to a marriage.

Trecker ⊕ ['trɛkər] *m* (-s/-) tractor.

Treff [trɛf] *n* (-s/-s) *cards:* club(s *pl.*).

treffen[1] ['trɛfən] (*irr.*, ge-) **1.** *v/t.* (h) hit (*a. fig.*), strike; concern, *disadvantageously:* affect; meet; *nicht* ~ miss; *e-e Entscheidung* ~ come to a decision; *Maßnahmen* ~ take measures *or* steps; *Vorkehrungen* ~ take precautions *or* measures; *sich* ~ happen; meet; gather, assemble; *a.* have an appointment (*mit* with), I have a date (with); *das trifft sich gut!* that's lucky!, how fortunate!; *sich getroffen fühlen* feel hurt; *wen trifft die Schuld?* who is to blame?; *das Los traf ihn* the lot fell on him; *du bist gut getroffen paint., phot.* this is a good likeness of you; *vom Blitz getroffen* struck by lightning; **2.** *v/i.* (h) hit; **3.** *v/i.* (sein): ~ *auf* (*acc.*) meet with; encounter (*a.* ✕).

Treffen[2] [~] *n* (-s/-) meeting; rally; gathering; ✕ encounter; '**2d** *adj. remark:* appropriate, to the point.

'**Treff**|**er** *m* (-s/-) hit (*a. fig.*); prize; '~**punkt** *m* meeting-place.

Treibeis ['traɪp?-] *n* drift-ice.

treiben[1] ['traɪbən] (*irr.*, ge-) *v/t.* (h) drive; ⊕ put in motion, propel; drift (*smoke, snow*); put forth (*leaves*); force (*plants*); *fig.* impel, urge, press (*j-n zu inf.* s.o. to *inf.*); carry on (*business, trade*); *Musik* (*Sport*) ~ go in for music (sports); *Sprachen* ~ study languages; *es zu weit* ~ go too far; *wenn er es weiterhin so treibt* if he carries *or* goes on like that; *was treibst du da?* what are you doing there?; **2.** *v/i.* (sein) drive; float, drift; **3.** *v/i.* (h) 🌑 shoot; *dough:* ferment, work.

Treiben[2] [~] *n* (-s/*no pl.*) driving; doings *pl.*, goings-on *pl.*; *geschäftiges* ~ bustle; '**2d** *adj.*: ~*e Kraft* driving force.

'**Treib**|**haus** ['traɪp-] *n* hothouse; '~**holz** *n* drift-wood; '~**jagd** *f* battue; '~**riemen** *m* driving-belt; '~**stoff** *m* fuel; propell|ant, -ent (*of rocket*).

trenn|**en** ['trɛnən] *v/t.* (ge-, h) separate, sever; rip (*seam*); *teleph.*, ⚡ cut off, disconnect; isolate, segregate; *sich* ~ separate (*von* from), part (*from or with* s.o.; with

s.th.); '**2schärfe** *f* radio: selectivity; '**2ung** *f* (-/-en) separation; disconne|xion, -ction; segregation (*of races, etc.*); '**2(ungs)wand** *f* partition (wall).   (-bit.)

Trense ['trɛnzə] *f* (-/-n) snaffle|

Treppe ['trɛpə] *f* (-/-n) staircase, stairway, (*e-e* a flight *or* pair of) stairs *pl.*; *zwei* ~*n hoch* on the second floor, *Am.* on the third floor.

'**Treppen**|**absatz** *m* landing; '~**geländer** *n* banisters *pl.*; '~**haus** *n* staircase; '~**stufe** *f* stair, step.

Tresor [trɛ'zoːr] *m* (-s/-e) safe; *bank:* strong-room, vault.

treten ['treːtən] (*irr.*, ge-) **1.** *v/i.* (h) tread, step (*j-n* on *or* *j-m auf die Zehen* on s.o.'s toes); **2.** *v/i.* (sein) tread, step (*j-m auf die Zehen* on s.o.'s toes); walk; *ins Haus* ~ enter the house; *j-m unter die Augen* ~ appear before s.o., face s.o.; *j-m zu nahe* ~ offend s.o.; *zu j-m* ~ step *or* walk up to s.o.; *über die Ufer* ~ overflow its banks; **3.** *v/t.* (h) tread; kick; *mit Füßen* ~ trample upon.

treu *adj.* [trɔʏ] faithful, loyal; '**2bruch** *m* breach of faith, perfidy; '**2e** *f* (-/*no pl.*) fidelity, faith(ful)ness), loyalty; '**2händer** ['~hɛndər] *m* (-s/-) trustee; '~**herzig** *adj.* guileless; ingenuous, simpleminded; '~**los** *adj.* faithless (*gegen* to), disloyal (to); perfidious.

Tribüne [tri'byːnə] *f* (-/-n) platform; *sports, etc.*: (grand) stand.

Tribut [tri'buːt] *m* (-[e]s/-e) tribute.

Trichter ['trɪçtər] *m* (-s/-) funnel; *made by bomb, shell, etc.*: crater; horn (*of wind instruments, etc.*).

Trick [trɪk] *m* (-s/-e, -s) trick; '~**film** *m* animation, animated cartoon.

Trieb [triːp] **1.** *m* (-[e]s/-e) 🌑 sprout, (new) shoot; driving force; impulse; instinct; (sexual) urge; desire; **2.** ♀ *pret. of treiben*; '~**feder** *f* main-spring; *fig.* driving force, motive; '~**kraft** *f* motive power; *fig.* driving force, motive; '~**wagen** 🚃 *m* rail-car, rail-motor; '~**werk** ⊕ *n* gear (drive), (driving) mechanism, transmission; engine.

triefen ['triːfən] *v/i.* ([*irr.*,] ge-, h) drip (*von* with); *eye:* run.

triftig *adj.* ['trɪftɪç] valid.

Trigonometrie ♭ [trigonome'tri:] *f* (-/*no pl.*) trigonometry.

Trikot [tri'ko:] (-s/-s) **1.** *m* stockinet; **2.** *n* tights *pl.*; vest; **ʼagen** [ˌˌo'ta:-ʒən] *f*/*pl.* hosiery.

Triller ♪ ['trilər] *m* (-s/-) trill, shake, quaver; **ʼn** ♪ *v*/*i.* and *v*/*t.* (ge-, h) trill, shake, quaver; *bird: a.* warble.

trink|bar *adj.* ['triŋkba:r] drinkable; **ʼbecher** *m* drinking-cup; **ʼen** (*irr.*, ge-, h) **1.** *v*/*t.* drink; take, have (*tea, etc.*); **2.** *v*/*i.* drink; ~ *auf* (*acc.*) drink to, toast; **ʼer** *m* (-s/-) drinker; drunkard; **ʼgelage** *n* drinking-bout; **ʼgeld** *n* tip, gratuity; *j-m e-e Mark ~ geben* tip s.o. one mark; **ʼglas** *n* drinking-glass; **ʼhalle** *f at spa:* pump-room; **ʼkur** *f:* e-e ~ *machen* drink the waters; **ʼspruch** *m* toast; **ʼwasser** *n* (-s/*no pl.*) drinking-water.

Trio ['tri:o] *n* (-s/-s) trio (*a.* ♪).

trippeln ['tripəln] *v*/*i.* (ge-,sein) trip.

Tritt [trit] *m* (-[e]s/-e) tread, step; footprint; *noise:* footfall, (foot)step; kick; ⊕ treadle; *s.* Trittbrett, Trittleiter; *im* (*falschen*) ~ (in or out of) step; ~ *halten* keep step; **ʼbrett** *n* step, footboard; *mot.* running-board; **ʼleiter** *f* stepladder, (e-e a pair or set of) steps *pl.*

Triumph [tri'umf] *m* (-[e]s/-e) triumph; **al** *adj.* [ˌˌ'fa:l] triumphant; **bogen** *m* triumphal arch; **ieren** [ˌˌ'fi:rən] *v*/*i.* (no -ge-, h) triumph (*über acc.* over).

trocken *adj.* ['trɔkən] dry (*a.* fig.); *soil, land:* arid; **ʼdock** ⊕ *n* dry dock; **ʼhaube** *f* (hood of) hair-drier; **ʼheit** *f* (-/*no pl.*) dryness; drought, aridity; **ʼlegen** *v*/*t.* (sep., -ge-, h) dry up; drain (*land*); change the napkins of, *Am.* change the diapers of (*baby*); **ʼobst** *n* dried fruit.

trocknen ['trɔknən] (ge-) **1.** *v*/*i.* (sein) dry; **2.** *v*/*t.* (h) dry.

Troddel ['trɔdəl] *f* (-/-n) tassel.

Trödel F ['trø:dəl] *m* (-s/*no pl.*) second-hand articles *pl.*; lumber, *Am.* junk; rubbish; **ʼn** F fig. *v*/*i.* (ge-, h) dawdle, loiter.

Trödler ['trø:dlər] *m* (-s/-) second-hand dealer, *Am.* junk dealer, junkman; fig. dawdler, loiterer.

troff [trɔf] *pret. of* triefen.

Trog¹ [tro:k] *m* (-[e]s/Ꞌe) trough.

trog² [ˌˌ] *pret. of* trügen.

Trommel ['trɔməl] *f* (-/-n) drum; ⊕ *a.* cylinder, barrel; **ʼfell** *n* drumskin; *anat.* ear-drum; **ʼn** *v*/*i.* and *v*/*t.* (ge-, h) drum.

Trommler ['trɔmlər] *m* (-s/-) drummer.

Trompete [trɔm'pe:tə] *f* (-/-n) trumpet; **ʼn** *v*/*i.* and *v*/*t.* (no -ge-, h) trumpet; **r** *m* (-s/-) trumpeter.

Tropen ['tro:pən]: *die* ~ *pl.* the tropics *pl.*

Tropf F [trɔpf] *m* (-[e]s/Ꞌe) simpleton; *armer* ~ poor wretch.

tröpfeln ['trœpfəln] (ge-) **1.** *v*/*i.* (h) drop, drip, trickle; *tap: a.* leak; *es tröpfelt rain:* a few drops are falling; **2.** *v*/*i.* (sein): ~ *aus or von* trickle or drip from; **3.** *v*/*t.* (h) drop, drip.

tropfen¹ ['trɔpfən] (ge-) **1.** *v*/*i.* (h) drop, drip, trickle; *tap: a.* leak; *candle:* gutter; **2.** *v*/*i.* (sein): ~ *aus or von* trickle or drip from; **3.** *v*/*t.* (h) drop, drip.

Tropfen² [ˌˌ] *m* (-s/-) drop; *ein* ~ *auf den heißen Stein* a drop in the ocean or bucket; **ʼförmig** *adj.* ['ˌˌfœrmiç] drop-shaped; **ʼweise** *adv.* drop by drop, by drops.

Trophäe [tro'fɛ:ə] *f* (-/-n) trophy.

tropisch *adj.* ['tro:piʃ] tropical.

Trosse ['trɔsə] *f* (-/-n) cable; ♪ *a.* hawser.

Trost [tro:st] *m* (-es/*no pl.*) comfort, consolation; *das ist ein schlechter* ~ that is cold comfort; *du bist wohl nicht* (*recht*) *bei* ~! F you must be out of your mind!

tröst|en ['trø:stən] *v*/*t.* (ge-, h) console, comfort; *sich* ~ console o.s. (*mit* with); ~ *Sie sich!* be of good comfort!, cheer up!; **ʼlich** *adj.* comforting.

'trost|los *adj.* disconsolate, inconsolable; *land, etc.:* desolate; fig. wretched; **ʼlosigkeit** *f* (-/*no pl.*) desolation; fig. wretchedness; **ʼpreis** *m* consolation prize, booby prize; **ʼreich** *adj.* consolatory, comforting.

Trott [trɔt] *m* (-[e]s/-e) trot; F fig. jogtrot, routine; **el** F *m* (-s/-) idiot, fool, ninny; **ʼen** *v*/*i.* (ge-, sein) trot.

trotz [trɔts] **1.** *prp.* (gen.) in spite of, despite; ~ *alledem* for all that; **2.** ꞔ *m* (-es/*no pl.*) defiance; obstinacy; **dem** *cj.* [ˌˌ'de:m] nevertheless; (al)though; **en** *v*/*i.* (ge-, *h*) (*dat.*) defy, dare; brave (*danger*); be obstinate; sulk; **⁓ig** *adj.* defiant; obstinate; sulky.

trüb *adj.* [try:p], **⁓e** *adj.* ['⁓bə] liquid: muddy, turbid, thick; *mind, thinking*: confused, muddy, turbid; *eyes, etc.*: dim, dull; *weather*: dull, cloudy, dreary (*all a. fig.*); *experiences*: sad.

Trubel ['tru:bəl] *m* (-s/*no pl.*) bustle.

trüben ['try:bən] *v/t.* (ge-, h) make thick *or* turbid *or* muddy; dim; darken; spoil (*pleasures, etc.*); blur (*view*); dull (*mind*); *sich ⁓ liquid*: become thick *or* turbid *or* muddy; dim, darken; *relations*: become strained.

Trüb|sal ['try:pza:l] *f* (-/⁓-e): **⁓** *blasen* mope; F be in the dumps, have the blues; **'⁓selig** *adj.* sad, gloomy, melancholy, wretched, miserable, dreary; **'⁓sinn** *m* (-[e]s/*no pl.*) melancholy, sadness, gloom; **'⁓sinnig** *adj.* melancholy, gloomy, sad; **⁓ung** ['⁓buŋ] *f* (-/-en) liquid: muddiness, turbidity (*both a. fig.*); dimming, darkening.

Trüffel ♀ ['tryfəl] *f* (-/-n), F *m* (-s/-) truffle.

Trug[1] [tru:k] *m* (-[e]s/*no pl.*) deceit, fraud; delusion (*of senses*).

trug[2] [⁓] *pret. of* tragen.

Trugbild *n* phantom; illusion.

trüg|en ['try:gən] (*irr.*, ge-, h) **1.** *v/t.* deceive; **2.** *v/i.* be deceptive; **⁓erisch** *adj.* deceptive, delusive; treacherous.

'Trugschluß *m* fallacy, false conclusion.

Truhe ['tru:ə] *f* (-/-n) chest, trunk; *radio, etc.*: cabinet, console.

Trümmer ['trymər] *pl.* ruins *pl.*; rubble, debris, ⚓, ⚒ wreckage; **'⁓haufen** *m* heap of ruins *or* rubble.

Trumpf [trumpf] *m* (-[e]s/⁓e) *cards*: trump (card) (*a. fig.*); *s-n ⁓ ausspielen* play one's trump card.

Trunk [truŋk] *m* (-[e]s/⁓e) drink; draught; drinking; **'⁓en** *adj.* drunken; *pred.* drunk (*a. fig. von, vor* with); intoxicated; **⁓enbold** *contp.* ['⁓bɔlt] *m* (-[e]s/-e) drunkard, sot; **'⁓enheit** *f* (-/*no pl.*) drunkenness, intoxication; *⁓ am Steuer* ☲ drunken driving, drunkenness at the wheel; **'⁓sucht** *f* alcoholism, dipsomania; **'⁓süchtig** *adj.* addicted to drink, given to drinking.

Trupp [trup] *m* (-s/-s) troop, band, gang; ⚔ detachment.

'Truppe *f* (-/-n) ⚔ troop, body; ⚔ unit; *thea.* company, troupe; **⁓n** *pl.* ⚔ troops *pl.*, forces *pl.*; *die ⁓n pl.* ⚔ the (fighting) services *pl.*, the armed forces *pl.*

'Truppen|gattung *f* arm, branch, division; **'⁓schau** *f* military review; **'⁓transporter** ⚓, ⚒ *m* (troop-)transport; **'⁓übungsplatz** *m* training area.

Truthahn *orn.* ['tru:t-] *m* turkey (-cock).

Tschech|e ['tʃɛçə] *m* (-n/-n), **'⁓in** *f* (-/-nen) Czech; **'⁓isch** *adj.* Czech.

Tube ['tu:bə] *f* (-/-n) tube.

tuberkul|ös ⚕ *adj.* [tuberku'lø:s] tuberculous, tubercular; **⁓ose** *f* [⁓o:zə] *f* (-/-n) tuberculosis.

Tuch [tu:x] *n* **1.** (-[e]s/-e) cloth; fabric; **2.** (-[e]s/⁓er) *head covering*: kerchief; shawl, scarf; *round neck*: neckerchief; duster; rag; **'⁓fühlung** *f* (-/*no pl.*) close touch.

tüchtig ['tyçtiç] **1.** *adj.* able, fit; clever; proficient; efficient; excellent; good; thorough; **2.** *adv.* vigorously; thoroughly; F awfully; **'⁓keit** *f* (-/*no pl.*) ability, fitness; cleverness; proficiency; efficiency; excellency.

'Tuchwaren *f/pl.* drapery, cloths *pl.*

Tück|e ['tykə] *f* (-/-n) malice, spite; **'⁓isch** *adj.* malicious, spiteful; treacherous.

tüfteln F ['tyftəln] *v/i.* (ge-, h) puzzle (*an dat.* over).

Tugend ['tu:gənt] *f* (-/-en) virtue; **⁓bold** ['⁓bɔlt] *m* (-[e]s/-e) paragon of virtue; **'⁓haft** *adj.* virtuous.

Tüll [tyl] *m* (-s/-e) tulle.

Tulpe ♀ ['tulpə] *f* (-/-n) tulip.

tummel|n ['tuməln] *v/refl.* (ge-, h) *children*: romp; hurry; bestir o.s.; **'⁓platz** *m* playground; *fig.* arena.

Tümmler ['tymlər] *m* (-s/-) *orn.* tumbler; *zo.* porpoise.

Tumor ⚕ ['tu:mɔr] *m* (-s/-en) tumo(u)r.

Tümpel ['tympəl] *m* (-s/-) pool.

Tumult [tu'mult] *m* (-[e]s/-e) tumult; riot, turmoil, uproar; row.

tun [tu:n] **1.** *v/t.* (*irr.*, ge-, h) do; make; put (*to school, into the bag, etc.*); *dazu ⁓* add to it; contribute; *ich kann nichts dazu ⁓* I cannot help it; *es ist mir darum zu ⁓* I am anxious about (it); zu ~ haben have to do; be busy; es tut nichts it doesn't matter; **2.** v/i. (irr., ge-, h) do; make; so ~ als ob make as if; pretend to inf.; das tut gut! that is a comfort!; that's good!; **3.** ⚲ n (-s/no pl.) doings pl.; proceedings pl.; action; ~ und Treiben ways and doings pl.

Tünche ['tynçə] f (-/-n) whitewash (a. fig.); '⚲n v/t. (ge-, h) whitewash.

Tunichtgut ['tu:niçtgu:t] m (-, -[e]s/-e) ne'er-do-well, good-for-nothing.

Tunke ['tuŋkə] f (-/-n) sauce; '⚲n v/t. (ge-, h) dip, steep.

tunlichst adv. ['tu:nliçst] if possible.

Tunnel ['tunəl] m (-s/-, -s) tunnel; subway.

Tüpfel ['typfəl] m, n (-s/-) dot, spot; '⚲n v/t. (ge-, h) dot, spot.

tupfen ['tupfən] **1.** v/t. (ge-, h) dab; dot, spot; **2.** ⚲ m (-s/-) dot, spot.

Tür [ty:r] f (-/-en) door; mit der ~ ins Haus fallen blurt (things) out; j-n vor die ~ setzen turn s.o. out; vor der ~ stehen be near or close at hand; zwischen ~ und Angel in passing; '⚲angel f (door-)hinge.

Turbine ⊕ [tur'bi:nə] f (-/-n) turbine; **⚲nflugzeug** n turbo-jet.

Turbo-Prop-Flugzeug ['turbo-'prɔp-] n turbo-prop.

Tür|flügel m leaf (of a door); '⚲füllung f (door-)panel; '⚲griff m door-handle.

Türk|e ['tyrkə] m (-n/-n) Turk; '⚲in f (-/-nen) Turk(ish woman); '⚲is min. [~'ki:s] m (-es/-e) turquoise; '⚲isch adj. Turkish.

'Türklinke f door-handle; latch.

Turm [turm] m (-[e]s/ᵘe) tower; a. steeple (of church); chess: castle, rook.

Türm|chen ['tyrmçən] n (-s/-) tur-

ret; '⚲en (ge-) **1.** v/t. (h) pile up; sich ~ tower; **2.** F v/i. (sein) bolt, F skedaddle, Am. sl. a. skiddoo.

'turm|hoch adv.: j-m ~ überlegen sein stand head and shoulders above s.o.; '⚲spitze f spire; '⚲springen n (-s/no pl.) swimming: high diving; '⚲uhr f tower-clock, church-clock.

turnen ['turnən] **1.** v/i. (ge-, h) do gymnastics; **2.** ⚲ n (-s/no pl.) gymnastics pl.

'Turn|er m (-s/-), '⚲erin f (-/-nen) gymnast; '⚲gerät n gymnastic apparatus; '⚲halle f gym(nasium); '⚲hemd n (gym-)shirt; '⚲hose f shorts pl.

Turnier [tur'ni:r] n (-s/-e) tournament.

'Turn|lehrer m gym master; '⚲lehrerin f gym mistress; '⚲schuh m gym-shoe; '⚲stunde f gym lesson; '⚲unterricht m instruction in gymnastics; '⚲verein m gymnastic or athletic club.

'Tür|pfosten m door-post; '⚲rahmen m door-case, door-frame; '⚲schild n door-plate.

Tusche ['tuʃə] f (-/-n) India(n) or Chinese ink; '⚲n v/i. (ge-, h) whisper; '⚲n v/t. (ge-, h) draw in India(n) ink.

Tüte ['ty:tə] f (-/-n) paper-bag.

tuten ['tu:tən] v/i. (ge-, h) toot(le); mot. honk, blow one's horn.

Typ [ty:p] m (-s/-en) type; ⊕ a. model; '⚲e f (-/-n) typ. type; F fig. (queer) character.

Typhus 𝕤 ['ty:fus] m (-/no pl.) typhoid (fever).

'typisch adj. typical (für of).

Tyrann [ty'ran] m (-en/-en) tyrant; ⚲ei [~'naɪ] f (-/no pl.) tyranny; ⚲isch adj. [ty'raniʃ] tyrannical; ⚲isieren [~i'zi:rən] v/t. (no -ge-, h) tyrannize (over) s.o., oppress, bully.

U

U-Bahn ['u:-] f s. Untergrundbahn.

übel ['y:bəl] **1.** adj. evil, bad; nicht ~ not bad, pretty good; mir ist ~ I am or feel sick; **2.** adv. ill; ~ gelaunt sein be in a bad mood; es gefällt mir nicht ~ I rather like it;

3. ⚲ n (-s/-) evil; s. Übelstand; das kleinere ~ wählen choose the lesser evil; '⚲gelaunt adj. ill-humo(u)red; '⚲keit f (-/-en) sickness, nausea; '⚲nehmen v/t. (irr. nehmen, sep., -ge-, h) take s.th. ill or amiss; '⚲-

stand *m* grievance; **'2täter** *m* evil-doer, wrongdoer.

'übelwollen 1. *v/i.* (*sep.*, -ge-, *h*): *j-m* ~ wish s.o. ill; be ill-disposed towards s.o.; **2.** ♀ *n* (-*s/no pl.*) ill will, malevolence; **~d** *adj.* malevolent.

üben ['y:bən] (ge-, *h*) **1.** *v/t.* exercise; practi|se, *Am. a.* -ce; *Geduld* ~ exercise patience; *Klavier* ~ practise the piano; **2.** *v/i.* exercise; practi|se, *Am. a.* -ce.

über ['y:bər] **1.** *prp.* (*dat.*; *acc.*) over, above; across (*river, etc.*); via, by way of (*Munich, etc.*); *sprechen* ~ (*acc.*) talk about *or* of; ~ *Politik sprechen* talk politics; *nachdenken* ~ (*acc.*) think about *or* of; *ein Buch schreiben* ~ (*acc.*) write a book on; ~ *Nacht bleiben bei* stay overnight at; ~ *s-e Verhältnisse leben* live beyond one's income; ~ *kurz oder lang* sooner *or* later; **2.** *adv.*: *die ganze Zeit* ~ all along; *j-m in et.* ~ *sein* excel s.o. in s.th.

über'all *adv.* everywhere, anywhere, *Am. a.* all over.

über|'anstrengen *v/t.* (*no* -ge-, *h*) overstrain; *sich* ~ overstrain o.s.; **~'arbeiten** *v/t.* (*no* -ge-, *h*) retouch (*painting, etc.*); revise (*book, etc.*); *sich* ~ overwork o.s.

überaus *adv.* ['y:bər⁹-] exceedingly, extremely.

'überbelichten *phot.* *v/t.* (*no* -ge-, *h*) over-expose.

über'bieten *v/t.* (*irr.* bieten, *no* -ge-, *h*) at auction: outbid; *fig.*: beat; surpass.

Überbleibsel ['y:bərblaipsəl] *n* (-*s*/-) remnant, *Am.* F *a.* holdover; ~ *pl. a.* remains *pl.*

'Überblick *fig.* *m* survey, general view (*both*: über *acc.* of).

über|'blicken *v/t.* (*no* -ge-, *h*) overlook; *fig.* survey, have a general view of; **~'bringen** *v/t.* (*irr.* bringen, *no* -ge-, *h*) deliver; **2'bringer** *m* (-*s*/-) bearer; **~'brücken** *v/t.* (*no* -ge-, *h*) bridge; *fig.* bridge over *s.th.*; **~'dachen** *v/t.* (*no* -ge-, *h*) roof over; **~'dauern** *v/t.* (*no* -ge-, *h*) outlast, outlive; **~'denken** *v/t.* (*irr.* denken, *no* -ge-, *h*) think *s.th.* over.

über'dies *adv.* besides, moreover.

über'drehen *v/t.* (*no* -ge-, *h*) overwind (*watch, etc.*); strip (*screw*).

'Überdruck *m* **1.** (-[e]s/-e) overprint; ♉ *a.* surcharge; **2.** ⊕ (-[e]s/ᵘe) overpressure.

Über|druß ['y:bərdrus] *m* (*Überdrusses/no pl.*) satiety; *bis zum* ~ to satiety; **2drüssig** *adj.* (*gen.*) ['ᵧ-sıç] disgusted with, weary *or* sick of.

Übereif|er ['y:bər⁹-] *m* over-zeal; **2rig** *adj.* ['y:bər⁹-] over-zealous.

über'eil|en *v/t.* (*no* -ge-, *h*) precipitate, rush; *sich* ~ hurry too much; **~t** *adj.* precipitate, rash.

übereinander [y:bər⁹aı'nandər] *adv.* one upon the other; **~schlagen** *v/t.* (*irr.* schlagen, *sep.*, -ge-, *h*) cross (*one's legs*).

über'ein|kommen *v/i.* (*irr.* kommen, *sep.*, -ge-, *sein*) agree; **2kommen** *n* (-*s*/-), **2kunft** [~kunft] *f* (-/⁸e) agreement; **~stimmen** *v/i.* (*sep.*, -ge-, *h*) *p.* agree (*mit* with); *thing*: correspond (with, to); **2stimmung** *f* agreement; correspondence; *in* ~ *mit* in agreement *or* accordance with.

über|'fahren 1. ['~faːrən] *v/i.* (*irr.* fahren, *sep.*, -ge-, *sein*) cross; **2.** [~'faːrən] *v/t.* (*irr.* fahren, *no* -ge-, *h*) run over; disregard (*traffic sign, etc.*); **'2fahrt** *f* passage; crossing.

'Überfall *m* ✗ surprise; ✗ invasion (*auf acc.* of); ✗ raid; hold-up; assault ([up]on).

über'fallen *v/t.* (*irr.* fallen, *no* -ge-, *h*) ✗ surprise; ✗ invade; ✗ raid; hold up; assault.

'über'fällig *adj.* overdue; **'2fallkommando** *n* flying squad, *Am.* riot squad.

über'fliegen *v/t.* (*irr.* fliegen, *no* -ge-, *h*) fly over *or* across; *fig.* glance over, skim (through); *den Atlantik* ~ fly (across) the Atlantic.

'überfließen *v/i.* (*irr.* fließen, *sep.*, -ge-, *sein*) overflow.

über'flügeln *v/t.* (*no* -ge-, *h*) outflank; *fig.* outstrip, surpass.

'Über|fluß *m* (*Überflusses/no pl.*) abundance (*an dat.* of); superfluity (of); ~ *haben an* (*dat.*) abound in; **2flüssig** *adj.* superfluous; redundant.

über'fluten *v/t.* (*no* -ge-, *h*) overflow, flood (*a. fig.*).

'Überfracht *f* excess freight.

über'führen *v/t.* **1.** ['~fy:rən] (*sep.*, -ge-, *h*) convey (*dead body*);

U
V

2. [ˌ[~]fy:rən] (no -ge-, h) s. 1; ⚖
convict (gen. of); **2führung** f
(-/-en) conveyance (of dead body);
bridge, Am. overpass; ⚖ convic-
tion (gen. of). [dat. of).\
'Überfülle f superabundance (an)
über'füllen v/t. (no -ge-, h) over-
fill; cram; overcrowd; **sich den
Magen** ~ glut o.s.; **'**füttern** v/t.
(no -ge-, h) overfeed.
'Übergabe f delivery; handing
over; surrender (a. ✗).
'Übergang m bridge; 🚂 crossing;
fig. transition (a. ♪); esp. ⚖ devolu-
tion; **'**sstadium** n transition stage.
über'geben** v/t. (irr. geben, no
-ge-, h) deliver up; hand over; surrender (a. ✗); **sich ~** vomit, be
sick; **gehen 1.** ['**~ge:ən]** v/i. (irr.
gehen, sep., -ge-, sein) pass over;
work, duties: devolve (auf acc.
[up]on); **~ in** (acc.) pass into; **~ zu
et.** proceed to s.th.; **2.** [ˌ[~]ge:ən]
v/t. (irr. gehen, no -ge-, h) pass over,
ignore.
'Übergewicht n (-[e]s no pl.) over-
weight; fig. a. preponderance (über
acc. over).
über'gießen** v/t. (irr. gießen, no
-ge-, h): **mit Wasser ~** pour water
over s.th.; **mit Fett ~** baste (roasting
meat).
'über|greifen v/i. (irr. greifen, sep.,
-ge-, h): **~ auf** (acc.) encroach (up-)
on (s.o.'s rights); fire, epidemic, etc.:
spread to; **2griff** m encroachment
(auf acc. [up]on), inroad (on); **'**haben** F v/t. (irr. haben, sep., -ge-, h)
have (coat, etc.) on; fig. have enough
of, sl. be fed up with.
über'handnehmen v/i. (irr. nehmen, sep., -ge-, h) be rampant,
grow or wax rife.
'überhängen 1. v/i. (irr. hängen,
sep., -ge-, h) overhang; **2.** v/t. (sep.,
-ge-, h) put (coat, etc.) round
one's shoulders; sling (rifle) over
one's shoulder.
über'häufen** v/t. (no -ge-, h): **~
mit** swamp with (letters, work, etc.);
overwhelm with (inquiries, etc.).
über'haupt adv.: **wer will denn ~,
daß er kommt?** who wants him to
come anyhow?; **wenn ~** if at all; **~
nicht** not at all; **~ kein** no ... what-
ever.
überheblich adj. [y:bər'he:plıç]
presumptuous, arrogant; **2keit** f

(-/**~**-en) presumption, arrogance.
über'hitzen v/t. (no -ge-, h) over-
heat (a. 🛠); ⊕ superheat; **'holen**
v/t. (no -ge-, h) overtake (a. mot.);
esp. sports: outstrip (a. fig.); over-
haul, esp. Am. a. service; **~'holt**
adj. outmoded; pred. a. out of date;
~'hören v/t. (no -ge-, h) fail to
hear, miss; ignore.
'überirdisch adj. supernatural; un-
earthly.
'überkippen v/i. (sep., -ge-, sein) p.
overbalance, lose one's balance.
über'kleben v/t. (no -ge-, h) paste
over.
'Überkleidung f outer garments pl.
'überklug adj. would-be wise,
sapient.
'überkochen v/i. (sep., -ge-, sein)
boil over; F leicht ~ be very irritable.
über'kommen** v/t. (irr. kommen,
no -ge-, h): **Furcht überkam ihn** he
was seized with fear; **~'laden** v/t.
(irr. laden, no -ge-, h) overload;
overcharge (battery, picture, etc.).
'Überland|flug m cross-country
flight; **'~zentrale** ⚡ f long-distance
power-station.
über'lassen** v/t. (irr. lassen, no
-ge-, h): **j-m et. ~** let s.o. have s.th.;
fig. leave s.th. to s.o.; **j-n sich selbst
~** leave s.o. to himself; **j-n s-m
Schicksal ~** leave or abandon s.o. to
his fate; **~'lasten** v/t. (no -ge-, h)
overload; fig. overburden.
über'laufen 1. ['**~laufən]** v/i. (irr.
laufen, sep., -ge-, sein) run over;
boil over; ✗ desert (zu to);
2. [ˌ[~]'laufən] v/t. (irr. laufen, no
-ge-, h): **es überlief mich kalt** a
shudder passed over me; **überlaufen
werden von** doctor, etc.: be besieged
by (patients, etc.); **3.** adj. [ˌ[~]'laufən]
place, profession, etc.: overcrowded;
2läufer m ✗ deserter; pol. rene-
gade, turncoat.
'überlaut adj. too loud.
über'leben** (no -ge-, h) **1.** v/t.
survive, outlive; **2.** v/i. survive; **2de**
m, f (-n/-n) survivor.
'überlebensgroß adj. bigger than
life-size(d).
überlebt adj. [y:bər'le:pt] outmoded, disused, out of date.
'überlegen¹ F v/t. (sep., -ge-, h)
give (child) a spanking.
über'leg|en² 1. v/t. and v/refl. (no

-ge-, h) consider, reflect upon, think about; *ich will es mir ~* I will think it over; *es sich anders ~* change one's mind; **2.** *v/i.* (*no -ge-, h*): *er überlegt noch* he hasn't made up his mind yet; **3.** *adj.* superior (*dat.* to; *an dat.* in); **2enheit** *f* (*-/no pl.*) superiority; preponderance; **~t** *adj.* [~kt] deliberate; prudent; **2ung** [~guŋ] *f* (*-/-en*) consideration, reflection; *nach reiflicher ~* after mature deliberation.

über'lesen *v/t.* (*irr. lesen, no -ge-, h*) read *s.th.* through quickly, run over *s.th.*; overlook.

über'liefer|n *v/t.* (*no -ge-, h*) hand down *or* on (*dat.* to); **2ung** *f* tradition.

über'listen *v/t.* (*no -ge-, h*) outwit, F outsmart.

'Über|macht *f* (*-/no pl.*) superiority; *esp.* ✗ superior forces *pl.*; *in der ~ sein* be superior in numbers; **'2mächtig** *adj.* superior.

über'malen *v/t.* (*no -ge-, h*) paint out; **~'mannen** *v/t.* (*no -ge-, h*) overpower, overcome, overwhelm (*all. a. fig.*).

'Über|maß *n* (*-es/no pl.*) excess (*an dat.* of); **'2mäßig 1.** *adj.* excessive; immoderate; **2.** *adv.* excessively, *Am. a.* overly; *~ trinken* drink to excess.

'Übermensch *m* superman; **'2lich** *adj.* superhuman.

über'mittel|n *v/t.* (*no -ge-, h*) transmit; convey; **2lung** *f* (*-/-en*) transmission; conveyance.

'übermorgen *adv.* the day after tomorrow.

über'müd|et *adj.* overtired; **2ung** *f* (*-/~-en*) overfatigue.

'Über|mut *m* wantonness; frolicsomeness; **2mütig** *adj.* ['~my:tiç] wanton; frolicsome.

'übernächst *adj. the* next but one; *~e Woche* the week after next.

über'nacht|en *v/i.* (*no -ge-, h*) stay overnight (*bei at a friend's* [*house*], *with friends*), spend the night (*at, with*); **2ung** *f* (*-/-en*) spending the night; *~ und Frühstück* bed and breakfast.

Übernahme ['y:bərna:mə] *f* (*-/-n*) field of application *s.* übernehmen 1: taking over; undertaking; assumption; adoption.

'übernatürlich *adj.* supernatural.

übernehmen *v/t.* **1.** [~'ne:mən] (*irr. nehmen, no -ge-, h*) take over (*business, etc.*); undertake (*responsibility, etc.*); take (*lead, risk, etc.*); assume (*direction of business, office, etc.*); adopt (*idea, custom, etc.*); *sich ~* overreach o.s.; **2.** ✗ ['~ne:mən] (*irr. nehmen, sep., -ge-, h*) slope, shoulder (*arms*).

'über|ordnen *v/t.* (*sep., -ge-, h*): *j-n j-m ~* set s.o. over s.o.; **'~parteilich** *adj.* non-partisan; **'2produktion** *f* over-production.

über'prüf|en *v/t.* (*no -ge-, h*) reconsider; verify; check; review; screen *s.o.*; **2ung** *f* reconsideration; checking; review.

über|'queren *v/t.* (*no -ge-, h*) cross; **~'ragen** *v/t.* (*no -ge-, h*) tower above (*a. fig.*), overtop; *fig.* surpass.

überrasch|en [y:bər'raʃən] *v/t.* (*no -ge-, h*) surprise; catch (*bei at, in*); **2ung** *f* (*-/-en*) surprise.

über'red|en *v/t.* (*no -ge-, h*) persuade (*zu inf.* to *inf.*, into *ger.*); talk (*into ger.*); **2ung** *f* (*-/~-en*) persuasion.

über'reich|en *v/t.* (*no -ge-, h*) present; **2ung** *f* (*-/~-en*) presentation.

über|'reizen *v/t.* (*no -ge-, h*) over-excite; **~'reizt** *adj.* overstrung; **~'rennen** *v/t.* (*irr. rennen, no -ge-, h*) overrun.

'Überrest *m* remainder; **~e** *pl.* remains *pl.*; *sterbliche ~e pl.* mortal remains *pl.*

über'rump|eln *v/t.* (*no -ge-, h*) (take by) surprise; **2(e)lung** *f* (*-/~-en*) surprise.

über'rund|en *v/t.* (*no -ge-, h*) *sports:* lap; *fig.* surpass; **2ung** *f* (*-/-en*) lapping.

übersät *adj.* [y:bər'zɛ:t] studded, dotted.

über'sättig|en *v/t.* (*no -ge-, h*) surfeit (*a. fig.*); 🜍 supersaturate; **2ung** *f* (*-/-en*) surfeit (*a. fig.*); 🜍 supersaturation.

'Überschallgeschwindigkeit *f* supersonic speed.

über|'schatten *v/t.* (*no -ge-, h*) overshadow (*a. fig.*); **~'schätzen** *v/t.* (*no -ge-, h*) overrate, overestimate.

'Überschlag *m* *gymnastics:* somersault; 🜨 loop; 🗲 flashover; *fig.*

estimate, approximate calculation; **~en** (*irr. schlagen*) **1.** ['~ʃlɑ:gən] *v/t.* (*sep., -ge-, h*) cross (*one's legs*); **2.** ['~ʃlɑ:gən] *v/i.* (*sep., -ge-, sein*) *voice:* become high-pitched; **3.** [~'ʃlɑ:gən] *v/t.* (*no -ge-, h*) skip (*page, etc.*); make a rough estimate of (*cost, etc.*); *sich ~* fall head over heels; *car, etc.:* (be) turn(ed) over; ✈ loop the loop; *voice:* become high-pitched; *sich ~ vor* (*dat.*) outdo (*one's friendliness, etc.*); **4.** *adj.* [~'ʃlɑ:gən] lukewarm, tepid.

'**über|schnappen** *v/i.* (*sep., -ge-, sein*) *voice:* become high-pitched; F *p.* go mad, turn crazy.

über|'schneiden *v/refl.* (*irr. schneiden, no -ge-, h*) overlap; intersect; **~'schreiben** *v/t.* (*irr. schreiben, no -ge-, h*) superscribe, entitle; make *s.th.* over (*dat.* to); **~'schreiten** *v/t.* (*irr. schreiten, no -ge-, h*) cross; transgress (*limit, bound*); infringe (*rule, etc.*); exceed (*speed limit, one's instructions, etc.*); *sie hat die 40 bereits überschritten* she is on the wrong side of 40.

'**Über|schrift** *f* heading, title; headline; '**~schuh** *m* overshoe; '**Über|schuß** *m* surplus, excess; profit; **Qschüssig** *adj.* ['~ʃysiç] surplus, excess.

über'schütten *v/t.* (*no -ge-, h*): *~ mit* pour (*water, etc.*) on; *fig.:* overwhelm with (*inquiries, etc.*); shower (*gifts, etc.*) upon.

überschwemm|en [y:bər'ʃvɛmən] *v/t.* (*no -ge-, h*) inundate, flood (*both a. fig.*); **Qung** *f* (*-/-en*) inundation, flood(ing).

überschwenglich *adj.* ['y:bərʃvɛŋliç] effusive, gushy.

'**Übersee:** *nach ~ gehen* go overseas; '**~dampfer** ⚓ *m* transoceanic steamer; '**~handel** *m* (*-s/no pl.*) oversea(s) trade.

über'sehen *v/t.* (*irr. sehen, no -ge-, h*) survey; overlook (*printer's error, etc.*); *fig.* ignore, disregard.

über'send|en *v/t.* [*irr. senden,*] *no -ge-, h*) send, transmit; consign; **Qung** *f* sending, transmission; ✞ consignment.

'**übersetzen**[1] *v/i.* (*sep., -ge-*) **1.** *v/i.* (*sein*) cross; **2.** *v/t.* (*h*) ferry.

über'setz|en[2] *v/t.* (*no -ge-, h*) translate (*in acc. into*), render (into); ⊕ gear; **Qer** *m* (*-s/-*) translator.

Qung *f* (*-/-en*) translation (*aus* from; *in acc.* into); rendering; ⊕ gear(ing), transmission.

'**Übersicht** *f* (*-/-en*) survey (*über acc.* of); summary; '**Qlich** *adj.* clear(ly arranged).

über|siedeln ['y:bərzi:dəln] *v/i.* (*sep., -ge-, sein and* [~'zi:dəln] *v/i.* (*no -ge-, sein*) remove (*nach* to); **Qsiedelung** [~'zi:dəluŋ] *f* (*-/-en*), **Qsiedlung** ['~zi:dluŋ, ~'zi:dluŋ] *f* (*-/-en*) removal (*nach* to).

'**übersinnlich** *adj.* transcendental; *forces:* psychic.

über'spann|en *v/t.* (*no -ge-, h*) cover (*mit* with); *den Bogen ~* go too far; **~t** *adj.* extravagant; *p.* eccentric; *claims, etc.:* exaggerated; **Qtheit** *f* (*-/~ -en*) extravagance; eccentricity.

über'spitzt *adj.* oversubtle; exaggerated.

überspringen 1. ['~ʃpriŋən] *v/i.* (*irr. springen, sep., -ge-, sein*) ⚡ *spark:* jump; *in a speech, etc.:* ~ *von ... zu ...* jump *or* skip from (*one subject*) to (*another*); **2.** [~'ʃpriŋən] *v/t.* (*irr. springen, no -ge-, h*) jump, clear; skip (*page, etc.*); jump (*class*).

überstehen (*irr. stehen*) **1.** ['~ʃte:ən] *v/i.* (*sep., -ge-, h*) jut (out *or* forth), project; **2.** [~'ʃte:ən] *v/t.* (*no -ge-, h*) survive (*misfortune, etc.*); weather (*crisis*); get over (*illness*).

über|'steigen *v/t.* (*irr. steigen, no -ge-, h*) climb over; *fig.* exceed; **~'stimmen** *v/t.* (*no -ge-, h*) outvote, vote down.

'**überstreifen** *v/t.* (*sep., -ge-, h*) slip *s.th.* over.

überströmen 1. ['~ʃtrø:mən] *v/i.* (*sep., -ge-, sein*) overflow (*vor dat.* with); **2.** [~'ʃtrø:mən] *v/t.* (*no -ge-, h*) flood, inundate.

'**Überstunden** *f/pl.* overtime; *~ machen* work overtime.

über'stürz|en *v/t.* (*no -ge-, h*) rush, hurry (up *or* on); *sich ~* act rashly; *events:* follow in rapid succession; **~t** *adj.* precipitate, rash; **Qung** *f* (*-/~ -en*) precipitancy.

über|'teuern *v/t.* (*no -ge-, h*) overcharge; **~'tölpeln** *v/t.* (*no -ge-, h*) dupe, take in; **~'tönen** *v/t.* (*no -ge-, h*) drown.

Übertrag ✞ ['y:bərtrɑ:k] *m* (*-[e]s/-*ᵉe) carrying forward; sum carried forward.

über'trag|bar adj. transferable; † negotiable; ⚖ communicable; **~en** [~gən] **1.** v/t. (irr. tragen, no -ge-, h) † carry forward; make over (property) (auf acc. to); ⚖ transfuse (blood); delegate (rights, etc.) (dat. to); render (book, etc.) (in acc. into); transcribe (s.th. written in shorthand); ⚖, ⊕, phys., radio: transmit; radio: a. broadcast; im Fernsehen ~ televise; ihm wurde eine wichtige Mission ~ he was charged with an important mission; **2.** adj. figurative; **2ung** [~gun] f (-/-en) field of application s. übertragen 1: carrying forward; making over; transfusion; delegation; rendering, free translation; transcription; transmission; broadcast; ~ im Fernsehen telecast.

über'treffen v/t. (irr. treffen, no -ge-, h) excel s.o. (an dat. in; in dat. in, at); surpass (in), exceed (in).

über'treib|en (irr. treiben, no -ge-, h) **1.** v/t. overdo; exaggerate, overstate; **2.** v/i. exaggerate, draw the long bow; **2ung** f (-/-en) exaggeration, overstatement.

'übertreten¹ v/i. (irr. treten, sep., -ge-, sein) sports: cross the take-off line; fig. go over (zu to); zum Katholizismus ~ turn Roman Catholic.

über'tret|en² v/t. (irr. treten, no -ge-, h) transgress, violate, infringe (law, etc.); sich den Fuß ~ sprain one's ankle; **2ung** f (-/-en) transgression, violation, infringement.

'Übertritt m going over (zu to); eccl. conversion (to).

über'völker|n [y:bər'fœlkərn] v/t. (no -ge-, h) over-populate; **2ung** f (-/~-en) over-population.

über'vorteilen v/t. (no -ge-, h) overreach, F do.

über'wach|en v/t. (no -ge-, h) supervise, superintend; control; police: keep under surveillance, shadow; **2ung** f (-/~-en) supervision, superintendence; control; surveillance.

überwältigen [y:bər'vɛltigən] v/t. (no -ge-, h) overcome, overpower, overwhelm (all a. fig.); **~d** fig. adj. overwhelming.

über'weis|en v/t. (irr. weisen, no -ge-, h) remit (money) (an dat. or acc. to); (zur Entscheidung etc.) ~ refer (to); **2ung** f (-/-en) remittance; reference (an acc. to); parl. devolution.

überwerfen (irr. werfen) **1.** ['~vɛrfən] v/t. (sep., -ge-, h) slip (coat) on; **2.** [~'vɛrfən] v/refl. (no -ge-, h) fall out (mit with).

über'wieg|en (irr. wiegen, no -ge-, h) **1.** v/t. outweigh; **2.** v/i. preponderate; predominate; **~end** adj. preponderant; predominant; **~winden** v/t. (irr. winden, no -ge-, h) overcome (a. fig.), subdue; sich ~ zu inf. bring o.s. to inf.; **~wintern** v/i. (no -ge-, h) (pass the) winter.

'Über|wurf m wrap; **'~zahl** f (-/~-en) numerical superiority; in der ~ superior in numbers; **2zählig** adj. ['~tsɛ:liç] supernumerary; surplus.

über'zeug|en v/t. (no -ge-, h) convince (von of); satisfy (of); **2ung** f (-/-en) conviction.

über'ziehe|n v/t. (irr. ziehen) **1.** ['~tsi:ən] (sep., -ge-, h) put on; **2.** [~'tsi:ən (no -ge-, h) cover; put clean sheets on (bed); † overdraw (account); sich ~ sky: become overcast; **2r** m (-s/-) overcoat, topcoat.

'Überzug m cover; case, tick; ⊕ coat(ing). [ary: normal.]

üblich adj. ['y:pliç] usual, custom-|

U-Boot ♣, ⚔ ['u:~] n submarine, in Germany: a. U-boat.

übrig adj. ['y:briç] left, remaining; die ~e Welt the rest of the world; die ~en pl. the others pl., the rest; im ~en for the rest; by the way; ~ haben have s.th. left; keine Zeit ~ haben have no time to spare; etwas ~ haben für care for, have a soft spot for; ein ~es tun go out of one's way; **'~bleiben** v/i. (irr. bleiben, sep., -ge-, sein) be left; remain; es blieb ihm nichts anderes übrig he had no (other) alternative (als but); **~ens** adv. ['~gəns] by the way; **~lassen** ['~ç~] v/t. (irr. lassen, sep., -ge-, h) leave; viel zu wünschen ~ leave much to be desired.

'Übung f (-/-en) exercise; practice; drill; **'~shang** m skiing: nursery slope.

Ufer ['u:fər] n (-s/-) shore (of sea, lake); bank (of river, etc.).

Uhr [u:r] f (-/-en) clock; watch; um vier ~ at four o'clock; **'~armband** n (-[e]s/~er) watch-strap; **'~feder** f watch-spring; '**~macher** m (-s/-) watch-maker; '**~werk** n clockwork; watch-work; '**~zeiger** m hand (of clock or watch); '**~zeigersinn** m (-[e]s/no pl.): im ~ clockwise; entgegen dem ~ counter-clockwise.

Uhu orn. ['u:hu:] m (-s/-s) eagle-owl.

Ulk [ulk] m (-[e]s/-e) fun, lark; '**2en** v/i. (ge-, h) (sky)lark, joke; '**2ig** adj. funny.

Ulme ♀ ['ulmə] f (-/-n) elm.

Ultimatum [ulti'ma:tum] n (-s/Ultimaten, -s) ultimatum; j-m ein ~ stellen deliver an ultimatum to s.o.

Ultimo † ['ultimo] m (-s/-s) last day of the month.

Ultrakurzwelle phys. [ultra'-] f ultra-short wave, very-high-frequency wave.

um [um] 1. prp. (acc.) round, about; ~ vier Uhr at four o'clock; ~ sein Leben laufen run for one's life; et. ~ einen Meter verfehlen miss s.th. by a metre; et. ~ zwei Mark verkaufen sell s.th. at two marks; 2. prp. (gen.): ~ seinetwillen for his sake; 3. cj.: ~ so besser all the better, so much the better; ~ so mehr (weniger) all the more (less); ~ zu (in order) to; 4. adv.: er drehte sich ~ he turned round.

um|ändern ['um?-] v/t. (sep., -ge-, h) change, alter; **~arbeiten** ['um?-] v/t. (sep., -ge-, h) make over (coat, etc.); revise (book, etc.); ~ zu make into.

um'arm|en v/t. (no -ge-, h) hug, embrace; sich ~ embrace; **2ung** f (-/-en) embrace, hug.

'**Umbau** m (-[e]s/-e, -ten) rebuilding; reconstruction; '**2en** v/t. (sep., -ge-, h) rebuild; reconstruct.

'**umbiegen** v/t. (irr. biegen, sep., -ge-, h) bend; turn up or down.

'**umbild|en** v/t. (sep., -ge-, h) remodel, reconstruct; reorganize, reform; reshuffle (cabinet); '**2ung** f (-/-en) remodel(l)ing, reconstruction; reorganization, pol. reshuffle.

um|binden v/t. (irr. binden, sep., -ge-, h) put on (apron, etc.); '**~blättern** (sep., -ge-, h) 1. v/t. turn over; 2. v/i. turn over the page; **~brechen** v/t. (irr. brechen) 1. ['~brɛçən] (sep., -ge-, h) dig, break up (ground). 2. typ. [~'brɛçən] (no -ge-, h) make up; '**~bringen** v/t. (irr. bringen, sep., -ge-, h) kill; sich ~ kill o.s.;

'**2bruch** m typ. make-up; fig.: upheaval; radical change; '**~buchen** v/t. (sep., -ge-, h) † transfer or switch to another account; book for another date; '**~disponieren** v/i. (sep., no -ge-, h) change one's plans.

'**umdreh|en** v/t. (sep., -ge-, h) turn; s. Spieß; sich ~ turn round; **2ung** [um?-] f (-/-en) turn; phys., ⊕ rotation, revolution.

um|fahren (irr. fahren) 1. ['~fa:rən] v/t. (sep., -ge-, h) run down; 2. ['~fa:rən] v/i. (sep., -ge-, sein) go a roundabout way; 3. [~'fa:rən] v/t. (no -ge-, h) drive round; ♣ sail round; ♣ double (cape); '**~fallen** v/i. (irr. fallen, sep., -ge-, sein) fall; collapse; tot ~ drop dead.

'**Umfang** m (-[e]s/no pl.) circumference, circuit; perimeter; girth (of body, tree, etc.); fig.: extent; volume; in großem ~ on a large scale; '**2reich** adj. extensive; voluminous; spacious.

um'fass|en v/t. (no -ge-, h) clasp; embrace (a. fig.); ✗ envelop; fig. comprise, cover, comprehend; **~d** adj. comprehensive, extensive; sweeping, drastic.

'**umform|en** v/t. (sep., -ge-, h) remodel, recast, transform (a. ⚡); ⚡ convert; '**2er** ⚡ m (-s/-) transformer; converter.

'**Umfrage** f poll; öffentliche ~ public opinion poll.

'**Umgang** m 1. (-[e]s/=e) △ gallery, ambulatory; eccl. procession (round the fields, etc.); 2. (-[e]s/no pl.) intercourse (mit with); company; ~ haben mit associate with.

umgänglich adj. ['umgɛnliç] sociable, companionable, affable.

'**Umgangs|formen** f/pl. manners pl.; '**~sprache** f colloquial usage; in der deutschen ~ in colloquial German.

um'garnen v/t. (no -ge-, h) ensnare.

um'geb|en v/t. (irr. geben, no -ge-, h) surround; mit e-r Mauer ~ wall in; 2. adj. surrounded (von with, by) (a. fig.); **2ung** f (-/-en) environs pl. (of town, etc.); surroundings pl., environment (of place, person, etc.).

umgeh|en (irr. gehen) 1. ['~ge:ən] v/i. (sep., -ge-, sein) make a detour; rumour, etc.: go about, be afloat;

ghost: walk; ~ *mit* use *s.th.*; deal with *s.o.*; keep company with; *ein Gespenst soll im Schlosse* ~ the castle is said to be haunted; **2.** [ˈ~ɡeːən] *v/t.* (*no* -ge-, *h*) go round; ✕ flank; bypass (*town*, etc.); *fig.* avoid, evade; circumvent, elude (*law*, etc.); **~end** *adj.* immediate; **₂ungsstraße** [umˈɡeːuŋs-] *f* by-pass.

umgekehrt [ˈumɡəˌkeːrt] **1.** *adj.* reverse; inverse, inverted; *in ~er Reihenfolge* in reverse order; *im ~en Verhältnis zu* in inverse proportion to; **2.** *adv.* vice versa.

'umgraben *v/t.* (*irr.* graben, sep., -ge-, *h*) dig (up).

um'grenzen *v/t.* (*no* -ge-, *h*) en-circle; enclose; *fig.* circumscribe, limit.

'umgruppier|en *v/t.* (sep., *no* -ge-, *h*) regroup; **'₂ung** *f* (-/-en) regrouping.

'um|haben F *v/t.* (*irr.* haben, sep., -ge-, *h*) have (*coat*, etc.) on; **'₂hang** *m* wrap; cape; **'~hängen** *v/t.* (sep., -ge-, *h*) rehang (*pictures*); sling (*rifle*) over one's shoulder; *sich den Mantel* ~ put one's coat round one's shoulders; **'~hauen** *v/t.* (*irr.* hauen, sep., -ge-, *h*) fell, cut down; F: *die Nachricht hat mich umge-hauen* I was bowled over by the news.

um'her|blicken *v/i.* (sep., -ge-, *h*) look about (one); **~streifen** *v/i.* (sep., -ge-, sein) rove.

um'hinkönnen *v/i.* (*irr.* können, sep., -ge-, *h*): *ich kann nicht umhin, zu sagen* I cannot help saying.

um'hüll|en *v/t.* (*no* -ge-, *h*) wrap up (*mit* in), envelop (in); **₂ung** *f* (-/-en) wrapping, wrapper, envelop-ment.

Umkehr [ˈumkeːr] *f* (-/*no pl.*) return; **'₂en** (sep., -ge-) **1.** *v/i.* (sein) return, turn back; **2.** *v/t.* (*h*) turn out (*one's pocket*, etc.); invert (*a.* ♪); reverse (*a.* ✂, ♫); **'~ung** *f* (-/-en) reversal; inversion.

'umkippen (sep., -ge-) **1.** *v/t.* (*h*) upset, tilt; **2.** *v/i.* (sein) upset, tilt (over); F faint.

um'klammer|n *v/t.* (*no* -ge-, *h*) clasp; *boxing*: clinch; **₂ung** *f* (-/-en) clasp; *boxing*: clinch.

'umkleid|en *v/refl.* (sep., -ge-, *h*) change (one's clothes); **'₂eraum** *m* dressing-room.

'umkommen *v/i.* (*irr.* kommen, sep., -ge-, sein) be killed (*bei* in), die (in), perish (in); *vor Lange-weile* ~ die of boredom.

'Umkreis *m* (-es/*no pl.*) ⅍ circum-scribed circle; *im ~ von* within a radius of.

um'kreisen *v/t.* (*no* -ge-, *h*) circle round.

'um|krempeln *v/t.* (sep., -ge-, *h*) tuck up (*shirt-sleeves*, etc.); change (*plan*, etc.); (*völlig*) ~ turn *s.th.* in-side out; **'~laden** *v/t.* (*irr.* laden, sep., -ge-, *h*) reload; ✝, ⚓ trans-ship.

'Umlauf *m* circulation; *phys.*, ⊕ rotation; circular (letter); *in ~ set-zen* or *bringen* circulate, put into circulation; *im ~ sein* circulate, be in circulation; *rumours*: *a.* be afloat; *außer ~ setzen* withdraw from cir-culation; **'~bahn** *f* orbit; **₂en** (*irr.* laufen) **1.** [ˈ~laufən] *v/t.* (sep., -ge-, *h*) knock over; **2.** [ˈ~laufən] *v/i.* (sep., -ge-, sein) circulate; make a detour; **3.** [~ˈlaufən] *v/t.* (*no* -ge-, *h*) run round.

'Umlege|kragen *m* turn-down collar; **'₂n** *v/t.* (sep., -ge-, *h*) lay down; ⊕ throw (*lever*); *storm*, etc.: beat down (*wheat*, etc.); re-lay (*cable*, etc.); put (*coat*, etc.) round one's shoulders; apportion (*costs*, etc.); *fig. sl.* do *s.o.* in.

'umleit|en *v/t.* (sep., -ge-, *h*) divert; **₂ung** *f* diversion, detour.

'umliegend *adj.* surrounding, cir-cumjacent.

um'nacht|et *adj.*: *geistig ~* men-tally deranged; **₂ung** *f* (-/⚘-en): *geistige ~* mental derangement.

'um|packen *v/t.* (sep., -ge-, *h*) re-pack; **~pflanzen** *v/t.* **1.** [ˈ~pflan-tsən] (sep., -ge-, *h*) transplant; **2.** [~ˈpflantsən] (*no* -ge-, *h*): ~ *mit* plant *s.th.* round with; **'~pflügen** *v/t.* (sep., -ge-, *h*) plough, *Am.* plow.

um'rahmen *v/t.* (*no* -ge-, *h*) frame; *musikalisch ~* put into a musical setting.

umrand|en [umˈrandən] *v/t.* (*no* -ge-, *h*) edge, border; **₂ung** *f* (-/-en) edge, border.

um'ranken *v/t.* (*no* -ge-, *h*) twine (*mit* with).

'umrechn|en *v/t.* (sep., -ge-, *h*) convert (*in acc.* into); **'₂ung** *f* (-/*no* *pl.*) conversion; '**⸚ungskurs** *m* rate of exchange.

umreißen *v/t.* (*irr. reißen*) **1.** ['⸚raisən] (*sep., -ge-, h*) pull down; knock *s.o.* over; **2.** [⸚'raisən] (*no -ge-, h*) outline. [round (*a. fig.*).\

um'ringen *v/t.* (*no -ge-, h*) sur-)

'**Um**|**riß** *m* outline (*a. fig.*), contour; '**⸚rühren** *v/t.* (*sep., -ge-, h*) stir; '**⸚satteln** (*sep., -ge-, h*) **1.** *v/t.* resaddle; **2.** F *fig. v/i.* change one's studies *or* occupation; **⸚ von ... auf** (*acc.*) change from ... to ...; '**⸚satz ✝** *m* turnover; sales *pl.*; return(s *pl.*); *stock exchange*: business done.

'**umschalt**|**en** (*sep., -ge-, h*) **1.** *v/t.* ⊕ change over; ⚡ commutate; ⚡, ⊕ switch; **2.** ⚡, ⊕ *v/i.* switch over; '**⸚er** *m* ⚡ change-over switch; '**⸚er** ⚡ commutator; '**⸚ung** *f* (*-/-en*) ⊕ change-over; ⚡ commutation.

'**Umschau** *f* (*-/no pl.*): **⸚ halten nach** look out for, be on the look-out for; '**⸚en** *v/refl.* (*sep., -ge-, h*) look round (*nach for*); look about (for) (*a. fig.*), look about one.

'**umschicht**|**en** *v/t.* (*sep., -ge-, h*) pile afresh; *fig.* regroup (*a.* ✝); '**⸚ig** *adv.* by or in turns; '**⸚ung** *fig. f* (*-/-en*) regrouping; **soziale ⸚en** *pl.* social upheavals *pl.*

um'schiff|**en** *v/t.* (*no -ge-, h*) circumnavigate; double (*cape*); **⸚ung** *f* (*-/⸚-en*) circumnavigation; doubling.

'**Umschlag** *m* envelope; cover, wrapper; jacket; turn-up, *Am. a.* cuff (*of trousers*); ⚕ compress; ⚕ poultice; trans-shipment (*of goods*); *fig.* change, turn; '**⸚en** (*irr. schlagen, sep., -ge-*) **1.** *v/t.* (*h*) knock *s.o.* down; cut down, fell (*tree*); turn (*leaf*); turn up (*sleeves, etc.*); turn down (*collar*); trans-ship (*goods*); **2.** *v/i.* (*sein*) turn over, upset; ⚓ capsize, upset; *wine, etc.*: turn sour; *fig.* turn (*in acc.* into); '**⸚hafen** *m* port of trans-shipment.

um'schließen *v/t.* (*irr. schließen, no -ge-, h*) embrace, surround (*a.* ✕), enclose; ✝ invest; **⸚schlingen** *v/t.* (*irr. schlingen, no -ge-, h*) embrace.

'**um**|**schmeißen** F *v/t.* (*irr. schmeißen, sep., -ge-, h*) *s.* umstoßen; '**⸚schnallen** *v/t.* (*sep., -ge-, h*) buckle on.

umschreib|**en** *v/t.* (*irr. schreiben*) **1.** ['⸚ʃraibən] (*sep., -ge-, h*) rewrite; transfer (*property, etc.*) (*auf acc.* to); **2.** [⸚'ʃraibən] (*no -ge-, h*) ᴀ circumscribe; paraphrase; **⸚ung** *f* (*-/-en*) **1.** ['⸚ʃraibuŋ] rewriting; transfer (*auf acc.* to); **2.** [⸚'ʃraibuŋ] ᴀ circumscription; paraphrase.

'**Umschrift** *f* circumscription; *phonetics:* transcription.

'**umschütten** *v/t.* (*sep., -ge-, h*) pour into another vessel; spill.

'**Um**|**schweife** *pl.*: **⸚ machen** beat about the bush; **ohne ⸚** point-blank; '**⸚schwenken** *fig. v/i.* (*sep., -ge-, sein*) veer or turn round; '**⸚schwung** *fig. m* revolution; revulsion (*of public feeling, etc.*); change (*in the weather, etc.*); reversal (*of opinion, etc.*).

um'segeln *v/t.* (*no -ge-, h*) sail round; double (*cape*); circumnavigate (*globe, world*); **⸚(e)lung** *f* (*-/-en*) sailing round (*world, etc.*); doubling; circumnavigation.

'**um**|**sehen** *v/refl.* (*irr. sehen, sep., -ge-, h*) look round (*nach for*); look about (for) (*a. fig.*), look about one; '**⸚sein** F *v/i.* (*irr. sein, sep., -ge-, sein*) *time:* be up; *holidays, etc.:* be over; '**⸚setzen** *v/t.* (*sep., -ge-, h*) transpose (*a.* ♪); ♪ transplant; ✝ turn over; spend (*money*) (*in acc.* on *books, etc.*); **in die Tat ⸚** realize, convert into fact.

'**Umsicht** *f* (*-/no pl.*) circumspection; '**⸚ig** *adj.* circumspect.

'**umsied**|**eln** (*sep., -ge-*) **1.** *v/t.* (*h*) resettle; **2.** *v/i.* (*sein*) (re)move (*nach, in acc.* to); '**⸚lung** *f* (*-/⸚-en*) resettlement; evacuation; removal.

um'sonst *adv.* gratis, free of charge; in vain; to no purpose; **nicht ⸚** not without good reason.

umspann|**en** *v/t.* **1.** ['⸚ʃpanən] (*sep., -ge-, h*) change (*horses*); ⚡ transform; **2.** [⸚'ʃpanən] (*no -ge-, h*) span; *fig. a.* embrace; '**⸚er** ⚡ *m* (*-s/-*) transformer.

'**umspringen** *v/i.* (*irr. springen, sep., -ge-, sein*) shift, veer (round); **⸚ mit** treat badly, *etc.*

'**Umstand** *m* circumstance; fact, detail; **unter diesen Umständen** *in or under the circumstances*; **unter keinen Umständen** *in or under no circumstances*, on no account; **unter Umständen** possibly; **ohne**

U V

Umstände without ceremony; *in anderen Umständen sein* be in the family way.

umständlich *adj.* ['ʊmʃtɛntliç] *story, etc.*: long-winded; *method, etc.*: roundabout; *p.* fussy; *das ist (mir) viel zu ~* that is far too much trouble (for me); 'Ωkeit *f* (-/ℝ-en) long-windedness; fussiness.

'**Umstands|kleid** *n* maternity robe; '**~wort** *gr. n* (-[e]s/~er) adverb.

'**umstehend 1.** *adj.*: *auf der ~en Seite* overleaf; **2.** *adv.* overleaf; Ωen ['~dən] *pl.* the bystanders *pl.*

'**Umsteige|karte** *f* transfer; Ωn *v/i.* (*irr.* steigen, *sep.*, -ge-, *sein*) change (*nach* for); 🚋 *a.* change trains (for).

Umsteigekarte ['ʊmʃtaɪk-] *f s. Umsteigekarte.*

umstell|en *v/t.* **1.** ['~ʃtɛlən] (*sep.*, -ge-, *h*) transpose (*a. gr.*); shift (*furniture*) about or round; convert (*currency, production*) (*auf acc.* to); *sich ~* change one's attitude; accommodate o.s. to new conditions; adapt o.s. (*auf acc.* to); **2.** [~'ʃtɛlən] (*no* -ge-, *h*) surround; Ωung ['~ʃtɛluŋ] *f* transposition; *fig.*: conversion; adaptation; change.

'**um|stimmen** *v/t.* (*sep.*, -ge-, *h*) ♪ tune to another pitch; *j-n ~* change s.o.'s mind, bring s.o. round; '**~stoßen** *v/t.* (*irr.* stoßen, *sep.*, -ge-, *h*) knock over; upset; *fig.* annul; 🚋 overrule, reverse; upset (*plan*).

um|'stricken *fig. v/t.* (*no* -ge-, *h*) ensnare; **~stritten** *adj.* [~'ʃtrɪtən] disputed, contested; controversial.

'**Um|sturz** *m* subversion, overturn; Ωstürzen (*sep.*, -ge-, *h*) **1.** *v/t.* (*h*) upset, overturn (*a. fig.*); *fig.* subvert; **2.** *v/i.* (*sein*) upset, overturn; fall down; Ωstürzlerisch *adj.* ['~lərɪʃ] subversive.

'**Umtausch** *m* (-es/ℝ-e) exchange; ♥ conversion (*of currency, etc.*); Ωen *v/t.* (*sep.*, -ge-, *h*) exchange (*gegen* for); ♥ convert.

'**umtun** F *v/t.* (*irr.* tun, *sep.*, -ge-, *h*) put (*coat, etc.*) round one's shoulders; *sich ~ nach* look about for.

'**umwälz|en** *v/t.* (*sep.*, -ge-, *h*) roll round; *fig.* revolutionize; '**~end** *adj.* revolutionary; Ωung *fig. f* (-/-en) revolution, upheaval.

'**umwand|eln** *v/t.* (*sep.*, -ge-, *h*) transform (*in acc.* into); ♪, ♥ con-

vert (into); 🚋 commute (into); 'Ωlung *f* transformation; ♪, ♥ conversion; 🚋 commutation.

'**um|wechseln** *v/t.* (*sep.*, -ge-, *h*) change; '**Ωweg** *m* roundabout way or route; detour; *auf ~en* in a roundabout way; '**~wehen** *v/t.* (*sep.*, -ge-, *h*) blow down or over; 'Ωwelt *f* (-/ℝ-en) environment; '**~wenden 1.** *v/t.* (*sep.*, -ge-, *h*) turn over; **2.** *v/refl.* ([*irr.* wenden], *sep.*, -ge-, *h*) look round (*nach* for).

um|'werben *v/t.* (*irr.* werben, *no* -ge-, *h*) court, woo.

'**umwerfen** *v/t.* (*irr.* werfen, *sep.*, -ge-, *h*) upset (*a. fig.*), overturn; *sich e-n Mantel ~* throw a coat round one's shoulders.

um|'wickeln *v/t.* (*no* -ge-, *h*): *et. mit Draht ~* wind wire round s.th.; **~wölken** [~'vœlkən] *v/refl.* (*no* -ge-, *h*) cloud over (*a. fig.*); **~zäunen** [~'tsɔynən] *v/t.* (*no* -ge-, *h*) fence (in).

umziehen (*irr.* ziehen) **1.** ['~tsiːən] *v/i.* (*sep.*, -ge-, *sein*) (re)move (*nach* to); move house; **2.** [~'tsiːən] *v/refl.* (*sep.*, -ge-, *h*) change (one's clothes); **3.** [~'tsiːən] *v/refl.* (*no* -ge-, *h*) cloud over.

umzingeln [ʊm'tsɪŋəln] *v/t.* (*no* -ge-, *h*) surround, encircle.

'**Umzug** *m* procession; move (*nach* to), removal (*to*); change of residence.

unab|änderlich *adj.* [ʊn'ʔapʔɛndərliç] unalterable; **~hängig** ['~hɛŋiç] **1.** *adj.* independent (*von* of); **2.** *adv.*: *~ von* irrespective of; 'Ωhängigkeit *f* (-/*no pl.*) independence (*von* of); '**~kömmlich** *adj.* ['~kœmliç]: *er ist im Moment ~* we cannot spare him at the moment, we cannot do without him at the moment; **~lässig** *adj.* incessant, unremitting; **~sehbar** *adj.* [~'zeːbaːr] incalculable; *in ~er Ferne* in a distant future; '**~sichtlich** *adj.* unintentional; inadvertent; '**~wendbar** *adj.* [~'vɛntbaːr] inevitable, inescapable.

unachtsam *adj.* ['ʊnʔ-] careless, heedless; Ωkeit *f* (-/ℝ-en) carelessness, heedlessness.

unähnlich *adj.* ['ʊnʔ-] unlike, dissimilar (*dat.* to).

unan|fechtbar *adj.* [ʊn'ʔan-] unimpeachable, unchallengeable, incontestable; **'~gebracht** *adj.* inappropriate; *pred. a.* out of place; **'~gefochten 1.** *adj.* undisputed; unchallenged; **2.** *adv.* without any hindrance; **'~gemessen** *adj.* unsuitable; improper; inadequate; **'~genehm** *adj.* disagreeable, unpleasant; awkward; troublesome; **~'nehmbar** *adj.* unacceptable (*für* to); **'2nehmlichkeit** *f* (-/-en) unpleasantness; awkwardness; troublesomeness; *~en pl.* trouble, inconvenience; **'~sehnlich** *adj.* unsightly; plain; **'~ständig** *adj.* indecent; obscene; **'2ständigkeit** *f* (-/-en) indecency; obscenity; **~'tastbar** *adj.* unimpeachable; inviolable.

unappetitlich *adj.* ['un?-] *food, etc.*: unappetizing; *sight, etc.*: distasteful, ugly.

Unart ['un?-] **1.** *f* bad habit; **2.** *m* (-[e]s/-e) naughty child; **'2ig** *adj.* naughty; **'~igkeit** *f* (-/-en) naughty behavio(u)r, naughtiness.

unauf|dringlich *adj.* ['un?auf-] unobtrusive; unostentatious; **'~fällig** *adj.* inconspicuous; unobtrusive; **~findbar** *adj.* [~'fintba:r] undiscoverable, untraceable; **~gefordert** ['~gəfɔrdərt] **1.** *adj.* unasked; **2.** *adv.* without being asked, of one's own accord; **~'hörlich** *adj.* incessant, continuous, uninterrupted; **'~merksam** *adj.* inattentive; **'2merksamkeit** *f* (-/-en) inattention, inattentiveness; **'~richtig** *adj.* insincere; **'2richtigkeit** *f* (-/-en) insincerity; **~schiebbar** *adj.* [~'ʃi:pba:r] urgent; *~ sein* brook no delay.

unaus|bleiblich *adj.* [un?aus'blaɪpliç] inevitable; *das war ~* that was bound to happen; **~'führbar** *adj.* impracticable; **~geglichen** *adj.* ['~gəgliçən] unbalanced (*a.* ⚕); **~'löschlich** *adj.* indelible; *fig. a.* inextinguishable; **~'sprechlich** *adj.* unutterable; unspeakable; inexpressible; **~'stehlich** *adj.* unbearable, insupportable.

unbarmherzig *adj.* merciless, unmerciful; **'2keit** *f* (-/*no pl.*) mercilessness, unmercifulness.

unbe|absichtigt *adj.* ['unbə?apziçtiçt] unintentional, undesigned; **'~achtet** *adj.* unnoticed; **~anstandet** *adj.* ['unbə?-] unopposed, not objected to; **'~baut** *adj.* ✐ untilled; *land*: undeveloped; **'~dacht** *adj.* inconsiderate; imprudent; **'~denklich 1.** *adj.* unobjectionable; **2.** *adv.* without hesitation; **'~deutend** *adj.* insignificant; slight; **'~dingt 1.** *adj.* unconditional; *obedience, etc.*: implicit; **2.** *adv.* by all means; under any circumstances; **~'fahrbar** *adj.* impracticable, impassable; **'~fangen** *adj.* unprejudiced, unbias(s)ed; ingenuous; unembarrassed; **'~friedigend** *adj.* unsatisfactory; **~friedigt** *adj.* ['~çt] dissatisfied; disappointed; **'~fugt** *adj.* unauthorized; incompetent; **'2fugte** *m* (-n/-n) unauthorized person; *~n ist der Zutritt verboten!* no trespassing!; **'~gabt** *adj.* untalented; **~'greiflich** *adj.* inconceivable, incomprehensible; **'~grenzt** *adj.* unlimited; boundless; **'~gründet** *adj.* unfounded; **'2hagen** *n* uneasiness; discomfort; **'~haglich** *adj.* uneasy; uncomfortable; **~helligt** *adj.* [~'hɛliçt] unmolested; **'~herrscht** *adj.* lacking self-control; **'2herrschtheit** *f* (-/*no pl.*) lack of self-control; **'~hindert** *adj.* unhindered, free; **~holfen** *adj.* ['~bəhɔlfən] clumsy, awkward; **'2holfenheit** *f* (-/*no pl.*) clumsiness, awkwardness; **~'irrt** *adj.* unswerving; **'~kannt** *adj.* unknown; *~e Größe* 𝔄 unknown quantity (*a. fig.*); **~'kümmert** *adj.* unconcerned (*um, wegen* about), careless (of, about); **'~lebt** *adj.* inanimate; *street, etc.*: unfrequented; **~'lehrbar** *adj.*: *~ sein* take no advice; **'~liebt** *adj.* unpopular; *sich ~ machen* get o.s. disliked; **'~mannt** *adj.* unmanned; **'~merkt** *adj.* unnoticed; **'~mittelt** *adj.* impecunious, without means; **~nommen** *adj.* [~'nɔmən]: *es bleibt ihm ~ zu inf.* he is at liberty to *inf.*; **'~nutzt** *adj.* unused; **'~quem** *adj.* uncomfortable; inconvenient; **'2quemlichkeit** *f* lack of comfort; inconvenience; **'~rechtigt** *adj.* unauthorized; unjustified; **~schadet** *prp.* (*gen.*) [~'ʃa:dət] without prejudice to; **~schädigt** *adj.* ['~çt] uninjured, undamaged; **'~scheiden** *adj.* immodest; **~scholten** *adj.* ['~ʃɔltən] blameless, irreproachable; **'~schränkt** *adj.* unrestricted; absolute; **~schreiblich**

adj. [~'raɪplɪç] indescribable; **~'sehen** *adv.* unseen; without inspection; **'~setzt** *adj.* unoccupied; vacant; **~siegbar** *adj.* [~'ziːkbaːr] invincible; **'~sonnen** *adj.* thoughtless, imprudent; rash; **'2sonnenheit** *f* (-/-en) thoughtlessness; rashness; **'~ständig** *adj.* inconstant; unsteady; *weather:* changeable, unsettled (*a.* ♉); *p.* erratic; **'2ständigkeit** *f* (-/no pl.) inconstancy; changeability; **~stätigt** *adj.* ['~çt] unconfirmed; *letter, etc.:* unacknowledged; **~'stechlich** *adj.* incorruptible, unbribable; **2'stechlichkeit** *f* (-/no pl.) incorruptibility; **'~stimmt** *adj.* indeterminate (*a.* ♈); indefinite (*a.* gr.); uncertain; *feeling, etc.:* vague; **'2stimmtheit** *f* (-/no pl.) indeterminateness, indetermination; indefiniteness; uncertainty; vagueness; **~'streitbar** *adj.* incontestable; indisputable; **'~stritten** *adj.* uncontested, undisputed; **'~teiligt** *adj.* unconcerned (*an dat.* in); indifferent; **~'trächtlich** *adj.* inconsiderable, insignificant. [flexible.\

unbeugsam *adj.* [un'bɔʏkzaːm] in-\
'unbe|wacht *adj.* unwatched, unguarded (*a. fig.*); **'~waffnet** *adj.* unarmed; *eye:* naked; **'~weglich** *adj.* immovable; motionless; **'~wiesen** *adj.* unproven; **'~wohnt** *adj.* uninhabited; unoccupied, vacant; **'~wußt** *adj.* unconscious; **~'zähmbar** *adj.* indomitable.

'Un|bilden *pl.:* ~ *der Witterung* inclemency of the weather; **'~bildung** *f* lack of education.

'un|billig *adj.* unfair; **'~blutig 1.** *adj.* bloodless; **2.** *adv.* without bloodshed.

unbotmäßig *adj.* ['unboːt-] insubordinate; **'2keit** *f* (-/-en) insubordination.

'un|brauchbar *adj.* useless; **'~christlich** *adj.* unchristian.

und *cj.* [unt] and; F: *na* ~? so what?
'Undank *m* ingratitude; **'2bar** *adj.* ungrateful (*gegen* to); *task, etc.:* thankless; **'~barkeit** *f* ingratitude, ungratefulness; *fig.* thanklessness.

un|'denkbar *adj.* unthinkable; inconceivable; **~'denklich** *adj.:* seit **~en** *Zeiten* from time immemorial; **'~deutlich** *adj.* indistinct; *speech:* *a.* inarticulate; *fig.* vague, indis-

tinct; **'~deutsch** *adj.* un-German; **'~dicht** *adj.* leaky; **'2ding** *n:* es wäre ein ~, zu behaupten, daß ... it would be absurd to claim that ...
'unduldsam *adj.* intolerant; **'2keit** *f* intolerance.

undurch|'dringlich *adj.* impenetrable; *countenance:* impassive; **~'führbar** *adj.* impracticable; **'~lässig** *adj.* impervious, impermeable; **'~sichtig** *adj.* opaque; *fig.* mysterious.

uneben *adj.* ['un⁹-] *ground:* uneven, broken; *way, etc.:* bumpy; **'2heit** *f* **1.** (-/no pl.) unevenness; **2.** (-/-en) bump.

un|echt *adj.* ['un⁹-] *jewellery, etc.:* imitation; *hair, teeth, etc.:* false; *money, jewellery, etc.:* counterfeit; *picture, etc.:* fake; ♈ *fraction:* improper; **'~ehelich** *adj.* illegitimate.

Unehr|e ['un⁹-] *f* dishono(u)r; *j-m* ~ *machen* discredit s.o.; **'2enhaft** *adj.* dishono(u)rable; **'2lich** *adj.* dishonest; **'~lichkeit** *f* dishonesty.

uneigennützig *adj.* ['un⁹-] disinterested, unselfish.

uneinig *adj.* ['un⁹-]: ~ *sein* be at variance (*mit* with); disagree (*über* acc. on); **'2keit** *f* variance, disagreement.

un|ein'nehmbar *adj.* impregnable; **'~empfänglich** *adj.* insusceptible (*für* of, to).

unempfindlich *adj.* ['un⁹-] insensitive (*gegen* to); **'2keit** *f* insensitiveness (*gegen* to).

un'endlich 1. *adj.* endless, infinite (*both a. fig.*); **2.** *adv.* infinitely (*a. fig.*); ~ *lang* endless; ~ *viel* no end of (*money, etc.*); **2keit** *f* (-/no pl.) endlessness, infinitude, infinity (*al. a. fig.*).

unent|'behrlich *adj.* [un⁹ent'beːrlɪç] indispensable; **~'geltlich 1.** *adj.* gratuitous, gratis; **2.** *adv.* gratis, free of charge; **~'rinnbar** *adj.* ineluctable; **'~schieden 1.** *adj.* undecided; ~ *enden* game: end in a draw *or* tie; **2.** ♈ *n* (-s/-) draw, tie; **'~schlossen** *adj.* irresolute; **'2schlossenheit** *f* irresoluteness, irresolution; **~schuldbar** *adj.* [~'ʃultbaːr] inexcusable; **~wegt** *adv.* [~'veːkt] untiringly; continuously; **~'wirrbar** *adj.* inextricable.

uner|'bittlich *adj.* [un⁹er'bɪtlɪç] inexorable; *fact:* stubborn; **'~fahrer**

adj. inexperienced; **ˬfindlich** *adj.* [ˬ'fɪntlɪç] incomprehensible; **ˬforschlich** *adj.* inscrutable; **ˬfreulich** *adj.* unpleasant; **ˬfüllbar** *adj.* unrealizable; **ˬgiebig** *adj.* unproductive (*an dat.* of); **ˬheblich** *adj.* irrelevant (*für* to); inconsiderable; **ˬhört** *adj.* **1.** [ˬhøːɪt] unheard; **2.** [ˬ'høːɪt] unheard-of, outrageous; **ˬkannt** *adj.* unrecognized; **ˬklärlich** *adj.* inexplicable; **ˬläßlich** *adj.* [ˬ'lɛslɪç] indispensable (*für* to, for); **ˬlaubt** *adj.* ['ˬlaupt] unauthorized; illegal, illicit; **ˬe** *Handlung* 🏛 tort; **ˬledigt** *adj.* ['ˬleːdɪçt] unsettled (*a.* ✝); **ˬmeßlich** *adj.* [ˬ'mɛslɪç] immeasurable, immense; **ˬmüdlich** *adj.* [ˬ'myːtlɪç] *p.* indefatigable, untiring; *efforts, etc.*: untiring, unremitting; **ˬquicklich** *adj.* unpleasant, unedifying; **ˬreichbar** *adj.* inattainable; inaccessible; *pred. a.* above or beyond or out of reach; **ˬreicht** *adj.* unrival(l)ed, unequal(l)ed; **ˬsättlich** *adj.* [ˬ'zɛtlɪç] insatiable, insatiate; **ˬschöpflich** *adj.* inexhaustible.

ˬerschrocken *adj.* ['un⁹-] intrepid, fearless; **2heit** *f* (-/*no pl.*) intrepidity, fearlessness.

ˬerschütterlich *adj.* [un⁹ɛr'ʃytɛrlɪç] unshakable; **ˬschwinglich** *adj.* *price*: prohibitive; *pred. a.* above or beyond or out of reach (*für* of); **ˬsetzlich** *adj.* irreplaceable; *loss, etc.*: irreparable; **ˬträglich** *adj.* intolerable, unbearable; **ˬwartet** *adj.* unexpected; **ˬwünscht** *adj.* undesirable, undesired.

unfähig *adj.* incapable (*zu inf.* or *ger.*); unable (to *inf.*); inefficient; **2keit** *f* incapability (*zu inf.* of *ger.*); inability (to *inf.*); inefficiency.

Unfall *m* accident; *e-n* **ˬ** *haben* meet with *or* have an accident; **ˬstation** *f* emergency ward; **ˬversicherung** *f* accident insurance.

ˬn|faßlich *adj.* incomprehensible, inconceivable; *das ist mir* **ˬ** that is beyond me.

ˬn|fehlbar *adj.* infallible (*a. eccl.*); *decision, etc.*: unimpeachable; *instinct, etc.*: unfailing; **2.** *adv.* without fail; inevitably; **2keit** *f* (-/*no pl.*) infallibility.

ˬun|fein *adj.* indelicate; *pred. a.* lacking in refinement; **ˬfern** *prp.* (*gen. or von*) not far from; **ˬfertig** *adj.* unfinished; *fig. a.* half-baked; **ˬflätig** *adj.* ['ˬflɛːtɪç] dirty, filthy.

unfolgsam *adj.* disobedient; **2keit** *f* disobedience.

un|förmig *adj.* ['unfœrmɪç] misshapen; shapeless; **ˬfrankiert** *adj.* unstamped; **ˬfrei** *adj.* not free; 🏛 unstamped; **ˬfreiwillig** *adj.* involuntary; *humour*: unconscious; **ˬfreundlich** *adj.* unfriendly (*zu* with), unkind (to); *climate, weather*: inclement; *room, day*: cheerless; **2friede(n)** *m* discord.

unfruchtbar *adj.* unfruitful, sterile; **2keit** *f* (-/*no pl.*) unfruitfulness; sterility.

Unfug ['unfuːk] *m* (-[e]s/*no pl.*) mischief.

Ungar ['uŋgar] *m* (-n/-n) Hungarian; **2isch** *adj.* Hungarian.

ungastlich *adj.* inhospitable.

unge|achtet *prp.* (*gen.*) ['uŋgə⁹axtət] regardless of; despite; **ˬahnt** *adj.* ['uŋgə⁹-] undreamt-of; unexpected; **ˬbärdig** *adj.* ['ˬbɛːrdɪç] unruly; **ˬbeten** *adj.* uninvited, unasked; **ˬer** *Gast* intruder, *sl.* gatecrasher; **ˬbildet** *adj.* uneducated; **ˬbräuchlich** *adj.* unusual; **ˬbraucht** *adj.* unused; **ˬbührlich** *adj.* improper, undue, unseemly; **ˬbunden** *adj.* *book*: unbound; *fig.*: free; single; **ˬdeckt** *adj.* *table*: unlaid; *sports*, ✝: uncovered; *paper currency*: fiduciary.

'Ungeduld *f* impatience; **2ig** *adj.* impatient.

'ungeeignet *adj.* unfit (*für* for *s.th.*, *to do s.th.*); *p. a.* unqualified; *moment*: inopportune.

ungefähr ['uŋgəfɛːr] **1.** *adj.* approximate, rough; **2.** *adv.* approximately, roughly, about, *Am.* F *a.* around; *von* **ˬ** by chance; **ˬdet** *adj.* unendangered, safe; **ˬlich** *adj.* harmless; *pred. a.* not dangerous.

'unge|fällig *adj.* disobliging; **ˬhalten** *adj.* displeased (*über acc.* at); **ˬhemmt 1.** *adj.* unchecked; **2.** *adv.* without restraint; **ˬheuchelt** *adj.* unfeigned.

ungeheuer ['uŋgəhɔyər] **1.** *adj.* vast, huge, enormous; **2.** **2** *n* (-s/-) monster; **ˬlich** *adj.* [ˬ'hɔyərlɪç] monstrous.

'**ungehobelt** adj. not planed; fig. uncouth, rough.

'**ungehörig** adj. undue, improper; '2keit f (-/ -en) impropriety.

'**ungehorsam 1.** adj. disobedient; **2.** 2 m disobedience.

'**unge|künstelt** adj. unaffected; '~kürzt adj. unabridged.

'**ungelegen** adj. inconvenient, inopportune; '2heiten f/pl. inconvenience; trouble; j-m ~ machen put s.o. to inconvenience.

'**unge|lehrig** adj. indocile; '~lenk adj. awkward, clumsy; '~lernt adj. unskilled; '~mütlich adj. uncomfortable; room: a. cheerless; p. nasty; '~nannt adj. unnamed; p. anonymous.

'**ungenau** adj. inaccurate, inexact; '2igkeit f inaccuracy, inexactness.

'**ungeniert** adj. free and easy, unceremonious; undisturbed.

unge|nießbar adj. ['ungəni:sbɑ:r] uneatable; undrinkable; F p. unbearable, pred. a. in a bad humo(u)r; '~nügend adj. insufficient; '~pflegt adj. unkempt; '~rade adj. odd; '~raten adj. spoilt, undutiful.

'**ungerecht** adj. unjust (gegen to); '2igkeit f (-/-en) injustice.

'**un|gern** adv. unwillingly, grudgingly; reluctantly; '~geschehen adj.: ~ machen undo s.th.

'**Ungeschick** n (-[e]s/no pl.), '~lichkeit f awkwardness, clumsiness, maladroitness; '2t adj. awkward, clumsy, maladroit.

unge|schlacht adj. ['ungəʃlaxt] hulking; uncouth; '~schliffen adj. unpolished, rough (both a. fig.); '~schminkt adj. not made up; fig. unvarnished.

'**ungesetzlich** adj. illegal, unlawful, illicit; '2keit f (-/-en) illegality, unlawfulness.

'**unge|sittet** adj. uncivilized; unmannerly; '~stört adj. undisturbed, uninterrupted; '~straft 1. adj. unpunished; 2. adv. with impunity; ~ davonkommen get off or escape scot-free.

ungestüm ['ungəʃty:m] 1. adj. impetuous; violent; 2. 2 n (-[e]s/no pl.) impetuosity; violence.

'**unge|sund** adj. climate: unhealthy; appearance: a. unwholesome; food: unwholesome; '~teilt adj. undivided (a. fig.); '~trübt adj.

['~try:pt] untroubled; unmixed; 2tüm ['~ty:m] n (-[e]s/-e) monster; '~übt adj. ['~?y:pt] untrained; inexperienced; '~waschen adj. unwashed.

'**ungewiß** adj. uncertain; j-n im ungewissen lassen keep s.o. in suspense; '2heit f (-/ -en) uncertainty; suspense.

'**unge|wöhnlich** adj. unusual, uncommon; '~wohnt adj. unaccustomed; unusual; '~zählt adj. numberless, countless; 2ziefer ['~tsi:fər] n (-s/-) vermin; '~ziemend adj. improper, unseemly; '~zogen adj. ill-bred, rude, uncivil; child: naughty; '~zügelt adj. unbridled.

'**ungezwungen** adj. unaffected; easy; '2heit f (-/ -en) unaffectedness, ease, easiness.

'**Unglaube(n)** m unbelief, disbelief.

'**ungläubig** adj. incredulous, unbelieving (a. eccl.); infidel; '2e m, f unbeliever; infidel.

unglaub|lich adj. [un'glauplɪç] incredible; '~würdig adj. p. untrustworthy; thing: incredible; ~e Geschichte cock-and-bull story.

'**ungleich 1.** adj. unequal, different; uneven; unlike; 2. adv. (by) far, much; '~artig adj. heterogeneous; '2heit f difference, inequality; unevenness; unlikeness; '~mäßig adj. uneven; irregular.

'**Unglück** n (-[e]s/ -e) misfortune; bad or ill luck; accident; calamity; disaster; misery; '2lich adj. unfortunate, unlucky; unhappy; 2licher'weise adv. unfortunately, unluckily; '2selig adj. unfortunate; disastrous.

'**Unglücks|fall** m misadventure; accident; '~rabe F m unlucky fellow.

'**Un|gnade** f (-/no pl.) disgrace, disfavo(u)r; in ~ fallen bei fall into disgrace with, incur s.o.'s disfavo(u)r; '2gnädig adj. ungracious, unkind.

'**ungültig** adj. invalid; ticket: not available; money: not current; jur. (null and) void; '2keit f invalidity; jur. a. voidness.

'**Un|gunst** f disfavo(u)r; inclemency (of weather); zu meinen ~en to my disadvantage; '2günstig adj. unfavo(u)rable; disadvantageous.

'**un|gut** adj.: ~es Gefühl misgiving

nichts für ~*!* no offen|ce, *Am.* -se!; '**~haltbar** *adj. shot:* unstoppable; *theory, etc.:* untenable; '**~handlich** *adj.* unwieldy, bulky.

'**Unheil** *n* mischief; disaster, calamity; '**2bar** *adj.* incurable; '**2voll** *adj.* sinister, ominous.

unheimlich 1. *adj.* uncanny (*a. fig.*), weird; sinister; F *fig.* tremendous; terrific; **2.** F *fig. adv.:* ~ *viel* heaps of, an awful lot of.

unhöflich *adj.* impolite, uncivil; '**2keit** *f* impoliteness, incivility.

Unhold ['unhɔlt] *m* (-[e]s/-e) fiend.

'**un|hörbar** *adj.* inaudible; '**~hygienisch** *adj.* unsanitary, insanitary.

Uni ['uni] *f* (-/-s) F varsity.

Uniform [uni'fɔrm] *f* (-/-en) uniform.

Unikum ['u:nikum] *n* (-s/*Unika*, -s) unique (thing); queer fellow.

uninteress|ant *adj.* ['un?-] uninteresting, boring; '**~iert** *adj.* uninterested (*an dat.* in).

Universität [univerzi'tɛ:t] *f* (-/-en) university.

Universum [uni'vɛrzum] *n* (-s/*no pl.*) universe.

Unke ['uŋkə] *f* (-/-n) *zo.* fire-bellied toad; F *fig.* croaker; '**2n** F *v/i.* (ge-, h) croak.

'**unkennt|lich** *adj.* unrecognizable; '**2lichkeit** *f* (-/*no pl.*): *bis zur* ~ past all recognition; '**2nis** *f* (-/*no pl.*) ignorance.

unklar *adj.* not clear; *meaning, etc.:* obscure; *answer, etc.:* vague; *im* ~*en sein* to be in the dark (*über acc.* about); '**2heit** *f* want of clearness; vagueness; obscurity.

unklug *adj.* imprudent, unwise.

Unkosten *pl.* cost(s *pl.*), expenses *pl.*; *sich in* (*große*) ~ *stürzen* go to great expense.

'**Unkraut** *n* weed.

un|kündbar *adj.* ['unkyntba:r] *loan, etc.:* irredeemable; *employment:* permanent; '**~kundig** *adj.* ['~kundiç] ignorant (*gen.* of); '**~längst** *adv.* lately, recently, the other day; '**~lauter** *adj. competition:* unfair; '**~leidlich** *adj.* intolerable, insufferable; '**~leserlich** *adj.* illegible; '**~leugbar** *adj.* ['~lɔykba:r] undeniable; '**~logisch** *adj.* illogical; '**~lösbar** *adj.* unsolvable, insoluble.

Unlust *f* (-/*no pl.*) reluctance (*zu*

inf. to *inf.*); '**2ig** *adj.* reluctant.

'**un|manierlich** *adj.* unmannerly; '**~männlich** *adj.* unmanly; '**~maßgeblich** *adj.* ['~ge:pliç]: *nach m-r* ~*en Meinung* in my humble opinion; '**~mäßig** *adj.* immoderate; intemperate; '**2menge** *f* enormous *or* vast quantity *or* number.

'**Unmensch** *m* monster, brute; '**2lich** *adj.* inhuman, brutal; '**~lichkeit** *f* inhumanity, brutality.

'**un|mißverständlich** *adj.* unmistakable; '**~mittelbar** *adj.* immediate, direct; '**~möbliert** *adj.* unfurnished; '**~modern** *adj.* unfashionable, outmoded.

unmöglich *adj.* impossible; '**2keit** *f* impossibility.

'**Unmoral** *f* immorality; '**2isch** *adj.* immoral.

'**unmündig** *adj.* under age.

'**un|musikalisch** *adj.* unmusical; '**2mut** *m* (-[e]s/*no pl.*) displeasure (*über acc.* at, over); '**~nachahmlich** *adj.* inimitable; '**~nachgiebig** *adj.* unyielding; '**~nachsichtig** *adj.* strict, severe; inexorable; '**~nahbar** *adj.* inaccessible, unapproachable; '**~natürlich** *adj.* unnatural; affected; '**~nötig** *adj.* unnecessary, needless; '**~nütz** *adj.* useless; '**~ordentlich** *adj.* ['un?-] untidy; *room, etc.:* a. disorderly; **2ordnung** ['un?-] *f* disorder, mess.

'**unpartei|isch** *adj.* impartial, unbias(s)ed; '**2ische** *m* (-n/-n) referee; umpire; '**2lichkeit** *f* impartiality.

'**un|passend** *adj.* unsuitable; improper; inappropriate; '**~passierbar** *adj.* impassable.

unpäßlich *adj.* ['unpɛsliç] indisposed, unwell; '**2keit** *f* (-/-en) indisposition.

'**un|persönlich** *adj.* impersonal (*a. gr.*); '**~politisch** *adj.* unpolitical; '**~praktisch** *adj.* unpractical, *Am. a.* impractical; '**2rat** *m* (-[e]s/*no pl.*) filth; rubbish; ~ *wittern* smell a rat.

'**unrecht 1.** *adj.* wrong; ~ *haben* be wrong; *j-m* ~ *tun* wrong s.o.; **2.** **2** *n* (-[e]s/*no pl.*): *mit or zu* ~ wrongly; *ihm ist* ~ *geschehen* he has been wronged; '**~mäßig** *adj.* unlawful; '**2mäßigkeit** *f* unlawfulness.

'**unreell** *adj.* dishonest; unfair.

'**unregelmäßig** *adj.* irregular (*a. gr.*); '**2keit** *f* (-/-en) irregularity.

U
V

'unreif *adj.* unripe, immature (*both a. fig.*); **'2e** *f* unripeness, immaturity (*both a. fig.*).

'un|rein *adj.* impure (*a. eccl.*); unclean (*a. fig.*); **~reinlich** *adj.* uncleanly; **~'rettbar** *adv.*: **~** verloren irretrievably lost; **~richtig** *adj.* incorrect, wrong.

Unruh ['unru:] *f* (-/-en) balance (-wheel); **'~e** *f* (-/-n) restlessness, unrest (*a. pol.*); uneasiness; disquiet(ude); flurry; alarm; **~n** *pl.* disturbances, riots *pl.*; **2ig** *adj.* restless; uneasy; *sea*: rough, choppy.

'unrühmlich *adj.* inglorious.

uns *pers. pron.* [uns] us; *dat.*: *a.* to us; **~** (*selbst*) ourselves, *after prp.*: us; *ein Freund von* **~** a friend of ours.

'un|sachgemäß *adj.* inexpert; **'~sachlich** *adj.* not objective; personal; **~säglich** *adj.* [~'ze:klɪç] unspeakable; untold; **~sanft** *adj.* ungentle; **~sauber** *adj.* dirty; *fig. a.* unfair (*a. sports*); **'~schädlich** *adj.* innocuous, harmless; **~scharf** *adj.* blurred; *pred. a.* out of focus; **~'schätzbar** *adj.* inestimable, invaluable; **~'scheinbar** *adj.* plain, *Am. a.* homely.

'unschicklich *adj.* improper, indecent; **2keit** *f* (-/-en) impropriety, indecency.

unschlüssig *adj.* ['unʃlʏsɪç] irresolute; **2keit** *f* (-/*no pl.*) irresoluteness, irresolution.

'un|schmackhaft *adj.* insipid; unpalatable, unsavo(u)ry; **'~schön** *adj.* unlovely, unsightly; *fig.* unpleasant.

'Unschuld *f* (-/*no pl.*) innocence; **2ig** *adj.* innocent (*an dat.* of).

'unselbständig *adj.* dependent (on others); **'2keit** *f* (lack of in)dependence.

unser ['unzər] **1.** *poss. pron.* our; *der* (*die*, *das*) **~e** ours; *die* **~en** *pl.* our relations *pl.*; **2.** *pers. pron.* of us; *wir waren* **~** *drei* there were three of us.

'unsicher *adj.* unsteady; unsafe, insecure; uncertain; **'2heit** *f* unsteadiness; insecurity, unsafeness; uncertainty.

'unsichtbar *adj.* invisible.

'Unsinn *m* (-[e]s/*no pl.*) nonsense; **'2ig** *adj.* nonsensical.

'Unsitt|e *f* bad habit; abuse; **2lich**

adj. immoral; indecent (*a. ſſ*); **'~lichkeit** *f* (-/-en) immorality.

'un|solid(e) *adj.* easy-going; *life*: dissipated; **✝** unreliable; **'~sozial** *adj.* unsocial, antisocial; **'~sportlich** *adj.* unsportsmanlike; unfair (*gegenüber* to).

'unstatthaft *adj.* inadmissible.

'unsterblich *adj.* immortal.

Un'sterblichkeit *f* immortality.

'un|stet *adj.* unsteady; *character*, *life*: unsettled; **2stimmigkeit** ['~ʃtɪmɪçkaɪt] *f* (-/-en) discrepancy; dissension; **~sträflich** *adj.* blameless; **'~streitig** *adj.* incontestable; **~'sympathisch** *adj.* disagreeable; *er ist mir* **~** I don't like him; **'~tätig** *adj.* inactive; idle.

'untauglich *adj.* unfit (*a. ✕*); unsuitable; **'2keit** *f* (-/*no pl.*) unfitness (*a. ✕*).

un'teilbar *adj.* indivisible.

unten *adv.* ['untən] below; downstairs; *von oben bis* **~** from top to bottom.

unter ['untər] **1.** *prp.* (*dat.*; *acc.*) below, under; among; **~** *anderem* among other things; **~** *zehn Mark* (for) less than ten marks; **~** *Null* below zero; **~** *aller Kritik* beneath contempt; **~** *diesem Gesichtspunkt* from this point of view; **2.** *adj.* lower; inferior; *die* **~en** *Räume* the downstair(s) rooms.

Unter|abteilung ['untər?-] *f* subdivision; **~arm** ['untər?-] *m* forearm; **'~bau** *m* (-[e]s/-ten) ⚒ substructure (*a. 🛤*), foundation.

unter'|bieten *v/t.* (*irr. bieten, no* -ge-, *h*) underbid; **✝** undercut, undersell (*competitor*); lower (*record*); **~'binden** *v/t.* (*irr. binden, no* -ge-, *h*) 🩺 ligature; *fig.* stop; **~'bleiben** *v/i.* (*irr. bleiben, no* -ge-, *sein*) remain undone; not to take place.

unter'brech|en *v/t.* (*irr. brechen, no* -ge-, *h*) interrupt (*a. ∮*); break, *Am. a.* stop over; ∮ break (*circuit*); **2ung** *f* (-/-en) interruption; break, *Am. a.* stopover. [mit-]

unter'breiten *v/t.* (*no* -ge-, *h*) sub-)

'unterbringen *v/t.* (*irr. bringen, sep.*, -ge-, *h*) place (*a. ✝*); accommodate, lodge; **'2ung** *f* (-/-en) accommodation; **✝** placement.

unter'dessen *adv.* [untər'dɛsən] (in the) meantime, meanwhile.

unter'drück|en *v/t.* (*no* -ge-, *h*) oppress (*subjects, etc.*); repress (*revolt, sneeze, etc.*); suppress (*rising, truth, etc.*); put down (*rebellion, etc.*); **2ung** *f* (-/-en) oppression; repression; suppression; putting down.

unterernähr|t *adj.* ['untər⁹-] underfed, undernourished; **2ung** *f* (-/no pl.) underfeeding, malnutrition.

Unter'führung *f* subway, *Am.* underpass.

'Untergang *m* (-[e]s/≈⁀e) *ast.* setting; ⚓ sinking; *fig.* ruin.

Unter'gebene *m* (-n/-n) inferior, subordinate; *contp.* underling.

'untergehen *v/i.* (*irr. gehen, sep.*, -ge-, *sein*) *ast.* set; ⚓ sink, founder; *fig.* be ruined.

untergeordnet *adj.* ['untərgə⁹ɔrd-nət] subordinate; *importance:* secondary.   [underweight.]

'Untergewicht *n* (-[e]s/no pl.)∤

unter'graben *fig. v/t.* (*irr. graben, no* -ge-, *h*) undermine.

'Untergrund *m* (-[e]s/no pl.) subsoil; **'_bahn** *f* underground (railway), *in London:* tube; *Am.* subway; **'_bewegung** *f* underground movement.

unterhalb *prp.* (*gen.*) below, underneath.

Unterhalt *m* (-[e]s/no pl.) support, subsistence, livelihood; maintenance.

unter'halt|en *v/t.* (*irr. halten, no* -ge-, *h*) maintain; support; entertain, amuse; *sich ~* converse (*mit* with; *über acc.* on, about); talk (with; on, about); *sich gut ~* enjoy o.s.; **2ung** *f* maintenance, upkeep; conversation, talk; entertainment.

'Unterhändler *m* negotiator; ✗ Parlementaire.

'Unter|haus *parl. n* (-es/no pl.) House of Commons; **'_hemd** *n* vest, undershirt; **'_holz** *n* (-es/no pl.) underwood, brushwood; **'_hose** *f* (e-e a pair of) drawers *pl.*, pants *pl.*; **2irdisch** *adj.* subterranean, underground (*both a. fig.*).

unter'joch|en *v/t.* (*no* -ge-, *h*) subjugate, subdue; **2ung** *f* (-/-en) subjugation.

'Unter|kiefer *m* lower jaw; **'_kleid** *n* slip; **'_kleidung** *f* underclothes *pl.*, underclothing, underwear.

'unterkommen 1. *v/i.* (*irr. kommen, sep.*, -ge-, *sein*) find accommodation; find employment; **2.** **2** *n* (-s/⟨⁀* -) accommodation; employment, situation.

'unter|kriegen F *v/t.* (*sep.*, -ge-, *h*) bring to heel; *sich nicht ~ lassen* not to knuckle down or under; **2kunft** ['_kunft] *f* (-/⁀e) accommodation, lodging; ✗ quarters *pl.*; **'2lage** *f* base; pad; *fig.:* voucher; **_n** *pl.* documents *pl.*; data *pl.*

unter'lass|en *v/t.* (*irr. lassen, no* -ge-, *h*) omit (*zu tun* doing, to do); neglect (to do, doing); fail (to do); **2ung** *f* (-/-en) omission; neglect; failure; **2ungssünde** *f* sin of omission.

'unterlegen¹ *v/t.* (*sep.*, -ge-, *h*) lay or put under; give (*another meaning*).

unter'legen² *adj.* inferior (*dat.* to); **2e** *m* (-n/-n) loser; underdog; **2heit** *f* (-/no pl.) inferiority.

'Unterleib *m* abdomen, belly.

unter'liegen *v/i.* (*irr. liegen, no* -ge-, *sein*) be overcome (*dat.* by); be defeated (by), *sports:* a. lose (to); *fig.:* be subject to; be liable to; *es unterliegt keinem Zweifel, daß ...* there is no doubt that ...

'Unter|lippe *f* lower lip; **'_mieter** *m* subtenant, lodger, *Am. a.* roomer.

unter'nehmen 1. *v/t.* (*irr. nehmen, no* -ge-, *h*) undertake; take (*steps*); **2.** **2** *n* (-s/-) enterprise; † *a.* business; ✗ operation.

unter'nehm|end *adj.* enterprising; **2er** † *m* (-s/-) entrepreneur; contractor; employer; **2ung** *f* (-/-en) enterprise, undertaking; ✗ operation; **_ungslustig** *adj.* enterprising.

'Unter|offizier ✗ *m* non-commissioned officer; **'2ordnen** *v/t.* (*sep.*, -ge-, *h*) subordinate (*dat.* to); *sich ~* submit (to).

Unter'redung *f* (-/-en) conversation, conference.

Unterricht ['untərriçt] *m* (-[e]s/⁀ -e) instruction, lessons *pl.*

unter'richten *v/t.* (*no* -ge-, *h*): *~ in* (*dat.*) instruct in, teach (*English, etc.*); *~ von* inform *s.o.* of.

'Unterrichts|ministerium *n* ministry of education; **'_stunde** *f* lesson, (teaching) period; **'_wesen** *n* (-s/no pl.) education; teaching.

'Unterrock *m* slip.

unter'sagen v/t. (no -ge-, h) forbid (j-m et. s.o. to do s.th.).

'Untersatz m stand; saucer.

unter'schätzen v/t. (no -ge-, h) undervalue; underestimate, underrate.

unter'scheid|en v/t. and v/i. (irr. scheiden, no -ge-, h) distinguish (zwischen between; von from); sich ~ differ (von from); 2ung f distinction.

'Unterschenkel m shank.

'unterschieb|en v/t. (irr. schieben, sep., -ge-, h) push under; fig.: attribute (dat. to); substitute (statt for); '2ung f substitution.

Unterschied ['untərʃiːt] m (-[e]s/-e) difference; distinction; zum ~ von in distinction from or to; 2lich adj. different; differential; variable, varying; 2slos adj. indiscriminate; undiscriminating.

unter'schlag|en v/t. (irr. schlagen, no -ge-, h) embezzle; suppress (truth, etc.); 2ung f (-/-en) embezzlement; suppression.

'Unterschlupf m (-[e]s/ᵘe, -e) shelter, refuge.

unter'schreiben v/t. and v/i. (irr. schreiben, no -ge-, h) sign.

'Unterschrift f signature.

'Untersee|boot ⚓, ✈ n s. U-Boot; '~kabel n submarine cable.

unter'setzt adj. thick-set, squat.

unterst adj. ['untərst] lowest, undermost.

'Unterstand ✖ m shelter, dug-out.

unter'stehen (irr. stehen, no -ge-, h) **1.** v/i. (dat.) be subordinate to; be subject to (law, etc.); **2.** v/refl. dare; untersteh dich! don't you dare!; ~stellen v/t. **1.** ['~ʃtɛlən] (sep., -ge-, h) put or place under; garage (car); sich ~ take shelter (vor dat. from); **2.** [~'ʃtɛlən] (no -ge-, h) (pre)suppose, assume; impute (dat. to); j-m ~ ✖ put (troops, etc.) under s.o.'s command; 2'stellung f (-/-en) assumption, supposition; imputation; ~'streichen v/t. (irr. streichen, no -ge-, h) underline, underscore (both a. fig.).

unter'stütz|en v/t. (no -ge-, h) support; back up; 2ung f (-/-en) support (a. ✖); assistance, aid; relief.

unter'such|en v/t. (no -ge-, h) examine (a. ✈); inquire into, investigate (a. ⚖); explore; ⚖ try;

analy|se, Am. -ze (a. 🜨); 2ung f (-/-en) examination (a. ✈); inquiry (gen. into), investigation (a. ⚖); exploration; analysis (a. 🜨).

Unter'suchungs|gefangene m prisoner on remand; ~gefängnis n remand prison; ~haft f detention on remand; ~richter m investigating judge.

Untertan ['untərtaːn] m (-s, -en/-en) subject. [missive.\]

untertänig adj. ['untərtɛːnɪç] sub-\

'Unter|tasse f saucer; 2tauchen (sep., -ge-) **1.** v/t. show, dip; duck; fig. disappear; **2.** v/t. (h) duck.

'Unterteil n, m lower part.

unter'teil|en v/t. (no -ge-, h) subdivide; 2ung f subdivision.

'Unter|titel m subheading; subtitle; a. caption (of film); '~ton m undertone; 2vermieten v/t. (no -ge-, h) sublet.

unter'wander|n pol. v/t. (no -ge-, h) infiltrate; 2ung pol. f infiltration.

'Unterwäsche f s. Unterkleidung.

unterwegs adv. [untər've:ks] on the or one's way.

unter'weis|en v/t. (irr. weisen, no -ge-, h) instruct (in dat. in); 2ung f instruction.

'Unterwelt f underworld (a. fig.).

unter'werf|en v/t. (irr. werfen, no -ge-, h) subdue (dat. to), subjugate (to); subject (to); submit (to); sich ~ submit (to); 2ung f (-/-en) subjugation, subjection; submission (unter acc. to).

unterworfen adj. [untər'vɔrfən] subject (dat. to).

unterwürfig adj. [untər'vyrfɪç] submissive; subservient; 2keit f (-/no pl.) submissiveness; subservience.

unter'zeichn|en v/t. (no -ge-, h) sign; 2er m signer, the undersigned; subscriber (gen. to); signatory (gen. to treaty); 2erstaat m signatory state; 2ete m, f (-n/-n) the undersigned; 2ung f signature, signing.

unterziehen v/t. (irr. ziehen) **1.** ['~tsi:ən] (sep., -ge-, h) put on underneath; **2.** [~'tsi:ən] (no -ge-, h) subject (dat. to); sich e-r Operation ~ undergo an operation; sich e-r Prüfung ~ go in or sit for an examination; sich der Mühe ~ zu inf. take the trouble to inf.

'Untiefe f shallow, shoal.

'Untier n monster (a. fig.).

un|tilgbar *adj.* [un'tilkbɑːr] indelible; † *government annuities:* irredeemable; ~'**tragbar** *adj.* unbearable, intolerable; *costs:* prohibitive; ~'**trennbar** *adj.* inseparable.

'**untreu** *adj.* untrue (*dat.* to), disloyal (to); *husband, wife:* unfaithful (to); '2**e** *f* disloyalty; unfaithfulness, infidelity.

un|'tröstlich *adj.* inconsolable, disconsolate; ~**trüglich** *adj.* [~'tryːklɪç] infallible, unerring.

'**Untugend** *f* vice, bad habit.

unüber|legt *adj.* ['unˀyːbər-] inconsiderate, thoughtless; ~**sicht-lich** *adj.* badly arranged; difficult to survey; involved; *mot. corner:* blind; ~'**trefflich** *adj.* unsurpassable; ~**windlich** *adj.* [~'vɪntlɪç] invincible; *fortress:* impregnable; *obstacle, etc.:* insurmountable; *difficulties, etc.:* insuperable.

unum|gänglich *adj.* [un ˀum'ɡɛŋlɪç] absolutely necessary; ~**schränkt** *adj.* [~'ʃrɛŋkt] absolute; ~**stößlich** *adj.* [~'ʃtøːslɪç] irrefutable; incontestable; irrevocable; ~**wunden** *adj.* ['~vʊndən] frank, plain.

ununterbrochen *adj.* ['unˀʊntər-brɔxən] uninterrupted; incessant.

unver|'änderlich *adj.* unchangeable; invariable; ~'**antwortlich** *adj.* irresponsible; inexcusable; ~'**besserlich** *adj.* incorrigible; '~**bindlich** *adj.* not binding or obligatory; *answer, etc.:* non-committal; ~**blümt** *adj.* [~'blyːmt] plain, blunt; ~**bürgt** *adj.* [~'byrkt] unwarranted; *news:* unconfirmed; '~**dächtig** *adj.* unsuspected; '~**daulich** *adj.* indigestible (*a. fig.*); '~**dient** *adj.* undeserved; '~**dorben** *adj.* unspoiled, unspoilt; *fig.:* uncorrupted; pure, innocent; '~**drossen** *adj.* indefatigable, unflagging; '~**dünnt** *adj.* undiluted, *Am. a.* straight; ~'**einbar** *adj.* incompatible; '~**fälscht** *adj.* unadulterated; *fig.* genuine; ~**fänglich** *adj.* ['~fɛŋlɪç] not captious; ~**froren** *adj.* ['~froːrən] unabashed, impudent; '2**frorenheit** *f* (-/-en) impudence, F cheek; '~**gänglich** *adj.* imperishable; ~**geßlich** *adj.* unforgettable; ~'**gleichlich** *adj.* incomparable; '~**hältnismäßig** *adj.* disproportionate; ~'**heiratet** *adj.* un-

married, single; '~**hofft** *adj.* unhoped-for, unexpected; '~**hohlen** *adj.* unconcealed; '~**käuflich** *adj.* unsal(e)able; not for sale; ~'**kenn-bar** *adj.* unmistakable; ~'**letzbar** *adj.* invulnerable; *fig. a.* inviolable; ~**meidlich** *adj.* [~'maɪtlɪç] inevitable; '~**mindert** *adj.* undiminished; '~**mittelt** *adj.* abrupt.

'**Unvermögen** *n* (-s/no pl.) inability; impotence; '2**d** *adj.* impecunious, without means.

'**unvermutet** *adj.* unexpected.

'**Unver|nunft** *f* unreasonableness, absurdity; '2**nünftig** *adj.* unreasonable, absurd; '2**richteterdinge** *adv.* without having achieved one's object.

'**unverschämt** *adj.* impudent, impertinent; '2**heit** *f* (-/-en) impudence, impertinence.

'**unver|schuldet** *adj.* not in debt; through no fault of mine, *etc.*; '~**sehens** *adv.* unawares, suddenly, all of a sudden; ~**sehrt** *adj.* ['~zeːrt] uninjured; ~**söhnlich** *adj.* implacable, irreconcilable; '~**sorgt** *adj.* unprovided for; '2**stand** *m* injudiciousness; folly, stupidity; '~**stän-dig** *adj.* injudicious; foolish; '~**ständlich** *adj.* unintelligible; incomprehensible; *das ist mir ~* that is beyond me; '~**sucht** *adj.*: *nichts ~ lassen* leave nothing undone; ~'**träglich** *adj.* unsociable; quarrelsome; '~**wandt** *adj.* steadfast; ~**wundbar** *adj.* [~'vʊntbɑːr] invulnerable; ~**wüstlich** *adj.* [~'vyːstlɪç] indestructible; *fig.* irrepressible; ~**zagt** *adj.* ['~tsaːkt] intrepid, undaunted; ~'**zeihlich** *adj.* unpardonable; ~'**zinslich** *adj.* bearing no interest; non-interest-bearing; ~**züglich** *adj.* [~'tsyːklɪç] immediate, instant.

'**unvollendet** *adj.* unfinished.

'**unvollkommen** *adj.* imperfect; '2**heit** *f* imperfection.

'**unvollständig** *adj.* incomplete; '2**keit** *f* (-/no pl.) incompleteness.

'**unvorbereitet** *adj.* unprepared; extempore.

'**unvoreingenommen** *adj.* unbias(s)ed, unprejudiced; '2**heit** *f* freedom from prejudice.

'**unvor|hergesehen** *adj.* unforeseen; '~**schriftsmäßig** *adj.* irregular.

unvorsichtig *adj.* incautious; imprudent; '2keit *f* incautiousness; imprudence.

unvor|stellbar *adj.* unimaginable; '~teilhaft *adj.* unprofitable; *dress, etc.*: unbecoming. [truth.]

'unwahr *adj.* untrue; '2heit *f* un-]

'unwahrscheinlich *adj.* improbable, unlikely; '2keit *f* (-/-en) improbability, unlikelihood.

'un|wegsam *adj.* pathless, impassable; '~weit *prp.* (*gen. or von*) not far from; '2wesen *n* (-s/*no pl.*) nuisance; *sein* ~ *treiben* be up to one's tricks; '~wesentlich *adj.* unessential, immaterial (*für* to); '2wetter *n* thunderstorm; '~wichtig *adj.* unimportant, insignificant.

unwider|legbar *adj.* [unvi:dər'le:kba:r] irrefutable; ~**ruflich** *adj.* irrevocable (*a.* ✝).

unwider'stehlich *adj.* irresistible; 2keit *f* (-/*no pl.*) irresistibility.

unwieder'bringlich *adj.* irretrievable.

'Unwill|e *m* (-ns/*no pl.*), ~**en** *m* (-s/*no pl.*) indignation (*über acc.* at), displeasure (at, over); '2ig *adj.* indignant (*über acc.* at), displeased (at, with); unwilling; '2kürlich *adj.* involuntary.

'unwirklich *adj.* unreal.

'unwirksam *adj.* ineffective, inefficient; *laws, rules, etc.*: inoperative; ⚗ inactive; '2keit *f* (-/*no pl.*) ineffectiveness, inefficiency; ⚗ inactivity.

unwirsch *adj.* ['unvirʃ] testy.

'unwirt|lich *adj.* inhospitable, desolate; '~schaftlich *adj.* uneconomic(al).

'unwissen|d *adj.* ignorant; '2heit *f* (-/*no pl.*) ignorance; '~tlich *adj.* unwitting, unknowing.

'unwohl *adj.* unwell, indisposed; '2sein *n* (-s/*no pl.*) indisposition.

'unwürdig *adj.* unworthy (*gen.* of).

un|zählig *adj.* [un'tsɛ:lɪç] innumerable; '2zart *adj.* indelicate.

Unze *f* ['untsə] *f* (-/-n) ounce.

'Unzeit *f*: *zur* ~ inopportunely; '2gemäß *adj.* old-fashioned; inopportune; '2ig *adj.* untimely; unseasonable; *fruit*: unripe.

unzer|brechlich *adj.* unbreakable; ~**reißbar** *adj.* untearable; ~**störbar** *adj.* indestructible; ~**trennlich** *adj.* inseparable.

'un|ziemlich *adj.* unseemly; '2zucht *f* (-/*no pl.*) lewdness; ⚖ sexual offen|ce, *Am.* -se; '~züchtig *adj.* lewd; obscene.

'unzufrieden *adj.* discontented (*mit* with), dissatisfied (with, at); '2heit *f* discontent, dissatisfaction.

'unzugänglich *adj.* inaccessible.

'unzulänglich *adj.* ['untsulɛnlɪç] insufficient; '2keit *f* (-/-en) insufficiency; shortcoming.

'unzulässig *adj.* inadmissible; *esp.* ⚖ influence: undue.

'unzurechnungsfähig *adj.* irresponsible; '2keit *f* irresponsibility.

'unzu|reichend *adj.* insufficient; '~sammenhängend** *adj.* incoherent; '~träglich** *adj.* unwholesome; '~treffend** *adj.* incorrect; inapplicable (*auf acc.* to).

'unzuverlässig *adj.* unreliable, untrustworthy; *friend: a.* uncertain; '2keit *f* unreliability, untrustworthiness.

'unzweckmäßig *adj.* inexpedient; '2keit *f* inexpediency.

'un|zweideutig *adj.* unequivocal; unambiguous; '~zweifelhaft 1.** *adj.* undoubted, undubitable; **2.** *adv.* doubtless.

üppig *adj.* ['ʏpɪç] ♀ luxuriant, exuberant, opulent; *food*: luxurious, opulent; *figure*: voluptuous; '2keit *f* (-/♀-en) luxuriance, luxuriancy, exuberance; voluptuousness.

ur|alt *adj.* ['u:r'alt] very old; (as) old as the hills; '2aufführung ['u:r'?-] *f* world première.

Uran [u'ra:n] *n* (-s/*no pl.*) uranium.

urbar *adj.* ['u:rba:r] arable, cultivable; ~ *machen* reclaim; '2machung *f* (-/-en) reclamation.

'Ur|bevölkerung *f* aborigines *pl.*; '~bild** *n* original, prototype; '~eigen** *adj.* one's very own; '~enkel** *m* great-grandson; '~eltern** *pl.* great-grandparents *pl.*; '~großmutter** *f* great-grandmother; '~großvater** *m* great-grandfather.

'Urheber *m* (-s/-) author; '~recht** *n* copyright (*an dat.* in); '~schaft** *f* (-/*no pl.*) authorship.

Urin [u'ri:n] *m* (-s/-e) urine; **2ieren** [-i'ni:rən] *v/i.* (*no* -ge-, *h*) urinate.

'Urkund|e *f* document; deed; '~enfälschung** *f* forgery of documents; 2lich *adj.* ['~tlɪç] documentary.

Urlaub ['uːrlaup] *m* (-[e]s/-e) leave (of absence) (*a.* ✕); holiday(s *pl.*), *esp. Am.* vacation; **~er** ['ˌʌbər] *m* (-s/-) holiday-maker, *esp. Am.* vacationist, vacationer.

Urne ['urnə] *f* (-/-n) urn; ballot-box.

'**ur**|**plötzlich 1.** *adj.* very sudden, abrupt; **2.** *adv.* all of a sudden; '**2sache** *f* cause; reason; *keine ~!* don't mention it, *Am. a.* you are welcome; '**~sächlich** *adj.* causal; '**2schrift** *f* original (text); '**2-sprung** *m* origin, source; **~sprünglich** *adj.* ['ˌʃpryŋlɪç] original; '**2stoff** *m* primary matter.

Urteil ['urtaıl] *n* (-s/-e) judg(e)-ment; ⚖ *a.* sentence; *meinem ~ nach* in my judg(e)ment; *sich ein ~ bilden* form a judg(e)ment (*über acc.* of, on); '**2en** *v/i.* (ge-, *h*) judge (*über acc.* of; *nach* by, from); '**~s-kraft** *f* (-/✕e) discernment.

'**Ur**|**text** *m* original (text); '**~wald** *m* primeval *or* virgin forest; **2-wüchsig** *adj.* ['ˌvyːksɪç] original; *fig.*: natural; rough; '**2zeit** *f* primitive times *pl.*   [sils *pl.*]

Utensilien [uten'ziːljən] *pl.* uten-

Utop|**ie** [uto'piː] *f* (-/-n) Utopia; **2isch** *adj.* [u'toːpiʃ] Utopian, utopian.

V

Vagabund [vaga'bunt] *m* (-en/-en) vagabond, vagrant, tramp, *Am.* hobo, F bum.

Vakuum ['vaːkuˀum] *n* (-s/*Vakua*, *Vakuen*) vacuum.

Valuta [va'luːta] *f* (-/*Valuten*) value; currency.

Vanille [va'nɪljə] *f* (-/no *pl.*) vanilla.

variabel *adj.* [vari'aːbəl] variable.

Varia|**nte** [vari'antə] *f* (-/-n) variant; **~tion** [ˌʌ'tsjoːn] *f* (-/-en) variation.

Varieté [varie'teː] *n* (-s/-s), **~thea-ter** *n* variety theatre, music-hall, *Am.* vaudeville theater.

variieren [vari'iːrən] *v/i.* and *v/t.* (no -ge-, *h*) vary.

Vase ['vaːzə] *f* (-/-n) vase.

Vater ['faːtər] *m* (-s/✕) father; '**~land** *n* native country *or* land, mother country; '**~landsliebe** *f* patriotism.   [paternal.]

väterlich *adj.* ['fɛːtərlɪç] fatherly,

'**Vater**|**schaft** *f* (-/no *pl.*) paternity, fatherhood; '**~unser** *eccl.* *n* (-s/-) Lord's Prayer.

Vati ['faːti] *m* (-s/-s) dad(dy).

Veget|**arier** [vege'taːrjər] *m* (-s/-) vegetarian; **2arisch** *adj.* vegetarian; **~ation** [ˌʌ'tsjoːn] *f* (-/-en) vegetation; **2ieren** [ˌʌ'tiːrən] *v/i.* (no -ge-, *h*) vegetate.

Veilchen ♣ ['faɪlçən] *n* (-s/-) violet.

Vene *anat.* ['veːnə] *f* (-/-n) vein.

Ventil [vɛn'tiːl] *n* (-s/-e) valve (*a.* ♪); ♪ stop (*of organ*); *fig.* vent,

outlet; **~ation** [ˌʌila'tsjoːn] *f* (-/-en) ventilation; **~ator** [ˌʌi'laːtər] *m* (-s/-en) ventilator, fan.

verab|**folgen** [fɛr'ap-] *v/t.* (no -ge-, *h*) deliver; give; ✞ administer (*medicine*); **~reden** *v/t.* (no -ge-, *h*) agree upon, arrange; appoint, fix (*time, place*); *sich ~* make an appointment, *Am.* F (have a) date; **2redung** *f* (-/-en) agreement; arrangement; appointment, *Am.* F date; **~reichen** *v/t.* (no -ge-, *h*) *s.* verabfolgen; **~scheuen** *v/t.* (no -ge-, *h*) abhor, detest, loathe; **~schieden** [ˌʌ'ʃiːdən] *v/t.* (no -ge-, *h*) dismiss; retire (*officer*); ✕ discharge (*troops*); *parl.* pass (*bill*); *sich ~* take leave (*von* of), say good-bye (*to*); **2schiedung** *f* (-/-en) dismissal; discharge; passing.

ver|'**achten** *v/t.* (no -ge-, *h*) despise; **~ächtlich** *adj.* [ˌʌ'ɛçtlɪç] contemptuous; contemptible; **2ach-tung** *f* contempt; **~allgemeinern** [ˌʌˀalgə'maɪnərn] *v/t.* (no -ge-, *h*) generalize; **~'altet** *adj.* antiquated, obsolete, out of date.

Veranda [ve'randa] *f* (-/*Veranden*) veranda(h), *Am. a.* porch.

veränder|**lich** *adj.* [fɛr'ɛndərlɪç] changeable; variable (*a.* ♈, *gr.*); **~n** *v/t.* and *v/refl.* (no -ge-, *h*) alter, change; vary; **2ung** *f* change, alteration (*in dat.* in; *an dat.* to); variation.   [timidated, scared.]

verängstigt *adj.* [fɛr'ɛŋstɪçt] in-

ver'anlag|en v/t. (no -ge-, h) of taxation: assess; **~t** adj. [.kt] talented; **2ung** [.gun] f (-/-en) assessment; fig. talent(s pl.); ⚕ predisposition.

ver'anlass|en v/t. (no -ge-, h) cause, occasion; arrange; **2ung** f (-/-en) occasion, cause; auf m-e ~ at my request or suggestion.

ver|'anschaulichen v/t. (no -ge-, h) illustrate; **~'anschlagen** v/t. (no -ge-, h) rate, value, estimate (all: auf acc. at).

ver'anstalt|en v/t. (no -ge-, h) arrange, organize; give (concert, ball, etc.); **2ung** f (-/-en) arrangement; event; sports: event, meeting, Am. meet.

ver'antwort|en v/t. (no -ge-, h) take the responsibility for; account for; **~lich** adj. responsible; j-n ~ machen für hold s.o. responsible for.

Ver'antwortung f (-/-en) responsibility; die ~ tragen be responsible; zur ~ ziehen call to account; **2slos** adj. irresponsible.

ver|'arbeiten v/t. (no -ge-, h) work up; ⊕ process, manufacture (both: zu into); digest (food) (a. fig.); **~'ärgern** v/t. (no -ge-, h) vex, annoy.

ver|'armen v/i. (no -ge-, sein) become poor; **~t** adj. impoverished.

ver|'ausgaben v/t. (no -ge-, h) spend (money); sich ~ run short of money; fig. spend o.s.; **~'äußern** v/t. (no -ge-, h) sell; alienate.

Verb gr. [vɛrp] n (-s/-en) verb.

Ver'band m (-[e]s/-e) ⚕ dressing, bandage; association, union; ✕ formation, unit; **~(s)kasten** m first-aid box; **~(s)zeug** n dressing (material).

ver'bann|en v/t. (no -ge-, h) banish (a. fig.), exile; **2ung** f (-/-en) banishment, exile.

ver|barrikadieren [fɛrbarika'di:-rən] v/t. (no -ge-, h) barricade; block (street, etc.); **~'bergen** v/t. (irr. bergen, no -ge-, h) conceal, hide.

ver'besser|n v/t. (no -ge-, h) improve; correct; **2ung** f improvement; correction.

ver'beug|en v/refl. (no -ge-, h) bow (vor dat. to); **2ung** f bow.

ver|'biegen v/t. (irr. biegen, no

-ge-, h) bend, twist, distort; **~'bieten** v/t. (irr. bieten, no -ge-, h) forbid, prohibit; **~'billigen** v/t. (no -ge-, h) reduce in price, cheapen.

ver'bind|en v/t. (irr. binden, no -ge-, h) ⚕ dress; tie (together); bind (up); link (mit to); join, unite, combine; connect (a. teleph.); teleph. put s.o. through (mit to); j-m die Augen ~ blindfold s.o.; ~ join, unite, combine (a. ⚕); ich bin Ihnen sehr verbunden I am greatly obliged to you; falsch verbunden! teleph. wrong number!; **~lich** adj. [.tliç] obligatory, obliging; **2lichkeit** f (-/-en) obligation, liability; obligingness, civility.

Ver'bindung f union; alliance; combination; association (of ideas); connexion, (Am. only) connection (a. teleph., 🚂, ⚓, ⊕); relation; communication (a. teleph.); 🧪 compound; geschäftliche ~ business relations pl.; teleph.: ~ bekommen (haben) get (be) through; die ~ verlieren mit lose touch with; in ~ bleiben (treten) keep (get) in touch (mit with); sich in ~ setzen mit communicate with, esp. Am. contact s.o.; **~sstraße** f communication road, feeder road; **~stür** f communication door.

ver|bissen adj. [fɛr'bisən] dogged; crabbed; **~'bitten** v/refl. (irr. bitten, no -ge-, h): das verbitte ich mir! I won't suffer or stand that!

ver'bitter|n v/t. (no -ge-, h) embitter; **2ung** f (-/⚕-en) bitterness (of heart).

verblassen [fɛr'blasən] v/i. (no -ge-, sein) fade (a. fig.).

Verbleib [fɛr'blaip] m (-[e]s/no pl.) whereabouts sg., pl.; **2en** [.bən] v/i. (irr. bleiben, no -ge-, sein) be left, remain.

ver'blend|en v/t. (no -ge-, h) ⚛ face (wall, etc.); fig. blind, delude; **2ung** f (-/⚕-en) ⚛ facing; fig. blindness, delusion. [faded.]

verblichen adj. [fɛr'bliçən] colour:|

verblüff|en [fɛr'blyfən] v/t. (no -ge-, h) amaze; perplex, puzzle; dumbfound; **2ung** f (-/⚕-en) amazement, perplexity.

ver|'blühen v/i. (no -ge-, sein) fade, wither; **~'bluten** v/i. (no -ge-, sein) bleed to death.

ver'borgen *adj.* hidden; secret; **Ꭲheit** *f* (-/*no pl.*) concealment; secrecy.

Verbot [fɛrˈboːt] *n* (-[e]s/-e) prohibition; **Ꭲen** *adj.* forbidden, prohibited; *Rauchen* ~ no smoking.

Ver'brauch *m* (-[e]s/ᴿ ⁼e) consumption (*an dat.* of); **Ꭲen** *v/t.* (*no* -ge-, *h*) consume, use up; wear out; **Ꭲer** *m* (-s/-) consumer; **Ꭲt** *adj.* air: stale; *p.* worn out.

Ver'brechen 1. *v/t.* (*irr. brechen*, *no* -ge-, *h*) commit; *was hat er verbrochen?* what is his offen|ce, *Am.* -se?, what has he done?; **2.** ᎒ *n* (-s/-) crime, offen|ce, *Am.* -se.

Ver'brecher *m* (-s/-) criminal; **Ꭲisch** *adj.* criminal; **Ꭲtum** *n* (-s/*no pl.*) criminality.

ver'breit|en *v/t.* (*no* -ge-, *h*) spread, diffuse; shed (*light, warmth, happiness*); *sich* ~ spread; *sich* ~ *über* (*acc.*) enlarge (up)on (*theme*); **Ꭲern** *v/t. and v/refl.* (*no* -ge-, *h*) widen, broaden; **Ꭲung** *f* (-/ᴿ -en) spread (-ing), diffusion.

ver'brenn|en (*irr. brennen*, *no* -ge-) **1.** *v/i.* (*sein*) burn; **2.** *v/t.* (*h*) burn (up); cremate (*corpse*); **Ꭲung** *f* (-/-en) burning, combustion; cremation (*of corpse*); *wound*: burn.

ver'bringen *v/t.* (*irr. bringen*, *no* -ge-, *h*) spend, pass.

verbrüder|n [fɛrˈbryːdərn] *v/refl.* (*no* -ge-, *h*) fraternize; **Ꭲung** *f* (-/-en) fraternization.

ver'brühen *v/t.* (*no* -ge-, *h*) scald; *sich* ~ scald o.s.; **Ꭲbuchen** *v/t.* (*no* -ge-, *h*) book.

Verbum *gr.* [ˈvɛrbum] *n* (-s/*Verba*) verb.

verbünden [fɛrˈbyndən] *v/refl.* (*no* -ge-, *h*) ally o.s. (*mit* to, with).

Verbundenheit [fɛrˈbundənhaɪt] *f* (-/*no pl.*) bonds *pl.*, ties *pl.*; solidarity; affection.

Ver'bündete *m, f* (-n/-n) ally, confederate; *die* ~*n pl.* the allies *pl.*

ver'bürgen *v/t.* (*no* -ge-, *h*) guarantee, warrant; *sich* ~ *für* answer *or* vouch for; **Ꭲbüßen** *v/t.* (*no* -ge-, *h*): *e-e Strafe* ~ serve a sentence, serve (one's) time.

Verdacht [fɛrˈdaxt] *m* (-[e]s/*no pl.*) suspicion; *in* ~ *haben* suspect.

verdächtig *adj.* [fɛrˈdɛçtɪç] suspected (*gen.* of); *pred.* suspect; suspicious; **Ꭲen** [~ɡən] *v/t.* (*no*

-ge-, *h*) suspect *s.o.* (*gen.* of); cast suspicion on; **Ꭲung** [~ɡuŋ] *f* (-/-en) suspicion; insinuation.

verdamm|en [fɛrˈdamən] *v/t.* (*no* -ge-, *h*) condemn, damn (*a. eccl.*); **Ꭲnis** *f* (-/*no pl.*) damnation; **Ꭲt 1.** *adj.* damned; F: ~*!* damn (it)!, confound it!; **-2.** F *adv.:* ~ *kalt* beastly cold; **Ꭲung** *f* (-/ᴿ -en) condemnation, damnation.

ver|'dampfen (*no* -ge-) *v/t.* (*h*) *and v/i.* (*sein*) evaporate; **Ꭲ'danken** *v/t.* (*no* -ge-, *h*): *j-m et.* ~ owe s.th. to s.o. [*ben.*\]

verdarb [fɛrˈdarp] *pret. of verder-*\]

verdau|en [fɛrˈdaʊən] *v/t.* (*no* -ge-, *h*) digest; **Ꭲlich** *adj.* digestible; *leicht* ~ easy to digest, light; **Ꭲung** *f* (-/*no pl.*) digestion; **Ꭲungsstörung** *f* indigestion.

Ver'deck *n* (-[e]s/-e) ⚓ deck; hood (*of carriage, car, etc.*); top (*of vehicle*); **Ꭲen** *v/t.* (*no* -ge-, *h*) cover, conceal, hide.

ver'denken *v/t.* (*irr. denken*, *no* -ge-, *h*): *ich kann es ihm nicht* ~, *daß I* cannot blame him for *ger.*

Verderb [fɛrˈdɛrp] *m* (-[e]s/*no pl.*) ruin; **Ꭲen** [~bən] **1.** *v/i.* (*irr.*, *no* -ge-, *sein*) spoil (*a. fig.*); rot; *meat, etc.*: go bad; *fig.* perish; **2.** *v/t.* (*irr.*, *no* -ge-, *h*) spoil; *fig. a.:* corrupt; ruin; *er will es mit niemandem* ~ he tries to please everybody; *sich den Magen* ~ upset one's stomach; **Ꭲen** [~bən] *n* (-s/*no pl.*) ruin; **Ꭲlich** *adj.* [~plɪç] pernicious; *food:* perishable; **Ꭲnis** [~pnɪs] *f* (-/ᴿ -se) corruption; depravity; **Ꭲt** *adj.* [~pt] corrupted, depraved.

ver|'deutlichen *v/t.* (*no* -ge-, *h*) make plain *or* clear; **Ꭲ'dichten** *v/t.* (*no* -ge-, *h*) condense; *sich* ~ condense; *suspicion:* grow stronger; **Ꭲ'dicken** *v/t. and v/refl.* (*no* -ge-, *h*) thicken; **Ꭲ'dienen** *v/t.* (*no* -ge-, *h*) merit, deserve; earn (*money*).

Ver'dienst (-es/-e) **1.** *m* gain, profit; earnings *pl.*; **2.** *n* merit; *es ist sein* ~, *daß* it is owing to him that; **Ꭲvoll** *adj.* meritorious, deserving; **Ꭲspanne** † *f* profit margin.

ver|'dient *adj. p.* of merit; (well-) deserved; *sich* ~ *gemacht haben um* deserve well of; **Ꭲ'dolmetschen** *v/t.* (*no* -ge-, *h*) interpret (*a. fig.*); **Ꭲ'doppeln** *v/t. and v/refl.* (*no* -ge-, *h*) double.

verdorben [fɛr'dɔrbən] **1.** p.p. of verderben; **2.** adj. meat: tainted; stomach: disordered, upset; fig. corrupt, depraved.

ver|dorren [fɛr'dɔrən] v/i. (no -ge-, sein) wither (up); **~'drängen** v/t. (no -ge-, h) push away, thrust aside; fig. displace; psych. repress; **~'drehen** v/t. (no -ge-, h) distort, twist (both a. fig.); roll (eyes); fig. pervert; j-m den Kopf ~ turn s.o.'s head; **~'dreht** F fig. adj. crazy; **~'dreifachen** v/t. and v/refl. (no -ge-, h) triple.

verdrießen [fɛr'driːsən] v/t. (irr., no -ge-, h) vex, annoy; **~lich** adj. vexed, annoyed; sulky; thing: annoying.

ver|droß [fɛr'drɔs] pret. of verdrießen; **~drossen** [~'drɔsən] **1.** p.p. of verdrießen; **2.** adj. sulky; listless.

ver|drucken typ. v/t. (no -ge-, h) misprint.

Verdruß [fɛr'drus] m (Verdrusses/% Verdrusse) vexation, annoyance.

ver|dummen (no -ge-) **1.** v/t. (h) make stupid; **2.** v/i. (sein) become stupid.

ver|dunk|eln v/t. (no -ge-, h) darken, obscure (both a. fig.); black out (window); sich ~ darken; **♀(e)lung** f (-/%-en) darkening; obscuration; black-out; ⚖ collusion.

ver|'dünnen v/t. (no -ge-, h) thin; dilute (liquid); **~'dunsten** v/i. (no -ge-, sein) volatilize, evaporate; **~'dursten** v/i. (no -ge-, sein) die of thirst; **~dutzt** adj. [~'dutst] nonplussed.

ver|ed|eln v/t. (no -ge-, h) ennoble; refine; improve; ⚘ graft; process (raw materials); **♀(e)lung** f (-/% -en) refinement; improvement; processing.

ver|ehr|en v/t. (no -ge-, h) revere, venerate; worship; admire, adore; **♀er** m (-s/-) worship(p)er; admirer, adorer; **♀ung** f (-/%-en) reverence, veneration; worship; adoration.

vereidigen [fɛr'aidigən] v/t. (no -ge-, h) swear (witness); at entrance into office: swear s.o. in.

Verein [fɛr'ain] m (-[e]s/-e) union; society, association; club.

ver|einbar adj. compatible (mit with), consistent (with); **~en** v/t.

(no -ge-, h) agree upon, arrange; **♀ung** f (-/-en) agreement, arrangement.

ver|einen v/t. (no -ge-, h) s. vereinigen.

ver|einfach|en v/t. (no -ge-, h) simplify; **♀ung** f (-/-en) simplification.

ver|einheitlichen v/t. (no -ge-, h) unify, standardize.

ver|einig|en v/t. (no -ge-, h) unite, join; associate; sich ~ unite, join; associate o.s.; **♀ung** f **1.** (-/%-en) union; **2.** (-/-en) union; society, association.

ver|ein|samen v/i. (no -ge-, sein) grow lonely or solitary; **~zelt** adj. isolated; sporadic.

ver|'eiteln v/t. (no -ge-, h) frustrate; **~'ekeln** v/t. (no -ge-, h): er hat mir das Essen verekelt he spoilt my appetite; **~'enden** v/i. (no -ge-, sein) animals: die, perish; **~enge(r)n** [~'ɛŋə(r)n] v/t. and v/refl. (no -ge-, h) narrow.

ver|erb|en v/t. (no -ge-, h) leave, bequeath; biol. transmit; sich ~ be hereditary; sich ~ auf (acc.) descend (up)on; **♀ung** f (-/%-en) biol. transmission; physiol. heredity; **♀ungslehre** f genetics.

verewig|en [fɛr'eːvigən] v/t. (no -ge-, h) perpetuate; **~t** adj. [~çt] deceased, late.

ver|fahren 1. v/i. (irr. fahren, no -ge-, sein) proceed; ~ mit deal with; **2.** v/t. (irr. fahren, no -ge-, h) mismanage, muddle, bungle; sich ~ miss one's way; **3.** ♀ n (-s/-) procedure; proceeding(s pl. ⚖); ⊕ process.

Ver|fall m (-[e]s/no pl.) decay, decline; dilapidation (of house, etc.); ⚖ forfeiture; expiration; maturity (of bill of exchange); **♀en 1.** v/i. (irr. fallen, no -ge-, sein) decay; house: dilapidate; document, etc.: expire; pawn: become forfeited; right: lapse; bill of exchange: fall due; sick person: waste away; ~ auf (acc.) hit upon (idea, etc.); ~ in (acc.) fall into; j-m ~ become s.o.'s slave; **2.** adj. ruinous; addicted (dat. to drugs, etc.); **~serscheinung** [fɛr'fals⁹-/] f symptom of decline; **~tag** m day of payment.

ver|'fälschen v/t. (no -ge-, h) falsify; adulterate (wine, etc.); **~fäng-**

lich adj. [ˌ'feŋliç] question: captious, insidious; risky; embarrassing; **ˌ'färben** v/refl. (no -ge-, h) change colo(u)r.

ver'fass|en v/t. (no -ge-, h) compose, write; **2er** m (-s/-) author.

Ver'fassung f state, condition; pol. constitution; disposition (of mind); **2smäßig** adj. constitutional; **2s-widrig** adj. unconstitutional.

ver|'faulen v/i. (no -ge-, sein) rot, decay; **ˌ'fechten** v/t. (irr. fechten, no -ge-, h) defend, advocate.

ver'fehl|en v/t. (no -ge-, h) miss; **2ung** f (-/-en) offen|ce, Am. -se.

ver'feind|en [fer'faɪndən] v/t. (no -ge-, h) make enemies of; sich ~ mit make an enemy of; **ˌfeinern** [ˌ'faɪnərn] v/t. and v/refl. (no -ge-, h) refine; **ˌfertigen** [ˌ'fertɪgən] v/t. (no -ge-, h) make, manufacture, compose.

ver'film|en v/t. (no -ge-, h) film, screen; **2ung** f (-/-en) film-version.

ver|'finstern v/t. (no -ge-, h) darken, obscure; sich ~ darken; **ˌ'flachen** (no -ge-) v/i. (sein and v/refl. (h) (become) shallow (a. fig.); **ˌ'flechten** v/t. (irr. flechten, no -ge-, h) interlace; fig. involve; **ˌ'fliegen** (irr. fliegen, no -ge-) **1.** v/i. (sein) evaporate; time: fly; fig. vanish; **2.** v/refl. (h) bird: stray; ✈ lose one's bearings, get lost; **ˌ'fließen** v/i. (irr. fließen, no -ge-, sein) colours: blend; time: elapse; **ˌflossen** adj. [ˌ'flɔsən] time: past; F ein ˌer Freund a late friend, an ex-friend.

ver'fluch|en v/t. (no -ge-, h) curse, Am. F cuss; **ˌt** adj. damned; ~! damn (it)!, confound it!

ver'flüchtigen [fer'flʏçtɪgən] v/t. (no -ge-, h) volatilize; sich ~ evaporate (a. fig.); F fig. vanish; **ˌflüssigen** [ˌ'flʏsɪgən] v/t. and v/refl. (no -ge-, h) liquefy.

ver'folg|en v/t. (no -ge-, h) pursue, persecute; follow (tracks); trace; thoughts, dream: haunt; gerichtlich ~ prosecute; **2er** m (-s/-) pursuer; persecutor; **2ung** f (-/-en) pursuit; persecution; pursuance; gerichtliche ~ prosecution; **2ungswahn** ⚕ m persecution mania.

ver|frachten [fer'fraxtən] v/t. (no -ge-, h) freight, Am. a. ship (goods);

⚓ ship; F j-n ~ in (acc.) bundle s.o. in(to) (train, etc.); **ˌ'froren** adj. chilled through; **ˌ'früht** adj. premature.

verfüg|bar adj. [fer'fy:kbaːr] available; **ˌen** [ˌgən] (no -ge-, h) **1.** v/t. decree, order; **2.** v/i.: ~ über (acc.) have at one's disposal; dispose of; **2ung** [ˌguŋ] f (-/-en) decree, order; disposal; j-m zur ~ stehen (stellen) be (place) at s.o.'s disposal.

ver'führ|en v/t. (no -ge-, h) seduce; **2er** m (-s/-) seducer; **ˌerisch** adj. seductive; enticing, tempting; **2ung** f seduction.

vergangen adj. [fer'gaŋən] gone, past; im ˌen Jahr last year; **2heit** f (-/-en) past; gr. past tense.

vergänglich adj. [fer'gɛŋliç] transient, transitory.

vergas|en [fer'gaːzən] v/t. (no -ge-, h) gasify; gas s.o.; **2er** mot. m (-s/-) carburet(t)or.

vergaß [fer'gaːs] pret. of vergessen.

ver'geb|en v/t. (irr. geben, no -ge-, h) give away (an j-n to s.o.); confer (on), bestow (on); place (order); forgive; sich et. ~ compromise one's dignity; **ˌens** adv. [ˌs] in vain; **ˌlich** [ˌpliç] **1.** adj. vain; **2.** adv. in vain; **2ung** [ˌbuŋ] f (-/ˌ-en) bestowal, conferment (both: an acc. on); forgiveness, pardon.

vergegenwärtigen [ferge·gən'vertɪgən] v/t. (no -ge-, h) represent; sich et. ~ visualize s.th.

ver'geh|en 1. v/i. (irr. gehen, no -ge-, sein) pass (away); fade (away); ~ vor (dat.) die of; **2.** v/refl. (irr. gehen, no -ge-, h): sich an j-m ~ assault s.o.; violate s.o.; sich gegen das Gesetz ~ offend against or violate the law; **3.** 2 n (-s/-) offen|ce, Am. -se.

ver'gelt|en v/t. (irr. gelten, no -ge-, h) repay, requite; reward; retaliate; **2ung** f (-/-en) requital; retaliation, retribution.

vergessen [fer'gɛsən] **1.** v/t. (irr., no -ge-, h) forget; leave; **2.** p.p. of **1**; **2heit** f (-/no pl.): in ~ geraten sink or fall into oblivion.

vergeßlich adj. [fer'gɛsliç] forgetful.

vergeud|en [fer'gɔʏdən] v/t. (no -ge-, h) dissipate, squander, waste (*time, money*); ~ung *f* (-/~-en) waste.

vergewaltig|en [fɛrgə'valtigən] *v/t.* (*no* -ge-, *h*) violate; rape; ~ung *f* (-/-en) violation; rape.

ver|gewissern [fɛrgə'wisərn] *v/refl.* (*no* -ge-, *h*) make sure (e-r Sache of s.th.); ~'gießen *v/t.* (*irr.* gießen, *no* -ge-, *h*) shed (*tears, blood*); spill (*liquid*).

ver'gift|en *v/t.* (*no* -ge-, *h*) poison (*a. fig.*); sich ~ take poison; ~ung *f* (-/-en) poisoning.

Vergißmeinnicht ♀ [fɛr'gismaɪnɪçt] *n* (-[e]s/-[e]) forget-me-not.

vergittern [fɛr'gitərn] *v/t.* (*no* -ge-, *h*) grate.

Vergleich [fɛr'glaɪç] *m* (-[e]s/-e) comparison; ⚖: agreement; compromise, composition; ~bar *adj.* comparable (*mit* to); ~en *v/t.* (*irr.* gleichen, *no* -ge-, *h*) compare (*mit* with, to); sich ~ mit come to terms with; verglichen mit as against, compared to; ~sweise *adv.* comparatively.

vergnügen [fɛr'gny:gən] **1.** *v/t.* (*no* -ge-, *h*) amuse; sich ~ enjoy o.s.; **2.** ♀ *n* (-s/-) pleasure, enjoyment; entertainment; ~ finden an (*dat.*) take pleasure in; viel ~! have a good time! [gay.⎸

vergnügt *adj.* [fɛr'gny:kt] merry,⎸ **Ver'gnügung** *f* (-/-en) pleasure, amusement, entertainment; ~s-reise *f* pleasure-trip; tour; ♀s-süchtig *adj.* pleasure-seeking.

ver|golden [fɛr'gɔldən] *v/t.* (*no* -ge-, *h*) gild; ~göttern *fig.* [~'gœtərn] *v/t.* (*no* -ge-, *h*) idolize, adore; ~'graben *v/t.* (*irr.* graben, *no* -ge-, *h*) bury (*a. fig.*); sich ~ bury o.s.; ~'greifen *v/refl.* (*irr.* greifen, *no* -ge-, *h*) sprain (*one's hand, etc.*); sich ~ an (*dat.*) lay (violent) hands on, attack, assault; embezzle (*money*); encroach upon (*s.o.'s property*); ~griffen *adj.* [~'grifən] *goods*: sold out; *book*: out of print.

vergrößer|n [fɛr'grø:sərn] *v/t.* (*no* -ge-, *h*) enlarge (*a. phot.*); opt. magnify; sich ~ enlarge; ♀ung *f* **1.** (-/-en) phot. enlargement; opt. magnification; **2.** (-/~-en) enlargement; increase; extension; ♀ungs-glas *n* magnifying glass.

Vergünstigung [fɛr'gynstigun] *f* (-/-en) privilege.

vergüt|en [fɛr'gy:tən] *v/t.* (*no* -ge-, *h*) compensate (*j-m et.* s.o. for s.th.); reimburse (*money spent*); ♀ung *f* (-/-en) compensation; reimbursement.

ver'haft|en *v/t.* (*no* -ge-, *h*) arrest; ♀ung *f* (-/-en) arrest.

ver'halten 1. *v/t.* (*irr.* halten, *no* -ge-, *h*) keep back; catch *or* hold (*one's breath*); suppress, check; sich ~ thing: be; *p.* behave; sich ruhig ~ keep quiet; **2.** ♀ *n* (-s/*no pl.*) behavio(u)r, conduct.

Verhältnis [fɛr'hɛltnɪs] *n* (-ses/-se) proportion, rate; relation(s *pl.*) (zu with); F liaison, love-affair; F mistress; ~se *pl.* conditions *pl.*, circumstances *pl.*; means *pl.*; ♀mäßig *adv.* in proportion; comparatively; ~wort *gr. n* (-[e]s/=er) preposition.

Ver'haltungsmaßregeln *f/pl.* instructions *pl.*

ver'hand|eln (*no* -ge-, *h*) **1.** *v/i.* negotiate, treat (*über* acc., *wegen* for); ⚖ try (*über* et. s.th.); **2.** *v/t.* discuss; ♀lung *f* negotiation; discussion; ⚖ trial, proceedings *pl.*

ver'häng|en *v/t.* (*no* -ge-, *h*) cover (over), hang; inflict (*punishment*) (*über* acc. upon); ♀nis *n* (-ses/-se) fate; ~nisvoll *adj.* fatal; disastrous.

ver|härmt *adj.* [fɛr'hɛrmt] careworn; ~'harren] *v/i.* (*no* -ge-, *h*, sein) persist (*auf* dat., *bei, in* dat. in), stick (to); ~'härten *v/t.* and *v/refl.* (*no* -ge-, *h*) harden; ~'haßt *adj.* [~'hast] hated; hateful, odious; ~'hätscheln [~'hɛtʃəln] *v/t.* (*no* -ge-, *h*) coddle, pamper, spoil; ~'hauen *v/t.* (*irr.* hauen, *no* -ge-, *h*) thrash.

verheer|en [fɛr'he:rən] *v/t.* (*no* -ge-, *h*) devastate, ravage, lay waste; ~end *fig. adj.* disastrous; ♀ung *f* (-/-en) devastation.

ver|hehlen [fɛr'he:lən] *v/t.* (*no* -ge-, *h*) *s.* verheimlichen; ~'heilen *v/i.* (*no* -ge-, sein) heal (up).

ver'heimlich|en *v/t.* (*no* -ge-, *h*) hide, conceal; ♀ung *f* (-/-en) concealment.

ver'heirat|en *v/t.* (*no* -ge-, *h*) marry (*mit* to); sich ~ marry; ♀ung *f* (-/~-en) marriage.

ver'heiß|en *v/t.* (*irr.* heißen, *no* -ge-, *h*) promise; ♀ung *f* (-/-en) promise; ~ungsvoll *adj.* promising.

ver'helfen *v/i.* (*irr.* helfen, *no* -ge-,

h): j-m zu et. ~ help s.o. to s.th.
ver'herrlich|en v/t. (no -ge-, h) glorify; ₤ung f (-/✆-en) glorification.

ver|'hetzen v/t. (no -ge-, h) instigate; ~'**hexen** v/t. (no -ge-, h) bewitch.

ver'hinder|n v/t. (no -ge-, h) prevent; ₤ung f (-/✆-en) prevention.

ver'höhn|en v/t. (no -ge-, h) deride, mock (at), taunt; ₤ung f (-/-en) derision, mockery.

Verhör 🏛 [fɛr'høːr] n (-[e]s/-e) interrogation, questioning (of prisoners, etc.); examination; ₤en v/t. (no -ge-, h) examine, hear; interrogate; sich ~ hear it wrong.

ver|'hüllen v/t. (no -ge-, h) cover, veil; ~'**hungern** v/i. (no -ge-, sein) starve; ~'**hüten** v/t. (no -ge-, h) prevent.

ver'irr|en v/refl. (no -ge-, h) go astray, lose one's way; ~t adj.: ~es Schaf stray sheep; ₤ung fig. f (-/-en) aberration; error.

ver'jagen v/t. (no -ge-, h) drive away.

verjähr|en 🏛 [fɛr'jɛːrən] v/i. (no -ge-, sein) become prescriptive; ₤ung f (-/-en) limitation, (negative) prescription.

verjüngen [fɛr'jyŋən] v/t. (no -ge-, h) make young again, rejuvenate; reduce (scale); sich ~ grow young again, rejuvenate; taper off.

Ver'kauf m sale; ₤en v/t. (no -ge-, h) sell; zu ~ for sale; sich gut ~ sell well.

Ver'käuf|er m seller; vendor; shop-assistant, salesman, Am. a. (sales)clerk; ~**erin** f (-/-nen) seller; vendor; shop-assistant, saleswoman, shop girl, Am. a. (sales)clerk; ₤lich adj. sal(e)able; for sale.

Ver'kaufs|automat m slot-machine, vending machine; ~**schlager** m best seller.

Verkehr [fɛr'keːr] m (-[e]s/✆-e) traffic; transport(ation); communication; correspondence; ⚓, ✈, ✍, etc.: service; commerce, trade; intercourse (a. sexually); aus dem ~ ziehen withdraw from service; withdraw (money) from circulation; ₤en (no -ge-, h) **1.** v/t. convert (in acc. into), turn (into); **2.** v/i. ship, bus, etc.: run, ply (zwischen dat. between); bei j-m ~ go to or visit

s.o.'s house; ~ in (dat.) frequent (public house, etc.); ~ mit associate or mix with; have (sexual) intercourse with.

Ver'kehrs|ader f arterial road; ~**ampel** f traffic lights pl., traffic signal; ~**büro** n tourist bureau; ~**flugzeug** n air liner; ~**insel** f refuge, island; ~**minister** m minister of transport; ~**mittel** n (means of) conveyance or transport, Am. transportation; ~**polizist** m traffic policeman or constable, sl. traffic cop; ₤**reich** adj. congested with traffic, busy; ~**schild** n traffic sign; ~**schutzmann** m s. Verkehrs-polizist; ~**stauung** f, ~**stockung** f traffic block, traffic jam; ~**störung** f interruption of traffic; 🚑, etc.: breakdown; ~**straße** f thoroughfare; ~**teilnehmer** m road user; ~**unfall** m traffic accident; ~**verein** m tourist agency; ~**verhältnisse** pl. traffic conditions pl.; ~**vorschrift** f traffic regulation; ~**wesen** n (-s/no pl.) traffic; ~**zeichen** n traffic sign.

ver|'kehrt adj. inverted, upside down; fig. wrong; ~'**kennen** v/t. (irr. kennen, no -ge-, h) mistake; misunderstand, misjudge.

Ver'kettung f (-/-en) concatenation (a. fig.).

ver|'klagen 🏛 v/t. (no -ge-, h) sue (auf acc., wegen for); bring an action against s.o.; ~'**kleben** v/t. (no -ge-, h) paste s.th. up.

ver'kleid|en v/t. (no -ge-, h) disguise; ⊕: line; face; wainscot; encase; sich ~ disguise o.s.; ₤ung f (-/-en) disguise; ⊕: lining; facing; panel(l)ing, wainscot(t)ing.

verkleiner|n [fɛr'klaınərn] v/t. (no -ge-, h) make smaller, reduce, diminish; fig. belittle, derogate; ₤ung f (-/-en) reduction, diminution; fig. derogation.

ver|'klingen v/i. (irr. klingen, no -ge-, sein) die away; ~'**köchern** [~'kœçərn] (no -ge-) **1.** v/t. (h) ossify; **2.** v/i. (sein) ossify; fig. a. fossilize; ~'**knoten** v/t. (no -ge-, h) knot; ~'**knüpfen** v/t. (no -ge-, h) knot or tie (together); fig. connect, combine; ~'**kohlen** (no -ge-) **1.** v/t. (h) carbonize; char; F: j-n ~ pull s.o.'s leg; **2.** v/i. (sein) char; ~'**kommen 1.** v/i. (irr. kommen, no -ge-,

U
V

sein) decay; *p.*: go downhill *or* to the dogs; become demoralized; **2.** *adj.* decayed; depraved, corrupt; **~'korken** *v/t.* (*no* -ge-, *h*) cork (up).

ver'körper|n *v/t.* (*no* -ge-, *h*) personify, embody; represent; *esp. thea.* impersonate; **2ung** *f* (-/-en) personification, embodiment; impersonation.

ver|'krachen F *v/refl.* (*no* -ge-, *h*) fall out (*mit* with); **~'krampft** *adj.* cramped; **~'kriechen** *v/refl.* (*irr. kriechen, no* -ge-, *h*) hide; **~- 'krümmt** *adj.* crooked; **~krüppelt** *adj.* [~'krypəlt] crippled; stunted; **~krustet** *adj.* [~'krustət] (en)crusted; caked; **~'kühlen** *v/refl.* (*no* -ge-, *h*) catch (*a*) cold.

ver'kümmer|n *v/i.* (*no* -ge-, *sein*) ♀, 🐾 become stunted; 🐾 atrophy; *fig.* waste away; **~t** *adj.* stunted; atrophied; rudimentary (*a. biol.*).

verkünd|en [fer'kyndən] *v/t.* (*no* -ge-, *h*), **~igen** *v/t.* (*no* -ge-, *h*) announce; publish, proclaim; pronounce (*judgement*); **2igung** *f*, **2ung** *f* (-/-en) announcement; proclamation; pronouncement.

ver|'kuppeln *v/t.* (*no* -ge-, *h*) ⊕ couple; *fig.* pander; **~'kürzen** *v/t.* (*no* -ge-, *h*) shorten; abridge; beguile (*time, etc.*); **~'lachen** *v/t.* (*no* -ge-, *h*) laugh at; **~'laden** *v/t.* (*irr. laden, no* -ge-, *h*) load, ship; 🚂 entrain (*esp. troops*).

Verlag [fer'la:k] *m* (-[e]s/-e) publishing house; the publishers *pl.*; *im ~ von* published by.

ver|'lagern *v/t.* (*no* -ge-, *h*) displace, shift; *sich ~* shift.

Ver'lags|buchhändler *m* publisher; **~buchhandlung** *f* publishing house; **~recht** *n* copyright.

ver'langen **1.** *v/t.* (*no* -ge-, *h*) demand; require; desire; **2.** *v/i.* (*no* -ge-, *h*): *~ nach* ask for; long for; **3.** 2 *n* (-s/-, -) desire; longing (*nach* for); demand, request; *auf ~* by request, 🕂 on demand; *auf ~ von* at the request of, at *s.o.*'s request.

verlänger|n [fer'lɛŋərn] *v/t.* (*no* -ge-, *h*) lengthen; prolong, extend; **2ung** *f* (-/-en) lengthening; prolongation, extension.

ver'langsamen *v/t.* (*no* -ge-, *h*) slacken, slow down.

ver'lassen *v/t.* (*irr. lassen, no* -ge-, *h*) leave; forsake, abandon, desert;

sich ~ auf (*acc.*) rely on; **2heit** *f* (-/*no pl.*) abandonment; loneliness.

verläßlich *adj.* [fer'lɛslɪç] reliable.

Ver'lauf *m* lapse, course (*of time*); progress, development (*of matter*); course (*of disease, etc.*); *im ~* (*gen.*) *or von* in the course of; *e-n schlimmen ~ nehmen* take a bad turn; **2en** (*irr. laufen, no* -ge-) **1.** *v/i.* (*sein*) *time*: pass, elapse; *matter*: take its course; turn out, develop; *road, etc.*: run, extend; **2.** *v/refl.* (*h*) lose one's way, go astray; *crowd*: disperse; *water*: subside.

ver'lauten *v/i.* (*no* -ge-, *sein*): *~ lassen* give to understand, hint; *wie verlautet* as reported.

ver'leb|en *v/t.* (*no* -ge-, *h*) spend, pass; **~t** *adj.* [~pt] worn out.

ver'leg|en **1.** *v/t.* (*no* -ge-, *h*) mislay; transfer, shift, remove; ⊕ lay (*cable, etc.*); bar (*road*); put off, postpone; publish (*book*); *sich ~ auf* (*acc.*) apply o.s. to; **2.** *adj.* embarrassed; at a loss (*um* for *answer, etc.*); **2enheit** *f* (-/~-en) embarrassment; difficulty; predicament; **2er** *m* (-s/-) publisher; **2ung** *f* (-/-en) transfer, removal; ⊕ laying; *time*: postponement.

ver'leiden *v/t.* (*no* -ge-, *h*) *s. verekeln.*

ver'leih|en *v/t.* (*irr. leihen, no* -ge-, *h*) lend, *Am. a.* loan; hire *or* let out; bestow (*right, etc.*) (*j-m* on *s.o.*); award (*price*); **2ung** *f* (-/-en) lending, loan; bestowal.

ver|'leiten *v/t.* (*no* -ge-, *h*) mislead; induce; seduce; 🕇🕇 suborn; **~'lernen** *v/t.* (*no* -ge-, *h*) unlearn, forget; **~'lesen** *v/t.* (*irr. lesen, no* -ge-, *h*) read out; call (*names*) over; pick (*vegetables, etc.*); *sich ~* read wrong.

verletz|en [fer'lɛtsən] *v/t.* (*no* -ge-, *h*) hurt, injure; *fig. a.*: offend; violate; **~end** *adj.* offensive; **2te** [~tə] *m*, *f* (-n/-n) injured person; *die ~n pl.* the injured *pl.*; **2ung** *f* (-/-en) hurt, injury, wound; *fig.* violation.

ver'leugn|en *v/t.* (*no* -ge-, *h*) deny; disown; renounce (*belief, principle, etc.*); *sich ~ lassen* have o.s. denied (*vor j-m* to *s.o.*); **2ung** *f* (-/-en) denial; renunciation.

verleumd|en [fer'lɔʏmdən] *v/t.* (*no* -ge-, *h*) slander, defame; **~erisch** *adj.* slanderous; **2ung** *f* (-/-en) slander, defamation, *in writing*: libel.

ver'lieb|en v/refl.(no -ge-, h): sich ~ in (acc.) fall in love with; **~t** adj. [~pt] in love (in acc. with); amorous; **2theit** f (-/%-en) amorousness.

verlieren [fer'li:rən] (irr., no -ge-, h) **1.** v/t. lose; shed (leaves, etc.); sich ~ lose o.s.; disappear; **2.** v/i. lose.

ver'lob|en v/t. (no -ge-, h) engage (mit to); sich ~ become engaged; **2te** [~ptə] (-n/-n) **1.** m fiancé; die ~n pl. the engaged couple sg.; **2.** f fiancée; **2ung** [~buŋ] f (-/-en) engagement.

ver'lock|en v/t. (no -ge-, h) allure, entice; tempt; **~end** adj. tempting; **2ung** f (-/-en) allurement, enticement.

verlogen adj. [fɛr'lo:gən] mendacious; **2heit** f (-/%-en) mendacity.

verlor [fɛr'lo:r] pret. of verlieren; **~en 1.** p.p. of verlieren; **2.** adj. lost; fig. forlorn; **~e** Eier poached eggs; **~engehen** (irr. gehen, sep., -ge-, sein) be lost.

ver'los|en v/t. (no -ge-, h) raffle; **2ung** f (-/-en) lottery, raffle.

ver'löten v/t. (no -ge-, h) solder.

Verlust [fɛr'lust] m (-es/-e) loss; ~e pl. ✗ casualties pl.

ver'machen v/t. (no -ge-, h) bequeath, leave s.th. (dat. to).

Vermächtnis [fɛr'mɛçtnɪs] n (-ses/ -se) will; legacy; bequest.

vermähl|en [fɛr'mɛ:lən] v/t. (no -ge-, h) marry (mit to); sich ~ (mit) marry (s.o.); **2ung** f (-/-en) wedding, marriage.

ver'mehr|en v/t. (no -ge-, h) increase (um by), augment; multiply; add to; durch Zucht ~ propagate; breed; sich ~ increase, augment; multiply (a. biol.); propagate (itself), zo. breed; **2ung** f (-/%-en) increase; addition (gen. to); propagation.

ver'meid|en v/t. (irr. meiden, no -ge-, h) avoid; **2ung** f (-/%-en) avoidance.

ver|meintlich adj. [fɛr'maɪntlɪç] supposed; **~mengen** v/t. (no -ge-, h) mix, mingle, blend.

Vermerk [fɛr'mɛrk] m (-[e]s/-e) note, entry; **2en** v/t. (no -ge-, h) note down, record.

ver'mess|en 1. v/t. (irr. messen, no -ge-, h) measure; survey (land); **2.** adj. presumptuous; **2enheit** f (-/%-en) presumption; **2ung** f (-/-en) measurement; survey (of land).

ver'miete|n v/t. (no -ge-, h) let, esp. Am. rent; hire (out); **2te** f lease; zu ~ on or for hire; Haus zu ~ house to (be) let; **2r** m landlord; **2** lessor; letter, hirer.

ver'mindern v/t. (no -ge-, h) diminish, lessen; reduce, cut.

ver'misch|en v/t. (no -ge-, h) mix, mingle, blend; **~t** adj. mixed; news, etc.: miscellaneous; **2ung** f (-/%-en) mixture.

ver'mi|ssen v/t. (no -ge-, h) miss; **~ßt** adj. [~'mɪst] missing; **2ßte** m, f (-n/-n) missing person; die ~n pl. the missing pl.

vermitt|eln [fɛr'mɪtəln] (no -ge-, h) **1.** v/t. mediate (settlement, peace); procure, get; give (impression, etc.); impart (knowledge) (j-m to s.o.); **2.** v/i. mediate (zwischen dat. between); intercede (bei with, für for), intervene; **2ler** m mediator; go-between; † agent; **2lung** f (-/-en) mediation; intercession, intervention; teleph. (telephone) exchange.

ver'modern v/i. (no -ge-, sein) mo(u)lder, decay, rot.

ver'mögen 1. v/t. (irr. mögen, no -ge-, h): ~ zu inf. be able to inf.; et. ~ bei j-m have influence with s.o.; **2.** 2 n (-s/-) ability, power; property; fortune; means pl.; **2** assets pl.; **~d** adj. wealthy; pred. well off; **2sverhältnisse** pl. pecuniary circumstances pl.

vermut|en [fɛr'mu:tən] v/t. (no -ge-, h) suppose, presume, Am. a. guess; conjecture, surmise; **~lich 1.** adj. presumable; **2.** adv. presumably; I suppose; **2ung** f (-/-en) supposition, presumption; conjecture, surmise.

vernachlässig|en [fɛr'na:xlɛsigən] v/t. (no -ge-, h) neglect; **2ung** f (-/%-en) neglect(ing).

ver'narben v/i. (no -ge-, sein) cicatrize, scar over. [with.\

ver'narrt adj.: ~ in (acc.) infatuated\

ver'nehm|en v/t. (irr. nehmen, no -ge-, h) hear, learn; examine, interrogate; **~lich** adj. audible, distinct;

2ung ⚖ *f* (-/-en) interrogation, questioning; examination.

ver'neig|en *v/refl.* (*no -ge-, h*) bow (*vor dat.* to); **2ung** *f* bow.

vernein|en [fɛr'naɪnən] (*no -ge-, h*) **1.** *v/t.* answer in the negative; deny; **2.** *v/i.* answer in the negative; **~end** *adj.* negative; **2ung** *f* (-/-en) negation; denial; *gr.* negative.

vernicht|en [fɛr'nɪçtən] *v/t.* (*no -ge-, h*) annihilate; destroy; dash (*hopes*); **~end** *adj.* destructive (*a. fig.*); *look:* withering; *criticism:* scathing; *defeat, reply:* crushing; **2ung** *f* (-/⅋-en) annihilation; destruction.

ver'nickeln [fɛr'nɪkəln] *v/t.* (*no -ge-, h*) nickel(-plate); **~'nieten** *v/t.* (*no -ge-, h*) rivet.

Vernunft [fɛr'nʊnft] *f* (-/*no pl.*) reason; **~** *annehmen* listen to or hear reason; *j-n zur* **~** *bringen* bring s.o. to reason or to his senses.

vernünftig *adj.* [fɛr'nʏnftɪç] rational; reasonable; sensible.

ver'öden (*no -ge-*) **1.** *v/t.* (*h*) make desolate; **2.** *v/i.* (*sein*) become desolate.

ver'öffentlich|en *v/t.* (*no -ge-, h*) publish; **2ung** *f* (-/-en) publication.

ver'ordn|en *v/t.* (*no -ge-, h*) decree; order (*a. ⚕*); **~** prescribe (*j-m* to or for s.o.); **2ung** *f* decree, order; **⚕** prescription.

ver'pachten *v/t.* (*no -ge-, h*) rent, ⚖ lease (*building, land*).

Ver'pächter *m* landlord, ⚖ lessor.

ver'pack|en *v/t.* (*no -ge-, h*) pack (up); wrap up; **2ung** *f* packing (*material*); wrapping.

ver'passen *v/t.* (*no -ge-, h*) miss (*train, opportunity, etc.*); **~patzen** F [~'patsən] *v/t.* (*no -ge-, h*) *s.* verpfuschen; **~'pesten** *v/t.* (*no -ge-, h*) *fumes:* contaminate (*the air*); **~'pfänden** *v/t.* (*no -ge-, h*) pawn, pledge (*a. fig.*); mortgage.

ver'pflanz|en *v/t.* (*no -ge-, h*) transplant (*a. ⚕*); **2ung** *f* transplantation; **⚕** *a.* transplant.

ver'pfleg|en *v/t.* (*no -ge-, h*) board; supply with food, victual; **2ung** *f* (-/⅋-en) board; food-supply; provisions *pl.*

ver'pflicht|en *v/t.* (*no -ge-, h*) oblige; engage; **2ung** *f* (-/-en) obligation; duty; †, ⚖ liability; engagement, commitment.

ver'pfusch|en F *v/t.* (*no -ge-, h*) bungle, botch; make a mess of; **~t** *adj. life:* ruined, wrecked.

ver'pönt *adj.* [fɛr'pøːnt] taboo; **~'prügeln** F *v/t.* (*no -ge-, h*) thrash, flog, F wallop; **~'puffen** *fig. v/i.* (*no -ge-, sein*) fizzle out.

Ver'putz ⚠ *m* (-es/⅋-e) plaster; **2en** ⚠ *v/t.* (*no -ge-, h*) plaster.

ver'quicken [fɛr'kvɪkən] *v/t.* (*no -ge-, h*) mix up; **~'quollen** *adj. wood:* warped; *face:* bloated; *eyes:* swollen; **~rammeln** [~'raməln] *v/t.* (*no -ge-, h*) bar(ricade).

Verrat [fɛr'raːt] *m* (-[e]s/*no pl.*) betrayal (*an dat.* of); treachery (to); ⚖ treason (to); **2en** *v/t.* (*irr. raten, no -ge-, h*) betray, give *s.o.* away; give away (*secret*); *sich* **~** betray o.s., give o.s. away.

Verräter [fɛr'rɛːtər] *m* (-s/-) traitor (*an dat.* to); **2isch** *adj.* treacherous; *fig.* telltale.

ver'rechn|en *v/t.* (*no -ge-, h*) reckon up; charge; settle; set off (*mit* against); account for (*j.*); **~** *mit* offset against; *sich* **~** miscalculate, make a mistake (*a. fig.*); *fig.* be mistaken; *sich um e-e Mark* **~** be one mark out; **2ung** *f* settlement; clearing; booking or charging (*to account*); **2ungsscheck** *m* collection-only cheque or *Am.* check.

ver'regnet *adj.* rainy, rain-spoilt.

ver'reis|en *v/i.* (*no -ge-, sein*) go on a journey; **~t** *adj.* out of town; (*geschäftlich*) **~** away (on business).

verrenk|en [fɛr'rɛŋkən] *v/t.* (*no -ge-, h*) ⚕: wrench; dislocate, luxate; *sich et.* **~** dislocate or luxate s.th.; *sich den Hals* **~** crane one's neck; **2ung** ⚕ *f* (-/-en) dislocation, luxation.

ver'richten *v/t.* (*no -ge-, h*) do, perform; execute; *sein Gebet* **~** say one's prayer(s); **~'riegeln** *v/t.* (*no -ge-, h*) bolt, bar.

verringer|n [fɛr'rɪŋərn] *v/t.* (*no -ge-, h*) diminish, lessen; reduce, cut; *sich* **~** diminish, lessen; **2ung** *f* (-/-en) diminution; reduction, cut.

ver'rosten *v/i.* (*no -ge-, sein*) rust; **~rotten** [~'rɔtən] *v/i.* (*no -ge-, sein*) rot.

ver'rück|en *v/t.* (*no -ge-, h*) displace, (re)move, shift; **~t** *adj.* mad, crazy (*both a. fig.: nach* about); *wie* **~** like mad; *j-n* **~** *machen* drive s.o. mad; **2te** (-n/-n) **1.** m lunatic, madman; **2.** f lunatic, madwoman; **2theit** f (-/-en) madness; foolish action; craze.

Ver'ruf m (-[e]s/no pl.): in ~ bringen bring discredit (up)on; in ~ kommen get into discredit; **2en** adj. ill-reputed, ill-famed.

ver'rutsch|en v/i. (no -ge-, sein) slip; **~t** adj. not straight.

Vers [fɛrs] m (-es/-e) verse.

ver'sagen 1. v/t. (no -ge-, h) refuse, deny (j-m et. s.o. s.th.); sich et. ~ deny o.s. s.th.; **2.** v/i. (no -ge-, h) fail, break down; gun: misfire; **3.** 2 n (-s/no pl.) failure. [fer. fail-|

ver'sager m (-s/-) misfire; p. fail-

ver'salzen v/t. (irr. salzen,] no -ge-, h) oversalt; F fig. spoil.

ver'samm|eln v/t. (no -ge-, h) assemble; sich ~ assemble, meet; **2lung** f assembly, meeting.

Versand [fɛr'zant] m (-[e]s/no pl.) dispatch, Am. a. shipment; mailing; ~ ins Ausland a. export(ation); **~abteilung** f forwarding department; **~geschäft** n, **~haus** n mailorder business or firm or house.

ver'säum|en v/t. (no -ge-, h) neglect (one's duty, etc.); miss (opportunity, etc.); lose (time); ~ zu inf. fail or omit to inf.; **2nis** n (-ses/-se) neglect, omission, failure.

ver'|schachern F v/t. (no -ge-, h) barter (away); **~'schaffen** v/t. (no -ge-, h) procure, get; sich ~ obtain, get; raise (money); sich Respekt ~ make o.s. respected; **~'schämt** adj. bashful; **~'schanzen** v/refl. (no -ge-, h) entrench o.s.; sich ~ hinter (dat.) (take) shelter behind; **~'schärfen** v/t. (no -ge-, h) heighten, intensify; aggravate; sich ~ get worse; **~'scheiden** v/i. (irr. scheiden, no -ge-, sein) pass away; **~'schenken** v/t. (no -ge-, h) give s.th. away; make a present of s.th.; **~'scherzen** v/t. and v/refl. (no -ge-, h) forfeit; **~'scheuchen** v/t. (no -ge-, h) frighten or scare away; fig. banish; **~'schicken** v/t. (no -ge-, h) send (away), dispatch, forward.

ver'schieb|en v/t. (irr. schieben, no -ge-, h) displace, shift, (re)move, ⚙ shunt; put off, postpone; F fig. ⚙ sell underhand; sich ~ shift; **2ung** f shift(ing); postponement.

verschieden adj. [fɛr'ʃiːdən] differ-

ent (von from); dissimilar, unlike; aus ~en Gründen for various or several reasons; Verschiedenes various things pl., esp. ⚙ sundries pl.; **~artig** adj. of a different kind, various; **2heit** f (-/-en) difference; diversity, variety; **~tlich** adv. repeatedly; at times.

ver'schiff|en v/t. (no -ge-, h) ship; **2ung** f (-/⚙-en) shipment.

ver'schimmeln v/i. (no -ge-, sein) get mo(u)ldy, Am. mo(u)ld; **~'schlafen 1.** v/t. (irr. schlafen, no -ge-, h) miss by sleeping; sleep (afternoon, etc.) away; sleep off (headache, etc.); **2.** v/i. (irr. schlafen, no -ge-, h) oversleep (o.s.); **3.** adj. sleepy, drowsy.

Ver'schlag m shed; box; crate; **2en** [~gən] **1.** v/t. (irr. schlagen, no -ge-, h) board up; nail up; es ver schlug ihm die Sprache it dum(b)-founded him; **2.** adj. cunning; eyes: a. shifty; **~enheit** f (-/no pl.) cunning.

verschlechter|n [fɛr'ʃlɛçtərn] v/t. (no -ge-, h) deteriorate, make worse; sich ~ deteriorate, get worse; **2ung** f (-/⚙-en) deterioration; change for the worse.

ver'schleiern v/t. (no -ge-, h) veil (a. fig.).

Verschleiß [fɛr'ʃlaɪs] m (-es/⚙-e) wear (and tear); **2en** v/t. ([irr.,] no -ge-, h) wear out.

ver'|schleppen v/t. (no -ge-, h) carry off; pol. displace (person); abduct; kidnap; delay, protract; neglect (disease); **~'schleudern** v/t. (no -ge-, h) dissipate, waste; ⚙ sell at a loss, sell dirt-cheap; **~'schließen** v/t. (irr. schließen, no -ge-, h) shut, close; lock (door); lock up (house).

verschlimmern [fɛr'ʃlɪmərn] v/t. (no -ge-, h) make worse, aggravate; sich ~ get worse.

ver'schlingen v/t. (irr. schlingen, no -ge-, h) devour; wolf (down) (one's food); intertwine, entwine, interlace; sich ~ intertwine, entwine, interlace.

verschli|ß [fɛr'ʃlɪs] pret. of ver schleißen; **~ssen** [~sən] p.p. of ver schleißen.

verschlossen adj. [fɛr'ʃlɔsən] closed, shut; fig. reserved; **2heit** f (-/no pl.) reserve.

ver'schlucken v/t. (no -ge-, h) swallow (up); sich ~ swallow the wrong way.

Ver'schluß m lock; clasp; lid; plug; stopper (of bottle); seal; fastener, fastening; phot. shutter; unter ~ under lock and key.

ver|'schmachten v/i. (no -ge-, sein) languish, pine away; vor Durst ~ die or be dying of thirst, be parched with thirst; ~'schmähen v/t. (no -ge-, h) disdain, scorn.

ver'schmelz|en (irr. schmelzen, no -ge-) v/t. (h) and v/i. (sein) melt, fuse (a. fig.); blend; fig.: amalgamate; merge (mit in, into); 2ung f (-/-en) fusion; † merger; fig. amalgamation.

ver|'schmerzen v/t. (no -ge-, h) get over (the loss of); ~'schmieren v/t. (no -ge-, h) smear (over); blur; ~schmitzt adj. [~'ſmitst] cunning; roguish; arch; ~'schmutzen (no -ge-) 1. v/t. (h) soil, dirty; pollute (water); 2. v/i. (sein) get dirty; ~'schnaufen F v/i. and v/refl. (no -ge-, h) stop for breath; ~'schneiden v/t. (irr. schneiden, no -ge-) cut badly; blend (wine, etc.); geld, castrate; ~'schneit adj. covered with snow; mountains: a. snow-capped; roofs: a. snow-covered.

Ver'schnitt m (-[e]s/no pl.) blend.

ver'schnupf|en F fig. v/t. (no -ge-, h) nettle, pique; ~t ♣ adj.: ~ sein have a cold.

ver|'schnüren v/t. (no -ge-, h) tie up, cord; ~schollen adj. [~'ſɔlən] not heard of again; missing; ⚔ presumed dead; ~'schonen v/t. (no -ge-, h) spare; j-n mit et. ~ spare s.o. s.th.

verschöne(r)n [fɛr'ſøːnə(r)n] v/t. (no -ge-, h) embellish, beautify; 2rung f (-/-en) embellishment.

ver|'schossen adj. [fɛr'ſɔsən] colour: faded; F ~ sein in (acc.) be madly in love with; ~schränken [~'ſrɛŋkən] v/t. (no -ge-, h) cross, fold (one's arms).

ver'schreib|en v/t. (irr. schreiben, no -ge-, h) use up (in writing); ⚕ prescribe (j-m for s.o.); ⚖ assign (j-m to s.o.); sich ~ make a slip of the pen; sich e-r Sache ~ devote o.s. to s.th.; 2ung f (-/-en) assignment; prescription.

ver|schroben adj. [fɛr'ſroːbən] ec-

centric, queer, odd; ~'schrotten v/t. (no -ge-, h) scrap; ~schüchtert adj. [~'ſyçtərt] intimidated.

ver'schulden 1. v/t. (no -ge-, h) be guilty of; be the cause of; 2. 2 n (-s/no pl.) fault.

ver|'schuldet adj. indebted, in debt; ~'schütten v/t. (no -ge-, h) spill (liquid); block (up) (road); bury s.o. alive; ~schwägert adj. [~'ſvɛːgərt] related by marriage; ~'schweigen v/t. (irr. schweigen, no -ge-, h) conceal (j-m et. s.th. from s.o.).

verschwend|en [fɛr'ſvɛndən] v/t. (no -ge-, h) waste, squander (an acc. on); lavish (on); 2er m (-s/-) spendthrift, prodigal; ~erisch adj. prodigal, lavish (both: mit of); wasteful; 2ung f (-/-en) waste; extravagance.

verschwiegen adj. [fɛr'ſviːgən] discreet; place: secret, secluded; 2heit f (-/no pl.) discretion; secrecy.

ver|'schwimmen v/i. (irr. schwimmen, no -ge-, sein) become indistinct or blurred; ~'schwinden v/i. (irr. schwinden, no -ge-, sein) disappear, vanish; F verschwinde! go away!, sl. beat it!; 2'schwinden n (-s/no pl.) disappearance; ~schwommen adj. [~'ſvɔmən] vague (a. fig.); blurred; fig. woolly.

ver'schwör|en v/refl. (irr. schwören, no -ge-, h) conspire; 2er m (-s/-) conspirator; 2ung f (-/-en) conspiracy, plot.

ver'seh|en 1. v/t. (irr. sehen, no -ge-, h) fill (an office); look after (house, etc.); mit et. ~ furnish or supply with; sich ~ make a mistake; ehe man sich's versieht all of a sudden; 2. 2 n (-s/-) oversight, mistake, slip; aus ~ = ~tlich adv. by mistake; inadvertently. [disabled person.]

Versehrte [fɛr'zeːrtə] m (-n/-n))

ver'send|en v/t. ([irr. senden,] no -ge-, h) send, dispatch, forward, Am. ship; by water: ship; ins Ausland ~ a. export; 2ung f (-/-en) dispatch, shipment, forwarding.

ver|'sengen v/t. (no -ge-, h) singe; scorch; ~'senken v/t. (no -ge-, h) sink; sich ~ in (acc.) immerse o.s. in; ~sessen adj. [~'zɛsən]: ~ auf (acc.) bent on, mad after.

ver'setz|en v/t. (no -ge-, h) displace, remove; transfer (*officer*); *at school*: remove, move up, *Am.* promote; transplant (*tree, etc.*); pawn, pledge; F *fig.* stand (*lover, etc.*) up; ~ *in* (*acc.*) put *or* place into (*situation, condition*); *j-m e-n Schlag* ~ give *or* deal s.o. a blow; *in Angst* ~ frighten *or* terrify *s.o.*; *in den Ruhestand* ~ pension *s.o.* off, retire *s.o.*; *versetzt werden* be transferred; *at school*: go up; ~ *Sie sich in m-e Lage* put *or* place yourself in my position; *Wein mit Wasser* ~ mix wine with water, add water to wine; *et.* ~ reply s.th.; ⚌**ung** *f* (-/-en) removal; transfer; *at school*: remove, *Am.* promotion.

ver'seuch|en *v/t.* (*no* -ge-, *h*) infect; contaminate; ⚌**ung** *f* (-/⚌-en) infection; contamination.

ver'sicher|n *v/t.* (*no* -ge-, *h*) assure (*a. one's life*); protest, affirm; insure (*one's property or life*); *sich* ~ insure *or* assure o.s.; *sich* ~ (, *daß*) make *or* make sure (that); ⚌**te** *m, f* (-n/-n) insurant, *the* insured *or* assured, policy-holder; ⚌**ung** *f* assurance, affirmation; insurance; (life-)assurance; insurance company.

Ver'sicherungs|gesellschaft *f* insurance company; ~**police** *f*, ~**schein** *m* policy of assurance, insurance policy.

ver'sicker|n *v/i.* (*no* -ge-, *sein*) trickle away; ~**siegeln** *v/t.* (*no* -ge-, *h*) seal (up); ~**siegen** *v/i.* (*no* -ge-, *sein*) dry up, run dry; ~**silbern** *v/t.* (*no* -ge-, *h*) silver; F *fig.* realize, convert into cash; ~**'sinken** *v/i.* (*irr. sinken, no* -ge-, *sein*) sink; *s.* **versunken**; ~**sinnbildlichen** *v/t.* (*no* -ge-, *h*) symbolize.

Version [vɛr'zjoːn] *f* (-/-en) version.

'Versmaß *n* met|re, *Am.* -er.

versöhn|en [fɛr'zøːnən] *v/t.* (*no* -ge-, *h*) reconcile (*mit* to, with); *sich* (*wieder*) ~ become reconciled; ~**lich** *adj.* conciliatory; ⚌**ung** *f* (-/⚌-en) reconciliation.

ver'sorg|en *v/t.* (*no* -ge-, *h*) provide (*mit* with), supply (with); take care of, look after; ~**t** *adj.* [⚌kt] provided for; ⚌**ung** [⚌guŋ] *f* (-/-en) providing (*mit* with), supplying (with); supply, provision.

ver'spät|en *v/refl.* (*no* -ge-, *h*) be late; ~**et** *adj.* belated, late, *Am.*

tardy; ⚌**ung** *f* (-/-en) lateness, *Am.* tardiness; ~ *haben* be late; *mit 2 Stunden* ~ two hours behind schedule.

ver'|speisen *v/t.* (*no* -ge-, *h*) eat (up); ~**'sperren** *v/t.* (*no* -ge-, *h*) lock (up); bar, block (up), obstruct (*a. view*); ~**'spielen** *v/t.* (*no* -ge-, *h*) at cards, *etc.*: lose (*money*); ~**spielt** *adj.* playful; ~**'spotten** *v/t.* (*no* -ge-, *h*) scoff at, mock (at), deride, ridicule; ~**'sprechen** *v/t.* (*irr. sprechen, no* -ge-, *h*) promise; *sich* ~ make a mistake in speaking; *sich viel* ~ *von* expect much of; ⚌**'sprechen** *n* (-s/⚌-) promise; ~**'sprühen** *v/t.* (*no* -ge-, *h*) spray; ~**'spüren** *v/t.* (*no* -ge-, *h*) feel; perceive, be conscious of.

ver'staatlich|en *v/t.* (*no* -ge-, *h*) nationalize; ⚌**ung** *f* (-/⚌-en) nationalization.

Verstand [fɛr'ʃtant] *m* (-[e]s/*no pl.*) understanding, intelligence, intellect, brains *pl.*; mind, wits *pl.*; reason; (common) sense.

Verstandes|kraft [fɛr'ʃtandəs-] *f* intellectual power *or* faculty; ⚌**mäßig** *adj.* rational; intellectual; ~**mensch** *m* matter-of-fact person.

verständ|ig *adj.* [fɛr'ʃtɛndɪç] intelligent; reasonable, sensible; judicious; ~**igen** [⚌gən] *v/t.* (*no* -ge-, *h*) inform (*von* of), notify (of); *sich mit j-m* ~ make o.s. understood to s.o.; come to an understanding with s.o.; ⚌**igung** [⚌guŋ] *f* (-/⚌-en) information; understanding, agreement; *teleph.* communication; ~**lich** *adj.* [⚌tlɪç] intelligible; understandable; *j-m et.* ~ *machen* make s.th. clear to s.o.; *sich* ~ *machen* make o.s. understood.

Verständnis [fɛr'ʃtɛntnɪs] *n* (-ses/⚌-se) comprehension, understanding; insight; appreciation (*für* of); ~ *haben für* appreciate; ⚌**los** *adj.* uncomprehending; *look, etc.*: blank; unappreciative; ⚌**voll** *adj.* understanding; appreciative; sympathetic; *look*: knowing.

ver'stärk|en *v/t.* (*no* -ge-, *h*) strengthen, reinforce (*a.* ⊕, ✕); amplify (*radio signals, etc.*); intensify; ⚌**er** *m* (-s/-) in radio, *etc.*: amplifier; ⚌**ung** *f* (-/⚌-en) strengthening, reinforcement (*a.* ✕); amplification; intensification.

U
V

ver'staub|en v/i. (no -ge-, sein) get dusty; **~t** adj. [~pt] dusty.

ver'stauch|en ✘ v/t. (no -ge-, h) sprain; sich den Fuß ~ sprain one's foot; **♀ung** ✘ f (-/-en) sprain.

ver'stauen v/t. (no -ge-, h) stow away.

Versteck [fɛr'ʃtɛk] n (-[e]s/-e) hiding-place; for gangsters, etc.: Am. F a. hide-out; ~ spielen play at hide-and-seek; **♀en** v/t. (no -ge-, h) hide, conceal; sich ~ hide.

ver'stehen v/t. (irr. stehen, no -ge-, h) understand, see, F get; comprehend; realize; know (language); es ~ zu inf. know how to inf.; Spaß ~ take a joke; zu ~ geben intimate; ~ Sie? do you see?; ich ~! I see!; verstanden? (do you) understand?, F (do you) get me?; falsch ~ misunderstand; ~ Sie mich recht! don't misunderstand me!; was ~ Sie unter (dat.)? what do you mean or understand by ...?; er versteht et. davon he knows a thing or two about it; sich ~ understand one another; sich ~ auf (acc.) know well, be an expert at or in; sich mit j-m gut ~ get on well with s.o.; es versteht sich von selbst it goes without saying.

ver'steifen v/t. (no -ge-, h) ⊕ strut, brace; stiffen; sich ~ stiffen; sich ~ auf (acc.) make a point of, insist on.

ver'steiger|n v/t. (no -ge-, h) (sell by or Am. at) auction; **♀ung** f (sale by or Am. at) auction, auction-sale.

ver'steinern (no -ge-) v/t. (h) and v/i. (sein) turn into stone, petrify (both a. fig.).

ver'stell|bar adj. adjustable; **~en** v/t. (no -ge-, h) shift; adjust; disarrange; bar, block (up), obstruct; disguise (voice, etc.); sich ~ play or act a part; dissemble, feign; **♀ung** f (-/~-en) disguise; dissimulation.

ver|'steuern v/t. (no -ge-, h) pay duty or tax on; **~stiegen** fig. adj. [~'ʃtiːɡən] eccentric.

ver'stimm|en v/t. (no -ge-, h) put out of tune; fig. put out of humo(u)r; **~t** adj. out of tune; fig. out of humo(u)r, F cross; **♀ung** f ill humo(u)r; disagreement; ill feeling.

ver'stockt adj. stubborn, obdurate; **♀heit** f (-/no pl.) obduracy.

verstohlen adj. [fɛr'ʃtoːlən] furtive.

ver'stopf|en v/t. (no -ge-, h) stop (up); clog, block (up), obstruct; jam, block (passage, street); ✘ constipate; **♀ung** ✘ f (-/~-en) constipation.

verstorben adj. [fɛr'ʃtɔrbən] late, deceased; **♀e** m, f (-n/-n) the deceased, Am. ⚖ a. decedent; die ~n pl. the deceased pl., the departed pl.

ver'stört adj. scared; distracted, bewildered; **♀heit** f (-/no pl.) distraction, bewilderment.

Ver'stoß m offen|ce, Am. -se; contravention (gegen of law); infringement (on trade name, etc.); blunder; **♀en** (irr. stoßen, no -ge-, h) 1. v/t. expel (aus from); repudiate, disown (wife, child, etc.); 2. v/i.: ~ gegen offend against; contravene (law); infringe (rule, etc.).

ver|'streichen (irr. streichen, no -ge-) 1. v/i. (sein) time: pass, elapse; expire; 2. v/t. (h) spread (butter, etc.); **~'streuen** v/t. (no -ge-, h) scatter.

verstümmel|n [fɛr'ʃtyməln] v/t. (no -ge-, h) mutilate; garble (text, etc.); **♀ung** f (-/-en) mutilation.

ver'stummen v/i. (no -ge-, sein) grow silent or dumb.

Verstümmlung [fɛr'ʃtymluŋ] f (-/-en) mutilation.

Versuch [fɛr'zuːx] m (-[e]s/-e) attempt, trial; phys., etc.: experiment; e-n ~ machen mit give s.o. or s.th. a trial; try one's hand at s.th.; have a go at s.th.; **♀en** v/t. (no -ge-, h) try, attempt; taste; j-n ~ tempt s.o.; es ~ mit give s.o. or s.th. a trial.

Ver'suchs|anstalt f research institute; **~kaninchen** fig. n guinea-pig; **♀weise** adv. by way of trial or (an) experiment; on trial; **~zweck** m: zu ~en pl. for experimental purposes pl.

Ver'suchung f (-/-en) temptation; j-n in ~ bringen tempt s.o.; in ~ sein be tempted.

ver|'sündigen v/refl. (no -ge-, h) sin (an dat. against); **~sunken** fig. adj. [~'zuŋkən]: ~ in (acc.) absorbed or lost in; **~'süßen** v/t. (no -ge-, h) sweeten.

ver'tag|en v/t. (no -ge-, h) adjourn; parl. prorogue; sich ~ adjourn, Am.

a. recess; **2ung** *f* adjournment; *parl.* prorogation.

ver'tauschen *v/t.* (*no* -ge-, *h*) exchange (*mit* for).

verteidig|en [fɛr'taɪdɪgən] *v/t.* (*no* -ge-, *h*) defend; *sich ~* defend o.s.; **2er** *m* (-s/-) defender; *tt, fig.* advocate; *tt* counsel for the defen|ce, *Am.* -se, *Am.* attorney for the defendant *or* defense; *football:* fullback; **2ung** *f* (-/~-en) defen|ce, *Am.* -se.

Ver'teidigungs|bündnis *n* defensive alliance; **~minister** *m* minister of defence; *Brt.* Minister of Defence, *Am.* Secretary of Defense; **~ministerium** *n* ministry of defence; *Brt.* Ministry of Defence, *Am.* Department of Defense.

ver'teil|en *v/t.* (*no* -ge-, *h*) distribute; spread (*colour, etc.*); **2er** *m* (-s/-) distributor; **2ung** *f* (-/~-en) distribution.

ver'teuern *v/t.* (*no* -ge-, *h*) raise *or* increase the price of.

ver'tief|en *v/t.* (*no* -ge-, *h*) deepen (*a. fig.*); *sich ~* deepen; *sich ~ in* (*acc.*) plunge in(to); become absorbed in; **2ung** *f* (-/~-en) hollow, cavity; recess.

vertikal *adj.* [vɛrti'kɑːl] vertical.

ver'tilg|en *v/t.* (*no* -ge-, *h*) exterminate; F consume, eat (up) (*food*); **2ung** *f* (-/~-en) extermination.

ver'tonen ♪ *v/t.* (*no* -ge-, *h*) set to music.

Vertrag [fɛr'trɑːk] *m* (-[e]s/~e) agreement, contract; *pol.* treaty; **2en** [~gən] *v/t.* (*irr.* tragen, *no* -ge-, *h*) endure, bear, stand; *diese Speise kann ich nicht ~* this food does not agree with me; *sich ~ things:* be compatible *or* consistent; *colours:* harmonize; *p.:* agree; get on with one another; *sich wieder ~* be reconciled, make it up; **2lich** [~klɪç] **1.** *adj.* contractual, stipulated; **2.** *adv.* as stipulated; *~ verpflichtet sein* be bound by contract; *sich ~ verpflichten* contract (*zu* for *s.th.*; *zu inf.* to *inf.*).

verträglich *adj.* [fɛr'trɛːklɪç] sociable.

Ver'trags|bruch *m* breach of contract; **2brüchig** *adj.*: *~ werden* commit a breach of contract; **~entwurf** *m* draft agreement; **~partner** *m* party to a contract.

ver'trauen 1. *v/i.* (*no* -ge-, *h*) trust (*j-m s.o.*); *~ auf* (*acc.*) trust *or* confide in; **2.** **2** *n* (-s/*no pl.*) confidence, trust; *im ~* confidentially, between you and me; **~erweckend** *adj.* inspiring confidence; promising.

Ver'trauens|bruch *m* breach *or* betrayal of trust; **~frage** *parl.* *f:* *die ~ stellen* put the question of confidence; **~mann** *m* (-[e]s/~er, *Vertrauensleute*) spokesman; shop-steward; confidential agent; **~sache** *f:* *das ist ~* that is a matter of confidence; **~stellung** *f* position of trust; **2voll** *adj.* trustful, trusting; **~votum** *parl.* *n* vote of confidence; **2würdig** *adj.* trustworthy, reliable.

ver'traulich *adj.* confidential, in confidence; intimate, familiar; **2keit** *f* (-/-en) confidence; intimacy, familiarity.

ver'traut *adj.* intimate, familiar; **2e** (-n/-n) **1.** *m* confidant, intimate friend; **2.** *f* confidante, intimate friend; **2heit** *f* (-/~-en) familiarity.

ver'treib|en *v/t.* (*irr.* treiben, *no* -ge-, *h*) drive away; expel (*aus* from); turn out; ✝ sell, distribute (*goods*); *sich die Zeit ~* pass one's time, kill time; **2ung** *f* (-/~-en) expulsion.

ver'tret|en *v/t.* (*irr.* treten, *no* -ge-, *h*) represent (*s.o., firm, etc.*); substitute for *s.o.*; attend to, look after (*s.o.'s interests*); hold (*view*); *parl.* sit for (*borough*); answer for *s.th.*; *j-s Sache ~ tt* plead s.o.'s case *or* cause; *sich den Fuß ~* sprain one's foot; F *sich die Beine ~* stretch one's legs; **2er** *m* (-s/-) representative; ✝ *a.* agent, proxy, agent; substitute, deputy; exponent; (sales) representative; door-to-door salesman; commercial travel(l)er, *esp. Am.* travel(l)ing salesman; **2ung** *f* (-/-en) representation (*a. pol.*); agency; *in office:* substitution; *in ~* by proxy; *gen.:* acting for.

Vertrieb ✝ [fɛr'triːp] *m* (-[e]s/-e) sale; distribution; **~ene** [~bənə] *m,f* (-n/-n) expellee.

ver'trocknen *v/i.* (*no* -ge-, *sein*) dry up; **~trödeln** F *v/t.* (*no* -ge-, *h*) dawdle away, waste (*time*); **~trösten** *v/t.* (*no* -ge-, *h*) put off; **~tuschen** F *v/t.* (*no* -ge-, *h*) hush up; **~übeln** *v/t.* (*no* -ge-, *h*) take *s.th.*

amiss; **~'üben** v/t. (no -ge-, h) commit, perpetrate.

ver'unglück|en v/i. (no -ge-, sein) meet with or have an accident; F fig. fail, go wrong; tödlich ~ be killed in an accident; **2te** m, f (-n/-n) casualty.

verun|reinigen [fer'unraınigən] v/t. (no -ge-, h) soil, dirty; defile; contaminate (air); pollute (water); **~stalten** [~ʃtaltən] v/t. (no -ge-, h) disfigure.

ver'untreu|en v/t. (no -ge-, h) embezzle; **2ung** f (-/-en) embezzlement.

ver'ursachen v/t. (no -ge-, h) cause.

ver'urteil|en v/t. (no -ge-, h) condemn (zu to) (a. fig.), sentence (to); convict (wegen of); **2te** m, f (-n/-n) convict; **2ung** f (-/-en) condemnation (a. fig.), conviction.

ver|vielfältigen [fer'fi:lfɛltıgən] v/t. (no -ge-, h) manifold; **~vollkomm-nen** [~'fɔlkɔmnən] v/t. (no -ge-, h) perfect; sich ~ perfect o.s.

vervollständig|en [fer'fɔlʃtɛndıgən] v/t. (no -ge-, h) complete; **2ung** f (-/~-en) completion.

ver|'wachsen 1. v/i. (irr. wachsen, no -ge-, sein): miteinander ~ grow together; **2.** adj. deformed; ♬ humpbacked, hunchbacked; ~'wackeln phot. v/t. (no -ge-, h) blur.

ver'wahr|en v/t. (no -ge-, h) keep; sich ~ gegen protest against; **~lost** adj. [~lo:st] child, garden, etc.: uncared-for, neglected; degenerate; **2ung** f keeping; charge; custody; fig. protest; **j-m et. in ~ geben** give s.th. into s.o.'s charge; **in ~ nehmen** take charge of. [fig. deserted.]

verwaist adj. [fer'vaıst] orphan(ed);)

ver'walt|en v/t. (no -ge-, h) administer, manage; **2er** m (-s/-) administrator, manager; steward (of estate); **2ung** f (-/-en) administration; management.

ver'wand|eln v/t. (no -ge-, h) change, turn, transform; sich ~ change (all: in acc. into); **2lung** f (-/-en) change; transformation.

verwandt adj. [fer'vant] related (mit to); languages, tribes, etc.: kindred; languages, sciences: cognate (with); pred. akin to (a. fig.); **2e** m, f (-n/-n) relative, relation; **2schaft** f (-/-en) relationship; re-

lations pl.; geistige ~ congeniality.

ver'warn|en v/t. (no -ge-, h) caution; **2ung** f caution.

ver'wässern v/t. (no -ge-, h) water (down), dilute; fig. water down, dilute.

ver'wechs|eln v/t. (no -ge-, h) mistake (mit for); confound, mix up, confuse (all: mit with); **2(e)-lung** f (-/-en) mistake; confusion.

verwegen adj. [fer've:gən] daring, bold, audacious; **2heit** f (-/~-en) boldness, audacity, daring.

ver|'wehren v/t. (no -ge-, h): j-m et. ~ (de)bar s.o. from (doing) s.th.; **den Zutritt ~** deny or refuse admittance (zu to); ~'weichlicht adj. effeminate, soft.

ver'weiger|n v/t. (no -ge-, h) deny, refuse; disobey (order); **2ung** f denial, refusal.

ver'weilen v/i. (no -ge-, h) stay, linger; bei et. ~ dwell (up)on s.th.

Verweis [fer'vaıs] m (-es/-e) reprimand; rebuke, reproof; reference (auf acc. to); **2en** [~zən] v/t. (irr. weisen, no -ge-, h): j-n des Landes ~ expel s.o. from Germany, etc.; j-m et. ~ reprimand s.o. for s.th.; j-n ~ auf (acc.) or an (acc.) refer s.o. to.

ver'welken v/i. (no -ge-, sein) fade, wither (up).

ver'wend|en v/t. (irr. wenden,) no -ge-, h) employ, use; apply (für for); spend (time, etc.) (auf acc. on); sich bei j-m ~ für intercede with s.o. for; **2ung** f (-/~-en) use, employment; application; keine ~ haben für have no use for.

ver'werf|en v/t. (irr. werfen, no -ge-, h) reject; ♫ quash (verdict); **~lich** adj. abominable.

ver'werten v/t. (no -ge-, h) turn to account, utilize.

verwes|en [fer've:zən] v/i. (no -ge-, sein) rot, decay; **2ung** f (-/~-en) decay.

ver'wick|eln v/t. (no -ge-, h) entangle (in acc. in); sich ~ entangle o.s. (in) (a. fig.); ~elt fig. adj. complicated; **2(e)lung** f (-/-en) entanglement; fig. a. complication.

ver'wilder|n v/i. (no -ge-, sein) run wild; sich ~ wild; **~t** adj. garden, etc.: uncultivated, weed-grown; fig. wild, unruly. [-ge-, h) get over s.th.)

ver'winden v/t. (irr. winden, no)

ver'wirklich|en v/t. (no -ge-, h) realize; sich ~ be realized, esp. Am. materialize; come true; 2ung f (-/~-en) realization.

ver'wirr|en v/t. (no -ge-, h) entangle; j-n ~ confuse s.o.; embarrass s.o.; ~t fig. adj. confused; embarrassed; 2ung fig. f (-/-en) confusion.

ver'wischen v/t. (no -ge-, h) wipe or blot out; efface (a. fig.); blur, obscure; cover up (one's tracks).

ver'wittern geol. v/i. (no -ge-, sein) weather; ~t adj. geol. weathered; weather-beaten (a. fig.).

ver'witwet adj. widowed.

verwöhn|en [fɛr'vø:nən] v/t. (no -ge-, h) spoil; ~t adj. fastidious, particular.

verworren adj. [fɛr'vɔrən] ideas, etc.: confused; situation, plot: intricate.

verwund|bar adj. [fɛr'vuntba:r] vulnerable (a. fig.); ~en [~dən] v/t. (no -ge-, h) wound.

ver'wunder|lich adj. astonishing; 2ung f (-/~-en) astonishment.

Ver'wund|ete ✕ m (-n/-n) wounded (soldier), casualty; ~ung f (-/-en) wound, injury.

ver'wünsch|en v/t. (no -ge-, h) curse; 2ung f (-/-en) curse.

ver'wüst|en v/t. (no -ge-, h) lay waste, devastate, ravage (a. fig.); 2ung f (-/-en) devastation, ravage.

verzag|en [fɛr'tsa:gən] v/i. (no -ge-, h) despond (an dat. of); ~t adj. [~kt] despondent; 2theit [~kt-] f (-/no pl.) despondence, -cy.

ver|'zählen v/refl. (no -ge-, h) miscount; ~zärteln [~'tsɛːrtəln] v/t. (no -ge-, h) coddle, pamper; ~'zaubern v/t. (no -ge-, h) bewitch, enchant, charm; ~'zehren v/t. (no -ge-, h) consume (a. fig.).

ver'zeichn|en v/t. (no -ge-, h) note down; record; list; fig. distort; ~ können, zu ~ haben score (success, etc.), ~et paint. adj. out of drawing; 2is n (-ses/-se) list, catalog(ue); register; inventory; index (of book); table, schedule.

verzeih|en [fɛr'tsaɪən] (irr. zeihen, h) 1. v/i. pardon, forgive; ~ Sie! I beg your pardon!; excuse me!; sorry!; 2. v/t. pardon, forgive (j-m et. s.o. s.th.).; ~lich adj. pardonable; 2ung f (-/no pl.) pardon; ~! I beg your pardon!, sorry!

ver'zerr|en v/t. (no -ge-, h) distort; sich ~ become distorted; 2ung f distortion.

ver'zetteln v/t. (no -ge-, h) enter on cards; sich ~ fritter away one's energies.

Verzicht [fɛr'tsɪçt] m (-[e]s/-e) renunciation (auf acc. of); 2en v/i. (no -ge-, h) renounce (auf et. s.th.); do without (s.th.).

verzieh v/t. pret. of verzeihen.

ver'ziehen¹ (irr. ziehen, no -ge-) 1. v/i. (sein) (re)move (nach to); 2. v/t. (h) spoil (child); distort; das Gesicht ~ make a wry face, screw up one's face, grimace; ohne e-e Miene zu ~ without betraying the least emotion; sich ~ wood: warp; crowd, clouds: disperse; storm, clouds: blow over; F disappear.

ver'ziehen² p.p. of verzeihen.

ver'zier|en v/t. (no -ge-, h) adorn, decorate; 2ung f (-/-en) decoration; ornament.

verzins|en [fɛr'tsɪnzən] v/t. (no -ge-, h) pay interest on; sich ~ yield interest; 2ung f (-/~-en) interest.

ver'zöger|n v/t. (no -ge-, h) delay, retard; sich ~ be delayed; 2ung f (-/-en) delay, retardation.

ver'zollen v/t. (no -ge-, h) pay duty on; haben Sie et. zu ~? have you anything to declare?

verzück|t adj. [fɛr'tsʏkt] ecstatic, enraptured; 2ung f (-/~-en) ecstasy, rapture; in ~ geraten go into ecstasies (wegen over).

Ver'zug m (-[e]s/no pl.) delay; ✝ default; in ~ geraten ✝ come in default; im ~ sein (be in) default.

ver'zweif|eln v/i. (no -ge-, h, sein) despair (an dat. of); es ist zum Verzweifeln it is enough to drive one mad; ~elt adj. hopeless; desperate; 2lung [~luŋ] f (-/no pl.) despair; j-n zur ~ bringen drive s.o. to despair.

verzweig|en [fɛr'tsvaɪgən] v/refl. (no -ge-, h) ramify; trees: branch (out); road: branch; business firm, etc.: branch out; 2ung f (-/-en) ramification; branching.

verzwickt adj. [fɛr'tsvɪkt] intricate, complicated.

Veteran [vete'ra:n] m (-en/-en) ✕ veteran (a. fig.), ex-serviceman.

Veterinär [veteri'nɛ:r] m (-s/-e) veterinary (surgeon), F vet.

Veto ['ve:to] n (-s/-s) veto; ein ~

U
V

einlegen gegen put a veto on, veto *s.th.*

Vetter ['fɛtər] *m* (-s/-n) cousin; '**~nwirtschaft** *f* (-/*no pl.*) nepotism.

vibrieren [vi'briːrən] *v/i.* (*no* -ge-, *h*) vibrate.

Vieh [fiː] *n* (-[e]s/*no pl.*) livestock, cattle; animal, brute, beast; F *fig.* brute, beast; '**~bestand** *m* livestock; '**~händler** *m* cattle-dealer; '**~hof** *m* stockyard; '**Qisch** *adj.* bestial, beastly, brutal; '**~wagen** 🚃 *m* stock-car; '**~weide** *f* pasture; '**~zucht** *f* stock-farming, cattle-breeding; '**~züchter** *m* stock-breeder, stock-farmer, cattle-breeder, *Am. a.* rancher.

viel [fiːl] **1.** *adj.* much; *~e pl.* many; a lot (of), lots of; plenty of (*cake, money, room, time, etc.*); *das ~e Geld* all that money; *seine ~en Geschäfte pl.* his numerous affairs *pl.*; *sehr ~e pl.* a great many *pl.*; *ziemlich ~ a* good deal of; *ziemlich ~e pl.* a good many *pl.*; *~ zuviel* far too much; *sehr ~ a* great *or* good deal; **2.** *adv.* much; *~ besser* much *or* a good deal better; *et. ~ lieber tun* prefer to do a th.

viel|beschäftigt *adj.* ['fiːlbəʃɛftiçt] very busy; '**~deutig** *adj.* ambiguous; **~erlei** *adj.* ['~ərˈlaɪ] of many kinds, many kinds of; multifarious; **~fach** ['~fax] **1.** *adj.* multiple; **2.** *adv.* in many cases, frequently; **~fältig** *adj.* ['~fɛltiç] multiple, manifold, multifarious; '**~leicht** *adv.* perhaps, maybe; **~mals** *adv.* ['~maːls]: *ich danke Ihnen ~* many thanks, thank you very much; *sie läßt (dich) ~ grüßen* she sends you her kind regards; *ich bitte ~ um Entschuldigung* I am very sorry, I do beg your pardon; **~mehr** *cj.* rather; '**~sagend** *adj.* significant, suggestive; **~seitig** *adj.* ['~zaɪtiç] many-sided, versatile; '**~versprechend** *adj.* (very) promising.

vier *adj.* [fiːr] four; *zu ~t* four of us *or* them; *auf allen ~en* on all fours; *unter ~ Augen* confidentially, privately; *um halb ~* at half past three; '**~beinig** *adj.* four-legged; '**Qeck** *n* square, quadrangle; '**~eckig** *adj.* square, quadrangular; **~erlei** *adj.* ['~ərˈlaɪ] of four different kinds, four kinds of; **~fach** *adj.* ['~fax] fourfold; **~e** *Ausfertigung* four

copies; **Qfüßer** *zo.* ['~fyːsər] *m* (-s/-) quadruped; **~füßig** *adj.* ['~fyːsɪç] four-footed; *zo.* quadruped; **Qfüßler** *zo.* ['~fyːslər] *m* (-s/-) quadruped; **~händig** ♪ *adv.* ['~hɛndiç]: *~ spielen* play a duet; **~jährig** *adj.* ['~jɛːriç] four-year-old, of four; **Qlinge** ['~liŋə] *m/pl.* quadruplets *pl.*, F quads *pl.*; '**~mal** *adv.* four times; **~schrötig** *adj.* ['~ʃrøːtiç] square-built, thickset; '**~seitig** *adj.* ['~zaɪtiç] four-sided; Ⱥ quadrilateral; **Qsitzer** *esp. mot. m* (-s/-) four-seater; **~stöckig** *adj.* ['~ʃtœkiç] four-storeyed, four-storied; **Qtaktmotor** *mot. m* four-stroke engine; '**~te** *adj.* fourth; '**~teilen** *v/t.* (ge-, *h*) quarter.

Viertel ['fɪrtəl] *n* (-s/-) fourth (part); quarter; *~ fünf, (ein) ~ nach vier* a quarter past four; *drei ~ vier* a quarter to four; '**~jahr** *n* three months *pl.*, quarter (of a year); **Qjährlich, Qjährlich 1.** *adj.* quarterly; **2.** *adv.* every three months, quarterly; '**~note** ♪ *f* crotchet, *Am. a.* quarter note; '**~pfund** *n*, '**~pfund** *n* quarter of a pound; '**~stunde** *f* quarter of an hour, *Am.* quarter hour.

vier|tens *adv.* ['fɪrtəns] fourthly; **Q'viertaltakt** ♪ *m* common time.

vierzehn *adj.* ['fɪrtseːn] fourteen; *~ Tage pl.* a fortnight, *Am.* two weeks *pl.*; '**~te** *adj.* fourteenth.

vierzig *adj.* ['fɪrtsiç] forty; '**~ste** *adj.* fortieth. [*vicar.*]

Vikar *eccl.* [vi'kaːr] *m* (-s/-e) curate;]

Villa ['vɪla] *f* (-/*Villen*) villa.

violett *adj.* [vio'lɛt] violet.

Violine ♪ [vio'liːnə] *f* (-/-n) violin.

Viper *zo.* ['viːpər] *f* (-/-n) viper.

virtuos *adj.* [virtu'oːs] masterly;
Qe [~zə] *m* (-n/-n), **Qin** [~zin] *f* (-/-nen) virtuoso; **Qität** [~ozi'tɛːt] *f* (-/*no pl.*) virtuosity.

Virus 🧫 ['viːrʊs] *n*, *m* (-/*Viren*) virus.

Vision [vi'zjoːn] *f* (-/-en) vision.

Visitation [vizita'tsjoːn] *f* (-/-en) search; inspection.

Visite 🩺 [vi'ziːtə] *f* (-/-n) visit. **~nkarte** *f* visiting-card, *Am.* calling card.

Visum ['viːzʊm] *n* (-s/*Visa, Visen*) visa, visé.

Vitalität [vitali'tɛːt] *f* (-/*no pl.*) vitality. [min.]

Vitamin [vita'miːn] *n* (-s/-e) vita-

Vize|kanzler ['fi:tsə-] *m* vice-chancellor; '**~könig** *m* viceroy; '**~konsul** *m* vice-consul; '**~präsident** *m* vice-president.

Vogel ['fo:gəl] *m* (-s/ᵘ) bird; F e-n ~ haben have a bee in one's bonnet, *sl.* have bats in the belfry; den ~ *abschießen* carry off the prize, *Am. sl.* take the cake; '**~bauer** *n, m* (-s/-) bird-cage; '**~flinte** *f* fowling-piece; '**²frei** *adj.* outlawed; '**~futter** *n* food for birds, bird-seed; '**~kunde** *f* (-/*no pl.*) ornithology; '**~liebhaber** *m* bird-fancier; '**~nest** *n* bird's nest, bird-nest; '**~perspektive** *f* (-/*no pl.*), '**~schau** *f* (-/*no pl.*) bird's-eye view; '**~scheuche** *f* (-/-n) scarecrow (*a. fig.*); ~'**Strauß-Politik** *f* ostrich policy; ~ *betreiben* hide one's head in the sand (like an ostrich); '**~warte** *f* ornithological station; '**~zug** *m* passage *or* migration of birds.

Vokab|el [vo'ka:bəl] *f* (-/-n) word; **~ular** [~abu'la:r] *n* (-s/-e) vocabulary.

Vokal *ling.* [vo'ka:l] *m* (-s/-e) vowel.

Volk [fɔlk] *n* **1.** (-[e]s/ᵘer) people; nation; swarm (*of bees*); covey (*of partridges*); **2.** (-[e]s/*no pl.*) populace, *the* common people; *contp. the* common or vulgar herd; *der Mann aus dem ~e* the man in the street *or Am.* on the street.

Völker|bund ['fœlkər-] *m* (-[e]s/*no pl.*) League of Nations; '**~kunde** *f* (-/*no pl.*) ethnology; '**~recht** *n* (-[e]s/*no pl.*) international law, law of nations; '**~wanderung** *f* age of national migrations.

'**Volks|abstimmung** *pol. f* plebiscite; '**~ausgabe** *f* popular edition (*of book*); '**~bücherei** *f* free *or* public library; '**~charakter** *m* national character; '**~dichter** *m* popular *or* national poet; '**~entscheid** *pol.* ['~ɛntʃaɪt] *m* (-[e]s/-e) referendum; plebiscite; '**~fest** *n* fun fair, amusement park *or* grounds *pl.*; public merry-making; national festival; '**~gunst** *f* popularity; '**~herrschaft** *f* democracy; '**~hochschule** *f* adult education (courses *pl.*); '**~lied** *n* folk-song; '**~menge** *f* crowd (*of people*), multitude; '**~partei** *f* people's party; '**~republik** *f* people's republic; '**~schule** *f* elementary *or* primary school, *Am.*

a. grade school; '**~schullehrer** *m* elementary *or* primary teacher, *Am.* grade teacher; '**~sprache** *f* vernacular; '**~stamm** *m* tribe, race; '**~stück** *thea. n* folk-play; '**~tanz** *m* folk-dance; '**~tracht** *f* national costume; **²tümlich** *adj.* ['~ty:mlɪç] national; popular; '**~versammlung** *f* public meeting; '**~vertreter** *parl. m* deputy, representative; member of parliament; *Brt.* Member of Parliament, *Am.* Representative; '**~vertretung** *parl. f* representation of the people; parliament; '**~wirt** *m* (political) economist; '**~wirtschaft** *f* economics, political economy; **~wirtschaftler** ['~tlər] *m* (-s/-) *s.* Volkswirt; '**~zählung** *f* census.

voll [fɔl] **1.** *adj.* full; filled; whole, complete, entire; *figure, face:* full, round; *figure:* buxom; ~er Knospen full of buds; *aus ~em Halse* at the top of one's voice; *aus ~em Herzen* from the bottom of one's heart; *in ~er Blüte* in full blossom; *in ~er Fahrt* at full speed; *mit ~en Händen* lavishly, liberally; *mit ~em Recht* with perfect right; *um das Unglück ~zumachen* to make things worse; **2.** *adv.* fully, in full; ~ *und ganz* fully, entirely; *j-n nicht für ~ ansehen or nehmen* have a poor opinion of s.o., think little of s.o.

'**voll|auf** *adv.*, ~'**auf** *adv.* abundantly, amply, F plenty; '**~automatisch** *adj.* fully automatic; '**²bad** *n* bath; '**²bart** *m* beard; '**²beschäftigung** *f* full employment; '**²besitz** *m* full possession; '**²blut(pferd)** *zo. n* thoroughbred (horse); '**~bringen** *v/t.* (*irr.* bringen, *no* -ge-, h) accomplish, achieve; perform; '**²dampf** *m* full steam; F: *mit* ~ *at or* in full blast; ~'**enden** *v/t.* (*no* -ge-, h) finish, complete; ~'**endet** *adj.* perfect; **~ends** *adv.* ['~ɛnts] entirely, wholly, altogether; **²endung** *f* (-/-en) finishing, completion; *fig.* perfection.

Völlerei [fœlə'raɪ] *f* (-/-en) gluttony.

voll|führen *v/t.* (*no* -ge-, h) execute, carry out; '**~füllen** *v/t.* (*sep.*, -ge-, h) fill (up); '**~gas** *mot. n:* ~ *geben* open the throttle; *mit* ~ with the throttle full open; at full speed; **~gepfropft** *adj.* ['~gəpfrɔpft] crammed, packed; '~**gießen** v/t. (irr. gießen, sep., -ge-, h) fill (up); '2**gummi** n, m solid rubber.

völlig adj. ['fœliç] entire, complete; silence, calm, etc.: dead.

voll|**jährig** adj. ['fɔljɛːriç]: ~ sein be of age; ~ werden come of age; '2**jährigkeit** f (-/no pl.) majority; **~kommen** adj. perfect; 2**kommenheit** f (-/%-en) perfection; '2**kornbrot** n whole-meal bread; '~**machen** v/t. (sep., -ge-, h) fill (up); F soil, dirty; um das Unglück vollzumachen to make things worse; '2**macht** f (-/-en) full power, authority; ⚖ power of attorney; ~ haben be authorized; '2**matrose** ⚓ m able-bodied seaman; '2**milch** f whole milk; '2**mond** m full moon; '~**packen** v/t. (sep., -ge-, h) stuff, cram; '2**pension** f (-/-en) full board; '~**schenken** v/t. (sep., -ge-, h) fill (up); '~**schlank** adj. stout, corpulent; '~**ständig** adj. complete; '~**stopfen** v/t. (sep., -ge-, h) stuff, cram; sich ~ stuff o.s.; sich die Taschen ~ stuff one's pockets; ~**strecken** v/t. (no -ge-, h) execute; 2**streckung** f (-/-en) execution; '~**tönend** adj. sonorous, rich; '2**treffer** m direct hit; '2**versammlung** f plenary meeting or assembly; General Assembly (of the United Nations); '~**wertig** adj. equivalent, equal in value; full; '~**zählig** adj. complete; ~**ziehen** v/t. (irr. ziehen, no -ge-, h) execute; consummate (marriage); sich ~ take place; 2**ziehung** f (-/%-en), 2**zug** m (-[e]s/no pl.) execution.

Volontär [volɔnˈtɛːr] m (-s/-e) unpaid assistant.

Volt ⚡ [volt] n (-, -[e]s/-) volt.

Volumen [voˈluːmən] n (-s/-, Volumina) volume.

vom prp. [fɔm] = von dem

von prp. (dat.) [fɔn] space, time: from; instead of gen.: of; passive: by; ~ Hamburg from Hamburg; ~ nun an from now on; ~ morgen an from tomorrow (on), beginning tomorrow; ein Freund ~ mir a friend of mine; die Einrichtung ~ Schulen the erection of schools; ~ dem or vom Apfel essen eat (some) of the apple; der Herzog ~ Edinburgh the Duke of Edinburgh; ein Gedicht ~ Schiller a poem by

Schiller; ~ selbst by itself; ~ selbst, ~ sich aus by oneself; ~ drei Meter Länge three metres long; ein Betrag ~ 300 Mark a sum of 300 marks; e-e Stadt ~ 10 000 Einwohnern a town of 10,000 inhabitants; reden ~ talk of or about s.th.; speak on (scientific subject); ~ mir aus as far as I am concerned; I don't mind, for all I care; das ist nett ~ ihm that is nice of him; ich habe ~ ihm gehört I have heard of him; ~**statten** adv. ['~ʃtatən]: gut ~ gehen go well. [~'ʃtatn]: gut ~ gehen go well.

vor prp. (dat.; acc.) [foːr] space: in front of, before; time: before; ~ langer Zeit a time long ago; ~ einigen Tagen a few days ago; (heute) ~ acht Tagen a week ago (today); am Tage ~ (on) the day before, on the eve of; 5 Minuten ~ 12 five minutes to twelve, Am. five minutes of twelve; fig. at the eleventh hour; ~ der Tür stehen be imminent, be close at hand; ~ e-m Hintergrund against a background; ~ Zeugen in the presence of witnesses; ~ allen Dingen above all; (dicht) ~ dem Untergang stehen be on the brink or verge of ruin; ~ Hunger sterben die of hunger; ~ Kälte zittern tremble with cold; schützen (verstecken) ~ protect (hide) from or against; ~ sich gehen take place, pass off; ~ sich hin lächeln smile to o.s.; sich fürchten ~ be afraid of, fear. **Vor**|**abend** ['foːrʔ-] m eve; '~**ahnung** f presentiment, foreboding.

voran adv. [foˈran] at the head (dat. of), in front (of); before; Kopf ~ head first; ~**gehen** v/i. (irr. gehen, sep., -ge-, sein) lead the way; precede; ~**kommen** v/i. (irr. kommen, sep., -ge-, sein) make progress; fig. get on (in life).

Voran|**schlag** ['foːr ʔan-] m (rough) estimate; '~**zeige** f advance notice; film: trailer.

vorarbeite|**n** ['foːrʔ-] v/t. and v/i. (sep., -ge-, h) work in advance; '2**r** m foreman.

voraus adv. [foˈraus] in front (dat. of), ahead (of); im ~ in advance, beforehand; ~**bestellen** v/t. (sep., no -ge-, h) s. vorbestellen; ~**bezahlen** v/t. (sep., no -ge-, h) pay in advance, prepay; ~**gehen** v/i. (irr. gehen, sep., -ge-, sein) go on before; s. vorangehen; 2**sage** f prediction;

prophecy; forecast (*of weather*); **~sagen** v/t. (*sep.*, -ge-, *h*) foretell, predict; prophesy; forecast (*weather*, *etc.*); **~schicken** v/t. (*sep.*, -ge-, *h*) send on in advance; *fig.* mention beforehand, premise; **~sehen** v/t. (*irr.* sehen, *sep.*, -ge-, *h*) foresee; **~setzen** v/t. (*sep.*, -ge-, *h*) (pre)suppose, presume, assume; vorausgesetzt, daß provided that; **2setzung** f (-/-en) (pre)supposition, assumption; prerequisite; **2sicht** f foresight; aller ~ nach in all probability; **~sichtlich** adj. presumable, probable, likely; **2zahlung** f advance payment or instal(l)ment.

'**Vor|bedacht 1.** m (-[e]s/no pl.): mit ~ deliberately, on purpose; **2.** ⌀ adj. premeditated; **~bedeutung** f foreboding, omen, portent; '**~bedingung** f prerequisite.

Vorbehalt ['fo:rbəhalt] m (-[e]s/-e) reservation, reserve; '**2en 1.** v/t. (*irr.* halten, *sep.*, no -ge-, *h*): sich ~ reserve (*right, etc.*); **2.** adj.: Änderungen ~ subject to change (without notice); '**2los** adj. unreserved, unconditional.

vorbei [fɔr'baɪ] *space*: along, by, past (*all:* an dat. s.o., s.th.); *time:* over, gone; 3 Uhr ~ past three (o'clock); **~fahren** v/i. (*irr.* fahren, *sep.*, -ge-, sein) drive past; **~gehen** v/i. (*irr.* gehen, *sep.*, -ge-, sein) pass, go by; *pain:* pass (off); *storm:* blow over; ~ an (dat.) pass by; im Vorbeigehen in passing; **~kommen** v/i. (*irr.* kommen, *sep.*, -ge-, sein) pass by; F drop in; F ~ an (dat.) get past (*obstacle, etc.*); **~lassen** v/t. (*irr.* lassen, *sep.*, -ge-, *h*) let pass.

'**Vorbemerkung** f preliminary remark or note.

'**vorbereit|en** v/t. (*sep.*, no -ge-, *h*) prepare (für, auf acc. for); '**2ung** f preparation (für, auf acc. for).

'**Vorbesprechung** f preliminary discussion or talk.

'**vor|bestellen** v/t. (*sep.*, no -ge-, *h*) order in advance; book (*room, etc.*); '**~bestraft** adj. previously convicted.

'**vorbeug|en** (*sep.*, -ge-, *h*) **1.** v/t. prevent (e-r Sache s.th.); **2.** v/t. and v/refl. bend forward; '**~end** adj. preventive; ✚ a. prophylactic; '**2ung** f prevention.

'**Vorbild** n model; pattern; example; prototype; '**2lich** adj. exemplary; **~ung** ['~duŋ] f preparatory training.

'**vor|bringen** v/t. (*irr.* bringen, *sep.*, -ge-, *h*) bring forward, produce; advance (*opinion*); ⚖ prefer (*charge*); utter, say, state; '**~datieren** v/t. (*sep.*, no -ge-, *h*) post-date.

vorder adj. ['fɔrdər] front, fore.

'**Vorder|achse** f front axle; '**~ansicht** f front view; '**~bein** n foreleg; '**~fuß** m forefoot; '**~grund** m foreground (a. fig.); '**~haus** n front building; '**~mann** m man in front (*of s.o.*); '**~rad** n front wheel; **~radantrieb** mot. ['fɔrdərra:t?-] m front-wheel drive; '**~seite** f front (side); obverse (*of coin*); '**~sitz** m front seat; '**2st** adj. foremost; '**~teil** n, m front (part); '**~tür** f front door; '**~zahn** m front tooth; '**~zimmer** n front room.

'**vordräng|en** v/refl. (*sep.*, -ge-, *h*) press or push forward.

'**vordring|en** v/i. (*irr.* dringen, *sep.*, -ge-, sein) advance; '**~lich** adj. urgent.   [blank.]

'**Vordruck** m (-[e]s/-e) form, Am. a.

voreilig adj. ['fo:r?-] hasty, rash, precipitate; **~e Schlüsse ziehen** jump to conclusions.

voreingenommen adj. ['fo:r?-] prejudiced, bias(s)ed; '**2heit** f (-/no pl.) prejudice, bias.

vor|enthalten ['fo:r?-] v/t. (*irr.* halten, *sep.*, no -ge-, *h*) keep back, withhold (*j-m et.* s.th. from s.o.); **2entscheidung** ['fo:r?-] f preliminary decision; **~erst** adv. ['fo:r?-] for the present, for the time being.

Vorfahr ['fo:rfa:r] m (-en/-en) ancestor.

'**vorfahr|en** v/i. (*irr.* fahren, *sep.*, -ge-, sein) drive up; pass; den Wagen ~ lassen order the car; '**2t(srecht** n) f right of way, priority.

'**Vorfall** m incident, occurrence, event; '**2en** v/i. (*irr.* fallen, *sep.*, -ge-, sein) happen, occur.

'**vorfinden** v/t. (*irr.* finden, *sep.*, -ge-, *h*) find.

'**Vorfreude** f anticipated joy.

'**vorführ|en** v/t. (*sep.*, -ge-, *h*) bring forward, produce; bring (dat. before); show, display, exhibit; demonstrate (use of s.th.); show, present (*film*); '**2er** m projectionist (*in cinema theatre*); '**Ꞩung** f presentation, showing; ⊕ demonstration; ⚔ production (*of prisoner*); *thea., film*: performance.

'**Vor|gabe** f *sports*: handicap; *athletics*: stagger; *golf, etc.*: odds *pl.*; '**⸗gang** m incident, occurrence, event; facts *pl.*; file, record(s *pl.*); *biol.*, ⊕ process; **⸗gänger** ['⸗gɛŋər] m (-s/-), '**⸗gängerin** f (-/-nen) predecessor; '**⸗garten** m front garden.

'**vorgeben** v/t. (*irr.* geben, *sep.*, -ge-, h) *sports*: give (*j-m* s.o.); *fig.* pretend, allege.

'**Vor|gebirge** n promontory, cape, headland; foot-hills *pl.*; '**⸗gefühl** n presentiment, foreboding.

'**vorgehen 1.** v/i. (*irr.* gehen, *sep.*, -ge-, sein) ⚔ advance; F lead the way; go on before; *watch, clock*: be fast, gain (*fünf Minuten* five minutes); take precedence (*dat.* of, over), be more important (than); take action, act; proceed (*a.* ⚔; *gegen* against); go on, happen, take place; **2.** Ꞩ n (-s/*no pl.*) action, proceeding.

'**Vor|geschmack** m (-[e]s/*no pl.*) foretaste; **⸗gesetzte** ['⸗gəzɛtstə] m (-n/-n) superior; *esp. Am.* F boss; '**Ꞩgestern** adv. the day before yesterday; '**Ꞩgreifen** v/i. (*irr.* greifen, *sep.*, -ge-, h) anticipate (*j-m* or *e-r Sache* s.o. *or* s.th.).

'**vorhaben 1.** v/t. (*irr.* haben, *sep.*, -ge-, h) intend, mean; be going to do s.th.; *nichts* ~ be at a loose end; *haben Sie heute abend et. vor?* have you anything on tonight?; *was hat er jetzt wieder vor?* what is he up to now?; *was hast du mit ihm vor?* what are you going to do with him?; **2.** Ꞩ n (-s/-) intention, purpose, ⚔ intent; plan; project.

'**Vorhalle** f vestibule, (entrance-)hall; lobby; porch.

'**vorhalt|en** (*irr.* halten, *sep.*, -ge-, h) **1.** v/t.: *j-m* et. ~ hold s.th. before s.o.; *fig.* reproach s.o. with s.th.; **2.** v/i. last; '**Ꞩung** f remonstrance; *j-m* ⸗en machen remonstrate with s.o. (*wegen* on).

'**vorhanden** adj. [for'handən] at hand, present; available (*a.* †); † on hand, in stock; ~ sein exist; **Ꞩ-sein** n presence, existence.

'**Vor|hang** m curtain; '**⸗hänge-schloß** n padlock.

'**vorher** adv. before, previously; in advance, beforehand.

vor'her|bestellen v/t. (*sep.*, *no* -ge-, h) s. vorbestellen; **⸗bestimmen** v/t. (*sep.*, *no* -ge-, h) determine beforehand, predetermine; **⸗gehen** v/i. (*irr.* gehen, *sep.*, -ge-, sein) precede; **⸗ig** adj. preceding, previous.

'**Vorherr|schaft** f predominance; '**Ꞩschen** v/i. (*sep.*, -ge-, h) predominate, prevail; '**Ꞩschend** adj. predominant, prevailing.

Vor'her|sage f s. Voraussage; **Ꞩgen** v/t. (*sep.*, -ge-, h) s. voraussagen; **Ꞩsehen** v/t. (*irr.* sehen, *sep.*, -ge-, h) foresee; **Ꞩwissen** v/t. (*irr.* wissen, *sep.*, -ge-, h) know beforehand, foreknow.

'**vor|hin** adv., ⸗**hin** adv. a short while ago, just now.

'**Vor|hof** m outer court, forecourt; *anat.* auricle (*of heart*); **⸗hut** ⚔ f vanguard.

'**vor|ig** adj. last; **⸗jährig** adj. ['⸗jɛːrɪç] of last year, last year's.

'**Vor|kämpfer** m champion, pioneer; '**⸗kehrung** f (-/-en) precaution; **⸗en treffen** take precautions; '**⸗kenntnisse** f/pl. preliminary or basic knowledge (*in dat.* of); guten ⸗n in (*dat.*) well grounded in.

'**vorkommen 1.** v/i. (*irr.* kommen, *sep.*, -ge-, sein) be found; occur, happen; *es kommt mir vor* it seems to me; **2.** Ꞩ n (-s/-) occurrence.

'**Vor|kommnis** n (-ses/-se) occurrence; event; '**⸗kriegszeit** f prewar times *pl.*

'**vorlad|en** v/t. (*irr.* laden, *sep.*, -ge-, h) summon; '**Ꞩung** ⚔ f summons.

'**Vorlage** f copy; pattern; *parl.* bill; presentation; production (*of document*); *football*: pass.

'**vorlassen** v/t. (*irr.* lassen, *sep.*, -ge-, h) let s.o. pass, allow s.o. to pass; admit.

'**Vorläuf|er** m, '**⸗erin** f (-/-nen) forerunner; '**Ꞩig 1.** adj. provisional, temporary; **2.** adv. provisionally, temporarily; for the present, for the time being.

'**vorlaut** adj. forward, pert.

'**Vorleben** n past (life), antecedents *pl.*

'**vorlege|n** v/t. (*sep.*, -ge-, h) put (*lock*) on; produce (*document*); submit (*plans, etc. for discussion, etc.*); propose (*plan, etc.*); present (*bill, etc.*); j-m et. ~ lay or place or put s.th. before s.o.; show s.o. s.th.; *at table:* help s.o. to s.th.; j-m e-e Frage ~ put a question to s.o.; *sich* ~ lean forward; **'²r** m (-s/-) rug.

'vorles|en v/t. (*irr. lesen, sep.,* -ge-, h) read aloud; j-m et. ~ read (out) s.th. to s.o.; **'²ung** f lecture (*über acc.* on; *vor dat.* to); e-e ~ halten (give a) lecture.

'vorletzt adj. last but one; ~e Nacht the night before last.

'Vorlieb|e f (-/*no pl.*) predilection, preference; **²nehmen** [~'li:p-] v/i. (*irr. nehmen, sep.,* -ge-, h) be satisfied (*mit* with); ~ *mit dem, was da ist at meals:* take pot luck.

'vorliegen v/i. (*irr. liegen, sep.,* -ge-, h) lie before s.o.; be there, exist; *da muß ein Irrtum* ~ there must be a mistake; *was liegt gegen ihn vor?* what is the charge against him?; **'~d** adj. present, in question.

'vor|lügen v/t. (*irr. lügen, sep.,* -ge-, h): j-m et. ~ tell s.o. a lie; **'~machen** v/t. (*sep.,* -ge-, h): j-m et. ~ show s.o. how to do s.th.; *fig.* impose upon s.o.; *sich (selbst)* et. ~ fool o.s.

'Vormacht f (-/~*e*), **'~stellung** f predominance; supremacy; hegemony.

'Vormarsch ✕ m advance.

'vormerken v/t. (*sep.,* -ge-, h) note down, make a note of; reserve; *sich* ~ *lassen für* put one's name down for.

'Vormittag m morning, forenoon; **'²s** adv. in the morning.

'Vormund m (-[e]s/-e, ~er) guardian; **'~schaft** f (-/-en) guardianship.

vorn adv. [fɔrn] in front; *nach* ~ forward; *von* ~ from the front; *ich sah sie von* ~ I saw her face; *von* ~ *anfangen* begin at the beginning; *noch einmal von* ~ *anfangen* begin anew, make a new start.

'Vorname m Christian name, first name, *Am.* a. given name.

vornehm ['foːrneːm] **1.** adj. of (superior) rank, distinguished; aristocratic; noble; fashioanble; ~e Gesinnung high character; **2.** adv.: ~ tun give o.s. airs; **'~en** v/t. (*irr. nehmen, sep.,* -ge-, h) take s.th. in

hand; deal with; make (*changes, etc.*); take up (*book*) F *sich* j-n ~ take s.o. to task (*wegen* for, about); *sich* ~ resolve (up)on s.th.; resolve (*zu inf.* to inf.), make up one's mind (*to inf.*); *sich vorgenommen haben* a. be determined (*zu inf.* to inf.); **'²heit** f (~/*no pl.*) refinement; elegance; high-mindedness.

'vorn|herein adv., **'~he'rein** adv.: *von* ~ from the first or start or beginning.

Vorort ['foːrʔ-] m (-[e]s/-e) suburb; **'~(s)verkehr** m suburban traffic; **'~(s)zug** m local (train).

'Vor|posten m outpost (a. ✕); **'~rang** m (-[e]s/*no pl.*) precedence (*vor dat.* of, over); priority (over); **'~rat** m store, stock (*an dat.* of); *Vorräte pl.* a. provisions *pl.*, supplies *pl.*; ✝ a. on hand, in stock; **'²rechnen** v/t. (*sep.,* -ge-, h) reckon up (j-m to s.o.); **'~recht** n privilege; **'~rede** f preface, introduction; **'~redner** m previous speaker; **'~richtung** ⊕ f contrivance, device; **'²rücken** (*sep.,* -ge-) **1.** v/t. (h) move (*chair, etc.*) forward; **2.** v/i. (*sein*) advance; **'~runde** f *sports:* preliminary round; **'²sagen** v/i. (*sep.,* -ge-, h): j-m ~ prompt s.o.; **'~saison** f off or dead season; **'~satz** m intention, purpose, design; **'²sätzlich** adj. ['~zetsliç] intentional, deliberate; ~er Mord ࢘ wil(l)ful murder; **'~schein** m: zum ~ bringen bring forward, produce; zum ~ kommen appear, turn up; **'²schieben** v/t. (*irr. schieben, sep.,* -ge-, h) push s.th. forward; slip (*bolt*); s. vorschützen; **'²schießen** v/t. (*irr. schießen, sep.,* -ge-, h) advance (*money*).

'Vorschlag m proposition, proposal; suggestion; offer; **²en** ['~gən] v/t. (*irr. schlagen, sep.,* -ge-, h) propose; suggest; offer.

'Vor|schlußrunde f *sports:* semifinal; **'²schnell** adj. hasty; rash; **'²schreiben** v/t. (*irr. schreiben, sep.,* -ge-, h): j-m et. ~ write s.th. out for s.o.; *fig.* prescribe; **'Vorschrift** f direction, instruction; prescription (*esp.* ࢙); order (a. ࢙); regulation(s *pl.*); **'²smäßig** adj. according to regulations; ~e Kleidung regulation dress; **'²swidrig**

adj. and adv. contrary to regulations.

'Vor|schub *m*: ~ leisten (*dat.*) countenance (*fraud, etc.*); further, encourage; ⚖ aid and abet; '~schule *f* preparatory school; '~schuß *m* advance; *for barrister:* retaining fee, retainer; '≈schützen *v/t.* (*sep.,* -ge-, h) pretend, plead (*sickness, etc. as excuse*); '≈schweben *v/i.* (*sep.,* -ge-, h): mir schwebt et. vor I have s.th. in mind.

'vorseh|en *v/t.* (*irr. sehen, sep.,* -ge-, h) plan; design; ⚖ provide; sich ~ take care, be careful; sich ~ vor (*dat.*) guard against; '≈ung *f* (-/‰ -en) providence.

'vorsetzen *v/t.* (*sep.,* -ge-, h) put forward; place *or* put *or* set before, offer:

'Vorsicht *f* caution; care; ~! caution!, danger!; look out!, be careful!; ~, Glas! Glass, with care!; ~, Stufe! mind the step!; '≈ig *adj.* cautious; careful; ~! F steady!

'vorsichts|halber *adv.* as a precaution; '≈maßnahme *f,* '≈maßregel *f* precaution(ary measure); ~n treffen take precautions.

'Vorsilbe *gr. f* prefix.

'vorsingen *v/t.* (*irr. singen, sep.,* -ge-, h): j-m et. ~ sing s.th. to s.o.

'Vorsitz *m* (-es/*no pl.*) chair, presidency; den ~ führen *or* haben be in the chair, preside (*bei* over; at); den ~ übernehmen take the chair; ~ende ['~ǝndǝ] (-n/-n) **1.** *m* chairman, president; **2.** *f* chairwoman.

'Vorsorg|e *f* (-/*no pl.*) provision, providence; precaution; ~ treffen make provision; '≈en *v/i.* (*sep.,* -ge-, h) provide; ≈lich ['~klɪç] **1.** *adj.* precautionary; **2.** *adv.* as a precaution.

'Vorspeise *f* appetizer, hors d'œuvre.

'vorspiegel|eln *v/t.* (*sep.,* -ge-, h) pretend; j-m et. ~ delude s.o. (with false hopes, *etc.*); '≈(e)lung *f* preten|ce, *Am.* -se.

'Vorspiel *n* prelude; '≈en *v/t.* (*sep.,* -ge-, h): j-m et. ~ play s.th. to s.o.

'vor|sprechen *v/i.* (*irr. sprechen, sep.,* -ge-, h) **1.** *v/t.* pronounce (j-m et. s.th. to *or* for s.o.); **2.** *v/i.* call (*bei* on *s.o.*; *at an office*); *thea.* audition; '~springen *v/i.* (*irr. springen, sep.,* -ge-, sein) jump forward; project; '≈sprung *m* △ projection;

sports: lead; *fig.* start, advantage (*vor dat.* of); '≈stadt *f* suburb; '~städtisch *adj.* suburban; '≈stand *m* board of directors, managing directors *pl.*

'vorsteh|en *v/i.* (*irr. stehen, sep.,* -ge-, h) project, protrude; *fig.*: direct; manage (both: e-r Sache s.th.); '≈er *m* director, manager; head, chief.

'vorstell|en *v/t.* (*sep.,* -ge-, h) put forward; put (*clock*) on; introduce (j-n j-m s.o. to s.o.); mean, stand for; represent; sich ~ bei have an interview with; sich et. ~ imagine *or* fancy s.th.; '≈ung *f* introduction, presentation; interview (*of applicant for post*); *thea.* performance; *fig.*: remonstrance; idea, conception; imagination; '≈ungsvermögen *n* imagination.

'Vor|stoß ✗ *m* thrust, advance; '~strafe *f* previous conviction; '≈-strecken *v/t.* (*sep.,* -ge-, h) thrust out, stretch forward; advance (*money*); '~stufe *f* first step *or* stage; '≈täuschen *v/t.* (*sep.,* -ge-, h) feign, pretend.

Vorteil ['fɔrtaɪl] *m* advantage (*a. sports*); profit; *tennis:* (ad)vantage; '≈haft *adj.* advantageous (*für* to), profitable (to).

Vortrag ['fo:rtra:k] *m* (-[e]s/~e) performance; execution (*a. ♪*); recitation (*of poem*); ♪ recital; lecture; report; ✝ balance carried forward; e-n ~ halten (give a) lecture (*über acc.* on); ≈en ['~gǝn] *v/t.* (*irr. tragen, sep.,* -ge-, h) ✝ carry forward; report on; recite (*poem*); perform, *sing ♪* execute; lecture on; state, express (*opinion*); ~ende ['~gǝndǝ] *m* (-n/-n) performer; lecturer; speaker.

vor|trefflich *adj.* [fo:r'trefliç] excellent; '~treten *v/i.* (*irr. treten, sep.,* -ge-, sein) step forward; *fig.* project, protrude, stick out; '≈tritt *m* (-[e]s/*no pl.*) precedence.

vorüber *adv.* [fo'ry:bər] *space:* by, past; *time:* gone by, over; ~gehen *v/i.* (*irr. gehen, sep.,* -ge-, sein) pass, go by; ~gehend *adj.* passing; temporary; ≈gehende [~də] *m* (-n/-n) passer-by; ~ziehen *v/i.* (*irr. ziehen, sep.,* -ge-, sein) march past, pass by; *storm:* blow over.

Vor|übung ['fo:r?-] *f* preliminary

practice; **~untersuchung** ☆ ['fo:r?-] f preliminary inquiry.
Vorurteil ['fo:r?-] n prejudice; **'2s-los** adj. unprejudiced, unbias(s)ed.
'Vor|verkauf thea. m booking in advance; im ~ bookable (bei at); **'2verlegen** v/t. (sep., no -ge-, h) advance; **'~wand** m (-[e]s/=e) pretext, preten|ce, Am. -se.
vorwärts adv. ['fo:rverts] forward, onward; on; ~! go ahead!; **'~kommen** v/i. (irr. kommen, sep., -ge-, sein) (make) progress; fig. make one's way, get on (in life).
vorweg adv. [for'vek] beforehand; **~nehmen** v/t. (irr. nehmen, sep., -ge-, h) anticipate.
'vor|weisen v/t. (irr. weisen, sep., -ge-, h) produce, show; **'~werfen** v/t. (irr. werfen, sep., -ge-, h) throw or cast before; j-m et. ~ reproach s.o. with s.th.; **'~wiegend 1.** adj. predominant, preponderant; **2.** adv. predominantly, chiefly, mainly, mostly; **'~witzig** adj. forward, pert; inquisitive.
'Vorwort n (-[e]s/-e) preface (by author); foreword.
'Vorwurf m reproach; subject (of drama, etc.); j-m e-n ~ or Vorwürfe machen reproach s.o. (wegen with); **'2svoll** adj. reproachful.
'vor|zählen v/t. (sep., -ge-, h) enumerate, count out (both: j-m to s.o.); **2zeichen** n omen; **'~zeichnen** v/t. (sep., -ge-, h): j-m et. ~ draw or sketch s.th. for s.o.; show s.o. how to draw s.th.; fig. mark out, destine; **'~zeigen** v/t. (sep., -ge-, h) produce, show.
'Vorzeit f antiquity; in literature often: times of old, days of yore; **'2ig** adj. premature.
'vor|ziehen v/t. (irr. ziehen, sep., -ge-, h) draw forth; draw (curtains); fig. prefer; **'2zimmer** n antechamber, anteroom; waiting-room; **'2-zug** fig. m preference; advantage; merit; priority; **~züglich** adj. [~-'tsy:kliç] excellent, superior, exquisite.
'Vorzugs|aktie f preference share or stock, Am. preferred stock; **'~preis** m special price; **'2weise** adv. preferably; chiefly.
Votum ['vo:tum] n (-s/Voten, Vota) vote.
vulgär adj. [vul'gɛ:r] vulgar.
Vulkan [vul'ka:n] m (-s/-e) volcano; **2isch** adj. volcanic.

W

Waag|e ['va:gə] f (-/-n) balance, (e-e a pair of) scales pl.; die ~ halten (dat.) counterbalance; **'2erecht** adj., **2recht** adj. ['va:k-] horizontal, level; **2schale** ['va:k-] f scale.
Wabe ['va:bə] f (-/-n) honeycomb.
wach adj. (vax) awake; hell~ wide awake; ~ werden awake, wake up; **'2e** f (-/-n) watch; guard; guardhouse, guardroom; police-station; sentry, sentinel; ~ haben be on guard; ~ halten keep watch; **'~en** v/i. (ge-, h) (keep) watch (über acc. over); sit up (bei with); **'2hund** m watch-dog.
Wacholder ♀ [va'xɔldər] m (-s/-) juniper.
wach|rufen v/t. (irr. rufen, sep., -ge-, h) rouse, evoke; **'~rütteln** v/t. (sep., -ge-, h) rouse (up); fig. rouse, shake up.
Wachs [vaks] n (-es/-e) wax.
'wachsam adj. watchful, vigilant; **'2keit** f (-/no pl.) watchfulness, vigilance.
wachsen[1] ['vaksən] v/i. (irr., ge-, sein) grow; fig. increase.
wachsen[2] [~] v/t. (ge-, h) wax.
wächsern adj. ['vɛksərn] wax; fig. waxen, waxy.
'Wachs|kerze f, **'~licht** n wax candle; **'~tuch** n waxcloth, oilcloth.
Wachstum ['vakstu:m] n (-s/no pl.) growth; fig. increase.
Wächte mount. ['vɛçtə] f (-/-n) cornice.
Wachtel orn. ['vaxtəl] f (-/-n) quail.
Wächter ['vɛçtər] m (-s/-) watcher, guard(ian); watchman.
'Wacht|meister m sergeant; **'~turm** m watch-tower.
wackel|ig adj. ['vakəliç] shaky (a. fig.), tottery; furniture, etc.: rickety;

W

tooth, etc.: loose; '2kontakt ∉ m loose connexion *or* (*Am. only*) connection; '~n *v/i.* (ge-, *h*) shake; *table, etc.*: wobble; *tooth, etc.*: be loose; *tail, etc.*: wag; ~ mit wag *s.th.*

wacker *adj.* ['vakər] honest, upright; brave, gallant.

wacklig *adj.* ['vakliç] s. *wackelig.*

Wade ['vɑːdə] *f* (-/-n) calf; '~nbein *anat. f* fibula.

Waffe ['vafə] *f* (-/-n) weapon (*a. fig.*); ~n *pl. a.* arms.

Waffel ['vafəl] *f* (-/-n) waffle; wafer.

'**Waffen|fabrik** *f* armaments factory, *Am. a.* armory; '~gattung *f* arm; '~gewalt *f* (-/*no pl.*): mit ~ by force of arms; '2los *adj.* weaponless, unarmed; '~schein *m* firearm certificate, *Am.* gun license; '~still-stand *m* armistice (*a. fig.*), truce.

Wage|hals ['vɑːgəhals] *m* daredevil; '2halsig *adj.* daring, foolhardy; *attr. a.* daredevil; '~mut *m* daring.

wagen¹ ['vɑːgən] *v/t.* (ge-, *h*) venture; risk, dare; *sich* ~ venture (*an acc.* [up]on).

Wagen² [~] *m* (-s/-, ⸚) carriage (*a.* 🚗); *Am.* 🚗 car; 🚂 coach; wag-(g)on; cart; car; lorry, truck; van.

wägen ['vɛːgən] *v/t.* ([*irr.*,] ge-, *h*) weigh (*a. fig.*).

'**Wagen|heber** *m* (-s/-) (lifting) jack; '~park *m* (-[e]s/*no pl.*) fleet of vehicles; '~schmiere *f* grease; '~spur *f* rut.

Waggon 🚃 [va'gõː] *m* (-s/-s) (railway) carriage, *Am.* (railroad) car.

wag|halsig *adj.* ['vɑːkhalsiç] s. *wagehalsig*; '2nis *n* (-ses/-se) venture, risk.

Wahl [vɑːl] *f* (-/-en) choice; alternative; selection; *pol.* election; e-e ~ *treffen* make a choice; *s-e* ~ *treffen* take one's choice; *ich hatte keine (andere)* ~ I had no choice.

wählbar ['vɛːlbaːr] *adj.* eligible; '2keit *f* (-/*no pl.*) eligibility.

wahl|berechtigt ['vɑːlbərɛçtiçt] entitled to vote; '2beteiligung *f* percentage of voting, F turn-out; '2bezirk *m* constituency.

'**wählen** (ge-, *h*) **1.** *v/t.* choose; *pol.* elect; *teleph.* dial; **2.** *v/i.* choose, take one's choice; *teleph.* dial (the number).

'**Wahlergebnis** *n* election return.

'**Wähler** *m* (-s/-) elector, voter; '2isch *adj.* particular (*in dat.* in, about, as to), nice (about), fastidious, F choosy; '~schaft *f* (-/-en) constituency, electorate.

'**Wahl|fach** *n* optional subject, *Am. a.* elective; '2fähig *adj.* having a vote; eligible; '~gang *m* ballot; '~kampf *m* election campaign; '~kreis *m* constituency; '~lokal *n* polling station; '2los *adj.* indiscriminate; '~recht *n* (-[e]s/*no pl.*) franchise; '~rede *f* electoral speech.

'**Wahlscheibe** *teleph. f* dial.

'**Wahl|spruch** *m* device, motto; '~stimme *f* vote; '~urne *f* ballotbox; '~versammlung *f* electoral rally; '~zelle *f* polling-booth; '~zettel *m* ballot, voting-paper.

Wahn [vɑːn] *m* (-[e]s/*no pl.*) delusion, illusion; mania; '~sinn *m* (-[e]s/*no pl.*) insanity, madness (*both a. fig.*); '2sinnig *adj.* insane, mad (*vor dat.* with) (*both a. fig.*); ~sinnige ['~gə] *m* (-n/-n) madman, lunatic; '~vorstellung *f* delusion, hallucination; '~witz *m* (-es/*no pl.*) madness, insanity; '2-witzig *adj.* mad, insane.

wahr *adj.* [vɑːr] true; real; genuine; '~en *v/t.* (ge-, *h*) safeguard (*interests, etc.*); maintain (*one's dignity*); *den Schein* ~ keep up *or* save appearances.

währen ['vɛːrən] *v/i.* (ge-, *h*) last, continue.

'**während 1.** *prp.* (*gen.*) during; pending; **2.** *cj.* while, whilst; while, whereas.

'**wahrhaft** *adv.* really, truly, indeed; '~ig [~'haftiç] **1.** *adj.* truthful, veracious; **2.** *adv.* really, truly, indeed.

'**Wahrheit** *f* (-/-en) truth; *in* ~ in truth; *j-m die* ~ *sagen* give s.o. a piece of one's mind; '2sgetreu *adj.* true, faithful; '~sliebe *f* (-/*no pl.*) truthfulness, veracity; '2sliebend *adj.* truthful, veracious.

'**wahr|lich** *adv.* truly, really; '~nehmbar *adj.* perceivable, perceptible; '~nehmen *v/t.* (*irr. nehmen, sep.,* -ge-, *h*) perceive, notice; avail o.s. of (*opportunity*); safeguard (*interests*); '2nehmung *f* (-/-en) perception, observation; '~sagen *v/i.* (*sep.,* -ge-, *h*) tell *or* read fortunes;

sich ~ *lassen* have one's fortune told; '2**sagerin** f (-/-nen) fortune-teller; ~**scheinlich 1.** *adj.* probable; likely; **2.** *adv.*: *ich werde* ~ *gehen* I am likely to go; 2'**schein-lichkeit** f (-/⚲-en) probability, likelihood; *aller* ~ *nach* in all probability *or* likelihood.

'**Wahrung** f (-/no *pl.*) maintenance; safeguarding.

'**Währung** ['vɛːruŋ] f (-/-en) currency; standard; '~**sreform** f currency *or* monetary reform.

'**Wahrzeichen** n landmark.

Waise ['vaizə] f (-/-n) orphan; '~**n-haus** n orphanage.

Wal *zo.* [vɑːl] m (-[e]s/-e) whale.

Wald [valt] m (-[e]s/⸚er) wood, forest; '~**brand** m forest fire; 2**ig** *adj.* ['~dɪç] wooded, woody; 2**reich** *adj.* ['~t-] rich in forests; ~**ung** ['~duŋ] f (-/-en) forest.

Walfänger ['vɑːlfɛŋər] m (-s/-) whaler.

walken ['valkən] v/t. (ge-, h) full (*cloth*); mill (*cloth*, *leather*).

Wall [val] m (-[e]s/⸚e) ✗ rampart (*a. fig.*); dam; mound.   [ing.]

Wallach ['valax] m (-[e]s/-e) geld-]

wallen ['valən] v/i. (ge-, h, sein) hair, articles of dress, etc.: flow; simmer; boil (*a. fig.*).

wall|fahren ['valfɑːrən] v/i. (ge-, sein) (go on a) pilgrimage; 2**fahrer** m pilgrim; 2**fahrt** f pilgrimage; '~**fahrten** v/i. (ge-, sein) (go on a) pilgrimage.

'**Wallung** f (-/-en) ebullition; ⚕ congestion; (*Blut*) *in* ~ *bringen* make *s.o.'s* blood boil, enrage.

Walnuß ['val-] f walnut; '~**baum** ⚜ m walnut(-tree).

Walroß *zo.* ['val-] n walrus.

walten ['valtən] v/i. (ge-, h): *s-s Amtes* ~ attend to one's duties; *Gnade* ~ *lassen* show mercy.

Walze ['valtsə] f (-/-n) roller, cylinder; ⊕ *a.* roll; ⊕, ♪ barrel; 2**n** v/t. (ge-, h) roll (*a.* ⊕).

wälzen ['vɛltsən] v/t. (ge-, h) roll; roll (*problem*) round in one's mind; shift (*blame*) (*auf acc.* [up]on); *sich* ~ roll; wallow (*in mud, etc.*); welter (*in blood, etc.*).

Walzer ♪ ['valtsər] m (-s/-) waltz.

Wand [vant] **1.** f (-/⸚e) wall; partition; **2.** 2 *pret. of* winden.

Wandel ['vandəl] m (-s/no *pl.*)

change; '2**bar** *adj.* changeable; variable; '2**n** (ge-) **1.** v/i. (sein) walk; **2.** v/i./*refl.* (h) change.

Wander|er ['vandərər] m (-s/-) wanderer; hiker; '~**leben** n (-s/no *pl.*) vagrant life; 2**n** v/i. (ge-, sein) wander; hike; '~**niere** ⚕ f floating kidney; '~**prediger** m itinerant preacher; '~**preis** m challenge trophy; '~**schaft** f (-/no *pl.*) wanderings *pl.*; *auf (der)* ~ on the tramp; '~**ung** f (-/-en) walking-tour; hike.

'**Wand|gemälde** n mural (painting); '~**kalender** m wall-calendar; '~**karte** f wall-map.

Wandlung f (-/-en) change, transformation; *eccl.* transubstantiation; ⚖ rehibition.

'**Wand|schirm** m folding-screen; '~**schrank** m wall-cupboard; '~**spiegel** m wall-mirror; '~**tafel** f blackboard; '~**teppich** m tapestry; '~**uhr** f wall-clock.

wandte ['vantə] *pret. of* wenden 2.

Wange ['vaŋə] f (-/-n) cheek.

Wankel|mut ['vaŋkəlmuːt] m fickleness, inconstancy; 2**mütig** *adj.* ['~myːtɪç] fickle, inconstant.

wanken ['vaŋkən] v/i. (ge-, h, sein) totter, stagger (*a. fig.*); *house, etc.*: rock; *fig.* waver.

wann *adv.* [van] when; *s.* dann; *seit* ~? how long?, since when?

Wanne ['vanə] f (-/-n) tub; bath (-tub), F tub; '~**nbad** n bath, F tub.

Wanze *zo.* ['vantsə] f (-/-n) bug, *Am. a.* bedbug.

Wappen ['vapən] n (-s/-) (coat of) arms *pl.*; '~**kunde** f (-/no *pl.*) heraldry; '~**schild** m, n escutcheon; '~**tier** n heraldic animal.

wappnen *fig.* ['vapnən] v/*refl.* (ge-, h): *sich* ~ *gegen* be prepared for; *sich mit Geduld* ~ have patience.

war [vɑːr] *pret. of* sein[1].

warb [varp] *pret. of* werben.

Ware ['vɑːrə] f (-/-n) commodity, article of trade; ~*n pl. a.* goods *pl.*, merchandise, wares *pl.*

'**Waren|aufzug** m hoist; '~**bestand** m stock (on hand); '~**haus** n department store; '~**lager** n stock; warehouse, *Am. a.* stock room; '~**probe** f sample; '~**zeichen** n trade mark.

warf [varf] *pret. of* werfen.

warm *adj.* [varm] warm (*a. fig.*); *meal:* hot; *schön* ~ nice and warm.

Wärme ['vermə] *f* (-/~ -n) warmth; *phys.* heat; '~**grad** *m* degree of heat; '**2n** *v/t.* (ge-, *h*) warm; *sich die Füße* ~ warm one's feet.

'**Wärmflasche** *f* hot-water bottle.

'**warmherzig** *adj.* warm-hearted.

Warm'wasser|heizung *f* hot-water heating; ~**versorgung** *f* hot-water supply.

warn|en ['varnən] *v/t.* (ge-, *h*) warn (*vor dat.* of, against), caution (against); '**2signal** *n* danger-signal (*a. fig.*); '**2streik** *m* token strike; '**2ung** *f* (-/-en) warning, caution; **2ungstafel** ['varnuŋs-] *f* notice-board.

Warte *fig.* ['vartə] *f* (-/-n) point of view.

warten ['vartən] *v/i.* (ge-, *h*) wait (*auf acc.* for); be in store (for *s.o.*); *j-n* ~ *lassen* keep s.o. waiting.

Wärter ['vertər] *m* (-s/-) attendant; keeper; (male) nurse.

'**Warte|saal** *m*, '~**zimmer** *n* waiting-room.

Wartung ⊕ ['vartuŋ] *f* (-/~ -en) maintenance.

warum *adv.* [va'rum] why.

Warze ['vartsə] *f* (-/-n) wart; nipple.

was [vas] **1.** *interr. pron.* what; ~ *kostet das Buch?* how much is this book?; F ~ *rennst du denn so (schnell)?* why are you running like this?; ~ *für (ein) ...!* what a(n) ...!; ~ *für ein ...?* what ...?; **2.** *rel. pron.* what; ~ *(auch immer), alles* ~ *...; ...,* ~ *ihn völlig kalt ließ ...* which left him quite cold; **3.** F *indef. pron.* something; *ich will dir mal* ~ *sagen* I'll tell you what.

wasch|bar *adj.* ['vaʃbɑːr] washable; '**2becken** *n* wash-basin, *Am.* wash-bowl.

Wäsche ['vɛʃə] *f* (-/-n) wash(ing); laundry; linen (*a. fig.*); underwear; *in der* ~ *sein* be at the wash; *sie hat heute große* ~ she has a large wash today.

waschecht *adj.* ['vaʃʔ-] washable; *colour:* a. fast; *fig.* dyed-in-the-wool.

'**Wäsche|klammer** *f* clothes-peg, clothes-pin; '~**leine** *f* clothes-line.

'**waschen** *v/t.* (*irr.*, ge-, *h*) wash;

---

sich ~ (have a) wash; *sich das Haar or den Kopf* ~ wash *or* shampoo one's hair *or* head; *sich gut* ~ (*lassen*) wash well.

Wäscher|ei [vɛʃə'raɪ] *f* (-/-en) laundry; '~**in** *f* (-/-nen) washer-woman, laundress.

'**Wäscheschrank** *m* linen closet.

'**Wasch|frau** *f* s. *Wäscherin;* '~**haus** *n* wash-house; '~**kessel** *m* copper; '~**korb** *m* clothes-basket; '~**küche** *f* wash-house; '~**lappen** *m* face-cloth, *Am.* washrag, wash-cloth; '~**maschine** *f* washing ma-chine, washer; '~**pulver** *n* wash-ing powder; '~**raum** *m* lavatory, *Am.* a. washroom; '~**schüssel** *f* wash-basin; '~**tag** *m* wash(ing)-day; '~**ung** *f* (-/-en) wash; ablution; '~**weib** *contp. n* gossip; '~**wanne** *f* wash-tub.

Wasser ['vasər] *n* (-s/-, ⸚) water; ~ *lassen* make water; *zu* ~ *und zu Land(e)* by sea and land; '~**ball** *m* **1.** beach-ball; water-polo ball; **2.** (-[e]s/*no pl.*) water-polo; '~**ball-spiel** *n* **1.** (-[e]s/*no pl.*) water-polo; **2.** water-polo match; '~**behälter** *m* reservoir, water-tank; '~**blase** *f* water-blister; '~**dampf** *m* steam; '**2dicht** *adj.* waterproof; water-tight; '~**eimer** *m* water-pail, bucket; '~**fall** *m* waterfall, cascade; cataract; '~**farbe** *f* water-colo(u)r; '~**flugzeug** *n* waterplane, seaplane; '~**glas** *n* **1.** tumbler; **2.** ⸚ (-es/*no pl.*) water-glass; '~**graben** *m* ditch; '~**hahn** *m* tap, *Am.* a. faucet; '~**hose** *f* waterspout.

wässerig *adj.* ['vesəriç] watery; washy (*a. fig.*); *j-m den Mund* ~ *machen* make s.o.'s mouth water.

'**Wasser|kanne** *f* water-jug, ewer; '~**kessel** *m* kettle; '~**klosett** *n* water-closet, W.C.; '~**kraft** *f* water-power; '~**kraftwerk** *n* hy-droelectric power station *or* plant, water-power station; '~**krug** *m* water-jug, ewer; '~**kur** *f* water-cure, hydropathy; '~**lauf** *m* water-course; '~**leitung** *f* water-supply; '~**leitungsrohr** *n* water-pipe; '~**mangel** *m* shortage of water; '**2n** *v/i.* (ge-, *h*) alight on water; splash down. [(*salted herring, etc.*).]

wässern ['vesərn] *v/t.* (ge-, *h*) soak]

'**Wasser|pflanze** *f* aquatic plant; '~**rinne** *f* gutter; '~**rohr** *n* water-

W

pipe; '~schaden *m* damage caused by water; '~scheide *f* watershed, *Am. a.* divide; '2scheu *adj.* afraid of water; '~schlauch *m* water-hose; '~spiegel *m* water-level; '~sport *m* aquatic sports *pl.*; '~spülung *f* (*-/-en*) flushing (system); '~stand *m* water-level; '~standsanzeiger ['vasərʃtants⁹-] *m* water-gauge; '~stiefel *m/pl.* waders *pl.*; '~stoff 🜍 *m* (*-[e]s/no pl.*) hydrogen; '~stoffbombe *f* hydrogen bomb, H-bomb; '~strahl *m* jet of water; '~straße *f* waterway; '~tier *n* aquatic animal; '~verdrängung *f* (*-/-en*) displacement; '~versorgung *f* water-supply; '~waage *f* spirit-level, water-level; '~weg *m* waterway; *auf dem* ~ by water; '~welle *f* water-wave; '~werk *n* waterworks *sg.*, *pl.*; '~zeichen *n* watermark.

wäßrig *adj.* ['vɛsriç] *s.* wässerig.

waten ['vɑːtən] *v/i.* (*ge-, sein*) wade.

watscheln ['vɑːtʃəln] *v/i.* (*ge-, sein, h*) waddle.

Watt ⚡ [vat] *n* (*-s/-*) watt.

Watt|e ['vatə] *f* (*-/-n*) cotton-wool; surgical cotton; wadding; '~ebausch *m* wad; '2ieren [~'tiːrən] *v/t.* wad, pad.

weben ['veːbən] *v/t. and v/i.* ([*irr.*], *ge-, h*) weave.

Weber *m* (*-s/-*) weaver; ~ei [~'rai] *f* **1.** (*-/no pl.*) weaving; **2.** (*-/-en*) weaving-mill.

Webstuhl ['veːpʃtuːl] *m* loom.

Wechsel ['vɛksəl] *m* (*-s/-*) change; allowance; ✝ bill (*of exchange*); *hunt.* runway; *eigener* ~ ✝ promissory note; '~beziehung *f* correlation; '~fälle [~'fɛlə] *pl.* vicissitudes *pl.*; '~fieber 🜍 *n* (*-s/no pl.*) intermittent fever; malaria; '~frist ✝ *f* usance; '~geld *n* change; '~kurs *m* rate of exchange; '~makler ✝ *m* bill-broker; '2n (*ge-, h*) **1.** *v/t.* change; vary; exchange (*words, etc.*); *den Besitzer* ~ change hands; *die Kleider* ~ change (one's clothes); **2.** *v/i.* change; vary; alternate; '~nehmer ✝ *m* (*-s/-*) payee; 2seitig *adj.* ['~zaitiç] mutual, reciprocal; '~strom ⚡ *m* alternating current; '~stube *f* exchange office; '2weise *adv.* alternately, by *or* in turns; '~wirkung *f* interaction.

wecke|n ['vɛkən] *v/t.* (*ge-, h*) wake

(up), waken; arouse (*a. fig.*); '2r *m* (*-s/-*) alarm-clock.

wedeln ['veːdəln] *v/i.* (*ge-, h*): ~ *mit* wag (*tail*).

weder *cj.* ['veːdər]: ~ ... *noch* neither ... nor.

Weg¹ [veːk] *m* (*-[e]s/-e*) way (*a. fig.*); road (*a. fig.*); path; route; walk; *auf halbem* ~ half-way; *am* ~e by the roadside; *aus dem* ~e *gehen* steer clear of; *aus dem* ~e *räumen* remove (*a. fig.*); *in die* ~e *leiten* set on foot, initiate.

weg² *adv.* [vɛk] away, off; gone; *geh* ~! be off (with you!); ~ *mit ihm!* off with him!; *Hände* ~! hands off!; F *ich muß* ~ I must be off; F *ganz* ~ *sein* be quite beside o.s.; '~bleiben F *v/i.* (*irr. bleiben, sep., -ge-, sein*) stay away; be omitted; '~bringen *v/t.* (*irr. bringen, sep., -ge-, h*) take away; *a.* remove (*things*).

wegen *prp.* (*gen.*) ['veːgən] because of, on account of, owing to.

weg|fahren ['vɛk-] (*irr. fahren, sep., -ge-*) **1.** *v/t.* (*h*) remove; cart away; **2.** *v/i.* (*sein*) leave; '~fallen *v/i.* (*irr. fallen, sep., -ge-, sein*) be omitted; be abolished; '2gang *m* (*-[e]s/no pl.*) going away, departure; '~gehen *v/i.* (*irr. gehen, sep., -ge-, sein*) go away *or* off; *merchandise*: sell; '~haben F *v/t.* (*irr. haben, sep., -ge-, h*): e-n ~ be tight; have a screw loose; *er hat noch nicht weg, wie man es machen muß* he hasn't got the knack of it yet; '~jagen *v/t.* (*sep., -ge-, h*) drive away; '~kommen F *v/i.* (*irr. kommen, sep., -ge-, sein*) get away; be missing; *gut* (*schlecht*) ~ come off well (badly); *mach, daß du wegkommst!* be off (with you)!; '~lassen *v/t.* (*irr. lassen, sep., -ge-, h*) let *s.o.* go; leave out, omit; '~laufen *v/i.* (*irr. laufen, sep., -ge-, sein*) run away; '~legen *v/t.* (*sep., -ge-, h*) put away; '~machen *v/t.* (*sep., -ge-, h*) remove; *a.* take out (*stains*); '~müssen F *v/i.* (*irr. müssen* 1, *sep., -ge-, h*): *ich muß weg* I must be off; 2nahme ['~nɑːmə] *f* (*-/-n*) taking (away); '~nehmen *v/t.* (*irr. nehmen, sep., -ge-, h*) take up, occupy (*time, space*); *j-m et.* ~ take s.th. away from s.o.; '~raffen *fig. v/t.* (*sep., -ge-, h*) carry off.

Wegrand ['ve:k-] *m* wayside.
weg|räumen ['vɛk-] *v/t.* (*sep.*, *-ge-*, h) clear away, remove; '**~schaffen** *v/t.* (*sep.*, *-ge-*, h) remove; '**~schik-ken** *v/t.* (*sep.*, *-ge-*, h) send away or off; '**~sehen** *v/i.* (*irr. sehen*, *sep.*, *-ge-*, h) look away; ~ **über** (*acc.*) overlook, shut one's eyes to; ~ **über** (*acc.*) disregard, ignore; '**~setzen** *v/t.* (*sep.*, *-ge-*, h) put away; *sich* ~ **über** (*acc.*) disregard, ignore; '**~streichen** *v/t.* (*irr. streichen*, *sep.*, *-ge-*, h) strike off or out; '**~tun** *v/t.* (*irr. tun*, *sep.*, *-ge-*, h) put away or aside.
Wegweiser ['ve:kvaɪzər] *m* (*-s/-*) signpost, finger-post; *fig.* guide.
weg|wenden ['vɛk-] *v/t.* (*[irr. wenden*,] *sep.*, *-ge-*, h) turn away, avert (*one's eyes*); *sich* ~ turn away; '**~werfen** *v/t.* (*irr. werfen*, *sep.*, *-ge-*, h) throw away; '**~werfend** *adj.* disparaging; '**~wischen** *v/t.* (*sep.*, *-ge-*, h) wipe off; '**~ziehen** (*irr. ziehen*, *sep.*, *-ge-*) **1.** *v/t.* (h) pull or draw away; **2.** *v/i.* (sein) (re)move.
weh [ve:] **1.** *adj.* sore; **2.** *adv.*: ~ tun ache, hurt; *j-m* ~ tun pain or hurt s.o.; *fig.* a. grieve s.o.; *sich* ~ tun hurt o.s.; *mir tut der Finger* ~ my finger hurts.
Wehen¹ ['ve:ən] *f/pl.* labo(u)r, travail.
wehen² [~] (*ge-*, h) **1.** *v/t.* blow; **2.** *v/i.* blow; *es weht ein starker Wind* it is blowing hard.
'**weh|klagen** *v/i.* (*ge-*, h) lament (*um* for, over); '**~leidig** *adj.* snivel(l)ing; *voice*: plaintive; '**2mut** *f* (*-/no pl.*) wistfulness; '**~mütig** *adj.* ['~my:-tiç] wistful.
Wehr [ve:r] **1.** *f* (*-/-en*): *sich zur* ~ setzen offer resistance (*gegen* to), show fight; **2.** *n* (*-[e]s/-e*) weir; '**~dienst** ⚔ *m* military service; '**2en** *v/refl.* (*ge-*, h) defend o.s.; offer resistance (*gegen* to); '**2fähig** ⚔ *adj.* able-bodied; '**2los** *adj.* defenceless, *Am.* defenseless; '**~pflicht** ⚔ *f* (*-/no pl.*) compulsory military service, conscription; '**2-pflichtig** ⚔ *adj.* liable to military service.
Weib [vaɪp] *n* (*-[e]s/-er*) woman; wife; '**~chen** *zo. n* (*-s/-*) female.
Weiber|feind ['vaɪbər-] *m* woman-hater; '**~held** *contp. m* ladies' man; '**~volk** F *n* (*-[e]s/no pl.*) womenfolk.

weib|isch *adj.* ['vaɪbɪʃ] womanish, effeminate; '**~lich** *adj.* ['~p-] female; *gr.* feminine; *womanly*, feminine.
weich *adj.* [vaɪç] soft (*a. fig.*); *meat*, *etc.*: tender; *egg*: soft-boiled; ~ *werden* soften; *fig.* relent.
Weiche¹ 🚂 ['vaɪçə] *f* (*-/-n*) switch; ~*n pl.* points *pl.*
Weiche² *anat.* [~] *f* (*-/-n*) flank, side.
weichen¹ ['vaɪçən] *v/i.* (*irr.*, *ge-*, sein) give way, yield (*dat.* to); *nicht von der Stelle* ~ not to budge an inch; *j-m nicht von der Seite* ~ stick to s.o.
weichen² [~] *v/i.* (*ge-*, h, sein) soak.
'**Weichensteller** 🚂 *m* (*-s/-*) points-man, switch-man.
'**weich|herzig** *adj.* soft-hearted, tender-hearted; '**~lich** *adj.* some-what soft; *fig.* effeminate; '**2ling** ['~lɪŋ] *m* (*-s/-e*) weakling, milksop, molly(-coddle), *sl.* sissy; '**2tier** *n* mollusc.
Weide¹ ♀ ['vaɪdə] *f* (*-/-n*) willow.
Weide² ✿ [~] *f* (*-/-n*) pasture; *auf der* ~ out at grass; '**~land** *n* pas-ture(-land); '**2n** (*ge-*, h) **1.** *v/t.* feed, pasture, graze; *sich* ~ *an* (*dat.*) gloat over; feast on; **2.** *v/i.* pasture, graze.
'**Weiden|korb** *m* wicker basket, osier basket; '**~rute** *f* osier switch.
weidmännisch *hunt. adj.* ['vaɪt-mɛnɪʃ] sportsmanlike.
weiger|n ['vaɪgərn] *v/refl.* (*ge-*, h) refuse, decline; '**2ung** *f* (*-/-en*) refusal.
Weihe *eccl.* ['vaɪə] *f* (*-/-n*) con-secration; ordination; '**2n** *eccl. v/t.* (*ge-*, h) consecrate; *j-n zum Prie-ster* ~ ordain s.o. priest.
Weiher ['vaɪər] *m* (*-s/-*) pond.
'**weihevoll** *adj.* solemn.
Weihnachten ['vaɪnaxtən] *n* (*-s/no pl.*) Christmas, Xmas.
'**Weihnachts|abend** *m* Christmas eve; '**~baum** *m* Christmas-tree; '**~ferien** *pl.* Christmas holidays *pl.*; '**~fest** *n* Christmas; '**~geschenk** *n* Christmas present; '**~gratifika-tion** *f* Christmas bonus; '**~karte** *f* Christmas card; '**~lied** *n* carol, Christmas hymn; '**~mann** *m* Father Christmas, Santa Claus; '**~markt** *m* Christmas fair; '**~zeit** *f* (*-/no pl.*) Christmas(-tide) (*in Germany beginning on the first Advent Sunday*).

'**Weih|rauch** *eccl. m* incense; '**~-wasser** *eccl. n* (-s/*no pl.*) holy water.

weil *cj.* [vaɪl] because, since, as.

Weil|chen ['vaɪlçən] *n* (-s/-): *ein ~* a little while, a spell; '**~e** *f* (-/*no pl.*): *e-e ~* a while.

Wein [vaɪn] *m* (-[e]s/-e): 💍 vine; *wilder ~* 💍 Virginia creeper; '**~bau** *m* (-[e]s/*no pl.*) vine-growing, viticulture; '**~beere** *f* grape; '**~berg** *m* vineyard; '**~blatt** *n* vine-leaf.

wein|en ['vaɪnən] *v/i.* (ge-, h) weep (*um, vor dat.* for), cry (*vor dat.* for *joy, etc.*, *with hunger, etc.*); '**~erlich** *adj.* tearful, lachrymose; whining.

Wein|ernte *f* vintage; '**~essig** *m* vinegar; '**~faß** *n* wine-cask; '**~flasche** *f* wine-bottle; '**~geist** *m* (-[e]s/-e) spirit(*s pl.*) of wine; '**~glas** *n* wineglass; '**~handlung** *f* wine-merchant's shop; '**~karte** *f* wine-list; '**~keller** *m* wine-vault; '**~kelter** *f* winepress; '**~kenner** *m* connoisseur of *or* in wines.

Weinkrampf 💊 *m* paroxysm of weeping.

'**Wein|kühler** *m* wine-cooler; '**~lese** *f* vintage; '**~presse** *f* winepress; '**~ranke** *f* vine-tendril; '**~rebe** *f* vine; '**2rot** *adj.* claret-colo(u)red; '**~stock** *m* vine; '**~traube** *f* grape, bunch of grapes.

weise[1] ['vaɪzə] **1.** *adj.* wise; sage; **2.** 💍 *m* (-n/-n) wise man, sage.

Weise[2] [~] *f* (-/-n) 💍 melody, tune; *fig.* manner, way; *auf diese ~* in this way.

weisen ['vaɪzən] (*irr.*, ge-, h) **1.** *v/t.*: *j-m die Tür ~* show s.o. the door; *von der Schule ~* expel from school; *von sich ~* reject (*idea, etc.*); deny (*charge, etc.*); **2.** *v/i.*: *~ auf* (*acc.*) point at *or* to.

Weis|heit ['vaɪshaɪt] *f* (-/💊-en) wisdom; *am Ende s-r ~ sein* be at one's wit's end; '**~heitszahn** *m* wisdom-tooth; '**2machen** *v/t.* (sep., -ge-, h): *j-m et. ~* make s.o. believe s.th.

weiß *adj.* [vaɪs] white; '**2blech** *n* tin(-plate); '**2brot** *n* white bread; '**2e** *m* (-n/-n) white (man); '**~en** *v/t.* (ge-, h) whitewash; '**2glühend** *adj.* white-hot, incandescent; '**2kohl** *m* white cabbage; '**~lich** *adj.* whitish; '**2waren** *pl.* linen goods *pl.*; '**2wein** *m* white wine.

Weisung ['vaɪzʊŋ] *f* (-/-en) direction, directive.

weit [vaɪt] **1.** *adj.* distant (*von* from); *world, garment:* wide; *area, etc.:* vast; *garment:* loose; *journey, way:* long; *conscience:* elastic; **2.** *adv.:* ~ *entfernt* far away; ~ *entfernt von a.* a long distance from; *fig.* far from; ~ *und breit* far and wide; ~ *über sechzig (Jahre alt)* well over sixty; *bei ~em* (by) far; *von ~em* from a distance.

weit|ab ['vaɪt'-] *adv.* far away (*von* from); '**~'aus** *adv.* (by) far, much; '**2blick** *m* (-[e]s/*no pl.*) far-sightedness; '**2blickend** *adj.* far-sighted, far-seeing; '**~en** *v/t. and v/refl.* (ge-, h) widen.

'**weiter 1.** *adj. particulars, etc.:* further; *charges, etc.:* additional, extra; ~*e fünf Wochen* another five weeks; *bis auf ~es* until further notice; *ohne ~es* without any hesitation; off-hand; **2.** *adv.* furthermore, moreover; ~*!* go on!; *nichts ~* nothing more; *und so ~* and so on; *bis hierher und nicht ~* so far and no farther; '**2e** *n* (-n/*no pl.*) *the* rest; *further details pl.*

'**weiter|befördern** *v/t.* (sep., *no* -ge-, h) forward; '**~bestehen** *v/i.* (*irr. stehen*, sep., *no* -ge-, h) continue to exist, survive; '**~bilden** *v/t.* (sep., -ge-, h) give s.o. further education; *sich ~* improve one's knowledge; continue one's education; '**~geben** *v/t.* (*irr. geben*, sep., -ge-, h) pass (*dat., an acc.* to); '**~gehen** *v/i.* (*irr. gehen*, sep., -ge-, sein) pass *or* move on, walk along; *fig.* continue, go on; '**~'hin** *adv.* in (the) future; furthermore; *et. ~ tun* continue doing *or* to do s.th.; '**~kommen** *v/i.* (*irr. kommen*, sep., -ge-, sein) get on; '**~können** *v/i.* (*irr. können*, sep., -ge-, h) be able to go on; '**~leben** *v/i.* (sep., -ge-, h) live on, survive (*a. fig.*); '**~machen** *v/t. and v/i.* (sep., -ge-, h) carry on.

'**weit|gehend** *adj. powers:* large; *support:* generous; '**2gereist** *adj.* travel(l)ed; '**~greifend** *adj.* far-reaching; '**~herzig** *adj.* broad-minded; '**~hin** *adv.* far off; '**~läufig** ['~lɔyfɪç] **1.** *adj. house, etc.:* spacious; *story, etc.:* detailed; *relative:* distant; *adv.:* ~ *erzählen* (tell in) detail; *er ist ~ verwandt mit mir*

he is a distant relative of mine;
'⁓reichend *adj.* far-reaching; '⁓-
schweifig *adj.* diffuse, prolix;
'⁓sichtig *adj.* ⚕ far-sighted; *fig. a.*
far-seeing; '2sichtigkeit ⚕ *f*
(-/⁊-en) far-sightedness; '2sprung
m (-[e]s/no *pl.*) long jump, *Am.*
broad jump; '⁓tragend *adj.* ✕
long-range; *fig.* far-reaching; '⁓ver-
breitet *adj.* widespread.

Weizen ⚘ ['vaɪtsən] *m* (-s/-)
wheat; '⁓brot *n* wheaten bread;
'⁓mehl *n* wheaten flour.

welch [vɛlç] 1. *interr. pron.* what;
which; ⁓er? which one?; ⁓er von
beiden? which of the two?; 2. *rel.
pron.* who, that; which, that; 3. F
indef. pron.: es gibt ⁓e, die sagen,
daß ... there are some who say
that ...; es sollen viele Ausländer
hier sein, hast du schon ⁓e gesehen?
many foreigners are said to be here,
have you seen any yet?

welk *adj.* [vɛlk] faded, withered;
skin: flabby, flaccid; '⁓en *v/i.* (ge-,
sein) fade, wither. [iron.]

Wellblech ['vɛlblɛç] *n* corrugated

Welle ['vɛlə] *f* (-/-n) wave (*a. fig.*);
⊕ shaft.

'wellen *v/t. and v/refl.* (ge-, h)
wave; '2bereich ⚡ *m* wave-range;
⁓förmig *adj.* ['⁓fœrmıç] undulat-
ing, undulatory; '2länge ⚡ *f* wave-
length; '2linie *f* wavy line; '2rei-
ten *n* (-s/no *pl.*) surf-riding.

'wellig *adj.* wavy.

'Wellpappe *f* corrugated cardboard
or paper.

Welt [vɛlt] *f* (-/-en) world; die ganze
⁓ the whole world, all the world;
auf der ⁓ in the world, auf der ganzen ⁓ all over the world; zur ⁓ bringen give birth to, bring into the
world.

'Welt|all *n* universe, cosmos; '⁓an-
schauung *f* Weltanschauung; '⁓-
ausstellung *f* world fair; '2be-
kannt *adj.* known all over the
world; '2berühmt *adj.* world-
famous; '⁓bürger *m* cosmopolite;
'2erschütternd *adj.* world-shak-
ing; '2fremd *adj.* wordly innocent;
'⁓friede(n) *m* universal peace; '⁓ge-
schichte *f* (-/no *pl.*) universal
history; '2gewandt *adj.* knowing
the ways of the world; '⁓handel ♱
m (-s/no *pl.*) world trade; '⁓karte *f*
map of the world; '2klug *adj.*

wordly-wise; '⁓krieg *m* world war;
der zweite ⁓ World War II; '⁓lage
f international situation; '⁓lauf *m*
course of the world; '2lich 1. *adj.*
wordly; secular, temporal; 2. *adv.*:
⁓ gesinnt wordly-minded; '⁓litera-
tur *f* world literature; '⁓macht
f world-power; '2männisch *adj.*
['⁓mɛnıʃ] man-of-the-world; '⁓-
markt *m* (-[e]s/no *pl.*) world market; '⁓meer *n* ocean; '⁓meister *m*
world champion; '⁓meisterschaft
f world championship; '⁓raum *m*
(-[e]s/no *pl.*) (outer) space; '⁓reich
n universal empire; das Britische ⁓
the British Empire; '⁓reise *f*
journey round the world; '⁓rekord
m world record; '⁓ruf *m* (-[e]s/no
pl.) world-wide reputation; '⁓-
schmerz *m* Weltschmerz; '⁓spra-
che *f* world *or* universal language;
'⁓stadt *f* metropolis; '2weit *adj.*
world-wide; '⁓wunder *n* wonder
of the world.

Wende ['vɛndə] *f* (-/-n) turn (*a.
swimming*); *fig. a.* turning-point;
'⁓kreis *m* geogr. tropic; *mot.* turn-
ing-circle.

Wendeltreppe ['vɛndəl-] *f* winding
staircase, (e-e a flight of) winding
stairs *pl.*, spiral staircase.

'Wende|marke *f* sports: turning-
point; '2n 1. *v/t.* (ge-, h) turn (*coat,
etc.*); turn (*hay*) about; 2. *v/refl.*
(*irr.*,) ge-, h): sich ⁓ an (*acc.*) turn
to; address o.s. to; apply to (*wegen*
for); 3. *v/i.* (ge-, h) ⚓, *mot.* turn;
bitte ⁓! please turn over!; '⁓punkt
m turning-point.

'wend|ig *adj.* nimble, agile (*both a.
fig.*); *mot.*, ⚓ easily steerable; *mot.*
flexible; '2ung *f* (-/-en) turn (*a.
fig.*); ✕ facing; *fig.*: change; expression; idiom.

wenig ['ve:nıç] 1. *adj.* little; ⁓e *pl.*
few *pl.*; ⁓er less; ⁓er *pl.* fewer; ein
klein ⁓ Geduld a little bit of patience;
das ⁓e the little; 2. *adv.* little; ⁓er
less; ⁓ a. minus; am ⁓sten least
(of all); '2keit *f* (-/-en): meine ⁓
my humble self; '⁓stens *adv.*
['⁓stəns] at least.

wenn *cj.* [vɛn] when; if; ⁓ ... nicht
if ... not, unless; ⁓ auch (al)though,
even though; ⁓ auch noch so however; und ⁓ nun ...? what if ...?;
wie wäre es, ⁓ wir jetzt heimgingen?
what about going home now?

wer [ve:r] **1.** *interr. pron.* who; which; ~ *von euch?* which of you?; **2.** *rel. pron.* who; ~ *auch (immer)* who(so)ever; **3.** F *indef. pron.* somebody; anybody; *ist schon* ~ *gekommen?* has anybody come yet?

Werbe|abteilung ['verbǝ-] *f* advertising or publicity department; '**_film** *m* advertising film.

'**werb|en** (*irr.*, ge-, h) **1.** *v/t.* canvass (*votes*, *subscribers*, *etc.*); ⚔ recruit, enlist; **2.** *v/i.* ~ *für* advertise, *Am. a.* advertize; make propaganda for; canvass for; '**_ung** *f* (-/-en) advertising, publicity, *Am. a.* advertizing; propaganda; canvassing; ⚔ enlistment, recruiting.

Werdegang ['ve:rdǝ-] *m* career; ⊕ process of manufacture.

'**werden 1.** *v/i.* (*irr.*, ge-, sein) become, get; grow; turn (*pale*, *sour*, *etc.*); *was ist aus ihm geworden?* what has become of him?; *was will er (einmal)* ~? what is he going to be?; **2.** ♀ *n* (-s/*no pl.*): *noch im* ~ *sein* be in embryo.

werfen ['verfǝn] (*irr.*, ge-, h) **1.** *v/t.* throw (*nach at*); *zo.* throw (*young*); cast (*shadow*, *glance*, *etc.*); *Falten* ~ fall in folds; set badly; **2.** *v/i.* throw; *zo.* litter; ~ *mit* throw (*auf acc.*, *nach at*). [dockyard.|

Werft ⚓ [verft] *f* (-/-en) shipyard,|

Werk [verk] *n* (-[e]s/-e) work; act; ⊕ works *pl.*; works *sg.*, *pl.*, factory; *das* ~ *e-s Augenblicks* the work of a moment; *zu* ~*e gehen* proceed; '**_bank** ⊕ *f* work-bench; '**_meister** *m* foreman; *Am.* (*-/=en*) workshop; '**_statt** ['~ʃtat] *f* (*-/=en*) workshop; '**_tag** *m* workday; '**_tätig** *adj.* working; '**_zeug** *n* tool; implement; instrument.

Wermut ['ve:rmu:t] *m* (-[e]s/*no pl.*) ♀ vermouth; verm(o)uth.

wert [ve:rt] **1.** *adj.* worth; worthy (*gen.* of); ~, *getan zu werden* worth doing; **2.** ♀ *m* (-[e]s/-e) value (*a.* ♣, ♠, *phys.*, *fig.*); worth (*a. fig.*); *Briefmarken im* ~ *von 2 Schilling* 2 shillings' worth of stamps; *großen* ~ *legen auf* (*acc.*) set a high value (up)on.

'**Wert|brief** *m* money-letter; '♀**en** *v/t.* (ge-, h) value; appraise; '**_gegenstand** *m* article of value; '**_los** *adj.* worthless, valueless; '**_papiere** *n/pl.* securities *pl.*; '**_sachen** *pl.* valuables *pl.*; '**_ung** *f* (-/-en)

valuation; appraisal; *sports*: score; '♀**voll** *adj.* valuable, precious.

Wesen ['ve:zǝn] *n* **1.** (-s/*no pl.*) entity, essence; nature, character; *viel* ~*s machen um* make a fuss of; **2.** (-s/-) being; creature; '♀**los** *adj.* unreal; '♀**tlich** *adj.* essential, substantial.

weshalb [vɛs'halp] **1.** *interr. pron.* why; **2.** *cj.* that's why.

Wespe *zo.* ['vɛspǝ] *f* (-/-n) wasp.

West *geogr.* [vɛst] west; '**_en** *m* (-s/*no pl.*) west; *the* West.

Weste ['vɛstǝ] *f* (-/-n) waistcoat, ♣ *and Am.* vest; *e-e reine* ~ *haben* have a clean slate.

'**west|lich** *adj.* west; westerly; western; '♀**wind** *m* (west(erly) wind.

Wett|bewerb ['vɛtbǝverp] *m* (-[e]s/-e) competition (*a.* ♣); '**_büro** *n* betting office; '**_e** *f* (-/-n) wager, bet; *e-e* ~ *eingehen* lay or make a bet; '**_eifer** *m* emulation, rivalry; '♀**eifern** *v/i.* (ge-, h) vie (*mit* with; *in dat.* in; *um* for); '**_en** (ge-, h) **1.** *v/t.* wager, bet; *auf* (*acc.*): *mit j-m um et.* ~ wager or bet s.o. s.th.; ~ *auf* (*acc.*) wager or bet on, back.

Wetter[1] ['vɛtǝr] *n* (-s/-) weather.

Wetter[2] [~] *m* (-s/-) better.

'**Wetter|bericht** *m* weather-forecast; '♀**fest** *adj.* weather-proof; '**_karte** *f* weather-chart; '**_lage** *f* weather-conditions *pl.*; '**_leuchten** *n* (-s/*no pl.*) sheet-lightning; '**_vorhersage** *f* (-/-n) weather-forecast; '**_warte** *f* weather-station.

'**Wett|kampf** *m* contest, competition; '**_kämpfer** *m* contestant; '**_lauf** *m* race; '**_läufer** *m* racer, runner; '♀**machen** *v/t.* (*sep.*, -ge-, h) make up for; '**_rennen** *n* race; '**_rüsten** *n* (-s/*no pl.*) armament race; '**_spiel** *n* match, game; '**_streit** *m* contest. [sharpen.|

wetzen ['vɛtsǝn] *v/t.* (ge-, h) whet,|

wich [viç] *pret. of* weichen[1].

Wichse ['viksǝ] *f* **1.** (-/-n) blacking; polish; **2.** F *fig.* (-/*no pl.*) thrashing; '♀**n** *v/t.* (ge-, h) black; polish.

wichtig *adj.* ['viçtiç] important; *sich* ~ *machen* show off; '**_keit** *f* (-/♣ -en) importance; ♀**tuer** ['~tu:-ǝr] *m* (-s/-) pompous fellow; '**_tuerisch** *adj.* pompous.

Wickel ['vikǝl] *m* (-s/-) roll(er); ♣: compress; packing; '♀**n** *v/t.* (ge-, h) wind; swaddle (*baby*); wrap.

W

Widder zo. ['vidər] m (-s/-) ram.
wider prp. (acc.) ['vi:dər] against, contrary to; '**borstig** adj. crossgrained; ~'**fahren** v/i. (irr. fahren, no -ge-, sein) happen (dat. to); '**2haken** m barb; **2hall** ['~hal] m (-[e]s/-e) echo, reverberation; fig. response; '**hallen** v/i. (sep., -ge-, h) (re-)echo (von with), resound (with); ~'**legen** v/t. (no -ge-, h) refute, disprove; '**lich** adj. repugnant, repulsive; disgusting; '~**natürlich** adj. unnatural; '~**rechtlich** adj. illegal, unlawful; '~**rede** f contradiction; '**2ruf** m ⚜ revocation; retraction; ~'**rufen** v/t. (irr. rufen, no -ge-, h) revoke; retract (a. ⚜); ~'**ruflich** adj. revocable; **2sacher** ['~zaxər] m (-s/-) adversary; '**2schein** m reflection; ~'**setzen** v/refl. (no -ge-, h): sich e-r Sache ~ oppose or resist s.th.; ~'**setzlich** adj. refractory; insubordinate; '~**sinnig** adj. absurd; '**spenstig** adj. ['~ʃpɛnstiç] refractory; '**2spenstigkeit** f (-/~-en) refractoriness; '~**spiegeln** v/t. (sep., -ge-, h) reflect (a. fig.); sich ~ in (dat.) be reflected in; ~'**sprechen** v/i. (irr. sprechen, no -ge-, h): j-m ~ contradict s.o.; '**2spruch** m contradiction; opposition; im ~ zu in contradiction to; ~**sprüchlich** adj. ['~ʃpry:çliç] contradictory; '~**spruchslos 1.** adj. uncontradicted; **2.** adv. without contradiction; '**2stand** m resistance (a. ⚡); opposition; ~ leisten offer resistance (dat. to); auf heftigen ~ stoßen meet with stiff opposition; '~**standsfähig** adj. resistant (a. ⊕); ~'**stehen** v/i. (irr. stehen, no -ge-, h) resist (e-r Sache s.th.); ~'**streben** v/i. (no -ge-, h): es widerstrebt mir, dies zu tun I hate doing or to do that, I am reluctant to do that; ~'**strebend** adj. reluctantly; '**2streit** m (-[e]s/~-e) antagonism; fig. conflict; ~'**wärtig** adj. ['~vɛrtiç] unpleasant, disagreeable; disgusting; '**2wille** m aversion (gegen to, for, from); dislike (to, of, for); disgust (at, for); reluctance, unwillingness; '~**willig** adj. reluctant, unwilling.
widm|en ['vitmən] v/t. (ge-, h) dedicate; '**2ung** f (-/-en) dedication.

widrig adj. ['vi:driç] adverse; ~**enfalls** adv. ['~gən'-] failing which, in default of which.
wie [vi:] **1.** adv. how; ~ alt ist er? what is his age?; ~ spät ist es? what is the time?; **2.** cj.: ein Mann ~ er a man such as he, a man like him; ~ er dies hörte hearing this; ich hörte, ~ er es sagte I heard him saying so.
wieder adv. ['vi:dər] again, anew; immer ~ again and again; **2'aufbau** m (-[e]s/no pl.) reconstruction; rebuilding; ~'**aufbauen** v/t. (sep., -ge-, h) reconstruct; ~'**aufleben** v/i. (sep., -ge-, sein) revive; **2'aufleben** n (-s/no pl.) revival; **2'aufnahme** f resumption; ~'**aufnehmen** v/t. (irr. nehmen, sep., -ge-, h) resume; **2beginn** m recommencement; re-opening; ~'**bekommen** v/t. (irr. kommen, sep., no -ge-, h) get back; ~'**beleben** v/t. (sep., no -ge-, h) resurrect; **2'belebung** f (-/-en) revival; fig. a. resurrection; **2'belebungsversuch** m attempt at resuscitation; ~'**bringen** v/t. (irr. bringen, sep., -ge-, h) bring back; restore, give back; ~'**einsetzen** v/t. (sep., -ge-, h) restore; ~'**einstellen** v/t. (sep., -ge-, h) re-engage; **2er-greifung** f reseizure; ~'**erkennen** v/t. (irr. kennen, sep., no -ge-, h) recognize (an dat. by); ~'**erstatten** v/t. (sep., no -ge-, h) restore; reimburse, refund (money); ~'**geben** v/t. (irr. geben, sep., -ge-, h) give back, return; render, reproduce; ~'**gutmachen** v/t. (sep., -ge-, h) make up for; **2'gutmachung** f (-/-en) reparation; ~'**herstellen** v/t. (sep., -ge-, h) restore; ~**holen** v/t. (h) **1.** [~'ho:lən] (no -ge-) repeat; **2.** ['~ho:lən] (sep., -ge-) fetch back; **2'holung** f (-/-en) repetition; ~**käuen** ['~kɔʏən] (sep., -ge-, h) **1.** v/i. ruminate, chew the cud; **2.** F fig. v/t. repeat over and over; **2kehr** ['~ke:r] f (-/no pl.) return; recurrence; '~**kehren** v/i. (sep., -ge-, sein) return; recur; '~**kommen** v/i. (irr. kommen, sep., -ge-, sein) come back; return; '~**sehen** v/t. and v/refl. (irr. sehen, sep., -ge-, h) see or meet again; **2sehen** n (-s/no pl.) meeting again; auf ~! good-bye!; '~**tun** v/t. (irr. tun, sep., -ge-, h) do again, repeat;

'**~um** *adv.* again, anew; '**~vereinigen** *v/t.* (*sep., no* -ge-, *h*) reunite; '**²vereinigung** *f* reunion; *pol.* reunification; '**²verheiratung** *f* remarriage; **²verkäufer** *m* reseller; retailer; '**²wahl** *f* re-election; '**~wählen** *v/t.* (*sep.,* -ge-, *h*) re-elect; **²zulassung** *f* readmission.

Wiege ['vi:gə] *f* (-/-n) cradle.

wiegen¹ ['vi:gən] *v/t. and v/i.* (*irr.,* ge-, *h*) weigh.

wiegen² [~] *v/t.* (ge-, *h*) rock; *in Sicherheit* ~ rock in security, lull into (a false sense of) security.

'**Wiegenlied** *n* lullaby.

wiehern ['vi:ərn] *v/i.* (ge-, *h*) neigh.

Wiener ['vi:nər] *m* (-s/-) Viennese; '**²isch** *adj.* Viennese.

wies [vi:s] *pret. of* weisen.

Wiese ['vi:zə] *f* (-/-n) meadow.

wie'so *interr. pron.* why; why so.

wie'viel *adv.* how much; ~ *pl.* how many *pl.*; ~**te** *adv.* [~tə]: *den ~ten haben wir heute?* what's the date today?

wild [vilt] **1.** *adj.* wild; savage; ~*es Fleisch* ☆ proud flesh; ~*e Ehe* concubinage; ~*er Streik* † wildcat strike; **2.** ♀ *n* (-[e]s/*no pl.*) game.

'**Wild**|**bach** *m* torrent; ~**bret** ['~brɛt] *n* (-s/*no pl.*) game; venison.

Wilde ['vildə] *m* (-n/-n) savage.

Wilder|**er** ['vildərər] *m* (-s/-) poacher; '**²n** *v/i.* (ge-, *h*) poach.

'**Wild**|**fleisch** *n s.* Wildbret; '**²-fremd** F *adj.* quite strange; '**~hüter** *m* gamekeeper; '**~leder** *n* buckskin; '**²ledern** *adj.* buckskin; doeskin; '**~nis** *f* (-/-se) wilderness, wild (*a. fig.*); '**~schwein** *n* wild-boar.

Wille ['vilə] *m* (-ns/♀,-n) will; *s-n ~n durchsetzen* have one's way; *gegen s-n ~n* against one's will; *j-m s-n ~n lassen* let s.o. have his (own) way; '**²nlos** *adj.* lacking will-power.

'**Willens**|**freiheit** *f* (-/*no pl.*) freedom of (the) will; '**~kraft** *f* (-/*no pl.*) will-power; '**~schwäche** *f* (-/*no pl.*) weak will; '**²stark** *adj.* strong-willed; '**~stärke** *f* (-/*no pl.*) strong will, will-power.

'**will**|**ig** *adj.* willing, ready; **~kommen** *adj.* welcome; **²kür** ['~ky:r] *f* (-/*no pl.*) arbitrariness; '**~kürlich** *adj.* arbitrary.

wimmeln ['viməln] *v/i.* (ge-, *h*) swarm (*von* with), teem (with).

wimmern ['vimərn] *v/i.* (ge-, *h*) whimper, whine.

Wimpel ['vimpəl] *m* (-s/-) pennant, pennon, streamer.

Wimper ['vimpər] *f* (-/-n) eyelash.

Wind [vint] *m* (-[e]s/-e) wind; '**~beutel** *m* cream-puff; F *fig.* windbag.

Winde ['vində] *f* (-/-n) windlass; reel.

Windel ['vindəl] *f* (-/-n) diaper, (baby's) napkin; ~*n pl. a.* swaddling-clothes *pl.*

'**winden** *v/t.* (*irr.,* ge-, *h*) wind; twist, twirl; make, bind (*wreath*); *sich* ~ *vor* (*dat.*) writhe with.

'**Wind**|**hose** *f* whirlwind, tornado; '**~hund** *m* greyhound; **²ig** *adj.* ['~diç] windy; F *fig. excuse:* thin, lame; '**~mühle** *f* windmill; '**~pocken** ♀ *pl.* chicken-pox; '**~richtung** *f* direction of the wind; '**~rose** ♣ *f* compass card; '**~schutzscheibe** *f* wind-screen, Am. windshield; '**~stärke** *f* wind velocity; '**²still** *adj.* calm; '**~stille** *f* calm; '**~stoß** *m* blast of wind, gust.

'**Windung** *f* (-/-en) winding, turn; bend (*of way, etc.*); coil (*of snake, etc.*).

Wink [viŋk] *m* (-[e]s/-e) sign; wave; wink; *fig.:* hint; tip.

Winkel ['viŋkəl] *m* (-s/-) ♣ angle; corner, nook; '**²ig** *adj.* angular; *street:* crooked; '**~zug** *m* subterfuge, trick, shift.

'**winken** *v/i.* (ge-, *h*) make a sign; beckon; *mit dem Taschentuch* ~ wave one's handkerchief.

winklig *adj.* ['viŋkliç] *s.* winkelig.

winseln ['vinzəln] *v/i.* (ge-, *h*) whimper, whine.

Winter ['vintər] *m* (-s/-) winter; *im* ~ in winter; '**²lich** *adj.* wintry; '**~schlaf** *m* hibernation; '**~sport** *m* winter sports *pl.*

Winzer ['vintsər] *m* (-s/-) vine-dresser; vine-grower; vintager.

winzig *adj.* ['vintsiç] tiny, diminutive.

Wipfel ['vipfəl] *m* (-s/-) top.

Wippe ['vipə] *f* (-/-n) seesaw; '**²n** *v/i.* (ge-, *h*) seesaw.

wir *pers. pron.* [vi:r] we; ~ *drei* the three of us.

Wirbel ['virbəl] *m* (-s/-) whirl, swirl; eddy; flurry (*of blows, etc.*); *anat.* vertebra; '**²ig** *adj.* giddy,

W

vertiginous; wild; '**2n** v/i. (ge-, h) whirl; drums: roll; '**~säule** anat. f spinal or vertebral column; '**~sturm** m cyclone, tornado, Am. a. twister; '**~tier** n vertebrate; '**~wind** m whirlwind (a. fig.).

wirk|en ['vɪrkən] (ge-, h) **1.** v/t. knit, weave; work (wonders); **2.** v/i.: ~ als act or function as; ~ auf (acc.) produce an impression on; beruhigend ~ have a soothing effect; '**~lich** adj. real, actual; true, genuine; '**2lichkeit** f (-/-en) reality; in ~ in reality; '**~sam** adj. effective, efficacious; '**2samkeit** f (-/~-en) effectiveness, efficacy; '**2ung** f (-/-en) effect.

'**Wirkungs|kreis** m sphere or field of activity; '**2los** adj. ineffective, inefficacious; '**~losigkeit** f (-/no pl.) ineffectiveness, inefficacy; '**2voll** adj. s. wirksam.

wirr [vɪr] adj. confused; speech: incoherent; hair: dishevel(l)ed; '**2en** pl. disorders pl.; troubles pl.; **2warr** ['~var] n (-s/no pl.) confusion, muddle.

Wirsingkohl ['vɪrzɪŋ-] m (-[e]s/no pl.) savoy.

Wirt [vɪrt] m (-[e]s/-e) host; landlord; innkeeper.

'**Wirtschaft** f (-/-en) housekeeping; economy; trade and industry; economics pl.; s. Wirtshaus; F mess; '**2en** v/i. (ge-, h) keep house; economize; F bustle (about); '**~erin** f (-/-nen) housekeeper; '**2lich** adj. economic; economical.

'**Wirtschafts|geld** n housekeeping money; '**~jahr** n financial year; '**~krise** f economic crisis; '**~politik** f economic policy; '**~prüfer** m (-s/-) chartered accountant, Am. certified public accountant.

'**Wirtshaus** n public house, F pub.

Wisch [vɪʃ] m (-es/-e) wisp (of straw, etc.); contp. scrap of paper; '**2en** v/t. (ge-, h) wipe.

wispern ['vɪspərn] v/t. and v/i. (ge-, h) whisper.

Wiß|begierde ['vɪs-] f (-/no pl.) thirst for knowledge; '**2begierig** adj. eager for knowledge.

wissen ['vɪsən] **1.** v/t. (irr., ge-, h) know; man kann nie ~ you never know, you never can tell; **2.** 2 n (-s/no pl.) knowledge; meines ~s to my knowledge, as far as I know.

'**Wissenschaft** f (-/-en) science; knowledge; '**~ler** m (-s/-) scholar; scientist; researcher; '**2lich** adj. scientific.

'**Wissens|drang** m (-[e]s/no pl.) urge or thirst for knowledge; '**2wert** adj. worth knowing.

'**wissentlich** adj. knowing, conscious.

wittern ['vɪtərn] v/t. (ge-, h) scent, smell; fig. a. suspect.

'**Witterung** f (-/~-en) weather; hunt. scent; **~sverhältnisse** ['~sferheltnɪsə] pl. meteorological conditions pl. [m (-s/-) widower.]

Witwe ['vɪtvə] f (-/-n) widow; '**~r**∫

Witz [vɪts] m **1.** (-es/no pl.) wit; **2.** (-es/-e) joke; ~e reißen crack jokes; '**~blatt** n comic paper; '**2ig** adj. witty; funny.

wo [vo:] **1.** adv. where?; **2.** cj.: F ach ~! nonsense!

wob [vo:p] pret. of weben.

wo'bei adv. at what?; at which; in doing so.

Woche ['vɔxə] f (-/-n) week; heute in e-r ~ today week.

'**Wochen|bett** n childbed; '**~blatt** n weekly (paper); '**~ende** n weekend; '**2lang 1.** adj.: nach ~em Warten after (many) weeks of waiting; **2.** adv. for weeks; '**~lohn** m weekly pay or wages pl.; '**~markt** m weekly market; '**~schau** f news-reel; '**~tag** m week-day.

wöchentlich ['vœçəntlɪç] **1.** adj. weekly; **2.** adv. weekly, every week; einmal ~ once a week.

Wöchnerin ['vœçnərɪn] f (-/-nen) woman in childbed.

wo'durch adv. by what?, how?; by which, whereby; **~'für** adv. for what?, what ... for?; (in return) for which. [gen¹.]

wog [vo:k] pret. of wägen and wie-∫

Woge ['vo:gə] f (-/-n) wave (a. fig.), billow; die ~n glätten pour oil on troubled waters; '**2n** v/i. (ge-, h) surge (a. fig.), billow; wheat: a. wave; heave.

wo'her adv. from where?, where ... from?; ~ wissen Sie das? how do you (come to) know that?; **~'hin** adv. where (... to)?

wohl [vo:l] **1.** adv. well; sich nicht ~ fühlen be unwell; ~ oder übel willy-nilly; leben Sie ~! farewell!; er wird ~ reich sein he is rich, I suppose;

2. ♀ n (-[e]s/no pl.): ~ und Wehe weal and woe; auf Ihr ~! your health!, here is to you!

'**Wohl**|**befinden** n well-being; good health; '**~behagen** n comfort, ease; '♀**behalten** adv. safe; '♀**bekannt** adj. well-known; '**~ergehen** n (-s/no pl.) welfare, prosperity; ♀**erzogen** adj. ['~ɛrtsoːɡən] well-bred, well-behaved; '**~fahrt** f (-/no pl.) welfare; public assistance; '**~gefallen** n (-s/no pl.) pleasure; sein ~ haben an (dat.) take delight in; '♀**gemeint** adj. well-meant, well-intentioned; ♀**gemut** adj. ['~ɡəmuːt] cheerful; '♀**genährt** adj. well-fed; '**~geruch** m scent, perfume; '♀**gesinnt** adj. well-disposed (j-m towards s.o.); '♀**habend** adj. well-to-do; '♀**ig** adj. comfortable; cosy, snug; '**~klang** m (-[e]s/no pl.) melodious sound, harmony; '♀**klingend** adj. melodious, harmonious; '**~laut** m s. Wohlklang; '**~leben** n (-s/no pl.) luxury; ♀**riechend** adj. fragrant; ♀**schmeckend** adj. savo(u)ry; '**~sein** n well-being; good health; '**~stand** m (-[e]s/no pl.) prosperity, wealth; '**~tat** f kindness, charity; fig. comfort, treat; '**~täter** m benefactor; '♀**tätig** adj. charitable, beneficient; '**~tätigkeit** f charity; ♀**tuend** adj. ['~tuːənt] pleasant, comfortable; '♀**tun** v/i. (irr. tun, sep., -ge-, h) do good; '♀**verdient** adj. well-deserved; p. of great merit; '**~wollen** n (-s/no pl.) goodwill; benevolence; favo(u)r; '♀**wollen** v/i. (sep., -ge-, h) be well-disposed (j-m towards s.o.).

wohn|**en** ['voːnən] v/i. (ge-, h) live (in dat. in, at; bei j-m with s.o.); reside (in, at; with); '♀**haus** n dwelling-house; block of flats, Am. apartment house; '**~haft** adj. resident, living; '**~lich** adj. comfortable; cosy, snug; '♀**ort** m dwelling-place, residence; esp. ⚖ domicile; '♀**sitz** m residence; mit ~ in residence in or at; ohne festen ~ without fixed abode; '♀**ung** f (-/-en) dwelling, habitation; flat, Am. apartment.

'**Wohnungs**|**amt** n housing office; '**~not** f housing shortage; '**~problem** n housing problem.

'**Wohn**|**wagen** m caravan, trailer; '**~zimmer** n sitting-room, esp. Am. living room.

wölb|**en** ['vœlbən] v/t. (ge-, h) vault; arch; sich ~ arch; '♀**ung** f (-/-en) vault, arch; curvature.

Wolf zo. [vɔlf] m (-[e]s/=e) wolf.

Wolke ['vɔlkə] f (-/-n) cloud.

'**Wolken**|**bruch** m cloud-burst; '**~kratzer** m (-s/-) skyscraper; '♀**los** adj. cloudless.

'**wolkig** adj. cloudy, clouded.

Woll|**decke** ['vɔl-] f blanket; '**~e** f (-/-n) wool.

wollen¹ ['vɔlən] (h) **1.** v/t. (ge-) wish, desire; want; lieber ~ prefer; nicht ~ refuse; er weiß, was er will he knows his mind; **2.** v/i. (ge-): ich will schon, aber ... I want to, but ...; **3.** v/aux. (no -ge-) be willing; intend, be going to; be about to; lieber ~ prefer; nicht ~ refuse; er hat nicht gehen ~ he refused to go.

woll|**en**² ['vɔlən] [~] wool(l)en; '**~ig** adj. wool(l)y; '♀**stoff** m wool(l)en.

Wol|**lust** ['vɔlʊst] f (-/=e) voluptuousness; ♀**lüstig** adj. ['~lʏstiç] voluptuous.

'**Wollwaren** pl. wool(l)en goods pl.

wo|**mit** adv. with what?, what ... with?; with which; '**~möglich** adv. perhaps, maybe.

Wonn|**e** ['vɔnə] f (-/-n) delight, bliss; '♀**ig** adj. delightful, blissful.

wo|**ran** adv. [voˈran]: ~ denkst du? what are you thinking of?; ich weiß nicht, ~ ich mit ihm bin I don't know what to make of him; ~ liegt es, daß ...? how is it that ...?; '**~rauf** adv. on what?, what ... on?; whereupon, after which; ~ wartest du? what are you waiting for?; '**~raus** adv. from what?; what ... of?; from which; '**~rin** adv. [~ˈrin] in what?; in which.

Wort [vɔrt] n **1.** (-[e]s/=er) word; er kann seine Wörter noch nicht he hasn't learnt his words yet; **2.** (-[e]s/-e) word; term, expression; ums ~ bitten ask permission to speak; das ~ ergreifen begin to speak; parl. rise to speak, address the House, esp. Am. take the floor; das ~ führen be the spokesman; ~ halten keep one's word; '♀**brüchig** adj.: er ist ~ geworden he has broken his word.

'**Wörter**|**buch** ['vœrtər-] n dictionary; '**~verzeichnis** n vocabulary, list of words.

'**Wort**|**führer** m spokesman; '♀**getreu** adj. literal; '♀**karg** adj. taci-

W

turn; **~klauberei** [.'klaubə'raɪ] *f* (-/-en) word-splitting; **'~laut** *m* (-[e]s/*no pl.*) wording; text. [eral.]
wörtlich *adj.* ['vœrtliç] verbal, lit-)
'Wort|schatz *m* (-es/*no pl.*) vocabulary; **~schwall** *m* (-[e]s/*no pl.*) verbiage; **~spiel** *n* pun (*über acc.*, *mit* [up]on), play upon words; **~stellung** *gr. f* word order, order of words; **~stamm** *ling. m* stem; **~streit** *m*, **~wechsel** *m* dispute.
wo|rüber *adv.* [vo:'ry:bər] over *or* upon what?, what ... over *or* about *or* on?; over *or* upon which, about which; **~rum** *adv.* [.'rum] about what?, what ... about?; about *or* for which; ~ *handelt es sich?* what is it about?; **~runter** *adv.* [.'rʊntər] under *or* among what?, what ... under?; under *or* among which; **~von** *adv.* of *or* from what?, what ... from *or* of?; about what?, what ... about?; of *or* from which; **~vor** *adv.* of what?, what ... of?; of which; **~zu** *adv.* for what?, what ... for?; for which.
Wrack [vrak] *n* (-[e]s/-e, -s) ⚓ wreck (*a. fig.*).
wrang [vraŋ] *pret. of* wringen.
wring|en ['vriŋən] *v/t.* (*irr.*, ge-, h) wring; **~maschine** *f* wringing-machine.
Wucher ['vu:xər] *m* (-s/*no pl.*) usury; ~ *treiben* practise usury; **~er** *m* (-s/-) usurer; **~gewinn** *m* excess profit; **~isch** *adj.* usurious; **~n** *v/i.* (ge-, h) grow exuberantly; **~ung** *f* (-/-en) ♀ exuberant growth; ♬ growth; **~zinsen** *m/pl.* usurious interest.
Wuchs [vu:ks] **1.** *m* (-es/⁰e) growth; figure, shape; stature. **2.** ♀ *pret. of* wachsen.
Wucht [vuxt] *f* (-/♬-en) weight; force; **'~ig** *adj.* heavy.
Wühl|arbeit *fig.* ['vy:l-] *f* insidious agitation, subversive activity; **~en** *v/i.* (ge-, h) dig; *pig:* root; *fig.* agitate; ~ *in* (*dat.*) rummage (about) in; **~er** *m* (-s/-) agitator.
Wulst [vulst] *m* (-es/⁰e), *f* (-/⁰e) roll; bulge; ⚠ roll(-mo[u]lding); ⊕ bead; **'~ig** *adj. lips:* thick.
wund [vunt] *adj.* (ge-, h) sore; **~e Stelle** sore; **~er Punkt** tender spot; **~e** ['~də] *f* (-/-n) wound; *alte* **~n** *wieder auf-reißen* reopen old sores.
Wunder ['vundər] *n* (-s/-) miracle;

fig. a. wonder, marvel; ~ *wirken* *pills, etc.:* work marvels; *kein* ~, *wenn man bedenkt ...* no wonder, considering ...; **'2bar** *adj.* miraculous; *fig. a.* wonderful, marvel-(l)ous; **~kind** *n* infant prodigy; **'2lich** *adj.* queer, odd; **'2n** *v/t.* (ge-, h) surprise, astonish; *sich* ~ *be surprised or astonished* (*über acc.* at); **2'schön** *adj.* very beautiful; **~tat** *f* wonder, miracle; **'~täter** *m* wonder-worker; **2tätig** *adj.* wonder-working; **2voll** *adj.* wonderful; **'~werk** *n* marvel, wonder.
'Wund|fieber ⚕ *n* wound-fever; **~starrkrampf** ⚕ *m* tetanus.
Wunsch [vunʃ] *m* (-es/⁰e) wish, desire; request; *auf* ~ by *or* on request; *if desired*; *nach* ~ as desired; *mit den besten Wünschen zum Fest* with the compliments of the season.
Wünschelrute ['vynʃəl-] *f* divining-rod, dowsing-rod; **~ngänger** ['~gɛŋər] *m* (-s/-) diviner, dowser.
wünschen ['vynʃən] *v/t.* (ge-, h) wish, desire; *wie Sie* ~ as you wish; *was* ~ *Sie?* what can I do for you?; **~swert** *adj.* desirable.
'wunsch|gemäß *adv.* as requested *or* desired, according to one's wishes; **'2zettel** *m* list of wishes.
wurde ['vurdə] *pret. of* werden.
Würde ['vyrdə] *f* (-/-n) dignity; *unter seiner* ~ beneath one's dignity; **2los** *adj.* undignified; **~nträger** *m* dignitary; **2voll** *adj.* dignified; grave.
'würdig *adj.* worthy (*gen.* of); dignified; grave; **~en** ['~gən] *v/t.* (ge-, h) appreciate, value; mention hono(u)rably; laud, praise; *j-n keines Blickes* ~ ignore s.o. completely; **2ung** ['~guŋ] *f* (-/-en) appreciation, valuation.
Wurf [vurf] *m* (-[e]s/⁰e) throw, cast; *zo.* litter.
Würfel ['vyrfəl] *m* (-s/-) die; cube (*a.* ♉); **~becher** *m* dice-box; **2n** *v/i.* (ge-, h) (play) dice; **~spiel** *n* game of dice; **~zucker** *m* lump sugar. [tile.]
'Wurfgeschoß *n* missile, projec-)
würgen ['vyrgən] (ge-, h) **1.** *v/t.* choke, strangle; **2.** *v/i.* choke; retch.
Wurm *zo.* [vurm] *m* (-[e]s/⁰er) worm; **'2en** F *v/t.* (ge-, h) vex; rankle (*in* s.o.'s mind); **'2-stichig** *adj.* worm-eaten.

Wurst [vurst] f (-/⸚e) sausage; F *das ist mir ganz ~* I don't care a rap.

Würstchen ['vyrstçən] n (-s/-) sausage; *heißes ~* hot sausage, *Am.* hot dog.

Würze ['vyrtsə] f (-/-n) seasoning, flavo(u)r; spice, condiment; *fig.* salt.

Wurzel ['vurtsəl] f (-/-n) root (a. gr., Å); *~ schlagen* strike or take root (a. *fig.*); '**Qn** v/i. (ge-, h) (strike or take) root; *~ in* (dat.) take one's root in, be rooted in.

'**würz|en** v/t. (ge-, h) spice, season, flavo(u)r; '**~ig** adj. spicy, well-seasoned, aromatic.

wusch [vuːʃ] pret. of waschen.

wußte ['vustə] pret. of wissen.

Wust F [vuːst] m (-es/no pl.) tangled mass; rubbish; mess.

wüst adj. [vyːst] desert, waste; confused; wild, dissolute; rude; '**Qe** f (-/-n) desert, waste; **Qling** ['~liŋ] m (-s/-e) debauchee, libertine, rake.

Wut [vuːt] f (-/no pl.) rage, fury; *in ~* in a rage; '**~anfall** m fit of rage.

wüten ['vyːtən] v/i. (ge-, h) rage (a. *fig.*); '**~d** adj. furious, enraged (*über acc.* at; *auf acc.* with), *esp. Am.* F a. mad (*über acc.*, *auf acc.* at).

Wüterich ['vyːtəriç] m (-[e]s/-e) berserker; bloodthirsty man. [rage.]

'**wutschnaubend** adj. foaming with

X, Y

X-Beine ['iks-] n/pl. knock-knees pl.; '**X-beinig** adj. knock-kneed.

x-beliebig adj. [iksbə'liːbiç] any (... you please); *jede(r, -s) ~e* ... any ...

x-mal adv. ['iks-] many times, *sl.* umpteen times.

X-Strahlen ['iks-] m/pl. X-rays pl.

x-te adj. ['ikstə]: *zum ~n Male* for the umpteenth time.

Xylophon ♪ [ksylo'foːn] n (-s/-e) xylophone.

Yacht ⚓ [jaxt] f (-/-en) yacht.

Z

Zacke ['tsakə] f (-/-n) s. Zacken.

'**Zacken 1.** m (-s/-) (sharp) point; prong; tooth (*of comb, saw, rake*); jag (*of rock*); **2.** ♀ v/t. (ge-, h) indent, notch; jag.

'**zackig** adj. indented, notched; *rock:* jagged; pointed; ⚔ F *fig.* smart.

zaghaft adj. ['tsaːkhaft] timid; '**Qig-keit** f (-/no pl.) timidity.

zäh adj. [tsɛː] tough, tenacious (*both a. fig.*); *liquid:* viscid, viscous; *fig.* dogged; '**~flüssig** adj. viscid, viscous, sticky; '**Qigkeit** f (-/no pl.) toughness, tenacity (*both a. fig.*); viscosity; *fig.* doggedness.

Zahl [tsaːl] f (-/-en) number; figure, cipher; '**Qbar** adj. payable.

'**zählbar** adj. countable.

zahlen ['tsaːlən] (ge-, h) **1.** v/i. pay; *at restaurant:* ~ *(, bitte)!* the bill, please!, *Am.* the check, please!; **2.** v/t. pay.

zählen ['tsɛːlən] (ge-, h) **1.** v/t. count, number; ~ *zu* count or number among; **2.** v/i. count; ~ *auf* (*acc.*) count (up)on, rely (up)on.

'**Zahlen|lotto** n s. Lotto; '**Qmäßig 1.** adj. numerical; **2.** adv.: *j-m ~ überlegen sein* outnumber s.o.

'**Zähler** m (-s/-) counter; Å numerator; *for gas, etc.:* meter.

'**Zahl|karte** f money-order form (*for paying direct into the postal cheque account*); '**Qlos** adj. numberless, innumerable, countless; '**~meister** ⚔ m paymaster; '**Qreich 1.** adj. numerous; **2.** adv. in great number; '**~tag** m pay-day; '**~ung** f (-/-en) payment.

'**Zählung** f (-/-en) counting.

'**Zahlungs|anweisung** f order to pay; '**~aufforderung** f request for payment; '**~bedingungen** f/pl. terms pl. of payment; '**~befehl** m order to pay; '**~einstellung** f suspension of payment; **'2fähig** *adj.* solvent; **'2fähigkeit** *f* solvency; **'2frist** *f* term for payment; **'2mittel** *n* currency; *gesetzliches* ~ legal tender; **'2schwierigkeiten** *f/pl.* financial *or* pecuniary difficulties *pl.*; **'2termin** *m* date of payment; **'2unfähig** *adj.* insolvent; **'2unfähigkeit** *f* insolvency.

'Zahlwort *gr. n* (-[e]s/-er) numeral.

zahm *adj.* [tsɑːm] tame (*a. fig.*), domestic(ated).

zähm|en ['tsɛːmən] *v/t.* (ge-, h) tame (*a. fig.*), domesticate; **'2ung** *f* (-/~-en) taming (*a. fig.*), domestication.

Zahn [tsɑːn] *m* (-[e]s/⸚e) tooth; ⊕ tooth, cog; *Zähne bekommen* cut one's teeth; **'~arzt** *m* dentist, dental surgeon; **'~bürste** *f* toothbrush; **'~creme** *f* tooth-paste; **'2en** *v/i.* (ge-, h) teethe, cut one's teeth; **'~ersatz** *m* denture; **'~fäule** *&* ['~fɔylə] *f* (-/no pl.) dental caries; **'~fleisch** *n* gums *pl.*; **'~füllung** *f* filling, stopping; **'~geschwür** *&* *n* gumboil; **'~heilkunde** *f* dentistry; **'2los** *adj.* toothless; **'~lücke** *f* gap between the teeth; **'~pasta** ['~pasta] *f* (-/Zahnpasten), **'~paste** *f* tooth-paste; **'~rad** ⊕ *n* cog-wheel; **'~radbahn** *f* rack-railway; **'~schmerzen** *m/pl.* toothache; **'~stocher** *m* (-s/-) toothpick.

Zange ['tsaŋə] *f* (-/-n) (e-e a pair of) tongs *pl.* or pliers *pl.* or pincers *pl.*; *&*, *zo.* forceps *sg.*, *pl.*

Zank [tsaŋk] *m* (-[e]s/no pl.) quarrel, F row; **'~apfel** *m* bone of contention; **'2en** (ge-, h) **1.** *v/i.* scold (*mit j-m s.o.*); **2.** *v/refl.* quarrel, wrangle.

zänkisch ['tsɛŋkiʃ] *adj.* quarrelsome.

Zäpfchen ['tsɛpfçən] *n* (-s/-) small peg; *anat.* uvula.

Zapfen ['tsapfən] **1.** *m* (-s/-) plug, peg, pin; bung (*of barrel*); pivot; *♀* cone; **2.** *♀* *v/t.* (ge-, h) tap; **'~streich** *⚔ m* tattoo, retreat, *Am. a.* taps *pl.*

'Zapf|hahn *m* tap, *Am.* faucet; **'~säule** *mot. f* petrol pump.

zappel|ig *adj.* ['tsapəliç] fidgety; **'~n** *v/i.* (ge-, h) struggle; fidget.

zart *adj.* [tsɑːrt] tender; soft; gentle; delicate; **'~fühlend** *adj.* delicate; **'2gefühl** *n* (-[e]s/no pl.) delicacy (*of feeling*).

zärtlich *adj.* ['tsɛːrtliç] tender; fond, loving; **'2keit** *f* **1.** (-/no pl.) tenderness; fondness; **2.** (-/-en) caress.

Zauber ['tsaubər] *m* (-s/-) spell, charm, magic (*all a. fig.*); *fig.*: enchantment; glamo(u)r; **'~ei** [~'rai] *f* (-/-en) magic, sorcery; witchcraft; conjuring; **'~er** *m* (-s/-) sorcerer, magician; conjurer; **'~flöte** *f* magic flute; **'~formel** *f* spell; **'2haft** *adj.* magic(al); *fig.* enchanting; **'~in** *f* (-/-nen) sorceress, witch; *fig.* enchantress; **'~kraft** *f* magic power; **'~kunststück** *n* conjuring trick; **'2n** (ge-, h) **1.** *v/i.* practise magic *or* witchcraft; do conjuring tricks; **2.** *v/t.* conjure; **'~spruch** *m* spell; **'~stab** *m* (magic) wand; **'~wort** *n* (-[e]s/-e) magic word, spell.

zaudern ['tsaudərn] *v/i.* (ge-, h) hesitate; linger, delay.

Zaum [tsaum] *m* (-[e]s/⸚e) bridle; *im* ~ *halten* keep in check.

zäumen ['tsɔymən] *v/t.* (ge-, h) bridle.

'Zaumzeug *n* bridle.

Zaun [tsaun] *m* (-[e]s/⸚e) fence; **'~gast** *m* deadhead; **'~könig** *orn. m* wren; **'~pfahl** *m* pale.

Zebra *zo.* ['tseːbra] *n* (-s/-s) zebra; **'~streifen** *m* zebra crossing.

Zech|e ['tsɛçə] *f* (-/-n) score, reckoning, bill; *⚒* mine; coal-pit, colliery; F *die* ~ *bezahlen* foot the bill, F stand treat; **'2en** *v/i.* (ge-, h) carouse, tipple; **'~gelage** *n* carousal, carouse; **'~preller** *m* (-s/-) bilk(er).

Zeh [tse:] *m* (-[e]s/-en), **'~e** *f* (-/-n) toe; **'~enspitze** *f* point *or* tip of the toe; *auf* ~*n* on tiptoe.

zehn *adj.* [tse:n] ten; **'2er** *m* (-s/-) ten; *coin:* F ten-pfennig piece; **'~fach** *adj.* ['~fax] tenfold; **~jährig** *adj.* ['~jɛːriç] ten-year-old, of ten (years); **'2kampf** *m sports:* decathlon; **'~mal** *adv.* ten times; **~te** ['~tə] **1.** *adj.* tenth; **2.** *2* † *m* (-n/-n) tithe; **2tel** ['~təl] *n* (-s/-) tenth (part); **~tens** *adv.* ['~təns] tenthly.

zehren ['tse:rən] *v/i.* (ge-, h) make thin; ~ *von* live on *s.th.*; *fig.* live off (*the capital*); ~ *an* prey (up)on (*one's mind*); undermine (*one's health*).

Zeichen ['tsaiçən] *n* (-s/-) sign; token; mark; indication; symptom;

signal; zum ~ (gen.) in sign of, as a sign of; '~block m drawing-block; '~brett n drawing-board; '~lehrer m drawing-master; '~papier n drawing-paper; '~setzung gr. f (-/no pl.) punctuation; '~sprache f sign-language; '~stift m pencil, crayon; '~trickfilm m animation, animated cartoon; '~unterricht m drawing-lessons pl.

zeichn|en ['tsaiçnən] (ge-, h) 1. v/t. draw (plan, etc.); design (pattern); mark; sign; subscribe (sum of money) (zu to); subscribe for (shares); 2. v/i. draw; sie zeichnet gut she draws well; 'Ser m (-s/-) draftsman, draughtsman; designer; subscriber (gen. for shares); 'Sung f (-/-en) drawing; design; illustration; zo. marking (of skin, etc.); subscription.

Zeige|finger ['tsaigə-] m forefinger, index (finger); 'Sn (ge-, h) 1. v/t. show; point out; indicate; demonstrate; sich ~ appear; 2. v/i.: ~ auf (acc.) point at; ~ nach point to; '~r m (-s/-) hand (of clock, etc.); pointer (of dial, etc.); '~stock m pointer.

Zeile ['tsailə] f (-/-en) line; row; j-m ein paar ~n schreiben drop s.o. a line or a few lines. [siskin.]

Zeisig orn. ['tsaiziç] m (-[e]s/-e)

Zeit [tsait] f (-/-en) time; epoch, era, age; period, space (of time); term; freie ~ spare time; mit der ~ in the course of time; von ~ zu ~ from time to time; vor langer ~ long ago, a long time ago; zur ~ (gen.) in the time of; at (the) present; zu meiner ~ in my time; zu s-r ~ in due course (of time); das hat ~ there is plenty of time for that; es ist höchste ~ it is high time; j-m ~ lassen give s.o. time; laß dir ~! take your time!; sich die ~ vertreiben pass the time, kill time.

'Zeit|abschnitt m epoch, period; '~alter n age; '~angabe f exact date and hour; date; '~aufnahme phot. f time-exposure; '~dauer f length of time, period (of time); '~enfolge gr. f sequence of tenses; '~geist m (-es/no pl.) spirit of the time(s), zeitgeist; 'Sgemäß adj. modern, up-to-date; 'Sgenosse m contemporary; Sgenössisch adj. ['~gənœsiʃ] contemporary; '~geschichte f contemporary history;

'~gewinn m gain of time; 'Sig 1. adj. early; 2. adv. on time; '~karte f season-ticket, Am. commutation ticket; '~lang f: e-e ~ for some time, for a while; 'Slebens adv. for life, all one's life; 'Slich 1. adj. temporal; 2. adv. as to time; ~ zusammenfallen coincide; 'Slos adj. timeless; '~lupe phot. f slow motion; '~lupenaufnahme phot. f slow-motion picture; 'Snah adj. current, up-to-date; '~ordnung f chronological order; '~punkt m moment; time; date; '~rafferaufnahme phot. f time-lapse photography; 'Sraubend adj. time-consuming; pred. a. taking up much time; '~raum m space (of time), period; '~rechnung f chronology; era; '~schrift f journal, periodical, magazine; review; '~tafel f chronological table.

'Zeitung f (-/-en) (news)paper, journal.

'Zeitungs|abonnement n subscription to a paper; '~artikel m newspaper article; '~ausschnitt m (press or newspaper) cutting, (Am. only) (newspaper) clipping; ~kiosk ['~kiosk m (-[e]s/-e) news-stand; '~notiz f press item; '~papier n newsprint; '~verkäufer m newsvendor; news-boy, news-man; '~wesen n journalism, the press.

'Zeit|verlust m loss of time; '~verschwendung f waste of time; ~vertreib ['~fɛrtraip] m (-[e]s/-e) pastime; zum ~ to pass the time; 'Sweilig adj. ['~vailiç] temporary; 'Sweise adv. for a time; at times, occasionally; '~wort gr. n (-[e]s/-er) verb; '~zeichen n time-signal.

Zell|e ['tsɛlə] f (-/-n) cell; '~stoff m, ~ulose ⊕ [~u'lo:zə] f (-/-n) cellulose.

Zelt [tsɛlt] n (-[e]s/-e) tent; 'Sen v/i. (ge-, h) camp; '~leinwand f canvas; '~platz m camping-ground.

Zement [tse'mɛnt] m (-[e]s/-e) cement; Sieren [~'ti:rən] v/t. (no -ge-, h) cement. [(a.fig.)]

Zenit [tse'ni:t] m (-[e]s/no pl.) zenith

zens|ieren [tsɛn'zi:rən] v/t. (no -ge-, h) censor (book, etc.); at school: mark, Am. a. grade; 'Sor ['~or] m (-s/-en) censor; Sur [~'zu:r] f 1. (-/no pl.) censorship; 2. (-/-en) at school: mark, Am. a. grade;

Z

(school) report, *Am.* report card.
Zentimeter [tsɛnti'-] *n, m* centimet|re, *Am.* -er.
Zentner ['tsɛntnər] *m* (-s/-) (*Brt. appr.*) hundredweight.
zentral *adj.* [tsɛn'trɑ:l] central; ℒe *f* (-/-n) central office; *teleph.* (telephone) exchange, *Am. a.* central; ℒheizung *f* central heating.
Zentrum ['tsɛntrum] *n* (-s/Zentren) cent|re, *Am.* -er. [*Am.* -er.\]
Zepter ['tsɛptər] *n* (-s/-) scept|re,\]
zer|'**beißen** [tsɛr'-] *v/t.* (*irr. beißen, no -ge-, h*) bite to pieces; ∼'**bersten** *v/i.* (*irr. bersten, no -ge-, sein*) burst asunder.
zer|'**brech**|**en** (*irr. brechen, no -ge-*) **1.** *v/t.* (h) break (to pieces); sich den Kopf ∼ rack one's brains; **2.** *v/i.* (sein) break; ∼**lich** *adj.* breakable, fragile.
zer|'**bröckeln** *v/t.* (h) *and v/i.* (sein) (*no -ge-*) crumble; ∼'**drücken** *v/t.* (*no -ge-, h*) crush; crease (*dress*).
Zeremon|**ie** [tseremo'ni:, ∼'mo:njə] *f* (-/-n) ceremony; ℒ**iell** *adj.* [∼o'njɛl] ∼o'njɛl] ceremonial; ∼**iell** [∼o'njɛl] *n* (-s/-e) ceremonial.
zer|'**fahren** *adj.* road: rutted; *p.:* flighty, giddy; scatter-brained; absent-minded.
Zer'fall *m* (-[e]s/no pl.) ruin, decay; disintegration; ℒen *v/i.* (*irr. fallen, no -ge-, sein*) fall to pieces, decay; disintegrate; *in mehrere Teile* ∼ fall into several parts.
zer|'**fetzen** *v/t.* (*no -ge-, h*) tear in *or* to pieces; ∼'**fleischen** *v/t.* (*no -ge-, h*) mangle; lacerate; ∼'**fließen** *v/i.* (*irr. fließen, no -ge-, sein*) melt (away); *ink, etc.:* run; ∼'**fressen** *v/t.* (*irr. fressen, no -ge-, h*) eat away; ℳ corrode; ∼'**gehen** *v/i.* (*irr. gehen, no -ge-, sein*) melt, dissolve; ∼'**gliedern** *v/t.* (*no -ge-, h*) dismember; *anat.* dissect; *fig.* analy|se, *Am.* -ze; ∼'**hacken** *v/t.* (*no -ge-, h*) cut (in)to pieces; mince, chop (up) (*wood, meat*); ∼'**kauen** *v/t.* (*no -ge-, h*) chew; ∼'**kleinern** *v/t.* (*no -ge-, h*) mince (*meat*); chop up (*wood*); grind.
zer'knirsch|**t** *adj.* contrite; ℒ**ung** *f* (-/∼-en) contrition.
zer|'**knittern** *v/t.* (*no -ge-, h*) (c)rumple, wrinkle, crease; ∼'**knüllen** *v/t.* (*no -ge-, h*) crumple up (*sheet of paper*); ∼'**kratzen** *v/t.* (*no*

-ge-, h) scratch; ∼'**krümeln** *v/t.* (*no -ge-, h*) crumble; ∼'**lassen** *v/t.* (*irr. lassen, no -ge-, h*) melt; ∼'**legen** *v/t.* (*no -ge-, h*) take apart *or* to pieces; carve (*joint*); ℳ, *gr., fig.* analy|se, *Am.* -ze; ∼'**lumpt** *adj.* ragged, tattered; ∼'**mahlen** *v/t.* (*irr. mahlen, no -ge-, h*) grind; **∼malmen** [∼'malmən] *v/t.* (*no -ge-, h*) crush; crunch; ∼'**mürben** *v/t.* (*no -ge-, h*) wear down *or* out; ∼'**platzen** *v/i.* (*no -ge-, sein*) burst; explode; ∼'**quetschen** *v/t.* (*no -ge-, h*) crush, squash; mash (*esp. potatoes*).
Zerrbild ['tsɛr-] *n* caricature.
zer|'**reiben** *v/t.* (*irr. reiben, no -ge-, h*) rub to powder, grind down, pulverize; ∼'**reißen** *v/t.* (*irr. reißen, no -ge-*) **1.** *v/t.* (h) tear, rip up; *in Stücke* ∼ tear to pieces; **2.** *v/i.* (sein) tear; *rope, string:* break.
zerren ['tsɛrən] (ge-, h) **1.** *v/t.* tug, pull; drag; ℳ strain; **2.** *v/i.:* ∼ *an* (*dat.*) pull at.
zer|'**rinnen** *v/i.* (*irr. rinnen, no -ge-, sein*) melt away; *fig.* vanish.
'**Zerrung** ℳ *f* (-/-en) strain.
zer|'**rütten** [tsɛr'rytən] *v/t.* (*no -ge-, h*) derange, unsettle; disorganize; ruin, shatter (*one's health or nerves*); wreck (*marriage*); ∼'**sägen** *v/t.* (*no -ge-, h*) saw up; ∼'**schellen** [∼'ʃɛlən] *v/i.* (*no -ge-, sein*) be dashed *or* smashed; ⚓ be wrecked; ✈ crash; ∼'**schlagen 1.** *v/t.* (*irr. schlagen, no -ge-, h*) break *or* smash (to pieces); *sich* ∼ come to nothing; **2.** *adj.* battered; *fig.* knocked up; ∼'**schmettern** *v/t.* (*no -ge-, h*) smash, dash, shatter; ∼'**schneiden** *v/t.* (*irr. schneiden, no -ge-, h*) cut in two; cut up, cut to pieces.
zer|'**setz**|**en** *v/t.* and *v/refl.* (*no -ge-, h*) decompose; ℒ**ung** *f* (-/∼-en) decomposition.
zer|'**spalten** *v/t.* ([*irr. spalten,*] *no -ge-, h*) cleave, split; ∼'**splittern** (*no -ge-*) **1.** *v/t.* (h) split (up), splinter; fritter away (*one's energy, etc.*); **2.** *v/i.* (sein) split (up), splinter; ∼'**sprengen** *v/t.* (*no -ge-, h*) burst (asunder); disperse (*crowd*); ∼'**springen** *v/i.* (*irr. springen, no -ge-, sein*) burst; *glass:* crack; *mein Kopf zerspringt mir* I've got a splitting headache; ∼'**stampfen** *v/t.* (*no -ge-, h*) crush; pound.

Z

zer'stäub|en v/t. (no -ge-, h) spray; **2er** m (-s/-) sprayer, atomizer.

zer'stör|en v/t. (no -ge-, h) destroy; **2er** m (-s/-) destroyer (a. ⊕.) **2ung** f destruction.

zer'streu|en v/t. (no -ge-, h) disperse, scatter; dissipate (doubt, etc.); fig. divert; sich ~ disperse, scatter; fig. amuse o.s.; ~t fig. adj. absent(-minded); **2theit** f (-/~-en) absent-mindedness; **2ung** f **1.** (-/-en) dispersion; diversion, amusement; **2.** phys. (-/no pl.) dispersion (of light).

zerstückeln [tsɛr'ʃtykəln] v/t. (no -ge-, h) cut up, cut (in)to pieces; dismember (body, etc.).

zer'teilen v/t. and v/refl. (no -ge-, h) divide (in acc. into); **~'trennen** v/t. (no -ge-, h) rip (up) (dress); **~'treten** (irr. treten, no -ge-, h) tread down; crush; tread or stamp out (fire); **~'trümmern** v/t. (no -ge-, h) smash.

Zerwürfnis [tsɛr'vyrfnis] n (-ses/-se) dissension, discord.

Zettel ['tsɛtəl] m (-s/-) slip of paper; scrap of paper; note; ticket; label, sticker; tag; s. Anschlagzettel; s. Theaterzettel; **~kartei** f, **~kasten** m card index.

Zeug [tsɔyk] n (-[e]s/-e) stuff (a. fig. contp.); material; cloth; tools pl.; things pl.

Zeuge ['tsɔygə] m (-n/-n) witness; **2n** (ge-, h) **1.** v/i. witness; ⚖ give evidence; für (gegen, von) et. ~ testify for (against, of) s.th.; ~ von be evidence of, bespeak (courage, etc.); **2.** v/t. beget.

Zeugin ['tsɔygin] f (-/-nen) (female) witness.

Zeugnis ['tsɔyknis] n (-ses/-se) ⚖ testimony, evidence; certificate; (school) report, Am. report card.

Zeugung ['tsɔygʊŋ] f (-/-en) procreation; **2sfähig** adj. capable of begetting; **~skraft** f generative power; **2sunfähig** adj. ['tsɔygʊŋs²-] impotent.

Zick|lein zo. ['tsiklain] n (-s/-) kid; **~zack** ['~tsak] m (-[e]s/-e) zigzag; im ~ fahren etc. zigzag.

Ziege zo. ['tsiːgə] f (-/-n) (she-)goat; nanny(-goat).

Ziegel ['tsiːgəl] m (-s/-) brick; tile (of roof); **~dach** n tiled roof; **~ei** [~'lai] f (-/-en) brickworks sg., pl., brickyard; **~stein** m brick.

'Ziegen|bock zo. m he-goat; **~fell** n goatskin; **~hirt** m goatherd; **~leder** n kid(-leather); **~peter** ⚕ m (-s/-) mumps.

Ziehbrunnen ['tsiː-] m draw-well.

ziehen ['tsiːən] (irr., ge-) **1.** v/t. (h) pull, draw; draw (line, weapon, lots, conclusion, etc.); drag; ✔ cultivate; zo. breed; take off (hat); dig (ditch); draw, extract (tooth); ⚕ extract (root of number); Blasen ~ ⚕ raise blisters; e-n Vergleich ~ draw or make a comparison; j-n ins Vertrauen ~ take s.o. into one's confidence; in Erwägung ~ take into consideration; in die Länge ~ draw out; fig. protract; Nutzen ~ aus derive profit or benefit from; an sich ~ draw to one; Aufmerksamkeit etc. auf sich ~ attract attention, etc.; et. nach sich ~ entail or involve s.th.; **2.** v/i. (h) pull (an dat. at); chimney, cigar, etc.: draw; puff (an e-r Zigarre at a cigar); tea: infuse, draw; play: draw (large audiences); F ✔ goods: draw (customers), take; es zieht there is a draught, Am. there is a draft; **3.** v/i. (sein) move, go; march; (re)move (nach to); birds: migrate; ✔ extend, stretch, run; wood: warp; sich in die Länge ~ drag on.

'Zieh|harmonika ♪ f accordion; **~ung** f (-/-en) drawing (of lots).

Ziel [tsiːl] n (-[e]s/-e) aim (a. fig.); mark; sports: winning-post, goal (a. fig.); target; ✗ objective; destination (of voyage); fig. end, purpose, target, object(ive); term; sein ~ erreichen gain one's end(s pl.); über das ~ hinausschießen overshoot the mark; zum ~e führen succeed, be successful; sich zum ~ setzen zu inf. aim at ger., Am. aim to inf.; **~band** n sports: tape; **2bewußt** adj. purposeful; **2en** v/i. (ge-, h) (take) aim (auf acc. at); **~fernrohr** n telescopic sight; **2los** adj. aimless, purposeless; **~scheibe** f target, butt; ~ des Spottes butt or target (of derision); **2strebig** adj. purposive.

ziemlich ['tsiːmlic] **1.** adj. fair, tolerable; considerable; **2.** adv.

Z

pretty, fairly, tolerably, rather; about.

Zier [tsiːr] f (-/no pl.), **~de** [ˈ~də] f (-/-n) ornament; fig. a. hono(u)r (für to); **'2en** v/t. (ge-, h) ornament, adorn; decorate; sich ~ be affected; esp. of woman: be prudish; refuse; **'2lich** adj. delicate; neat; graceful, elegant; **'~lichkeit** f (-/~ -en) delicacy; neatness; gracefulness, elegance; **'~pflanze** f ornamental plant.

Ziffer [ˈtsifər] f (-/-n) figure, digit; **'~blatt** n dial(-plate); face.

Zigarette [tsigaˈretə] f (-/-n) cigaret(te); **~nautomat** [~nʔ-] m cigarette slot-machine; **~netui** [~nʔ-] n cigarette-case; **~nspitze** f cigarette-holder; **~nstummel** m stub, Am. a. butt.

Zigarre [tsiˈgarə] f (-/-n) cigar.

Zigeuner [tsiˈgɔʏnər] m (-s/-), **~in** f (-/-nen) gipsy, gypsy.

Zimmer [ˈtsimər] n (-s/-) room; apartment; **'~antenne** f radio, etc.: indoor aerial, Am. a. indoor antenna; **'~einrichtung** f furniture; **'~flucht** f suite (of rooms); **'~mädchen** n chamber-maid; **'~mann** m (-[e]s/Zimmerleute) carpenter; **'2n** (ge-, h) **1.** v/t. carpenter; fig. frame; **2.** v/i. carpenter; **'~pflanze** f indoor plant; **'~vermieterin** f (-/-nen) landlady. [prudish; affected.]

zimperlich adj. [ˈtsimpərliç] prim;]

Zimt [tsimt] m (-[e]s/-e) cinnamon.

Zink [tsiŋk] n (-[e]s/no pl.) zinc; **'~blech** n sheet zinc.

Zinke [ˈtsiŋkə] f (-/-n) prong; tooth (of comb or fork); **'~n** m (-s/-) s. Zinke.

Zinn [tsin] n (-[e]s/no pl.) tin.

Zinne [ˈtsinə] f (-/-n) pinnacle; ⚔ battlement.

Zinnober [tsiˈnoːbər] m (-s/-) cinnabar; **2rot** adj. vermilion.

Zins [tsins] m (-es/-en) rent; tribute; mst **~en** pl. interest; **~en tragen** yield or bear interest; **'2bringend** adj. bearing interest; **~eszins** [ˈ~zəs-] m compound interest; **'2frei** adj. rent-free; free of interest; **'~fuß** m, **'~satz** m rate of interest.

Zipf|el [ˈtsipfəl] m (-s/-) tip, point, end; corner (of handkerchief, etc.); lappet (of garment); **'2elig** adj. having points or ends; **'~elmütze** f jelly-bag cap; nightcap.

Zirkel [ˈtsirkəl] m (-s/-) circle (a. fig.); ⚒ (ein a pair of) compasses pl. or dividers pl.

zirkulieren [tsirkuˈliːrən] v/i. (no -ge-, h) circulate.

Zirkus [ˈtsirkus] m (-/-se) circus.

zirpen [ˈtsirpən] v/i. (ge-, h) chirp, cheep.

zisch|eln [ˈtsiʃəln] v/t. and v/i. (ge-, h) whisper; **'~en** v/i. (ge-, h) hiss; whiz(z).

ziselieren [tsizeˈliːrən] v/t. (no -ge-, h) chase.

Zit|at [tsiˈtaːt] n (-[e]s/-e) quotation; **2ieren** [~ˈtiːrən] v/t. (no -ge-, h) summon; quote.

Zitrone [tsiˈtroːnə] f (-/-n) lemon; **~nlimonade** f lemonade; lemon squash; **~npresse** f lemon-squeezer; **~nsaft** m lemon juice.

zittern [ˈtsitərn] v/i. (ge-, h) tremble, shake (vor dat. with).

zivil [tsiˈviːl] **1.** adj. civil; civilian; price: reasonable; **2.** ♀ n (-s/no pl.) civilians pl.; s. Zivilkleidung; **2bevölkerung** f civilian population, civilians pl.; **2isation** [~iliˈzaˈtsjoːn] f (-/~-en) civilization; **~isieren** [~iliˈziːrən] v/t. (no -ge-, h) civilize; **2ist** [~iˈlist] m (-en/-en) civilian; **2kleidung** f civilian or plain clothes pl.

Zofe [ˈtsoːfə] f (-/-n) lady's maid.

zog [tsoːk] pret. of ziehen.

zögern [ˈtsøːgərn] **1.** v/i. (ge-, h) hesitate; linger; delay; **2.** ♀ n (-s/no pl.) hesitation; delay.

Zögling [ˈtsøːkliŋ] m (-s/-e) pupil.

Zoll [tsɔl] m **1.** (-[e]s/-) inch; **2.** (-[e]s/ᵗe) customs pl., duty; the Customs pl.; **'~abfertigung** f customs clearance; **'~amt** n customhouse; **'~beamte** m customs officer; **'~behörde** f the Customs pl.; **'~erklärung** f customs declaration; **'2frei** adj. duty-free; **'~kontrolle** f customs examination; **'2pflichtig** adj. liable to duty; **'~stock** m footrule; **'~tarif** m tariff.

Zone [ˈtsoːnə] f (-/-n) zone.

Zoo [tsoː] m (-[s]/-s) zoo.

Zoolog|e [tsoˈoˈloːgə] m (-n/-n) zoologist; **~ie** [~oˈgiː] f (-/no pl.) zoology; **2isch** adj. [~ˈloːgiʃ] zoological.

Zopf [tsɔpf] m (-[e]s/ᵗe) plait, tress; pigtail; alter ~ antiquated ways pl. or custom.

Zorn [tsɔrn] *m* (-[e]s/*no pl.*) anger; **ˈ2ig** *adj.* angry (*auf* j-n with s.o.; *auf* et. at s.th.).

Zote [ˈtsoːtə] *f* (-/-n) filthy *or* smutty joke, obscenity.

Zott|el [ˈtsɔtəl] *f* (-/-n) tuft (of hair); tassel; **ˈ2(e)lig** *adj.* shaggy.

zu [tsuː] **1.** *prp.* (*dat.*) *direction:* to, towards, up to; at, in; on; in addition to, along with; *purpose:* for; ~ *Beginn* at the beginning *or* outset; ~ *Weihnachten* at Christmas; *zum ersten Mal* for the first time; ~ *e-m ... Preise* at a ... price; ~ *meinem Erstaunen* to my surprise; ~ *Wasser* by water; ~ *zweien* by twos; *zu Tausenden* by thousands; ~ *Wasser* by water; ~ *zweien* by twos; *zum Beispiel* for example; **2.** *adv.* too; *direction:* towards, to; *F* closed, shut; *with inf.:* to; *ich habe* ~ *arbeiten* I have to work.

ˈzubauen *v/t.* (*sep.*, -ge-, *h*) build up *or* in; block.

Zubehör [ˈtsuːbəhøːr] *n, m* (-[e]s/-e) appurtenances *pl.*, fittings *pl.*, *Am.* F fixings *pl.*; *esp.* ⊕ accessories *pl.*

ˈzubereit|en *v/t.* (*sep.*, *no* -ge-, *h*) prepare; **ˈ2ung** *f* preparation.

ˈzu|billigen *v/t.* (*sep.*, -ge-, *h*) grant; **ˈ~binden** *v/t.* (*irr.* binden, *sep.*, -ge-, *h*) tie up; **ˈ~blinzeln** *v/i.* (*sep.*, -ge-, *h*) wink at s.o.; **ˈ~bringen** *v/t.* (*irr.* bringen, *sep.*, -ge-, *h*) pass, spend (*time*).

Zucht [tsuxt] *f* **1.** (-/*no pl.*) discipline; breeding, rearing; *rearing of bees, etc.*: culture; ♀ cultivation; **2.** (-/-en) breed, race; **ˈ~bulle** *zo.* *m* bull (*for breeding*).

züчht|en [ˈtsʏçtən] *v/t.* (*ge-*, *h*) breed (*animals*); grow, cultivate (*plants*); **ˈ2er** *m* (-s/-) breeder (*of animals*); grower (*of plants*).

ˈZucht|haus *n* penitentiary; *punishment:* penal servitude; **ˈ~häusler** [ˈ~hɔʏslər] *m* (-s/-) convict; **ˈ~hengst** *zo.* *m* stud-horse, stallion.

züchtig *adj.* [ˈtsʏçtiç] chaste, modest; **ˈ~en** [ˈ~gən] *v/t.* (*ge-*, *h*) flog.

ˈzucht|los *adj.* undisciplined; **ˈ2losigkeit** *f* (-/♀-en) want of discipline; **ˈ2stute** *zo.* *f* brood-mare.

zucken [ˈtsukən] *v/i.* (*ge-*, *h*) jerk; move convulsively, twitch (*all: mit et.* s.th.); *with pain:* wince; *lightning:* flash.

zücken [ˈtsʏkən] *v/t.* (*ge-*, *h*) draw (*sword*); F pull out (*purse, pencil*).

Zucker [ˈtsukər] *m* (-s/*no pl.*) sugar; **ˈ~dose** *f* sugar-basin, *Am.* sugar bowl; **ˈ~erbse** ♀ *f* green pea; **ˈ~guß** *m* icing, frosting; **ˈ~hut** *m* sugar-loaf; **ˈ2ig** *adj.* sugary; **ˈ2krank** *adj.* diabetic; **ˈ2n** *v/t.* (*ge-*, *h*) sugar; **ˈ~rohr** ♀ *n* sugar-cane; **ˈ~rübe** ♀ *f* sugar-beet; **ˈ2süß** *adj.* (as) sweet as sugar; **ˈ~wasser** *n* sugared water; **ˈ~zange** *f* (e-e a pair of) sugar-tongs *pl.*

zuckrig *adj.* [ˈtsukriç] sugary.

ˈZuckung ⚕ *f* (-/-en) convulsion.

ˈzudecken *v/t.* (*sep.*, -ge-, *h*) cover (up).

zudem *adv.* [tsuˈdeːm] besides, moreover.

ˈzu|drehen *v/t.* (*sep.*, -ge-, *h*) turn off (*tap*); j-m den Rücken ~ turn one's back on s.o.; **ˈ~dringlich** *adj.* importunate, obtrusive; **ˈ~drücken** *v/t.* (*sep.*, -ge-, *h*) close, shut; **ˈ~erkennen** *v/t.* (*irr.* kennen, *sep.*, *no* -ge-, *h*) award (a. ⚖); adjudge (*dat.* to) (a. ⚖).

zuerst *adv.* [tsuˈ-] first (of all); at first; *er kam* ~ *an* he was the first to arrive.

ˈzufahr|en *v/i.* (*irr.* fahren, *sep.*, -ge-, *sein*) drive on; ~ *auf* (*acc.*) drive to (-wards); *fig.* rush at s.o.; **ˈ2t** *f* approach, drive, *Am.* driveway; **ˈ2tsstraße** *f* approach (road).

ˈZufall *m* chance, accident; *durch* ~ by chance, by accident; **ˈ2en** *v/i.* (*irr.* fallen, *sep.*, -ge-, *sein*) *eyes:* be closing (*with sleep*); *door:* shut (*of itself*); j-m ~ fall to s.o.('s share).

ˈzufällig **1.** *adj.* accidental; *attr.* chance; casual; **2.** *adv.* accidentally, by chance.

ˈzufassen *v/i.* (*sep.*, -ge-, *h*) seize (hold of) s.th.; (*mit*) ~ lend *or* give a hand.

ˈZuflucht *f* (-/♀ ~e) refuge, shelter, resort; *s-e* ~ *nehmen zu* have recourse to s.th., take refuge in s.th.

ˈZufluß *m* afflux; influx (a. ⚕); affluent, tributary (*of river*); ⚕ supply.

ˈzuflüstern *v/t.* (*sep.*, -ge-, *h*): j-m et. ~ whisper s.th. to s.o.

zufolge *prp.* (*gen.; dat.*) [tsuˈfɔlgə] according to.

zufrieden *adj.* [tsuˈ-] content(ed), satisfied; **2heit** *f* (-/*no pl.*) contentment, satisfaction; **ˈ~lassen** *v/t.* (*irr.* lassen, *sep.*, -ge-, *h*) let s.o. alone;

Z

~stellen v/t. (sep., -ge-, h) satisfy; **~stellend** adj. satisfactory.

'**zu|frieren** v/i. (irr. frieren, sep., -ge-, sein) freeze up or over; '**~fügen** v/t. (sep., -ge-, h) add; do, cause; inflict (wound, etc.) (j-m [up]on s.o.); **2fuhr** ['~fu:r] f (-/-en) supply; supplies pl.; influx; '**~führen** v/t. (sep., -ge-, h) carry, lead, bring; ⊕ feed; supply (a. ⊕).

Zug [tsu:k] m (-[e]s/⁄e) draw(ing), pull(ing); ⊕ traction; ⚒ expedition, campaign; procession; migration (of birds); drift (of clouds); range (of mountains); 🚂 train; feature; trait (of character); bent, tendency, trend; draught, Am. draft (of air); at chess: move; drinking; draught, Am. draft; at cigarette, etc.: puff.

'**Zu|gabe** f addition; extra; thea. encore; '**~gang** m entrance; access; approach; **2gänglich** adj. ['~gen-liç] accessible (für to); '**2geben** v/t. (irr. geben, sep., -ge-, h) add; fig.: allow; confess; admit.

zugegen adj. (tsu'-] present (bei at.).
'**zugehen** v/i. (irr. gehen, sep., -ge-, sein) door, etc.: close, shut; p. move on, walk faster; happen; auf j-n ~ go up to s.o., move or walk towards s.o.

'**Zugehörigkeit** f (-/no pl.) membership (zu to) (society, etc.); belonging (to).

'**Zügel** ['tsy:gəl] m (-s/-) rein; bridle (a. fig.); '**2los** adj. unbridled; fig.: unrestrained; licentious; '**2n** v/t. (ge-, h) rein (in); fig. bridle, check.

'**Zuge|ständnis** n concession; '**2-stehen** v/t. (irr. stehen, sep., -ge-, h) concede.

'**zugetan** adj. attached (dat. to).
'**Zugführer** 🚂 m guard, Am. conductor.   [-ge-, h) add.]
'**zugießen** v/t. (irr. gießen, sep.,)
zug|ig adj. ['tsu:giç] draughty, Am. drafty; **2kraft** ['~k-] f ⊕ traction; fig. attraction, draw, appeal; **~kräf-tig** adj. ['~k-]: ~ sein be a draw.

zugleich adv. [tsu'-] at the same time; together.

'**Zug|luft** f (-/no pl.) draught, Am. draft; '**~maschine** f traction-engine, tractor; '**~pflaster** n blister.

'**zu|greifen** v/i. (irr. greifen, sep., -ge-, h) grasp or grab at s.th.; at

table: help o.s.; lend a hand; '**2griff** m grip, clutch.

zugrunde adv. [tsu'grundə]: ~ gehen perish; ~ richten ruin.

'**Zugtier** n draught animal, Am. draft animal.

zu|gunsten prp. (gen.) [tsu'gunstən] in favo(u)r of; **~'gute** adv.: j-m et. ~ halten give s.o. credit for s.th.; ~ kommen be for the benefit (dat.)

'**Zugvogel** m bird of passage. [of).]

'**zu|halten** v/t. (irr. halten, sep., -ge-, h) hold (door) to; sich die Ohren ~ stop one's ears.   [home.]

Zuhause [tsu'hauzə] n (-/no pl.))
'**zu|heilen** v/i. (sep., -ge-, sein) heal up, skin over; '**~hören** v/i. (sep., -ge-, h) listen (dat. to).

'**Zuhörer** m hearer, listener; ~ pl. audience; '**~schaft** f (-/⁄-en) audience.

'**zu|jubeln** v/i. (sep., -ge-, h) cheer; '**~kleben** v/t. (sep., -ge-, h) paste or glue up; gum (letter) down; '**~knallen** v/t. (sep., -ge-, h) bang, slam (door, etc.); '**~knöpfen** v/t. (sep., -ge-, h) button (up); '**~kommen** v/i. (irr. kommen, sep., -ge-, sein): auf j-n ~ come up to s.o.; j-m ~ be due to s.o.; j-m et. ~ lassen let s.o. have s.th.; send s.o. s.th.; '**~korken** v/t. (sep., -ge-, h) cork (up).

Zu|kunft ['tsu:kunft] f (-/no pl.) future; gr. future (tense); '**2künftig 1.** adj. future; ~er Vater father-to-be; **2.** adv. in future.

'**zu|lächeln** v/i. (sep., -ge-, h) smile at or (up)on; '**2lage** f extra pay, increase; rise, Am. raise (in salary or wages); '**~langen** v/i. (sep., -ge-, h) at table: help o.s.; '**~lassen** v/t. (irr. lassen, sep., -ge-, h) leave (door) shut; keep closed; fig.: admit s.o.; license; allow, suffer; admit of (only one interpretation, etc.); '**~lässig** adj. admissible, allowable; '**2lassung** f (-/-en) admission; permission; licen|ce, Am. -se.

'**zulegen** v/t. (sep., -ge-, h) add; F sich et. ~ get o.s. s.th.

zuleide adv. ['tsu'laɪdə]: j-m et. ~ tun do s.o. harm, harm or hurt s.o.

'**zuleiten** v/t. (sep., -ge-, h) let in (water, etc.); conduct to; pass on to s.o.

zu|letzt adv. [tsu'-] finally, at last; er kam ~ an he was the last to arrive; **⁀liebe** adv.: j-m ⁀ for s.o.'s sake.

zum prp. [tsum] = zu dem.

'**zumachen** v/t. (sep., -ge-, h) close, shut; button (up) (coat); fasten.

zumal cj. [tsu'-] especially, particularly. [up.]

'**zumauern** v/t. (sep., -ge-, h) wall]

zumut|en ['tsu:mu:tən] v/t. (sep., -ge-, h): j-m et. ⁀ expect s.th. of s.o.; sich zuviel ⁀ overtask o.s., overtax one's strength, etc.; **⁀ung** f (-/-en) exacting demand, exaction; fig. impudence.

zunächst [tsu'-] **1.** prp. (dat.) next to; **2.** adv. first of all; for the present.

'**zu|nageln** v/t. (sep., -ge-, h) nail up; '**⁀nähen** v/t. (sep., -ge-, h) sew up; **⁀nahme** ['⁀na:mə] f (-/-n) increase, growth; '**⁀name** m surname.

zünden ['tsyndən] v/i. (ge-, h) kindle; esp. mot. ignite; fig. arouse enthusiasm.

Zünd|holz ['tsynt-] n match; '**⁀kerze** mot. f spark(ing)-plug, Am. spark plug; '**⁀schlüssel** mot. m ignition key; '**⁀schnur** f fuse; '**⁀stoff** fig. m fuel; **⁀ung** mot. ['⁀duŋ] f (-/-en) ignition.

zunehmen v/i. (irr. nehmen, sep., -ge-, h) increase (an dat. in); grow; put on weight; moon: wax; days: grow longer.

zuneig|en (sep., -ge-, h) **1.** v/i. incline to(wards); **2.** v/refl. incline to(wards); sich dem Ende ⁀ draw to a close; '**⁀ung** f (-/⁀-en) affection.

Zunft [tsunft] f (-/⁀e) guild, corporation.

Zunge ['tsuŋə] f (-/-n) tongue.

züngeln ['tsyŋəln] v/i. (ge-, h) play with its tongue; flame: lick.

zungen|fertig adj. voluble; '**⁀fertigkeit** f (-/no pl.) volubility; '**⁀spitze** f tip of the tongue.

zunichte adv. [tsu'niçtə]: ⁀ machen or werden bring or come to nothing.

'**zunicken** v/i. (sep., -ge-, h) nod to.

zu|nutze adv. [tsu'nutsə]: sich et. ⁀ machen turn s.th. to account, utilize s.th.; **⁀'oberst** adv. at the top, uppermost.

zupfen ['tsupfən] (ge-, h) **1.** v/t. pull, tug, twitch; **2.** v/i. pull, tug, twitch (all: an dat. at).

zur prp. [tsu:r] = zu der.

'**zurechnungsfähig** adj. of sound mind; ⁀⁀ responsible; '**⁀keit** ⁀⁀ f (-/no pl.) responsibility.

zurecht|finden [tsu'-] v/refl. (irr. finden, sep., -ge-, h) find one's way; **⁀kommen** v/i. (irr. kommen, sep., -ge-, sein) arrive in time; ⁀ (mit) get on (well) (with); manage s.th.; **⁀legen** v/t. (sep., -ge-, h) arrange; sich e-e Sache ⁀ think s.th. out; **⁀machen** F v/t. (sep., -ge-, h) get ready, prepare, Am. F fix; adapt (für to, for purpose); sich ⁀ of woman: make (o.s.) up; **⁀weisen** v/t. (irr. weisen, sep., -ge-, h) reprimand; **⁀weisung** f reprimand.

'**zu|reden** v/i. (sep., -ge-, h): j-m ⁀ try to persuade s.o.; encourage s.o.; '**⁀reiten** v/t. (irr. reiten, sep., -ge-, h) break in; '**⁀riegeln** v/t. (sep., -ge-, h) bolt (up).

zürnen ['tsyrnən] v/i. (ge-, h) be angry (j-m with s.o.).

zurück adv. [tsu'ryk] back; backward(s); behind; **⁀behalten** v/t. (irr. halten, sep., no -ge-, h) keep back, retain; **⁀bekommen** v/t. (irr. kommen, sep., no -ge-, h) get back; **⁀bleiben** v/i. (irr. bleiben, sep., -ge-, sein) remain or stay behind; fall behind, lag; **⁀blicken** v/i. (sep., -ge-, h) look back; **⁀bringen** v/t. (irr. bringen, sep., -ge-, h) bring back; **⁀datieren** v/t. (sep., no -ge-, h) date back, antedate; **⁀drängen** v/t. (sep., -ge-, h) push back; fig. repress; **⁀erobern** v/t. (sep., no -ge-, h) reconquer; **⁀erstatten** v/t. (sep., no -ge-, h) restore, return; refund (expenses); **⁀fahren** (irr. fahren, sep., -ge-) **1.** v/i. (sein) drive back; fig. start; **2.** v/t. (h) drive back; **⁀fordern** v/t. (sep., -ge-, h) reclaim; **⁀führen** v/t. (sep., -ge-, h) lead back; ⁀ auf (acc.) reduce to (rule, etc.); refer to (cause, etc.); **⁀geben** v/t. (irr. geben, sep., -ge-, h) give back, return, restore; **⁀gehen** v/i. (irr. gehen, sep., -ge-, sein) go back; return; **⁀gezogen** adj. retired; **⁀greifen** fig. v/i. (irr. greifen, sep., -ge-, h): ⁀ auf (acc.) fall back (up)on; **⁀halten** (irr. halten, sep., -ge-, h) **1.** v/t. hold back; **2.** v/i.: ⁀ mit keep back; **⁀haltend** adj. reserved; **⁀haltung** f (-/⁀-en) reserve; **⁀kehren** v/i. (sep., -ge-, sein) return; **⁀kommen**

v/i. (irr. kommen, sep., -ge-, sein) come back; return (*fig. auf acc.* to); **~lassen** *v/t. (irr. lassen, sep., -ge-, h)* leave (behind); **~legen** *v/t. (sep., -ge-, h)* lay aside; cover (*distance, way*); **~nehmen** *v/t. (irr. nehmen, sep., -ge-, h)* take back; withdraw, retract (*words, etc.*); **~prallen** *v/i. (sep., -ge-, sein)* rebound; start; **~rufen** *v/t. (irr. rufen, sep., -ge-, h)* call back; *sich ins Gedächtnis* ~ recall; **~schicken** *v/t. (sep., -ge-, h)* send back; **~schlagen** *(irr. schlagen, sep., -ge-, h)* 1. *v/t.* drive (*ball*) back; repel (*enemy*); turn down (*blanket*); 2. *v/i.* strike back; **~schrecken** *v/i. (sep., -ge-, sein)* 1. *(irr. schrecken)* shrink back (*vor dat. from spectacle, etc.*); 2. shrink (*vor dat. from work, etc.*); **~setzen** *v/t. (sep., -ge-, h)* put back; *fig.* slight, neglect; **~stellen** *v/t. (sep., -ge-, h)* put back (*a. clock*); *fig.* defer, postpone; **~strahlen** *v/t. (sep., -ge-, h)* reflect; **~streifen** *v/t. (sep., -ge-, h)* turn or tuck up (*sleeve*); **~treten** *v/i. (irr. treten, sep., -ge-, sein)* step or stand back; *fig.:* recede; resign; withdraw; **~weichen** *v/i. (irr. weichen, sep., -ge-, sein)* fall back; recede (*a. fig.*); **~weisen** *v/t. (irr. weisen, sep., -ge-, h)* decline, reject; repel (*attack*); **~zahlen** *v/t. (sep., -ge-, h)* pay back (*a. fig.*); **~ziehen** *(irr. ziehen, sep., -ge-)* 1. *v/t. (h)* draw back; *fig.* withdraw; *sich* ~ retire, withdraw; ✗ retreat; 2. *v/i. (sein)* move or march back.

'Zuruf *m (a. fig.)* call; **'2en** *v/t. (irr. rufen, sep., -ge-, h)* call (out), shout (*j-m et. s.th. to s.o.*).

'Zusage *f* promise; assent; **'2en** *(sep., -ge-, h)* 1. *v/t.* promise; 2. *v/i.* promise to come; *j-m* ~ *food, etc.:* agree with s.o.; accept s.o.'s invitation; suit s.o.

zusammen *adv.* [tsu'zamən] together; at the same time; *alles* ~ (all) in all; ~ *betragen* amount to, total (up to); **2arbeit** *f (-/no pl.)* co-operation; team-work; **~arbeiten** *v/i. (sep., -ge-, h)* work together; co-operate; **~beißen** *v/t. (irr. beißen, sep., -ge-, h): die Zähne* ~ set one's teeth; **~brechen** *v/i. (irr. brechen, sep., -ge-, sein)* break down; collapse; **2bruch** *m* breakdown; collapse; **~drücken** *v/t.*

(sep., -ge-, h) compress, press together; **~fahren** *fig. v/i. (irr. fahren, sep., -ge-, sein)* start (*bei at; vor dat.* with); **~fallen** *v/i. (irr. fallen, sep., -ge-, sein)* fall in, collapse; coincide; **~falten** *v/t. (sep., -ge-, h)* fold up; **~fassen** *v/t. (sep., -ge-, h)* summarize, sum up; **2fassung** *f (-/-en)* summary; **~fügen** *v/t. (sep., -ge-, h)* join (together); **~halten** *(irr. halten, sep., -ge-, h)* 1. *v/t.* hold together; 2. *v/i.* hold together; *friends:* F stick together; **2hang** *m* coherence, coherency; connection; context; **~hängen** *(sep., -ge-, h)* 1. *v/i. (irr. hängen)* cohere; *fig.* be connected; 2. *v/t.* hang together; **~klappen** *v/t. (sep., -ge-, h)* fold up; close (*clasp-knife*); **~kommen** *v/i. (irr. kommen, sep., -ge-, sein)* meet; **2kunft** [~kʊnft] *f (-/-̈e)* meeting; **~laufen** *v/i. (irr. laufen, sep., -ge-, sein)* run or crowd together; ⚕ converge; *milk:* curdle; **~legen** *v/t. (sep., -ge-, h)* lay together; fold up; club (*money*) (together); **~nehmen** *fig. v/t. (irr. nehmen, sep., -ge-, h)* collect (*one's wits*); *sich* ~ be on one's good behavio(u)r; pull o.s. together; **~packen** *v/t. (sep., -ge-, h)* pack up; **~passen** *v/i. (sep., -ge-, h)* match, harmonize; **~rechnen** *v/t. (sep., -ge-, h)* add up; **~reißen** F *v/refl. (irr. reißen, sep., -ge-, h)* pull o.s. together; **~rollen** *v/t. and v/refl. (sep., -ge-, h)* coil (up); **~rotten** *v/refl. (sep., -ge-, h)* band together; **~rücken** *(sep., -ge-)* 1. *v/t. (h)* move together; 2. *v/i. (sein)* close up; **~schlagen** *(irr. schlagen, sep., -ge-)* 1. *v/t. (h)* clap (*hands*) (together); F smash to pieces; beat *s.o.* up; 2. *v/i. (sein):* ~ *über (dat.)* close over; **~schließen** *v/refl. (irr. schließen, sep., -ge-, h)* join; unite; **2schluß** *m* union; **~schrumpfen** *v/i. (sep., -ge-, sein)* shrivel (up), shrink; **~setzen** *v/t. (sep., -ge-, h)* put together; compose; compound (*a. ⚛, word*); ⊕ assemble; *sich* ~ *aus* consist of; **2setzung** *f (-/-en)* composition; compound; ⊕ assembly; **~stellen** *v/t. (sep., -ge-, h)* put together; compile; combine; **2stoß** *m* collision (*a. fig.*); ✗ encounter; *fig.* clash; **~stoßen** *v/i. (irr. stoßen, sep., -ge-, sein)* collide (*a. fig.*); adjoin; *fig.* clash;

Z

~ mit knock (heads, etc.) together; ~stürzen v/i. (sep., -ge-, sein) collapse; house, etc.: fall in; ~tragen v/t. (irr. tragen, sep., -ge-, h) collect; compile (notes); ~treffen v/i. (irr. treffen, sep., -ge-, sein) meet; coincide; 2treffen n (-s/no pl.) meeting; encounter (of enemies); coincidence; ~treten v/i. (irr. treten, sep., -ge-, sein) meet; parl. a. convene; ~wirken v/i. (sep., -ge-, h) co-operate; 2wirken n (-s/no pl.) co-operation; ~zählen v/t. (sep., -ge-, h) add up, count up; ~ziehen v/t. (irr. ziehen, sep., -ge-, h) draw together; contract; concentrate (troops); sich ~ contract.

'Zusatz m addition; admixture; metall. alloy; supplement.

zusätzlich adj. ['tsuːzetsliç] additional.

'zuschau|en v/i. (sep., -ge-, h) look on (e-r Sache at s.th.); j-m ~ watch s.o. (bei s.th. doing s.th.); '2er m (-s/-) spectator, looker-on, onlooker; '2erraum thea. m auditorium.

'zuschicken v/t. (sep., -ge-, h) send (dat. to); mail; consign (goods).

'Zuschlag m addition; extra charge; excess fare; ⚹ surcharge; at auction: knocking down; 2en ['~gən] (irr. schlagen, sep., -ge-) 1. v/i. (h) strike; 2. v/i. (sein) door: slam (to); 3. v/t. (h) bang, slam (door) (to); at auction: knock down (dat. to).

'zu|schließen v/t. (irr. schließen, sep., -ge-, h) lock (up); '~schnallen v/t. (sep., -ge-, h) buckle (up); '~schnappen (sep., -ge-) 1. v/i. (h) dog: snap; 2. v/i. (sein) door: snap to; '~schneiden v/t. (irr. schneiden, sep., -ge-, h) cut up; cut (suit) (to size); '2schnitt m (-[e]s/✗-e) cut; style; '~schnüren v/t. (sep., -ge-, h) lace up; cord up; '~schrauben v/t. (sep., -ge-, h) screw up or tight; '~schreiben v/t. (irr. schreiben, sep., -ge-, h): j-m et. ~ ascribe or attribute s.th. to s.o.; '2schrift f letter.

zuschulden adv. ['tsu'-]: sich et. ~ kommen lassen make o.s. guilty of s.th.

'Zu|schuß m allowance; subsidy, grant (of government); '2schütten v/t. (sep., -ge-, h) fill up (ditch); F add; '2sehen v/i. (irr. sehen, sep., -ge-, h) s. zuschauen; daß see (to

it) that; 2sehends adv. ['~ts] visibly; '2senden v/t. ([irr. senden,] sep., -ge-, h) s. zuschicken; '2setzen (sep., -ge-, h) 1. v/t. add; lose (money); 2. v/i. lose money; j-m ~ press s.o. hard.

'zusicher|n v/t. (sep., -ge-, h): j-m et. ~ assure s.o. of s.th.; promise s.o. s.th.; '2ung f promise, assurance.

'zu|spielen v/t. (sep., -ge-, h) sports: pass (ball) (dat. to); '~spitzen (sep., -ge-, h) point; sich ~ taper (off); fig. come to a crisis; '2spruch m (-[e]s/no pl.) encouragement; consolation; ✝ custom; '2stand m condition, state; in gutem ~ house: in good repair.

zustande adv. [tsu'ʃtandə]: ~ bringen bring about; ~ kommen come about; nicht ~ kommen not to come off. [(-/-en) competence.)

'zuständig adj. competent; '2keit f)

zustatten adv. [tsu'ʃtatən]: j-m ~ kommen be useful to s.o.

'zustehen v/i. (irr. stehen, sep., -ge-, h) be due (dat. to).

'zustell|en v/t. (sep., -ge-, h) deliver (a. ⚹); ⚖ serve (j-m on s.o.); '2ung f delivery; ⚖ service.

'zustimm|en v/i. (sep., -ge-, h) agree (dat.: to s.th.; with s.o.); consent (to s.th.); '2ung f consent.

'zustoßen fig. v/i. (irr. stoßen, sep., -ge-, sein): j-m ~ happen to s.o.

zutage adv. [tsu'taːgə]: ~ treten come to light.

Zutaten ['tsuːtaːtən] f/pl. ingredients pl. (of food); trimmings pl. (of dress). [fall to s.o.'s share.)

zuteil adv. [tsu'taɪl]: j-m ~ werden)

'zuteil|en v/t. (sep., -ge-, h) allot, apportion; '2ung f allotment, apportionment; ration.

'zutragen v/refl. (irr. tragen, sep., -ge-, h) happen.

'zutrauen 1. v/t. (sep., -ge-, h): j-m et. ~ credit s.o. with s.th.; sich zuviel ~ overrate o.s.; 2. 2 n (-s/no pl.) confidence (zu in).

'zutraulich adj. confiding, trustful, trusting; animal: friendly, tame.

'zutreffen v/i. (irr. treffen, sep., -ge-, h) be right, be true; ~ auf (acc.) be true of; '~d adj. right, correct; applicable.

'zutrinken v/i. (irr. trinken, sep., -ge-, h): j-m ~ drink to s.o.

Z

'Zutritt *m* (-[e]s/*no pl.*) access; admission; ~ *verboten!* no admittance! [bottom.]

zuunterst *adv.* [tsu-] right at the

zuverlässig *adj.* ['tsu:ferlɛsiç] reliable; certain; **'2keit** *f* (-/*no pl.*) reliability; certainty.

Zuversicht ['tsu:ferziçt] *f* (-/*no pl.*) confidence; **2lich** *adj.* confident.

zuviel *adv.* [tsu'-] too much; e-r ~ one too many.

zuvor *adv.* [tsu'-] before, previously; first; **~kommen** v/i. (*irr. kommen*, *sep.*, -ge-, *sein*): j-m ~ anticipate s.o.; e-r *Sache* ~ anticipate *or* prevent s.th.; **~kommend** *adj.* obliging; courteous.

Zuwachs ['tsu:vaks] *m* (-es/*no pl.*) increase; **2en** v/i. (*irr. wachsen*, *sep.*, -ge-, *sein*) become overgrown; *wound*: close.

zu|wege *adv.* [tsu've:gǝ]: ~ *bringen* bring about; **~weilen** *adv.* sometimes.

'zu|weisen v/t. (*irr. weisen*, *sep.*, -ge-, *h*) assign; **~wenden** v/t. (*irr. wenden*) *sep.*, -ge-, *h*) (*dat.*) turn to(wards); *fig.*: give; bestow on; *sich* ~ (*dat.*) turn to(wards).

zuwenig *adv.* [tsu'-] too little.

'zuwerfen v/t. (*irr. werfen*, *sep.*, -ge-, *h*) fill up (*pit*); slam (*door*) (to); j-m ~ throw (*ball, etc.*) to s.o.; cast (*look*) at s.o.

zuwider *prp.* (*dat.*) [tsu'-] contrary to, against; repugnant; distasteful; **~handeln** v/i. (*sep.*, -ge-, *h*) (*dat.*) act contrary *or* in opposition to; *esp.* ⚖ contravene; **2handlung** ⚖ *f* contravention.

'zu|winken v/i. (*sep.*, -ge-, *h*) (*dat.*) wave to; beckon to; **~zahlen** v/t. (*sep.*, -ge-, *h*) pay extra; **~zählen** v/t. (*sep.*, -ge-, *h*) add; **~ziehen** (*irr. ziehen*, *sep.*, -ge-) **1.** v/t. (*h*) draw together; draw (*curtains*); consult (*doctor, etc.*); *sich* ~ incur (*s.o.'s displeasure etc.*); ⚕ catch (*disease*); **2.** v/i. (*sein*) move in; **~züglich** *prp.* (*gen.*) ['tsy:k-] plus.

Zwang [tsvaŋ] **1.** *m* (-[e]s/⸚e) compulsion, coercion; constraint; ⚖ duress(e); force; *sich* ~ *antun* check *or* restrain o.s.; **2.** 2 *pret. of zwingen*.

zwängen ['tsvɛŋǝn] v/t. (ge-, *h*) press, force.

'zwanglos *fig. adj.* free and easy,

informal; **2igkeit** *f* (-/-en) ease, informality.

'Zwangs|arbeit *f* hard labo(u)r; **~jacke** *f* strait waistcoat *or* jacket; **~lage** *f* embarrassing situation; **2läufig** *fig. adj.* ['~lɔyf-] necessary; **~maßnahme** *f* coercive measure; **~vollstreckung** ⚖ *f* distraint, execution; **~vorstellung** ⚕ *f* obsession, hallucination; **2weise** *adv.* by force; **~wirtschaft** *f* (-/⚐ -en) controlled economy.

zwanzig *adj.* ['tsvantsiç] twenty; **~ste** *adj.* ['~stǝ] twentieth.

zwar *cj.* [tsva:r] indeed, it is true; *und* ~ and that, that is.

Zweck [tsvɛk] *m* (-[e]s/-e) aim, end, object, purpose; design; *keinen* ~ *haben* be of no use; s-n ~ *erfüllen* answer its purpose; *zu dem* ~ (*gen.*) for the purpose of; **2dienlich** *adj.* serviceable, useful, expedient.

Zwecke ['tsvɛkǝ] *f* (-/-n) tack; drawing-pin, *Am.* thumbtack.

'zweck|los *adj.* aimless, purposeless; useless; **~mäßig** *adj.* expedient; suitable; **2mäßigkeit** *f* (-/*no pl.*) expediency.

zwei *adj.* [tsvai] two; **~beinig** *adj.* two-legged; **2bettzimmer** *n* double (bedroom); **~deutig** *adj.* ['~dɔy-tiç] ambiguous; suggestive; **~erlei** *adj.* ['~ɔr'lai] of two kinds, two kinds of; **~fach** *adj.* ['~fax] double, twofold.

Zweifel ['tsvaifǝl] *m* (-s/-) doubt; **2haft** *adj.* doubtful, dubious; **2los** *adj.* doubtless; **2n** v/i. (ge-, *h*) doubt (*an e-r Sache* s.th.; *an j-m* s.o.).

Zweig [tsvaik] *m* (-[e]s/-e) branch (*a. fig.*); *kleiner* ~ twig; **~geschäft** *n*, **~niederlassung** *f*, **~stelle** *f* branch.

zwei|jährig *adj.* ['tsvaijɛ:riç] two-year-old, of two (years); **2kampf** *m* duel, single combat; **~mal** *adv* twice; **~malig** *adj.* (twice) repeated; **2motorig** *adj.* ['~moto:riç] two-*or* twin-engined; **~reihig** *adj.* having two rows; *suit*: double-breasted; **~schneidig** *adj.* double *or* two-edged (*both a. fig.*); **~seitig** *adj.* two-sided; *contract, etc.* bilateral; *fabric*: reversible; **2sitzer** *esp. mot. m* (-s/-) two-seater **~sprachig** *adj.* bilingual; **~stimmig** *adj.* for two voices; **~stöckig**

adj. ['ʃtœkiç] two-stor|eyed, -ied; '⁓stufig ⊕ *adj.* two-stage; ⁓stündig *adj.* ['⁓ʃtyndiç] of *or* lasting two hours, two-hour.

zweit *adj.* [tsvaɪt] second; *ein* ⁓er another; *aus* ⁓er Hand second-hand; *zu* ⁓ by twos; *wir sind zu* ⁓ there are two of us.   [engine.]

'Zweitaktmotor *mot. m* two-stroke)

'zweit'best *adj.* second-best.

'zweiteilig *adj. garment:* two-piece.

'zweitens *adv.* ['tsvaɪtəns] secondly.

'zweitklassig *adj.* second-class, second-rate.

Zwerchfell *anat.* ['tsverç-] *n* diaphragm.

Zwerg [tsverk] *m* (-[e]s/-e) dwarf; ⁓enhaft *adj.* ['⁓gən-] dwarfish.

Zwetsch(g)e ['tsvetʃ(g)ə] *f* (-/-n) plum.

Zwick|el ['tsvikəl] *m* (-s/-) *sewing:* gusset; '⁓en *v/t. and v/i.* (ge-, h) pinch, nip; '⁓er *m* (-s/-) (*ein* a pair of) eye-glasses *pl.*, pince-nez; '⁓mühle *fig. f* dilemma, quandary, fix.

Zwieback ['tsvi:bak] *m* (-[e]s/⁓e, -e) rusk, zwieback.

Zwiebel ['tsvi:bəl] *f* (-/-n) onion; bulb (*of flowers, etc.*).

Zwie|gespräch ['tsvi:-] *n* dialog(ue); '⁓licht *n* (-[e]s/*no pl.*) twilight; '⁓spalt *m* (-[e]s/-e, ⁓e) disunion; conflict; ⁓spältig *adj.* ['⁓ʃpɛltiç] disunited; *emotions:* conflicting; '⁓tracht *f* (-/*no pl.*) discord.

Zwilling|e ['tsvilɪŋə] *m/pl.* twins *pl.*; '⁓sbruder *m* twin brother; '⁓sschwester *f* twin sister.

Zwinge ['tsvɪŋə] *f* (-/-n) ferrule (*of stick, etc.*); ⊕ clamp; '⁓n *v/t.* (*irr.*, ge-, h) compel, constrain; force; '⁓nd *adj.* forcible; *arguments:* cogent, compelling; imperative; '⁓r *m* (-s/-) outer court; kennel(s *pl.*); bear-pit.

zwinkern ['tsviŋkərn] *v/i.* (ge-, h) wink, blink.

Zwirn [tsvirn] *m* (-[e]s/-e) thread, cotton; '⁓sfaden *m* thread.

zwischen *prp.* (*dat.; acc.*) ['tsviʃən] between (*two*); among (*several*); '⁓bilanz ✝ *f* interim balance; '⁓deck ⚓ *n* steerage; ⁓'durch F *adv.* in between; for a change; '⁓ergebnis *n* provisional result; '⁓fall *m* incident; '⁓händler ✝ *m* middleman; '⁓landung ✈ *f* intermediate landing, stop, *Am. a.* stopover; (*Flug*) *ohne* ⁓ non-stop (flight); '⁓pause *f* interval, intermission; '⁓prüfung *f* intermediate examination; '⁓raum *m* space, interval; '⁓ruf *m* (loud) interruption; '⁓spiel *n* interlude; '⁓staatlich *adj.* international; *Am. between States:* interstate; '⁓station *f* intermediate station; '⁓stecker ⚡ *m* adapter; '⁓stück *n* intermediate piece, connexion, (*Am. only*) connection; '⁓stufe *f* intermediate stage; '⁓wand *f* partition (wall); '⁓zeit *f* interval; *in der* ⁓ in the meantime.

Zwist [tsvɪst] *m* (-es/-e), '⁓igkeit *f* (-/-en) discord; disunion; quarrel.

zwitschern ['tsvɪtʃərn] *v/i.* (ge-, h) twitter, chirp.

Zwitter ['tsvɪtər] *m* (-s/-) hermaphrodite.

zwölf *adj.* [tsvœlf] twelve; *um* ⁓ (*Uhr*) at twelve (o'clock); (*um*) ⁓ Uhr mittags (at) noon; (*um*) ⁓ Uhr nachts (at) midnight; 2'fingerdarm *anat. m* duodenum; ⁓te *adj.* ['⁓tə] twelfth.

Zyankali [tsyan'ka:li] *n* (-s/*no pl.*) potassium cyanide.

Zyklus ['tsy:klus, 'tsyk-] *m* (-/Zyklen) cycle; course, set (*of lectures, etc.*).

Zylind|er [tsi'lindər, tsy'-] *m* (-s/-) ⚓, ⊕ cylinder; chimney (*of lamp*); top hat; 2risch *adj.* [⁓driʃ] cylindrical.

Zyni|ker ['tsy:nikər] *m* (-s/-) cynic; 2isch *adj.* cynical; ⁓smus [tsy-'nismus] *m* (-/Zynismen) cynicism.

Zypresse ♀ [tsy'prɛsə] *f* (-/-n) cypress.

Zyste ⚕ ['tsystə] *f* (-/-n) cyst.

PART II

ENGLISH-GERMAN
DICTIONARY

A

a [ə, *betont*: eɪ], *vor Vokal*: **an** [ən, *betont*: æn] *unbestimmter Artikel*: ein(e); per, pro, je; *not* a(n) kein(e); *all of a size* alle gleich groß; £ *10 a year* zehn Pfund im Jahr; *twice a week* zweimal die od. in der Woche.

A 1 F [ˈeɪˈwʌn] Ia, prima.

a·back [əˈbæk]: *taken ~ fig.* überrascht, verblüfft; bestürzt.

a·ban·don [əˈbændən] auf-, preisgeben; verlassen; überlassen; **~ed**: *be found ~* verlassen aufgefunden werden (*Fahrzeug etc.*).

a·base [əˈbeɪs] erniedrigen, demütigen; **~·ment** [~mənt] Erniedrigung *f*, Demütigung *f*.

a·bashed [əˈbæʃt] verlegen.

a·bate [əˈbeɪt] *v/t.* verringern; *Mißstand* abstellen; *v/i.* abnehmen, nachlassen; **~·ment** [~mənt] Verminderung *f*; Abschaffung *f*.

ab·at·toir [ˈæbətwɑː] Schlachthof *m*.

ab·bess [ˈæbɪs] Äbtissin *f*.

ab·bey [ˈæbɪ] Kloster *n*; Abtei *f*.

ab·bot [ˈæbət] Abt *m*.

ab·bre·vi·ate [əˈbriːvɪeɪt] (ab)kürzen; **~·a·tion** [əbriːvɪˈeɪʃn] Abkürzung *f*, Kurzform *f*.

ABC [ˈeɪbiːˈsiː] Abc *n*, Alphabet *n*.

ABC weap·ons *pl.* ABC-Waffen *pl.*

ab·di·cate [ˈæbdɪkeɪt] *Amt, Recht etc.* aufgeben; entsagen *auf (acc.)*; ~ (*from*) *the throne* abdanken; **~·ca·tion** [æbdɪˈkeɪʃn] Verzicht *m*; Abdankung *f*.

ab·do·men *anat.* [ˈæbdəmən] Unterleib *m*; **ab·dom·i·nal** *anat.* [æbˈdɒmɪnl] Unterleibs...

ab·duct ɪ̯ɪ̯ [æbˈdʌkt] *j-n* entführen.

a·bet [əˈbet] (-*tt*-): *aid and* ~ *Jur.* Beihilfe leisten (*dat.*); begünstigen; **~·tor** [~ə] Anstifter *m*; (Helfers)Helfer *m*.

a·bey·ance [əˈbeɪəns] Unentschiedenheit *f*; *in* ~ ɪ̯ɪ̯ in der Schwebe.

ab·hor [əbˈhɔː] (-*rr*-) verabscheuen; **~·rence** [əbˈhɒrəns] Abscheu *m (of vor dat.)*; **~·rent** [~t] zuwider (*to dat.*); abstoßend.

a·bide [əˈbaɪd] *v/i.*: ~ *by the law, etc.* sich an das Gesetz *etc.* halten; *v/t.*: *I can't ~ him* ich kann ihn nicht ausstehen.

a·bil·i·ty [əˈbɪlətɪ] Fähigkeit *f*.

ab·ject □ [ˈæbdʒekt] verächtlich, erbärmlich; *in ~ poverty* in äußerster Armut.

ab·jure [əbˈdʒʊə] abschwören; entsagen (*dat.*).

a·blaze [əˈbleɪz] in Flammen; *fig.* glänzend, funkelnd (*with* vor *dat.*).

a·ble □ [ˈeɪbl] fähig; geschickt; *be ~ to do* imstande sein zu tun; tun können; **~·bod·ied** kräftig; ~ *seaman* Vollmatrose *m*.

ab·nor·mal □ [æbˈnɔːml] abnorm, ungewöhnlich; anomal.

a·board [əˈbɔːd] an Bord; *all~!* ⚓ alle Mann od. Reisenden an Bord!; 🚂 alles einsteigen!; ~ *a bus* in e-m Bus; *go* ~ *a train* in e-n Zug einsteigen.

a·bode [əˈbəʊd] *a. place of ~* Aufenthaltsort *m*, Wohnsitz *m*; *of (od. with) no fixed ~* ohne festen Wohnsitz.

a·bol·ish [əˈbɒlɪʃ] abschaffen, aufheben.

ab·o·li·tion [æbəˈlɪʃn] Abschaffung *f*, Aufhebung *f*; **~·ist** *hist.* [~ʃənɪst] Gegner *m* der Sklaverei.

A-bomb [ˈeɪbɒm] = *atom(ic) bomb.*

a·bom·i·na·ble □ [əˈbɒmɪnəbl] abscheulich, scheußlich; **~·nate** [~eɪt] verabscheuen; **~·na·tion** [əbɒmɪˈneɪʃn] Abscheu *m*.

ab·o·rig·i·nal [æbəˈrɪdʒənl] **1.** □ eingeboren, Ur...; **2.** Ureinwohner *m*; **~·ne** [~niː] Ureinwohner *m (bsd. Australiens)*.

a·bort [əˈbɔːt] ⚕ e-e Fehlgeburt herbeiführen bei od. haben; *Raumflug etc.* abbrechen; *fig.* fehlschlagen, scheitern; **a·bor·tion** ⚕ [~ʃn] Fehlgeburt *f*; Schwangerschaftsunterbrechung *f*, -abbruch *m*, Abtreibung *f*; *have an ~* abtreiben (lassen); **a·bor·tive** □ *fig.* [~ɪv] mißlungen, erfolglos.

a·bound [əˈbaʊnd] reichlich vorhanden sein; Überfluß haben, reich sein (*in an dat.*); voll sein (*with* von).

a·bout [əˈbaʊt] **1.** *prp.* um (...herum);

bei (*dat.*); (irgendwo) herum in (*dat.*); um, gegen, etwa; im Begriff, dabei; über (*acc.*); *I had no money ~ me* ich hatte kein Geld bei mir; *what are you ~?* was macht ihr da?; **2.** *adv.* herum, umher; in der Nähe; etwa, ungefähr.

a·bove [ə'bʌv] **1.** *prp.* über, oberhalb; *fig.* über, erhaben über; *~ all* vor allem; **2.** *adv.* oben; darüber; **3.** *adj.* obig, obenerwähnt.

a·breast [ə'brest] nebeneinander; *keep ~d. be ~ of fig.* Schritt halten mit.

a·bridge [ə'brɪdʒ] (ab-, ver)kürzen; **a·bridg(e)·ment** [~mənt] (Ab-, Ver)Kürzung *f*; Kurzfassung *f*; Abriß *m*.

a·broad [ə'brɔːd] im *od.* ins Ausland; überall(hin); *the news soon spread ~* die Nachricht verbreitete sich rasch.

a·brupt □ [ə'brʌpt] abrupt; jäh; zusammenhanglos; schroff.

ab·scess ♯ ['æbsɪs] Abszeß *m*.

ab·scond [əb'skɒnd] sich davonmachen.

ab·sence ['æbsəns] Abwesenheit *f*; Mangel *m*.

ab·sent 1. □ ['æbsənt] abwesend; fehlend; nicht vorhanden; *be ~* fehlen (*from school* in der Schule; *from work* am Arbeitsplatz); **2.** [æb'sent]: *~ o.s. from* fernbleiben (*dat.*) *od.* von; **~-mind·ed** □ ['æbsənt'maɪndɪd] zerstreut, geistesabwesend.

ab·so·lute □ ['æbsəluːt] absolut; unumschränkt; vollkommen; ♫ rein, unvermischt; unbedingt.

ab·so·lu·tion *eccl.* [æbsə'luːʃn] Absolution *f*.

ab·solve [əb'zɒlv] frei-, lossprechen; △ *nicht* absolvieren.

ab·sorb [əb'sɔːb] absorbieren, auf-, einsaugen; *fig.* ganz in Anspruch nehmen; **~·ing** *fig.* [~ɪŋ] fesselnd, packend.

ab·sorp·tion [əb'sɔːpʃn] Absorption *f*; *fig.* Vertieftsein *n*.

ab·stain [əb'steɪn] sich enthalten (*from gen.*).

ab·ste·mi·ous □ [æb'stiːmɪəs] enthaltsam; mäßig.

ab·sten·tion [əb'stenʃn] Enthaltung *f*; *pol.* Stimmenthaltung *f*.

ab·sti·nence ['æbstɪnəns] Abstinenz *f*, Enthaltsamkeit *f*; **~·nent** □ [~t] abstinent, enthaltsam.

ab·stract 1. □ ['æbstrækt] abstrakt; **2.** [~] *das* Abstrakte; Auszug *m*; **3.** [æb'strækt] abstrahieren; entwenden; *e-n wichtigen Punkt aus e-m Buch etc.* herausziehen; **~·ed** □ *fig.* zerstreut; **ab·strac·tion** [~kʃn] Abstraktion *f*; abstrakter Begriff.

ab·struse □ [æb'struːs] dunkel, schwer verständlich.

ab·surd □ [əb'sɜːd] absurd; lächerlich.

a·bun·dance [ə'bʌndəns] Überfluß *m*; Fülle *f*; Überschwang *m*; **~·dant** □ [~t] reich(lich).

a·buse 1. [ə'bjuːs] Mißbrauch *m*; Beschimpfung *f*; **2.** [~z] mißbrauchen; beschimpfen; **a·bu·sive** □ [~sɪv] ausfallend, Schimpf-.

a·but [ə'bʌt] (-*tt*-) (an)grenzen (*on an*).

a·byss [ə'bɪs] Abgrund *m* (*a. fig.*).

ac·a·dem·ic [ækə'demɪk] **1.** Hochschullehrer *m*; △ *nicht Akademiker*; **2.** (*~ally*) akademisch; **ac·a·de·mi·cian** [əkædə'mɪʃn] Akademiemitglied *n*; △ *nicht Akademiker.*

a·cad·e·my [ə'kædəmɪ] Akademie *f*; *~ of music* Musikhochschule.

ac·cede [æk'siːd]: *~ to* zustimmen (*dat.*); *Amt* antreten; *Thron* besteigen.

ac·cel·e·rate [ək'seləreɪt] *v/t.* beschleunigen; *v/i.* schneller werden, *mot. a.* beschleunigen, Gas geben; **~·ra·tion** [əkselə'reɪʃn] Beschleunigung *f*; **~·ra·tor** [ək'seləreɪtə] Gaspedal *n*.

ac·cent 1. ['æksənt] Akzent *m* (*a. gr.*); **2.** [æk'sent] = **ac·cen·tu·ate** [æk'sentjʊeɪt] akzentuieren, betonen.

ac·cept [ək'sept] annehmen, akzeptieren; hinnehmen; **ac·cep·ta·ble** □ [~əbl] annehmbar; **~·ance** [~əns] Annahme *f*; Aufnahme *f*.

ac·cess ['ækses] Zugang *m* (*to zu*); *fig.* Zutritt *m* (*to bei, zu*); *easy of ~* zugänglich (*Person*); *~ road* Zufahrtsstraße *f*; (*Autobahn*)Zubringerstraße *f*.

ac·ces·sa·ry ♯♯ [æk'sesərɪ] *s. accessory 2* ♯♯.

ac·ces·si·ble □ [ək'sesəbl] (leicht) zugänglich; **~·sion** [~ʃn] Zuwachs *m*, Zunahme *f*; Antritt *m* (*e-s Amtes*); *~ to power* Machtübernahme *f*; *~ to the throne* Thronbesteigung *f*.

ac·ces·so·ry [ək'sesərɪ] **1.** zusätzlich; **2.** ♯♯ Komplize *m*, -zin *f*, Mitschuldige(r *m*) *f*; *mst accessories pl.* Zubehör *n*, *Mode a.* Accessoires *pl.*; ⊕ Zubehör(teile *pl.*) *n.*

ac·ci·dent [ˈæksɪdənt] Zufall *m*; (Un-)(glücks)fall *m*; *by* ~ zufällig; **~·den·tal** □ [æksɪˈdentl] zufällig; versehentlich.

ac·claim [əˈkleɪm] freudig begrüßen.

ac·cla·ma·tion [ækləˈmeɪʃn] lauter Beifall; Lob *n.*

ac·cli·ma·tize [əˈklaɪmətaɪz] (sich) akklimatisieren *od.* eingewöhnen.

ac·com·mo·date [əˈkɒmədeɪt] (sich) anpassen (*to dat. od. an acc.*); unterbringen, beherbergen; Platz haben für; *j-m* aushelfen (*with* mit *Geld*); **~·da·tion** [əkɒməˈdeɪʃn] Anpassung *f*; Unterbringung *f*, (Platz *m* für) Unterkunft *f*, Quartier *n.*

ac·com·pa·ni·ment ♪ [əˈkʌmpənɪmənt] Begleitung *f*; **~·ny** [əˈkʌmpənɪ] begleiten (*a. ♪*); *accompanied with* verbunden mit.

ac·com·plice [əˈkʌmplɪs] Kompli|ze *m*, -zin *f.*

ac·com·plish [əˈkʌmplɪʃ] vollenden; ausführen; *Zweck* erreichen; **~·ed** vollendet, perfekt; **~·ment** [~mənt] Vollendung *f*, Ausführung *f*, Fähigkeit *f*, Talent *n.*

ac·cord [əˈkɔːd] 1. Übereinstimmung *f*; △ *nicht* Akkord; *of one's own* ~ aus eigenem Antrieb; *with one* ~ einstimmig; 2. *v/i.* übereinstimmen; *v/t.* gewähren; **~·ance** [~əns] Übereinstimmung *f*; *in* ~ *with* laut (*gen.*), gemäß (*dat.*); **~·ant** [~t] übereinstimmend; **~·ing** [~ɪŋ]: ~ *to* gemäß (*dat.*), nach; **~·ing·ly** [~ɪŋlɪ] (dem-)entsprechend.

ac·cost [əˈkɒst] *j-n bsd. auf der Straße* ansprechen.

ac·count [əˈkaʊnt] 1. *econ.* Rechnung *f*, Berechnung *f*; *econ.* Konto *n*; Rechenschaft *f*; Bericht *m*; *by all* ~s nach allem, was man so hört; *of no* ~ ohne Bedeutung; *on no* ~ auf keinen Fall; *on* ~ *of* wegen; *take into* ~, *take* ~ *of* in Betracht *od.* Erwägung ziehen, berücksichtigen; *turn s.th. to* (*good*) ~ et. (gut) ausnutzen; *keep* ~s die Bücher führen; *call to* ~ zur Rechenschaft ziehen; *give* (*an*) ~ *of* Rechenschaft ablegen über (*acc.*); *give an* ~ *of* Bericht erstatten über (*acc.*); 2. *v/i.*: ~ *for* Rechenschaft über *et.* ablegen; (sich) erklären; **ac·coun·ta·ble** □ [~əbl] verant-

wortlich; erklärlich; **ac·coun·tant** [~ənt] Buchhalter *m*; **~·ing** [~ɪŋ] Buchführung *f.*

ac·cu·mu·late [əˈkjuːmjʊleɪt] (sich) (an)häufen *od.* ansammeln; **~·la·tion** [əkjuːmjʊˈleɪʃn] Ansammlung *f.*

ac·cu·ra·cy [ˈækjʊrəsɪ] Genauigkeit *f*; **~·rate** □ [~rət] genau; richtig.

ac·cu·sa·tion [ækjuːˈzeɪʃn] Anklage *f*; An-, Beschuldigung *f.*

ac·cu·sa·tive *gr.* [əˈkjuːzətɪv] *a.* ~ *case* Akkusativ *m.*

ac·cuse [əˈkjuːz] anklagen; beschuldigen; *the* ~*d* der *od.* die Angeklagte, die Angeklagten; **ac·cus·er** [~ə] Ankläger(in); **ac·cus·ing** □ [~ɪŋ] anklagend, vorwurfsvoll.

ac·cus·tom [əˈkʌstəm] gewöhnen (*to* an *acc.*); **~·ed** gewohnt, üblich; gewöhnt (*to* an *acc.*, zu *inf.*).

ace [eɪs] As *n* (*a. fig.*); *have an* ~ *up one's sleeve*, *Am. have an* ~ *in the hole fig.* (noch) e-n Trumpf in der Hand haben; *within an* ~ um ein Haar.

ache [eɪk] 1. schmerzen, weh tun; 2. *anhaltender* Schmerz.

a·chieve [əˈtʃiːv] zustande bringen; *Ziel* erreichen; **~·ment** [~mənt] Zustandebringen *n*, Ausführung *f*; Leistung *f.*

ac·id [ˈæsɪd] 1. sauer; *fig.* beißend, bissig; ~ *rain* saurer Regen; 2. 🏭 Säure *f*; **a·cid·i·ty** [əˈsɪdətɪ] Säure *f.*

ac·knowl·edge [əkˈnɒlɪdʒ] anerkennen; zugeben; *Empfang* bestätigen; **ac·knowl·edg(e)·ment** [~mənt] Anerkennung *f*; (Empfangs)Bestätigung *f*; Eingeständnis *n.*

a·corn ♀ [ˈeɪkɔːn] Eichel *f.*

a·cous·tics [əˈkuːstɪks] *pl.* Akustik *f* (*e-s Raumes*).

ac·quaint [əˈkweɪnt] bekannt machen; ~ *s.o. with s.th.* j-m et. mitteilen; *be* ~*ed with* kennen; **~·ance** [~əns] Bekanntschaft *f*; Bekannte(r *m*) *f.*

ac·qui·esce [ækwɪˈes] (*in*) hinnehmen (*acc.*); einwilligen (in *acc.*).

ac·quire [əˈkwaɪə] erwerben; sich aneignen (*Kenntnisse*).

ac·qui·si·tion [ækwɪˈzɪʃn] Erwerb *m*; Erwerbung *f*; Errungenschaft *f.*

ac·quit [əˈkwɪt] (*-tt-*) 🏛 *j-n* freisprechen (*of a charge* von e-r Anklage); ~ *o.s. of e-e Pflicht* erfüllen; ~ *o.s. well* s-e Sache gut machen; **~·tal** 🏛 [~tl] Freispruch *m.*

a·cre ['eɪkə] Acre m (4047 qm).

ac·rid ['ækrɪd] scharf, beißend.

a·cross [ə'krɒs] **1.** adv. (quer) hin- od. herüber; querdurch; drüben; auf der anderen Seite od. auf der anderen Seite über Kreuz; **2.** prp. (quer) über (acc.); (quer) durch; auf der anderen Seite von (od. gen.), jenseits (gen.); über (dat.); come ~, run ~ stoßen auf (acc.).

act [ækt] **1.** v/i. handeln; sich benehmen; wirken; funktionieren; (Theater) spielen (a. fig.), auftreten; v/t. thea. spielen (a. fig.), Stück aufführen; ~ out szenisch darstellen, vorspielen; **2.** Handlung f, Tat f, Maßnahme f, Akt m; thea. Akt m; Gesetz n, Beschluß m; Urkunde f, Vertrag m; **~·ing** ['æktɪŋ] **1.** Handeln n; Spiel(en) n; **2.** tätig; amtierend.

ac·tion ['ækʃn] Handlung f (a. thea.), Tat f; Action f (spannende Handlung); Aktion f; Tätigkeit f, Funktion f; (Ein)Wirkung f; ⚖ Klage f, Prozeß m; ⚔ Gefecht n, Kampfhandlung f; ⊕ Mechanismus m; take ~ Schritte unternehmen, handeln.

ac·tive ['æktɪv] aktiv; tätig, rührig, lebhaft, rege; wirksam; econ. lebhaft; ~ voice gr. Aktiv n, Tatform f; **ac·tiv·ist** [~vɪst] Aktivist(in); **ac·tiv·i·ty** [æk'tɪvətɪ] Tätigkeit f; Aktivität f; Betriebsamkeit f; bsd. econ. Lebhaftigkeit f.

ac·tor ['æktə] Schauspieler m; **ac·tress** [~trɪs] Schauspielerin f.

ac·tu·al □ ['æktʃʊəl] wirklich, tatsächlich, eigentlich; △ nicht aktuell.

a·cute □ [ə'kju:t] (~r, ~st) spitz; scharf(sinnig); brennend (Frage); 🗲 akut.

ad F [æd] = advertisement.

ad·a·mant □ fig. ['ædəmənt] unerbittlich.

a·dapt [ə'dæpt] anpassen (to dat. od. an acc.); Text bearbeiten (from nach); ⊕ umstellen (to auf acc.); umbauen (to für); **ad·ap·ta·tion** [ædæp'teɪʃn] Anpassung f; Bearbeitung f; **a·dapt·er, a·dapt·or** f [ə'dæptə] Adapter m.

add [æd] v/t. hinzufügen; ~ up zusammenzählen, addieren; v/i.: ~ to vermehren, beitragen zu, hinzukommen zu; ~ up fig. F e-n Sinn ergeben.

ad·dict ['ædɪkt] Süchtige(r m) f; alcohol (drug) ~ Alkohol- (Drogen-od. Rauschgift)Süchtige(r m) f; Fuß-

ball- etc. Fanatiker(in), Film- etc. Narr m; **~ed** [ə'dɪktɪd] süchtig, abhängig (to von); be ~ to alcohol (drugs, television, etc.) alkohol-(drogen-, fernseh- etc.)süchtig sein; **ad·dic·tion** [~ʃn] Sucht f, Zustand a. Süchtigkeit f.

ad·di·tion [ə'dɪʃn] Hinzufügen n; Zusatz m; Zuwachs m; Anbau m; 🅰 Addition f; in ~ außerdem, noch; in ~ to außer (dat.); **~al** [~l] zusätzlich.

ad·dress [ə'dres] **1.** Worte richten (to an acc.), j-n anreden od. ansprechen; **2.** Adresse f, Anschrift f; Rede f; Ansprache f; **~ee** [ædre'si:] Empfänger(in).

ad·ept ['ædept] **1.** erfahren, geschickt (at, in in dat.); **2.** Meister m, Experte m (at, in in dat.).

ad·e·qua·cy ['ædɪkwəsɪ] Angemessenheit f; **~quate** □ [~kwət] angemessen.

ad·here [əd'hɪə] (to) kleben, haften (an dat.); fig. festhalten (an dat.); **ad·her·ence** [~rəns] Anhaften n; fig. Festhalten n; **ad·her·ent** [~rənt] Anhänger(in).

ad·he·sive [əd'hi:sɪv] **1.** □ klebend; ~ plaster Heftpflaster n; ~ tape Klebestreifen m; Am. Heftpflaster n; **2.** Klebstoff m.

ad·ja·cent □ [ə'dʒeɪsnt] angrenzend, anstoßend (to an acc.); benachbart.

ad·jec·tive gr. ['ædʒɪktɪv] Adjektiv n, Eigenschaftswort n.

ad·join [ə'dʒɔɪn] (an)grenzen an (acc).

ad·journ [ə'dʒɜ:n] verschieben, (v/i. sich) vertagen; **~ment** [~mənt] Vertagung f, -schiebung f.

ad·just [ə'dʒʌst] anpassen; in Ordnung bringen; Streit beilegen; Mechanismus u. fig. einstellen (to auf acc.); **~ment** [~mənt] Anpassung f; Ordnung f; ⊕ Einstellung f; Beilegung f.

ad·min·is·ter [əd'mɪnɪstə] verwalten; spenden; Arznei geben, verabreichen; ~ justice Recht sprechen; **~·tra·tion** [ədmɪnɪ'streɪʃn] Verwaltung f; pol. bsd. Am. Regierung f; bsd. Am. Amtsperiode f (e-s Präsidenten); **~·tra·tive** [əd'mɪnɪstrə-tɪv] Verwaltungs...; **~·tra·tor** [~reɪtə] Verwaltungsbeamte(r) m.

ad·mi·ra·ble □ ['ædmərəbl] bewundernswert; großartig.

ad·mi·ral ['ædmrəl] Admiral m.

affair

ad·mi·ra·tion [ædmə'reɪʃn] Bewunderung f.

ad·mire [əd'maɪə] bewundern, verehren; **ad·mir·er** [~rə] Verehrer m.

ad·mis·si·ble □ [əd'mɪsəbl] zulässig; **~sion** [~ʃn] Zulassung f; Eintritt(sgeld n) m; Eingeständnis n; ~ free Eintritt frei.

ad·mit [əd'mɪt] (-tt-) v/t. (her)einlassen (to, into in acc.), eintreten lassen; zulassen (to zu); zugeben; **~tance** [~əns] Einlaß m, Ein-, Zutritt m; no ~ Zutritt verboten.

ad·mix·ture [æd'mɪkstʃə] Beimischung f, Zusatz m.

ad·mon·ish [əd'mɒnɪʃ] ermahnen; warnen (of, against vor dat.); **ad·mo·ni·tion** [ædmə'nɪʃn] Ermahnung f; Warnung f.

a·do [ə'duː] (pl. -dos) Getue n, Lärm m; without much od. more od. further ~ ohne weitere Umstände.

ad·o·les·cence [ædə'lesns] Adoleszenz f, Reifezeit f; **~cent** [~t] **1.** jugendlich, heranwachsend; **2.** Jugendliche(r m) f.

a·dopt [ə'dɒpt] adoptieren; sich zu eigen machen, übernehmen; **~ed child** Adoptivkind n; **a·dop·tion** [~pʃn] Adoption f; **a·dop·tive** □ [~tɪv] Adoptiv...; angenommen; ~ child Adoptivkind n; ~ parents pl. Adoptiveltern pl.

a·dor·a·ble □ [ə'dɔːrəbl] anbetungswürdig; F entzückend; **ad·o·ra·tion** [ædə'reɪʃn] Anbetung f, Verehrung f; **a·dore** [ə'dɔː] anbeten, verehren.

a·dorn [ə'dɔːn] schmücken, zieren; **~ment** [~mənt] Schmuck m.

a·droit □ [ə'drɔɪt] geschickt.

ad·ult ['ædʌlt] **1.** erwachsen; **2.** Erwachsene(r m) f; ~ education Erwachsenenbildung f.

a·dul·ter·ate [ə'dʌltəreɪt] verfälschen; **~er** [~rə] Ehebrecher m; **~ess** [~rɪs] Ehebrecherin f; **~ous** □ [~rəs] ehebrecherisch; **~y** [~rɪ] Ehebruch m.

ad·vance [əd'vɑːns] **1.** v/i. vorrücken, -dringen; vorrücken (Zeit); steigen; Fortschritte machen; v/t. vorrücken; Ansicht etc. vorbringen; Geld vorauszahlen; vorschießen; (be)fördern; Preis erhöhen; beschleunigen; **2.** Vorrücken n, Vorstoß m (a. fig.); Fortschritt m; Vorschuß m; Erhöhung f; in ~ im voraus; **~d** fortgeschritten; ~ for one's years weit od.

reif für sein Alter; **~ment** [~mənt] Förderung f; Fortschritt m.

ad·van·tage [əd'vɑːntɪdʒ] Vorteil m; Überlegenheit f; Gewinn m; take ~ of ausnutzen; **~ta·geous** □ [ædvən'teɪdʒəs] vorteilhaft.

ad·ven·ture [əd'ventʃə] Abenteuer n, Wagnis n; Spekulation f; **~tur·er** [~rə] Abenteurer m; Spekulant m; **~tur·ess** [~rɪs] Abenteu(r)erin f; **~tur·ous** □ [~rəs] abenteuerlich; verwegen, kühn.

ad·verb gr. ['ædvɜːb] Adverb n, Umstandswort n.

ad·ver·sa·ry ['ædvəsərɪ] Gegner(in), Feind(in); **ad·verse** □ ['ædvɜːs] widrig; feindlich; ungünstig, nachteilig (to für dat.); **ad·ver·si·ty** [əd'vɜːsə-tɪ] Unglück n.

ad·ver·tise ['ædvətaɪz] ankündigen, bekanntmachen, inserieren; Reklame machen (für); **~tise·ment** [əd'vɜːtɪsmənt] Anzeige f, Ankündigung f, Inserat n; Reklame f; **~tis·ing** ['ædvətaɪzɪŋ] **1.** Reklame f, Werbung f; **2.** Anzeigen..., Reklame..., Werbe...; ~ agency Anzeigenannahme f; Werbeagentur f.

ad·vice [əd'vaɪs] Rat(schlag) m; Nachricht f, Meldung f; take medical ~ e-n Arzt zu Rate ziehen; take my ~ hör auf mich.

ad·vis·a·ble □ [əd'vaɪzəbl] ratsam; **ad·vise** [əd'vaɪz] v/t. j-n beraten; j-m raten; bsd. econ. benachrichtigen, avisieren; v/i. sich beraten; **ad·vis·er**, Am. a. **ad·vi·sor** [~ə] Berater m; **ad·vi·so·ry** [~ərɪ] beratend.

ad·vo·cate 1. ['ædvəkət] Anwalt m; Verfechter m; Befürworter m; **2.** [~keɪt] verteidigen, befürworten.

aer·i·al ['eərɪəl] **1.** □ luftig; Luft...; ~ view Luftaufnahme f; **2.** Antenne f.

ae·ro- ['eərəʊ] Aero..., Luft...

aer·o·bics [eə'rəʊbɪks] sg. Sport: Aerobic n; **~drome** bsd. Brt. ['eərə-drəʊm] Flugplatz m; **~dy·nam·ic** [eərəʊdə'næmɪk] (~ally) aerodynamisch; **~dy·nam·ics** sg. Aerodynamik f; **~nau·tics** [eərə'nɔːtɪks] sg. Luftfahrt f; **~plane** Brt. ['eərə-pleɪn] Flugzeug n.

aes·thet·ic [iːs'θetɪk] ästhetisch; **~s** sg. Ästhetik f.

a·far [ə'fɑː] fern, weit (weg).

af·fa·ble □ ['æfəbl] leutselig.

af·fair [ə'feə] Geschäft n, Angelegenheit f, Sache f; F Ding n,

Sache *f*; Liebesaffäre *f*, Verhältnis *n*.

af·fect [ə'fekt] (ein- *od.* sich aus-) wirken auf (*acc.*); rühren; *Gesundheit* angreifen; lieben, vorziehen; nachahmen; vortäuschen; **af·fec·ta·tion** [æfek'teɪʃn] Vorliebe *f*; Affektiertheit *f*; Verstellung *f*; □ gerührt; befallen (*von Krankheit*); angegriffen (*Augen etc.*); geziert, affektiert; **af·fec·tion** [ʌkʃn] Zuneigung *f*; **af·fec·tion·ate** □ [ʌʃnət] liebevoll.

af·fil·i·ate [ə'fɪlɪeɪt] *als Mitglied* aufnehmen; angliedern; ∼**d** *company econ.* Tochtergesellschaft *f*.

af·fin·i·ty [ə'fɪnətɪ] (geistige) Verwandtschaft *f*; ♣ Affinität *f*; Neigung *f* (*for, to* zu).

af·firm [ə'fɜːm] versichern; beteuern; bestätigen; **af·fir·ma·tion** [æfə'meɪʃn] Versicherung *f*; Beteuerung *f*; Bestätigung *f*; **af·fir·ma·tive** [ə'fɜːmətɪv] **1.** □ bejahend; **2.** *answer in the* ∼ bejahen.

af·fix [ə'fɪks] (*to*) anheften, -kleben (an *acc.*), befestigen (an *dat.*); bei-, hinzufügen (*dat.*).

af·flict [ə'flɪkt] betrüben, heimsuchen, plagen; **af·flic·tion** [ʌkʃn] Betrübnis *f*; Gebrechen *n*; Elend *n*, Not *f*.

af·flu·ence ['æfluəns] Überfluß *m*; Wohlstand *m*; ∼**ent** [ʌt] **1.** □ reich (-lich); ∼ *society* Wohlstandsgesellschaft *f*; **2.** Nebenfluß *m*.

af·ford [ə'fɔːd] sich leisten, gewähren, bieten; *I can* ∼ *it* ich kann es mir leisten.

af·front [ə'frʌnt] **1.** beleidigen; **2.** Beleidigung *f*.

a·field [ə'fiːld] im Feld; (weit) weg.

a·float [ə'fləʊt] ♣ *u. fig.* flott; schwimmend; auf See; *set* ∼ ♣ flottmachen; in Umlauf bringen.

a·fraid [ə'freɪd] *be* ∼ *of* sich fürchten *od.* Angst haben vor (*dat.*); *I'm* ∼ *she won't come* ich fürchte, sie wird nicht kommen; *I'm* ∼ *I must go now* leider muß ich jetzt gehen.

a·fresh [ə'freʃ] von neuem.

Af·ri·can ['æfrɪkən] **1.** afrikanisch; **2.** Afrikaner(in); *Am. a.* Neger(in).

af·ter ['ɑːftə] **1.** *adv.* hinterher, nachher, danach; **2.** *prp.* nach; hinter (*dat.*) ... her; ∼ *all* schließlich (doch); **3.** *cj.* nachdem; **4.** *adj.* später; Nach...; ∼**ef·fect** ♣ Nachwirkung *f*

(*a. fig.*); *fig.* Folge *f*; ∼**glow** Abendrot *n*; ∼**math** [ʌmæθ] Nachwirkungen *pl.*, Folgen *pl.*; ∼**noon** [ɑːftə'nuːn] Nachmittag *m*; *this* ∼ heute nachmittag; *good* ∼*!* guten Tag!; ∼**taste** ['ɑːfəteɪst] Nachgeschmack *m*; ∼**thought** nachträglicher Einfall; ∼**wards**, *Am. a.* ∼**ward** [ʌwəd(z)] nachher, später.

a·gain [ə'gen] wieder(um); ferner; ∼ *and* ∼, *time and* ∼ immer wieder; *as much* ∼ noch einmal soviel.

a·gainst [ə'genst] gegen; räumlich: gegen; an, vor (*dat. od. acc.*); *fig.* im Hinblick auf (*acc.*); *as* ∼ verglichen mit; *he was* ∼ *it* er war dagegen.

age [eɪdʒ] **1.** (Lebens)Alter *n*; Zeit (-alter *n*) *f*; Menschenalter *n*; (*old*) ∼ (hohes) Alter; (*come*) *of* ∼ mündig *od.* volljährig (werden); *be over* ∼ die Altersgrenze überschritten haben; *under* ∼ minderjährig; unmündig; *wait for* ∼ F e-e Ewigkeit warten; **2.** alt werden *od.* machen; ∼**d** ['eɪdʒɪd] alt, betagt; [eɪdʒd]: ∼ *twenty* 20 Jahre alt; ∼**less** ['eɪdʒlɪs] zeitlos; ewig jung.

a·gen·cy ['eɪdʒənsɪ] Tätigkeit *f*; Vermittlung *f*; Agentur *f*, Büro *n*.

a·gen·da [ə'dʒendə] Tagesordnung *f*.

a·gent ['eɪdʒənt] Handelnde(r *m*) *f*; (Stell)Vertreter(in); Agent *m* (*a. pol.*); Wirkstoff *m*, Mittel *n*, Agens *n*.

ag·glom·er·ate [ə'glɒməreɪt] (sich) zusammenballen; (sich) (an)häufen.

ag·gra·vate ['ægrəveɪt] erschweren, verschlimmern; F ärgern.

ag·gre·gate 1. ['ægrɪgeɪt] (sich) anhäufen; vereinigen (to mit); sich belaufen auf (*acc.*); **2.** □ [ʌgət] (an)gehäuft; gesamt; **3.** [ʌ] Anhäufung *f*; Gesamtmenge *f*, Summe *f*; Aggregat *n*.

ag·gres|sion [ə'greʃn] Angriff *m*; ∼**sive** □ [ʌsɪv] aggressiv, Angriffs...; *fig.* energisch; ∼**sor** [ʌsə] Angreifer *m*.

ag·grieved [ə'griːvd] verletzt, gekränkt.

a·ghast [ə'gɑːst] entgeistert, entsetzt.

ag·ile □ ['ædʒaɪl] flink, behend; **a·gil·i·ty** [ə'dʒɪlətɪ] Behendigkeit *f*.

ag·i|tate ['ædʒɪteɪt] *v/t.* hin u. her bewegen, schütteln; *fig.* aufregen; erörtern; *v/i.* agitieren; ∼**ta·tion** [ædʒɪ'teɪʃn] heftige Bewegung, Erschütterung *f*; Aufregung *f*; Agita-

alien

tion *f*; **~ta·tor** [ˈædʒɪteɪtə] Agitator *m*, Aufwiegler *m*.

a·glow [əˈgləʊ] glühend; *be ~* strahlen (*with* vor).

a·go [əˈgəʊ]: *a year ~* vor e-m Jahr.

ag·o·nize [ˈægənaɪz] (sich) quälen.

ag·o·ny [ˈægənɪ] heftiger Schmerz, *a. seelische* Qual; Pein *f*; Agonie *f*, Todeskampf *m*.

a·grar·i·an [əˈgreərɪən] Agrar...

a·gree [əˈgriː] *v/i.* übereinstimmen; sich vertragen; einig werden; sich einigen (*on, upon* über *acc.*); übereinkommen (*~ to* zustimmen (*dat.*), einverstanden sein mit; **~·a·ble** □ [əˈgrɪəbl] (*to*) angenehm (für); übereinstimmend (mit); **~·ment** [əˈgriːmənt] Übereinstimmung *f*; Vereinbarung *f*; Abkommen *n*; Vertrag *m*.

ag·ri·cul·tur·al [ægrɪˈkʌltʃərəl] landwirtschaftlich; **~e** [ˈægrɪkʌltʃə] Landwirtschaft *f*; **~·ist** [ægrɪˈkʌltʃərɪst] Landwirt *m*.

a·ground ⚓ [əˈgraʊnd] gestrandet; *run ~* stranden, auf Grund laufen.

a·head [əˈhed] vorwärts, voraus; vorn; *go ~!* nur zu!, mach nur!; *straight ~* geradeaus.

aid [eɪd] **1.** helfen (*dat.*; *in* bei *et.*); fördern; **2.** Hilfe *f*, Unterstützung *f*.

ail [eɪl] *v/i* kränkeln; *v/t.* schmerzen, weh tun (*dat.*); *what ~s him?* was fehlt ihm?; **~·ing** [ˈeɪlɪŋ] leidend; **~·ment** [~mənt] Leiden *n*.

aim [eɪm] **1.** *v/i.* zielen (*at auf acc.*; nach); ~ *at fig.* beabsichtigen; *be ~ing to do s.th.* vorhaben, et. zu tun; *v/t.* ~ *at* Waffe etc. richten auf *od.* gegen (*acc.*); **2.** Ziel *n* (*a. fig.*); Absicht *f*; *take ~ at* zielen auf (*acc.*) *od.* nach; **~·less** □ [ˈeɪmlɪs] ziellos.

air¹ [eə] **1.** Luft *f*; Luftzug *m*; Miene *f*, Aussehen *n*; *by ~* auf dem Luftwege; *in the open ~* im Freien; *on the ~* im Rundfunk *od.* Fernsehen; *be on the ~* senden (*Sender*); *go off the ~* die Sendung beenden (*Person*); *sein* Programm beenden (*Sender*); *give o.s. ~s, put on ~s* vornehm tun; **2.** (aus)lüften; *fig.* an die Öffentlichkeit bringen; erörtern.

air² ♩ [ʌ] Arie *f*, Weise *f*, Melodie *f*.

air|base ✕ [ˈeəbeɪs] Luftstützpunkt *m*; **~·bed** Luftmatratze *f*; **~·borne** in der Luft (*Flugzeug*); ✕ Luftlande...; **~·brake** ⊕ Druckluftbremse *f*; **~-con·di·tioned** mit Klimaanlage;

~·craft (*pl.* -craft) Flugzeug *n*; **~·craft car·ri·er** Flugzeugträger *m*; **~·field** Flugplatz *m*; **~·force** ✕ Luftwaffe *f*; **~ host·ess** ✈ Stewardess *f*; **~·jack·et** Schwimmweste *f*; **~·lift** ✈ Luftbrücke *f*; **~·line** ✈ Fluggesellschaft *f*; **~·lin·er** ✈ Verkehrsflugzeug *n*; **~·mail** Luftpost *f*; *by ~* mit Luftpost; **~·man** (*pl.* -men) Flieger *m* (*Luftwaffe*); **~·plane** Am. Flugzeug *n*; **~·pock·et** ✈ Luftloch *n*; **~·pol·lu·tion** Luftverschmutzung *f*; **~·port** Flughafen *m*; **~ raid** Luftangriff *m*; **~·raid pre·cau·tions** *pl.* Luftschutz *m*; **~·raid shel·ter** Luftschutzraum *m*; **~·route** ✈ Flugroute *f*; **~·sick** luftkrank; **~·space** Luftraum *m*; **~·strip** (behelfsmäßige) Start- u. Landebahn; **~ ter·mi·nal** Flughafenabfertigungsgebäude *n*; **~·tight** luftdicht; **~ traf·fic** Flugverkehr *m*; **~·traf·fic con·trol** ✈ Flugsicherung *f*; **~·traf·fic con·trol·ler** ✈ Fluglotse *m*; **~·way** ✈ Fluggesellschaft *f*; **~·wor·thy** flugtüchtig.

air·y □ [ˈeərɪ] (-ier, -iest) luftig; *contp.* überspannt.

aisle *arch.* [aɪl] Seitenschiff *n*; Gang *m*.

a·jar [əˈdʒɑː] halb offen, angelehnt.

a·kin [əˈkɪn] verwandt (*to* mit).

a·lac·ri·ty [əˈlækrətɪ] Munterkeit *f*; Bereitwilligkeit *f*; Eifer *m*.

a·larm [əˈlɑːm] **1.** Alarm(zeichen *n*) *m*; Wecker *m*; Angst *f*; **2.** alarmieren; beunruhigen; **~ clock** Wecker *m*.

al·bum [ˈælbəm] Album *n*.

al·bu·mi·nous [ælˈbjuːmɪnəs] eiweißhaltig.

al·co·hol [ˈælkəhɒl] Alkohol *m*; **~·ic** [ælkəˈhɒlɪk] **1.** alkoholisch; **2.** Alkoholiker(in); **~·is·m** [ˈælkəhɒlɪzəm] Alkoholismus *m*.

al·cove [ˈælkəʊv] Nische *f*; Laube *f*.

al·der·man [ˈɔːldəmən] (*pl.* -men) Ratsherr *m*, Stadtrat *m*.

ale [eɪl] Ale *n* (*helles, obergäriges Bier*).

a·lert [əˈlɜːt] **1.** □ wachsam; munter; **2.** Alarm(bereitschaft *f*) *m*; *on the ~* auf der Hut; *in* Alarmbereitschaft; **3.** warnen (*to* vor *dat.*), alarmieren.

al·i·bi [ˈælɪbaɪ] Alibi *n*; F Entschuldigung *f*, Ausrede *f*.

a·li·en [ˈeɪljən] **1.** fremd; ausländisch; **2.** Fremde(r *m*) *f*, Ausländer(in);

~ate [~eɪt] veräußern; entfremden (*from dat.*).

a·light [əˈlaɪt] **1.** in Flammen; erhellt; **2.** ab-, aussteigen; ✈ niedergehen, landen; sich niederlassen (*on, upon* auf *dat. od. acc.*).

a·lign [əˈlaɪn] (sich) ausrichten (*with* nach); ~ *o.s. with* sich anschließen an (*acc.*).

a·like [əˈlaɪk] **1.** *adj.* gleich; **2.** *adv.* gleich, ebenso.

al·i·men·ta·ry [ælɪˈmentərɪ] nahrhaft; ~ *canal* Verdauungskanal *m.*

al·i·mo·ny ✝ [ˈælɪmənɪ] Unterhalt *m.*

alive [əˈlaɪv] lebendig; (noch) am Leben; empfänglich (*to* für); lebhaft; belebt (*with* von).

all [ɔːl] **1.** *adj.* all; ganz; jede(r, -s); **2.** *pron.* alles; alle *pl.*; **3.** *adv.* ganz, völlig; *Wendungen:* ~ *at once* auf einmal; ~ *the better* desto besser; ~ *but* beinahe, fast; ~ *in Am.* F fertig, ganz erledigt; ~ *right* (alles) in Ordnung; *for* ~ dessenungeachtet, trotzdem; *for* ~ *(that) I care* meinetwegen; *for* ~ *I know* soviel ich weiß; *at* ~ überhaupt; *not at* ~ überhaupt nicht; *the score was two* ~ ~ das Spiel stand zwei zu zwei.

all-A·mer·i·can [ˈɔːləˈmerɪkən] rein amerikanisch; die ganzen USA vertretend.

al·lay [əˈleɪ] beruhigen; lindern.

al·le·ga·tion [ælɪˈɡeɪʃn] *unerwiesene* Behauptung.

al·lege [əˈledʒ] behaupten; **~d** ☐ angeblich.

al·le·giance [əˈliːdʒəns] (Untertanen)Treue *f.*

al·ler·gic [əˈlɜːdʒɪk] allergisch; **~gy** [ˈælədʒɪ] Allergie *f.*

al·le·vi·ate [əˈliːvɪeɪt] lindern, vermindern.

al·ley [ˈælɪ] (enge *od.* schmale) Gasse; Garten-, Parkweg *m; Bowling, Kegeln:* Bahn *f;* △ *nicht* Allee.

al·li·ance [əˈlaɪəns] Bündnis *n.*

al·lo·cate [ˈæləkeɪt] zuteilen, anweisen; **~ca·tion** [æləˈkeɪʃn] Zuteilung *f.*

al·lot [əˈlɒt] (*-tt-*) zuteilen, an-, zuweisen; **~ment** [~mənt] Zuteilung *f;* Parzelle *f.*

al·low [əˈlaʊ] erlauben, bewilligen, gewähren; zugeben; ab-, anrechnen; vergüten; ~ *for* berücksichtigen (*acc.*); **~a·ble** ☐ [əˈlaʊəbl] erlaubt,

zulässig; **~ance** Erlaubnis *f;* Bewilligung *f;* Taschengeld *n,* Zuschuß *m;* Vergütung *f; fig.* Nachsicht *f; make* ~(*s*) *for s.th.* et. in Betracht ziehen.

al·loy 1. [ˈælɔɪ] Legierung *f;* **2.** [əˈlɔɪ] legieren.

all-round [ˈɔːlraʊnd] vielseitig; **~er** [ˈɔːlˈraʊndə] Alleskönner *m; Sport:* Allroundsportler *m,* -spieler *m.*

al·lude [əˈluːd] anspielen (*to* auf *acc.*).

al·lure [əˈljʊə] (an-, ver)locken; **~ment** [~mənt] Verlockung *f.*

al·lu·sion [əˈluːʒn] Anspielung *f.*

al·ly 1. [əˈlaɪ] (sich) vereinigen, verbünden (*to, with* mit); **2.** [ˈælaɪ] Verbündete(r *m*) *f,* Bundesgenoss|e *m,* -in *f;* the Allies *pl.* die Alliierten *pl.*

al·ma·nac [ˈɔːlmənæk] Almanach *m.*

al·might·y [ɔːlˈmaɪtɪ] allmächtig; *der* Allmächtige.

al·mond ♀ [ˈɑːmənd] Mandel *f.*

al·mo·ner Brt. [ˈɑːmənə] Sozialarbeiter(in) im Krankenhaus.

al·most [ˈɔːlməʊst] fast, beinah(e).

alms [ɑːmz] *pl.* Almosen *n.*

a·loft [əˈlɒft] (hoch) (dr)oben.

a·lone [əˈləʊn] allein; *let od. leave* ~ in Ruhe *od.* bleiben lassen; *let* ~ ... abgesehen von ...

a·long [əˈlɒŋ] **1.** *adv.* weiter, vorwärts; da; dahin; *all* ~ die ganze Zeit; ~ *with* (zusammen) mit; *come* ~ mitkommen, -gehen; *get* ~ vorwärts-, weiterkommen; auskommen, sich vertragen (*with s.o.* mit j-m); *take* ~ mitnehmen; **2.** *prp.* entlang, längs; **~side** [~ˈsaɪd] Seite an Seite; neben.

a·loof [əˈluːf] abseits; reserviert, zurückhaltend.

a·loud [əˈlaʊd] laut.

al·pha·bet [ˈælfəbɪt] Alphabet *n.*

al·pine [ˈælpaɪn] alpin, (Hoch)Gebirgs...

al·read·y [ɔːlˈredɪ] bereits, schon.

al·right [ɔːlˈraɪt] = *all right.*

al·so [ˈɔːlsəʊ] auch, ferner; △ *nicht also.*

al·tar [ˈɔːltə] Altar *m.*

al·ter [ˈɔːltə] (sich) (ver)ändern; ab-, umändern; **~a·tion** [ɔːltəˈreɪʃn] Änderung *f* (*to an dat.*), Veränderung *f.*

al·ter|nate 1. [ˈɔːltəneɪt] abwechseln (lassen); *alternating current* ⚡ Wechselstrom *m;* **2.** ☐ [ɔːlˈtɜːnət] abwechselnd; **3.** *Am.* [~] Stellvertreter *m;* **~na·tion** [ɔːltəˈneɪʃn] Abwechslung *f;* Wechsel *m;* **~na·tive**

[ɔːlˈtɜːnətɪv] **1.** □ alternativ, wahlweise; ∼ *society* alternative Gesellschaft; **2.** Alternative *f*, Wahl *f*, Möglichkeit *f*.

al·though [ɔːlˈðəʊ] obwohl, obgleich.

al·ti·tude [ˈæltɪtjuːd] Höhe *f*; *at an* ∼ in e-r Höhe von.

al·to·geth·er [ɔːltəˈgeðə] im ganzen, insgesamt; ganz (u. gar), völlig.

a·lu·min·i·um [əljuˈmɪnjəm], *Am.* **a·lu·mi·num** [əˈluːmɪnəm] Aluminium *n*.

al·ways [ˈɔːlweɪz] immer, stets.

am [æm; *im Satz* əm] *1. sg. pres. von* *be.*

a·mal·gam·ate [əˈmælgəmeit] amalgamieren; verschmelzen.

a·mass [əˈmæs] an-, aufhäufen.

am·a·teur [ˈæmətə] Amateur *m*; Dilettant(in).

a·maze [əˈmeɪz] in Erstaunen setzen, verblüffen; ∼**·ment** [∼mənt] Staunen *n*, Verblüffung *f*; **a·maz·ing** □ [∼ɪŋ] erstaunlich, verblüffend.

am·bas·sa·dor *pol.* [æmˈbæsədə] Botschafter *m* (*to* in e-m *Land*); Gesandte(r) *m*; ∼**·dress** *pol.* [∼drɪs] Botschafterin *f* (*to* in e-m *Land*).

am·ber *min.* [ˈæmbə] Bernstein *m*.

am·bi·gu·i·ty [æmbɪˈgjuːɪtɪ] Zwei-, Mehrdeutigkeit *f*; **am·big·u·ous** □ [æmˈbɪgjʊəs] zwei-, vieldeutig; doppelsinnig.

am·bi·tion [æmˈbɪʃn] Ehrgeiz *m*; Streben *n*; ∼**·tious** □ [∼ʃəs] ehrgeizig; begierig (*of* nach).

am·ble [ˈæmbl] **1.** Paßgang *m*; **2.** im Paßgang gehen *od.* reiten; schlendern.

am·bu·lance [ˈæmbjʊləns] ✕ Feldlazarett *n*; Krankenwagen *m*.

am·bush [ˈæmbʊʃ] **1.** Hinterhalt *m*; *be od. lie in* ∼ *for s.o.* j-m auflauern; **2.** auflauern (*dat.*); überfallen.

a·me·lio·rate [əˈmiːljəreit] *v/t.* verbessern; *v/i.* besser werden.

a·men *int.* [ɑːˈmen] amen.

a·mend [əˈmend] verbessern, berichtigen; *Gesetz* abändern, ergänzen; ∼**·ment** [∼mənt] Besserung *f*; Verbesserung *f*; *parl.* Abänderungs-, Ergänzungsantrag *m* (*zu* e-m *Gesetz*); *Am.* Zusatzartikel *m* zur Verfassung; ∼**s** *pl.* (Schaden)Ersatz *m*; *make* ∼ Schadenersatz leisten; *make* ∼ *to s.o. for s.th.* j-n für et. entschädigen.

a·men·i·ty [əˈmiːnətɪ] *oft* amenities

pl. Annehmlichkeiten *pl.*

A·mer·i·can [əˈmerɪkən] **1.** amerikanisch; ∼ *plan* Vollpension *f*; **2.** Amerikaner(in); ∼**·ism** [∼ɪzəm] Amerikanismus *m*; ∼**·ize** [∼aɪz] (sich) amerikanisieren.

a·mi·a·ble □ [ˈeɪmjəbl] liebenswürdig, freundlich.

am·i·ca·ble □ [ˈæmɪkəbl] freundschaftlich; gütlich.

a·mid(st) [əˈmɪd(st)] inmitten (*gen.*), (mitten) in *od.* unter.

a·miss [əˈmɪs] verkehrt, falsch, übel; *take* ∼ übelnehmen.

am·mo·ni·a [əˈməʊnjə] Ammoniak *n*.

am·mu·ni·tion [æmjʊˈnɪʃn] Munition *f*.

am·nes·ty [ˈæmnɪstɪ] **1.** Amnestie *f* (*Straferlaß*); **2.** begnadigen.

a·mok [əˈmɒk]: *run* ∼ Amok laufen.

a·mong(st) [əˈmʌŋ(st)] (mitten) unter, zwischen.

am·o·rous □ [ˈæmərəs] verliebt (*of* in *acc.*).

a·mount [əˈmaʊnt] **1.** (*to*) sich belaufen (auf *acc.*); hinauslaufen (auf *acc.*); **2.** Betrag *m*, (Gesamt)Summe *f*; Menge *f*.

am·ple □ [ˈæmpl] (∼*r*, ∼*st*) weit, groß, geräumig; reichlich, beträchtlich.

am·pli·fi·ca·tion [æmplɪfɪˈkeɪʃn] Erweiterung *f*; *rhet.* weitere Ausführung; *phys.* Verstärkung *f*; ∼**·fi·er** ⚡ [ˈæmplɪfaɪə] Verstärker *m*; ∼**·fy** [∼faɪ] erweitern; ⚡ verstärken; weiter ausführen; ∼**·tude** [∼tjuːd] Umfang *m*, Weite *f*, Fülle *f*.

am·pu·tate [ˈæmpjʊteit] amputieren.

a·muck [əˈmʌk] = amok.

a·muse [əˈmjuːz] (*o.s.* sich) amüsieren, unterhalten, belustigen; ∼**·ment** [∼mənt] Unterhaltung *f*, Vergnügen *n*, Zeitvertreib *m*; **a·mus·ing** □ [∼ɪŋ] amüsant, unterhaltend.

an [æn, ən] *unbestimmter Artikel vor vokalisch anlautenden Wörtern:* ein(e).

a·nae·mi·a ⚕ [əˈniːmjə] Blutarmut *f*, Anämie *f*.

an·aes·thet·ic [ænɪsˈθetɪk] **1.** (∼*ally*) betäubend, Narkose...; **2.** Betäubungsmittel *n*.

a·nal *anat.* [ˈeɪnl] anal, Anal...

a·nal·o·gous □ [əˈnæləgəs] analog, entsprechend; ∼**·gy** [∼dʒɪ] Analogie *f*, Entsprechung *f*.

an·a·lyse *bsd. Brt.*, *Am.* **-lyze** ['ænə-laɪz] analysieren; zerlegen; **a·nal·y·sis** [ə'næləsɪs] (*pl.* -ses [-siːz]) Analyse *f*.

an·arch·y ['ænəkɪ] Anarchie *f*, Gesetzlosigkeit *f*; Chaos *n*.

a·nat·o|mize [ə'nætəmaɪz] *~* zergliedern; zerlegen; *~my* [~ɪ] Anatomie *f*; Zergliederung *f*, Analyse *f*.

an·ces|tor ['ænsestə] Vorfahr *m*, Ahn *m*; **~·tral** [æn'sestrəl] angestammt; **~tress** ['ænsestrɪs] Ahne *f*; **~try** [~rɪ] Abstammung *f*; Ahnen *pl*.

an·chor ['æŋkə] **1.** Anker *m*; *at ~* vor Anker; **2.** verankern; **~age** [~rɪdʒ] Ankerplatz *m*.

an·cho·vy *zo.* ['æntʃəvɪ] An(s)chovis *f*, Sardelle *f*.

an·cient ['eɪnʃənt] **1.** alt, antik; uralt; **2.** *the ~s pl. hist.* die Alten, die antiken Klassiker.

and [ænd, ənd] und.

a·ne·mi·a *Am.* = anaemia.

an·es·thet·ic *Am.* = anaesthetic.

a·new [ə'njuː] von neuem.

an·gel ['eɪndʒəl] Engel *m*; △ *nicht* Angel.

an·ger ['æŋgə] **1.** Zorn *m*, Ärger *m* (*at* über *acc.*); **2.** erzürnen, (ver)ärgern.

an·gi·na *~* [æn'dʒaɪnə] Angina *f*, Halsentzündung *f*.

an·gle ['æŋgl] **1.** Winkel *m*; *fig.* Standpunkt *m*; **2.** angeln (*for* nach); **~r** [~ə] Angler(in).

An·gli·can ['æŋglɪkən] **1.** *eccl.* anglikanisch; *Am.* britisch, englisch; **2.** *eccl.* Anglikaner(in).

An·glo-Sax·on ['æŋgləʊ'sæksən] **1.** angelsächsisch; **2.** Angelsachse *m*; *ling.* Altenglisch *n*.

an·gry ['æŋgrɪ] □ (*-ier*, *-iest*) zornig, verärgert, böse (*at*, *with* über *acc.*, *mit dat.*).

an·guish ['æŋgwɪʃ] (Seelen)Qual *f*, Schmerz *m*; **~ed** [~ʃt] qualvoll.

an·gu·lar □ ['æŋgjʊlə] winkelig, Winkel...; knochig.

an·i·mal ['ænɪml] **1.** Tier *n*; **2.** tierisch.

an·i|mate ['ænɪmeɪt] beleben, beseelen; aufmuntern, anregen; △ *nicht* animieren; **~·ma·ted** lebendig; lebhaft, angeregt; **~** *cartoon* Zeichentrickfilm *m*; **~·ma·tion** [ænɪ'meɪʃn] Leben *n*, Lebhaftigkeit *f*, Feuer *n*; Animation *f*, Herstellung *f* von (Zeichen)Trickfilmen; (Zeichen)Trickfilm *m*.

an·i·mos·i·ty [ænɪ'mɒsətɪ] Animosität *f*, Feindseligkeit *f*.

an·kle *anat.* ['æŋkl] (Fuß)Knöchel *m*.

an·nals ['ænlz] *pl.* Jahrbücher *pl*.

an·nex 1. [ə'neks] anhängen; annektieren; **2.** ['æneks] Anhang *m*; Anbau *m*; **~·a·tion** [ænek'seɪʃn] Annexion *f*, Einverleibung *f*.

an·ni·hi·late [ə'naɪəleɪt] vernichten.

an·ni·ver·sa·ry [ænɪ'vɜːsərɪ] Jahrestag *m*; Jahresfeier *f*.

an·no|tate ['ænəʊteɪt] mit Anmerkungen versehen; kommentieren; **~·ta·tion** [ænəʊ'teɪʃn] Kommentieren *n*; Anmerkung *f*.

an·nounce [ə'naʊns] ankündigen; bekanntgeben; *Rundfunk*, *TV*: ansagen; durchsagen; △ *nicht* annoncieren; **~·ment** [~mənt] Ankündigung *f*; Bekanntgabe *f*; *Rundfunk*, *TV*: Ansage *f*; Durchsage *f*; **an·nounc·er** [~ə] *Rundfunk*, *TV*: Ansager(in), Sprecher(in).

an·noy [ə'nɔɪ] ärgern; belästigen; **~·ance** [~əns] Störung *f*, Belästigung *f*; Ärgernis *n*; **~·ing** [~ɪŋ] ärgerlich, lästig.

an·nu·al ['ænjʊəl] **1.** □ jährlich; Jahres...; **2.** ♀ einjährige Pflanze; Jahrbuch *n*.

an·nu·i·ty [ə'njuːɪtɪ] (Jahres)Rente *f*.

an·nul [ə'nʌl] (*-ll-*) für ungültig erklären, annullieren; **~·ment** [~mənt] Annullierung *f*, Aufhebung *f*.

an·o·dyne *~* ['ænədaɪn] **1.** schmerzstillend; **2.** schmerzstillendes Mittel.

a·noint [ə'nɔɪnt] salben.

a·nom·a·lous □ [ə'nɒmələs] anomal, abnorm, regelwidrig.

a·non·y·mous □ [ə'nɒnɪməs] anonym, ungenannt.

an·o·rak ['ænəræk] Anorak *m*.

an·oth·er [ə'nʌðə] ein anderer; ein zweiter; noch eine(r, -s).

an·swer ['ɑːnsə] **1.** *v/t. et.* beantworten; *j-m* antworten; entsprechen (*dat.*); *Zweck* erfüllen; ⊕ *dem Steuer* gehorchen; *e-r Vorladung* Folge leisten; *e-r Beschreibung* entsprechen; ~ *the bell od. door* (die Haustür) aufmachen; ~ *the telephone* ans Telefon gehen; *v/i.* antworten (*to* auf *acc.*); entsprechen (*to dat.*); ~ *back* freche Antworten geben; widersprechen; ~ *for* einstehen für; **2.** Antwort *f* (*to* auf *acc.*); **~·a·ble** [~rəbl] verantwortlich.

ant *zo.* [ænt] Ameise *f*.

an·tag·o·nis·m [æn'tægənɪzəm] Widerstreit *m*; Widerstand *m*; Feindschaft *f*; **~nist** [~ɪst] Gegner(in); **~nize** [~naɪz] ankämpfen gegen; sich *j-n* zum Feind machen.

an·te·ced·ent [æntɪ'si:dənt] **1.** □ vorhergehend, früher (*to* als); **~s** *pl.* Vorgeschichte *f*; Vorleben *n*.

an·te·lope *zo.* ['æntɪləʊp] Antilope *f*.

an·ten·na¹ *zo.* [æn'tenə] (*pl. -nae* [-niː]) Fühler *m*.

an·ten·na² *Am.* [~] Antenne *f*.

an·te·ri·or [æn'tɪərɪə] vorhergehend, früher (*to* als); vorder.

an·te·room ['æntɪrʊm] Vorzimmer *n*; Wartezimmer *n*.

an·them ♪ ['ænθəm] Hymne *f*.

an·ti- ['æntɪ] Gegen..., gegen ... eingestellt *od.* wirkend, Anti..., anti...; **~air·craft** ✕ Flieger-, Flugabwehr...; **~bi·ot·ic** [~baɪ'ɒtɪk] Antibiotikum *n*.

an·tic·i·pate [æn'tɪsɪpeɪt] vorwegnehmen; zuvorkommen (*dat.*); voraussehen, (-)ahnen; erwarten; **an·tic·i·pa·tion** [æntɪsɪ'peɪʃn] Vorwegnahme *f*; Zuvorkommen *n*; Voraussicht *f*; Erwartung *f*; *in* ~ im voraus.

an·ti·clock·wise *Brt.* [æntɪ'klɒkwaɪz] entgegen dem Uhrzeigersinn.

an·tics ['æntɪks] *pl.* Gekasper *n*; Mätzchen *pl.*; △ *nicht* antik, Antike.

an·ti·dote ['æntɪdəʊt] Gegengift *n*, -mittel *n*; **~freeze** Frostschutzmittel *n*; **~mis·sile** ✕ [æntɪ'mɪsaɪl] Raketenabwehr...

an·tip·a·thy [æn'tɪpəθɪ] Abneigung *f*.

an·ti·quat·ed ['æntɪkweɪtɪd] veraltet, altmodisch.

an·tique [æn'tiːk] **1.** antik, alt; **2.** Antiquität *f*; △ *nicht* Antike; ~ *dealer* Antiquitätenhändler(in); ~ *shop*, *bsd. Am.* ~ *store* Antiquitätenladen *m*; **an·tiq·ui·ty** [æn'tɪkwɒtɪ] Altertum *n*, Vorzeit *f*.

an·ti·sep·tic [æntɪ'septɪk] **1.** antiseptisch; **2.** antiseptisches Mittel.

ant·lers ['æntləz] *pl.* Geweih *n*.

a·nus *anat.* ['eɪnəs] After *m*.

an·vil ['ænvɪl] Amboß *m*.

anx·i·e·ty [æŋ'zaɪətɪ] Angst *f*; Sorge *f* (*for* um); ❀ Beklemmung *f*.

anx·ious □ ['æŋkʃəs] besorgt, beunruhigt (*about* wegen); △ *nicht* ängstlich; begierig, gespannt (*for* auf *acc.*); bestrebt (*to do* zu tun).

an·y ['enɪ] **1.** *adj. u. pron.* (irgend-) eine(r, -s), (irgend)welche(r, -s); (irgend) etwas; jede(r, -s) (beliebige); einige *pl.*, welche *pl.*; *not* ~ keiner; **2.** *adv.* irgend(wie), ein wenig, etwas, (noch) etwas; **~bod·y** (irgend) jemand; jeder; **~how** irgendwie; trotzdem, jedenfalls; wie dem auch sei; **~one** = anybody; **~thing** (irgend) etwas; alles; ~ *but* alles andere als; ~ *else*? sonst noch etwas?; *not* ~ nichts; **~way** = anyhow; **~where** irgendwo(hin); überall.

a·part [ə'pɑːt] einzeln, getrennt, für sich; beiseite; △ *nicht* apart; ~ *from* abgesehen von.

a·part·heid [ə'pɑːtheɪt] Apartheid *f*, Politik *f* der Rassentrennung.

a·part·ment [ə'pɑːtmənt] Zimmer *n*; *Am.* Wohnung *f*; **~s** *pl.* *Brt.* (möblierte) (Miet)Wohnung *f*; ~ *house* *Am.* Mietshaus *n*.

ap·a·thet·ic [æpə'θetɪk] (~*ally*) apathisch, teilnahmslos, gleichgültig; **~thy** ['æpəθɪ] Apathie *f*, Teilnahmslosigkeit *f*, Gleichgültigkeit *f*.

ape [eɪp] **1.** *zo.* (Menschen)Affe *m*; **2.** nachäffen.

a·pe·ri·ent [ə'pɪərɪənt] Abführmittel *n*.

ap·er·ture ['æpətjʊə] Öffnung *f*.

a·pi·a·ry ['eɪpɪərɪ] Bienenhaus *n*; **~cul·ture** [~ɪkʌltʃə] Bienenzucht *f*.

a·piece [ə'piːs] für jedes *od.* pro Stück, je.

a·pol·o·get·ic [əpɒlə'dʒetɪk] (~*ally*) verteidigend; rechtfertigend; entschuldigend; **~gize** [ə'pɒlədʒaɪz] sich entschuldigen (*for* für; *to* bei); **~gy** [~ɪ] Entschuldigung *f*; Rechtfertigung *f*; *make od. offer s.o. an* ~ (*for s.th.*) sich bei j-m (für et.) entschuldigen.

ap·o·plex·y ['æpəpleksɪ] Schlag(anfall) *m*.

a·pos·tle [ə'pɒsl] Apostel *m*.

a·pos·tro·phe *ling.* [ə'pɒstrəfɪ] Apostroph *m*.

ap·pal(**l**) [ə'pɔːl] (*-ll-*) erschrecken, entsetzen; **~ling** □ [~ɪŋ] erschreckend, entsetzlich.

ap·pa·ra·tus [æpə'reɪtəs] Apparat *m*, Vorrichtung *f*, Gerät *n*.

ap·par·el [ə'pærəl] Kleidung *f*.

ap·par·ent □ [ə'pærənt] sichtbar; anscheinend; offenbar.

ap·pa·ri·tion [æpə'rɪʃn] Erscheinung *f*, Gespenst *n*.

ap·peal [ə'piːl] **1.** ⚖ Berufung *od.*

Revision einlegen, Einspruch erheben, Beschwerde einlegen; appellieren, sich wenden (*to* an·*acc.*); ~ *to* gefallen (*dat.*), zusagen (*dat.*), wirken *auf* (*acc.*); *j-n* dringend bitten (*for* um); **2.** ⚖ Revision *f*, Berufung *f*; Beschwerde *f*; Einspruch *m*; Appell *m* (*to* an *acc.*), Aufruf *m*; △ *nicht* ⚔ *Appell;* Wirkung *f*, Reiz *m*; Bitte *f* (*to* an *acc.*; *for* um); ~ *for mercy* ⚖ Gnadengesuch *n*; **~·ing** □ [~ɪŋ] flehend; ansprechend.

ap·pear [ə'pɪə] (er)scheinen; sich zeigen; *öffentlich* auftreten; sich ergeben *od.* herausstellen; **~·ance** [~rəns] Erscheinen *n*; Auftreten *n*; Äußere(s) *n*, Erscheinung *f*, Aussehen *n*; Anschein *m*, äußerer Schein; *to all* ~(*s*) allem Anschein nach.

ap·pease [ə'piːz] beruhigen; beschwichtigen; stillen; mildern; beilegen.

ap·pend [ə'pend] an-, hinzu-, beifügen; **~·age** [~ɪdʒ] Anhang *m*, Anhängsel *n*, Zubehör *n*.

ap·pen·di·ci·tis ✦ [əpendɪ'saɪtɪs] Blinddarmentzündung *f*; **~·dix** [ə'pendɪks] (*pl. -dixes, -dices* [-dɪsiːz]) Anhang *m*; *a. vermiform* ~ ✦ Wurmfortsatz *m*, Blinddarm *m*.

ap·per·tain [æpə'teɪn] gehören (*to* zu).

ap·pe·tite ['æpɪtaɪt] (*for*) Appetit *m* (auf *acc.*); *fig.* Verlangen *n* (nach); **~·tiz·er** [~zə] Appetithappen *m*, pikante Vorspeise; **~·tiz·ing** □ [~ɪŋ] appetitanregend.

ap·plaud [ə'plɔːd] applaudieren, Beifall spenden; loben; **ap·plause** [~z] Applaus *m*, Beifall *m*.

ap·ple ⚘ ['æpl] Apfel *m*; ~*·cart: upset s.o.'s* ~ ⊦ *j-s* Pläne über den Haufen werfen; ~ **pie** (*warmer*) gedeckter Apfelkuchen; *in* ~*·pie order* ⊦ in schönster Ordnung; ~ **sauce** Apfelmus *n*; *Am. sl.* Schmus *m*, Quatsch *m*.

ap·pli·ance [ə'plaɪəns] Vorrichtung *f*; Gerät *n*; Mittel *n*.

ap·plic·a·ble □ ['æplɪkəbl] anwendbar (*to auf acc.*).

ap·pli·cant ['æplɪkənt] Antragsteller(in), Bewerber(in) (*for* um); **~·ca·tion** [æplɪ'keɪʃn] Anwendung *f* (*to auf acc.*); Bedeutung *f* (für); Gesuch *n* (*for* um); Bewerbung *f* (*for* um).

ap·ply [ə'plaɪ] *v/t.* (*to*) (auf)legen,

auftragen (auf *acc.*); anwenden (auf *acc.*); verwenden (für); ~ *o.s. to* sich widmen (*dat.*); *v/i.* (*to*) passen, zutreffen, sich anwenden lassen (auf *acc.*); gelten (für); sich wenden (an *acc.*); sich bewerben (*for* um), beantragen (*for acc.*).

ap·point [ə'pɔɪnt] bestimmen, festsetzen; verabreden; ernennen (*s.o. governor* j-n zum ...); berufen (*to auf e-n Posten*); **~·ment** [~mənt] Bestimmung *f*; Verabredung *f*; Termin *m* (*geschäftlich, beim Arzt etc.*); Ernennung *f*, Berufung *f*; Stelle *f*; ~ *book* Terminkalender *m*.

ap·por·tion [ə'pɔːʃn] ver-, zuteilen; **~·ment** [~mənt] Ver-, Zuteilung *f*.

ap·prais·al [ə'preɪzl] (Ab)Schätzung *f*; **~·e** [ə'preɪz] (ab)schätzen, taxieren.

ap·pre·cia·ble □ [ə'priːʃəbl] nennenswert, spürbar; **~·ci·ate** [~ʃɪeɪt] *v/t.* schätzen, würdigen; dankbar sein für; *v/i.* im Wert steigen; **~·ci·a·tion** [əpriːʃɪ'eɪʃn] Schätzung *f*, Würdigung *f*; Anerkennung *f*; Verständnis *n* (*of* für); Einsicht *f*; Dankbarkeit *f*; *econ.* Wertsteigerung *f*.

ap·pre·hend [æprɪ'hend] ergreifen, fassen; begreifen; befürchten; **~·hen·sion** [~ʃn] Ergreifung *f*, Festnahme *f*; Besorgnis *f*; **~·hen·sive** □ [~sɪv] ängstlich, besorgt (*for* um; *that* daß).

ap·pren·tice [ə'prentɪs] **1.** Auszubildende(r *m*) *f*, Lehrling *m*; **2.** in die Lehre geben; **~·ship** [~ʃɪp] Lehrzeit *f*, Lehre *f*, Ausbildung *f*.

ap·proach [ə'prəʊtʃ] **1.** *v/i.* näherkommen, sich nähern; *v/t.* sich nähern (*dat.*); herangehen *od.* herantreten an (*acc.*); **2.** (Heran)Nahen *n*; Ein-, Zu-, Auffahrt *f*; Annäherung *f*; Methode *f*.

ap·pro·ba·tion [æprə'beɪʃn] Billigung *f*, Beifall *m*.

ap·pro·pri·ate 1. [ə'prəʊprɪeɪt] sich aneignen; verwenden; *parl.* bewilligen; **2.** □ [~ɪt] (*for, to*) angemessen (*dat.*), passend (für, zu).

ap·prov·al [ə'pruːvl] Billigung *f*; Anerkennung *f*, Beifall *m*; **~·e** [~v] billigen, anerkennen; **~·ed** bewährt.

ap·prox·i·mate 1. [ə'prɒksɪmeɪt] sich nähern; **2.** □ [~mət] annähernd, ungefähr.

a·pri·cot ⚘ ['eɪprɪkɒt] Aprikose *f*.

A·pril ['eɪprəl] April *m*.

a·pron ['eɪprən] Schürze *f*; **~·string**

Schürzenband *n*; *be tied to one's wife's (mother's)* ~s *fig.* unterm Pantoffel stehen (der Mutter am Schürzenzipfel hängen).

apt □ [æpt] geeignet, passend; treffend; begabt; ~ *to* geneigt zu; **ap·ti·tude** ['æptɪtjuːd] *(for)* Begabung *f* (für), Befähigung *f* (für), Talent *n* (zu); ~ *test* Eignungsprüfung *f*.

a·quat·ic [ə'kwætɪk] Wassertier *n*, -pflanze *f*; ~s *sg.* Wassersport *m*.

aq·ue·duct ['ækwɪdʌkt] Aquädukt *m*.

aq·ui·line ['ækwɪlaɪn] Adler...; gebogen; ~ *nose* Adlernase *f*.

Ar·ab ['ærəb] Araber(in); **Ar·a·bic** [~ɪk] **1.** arabisch; **2.** *ling.* Arabisch *n*.

ar·a·ble ['ærəbl] anbaufähig; Acker...

ar·bi·tra·ry □ ['ɑːbɪtrərɪ] willkürlich, eigenmächtig; **~trate** [~reɪt] entscheiden, schlichten; **~tra·tion** [ɑːbɪ'treɪʃn] Schlichtung *f*; **~tra·tor** ['ɑːbɪtreɪtə] Schiedsrichter *m*; Schlichter *m*.

ar·bo·u)r ['ɑːbə] Laube *f*.

arc [ɑːk] (⚡ Licht)Bogen *m*; **ar·cade** [ɑː'keɪd] Arkade *f*, Bogen-, Laubengang *m*; Durchgang *m*, Passage *f*.

arch¹ [ɑːtʃ] **1.** Bogen *m*; Gewölbe *n*; *anat.* Rist *m*, Spann *m* (*Fuß*); **2.** (sich) wölben; krümmen; ~ *over* überwölben.

arch² [~] erste(r, -s), oberste(r, -s), Haupt..., Erz...

arch³ □ [~] schelmisch.

ar·cha·ic [ɑː'keɪɪk] (⚓ *ally*) veraltet.

arch|an·gel ['ɑːkeɪndʒəl] Erzengel *m*; **~bish·op** ['ɑːtʃbɪʃəp] Erzbischof *m*.

ar·cher ['ɑːtʃə] Bogenschütze *m*; **~·y** [~rɪ] Bogenschießen *n*.

ar·chi·tect ['ɑːkɪtekt] Architekt *m*; Urheber(in), Schöpfer(in); **~tec·ture** [~ktʃə] Architektur *f*, Baukunst *f*.

ar·chives ['ɑːkaɪvz] *pl.* Archiv *n*.

arch·way ['ɑːtʃweɪ] (Bogen)Gang *m*.

arc·tic ['ɑːktɪk] **1.** arktisch, nördlich, Nord...; Polar...; **2.** *Am.* wasserdichter Überschuh.

ar·dent □ ['ɑːdənt] heiß, glühend; *fig.* leidenschaftlich, heftig; eifrig.

ar·do(u)r *fig.* ['ɑːdə] Leidenschaft (-lichkeit) *f*, Heftigkeit *f*, Feuer *n*; Eifer *m*.

ar·du·ous □ ['ɑːdjʊəs] mühsam; zäh.

are [ɑː, *unbetont:* ə] *pres. pl. u. 2. sg. von* be.

ar·e·a ['eərɪə] Areal *n*; (Boden)Fläche *f*, Flächenraum *m*; Gegend *f*, Gebiet *n*, Zone *f*; Bereich *m*; ~ *code Am. teleph.* Vorwählnummer *f*, Vorwahl *f*.

Ar·gen·tine ['ɑːdʒəntaɪn] **1.** argentinisch; **2.** Argentinier(in).

a·re·na [ə'riːnə] Arena *f*.

ar·gue ['ɑːgjuː] *v/t.* (das Für u. Wider) erörtern, diskutieren; *v/i.* streiten; argumentieren, Gründe (für u. wider) anführen, Einwendungen machen.

ar·gu·ment ['ɑːgjʊmənt] Argument *n*, Beweis(grund) *m*; Streit *m*, Wortwechsel *m*, Auseinandersetzung *f*.

ar·id □ ['ærɪd] dürr, trocken (*a. fig.*).

a·rise [ə'raɪz] *(arose, arisen)* entstehen; auftauchen, -treten, -kommen; **a·ris·en** [ə'rɪzn] *p.p von* arise.

ar·is·toc·ra·cy [ærɪ'stɒkrəsɪ] Aristokratie *f*, Adel *m*; **~to·crat** ['ærɪstəkræt] Aristokrat(in); **~to·crat·ic** (~*ally*) [ærɪstə'krætɪk] aristokratisch.

a·rith·me·tic [ə'rɪθmətɪk] Rechnen *n*.

ark [ɑːk] Arche *f*.

arm¹ [ɑːm] Arm *m*; Ärmelloch *f*; *keep s.o. at* ~'*s length* sich j-n vom Leibe halten; *infant in* ~s Säugling *m*.

arm² [~] *mst* ~s *pl.* Waffen *pl.*; Waffengattung *f*; ~s *control* Rüstungskontrolle *f*; ~s *race* Wettrüsten *n*, Rüstungswettlauf *m*; *up in* ~s kampfbereit; *fig.* in Harnisch; **2.** (sich) bewaffnen; (sich) wappnen *od.* rüsten.

ar·ma·da [ɑː'mɑːdə] Kriegsflotte *f*.

ar·ma·ment ['ɑːməmənt] (Kriegsaus)Rüstung *f*; Aufrüstung *f*.

ar·ma·ture ⚡ ['ɑːmətjʊə] Anker *m*.

arm·chair ['ɑːm't∫eə] Lehnstuhl *m*, Sessel *m*.

ar·mi·stice ['ɑːmɪstɪs] Waffenstillstand *m* (*a. fig.*).

ar·mo(u)r ['ɑːmə] **1.** ✗ Rüstung *f*, Panzer *m* (*a. fig., zo.*); **2.** panzern; ~*ed car* gepanzertes Fahrzeug (*für Geldtransporte etc.*); **~·y** [~rɪ] Waffenkammer *f*; Waffenfabrik *f*.

arm·pit ['ɑːmpɪt] Achselhöhle *f*.

ar·my ['ɑːmɪ] Heer *n*, Armee *f*; *fig.* Menge *f*; ~ *chaplain* Militärgeistliche(r) *m*.

a·ro·ma [ə'rəʊmə] Aroma *n*, Duft *m*; **ar·o·mat·ic** [ærə'mætɪk] (~*ally*) aromatisch, würzig.

a·rose [əˈrəʊz] *pret. von* arise.

a·round [əˈraʊnd] **1.** *adv.* (rings)herum, (rund)herum, ringsumher, überall; umher, herum; in der Nähe; da; **2.** *prp.* um, um... herum, rund um; in (*dat.*) ... herum; ungefähr, etwa.

a·rouse [əˈraʊz] (auf)wecken; *fig.* aufrütteln, erregen.

ar·range [əˈreɪndʒ] (an)ordnen; in die Wege leiten, arrangieren; vereinbaren, ausmachen; ♪ arrangieren, bearbeiten (*a. thea.*); **~ment** [~mənt] Anordnung *f*, Zusammenstellung *f*, Verteilung *f*, Disposition *f*; Vereinbarung *f*, Absprache *f*; ♪ Arrangement *n*, Bearbeitung *f* (*a. thea.*); make ~s Vorkehrungen *od.* Vorbereitungen treffen.

ar·ray [əˈreɪ] ✕ Schlachtordnung *f*; Schar *f*, Aufgebot *n*.

ar·rear [əˈrɪə] *mst* ~s *pl.* Rückstand *m*, Rückstände *pl.*; Schulden *pl.*

ar·rest [əˈrest] **1.** ⚖ Verhaftung *f*, Festnahme *f*; △ *nicht* Arrest (*Schule etc.*); **2.** ⚖ verhaften, festnehmen, an-, aufhalten; *fig.* fesseln.

ar·riv·al [əˈraɪvl] Ankunft *f*; Erscheinen *n*; Ankömmling *m*; ~s *pl.* ankommende Züge *pl. od.* Schiffe *pl. od.* Flugzeuge *pl.*; **ar·rive** [~v] (an)kommen, eintreffen, erscheinen; ~ at *fig.* erreichen (*acc.*).

ar·ro|gance [ˈærəgəns] Arroganz *f*, Anmaßung *f*, Überheblichkeit *f*; **~gant** □ [~t] arrogant, anmaßend, überheblich.

ar·row [ˈærəʊ] Pfeil *m*; **~head** Pfeilspitze *f*.

ar·se·nal [ˈɑːsənl] Arsenal *n*, Zeughaus *n.*

ar·se·nic ⚗ [ˈɑːsnɪk] Arsen *n.*

ar·son ⚖ [ˈɑːsn] Brandstiftung *f*.

art [ɑːt] Kunst *f*; *fig.* List *f*; Kniff *m*; △ *nicht* Art; ~s *pl.* Geisteswissenschaften *pl.*; Faculty of ♀s, *Am.* ♀s Department philosophische Fakultät *f*.

ar·te·ri·al [ɑːˈtɪərɪəl] *anat.* Schlagader...; ~ road Hauptstraße *f*; **ar·te·ry** [ˈɑːtərɪ] *anat.* Arterie *f*, Schlag-, Pulsader *f*; *fig.* Verkehrsader *f*.

art·ful □ [ˈɑːtfl] schlau, verschmitzt.

ar·ti·cle [ˈɑːtɪkl] Artikel *m* (*a. gr.*).

ar·tic·u|late 1. [ɑːˈtɪkjʊlɪt] deutlich (aus)sprechen; zusammenfügen; **2.** □ [~lət] deutlich; ♀, *zo.* gegliedert; **~la·tion** [ɑːtɪkjʊˈleɪʃn] (deutliche)

Aussprache; *anat.* Gelenk(verbindung *f*) *n.*

ar·ti|fice [ˈɑːtɪfɪs] Kunstgriff *m*, List *f*; **~fi·cial** □ [ɑːtɪˈfɪʃl] künstlich, Kunst...; ~ person juristische Person.

ar·til·le·ry [ɑːˈtɪlərɪ] Artillerie *f*.

ar·ti·san [ɑːtɪˈzæn] Handwerker *m.*

art·ist [ˈɑːtɪst] Künstler(in); variety ~ Artist(in); **ar·tis·tic** [ɑːˈtɪstɪk] (~ally) künstlerisch, Kunst...

art·less □ [ˈɑːtlɪs] ungekünstelt, schlicht; arglos.

as [æz, əz] **1.** *adv.* so, ebenso; wie; (*in der Eigenschaft*) als; **2.** *cj.* (ge)rade) wie, so wie; ebenso wie; als, während; obwohl, obgleich; da, weil; *besondere Wendungen:* ~ ... ~ (eben)so ... wie; ~ for, ~ to was ... (an)betrifft; ~ from *von e-m Zeitpunkt an*, ab; ~ it were sozusagen; ~ Hamlet als Hamlet.

as·cend [əˈsend] *v/i.* (auf-, empor-, hinauf)steigen; *v/t.* be-, ersteigen; Fluß *etc.* hinauffahren.

as·cen|dan·cy, ~den·cy [əˈsendənsɪ] [~nsɪ] Überlegenheit *f*, Einfluß *m*; **~sion** [~ʃn] Aufsteigen *n* (*bsd. ast.*); Aufstieg *m* (*e-s Ballons etc.*); ♀ (Day) Himmelfahrt(stag *m*) *f*; **~t** [~t] Aufstieg *m*; Steigung *f.*

as·cer·tain [æsəˈteɪn] ermitteln.

as·cet·ic [əˈsetɪk] (~ally) asketisch.

as·cribe [əˈskraɪb] zuschreiben (*to dat.*).

a·sep·tic ⚕ [æˈseptɪk] **1.** aseptisch, keimfrei; **2.** aseptisches Mittel.

ash¹ [æʃ] ♀ Esche *f*; Eschenholz *n.*

ash² [~] *a.* ~es *pl.* Asche *f*; Ash Wednesday Aschermittwoch *m.*

a·shamed [əˈʃeɪmd] beschämt; be ~ of sich schämen für (*od. gen.*).

ash can *Am.* [~kæn] = dustbin.

ash·en [ˈæʃn] Aschen...; aschfahl.

a·shore [əˈʃɔː] *am od.* ans Ufer *od.* Land; run ~ stranden.

ash|tray [ˈæʃtreɪ] Asch(en)becher *m*; **~y** [~ɪ] (-ier, -iest) = ashen.

A·sian [ˈeɪʃn, ˈeɪʒn], **A·si·at·ic** [eɪʃɪˈætɪk] **1.** asiatisch; **2.** Asiat(in).

a·side [əˈsaɪd] **1.** beiseite (*a. thea.*), seitwärts; ~ from *Am.* abgesehen von; **2.** *thea.* Aparte *n.*

ask [ɑːsk] *v/t.* fragen (*s.th.* nach s.): verlangen (*of, from s.o.* von j-m); bitten (*s.o.* [for] *s.th.* j. um et.; *that* darum, daß); erbitten; ~ (*s.o.*) a question (j-m) e-e Frage stellen;

v/i.: ~ *for* bitten um; fragen nach; *he* ~*ed for it od. for* trouble er wollte es ja so haben; *to be had for the* ~*ing* umsonst zu haben.

a·skance [əˈskæns]: *look* ~ *at s.o.* j-n von der Seite ansehen; j-n schief *od.* mißtrauisch ansehen.

a·skew [əˈskjuː] schief.

a·sleep [əˈsliːp] schlafend; *be (fast, sound)* ~ *(fest)* schlafen; *fall* ~ einschlafen.

as·par·a·gus ♀ [əˈspærəgəs] Spargel *m*.

as·pect [ˈæspekt] Lage *f*; Aspekt *m*, Seite *f*, Gesichtspunkt *m*.

as·phalt [ˈæsfælt] **1.** Asphalt *m*; **2.** asphaltieren.

as·pic [ˈæspɪk] Aspik *m*, Gelee *n*.

as·pi·rant [əˈspaɪərənt] Bewerber(in) *m*; ~·**ra·tion** [æspəˈreɪʃn] Ambition *f*, Bestrebung *f*.

as·pire [əˈspaɪə] streben, trachten (*to, after* nach).

ass *zo.* [æs] Esel *m*; △ *nicht* As.

as·sail [əˈseɪl] angreifen; *be* ~*ed with* doubts von Zweifeln befallen werden; **as·sai·lant** [~ənt] Angreifer(in).

as·sas·sin [əˈsæsɪn] Mörder(in) (aus politischen Gründen), Attentäter(in); ~·**ate** *bsd. pol.* [~eɪt] ermorden; *be* ~*d* e-m Attentat *od.* Mordanschlag zum Opfer fallen; ~·**a·tion** [əsæsɪˈneɪʃn] (*of*) *bsd.* politischer Mord (*an dat.*), Ermordung *f* (*gen.*), (geglücktes) Attentat (auf *acc.*).

as·sault [əˈsɔːlt] **1.** Angriff *m*; **2.** angreifen, überfallen; ♈ tätlich angreifen *od.* beleidigen.

as·say [əˈseɪ] **1.** (Erz-, Metall)Probe *f*; **2.** *v/t.* prüfen, untersuchen.

as·sem·blage [əˈsemblɪdʒ] (An-)Sammlung *f*; ⊕ Montage *f*; ~·**ble** [~bl] (sich) versammeln; ⊕ montieren; ~·**bly** [~ɪ] Versammlung *f*, Gesellschaft *f*; ⊕ Montage *f*; ~ *line* ⊕ Fließband *n*.

as·sent [əˈsent] **1.** Zustimmung *f*; **2.** (*to*) zustimmen (*dat.*); billigen.

as·sert [əˈsɜːt] behaupten; geltend machen; ~ *o.s.* sich behaupten *od.* durchsetzen; **as·ser·tion** [əˈsɜːʃn] Behauptung *f*; Erklärung *f*; Geltendmachung *f*.

as·sess [əˈses] *Kosten etc.* festsetzen; (zur Steuer) veranlagen (*at* mit); *fig.* abschätzen, beurteilen; ~·**ment** [~mənt] Festsetzung *f*; (Steuer-)

Veranlagung *f*; *fig.* Einschätzung *f*.

as·set [ˈæset] *econ.* Aktivposten *m*; *fig.* Plus *n*, Gewinn *m*; ~*s pl.* Vermögen *n*; *econ.* Aktiva *pl.*; ♈ Konkursmasse *f*.

as·sid·u·ous □ [əˈsɪdjʊəs] emsig, fleißig; aufmerksam.

as·sign [əˈsaɪn] an-, zuweisen; bestimmen; zuschreiben; **as·sig·na·tion** [æsɪgˈneɪʃn] (*bsd.* heimliches) Treffen (*e-s Liebespaares*); = ~·**ment** [əˈsaɪnmənt] An-, Zuweisung *f*; Aufgabe *f*; Auftrag *m*; ♈ Übertragung *f*.

as·sim·i·late [əˈsɪmɪleɪt] (sich) angleichen *od.* anpassen (*to, with dat.*); ~·**la·tion** [əsɪmɪˈleɪʃn] Assimilation *f*, Angleichung *f*, Anpassung *f*.

as·sist [əˈsɪst] *j-m* beistehen, helfen; unterstützen; ~·**ance** [~əns] Beistand *m*, Hilfe *f*; **as·sis·tant** [~t] **1.** stellvertretend, Hilfs...; **2.** Assistent(in), Mitarbeiter(in); *shop* ~ *Brt.* Verkäufer(in).

as·siz·es *Brt. hist.* [əˈsaɪzɪz] *pl.* Sitzung(en *pl.*) *f* des periodischen Geschworenengerichts.

as·so·ci·ate 1. [əˈsəʊʃɪeɪt] vereinigen, -binden; assoziieren; ~ *with* verkehren mit; **2.** [~ʃɪət] verbunden; ~ *member* außerordentliches Mitglied; **3.** [~] Kollege *m*, -in *f*; Teilhaber(in); ~·**a·tion** [əsəʊsɪˈeɪʃn] Vereinigung *f*, Verbindung *f*; Verein *m*; Assoziation *f*.

as·sort [əˈsɔːt] sortieren, aussuchen, zusammenstellen; ~·**ment** [~mənt] Sortieren *n*; *econ.* Sortiment *n*, Auswahl *f*.

as·sume [əˈsjuːm] annehmen; vorgeben; übernehmen; **as·sump·tion** [əˈsʌmpʃn] Annahme *f*; Übernahme *f*; ⚸ (*Day*) *eccl.* Mariä Himmelfahrt *f*.

as·sur·ance [əˈʃʊərəns] Zu-, Versicherung *f*; Zuversicht *f*; Sicherheit *f*, Gewißheit *f*; Selbstsicherheit *f*; (*life*) ~ *bsd. Brt.* (Lebens)Versicherung *f*; ~·**e** [əˈʃʊə] versichern; *bsd. Brt. j-s Leben* versichern; ~·**ed 1.** (*adv.* ~·**ed·ly** [~rɪdlɪ]) sicher; **2.** Versicherte(r *m*) *f*.

asth·ma ♈ [ˈæsmə] Asthma *n*.

a·stir [əˈstɜː] auf(gestanden); auf den Beinen; voller *od.* in Aufregung.

as·ton·ish [əˈstɒnɪʃ] in Erstaunen setzen; *be* ~*ed* erstaunt sein (*at über acc.*); ~·**ing** □ [~ɪŋ] erstaunlich;

~·ment [~mənt] (Er)Staunen *n*, Verwunderung *f*.

as·tound [əˈstaʊnd] verblüffen.

a·stray [əˈstreɪ]: *go* ~ vom Weg abkommen; *fig.* auf Abwege geraten; irregehen; *lead* ~ *fig.* irreführen, verleiten; vom rechten Weg abbringen.

a·stride [əˈstraɪd] rittlings (*of* auf *dat.*).

as·trin·gent ✍ [əˈstrɪndʒənt] **1.** □ adstringierend; **2.** Adstringens *n*.

as·trol·o·gy [əˈstrɒlədʒɪ] Astrologie *f*.

as·tro·naut [ˈæstrənɔːt] Astronaut *m*, (Welt)Raumfahrer *m*.

as·tron·o·my [əˈstrɒnəmɪ] Astronomie *f*.

as·tute □ [əˈstjuːt] scharfsinnig; schlau; **~·ness** [~nɪs] Scharfsinn *m*.

a·sun·der [əˈsʌndə] auseinander; entzwei.

a·sy·lum [əˈsaɪləm] Asyl *n*.

at [æt, *unbetont:* ət] *prp.* an; auf; aus; bei; für; in; mit; nach; über; um; von; vor; zu; ~ *school* in der Schule; ~ *the age of* im Alter von.

ate [et] *pret. von eat* 1.

a·the·is·m [ˈeɪθɪɪzəm] Atheismus *m*.

ath|lete [ˈæθliːt] (*bsd.* Leicht)Athlet *m*; **~·let·ic** [æθˈletɪk] (*~ally*) athletisch; **~·let·ics** *sg. od. pl.* (*bsd.* Leicht)Athletik *f*.

At·lan·tic [ətˈlæntɪk] **1.** atlantisch; **2.** *a.* ~ *Ocean* Atlantik *m*.

at·mo·sphere [ˈætməsfɪə] Atmosphäre *f* (*a. fig.*); **~·spher·ic** [ætməsˈferɪk] (*~ally*) atmosphärisch.

at·om [ˈætəm] Atom *n* (*a. fig.*); ~ **bomb** Atombombe *f*.

a·tom·ic [əˈtɒmɪk] (*~ally*) atomar, Atom...; ~ **age** Atomzeitalter *n*; ~ **bomb** Atombombe *f*; ~ **en·er·gy** Atomenergie *f*; ~ **pile** Atomreaktor *m*; ~ **pow·er** Atomkraft *f*; **~·pow·ered** atomgetrieben; ~ **waste** Atommüll.

at·om·ize [ˈætəmaɪz] in Atome auflösen; atomisieren; zerstäuben; **~·iz·er** [~ə] Zerstäuber *m*.

a·tone [əˈtəʊn]: ~ *for et.* wiedergutmachen; **~·ment** [~mənt] Buße *f*, Sühne *f*.

a·tro·cious □ [əˈtrəʊʃəs] scheußlich, gräßlich; grausam; **~·ci·ty** [əˈtrɒsətɪ] Scheußlichkeit *f*, Gräßlichkeit *f*; Greueltat *f*, Greuel *m*.

at·tach [əˈtætʃ] *v/t.* (*to*) anheften, ankleben (an *acc.*), befestigen, anbrin-

gen (an *dat.*); Wert, Wichtigkeit *etc.* beimessen (*dat.*); ~ *o.s. to* sich anschließen (*dat.*, an *acc.*); **~ed** zugetan; **~·ment** [~mənt] Befestigung *f*; ~ *for*, ~ *to* Bindung *f* an (*acc.*); Anhänglichkeit *f* an (*acc.*), Neigung *f* zu.

at·tack [əˈtæk] **1.** angreifen (*a. fig.*); befallen (*Krankheit*); *Arbeit* in Angriff nehmen; **2.** Angriff *m*; ✍ Anfall *m*; Inangriffnahme *f*.

at·tain [əˈteɪn] Ziel erreichen, erlangen; **~·ment** [~mənt] Erreichung *f*; Erlangen *n*; **~s** *pl.* Kenntnisse *pl.*, Fertigkeiten *pl.*

at·tempt [əˈtempt] **1.** versuchen; **2.** Versuch *m*; Attentat *n*.

at·tend [əˈtend] *v/t.* begleiten; bedienen; pflegen; ✍ behandeln; *j-m* aufwarten; beiwohnen (*dat.*), anwesend sein bei, teilnehmen an, *Schule etc.* besuchen; *e-e Vorlesung etc.* hören; *v/i.* achten, hören (*to* auf *acc.*); ~ *to* erledigen; **~·ance** [~əns] Begleitung *f*; Dienst *m*; (Auf)Wartung *f*, Pflege *f*; ✍ Behandlung *f*; Anwesenheit *f* (*at* bei); Besuch *m* (*der Schule etc.*); Besucher(zahl *f*) *pl.*; **~·ant** [~t] Aufseher(in); ⊕ Bedienungsmann *m*.

at·ten|tion [əˈtenʃn] Aufmerksamkeit *f* (*a. fig.*); **~·tive** □ [~tɪv] aufmerksam.

at·tic [ˈætɪk] Dachboden *m*; Dachstube *f*.

at·tire [əˈtaɪə] **1.** kleiden; **2.** Kleidung *f*.

at·ti·tude [ˈætɪtjuːd] (Ein)Stellung *f*; Haltung *f*.

at·tor·ney [əˈtɜːnɪ] Bevollmächtigte(r) *m*; *Am.* Rechtsanwalt *m*; *power of* ~ Vollmacht *f*; ♀ *General Brt.* erster Kronanwalt; *Am.* Justizminister *m*.

at·tract [əˈtrækt] anziehen, *Aufmerksamkeit* erregen; *fig.* reizen; **at·trac·tion** [~kʃn] Anziehung(skraft) *f*, Reiz *m*; Attraktion *f*, *thea. etc.* Zugnummer *f*, -stück *n*; **at·trac·tive** [~tɪv] anziehend; attraktiv; reizvoll; **at·trac·tive·ness** [~nɪs] Reiz *m*.

at·trib·ute[1] [əˈtrɪbjuːt] beimessen, zuschreiben; zurückführen (*to* auf *acc.*).

at·tri·bute[2] [ˈætrɪbjuːt] Attribut *n* (*a. gr.*), Eigenschaft *f*, Merkmal *n*.

at·tune [əˈtjuːn]: ~ *to fig.* einstellen auf (*acc.*).

au·burn ['ɔ:bən] kastanienbraun.

auc·tion ['ɔ:kʃn] 1. Auktion f; sell by (Am. at) ~ versteigern; put up for (Am. at) ~ zur Versteigerung anbieten; 2. mst ~ off versteigern; ~·tio·neer [ɔ:kʃə'nɪə] Auktionator m.

au·da·cious □ [ɔ:'deɪʃəs] kühn; dreist; ~·ci·ty [ɔ:'dæsətɪ] Kühnheit f; Dreistigkeit f.

au·di·ble □ ['ɔ:dəbl] hörbar.

au·di·ence ['ɔ:djəns] Publikum n, Zuhörer(schaft f) pl., Zuschauer pl., Besucher pl., Leser(kreis m) pl.; Audienz f; give ~ to Gehör schenken (dat.).

au·di·o·cas·sette ['ɔ:dɪəʊkæ'set] Text-, Tonkassette f; ~·vis·u·al ['ɔ:dɪəʊ'vɪʒʊəl]: ~ aids pl. audiovisuelle Unterrichtsmittel pl.

au·dit econ. ['ɔ:dɪt] 1. Bücherrevision f; 2. Rechnungen prüfen; au·di·tor [~ə] (Zu)Hörer(in); econ. Bücherrevisor m, Buchprüfer m; au·di·to·ri·um [ɔ:dɪ'tɔ:rɪəm] Zuschauerraum m; Am. Vortrags-, Konzertsaal m.

au·ger ⊕ ['ɔ:gə] großer Bohrer.

aught [ɔ:t] (irgend) etwas; for ~ I care meinetwegen; for ~ I know soviel ich weiß.

aug·ment [ɔ:g'ment] vergrößern.

au·gur ['ɔ:gə]: ~ ill (well) ein schlechtes (gutes) Zeichen od. Omen sein (for für).

Au·gust [1] ['ɔ:gəst] August m.

au·gust [2] □ [ɔ:'gʌst] erhaben.

aunt [ɑ:nt] Tante f; ~·ie, ~·y ['ɑ:ntɪ] Tantchen n.

aus·pices ['ɔ:spɪsɪz] pl. Schirmherrschaft f; ~·pi·cious □ [ɔ:'spɪʃəs] günstig.

aus·tere □ [ɒ'stɪə] streng; herb; hart; einfach; ~·ter·i·ty [ɒ'sterətɪ] Strenge f; Härte f; Einfachheit f.

Aus·tra·li·an [ɒ'streɪljən] 1. australisch; 2. Australier(in).

Aus·tri·an ['ɒstrɪən] 1. österreichisch; 2. Österreicher(in).

au·then·tic □ [ɔ:'θentɪk] (~ally) authentisch; zuverlässig; echt.

au·thor ['ɔ:θə] Urheber(in); Autor(in), Verfasser(in); ~·i·ta·tive □ [ɔ:'θɒrɪtətɪv] maßgebend; gebieterisch; zuverlässig; ~·i·ty □ [~'rɒtɪ] Autorität f; (Amts)Gewalt f; Nachdruck m, Gewicht n; Vollmacht f; Einfluß m (over auf acc.); Ansehen n; Quelle f; Fachmann m; mst authorities pl. Behörde f; ~·ize

['ɔ:θəraɪz] j-n autorisieren, ermächtigen, bevollmächtigen, berechtigen; et. gutheißen; ~·ship [~ʃɪp] Urheberschaft f.

au·to·graph ['ɔ:təgrɑ:f] Autogramm n.

au·to·mat TM ['ɔ:təmæt] Automatenrestaurant n (in den USA).

au·to·mate ['ɔ:təmeɪt] automatisieren; ~·mat·ic [ɔ:tə'mætɪk] (~ally) 1. automatisch; 2. Selbstladepistole f, -gewehr n; mot. Auto n mit Automatik; ~·ma·tion [~'meɪʃn] Automation f; ~·m·a·ton fig. [ɔ:'tɒmətən] (pl. -ta [-tə], -tons) Roboter m.

au·to·mo·bile bsd. Am. ['ɔ:təməbi:l] Auto n, Automobil n.

au·ton·o·my [ɔ:'tɒnəmɪ] Autonomie f.

au·tumn ['ɔ:təm] Herbst m; au·tum·nal □ [ɔ:'tʌmnəl] herbstlich, Herbst...

aux·il·i·a·ry [ɔ:g'zɪljərɪ] helfend, Hilfs...

a·vail [ə'veɪl] 1. ~ o.s. of sich e-r Sache bedienen, et. nutzen; 2. Nutzen m; of od. to no ~ nutzlos; a·vai·la·ble □ [~əbl] verfügbar, vorhanden; erreichbar; econ. lieferbar, vorrätig, erhältlich.

av·a·lanche ['ævəlɑ:nʃ] Lawine f.

av·a·rice ['ævərɪs] Habsucht f; ~·ri·cious □ [ævə'rɪʃəs] habgierig, -süchtig.

a·venge [ə'vendʒ] rächen; a·veng·er [~ə] Rächer(in).

av·e·nue ['ævənju:] Allee f; Boulevard m, Prachtstraße f.

a·ver [ə'vɜ:] (-rr-) behaupten.

av·e·rage ['ævərɪdʒ] 1. Durchschnitt m; ⚓ Havarie f; 2. □ durchschnittlich, Durchschnitts...; 3. durchschnittlich betragen (ausmachen, haben, leisten, erreichen etc.); a. ~ out den Durchschnitt ermitteln.

a·verse □ [ə'vɜ:s] abgeneigt (to dat.); a·ver·sion [~ʃn] Widerwille m, Abneigung f.

a·vert [ə'vɜ:t] abwenden (a. fig.).

a·vi·a·ry ['eɪvɪərɪ] Vogelhaus n, Voliere f.

a·vi·a·tion ✈ [eɪvɪ'eɪʃn] Luftfahrt f; ~·tor ['eɪvɪeɪtə] Flieger m.

av·id □ ['ævɪd] gierig (for nach); begeistert, passioniert.

a·void [ə'vɔɪd] (ver)meiden; ausweichen; ~·ance [~əns] Vermeidung f.

a·vow [ə'vaʊ] bekennen, (ein)gestehen; anerkennen; **~al** [~əl] Bekenntnis *n*, (Ein)Geständnis *n*; **~ed·ly** [~ɪdlɪ] eingestandenermaßen.

a·wait [ə'weɪt] erwarten.

a·wake [ə'weɪk] **1.** wach, munter; *be ~ to* sich e-r *Sache* (voll) bewußt sein; **2.** *a.* **a·wak·en** [~ən] (*awoke od. awaked, awaked od. awoken*) *v/t.* (auf)wecken; *~ s.o. to s.th.* j-m et. zum Bewußtsein bringen; *v/i.* auf-, erwachen; **a·wak·en·ing** [~ənɪŋ] Erwachen *n*.

a·ward [ə'wɔːd] **1.** Belohnung *f*; Preis *m*, Auszeichnung *f*; **2.** zuerkennen, *Preis etc.* verleihen.

a·ware [ə'weə]: *be ~ of s.th.* von et. wissen, sich e-r *Sache* bewußt sein; *become ~ of s.th.* et. gewahr werden *od.* merken.

a·way [ə'weɪ] (hin)weg, fort; entfernt; immer weiter, d(a)rauflos; *Sport:* auswärts; *~* (*game*) Auswärtsspiel *n*; *~* (*win*) Auswärtssieg *m*.

awe [ɔː] **1.** Ehrfurcht *f*, Scheu *f*, Furcht *f*; **2.** (Ehr)Furcht einflößen (*dat.*).

aw·ful □ ['ɔːfl] furchtbar, schrecklich.

a·while [ə'waɪl] e-e Weile.

awk·ward □ [~kwəd] ungeschickt, unbeholfen, linkisch; unangenehm; dumm, ungünstig (*Zeitpunkt etc.*).

awl [ɔːl] Ahle *f*, Pfriem *m*.

aw·ning ['ɔːnɪŋ] Plane *f*; Markise *f*.

a·woke [ə'wəuk] *pret. von awake 2; a.* **a·wok·en** [~ən] *p.p. von awake 2.*

a·wry [ə'raɪ] schief; *fig.* verkehrt.

ax(e) [æks] Axt *f*, Beil *n*.

ax·is ['æksɪs] (*pl. -es* [-siːz]) Achse *f*.

ax·le ⊕ ['æksl] *a.* **~-tree** (Rad)Achse *f*, Welle *f*.

aye [aɪ] Ja *n*; *parl.* Jastimme *f*; *the ~s have it* der Antrag ist angenommen.

az·ure ['æʒə] azur-, himmelblau.

B

bab·ble ['bæbl] **1.** stammeln; plappern, schwatzen; plätschern (*Bach*); **2.** Geplapper *n*, Geschwätz *n*.

babe [beɪb] kleines Kind, Baby *n*; *Am.* F Puppe *f* (*Mädchen*).

ba·boon *zo.* [bə'buːn] Pavian *m*.

ba·by ['beɪbɪ] **1.** Säugling *m*, kleines Kind, Baby *n*; *Am.* F Puppe *f* (*Mädchen*); **2.** Baby..., Kinder...; klein; *~* **car·riage** *Am.* Kinderwagen *m*; **~·hood** [~hʊd] frühe Kindheit, Säuglingsalter *n*; **~-mind·er** *Brt.* [~maɪndə] Tagesmutter *f*; **~-sit** (-*tt-*; -*sat*) babysitten; **~-sit·ter** [~ə] Babysitter(in).

bach·e·lor ['bætʃələ] Junggeselle *m*; *univ.* Bakkalaureus *m* (*Grad*).

back [bæk] **1.** Rücken *m*; Rückseite *f*; Rücklehne *f*; Hinterende *n*; *Fußball:* Verteidiger *m*; **2.** *adj.* Hinter..., Rück..., hintere(r, -s), rückwärtig; entlegen; rückläufig; rückständig; alt, zurückliegend (*Zeitung etc.*); **3.** *adv.* zurück; rückwärts; **4.** *v/t.* mit e-m Rücken versehen; (*a. ~ up*) unterstützen; hinten grenzen an

(*acc.*); zurückbewegen, zurückstoßen mit (*Auto*); wetten *od.* setzen auf (*acc.*); *econ. Scheck* indossieren; *v/i.* sich rückwärts bewegen, zurückgehen *od.* -treten *od.* -fahren, *mot. a.* zurückstoßen; **~ al·ley** *Am.* finstere Seitengasse; **~·bite** ['bækbaɪt] (*-bit, -bitten*) verleumden; **~·bone** Rückgrat *n*; **~·break·ing** [~ɪŋ] erschöpfend, mörderisch (*Arbeit*); **~·comb** *Haar* toupieren; **~·er** [~ə] Unterstützer(in); Wetter(in); **~·fire** *mot.* Früh-, Fehlzündung *f*; **~·ground** Hintergrund *m*; **~·hand** *Sport:* Rückhand *f*; **~·ing** [~ɪŋ] Unterstützung *f*; ⊕ versteifende Ausfütterung, Verstärkung *f*; ♪ Begleitung *f* (*e-s Popsängers*); **~ num·ber** alte Nummer (*e-r Zeitung*); **~ seat** Rücksitz *m*; **~·side** Gesäß *n*, Hintern *m*, Po *m*; **~ stairs** Hintertreppe *f*; **~ street** Seitenstraße *f*; **~·stroke** *Sport:* Rückenschwimmen *n*; **~·talk** *Am.* F freche Antwort(en *pl.*); **~·track** *fig.* e-n Rückzieher machen; **~·ward** [~wəd] **1.** *adj.* Rück-

(wärts)...; langsam; zurückgeblieben; rückständig; zurückhaltend; **2.** *adv.* (*a.* **~wards** [~wədz]) rückwärts, zurück; **~yard** *Brt.* Hinterhof *m*; *Am.* Garten *m* hinter dem Haus.

ba·con ['beɪkən] Speck *m*.

bac·te·ri·a *biol.* [bæk'tɪərɪə] *pl.* Bakterien *pl.*

bad □ [bæd] (*worse, worst*) schlecht, böse, schlimm; *go* **~** schlecht werden, verderben; *he is in a* **~** *way* es geht ihm schlecht, er ist übel dran; *he is* **~***ly off* es geht ihm sehr schlecht; **~***ly wounded* schwerverwundet; *want* **~***ly* F dringend brauchen.

bade [beɪd] *pret. von bid 1.*

badge [bædʒ] Abzeichen *n*; Dienstmarke *f*.

bad·ger ['bædʒə] **1.** *zo.* Dachs *m*; **2.** plagen, *j-m* zusetzen.

bad·lands ['bædlændz] *pl.* Ödland *n*.

baf·fle ['bæfl] *j-n* verwirren; *Plan etc.* vereiteln, durchkreuzen.

bag [bæg] **1.** Beutel *m*, Sack *m*; Tüte *f*; Tasche *f*; **~** *and baggage* (mit) Sack und Pack; **2.** (*-gg-*) in e-n Beutel *etc.* tun; in e-n Beutel verpacken *od.* abfüllen; *hunt.* zur Strecke bringen; (sich) bauschen.

bag·gage *bsd. Am.* ['bægɪdʒ] (Reise-) Gepäck *n*; **~ car** 🚃 Gepäckwagen *m*; **~ check** *Am.* Gepäckschein *m*; **~ room** *Am.* Gepäckaufbewahrung *f*.

bag·gy F ['bægɪ] (*-ier, -iest*) sackartig; schlaff (herunterhängend); ausgebeult (*Hose*).

bag·pipes ['bægpaɪps] *pl.* Dudelsack *m*.

bail [beɪl] **1.** Bürge *m*; Bürgschaft *f*; Kaution *f*; *admit to* **~** ⚖ gegen Kaution freilassen; *go od.* *stand* **~** *for s.o.* ⚖ für *j-n* Kaution stellen; **2.** **~** *out* ⚖ *j-n* gegen Kaution freibekommen; *Am.* 🪂 (mit dem Fallschirm) abspringen.

bai·liff ['beɪlɪf] ⚖ *bsd.* Gerichtsvollzieher *m*; (Guts)Verwalter *m*.

bait [beɪt] **1.** Köder *m* (*a. fig.*); **2.** mit e-m Köder versehen; *fig.* ködern; *fig.* quälen, piesacken.

bake [beɪk] backen, im (Back)Ofen braten; *Ziegel* brennen; dörren; **~***d beans pl.* Bohnen *pl.* in Tomatensoße; **~***d potatoes pl. ungeschälte, im Ofen gebackene Kartoffeln*; Folienkartoffeln *pl.*; **bak·er** ['beɪkə] Bäcker

m; **bak·er·y** [~ərɪ] Bäckerei *f*; **bak·ing-pow·der** [~ɪŋpaʊdə] Backpulver *n*.

bal·ance ['bæləns] **1.** Waage *f*; Gleichgewicht *n* (*a. fig.*); Harmonie *f*; *econ.* Bilanz *f*; *econ.* Saldo *m*, Kontostand *m*, Guthaben *n*; F Rest *m*; *a.* **~ wheel** Unruh *f* (*der Uhr*); *keep one's* **~** das Gleichgewicht halten; *lose one's* **~** das Gleichgewicht verlieren; *fig.* die Fassung verlieren; **~** *of payments econ.* Zahlungsbilanz *f*; **~** *of power pol.* Kräftegleichgewicht *n*; **~** *of trade* (Außen)Handelsbilanz *f*; **2.** *v/t.* (ab-, er)wägen; im Gleichgewicht halten, balancieren; ausgleichen; *v/i.* balancieren, sich ausgleichen.

bal·co·ny ['bælkənɪ] Balkon *m* (*a. thea.*).

bald □ [bɔːld] kahl; *fig.* dürftig; *fig.* unverblümt; △ *nicht bald*.

bale¹ *econ.* [beɪl] Ballen *m*.

bale² *Brt.* 🪂 [~]: **~** *out* (mit dem Fallschirm) abspringen.

bale·ful □ ['beɪlfl] verderblich; unheilvoll; haßerfüllt (*Blick*).

balk [bɔːk] **1.** 🜛 (Furchen)Rain *m*; Balken *m*; Hindernis *n*; **2.** *v/t.* (ver-) hindern, vereiteln; *v/i.* stutzen, scheuen.

ball¹ [bɔːl] **1.** Ball *m*; Kugel *f*; *anat.* (Hand-, Fuß)Ballen *m*; Knäuel *m*, *n*; Kloß *m*; **~***s pl.* V Eier *pl.* (*Hoden*); *keep the* **~** *rolling* das Gespräch *od.* die Sache in Gang halten; *play* **~** F mitmachen; **2.** (sich) (zusammen-) ballen.

ball² [~] Ball *m*, Tanzveranstaltung *f*.

bal·lad ['bæləd] Ballade *f*; Lied *n*.

bal·last ['bæləst] **1.** Ballast *m*; Schotter *m*; **2.** mit Ballast beladen; beschottern.

ball-bear·ing ⊕ ['bɔːl'beərɪŋ] Kugellager *n*.

bal·let ['bæleɪ] Ballett *n*.

bal·lis·tics ✕, *phys.* [bə'lɪstɪks] *sg.* Ballistik *f*.

bal·loon [bə'luːn] **1.** Ballon *m*; **2.** im Ballon aufsteigen; sich blähen.

bal·lot ['bælət] **1.** Wahl-, Stimmzettel *m*; geheime Wahl; **2.** (geheim) abstimmen; **~** *for* losen um; **~-box** Wahlurne *f*.

ball-point (pen) ['bɔːlpɔɪnt('pen)] Kugelschreiber *m*.

ball·room ['bɔːlrʊm] Ball-, Tanzsaal *m*.

balm [bɑːm] Balsam m (a. fig.).
balm·y □ ['bɑːmɪ] (-ier, -iest) lind, mild (Wetter); bsd. Am. sl. bekloppt, verrückt.
ba·lo·ney Am. sl. [bə'ləʊnɪ] Quatsch m.
bal·us·trade [bælə'streɪd] Balustrade f, Brüstung f, Geländer n.
bam·boo [bæm'buː] (pl. -boos) Bambus(rohr n) m.
bam·boo·zle F [bæm'buːzl] betrügen, übers Ohr hauen.
ban [bæn] 1. (amtliches) Verbot, Sperre f; eccl. Bann m; 2. (-nn-) verbieten.
ba·nal [bə'nɑːl] banal, abgedroschen.
ba·na·na ♀ [bə'nɑːnə] Banane f.
band [bænd] 1. Band n; Streifen m; Schar f, Gruppe f; (bsd. Räuber)Bande f; ♪ Kapelle f, (Tanz-, Unterhaltungs)Orchester n, (Jazz-, Rock-) Band f; 2. ~ together sich zusammentun od. zusammenrotten.
ban·dage ['bændɪdʒ] 1. Binde f; Verband m; 2. bandagieren; verbinden.
ban·dit ['bændɪt] Bandit m.
band|-mas·ter ['bændmɑːstə] Kapellmeister m; ~·stand Musikpavillon m, -podium n; ~·wag·on Am. Wagen m mit Musikkapelle; jump on the ~ sich der erfolgversprechenden Sache anschließen.
ban·dy¹ ['bændɪ]: ~ words (with s.o.) sich (mit j-m) streiten; ~ about od. Gerüchte etc. in Umlauf setzen od. weitererzählen.
ban·dy² [~] (-ier, -iest) krumm; ~-legged säbel-, O-beinig.
bane [beɪn] Ruin m, Fluch m; ~·ful □ ['beɪnfl] verderblich.
bang [bæŋ] 1. heftiger Schlag; Knall m; mst ~s pl. Ponyfrisur f; 2. dröhnend (zu)schlagen.
ban·ish ['bænɪʃ] verbannen; ~·ment [~mənt] Verbannung f.
ban·is·ter ['bænɪstə] a. ~s pl. Treppengeländer.
bank [bæŋk] 1. Damm m; Ufer n; (Fels-, Sand-, Wolken-, ♣ Blutetc.)Bank f; econ. Bank(haus n) f; ~ of issue Notenbank f; △ nicht Sitz-Bank; 2. v/t. eindämmen; econ. Geld auf e-r Bank einzahlen; ♣ Blut etc. konservieren u. aufbewahren; v/i. econ. Bankgeschäfte machen; econ. ein Bankkonto haben; ~ on sich verlassen auf (acc.); ~·bill ['bæŋkbɪl]

Bankwechsel m; Am. = banknote; ~·book Kontobuch n, a. Sparbuch n; ~·er [~ə] Bankier m; ~ hol·i·day Brt. Bankfeiertag m (gesetzlicher Feiertag); ~·ing [~ɪŋ] Bankgeschäft n, Bankwesen n; attr. Bank...; ~·note Banknote f, Geldschein m; ~ rate Diskontsatz m.
bank·rupt ⅀⅀ ['bæŋkrʌpt] 1. Zahlungsunfähige(r m) f; 2. bankrott, zahlungsunfähig; go ~ in Konkurs gehen, Bankrott machen; 3. bankrott machen; ~·cy ⅀⅀ [~sɪ] Bankrott m, Konkurs m.
ban·ner ['bænə] Banner n; Fahne f.
banns [bænz] pl. Aufgebot n.
ban·quet ['bæŋkwɪt] Bankett n, Festessen n.
ban·ter ['bæntə] necken.
bap|tis·m ['bæptɪzəm] Taufe f; ~·tize [bæp'taɪz] taufen.
bar [bɑː] 1. Stange f, Stab m; Barren m; Riegel m; Schranke f; Sandbank f; (Ordens)Spange f; ♪ Takt(strich) m; dicker Strich; ⅀⅀ (Gerichts-) Schranke f; ⅀⅀ Anwaltschaft f; Bar f (im Hotel etc.); fig. Hindernis n; 2. (-rr-) zu-, verriegeln; versperren; einsperren; (ver)hindern; ausschließen.
barb [bɑːb] Widerhaken m.
bar·bar·i·an [bɑː'beərɪən] 1. barbarisch; 2. Barbar(in).
bar·be·cue ['bɑːbɪkjuː] 1. Bratrost m, Grill m; Grillfleisch n (bsd. Ochse); Grillparty f; 2. bsd. Ochse auf dem Rost braten, grillen.
barbed wire [bɑːbd 'waɪə] Stacheldraht m.
bar·ber ['bɑːbə] (Herren)Friseur m.
bare [beə] 1. (~r, ~st) nackt, bloß; kahl; bar, leer; 2. entblößen; ~·faced □ ['beəfeɪst] frech; ~·foot, ~·footed barfuß; ~·head·ed barhäuptig; ~·ly [~lɪ] kaum.
bar·gain ['bɑːgɪn] 1. Vertrag m, Abmachung f; Geschäft n, Handel m, Kauf m; vorteilhafter Kauf; a (dead) ~ spottbillig; it's a ~! abgemacht!; into the ~ obendrein; 2. (ver)handeln; übereinkommen; ~ sale Ausverkauf m.
barge [bɑːdʒ] 1. Flußboot n, Lastkahn m; Hausboot n; 2. ~ in(to) hereinplatzen in (acc.).
bark¹ [bɑːk] ♀ Borke f, Rinde f; 2. abrinden; Knie abschürfen.
bark² [~] 1. bellen; ~ up the wrong

bay

tree F auf dem Holzweg sein; an der falschen Adresse sein; **2.** Bellen *n*.

bar·ley ♀ ['bɑːlɪ] Gerste *f*; Graupe *f*.

barn [bɑːn] Scheune *f*; (Vieh)Stall *m*; **~storm** *Am. pol.* ['bɑːnstɔːm] herumreisen u. (Wahl)Reden halten.

ba·rom·e·ter [bə'rɒmɪtə] Barometer *n*.

bar·on ['bærən] Baron *m*; Freiherr *m*; **~ess** [~ɪs] Baronin *f*; Freifrau *f*.

bar·racks ['bærəks] *sg.* ⚔ Kaserne *f*; *contp.* Mietskaserne *f*; △ *nicht Baracke*.

bar·rage ['bærɑːʒ] Staudamm *m*; ⚔ Sperrfeuer *n*; *fig.* Hagel *m*, (Wort-, Rede)Schwall *m*.

bar·rel ['bærəl] **1.** Faß *n*, Tonne *f*; (*Gewehr*)Lauf *m*; ⊕ Trommel *f*, Walze *f*; **2.** in Fässer füllen; **~or·gan** ♪ Drehorgel *f*.

bar·ren □ ['bærən] unfruchtbar; dürr, trocken; tot (*Kapital*).

bar·ri·cade [bærɪ'keɪd] **1.** Barrikade *f*; **2.** verbarrikadieren; sperren.

bar·ri·er ['bærɪə] Schranke *f* (*a. fig.*), Barriere *f*, Sperre *f*; Hindernis *n*.

bar·ris·ter *Brt.* ['bærɪstə] (plädierender) Rechtsanwalt, Barrister *m*.

bar·row ['bærəʊ] Karre *f*.

bar·ter ['bɑːtə] **1.** Tausch(handel) *m*; **2.** tauschen (*for gegen*).

base¹ ['beɪs] (*~r, ~st*) gemein.

base² [~] **1.** Basis *f*; Grundlage *f*; Fundament *n*; Fuß *m*; 🎵 Base *f*; ⚔Standort *m*; ⚔ Stützpunkt *m*; **2.** gründen, stützen (*on, upon* auf *acc.*).

base|ball ['beɪsbɔːl] Baseball(spiel *n*) *m*; **~board** *Am.* Scheuerleiste *f*; **~less** ['beɪslɪs] grundlos; **~ment** [~mənt] Fundament *n*; Kellergeschoß *n*.

base·ness ['beɪsnɪs] Gemeinheit *f*.

bash·ful □ ['bæʃfl] schüchtern.

ba·sic¹ ['beɪsɪk] **1.** grundlegend, Grund...; 🎵 basisch; **2.** **~s** *pl.* Grundlagen *pl.*

BA·SIC² [~] BASIC *n* (*e-e Computersprache*).

ba·sic·al·ly ['beɪsɪkəlɪ] im Grunde.

ba·sin ['beɪsn] Becken *n*, Schale *f*, Schüssel *f*; Tal-, Wasser-, Hafenbecken *n*.

ba·sis ['beɪsɪs] (*pl.* -*ses* [-siːz]) Basis *f*; Grundlage *f*.

bask [bɑːsk] sich sonnen (*a. fig.*).

bas·ket ['bɑːskɪt] Korb *m*; **~ball** Basketball(spiel *n*) *m*.

bass¹ ♪ [beɪs] Baß *m*.

bass² *zo.* [bæs] (Fluß-, See)Barsch *m*.

bas·tard ['bɑːstəd] **1.** □ unehelich; unecht; Bastard...; **2.** Bastard *m*.

baste¹ [beɪst] *Braten* mit Fett begießen.

baste² [~] (an)heften.

bat¹ [bæt] *zo.* Fledermaus *f*; *as blind as a ~* stockblind.

bat² [~] *Sport:* **1.** Schlagholz *n*, Schläger *m*; **2.** (*-tt-*) *den Ball* schlagen; am Schlagen *od.* dran sein.

batch [bætʃ] Schub *m* (*Brote*); Stoß *m*, Stapel *m* (*Briefe etc.*).

bate [beɪt]: *with ~d breath* mit angehaltenem Atem.

bath [bɑːθ] **1.** (*pl.* baths [~ðz]) (Wannen)Bad *n*; *have a ~ Brt., take a ~ Am.* baden, ein Bad nehmen; **~s** *pl.* Bad *n*; Badeanstalt *f*; Badeort *m*; **2.** *Brt. v/t. Kind etc.* baden; *v/i.* baden, ein Bad nehmen.

bathe [beɪð] *v/t. Wunde etc.*, *bsd. Am. Kind etc.* baden; *v/i.* baden; schwimmen; *bsd. Am.* baden, ein Bad nehmen.

bath·ing ['beɪðɪŋ] Baden *n*; *attr.* Bade...; **~suit** Badeanzug *m*.

bath|robe ['bɑːθrəʊb] Bademantel *m*; *Am.* Morgen-, Schlafrock *m*; **~room** Badezimmer *n*; (Wasch)Raum *m*; **~tow·el** Badetuch *n*; **~tub** Badewanne *f*.

bat·on ['bætɒn] Stab *m*; ♪ Taktstock *m*; Schlagstock *m*, Gummiknüppel *m*.

bat·tal·i·on ⚔ [bə'tæljən] Bataillon *n*.

bat·ten ['bætn] Latte *f*.

bat·ter ['bætə] **1.** *Sport:* Schläger *m*; Rührteig *m*; **2.** heftig schlagen; *Ehefrau, Kind etc.* mißhandeln; verbeulen; **~** *down od. in Tür* einschlagen; **~y** [~rɪ] Batterie *f*; *assault and* **~** 🎵 tätlicher Angriff; **~y-op·er·at·ed** batteriebetrieben.

bat·tle ['bætl] **1.** Schlacht *f* (*of* bei); **2.** streiten, kämpfen; **~ax(e)** Streitaxt *f*; F alter Drachen (*bösartige Frau*); **~field, ~ground** Schlachtfeld *n*; **~ments** [~mənts] *pl.* Zinnen *pl.*; **~plane** ⚔ Kampfflugzeug *n*; **~ship** ⚔ Schlachtschiff *n*.

baulk [bɔːk] = *balk*.

Ba·var·i·an [bə'veərɪən] **1.** bay(e)risch; **2.** Bayer(in).

bawd·y ['bɔːdɪ] (*-ier, -iest*) obszön.

bawl [bɔːl] brüllen, schreien, grölen; **~** *out Befehl* brüllen.

bay¹ [beɪ] **1.** rotbraun; **2.** Braune(r) *m* (*Pferd*).

bay² [ˌ] Bai f, Bucht f; Erker m.

bay³ ⚓ [ˌ] a. ~ tree Lorbeer(baum) m.

bay⁴ [ˌ] 1. bellen, Laut geben (*Hund*); 2. *hold od.* keep *at* ~ *j*-n in Schach halten; *et.* von sich fernhalten.

bay·o·net ⚔ ['beɪənɪt] Bajonett n.

bay·ou *Am.* ['baɪuː] sumpfiger Fluß-arm.

bay win·dow ['beɪˈwɪndəʊ] Erker-fenster n; *Am. sl.* Vorbau m (*Bauch*).

ba·za(a)r [bəˈzɑː] Basar m.

be [biː, bɪ] (*was od.* were, been) sein; *zur Bildung des Passivs:* werden; stattfinden; werden (*beruflich:*); he wants to ~ ... er möchte ... werden; how much are the shoes? was ko-sten die Schuhe? ~ reading beim Lesen sein, gerade lesen; there is, there are es gibt.

beach [biːtʃ] 1. Strand m; 2. ⚓ auf den Strand setzen *od.* ziehen; ~ ball Wasserball m; ~ bug·gy m; ~comb·er *fig.* ['biːtʃ-kəʊmə] Nichtstuer m.

bea·con ['biːkən] Leuchtfeuer n; Funkfeuer n.

bead [biːd] (*Glas- etc.*)Perle f; Tropfen m; ~s pl. a. Rosenkranz m; ~y ['biːdɪ] (*-ier, -iest*) klein, rund u. glänzend (*Augen*).

beak [biːk] Schnabel m; ⊕ Tülle f.

bea·ker ['biːkə] Becher m.

beam [biːm] 1. Balken m; Waage-balken m; Strahl m; ⚡ (Funk)Leit-, Richtstrahl m; 2. ausstrahlen; strah-len (*a. fig.* with vor *dat.*).

bean [biːn] ⚓ Bohne f; *Am. sl.* Birne f (*Kopf*); be full of ~s F voller Le-ben(skraft) stecken.

bear¹ zo. [beə] Bär m.

bear² [ˌ] (bore, borne *od. pass.* gebo-ren [*werden*]: born) v/t. tragen; ge-bären; *ein Gefühl* hegen; ertragen; aushalten; *mst negativ:* ausstehen, leiden; ~ down überwinden, bewäl-tigen; ~out bestätigen; v/i. tragen; zo. trächtig sein; ~·a·ble □ ['beərəbl] erträglich.

beard [bɪəd] Bart m; ⚓ Grannen pl.; ~·ed ['bɪədɪd] bärtig.

bear·er ['beərə] Träger(in); econ. Überbringer(in), (*Wertpapier*)Inha-ber(in).

bear·ing ['beərɪŋ] (Er)Tragen n; Be-tragen n; *fig.* Beziehung f; Lage f, Richtung f, Orientierung f; take one's ~s sich orientieren; lose one's ~s die Orientierung verlieren.

beast [biːst] Vieh n, Tier n; Bestie f; ~·ly ['biːstlɪ] (*-ier, -iest*) scheußlich.

beat [biːt] 1. (beat, beaten *od.* beat) v/t. schlagen; (ver)prügeln; besie-gen; übertreffen; ~ it! F hau ab!; that ~s all! das ist doch der Gipfel *od.* die Höhe!; that ~s me das ist mir zu hoch; ~ down econ. Preis drücken, herunterhandeln; ~ out Melodie etc. trommeln; Feuer ausschlagen; ~ up j-n zusammenschlagen; v/i. schla-gen; ~ about the bush wie die Katze um den heißen Brei herumschlei-chen; 2. Schlag m; ♪ Takt(schlag) m; Jazz: Beat m; Pulsschlag m; Runde f, Revier n (*e-s Polizisten*); 3. (dead) ~ F wie erschlagen, fix u. fertig; ~·en ['biːtn] p.p. von beat 1; vielbegangen (*Weg*); off the ~ track abgelegen; *fig.* ungewohnt.

beau·ti·cian [bjuːˈtɪʃn] Kosmetikerin f; ~·ful □ ['bjuːtəfl] schön; ~·fy [ˌ·ɪfaɪ] schön(er) machen.

beau·ty ['bjuːtɪ] Schönheit f; Sleep-ing ⚓ Dornrös-chen n; ~ parlo(u)r, ~ shop Schönheitssalon m.

bea·ver ['biːvə] zo. Biber m; Biber-pelz m.

be·came [bɪˈkeɪm] pret. von become.

be·cause [bɪˈkɒz] weil; ~ of wegen.

beck·on ['bekən] (zu)winken.

be·come [bɪˈkʌm] (-came, -come) v/i. werden (of aus) v/t. sich schik-ken für; j-m stehen, j-n kleiden; △ nicht bekommen; **be·com·ing** □ [ˌ·ɪŋ] passend; schicklich; kleidsam.

bed [bed] 1. Bett n; Lager n (*e-s Tieres*); ⚘ Beet n; Unterlage f; ~ and breakfast Zimmer n mit Frühstück; 2. (-dd-): ~ down sein Nachtlager aufschlagen; ~·clothes ['bedkləʊðz] pl. Bettwäsche f; ~·ding [ˌ·ɪŋ] Bett-zeug n; Streu f.

bed·lam ['bedləm] Tollhaus n.

bed·rid·den ['bedrɪdn] bettlägerig; ~·room Schlafzimmer n; ~·side: at the ~ am (a. Kranken)Bett; ~ lamp Nachttischlampe f; ~·sit F, ~·sit·ter [ˌ·ə], ~·sit·ting room [ˌ·ɪŋ] Brt. möbliertes Zimmer; Einzimmerap-partement n; ~·spread Tagesdecke f; ~·stead Bettgestell n; ~·time Schlafenszeit f.

bee [biː] zo. Biene f; have a ~ in one's bonnet F e-n Tick haben.

beech ⚓ [biːtʃ] Buche f; ~·nut Buch-ecker f.

beef [biːf] 1. Rindfleisch n; 2. F

B

meckern (*about* über *acc.*); ~ **tea** Fleischbrühe *f*; ~**y** ['bi:fɪ] (*-ier, -iest*) fleischig; kräftig, bullig.

bee|hive ['bi:haɪv] Bienenkorb *m*, -stock *m*; ~**keep·er** Bienenzüchter *m*, Imker *m*; ~**line** kürzester Weg; *make a* ~ *for* schnurstracks losgehen auf (*acc.*).

been [bi:n, bɪn] *p.p. von* be.

beer [bɪə] Bier *n*.

beet ♀ [bi:t] (Runkel)Rübe *f*, Bete *f*; *Am.* = beetroot.

bee·tle¹ *zo.* ['bi:tl] Käfer *m*.

bee·tle² [~] **1.** überhängend; buschig (*Brauen*); **2.** *v/i.* überhängen.

beet·root ♀ ['bi:tru:t] Rote Bete *od.* Rübe.

be·fall [bɪ'fɔ:l] (*-fell, -fallen*) *v/t.* j-m zustoßen; △ *nicht befallen*; *v/i.* sich ereignen.

be·fit [bɪ'fɪt] (*-tt-*) sich schicken für.

be·fore [bɪ'fɔ:] **1.** *adv. räumlich:* vorn, voran; *zeitlich:* vorher, früher, schon (früher); **2.** *cj.* bevor, ehe, bis; **3.** *prp.* vor; ~**hand** zuvor, (im) voraus.

be·friend [bɪ'frend] sich *j-s* annehmen; △ *nicht befreunden*.

beg [beg] (*-gg-*) *v/t. et.* erbetteln; erbitten (*of* von), bitten um; *j-n* bitten; *v/i.* betteln; bitten, flehen; betteln gehen; sich erlauben.

be·gan [bɪ'gæn] *pret. von* begin.

be·get [bɪ'get] (*-tt-, -got, -gotten*) (er)zeugen.

beg·gar ['begə] **1.** Bettler(in); F Kerl *m*; **2.** arm machen; *fig.* übertreffen; *it* ~*s all description* es spottet jeder Beschreibung.

be·gin [bɪ'gɪn] (*-nn-, began, begun*) beginnen, anfangen; ~**ner** [~ə] Anfänger(in); ~**ning** Beginn *m*, Anfang *m*.

be·gone *int.* [bɪ'gɒn] fort!

be·got [bɪ'gɒt] *pret. von* beget; ~**ten** [~tn] *p.p. von* beget.

be·grudge [bɪ'grʌdʒ] mißgönnen.

be·guile [bɪ'gaɪl] täuschen; betrügen (*of, out of* um); sich *die Zeit* vertreiben.

be·gun [bɪ'gʌn] *p.p. von* begin.

be·half [bɪ'hɑ:f]: *on* (*Am. a. in*) ~ *of* im Namen von (*od. gen.*).

be·have [bɪ'heɪv] sich (gut) benehmen.

be·hav·io(u)r [bɪ'heɪvjə] Benehmen *n*, Betragen *n*, Verhalten *n*; ~**al** *psych.* [~rəl] Verhaltens...

be·head [bɪ'hed] enthaupten.

be·hind [bɪ'haɪnd] **1.** *adv.* hinten, dahinter; zurück; **2.** *prp.* hinter; **3.** F Hinterteil *n*, Hintern *m*; ~**hand** im Rückstand.

be·hold [bɪ'həʊld] (*-held*) **1.** erblicken, sehen; △ *nicht behalten*; **2.** *int.* siehe (da)!; △ [~ə] Betrachter(in).

be·ing ['bi:ɪŋ] (Da)Sein *n*; Wesen *n*; *in* ~ wirklich (vorhanden).

be·lat·ed [bɪ'leɪtɪd] verspätet.

belch [beltʃ] **1.** aufstoßen, rülpsen; ausspeien; **2.** Rülpser *m*.

be·lea·guer [bɪ'li:gə] belagern.

bel·fry ['belfrɪ] Glockenturm *m*, -stuhl *m*.

Bel·gian ['beldʒən] **1.** belgisch; **2.** Belgier(in).

be·lie [bɪ'laɪ] Lügen strafen.

be·lief [bɪ'li:f] Glaube *m* (*in an acc.*).

be·lie·va·ble □ [bɪ'li:vəbl] glaubhaft.

be·lieve [bɪ'li:v] glauben (*in an acc.*); ~**liev·er** *eccl.* [~ə] Gläubige(r *m*) *f*.

be·lit·tle *fig.* [bɪ'lɪtl] herabsetzen.

bell [bel] Glocke *f*; Klingel *f*; ~**boy** *Am.* ['belbɔɪ] (Hotel)Page *m*.

belle [bel] Schöne *f*, Schönheit *f*.

bell·hop *Am.* ['belhɒp] (Hotel)Page *m*.

-bel·lied ['belɪd] ...bäuchig.

bel·lig·er·ent [bɪ'lɪdʒərənt] **1.** kriegführend; streit-, kampflustig; aggressiv; **2.** kriegführendes Land.

bel·low ['beləʊ] **1.** brüllen; **2.** Gebrüll *n*; ~**s** *pl.* Blasebalg *m*.

bel·ly ['belɪ] **1.** Bauch *m*; **2.** bauchen; (an)schwellen; bauschen; ~**ache** F Bauchweh *n*.

be·long [bɪ'lɒŋ] gehören, ~ *to* gehören *dat. od.* zu; ~**ings** [~ɪŋz] *pl.* Habseligkeiten *pl.*

be·loved [bɪ'lʌvd] **1.** (innig) geliebt; **2.** Geliebte(r *m*) *f*.

be·low [bɪ'ləʊ] **1.** *adv.* unten; **2.** *prp.* unter.

belt [belt] **1.** Gürtel *m*; ✕ Koppel *n*; Zone *f*, Gebiet *n*; ⊕ Treibriemen *m*; **2.** *a.* ~ *up* den Gürtel (*gen.*) zumachen; ~**ed** [belt ɪd] mit e-m Gürtel.

be·moan [bɪ'məʊn] betrauern, beklagen.

bench [bentʃ] (Sitz)Bank *f*; Richterbank *f*; Richter *m od. pl.*; Werkbank *f*.

bend [bend] **1.** Biegung *f*, Kurve *f*; *drive s.o. round the* ~ F j-n noch wahnsinnig machen; **2.** (*bent*) (sich) biegen; *Gedanken etc.* richten (*to, on* auf *acc.*); (sich) beugen; sich neigen.

be·neath [bɪ'niːθ] = below.

ben·e·dic·tion [benɪ'dɪkʃn] Segen *m*.

ben·e·fac·tor ['benɪfæktə] Wohltäter *m*.

be·nef·i·cent □ [bɪ'nefɪsnt] wohltätig.

ben·e·fi·cial □ [benɪ'fɪʃl] wohltuend, zuträglich, nützlich.

ben·e·fit ['benɪfɪt] **1.** Nutzen *m*, Vorteil *m*; Wohltätigkeitsveranstaltung *f*; (*Sozial-, Versicherungs- etc*.)Leistung *f*; Rente *f*; Unterstützung *f*; **2.** nützen; begünstigen; ~ *by od*. *from* Vorteil haben von *od*. durch, Nutzen ziehen aus.

be·nev·o·lence [bɪ'nevələns] Wohlwollen *n*; **~·lent** □ [~lt] wohlwollend; gütig, mildtätig.

be·nign □ [bɪ'naɪn] freundlich, gütig; *&* gutartig.

bent [bent] **1.** *pret. u. p.p. von* bend 2; ~ *on doing* entschlossen zu tun; **2.** *fig*. Hang *m*, Neigung *f*; Veranlagung *f*.

ben·zene *⚗* ['benziːn] Benzol *n*.

ben·zine *⚗* ['benziːn] Leichtbenzin *n*; △ *nicht* Benzin.

be·queath *⚖* [bɪ'kwiːð] vermachen.

be·quest *⚖* [bɪ'kwest] Vermächtnis *n*.

be·reave [bɪ'riːv] (*bereaved od*. *bereft*) berauben.

be·reft [bɪ'reft] *pret. u. p.p. von* bereave.

be·ret ['bereɪ] Baskenmütze *f*.

ber·ry *⚘* ['berɪ] Beere *f*.

berth [bɜːθ] **1.** *⚓* Liege-, Ankerplatz *m*; *⚓* Koje *f*; *🛏*(Schlafwagen)Bett *n*; **2.** *v/t*. *⚓* vor Anker legen; *v/i*. *⚓* anlegen.

be·seech [bɪ'siːtʃ] (*besought od*. *beseeched*) (inständig) bitten (um); anflehen.

be·set [bɪ'set] (*-tt-*; *beset*) heimsuchen, bedrängen; ~ *with difficulties* mit vielen Schwierigkeiten verbunden; △ *nicht besetzen*.

be·side *prp*. [bɪ'saɪd] neben; ~ *o.s.* außer sich (*with* vor); ~ *the point*, ~ *the question* nicht zur Sache gehörig; **~s** [~z] **1.** *adv*. außerdem; **2.** *prp*. abgesehen von, außer.

be·siege [bɪ'siːdʒ] belagern; △ *nicht besiegen*.

be·smear [bɪ'smɪə] beschmieren.

be·sought [bɪ'sɔːt] *pret. u. p.p. von* beseech.

be·spat·ter [bɪ'spætə] bespritzen.

best [best] **1.** *adj*. (*sup. von* good 1) beste(r, -s) höchste(r, -s), größte(r, -s), meiste; ~ *man* Trauzeuge *m* (*des Bräutigams*); **2.** *adv*. (*sup. von* well[2] 1) am besten; **3.** *der, die, das* Beste; *All the* ~! Alles Gute!, Viel Glück!; *to the* ~ *of* ... nach bestem ...; *make the* ~ *of* das Beste machen aus; *at* ~ bestenfalls; *be at one's* ~ in Hochod. Höchstform sein.

bes·ti·al □ ['bestjəl] tierisch, viehisch.

be·stow [bɪ'stəʊ] geben, schenken, verleihen (*on, upon dat*.).

best·sell·er [best'selə] Bestseller *m*, Verkaufsschlager *m* (*bsd. Buch*).

bet [bet] **1.** Wette *f*; **2.** (*-tt-; bet od. betted*) wetten; *you* ~ F und ob!

be·tray [bɪ'treɪ] verraten (*a. fig*.); verleiten; **~·al** [~l] Verrat *m*; **~·er** [~ə] Verräter(in).

bet·ter ['betə] **1.** *adj*. (*comp. von* good 1) besser; *he is* ~ es geht ihm besser; **2.** *das* Bessere; **~s** *pl*. Höherstehende *pl*., Vorgesetzte *pl*.; *get the* ~ *of* die Oberhand gewinnen über (*acc*.); *et*. überwinden; **3.** *adv*. (*comp. von* well[2] 1) besser; mehr; *so much the* ~ desto besser; *you had* ~ (*Am*. F *you* ~) *go* es wäre besser, wenn du gingest; **4.** *v/t*. verbessern; *v/i*. sich bessern.

be·tween [bɪ'twiːn] **1.** *adv*. dazwischen; *few and far* ~ F (ganz) vereinzelt; **2.** *prp*. zwischen; unter; *you and me* ~ unter uns *od*. im Vertrauen (gesagt).

bev·el ['bevl] (*bsd. Brt. -ll-, Am. -l-*) abkanten, abschrägen.

bev·er·age ['bevərɪdʒ] Getränk *n*.

bev·y ['bevɪ] Schwarm *m*, Schar *f*.

be·wail [bɪ'weɪl] be-, wehklagen.

be·ware [bɪ'weə] (*of*) sich in acht nehmen (vor *dat*.), sich hüten (vor *dat*.); △ *nicht bewahren*; ~ *of the dog!* Warnung vor dem Hunde!

be·wil·der [bɪ'wɪldə] verwirren, irremachen; **~·ment** [~mənt] Verwirrung *f*.

be·witch [bɪ'wɪtʃ] bezaubern, behexen.

be·yond [bɪ'jɒnd] **1.** *adv*. darüber hinaus; **2.** *prp*. jenseits; über ... (*acc*.) hinaus.

bi- [baɪ] zwei(fach, -mal).

bi·as ['baɪəs] **1.** *adj. u. adv*. schief, schräg; **2.** Neigung *f*; Vorurteil *n*; **3.** (*-s-, -ss-*) *mst ungünstig* beeinflussen; **~**(s)*ed bsd*. *⚖* befangen.

bi·ath|lete [bar'æθliːt] *Sport*: Biathlet *m*; **~lon** [~ən] *Sport*: Biathlon *n*.
bib [bɪb] (Sabber)Lätzchen *n*.
Bi·ble ['baɪbl] Bibel *f*.
bib·li·cal □ ['bɪblɪkl] biblisch, Bibel…
bib·li·og·ra·phy [bɪblɪ'ɒɡrəfɪ] Bibliographie *f*.
bi·car·bon·ate ⌒ [baɪ'kɑːbənɪt] *a.* ~ *of soda* doppeltkohlensaures Natron.
bi·cen|te·na·ry [baɪsen'tiːnərɪ] *Am.* **~ten·ni·al** [~'tenɪəl] Zweihundertjahrfeier *f*, zweihundertjähriges Jubiläum.
bi·ceps *anat.* ['baɪseps] Bizeps *m*.
bick·er ['bɪkə] (sich) zanken; flackern; plätschern; prasseln.
bi·cy·cle ['baɪsɪkl] **1.** Fahrrad *n*; **2.** radfahren, radeln.
bid [bɪd] **1.** (*-dd-*; *bid od. bade, bid od. bidden*) gebieten, befehlen; (ent)bieten; *Karten*: reizen; ~ *farewell* Lebewohl sagen; **2.** *econ.* Gebot *n*, Angebot *n*; *Karten*: Reizen *n*; **~den** ['bɪdn] *p.p. von bid 1.*
bide [baɪd] (*bode od. bided, bided*) ~ *one's time* den rechten Augenblick abwarten.
bi·en·ni·al □ [baɪ'enɪəl] zweijährlich; zweijährig (*Pflanzen*); **~ly** [~lɪ] alle zwei Jahre.
bier [bɪə] (Toten)Bahre *f*; △ *nicht* Bier.
big [bɪɡ] (*-gg-*) groß; erwachsen; (hoch)schwanger; F wichtig(tuerisch); ~ *business* Großunternehmertum *n*; ~ *shot* F hohes Tier (*Person*); *talk* ~ den Mund vollnehmen.
big·a·my ['bɪɡəmɪ] Bigamie *f*.
big·ot ['bɪɡət] selbstgerechte *od.* intolerante Person; **~ed** selbstgerecht, intolerant.
big·wig F ['bɪɡwɪɡ] hohes Tier (*Person*).
bike F [baɪk] (Fahr)Rad *n*.
bi·lat·er·al □ [baɪ'lætərəl] bilateral.
bile [baɪl] Galle *f* (*a. fig.*).
bi·lin·gual [baɪ'lɪŋɡwəl] zweisprachig.
bil·i·ous □ ['bɪljəs] gallig; *fig.* gereizt.
bill¹ [bɪl] Schnabel *m*; Spitze *f*.
bill² [~] *econ.* **1.** Rechnung *f*; *pol.* Gesetzentwurf *m*; ⚖ Klageschrift *f*; *a.* ~ *of exchange econ.* Wechsel *m*; Plakat *n*; *Am.* Banknote *f*, Geldschein *m*; ~ *of fare* Speisekarte *f*; ~ *of*

lading Seefrachtbrief *m*, Konnossement *n*; ~ *of sale* ⚖ Verkaufsurkunde *f*; **2.** (durch Anschlag) ankündigen.
bill·board *Am.* ['bɪlbɔːd] Reklametafel *f*.
bill·fold *Am.* ['bɪlfəʊld] Brieftasche *f*.
bil·li·ards ['bɪljədz] *sg.* Billiard(spiel) *n*.
bil·li·on ['bɪljən] Milliarde *f*.
bil·low ['bɪləʊ] Woge *f*; (*Rauch- etc.*) Schwade *f*; **~y** [~ɪ] wogend; in Schwaden ziehend; gebläht, gebauscht.
bil·ly *Am.* ['bɪlɪ] (Gummi)Knüppel *m*; **~goat** *zo.* Ziegenbock *m*.
bin [bɪn] (großer) Behälter.
bind [baɪnd] (*bound*) *v/t.* (an-, ein-, um-, auf-, fest-, ver)binden; *a.* vertraglich binden, verpflichten; *Saum* einfassen; *v/i.* binden; **~er** ['baɪndə] (*bsd. Buch*)Binder(in); Einband *m*, (Akten- *etc.*)Deckel *m*, Hefter *m*; **~ing** [~ɪŋ] **1.** bindende, verbindlich; **2.** (*Buch*)Einband *m*; Einfassung *f*, Borte *f*.
bi·noc·u·lars [bɪ'nɒkjʊləz] *pl.* Feldstecher *m*, Fern-, Opernglas *n*.
bi·o·chem·is·try [baɪəʊ'kemɪstrɪ] Biochemie *f*.
bi·og·ra·pher [baɪ'ɒɡrəfə] Biograph *m*; **~phy** [~ɪ] Biographie *f*.
bi·o·log·i·cal □ [baɪəʊ'lɒdʒɪkl] biologisch; **bi·ol·o·gy** [baɪ'ɒlədʒɪ] Biologie *f*.
bi·ped *zo.* ['baɪped] Zweifüßer *m*.
birch [bɜːtʃ] **1.** ♀ Birke *f*; (Birken-)Rute *f*; **2.** (mit der Rute) züchtigen.
bird [bɜːd] Vogel *m*; ~ *of prey* Raubvogel *m*; ~ *sanctuary* Vogelschutzgebiet *n*; **~'s-eye** ['bɜːdzaɪ]: ~ *view* Vogelperspektive *f*.
bi·ro *TM* ['baɪrəʊ] (*pl. -ros*) Kugelschreiber *m*.
birth [bɜːθ] Geburt *f*; Ursprung *m*, Entstehung *f*; Herkunft *f*; *give* ~ *to* gebären, zur Welt bringen; ~ *control* Geburtenregelung *f*; **~day** ['bɜːθdeɪ] Geburtstag *m*; **~mark** Muttermal *n*; **~place** Geburtsort *m*; ~ *rate* Geburtenziffer *f*.
bis·cuit *Brt.* ['bɪskɪt] Keks *m*, *n*, Plätzchen *n*; △ *nicht Biskuit.*
bish·op ['bɪʃəp] Bischof *m*; *Schach*: Läufer *m*; **~ric** [~rɪk] Bistum *n*.
bi·son *zo.* ['baɪsn] Bison *m*, Amer. Büffel; Europäischer Wisent *m*.
bit [bɪt] **1.** Bißchen *n*, Stück(chen) *n*;

Gebiß n (am Zaum); (Schlüssel)Bart m; Computer: Bit n; a (little) ~ ein (kleines) bißchen; **2.** pret. von bite 2.

bitch [bɪtʃ] zo. Hündin f; contp. Miststück n, -weib n.

bite [baɪt] **1.** Beißen n; Biß m; Bissen m, Happen m; ⊕ Fassen n; **2.** (bit, bitten) (an)beißen; stechen (Insekt); brennen (Pfeffer); schneiden (Kälte); beißen (Rauch); ⊕ fassen; fig. verletzen.

bit·ten ['bɪtn] p.p. von bite 2.

bit·ter ['bɪtə] **1.** ☐ bitter; fig. verbittert; **2.** ~s pl. Magenbitter m.

biz F[bɪz] = business.

blab F [blæb] (-bb-) (aus)schwatzen.

black [blæk] **1.** ☐ schwarz; dunkel; finster; ~ eye blaues Auge; have s.th. in ~ and white et. schwarz auf weiß haben u. die besitzen; be ~ and blue blaue Flecken haben; beat s.o. ~ and blue j-n grün u. blau schlagen; **2.** schwärzen; wichsen; ~ out verdunkeln; **3.** Schwarz m; Schwärze f; Schwarze(r m) f, Neger(in); ~·ber·ry ♀ ['blækberɪ] Brombeere f; ~·bird zo. Amsel f; ~·board (Schul-, Wand)Tafel f; △ nicht Schwarzes Brett; ~·en [~ən] v/t. schwärzen; fig. anschwärzen; v/i. schwarz werden; ~·guard ['blægɑːd] **1.** Lump m, Schuft m; **2.** ☐ gemein, schuftig; ~·head ﹖ Mitesser m; ~·ice Glatteis n; ~·ing [~ɪŋ] schwarze Schuhwichse; ~·ish ☐ [~ʃ] schwärzlich; ~·jack bsd. Am. Totschläger m (Waffe); ~·leg Br. Streikbrecher m; ~·let·ter print. Fraktur f; ~·mail **1.** Erpressung f; **2.** j-n erpressen; ~·mail·er [~ə] Erpresser(in); ~ mar·ket schwarzer Markt; ~·ness [~nɪs] Schwärze f; ~·out Verdunkelung f; thea., ﹖, Raumfahrt: Blackout n, m; ﹖ Ohnmacht f; ~ pud·ding Blutwurst f; ~ sheep fig. schwarzes Schaf; ~·smith Grobschmied m.

blad·der anat. ['blædə] Blase f.

blade [bleɪd] ♀ Blatt n, Halm m; (Säge-, Schulter- etc.)Blatt n; (Propeller)Flügel m; Klinge f.

blame [bleɪm] **1.** Tadel m; Schuld f; **2.** tadeln; be to ~ for schuld sein an (dat.); △ nicht blamieren; ~·less ☐ [~lɪs] untadelig.

blanch [blɑːntʃ] bleichen; erbleichen (lassen).

blanc·mange [blə'mɒnʒ] Pudding m.

bland ☐ [blænd] mild, sanft.

blank [blæŋk] **1.** ☐ leer; unausgefüllt, unbeschrieben; econ. Blanko...; verdutzt; △ nicht blank (glänzend); ~ cartridge ✗ Platzpatrone f; ~ cheque (Am. check) econ. Blankoscheck m; **2.** Leere f; leerer Raum, Lücke f; unbeschriebenes Blatt, Formular n; Lotterie: Niete f.

blan·ket ['blæŋkɪt] **1.** (Woll)Decke f; wet ~ Spielverderber m; **2.** zudecken.

blare [bleə] brüllen, plärren (Radio etc.), schmettern (Trompete).

blas|pheme [blæs'fiːm] lästern; ~·phe·my ['blæsfəmɪ] Gotteslästerung f.

blast [blɑːst] **1.** Windstoß m; Ton m (e-s Blasinstruments); ⊕ Gebläse(luft f) n; Druckwelle f; ♀ Mehltau m; **2.** v/t. vernichten; sprengen; ~ off (into space) Rakete, Astronauten in den Weltraum schießen; v/i.: ~ off abheben, starten (Rakete); ~·! verdammt!; ~·fur·nace ⊕ ['blɑːstfɜː-nɪs] Hochofen m; ~·off Start m (Rakete).

bla·tant ☐ ['bleɪtənt] lärmend; kraß; unverhohlen.

blaze [bleɪz] **1.** Flamme(n pl.) f, Feuer n; heller Schein; fig. Ausbruch m; go to ~s! zum Teufel mit dir!; **2.** brennen, flammen, lodern; leuchten; △ nicht blasen.

blaz·er ['bleɪzə] Blazer m.

bla·zon ['bleɪzn] Wappen n.

bleach [bliːtʃ] bleichen.

bleak ☐ [bliːk] öde, kahl; rauh; fig. trüb, freudlos, finster.

blear·y ☐ ['blɪərɪ] (-ier, -iest) trübe, verschwommen; ~·eyed mit trüben Augen; verschlafen.

bleat [bliːt] **1.** Blöken n; **2.** blöken.

bled [bled] pret. u. p.p. von bleed.

bleed [bliːd] (bled) v/i. bluten; v/t. ﹖ zur Ader lassen; fig. F schröpfen; ~·ing ['bliːdɪŋ] **1.** ﹖ Bluten n, Blutung f; ﹖ Aderlaß m; **2.** sl. verflixt.

bleep [bliːp] **1.** Piepton m; **2.** j-n anpiepsen (über Funkrufempfänger).

blem·ish ['blemɪʃ] **1.** (a. Schönheits-) Fehler m; Makel m; **2.** entstellen.

blend [blend] **1.** (sich) (ver)mischen; Wein etc. verschneiden; △ nicht blenden; **2.** Mischung f; econ. Verschnitt m; ~·er ['blendə] Mixer m, Mixgerät n.

bless [bles] (blessed od. blest) segnen; preisen; be ~ed with gesegnet sein mit; (God) ~ you! alles Gute!

Gesundheit!; ~ *me!*, ~ my heart!, ~
my soul! F du meine Güte!; **~ed** *adj.*
□ ['blesɪd] glückselig, gesegnet;
~ing [~ɪŋ] Segen *m.*

blest [blest] *pret. u. p.p. von* bless.

blew [bluː] *pret. von* blow² 1.

blight [blaɪt] 1. ♀ Mehltau *m.; fig.*
Gifthauch *m;* 2. vernichten.

blind □: [blaɪnd] 1. blind (*fig. to*
gegen[über]); verborgen, geheim;
schwererkennbar; ~ *alley* Sackgasse *f;*
~*ly fig.* blindlings; 2. Rouleau *n,*
Rollo *n; the* ~ *pl.* die Blinden *pl.;* 3.
blenden; *fig.* blind machen (*to* für,
gegen); **~ers** *Am.* ['blaɪndəz] *pl.*
Scheuklappen *pl.;* **~fold** 1. blindlings; 2. *j-m* die Augen verbinden; 3.
Augenbinde *f;* **~worm** *zo.* Blindschleiche *f.*

blink [blɪŋk] 1. Blinzeln *n;* Schimmer
m; 2. *v/i.* blinzeln, zwinkern; blinken; schimmern; *v/t. fig.* ignorieren;
~ers ['blɪŋkəz] *pl.* Scheuklappen *pl.*

bliss [blɪs] Seligkeit *f,* Wonne *f.*

blis·ter ['blɪstə] 1. Blase *f* (*auf der
Haut, im Lack*); ♣ Zugpflaster *n;* 2.
Blasen hervorrufen auf (*dat.*); Bla-
sen ziehen.

blitz [blɪts] 1. heftiger (Luft)Angriff;
2. schwer bombardieren; △ *nicht*
Blitz; blitzen.

bliz·zard ['blɪzəd] Schneesturm *m.*

bloat·ed ['bloʊtɪd] (an)geschwollen,
(auf)gedunsen; *fig.* aufgeblasen;
~er [~ə] Bückling *m.*

block [blɒk] 1. Block *m,* Klotz *m;*
Baustein *m;* Verstopfung *f,* (Ver-
kehrs)Stockung *f; a.* ~ *of flats* Brt.
Wohn-, Mietshaus *n; Am.* (Häuser-)
Block *m;* 2. formen; verhindern; *a.* ~
up (ab-, ver)sperren, blockieren.

block·ade [blɒ'keɪd] 1. Blockade *f;* 2.
blockieren.

block·head ['blɒkhed] Dummkopf
m; **~ let·ters** *pl.* Blockschrift *f.*

bloke *Brt.* F [bloʊk] Kerl *m.*

blond [blɒnd] 1. Blonde(r) *m;* 2.
blond; hell (*Haut*); **~e** [~] 1. blond; 2.
Blondine *f.*

blood [blʌd] Blut *n; fig.* Blut *n;*
Abstammung *f; attr.* Blut...; *in cold*
~ kaltblütig; **~-cur·dling** ['blʌdkɜː-
dlɪŋ] grauenhaft; **~shed** Blutvergie-
ßen *n;* **~shot** blutunterlaufen;
~thirst·y □ blutdürstig; **~ves·sel**
anat. Blutgefäß *n;* **~y** □ [~ɪ] (*-ier,
-iest*) blutig; *Brt.* F verdammt, verflucht.

bloom [bluːm] 1. *poet.* Blume *f,* Blüte
f; fig. Blüte(zeit) *f;* △ *nicht allg.*
Blume; 2. blühen; *fig.* (er)strahlen.

blos·som ['blɒsəm] 1. Blüte *f;* 2.
blühen.

blot [blɒt] 1. Klecks *m; fig.* Makel *m;*
2. (*-tt-*) *v/t.* beklecksen, beflecken;
(ab)löschen; ausstreichen; *v/i.*
klecksen.

blotch [blɒtʃ] Klecks *m;* Hautfleck *m;*
~y ['blɒtʃɪ] (*-ier, -iest*) fleckig
(*Haut*).

blot·ter ['blɒtə] (Tinten)Löscher *m;*
Am. Eintragungsbuch *n;* **~ting-
pa·per** [~ɪŋpeɪpə] Löschpapier *n.*

blouse [blaʊz] Bluse *f.*

blow¹ [bloʊ] Schlag *m,* Stoß *m.*

blow² [~] 1. (*blew, blown*) *v/i.* blasen,
wehen; schnaufen; platzen (*Reifen*);
⚡ durchbrennen (*Sicherung*); ~ *up* in
die Luft fliegen; *v/t.* blasen, wehen;
~ *one's nose* sich die Nase putzen; ~
one's top F an die Decke gehen (*vor
Wut*); ~ *out* ausblasen; ~ *up* sprengen; *Foto* vergrößern; 2. Blasen *n,*
Wehen *n;* **~-dry** ['bloʊdraɪ] fönen;
~fly *zo.* Schmeißfliege *f;* **~n** [bloʊn]
p.p. von blow² 1; **~pipe** ['bloʊpaɪp]
⊕ Lötrohr *n;* Blasrohr *n;* **~-up** Explosion *f; phot.* Vergrößerung *f.*

blud·geon ['blʌdʒən] Knüppel *m.*

blue [bluː] 1. blau; F melancholisch,
traurig, schwermütig; 2. Blau *n; out
of the* ~ *fig.* aus heiterem Himmel;
~ber·ry ♀ ['bluːbərɪ] Blau-, Heidelbeere *f;* **~bot·tle** *zo.* Schmeißfliege
f; **~col·lar work·er** (Fabrik)Arbei-
ter(in).

blues [bluːz] *pl. od. sing.* ♪ Blues *m;* F
Melancholie *f; have the* ~ F den
Moralischen haben.

bluff [blʌf] 1. □ schroff, steil; derb;
2. Steilufer *n;* Bluff *m;* 3. bluffen.

blu·ish ['bluːɪʃ] bläulich.

blun·der ['blʌndə] 1. Fehler *m,*
Schnitzer *m;* 2. e-n (groben) Fehler
machen; stolpern; verpfuschen; △
nicht plündern.

blunt [blʌnt] 1. □ stumpf (*a. fig.*);
grob, rauh; 2. abstumpfen; **~ly**
['blʌntlɪ] frei heraus.

blur [blɜː] 1. Fleck *m;* undeutlicher
Eindruck, verschwommene Vorstellung; 2. (*-rr-*) *v/t.* beflecken; verwi-
schen, -schmieren; *phot., TV* ver-
wackeln, -zerren; *Sinn* trüben.

blurt [blɜːt]: ~ *out* herausplatzen
mit.

blush

blush [blʌʃ] **1.** Schamröte *f*; Erröten *n*; **2.** erröten, rot werden.

blus·ter ['blʌstə] **1.** Brausen *n*, Toben *n* (*a. fig.*); *fig.* Poltern *n*; **2.** brausen; *fig.* poltern, toben.

boar *zo.* [bɔː] Eber *m*; Keiler *m*.

board [bɔːd] **1.** Brett *n*; (Anschlag-) Brett *n*; Konferenztisch *m*; Ausschuß *m*, Kommission *f*; Behörde *f*; Verpflegung *f*; Pappe *f*, Karton *m*; *Sport*: (Surf)Board *n*; △ *nicht* Bücher-Bord; on ~ a train in e-m Zug; ~ of directors *econ.* Verwaltungsrat *m*; ♀ of Trade Brt. Handelsministerium *n*, *Am.* Handelskammer *f*; **2.** *v/t.* dielen, verschalen; beköstigen; an Bord gehen; ♣ entern; einsteigen in (*ein Fahr- od. Flugzeug*); *v/i.* in Kost sein, wohnen; **~er** ['bɔːdə] Kostgänger(in); Pensionsgast *m*; Internatsschüler(in); **~ing-house** [~ɪŋhaʊs] Pension *f*, Fremdenheim *n*; **~ing-school** [~ɪŋskuːl] Internat *n*; **~walk** *bsd. Am.* Strandpromenade *f*.

boast [bəʊst] **1.** Prahlerei *f*; **2.** (*of, about*) sich rühmen (*gen.*), prahlen (mit); **~ful** [~bəʊstfl] prahlerisch.

boat [bəʊt] **1.** Boot *n*; Schiff *n*; **~ing** ['bəʊtɪŋ] Bootsfahrt *f*.

bob [bɒb] **1.** Quaste *f*; Ruck *m*; Knicks *m*; kurzer Haarschnitt; *Brt. F hist.* Schilling *m*; **2.** (-**bb**-) *v/t.* Haar kurz schneiden; ~bed hair Bubikopf *m*; *v/i.* springen, tanzen; knicksen.

bob·bin ['bɒbɪn] Spule *f* (*a. ⚡*).

bob·by *Brt. F* ['bɒbɪ] Bobby *m* (*Polizist*).

bob·sleigh ['bɒbsleɪ] *Sport*: Bob *m*.

bode [bəʊd] *pret. von* bide.

bod·ice ['bɒdɪs] Mieder *n*; Oberteil *n* (*e-s Kleides*).

bod·i·ly ['bɒdɪlɪ] körperlich.

bod·y ['bɒdɪ] Körper *m*, Leib *m*; Leiche *f*; Körperschaft *f*; Hauptteil *m*; *mot.* Karosserie *f*; ✕ Truppenkörper *m*; **~guard** Leibwache *f*; **~work** Karosserie *f*.

Boer ['bəʊə] Bure *m*; *attr.* Buren...

bog [bɒg] **1.** Sumpf *m*, Moor *n*; **2.** (-**gg**-): get ~ged down *fig.* sich festfahren.

bo·gus ['bəʊgəs] falsch; Schwindel...

boil[1] ✚ [bɔɪl] Geschwür *n*, Furunkel *m, n.*

boil[2] [~] **1.** kochen, sieden; **2.** Kochen *n*, Sieden *n*; **~er** ['bɔɪlə] (Dampf-)

Kessel *m*; Boiler *m*; **~er suit** Overall *m*; **~ing** [~ɪŋ] kochend, siedend; **~ing-point** Siedepunkt *m* (*a. fig.*).

bois·ter·ous ☐ ['bɔɪstərəs] ungestüm; heftig, laut; lärmend.

bold ☐ [bəʊld] kühn; keck, dreist, unverschämt; steil; as ~ as brass F frech wie Oskar; **~ness** ['bəʊldnɪs] Kühnheit *f*; Keckheit *f*; Dreistigkeit *f*.

bol·ster ['bəʊlstə] **1.** Keilkissen *n*; Nackenrolle *f*; △ *nicht* Polster; **2.** ~ up *fig.* (unter)stützen, *j-m* Mut machen.

bolt [bəʊlt] **1.** Bolzen *m*; Riegel *m*; Blitz(strahl) *m*; plötzlicher Satz, Fluchtversuch *m*; **2.** *adv.* ~ upright kerzengerade; **3.** *v/t.* verriegeln; *F* hinunterschlingen; *v/i.* davonlaufen, ausreißen; scheuen, durchgehen (*Pferd*).

bomb [bɒm] **1.** Bombe *f*; the ~ die Atombombe; **2.** bombardieren.

bom·bard [bɒm'bɑːd] bombardieren (*a. fig.*).

bomb-proof ['bɒmpruːf] bombensicher; **~shell** Bombe *f* (*a. fig.*).

bond [bɒnd] *econ.* Schuldverschreibung *f*, Obligation *f*; ⊕ Haftfestigkeit *f*; **~s** *pl.* Bande (*der Freundschaft etc.*); in ~ *econ.* unter Zollverschluß; **~age** *lit.* ['bɒndɪdʒ] Hörigkeit *f*; Knechtschaft *f*.

bone [bəʊn] **1.** Knochen *m*; Gräte *f*; △ *nicht* Bein; **~s** *pl. a.* Gebeine *pl.*; ~ of contention Zankapfel *m*; have a ~ to pick with s.o. mit *j-m* ein Hühnchen zu rupfen haben; make no ~s about nicht lange fackeln mit; keine Skrupel haben hinsichtlich (*gen.*); **2.** die Knochen auslösen (aus); entgräten.

bon·fire ['bɒnfaɪə] Feuer *n* im Freien; Freudenfeuer *n*.

bon·net ['bɒnɪt] Haube *f*; *Brt.* Motorhaube *f*.

bon·ny *bsd. schott.* ['bɒnɪ] (*-ier, -iest*) hübsch; rosig (*Baby*); gesund.

bo·nus *econ.* ['bəʊnəs] Bonus *m*, Prämie *f*; Gratifikation *f*.

bon·y ['bəʊnɪ] (*-ier, -iest*) knöchern; knochig.

boob *sl.* [buːb] Blödmann *m*; *Brt.* (grober) Fehler; **~s** *pl.* F Titten *pl.* (*Busen*).

boo·by ['buːbɪ] Trottel *m*.

book [bʊk] **1.** Buch *n*; Heft *n*; Liste *f*; Block *m*; **2.** buchen; eintragen;

Fahrkarte etc. lösen; *Platz etc.* (vor-) bestellen, reservieren lassen; *Gepäck* aufgeben; ~ *in bsd. Brt.* sich (*im Hotel*) eintragen; ~ *in at* absteigen in (*dat.*); ~*ed up* ausgebucht, -verkauft, belegt (*Hotel*); ~**case** ['bʊkeɪs] Bücherschrank *m*; ~**ing** [~ɪŋ] Buchen *n*, (Vor)Bestellung *f*; ~**ing-clerk** Schalterbeamt(e)r *m*; ~**ing-office** Fahrkartenausgabe *f*, -schalter *m*; *thea.* Kasse *f*; ~**keep·er** Buchhalter(in); ~**keep·ing** Buchhaltung *f*, -führung *f*; ~**let** [~lɪt] Büchlein *n*, Broschüre *f*; ~**mark(·er)** [~ə] Lesezeichen *n*; ~**sell·er** Buchhändler(in); ~**shop,** *Am.* ~**store** Buchhandlung *f*.

boom[1] [bu:m] **1.** *econ.* Boom *m*, Aufschwung *m*, Hochkonjunktur *f*, Hausse *f*; **2.** in die Höhe treiben *od.* gehen.

boom[2] [~] dröhnen, donnern.

boon [bu:n] Segen *m*, Wohltat *f*.

boor *fig.* [bʊə] Bauer *m*, Lümmel *m*; ~**ish** □ ['bʊərɪʃ] bäuerisch, ungehobelt.

boost [bu:st] hochschieben; *Preise in die Höhe treiben*; *Wirtschaft* ankurbeln; verstärken (*a. ⚡*); *fig.* fördern, Auftrieb geben.

boot[1] [bu:t]: *to* ~ obendrein.

boot[2] [~] Stiefel *m*; *Brt. mot.* Kofferraum *m*; △ *nicht Boot*; ~**ee** ['bu:ti:] (*Damen*)Halbstiefel *m*.

booth [bu:ð] (*Markt- etc.*)Bude *f*; (*Messe*)Stand *m*; (*Wahl-, etc.*) Kabine *f*; (*Fernsprech*)Zelle *f*.

boot|lace ['bu:tleɪs] Schnürsenkel *m*; ~**leg·ger** [~legə] Alkoholschmuggler *m*.

boot·y ['bu:tɪ] Beute *f*, Raub *m*.

booze F [bu:z] **1.** saufen; **2.** Alkohol *m* (*Getränk*); Sauferei *f*.

bop·per ['bɒpə] = *teeny-bopper.*

bor·der ['bɔ:də] **1.** Rand *m*, Saum *m*, Einfassung *f*; Rabatte *f*; Grenze *f*; **2.** einfassen; (um)säumen; grenzen (*on, upon an acc.*).

bore[1] [bɔ:] **1.** Bohrloch *n*; Kaliber *n*; *fig.* langweiliger Mensch; langweilige Sache; *Brt.* F lästige Sache; **2.** bohren; langweilen; *j-m* lästig sein.

bore[2] [~] *pret. von bear*[2].

bor·ing □ ['bɔ:rɪŋ] langweilig.

born [bɔ:n] *p.p. von bear*[2] geboren.

borne [bɔ:n] *p.p. von bear*[2] tragen.

bor·ough ['bʌrə] Stadtteil *m*; Stadtgemeinde *f* od. Stadtbezirk *m*.

bor·row ['bɒrəʊ] (sich) *et.* borgen *od.* (aus)leihen; △ *nicht j-m et.* borgen.

bos·om ['bʊzəm] Busen *m*; *fig.* Schoß *m*.

boss F [bɒs] **1.** Boss *m*, Chef *m*; *bsd. Am. pol.* (Partei-, Gewerkschafts-) Bonze *m*; **2.** *a.* ~ *about*, ~ *around* herumkommandieren; ~**y** F ['bɒsɪ] (*-ier, -iest*) herrisch.

bo·tan·i·cal □ [bə'tænɪkl] botanisch; **bot·a·ny** ['bɒtənɪ] Botanik *f*.

botch [bɒtʃ] **1.** Pfusch(arbeit *f*) *m*; **2.** verpfuschen.

both [bəʊθ] beide(s); ~ *... and* sowohl ... als (auch).

both·er ['bɒðə] **1.** Belästigung *f*, Störung *f*, Plage *f*, Mühe *f*; **2.** belästigen, stören, plagen; *don't* ~*!* bemühen Sie sich nicht!

bot·tle ['bɒtl] **1.** Flasche *f*; **2.** in Flaschen abfüllen; ~**neck** Flaschenhals *m*, Engpaß *m* (*e-r Straße*) (*a. fig.*).

bot·tom ['bɒtəm] unterster Teil, Boden *m*, Fuß *m*, Unterseite *f*; Grund *m*; F Hintern *m*, Popo *m*; *be at the* ~ *of hinter e-r Sache* stecken; *get to the* ~ *of s.th.* e-r Sache auf den Grund gehen.

bough [baʊ] Ast *m*, Zweig *m*.

bought [bɔ:t] *pret. u. p.p. von buy.*

boul·der ['bəʊldə] Geröllblock *m*, Findling *m*.

bounce [baʊns] **1.** Aufprall(en *n*) *m*, Aufspringen *n* (*e-s Balles etc.*); Schwung *m* (*Lebensfreude, -kraft*); **2.** aufprallen *od.* springen (*lassen*) (*Ball*); F platzen (*ungedeckter Scheck*); *she* ~*d the baby on her knee* sie ließ das Kind auf den Knien reiten; **bounc·ing** ['baʊnsɪŋ] stramm (*Baby*).

bound[1] [baʊnd] **1.** *pret. u. p.p. von bind*; **2.** *adj.* verpflichtet; bestimmt, unterwegs (*for nach*).

bound[2] [~] *mst* ~*s pl.* Grenze *f*, *fig. a.* Schranke *f*.

bound[3] [~] **1.** Sprung *m*; **2.** (hoch-) springen; auf-, abprallen.

bound·a·ry ['baʊndərɪ] Grenze *f*.

bound·less □ ['baʊndlɪs] grenzenlos.

boun·te·ous □ ['baʊntɪəs], ~**·ti·ful** □ [~fl] freigebig, reichlich.

boun·ty ['baʊntɪ] Mildtätigkeit *f*, Freigebigkeit *f*; Spende *f*; Prämie *f*.

bou·quet [bʊ'keɪ] Bukett *n*, Strauß *m*; Blume *f* (*des Weins*).

B

B

bout [baʊt] *Boxen, Ringen, Fechten*: Kampf *m*; (Verhandlungs)Runde *f*; ✠ Anfall *m*; (Trink)Gelage *n*.

bou·tique [buːˈtiːk] Boutique *f*.

bow¹ [baʊ] **1.** Verbeugung *f*; **2.** *v/i.* sich verbeugen *od.* -neigen (*to* vor *dat.*); *fig.* sich beugen *od.* unterwerfen (*to dat.*); *v/t.* biegen; beugen, neigen.

bow² ⚓ [~] Bug *m*.

bow³ [bəʊ] **1.** Bogen *m*; Schleife *f*; **2.** geigen; *~-legged* O-beinig.

bow·els [ˈbaʊəlz] *pl. anat.* Eingeweide *pl.*; *das* Innere.

bowl¹ [bəʊl] Schale *f*, Schüssel *f*; Napf *m*; (Pfeifen)Kopf *m*; *geogr.* Becken *n*; *Am.* Stadion *n*; △ *nicht* Bowle (*Getränk*).

bowl² [~] **1.** (*Bowling-, Kegel- etc.*) Kugel *f*; **2.** *v/t.* rollen; *Bowlingkugel, Kricketball* werfen; *v/i.* bowlen, Bowling spielen; kegeln; *Kricket*: werfen; *~·ing* [ˈbəʊlɪŋ] Bowling *n*; Kegeln *n*.

box¹ [bɒks] ♀ Buchsbaum *m*; Kasten *m*, Kiste *f*; Büchse *f*; Schachtel *f*; ⊕ Gehäuse *n*; *thea.* Loge *f*; Box *f*; **2.** in Kästen *etc.* tun.

box² [~] *Sport*: boxen; ~ *s.o.'s ears* j-n ohrfeigen; **2.** ~ *on the ear* Ohrfeige *f*; *~·er* [ˈbɒksə] Boxer *m*; *~·ing* [~ɪŋ] Boxen *n*, Boxsport *m*; **2·ing Day** *Brt.* der zweite Weihnachtsfeiertag.

box-of·fice [ˈbɒksɒfɪs] Theaterkasse *f*.

boy [bɔɪ] Junge *m*, Knabe *m*, Bursche *m*; *~friend* Freund *m*; ~ *scout* Pfadfinder *m*.

boy·cott [ˈbɔɪkɒt] boykottieren.

boy|hood [ˈbɔɪhʊd] Knabenalter *n*, Kindheit *f*, Jugend(zeit) *f*; *~·ish* □ [ˈbɔɪɪʃ] jungenhaft.

bra [brɑː] BH *m* (Büstenhalter).

brace [breɪs] **1.** ⊕ Strebe *f*, Stützbalken *m*; Klammer *f*; Paar *n* (*a. Wild, Geflügel*); (*a. a pair of*) *~s pl. Brt.* Hosenträger *pl.*; **2.** verstreben, -steifen, stützen; spannen; *fig.* stärken.

brace·let [ˈbreɪslɪt] Armband *n*.

brack·et [ˈbrækɪt] **1.** ⊕ Träger *m*, Halter *m*, Stütze *f*; (Wand)Arm *m* (*e-r Leuchte*); Winkelstütze *f*; *arch.* Konsole *f*; *print.* (*mst* eckige) Klammer; (*bsd. Alters-, Steuer*)Klasse *f*; *lower income* ~ niedrige Einkommensgruppe; **2.** einklammern; *fig.* gleichstellen.

brack·ish [ˈbrækɪʃ] brackig, salzig.

brag [bræg] **1.** Prahlerei *f*; **2.** (*-gg-*) prahlen (*about, of* mit).

brag·gart [ˈbrægət] **1.** Prahler *m*; **2.** prahlerisch.

braid [breɪd] **1.** (Haar)Flechte *f*, Zopf *m*; Borte *f*, Tresse *f*; **2.** flechten; Borte besetzen.

brain [breɪn] *anat.* Gehirn *n*; *oft ~s pl. fig.* Gehirn *n*, Verstand *m*, Intelligenz *f*, Kopf *m*; *~s trust Brt.*, *Am.* ~ **trust** [ˈbreɪn(z)trʌst] Gehirntrust *m* (*bsd. politische od. wirtschaftliche Beratergruppe*); *~·wash* j-n e-r Gehirnwäsche unterziehen; *~·wash·ing* Gehirnwäsche *f*; *~·wave* F Geistesblitz *m*.

brake [breɪk] **1.** ⊕ Bremse *f*; **2.** bremsen.

bram·ble ♀ [ˈbræmbl] Brombeerstrauch *m*.

bran [bræn] Kleie *f*.

branch [brɑːntʃ] **1.** Ast *m*, Zweig *m*; Fach *n*; Linie *f* (*des Stammbaumes*); Zweigstelle *f*; **2.** sich verzweigen; abzweigen.

brand [brænd] **1.** *econ.* (Handels-, Schutz)Marke *f*, Warenzeichen *n*; Sorte *f*, Klasse *f* (*e-r Ware*); Brandmal *n*; △ *nicht* Brand; ~ **name** Markenbezeichnung *f*, -name *m*; **2.** einbrennen; brandmarken.

bran·dish [ˈbrændɪʃ] schwingen.

bran(d)-new [ˈbræn(d)ˈnjuː] nagelneu.

bran·dy [ˈbrændɪ] Kognak *m*, Weinbrand *m*.

brass [brɑːs] Messing *n*; F Unverschämtheit *f*; ~ **band** Blaskapelle *f*; ~ **knuckles** *pl. Am.* Schlagring *m*.

bras·sière [ˈbræsɪə] Büstenhalter *m*.

brat *contp.* [bræt] Balg *m, n*, Gör *n* (*Kind*).

brave [breɪv] **1.** □ (*~r, ~st*) tapfer, mutig, unerschrocken; △ *nicht* brav; **2.** trotzen; mutig begegnen (*dat.*); **brav·er·y** [ˈbreɪvərɪ] Tapferkeit *f*.

brawl [brɔːl] **1.** Krawall *m*; Rauferei *f*; **2.** Krawall machen; raufen.

brawn·y [ˈbrɔːnɪ] (*-ier, -iest*) muskulös.

bray [breɪ] **1.** Eselsschrei *m*; **2.** schreien; schmettern; dröhnen.

bra·zen □ [ˈbreɪzn] unverschämt, unverfroren, frech.

Bra·zil·ian [brəˈzɪljən] **1.** brasilianisch; **2.** Brasilianer(in).

breach [briːtʃ] **1.** Bruch *m*; *fig.* Verletzung *f*; Bresche *f*; **2.** e-e Bresche schlagen in (*acc.*).

bread [bred] Brot *n*; brown ~ Schwarzbrot *n*; *know which side one's ~ is buttered* F s-n Vorteil (er)kennen.

breadth [bredθ] Breite *f*, Weite *f*; *fig.* Größe *f*; (*Tuch*)Bahn *f*.

break [breɪk] **1.** Bruch *m*; Lücke *f*; Pause *f* (*Brt. a. Schule*), Unterbrechung *f*; *econ.* (*Preis- etc.*)Sturz *m*; (*Tages*)Anbruch *m*; *fig.* Zäsur *f*, Einschnitt *m*; *bad* ~ F Pech *n*; *lucky* ~ F Dusel *m*, Schwein *n* (*Glück*); *without a* ~ ununterbrochen; **2.** (*broke*, *broken*) *v/t.* ab-, auf-, durchbrechen; *v/t.* (zer)brechen; unterbrechen; übertreten; *Tier* abrichten, *Pferd* zureiten; *Bank* sprengen; *Vorrat* anbrechen; *Nachricht* (schonend) mitteilen; ruinieren; *v/i.* brechen; eindringen *od.* -brechen in (*acc.*); (zer)brechen; aus-, los-, an-, auf-, hervorbrechen; umschlagen (*Wetter*); *mit Adverbien*: ~ *away* abbrechen; sich losmachen *od.* losreißen; ~ *down* ein-, niederreißen, *Haus* abbrechen; zusammenbrechen (*a. fig.*); versagen; ~ *in* einbrechen, -dringen; ~ *off* abbrechen; *fig. a.* Schluß machen mit; ~ *out* ausbrechen; ~ *through* durchbrechen; *fig.* den Durchbruch schaffen; ~ *up* abbrechen, beendigen, schließen; (sich) auflösen; zerbrechen, auseinandergehen (*Ehe etc.*); **~·a·ble** ['breɪkəbl] zerbrechlich; **~·age** [~ɪdʒ] Bruch *m*; **~·a·way** Trennung *f*, Bruch *m*; *Brt.* Splitter...; **~·down** Zusammenbruch *m* (*a. fig.*); ⊕ Maschinenschaden *m*; *mot.* Panne *f*.

break·fast ['brekfəst] **1.** Frühstück *n*; **2.** frühstücken.

break|through *fig.* ['breɪkθruː] Durchbruch *m*; **~·up** Auflösung *f*; Zerfall *m*; Zerrüttung *f*; Zusammenbruch *m*.

breast [brest] Brust *f*; Busen *m*; *fig.* Herz *n*; *make a clean* ~ *of s.th.* et. offen gestehen; **~·stroke** ['breststrəʊk] *Sport*: Brustschwimmen *n*.

breath [breθ] Atem(zug) *m*; Hauch *m*; *waste one's* ~ s-e Worte verschwenden.

breath·al·lyse, *Am.* **-lyze** ['breθəlaɪz] *Verkehrsteilnehmer* (ins Röhrchen) blasen *od.* pusten lassen; **~·lys·er**,

Am. **-lyz·er** [~ə] Alkoholtestgerät *n*, F Röhrchen *n*.

breathe [briːð] *v/i.* atmen; leben; *v/t.* (aus-, ein)atmen; hauchen, flüstern.

breath|less □ ['breθlɪs] atemlos; **~·tak·ing** atemberaubend.

bred [bred] *pret. u. p.p. von breed 2.*

breech·es ['brɪtʃɪz] *pl.* Knie-, Reithosen *pl.*

breed [briːd] **1.** Zucht *f*, Rasse *f*; (*Menschen*)Schlag *m*; **2.** (*bred*) *v/t.* erzeugen; auf-, erziehen; züchten; *v/i.* sich fortpflanzen; **~·er** ['briːdə] Züchter(in); Zuchttier *n*; **~·ing** [~ɪŋ] (*Tier*)Zucht *f*; Erziehung *f*; (*gutes*) Benehmen.

breeze [briːz] Brise *f*; **breez·y** ['briːzɪ] (*-ier, -iest*) windig, luftig; heiter, unbeschwert.

breth·ren ['breðrən] *pl.* Brüder *pl.*

brev·i·ty ['brevətɪ] Kürze *f*.

brew [bruː] **1.** *v/t. u. v/i.* brauen; zubereiten; *fig.* ausbrechen; **2.** Gebräu *n*; **~·er** ['bruːə] (*Bier*)Brauer *m*; **~·er·y** ['brʊərɪ] Brauerei *f*.

bri·ar ['braɪə] = brier.

bribe [braɪb] **1.** Bestechung(sgeld *n*, -geschenk *n*) *f*; **2.** bestechen; **brib·er·y** ['braɪbərɪ] Bestechung *f*.

brick [brɪk] **1.** Ziegel(stein) *m*; *drop a* ~ *Brt.* F ins Fettnäpfchen treten; **2.** ~ *up od.* in zumauern; **~·lay·er** ['brɪkleɪə] Maurer *m*; **~·works** *sg.* Ziegelei *f*.

brid·al □ ['braɪdl] Braut...

bride [braɪd] Braut *f*; **~·groom** ['braɪdɡrʊm] Bräutigam *m*; **~·s·maid** [~zmeɪd] Brautjungfer *f*.

bridge [brɪdʒ] **1.** Brücke *f*; **2.** e-e Brücke schlagen über (*acc.*); *fig.* überbrücken.

bri·dle ['braɪdl] **1.** Zaum *m*; Zügel *m*; **2.** *v/t.* (auf)zäumen; zügeln; *v/i. a.* ~ *up* den Kopf zurückwerfen; **~·path** Reitweg *m*.

brief [briːf] **1.** □ kurz, bündig; **2.** ⚖ schriftliche Instruktion; △ *nicht* Brief; **3.** kurz zusammenfassen; instruieren; **~·case** ['briːfkeɪs] Aktenmappe *f*.

briefs [briːfs] *pl.* (*a pair of* ~ ein) Slip (*kurze Unterhose*).

bri·er ♀ ['braɪə] Dorn-, Hagebuttenstrauch *m*; Wilde Rose.

bri·gade ⚔ [brɪˈɡeɪd] Brigade *f*.

bright □ [braɪt] hell, glänzend; klar; heiter; lebhaft; gescheit; △ *nicht* breit; **~·en** ['braɪtn] *v/t.* auf-, erhellen; polieren; aufheitern; v/i. sich aufhellen; ~**ness** [~nɪs] Helligkeit f; Glanz m; Klarheit f; Heiterkeit f; Aufgeweckheit f, Intelligenz f.

bril·liance, ~·**lian·cy** ['brɪljəns, ~sɪ] Glanz m; durchdringender Verstand; ~·**liant** [~t] **1.** □ glänzend; hervorragend, brillant; **2.** Brillant m.

brim [brɪm] **1.** Rand m; Krempe f; **2.** (-mm-) bis zum Rande füllen od. voll sein; ~·**ful(l)** ['brɪm'fʊl] randvoll.

brine [braɪn] Salzwasser n; Sole f.

bring [brɪŋ] (brought) (mit-, her-) bringen; △ nicht fort-, wegbringen; j-n veranlassen; Klage erheben; Grund etc. vorbringen; ~ about zustande bringen; bewirken; ~ back zurückbringen; ~ forth hervorbringen; ~ home to j-n überzeugen; ~ in (her)einbringen; ⚖ Spruch fällen; ~ off et. fertigbringen, schaffen; ~ on verursachen; ~ out herausbringen; ~ round wieder zu sich bringen; Kranken durchbringen; ~ up auf-, großziehen; erziehen; zur Sprache bringen; bsd. Brt. et. (er)brechen.

brink [brɪŋk] Rand m (a. fig.).

brisk □ [brɪsk] lebhaft, munter; frisch; flink; belebend.

bris·tle ['brɪsl] **1.** Borste f; **2.** (sich) sträuben; hochfahren, zornig werden; ~ with fig. starren von; ~·**tly** [~ɪ] (-ier, -iest) stopp(e)lig, Stoppel...

Brit·ish ['brɪtɪʃ] britisch; the ~ pl. die Briten m.

brit·tle ['brɪtl] zerbrechlich, spröde.

broach [brəʊtʃ] Thema anschneiden.

broad □ [brɔːd] breit; weit; hell (Tag); deutlich (Wink etc.); derb (Witz); allgemein; weitherzig; liberal; ~·**cast** ['brɔːdkɑːst] **1.** (-cast od. -casted) fig. Nachricht verbreiten; im Rundfunk od. Fernsehen bringen, ausstrahlen, übertragen; senden; im Rundfunk od. Fernsehen sprechen od. auftreten; **2.** Rundfunk-, Fernsehsendung f; ~·**cast·er** [~ə] Rundfunk-, Fernsehsprecher(in); ~·**en** [~dn] verbreitern, erweitern; ~ **jump** Am. Sport: Weitsprung m; ~·**mind·ed** liberal.

bro·cade [brə'keɪd] Brokat m.

bro·chure ['brəʊʃə] Broschüre f, Prospekt m.

brogue [brəʊg] derber Straßenschuh.

broil bsd. Am. [brɔɪl] = grill 1.

broke [brəʊk] **1.** pret. von break 2;

2. F pleite, abgebrannt; **bro·ken** ['brəʊkən] **1.** p.p. von break 2; **2.** ~ health zerrüttete Gesundheit; ~·**hearted** verzweifelt, untröstlich.

bro·ker econ. ['brəʊkə] Makler m.

bron·co Am. ['brɒŋkəʊ] (pl. -cos) (halb)wildes Pferd.

bronze [brɒnz] **1.** Bronze f; **2.** bronzen, Bronze...; **3.** bronzieren.

brooch [brəʊtʃ] Brosche f, Spange f.

brood [bruːd] **1.** Brut f; attr. Brut...; **2.** brüten (a. fig.); ~·**er** ['bruːdə] Brutkasten m.

brook [brʊk] Bach m.

broom [bruːm] Besen m; ~·**stick** ['bruːmstɪk] Besenstiel m.

broth [brɒθ] Fleischbrühe f.

broth·el ['brɒθl] Bordell n.

broth·er ['brʌðə] Bruder m; ~(s) sister(s) Geschwister pl.; ~·**hood** [~hʊd] Bruderschaft f; Brüderlichkeit f; ~·**in-law** [~rɪnlɔː] (pl. -s-in-law) Schwager m; ~·**ly** [~lɪ] brüderlich.

brought [brɔːt] pret. u. p.p. von bring.

brow [braʊ] (Augen)Braue f; Stirn f; Rand m (e-s Steilhanges); ~·**beat** ['braʊbiːt] (-beat, -beaten) einschüchtern; tyrannisieren.

brown [braʊn] **1.** braun; **2.** Braun n; **3.** bräunen; braun werden.

browse [braʊz] **1.** Grasen n; fig. Schmökern n; **2.** grasen, weiden; fig. schmökern.

bruise [bruːz] **1.** ⚕ Quetschung f, Prellung f, Bluterguß m; **2.** (zer-) quetschen; j-n grün u. blau schlagen.

brunch F [brʌntʃ] Brunch m (spätes reichliches Frühstück, das das Mittagessen ersetzt).

brunt [brʌnt]: bear the ~ of die Hauptlast von et. tragen.

brush [brʌʃ] **1.** Bürste f; Pinsel m; (Fuchs)Rute f; Scharmützel n; Unterholz n; **2.** bürsten; fegen; streifen; ~ against s.o. j-n streifen; ~ away, ~ off wegbürsten, abwischen; ~ aside, ~ away fig. et. abtun; ~ up Kenntnisse aufpolieren, -frischen; ~·**up** ['brʌʃʌp]: give one's English a ~ s-e Englischkenntnisse aufpolieren; ~·**wood** Gestrüpp n, Unterholz n.

brusque □ [brʊsk] brüsk, barsch.

Brus·sels sprouts ♣ ['brʌsl'spraʊts] pl. Rosenkohl m.

bru·tal □ ['bruːtl] viehisch; brutal; roh; ~·**i·ty** [bruː'tælətɪ] Brutalität f,

Roheit *f*; **brute** [bru:t] **1.** tierisch; unvernünftig; brutal, roh; **2.** Vieh *n*; F Untier *n*, Scheusal *n*.

bub·ble [ˈbʌbl] **1.** Blase *f*; *fig.* Schwindel *m*; **2.** sprudeln.

buc·ca·neer [bʌkəˈnɪə] Seeräuber *m*.

buck [bʌk] **1.** *zo.* Bock *m*; *Am. sl.* Dollar *m*; **2.** *v/i.* bocken; ~ *up!* Kopf hoch!; *v/t.* ~ *off Reiter* (durch Bocken) abwerfen.

buck·et [ˈbʌkɪt] Eimer *m*, Kübel *m*.

buck·le [ˈbʌkl] **1.** Schnalle *f*, Spange *f*; △ *nicht* Buckel; **2.** *v/t. a.* ~ *up* zu-, festschnallen; ~ *on* anschnallen; *v/i.* ⊕ sich (ver)biegen; ~ *down to a task* F sich hinter e-e Aufgabe klemmen.

buck|shot *hunt.* [ˈbʌkʃɒt] Rehposten *m*; ~**skin** Wildleder *n*.

bud [bʌd] **1.** ♀ Knospe *f*; *fig.* Keim *m*; **2.** (-dd-) *v/i.* knospen, keimen; *a* ~*ding lawyer* ein angehender Jurist.

bud·dy *Am.* F [ˈbʌdɪ] Kamerad *m*.

budge [bʌdʒ] (sich) bewegen.

bud·ger·i·gar *zo.* [ˈbʌdʒərɪgɑ:] Wellensittich *m*.

budg·et [ˈbʌdʒɪt] Vorrat *m*; Staatshaushalt *m*; Etat *m*, Finanzen *pl.*

bud·gie *zo.* F [ˈbʌdʒɪ] = *budgerigar*.

buff¹ [bʌf] **1.** Ochsenleder *n*; Lederfarbe *f*; **2.** lederfarben.

buff² F [~] Film- *etc.* Fan *m*.

buf·fa·lo *zo.* [ˈbʌfələu] (*pl. -loes, -los*) Büffel *m*.

buff·er [ˈbʌfə] ⊕ Puffer *m*; Prellbock *m* (*a. fig.*).

buf·fet¹ [ˈbʌfɪt] **1.** (Faust)Schlag *m*; **2.** schlagen; ~ *about* durchrütteln, -schütteln.

buf·fet² [~] Büfett *n*, Anrichte *f*.

buf·fet³ [ˈbufeɪ] Büfett *n*, Theke *f*; Tisch mit Speisen u. Getränken.

buf·foon [bəˈfu:n] Possenreißer *m*.

bug [bʌg] **1.** *zo.* Wanze *f*; *Am. zo.* Insekt *n*; F Bazillus *m*; F Abhörvorrichtung *f*, Wanze *f*; *Computer*: Fehler *m* im Programm (*in Soft- od. Hardware*); **2.** (*-gg-*) F Gespräch abhören; F Wanzen anbringen in (*dat.*); *Am.* F ärgern, wütend machen.

bug·gy [ˈbʌgɪ] *mot.* Buggy *m* (*Freizeitauto*); *Am.* Kinderwagen *m*.

bu·gle [ˈbju:gl] Wald-, Signalhorn *n*.

build [bɪld] **1.** (*built*) (er)bauen, errichten; △ *nicht* bilden; **2.** Körperbau *m*, Figur *f*; ~**er** [ˈbɪldə] Erbauer *m*, Baumeister *m*; Bauunternehmer

m; ~**ing** [~ɪŋ] (Er)Bauen *n*; Bau *m*, Gebäude *n*; *attr.* Bau...

built [bɪlt] *pret. u. p.p. von build 1.*

bulb [bʌlb] ♀ Zwiebel *f*, Knolle *f*; ⚡ (Glüh)Birne *f*.

bulge [bʌldʒ] **1.** (Aus)Bauchung *f*; Anschwellung *f*; **2.** sich (aus)bauchen; hervorquellen.

bulk [bʌlk] Umfang *m*; Masse *f*; Hauptteil *m*; ♣ Ladung *f*; *in ~ econ.* lose; in großer Menge; ~**y** [ˈbʌlkɪ] (*-ier, -iest*) umfangreich; unhandlich, sperrig.

bull¹ *zo.* [bul] Bulle *m*, Stier *m*.

bull² [~] päpstliche Bulle.

bull·dog *zo.* [ˈbuldɒg] Bulldogge *f*.

bull|doze [ˈbuldəuz] terrorisieren; ~**doz·er** ⊕ [~ə] Bulldozer *m*, Planierraupe *f*.

bul·let [ˈbulɪt] Kugel *f*; ~**-proof** kugelsicher.

bul·le·tin [ˈbulɪtɪn] Bulletin *n*, Tagesbericht *m*; ~ *board Am.* Schwarzes Brett.

bul·lion [ˈbuljən] Gold-, Silberbarren *m*; Gold-, Silberlitze *f*.

bul·ly [ˈbulɪ] **1.** Maulheld *m*; Tyrann *m*; **2.** einschüchtern, tyrannisieren.

bul·wark [ˈbulwək] Bollwerk *n* (*a. fig.*).

bum *Am.* F [bʌm] **1.** Nichtstuer *m*, Herumtreiber *m*; Gammler *m*; **2.** *v/t.* (*-mm-*) schnorren; ~ *around* herumgammeln.

bum·ble-bee *zo.* [ˈbʌmblbi:] Hummel *f*.

bump [bʌmp] **1.** heftiger Schlag *od.* Stoß; Beule *f*; **2.** stoßen; zusammenstoßen (mit), rammen; ~ *into fig. j-n* zufällig treffen; ~ *off* F *j-n* umlegen, umbringen.

bum·per¹ [ˈbʌmpə] **1.** volles Glas (*Wein*); **2.** riesig; ~ *crop* Rekordernte *f*.

bum·per² *mot.* [~] Stoßstange *f*; ~*-to-~* Stoßstange an Stoßstange.

bump·y [ˈbʌmpɪ] (*-ier, -iest*) holp(e)rig.

bun [bʌn] süßes Brötchen; (Haar-)Knoten *m*.

bunch [bʌntʃ] **1.** Bund *n*, Büschel *n*; Haufen *m*; ~ *of grapes* Weintraube *f*; **2.** *a.* ~ *up* bündeln.

bun·dle [ˈbʌndl] **1.** Bündel *n* (*a. fig.*), Bund *n*; **2.** *v/t. a.* ~ *up* bündeln.

bung [bʌŋ] Spund *m*.

bun·ga·low [ˈbʌŋgələu] Bungalow *m*.

bun·gle [ˈbʌŋgl] **1.** Stümperei *f*,

B

Pfusch(arbeit f) m; **2.** (ver)pfuschen.

bun·ion ⚕ ['bʌnjən] entzündeter Fußballen.

bunk [bʌŋk] Schlafkoje f.

bun·ny ['bʌnɪ] Häschen n.

buoy ⚓ [bɔɪ] **1.** Boje f; **2.** ~ed up fig. von neuem Mut erfüllt; **~ant** □ ['bɔɪənt] schwimmfähig; tragend (Wasser etc.); fig. heiter.

bur·den ['bɜːdn] **1.** Last f; Bürde f; ⚓ Tragfähigkeit f; **2.** belasten; **~some** [~səm] lästig, drückend.

bu·reau ['bjʊərəʊ] (pl. -reaux, -reaus) Büro n, Geschäftszimmer n; Brt. Schreibtisch m, -pult n; Am. (bsd. Spiegel)Kommode f; **~·cra·cy** [bjʊəˈrɒkrəsɪ] Bürokratie f.

bur·glar ['bɜːglə] Einbrecher m; **~·glar·ize** Am. [~raɪz] = burgle; **~·glar·y** [~rɪ] Einbruch(sdiebstahl) m; **~·gle** [~gl] einbrechen (in acc.).

bur·i·al ['berɪəl] Begräbnis n.

bur·ly ['bɜːlɪ] (-ier, -iest) stämmig, kräftig.

burn [bɜːn] **1.** ⚕ Brandwunde f; verbrannte Stelle; **2.** (burnt od. burned) (ver-, an)brennen; ~ down ab-, niederbrennen; ~ out ausbrennen; ~ up auflodern; verbrennen; verglühen (Rakete etc.); **~·ing** ['bɜːnɪŋ] brennend (a. fig.).

bur·nish ['bɜːnɪʃ] polieren.

burnt [bɜːnt] pret. u. p.p. von burn 2.

burp F [bɜːp] rülpsen, aufstoßen; ein Bäuerchen machen (lassen) (Baby).

bur·row ['bʌrəʊ] **1.** Höhle f, Bau m; **2.** (sich ein-, ver)graben.

burst [bɜːst] **1.** Bersten n; Riß m; fig. Ausbruch m; **2.** (burst) v/i. bersten, platzen; zerspringen; explodieren; ~ from sich losreißen von; ~ in on od. upon hereinplatzen bei j-m; ~ into tears in Tränen ausbrechen; ~ out herausplatzen; v/t. (auf)sprengen.

bur·y ['berɪ] be-, vergraben; beerdigen.

bus [bʌs] (pl. -es, -ses) (Omni)Bus m.

bush [bʊʃ] Busch m; Gebüsch n.

bush·el ['bʊʃl] Scheffel m (= Brt. 36,37 l, Am. 35,24 l).

bush·y ['bʊʃɪ] (-ier, -iest) buschig.

busi·ness ['bɪznɪs] Geschäft n; Beschäftigung f; Beruf m; Angelegenheit f; Aufgabe f; econ. Handel m; ~ of the day Tagesordnung f; on ~ geschäftlich; you have no ~ doing

(od. to do) that Sie haben kein Recht, das zu tun; this is none of your ~ das geht Sie nichts an; s. mind 2; **~ hours** pl. Geschäftszeit f; **~·like** geschäftsmäßig, sachlich; **~·man** (pl. -men) Geschäftsmann m; **~ trip** Geschäftsreise f; **~·wom·an** (pl. -women) Geschäftsfrau f.

bust¹ [bʌst] Büste f.

bust² Am. F [~] Pleite f.

bus·tle ['bʌsl] **1.** Geschäftigkeit f; geschäftiges Treiben; **2.** ~ about geschäftig hin u. her eilen.

bus·y □ ['bɪzɪ] **1.** (-ier, -iest) beschäftigt; geschäftig; fleißig (at bei, an dat.); lebhaft; Am. teleph. besetzt; **2.** (mst ~ o.s. sich) beschäftigen (with mit); **~·bod·y** aufdringlicher Mensch, Gschaftlhuber m.

but [bʌt, bət] **1.** cj. aber, jedoch, sondern; außer, als; ohne daß; dennoch; a. ~ that daß nicht; he could not ~ laugh er mußte einfach lachen; **2.** prp. außer; all ~ him alle außer ihm; the last ~ one der vorletzte; the next ~ one der übernächste; nothing ~ nichts als; ~ for wenn nicht ... gewesen wäre, ohne; **3.** nach Negation: der (die od. das) nicht; there is no one ~ knows es gibt niemand, der es nicht weiß; **4.** adv. nur; erst, gerade; all ~ fast, beinahe.

butch·er ['bʊtʃə] **1.** Fleischer m, Metzger m; **2.** (fig. ab-, hin)schlachten; **~·y** [~rɪ] Schlachthaus n; fig. Gemetzel n.

but·ler ['bʌtlə] Butler m.

butt¹ [bʌt] Stoß m; (dickes) Ende (e-s Baumes etc.); Stummel m, Kippe f; (Gewehr)Kolben m; Schießstand m; fig. Zielscheibe f; **2.** (mit dem Kopf) stoßen; ~ in F sich einmischen (on in acc.).

butt² [~] Wein-, Bierfaß n; Regentonne f.

but·ter ['bʌtə] **1.** Butter f; F Schmeichelei f; **2.** mit Butter bestreichen; **~·cup** ⚘ Butterblume f; **~·fly** zo. Schmetterling m; **~·y** [~rɪ] butter(-artig), Butter...

but·tocks ['bʌtəks] pl. Gesäß n, F od. zo. Hinterteil n.

but·ton ['bʌtn] **1.** Knopf m; ⚘ Knospe f; **2.** mst ~ up zuknöpfen; **~·hole** Knopfloch n.

but·tress ['bʌtrɪs] **1.** Strebepfeiler m; fig. Stütze f; **2.** (unter)stützen.

bux·om ['bʌksəm] drall, stramm.

buy [baɪ] **1.** F Kauf *m;* **2.** (*bought*) *v/t.* (an-, ein)kaufen (*of, from* von; *at* bei); ~ **out** *j-n* abfinden, auszahlen; *Firma* aufkaufen; ~ **up** aufkaufen; **~er** [ˈbaɪə] (Ein)Käufer(in).

buzz [bʌz] **1.** Summen *n,* Surren *n;* Stimmengewirr *n;* **2.** *v/i.* summen, surren; ~ **about** herumschwirren; ~ **off!** *Brt.* F schwirr ab!, hau ab!

buz·zard *zo.* [ˈbʌzəd] Bussard *m.*

buzz·er *ℰ* [ˈbʌzə] Summer *m.*

by [baɪ] **1.** *prp. räumlich:* bei; an, neben; *Richtung:* durch, über; an (*dat.*) entlang *od.* vorbei; *zeitlich:* an, bei; *spätestens* bis; *bis zu; Urheber, Ursache:* von, durch (*bsd. beim Passiv*); *Mittel, Werkzeug:* durch, mit; *Art u. Weise:* bei; *Schwur:* bei; *Maß:* um, bei; *Richtschnur:* gemäß, nach; ~ *the dozen* dutzendweise; ~ *o.s.* allein; ~ *land* zu Lande; ~ *rail* per

Bahn; *day* ~ *day* Tag für Tag; ~ *twos* zu zweien; **2.** *adv.* dabei; vorbei; beiseite; ~ *and* ~ bald; nach u. nach; ~ *the* ~ nebenbei bemerkt; ~ *and large* im großen u. ganzen.

by- [baɪ] Neben...; Seiten...

bye, **bye-bye** [ˈ~ˈbaɪ] *int.* F [baɪ], *a.* Wiedersehen!, Tschüs!

by|-e·lec·tion [ˈbaɪɪlekʃn] Nachwahl *f;* **~gone 1.** vergangen; **2.** *let* ~*s be* ~*s* laß(t) das Vergangene ruhen; **~pass 1.** Umgehungsstraße *f; ℱ* Bypass *m;* **2.** umgehen; vermeiden; **~path** Seitenstraße *f;* **~prod·uct** Nebenprodukt *n;* **~road** Seitenstraße *f;* **~stand·er** Zuschauer(in); **~street** Neben-, Seitenstraße *f.*

byte [baɪt] *Computer:* Byte *n.*

by|way [ˈbaɪweɪ] Seitenstraße *f;* **~word** Sprichwort *n;* Inbegriff *m;* *be a* ~ *for* gleichbedeutend sein mit.

C

cab [kæb] Droschke *f,* Taxi *n;* Führerrstand *m* (*Lokomotive*); Fahrerhaus *n* (*Lastwagen*), Führerhaus *n* (*a. Kran*).

cab·bage ♀ [ˈkæbɪdʒ] Kohl *m.*

cab·in [ˈkæbɪn] Hütte *f;* ♣ Kabine *f* (*a. Seilbahn*), Kajüte *f;* ✈ Kanzel *f;* **~boy** ♣ junger Kabinensteward; ~ **cruis·er** ♣ Kabinenkreuzer *m.*

cab·i·net [ˈkæbɪnɪt] *pol.* Kabinett *n;* Schrank *m,* Vitrine *f;* (Radio)Gehäuse *n;* ~ **meeting** Kabinettssitzung *f;* **~mak·er** Kunsttischler *m.*

ca·ble [ˈkeɪbl] **1.** Kabel *n;* ♣ Ankertau *n;* **2.** telegrafieren; *j-m* Geld telegrafisch anweisen; **~car** Seilbahn: Kabine *f,* Wagen *m;* **~gram** [~græm] (Übersee)Telegramm *n;* ~ **tel·e·vi·sion** Kabelfernsehen *n.*

cab|-rank [ˈkæbræŋk], **~stand** Taxi-, Droschkenstand *m.*

ca·ca·o ♀ [kəˈkɑːəʊ] (*pl. -os*) Kakaobaum *m,* -bohne *f.*

cack·le [ˈkækl] **1.** Gegacker *n,* Geschnatter *n;* **2.** gackern, schnattern.

cad ✎ [kæd] Schuft *m,* Schurke *m.*

ca·dav·er *ℱ* [kəˈdeɪvə] Leichnam *m;* △ *nicht Kadaver.*

ca·dence [ˈkeɪdəns] ♪ Kadenz *f;* Tonfall *m;* Rhythmus *m.*

ca·det ✗ [kəˈdet] Kadett *m.*

caf·é, **caf·e** [ˈkæfeɪ] Café *n.*

caf·e·te·ri·a [kæfɪˈtɪərɪə] Selbstbedienungsrestaurant *n.*

cage [keɪdʒ] **1.** Käfig *m;* ✗ Förderkorb *m;* **2.** einsperren.

cag·ey □ F [ˈkeɪdʒɪ] (*-gier, -giest*) verschlossen; vorsichtig; *Am.* schlau, gerissen.

ca·jole [kəˈdʒəʊl] *j-m* schmeicheln; *j-n* beschwatzen.

cake [keɪk] **1.** Kuchen *m,* Torte *f;* Tafel *f* (*Schokolade*), Riegel *m* (*Seife*); **2.** ~*d with mud* schmutzverkrustet.

ca·lam·i·tous □ [kəˈlæmɪtəs] katastrophal; **~ty** [~tɪ] großes Unglück, Katastrophe *f.*

cal·cu·late [ˈkælkjʊleɪt] *v/t.* kalkulieren; be-, aus-, errechnen; *Am.* F vermuten; *v/i.* rechnen (*on, upon* mit, auf *acc.*); **~la·tion** [kælkjʊˈleɪʃn] Berechnung *f* (*a. fig.*), Ausrechnung *f; econ.* Kalkulation *f;* Überlegung *f;* **~la·tor** [ˈkælkjʊleɪtə] Rechner *m* (*Gerät*).

caldron

cal·dron [ˈkɔːldrən] = cauldron.

cal·en·dar [ˈkælɪndə] **1.** Kalender *m*; Liste *f*; **2.** registrieren.

calf¹ [kɑːf] (*pl.* calves [~vz]) Wade *f*.

calf² [~] (*pl.* calves) Kalb *n*; ~**skin** Kalb(s)fell *n*.

cal·i·bre, *Am.* **-ber** [ˈkælɪbə] Kaliber *n*.

cal·i·co [ˈkælɪkəʊ] (*pl.* -coes, -cos) Kaliko *m*.

call [kɔːl] **1.** Ruf *m*; *teleph.* Anruf *m*, Gespräch *n*; Ruf *m*, Berufung *f* (*to* in *ein Amt*; *auf e-n Lehrstuhl*); Aufruf *m*, Aufforderung *f*; Signal *n*; (kurzer) Besuch; Kündigung *f* (*von Geldern*); *on* ~ auf Abruf; *make a* ~ telefonieren; **2.** *v/t.* (herbei)rufen; (ein)berufen; *teleph.* j-n anrufen; berufen, ernennen (*to* zu); nennen; *Aufmerksamkeit lenken* (*to* auf *acc.*); *be* ~*ed* heißen; ~ *s.o. names* j-n beschimpfen, beleidigen; ~ *up teleph.* anrufen; *v/i.* rufen; *teleph.* anrufen; e-n (kurzen) Besuch machen (*on s.o.*, *at s.o.'s* [*house*] bei j-m); ~ *at a port* e-n Hafen anlaufen; ~ *for* rufen nach; *et.* anfordern; *et.* abholen; *to be* ~*ed for* postlagernd; ~ *on s.o.* j-n besuchen; ~ *on*, ~ *upon* sich an j-n wenden (*for* wegen); appellieren an (*acc.*) (*to do* zu tun); ~**box** [ˈkɔːlbɒks] *Am.* Fernsprechzelle *f*; ~**er** [ˈkɔːlə] *teleph.* Anrufer(in); Besucher(in); ~**girl** Callgirl *n*; ~**ing** [~ɪŋ] Rufen *n*; Berufung *f*; Beruf *m*.

cal·lous □ [ˈkæləs] schwielig; *fig.* dickfellig, herzlos.

cal·low [ˈkæləʊ] nackt (*ungefiedert*); *fig.* unerfahren.

calm [kɑːm] **1.** □ still, ruhig; **2.** (Wind)Stille *f*, Ruhe *f*; **3.** *oft* ~ *down* besänftigen, sich beruhigen.

cal·o·rie *phys.* [ˈkælərɪ] Kalorie *f*; ~**con·scious** kalorienbewußt.

ca·lum·ni·ate [kəˈlʌmnɪeɪt] verleumden; **cal·um·ny** [ˈkæləmnɪ] Verleumdung *f*.

calve [kɑːv] kalben.

calves [kɑːvz] *pl. von calf¹*, ².

cam·bric [ˈkeɪmbrɪk] Kambrik *m* (*feines Gewebe*).

came [keɪm] *pret. von* come.

cam·el *zo.*, ⚓ [ˈkæml] Kamel *n*.

cam·e·ra [ˈkæmərə] Kamera *f*, Fotoapparat *m*; 🏛️ *unter Ausschluß der Öffentlichkeit*.

cam·o·mile ♣ [ˈkæməmaɪl] Kamille *f*.

cam·ou·flage ✕ [ˈkæmʊflɑːʒ] **1.** Tarnung *f*; **2.** tarnen.

camp [kæmp] **1.** Lager *n*; ✕ Feldlager *n*; ~ *bed* Feldbett *n*; **2.** lagern; ~ *out* zelten, campen.

cam·paign [kæmˈpeɪn] **1.** ✕ Feldzug *m*; *fig.* Kampagne *f*, Feldzug *m*, Aktion *f*; *pol.* Wahlkampf *m*; **2.** ✕ *an e-m Feldzug teilnehmen*; *fig.* kämpfen, *zu Felde ziehen*; *pol.* sich am Wahlkampf beteiligen, Wahlkampf machen; *Am.* kandidieren (*for* für).

camp|ground [ˈkæmpɡraʊnd], ~**site** Lagerplatz *m*; Zelt-, Campingplatz *m*.

cam·pus [ˈkæmpəs] Campus *m*, Universitätsgelände *n*.

can¹ *v/aux.* [kæn, kən] (*pret.* could; *verneint:* cannot, can't) ich, du *etc.* kann(st) *etc.*; dürfen, können.

can² [~] **1.** Kanne *f*; (Blech-, Konserven)Dose *f*, (-)Büchse *f*; **2.** (-nn-) (*in Büchsen*) einmachen, eindosen.

Ca·na·di·an [kəˈneɪdjən] **1.** kanadisch; **2.** Kanadier(in).

ca·nal [kəˈnæl] Kanal *m* (*a. anat.*).

ca·nard [kæˈnɑːd] (Zeitungs)Ente *f*.

ca·nar·y *zo.* [kəˈneərɪ] Kanarienvogel *m*.

can·cel [ˈkænsl] (*bsd. Brt.* -ll-, *Am.* -l-) (durch-, aus)streichen; entwerten; rückgängig machen; absagen; *be* ~(*l*)*ed* ausfallen.

can·cer *ast.*, 🎗️ [ˈkænsə] Krebs *m*; ~**ous** [~rəs] krebsartig; krebsbefallen.

can·did □ [ˈkændɪd] aufrichtig, offen.

can·di·date [ˈkændɪdət] Kandidat(in) (*for* für), Bewerber(in) (*for* um).

can·died [ˈkændɪd] kandiert.

can·dle [ˈkændl] Kerze *f*; Licht *n*; *burn the* ~ *at both ends* mit s-r Gesundheit Raubbau treiben; ~**stick** Kerzenleuchter *m*.

can·do(u)r [ˈkændə] Aufrichtigkeit *f*, Offenheit *f*.

can·dy [ˈkændɪ] **1.** Kandis(zucker) *m*; *Am.* Süßigkeiten *pl.*; **2.** *v/t.* kandieren.

cane [keɪn] **1.** ♣ Rohr *n*; (Rohr)Stock *m*; **2.** (*mit dem Stock*) züchtigen.

ca·nine [ˈkeɪnaɪn] Hunde...

canned *Am.* [kænd] Dosen..., Büchsen...

can·ner·y *Am.* [ˈkænərɪ] Konservenfabrik *f*.

can·ni·bal [ˈkænɪbl] Kannibale *m*.

can·non [ˈkænən] Kanone *f*.

can·not [ˈkænɒt] *s.* can¹.

can·ny [ˈkænɪ] (*-ier, -iest*) gerissen, schlau.

ca·noe [kəˈnuː] **1.** Kanu *n*, Paddelboot *n*; **2.** Kanu fahren, paddeln.

can·on [ˈkænən] Kanon *m*; Regel *f*, Richtschnur *f*; **~·ize** [~aɪz] heiligsprechen.

can·o·py [ˈkænəpɪ] Baldachin *m*; *arch.* Vordach *n*.

cant [kænt] Fachsprache *f*; Gewäsch *n*; frömmlerisches Gerede.

can't [kɑːnt] = cannot.

can·tan·ker·ous □ [kænˈtæŋkərəs] zänkisch, mürrisch.

can·teen [kænˈtiːn] ✕ Feldflasche *f*; Kantine *f*; ✕ Kochgeschirr *n*; Besteck(kasten *m*) *n*.

can·ter [ˈkæntə] **1.** Kanter *m* (*kurzer, leichter Galopp*); **2.** kantern.

can·vas [ˈkænvəs] Segeltuch *n*; Zelt-, Packleinwand *f*; Segel *pl.*; *paint.* Leinwand *f*; Gemälde *n*.

can·vass [~] **1.** *pol.* Wahlfeldzug *m*; *econ.* Werbefeldzug *m*; **2.** *v/t.* eingehend untersuchen *od.* erörtern *od.* prüfen; *v/i.* werben um (*Stimmen*); *v/i. pol.* e-n Wahlfeldzug veranstalten.

can·yon [ˈkænjən] Cañon *m*.

cap [kæp] **1.** Kappe *f*; Mütze *f*; Haube *f*; *arch.* Aufsatz *m*; Zündkapsel *f*; ✚ Pessar *n*; **2.** (*-pp-*) (mit e-r Kappe *etc.*) bedecken; *fig.* krönen; übertreffen.

ca·pa·bil·i·ty [keɪpəˈbɪlətɪ] Fähigkeit *f*; **~·ble** □ [ˈkeɪpəbl] fähig (*of* zu).

ca·pa·cious □ [kəˈpeɪʃəs] geräumig; **ca·pac·i·ty** [kəˈpæsətɪ] (Raum)Inhalt *m*; Fassungsvermögen *n*; Kapazität *f*; Aufnahmefähigkeit *f*; *geistige* (*od.* ⊕ Leistungs)Fähigkeit *f* (*for ger.* zu *inf.*); in my ~ as in meiner Eigenschaft als.

cape¹ [keɪp] Kap *n*, Vorgebirge *n*.

cape² [~] Cape *n*, Umhang *m*.

ca·per [ˈkeɪpə] **1.** Kapriole *f*, Luftsprung *m*; *cut* ~*s* = **2.** Freuden- *od.* Luftsprünge machen.

ca·pil·la·ry *anat.* [kəˈpɪlərɪ] Haar-, Kapillargefäß *n*.

cap·i·tal [ˈkæpɪtl] **1.** □ Kapital...; Tod(es)...; *jur.* Haupt...; großartig, prima; ~ *crime* Kapitalverbrechen *n*; ~ *punishment* Todesstrafe *f*; **2.** Hauptstadt *f*; Kapital *n*; *mst* ~ *letter*

Großbuchstabe *m*; **~·is·m** [~ɪzəm] Kapitalismus *m*; **~·ist** [~ɪst] Kapitalist *m*; **~·ize** [~əlaɪz] kapitalisieren; groß schreiben.

ca·pit·u·late [kəˈpɪtjʊleɪt] kapitulieren (*to* vor *dat.*).

ca·price [kəˈpriːs] Laune *f*; **ca·pri·cious** □ [~ɪʃəs] kapriziös, launisch.

Cap·ri·corn *ast.* [ˈkæprɪkɔːn] Steinbock *m*.

cap·size [kæpˈsaɪz] *v/i.* kentern; *v/t.* zum Kentern bringen.

cap·sule [ˈkæpsjuːl] Kapsel *f*; (Raum)Kapsel *f*.

cap·tain [ˈkæptɪn] (An)Führer *m*; Kapitän *m*; ✕ Hauptmann *m*.

cap·tion [ˈkæpʃn] Überschrift *f*, Titel *m*; Bildunterschrift *f*; *Film:* Untertitel *m*.

cap·ti·vate *fig.* [ˈkæptɪveɪt] gefangennehmen, fesseln; **~·tive** [ˈkæptɪv] **1.** gefangen; gefesselt; *hold* ~ gefangenhalten; *take* ~ gefangennehmen; **2.** Gefangene(*r m*) *f*; **~·tiv·i·ty** [kæpˈtɪvətɪ] Gefangenschaft *f*.

cap·ture [ˈkæptʃə] **1.** Eroberung *f*; Gefangennahme *f*; **2.** fangen; erobern; erbeuten; ⚓ kapern.

car [kɑː] Auto *n*, Wagen *m*; (Eisenbahn-, Straßenbahn)Wagen *m*; Gondel *f* (*e-s Ballons etc.*); Kabine *f* (*e-s Aufzugs*); *by* ~ mit dem Auto, im Auto.

car·a·mel [ˈkærəmel] Karamel *m*; Karamelle *f*.

car·a·van [ˈkærəvæn] Karawane *f*; *Brt.* Wohnwagen *m*, -anhänger *m*; ~ *site* Campingplatz *m* für Wohnwagen.

car·a·way ♀ [ˈkærəweɪ] Kümmel *m*.

car·bine ✕ [ˈkɑːbaɪn] Karabiner *m*.

car·bo·hy·drate ⚗ [ˈkɑːbəʊˈhaɪdreɪt] Kohle(n)hydrat *n*.

car·bon [ˈkɑːbən] ⚗ Kohlenstoff *m*; *a.* ~ *copy* Durchschlag *m*; *a.* ~ *paper* Kohlepapier *n*.

car·bu·ret·tor, *a.* **-ret·er** *bsd. Brt.*, *Am.* **-ret·or**, *a.* **-ret·er** ⊕ [kɑːbjʊˈretə] Vergaser *m*.

car·case, *esp. Brt.* **car·cass** [ˈkɑːkəs] Kadaver *m*, Aas *n*; *Fleischerei:* Rumpf *m*.

card [kɑːd] Karte *f*; *have a* ~ *up one's sleeve fig.* (noch) e-n Trumpf in der Hand haben; **~·board** [ˈkɑːdbɔːd] Pappe *f*; ~ *box* Pappkarton *m*.

car·di·ac ✚ [ˈkɑːdɪæk] Herz...

car·di·gan [ˈkɑːdɪgən] Strickjacke *f*.

car·di·nal [ˈkɑːdɪnl] **1.** □ Grund...,

Haupt..., Kardinal...; scharlachrot; ~ *number* Grundzahl *f*; **2.** *eccl.* Kardinal *m*.

card-in|dex ['kɑːdɪndeks] Kartei *f*.
card-sharp-er ['kɑːdʃɑːpə] Falschspieler *m*.
care [keə] **1.** Sorge *f*; Sorgfalt *f*; Vorsicht *f*; Obhut *f*, Pflege *f*; *medical* ~ ärztliche Behandlung; ~ *of* (*abbr. c/o*) ... per Adresse, bei ...; *take* ~ *of* aufpassen auf (*acc.*); *with* ~! Vorsicht!; **2.** Lust haben (*to inf.* zu); ~ *for* sorgen für, sich kümmern um; sich etwas machen aus; *I don't* ~! F meinetwegen!; *I couldn't* ~ *less* F es ist mir völlig egal; *well* ~*d-for* gepflegt.
ca-reer [kə'rɪə] **1.** Karriere *f*, Laufbahn *f*; Berufs...; Karriere...; **3.** rasen.
care-free ['keəfriː] sorgenfrei, sorglos.
care-ful □ ['keəfl] vorsichtig; sorgsam bedacht (*of* auf *acc.*); sorgfältig; *be* ~! gib acht!; ~**ness** [~nɪs] Vorsicht *f*; Sorgfalt *f*.
care-less □ ['keəlɪs] sorglos; nachlässig; unachtsam; leichtsinnig; ~**ness** [~nɪs] Sorglosigkeit *f*; Nachlässigkeit *f*; Fahrlässigkeit *f*.
ca-ress [kə'res] **1.** Liebkosung *f*; **2.** liebkosen, streicheln.
care-tak-er ['keəteɪkə] Hausmeister *m*; (*Haus- etc.*)Verwalter *m*.
care-worn ['keəwɔːn] abgehärmt.
car-go ['kɑːgəʊ] (*pl.* -goes, *Am. a.* -gos) Ladung *f*.
car-i-ca|ture ['kærɪkətjʊə] **1.** Karikatur *f*; **2.** karikieren; ~**tur-ist** [~rɪst] Karikaturist *m*.
car-mine ['kɑːmaɪn] Karmin(rot) *m*.
car-nal □ ['kɑːnl] fleischlich; sinnlich.
car-na-tion [kɑː'neɪʃn] ⚘ (Garten-)Nelke *f*; Blaßrot *n*.
car-ni-val ['kɑːnɪvl] Karneval *m*.
car-niv-o-rous ⚘ *zo.* [kɑː'nɪvərəs] fleischfressend.
car-ol ['kærəl] Weihnachtslied *n*.
carp *zo.* [kɑːp] Karpfen *m*.
car-park *Brt.* ['kɑːpɑːk] Parkplatz *m*; Parkhaus *n*.
car-pen|ter ['kɑːpɪntə] Zimmermann *m*; ~**try** [~rɪ] Zimmerhandwerk *n*; Zimmermannsarbeit *f*.
car-pet ['kɑːpɪt] **1.** Teppich *m*; *bring on the* ~ aufs Tapet bringen; **2.** mit e-m Teppich belegen.

car|pool ['kɑːpuːl] Fahrgemeinschaft *f*; ~**port** überdachter Abstellplatz *m* (*für Autos*).
car-riage ['kærɪdʒ] Beförderung *f*, Transport *m*; Fracht(gebühr) *f*; Kutsche *f*; *Brt.* 🚃 (Personen-)Wagen *m*; ⊕ Fahrgestell *n* (*a.* ✱); (Körper-)Haltung *f*; ~**way** Fahrbahn *f*.
car-ri-er ['kærɪə] Spediteur *m*, Fuhrmann *m*; Gepäckträger *m*; ~**bag** Trag(e)tasche *f*, -tüte *f*; ~ **pi-geon** Brieftaube *f*.
car-ri-on ['kærɪən] Aas *n*; *attr.* Aas...
car-rot ⚘ ['kærət] Karotte *f*, Möhre, Mohrrübe *f*.
car-ry ['kærɪ] *v/t. wohin* bringen, führen, tragen (*a. v/i.*), fahren, befördern; (*bei sich*) haben *od.* tragen; *Ansicht* durchsetzen; *Gewinn, Preis* davontragen; *Ernte, Zinsen* tragen; (weiter)führen, *Mauer* ziehen; *Antrag* durchbringen; *be carried* angenommen werden (*Antrag*); ~ *the day* den Sieg davontragen; ~ *s.th. too far* et. übertreiben, et. zu weit treiben; *get carried away fig.* die Kontrolle über sich verlieren; ~ *forward*, ~ *over econ.* übertragen; ~ *on* fortsetzen, weiterführen; *Geschäft etc.* betreiben; ~ *out*, ~ *through* durchführen, ausführen; ~**cot** *Brt.* ['kærɪkɒt] (Baby)Trag(e)tasche *f*.
cart [kɑːt] **1.** Karren *m*; Wagen *m*; *put the* ~ *before the horse fig.* das Pferd beim Schwanz aufzäumen; **2.** karren, fahren.
car-ti-lage *anat.* ['kɑːtɪlɪdʒ] Knorpel *m*.
car-ton ['kɑːtən] Karton *m*; *a* ~ *of cigarettes* e-e Stange Zigaretten.
car-toon [kɑː'tuːn] Cartoon *m*, *n*; Karikatur *f*; Zeichentrickfilm *m*; ~**ist** [~ɪst] Karikaturist *m*.
car-tridge ['kɑːtrɪdʒ] Patrone *f*; *phot.* (Film)Patrone *f* (*e-r Kleinbildkamera*), (Film)Kassette *f* (*e-r Film- od. Kassettenkamera*); ~**pen** Patronenfüllhalter *m*.
cart-wheel ['kɑːtwiːl] Wagenrad *n*; *turn* ~*s* radschlagen.
carve [kɑːv] *Fleisch* vorschneiden, zerlegen; schnitzen; meißeln; **carv-er** ['kɑːvə] (Holz)Schnitzer *m*; Bildhauer *m*; Tranchierer *m*; Tranchiermesser *n*; **carv-ing** [~ɪŋ] Schnitzerei *f*.
car wash ['kɑːwɒʃ] Autowäsche *f*; Waschanlage *f*, -straße *f*.

cas·cade [kæˈskeɪd] Wasserfall *m*.

case[1] [keɪs] **1.** Behälter *m*; Kiste *f*, Kasten *m*; Etui *n*; Gehäuse *n*; Schachtel *f*; (*Glas*)Schrank *m*; (*Kissen*)Bezug *m*; ⊕ Verkleidung *f*; **2.** in ein Gehäuse *od.* Etui stecken; ⊕ verkleiden.

case[2] [~] Fall *m* (*a.* ⚕); *gr.* Kasus *m*, Fall *m*; ⚕ (Krankheits)Fall *m*, Patient(in); F komischer Kauz; Sache *f*, Angelegenheit *f*.

case·ment [ˈkeɪsmənt] Fensterflügel *m*; *a.* ~ *window* Flügelfenster *n*.

cash [kæʃ] **1.** Bargeld *n*; Zahlung *f*; ~ *down* gegen bar; ~ *on delivery* Lieferung *f* gegen bar; (per) Nachnahme *f*; **2.** *Scheck etc.* einlösen; **~book** [ˈkæʃbʊk] Kassenbuch *n*; **~desk** Kasse *f* (*im Warenhaus etc.*); **~di·spens·er** Geldautomat *m*, Bankomat *m*; **~ier** [kæˈʃɪə] Kassierer(in); ~'s desk *of office* Kasse *f*; **~less** [~lɪs] bargeldlos; **~o·mat** [kæʃəʊˈmæt] = ~ *dispenser* *f*; **~ re·gis·ter** Registrierkasse *f*.

cas·ing [ˈkeɪsɪŋ] (Schutz)Hülle *f*; Verschalung *f*, -kleidung *f*, Gehäuse *n*.

cask [kɑːsk] Faß *n*.

cas·ket [ˈkɑːskɪt] Kästchen *n*; *Am.* Sarg *m*.

cas·se·role [ˈkæsərəʊl] Kasserolle *f*.

cas·sette [kəˈset] (Film-, Band-*etc.*)Kassette *f*; ∆ *nicht* Geld- *etc.* Kassette; **~ deck** Kassettendeck *n*; **~ra·di·o** Radiorecorder *m*; **~re·cord·er** Kassettenrecorder *m*.

cas·sock *eccl.* [ˈkæsək] Soutane *f*.

cast [kɑːst] **1.** Wurf *m*; ⊕ Guß(form *f*) *m*; Abguß *m*, Abdruck *m*; Schattierung *f*, Anflug *m*; Form *f*, Art *f*; Auswerfen *n* (*der Angel etc.*); *thea.* Besetzung *f*; **2.** (*cast*) *v/t.* (ab-, aus-, hin-, um-, weg)werfen; *zo.* Haut *etc.* abwerfen; *Zähne etc.* verlieren; verwerfen; gestalten; ⊕ gießen; *a.* ~ *up* ausrechnen, zusammenzählen; *thea. Stück* besetzen; *Rollen* verteilen (*to an acc.*); *be* ~ *in a lawsuit* ⚖ e-n Prozeß verlieren; ~ *lots* losen (*for* um); ~ *in one's lot with s.o.* j-s Los teilen; ~ *aside Gewohnheit etc.* ablegen; *Freund etc.* fallenlassen; ~ *away* wegwerfen; *be* ~ *away* ⚓ verschlagen werden; *be* ~ *down* niedergeschlagen sein; ~ *off Kleidung* ausrangieren; *Freund etc.* fallenlassen; *Stricken etc.: Maschen* abnehmen;

v/i. ⊕ sich gießen lassen; sich (ver-)werfen (*Holz*); ~ *about for*, ~ *around for* suchen (nach), *fig. a.* sich umsehen nach.

cas·ta·net [kæstəˈnet] Kastagnette *f*.

cast·a·way [ˈkɑːstəweɪ] **1.** ausgestoßen; ausrangiert, abgelegt (*Kleidung etc.*); ⚓ schiffbrüchig; **2.** Ausgestoßene(r *m f*); ⚓ Schiffbrüchige(r *m f*).

caste [kɑːst] Kaste *f* (*a. fig.*).

cast·er [ˈkɑːstə] = *castor*[2].

cas·ti·gate [ˈkæstɪgeɪt] züchtigen; *fig.* geißeln.

cast i·ron [ˈkɑːstˈaɪən] Gußeisen *n*; **cast-i·ron** gußeisern.

cas·tle [ˈkɑːsl] Burg *f*, Schloß *n*; *Schach:* Turm *m*.

cast·or[1] [ˈkɑːstə]: ~ *oil* Rizinusöl *n*.

cast·or[2] [~] Laufrolle *f* (*unter Möbeln*); (Salz-, Zucker- *etc.*)Streuer *m*.

cas·trate [kæˈstreɪt] kastrieren.

cas·u·al ☐ [ˈkæʒjʊəl] zufällig; gelegentlich; flüchtig; lässig; ~ *wear* Freizeitkleidung *f*; **~ty** [~tɪ] Unfall *m*; Verunglückte(r *m f*), Opfer *n*; ✕ Verwundete(r) *m*, Gefallene(r) *m*; *casualties pl.* Opfer *pl.*, ✕ *mst* Verluste *pl.*; ~ *ward*, ~ *department* Unfallstation *f*.

cat *zo.* [kæt] Katze *f*.

cat·a·logue, *Am.* **-log** [ˈkætəlɒg] **1.** Katalog *m*; *Am. univ.* Vorlesungsverzeichnis *n*; **2.** katalogisieren.

cat·a·pult [ˈkætəpʌlt] *Brt.* Schleuder *f*; Katapult *n*, *m*.

cat·a·ract [ˈkætərækt] Wasserfall *m*; Stromschnelle *f*; ⚕ grauer Star.

ca·tarrh ⚕ [kəˈtɑː] Katarrh *m*; Schnupfen *m*.

ca·tas·tro·phe [kəˈtæstrəfɪ] Katastrophe *f*.

catch [kætʃ] **1.** Fangen *n*; Fang *m*, Beute *f*; Stocken *n* (*des Atems*); Halt *m*, Griff *m*; ⊕ Haken *m*; (Tür)Klinke *f*; Verschluß *m*; *fig.* Haken *m*; **2.** (*caught*) *v/t.* (auf-, ein)fangen; packen, fassen, ergreifen; überraschen, ertappen; *Blick etc.* auffangen; *Zug etc.* (noch) kriegen; erwischen; erfassen, verstehen; einfangen (*Atmosphäre*); sich *e-e Krankheit* holen; ~ (*a*) *cold* sich erkälten; ~ *the eye* ins Auge fallen; ~ *s.o.'s eye* j-s Aufmerksamkeit auf sich lenken; ~ *s.o. up* einholen; *be caught up in* verwickelt sein in (*acc.*); **3.** *v/i.* sich verfangen, hängenbleiben; fassen, greifen; ineinandergreifen (*Räder*);

klemmen; einschnappen (*Schloß etc.*); ~ on F einschlagen, Anklang finden; F kapieren; ~ up with einholen; ~**er** ['kætʃə] Fänger *m*; ~**ing** [~ɪŋ] packend; ⚕ ansteckend; ~**word** Schlagwort *n*; Stichwort *n*; ~**y** □ [~ɪ] (*-ier, -iest*) eingängig (*Melodie*).

cat·e·chis·m ['kætɪkɪzəm] Katechismus *m*.

cat·e·gor·i·cal □ [kætɪ'gɒrɪkl] kategorisch; ~**go·ry** ['kætɪgɔrɪ] Kategorie *f*.

ca·ter ['keɪtə]: ~ *for* Speisen u. Getränke liefern für; *fig.* sorgen für.

cat·er·pil·lar ['kætəpɪlə] *zo.* Raupe *f*; *TM* Raupenfahrzeug *n*; ~ *tractor TM* Raupenschlepper *m*.

cat·gut ['kætɡʌt] Darmsaite *f*.

ca·the·dral [kə'θiːdrəl] Dom *m*, Kathedrale *f*.

Cath·o·lic ['kæθəlɪk] **1.** katholisch; **2.** Katholik(in).

cat·kin ⚘ ['kætkɪn] Kätzchen *n*.

cat|tle ['kætl] Vieh *n*; ~**ty** F ['kætɪ] (*-ier, iest*) boshaft, gehässig.

caught [kɔːt] *pret. u. p.p. von catch* 2.

caul·dron ['kɔːldrən] großer Kessel.

cau·li·flow·er ⚘ ['kɒlɪflaʊə] Blumenkohl *m*.

caus·al □ ['kɔːzl] ursächlich.

cause [kɔːz] **1.** Ursache *f*; Grund *m*; ⚖ Klagegrund *m*; ⚖ Fall *m*, Sache *f*, Angelegenheit *f*, Sache *f*; **2.** verursachen; veranlassen; ~**less** □ [~zlɪs] grundlos.

cause·way ['kɔːzweɪ] Damm *m*.

caus|tic ['kɔːstɪk] (~*ally*) ätzend; *fig.* beißend, scharf.

cau|tion ['kɔːʃn] **1.** Vorsicht *f*; Warnung *f*; Verwarnung *f*; △ *nicht Kaution*; **2.** warnen; verwarnen; ⚖ zu belehren.

cau·tious □ ['kɔːʃəs] behutsam, vorsichtig; ~**ness** [~nɪs] Behutsamkeit *f*, Vorsicht *f*.

cav·al·ry *bsd. hist.* ✗ ['kævlrɪ] Kavallerie *f*.

cave [keɪv] **1.** Höhle *f*; **2.** *v/i.* ~ *in* einstürzen; klein beigeben.

cav·ern ['kævən] (große) Höhle; ~**ous** *fig.* [~əs] hohl.

cav·i·ty ['kævətɪ] Höhle *f*; Loch *n*.

caw [kɔː] **1.** krächzen; **2.** Krächzen *n*.

cease [siːs] *v/i.* aufhören, zu Ende gehen; *v/t.* aufhören (*to do, doing* zu tun); ~**fire** ✗ ['siːsfaɪə] Feuereinstellung *f*; Waffenruhe *f*; ~**less** □ [~lɪs] unaufhörlich.

cede [siːd] abtreten, überlassen.

ceil·ing ['siːlɪŋ] (Zimmer-)Decke *f*; *fig.* Höchstgrenze *f*; ~ *price* Höchstpreis *m*.

cel·e|brate ['selɪbreɪt] feiern; ~**brated** gefeiert, berühmt (*for* für, wegen); ~**bra·tion** [selɪ'breɪʃn] Feier *f*.

ce·leb·ri·ty [sɪ'lebrətɪ] Berühmtheit *f*.

ce·ler·i·ty [sɪ'lerətɪ] Geschwindigkeit *f*.

cel·er·y ⚘ ['selərɪ] Sellerie *m, f*.

ce·les·tial □ [sɪ'lestjəl] himmlisch.

cel·i·ba·cy ['selɪbəsɪ] Ehelosigkeit *f*.

cell [sel] Zelle *f*; ⚡ *a.* Element *n*.

cel·lar ['selə] Keller *m*.

cel|list ♪ ['tʃelɪst] Cellist(in); ~**lo** ♪ [~əʊ] (*pl. -los*) (Violon)Cello *n*.

cel·lo·phane *TM* ['seləʊfeɪn] Zellophan *n*.

cel·lu·lar ['seljʊlə] Zell(en)...

Cel·tic ['keltɪk] keltisch.

ce·ment [sɪ'ment] **1.** Zement *m*; Kitt *m*; **2.** zementieren; (ver)kitten.

cem·e·tery ['semɪtrɪ] Friedhof *m*.

cen|sor ['sensə] **1.** Zensor *m*; **2.** zensieren; ~**ship** [~ʃɪp] Zensur *f*.

cen·sure ['senʃə] **1.** Tadel *m*, Verweis *m*; △ *nicht Zensur*; **2.** tadeln.

cen·sus ['sensəs] Volkszählung *f*.

cent [sent] Hundert *n*; *Am.* Cent *m* (= $^{1}/_{100}$ *Dollar*); *per* ~ Prozent *n*.

cen·te·na·ry [sen'tiːnərɪ] Hundertjahrfeier *f*, hundertjähriges Jubiläum.

cen·ten·ni·al [sen'tenjəl] **1.** hundertjährig; **2.** *Am.* = *centenary*.

cen·ter *Am.* ['sentə] = *centre*.

cen·ti|grade ['sentɪɡreɪd]: *10 degrees* ~ 10 Grad Celsius; ~**me·tre**, *Am.* ~**me·ter** Zentimeter *m, n*; ~**pede** *zo.* [~piːd] Tausendfüß(l)er *m*.

cen·tral □ ['sentrəl] zentral; Haupt..., Zentral...; Mittel...; ~ *heating* Zentralheizung *f*; ~**ize** [~aɪz] zentralisieren.

cen·tre, *Am.* **-ter** ['sentə] **1.** Zentrum *n*, Mittelpunkt *m*; ~ *of gravity phys.* Schwerpunkt *m*; **2.** (sich) konzentrieren; zentrieren.

cen·tu·ry ['sentʃʊrɪ] Jahrhundert *n*.

ce·ram·ics [sɪ'ræmɪks] *pl.* Keramik *f*, keramische Erzeugnisse *pl.*

ce·re·al ['sɪərɪəl] **1.** Getreide...; **2.** Getreide(pflanze) *n*; Getreideflok-

chapter

ken(gericht n) pl., Frühstückskost f (aus Getreide).

cer·e·bral anat. ['serɪbrəl] Gehirn...

cer·e·mo|ni·al [serɪ'məʊnjəl] 1. □ zeremoniell; 2. Zeremoniell n; **~ni·ous** □ [~jəs] zeremoniell; förmlich; **~ny** ['serɪmənɪ] Zeremonie f; Feier(lichkeit) f; Förmlichkeit(en pl.) f.

cer·tain □ ['sɜ:tn] sicher, gewiß; zuverlässig; bestimmt; gewisse(r, -s); **~ly** [~lɪ] sicher, gewiß; in Antworten: sicherlich, bestimmt, natürlich; **~ty** [~tɪ] Sicherheit f, Bestimmtheit f, Gewißheit f.

cer|tif·i·cate 1. [sə'tɪfɪkət] Zeugnis n; Bescheinigung f; ~ of birth Geburtsurkunde f; General ♀ of Education advanced level (A level) Brt. Schule: etwa Abitur(zeugnis) n; General ♀ of Education ordinary level (O level) Schule: etwa mittlere Reife; medical ~ ärztliches Attest; 2. [~keɪt] bescheinigen; **~ti·fy** ['sɜ:tɪfaɪ] bescheinigen; beglaubigen.

cer·ti·tude ['sɜ:tɪtju:d] Sicherheit f, Bestimmtheit f, Gewißheit f.

ces·sa·tion [se'seɪʃn] Aufhören n.

chafe [tʃeɪf] v/t. (auf)scheuern, wund scheuern; ärgern; v/i. sich aufscheuern od. wund scheuern; scheuern; sich ärgern.

chaff [tʃɑːf] 1. Spreu f; Häcksel n; F Neckerei f; 2. F necken.

chaf·finch zo. ['tʃæfɪntʃ] Buchfink m.

chag·rin ['ʃægrɪn] 1. Ärger m; 2. ärgern.

chain [tʃeɪn] 1. Kette f; fig. Fessel f; ~ reaction Kettenreaktion f; ~ smoke Kette rauchen; ~ smoker Kettenraucher m; ~ store Kettenladen m; 2. (an)ketten; fesseln.

chair [tʃeə] Stuhl m; Lehrstuhl m; Vorsitz m; be in the ~ den Vorsitz führen; ~ lift ['tʃeəlɪft] Sessellift m; **~man** (pl. -men) Vorsitzende(r) m, Präsident m; **~man·ship** [~ʃɪp] Vorsitz m; **~wom·an** (pl. -women) Vorsitzende f.

chal·ice ['tʃælɪs] Kelch m.

chalk [tʃɔːk] 1. Kreide f; 2. mit Kreide schreiben od. zeichnen; ~ up Sieg verbuchen.

chal·lenge ['tʃælɪndʒ] 1. Herausforderung f; ✗ Anruf m; bsd. ⚖ Ablehnung f; 2. herausfordern; anrufen; ablehnen; anzweifeln.

cham·ber ['tʃeɪmbə] parl., zo., ⚘, ⊕, Kammer f; ~s pl. Geschäfts-

räume pl.; **~maid** Zimmermädchen n.

cham·ois ['ʃæmwɑ:] Gemse f; a. ~ leather [mst. 'ʃæmɪleðə] Wildleder n.

champ F [tʃæmp] = champion (Sport).

cham·pagne [ʃæm'peɪn] Champagner m.

cham·pi·on ['tʃæmpjən] 1. Verfechter m, Fürsprecher m; Sport: Sieger m; Meister m; 2. verfechten, eintreten für, verteidigen; 3. Meister...; **~ship** Sport: Meisterschaft f.

chance [tʃɑːns] 1. Zufall m; Schicksal n; Risiko n; Chance f, (günstige) Gelegenheit; Aussicht f (of auf acc.); Möglichkeit f; by ~ zufällig; take a ~ es darauf ankommen lassen; take no ~s nichts riskieren (wollen); 2. zufällig; 3. v/i. (unerwartet) eintreten od. geschehen; I ~d to meet her zufällig traf ich sie; v/t. riskieren.

chan·cel·lor ['tʃɑːnsələ] Kanzler m.

chan·de·lier [ʃændə'lɪə] Kronleuchter m.

change [tʃeɪndʒ] 1. Veränderung f, Wechsel m; Abwechslung f; Wechselgeld n; Kleingeld n; for a ~ zur Abwechslung; ~ for the better (worse) Besserung f (Verschlechterung f); 2. v/t. (ver)ändern, umändern; (aus)wechseln; (aus-, ver)tauschen (for gegen); mot. ⊕ schalten; ~ over umschalten; umstellen; ~ trains umsteigen; v/i. sich (ver)ändern, wechseln; sich umziehen; **~a·ble** □ ['tʃeɪndʒəbl] veränderlich; **~less** □ [~lɪs] unveränderlich; **~o·ver** Umstellung f.

chan·nel ['tʃænl] 1. Kanal m; Flußbett n; Rinne f; (Fernseh- etc.)Kanal m, (-)Programm n; fig. Kanal m, Weg m; 2. (bsd. Brt. -ll-; Am. -l-) furchen; aushöhlen; fig. lenken.

chant [tʃɑːnt] 1. (Kirchen)Gesang m; Singsang m; 2. singen; in Sprechchören rufen; Sprechchöre anstimmen.

cha·os ['keɪɒs] Chaos n.

chap[1] [tʃæp] 1. Riß m, Sprung m; 2. (-pp-) rissig machen od. werden.

chap[2] [~] Bursche m, Kerl m, Junge m.

chap[3] [~] Kinnbacke(n m) f; Maul n.

chap·el ['tʃæpl] Kapelle f; Gottesdienst m.

chap·lain ['tʃæplɪn] Kaplan m.

chap·ter ['tʃæptə] Kapitel n.

char [tʃɑː] (*-rr-*) verkohlen.

char·ac·ter ['kærəktə] Charakter *m*; Eigenschaft *f*; Schrift(zeichen *n*) *f*; Persönlichkeit *f*; *Roman etc.*: Figur *f*, Gestalt *f*; *thea.* Rolle *f*; (*bsd.* guter) Ruf; Zeugnis *n*; **~·is·tic** [kærəktə'rɪs-tɪk] **1.** (*~ally*) charakteristisch (of für); **2.** Kennzeichen *n*; **~·ize** ['kærəktəraɪz] charakterisieren.

char·coal ['tʃɑːkəʊl] Holzkohle *f*.

charge [tʃɑːdʒ] **1.** Ladung *f*; (Spreng)Ladung *f*; *bsd. fig.* Last *f*; Verantwortung *f*; Aufsicht *f*, Leitung *f*; Obhut *f*; Schützling *m*; ✕ Angriff *m*; Beschuldigung *f*, ⚖ *a.* (Punkt *m* der) Anklage *f*; Preis *m*, Kosten *pl.*; Gebühr *f*; *free of ~* kostenlos; *be in ~ of* verantwortlich sein für; *have ~ of* in Obhut *od.* Verwahrung haben, betreuen; *take ~ die Leitung etc.* übernehmen, die Sache in die Hand nehmen; **2.** *v/t.* laden, beladen, belasten; beauftragen; belehren; ⚖ beschuldigen, anklagen (*with gen.*); in Rechnung stellen; berechnen, (als Preis) fordern; ✕ angreifen; *v/i.* stürmen; *~ at s.o.* auf j-n losgehen.

char·i·ot *poet. od. hist.* ['tʃærɪət] Streit-, Triumphwagen *m*.

char·i·ta·ble □ ['tʃærɪtəbl] mild (-tätig), wohltätig.

char·i·ty ['tʃærətɪ] Nächstenliebe *f*; Wohltätigkeit *f*; Güte *f*; Nachsicht *f*; milde Gabe.

char·la·tan ['ʃɑːlətən] Scharlatan *m*; Quacksalber *m*, Kurpfuscher *m*.

charm [tʃɑːm] **1.** Zauber *m*; Charme *m*, Reiz *m*; Talisman *m*, Amulett *n*; **2.** bezaubern, entzücken; **~·ing** □ ['tʃɑːmɪŋ] charmant, bezaubernd.

chart [tʃɑːt] **1.** ⚓ Seekarte *f*; Tabelle *f*; *~s pl.* Charts *pl.*, Hitliste(n *pl.*) *f*; **2.** auf e-r Karte einzeichnen.

char·ter ['tʃɑːtə] **1.** Urkunde *f*, Freibrief *m*; Chartern *n*; **2.** konzessionieren; ⚓, ✈ chartern, mieten; **~ flight** Charterflug *m*.

char·wom·an ['tʃɑːwʊmən] (*pl. -women*) Putzfrau *f*, Raumpflegerin *f*.

chase [tʃeɪs] **1.** Jagd *f*; Verfolgung *f*; gejagtes Wild; **2.** jagen, hetzen; Jagd machen auf (*acc.*); rasen, rennen.

chas·m ['kæzəm] Kluft *f*, Abgrund *m* (*a. fig.*); Riß *m*, Spalte *f*.

chaste □ [tʃeɪst] rein, keusch, unschuldig; schlicht (*Stil*).

chas·tise [tʃæs'taɪz] züchtigen.

chas·ti·ty ['tʃæstətɪ] Keuschheit *f*.

chat [tʃæt] **1.** Geplauder *n*, Schwätzchen *n*, Plauderei *f*; **2.** plaudern.

chat·tels ['tʃætlz] *pl. mst goods and ~* bewegliches Eigentum.

chat·ter ['tʃætə] **1.** plappern; schnattern; klappern; **2.** Geplapper *n*; Klappern *n*; **~·box** F Plappermaul *n*; **~·er** [~rə] Schwätzer(in).

chat·ty ['tʃætɪ] (*-ier, -iest*) gesprächig.

chauf·feur ['ʃəʊfə] Chauffeur *m*.

chau·vi F ['ʃəʊvɪ] Chauvi *m*; **~·vin·ist** [~nɪst] Chauvinist *m*.

cheap □ [tʃiːp] billig; *fig.* schäbig, gemein; **~·en** ['tʃiːpən] (sich) verbilligen; *fig.* herabsetzen.

cheat [tʃiːt] **1.** Betrug *m*, Schwindel *m*; Betrüger(in); **2.** betrügen.

check [tʃek] **1.** Schach(stellung *f*) *n*; Hemmnis *n*, Hindernis *n* (on für); Einhalt *m*; Kontrolle *f* (on gen.); Kontrollabschnitt *m*, -schein *m*; *Am.* Gepäckschein *m*; *Am.* Garderobenmarke *f*; *Am. econ. = cheque*; *Am.* Rechnung *f* (*im Restaurant od. Kaufhaus*); karierter Stoff; **2.** *v/i.* an-, innehalten; *Am.* ⚓ in Schach ausstellen; *~ in* sich (*in e-m Hotel*) anmelden; einstempeln; ✈ einchecken; *~ out* (*aus e-m Hotel*) abreisen; ausstempeln; *~ up* (*on*) F (*e-e Sache*) nachprüfen, (*e-e Sache, j-n*) überprüfen; *v/t.* hemmen, hindern, aufhalten; zurückhalten; kontrollieren, über-, nachprüfen; *Am. auf e-r Liste* abhaken; *Am. Kleider* in der Garderobe abgeben; *Am.* Gepäck aufgeben; **~ card** *Am. econ.* ['tʃekkɑːd] Scheckkarte *f*; **~ed** [~t] kariert; **~ers** *Am.* [~əz] *sg.* Damespiel *n*; **~ in** Anmeldung *f* (*in e-m Hotel*); Einstempeln *n*; ✈ Einchecken *n*; *~ counter od. desk* ✈ Abfertigungsschalter *m*; **~ ing ac·count** *Am. econ.* Girokonto *n*; **~·list** Check-, Kontroll-, Vergleichsliste *f*; **~·mate 1.** (Schach)Matt *n*; **2.** (schach)matt setzen; **~·out** Abreise *f* (*aus e-m Hotel*); Ausstempeln *n*; *a. ~ counter* Kasse *f* (*bsd. im Supermarkt*); **~·point** Kontrollpunkt *m*; **~·room** *Am.* Garderobe *f*; Gepäckaufbewahrung *f*; **~ up** Überprüfung *f*, Kontrolle *f*; ✈ Check-up *m*, (umfangreiche) Vorsorgeuntersuchung *f*.

cheek [tʃiːk] Backe *f*, Wange *f*;

chloroform

Unverschämtheit f; **~·y** □ F ['tʃi:kɪ] (-ier, -iest) frech.

cheer [tʃɪə] 1. Stimmung f, Fröhlichkeit f; Hoch(ruf m) n, Beifall(sruf) m; **~s!** prost!; *three* **~s!** dreimal hoch!; 2. v/t. mit Beifall begrüßen; a. **~** *on* anspornen; a. **~** *up* aufheitern; v/i. hoch rufen, jubeln; a. **~** *up* Mut fassen; **~** *up!* Kopf hoch!; **~·ful** □ ['tʃɪəfl] vergnügt; **~·i·o** *int.* F [ˌʌrɪˈəʊ] mach's gut!, tschüs!; **~·less** □ [ˌʌlɪs] freudlos; **~·y** □ [ˌʌrɪ] (-ier, -iest) vergnügt.

cheese [tʃiːz] Käse m.

chee·tah zo. ['tʃiːtə] Gepard m.

chef [ʃef] Küchenchef m; Koch m; △ *nicht* Chef.

chem·i·cal ['kemɪkl] 1. □ chemisch; 2. Chemikalie f.

che·mise [ʃəˈmiːz] (Damen)Hemd n.

chem|ist ['kemɪst] Chemiker(in); Apotheker(in); Drogist(in); **~'s** *shop* Apotheke f; Drogerie f; **~·is·try** [ˌʌrɪ] Chemie f.

cheque *Brt. econ.* [tʃek] (*Am. check*) Scheck m; *crossed* **~** Verrechnungsscheck m; **~ ac·count** *Brt. econ.* Girokonto n; **~ card** *Brt. econ.* Scheckkarte f.

chequ·er *Brt.* ['tʃekə] Karomuster n.

cher·ish ['tʃerɪʃ] *Andenken* a·n etc. hochhalten; hegen, pflegen.

cher·ry 🌸 ['tʃerɪ] Kirsche f.

chess [tʃes] Schach(spiel) n; *a game of* **~** e-e Partie Schach; **~·board** ['tʃesbɔːd] Schachbrett n; **~·man** (*pl. -men*), **~ piece** Schachfigur f.

chest [tʃest] Kiste f, Kasten m, Truhe f; *anat.* Brustkasten m; *get s.th. off one's* **~** F et. od. von der Seele reden; **~** *of drawers* Kommode f.

chest·nut ['tʃesnʌt] 1. 🌰 Kastanie f; 2. kastanienbraun.

chew [tʃuː] kauen; nachsinnen, grübeln (*on, over* über *acc.*); **~·ing·gum** ['tʃuːɪŋɡʌm] Kaugummi m.

chick [tʃɪk] Küken n, junger Vogel; F Biene f, Puppe f (*Mädchen*).

chick·en ['tʃɪkɪn] Huhn n; Küken n; (*Brat*)Hähnchen n, (-)Hühnchen n; **~·heart·ed** furchtsam, feige; **~·pox** 🔹 [ˌʌpɒks] Windpocken pl.

chic·o·ry 🌸 ['tʃɪkərɪ] Chicorée f, m.

chief [tʃiːf] 1. □ oberste(r, -s), Ober..., Haupt...; wichtigste(r, -s); *clerk* Bürovorsteher m; 2. Oberhaupt n, Chef m; Häuptling m; *...-in-chief* Ober...; **~·ly** ['tʃiːflɪ]

hauptsächlich; **~·tain** [ˌʌtən] Häuptling m.

chil·blain ['tʃɪlbleɪn] Frostbeule f.

child [tʃaɪld] (*pl. children*) Kind n; *from a* **~** von Kindheit an; *with* **~** schwanger; **~ a·buse** 🔹 Kindesmißhandlung f; **~·birth** [tʃaɪldbɜːθ] Geburt f, Niederkunft f; **~·hood** [ˌʌhʊd] Kindheit f; **~·ish** □ [ˌʌʃ] kindisch; kindlich; **~·like** kindlich; **~·mind·er** *Brt.* [ˌʌmaɪndə] Tagesmutter f; **chil·dren** ['tʃɪldrən] *pl. v.* child.

chill [tʃɪl] 1. eisig, frostig; 2. Frost m, Kälte f; 🔹 Fieberschauer m; Erkältung f; 3. abkühlen; *j-n* frösteln lassen; **~ed** gekühlt; **~·y** ['tʃɪlɪ] (-ier, -iest) kalt, frostig.

chime [tʃaɪm] 1. Glockenspiel n; Geläut n; *fig.* Einklang m; 2. läuten; **~** *in* sich (ins Gespräch) einmischen.

chim·ney ['tʃɪmnɪ] Schornstein m; Rauchfang m; (Lampen)Zylinder m; **~·sweep** Schornsteinfeger m.

chimp zo. [tʃɪmp], **chim·pan·zee** zo. [ˌʌənˈziː] Schimpanse m.

chin [tʃɪn] 1. Kinn n; (*keep your*) **~** *up!* Kopf hoch!, halte die Ohren steif!

chi·na ['tʃaɪnə] Porzellan n.

Chi·nese [tʃaɪˈniːz] 1. chinesisch; 2. Chinese m, -in f; *ling.* Chinesisch n; *the* **~** *pl.* die Chinesen pl.

chink [tʃɪŋk] Ritz m, Spalt m.

chip [tʃɪp] 1. Splitter m, Span m, Schnitzel n, m ; dünne Scheibe; Spielmarke f; *Computer:* Chip m; *have a* **~** *on one's shoulder* F sich ständig angegriffen fühlen; e-n Komplex haben (*about* wegen); **~s** *pl. Brt.* Pommes frites *pl.*; *Am.* (Kartoffel)Chips *pl.*; 2. (-*pp-*) v/t. schnitzeln; an-, abschlagen; v/i. abbröckeln; **~·munk** zo. ['tʃɪpmʌŋk] nordamerikanisches gestreiftes Eichhörnchen.

chirp [tʃɜːp] 1. zirpen, zwitschern, piepsen; 2. Gezirp n, Zwitschern n, Piepsen n.

chis·el ['tʃɪzl] 1. Meißel m; 2. (*bsd. Brt. -ll-, Am. -l-*) meißeln.

chit-chat ['tʃɪttʃæt] Plauderei f.

chiv·al|rous □ ['ʃɪvlrəs] ritterlich; **~·ry** [ˌʌɪ] *hist.* Rittertum n; Ritterlichkeit f.

chive(s *pl.*) 🌸 [tʃaɪv(z)] Schnittlauch m.

chlo|ri·nate ['klɔːrɪneɪt] *Wasser etc.* chloren; **~·rine** 🔹 [ˌʌriːn] Chlor n; **chlor·o·form** ['klɒrəfɔːm]

chocolate

1. $\curvearrowright$, $\textit{\&}$ Chloroform n; 2. chloroformieren.

choc·o·late ['tʃɒkələt] Schokolade f; Praline f; ~s pl. Pralinen pl., Konfekt n.

choice [tʃɔɪs] 1. Wahl f; Auswahl f; 2. □ auserlesen, ausgesucht, vorzüglich.

choir ['kwaɪə] Chor m.

choke [tʃəʊk] 1. v/t. (er)würgen, (a. v/i.) ersticken; ~ *back* Ärger etc. unterdrücken, Tränen zurückhalten; ~ *down* hinunterwürgen; a. ~ *up* verstopfen; 2. mot. Choke m, Luftklappe f.

choose [tʃuːz] (*chose, chosen*) (aus-) wählen, aussuchen; ~ *to do* vorziehen zu tun.

chop [tʃɒp] 1. Hieb m, Schlag m; Kotelett n; 2. (*-pp-*) v/t. hauen, hacken, zerhacken; ~ *down* fällen; v/i. hacken; ~**per** ['tʃɒpə] Hackmesser n, -beil n; F Hubschrauber m; Am. sl. Maschinengewehr n; ~**py** [~ɪ] (*-ier, -iest*) unruhig (*See*); ~**stick** Eßstäbchen n.

cho·ral □ ['kɔːrəl] Chor...; ~**(e)** ♪ [kɒ'rɑːl] Choral m.

chord ♪ [kɔːd] Saite f; Akkord m.

chore Am. [tʃɔː] schwierige od. unangenehme Aufgabe; mst ~s pl. Hausarbeit f.

cho·rus ['kɔːrəs] Chor m; Kehrreim m, Refrain m; Tanzgruppe f (e-r *Revue*).

chose [tʃəʊz] pret. von choose; **chosen** ['tʃəʊzn] p.p. von choose.

Christ [kraɪst] Christus m; ⚠ nicht der Christ.

chris·ten ['krɪsn] taufen; ~**ing** [~ɪŋ] Taufe f; attr. Tauf...

Chris·tian ['krɪstjən] 1. christlich; ~ *name* Vorname m; 2. Christ(in); ~**ti·an·i·ty** [krɪstɪˈænətɪ] Christentum n.

Christ·mas ['krɪsməs] Weihnachten n u. pl.; at ~ zu Weihnachten; ~ **Day** der erste Weihnachtsfeiertag; ~ **Eve** Heiliger Abend.

chrome [krəʊm] Chrom n; **chro·mi·um** $\curvearrowright$ ['krəʊmjəm] Chrom n; ~**plated** verchromt.

chron·ic ['krɒnɪk] (*~ally*) chronisch (mst $\textit{\&}$); dauernd; ~**i·cle** [~l] 1. Chronik f; 2. aufzeichnen.

chron·o·log·i·cal □ [krɒnəˈlɒdʒɪkl] chronologisch; **chro·nol·o·gy** [krəˈnɒlədʒɪ] Zeitrechnung f; Zeitfolge f.

chub·by F ['tʃʌbɪ] (*-ier, -iest*) rundlich; pausbäckig.

chuck F [tʃʌk] werfen, schmeißen; ~ *out* j-n rausschmeißen; et. wegschmeißen; ~ *up Job* etc. hinschmeißen.

chuck·le ['tʃʌkl] 1. ~ (*to o.s.*) (still-vergnügt) in sich hineinlachen; 2. leises Lachen.

chum F [tʃʌm] Kamerad m, Kumpel m; ~**my** F ['tʃʌmɪ] (*-ier, -iest*) dick befreundet.

chump [tʃʌmp] Holzklotz m; F Trottel m.

chunk [tʃʌnk] Klotz m, Klumpen m.

church [tʃɜːtʃ] Kirche f; attr. Kirch(en)...; ~ *service* Gottesdienst m; ~**war·den** ['tʃɜːˈwɔːdn] Kirchenvorsteher m; ~**yard** Kirchhof m.

churl·ish □ ['tʃɜːlɪʃ] grob, flegelhaft.

churn [tʃɜːn] 1. Butterfaß n; 2. buttern; aufwühlen.

chute [ʃuːt] Stromschnelle f; Rutsche f, Rutschbahn f; F Fallschirm m.

ci·der ['saɪdə] (*Am. hard* ~) Apfelwein m; (*sweet*) ~ Am. Apfelmost m, -saft m.

ci·gar [sɪˈɡɑː] Zigarre f.

cig·a·rette, Am. a. **-ret** [sɪɡəˈret] Zigarette f.

cinch F [sɪntʃ] todsichere Sache.

cin·der ['sɪndə] Schlacke f; ~s pl. Asche f; **Cin·de·rel·la** [sɪndəˈrelə] Aschenbrödel n, -puttel n; ~**path**, ~**track** Sport: Aschenbahn f.

cin·e·cam·e·ra ['sɪnɪkæmərə] (Schmal)Filmkamera f; ~**film** Schmalfilm m.

cin·e·ma Brt. ['sɪnəmə] Kino n; Film m.

cin·na·mon ['sɪnəmən] Zimt m.

ci·pher ['saɪfə] Ziffer f; Null f (a. fig.); Geheimschrift f, Chiffre f.

cir·cle ['sɜːkl] 1. Kreis m; Bekanntenetc. Kreis m; fig. Kreislauf m; thea. Rang m; Ring m; 2. (um)kreisen.

cir·cuit ['sɜːkɪt] Kreislauf m; $\textit{\&}$ Stromkreis m; Rundreise f; Sport: Zirkus m; short ~, $\textit{\&}$ Kurzschluß m; ~**cu·i·tous** □ [səˈkjuːɪtəs] weitschweifig; ~ *route* Umweg m.

cir·cu·lar ['sɜːkjʊlə] 1. □ kreisförmig; Kreis...; ~ *letter* Rundschreiben n; 2. Rundschreiben n, Umlauf m.

cir·cu·late ['sɜːkjʊleɪt] v/i. umlaufen, zirkulieren; v/t. in Umlauf setzen;

~·lat·ing [~ɪŋ]: ~ *library* Leihbücherei *f*; **~·la·tion** [sɜːkjuˈleɪʃn] Zirkulation *f*, Kreislauf *m*; (Blut)Kreislauf *m*; *fig.* Umlauf *m*; Verbreitung *f*; Auflage(nhöhe) *f* (*e-r Zeitung*, *e-s Buches etc.*).

cir·cum-... [ˈsɜːkəm] (her)um; **~·fer·ence** [səˈkʌmfərəns] (Kreis)Umfang *m*, Peripherie *f*; **~·navi·gate** [sɜːkəmˈnævɪgeɪt] umschiffen; **~scribe** [ˈsɜːkəmskraɪb] ⩑ umschreiben; *fig.* begrenzen; **~spect** □ [~spekt] um-, vorsichtig; **~stance** [~stəns] Umstand *m*, Einzelheit *f*; **~s** *pl.* a. Verhältnisse *pl.*; *in od. under no ~s* unter keinen Umständen, auf keinen Fall; *in od. under the ~s* unter diesen Umständen; **~stan·tial** □ [sɜːkəmˈstænʃl] umständlich; *~ evidence* ⚖ Indizien(beweis *m*) *pl.*; **~vent** [~ˈvent] überlisten; vereiteln.

cir·cus [ˈsɜːkəs] Zirkus *m*; (runder) Platz.

cis·tern [ˈsɪstən] Wasserbehälter *m*; Spülkasten *m* (*in der Toilette*).

ci·ta·tion [saɪˈteɪʃn] ⚖ Vorladung *f*; Anführung *f*, Zitat *n*; **cite** [saɪt] ⚖ vorladen; anführen; zitieren.

cit·i·zen [ˈsɪtɪzn] (Staats)Bürger(in); Städter(in); **~ship** [~ʃɪp] Bürgerrecht *n*; Staatsbürgerschaft *f*.

cit·y [ˈsɪtɪ] **1.** (Groß)Stadt *f*; *the ⊊ die* (Londoner) City; **2.** städtisch, Stadt...; *~ centre Brt.* Innenstadt *f*, City *f*; *~ council(l)or* Stadtrat(smitglied *n*) *m*; *~ editor Am.* Lokalredakteur *m*; *Brt.* Wirtschaftsredakteur *m*; *~ hall* Rathaus *n*; *bsd. Am.* Stadtverwaltung *f*.

civ·ic [ˈsɪvɪk] (staats)bürgerlich; städtisch; **~s** *sg.* Staatsbürgerkunde *f*.

civ·il [ˈsɪvl] staatlich, Staats...; (staats)bürgerlich; Bürger...; Zivil...; ⚖ zivilrechtlich; höflich; *~ rights pl.* (Staats)Bürgerrechte *pl.*; *~ rights activist* Bürgerrechtler(in); *~ rights movement* Bürgerrechtsbewegung *f*; *~ servant* Staatsbeamte(r) *m*; *~ service* Staatsdienst *m*, öffentlicher Dienst *m*; Beamtenschaft *f*; *~ war* Bürgerkrieg *m*.

ci·vil·ian [sɪˈvɪljən] Zivilist *m*; **~·ty** [~ˈlətɪ] Höflichkeit *f*.

civ·i·li·za·tion [sɪvɪlaɪˈzeɪʃn] Zivilisation *f*, Kultur *f*; **~ze** [ˈsɪvɪlaɪz] zivilisieren.

clad [klæd] **1.** *pret. u. p.p. von* clothe; **2.** *adj.* gekleidet.

claim [kleɪm] **1.** Anspruch *m*; Anrecht *n* (*to auf acc.*); Forderung *f*; *Am.* Stück *n* Staatsland; *Am.* Claim *m*; **2.** beanspruchen; fordern; behaupten; **clai·mant** [ˈkleɪmənt] Ansprucherhebende(r *m*) *f*.

clair·voy·ant [kleəˈvɔɪənt] Hellseher(in).

clam·ber [ˈklæmbə] klettern.

clam·my □ [ˈklæmɪ] (-ier, -iest) feuchtkalt, klamm.

clam·o(u)r [ˈklæmə] **1.** Geschrei *n*, Lärm *m*; **2.** schreien (*for* nach).

clamp ⊕ [klæmp] **1.** Klammer *f*; **2.** mit Klammer(n) befestigen.

clan [klæn] Clan *m*, Sippe *f* (*a. fig.*).

clan·des·tine □ [klænˈdestɪn] heimlich, Geheim...

clang [klæŋ] **1.** Klang *m*, Geklirr *n*; **2.** schallen; klirren (lassen).

clank [klæŋk] **1.** Gerassel *n*, Geklirr *n*; **2.** rasseln *od.* klirren (mit).

clap [klæp] **1.** Klatschen *n*, Schlag *m*, Klaps *m*; **2.** (-pp-) schlagen *od.* klatschen (mit).

clar·et [ˈklærət] roter Bordeaux; Rotwein *m*; Weinrot *n*; *sl.* Blut *n*.

clar·i·fy [ˈklærɪfaɪ] *v/t.* (auf)klären, erhellen, klarstellen; *v/i.* sich (auf)klären, klar werden.

clar·i·net [klærɪˈnet] Klarinette *f*.

clar·i·ty [ˈklærətɪ] Klarheit *f*.

clash [klæʃ] **1.** Geklirr *n*; Zusammenstoß *m*; Widerstreit *m*, Konflikt *m*; **2.** klirren (mit); zusammenstoßen; nicht zusammenpassen *od.* harmonieren.

clasp [klɑːsp] **1.** Haken *m*, Klammer *f*; Schnalle *f*, Spange *f*; *fig.* Umklammerung *f*, Umarmung *f*; **2.** ein-, zuhaken; *fig.* umklammern, umfassen; **~·knife** [ˈklɑːspnaɪf] Taschenmesser *n*.

class [klɑːs] **1.** Klasse *f*; (Bevölkerungs)Schicht *f*; (Schul)Klasse *f*; (Unterrichts)Stunde *f*; Kurs *m*; *Am. univ.* Studenten *pl.* *e-s Jahrgangs*; *~mate* Mitschüler(in); *~room* Klassenzimmer *n*; **2.** (in Klassen) einteilen, einordnen.

clas·sic [ˈklæsɪk] **1.** Klassiker *m*; **2.** *adj.* (*~ally*) erstklassig; klassisch; **~·si·cal** □ [~kl] klassisch.

clas·si·fi·ca·tion [klæsɪfɪˈkeɪʃn] Klassifizierung *f*, Einteilung *f*; **~fy** [ˈklæsɪfaɪ] klassifizieren, einstufen.

clat·ter ['klætə] 1. Geklapper *n*; 2. klappern (mit).

clause [klɔːz] *gr* Klausel *f*, Bestimmung *f*; *gr.* Satz(teil *n*) *m*.

claw [klɔː] 1. Klaue *f*, Kralle *f*, Pfote *f*; (*Krebs*)Schere *f*; 2. (zer)kratzen; umkrallen, packen.

clay [kleɪ] Ton *m*; Erde *f*.

clean [kliːn] 1. *adj.* □ rein; sauber, glatt, eben; *sl.* clean (*nicht mehr drogenabhängig*); 2. *adv.* völlig, ganz u. gar; 3. reinigen, säubern, putzen; ~ out reinigen; ~ up gründlich reinigen; aufräumen; ~·er ['kliːnə] Reiniger *m*; Rein(e)machefrau *f*; *mst* ~s *pl.*, ~'s (chemische) Reinigung (*Geschäft*); ~·ing ['kliːnɪŋ] Reinigung *f*, Putzen *n*; *do the* ~ saubermachen, putzen; *spring-cleaning* Frühjahrsputz *m*; ~·li·ness ['klenlɪnɪs] Reinlichkeit *f*; ~·ly 1. *adv.* ['kliːnlɪ] rein; sauber; 2. *adj.* ['klenlɪ] (-*ier*, -*iest*) reinlich.

cleanse [klenz] reinigen, säubern; **cleans·er** ['klenzə] Reinigungsmittel *n*.

clear [klɪə] 1. □ klar; hell; rein; frei (*of* von); ganz, voll; *econ.* rein, netto; 2. *v/t.* reinigen (*of, from* von); *Wald* lichten, roden; wegräumen (*a.* ~ *away*); *Tisch* abräumen; räumen, leeren; *Hindernis* nehmen; *econ.* verzollen; ✝ freisprechen; ~ *out* säubern; ausräumen; *a.* wegtun; ~ *up* aufräumen; aufklären; *v/i.* aufklaren (*Wetter*); ~ *out* ✝ abhauen; ~ *up* aufräumen; sich aufhellen, aufklaren (*Wetter*); ~·ance ['klɪərəns] Räumung *f*; Rodung *f*; ⊕ lichter Abstand; *econ.* Zollabfertigung *f*; Freigabe *f*; ⚓ Auslaufgenehmigung *f*; ~·ing [~rɪŋ] Aufklärung *f*; Lichtung *f*, Rodung *f*.

cleave [kliːv] (*cleaved od. cleft od. clove, cleaved od. cleft od. cloven*) spalten.

cleav·er ['kliːvə] Hackmesser *n*.

clef ♪ [klef] Schlüssel *m*.

cleft [kleft] 1. Spalt *m*, Spalte *f*; 2. *pret. u. p.p. von* cleave.

clem·en·cy ['klemənsɪ] Milde *f*, Gnade *f*; ~·t □ [~t] mild.

clench [klentʃ] *Lippen etc.* (fest) zusammenpressen; *Zähne* zusammenbeißen; *Faust* ballen.

cler·gy ['klɜːdʒɪ] Geistlichkeit *f*; ~·man (*pl.* -*men*) Geistliche(r) *m*.

cler·i·cal □ ['klerɪkl] geistlich; Schreib(er)...

clerk [klɑːk] Schriftführer(in); Sekretär(in); kaufmännische(r) Angestellte(r), (Büro- *etc.*) Angestellte(r *m*) *f*, (Bank-, Post)Beamt|e(r) *m*, -in *f*; *Am.* Verkäufer(in).

clev·er □ ['klevə] klug, gescheit; geschickt.

click [klɪk] 1. Klicken *n*, Knacken *n*; ⊕ Sperrhaken *m*, -klinke *f*; 2. klicken, knacken; zu-, einschnappen; *mit der Zunge* schnalzen.

cli·ent ['klaɪənt] ✝ Klient(in), Mandant(in); Kund|e *m*, -in *f*.

cliff [klɪf] Klippe *f*, Felsen *m*.

cli·mate ['klaɪmɪt] Klima *n*.

cli·max ['klaɪmæks] 1. *rhet.* Steigerung *f*; Gipfel *m*, Höhepunkt *m*, *physiol. a.* Orgasmus *m*; 2. (sich) steigern.

climb [klaɪm] klettern; (er-, be)steigen; ~·er ['klaɪmə] Kletterer *m*, Bergsteiger(in); *fig.* Aufsteiger *m*; ♣ Kletterpflanze *f*; ~·ing [~ɪŋ] Klettern *n*; *attr.* Kletter...

clinch [klɪntʃ] 1. ⊕ Vernietung *f*; *Boxen*: Clinch *m*; ✝ Umarmung *f*; 2. *v/t.* ⊕ vernieten; festmachen; (vollends) entscheiden; *v/i. Boxen*: clinchen.

cling [klɪŋ] (*clung*) (*to*) festhalten (an *dat.*), sich klammern (an *acc.*); sich (an)schmiegen (an *acc.*).

clin·ic ['klɪnɪk] Klinik *f*; ~·i·cal □ [~l] klinisch.

clink [klɪŋk] 1. Klirren *n*, Klingen *n*; 2. klingen *od.* klirren (lassen); klimpern mit.

clip¹ [klɪp] 1. Schneiden *n*; Schur *f*; ✝ (Faust)Schlag *m*; 2. (-*pp*-) (be)schneiden; ab-, ausschneiden; *Schafe etc.* scheren.

clip² [~] 1. Klipp *m*, Klammer *f*, Spange *f*; 2. (-*pp*-) *a.* ~ *on* befestigen, anklammern.

clip|per ['klɪpə]: (*a pair of*) ~s *pl.* (e-e) Haarschneide-, Schermaschine *f*; (*Nagel- etc.*) Schere *f*; ⚓ Klipper *m*; ✈ Clipper *m*; ~·pings [~ɪŋz] *pl.* Abfälle *pl.*, Schnitzel *pl.*; *bsd. Am.* (*Zeitungs- etc.*) Ausschnitte *pl.*

clit·o·ris *anat.* ['klɪtərɪs] Klitoris *f*.

cloak [kləʊk] 1. Mantel *m*; 2. *fig.* verhüllen; ~·room ['kləʊkrʊm] Garderobe *f*; *Brt.* Toilette *f*.

clock [klɒk] 1. (Wand-, Stand-Turm)Uhr *f*; 2. die Zeit (*e-s Läufers*) stoppen; ~ *in*, ~ *on* einstempeln; ~ *out*, ~ *off* ausstempeln; ~·wise ['klɒkwaɪz] im Uhrzeigersinn; **~work** Uhrwerk *n*; *like* ~ wie am Schnürchen.

clod [klɒd] (Erd)Klumpen *m*.

clog [klɒg] **1.** Klotz *m*; Holzschuh *m*, Pantine *f*; **2.** (*-gg-*) (be)hindern, hemmen; (sich) verstopfen; klumpig werden.

clois·ter ['klɔɪstə] Kreuzgang *m*; Kloster *n*.

close 1. *adj.* □ [kləʊs] knapp, kurz, geschlossen, *nur pred.*: zu; verborgen; verschwiegen; knapp; nah; eng; knapp, kurz, bündig; dicht; genau (*Übersetzung*); schwül; geizig, knaus(e)rig; *keep a ~ watch on* scharf im Auge behalten (*acc.*); ~ *fight* Handgemenge *n*; ~ *season* *hunt.* Schonzeit *f*; **2.** *adv.* eng, nahe, dicht; ~ *by*, ~ *to* ganz in der Nähe, nahe *od.* dicht bei; **3.** [kləʊz] Schluß *m*; (Ab)Schluß *m*; *come od.* *draw to a* ~ sich dem Ende nähern; [kləʊs] Einfriedung *f*; Hof *m*; **4.** [kləʊz] *v/t.* (ab-, ver-, zu)schließen; *Straße* (ab)sperren; *v/i.* (sich) schließen; *handgemein werden*; *mit Adverbien:* ~ *down* schließen; stillegen; stillgelegt werden; *Rundfunk*, *TV*: das Programm beenden, Sendeschluß haben; ~ *in* bedrohlich nahekommen; hereinbrechen (*Nacht*); kürzer werden (*Tage*); ~ *up* (ab-, ver-, zu)schließen; blockieren; aufschließen, -rücken; ~**d** geschlossen, *pred.* zu.

clos·et ['klɒzɪt] **1.** (Wand)Schrank *m*; △ *nicht* Klosett; **2.** *be* ~*ed with mit* *j-m* geheime Besprechungen führen.

close-up ['kləʊsʌp] *phot.*, *Film*: Großaufnahme *f*.

clos·ing-time ['kləʊzɪŋtaɪm] Laden-, Geschäftsschluß *m*; Polizeistunde *f* (*e-s Pubs*).

clot [klɒt] **1.** Klumpen *m*, Klümpchen *n*; *Brt.* F Trottel *m*; **2.** (*-tt-*) gerinnen; Klumpen bilden.

cloth [klɒθ] (*pl.* cloths [~θs, ~ðz]) Stoff *m*, Tuch *n*; Tischtuch *n*; *the* ~ der geistliche Stand; *lay the* ~ den Tisch decken; ~*-bound* in Leinen gebunden.

clothe [kləʊð] (*clothed od. clad*) (an-, be)kleiden; einkleiden.

clothes [kləʊðz] *pl.* Kleider *pl.*, Kleidung *f*; Wäsche *f*; ~**bas·ket** ['kləʊðzbɑːskɪt] Wäschekorb *m*; ~**horse** Wäscheständer *m*; ~**line** Wäscheleine *f*; ~**peg** *Brt.*, *Am.*

~**pin** Wäscheklammer *f*.

cloth·ing ['kləʊðɪŋ] (Be)Kleidung *f*.

cloud [klaʊd] **1.** Wolke *f* (*a. fig.*); Trübung *f*, Schatten *m*; **2.** (sich) bewölken (*a. fig.*); (sich) trüben; **~burst** ['klaʊdbɜːst] Wolkenbruch *m*; ~**less** □ [~lɪs] wolkenlos; ~**y** □ [~ɪ] (*-ier*, *-iest*) wolkig, bewölkt; Wolken...; trüb; unklar.

clout F [klaʊt] Schlag *m*; *bsd. Am.* Macht *f*, Einfluß *m*.

clove[1] [kləʊv] (Gewürz)Nelke *f*; ~ *of garlic* Knoblauchzehe *f*.

clove[2] [~] *pret. von* cleave[1]; **clo·ven** ['kləʊvn] **1.** *p.p. von* cleave[1]; **2.** ~ *hoof zo.* Huf *m* der Paarzeher.

clo·ver ♧ ['kləʊvə] Klee *m*.

clown [klaʊn] Clown *m*, Hanswurst *m*; Bauer *m*, ungehobelter Kerl; ~**ish** □ ['klaʊnɪʃ] clownisch.

club [klʌb] **1.** Keule *f*; (Gummi-) Knüppel *m*; (Golf)Schläger *m*; Klub *m*; ~*s pl.* Karten: Kreuz *n*; **2.** (*-bb-*) *v/t.* einknüppeln auf (*acc.*), (nieder-) knüppeln; *v/i.*: ~ *together* sich zusammentun; ~**foot** (*pl. -feet*) ['klʌbfʊt] Klumpfuß *m*.

cluck [klʌk] **1.** gackern; glucken; **2.** Gackern *n*; Glucken *n*.

clue [kluː] Anhaltspunkt *m*, Fingerzeig *m*, Spur *f*.

clump [klʌmp] **1.** Klumpen *m*; (*Baum- etc.*)Gruppe *f*; **2.** trampeln.

clum·sy □ ['klʌmzɪ] (*-ier, -iest*) unbeholfen, ungeschickt, plump.

clung [klʌŋ] *pret. u. p.p. von* cling.

clus·ter ['klʌstə] **1.** Traube *f*; Büschel *n*; Haufen *m*; **2.** büschelartig wachsen; sich drängen.

clutch [klʌtʃ] **1.** Griff *m*; ⊕ Kupplung *f*; Klaue *f*; **2.** (er)greifen.

clut·ter ['klʌtə] **1.** Wirrwarr *m*; Unordnung *f*; **2.** *a.* ~ *up* zu voll machen *od.* stellen; überladen.

coach [kəʊtʃ] **1.** Kutsche *f*; *Brt.* 🚌 (Personen)Wagen *m*; Omnibus, *bsd.* Reisebus *m*; Einpauker *m*; *Sport*: Trainer *m*; **2.** einpauken; *Sport*: trainieren; ~**man** ['kəʊtʃmən] (*pl. -men*) Kutscher *m*.

co·ag·u·late [kəʊˈægjʊleɪt] gerinnen (lassen).

coal [kəʊl] (Stein)Kohle *f*; *carry* ~*s to Newcastle* Eulen nach Athen tragen.

co·a·lesce [kəʊəˈles] verschmelzen, zusammenwachsen; sich vereinigen *od.* verbinden.

co·a·li·tion [kəʊə'lɪʃn] **1.** *pol.* Koalition *f*; Bündnis *n*, Zusammenschluß *m*; **2.** *pol.* Koalitions...

coal|-mine ['kəʊlmaɪn], **~-pit** Kohlengrube *f*.

coarse □ [kɔːs] (*~r*, *~st*) grob; ungeschliffen.

coast [kəʊst] **1.** Küste *f*; *Am.* Rodelbahn *f*; **2.** die Küste entlangfahren; im Leerlauf (*Auto*) *od.* im Freilauf (*Fahrrad*) fahren; *Am.* rodeln; **~·er** ['kəʊstə] *Am.* (Rodel)Schlitten; ♎ Küstenfahrer *m*; **~ guard** Küstenwache *f*; **~·guard** Angehörige(r) *m* der Küstenwache; **~·line** Küstenlinie *f*, -strich *m*.

coat [kəʊt] **1.** Jackett *n*, Jacke *f*, Rock *m*; Mantel *m*; *zo.* Pelz *m*, Fell *n*, Haut *f*, Gefieder *n*; Überzug *m*, Anstrich *m*, Schicht *f*; *~ of arms* Wappen (-schild *m*, *n*) *n*; **2.** überziehen, beschichten; (an)streichen; **~·hang·er** ['kəʊthæŋə] Kleiderbügel *m*; **~·ing** ['kəʊtɪŋ] Überzug *m*, Anstrich *m*, Schicht *f*; Mantelstoff *m*.

coax [kəʊks] überreden, beschwatzen.

cob [kɒb] kleines starkes Pferd; Schwan *m*; Maiskolben *m*.

cob|bled ['kɒbld]: *~ street* Straße *f* mit Kopfsteinpflaster; **~·bler** [*~ə*] (Flick)Schuster *m*; Stümper *m*.

cob·web ['kɒbweb] Spinn(en)gewebe *n*.

co·caine [kəʊ'keɪn] Kokain *n*.

cock [kɒk] **1.** *zo. etc.* Hahn *m*; (An-) Führer *m*; Heuhaufen *m*; **2.** *a. ~ up* aufrichten; *Gewehrhahn* spannen.

cock·a·too *zo.* [kɒkə'tuː] Kakadu *m*.

cock·chaf·er ['kɒktʃeɪfə] Maikäfer *m*.

cock|-eyed F ['kɒkaɪd] schielend; (krumm u.) schief.

cock|ney ['kɒknɪ] *mst* ♀ Cockney *m*, waschechter Londoner.

cock|pit ['kɒkpɪt] ✈, ♎ Cockpit *n* (*a. e-s Rennwagens*); Hahnenkampfplatz *m*.

cock·roach *zo.* ['kɒkrəʊtʃ] Schabe *f*.

cock·sure F ['kɒk'ʃʊə] absolut sicher; anmaßend; **~·tail** Cocktail *m*; **~·y** □ F ['kɒkɪ] (*-ier*, *-iest*) großspurig, anmaßend.

co·co ♀ ['kəʊkəʊ] (*pl. -cos*) Kokospalme *f*.

co·coa ['kəʊkəʊ] Kakao *m*.

co·co·nut ['kəʊkənʌt] Kokosnuß *f*.

co·coon [kə'kuːn] (*Seiden*)Kokon *m*.

cod *zo.* [kɒd] Kabeljau *m*, Dorsch *m*.

cod·dle ['kɒdl] verhätscheln.

code [kəʊd] **1.** Gesetzbuch *n*; Kodex *m*; (*Telegramm-*)Schlüssel *m*; Code *m*, Chiffre *f*; **2.** verschlüsseln, kodieren, chiffrieren.

cod|fish *zo.* ['kɒdfɪʃ] = *cod*; **~·liv·er oil** Lebertran *m*.

co-ed F ['kəʊ'ed] Schülerin *f od.* Studentin *f* e-r gemischten Schule; **~·u·ca·tion** [kəʊedjuː'keɪʃn] Koedukation *f*, Gemeinschaftserziehung *f*.

co·erce [kəʊ'ɜːs] (er)zwingen.

co·ex·ist [kəʊɪg'zɪst] gleichzeitig *od.* nebeneinander bestehen *od.* leben; **~·ence** [*~*əns] Koexistenz *f*.

cof·fee ['kɒfɪ] Kaffee *m*; **~ bean** Kaffeebohne *f*; **~·pot** Kaffeekanne *f*; **~·set** Kaffeeservice *n*; **~·ta·ble** Couchtisch *m*.

cof·fer ['kɒfə] (Geld- *etc.*)Kasten *m*.

cof·fin ['kɒfɪn] Sarg *m*.

cog ⊕ [kɒg] (Rad)Zahn *m*.

co·gent □ ['kəʊdʒənt] zwingend.

cog·i·tate ['kɒdʒɪteɪt] (nach)denken.

cog·wheel ⊕ ['kɒgwiːl] Zahnrad *n*.

co·her|ence [kəʊ'hɪərəns] Zusammenhang *m*; **~·ent** □ [*~*t] zusammenhängend.

co·he|sion [kəʊ'hiːʒn] Zusammenhalt *m*; **~·sive** [*~*sɪv] (fest) zusammenhaltend.

coif·fure [kwɑː'fjʊə] Frisur *f*.

coil [kɔɪl] **1.** *a. ~ up* aufwickeln; (sich) zusammenrollen; **2.** Rolle *f*; Spirale *f*; Wicklung *f*; Spule *f*; Windung *f*; ⊕ (Rohr)Schlange *f*.

coin [kɔɪn] **1.** Münze *f*; **2.** prägen (*a. fig.*); münzen.

co·in|cide [kəʊɪn'saɪd] zusammentreffen; übereinstimmen; **~·ci·dence** [kəʊ'ɪnsɪdəns] Zusammentreffen *n*; Zufall *m*; *fig.* Übereinstimmung *f*.

coke[1] [kəʊk] Koks *m* (*a. sl. = Kokain*).

Coke[2] TM F [*~*] Coke *n*, Cola *n*, *f*, Coca *n*, *f* (*Coca-Cola*).

cold [kəʊld] **1.** □ kalt; **2.** Kälte *f*, Frost *m*; Erkältung *f*; **~·blood·ed** [*~*'blʌdɪd] kaltblütig; **~·heart·ed** kalt-, hartherzig; **~·ness** ['kəʊldnɪs] Kälte *f*; **~ war** *pol.* kalter Krieg.

cole·slaw ['kəʊlslɔː] Krautsalat *m*.

col·ic ✚ ['kɒlɪk] Kolik *f*.

col·lab·o·rate [kə'læbəreɪt] zusammenarbeiten; **~·ra·tion** [kəlæbə'reɪʃn] Zusammenarbeit *f*; *in ~* with gemeinsam mit.

col|lapse [kə'læps] **1.** zusammen-, einfallen; zusammenbrechen; **2.** Zusammenbruch *m*; **~lap·si·ble** [~əbl] zusammenklappbar.

col·lar ['kɒlə] **1.** Kragen *m*; Halsband *n*; Kummet *n*; **2.** beim Kragen packen; *j-n* festnehmen, F schnappen; **~bone** *anat.* Schlüsselbein *n*.

col|league ['kɒli:g] Kolleg|e *m*, -in *f*, Mitarbeiter(in).

col|lect 1. *eccl.* ['kɒlekt] Kollekte *f*; **2.** *v/t.* [kə'lekt] (ein)sammeln; *Gedanken etc.* sammeln; einkassieren; abholen; *v/i.* sich (ver)sammeln; **~lect·ed** □ *fig.* gesammelt; **~lec·tion** [~kʃn] Sammlung *f*; *econ.* Eintreibung *f*; *eccl.* Kollekte *f*; **~lec·tive** □ [~tiv] gesammelt; Sammel...; **~ bargaining** *econ.* Tarifverhandlungen *pl.*; **~lec·tive·ly** [~li] insgesamt; zusammen; **~lec·tor** [~ə] Sammler(in); Steuereinnehmer *m*; ⛴ Fahrkartennehmer *m*; ⚡ Stromabnehmer *m*.

col|lege ['kɒlidʒ] College *n* (*Teil e-r Universität*); Hochschule *f*; höhere Lehranstalt.

col·lide [kə'laɪd] zusammenstoßen.

col|li·er ['kɒliə] Bergmann *m*; ⚓ Kohlenschiff *n*; **~lie·ry** [~jəri] Kohlengrube *f*.

col·li·sion [kə'liʒn] Zusammenstoß *m*, -prall *m*, Kollision *f*.

col·lo·qui·al □ [kə'ləʊkwiəl] umgangssprachlich, familiär.

col·lo·quy ['kɒləkwi] Gespräch *n*.

co·lon ['kəʊlən] Doppelpunkt *m*.

colo·nel ['kɜ:nl] Oberst *m*.

co·lo·ni·al □ [kə'ləʊnjəl] Kolonial...; **~is·m** *pol.* [~lɪzəm] Kolonialismus *m*.

col·o|nize ['kɒlənaɪz] kolonisieren, besiedeln; sich ansiedeln; **~ny** [~ni] Kolonie *f*; Siedlung *f*.

co·los·sal □ [kə'lɒsl] kolossal, riesig.

col·o·(u)r ['kʌlə] **1.** Farbe *f*; *fig.* Anschein *m*; Vorwand *m*; **~s** *pl.* Fahne *f*, Flagge *f*; *what* ~ *is* ...? welche Farbe hat ...?; **2.** *v/t.* färben; an-, bemalen, anstreichen; *fig.* beschönigen; *v/i.* sich (ver)färben; erröten; **~bar** Rassenschranke *f*; **~blind** farbenblind; **~ed 1.** bunt; farbig; ~ *man* Farbige(r) *m*; **2.** *oft contp.* Farbige(r *m*) *f*); **~fast** farbecht; **~film** *phot.* Farbfilm *m*; **~ful** [~fl] farbenreich, -freudig; lebhaft; **~ing** [~rɪŋ] Färbemittel *n*; Gesichtsfarbe *f*;

fig. Beschönigung *f*; **~less** □ [~lɪs] farblos; **~ line** Rassenschranke *f*; **~ set** Farbfernseher *m*; **~ tel·e·vi·sion** Farbfernsehen *n*.

colt [kəʊlt] Hengstfüllen *n*, -fohlen *n*.

col·umn ['kɒləm] Säule *f*; *print.* Spalte *f*; ✕ Kolonne *f*; **~ist** [~nist] Kolumnist(in).

comb [kəʊm] **1.** Kamm *m*; (Flachs-) Hechel *f*; **2.** *v/t.* kämmen; striegeln; *Flachs* hecheln.

com|bat ['kɒmbæt] **1.** Kampf *m*; *single* ~ Zweikampf *m*; **2.** (*-tt-, Am. a. -t-*) kämpfen gegen, bekämpfen; **~ba·tant** [~ənt] Kämpfer *m*.

com|bi·na·tion [kɒmbɪ'neɪʃn] Verbindung *f*; *mst* **~s** *pl.* Hemdhose *f* mit langem Bein; **~bine** [kəm'baɪn] (sich) verbinden *od.* vereinigen.

com·bus|ti·ble [kəm'bʌstəbl] **1.** brennbar; **2.** Brennstoff *m*, -material *n*; **~tion** [~tʃən] Verbrennung *f*.

come [kʌm] (*came, come*) kommen; *to* ~ künftig, kommend; ~ *about* geschehen, passieren; ~ *across* auf *j-n od. et.* stoßen; F ankommen (*Rede etc.*); ~ *along* mitkommen; ~ *apart* auseinanderfallen; ~ *at* auf *j-n od. et.* losgehen; ~ *back* zurückkommen; ~ *by et.* kommen; ~ *down* herunterkommen (*a. fig.*); einstürzen; sinken (*Preis*); überliefert werden; ~ *down with* F erkranken an (*dat.*); ~ *for* abholen kommen, kommen wegen; ~ *loose* sich ablösen, abgehen; ~ *off* ab-, losgehen, sich lösen; stattfinden; ~ *on!* los!, vorwärts!, komm!; ~ *over* vorbeikommen (*Besucher*); ~ *round* vorbeikommen (*Besucher*); wiederkehren; F wieder zu sich kommen; anders überlegen; ~ *through* durchkommen; *Krankheit etc.* überstehen, -leben; ~ *to* sich belaufen auf; wieder zu sich kommen; *what's the world coming to?* wohin ist die Welt geraten?; ~ *to see* besuchen; ~ *up to* entsprechen (*dat.*), heranreichen an (*acc.*); **~back** ['kʌmbæk] Comeback *n*.

co·me·di·an [kə'mi:djən] Komödiendienschauspieler(in); Komiker(in); Lustspieldichter *m*.

com·e·dy ['kɒmədi] Komödie *f*, Lustspiel *n*.

come·ly ['kʌmli] (*-ier, -iest*) attraktiv, gutaussehend.

com·fort ['kʌmfət] **1.** Behaglichkeit *f*; Trost *m*; Wohltat *f*, Erquickung *f*;

a. ~s *pl.* Komfort *m*; **2.** trösten;
com·for·ta·ble □ [~əbl] komfortabel, behaglich, bequem; tröstlich; **~er** [~ə] Tröster *m*; Wollschal *m*; *bsd. Brt.* Schnuller *m*; *Am.* Steppdecke *f*; **~·less** □ [~lɪs] unbequem; trostlos; **~·sta·tion** *Am.* Bedürfnisanstalt *f*.

com·ic ['kɒmɪk] (~ally) komisch; Komödien..., Lustspiel...

com·i·cal □ ['kɒmɪkl] komisch, spaßig.

com·ics ['kɒmɪks] *pl.* Comics *pl.*, Comic-Hefte *pl.*

com·ing ['kʌmɪŋ] **1.** kommend; künftig; **2.** Kommen *n*.

com·ma ['kɒmə] Komma *n*.

com·mand [kə'mɑːnd] **1.** Herrschaft *f*, Beherrschung *f* (*a. fig.*); Befehl *m*; ✗ Kommando *n*; *be* (*have*) *at* ~ zur Verfügung stehen (haben); **2.** befehlen; ✗ kommandieren; verfügen über (*acc.*); beherrschen; **~·er** [~ə] ✗ Kommandeur *m*, Befehlshaber *m*; ⚓ Fregattenkapitän *m*; **~·er-in-chief** ✗ [~ərɪn'tʃiːf] (*pl.* commanders-in-chief) Oberbefehlshaber *m*; **~·ing** □ [kə'mɑːndɪŋ] kommandierend, befehlshabend; gebieterisch; **~·ment** [~mənt] Gebot *n*; **~·mod·ule** *Raumfahrt:* Kommandokapsel *f*.

com·man·do ✗ [kə'mɑːndəʊ] (*pl. -dos, -does*) Kommando *n*.

com·mem·o·rate [kə'meməreɪt] gedenken (*gen.*), *j-s* Gedächtnis feiern; **~·ra·tion** [kəmemə'reɪʃn]: *in* ~ *of* zum Gedenken *od.* Gedächtnis an (*acc.*); **~·ra·tive** □ [kə'memərətɪv] Gedenk..., Erinnerungs...

com·mence [kə'mens] anfangen, beginnen; **~·ment** [~mənt] Anfang *m*, Beginn *m*.

com·mend [kə'mend] empfehlen; anvertrauen.

com·ment ['kɒment] **1.** Kommentar *m*; Erläuterung *f*; Bemerkung *f*; Stellungnahme *f*; *no* ~! kein Kommentar!; **2.** (*on, upon*) erläutern (*acc.*); sich (kritisch) äußern (über *acc.*); **~·men·ta·ry** ['kɒmentərɪ] Kommentar *m*; **~·men·tate** [~eɪt]: ~ *on Rundfunk, TV:* kommentieren (*acc.*); **~·men·ta·tor** [~ə] Kommentator *m*, *Rundfunk, TV:* a. Reporter *m*.

com·merce ['kɒmɜːs] Handel *m*; Verkehr *m*.

com·mer·cial □ [kə'mɜːʃl] **1.** kauf-

männisch, Handels..., Geschäfts...; handelsüblich; ~ *travel(l)er* Handlungsreisende(r) *m*; **2.** *Rundfunk, TV:* Werbespot *m*, -sendung *f*; **~·ize** [~[ə]laɪz] kommerzialisieren, vermarkten.

com·mis·e·rate [kə'mɪzəreɪt]: ~ *with* Mitleid empfinden mit; **~·ra·tion** [kəmɪzə'reɪʃn] Mitleid *n* (*for* mit).

com·mis·sa·ry ['kɒmɪsərɪ] Kommissar *m*.

com·mis·sion [kə'mɪʃn] **1.** Auftrag *m*; Übertragung *f* (*von Macht etc.*); Begehung *f* (*e-s Verbrechens*); Provision *f*; Kommission *f*; ✗ (Offiziers-)Patent *n*; **2.** beauftragen, bevollmächtigen; *et.* in Auftrag geben; *j-n* zum Offizier ernennen; *Schiff* in Dienst stellen; **~·er** [~ə] Bevollmächtigte(r *m*) *f*; (Regierungs)Kommissar *m*.

com·mit [kə'mɪt] (*-tt-*) anvertrauen, übergeben; 🏛 *j-n* einweisen; 🏛 *j-n* übergeben; *Verbrechen* begehen; bloßstellen; ~ (*o.s.*) sich verpflichten; **~·ment** [~mənt] Verpflichtung *f*; **~·tal** 🏛 [~l] Einweisung *f*; **~·tee** [~ɪ] Ausschuß *m*, Komitee *n*.

com·mod·i·ty [kə'mɒdɪtɪ] Ware *f*, Gebrauchsartikel *m*.

com·mon ['kɒmən] **1.** □ allgemein; gewöhnlich; gemein(sam), gemeinschaftlich; öffentlich; gewöhnlich, minderwertig; F ordinär; ⚖ *Council* Gemeinderat *m*; **2.** Gemeindeland *n*; *in* ~ gemeinsam; *in* ~ *with* genau wie; **~·er** [~ə] Bürgerliche(r *m*) *f*; ~ *law* (ungeschriebenes englisches) Gewohnheitsrecht; ⚖ *Mar·ket econ. pol.* Gemeinsamer Markt; **~·place 1.** Gemeinplatz *m*; **2.** alltäglich; abgedroschen; **~s** *pl. das* gemeine Volk; *House of* ⚖ *parl.* Unterhaus *n*; ~ *sense* gesunder Menschenverstand; **~·wealth** [~welθ] Gemeinwesen *n*, Staat *m*; Republik *f*; *the* ⚖ (*of Nations*) das Commonwealth.

com·mo·tion [kə'məʊʃn] Aufruhr *m*, Erregung *f*.

com·mu·nal □ ['kɒmjʊnl] Gemeinde...; Gemeinschafts...

com·mune 1. [kə'mjuːn] sich vertraulich besprechen; **2.** ['kɒmjuːn] Kommune *f*; Gemeinde *f*.

com·mu·ni·cate [kə'mjuːnɪkeɪt] *v/t.* mitteilen; *v/i.* sich besprechen; sich in Verbindung setzen (*with* s.o. mit j-m); (*durch e-e Tür*) verbunden

435

complicate

sein; **~·ca·tion** [kəmjuːˈkeɪʃn] Mitteilung *f*; Verständigung *f*; Verbindung *f*, **~s** *pl.* Verbindung *f*, Verkehrswege *pl.*; **~s** *satellite* Nachrichtensatellit *m*; **~·ca·tive** □ [kəˈmjuːnɪkətɪv] mitteilsam, gesprächig.

com·mu·nion [kəˈmjuːnjən] Gemeinschaft *f*; ♀ *eccl.* Kommunion *f*, Abendmahl *n*.

com·mu·nis|m [ˈkɒmjunɪzəm] Kommunismus *m*; **~t** [~ɪst] 1. Kommunist(in); 2. kommunistisch.

com·mu·ni·ty [kəˈmjuːnɪtɪ] Gemeinschaft *f*; Gemeinde *f*; Staat *m*.

com|mute [kəˈmjuːt] ⚖ Strafe *mildernd* umwandeln; ⚙ *etc.* pendeln; **~·mut·er** [~ə] Pendler(in); **~ train** Pendler-, Vorort-, Nahverkehrszug *m*.

com·pact 1. [ˈkɒmpækt] Vertrag *m*; Puderdose *f*; *Am. mot.* Kompaktauto *n*; 2. [kəmˈpækt] *adj.* dicht, fest; knapp, bündig; **~ disc** Compact Disc *f* (*Schallplatte*); 3. *v/t.* fest verbinden.

com·pan|ion [kəmˈpænjən] Begleiter(in); Gefährt|e *m*, -in *f*; Gesellschafter(in); Handbuch *n*, Leitfaden *m*; **~·io·na·ble** □ [~əbl] gesellig; **~·ion·ship** [~ʃɪp] Gesellschaft *f*.

com·pa·ny [ˈkʌmpənɪ] Gesellschaft *f*; Begleitung *f*; ✕ Kompanie *f*; *econ.* (Handels)Gesellschaft *f*; ♣ Mannschaft *f*; *thea.* Truppe *f*; *have* **~** Gäste haben; *keep* **~** *with* verkehren mit.

com·pa·ra·ble □ [ˈkɒmpərəbl] vergleichbar; **~·par·a·tive** [kəmˈpærətɪv] 1. □ vergleichend; verhältnismäßig; 2. *a.* **~ degree** *gr.* Komparativ *m*; **~·pare** [~ˈpeə] 1. *beyond* **~**, *without* **~**, *past* **~** unvergleichlich; 2. *v/t.* vergleichen; (*as*) **~d with** im Vergleich zu; *v/i.* sich vergleichen (lassen); **~·pa·ri·son** [~ˈpærɪsn] Vergleich *m*.

com·part·ment [kəmˈpɑːtmənt] Abteilung *f*, Fach *n*; 🚆 Abteil *n*.

com|pass [ˈkʌmpəs] Bereich *m*; ♪ Umfang *m*; Kompaß *m*; *pair of* **~es** *pl.* Zirkel *m*; **~·pas·sion** [kəmˈpæʃn] Mitleid *n*; **~·ate** [~ət] mitleidig.

com·pat·i·ble □ [kəmˈpætəbl] vereinbar; ⚙ verträglich; passend.

com·pat·ri·ot [kəmˈpætrɪət] Landsmann *m*, -männin *f*.

com·pel [kəmˈpel] (*-ll-*) (er)zwingen; **~·ling** □ [~ɪŋ] zwingend.

com·pen|sate [ˈkɒmpenseɪt] *j-n* entschädigen; *et.* ersetzen; ausgleichen; **~·sa·tion** [kɒmpenˈseɪʃn] Ersatz *m*; Ausgleich *m*; (Schaden)Ersatz *m*, Entschädigung *f*; *Am.* Bezahlung *f*, Gehalt *n*.

com|père, **~·pere** *Brt.* [ˈkɒmpeə] Conférencier *m*; 2. konferieren, ansagen.

com·pete [kəmˈpiːt] sich (mit)bewerben (*for* um); konkurrieren.

com·pe|tence, **~·ten·cy** [ˈkɒmpɪtəns] Können *n*, Fähigkeit *f*; ⚖ Zuständigkeit *f*; **~·tent** □ [~t] hinreichend; (leistungs)fähig, tüchtig; sachkundig.

com·pe·ti·tion [kɒmpɪˈtɪʃn] Wettbewerb *m*; Konkurrenz *f*.

com·pet·i|tive □ [kəmˈpetɪtɪv] konkurrierend; **~·tor** [~ə] Mitbewerber(in); Konkurrent(in); *Sport:* (Wettbewerbs)Teilnehmer(in).

com·pile [kəmˈpaɪl] zusammentragen, zusammenstellen, sammeln.

com·pla|cence, **~·cen·cy** [kəmˈpleɪsns, ~sɪ] Selbstzufriedenheit *f*, -gefälligkeit *f*; **~·cent** □ [~nt] selbstzufrieden, -gefällig.

com·plain [kəmˈpleɪn] sich beklagen *od.* beschweren; klagen (*of* über *acc.*); **~t** [~t] Klage *f*; Beschwerde *f*, 🅂 *a.* Leiden *n*.

com·plai·sant □ [kəmˈpleɪzənt] gefällig, entgegenkommend.

com·ple|ment 1. [ˈkɒmplɪmənt] Ergänzung *f*; *a. full* **~** volle Anzahl; 2. [~mənt] ergänzen; **~·men·ta·ry** [kɒmplɪˈmentərɪ] (sich gegenseitig) ergänzend.

com|plete [kəmˈpliːt] 1. □ vollständig, ganz, völlig, vollkommen; vollzählig; 2. vervollständigen; vervollkommnen; abschließen; **~·ple·tion** [~iːʃn] Vervollständigung *f*; Abschluß *m*; Erfüllung *f*.

com·plex [ˈkɒmpleks] 1. □ zusammengesetzt; komplex, vielschichtig, kompliziert; 2. Gesamtheit *f*; Komplex *m* (*a. psych.*); **~·ion** [kəmˈplekʃn] Aussehen *n*, Charakter *m*; Gesichtsfarbe *f*, Teint *m*; **~·i·ty** [~sətɪ] Vielschichtigkeit *f*.

com·pli|ance [kəmˈplaɪəns] Einwilligung *f*; Einverständnis *n*; *in* **~** *with* gemäß; **~·ant** □ [~t] willfährig, unterwürfig.

com·pli·cate [ˈkɒmplɪkeɪt] kompli-

C

zieren; **~cat·ed** kompliziert; **~ca·tion** [kɒmplɪˈkeɪʃn] Komplikation f (a. 🖈); Kompliziertheit f.

com·plic·i·ty [kəmˈplɪsətɪ] Mitschuld f (in an dat.).

com·pli·ment 1. [ˈkɒmplɪmənt] Kompliment n; Empfehlung f; Gruß m; **2.** [~ment] v/t. (on) beglückwünschen (zu); j-m ein Kompliment machen (wegen); **~men·ta·ry** [kɒmplɪˈmentərɪ] höflich.

com·ply [kəmˈplaɪ] sich fügen; nachkommen, entsprechen (with dat.).

com·po·nent [kəmˈpəʊnənt] Bestandteil m; ⊕, ⚡ Bauelement n.

com·pose [kəmˈpəʊz] zusammensetzen od. -stellen; ♪ komponieren; verfassen; ordnen; print. (ab)setzen; ~ o.s. sich beruhigen; **~posed** □ ruhig, gesetzt; **~pos·er** [~ə] Komponist(in) f; Verfasser(in); **~pos·ite** [ˈkɒmpəzɪt] zusammengesetzt, gemischt; **~po·si·tion** [kɒmpəˈzɪʃn] Zusammensetzung f; Abfassung f; Komposition f; Schriftstück n, Dichtung f; Aufsatz m; **~po·sure** [kəmˈpəʊʒə] Fassung f, (Gemüts-) Ruhe f.

com·pound¹ [ˈkɒmpaʊnd] Lager n; Gefängnishof m; (Tier)Gehege n.

com·pound² 1. [~] zusammengesetzt; ~ interest Zinseszinsen pl.; **2.** Zusammensetzung f; Verbindung f; gr. zusammengesetztes Wort; **3.** [kəmˈpaʊnd] v/t. zusammensetzen; steigern, bsd. verschlimmern.

com·pre·hend [kɒmprɪˈhend] umfassen; begreifen, verstehen.

com·pre·hen·si·ble □ [kɒmprɪˈhensəbl] verständlich; **~sion** [~ʃn] Begreifen n, Verständnis n; Fassungskraft f, Begriffsvermögen n, Verstand m, Einsicht f; past~ unfaßbar, unfaßlich; **~sive** [~sɪv] **1.** □ umfassend; **2.** a. ~ school Brt. Gesamtschule f.

com·press [kəmˈpres] zusammendrücken; ~ed air Druckluft f; **~pres·sion** [~ʃn] phys. Verdichtung f; ⊕ Druck m.

com·prise [kəmˈpraɪz] einschließen, umfassen, enthalten.

com·pro·mise [ˈkɒmprəmaɪz] **1.** Kompromiß m, n; **2.** v/t. (o.s. sich) bloßstellen; v/i. e-n Kompromiß schließen.

com·pul·sion [kəmˈpʌlʃn] Zwang m; **~sive** □ [~sɪv] zwingend, Zwangs...;

psych. zwanghaft; **~so·ry** □ [~sərɪ] obligatorisch; Zwangs...; Pflicht...

com·punc·tion [kəmˈpʌŋkʃn] Gewissensbisse pl.; Reue f; Bedenken pl.

com·pute [kəmˈpjuːt] (be-, er)rechnen; schätzen.

com·put·er [kəmˈpjuːtə] Computer m, Rechner m; **~con·trolled** computergesteuert; **~ize** [~raɪz] mit Computern ausstatten, auf Computer umstellen; Information in e-m Computer speichern.

com·rade [ˈkɒmreɪd] Kamerad m; (Partei)Genosse m.

con¹ abbr. [kɒn] = contra.

con² F [~] (-nn-) reinlegen, betrügen.

con·ceal [kənˈsiːl] verbergen; verheimlichen.

con·cede [kənˈsiːd] zugestehen, einräumen; gewähren; nachgeben.

con·ceit [kənˈsiːt] Einbildung f, Dünkel m; gesuchte Metapher; **~ed** □ eingebildet (of auf acc.).

con·ceiv·a·ble □ [kənˈsiːvəbl] denkbar, begreiflich; **~ve** [kənˈsiːv] v/i. schwanger werden; v/t. Kind empfangen; sich denken; planen, ausdenken.

con·cen·trate [ˈkɒnsəntreɪt] **1.** (sich) zusammenziehen, vereinigen; (sich) konzentrieren. **2.** Konzentrat n.

con·cept [ˈkɒnsept] Begriff m; Gedanke m; △ nicht Konzept.

con·cep·tion [kənˈsepʃn] Begreifen n; Vorstellung f, Begriff m, Idee f; biol. Empfängnis f.

con·cern [kənˈsɜːn] **1.** Angelegenheit f; Interesse n; Sorge f; Beziehung f (with zu); Geschäft n, (industrielles) Unternehmen; △ nicht Konzern; **2.** betreffen, angehen, interessieren; beunruhigen; interessieren, beschäftigen; **~ed** □ interessiert, beteiligt (in an dat.); besorgt; **~ing** prp. [~ɪŋ] betreffend, über, wegen, hinsichtlich.

con·cert [ˈkɒnsət] Konzert n; ♪ [~sɜːt] Einverständnis n; **~ed** □ [kənˈsɜːtɪd] gemeinsam; ♪ mehrstimmig.

con·ces·sion [kənˈseʃn] Zugeständnis n; Konzession f.

con·cil·i·ate [kənˈsɪlɪeɪt] aus-, versöhnen; **~a·to·ry** [~ɪətərɪ] versöhnlich, vermittelnd.

con·cise □ [kənˈsaɪs] kurz, bündig, knapp; **~ness** [~nɪs] Kürze f.

con·clude [kən'klu:d] schließen, beschließen, beenden; abschließen; folgern, schließen (*from* aus); sich entscheiden; *to be* ~*d* Schluß folgt.

con·clu·sion [kən'klu:ʒn] Schluß *m*, Ende *n*; Abschluß *m*; Schluß *m*, (Schluß)Folgerung *f*; Beschluß *m*; *s. jump*; ~**sive** □ [~sɪv] überzeugend; endgültig.

con|coct [kən'kɒkt] zusammenbrauen; *fig.* aushecken, sich ausdenken; ~**coc·tion** [~kʃn] Gebräu *n*; *fig.* Erfindung *f.*

con·cord ['kɒnkɔ:d] Eintracht *f*; Übereinstimmung *f* (*a. gr.*); ♪ Harmonie *f.*

con·course ['kɒnkɔ:s] Zusammen-, Auflauf *m*; Menge *f*; freier Platz.

con·crete ['kɒnkri:t] **1.** □ fest; konkret; Beton...; **2.** Beton *m*; **3.** betonieren.

con·cur [kən'kɜ:] (-*rr*-) übereinstimmen; ~**rence** [~'kʌrəns] Zusammentreffen *n*; Übereinstimmung *f*; △ *nicht* Konkurrenz.

con·cus·sion [kən'kʌʃn]: ~ *of the brain* ♂ Gehirnerschütterung *f.*

con|demn [kən'dem] verdammen; *t⁄* *u. fig.* verurteilen (*to death* zum Tode); für unbewohnbar *etc.* unbewohnbar *etc.* erklären; ~**dem·na·tion** [kɒndem'neɪʃn] *t⁄* *u. fig.* Verurteilung *f*; Verdammung *f*, Mißbilligung *f.*

con|den·sa·tion [kɒnden'seɪʃn] Verdichtung *f*; ~**dense** [kən'dens] (sich) verdichten; ⊕ kondensieren; zusammenziehen, kürzen; ~**dens·er** ⊕ [~ə] Kondensator *m.*

con·de|scend [kɒndɪ'send] sich herablassen, geruhen; ~**scen·sion** [~ʃn] Herablassung *f.*

con·di·ment ['kɒndɪmənt] Würze *f.*

con·di·tion [kən'dɪʃn] **1.** Zustand *m*; (körperlicher *od.* Gesundheits)Zustand *m*; *Sport:* Kondition, Form *f*; Bedingung *f*; ~*s pl.* Verhältnisse *pl.*, Umstände *pl.*; *on* ~ *that* unter der Bedingung, daß; *out of* ~ in schlechter Verfassung, in schlechtem Zustand; **2.** bedingen; in e-n bestimmten Zustand bringen; ~**al** [~l] **1.** □ bedingt (*on, upon* durch); Bedingungs...; **2.** *a.* ~ *clause gr.* Bedingungs-, Konditionalsatz *m*; *a.* ~ *mood gr.* Konditional *m.*

con|dole [kən'dəʊl] kondolieren (*with dat.*); ~**do·lence** [~əns] Beileid *n.*

con·done [kən'dəʊn] verzeihen, vergeben.

con·du·cive [kən'dju:sɪv] dienlich, förderlich (*to dat.*).

con|duct 1. ['kɒndʌkt] Führung *f*; Verhalten *n*, Betragen *n*; **2.** [kən'dʌkt] führen; ♪ dirigieren; ~*ed tour (of)* Führung *f* (durch); Gesellschaftsreise (durch); ~**duc·tion** [~kʃn] Leitung *f*; ~**duc·tor** [~tə] Führer *m*; Leiter *m*; Schaffner *m*; *Am.* 🚋 Zugbegleiter *m*; ♪ (Orchester)Dirigent *m*, (Chor)Leiter *m*; ⚡ Blitzableiter *m.*

cone [kəʊn] Kegel *m*; Eistüte *f*; ♀ Zapfen *m.*

con·fec·tion [kən'fekʃn] Konfekt *n*; △ *nicht* Konfektion; ~**er** [~nə] Konditor *m*; ~**e·ry** [~ərɪ] Süßigkeiten *pl.*, Süß-, Konditoreiwaren *pl.*; Konfekt *n*; Konditorei *f*; Süßwarengeschäft *n.*

con·fed·e|ra·cy [kən'fedərəsɪ] Bündnis *n*; *the* ~ *Am. hist.* die Konföderation; ~**rate 1.** [~rət] verbündet; **2.** [~] Bundesgenosse *m*; **3.** [~reɪt] (sich) verbünden; ~**ra·tion** [kənfedə'reɪʃn] Bund *m*, Bündnis *n*; Staatenbund *m.*

con·fer [kən'fɜ:] (-*rr*-) *v/t.* übertragen, verleihen; *v/i.* sich besprechen.

con·fe·rence ['kɒnfərəns] Konferenz *f.*

con|fess [kən'fes] bekennen, gestehen; beichten; ~**fes·sion** [~ʃən] Geständnis *n*; Bekenntnis *n*; Beichte *f*; ~**fes·sion·al** [~nl] Beichtstuhl *m*; ~**fes·sor** [~esə] Bekenner *m*; Beichtvater *m.*

con·fide [kən'faɪd] *v/t.* anvertrauen; *v/i.:* ~ *in s.o.* j-m vertrauen.

con·fi·dence ['kɒnfɪdəns] Vertrauen *n*; Zuversicht *f*; ~ *man* (*pl. -men*) Betrüger *m*; ~ *trick* aufgelegter Schwindel.

con·fi·dent □ ['kɒnfɪdənt] zuversichtlich; ~**den·tial** □ [kɒnfɪ'denʃl] vertraulich.

con·fid·ing □ [kən'faɪdɪŋ] vertrauensvoll.

con·fine [kən'faɪn] begrenzen; beschränken; einsperren; *be* ~*d of* entbunden werden von; *be* ~*d to bed* das Bett hüten müssen; ~**ment** [~mənt] Haft *f*; Beschränkung *f*; Entbindung *f.*

con|firm [kən'fɜ:m] (be)kräftigen; bestätigen; *eccl.* konfirmieren; *eccl.*

C

firmen; **~fir·ma·tion** [kɒnfə-
ˈmeɪʃn] Bestätigung f; eccl. Kon-
firmation f; eccl. Firmung f.
con·fis|cate [ˈkɒnfɪskeɪt] beschlag-
nahmen; **~ca·tion** [kɒnfɪˈskeɪʃn]
Beschlagnahme f.
con·fla·gra·tion [kɒnfləˈgreɪʃn] (bsd.
Groß)Brand.
con·flict 1. [ˈkɒnflɪkt] Konflikt m; 2.
[kənˈflɪkt] in Konflikt stehen; **~ing**
[~ɪŋ] widersprüchlich.
con·form [kənˈfɔːm] (sich) anpassen
(to dat., an acc.).
con·found [kənˈfaʊnd] j-n verwirren,
-blüffen; ~ it! F verdammt!; **~ed** □
F verdammt.
con|front [kənˈfrʌnt] gegenübertre-
ten, -stehen (dat.); sich stellen
(dat.); konfrontieren; **~fron·ta-
tion** [kɒnfrʌnˈteɪʃn] Konfrontation
f.
con|fuse [kənˈfjuːz] verwechseln;
verwirren; **~fused** □ verwirrt; verlegen; verworren; **~fu·sion** [~uːʒn]
Verwirrung f; Verlegenheit f; Ver-
wechslung f.
con·geal [kənˈdʒiːl] erstarren (lassen); gerinnen (lassen).
con|gest·ed [kənˈdʒestɪd] überfüllt;
verstopft; **~ges·tion** [~tʃən] Blutan-
drang m; a. traffic ~ Verkehrs-
stockung f, -stauung f.
con·glom·e·ra·tion [kənɡlɒməˈreɪʃn]
Anhäufung f; Konglomerat n.
con·grat·u·late [kənˈɡrætjuleɪt] beglückwünschen, j-m gratulieren;
~la·tion [kənɡrætjʊˈleɪʃn] Glückwunsch m; ~s! ich gratuliere!, herzlichen Glückwunsch!
con·gre|gate [ˈkɒnɡrɪɡeɪt] (sich)
(ver)sammeln; **~ga·tion** [kɒnɡrɪ-
ˈɡeɪʃn] Versammlung f; eccl. Gemeinde f.
con·gress [ˈkɒnɡres] Kongreß m; ♀
Am. parl. der Kongreß; ♀-**man** (pl.
-men) Am. parl. Kongreßabgeord-
nete(r) m; ♀-**wom·an** (pl. -women)
Am. parl. Kongreßabgeordnete f.
con|ic bsd. ⊕ [ˈkɒnɪk], **~i·cal** □ [~kl]
konisch, kegelförmig.
co·ni·fer ♀ [ˈkɒnɪfə] Nadelbaum m.
con·jec·ture [kənˈdʒektʃə] 1. Mut-
maßung f; 2. mutmaßen.
con·ju·gal ♀ [ˈkɒndʒʊɡl] ehelich.
con·ju|gate gr. [ˈkɒndʒʊɡeɪt] kon-
jugieren, beugen; **~ga·tion** gr.
[kɒndʒʊˈɡeɪʃn] Konjugation f, Beugung f.

con·junc·tion [kənˈdʒʌŋkʃn] Verbindung f; gr. Konjunktion f.
con·junc·ti·vi·tis ♉ [kəndʒʌŋktɪˈvaɪ-
tɪs] Bindehautentzündung f.
con|jure [ˈkʌndʒə] Teufel etc. be-
schwören; zaubern; **~jur·er** [~rə]
Zauber|er m, -in f, Zauberkünst-
ler(in); **~jur·ing trick** [~rɪŋ trɪk]
Zauberkunststück n; **~jur·or** [~rə]
= conjurer.
con|nect [kəˈnekt] verbinden; ⚡ an-
schließen, (zu)schalten; 🚍, 🚋 etc.
Anschluß haben (with an acc.);
~nect·ed □ verbunden; (logisch)
zusammenhängend (Rede etc.); be
well ~ gute Beziehungen haben;
~nec·tion, Brt. a. **~nex·ion** [~kʃn]
Verbindung f; ⚡ Schaltung f; Anschluß m; Zusammenhang m; Verwandtschaft f.
con|quer [ˈkɒŋkə] erobern; (be)sie-
gen; **~or** [~rə] Eroberer m.
con·quest [ˈkɒŋkwest] Eroberung f
(a. fig.); erobertes Gebiet; Besiegung f; Bezwingung f.
con·science [ˈkɒnʃəns] Gewissen n.
con·sci·en·tious □ [kɒnʃɪˈenʃəs] gewissenhaft; Gewissens...; ~ objector
Wehrdienstverweigerer m (aus Überzeugung); **~ness** [~nɪs] Gewissen-
haftigkeit f.
con·scious □ [ˈkɒnʃəs] bei Bewußtsein; bewußt; be ~ of sich bewußt
sein (gen.); **~ness** [~nɪs] Bewußtsein
n.
con|script ✗ 1. [kənˈskrɪpt] einzie-
hen, -berufen; 2. [ˈkɒnskrɪpt] Wehr-
pflichtige(r) m; **~scrip·tion** ✗
[kənˈskrɪpʃn] Einberufung f, Einzie-
hung f.
con·se|crate [ˈkɒnsɪkreɪt] weihen,
einsegnen; widmen; **~cra·tion**
[kɒnsɪˈkreɪʃn] Weihe f; Einsegnung
f.
con·sec·u·tive □ [kənˈsekjʊtɪv] aufeinanderfolgend; fortlaufend.
con·sent [kənˈsent] 1. Zustimmung f;
2. einwilligen, zustimmen.
con·se|quence [ˈkɒnsɪkwəns] Folge f,
Konsequenz f; Einfluß m; Bedeutung f; **~quent·ly** [~tlɪ] folglich,
daher.
con·ser|va·tion [kɒnsəˈveɪʃn] Erhal-
tung f; Naturschutz m; Umwelt-
schutz m; **~tion·ist** [~ʃnɪst] Natur-
schützer(in); Umweltschützer(in);
~tive □ [kənˈsɜːvətɪv] 1. erhaltend;
konservativ; vorsichtig; 2. ♀ pol.

Konservative(r *m*) *f*; **~·to·ry** [kɒn-'sɜːtəri] Treib-, Gewächshaus *n*; ♪ Konservatorium *n*; **con·serve** [kən-'sɜːv] erhalten.

con·sid|er [kən'sɪdə] *v/t.* betrachten; sich überlegen, erwägen; in Betracht ziehen, berücksichtigen; meinen; *v/i.* nachdenken, überlegen; **~·e·ra·ble** □ [~rəbl] ansehnlich, beträchtlich; **~·e·ra·bly** [~rə·bli] ziemlich, (sehr) viel; **~·er·ate** □ [~rət] rücksichtsvoll; **~·e·ra·tion** [kənsɪdə'reɪʃn] Betrachtung *f*, Erwägung *f*, Überlegung *f*; Rücksicht *f*; Gesichtspunkt *m*; *take into ~* in Erwägung *od.* in Betracht ziehen, berücksichtigen; **~·er·ing** □ [kən-'sɪdərɪŋ] **1.** *prp.* in Anbetracht (*gen.*); **2.** *adv.* F den Umständen entsprechend.

con·sign [kən'saɪn] übergeben; anvertrauen; *econ.* Waren zusenden; **~·ment** *econ.* [~mənt] Über-, Zusendung *f*; (Waren)Sendung *f*.

con·sist [kən'sɪst]: *~ in* bestehen in (*dat.*); *~ of* bestehen *od.* sich zusammensetzen aus.

con·sis|tence, **~·ten·cy** [kən'sɪstəns, ~sɪ] Konsistenz *f*, Beschaffenheit *f*; Übereinstimmung *f*, Konsequenz *f*; **~·tent** □ [~ənt] übereinstimmend, vereinbar (*with* mit); konsequent; *Sport etc.*: beständig (*Leistung*).

con|so·la·tion [kɒnsə'leɪʃn] Trost *m*; **~·sole** [kən'səʊl] trösten.

con·sol·i·date [kən'sɒlɪdeɪt] festigen; *fig.* zusammenschließen, -legen.

con·so·nant ['kɒnsənənt] **1.** □ übereinstimmend; **2.** *gr.* Konsonant *m*, Mitlaut *m*.

con·spic·u·ous □ [kən'spɪkjʊəs] sichtbar; auffallend; hervorragend; *make o.s. ~* sich auffällig benehmen.

con|spi·ra·cy [kən'spɪrəsɪ] Verschwörung *f*; **~·spi·ra·tor** [~tə] Verschwörer *m*; **~·spire** [~'spaɪə] sich verschwören.

con|sta·ble *Brt.* ['kʌnstəbl] Polizist *m* (auf Streife), Wachtmeister *m*; **~·stab·u·la·ry** [kən'stæbjʊlərɪ] Polizei(truppe) *f*.

con|stan·cy ['kɒnstənsɪ] Standhaftigkeit *f*; Beständigkeit *f*; **~·stant** □ [~t] beständig, unveränderlich, treu.

con·ster·na·tion [kɒnstə'neɪʃn] Bestürzung *f*.

con·sti|pat·ed ♂ ['kɒnstɪpeɪtɪd] ver-

stopft; **~·pa·tion** ♂ [kɒnstɪ'peɪʃn] Verstopfung *f*.

con·sti·tu|en·cy [kən'stɪtjʊənsɪ] Wählerschaft *f*; Wahlkreis *m*; **~·ent** [~t] **1.** e-n (Bestand)Teil bildend; *pol.* konstituierend; **2.** (wesentlicher) Bestandteil; *pol.* Wähler(in).

con·sti·tute ['kɒnstɪtjuːt] ein-, errichten; ernennen; bilden, ausmachen.

con·sti·tu·tion [kɒnstɪ'tjuːʃn] *pol.* Verfassung *f*; Konstitution *f*, körperliche Verfassung *f*; Zusammensetzung *f*; **~·al** □ [~nl] **1.** □ konstitutionell; *pol.* verfassungsmäßig; **2.** (Verdauungs)Spaziergang *m*.

con·strain [kən'streɪn] zwingen; **~·ed** gezwungen, unnatürlich; **~·t** [~t] Zwang *m*.

con|strict [kən'strɪkt] zusammenziehen; **~·stric·tion** [~kʃn] Zusammenziehung *f*.

con|struct [kən'strʌkt] bauen, errichten, konstruieren; *fig.* bilden; **~·struc·tion** [~kʃn] Konstruktion *f*; Bau *m*; *fig.* Auslegung *f*; *~ site* Baustelle *f*; **~·struc·tive** □ [~tɪv] aufbauend, schöpferisch, konstruktiv, positiv; **~·struc·tor** [~ə] Erbauer *m*, Konstrukteur *m*.

con·strue [kən'struː] *gr.* konstruieren; auslegen, auffassen.

con|sul ['kɒnsəl] Konsul *m*; **~·general** Generalkonsul *m*; **~·su·late** [~sjʊlət] Konsulat *n* (*a. Gebäude*).

con·sult [kən'sʌlt] *v/t.* konsultieren, um Rat fragen; in e-m Buch nachschlagen; *v/i.* sich beraten.

con·sul|tant [kən'sʌltənt] (fachmännische[r]) Berater(in); *Brt.* Facharzt *m* (*an e-m Krankenhaus*); **~·ta·tion** [kɒnsl'teɪʃn] Konsultation *f*, Beratung *f*, Rücksprache *f*; *~ hour* Sprechstunde *f*; **~·ta·tive** [kən'sʌltətɪv] beratend.

con|sume [kən'sjuːm] *v/t.* essen, trinken; verbrauchen; zerstören, vernichten (*durch Feuer*); verzehren (*durch Haß etc.*); **~·sum·er** [~ə] *econ.* Verbraucher(in).

con·sum|mate 1. □ [kən'sʌmɪt] vollendet; **2.** ['kɒnsəmeɪt] vollenden.

con·sump|tion [kən'sʌmpʃn] Verbrauch *m*; *veraltet* ♂ Schwindsucht *f*; **~·tive** □ [~tɪv] verzehrend; *veraltet* ♂ schwindsüchtig.

con·tact ['kɒntækt] **1.** Berührung *f*; Kontakt *m*; *make ~s* Verbindungen

C

anknüpfen *od.* herstellen; ~ *lenses pl.* Haft-, Kontaktschalen *pl.*; **2.** sich in Verbindung setzen mit, Kontakt aufnehmen mit.

con·ta·gious ☐ *⚕* [kən'teɪdʒəs] ansteckend (*a. fig.*).

con·tain [kən'teɪn] enthalten, (um-)fassen; ~ *o.s.* an sich halten, sich beherrschen; **~er** [~ə] Behälter *m*; *econ.* Container *m*; **~er·ize** *econ.* [~əraɪz] (auf) Containerbetrieb umstellen; in Containern transportieren.

con·tam·i·nate [kən'tæmɪneɪt] verunreinigen; infizieren, vergiften; (*a.* radioaktiv) verseuchen; **~na·tion** [kəntæmɪ'neɪʃn] Verunreinigung *f*; Vergiftung *f*; (*a.* radioaktive) Verseuchung.

con·tem·plate ['kɒntempleɪt] betrachten; beabsichtigen, vorhaben; **~pla·tion** [kɒntem'pleɪʃn] Betrachtung *f*; Nachdenken *n*; **~pla·tive** ☐ ['kɒntempleɪtɪv] nachdenklich; [kən'templətɪv] beschaulich.

con·tem·po·ra·ne·ous ☐ [kəntempə'reɪnjəs] gleichzeitig; **~ry** [kən'tempərərɪ] **1.** zeitgenössisch; **2.** Zeitgenoss|e *m*, -in *f*.

con·tempt [kən'tempt] Verachtung *f*; **~temp·ti·ble** ☐ [~əbl] verachtenswert; **~temp·tu·ous** ☐ [~juəs] geringschätzig, verächtlich.

con·tend [kən'tend] *v/i.* kämpfen, ringen (*for* um); *v/t.* behaupten; **~er** [~ə] *bsd.* Sport: Wettkämpfer(in).

con·tent [kən'tent] **1.** zufrieden; **2.** befriedigen; ~ *o.s.* sich begnügen; **3.** Zufriedenheit *f*; *to one's heart's* ~ nach Herzenslust; ['kɒntent] Gehalt *m*; **~s** *pl.* (*stofflicher*) Inhalt; **~ed** ☐ [kən'tentɪd] zufrieden.

con·ten·tion [kən'tenʃn] Streit *m*; Argument *n*, Behauptung *f*.

con·tent·ment [kən'tentmənt] Zufriedenheit *f*.

con·test 1. ['kɒntest] Streit *m*; Wettkampf *m*; **2.** [kən'test] sich bewerben um, kandidieren für; (be)streiten, anfechten; um *et.* streiten; **~tes·tant** [~ənt] Wettkämpfer(in), (Wettkampf)Teilnehmer(in).

con·text ['kɒntekst] Zusammenhang *m*.

con·ti·nent ['kɒntɪnənt] **1.** ☐ enthaltsam, mäßig; **2.** Kontinent *m*, Erdteil *m*; *the* ⁎ *Brt.* das (europäische) Festland; **~nen·tal** [kɒntɪ'nentl] **1.** ☐

kontinental, Kontinental...; **2.** Kontinentaleuropäer(in).

con·tin·gen|cy [kən'tɪndʒənsɪ] Zufälligkeit *f*; Möglichkeit *f*, Eventualität *f*; **~t** [~t] **1.** ☐: *be* ~ *on od. upon* abhängen von; **2.** Kontingent *n*.

con·tin·u·al ☐ [kən'tɪnjʊəl] fortwährend, unaufhörlich; **~u·a·tion** [kəntɪnjʊ'eɪʃn] Fortsetzung *f*; Fortdauer *f*; ~ *school* Fortbildungsschule *f*; ~ *training* berufliche Fortbildung; **~ue** [kən'tɪnjuː] *v/t.* fortsetzen, -fahren mit; beibehalten; *to be* ~*d* Fortsetzung folgt; *v/i.* fortdauern, andauern, anhalten; fortfahren, weitermachen; **con·ti·nu·i·ty** [kɒntɪ'njuːətɪ] Kontinuität *f*; **~u·ous** ☐ [kən'tɪnjʊəs] ununterbrochen; ~ *form gr.* Verlaufsform *f*.

con·tort [kən'tɔːt] verdrehen; verzerren; **~tor·tion** [~ʃn] Verdrehung *f*; Verzerrung *f*.

con·tour ['kɒntʊə] Umriß *m*.

con·tra ['kɒntrə] wider, gegen.

con·tra·band *econ.* ['kɒntrəbænd] unter Ein- *od.* Ausfuhrverbot stehende Ware.

con·tra·cep|tion *⚕* [kɒntrə'sepʃn] Empfängnisverhütung *f*; **~tive** *⚕* [~tɪv] empfängnisverhütend(es Mittel).

con|tract 1. [kən'trækt] *v/t.* zusammenziehen; sich *e-e Krankheit* zuziehen; *Schulden* machen; *e-e Ehe etc.* schließen; *v/i.* sich zusammenziehen, schrumpfen; *⚕* e-n Vertrag schließen; sich vertraglich verpflichten; **2.** ['kɒntrækt] Kontrakt *m*, Vertrag *m*; **~trac·tion** [kən'trækʃn] Zusammenziehung *f*; *gr.* Kurzform *f*; **~trac·tor** [~ə]: *a. building* ~ Bauunternehmer *m*.

con·tra·dict [kɒntrə'dɪkt] widersprechen (*dat.*); **~dic·tion** [~kʃn] Widerspruch *m*; **~dic·to·ry** ☐ [~tərɪ] (sich) widersprechend.

con·tra·ry ['kɒntrərɪ] **1.** ☐ entgegengesetzt; widrig; ~ *to* im Gegensatz zu; ~ *to expectations* wider Erwarten; **2.** Gegenteil *n*; *on the* ~ im Gegenteil.

con·trast 1. ['kɒntrɑːst] Gegensatz *m*; Kontrast *m*; **2.** [kən'trɑːst] *v/t.* gegenüberstellen, vergleichen; *v/i.* sich unterscheiden, abstechen (*with* von).

con·trib·ute [kən'trɪbjuːt] beitragen, -steuern; spenden (*to* für); **~tri-**

bu·tion [kɒntrɪˈbjuːʃn] Beitrag *m*; Spende *f*; **~trib·u·tor** [kənˈtrɪbjʊtə] Beitragende(r *m*) *f*; Mitarbeiter(in) (*an e-r Zeitung*); **~trib·u·to·ry** [~ərɪ] beitragend.

con|trite □ [ˈkɒntraɪt] zerknirscht; **~tri·tion** [kənˈtrɪʃn] Zerknirschung *f*.

con·trive [kənˈtraɪv] ersinnen, (sich) ausdenken, planen; zustande bringen; es fertigbringen (*to inf. zu inf.*); **~d** gekünstelt (*Freundlichkeit etc.*).

con·trol [kənˈtrəʊl] **1.** Kontrolle *f*, Herrschaft *f*, Macht *f*, Gewalt *f*; Beherrschung *f*; Aufsicht *f*; ⊕ Steuerung *f*; *mst* **~s** *pl.* ⊕ Steuervorrichtung *f*; △ *nicht Kontrolle (Überprüfung)*; *lose* **~** die Herrschaft *od.* Gewalt *od.* Kontrolle verlieren; **2.** (-*ll*-) beherrschen, die Kontrolle haben über (*acc.*); *e-r Sache* Herr werden, (erfolgreich) bekämpfen; kontrollieren, überwachen; *econ.* (staatlich) lenken, *Preise* binden; **~**, ⊕ steuern, regeln, regulieren; △ *nicht kontrollieren (überprüfen)*; **~ desk** *f*, ⊕ Schalt-, Steuerpult *n*; **~ pan·el** *f* Schalttafel *f*; Bedienungsfeld *n*; **~ tow·er** ✈ Kontrollturm *m*, Tower *m*.

con·tro·ver|sial □ [kɒntrəˈvɜːʃl] umstritten; **~sy** [ˈkɒntrəvɜːsɪ] Kontroverse *f*, Streit *m*.

con·tuse [kənˈtjuːz] quetschen.

con·va|lesce [kɒnvəˈles] gesund werden, genesen; **~les·cence** [~ns] Rekonvaleszenz *f*, Genesung *f*; **~les·cent** [~t] **1.** □ genesend; **2.** Rekonvaleszent(in), Genesende(r *m*) *f*.

con·vene [kənˈviːn] (sich) versammeln; zusammentreten (*Parlament etc.*); einberufen.

con·ve·ni|ence [kənˈviːnjəns] Bequemlichkeit *f*; Angemessenheit *f*; Vorteil *m*; *Brt.* Toilette *f*; *all* (*modern*) **~s** *pl.* aller Komfort; *at your earliest* **~** möglichst bald; **~ent** □ [~t] bequem; günstig.

con·vent [ˈkɒnvənt] (Nonnen)Kloster *n*.

con·ven·tion [kənˈvenʃn] Versammlung *f*; Konvention *f*, Übereinkommen *n*, Abkommen *n*; Sitte *f*; **~al** □ [~nl] herkömmlich, konventionell.

con·verge [kənˈvɜːdʒ] konvergieren; zusammenlaufen, -strömen.

con·ver·sant [kənˈvɜːsənt] vertraut.

con·ver·sa·tion [kɒnvəˈseɪʃn] Gespräch *n*, Unterhaltung *f*; **~al** □ [~nl] Unterhaltungs...; umgangssprachlich.

con·verse 1. □ [ˈkɒnvɜːs] umgekehrt; **2.** [kənˈvɜːs] sich unterhalten.

con·ver·sion [kənˈvɜːʃn] Um-, Verwandlung *f*; *econ.* ⊕ Umstellung *f*; ⊕ Umbau *m*; *⚡* Umformung *f*; *eccl.* Konversion *f*; *pol.* Übertritt *m*; *econ.* Konvertierung *f*; Umstellung *f* (*e-r Währung etc.*).

con|vert 1. [ˈkɒnvɜːt] Bekehrte(r *m*) *f*, *eccl. a.* Konvertit(in); **2.** [kənˈvɜːt] (sich) um- *od.* verwandeln; *econ.* ⊕ umstellen (*to auf acc.*); ⊕ umbauen (*into zu*); *⚡* umformen; *eccl.* bekehren; *econ.* konvertieren, umwandeln; *Währung etc.* umstellen; **~vert·er** *⚡* [~ə] Umformer *m*; **~vert·i·ble 1.** □ [~əbl] um-, verwandelbar; *econ.* konvertierbar; **2.** *mot.* Kabrio(lett) *n*.

con·vey [kənˈveɪ] befördern, transportieren, bringen; überbringen; -mitteln; übertragen; mitteilen; **~ance** [~əns] Beförderung *f*, Transport *m*; Übermittlung *f*; Verkehrsmittel *n*; *jur.* Übertragung *f*; **~er, ~or** ⊕ [~ə] = **~er belt** Förderband *n*.

con|vict 1. [ˈkɒnvɪkt] Strafgefangene(r *m*), Sträfling *m*; **2.** *jur.* [kənˈvɪkt] *j-n* überführen; **~vic·tion** [~kʃn] *jur.* Verurteilung *f*; Überzeugung *f*.

con·vince [kənˈvɪns] überzeugen.

con·viv·i·al □ [kənˈvɪvɪəl] gesellig.

con·voy [ˈkɒnvɔɪ] **1.** ✠ Geleitzug *m*, Konvoi *m*; (Wagen)Kolonne *f*; (Geleit)Schutz *m*; **2.** Geleitschutz geben (*dat.*), eskortieren.

con·vul|sion *⚘* [kənˈvʌlʃn] Zuckung *f*, Krampf *m*; **~sive** □ [~sɪv] krampfhaft, -artig, konvulsiv.

coo [kuː] gurren.

cook [kʊk] **1.** Koch *m*; Köchin *f*; **2.** kochen; F *Bericht etc.* frisieren; **~ up** F sich ausdenken, erfinden; **~book** *Am.* [ˈkʊkbʊk] Kochbuch *n*; **~er** *Brt.* [~ə] Ofen *m*, Herd *m*; **~er·y** [~ərɪ] Kochen *n*; Kochkunst *f*; **~ book** *Brt.* Kochbuch *n*; **~ie** *Am.* [~ɪ] (süßer) Keks, Plätzchen *n*; **~ing** [ɪŋ] Küche *f* (*Kochweise*); **~y** *Am.* [~ɪ] = *cookie*.

cool [kuːl] **1.** □ kühl; *fig.* kaltblütig, gelassen; unverfroren; *bsd. Am.* F klasse, prima, cool; **2.** Kühle *f*; F

(Selbst)Beherrschung f; **3.** (sich) abkühlen; ~ **down,** ~ **off** sich beruhigen.

coon zo. F [ku:n] Waschbär m.

coop [ku:p] **1.** Hühnerstall m; **2.** ~ **up,** ~ **in** einsperren, -pferchen.

co-op F [ˈkəʊɒp] Co-op m (Genossenschaft u. Laden).

co(-)op·e|rate [kəʊˈɒpəreɪt] mitwirken; zusammenarbeiten; ~**ra·tion** [kəʊpəˈreɪʃn] Mitwirkung f; Zusammenarbeit f; ~**ra·tive** [kəʊˈɒpərətɪv] **1.** □ zusammenarbeitend; mitarbeitend; **2.** a. ~ **society** Genossenschaft f; Co-op m, Konsumverein m; a. ~ **store** Co-op m, Konsumladen m; ~**ra·tor** [ˌreɪtə] Mitarbeiter(in).

co(-)or·di|nate 1. □ [kəʊˈɔːdɪnət] koordiniert, gleichgeordnet; **2.** [ˌneɪt] koordinieren, aufeinander abstimmen; ~**na·tion** [kəʊɒˈdɪˈneɪʃn] Koordination f; harmonisches Zusammenspiel.

cop F [kɒp] Bulle m (Polizist).

cope [kəʊp]: ~ **with** gewachsen sein, fertig werden mit.

cop·i·er [ˈkɒpɪə] Kopiergerät n, Kopierer m; = copyist.

co·pi·ous □ [ˈkəʊpjəs] reich(lich); weitschweifig.

cop·per¹ [ˈkɒpə] **1.** min. Kupfer n; Kupfermünze f; **2.** kupfern, Kupfer...

cop·per² F [~] Bulle m (Polizist).

cop·pice, copse [ˈkɒpɪs, kɒps] Unterholz n, Dickicht n.

cop·y [ˈkɒpɪ] **1.** Kopie f; Abschrift f; Nachbildung f; Durchschlag m; Muster n; Exemplar n (e-s Buches); (Zeitungs)Nummer f; druckfertiges Manuskript; fair od. clean ~ Reinschrift f; **2.** kopieren; abschreiben; Computer: Daten übertragen; nachbilden; nachahmen; ~**book** Schreibheft n; ~**ing** [~ɪŋ] Kopier...; ~**ist** [~ɪst] Abschreiber m, Kopist m; ~**right** Urheberrecht n, Copyright n.

cor·al zo. [ˈkɒrəl] Koralle f.

cord [kɔːd] **1.** Schnur f, Strick m; anat. Band n, Schnur f, Strang m; **2.** (zu)schnüren, binden.

cor·di·al [ˈkɔːdjəl] **1.** □ herzlich; ⚕ stärkend; **2.** belebendes Mittel, Stärkungsmittel n; Fruchtsaftkonzentrat n; Likör m; ~**i·ty** [kɔːdɪˈælətɪ] Herzlichkeit f.

cor·don [ˈkɔːdn] **1.** Kordon m, Po-

stenkette f; **2.** ~ **off** abriegeln, absperren.

cor·du·roy [ˈkɔːdərɔɪ] Kord(samt) m; (a pair of) ~**s** pl. (e-e) Kordhose.

core [kɔː] **1.** Kerngehäuse n; fig. Herz n, Mark n, Kern m, Kern f; **2.** entkernen.

cork [kɔːk] **1.** Kork m; **2.** a. ~ **up** zu-, verkorken; ~**screw** [ˈkɔːkskruː] Korkenzieher m.

corn [kɔːn] **1.** (Samen-, Getreide-)Korn n; Getreide n; a. Indian ~ Am. Mais m; ⚕ Hühnerauge n. **2.** (ein)pökeln.

cor·ner [ˈkɔːnə] **1.** Ecke f; Winkel m; Kurve f; Fußball etc.: Eckball m, Ecke f; fig. schwierige Lage, Klemme f, Enge f; **2.** Eck...; ~**kick** Fußball: Eckstoß m; **3.** in die Ecke (fig. Enge) treiben; econ. aufkaufen; ~**ed** ...eckig.

cor·net [ˈkɔːnɪt] ♪ Kornett n; Brt. Eistüte f.

corn·flakes [ˈkɔːnfleɪks] pl. Cornflakes pl.

cor·nice arch. [ˈkɔːnɪs] Gesims n, Sims m.

cor·o·na·ry anat. [ˈkɒrənərɪ] koronar; ~ **artery** Koronar-, Kranzarterie f.

cor·o·na·tion [kɒrəˈneɪʃn] **1.** Krönung f.

cor·o·ner ⚖ [ˈkɒrənə] Coroner m (richterlicher Beamter zur Untersuchung der Todesursache in Fällen gewaltsamen od. unnatürlichen Todes); ~'s inquest gerichtliches Verfahren zur Untersuchung der Todesursache.

cor·o·net [ˈkɒrənɪt] Adelskrone f.

cor·po|ral [ˈkɔːpərəl] **1.** □ körperlich; **2.** ✕ Unteroffizier m; ~**ra·tion** [kɔːpəˈreɪʃn] Körperschaft f; Stadtverwaltung f; Vereinigung f, Gesellschaft f; Am. Aktiengesellschaft f.

corpse [kɔːps] Leichnam m, Leiche f.

cor·pu|lence, ~len·cy [ˈkɔːpjʊləns, ~sɪ] Beleibtheit f; ~**lent** [~t] beleibt.

cor·ral Am. [kɔːˈrɑːl, Am. kəˈræl] Korral m, Hürde f, Pferch m; **2.** (-ll-) Vieh in e-n Pferch treiben.

cor·rect [kəˈrekt] **1.** adj. □ korrekt, richtig; **2.** v/t. korrigieren; zurechtweisen; strafen; ~**rec·tion** [~kʃn] Berichtigung f; Korrektur f; Verweis m; Strafe f; house of ~ (Jugend-)Strafanstalt f; ~ (~)Gefängnis n.

cor·re|spond [kɒrɪˈspɒnd] entsprechen (with, to dat.); korrespondieren; ~**spon·dence** [~əns] Übereinstimmung *f*; Korrespondenz *f*, Briefwechsel *m*; ~ *course* Fernkurs *m*; ~**spon·dent** [~t] 1. □ entsprechend; 2. Briefpartner(in); Korrespondent(in); ~**spon·ding** □ [~ɪŋ] entsprechend.

cor·ri·dor [ˈkɒrɪdɔ:] Korridor *m*, Gang *m*; ~ *train* D-Zug *m*.

cor·rob·o·rate [kəˈrɒbəreɪt] bekräftigen, bestätigen.

cor|rode [kəˈrəʊd] zerfressen; korrodieren; ~**ro·sion** [~ʒn] Zerfressen *n*; ⊕ Korrosion *f*; Rost *m*; ~**ro·sive** [~sɪv] 1. □ zerfressend, ätzend; 2. Korrosions-, Ätzmittel *n*.

cor·ru·gate [ˈkɒrʊgeɪt] runzeln; ⊕ wellen, riefen; ~*d iron* Wellblech *n*.

cor|rupt [kəˈrʌpt] 1. □ verdorben; korrupt, bestechlich, käuflich; 2. *v/t.* verderben; bestechen; *v/i.* verderben; ~**rupt·i·ble** □ [~əbl] verderblich; korrupt, bestechlich, käuflich; ~**rup·tion** [~pʃn] Verdorbenheit, Verworfenheit *f*; Fäulnis *f*; Korruption *f*, Bestechlichkeit *f*; Verfälschung *f*.

cor·set [ˈkɔ:sɪt] Korsett *n*.

cos|met·ic [kɒzˈmetɪk] 1. (~*ally*) kosmetisch, Schönheits...; 2. kosmetisches Mittel, Schönheitsmittel *n*; ~**me·ti·cian** [kɒzməˈtɪʃn] Kosmetiker(in).

cos·mo·naut [ˈkɒzmənɔ:t] Kosmonaut *m*, (sowjetischer) (Welt)Raumfahrer.

cos·mo·pol·i·tan [kɒzməˈpɒlɪtən] 1. kosmopolitisch; 2. Weltbürger(in).

cost [kɒst] 1. Preis *m*; Kosten *pl.*; Schaden *m*; △ *nicht Kost (Essen)*; ~ *of living* Lebenshaltungskosten *pl.*; 2. (*cost*) kosten; ~**ly** [ˈkɒstlɪ] (*-ier, -iest*) kostspielig; teuer erkauft.

cos·tume [ˈkɒstju:m] Kostüm *n*, Kleidung *f*, Tracht *f*.

co·sy [ˈkəʊzɪ] 1. □ (*-ier, -iest*) behaglich, gemütlich; 2. = *egg-cosy, tea-cosy*.

cot [kɒt] Feldbett *n*; *Brt.* Kinderbett *n*.

cot|tage [ˈkɒtɪdʒ] Cottage *n*, (kleines) Landhaus; *Am.* Ferienhaus *n*, -häuschen *n*; ~ *cheese* Hüttenkäse *m*; ~**tag·er** [~ə] Cottagebewohner(in); *Am.* Urlauber(in) in e-m Ferienhaus.

cot·ton [ˈkɒtn] 1. Baumwolle *f*; Baumwollstoff *m*; (Baumwoll)Garn *n*, (-)Zwirn *m*; 2. baumwollen,

Baumwoll...; 3. ~ *on to et.* kapieren, verstehen; ~**wood** ♀ *e-e* amer. Pappel; ~ *wool Brt.* (Verband)Watte *f*.

couch [kaʊtʃ] 1. Couch *f*, Sofa *n*; Liege *f*; 2. (ab)fassen, formulieren.

cou·chette 🚆 [ku:ˈʃet] Liegewagenplatz *m*; *a.* ~ *coach* Liegewagen *m*.

cou·gar *zo.* [ˈku:gə] Puma *m*.

cough [kɒf] 1. Husten *m*; 2. husten.

could [kʊd] *pret. von can*[1].

coun|cil [ˈkaʊnsl] Rat(sversammlung *f*) *m*; ~ *house Brt.* gemeindeeigenes Wohnhaus (*mit niedrigen Mieten*); ~**ci(l)·lor** [~sələ] Ratsmitglied *n*, Stadtrat *m*, Stadträtin *f*.

coun|sel [ˈkaʊnsl] 1. Beratung *f*; Rat(schlag) *m*; *Brt.* 🏛 (Rechts)Anwalt *m*; ~ *for the defence* (*Am. defense*) Verteidiger *m*; ~ *for the prosecution* Anklagevertreter *m*; 2. (*bsd. Brt. -ll-, Am. -l-*) *j-n* beraten; *j-m* raten; ~**se(l)·lor** [~sələ] Berater *m*; *a.* ~*-at-law Am.* 🏛 (Rechts)Anwalt *m*.

count[1] [kaʊnt] Graf *m* (*nicht britisch*).

count[2] [~] 1. Rechnung *f*, Zählung *f*; 🏛 Anklagepunkt *m*; 2. *v/t.* zählen; aus-, berechnen; *fig.* halten für; ~ *down* Geld hinzählen; *a.* *v/i.* den Countdown durchführen (für *e-e* Rakete etc.), letzte (Start)Vorbereitungen treffen (für); *v/i.* zählen; rechnen; (*on, upon*) zählen, sich verlassen (auf *acc.*); gelten (*for little* wenig); ~**down** [ˈkaʊntdaʊn] Countdown *m*, *n* (*beim Raketenstart etc.*), letzte (Start)Vorbereitungen *pl.*

coun·te·nance [ˈkaʊntɪnəns] Gesichtsausdruck *m*; Fassung *f*.

count·er[1] [ˈkaʊntə] Zähler *m*; Zählgerät *n*; *Brt.* Spielmarke *f*.

coun·ter[2] [~] Ladentisch *m*; Theke *f*; (Bank-, Post)Schalter *m*.

coun·ter[3] [~] 1. (ent)gegen, Gegen...; 2. entgegentreten (*dat.*), entgegnen (*dat.*); bekämpfen; abwehren.

coun·ter·act [kaʊntərˈrækt] entgegenwirken (*dat.*); neutralisieren; bekämpfen.

coun·ter·bal·ance 1. [ˈkaʊntəbæləns] Gegengewicht *n*; 2. [kaʊntəˈbæləns] aufwiegen, ausgleichen.

coun·ter·clock·wise *Am.* [kaʊntəˈklɒkwaɪz] = *anticlockwise*.

coun·ter·es·pi·o·nage [ˈkaʊntərˈespɪənɑ:ʒ] Spionageabwehr *f*.

coun·ter·feit [ˈkaʊntəfɪt] 1. □ nachgemacht, falsch, unecht; **2.** Fälschung f; Falschgeld n; **3.** Geld, Unterschrift etc. fälschen.

~s martial, **~ martials**) Kriegsgericht n; **~·mar·tial** [~'mɑ:ʃl] (bsd. Brt. -**ll**-, Am. -**l**-) vor ein Kriegsgericht stellen; **~·room** Gerichtssaal m; **~·ship** ['kɔ:tʃɪp] Werben n; **~·yard** Hof m.

coun·ter·foil ['kauntəfɔɪl] Kontrollabschnitt m.

coun·ter·mand [kauntə'mɑ:nd] widerrufen; Ware abbestellen.

coun·ter·pane ['kauntəpeɪn] = bedspread.

coun·ter·part ['kauntəpɑ:t] Gegenstück n; genaue Entsprechung.

coun·ter·sign ['kauntəsaɪn] gegenzeichnen, mit unterschreiben.

coun·tess ['kauntɪs] Gräfin f.

count·less ['kauntlɪs] zahllos.

coun·try ['kʌntrɪ] **1.** Land n; Gegend f; Heimatland n; **2.** Land..., ländlich; **~·man** (pl. -men) Landbewohner m; Bauer m; a. fellow **~** Landsmann m; **~ road** Landstraße f; **~·side** (ländliche) Gegend; Landschaft f; **~·wom·an** (pl. -women) Landbewohnerin f; Bäuerin f; a. fellow **~** Landsmännin f.

coun·ty ['kauntɪ] Brt. Grafschaft f; Am. (Land)Kreis m (einzelstaatlicher Verwaltungsbezirk); **~ seat** Am. Kreis(haupt)stadt f; **~ town** Brt. Grafschaftshauptstadt f.

coup [ku:] Coup m; Putsch m.

cou·ple ['kʌpl] **1.** Paar n; a **~** of F ein paar; **2.** (zusammen)koppeln; ⊕ kuppeln; zo. (sich) paaren.

coup·ling ['kʌplɪŋ] Kupplung f.

cou·pon ['ku:pɒn] Gutschein m; Kupon m, Bestellzettel m.

cour·age ['kʌrɪdʒ] Mut m; **cou·ra·geous** □ [kə'reɪdʒəs] mutig, beherzt.

cou·ri·er ['kʊrɪə] Kurier m; Eilbote m; Reiseleiter m.

course [kɔ:s] **1.** Lauf m, Gang m; Weg m; ♏, ✈, fig. Kurs m; Sport: (Renn-) Bahn f, (-)Strecke f, (Golf)Platz m; Gang m (Speisen); Reihe f; Folge f; Kurs m; ♨ Kur f; of **~** natürlich, selbstverständlich; **2.** hetzen, jagen; strömen (Tränen etc.).

court [kɔ:t] **1.** Hof m (a. e.-s Fürsten); kleiner Platz; Sport: Platz m, (Spiel)Feld n; ⚖ Gericht(shof m) n; Gerichtssaal m; **2.** j-m den Hof machen; werben um.

cour·te·ous □ ['kɜ:tjəs] höflich; **~·sy** [~ɪsɪ] Höflichkeit f; Gefälligkeit f.

court|-**house** ['kɔ:thaus] Gerichtsgebäude n; **~·ier** [~jə] Höfling m; **~·ly** [~lɪ] höfisch; höflich; **~ mar·tial** (pl.

cous·in ['kʌzn] Cousin m, Vetter m; Cousine f, Kusine f.

cove [kəʊv] kleine Bucht.

cov·er ['kʌvə] **1.** Decke f; Deckel m; (Buch)Deckel m, Einband m; Umschlag m; Hülle f; Schutzhaube f, -platte f; Abdeckhaube f; Briefumschlag m; Deckung f; Schutz m; Dickicht n; Decke f; fig. (Be-)reifung f);fig. Deckmantel m; take **~** in Deckung gehen; under plain **~** in neutralem Umschlag m; under separate **~** mit getrennter Post; **2.** (be-, zu)decken; einschlagen, -wickeln; verbergen, -decken; schützen; Weg zurücklegen; decken; mit e-r Schußwaffe zielen auf (acc.); ⚔ Gelände bestreichen; umfassen; fig. erfassen; Presse, Rundfunk, TV: berichten über (acc.); **~** up ab-, zudecken; fig. verbergen, -heimlichen; **~** up for s.o. j-n decken; **~·age** [~rɪdʒ] Berichterstattung f (of über acc.); **~ girl** Covergirl n, Titelblattmädchen n; **~·ing** [~rɪŋ] Decke f; Überzug m; (Fußboden)Belag m; **~ sto·ry** Titelgeschichte f.

cov·ert □ ['kʌvət] heimlich, versteckt.

cov·et ['kʌvɪt] begehren; **~·ous** □ [~əs] (be)gierig; habsüchtig.

cow[1] zo. [kaʊ] Kuh f.

cow[2] [~] einschüchtern, ducken.

cow·ard ['kauəd] **1.** □ feig(e); **2.** Feigling m; **~·ice** [~ɪs] Feigheit f; **~·ly** [~lɪ] feig(e).

cow·boy ['kaʊbɔɪ] Cowboy m.

cow·er ['kauə] kauern; sich ducken.

cow·herd ['kauhɜ:d]Kuhhirt m; **~·hide** Rind(s)leder n; **~·house** Kuhstall m.

cowl [kaʊl] Mönchskutte f (mit Kapuze); Kapuze f; Schornsteinkappe f.

cow|**shed** ['kaʊʃed] Kuhstall m; **~·slip** ♀ Schlüsselblume f; Am. Sumpfdotterblume f.

cox [kɒks] = coxswain.

cox·comb ['kɒkskəʊm] Geck m.

cox·swain ['kɒkswein, ♏ mst 'kɒksn] Bootsführer m; Rudern: Steuermann m.

coy □ [kɔɪ] schüchtern; spröde.

coy·ote zo. [ˈkɔɪəʊt] Kojote m, Prärie-wolf m.

co·zy Am. □ [ˈkəʊzɪ] (-ier, -iest) = cosy.

crab [kræb] Krabbe f, Taschenkrebs m; F Nörgler(in).

crack [kræk] **1.** Krach m, Knall m; Spalte f, Spalt m, Schlitz m; F derber Schlag; F Versuch m; Witz m; **2.** erstklassig; **3.** v/t. knallen mit, knacken lassen; zerbrechen, (zer-)sprengen; schlagen, hauen; (auf-)knacken; ~ a joke e-n Witz reißen; v/i. krachen, knallen, knacken; (zer-)springen, (-)platzen; überschlagen (Stimme); a. ~ up fig. zusammenbrechen; get ~ing F loslegen; **~·er** [ˈkrækə] Cracker m, Kräcker m (ungesüßtes, keksartiges Kleingebäck); Schwärmer m, Frosch m (Feuerwerkskörper); **~·le** [ˌkl] knattern, knistern, krachen.

cra·dle [ˈkreɪdl] **1.** Wiege f; fig. Kindheit f; **2.** wiegen; betten.

craft¹ [krɑːft] ⊕ Boot(e pl.) n, Schiff(e pl.) n; ✈ Flugzeug(e pl.) n; (Welt)Raumfahrzeug(e pl.) n.

craft² [ˌ] Handwerk n, Gewerbe n; Schlauheit f, List f; ⚠ nicht Kraft; **~s·man** [ˈkrɑːftsmən] (pl. -men) (Kunst)Handwerker m; **~·y** □ [ˌɪ] (-ier, -iest) gerissen, listig, schlau.

crag [kræg] Klippe f, Felsenspitze f.

cram [kræm] (-mm-) (voll)stopfen; nudeln, mästen; mit j-m pauken; für e-e Prüfung pauken.

cramp [kræmp] **1.** Krampf m; ⊕ Klammer f; fig. Fessel f; **2.** einengen, hemmen.

cran·ber·ry ♀ [ˈkrænbərɪ] Preiselbeere f.

crane [kreɪn] **1.** zo. Kranich m; ⊕ Kran m; **2.** den Hals recken; ~ one's neck sich den Hals verrenken (for nach).

crank [kræŋk] **1.** ⊕ Kurbel f; ⊕ Schwengel m; F Spinner m, komischer Kauz; **2.** (an)kurbeln; **~·shaft** ⊕ [ˈkræŋkʃɑːft] Kurbelwelle f; **~·y** □ [ˌɪ] (-ier, -iest) wacklig; verschroben; Am. schlechtgelaunt.

cran·ny [ˈkrænɪ] Riß m, Ritze f.

crape [kreɪp] Krepp m, Flor m.

craps Am. [kræps] sg. ein Würfelspiel.

crash [kræʃ] **1.** Krach(en n) m; Unfall m, Zusammenstoß m; ✈ Absturz m; bsd. econ. Zusammenbruch m, (Börsen)Krach m; **2.** v/t. zertrüm-

mern; e-n Unfall haben mit; ✈ abstürzen mit; v/i. (krachend) zerbersten, -brechen; krachend einstürzen, zusammenkrachen; bsd. econ. zusammenbrechen; krachen (against, into gegen); mot. zusammenstoßen, verunglücken; ✈ abstürzen; **3.** Schnell..., Sofort...; **~·bar·ri·er** [ˈkræʃbærɪə] Leitplanke f; **~ course** Schnell-, Intensivkurs m; **~ di·et** radikale Schlankheitskur; **~ hel·met** Sturzhelm m; **~·land** ✈ e-e Bruchlandung machen (mit); **~ land·ing** ✈ Bruchlandung f.

crate [kreɪt] (Latten)Kiste f.

cra·ter [ˈkreɪtə] Krater m; Trichter m.

crave [kreɪv] v/t. dringend bitten od. flehen um; v/i. sich sehnen (for nach); **crav·ing** [ˈkreɪvɪŋ] heftiges Verlangen.

craw·fish zo. [ˈkrɔːfɪʃ] Flußkrebs m.

crawl [krɔːl] **1.** Kriechen n; **2.** kriechen; schleichen; wimmeln; kribbeln; Schwimmen: kraulen; it makes one's flesh ~ man bekommt e-e Gänsehaut davon.

cray·fish zo. [ˈkreɪfɪʃ] Flußkrebs m.

cray·on [ˈkreɪən] Zeichenstift m, Pastellstift m.

craze [kreɪz] Verrücktheit f, F Fimmel m; be the ~ Mode sein; **cra·zy** □ [ˈkreɪzɪ] (-ier, -iest) verrückt (about nach).

creak [kriːk] knarren, quietschen.

cream [kriːm] **1.** Rahm m, Sahne f; Creme f, das Beste; **2.** a. ~ off den Rahm abschöpfen von, absahnen (a. fig.); **~·er·y** [ˈkriːmərɪ] Molkerei f; Milchgeschäft n; **~·y** □ [ˌɪ] (-ier, -iest) sahnig; weich.

crease [kriːs] **1.** (Bügel)Falte f; **2.** (zer)knittern.

cre·ate [kriːˈeɪt] (er)schaffen; hervorrufen; verursachen; kreieren; **~·a·tion** [ˌˈeɪʃn] (Er)Schaffung f; Erzeugung f; Schöpfung f; **~·a·tive** □ [ˌˈeɪtɪv] schöpferisch; **~·a·tor** [ˌə] Schöpfer m; Er/Schaffer m; **crea·ture** [ˈkriːtʃə] Geschöpf n; Kreatur f.

crèche [kreɪʃ] (Kinder)Krippe f.

cre·dence [ˈkriːdns] Glaube m; **~·den·tials** [krɪˈdenʃlz] pl. Beglaubigungsschreiben n; Referenzen pl.; Zeugnisse pl.; (Ausweis)Papiere pl.

cred·i·ble □ [ˈkredəbl] glaubwürdig; glaubhaft.

cred|it [ˈkredɪt] **1.** Glaube(n) *m*; Ruf *m*, Ansehen *n*; Verdienst *n*; *econ.* Guthaben *n*; *econ.* Kredit *m*; ~ **card** *econ.* Kreditkarte *f*; **2.** *j-m* glauben; *j-m* trauen; *econ.* gutschreiben; ~ **s.o. with s.th.** j-m et. zutrauen; j-m et. zuschreiben; ~**i·ta·ble** □ [~əbl] achtbar, ehrenvoll (*to* für); ~**i·tor** [~ə] Gläubiger *m*; ~**u·lous** □ [~jʊləs] leichtgläubig.

creed [kri:d] Glaubensbekenntnis *n*.
creek [kri:k] *Brt.* kleine Bucht; *Am.* Bach *m*.
creel [kri:l] Fischkorb *m*.
creep [kri:p] (*crept*) kriechen; schleichen (*a. fig.*); ~ **in** (sich) hinein- od. hereinschleichen; sich einschleichen (*Fehler etc.*); **it makes my flesh** ~ ich bekomme e-e Gänsehaut davon; ~**er** ♀ [ˈkri:pə] Kriech-, Kletterpflanze *f*; ~**s** *pl.* F: **the sight gave me the** ~ bei dem Anblick bekam ich e-e Gänsehaut.
crept [krept] *pret. u. p.p. von creep*.
cres·cent [ˈkresnt] **1.** zunehmend; halbmondförmig; **2.** Halbmond *m*.
cress ♀ [kres] Kresse *f*.
crest [krest] (Hahnen-, Berg- *etc.*) Kamm *m*; Mähne *f*; Federbusch *m*; *family* ~ Heraldik: Familienwappen *n*; ~**fal·len** [ˈkrestfɔ:lən] niedergeschlagen.
cre·vasse [krɪˈvæs] (Gletscher)Spalte *f*; *Am.* Deichbruch *m*.
crev·ice [ˈkrevɪs] Riß *m*, Spalte *f*.
crew[1] [kru:] ♣, ✈ Besatzung *f*, ♣ *a.* Mannschaft *f*; (*Arbeits*)Gruppe *f*; Belegschaft *f*.
crew[2] [~] *pret. von crow* 2.
crib [krɪb] **1.** Krippe *f*; *Am.* Kinderbett *n*; F *Schule*: Klatsche *f*, Spickzettel *m*; **2.** (-*bb*-) F abschreiben, spicken.
crick [krɪk]: **a** ~ **in one's back** (*neck*) ein steifer Rücken (Hals).
crick·et [ˈkrɪkɪt] *zo.* Grille *f*; *Sport*: Kricket *n*; **not** ~ F nicht fair.
crime [kraɪm] ⚖ Verbrechen *n*; *coll.* Verbrechen *pl.*; ~ **novel** Kriminalroman *m*.
crim·i·nal [ˈkrɪmɪnl] **1.** □ verbrecherisch; Kriminal..., Straf...; **2.** Verbrecher(in), Kriminelle(r *m*) *f*.
crimp [krɪmp] kräuseln.
crim·son [ˈkrɪmzn] karmesinrot; puterrot.
cringe [krɪndʒ] sich ducken.
crin|kle [ˈkrɪŋkl] **1.** Falte *f*, *im Ge-*

sicht: Fältchen *n*; **2.** (sich) kräuseln; knittern.
crip·ple [ˈkrɪpl] **1.** Krüppel *m*; **2.** zum Krüppel machen; *fig.* lähmen.
cri·sis [ˈkraɪsɪs] (*pl.* -*ses* [-si:z]) Krisis *f*, Krise *f*; *Wende-*, Höhepunkt *m*.
crisp [krɪsp] **1.** □ kraus; knusp(e)rig, mürbe (*Gebäck*); frisch; klar; steif; **2.** (sich) kräuseln; knusp(e)rig machen *od.* werden; **3.** ~**s** *pl.*, *a.* potato ~**s** *pl. Brt.* (Kartoffel)Chips *pl.*; ~**bread** [ˈkrɪspbred] Knäckebrot *n*.
criss-cross [ˈkrɪskrɒs] **1.** Netz *n* sich schneidender Linien; **2.** (durch-) kreuzen.
cri·te·ri·on [kraɪˈtɪərɪən] (*pl.* -*ria* [-rɪə], -*rions*) Kriterium *n*.
crit|ic [ˈkrɪtɪk] Kritiker(in); △ *nicht Kritik*; ~**i·cal** □ [~kl] kritisch; bedenklich; ~**i·cis·m** [~ɪsɪzəm] Kritik *f* (*of an dat.*); ~**i·cize** [~saɪz] kritisieren; kritisch beurteilen; tadeln.
cri·tique [krɪˈti:k] kritischer Essay, Kritik *f*.
croak [krəʊk] krächzen; quaken.
cro·chet [ˈkrəʊʃeɪ] **1.** Häkelei *f*; Häkelarbeit *f*; **2.** häkeln.
crock·e·ry [ˈkrɒkərɪ] Geschirr *n*.
croc·o·dile *zo.* [ˈkrɒkədaɪl] Krokodil *n*.
crone F [krəʊn] altes Weib.
cro·ny F [ˈkrəʊnɪ] alter Freund.
crook [krʊk] **1.** Krümmung *f*; Haken *m*; Hirtenstab *m*; F Gauner *m*; **2.** (sich) krümmen od. (ver)biegen; ~**ed** [ˈkrʊkɪd] krumm; bucklig; F unehrlich; [krʊkt] Krück...
croon [kru:n] schmalzig singen; summen; ~**er** [ˈkru:nə] Schnulzensänger(in).
crop [krɒp] **1.** *zo.* Kropf *m*; Peitschenstiel *m*; Reitpeitsche *f*; (*Feld-*)Frucht *f*, *bsd.* Getreide *n*; Ernte *f*; kurzer Haarschnitt; **2.** (-*pp*-) abfressen, abweiden; *Haar* kurz schneiden; ~ **up** *fig.* plötzlich auftauchen.
cross [krɒs] **1.** Kreuz *n* (*a. fig. Leiden*); Kreuzung *f*; **2.** □ sich kreuzend, quer (liegend, laufend *etc.*); ärgerlich, böse; entgegengesetzt; Kreuz..., Quer..., **3.** *v/t.* kreuzen; überqueren; *fig.* durchkreuzen; *j-m* in die Quere kommen; ~ **off**, ~ **out** aus-, durchstreichen; ~ **o.s.** sich bekreuzigen; **keep one's fingers** ~**ed** den Daumen halten; *v/i.* sich kreuzen; ~**bar** [ˈkrɒsbɑ:] *Fußball*: Torlatte *f*; ~**breed** (Rassen)Kreuzung

f; **~coun·try** Querfeldein..., Gelände...; ~ *skiing* Skilanglauf m; **~ex·am·i·na·tion** Kreuzverhör n; **~ex·am·ine** ins Kreuzverhör nehmen; **~eyed** schielend; *be* ~ schielen; **~ing** [~ɪŋ] Kreuzung f; Übergang m; ✠ Überfahrt f; **~road** Querstraße f; **~roads** pl. od. sg. Straßenkreuzung f; fig. Scheideweg m; **~sec·tion** Querschnitt m; **~walk** Am. Fußgängerüberweg m; **~wise** kreuzweise; **~word (puz·zle)** Kreuzworträtsel n.

crotch [krɒtʃ] Schritt m (*des Körpers, der Hose*).

crotch·et ['krɒtʃɪt] Haken m; *bsd.* Br. ♪ Viertelnote f.

crouch [krautʃ] 1. sich ducken; 2. Hockstellung f.

crow [krəʊ] 1. zo. Krähe f; Krähen n; 2. (*crowed.* crew, crowed) krähen; (*crowed*) F prahlen (*about* mit).

crow·bar ['krəʊbɑː] Brecheisen n.

crowd [kraʊd] 1. Masse f, Menge f, Gedränge n; F Bande f; 2. sich drängen; *Straßen etc.* bevölkern; vollstopfen; **~ed** ['kraʊdɪd] überfüllt, voll.

crown [kraʊn] 1. Krone f; Kranz m; Gipfel m; Scheitel m; 2. krönen; *Zahn* überkronen; *to* ~ *all* zu allem Überfluß.

cru·cial □ ['kruːʃl] entscheidend, kritisch.

cru·ci·fix ['kruːsɪfɪks] Kruzifix n; **~fix·ion** [kruːsɪ'fɪkʃn] Kreuzigung f; **~fy** ['kruːsɪfaɪ] kreuzigen.

crude □ [kruːd] roh; unfertig; unreif; unfein; grob; Roh...; grell.

cru·el □ ['krʊəl] (*-ll-*) grausam; roh, gefühllos; **~ty** ['krʊəltɪ] Grausamkeit f; ~ *to animals* Tierquälerei f; ~ *to children* Kindesmißhandlung f.

cru·et ['kruːɪt] Essig-, Ölfläschchen n.

cruise ✠ [kruːz] 1. Kreuzfahrt f, Seereise f; ~ *missile* ⚔ Marschflugkörper m; 2. kreuzen, e-e Kreuzfahrt machen; mit Reisegeschwindigkeit fliegen od. fahren; **cruis·er** ['kruːzə] ✠ ⚔ Kreuzer m; Jacht f; Kreuzfahrtschiff n; Am. (Funk-)Streifenwagen m.

crumb [krʌm] 1. Krume f; Brocken m; 2. panieren; zerkrümeln; **crum·ble** ['krʌmbl] (zer)bröckeln; fig. zugrunde gehen.

crum·ple ['krʌmpl] v/t. zerknittern;

v/i. knittern; zusammengedrückt werden.

crunch [krʌntʃ] (zer)kauen; zermalmen; knirschen.

cru·sade [kruː'seɪd] Kreuzzug m (*a. fig.*); **~sad·er** hist. [~ə] Kreuzfahrer m.

crush [krʌʃ] 1. Druck m; Gedränge n; (*Frucht*)Saft m; F Schwärmerei f; *have a* ~ *on s.o.* in j-n verliebt od. verknallt sein; 2. v/t. (zer-, aus)quetschen; zermalmen; fig. vernichten; v/i. sich drängen; **~bar·ri·er** ['krʌʃbærɪə] Barriere f, Absperrung f.

crust [krʌst] 1. Kruste f; Rinde f; 2. verkrusten; verharschen.

crus·ta·cean zo. [krʌ'steɪʃn] Krebs-, Krusten-, Schalentier n.

crust·y □ ['krʌstɪ] (*-ier, -iest*) krustig; fig. mürrisch, barsch.

crutch [krʌtʃ] Krücke f.

cry [kraɪ] 1. Schrei m; Geschrei n; Ruf m; Weinen n; Gebell n; 2. schreien; (aus)rufen; weinen; ~ *for* verlangen nach.

crypt [krɪpt] Gruft f; **cryp·tic** ['krɪptɪk] (*~ally*) verborgen, geheim; rätselhaft.

crys·tal ['krɪstl] Kristall m; Am. Uhrglas n; **~line** [~təlaɪn] kristallen; **~lize** [~aɪz] kristallisieren.

cub [kʌb] 1. Junge(s) n; Flegel m; Anfänger m; 2. (Junge) werfen.

cube [kjuːb] Würfel m (*a. A̸*); phot. Blitzwürfel m; A̸ Kubikzahl f; ~ *root* A̸ Kubikwurzel f; **cu·bic** ['kjuːbɪk] (*~ally*), **cu·bi·cal** □ [~kl] würfelförmig, kubisch; Kubik...

cu·bi·cle ['kjuːbɪkl] Kabine f.

cuck·oo zo. ['kʊkuː] (*pl. -oos*) Kuckuck m.

cu·cum·ber ['kjuːkʌmbə] Gurke f; *as cool as a* ~ fig. eiskalt, gelassen.

cud [kʌd] wiedergekäutes Futter; *chew the* ~ wiederkäuen; fig. überlegen.

cud·dle ['kʌdl] v/t. an sich drücken; schmusen (mit).

cud·gel ['kʌdʒəl] 1. Knüppel m; 2. (*bsd. Brt. -ll-, Am. -l-*) prügeln.

cue [kjuː] Billard: Queue n; thea. etc., a. fig. Stichwort n; Wink m.

cuff [kʌf] 1. Manschette f; Handschelle f; (Ärmel-, Am. a. Hosen-) Aufschlag m; Schlag m (mit der offenen Hand); Klaps m; 2. (mit der flachen Hand) schlagen.

cui·sine [kwiˈziːn] Küche f (*Kochkunst*).

cul·mi·nate [ˈkʌlmɪneɪt] gipfeln (*in* in *dat.*).

cu·lottes [kjuˈlɒts] *pl.* (*a pair of* ein) Hosenrock m.

cul·pa·ble □ [ˈkʌlpəbl] strafbar.

cul·prit [ˈkʌlprɪt] Angeklagte(r m) f; Schuldige(r m) f; Täter(in).

cul·ti·vate [ˈkʌltɪveɪt] ✔ kultivieren, bestellen, an-, bebauen; *Freundschaft etc.* pflegen; **~·vat·ed** ✔ bebaut; *fig.* gebildet, kultiviert; **~·va·tion** [↓ˈveɪʃn] ✔ Kultivierung f, (An-, Acker)Bau m; *fig.* Pflege f.

cul·tu·ral □ [ˈkʌltʃərəl] kulturell; Kultur...

cul·ture [ˈkʌltʃə] Kultur f; Zucht f; **~d** kultiviert (*a. fig.*); Zucht...

cum·ber·some [ˈkʌmbəsəm] lästig, hinderlich; klobig.

cu·mu·la·tive □ [ˈkjuːmjʊlətɪv] sich (an-, auf)häufend, anwachsend; Zusatz...

cun·ning [ˈkʌnɪŋ] 1. □ schlau, listig, gerissen; geschickt; *Am.* niedlich; 2. List f, Schlauheit f, Gerissenheit f; Geschicklichkeit f.

cup [kʌp] 1. Tasse f; Becher m; Schale f; Kelch m; *Sport:* Cup m, Pokal m; **~ final** Pokalendspiel n; **~ winner** Pokalsieger m; 2. (*-pp-*) *die* Hand hohl machen; *she* **~ped** *her chin in her hand* sie stützte das Kinn in die Hand; **~·board** [ˈkʌbəd] (Geschirr-, Speise-, *Brt. a.* Wäsche-, Kleider-) Schrank m; **~ bed** Schrankbett n.

cu·pid·i·ty [kjuːˈpɪdətɪ] Habgier f.

cu·po·la [ˈkjuːpələ] Kuppel m.

cur [kɜː] Köter m; Schurke m.

cu·ra·ble [ˈkjʊərəbl] heilbar.

cu·rate [ˈkjʊərət] Hilfsgeistliche(r) m.

curb [kɜːb] 1. Kandare f (*a. fig.*); *bsd. Am.* = kerb(*stone*) f; 2. an die Kandare legen (*a. fig.*); *fig.* zügeln.

curd [kɜːd] 1. Quark m; 2. *mst* **cur·dle** [ˈkɜːdl] gerinnen (lassen); *the sight made my blood* **~** bei dem Anblick erstarrte mir das Blut in den Adern.

cure [kjʊə] 1. Kur f; Heilmittel n; Heilung f; Seelsorge f; Pfarre f; 2. heilen; pökeln; räuchern; trocknen.

cur·few [ˈkɜːfjuː] Ausgangsverbot n, -sperre f.

cu·ri·o [ˈkjʊərɪəʊ] (*pl. -os*) Rarität f; **~·os·i·ty** [kjʊərɪˈɒsətɪ] Neugier f; Rarität f; **~·ous** □ [ˈkjʊərɪəs] neu-

gierig; wißbegierig; seltsam, merkwürdig.

curl [kɜːl] 1. Locke f; 2. (sich) kräuseln *od.* locken; **~·er** [ˈkɜːlə] Lockenwickler m; **~·y** [↓ɪ] (*-ier, -iest*) gekräuselt; gelockt, lockig.

cur·rant [ˈkʌrənt] ♀ Johannisbeere f; Korinthe f.

cur·ren·cy [ˈkʌrənsɪ] Umlauf m; *econ.* Laufzeit f; *econ.* Währung f; *foreign* **~** Devisen *pl.*; **~·rent** [↓t] 1. □ umlaufend; *econ.* gültig (*Geld*); allgemein (bekannt); geläufig; laufend (*Jahr etc.*); gegenwärtig, aktuell; 2. Strom m (*a.* ⚡); Strömung f (*a. fig.*); (*Luft*)Zug m; **~·rent account** *econ.* Girokonto n.

cur·ric·u·lum [kəˈrɪkjʊləm] (*pl. -la* [-lə], *-lums*) Lehr-, Stundenplan m; **~ vi·tae** [↓ˈvaːtiː] Lebenslauf m.

cur·ry¹ [ˈkʌrɪ] Curry m, n.

cur·ry² [↓] *Pferd* striegeln.

curse [kɜːs] 1. Fluch m; △ *nicht* Kurs; 2. (ver)fluchen; strafen; **curs·ed** □ [ˈkɜːsɪd] verflucht.

cur·sor [ˈkɜːsə] ⚙ Läufer m, Schieber m (*am Rechenschieber*); *Computer:* Positionsanzeiger m (*auf dem Bildschirm*).

cur·so·ry □ [ˈkɜːsrɪ] flüchtig, oberflächlich.

curt □ [kɜːt] kurz, knapp; barsch.

cur·tail [kɜːˈteɪl] beschneiden; *fig.* beschränken; kürzen (*of* um).

cur·tain [ˈkɜːtn] 1. Vorhang m, Gardine f; *draw the* **~s** den Vorhang *od.* die Vorhänge zuziehen *od.* aufziehen; 2. **~ off** mit Vorhängen abteilen.

curt·s(e)y [ˈkɜːtsɪ] 1. Knicks m; 2. knicksen (*to* vor *dat.*).

cur·va·ture [ˈkɜːvətʃə] Krümmung f.

curve [kɜːv] 1. Kurve f; Krümmung f; 2. (sich) krümmen *od.* biegen.

cush·ion [ˈkʊʃn] 1. Kissen n, Polster n; *Billardtisch:* Bande f; 2. polstern.

cuss F [kʌs] 1. Fluch m; 2. (ver)fluchen.

cus·tard [ˈkʌstəd] Eiercreme f.

cus·to·dy [ˈkʌstədɪ] Haft f; Gewahrsam m; Obhut f.

cus·tom [ˈkʌstəm] Gewohnheit f, Brauch m, Sitte f; *econ.* Kundschaft f; **~·a·ry** □ [↓ərɪ] gewöhnlich, üblich; **~-built** nach Kundenangaben gefertigt; **~·er** [↓ə] Kunde m, -in f; F Bursche m; **~·house** Zollamt n; **~-made** maßgefertigt, Maß...

cus·toms [ˈkʌstəmz] *pl.* Zoll m; **~**

clear·ance Zollabfertigung *f*; ~ **of·fi·cer,** ~ **of·fi·cial** Zollbeamte(r) *m*.

cut [kʌt] **1.** Schnitt *m*; Hieb *m*; Stich *m*; (Schnitt)Wunde *f*; Einschnitt *m*; Graben *m*; Kürzung *f*; Ausschnitt *m*; Wegabkürzung *f* (*mst short-~*); (*Holz*)Schnitt *m*; (*Kupfer*)Stich *m*; Schliff *m*; Schnitte *f*, Scheibe *f*; *Karten*: Abheben *n*; *cold* ~*s pl. Küche*: Aufschnitt *m*; *give s.o. the* ~ *direct* F j-n ostentativ schneiden; **2.** (*-tt-*; *cut*) schneiden; schnitzen; gravieren; ab-, an-, auf-, aus-, be-, durch-, zer-, zuschneiden; kürzen; *Edelstein etc.* schleifen; *Karten* abheben; *j-n beim Begegnen* schneiden; ~ *teeth* zahnen; ~ *short j-n* unterbrechen; ~ *across* quer durch... gehen (*um abzukürzen*); ~ *back Pflanze* beschneiden, stutzen; kürzen; einschränken; herabsetzen; ~ *down Bäume* fällen; verringern, einschränken, reduzieren; ~ *in* F sich einschalten; ~ *in on s.o. mot.* j-n schneiden; ~ *off* abschneiden; *teleph.* *Teilnehmer* trennen; *j-n* enterben; ~ *out* ausschneiden; *Am.* Vieh aussondern (*aus der Herde*); *fig. j-n* ausstechen; *be* ~ *out for* das Zeug zu et. haben; ~ *up* zerschneiden; *be* ~ *up* F tief betrübt sein; ~**back** [ˈkʌtbæk] Kürzung *f*; Herabsetzung *f*, Verringerung *f*.

cute □ F [kjuːt] (~*r*, ~*st*) schlau; *Am.* niedlich; süß.

cu·ti·cle [ˈkjuːtɪkl] Nagelhaut *f*.

cut·ler·y [ˈkʌtlərɪ] (Tisch-, Eß)Besteck *n*.

cut·let [ˈkʌtlɪt] Schnitzel *n*; Hacksteak *n*.

cut|-price *econ.* [ˈkʌtpraɪs], ~**rate** ermäßigt, herabgesetzt; Billig...; ~**ter** [~ə] (Blech-, Holz)Schneider *m*; Schnitzer *m*; Zuschneider(in); (Glas- *etc.*)Schleifer *m*; *Film:* Cutter(in); ⊕ Schneidewerkzeug *n*, -maschine *f*; ⚓ Kutter *m*; *Am.* leichter Schlitten; ~**throat** Mörder *m*; Killer *m*; ~**ting** [~ɪŋ] **1.** □ schneidend; scharf; ⊕ Schneid..., Fräs...; **2.** Schneiden *n*; 🚂 *etc.* Einschnitt *m*; ♀ Steckling *m*; *bsd. Brt.* (*Zeitungs-*)Ausschnitt *m*; ~*s pl.* Schnipsel *pl.*; ⊕ Späne *pl.*

cy·cle¹ [ˈsaɪkl] Zyklus *m*; Kreis(lauf) *m*; Periode *f*.

cy·cle² [~] **1.** Fahrrad *n*; **2.** radfahren; **cy·clist** [~lɪst] Radfahrer(in); Motorradfahrer(in).

cy·clone [ˈsaɪkləʊn] Wirbelsturm *m*.

cyl·in·der [ˈsɪlɪndə] Zylinder *m*, Walze *f*; ⊕ Trommel *f*.

cym·bal ♪ [ˈsɪmbl] Becken *n*.

cyn|ic [ˈsɪnɪk] Zyniker *m*; ~**i·cal** □ [~kl] zynisch.

cy·press ♀ [ˈsaɪprɪs] Zypresse *f*.

cyst ⚕ [sɪst] Zyste *f*.

czar *hist.* [zɑː] = *tsar.*

Czech [tʃek] **1.** tschechisch; **2.** Tscheche|e *m*, -in *f*; *ling.* Tschechisch *n*.

Czech·o·slo·vak [ˈtʃekəʊˈsləʊvæk] **1.** Tschechoslowake|e *m*, -in *f*; **2.** tschechoslowakisch.

D

dab [dæb] **1.** Klaps *m*; Tupfen *m*, Klecks *m*; **2.** (*-bb-*) leicht schlagen *od.* klopfen; be-, abtupfen.

dab·ble [ˈdæbl] bespritzen; betupfen; plätschern; sich oberflächlich *od.* (*contp.*) in dilettantischer Weise befassen (*at*, *in* mit).

dachs·hund *zo.* [ˈdækshʊnd] Dackel *m*.

dad F [dæd], ~**dy** F [ˈdædɪ] Papa *m*, Vati *m*.

dad·dy-long-legs *zo.* [ˈdædɪˈlɒŋlegz] Schnake *f*; *Am.* Weberknecht *m*.

daf·fo·dil ♀ [ˈdæfədɪl] gelbe Narzisse.

daft F [dɑːft] blöde, doof.

dag·ger [ˈdægə] Dolch *m*; *be at* ~*s drawn fig.* auf Kriegsfuß stehen.

dai·ly [ˈdeɪlɪ] **1.** täglich; **2.** Tageszeitung *f*; Putzfrau *f*.

dain·ty [ˈdeɪntɪ] **1.** □ (*-ier*, *-iest*) lecker; zart; zierlich, niedlich, reizend; wählerisch; **2.** Leckerbissen *m.*

dair·y ['deərɪ] Molkerei *f;* Milchwirtschaft *f;* Milchgeschäft *n;* ~ **cattle** Milchvieh *n;* ~**man** (*pl. -men*) Melker *m;* Milchmann *m.*

dai·sy ['deɪzɪ] Gänseblümchen *n.*

dale *dial. od. poet.* [deɪl] Tal *n.*

dal·ly ['dælɪ] (ver)trödeln; schäkern.

dam¹ *zo.* [dæm] Mutter(tier *n*) *f.*

dam² [~] **1.** Deich *m,* (Stau)Damm *m;* **2.** (*-mm-*) *a.* ~ *up* stauen, (ab-, ein-)dämmen (*a. fig.*).

dam·age ['dæmɪdʒ] **1.** Schaden *m,* (Be)Schädigung *f;* ~s *pl.* ⚖ Schadenersatz *m;* **2.** (be)schädigen.

dam·ask ['dæməsk] Damast *m.*

dame *Am.* F [deɪm] Weib *n;* △ *nicht* Dame.

damn [dæm] **1.** verdammen; verurteilen; ~ (*it*)! F verflucht!, verdammt!; **2.** *adj. u. adv.* F = damned; **3.** *I don't care a* ~ F das ist mir völlig gleich(gültig) *od.* egal; **dam·na·tion** [dæm'neɪʃn] Verdammung *f;* Verurteilung *f;* ~**ed** F [dæmd] verdammt; ~**ing** ['dæmɪŋ] vernichtend, belastend.

damp [dæmp] **1.** ☐ feucht, klamm; **2.** Feuchtigkeit *f;* **3.** *a.* ~**en** ['dæmpən] an-, befeuchten; dämpfen; ~**ness** [~nɪs] Feuchtigkeit *f.*

dance [dɑːns] **1.** Tanz *m;* Tanz(veranstaltung *f*) *m;* **2.** tanzen (lassen); **danc·er** ['dɑːnsə] Tänzer(in); **dancing** [~ɪŋ] Tanzen *n; attr.* Tanz...

dan·de·li·on ⚘ ['dændɪlaɪən] Löwenzahn *m.*

dan·dle ['dændl] wiegen, schaukeln.

dan·druff ['dændrʌf] (Kopf)Schuppen *pl.*

Dane [deɪn] Dän|e *m,* -in *f.*

dan·ger ['deɪndʒə] **1.** Gefahr *f; be in* ~ *of doing s.th.* Gefahr laufen et. zu tun; *be out of* ~ 🕱 über den Berg sein; **2.** Gefahren...; ~ *area,* ~ *zone* Gefahrenzone *f,* -bereich *m;* ~**ous** ☐ [~rəs] gefährlich.

dan·gle ['dæŋgl] baumeln (lassen).

Da·nish ['deɪnɪʃ] **1.** dänisch; **2.** *ling.* Dänisch *n.*

dank [dæŋk] feucht, naß(kalt).

dap·per ['dæpə] adrett; flink.

dap·pled ['dæpld] scheckig.

dare [deə] *v/i.* es wagen; *I* ~ *say, I* ~*say* ich glaube wohl; allerdings; *v/t. et.* wagen; *j-n* herausfordern; trotzen (*dat.*); ~**·dev·il** ['deədevl]

Draufgänger *m,* Teufelskerl *m;* **dar·ing** ☐ [~rɪŋ] **1.** kühn; waghalsig; **2.** Mut *m,* Kühnheit *f.*

dark [dɑːk] **1.** ☐ dunkel; brünett; geheim(nisvoll); trüb(selig); **2.** Dunkel(heit *f*) *n; before* (*at, after*) ~ vor (bei, nach) Einbruch der Dunkelheit; *keep s.o. in the* ~ *about s.th.* j-n über et. im ungewissen lassen; ⚱ **Ag·es** *pl. das* frühe Mittelalter; ~**en** ['dɑːkən] (sich) verdunkeln *od.* verfinstern; ~**ness** [~nɪs] Dunkelheit *f,* Finsternis *f.*

dar·ling ['dɑːlɪŋ] **1.** Liebling *m;* **2.** Lieblings...; geliebt.

darn [dɑːn] stopfen, ausbessern.

dart [dɑːt] **1.** Wurfspieß *m;* Wurfpfeil *m;* Sprung *m,* Satz *m;* ~s *sg.* Darts *n* (*Wurfpfeilspiel*); ~**board** Dartsscheibe *f;* **2.** *v/t.* werfen, schleudern; *v/i.* schießen, stürzen.

dash [dæʃ] Schlag *m;* Klatschen *n;* Schwung *m;* Ansturm *m; fig.* Anflug *m;* Prise *f;* Schuß *m* (*Rum etc.*); (Feder)Strich *m;* Gedankenstrich *m; Sport:* Sprint *m;* **2.** *v/t.* schlagen, werfen, schleudern, schmettern; *Hoffnung* zunichte machen; *v/i.* stürzen, stürmen, jagen, rasen; schlagen; ~**board** *mot.* ['dæʃbɔːd] Armaturenbrett *n;* ~**ing** ☐ [~ɪŋ] schneidig, forsch; flott, F fesch.

da·ta ['deɪtə] *pl., a. sg.* Daten *pl.,* Einzelheiten *pl.,* Angaben *pl.,* Unterlagen *pl.; Computer:* Daten *pl.;* ~ **bank** Datenbank *f;* ~ **in·put** Dateneingabe *f;* ~ **out·put** Datenausgabe *f;* ~ **pro·cess·ing** Datenverarbeitung *f;* ~ **pro·tec·tion** Datenschutz *m;* ~ **typ·ist** Datentypist(in).

date¹ ⚘ [deɪt] Dattel *f.*

date² [~] Datum *n;* Zeit(punkt *m*) *f;* Termin *m;* Verabredung *f; Am.* 🕱 (Verabredungs)Partner(in); *out of* ~ veraltet, unmodern; *up to* ~ zeitgemäß, modern, auf dem laufenden; **2.** datieren; *Am.* F sich verabreden mit, ausgehen mit, (*regelmäßig*) gehen mit; **dat·ed** ['deɪtɪd] veraltet, überholt.

da·tive *gr.* ['deɪtɪv] *a.* ~ *case* Dativ *m,* dritter Fall.

daub [dɔːb] (be)schmieren; (be)klecksen.

daugh·ter ['dɔːtə] Tochter *f;* ~-**in-law** [~rɪnlɔː] (*pl. daughters-in-law*) Schwiegertochter *f.*

daunt [dɔːnt] entmutigen; ~**less** ['dɔːntlɪs] furchtlos, unerschrocken.

decay

daw zo. [dɔ:] Dohle f.
daw·dle F ['dɔːdl] (ver)trödeln.
dawn [dɔːn] **1.** (Morgen)Dämmerung f, Tagesanbruch m; **2.** dämmern, tagen; it ~ed on od. upon him fig. es wurde ihm langsam klar.
day [deɪ] Tag m; oft ~s pl. (Lebens-)Zeit f; ~ off (dienst)freier Tag; carry od. win the ~ den Sieg davontragen; any ~ jederzeit; these ~s heutzutage; the other ~ neulich; this ~ week heute in e-r Woche; heute vor e-r Woche; let's call it a ~! machen wir Schluß für heute!, Feierabend!; ~break ['deɪbreɪk] Tagesanbruch m; ~light Tageslicht n; in broad ~ am hellichten Tag; ~time: in the ~ am Tag, bei Tage.
daze [deɪz] **1.** blenden; betäuben; **2.** in a ~ benommen, betäubt.
dead [ded] **1.** tot; unempfindlich (to für); matt (Farbe etc.); blind (Fenster etc.); erloschen (Feuer); schal (Getränk); tief (Schlaf); econ. still, ruhig, flau; econ. tot (Kapital etc.); völlig, absolut, total; ~ bargain Spottpreis m; ~ letter unzustellbarer Brief; ~ loss Totalverlust m; a ~ shot ein Meisterschütze; **2.** adv. gänzlich, völlig, total; plötzlich, abrupt; genau, (haar)scharf; ~ tired todmüde; ~ against ganz u. gar gegen; **3.** the ~ der, die, das Tote; die Toten pl.; in the ~ of winter im tiefsten Winter; in the ~ of night mitten in der Nacht; ~cen·tre, Am. ~ cen·ter genaue Mitte; ~en ['dedn] abstumpfen; dämpfen; (ab)schwächen; ~ end Sackgasse f (a. fig.); ~ heat Sport: totes Rennen; ~line Am. Sperrlinie f, Todesstreifen m (im Gefängnis); letzter (Ablieferungs)Termin; Stichtag m; ~lock fig. toter Punkt; ~locked fig. festgefahren (Verhandlungen); ~ly [ˌlɪ] (-ier, -iest) tödlich.
deaf [def] **1.** □ taub; ~ and dumb taubstumm; **2.** the ~ pl. die Tauben pl.; ~en ['defn] taub machen; betäuben.
deal [diːl] **1.** Teil m; Menge f; Karten: Geben n; F Geschäft n; Abmachung f; a good ~ ziemlich viel; a great ~ sehr viel; **2.** (dealt) v/t. (aus-, ver-, zu)teilen; Karten: geben; e-n Schlag versetzen; v/i. handeln (in mit e-r Ware); sl. dealen (mit Rauschgift handeln); Karten: geben; ~ with sich befassen mit, behandeln; econ. Han-

del treiben mit, in Geschäftsverbindung stehen mit; ~er ['diːlə] econ. Händler(in); Karten: Geber(in); sl. Dealer m (Rauschgifthändler); ~ing [ˌɪŋ] Verhalten n, Handlungsweise f; econ. Geschäftsgebaren n; ~s pl. Umgang m, (Geschäfts)Beziehungen pl.; ~t [delt] pret. u. p.p. von deal 2.
dean [diːn] Dekan m.
dear [dɪə] **1.** □ teuer; lieb; **2.** Liebste(r m) f, Schatz m; my ~ m-e Liebe, mein Lieber; **3.** int. (oh) ~!, ~ ~!, ~ me! F du liebe Zeit!, ach herrje!; ~ly ['dɪəlɪ] innig, von ganzem Herzen; teuer (im Preis).
death [deθ] Tod m; Todesfall m; ~bed ['deθbed] Sterbebett n; ~less [ˌlɪs] unsterblich; ~ly [ˌlɪ] (-ier, -iest) tödlich; ~war·rant ⚖ Hinrichtungsbefehl m; fig. Todesurteil n.
de·bar [dɪˈbɑː] (-rr-): ~ from doing s.th. j-n hindern et. zu tun.
de·base [dɪˈbeɪs] erniedrigen.
de·ba·ta·ble [dɪˈbeɪtəbl] strittig; umstritten; **de·bate** [dɪˈbeɪt] **1.** Debatte f; **2.** debattieren; erörtern; et. überlegen.
de·bil·i·tate [dɪˈbɪlɪteɪt] schwächen.
deb·it econ. ['debɪt] **1.** Debet n, Soll n; (Konto)Belastung f; ~ and credit Soll u. Haben n; **2.** j-n, ein Konto belasten.
deb·ris ['debriː] Trümmer pl.
debt [det] Schuld f; be in ~ verschuldet sein; be out of ~ schuldenfrei sein; ~or ['detə] Schuldner(in).
de·bug ⊕ [diːˈbʌg] (-gg-) Fehler beseitigen (a. Computer).
de·bunk ['diːˈbʌŋk] den Nimbus nehmen (dat.).
dé·but, bsd. Am. **de·but** ['deɪbuː] Debüt n.
dec·ade ['dekeɪd] Jahrzehnt n.
dec·a|dence ['dekədəns] Dekadenz f, Verfall m; ~dent [ˌt] dekadent.
de·caf·fein·at·ed [ˈdiːˈkæfmeɪtɪd] koffeinfrei.
de·camp [dɪˈkæmp] bsd. ⚔ das Lager abbrechen; F verschwinden.
de·cant [dɪˈkænt] abgießen; umfüllen; ~er [ˌə] Karaffe f.
de·cath|lete [dɪˈkæθliːt] Sport: Zehnkämpfer m; ~lon [ˌlɔn] Sport: Zehnkampf m.
de·cay [dɪˈkeɪ] **1.** Verfall m; Zerfall m; Fäule f; **2.** verfallen; (ver)faulen;

de·cease bsd. ⚖ [dɪˈsiːs] **1.** Tod *m*, Ableben *n*; **2.** sterben; **~d** bsd. ⚖ **1.** the ~ der *od.* die Verstorbene; die Verstorbenen *pl.*; **2.** ver-, gestorben.

de·ceit [dɪˈsiːt] Täuschung *f*; Betrug *m*; **~·ful** □ [~fl] falsch; betrügerisch.

de·ceive [dɪˈsiːv] betrügen; täuschen; **de·ceiv·er** [~ə] Betrüger(in).

De·cem·ber [dɪˈsembə] Dezember *m*.

de·cen·cy [ˈdiːsnsɪ] Anstand *m*; **~t** □ [~t] anständig; F annehmbar, (ganz) anständig; F nett; △ *nicht* dezent.

de·cep·tion [dɪˈsepʃn] Täuschung *f*; **~·tive** □ [~tɪv]: be ~ täuschen, trügen (*Sache*).

de·cide [dɪˈsaɪd] (sich) entscheiden; bestimmen; sich entschließen; **de·cid·ed** □ entschieden; bestimmt; entschlossen.

dec·i·mal [ˈdesɪml] *a.* ~ *fraction* Dezimalbruch *m*; *attr.* Dezimal...

de·ci·pher [dɪˈsaɪfə] entziffern.

de·ci·sion [dɪˈsɪʒn] Entscheidung *f*; Entschluß *m*; Entschlossenheit *f*; *make a* ~ e-e Entscheidung treffen; *reach an* ~ *od.* come to a ~ zu e-m Entschluß kommen; **~·sive** □ [dɪˈsaɪsɪv] entscheidend; ausschlaggebend; entschieden.

deck [dek] **1.** ⚓ Deck *n* (*a. e-s Busses*); *Am.* Pack *m* Spielkarten; Laufwerk *n* (*e-s Plattenspielers*); *tape* ~ Tapedeck *n*; **2.** ~ *out* schmücken; **~·chair** [ˈdektʃeə] Liegestuhl *m*.

de·claim [dɪˈkleɪm] deklamieren, vortragen.

de·clar·a·ble [dɪˈkleərəbl] zollpflichtig.

dec·la·ra·tion [dekləˈreɪʃn] Erklärung *f*; Zollerklärung *f*.

de·clare [dɪˈkleə] (sich) erklären, bekanntgeben; behaupten; deklarieren, verzollen.

de·clen·sion gr. [dɪˈklenʃn] Deklination *f*.

dec·li·na·tion [deklɪˈneɪʃn] Neigung *f*; Abweichung *f*; **de·cline** [dɪˈklaɪn] **1.** Abnahme *f*; Niedergang *m*, Verfall *m*; **2.** *v/t.* neigen; (höflich) ablehnen; *gr.* deklinieren; *v/i.* sich neigen; abnehmen; verfallen.

de·cliv·i·ty [dɪˈklɪvətɪ] Abhang *m*.

de·clutch *mot.* [ˈdiːˈklʌtʃ] auskuppeln.

de·code [ˈdiːˈkoud] entschlüsseln.

de·com·pose [diːkəmˈpouz] zerlegen; (sich) zersetzen; verwesen.

dec·o·rate [ˈdekəreɪt] verzieren, schmücken; tapezieren; (an)streichen; dekorieren; **~·ra·tion** [dekəˈreɪʃn] Verzierung *f*, Schmuck *m*; Dekoration *f*; Orden *m*; **~·ra·tive** □ [ˈdekərətɪv] dekorativ; Zier...; **~·ra·tor** [~reɪtə] Dekorateur *m*; Maler *m* u. Tapezierer *m*.

dec·o·rous □ [ˈdekərəs] anständig; **de·co·rum** [dɪˈkɔːrəm] Anstand *m*.

de·coy 1. [ˈdiːkɔɪ] Lockvogel *m* (*a. fig.*); Köder *m* (*a. fig.*); **2.** [dɪˈkɔɪ] ködern; locken (*into* in *acc.*); verleiten (*into* zu).

de·crease 1. [ˈdiːkriːs] Abnahme *f*; **2.** [diːˈkriːs] (sich) vermindern.

de·cree [dɪˈkriː] **1.** Dekret *n*, Verordnung *f*, Erlaß *m*; ⚖ Entscheid *m*; **2.** ⚖ entscheiden; verordnen, verfügen.

ded·i·cate [ˈdedɪkeɪt] widmen; **~·cat·ed** engagiert; **~·ca·tion** [dedɪˈkeɪʃn] Widmung *f*; Hingabe *f*.

de·duce [dɪˈdjuːs] ableiten; folgern.

de·duct [dɪˈdʌkt] abziehen; einbehalten; **de·duc·tion** [~kʃn] Abzug *m*; *econ. a.* Rabatt *m*; Schlußfolgerung *f*, Schluß *m*.

deed [diːd] **1.** Tat *f*; Heldentat *f*; ⚖ (Vertrags-, bsd. Übertragungs-)Urkunde *f*; **2.** *Am.* ⚖ urkundlich übertragen (*to dat.*, auf *acc.*).

deem [diːm] *v/t.* halten für; *v/i.* denken, urteilen (*of* über *acc.*).

deep [diːp] **1.** □ tief; gründlich; schlau; vertieft; dunkel (*a. fig.*); verborgen; **2.** Tiefe *f*; poet. Meer *n*; **~·en** [ˈdiːpən] (sich) vertiefen; (sich) verstärken; **~·freeze** [-froze, -frozen] [ˈdiːpən] tiefkühlen, einfrieren; **2.** Tiefkühl-, Gefriergerät *n*; **3.** Tiefkühl..., Gefrier...; ~ *cabinet* Tiefkühl-, Gefriertruhe *f*; **~·fro·zen** tiefgefroren; ~ *food* Tiefkühlkost *f*; **~·fry** fritieren; **~·ness** [~nɪs] Tiefe *f*.

deer zo. [dɪə] Rotwild *n*; Hirsch *m*.

de·face [dɪˈfeɪs] entstellen; unkenntlich machen; ausstreichen.

def·a·ma·tion [defəˈmeɪʃn] Verleumdung *f*; **de·fame** [dɪˈfeɪm] verleumden.

de·fault [dɪˈfɔːlt] **1.** Nichterscheinen *n* vor Gericht; *Sport*: Nichtantreten *n*; *econ.* Verzug *m*; **2.** s-n *etc.* Verbindlichkeiten nicht nachkommen; im Verzug sein; nicht (vor Gericht) erscheinen; *Sport*: nicht antreten.

de·feat [dɪˈfiːt] **1.** Niederlage *f*; Besiegung *f*; Vereitelung *f*; **2.** besiegen; vereiteln, zunichte machen.

de·fect [dɪ'fekt] Defekt *m*, Fehler *m*; Mangel *m*; **de·fec·tive** □ [~ɪv] mangelhaft; schadhaft, defekt.

de·fence, *Am.* **de·fense** [dɪ'fens] Verteidigung *f*; Schutz *m*; *witness for the* ~ Entlastungszeuge *m*; **~·less** [~lɪs] schutzlos, wehrlos.

de·fend [dɪ'fend] *(from, against)* verteidigen (gegen), schützen (vor *dat.*, gegen); **de·fen·dant** [~ənt] Angeklagte(r *m*) *f*; Beklagte(r *m*) *f*; **de·fend·er** [~ə] Verteidiger(in).

de·fen·sive [dɪ'fensɪv] **1.** Defensive *f*, Verteidigung *f*, Abwehr *f*; **2.** □ defensiv; Verteidigungs..., Abwehr...

de·fer [dɪ'fɜː] *(-rr-)* auf-, verschieben; *Am.* ✕ (vom Wehrdienst) zurückstellen; sich fügen, nachgeben.

def·er·ence ['defərəns] Ehrerbietung *f*; Nachgiebigkeit *f*; **~·en·tial** □ [defə'renʃl] ehrerbietig.

de·fi·ance [dɪ'faɪəns] Herausforderung *f*; Trotz *m*; **~·ant** □ [~t] herausfordernd; trotzig.

de·fi·cien·cy [dɪ'fɪʃnsɪ] Unzulänglichkeit *f*; Mangel *m*; = *deficit*; **~·t** □ [~t] mangelhaft, unzureichend.

def·i·cit *econ.* ['defɪsɪt] Fehlbetrag *m*.

de·file 1. [dɪ'faɪl] Engpaß *m*; **2.** [dɪ'faɪl] beschmutzen.

de·fine [dɪ'faɪn] definieren; erklären, genau bestimmen; **def·i·nite** □ ['defɪnɪt] bestimmt; deutlich; genau; **def·i·ni·tion** [defɪ'nɪʃn] Definition *f*, (Begriffs)Bestimmung *f*, Erklärung *f*; **de·fin·i·tive** □ [dɪ'fɪnɪtɪv] endgültig; maßgeblich.

de·flect [dɪ'flekt] ablenken; abweichen.

de·form [dɪ'fɔːm] entstellen, verunstalten; **~ed** deformiert, verunstaltet; verwachsen; **de·for·mi·ty** [~ətɪ] Entstelltheit *f*; Mißbildung *f*.

de·fraud [dɪ'frɔːd] betrügen (*of* um).

de·frost [diː'frɒst] *v/t.* *Windschutzscheibe* entfrosten; *Kühlschrank etc.* abtauen; *Tiefkühlkost* auftauen; *v/i.* ab-, auftauen.

deft □ [deft] gewandt, flink.

de·fy [dɪ'faɪ] herausfordern; trotzen (*dat.*).

de·gen·er·ate 1. [dɪ'dʒenəreɪt] entarten; **2.** [~rət] entartet.

deg·ra·da·tion [degrə'deɪʃn] Erniedrigung *f*; **de·grade** [dɪ'greɪd] *v/t.* erniedrigen, demütigen;

de·gree [dɪ'griː] Grad *m*; Stufe *f*, Schritt *m*; Rang *m*, Stand *m*; *by* ~*s* allmählich; *take one's* ~ e-n akademischen Grad erwerben, promovieren.

de·hy·drat·ed ['diː'haɪdreɪtɪd] Trokken...

de·i·fy ['diːɪfaɪ] vergöttern; vergöttlichen.

deign [deɪn] sich herablassen.

de·i·ty ['diːɪtɪ] Gottheit *f*.

de·ject·ed □ [dɪ'dʒektɪd] niedergeschlagen, mutlos, deprimiert; **~·tion** [~kʃn] Niedergeschlagenheit *f*.

de·lay [dɪ'leɪ] **1.** Aufschub *m*; Verzögerung *f*; **2.** *v/t.* ver-, aufschieben; verzögern; aufhalten; *v/i.* ~ *in doing s.th.* es verschieben, et. zu tun.

del·e·gate 1. ['delɪgeɪt] abordnen; übertragen; **2.** [~gət] (*Am. parl.* Kongreß)Abgeordnete(r *m*) *f*; **~·ga·tion** [delɪ'geɪʃn] Abordnung *f*; *Am. parl.* Kongreßabgeordnete *pl.*

de·lete [dɪ'liːt] tilgen, (aus)streichen, (aus)radieren.

de·lib·e·rate 1. [dɪ'lɪbəreɪt] *v/t.* überlegen, erwägen; *v/i.* nachdenken; beraten; **2.** □ [~rət] bedachtsam; wohlüberlegt; vorsätzlich; **~·ra·tion** [dɪlɪbə'reɪʃn] Überlegung *f*; Beratung *f*; Bedächtigkeit *f*.

del·i·ca·cy ['delɪkəsɪ] Delikatesse *f*, Leckerbissen *m*; Zartheit *f*; Schwächlichkeit *f*; Feingefühl *n*; **~·cate** □ [~kət] schmackhaft, lecker; zart; fein; schwach; heikel; empfindlich; feinfühlig; wählerisch; **~·ca·tes·sen** [delɪkə'tesn] Delikatessen *pl.*, Feinkost *f*; Delikatessen-, Feinkostgeschäft *n*.

de·li·cious □ [dɪ'lɪʃəs] köstlich.

de·light [dɪ'laɪt] **1.** Lust *f*, Freude *f*, Wonne *f*; **2.** entzücken, (sich) erfreuen; ~ *in* (große) Freude haben an (*dat.*); **~·ful** □ [~fl] entzückend.

de·lin·e·ate [dɪ'lɪnɪeɪt] entwerfen; schildern.

de·lin·quen·cy [dɪ'lɪŋkwənsɪ] Kriminalität *f*; Straftat *f*; **~·t** [~t] **1.** straffällig; **2.** Straffällige(r *m*) *f*; *s. juvenile 1.*

de·lir·i·ous □ [dɪ'lɪrɪəs] ⚕ phantasierend; wahnsinnig; **~·um** [~əm] Delirium *n*.

de·liv·er [dɪ'lɪvə] befreien; über-, aus-, abliefern; *bsd. econ.* liefern; *Botschaft* ausrichten; äußern; *Rede etc.* halten; *Schlag* austeilen; werfen;

D

🏵 entbinden; *be* ~*ed of a child* entbunden werden, entbinden; **~ance** [~rəns] Befreiung *f*; (Meinungs)Äußerung *f*; **~er** [~rə] Befreier(in); Überbringer(in); **~y** [~rɪ] (Ab-, Aus)Lieferung *f*; 😃 Zustellung *f*; Übergabe *f*; Halten *n* (*e-r Rede etc.*); 🏵 Entbindung *f*; **~y van** *Brt.* Lieferwagen *m*.

dell [del] kleines Tal.

de·lude [dɪ'lu:d] täuschen; verleiten.

del·uge ['delju:dʒ] **1.** Überschwemmung *f*; **2.** überschwemmen.

de·lu|sion [dɪ'lu:ʒn] Täuschung *f*, Verblendung *f*, Wahn *m*; **~sive** □ [~sɪv] trügerisch, täuschend.

de·mand [dɪ'mɑ:nd] **1.** Verlangen *n*; Forderung *f*; Aufforderung (*on* an *acc.*), Inanspruchnahme *f* (*on gen.*); *econ.* Nachfrage *f*, Bedarf *m*; ⚖ Rechtsanspruch *m*; **2.** verlangen, fordern; erfordern; **~ing** □ [~ɪŋ] fordernd; anspruchsvoll; schwierig.

de·mean [dɪ'mi:n]: ~ *o.s.* sich benehmen; sich erniedrigen; **de·mea·no(u)r** [~ə] Benehmen *n*.

de·ment·ed □ [dɪ'mentɪd] wahnsinnig.

dem·i- ['demɪ] Halb...

dem·i·john ['demɪdʒɒn] große Korbflasche, Glasballon *m*.

de·mil·i·ta·rize [di:'mɪlɪtəraɪz] entmilitarisieren.

de·mo·bi·lize [di:'məʊbɪlaɪz] demobilisieren.

de·moc·ra·cy [dɪ'mɒkrəsɪ] Demokratie *f*.

dem·o·crat ['deməkræt] Demokrat(in); **~ic** [demə'krætɪk] (~*ally*) demokratisch.

de·mol·ish [dɪ'mɒlɪʃ] demolieren; ab-, ein-, niederreißen; zerstören; **dem·o·li·tion** [demə'lɪʃn] Demolierung *f*; Niederreißen *n*, Abbruch *m*.

de·mon ['di:mən] Dämon *m*; Teufel *m*.

dem·on|strate ['demənstreɪt] anschaulich darstellen; beweisen; demonstrieren; **~stra·tion** [demən'streɪʃn] Demonstration *f*, Kundgebung *f*; Demonstration *f*, Vorführung *f*; anschauliche Darstellung; Beweis *m*; (Gefühls)Äußerung *f*; **de·mon·stra·tive** □ [dɪ'mɒnstrətɪv] überzeugend; demonstrativ; *be* ~ s-e Gefühle (offen) zeigen; **~stra·tor** ['demənstreɪtə] Demonstrant(in); Vorführer(in).

de·mote [di:'məʊt] degradieren.

de·mur [dɪ'mɜ:] (*-rr-*) Einwendungen machen.

de·mure □ [dɪ'mjʊə] ernst; prüde.

den [den] Höhle *f*, Bau *m*; Bude *f*; Arbeitszimmer *n*.

de·ni·al [dɪ'naɪəl] Leugnen *n*; Verneinung *f*; abschlägige Antwort.

den·ims ['denɪmz] *pl.* Overall *m od.* Jeans *pl.* aus Köper.

de·nom·i·na·tion [dɪnɒmɪ'neɪʃn] *eccl.* Sekte *f*; *eccl.* Konfession *f*; *econ.* Nennwert *m* (*von Banknoten etc.*).

de·note [dɪ'nəʊt] bezeichnen; bedeuten.

de·nounce [dɪ'naʊns] anzeigen; brandmarken; *Vertrag* kündigen.

dense □ [dens] (~*r*, ~*st*) dicht, dick (*Nebel*); beschränkt; **den·si·ty** ['densətɪ] Dichte *f*.

dent [dent] **1.** Beule *f*, Delle *f*; Kerbe *f*; **2.** ver-, einbeulen.

den|tal ['dentl] Zahn...; ~ *plaque* Zahnbelag *m*; ~ *plate* Zahnprothese *f*; ~ *surgeon* Zahnarzt *m*; **~tist** [~ɪst] Zahnarzt *m*, -ärztin *f*; **~tures** [~ʃəz] *pl.* (künstliches) Gebiß.

de·nun·ci·a·tion [dɪnʌnsɪ'eɪʃn] Anzeige *f*, Denunziation *f*; **~tor** [dɪ'nʌnsɪeɪtə] Denunziant(in).

de·ny [dɪ'naɪ] ab-, bestreiten, (ab-)leugnen; verweigern, abschlagen; *j-n* abweisen.

de·part [dɪ'pɑ:t] abreisen; abfahren, abfliegen; abweichen.

de·part·ment [dɪ'pɑ:tmənt] Abteilung *f*; Bezirk *m*; *econ.* Branche *f*; *pol.* Ministerium *n*; ♀ *of Defense Am.* Verteidigungsministerium *n*; ♀ *of the Environment Brt.* Umweltschutzministerium *n*; ♀ *of the Interior Am.* Innenministerium *n*; ♀ *of State Am.*, State ♀ *Am.* Außenministerium *n*; **~ store** Warenhaus *n*.

de·par·ture [dɪ'pɑ:tʃə] Abreise *f*, 🚢 *etc.* Abfahrt *f*, ✈ Abflug *m*; Abweichung *f*; **~ gate** ✈ Flugsteig *m*; **~ lounge** ✈ Abflughalle *f*.

de·pend [dɪ'pend]: ~ *on*, ~ *upon* abhängen von; angewiesen sein *auf* (*acc.*); sich verlassen auf (*acc.*); ankommen auf (*acc.*); *it* ~*s* F es kommt (ganz) darauf an.

de·pen|da·ble [dɪ'pendəbl] zuverlässig; **~dant** [~ənt] Abhängige(r *m*) *f*; *bsd.* (Familien)Angehörige(r *m*) *f*; **~dence** [~əns] Abhängigkeit *f*; Vertrauen *n*; **~den·cy** [~ənsɪ] *pol.*

Schutzgebiet n; **~dent** [~ənt] **1.** □ (on) abhängig (von); angewiesen (auf acc.); **2.** Am. = dependant.

de·pict [dɪ'pɪkt] darstellen; schildern.

de·plor|a·ble □ [dɪ'plɔːrəbl] bedauerlich, beklagenswert; **~e** [dɪ-'plɔː] beklagen, bedauern.

de·pop·u·late [diː'pɒpjʊleɪt] (sich) entvölkern.

de·port [dɪ'pɔːt] Ausländer abschieben; ~ o.s. sich gut etc. benehmen; **~ment** [~mənt] Benehmen n.

de·pose [dɪ'pəʊz] absetzen; ⚖ unter Eid aussagen.

de·pos|it [dɪ'pɒzɪt] **1.** Ablagerung f; Lager n; (Bank)Einlage f; Hinterlegung f; Anzahlung f; make a ~ e-e Anzahlung leisten; ~ account f/t Termineinlagekonto n; **2.** (nieder-, ab-, hin)legen; Geld einzahlen; Betrag anzahlen; hinterlegen; (sich) ablagern; **dep·o·si·tion** [depə'zɪʃn] Absetzung f; (zu Protokoll gegebene) eidliche Aussage; **~i·tor** [dɪ-'pɒzɪtə] Hinterleger(in); Einzahler(in); Kontoinhaber(in).

dep·ot ['depəʊ] Depot n; Lagerhaus n; Am. ['diːpəʊ] Bahnhof m.

de·prave [dɪ'preɪv] moralisch verderben.

de·pre·ci·ate [dɪ'priːʃɪeɪt] Wert mindern.

de·press [dɪ'pres] (nieder)drücken; Preise etc. senken, drücken; deprimieren, bedrücken; **~ed** deprimiert, niedergeschlagen; **de·pres·sion** [~eʃn] Vertiefung f, Senke f; Depression f, Niedergeschlagenheit f; econ. Depression f, Flaute f, Wirtschaftskrise f; ⚡ Schwäche f.

de·prive [dɪ'praɪv]: ~ s.o. of s.th. j-m et. entziehen od. nehmen; **~d** benachteiligt, unterprivilegiert.

depth [depθ] Tiefe f; attr. Tiefen...

dep·u|ta·tion [depjʊ'teɪʃn] Abordnung f; **~tize** ['depjʊtaɪz]: ~ for s.o. j-n vertreten; **~ty** [~ɪ] parl. Abgeordnete(r m) f; Stellvertreter(in), Beauftragte(r m) f, Bevollmächtigte(r m) f; a. ~ sheriff Am. Hilfssheriff m.

de·rail ⛏ [dɪ'reɪl] v/i. entgleisen; v/t. zum Entgleisen bringen.

de·range [dɪ'reɪndʒ] in Unordnung bringen; stören; verrückt od. wahnsinnig machen; **~d** geistesgestört.

der·e·lict ['derɪlɪkt] verlassen; nachlässig.

de·ride [dɪ'raɪd] verlachen, -spotten; **de·ri·sion** [dɪ'rɪʒn] Hohn m, Spott m; **de·ri·sive** □ [dɪ'raɪsɪv] spöttisch, höhnisch.

de·rive [dɪ'raɪv] herleiten; et. gewinnen (from aus); Nutzen etc. ziehen (from aus).

de·rog·a·to·ry □ [dɪ'rɒgətərɪ] abfällig, geringschätzig.

der·rick ['derɪk] ⊕ Derrickkran m; ⚓ Ladebaum m; Bohrturm m.

de·scend [dɪ'send] (her-, hin)absteigen, herunter-, hinuntersteigen, herabkommen; 🛫 niedergehen; (ab)stammen; ~ on, ✕ upon herfallen über (acc.); einfallen in (acc.); **de·scen·dant** [~ənt] Nachkomme m.

de·scent [dɪ'sent] Herab-, Hinuntersteigen n, Abstieg m; 🛫 Niedergehen n; Abhang m; Gefälle n; Abstammung f; fig. Niedergang m, Abstieg m.

de·scribe [dɪ'skraɪb] beschreiben.

de·scrip|tion [dɪ'skrɪpʃn] Beschreibung f, Schilderung f; Art f; **~tive** □ [~tɪv] beschreibend; anschaulich.

des·e·crate ['desɪkreɪt] entweihen.

de·seg·re·gate [diː'segrɪgeɪt] die Rassentrennung aufheben in (dat.).

des·ert¹ ['dezət] **1.** Wüste f; **2.** Wüsten...

de·sert² [dɪ'zɜːt] v/t. verlassen; v/i. desertieren; **~er** ✕ [~ə] Deserteur m, Fahnenflüchtige(r) m; **de·ser·tion** [~ʃn] (⚖ a. böswilliges) Verlassen; ✕ Fahnenflucht f.

de·serve [dɪ'zɜːv] verdienen; **de·serv·ed·ly** [~ɪdlɪ] mit Recht; **de·serv·ing** [~ɪŋ] würdig (of gen.); verdienstvoll, verdient.

de·sign [dɪ'zaɪn] **1.** Plan m; Entwurf m, Zeichnung f; Muster n; Vorhaben n, Absicht f; have ~s on od. against et. (Böses) im Schilde führen gegen; **2.** entwerfen, ⊕ konstruieren; gestalten; planen; bestimmen.

des·ig·nate ['dezɪgneɪt] bezeichnen; ernennen, bestimmen; **~na·tion** [dezɪg'neɪʃn] Bezeichnung f; Bestimmung f, Ernennung f.

de·sign·er [dɪ'zaɪnə] (Muster)Zeichner(in); Designer(in); ⊕ Konstrukteur m; (Mode)Schöpfer(in).

de·sir|a·ble □ [dɪ'zaɪərəbl] wünschenswert; angenehm; **~e** [dɪ'zaɪə]

1. Wunsch *m*, Verlangen *n*; Begierde *f*; 2. verlangen, wünschen; begehren; **~ous** □ [~rəs] begierig.

de·sist [dɪ'zɪst] ablassen (*from* von).

desk [desk] Pult *n*; Schreibtisch *m*.

des·o·late □ ['desələt] einsam; verlassen; öde.

de·spair [dɪ'speə] 1. Verzweiflung *f*; 2. verzweifeln (*of an dat.*); **~ing** □ [~rɪŋ] verzweifelt.

de·spatch [dɪ'spætʃ] = dispatch.

des·per|ate □ ['despərət] verzweifelt; hoffnungslos; F schrecklich; **~a·tion** [despə'reɪʃn] Verzweiflung *f*.

des·pic·a·ble □ ['despɪkəbl] verachtenswert, verabscheuungswürdig.

de·spise [dɪ'spaɪz] verachten.

de·spite [dɪ'spaɪt] 1. Verachtung *f*; *in ~ of* zum Trotz, trotz; 2. *prp. a. ~ of* trotz.

de·spon·dent □ [dɪ'spɒndənt] mutlos, verzagt.

des·pot ['despɒt] Despot *m*, Tyrann *m*; **~·is·m** [~pɒtɪzəm] Despotismus *m*.

des·sert [dɪ'zɜːt] Nachtisch *m*, Dessert *n*; *attr.* Dessert...

des|ti·na·tion [destɪ'neɪʃn] Bestimmung(sort *m*) *f*; **~·tined** ['destɪnd] bestimmt; **~·ti·ny** [~ɪ] Schicksal *n*.

des·ti·tute □ ['destɪtjuːt] mittellos, notleidend; *~ of* bar (*gen.*), ohne.

de·stroy [dɪ'strɔɪ] zerstören, vernichten; töten, *Tier a.* einschläfern; **~·er** [~ə] Zerstörer(in); ♣ ✕ Zerstörer *m*.

de·struc|tion [dɪ'strʌkʃn] Zerstörung *f*, Vernichtung *f*; Tötung *f*, *e·s Tiers a.* Einschläferung *f*; **~·tive** □ [~tɪv] zerstörend, vernichtend; zerstörerisch.

des·ul·to·ry □ ['desəltərɪ] unstet; planlos; oberflächlich.

de·tach [dɪ'tætʃ] losmachen, (ab)lösen; absondern; ✕ abkommandieren; **~ed** einzeln (stehend); unvoreingenommen, distanziert; **~·ment** [~mənt] Loslösung *f*; (Ab)Trennung *f*; ✕ (Sonder)Kommando *n*.

de·tail ['diːteɪl] 1. Detail *n*, Einzelheit *f*; eingehende Darstellung; ✕ (Sonder)Kommando *n*; *in ~* ausführlich; 2. genau schildern; ✕ abkommandieren; **~ed** detailliert, ausführlich.

de·tain [dɪ'teɪn] aufhalten; *j-n* in (Untersuchungs)Haft (be)halten.

de·tect [dɪ'tekt] entdecken; (auf)finden; **de·tec·tion** [~kʃn] Entdeckung

f; **de·tec·tive** [~tɪv] Kriminalbeamte(r) *m*, Detektiv *m*; *~ novel, ~ story* Kriminalroman *m*.

de·ten·tion [dɪ'tenʃn] Vorenthaltung *f*; Aufhaltung *f*; Haft *f*.

de·ter [dɪ'tɜː] (*-rr-*) abschrecken (*from* von).

de·ter·gent [dɪ'tɜːdʒənt] Reinigungsmittel *n*; Waschmittel *n*; Geschirrspülmittel *n*.

de·te·ri·o·rate [dɪ'tɪərɪəreɪt] (sich) verschlechtern; verderben; entarten.

de·ter|mi·na·tion [dɪtɜːmɪ'neɪʃn] Entschlossenheit *f*; Entscheidung *f*; Entschluß *m*; **~·mine** [dɪ'tɜːmɪn] bestimmen; (sich) entscheiden; sich entschließen; **~·mined** entschlossen.

de·ter|rence [dɪ'terəns] Abschreckung *f*; **~·rent** [~t] 1. abschreckend; 2. Abschreckungsmittel *n*.

de·test [dɪ'test] verabscheuen; **~·a·ble** □ [~əbl] abscheulich.

de·throne [dɪ'θrəʊn] entthronen.

de·to·nate ['detəneɪt] explodieren (lassen).

de·tour ['diːtʊə] Umweg *m*; Umleitung *f*.

de·tract [dɪ'trækt]: *~ from s.th.* et. beeinträchtigen, et. schmälern.

de·tri·ment ['detrɪmənt] Schaden *m*.

deuce [djuːs] Zwei *f* (*im Spiel*); *Tennis:* Einstand *m*; F Teufel *m*; *how the ~* wie zum Teufel.

de·val·u|a·tion ['diːvæljuˈeɪʃn] Abwertung *f*; **~·e** ['diːˈvæljuː] abwerten.

dev·a|state ['devəsteɪt] verwüsten; **~·stat·ing** □ [~ɪŋ] verheerend, -nichtend; F umwerfend; **~·sta·tion** [devəˈsteɪʃn] Verwüstung *f*.

de·vel·op [dɪ'veləp] (sich) entwickeln; (sich) entfalten; *Gelände* erschließen; *Altstadt etc.* sanieren; ausbauen; (sich) zeigen; **~·er** [~ə] *phot.* Entwickler *m*; (Stadt)Planer *m*; **~·ing** [~ɪŋ] Entwicklungs...; *~ country econ.* Entwicklungsland *n*; **~·ment** [~mənt] Entwicklung *f*; Entfaltung *f*; Erschließung *f*; Ausbau *m*; *~ aid econ.* Entwicklungshilfe *f*.

de·vi|ate ['diːvɪeɪt] abweichen; **~·a·tion** [diːvɪ'eɪʃn] Abweichung *f*.

de·vice [dɪ'vaɪs] Vor-, Einrichtung *f*, Gerät *n*; Erfindung *f*; Plan *m*; Kunstgriff *m*, Kniff *m*; Devise *f*, Motto *n*; *leave s.o. to his own ~s* j-n sich selbst überlassen.

dev·il ['devl] Teufel m (a. fig.); **~ish** □ [~ɪʃ] teuflisch.

de·vi·ous □ ['di:vjəs] abwegig; gewunden; unaufrichtig; *take a ~ route* e-n Umweg machen.

de·vise □ [dɪ'vaɪz] ausdenken, ersinnen; ⚖ℒ⁴ vermachen.

de·void [dɪ'vɔɪd]: *~ of* bar (*gen.*), ohne.

de·vote [dɪ'vəʊt] widmen, *et.* hingeben, opfern (*to dat.*); △ *nicht* devot; **de·vot·ed** □ ergeben; eifrig; begeistert; zärtlich; **dev·o·tee** [devəʊ'ti:] begeisterter Anhänger; **de·vo·tion** [dɪ'vəʊʃn] Ergebenheit f; Hingabe f; Frömmigkeit f, Andacht f.

de·vour [dɪ'vaʊə] verschlingen.

de·vout □ [dɪ'vaʊt] andächtig; fromm; sehnlichst.

dew [dju:] Tau m; **~y** ['dju:ɪ] (*-ier, -iest*) (tau)feucht.

dex·ter·i·ty [dek'sterətɪ] Gewandtheit f; Geschick n; **~ter·ous**, **~trous** □ ['dekstrəs] gewandt.

di·ag·nose ['daɪəɡnəʊz] diagnostizieren; **~no·sis** [daɪəɡ'nəʊsɪs] (*pl. -ses* [-si:z]) Diagnose f.

di·a·gram ['daɪəɡræm] graphische Darstellung, Schema n, Plan m.

di·al ['daɪəl] **1.** Zifferblatt n; teleph. Wählscheibe f; ⊕ Skala f; **2.** (*bsd. Brt. -ll-, Am. -l-*) teleph. wählen; *~ direct* durchwählen (*to* nach); *direct ~(l)ing* Durchwahl f.

di·a·lect ['daɪəlekt] Dialekt m; Mundart f.

di·a·logue, *Am.* **-log** ['daɪəlɒɡ] Dialog m, Gespräch n.

di·am·e·ter [daɪ'æmɪtə] Durchmesser m; *in ~* im Durchmesser.

di·a·mond ['daɪəmənd] Diamant m; Rhombus m; *Baseball:* Spielfeld n; *Karten:* Karo n.

di·a·per *Am.* ['daɪəpə] Windel f.

di·a·phragm ['daɪəfræm] anat. Zwerchfell n; opt. Blende f; teleph. Membran(e) f.

di·ar·rh(o)e·a 𝒮⁴ [daɪə'rɪə] Durchfall m.

di·a·ry ['daɪərɪ] Tagebuch n.

dice [daɪs] **1.** pl. von die²; **2.** würfeln; **~box** ['daɪsbɒks], **~cup** Würfelbecher m.

dick *Am. sl.* [dɪk] Schnüffler m (*Detektiv*).

dick·(e)y(-bird) ['dɪkɪ(bɜːd)] Piepvögelchen n.

dic|tate [dɪk'teɪt] diktieren; fig. vorschreiben; **~ta·tion** [~ʃn] Diktat n.

dic·ta·tor [dɪk'teɪtə] Diktator m; **~ship** [~ʃɪp] Diktatur f.

dic·tion ['dɪkʃn] Ausdruck(sweise f) m, Stil m.

dic·tion·a·ry ['dɪkʃnrɪ] Wörterbuch n.

did [dɪd] pret. von do.

die¹ [daɪ] sterben; umkommen; untergehen; absterben; *~ away* sich legen (*Wind*); verklingen (*Ton*); verlöschen (*Licht*); *~ down* nachlassen; herunterbrennen; schwächer werden; *~ off* wegsterben; *~ out* aussterben (*a. fig.*).

die² [~] (*pl. dice* [daɪs]) Würfel m; (*pl. dies* [daɪz]) Prägestock m, -stempel m.

die-hard ['daɪhɑːd] Reaktionär m.

di·et ['daɪət] **1.** Diät f; Nahrung f, Kost f; *be on a ~* diät leben; **2.** diät leben.

dif·fer ['dɪfə] sich unterscheiden; anderer Meinung sein (*with, from* als); abweichen.

dif·fer|ence ['dɪfrəns] Unterschied m; Differenz f; Meinungsverschiedenheit f; **~ent** □ [~t] verschieden; andere(r, -s); anders (*from* als); **~ren·ti·ate** [dɪfə'renʃɪeɪt] (sich) unterscheiden.

dif·fi|cult ['dɪfɪkəlt] schwierig; **~cul·ty** [~ɪ] Schwierigkeit f.

dif·fi|dence ['dɪfɪdəns] Schüchternheit f; **~dent** □ [~t] schüchtern.

dif|fuse 1. fig. [dɪ'fju:z] verbreiten; **2.** □ [~s] weitverbreitet, zerstreut (*bsd. Licht*); weitschweifig; **~fu·sion** [~ʒn] Verbreitung f.

dig [dɪɡ] **1.** (*-gg-; dug*) graben (in *dat.*); oft *~ up* umgraben; oft *~ up*, *~ out* ausgraben (*a. fig.*); **2.** F Ausgrabung(sstätte) f; F Puff m, Stoß m; *~s* pl. Brt. F Bude f, (Studenten)Zimmer n.

di·gest 1. [dɪ'dʒest] v/t. verdauen (*a. fig.*); ordnen; v/i. verdauen; verdaulich sein; **2.** ['daɪdʒest] Abriß m; Auslese f, Auswahl f; **~i·ble** [dɪ'dʒestəbl] verdaulich; **di·ges·tion** [~tʃən] Verdauung f; **di·ges·tive** □ [~tɪv] verdauungsfördernd.

dig·ger ['dɪɡə] (*bsd. Gold*)Gräber m.

di·git ['dɪdʒɪt] Ziffer f; *three-~ number* dreistellige Zahl; **di·gi·tal** □ [~tl] digital, Digital...; *~ clock*, *~ watch* Digitaluhr f.

D

dig·ni·fied ['dɪgnɪfaɪd] würdevoll, würdig.

dig·ni·ta·ry ['dɪgnɪtərɪ] Würdenträger(in).

dig·ni·ty ['dɪgnɪtɪ] Würde f.

di·gress [daɪ'gres] abschweifen.

dike¹ [daɪk] 1. Deich m, Damm m; Graben m; 2. eindeichen, -dämmen.

dike² sl. [~] Lesbe f (Lesbierin).

di·lap·i·dat·ed [dɪ'læpɪdeɪtɪd] verfallen, baufällig, klapp(e)rig.

di·late [daɪ'leɪt] (sich) ausdehnen; Augen weit öffnen; **dil·a·to·ry** □ ['dɪlətərɪ] verzögernd, hinhaltend; aufschiebend; langsam.

dil·i‖gence ['dɪlɪdʒəns] Fleiß m; ~**gent** [~nt] fleißig, emsig.

di·lute [daɪ'lju:t] 1. verdünnen; verwässern; 2. verdünnt.

dim [dɪm] 1. □ (-mm-) trüb(e); dunkel; matt; 2. (-mm-) (sich) verdunkeln; abblenden; (sich) trüben; matt werden.

dime Am. [daɪm] Zehncentstück n.

di·men·sion [dɪ'menʃn] Dimension f, Abmessung f; ~s pl. a. Ausmaß n; ~**al** [~ʃnl] dimensional; three-~ dreidimensional.

di·min·ish [dɪ'mɪnɪʃ] (sich) vermindern; abnehmen.

di·min·u·tive □ [dɪ'mɪnjʊtɪv] klein, winzig.

dim·ple ['dɪmpl] Grübchen n.

din [dɪn] Getöse n, Lärm m.

dine [daɪn] (zu Mittag, zu Abend) essen, speisen; bewirten; ~ in od. out zu Hause od. auswärts essen; **din·er** ['daɪnə] Speisende(r m) f; Gast m (im Restaurant); bsd. Am. ⬤ Speisewagen m; Am. Speiselokal n.

din·gy □ ['dɪndʒɪ] (-ier, -iest) schmutzig.

din·ing‖ car ⬤ ['daɪnɪŋkɑ:] Speisewagen m; ~ **room** Eß-, Speisezimmer n.

din·ner ['dɪnə] (Mittag-, Abend)Essen n; Festessen n; ~**jack·et** Smoking m; ~**par·ty** Tischgesellschaft f; ~**ser·vice**, ~**set** Speiseservice n, Tafelgeschirr n.

dint [dɪnt] 1. Beule f; by ~ of kraft, vermöge (gen.); 2. ver-, einbeulen.

dip [dɪp] 1. (-pp-) v/t. (ein)tauchen; senken; schöpfen; ~ the headlights bsd. Brt. mot. abblenden; v/i. (unter)tauchen; sinken; sich neigen, sich senken; 2. (Ein-, Unter)Tauchen n; F kurzes Bad; Senkung f,

Neigung f; Gefälle n; Dip m (Soße).

diph·ther·i·a 🜊 [dɪf'θɪərɪə] Diphtherie f.

di·plo·ma [dɪ'pləʊmə] Diplom n.

di·plo·ma·cy [dɪ'pləʊməsɪ] Diplomatie f.

dip·lo·mat ['dɪpləmæt] Diplomat m; ~**ic** [dɪplə'mætɪk] (~ally) diplomatisch.

di·plo·ma·tist fig. [dɪ'pləʊmətɪst] Diplomat(in).

dip·per ['dɪpə] Schöpfkelle f.

dire ['daɪə] (~r, ~st) gräßlich, schrecklich.

di·rect [dɪ'rekt] 1. adj. □ direkt; gerade; unmittelbar; offen, aufrichtig; ~ current ⚡ Gleichstrom m; ~ train durchgehender Zug; 2. adv. direkt, unmittelbar; 3. richten; lenken, steuern; leiten; anordnen; j-n anweisen; j-m den Weg zeigen; Brief adressieren; Regie führen bei.

di·rec·tion [dɪ'rekʃn] Richtung f; Leitung f, Führung f; Adresse f (e-s Briefes etc.); Film etc.: Regie f; mst ~s pl. Anweisung f, Anleitung f; ~s for use Gebrauchsanweisung f; △ nicht Direktion; ~**find·er** [~faɪndə] (Funk)Peiler m, Peilempfänger m; ~**in·di·ca·tor** mot. Fahrtrichtungsanzeiger m, Blinker m; 🚂 Kursweiser m.

di·rec·tive [dɪ'rektɪv] richtungweisend, leitend.

di·rect·ly [dɪ'rektlɪ] 1. adv. sofort; 2. cj. sobald, sowie.

di·rec·tor [dɪ'rektə] Direktor m; Film etc.: Regisseur m; board of ~s Aufsichtsrat m.

di·rec·to·ry [dɪ'rektərɪ] Adreßbuch n; telephone ~ Telefonbuch n.

dirge [dɜ:dʒ] Klagelied n.

dir·i·gi·ble ['dɪrɪdʒəbl] 1. lenkbar; 2. lenkbares Luftschiff n.

dirt [dɜ:t] Schmutz m; (lockere) Erde; ~**-cheap** F ['dɜ:t'tʃi:p] spottbillig; ~**y** [~ɪ] 1. □ (-ier, -iest) schmutzig (a. fig.); 2. beschmutzen; schmutzig werden.

dis·a·bil·i·ty [dɪsə'bɪlətɪ] Unfähigkeit f.

dis·a·ble [dɪs'eɪbl] (✗ kampf)unfähig machen; ✗ dienstuntauglich machen; ~**d** 1. arbeits-, erwerbsunfähig, invalid(e); ✗ dienstuntauglich; ✗ kriegsversehrt; körperlich od. geistig behindert; 2. the ~ pl. die Behinderten pl.

dis·ad·van|tage [dɪsəd'vɑːntɪdʒ] Nachteil *m*; Schaden *m*; **~ta·geous** □ [dɪsædvɑːn'teɪdʒəs] nachteilig, ungünstig.

dis·a·gree [dɪsə'griː] nicht übereinstimmen; uneinig sein; nicht bekommen (*with* s.o. j-m); **~a·ble** □ [~əbl] unangenehm; **~ment** [~iːmənt] Verschiedenheit *f*, Unstimmigkeit *f*; Meinungsverschiedenheit *f*.

dis·ap·pear [dɪsə'pɪə] verschwinden; **~ance** [~rəns] Verschwinden *n*.

dis·ap·point [dɪsə'pɔɪnt] *j-n* enttäuschen; *Hoffnungen etc.* zunichte machen; **~ment** [~mənt] Enttäuschung *f*.

dis·ap·prov|al [dɪsə'pruːvl] Mißbilligung *f*; **~e** [dɪsə'pruːv] mißbilligen; dagegen sein.

dis|arm [dɪs'ɑːm] *v/t.* entwaffnen (*a. fig.*); *v/i.* ⚔ *pol.* abrüsten; **~ar·ma·ment** [~əmənt] Entwaffnung *f*; ⚔ *pol.* Abrüstung *f*.

dis·ar·range [dɪsə'reɪndʒ] in Unordnung bringen.

dis·ar·ray [dɪsə'reɪ] Unordnung *f*.

di·sas|ter [dɪ'zɑːstə] Unglück(sfall *m*) *n*, Katastrophe *f*; **~trous** □ [~trəs] katastrophal, verheerend.

dis·band [dɪs'bænd] (sich) auflösen.

dis·be|lief [dɪsbɪ'liːf] Unglaube *m*; Zweifel *m* (*in an dat.*); **~lieve** [~iːv] *et.* bezweifeln, nicht glauben.

disc [dɪsk] Scheibe *f* (*a. anat.*, *zo.*, ⊕); (Schall)Platte *f*; Parkscheibe *f*; △ *nicht Diskus*; *slipped* **~** ❀ Bandscheibenvorfall *m*.

dis·card [dɪ'skɑːd] *Karten, Kleid etc.* ablegen; *Freund etc.* fallenlassen.

di·scern [dɪ'sɜːn] wahrnehmen, erkennen; **~ing** □ [~ɪŋ] kritisch, scharfsichtig; **~ment** [~mənt] Einsicht *f*; Scharfblick *m*; Wahrnehmen *n*.

dis·charge [dɪs'tʃɑːdʒ] **1.** *v/t.* ent-, ausladen; *j-n* befreien, entbinden; *j-n* entlassen; *Gewehr etc.* abfeuern; von sich geben, ausströmen, -senden; ❀ absondern; *Pflicht etc.* erfüllen; *Zorn etc.* auslassen (*on an dat.*); *Schuld* bezahlen; *Wechsel* einlösen; münden (*Fluß*); ❀ eitern; **2.** Entladung *f* (*e-s Schiffes etc.*); Abfeuern *n* (*e-s Gewehrs etc.*); Ausströmen *n*; ❀ Absonderung *f*; ❀ Ausfluß *m*; Ausstoßen *n*; ⚡ Entladung *f*; Entlassung

f; Entlastung *f*; Erfüllung *f* (*e-r Pflicht*).

di·sci·ple [dɪ'saɪpl] Schüler *m*; Jünger *m*.

dis·ci·pline [dɪsɪplɪn] **1.** Disziplin *f*; Bestrafung *f*; **2.** disziplinieren; bestrafen; *well* **~d** diszipliniert; *badly* **~d** disziplinlos, undiszipliniert.

disc jock·ey [dɪskdʒɒkɪ] Disk-, Discjockey *m*.

dis·claim [dɪs'kleɪm] ab-, bestreiten; *Verantwortung* ablehnen; 🏛 verzichten auf (*acc.*).

dis|close [dɪs'kləʊz] bekanntgeben, -machen; enthüllen, aufdecken; **~clo·sure** [~əʊʒə] Enthüllung *f*.

dis·co F [dɪskəʊ] **1.** (*pl.* -cos) Disko *f* (*Diskothek*); **2.** Disko...; **~** *sound* Diskosound *m*.

dis·col·o(u)r [dɪs'kʌlə] (sich) verfärben.

dis·com·fort [dɪs'kʌmfət] **1.** Unbehagen *n*; Beschwerden *pl.*; **2.** *j-m* Unbehagen verursachen.

dis·con·cert [dɪskən'sɜːt] aus der Fassung bringen.

dis·con·nect [dɪskə'nekt] trennen (*a.* ⚡); ⊕ auskuppeln; 🔌 *Gerät* abschalten; *Gas, Strom, Telefon* abstellen; *teleph.* Gespräch unterbrechen; **~ed** □ zusammenhang(s)los.

dis·con·so·late □ [dɪs'kɒnsəlɪt] untröstlich, tieftraurig.

dis·con·tent [dɪskən'tent] Unzufriedenheit *f*; **~ed** □ unzufrieden.

dis·con·tin·ue [dɪskən'tɪnjuː] aufgeben, aufhören mit; unterbrechen.

dis·cord [dɪskɔːd], **~ance** [dɪs'kɔːdəns] Uneinigkeit *f*; ♪ Mißklang *m*; **~ant** □ [~t] nicht übereinstimmend; ♪ unharmonisch, mißtönend.

dis·co·theque [dɪskətek] Diskothek *f*.

dis·count [dɪskaʊnt] **1.** *econ.* Diskont *m*; Abzug *m*, Rabatt *m*; **2.** *econ.* diskontieren; abziehen, abrechnen; *Nachricht* mit Vorsicht aufnehmen.

dis·cour·age [dɪs'kʌrɪdʒ] entmutigen; abschrecken; **~ment** [~mənt] Entmutigung *f*; Hindernis *n*, Schwierigkeit *f*.

dis·course 1. [dɪskɔːs] Rede *f*; Abhandlung *f*; Predigt *f*; **2.** [dɪs'kɔːs] e-n Vortrag halten (*on, upon* über *acc.*).

dis·cour·te|ous □ [dɪs'kɜːtjəs] unhöflich; **~sy** [~təsɪ] Unhöflichkeit *f*.

dis·cov|er [dɪ'skʌvə] entdecken; aus-

findig machen; feststellen; **~·e·ry**
[~ərɪ] Entdeckung f.

dis·cred·it [dɪsˈkredɪt] **1.** Zweifel m;
Mißkredit m, schlechter Ruf; **2.**
nicht glauben; in Mißkredit bringen.

di·screet □ [dɪˈskriːt] besonnen, vorsichtig; diskret, verschwiegen.

di·screp·an·cy [dɪˈskrepənsɪ] Widerspruch m, Unstimmigkeit f.

di·scre·tion [dɪˈskreʃn] Besonnenheit f, Klugheit f; Takt m; Verschwiegenheit f; Belieben n.

di·scrim·i·nate [dɪˈskrɪmɪneɪt] unterscheiden; ~ *against* benachteiligen; **~·nat·ing** □ [~ɪŋ] unterscheidend; kritisch, urteilsfähig; **~·na·
tion** [dɪskrɪmɪˈneɪʃn] Unterscheidung f; unterschiedliche (bsd. nachteilige) Behandlung; ⊕ loskuppeln.

dis·cus [ˈdɪskəs] *Sport:* Diskus m; ~
throw Diskuswerfen n; ~ *thrower*
Diskuswerfer(in).

di·scuss [dɪˈskʌs] diskutieren, erörtern, besprechen; **di·scus·sion**
[~ʌʃn] Diskussion f, Besprechung f.

dis·dain [dɪsˈdeɪn] **1.** Verachtung f; **2.**
geringschätzen, verachten; verschmähen.

dis·ease [dɪˈziːz] Krankheit f; **~d**
krank.

dis·em·bark [ˈdɪsɪmˈbaːk] v/t. ausschiffen; v/i. von Bord gehen.

dis·en·chant·ed [dɪsɪnˈtʃaːntɪd]: *be ~
with* sich keinen Illusionen mehr
hingeben über (acc.).

dis·en·gage [dɪsɪnˈgeɪdʒ] (sich) freimachen od. lösen; ⊕ loskuppeln.

dis·en·tan·gle [ˈdɪsɪnˈtæŋgl] entwirren; herauslösen (from aus).

dis·fa·vo·u·r [ˈdɪsˈfeɪvə] Mißfallen
n; Ungnade f.

dis·fig·ure [dɪsˈfɪgə] entstellen.

dis·grace [dɪsˈgreɪs] **1.** Ungnade f;
Schande f; **2.** Schande bringen über
(acc.), j-m Schande bereiten; *be ~d*
in Ungnade fallen; **~·ful** □ [~fl]
schändlich; skandalös.

dis·guise [dɪsˈgaɪz] **1.** verkleiden (as
als); verstellen; verschleiern, -bergen; **2.** Verkleidung f; Verstellung f;
Verschleierung f; thea. u. fig. Maske
f; in ~ maskiert, verkleidet; fig. verkappt; *in ~ of* verkleidet als.

dis·gust [dɪsˈgʌst] **1.** Ekel m, Abscheu
m; **2.** (an)ekeln; empören, entrüsten;
~·ing □ [~ɪŋ] ekelhaft.

dish [dɪʃ] **1.** flache Schüssel; (Ser

vier)Platte f; Gericht n, Speise f; *the
~es pl.* das Geschirr; **2.** ~ *up*
anrichten; auftischen, -tragen; ~ *out*
F austeilen; **~·cloth** [ˈdɪʃklɒθ] Geschirrspültuch n.

dis·heart·en [dɪsˈhaːtn] entmutigen.

di·shev·el(l)ed [dɪˈʃevld] zerzaust.

dis·hon·est □ [dɪsˈɒnɪst] unehrlich,
unredlich; **~·y** [~ɪ] Unredlichkeit f.

dis·hon·o·u·r [dɪsˈɒnə] **1.** Unehre f,
Schande f; **2.** entehren; schänden;
econ. *Wechsel* nicht honorieren od.
einlösen; **~·o·u·ra·ble** □ [~rəbl]
schändlich, unehrenhaft.

dish·rag [ˈdɪʃræg] = dishcloth;
~·wash·er Spüler(in); Geschirrspülmaschine f, -spüler m; **~·wa·ter**
Spülwasser n.

dis·il·lu·sion [dɪsɪˈluːʒn] **1.** Ernüchterung f, Desillusion f; **2.** ernüchtern, desillusionieren; *be ~ed with*
sich keinen Illusionen mehr hingeben über (acc.).

dis·in·clined [ˈdɪsɪnˈklaɪnd] abgeneigt.

dis·in·fect [ˈdɪsɪnˈfekt] desinfizieren;
~·fec·tant [~ənt] Desinfektionsmittel n.

dis·in·her·it [dɪsɪnˈherɪt] enterben.

dis·in·te·grate [dɪsˈɪntɪgreɪt] (sich)
auflösen; ver-, zerfallen.

dis·in·ter·est·ed □ [dɪsˈɪntrəstɪd]
uneigennützig, selbstlos; objektiv,
unvoreingenommen; △ *mst nicht*
desinteressiert.

disk [dɪsk] bsd. Am. = Brt. disc;
Computer: Diskette f; ~ *drive* Diskettenlaufwerk n, F Floppy f.

disk·ette [ˈdɪsket, dɪsˈket] *Computer:*
Diskette f.

dis·like [dɪsˈlaɪk] **1.** Abneigung f, Widerwille m (of, for gegen); *take a ~ to
s.o.* gegen j-n e-e Abneigung fassen;
2. nicht mögen.

dis·lo·cate [ˈdɪsləkeɪt] ⚕ verrenken;
verlagern.

dis·lodge [dɪsˈlɒdʒ] vertreiben, verjagen; entfernen; *Stein etc.* lösen.

dis·loy·al □ [ˈdɪsˈlɔɪəl] treulos.

dis·mal □ [ˈdɪzməl] trüb(e), trostlos,
elend.

dis·man·tle [dɪsˈmæntl] abbrechen,
niederreißen; ⚓ abtakeln; ⚓ abwracken; ⊕ demontieren.

dis·may [dɪsˈmeɪ] **1.** Schrecken m,
Bestürzung f; *in ~, with ~* bestürzt;
to one's ~ zu m-m Entsetzen; **2.** v/t.
erschrecken, bestürzen.

dis·miss [dɪsˈmɪs] v/t. entlassen; wegschicken; ablehnen; *Thema etc.* fallenlassen; ⚖ abweisen; **~al** [~l] Entlassung *f*; Aufgabe *f*; ⚖ Abweisung *f*.

dis·mount [ˈdɪsˈmaʊnt] v/t. aus dem Sattel heben; *Reiter* abwerfen; demontieren; ⊕ auseinandernehmen; v/i. absteigen, absitzen (*from* von *Fahrrad, Pferd etc.*).

dis·o·be·di·ence [dɪsəˈbiːdjəns] Ungehorsam *m*; **~ent** ☐ [~t] ungehorsam.

dis·o·bey [ˈdɪsəˈbeɪ] nicht gehorchen, ungehorsam sein (gegen).

dis·or·der [dɪsˈɔːdə] **1.** Unordnung *f*; Aufruhr *m*; 𝔰 Störung *f*; **2.** in Unordnung bringen; 𝔰 angreifen; **~ly** [~lɪ] unordentlich; ordnungswidrig; unruhig; aufrührerisch.

dis·or·gan·ize [dɪsˈɔːgənaɪz] durcheinanderbringen; desorganisieren.

dis·own [dɪsˈəʊn] nicht anerkennen; *Kind* verstoßen; ablehnen.

di·spar·age [dɪˈspærɪdʒ] verächtlich machen, herabsetzen; geringschätzen.

di·spar·i·ty [dɪˈspærətɪ] Ungleichheit *f*; **~ of** od. **in age** Altersunterschied *m*.

dis·pas·sion·ate ☐ [dɪˈspæʃnət] leidenschaftslos; objektiv.

di·spatch [dɪˈspætʃ] **1.** schnelle Erledigung *f*; (Ab)Sendung *f*; Abfertigung *f*; Eile *f*; (Eil)Botschaft *f*; Bericht *m* (*e-s Korrespondenten*); **2.** schnell erledigen; absenden, abschicken, *Telegramm* aufgeben, abfertigen.

di·spel [dɪˈspel] (*-ll-*) *Menge etc.* zerstreuen (*a. fig.*), *Nebel* zerteilen.

di·spen·sa·ble [dɪˈspensəbl] entbehrlich; **~ry** [~rɪ] Werks-, Krankenhaus-, Schul-, ✕ Lazarettapotheke *f*.

dis·pen·sa·tion [dɪspenˈseɪʃn] Austeilung *f*; Befreiung *f* (*with* von); Dispens *m*; *göttliche* Fügung.

di·spense [dɪˈspens] austeilen; *Recht* sprechen; *Arzneien* zubereiten u. abgeben; **~ with** auskommen ohne; überflüssig machen; **di·spens·er** [~ə] Spender *m*, *für Klebestreifen a.* Abroller *m*, (*Briefmarken- etc.*)Automat *m*.

di·sperse [dɪˈspɜːs] verstreuen; (sich) zerstreuen.

di·spir·it·ed [dɪˈspɪrɪtɪd] entmutigt.

dis·place [dɪsˈpleɪs] verschieben; ablösen, entlassen; verschleppen; ersetzen; verdrängen.

di·splay [dɪˈspleɪ] **1.** Entfaltung *f*; (Her)Zeigen *n*; (protzige) Zurschaustellung; Sichtanzeige *f*; *econ.* Display *n*, Auslage *f*; **be on ~** ausgestellt sein; **2.** entfalten; zur Schau stellen; zeigen.

dis·please [dɪsˈpliːz] *j-m* mißfallen; **~pleased** ungehalten; **~plea·sure** [~pleʒə] Mißfallen *n*.

dis·po·sa·ble [dɪˈspəʊzəbl] Einweg...; Wegwerf...; **~pos·al** [~zl] Beseitigung *f* (*von Müll etc.*), Entsorgung *f*; Verfügung(srecht *n*) *f*; **be** (*put*) **at s.o.'s ~** *j-m* zur Verfügung stehen (stellen); **~pose** [~əʊz] v/t. (an)ordnen, einrichten; geneigt machen, veranlassen; v/i. **~ of** verfügen über (*acc.*); erledigen; loswerden; beseitigen; **~posed** geneigt; ...gesinnt; **~po·si·tion** [dɪspəˈzɪʃn] Disposition *f*; Anordnung *f*; Neigung *f*; Veranlagung *f*, Art *f*.

dis·pos·sess [ˈdɪspəˈzes] enteignen, vertreiben; berauben (*of gen.*).

dis·pro·por·tion·ate ☐ [ˈdɪsprəˈpɔː-nət] unverhältnismäßig.

dis·prove [ˈdɪsˈpruːv] widerlegen.

di·spute [dɪˈspjuːt] **1.** Disput *m*, Kontroverse *f*; Streit *m*; Auseinandersetzung *f*; **2.** streiten (über *acc.*); bezweifeln.

dis·qual·i·fy [dɪsˈkwɒlɪfaɪ] unfähig od. untauglich machen; für untauglich erklären; *Sport:* disqualifizieren.

dis·qui·et [dɪsˈkwaɪət] beunruhigen.

dis·re·gard [ˈdɪsrɪˈɡɑːd] **1.** Nichtbeachtung *f*; Mißachtung *f*; **2.** nicht beachten.

dis·rep·u·ta·ble ☐ [dɪsˈrepjʊtəbl] übel; verrufen; **~re·pute** [ˈdɪsrɪ-ˈpjuːt] schlechter Ruf.

dis·re·spect [ˈdɪsrɪˈspekt] Respektlosigkeit *f*; Unhöflichkeit *f*; **~ful** ☐ [~fl] respektlos; unhöflich.

dis·rupt [dɪsˈrʌpt] unterbrechen.

dis·sat·is·fac·tion [ˈdɪssætɪsˈfækʃn] Unzufriedenheit *f*; **~fy** [ˈdɪsˈsætɪsfaɪ] nicht befriedigen; *j-m* mißfallen.

dis·sect [dɪˈsekt] zerlegen, -gliedern.

dis·sem·ble [dɪˈsembl] v/t. verbergen; v/i. sich verstellen, heucheln.

dis·sen·sion [dɪˈsenʃn] Meinungsverschiedenheit(en *pl.*) *f*, Differenz(en *pl.*) *f*; Uneinigkeit *f*; **~t** [~t]

D

1. abweichende Meinung; 2. anderer Meinung sein *(from* als); **~t·er** [~ə] Andersdenkende(r *m*) *f*.

dis·si·dent [ˈdɪsɪdənt] 1. andersdenkend; 2. Andersdenkende(r *m*) *f*; *pol.* Dissident(in), Regime-, Systemkritiker(in).

dis·sim·i·lar □ [ˈdɪˈsɪmɪlə] (*to*) unähnlich (*dat.*); verschieden (von).

dis·sim·u·la·tion [dɪsɪmjʊˈleɪʃn] Verstellung *f*.

dis·si|pate [ˈdɪsɪpeɪt] (sich) zerstreuen; verschwenden; **~·pat·ed** ausschweifend, zügellos.

dis·so·ci·ate [dɪˈsəʊʃɪeɪt] trennen; ~ *o.s.* sich distanzieren, abrücken.

dis·so|lute □ [ˈdɪsəluːt] ausschweifend, zügellos; **~·lu·tion** [dɪsəˈluːʃn] Auflösung *f*; Zerstörung *f*; *jjf* Aufhebung *f*, Annullierung *f*.

dis·solve [dɪˈzɒlv] *v/t.* (auf)lösen; schmelzen; *v/i.* sich auflösen.

dis·so·nant □ [ˈdɪsənənt] ♪ dissonant, mißtönend; *fig.* unstimmig.

dis·suade [dɪˈsweɪd] *j-m* abraten (*from* von).

dis|tance [ˈdɪstəns] 1. Abstand *m*; Entfernung *f*, Ferne *f*; Strecke *f*; *fig.* Distanz *f*, Zurückhaltung *f*; *at a* ~ von weitem; in einiger Entfernung; *keep s.o. at a* ~ j-m gegenüber reserviert sein; ~ *race Sport:* Langstreckenlauf *m*; ~ *runner Sport:* Langstreckenläufer(in); 2. hinter sich lassen; **~·tant** □ [~t] entfernt; fern; zurückhaltend; *Fern...;* ~ *control* Fernsteuerung *f*.

dis·taste [dɪsˈteɪst] Widerwille *m*, Abneigung *f*; **~·ful** □ [~fl]: *be* ~ *to s.o.* j-m zuwider sein.

dis·tem·per [dɪˈstempə] Krankheit *f* (*bsd. von Tieren*); (Hunde)Staupe *f*.

dis·tend [dɪˈstend] (sich) (aus)dehnen; (auf)blähen; sich weiten.

dis·til(l) [dɪˈstɪl] (*-ll-*) herabtropfen (lassen); ♫ destillieren; **dis·til·le·ry** [~ərɪ] (Branntwein)Brennerei *f*.

dis|tinct □ [dɪˈstɪŋkt] verschieden; getrennt; deutlich, klar, bestimmt; **~·tinc·tion** [~kʃn] Unterscheidung *f*; Unterschied *m*; Auszeichnung *f*; Rang *m*; **~·tinc·tive** □ [~tɪv] unterscheidend; kennzeichnend, bezeichnend.

dis·tin·guish [dɪˈstɪŋgwɪʃ] unterscheiden; auszeichnen; ~ *o.s.* sich auszeichnen; **~ed** berühmt; ausgezeichnet; vornehm.

dis·tort [dɪˈstɔːt] verdrehen; verzerren.

dis·tract [dɪˈstrækt] ablenken; zerstreuen; beunruhigen; verwirren; verrückt machen; **~ed** □ beunruhigt, besorgt; (*by, with*) außer sich (vor *dat.*); wahnsinnig (vor *Schmerzen etc.*); **dis·trac·tion** [~kʃn] Ablenkung *f*; Zerstreutheit *f*; Verwirrung *f*; Zerstreuung *f*; Raserei *f*.

dis·traught [dɪˈstrɔːt] = *distracted.*

dis·tress [dɪˈstres] 1. Qual *f*; Kummer *m*, Sorge *f*; Elend *n*, Not *f*; 2. in Not bringen; quälen; beunruhigen; betrüben; *j-n* erschöpfen; **~ed** beunruhigt, besorgt; betrübt; notleidend; ~ *area Brt.* Notstandsgebiet *n*.

dis·trib|ute [dɪˈstrɪbjuːt] ver-, aus-, zuteilen; einteilen; verbreiten; **~·tri·bu·tion** [dɪstrɪˈbjuːʃn] Ver-, Austeilung *f*; Verleih *m* (*von Filmen*); Verbreitung *f*; Einteilung *f*.

dis·trict [ˈdɪstrɪkt] Bezirk *m*; Gegend *f*.

dis·trust [dɪsˈtrʌst] 1. Mißtrauen *n*; 2. mißtrauen (*dat.*); **~·ful** □ [~fl] mißtrauisch.

dis·turb [dɪˈstɜːb] stören; beunruhigen; **~ance** [~əns] Störung *f*; Unruhe *f*; ~ *of the peace jjf* Störung *f* der öffentlichen Sicherheit u. Ordnung; *cause a* ~ für Unruhe sorgen; ruhestörenden Lärm machen; **~ed** geistig gestört; verhaltensgestört.

dis·used [ˈdɪsˈjuːzd] nicht mehr benutzt (*Maschine etc.*), stillgelegt (*Bergwerk etc.*).

ditch [dɪtʃ] Graben *m*.

di·van [dɪˈvæn, *Am.* ˈdaɪvæn] Diwan *m*; ~ *bed* Bettcouch *f*.

dive [daɪv] 1. (*dived od. Am. a. dove, dived*) (unter)tauchen; *vom Sprungbrett* springen; *e-n Hecht- od. Kopfsprung machen; hechten (*for* nach); *e-n Sturzflug machen;* 2. *Schwimmen:* Springen *n*; Kopf-, Hechtsprung *m*; Sturzflug *m*; F Spelunke *f*; **div·er** [ˈdaɪvə] Taucher(in); *Sport:* Wasserspringer(in).

di·verge [daɪˈvɜːdʒ] auseinanderlaufen; abweichen; **di·ver·gence** [~əns] Abweichung *f*; **di·ver·gent** □ [~t] abweichend.

di·vers [ˈdaɪvɜːz] mehrere.

di·verse □ [daɪˈvɜːs] verschieden; mannigfaltig; **di·ver·si·fy** [~sɪfaɪ] verschieden(artig) *od.* abwechslungsreich gestalten; **di·ver·sion**

[~ɜːʃn] Ablenkung f; Zeitvertreib m; **di·ver·si·ty** [~ɜːsətɪ] Verschiedenheit f; Mannigfaltigkeit f.

di·vert [daɪˈvɜːt] ablenken; j-n zerstreuen, unterhalten; Verkehr umleiten.

di·vide [dɪˈvaɪd] 1. v/t. teilen; ver-, aus-, aufteilen; trennen; einteilen; Ⱥ dividieren (by durch); v/i. sich teilen; zerfallen; Ⱥ sich dividieren lassen; sich trennen od. auflösen; 2. geogr. Wasserscheide f; **di·vid·ed** geteilt; ~ highway Am. Schnellstraße f; ~ skirt Hosenrock m.

div·i·dend econ. [ˈdɪvɪdend] Dividende f.

di·vid·ers [dɪˈvaɪdəz] pl. (a pair of ~ ein) Stechzirkel m.

di·vine [dɪˈvaɪn] 1. □ (~r, ~st) göttlich; ~ service Gottesdienst m; 2. Geistliche(r) m; 3. weissagen; ahnen.

div·ing [ˈdaɪvɪŋ] Tauchen n; Sport: Wasserspringen n; attr. Tauch..., Taucher...; ⚓ Sturzflug...; ~board Sprungbrett n; ~suit Taucheranzug m.

di·vin·i·ty [dɪˈvɪnətɪ] Gottheit f; Göttlichkeit f; Theologie f.

di·vis·i·ble □ [dɪˈvɪzəbl] teilbar; **di·vi·sion** [~ˈvɪʒn] Teilung f; Trennung f; Abteilung f; ✕, Ⱥ Division f.

di·vorce [dɪˈvɔːs] 1. (Ehe)Scheidung f; get a ~ geschieden werden (from von); 2. Ehe scheiden; sie scheiden lassen von; they have been ~d sie haben sich scheiden lassen; **di·vor·cee** [dɪvɔːˈsiː] Geschiedene(r m) f.

diz·zy □ [ˈdɪzɪ] (-ier, -iest) schwind(e)lig.

do [duː] (did, done) v/t. tun, machen; (zu)bereiten; Zimmer aufräumen; Geschirr abwaschen; Rolle spielen; Wegstrecke zurücklegen, schaffen; ~ you know him? – no, I don't kennst du ihn? – nein; what can I ~ for you? was kann ich für Sie tun?, womit kann ich (Ihnen) dienen?; ~ London F London besichtigen; have one's hair done sich die Haare machen od. frisieren lassen; have done reading fertig sein mit Lesen; v/i. tun, handeln; sich befinden; genügen; that will ~ das genügt; how ~ you ~? guten Tag! (bei der Vorstellung); ~ be quick beeile dich doch; ~ you like London? – I ~ gefällt Ihnen London? – ja; ~ well s-e Sache gut machen; gute

Geschäfte machen; mit Adverbien u. Präpositionen: ~ away with beseitigen, weg-, abschaffen; I'm done in F ich bin geschafft; ~ up Kleid etc. zumachen; Haus etc. instand setzen; Päckchen zurechtmachen; ~ o.s. up sich zurechtmachen; I'm done up F ich bin geschafft; I could ~ with ... ich könnte ... brauchen od. vertragen; ~ without auskommen od. sich behelfen ohne.

do·cile □ [ˈdəʊsaɪl] gelehrig; fügsam.

dock¹ [dɒk] stutzen, kupieren; fig. kürzen.

dock² [~] 1. ⚓ Dock n; Kai m, Pier m; ☆ Anklagebank f; ~ off Schiff (ein-) docken; Raumschiff koppeln; v/i. ⚓ anlegen; andocken, ankoppeln (Raumschiff); ~ing [~ɪŋ] F Docking n, Ankopp(e)lung f (von Raumschiffen); ~yard ⚓ (bsd. Brt. Marine)Werft f.

doc·tor [ˈdɒktə] 1. Doktor m; Arzt m; 2. F (ver)fälschen.

doc·trine [ˈdɒktrɪn] Doktrin f, Lehre f.

doc·u·ment 1. [ˈdɒkjʊmənt] Urkunde f; 2. [~ment] (urkundlich) belegen.

doc·u·men·ta·ry [dɒkjʊˈmentrɪ] 1. urkundlich; Film etc.: Dokumentar...; 2. Dokumentarfilm m.

dodge [dɒdʒ] 1. Sprung m zur Seite, Kniff m, Trick m; 2. (rasch) zur Seite springen, ausweichen; F sich drücken (vor dat.).

doe zo. [dəʊ] Hirschkuh f; Rehgeiß f, Ricke f; Häsin f.

dog [dɒg] 1. zo. Hund m; 2. (-gg-) j-n beharrlich verfolgen; **~-eared** [ˈdɒgɪəd] mit Eselsohren (Buch); **~ged** □ verbissen, hartnäckig.

dog·ma [ˈdɒgmə] Dogma n; Glaubenssatz m; **~t·ic** [dɒgˈmætɪk] (~ally) dogmatisch.

dog-tired F [ˈdɒgˈtaɪəd] hundemüde.

do·ings [ˈduːɪŋz] pl. Handlungen pl., Taten pl., Tätigkeit f; Begebenheiten pl.; Treiben n, Betragen n.

do-it-your·self [duːɪtjɔːˈself] 1. Heimwerken n; 2. Heimwerker...

dole [dəʊl] 1. milde Gabe; Brt. F Stempelgeld n; be od. go on the ~ Brt. F stempeln gehen; 2. ~ out sparsam ver- od. austeilen.

dole·ful □ [ˈdəʊlfl] trübselig.

doll [dɒl] Puppe f.

D

dol·lar ['dɒlə] Dollar *m*.

dol·phin *zo.* ['dɒlfɪn] Delphin *m*.

do·main [dəʊ'meɪn] Domäne *f*; *fig.* Gebiet *n*, Bereich *m*.

dome [dəʊm] Kuppel *f*; △ *nicht* Dom; **~d** gewölbt.

Domes·day Book ['du:mzdeɪbʊk] *Reichsgrundbuch Englands* (1086).

do·mes|tic [də'mestɪk] **1.** (~ally) häuslich; inländisch, einheimisch; zahm; ~ *animal* Haustier *n*; ~ *flight* ✈ Inlandsflug *m*; ~ *trade* Binnenhandel *m*; **2.** Hausangestellte(r *m f*); **~·ti·cate** [~eɪt] zähmen.

dom·i·cile ['dɒmɪsaɪl] Wohnsitz *m*.

dom·i|nant ['dɒmɪnənt] (vor-) herrschend; [~eɪt] (be)herrschen; **~·na·tion** [dɒmɪ'neɪʃn] Herrschaft *f*; **~·neer·ing** [~'nɪərɪŋ] herrisch, tyrannisch; überheblich.

do·min·ion [də'mɪnjən] Herrschaft *f*; (Herrschafts)Gebiet *n*; ♀ Dominion *n* (*im Brit. Commonwealth*).

don [dɒn] anziehen; *Hut* aufsetzen.

do·nate [dəʊ'neɪt] schenken, stiften; **do·na·tion** [~eɪʃn] Schenkung *f*.

done [dʌn] **1.** *p.p. von* do; **2.** *adj.* getan; erledigt; fertig; gar *gekocht*.

don·key ['dɒŋkɪ] *zo.* Esel *m*; *attr.* Hilfs-.

do·nor ['dəʊnə] (♀ *bsd.* Blut-, Organ)Spender(in).

doom [du:m] **1.** Schicksal *n*, Verhängnis *n*; **2.** verurteilen, -dammen; **~s·day** ['du:mzdeɪ]: *till* ~ F bis zum Jüngsten Tag.

door [dɔ:] Tür *f*; Tor *n*; *next* ~ nebenan; **~·han·dle** [dɔ:hændl] Türklinke *f*; **~·keep·er** Pförtner *m*; **~·man** (*pl. -men*) (livrierter) Portier; **~·step** Türstufe *f*; **~·way** Türöffnung *f*, (Tür)Eingang *m*.

dope [dəʊp] **1.** Schmiere *f*; *bsd.* ✈ Lack *m*; F Stoff *m*, Rauschgift *n*; F Betäubungsmittel *n*; *Sport*: Dopingmittel *n*; *Am.* F Rauschgiftsüchtige(r *m*) *f*; *sl.* Trottel *m*; *sl.* (vertrauliche) Informationen *f*, Geheimtip *m*; **2.** ✈ lackieren; F *j-m* Stoff geben; *Sport*: dopen; **~ ad·dict**, **~ fiend** F Rauschgift-, Drogensüchtige(r *m*) *f*; **~ test** Dopingkontrolle *f*.

dorm F [dɔ:m] = *dormitory*.

dor·mant *mst fig.* ['dɔ:mənt] schlafend, ruhend; untätig.

dor·mer (win·dow) ['dɔ:mə('wɪndəʊ)] stehendes Dachfenster.

dor·mi·to·ry ['dɔ:mɪtrɪ] Schlafsaal *m*; *bsd. Am.* Studentenwohnheim *n*.

dose [dəʊs] **1.** Dosis *f*; △ *nicht* Dose; **2.** *j-m* e-e Medizin geben.

dot [dɒt] **1.** Punkt *m*; Fleck *m*; *on the* ~ F auf die Sekunde pünktlich; **2.** (*-tt-*) punktieren; tüpfeln; *fig.* sprenkeln; **~ted line** punktierte Linie.

dote [dəʊt]: ~ *on*, ~ *upon* vernarrt sein in (*acc.*), abgöttisch lieben (*acc.*); **dot·ing** ['dəʊtɪŋ] vernarrt.

dou·ble ['dʌbl] **1.** doppelt; zu zweien; gekrümmt; zweideutig; *Doppelte(s) n*; *Doppelgänger(in)*; *Film, TV*: Double *n*; *mst* ~s *sg., pl. Tennis*: Doppel *n*; *men's od. women's* ~s *sg., pl.* Herren- *od.* Damendoppel *n*; **3.** (sich) verdoppeln; *Film, TV*: *j-n* doubeln; *a.* ~ *up* falten; *Decke* zusammenlegen; ~ *back* kehrtmachen; ~ *up* zusammenkrümmen; sich krümmen (*with vor dat.*); **~·breast·ed** zweireihig (*Jakkett*); **~·check** genau nachprüfen; **~·chin** Doppelkinn *n*; **~·cross** ein doppeltes *od.* falsches Spiel treiben mit; **~·deal·ing 1.** betrügerisch; **2.** Betrug *m*; **~·deck·er** [~ə] Doppeldecker *m*; **~·edged** zweischneidig; zweideutig; **~·en·try** *econ.* doppelte Buchführung; **~ fea·ture** *Film*: Doppelprogramm *n*; **~·head·er** *m*. [~ə] Doppelveranstaltung *f*; **~·park** *mot.* in zweiter Reihe parken; **~·quick** F im Eiltempo, fix.

doubt [daʊt] **1.** *v/i.* zweifeln; *v/t.* bezweifeln; mißtrauen (*dat.*); **2.** Zweifel *m*; *be in* ~ *about* Zweifel haben an (*dat.*); *no* ~ ohne Zweifel; **~·ful** ['daʊtfl] zweifelhaft; **~·less** [~lɪs] ohne Zweifel.

douche [du:ʃ] **1.** Spülung *f* (*a.* ✿); Spülapparat *m*; △ *nicht* Dusche; **2.** spülen (*a.* ✿); △ *nicht* duschen.

dough [dəʊ] Teig *m*; ~ **nut** ['dəʊnʌt] Krapfen *m*, Berliner (Pfannkuchen) *m*, Schmalzkringel *m*.

dove[1] *zo.* [dʌv] Taube *f*.

dove[2] *Am.* [dəʊv] *pret. von* dive 1.

dow·el ⊕ ['daʊəl] Dübel *m*.

down[1] [daʊn] Daunen *pl.*; Flaum *m*; Düne *f*; ~s *pl.* Hügelland *n*.

down[2] [~] **1.** *adv.* nach unten, her-, hinunter, her-, hinab, abwärts; unten; **2.** *prp.* her-, hinab, her-, hinunter; ~ *the river* flußabwärts; **3.** *adj.* nach unten gerichtet; deprimiert, niedergeschlagen; ~ *platform* Abfahrtsbahnsteig *m* (*in London*); ~

train Zug *m* (von London fort); **4.** *v/t.* niederschlagen; *Flugzeug* abschießen; F *Getränk* runterkippen; ~ *tools* die Arbeit niederlegen, in den Streik treten; ~**cast** [ˈdaʊnkɑːst] niedergeschlagen; ~**fall** Platzregen *m*; *fig.* Sturz *m*; ~**heart·ed** □ niedergeschlagen; ~**hill 1.** *adv.* bergab; **2.** *adj.* abschüssig; *Skisport:* Abfahrts...; **3.** Abhang *m*; *Skisport:* Abfahrt *f*; ~**pay·ment** *econ.* Anzahlung *f*; ~**pour** Regenguß *m*, Platzregen *m*; ~**right 1.** *adv.* völlig, ganz u. gar, ausgesprochen; **2.** *adj.* glatt (*Lüge etc.*); ausgesprochen; ~**stairs** die Treppe her- *od.* hinunter; (nach) unten; ~**stream** stromabwärts; ~**to-earth** realistisch; ~**town** *Am.* **1.** *adv.* im *od.* ins Geschäftsviertel; **2.** *adj.* im Geschäftsviertel (gelegen *od.* tätig); **3.** Geschäftsviertel *n*, Innenstadt *f*, City *f*; ~**ward(s)** [ˌwəd(z)] abwärts, nach unten.

down·y [ˈdaʊnɪ] (*-ier, -iest*) flaumig.

dow·ry [ˈdaʊərɪ] Mitgift *f*.

doze [dəʊz] **1.** dösen, ein Nickerchen machen; **2.** Nickerchen *n*.

doz·en [ˈdʌzn] Dutzend *n*.

drab [dræb] trist; düster; eintönig.

draft [drɑːft] **1.** Entwurf *m*; *econ.* Tratte *f*; Abhebung *f* (*von Geld*); ✕ (Sonder)Kommando *n*; *Am.* ✕ Einberufung *f*; *bsd. Brit.* = *draught*; **2.** entwerfen; aufsetzen; ✕ abkommandieren; *Am.* ✕ einziehen, -berufen; ~**ee** *Am.* ✕ [drɑːfˈtiː] Wehrdienstpflichtige(r) *m*; ~**s·man** *bsd. Am.* [ˈdrɑːftsmən] (*pl. -men*) *s.* draughtsman; ~**y** *Am.* [ˌɪ] (*-ier, -iest*) *s.* draughty.

drag [dræg] **1.** Schleppen *n*, Zerren *n*; ⚓ Schleppnetz *n*; Egge *f*; Schlepp-, Zugseil *n*; *fig.* Hemmschuh *m*; F *et.* Langweiliges *n*; **2.** (*-gg-*) (sich) schleppen, zerren, ziehen, schleifen; *a.* ~ *behind* zurückbleiben, nachhinken; ~ *on* weiterschleppen; *fig.* sich dahinschleppen; *fig.* sich in die Länge ziehen; ~**lift** [ˈdræglɪft] Schlepplift *m*.

drag·on [ˈdrægən] Drache *m*; ~**fly** *zo.* Libelle *f*.

drain [dreɪn] **1.** Abfluß(kanal *m*, -rohr *n*) *m*; Entwässerungsgraben *m*; *fig.* Belastung *f*; **2.** *v/t.* abfließen lassen; entwässern; austrinken, leeren; *fig.* aufbrauchen, -zehren; *v/i.* ~ *off, ~ away* abfließen, ablaufen;

~**age** [ˈdreɪnɪdʒ] Abfließen *n*, Ablaufen *n*; Entwässerung(sanlage *f*, -ssystem *n*) *f*; Abwasser *n*; ~**pipe** Abflußrohr *n*.

drake *zo.* [dreɪk] Enterich *m*, Erpel *m*; △ *nicht Drache*.

dram F [dræm] Schluck *m*.

dra·ma [ˈdrɑːmə] Drama *n*; ~**mat·ic** [drəˈmætɪk] (~*ally*) dramatisch; ~**m·a·tist** [ˈdræmətɪst] Dramatiker *m*; ~**m·a·tize** [ˌtaɪz] dramatisieren.

drank [dræŋk] *pret. von* drink 2.

drape [dreɪp] **1.** drapieren; in Falten legen; **2.** *mst* ~*s pl. Am.* Gardinen *pl.*; ~**er·y** [ˈdreɪpərɪ] Textilhandel *m*; Stoffe *pl.*; Faltenwurf *m*.

dras·tic [ˈdræstɪk] (~*ally*) drastisch.

draught [drɑːft] (Luft)Zug *m*; Zug *m*, Schluck *m*; Fischzug *m*; ⚓ Tiefgang *m*; ~*s sg.* Brt. Damespiel *n*; ~ *beer* Faßbier *n*; ~**horse** [ˈdrɑːfthɔːs] Zugpferd *n*; ~**s·man** [ˌsmən] (*pl. -men*) Brt. Damestein *m*; ⊕ (Konstruktions-, Muster)Zeichner *m*; ~**y** [ˌɪ] (*-ier, -iest*) zugig.

draw [drɔː] **1.** (drew, drawn) ziehen; an-, auf-, ein-, zuziehen; 🝙 *Blut* abnehmen; *econ. Geld* abheben; *Tränen* hervorlocken; *Kunden etc.* anziehen, anlocken; *j-s Aufmerksamkeit* lenken (*to* auf *acc.*); *Bier* abzapfen; ausfischen; *Tier* ausnehmen, -weiden; *Luft* schöpfen; ziehen (lassen) (*Tee*); (in Worten) schildern; *Schriftstück* ab-, verfassen; *fig.* entlocken; zeichnen, malen, ziehen; Zug haben (*Kamin*); sich zusammenziehen; sich nähern (*to dat.*); *Sport:* unentschieden spielen; ~ *near* sich nähern; ~ *on, ~ upon* in Anspruch nehmen; ~ *out* in die Länge ziehen; ~ *up Schriftstück* aufsetzen; halten; vorfahren; **2.** Zug *m* (*Ziehen*); *Lotterie:* Ziehung *f*; *Sport:* Unentschieden *n*; Attraktion *f*, (Kassen)Schlager *m*; ~**back** [ˈdrɔːbæk] Nachteil *m*, Hindernis *n*; ~**er** [ˈdrɔːə] Zeichner *m*; *econ.* Aussteller *m*, Trassant *m* (*e-s Wechsels*); [drɔː] Schubfach *n*, -lade *f*; (*a pair of*) ~*s pl.* (eine) Unterhose; (ein) (Damen-) Schlüpfer *m*; *mst chest of* ~*s* Kommode *f*.

draw·ing [ˈdrɔːɪŋ] Ziehen *n*; Zeichnen *n*; Zeichnung *f*; ~**ac·count** *econ.* Girokonto *n*; ~**board** Reißbrett *n*; ~**pin** Brt. Reißzwecke *f*, -nagel *m*, Heftzwecke *f*; **~room** = *living room*; Salon *m*.

drawl [drɔːl] 1. gedehnt sprechen; 2. gedehntes Sprechen.

drawn [drɔːn] 1. *p.p. von* draw 1; 2. *adj. Sport*: unentschieden; abgespannt.

dread [dred] 1. (große) Angst, Furcht *f*; 2. (sich) fürchten; **~ful** □ ['dredfl] schrecklich, furchtbar.

dream [driːm] 1. Traum *m*; 2. (*dreamed od.* dreamt) träumen; **~er** ['driːmə] Träumer(in); **~t** [dremt] *pret. u. p.p. von* dream 2; **~y** □ ['driːmɪ] (*-ier, -iest*) träumerisch, verträumt.

drear·y □ ['drɪərɪ] (*-ier, -iest*) trübselig; trüb(e); langweilig.

dredge [dredʒ] 1. Schleppnetz *n*; Bagger(maschine *f*) *m*; 2. (aus)baggern.

dregs [dregz] *pl.* Bodensatz *m*; *fig.* Abschaum *m*.

drench [drentʃ] durchnässen.

dress [dres] 1. Anzug *m*; Kleidung *f*; Kleid *n*; 2. (sich) ankleiden *od.* anziehen; schmücken, dekorieren; zurechtmachen; *Speisen* zubereiten; *Salat* anmachen; Abendkleidung anziehen; ✗ verbinden; frisieren; **~ down** *j-m* e-e Standpauke halten; **~ up** (sich) fein machen; sich kostümieren *od.* verkleiden (*bsd. Kinder*); **~ cir·cle** *thea.* ['dres'sɜːkl] erster Rang; **~ de·sign·er** Modezeichner(in); **~er** [~ə] Anrichte *f*; Toilettentisch *m*.

dress·ing ['dresɪŋ] An-, Zurichten *n*; Ankleiden *n*; ✗ Verband *m*; Appretur *f*; Dressing *n* (*Salatsoße*); Füllung *f*; **~-down** Standpauke *f*; **~ gown** Morgenrock *m*, *-mantel m*; *Sport*: Bademantel *m*; **~-ta·ble** Toilettentisch *m*.

dress·mak·er ['dresmeɪkə] (Damen-) Schneider(in).

drew [dru:] *pret. von* draw 1.

drib·ble ['drɪbl] tröpfeln (lassen); sabbern, geifern; *Fußball*: dribbeln.

dried [draɪd] getrocknet, Dörr-.

dri·er ['draɪə] = dryer.

drift [drɪft] 1. (Dahin)Treiben *n*; (Schnee)Verwehung *f*; (Schnee-, Sand)Wehe *f*; *fig.* Tendenz *f*; 2. (dahin)treiben; wehen; aufhäufen.

drill [drɪl] 1. Drillbohrer *m*; Furche *f*; ✔ Drill-, Sämaschine *f*; ✗ Drill *m* (*a. fig.*); ✗ Exerzieren *n*; 2.

bohren; ✗, *fig.* drillen, einexerzieren.

drink [drɪŋk] 1. Getränk *n*; 2. (*drank, drunk*) trinken; **~ to** *s.o.* j-m zuprosten *od.* zutrinken; **~er** ['drɪŋkə] Trinker(in).

drip [drɪp] 1. Tröpfeln *n*; ✗ Tropf *m*; 2. (*-pp-*) tropfen *od.* tröpfeln (lassen); triefen; **~-dry shirt** [drɪp'draɪ ʃɜːt] bügelfreies Hemd; **~ping** ['drɪpɪŋ] Bratenfett *n*.

drive [draɪv] 1. (Spazier)Fahrt *f*; Auffahrt *f*; Fahrweg *m*; ⊕ Antrieb *m*; *mot.* (Links- *etc.*)Steuerung *f*; *psych.* Trieb *m*; *fig.* Kampagne *f*; *fig.* Schwung *m*, Elan *m*, Dynamik *f*; 2. (*drove, driven*) *v/t.* (an-, ein)treiben; *Auto etc.* fahren, lenken, steuern; (im Auto *etc.*) fahren; ⊕ (an)treiben; zwingen; *a.* **~ off** vertreiben; *v/i.* treiben; (Auto) fahren; **~ off** wegfahren; *what are you driving at?* F worauf wollen Sie hinaus?

drive-in ['draɪvɪn] 1. Auto...; **~ cinema**, *Am.* **~ motion-picture theater** Autokino *n*; 2. Autokino *n*; Drive-in-Restaurant *n*; Autoschalter *m*, Drive-in-Schalter *m* (*e-r Bank*).

driv·el ['drɪvl] 1. (*bsd. Brt. -ll-, Am. -l-*) faseln; 2. Geschwätz *n*, Gefasel *n*.

driv·en ['drɪvn] *p.p. von* drive 2.

driv·er ['draɪvə] *mot.* Fahrer(in); (*Lokomotiv*)Führer *m*; **~'s li·cense** *Am.* Führerschein *m*.

driv·ing ['draɪvɪŋ] (an)treibend; ⊕ Antriebs..., Treib..., Trieb...; *mot.* Fahr...; **~ li·cence** Führerschein *m*.

driz·zle ['drɪzl] 1. Sprühregen *m*; 2. sprühen, nieseln.

drone [drəun] 1. *zo.* Drohne *f* (*a. fig.*); 2. summen; dröhnen.

droop [dru:p] (schlaff) herabhängen; den Kopf hängenlassen; schwinden.

drop [drɒp] 1. Tropfen *m*; Fallen *n*, Fall *m*; *fig.* Fall *m*, Sturz *m*; Bonbon *m*, *n*; *fruit* *~s pl.* Drops *m*, *n od. pl.*; 2. (*-pp-*) *v/t.* tropfen (lassen); fallen lassen; *Bemerkung, Thema etc.* fallenlassen; *Brief* einwerfen; *Fahrgast* absetzen; senken; **~** *s.o.* **a few lines** *pl.* j-m ein paar Zeilen schreiben; *v/i.* tropfen; (herab-, herunter)fallen; umsinken, fallen; **~ in** (kurz) hereinschauen; **~ off** abfallen; zurückgehen, nachlassen; F einnicken;

~ **out** herausfallen; aussteigen (of aus); *a.* ~ **out of school** (*university*) die Schule (das Studium) abbrechen; **~out** ['drɒpaʊt] Drop-out *m*, Aussteiger *m* (*aus der Gesellschaft*); (Schul-, Studien)Abbrecher *m*.

drought [draʊt] Trockenheit *f*, Dürre *f*.

drove [drəʊv] **1.** Herde *f* (*Vieh*); Schar *f* (*Menschen*); **2.** *pret. von* drive 2.

drown [draʊn] *v/t.* ertränken; überschwemmen; *fig.* übertönen; *v/i.* ertrinken.

drowse [draʊz] dösen; ~ **off** eindösen; **drow·sy** ['draʊzɪ] (*-ier, -iest*) schläfrig; einschläfernd.

drudge [drʌdʒ] sich (ab)placken, schuften; **drudg·e·ry** ['drʌdʒərɪ] (stumpfsinnige) *od.* drogensüchtige(r *m*) *f*; Inhaber(in) e-s Drugstores; **~·store** *Am.* Apotheke *f*; Drugstore *m*.

drug [drʌɡ] **1.** Arzneimittel *n*, Medikament *n*; Droge *f*, Rauschgift *n*; be on (off) ~s rauschgift- *od.* drogensüchtig (clean) sein; **2.** (*-gg-*) j-m Medikamente geben; *j-n* unter Drogen setzen; ein Betäubungsmittel beimischen (*dat.*); betäuben (*a. fig.*); ~ **a·buse** Drogenmißbrauch *m*; Medikamentenmißbrauch *m*; ~ **ad·dict** Drogen-, Rauschgiftsüchtige(r *m*) *f*; **~·gist** *Am.* ['drʌɡɪst] Apotheker(in); Inhaber(in) e-s Drugstores; **~·store** *Am.* Apotheke *f*; Drugstore *m*.

drum [drʌm] **1.** ♪ Trommel *f*; *anat.* Trommelfell *n*; **~s** *pl.* ♪ Schlagzeug *n*; **2.** (*-mm-*) trommeln; **~·mer** ♪ ['drʌmə] Trommler *m*; Schlagzeuger *m*.

drunk [drʌŋk] **1.** *p.p. von* drink 2; **2.** *adj.* betrunken; get ~ sich betrinken; **3.** Betrunkene(r *m*) *f*; = **~·ard** ['drʌŋkəd] Trinker(in), Säufer(in); **~·en** *adj.* [~ən] betrunken; ~ **driving** Trunkenheit *f* am Steuer.

dry [draɪ] **1.** □ (*-ier, -iest*) trocken; trocken, herb (*Wein*); F durstig; F trocken (*ohne Alkohol*); ~ **goods** *pl.* Textilien *f pl.*; **2.** trocknen; dörren; ~ **up** austrocknen; versiegen; **~·clean** ['draɪ'kliːn] chemisch reinigen; ~ **clean·er's** chemische Reinigung; **~·er** [~ə] *a.* drier Trockenapparat *m*, Trockner *m*.

du·al □ ['djuːəl] doppelt, Doppel...; ~ **carriageway** *Brt.* Schnellstraße *f* (*mit Mittelstreifen*).

dub [dʌb] (*-bb-*) Film synchronisieren.

du·bi·ous □ ['djuːbjəs] zweifelhaft.

duch·ess ['dʌtʃɪs] Herzogin *f*.

duck [dʌk] **1.** *zo.* Ente *f*; Ducken *n*; F Schatz *m* (*Anrede, oft unübersetzt*); **2.** (unter)tauchen; (sich) ducken; **~·ling** *zo.* ['dʌklɪŋ] Entchen *n*.

due [djuː] **1.** zustehend; gebührend; gehörig, angemessen; fällig; *zeitlich* fällig, erwartet; *in* ~ **time** zur rechten Zeit; ~ **to** wegen (*gen.*); be ~ **to** j-m gebühren, zustehen; kommen von, zurückzuführen sein auf; **2.** *adv.* direkt, genau; **3.** Recht *n*, Anspruch *m*; **~s** *pl.* Gebühr(en *pl.*) *f*; Beitrag *m*.

du·el ['djuːəl] **1.** Duell *n*; **2.** (*bsd. Brt. -ll-, Am. -l-*) sich duellieren.

dug [dʌɡ] *pret. u. p.p. von* dig 1.

duke [djuːk] Herzog *m*.

dull [dʌl] **1.** □ dumm; träge, schwerfällig; stumpf; matt (*Auge etc.*); schwach (*Gehör*); langweilig; abgestumpft, teilnahmslos; dumpf; trüb(e); *econ.* flau; **2.** stumpf machen *od.* werden; (sich) trüben; mildern, dämpfen; *Schmerz* betäuben; *fig.* abstumpfen.

du·ly *adv.* ['djuːlɪ] ordnungsgemäß; gebührend; rechtzeitig.

dumb □ [dʌm] stumm; sprachlos; *bsd. Am.* F doof, dumm, blöd; **dum(b)·found·ed** ['dʌm'faʊndɪd] verblüfft, sprachlos.

dum·my ['dʌmɪ] Attrappe *f*; Kleider-, Schaufensterpuppe *f*; Dummy *m*, Puppe *f* (*für Unfalltests*); *Brt.* Schnuller *m*; *attr.* Schein...

dump [dʌmp] **1.** *v/t.* (hin)plumpsen *od.* (hin)fallen lassen; auskippen; *Schutt etc.* abladen; *econ. Waren zu* Dumpingpreisen verkaufen; **2.** Plumps *m*; (Schutt-, Müll)Abladeplatz *m*; ✕ Depot *n*, Lager(platz *m*) *n*; **~·ing** *econ.* ['dʌmpɪŋ] Dumping *n*, Ausfuhr *f* zu Schleuderpreisen.

dune [djuːn] Düne *f*.

dung [dʌŋ] **1.** Dung *m*; **2.** düngen.

dun·ga·rees [dʌŋɡə'riːz] *pl.* (a pair of ~ e-e) Arbeitshose.

dun·geon ['dʌndʒən] (Burg)Verlies *n*.

dunk F [dʌŋk] (ein)tunken.

dupe [djuːp] anführen, täuschen.

du·plex ['djuːpleks] doppelt, Doppel...; ~ (*apartment*) *Am.* Maison(n)ette(wohnung) *f*; ~ (*house*) *Am.* Doppel-, Zweifamilienhaus *n*.

du·pli·cate 1. ['djuːplɪkət] doppelt; ~ **key** Zweit-, Nachschlüssel *m*; **2.** [~]

Duplikat n; Zweit-, Nachschlüssel m; **3.** [⁓keɪt] doppelt ausfertigen; kopieren, vervielfältigen.

du·plic·i·ty [djuː'plɪsətɪ] Doppelzüngigkeit f.

dur·a·ble ☐ ['djʊərəbl] haltbar; dauerhaft; **du·ra·tion** [djʊə'reɪʃn] Dauer f.

du·ress [djʊə'res] Zwang m.

dur·ing prp. ['djʊərɪŋ] während.

dusk [dʌsk] (Abend)Dämmerung f; **⁓y** ☐ ['dʌskɪ] (-ier, -iest) dämmerig, düster (a. fig.); schwärzlich.

dust [dʌst] **1.** Staub m; **2.** v/t. abstauben; (be)streuen; v/i. Staub wischen, abstauben; **⁓bin** Brt. ['dʌstbɪn] Abfall-, Mülleimer m; Abfall-, Mülltonne f; **⁓·cart** Brt. Müllwagen m; **⁓·er** [⁓ə] Staublappen m, -wedel m; Schule: Tafelschwamm m, -tuch m; **⁓·cov·er, ⁓·jack·et** Schutzumschlag m (e-s Buches); **⁓·man** (pl. -men) Brt. Müllmann m; **⁓·y** [⁓ɪ] (-ier, -iest) staubig.

Dutch [dʌtʃ] **1.** adj. holländisch; **2.** adv.: go ⁓ getrennte Kasse machen; **3.** ling. Holländisch n; the ⁓ die Holländer pl.

du·ty ['djuːtɪ] Pflicht f; Ehrerbietung f; econ. Abgabe f; Zoll m; Dienst m; be on ⁓ Dienst haben; be off ⁓ dienstfrei haben; **⁓·free** zollfrei.

dwarf [dwɔːf] **1.** (pl. dwarfs [⁓fs], dwarves [⁓vz]) Zwerg(in) f; **2.** verkleinern, klein erscheinen lassen.

dwell [dwel] (dwelt od. dwelled) wohnen; verweilen (on, upon bei); **⁓·ing** ['dwelɪŋ] Wohnung f.

dwelt [dwelt] pret. u. p.p. von dwell.

dwin·dle ['dwɪndl] (dahin)schwinden, abnehmen.

dye [daɪ] **1.** Farbe f; of the deepest ⁓ fig. von der übelsten Sorte; **2.** färben.

dy·ing ['daɪɪŋ] **1.** sterbend; Sterbe...; **2.** Sterben n.

dyke [daɪk] = dike[1, 2].

dy·nam·ic [daɪ'næmɪk] dynamisch, kraftgeladen; **⁓s** mst sg. Dynamik f.

dy·na·mite ['daɪnəmaɪt] **1.** Dynamit n; **2.** (mit Dynamit) sprengen.

dys·en·te·ry ⚕ ['dɪsntrɪ] Ruhr f.

dys·pep·si·a ⚕ [dɪs'pepsɪə] Verdauungsstörung f.

E

each [iːtʃ] jede(r, -s); ⁓ other einander, sich; je, pro Person, pro Stück.

ea·ger ☐ ['iːgə] begierig; eifrig; **⁓·ness** ['iːgənɪs] Begierde f; Eifer m.

ea·gle ['iːgl] zo. Adler m; Am. hist. Zehndollarstück n; **⁓·eyed** scharfsichtig.

ear [ɪə] Ähre f; anat. Ohr n; Öhr n; Henkel m; keep an ⁓ to the ground die Ohren offenhalten; **⁓·drum** anat. ['ɪədrʌm] Trommelfell n; **⁓·ed** mit (...) Ohren, ...ohrig.

earl [ɜːl] englischer Graf.

ear·lobe ['ɪələʊb] Ohrläppchen n.

ear·ly ['ɜːlɪ] früh; Früh...; Anfangs..., erste(r, -s); bald(ig); as ⁓ as May schon im Mai; as ⁓ as possible so bald wie möglich; ⁓ bird Frühaufsteher(in) f; ⁓ warning system ✕ Frühwarnsystem n.

ear·mark ['ɪəmɑːk] **1.** Kennzeichen n; Merkmal n; **2.** kennzeichnen; zurücklegen (for für).

earn [ɜːn] verdienen; einbringen.

ear·nest ['ɜːnɪst] **1.** ☐ ernst(lich, -haft); ernstgemeint; **2.** Ernst m; in ⁓ im Ernst; ernsthaft.

earn·ings ['ɜːnɪŋz] pl. Einkommen n.

ear|phones ['ɪəfəʊnz] pl. Ohrhörer pl.; Kopfhörer pl.; **⁓·piece** teleph. Hörmuschel f; **⁓·ring** Ohrring m; **⁓·shot**: within (out of) ⁓ in (außer) Hörweite.

earth [ɜːθ] **1.** Erde f; Land n; **2.** v/t. ⚡ erden; **⁓·en** ['ɜːθn] irden; **⁓·en·ware** ['ɜːθnweə] **1.** Töpferware f; Steingut n; **2.** irden; **⁓·ly** ['ɜːθlɪ] irdisch; F denkbar; **⁓·quake** Erdbeben n; **⁓·worm** zo. Regenwurm m.

ease [iːz] **1.** Bequemlichkeit f, Behagen n; Ruhe f; Ungezwungenheit f;

Leichtigkeit *f*; *at ~* bequem, behaglich; *ill at ~* unruhig; befangen; **2.** *v/t.* erleichtern; lindern; beruhigen; bequem(er) machen; *v/i. ~ off, ~ up* nachlassen, sich entspannen (*Lage*); (bei der Arbeit) kürzertreten.

ea·sel ['i:zl] Staffelei *f*.

east [i:st] **1.** Ost(en *m*); *the ♀* der Osten, die Oststaaten *pl.* (*der USA*); *pol.* der Osten; der Orient; **2.** Ost..., östlich; **3.** ostwärts, nach Osten.

Eas·ter ['i:stə] Ostern *n*; *attr.* Oster...

eas·ter·ly ['i:stəlɪ] östlich, Ost...; nach Osten; **east·ern** [~n] östlich, Ost...; **east·ward(s)** [~wəd(z)] östlich, nach Osten.

eas·y ['i:zɪ] □ (*-ier, -iest*) leicht, einfach; bequem; frei von Schmerzen; gemächlich, gemütlich; ruhig; ungezwungen; *in ~ circumstances* wohlhabend; *on ~ street Am.* in guten Verhältnissen; *go ~, take it ~* sich Zeit lassen, langsam tun; sich nicht aufregen; *take it ~!* immer mit der Ruhe!; *~ chair* Sessel *m*; *~·go·ing* gelassen.

eat [i:t] **1.** (*ate, eaten*) essen; (zer)fressen; *~ out* auswärts essen; **2.** *~s* *pl.* F Fressalien *pl.*; **ea·ta·ble** ['i:təbl] **1.** eß-, genießbar; **2.** *~s* *pl.* Eßwaren *pl.*; *~·en* ['i:tn] *p.p. von eat 1*; *~·er* [~ə] Esser(in).

eaves [i:vz] *pl.* Dachrinne *f*, Traufe *f*; *~·drop* ['i:vzdrɒp] (*-pp-*) (heimlich) lauschen *od.* horchen.

ebb [eb] **1.** Ebbe *f*; *fig.* Tiefstand *m*; *fig.* Abnahme *f*; **2.** verebben; *fig.* abnehmen, sinken; *~ tide* ['eb'taɪd].

eb·o·ny ['ebənɪ] Ebenholz *n*.

ec·cen·tric [ɪk'sentrɪk] **1.** (*~ally*) exzentrisch; überspannt; **2.** Exzentriker *m*, Sonderling *m*.

ec·cle·si·as·tic [ɪklɪːzɪ'æstɪk] (*~ally*), *~·ti·cal* [~kl] geistlich, kirchlich.

ech·o ['ekəʊ] **1.** (*pl. -oes*) Echo *n*; **2.** widerhallen; *fig.* echoen, nachsprechen.

e·clipse [ɪ'klɪps] **1.** *ast.* Finsternis *f*; **2.** verfinstern; *be ~d by fig.* verblassen neben (*dat.*).

e·co·cide ['i:kəsaɪd] Umweltzerstörung *f*.

e·co·lo·gi·cal [i:kə'lɒdʒɪkl] ökologisch; *~·lo·gist* [i:'kɒlədʒɪst] Ökologe *m*; *~·lo·gy* [~ɪ] Ökologie *f*.

e·co·nom·ic [i:kə'nɒmɪk] (*~ally*) wirtschaftlich, Wirtschafts...; *~ aid*

Wirtschaftshilfe *f*; *~ growth* Wirtschaftswachstum *n*; *~·i·cal* □ [~kl] wirtschaftlich, sparsam; *~·ics sg.* Volkswirtschaft(slehre) *f*.

e·con·o·mist [ɪ'kɒnəmɪst] Volkswirt *m*; *~·mize* [~aɪz] sparsam wirtschaften (mit); *~·my* [~ɪ] **1.** Wirtschaft *f*; Wirtschaftlichkeit *f*, Sparsamkeit *f*; Einsparung *f*; **2.** Spar...; *~ class ✈* Economyklasse *f*.

e·co·sys·tem ['i:kəʊsɪstəm] Ökosystem *n*.

ec·sta·sy ['ekstəsɪ] Ekstase *f*, Verzückung *f*; *~·tic* [ɪk'stætɪk] (*~ally*) verzückt.

ed·dy ['edɪ] **1.** Wirbel *m*; **2.** wirbeln.

edge [edʒ] **1.** Schneide *f*; Rand *m*; Kante *f*; Schärfe *f*; △ *nicht* (*Straßen-, Haus*)*Ecke*; *be on ~* nervös *od.* gereizt sein; **2.** schärfen; (um)säumen; (sich) drängen; *~·ways, ~·wise* ['edʒweɪz, ~waɪz] seitlich, von der Seite.

edg·ing ['edʒɪŋ] Einfassung *f*; Rand *m*.

edg·y ['edʒɪ] (*-ier, -iest*) scharf(kantig); F gereizt.

ed·i·ble ['edɪbl] eßbar.

e·dict ['i:dɪkt] Edikt *n*.

ed·i·fice ['edɪfɪs] Gebäude *n*.

ed·i·fy·ing □ ['edɪfaɪɪŋ] erbaulich.

ed·it ['edɪt] *Text* herausgeben, redigieren; *Zeitung* als Herausgeber leiten; **e·di·tion** [ɪ'dɪʃn] (*Buch*)Ausgabe *f*; Auflage *f*; **ed·i·tor** ['edɪtə] Herausgeber(in); Redakteur(in); **ed·i·to·ri·al** [edɪ'tɔːrɪəl] **1.** Leitartikel *m*; **2.** □ Redaktions...

ed·u·cate ['edjuːkeɪt] erziehen; unterrichten; *~·cat·ed* gebildet; *~·ca·tion* [edjuː'keɪʃn] Erziehung *f*; (Aus)Bildung *f*; Bildungs-, Schulwesen *n*; *Ministry of ♀* Unterrichtsministerium *n*; *~·ca·tion·al* □ [~nl] erzieherisch, Erziehungs...; Bildungs...; *~·ca·tor* ['edjuːkeɪtə] Erzieher(in).

eel *zo.* [i:l] Aal *m*.

ef·fect [ɪ'fekt] **1.** Wirkung *f*; Erfolg *m*, Ergebnis *n*; Auswirkung *f* (*on pl.*); Effekt *m*, Eindruck *m*; ⊕ Leistung *f*; *~s pl. econ.* Effekten *pl.*; persönliche Habe; *be of ~* Wirkung haben; *take ~* in Kraft treten; *in ~* tatsächlich, praktisch; *to the ~* des Inhalts; **2.** bewirken; ausführen; **ef·fec·tive** □ [~ɪv] wirksam; eindrucksvoll; tatsächlich, wirklich; ⊕ nutzbar; ~ **date** Tag *m* des Inkrafttretens.

ef·fem·i·nate □ [ɪˈfemɪnət] verweichlicht; weibisch.

ef·fer|vesce [efəˈves] brausen, sprudeln; **~·ves·cent** [~nt] sprudelnd, schäumend.

ef·fi·cien|cy [ɪˈfɪʃənsɪ] Leistung(sfähigkeit) *f*; ~ **engineer**, ~ **expert** *econ.* Rationalisierungsfachmann *m*; **~t** □ [~t] wirksam; leistungsfähig, tüchtig.

ef·flu·ent [ˈefluənt] Abwasser *n*, Abwässer *pl.*

ef·fort [ˈefət] Anstrengung *f*, Bemühung *f (at um)*; Mühe *f; without* ~ = **~·less** □ [~lɪs] mühelos, ohne Anstrengung.

ef·fron·te·ry [ɪˈfrʌntərɪ] Frechheit *f*.

ef·fu·sive □ [ɪˈfjuːsɪv] überschwenglich.

egg[1] [eg]: ~ **on** anstacheln.

egg[2] [~] Ei *n; put all one's* ~s *in one basket* alles auf eine Karte setzen; *as sure as* ~s *is* ~s *f* todsicher; **~·co·sy** [ˈegkəʊzɪ] Eierwärmer *m*; **~·cup** Eierbecher *m*; **~·head** F Eierkopf *m (Intellektueller)*.

e·go·is|m [ˈegəʊɪzəm] Egoismus *m*, Selbstsucht *f*; **~t** [~ɪst] Egoist(in), selbstsüchtiger Mensch.

ego·tis|m [ˈegəʊtɪzəm] Egotismus *m*, Selbstgefälligkeit *f*; **~t** [~ɪst] Egotist(in), selbstgefälliger *od.* geltungsbedürftiger Mensch.

E·gyp·tian [ɪˈdʒɪpʃn] **1.** ägyptisch; **2.** Ägypter(in).

ei·der·down [ˈaɪdədaʊn] Eiderdaunen *pl.*; Daunendecke *f*.

eight [eɪt] **1.** acht; **2.** Acht *f*; **eigh·teen** [ˈeɪˈtiːn] **1.** achtzehn; **2.** Achtzehn *f*; **eigh·teenth** [~θ] achtzehnte(r, -s); **~·fold** [ˈeɪtfəʊld] achtfach; **~·h** [eɪtθ] **1.** achte(r, -s); **2.** Achtel *n*; **~·h·ly** [ˈeɪtθlɪ] achtens; **eigh·ti·eth** [ˈeɪtɪɪθ] achtzigste(r, -s); **eigh·ty** [ˈeɪtɪ] **1.** achtzig; **2.** Achtzig *f*.

ei·ther [ˈaɪðə; *Am.* ˈiːðə] jede(r, -s) *(von zweien)*; eine(r, -s) *(von zweien)*; beides; ~ ... *or* entweder ... oder; *not* ~ auch nicht.

e·jac·u·late [ɪˈdʒækjʊleɪt] *v/t. Worte etc.* aus-, hervorstoßen; *physiol. Samen* ausstoßen; *v/i. physiol.* ejakulieren, e-n Samenerguß haben.

e·ject [ɪˈdʒekt] vertreiben; hinauswerfen; entlassen, -fernen *(from aus e-m Amt)*.

eke [iːk]: ~ *out Vorräte etc.* strecken; *Einkommen* aufbessern; ~ *out a living* sich (mühsam) durchschlagen.

e·lab·o·rate 1. □ [ɪˈlæbərət] sorgfältig (aus)gearbeitet; kompliziert; **2.** [~reɪt] sorgfältig ausarbeiten.

e·lapse [ɪˈlæps] verfließen, -streichen.

e·las·tic [ɪˈlæstɪk] **1.** (~*ally*) elastisch, dehnbar; ~ *band Brt.* = **2.** Gummiring *m*, -band *n*; **~·ti·ci·ty** [elæˈstɪsətɪ] Elastizität *f*.

e·lat·ed [ɪˈleɪtɪd] begeistert, stolz.

el·bow [ˈelbəʊ] **1.** Ellbogen *m*; Biegung *f*; ⊕ Knie *n; at one's* ~ bei der Hand; *out at* ~s *fig.* heruntergekommen; **2.** mit den Ellbogen (weg)stoßen; ~ *one's way through* sich (mit den Ellbogen) e-n Weg bahnen durch.

el·der[1] ♀ [ˈeldə] Holunder *m*.

el·der[2] [~] **1.** ältere(r, -s); **2.** der, die Ältere; (Kirchen)Älteste(r) *m*; **~·ly** [~lɪ] ältlich, ältere(r, -s).

el·dest [ˈeldɪst] älteste(r, -s).

e·lect [ɪˈlekt] **1.** gewählt; **2.** (aus-, er)wählen.

e·lec·tion [ɪˈlekʃn] **1.** Wahl *f*; **2.** *pol.* Wahl...; **~·tor** [~tə] Wähler(in); *Am. pol.* Wahlmann *m; hist.* Kurfürst *m*; **~·to·ral** [~ərəl] Wahl..., Wähler...; ~ *college Am. pol.* Wahlmänner *pl.*; **~·to·rate** *pol.* [~ərət] Wähler(schaft *f*) *pl.*

e·lec·tric [ɪˈlektrɪk] (~*ally*) elektrisch, Elektro...; *fig.* elektrisierend; **~·tri·cal** □ [~kl] elektrisch; Elektro...; ~ *engineer* Elektroingenieur *m*, -techniker *m*; **~·tric chair** elektrischer Stuhl; **~·tri·cian** [ɪlekˈtrɪʃn] Elektriker *m*; **~·tri·ci·ty** [~ɪsətɪ] Elektrizität *f*.

e·lec·tri·fy [ɪˈlektrɪfaɪ] elektrifizieren; elektrisieren *(a. fig.)*.

e·lec·tro- [ɪˈlektrəʊ] Elektro...

e·lec·tro·cute [ɪˈlektrəkjuːt] auf dem elektrischen Stuhl hinrichten; durch elektrischen Strom töten.

e·lec·tron [ɪˈlektrɒn] Elektron *n*.

e·lec·tron·ic [ɪlekˈtrɒnɪk] **1.** (~*ally*) elektronisch, Elektronen...; ~ *data processing* elektronische Datenverarbeitung; **2.** ~s *sg.* Elektronik *f*; *pl.* Elektronik *f (e-s Geräts)*.

el·e·gance [ˈelɪgəns] Eleganz *f*; **~·gant** □ [~t] elegant; geschmackvoll; erstklassig.

el·e|ment [ˈelɪmənt] Element *n*; Urstoff *m*; (Grund)Bestandteil *m*; ~s *pl*. Anfangsgründe *pl*., Grundlage(n *pl*.) *f*; Elemente *pl*., Naturkräfte *pl*.; **~men·tal** □ [elɪˈmentl] elementar; wesentlich.

el·e·men·ta·ry □ [elɪˈmentərɪ] elementar; Anfangs..; ~ **school** *Am*. Grundschule *f*.

el·e·phant *zo*. [ˈelɪfənt] Elefant *m*.

el·e·vate [ˈelɪveɪt] erhöhen; *fig*. erheben; **~·vat·ed** erhöht; *fig*. gehoben, erhaben; ~ (*railroad*) *Am*. Hochbahn *f*; **~·va·tion** [elɪˈveɪʃn] Erhebung *f*; Erhöhung *f*; Höhe *f*; Erhabenheit *f*; **~·va·tor** ⊕ [ˈelɪveɪtə] *Am*. Lift *m*, Fahrstuhl *m*, Aufzug *m*; ✈ Höhenruder *n*.

e·lev·en [ɪˈlevn] **1.** elf; **2.** Elf *f*; **~th** [~θ] **1.** elfte(r, -s); **2.** Elftel *n*.

elf [elf] (*pl. elves*) Elf(e *f*) *m*; Kobold *m*.

e·li·cit [ɪˈlɪsɪt] *et*. entlocken (*from dat*.); ans (Tages)Licht bringen.

el·i·gi·ble □ [ˈelɪdʒəbl] geeignet, annehmbar, akzeptabel; berechtigt.

e·lim·i·nate [ɪˈlɪmɪneɪt] entfernen, beseitigen; ausscheiden; **~·na·tion** [ɪlɪmɪˈneɪʃn] Entfernung *f*, Beseitigung *f*; Ausscheidung *f*.

é·lite [eɪˈliːt] Elite *f*; Auslese *f*.

elk *zo*. [elk] Elch *m*.

el·lipse ⩕ [ɪˈlɪps] Ellipse *f*.

elm ♣ [elm] Ulme *f*, Rüster *f*.

el·o·cu·tion [eləˈkjuːʃn] Vortrag(skunst *f*, -sweise) *f* *m*; Sprechtechnik *f*.

e·lon·gate [ˈiːlɒŋɡeɪt] verlängern.

e·lope [ɪˈləʊp] (mit s-m *od*. s-r Geliebten) ausreißen *od*. durchbrennen.

e·lo·quence [ˈeləkwəns] Beredsamkeit *f*; **~·quent** □ [~t] beredt.

else [els] sonst, weiter; anderer(r, -s); **~·where** [ˈelsˈweə] anderswo(hin).

e·lu·ci·date [ɪˈluːsɪdeɪt] erklären.

e·lude [ɪˈluːd] geschickt entgehen, ausweichen, sich entziehen (*alle dat*.); *fig*. nicht einfallen (*dat*.).

e·lu·sive □ [ɪˈluːsɪv] schwerfaßbar.

elves [elvz] *pl*. *von* elf.

e·ma·ci·ated [ɪˈmeɪʃɪeɪtɪd] abgezehrt, ausgemergelt.

em·a|nate [ˈeməneɪt] ausströmen; ausgehen (*from* von); **~·na·tion** [eməˈneɪʃn] Ausströmen *n*; *fig*. Ausstrahlung *f*.

e·man·ci|pate [ɪˈmænsɪpeɪt] emanzipieren; befreien; **~·pa·tion** [ɪmænsɪˈpeɪʃn] Emanzipation *f*; Befreiung *f*.

em·balm [ɪmˈbɑːm] (ein)balsamieren.

em·bank·ment [ɪmˈbæŋkmənt] Eindämmung *f*; (Erd)Damm *m*; (Bahn-, Straßen)Damm *m*; Uferstraße *f*.

em·bar·go [emˈbɑːɡəʊ] (*pl. -goes*) Embargo *n*, (Hafen-, Handels)Sperre *f*.

em·bark [ɪmˈbɑːk] ♣, ✈ an Bord nehmen *od*. gehen, ♣ *a*. (sich) einschiffen; *Waren* verladen; ~ **on**, ~ **upon** *et*. anfangen *od*. beginnen.

em·bar·rass [ɪmˈbærəs] in Verlegenheit bringen, verlegen machen, in e-e peinliche Lage versetzen; **~·ing** □ [~ɪŋ] unangenehm, peinlich; **~·ment** [~mənt] Verlegenheit *f*.

em·bas·sy [ˈembəsɪ] Botschaft *f*.

em·bed [ɪmˈbed] (*-dd-*) (ein)betten, (ein)lagern.

em·bel·lish [ɪmˈbelɪʃ] verschönern; *fig*. ausschmücken, beschönigen.

em·bers [ˈembəz] *pl*. Glut *f*.

em·bez·zle [ɪmˈbezl] unterschlagen; **~·ment** [~mənt] Unterschlagung *f*.

em·bit·ter [ɪmˈbɪtə] verbittern.

em·blem [ˈembləm] Sinnbild *n*; Wahrzeichen *n*.

em·bod·y [ɪmˈbɒdɪ] verkörpern; enthalten.

em·bo·lis·m ⚕ [ˈembəlɪzəm] Embolie *f*.

em·brace [ɪmˈbreɪs] **1.** (sich) umarmen; einschließen; **2.** Umarmung *f*.

em·broi·der [ɪmˈbrɔɪdə] (be)sticken; *fig*. ausschmücken; **~·y** [~ərɪ] Stickerei *f*; *fig*. Ausschmückung *f*.

em·broil [ɪmˈbrɔɪl] (in Streit) verwickeln; verwirren.

e·men·da·tion [iːmənˈdeɪʃn] Verbesserung *f*, Berichtigung *f*.

em·er·ald [ˈemərəld] **1.** Smaragd *m*; **2.** smaragdgrün.

e·merge [ɪˈmɜːdʒ] auftauchen; hervorgehen; *fig*. sich erheben; sich zeigen.

e·mer|gen·cy [ɪˈmɜːdʒənsɪ] Not (-lage) *f*, -fall *m*, -stand *m*; *attr*. Not...; ~ **brake** Notbremse *f*; ~ **call** Notruf *m*; ~ **exit** Notausgang *m*; ~ **landing** ✈ Notlandung *f*; ~ **number** Notruf(nummer *f*) *m*; ~ **ward** ♣ Notaufnahme *f*; **~·gent** [~t] auftauchend; *fig*. (jung u.) aufstrebend (*Nationen*).

em·i|grant [ˈemɪɡrənt] Auswanderer *m*, *bsd. pol*. Emigrant(in); **~·grate** [~reɪt] auswandern, *bsd. pol*. emigrieren; **~·gra·tion** [emɪˈgreɪʃn] Auswanderung f, bsd. pol. Emigration f.

em·i·nence [ˈemɪnəns] (An)Höhe f; hohe Stellung; Ruhm m, Bedeutung f; ♀ Eminenz f (Titel); **~·nent** □ [~t] fig. ausgezeichnet, hervorragend; **~·nent·ly** [~lɪ] ganz besonders, äußerst.

e·mit [ɪˈmɪt] (-tt-) aussenden, -stoßen, -strahlen, -strömen; von sich geben.

e·mo·tion [ɪˈməʊʃn] (Gemüts)Bewegung f, Gefühl(sregung f) n; Rührung f; **~·al** [~l] emotional; gefühlsmäßig; gefühlsbetont; **~·al·ly** [~lɪ] emotional, gefühlsmäßig; **~ disturbed** seelisch gestört; **~ ill** gemütskrank; **~·less** [~lɪs] gefühllos; unbewegt.

em·pe·ror [ˈempərə] Kaiser m.

em·pha|sis [ˈemfəsɪs] (pl. -ses [-siːz]) Gewicht n; Nachdruck m; **~·size** [~saɪz] nachdrücklich betonen; **~·t·ic** [ɪmˈfætɪk] (~ally) nachdrücklich; deutlich; bestimmt.

em·pire [ˈempaɪə] (Kaiser)Reich n; Herrschaft f; **the British ♀** das britische Weltreich.

em·pir·i·cal □ [emˈpɪrɪkl] erfahrungsgemäß.

em·ploy [ɪmˈplɔɪ] 1. beschäftigen, anstellen; an-, verwenden, gebrauchen; 2. Beschäftigung f; **in the ~ of** angestellt bei; **~·ee** [emplɔɪˈiː] Angestellte(r m) f, Arbeitnehmer(in); **~·er** [~ˈplɔɪə] Arbeitgeber(in); **~·ment** [~mənt] Beschäftigung f, Arbeit f; **~ agency**, **~ bureau** Stellenvermittlung(sbüro n) f; **~ market** Arbeits-, Stellenmarkt m; **~ service agency** Brt. Arbeitsamt n.

em·pow·er [ɪmˈpaʊə] ermächtigen; befähigen.

em·press [ˈemprɪs] Kaiserin f.

emp|ti·ness [ˈemptɪnɪs] Leere f (a. fig.); **~·ty** □ [ˈemptɪ] 1. (-ier, -iest) leer (a. fig.); **~ of** ohne; 2. (aus-, ent)leeren; sich leeren.

em·u·late [ˈemjʊleɪt] wetteifern mit; nacheifern (dat.); es gleichtun (dat.).

e·mul·sion [ɪˈmʌlʃn] Emulsion f.

en·a·ble [ɪˈneɪbl] befähigen; es j-m ermöglichen; ermächtigen.

en·act [ɪˈnækt] verfügen, -ordnen; Gesetz erlassen; thea. aufführen.

e·nam·el [ɪˈnæml] 1. Email(le f) n; anat. (Zahn)Schmelz m; Glasur f,

Lack m; Nagellack m; 2. (bsd. Brt. -ll-, Am. -l-) emaillieren; glasieren; lackieren.

en·am·o·u)red [ɪˈnæməd]: **~ of** verliebt in.

en·camp·ment bsd. ⚔ [ɪnˈkæmpmənt] (Feld)Lager n.

en·cased [ɪnˈkeɪst]: **~ in** gehüllt in (acc.).

en·chant [ɪnˈtʃɑːnt] bezaubern; **~·ing** □ [~ɪŋ] bezaubernd; **~·ment** [~mənt] Bezauberung f; Zauber m.

en·cir·cle [ɪnˈsɜːkl] einkreisen, umzingeln; umfassen, umschlingen.

en·close [ɪnˈkləʊz] einzäunen; einschließen; beifügen; **en·clo·sure** [~əʊʒə] Einzäunung f; eingezäuntes Grundstück; Anlage f (zu e-m Brief).

en·com·pass [ɪnˈkʌmpəs] umgeben.

en·coun·ter [ɪnˈkaʊntə] 1. Begegnung f; Gefecht n; 2. begegnen (dat.); auf Schwierigkeiten etc. stoßen; mit j-m feindlich zusammenstoßen.

en·cour·age [ɪnˈkʌrɪdʒ] ermutigen; fördern; **~·ment** [~mənt] Ermutigung f; Anfeuerung f; Unterstützung f.

en·croach [ɪnˈkrəʊtʃ] (on, upon) eingreifen (in j-s Recht etc.), eindringen (in acc.); über Gebühr in Anspruch nehmen (acc.); **~·ment** [~mənt] Ein-, Übergriff m.

en·cum|ber [ɪnˈkʌmbə] belasten; (be)hindern; **~·brance** [~brəns] Last f, Belastung f, Hindernis n, Behinderung f; **without ~** ohne (Familien-)Anhang.

en·cy·clo·p(a)e·di·a [ensaɪkləˈpiːdjə] Enzyklopädie f.

end [end] 1. Ende n; Ziel n, Zweck m; **no ~ of** unendlich viel(e), unzählige; **in the ~** am Ende, schließlich; **on ~** aufrecht; **stand on ~** zu Berge stehen (Haare); **to no ~** vergebens; **go off the deep ~** fig. in die Luft gehen; **make both ~s meet** gerade auskommen; 2. enden; beend(ig)en.

en·dan·ger [ɪnˈdeɪndʒə] gefährden.

en·dear [ɪnˈdɪə] beliebt machen (to s.o. bei j-m); **~·ing** □ [~rɪŋ] gewinnend; liebenswert; **~·ment** [~mənt] Liebkosung f; term of **~** Kosewort n.

end|ing [ˈendɪŋ] Ende n; Schluß m; gr. Endung f; **~·less** □ [~lɪs] endlos, unendlich; ⊕ ohne Ende.

en·dive ♧ ['endɪv] Endivie f.

en·dorse [ɪn'dɔːs] *econ. Scheck etc.* indossieren; *et.* vermerken (*on auf der Rückseite e-r Urkunde*); gutheißen; **~ment** [~mənt] Aufschrift f, Vermerk m; *econ.* Indossament n.

en·dow [ɪn'dau] *fig.* ausstatten; ~ *s.o. with s.th.* j-m et. stiften; **~ment** [~mənt] Stiftung f; *mst* ~s pl. Begabung f, Talent n.

en·dur·ance [ɪn'djuərəns] Ausdauer f; Ertragen n; *beyond* ~, *past* ~ unerträglich; ~ *test* [~'djuə] ertragen.

en·e·my ['enəmɪ] **1.** Feind m; *the* ♀ der Teufel; **2.** feindlich.

en·er·get·ic [enə'dʒetɪk] (~*ally*) energisch; **~gy** ['enədʒɪ] Energie f; ~ *crisis* Energiekrise f.

en·fold [ɪn'fəʊld] einhüllen; umfassen.

en·force [ɪn'fɔːs] (mit Nachdruck, *a.* gerichtlich) geltend machen; erzwingen; aufzwingen (*upon dat.*); durchführen; **~ment** [~mənt] Erzwingung f; Geltendmachung f; Durchführung f.

en·fran·chise [ɪn'fræntʃaɪz] j-m das Wahlrecht verleihen; j-m die Bürgerrechte verleihen.

en·gage [ɪn'geɪdʒ] *v/t.* anstellen; verpflichten; *Künstler etc.* engagieren; in Anspruch nehmen; ✕ angreifen; *be* ~*d* verlobt sein (*to mit*); beschäftigt sein (*in mit*); besetzt sein; ~ *the clutch mot.* e-n Gang einlegen; *v/i.* sich verpflichten (*to do zu tun*); garantieren (*for für*); sich beschäftigen (*in mit*); ✕ angreifen; ⊕ greifen (*Zahnräder*); **~ment** [~mənt] Verpflichtung f; Verlobung f; Verabredung f; Beschäftigung f; ✕ Gefecht n; ⊕ Ineinandergreifen n.

en·gag·ing □ [ɪn'geɪdʒɪŋ] einnehmend; gewinnend (*Lächeln etc.*).

en·gine ['endʒɪn] Maschine f; Motor m; ⬚ Lokomotive f; **~·driv·er** *Brt.* 🚂 Lokomotivführer m.

en·gi·neer [endʒɪ'nɪə] **1.** Ingenieur m; Techniker m; Mechaniker m; *Am.* 🚂 Lokomotivführer m; ✕ Pionier m; **2.** als Ingenieur tätig sein; bauen; **~·ing** [~rɪŋ] **1.** Maschinen-u. Gerätebau m; Ingenieurwesen n; **2.** technisch; Ingenieur...

En·glish ['ɪŋglɪʃ] **1.** englisch; **2.** *ling.* Englisch n; *the* ~ pl. die Engländer pl.; *in plain* ~ *fig.* unverblümt; **~·man** (pl. -men) Engländer m;

~·wom·an (pl. -women) Engländerin f.

en·grave [ɪn'greɪv] (ein)gravieren, (-)meißeln, (-)schnitzen; *fig.* einprägen; **en·grav·er** [~ə] Graveur m; **en·grav·ing** [~ɪŋ] (Kupfer-, Stahl-)Stich m; Holzschnitt m.

en·grossed [ɪn'grəʊst] (*in*) (voll) in Anspruch genommen (von), vertieft, -sunken (*in acc.*).

en·gulf [ɪn'gʌlf] verschlingen (*a. fig.*).

en·hance [ɪn'hɑːns] erhöhen.

e·nig·ma [ɪ'nɪgmə] Rätsel n; **en·ig·mat·ic** [enɪg'mætɪk] (~*ally*) rätselhaft.

en·joy [ɪn'dʒɔɪ] sich erfreuen an (*dat.*); genießen; *did you* ~ *it?* hat es Ihnen gefallen?; ~ *o.s.* sich amüsieren, sich gut unterhalten; ~ *yourself!* viel Spaß!; *I* ~ *my dinner es* schmeckt mir; **~·a·ble** □ [~əbl] angenehm, erfreulich; **~·ment** [~mənt] Genuß m, Freude f.

en·large [ɪn'lɑːdʒ] (sich) vergrößern *od.* erweitern, ausdehnen; *phot.* vergrößern; sich vergrößern lassen; sich verbreiten *od.* auslassen (*on, upon über acc.*); **~·ment** [~mənt] Erweiterung f; Vergrößerung f (*a. phot.*).

en·light·en [ɪn'laɪtn] *fig.* erleuchten; j-n aufklären; **~·ment** [~mənt] Aufklärung f.

en·list [ɪn'lɪst] *v/t.* ✕ anwerben; j-n gewinnen; ~*ed men* pl. *Am.* ✕ Unteroffiziere pl. und Mannschaften pl.; *v/i.* sich freiwillig melden.

en·liv·en [ɪn'laɪvn] beleben.

en·mi·ty ['enmɪtɪ] Feindschaft f.

en·no·ble [ɪ'nəʊbl] adeln; veredeln.

e·nor·mi·ty [ɪ'nɔːmətɪ] Ungeheuerlichkeit f; **~·mous** □ [~əs] ungeheuer.

e·nough [ɪ'nʌf] genug.

en·quire, en·qui·ry [ɪn'kwaɪə, ~rɪ] = *inquire, inquiry.*

en·rage [ɪn'reɪdʒ] wütend machen; ~*d* wütend (*at über acc.*).

en·rap·ture [ɪn'ræptʃə] entzücken, hinreißen; ~*d* entzückt, hingerissen.

en·rich [ɪn'rɪtʃ] be-, anreichern.

en·rol(l) [ɪn'rəʊl] (-*ll-*) *v/t.* j-n in e-e Liste eintragen, *univ.* j-n immatrikulieren; ✕ anwerben; aufnehmen; *v/i.* sich einschreiben (lassen), *univ.* sich immatrikulieren; **~·ment** [~mənt] Eintragung f, -schreibung f, *univ.* Immatrikulation f; *bsd.* ✕ Anwerbung f; Einstellung f; Aufnahme f; Schüler-, Studenten-, Teilnehmerzahl f.

en·sign ['ensain] Fahne f; Flagge f; Abzeichen n; Am. ♣ ['ensn] Leutnant m zur See.

en·sue [in'sju:] (darauf, nach)folgen.

en·sure [in'ʃʊə] sichern.

en·tail [in'teil] ⚖ als Erbgut vererben; fig. mit sich bringen.

en·tan·gle [in'tæŋgl] verwickeln; **~ment** [~mənt] Verwicklung f; ⚔ Drahtverhau m.

en·ter ['entə] v/t. (hinein)gehen, (-)kommen in (acc.), (ein)treten in (acc.), betreten; einsteigen od. einfahren etc. in (acc.); eindringen in (acc.); econ. eintragen, (ver)buchen; Protest erheben; Namen eintragen, -schreiben; j-n aufnehmen; Sport: melden, nennen; ~ s.o. at school j-n zur Schule anmelden; v/i. eintreten, herein-, hineinkommen, -gehen; in ein Land einweisen; Sport: sich melden (for für); ~ into fig. eingehen auf (acc.); ~ on od. upon an inheritance e-e Erbschaft antreten.

en·ter·prise ['entəpraiz] Unternehmen n (a. econ.); econ. Unternehmertum n; Unternehmungsgeist m; **~pris·ing** □ [~iŋ] unternehmungslustig; wagemutig; kühn.

en·ter·tain [entə'tein] unterhalten; bewirten; in Erwägung ziehen; Zweifel etc. hegen; **~er** [~ə] Entertainer(in), Unterhaltungskünstler(in); **~ment** [~mənt] Unterhaltung f; Entertainment n; Bewirtung f.

en·thral(l) fig. [in'θrɔ:l] (-ll-) fesseln, bezaubern.

en·throne [in'θrəʊn] inthronisieren.

en·thu·si·asm [in'θju:ziæzəm] Begeisterung f; **~t** [~st] Enthusiast(in); **~tic** [inθju:zi'æstik] (~ally) begeistert.

en·tice [in'tais] (ver)locken; **~ment** [~mənt] Verlockung f, Reiz m.

en·tire □ [in'taiə] ganz, vollständig; ungeteilt; **~ly** [~li] völlig; ausschließlich.

en·ti·tle [in'taitl] betiteln; berechtigen (to zu).

en·ti·ty ['entəti] Wesen n; Dasein n.

en·trails ['entreilz] pl. Eingeweide pl.; fig. das Innere.

en·trance ['entrəns] Eintritt m; Einfahrt f; Eingang m; Einlaß m.

en·treat [in'tri:t] inständig bitten,

anflehen; **en·trea·ty** [~ı] dringende od. inständige Bitte.

en·trench ⚔ [in'trentʃ] verschanzen (a. fig.).

en·trust [in'trʌst] anvertrauen (s.th. to s.o. j-m et.); betrauen.

en·try ['entri] Einreise f; Einlaß m; Zutritt m; Eingang m; Einfahrt f; Beitritt m (into zu); Eintragung f; Sport: Meldung f, Nennung f; ~ permit Einreisegenehmigung f; ~ visa Einreisevisum n; book-keeping by double (single) ~ econ. doppelte (einfache) Buchführung; no ~! Zutritt verboten!, mot. keine Einfahrt!

en·twine [in'twain] ineinanderschlingen.

e·nu·me·rate [i'nju:məreit] aufzählen.

en·vel·op [in'veləp] (ein)hüllen, einwickeln.

en·ve·lope ['envələʊp] Briefumschlag m.

en·vi·a·ble □ ['enviəbl] beneidenswert; **~ous** □ [~əs] neidisch.

en·vi·ron·ment [in'vaiərənmənt] Umgebung f, sociol. a. Milieu n; Umwelt f (a. sociol.); **~men·tal** □ [invaiərən'mentl] sociol. Milieu...; Umwelt...; ~ law Umweltschutzgesetz n; ~ pollution Umweltverschmutzung f; **~men·tal·ist** [~'əlist] Umweltschützer(in); **~s** ['envirənz] pl. Umgebung f (e-r Stadt).

en·vis·age [in'vizidʒ] sich et. vorstellen.

en·voy ['envɔi] Gesandte(r) m.

en·vy ['envi] 1. Neid m; 2. beneiden.

ep·ic ['epik] 1. episch; 2. Epos n.

ep·i·dem·ic [epi'demik] 1. (~ally) seuchenartig; ~ disease = 2. Epidemie f, Seuche f.

ep·i·der·mis [epi'dɜ:mis] Oberhaut f.

ep·i·lep·sy ⚕ ['epilepsi] Epilepsie f.

ep·i·logue, Am. a. **-log** ['epilɔg] Nachwort n.

e·pis·co·pal □ eccl. [i'piskəpl] bischöflich.

ep·i·sode ['episəʊd] Episode f.

ep·i·taph ['epita:f] Grabinschrift f; Gedenktafel f.

e·pit·o·me [i'pitəmi] Verkörperung f, Inbegriff m.

e·poch ['i:pɒk] Epoche f, Zeitalter n.

eq·ua·ble □ ['ekwəbl] ausgeglichen (a. Klima).

e·qual ['i:kwəl] 1. □ gleich; gleichmäßig; ~ *to* fig. gewachsen (*dat.*); ~ *opportunities pl.* Chancengleichheit f; ~ *rights pl. for women* Gleichberechtigung f der Frau; 2. Gleiche(r m) f; 3. (bsd. Brt. -ll-, Am. -l-) gleichen (dat.); **~·i·ty** [i:'kwɒlətɪ] Gleichheit f; **~·i·za·tion** [i:kwəlaɪ-'zeɪʃn] Gleichstellung f; Ausgleich m; **~·ize** [i:'kwəlaɪz] gleichmachen, -stellen, angleichen; *Sport*: ausgleichen.

e·qua·nim·i·ty [i:kwə'nɪmətɪ] Gleichmut m.

e·qua·tion [ɪ'kweɪʒn] Ausgleich m; ⅋ Gleichung f.

e·qua·tor [ɪ'kweɪtə] Äquator m.

e·qui·lib·ri·um [i:kwɪ'lɪbrɪəm] Gleichgewicht n.

e·quip [ɪ'kwɪp] (-pp-) ausrüsten; **~·ment** [~mənt] Ausrüstung f; Einrichtung f.

eq·ui·ty ['ekwətɪ] Gerechtigkeit f, Billigkeit f.

e·quiv·a·lent [ɪ'kwɪvələnt] 1. □ gleichwertig; gleichbedeutend (*to* mit); 2. Äquivalent n, Gegenwert m.

e·quiv·o·cal □ [ɪ'kwɪvəkl] zweideutig; zweifelhaft.

e·ra ['ɪərə] Zeitrechnung f; Zeitalter n.

e·rad·i·cate [ɪ'rædɪkeɪt] ausrotten.

e·rase [ɪ'reɪz] ausradieren, -streichen, löschen (*a. Tonband*); fig. auslöschen; **e·ras·er** [~ə] Radiergummi m.

ere [eə] 1. *cj.* ehe, bevor; 2. *prp.* vor (dat.).

e·rect [ɪ'rekt] 1. □ aufrecht; 2. aufrichten; *Denkmal etc.* errichten; aufstellen; **e·rec·tion** [~kʃn] Errichtung f; physiol. Erektion f.

er·mine zo. ['ɜ:mɪn] Hermelin n.

e·ro·sion [ɪ'rəʊʒn] Zerfressen n; geol. Erosion f, Auswaschung f.

e·rot·ic [ɪ'rɒtɪk] (~ally) erotisch; **~·cis·m** [~ɪsɪzəm] Erotik f.

err [ɜ:] (sich) irren.

er·rand ['erənd] Botengang m, Auftrag m, Besorgung f; *go on* od. *run an* ~ e-e Besorgung machen; **~·boy** Laufbursche m.

er·rat·ic [ɪ'rætɪk] (~ally) sprunghaft, unstet, unberechenbar.

er·ro·ne·ous □ [ɪ'rəʊnjəs] irrig.

er·ror ['erə] Irrtum m, Fehler m; **~s** *excepted* Irrtümer vorbehalten.

e·rupt [ɪ'rʌpt] ausbrechen (*Vulkan etc.*); durchbrechen (*Zähne*); **e·rup·-**

tion [~pʃn] (*Vulkan*)Ausbruch m; ⚕ Ausbruch m e-s Ausschlags; ⚕ Ausschlag m.

es·ca·late ['eskəleɪt] eskalieren (*Krieg etc.*); steigen, in die Höhe gehen (*Preise*); **~·la·tion** [eskə'leɪʃn] Eskalation f.

es·ca·la·tor ['eskəleɪtə] Rolltreppe f.

es·ca·lope ['eskələʊp] (*bsd. Wiener*) Schnitzel n.

es·cape [ɪ'skeɪp] 1. entgehen; entkommen, -rinnen; entweichen; *j-m* entfallen; 2. Entrinnen n; Entweichen n; Flucht f; *have a narrow* ~ mit knapper Not davonkommen; ~ *chute* ⚓ Notrutsche f.

es·cort 1. ['eskɔːt] ✕ Eskorte f; Geleit(schutz m) n; 2. [ɪ'skɔːt] ✕ eskortieren; ✕, ⚓ Geleit(schutz) geben; geleiten.

es·cutch·eon [ɪ'skʌtʃən] Wappenschild m, n.

es·pe·cial [ɪ'speʃl] besondere(r, -s); vorzüglich; **~·ly** [~lɪ] besonders.

es·pi·o·nage [espɪə'nɑːʒ] Spionage f.

es·pla·nade [esplə'neɪd] (*bsd.* Strand)Promenade f.

es·pres·so [e'spresəʊ] (*pl. -sos*) Espresso m (*Kaffee*).

Es·quire [ɪ'skwaɪə] (*abbr. Esq.*) *auf Briefen*: *John Smith Esq.* Herrn John Smith.

es·say 1. [e'seɪ] versuchen; probieren; 2. ['eseɪ] Versuch m; Aufsatz m, kurze Abhandlung, Essay m, n.

es·sence ['esns] Wesen n (*e-r Sache*); Essenz f; Extrakt m.

es·sen·tial [ɪ'senʃl] 1. □ (*to* für) wesentlich; wichtig; 2. *mst ~s pl. das* Wesentliche; **~·ly** [~lɪ] im wesentlichen, in der Hauptsache.

es·tab·lish [ɪ'stæblɪʃ] festsetzen; errichten, gründen; einrichten; *j-n* einsetzen; ~ *o.s.* sich niederlassen; *2ed Church* Staatskirche f; **~·ment** [~mənt] Er-, Einrichtung f; Gründung f; *the 2* das Establishment, die etablierte Macht, die herrschende Schicht.

es·tate [ɪ'steɪt] (*großes*) Grundstück, Landsitz m, Gut n; ⚖ Besitz m, (Erb)Masse f, Nachlaß m; *housing* ~ (Wohn)Siedlung f; *industrial* ~ Industriegebiet n; *real* ~ Liegenschaften pl.; (*Am. real*) ~ **a·gent** Grundstücks-, Immobilienmakler m; ~ **car** Brt. mot. Kombiwagen m.

es·teem [ɪ'stiːm] 1. Achtung f, Ansehen *n* (*with* bei); **2.** achten, (hoch-) schätzen; ansehen *od.* betrachten als.

es·thet·ic(s) *Am.* [es'θetɪk(s)] = aesthetic(s).

es·ti·ma·ble ['estɪməbl] schätzenswert.

es·ti·mate 1. ['estɪmeɪt] (ab-, ein-) schätzen; veranschlagen; **2.** [~mɪt] Schätzung *f*; (Kosten)Voranschlag *m*; **~·ma·tion** [estɪ'meɪʃn] Schätzung *f*; Meinung *f*; Achtung *f*.

es·trange [ɪ'streɪndʒ] entfremden.

es·tu·a·ry ['estjʊərɪ] *den Gezeiten ausgesetzte* weite Flußmündung.

etch [etʃ] ätzen; radieren; **~·ing** ['etʃɪŋ] Radierung *f*; Kupferstich *m*.

e·ter·nal [ɪ'tɜːnl] immerwährend, ewig; **~·ni·ty** [~ətɪ] Ewigkeit *f*.

e·ther ['iːθə] Äther *m*; **e·the·re·al** [iː'θɪərɪəl] ätherisch (*a. fig.*).

eth|i·cal □ ['eθɪkl] sittlich, ethisch; **~·ics** [~s] *sg.* Sittenlehre *f*, Ethik *f*.

Eu·ro- ['jʊərəʊ] europäisch, Euro...

Eu·ro·pe·an [jʊərə'pɪən] **1.** europäisch; **~** (*Economic*) *Community* Europäische (Wirtschafts)Gemeinschaft; **2.** Europäer(in).

e·vac·u·ate [ɪ'vækjʊeɪt] entleeren; evakuieren; *Haus etc.* räumen.

e·vade [ɪ'veɪd] (geschickt) ausweichen (*dat.*); umgehen.

e·val·u·ate [ɪ'væljʊeɪt] schätzen; abschätzen, bewerten, beurteilen.

ev·a·nes·cent [iːvə'nesnt] vergänglich.

e·van·gel·i·cal □ [iːvæn'dʒelɪkl] evangelisch.

e·vap·o·rate [ɪ'væpəreɪt] verdunsten, -dampfen (lassen); **~d** *milk* Kondensmilch *f*; **~·ra·tion** [ɪvæpə'reɪʃn] Verdunstung *f*, -dampfung *f*.

e·va·sion [ɪ'veɪʒn] Entkommen *n*; Umgehung *f*, Vermeidung *f*; Ausflucht *f*; **~·sive** [~sɪv] ausweichend; *be* **~** ausweichen.

eve [iːv] Vorabend *m*; Vortag *m*; *on the* **~** *of* unmittelbar vor (*dat.*), am Vorabend (*gen.*).

e·ven ['iːvn] **1.** *adj.* □ eben, gleich; gleichmäßig; ausgeglichen; glatt; gerade (*Zahl*); unparteiisch; *get* **~** *with s.o. fig.* mit j-m abrechnen; **2.** *adv.* selbst, sogar, auch; *not* **~** nicht einmal; **~** *though*, **~** *if* wenn auch; **3.** ebnen, glätten; **~** *out* sich einpendeln.

eve·ning ['iːvnɪŋ] Abend *m*; **~** *class*-

es pl. Abendkurs *m*; **~** *dress* Gesellschaftsanzug *m*; Frack *m*, Smoking *m*; Abendkleid *n*.

e·ven·song ['iːvnsɒŋ] Abendgottesdienst *m*.

e·vent [ɪ'vent] Ereignis *n*, Vorfall *m*; sportliche Veranstaltung; *Sport:* Disziplin *f*; *Sport:* Wettbewerb *m*; *at all* **~***s* auf alle Fälle; *in the* **~** *of* im Falle (*gen.*); **~·ful** [~fl] ereignisreich.

e·ven·tu·al □ [ɪ'ventʃʊəl] schließlich; △ *nicht eventuell;* **~·ly** schließlich, endlich.

ev·er ['evə] je, jemals; immer; **~** *so* noch so (sehr); *as soon as* **~** *I* sobald ich nur irgend kann; **~** *after*, **~** *since* von der Zeit an, seitdem; **~** *and again* dann u. wann, hin u. wieder; *for* **~** für immer, auf ewig; *Yours* **~**, ... Viele Grüße, Dein(e) *od.* Ihr(e), ... (*Briefschluß*); **~·glade** *Am.* sumpfiges Flußgebiet; **~·green 1.** immergrün; unverwüstlich, *bsd.* immer wieder gern gehört; **~** *song* Evergreen *m*; **2.** immergrüne Pflanze; **~·last·ing** □ ewig; dauerhaft; **~·more** [~'mɔː] immerfort.

ev·ery ['evrɪ] jede(r, -s); alle(r, -s); **~** *now and then* dann u. wann; **~** *one of* them jeder von ihnen; **~** *other day* jeden zweiten Tag, alle zwei Tage; **~·bod·y** jeder(mann); **~·day** Alltags...; **~·one** jeder(mann); **~·thing** alles; **~·where** überall; überallhin.

e·vict [ɪ'vɪkt] ṣ̌t̞ zur Räumung zwingen; *j-n* gewaltsam vertreiben.

ev·i·dence ['evɪdəns] **1.** Beweis(material *n*) *m*, Beweise *pl.*; (Zeugen-) Aussage *f*; *give* **~** (als Zeuge) aussagen; *in* **~** als Beweis; deutlich sichtbar; **2.** be-, nachweisen, zeugen von; **~·dent** □ [~t] augenscheinlich, offenbar, klar.

e·vil ['iːvl] **1.** □ (*bsd. Brt. -ll-, Am. -l-*) übel, schlimm, böse; *the* ♀ *One* der Böse (*Teufel*); **2.** Übel *n*; das Böse; **~·mind·ed** [~'maɪndɪd] bösartig.

e·vince [ɪ'vɪns] zeigen, bekunden.

e·voke [ɪ'vəʊk] (herauf)beschwören; *Erinnerungen* wachrufen.

ev·o·lu·tion [iːvə'luːʃn] Evolution *f*, Entwicklung *f*.

e·volve [ɪ'vɒlv] (sich) entwickeln.

ewe *zo.* [juː] Mutterschaf *n*.

ex [eks] *prp. econ.* ab *Fabrik etc.*; *Börse:* ohne.

ex- [~] ehemalig, früher.

ex·act [ɪg'zækt] **1.** □ genau; **2.** *Zah-*

lung eintreiben; *Gehorsam* fordern; **~ing** [~ɪŋ] streng, genau; **~i·tude** [~ɪtjuːd] = *exactness*; **~ly** [~lɪ] exakt, genau; *als Antwort:* ganz recht, genau; **~ness** [~nɪs] Genauigkeit *f*.

ex·ag·ge|rate [ɪg'ædʒəreɪt] übertreiben; **~ra·tion** [ɪgædʒə'reɪʃn] Übertreibung *f*.

ex·alt [ɪg'zɔːlt] erhöhen, erheben; preisen; **ex·al·ta·tion** [egzɔːl'teɪʃn] Begeisterung *f*.

ex·am F [ɪg'zæm] Examen *n*.

ex·am|i·na·tion [ɪgzæmɪ'neɪʃn] Examen *n*, Prüfung *f*; Untersuchung *f*; Vernehmung *f*; **~ine** [ɪg'zæmɪn] untersuchen, (*ärztlich*) vernehmen, -hören; *Schule etc.:* prüfen (*in* in *dat.*; *on* über *acc.*).

ex·am·ple [ɪg'zɑːmpl] Beispiel *n*; Vorbild *n*, Muster *n*; *for* ~ zum Beispiel.

ex·as·pe|rate [ɪg'zæspəreɪt] wütend machen; **~rat·ing** □ [~ɪŋ] ärgerlich.

ex·ca·vate [ˈekskəveɪt] ausgraben, -heben, -schachten.

ex·ceed [ɪk'siːd] überschreiten; übertreffen; **~ing** □ [~ɪŋ] übermäßig; **~ing·ly** [~lɪ] außerordentlich, überaus.

ex·cel [ɪk'sel] (*-ll-*) *v/t.* übertreffen; *v/i.* sich auszeichnen; **~·lence** [ˈeksələns] ausgezeichnete Qualität; hervorragende Leistung; **Ex·cel·len·cy** [~ənsɪ] Exzellenz *f*; **~·lent** □ [~ənt] ausgezeichnet, hervorragend.

ex·cept [ɪk'sept] **1.** ausnehmen, -schließen; **2.** *prp.* ausgenommen, außer; ~ *for* abgesehen von; **~ing** *prp.* [~ɪŋ] ausgenommen.

ex·cep·tion [ɪk'sepʃn] Ausnahme *f*; Einwendung *f*, Einwand *m* (*to* gegen); *by way of* ~ ausnahmsweise; *make an* ~ e-e Ausnahme machen; *take* ~ *to* Anstoß nehmen an (*dat.*); **~al** □ [~nl] außergewöhnlich; **~al·ly** [~ʃnəlɪ] un-, außergewöhnlich.

ex·cerpt [ˈeksɜːpt] Auszug *m*.

ex·cess [ɪk'ses] Übermaß *n*; Überschuß *m*; Ausschweifung *f*; *attr.* Mehr...; ~ *fare* (Fahrpreis)Zuschlag *m*; ~ *baggage bsd. Am.*, ~ *luggage bsd. Brt.* 🗲 Übergepäck *n*; ~ *postage* Nachgebühr *f*; **ex·ces·sive** □ [~ɪv] übermäßig, übertrieben.

ex·change [ɪks'tʃeɪndʒ] **1.** (aus-, ein-, um)tauschen (*for* gegen); wechseln; **2.** (Aus-, Um)Tausch *m*; (*bsd.* Geld-)

Wechsel *m*; *a. bill of* ~ Wechsel *m*; Börse *f*; Wechselstube *f*; Fernsprechamt *n*; *foreign* ~(*s pl.*) Devisen *pl.*; *rate of* ~, ~ *rate* Wechselkurs *m*; ~ *office* Wechselstube *f*; ~ *student* Austauschstudent(in), -schüler(in).

ex·cheq·uer [ɪks'tʃekə] Staatskasse *f*; *Chancellor of the* 🗲 *Brt.* Schatzkanzler *m*, Finanzminister *m*.

ex·cise¹ [ˈeksaɪz] Verbrauchssteuer *f*.

ex·cise² 🗲 [~] herausschneiden.

ex·ci·ta·ble [ɪk'saɪtəbl] reizbar, (leicht) erregbar.

ex·cite [ɪk'saɪt] er-, anregen; reizen; **ex·cit·ed** □ erregt, aufgeregt; **ex·cite·ment** [~mənt] Auf-, Erregung *f*; Reizung *f*; **ex·cit·ing** □ [~ɪŋ] erregend, aufregend, spannend.

ex·claim [ɪk'skleɪm] (aus)rufen.

ex·cla·ma·tion [ekskləˈmeɪʃn] Ausruf *m*, (Auf)Schrei *m*; ~ *mark*, *Am. a.* ~ *point* Ausrufe-, Ausrufungszeichen *n*.

ex·clude [ɪk'skluːd] ausschließen.

ex·clu·sion [ɪk'skluːʒn] Ausschließung *f*, Ausschluß *m*; **~·sive** □ [~sɪv] ausschließlich; exklusiv; Exklusiv...; ~ *of* abgesehen von, ohne.

ex·com·mu·ni|cate [ekskəˈmjuːnɪkeɪt] exkommunizieren; **~·ca·tion** [ˈekskəmjuːnɪˈkeɪʃn] Exkommunikation *f*.

ex·cre·ment [ˈekskrɪmənt] Kot *m*.

ex·crete [ekˈskriːt] ausscheiden.

ex·cru·ci·at·ing □ [ɪkˈskruːʃɪeɪtɪŋ] entsetzlich, scheußlich.

ex·cur·sion [ɪk'skɜːʃn] Ausflug *m*.

ex·cu·sa·ble □ [ɪk'skjuːzəbl] entschuldbar; **ex·cuse 1.** [ɪk'skjuːz] entschuldigen; ~ *me* entschuldige(n Sie); **2.** [~uːs] Entschuldigung *f*.

ex·e·cute [ˈeksɪkjuːt] ausführen; vollziehen; ♪ vortragen; hinrichten; *Testament* vollstrecken; **~·cu·tion** [eksɪ'kjuːʃn] Ausführung *f*; Vollziehung *f*; (Zwangs)Vollstreckung *f*; Hinrichtung *f*; ♪ Vortrag *m*; *put od.* *carry a plan into* ~ e-n Plan ausführen *od.* verwirklichen; **~·cu·tion·er** [~ʃnə] Henker *m*, Scharfrichter *m*; **~·c·u·tive** [ɪg'zekjʊtɪv] **1.** □ vollziehend, ausübend, *pol.* Exekutiv...; *econ.* leitend; ~ *board* Vorstand *m*; ~ *committee* Exekutivausschuß *m*; **2.** *pol.* Exekutive *f*, vollziehende Gewalt; *econ.* leitender Angestellter; **~·c·u·tor** [~ə] Erbschaftsverwalter *m*, Testamentsvollstrecker *m*.

E

ex·em·pla·ry □ [ɪgˈzemplərɪ] vorbildlich.

ex·em·pli·fy [ɪgˈzemplɪfaɪ] veranschaulichen.

ex·empt [ɪgˈzempt] **1.** befreit, frei; **2.** ausnehmen, befreien.

ex·er·cise [ˈeksəsaɪz] **1.** Übung *f*; Ausübung *f*, *Schule*: Übung (*Arbeit*) *f*, Schulaufgabe *f*; ✕ Manöver *n*; (körperliche) Bewegung; *do one's* ∼*s* Gymnastik machen; *take* ∼ *sich Bewegung machen*; *Am.* ∼*s pl.* Feierlichkeiten *pl.*; ∼ *book* Schul-, Schreibheft *n*; **2.** üben; ausüben; (sich) bewegen; sich Bewegung machen; ✕ exerzieren.

ex·ert [ɪgˈzɜːt] *Einfluß etc.* ausüben; ∼ *o.s.* sich anstrengen od. bemühen; **ex·er·tion** [∼ɜːʃn] Ausübung *f*; Anstrengung *f*, Strapaze *f*.

ex·hale [eksˈheɪl] ausatmen; *Gas, Geruch etc.* verströmen; *Rauch* ausstoßen.

ex·haust [ɪgˈzɔːst] **1.** erschöpfen; entleeren; auspumpen; **2.** ⊕ Abgas *n*, Auspuffgase *pl.*; Auspuff *m*; ∼ *fumes pl.* Abgase *pl.*; ∼ *pipe* Auspuffrohr *n*; ∼**ed** erschöpft (*a. fig.*); vergriffen (*Auflage*); **ex·haus·tion** [∼tʃən] Erschöpfung *f*; **ex·haus·tive** □ [∼tɪv] erschöpfend.

ex·hib·it [ɪgˈzɪbɪt] **1.** ausstellen; ⚖ vorzeigen, *Beweise* beibringen; *fig.* zeigen; **2.** Ausstellungsstück *n*; Beweisstück *n*; **ex·hi·bi·tion** [eksɪˈbɪʃn] Ausstellung *f*; Zurschaustellung *f*; *Brt.* Stipendium *n*.

ex·hil·a·rate [ɪgˈzɪləreɪt] auf-, erheitern.

ex·hort [ɪgˈzɔːt] ermahnen.

ex·ile [ˈeksaɪl] **1.** Verbannung *f*; Exil *n*; Verbannte(r *m*) *f*; im Exil Lebende(r *m*) *f*; **2.** in die Verbannung od. ins Exil schicken.

ex·ist [ɪgˈzɪst] existieren; vorhanden sein; leben; bestehen; ∼**ence** [∼əns] Existenz *f*; Vorhandensein *n*, Vorkommen *n*; Leben *n*, Dasein *n*; △ *nicht Existenz* (*Lebensunterhalt*); ∼**ent** [∼t] vorhanden.

ex·it [ˈeksɪt] **1.** Abgang *m*; Ausgang *m*; (*Autobahn*)Ausfahrt *f*; Ausreise *f*; **2.** *thea.* (geht) ab.

ex·o·dus [ˈeksədəs] Auszug *m*; Abwanderung *f*; *general* ∼ allgemeiner Aufbruch.

ex·on·e·rate [ɪgˈzɒnəreɪt] entlasten, entbinden, befreien.

ex·or·bi·tant □ [ɪgˈzɔːbɪtənt] übertrieben, maßlos; unverschämt (*Preis etc.*).

ex·or·cize [ˈeksɔːsaɪz] *böse Geister* beschwören, austreiben (*from* aus); befreien (*of* von).

ex·ot·ic [ɪgˈzɒtɪk] (∼*ally*) exotisch; fremdländisch; fremd(artig).

ex·pand [ɪkˈspænd] (sich) ausbreiten; (sich) ausdehnen *od.* erweitern; ∼ *on* sich auslassen über (*acc.*); **ex·panse** [∼s] Ausdehnung *f*, Weite *f*; **ex·pan·sion** [∼ʃn] Ausbreitung *f*; *phys.* Ausdehnen *f*; *fig.* Erweiterung *f*, Ausweitung *f*; **ex·pan·sive** □ [∼sɪv] ausdehnungsfähig; ausgedehnt, weit; *fig.* mitteilsam.

ex·pat·ri·ate [eksˈpætrɪeɪt] *j-n* ausbürgern, *j-m* die Staatsangehörigkeit aberkennen.

ex·pect [ɪkˈspekt] erwarten; F annehmen; *be* ∼*ing* in anderen Umständen sein; **ex·pec·tant** □ [∼ənt] erwartend (*of acc.*); ∼ *mother* werdende Mutter; **ex·pec·ta·tion** [ekspekˈteɪʃn] Erwartung *f*; Hoffnung *f*, Aussicht *f*.

ex·pe·di·ent [ɪkˈspiːdjənt] **1.** □ zweckmäßig; ratsam; **2.** (Hilfs-) Mittel *n*, (Not)Behelf *m*.

ex·pe·di·tion [ekspɪˈdɪʃn] Eile *f*; ✕ Feldzug *m*; (Forschungs)Reise *f*, Expedition *f*; ∼**tious** □ [∼ʃəs] schnell.

ex·pel [ɪkˈspel] (*-ll-*) ausstoßen; vertreiben, -jagen; hinauswerfen, ausschließen.

ex·pend [ɪkˈspend] *Geld* ausgeben; aufwenden; verbrauchen; **ex·pen·di·ture** [∼dɪtʃə] Ausgabe *f*; Aufwand *m*; **ex·pense** [ɪkˈspens] Ausgabe *f*; Kosten *pl.*; ∼*s pl.* Unkosten *pl.*, Spesen *pl.*, Auslagen *pl.*; *at the* ∼ *of* auf Kosten (*gen.*); *at any* ∼ um jeden Preis; **ex·pen·sive** □ [∼sɪv] kostspielig, teuer.

ex·pe·ri·ence [ɪkˈspɪərɪəns] **1.** Erfahrung *f*; (Lebens)Praxis *f*; Erlebnis *n*; **2.** erfahren, erleben; ∼**d** erfahren.

ex·per·i·ment 1. [ɪkˈsperɪmənt] Versuch *m*; **2.** [∼ment] experimentieren; ∼**men·tal** □ [eksperɪˈmentl] Versuchs-...

ex·pert [ˈekspɜːt] **1.** [*pred.* eksˈpɜːt] erfahren, geschickt; fachmännisch; **2.** Fachmann *m*; Sachverständige(r *m*) *f*.

ex·pi·ra·tion [ekspɪˈreɪʃn] Ausatmung *f*; Ablauf *m*, Ende *n*; **ex·pire** [ık'spaıǝ] ausatmen; sein Leben *od.* s-n Geist aushauchen; ablaufen, verfallen, erlöschen.

ex·plain [ık'spleın] erklären, erläutern; *Gründe* auseinandersetzen.

ex·pla·na·tion [eksplǝ'neıʃn] Erklärung *f*; Erläuterung *f*; **ex·plan·a·to·ry** □ [ık'splænǝtǝrı] erklärend.

ex·pli·ca·ble □ ['eksplıkǝbl] erklärlich.

ex·pli·cit □ [ık'splısıt] deutlich.

ex·plode [ık'splǝud] explodieren (lassen); *fig.* ausbrechen (*with in acc.*), platzen (*with* vor); *fig.* sprunghaft ansteigen.

ex·ploit 1. ['eksplɔıt] Heldentat *f*; **2.** [ık'splɔıt] ausbeuten; *fig.* ausnutzen; **ex·ploi·ta·tion** [eksplɔı'teıʃn] Ausbeutung *f*, Auswertung *f*, Verwertung *f*, Abbau; *fig.* Ausnutzung *f*.

ex·plo·ra·tion [eksplǝ'reıʃn] Erforschung *f*; **ex·plore** [ık'splɔ:] erforschen; **ex·plor·er** [⌣rǝ] Forscher(in); Forschungsreisende(r *m*) *f*.

ex·plo·sion [ık'splǝuʒn] Explosion *f*; *fig.* Ausbruch *m*; *fig.* sprunghafter Anstieg; **∼·sive** [⌣ǝusıv] **1.** □ explosiv; *fig.* aufbrausend; *fig.* sprunghaft ansteigend; **2.** Sprengstoff *m*.

ex·po·nent [ek'spǝunǝnt] Exponent *m*; Vertreter *m*.

ex·port 1. [ek'spɔ:t] exportieren, ausführen; **2.** ['ekspɔ:t] Export(artikel) *m*, Ausfuhr(artikel *m*) *f*; **ex·por·ta·tion** [ekspɔ:'teıʃn] Ausfuhr *f*.

ex·pose [ık'spǝuz] aussetzen; *phot.* belichten; ausstellen; *fig.* entlarven, bloßstellen, *et.* aufdecken; **ex·po·si·tion** [ekspǝ'zıʃn] Ausstellung *f*.

ex·po·sure [ık'spǝuʒǝ] Aussetzen *n*; Ausgesetztsein *n*; *fig.* Bloßstellung *f*; Aufdeckung *f*; Enthüllung *f*, Entlarvung *f*; *phot.* Belichtung *f*; *phot.* Aufnahme *f*; ∼ *meter* Belichtungsmesser *m*.

ex·pound [ık'spaund] erklären, auslegen.

ex·press [ık'spres] **1.** □ ausdrücklich, deutlich; Expreß..., Eil...; ∼ *company Am.* (Schnell)Transportunternehmen *n*; ∼ *train* Schnellzug *m*; **2.** Eilbote *m*; Schnellzug *m*; *by* ∼ = **3.** *adv.* durch Eilboten; als Eilgut; **4.** äußern; ausdrücken; auspressen; **ex·pres·sion** [⌣eʃn] Ausdruck *m*; **ex·pres·sion·less** □ [⌣lıs] ausdruckslos; **ex·pres·sive** □ [⌣sıv]

ausdrückend (*of acc.*); ausdrucksvoll; **∼·ly** [⌣lı] ausdrücklich, eigens; **∼·way** *bsd. Am.* Schnellstraße *f*.

ex·pro·pri·ate [eks'prǝuprıeıt] enteignen.

ex·pul·sion [ık'spʌlʃn] Vertreibung *f*; Ausweisung *f*.

ex·pur·gate ['ekspǝ:geıt] reinigen.

ex·qui·site □ ['ekskwızıt] auserlesen, vorzüglich; fein; heftig.

ex·tant [ek'stænt] (noch) vorhanden.

ex·tend [ık'stend] *v/t.* ausdehnen; ausstrecken; erweitern; verlängern; *Hilfe etc.* gewähren; ✕ ausschwärmen lassen; *v/i.* sich erstrecken.

ex·ten·sion [ık'stenʃn] Ausdehnung *f*; Erweiterung *f*; Verlängerung *f*; Aus-, Anbau *m*; *teleph.* Nebenanschluß *m*, Apparat *m*; ∼ *cord ⏚* Verlängerungsschnur *f*; **∼·sive** [⌣sıv] ausgedehnt, umfassend.

ex·tent [ık'stent] Ausdehnung *f*, Weite *f*, Größe *f*, Umfang *m*; Grad *m*; *to the* ∼ *of* bis zum Betrag von; *to some od. a certain* ∼ bis zu e-m gewissen Grade, einigermaßen.

ex·ten·u·ate [ek'stenjueıt] abschwächen, mildern; beschönigen; *extenuating circumstances pl.* 🏛 mildernde Umstände *pl.*

ex·te·ri·or [ek'stıǝrıǝ] **1.** äußerlich, äußere(r, -s), Außen...; **2.** *das* Äußere; *Film*: Außenaufnahme *f*.

ex·ter·mi·nate [ek'stɜ:mıneıt] ausrotten (*a. fig.*), vernichten, *Ungeziefer, Unkraut a.* vertilgen.

ex·ter·nal □ [ek'stɜ:nl] äußere(r, -s), äußerlich, Außen...

ex·tinct [ık'stıŋkt] erloschen; ausgestorben; **ex·tinc·tion** [⌣kʃn] Erlöschen *n*; Aussterben *n*, Untergang *m*; (Aus)Löschen *n*; Vernichtung *f*, Zerstörung *f*.

ex·tin·guish [ık'stıŋgwıʃ] (aus)löschen; vernichten; **∼·er** [⌣ǝ] (Feuer-)Löschgerät *n*.

ex·tort [ık'stɔ:t] erpressen (*from* von); **ex·tor·tion** [⌣ʃn] Erpressung *f*.

ex·tra ['ekstrǝ] **1.** *adj.* Extra..., außer..., Außer...; Neben..., Sonder...; ∼ *pay* Zulage *f*; ∼ *time Sport:* (Spiel)Verlängerung *f*; **2.** *adv.* besonders; **3.** *et.* Zusätzliches, Extra *n*; Zuschlag *m*; Extrablatt *n*; *thea., Film:* Statist(in).

ex·tract 1. ['ekstrækt] Auszug *m*; **2.** [ık'strækt] (heraus)ziehen; herauslocken; ab-, herleiten; **ex·trac·tion** [~kʃn] (Heraus)Ziehen n; Herkunft f.

ex·tra|dite ['ekstrədait] ausliefern; j-s Auslieferung erwirken; **~di·tion** [ekstrə'dɪʃn] Auslieferung f.

extra·or·di·na·ry □ [ik'strɔːdnrɪ] außerordentlich; ungewöhnlich; außerordentlich, Sonder...

ex·tra·ter·res·tri·al □ ['ekstrətɪ're-striəl] außerirdisch.

ex·trav·a|gence [ik'strævəgəns] Übertriebenheit f; Verschwendung f; Extravaganz f; **~gant** □ [~t] übertrieben, überspannt; verschwenderisch; extravagant.

ex·treme [ik'striːm] **1.** □ äußerste(r, -s), größte(r, -s), höchste(r, -s); außergewöhnlich; **2.** das Äußerste; Extrem n; höchster Grad; **~·ly** [~lɪ] äußerst, höchst.

ex·trem|is·m bsd. pol. [ik'striːmɪzm] Extremismus m; **~ist** [~ɪst] Extremist(in).

ex·trem·i·ty [ik'stremətɪ] das Äußerste; höchste Not; äußerste Maßnahme; extremities pl. Gliedmaßen pl., Extremitäten pl.

ex·tri·cate ['ekstrikeit] herauswinden, -ziehen, befreien.

ex·tro·vert ['ekstrəʊvɜːt] Extrovertierte(r m) f.

ex·u·be|rance [ig'zjuːbərəns] Fülle f; Überschwang m; **~rant** □ [~t] reichlich, üppig; überschwenglich; ausgelassen.

ex·ult [ig'zʌlt] frohlocken, jubeln.

eye [ai] **1.** Auge n; Blick m; Öhr n; Öse f; see ~ to ~ with s.o. mit j-m völlig übereinstimmen; be up to the ~s in work bis über die Ohren in Arbeit stecken; with an ~ to s.th. im Hinblick auf et.; **2.** ansehen; mustern; **~·ball** ['aibɔːl] Augapfel m; **~·brow** Augenbraue f; **~·catch·ing** [~ɪŋ] ins Auge fallend, auffallend; **~d** ...äugig; **~·glass** Augenglas n; (a pair of) **~es** pl. (e-e) Brille; **~·lash** Augenwimper f; **~·lid** Augenlid n; **~·lin·er** Eyeliner m; **~·o·pen·er:** that was an ~ to me das hat mir die Augen geöffnet; **~·shad·ow** Lidschatten m; **~·sight** Augen(licht n) pl., Sehkraft f; **~·strain** Ermüdung f od. Überanstrengung f der Augen; **~·wit·ness** Augenzeug|e m, -in f.

F

fa·ble ['feibl] Fabel f; Sage f; Lüge f.
fab|ric ['fæbrik] Gewebe n, Stoff m; Bau m; Gebäude n; Struktur f; △ nicht Fabrik; **~·ri·cate** [~eit] fabrizieren (mst fig. = erdichten, fälschen).
fab·u·lous □ ['fæbjʊləs] sagenhaft, der Sage angehörend; sagen-, fabelhaft.
fa·çade arch. [fə'sɑːd] Fassade f.
face [feis] **1.** Gesicht n; Gesicht(sausdruck m) n, Miene f; (Ober)Fläche f; Vorderseite f; Zifferblatt n; ~ to ~ with Auge in Auge mit; save od. lose one's ~ das Gesicht wahren od. verlieren; on the ~ of it auf den ersten Blick; pull a long ~ ein langes Gesicht machen; have the ~ to do s.th. die Stirn haben, et. zu tun; **2.** v/t. ansehen; gegenüberstehen (dat.); (hinaus)gehen auf (acc.); die Stirn bieten (dat.); einfassen; arch. beklei-

den; v/i. ~ about sich umdrehen; **~·cloth** ['feiskloθ] Waschlappen m; **~d** in Zssgn: mit (e-m) ... Gesicht; **~·flan·nel** Brt. = face-cloth; **~·lift·ing** [~ɪŋ] Facelifting n, Gesichtsstraffung f; fig. Renovierung f, Verschönerung f.
fa·ce·tious □ [fə'siːʃəs] witzig.
fa·cial ['feiʃl] **1.** □ Gesichts...; **2.** Kosmetik: Gesichtsbehandlung f.
fa·cile ['fæsail] leicht; oberflächlich.
fa·cil·i·tate [fə'sɪliteit] erleichtern.
fa·cil·i·ty [~əti] Leichtigkeit f; Oberflächlichkeit f; mst facilities pl. Erleichterung(en pl.) f; Einrichtung(en pl.) f, Anlage(n pl.) f.
fac·ing ['feisiŋ] ⊕ Verkleidung f; ~s pl. Schneiderei: Besatz m.
fact [fækt] Tatsache f, Wirklichkeit f, Wahrheit f; Tat f; in ~ in der Tat, tatsächlich.

fac·tion *bsd. pol.* ['fækʃn] Splittergruppe *f*; Zwietracht *f*.

fac·ti·tious □ [fæk'tɪʃəs] künstlich.

fac·tor ['fæktə] *fig.* Umstand *m*, Moment *n*, Faktor *m*; Agent *m*; *Schott.* Verwalter *m*.

fac·to·ry ['fæktrɪ] Fabrik *f*.

fac·ul·ty ['fækəltɪ] Fähigkeit *f*; Kraft *f*; *fig.* Gabe *f*; *univ.* Fakultät *f*.

fad [fæd] Mode(erscheinung, -torheit) *f*; (vorübergehende) Laune.

fade [feɪd] (ver)welken (lassen), verblassen; schwinden; immer schwächer werden (*Person*); △ *nicht fade*; *Film, Rundfunk, TV*: ~ *in* auf- od. eingeblendet werden; auf- od. einblenden; ~ *out* aus- od. abgeblendet werden; aus- od. abblenden.

fag¹ [fæg] F Plackerei *f*, Schinderei *f*; *Brt. Schule*: Schüler, der für e-n älteren Dienste verrichtet.

fag² *sl.* [~] *Brt.* Glimmstengel *m* (*Zigarette*); *Am.* Schwule(r) *m* (*Homosexueller*).

fail [feɪl] **1.** *v/i.* versagen; mißlingen, fehlschlagen; versiegen; nachlassen; Bankrott machen; durchfallen (*Kandidat*); *v/t.* im Stich lassen, verlassen; *j-n in e-r Prüfung* durchfallen lassen; *he ~ed to come* er kam nicht; *he cannot ~ to* er muß (einfach); 2. *without ~* mit Sicherheit, ganz bestimmt; **~ing** ['feɪlɪŋ] **1.** Fehler *m*, Schwäche *f*; in Ermang(e)lung (*gen.*); **~ure** [~jə] Fehlen *n*; Ausbleiben *n*; Versagen *n*; Fehlschlag *m*, Mißerfolg *m*; Verfall *m*; Versäumnis *n*; Bankrott *m*; Versager *m*.

faint [feɪnt] **1.** □ schwach, matt; *2.* ohnmächtig werden, in Ohnmacht fallen (*with vor*); **3.** Ohnmacht *f*; **~hearted** □ ['feɪnt'hɑːtɪd] verzagt.

fair¹ [feə] **1.** *adj.* □ gerecht, ehrlich, anständig, fair; ordentlich, schön (*Wetter*), günstig (*Wind*); reichlich; hell (*Haut, Haar, Teint*), blond (*Haar*); freundlich; sauber, in Reinschrift; schön, hübsch, nett; *2. adv.* gerecht, ehrlich, anständig, fair; in Reinschrift; direkt.

fair² [~] (Jahr)Markt *m*; Volksfest *n*; Ausstellung *f*, Messe *f*.

fair|ly ['feəlɪ] ziemlich; völlig; **~ness** [~nɪs] Schönheit *f*; Blondheit *f*; Anständigkeit *f*, *bsd. Sport*: Fairneß *f*; Ehrlichkeit *f*; Gerechtigkeit *f*.

fai·ry ['feərɪ] Fee *f*; Zauberin *f*; Elf(e

f) *m*; **~land** Feen-, Märchenland *n*; **~-tale** Märchen *n* (*a. fig.*):

faith [feɪθ] Glaube *m*; Vertrauen *n*; Treue *f*; **~ful** □ ['feɪθfl] treu; ehrlich; *Yours ~ly* Mit freundlichen Grüßen (*Briefschluß*); **~less** □ [~lɪs] treulos; ungläubig.

fake [feɪk] **1.** Schwindel *m*; Fälschung *f*; Schwindler *m*; **2.** fälschen; imitieren, nachmachen; vortäuschen, simulieren; **3.** gefälscht.

fal·con *zo.* ['fɔːlkən] Falke *m*.

fall [fɔːl] **1.** Fall(en *n*) *m*; Sturz *m*; Verfall *m*; Einsturz *m*; *Am.* Herbst *m*; Sinken *n* (*der Preise etc.*); Gefälle *n*; *mst* ~*s pl.* Wasserfall *m*; △ *nicht gr.*, ~⁸, ~ *Fall*; *2.* (*fell, fallen*) fallen, stürzen; ab-, einfallen; sinken; sich legen (*Wind*); *in e-n Zustand* verfallen; ~ *ill* od. *sick* krank werden; ~ *in love* sich verlieben in (*acc.*); ~ *short of* den *Erwartungen etc.* nicht entsprechen; ~ *back* zurückweichen; ~ *back on* *fig.* zurückgreifen auf (*acc.*); ~ *for* hereinfallen auf (*j-n, et.*); *fig.* sich in *j-n* verknallen; ~ *off* zurückgehen (*Geschäfte, Zuschauerzahlen etc.*), nachlassen; ~ *on* herfallen über (*acc.*); ~ *out* sich streiten (*with* mit); ~ *through* durchfallen (*a. fig.*); ~ *to* reinhauen, tüchtig zugreifen (*beim Essen*).

fal·la·cious □ [fə'leɪʃəs] trügerisch.

fal·la·cy ['fæləsɪ] Trugschluß *m*.

fall·en ['fɔːlən] *p.p. von* fall 2.

fall guy *Am.* F ['fɔːlgaɪ] *der* Lackierte, *der* Dumme.

fal·li·ble □ ['fæləbl] fehlbar.

fal·ling star *ast.* ['fɔːlɪŋstɑː] Sternschnuppe *f*.

fall-out ['fɔːlaʊt] Fallout *m*, radioaktiver Niederschlag *m*.

fal·low ['fæləʊ] *zo.* falb; ✧ brach(liegend).

false □ [fɔːls] falsch; **~hood** ['fɔːlshʊd], **~ness** [~nɪs] Falschheit *f*; Unwahrheit *f*.

fal·si|fi·ca·tion [fɔːlsɪfɪ'keɪʃn] (Ver-)Fälschung *f*; **~fy** ['fɔːlsɪfaɪ] (ver)fälschen; **~ty** [~tɪ] Falschheit *f*, Unwahrheit *f*.

fal·ter ['fɔːltə] schwanken, stocken (*Stimme*); stammeln; *fig.* zaudern.

fame [feɪm] Ruf *m*, Ruhm *m*; **~d** berühmt (*for* wegen).

fa·mil·i·ar [fə'mɪljə] **1.** □ vertraut; gewohnt; familiär; **2.** Vertraute(r *m*) *f*; **~i·ty** [fəmɪlɪ'ærətɪ] Vertrautheit *f;* (plumpe) Vertraulichkeit; **~ize** [fə'mɪljəraɪz] vertraut machen.

fam·i·ly ['fæməlɪ] **1.** Familie *f;* **2.** Familien..., Haus...; *be in the ~ way* F in anderen Umständen sein; *~ allowance* Kindergeld *n;* **~ planning** Familienplanung *f;* **~ tree** Stammbaum *m.*

fam|ine ['fæmɪn] Hungersnot *f;* Knappheit *f* (*of an dat.*); **~ished** [~ʃt] verhungert; *be ~* F am Verhungern sein.

fa·mous □ ['feɪməs] berühmt; △ *nicht famos.*

fan¹ [fæn] **1.** Fächer *m;* Ventilator *m;* ~ *belt* ⊕ Keilriemen *m;* **2.** (-*nn-*) (zu)fächeln; an-, *fig.* entfachen.

fan² [~] (*Sport- etc.*)Fan *m;* ~ *club* Fanklub *m;* ~ *mail* Verehrerpost *f.*

fa·nat|ic [fə'nætɪk] **1.** (*~ally*), *a.* **~·i·cal** □ [~kl] fanatisch; **2.** Fanatiker(in).

fan·ci·er ['fænsɪə] (*Tier-, Pflanzen-*) Liebhaber(in), (-)Züchter(in).

fan·ci·ful □ ['fænsɪfl] phantastisch.

fan·cy ['fænsɪ] **1.** Phantasie *f;* Einbildung(skraft) *f;* Schrulle *f;* Vorliebe *f;* Liebhaberei *f;* **2.** Phantasie...; Mode...; ~ *ball* Kostümfest *n,* Maskenball *m;* ~ *dress* (Masken)Kostüm *n;* ~ *goods pl.* Modeartikel *pl.,* -waren *pl.;* **3.** sich einbilden; Gefallen finden an (*dat.*); *just ~!* denken Sie nur!; **~-free** frei u. ungebunden; **~ work** feine Handarbeit, Stickerei *f.*

fang [fæŋ] Reiß-, Fangzahn *m;* Hauer *m;* Giftzahn *m.*

fan|tas·tic [fæn'tæstɪk] (*~ally*) phantastisch; **~·ta·sy** ['fæntəsɪ] Phantasie *f.*

far [faː] (*farther, further; farthest, furthest*) **1.** *adj.* fern, entfernt, weit; **2.** *adv.* fern; weit; (sehr) viel; *as ~ as* bis; *in so ~ as* insofern als; **~·a·way** ['faːrəweɪ] weit entfernt.

fare [feə] **1.** Fahrgeld *n;* Fahrgast *m;* Verpflegung *f,* Kost *f;* **2.** *gut* leben; *he ~d well* es (er)ging ihm gut; **~well** ['feə'wel] **1.** *int.* lebe (lebt) Sie wohl!; **2.** Abschied *m,* Lebewohl *n.*

far-fetched *fig.* ['faː'fetʃt] weithergeholt, gesucht.

farm [faːm] **1.** Bauernhof *m,* Gut *n,* Gehöft *n,* Farm *f;* Züchterei *f; chicken ~* Hühnerfarm *f;* **2.** (ver-)pachten; *Land, Hof* bewirtschaften; *Geflügel etc.* züchten; **~·er** ['faːmə] Bauer *m,* Landwirt *m,* Farmer

m; (*Geflügel- etc.*)Züchter *m;* Pächter *m;* **~·hand** Landarbeiter(in); **~·house** Bauernhaus *n;* **~·ing** [~ɪŋ] **1.** Acker..., landwirtschaftlich; **2.** Landwirtschaft *f;* **~·stead** Bauernhof *m,* Gehöft *n;* **~·yard** Wirtschaftshof *n* (*e-s Bauernhofs*).

far|-off ['faː'ɒf] entfernt, fern; **~·sight·ed** *bsd. Am.* weitsichtig; *fig.* weitblickend.

far·ther ['faːðə] *comp. von far,* **~·thest** ['faːðɪst] *sup. von far.*

fas·ci·nate ['fæsɪneɪt] faszinieren; **~·nat·ing** □ [~ɪŋ] faszinierend; **~·na·tion** [fæsɪ'neɪʃn] Zauber *m,* Reiz *m,* Faszination *f.*

fas·cis|m *pol.* ['fæʃɪzəm] Faschismus *m;* **~t** *pol.* [~ɪst] **1.** Faschist *m;* **2.** faschistisch.

fash·ion ['fæʃn] Mode *f;* Art *f;* feine Lebensart; Form *f;* Schnitt *m;* *in* (*out of*) ~ (un)modern; ~ *parade,* ~ *show* Mode(n)schau *f;* **2.** gestalten; *Kleid* machen; **~·a·ble** □ [~nəbl] modern, elegant.

fast¹ [faːst] **1.** Fasten *n;* **2.** fasten.

fast² [~] schnell; fest; treu; echt, beständig (*Farbe*); flott; △ *nicht fast; be ~* vorgehen (*Uhr*); **~·back** *mot.* ['faːstbæk] (Wagen *m* mit) Fließheck *n;* **~ breed·er, ~ breed·er re·ac·tor** *phys.* schneller Brüter; **~ food** Schnellgericht(e *pl.*) *n;* **~-food res·tau·rant** Schnellimbiß *m,* -gaststätte *f;* **~ lane** *mot.* Überholspur *f.*

fas·ten ['faːsn] *v/t.* befestigen; anheften; fest zumachen; zubinden; *Augen etc.* heften (*on, upon* auf *acc.*); *v/i.* schließen (*Tür*); △ *nicht fassen;* ~ *on,* ~ *upon* sich klammern an (*acc.*); *fig.* sich stürzen auf (*acc.*); **~·er** [~ə] Verschluß *m,* Halter *m;* **~·ing** [~ɪŋ] Verschluß *m,* Halterung *f.*

fas·tid·i·ous □ [fə'stɪdɪəs] anspruchsvoll, heikel, wählerisch, verwöhnt.

fat [fæt] **1.** □ (-*tt-*) fett; dick; fettig; **2.** Fett *n;* **3.** (-*tt-*) fett machen *od.* werden; mästen.

fa·tal □ ['feɪtl] verhängnisvoll, fatal (*to* für); Schicksals...; tödlich; **~·i·ty** [fə'tælətɪ] Verhängnis *n;* Unglücks-, Todesfall *m;* Todesopfer *n.*

fate [feɪt] Schicksal *n;* Verhängnis *n.*

fa·ther ['faːðə] Vater *m;* ♀ **Christ·mas** *bsd. Brt.* der Weihnachtsmann, der Nikolaus; **~·hood** [~hʊd] Vaterschaft *f;* **~-in-law** [~rɪnlɔː] (*pl.*

fathers-in-law) Schwiegervater *m*; **~·less** [~lɪs] vaterlos; **~·ly** [~lɪ] väterlich.

fath·om ['fæðəm] **1.** ⚓ Faden *m* (*Tiefenmaß*); **2.** ⚓ loten; *fig.* ergründen; **~·less** [~lɪs] unergründlich.

fa·tigue [fə'tiːg] **1.** Ermüdung *f*; Strapaze *f*; **2.** ermüden.

fat|ten ['fætn] fett machen *od.* werden; mästen; *Boden* düngen; **~·ty** [~tɪ] (*-ier, -iest*) fett(ig).

fat·u·ous □ ['fætjʊəs] albern.

fau·cet *Am.* ['fɔːsɪt] (Wasser)Hahn *m*.

fault [fɔːlt] Fehler *m*; Defekt *m*; Schuld *f*; *find* ~ *with* et. auszusetzen haben an (*dat.*); *be at* ~ Schuld haben; **~·less** □ [~lɪs] fehlerfrei, -los; **~·y** □ [~tɪ] (*-ier, -iest*) fehlerhaft, *a.* defekt.

fa·vo(u)r ['feɪvə] **1.** Gunst *f*; Gefallen *m*; Begünstigung *f*; *in* ~ *of* zugunsten von *od. gen.*; *do s.o. a* ~ j-m ein Gefallen tun; **2.** begünstigen; bevorzugen, vorziehen; wohlwollend gegenüberstehen; *Sport:* favorisieren; beehren; **fa·vo(u)r·a·ble** □ [~rəbl] günstig; **fa·vo(u)r·ite** [~rɪt] **1.** Liebling *m*; *Sport:* Favorit *m*; **2.** Lieblings...

fawn¹ [fɔːn] **1.** *zo.* (Reh)Kitz *n*; Rehbraun *n*; **2.** rehbraun.

fawn² [~] (*mit dem Schwanz*) wedeln (*Hund*); *fig.* katzbuckeln (*on, upon* vor *dat.*).

fear [fɪə] **1.** Furcht *f* (*of* vor *dat.*); Befürchtung *f*; Angst *f*; **2.** (be)fürchten; sich fürchten vor (*dat.*); **~·ful** □ ['fɪəfl] furchtsam; furchtbar; **~·less** □ [~lɪs] furchtlos.

fea·si·ble □ ['fiːzəbl] durchführbar.

feast [fiːst] **1.** *eccl.* Fest *n*, Feiertag *m*; Festessen *n*; *fig.* Fest *n*, (Hoch)Genuß *m*; **2.** *v/t.* festlich bewirten; *v/i.* sich gütlich tun (*on* an *dat.*).

feat [fiːt] (Helden)Tat *f*; Kunststück *n*.

feath·er ['feðə] **1.** Feder *f*; *a.* ~*s* Gefieder *n*; *birds of a* ~ Leute vom gleichen Schlag; *in high* ~ (bei) bester Laune; *in Hochform*; **2.** mit Federn schmücken; **~ bed** Matratze *f* mit Feder- *od.* Daunenfüllung; △ *nicht Federbett*; **~·bed** (*-dd-*) verwöhnen; **~·brained**, **~·head·ed** unbesonnen; albern; **~·ed** be-, gefiedert; **~·weight** *Sport:* Federgewicht(ler *m*) *n*; Leichtgewicht *n* (*Person*); *fig.* unbedeutende Person;

---

et. Belangloses; **~·y** [~rɪ] be-, gefiedert; feder(art)ig.

fea·ture ['fiːtʃə] **1.** (Gesichts-, Grund-, Haupt-, Charakter)Zug *m*; (charakteristisches) Merkmal; *Rundfunk, TV:* Feature *n*; *a.* ~ *article*, ~ *story* Zeitung: Feature *n*; *a.* ~ *film* Haupt-, Spielfilm *m*; **~·s** *pl.* Gesicht *n*; **2.** kennzeichnen; sich auszeichnen durch; groß herausbringen *od.* -stellen; *Film:* in der Hauptrolle zeigen.

Feb·ru·a·ry ['februərɪ] Februar *m*.

fed [fed] *pret. u. p.p. von* feed 2.

fed·e·ral □ ['fedərəl] Bundes...; *USA:* Zentral..., Unions..., National...; ♀ *Bureau of Investigation* (*abbr. FBI*) *amer.* Bundeskriminalpolizei; ~ *government* Bundesregierung *f*; **~·rate** [~eɪt] (sich) zu e-m (Staaten)Bund zusammenschließen; **~·ra·tion** [fedə'reɪʃn] Föderation *f* (*a. econ., pol.*); (politischer) Zusammenschluß; *econ.* (Dach)Verband *m*; *pol.* Staatenbund *m*.

fee [fiː] Gebühr *f*; Honorar *n*; (Mitglieds)Beitrag *m*; Eintrittsgeld *n*.

fee·ble □ ['fiːbl] (*~r, ~st*) schwach.

feed [fiːd] **1.** Futter *n*; Nahrung *f*; Fütterung *f*; ⊕ Zuführung *f*, Speisung *f*; **2.** (*fed*) *v/t.* füttern; ernähren; ⊕ (ein)speisen; weiden lassen; *be fed up with* et. *od.* j-n satt haben; *well fed* wohlgenährt; *v/i.* essen; sich ernähren; weiden; **~·back** ['fiːdbæk] ⚡, *Kybernetik:* Feedback *n*, Rückkopplung *f*; *Rundfunk, TV:* Feedback *n* (*mögliche Einflußnahme des Publikums auf eine laufende e-r Sendung*); Zurückleitung *f* (*von Informationen*) (*to an acc.*); **~·er** [~ə] Fütterer *m*; *Am.* Viehmäster *m*; Esser(in); **~·er road** Zubringer (-straße *f*) *m*; **~·ing-bot·tle** [~ɪŋbɒtl] (Säuglings-, Saug)Flasche *f*.

feel [fiːl] **1.** (*felt*) (sich) fühlen; befühlen; empfinden; sich anfühlen; *I* ~ *like doing* ich möchte am liebsten tun; **2.** Gefühl *n*; Empfindung *f*; **~·er** *zo.* ['fiːlə] Fühler *m*; **~·ing** [~ɪŋ] Gefühl *n*.

feet [fiːt] *pl. von* foot 1.

feign [feɪn] *Interesse etc.* vortäuschen, *Krankheit a.* simulieren.

feint [feɪnt] Finte *f*; ✗ Täuschungsmanöver *n*.

fell [fel] **1.** *pret. von* fall 2; **2.** niederschlagen; fällen.

fellow

fel·low [ˈfeləʊ] **1.** Gefährt|e m, -in f, Kamerad(in); Gleiche(r, -s); Gegenstück n; univ. Fellow m, Mitglied n e-s College; Kerl m, Bursche m, Mensch m; old ~ F alter Junge; the ~ of a glove der andere Handschuh; **2.** Mit...; ~ being Mitmensch m; ~ countryman Landsmann m; ~ travel(l)er Mitreisende(r) m, Reisegefährte m; ~**ship** [~ʃɪp] Gemeinschaft f; Kameradschaft f.

fel·o·ny 🏛 [ˈfelənɪ] (schweres) Verbrechen, Kapitalverbrechen n.

felt[1] [felt] pret. u. p.p. von feel 1.

felt[2] [~] Filz m; ~ tip, ~-tip(ped) pen Filzschreiber m, -stift m.

fe·male [ˈfiːmeɪl] **1.** weiblich; ~ Weib n; zo. Weibchen n.

fem·i·nine □ [ˈfemɪnɪn] weiblich, Frauen...; weibisch; ~**nis·m** [~ɪzəm] Feminismus m; ~**nist** [~ɪst] **1.** Feminist(in); **2.** feministisch.

fen [fen] Fenn n, Moor n; Marsch f.

fence [fens] **1.** Zaun m; F Hehler m; **2.** v/t. ~ in ein-, umzäunen; einsperren; ~ off abzäunen; v/i. Sport: fechten; sl. Hehlerei treiben; **fenc·er** [ˈfensə] Sport: Fechter m; **fenc·ing** [~ɪŋ] Einfriedung f; Sport: Fechten n; attr. Fecht...

fend [fend]: ~ off abwehren; ~ for o.s. für sich selbst sorgen; ~**er** [ˈfendə] Schutzvorrichtung f; Schutzblech n; Am. mot. Kotflügel m; Kamingitter n, -vorsetzer m.

fen·nel 🌿 [ˈfenl] Fenchel m.

fer·ment 1. [ˈfɜːment] Ferment n; Gärung f; **2.** [fəˈment] gären (lassen); ~**men·ta·tion** [fɜːmenˈteɪʃn] Gärung f.

fern [fɜːn] Farn(kraut n) m.

fe·ro·cious □ [fəˈrəʊʃəs] wild; grausam; ~**ci·ty** [fəˈrɒsətɪ] Wildheit f.

fer·ret [ˈferɪt] **1.** zo. Frettchen n; fig. Spürhund m; **2.** herumstöbern; ~ out aufspüren, -stöbern.

fer·ry [ˈferɪ] **1.** Fähre f; **2.** übersetzen; ~**boat** Fährboot n, Fähre f; ~**man** (pl. -men) Fährmann m.

fer·tile □ [ˈfɜːtaɪl] fruchtbar; reich (of, in an dat.); ~**til·i·ty** [fəˈtɪlətɪ] Fruchtbarkeit f (a. fig.); ~**ti·lize** [ˈfɜːtɪlaɪz] fruchtbar machen; befruchten; düngen; ~**ti·liz·er** [~ə] (bsd. Kunst)Dünger m, Düngemittel n.

fer·vent □ [ˈfɜːvənt] heiß; inbrünstig, glühend; leidenschaftlich.

fer·vo(u)r [ˈfɜːvə] Glut f; Inbrunst f.

fes·ter [ˈfestə] eitern; verfaulen.

fes·ti·val [ˈfestəvl] Fest n; Feier f; Festspiele pl.; ~**tive** [~tɪv] festlich; ~**tiv·i·ty** [feˈstɪvətɪ] Festlichkeit f.

fes·toon [feˈstuːn] Girlande f.

fetch [fetʃ] holen; Preis erzielen; Seufzer ausstoßen; ~**ing** □ F [ˈfetʃɪŋ] reizend.

fet·id □ [ˈfetɪd] stinkend.

fet·ter [ˈfetə] **1.** Fessel f; **2.** fesseln.

feud [fjuːd] Fehde f; Lehen n; ~**al** □ [ˈfjuːdl] feudal, Lehns...; **feu·dal·is·m** [~əlɪzəm] Feudalismus m, Feudalsystem n.

fe·ver [ˈfiːvə] Fieber n; ~**ish** □ [~rɪʃ] fieb(e)rig; fig. fieberhaft.

few [fjuː] wenige; a ~ ein paar, einige; no ~er than nicht weniger als; quite a ~, a good ~ e-e ganze Menge.

fi·an·cé [fɪˈɑːnseɪ] Verlobte(r) m; ~**e** [~] Verlobte f.

fib F [fɪb] **1.** Flunkerei f, Schwindelei f; **2.** (-bb-) schwindeln, flunkern.

fi·bre, Am. **-ber** [ˈfaɪbə] Faser f; Charakter m; **fi·brous** [ˈfaɪbrəs] faserig.

fick·le [ˈfɪkl] wankelmütig; unbeständig; ~**ness** [~nɪs] Wankelmut m.

fic·tion [ˈfɪkʃn] Erfindung f; Prosaliteratur f, Belletristik f; Romane pl.; ~**al** □ [~l] erdichtet; Roman...

fic·ti·tious □ [fɪkˈtɪʃəs] erfunden.

fid·dle □ [ˈfɪdl] **1.** Fiedel f, Geige f; play first (second) ~ bsd. fig. die erste (zweite) Geige spielen; (as) fit as a ~ kerngesund; **2.** ♪ fiedeln; a. ~ about od. around (with) herumfingern (an dat.), spielen (mit); ~**r** [~ə] Geiger(in); ~**sticks** int. dummes Zeug!

fi·del·i·ty [fɪˈdelətɪ] Treue f; Genauigkeit f.

fidg·et F [ˈfɪdʒɪt] **1.** nervöse Unruhe f; **2.** nervös machen od. sein; ~**y** [~ɪ] zapp(e)lig, nervös.

field [fiːld] Feld n; (Spiel)Platz m; Arbeitsfeld n; Gebiet n; Bereich m; hold the ~ das Feld behaupten; ~ e·vents pl. Sport: Sprung- u. Wurfdisziplinen pl.; ~**glass·es** pl. (a pair of ~ ein) Feldstecher m od. Fernglas n; ~ **mar·shal** ✕ Feldmarschall m; ~ **of·fi·cer** ✕ Stabsoffizier m; ~ **sports** pl. Sport m im Freien (bsd. Jagen, Schießen, Fischen); ~**work** praktische (wissenschaftliche) Arbeit, Archäologie etc.: a. Arbeit f im Gelände; *Markt-, Meinungsforschung*: Feldarbeit *f*.

fiend [fiːnd] Satan *m*, Teufel *m*; *in Zssgn*: Süchtige(r *m*) *f*; Fanatiker(in); △ *nicht* Feind; **~ish** □ ['fiːndʃ] teuflisch, boshaft.

fierce □ [fɪəs] (*~r*, *~st*) wild; scharf; heftig; **~ness** ['fɪəsnɪs] Wildheit *f*, Schärfe *f*; Heftigkeit *f*.

fi·e·ry □ ['faɪərɪ] (*-ier*, *-iest*) feurig; hitzig.

fif|teen ['fɪf'tiːn] **1.** fünfzehn; **2.** Fünfzehn *f*; **~teenth** [~'tiːnθ] fünfzehnte(r, -s); **~th** [fɪfθ] **1.** fünfte(r, -s); **2.** Fünftel *n*; **~th·ly** ['fɪfθlɪ] fünftens; **~ti·eth** ['fɪftɪɪθ] fünfzigste(r, -s); **~ty** [~tɪ] **1.** fünfzig; **2.** Fünfzig *f*; **~ty-fif·ty** F halbe-halbe.

fig ♀ [fɪg] Feige(nbaum *m*) *f*.

fight [faɪt] **1.** Kampf *m*; ✗ Gefecht *n*; Schlägerei *f*; *Boxen*: Kampf *m*, Fight *m*; Kampflust *f*; **2.** (*fought*) *v/t*. bekämpfen; kämpfen gegen *od*. mit, *Sport*: *a*. boxen gegen; *v/i*. kämpfen, sich schlagen; *Sport*: boxen; **~er** ['faɪtə] Kämpfer *m*; *Sport*: Boxer *m*, Fighter *m*; *a*. ~ plane ✗ Jagdflugzeug *n*; **~ing** [~ɪŋ] Kampf *m*.

fig·u·ra·tive □ ['fɪgjʊrətɪv] bildlich.

fig·ure ['fɪgə] **1.** Figur *f*; Gestalt *f*; Zahl *f*, Ziffer *f*; Preis *m*; *be good at* ~s ein guter Rechner sein; **2.** *v/t*. abbilden, darstellen; *Am*. F meinen, glauben; sich *er*. vorstellen; ~ *out* rauskriegen; *Problem* lösen; verstehen; ~ *up* zusammenzählen; *v/i*. erscheinen, vorkommen; ~ *on bsd*. *Am*. rechnen mit; ~ **skat·er** *Sport*: Eiskunstläufer(in); ~ **skat·ing** *Sport*: Eiskunstlauf *m*.

fil·a·ment ['fɪləmənt] Faden *m*, Faser *f*; ♀ Staubfaden *m*; ⚡ Glüh-, Heizfaden *m*.

fil·bert ♀ ['fɪlbət] Haselnuß *f*.

filch F [fɪltʃ] klauen, stibitzen.

file¹ [faɪl] **1.** Ordner *m*, Karteikasten *m*; Akte *f*, Akten *pl*., Ablage *f*; *Computer*: Datei *f*; Reihe *f*; ✗ Rotte *f*; *on* ~ bei den Akten; **2.** *v/t*. *Briefe etc*. einordnen, ablegen, zu den Akten nehmen; *Antrag* einlegen, *Berufung* einlegen; *v/i*. hintereinander marschieren.

file² [~] **1.** Feile *f*; **2.** feilen.

fi·li·al □ ['fɪljəl] kindlich, Kindes..

fil·ing ['faɪlɪŋ] Ablegen *n* (*von Briefen etc.*); ~ *cabinet* Aktenschrank *m*.

fill [fɪl] **1.** (sich) füllen; an-, aus-, erfüllen; *Auftrag* ausführen; ~ *in* einsetzen; *Am. a.* ~ *out* Formular ausfüllen; ~ *up* vollfüllen; sich füllen; ~ *her up!* F volltanken, bitte!; **2.** Füllung *f*; *eat one's* ~ sich satt essen.

fil·let, *Am. a.* **fil·et** ['fɪlɪt] Filet *n*.

fill·ing ['fɪlɪŋ] Füllung *f*; 𝒳 (Zahn-)Plombe *f*; (*-*)Füllung *f*; ~ *station* Tankstelle *f*.

fil·ly ['fɪlɪ] Stutenfohlen *n*; *fig*. wilde Hummel (*Mädchen*).

film [fɪlm] **1.** Häutchen *n*; Membran(e) *f*; Film *m* (*a. phot. u. bsd. Brt. Kinofilm*); Trübung *f* (*des Auges*); Nebelschleier *m*; *take od. shoot a* ~ e-n Film drehen; **2.** (ver)filmen; sich verfilmen lassen.

fil·ter ['fɪltə] **1.** Filter *m*; **2.** filtern; **~ tip** Filter *m*; Filterzigarette *f*; **~-tipped:** ~ *cigarette* Filterzigarette *f*.

filth [fɪlθ] Schmutz *m*; **~y** □ ['fɪlθɪ] (*-ier, -iest*) schmutzig; *fig*. unflätig.

fin [fɪn] *zo*. Flosse *f* (*a. sl.* = Hand).

fi·nal ['faɪnl] **1.** □ letzte(r, -s); End..., Schluß...; endgültig; ~ *storage* Endlagerung *f* (*von Atommüll etc.*); **2.** *Sport*: Finale *n*, Endkampf, -lauf *m*, -runde *f*, -spiel *n*; *mst* ~s *pl*. Schlußexamen, -prüfung *f*; **~ist** [~nəlɪst] *Sport*: Finalist(in), Endkampfteilnehmer(in); **~ly** [~lɪ] endlich, schließlich; endgültig.

fi·nance [faɪ'næns] **1.** Finanzwesen *n*; ~s *pl*. Finanzen *pl*.; **2.** *v/t*. finanzieren; *v/i*. Geldgeschäfte machen; **fi·nan·cial** □ [~n∫l] finanziell; **fi·nan·cier** [~nsɪə] Finanzier *m*.

finch *zo*. [fɪntʃ] Fink *m*.

find [faɪnd] **1.** (*found*) finden; (an-)treffen; auf-, herausfinden; 𝕥𝕥 *j-n* für (*nicht*) *schuldig* erklären; beschaffen; versorgen; **2.** Fund *m*, Entdeckung *f*; **~ings** ['faɪndɪŋz] *pl*. Befund *m*; 𝕥𝕥 Feststellung *f*, Spruch *m*.

fine¹ □ [faɪn] **1.** *adj*. (*~r, ~st*) schön; fein; verfeinert; rein; spitz, dünn; scharf; geziert; vornehm; *I'm* ~ mir geht es gut; **2.** *adv*. gut, bestens.

fine² [~] **1.** Geldstrafe *f*, Bußgeld *n*; **2.** zu e-r Geldstrafe verurteilen.

fi·ne·ry ['faɪnərɪ] Glanz *m*; Putz *m*, Staat *m*.

fin·ger ['fɪŋgə] **1.** Finger *m*; *s. cross* **2**; **2.** betasten, (herum)fingern an (*dat.*); **~nail** Fingernagel *m*; **~print** Fingerabdruck *m*; **~tip** Fingerspitze *f*.

fin·i·cky ['fɪnɪkɪ] wählerisch.

fin·ish ['fɪnɪʃ] **1.** v/t. beenden, vollenden; fertigstellen; abschließen; vervollkommnen; erledigen; v/i. enden, aufhören; ~ **with** mit j-m, et. Schluß machen; **have** ~ed **with** j-n, et. nicht mehr brauchen; **2.** Vollendung f, letzter Schliff; Sport: Endspurt m, Finish m; Ziel n; ~**ing line** [~ɪŋlaɪn] Sport: Ziellinie f.

Finn [fɪn] Finn|e m, -in f; ~**ish** ['fɪnɪʃ] **1.** finnisch; **2.** ling. Finnisch n.

fir ♀ [fɜː] a. ~**tree** Tanne f; ~**cone** [~kəʊn] Tannenzapfen m.

fire ['faɪə] **1.** Feuer n; be on ~ in Flammen stehen, brennen; catch ~ Feuer fangen, in Brand geraten; set on ~, set ~ to anzünden; **2.** v/t. anentzünden; fig. anfeuern; abfeuern; Ziegel etc. brennen; F rausschmeißen (entlassen); heizen; v/i. Feuer fangen (a. fig.); feuern; ~**a·larm** [~əlɑːm] Feueralarm m; ~**arms** pl. Feuer-, Schußwaffen pl.; ~ **bri·gade** Feuerwehr f; ~**crack·er** Frosch m (Feuerwerkskörper); ~ **de·part·ment** Am. Feuerwehr f; ~**en·gine** [~rendʒɪn] (Feuer)Spritze f; ~**es·cape** [~rɪskeɪp] Feuerleiter f; -treppe f; ~**ex·tin·guish·er** [~rɪkstɪŋgwɪʃə] Feuerlöscher m; ~**guard** Kamingitter n; ~**man** Feuerwehrmann m; Heizer m; ~**place** (offener) Kamin; ~**plug** Hydrant m; ~**proof** feuerfest; ~**rais·ing** Brt. [~ɪŋ] Brandstiftung f; ~**side** Herd m; Kamin m; ~ **sta·tion** Feuerwache f; ~**wood** Brennholz n; ~**works** pl. Feuerwerk n.

fir·ing squad ⚔ ['faɪərɪŋskwɒd] Exekutionskommando n.

firm[1] [fɜːm] fest; derb; standhaft; △ nicht firm.

firm[2] [~] Firma f, Betrieb m, Unternehmen n.

first [fɜːst] **1.** adj. □ erste(r, -s); beste(r, -s); **2.** adv. erstens; zuerst; ~ of all an erster Stelle; zu allererst; Erste(r, -s); at ~ zuerst, anfangs; from the ~ von Anfang an; ~ **aid** Erste Hilfe; ~**aid** ['fɜːsteɪd] Erste-Hilfe-...; ~ **kit** Verband(s)kasten m, -zeug n; ~**born** erstgeborene(r, -s), älteste(r, -s); ~ **class** 1. Klasse (e-s Verkehrsmittels); ~**class** erstklassig; ~**ly** [~lɪ] erstens; ~**hand** aus erster Hand; ~ **name** Vorname m; Beiname m; ~**rate** erstklassig.

firth [fɜːθ] Förde f, Meeresarm m.

fish [fɪʃ] **1.** Fisch(e pl.) m; a queer ~ F ein komischer Kauz; **2.** fischen, angeln; ~ **around** kramen (for nach); ~**bone** ['fɪʃbəʊn] Gräte f.

fish·er·man ['fɪʃəmən] (pl. -men) Fischer m; ~**er·y** [~rɪ] Fischerei f.

fish·ing ['fɪʃɪŋ] Fischen n, Angeln n; ~**line** Angelschnur f; ~**rod** Angelrute f; ~**tack·le** Angelgerät n.

fish·mon·ger Brt. ['fɪʃmʌŋgə] Fischhändler m; ~ **y** □ [~ɪ] (-ier, -iest) Fisch...; F verdächtig, faul.

fis·sile ⊕ ['fɪsaɪl] spaltbar; ~**sion** ['fɪʃn] Spaltung f; ~**sure** ['fɪʃə] Spalt m, Riß m.

fist [fɪst] Faust f.

fit[1] [fɪt] **1.** □ (-tt-) geeignet, passend; tauglich; Sport: fit, in (guter) Form; **2.** (-tt-; fitted, Am. a. fit) v/t. passen für od. dat.; anpassen, passend machen; befähigen; geeignet machen (for, to für, zu); ~ in j-m e-n Termin geben, j-n, et. einschieben; a. ~ on anprobieren; a. ~ out ausrüsten, -statten, einrichten, versehen (with mit); a. ~ up ausrüsten, -statten, einrichten; montieren; v/i. passen; sitzen (Kleid); **3.** Sitz m (Kleid).

fit[2] [~] Anfall m; ⚕ Ausbruch m; Anwandlung f; by ~s and starts ruckweise; give s.o. a ~ F j-n auf die Palme bringen; j-m e-n Schock versetzen.

fit·ful □ ['fɪtfl] ruckartig; fig. unstet; ~**ness** [~nɪs] Tauglichkeit f; bsd. Sport: Fitneß f, (gute) Form; ~**ted** zugeschnitten, nach Maß (gearbeitet); Einbau...; ~ carpet Spannteppich m, Teppichboden m; ~ kitchen Einbauküche f; ~**ter** [~ə] Monteur m; Installateur m; ~**ting** [~ɪŋ] **1.** passend; **2.** Montage f; Anprobe f; ~s pl. Einrichtung f; Armaturen pl.

five [faɪv] **1.** fünf; **2.** Fünf f.

fix [fɪks] **1.** v/t. befestigen, anheften, fixieren; Blick etc. heften, richten (on auf acc.); fesseln; aufstellen; bestimmen, festsetzen; reparieren, instand setzen; bsd. Am. et. zurechtmachen, ein Essen zubereiten; △ nicht fix; ~ up in Ordnung bringen, regeln; j-n unterbringen; v/i. fest werden; ~ on sich entschließen für od. zu; **2.** F Klemme f; sl. Schuß m (Heroin etc.); ~**ed** □ fest; bestimmt; starr; ~**ing** ['fɪksɪŋ] Befestigen n;

Instandsetzen *n*; Fixieren *n*; Aufstellen *n*, Montieren *n*; Besatz *m*, Verstärkung *f*; *Am.* ~s *pl.* Zubehör *n*, Ausrüstung *f*; ~**ture** [~st[ə] fest angebrachtes Zubehörteil, feste Anlage; Inventarstück *n*; *lighting* ~ Beleuchtungskörper *m*.

fizz [fiz] **1.** zischen, sprudeln; **2.** Zischen *n*; F Schampus *m* (*Sekt*).

flab·ber·gast F ['flæbəga:st] verblüffen; *be* ~*ed* ganz platt sein.

flab·by □ ['flæbi] (*-ier, -iest*) schlaff.

flac·cid □ ['flæksid] schlaff, schlapp.

flag [flæg] **1.** Flagge *f*; Fahne *f*; Fliese *f*; ♀ Schwertlilie *f*; **2.** (*-gg-*) beflaggen; durch Flaggen signalisieren; mit Fliesen belegen; ermatten; mutlos werden; ~**pole** ['flægpəul] = *flagstaff.*

fla·grant □ ['fleigrənt] abscheulich; berüchtigt; offenkundig.

flag|staff ['flægsta:f] Fahnenstange *f*, -mast *m*; ~**stone** Fliese *f*.

flair [fleə] Talent *n*; Gespür *n*, (feine) Nase.

flake [fleik] **1.** Flocke *f*; Schicht *f*; **2.** (sich) flocken; abblättern; **flak·y** ['fleiki] (*-ier, -iest*) flockig; blätt(e)rig; ~ *pastry* Blätterteig *m*.

flame [fleim] **1.** Flamme *f* (*a. fig.*); *be in* ~*s* in Flammen stehen; **2.** flammen, lodern.

flam·ma·ble *Am. u.* ⊕ ['flæməbl] = *inflammable.*

flan [flæn] Obst-, Käsekuchen *m*.

flank [flæŋk] **1.** Flanke *f*; **2.** flankieren.

flan·nel ['flænl] Flanell *m*; Waschlappen *m*; ~*s pl.* Flanellhose *f*.

flap [flæp] **1.** (Ohr)Läppchen *n*; Rockschoß *m* (*Hut*)Krempe *f*; Klappe *f*; Klaps *m*; (Flügel)Schlag *m*; **2.** *v/t.* (*-pp-*) klatschen(d schlagen); *v/i.* lose herabhängen; flattern.

flare [fleə] **1.** flackern; sich nach außen erweitern; sich bauschen; ~ *up* aufflammen; *fig.* aufbrausen; **2.** flackerndes Licht; Lichtsignal *n*.

flash [flæʃ] **1.** Aufblitzen *n*, -leuchten *n*, Blitz *m*; *Rundfunk etc.*: Kurzmeldung *f*; *phot.* F Blitz *m* (*Blitzlicht*); *bsd. Am.* F Taschenlampe *f*; *like a* ~ wie der Blitz; *in a* ~ im Nu; ~ *of lightning* Blitzstrahl *m*; **2.** (auf)blitzen; auflodern (lassen); *Blick etc.* werfen; flitzen; funken; telegrafieren; *it* ~*ed on me* mir kam plötzlich der Gedanke; ~**back** ['flæʃbæk]

Film, Roman: Rückblende *f*; ~**light** *phot.* Blitzlicht *n*; ♣ Leuchtfeuer; *bsd. Am.* Taschenlampe *f*; ~**y** □ [~i] (*-ier, -iest*) auffallend, -fällig.

flask [fla:sk] Taschenflasche *f*; Thermosflasche *f*.

flat [flæt] **1.** □ (*-tt-*) flach, platt; schal; *econ.* flau; klar; glatt; *mot.* platt (*Reifen*); ♩ erniedrigt (*Note*); ~ *price* Einheitspreis *m*; **2.** *adv.* glatt; völlig; *fall* ~ danebengehen; *sing* ~ zu tief singen; **3.** Fläche *f*, Ebene *f*; Flachland *n*; Etage *f*, (Miet)Wohnung *f*; ♪ B *n*; F Simpel *m*; *bsd. Am. mot.* Reifenpanne *f*, Plattfuß *m*; ~**foot** ['flætfut] (*pl.* -feet) *sl.* Bulle *m* (*Polizist*); ~**foot·ed** plattfüßig; ~**i·ron** Plätteisen *n*; ~**ten** [~tn] (sich) ab-, verflachen.

flat·ter ['flætə] schmeicheln (*dat.*); △ *nicht flattern;* ~**er** [~rə] Schmeichler(in); ~**y** [~ri] Schmeichelei *f*.

fla·vo(u)r ['fleivə] **1.** Geschmack *m*; Aroma *n*; Blume *f* (*Wein*); *fig.* Beigeschmack *m*; Würze *f*; **2.** würzen; ~**ing** [~əriŋ] Würze *f*, Aroma *n*; ~**less** [~lis] geschmacklos, fad.

flaw [flɔ:] **1.** Sprung *m*, Riß *m*; Fehler *m*; ♣ Bö *f*; **2.** zerbrechen; beschädigen; ~**less** □ ['flɔ:lis] fehlerlos.

flax ♀ [flæks] Flachs *m*, Lein *m*.

flea *zo.* [fli:] Floh *m*.

fleck [flek] Fleck(en) *m*; Tupfen *m*.

fled [fled] *pret. u. p.p. von flee.*

fledged [fledʒd] flügge; **fledg(e)·ling** ['fledʒliŋ] Jungvogel *m*; *fig.* Grünschnabel *m*.

flee [fli:] (*fled*) fliehen; meiden.

fleece [fli:s] **1.** Vlies *n*; **2.** scheren; **fleec·y** ['fli:si] (*-ier, -iest*) wollig, flockig.

fleet [fli:t] **1.** □ schnell; **2.** ♣ Flotte *f*; ♀ *Street das Londoner Presseviertel; die (Londoner) Presse.*

flesh [fleʃ] *lebendiges* Fleisch; ~**y** ['fleʃi] (*-ier, -iest*) fleischig; dick.

flew [flu:] *pret. von fly 2.*

flex¹ *bsd. anat.* [fleks] biegen.

flex² *bsd. Brit.* ≠ [~] (Anschluß-, Verlängerungs)Kabel *n*, (-)Schnur *f*.

flex·i·ble □ ['fleksəbl] flexibel, biegsam; *fig.* anpassungsfähig.

flick [flik] schnippen; schnellen.

flick·er ['flikə] **1.** flackern; flattern; flimmern; **2.** Flackern *n*, Flimmern *n*; Flattern *n*; *Am.* Buntspecht *m*.

fli·er ['flaiə] = *flyer.*

flight [flait] Flucht *f*; Flug *m* (*a. fig.*);

Schwarm m (Vögel etc.; a. ✈, ✗); a. ~ of stairs Treppe f; put to ~ in die Flucht schlagen; take (to) ~ die Flucht ergreifen; **~less** zo. [~lɪs] flugunfähig; **~y** □ ['flaɪtɪ] (-ier, -iest) launisch.

flim·sy ['flɪmzɪ] (-ier, -iest) dünn; zart; fig. fadenscheinig.

flinch [flɪntʃ] zurückweichen; zucken.

fling [flɪŋ] 1. Wurf m; Schlag m; have one's od. a ~ sich austoben; 2. (flung) v/i. eilen; ausschlagen (Pferd); fig. toben; v/t. werfen, schleudern; ~ o.s. sich stürzen; ~ open aufreißen.

flint [flɪnt] Feuerstein m.

flip [flɪp] 1. Klaps m; Ruck m; 2. (-pp-) schnippen, schnipsen.

flip·pant □ ['flɪpənt] respektlos, schnodd(e)rig.

flip·per ['flɪpə] zo. Flosse f; Sport: (Schwimm)Flosse f.

flirt [flɜːt] 1. flirten; = flip 2; 2. be a ~ gern flirten; **flir·ta·tion** [flɜː'teɪʃn] Flirt m.

flit [flɪt] (-tt-) flitzen, huschen.

float [fləʊt] 1. Schwimmer m; Floß n; Plattformwagen m; 2. v/t. überfluten; flößen; tragen (Wasser); ⚓ flott machen; fig. in Gang bringen; econ. Gesellschaft gründen; econ. Wertpapiere etc. in Umlauf bringen; verbreiten; v/i. schwimmen, treiben; schweben; umlaufen, in Umlauf sein; **~ing** ['fləʊtɪŋ] 1. schwimmend, treibend, Schwimm...; econ. umlaufend (Geld etc.); flexibel (Wechselkurs); frei konvertierbar (Währung); ~ voter pol. Wechselwähler m; 2. econ. Floating n.

flock [flɒk] 1. Herde f (bsd. Schafe od. Ziegen) (a. fig.); Schar f; △ nicht Flocke; 2. sich scharen; zs.-strömen.

floe [fləʊ] (treibende) Eisscholle.

flog [flɒg] (-gg-) peitschen; prügeln; **~ging** ['flɒgɪŋ] Tracht f Prügel.

flood [flʌd] 1. a. ~-tide Flut f; Überschwemmung f; 2. überfluten, überschwemmen; **~·gate** ['flʌdgeɪt] Schleusentor n; **~·light** ⚡ Flutlicht n.

floor [flɔː] 1. (Fuß)Boden m; Stock (-werk n) m; Tanzfläche f; ✗ Tenne f; first ~ Brt. erster Stock; Am. Erdgeschoß n; second ~ Brt. zweiter Stock, Am. erster Stock; ~ leader Am. parl. Fraktionsvorsitzende(r) m; ~ show Nachtklubvor-

stellung f; take the ~ das Wort ergreifen; 2. dielen; zu Boden schlagen; verblüffen; **~·board** ['flɔːbɔːd] (Fußboden)Diele f; **~cloth** Putzlappen m; **~ing** [~rɪŋ] Dielung f; Fußboden m; **~ lamp** Stehlampe f; **~·walk·er** Am. = shopwalker.

flop [flɒp] 1. (-pp-) schlagen; flattern; (hin)plumpsen; sich fallen lassen; F durchfallen, danebengehen, ein Reinfall sein; 2. Plumps m; F Flop m, Mißerfolg m, Reinfall m, Pleite f; Versager m.

flor·id □ ['flɒrɪd] rot, gerötet.

flor·ist ['flɒrɪst] Blumenhändler m.

flounce[1] [flaʊns] Volant m.

flounce[2] [~]: ~ off davonstürzen.

floun·der[1] zo. ['flaʊndə] Flunder f.

floun·der[2] [~] zappeln; strampeln; fig. sich verhaspeln.

flour ['flaʊə] (feines) Mehl.

flour·ish ['flʌrɪʃ] 1. Schnörkel m; schwungvolle Bewegung; ♪ Tusch m; 2. v/i. blühen, gedeihen; v/t. schwenken.

flout [flaʊt] (ver)spotten.

flow [fləʊ] 1. Fließen n, Strömen n (beide a. fig.), Rinnen n; Fluß m, Strom m (beide a. fig.); ⚓ Flut f; 2. fließen, strömen, rinnen; wallen (Haar).

flow·er ['flaʊə] 1. Blume f; Blüte f (a. fig.); Zierde f; 2. blühen; **~·bed** Blumenbeet n; **~·pot** Blumentopf m; **~y** [~rɪ] (-ier, -iest) Blumen...; fig. blumig (Stil).

flown [fləʊn] p.p. von fly 2.

fluc·tu·ate ['flʌktjʊeɪt] schwanken; **~·a·tion** [flʌktjʊ'eɪʃn] Schwankung f.

flu F [fluː] Grippe f.

flue [fluː] Rauchfang m, Esse f.

flu·en·cy fig. ['fluːənsɪ] Fluß m; **~t** □ [~t] fließend; flüssig; gewandt (Redner).

fluff [flʌf] 1. Flaum m; Flocke f; fig. Schnitzer m; 2. Kissen aufschütteln; Federn aufplustern (Vogel); **~y** ['flʌfɪ] (-ier, -iest) flaumig; flockig.

flu·id ['fluːɪd] 1. flüssig; 2. Flüssigkeit f.

flung [flʌŋ] pret. u. p.p. von fling 2.

flunk Am. fig. F [flʌŋk] durchfallen (lassen).

flu·o·res·cent [flʊə'resnt] fluoreszierend.

flur·ry ['flʌrɪ] Nervosität f; Bö f;

Am. a. (Regen)Schauer *m*; Schnee-
gestöber *n*.

flush [flʌʃ] **1.** ⊕ in gleicher Ebene;
reichlich; (über)voll; **2.** Erröten *n*;
Erregung *f*; Spülung *f*; (Wasser-)
Spülung *f* (*in der Toilette*); **3.** *v/t. a.* ~
out (aus)spülen; ~ **down** hinunter-
spülen; ~ **the toilet** spülen; *v/i.* erröten, rot werden; spülen (*Toilette od.
Toilettenbenutzer*).

flus·ter ['flʌstə] **1.** Aufregung *f*; **2.**
nervös machen, durcheinanderbrin-
gen.

flute [fluːt] **1.** ♪ Flöte *f*; Falte *f*; **2.** (auf
der) Flöte spielen; riefeln; fälteln.

flut·ter ['flʌtə] **1.** Geflatter *n*; Erregung *f*; ✝ Spekulation *f*; **2.** *v/t.*
aufregen; *v/i.* flattern.

flux *fig.* [flʌks] Fluß *m*.

fly [flaɪ] **1.** *zo.* Fliege *f*; Flug *m*;
Hosenschlitz *m*; Zeltklappe *f*; **2.**
(*flew, flown*) fliegen (lassen); stürmen, stürzen; flattern, wehen; ver-
fliegen (*Zeit*); *Drachen* steigen lassen; ✈ überfliegen; ~ **at** *s.o.* auf j-n
losgehen; ~ **into a passion** od. **rage**
in Wut geraten; **~·er** ['flaɪə] Flieger
m; *Am.* Flugblatt *n*, Reklamezettel
m; **~·ing** [~ɪŋ] fliegend; Flug...; ~
saucer fliegende Untertasse; ~
squad Überfallkommando *n* (*der
Polizei*); **~·o·ver** *Brt.* (Straßen-, Eisenbahn)Überführung *f*; **~·weight**
Boxen: Fliegengewicht(ler *m*) *n*;
~·wheel Schwungrad *n*.

foal *zo.* [fəʊl] Fohlen *n*.

foam [fəʊm] **1.** Schaum *m*; ~ **rubber**
Schaumgummi *m*; **2.** schäumen; **~·y**
['fəʊmɪ] (*-ier, -iest*) schaumig.

fo·cus ['fəʊkəs] **1.** (*pl.* -*cuses*, -*ci*
[-saɪ]) (sich) im Brennpunkt vereini-
gen; *opt.* einstellen (*a. fig.*); konzentrieren.

fod·der ['fɒdə] (Trocken)Futter *n*.

foe *poet.* [fəʊ] Feind *m*, Gegner *m*.

fog [fɒg] **1.** (dichter) Nebel; *fig.* Um-
nebelung *f*; *phot.* Schleier *m*; **2.**
(*-gg-*) *mst fig.* umnebeln; *phot.* verschleiern; **~·gy** □ ['fɒgɪ] (*-ier, -iest*)
neb(e)lig; *fig.* verschwommen.

foi·ble *fig.* ['fɔɪbl] (kleine) Schwäche *f*.

foil[1] [fɔɪl] Folie *f*; *fig.* Hintergrund *m*.

foil[2] [~] vereiteln.

foil[3] [~] *Fechten:* Florett *n*.

fold[1] [fəʊld] **1.** Schafhürde *f*; *fig.*
Herde *f*; **2.** einpferchen.

fold[2] [~] **1.** Falte *f*; Falz *m*; **2.** ...fach,
...fältig; **3.** *v/t.* falten; falzen; *Arme*

kreuzen; ~ (**up**) einwickeln; *v/i.* sich
falten; *Am.* ✝ eingehen; **~·er** ['fəʊldə]
Mappe *f*, Schnellhefter *m*; Faltpro-
spekt *m*.

fold·ing ['fəʊldɪŋ] zusammenlegbar;
Klapp...; ~ **bed** Klappbett *n*; ~
bi·cy·cle Klapprad *n*; ~ **boat** Falt-
boot *n*; ~ **chair** Klappstuhl *m*; ~
door(s *pl.*) Falttür *f*.

fo·li·age ['fəʊlɪɪdʒ] Laub(werk) *n*.

folk [fəʊk] *pl.* Leute *pl.*; *adj. Volks-* *F m-e*
etc. Leute *pl.* (*Angehörige*); △ *nicht
Volk*; **~·lore** ['fəʊklɔː] Volkskunde *f*;
Volkssagen *pl.*; **~·song** Volkslied *n*;
Folksong *m*.

fol·low ['fɒləʊ] folgen (*dat.*); folgen
auf (*acc.*); be-, verfolgen; *s-m Beruf
etc.* nachgehen; ~ **through** *Plan etc.*
bis zum Ende durchführen; ~ **up** *e-r
Sache* nachgehen; *e-e Sache* weiter-
verfolgen; **~·er** [~ə] Nachfolger(in);
Verfolger(in); Anhänger(in); **~·ing**
[~ɪŋ] **1.** Anhängerschaft *f*, Anhänger
pl.; Gefolge *n*; *the* ~ das Folgende;
die Folgenden *pl.*; **2.** folgende(r, -s);
3. im Anschluß an (*acc.*).

fol·ly ['fɒlɪ] Torheit *f*; Narrheit *f*.

fond □ [fɒnd] zärtlich; vernarrt (*of* in
acc.); *be* ~ *of* gern haben, lieben;
fon·dle ['fɒndl] liebkosen; streicheln; (ver)hätscheln; **~·ness** [~nɪs]
Liebe *f*, Zuneigung *f*; Vorliebe *f*.

font [fɒnt] Taufstein *m*; *Am.* Quelle *f*.

food [fuːd] Speise *f*, Nahrung *f*;
Essen *n*; Futter *n*; Lebensmittel *pl.*

fool [fuːl] **1.** Narr *m*, Närrin *f*,
Dummkopf *m*; *make a* ~ *of s.o.* j-n
zum Narren halten; *make a* ~ *of o.s.*
sich lächerlich machen; **2.** *Am.* F
närrisch, dumm; **3.** *v/t.* narren; betrügen (*out of* um *et.*); ~ **away** F
vertrödeln; *v/i.* herumalbern; (herum)spielen; ~(**a**)**round** *bsd. Am.* Zeit
vertrödeln.

fool·e·ry ['fuːlərɪ] Torheit *f*; **~·har·dy**
□ [~hɑːdɪ] tollkühn; **~·ish** □ [~ɪʃ]
dumm, töricht; unklug; **~·ish·ness**
[~ɪʃnɪs] Dummheit *f*; **~·proof** kin-
derleicht; todsicher.

foot [fʊt] **1.** (*pl.* **feet**) Fuß *m* (*a. Maß
= 0,3048 m*); Fußende *n*; ✗ Infante-
rie *f*; *on* ~ zu Fuß; im Gange, in
Gang; **2.** *mst* ~ **up** addieren; ~ *it* zu
Fuß gehen; **~·ball** ['fʊtbɔːl] *Brt.*
Fußball(spiel *n*) *m*; *Am.* Football
(-spiel *n*) *m*; *Brt.* Fußball *m*; *Am.*
Football-Ball *m*; **~·board** Trittbrett

n; **~bridge** Fußgängerbrücke f; **~fall** Tritt m, Schritt m (*Geräusch*); **~gear** Schuhwerk n; **~hold** fester Stand; *fig.* Halt m.

foot·ing ['fʊtɪŋ] Halt m, Stand m; Grundlage f, Basis f; Stellung f; fester Fuß; Verhältnis n; ✕ Zustand m; Endsumme f; *on a friendly ~ with s.o.* ein gutes Verhältnis zu j-m haben; *lose one's ~* ausgleiten.

foot|lights *thea.* ['fʊtlaɪts] *pl.* Rampenlicht(er *pl.*) n; Bühne f; **~loose** frei, unbeschwert; **~ and fancy-free** frei u. ungebunden; **~path** (Fuß-)Pfad m; **~print** Fußabdruck m; **~s** *pl. a.* Fußspur(en *pl.*) f; **~sore** wund an den Füßen; **~step** Tritt m, Schritt m; Fußstapfe f; **~wear** = footgear.

fop [fɒp] Geck m, Fatzke m.

for [fɔ:, fə] **1.** *prp.* meist für; *Zweck, Ziel, Richtung:* zu; nach; *warten, hoffen etc.* auf (*acc.*); *sich sehnen etc.* nach; *Grund, Anlaß:* aus, vor (*dat.*), wegen; *Zeitdauer:* ~ *three days* drei Tage (lang); seit drei Tagen; *Entfernung: I walked ~ a mile* ich ging eine Meile (weit); *Austausch:* (an)statt; *in der Eigenschaft* als; *I ~ one* ich zum Beispiel; ~ *sure* sicher!, gewiß!; **2.** *cj.* denn.

for·age ['fɒrɪdʒ] *a.* ~ *about* (herum-) stöbern, (-)wühlen (*in* in *dat.*; *for* nach).

for·ay ['fɒreɪ] räuberischer Einfall.

for·bear¹ [fɔ:'beə] (*-bore, -borne*) *v/t.* unterlassen; *v/i.* sich enthalten (*from gen.*); Geduld haben.

for·bear² ['fɔːbeə] Vorfahr m.

for·bid [fə'bɪd] (*-dd-; -bade od. -bad* [-bæd], *-bidden od. -bid*) verbieten; hindern; **~ding** □ [~ɪŋ] abstoßend.

force [fɔːs] **1.** Stärke f, Kraft f, Gewalt f; Nachdruck m; Zwang m; Heer n; Streitmacht f; *in ~* in großer Zahl *od.* Menge; *the (police)* ~ die Polizei; *armed* ~s *pl.* (Gesamt)Streitkräfte *pl.*; *come (put) in(to)* ~ in Kraft treten (setzen); **2.** zwingen, nötigen; erzwingen; aufzwingen; Gewalt antun (*dat.*); beschleunigen; aufbrechen; künstlich reif machen; ~ *open* aufbrechen; **~d:** ~ *landing* Notlandung f; ~ *march* bsd. ✕ Gewaltmarsch m; **~ful** □ ['fɔːsfl] energisch, kraftvoll (*Person*); eindrucksvoll, überzeugend.

for·ceps 🔬 ['fɔːseps] Zange f.

for·ci·ble □ ['fɔːsəbl] gewaltsam; Zwangs...; eindringlich; wirksam.

ford [fɔːd] **1.** Furt f; **2.** durchwaten.

fore [fɔː] **1.** *adv.* vorn; **2.** Vorderteil m, n; *come to the* ~ sich hervortun; **3.** *adj.* vorder; Vorder...; **~arm** ['fɔːrɑːm] Unterarm m; **~bear** [fɔː'beə] = forebear²; **~bod·ing** [fɔː'bəʊdɪŋ] (böses) Vorzeichen; Ahnung f; **~cast** ['fɔːkɑːst] **1.** Vorhersage f; **2.** (*-cast od. -casted*) vorhersagen; voraussagen; **~fa·ther** Vorfahr m; **~fin·ger** Zeigefinger m; **~foot** (*pl. -feet*) zo. Vorderfuß m; **~gone** ['fɔːgɒn] von vornherein feststehend; ~ *conclusion* ausgemachte Sache, Selbstverständlichkeit f; **~ground** ['fɔːgraʊnd] Vordergrund m; **~hand 1.** *Sport:* Vorhand(schlag m) f; **2.** *Sport:* Vorhand...; **~head** ['fɒrɪd] Stirn f.

for·eign ['fɒrən] fremd, ausländisch, -wärtig, Auslands...; Außen...; ~ *affairs* Außenpolitik f; ~ *language* Fremdsprache f; ~ *minister pol.* Außenminister m; ♀ *Office Brt. pol.* Außenministerium n; ~ *policy* Außenpolitik f; ♀ *Secretary Brt. pol.* Außenminister m; ~ *trade econ.* Außenhandel m; ~ *worker* Gastarbeiter m; **~er** [~ə] Ausländer(in), Fremde(r m) f.

fore|knowl·edge ['fɔː'nɒlɪdʒ] Vorherwissen n; **~leg** zo. ['fɔːleg] Vorderbein n; **~man** (*pl. -men*) ⚖ Obmann m; Vorarbeiter m, (Werk-) Meister m, Polier m, ⚒ Steiger m; **~most** vorderste(r, -s), erste(r, -s); **~name** Vorname m; **~run·ner** Vorläufer(in); **~see** [fɔː'siː] (*-saw, -seen*) vorhersehen; **~shad·ow** ahnen lassen, andeuten; **~sight** ['fɔːsaɪt] *fig.* Weitblick m, (weise) Voraussicht.

for·est ['fɒrɪst] **1.** Wald m (*a. fig.*), Forst m; ~ *ranger Am.* Förster m; **2.** aufforsten.

fore·stall [fɔː'stɔːl] *et.* vereiteln; j-m zuvorkommen.

for·est|er ['fɒrɪstə] Förster m; Waldarbeiter m; **~ry** [~rɪ] Forstwirtschaft f; Waldgebiet n.

fore|taste ['fɔːteɪst] Vorgeschmack m; **~tell** [fɔː'tel] (*-told*) vorhersagen; **~thought** ['fɔːθɔːt] Vorsorge f, -bedacht m.

for·ev·er, for ev·er [fə'revə] für immer.

fore|wom·an (*pl.* -women) Aufseherin *f*; Vorarbeiterin *f*; **~word** Vorwort *n*.

for·feit ['fɔːfɪt] **1.** Verwirkung *f*; Strafe *f*; Pfand *n*; **2.** verwirken; einbüßen.

forge¹ [fɔːdʒ] *mst* ~ *ahead* sich vor(wärts)arbeiten.

forge² [~] **1.** Schmiede *f*; **2.** schmieden (*fig. sich ausdenken*); fälschen; **forg·er** ['fɔːdʒə] Fälscher; **for·ge·ry** [~ərɪ] Fälschen *n*; Fälschung *f*.

for·get [fə'get] (*-got, -gotten*) vergessen; **~·ful** □ [~fl] vergeßlich; **~·me-not** ♣ Vergißmeinnicht *n*.

for·give [fə'gɪv] (*-gave, -given*) vergeben, -zeihen; *Schuld* erlassen; **~·ness** [~nɪs] Verzeihung *f*; **for·giv·ing** □ [~ɪŋ] versöhnlich; nachsichtig.

for·go [fɔː'gəʊ] (*-went, -gone*) verzichten auf (*acc.*).

fork [fɔːk] **1.** (Eß-, Heu-, Mist-*etc.*)Gabel *f*; **2.** (sich) gabeln; **~ed** gegabelt, gespalten; **~·lift** ['fɔːklɪft], *a.* **~ truck** Gabelstapler *m*.

for·lorn [fə'lɔːn] verloren, -lassen.

form [fɔːm] **1.** Form *f*; Gestalt *f*; Formalität *f*; Formular *n*; (Schul-)Bank *f* (Schul)Klasse *f*; Kondition *f*; geistige Verfassung; **2.** (sich) formen, (sich) bilden, gestalten; ✕ (sich) aufstellen.

form·al □ ['fɔːml] förmlich; formell; äußerlich; **for·mal·i·ty** [fɔː'mælətɪ] Förmlichkeit *f*; Formalität *f*.

for·ma|tion [fɔː'meɪʃn] Bildung *f*; **~·tive** ['fɔːmətɪv] bildend; gestaltend; ~ *years pl.* Entwicklungsjahre *pl.*

for·mer ['fɔːmə] vorig, früher; ehemalig, vergangen; erstere(r, -s); jene(r, -s); **~·ly** [~lɪ] ehemals, früher.

for·mi·da·ble □ ['fɔːmɪdəbl] furchtbar, schrecklich; ungeheuer.

for·mu|la ['fɔːmjʊlə] (*pl.* -las, -lae [-liː]) Formel *f*; Rezept *n* (*zur Zubereitung*); ⚠ *nicht Formular*; **~·late** [~leɪt] formulieren.

for|sake [fə'seɪk] (*-sook, -saken*) aufgeben; verlassen; **~·sak·en** [~ən] *p.p. von forsake*; **~·sook** [fə'sʊk] *pret. von forsake*; **~·swear** [fɔː'sweə] (*-swore, -sworn*) abschwören, entsagen.

fort ✕ [fɔːt] Fort *n*, Festung *f*.

forth [fɔːθ] vor(wärts), voran; heraus, hinaus, hervor; weiter, fort;

~·com·ing ['fɔː'θkʌmɪŋ] erscheinend; bereit; bevorstehend; *F* entgegenkommend; **~·with** [~'wɪθ] sogleich.

for·ti·eth ['fɔːtɪɪθ] vierzigste(r, -s).

for·ti|fi·ca·tion [fɔːtɪfɪ'keɪʃn] Befestigung *f*; **~·fy** ['fɔːtɪfaɪ] ✕ befestigen; *fig.* (ver)stärken; **~·tude** [~tjuːd] Seelenstärke *f*; Tapferkeit *f*.

fort·night ['fɔːtnaɪt] vierzehn Tage.

for·tress [fɔːtrɪs] Festung *f*.

for·tu·i·tous □ [fɔː'tjuːɪtəs] zufällig.

for·tu·nate ['fɔːtʃnət] glücklich; *be* ~ Glück haben; **~·ly** [~lɪ] glücklicherweise.

for·tune ['fɔːtʃn] Glück *n*; Schicksal *n*; Zufall *m*; Vermögen *n*; **~·tell·er** Wahrsager(in).

for·ty ['fɔːtɪ] **1.** vierzig; **~·niner** *Am. kalifornischer Goldsucher von 1849*; ~ *winks pl. F* Nickerchen *pl.*; **2.** Vierzig *f*.

for·ward ['fɔːwəd] **1.** *adj.* vorder; bereit(willig); fortschrittlich; vorwitzig, keck; **2.** *adv. a.* **~s** vor(wärts); **3.** *Fußball:* Stürmer *m*; **4.** befördern, (ver)senden, schicken; *Brief etc.* nachsenden; **~·ing a·gent** [~ɪŋeɪdʒənt] Spediteur *m*.

fos·ter·child ['fɒstətʃaɪld] (*pl.* -children) Pflegekind *n*; **~·par·ents** *pl.* Pflegeeltern *pl.*

fought [fɔːt] *pret. u. p.p. von fight* 2.

foul [faʊl] **1.** □ stinkend, widerlich, schlecht, übel(riechend); schlecht, stürmisch (*Wetter*); widrig (*Wind*); *Sport:* regelwidrig, unfair; *fig.* widerlich, ekelhaft; *fig.* abscheulich, gemein; ⚠ *nicht faul*; **2.** *Sport:* Foul *n*, Regelverstoß *m*; **3.** *a.* ~ *up* be-, verschmutzen, verunreinigen; *Sport:* foulen.

found [faʊnd] **1.** *pret. u. p.p. von find* 1; **2.** (be)gründen; stiften; ⊕ gießen.

foun·da·tion [faʊn'deɪʃn] *arch.* Grundmauer *f*, Fundament *n*; *fig.* Gründung *f*, Errichtung *f*; (gemeinnützige) Stiftung; *fig.* Grund(lage *f*) *m*, Basis *f*.

found·er¹ ['faʊndə] Gründer(in), Stifter(in).

found·er² [~] ⚓ sinken; *fig.* scheitern.

found·ling ['faʊndlɪŋ] Findling *m*.

foun·dry ⊕ ['faʊndrɪ] Gießerei *f*.

foun·tain ['faʊntɪn] Quelle *f*; Springbrunnen *m*; ~ **pen** Füllfederhalter *m*.

four [fɔː] 1. vier; 2. Vier f; *Rudern:* Vierer m; *on all* ~s auf allen vieren; ~**square** [fɔːˈskweə] viereckig; *fig.* unerschütterlich; ~**stroke** [ˈfɔː-strəʊk] *mot.* Viertakt...; ~**teen** [ˈfɔːˈtiːn] 1. vierzehn; 2. Vierzehn f; ~**teenth** [~ˈtiːnθ] vierzehnte(r, -s); ~**th** [fɔːθ] 1. vierte(r, -s); 2. Viertel n; ~**th·ly** [ˈfɔːθlɪ] viertens.

fowl [faʊl] Geflügel n; Huhn n; Vogel m; ~**ing piece** [ˈfaʊlɪŋpiːs] Vogelflinte f.

fox [fɒks] 1. Fuchs m; 2. überlisten; ~**glove** ♀ [ˈfɒksglʌv] Fingerhut m; ~**y** [~sɪ] (*-ier, -iest*) fuchsartig; schlau, gerissen.

frac·tion [ˈfrækʃn] Bruch(teil) m; △ *nicht parl.* Fraktion.

frac·ture [ˈfræktʃə] 1. (*bsd.* Knochen-)Bruch m; 2. brechen.

fra·gile [ˈfrædʒaɪl] zerbrechlich.

frag·ment [ˈfrægmənt] Bruchstück n.

fra·grance [ˈfreɪɡrəns] Wohlgeruch m, Duft m; ~**grant** □ [~t] wohlriechend.

frail □ [freɪl] ge-, zerbrechlich; zart, schwach; ~**ty** [ˈfreɪltɪ] Zartheit f; Zerbrechlichkeit f; Schwäche f.

frame [freɪm] 1. Rahmen m; Gerippe n; Gerüst n; (Brillen)Gestell n; Körper m; (An)Ordnung f; *phot.* (Einzel)Bild n; ✔ Frühbeetkasten m; ~ *of mind* Gemütsverfassung f, Stimmung f; 2. bilden, formen, bauen; entwerfen; (ein)rahmen; sich entwickeln; ~**up** *bsd. Am.* F [ˈfreɪmʌp] abgekartetes Spiel; ~**work** ⊕ Gerippe n; Rahmen m; *fig.* Struktur f, System n.

fran·chise ⚖ [ˈfræntʃaɪz] Wahlrecht n; Bürgerrecht n; *bsd. Am.* Konzession f.

frank [fræŋk] 1. □ frei(mütig), offen; 2. *Brief* maschinell frankieren.

frank·furter [ˈfræŋkfɜːtə] Frankfurter Würstchen n.

frank·ness [ˈfræŋknɪs] Offenheit f.

fran·tic [ˈfræntɪk] (~ally) wahnsinnig.

fra·ter·nal □ [frəˈtɜːnl] brüderlich; ~**ni·ty** [~nətɪ] Brüderlichkeit f; Bruderschaft f; *Am. univ.* Verbindung f.

fraud [frɔːd] Betrug m; F Schwindel m; ~**u·lent** □ [ˈfrɔːdjʊlənt] betrügerisch.

fray [freɪ] (sich) abnutzen; (sich) durchscheuern, (sich) ausfransen.

freak [friːk] 1. Mißbildung f, Mißge-

burt f, Monstrosität f; außergewöhnlicher Umstand; Grille f, Laune f; *mst in Zssgn:* Süchtige(r m) f; Freak m, Narr m, Fanatiker m; ~ *of nature* Laune f der Natur; *film* ~ Kinonarr m, -fan m; 2. ~ *out sl.* ausflippen.

freck·le [ˈfrekl] Sommersprosse f; ~**d** [~d] sommersprossig.

free [friː] 1. □ (~r, ~st) frei; freigebig (*of* mit); freiwillig; *he is* ~ *to inf.* es steht ihm frei, zu *inf.*; ~ *and easy* zwanglos; sorglos; *make* ~ sich Freiheiten erlauben; *set* ~ freilassen; 2. (*freed*) befreien; freilassen, et. freimachen; ~**dom** [ˈfriːdəm] Freiheit f; freie Benutzung; Offenheit f; Zwanglosigkeit f; (plumpe) Vertraulichkeit; ~ *of a city* (Ehren)Bürgerrecht n; ~**hold·er** Grundeigentümer m; ~**lance** frei(beruflich tätig), freischaffend; ♫**ma·son** Freimaurer m; ~**way** *Am.* Schnellstraße f; ~**wheel** ⊕ [friːˈwiːl] 1. Freilauf m; 2. im Freilauf fahren.

freeze [friːz] 1. (*froze, frozen*) v/i. (ge)frieren; erstarren; v/t. gefrieren lassen; *Fleisch etc.* einfrieren, tiefkühlen; *econ. Preise etc.* einfrieren; 2. Frost m, Kälte f; *econ. pol.* Einfrieren n; *wage* ~, *on wages* Lohnstopp m; ~**dry** [friːzˈdraɪ] gefriertrocknen; **freez·er** [ˈfriːzə] a. *deep* ~ Gefriertruhe f, Tiefkühl-, Gefriergerät n; Gefrierfach n; **freez·ing** [~ɪŋ] eisig; ⊕ Gefrier...; ~ *compartment* Gefrier-, Tiefkühlfach n; ~ *point* Gefrierpunkt m.

freight [freɪt] 1. Fracht(geld n) f; *attr. Am.* Güter...; 2. be-, verfrachten; ~ **car** *Am.* 🚃 [ˈfreɪtkɑː] Güterwagen m; ~**er** [~ə] Frachter m, Frachtschiff n; Fracht-, Transportflugzeug n; ~ **train** *Am.* Güterzug m.

French [frentʃ] 1. französisch; *take* ~ *leave* heimlich weggehen; ~ *doors pl. Am.* = *French window(s pl.)*; ~ *fries pl. bsd. Am.* Pommes frites *pl.*; ~ *window(s pl.)* Terrassen-, Balkontür f; 2. *ling.* Französisch n; *the* ~ *pl.* die Franzosen *pl.*; ~**man** [ˈfrentʃmən] (*pl. -men*) Franzose m.

fren·zied [ˈfrenzɪd] wahnsinnig; ~**zy** [~ɪ] wilde Aufregung; Ekstase f; Raserei f.

fre·quen·cy [ˈfriːkwənsɪ] Häufigkeit f; ⚡ Frequenz f; ~**t** 1. □ [~t] häufig; 2. [frɪˈkwent] (oft) besuchen.

fresh □ [freʃ] frisch; neu; unerfahren; *Am.* F frech; **~en** ['freʃn] frisch machen *od.* werden; **~** *up* neuer *od.* schöner machen; **~** (*o.s.*) *up* sich frisch machen; **~man** (*pl. -men*) *univ.* Student *m* im ersten Jahr; **~ness** [~nɪs] Frische *f*; Neuheit *f*; Unerfahrenheit *f*; **~ wa·ter** Süßwasser *n*; **~wa·ter** Süßwasser...

fret [fret] 1. Aufregung *f*; Ärger *m*; ♪ Bund *m*, Griffleiste *f*; 2. (*-tt-*) zerfressen; (sich) ärgern; (sich) grämen; **~** *away*, **~** *out* aufreißen.

fret·ful □ ['fretfl] ärgerlich.

fret·saw ['fretsɔː] Laubsäge *f*.

fret·work ['fretwɜːk] (geschnitztes) Gitterwerk; Laubsägearbeit *f*.

fri·ar ['fraɪə] Mönch *m*.

fric·tion ['frɪkʃn] Reibung *f* (*a. fig.*).

Fri·day ['fraɪdɪ] Freitag *m*.

fridge F [frɪdʒ] Kühlschrank *m*.

friend [frend] Freund(in); Bekannte(r *m*) *f*; *make* ~s with sich anfreunden mit, Freundschaft schließen mit; **~ly** ['frendlɪ] freund(schaft)lich; **~ship** [~ʃɪp] Freundschaft *f*.

frig·ate ♣ ['frɪgɪt] Fregatte *f*.

fright [fraɪt] Schreck(en) *m*; *fig.* Vogelscheuche *f*; **~en** ['fraɪtn] erschrecken; *be* ~*ed of s.th.* vor et. Angst haben; **~en·ing** [~ɪŋ] furchterregend; **~ful** □ [~fl] schrecklich.

fri·gid □ ['frɪdʒɪd] kalt, frostig; *psych.* frigid(e).

frill [frɪl] Krause *f*, Rüsche *f*.

fringe [frɪndʒ] 1. Franse *f*; Rand *m*; Ponyfrisur *f*; ~ *benefits pl. econ.* Gehalts-, Lohnnebenleistungen *pl.*; ~ *event* Randveranstaltung *f*; ~ *group* Soziologie: Randgruppe *f*; 2. mit Fransen besetzen.

Fri·si·an ['frɪzɪən] friesisch.

frisk [frɪsk] 1. Luftsprung *m*; 2. herumtollen; F filzen; *j-n, et.* durchsuchen; **~y** □ ['frɪskɪ] (*-ier, -iest*) lebhaft, munter.

frit·ter ['frɪtə] 1. Pfannkuchen *m*, Krapfen *m*. 2. ~ *away* vertun, -trödeln, -geuden.

fri·vol·i·ty [frɪ'vɒlətɪ] Frivolität *f*, Leichtfertigkeit *f*; **friv·o·lous** □ ['frɪvələs] frivol, leichtfertig.

friz·zle ['frɪzl] *Küche:* brutzeln.

frizz·y □ ['frɪzɪ] (*-ier, -iest*) gekräuselt, kraus (*Haar*).

fro [frəʊ]: *to and* ~ hin und her.

frock [frɒk] Kutte *f*; (*Frauen*)Kleid *n*; Kittel *m*; Gehrock *m*.

frog *zo.* [frɒg] Frosch *m*; **~man** ['frɒgmən] (*pl. -men*) Froschmann *m*.

frol·ic ['frɒlɪk] 1. Herumtoben *n*, -tollen *n*; Ausgelassenheit *f*; Streich *m*, Jux *m*; 2. (*-ck-*) herumtoben, -tollen; **~some** □ [~səm] lustig, fröhlich.

from [frɒm, frəm] von; aus, von ... her; von ... (an); aus, vor, wegen; nach, gemäß; *defend* ~ schützen vor (*dat.*); ~ *amidst* mitten aus.

front [frʌnt] 1. Stirn *f*; Vorderseite *f*; ✕ Front *f*; Hemdbrust *f*; Strandpromenade *f*; Kühnheit *f*, Frechheit *f*; *at the* ~, *in* ~ vorn; *in* ~ *of räumlich* vor; 2. Vorder...; ~ *door* Haustür *f*; ~ *entrance* Vordereingang *m*; 3. *a.* ~ *on*, ~ *towards* die Front haben von; gegenüberstehen, gegenübertreten (*dat.*); **~age** ['frʌntɪdʒ] (Vorder-) Front *f* (*e-s Hauses*); **~al** □ [~tl] Stirn...; Front..., Vorder...

fron·tier [frʌn'tɪə] (Landes)Grenze *f*; *Am. hist.* Grenzland *n*, Grenze *f* (*zum Wilden Westen*); *attr.* Grenz...

front| page ['frʌntpeɪdʒ] *Zeitung:* Titelseite *f*; **~-wheel drive** *mot.* Vorderradantrieb *m*.

frost [frɒst] 1. Frost *m*; *a. hoar* ~, *white* ~ Reif *m*; 2. (mit Zucker) bestreuen, glasieren, mattieren; ~*ed glass* Milchglas *n*; **~bite** ['frɒstbaɪt] Erfrierung *f*; **~bit·ten** erfroren; **~y** □ [~ɪ] (*-ier, -iest*) eisig, frostig (*a. fig.*).

froth [frɒθ] 1. Schaum *m*; 2. schäumen; zu Schaum schlagen; **~y** □ ['frɒθɪ] (*-ier, -iest*) schäumend, schaumig; *fig.* seicht.

frown [fraʊn] 1. Stirnrunzeln *n*; finsterer Blick; 2. *v*/*i.* die Stirn runzeln; finster blicken; ~ *on od. upon s.th.* et. mißbilligen.

froze [frəʊz] *pret. von* freeze 1; **fro·zen** ['frəʊzn] 1. *p.p. von* freeze 1; 2. *adj.* (eis)kalt; (ein-, zu)gefroren; Gefrier...; ~ *food* Tiefkühlkost *f*.

fru·gal □ ['fruːgl] einfach; sparsam.

fruit [fruːt] 1. Frucht *f*; Früchte *pl.*; Obst *n*; 2. Frucht tragen; **~er·er** ['fruːtərə] Obsthändler *m*; **~ful** □ [~fl] fruchtbar; **~less** □ [~lɪs] unfruchtbar; **~y** [~ɪ] (*-ier, -iest*) frucht-, obstartig; fruchtig (*Wein*); klangvoll, sonor (*Stimme*).

frus|trate [frʌˈstreɪt] vereiteln; enttäuschen; frustrieren; **~·tra·tion** [~eɪʃn] Vereitelung f; Enttäuschung f; Frustration f.

fry [fraɪ] **1.** Gebratene(s) n; Fischbrut f; **2.** braten, backen; **~·ing-pan** [ˈfraɪŋpæn] Bratpfanne f.

fuch·sia ♀ [ˈfjuːʃə] Fuchsie f.

fuck V [fʌk] **1.** ficken, vögeln; ~ it! Scheiße!; get ~ed! der Teufel soll dich holen!; **2.** int. Scheiße!; **~·ing** V [ˈfʌkɪŋ] Scheiß..., verflucht, -dammt (oft nur verstärkend); ~ hell! verdammte Scheiße!

fudge [fʌdʒ] **1.** F zurechtpfuschen; **2.** Unsinn m; Art Fondant m.

fu·el [ˈfjʊəl] **1.** Brennmaterial n; Betriebs-, mot. Kraftstoff m; **2.** (bsd. Brt. -ll-, Am. -l-) mot., ✈ (auf)tanken.

fu·gi·tive [ˈfjuːdʒɪtɪv] **1.** flüchtig (a. fig.); **2.** Flüchtling m.

ful·fil, Am. a. **-fill** [fʊlˈfɪl] (-ll-) erfüllen; vollziehen; **~·ment** [~mənt] Erfüllung f.

full [fʊl] **1.** □ voll; Voll...; vollständig, völlig; reichlich; ausführlich; of ~ age volljährig; **2.** adv. völlig, ganz; genau; **3.** das Ganze; Höhepunkt m; in ~ völlig; ausführlich; to the ~ vollständig; **~·blood·ed** [ˈfʊlblʌdɪd] vollblütig; kräftig; reinrassig; **~ dress** Gesellschaftsanzug m; **~ dress** formell; Gala...; **~·fledged** Am. = fully-fledged; **~·grown** ausgewachsen; **~·length** in voller Größe; bodenlang; abendfüllend (Film etc.); **~ moon** Vollmond m; **~ stop** ling. Punkt m; ~ time Sport: Spielende n; **~·time** ganztägig, Ganztags...; ~ job Ganztagsbeschäftigung f.

ful·ly [ˈfʊlɪ] voll, völlig, ganz; **~·fledged** flügge; fig. richtig; **~·grown** Brt. = full-grown.

fum·ble [ˈfʌmbl] tasten; fummeln.

fume [fjuːm] **1.** rauchen; aufgebracht sein; **2.** ~s pl. Dämpfe pl., Dünste pl.

fu·mi·gate [ˈfjuːmɪɡeɪt] ausräuchern, desinfizieren.

fun [fʌn] Scherz m, Spaß m; make ~ of sich lustig machen über (acc.).

func·tion [ˈfʌŋkʃn] **1.** Funktion f; Beruf m; Tätigkeit f; Aufgabe f; Feierlichkeit f; **2.** funktionieren; **~·a·ry** [~ərɪ] Funktionär m.

fund [fʌnd] **1.** Fonds m; ~s pl. Staatspapiere pl.; Geld(mittel pl.) n; a ~ of fig. ein Vorrat an (dat.); **2.** Schuld fundieren; Geld anlegen; das Kapital aufbringen für.

fun·da·men·tal □ [fʌndəˈmentl] **1.** grundlegend; Grund...; **2.** ~s pl. Grundlage f, -züge pl., -begriffe pl.

fu·ne|ral [ˈfjuːnərəl] Beerdigung f; attr. Trauer..., Begräbnis...; **~·re·al** □ [fjuːˈnɪərɪəl] traurig, düster.

fun-fair [ˈfʌnfeə] Rummelplatz m.

fu·nic·u·lar [fjuːˈnɪkjʊlə] a. ~ railway (Draht)Seilbahn f.

fun·nel [ˈfʌnl] Trichter m; Rauchfang m; ♣, 🚂 Schornstein m.

fun·nies Am. [ˈfʌnɪz] pl. Comics pl.

fun·ny □ [ˈfʌnɪ] (-ier, -iest) lustig, spaßig, komisch.

fur [fɜː] **1.** Pelz m; Belag m (auf der Zunge); Kesselstein m; ~s pl. Pelzwaren pl.; **2.** mit Pelz besetzen od. füttern.

fur·bish [ˈfɜːbɪʃ] putzen, polieren.

fu·ri·ous □ [ˈfjʊərɪəs] wütend; wild.

furl [fɜːl] Fahne, Segel auf-, einrollen; Schirm zusammenrollen.

fur·lough ✕ [ˈfɜːləʊ] Urlaub m.

fur·nace [ˈfɜːnɪs] Schmelz-, Hochofen m; (Heiz)Kessel m.

fur·nish [ˈfɜːnɪʃ] versehen (with mit); et. liefern; möblieren; ausstatten.

fur·ni·ture [ˈfɜːnɪtʃə] Möbel pl., Einrichtung f; Ausstattung f; sectional ~ Anbaumöbel pl.

fur·ri·er [ˈfʌrɪə] Kürschner m.

fur·row [ˈfʌrəʊ] **1.** Furche f; **2.** furchen.

fur·ry [ˈfɜːrɪ] aus Pelz, pelzartig; belegt (Zunge).

fur·ther [ˈfɜːðə] **1.** comp. von far; **2.** fördern; **~·ance** [~rəns] Förderung f; **~·more** [~ˈmɔː] ferner, überdies; **~·most** [~məʊst] weiteste(r, -s), entfernteste(r, -s).

fur·thest [ˈfɜːðɪst] sup. von far.

fur·tive □ [ˈfɜːtɪv] verstohlen.

fu·ry [ˈfjʊərɪ] Raserei f, Wut f; Furie f.

fuse [fjuːz] **1.** schmelzen; ⚡ durchbrennen; ⚡ Sicherung f; Zünder m; Zündschnur f.

fu·se·lage ✈ [ˈfjuːzɪlɑːʒ] (Flugzeug-) Rumpf m.

fu·sion [ˈfjuːʒn] Verschmelzung f, Fusion f; nuclear ~ Kernfusion f.

fuss F [fʌs] **1.** Lärm m; Wesen n; Getue n; **2.** viel Aufhebens machen (about um, von); (sich) aufregen; **~·y**

☐ ['fʌsɪ] (-ier, -iest) aufgeregt, hektisch; kleinlich, pedantisch; heikel, wählerisch.

fus·ty ['fʌstɪ] (-ier, -iest) muffig; *fig.* verstaubt.

fu·tile ☐ ['fju:taɪl] nutz-, zwecklos.

fu·ture ['fju:tʃə] **1.** (zu)künftig; **2.** Zukunft *f*; *gr.* Futur *n*, Zukunft *f*; *in* ~ in Zukunft, künftig.

fuzz[1] [fʌz] **1.** feiner Flaum; Fusseln *pl.*; **2.** fusseln, (zer)fasern.

fuzz[2] *sl.* [~] Bulle *m* (*Polizist*).

G

gab F [gæb] Geschwätz *n*; *have the gift of the* ~ ein gutes Mundwerk haben.

gab·ar·dine ['gæbədi:n] Gabardine *m* (*Wollstoff*).

gab·ble ['gæbl] **1.** Geschnatter *n*, Geschwätz *n*; **2.** schnattern, schwatzen.

gab·er·dine ['gæbədi:n] *hist.* Kaftan *m* (*der Juden*); = gabardine.

ga·ble *arch.* ['geɪbl] Giebel *m*.

gad F [gæd] (-dd-): ~ about, ~ around (viel) unterwegs sein (in *dat.*).

gad·fly *zo.* ['gædflaɪ] Bremse *f*.

gad·get ⊕ ['gædʒɪt] Apparat *m*, Gerät *n*, Vorrichtung *f*; *oft contp.* technische Spielerei.

gag [gæg] **1.** Knebel *m* (*a. fig.*); F Gag *m*; **2.** (-gg-) knebeln; *fig.* mundtot machen.

gage *Am.* [geɪdʒ] = gauge; △ *nicht* Gage.

gai·e·ty ['geɪətɪ] Fröhlichkeit *f*.

gai·ly ['geɪlɪ] *adv. von* gay 1.

gain [geɪn] **1.** Gewinn *m*; Vorteil *m*; **2.** gewinnen; erreichen; bekommen; zunehmen an (*dat.*); vorgehen (um) (*Uhr*); ~ in zunehmen an (*dat.*).

gait [geɪt] Gang(art *f*) *m*; Schritt *m*.

gai·ter ['geɪtə] Gamasche *f*.

gal F [gæl] Mädel *n*.

gal·ax·y *ast.* ['gæləksɪ] Milchstraße *f*, Galaxis *f*.

gale [geɪl] Sturm *m*.

gall [gɔ:l] **1.** *veraltet* Galle *f*; wundgeriebene Stelle; F Frechheit *f*; **2.** wund reiben; ärgern.

gal·lant ['gælənt] stattlich; tapfer; galant, höflich; ~**lan·try** [~rɪ] Tapferkeit *f*; Galanterie *f*.

gal·le·ry ['gælərɪ] Galerie *f*; Empore *f*.

gal|ley ['gælɪ] ⊕ Galeere *f*; ⊕ Kom-

büse *f*; *a.* ~ *proof print.* Fahne(nabzug *m*) *f*.

gal·lon ['gælən] Gallone *f* (4,54 Liter, *Am.* 3,78 Liter).

gal·lop ['gæləp] **1.** Galopp *m*; **2.** galoppieren (lassen).

gal·lows ['gæləʊz] *sg.* Galgen *m*.

ga·lore [gə'lɔ:] in rauhen Mengen.

gam·ble ['gæmbl] **1.** (um Geld) spielen; **2.** F Glücksspiel *n*; ~**r** [~ə] Spieler(in).

gam·bol ['gæmbl] **1.** Luftsprung *m*; **2.** (*bsd. Brt.* -ll-, *Am.* -l-) (herum-) tanzen, (-)hüpfen.

game [geɪm] **1.** (Karten-, Ball-*etc.*)Spiel *n*; (einzelnes) Spiel (*a. fig.*); *hunt.* Wild *n*; Wildbret *n*; ~**s** *pl.* Spiele *pl.*; *Schule:* Sport *m*; **2.** mutig; bereit (*for* zu; *to do* zu tun); ~**keep·er** ['geɪmki:pə] Wildhüter *m*.

gam·mon *bsd. Brt.* ['gæmən] schwachgepökelter *od.* -geräucherter Schinken.

gan·der *zo.* ['gændə] Gänserich *m*.

gang [gæŋ] **1.** (Arbeiter)Trupp *m*; Gang *f*, Bande *f*; Clique *f*; Horde *f*; △ *nicht* der Gang; **2.** ~ up sich zusammentun, *contp.* sich zusammenrotten.

gang·ster ['gæŋstə] Gangster *m*.

gang·way ['gæŋweɪ] (Durch)Gang *m*; ⊕ Fallreep *n*; ⊕ Laufplanke *f*.

gaol [dʒeɪl], ~**bird** ['dʒeɪlbɜ:d], ~**er** [~ə] *s.* jail *etc.*

gap [gæp] Lücke *f*; Kluft *f*; Spalte *f*.

gape [geɪp] gähnen; klaffen; gaffen.

gar·age ['gærɑ:ʒ] **1.** Garage *f*; (Reparatur)Werkstatt *f* (u. Tankstelle *f*); **2.** Auto in e-r Garage ab- *od.* unterstellen; Auto in die Garage fahren.

gar·bage *bsd. Am.* ['gɑ:bɪdʒ] Abfall *m*, Müll *m*; ~ *can* Abfall-, Mülleimer *m;* Abfall-, Mülltonne *f;* ~ *truck* Müllwagen *m.*

gar·den ['gɑ:dn] **1.** Garten *m;* **2.** im Garten arbeiten; Gartenbau treiben; **~·er** [~ə] Gärtner(in); **~·ing** [~ɪŋ] Gartenarbeit *f.*

gar·gle ['gɑ:gl] **1.** gurgeln; **2.** Gurgeln *n;* Gurgelwasser *n.*

gar·ish □ ['geərɪʃ] grell, auffallend.

gar·land ['gɑ:lənd] Girlande *f.*

gar·lic ♀ ['gɑ:lɪk] Knoblauch *m.*

gar·ment ['gɑ:mənt] Gewand *n.*

gar·nish ['gɑ:nɪʃ] garnieren; zieren.

gar·ret ['gærət] Dachstube *f.*

gar·ri·son ✕ ['gærɪsn] Garnison *f.*

gar·ru·lous □ ['gærələs] schwatzhaft.

gar·ter ['gɑ:tə] Strumpfband *n;* *Am.* Socken-, Strumpfhalter *m.*

gas [gæs] **1.** Gas *n;* *Am.* F Benzin *n;* **2.** (-ss-) *v/t.* vergasen; *v/i.* F faseln; *a.* ~ *up Am.* F *mot.* (auf)tanken; **~·e·ous** ['gæsjəs] gasförmig.

gash [gæʃ] **1.** klaffende Wunde; Hieb *m;* Riß *m;* **2.** tief (ein)schneiden in *(acc.).*

gas·ket ⊕ ['gæskɪt] Dichtung *f.*

gas·light ['gæslaɪt] Gasbeleuchtung *f;* **~ me·ter** Gasuhr *f;* **~·o·lene**, **~·o·line** *Am.* ['~əliːn] Benzin *n.*

gasp [gɑ:sp] **1.** Keuchen *n,* schweres Atmen; **2.** keuchen; ~ *for breath* nach Luft schnappen, nach Atem ringen.

gas sta·tion *Am.* ['gæssteɪʃn] Tankstelle *f;* **~ stove** Gasofen *m,* -herd *m;* **~·works** *sg.* Gaswerk *n.*

gate [geɪt] Tor *n;* Pforte *f;* Schranke *f,* Sperre *f;* ✈ Flugsteig *m;* **~·crash** ['geɪtkræʃ] uneingeladen kommen *od.* (hin)gehen (zu); sich ohne zu bezahlen hinein- *od.* hereinschmuggeln; sich ohne zu bezahlen schmuggeln in *(acc.);* **~·post** Tor-, Türpfosten *m;* **~·way** Tor(weg *m) n,* Einfahrt *f.*

gath·er ['gæðə] **1.** *v/t.* (ein-, ver-)sammeln; ernten; pflücken; schließen *(from* aus); zusammenziehen, kräuseln; ~ *speed* schneller werden; *v/i.* sich (ver)sammeln; sich vergrößern; reifen *(Abszeß);* eitern *(Wunde);* **2.** Falte *f;* **~·ing** [~rɪŋ] Versammlung *f;* Zusammenkunft *f.*

gau·dy □ ['gɔːdɪ] (-*ier,* -*iest*) auffällig, bunt, grell *(Farbe);* protzig.

gauge [geɪdʒ] **1.** (Normal)Maß *n;* ⊕ Lehre *f;* ⊞ Spurweite *f;* Meßgerät *n;*

fig. Maßstab *m;* **2.** eichen; (aus)messen; *fig.* abschätzen.

gaunt □ [gɔːnt] hager; ausgemergelt.

gaunt·let ['gɔːntlɪt] Schutzhandschuh *m; fig.* Fehdehandschuh *m;* *run the* ~ Spießruten laufen.

gauze [gɔːz] Gaze *f.*

gave [geɪv] *pret. von give.*

gav·el ['gævl] Hammer *m (e-s Vorsitzenden od. Auktionators).*

gaw·ky ['gɔːkɪ] (-*ier,* -*iest*) unbeholfen, linkisch.

gay [geɪ] **1.** □ lustig, fröhlich; bunt, (farben)prächtig; F schwul *(homosexuell);* **2.** F Schwule(r) *m (homosexueller).*

gaze [geɪz] **1.** (starrer) Blick; △ *nicht* Gaze; **2.** starren; ~ *at* starren auf *(acc.),* anstarren.

ga·zette [gə'zet] Amtsblatt *n.*

ga·zelle *zo.* [gə'zel] Gazelle *f.*

gear [gɪə] **1** ⊕ Getriebe *n; mot.* Gang *m; mst in Zssgn:* Vorrichtung *f,* Gerät *n; in* ~ mit eingelegtem Gang; *out of* ~ im Leerlauf; *change* ~(*s*), *Am. shift* ~(*s*) *mot.* schalten; *landing* ~ ✈ Fahrgestell *n; steering* ~ ♨ Ruderanlage *f; mot.* Lenkung *f;* **2.** einschalten; ⊕ greifen; **~·le·ver** ['gɪəliːvə], *Am.* **~·shift** *mot.* Schalthebel *m.*

geese [giːs] *pl. von goose.*

geld·ing *zo.* ['geldɪŋ] Wallach *m.*

gem [dʒem] Edelstein *m;* Gemme *f; fig.* Glanzstück *n.*

gen·der ['dʒendə] *gr.* Genus *n,* Geschlecht *n; coll.* F Geschlecht *n.*

gen·er·al ['dʒenərəl] **1.** □ allgemein; allgemeingültig; ungefähr; Haupt..., General...; ♋ *Certificate of Education s. certificate* **1;** ~ *education od. knowledge* Allgemeinbildung *f;* ~ *election Brt. pol.* allgemeine Wahlen *pl.;* ~ *practitioner* praktischer Arzt; **2.** ✕ General *m;* Feldherr *m; in* ~ im allgemeinen; **~·i·ty** [dʒenə'rælətɪ] Allgemeinheit *f; die* große Masse; **~·ize** [~laɪz] verallgemeinern; **gen·er·al·ly** [~lɪ] im allgemeinen, überhaupt; gewöhnlich.

gen·er·ate ['dʒenəreɪt] erzeugen; **~·ra·tion** [dʒenə'reɪʃn] (Er)Zeugung *f;* Generation *f;* Menschenalter *n;* **~·ra·tor** ['dʒenəreɪtə] Erzeuger *m;* ⊕ Generator *m; bsd. Am. mot.* Lichtmaschine *f.*

gen·er·os·i·ty [dʒenə'rɒsətɪ] Großmut *f;* Großzügigkeit *f;* **~·rous** □ ['dʒenərəs] großmütig, großzügig.

ge·ni·al □ ['dʒiːnjəl] freundlich; angenehm; wohltuend; △ *nicht genial.*

gen·i·tive *gr.* ['dʒenɪtɪv] *a.* ~ *case* Genitiv *m*, zweiter Fall.

ge·ni·us ['dʒiːnjəs] Geist *m*; Genie *n*.

gent F [dʒent] Herr *m*; ~*s sg.* Brt. F Herrenklo *n*.

gen·teel □ [dʒen'tiːl] vornehm; elegant.

gen·tile ['dʒentail] **1.** heidnisch, nichtjüdisch; **2.** Heide *m*, -in *f*.

gen·tle □ ['dʒentl] (~*r*, ~*st*) sanft; mild; zahm; leise, sacht; vornehm; ~**man** (*pl.* -men) Herr *m*; Gentleman *m*; ~**man·ly** [~mənlɪ] gentlemanlike, vornehm; ~**ness** [~nɪs] Sanftheit *f*; Milde *f*, Güte *f*, Sanftmut *f*.

gen·try ['dʒentrɪ] niederer Adel; Oberschicht *f*.

gen·u·ine □ ['dʒenjʊɪn] echt; aufrichtig.

ge·og·ra·phy [dʒɪ'ɒɡrəfɪ] Geographie *f*.

ge·ol·o·gy [dʒɪ'ɒlədʒɪ] Geologie *f*.

ge·om·e·try [dʒɪ'ɒmətrɪ] Geometrie *f*.

germ *biol.*, ♀ [dʒɜːm] Keim *m*.

Ger·man ['dʒɜːmən] **1.** deutsch; **2.** Deutsche(r *m*) *f*; *ling.* Deutsch *n*.

ger·mi·nate ['dʒɜːmɪneɪt] keimen (lassen).

ger·und *gr.* ['dʒerənd] Gerundium *n*.

ges·tic·u·late [dʒe'stɪkjʊleɪt] gestikulieren; ~**la·tion** [dʒestɪkjʊ'leɪʃn] Gebärdenspiel *n*.

ges·ture ['dʒestʃə] Geste *f*, Gebärde *f*.

get [get] (-*tt*-; *got*, *got* od. Am. *gotten*) *v/t.* erhalten, bekommen, F kriegen; besorgen; holen; bringen; erwerben; verdienen; ergreifen, fassen, fangen; (veran)lassen; *mit adv. mst* bringen, machen; *have got* haben; *have got to* müssen; ~ *one's hair cut* sich die Haare schneiden lassen; ~ *by heart* auswendig lernen; *v/i.* gelangen, geraten, kommen; gehen; werden; ~ *ready* sich fertig machen; ~ *about* auf den Beinen sein; herumkommen; sich verbreiten (*Gerücht*); ~ *ahead* vorankommen; ~ *ahead of* übertreffen (*acc.*); ~ *along* vorwärtskommen; auskommen (*with* mit); ~ *at* herankommen an (*acc.*); sagen wollen; ~ *away* loskommen; entkommen; ~ *in* einsteigen (in); ~ *off*

aussteigen (aus); ~ *on* einsteigen (in); ~ *out* heraus-, hinausgehen; aussteigen (of aus); ~ *over* s.th. über et. hinwegkommen; ~ *to* kommen nach; ~ *together* zusammenkommen; ~ *up* aufstehen; ~**a·way** ['getəweɪ] Flucht *f*; ~ *car* Fluchtauto *n*; ~**up** Aufmachung *f*.

ghast·ly ['ɡaːstlɪ] (-*ier*, -*iest*) gräßlich; schrecklich; (toten)bleich; gespenstisch.

gher·kin ['ɡɜːkɪn] Gewürzgurke *f*.

ghost [ɡəʊst] Geist *m*, Gespenst *n*; *fig.* Spur *f*; ~**·ly** ['ɡəʊstlɪ] (-*ier*, -*iest*) geisterhaft.

gi·ant ['dʒaɪənt] **1.** riesig; **2.** Riese *m*.

gib·ber ['dʒɪbə] kauderwelschen; ~**ish** [~rɪʃ] Kauderwelsch *n*.

gib·bet ['dʒɪbɪt] Galgen *m*.

gibe [dʒaɪb] **1.** spotten (*at* über *acc.*); **2.** höhnische Bemerkung.

gib·lets ['dʒɪblɪts] *pl.* Hühner-, Gänseklein *n*.

gid·di·ness ['ɡɪdɪnɪs] ♂ Schwindel *m*; Unbeständigkeit *f*; Leichtsinn *m*; ~**·dy** □ ['ɡɪdɪ] (-*ier*, -*iest*) schwind(e)lig; leichtfertig; unbeständig; albern.

gift [ɡɪft] Geschenk *n*; Talent *n*; △ *nicht* Gift; ~**ed** ['ɡɪftɪd] begabt.

gi·gan·tic [dʒaɪ'ɡæntɪk] (~*ally*) gigantisch, riesenhaft, riesig, gewaltig.

gig·gle ['ɡɪɡl] **1.** kichern; **2.** Gekicher *n*.

gild [ɡɪld] (*gilded od. gilt*) vergolden; verschönen; ~*ed youth* Jeunesse *f* dorée.

gill [ɡɪl] *zo.* Kieme *f*; ♀ Lamelle *f*.

gilt [ɡɪlt] **1.** *pret. u. p.p. von* gild; **2.** Vergoldung *f*.

gim·mick F ['ɡɪmɪk] Trick *m*.

gin [dʒɪn] Gin *m* (*Wacholderschnaps*).

gin·ger ['dʒɪndʒə] **1.** Ingwer *m*; rötliches *od.* gelbliches Braun; **2.** rötlich *od.* gelblichbraun; ~**bread** Pfefferkuchen *m*; ~**·ly** [~lɪ] zimperlich; behutsam, vorsichtig.

gip·sy ['dʒɪpsɪ] Zigeuner(in).

gi·raffe *zo.* [dʒɪ'raːf] Giraffe *f*.

gir·der ⊕ ['ɡɜːdə] Tragbalken *m*.

gir·dle ['ɡɜːdl] Hüfthalter *m*, -gürtel *m*, Korselett *n*, Hüfthose *f*.

girl [ɡɜːl] Mädchen *n*; ~**friend** ['ɡɜːlfrend] Freundin *f*; ~ **guide** [~ɡaɪd] Pfadfinderin *f* (*in Großbritannien*); ~**hood** [~hʊd] Mädchenzeit *f*, Mädchenjahre *pl.*, Jugend(zeit) *f*; ~**ish** □ [~lɪʃ] mädchenhaft; Mäd-

G

chen...; ~ **scout** Pfadfinderin f (*in den USA*).

gi·ro ['dʒaɪrəʊ] **1.** Postscheckdienst m (*in Großbritannien*); **2.** Postscheck...

girth [gɜːθ] (Sattel)Gurt m; (a. Körper)Umfang m.

gist [dʒɪst] *das* Wesentliche.

give [gɪv] (*gave, given*) geben; ab-, übergeben; her-, hingeben; überlassen; zum besten geben; schenken; gewähren; von sich geben; ergeben; ~ *birth to* zur Welt bringen; ~ *away* her-, weggeben, verschenken; *j-n, et.* verraten; ~ *back* zurückgeben; ~ *in Gesuch* einreichen, *Prüfungsarbeit* abgeben; nachgeben; aufgeben; ~ *off Geruch* verbreiten; ausstoßen, -strömen; ~ *out* aus-, verteilen; zu Ende gehen (*Kräfte, Vorräte*); ~ *up* (es) aufgeben; aufhören mit; *j-n* ausliefern; ~ *o.s. up* sich (freiwillig) stellen (*to the police* der Polizei); ~ **and take** ['gɪvən'teɪk] (Meinungs)Austausch m; Kompromiß m, n; **giv·en** ['gɪvn] **1.** *p.p. von give*; **2.** *be* ~ *to* verfallen sein; neigen zu; **giv·en name** *Am.* Vorname m.

gla·cial ['gleɪsjəl] eisig; Eis...; Gletscher...; ~**ci·er** ['glæsjə] Gletscher m.

glad □ [glæd] (*-dd-*) froh, erfreut; freudig; ~**den** ['glædn] erfreuen.

glade [gleɪd] Lichtung f; *Am.* sumpfige Niederung.

glad|ly ['glædlɪ] gern(e); ~**ness** [~nɪs] Freude f.

glam|or·ous, -our·ous □ ['glæmərəs] bezaubernd; ~**o(u)r** ['glæmə] **1.** Zauber m, Glanz m, Reiz m; **2.** bezaubern.

glance [glɑːns] **1.** (schneller od. flüchtiger) Blick (*at* auf *acc.*); △ *nicht Glanz*; *at a* ~ mit e-m Blick; **2.** (auf)leuchten, (-)blitzen; *mst* ~ *off* abprallen; ~ *at* flüchtig ansehen; anspielen auf (*acc.*).

gland *anat.* [glænd] Drüse f.

glare [gleə] **1.** grelles Licht; wilder, starrer Blick; **2.** grell leuchten; wild blicken; (~ *at* an)starren.

glass [glɑːs] **1.** Glas n; Spiegel m; Opern-, Fernglas n; Barometer n; (a *pair of*) ~**es** pl. (e-e) Brille; **2.** gläsern; Glas...; **3.** (gläsern [(a *pair of*) gläsern] ['glɑːskeɪs] Vitrine f; Schaukasten m; ~**ful** [~fʊl] *ein* Glas(voll); ~**house** Treibhaus n; ⚔ F Bau m;

~**ware** Glas(waren pl.) n; ~**y** [~ɪ] (*-ier, -iest*) gläsern; glasig.

glaze [gleɪz] **1.** Glasur f; **2.** v/t. verglasen; glasieren; polieren; v/i. trüb(e) od. glasig werden (*Auge*); **gla·zi·er** ['gleɪzjə] Glaser m.

gleam [gliːm] **1.** Schimmer m, Schein m; **2.** schimmern.

glean [gliːn] v/t. sammeln; v/i. Ähren lesen.

glee [gliː] Fröhlichkeit f; ~**ful** □ ['gliːfl] ausgelassen, fröhlich.

glen [glen] Bergschlucht f.

glib □ [glɪb] (*-bb-*) gewandt; schlagfertig.

glide [glaɪd] **1.** Gleiten n; ⚔ Gleitflug m; **2.** (dahin)gleiten (lassen); ~ *en* Gleitflug machen; **glid·er** ⚔ ['glaɪdə] Segelflugzeug n; Segelflieger(in); **glid·ing** ⚔ [~ɪŋ] *das* Segelfliegen.

glim·mer ['glɪmə] **1.** Schimmer m; *min.* Glimmer m; **2.** schimmern.

glimpse [glɪmps] **1.** flüchtiger Blick (*at* auf *acc.*); Schimmer m; flüchtiger Eindruck; **2.** flüchtig (er)blicken.

glint [glɪnt] **1.** blitzen, glitzern; **2.** Lichtschein m.

glis·ten ['glɪsn] glitzern, glänzen.

glit·ter ['glɪtə] **1.** glitzern, funkeln, glänzen; **2.** Glitzern n, Funkeln n, Glanz m.

gloat [gləʊt]: ~ *over* sich hämisch *od.* diebisch freuen über (*acc.*); ~**ing** □ ['gləʊtɪŋ] hämisch, schadenfroh.

globe [gləʊb] (Erd)Kugel f; Globus m.

gloom [gluːm] Düsterkeit f; Dunkelheit f; gedrückte Stimmung, Schwermut f; ~**y** □ ['gluːmɪ] (*-ier, -iest*) dunkel; düster; schwermütig, traurig.

glo·ri·fy ['glɔːrɪfaɪ] verherrlichen; ~**ri·ous** □ [~ɪəs] herrlich; glorreich; ~**ry** [~ɪ] **1.** Ruhm m; Herrlichkeit f, Pracht f; Glorienschein m; **2.** ~ *in* sich freuen über (*acc.*).

gloss [glɒs] **1.** Glosse f, Bemerkung f; Glanz m; **2.** Glossen machen (zu); Glanz geben (*dat.*); ~ *over* beschönigen.

glos·sa·ry ['glɒsərɪ] Glossar n, Wörterverzeichnis n (*mit Erklärungen*).

gloss·y □ ['glɒsɪ] (*-ier, -iest*) glänzend.

glove [glʌv] Handschuh m; ~ *compartment* mot. Handschuhfach n.

glow [gləʊ] 1. Glühen *n*; Glut *f*; 2. glühen.

glow·er ['glaʊə] finster blicken.

glow-worm zo. ['glaʊwɜːm] Glühwürmchen *n*.

glu·cose ['gluːkəʊs] Traubenzucker *m*.

glue [gluː] 1. Leim *m*; 2. kleben.

glum □ [glʌm] (-*mm*-) bedrückt, niedergeschlagen.

glut [glʌt] (-*tt*-) übersättigen, -schwemmen; ~ *o.s. with od. on* sich vollstopfen mit.

glu·ti·nous □ ['gluːtɪnəs] klebrig.

glut·ton ['glʌtn] Unersättliche(r *m*) *f*; Vielfraß *m*; **~ous** □ [~əs] gefräßig; **~y** [~ɪ] Gefräßigkeit *f*.

gnarled [nɑːld] knorrig; knotig (*Hände*).

gnash [næʃ] knirschen (mit).

gnat zo. [næt] (Stech)Mücke *f*.

gnaw [nɔː] (zer)nagen; (zer)fressen.

gnome [nəʊm] Gnom *m*; Gartenzwerg *m*.

go [gəʊ] 1. (*went*, *gone*) gehen, fahren, fliegen; weggehen, aufbrechen, abfahren, abreisen; verkehren (*Fahrzeuge*); vergehen (*Zeit*); werden; führen (*to* nach); sich erstrecken, reichen (*to* bis zu); ausgehen, ablaufen, ausfallen; gehen, arbeiten, funktionieren, kaputtgehen; *let* ~ loslassen; ~ *shares* teilen; *I must be* ~*ing* ich muß weg *od.* fort; *~ to bed* ins Bett gehen; *~ to school* zur Schule gehen; *~ to see* besuchen; *~ ahead* vorangehen; vorausgehen, -fahren; *~ ahead with s.th.* et. durchführen, et. machen; *~ at* losgehen auf (*acc.*); *~ between* vermitteln (*zwischen*); *~ by* sich richten nach; *~ for holen*; *~ for a walk* e-n Spaziergang machen, spazierengehen; *~ in hineingehen*, eintreten; *~ in for an examination* e-e Prüfung machen; *~ off fortgehen*; *~ on weitergehen*, -fahren; *~ on* fortfahren (*doing zu tun*); *fig.* vor sich gehen, vorgehen; *~ out hinausgehen*; ausgehen (*with mit*) (*a. Licht etc.*); *~ through durchgehen*; durchmachen; *~ up steigen*; hinaufgehen, -steigen; *~ without* sich behelfen ohne, auskommen ohne; 2. F Mode *f*; Schwung *m*, Schneid *m*; *on the* ~ auf den Beinen; im Gange; *it is no* ~ es geht nicht; *in one* ~ auf Anhieb; *have a* ~ *at* es versuchen mit.

goad [gəʊd] 1. Stachelstock *m*; *fig.* Ansporn *m*; 2. *fig.* anstacheln.

go-a·head ['gəʊəhed] zielstrebig; unternehmungslustig.

goal [gəʊl] Mal *n*; Ziel *n*; *Fußball:* Tor *n*; **~·keep·er** ['gəʊlkiːpə] Torwart *m*.

goat zo. [gəʊt] Ziege *f*, Geiß *f*.

gob·ble ['gɒbl] 1. kollern (*Truthahn*); schlingen; *mst* ~ *up* verschlingen; 2. Kollern *n*; **~r** [~ə] Truthahn *m*; gieriger Esser.

go-be·tween ['gəʊbɪtwiːn] Vermittler(in), Mittelsmann *m*.

gob·let ['gɒblɪt] Kelchglas *n*; Pokal *m*, Becher *m*.

gob·lin ['gɒblɪn] Kobold *m*.

god [gɒd] *eccl.* ♀ Gott *m*; *fig.* Abgott *m*; **~child** ['gɒdtʃaɪld] (*pl. -children*) Patenkind *n*; **~dess** ['gɒdɪs] Göttin *f*; **~fa·ther** Pate *m* (*a. fig.*), Taufpate *m*; **~for·sak·en** *contp.* gottverlassen; **~head** Gottheit *f*; **~less** [~lɪs] gottlos; **~like** göttlich; **~ly** [~lɪ] (*-ier, -iest*) gottesfürchtig; fromm; **~moth·er** (Tauf)Patin *f*; **~pa·rent** (Tauf)Pate *m*, (-)Patin *f*; **~send** Geschenk *n* des Himmels.

go-get·ter F ['gəʊ'getə] Draufgänger *m*.

gog·gle ['gɒgl] 1. glotzen; 2. **~s** *pl.* Schutzbrille *f*; **~box** Brt. F Glotze *f* (*Fernseher*).

go·ing ['gəʊɪŋ] 1. gehend; im Gange (befindlich); *be* ~ *to inf.* im Begriff sein zu *inf.*, gleich tun wollen *od.* werden; 2. Gehen *n*; Vorwärtskommen *n*; Straßenzustand *m*; Geschwindigkeit *f*, Leistung *f*; **~s-on** [~z'ɒn] *pl.* Treiben *n*, Vorgänge *pl.*

gold [gəʊld] 1. Gold *n*; 2. golden; **~ dig·ger** *Am.* ['gəʊlddɪgə] Goldgräber *m*; **~en** *mst fig.* [~ən] golden, goldgelb; **~finch** zo. Stieglitz *m*; **~fish** zo. Goldfisch *m*; **~smith** Goldschmied *m*.

golf [gɒlf] 1. Golf(spiel) *n*; 2. Golf spielen; ~ *club* ['gɒlfklʌb] Golfschläger *m*; Golfklub *m*; **~ course**, **~ links** *pl. od. sg.* Golfplatz *m*.

gon·do·la ['gɒndələ] Gondel *f*.

gone [gɒn] 1. *p.p. von go* 1; 2. *adj.* fort; F futsch; vergangen; tot; F hoffnungslos.

good [gʊd] 1. (*better, best*) gut; artig; gütig; gründlich; ~ *at* geschickt *od.* gut in (*dat.*); 2. Nutzen *m*, Wert *m*,

Vorteil m; *das Gute, Wohl* n; *~s* pl. econ. Waren pl., Güter pl.; *that's no ~* das nützt nichts; *for ~* für immer; **~·by(e)** 1. [gʊdˈbaɪ]: *wish s.o. ~, say ~ to s.o.* j-m auf Wiedersehen sagen; 2. *int.* [gʊdˈbaɪ] (auf) Wiedersehen! ♀ **Fri·day** Karfreitag m; **~·hu·mo(u)red** □ gutgelaunt; gutmütig; **~·look·ing** [~ɪŋ] gutaussehend; **~·ly** [ˈgʊdlɪ] anmutig, hübsch; *fig.* ansehnlich; **~·na·tured** □ gutmütig; **~·ness** [~nɪs] Güte f; *das Beste*; *thank ~!* Gott sei Dank!; *(my) ~!, ~ gracious!* du meine Güte!, du lieber Himmel!; *for ~' sake* um Himmels willen!; *~ knows* weiß der Himmel; **~·will** Wohlwollen n; econ. Kundschaft f; econ. Firmenwert m.

good·y F [ˈgʊdɪ] Bonbon m n.

goose zo. [guːs] (pl. geese) Gans f (a. fig.).

goose·ber·ry ♀ [ˈgʊzbərɪ] Stachelbeere f.

goose·flesh [ˈguːsfleʃ], **~·pim·ples** pl. Gänsehaut f.

go·pher zo. [ˈgəʊfə] Taschenratte f; Am. Ziesel m.

gore [gɔː] durchbohren, aufspießen (*mit den Hörnern etc.*).

gorge [gɔːdʒ] 1. Kehle f, Schlund m; *enge* (Fels)Schlucht; 2. (ver)schlingen; (sich) vollstopfen.

gor·geous □ [ˈgɔːdʒəs] prächtig.

go·ril·la zo. [gəˈrɪlə] Gorilla m.

gor·y □ [ˈgɔːrɪ] (-ier, -iest) blutig; *fig.* blutrünstig.

gosh *int.* F [gɒʃ]: *by ~* Mensch!

gos·ling zo. [ˈgɒzlɪŋ] junge Gans.

go-slow Brt. econ. [gəʊˈsləʊ] Bummelstreik m.

Gos·pel eccl. [ˈgɒspəl] Evangelium n.

gos·sa·mer [ˈgɒsəmə] Altweibersommer m.

gos·sip [ˈgɒsɪp] 1. Klatsch m, Tratsch m; Klatschbase f; 2. klatschen, tratschen.

got [gɒt] pret. u. p.p. von get.

Goth·ic [ˈgɒθɪk] gotisch; Schauer...; *~ novel* Schauerroman m.

got·ten Am. [ˈgɒtn] p.p. von get.

gouge [gaʊdʒ] 1. ⊕ Hohlmeißel m; 2. *~ out* ⊕ ausmeißeln; *~ out s.o.'s eye* j-m ein Auge ausstechen.

gourd ♀ [gʊəd] Kürbis m.

gout ♂ [gaʊt] Gicht f.

gov·ern [ˈgʌvn] *v/t.* regieren, beherrschen; lenken, leiten; *v/i.* herrschen; **~·ess** [~ɪs] Erzieherin f; **~·ment** [~mənt] Regierung(sform) f; Herrschaft f (*of über* acc.); Ministerium n; attr. Staats...; **~·men·tal** [gʌvən-ˈmentl] Regierungs...; **gov·er·nor** [ˈgʌvənə] Gouverneur m; Direktor m, Präsident m; F Alte(r) m (*Vater, Chef*).

gown [gaʊn] 1. (Frauen)Kleid n; Robe f, Talar m; 2. kleiden.

grab [græb] 1. (-bb-) (*hastig od. gierig*) ergreifen, packen, fassen; 2. (*hastiger od. gieriger*) Griff; ⊕ Greifer m.

grace [greɪs] 1. Gnade f; Gunst f; (Gnaden)Frist f; Grazie f, Anmut f; Anstand m; Zier(de) f; Reiz m; Tischgebet n; Eure Hoheit (*Herzog[in]*); Eure Exzellenz (*Erzbischof*); 2. zieren, schmücken; begünstigen, auszeichnen; **~·ful** □ [ˈgreɪsfl] anmutig, **~·less** □ [~lɪs] ungraziös, linkisch; ungehobelt.

gra·cious □ [ˈgreɪʃəs] gnädig.

gra·da·tion [grəˈdeɪʃn] Abstufung f.

grade [greɪd] 1. Grad m, Rang m; Stufe f; Qualität f; bsd. Am. = gradient; Am. Schule: Klasse f; Note f; *make the ~* es schaffen, Erfolg haben; *~ crossing* bsd. Am. schienengleicher Bahnübergang; 2. abstufen; einstufen; ⊕ planieren.

gra·di·ent ⊕ etc. [ˈgreɪdjənt] Steigung f.

grad·u·al □ [ˈgrædjʊəl] stufenweise, allmählich; **~·al·ly** [~lɪ] nach u. nach; allmählich; **~·ate** 1. [~eɪt] graduieren; (sich) abstufen; die Abschlußprüfung machen; promovieren; 2. [~ət] univ. Hochschulabsolvent(in), Akademiker(in); Graduierte(r m) f; Am. Schulabgänger(in); **~·a·tion** [grædjʊˈeɪʃn] Gradeinteilung f; univ., Am. a. Schule: (Ab-)Schlußfeier f; univ. Erteilung f od. Erlangung f e-s akademischen Grades.

graft [grɑːft] 1. ✔ Pfropfreis n; Am. Schiebung f; Am. Schmiergelder pl.; 2. ✔ pfropfen; ✔ verpflanzen.

grain [greɪn] (Samen)Korn n; Getreide n; Gefüge n; fig. Natur f; Gran n (*Gewicht*).

gram [græm] Gramm n.

gram·mar [ˈgræmə] Grammatik f; **~ school** Brt. etwa (humanistisches) Gymnasium; Am. etwa Grundschule f.

gram·mat·i·cal □ [grəˈmætɪkl] grammatisch.

gramme [græm] = gram.

gra·na·ry [ˈgrænərɪ] Kornspeicher m.

grand [grænd] 1. fig. großartig; erhaben; groß; Groß…, Haupt…; ♀ Old Party Am. Republikanische Partei; 2. (pl. grand) F Riese m (1000 Dollar od. Pfund); ~child [ˈgræntʃaɪld] (pl. -children) Enkel(in).

gran·deur [ˈgrændʒə] Größe f, Hoheit f; Erhabenheit f.

grand·fa·ther [ˈgrænfɑːðə] Großvater m.

gran·di·ose □ [ˈgrændɪəʊs] großartig.

grand|moth·er [ˈgrænmʌðə] Großmutter f; ~·par·ents [~peərənts] pl. Großeltern pl.; ~ pi·an·o ♩ (pl. -os) (Konzert)Flügel m; ~stand Sport: Haupttribüne f.

grange [greɪndʒ] (kleiner) Gutshof.

gran·ny F [ˈgrænɪ] Oma f.

grant [grɑːnt] 1. Gewährung f, Unterstützung f; Stipendium n; 2. gewähren; bewilligen; verleihen; ⚖ übertragen; zugestehen; ~ed, but zugeben, aber; take for ~ed als selbstverständlich annehmen.

gran·u·lat·ed [ˈgrænjʊleɪtɪd] körnig, granuliert; ~ sugar Kristallzucker m; ~·ule [~juːl] Körnchen n.

grape [greɪp] Weinbeere f, -traube f; ~·fruit ♀ [ˈgreɪpfruːt] Grapefruit f, Pampelmuse f; ~·vine ♀ Weinstock m.

graph [græf] graphische Darstellung; ~·ic [ˈgræfɪk] (~ally) graphisch; anschaulich; ~ arts pl. Graphik f, graphische Kunst.

grap·ple [ˈgræpl] ringen, kämpfen; ~ with s.th. fig. sich mit et. herumschlagen.

grasp [grɑːsp] 1. Griff m; Bereich m; Beherrschung f; Fassungskraft f; 2. (er)greifen, packen; begreifen.

grass [grɑːs] Gras n; Rasen m; Weide(land n) f; sl. Grass n (Marihuana); ~·hop·per zo. [ˈgrɑːshɒpə] Heuschrecke f; ~ wid·ow Strohwitwe f; Am. geschiedene Frau; Am. (von ihrem Mann) getrennt lebende Frau; ~ wid·ow·er Strohwitwer m; Am. geschiedener Mann; Am. (von s-r Frau) getrennt lebender Mann; **gras·sy** [~ɪ] (-ier, -iest) grasbedeckt, Gras…

grate [greɪt] 1. (Kamin)Gitter n; (Feuer)Rost m; 2. reiben, raspeln; knirschen (mit); ~ on s.o.'s nerves an j-s Nerven zerren.

grate·ful □ [ˈgreɪtfl] dankbar.

grat·er [ˈgreɪtə] Reibe f.

grat·i·fi·ca·tion [grætɪfɪˈkeɪʃn] Befriedigung f; Freude f; △ nicht Gratifikation!; ~·fy [ˈgrætɪfaɪ] erfreuen; befriedigen.

grat·ing [ˈgreɪtɪŋ] kratzend, knirschend, quietschend; schrill; unangenehm.

grat·ing² [~] Gitter(werk) n.

grat·i·tude [ˈgrætɪtjuːd] Dankbarkeit f.

gra·tu·i·tous □ [grəˈtjuːɪtəs] unentgeltlich; freiwillig; ~·ty [~ˈtjuːətɪ] Abfindung f; Gratifikation f; Trinkgeld n.

grave¹ □ [greɪv] (~r, ~st) ernst; (ge)wichtig; gemessen.

grave² [~] Grab n; ~·dig·ger [ˈgreɪvdɪgə] Totengräber m (a. zo.).

grav·el [ˈgrævl] 1. Kies m; Schotter m; ⚕ Harngrieß m; 2. (bsd. Brt. -ll-, Am. -l-) mit Kies bestreuen.

grave·stone [ˈgreɪvstəʊn] Grabstein m; ~·yard Friedhof m.

grav·i·ta·tion [grævɪˈteɪʃn] phys. Schwerkraft f; fig. Hang m, Neigung f.

grav·i·ty [ˈgrævətɪ] Schwere f, Ernst m; phys. Schwerkraft f.

gra·vy [ˈgreɪvɪ] Bratensaft m; Bratensoße f.

gray bsd. Am. [greɪ] grau.

graze¹ [greɪz] Vieh weiden (lassen); (ab)weiden; (ab)grasen.

graze² [~] 1. streifen; schrammen; Haut (ab-, auf)schürfen, (auf)schrammen; 2. Abschürfung f, Schramme f.

grease 1. [griːs] Fett n; Schmiere f; 2. [griːz] (be)schmieren.

greas·y □ [ˈgriːzɪ] (-ier, -iest) fett(ig), ölig; schmierig.

great □ [greɪt] groß, Groß…; F großartig; ~·grand·child [greɪtˈgræntʃaɪld] (pl. -children) Urenkel(in); ~·grand·fa·ther Urgroßvater m; ~·grand·moth·er Urgroßmutter f; ~·grand·par·ents pl. Urgroßeltern pl.; ~·ly [ˈgreɪtlɪ] sehr; ~·ness [~nɪs] Größe f; Stärke f.

greed [griːd] Gier f; ~·y □ [ˈgriːdɪ] (-ier, -iest) gierig (for auf acc., nach); habgierig; gefräßig.

Greek [griːk] **1.** griechisch; **2.** Griech|e m, -in f; ling. Griechisch n.

green [griːn] **1.** □ grün (a. fig.); frisch (Fisch etc.); neu; Grün...; **2.** Grün n; Grünfläche f, Rasen m; ~s pl. grünes Gemüse, Blattgemüse n; ~**back** Am. F ['griːnbæk] Dollarschein m; ~**belt** Grüngürtel m (um e-e Stadt); ~**gro·cer** bsd. Brt. Obst- u. Gemüsehändler(in); ~**gro·cer·y** bsd. Brt. Obst- u. Gemüsehandlung f; ~**horn** Greenhorn m, Grünschnabel m; ~**house** Gewächs-, Treibhaus n; ~**ish** [~ɪʃ] grünlich.

greet [griːt] grüßen; ~**ing** ['griːtɪŋ] Begrüßung f, Gruß m; ~s pl. Grüße pl.

gre·nade ⚔ [grɪˈneɪd] Granate f.

grew [gruː] pret. von grow.

grey [greɪ] **1.** □ grau; **2.** Grau n; **3.** grau machen od. werden; ~**hound** zo. ['greɪhaʊnd] Windhund m.

grid [grɪd] **1.** Gitter n; ⚡ etc. Versorgungsnetz n; ⚡ Gitter...; **2.** ~**i·ron** ['grɪdaɪən] (Brat)Rost m.

grief [griːf] Gram m, Kummer m; come to ~ zu Schaden kommen.

griev|ance ['griːvns] Beschwerde f; Mißstand m; ~**e** [griːv] v/t. betrüben, bekümmern; j-m Kummer bereiten; v/i. bekümmert sein; ~ for trauern um; ~**ous** □ ['griːvəs] kränkend, schmerzlich; schlimm.

grill [grɪl] **1.** grillen; **2.** Grill m; Bratrost m; Gegrillte(s) n; a. ~-**room** m Grillroom m.

grim □ [grɪm] (-mm-) grimmig; schrecklich; erbittert; F schlimm.

gri·mace [grɪˈmeɪs] **1.** Fratze f, Grimasse f; **2.** Grimassen schneiden.

grime [graɪm] Schmutz m; Ruß m; **grim·y** □ ['graɪmɪ] (-ier, -iest) schmutzig; rußig.

grin [grɪn] **1.** Grinsen n; **2.** (-nn-) grinsen.

grind [graɪnd] **1.** (ground) (zer)reiben; mahlen; schleifen; Leierkasten etc. drehen; fig. schinden; mit den Zähnen knirschen; **2.** Schinderei f, Schufterei f; △ nicht Grind; ~**er** ['graɪndə] (Messer- etc.)Schleifer m; ⊕ Schleifmaschine f; ⊕ Mühle f; ~**stone** Schleifstein m.

grip [grɪp] **1.** (-pp-) packen, fassen (a. fig.); **2.** Griff m (a. fig.); fig. Gewalt f, Herrschaft f; Am. Reisetasche f.

gripes [graɪps] pl. Bauchschmerzen pl., Kolik f.

grip·sack Am. ['grɪpsæk] Reisetasche f.

gris·ly ['grɪzlɪ] (-ier, -iest) gräßlich, schrecklich.

gris·tle ['grɪsl] Knorpel m (im Fleisch).

grit [grɪt] **1.** Kies m; Sand(stein) m; fig. Mut m; **2.** (-tt-): ~ one's teeth die Zähne zusammenbeißen.

griz·zly (bear) ['grɪzlɪ(beə)] Grizzly (-bär) m, Graubär m.

groan [grəʊn] **1.** stöhnen, ächzen; **2.** Stöhnen n, Ächzen n.

gro·cer ['grəʊsə] Lebensmittelhändler m; ~**ies** [~rɪz] pl. Lebensmittel pl.; ~**y** [~ɪ] Lebensmittelgeschäft n.

grog·gy F ['grɒgɪ] (-ier, -iest) schwach od. wackelig (auf den Beinen).

groin anat. [grɔɪn] Leiste(ngegend) f.

groom [grʊm] **1.** Pferdepfleger m, Stallbursche m; = bridegroom; **2.** pflegen; j-n aufbauen, lancieren.

groove [gruːv] Rinne f, Furche f; Rille f, Nut f; groov·y sl. ['gruːvɪ] (-ier, -iest) klasse, toll.

grope [grəʊp] tasten; sl. Mädchen befummeln.

gross [grəʊs] **1.** □ dick, fett; grob, derb; econ. Brutto...; **2.** Gros n (12 Dutzend); in the ~ im ganzen.

gro·tesque □ [grəʊˈtesk] grotesk.

ground[1] [graʊnd] **1.** pret. u. p.p. von grind 1; **2.** ~ glass Mattglas n.

ground[2] [graʊnd] **1.** Grund m, Boden m; Gebiet n; (Spiel- etc.)Platz m; (Beweg- etc.)Grund m; ⚡ Erde f; ~s pl. Grundstück n, Park(s pl.) m, Gärten pl.; (Kaffee)Satz m; on the ~(s) of auf Grund (gen.); stand od. hold od. keep one's ~ sich behaupten; **2.** niederlegen; (be)gründen; j-m die Anfangsgründe beibringen; ⚡ erden; ~ **crew** ✈ Bodenpersonal n; ~ **floor** bsd. Brt. [graʊnd'flɔː] Erdgeschoß n; ~ **forc·es** ⚔ Bodentruppen pl., Landstreitkräfte pl.; ~**hog** zo. Amer. Waldmurmeltier n; ~**ing** [~ɪŋ] Am. ⚡ Erdung f; Grundlagen pl., -kenntnisse pl.; ~**less** □ [~lɪs] grundlos; ~**nut** Brt. ♀ Erdnuß f; ~ **staff** Brt. ✈ Bodenpersonal n; ~ **sta·tion** Raumfahrt: Bodenstation f; ~**work** Grundlage f.

group [gruːp] **1.** Gruppe f; **2.** (sich) gruppieren.

group·ie F ['gru:pɪ] Groupie *n (aufdringlicher weiblicher Fan)*.

group·ing ['gru:pɪŋ] Gruppierung *f*.

grove [grəʊv] Wäldchen *n*, Gehölz *n*.

grov·el ['grɒvl] *(bsd. Brt. -ll-, Am. -l-)* (am Boden) kriechen.

grow [grəʊ] *(grew, grown) v/i.* wachsen; werden; ~ *into* hineinwachsen in; werden, sich entwickeln zu; ~ *on j-m* lieb werden *od.* ans Herz wachsen; ~ *out of* herauswachsen aus; entstehen aus; ~ *up* aufwachsen, heranwachsen; sich entwickeln; *v/t.* ♣ anpflanzen, anbauen, züchten; **~er** ['grəʊə] Züchter *m*, Erzeuger *m*, *in Zssgn* ...bauer *m*.

growl [graʊl] knurren, brummen.

grown [grəʊn] **1.** *p.p. von* grow; **2.** *adj.* erwachsen; bewachsen; **~-up** ['grəʊnʌp] **1.** erwachsen; **2.** Erwachsene(r *m*) *f*; **growth** [grəʊθ] Wachstum *n*; (An)Wachsen *n*; Entwicklung *f*; Erzeugnis *n*; ♣ Gewächs *n*, Wucherung *f*.

grub [grʌb] **1.** *zo.* Raupe *f*, Larve *f*, Made *f*; F Futter *n (Essen)*; **2.** *(-bb-)* graben; sich abmühen; **~·by** ['grʌbɪ] *(-ier, -iest)* schmutzig.

grudge [grʌdʒ] **1.** Groll *m*; **2.** mißgönnen; ungern geben *od.* tun *etc.*

gru·el [grʊəl] Haferschleim *m*.

gruff □ [grʌf] grob, schroff, barsch.

grum·ble ['grʌmbl] **1.** murren; **2.** Murren *n*; **~r** *fig.* [~ə] Brummbär *m*.

grunt [grʌnt] **1.** grunzen; brummen; stöhnen; **2.** Grunzen *n*; Stöhnen *n*.

guar·an|tee [gærən'ti:] **1.** Garantie *f*; Bürgschaft *f*; Sicherheit *f*; Zusicherung *f*; **2.** (sich ver)bürgen für; garantieren; **~tor** [~'tɔ:] Bürge *m*, Bürgin *f*; **~ty** ['gærəntɪ] Garantie *f*; Bürgschaft *f*; Sicherheit *f*.

guard [gɑ:d] **1.** Wacht *f*; ⚔ Wache *f*; Wächter *m*, Wärter *m*; 🚂 Schaffner *m*; Schutz(vorrichtung *f*) *m*; 🚂*s pl.* Garde *f*; *be on* ~ Wache haben; *be on (off) one's* ~ (nicht) auf der Hut sein; **2.** *v/t.* bewachen, (be)schützen *(from vor dat.)*; *v/i.* sich hüten *(against vor dat.)*; **~·ed** □ ['gɑ:dɪd] vorsichtig, zurückhaltend; **~·i·an** [~jən] Hüter *m*, Wächter *m*; 🖚 Vormund *m*; *attr.* Schutz...; **~·i·an·ship** 🖚 [~ʃɪp] Vormundschaft *f*.

gue(r)·ril·la ⚔ [gə'rɪlə] Guerilla *m*; ~ *warfare* Guerillakrieg *m*.

guess [ges] **1.** Vermutung *f*; **2.** vermuten; schätzen; raten; *Am.* glau-

ben, denken; **~·ing game** Ratespiel *n*; **~·work** ['geswɜ:k] (reine) Vermutung(en *pl.*).

guest [gest] **1.** Gast *m*; **2.** Gast...; **~·house** ['gesthaʊs] (Hotel)Pension *f*, Fremdenheim *n*; **~·room** Gast-, Gäste-, Fremdenzimmer *n*.

guf·faw [gʌ'fɔ:] **1.** schallendes Gelächter *n*; **2.** schallend lachen.

guid·ance ['gaɪdns] Führung *f*; (An-)Leitung *f*.

guide [gaɪd] **1.** (Reise-, Fremden-)Führer(in); ⊕ Führung *f*; *a.* ~*book* (Reise- *etc.*)Führer *m (Buch)*; *a.* ~ *to London* ein London-Führer; *s. girl guide*; **2.** leiten; führen; lenken; **guid·ed mis·sile** ⚔ Lenkflugkörper *m*; **guid·ed tour** Führung *f*; **~·line** ['gaɪdlaɪn] Richtlinie *f*, -schnur *f (on gen.)*.

guild *hist.* [gɪld] Gilde *f*, Zunft *f*; **2·hall** ['gɪld'hɔ:l] Rathaus *n (von London)*.

guile [gaɪl] Arglist *f*; **~·ful** □ ['gaɪlfl] arglistig; **~·less** □ [~lɪs] arglos.

guilt [gɪlt] Schuld *f*; Strafbarkeit *f*; **~·less** □ ['gɪltlɪs] schuldlos, unkundig; **~·y** □ [~ɪ] *(-ier, -iest)* schuldig *(of gen.)*.

guin·ea ['gɪnɪ] Guinee *f (21 Schilling alter Währung)*; **~·pig** *zo.* Meerschweinchen *n*.

guise [gaɪz] Erscheinung *f*, Gestalt *f*; *fig.* Maske *f*.

gui·tar ♪ [gɪ'tɑ:] Gitarre *f*.

gulch *bsd. Am.* [gʌlʃ] tiefe Schlucht.

gulf [gʌlf] Meerbusen *m*, Golf *m*; Abgrund *m*; Strudel *m*.

gull *zo.* [gʌl] Möwe *f*.

gul·let *anat.* [gʌlɪt] Schlund *m*, Speiseröhre *f*, Gurgel *f*.

gulp [gʌlp] **1.** (großer) Schluck; **2.** *oft* ~ *down* Getränk hinunterstürzen, *Speise* hinunterschlingen.

gum [gʌm] **1.** Gummi *m*, *n*; Klebstoff *m*; ~, *Am.* ~*drop* Gummibonbon *m*, *n*; ~*s pl. anat.* Zahnfleisch *n*; *Am.* Gummischuhe *pl.*; **2.** *(-mm-)* gummieren; kleben.

gun [gʌn] **1.** Gewehr *n*; Flinte *f*; Geschütz *n*, Kanone *f*; *Am.* Revolver *m*; *big* ~ F *fig.* hohes Tier; **2.** *(-nn-)*: *mst* ~ *down* niederschießen; **~·bat·tle** Feuergefecht *n*, Schießerei *f*; **~·boat** ['gʌnbəʊt] Kanonenboot *n*; **~·fight** *Am.* = *gun battle*; **~·fire** Schüsse *pl.*; ⚔ Geschützfeuer *n*; **~·li·cence** Waffenschein *m*; **~·man**

(pl. -men) Bewaffnete(r) *m;* Revolverheld *m;* **~ner** ✕ [~ə] Kanonier *m;* **~point:** *at* ~ mit vorgehaltener Waffe, mit Waffengewalt; **~powder** Schießpulver *n;* **~run·ner** Waffenschmuggler *m;* **~run·ning** Waffenschmuggel *m;* **~shot** Schuß *m; within (out of)* ~ in (außer) Schußweite; **~smith** Büchsenmacher *m.*

gur·gle ['gɜːgl] 1. glucksen, gluckern, gurgeln; 2. Glucksen *n,* Gurgeln *n.*

gush [gʌʃ] 1. Schwall *m,* Strom *m (a. fig.);* 2. sich ergießen, schießen *(from* aus); *fig.* schwärmen.

gust [gʌst] Windstoß *m,* Bö *f.*

gut [gʌt] *anat.* Darm *m;* ♪ Darmsaite

f; **~s** *pl.* Eingeweide *pl.; das* Innere; *fig.* Schneid *m,* Mumm *m.*

gut·ter ['gʌtə] Dachrinne *f;* Gosse *f (a. fig.),* Rinnstein *m.*

guy F [gaɪ] Kerl *m,* Typ *m.*

guz·zle ['gʌzl] saufen; fressen.

gym F [dʒɪm] *= gymnasium;* gymnastics; **~na·si·um** [dʒɪm'neɪzjəm] Turn-, Sporthalle *f;* △ *nicht Gymnasium;* **~nas·tics** [~'næstɪks] *sg.* Turnen *n,* Gymnastik *f.*

gy·n(a)e·col·o·gist [gaɪnɪ'kɒlədʒɪst] Gynäkolog|e *m,* -in *f,* Frauenarzt *m,* -ärztin *f;* **~gy** [~dʒɪ] Gynäkologie *f,* Frauenheilkunde *f.*

gyp·sy *bsd. Am.* ['dʒɪpsɪ] = gipsy.

gy·rate [dʒaɪə'reɪt] kreisen, sich (im Kreis) drehen, (herum)wirbeln.

H

hab·er·dash·er ['hæbədæʃə] *Brt.* Kurzwarenhändler *m; Am.* Herrenausstatter *m;* **~y** [~rɪ] *Brt.* Kurzwaren(geschäft *n*) *pl.; Am.* Herrenbekleidungsartikel *pl.; Am.* Herrenmodengeschäft *n.*

hab·it ['hæbɪt] (An)Gewohnheit *f; bsd.* Ordenskleidung *f;* ~ *of mind* Geistesverfassung *f; drink has become a* ~ *with him* er kommt vom Alkohol nicht mehr los; **~i·ta·ble** □ [~əbl] bewohnbar.

ha·bit·u·al □ [hə'bɪtjʊəl] gewohnt, gewöhnlich; Gewohnheits...

hack¹ [hæk] (zer)hacken.

hack² [~] Reitpferd *n;* Mietpferd *n;* Klepper *m; a.* ~ *writer* Schreiberling *m;* **~neyed** ['hæknɪd] abgedroschen.

had [hæd] *pret. u. p.p. von* have.

had·dock *zo.* ['hædək] Schellfisch *m.*

h(a)e·mor·rhage ✗ ['heməridʒ] Blutung *f.*

hag *fig.* [hæg] häßliches altes Weib, Hexe *f.*

hag·gard □ ['hægəd] verhärmt.

hag·gle ['hægl] feilschen, schachern.

hail [heɪl] 1. Hagel *m;* (Zu)Ruf *m;* 2. (nieder)hageln, rufen; (be-)grüßen; ~ *from* stammen aus; **~stone** ['heɪlstəʊn] Hagelkorn *n;* **~storm** Hagelschauer *m.*

hair [heə] *einzelnes* Haar; *coll.* Haar *n,* Haare *pl.;* **~breadth** ['heəbredθ]: *by a* ~ um Haaresbreite; **~brush** Haarbürste *f;* **~cut** Haarschnitt *m;* **~do** *(pl. -dos)* F Frisur *f;* **~dress·er** Friseur *m,* Friseuse *f;* **~dri·er,** **dry·er** [~draɪə] Trockenhaube *f;* Haartrockner *m; TM* Fön *m;* **~grip** *Brt.* Haarklammer *f,* -klemme *f;* **~less** [~lɪs] ohne Haare, kahl; **~pin** Haarnadel *f;* ~ *bend* Haarnadelkurve *f;* **~rais·ing** [~reɪzɪŋ] haarsträubend; **~'s breadth** *= hairbreadth;* **~slide** *Brt.* Haarspange *f;* **~splitting** Haarspalterei *f;* **~spray** Haarspray *m,n;* **~style** Frisur *f;* ~ **styl·ist** Hair-Stylist *m,* Haarstilist *m,* Damenfriseur *m;* **~y** [~rɪ] *(-ier, -iest)* behaart; haarig.

hale [heɪl]: ~ *and hearty* gesund u. munter.

half [hɑːf] 1. *(pl. halves* [~vz]*)* Hälfte *f; by halves* nur halb; *go halves* halbe-halbe machen, teilen; 2. halb; ~ *an hour* e-e halbe Stunde; ~ *a pound* ein halbes Pfund; ~ *past ten* halb elf (Uhr); ~ *way up* auf halbe Höhe; **~back** [hɑːf'bæk] *Fußball:* Läufer *m;* **~breed** [~briːd] Halbblut *n;* **~broth·er** Halbbruder *m;* **~caste** Halbblut *n;* **~heart·ed** □

[~'hɑːtɪd] lustlos, lau; **~length:** ~ *portrait* Brustbild *n*; **~mast:** *fly at* ~ auf halbmast wehen; **~pen·ny** ['heɪpnɪ] (*pl.* -pennies, -pence) halber Penny; ~ **sis·ter** Halbschwester *f*; **~term** *Brt. univ. kurze Ferien in der Mitte e-s Trimesters*; **~time** ['hɑːftaɪm] *Sport:* Halbzeit *f*; **~way** halb; auf halbem Weg, in der Mitte; **~wit·ted** schwachsinnig.

hal·i·but *zo.* ['hælɪbət] Heilbutt *m*.

hall [hɔːl] Halle *f*, Saal *m*; Flur *m*, Diele *f*; Herrenhaus *n*; *univ.* Speisesaal *m*; ~ *of residence* Studentenwohnheim *n*.

hal·lo *Brt.* [hə'ləʊ] = *hello*.

hal·low ['hæləʊ] heiligen, weihen; 2**·e'en** [hæləʊ'iːn] Abend *m* vor Allerheiligen.

hal·lu·ci·na·tion [həluːsɪ'neɪʃn] Halluzination *f*.

hall·way *bsd. Am.* ['hɔːlweɪ] Halle *f*, Diele *f*; Korridor *m*.

ha·lo ['heɪləʊ] (*pl.* -loes, -los) *ast.* Hof *m*; Heiligenschein *m*.

halt [hɔːlt] 1. Halt(estelle *f*) *m*; Stillstand *m*; 2. (an)halten.

hal·ter ['hɔːltə] Halfter *m, n*; Strick *m*.

halve [hɑːv] halbieren; **~s** [hɑːvz] *pl. von half* 1.

ham [hæm] Schinken *m*; ~ *and eggs* Schinken mit (Spiegel)Ei.

ham·burg·er ['hæmbɜːgə] *Am.* Rinderhack *n*; *a.* 2 *steak* Hamburger *m*, Frikadelle *f* (*aus Rinderhack*).

ham·let ['hæmlɪt] Weiler *m*.

ham·mer ['hæmə] 1. Hammer *m*; 2. hämmern.

ham·mock ['hæmək] Hängematte *f*.

ham·per¹ ['hæmpə] (Trag)Korb *m* (*mit Deckel*); Geschenk-, Freßkorb *m*.

ham·per² [~] (be)hindern, stören.

ham·ster *zo.* ['hæmstə] Hamster *m*.

hand [hænd] 1. Hand *f* (*a. fig.*); Handschrift *f*; Handbreite *f*; (Uhr)Zeiger *m*; Mann *m*, Arbeiter *m*; *Karten:* Blatt *n*; *at* ~ bei der Hand; nahe bevorstehend; *at first* ~ aus erster Hand; *a good* (*poor*) ~ *at* (un)geschickt in (*dat.*); ~ *and glove* ein Herz und eine Seele; *change* ~s den Besitzer wechseln; *lend a* ~ (mit) anfassen; *off* ~ aus dem Handgelenk *od.* Stegreif; *on* ~ *econ.* vorrätig, auf

Lager; *bsd. Am.* zur Stelle, bereit; *on one's* ~s auf dem Hals; *on the one* ~ einerseits; *on the other* ~ andererseits; 2. ein-, aushändigen, (über)geben, (-)reichen; ~ *around* herumreichen; ~ *down* herunterreichen; vererben; ~ *in* et. hinein-, hereinreichen; *Prüfungsarbeit etc.* abgeben; *Bericht, Gesuch* einreichen; ~ *on* weiterreichen, -geben; ~ *out* aus-, verteilen; ~ *over* übergeben; aushändigen; ~ *up* hinauf-, heraufreichen; **~bag** ['hændbæg] Handtasche *f*; **~bill** Handzettel *m*, Flugblatt *n*; **~brake** ⊕ Handbremse *f*; **~cuffs** *pl.* Handschellen *pl.*; **~ful** [~fʊl] Handvoll *f*; F Plage *f*.

hand·i·cap ['hændɪkæp] 1. Handikap *n*; Vorgabe *f*; Vorgaberennen *n*, -spiel *n*, -kampf *m*; *fig.* Behinderung *f*, Benachteiligung *f*, Nachteil *m*; *s. mental, physical*; 2. (*-pp-*) (be)hindern, benachteiligen, belasten; *Sport:* mit Handikaps belegen; **~ped** 1. gehandikapt, behindert, benachteiligt; *s. mental, physical*; 2. *the* ~ *pl.* ⚕ die Behinderten *pl.*

hand·ker·chief ['hæŋkətʃɪf] (*pl.* -chiefs) Taschentuch *n*.

han·dle ['hændl] 1. Griff *m*; Stiel *m*; Henkel *m*; (*Pumpen- etc.*)Schwengel *m*; *fig.* Handhabe *f*; *fly off the* ~ F wütend werden; 2. anfassen; handhaben; behandeln; △ *nicht handeln*; **~bar(s** *pl.*) Lenkstange *f*.

hand|lug·gage ['hændlʌgɪdʒ] Handgepäck *n*; **~made** handgearbeitet; **~rail** Geländer *n*; **~shake** Händedruck *m*; **~some** □ ['hænsəm] (~*r*, ~*st*) ansehnlich; hübsch; anständig; **~work** Handarbeit *f*; **~writ·ing** Handschrift *f*; **~writ·ten** handgeschrieben; **~y** □ [~ɪ] (*-ier*, *-iest*) geschickt; handlich; nützlich; zur Hand; *come in* ~ sich als nützlich erweisen; sehr gelegen kommen.

hang¹ [hæŋ] (*hung*) *v/t.* hängen; auf-, einhängen; verhängen; hängenlassen; *Tapete* ankleben; *v/i.* hängen; schweben; sich neigen; ~ *about*, ~ *around* herumlungern; ~ *back* zögern; ~ *on* sich klammern (*to* an *acc.*) (*a. fig.*); ~ *up teleph.* einhängen, auflegen; *she hung up on me* sie legte einfach auf; 2. Fall *m*, Sitz *m* (*e-s Kleides etc.*); *get the* ~ *of* s.th. et. kapieren, den Dreh rauskriegen (bei et.).

H

hang² [~] (*hanged*) (auf)hängen; ~ **o.s.** sich erhängen.

han·gar ['hæŋə] Hangar *m*, Flugzeughalle *f*.

hang·dog ['hæŋdɒg] Armesünder...

hang·er ['hæŋə] Kleiderbügel *m*; ~ **on** *fig.* [~ər'ɒn] (*pl. hangers-on*) Klette *f*.

hang|·glid·er ['hæŋglaɪdə] (Flug-) Drachen *m*; Drachenflieger(in); ~ **glid·ing** [~ŋ] Drachenfliegen *n*.

hang·ing ['hæŋɪŋ] **1.** hängend; Hänge...; **2.** (Er)Hängen *n*; ~s Tapete *f*, Wandbehang *m*, Vorhang *m*.

hang·man ['hæŋmən] (*pl. -men*) Henker *m*.

hang·nail ⚕ ['hæŋneɪl] Niednagel *m*.

hang·o·ver F ['hæŋəʊvə] Katzenjammer *m*, Kater *m*.

han·ker ['hæŋkə] sich sehnen (*after*, *for* nach).

hap·haz·ard ['hæp'hæzəd] **1.** Zufall *m*; *at* ~ aufs Geratewohl; **2.** □ willkürlich, plan-, wahllos.

hap·pen ['hæpən] sich ereignen, geschehen; *he* ~*ed to be at home* er war zufällig zu Hause; ~ *on*, ~ *upon* zufällig treffen auf (*acc.*); ~ *in Am.* F hereinschneien; ~**ing** ['hæpnɪŋ] Ereignis *n*, Vorkommnis *n*; Happening *n*.

hap·pi|·ly ['hæpɪlɪ] glücklich(erweise); ~**ness** [~nɪs] Glück(seligkeit *f*) *n*.

hap·py □ ['hæpɪ] (*-ier, -iest*) glücklich; beglückt; erfreut; erfreulich; geschickt; treffend; F beschwipst; ~**go-luck·y** unbekümmert.

ha·rangue [hə'ræŋ] **1.** Strafpredigt *f*; **2.** *v/t.* j-m e-e Strafpredigt halten.

har·ass ['hærəs] belästigen, quälen.

har·bo(u)r ['hɑːbə] **1.** Hafen *m*; Zufluchtsort *m*; **2.** beherbergen; *Gedanken, Rache etc.* hegen.

hard [hɑːd] **1.** *adj.* □ hart; schwer; mühselig, streng; ausdauernd; fleißig; heftig; hart (*Droge*), *Getränk a.* stark; ~ *of hearing* schwerhörig; **2.** *adv.* stark; tüchtig; mit Mühe; ~ *by* nahe bei; ~ *up* in Not; ~**boiled** ['hɑːdbɔɪld] hart(gekocht); *fig.* hart, unsentimental, nüchtern; ~ *cash* Bargeld *n*; klingende Münze; ~**core** harter Kern (*e-r Bande etc.*); ~**core** zum harten Kern gehörend; hart (*Pornographie*); ~**cov·er** *print.* **1.** gebunden; **2.** Hard cover *n*, gebundene Ausgabe; ~**en** [~n] härten; hart ma-

chen *od.* werden; (sich) abhärten; *fig.* (sich) verhärten (*to* gegen); *econ.* sich festigen (*Preise*); ~ **hat** Schutzhelm *m* (*für Bauarbeiter etc.*); ~**head·ed** nüchtern, praktisch; *bsd. Am.* starr-, dickköpfig; ~ **la·bo(u)r** ⚖ Zwangsarbeit *f*; ~ **line** *bsd. pol.* harter Kurs; ~**line** *bsd. pol.* hart, kompromißlos; ~**heart·ed** □ hart (-herzig); ~**ly** [~lɪ] kaum; streng; mit Mühe; ~**ness** [~nɪs] Härte *f*; Schwierigkeit *f*; Not *f*; ~**ship** [~ʃɪp] Bedrängnis *f*, Not *f*; Härte *f*; ~ **shoul·der** *mot.* Standspur *f*; ~**ware** Eisenwaren *pl.*; Haushaltswaren *pl.*; *Computer:* Hardware *f* (*technisch-physikalische Teile*); *Sprachlabor:* Hardware *f*, technische Ausrüstung; **har·dy** □ [~ɪ] (*-ier, -iest*) kühn; widerstandsfähig, hart; abgehärtet; winterfest (*Pflanze*).

hare *zo.* [heə] Hase *m*; ~**bell** ♥ ['heəbel] Glockenblume *f*; ~**brained** verrückt (*Person, Plan*); ~**lip** *anat.* [~'lɪp] Hasenscharte *f*.

hark [hɑːk]: ~ *back* F zurückgreifen, -kommen, *a. zeitlich:* zurückgehen (*to* auf *acc.*).

harm [hɑːm] **1.** Schaden *m*; Unrecht *n*, Böse(s) *n*; **2.** beschädigen, verletzen; schaden, Leid zufügen (*dat.*); ~**ful** □ ['hɑːmfl] schädlich; ~**less** □ [~lɪs] harmlos; unschädlich.

har·mo|ni·ous □ [hɑː'məʊnjəs] harmonisch; ~**nize** ['hɑːmənaɪz] *v/t.* in Einklang bringen; *v/i.* harmonieren; ~**ny** [~ɪ] Harmonie *f*.

har·ness ['hɑːnɪs] **1.** Harnisch *m*; (*Pferde- etc.*)Geschirr *n*; *die in* ~ *fig.* in den Sielen sterben; **2.** anschirren; *Naturkräfte etc.* nutzbar machen.

harp [hɑːp] **1.** ♪ Harfe *f*; **2.** ♪ Harfe spielen; ~ *on fig.* herumreiten auf (*dat.*).

har·poon [hɑː'puːn] **1.** Harpune *f*; **2.** harpunieren.

har·row ✔ ['hærəʊ] **1.** Egge *f*; **2.** eggen.

har·row·ing □ ['hærəʊɪŋ] quälend, qualvoll, erschütternd.

harsh □ [hɑːʃ] rauh; herb; grell; streng; schroff; barsch.

hart *zo.* [hɑːt] Hirsch *m*.

har·vest ['hɑːvɪst] **1.** Ernte(zeit) *f*; (Ernte)Ertrag *m*; **2.** ernten; einbringen; ~**er** [~ə] *bsd.* Mähdrescher *m*.

has [hæz] **3.** *sg. pres. von* have.

hash¹ [hæʃ] **1.** Haschee *n*; *fig.* Durcheinander *n*; *make a ~ of* verpfuschen; 2. *Fleisch* zerhacken, -kleinern.

hash[2] F [~] Hasch *n* (*Haschisch*).

hash·ish ['hæʃiːʃ] Haschisch *n*.

hasp [hɑːsp] Schließband *n*, (Verschluß)Spange *f*.

haste [heɪst] Eile *f*; *make ~* sich beeilen; **has·ten** ['heɪsn] *j-n* antreiben; (sich be)eilen; *et.* beschleunigen; **hast·y** □ ['heɪstɪ] (*-ier, -iest*) (vor)eilig; hastig; hitzig, heftig.

hat [hæt] Hut *m*.

hatch[1] [hætʃ] *a. ~ out* ausbrüten; ausschlüpfen.

hatch[2] [~] ♏, 🗡 Luke *f*; Durchreiche *f* (*für Speisen*); **~·back** *mot.* ['hætʃbæk] (Wagen *m* mit) Hecktür *f*.

hatch·et ['hætʃɪt] (Kriegs)Beil *n*.

hatch·way ♏ ['hætʃweɪ] Luke *f*.

hate [heɪt] 1. Haß *m*; 2. hassen; **~·ful** □ ['heɪtfl] verhaßt; abscheulich; **ha·tred** [~rɪd] Haß *m*.

haugh·ti·ness ['hɔːtɪnɪs] Stolz *m*; Hochmut *m*; **~·ty** □ [~ɪ] stolz; hochmütig.

haul [hɔːl] 1. Ziehen *n*; (Fisch)Zug *m*; Transport(weg *m*) *m*; 2. ziehen; schleppen; transportieren; 🗡 fördern; ⚓ abdrehen.

haunch [hɔːntʃ] Hüfte *f*; *zo.* Keule *f*; *Am. a. ~es pl.* Gesäß *n*; *zo.* Hinterbacken *pl.*

haunt [hɔːnt] 1. Aufenthaltsort *m*; Schlupfwinkel *m*; 2. oft besuchen; heimsuchen; verfolgen; spuken in (*dat.*); **~·ing** □ ['hɔːntɪŋ] quälend; unvergeßlich, eindringlich.

have [hæv] (*had*) *v/t.* haben; bekommen; *Mahlzeit* einnehmen; *~ to do* tun müssen; *I had my hair cut* ich ließ mir die Haare schneiden; *he will ~ it that ...* er behauptet, daß ...; *I had better go* es wäre besser, wenn ich ginge; *I had rather go* ich möchte lieber gehen; *~ about one* bei *od.* an sich haben; *~ on* anhaben; *~ it out with* sich auseinandersetzen mit; *v/aux.* haben; *bei v/i. oft* sein; *~ come* gekommen sein.

ha·ven ['heɪvn] Hafen *m* (*mst fig.*).

hav·oc ['hævək] Verwüstung *f*; *play ~ with* verwüsten, zerstören; verheerend wirken auf (*acc.*), übel mitspielen (*dat.*).

haw ♏ [hɔː] Mehlbeere *f*.

Ha·wai·i·an [həˈwaɪən] 1. hawai-

isch; 2. Hawaiianer(in); *ling.* Hawaiisch *n*.

hawk[1] *zo.* [hɔːk] Habicht *m*, Falke *m*.

hawk[2] [~] hausieren (gehen) mit; auf der Straße verkaufen.

haw·thorn ♏ ['hɔːθɔːn] Weißdorn *m*.

hay [heɪ] 1. Heu *n*; 2. Heu machen; **~·cock** ['heɪkɒk] Heuhaufen *m*; **~ fe·ver** Heuschnupfen *m*; **~·loft** Heuboden *m*; **~·rick**, **~·stack** Heumiete *f*.

haz·ard ['hæzəd] 1. Zufall *m*; Gefahr *f*, Wagnis *n*; Hasard(spiel) *n*; 2. wagen; **~·ous** □ [~əs] gewagt.

haze [heɪz] Dunst *m*, feiner Nebel.

ha·zel ['heɪzl] 1. ♏ Haselnuß *f*, Hasel(nuß)strauch *m*; 2. (hasel)nußbraun; **~·nut** ♏ Haselnuß *f*.

haz·y □ ['heɪzɪ] (*-ier, -iest*) dunstig, diesig; *fig.* unklar.

H-bomb ☢ ['eɪtʃbɒm] H-Bombe *f*, Wasserstoffbombe *f*.

he [hiː] 1. er; 2. Er *m*; *zo.* Männchen *n*; 3. *adj. in Zssgn, bsd. zo.*: männlich, ...männchen *n*; **~-goat** Ziegenbock *m*.

head [hed] 1. Kopf *m* (*a. fig.*); Haupt *n* (*a. fig.*); *nach Zahlwort* (*pl. ~*): Kopf *m*, Person *f*, Stück *n* (*Vieh etc.*); Leiter(in); Chef *m*; Kopfende *n* (*e-s Bettes etc.*); Kopfseite *f* (*e-r Münze*); Gipfel *m*; Quelle *f*; Vorderteil *n*; ♏ Bug *m*; Hauptpunkt *m*, Abschnitt *m*; Überschrift *f*; *come to a ~* eitern (*Geschwür*); *fig.* sich zuspitzen, zur Entscheidung kommen; *get it into one's ~ that ...* es sich in den Kopf setzen, daß; *lose one's ~* den Kopf *od.* die Nerven verlieren; *~ over heels* Hals über Kopf; 2. Ober..., Haupt..., Chef..., oberste(r, -s), erste(r, -s); 3. *v/t.* (an)führen; an der Spitze von *et.* stehen; vorausgehen (*dat.*); mit *e-r* Überschrift versehen; *~ off* ablenken; *v/i.* gehen, fahren; sich bewegen (*for auf acc. ... zu*), lossteuern, zugehen (*for auf acc.*); ♏ zusteuern (*for auf acc.*); entspringen (*Fluß*); **~·ache** ['hedeɪk] Kopfweh *n*; **~·band** Stirnband *n*; **~·dress** Kopfschmuck *m*; **~·gear** Kopfbedeckung *f*; Zaumzeug *n*; **~·ing** [~ɪŋ] Brief-, Titelkopf *m*, Rubrik *f*; Überschrift *f*, Titel *m*; Kopfballspiel *n*; **~·land** [~lənd] Vorgebirge *n*, Kap *n*; **~·light** *mot.* Scheinwerfer(licht *n*) *m*; **~·line** Überschrift *f*; Schlagzeile *f*; **~s** *pl.* Rundfunk, *TV:* das Wichtigste in Schlagzeilen; **~·long 1.** *adj.* ungestüm; **2.** *adv.* kopfüber; **~·mas·ter** *Schule:* Direktor *m*, Rektor *m*; **~·mis·tress** *Schule:* Direktorin *f*, Rektorin *f*; **~·on** frontal; **~ collision** Frontalzusammenstoß *m*; **~·phones** *pl.* Kopfhörer *pl.*; **~·quar·ters** *pl.* ✕ Hauptquartier *n*; Zentrale *f*; **~·rest**, **~ re·straint** Kopfstütze *f*; **~·set** *bsd. Am.* Kopfhörer *pl.*; **~ start** *Sport:* Vorgabe *f*, *-*sprung (*a. fig.*); **~·strong** halsstarrig; **~·wa·ters** *pl.* Quellgebiet *n*; **~·way** *fig.* Fortschritt(e *pl.*) *m*; *make* ~ (gut) vorankommen; **~·word** Stichwort *n* (*in e-m Wörterbuch*); **~·y** □ [~ɪ] (*-ier, -iest*) ungestüm; voreilig; zu Kopfe steigend.

heal [hiːl] heilen; ~ *over*, ~ *up* (zu-) heilen.

health [helθ] Gesundheit *f*; **~ club** Fitneßclub *m*; **~ food** Reformkost *f*; **~ food shop** (*bsd. Am. store*) Reformhaus *n*; **~ insurance** Krankenversicherung *f*; **~ resort** Kurort *m*; **~ service** Gesundheitsdienst *m*; **~·ful** □ [ˈhelθfl] gesund; heilsam; **~·y** □ [~ɪ] (*-ier, -iest*) gesund.

heap [hiːp] **1.** Haufe(n) *m*; **2.** *a.* ~ *up* aufhäufen, *fig. a.* anhäufen.

hear [hɪə] (*heard*) hören; erfahren; anhören; *j-m* zuhören; erhören; *Zeugen* vernehmen; *Lektion* abhören; **~d** [hɜːd] *pret. u. p.p. von* hear; **~·er** [ˈhɪərə] (Zu)Hörer(in); **~·ing** [~rɪŋ] Gehör *n*; ⚖ Verhandlung *f*; ⚖ Vernehmung *f*; *bsd. pol.* Hearing *n*, Anhörung *f*; *within* (*out of*) ~ in (außer) Hörweite; **~·say** Gerede *n*; *by* ~ vom Hörensagen *n*.

hearse [hɜːs] Leichenwagen *m*.

heart [hɑːt] *anat.* Herz *n* (*a. fig.*); Innere(s) *n*; Kern *m*; *fig.* Liebling *m*, Schatz *m*; *by* ~ auswendig; *out of* ~ mutlos; *cross my* ~ Hand aufs Herz, auf Ehre u. Gewissen; *lay to* ~ sich zu Herzen nehmen; *lose* ~ den Mut verlieren; *take* ~ sich ein Herz fassen; **~·ache** [ˈhɑːteɪk] Kummer *m*; **~ at·tack** Herzanfall *m*; **~ Herzinfarkt** *m*; **~·beat** Herzschlag *m*; **~ break** Leid *n*, großer Kummer; **~ break·ing** □ [~ɪŋ] herzzerreißend; **~·brok·en** gebrochen, verzweifelt; **~·burn** ✿ Sodbrennen *n*; **~·en** [~n] ermutigen; **~ fail·ure** ✿ Herzinsuffizienz *f*; ✿ Herzversagen *n*; **~·felt** innig, tiefempfunden.

hearth [hɑːθ] Herd *m* (*a. fig.*).
heart|less □ [ˈhɑːtlɪs] herzlos; **~·rend·ing** □ [ˈhɑːtrendɪŋ] herzzerreißend; **~ trans·plant** ✿ Herzverpflanzung *f*, *-*transplantation *f*; **~·y** □ [~ɪ] (*-ier, -iest*) herzlich; aufrichtig; gesund; herzhaft.

heat [hiːt] **1.** Hitze *f*; Wärme *f*; Eifer *m*; *Sport:* Vorlauf *m*; *zo.* Läufigkeit *f*; **2.** heizen; (sich) erhitzen (*a. fig.*); **~·ed** □ [ˈhiːtɪd] erhitzt; *fig.* erregt; **~·er** ⊕ [~ə] Heizgerät *n*, Ofen *m*.

heath [hiːθ] Heide *f*; ✿ Heidekraut *n*.

hea·then [ˈhiːðn] **1.** Heide *m*, *-*in *f*; **2.** heidnisch.

heath·er ✿ [ˈheðə] Heidekraut *n*.

heat|ing [ˈhiːtɪŋ] Heizung *f*; *attr.* Heiz...; **~·proof**, **~·re·sis·tant**, **~·re·sist·ing** hitzebeständig; **~ shield** *Raumfahrt:* Hitzeschild *m*; **~·stroke** ✿ Hitzschlag *m*; **~ wave** Hitzewelle *f*.

heave [hiːv] **1.** Heben *n*; **2.** (*heaved*, *bsd.* ⚓ *hove*) *v/t.* heben; *Seufzer* ausstoßen; *Anker* lichten; *v/i.* sich heben u. senken, wogen.

heav·en [ˈhevn] Himmel *m*; **~·ly** [~ɪ] himmlisch.

heav·i·ness [ˈhevɪnɪs] Schwere *f*, Druck *m*; Schwerfälligkeit *f*; Schwermut *f*.

heav·y □ [ˈhevɪ] (*-ier, -iest*) schwer; schwermütig; schwerfällig; trüb; drückend; heftig (*Regen etc.*); unwegsam (*Straße*); Schwer...; **~ cur·rent** ⚡ Starkstrom *m*; **~·du·ty** ⊕ Hochleistungs...; strapazierfähig; **~·hand·ed** □ ungeschickt; **~·heart·ed** niedergeschlagen; **~ weight** *Boxen:* Schwergewicht(ler *m*) *n*.

He·brew [ˈhiːbruː] **1.** hebräisch; **2.** Hebräer(in), Jude *m*, Jüdin *f*; *ling.* Hebräisch *n*.

heck·le [ˈhekl] *j-m* zusetzen; *e-n* Redner durch Zwischenrufe *od.* -fragen aus der Fassung bringen *od.* in die Enge treiben.

hec·tic [ˈhektɪk] (*~ally*) hektisch.

hedge [hedʒ] **1.** Hecke *f*; **2.** *v/t.* mit *e-r* Hecke einfassen *od.* umgeben; *v/i.* ausweichen, sich nicht festlegen (wollen); **~·hog** *zo.* [ˈhedʒhɒg] Igel *m*; *Am.* Stachelschwein *n*; **~·row** Hecke *f*.

heed [hiːd] **1.** Beachtung *f*, Aufmerksamkeit *f*; *take* ~ *of*, *give od. pay* ~ *to* achtgeben auf (*acc.*), beachten; **2.** beachten, achten auf (*acc.*); **~·less** □

['hi:dlıs] unachtsam; unbekümmert (*of* um).

heel [hi:l] **1.** Ferse *f*; Absatz *m*; *Am. sl.* Lump *m*; *head over* ~*s* Hals über Kopf; *down at* ~ mit schiefen Absätzen; *fig.* abgerissen; schlampig; **2.** Absätze machen auf.

hef·ty ['heftı] (*-ier, -iest*) kräftig, stämmig; mächtig (*Schlag etc.*), gewaltig.

heif·er *zo.* ['hefə] Färse *f*, junge Kuh.

height [haıt] Höhe *f*; Höhepunkt *m*; ~**en** ['haıtn] erhöhen; vergrößern.

hei·nous □ ['heınəs] abscheulich.

heir [eə] Erbe *m*; ~ *apparent* rechtmäßiger Erbe; ~**ess** ['eərıs] Erbin *f*; ~**loom** ['eəlu:m] Erbstück *n*.

held [held] *pret. u. p.p. von* hold 2.

hel·i·cop·ter 🛩 ['helıkɒptə] Hubschrauber *m*, Helikopter *m*; ~**port** 🛩 Hubschrauberlandeplatz *m*.

hell [hel] **1.** Hölle *f*; *attr.* Höllen...; *what the* ~ ...? F was zum Teufel ...?; *raise* ~ F e-n Mordskrach schlagen; **2.** *int.* F verdammt!; verflucht!; ~**bent** ['helbent] ganz versessen, wie wild (*for*, on auf *acc.*); ~**ish** □ [~ıʃ] höllisch.

hel·lo *int.* [hə'ləʊ] hallo!

helm ⚓ [helm] Ruder *n*, Steuer *n*; ⚠ *nicht* Helm.

hel·met ['helmıt] Helm *m*.

helms·man ⚓ ['helmzmən] (*pl. -men*) Steuermann *m*.

help [help] **1.** Hilfe *f*; (Hilfs)Mittel *n*; (Dienst)Mädchen *n*; **2.** helfen; ~ *o.s.* sich bedienen, zulangen; *I cannot* ~ *it* ich kann es nicht ändern; *I could not* ~ *laughing* ich mußte einfach lachen; ~**er** ['helpə] Helfer(in); ~**ful** □ [~fl] hilfreich; nützlich; ~**ing** [~ıŋ] Portion *f* (*Essen*); ~**less** □ [~lıs] hilflos; ~**less·ness** [~nıs] Hilflosigkeit *f*.

hel·ter-skel·ter ['heltə'skeltə] **1.** *adv.* holterdiepolter, Hals über Kopf; **2.** *adj.* hastig, überstürzt; **3.** *Brt.* Rutschbahn *f*.

helve [helv] Stiel *m*, Griff *m*.

Hel·ve·tian [hel'vi:ʃən] Helvetier(in); *attr.* Schweizer...

hem [hem] **1.** Saum *m*; **2.** (*-mm-*) säumen; ~ *in* einschließen; **hem·i·sphere** *geogr.* ['hemısfıə] Halbkugel *f*, Hemisphäre *f*.

hem·line ['hemlaın] (Kleider)Saum *m*.

hem·lock 🌿 ['hemlɒk] Schierling *m*.

hemp 🌿 [hemp] Hanf *m*.

hem·stitch ['hemstıtʃ] Hohlsaum *m*.

hen [hen] *zo.* Henne *f*, Huhn *n*; Weibchen *n* (*von Vögeln*).

hence [hens] hieraus; daher; *a week* ~ *in od.* nach e-r Woche; ~**forth** ['hens'fɔ:θ], ~**for·ward** [~'fɔ:wəd] von nun an.

hen·house ['henhaʊs] Hühnerstall *m*; ~**pecked** unter dem Pantoffel (stehend).

her [hɜː, hə] sie; ihr; ihr(e); sich.

her·ald ['herəld] **1.** *hist.* Herold *m*; **2.** ankündigen; ~ *in* einführen; ~**ry** [~rı] Wappenkunde *f*, Heraldik *f*.

herb 🌿 [hɜːb] Kraut *n*; **her·ba·ceous** 🌿 [hɜː'beıʃəs] krautartig; ~ *border* (Stauden)Rabatte *f*; **herb·age** ['hɜːbıdʒ] Gras *n*; Weide *f*; **her·biv·o·rous** □ *zo.* [hɜː'bıvərəs] pflanzenfressend.

herd [hɜːd] **1.** Herde *f* (*a. fig.*), *wildlebender Tiere a.* Rudel *n*; **2.** *v/t.* Vieh hüten; *v/i. a.* ~ *together* in e-r Herde leben; sich zusammendrängen; ~**s·man** ['hɜːdzmən] (*pl. -men*) Hirt *m*.

here [hıə] hier; hierher; ~ *you are* hier(, bitte); ~*'s to you!* auf dein Wohl!

here·a·bout(s) ['hıərəbaʊt(s)] hier herum, in dieser Gegend; ~**af·ter** [hıər'ɑ:ftə] **1.** künftig; **2.** *das* Jenseits; ~**by** ['hıə'baı] hierdurch.

he·red·i·ta·ry [hı'redıtərı] erblich; Erb...; ~**ty** [~ı] Erblichkeit *f*; ererbte Anlagen *pl.*, Erbmasse *f*.

here·in ['hıər'ın] hierin; ~**of** [~'ɒv] hiervon.

her·e·sy ['herəsı] Häresie *f*, Ketzerei *f*; ~**tic** [~tık] Häretiker(in), Ketzer(in).

here·up·on ['hıərə'pɒn] hierauf; ~**with** hiermit.

her·i·tage ['herıtıdʒ] Erbschaft *f*.

her·mit ['hɜːmıt] Einsiedler *m*.

he·ro ['hıərəʊ] (*pl. -roes*) Held *m*; ~**ic** [hı'rəʊık] (~*ally*) heroisch; heldenhaft; Helden...

her·o·in ['herəʊın] Heroin *n*.

her·o·ine ['herəʊın] Heldin *f*; ~**is·m** [~ızəm] Heldenmut *m*, -tum *n*.

her·on *zo.* ['herən] Reiher *m*.

her·ring *zo.* ['herıŋ] Hering *m*.

hers [hɜːz] der, die, das ihr(ig)e; ihr.

her·self [hɜː'self] sie selbst; ihr selbst; sich; *by* ~ von selbst, allein, ohne Hilfe.

hes·i·tant ☐ ['hezɪtənt] zögernd, zaudernd, unschlüssig; **~·tate** [~eɪt] zögern, zaudern, unschlüssig sein, Bedenken haben; **~·ta·tion** [hezɪ'teɪʃn] Zögern n, Zaudern n, Unschlüssigkeit f; without ~ ohne zu zögern, bedenkenlos.

hew [hju:] (hewed, hewed od. hewn) hauen, hacken; ~ down fällen, umhauen; **~n** [hju:n] p.p. von hew.

hey int. [heɪ] ei!, hei!; he!, heda!

hey·day ['heɪdeɪ] Höhepunkt m, Blüte f.

hi int. [haɪ] hallo!; he!, heda!

hi·ber·nate zo. ['haɪbəneɪt] Winterschlaf halten.

hic·cup, ~·cough ['hɪkʌp] 1. Schluckauf m; 2. den Schluckauf haben.

hid [hɪd] pret. von hide²; **~·den** ['hɪdn] p.p. von hide².

hide¹ [haɪd] Haut f, Fell n.

hide² [~] (hid, hidden) (sich) verbergen, -stecken; **~-and-seek** ['haɪdn'si:k] Versteckspiel n; **~·a·way** [~əweɪ] Versteck n; **~·bound** engstirnig.

hid·e·ous ☐ ['hɪdɪəs] scheußlich.

hide·out ['haɪdaʊt] Versteck n.

hid·ing¹ f ['haɪdɪŋ] Tracht f Prügel.

hid·ing² [~] Versteck n, -bergen n, **~·place** Versteck n.

hi-fi ['haɪ'faɪ] 1. (pl. hi-fis) Hi-Fi n; Hi-Fi-Anlage f; 2. Hi-Fi-...

high [haɪ] 1. adj. ☐ hoch; vornehm; gut, edel (Charakter); stolz; hochtrabend; angegangen (Fleisch); extrem; stark; üppig, flott (Leben); F blau (betrunken); F high (im Drogenrausch; in euphorischer Stimmung); Haupt..., Hoch..., Ober...; with a ~ hand arrogant, anmaßend; in ~ spirits guter Laune; ~ society High-Society f; gehobene Gesellschaftsschicht; ♀ Tech = ♀ Technology Hochtechnologie f; ~ time höchste Zeit; ~ words heftige Worte; 2. meteor. Hoch n; 3. adv. hoch; stark, heftig; **~·ball** Am. ['haɪbɔːl] Highball m (Whisky-Cocktail); **~·brow** F 1. Intellektuelle(r m) f; 2. betont intellektuell; **~·class** erstklassig; **~·fi·del·i·ty** High-Fidelity f; **~·fi·del·i·ty** High-Fidelity-...; **~·grade** hochwertig; **~·hand·ed** ☐ anmaßend; **~·jump** Sport: Hochsprung m; ~ **jump·er** Sport: Hochspringer(in); **~·land** ['haɪlənd] mst ~s pl. Hochland n; **~·lights** pl. fig. Höhepunkte pl.; **~·ly** [~lɪ] hoch; sehr; speak~ of s.o. j-n loben; **~·mind·ed** hochgesinnt; hoch (Ideale); **~·ness** [~nɪs] Höhe f; fig. Hoheit f; **~·pitched** schrill (Ton); steil (Dach); **~·pow·ered** ⊕ Hochleistungs..., Groß..., stark; dynamisch; **~·pres·sure** meteor., ⊕ Hochdruck...; **~·rise** 1. Hoch..., Hochhaus...; 2. Hochhaus n; **~·road** Hauptstraße f; ~ **school** bsd. Am. High-School f; **~·street** Hauptstraße f; **~·strung** reizbar, nervös; ~ **tea** Brt. (frühes) Abendessen; ~ **wa·ter** Hochwasser n; **~·way** bsd. Am. od. ⚖ Highway m, Haupt(verkehrs)straße f; ♀ Code Brt. Straßenverkehrsordnung f; **~·way·man** (pl. -men) Straßenräuber m.

hi·jack ['haɪdʒæk] 1. Flugzeug entführen; j-n, Geldtransport etc. überfallen; 2. (Flugzeug)Entführung f; Überfall m; **~·er** [~ə] (Flugzeug)Entführer m, Luftpirat m; Räuber m.

hike F [haɪk] 1. wandern; 2. Wanderung f; Am. Erhöhung f (Preis etc.); **hik·er** ['haɪkə] Wanderer m; **hik·ing** [~ɪŋ] Wandern n.

hi·lar·i·ous ☐ [hɪ'leərɪəs] ausgelassen; **~·ty** [hɪ'lærətɪ] Ausgelassenheit f.

hill [hɪl] Hügel m, Berg m; **~·bil·ly** Am. F ['hɪlbɪlɪ] Hinterwäldler m; ~ **music** Hillbilly-Musik f; **~·ock** ['hɪlək] kleiner Hügel; **~·side** ['hɪl'saɪd] Hang m; **~·top** Gipfel m; **~·y** ['hɪlɪ] (-ier, -iest) hügelig.

hilt [hɪlt] Griff m (bsd. am Degen).

him [hɪm] ihn; ihm; sich; **~·self** [hɪm'self] sich; sich (selbst); (er, ihm, ihn) selbst; by ~ von selbst, allein, ohne Hilfe.

hind¹ zo. [haɪnd] Hirschkuh f.

hind² [~] Hinter...

hin·der¹ ['haɪndə] hintere(r, -s); Hinter...

hin·der² ['hɪndə] hindern (from an dat.); hemmen.

hind·most ['haɪndməʊst] hinterste(r, -s), letzte(r, -s).

hin·drance ['hɪndrəns] Hindernis n.

hinge [hɪndʒ] 1. Türangel f; Scharnier n; fig. Angelpunkt m; 2. ~ on, ~ upon fig. abhängen von.

hint [hɪnt] 1. Wink m; Anspielung f; take a ~ e-n Wink verstehen; 2. andeuten; anspielen (at auf acc.).

hin·ter·land ['hɪntəlænd] Hinterland *n*.

hip[1] *anat.* [hɪp] Hüfte *f*.

hip[2] ♀ [~] Hagebutte *f*.

hip·pie, hip·py ['hɪpɪ] Hippie *m*.

hip·po *zo.* F ['hɪpəʊ] (*pl. -pos*) = **~·pot·a·mus** *zo.* [hɪpə'pɒtəməs] (*pl. -muses, -mi* [-maɪ]) Fluß-, Nilpferd *n*.

hire ['haɪə] **1.** Miete *f*; Entgelt *n*, Lohn *m*; *for* ~ zu vermieten; frei (*Taxi*); ~ *car* Leih-, Mietwagen *m*; ~ *charge* Leihgebühr *f*; ~ *purchase Brt. econ.* Kauf *m* auf Raten- *od.* Teilzahlung; **2.** mieten; *j-n* anstellen; ~ *out* vermieten.

his [hɪz] sein(e); seine(r, -s).

hiss [hɪs] **1.** zischen; zischeln; *a.* ~ *at* auszischen; **2.** Zischen *n*.

his|to·ri·an [hɪ'stɔːrɪən] Historiker *m*; **~·tor·ic** [hɪ'stɒrɪk] (*~ally*) historisch, geschichtlich; **~·tor·i·cal** □ [~kl] historisch, geschichtlich; Geschichts...; **~·to·ry** ['hɪstərɪ] Geschichte *f*; ~ *of civilization* Kulturgeschichte *f*; *contemporary* ~ Zeitgeschichte *f*.

hit [hɪt] **1.** Schlag *m*, Stoß *m*; *fig.* (Seiten)Hieb *m*; (Glücks)Treffer *m*; Hit *m* (*Buch, Schlager etc.*); **2.** (*-tt-*; *hit*) schlagen, stoßen; treffen; auf *et.* stoßen; ~ *it off with* F sich vertragen mit; ~ *on*, ~ *upon* (zufällig) stoßen auf (*acc.*), finden; **~·and-run** [hɪtənd'rʌn] **1.** *a.* ~ *accident* Unfall *m* mit Fahrerflucht; **2.** ~ *driver* unflüchtiger Fahrer.

hitch [hɪtʃ] **1.** Ruck *m*; ♣ Knoten *m*; Schwierigkeit *f*, Problem *n*, Haken *m*; **2.** (ruckartig) ziehen, rücken; befestigen, festmachen, -haken, anbinden, ankoppeln; **~·hike** ['hɪtʃhaɪk] per Anhalter fahren, trampen; **~·hik·er** Anhalter(in), Tramper(in).

hith·er ['hɪðə] ~ *and thither* hierhin u. dorthin; **~·to** bisher.

hive [haɪv] Bienenstock *m*; Bienenschwarm *m*.

hoard [hɔːd] **1.** Vorrat *m*, Schatz *m*; **2.** *a.* ~ *up* horten, hamstern.

hoard·ing ['hɔːdɪŋ] Bauzaun *m*; *Brt.* Reklametafel *f*.

hoar·frost ['hɔː'frɒst] (Rauh)Reif *m*.

hoarse □ [hɔːs] (*~r, ~st*) heiser, rauh.

hoar·y ['hɔːrɪ] (*-ier, -iest*) (alters-)grau.

hoax [həʊks] **1.** Falschmeldung *f*; (übler) Scherz *m*; **2.** *j-n* hereinlegen.

hob·ble ['hɒbl] **1.** Hinken *n*, Humpeln *n*; **2.** *v/i.* humpeln, hinken (*a. fig.*); *v/t.* an den Füßen fesseln.

hob·by ['hɒbɪ] *fig.* Steckenpferd *n*, Hobby *n*; **~·horse** Steckenpferd *n*; Schaukelpferd *n*.

hob·gob·lin ['hɒbgɒblɪn] Kobold *m*.

ho·bo *Am.* ['həʊbəʊ] (*pl. -boes, -bos*) Wanderarbeiter *m*; Landstreicher *m*.

hock[1] [hɒk] Rheinwein *m*.

hock[2] *zo.* [~] Sprunggelenk *n*.

hock·ey ['hɒkɪ] *Brt., Am.* field ~ *Sport:* Hockey *n*; *Am.* Eishockey *n*.

hoe ✓ [həʊ] **1.** Hacke *f*; **2.** hacken.

hog [hɒg] (Mast)Schwein *n*; *Am.* Schwein *n*; **~·gish** □ ['hɒgɪʃ] schweinisch; gefräßig.

hoist [hɔɪst] **1.** (Lasten)Aufzug *m*, Winde *f*; **2.** hochziehen; hissen.

hold [həʊld] **1.** Halten *n*; Halt *m*; Griff *m*; Gewalt *f*, Macht *f*, Einfluß *m*; ♣ Lade-, Frachtraum *m*; *catch (od. get, lay, take, seize)* ~ *of* erfassen, ergreifen; sich aneignen; *keep* ~ *of* festhalten; **2.** (*held*) halten; (fest)halten; (zurück-, einbe)halten; abhalten (*from* von); an-, aufhalten; *Wahlen, Versammlung etc.* abhalten; *Sport:* Meisterschaft *etc.* austragen; beibehalten; innehaben; besitzen; *Amt* bekleiden; *Platz* einnehmen; *Rekord* halten; fassen, enthalten; behaupten, *Ansicht* vertreten; fesseln, in Spannung halten; stand-, aushalten; (sich) festhalten; sich verhalten; anhalten, andauern (*Wetter*); ~ *one's ground*, ~ *one's own* sich behaupten; ~ *the line teleph.* am Apparat bleiben; *a.* ~ *good* (weiterhin) gelten; ~ *still* stillhalten; ~ *against j-m et.* vorhalten *od.* vorwerfen; *j-m et.* übelnehmen; ~ *back* (sich) zurückhalten; *fig.* zurückhalten mit; ~ *forth* sich auslassen *od.* verbreiten (*on* über *acc*); ~ *off* (sich) fernhalten; *et.* aufschieben; ausbleiben; ~ *on* (sich) festhalten (*to* an *dat.*); aus-, durchhalten; andauern; *teleph.* am Apparat bleiben; ~ *on to et.* behalten; ~ *over* vertagen, -schieben; ~ *together* zusammenhalten; hinstellen (*as als Beispiel etc.*); ~ *up* hochheben; hochhalten; aufhalten, verzögern; *j-n, Bank etc.* überfallen; **~·all** ['həʊldɔːl] Reisetasche *f*; **~·er** [~ə] Pächter *m*; Halter *m* (*Gerät*); Inhaber(in) (*bsd. econ.*);

~ing [~ɪŋ] Halten n; Halt m; Pachtgut n; Besitz m; **~ company** econ. Holding-, Dachgesellschaft f; **~up** Verzögerung f, (a. Verkehrs-)Stockung f; (bewaffneter) (Raub-)Überfall m.

hole [həʊl] **1.** Loch n; Höhle f; F fig. Klemme f; **pick ~s in** bekritteln; **2.** aushöhlen; durchlöchern.

hol·i·day ['hɒlɪdɪ] Feiertag m; freier Tag; bsd. Brt. mst ~s pl. Ferien pl., Urlaub m; **~mak·er** Urlauber(in f) m.

hol·i·ness ['həʊlɪnɪs] Heiligkeit f; His ♀ Seine Heiligkeit (der Papst).

hol·ler Am. F ['hɒlə] schreien.

hol·low ['hɒləʊ] **1.** □ hohl; leer; falsch; **2.** Höhle f, (Aus)Höhlung f; (Land)Senke f; **3.** ~ **out** aushöhlen.

hol·ly ♀ ['hɒlɪ] Stechpalme f.

hol·o·caust ['hɒləkɔːst] Massenvernichtung f, -sterben n, (bsd. Brand-)Katastrophe f; the ♀ hist. der Holocaust.

hol·ster ['həʊlstə] (Pistolen)Halfter m, n.

ho·ly ['həʊlɪ] (-ier, -iest) heilig; ♀ Thursday Gründonnerstag m; ~ water Weihwasser n; ♀ Week Karwoche f.

home [həʊm] **1.** Heim n; Haus n, Wohnung f; Heimat f; Sport: Heimspiel n; Heimsieg m; at ~ zu Hause; **make oneself at ~** es sich bequem machen; **at ~ and abroad** im In- u. Ausland; **2.** adj. (ein)heimisch, inländisch; wirkungsvoll (Schlag etc.); **3.** adv. heim, nach Hause; zu Hause, daheim; im Ziel od. Schwarze; **strike ~** sitzen, treffen; **~ com·put·er** Heimcomputer m; ♀ **Coun·ties** pl. die an London angrenzenden Grafschaften; **~ e·co·nom·ics** ♀ Hauswirtschaft(slehre) f; **~felt** ['həʊmfelt] tief empfunden; **~less** [~lɪs] heimatlos; **~like** anheimelnd, gemütlich (with zu); **~ly** [~lɪ] (-ier, -iest) freundlich (with zu); vertraut; einfach; Am. unscheinbar, reizlos; **~made** selbstgemacht, Hausmacher...; ♀ **Of·fice** Brt. pol. Innenministerium m; ♀ **Sec·re·ta·ry** Brt. pol. Innenminister m; **~sick:** be ~ Heimweh haben; **~sick·ness** Heimweh n; **~stead** Gehöft n; ☆ in USA: Heimstätte f; **~ team** Sport: Gastgeber pl.; **~ward** [~wəd] **1.** adj. Heim..., Rück...; **2.** adv. Am. heimwärts, nach Hause; **~wards** [~wədz] adv. = homeward 2; **~work** Hausaufgabe(n pl.) f, Schularbeiten pl.

hom·i·cide ☆ ['hɒmɪsaɪd] Tötung f; Totschlag m; Mord m; Totschläger(in) m; Mörder(in); ~ **squad** Mordkommission f.

ho·mo F ['həʊməʊ] (pl. -mos) Homo m (Homosexueller).

ho·mo·ge·ne·ous □ [hɒməˈdʒiːnjəs] homogen, gleichartig.

ho·mo·sex·u·al [hɒməʊˈseksjʊəl] **1.** □ homosexuell; **2.** Homosexuelle(r m) f.

hone ⊕ [həʊn] feinschleifen.

hon·est □ ['ɒnɪst] ehrlich, rechtschaffen; aufrichtig; echt; **~es·ty** [~ɪ] Ehrlichkeit f, Rechtschaffenheit f; Aufrichtigkeit f.

hon·ey ['hʌnɪ] Honig m; fig. Liebling m; **~comb** [~kəʊm] (Honig)Wabe f; **~ed** [~ɪd] honigsüß; **~moon 1.** Flitterwochen pl.; **2.** s-e Hochzeitsreise machen.

honk mot. [hɒŋk] hupen.

hon·ky-tonk Am. sl. ['hɒŋkɪtɒŋk] Spelunke f.

hon·or·ar·y ['ɒnərərɪ] Ehren...; ehrenamtlich.

hon·o(u)r ['ɒnə] **1.** Ehre f; fig. Zierde f; ~s pl. besondere Auszeichnung(en pl.), Ehren pl.; Your ♀ Euer Ehren; **2.** (be)ehren; econ. honorieren; **~a·ble** □ [~rəbl] ehrenvoll; redlich; ehrbar; ehrenwert.

hood [hʊd] Kapuze f; mot. Verdeck n; Am. (Motor)Haube f; ⊕ Kappe f.

hood·lum Am. F ['huːdləm] Rowdy m; Ganove m.

hood·wink ['hʊdwɪŋk] j-n reinlegen.

hoof [huːf] (pl. hoofs [~fs], hooves [~vz]) Huf m.

hook [hʊk] **1.** Haken m; Angelhaken m; Sichel f; **by ~ or by crook** so oder so; **2.** (sich) (zu-, fest)haken; angeln (a. fig.) **~ed** krumm, Haken...; ♀ süchtig (on nach) (a. fig.); ~ on heroin (television) heroin- (fernseh)süchtig; **~y** ['hʊkɪ]: play ~ Am. F (bsd. die Schule) schwänzen.

hoo·li·gan ['huːlɪgən] Rowdy m; **~is·m** [~ɪzəm] Rowdytum n.

hoop [huːp] **1.** (Faß- etc.)Reif(en) m; ⊕ Ring m; **2.** Fässer binden.

hoot [huːt] **1.** Schrei m (der Eule); höhnischer, johlender Schrei; mot. Hupen n; **2.** v/i. heulen; johlen; mot. hupen; v/t. auspfeifen, auszischen.

Hoo·ver *TM* [ˈhuːvə] **1.** Staubsauger *m*; **2.** *mst* ♀ (staub)saugen, *Teppich etc. a.* absaugen.

hooves [huːvz] *pl. von* hoof.

hop¹ [hɒp] Sprung *m*; F Tanz *m*; **2.** (-*pp*-) hüpfen; springen (über *acc.*); *be* ~*ping mad* F e-e Stinkwut (im Bauch) haben.

hop² ♀ [~] Hopfen *m*.

hope [həʊp] **1.** Hoffnung *f*; **2.** hoffen (*for acc.*); ~ *in* vertrauen auf (*acc.*); ~**ful** □ [ˈhəʊpfl] hoffnungsvoll; ~**less** □ [~lɪs] hoffnungslos; verzweifelt.

horde [hɔːd] Horde *f*.

ho·ri·zon [həˈraɪzn] Horizont *m*.

hor·i·zon·tal □ [hɒrɪˈzɒntl] horizontal, waag(e)recht.

horn [hɔːn] Horn *n*; Schalltrichter *m*; *mot.* Hupe *f*; ~*s pl.* Geweih *n*; ~ *of plenty* Füllhorn *n*.

hor·net *zo.* [ˈhɔːnɪt] Hornisse *f*.

horn·y [ˈhɔːnɪ] (-*ier*, -*iest*) hornig, schwielig; V geil (*Mann*).

ho·ro·scope [ˈhɒrəskəʊp] Horoskop *n*.

hor·ri·ble □ [ˈhɒrəbl] schrecklich, furchtbar, scheußlich; F gemein; ~**rid** □ [ˈhɒrɪd] gräßlich, abscheulich; schrecklich; ~**ri·fy** [~faɪ] erschrecken; entsetzen; ~**ror** [~ə] Entsetzen *n*, Schauder *m*; Schrecken *m*; Greuel *m*.

horse [hɔːs] *zo.* Pferd *n*; Bock *m*, Gestell *n*; *wild* ~*s will not drag me there* keine zehn Pferde bringen mich dort hin; ~**back** [ˈhɔːsbæk]: *on* ~ zu Pferde, beritten; ~**chest·nut** ♀ Roßkastanie *f*; ~**hair** Roßhaar *n*; ~**man** (*pl. -men*) (geübter) Reiter; ~**man·ship** [~mənʃɪp] Reitkunst *f*; ~ **op·e·ra** F Western *m* (*Film*); ~**pow·er** *phys.* Pferdestärke *f*; ~**rac·ing** Pferderennen *n od. pl.*; ~**rad·ish** Meerrettich *m*; ~**shoe** Hufeisen *n*; ~**wom·an** (*pl. -women*) (geübte) Reiterin.

hor·ti·cul·ture [ˈhɔːtɪkʌltʃə] Gartenbau *m*.

hose¹ [həʊz] Schlauch *m*.

hose² [~] *pl.* Strümpfe *pl.*, Strumpfwaren *pl.*; △ *nicht* Hose.

ho·sier·y [ˈhəʊʒərɪ] Strumpfwaren *pl.*

hos·pi·ta·ble □ [ˈhɒspɪtəbl] gastfrei.

hos·pi·tal [ˈhɒspɪtl] Krankenhaus *n*, Klinik *f*; ✗ Lazarett *n*; *in* (*Am. in the*) ~ im Krankenhaus; ~**i·ty** [hɒspɪˈtælətɪ] Gastfreundschaft *f*, Gastlichkeit *f*; ~**ize** [ˈhɒspɪtəlaɪz] ins Krankenhaus einliefern *od.* -weisen.

host¹ [həʊst] Gastgeber *m*; (Gast-) Wirt *m*; *Rundfunk, TV:* Talkmaster *m*; Showmaster *m*; Moderator *m*; *your* ~ *was ...* durch die Sendung führte Sie ...

host² [~] Menge *f*, Masse *f*.

host³ *eccl.* [~] *oft* ♀ Hostie *f*.

hos·tage [ˈhɒstɪdʒ] Geisel *m, f*; *take s.o.* ~ j-n als Geisel nehmen.

hos·tel [ˈhɒstl] *bsd. Brt.* (*Studenten-, Arbeiter- etc.*) (Wohn)Heim *n*; *mst youth* ~ Jugendherberge *f*.

host·ess [ˈhəʊstɪs] Gastgeberin *f*; (Gast)Wirtin *f*; Hostess *f*; ✈ Stewardeß *f*.

hos·tile [ˈhɒstaɪl] feindlich (gesinnt); ~ *to foreigners* ausländerfeindlich; ~**til·i·ty** [hɒˈstɪlətɪ] Feindseligkeit *f* (*to gegen*).

hot [hɒt] (-*tt*-) heiß; scharf; beißend; hitzig, heftig; eifrig; warm (*Speise, Fährte*); F heiß, gestohlen; radioaktiv; ~**bed** [ˈhɒtbed] Mistbeet *n*; *fig.* Brutstätte *f*.

hotch·potch [ˈhɒtʃpɒtʃ] Mischmasch *m*; Gemüsesuppe *f*.

hot dog [hɒtˈdɒg] Hot dog *n, m*.

ho·tel [həʊˈtel] Hotel *n*.

hot·head [ˈhɒthed] Hitzkopf *m*; ~**house** Treibhaus *n*; ~ **line** *pol.* heißer Draht; ~**pot** Eintopf *m*; ~**spot** *bsd. pol.* Unruhe-, Krisenherd *m*; ~**spur** Hitzkopf *m*; ~**wa·ter** Heißwasser...; ~ *bottle* Wärmflasche *f*.

hound [haʊnd] **1.** Jagdhund *m*; *fig.* Hund *m*; **2.** jagen, hetzen.

hour [ˈaʊə] Stunde *f*; Zeit *f*, Uhr *f*; ~**ly** [~lɪ] stündlich.

house 1. [haʊs] Haus *n*; *the* ♀ das Unterhaus; die Börse; **2.** [haʊz] *v/t.* unterbringen; *v/i.* hausen; ~**a·gent** [ˈhaʊseɪdʒənt] Häusermakler *m*; ~**bound** *fig.* ans Haus gefesselt; ~**hold** Haushalt *m*; *attr.* Haushalts...; Haus...; ~**hold·er** Hausherr *m*; ~**hus·band** *bsd. Am.* Hausmann *m*; ~**keep·er** Haushälterin *f*; ~**keep·ing** Haushaltung *f*, Haushaltführung *f*; ~**maid** Hausmädchen *n*; ~**man** (*pl. -men*) *Brt.* ✗ Medizinalassistent *m*; △ *nicht* Hausmann; ~**warm·ing** (**par·ty**) [~wɔːmɪŋ(pɑːtɪ)] Einzugsparty *f*;

~wife ['hauswaɪf] (pl. -wives) Hausfrau f; ['hʌzɪf] Nähetui n; **~work** Hausarbeit f; △ nicht Hausaufgabe(n).

hous·ing ['hauzɪŋ] Unterbringung f; Wohnung f; ~ estate Brt. Wohnsiedlung f.

hove [həuv] pret. u. p.p. von heave 2.

hov·el ['hɒvl] Schuppen m; Hütte f.

hov·er ['hɒvə] schweben; lungern; fig. schwanken; **~craft** (pl. -craft[s]) Hovercraft n, Luftkissenfahrzeug n.

how [hau] wie; ~ do you do? bei der Vorstellung: guten Tag!; ~ about ...? wie steht's mit ...?

how·dy Am. int. F ['haudɪ] Tag!

how·ev·er [hau'evə] 1. adv. wie auch (immer), wenn auch noch so ...; 2. cj. (je)doch.

howl [haul] 1. heulen; brüllen; 2. Heulen n, Geheul n; **~er** F ['haulə] grober Schnitzer.

hub [hʌb] (Rad)Nabe f; fig. Mittel-Angelpunkt m.

hub·bub ['hʌbʌb] Tumult m.

hub·by F ['hʌbɪ] (Ehe)Mann m.

huck·le·ber·ry ♥ ['hʌklberɪ] amerikanische Heidelbeere.

huck·ster ['hʌkstə] Hausierer(in).

hud·dle ['hʌdl] 1. a. ~ together (sich) zusammendrängen, zusammenpressen; ~ (o.s.) up sich zusammenkauern; 2. (wirrer) Haufen, Wirrwarr m, Durcheinander n.

hue[1] [hju:] Farbe f; (Farb)Ton m.

hue[2] [~]: ~ and cry fig. großes Geschrei.

huff [hʌf] Verärgerung f; Verstimmung f; be in a ~ verärgert od. -stimmt sein.

hug [hʌg] 1. Umarmung f; 2. (-gg-) an sich drücken, umarmen; fig. festhalten an (dat.); sich dicht am Weg etc. halten.

huge [hju:dʒ] ungeheuer, riesig; **~ness** ['hju:dʒnɪs] ungeheure Größe.

hulk·ing ['hʌlkɪŋ] sperrig, klotzig; ungeschlacht, schwerfällig.

hull [hʌl] ♥ Schale f, Hülse f; ⚓ Rumpf m; 2. enthülsen; schälen.

hul·la·ba·loo ['hʌləbə'lu:] (pl. -loos) Lärm m.

hul·lo int. [hə'ləu] hallo!

hum [hʌm] (-mm-) summen; brummen.

hu·man ['hju:mən] 1. □ menschlich, Menschen...; △ nicht human; **~ly**

possible menschenmöglich; ~ being Mensch m; ~ rights pl. Menschenrechte pl.; 2. Mensch m; **~e** □ [hju:-'meɪn] human, menschenfreundlich; **~i·tar·i·an** [hju:mænɪ'teərɪən] 1. Menschenfreund m; 2. menschenfreundlich; **~i·ty** [hju:'mænətɪ] die Menschheit, die Menschen pl.; Humanität f, Menschlichkeit f; humanities pl. Geisteswissenschaften pl.; Altphilologie f.

hum·ble ['hʌmbl] 1. □ (~r, ~st) demütig; bescheiden; 2. erniedrigen; demütigen.

hum·ble-bee zo. ['hʌmblbi:] Hummel f.

hum·ble·ness ['hʌmblnɪs] Demut f.

hum·drum ['hʌmdrʌm] eintönig.

hu·mid ['hju:mɪd] feucht, naß; **~i·ty** [hju:'mɪdətɪ] Feuchtigkeit f.

hu·mil·i·ate [hju:'mɪlɪeɪt] erniedrigen, demütigen; **~a·tion** [hju:mɪ-lɪ'eɪʃn] Erniedrigung f, Demütigung f; **~ty** [hju:'mɪlətɪ] Demut f.

hum·ming·bird zo. ['hʌmɪŋbɜ:d] Kolibri m.

hu·mor·ous □ ['hju:mərəs] humoristisch, humorvoll; spaßig.

hu·mo(u)r ['hju:mə] 1. Laune f, Stimmung f; Humor m; das Spaßige; out of ~ schlecht gelaunt; 2. j-m s-n Willen lassen; eingehen auf (acc.).

hump [hʌmp] 1. Höcker m (e-s Kamels), Buckel m; 2. krümmen; Brt. F auf den Rücken nehmen, tragen; ~ o.s. Am. sl. sich ranhalten; **~back(ed)** ['hʌmpbæk(t)] = hunchback(ed).

hunch [hʌntʃ] 1. = hump 1; dickes Stück; Ahnung f, Gefühl n; 2. a. ~ up krümmen; **~back** ['hʌntʃbæk] Buckel m; Bucklige(r m) f; **~backed** buck(e)lig.

hun·dred ['hʌndrəd] 1. hundert; 2. Hundert n (Einheit); Hundert f (Zahl); **~th** [~θ] 1. hundertste(r, -s); 2. Hundertstel n; **~weight** in GB: appr. Zentner m (= 50,8 kg).

hung [hʌŋ] 1. pret. u. p.p. von hang[1]; 2. adj. abgehangen (Fleisch).

Hun·gar·i·an [hʌŋ'geərɪən] 1. ungarisch; 2. Ungar(in); ling. Ungarisch n.

hun·ger ['hʌŋgə] 1. Hunger m (a. fig.: for nach); 2. hungern (for, after nach); ~ strike Hungerstreik m.

hun·gry □ ['hʌŋgrɪ] (*-ier, -iest*) hungrig.

hunk [hʌŋk] dickes Stück.

hunt [hʌnt] **1.** Jagd *f* (*a. fig.: for* nach); Jagd(revier *n*) *f*; Jagd(gesellschaft) *f*; **2.** jagen; *Revier* bejagen; hetzen; ~ **out**, ~ **up** aufspüren; ~ *after*, ~ *for* Jagd machen auf (*acc.*); **~·er** ['hʌntə] Jäger *m*; Jagdpferd *n*; **~·ing** [~ɪŋ] Jagen *n*; *attr.* Jagd...; **~·ing-ground** Jagdrevier *n*.

hur·dle ['hɜːdl] *Sport:* Hürde *f* (*a. fig.*); **~r** [~ə] *Sport:* Hürdenläufer(in) *f*; **~race** *Sport:* Hürdenrennen *n*.

hurl [hɜːl] **1.** Schleudern *n*; **2.** schleudern; *Worte* ausstoßen.

hur·ri·cane ['hʌrɪkən] Hurrikan *m*, Wirbelsturm *m*; Orkan *m*.

hur·ried □ ['hʌrɪd] eilig; übereilt.

hur·ry ['hʌrɪ] **1.** (große) Eile, Hast *f*; *be in a (no)* ~ es (nicht) eilig haben; *not ... in a* ~ F nicht so bald, nicht so leicht; **2.** *v/t.* (an)treiben; drängen; *et.* beschleunigen; eilig schicken *od.* bringen; *v/i.* eilen, hasten; ~ **up** sich beeilen.

hurt [hɜːt] **1.** Schmerz *m*; Verletzung *f*, Wunde *f*; Schaden *m*; **2.** (*hurt*) verletzen, -wunden (*a. fig.*); schmerzen, weh tun; schaden (*dat.*); **~·ful** □ ['hɜːtfl] verletzend.

hus·band ['hʌzbənd] **1.** (Ehe)Mann *m*; **2.** haushalten mit; verwalten; **~·ry** [~rɪ] ✔ Landwirtschaft *f*; *fig.* Haushalten *n*, sparsamer Umgang (*of* mit).

hush [hʌʃ] **1.** *int.* still!; **2.** Stille *f*; **3.** zum Schweigen bringen; besänftigen, beruhigen; △ *nicht huschen*; ~ **up** vertuschen; **~ money** ['hʌʃmʌnɪ] Schweigegeld *n*.

husk [hʌsk] **1.** ✔ Hülse *f*, Schote *f*, Schale *f* (*a. fig.*); **2.** enthülsen; **hus·ky** ['hʌskɪ] **1.** □ (*-ier, -iest*) hülsig; trocken; heiser; F stramm, stämmig; **2.** F stämmiger Kerl.

hus·sy ['hʌsɪ] Fratz *m*, Göre *f*; Flittchen *n*.

hus·tle ['hʌsl] **1.** *v/t.* (an)rempeln; stoßen; drängen; *v/i.* (sich) drängen; hasten, hetzen; sich beeilen; **2.** ~ *and bustle* Gedränge *n*; Gehetze *n*; Getriebe *n*.

hut [hʌt] Hütte *f*; ✗ Baracke *f*.

hutch [hʌtʃ] (*bsd. Kaninchen*)Stall *m*.

hy·a·cinth ✿ ['haɪəsɪnθ] Hyazinthe *f*.

hy·ae·na *zo.* [haɪ'iːnə] Hyäne *f*.

hy·brid *biol.* ['haɪbrɪd] Bastard *m*, Mischling *m*, Kreuzung *f*; *attr.* Bastard...; Zwitter...; **~·ize** [~aɪz] kreuzen.

hy·drant ['haɪdrənt] Hydrant *m*.

hy·drau·lic [haɪ'drɔːlɪk] (~*ally*) hydraulisch; **~s** *sg.* Hydraulik *f*.

hy·dro- ['haɪdrəʊ] Wasser...; **~·car·bon** Kohlenwasserstoff *m*; **~·chlor·ic ac·id** [~rə'klɒrɪk'æsɪd] Salzsäure *f*; **~·foil** ⚓ [~fɔɪl] Tragflächen-, Tragflügelboot *n*; **~·gen** [~ədʒən] Wasserstoff *m*; **~·gen bomb** Wasserstoffbombe *f*; **~·plane** ✈ Wasserflugzeug *n*; ⚓ Gleitboot *n*.

hy·e·na *zo.* [haɪ'iːnə] Hyäne *f*.

hy·giene ['haɪdʒiːn] Hygiene *f*; **hy·gien·ic** [haɪ'dʒiːnɪk] (~*ally*) hygienisch.

hymn [hɪm] **1.** Hymne *f*; Lobgesang *m*; Kirchenlied *n*; **2.** preisen.

hy·per- ['haɪpə] hyper..., Hyper..., über..., höher, größer; **~·mar·ket** Groß-, Verbrauchermarkt *m*; **~·sen·si·tive** [haɪpə'sensətɪv] überempfindlich (*to* gegen).

hy·phen ['haɪfn] Bindestrich *m*; **~·ate** [~eɪt] mit Bindestrich schreiben.

hyp·no·tize ['hɪpnətaɪz] hypnotisieren.

hy·po·chon·dri·ac ['haɪpəʊ'kɒndrɪæk] Hypochonder *m*.

hy·poc·ri·sy [hɪ'pɒkrəsɪ] Heuchelei *f*; **hyp·o·crite** ['hɪpəkrɪt] Heuchler(in) *f*; Scheinheilige(r *m*) *f*; **hyp·o·crit·i·cal** □ [hɪpə'krɪtɪkl] heuchlerisch, scheinheilig.

hy·poth·e·sis [haɪ'pɒθɪsɪs] (*pl. -ses* [-siːz]) Hypothese *f*.

hys·te·ri·a ✱ [hɪ'stɪərɪə] Hysterie *f*; **~·ter·i·cal** □ [~'sterɪkl] hysterisch; **~·ter·ics** [~ɪks] *pl.* hysterischer Anfall; *go into* ~ hysterisch werden; F e-n Lachkrampf bekommen.

H

I

I [aɪ] ich; *it is* ~ ich bin es.
ice [aɪs] **1.** Eis *n*; **2.** gefrieren lassen; *a.* ~ *up* vereisen; *Kuchen* mit Zuckerguß überziehen; in Eis kühlen; **~age** ['aɪseɪdʒ] Eiszeit *f*; **~berg** [~bɜ:g] Eisberg *m* (*a. fig.*); **~bound** eingefroren; **~box** Eisfach *n*; *Am.* Kühlschrank *m*; **~cream** (Speise)Eis *n*; **~cube** Eiswürfel *m*; **~floe** Eisscholle *f*; **~lolly** *Brt.* Eis *n* am Stiel; **~rink** (Kunst)Eisbahn *f*; **~show** Eisrevue *f*.
i·ci·cle ['aɪsɪkl] Eiszapfen *m*.
ic·ing ['aɪsɪŋ] Zuckerguß *m*; Vereisung *f*.
i·cy □ ['aɪsɪ] (*-ier, -iest*) eisig (*a. fig.*); vereist.
i·dea [aɪ'dɪə] Idee *f*; Begriff *m*; Vorstellung *f*; Gedanke *m*; Meinung *f*; Ahnung *f*; Plan *m*; **~l** [~l] **1.** □ ideell; (nur) eingebildet; ideal; **2.** Ideal *n*; **~l·is·m** [~ɪzəm] Idealismus *m*; **~l·ize** [~aɪz] idealisieren.
i·den·ti·cal □ [aɪ'dentɪkl] identisch, gleich(bedeutend); **~fi·ca·tion** [aɪdentɪfɪ'keɪʃn] Identifizierung *f*; Ausweis *m*; **~fy** [aɪ'dentɪfaɪ] identifizieren; ausweisen; erkennen; **~ty** [~ətɪ] Identität *f*; Persönlichkeit *f*, Eigenart *f*; ~ *card* (Personal)Ausweis *m*, Kennkarte *f*; *Am.* ~ *tag* ✗ Erkennungsmarke *f*.
i·de·o·log·i·cal □ [aɪdɪə'lɒdʒɪkl] ideologisch; **~ol·o·gy** [aɪdɪ'ɒlədʒɪ] Ideologie *f*.
id·i·om ['ɪdɪəm] Idiom *n*; Redewendung *f*; **~o·mat·ic** [ɪdɪə'mætɪk] (*~ally*) idiomatisch.
id·i·ot ['ɪdɪət] Idiot(in), Schwachsinnige(r *m*) *f*; **~ic** [ɪdɪ'ɒtɪk] (*~ally*) blödsinnig.
i·dle ['aɪdl] **1.** □ (*~r, ~st*) müßig, untätig; träge, faul; *econ.* unproduktiv; tot; ungenutzt; beiläufig; ~ *hours pl.* Mußestunden *pl.*; **2.** *v/t.* *mst* ~ *away* vertrödeln; *v/i.* faulenzen; ⊕ leer laufen; **~ness** [~nɪs] Untätigkeit *f*, Müßiggang *m*; Faul-, Trägheit *f*; Muße *f*; Zwecklosigkeit *f*.
i·dol ['aɪdl] Idol *n* (*a. fig.*); Götzenbild *n*; **~a·trous** □ [aɪ'dɒlətrəs] abgöttisch; **~a·try** Götzenanbetung *f*; *fig.* abgöttische Verehrung *f*, Vergötterung *f*; **~ize** ['aɪdəlaɪz] abgöttisch verehren, vergöttern.

i·dyl·lic [aɪ'dɪlɪk] (*~ally*) idyllisch.
if [ɪf] **1.** wenn, falls; ob; **2.** Wenn *n*.
ig·nite [ɪg'naɪt] anzünden, (sich) entzünden; *mot.* zünden; **ig·ni·tion** [ɪg'nɪʃən] An-, Entzünden *n*; *mot.* Zündung *f*.
ig·no·ble □ [ɪg'nəʊbl] gemein, unehrenhaft.
ig·no·min·i·ous □ [ɪgnə'mɪnɪəs] schändlich, schimpflich.
ig·no·rance ['ɪgnərəns] Unwissenheit *f*; **ig·no·rant** [~t] unwissend; ungebildet; F ungehobelt; **ig·nore** [ɪg'nɔ:] ignorieren, nicht beachten; ⅍ verwerfen.
ill [ɪl] **1.** (*worse, worst*) krank; schlimm, schlecht, übel; böse; *fall* ~, *be taken* ~ krank werden; **2.** ~ *s pl.* Übel *n*, Mißstand *m*; **~ad·vised** □ ['ɪləd'vaɪzd] schlecht beraten; unbesonnen, unklug; **~bred** schlechterzogen; ungezogen; ~ *breed·ing* schlechtes Benehmen.
il·le·gal □ [ɪ'li:gl] unerlaubt; ⅍ illegal, ungesetzlich; ~ *parking* Falschparken *n*.
il·le·gi·ble □ [ɪ'ledʒəbl] unleserlich.
il·le·git·i·mate □ [ɪlɪ'dʒɪtɪmət] illegitim; unrechtmäßig; unehelich.
ill·fat·ed ['ɪl'feɪtɪd] unglücklich, Unglücks...; **~fa·vo(u)red** häßlich; **~hu·mo(u)red** schlechtgelaunt.
il·lib·e·ral □ [ɪ'lɪbərəl] engstirnig; intolerant; knaus(e)rig.
il·li·cit □ [ɪ'lɪsɪt] unerlaubt.
il·lit·e·rate [ɪ'lɪtərət] **1.** □ unwissend, ungebildet; **2.** Analphabet(in).
ill·judged ['ɪl'dʒʌdʒd] unbesonnen, unklug; **~man·nered** ungezogen, mit schlechten Umgangsformen; **~na·tured** □ boshaft, bösartig.
ill·ness ['ɪlnɪs] Krankheit *f*.
il·log·i·cal □ [ɪ'lɒdʒɪkl] unlogisch.
ill·tem·pered ['ɪl'tempəd] schlechtgelaunt, übellaunig; **~timed** ungelegen, unpassend, zur unrechten Zeit.
il·lu·mi·nate [ɪ'lju:mɪneɪt] be-, erleuchten (*a. fig.*); *fig.* erläutern, erklären; **~nat·ing** [~ɪŋ] Leucht...; *fig.* aufschlußreich; **~na·tion** [ɪlju:mɪ'neɪʃn] Er-, Beleuchtung *f*; *fig.* Erläuterung *f*, Erklärung *f*; **~s** *pl.* Illumination *f*, Festbeleuchtung *f*.
ill·use ['ɪl'ju:z] mißhandeln.

impenetrable

il·lu·sion [ɪ'lu:ʒn] Illusion f, Täuschung f; **~·sive** [~sɪv], **~·so·ry** □ [~sərɪ] illusorisch, trügerisch.

il·lus·trate ['ɪləstreɪt] illustrieren, bebildern; erläutern; **~·tra·tion** [ɪlə'streɪʃn] Erläuterung f; Illustration f; Bild n, Abbildung f; **~·tra·tive** □ ['ɪləstrətɪv] erläuternd.

il·lus·tri·ous □ [ɪ'lʌstrɪəs] berühmt.

ill will ['ɪl'wɪl] Feindschaft f.

im·age ['ɪmɪdʒ] Bild n; Statue f; Götzenbild n; Ebenbild n; Image n; **im·ag·e·ry** [~ərɪ] Bilder pl.; Bildersprache f, Metaphorik f.

i·ma·gi·na·ble □ ['ɪmædʒɪnəbl] denkbar; **~·ry** [~ərɪ] eingebildet, imaginär; **~·tion** [ɪmædʒɪ'neɪʃn] Einbildung(skraft) f; **~·tive** □ ['ɪmædʒɪnətɪv] ideen-, einfallsreich; **i·ma·gine** [ɪ'mædʒɪn] sich et. einbilden od. vorstellen od. denken.

im·bal·ance [ɪm'bæləns] Unausgewogenheit f; pol. etc. Ungleichgewicht n.

im·be·cile □ ['ɪmbɪsi:l] 1. schwachsinnig; 2. Schwachsinnige(r m) f; contp. Idiot m, Trottel m.

im·bibe [ɪm'baɪb] trinken; fig. sich zu eigen machen.

im·bue fig. [ɪm'bju:] durchdringen, erfüllen (with mit).

im·i·tate ['ɪmɪteɪt] nachahmen, imitieren; **~·ta·tion** [ɪmɪ'teɪʃn] 1. Nachahmung f; Imitation f; 2. nachgemacht, unecht, künstlich, Kunst...

im·mac·u·late □ [ɪ'mækjʊlət] unbefleckt, rein; fehlerlos.

im·ma·te·ri·al □ [ɪmə'tɪərɪəl] unkörperlich; unwesentlich (to für).

im·ma·ture □ [ɪmə'tjʊə] unreif.

im·mea·su·ra·ble □ [ɪ'meʒərəbl] unermeßlich.

im·me·di·ate □ [ɪ'mi:djət] unmittelbar; unverzüglich, sofortig; **~·ly** [~lɪ] 1. adv. sofort; 2. cj. sobald, sofort, als.

im·mense □ [ɪ'mens] riesig; fig. a. enorm, immens; prima, großartig.

im·merse [ɪ'mɜ:s] (ein-, unter)tauchen; fig. versenken od. vertiefen (in in acc.); **im·mer·sion** [~ʃn] Ein-, Untertauchen n; **~ heater** Tauchsieder m.

im·mi·grant ['ɪmɪgrənt] Einwanderer m, -in f; Immigrant(in); **~·grate** [~greɪt] v/i. einwandern; v/t. ansiedeln (into in dat.); **~·gra·tion** [ɪmɪ'greɪʃn] Einwanderung f, Immigration f.

im·mi·nent □ ['ɪmɪnənt] nahe bevorstehend; **~ danger** drohende Gefahr.

im·mo·bile [ɪ'məʊbaɪl] unbeweglich.

im·mod·e·rate □ [ɪ'mɒdərət] maßlos.

im·mod·est □ [ɪ'mɒdɪst] unbescheiden; unanständig.

im·mor·al □ [ɪ'mɒrəl] unmoralisch.

im·mor·tal [ɪ'mɔ:tl] 1. □ unsterblich; 2. Unsterbliche(r m) f; **~·i·ty** [ɪmɔ:'tælətɪ] Unsterblichkeit f.

im·mo·va·ble [ɪ'mu:vəbl] 1. □ unbeweglich; unerschütterlich; unnachgiebig; 2. **~s** pl. Immobilien pl.

im·mune [ɪ'mju:n] (against, from, to) immun (gegen); geschützt (gegen), frei (von); **im·mu·ni·ty** [~ətɪ] Immunität f; Unempfindlichkeit f.

im·mu·ta·ble □ [ɪ'mju:təbl] unveränderlich.

imp [ɪmp] Teufelchen n; Racker m.

im·pact ['ɪmpækt] (Zusammen)Stoß m; Anprall m; Einwirkung f.

im·pair [ɪm'peə] beeinträchtigen.

im·part [ɪm'pɑ:t] (to dat.) geben; mitteilen; vermitteln.

im·par·tial □ [ɪm'pɑ:ʃl] unparteiisch; **~·ti·al·i·ty** ['ɪmpɑ:ʃɪ'ælətɪ] Unparteilichkeit f, Objektivität f.

im·pass·a·ble □ [ɪm'pɑ:səbl] unpassierbar.

im·passe [æm'pɑ:s] Sackgasse f (a. fig.); fig. toter Punkt.

im·pas·sioned [ɪm'pæʃnd] leidenschaftlich.

im·pas·sive □ [ɪm'pæsɪv] teilnahmslos; unbewegt (Gesicht).

im·pa·tience [ɪm'peɪʃns] Ungeduld f; **~·tient** □ [~ʌt] ungeduldig.

im·peach [ɪm'pi:tʃ] anklagen (for, of, with gen.); anfechten, anzweifeln.

im·pec·ca·ble □ [ɪm'pekəbl] sünd(en)los; untadelig, einwandfrei.

im·pede [ɪm'pi:d] (be)hindern.

im·ped·i·ment [ɪm'pedɪmənt] Hindernis n.

im·pel [ɪm'pel] (-ll-) (an)treiben.

im·pend·ing [ɪm'pendɪŋ] nahe bevorstehend; **~ danger** drohende Gefahr.

im·pen·e·tra·ble □ [ɪm'penɪtrəbl] undurchdringlich; fig. unergründlich; fig. unzugänglich (to dat.).

im·per·a·tive [ɪm'perətɪv] 1. □ notwendig, dringend, unbedingt erforderlich; befehlend; gebieterisch; *gr.* imperativisch; 2. Befehl *m*; *a.* ~ *mood gr.* Imperativ *m*, Befehlsform *f*.

im·per·cep·ti·ble □ [ɪmpə'septəbl] unmerklich.

im·per·fect [ɪm'pɜ:fɪkt] 1. □ unvollkommen; unvollendet; 2. *a.* ~ *tense gr.* Imperfekt *n*.

im·pe·ri·al·is·m *pol.* [ɪm'pɪərɪəlɪzəm] Imperialismus *m*; **~t** *pol.* [~ɪst] Imperialist *m*.

im·per·il [ɪm'perəl] (*bsd. Brt. -ll-, Am. -l-*) gefährden.

im·pe·ri·ous □ [ɪm'pɪərɪəs] herrisch, gebieterisch; dringend.

im·per·me·a·ble □ [ɪm'pɜ:mjəbl] undurchlässig.

im·per·son·al □ [ɪm'pɜ:snl] unpersönlich.

im·per·so·nate [ɪm'pɜ:səneɪt] *thea. etc.* verkörpern, darstellen.

im·per·ti·nence [ɪm'pɜ:tɪnəns] Unverschämtheit *f*, Ungehörigkeit *f*, Frechheit *f*; **~nent** □ [~t] unverschämt, ungehörig, frech.

im·per·tur·ba·ble □ [ɪmpə'tɜ:bəbl] unerschütterlich, gelassen.

im·per·vi·ous □ [ɪm'pɜ:vjəs] unzugänglich (*to* für); undurchlässig.

im·pe·tu·ous □ [ɪm'petjʊəs] ungestüm, heftig; impulsiv.

im·pe·tus ['ɪmpɪtəs] Antrieb *m*, Schwung *m*.

im·pi·e·ty [ɪm'paɪətɪ] Gottlosigkeit *f*; Respektlosigkeit *f*.

im·pinge [ɪm'pɪndʒ]: ~ *on, ~ upon* sich auswirken auf (*acc.*), beeinflussen (*acc.*).

im·pi·ous □ ['ɪmpɪəs] gottlos; pietätlos; respektlos.

im·plac·a·ble □ [ɪm'plækəbl] unversöhnlich, unnachgiebig.

im·plant [ɪm'plɑ:nt] *&* einpflanzen; *fig.* einprägen.

im·ple·ment 1. ['ɪmplɪmənt] Werkzeug *n*; Gerät *n*; 2. [~ment] ausführen.

im·pli·cate ['ɪmplɪkeɪt] verwickeln; zur Folge haben; **~ca·tion** [ɪmplɪ'keɪʃn] Verwick(e)lung *f*; Implikation *f*, Einbeziehung *f*; Folgerung *f*.

im·pli·cit □ [ɪm'plɪsɪt] unausgesprochen; bedingungslos, blind (*Glaube etc.*).

im·plore [ɪm'plɔ:] inständig bitten, anflehen; (er)flehen.

im·ply [ɪm'plaɪ] implizieren, (mit) einbegreifen; bedeuten; andeuten.

im·po·lite □ [ɪmpə'laɪt] unhöflich.

im·pol·i·tic □ [ɪm'pɒlɪtɪk] unklug.

im·port 1. ['ɪmpɔ:t] *econ.* Import *m*, Einfuhr *f*; *econ.* Import-, Einfuhrartikel *m*; Bedeutung *f*; Wichtigkeit *f*; ~s *pl. econ.* (Gesamt)Import *m*, (-)Einfuhr *f*; Importgüter *pl.*; 2. [ɪm'pɔ:t] *econ.* importieren, einführen; bedeuten.

im·por·tance [ɪm'pɔ:təns] Bedeutung *f*, Wichtigkeit *f*; **~tant** □ [~t] bedeutend, wichtig; wichtigtuerisch.

im·por·ta·tion [ɪmpɔ:'teɪʃn] *s. import 1 econ.*

im·por·tu·nate □ [ɪm'pɔ:tjʊnət] lästig; zudringlich; **~tune** [ɪm'pɔ:tju:n] dringend bitten; belästigen.

im·pose [ɪm'pəʊz] *v/t.* auferlegen, -bürden, -drängen, -zwingen (*on, upon dat.*); *v/i.* ~ *on, ~ upon j-n* imponieren, *j-n* beeindrucken; *j-n* ausnutzen; sich *j-m* aufdrängen; *j-m* zur Last fallen; **im·pos·ing** □ [~ɪŋ] imponierend, eindrucksvoll, imposant.

im·pos·si·bil·i·ty [ɪmpɒsə'bɪlətɪ] Unmöglichkeit *f*; **~ble** □ [ɪm'pɒsəbl] unmöglich.

im·pos·tor [ɪm'pɒstə] Betrüger *m*.

im·po·tence ['ɪmpətəns] Unfähigkeit *f*; Hilflosigkeit *f*; Schwäche *f*; *&* Impotenz *f*; **~tent** □ [~t] unfähig; hilflos; schwach; *&* impotent.

im·pov·er·ish [ɪm'pɒvərɪʃ] arm machen; *Boden* auslaugen.

im·prac·ti·ca·ble □ [ɪm'præktɪkəbl] unbrauchbar; unpassierbar (*Straße*).

im·prac·ti·cal [ɪm'præktɪkl] unpraktisch; theoretisch; unbrauchbar.

im·preg·na·ble □ [ɪm'pregnəbl] uneinnehmbar; **~nate** ['ɪmpregneɪt] *biol.* schwängern; **⌖** sättigen; ⊕ imprägnieren.

im·press [ɪm'pres] (auf-, ein)drücken; (deutlich) klarmachen; einschärfen; *j-n* beeindrucken; *j-n mit et.* erfüllen; **im·pres·sion** [~ʃn] Eindruck *m*; *print.* Abdruck *m*; Abzug *m*; Auflage *f*; *be under the ~ that* den Eindruck haben, daß; **im·pres·sive** □ [~sɪv] eindrucksvoll.

im·print 1. [ɪmˈprɪnt] aufdrücken, -prägen; *fig.* einprägen (*on*, in *dat.*); **2.** [ˈɪmprɪnt] Eindruck *m*; Stempel *m* (*a. fig.*); *print.* Impressum *n*.

im·pris·on ᵗᵗ [ɪmˈprɪzn] inhaftieren; **~ment** ᵗᵗ [~mənt] Freiheitsstrafe *f*, Gefängnis(strafe *f*) *n*, Haft *f*.

im·prob·a·ble □ [ɪmˈprɒbəbl] unwahrscheinlich.

im·prop·er □ [ɪmˈprɒpə] ungeeignet, unpassend; unanständig, unschicklich (*Benehmen etc.*); ungenau.

im·pro·pri·e·ty [ɪmprəˈpraɪətɪ] Unschicklichkeit *f*.

im·prove [ɪmˈpruːv] *v/t.* verbessern; veredeln, -feinern; *v/i.* sich (ver)bessern; **~ on**, **~ upon** übertreffen; **~ment** (Ver)Besserung *f*; Fortschritt *m* (*on*, *upon* gegenüber *dat.*).

im·pro·vise [ˈɪmprəvaɪz] improvisieren.

im·pru·dent □ [ɪmˈpruːdənt] unklug.

im·pu·dence [ˈɪmpjʊdəns] Unverschämtheit *f*, Frechheit *f*; **~dent** □ [~t] unverschämt, frech.

im·pulse [ˈɪmpʌls] Impuls *m*, (An-)Stoß *m*; *fig.* (An)Trieb *m*; **im·pul·sive** □ [ɪmˈpʌlsɪv] (an)treibend; *fig.* impulsiv.

im·pu·ni·ty [ɪmˈpjuːnətɪ] Straflosigkeit *f*; *with* **~** ungestraft.

im·pure □ [ɪmˈpjʊə] unrein (*a. eccl.*), schmutzig; verfälscht; *fig.* schlecht, unmoralisch.

im·pute [ɪmˈpjuːt] zuschreiben (*to dat.*); **~** *s.th.* *to* s.o. j-n e-r Sache bezichtigen; j-m et. unterstellen.

in [ɪn] **1.** *prp.* in (*dat.*), innerhalb (*gen.*); an (*dat.*); (**~** *the morning*, **~** *number*, **~** *itself*, *professor* **~** *at the university*); auf (*dat.*); (**~** *the street*, **~** *English*); auf (*acc.*); (**~** *this manner*, **~** *English*); aus (*coat* **~** *velvet*); bei (**~** *Shakespeare*, **~** *crossing the road*); mit (*engaged* **~** *reading*, **~** *a word*); nach (**~** *my opinion*); über (*acc.*) (*rejoice* **~** *s.th.*); unter (*dat.*) (**~** *the circumstances*, **~** *the reign of*, *one* **~** *ten*); vor (*dat.*) (*cry out* **~** *alarm*); zu (*grouped* **~** *tens*, **~** *excuse*, **~** *honour of*); **~** *1989* 1989; **~** *that* ... insofern als, weil; **2.** *adv.* innen, drinnen; herein; hinein; in, in Mode; *be* **~** *for et.* zu erwarten haben; *e-e Prüfung etc.* vor sich haben; *be* **~** *with* gut mit

j-m stehen; **3.** *adj.* hereinkommend; Innen...

in·a·bil·i·ty [ɪnəˈbɪlətɪ] Unfähigkeit *f*.

in·ac·ces·si·ble □ [ɪnækˈsesəbl] unzugänglich, unerreichbar (*to* für *od. dat.*).

in·ac·cu·rate □ [ɪnˈækjʊrət] ungenau; unrichtig.

in·ac·tive □ [ɪnˈæktɪv] untätig; *econ.* lustlos, flau; ⚗ unwirksam; **~tiv·i·ty** [ɪnækˈtɪvɪtɪ] Untätigkeit *f*; *econ.* Lustlosigkeit *f*, Flauheit *f*; ⚗ Unwirksamkeit *f*.

in·ad·e·quate □ [ɪnˈædɪkwət] unangemessen; unzulänglich, ungenügend

in·ad·mis·si·ble □ [ɪnədˈmɪsəbl] unzulässig, unerlaubt.

in·ad·ver·tent □ [ɪnədˈvɜːtənt] unachtsam; unbeabsichtigt, versehentlich.

in·a·lien·a·ble □ [ɪnˈeɪljənəbl] unveräußerlich.

i·nane □ *fig.* [ɪˈneɪn] leer; albern.

in·an·i·mate □ [ɪnˈænɪmət] leblos; unbelebt (*Natur*); geistlos, langweilig.

in·ap·pro·pri·ate □ [ɪnəˈprəʊprɪət] unpassend, ungeeignet.

in·apt □ [ɪnˈæpt] ungeeignet, unpassend.

in·ar·tic·u·late □ [ɪnɑːˈtɪkjʊlət] unartikuliert, undeutlich (ausgesprochen), unverständlich; unfähig (, deutlich) zu sprechen.

in·as·much [ɪnəzˈmʌtʃ]: **~** *as* insofern als.

in·at·ten·tive □ [ɪnəˈtentɪv] unaufmerksam.

in·au·di·ble □ [ɪnˈɔːdəbl] unhörbar.

in·au·gu·ral [ɪˈnɔːgjʊrəl] Antrittsrede *f*; *attr.* Antritts...; **~rate** [~reɪt] (feierlich) einführen; einweihen; einleiten; **~ra·tion** [ɪnɔːgjʊˈreɪʃn] Amtseinführung *f*; Einweihung *f*; Beginn *m*; ♀ *Day Am.* Tag *m* der Amtseinführung des neugewählten Präsidenten der USA (*20. Januar*).

in·born [ˈɪnˈbɔːn] angeboren.

in·built [ˈɪnbɪlt] eingebaut, Einbau...

in·cal·cu·la·ble □ [ɪnˈkælkjʊləbl] unberechenbar.

in·can·des·cent □ [ɪnkænˈdesnt] (weiß)glühend.

in·ca·pa·ble □ [ɪnˈkeɪpəbl] unfähig, nicht imstande (*of doing* zu tun); hilflos.

in·ca·pa·ci·tate [ɪnkə'pæsɪteɪt] unfähig machen; **~ty** [~sətɪ] Unfähigkeit f.

in·car·nate [ɪn'kɑ:nət] *eccl.* fleischgeworden; *fig.* verkörpert.

in·cau·tious □ [ɪn'kɔ:ʃəs] unvorsichtig.

in·cen·di·a·ry [ɪn'sendjərɪ] **1.** Brand...; *fig.* aufwiegelnd, -hetzend; **2.** Brandstifter m; Aufwiegler m.

in·cense[1] ['ɪnsens] Weihrauch m.

in·cense[2] [ɪn'sens] in Wut bringen.

in·cen·tive [ɪn'sentɪv] Ansporn m, Antrieb m.

in·ces·sant □ [ɪn'sesnt] unaufhörlich.

in·cest ['ɪnsest] Inzest m, Blutschande f.

inch [ɪntʃ] **1.** Inch m (= 2,54 cm), Zoll m (a. fig.); by **~es** allmählich; *every* **~** durch u. durch; **2.** (sich) zentimeterweise od. sehr langsam bewegen.

in·ci·dence ['ɪnsɪdəns] Vorkommen n; **~dent** [~t] Vorfall m, Ereignis n, Vorkommnis n; **~den·tal** □ [ɪnsɪ'dentl] zufällig; gelegentlich; Neben...; beiläufig; **~ly** nebenbei.

in·cin·e·rate [ɪn'sɪnəreɪt] verbrennen; **~ra·tor** [~ə] Verbrennungsofen m; Verbrennungsanlage f.

in·cise [ɪn'saɪz] ein-, aufschneiden; einritzen, -schnitzen; **in·ci·sion** [ɪn'sɪʒn] (Ein)Schnitt m; **in·ci·sive** □ [ɪn'saɪsɪv] (ein)schneidend; scharf; **in·ci·sor** [~aɪzə] *anat.* Schneidezahn m.

in·cite [ɪn'saɪt] anspornen, anregen; anstiften; **~ment** [~mənt] Anregung f; Ansporn m; Anstiftung f.

in·clem·ent [ɪn'klemənt] rauh (*Klima*).

in·cli·na·tion [ɪnklɪ'neɪʃn] Neigung f (a. fig.); **in·cline** [ɪn'klaɪn] **1.** v/i. sich neigen, (schräg) abfallen; **~** *to fig.* zu et. neigen; v/t. neigen; geneigt machen; **2.** Gefälle n; (Ab)Hang m.

in·close [ɪn'kləʊz], **in·clos·ure** [~əʊ-ʒə] s. *enclose, enclosure.*

in·clude [ɪn'klu:d] einschließen; enthalten; **in·clud·ed** eingeschlossen; mit inbegriffen; *tax* **~** inklusive Steuer; **in·clud·ing** einschließlich; **in·clu·sion** [~ʒn] Einschluß m, Einbeziehung f; **in·clu·sive** □ [~sɪv] einschließlich, inklusive (*of gen.*); **~** *of* einschließen (*acc.*); **~** *terms pl.* Pauschalpreis m.

in·co·her·ence [ɪnkəʊ'hɪərəns] Zu-

sammenhang(s)losigkeit f; **~ent** □ [~t] (logisch) unzusammenhängend, unklar, unverständlich.

in·come *econ.* ['ɪnkʌm] Einkommen n, Einkünfte *pl.*; **~** *tax econ.* Einkommensteuer f.

in·com·ing ['ɪnkʌmɪŋ] hereinkommend; ankommend; nachfolgend, neu; **~** *orders pl. econ.* Auftragseingänge *pl.*

in·com·mu·ni·ca·tive □ [ɪnkə'mju:-nɪkətɪv] nicht mitteilsam, verschlossen.

in·com·pa·ra·ble □ [ɪn'kɒmpərəbl] unvergleichlich.

in·com·pat·i·ble □ [ɪnkəm'pætəbl] unvereinbar; unverträglich.

in·com·pe·tence [ɪn'kɒmpɪtəns] Unfähigkeit f; Inkompetenz f; **~tent** □ [~t] unfähig; nicht fach- od. sachkundig; unzuständig, inkompetent.

in·com·plete □ [ɪnkəm'pli:t] unvollständig; unvollkommen.

in·com·pre·hen·si·ble □ [ɪnkɒm-prɪ'hensəbl] unbegreiflich, unfaßbar; **~sion** [~ʃn] Unverständnis n.

in·con·cei·va·ble □ [ɪnkən'si:vəbl] unbegreiflich, unfaßbar; undenkbar.

in·con·clu·sive □ [ɪnkən'klu:sɪv] nicht überzeugend; ergebnis-, erfolglos.

in·con·gru·ous □ [ɪn'kɒŋgruəs] nicht übereinstimmend; nicht passend.

in·con·se|quent □ [ɪn'kɒnsɪkwənt] inkonsequent, folgewidrig; **~quen·tial** □ [ɪnkɒnsɪ'kwenʃl] unbedeutend.

in·con·sid·e·ra·ble □ [ɪnkən'sɪdə-rəbl] unbedeutend; **~er·ate** □ [~rət] unüberlegt; rücksichtslos.

in·con·sis·ten·cy [ɪnkən'sɪstənsɪ] Unvereinbarkeit f; Inkonsequenz f; **~tent** □ [~t] unvereinbar; widersprüchlich; unbeständig; inkonsequent.

in·con·so·la·ble □ [ɪnkən'səʊləbl] untröstlich.

in·con·spic·u·ous □ [ɪnkən'spɪk-juəs] unauffällig.

in·con·stant □ [ɪn'kɒnstənt] unbeständig, veränderlich.

in·con·ti·nent □ [ɪn'kɒntɪnənt] zügellos; *&* inkontinent.

in·con·ve·ni·ence [ɪnkən'vi:njəns] **1.** Unbequemlichkeit f; Unannehmlichkeit f; **2.** belästigen, stören;

∼ent □ [∼t] unbequem; ungelegen, lästig.

in·cor·po·rate [ɪnˈkɔːpəreɪt] (sich) verbinden *od.* -vereinigen *od.* zusammenschließen; *Idee etc.* einverleiben; aufnehmen, eingliedern, inkorporieren; *econ.*, ᵵᵵ als Gesellschaft eintragen (lassen); **∼rat·ed** *econ.*, ᵵᵵ (*Am.* Aktien)Gesellschaft eingetragen; **∼ra·tion** [ɪnkɔːpəˈreɪʃn] Vereinigung *f*, -bindung *f*, Zusammenschluß *m*; Eingliederung *f*; *econ.*, ᵵᵵ Eintragung *f* als (*Am.* Aktien)Gesellschaft.

in·cor·rect □ [ɪnkəˈrekt] unrichtig, falsch; inkorrekt.

in·cor·ri·gi·ble □ [ɪnˈkɒrɪdʒəbl] unverbesserlich.

in·cor·rup·ti·ble □ [ɪnkəˈrʌptəbl] unbestechlich; unvergänglich.

in·crease 1. [ɪnˈkriːs] zunehmen, (an)wachsen, (an)steigen, (sich) vergrößern *od.* -mehren *od.* erhöhen *od.* steigern *od.* verstärken; **2.** [ˈɪnkriːs] Zunahme *f*, Vergrößerung *f*; (An-)Wachsen *n*, Steigen *n*, Steigerung *f*; Zuwachs *m*; **in·creas·ing·ly** [ɪnˈkriːsɪŋlɪ] zunehmend, immer mehr; *∼ difficult* immer schwieriger.

in·cred·i·ble □ [ɪnˈkredəbl] unglaublich, unglaubhaft.

in·cre·du·li·ty [ɪnkrɪˈdjuːlətɪ] Ungläubigkeit *f*; **in·cred·u·lous** □ [ɪnˈkredjʊləs] ungläubig, skeptisch.

in·crim·i·nate [ɪnˈkrɪmɪneɪt] beschuldigen; *j-n* belasten.

in·cu·bate [ˈɪnkjʊbeɪt] ausbrüten; **∼ba·tor** [∼ə] Brutapparat *m*; Brutkasten *m*.

in·cum·bent □ [ɪnˈkʌmbənt] obliegend; *it is ∼ on her* es ist ihre Pflicht.

in·cur [ɪnˈkɜː] (-*rr*-) sich *et.* zuziehen, auf sich laden, geraten in (*acc.*); *Schulden* machen; *Verpflichtung* eingehen; *Verlust* erleiden.

in·cu·ra·ble □ [ɪnˈkjʊərəbl] unheilbar.

in·cu·ri·ous □ [ɪnˈkjʊərɪəs] nicht neugierig, gleichgültig, uninteressiert.

in·cur·sion [ɪnˈkɜːʃn] (feindlicher) Einfall; plötzlicher Angriff; Eindringen *n*.

in·debt·ed [ɪnˈdetɪd] *econ.* verschuldet; *fig.* (zu Dank) verpflichtet.

in·de·cent □ [ɪnˈdiːsnt] unanständig, anstößig; ᵵᵵ unsittlich, unzüchtig; **∼ assault** ᵵᵵ Sittlichkeitsverbrechen *n*.

in·de·ci·sion [ɪndɪˈsɪʒn] Unentschlossenheit *f*; **∼sive** □ [∼ˈsaɪsɪv] unbestimmt, ungewiß; unentschlossen, unschlüssig.

in·deed [ɪnˈdiːd] **1.** *adv.* in der Tat, tatsächlich, wirklich; allerdings; *thank you very much ∼!* vielen herzlichen Dank!; **2.** *int.* ach wirklich!

in·de·fat·i·ga·ble □ [ɪndɪˈfætɪgəbl] unermüdlich.

in·de·fen·si·ble □ [ɪndɪˈfensəbl] unhaltbar.

in·de·fi·na·ble □ [ɪndɪˈfaɪnəbl] undefinierbar, unbestimmbar.

in·def·i·nite □ [ɪnˈdefnət] unbestimmt; unbegrenzt; unklar.

in·del·i·ble □ [ɪnˈdelɪbl] unauslöschlich, untilgbar; *fig.* unvergeßlich; **∼ pencil** Kopier-, Tintenstift *m*.

in·del·i·cate □ [ɪnˈdelɪkət] unfein, derb; taktlos.

in·dem·ni·fy [ɪnˈdemnɪfaɪ] *j-n* entschädigen (*for* für); versichern; ᵵᵵ *j-m* Straflosigkeit zusichern; **∼ty** [∼ɔtɪ] Schadenersatz *m*, Entschädigung *f*, Abfindung *f*; Versicherung *f*; ᵵᵵ Straflosigkeit *f*.

in·dent [ɪnˈdent] einkerben, auszacken; *print.* Zeile einrücken; ᵵᵵ *Vertrag* mit Doppel ausfertigen; **∼ on s.o. for s.th.** bsd. Brt. econ. et. bei *j-m* bestellen.

in·den·tures *econ.*, ᵵᵵ [ɪnˈdentʃəz] *pl.* Ausbildungs-, Lehrvertrag *m*.

in·de·pen·dence [ɪndɪˈpendəns] Unabhängigkeit *f*; Selbständigkeit *f*; Auskommen *n*; ♀ *Day Am.* Unabhängigkeitstag *m* (4. *Juli*); **∼dent** □ [∼t] unabhängig; selbständig.

in·de·scri·ba·ble □ [ɪndɪˈskraɪbəbl] unbeschreiblich.

in·de·struc·ti·ble □ [ɪndɪˈstrʌktəbl] unzerstörbar; unverwüstlich.

in·de·ter·mi·nate □ [ɪndɪˈtɜːmɪnət] unbestimmt; unklar, vage.

in·dex [ˈɪndeks] **1.** (*pl.* -dexes, -dices [-dɪsiːz]) (Inhalts-, Namens-, Sach-, Stichwort)Verzeichnis *n*, Register *n*, Index *m*; Index-, Meßziffer *f*; ⊕ Zeiger *m*; Anzeichen *n*; *cost of living* ∼ Lebenshaltungskosten-Index *m*; **2.** mit e-m Indexverzeichnis versehen; in ein Verzeichnis aufnehmen; **∼ card** Karteikarte *f*; **∼ fin·ger** Zeigefinger *m*.

In·di·an [ˈɪndjən] **1.** indisch; indianisch, Indianer...; **2.** Inder(in); *a. American ∼, Red ∼* Indianer(in);

~ corn ♀ Mais *m*; **~ file:** *in ~* im Gänsemarsch; **~ pud·ding** Maismehlpudding *m*; **~ sum·mer** Altweiber-, Nachsommer *m*.

In·di·a rub·ber, in·di·a·rub·ber ['ɪndjə'rʌbə] Radiergummi *m*; *attr.* Gummi...

in·di·cate ['ɪndɪkeɪt] (an)zeigen; hinweisen *od.* -deuten auf (*acc.*); andeuten; *mot.* blinken; **~·ca·tion** [ɪndɪ'keɪʃn] (An)Zeichen *n*, Hinweis *m*, Andeutung *f*; **in·dic·a·tive** [ɪn'dɪkətɪv] *a.* ~ *mood gr.* Indikativ *m*; **~·ca·tor** ['ɪndɪkeɪtə] (An)Zeiger *m*; *mot.* Richtungsanzeiger *m*, Blinker *m*.

in·di·ces ['ɪndɪsiːz] *pl. von* index.

in·dict ɪ⅊ [ɪn'daɪt] anklagen (*for* wegen); **~·ment** ɪ⅊ [~mənt] Anklage *f*.

in·dif·fer|ence [ɪn'dɪfrəns] Gleichgültigkeit *f*, Interesselosigkeit *f*; **~·ent** □ [~t] gleichgültig (*to* gegen), interesselos (*to* gegenüber); durchschnittlich, mittelmäßig.

in·di·gent ['ɪndɪdʒənt] arm.

in·di·ges·ti·ble □ [ɪndɪ'dʒestəbl] unverdaulich; **~·tion** [~tʃən] Verdauungsstörung *f*, Magenverstimmung *f*.

in·dig·nant □ [ɪn'dɪgnənt] entrüstet, empört, ungehalten (*at, over, about* über *acc.*); **~·na·tion** [ɪndɪg'neɪʃn] Entrüstung *f*, Empörung *f* (*at, over, about* über *acc.*); **~·ni·ty** [ɪn'dɪgnətɪ] Demütigung *f*, unwürdige Behandlung.

in·di·rect □ [ɪndɪ'rekt] indirekt (*a. gr.*); *by ~ means* auf Umwegen.

in·dis|creet □ [ɪndɪ'skriːt] unbesonnen; taktlos; indiskret; **~·cre·tion** [~'kreʃn] Unbesonnenheit *f*; Taktlosigkeit *f*; Indiskretion *f*.

in·dis·crim·i·nate □ [ɪndɪ'skrɪmɪnət] unterschieds-, wahllos; willkürlich.

in·di·spen·sa·ble □ [ɪndɪ'spensəbl] unentbehrlich, unerläßlich.

in·dis|posed [ɪndɪ'spəʊzd] indisponiert; unpäßlich; abgeneigt; **~·po·si·tion** [ɪndɪspə'zɪʃn] Abneigung *f* (*to* gegen); Unpäßlichkeit *f*.

in·dis·pu·ta·ble □ [ɪndɪ'spjuːtəbl] unbestreitbar, unstreitig.

in·dis·tinct □ [ɪndɪ'stɪŋkt] undeutlich; unklar, verschwommen.

in·dis·tin·guish·a·ble □ [ɪndɪ'stɪŋgwɪʃəbl] nicht zu unterscheiden(d).

in·di·vid·u·al [ɪndɪ'vɪdjʊəl] **1.** □ persönlich; individuell; besondere(r, -s); einzeln, Einzel...; **2.** Individuum *n*, Einzelne(r *m*) *f*; **~·is·m** [~ɪzəm] Individualismus *m*; **~·ist** [~ɪst] Individualist(in); **~·i·ty** [ɪndɪvɪdjʊ'ælətɪ] Individualität *f*, (persönliche) Note; **~·ly** [ɪndɪ'vɪdjʊəlɪ] einzeln, jede(r, -s) für sich.

in·di·vis·i·ble □ [ɪndɪ'vɪzəbl] unteilbar.

in·do·lent □ ['ɪndələnt] träge, faul, arbeitsscheu; *⚕* schmerzlos.

in·dom·i·ta·ble □ [ɪn'dɒmɪtəbl] unbezähmbar, nicht unterzukriegen(d).

in·door ['ɪndɔː] zu *od.* im Hause (befindlich), Haus..., Zimmer..., Innen..., *Sport:* Hallen...; **~s** ['ɪn'dɔːz] zu *od.* im Hause; im *od.* ins Haus.

in·dorse [ɪn'dɔːs] = *endorse etc.*

in·duce [ɪn'djuːs] veranlassen; hervorrufen, bewirken; **~·ment** [~mənt] Anlaß *m*; Anreiz *m*, Ansporn *m*.

in·duct [ɪn'dʌkt] einführen, -setzen; **in·duc·tion** [~kʃn] Einführung *f*, Einsetzung *f* (*in Amt, Pfründe*); *⚡* Induktion *f*.

in·dulge [ɪn'dʌldʒ] nachsichtig sein gegen, gewähren lassen, *j-m* nachgeben; ~ *in s.th.* sich et. gönnen *od.* leisten; **in·dul·gence** [~əns] Nachsicht *f*, Nachgiebigkeit *f*; Schwäche *f*, Leidenschaft *f*; **in·dul·gent** □ [~nt] nachsichtig, -giebig.

in·dus·tri·al □ [ɪn'dʌstrɪəl] industriell, Industrie..., Gewerbe..., Betriebs...; ~ *area* Industriegebiet *n*; **~·ist** *econ.* [~əlɪst] Industrielle(r *m*) *f*; **~·ize** *econ.* [~əlaɪz] industrialisieren.

in·dus·tri·ous □ [ɪn'dʌstrɪəs] fleißig; *△ nicht Industrie...*

in·dus·try ['ɪndəstrɪ] *econ.* Industrie (-zweig *m*) *f*; Gewerbe(zweig *m*) *n*; Fleiß *m*.

in·ed·i·ble □ [ɪn'edɪbl] ungenießbar, nicht eßbar.

in·ef·fa·ble □ [ɪn'efəbl] unaussprechlich, unbeschreiblich.

in·ef·fec·tive □ [ɪnɪ'fektɪv], **~·tu·al** □ [~tʃʊəl] unwirksam, wirkungslos; untauglich.

in·ef·fi·cient □ [ɪnɪ'fɪʃnt] unfähig, untauglich; leistungsschwach, unproduktiv.

in·el·e·gant □ [ɪn'elɪgənt] unelegant; schwerfällig.

in·el·i·gi·ble □ [ɪn'elɪdʒəbl] nicht

wählbar; ungeeignet; nicht berechtigt; *bsd.* ✗ untauglich.

in·ept □ [ɪˈnept] unpassend; ungeschickt; albern, töricht.

in·e·qual·i·ty [ɪnɪˈkwɒlətɪ] Ungleichheit *f*.

in·ert □ [ɪˈnɜːt] *phys.* träge (*a. fig.*); 🜄 inaktiv; **in·er·tia** [ɪˈnɜːʃjə] Trägheit *f* (*a. fig.*).

in·es·ca·pa·ble [ɪnɪˈskeɪpəbl] unvermeidlich.

in·es·sen·tial [ɪnɪˈsenʃl] unwesentlich, unwichtig (*to* für).

in·es·ti·ma·ble □ [ɪnˈestɪməbl] unschätzbar.

in·ev·i·ta·ble □ [ɪnˈevɪtəbl] unvermeidlich; zwangsläufig.

in·ex·act □ [ɪnɪgˈzækt] ungenau.

in·ex·cu·sa·ble □ [ɪnɪkˈskjuːzəbl] unverzeihlich, unentschuldbar.

in·ex·haus·ti·ble □ [ɪnɪgˈzɔːstəbl] unerschöpflich; unermüdlich.

in·ex·o·ra·ble □ [ɪnˈeksərəbl] unerbittlich.

in·ex·pe·di·ent □ [ɪnɪkˈspiːdjənt] unzweckmäßig; nicht ratsam.

in·ex·pen·sive □ [ɪnɪkˈspensɪv] nicht teuer, billig, preiswert.

in·ex·pe·ri·ence [ɪnɪkˈspɪərɪəns] Unerfahrenheit *f*; **~d** unerfahren.

in·ex·pert □ [ɪnˈekspɜːt] unerfahren; ungeschickt.

in·ex·pli·ca·ble □ [ɪnɪkˈsplɪkəbl] unerklärlich.

in·ex·pres·si·ble □ [ɪnɪkˈspresəbl] unaussprechlich, unbeschreiblich; **~ve** [~sɪv] ausdruckslos.

in·ex·tri·ca·ble □ [ɪnˈekstrɪkəbl] unentwirrbar.

in·fal·li·ble □ [ɪnˈfæləbl] unfehlbar.

in·fa|mous □ [ˈɪnfəməs] berüchtigt; schändlich, niederträchtig; **~my** [~ɪ] Ehrlosigkeit *f*; Schande *f*; Niedertracht *f*.

in·fan|cy [ˈɪnfənsɪ] frühe Kindheit; ⚖ Minderjährigkeit *f*; *in its* **~** *fig.* in den Anfängen *od.* Kinderschuhen steckend; **~t** [~t] Säugling *m*; Kleinkind *n*; ⚖ Minderjährige(r *m*) *f*.

in·fan·tile [ˈɪnfəntaɪl] kindlich; Kindes..., Kinder...; infantil, kindisch.

in·fan·try ✗ [ˈɪnfəntrɪ] Infanterie *f*.

in·fat·u·at·ed [ɪnˈfætjʊeɪtɪd] vernarrt (*with* in *acc.*).

in·fect [ɪnˈfekt] ✿ *j-n, et.* infizieren, *j-n* anstecken (*a. fig.*); verseuchen, -unreinigen; **in·fec·tion** [~kʃn] ✿ Infektion *f*, Ansteckung *f* (*a. fig.*);

in·fec·tious □ [~kʃəs] ✿ infektiös, ansteckend (*a. fig.*).

in·fer [ɪnˈfɜː] (*-rr-*) folgern, schließen (*from* aus); **~ence** [ˈɪnfərəns] (Schluß)Folgerung *f*.

in·fe·ri·or [ɪnˈfɪərɪə] **1.** (*to*) untergeordnet (*dat.*), (*im Rang*) tieferstehend, niedriger, geringer (als); minderwertig; *be* **~** *to s.o.* *j-m* untergeordnet sein; *j-m* unterlegen sein; **2.** Untergebene(r *m*) *f*; **~i·ty** [ɪnfɪərɪˈɒrətɪ] Unterlegenheit *f*; geringerer Wert *od.* Stand, Minderwertigkeit *f*; **~** *complex psych.* Minderwertigkeitskomplex *m*.

in·fer|nal □ [ɪnˈfɜːnl] höllisch, Höllen...; **~no** [~əʊ] (*pl. -nos*) Inferno *n*, Hölle *f*.

in·fer·tile [ɪnˈfɜːtaɪl] unfruchtbar.

in·fest [ɪnˈfest] heimsuchen; verseuchen, befallen; *fig.* überschwemmen (*with* mit).

in·fi·del·i·ty [ɪnfɪˈdelətɪ] (*bsd.* eheliche) Untreue.

in·fil·trate [ˈɪnfɪltreɪt] *v/t.* eindringen in (*acc.*); einsickern in (*acc.*), durchdringen; *pol.* unterwandern; *pol.* einschleusen; *v/i.* eindringen (*into* in *acc.*); *pol.* unterwandern (*into* acc.), sich einschleusen (*into* in *acc.*).

in·fi·nite □ [ˈɪnfɪnət] unendlich.

in·fin·i·tive [ɪnˈfɪnətɪv] *a.* **~** *mood gr.* Infinitiv *m*, Nennform *f*.

in·fin·i·ty [ɪnˈfɪnətɪ] Unendlichkeit *f*.

in·firm □ [ɪnˈfɜːm] schwach; gebrechlich; **in·fir·ma·ry** [~ərɪ] Krankenhaus *n*; Krankenstube *f*, -zimmer *n* (*in Internaten etc.*); **in·fir·mi·ty** [~ətɪ] Schwäche *f* (*a. fig.*); Gebrechlichkeit *f*.

in·flame [ɪnˈfleɪm] entflammen (*mst fig.*); ✿ (sich) entzünden; erregen; erzürnen.

in·flam·ma|ble [ɪnˈflæməbl] leicht entzündlich; feuergefährlich; **~tion** ✿ [ɪnfləˈmeɪʃn] Entzündung *f*; **~to·ry** [ɪnˈflæmətərɪ] ✿ entzündlich; *fig.* aufrührerisch, Hetz...

in·flate [ɪnˈfleɪt] aufpumpen, -blasen, -blähen (*a. fig.*); *econ.* Preise *etc.* in die Höhe treiben; **in·fla·tion** [~ʃn] Aufblähung *f*; *econ.* Inflation *f*.

in·flect *gr.* [ɪnˈflekt] flektieren, beugen; **in·flec·tion** [~kʃn] *= inflexion*.

in·flex·i·ble □ [ɪnˈfleksəbl] unbiegsam, starr (*a. fig.*); *fig.* unbeugsam;

I J

~·ion *bsd. Brt.* [~k∫n] *gr.* Flexion *f*, Beugung *f*; ♪ Modulation *f*.

in·flict [ɪn'flɪkt] (*on, upon*) Leid etc. zufügen (*dat.*); *Wunde etc.* beibringen (*dat.*); *Schlag* versetzen (*dat.*); *Strafe* verhängen (über *acc.*); aufbürden, -drängen (*dat.*); **in·flic·tion** [~k∫n] Zufügung *f*; Verhängung *f* (*e-r Strafe*); Plage *f*.

in·flu·ence ['ɪnfloəns] **1.** Einfluß *m*; **2.** beeinflussen; **~·en·tial** □ [ɪnflo-'en∫l] einflußreich.

in·flu·en·za *♬* [ɪnflo'enzə] Grippe *f*.

in·flux ['ɪnflʌks] Einströmen *n*; *econ.* (*Waren*)Zufuhr *f*; *fig.* (Zu)Strom *m*.

in·form [ɪn'fɔ:m] benachrichtigen, unterrichten (*of* von), informieren (*of* über *acc.*); ~ *against od. on od. upon* s.o. j-n anzeigen; j-n denunzieren.

in·for·mal □ [ɪn'fɔ:ml] formlos, zwanglos; **~·i·ty** [ɪnfɔ:'mælətɪ] Formlosigkeit *f*; Ungezwungenheit *f*.

in·for·ma·tion [ɪnfə'meɪ∫n] Auskunft *f*; Nachricht *f*; Information *f*; ~ *storage Computer:* Datenspeicherung *f*; **~·tive** [ɪn'fɔ:mətɪv] informativ; lehrreich; mitteilsam.

in·form·er [ɪn'fɔ:mə] Denunziant(in); Spitzel *m*.

in·fre·quent □ [ɪn'fri:kwənt] selten.

in·fringe [ɪn'frɪndʒ]: ~ *on,* ~ *upon Rechte, Vertrag etc.* verletzen.

in·fu·ri·ate [ɪn'fjʊərɪeɪt] wütend machen.

in·fuse [ɪn'fju:z] *Tee* aufgießen; *fig.* einflößen; *fig.* erfüllen (*with* mit); **in·fu·sion** [~ʒn] Aufguß *m*, Tee *m*; Einflößen *n*; *♬* Infusion *f*.

in·ge·ni·ous □ [ɪn'dʒi:njəs] genial; geist-, sinnreich; erfinderisch; raffiniert; **~·nu·i·ty** [ɪndʒɪ'nju:ətɪ] Genialität *f*; Einfallsreichtum *m*.

in·gen·u·ous □ [ɪn'dʒenjʊəs] offen, aufrichtig; unbefangen; naiv.

in·got ['ɪŋɡət] (*Gold- etc.*)Barren *m*.

in·gra·ti·ate [ɪn'ɡreɪ∫ɪeɪt]: ~ *o.s. with* s.o. sich bei j-m beliebt machen.

in·grat·i·tude [ɪn'ɡrætɪtju:d] Undankbarkeit *f*.

in·gre·di·ent [ɪn'ɡri:dʒənt] Bestandteil *m*; *Küche:* Zutat *f*.

in·grow·ing ['ɪnɡrəʊɪŋ] nach innen wachsend; eingewachsen.

in·hab·it [ɪn'hæbɪt] bewohnen, leben in (*dat.*); **~·it·a·ble** [~əbl] bewohn-

bar; **~·i·tant** [~ənt] Bewohner(in); Einwohner(in).

in·hale [ɪn'heɪl] einatmen, *♬ a.* inhalieren.

in·her·ent □ [ɪn'hɪərənt] anhaftend; innewohnend, angeboren, eigen (*in dat.*).

in·her·it [ɪn'herɪt] erben; **~·i·tance** [~əns] Erbe *n*, Erbschaft *f*; *biol.* Vererbung *f*.

in·hib·it [ɪn'hɪbɪt] hemmen (*a. psych.*), hindern; **~·ed** *psych.* gehemmt; **in·hi·bi·tion** *psych.* [ɪnhɪ-'bɪ∫n] Hemmung *f*.

in·hos·pi·ta·ble □ [ɪn'hɒspɪtəbl] ungastlich; unwirtlich (*Gegend etc.*).

in·hu·man □ [ɪn'hju:mən] unmenschlich; **~·e** □ [ɪnhju:'meɪn] inhuman; menschenunwürdig.

in·im·i·cal □ [ɪ'nɪmɪkl] feindselig (*to* gegen); nachteilig (*to* für).

in·im·i·ta·ble □ [ɪ'nɪmɪtəbl] unnachahmlich.

i·ni·tial [ɪ'nɪ∫l] **1.** □ anfänglich, Anfangs...; **2.** Initiale *f*, (großer) Anfangsbuchstabe; **~·tial·ly** [~∫əlɪ] am *od.* zu Anfang; **~·ti·ate 1.** [~∫ɪət] Eingeweihte(r *m*) *f*; **2.** [~∫ɪeɪt] beginnen, in die Wege leiten; einführen, einweihen; aufnehmen; **~·ti·a·tion** [ɪnɪ∫ɪ'eɪ∫n] Einführung *f*; Aufnahme *f*; ~ *fee bsd. Am.* Aufnahmegebühr *f* (*Vereinigung*); **~·tia·tive** [ɪ'nɪ∫ɪətɪv] Initiative *f*; erster Schritt; Entschlußkraft *f*, Unternehmungsgeist *m*; *take the* ~ die Initiative ergreifen; *on one's own* ~ aus eigenem Antrieb.

in·ject *♬* [ɪn'dʒekt] injizieren, einspritzen; **in·jec·tion** *♬* [~k∫n] Injektion *f*, Spritze *f*.

in·ju·di·cious □ [ɪndʒu:'dɪ∫əs] unklug, unüberlegt.

in·junc·tion [ɪn'dʒʌŋk∫n] *tₜₜ* gerichtliche Verfügung *f*; ausdrücklicher Befehl.

in·jure ['ɪndʒə] verletzen, -wunden; (be)schädigen; schaden (*dat.*); kränken; **in·ju·ri·ous** □ [ɪn'dʒʊərɪəs] schädlich; beleidigend; *be* ~ *to* schaden (*dat.*); ~ *to health* gesundheitsschädlich; **in·ju·ry** ['ɪndʒərɪ] *♬* Verletzung *f*; Unrecht *n*; Schaden *m*; Kränkung *f*.

in·jus·tice [ɪn'dʒʌstɪs] Ungerechtigkeit *f*; Unrecht *n*; *do s.o. an* ~ j-m unrecht tun.

ink [ɪŋk] Tinte *f*; *mst printer's* ~

Druckerschwärze f; attr. Tinten...

ink·ling ['ɪŋklɪŋ] Andeutung f; dunkle od. leise Ahnung.

ink·pad ['ɪŋkpæd] Stempelkissen n; ~y [~ɪ] (-ier, -iest) voll Tinte, Tinten...; tinten-, pechschwarz.

in·laid ['ɪnleɪd] eingelegt, Einlege...; ~ work Einlegearbeit f.

in·land 1. adj. ['ɪnlənd] inländisch, einheimisch; Binnen...; **2.** [~] das Landesinnere; Binnenland n. **3.** adv. [ɪn'lænd] landeinwärts; ~ rev·e·nue Brt. Steuereinnahmen pl.; ⊘ **Rev·e·nue** Brt. Finanzamt n.

in·lay ['ɪnleɪ] Einlegearbeit f; (Zahn-) Füllung f, Plombe f.

in·let ['ɪnlet] Meeresarm m; Flußarm m; ⊕ Einlaß m.

in·mate ['ɪnmeɪt] Insassle m, -in f; Mitbewohner(in).

in·most ['ɪnməʊst] = innermost.

inn [ɪn] Gasthaus n, Wirtshaus n.

in·nate □ ['ɪ'neɪt] angeboren.

in·ner ['ɪnə] innere(r, -s); Innen...; verborgen; ~·most innerste(r, -s) (a. fig.).

in·nings ['ɪnɪŋz] (pl. innings) Kriket, Baseball: Spielzeit f (e-s Spielers od. e-r Mannschaft).

inn·keep·er ['ɪnkiːpə] Gastwirt(in).

in·no·cence ['ɪnəsns] Unschuld f; Harmlosigkeit f; Naivität f; ~·cent [~t] **1.** □ unschuldig; harmlos; arglos, naiv; **2.** Unschuldige(r m) f; Einfältige(r m) f.

in·noc·u·ous □ [ɪ'nɒkjʊəs] harmlos.

in·no·va·tion [ɪnəʊ'veɪʃn] Neuerung f.

in·nu·en·do [ɪnjuː'endəʊ] (pl. -does, -dos) (versteckte) Andeutung.

in·nu·me·ra·ble □ [ɪ'njuːmərəbl] unzählig, zahllos.

i·noc·u·late [ɪ'nɒkjʊleɪt] (ein)impfen; ~·la·tion ⚕ [ɪnɒkjʊ'leɪʃn] Impfung f.

in·of·fen·sive □ [ɪnə'fensɪv] harmlos.

in·op·e·ra·ble [ɪn'ɒpərəbl] ⚕ inoperabel, nicht operierbar; undurchführbar (Plan etc.).

in·op·por·tune □ [ɪn'ɒpətjuːn] inopportun, unangebracht, ungelegen.

in·or·di·nate □ [ɪ'nɔːdɪnət] unmäßig.

in·pa·tient ⚕ ['ɪnpeɪʃnt] stationärer Patient, stationäre Patientin.

in·put ['ɪnpʊt] Input m: econ. (von außen bezogene) Produktionsmittel pl.; Arbeitsaufwand m; Energiezufuhr f; ⚡ Eingang m (an Geräten); Computer: (Daten- od. Programm-) Eingabe f.

in·quest ⚖ ['ɪnkwest] gerichtliche Untersuchung; coroner's ~ s. coroner.

in·quir|e [ɪn'kwaɪə] fragen od. sich erkundigen (nach); ~ into untersuchen; **in·quir·ing** □ [~rɪŋ] forschend; wißbegierig; **in·quir·y** [~rɪ] Erkundigung f, Nachfrage f; Untersuchung f; Ermittlung f; make inquiries Erkundigungen einziehen.

in·qui·si·tion [ɪnkwɪ'zɪʃn] ⚖ Untersuchung f; Verhör n; eccl. hist. Inquisition f; **in·quis·i·tive** □ [ɪn'kwɪzətɪv] neugierig; wißbegierig.

in·road fig. ['ɪnrəʊd] (into, on) Eingriff m (in acc.); übermäßige Inanspruchnahme (gen.).

in·sane □ ['ɪn'seɪn] geisteskrank, wahnsinnig.

in·san·i·ta·ry [ɪn'sænɪtərɪ] unhygienisch.

in·san·i·ty [ɪn'sænətɪ] Geisteskrankheit f, Wahnsinn m.

in·sa·tia·ble □ [ɪn'seɪʃjəbl] unersättlich.

in·scribe [ɪn'skraɪb] (ein-, auf-) schreiben, einmeißeln, -ritzen; Buch mit e-r Widmung versehen.

in·scrip·tion [ɪn'skrɪpʃn] In-, Aufschrift f; Widmung f.

in·scru·ta·ble □ [ɪn'skruːtəbl] unerforschlich, unergründlich.

in·sect zo. ['ɪnsekt] Insekt n, Kerbtier n; **in·sec·ti·cide** [ɪn'sektɪsaɪd] Insektenvertilgungsmittel n, Insektizid n.

in·se·cure □ [ɪnsɪ'kjʊə] unsicher; nicht sicher od. fest.

in·sen·si·ble □ [ɪn'sensəbl] unempfindlich (to gegen); bewußtlos; unmerklich; gefühllos, gleichgültig; ~·tive [~sətɪv] unempfindlich, gefühllos (to gegen); unempfänglich.

in·sep·a·ra·ble □ [ɪn'sepərəbl] untrennbar; unzertrennlich.

in·sert 1. [ɪn'sɜːt] einfügen, -setzen, -führen, (hinein)stecken; Münze einwerfen; inserieren; **2.** ['ɪnsɜːt] Bei-, Einlage f; **in·ser·tion** [ɪn'sɜːʃn] Einfügen n, -setzen n, -führen n, Hineinstecken n; Einfügung f; Einwurf m (e-r Münze); Anzeige f, Inserat n.

inshore

in·shore ['ɪn'ʃɔ:] an *od.* nahe der Küste; Küsten...

in·side [ɪn'saɪd] **1.** Innenseite *f; das* Innere; *turn ~ out* umkrempeln; auf den Kopf stellen; **2.** *adj.* innere(r, -s), Innen...; Insider...; **3.** *adv.* im Innern, (dr)innen; ~ *of a week* F innerhalb e-r Woche; **4.** *prp.* innen in; in ... (hinein); **in·sid·er** [~ə] Eingeweihte(r *m*) *f*, Insider *m*.

in·sid·i·ous □ [ɪn'sɪdɪəs] heimtückisch.

in·sight ['ɪnsaɪt] Einsicht *f*, Einblick *m*; Verständnis *n*.

in·sig·ni·a [ɪn'sɪgnɪə] *pl.* Insignien *pl.*; Abzeichen *pl.*

in·sig·nif·i·cant [ɪnsɪg'nɪfɪkənt] bedeutungslos; unbedeutend.

in·sin·cere □ [ɪnsɪn'sɪə] unaufrichtig.

in·sin·u·ate [ɪn'sɪnjʊeɪt] andeuten, anspielen auf (*acc.*); **~·a·tion** [ɪnsɪnjʊ'eɪʃn] Anspielung *f*, Andeutung *f*.

in·sip·id [ɪn'sɪpɪd] geschmacklos, fad.

in·sist [ɪn'sɪst] bestehen, beharren (*on, upon* auf *dat.*); **in·sis·tence** [~əns] Bestehen *n*, Beharren *n*; Beharrlichkeit *f*; **in·sis·tent** □ [~t] beharrlich, hartnäckig.

in·so·lent □ ['ɪnsələnt] unverschämt.

in·sol·u·ble □ [ɪn'sɒljʊbl] unlöslich; unlösbar (*Problem etc.*).

in·sol·vent [ɪn'sɒlvənt] zahlungsunfähig, insolvent.

in·som·ni·a [ɪn'sɒmnɪə] Schlaflosigkeit *f*.

in·spect [ɪn'spekt] untersuchen, prüfen, nachsehen; besichtigen, inspizieren; **in·spec·tion** [~kʃn] Prüfung *f*, Untersuchung *f*, Kontrolle *f*; Inspektion *f*; **in·spec·tor** [~ktə] Aufsichtsbeamte(r) *m*, Inspektor *m*; (Polizei)Inspektor *m*, (-)Kommissar *m*.

in·spi·ra·tion [ɪnspə'reɪʃn] Inspiration *f*, Eingebung *f*; **in·spire** [ɪn'spaɪə] inspirieren; hervorrufen; *Hoffnung etc.* wecken; *Respekt etc.* einflößen.

in·stall [ɪn'stɔ:l] ⊕ installieren, einrichten, aufstellen, einbauen, *Leitung* legen; *in ein Amt etc.* einsetzen; **in·stal·la·tion** [ɪnstə'leɪʃn] ⊕ Installation *f*, Einrichtung *f*, -bau *m*; ⊕ fertige Anlage; Einsetzung *f*, -führung *f* (*in ein Amt*).

in·stal·ment, *Am. a.* **-stall-** [ɪn'stɔ:l-mənt] *econ.* Rate *f*; (Teil)Lieferung *f* (*e-s Buches etc.*); Fortsetzung *f* (*e-s Romans etc.*); Rundfunk, *TV :* (Sende)Folge *f*.

in·stance ['ɪnstəns] Beispiel *n*; (besonderer) Fall; ⊞ Instanz *f; for ~* zum Beispiel; *at s.o.'s ~* auf j-s Veranlassung (hin).

in·stant □ ['ɪnstənt] **1.** sofortig; unmittelbar; *econ.* Fertig...; ~ *coffee* löslicher *od.* Pulverkaffee, Instantkaffee *m*; **2.** Augenblick *m*; **in·stan·ta·ne·ous** □ [ɪnstən'teɪnjəs] sofortig, augenblicklich; Moment...; ~·ly ['ɪnstəntlɪ] sofort, unverzüglich.

in·stead [ɪn'sted] statt dessen, dafür; ~ *of* an Stelle von, (an)statt.

in·step *anat.* ['ɪnstep] Spann *m*, Rist *m*.

in·sti·gate ['ɪnstɪgeɪt] anstiften; aufhetzen; veranlassen; **~·ga·tor** [~ə] Anstifter(in); (Auf)Hetzer(in).

in·stil, *Am. a.* **-still** *fig.* [ɪn'stɪl] (*-ll-*) beibringen, einflößen (*into dat.*).

in·stinct ['ɪnstɪŋkt] Instinkt *m*; **in·stinc·tive** □ [ɪn'stɪŋktɪv] instinktiv.

in·sti·tute ['ɪnstɪtju:t] **1.** Institut *n*; (*gelehrte etc.*) Gesellschaft *f*; **2.** einrichten, gründen; einführen; einleiten; **~·tu·tion** [ɪnstɪ'tju:ʃn] Institut *n*, Anstalt *f*; Einführung *f*; Institution *f*, Einrichtung *f*.

in·struct [ɪn'strʌkt] unterrichten; belehren; *j-n* anweisen; **in·struc·tion** [~kʃn] Unterricht *m*; Anweisung *f*, Instruktion *f*; *Computer :* Befehl *m*; ~*s for use* Gebrauchsanweisung *f*; *operating* ~*s* Bedienungsanleitung *f*; **in·struc·tive** □ [~ktɪv] instruktiv, lehrreich; **in·struc·tor** [~ə] Lehrer *m*; Ausbilder *m*; *Am. univ.* Dozent *m*.

in·stru·ment ['ɪnstrʊmənt] Instrument *n*; Werkzeug *n* (*a. fig.*); ~ *panel* ⊕ Armaturenbrett *n*; **~·men·tal** □ [ɪnstrʊ'mentl] behilflich, dienlich; ♪ Instrumental...

in·sub·or·di·nate [ɪnsə'bɔ:dənət] aufsässig; **~·na·tion** ['ɪnsəbɔ:dɪ'neɪʃn] Auflehnung *f*.

in·suf·fe·ra·ble □ [ɪn'sʌfərəbl] unerträglich, unausstehlich.

in·suf·fi·cient □ [ɪnsə'fɪʃnt] unzulänglich, ungenügend.

in·su·lar □ ['ɪnsjʊlə] Insel...; *fig.* engstirnig.

in·sul·ate ['ɪnsjʊleɪt] isolieren; **~la·tion** [ɪnsjʊ'leɪʃn] Isolierung f; Isoliermaterial n.

in·sult 1. ['ɪnsʌlt] Beleidigung f; **2.** [ɪn'sʌlt] beleidigen.

in·sur·ance [ɪn'ʃʊərəns] Versicherung f; Versicherungssumme f; **~ company** Versicherungsgesellschaft f; **~ policy** Versicherungspolice f; **~e** [ɪn'ʃʊə] versichern (against gegen).

in·sur·gent [ɪn'sɜːdʒənt] **1.** aufständisch; **2.** Aufständische(r m) f.

in·sur·moun·ta·ble □ fig. [ɪnsə-'maʊntəbl] unüberwindlich.

in·sur·rec·tion [ɪnsə'rekʃn] Aufstand m.

in·tact [ɪn'tækt] unberührt; unversehrt, intakt.

in·tan·gi·ble □ [ɪn'tændʒəbl] nicht greifbar; unbestimmt.

in·te·gral □ ['ɪntɪɡrəl] ganz, vollständig; wesentlich; **~grate** [~eɪt] v/t. integrieren, zu e-m Ganzen zusammenfassen; einbeziehen, -gliedern; Am. die Rassenschranken aufheben zwischen; v/i. sich integrieren; **~grat·ed** einheitlich; ⊕ integrabaut; ohne Rassentrennung; **~gra·tion** [~'ɡreɪʃn] Integration f.

in·teg·ri·ty [ɪn'teɡrɪtɪ] Integrität f, Rechtschaffenheit f; Vollständigkeit f.

in·tel·lect ['ɪntəlekt] Intellekt m, Verstand m; **~tu·al** [ɪntə'lektjʊəl] **1.** □ intellektuell, Verstandes..., geistig; **2.** Intellektuelle(r m) f.

in·tel·li·gence [ɪn'telɪdʒəns] Intelligenz f, Verstand m; Nachrichten pl., Informationen pl.; a. **~ department** Geheimdienst m; **~gent** □ [~t] intelligent, klug.

in·tel·li·gi·ble □ [ɪn'telɪdʒəbl] verständlich (to für).

in·tem·per·ate □ [ɪn'tempərət] unmäßig, maßlos; trunksüchtig.

in·tend [ɪn'tend] beabsichtigen, vorhaben, planen; **~ed for** bestimmt für od. zu.

in·tense □ [ɪn'tens] intensiv; stark, heftig; angespannt; ernsthaft.

in·ten·si·fy [ɪn'tensɪfaɪ] intensivieren; (sich) verstärken; **~si·ty** [~sətɪ] Intensität f; **~sive** [~sɪv] intensiv; stark, heftig; **~ care unit** 🎖 Intensivstation f.

in·tent [ɪn'tent] **1.** □ gespannt, aufmerksam; **~ on** fest entschlossen zu (dat.); konzentriert auf (acc.); **2.**

Absicht f, Vorhaben n; to all **~s** and purposes in jeder Hinsicht; **in·ten·tion** [~ʃn] Absicht f; 🏛 Vorsatz m; **in·ten·tion·al** □ [~nl] absichtlich, vorsätzlich.

in·ter [ɪn'tɜː] (-rr-) bestatten.

in·ter- ['ɪntə] zwischen, Zwischen...; gegenseitig, einander.

in·ter·act [ɪntə'rækt] aufeinander (ein)wirken, sich gegenseitig beeinflussen.

in·ter·cede [ɪntə'siːd] vermitteln, sich einsetzen (with bei; for für).

in·ter·cept [ɪntə'sept] abfangen; aufhalten; **~cep·tion** [~pʃn] Abfangen n; Aufhalten n.

in·ter·ces·sion [ɪntə'seʃn] Fürbitte f, -sprache f.

in·ter·change 1. [ɪntə'tʃeɪndʒ] austauschen; **2.** ['ɪntətʃeɪndʒ] Austausch m; kreuzungsfreier Verkehrsknotenpunkt.

in·ter·course ['ɪntəkɔːs] Verkehr m; a. sexual **~** (Geschlechts)Verkehr m.

in·ter·dict 1. [ɪntə'dɪkt] untersagen, verbieten (s.th. to s.o. j-m et.; s.o. from doing j-m zu tun); **2.** ['ɪntə-dɪkt], **~dic·tion** [ɪntə'dɪkʃn] Verbot n.

in·terest ['ɪntrɪst] **1.** Interesse n (in an dat., für), (An)Teilnahme f; Nutzen m; econ. Anteil m, Beteiligung f; econ. Zins(en pl.) m; Interessenten pl., Interessengruppe(n pl.) f; take an **~** in sich interessieren für; **2.** interessieren (in für et.); **~ing** □ [~ɪŋ] interessant.

in·ter·face ['ɪntəfeɪs] Computer: Schnittstelle f.

in·ter·fere [ɪntə'fɪə] sich einmischen (with in acc.); stören; **~fer·ence** [~rəns] Einmischung f; Störung f.

in·te·ri·or [ɪn'tɪərɪə] **1.** □ innere(r, -s), Innen...; Binnen...; Inlands...; **~ decorator** Innenarchitekt(in); **2.** das Innere; Interieur n; pol. innere Angelegenheiten pl.; Department of the ♀ Am. Innenministerium n.

in·ter·ject [ɪntə'dʒekt] Bemerkung einwerfen; **~jec·tion** [~kʃn] Einwurf m; Ausruf m; ling. Interjektion f.

in·ter·lace [ɪntə'leɪs] (sich) (ineinander) verflechten.

in·ter·lock [ɪntə'lɒk] ineinandergreifen; (miteinander) verzahnen.

in·ter·lop·er ['ɪntələʊpə] Eindringling m.

in·ter·lude ['ɪntəluːd] Zwischenspiel *n*; Pause *f*; ~*s of bright weather* zeitweilig schön.

in·ter·me·di·a·ry [ɪntə'miːdjərɪ] Vermittler(in); ~**ate** □ [~ət] in der Mitte liegend, Mittel..., Zwischen...; ~*range missile* Mittelstreckenrakete *f*.

in·ter·ment [ɪn'tɜːmənt] Beerdigung *f*, Bestattung *f*.

in·ter·mi·na·ble □ [ɪn'tɜːmɪnəbl] endlos.

in·ter·mis·sion [ɪntə'mɪʃn] Aussetzen *n*, Unterbrechung *f*; *bsd. Am. thea., Film etc.:* Pause *f*.

in·ter·mit·tent □ [ɪntə'mɪtənt] (zeitweilig) aussetzend, periodisch (auftretend); ~ *fever* ⚕ Wechselfieber *n*.

in·tern¹ [ɪn'tɜːn] internieren.

in·tern² *Am.* ⚕ ['ɪntɜːn] Medizinalassistent(in).

in·ter·nal □ [ɪn'tɜːnl] innere(r, -s); einheimisch, Inlands...; ~*-combustion engine* Verbrennungsmotor *m*.

in·ter·na·tion·al [ɪntə'næʃənl] **1.** □ international; ~ *law* ⚖ Völkerrecht *n*; **2.** *Sport:* Internationale *m, f*, Nationalspieler(in); internationaler Wettkampf; Länderspiel *n*.

in·ter·po·late [ɪn'tɜːpəleɪt] einfügen.

in·ter·pose [ɪntə'pəʊz] *v/t.* Veto einlegen; *Wort* einwerfen; *v/i.* eingreifen.

in·ter|pret [ɪn'tɜːprɪt] auslegen, erklären, deuten, interpretieren; dolmetschen; ~**·pre·ta·tion** [ɪntɜːprɪ'teɪʃn] Auslegung *f*, Deutung *f*, Interpretation *f*; ~**·pret·er** [ɪn'tɜːprɪtə] Dolmetscher(in); Interpret(in).

in·ter·ro|gate [ɪn'terəɡeɪt] (be-, aus-) fragen; verhören; ~**·ga·tion** [ɪnterə'ɡeɪʃn] Befragung *f*; Verhör *m*; Frage *f*; *note od. mark od. point of* ~ *ling.* Fragezeichen *n*; ~**·ga·tive** □ [ɪntə'rɒɡətɪv] fragend, Frage...; *gr.* Interrogativ..., Frage...

in·ter|rupt [ɪntə'rʌpt] unterbrechen; ~**·rup·tion** [~pʃn] Unterbrechung *f*.

in·ter|sect [ɪntə'sekt] durchschneiden; sich schneiden *od.* kreuzen; ~**·sec·tion** [~kʃn] Schnittpunkt *m*; (Straßen- *etc.*)Kreuzung *f*.

in·ter·sperse [ɪntə'spɜːs] einstreuen, hier u. da einfügen.

in·ter·state *Am.* [ɪntə'steɪt] zwischen den einzelnen Bundesstaaten.

in·ter·twine [ɪntə'twaɪn] (sich ineinander) verschlingen.

in·ter·val ['ɪntəvl] Intervall *n* (*a.* ♪), Abstand *m*; Pause *f*; *at* ~*s of* in Abständen von.

in·ter|vene [ɪntə'viːn] einschreiten, intervenieren; dazwischenliegen; (unerwartet) dazwischenkommen; ~**·ven·tion** [~'venʃn] Eingreifen *n*, -griff *m*, Intervention *f*.

in·ter·view ['ɪntəvjuː] **1.** *Presse, TV:* Interview *n*; Unterredung *f*; (Vorstellungs)Gespräch *n*; **2.** *j-n* interviewen, befragen; (ein Vorstellungsgespräch führen mit; ~**er** [~ə] Interviewer(in); Leiter(in) e-s Vorstellungsgesprächs.

in·ter·weave [ɪntə'wiːv] (-*wove*, -*woven*) (miteinander) verweben, -flechten, -schlingen.

in·tes·tate ⚖ [ɪn'testeɪt]: *die* ~ *ohne* Testament sterben.

in·tes·tine *anat.* [ɪn'testɪn] Darm *m*; ~*s pl.* Eingeweide *pl.*

in·ti·ma·cy ['ɪntɪməsɪ] Intimität *f* (*a. sexuell*), Vertrautheit *f*; Vertraulichkeit *f*.

in·ti·mate¹ ['ɪntɪmət] **1.** □ intim (*a. sexuell*), vertraut; vertraulich; **2.** Vertraute(r *m*) *f*.

in·ti|mate² ['ɪntɪmeɪt] andeuten; ~**·ma·tion** [ɪntɪ'meɪʃn] Andeutung *f*.

in·tim·i·date [ɪn'tɪmɪdeɪt] einschüchtern; ~**·da·tion** [ɪntɪmɪ'deɪʃn] Einschüchterung *f*.

in·to ['ɪntʊ, 'ɪntə] in (*acc.*), in (*acc.*) ... hinein; gegen (*acc.*); A in (*acc.*); *4* ~ *20 goes five times* 4 geht fünfmal in 20.

in·tol·e·ra·ble □ [ɪn'tɒlərəbl] unerträglich.

in·tol·e|rance [ɪn'tɒlərəns] Intoleranz *f*, Unduldsamkeit (*of* gegen); ~**·rant** [~t] intolerant, unduldsam (*of* gegen).

in·to·na·tion [ɪntəʊ'neɪʃn] *gr.* Intonation *f*, Tonfall *m*; ♪ Intonation *f*.

in·tox·i|cant [ɪn'tɒksɪkənt] **1.** berauschend; **2.** *bsd.* berauschendes Getränk; ~**·cate** [~eɪt] berauschen (*a. fig.*), betrunken machen; ~**·ca·tion** [ɪntɒksɪ'keɪʃn] Rausch *m* (*a. fig.*).

in·trac·ta·ble □ [ɪn'træktəbl] unlenksam, eigensinnig; schwer zu handhaben(d).

in·tran·si·tive □ *gr.* [ɪn'trænsətɪv] intransitiv.

in·tra·ve·nous 🗲 [ɪntrə'viːnəs] intravenös.

in·trep·id □ [ɪn'trepɪd] unerschrocken.

in·tri·cate □ ['ɪntrɪkət] verwickelt, kompliziert.

in·trigue [ɪn'triːg] **1.** Intrige f; Machenschaft f; **2.** faszinieren, interessieren; intrigieren.

in·trin·sic [ɪn'trɪnsɪk] (~ally) wirklich, wahr, inner(lich).

in·tro·duce [ɪntrə'djuːs] vorstellen (to dat.), j-n bekannt machen (to mit); einführen; einleiten; **~duc·tion** [~'dʌkʃn] Vorstellung f; Einführung f; Einleitung f; letter of ~ Empfehlungsschreiben n; **~duc·to·ry** [~tərɪ] einleitend, Einführungs..., Einleitungs...

in·tro·spec·tion [ɪntrəʊ'spekʃn] Selbstbeobachtung f; **~tive** [~tɪv] selbstbeobachtend.

in·tro·vert psych. ['ɪntrəʊvɜːt] introvertierter Mensch; **~ed** psych. introvertiert, in sich gekehrt.

in·trude [ɪn'truːd] sich einmischen; sich ein- od. aufdrängen; stören; am I intruding? störe ich?; **in·trud·er** [~də] Eindringling m; **in·tru·sion** [~ʒn] Aufdrängen n; Einmischung f; Auf-, Zudringlichkeit f; Störung f; Verletzung f; **in·tru·sive** □ [~sɪv] aufdringlich.

in·tu·i·tion [ɪntjuː'ɪʃn] Intuition f; Ahnung f; **~tive** □ [ɪn'tjuːɪtɪv] intuitiv.

in·un·date ['ɪnʌndeɪt] überschwemmen, -fluten (a. fig.).

in·vade [ɪn'veɪd] eindringen in, einfallen in, ✗ a. einmarschieren in (acc.); fig. überlaufen, -schwemmen; **~r** [~ə] Eindringling m.

in·va·lid¹ ['ɪnvəlɪd] **1.** dienstunfähig; kränklich, invalide; Kranken...; **2.** Invalide m, f.

in·val·id² □ [ɪn'vælɪd] (rechts)ungültig; **~i·date** [~eɪt] Argument entkräften; ⚖ ungültig machen.

in·val·u·a·ble □ [ɪn'væljʊəbl] unschätzbar.

in·var·i·a·ble □ [ɪn'veərɪəbl] unveränderlich; **~bly** [~lɪ] ausnahmslos.

in·va·sion [ɪn'veɪʒn] Invasion f, Einfall m; fig. Eingriff m, Verletzung f.

in·vec·tive [ɪn'vektɪv] Schmähung f, Beschimpfung f.

in·vent [ɪn'vent] erfinden; **in·ven-tion** [~nʃn] Erfindung(sgabe) f; **in·ven·tive** □ [~tɪv] erfinderisch; **in·ven·tor** [~ə] Erfinder(in); **in·ven·to·ry** ['ɪnvəntrɪ] Inventar n; Bestandsverzeichnis n; Am. Inventur f.

in·verse ['ɪn'vɜːs] **1.** □ umgekehrt; **2.** Umkehrung f, Gegenteil n; **in·ver·sion** [ɪn'vɜːʃn] Umkehrung f; gr. Inversion f.

in·vert [ɪn'vɜːt] umkehren; gr. Satz etc. umstellen; **~ed commas** pl. Anführungszeichen pl.

in·ver·te·brate zo. [ɪn'vɜːtɪbrət] **1.** wirbellos; **2.** wirbelloses Tier.

in·vest [ɪn'vest] investieren, anlegen.

in·ves·ti·gate [ɪn'vestɪgeɪt] untersuchen; überprüfen; Untersuchungen od. Ermittlungen anstellen (into über acc.), nachforschen; **~ga·tion** [ɪnvestɪ'geɪʃn] Untersuchung f; Ermittlung f, Nachforschung f; **~ga·tor** [ɪn'vestɪgeɪtə] Untersuchungs-, Ermittlungsbeamte(r) m; private ~ Privatdetektiv m.

in·vest·ment econ. [ɪn'vestmənt] Investition f, (Kapital)Anlage f.

in·vet·er·ate □ [ɪn'vetərət] unverbesserlich; unversöhnlich; hartnäckig.

in·vid·i·ous □ [ɪn'vɪdɪəs] verhaßt; gehässig, boshaft, gemein; ungerecht.

in·vig·o·rate [ɪn'vɪgəreɪt] kräftigen, stärken, beleben.

in·vin·ci·ble □ [ɪn'vɪnsəbl] unbesiegbar; unüberwindlich.

in·vi·o·la·ble □ [ɪn'vaɪələbl] unverletzlich, unantastbar; **~te** [~lət] unverletzt; unversehrt.

in·vis·i·ble □ [ɪn'vɪzəbl] unsichtbar.

in·vi·ta·tion [ɪnvɪ'teɪʃn] Einladung f; Aufforderung f; **in·vite** [ɪn'vaɪt] einladen; auffordern; Gefahr etc. herausfordern; ~ s.o. in j-n hereinbitten; **in·vit·ing** □ [~ɪŋ] einladend, verlockend.

in·voice econ. ['ɪnvɔɪs] **1.** (Waren-) Rechnung f; Lieferschein m; **2.** in Rechnung stellen, berechnen.

in·voke [ɪn'vəʊk] anrufen; zu Hilfe rufen (acc.); appellieren an (acc.); Geist heraufbeschwören.

in·vol·un·ta·ry □ [ɪn'vɒləntərɪ] unfreiwillig; unabsichtlich; unwillkürlich.

in·volve [ɪn'vɒlv] verwickeln, hineinziehen (in in acc.); umfassen; zur Folge haben, mit sich bringen; be-

J

treffen; **∼d** kompliziert; betroffen (*Person*); **∼·ment** [∼mənt] Verwicklung *f*; Beteiligung *f*; Engagement *n*; (*Geld*)Verlegenheit *f*.

in·vul·ne·ra·ble □ [ɪn'vʌlnərəbl] unverwundbar; *fig.* unanfechtbar.

in·ward ['ɪnwəd] **1.** *adj.* innere(r, -s), innerlich; **2.** *adv. mst* ∼s einwärts, nach innen.

i·o·dine ↗ ['aɪədiːn] Jod *n*.

i·on *phys.* ['aɪən] Ion *n*.

IOU ['aɪəʊ'juː] (= *I owe you*) Schuldschein *m*.

I·ra·ni·an [ɪ'reɪnjən] **1.** iranisch, persisch; **2.** Iraner(in), Perser(in); *ling.* Iranisch *n*, Persisch *n*.

I·ra·qi [ɪ'rɑːkɪ] **1.** irakisch; **2.** Iraker(in); *ling.* Irakisch *n*.

i·ras·ci·ble □ [ɪ'ræsəbl] jähzornig.

i·rate [aɪ'reɪt] zornig, wütend.

ir·i·des·cent [ɪrɪ'desnt] schillernd.

i·ris ['aɪərɪs] *anat.* Regenbogenhaut *f*, Iris *f*; ♀ Schwertlilie *f*, Iris *f*.

I·rish ['aɪərɪʃ] **1.** irisch; **2.** *ling.* Irisch *n*; *the ∼ pl.* die Iren *pl.*; **∼·man** (*pl. -men*) Ire *m*; **∼·wom·an** (*pl. -women*) Irin *f*.

irk·some ['ɜːksəm] lästig, ärgerlich.

i·ron ['aɪən] **1.** Eisen *n*; *a. flat-∼* Bügeleisen *n*; ∼s *pl.* Hand- u. Fußschellen *pl.*; *strike while the ∼ is hot fig.* das Eisen schmieden, solange es heiß ist; **2.** eisern (*a. fig.*), Eisen..., aus Eisen; **3.** bügeln, plätten; ∼ *out fig. et.* ausbügeln, *Schwierigkeiten* beseitigen; **⌧ Cur·tain** *pol.* Eiserner Vorhang.

i·ron·ic [aɪ'rɒnɪk] (∼*ally*), **i·ron·i·cal** □ [∼kl] ironisch, spöttisch.

i·ron|ing ['aɪənɪŋ] Bügel-, Plättwäsche *f*; **∼·board** Bügel-, Plättbrett *n*; **∼ lung** ♬ eiserne Lunge; **∼·mon·ger** *Brt.* [∼mʌŋgə] Eisenwarenhändler *m*; **∼·mon·ger·y** *Brt.* [∼ərɪ] Eisenwaren *pl.*; **∼·works** *pl.* Eisenhütte *f*.

i·ron·y ['aɪərənɪ] Ironie *f*.

ir·ra·tion·al □ [ɪ'ræʃənl] irrational; unvernünftig; vernunftlos (*Tier*).

ir·re·con·cil·a·ble □ [ɪ'rekənsaɪləbl] unversöhnlich; unvereinbar.

ir·re·cov·er·a·ble □ [ɪrɪ'kʌvərəbl] unersetzlich; unwiederbringlich.

ir·re·fu·ta·ble □ [ɪ'refjʊtəbl] unwiderlegbar, nicht zu widerlegen(d).

ir·reg·u·lar □ [ɪ'regjʊlə] unregelmäßig; uneben; ungleichmäßig; regelwidrig; ungesetzlich; ungehörig.

ir·rel·e·vant □ [ɪ'reləvənt] irrele-

vant, nicht zur Sache gehörig; unerheblich, belanglos (*to* für).

ir·rep·a·ra·ble □ [ɪ'repərəbl] irreparabel, nicht wiedergutzumachen(d).

ir·re·place·a·ble □ [ɪrɪ'pleɪsəbl] unersetzlich.

ir·re·pres·si·ble □ [ɪrɪ'presəbl] nicht zu unterdrücken(d); unerschütterlich; un(be)zähmbar.

ir·re·proa·cha·ble □ [ɪrɪ'prəʊtʃəbl] einwandfrei, tadellos, untadelig.

ir·re·sis·ti·ble □ [ɪrɪ'zɪstəbl] unwiderstehlich.

ir·res·o·lute □ [ɪ'rezəluːt] unentschlossen.

ir·re·spec·tive □ [ɪrɪ'spektɪv]: ∼ *of* ungeachtet (*gen.*), ohne Rücksicht auf (*acc.*); unabhängig von.

ir·re·spon·si·ble □ [ɪrɪ'spɒnsəbl] unverantwortlich; verantwortungslos.

ir·re·trie·va·ble □ [ɪrɪ'triːvəbl] unwiederbringlich, unersetzlich; nicht wiedergutzumachen(d).

ir·rev·e·rent □ [ɪ'revərənt] respektlos.

ir·rev·o·ca·ble □ [ɪ'revəkəbl] unwiderruflich, unabänderlich, endgültig.

ir·ri·gate ['ɪrɪgeɪt] (künstlich) bewässern.

ir·ri·ta|ble □ ['ɪrɪtəbl] reizbar; **∼nt** [∼ənt] Reizmittel *n*; **∼te** [∼teɪt] reizen; ärgern; **∼t·ing** □ [∼tɪŋ] aufreizend; ärgerlich (*Sache*); **∼tion** [ɪrɪ'teɪʃn] Reizung *f*; Gereiztheit *f*, Ärger *m*.

is [ɪz] *3. sg. pres. von* be.

Is·lam ['ɪzlɑːm] der Islam.

is·land ['aɪlənd] Insel *f*; *a. traffic ∼* Verkehrsinsel *f*; **∼·er** [∼ə] Inselbewohner(in).

isle *poet.* [aɪl] Insel *f*.

is·let ['aɪlɪt] Inselchen *n*.

i·so|late ['aɪsəleɪt] absondern; isolieren; **∼·lat·ed** einsam, abgeschieden; einzeln; △ *nicht ∉ isoliert*; **∼·la·tion** [aɪsə'leɪʃn] Isolierung *f*; Absonderung *f*; ∼ *ward* ♬ Isolierstation *f*.

Is·rae·li [ɪz'reɪlɪ] **1.** israelisch; **2.** Israeli *m*, Bewohner(in) des Staates Israel.

is·sue ['ɪʃuː] **1.** Herauskommen *n*; Herausfließen *n*; Abfluß *m*; ♂ Nachkommen(schaft) *f*; *econ.* Ausgabe *f* (*von Banknoten etc.*); Erteilung *f* (*von Befehlen etc.*); *print.* Ausgabe *f*, Exemplar *n* (*e-s Buches*);

print. Ausgabe *f,* Nummer *f (e-r Zeitung); bsd.* ⚖ Streitfrage *f; fig.* Ausgang, Ergebnis *n; at ~* zur Debatte stehend; *point at ~* strittiger Punkt; **2.** *v/i.* herauskommen; ausfließen, -strömen; herkommen, -rühren *(from* von); *v/t. econ., Material etc.* ausgeben; *Befehl* erteilen; *Buch, Zeitung* herausgeben, veröffentlichen.

isth·mus ['ɪsməs] Landenge *f.*

it [ɪt] es; er, ihn, sie; *nach prp.: by ~* dadurch; *for ~* dafür.

I·tal·i·an [ɪ'tæljən] **1.** italienisch; **2.** Italiener(in); *ling.* Italienisch *n.*

i·tal·ics *print.* [ɪ'tælɪks] Kursivschrift *f.*

itch [ɪtʃ] **1.** ⚕ Krätze *f;* Jucken *n;* Verlangen *n;* **2.** jucken; *I ~ all over* es

juckt mich überall; *be ~ing to inf.* darauf brennen, zu *inf.*

i·tem ['aɪtəm] Punkt *m;* Gegenstand *m;* Posten *m,* Artikel *m; a. news ~* (Zeitungs)Notiz *f,* (kurzer) Artikel; *Rundfunk, TV:* (kurze) Meldung; *~ize* [~aɪz] einzeln angeben *od.* aufführen.

i·tin·er·ant □ [ɪ'tɪnərənt] reisend; umherziehend, Reise..., Wander...; *~ra·ry* [aɪ'tɪnərərɪ] Reiseroute *f;* Reisebeschreibung *f.*

its [ɪts] sein(e), ihr(e), dessen, deren.

it·self [ɪt'self] sich; (sich) selbst; *by ~* (für sich) allein; von selbst; *in ~* an sich.

i·vo·ry ['aɪvərɪ] Elfenbein *n.*

i·vy 🌿 ['aɪvɪ] Efeu *m.*

J

jab [dʒæb] **1.** (-bb-) stechen; (zu)stoßen; **2.** Stich *m,* Stoß *m;* F ⚕ Spritze *f.*

jab·ber ['dʒæbə] (daher)plappern.

jack [dʒæk] **1.** ⊕ Hebevorrichtung *f;* ⊕ Wagenheber *m;* ⚡ Klinke *f;* ⚡ Steckdose *f,* Buchse *f;* ♣ Gösch *f,* kleine Bugflagge; *Kartenspiel:* Bube *m;* **2.** *~ up Auto* aufbocken.

jack·al *zo.* ['dʒæko:l] Schakal *m.*

jack|ass ['dʒækæs] Esel *m (a. fig.); ~boots* ✕ Reitstiefel *pl.;* hohe Wasserstiefel *pl.; ~daw zo.* Dohle *f.*

jack·et ['dʒækɪt] Jacke *f,* Jackett *n;* ⊕ Mantel *m;* Schutzumschlag *m (e-s Buches); Am.* (Schall)Plattenhülle *f.*

jack|-knife ['dʒæknaɪf] **1.** (*pl. -knives*) Klappmesser *n;* **2.** zusammenklappen, -knicken; *~ of all trades* Alleskönner *m,* Hansdampf in allen Gassen; *~pot* Haupttreffer *m,* -gewinn *m; hit the ~* F den Haupttreffer machen; *fig.* das große Los ziehen.

jade [dʒeɪd] Jade *m, f;* Jadegrün *n.*

jag [dʒæg] Zacken *m; ~ged* □ ['dʒægɪd] gezackt; zackig.

jag·u·ar *zo.* ['dʒægjuə] Jaguar *m.*

jail [dʒeɪl] **1.** Gefängnis *n;* **2.** einsperren; *~bird* F ['dʒeɪlbɜ:d] Knastbru-

der *m; ~er* [~ə] Gefängnisaufseher *m; ~house Am.* Gefängnis *n.*

jam¹ [dʒæm] Konfitüre *f,* Marmelade *f.*

jam² [~] **1.** Gedränge *n,* Gewühl *n;* ⊕ Klemmen *n,* Blockierung *f;* Stauung *f,* Stockung *f; traffic ~* Verkehrsstau *m; be in a ~* F in der Klemme sein; **2.** (-mm-) ⊕ (sich) (ver)klemmen, blockieren; (hinein)zwängen, (-)stopfen; einklemmen; pressen, quetschen; *~ the brakes on, ~ on the brakes* auf die Bremse steigen.

jamb [dʒæm] (Tür-, Fenster)Pfosten *m.*

jam·bo·ree [dʒæmbə'ri:] Jamboree *n,* Pfadfindertreffen *n.*

jan·gle ['dʒæŋgl] klimpern *od.* klirren (mit); bimmeln (lassen).

jan·i·tor ['dʒænɪtə] Hausmeister *m.*

Jan·u·ar·y ['dʒænjʊərɪ] Januar *m.*

Jap·a·nese [dʒæpə'ni:z] **1.** japanisch; **2.** Japaner(in); *ling.* Japanisch *n; the ~ pl.* die Japaner *pl.*

jar¹ [dʒɑ:] **1.** Krug *m,* Topf *m;* (Marmelade- *etc.*)Glas *n.*

jar² [~] **1.** (-rr-) knarren, kreischen, quietschen; sich nicht vertragen; erschüttern (*a. fig.*); **2.** Knarren *n,*

Kreischen n, Quietschen n; Erschütterung f (a. fig.); Schock m.

jar·gon ['dʒɑːgən] Jargon m, Fachsprache f.

jaun·dice ❦ ['dʒɔːndɪs] Gelbsucht f; **~d** ❦ gelbsüchtig; fig. neidisch, eifersüchtig, voreingenommen.

jaunt [dʒɔːnt] **1.** Ausflug m, Spritztour f; **2.** e-n Ausflug machen; **jaun·ty** □ [∼ɪ] (-ier, -iest) munter, unbeschwert; flott.

jav·e·lin ['dʒævlɪn] Sport: Speer m; ∼ (throw[ing]), throwing the ∼ Speerwerfen n; ∼ thrower Speerwerfer(in).

jaw [dʒɔː] anat. Kinnbacken m, Kiefer m; ∼s pl. Rachen m; Maul n; Schlund m; ⊕ Backen pl.; **~bone** anat. ['dʒɔːbəʊn] Kieferknochen m.

jay zo. [dʒeɪ] Eichelhäher m; **~walk** ['dʒeɪwɔːk] unachtsam über die Straße gehen; **~walk·er** unachtsamer Fußgänger.

jazz ♪ [dʒæz] Jazz m.

jeal·ous □ ['dʒeləs] eifersüchtig (of auf acc.); neidisch; **~y** [∼sɪ] Eifersucht f; Neid m; △ nicht Jalousie.

jeans [dʒiːnz] pl. Jeans pl.

jeep TM [dʒiːp] Jeep m.

jeer [dʒɪə] **1.** Spott m; höhnische Bemerkung; **2.** spotten (at über acc.); verspotten, -höhnen.

jel·lied ['dʒelɪd] eingedickt (Fruchtsaft); in Gelee.

jel·ly ['dʒelɪ] **1.** Gallert(e f) n; Gelee n; **2.** gelieren; **~ ba·by** Brt. Gummibärchen n; **~ bean** Gummi-, Geleebonbon m, n; **~fish** zo. Qualle f.

jeop·ar|dize ['dʒepədaɪz] gefährden; **~dy** [∼ɪ] Gefahr f.

jerk [dʒɜːk] **1.** (plötzlicher) Ruck, Sprung m, Satz m; ❦ Zuckung f, Zucken n; **2.** (plötzlich) ziehen, zerren, reißen (an dat.); schleudern; schnellen; **~y** □ ['dʒɜːkɪ] (-ier, -iest) ruckartig; holprig; abgehackt (Sprache).

jer·sey ['dʒɜːzɪ] Pullover m.

jest [dʒest] **1.** Spaß m; **2.** scherzen; **~er** ['dʒestə] (Hof)Narr m.

jet [dʒet] **1.** (Wasser-, Gas- etc.)Strahl m; ⊕ Düse f; ∼ engine, ∼ plane; **2.** (-tt-) hervorschießen, (her)ausströmen; ✈ jetten; **~ en·gine** ⊕ Düsen-, Strahltriebwerk n; **~ lag** körperliche Anpassungsschwierigkeiten pl. durch die Zeitverschiebung bei weiten Flugreisen; **~ plane** Düsenflug-

zeug n, Jet m; **~-pro·pelled** ['dʒetprəpeld] mit Düsenantrieb, Düsen...; ∼ pro·pul·sion ⊕ Düsen-, Strahlantrieb m; **~ set** Jet-set m; **~ set·ter** Angehörige(r m) f des Jet-set.

jet·ty ⚓ ['dʒetɪ] Mole f; Pier m.

Jew [dʒuː] Jude m, Jüdin f; attr. Juden...

jew·el ['dʒuːəl] Juwel n, m, Edelstein m; Schmuckstück n; **~·ler**, Am. **~·er** [∼ə] Juwelier m; **~·lery**, Am. **~·ry** [∼lrɪ] Juwelen pl.; Schmuck m.

Jew|ess ['dʒuːɪs] Jüdin f; **~·ish** [∼ɪʃ] jüdisch.

jib ⚓ [dʒɪb] Klüver m.

jif·fy F ['dʒɪfɪ]: in a ∼ im Nu, sofort.

jig·saw ['dʒɪgsɔː] Laubsäge f; ∼ = **puz·zle** Puzzle(spiel) n.

jilt [dʒɪlt] Mädchen sitzenlassen; Liebhaber den Laufpaß geben.

jin·gle ['dʒɪŋgl] **1.** Geklingel n, Klimpern n; Spruch m, Vers m; advertising ∼ Werbespruch m; **2.** klingeln; klimpern (mit); klinge(l)n lassen.

jit·ters F ['dʒɪtəz] pl.: the ∼ Bammel m, das große Zittern.

job [dʒɒb] (ein Stück) Arbeit f; econ. Akkordarbeit f; Beruf m, Beschäftigung f, Stellung f, Stelle f, Arbeit f, Job m; Aufgabe f, Sache f; by the ∼ im Akkord; out of ∼ arbeitslos; **~·ber** Brt. ['dʒɒbə] Börsenspekulant m; **~·hop·ping** Am. [∼hɒpɪŋ] häufiger Arbeitsplatzwechsel; **~ hunt·er** Arbeit(s)suchende(r m) f; **~ hunt·ing**: be ∼ auf Arbeitssuche sein; **~·less** [∼lɪs] arbeitslos; **~ work** Akkordarbeit f.

jock·ey ['dʒɒkɪ] Jockei m.

joc·u·lar □ ['dʒɒkjʊlə] lustig; spaßig.

jog [dʒɒg] **1.** (leichter) Stoß, Schubs m; Sport: Dauerlauf m; Trott m; **2.** (-gg-) v/t. (an)stoßen, (fig. auf)rütteln; v/i. mst ∼ along, ∼ on dahintrotten, -zuckeln; Sport: Dauerlauf machen, joggen; **~·ging** ['dʒɒgɪŋ] Sport: Dauerlauf m, Jogging n, Joggen n.

join [dʒɔɪn] **1.** v/t. verbinden, zusammenfügen (to mit); vereinigen; sich anschließen (dat. od. an acc.), sich gesellen zu; eintreten in (acc.), beitreten; ∼ hands sich die Hände reichen; fig. sich zusammentun od.; v/i. sich verbinden od. vereinigen; ∼ in teilnehmen an (dat.), mitmachen bei, sich beteiligen an (dat.); ∼ up Soldat werden; **2.** Verbindungsstelle *f*, Naht *f*.

join·er ['dʒɔɪnə] Tischler *m*, Schreiner *m*; **~y** *bsd. Brt.* [~əri] Tischlerhandwerk *n*; Tischlerarbeit *f*.

joint [dʒɔɪnt] **1.** Verbindung(sstelle) *f*; Naht(stelle) *f*; *anat.*, ⊕ Gelenk *n*; ♥ Knoten *m*; *Brt.* Braten *m*; *sl.* Spelunke *f*; *sl.* Joint *m* (*Marihuanazigarette*); *out of* ~ ausgerenkt; *fig.* aus den Fugen; **2.** □ gemeinsam; Mit...; ~ *heir* Miterbe *m*; ~ *stock econ.* Aktienkapital *n*; **3.** verbinden, zusammenfügen; *Braten* zerlegen; **~ed** ['dʒɔɪntɪd] gegliedert; Glieder...; **~-stock** *econ.* Aktien...; ~ *company Brt.* Aktiengesellschaft *f*.

joke [dʒəʊk] **1.** Witz *m*; Scherz *m*, Spaß *m*; *practical* ~ Streich *m*; **2.** scherzen, Witze machen; **jok·er** ['dʒəʊkə] Spaßvogel *m*; *Kartenspiel:* Joker *m*.

jol·ly ['dʒɒlɪ] **1.** *adj.* (-*ier*, -*iest*) lustig, fidel, vergnügt; **2.** *adv. Brt.* F mächtig, sehr; ~ *good* prima.

jolt [dʒəʊlt] **1.** stoßen, rütteln, holpern; *fig.* aufrütteln; **2.** Ruck *m*, Stoß *m*; *fig.* Schock *m*.

jos·tle ['dʒɒsl] **1.** (an)rempeln; drängeln; **2.** Stoß *m*, Rempelei *f*; Zusammenstoß *m*.

jot [dʒɒt] **1.** *not a* ~ keine Spur, kein bißchen; **2.** (-*tt*-): ~ *down* schnell hinschreiben *od.* notieren.

jour·nal ['dʒɜːnl] Journal *n*; (Fach-) Zeitschrift *f*; (Tages)Zeitung *f*; Tagebuch *n*; **~·is·m** ['dʒɜːnəlɪzəm] Journalismus *m*; **~·ist** [~ɪst] Journalist(in).

jour·ney ['dʒɜːnɪ] **1.** Reise *f*; Fahrt *f*; **2.** reisen; **~·man** (*pl.* -men) Geselle *m*.

jo·vi·al □ ['dʒəʊvjəl] heiter, jovial.

joy [dʒɔɪ] Freude *f*; *for* ~ vor Freude; **~·ful** □ ['dʒɔɪful] freudig; erfreut; **~·less** □ [~lɪs] freudlos, traurig; **~·stick** ✈ Steuerknüppel *m* (F *a. für Computerspiele*).

ju·bi·lant ['dʒuːbɪlənt] jubelnd, überglücklich.

ju·bi·lee ['dʒuːbɪliː] Jubiläum *n*.

judge [dʒʌdʒ] **1.** ⚖ Richter *m*; Schieds-, Preisrichter *m*; Kenner(in), Sachverständige(r *m*) *f*; **2.** *v/i.* urteilen; *v/t.* ⚖ *Fall* verhandeln, die Verhandlung führen über (*acc.*); ⚖ ein Urteil fällen über (*acc.*); richten; beurteilen; halten für.

judg(e)·ment ['dʒʌdʒmənt] ⚖ Urteil *n*; Urteilsvermögen *n*; Meinung *f*, Ansicht *f*, Urteil *n*; *göttliches* (Straf-) Gericht; *pass* ~ *on* ein Urteil fällen über (*acc.*); ♀ *Day, Day of* ♀ *eccl.* Tag *m* des Jüngsten Gerichts.

ju·di·cial □ [dʒuːˈdɪʃl] ⚖ gerichtlich, Gerichts...; kritisch; unparteiisch.

ju·di·cia·ry ⚖ [dʒuːˈdɪʃɪərɪ] Richter (-stand *m*) *pl*.

ju·di·cious □ [dʒuːˈdɪʃəs] klug, weise.

jug [dʒʌg] Krug *m*, Kanne *f*.

jug·gle ['dʒʌgl] jonglieren (mit); manipulieren, *Bücher etc.* frisieren; **~r** [~ə] Jongleur *m*; Schwindler(in).

juice [dʒuːs] Saft *m*; *sl. mot.* Sprit *m*; **juic·y** □ ['dʒuːsɪ] (-*ier*, -*iest*) saftig; F pikant, gepfeffert.

juke·box ['dʒuːkbɒks] Musikbox *f*, Musikautomat *m*.

Ju·ly [dʒuːˈlaɪ] Juli *m*.

jum·ble ['dʒʌmbl] **1.** Durcheinander *n*; **2.** *a.* ~ *together*, ~ *up* durcheinanderbringen, -werfen; ~ *sale Brt.* Wohltätigkeitsbasar *m*.

jum·bo ['dʒʌmbəʊ] *a.* ~-*sized* riesig.

jump [dʒʌmp] **1.** Sprung *m*; *the* ~*s pl.* große Nervosität; *high* (*long*) ~ *Sport:* Hoch-(Weit)sprung *m*; *get the* ~ *on* F zuvorkommen; **2.** *v/i.* springen; zusammenzucken, -fahren, hochfahren; ~ *at the chance* mit beiden Händen zugreifen; ~ *to conclusions* übereilte Schlüsse ziehen; *v/t.* (hinweg)springen über (*acc.*); überspringen; springen lassen; ~ *the queue Brt.* sich vordränge(l)n; ~ *the lights* bei Rot über die Kreuzung fahren, F bei Rot drüberfahren; **~·er** ['dʒʌmpə] Springer(in); *Brt.* Pullover *m*; *Am.* Trägerkleid *n*; **~·ing jack** Hampelmann *m*; **~·y** [~ɪ] (-*ier*, -*iest*) nervös.

junc·tion ['dʒʌŋk∫n] Verbindung *f*; (Straßen)Kreuzung *f*; 🚆 Knotenpunkt *m*; **~·ture** [~kt∫ə]: *at this* ~ an dieser Stelle, in diesem Augenblick.

June [dʒuːn] Juni *m*.

jun·gle ['dʒʌŋgl] Dschungel *m*.

ju·ni·or ['dʒuːnjə] **1.** jüngere(r, -s); untergeordnet, rangniedriger; *Sport:* Junioren..., Jugend...; **2.** Jüngere(r *m*) *f*; F Junior *m*; *Am. univ.* Student (-in) im vorletzten Studienjahr.

junk [dʒʌŋk] ⚓ Dschunke *f*.

junk² F [~] Plunder *m*, alter Kram; *sl.* Stoff *m* (*bsd. Heroin*); ~ *food* kalo-

rienreiches aber minderwertiges Nahrungsmittel; **~·ie,** **~·y** *sl.* ['dʒʌŋkɪ] Fixer(in), Junkie *m;* **~ yard** Schrottplatz *m.*

jur·is·dic·tion ['dʒʊərɪs'dɪkʃn] Gerichtsbarkeit *f;* Zuständigkeit(sbereich *m*) *f.*

ju·ris·pru·dence ['dʒʊərɪs'pru:dəns] Rechtswissenschaft *f.*

ju·ror 🏛 ['dʒʊərə] Geschworene(r *m*) *f.*

ju·ry ['dʒʊərɪ] 🏛 *die* Geschworenen *pl.;* Jury *f,* Preisrichter *pl.;* **~·man** *(pl. -men)* 🏛 Geschworene(r) *m;* **~·wom·an** *(pl. -women)* 🏛 Geschworene *f.*

just □ [dʒʌst] **1.** *adj.* gerecht; berechtigt; angemessen; **2.** *adv.* gerade, (so)eben; gerade, genau, eben; gerade (noch), ganz knapp; nur, bloß; F

einfach, wirklich; **~** *now* gerade (jetzt); (so)eben.

jus·tice ['dʒʌstɪs] Gerechtigkeit *f;* Rechtmäßigkeit *f;* Berechtigung *f,* Recht *n;* Gerichtsbarkeit *f,* Justiz *f;* 🏛 Richter *m;* ♀ *of the Peace* Friedensrichter *m; court of* **~** Gericht(shof *m*) *n.*

jus·ti·fi·ca·tion [dʒʌstɪfɪ'keɪʃn] Rechtfertigung *f;* **~·fy** ['dʒʌstɪfaɪ] rechtfertigen.

just·ly ['dʒʌstlɪ] *mit od.* zu Recht.

jut [dʒʌt] *(-tt-):* **~** *out* vorspringen, hervorragen, -stehen.

ju·ve·nile ['dʒu:vənaɪl] **1.** jung, jugendlich; Jugend..., für Jugendliche; **~** *court* Jugendgericht *n;* **~** *delinquency* Jugendkriminalität *f;* **~** *delinquent* jugendlicher Straftäter *m;* **2.** Jugendliche(r *m*) *f.*

K

kan·ga·roo *zo.* [kæŋgə'ru:] *(pl. -roos)* Känguruh *n.*

keel ⚓ [ki:l] **1.** Kiel *m;* **2.** **~** *over* kieloben legen; umschlagen, kentern.

keen □ [ki:n] scharf *(a. fig.);* schneidend *(Kälte);* heftig; stark, groß *(Appetit etc.);* **~** *on* F scharf *od.* erpicht auf *(acc.); be* **~** *on hunting* ein leidenschaftlicher Jäger sein; **~·ness** ['ki:nnɪs] Schärfe *f;* Heftigkeit *f;* Scharfsinn *m.*

keep [ki:p] **1.** (Lebens)Unterhalt *m; for* **~** *s* F *my* Leben; **2.** *(kept) v/t.* (auf-, [bei]be-, er-, fest-, zurück-)halten; unterhalten, sorgen für; *Gesetze etc.* einhalten, befolgen; *Ware, Tagebuch* führen; *Geheimnis* für sich behalten; *Versprechen* halten, einlösen; (auf)bewahren; abhalten, hindern *(from* von); *Vieh* halten; *Bett* hüten; (be)schützen; **~** *s.o. company* j-m Gesellschaft leisten; **~** *company with* verkehren mit; **~** *one's head* die Ruhe bewahren; **~** *early hours* früh zu Bett gehen; **~** *one's temper* sich beherrschen; **~** *time* richtig gehen *(Uhr);* Takt, Schritt halten; **~** *s.o. waiting* j-n

warten lassen; **~** *away* fernhalten; **~** *s.th. from s.o.* j-m et. vorenthalten *od.* verschweigen *od.* verheimlichen; **~** *in* *Schüler* nachsitzen lassen; **~** *on Kleid* anbehalten, *Hut* aufbehalten; **~** *up* aufrechterhalten; *Mut* bewahren; instand halten; fortfahren mit, weitermachen; nicht schlafen lassen; **~** *it up* so weitermachen; *v/i.* bleiben; sich halten; fortfahren, weitermachen; **~** *doing* immer wieder tun; **~** *going* weitergehen; **~** *away* sich fernhalten; **~** *from doing s.th.* et. nicht tun; **~** *off* weg-, fernbleiben; **~** *on* fortfahren *(doing* zu tun); **~** *on talking* weiterreden; **~** *to* sich halten an *(acc.);* **~** *up* stehen bleiben; andauern, anhalten; **~** *up with* Schritt halten mit; **~** *up with the Joneses* nicht hinter den Nachbarn zurückstehen (wollen).

keep|er ['ki:pə] Wärter(in), Wächter(in), Aufseher(in); Verwalter(in); Inhaber(in); **~·ing** [~ɪŋ] Verwahrung *f;* Obhut *f; be in (out of)* **~** *with ...* (nicht) übereinstimmen mit ...; **~·sake** [~seɪk] Andenken *n (Geschenk).*

keg [keg] Fäßchen *n,* kleines Faß.

ken·nel ['kenl] Hundehütte *f*; ~s *pl.* Hundezwinger *m*; Hundepension *f*.

kept [kept] *pret. u. p.p. von* keep 2.

kerb [kɜːb], **~stone** ['kɜːbstəʊn] Bordstein *m*.

ker·chief ['kɜːtʃɪf] (Hals-, Kopf-) Tuch *n*.

ker·nel ['kɜːnl] Kern *m* (*a. fig.*).

ket·tle ['ketl] (Koch)Kessel *m*; **~drum** ♪ (Kessel)Pauke *f*.

key [kiː] **1.** Schlüssel *m*; (*Schreibmaschinen-, Klavier- etc.*)Taste *f*; (Druck)Taste *f*; ♪ Tonart *f*; *fig.* Ton *m*; *fig.* Schlüssel *m*, Lösung *f*; *attr.* Schlüssel...; **2.** anpassen (*to an acc.*); ~ed up nervös, aufgeregt, überdreht; **~board** ['kiːbɔːd] Klaviatur *f*; Tastatur *f*; **~hole** Schlüsselloch *n*; ~ **man** (*pl. -men*) Schlüsselfigur *f*; ~ **mon·ey** *Brt.* Abstand(ssumme *f*) *m* (*für e-e Wohnung*); **~note** ♪ Grundton *m*; *fig.* Grundgedanke *m*, Tenor *m*; ~ **ring** Schlüsselring *m*; **~stone** *arch.* Schlußstein *m*; *fig.* Grundpfeiler *m*; **~word** Schlüssel-, Stichwort *n*.

kick [kɪk] **1.** (Fuß)Tritt *m*; Stoß *m*; F Kraft *f*, Feuer *n*; F Nervenkitzel *m*; *get a ~ out of s.th.* e-n Riesenspaß an et. haben; *for ~s* (nur) zum Spaß; **2.** *v/t.* (mit dem Fuß) stoßen *od.* treten; *Fußball:* schießen, treten, kicken; ~ *off* von sich schleudern; ~ *out* hinauswerfen; ~ *up* hochschleudern; ~ *up a fuss od.* row F Krach schlagen; *v/i.* (mit dem Fuß) treten *od.* stoßen; (hinten) ausschlagen; strampeln; ~ *off Fußball:* anstoßen, den Anstoß ausführen; **~er** ['kɪkə] Fußballspieler *m*; **~off** Fußball: Anstoß *m*.

kid [kɪd] **1.** Zicklein *n*, Kitz *n*; Ziegenleder *n*; F Kind *n*; *o bother* F kleiner Bruder *m*; **2.** (*-dd-*) *v/t.* j-n aufziehen; ~ *s.o.* j-m et. vormachen; *v/i.* Spaß machen; *he is only ~ding* er macht ja nur Spaß; *no ~ding!* im Ernst!; ~ **glove** Glacéhandschuh *m* (*a. fig.*).

kid·nap ['kɪdnæp] (*-pp-, Am. a. -p-*) entführen, kidnappen; **~per**, *Am. a.* **~er** [~ə] Entführer(in), Kidnapper(in); **~ping**, *Am. a.* **~ing** [~ɪŋ] Entführung *f*, Kidnapping *n*.

kid·ney ['kɪdnɪ] *anat.* Niere *f* (*a. als Speise*); ~ **bean** ♥ Weiße Bohne; ~ **machine** künstliche Niere.

kill [kɪl] **1.** töten (*a. fig.*); umbringen; vernichten; beseitigen; *Tiere* schlach-

ten; *hunt.* erlegen, schießen; *be ~ed in an accident* tödlich verunglücken; ~ *time* die Zeit totschlagen; **2.** Tötung *f*; *hunt.* Jagdbeute *f*; **~er** ['kɪlə] Mörder(in), F Killer *m*; **~ing** □ [~ɪŋ] mörderisch, tödlich.

kiln [kɪln] Brenn-, Darrofen *m*.

ki·lo F ['kiːləʊ] (*pl. -los*) Kilo *n*.

kil·o·gram(me) ['kɪləgræm] Kilogramm *n*; **~me·tre**, *Am.* **~me·ter** Kilometer *m*.

kilt [kɪlt] Kilt *m*, Schottenrock *m*.

kin [kɪn] Verwandtschaft *f*, Verwandte *pl.*

kind [kaɪnd] **1.** □ gütig, freundlich, liebenswürdig, nett; **2.** Art *f*, Sorte *f*; Art *f*, Gattung *f*, Geschlecht *n*; △ *nicht* Kind; *pay in ~* in Naturalien zahlen; *fig.* mit gleicher Münze heimzahlen.

kin·der·gar·ten ['kɪndəgɑːtn] Kindergarten *m*.

kind-heart·ed ['kaɪnd'hɑːtɪd] gütig.

kin·dle ['kɪndl] anzünden; (sich) entzünden (*a. fig.*).

kin·dling ['kɪndlɪŋ] Material *n* zum Anzünden, Anmachholz *n*.

kind·ly ['kaɪndlɪ] *adj.* (*-ier, -iest*) *u. adv.* freundlich, liebenswürdig, nett; gütig; **~ness** ['kaɪ~] Güte *f*; Freundlichkeit *f*, Liebenswürdigkeit *f*; Gefälligkeit *f*.

kin·dred ['kɪndrɪd] **1.** verwandt; *fig.* gleichartig, ~ *spirits pl.* Gleichgesinnte *pl.*; **2.** Verwandtschaft *f*.

king [kɪŋ] König *m* (*a. fig. u. Schach, Kartenspiel*); **~dom** ['kɪŋdəm] Königreich *n*; *eccl.* Reich *n* Gottes; *animal* (*mineral, vegetable*) ~ Tier-(Mineral-, Pflanzen)reich *n*; **~ly** ['kɪŋlɪ] (*-ier, -iest*) königlich; **~size(d)** extrem groß.

kink [kɪŋk] Schleife *f*, Knoten *m*; *fig.* Schrulle *f*, Tick *m*, Spleen *m*; **~y** ['kɪŋkɪ] (*-ier, -iest*) schrullig, spleenig.

ki·osk ['kiːɒsk] Kiosk *m*; *Brt.* Telefonzelle *f*.

kip·per ['kɪpə] Räucherhering *m*.

kiss [kɪs] **1.** Kuß *m*; **2.** (sich) küssen.

kit [kɪt] Ausrüstung *f* (*a. ✕ u. Sport*); Werkzeug(e *pl.*) *n*; Werkzeugtasche *f*, -kasten *m*; Bastelsatz *m*; *s.* first-aid; **~bag** ['kɪtbæg] Seesack *m*.

kitch·en ['kɪtʃɪn] Küche *f*; *attr.* Küchen...; **~ette** [kɪtʃɪ'net] Kleinküche *f*, Kochnische *f*; ~ **gar·den** ['kɪtʃɪn'gɑːdn] Küchen-, Gemüsegarten *m*.

K

kite [kaɪt] (Papier-, Stoff)Drachen *m*; *zo.* Milan *m*.

kit·ten ['kɪtn] Kätzchen *n*.

knack [næk] Kniff *m*, Trick *m*, Dreh *m*; Geschick *n*, Talent *n*.

knave [neɪv] Schurke *m*, Spitzbube *m*; *Kartenspiel:* Bube *m*, Unter *m*.

knead [niːd] kneten; massieren.

knee [niː] Knie *n*; ⊕ Kniestück *n*; ~**cap** anat. ['niːkæp] Kniescheibe *f*; ~**-deep** knietief, bis an die Knie (reichend); ~**-joint** anat. Kniegelenk *n* (a. ⊕); **⌐l** [niːl] (*knelt, Am. a. kneeled*) knien (*to* vor *dat.*); ~**length** knielang (*Rock etc.*).

knell [nel] Totenglocke *f*.

knelt [nelt] *pret. u. p.p. von kneel.*

knew [njuː] *pret. von know.*

knick·er·bock·ers ['nɪkəbɒkəz] *pl.* Knickerbocker *pl.*, Kniehosen *pl.*; ~**s** *Brt.* F [⌐z] *pl.* (Damen)Schlüpfer *m.*

knick-knack ['nɪknæk] Nippsache *f.*

knife [naɪf] **1.** (*pl. knives* [⌐vz]) Messer *n*; **2.** schneiden; mit e-m Messer verletzen; erstechen.

knight [naɪt] **1.** Ritter *m*; *Schach:* Springer *m*; **2.** zum Ritter schlagen; ~**hood** ['naɪthʊd] Ritterwürde *f*, -stand *m*; Ritterschaft *f*.

knit [nɪt] (*-tt-; knit od. knitted*) *v/t.* stricken; *a.* ~ *together* zusammenfügen, verbinden; ~ *one's brows* die Stirn runzeln; *v/i.* stricken; zusammenwachsen (*Knochen*); ~**ting** ['nɪtɪŋ] Stricken *n*; Strickzeug *n*; *attr.* Strick...; ~**wear** Strickwaren *pl.*

knives [naɪvz] *pl. von knife 1.*

knob [nɒb] Knopf *m*, Knauf *m*; Buckel *m*; Brocken *m*.

knock [nɒk] **1.** Stoß *m*; Klopfen (*a. mot.*), Pochen *n*; *there is a* ~ es klopft; **2.** *v/i.* schlagen, pochen, klopfen; stoßen (*against, into* gegen); ~ *about,* ~ *around* F sich herumtreiben; F herumliegen; ~ *at the door* an die Tür klopfen; ~ *off* F Feierabend *od.* Schluß machen, aufhören; *v/t.* stoßen, schlagen; F schlechtmachen, verreißen; ~ *about,* ~ *around* herumstoßen, übel zurich-

ten; ~ *down* niederschlagen, umwerfen; um-, überfahren; *Auktion: et.* zuschlagen (*to* s.o. j-m); *Preis* herabsetzen; ⊕ auseinandernehmen, zerlegen; *Haus* abreißen; *Baum* fällen; *be* ~*ed down* überfahren werden; ~ *off* herunterstoßen; abschlagen; F aufhören mit; F hinhauen (*schnell erledigen*); *vom Preis* abziehen, nachlassen; *Brt.* F ausrauben; ~ *out* (her)ausschlagen, (her)ausklopfen; k.o. schlagen; *fig.* F umwerfen, schocken; *be* ~*ed out of* ausscheiden aus (*e-m Wettbewerb*); ~ *over* umwerfen, umstoßen; um-, überfahren; *be* ~*ed over* überfahren werden; ~ *up* hochschlagen; *Brt.* F rasch auf die Beine stellen, improvisieren; ~**er** ['nɒkə] Türklopfer *m*; ~**-kneed** [⌐'niːd] X-beinig; ~**-out** [⌐kaʊt] *Boxen:* Knockout *m*, K.o. *m.*

knoll [nəʊl] kleiner runder Hügel; △ *nicht* Knolle.

knot [nɒt] **1.** Knoten *m*; Astknorren *m*; ♟ Knoten *m*, Seemeile *f*; Gruppe *f*, Knäuel *m*, *n* (*Menschen*); **2.** (*-tt-*) (ver)knoten, (-)knüpfen; ~**ty** ['nɒtɪ] (*-ier, -iest*) knotig; knorrig; *fig.* verzwickt.

know [nəʊ] (*knew, known*) wissen; kennen; erfahren; (wieder)erkennen, unterscheiden; (es) können *od.* verstehen; ~ *French* Französisch können; *come to* ~ erfahren; *get to* ~ kennenlernen; ~ *one's business,* ~ *the ropes,* ~ *a thing or two,* ~ *what's what* F sich auskennen, Erfahrung haben; *you* ~ wissen Sie; ~**how** ['nəʊhaʊ] Know-how *n*, praktische (Sach-, Spezial)Kenntnis(se *pl.*) *f*; ~**ing** □ [⌐ɪŋ] klug; schlau; verständnisvoll; wissend; ~**ing·ly** [⌐lɪ] wissend; absichtlich, bewußt; ~**l-edge** ['nɒlɪdʒ] Kenntnis(se *pl.*) *f*; Wissen *n*; *to my* ~ meines Wissens; ~**n** [nəʊn] *p.p. von know*; bekannt; *make* ~ bekanntmachen.

knuck·le ['nʌkl] **1.** (Finger)Knöchel *m*; **2.** ~ *down to work* sich an die Arbeit machen.

Krem·lin ['kremlɪn]: *the* ~ der Kreml.

L

lab F [læb] Labor *n*.

la·bel ['leɪbl] **1.** Etikett *n*, Aufkleber *m*, Schild(chen) *n*; Aufschrift *f*, Beschriftung *f*; (Schall)Plattenfirma *f*; **2.** (*bsd. Brt. -ll-, Am. -l-*) etikettieren, beschriften; *fig.* abstempeln als.

la·bor·a·to·ry [ləˈbɒrətərɪ] Labor(atorium) *n*; ~ *assistant* Laborant(in).

la·bo·ri·ous □ [ləˈbɔːrɪəs] mühsam; schwerfällig (*Stil*).

la·bo(u)r ['leɪbə] **1.** (schwere) Arbeit, Mühe *f*; ♣ Wehen *pl.*; Arbeiter *pl.*, Arbeitskräfte *pl.*; *the* Labour Party; *hard* ~ ⚖ Zwangsarbeit *f*; **2.** Arbeiter..., Arbeits...; **3.** *v/i.* (schwer) arbeiten; sich abmühen, sich quälen; ~ *under* leiden unter (*dat.*), zu kämpfen haben mit; *v/t.* ausführlich behandeln; **~ed** schwerfällig (*Stil*); mühsam (*Atem etc.*); **~er** [~rə] *bsd. ungelernter* Arbeiter; **Labour Ex·change** *Brt.* F *od. hist.* Arbeitsamt *n*; **La·bour Par·ty** *pol.* Labour Party *f*; **la·bor u·ni·on** *Am. pol.* Gewerkschaft *f*.

lace [leɪs] **1.** Spitze *f*; Borte *f*; Schnürsenkel *m*; **2.** ~ *up* (zu-, zusammen-)schnüren; *Schuh* zubinden; ~*d with brandy* mit e-m Schuß Weinbrand.

la·ce·rate ['læsəreɪt] zerfleischen, -schneiden, -kratzen; aufreißen; *j-s Gefühle* verletzen.

lack [læk] **1.** (*of*) Fehlen *n* (von), Mangel *m* (an *dat.*); △ *nicht* Lack; *v/t.* nicht haben; *he* ~*s money* es fehlt ihm an Geld; *v/i. he* ~*ing* fehlt; *he is* ~*ing in courage* ihm fehlt der Mut; **~·lus·tre,** *Am.* **~·lus·ter** ['læklʌstə] glanzlos, matt.

la·con·ic [ləˈkɒnɪk] (~*ally*) lakonisch, wortkarg, kurz und prägnant.

lac·quer ['lækə] **1.** Lack *m*; Haarspray *m*, *n*; Nagellack *m*; **2.** lackieren.

lad [læd] Bursche *m*, Junge *m*.

lad·der ['lædə] Leiter *f*; *Brt.* Laufmasche *f*; **~·proof** (lauf)maschenfest (*Strumpf*).

la·den ['leɪdn] (schwer) beladen.

la·ding ['leɪdɪŋ] Ladung *f*, Fracht *f*.

la·dle ['leɪdl] **1.** (Schöpf-, Suppen-)Kelle *f*, Schöpflöffel *m*; **2.** ~ *out* *Suppe* austeilen.

la·dy ['leɪdɪ] Dame *f*; Lady *f* (*a. Titel*); ~ *doctor* Ärztin *f*; *Ladies*('), *Am. Ladies' room* Damentoilette *f*; **~·bird** *zo.* Marienkäfer *m*; **~·like** damenhaft; **~·ship** [~ʃɪp]: *her od. your* ~ Ihre Ladyschaft.

lag [læg] **1.** (*-gg-*) ~ *behind* zurückbleiben; sich verzögern; **2.** Verzögerung *f*; Zeitabstand *m*, -differenz *f*.

la·ger ['lɑːgə] Lagerbier *n*; △ *nicht Lager*.

la·goon [ləˈguːn] Lagune *f*.

laid [leɪd] *pret. u. p.p. von* lay³.

lain [leɪn] *p.p. von* lie² 2.

lair [leə] Lager *n*, Höhle *f*, Bau *m* (*e-s wilden Tieres*).

la·i·ty ['leɪətɪ] Laien *pl.*

lake [leɪk] See *m*.

lamb [læm] **1.** Lamm *n*; **2.** lammen.

lame [leɪm] **1.** □ lahm (*a. fig. = unbefriedigend*); **2.** lähmen.

la·ment [ləˈment] **1.** Wehklage *f*; Klagelied *n*; **2.** (be)klagen; (be)trauern; **lam·en·ta·ble** □ ['læməntəbl] beklagenswert; kläglich; **lam·en·ta·tion** [læmənˈteɪʃn] Wehklage *f*.

lamp [læmp] Lampe *f*; Laterne *f*.

lam·poon [læmˈpuːn] **1.** Schmähschrift *f*; **2.** verspotten, -unglimpfen.

lamp|post ['læmppəʊst] Laternenpfahl *m*; **~·shade** Lampenschirm *m*.

lance [lɑːns] Lanze *f*.

land [lænd] **1.** Land *n*; ✓ Land *n*, Boden *m*; Land-, Grundbesitz *m*; Land *n*, Staat *m*, Nation *f*; *by* ~ *auf dem Landweg*; ~*s pl.* Ländereien *pl.*; **2.** landen; *Fracht* löschen; F *j-n od. et.* erwischen, kriegen; F *in Schwierigkeiten etc.* bringen; **~·a·gent** ['lændeɪdʒənt] Gutsverwalter *m*; **~·ed** Land..., Grund...; **~·hold·er** Grundbesitzer(in).

land·ing ['lændɪŋ] Landung *f*; Anlegen *n* (*Schiff*); Anlegestelle *f*; Treppenabsatz *m*; Flur *m*, Gang *m* (*am Ende e-r Treppe*); **~·field** ✈ Landebahn *f*; **~·gear** ✈ Fahrgestell *n*; **~·stage** Landungsbrücke *f*, -steg *m*.

land|la·dy ['lænleɪdɪ] Vermieterin *f*; Wirtin *f*; **~·lord** [~lɔːd] Vermieter *m*; Wirt *m*; Hauseigentümer *m*; Grundbesitzer *m*; **~·lub·ber** ♣ *contp.* [~dlʌbə] Landratte (*f*); **~·mark** Grenzstein *m*; Orientierungspunkt *m*; Wahrzeichen *n*; *fig.* Markstein *m*; **~·own·er** Grundbesitzer(in);

~scape [ˈlænskeɪp] Landschaft *f* (*a. paint.*); **~slide** Erdrutsch *m* (*a. pol.*); *a ~ victory pol.* ein überwältigender Wahlsieg; **~slip** (kleiner) Erdrutsch.

lane [leɪn] Feldweg *m*; Gasse *f*, Sträßchen *n*; ♣ (Fahrt)Route *f*; ⚓ Flugschneise *f*; *mot.* Fahrbahn *f*, Spur *f*; *Sport:* (einzelne) Bahn.

lan·guage [ˈlæŋgwɪdʒ] Sprache *f*; ~ *laboratory* Sprachlabor *n*.

lan·guid □ [ˈlæŋgwɪd] matt; träg(e).

lank [læŋk] dünn, dürr; strähnig (*Haar*); **~y** □ [ˈlæŋkɪ] (*-ier*, *-iest*) schlaksig.

lan·tern [ˈlæntən] Laterne *f*.

lap¹ [læp] Schoß *m*.

lap² [~] 1. *Sport:* Runde *f*; 2. (*-pp-*) *Sport: Gegner* überrunden; *Sport:* e-e Runde zurücklegen; wickeln; einhüllen.

lap³ [~] (*-pp-*) *v/t.:* ~ *up* auflecken, -schlecken; *v/i.* plätschern (*against* gegen).

la·pel [ləˈpel] Revers *n, m*.

lapse [læps] 1. Verlauf *m* (*der Zeit*); (kleiner) Fehler *od.* Irrtum; ⚖ *Verfall* *m*; 2. verfallen; ⚖ verfallen, erlöschen; abfallen (*vom Glauben*).

lar·ce·ny ⚖ [ˈlɑːsənɪ] Diebstahl *m*.

larch ⚘ [lɑːtʃ] Lärche *f*.

lard [lɑːd] 1. Schweinefett *n*, -schmalz *n*; 2. *Fleisch* spicken; **lar·der** [ˈlɑːdə] Speisekammer *f*; Speiseschrank *m*.

large □ [lɑːdʒ] (*~r, ~st*) groß; umfassend, weitgehend, ausgedehnt; *at ~* in Freiheit, auf freiem Fuß; ganz allgemein; in der Gesamtheit; (sehr) ausführlich; **~ly** [ˈlɑːdʒlɪ] zum großen Teil; im wesentlichen; **~-minded** tolerant; **~ness** [~nɪs] Größe *f*.

lar·i·at *bsd. Am.* [ˈlærɪət] Lasso *n, m*.

lark¹ *zo.* [lɑːk] Lerche *f*.

lark² F [~] Jux *m*, Spaß *m*.

lark·spur ⚘ [ˈlɑːkspɜː] Rittersporn *m*.

lar·va *zo.* [ˈlɑːvə] (*pl. -vae* [-viː]) Larve *f*.

lar·ynx *anat.* [ˈlærɪŋks] Kehlkopf *m*.

las·civ·i·ous □ [ləˈsɪvɪəs] lüstern.

la·ser *phys.* [ˈleɪzə] Laser *m*; ~ *beam* Laserstrahl *m*.

lash [læʃ] 1. Peitschenschnur *f*; Peitschenhieb *m*; Wimper *f*; 2. peitschen, schlagen; (fest)binden; ~ *out* (wild) um sich schlagen; *fig.* heftig angreifen.

lass, ~ie [læs, ˈlæsɪ] Mädchen *n*.

las·si·tude [ˈlæsɪtjuːd] Mattigkeit *f*.

las·so [læˈsuː] (*pl. -sos, -soes*) Lasso *n, m*.

last¹ [lɑːst] 1. *adj.* letzte(r, -s); vorige(r, -s); äußerste(r, -s); neueste(r, -s); ~ *one* vorletzte(r, -s); ~ *night* gestern abend; 2. *der, die, das* Letzte; △ *nicht Last*; *at* ~ endlich; *to the* ~ bis zum Schluß; 3. *adv.* zuletzt; ~ *but not least* nicht zuletzt.

last² [~] (an-, fort)dauern; (sich) halten (*Farbe etc.*); (aus)reichen.

last³ [~] (Schuhmacher)Leisten *m*.

last·ing □ [ˈlɑːstɪŋ] dauerhaft; beständig.

last·ly [ˈlɑːstlɪ] schließlich, zum Schluß.

latch [lætʃ] Klinke *f*; Schnappschloß *n*; 2. ein-, zuklinken; **~key** [ˈlætʃkiː] Hausschlüssel *m*.

late □ [leɪt] (*~r, ~st*) spät; jüngste(r, -s), letzte(r, -s); frühere(r, -s), ehemalig; verstorben; *be* ~ zu spät kommen, sich verspäten; *at (the)* ~*st* spätestens; *as* ~ *as* noch, erst; *of* ~ kürzlich; ~*r on* später; **~ly** [ˈleɪtlɪ] kürzlich.

la·tent □ [ˈleɪtənt] verborgen, latent.

lat·er·al □ [ˈlætərəl] seitlich, Seiten...

lath □ [lɑːθ] Latte *f*.

lathe ⊕ [leɪð] Drehbank *f*.

la·ther [ˈlɑːðə] 1. (Seifen)Schaum *m*; 2. *v/t.* einseifen; *v/i.* schäumen.

Lat·in [ˈlætɪn] *ling.* lateinisch; romanisch; südländisch; 2. *ling.* Latein *n*; Roman|e *m*, -in *f*, Südländer(in).

lat·i·tude [ˈlætɪtjuːd] *geogr.* Breite *f*; *fig.* Spielraum *m*.

lat·ter [ˈlætə] letztere(r, -s) (*von zweien*); letzte(r, -s), spätere(r, -s); **~ly** [~lɪ] in letzter Zeit.

lat·tice [ˈlætɪs] Gitter *n*.

lau·da·ble □ [ˈlɔːdəbl] lobenswert.

laugh [lɑːf] 1. Lachen *n*, Gelächter *n*; 2. lachen; ~ *at* j-n auslachen; *have the last* ~ (am Ende) doch noch gewinnen; **~a·ble** □ [ˈlɑːfəbl] lächerlich; **~ter** [~tə] Lachen *n*, Gelächter *n*.

launch [lɔːntʃ] 1. *Schiff* vom Stapel laufen lassen; *Boot* aussetzen; schleudern; *Rakete* starten, abschießen; *fig.* in Gang bringen; 2. ♣ Barkasse *f*; = **~ing** [ˈlɔːntʃɪŋ] ♣ Stapellauf *m*; Abschuß *m* (*e-r Rakete*); *fig.*

Start(en *n*) *m*; ~ *pad* Abschußrampe *f*; ~ *site* Abschußbasis *f*.

laun|de·rette [lɔːndəˈret], *bsd. Am.* **~·dro·mat** [ˈlɔːndrəmæt] Waschsalon *m*, Münzwäscherei *f*; **~·dry** [ˌri] Wäscherei *f*; *schmutzige od. gewaschene* Wäsche.

laur·el ♣ [ˈlɔrəl] Lorbeer *m* (*a. fig.*).

lav·a·to·ry [ˈlævətəri] Toilette *f*, Klosett *n*; *public* ~ Bedürfnisanstalt *f*.

lav·en·der ♣ [ˈlævəndə] Lavendel *m*.

lav·ish [ˈlævɪʃ] **1.** □ freigebig, verschwenderisch; **2.** ~ *s.th. on s.o.* j-n mit et. überhäufen *od.* überschütten.

law [lɔː] Gesetz *n*; Recht *n*; (Spiel-) Regel *f*; Rechtswissenschaft *f*, Jura *pl.*; F *die* Polizei; ~ *and order* Recht *od.* Ruhe u. Ordnung; **~·a·bid·ing** [ˈlɔːbaɪdɪŋ] gesetzestreu; **~·court** Gericht(shof *m*) *n*; **~·ful** □ [ˌfl] gesetzlich; rechtmäßig, legitim; rechtsgültig; **~·less** □ [ˌlɪs] gesetzlos; gesetzwidrig; zügellos.

lawn [lɔːn] Rasen *m*.

law·suit [ˈlɔːsjuːt] Prozeß *m*; **~·yer** [ˌjə] (Rechts)Anwalt *m*, (-)Anwältin *f*.

lax □ [læks] locker, lax; schlaff; lasch; **~·a·tive** ♣ [ˈlæksətɪv] **1.** abführend; **2.** Abführmittel *n*.

lay[1] [leɪ] *pret. von* lie[2] 2.

lay[2] [~] *eccl.* weltlich; Laien...

lay[3] [~] (*laid*) *v/t.* legen; umlegen; *Plan* schmieden; *Tisch* decken; *Eier* legen; beruhigen, besänftigen; auferlegen; *Klage* vorbringen, *Anklage* erheben; *Wette* abschließen; *Summe* wetten; ~ *in* einlagern, sich eindecken mit; ~ *low* niederstrecken, -werfen; ~ *off econ.* Arbeiter vorübergehend entlassen, *Arbeit* einstellen; ~ *open* darlegen; ~ *out* ausbreiten; *Garten etc.* anlegen; entwerfen, planen; *print. Buch* gestalten; ~ *up Vorräte* hinlegen, sammeln; *be laid up* das Bett hüten müssen; *v/i.* (Eier) legen.

lay-by *Brt. mot.* [ˈleɪbaɪ] Parkbucht *f*, -streifen *m*; Park-, Rastplatz *m*.

lay·er [ˈleɪə] Lage *f*, Schicht *f*.

lay·man [ˈleɪmən] (*pl. -men*) Laie *m*.

lay-off *econ.* [ˈleɪɒf] vorübergehend Arbeitseinstellung, Feierschicht(en *pl.*) *f*; **~·out** Anlage *f*; Plan *m*; *print.* Layout *n*, Gestaltung *f*.

la·zy □ [ˈleɪzɪ] (*-ier, -iest*) faul, träg(e), langsam; müde *od.* faul machend.

lead[1] [led] ♠ Blei *n*; ♣ Lot *n*.

lead[2] [liːd] **1.** Führung *f*; Leitung *f*; Spitzenposition *f*; Beispiel *n*; *thea.* Hauptrolle *f*; *thea.* Hauptdarsteller(in); *Sport u. fig.* Führung *f*, Vorsprung *m*; *Kartenspiel:* Vorhand *f*; ⚡ Leitung *f*; (Hunde)Leine *f*; Hinweis *m*, Tip *m*, Anhaltspunkt *m*; **2.** (*led*) *v/t.* führen; leiten; (an)führen; verleiten, bewegen (*to* zu); *Karte* ausspielen; ~ *on* F j-n anführen; am Arm nehmen; *v/i.* führen; vorangehen; *Sport:* in Führung liegen; ~ *off* den Anfang machen; ~ *up to* führen zu, überleiten zu.

lead·en [ˈledn] bleiern (*a. fig.*), Blei...

lead·er [ˈliːdə] (An)Führer(in), Leiter(in); Erste(r *m*) *f*; *Brt.* Leitartikel *m*; **~·ship** [ˌʃɪp] Führung *f*, Leitung *f*.

lead-free [ˈledfriː] bleifrei.

lead·ing [ˈliːdɪŋ] leitend; führend; Haupt...

leaf [liːf] **1.** (*pl. leaves* [ˌvz]) Blatt *n*; (*Tür- etc.*)Flügel *m*; (*Tisch*)Klappe *f*; **2.** ~ *through* durchblättern; **~·let** [ˈliːflɪt] Prospekt *m*; Broschüre *f*, Informationsblatt *n*; Merkblatt *n*; **~·y** [ˌɪ] (*-ier, -iest*) belaubt.

league [liːg] Liga *f* (*a. hist. u. Sport*); Bund *m*.

leak [liːk] **1.** Leck *n*, undichte Stelle (*a. fig.*); **2.** lecken, leck sein; tropfen; ~ *out* auslaufen, -strömen, entweichen; *fig.* durchsickern; **~·age** [ˈliːkɪdʒ] Lecken *n*, Auslaufen *n*, -strömen *n*; *fig.* Durchsickern *n*; **~·y** [ˌɪ] (*-ier, -iest*) leck, undicht.

lean[1] [liːn] (*bsd. Brt. leant od. bsd. Am. leaned*) (sich) lehnen; (sich) stützen; (sich) neigen; ~ *on*, ~ *upon* sich verlassen auf (*acc.*).

lean[2] [~] **1.** mager; **2.** das Magere (*von gekochtem Fleisch*).

leant *bsd. Brt.* [lent] *pret u. p.p. von* lean[1].

leap [liːp] **1.** Sprung *m*, Satz *m*; **2.** (*leapt od. leaped*) (über)springen; ~ *at fig.* sich stürzen auf; **~·t** [lept] *pret. u. p.p. von* leap 2; ~ *year* [ˈliːpjɜː] Schaltjahr *n*.

learn [lɜːn] (*learned od. learnt*) (er-) lernen; erfahren, hören; **~·ed** [ˈlɜːnɪd] gelehrt; **~·er** [ˌə] Anfänger(in); Lernende(r *m*) *f*; *driver mot.* Fahrschüler(in); **~·ing** [ˌɪŋ] (Er)Lernen *n*; Gelehrsamkeit *f*; **~·t** [lɜːnt] *pret. u. p.p. von* learn.

lease [li:s] 1. Pacht f, Miete f; Pacht-, Mietvertrag m; 2. (ver)pachten, (ver)mieten.

leash [li:ʃ] (Hunde)Leine f.

least [li:st] 1. adj. (sup. von little 1) kleinste(r, -s), geringste(r, -s), wenigste(r, -s); 2. adv. (sup. von little 2) am wenigsten; ~ of all am allerwenigsten; 3. das Geringste, das Mindeste, das Wenigste; at ~ wenigstens; to say the ~ gelinde gesagt.

leath·er ['leðə] 1. Leder n; 2. ledern; Leder...

leave [li:v] 1. Erlaubnis f; a. ~ of absence Urlaub m; Abschied m; take (one's) ~ sich verabschieden; 2. (left) v/t. (hinter-, über-, übrig-, ver-, zurück)lassen; stehen-, liegenlassen; vergessen; vermachen, -erben; v/i. (fort-, weg)gehen, abreisen, abfahren, abfliegen.

leav·en ['levn] Sauerteig m; Hefe f.

leaves [li:vz] pl. von leaf 1; Laub n.

leav·ings ['li:vɪŋz] pl. Überreste pl.

lech·er·ous □ ['letʃərəs] lüstern.

lec|ture ['lektʃə] 1. univ. Vorlesung f; Vortrag m; Strafpredigt f; △ nicht Lektüre; 2. v/i. univ. e-e Vorlesung halten; e-n Vortrag halten; v/t. tadeln, abkanzeln; ~**tur·er** [~rə] univ. Dozent(in); Redner(in).

led [led] pret. u. p.p. von lead[2].

ledge [ledʒ] Leiste f; Sims m, n; Riff n; (Fels)Vorsprung m.

led·ger econ. ['ledʒə] Hauptbuch n.

leech [li:tʃ] zo. Blutegel m; fig. Blutsauger m, Schmarotzer m.

leek ♀ [li:k] Lauch m, Porree m.

leer [lɪə] 1. anzüglicher (Seiten)Blick; 2. anzüglich od. lüstern blicken; schielen (at nach).

lee|ward ♩ ['li:wəd] leewärts; ~**way** ♩ Abtrift f; fig. Rückstand m; fig. Spielraum m.

left[1] [left] pret. u. p.p. von leave[2].

left[2] [~] 1. adj. linke(r, -s); 2. adv. (nach) links; 3. Linke f (a. pol., Boxen), linke Seite; on od. to the ~ links; ~**hand** ['lefthænd] linke(r, -s); ~ drive mot. Linkssteuerung f; ~**hand·ed** □ ['left'hændɪd] linkshändig; für Linkshänder.

left|-lug·gage of·fice Brt. 🚉 ['left-'lʌgɪdʒɒfɪs] Gepäckaufbewahrung f; ~**o·vers** pl. (Speise)Reste pl.; ~**wing** pol. linke(r, -s), linksgerichtet.

leg [leg] Bein n; Keule f; (Stiefel-) Schaft m; ⚕ Schenkel m; pull s.o.'s ~ j-n auf den Arm nehmen (hänseln); stretch one's ~s sich die Beine vertreten.

leg·a·cy ['legəsɪ] Vermächtnis n.

le·gal □ ['li:gl] legal, gesetz-, rechtmäßig; gesetz-, rechtlich; juristisch; Rechts...; ~**ize** [~aɪz] legalisieren, rechtskräftig machen.

le·ga·tion [lɪ'geɪʃn] Gesandtschaft f.

le·gend ['ledʒənd] Legende f, Sage f; Bildunterschrift f; **le·gen·da·ry** [~ərɪ] legendär, sagenhaft.

leg·gings ['legɪŋz] pl. Gamaschen pl.; Beinlinge pl., -schutz m.

le·gi·ble □ ['ledʒəbl] leserlich.

le·gion fig. ['li:dʒən] Legion f, Heer n.

le·gis·la·tion [ledʒɪs'leɪʃn] Gesetzgebung f; ~**tive** pol. ['ledʒɪslətɪv] 1. □ gesetzgebend, legislativ; 2. Legislative f, gesetzgebende Gewalt; ~**tor** [~eɪtə] Gesetzgeber m.

le·git·i·mate □ [lɪ'dʒɪtɪmət] legitim; gesetz-, rechtmäßig; berechtigt; ehelich.

lei·sure ['leʒə] Muße f, Freizeit f; at ~ frei, unbeschäftigt; ohne Hast; ~**ly** [~lɪ] gemächlich.

lem·on ♀ ['lemən] Zitrone f; ~**ade** [lemə'neɪd] Zitronenlimonade f; ~ **squash** Zitronenwasser n.

lend [lend] (lent) j-m et. (ver-, aus)leihen, borgen; △ nicht sich et. leihen.

length [leŋθ] Länge f; Strecke f; (Zeit)Dauer f; at ~ endlich, schließlich; ausführlich; go to any od. great od. considerable ~ sehr weit gehen; ~**en** ['leŋθən] verlängern; länger werden; ~**ways** [~weɪz], ~**wise** [~waɪz] der Länge nach; ~**y** □ [~ɪ] (-ier, -iest) sehr lang.

le·ni·ent □ ['li:njənt] mild(e), nachsichtig.

lens opt. [lenz] Linse f.

lent[1] [lent] pret. u. p.p. von lend.

Lent[2] [~] Fastenzeit f.

len·til ♀ ['lentɪl] Linse f.

leop·ard zo. ['lepəd] Leopard m.

le·o·tard ['li:əʊta:d] (Tänzer)Trikot n; Gymnastikanzug m.

lep·ro·sy ⚕ ['leprəsɪ] Lepra f.

les·bi·an ['lezbɪən] 1. lesbisch; 2. Lesbierin f, F Lesbe f.

less [les] 1. adj. u. adv. (comp. von little 1, 2) kleiner, geringer, weniger; 2. prp. weniger, minus, abzüglich.

less·en ['lesn] (sich) vermindern od. -ringern; abnehmen; herabsetzen.

less·er [ˈlesə] kleiner, geringer.
les·son [ˈlesn] Lektion *f*; (Haus)Aufgabe *f*; (Unterrichts)Stunde *f*; *fig.* Lektion *f*, Lehre *f*; ~*s pl.* Unterricht *m*.
lest [lest] damit nicht; daß.
let [let] (*let*) lassen; vermieten, -pachten; ~ *alone* in Ruhe lassen; geschweige denn; ~ *down* herab-, herunterlassen; *Kleider* verlängern; *j-n* im Stich lassen; ~ *go* loslassen; ~ *o.s. go* sich gehenlassen; ~ *in* (her)einlassen; ~ *o.s. in for s.th.* sich et. aufhalsen *od.* einbrocken; ~ *s.o. in on s.th.* j-n in et. einweihen; ~ *off* abschießen; *j-n* laufenlassen; aussteigen lassen; ~ *out* hinauslassen; *Schrei* ausstoßen; ausplaudern; vermieten; ~ *up* aufhören.
le·thal □ [ˈliːθl] tödlich; Todes...
leth·ar·gy [ˈleθədʒɪ] Lethargie *f*.
let·ter [ˈletə] **1.** Buchstabe *m*; *print.* Type *f*; Brief *m*, Schreiben *n*; ~*s pl.* Literatur *f*; *attr.* Brief...; **2.** beschriften; **~-box** Briefkasten *m*; **~-card** Kartenbrief *m*; ~ **car·ri·er** *Am.* Briefträger *m*; **~ed** (literarisch) gebildet; **~·ing** [~rɪŋ] Beschriftung *f*.
let·tuce ♀ [ˈletɪs] (*bsd.* Kopf)Salat *m*.
leu·k(a)e·mia ⚕ [ljuːˈkiːmɪə] Leukämie *f*.
lev·el [ˈlevl] **1.** waag(e)recht; eben; gleich; ausgeglichen; *my* ~ *best* F mein möglichstes; ~ *crossing Brt.* schienengleicher Bahnübergang; **2.** Ebene *f*, ebene Fläche; (gleiche) Höhe, (*Wasser- etc.*)Spiegel *m*, (-)Stand *m*; Wasserwaage *f*; *fig.* Niveau *n*, Stand *m*, Stufe *f*; *sea* ~ Meeresspiegel *m*; *on the* ~ F ehrlich, aufrichtig; **3.** (*bsd. Brt. -ll-, Am. -l-*) ebnen, planieren; niederschlagen, fällen; ~ *at Waffe* richten auf (*acc.*); *Anklage* erheben gegen (*acc.*); **~-head·ed** vernünftig, nüchtern.
le·ver [ˈliːvə] Hebel *m*; **~·age** [~rɪdʒ] Hebelkraft *f*, -wirkung *f*.
lev·y [ˈlevɪ] **1.** Steuereinziehung *f*; Steuer *f*; ⚔ Aushebung *f*; **2.** *Steuern* einziehen, erheben; ⚔ ausheben.
lewd □ [ljuːd] unanständig, obszön; schmutzig.
li·a·bil·i·ty [laɪəˈbɪlətɪ] ⚖ Haftung *f*, Haftpflicht *f*; *liabilities pl.* Verbindlichkeiten *pl.*; *econ.* Passiva *pl.*
li·a·ble [ˈlaɪəbl] ⚖ haftbar, -pflichtig; *be* ~ *for* haften für; *be* ~ *to* neigen zu; anfällig sein für.
li·ar [ˈlaɪə] Lügner(in).
lib F [lɪb] *abbr. für liberation.*
li·bel ⚖ [ˈlaɪbl] **1.** Verleumdung *f od.* Beleidigung *f* (durch Veröffentlichung); **2.** (*bsd. Brt. -ll-, Am. -l-*) (schriftlich) verleumden *od.* beleidigen.
lib·e·ral [ˈlɪbərəl] **1.** □ liberal (*a. pol.*), aufgeschlossen; großzügig; reichlich; **2.** Liberale(r *m*) *f* (*a. pol.*); **~·i·ty** [lɪbəˈrælətɪ] Großzügigkeit *f*; Aufgeschlossenheit *f*.
lib·e|rate [ˈlɪbəreɪt] befreien; **~·ra·tion** [lɪbəˈreɪʃn] Befreiung *f*; **~·ra·tor** [ˈlɪbəreɪtə] Befreier *m*.
lib·er·ty [ˈlɪbətɪ] Freiheit *f*; *take liberties* sich Freiheiten herausnehmen; *be at* ~ frei sein.
li·brar·i·an [laɪˈbreərɪən] Bibliothekar(in); **li·bra·ry** [ˈlaɪbrərɪ] Bibliothek *f*; Bücherei *f*.
lice [laɪs] *pl. von louse.*
li·cence, *Am.* **-cense** [ˈlaɪsəns] Lizenz *f*, Konzession *f*; Freiheit *f*; Zügellosigkeit *f*; *license plate Am. mot.* Nummernschild *n*; *driving* ~ Führerschein *m*.
li·cense, -cence [~] e-e Lizenz *od.* Konzession erteilen; (amtlich) genehmigen *od.* zulassen.
li·cen·tious □ [laɪˈsenʃəs] ausschweifend, zügellos.
li·chen ♀, ⚕ [ˈlaɪkən] Flechte *f*.
lick [lɪk] **1.** Lecken *n*; Salzlecke *f*; **2.** *v/t.* (ab-, auf-, be)lecken; F verdreschen, -prügeln; F schlagen, besiegen; *v/i.* lecken; züngeln (*Flammen*).
lic·o·rice [ˈlɪkərɪs] = *liquorice.*
lid [lɪd] Deckel *m*; (Augen)Lid *n*.
lie[1] [laɪ] **1.** Lüge *f*; *give s.o. the* ~ j-n Lügen strafen; **2.** lügen.
lie[2] [~] **1.** Lage *f*; **2.** (*lay, lain*) liegen; ~ *behind fig.* dahinterstecken; ~ *down* sich hinlegen; *let sleeping dogs* ~ *fig.* daran rühren wir lieber nicht; **~-down** F [laɪˈdaʊn] Nickerchen *n*; **~-in** [ˈlaɪɪn]: *have a* ~ *Brt.* F sich gründlich ausschlafen.
lieu [ljuː]: *in* ~ statt dessen; *in* ~ *of* an Stelle von (*od. gen.*), anstatt (*gen.*).
lieu·ten·ant [lefˈtenənt; ⚓ leˈtenənt; *Am.* luːˈtenənt] Leutnant *m*.
life [laɪf] (*pl. lives* [~vz]) Leben *n*; Menschenleben *n*; Lebensbeschreibung *f*, Biographie *f*; *for* ~ fürs (ganze) Leben; *bsd.* ⚖ lebenslänglich; ~ *imprisonment*, ~ *sentence*

lebenslängliche Freiheitsstrafe; ~
as·sur·ance Lebensversicherung *f*;
~·belt ['laɪfbelt] Rettungsgürtel *m*;
~·boat Rettungsboot *n*; **~·guard** ✗
Leibgarde *f*; Bademeister *m*; Rettungsschwimmer *m*; ~ **in·sur·ance**
Lebensversicherung *f*; **~·jack·et**
Schwimmweste *f*; **~·less** □ [~lɪs]
leblos; matt, schwung-, lustlos;
~·like lebensecht; **~·long** lebenslang; ~ **pre·serv·er** *Am.* [~prɪzɜːvə]
Schwimmweste *f*; Rettungsgürtel
m; **~·time** Lebenszeit *f*.

lift [lɪft] **1.** (Hoch-, Auf)Heben *n*;
phys., ✈ Auftrieb *m*; *bsd. Brt.* Lift
m, Aufzug *m*, Fahrstuhl *m*; *give s.o.*
a ~ j-n aufmuntern; j-m Auftrieb
geben; j-n (im Auto) mitnehmen; **2.**
v/t. (hoch-, auf)heben; aufheben;
Verbot aufheben; *Gesichtshaut* straffen; F klauen, stehlen; *v/i.* sich heben (*Nebel*); ~ *off* abheben (*Rakete*
etc.); **~·off** ['lɪftɒf] Start *m*, Abheben
n (*Rakete etc.*).

lig·a·ture ['lɪgətʃʊə] Binde *f*; ✚ Verband *m*.

light[1] [laɪt] **1.** Licht *n* (*a. fig.*); Lampe
f; Leuchten *n*, Glanz *m*; Aspekt *m*,
Gesichtspunkt *m*; *Can you give me*
a ~, *please?* Haben Sie Feuer?; *put*
a ~ *to* anzünden; **2.** licht, hell; blond;
3. (*lit od. lighted*) *v/t.* ~ (*up*) beleuchten; anzünden; *v/i.* sich entzünden, brennen; ~ *up* aufleuchten.

light[2] *adj.* □ *u. adv.* [~] leicht (*a. fig.*);
make ~ *of et.* leichtnehmen.

light·en[1] ['laɪtn] *v/t.* erhellen; aufhellen; aufheitern; *v/i.* hell(er) werden,
sich aufhellen.

light·en[2] [~] leichter machen *od.* werden; erleichtern.

light·er ['laɪtə] Anzünder *m*; Feuerzeug *n*; ⏚ Leichter *m*.

light|-head·ed ['laɪthedɪd] benommen, benebelt; leichtfertig, töricht;
~·heart·ed □ fröhlich, unbeschwert; **~·house** Leuchtturm *m*.

light·ing ['laɪtɪŋ] Beleuchtung *f*; Anzünden *n*.

light|-mind·ed ['laɪt'maɪndɪd]
leichtfertig, **~·ness** ['laɪtnɪs] Leichtheit *f*; Leichtigkeit *f*.

light·ning ['laɪtnɪŋ] Blitz *m*; *attr.*
blitzschnell, Blitz...; ~ **con·duc·tor**,
Am. ~ **rod** ⚡ Blitzableiter *m*.

light·weight ['laɪtweɪt] *Boxen*:
Leichtgewicht(ler *m*) *n*.

like[1] [laɪk] **1.** gleich; ähnlich; (so) wie;

F als *ob*; ~ *that* so; *feel* ~ Lust haben
auf *od.* zu; *what is he* ~? wie ist er?;
that is just ~ *him!* das sieht ihm
ähnlich!; **2.** *der, die, das* gleiche, *et.*
Gleiches; *his* ~ seinesgleichen; *the* ~
dergleichen; *the* ~s *of you* Leute wie
du; *my* ~s *and dislikes* was ich mag
und was ich nicht mag; **3.** *v/t.* gern
haben, (gern) mögen; gern tun *etc.*;
how do you ~ *it?* wie gefällt es dir?;
wie findest du es?; *I* ~ *that!* iro. das
hab' ich gern!; *I should* ~ *to come* ich
würde gern kommen; *v/i.* wollen; *as*
you ~ wie du willst; *if you* ~ wenn Sie
wollen; **~·li·hood** ['laɪklɪhʊd] Wahrscheinlichkeit *f*; **~·ly** [~lɪ] **1.** *adj.*
(*-ier, -iest*) wahrscheinlich; geeignet; **2.** *adv.* wahrscheinlich; *not* ~!
F bestimmt nicht!

lik·en ['laɪkən] vergleichen (*to* mit).

like|ness ['laɪknɪs] Ähnlichkeit *f*;
(Ab)Bild *n*; Gestalt *f*; **~·wise** [~waɪz]
gleich-, ebenfalls; auch.

lik·ing ['laɪkɪŋ] (*for*) Vorliebe *f* (für),
Gefallen *n* (an *dat.*).

li·lac ['laɪlək] **1.** lila; **2.** ♀ Flieder *m*.

lil·y ['lɪlɪ] Lilie *f*; ~ *of the valley*
Maiglöckchen *n*; **~·white** schneeweiß.

limb [lɪm] (Körper)Glied *n*; Ast *m*.

lim·ber ['lɪmbə]: ~ *up* *Sport*:
Lockerungsübungen machen.

lime[1] [laɪm] Kalk *m*; Vogelleim *m*; △
nicht Leim.

lime[2] ♀ [~] Linde *f*; Limone *f*.

lime·light *fig.* ['laɪmlaɪt] Rampenlicht *n*.

lim·it ['lɪmɪt] **1.** *fig.* Grenze *f*; *within*
~s inGrenzen; *off* ~s *Am.* Zutritt
verboten (*to* für); *that is the* ~! F das
ist der Gipfel!, das ist (doch) die
Höhe!; *go to the* ~s bis zum Äußersten gehen; **2.** beschränken (*to* auf
acc.).

lim·i·ta·tion [lɪmɪ'teɪʃn] Ein-, Beschränkung *f*; *fig.* Grenze *f*.

lim·it·ed ['lɪmɪtɪd] beschränkt, begrenzt; ~ (*liability*) *company Brt.*
Gesellschaft *f* mit beschränkter Haftung; **~·less** □ [~lɪs] grenzenlos.

limp [lɪmp] **1.** hinken, humpeln; **2.**
Hinken *n*, Humpeln *n*; **3.** schlaff,
schwach, müde; weich.

lim·pid □ ['lɪmpɪd] klar, durchsichtig.

line [laɪn] **1.** Linie *f*; Zeile *f*; Vers *m*;
Strich *m*; Falte *f*, Runzel *f*, Furche *f*;
Reihe *f*; (Menschen)Schlange *f*;

(*Ahnen-* etc.)Reihe *f*, Linie *f*; (Bahn-, Verkehrs- etc.)Linie *f*, Strecke *f*; (Eisenbahn-, Verkehrs-etc.)Gesellschaft *f*; *tel.*, *teleph.* Leitung *f*; Branche *f*; Fach *n*, Gebiet *n*; *Sport*: (Ziel- etc.)Linie *f*; Leine *f*; (Angel)Schnur *f*; Äquator *m*; Richtung *f*; *econ.* Posten *m* (*Ware*); *fig.* Grenze *f*; ~*s pl. thea.* Rolle *f*, Text *m*; be in ~ for gute Aussichten haben auf (*acc.*); be in ~ with übereinstimmen mit; draw the ~ haltmachen, e-e Grenze ziehen (*at* bei); hold the ~ *teleph.* am Apparat bleiben; stand in ~ *Am.* Schlange stehen; **2.** lin(i)ieren; *Gesicht* furchen, zeichnen; *Weg* etc. säumen; *Kleid* füttern; ⊕ auskleiden; ~ up (sich) in e-r Reihe aufstellen.

lin·e·a·ments ['lɪnɪəmənts] *pl.* Gesichtszüge *pl.*

lin·e·ar ['lɪnɪə] linear, geradlinig; Längen...

lin·en ['lɪnɪn] **1.** Leinen *n*; (Bett-, Tisch- etc.)Wäsche *f*; **2.** leinen, Leinen...; **~clos·et**, **~cup·board** Wäscheschrank *m*.

lin·er ['laɪnə] Linien-, Passagierschiff *n*; Verkehrsflugzeug *n*; = eyeliner.

lin·ger ['lɪŋgə] zögern; verweilen, sich aufhalten; dahinsiechen; *a.* ~ on sich hinziehen.

lin·ge·rie ['lɛ̃:nʒəri:] Damenunterwäsche *f*.

lin·i·ment *pharm.* ['lɪnɪmənt] Liniment *n*, Einreibemittel *n*.

lin·ing ['laɪnɪŋ] Futter(stoff *m*) *n*; (Brems)Belag *m*; ⊕ Aus-, Verkleidung *f*.

link [lɪŋk] **1.** (Ketten)Glied *n*; Manschettenknopf *m*; *fig.* (Binde)Glied *n*, Verbindung *f*; **2.** (sich) verbinden; ~ up miteinander verbinden; *Raumschiff* (an)koppeln.

links [lɪŋks] *pl.* Dünen *pl.*; *a. golf* ~ Golfplatz *m*.

link-up [lɪŋkʌp] Zusammenschluß *m*, Verbindung *f*; Kopplung(smanöver *n*) *f* (*Raumschiff*).

lin·seed [lɪŋksi:d] ♀ Leinsamen *m*; ~ oil Leinöl *n*.

li·on *zo.* ['laɪən] Löwe *m*; **~·ess** *zo.* [~nɪs] Löwin *f*.

lip [lɪp] Lippe *f*; (Tassen- etc.)Rand *m*; *sl.* Unverschämtheit *f*; **~·stick** ['lɪpstɪk] Lippenstift *m*.

liq·ue·fy ['lɪkwɪfaɪ] (sich) verflüssigen.

liq·uid ['lɪkwɪd] **1.** flüssig; feucht (schimmernd) (*Augen*); **2.** Flüssigkeit *f*.

liq·ui·date ['lɪkwɪdeɪt] liquidieren (*a. econ.*); *Schuld(en)* tilgen.

liq·uid·ize ['lɪkwɪdaɪz] zerkleinern, pürieren (*im Mixer*); **~·iz·er** [~ə] Mixgerät *n*, Mixer *m*.

liq·uor ['lɪkə] *Brt.* alkoholisches Getränk; *Am.* Schnaps *m*; ⚠ *nicht* Likör.

liq·uo·rice ['lɪkərɪs] Lakritze *f*.

lisp [lɪsp] **1.** Lispeln *n*; **2.** lispeln.

list [lɪst] **1.** Liste *f*, Verzeichnis *n*; **2.** (in e-e Liste) eintragen; verzeichnen, auflisten.

lis·ten ['lɪsn] (*to*) lauschen, horchen (auf *acc.*); anhören (*acc.*); zuhören (*dat.*); hören (auf *acc.*); ~ in (im Radio) hören (*to acc.*); am Telefon mithören; **~·er** [~ə] Zuhörer(in); (Rundfunk)Hörer(in).

list·less ['lɪstlɪs] teilnahms-, lustlos.

lit [lɪt] *pret. u. p.p. von light[1] 3.*

lit·er·al ['lɪtərəl] (wort)wörtlich; buchstäblich; prosaisch.

lit·er·a·ry ['lɪtərərɪ] literarisch, Literatur...; **~·ture** [~rət∫ə] Literatur *f*.

lithe □ [laɪð] geschmeidig, gelenkig.

lit·i·ga·tion ⅌ ['lɪtɪ'geɪʃn] Prozeß *m*.

li·tre, *Am.* **-ter** ['li:tə] Liter *m*, *n*.

lit·ter ['lɪtə] **1.** Sänfte *f*; Tragbahre *f*, Trage *f*; Streu *f*; *zo.* Wurf *m*; Abfall *m*, *bsd.* herumliegendes Papier; Durcheinander *n*, Unordnung *f*; **2.** *v/t. zo.* Junge werfen; verstreuen; be ~ed with übersät sein mit; *v/i. zo.* Junge werfen; ~ **bas·ket**, ~ **bin** Abfallkorb *m*.

lit·tle ['lɪtl] **1.** *adj.* (less, least) klein; gering(fügig), unbedeutend; wenig; ~ one Kleiner *m*, Kleine *f*, Kleines *n* (*Kind*); **2.** *adv.* (less, least) wenig, kaum; überhaupt nicht; **3.** Kleinigkeit *f*; *a* ~ ein bißchen, etwas; ~ by ~ nach und nach; not *a* ~ nicht wenig.

live[1] [lɪv] *v/i.* leben; wohnen; ~ to see erleben; ~ off von ~ s-m *Kapital* etc. leben; auf *j-s* Kosten leben; ~ on leben von; ~ through durchmachen, -stehen; ~ up to s-m Ruf gerecht werden, s-n Grundsätzen gemäß leben; *Versprechen* halten, *Erwartungen* erfüllen; ~ with mit *j-m* zusammenleben; mit etc. leben; *v/t.* Leben führen; ~ s.th. down et. durch guten Lebenswandel vergessen lassen.

live[2] [laɪv] **1.** *adj.* lebend, lebendig;

wirklich, richtig; aktuell; glühend; scharf (*Munition*); ⚡ stromführend, geladen; *Rundfunk, TV*: direkt, Direkt..., live, Live..., Original...; **2.** *adv. Rundfunk, TV*: direkt, live, original.

live|li·hood ['laɪvlɪhʊd] (Lebens)Unterhalt *m*; **~·li·ness** [ˌnɪs] Lebhaftigkeit *f*; **~·ly** [ˌlɪ] (*-ier, -iest*) lebhaft, lebendig; aufregend; schnell; bewegt.

liv·er *anat.* ['lɪvə] Leber *f*.

liv·e·ry ['lɪvərɪ] Livree *f*; (*Amts-*) Tracht *f*.

lives [laɪvz] *pl. von* life.

live·stock ['laɪvstɒk] Vieh(bestand *m*) *n*.

liv·id □ ['lɪvɪd] bläulich; F fuchsteufelswild.

liv·ing ['lɪvɪŋ] **1.** □ lebend(ig); *the ~ image of* das genaue Ebenbild *gen.*; **2.** *das* Leben; Lebensweise *f*; Lebensunterhalt *m*; *eccl.* Pfründe *f*; *the ~ pl.* die Lebenden *pl.*; *standard of ~* Lebensstandard *m*; **~ room** Wohnzimmer *n*.

liz·ard *zo.* ['lɪzəd] Eidechse *f*.

load [ləʊd] **1.** Last *f* (*a. fig.*); Ladung *f*; Belastung *f*; **2.** (auf-, be)laden; *Schußwaffe* laden; *j-n* überhäufen (*with* mit); **~** *a camera* e-n Film einlegen; **~·ing** ['ləʊdɪŋ] Laden *n*; Ladung *f*, Fracht *f*; *attr.* Lade...

loaf¹ [ləʊf] (*pl. loaves* [ˌvz]) Laib *m* (*Brot*); Brot *n*.

loaf² [ˌ] herumlungern; **~·er** ['ləʊfə] Faulenzer(in).

loam [ləʊm] Lehm *m*; **~·y** ['ləʊmɪ] (*-ier, -iest*) lehmig.

loan [ləʊn] **1.** (Ver)Leihen *n*; Anleihe *f*; Darlehen *n*; Leihgabe *f*; *on ~* leihweise; **2.** *bsd. Am.* an *j-n* ausleihen.

loath □ [ləʊθ] abgeneigt; *be ~ to do s.th.* et. ungern tun; **~e** [ləʊð] sich ekeln vor (*dat.*); verabscheuen; **~·ing** ['ləʊðɪŋ] Ekel *m*; Abscheu *m*; **~·some** □ [ˌðsəm] abscheulich, ekelhaft; verhaßt.

loaves [ləʊvz] *pl. von* loaf¹.

lob·by ['lɒbɪ] **1.** Vorhalle *f*; *thea., Film*: Foyer *n*; *parl.* Wandelhalle *f*; *pol.* Lobby *f*, Interessengruppe *f*; **2.** *pol. Abgeordnete* beeinflussen.

lobe *anat.*, **~** [ləʊb] Lappen *m*; *a. ear~* Ohrläppchen *n*.

lob·ster *zo.* ['lɒbstə] Hummer *m*.

lo·cal □ ['ləʊkl] **1.** örtlich, Orts...;

lokal, Lokal...; **~** *government* Gemeindeverwaltung *f*; **2.** Einheimische(r *m*) *f*; *a.* **~** *train* Nahverkehrszug *m*; *the ~ Brt.* F *bsd.* die Stammkneipe; **~·i·ty** [ləʊˈkælətɪ] Örtlichkeit *f*; Lage *f*; **~·ize** ['ləʊkəlaɪz] lokalisieren.

lo·cate [ləʊˈkeɪt] *v/t.* ausfindig machen; orten; *be ~d* liegen, sich befinden; **lo·ca·tion** [ˌeɪʃn] Lage *f*; Standort *m*; Platz (*for* für); *Film*: Gelände *n* für Außenaufnahmen; *on ~* auf Außenaufnahme.

loch *schott.* [lɒk] See *m*.

lock¹ [lɒk] **1.** (*Tür-, Gewehr- etc.*) Schloß *n*; Schleuse(nkammer) *f*; ⊕ Sperrvorrichtung *f*; **2.** (ab-, verzu)schließen, zu-, versperren; umschließen, umfassen; sich schließen lassen; ⊕ blockieren; **~** *away* wegschließen; **~** *in* einschließen, -sperren; **~** *out* aussperren; **~** *up* abschließen; wegschließen; einsperren.

lock² [ˌ] (Haar)Locke *f*.

lock|er ['lɒkə] Schrank *m*, Spind *m*; Schließfach *n*; **~ room** Umkleideraum *m*; **~·et** [ˌɪt] Medaillon *n*; **~·out** *econ.* Aussperrung *f*; **~·smith** Schlosser *m*; **~·up** (Haft)Zelle *f*; Gefängnis *n*.

lo·co *Am. sl.* ['ləʊkəʊ] bekloppt.

lo·co·mo·tion [ləʊkəˈməʊʃn] Fortbewegung(sfähigkeit) *f*; **~·tive** ['ləʊkəməʊtɪv] **1.** (Fort)Bewegungs...; **2.** *a. ~ engine* Lokomotive *f*.

lo·cust *zo.* ['ləʊkəst] Heuschrecke *f*.

lodge [lɒdʒ] **1.** Häuschen *n*; Jagd-, Skihütte *f etc.*; Pförtnerhaus *n*, -loge *f*; (*Freimaurer*)Loge *f*; **2.** *v/i. bsd.* vorübergehend *od.* in Untermiete wohnen; stecken(bleiben) (*Kugel etc.*), (fest)sitzen; *v/t.* aufnehmen, beherbergen, unterbringen; *Kugel* jagen (*in* in *dat.*); *Schlag* versetzen; *Beschwerde* einlegen; *Klage* einreichen; **lodg·er** ['lɒdʒə] Untermieter(in); **lodg·ing** [ˌɪŋ] Unterkunft *f*; **~s** *pl. bsd.* möbliertes Zimmer.

loft [lɒft] (Dach)Boden *m*; Heuboden *m*; Empore *f*; **~·y** □ ['lɒftɪ] (*-ier, -iest*) hoch; erhaben; stolz.

log [lɒg] (Holz)Klotz *m*, (*gefällter*) Baumstamm; ♪ Log *n*; = **~·book** ['lɒgbʊk] ♪, ✈ Logbuch *n*; *mot.* Fahrtenbuch *n*; *Brt. mot.* Kraftfahrzeugbrief *m*; **~ cab·in** Blockhaus *n*, -hütte *f*; **~·ger·head** [ˌəhed]: *be at ~s* sich in den Haaren liegen.

lo·gic ['lɒdʒɪk] Logik *f*; **~al** □ [~kl] logisch.

loins [lɔɪnz] *pl. anat.* Lende *f*; *Kochkunst:* Lende(nstück *n*) *f*.

loi·ter ['lɔɪtə] trödeln, schlendern, bummeln; herumlungern.

loll [lɒl] (sich) rekeln *od.* lümmeln; **~out** heraushängen (*Zunge*).

lol·li·pop ['lɒlɪpɒp] Lutscher *m*; Eis *n* am Stiel; **~ man**, **~ woman** *Brt.* Schülerlotse *m*; **~·ly** F [~'lɒlɪ] Lutscher *m*; **ice(d) ~** Eis *n* am Stiel.

lone·li·ness ['ləʊnlɪnɪs] Einsamkeit *f*; **~·ly** [~lɪ] (*-ier, -iest*), **~some** □ [~səm] einsam.

long[1] [lɒŋ] **1.** (*e-e*) lange Zeit; *before ~* bald; *for ~* lange; *take ~* lange brauchen *od.* dauern; **2.** *adj.* lang; langfristig; *in the ~ run* schließlich; *be ~* lange brauchen *od.* dauern; **3.** *adv.* lang(e); *as od. so ~ as* solange, vorausgesetzt, daß; *~ ago* vor langer Zeit; *no ~er* nicht mehr, nicht länger; *so ~!* F bis dann!, tschüs!

long[2] [~] sich sehnen (*for* nach).

long·dis·tance ['lɒŋ'dɪstəns] Fern...; *Langstrecken...;* **~ call** *teleph.* Ferngespräch *n*; **~ runner** *Sport:* Langstreckenläufer *m*.

lon·gev·i·ty [lɒn'dʒevətɪ] Langlebigkeit *f*.

long·hand ['lɒŋhænd] Schreibschrift *f*.

long·ing ['lɒŋɪŋ] **1.** □ sehnsüchtig; **2.** Sehnsucht *f*, Verlangen *n*.

lon·gi·tude *geogr.* ['lɒndʒɪtjuːd] Länge *f*.

long jump ['lɒŋdʒʌmp] *Sport:* Weitsprung *m*; **~·shore·man** [~'ʃɔːmən] (*pl. -men*) Hafenarbeiter *m*; **~sight·ed** □ [lɒŋ'saɪtɪd] weitsichtig; **~stand·ing** seit langer Zeit bestehend; alt; **~term** langfristig, auf lange Sicht; **~ wave** *≠* Langwelle *f*; **~wind·ed** □ langatmig.

loo *Brt.* F [luː] Klo *n*.

look [lʊk] **1.** Blick *m*; Miene *f*, (Gesichts)Ausdruck *m*; (*good*) *~s pl.* gutes Aussehen; *have a ~ at s.th.* sich et. ansehen; *I don't like the ~ of it* es gefällt mir nicht; **2.** sehen, blicken, schauen (*at, on* auf *acc., nach*); nachsehen; *krank etc.* aussehen; aufpassen, achten; *nach e-r Richtung* liegen, gehen (*Fenster etc.*); *~ here!* schau mal (her); hör mal (zu)!; *~ like* aussehen wie; *it ~s as if* es sieht (so) aus, als ob; *~ after* aufpassen auf

(*acc.*), sich kümmern um, sorgen für; *~ ahead* nach vorne sehen; *fig.* vorausschauen; *~ around* sich umsehen; *~ at* ansehen; *~ back* sich umsehen; *fig.* zurückblicken; *~ down* herab-, heruntersehen (*a. fig. on s.o.* auf j-n); *~ for* suchen; *~ forward to* sich freuen auf (*acc.*); *~ in* F hereinsehen (*on bei*) (*als Besucher*); F *TV* fernsehen; *~ into* untersuchen, prüfen; *~ on* zusehen, -schauen (*dat.*); *~ on* to liegen zu, (hinaus)gehen auf (*acc.*) (*Fenster, etc.*); *~ on, ~ upon* betrachten, ansehen (*as* als); *~ out* hinaus-, heraussehen; aufpassen, sich vorsehen; Ausschau halten (*for* nach); *~ over et.* durchsehen; *j-n* mustern; *~ round* sich umsehen; *~ through et.* durchsehen; *~ up* aufblicken, -sehen; *et.* nachschlagen; *j-n* aufsuchen.

look·ing-glass ['lʊkɪŋglɑːs] Spiegel *m*.

look-out ['lʊkaʊt] Ausguck *m*; Ausschau *f*; *fig.* F Aussicht(en *pl.*) *f*; *that is my ~* F das ist meine Sache.

loom [luːm] **1.** Webstuhl *m*; **2.** *a. ~ up* undeutlich sichtbar werden *od.* auftauchen.

loop [luːp] **1.** Schlinge *f*, Schleife *f*; Schlaufe *f*; Öse *f*; *≫* Looping *m*, *n*; *Computer:* Programmschleife *f*; **2.** *v/t.* in Schleifen legen; schlingen; *v/i. e-e* Schleife machen; sich schlingen; **~hole** ['luːphəʊl] *≫* Schießscharte *f*; *fig.* Hintertürchen *n*; *a ~ in the law e-e* Gesetzeslücke.

loose [luːs] **1.** □ (*~r, ~st*) los(e); locker; weit; frei; ungenau; liederlich; *let ~* loslassen; freilassen; **2.** *be on the ~* frei herumlaufen; **loos·en** ['luːsn] (sich) lösen, (sich) lockern; *~ up Sport:* Lockerungsübungen machen.

loot [luːt] **1.** plündern; **2.** Beute *f*.

lop [lɒp] (*-pp-*) *Baum* beschneiden, stutzen; *~ off* abhauen, abhacken; **~sid·ed** □ ['lɒp'saɪdɪd] schief; einseitig.

lo·qua·cious □ [ləʊ'kweɪʃəs] redselig, geschwätzig.

lord [lɔːd] Herr *m*, Gebieter *m*; Lord *m*; *the ♀ der* Herr (*Gott*); *my ~* [mɪ'lɔːd] Mylord, Euer Gnaden, Euer Ehren (*Anrede*); *♀ Mayor Brt.* Oberbürgermeister *m*; *the ♀'s Prayer* das Vaterunser; *the ♀'s Supper* das Abendmahl; **~·ly** ['lɔːdlɪ]

(-ier, -iest) vornehm, edel; gebieterisch; hochmütig, arrogant; **~ship** [~ʃɪp]: *his od. your ~* seine od. Euer Lordschaft.

lore [lɔː] Kunde *f*; Überlieferungen *pl*.

lor·ry *Brt*. ['lɒrɪ] Last(kraft)wagen *m*, Lastauto *n*, Laster *m*; 🚊 Lore *f*.

lose [luːz] (*lost*) *v/t.* verlieren; verpassen, -säumen; *et.* nicht mitbekommen; nachgehen (*Uhr*); *j-n s-e Stellung kosten; ~ o.s.* sich verirren; sich verlieren; *v/i.* Verluste erleiden; verlieren; nachgehen (*Uhr*); **los·er** ['luːzə] Verlierer(in).

loss [lɒs] Verlust *m*; Schaden *m*; *at a ~ econ.* mit Verlust; *be at a ~* nicht mehr weiterwissen.

lost [lɒst] **1.** *pret. u. p.p. von lose*; **2.** *adj.* verloren; verlorengegangen; verirrt; verschwunden; verloren, -geudet (*Zeit*); versäumt (*Gelegenheit*); *be ~ in thought* in Gedanken versunken od. -tieft sein; *~ property office* Fundbüro *n*.

lot [lɒt] Los *n*; *econ.* Partie *f*, Posten (*Ware*) *m*; *bsd. Am.* Bauplatz *m*; *bsd. Am.* Parkplatz *m*; *bsd. Am.* Filmgelände *n*; F Gruppe *f*, Gesellschaft *f*; Los *n*, Schicksal *n*; △ *nicht Lot*; *the ~* F alles, das Ganze; *a ~ of* F, *~s of* F viel, e-e Menge; *~s of Am. od. ~s of* F jede Menge; *a bad ~* F ein übler Kerl; *cast od. draw ~s* losen.

loth [ləʊθ] = *loath*.

lo·tion ['ləʊʃn] Lotion *f*.

lot·te·ry ['lɒtərɪ] Lotterie *f*.

loud [laʊd] laut (*a. adv.*); *fig.* schreiend, grell (*Farben etc.*); **~·speak·er** ['laʊdspiːkə] Lautsprecher *m*.

lounge [laʊndʒ] **1.** faulenzen; herumlungern; schlendern; **2.** Bummel *m*; Wohnzimmer *n*; Aufenthaltsraum *m*, Lounge *f* (*e-s Hotels*); Warteraum *m*, Lounge *f* (*e-s Flughafens*); **~ suit** Straßenanzug *m*.

louse *zo.* [laʊs] (*pl. lice* [laɪs]) Laus *f*; **lou·sy** ['laʊzɪ] (-ier, -iest) verlaust; F miserabel, saumäßig.

lout [laʊt] Flegel *m*, Lümmel *m*.

lov·a·ble □ ['lʌvəbl] liebenswert; reizend.

love [lʌv] **1.** Liebe *f* (*of, for, to, towards* zu); Liebling *m*, Schatz *m*; *Brt.* m-e Liebe, mein Lieber, mein Liebes (*Anrede*); *Tennis:* null; *be in ~ with s.o.* in j-n verliebt sein; *fall in* ~ *with s.o.* sich in j-n verlieben; *make ~* sich lieben, miteinander schlafen; *give my ~ to her* grüße sie herzlich von mir; *send one's ~ to j-n* grüßen lassen; ~ *from* herzliche Grüße von (*Briefschluß*); **2.** lieben; gern mögen; **~·af·fair** Liebesaffäre *f*; **~·ly** ['lʌvlɪ] (-ier, -iest) lieblich, wunderschön, entzückend, reizend; **lov·er** [~ə] Liebhaber *m*, Geliebte(r) *m*; Geliebte *f*; Liebhaber(in), (*Tieretc.*)Freund(in).

lov·ing □ ['lʌvɪŋ] liebevoll, liebend.

low¹ [ləʊ] **1.** *adj.* nieder, niedrig (*a. fig.*); tief; gering(schätzig); knapp (*Vorrat*); gedämpft, schwach (*Licht*); schwach, matt; niedergeschlagen; *sozial* untere(r, -s), niedrig; gewöhnlich, niedrig (*denkend od. gesinnt*); gemein; tief (*Ton*); leise (*Ton, Stimme*); **2.** *adv.* niedrig; tief (*a. fig.*); leise; **3.** *meteor.* Tief(druckgebiet) *n*; Tiefstand *m*, -punkt *m*.

low² [ləʊ] brüllen, muhen (*Rind*).

low·brow F ['ləʊbraʊ] **1.** geistig Anspruchslose(r *m*) *f*; **2.** geistig anspruchslos.

low·er ['ləʊə] **1.** niedriger, tiefer; geringer; leiser; untere(r, -s), Unter...; **2.** *v/t.* herunterlassen; niedriger machen; *Augen, Stimme, Preis etc.* senken; (ab)schwächen; *Standard* herabsetzen; erniedrigen; ~ *o.s.* sich herablassen; sich demütigen; *v/i.* fallen, sinken.

low·land ['ləʊlənd] *mst ~s pl.* Tiefland *n*; **~·li·ness** [~lɪnɪs] Niedrigkeit *f*; Bescheidenheit *f*; **~·ly** [~lɪ] (-ier, -iest) niedrig; bescheiden; **~·necked** (tief) ausgeschnitten (*Kleid*); **~·pitched** ♪ tief; **~·pres·sure** *meteor.* Tiefdruck...; ⊕ Niederdruck...; **~·rise** *bsd. Am.* niedrig (gebaut); **~·spir·it·ed** niedergeschlagen.

loy·al □ ['lɔɪəl] loyal, treu; **~·ty** [~tɪ] Loyalität *f*, Treue *f*.

loz·enge ['lɒzɪndʒ] Raute *f*; Pastille *f*.

lu·bri·cant ['luːbrɪkənt] Schmiermittel *n*; **~·cate** [~keɪt] schmieren, ölen; **~·ca·tion** [luːbrɪˈkeɪʃn] Schmieren *n*, Ölen *n*.

lu·cid □ ['luːsɪd] klar; deutlich.

luck [lʌk] Schicksal *n*; Glück *n*; *bad ~, hard ~* Unglück *n*, Pech *n*; *good ~ Glück n; good ~! viel Glück!; be in (out of) ~* (kein) Glück haben; **~·i·ly** ['lʌkɪlɪ] glücklicherweise, zum Glück; **~·y** □ [~ɪ] (-ier, -iest) glücklich; Glücks...; _be_ ~ Glück haben.

lu·cra·tive □ ['lu:krətɪv] einträglich, lukrativ.

lu·di·crous □ ['lu:dɪkrəs] lächerlich.

lug [lʌɡ] (-_gg_-) zerren, schleppen.

lug·gage _bsd. Brt._ ['lʌɡɪdʒ] (Reise-) Gepäck _n_; ~ **car·ri·er** Gepäckträger _m (am Fahrrad)_; ~ **rack** Gepäcknetz _n_, -ablage _f_; ~ **van** _bsd. Brt._ Gepäckwagen _m_.

luke·warm ['lu:kwɔ:m] lau(warm); _fig._ lau, mäßig.

lull [lʌl] **1.** beruhigen; sich legen _od._ beruhigen; _mst_ ~ _to sleep_ einlullen; **2.** Pause _f_; Flaute _f (a. econ.)_, Windstille _f_.

lul·la·by ['lʌləbaɪ] Wiegenlied _n_.

lum·ba·go 𝓰 [lʌm'beɪɡəʊ] Hexenschuß _m_.

lum·ber ['lʌmbə] **1.** _bsd. Am._ Bau-, Nutzholz _n_; _bsd. Brt._ Gerümpel _n_; **2.** _v/t._ ~ _s.o. with s.th. Brt._ F j-m et. aufhalsen; _v/i._ rumpeln, poltern _(Wagen)_; schwerfällig gehen, trampeln; ~**jack**, ~**man** (_pl._ -**men**) _bsd. Am._ Holzfäller _m_, -arbeiter _m_; ~ **mill** Sägewerk _n_; ~ **room** Rumpelkammer _f_; ~**yard** Holzplatz _m_, -lager _n_.

lu·mi·na·ry ['lu:mɪnərɪ] Himmelskörper _m_; _fig._ Leuchte _f_, Koryphäe _f_; ~**nous** □ [~əs] leuchtend, Leucht...

lump [lʌmp] **1.** Klumpen _m_; Beule _f_; Stück _n_ (_Zucker etc._); △ _nicht_ Lump; _in the_ ~ in Bausch und Bogen; ~ _sugar_ Würfelzucker _m_; ~ _sum_ Pauschalsumme _f_; **2.** _v/t._ zusammentun, -stellen, -legen, -werfen, -fassen; _v/i._ Klumpen bilden; ~**y** □ [~ɪ] (-_ier_, -_iest_) klumpig.

lu·na·cy ['lu:nəsɪ] Wahnsinn _m_.

lu·nar ['lu:nə] Mond...; ~ _module_ Raumfahrt: Mond(lande)fähre _f_.

lu·na·tic ['lu:nətɪk] **1.** irr-, wahnsinnig; **2.** Irre(r _m_) _f_, Wahnsinnige(r _m_) _f_, Geisteskranke(r _m_) _f_.

lunch [lʌntʃ], _formell_ **lun·cheon** ['lʌntʃən] **1.** Lunch _m_, Mittagessen

_n_; **2.** zu Mittag essen; ~ **hour**, ~ **time** Mittagszeit _f_, -pause _f_.

lung _anat._ [lʌŋ] Lunge(nflügel _m_) _f_; _the_ ~_s pl._ die Lunge.

lunge [lʌndʒ] **1.** _Fechten:_ Ausfall _m_; **2.** _v/i. Fechten:_ e-n Ausfall machen (_at_ gegen); losstürzen (_at auf acc._).

lurch [lɜ:tʃ] **1.** taumeln, torkeln; **2.** _leave in the_ ~ im Stich lassen.

lure [ljʊə] **1.** Köder _m_; _fig._ Lockung _f_; **2.** ködern, (an)locken.

lu·rid □ ['ljʊərɪd] grell, schreiend (_Farben etc._); schockierend, widerlich.

lurk [lɜ:k] lauern; ~ _about_, ~ _around_ herumschleichen.

lus·cious □ ['lʌʃəs] köstlich, lecker; üppig; knackig (_Mädchen_).

lush [lʌʃ] saftig, üppig.

lust [lʌst] **1.** sinnliche Begierde, Lust _f_; Gier _f_; △ _nicht_ Lust (_Freude etc._); **2.** ~ _after_, ~ _for_ begehren; gierig sein nach.

lus|tre, _Am._ **-ter** ['lʌstə] Glanz _m_, Schimmer _m_; ~**trous** □ [~rəs] glänzend, schimmernd.

lust·y □ ['lʌstɪ] (-_ier_, -_iest_) kräftig, stark u. gesund, vital; kraftvoll.

lute ♪ [lu:t] Laute _f_.

Lu·ther·an ['lu:θərən] lutherisch.

lux·ate 𝓰 ['lʌkseɪt] verrenken.

lux·u·ri·ant □ [lʌɡ'zjʊərɪənt] üppig; ~**ri·ate** [~ieɪt] schwelgen (_in in dat._); ~**ri·ous** □ [~ɪəs] luxuriös, üppig, Luxus...; ~**ry** ['lʌkʃərɪ] Luxus _m_; Komfort _m_; Luxusartikel _m_; _attr._ Luxus...

lye [laɪ] Lauge _f_.

ly·ing ['laɪɪŋ] **1.** _p.pr. von_ lie[1] 2 _u._ lie[2] 2; **2.** _adj._ lügnerisch, verlogen; ~**in** [~'ɪn] Wochenbett _n_.

lymph 𝓰 [lɪmf] Lymphe _f_.

lynch [lɪntʃ] lynchen; ~ _law_ ['lɪntʃlɔ:] Lynchjustiz _f_.

lynx _zo._ [lɪŋks] Luchs _m_.

lyr|ic ['lɪrɪk] **1.** lyrisch; **2.** lyrisches Gedicht; ~_s pl._ Lyrik _f_; (Lied)Text _m_; ~**i·cal** □ [~kl] lyrisch, gefühlvoll; schwärmerisch.

M

ma F [mɑ:] Mama f, Mutti f.

ma'am [mæm] Majestät (Anrede für die Königin); (königliche) Hoheit (Anrede für Prinzessinnen); F [məm] gnä' Frau (Anrede).

mac Brt. F [mæk] = mackintosh.

ma·cad·am [mə'kædəm] Schotterdecke f (Straßenbau).

mac·a·ro·ni [mækə'rəʊnɪ] Makkaroni pl.

mac·a·roon [mækə'ru:n] Makrone f.

mach·i·na·tion [mækɪ'neɪʃn] (tückischer) Anschlag; ~s pl. Ränke pl.

ma·chine [mə'ʃi:n] 1. Maschine f; Mechanismus m; 2. maschinell herstellen od. drucken; mit der (Näh-)Maschine nähen; ~made maschinell hergestellt.

ma·chin|e·ry [mə'ʃi:nərɪ] Maschinen pl.; Maschinerie f; ~ist [~ɪst] Maschinenbauer m; Maschinist m; Maschinennäherin f.

mack Brt. F [mæk] = mackintosh.

mack·e·rel zo. ['mækrəl] Makrele f.

mack·in·tosh bsd. Brt. ['mækɪntɒʃ] Regenmantel m.

mac·ro- ['mækrəʊ] Makro..., (sehr) groß.

mad □ [mæd] wahnsinnig, verrückt; toll(wütig); F wütend; fig. wild; go ~, Am. get ~ verrückt od. wahnsinnig werden; drive s.o. ~ j-n verrückt od. wahnsinnig machen; like ~ wie toll, wie verrückt (arbeiten etc.).

mad·am ['mædəm] gnädige Frau, gnädiges Fräulein (Anrede).

mad|cap ['mædkæp] 1. verrückt; 2. verrückter Kerl; ~den [~n] verrückt od. rasend machen; ~den·ing □ [~ɪŋ] verrückt od. rasend machend.

made [meɪd] pret. u. p.p. von make 1; ~ of gold aus Gold.

mad|house ['mædhaʊs] Irrenhaus n; ~ly [~lɪ] wie verrückt, wie besessen; F irre, wahnsinnig; ~man (pl. -men) Wahnsinnige(r) m, Verrückte(r) m; ~ness [~nɪs] Wahnsinn m; (Toll)Wut f; ~wom·an (pl. -women) Wahnsinnige f, Verrückte f.

mag·a·zine [mægə'zi:n] Magazin n; (Munitions)Lager n; Zeitschrift f.

mag·got zo. ['mægət] Made f, Larve f.

Ma·gi ['meɪdʒaɪ] pl.: the (three) ~ die (drei) Weisen aus dem Morgenland, die Heiligen Drei Könige.

ma·gic ['mædʒɪk] 1. (~ally) a. ~al □ [~l] magisch, Zauber...; 2. Zauberei f; Zauber m; fig. Wunder n; **ma·gi·cian** [mə'dʒɪʃn] Zauberer m; Zauberkünstler m.

ma·gis|tra·cy ['mædʒɪstrəsɪ] Richteramt n; die Richter pl.; ~trate [~eɪt] (Polizei-, Friedens)Richter m; △ nicht Magistrat.

mag|na·nim·i·ty [mægnə'nɪmətɪ] Großmut m; ~nan·i·mous □ [mæg'nænɪməs] großmütig, hochherzig.

mag·net ['mægnɪt] Magnet m; ~ic [mæg'netɪk] (~ally) magnetisch, Magnet...

mag·nif|i·cence [mæg'nɪfɪsns] Pracht f, Herrlichkeit f; ~i·cent [~t] prächtig, herrlich.

mag·ni|fy ['mægnɪfaɪ] vergrößern; ~ing glass Vergrößerungsglas n, Lupe f; ~tude [~tju:d] Größe f; Wichtigkeit f.

mag·pie zo. ['mægpaɪ] Elster f.

ma·hog·a·ny [mə'hɒgənɪ] Mahagoni(holz) n.

maid [meɪd] veraltet od. lit. (junges) Mädchen n, (junge) unverheiratete Frau; (Dienst)Mädchen n, Hausangestellte f; old ~ alte Jungfer; ~ of all work Mädchen n für alles; ~ of honour Ehren-, Hofdame f; bsd. Am. (erste) Brautjungfer.

maid·en ['meɪdn] 1. = maid; 2. jungfräulich; unverheiratet; fig. Jungfern..., Erstlings...; ~ name Mädchenname m (e-r Frau); ~head veraltet Jungfräulichkeit f; ~hood lit. [~hʊd] Jungmädchenzeit f; ~ly [~lɪ] jungfräulich; mädchenhaft.

mail[1] [meɪl] (Ketten)Panzer m.

mail[2] [~] 1. Post(dienst m) f; Post(-sendung) f; by ~ mit der Post; 2. bsd. Am. mit der Post schicken, aufgeben; ~a·ble Am. ['meɪləbl] postversandfähig; ~bag Postsack m; Am. Posttasche f (e-s Briefträgers); ~box Am. Briefkasten m; ~ car·ri·er Am., ~man (pl. -men) Am. Briefträger m, Postbote m; ~ or·der Bestellung f (von Waren) durch die Post; ~or·der firm, bsd. Am. ~or·der house Versandgeschäft n, -haus n.

malign

maim [meɪm] verstümmeln, zum Krüppel machen.

main [meɪn] **1.** Haupt..., größte(r, -s), wichtigste(r, -s); hauptsächlich; by ~ force mit äußerster Kraft; ~ road Haupt(verkehrs)straße f; **2.** mar ~s pl. Haupt(gas-, -wasser-, -strom-)leitung f; (Strom)Netz n; in the ~ in der Hauptsache, im wesentlichen; ~**land** [~lənd] Festland n; ~**ly** [~lɪ] hauptsächlich; ~**spring** Triebfeder f (e-r Uhr); fig. Triebfeder f; ~**stay** ♣ Großstag n; fig. Hauptstütze f; ⚲ **Street** Am. provinziell-materialistisch; ⚲ **Street·er** Am. provinzieller Spießer.

main·tain [meɪnˈteɪn] (aufrecht)er-halten, beibehalten; instand halten, ⊕ a. warten; unterstützen; unterhal-ten; behaupten.

main·te·nance [ˈmeɪntənəns] Erhal-tung f; Unterhalt m; Instandhaltung f, ⊕ a. Wartung f.

maize bsd. Brt. ⚲ [meɪz] Mais m.

ma·jes·tic [məˈdʒestɪk] (~ally) maje-stätisch; ~**ty** [ˈmædʒəstɪ] Majestät f; Würde f, Hoheit f.

ma·jor [ˈmeɪdʒə] **1.** größere(r, -s); fig. a. bedeutend, wichtig; ⚲ voll-jährig; C ~ ♪ C-Dur n; ~ key ♪ Dur(tonart f) n; ~ league Am. Base-ball: oberste Spielklasse; ~ road Haupt(verkehrs)straße f; **2.** ⚔ Major m; ⚲ Volljährige(r m) f; Am. univ. Hauptfach n; ♪ Dur n; ~**gen·er·al** ⚔ Generalmajor m; ~**i·ty** [məˈdʒɒrətɪ] Mehrheit f, Mehrzahl f; ⚲ Volljährigkeit f; ⚔ Majorsrang m.

make [meɪk] **1.** (made) v/t. machen; anfertigen, herstellen, erzeugen; (zu)bereiten; bilden; (er)schaffen; (aus)machen; (er)geben; machen zu; ernennen zu; j-n lassen, veran-lassen zu, bringen zu, zwingen zu; verdienen; sich erweisen als, abge-ben; schätzen auf (acc.); ⸢ et. er-reichen, et. schaffen; Fehler ma-chen; Frieden etc. schließen; e-e Rede halten; ⸢ Strecke zurücklegen; Uhr-zeit feststellen; ~ s.th. do, ~ do with s.th. mit et. auskommen, sich mit et. behelfen; do you ~ one of us? ma-chen Sie mit?; what do you ~ of it? was halten Sie davon?; ~ friends with sich anfreunden mit; ~ good wieder-gutmachen; Versprechen etc. halten, erfüllen; ~ haste sich beeilen; ~ way Platz machen; vorwärtskommen;

v/i. sich anschicken (to do zu tun); sich begeben; führen, gehen (Weg etc.); mit Adverbien u. Präpositionen: ~ away with sich davonmachen mit (Geld etc.); beseitigen; ~ for zugehen auf (acc.); sich aufmachen nach; ~ into verarbeiten zu; ~ off sich davon-machen, sich aus dem Staub ma-chen; ~ out ausfindig machen; er-kennen; verstehen; entziffern; Rech-nung etc. ausstellen; ~ over Eigentum übertragen; ~ up ergänzen, vervoll-ständigen; zusammenstellen; bil-den, ausmachen; sich et. ausdenken; Streit beilegen; (sich) zurechtma-chen od. schminken; ~ up one's mind sich entschließen; be made up of bestehen aus, sich zusammenset-zen aus; ~ up (for) nach-, aufholen; für et. entschädigen; **2.** Mach-, Bau-art f; (Körper)Bau m; Form f; Fabri-kat n, Erzeugnis n; ~**be·lieve** [ˈmeɪkbɪliːv] Schein m, Vorwand m, Verstellung f; ⚲ [~ə] Hersteller m; ⚲ Schöpfer m (Gott); ~**shift 1.** Not-behelf m; **2.** behelfsmäßig, Be-helfs...; ~**up** typ. Umbruch m; Auf-machung f; Schminke f, Make-up n.

mak·ing [ˈmeɪkɪŋ] Machen n; Erzeu-gung f, Herstellung f; this will be the ~ of him damit ist er ein gemachter Mann; he has the ~s of er hat das Zeug od. die Anlagen zu.

mal- [mæl] s. bad(ly).

mal·ad·just·ed [mæləˈdʒʌstɪd] schlecht angepaßt od. angeglichen; ~**ment** [~mənt] schlechte Anpas-sung.

mal·ad·min·is·tra·tion [ˈmæləd-mɪnɪsˈtreɪʃn] schlechte Verwaltung; pol. Mißwirtschaft f.

mal·a·dy [ˈmælədɪ] Krankheit f.

mal·con·tent [ˈmælkəntent] **1.** unzu-frieden; **2.** Unzufriedene(r m) f.

male [meɪl] **1.** männlich; Männer...; **2.** Mann m; zo. Männchen n.

mal·e·dic·tion [mælɪˈdɪkʃn] Fluch m, Verwünschung f.

mal·e·fac·tor [ˈmælɪfæktə] Übeltäter m.

ma·lev·o·lence [məˈlevələns] Bos-heit f; ~**lent** □ [~t] feindlich.

mal·for·ma·tion [mælfɔːˈmeɪʃn] Mißbildung f.

mal·ice [ˈmælɪs] Bosheit f; Groll m.

ma·li·cious □ [məˈlɪʃəs] boshaft; böswillig; ~**ness** [~nɪs] Bosheit f.

ma·lign [məˈlaɪn] **1.** □ schädlich; **2.**

verleumden; **ma·lig·nant** □ [mə-ˈlɪgnənt] bösartig (*a.* 🞩); boshaft; **ma·lig·ni·ty** [~ətɪ] Bösartigkeit *f* (*a.* 🞩); Bosheit *f*.

mall *Am.* [mɔːl, mæl] Einkaufszentrum *n*.

mal·le·a·ble [ˈmælɪəbl] hämmerbar; *fig.* formbar, geschmeidig.

mal·let [ˈmælɪt] Holzhammer *m*; (Krocket-, Polo)Schläger *m*.

mal·nu·tri·tion [ˈmælnjuːˈtrɪʃn] Unterernährung *f*; Fehlernährung *f*.

mal·o·dor·ous □ [mælˈəʊdərəs] übelriechend.

mal·prac·tice 🜂 [ˈmælˈpræktɪs] ⚖ falsche Behandlung; Amtsvergehen *n*; Untreue (*im Amt etc.*).

malt [mɔːlt] Malz *n*.

mal·treat [mælˈtriːt] schlecht behandeln; mißhandeln.

ma·ma, mam·ma [məˈmɑː] Mama *f*, Mutti *f*.

mam·mal *zo.* [ˈmæml] Säugetier *n*.

mam·moth [ˈmæməθ] **1.** Mammut *n*; **2.** riesig.

mam·my *F* [ˈmæmɪ] Mami *f*; *Am. contp.* farbiges Kindermädchen.

man [mæn] **1.** [*in nachgestellten Zssgn:* -mən] (*pl. men* [men; *in nachgestellten Zssgn:* -mən]) Mann *m*; Mensch(en *pl.*) *m*; Menschheit *f*; Diener *m*; Angestellte(r) *m*; Arbeiter *m*; ✕ Mann *m*, (einfacher) Soldat; (Ehe)Mann *m*; *F* Freund *m*, *F* Geliebte(r) *m*; (Schach)Figur *f*; Damestein *m*; *the* ~ *in* (*Am. a. on*) *the street* der Mann auf der Straße, der Durchschnittsbürger; **2.** männlich; **3.** (*-nn-*)✕, ⚓ bemannen; ~ *o.s.* sich ermannen.

man·age [ˈmænɪdʒ] *v/t.* handhaben; verwalten; *Betrieb etc.* leiten *od.* führen; *Gut etc.* bewirtschaften; *Künstler, Sportler* managen; mit *j-m* fertig werden; *et.* fertigbringen; *F Arbeit, Essen etc.* bewältigen, schaffen; ~ *to inf.* es fertigbringen, zu *inf.*; *v/i.* die Aufsicht haben, das Geschäft führen; auskommen; *F* es schaffen; *F* es einrichten, es ermöglichen; ~·**a·ble** □ [~əbl] handlich; lenksam; ~·**ment** [~mənt] Verwaltung *f*; *econ.* Management *n*, Unternehmensführung *f*; *econ.* (Geschäfts)Leitung *f*, Direktion *f*; Bewirtschaftung *f*; Geschicklichkeit *f*, (kluge) Taktik; ~ *studies* Betriebswirtschaft *f*; *labo(u)r and* ~ Arbeitnehmer u. Arbeitgeber.

man·ag·er [ˈmænɪdʒə] Verwalter *m*; *econ.* Manager *m*; *econ.* Geschäftsführer *m*, Leiter *m*, Direktor *m*; *thea.* Intendant *m*; *thea.* Regisseur *m*; Manager *m* (*e-s Schauspielers etc.*); (Guts)Verwalter *m*; *Sport:* Cheftrainer *m*; *be a good* ~ gut *od.* sparsam wirtschaften können; ~·**ess** [mænɪ-dʒəˈres] Verwalterin *f*; *econ.* Managerin *f*; *econ.* Geschäftsführerin *f*, Leiterin *f*, Direktorin *f*; Managerin *f* (*e-s Schauspielers etc.*).

man·a·ge·ri·al *econ.* [mænəˈdʒɪərɪəl] geschäftsführend, leitend; ~ *position* leitende Stellung; ~ *staff* leitende Angestellte *pl.*

man·ag·ing *econ.* [ˈmænɪdʒɪŋ] geschäftsführend; Betriebs...

man|date [ˈmændeɪt] Mandat *n*; Befehl *m*; Auftrag *m*; Vollmacht *f*; ~·**da·to·ry** [~ətərɪ] vorschreibend, befehlend; obligatorisch.

mane [meɪn] Mähne *f*.

ma·neu·ver [məˈnuːvə] = *manoeuvre*.

man·ful □ [ˈmænfl] mannhaft, beherzt.

mange *vet.* [meɪndʒ] Räude *f*.

manger [ˈmeɪndʒə] Krippe *f*.

man·gle [ˈmæŋgl] **1.** (Wäsche)Mangel *f*; **2.** mangeln; übel zurichten, zerfleischen; *fig.* verstümmeln.

mang·y □ [ˈmeɪndʒɪ] (*-ier, -iest*) *vet.* räudig; *fig.* schäbig.

man·hood [ˈmænhʊd] Mannesalter *n*; Männlichkeit *f*; die Männer *pl.*

ma·ni·a [ˈmeɪnjə] Wahn(sinn) *m*; *fig.* (*for*) Sucht *f* (*nach*), Leidenschaft (*für*), Manie *f* (*für*); ~**c** [ˈmeɪnɪæk] Wahnsinnige(r *m*) *f*; *fig.* Fanatiker *m*.

man·i·cure [ˈmænɪkjʊə] **1.** Maniküre *f*; **2.** maniküren.

man·i|fest [ˈmænɪfest] **1.** □ offenbar, -kundig, deutlich (erkennbar); **2.** *v/t.* offenbaren, kundtun, deutlich zeigen; ⚓ Ladungsverzeichnis *n*; ~**·fes·ta·tion** [mænɪfeˈsteɪʃn] Offenbarung *f*; Kundgebung *f*; △ *nicht Manifest*; ~**·fes·to** [mænɪˈfestəʊ] (*pl. -tos, -toes*) Manifest *n*; *pol.* Grundsatzerklärung *f*, Programm *n* (*e-r Partei*).

man·i·fold [ˈmænɪfəʊld] **1.** □ mannigfaltig; **2.** vervielfältigen.

ma·nip·u|late [məˈnɪpjʊleɪt] manipulieren; (geschickt) handhaben; ~**·la·tion** [mənɪpjʊˈleɪʃn] Manipulation f; Handhabung f, Behandlung f, Verfahren n; Kniff m.

man|jack [mæn'dʒæk]: *every* ~ jeder einzelne; **~·kind** [mæn'kaind] die Menschheit, die Menschen *pl.*; ['mænkaind] die Männer *pl.*; **~·ly** ['mænli] (*-ier*, *-iest*) männlich; mannhaft.

man·ner ['mænə] Art f, Weise f, Art f u. Weise f; Stil(art f) m; Art f (*sich zu geben*); **~s** *pl.* Benehmen n, Manieren *pl.*; Sitten *pl.*; *in a* ~ gewissermaßen; **~ed** ...geartet; gekünstelt; **~·ly** [~li] manierlich, gesittet, anständig.

ma·noeu·vre, *Am.* **ma·neu·ver** [mə'nu:və] **1.** Manöver n (*a. fig.*); **2.** manövrieren (*a. fig.*).

man-of-war *veraltet* ['mænəv'wɔ:] (*pl.* men-of-war) Kriegsschiff n.

man·or *Brt.* ['mænə] *hist.* Rittergut n; (Land)Gut n; *jur.* Polizeibezirk m; *lord of the* ~ Gutsherr m; = **~-house** Herrenhaus n, -sitz m.

man·pow·er ['mænpauə] menschliche Arbeitskraft; Menschenpotential n; Arbeitskräfte pl.

man·ser·vant ['mænsɜ:vənt] (*pl.* menservants) Diener m.

man·sion ['mænʃn] (herrschaftliches) Wohnhaus.

man·slaugh·ter ☆ ['mænslɔ:tə] Totschlag m, fahrlässige Tötung.

man·tel|piece ['mæntlpi:s], **~·shelf** (*pl.* -shelves) Kaminsims m.

man·tle ['mæntl] **1.** ⊕ Glühstrumpf m; *fig.* Hülle f; *a* ~ *of snow* e-e Schneedecke; △ *nicht* Mantel; **2.** (sich) überziehen; einhüllen.

man·u·al ['mænjuəl] **1.** □ Hand...; mit der Hand (gemacht); **2.** Handbuch n.

man·u·fac·ture [mænju'fæktʃə] **1.** Herstellung f, Fabrikation f; Fabrikat n; **2.** (an-, ver)fertigen, erzeugen, herstellen, fabrizieren; verarbeiten; **~·tur·er** [~rə] Hersteller m, Erzeuger m; Fabrikant m; **~·tur·ing** [~ɪŋ] Herstellungs...; Fabrik...; Gewerbe...; Industrie...

ma·nure [mə'njuə] **1.** Dünger m, Mist m, Dung m; **2.** düngen.

man·u·script ['mænjuskript] Manuskript n; Handschrift f.

man·y ['meni] **1.** (*more, most*) viel(e); ~ (*a*) manche(r, -s), manch eine(r, -s); ~ *times* oft; *as* ~ ebensoviel(e); *be one too* ~ *for s.o.* j-m überlegen sein; **2.** viele; Menge f; a

---

good ~ ziemlich viel(e); *a great* ~ sehr viele.

map [mæp] **1.** (Land- *etc.*)Karte f; (Stadt- *etc.*)Plan m; △ *nicht* Mappe; **2.** (-*pp*-) e-e Karte machen von; auf e-r Karte eintragen; ~ *out* *fig.* planen; einteilen.

ma·ple ♀ ['meipl] Ahorn m.

mar [mɑ:] (-*rr*-) schädigen; verderben.

ma·raud [mə'rɔ:d] plündern.

mar·ble ['mɑ:bl] **1.** Marmor m; Murmel f; **2.** marmorn.

March¹ [mɑ:tʃ] März m.

march² [~] **1.** Marsch m; *fig.* Fortgang m; *the* ~ *of events* der Lauf der Dinge; **2.** marschieren (lassen); *fig.* fort-, vorwärtsschreiten.

mar·chio·ness ['mɑ:ʃənis] Marquise f.

mare [meə] Stute f; △ *nicht* Mähre; **~'s** *nest* *fig.* Schwindel m; (Zeitungs)Ente f.

mar·ga·rine [mɑ:dʒə'ri:n], *Brt.* F **marge** [mɑ:dʒ] Margarine f.

mar·gin ['mɑ:dʒin] Rand m (*a. fig.*); Grenze f (*a. fig.*); Spielraum m; Verdienst-, Gewinn-, Handelsspanne f; *by a narrow* ~ *fig.* mit knapper Not; **~·al** □ [~l] am Rande (befindlich); Rand...; ~ *note* Randbemerkung f.

ma·ri·na [mə'ri:nə] Boots-, Jachthafen m.

ma·rine [mə'ri:n] Marine f; △ *nicht* (Kriegs)Marine; ☆, ✗ Marineinfanterist m; *paint.* Seestück n; *attr.* See...; Meeres...; Marine...; Schiffs...; **mar·i·ner** ['mærinə] Seemann m.

mar·i·tal □ ['mæritl] ehelich, Ehe...; ~ *status* ☆ Familienstand m.

mar·i·time ['mæritaim] an der See liegend *od.* lebend; See...; Küsten...; Schiffahrts...

mark¹ [mɑ:k] (deutsche) Mark; △ *nicht* das Mark.

mark² [~] **1.** Marke f, Markierung f, Bezeichnung f; Zeichen n (*a. fig.*); Merkmal n; (Körper)Mal n; Fleck m (*a. fig.*); (Fuß-, Brems- *etc.*)Spur f (*a. fig.*); (Fabrik-, Waren)Zeichen n, (Schutz-, Handels)Marke f; *econ.* Preisangabe f; (Schul)Note f, Zensur f; Punkt m; *Sport:* Startlinie f; *fig.* Norm f; *fig.* Bedeutung f, Rang m; *a man of* ~ e-e bedeutende Persönlichkeit; *be up to the* ~ gesund-

heitlich auf der Höhe sein; *be wide of the ~ fig.* sich gewaltig irren; den Kern der Sache nicht treffen; *hit the ~ fig.* (ins Schwarze) treffen; *miss the ~* danebenschießen; *fig.* sein Ziel verfehlen; **2.** *v/t.* (be)zeichnen; markieren; kennzeichnen; be(ob)achten, achtgeben auf (*acc.*); sich *et.* merken; Zeichen hinterlassen auf (*dat.*); *Schule:* benoten, zensieren; notieren, vermerken; *econ. Waren* auszeichnen; *econ.* den Preis festsetzen; *Sport:* s-n Gegenspieler decken; *~ my words* denke an m-e Worte; *to ~ the occasion* zur Feier des Tages; *~ time* auf der Stelle treten (*a. fig.*); *~ down* notieren, vermerken; *econ. im Preis* herabsetzen; *~ off* abgrenzen; *bsd. auf e-r Liste* abhaken; *~ out durch Striche etc.* markieren, bezeichnen; *~ up econ. im Preis* heraufsetzen; *v/i.* markieren; achtgeben, aufpassen; *Sport:* decken; **~ed** □ auffallend; merklich; ausgeprägt.

mar·ket ['mɑːkɪt] **1.** Markt(platz) *m*; *Am.* (Lebensmittel)Geschäft *n*, Laden *m*; *econ.* Absatz *m*; *econ.* (*for*) Nachfrage *f* (nach), Bedarf *m* (an); *in the ~* auf dem Markt; *be on the ~* (zum Verkauf) angeboten werden; *play the ~* (an der Börse) spekulieren; **2.** *v/t.* auf den Markt bringen; verkaufen; *v/i. bsd. Am.* go *~ing* einkaufen gehen; **~a·ble** □ [~əbl] marktfähig, -gängig; **~ gar·den** *Brt.* Handelsgärtnerei *f*; **~ing** [~ɪŋ] *econ.* Marketing *n*, Absatzpolitik *f*; Marktbesuch *m*.

marks·man ['mɑːksmən] (*pl. -men*) guter Schütze.

mar·ma·lade ['mɑːməleɪd] *bsd.* Orangenmarmelade *f*.

mar·mot *zo.* ['mɑːmət] Murmeltier *n.*

ma·roon [mə'ruːn] **1.** kastanienbraun; **2.** *auf e-r einsamen Insel* aussetzen; **3.** Leuchtrakete *f.*

mar·quee [mɑː'kiː] Festzelt *n.*

mar·quis ['mɑːkwɪs] Marquis *m.*

mar·riage ['mærɪdʒ] Heirat *f*, Hochzeit *f*; Ehe(stand *m*) *f*; *civil ~* standesamtliche Trauung; **mar·ria·gea·ble** [~dʒəbl] heiratsfähig; **~ ar·ti·cles** *pl.* Ehevertrag *m*; **~ cer·tif·i·cate**, **~ lines** *pl. bsd. Brt.* F Trauschein *m*; **~ por·tion** Mitgift *f.*

mar·ried ['mærɪd] verheiratet; ehe-

lich, Ehe...; *~ couple* Ehepaar *n*; *~ life* Ehe(leben *n*) *f.*

mar·row ['mærəʊ] *anat.* (Knochen-)Mark *n*; *fig.* Kern *m, das* Wesentlichste; (*vegetable*) ~ *Brt.* ♣ Kürbis *m.*

mar·ry ['mærɪ] *v/t.* (ver)heiraten; *eccl.* trauen; *get married to* sich verheiraten mit; *v/i.* (sich ver)heiraten.

marsh [mɑːʃ] Sumpf *m*; Morast *m.*

mar·shal ['mɑːʃl] **1.** ✕ Marschall *m*; *hist.* Hofmarschall *m*; Zeremonienmeister *m*; *Am.* Branddirektor *m*; *Am.* Polizeidirektor *m*; *Am.* Bezirkspolizeichef *m*; *US ~ Am.* (Bundes-)Vollzugsbeamte(r) *m*; **2.** (*bsd. Brt. -ll-, Am. -l-*) ordnen, aufstellen; führen; 🚂 (Zug) zusammenstellen.

marsh·y ['mɑːʃɪ] (*-ier, -iest*) sumpfig, morastig.

mart [mɑːt] Markt *m*; Auktionsraum *m.*

mar·ten *zo.* ['mɑːtɪn] Marder *m.*

mar·tial □ ['mɑːʃl] kriegerisch; militärisch; Kriegs...; *~ law* ✕ Kriegsrecht *n*; (*state of*) *~ law* ✕ Ausnahmezustand *m.*

mar·tyr ['mɑːtə] **1.** Märtyrer(in) (*to gen.*); **2.** (zu Tode) martern.

mar·vel ['mɑːvl] **1.** Wunder *n, et.* Wunderbares; **2.** (*bsd. Brt. -ll-, Am. -l-*) sich wundern; **~·(l)ous** □ ['mɑːvələs] wunderbar; erstaunlich.

mar·zi·pan [mɑːzɪ'pæn] Marzipan *n.*

mas·ca·ra [mæ'skɑːrə] Wimperntusche *f.*

mas·cot ['mæskət] Maskottchen *n.*

mas·cu·line ['mæskjʊlɪn] männlich; Männer...

mash [mæʃ] **1.** Gemisch *n*; Maische *f*; Mengfutter *n*; **2.** zerdrücken; (ein)maischen; *~ed potatoes* *pl.* Kartoffelbrei *m.*

mask [mɑːsk] **1.** Maske *f*; **2.** maskieren; *fig.* verbergen; tarnen; *~ed* maskiert; *~ ball* Maskenball *m.*

ma·son ['meɪsn] Steinmetz *m*; *Am.* Maurer *m*; *mst* 🌑 Freimaurer *m*; **~·ry** [~rɪ] Mauerwerk *n.*

masque *thea. hist.* [mɑːsk] Maskenspiel *n*; △ *nicht* Maske.

mas·que·rade [mæskə'reɪd] **1.** Maskenball *m*; *fig.* Maske, *f* Verkleidung *f*; **2.** *fig.* sich maskieren.

mass [mæs] **1.** *eccl. a.* 🌑 Messe *f*; Masse *f*; Menge *f*; *the ~es pl.* die (breite) Masse; ~ media *pl.* Massenmedien *pl.*; ~ meeting Massenversammlung *f*; **2.** (sich) (an)sammeln.

mas·sa·cre ['mæsəkə] **1.** Blutbad *n*; **2.** niedermetzeln.

mas·sage ['mæsɑ:ʒ] **1.** Massage *f*; **2.** massieren.

mas·sif ['mæsi:f] (Gebirgs)Massiv *n*.

mas·sive ['mæsiv] massiv; groß u. schwer; *fig.* gewaltig.

mast ✠ [mɑːst] Mast *m*.

mas·ter ['mɑːstə] **1.** Meister *m*; Herr *m* (*a. fig.*); Gebieter *m*; *bsd.* Brt. Lehrer *m*; Kapitän *m* (*e-s Handelsschiffs*); (junger) Herr (*Anrede*); *univ.* Rektor *m* (*e-s College*); ♀ of Arts (*abbr.* MA) Magister *m* Artium; ~ of ceremonies *bsd.* Am. Conférencier *m*; **2.** Meister...; Haupt..., hauptsächlich; *fig.* führend; **3.** Herr sein *od.* herrschen über (*acc.*); *Sprache etc.* meistern, beherrschen; **~build·er** Baumeister *m*; **~ful** □ [~fl] herrisch; meisterhaft; **~key** Hauptschlüssel *m*; **~ly** [~lɪ] meisterhaft, virtuos; **~piece** Meisterstück *n*; **~ship** [~ʃɪp] Meisterschaft *f*; Herrschaft *f*; *bsd.* Brt. Lehramt *n*; **~y** [~rɪ] Herrschaft *f*; Überlegenheit *f*, Oberhand *f*; Meisterschaft *f*; Beherrschung *f*.

mas·ti·cate ['mæstɪkeɪt] (zer)kauen.

mas·tur·bate ['mæstəbeɪt] masturbieren.

mat [mæt] **1.** Matte *f*; Deckchen *n*; Unterlage *f*, -setzer *m*; **2.** (-*tt*-) (sich) verflechten, (sich) -filzen; *fig.* bedecken; **3.** mattiert, matt.

match¹ [mætʃ] Zünd-, Streichholz *n*.

match² [~] **1.** der, die, das gleiche; Partie *f*, Wettspiel *n*, -kampf *m*, Treffen *n*, Match *n*, *m*; Heirat *f*; be a ~ for j-m gewachsen sein; find a ~ meet one's ~ s-n Meister finden; **2.** *v/t.* passend machen, anpassen; passen zu; et. Passendes finden od. geben zu; es aufnehmen mit; passend verheiraten; be well ~ed gut zusammenpassen; *v/i.* zusammenpassen; *gloves to* ~ dazu passende Handschuhe.

match·box ['mætʃbɒks] Zünd-, Streichholzschachtel *f*; ~ car TM Matchbox-Auto *n*.

match·less □ ['mætʃlɪs] unvergleichlich, einzigartig; **~mak·er** Ehestifter(in).

mate¹ [meɪt] *s.* checkmate.

mate² [~] **1.** Gefährt|e *m*, -in *f*; (Arbeits)Kamerad(in); Gatt|e *m*, -in *f*; Männchen *n*, Weibchen *n* (*von Tieren*); Gehilf|e *m*, -in *f*; ✠ Maat *m*; **2.** (sich) verheiraten; (sich) paaren.

ma·te·ri·al □ [məˈtɪərɪəl] **1.** materiell; körperlich; materialistisch; wesentlich; **2.** Material *n*; Stoff *m*; Werkstoff *m*; writing ~s *pl.* Schreibmaterial(ien *pl.*) *n*.

ma·ter|nal □ [məˈtɜːnl] mütterlich, Mutter...; mütterlicherseits; **~ni·ty** [~ətɪ] **1.** Mutterschaft *f*; **2.** Schwangerschafts..., Umstands...; ~ hospital Entbindungsklinik *f*; ~ ward Entbindungsstation *f*.

math *Am.* F [mæθ] Mathe *f* (*Mathematik*).

math·e|ma·ti·cian [mæθəməˈtɪʃn] Mathematiker *m*; **~·mat·ics** [~ˈmætɪks] *mst sg.* Mathematik *f*.

maths Brt. F [mæθs] Mathe *f* (*Mathematik*).

mat·i·née *thea.*, ♪ ['mætɪneɪ] Nachmittagsvorstellung *f*, Frühvorstellung *f*; △ nicht Matinee.

ma·tric·u·late [məˈtrɪkjʊleɪt] (sich) immatrikulieren (lassen).

mat·ri|mo·ni·al □ [mætrɪˈməʊnjəl] ehelich, Ehe...; **~ny** ['mætrɪmənɪ] Ehe(stand *m*) *f*.

ma·trix ⊕ ['meɪtrɪks] (*pl.* -trices [-trɪsiːz], -trixes) Matrize *f*.

ma·tron ['meɪtrən] Matrone *f*; Hausmutter *f*; Brt. Oberschwester *f*.

mat·ter ['mætə] **1.** Materie *f*, Material *n*, Substanz *f*, Stoff *m*; ♨ Eiter *m*; Gegenstand *m*; Sache *f*; Angelegenheit *f*; Anlaß *m*, Veranlassung *f* (*for* zu); *printed* ~ ♦ Drucksache *f*; *what's the* ~ (*with you*)? was ist los (mit Ihnen)?; *no* ~ es hat nichts zu sagen; *no* ~ *who* gleichgültig, wer; *a* ~ *of course* e-e Selbstverständlichkeit; *for that* ~, *for the* ~ *of that* was das betrifft; *a* ~ *of fact* e-e Tatsache; **2.** von Bedeutung sein; *it doesn't* ~ es macht nichts; **~-of-fact** sachlich, nüchtern.

mat·tress ['mætrɪs] Matratze *f*.

ma·ture [məˈtjʊə] **1.** □ (~*r*, ~*st*) reif (*a. fig.*); *econ.* fällig; *fig.* reiflich erwogen; **2.** *v/t.* zur Reife bringen; *v/i.* reifen; *econ.* fällig werden; **ma·tu·ri·ty** [~rətɪ] Reife *f*; *econ.* Fälligkeit *f*.

maud·lin □ ['mɔːdlɪn] rührselig.

maul [mɔːl] übel zurichten, roh umgehen mit; *fig.* verreißen.

Maun·dy Thurs·day *eccl.* ['mɔːndɪ 'θɜːzdɪ] Gründonnerstag *m.*

mauve [məʊv] **1.** Malvenfarbe *f*; **2.** hellviolett.

maw *zo.* [mɔː] (Tier)Magen *m*, *bsd.* Labmagen *m*; Rachen *m*; Kropf *m.*

mawk·ish □ ['mɔːkɪʃ] rührselig, sentimental.

max·i ['mæksɪ] **1.** Maximode *f*; Maximantel *m*, -kleid *n*, -rock *m*; **2.** Maxi...

max·i- ['mæksɪ] Maxi..., riesig, Riesen...

max·im ['mæksɪm] Grundsatz *m.*

May[1] [meɪ] Mai *m.*

may[2] *v/aux.* [ ] (*pret.* might) mögen, können, dürfen.

may·be ['meɪbɪ] vielleicht.

may·-bee·tle *zo.* ['meɪbiːtl], **~bug** *zo.* Maikäfer *m.*

May Day ['meɪdeɪ] der 1. Mai.

mayor [meə] Bürgermeister *m*; △ *nicht* Major.

may·pole ['meɪpəʊl] Maibaum *m.*

maze [meɪz] Irrgarten *m*, Labyrinth *n*; *fig.* Verwirrung *f*; *in a* ~ = **~d** [meɪzd] verwirrt.

me [miː, *unbetont*: mɪ] mich; mir; F ich.

mead[1] [miːd] Met *m.*

mead[2] *poet.* [ ] = meadow.

mead·ow ['medəʊ] Wiese *f.*

mea·gre, *Am.* **-ger** □ ['miːgə] mager (*a. fig.*); dürr; dürftig.

meal [miːl] Mahl(zeit *f*) *n*; Essen *n*; Mehl *n.*

mean[1] □ [miːn] gemein, niedrig, gering; armselig; knauserig; schäbig; *Am.* boshaft, ekelhaft.

mean[2] [ ] **1.** mittel, mittlere(r, -s) Mittel..., Durchschnitts...; **2.** Mitte *f*; ~*s pl.* (Geld)Mittel *pl.*; (*a. sg.*) Mittel *n*; *by all* ~*s* auf alle Fälle, unbedingt; *by no* ~*s* keineswegs; *by* ~*s of* mittels (*gen.*).

mean[3] [ ] (*meant*) meinen, beabsichtigen; bestimmen; bedeuten; ~ *well* (*ill*) es gut (schlecht) meinen.

mean·ing ['miːnɪŋ] **1.** □ bedeutsam; **2.** Sinn *m*, Bedeutung *f*; △ *nicht* Meinung; **~ful** [~fʊl] bedeutungsvoll; sinnvoll; **~less** [~lɪs] bedeutungslos; sinnlos.

meant [ment] *pret. u. p.p. von* mean[3].

mean|time ['miːntaɪm] **1.** mittlerweile, inzwischen; **2.** *in the* ~ inzwischen; **~while** = meantime.

mea·sles 𝔉 [ ] *sg.* Masern *pl.*

mea·su·ra·ble □ ['meʒərəbl] meßbar.

mea·sure ['meʒə] **1.** Maß *n*; Maß *n*, Meßgerät *n*; 𝄞 Takt *m*; Maßnahme *f*; *fig.* Maßstab *m*; ~ *of capacity* Hohlmaß *n*; *beyond* ~ über alle Maßen; *in a great* ~ großenteils; *made to* ~ nach Maß gemacht; *take* ~*s* Maßnahmen treffen *od.* ergreifen; **2.** (ab-, aus-, ver)messen; *j-m* Maß nehmen; ~ *up to* den Ansprüchen (*gen.*) genügen; **~d** gemessen; wohlüberlegt; maßvoll; **~less** □ [~lɪs] unermeßlich; **~ment** [~mənt] Messung *f*; Maß *n.*

meat [miːt] Fleisch *n*; *fig.* Gehalt *m*; *cold* ~ kalte Platte; **~y** ['miːtɪ] (-*ier*, -*iest*) fleischig; *fig.* gehaltvoll.

me·chan|ic [mɪ'kænɪk] Handwerker *m*; Mechaniker *m*; **~i·cal** □ [~kl] mechanisch; Maschinen...; **~ics** *phys. mst sg.* Mechanik *f.*

mech·a·nis·m ['mekənɪzm] Mechanismus *m*; **~nize** [~aɪz] mechanisieren; **~d** ⚔ motorisiert; Panzer...

med·al ['medl] Medaille *f*; Orden *m*; **~(l)ist** [~lɪst] *Sport*: Medaillengewinner(in).

med·dle ['medl] sich einmischen (*with*, *in* in *acc.*); **~some** [~səm] zudringlich.

me·di·a ['miːdjə] *pl.* die Medien *pl.* (*Zeitung, Fernsehen, Rundfunk*).

med·i·ae·val □ [medɪ'iːvl] = medieval.

me·di·al □ ['miːdjəl] Mittel...

me·di·an ['miːdjn] die Mitte bildend *od.* einnehmend, Mittel...

me·di·ate ['miːdɪeɪt] vermitteln; **~a·tion** [miːdɪ'eɪʃn] Vermittlung *f*; **~a·tor** ['miːdɪeɪtə] Vermittler *m.*

med·i·cal □ ['medɪkl] medizinisch, ärztlich; ~ *certificate* ärztliches Attest; ~ *man* F Doktor *m* (*Arzt*).

med·i·cate ['medɪkeɪt] medizinisch behandeln; mit Arzneistoff(en) versetzen; **~d** *bath* medizinisches Bad.

me·dic·i·nal □ [me'dɪsɪnl] medizinisch; heilend, Heil...; *fig.* heilsam.

medi·cine ['medsɪn] Medizin *f* (*Heilkunde, Arznei*).

me·di·e·val □ [medɪ'iːvl] mittelalterlich.

me·di·o·cre [miːdɪ'əʊkə] mittelmäßig, zweitklassig.

med·i·tate ['medɪteɪt] v/i. nachdenken, überlegen, meditieren; v/t. im Sinn haben, planen, erwägen; **~ta·tion** [medɪ'teɪʃn] Nachdenken n; Meditation f; **~ta·tive** □ ['medɪtətɪv] nachdenklich, meditativ.

Med·i·ter·ra·ne·an [medɪtə'reɪnjən] Mittelmeer...

me·di·um ['miːdjəm] **1.** (pl. -dia [-djə], -diums) Mitte f; Mittel n; Vermittlung f; Medium n; (Lebens-)Element n; **2.** mittlere(r, -s), Mittel..., Durchschnitts...

med·ley ['medlɪ] Gemisch n; ♪ Medley n, Potpourri n.

meek □ [miːk] sanft-, demütig, bescheiden; **~ness** ['miːknɪs] Sanft-, Demut f.

meer·schaum ['mɪəʃəm] Meerschaum(pfeife f) m.

meet [miːt] (met) v/t. treffen (auf acc.); begegnen (dat.); abholen; stoßen auf (den Gegner); e-m Wunsch, e-r Verpflichtung etc. nachkommen; j-n kennenlernen; Am. j-m vorgestellt werden; fig. j-m entgegenkommen; v/i. sich treffen; zusammenstoßen; sich versammeln; sich kennenlernen; Sport: sich begegnen; **~ with** stoßen auf (acc.); erleiden; **~ing** ['miːtɪŋ] Begegnung f; (Zusammen)Treffen n; Versammlung f; Tagung f.

mel·an·chol·y ['melənkəlɪ] **1.** Melancholie f, Schwermut f; **2.** melancholisch, traurig.

me·li·o·rate ['miːljəreɪt] (sich) (ver-)bessern.

mel·low ['meləʊ] **1.** □ mürbe; reif; weich; mild; **2.** reifen (lassen) od. weich machen od. werden; (sich) mildern.

me·lo·di·ous □ [mɪ'ləʊdjəs] melodisch.

mel·o·dra·mat·ic [meləʊdrə'mætɪk] melodramatisch; **~dy** ['melədɪ] Melodie f; Lied n.

mel·on ♀ ['melən] Melone f.

melt [melt] (zer)schmelzen; fig. zerfließen; Gefühl erweichen.

mem·ber ['membə] (Mit)Glied n; Angehörige(r m) f; ♀ of Parliament parl. Mitglied n des Unterhauses; **~ship** [~ʃɪp] Mitgliedschaft f; Mitgliederzahl f; **~ card** Mitgliedsausweis m.

mem·brane ['membreɪn] Membran(e) f, Häutchen n.

me·men·to [mɪ'mentəʊ] (pl. -toes,

-tos) Mahnzeichen n; Andenken n.

mem·o ['meməʊ] (pl. -os) = **memorandum**.

mem·oir ['memwɑː] Denkschrift f; **~s** pl. Memoiren pl.

mem·o·ra·ble □ ['memərəbl] denkwürdig.

mem·o·ran·dum [memə'rændəm] (pl. -da [-də], -dums) Notiz f; pol. Note f; ⚖ Schriftsatz m.

me·mo·ri·al [mɪ'mɔːrɪəl] Denkmal n (to für); Gedenkfeier f; Denkschrift f, Eingabe f; attr. Gedächtnis..., Gedenk...

mem·o·rize ['meməraɪz] auswendig lernen, memorieren.

mem·o·ry ['memərɪ] Gedächtnis n; Erinnerung f; Andenken n; Computer: Speicher m; commit to **~** auswendig lernen; in **~** of zum Andenken an (acc.).

men [men] pl. von **man** 1; Mannschaft f.

men·ace ['menəs] **1.** (be)drohen; **2.** (Be)Drohung f; drohende Gefahr.

mend [mend] **1.** v/t. (ver)bessern; ausbessern, flicken; besser machen; **~ one's ways** sich bessern; v/i. sich bessern; **2.** ausgebesserte Stelle; on the **~** auf dem Wege der Besserung.

men·da·cious □ [men'deɪʃəs] lügnerisch, verlogen; unwahr.

men·di·cant ['mendɪkənt] **1.** bettelnd, Bettel...; **2.** Bettler(in); Bettelmönch m.

me·ni·al ['miːnjəl] **1.** □ knechtisch; niedrig; **2.** contp. Diener(in), Knecht m.

men·in·gi·tis ⚕ [menɪn'dʒaɪtɪs] Meningitis f, Hirnhautentzündung f.

men·stru·ate physiol. ['menstrʊeɪt] menstruieren, die Regel od. Periode haben.

men·tal □ ['mentl] geistig, Geistes...; bsd. Brt. ☞ geisteskrank, -gestört; **~ arithmetic** Kopfrechnen n; **~ handicap** geistige Behinderung; **~ home**, **~ hospital** Nervenklinik f; **~ly handicapped** geistig behindert; **~i·ty** [men'tælətɪ] Mentalität f.

men·tion ['menʃn] **1.** Erwähnung f; **2.** erwähnen; don't **~** it! bitte (sehr)!

men·u ['menjuː] Speise(n)karte f; Speisenfolge f; △ nicht Menü.

mer·can·tile ['mɜːkəntaɪl] kaufmännisch, Handels...

mer·ce·na·ry ['mɜːsɪnərɪ] **1.** feil,

käuflich; gedungen; gewinnsüchtig; 2. ⚔ Söldner *m*.

mer·cer ['mɜːsə] Seiden-, Stoffhändler *m*.

mer·chan·dise ['mɜːtʃəndaɪz] Ware(n *pl.*) *f*.

mer·chant ['mɜːtʃənt] 1. Kaufmann *m; bsd. Am.* Ladenbesitzer *m*, Krämer *m*; 2. Handels..., Kaufmanns...; **~·man** (*pl. -men*) Handelsschiff *n*.

mer·ci·ful □ ['mɜːsɪfl] barmherzig; **~·less** □ [~lɪs] unbarmherzig.

mer·cu·ry ['mɜːkjʊrɪ] Quecksilber *n*.

mer·cy ['mɜːsɪ] Barmherzigkeit *f*; Gnade *f*; *be at the ~ of s.o.* j-m auf Gedeih u. Verderb ausgeliefert sein.

mere [mɪə] (*~r, ~st*) rein; bloß; **~·ly** ['mɪəlɪ] bloß, nur, lediglich.

mer·e·tri·cious □ [merɪ'trɪʃəs] protzig; bombastisch (*Stil*).

merge [mɜːdʒ] verschmelzen (*in* mit); *econ.* fusionieren; **merg·er** ['mɜːdʒə] Verschmelzung *f*; *econ.* Fusion *f*.

me·rid·i·an [mə'rɪdɪən] *geogr.* Meridian *m; fig.* Gipfel *m*.

mer·it ['merɪt] 1. Verdienst *n;* Wert *m;* Vorzug *m; ~s pl.* ⚖ Hauptpunkte *pl.*, Wesen *n* (*e-r Sache*); 2. verdienen; **~·i·to·ri·ous** □ [merɪ'tɔːrɪəs] verdienstvoll.

mer·maid ['mɜːmeɪd] Nixe *f*.

mer·ri·ment ['merɪmənt] Lustigkeit *f*; Belustigung *f*.

mer·ry □ ['merɪ] (*-ier, -iest*) lustig, fröhlich; *make ~* lustig sein, feiern; **~ an·drew** Hanswurst *m;* **~-go-round** Karussell *n;* **~·mak·ing** [~meɪkɪŋ] Feiern *n*.

mesh [meʃ] 1. Masche *f; fig. oft ~es pl.* Netz *n; be in ~* ⊕ (ineinander-)greifen; 2. in *e-m* Netz fangen.

mess[1] [mes] 1. Unordnung *f;* Schmutz *m,* F Schweinerei *f;* F Patsche *f;* ⚔ usw. *Essen n;* Messe *f; make a ~ of* verpfuschen; 2. *v/t.* in Unordnung bringen; verpfuschen; *v/i. ~ about, ~ around* F herummurksen; sich herumtreiben.

mess[2] [~] Kasino *n,* Messe *f;* △ *nicht eccl.* Messe.

mes·sage ['mesɪdʒ] Botschaft *f* (*to an acc.*); Mitteilung *f,* Bescheid *m*.

mes·sen·ger ['mesɪndʒə] Bote *m*.

mess·y □ ['mesɪ] (*-ier, -iest*) unordentlich; unsauber, schmutzig.

met [met] *pret. u. p.p. von* meet.

met·al ['metl] 1. Metall *n;* Brt.

Schotter *m;* 2. (*bsd. Brt. -ll-, Am. -l-*) beschottern; **me·tal·lic** [mɪ'tælɪk] (*~ally*) metallisch, Metall...; **~·lur·gy** [mɛˈtælədʒɪ] Hüttenkunde *f*.

met·a·mor·phose [metə'mɔːfəʊz] verwandeln, umgestalten.

met·a·phor ['metəfə] Metapher *f*.

me·te·or ['miːtjə] Meteor *m;* **me·te·o·rol·o·gy** [miːtjə'rɒlədʒɪ] Meteorologie *f,* Wetterkunde *f*.

me·ter ⊕ ['miːtə] Messer *m,* Meßgerät *n,* Zähler; △ *Brt. nicht* Meter.

meth·od ['meθəd] Methode *f;* Art *f* u. Weise *f;* Verfahren *n;* Ordnung *f,* System *n;* **me·thod·ic** [mɪ'θɒdɪk] (*~ally*), **me·thod·i·cal** □ [~kl] methodisch, planmäßig; überlegt.

me·tic·u·lous □ [mɪ'tɪkjʊləs] peinlich genau, übergenau.

me·tre, *Am. -ter* ['miːtə] Meter *m, n;* Versmaß *n*.

met·ric ['metrɪk] (*~ally*) metrisch; Maß...; Meter...; *~ system* metrisches (Maß- u. Gewichts)System.

me·trop·o·lis [mɪ'trɒpəlɪs] Metropole *f,* Hauptstadt *f;* **met·ro·pol·i·tan** [metrə'pɒlɪtən] hauptstädtisch.

met·tle ['metl] Eifer *m,* Mut *m,* Feuer *n; be on one's ~* sein Bestes tun.

mews *Brt.* [mjuːz] *sg. veraltet* Stallungen *pl.; daraus entstandene* Garagen *pl. od.* Wohnungen *pl.*

Mex·i·can ['meksɪkən] 1. mexikanisch; 2. Mexikaner(in).

mi·aow [miː'aʊ] miauen.

mice [maɪs] *pl. von* mouse.

Mich·ael·mas ['mɪklməs] Michaelstag *m,* Michaeli(s) *n* (*29. September*).

mi·cro- ['maɪkrəʊ] Mikro..., (sehr) klein.

mi·cro·phone ['maɪkrəfəʊn] Mikrophon *n;* **~·pro·ces·sor** Mikroprozessor *m;* **~·scope** Mikroskop *n*.

mid [mɪd] mittlere(r, -s), Mitt(el)...; *in ~air* (mitten) in der Luft; **~·day** ['mɪddeɪ] 1. Mittag *m;* 2. mittägig; Mittag(s)...

mid·dle ['mɪdl] 1. Mitte *f;* Mitte *f* (*des Leibes*), Taille *f;* △ *nicht* Mittel; 2. mittlere(r, -s), Mittel...; **~·aged** mittleren Alters; **2 Ag·es** *pl.* Mittelalter *n;* **~·class** Mittelstands...; **~ class**(**·es** *pl.*) Mittelstand *m;* **~·man** (*pl. -men*) Mittelsmann *m;* **~ name** zweiter Vorname *m;* **~·sized** mittelgroß; **~ weight** *Boxen:* Mittelgewicht(ler *m*) *n*.

mid·dling ['mɪdlɪŋ] mittelmäßig, Mittel...; leidlich.

midge zo. [mɪdʒ] kleine Mücke; **midg·et** ['mɪdʒɪt] Zwerg m, Knirps m.

mid·land ['mɪdlənd] binnenländisch; **~most** mittelste(r, -s); innerste(r, -s); **~night** Mitternacht f; **~riff** anat. ['mɪdrɪf] Zwerchfell n; **~ship·man** (pl. -men) Midshipman m; Brt. unterster Marineoffiziersrang; Am. Seeoffiziersanwärter m; **~st** [mɪdst] Mitte f; in the ~ of mitten in (dat.); **~sum·mer** ast. Sommersonnenwende f; Hochsommer m; **~way 1.** adj. in der Mitte befindlich, mittlere(r, -s); **2.** adv. auf halbem Wege; **~wife** (pl. -wives) Hebamme f; **~wif·er·y** [~wɪfərɪ] Geburtshilfe f; **~win·ter** ast. Wintersonnenwende f; Mitte f des Winters; in ~ mitten im Winter.

mien lit. [miːn] Miene f.

might [maɪt] **1.** Macht f, Gewalt f, Kraft f; with ~ and main mit aller Kraft od. Gewalt; **2.** pret. von may²; **~y** □ ['maɪtɪ] (-ier, -iest) mächtig, gewaltig.

mi·grate [maɪˈgreɪt] (aus)wandern, (fort)ziehen (a. zo.); **mi·gra·tion** [~ʃn] Wanderung f; **mi·gra·to·ry** ['maɪgrətərɪ] wandernd; zo. Zug...

mike F [maɪk] Mikro n (Mikrophon).

mil·age ['maɪlɪdʒ] = mileage.

mild □ [maɪld] mild; sanft; gelind; leicht.

mil·dew ♀ ['mɪldjuː] Mehltau m.

mild·ness ['maɪldnɪs] Milde f.

mile [maɪl] Meile f (1,609 km).

mile·age ['maɪlɪdʒ] zurückgelegte Meilenzahl od. Fahrtstrecke, Meilenstand m; a. ~ allowance Meilen-, appr. Kilometergeld n.

mile·stone ['maɪlstəʊn] Meilenstein m (a. fig.).

mil·i·tant □ ['mɪlɪtənt] militant; streitend; streitbar, kriegerisch; **~ta·ry** [~ərɪ] **1.** □ militärisch, Militär...; Heeres..., Kriegs...; ♀ Government Militärregierung f; **2.** das Militär, Soldaten pl., Truppen pl.

mi·li·tia [mɪˈlɪʃə] Miliz f, Bürgerwehr f.

milk [mɪlk] **1.** Milch f; it's no use crying over spilt ~ geschehen ist geschehen; **2.** v/t. melken; v/i. melken; Milch geben; **~maid** ['mɪlkmeɪd] Melkerin f; Milchmädchen n;

~man (pl. -men) Milchmann m; **~pow·der** Milchpulver n; **~shake** Milchmixgetränk n; **~sop** Weichling m, Muttersöhnchen n; **~y** [~kɪ] (-ier, -iest) milchig; Milch...; ♀ Way ast. Milchstraße f.

mill¹ [mɪl] **1.** Mühle f; Fabrik f, Spinnerei f; **2.** Korn etc. mahlen; ⊕ fräsen; Münze rändeln.

mill² Am. [~] ¹/₁₀₀₀ Dollar n.

mil·le·pede zo. ['mɪlɪpiːd] Tausendfüß(l)er m.

mill·er ['mɪlə] Müller m.

mil·let ['mɪlɪt] Hirse f.

mil·li·ner ['mɪlɪnə] Hut-, Putzmacherin f, Modistin f; **~ne·ry** [~rɪ] Putz-, Modewaren(geschäft n) pl.

mil·lion ['mɪljən] Million f; **~aire** [mɪljəˈneə] Millionär(in); **~th** ['mɪljənθ] **1.** millionste(r, -s); **2.** Millionstel n.

mil·li·pede zo. ['mɪlɪpiːd] = millepede.

mill|·pond ['mɪlpɒnd] Mühlteich m; **~stone** Mühlstein m.

milt [mɪlt] Milch f (der Fische).

mim·ic ['mɪmɪk] **1.** mimisch; Schein...; **2.** Imitator m; **3.** (-ck-) nachahmen; nachäffen; **~ry** [~rɪ] Nachahmung f; zo. Mimikry f.

mince [mɪns] **1.** v/t. zerhacken, -stückeln; he does not ~ matters er nimmt kein Blatt vor den Mund; v/i. sich zieren; **2.** a. ~d meat Hackfleisch n; **~meat** ['mɪnsmiːt] e-e süße Pastetenfüllung; ~ pie mit mincemeat gefüllte Pastete; **minc·er** [~ə] Fleischwolf m.

mind [maɪnd] **1.** Sinn m, Gemüt n, Herz n; Geist m (a. phls.); Verstand m; Meinung f, Ansicht f; Absicht f; Neigung f, Lust f; Gedächtnis n; to my ~ meiner Ansicht nach; out of one's ~, not in one's right ~ von Sinnen; change one's ~ sich anders besinnen; bear od. keep s.th. in ~ (immer) an et. denken; have (half) a ~ to (beinahe) Lust haben zu; have s.th. on one's ~ et. auf dem Herzen haben; make up one's ~ sich entschließen; s. presence; **2.** merken od. achten auf (acc.); sich kümmern um; etwas (einzuwenden) haben gegen; ~! gib acht!; never ~! macht nichts!; ~ the step! Achtung, Stufe!; I don't ~ (it) ich habe nichts dagegen; do you ~ if I smoke? stört es Sie, wenn ich rauche?; would you ~ taking off your hat? würden Sie bitte den Hut abnehmen?; ~ your own business! kümmern Sie sich um Ihre Angelegenheiten!; **~ful** □ ['maɪndfl] (of) eingedenk (gen.); achtsam (auf acc.); **~less** □ [~lɪs] (of) unbekümmert (um), ohne Rücksicht (auf acc.).

mine¹ [maɪn] der, die, das meinige od. meine.

mine² [~] **1.** Bergwerk n, Mine f, Zeche f, Grube f; ✕ Mine f; fig. Fundgrube f; △ nicht (Kugelschreiber- etc.)Mine(; **2.** v/i. graben; minieren; v/t. graben in (dat.); ✕ fördern; ✕ verminen; **min·er** ['maɪnə] Bergmann m.

min·e·ral ['mɪnərəl] **1.** Mineral n; ~s pl. Brt. Mineralwasser n; **2.** mineralisch, Mineral...

min·gle ['mɪŋgl] v/t. (ver)mischen; v/i. sich mischen od. mengen (with unter).

min·i¹ ['mɪnɪ] **1.** Minimode f; Minimantel m, -kleid m, -rock m; **2.** Mini...

min·i- ['mɪnɪ] Mini..., Klein(st)...

min·i·a·ture ['mɪnjət∫ə] **1.** Miniatur(gemälde n) f; **2.** in Miniatur; Miniatur...; Klein...; ~ camera Kleinbildkamera f.

min·i·mize ['mɪnɪmaɪz] auf ein Mindestmaß herabsetzen; als geringfügig hinstellen, bagatellisieren; **~mum** [~əm] **1.** (pl. -ma [-mə], -mums) Minimum n, Mindestmaß n, -betrag m; **2.** niedrigste(r, -s), minimal, Mindest...

min·ing ['maɪnɪŋ] Bergbau m; attr. Berg(bau)..., Bergwerks...; Gruben...

min·i·on contp. ['mɪnjən] Lakai m, Kriecher m.

min·i·skirt ['mɪnɪskɜːt] Minirock m.

min·is·ter ['mɪnɪstə] **1.** Geistliche(r) m; Minister m; Gesandte(r) m; **2.** ~ to helfen (dat.), unterstützen (acc.).

min·is·try ['mɪnɪstrɪ] geistliches Amt; Ministerium n; Regierung f.

mink zo. [mɪŋk] Nerz m.

mi·nor ['maɪnə] **1.** kleinere(r, -s), geringere(r, -s); fig. a. unbedeutend, geringfügig; ✝✝ minderjährig; A ♪ a-Moll n; ~ key ♪ Moll(tonart f) n; ~ league Am. Baseball: untere Spielklasse; **2.** ✝✝ Minderjährige(r m) f; Am. univ. Nebenfach n; ♪ Moll n;

~·i·ty [maɪˈnɒrɪtɪ] Minderheit f; ✝✝ Minderjährigkeit f.

min·ster ['mɪnstə] Münster n.

min·strel ['mɪnstrəl] Minnesänger m; Varietékünstler, der als Neger geschminkt auftritt.

mint¹ [mɪnt] **1.** Münze f, Münzamt n; a ~ of money e-e Menge Geld; **2.** münzen, prägen.

mint² ♀ [~] Minze f.

min·u·et ♪ [mɪnjʊˈet] Menuett n.

mi·nus ['maɪnəs] **1.** prp. minus, weniger; F ohne; **2.** adj. negativ.

min·ute¹ ['mɪnɪt] Minute f; Augenblick m; in a ~ sofort; just a ~ Moment mal!; ~s pl. Protokoll n.

mi·nute² □ [maɪˈnjuːt] sehr klein, winzig; unbedeutend; sehr genau; **~ness** [~nɪs] Kleinheit f; Genauigkeit f.

mir·a·cle ['mɪrəkl] Wunder n (übernatürliches Ereignis); **mi·rac·u·lous** □ [mɪˈrækjʊləs] wunderbar.

mi·rage ['mɪrɑːʒ] Luftspiegelung f.

mire ['maɪə] **1.** Sumpf m; Schlamm m; Kot m; **2.** mit Schlamm od. Schmutz bedecken.

mir·ror ['mɪrə] **1.** Spiegel m; **2.** (wider)spiegeln (a. fig.).

mirth [mɜːθ] Fröhlichkeit f, Heiterkeit f; **~ful** □ ['mɜːθfl] fröhlich, heiter; **~less** □ [~lɪs] freudlos.

mir·y ['maɪərɪ] (-ier, -iest) sumpfig, schlammig.

mis- [mɪs] miß..., falsch, schlecht.

mis·ad·ven·ture ['mɪsədˈvent∫ə] Mißgeschick n; Unglück(sfall m) n.

mis·an·thrope ['mɪzənθrəʊp], **~thro·pist** [mɪˈzænθrəpɪst] Menschenfeind m.

mis·ap·ply ['mɪsəˈplaɪ] falsch anwenden.

mis·ap·pre·hend ['mɪsæprɪˈhend] mißverstehen.

mis·ap·pro·pri·ate ['mɪsəˈprəʊprɪeɪt] unterschlagen, veruntreuen.

mis·be·have ['mɪsbɪˈheɪv] sich schlecht benehmen.

mis·cal·cu·late [mɪsˈkælkjʊleɪt] falsch berechnen; sich verrechnen.

mis·car·riage [mɪsˈkærɪdʒ] Mißlingen n; Verlust m, Fehlleitung f (von Briefen etc.); ✝ Fehlgeburt f; ~ of justice Fehlspruch m, -urteil n; **~ry** [~ɪ] mißlingen, scheitern; verlorengehen (Brief); ✝ e-e Fehlgeburt haben.

mis·cel·la·ne·ous □ [mɪsɪˈleɪnjəs]

ge-, vermischt; verschiedenartig;
~·ny [mɪˈseləni] Gemisch n; Sammelband m.

mis·chief [ˈmɪstʃif] Schaden m; Unfug m; Mutwille m, Übermut m; **~maker** Unheil-, Unruhestifter(in).

mis·chie·vous □ [ˈmɪstʃivəs] schädlich; boshaft, mutwillig; schelmisch.

mis·con·ceive [ˈmɪskənˈsiːv] falsch auffassen, mißverstehen.

mis·con·duct 1. [mɪsˈkɒndʌkt] schlechtes Benehmen; Eheverfehlung f; schlechte Verwaltung; **~** [ˈmɪskənˈdʌkt] schlecht verwalten; **~ o.s.** sich schlecht benehmen; e-n Fehltritt begehen.

mis·con·strue [ˈmɪskənˈstruː] falsch auslegen, mißdeuten.

mis·deed [ˈmɪsˈdiːd] Missetat f, Vergehen n; Verbrechen n.

mis·de·mea·no(u)r ⚖ [ˈmɪsdɪˈmiːnə] Vergehen n.

mis·di·rect [ˈmɪsdɪˈrekt] fehl-, irreleiten; e-n Brief etc. falsch adressieren.

mis·do·ing [ˈmɪsduːɪŋ] mst **~s** pl. = misdeed.

mise en scène thea. [ˈmiːzɑ̃ːnˈseɪn] Inszenierung f.

mi·ser [ˈmaɪzə] Geizhals m.

mis·e·ra·ble □ [ˈmɪzərəbl] elend; unglücklich; erbärmlich.

mi·ser·ly [ˈmaɪzəli] geizig,   F knick(e)rig.

mis·e·ry [ˈmɪzəri] Elend n, Not f.

mis·fire [ˈmɪsˈfaɪə] versagen (Waffe); mot. fehlzünden, aussetzen.

mis·fit [ˈmɪsfɪt] schlechtsitzendes Kleidungsstück; Außenseiter m, Einzelgänger m.

mis·for·tune [mɪsˈfɔːtʃən] Unglück(sfall m) n; Mißgeschick n.

mis·giv·ing [ˈmɪsˈgɪvɪŋ] böse Ahnung, Befürchtung f.

mis·guide [ˈmɪsˈgaɪd] fehl-, irreleiten.

mis·hap [ˈmɪshæp] Unglück n; Unfall m; Mißgeschick n; Panne f.

mis·lay [mɪsˈleɪ] (-laid) et. verlegen.

mis·lead [mɪsˈliːd] (-led) irreführen; verleiten.

mis·man·age [ˈmɪsˈmænɪdʒ] schlecht verwalten od. führen od. handhaben.

mis·place [ˈmɪsˈpleɪs] an e-e falsche Stelle legen od. setzen; et. verlegen; falsch anbringen.

mis·print 1. [mɪsˈprɪnt] verdrucken; **2.** [ˈmɪsprɪnt] Druckfehler m.

mis·read [ˈmɪsˈriːd] (-read [-red]) falsch lesen od. deuten.

mis·rep·re·sent [ˈmɪsreprɪˈzent] falsch darstellen, verdrehen.

miss¹ [mɪs] (mit nachfolgendem Namen 2) Fräulein n.

miss² [~] **1.** Fehlschlag m, -schuß m, -stoß m, -wurf m; Versäumen n, Entrinnen n; **2.** v/t. (ver)fehlen; verfehlen, -passen, -säumen; auslassen, übergehen; übersehen; überhören; he **~** ... ihm entging ...; v/i. nicht treffen; mißglücken.

mis·shap·en [ˈmɪsˈʃeɪpən] mißgebildet.

mis·sile [ˈmɪsaɪl, Am. ˈmɪsəl] **1.** (Wurf)Geschoß n; ✕ Rakete f; **2.** ✕ Raketen...

miss·ing [ˈmɪsɪŋ] fehlend; weg, nicht da; ✕ vermißt; be **~** fehlen, weg sein (Sache); vermißt sein od. werden.

mis·sion [ˈmɪʃn] pol. Auftrag m; (innere) Berufung, Sendung f, Lebensziel n; pol. Gesandtschaft f; eccl., pol. Mission f; ✕ Einsatz m, (Kampf-) Auftrag m; **~·a·ry** [ˈmɪʃənrɪ] **1.** Missionar m; **2.** Missions...

mis·sive [ˈmɪsɪv] Sendschreiben n.

mis·spell [ˈmɪsˈspel] (-spelt od. -spelled) falsch buchstabieren od. schreiben.

mis·spend [ˈmɪsˈspend] (-spent) falsch verwenden; vergeuden.

mist [mɪst] **1.** (feiner od. leichter) Nebel; △ nicht Mist; **2.** (um)nebeln; sich trüben; beschlagen.

mis·take [mɪsˈteɪk] **1.** (-took, -taken) sich irren; verkennen; mißverstehen; verwechseln (for mit); **2.** Mißverständnis n; Irrtum m; Versehen n; Fehler m; **~·tak·en** □ [~ən] irrig, falsch (verstanden); be **~** sich irren.

mis·ter [ˈmɪstə] (mit nachfolgendem Namen 2) Herr m (abbr. **Mr**).

mis·tle·toe ♀ [ˈmɪsltəʊ] Mistel f.

mis·tress [ˈmɪstrɪs] Herrin f; Frau f des Hauses; bsd. Brt. Lehrerin f; Geliebte f; Meisterin f.

mis·trust [ˈmɪsˈtrʌst] **1.** mißtrauen (dat.); **2.** Mißtrauen n; **~·ful** □ [~fl] mißtrauisch.

mist·y □ [ˈmɪstɪ] (-ier, -iest) neb(e)lig; unklar.

M

mis·un·der·stand ['mɪsʌndə'stænd] (*-stood*) mißverstehen; *v/i* nicht verstehen; **~·ing** [~ɪŋ] Mißverständnis *n*.

mis|us·age [mɪs'ju:zɪdʒ] Mißbrauch *m*; Mißhandlung *f*; **~·use** 1. ['mɪs-'ju:z] mißbrauchen, -handeln; 2. [~s] Mißbrauch *m*.

mite [maɪt] *zo.* Milbe *f*; Würmchen *n* (*Kind*); Heller *m*; *fig.* Scherflein *n*.

mit·i·gate ['mɪtɪgeɪt] mildern, lindern.

mi·tre, *Am.* **-ter** ['maɪtə] Mitra *f*, Bischofsmütze *f*.

mitt [mɪt] *Baseball:* (Fang)Handschuh *m*; *sl.* Boxhandschuh *m*; = mitten.

mit·ten ['mɪtn] Fausthandschuh *m*; Halbhandschuh *m* (*ohne Finger*).

mix [mɪks] (sich) (ver)mischen; mixen; verkehren (*with* mit); *~ed* gemischt; *fig.* zweifelhaft; *~ed school bsd. Brt.* Koedukationsschule *f*; *~ up* durcheinanderbringen; *be ~ed up with* in *e-e* Sache verwickelt sein; **~·ture** ['mɪkstʃə] Mischung *f*.

moan [məʊn] 1. Stöhnen *n*; 2. stöhnen.

moat [məʊt] Burg-, Stadtgraben *m*.

mob [mɒb] 1. Mob *m*, Pöbel *m*; 2. (*-bb-*) (lärmend) bedrängen; (in *e-r* Rotte) herfallen über (*acc.*) *od.* angreifen.

mo·bile ['məʊbaɪl] beweglich; ✕ mobil, motorisiert; lebhaft (*Gesichtszüge*); *~ home bsd. Am.* Wohnwagen *m*.

mo·bi·li·za·tion ✕ [məʊbɪlaɪ'zeɪʃn] Mobilmachung *f*; **~·ze** ✕ ['məʊbɪlaɪz] mobil machen.

moc·ca·sin ['mɒkəsɪn] weiches Leder; Mokassin *m* (*Schuh*).

mock [mɒk] 1. Spott *m*; 2. Schein...; falsch, nachgemacht; 3. *v/t.* verspotten; nachmachen; täuschen; spotten (*gen.*); *v/i.* spotten (*at* über *acc.*); **~·e·ry** ['mɒkərɪ] Spott *m*, Hohn *m*, Spötterei *f*; Gespött *n*; Nachäfferei *f*; **~·ing-bird** *zo.* [~ɪŋbɜ:d] Spottdrossel *f*.

mode [məʊd] (Art *f* u.) Weise *f*; (Erscheinungs)Form *f*; Mode *f*, Brauch *m*; △ *nicht* (*Damen- etc.*) Mode.

mod·el ['mɒdl] 1. Modell *n*; Muster *n*; Vorbild *n*; Mannequin *n*, (Foto-)Modell *n*; *male ~* Dressman *m*; 2. Muster...; 3. *v/t. bsd. Brt.* (*-ll-*, *Am.* *-l-*) modellieren; (ab)formen; *Klei-*

der etc. vorführen; *fig.* formen, bilden; *v/i.* (*e-m Künstler*) Modell stehen; als Mannequin *od.* (Foto)Modell arbeiten.

mod·e|rate 1. □ ['mɒdərət] (mittel-)mäßig; gemäßigt; vernünftig, angemessen; 2. [~reɪt] (sich) mäßigen; **~·ra·tion** [mɒdə'reɪʃn] Mäßigung *f*; Mäßigkeit *f*.

mod·ern ['mɒdən] modern, neu; **~·ize** [~aɪz] modernisieren.

mod·est □ ['mɒdɪst] bescheiden; anständig, sittsam; **~·es·ty** [~ɪ] Bescheidenheit *f*.

mod·i·fi·ca·tion [mɒdɪfɪ'keɪʃn] Abänderung, Veränderung *f*; Einschränkung *f*; **~·fy** ['mɒdɪfaɪ] (ab)ändern; mildern.

mods *Brt.* [mɒdz] *pl.* betont dandyhaft gekleidete Halbstarke *pl.*

mod·u·late ['mɒdjʊleɪt] modulieren.

mod·ule ['mɒdju:l] Verhältniszahl *f*; ⊕ Baueinheit *f*; ⊕ Modul *n* (*austauschbare Funktionseinheit*), & *a.* Baustein *m*; *Raumfahrt:* (Kommando- *etc.*)Kapsel *f*.

moi·e·ty ['mɔɪətɪ] Hälfte *f*; Teil *m*.

moist [mɔɪst] feucht; **~·en** ['mɔɪsn] *v/t.* be-, anfeuchten; *v/i.* feucht werden; **mois·ture** [~stʃə] Feuchtigkeit *f*.

mo·lar ['məʊlə] Backenzahn *m*.

mo·las·ses [mə'læsɪz] *sg.* Melasse *f*; *Am.* Sirup *m*.

mole[1] *zo.* [məʊl] Maulwurf *m*.

mole[2] [~] Muttermal *n*.

mole[3] [~] Mole *f*, Hafendamm *m*.

mol·e·cule ['mɒlɪkju:l] Molekül *n*.

mole·hill ['məʊlhɪl] Maulwurfshügel *m*; *make a mountain out of a ~* aus *e-r* Mücke *e-n* Elefanten machen.

mo·lest [məʊ'lest] belästigen.

mol·li·fy ['mɒlɪfaɪ] besänftigen, beruhigen.

mol·ly·cod·dle ['mɒlɪkɒdl] 1. Weichling *m*, Muttersöhnchen *n*; 2. verweichlichen, -zärteln.

mol·ten ['məʊltən] geschmolzen.

mom *Am.* F [mɒm] Mami *f*, Mutti *f*.

mo·ment ['məʊmənt] Moment *m*, Augenblick *m*; Bedeutung *f*; = *momentum*; **mo·men·ta·ry** □ [~ərɪ] momentan, augenblicklich; vorübergehend; **mo·men·tous** □ [mə'mentəs] bedeutend, folgenschwer; △ *nicht momentan*; **mo·men·tum** *phys.* [~əm] (*pl.* *-ta* [-tə], *-tums*) Moment *n*; Triebkraft *f*.

mon|arch ['mɒnək] Monarch(in); **~ar·chy** [~ɪ] Monarchie f.

mon·as·tery ['mɒnəstrɪ] (Mönchs-) Kloster m.

Mon·day ['mʌndɪ] Montag m.

mon·e·ta·ry econ. ['mʌnɪtərɪ] Währungs...; Geld...

mon·ey ['mʌnɪ] Geld n; ready ~ Bargeld n; **~-box** Sparbüchse f; **~-chang·er** [~ʧeɪndʒə] (Geld)Wechsler m (Person); Am. Wechselautomat m; **~ or·der** Postanweisung f.

mon·ger ['mʌŋgə] mst in Zusammensetzungen: Händler m, Krämer m.

mon·grel ['mʌŋgrəl] Mischling m, Bastard m; attr. Bastard...

mon·i·tor ['mɒnɪtə] ⊕, TV: Monitor m; Schule: (Klassen)Ordner m.

monk [mʌŋk] Mönch m.

mon·key ['mʌŋkɪ] 1. zo. Affe m; ⊕ Rammblock m; put s.o.'s ~ up F j-n auf die Palme bringen; ~ business F fauler Zauber; 2. ~ about, ~ around F (herum)albern; ~ (about od. around) with F herummurksen an (dat.); **~-wrench** ⊕ Engländer m (Schraubenschlüssel); throw a ~ into s.th. Am. et. über den Haufen werfen.

monk·ish ['mʌŋkɪʃ] mönchisch.

mon·o F ['mɒnəʊ] (pl. -os) Radio etc.: Mono n; Monogerät n; attr. Mono...

mon·o- ['mɒnəʊ] ein(fach), einzeln.

mon·o·cle ['mɒnəkl] Monokel n.

mo·nog·a·my [mɒ'nɒgəmɪ] Einehe f.

mon·o|logue, Am. a. **~log** ['mɒnəlɒg] Monolog m.

mo·nop·o|list [mə'nɒpəlɪst] Monopolist m; **~lize** [~aɪz] monopolisieren; fig. an sich reißen; **~ly** [~ɪ] Monopol n (of auf acc.).

mo·not·o|nous [mə'nɒtnəs] monoton, eintönig; **~ny** [~ɪ] Monotonie f.

mon·soon [mɒn'su:n] Monsun m.

mon·ster ['mɒnstə] Ungeheuer n (a. fig.); Monstrum n; attr. Riesen...

mon|stros·i·ty [mɒn'strɒsətɪ] Ungeheuer(lichkeit f) n; **~strous** □ ['mɒnstrəs] ungeheuer(lich), gräßlich.

month [mʌnθ] Monat m; this day ~ heute in e-m Monat; **~ly** ['mʌnθlɪ] 1. monatlich; Monats...; 2. Monatsschrift f.

mon·u·ment ['mɒnjʊmənt] Denkmal n; **~al** □ [mɒnjʊ'mentl] monumental; großartig; Gedenk...

moo [mu:] muhen.

mood [mu:d] Stimmung f, Laune f; ~s pl. schlechte Laune; **~y** □ ['mu:dɪ] (-ier, -iest) launisch; übellaunig; niedergeschlagen.

moon [mu:n] 1. Mond m; once in a blue ~ F alle Jubeljahre (einmal); 2. ~ about, ~ around F herumirren; träumen, dösen; **~·light** ['mu:nlaɪt] Mondlicht n, -schein m; **~·lit** mondhell; **~·struck** mondsüchtig; ~ walk Mondspaziergang m.

Moor[1] [mʊə] Maure m, Mohr m.

moor[2] [~] Moor n; Ödland n, Heideland n.

moor[3] ⚓ [~] vertäuen; **~ings** ⚓ ['mʊərɪŋz] pl. Vertäuung f; Liegeplatz m.

moose zo. [mu:s] nordamerikanischer Elch.

mop [mɒp] 1. Mop m; (Haar)Wust m; 2. (-pp-) auf-, abwischen.

mope [məʊp] den Kopf hängen lassen.

mo·ped Brt. mot. ['məʊped] Moped n.

mor·al ['mɒrəl] 1. □ moralisch; Moral..., Sitten...; 2. Moral f; Lehre f; ~s pl. Sitten pl.; **mo·rale** [mɒ'rɑ:l] bsd. ⚔ Moral f, Stimmung f, Haltung f; **mo·ral·i·ty** [mə'rælətɪ] Moralität f; Sittlichkeit f, Moral f; **mor·al·ize** ['mɒrəlaɪz] moralisieren.

mo·rass [mə'ræs] Morast m, Sumpf m.

mor·bid □ ['mɔ:bɪd] krankhaft.

more [mɔ:] mehr; noch (mehr); no ~ nicht mehr; no ~ than ebensowenig wie; once ~ noch einmal, wieder; (all) the ~ so (nur) um so mehr; so much the ~ as um so mehr als.

mo·rel ⚘ [mɒ'rel] Morchel f.

more·o·ver [mɔ:'rəʊvə] außerdem, überdies, weiter, ferner.

morgue [mɔ:g] Am. Leichenschauhaus n; F (Zeitungs)Archiv n.

morn·ing ['mɔ:nɪŋ] Morgen m; Vormittag m; good ~! guten Morgen!; in the ~ morgens; morgen früh; tomorrow ~ morgen früh; ~·dress Anzug m (für offizielle Anlässe).

mo·ron ['mɔ:rɒn] Schwachsinnige(r m) f; contp. Idiot m.

mo·rose □ [mə'rəʊs] mürrisch.

mor|phi·a ['mɔ:fjə], **~phine** ['mɔ:fi:n] Morphium n.

mor·sel ['mɔ:sl] Bissen m; Stückchen n, das bißchen.

M

mor·tal ['mɔːrtl] **1.** ☐ sterblich; tödlich; Tod(es)...; **2.** Sterbliche(r *m*) *f*; **~·i·ty** [mɔː'tælətɪ] Sterblichkeit *f*.

mor·tar ['mɔːtə] Mörser *m*; Mörtel *m*.

mort·gage ['mɔːgɪdʒ] **1.** Hypothek *f*; **2.** verpfänden; **~·gag·ee** [mɔːgə'dʒiː] Hypothekengläubiger *m*; **~·gag·er** ['mɔːgɪdʒə], **~·ga·gor** [mɔːgə'dʒɔː] Hypothekenschuldner *m*.

mor·tice ⊕ ['mɔːtɪs] = mortise.

mor·ti·cian *Am.* [mɔː'tɪʃn] Leichenbestatter *m*.

mor·ti·fi·ca·tion [mɔːtɪfɪ'keɪʃn] Kränkung *f*; Ärger *m*; **~·fy** ['mɔːtɪfaɪ] kränken; ärgern.

mor·tise ⊕ ['mɔːtɪs] Zapfenloch *n*.

mor·tu·a·ry ['mɔːtjʊərɪ] Leichenhalle *f*.

mo·sa·ic [mə'zeɪɪk] Mosaik *n*.

mosque [mɒsk] Moschee *f*.

mos·qui·to *zo.* [mə'skiːtəʊ] (*pl. -toes*) Moskito *m*; Stechmücke *f*.

moss ⚘ [mɒs] Moos *n*; **~·y** ⚘ ['mɒsɪ] (*-ier, -iest*) moosig, bemoost.

most [məʊst] **1.** *adj.* ☐ meiste(r, -s); die meisten; ~ *people pl.* die meisten Leute *pl.*; **2.** *adv.* am meisten; *vor adj.:* höchst, äußerst; *zur Bildung des Superlativs:* the ~ *important point* der wichtigste Punkt; **3.** *das* meiste, *das* Höchste; die meiste; die meisten *pl.*; at (the) ~ höchstens; *make the* ~ *of* möglichst ausnutzen; △ *nicht* Most; **~·ly** ['məʊstlɪ] hauptsächlich, meistens.

mo·tel [məʊ'tel] Motel *n*.

moth *zo.* [mɒθ] Motte *f*; **~·eat·en** ['mɒθiːtn] mottenzerfressen.

moth·er ['mʌðə] **1.** Mutter *f*; **2.** bemuttern; **~ coun·try** Vater-, Heimatland *n*; Mutterland *n*; **~·hood** [∼hʊd] Mutterschaft *f*; **~·in-law** [∼rɪnlɔː] (*pl. mothers-in-law*) Schwiegermutter *f*; **~·ly** [∼lɪ] mütterlich; **~-of-pearl** [∼rəv'pɜːl] Perlmutter *f*, Perlmutt *n*; **~ tongue** Muttersprache *f*.

mo·tif [məʊ'tiːf] (Leit)Motiv *n*.

mo·tion ['məʊʃn] **1.** Bewegung *f*; Gang *m* (*a.* ⊕); *parl.* Antrag *m*; ✻ Stuhlgang *m*, *oft* ~s *pl.* Stuhl *m*; *v/t. j-m* (zu)winken; *j-m* ein Zeichen geben; *v/i.* winken; **~·less** [∼lɪs] bewegungslos; **~ pic·ture** Film *m*.

mo·ti·vate ['məʊtɪveɪt] motivieren, begründen; **~·va·tion** [məʊtɪ'veɪʃn] Motivierung *f*, Begründung *f*; Motivation *f*.

mo·tive ['məʊtɪv] **1.** Motiv *n*, Beweggrund *m*; **2.** bewegend, treibend (*a. fig.*); **3.** veranlassen.

mot·ley ['mɒtlɪ] bunt, scheckig.

mo·tor ['məʊtə] **1.** Motor *m*; Kraftwagen *m*, Auto(mobil) *n*; *anat.* Muskel *m*; *fig.* treibende Kraft; **2.** motorisch; bewegend; Motor...; Kraft...; Auto...; **3.** (*in e-m Kraftfahrzeug*) fahren; **~ bi·cy·cle** Motorrad *n*; *Am.* Moped *n*; *Am.* Mofa *n*; **~·bike** F Motorrad *n*; *Am.* Moped *n*; *Am.* Mofa *n*; **~·boat** Motorboot *n*; **~ bus** Autobus *m*; **~·cade** [∼keɪd] Auto-kolonne *f*; **~ car** (Kraft)Wagen *m*, Kraftfahrzeug *n*, Auto(mobil) *n*; **~ coach** Reisebus *m*; **~ cy·cle** Motorrad *n*; **~·cy·clist** Motorradfahrer(in); **~·ing** [∼rɪŋ] Autofahren *n*; *school of* ~ Fahrschule *f*; **~·ist** [∼rɪst] Kraft-, Autofahrer(in); **~·ize** [∼raɪz] motorisieren; **~ launch** Motorbarkasse *f*; **~·way** *Brt.* Autobahn *f*.

mot·tled ['mɒtld] gefleckt.

mo(u)ld [məʊld] ⚘ Gartenerde *f*; Humus(boden) *m*; Schimmel *m*, Moder *m*; ⊕ (Guß)Form *f* (*a. fig.*); *geol.* Abdruck *m*; Art *f*; **2.** formen, gießen (*on, upon* nach).

mo(u)l·der ['məʊldə] zerfallen.

mo(u)ld·ing *arch.* ['məʊldɪŋ] Fries *m*.

mo(u)ld·y ['məʊldɪ] (*-ier, -iest*) schimm(e)lig, dumpfig, mod(e)rig.

mo(u)lt [məʊlt] (sich) mausern; *Haare* verlieren.

mound [maʊnd] Erdhügel *m*, -wall *m*.

mount [maʊnt] **1.** Berg *m*; Reitpferd *n*; **2.** *v/i.* (auf-, hoch)steigen; aufsitzen, aufs Pferd steigen; *v/t.* be-, ersteigen; montieren; aufziehen, -kleben; *Edelstein* fassen; **~ed police** berittene Polizei.

moun·tain ['maʊntɪn] **1.** Berg *m*; ~s *pl.* Gebirge *n*; **2.** Berg..., Gebirgs...; **~·eer** [maʊntɪ'nɪə] Bergbewohner(in); Bergsteiger(in); **~·eer·ing** [∼rɪŋ] Bergsteigen *n*; **~·ous** ['maʊntɪnəs] bergig, gebirgig.

moun·te·bank ['maʊntɪbæŋk] Marktschreier *m*, Scharlatan *m*.

mourn [mɔːn] (be)trauern; trauern um; **~·er** ['mɔːnə] Trauernde(r *m*) *f*; **~·ful** ☐ [∼fl] traurig; Trauer...; **~·ing** [∼ɪŋ] Trauer *f*; *attr.* Trauer...

mouse [maʊs] (*pl. mice* [maɪs]) Maus *f*.

multiplication

mous·tache [mə'stɑ:ʃ], *Am.* **mus·tache** ['mʌstæʃ] Schnurrbart *m*.

mouth [maʊθ] (*pl.* mouths [maʊðz]) Mund *m*; Maul *n*; Mündung *f*; Öffnung *f*; **~·ful** ['maʊθful] Mundvoll *m*; **~·or·gan** Mundharmonika *f*; **~·piece** Mundstück *n*; *fig.* Sprachrohr *n*.

mov·a·ble □ ['mu:vəbl] beweglich.

move [mu:v] **1.** *v/t.* (fort)bewegen; in Bewegung setzen; (weg)rücken; (an)treiben; *Schach:* e-n Zug machen mit; *et.* beantragen; *j-n* er-, aufregen; *fig.* bewegen, rühren, ergreifen; **~ down** *Schüler* zurückstufen; **~ up** *Schüler* versetzen; **~ house** *Brt.* umziehen; **~ heaven and earth** Himmel und Hölle in Bewegung setzen; *v/i.* sich (fort)bewegen; sich rühren; *Schach:* ziehen; (um)ziehen (**to** nach) (*Mieter*); *♂* sich entleeren (*Darm*); *fig.* voran-, fortschreiten; **~ away** weg-, fortziehen; **~ for** *s.th.* et. beantragen; **~** einziehen; anrücken (*Polizei etc.*); vorgehen (**on** gegen *Demonstranten etc.*); **~ on** weitergehen; **~ out** ausziehen; **2.** (Fort-) Bewegung *f*, Aufbruch *m*; Umzug *m*; *Schach:* Zug *m*; *fig.* Schritt *m*; **on the ~** in Bewegung; auf den Beinen; **get a ~ on!** Tempo!, mach(t) schon!, los!; **make a ~** aufbrechen; *fig.* handeln; **~·a·ble** □ ['mu:vəbl] = *movable*; **~·ment** [~mənt] Bewegung *f*; Bestrebung *f*, Tendenz *f*, Richtung *f*; *♩* Tempo *n*; *♩* Satz *m*; ⊕ (Geh-)Werk *n*; *♂* Stuhl(gang) *m*.

mov·ie *bsd. Am.* F ['mu:vɪ] Film *m*; **~s** *pl.* Kino *n*.

mov·ing □ ['mu:vɪŋ] bewegend (*a. fig.*); sich bewegend, beweglich; **~ staircase** Rolltreppe *f*.

mow [məʊ] (*~ed, ~n od. ~ed*) mähen; **~·er** ['məʊə] Mäher(in); Mähmaschine *f*, *bsd.* Rasenmäher *m*; **~·ing·ma·chine** [~ɪŋməʃiːn] Mähmaschine *f*; **~·n** [məʊn] *p.p. von* mow.

much [mʌtʃ] **1.** *adj.* (*more, most*) viel; **2.** *adv.* sehr; *in Zssgn:* viel...; *vor comp.:* viel; *vor sup.:* bei weitem; fast; **~ as I would like** so gern ich möchte; **I thought as ~** das dachte ich mir; **3.** Menge *f*, große Sache, Besondere(s) *n*; **make ~ of** viel Wesens machen von; **I am not ~ of a dancer** F ich bin kein großer Tänzer.

muck [mʌk] Mist *m* (F *a. fig.*); **~·rake** ['mʌkreɪk] **1.** Mistgabel *f*; **2.** Skanda-

le aufdecken; *contp.* im Schmutz wühlen.

mu·cus ['mjuːkəs] (Nasen)Schleim *m*.

mud [mʌd] Schlamm *m*; Kot *m*, Schmutz *m* (*a. fig.*).

mud·dle ['mʌdl] **1.** *v/t.* verwirren; *a.* **~ up, ~ together** durcheinanderbringen; F benebeln; *v/i.* pfuschen, stümpern; **~ through** F sich durchwursteln; **2.** Durcheinander *n*; Verwirrung *f*.

mud·dy □ ['mʌdɪ] (*-ier, -iest*) schlammig; trüb; **~·guard** Kotflügel *m*; Schutzblech *n*.

muff [mʌf] Muff *m*.

muf·fin ['mʌfɪn] Muffin *n* (*rundes heißes Teegebäck, mst mit Butter gegessen*).

muf·fle ['mʌfl] *oft* **~ up** ein-, umhüllen, umwickeln; *Stimme etc.* dämpfen; **~·r** [~ə] (dicker) Schal; *Am. mot.* Auspufftopf *m*.

mug[1] [mʌg] Krug *m*; Becher *m*.

mug[2] F [mʌg] (*-gg-*) überfallen u. ausrauben; **~·ger** F ['mʌgə] Straßenräuber *m*; **~·ging** F [~ɪŋ] Raubüberfall *m* (*auf der Straße*).

mug·gy ['mʌgɪ] schwül.

mug·wump *Am. iro.* ['mʌgwʌmp] hohes Tier (*Person*); *pol.* Unabhängige(r) *m*.

mu·lat·to [mjuː'lætəʊ] (*pl. -tos, Am. -toes*) Mulatt|e *m*, -in *f*.

mul·ber·ry ♀ ['mʌlbərɪ] Maulbeerbaum *m*; Maulbeere *f*.

mule [mjuːl] *zo.* Maultier *n*, -esel *m*; störrischer Mensch; **mu·le·teer** [mjuːlɪ'tɪə] Maultiertreiber *m*.

mull[1] [mʌl] Mull *m*.

mull[2] [~]: **~ over** überdenken.

mulled [mʌld]: **~ claret, ~ wine** Glühwein *m*.

mul·li·gan *Am.* F ['mʌlɪgən] Eintopfgericht *n*.

mul·li·on *arch.* ['mʌljən] Mittelpfosten *m* (*am Fenster*).

mul·ti- ['mʌltɪ] viel..., mehr..., ...reich, Mehrfach..., Multi...

mul·ti·far·i·ous □ [mʌltɪ'feərɪəs] mannigfaltig; **~·form** ['mʌltɪfɔːm] vielförmig, -gestaltig; **~·lat·er·al** [mʌltɪ'lætərəl] vielseitig; *pol.* multilateral, mehrseitig; **~·ple** ['mʌltɪpl] **1.** vielfach; **2.** *&* Vielfache(s) *n*; **~·pli·ca·tion** [mʌltɪplɪ'keɪʃn] Vervielfachung *f*; Vermehrung *f*; *&* Multiplikation *f*; **~ table** Einmaleins

M

n; **~·pli·ci·ty** [~'plɪsətɪ] Vielfalt f; **~·ply** ['mʌltɪplaɪ] (sich) vermehren (a. biol.); vervielfältigen; ♣ multiplizieren, malnehmen (by mit); **~·tude** [~tjuːd] Vielheit f; Menge f; **~·tu·di·nous** [mʌltɪ'tjuːdɪnəs] zahlreich.

mum¹ [mʌm] **1.** still; **2.** pst!

mum² Brt. F [~] Mami f, Mutti f.

mum·ble ['mʌmbl] murmeln, nuscheln; mümmeln (mühsam essen).

mum·mer·y contp. ['mʌmərɪ] Mummenschanz m.

mum·mi·fy ['mʌmɪfaɪ] mumifizieren.

mum·my¹ ['mʌmɪ] Mumie f.

mum·my² Brt. F [~] Mami f, Mutti f.

mumps ✻ [mʌmps] sg. Ziegenpeter m, Mumps m.

munch [mʌntʃ] geräuschvoll od. schmatzend kauen; mampfen.

mun·dane □ [mʌn'deɪn] weltlich.

mu·ni·ci·pal □ [mjuː'nɪsɪpl] städtisch, Stadt..., kommunal, Gemeinde...; **~·i·ty** [mjuːnɪsɪ'pælətɪ] Stadt f mit Selbstverwaltung; Stadtverwaltung f.

mu·nif·i·cence [mjuː'nɪfɪsns] Freigebigkeit f; **~·cent** [~t] freigebig.

mu·ni·tions ✗ [mjuː'nɪʃnz] pl. Munition f.

mu·ral ['mjʊərəl] **1.** Wandgemälde n; **2.** Mauer..., Wand...

mur·der ['mɜːdə] **1.** Mord m; **2.** (er)morden; fig. ✗ verhunzen; **~·er** [~rə] Mörder m; **~·ess** [~rɪs] Mörderin f; **~·ous** □ [~rəs] mörderisch; Mord...

murk·y □ ['mɜːkɪ] (-ier, -iest) dunkel, finster.

mur·mur ['mɜːmə] **1.** Murmeln f; Gemurmel n; Murren n; **2.** murmeln; murren.

mur·rain ['mʌrɪn] Viehseuche f.

mus·cle ['mʌsl] Muskel m; **~·cle-bound:** be ~ bei Gewichtheben etc.: e-e starke, aber erstarrte Muskulatur haben; **~·cu·lar** ['mʌskjʊlə] Muskel...; muskulös.

Muse¹ [mjuːz] Muse f.

muse² [~] (nach)sinnen, (-)grübeln.

mu·se·um [mjuː'zɪəm] Museum n.

mush [mʌʃ] Brei m, Mus n; Am. Maisbrei m.

mush·room ['mʌʃrʊm] **1.** ♀ Pilz m, bsd. Champignon m; **2.** rasch wachsen; ~ up (wie Pilze) aus dem Boden schießen.

mu·sic ['mjuːzɪk] Musik f; Musikstück n; Noten pl.; set to ~ vertonen; **~·al** [~əl] **1.** Musical n; **2.** □ musikalisch; Musik...; wohlklingend; ~ box bsd. Brt. Spieldose f; ~ **box** bsd. Am. Spieldose f; **~·hall** Brt. Varieté(-theater) n; **mu·si·cian** [mjuː'zɪʃn] Musiker(in); **~·stand** Notenständer m; **~·stool** Klavierstuhl m.

musk [mʌsk] Moschus m, Bisam m; **~·deer** zo. ['mʌsk'dɪə] Moschustier n.

mus·ket ✗ hist. ['mʌskɪt] Muskete f.

musk·rat ['mʌskræt] zo. Bisamratte f; Bisampelz m.

mus·lin ['mʌzlɪn] Musselin m.

mus·quash ['mʌskwɒʃ] zo. Bisamratte f; Bisampelz m.

muss Am. F [mʌs] Durcheinander n.

mus·sel ['mʌsl] (Mies)Muschel f.

must¹ [mʌst] **1.** v/aux. ich, du etc. muß(t) etc., darf(st) etc., pret. mußte(st) etc., durfte(st) etc.; I ~ not (F mustn't) ich darf nicht; **2.** Muß n.

must² [~] Schimmel m, Moder m.

must³ [~] Most m.

mus·tache Am. ['mʌstæʃ] = moustache.

mus·ta·chi·o [mə'stɑːʃɪəʊ] (pl. -os) mst ~s pl. Schnauzbart m.

mus·tard ['mʌstəd] Senf m.

mus·ter ['mʌstə] **1.** ✗ Musterung f; pass ~ fig. Zustimmung finden (with bei); △ nicht (Stoff- etc.)Muster; **2.** ✗ mustern; a. ~ up Mut etc. aufbieten, zusammennehmen; △ nicht Stoff etc. mustern.

must·y □ ['mʌstɪ] (-ier, -iest) mod(e)rig, muffig.

mu·ta·ble □ ['mjuːtəbl] veränderlich; fig. wankelmütig; **~·tion** [mjuː'teɪʃn] Veränderung f; biol. Mutation f.

mute [mjuːt] **1.** □ stumm; **2.** Stumme(r m) f; Statist(in); **3.** dämpfen.

mu·ti·late ['mjuːtɪleɪt] verstümmeln.

mu·ti·neer [mjuːtɪ'nɪə] Meuterer m; **~·nous** □ ['mjuːtɪnəs] meuterisch; rebellisch; **~·ny** [~ɪ] **1.** Meuterei f; **2.** meutern.

mut·ter ['mʌtə] **1.** Gemurmel n; Murren n; **2.** murmeln; murren.

mut·ton ['mʌtn] Hammel-, Schaffleisch n; leg of ~ Hammelkeule f; ~ **chop** Hammelkotelett n.

mu·tu·al □ ['mjuːtʃʊəl] gegenseitig; gemeinsam.

M

muz·zle ['mʌzl] **1.** zo. Maul n, Schnauze f; Mündung f (e-r Feuerwaffe); Maulkorb m; **2.** e-n Maulkorb anlegen (dat.); fig. den Mund stopfen (dat.).

my [mai] mein(e).

myrrh ♀ [mɜː] Myrrhe f.

myr·tle ♀ ['mɜːtl] Myrte f.

my·self [mai'self] (ich) selbst; mir; mich; by ~ allein.

mys·te·ri·ous □ [mi'stiəriəs] geheimnisvoll, mysteriös; **~·ry** ['mistəri] Mysterium n; Geheimnis n; Rätsel n.

mys·tic ['mistik] **1.** a. **~·ti·cal** □ [~kl] mystisch; geheimnisvoll; **2.** Mystiker(in); **~·ti·fy** [~fai] täuschen; verwirren; in Dunkel hüllen.

myth [miθ] Mythe f, Mythos m, Sage f.

N

nab F [næb] (-bb-) schnappen, erwischen.

na·cre ['neikə] Perlmutt(er f) n.

na·dir ['neidiə] ast. Nadir m (Fußpunkt); fig. Tiefpunkt m.

nag [næg] **1.** F Gaul m, Klepper m; **2.** (-gg-) v/i. nörgeln; ~ at herumnörgeln an; v/t. bekritteln; ⚠ nicht nagen.

nail [neil] **1.** (Finger-, Zehen)Nagel m; ⊕ Nagel m; zo. Kralle f, Klaue f; **2.** (an-, fest)nageln; Augen etc. heften (to auf acc.); ~ **e·nam·el**, **pol·ish** Am. Nagellack m; ~ **scissors** pl. Nagelschere f; ~ **var·nish** Brt. Nagellack m.

na·ïve □ [nɑː'iːv], **na·ive** □ [neiv] naiv; ungekünstelt.

na·ked □ ['neikid] nackt, bloß; kahl; fig. ungeschminkt; schutz-, wehrlos; **~·ness** [~nis] Nacktheit f, Blöße f; Kahlheit f; Schutz-, Wehrlosigkeit f; fig. Ungeschminktheit f.

name [neim] **1.** Name m; Ruf m; by the ~ of... namens ...; what's your ~? wie heißen Sie?; call s.o. ~s j-n beschimpfen; **2.** (be)nennen; erwähnen; ernennen zu; **~·less** □ ['neimlis] namenlos; unbekannt; **~·ly** [~li] nämlich; **~·plate** Namens-, Tür-, Firmenschild n; **~·sake** [~seik] Namensvetter m.

nan·ny ['næni] Kindermädchen n; **~·goat** zo. Ziege f.

nap¹ [næp] (Tuch)Noppe f.

nap² [~] **1.** Schläfchen n; have od. take a ~ = 2; **2.** (-pp-) ein Nickerchen machen.

nape [neip] mst ~ of the neck Genick n, Nacken m.

nap|kin ['næpkin] Serviette f; Brt. Windel f; **~·py** Brt. F [~i] Windel f.

nar·co·sis ✻ [nɑː'kəusis] (pl. -ses [-siːz]) Narkose f.

nar·cot·ic ✻ [nɑː'kɒtik] **1.** (~ally) narkotisch, betäubend, einschläfernd; Rauschgift...; ~ **addiction** Rauschgiftsucht f; ~ **drug** Rauschgift n; **2.** Betäubungsmittel n; Rauschgift n; **~s squad** Rauschgiftdezernat n.

nar|rate [nə'reit] erzählen; **~·ra·tion** [~ʃn] Erzählung f; **~·ra·tive** ['nærətiv] **1.** □ erzählend; **2.** Erzählung f; **~·ra·tor** [nə'reitə] Erzähler(in).

nar·row ['nærəu] **1.** eng, schmal; beschränkt; knapp (Mehrheit, Entkommen); engherzig; **2.** ~**s** pl. Engpaß m; Meerenge f; **3.** (sich) verengen; beschränken; einengen; Maschen abnehmen; **~·chest·ed** schmalbrüstig; **~·mind·ed** □ engherzig, -stirnig, beschränkt; **~·ness** [~nis] Enge f; Beschränktheit f (a. fig.); Engherzigkeit f.

na·sal □ ['neizl] nasal; Nasen...

nas·ty □ ['nɑːsti] (-ier, -iest) schmutzig; garstig; eklig, widerlich; böse; häßlich; abstoßend, unangenehm.

na·tal ['neitl] Geburts...

na·tion ['neiʃn] Nation f; Volk n.

na·tion·al ['næʃənl] **1.** □ national, National..., Landes..., Volks..., Staats...; **2.** Staatsangehörige(r m) f; **~·i·ty** [næʃə'næləti] Nationalität f, Staatsangehörigkeit f; **~·ize**

['næʃnəlaɪz] naturalisieren, einbürgern; verstaatlichen.

na·tion-wide ['neɪʃnwaɪd] die ganze Nation umfassend, landesweit.

na·tive ['neɪtɪv] **1.** □ angeboren; heimatlich, Heimat...; eingeboren; einheimisch; ~ **language** Muttersprache f; **2.** Eingeborene(r m) f; ~**born** gebürtig.

Na·tiv·i·ty eccl. [nə'tɪvətɪ] Geburt f (Christi).

nat·u·ral □ ['nætʃrəl] natürlich; angeboren; ungezwungen; unehelich (Kind); ~ **sience** Naturwissenschaft f; ~**ist** [~ɪst] Naturwissenschaftler(in), bsd. Biologe m; phls. Naturalist(in); ~**ize** [~aɪz] einbürgern; ~**ness** [~nɪs] Natürlichkeit f.

na·ture ['neɪtʃə] Natur f; ~ **reserve** Naturschutzgebiet n; ~ **trail** Naturlehrpfad m.

-na·tured ['neɪtʃəd] in Zssgn: ...artig, ...mütig.

naught [nɔːt] Null f; set at ~ et. ignorieren, in den Wind schlagen.

naugh·ty □ ['nɔːtɪ] (-ier, -iest) unartig, frech, ungezogen.

nau·se|a ['nɔːsjə] Übelkeit f, Ekel m; ~**ate** ['nɔːsɪeɪt] ~ s.o. (bei) j-m Übelkeit verursachen; be ~d sich ekeln; ~**at·ing** [~ɪŋ] ekelerregend; ~**ous** □ ['nɔːsjəs] ekelhaft.

nau·ti·cal □ ['nɔːtɪkl] nautisch, See...

na·val ⚓ ['neɪvl] See...; Marine...; ~ **base** Flottenstützpunkt m.

nave¹ arch. [neɪv] (Kirchen)Schiff n.

nave² [neɪv] (Rad)Nabe f.

na·vel ['neɪvl] anat. Nabel m; ~ Mittelpunkt m.

nav·i|ga·ble □ ['nævɪgəbl] schiffbar; fahrbar; lenkbar; ~**gate** [~eɪt] v/i. fahren, segeln; steuern; v/t. See etc. befahren; steuern; ~**ga·tion** [nævɪ'geɪʃən] Schiffahrt f; Navigation f; ~**ga·tor** ['nævɪgeɪtə] ⚓ Seefahrer m; ⚓ Steuermann m; ✈ Navigator m.

na·vy ['neɪvɪ] Kriegsmarine f.

nay Nein n; parl. Neinstimme f; the ~s have it der Antrag ist abgelehnt.

near [nɪə] **1.** adj. u. adv. nahe; kurz (Weg); nahe (verwandt); eng (befreundet od. vertraut); knapp; genau, wörtlich; sparsam, geizig; ~ at hand dicht dabei; **2.** prp. nahe, in der Nähe (von), nahe an (dat.) od. bei; **3.** sich nähern (dat.); ~**by** ['nɪəbaɪ] in der Nähe (gelegen); nahe; ~**ly** [~lɪ]

nahe; fast, beinahe; annähernd; genau; ~**ness** [~nɪs] Nähe f; ~**side** mot. Beifahrerseite f; ~ **door** Beifahrertür f; ~**sight·ed** kurzsichtig.

neat □ [niːt] ordentlich; sauber; gepflegt; hübsch, adrett; geschickt; rein; bsd. Brt. pur (Whisky etc.); ~**ness** ['niːtnɪs] Sauberkeit f; Gefälligkeit f; Gewandtheit f; Reinheit f.

neb·u·lous □ ['nebjʊləs] neb(e)lig.

ne·ces|sa·ry □ ['nesəsərɪ] **1.** notwendig; unvermeidlich; **2.** mst necessaries pl. Bedürfnisse pl.; ~**si·tate** [nɪ'sesɪteɪt] et. erfordern, verlangen; ~**si·ty** [~ətɪ] Notwendigkeit f; Bedürfnis n; Not f.

neck [nek] **1.** (a. Flaschen)Hals m; Nacken m, Genick n; Ausschnitt m (Kleid); ~ and ~ Kopf an Kopf; ~ or nothing auf Biegen od. Brechen; **2.** F (ab)knutschen, knutschen od. schmusen (mit); △ mst necken; ~**band** ['nekbænd] Halsbund f; ~**er·chief** ['nekətʃɪf] Halstuch n; ~**ing** F [~ɪŋ] Geschmuse n, Geknutsche n; ~**lace** ['neklɪs], ~**let** [~lɪt] Halskette f; ~**line** (Kleid)Ausschnitt m; ~**tie** Am. Krawatte f, Schlips m.

nec·ro·man·cy ['nekrəʊmænsɪ] Zauberei f.

née, Am. a. **nee** [neɪ] vor dem Mädchennamen: geborene.

need [niːd] **1.** Not f; Notwendigkeit f; Bedürfnis n; Mangel m, Bedarf m; be od. stand in ~ of dringend brauchen; **2.** nötig haben, brauchen, bedürfen (gen.); müssen, brauchen; ~**ful** ['niːdfl] notwendig.

nee·dle ['niːdl] **1.** Nadel f; Zeiger m; **2.** nähen; fig. F aufziehen, reizen; fig. anstacheln.

need·less □ ['niːdlɪs] unnötig.

nee·dle|wom·an ['niːdlwʊmən] (pl. -women) Näherin f; ~**work** Handarbeit f.

need·y □ ['niːdɪ] (-ier, -iest) bedürftig, arm.

ne·far·i·ous □ [nɪ'feərɪəs] schändlich.

ne·gate [nɪ'geɪt] verneinen; **ne·ga·tion** [~ʃn] Verneinung f; Nichts n; **neg·a·tive** ['negətɪv] **1.** □ negativ; verneinend; **2.** Verneinung f; phot. Negativ n; answer in the ~ verneinen; **3.** verneinen; ablehnen.

ne·glect [nɪ'glekt] **1.** Vernachlässigung f; Nachlässigkeit f; **2.** vernachlässigen; ~**ful** □ [~fl] nachlässig.

neg·li|gence [ˈneglɪdʒəns] Nachlässigkeit f; **~gent** □ [~t] nachlässig.
neg·li·gi·ble [ˈneglɪdʒəbl] nebensächlich; unbedeutend.
ne·go·ti|ate [nɪˈɡəʊʃɪeɪt] verhandeln (über *acc.*); zustande bringen; bewältigen; *Wechsel* begeben; **~a·tion** [nɪɡəʊʃɪˈeɪʃn] Begebung f (*e-s Wechsels etc.*); Ver-, Unterhandlung f, Bewältigung f; **~a·tor** [nɪˈɡəʊʃɪeɪtə] Unterhändler m.
Ne·gress [ˈniːɡrɪs] Negerin f; **Ne·gro** [~əʊ] (*pl.* -groes) Neger m.
neigh [neɪ] 1. Wiehern n; 2. wiehern.
neigh·bo(u)r [ˈneɪbə] Nachbar(in); Nächste(r m) f; **~hood** [~hʊd] Nachbarschaft f, Umgebung f, Nähe f; **~ing** [~rɪŋ] benachbart; **~ly** [~lɪ] nachbarlich, freundlich; **~ship** [~ʃɪp] Nachbarschaft f.
nei·ther [ˈnaɪðə, *Am.* ˈniːðə] 1. keine(r, -s) (von beiden); 2. noch, auch nicht; **~** ... *nor* ... weder ... noch ...
ne·on [ˈniːən] Neon n; **~** *lamp* Neonlampe f; **~** *sign* Leuchtreklame f.
neph·ew [ˈnevjuː] Neffe m.
nerve [nɜːv] 1. Nerv m; Sehne f; (*Blatt*)Rippe f; Kraft f, Mut m; Dreistigkeit f; *lose one's* **~** den Mut verlieren; *get on s.o.'s* **~** *s* j-m auf die Nerven gehen; *you've got a* **~** ! F Sie haben Nerven!; 2. kräftigen; ermutigen; △ *nicht nerven*; **~less** □ [ˈnɜːvlɪs] kraftlos.
ner·vous □ [ˈnɜːvəs] Nerven...; nervös; nervig, kräftig; **~ness** [~nɪs] Nervigkeit f, Nervosität f.
nest [nest] 1. Nest n (*a. fig.*); 2. nisten.
nes·tle [ˈnesl] (sich) (an)schmiegen *od.* kuscheln (*to, against* an *acc.*); a. **~** *down* sich behaglich niederlassen.
net¹ [net] 1. Netz n; 2. (*-tt-*) mit e-m Netz fangen *od.* umgeben.
net² [~] 1. netto; Rein...; 2. (*-tt-*) netto einbringen.
neth·er [ˈneðə] niedere(r, -s); Unter...
net·tle [ˈnetl] 1. ♥ Nessel f; 2. ärgern.
net·work [ˈnetwɜːk] (Straßen-, Kanal- *etc.*)Netz n; *Rundfunk*: Sendernetz n, -gruppe f.
neu·ro·sis ♣ [njʊəˈrəʊsɪs] (*pl.* -ses [-siːz]) Neurose f.
neu·ter [ˈnjuːtə] 1. geschlechtslos; *gr.* sächlich; 2. kastriertes Tier; *gr.* Neutrum n.

neu·tral [ˈnjuːtrəl] 1. neutral; unparteiisch; **~** *gear mot.* Leerlauf(gang) m; 2. Neutrale(r m) f; Null(punkt m) f; *mot.* Leerlauf(stellung f) m; **~i·ty** [njuːˈtrælətɪ] Neutralität f; **~ize** [ˈnjuːtrəlaɪz] neutralisieren.
neu·tron *phys.* [ˈnjuːtrɒn] Neutron n; **~** *bomb* ⚔ Neutronenbombe f.
nev·er [ˈnevə] nie(mals); gar nicht; **~more** [~ˈmɔː] nie wieder; **~theless** [nevəðəˈles] nichtsdestoweniger, dennoch.
new [njuː] neu; frisch; unerfahren; **~born** [ˈnjuːbɔːn] neugeboren; **~comer** [~ˈkʌmə] Neuankömmling m; Neuling m; **~ly** [ˈnjuːlɪ] neulich; neu.
news [njuːz] *mst sg.* Neuigkeit(en *pl.*) f, Nachricht(en *pl.*) f; **~agent** [ˈnjuːzeɪdʒənt] Zeitungshändler m; **~boy** Zeitungsjunge m, -austräger m; **~cast** *Rundfunk, TV*: Nachrichtensendung f; **~cast·er** *Rundfunk, TV*: Nachrichtensprecher(in); **~deal·er** *Am.* Zeitungshändler m; **~mon·ger** Klatschmaul n; **~pa·per** [~speɪpə] Zeitung f; *attr.* Zeitungs...; **~print** [~zprɪnt] Zeitungspapier n; **~reel** *Film*: Wochenschau f; **~room** Nachrichtenredaktion f; **~stand** Zeitungskiosk m.
new year [ˈnjuːˈjɜː] Neujahr n, das neue Jahr; *New Year's Day* Neujahrstag m; *New Year's Eve* Silvester m, n.
next [nekst] 1. *adj.* nächste(r, -s); (*the*) **~** *day* am nächsten Tag; **~** *to* gleich neben *od.* nach; *fig.* fast; **~** *but one* übernächste(r, -s); **~** *door to fig.* beinahe, fast; 2. *adv.* als nächste(r, -s), gleich darauf; das nächste Mal; 3. *der, die, das* Nächste; **~-door** benachbart, nebenan; **~** *of kin der, die* nächste Verwandte, *die* nächsten Angehörigen *pl.*
nib·ble [ˈnɪbl] *v/t.* knabbern an (*dat.*); *v/i.* a. **~** *at* nagen *od.* knabbern an (*dat.*); *fig.* (herum)kritteln an (*dat.*).
nice □ [naɪs] (~r, ~st) fein; wählerisch; (peinlich) genau; heikel; nett; sympathisch; schön; hübsch; **~ly** [ˈnaɪslɪ] (sehr) gut; **ni·ce·ty** [~ətɪ] Feinheit f; Genauigkeit f; Spitzfindigkeit f.
niche [nɪtʃ] Nische f.
nick [nɪk] 1. Kerbe f; *in the* **~** *of time* im richtigen Augenblick; im letzten

Moment; 2. (ein)kerben; *Brt. sl. j-n*
schnappen.

nick·el ['nɪkl] 1. *min.* Nickel *m* (*Am. a.*
Fünfcentstück); 2. vernickeln.

nick-nack ['nɪknæk] = *knick-knack*.

nick·name ['nɪkneɪm] 1. Spitzname
m; 2. *j-m* den Spitznamen ... geben.

niece [niːs] Nichte *f.*

nif·ty F ['nɪftɪ] (*-ier, -iest*) hübsch,
schick, fesch; stinkend.

nig·gard ['nɪgəd] Geizhals *m*; **~·ly**
[∼lɪ] geizig, knaus(e)rig; karg.

night [naɪt] Nacht *f*; Abend *m*; *at ∼*,
by ∼, in the ∼ nachts; **~·cap** ['naɪt-
kæp] Nachtmütze *f*; Schlaftrunk *m*;
~·club Nachtklub *m*, -lokal *n*; **~·
dress** (Damen-, Kinder)Nacht-
hemd *n*; **~·fall** Einbruch *m* der
Nacht; **~·gown** *bsd. Am.*, **~·ie** F [∼ɪ]
= *nightdress*; **night·in·gale** *zo.*
[∼ɪŋgeɪl] Nachtigall *f*; **~·ly** [∼lɪ]
nächtlich; jede Nacht *od.* jeden
Abend (stattfindend); **~·mare** Alptraum *m*; **~ school** Abendschule *f*;
~·shirt (Herren)Nachthemd *n*; **~·y**
[∼ɪ] = *nightie*.

nil [nɪl] *bsd. Sport*: Nichts *n*, Null *f.*

nim·ble ◻ ['nɪmbl] (*∼r, ∼st*) flink,
behend(e).

nine [naɪn] 1. neun; *∼ to five* normale
Dienststunden; *a ∼-to-five job* e-e
(An)Stellung mit geregelter Arbeitszeit; 2. Neun *f*; **~·pin** ['naɪnpɪn]
Kegel *m*; **~s** *sg.* Kegeln *n*; **~·teen**
['naɪn'tiːn] 1. neunzehn; 2. Neunzehn *f*; **~·teenth** [∼θ] neunzehnte(r,
-s); **~·ti·eth** ['naɪntɪɪθ] neunzigste(r,
-s); **~·ty** ['naɪntɪ] 1. neunzig; 2.
Neunzig *f.*

nin·ny F ['nɪnɪ] Dummkopf *m.*

ninth [naɪnθ] 1. neunte(r, -s); 2.
Neuntel *n*; **~·ly** ['naɪnθlɪ] neuntens.

nip [nɪp] 1. Kneifen *n*; ⊕ Knick *m*;
scharfer Frost; Schlückchen *n*; 2.
(*-pp-*) kneifen, klemmen; schneiden
(*Kälte*); *sl.* flitzen; nippen (*an dat.*);
∼ in the bud im Keim ersticken.

nip·per ['nɪpə] *zo.* (*Krebs*)Schere *f*;
(*a pair of*) **~s** *pl.* (e-e) (Kneif)Zange.

nip·ple ['nɪpl] Brustwarze *f.*

ni·tre, *Am.* **-ter** ♔ ['naɪtə] Salpeter *m.*

ni·tro·gen ♔ ['naɪtrədʒən] Stickstoff
m.

no [nəʊ] 1. *adj.* kein(e); *at ∼ time* nie;
in ∼ time im Nu; *∼ one* keiner; 2. *adv.*
nein; nicht; 3. (*pl.* noes) Nein *n.*

no·bil·i·ty [nəʊ'bɪlətɪ] Adel *m* (*a.*
fig.).

no·ble ['nəʊbl] 1. ◻ (*∼r, ∼st*) adlig;
edel; vornehm; vortrefflich; △ *nicht*
nobel; 2. Adlige(r *m*) *f*; **~·man** (*pl.*
-men) Adlige(r) *m*; **~·mind·ed** edel-
mütig.

no·bod·y ['nəʊbədɪ] niemand, keiner.

noc·tur·nal [nɒk'tɜːnl] Nacht...

nod [nɒd] 1. (*-dd-*) nicken (mit); (*im*
Sitzen) schlafen; sich neigen; *∼ off*
einnicken; **~·ding** *acquaintance*
oberflächliche Bekanntschaft; 2.
Nicken *n*, Wink *m.*

node [nəʊd] Knoten *m* (*a.* ♀, ♗, *ast.*);
♐ Überbein *n*, (*Gicht*)Knoten *m.*

noise [nɔɪz] 1. Lärm *m*; Geräusch *n*;
Geschrei *n*; *big ∼ contp.* großes Tier
(*Person*); 2. ∼ *abroad* (*about,*
around) verbreiten; **~·less** ◻
['nɔɪzlɪs] geräuschlos.

noi·some ['nɔɪsəm] schädlich; unangenehm; widerlich (*Geruch*).

nois·y ◻ ['nɔɪzɪ] (*-ier, -iest*) geräuschvoll; laut; lärmend; grell, aufdringlich (*Farbe*).

nom·i·nal ◻ ['nɒmɪnl] nominell;
(nur) dem Namen nach (vorhanden); namentlich; *∼ value econ.*
Nennwert *m*; **~·nate** [∼eɪt] ernennen; nominieren, (zur Wahl) vorschlagen; **~·na·tion** [nɒmɪ'neɪʃn]
Ernennung *f*, Nominierung *f*, Aufstellung *f* (*e-s Kandidaten*); **~·nee**
[∼'niː] Kandidat(in).

nom·i·na·tive *gr.* ['nɒmɪnətɪv] *a.* ∼
case Nominativ *m*, erster Fall.

non- [nɒn] *in Zssgn*: nicht..., Nicht...,
un...

no·nage ['nəʊnɪdʒ] Minderjährigkeit
f.

non-al·co·hol·ic ['nɒnælkə'hɒlɪk] alkoholfrei.

non-a·ligned *pol.* [nɒnə'laɪnd] block-
frei.

nonce [nɒns]: *for the ∼* nur für diesen
Fall.

non-com·mis·sioned ['nɒnkə-
'mɪʃnd] nicht bevollmächtigt; *∼ offi-*
cer ✗ Unteroffizier *m.*

non-com·mit·tal ['nɒnkə'mɪtl] un-
verbindlich.

non-con·duc·tor *bsd.* ♐ ['nɒnkən-
dʌktə] Nichtleiter *m.*

non·con·form·ist ['nɒnkən'fɔːmɪst]
Nonkonformist(in); ♀ *Brt. eccl.* Dis-
sident(in).

non·de·sript ['nɒndɪskrɪpt] nichtssagend; schwer zu beschreiben(d).

none [nʌn] **1.** keine(r, -s); nichts; **2.** keineswegs, gar nicht; ~ *the less* nichtsdestoweniger.

non-en-ti-ty [nɒn'nentətɪ] Nichtsein *n*; Unding *n*, Nichts *n*; *fig.* Null *f*.

non-ex-ist-ence ['nɒnɪɡ'zɪstəns] Nicht(vorhanden)sein *n*; Fehlen *n*.

non-fic-tion ['nɒn'fɪk∫n] Sachbücher *pl*.

non-par-ty [nɒn'pɑːtɪ] parteilos.

non-per-form-ance ['nɒnpə'fɔːməns] Nichterfüllung *f*.

non-plus ['nɒn'plʌs] **1.** Verlegenheit *f*; **2.** (*-ss-*) *j-n* (völlig) verwirren.

non-pol-lut-ing ['nɒnpə'luːtɪŋ] umweltfreundlich, ungiftig.

non-res-i-dent ['nɒn'rezɪdənt] nicht im Haus *od.* am Ort wohnend.

non|sense ['nɒnsəns] Unsinn *m*; **~sen-si-cal** □ [nɒn'sensɪkl] unsinnig.

non-skid ['nɒn'skɪd] rutschfest.

non-smoker ['nɒn'sməʊkə] Nichtraucher(in); 🚂 Nichtraucher(abteil *n*) *m*.

non-stop ['nɒn'stɒp] Nonstop..., ohne Halt, durchgehend (*Zug*), ohne Zwischenlandung (*Flugzeug*).

non-u-ni-on ['nɒn'juːnjən] nicht (gewerkschaftlich) organisiert.

non-vi-o-lence ['nɒn'vaɪələns] (Politik *f* der) Gewaltlosigkeit *f*.

noo-dle ['nuːdl] Nudel *f*.

nook [nʊk] Ecke *f*, Winkel *m*.

noon [nuːn] Mittag *m*; *at (high)* ~ um 12 Uhr mittags; **~day** ['nuːndeɪ], **~tide,** ~time *Am.* = noon.

noose [nuːs] **1.** Schlinge *f*; **2.** mit der Schlinge fangen; schlingen.

nope F [nəʊp] ne(e), nein.

nor [nɔː] noch; auch nicht.

norm [nɔːm] Norm *f*, Regel *f*; Muster *n*; Maßstab *m*; **nor-mal** □ ['nɔːml] normal; **nor-mal-ize** [~ə-laɪz] normalisieren; normen.

north [nɔːθ] **1.** Nord(*en m*); **2.** nördlich, Nord...; **~east** ['nɔː'θiːst] **1.** Nordost(*en m*); **2.** *a.* **~east-ern** [~ən] nordöstlich; **nor-ther-ly** ['nɔːðəlɪ], **nor-thern** [~ən] nördlich, Nord...; **~ward(s)** ['nɔːθwəd(z)] *adv.* nördlich, nordwärts; **~west** ['nɔː'θwest] **1.** Nordwest(*en m*); **2.** *a.* **~west-ern** [~ən] nordwestlich.

Nor-we-gian [nɔː'wiːdʒən] **1.** norwegisch; **2.** Norweger(in); *ling.* Norwegisch *n*.

nose [nəʊz] **1.** Nase *f*; Spitze *f*;

Schnauze *f*; **2.** *v/t.* riechen; ~ *one's way* vorsichtig fahren; *v/i.* schnüffeln; **~bleed** ['nəʊzbliːd] Nasenbluten *n*; *have a* ~ Nasenbluten haben; **~cone** Raketenspitze *f*; **~dive** ✈ Sturzflug *m*; **~gay** [~ɡeɪ] Sträußchen *n*.

nos-ey ['nəʊzɪ] = nosy.

nos-tal-gia [nɒ'stældʒɪə] Nostalgie *f*, Sehnsucht *f*.

nos-tril ['nɒstrəl] Nasenloch *n*, *bsd. zo.* Nüster *f*.

nos-y F ['nəʊzɪ] (*-ier, -iest*) neugierig.

not [nɒt] nicht; ~ *a* kein(e).

no-ta-ble ['nəʊtəbl] **1.** □ bemerkenswert; **2.** angesehene Person.

no-ta-ry ['nəʊtərɪ] *mst* ~ *public* Notar *m*.

no-ta-tion [nəʊ'teɪ∫n] Bezeichnung *f*.

notch [nɒt∫] **1.** Kerbe *f*, Einschnitt *m*; Scharte *f*; *Am. geol.* Engpaß *m*; **2.** (ein)kerben.

note [nəʊt] **1.** Zeichen *n*; Notiz *f*; *print.* Anmerkung *f*; Briefchen *n*, Zettel *m*; *bsd. Brt.* Banknote *f*; (*bsd.* Schuld)Schein *m*; Diplomatie, ♪: Note *f*; △ *nicht* (*Schul*)Note; ♪ Ton *m* (*a. fig.*); *fig.* Ruf *m*; Beachtung *f*; *take* ~*s* sich Notizen machen; **2.** bemerken; (besonders) beachten *od.* achten auf (*acc.*); besonders erwähnen; *a.* ~ *down* niederschreiben, notieren; **~book** ['nəʊtbʊk] Notizbuch *n*; **not-ed** bekannt, berühmt (*for wegen*); **~pa-per** Briefpapier *n*; **~wor-thy** bemerkenswert.

noth-ing ['nʌθɪŋ] **1.** nichts; **2.** Nichts *n*; Null *f*; ~ *but* nichts als, nur; *for* ~ umsonst; *good for* ~ zu nichts zu gebrauchen; *come to* ~ zunichte werden; *to say* ~ *of* ganz zu schweigen von; *there is* ~ *like* es geht nichts über (*acc.*).

no-tice ['nəʊtɪs] **1.** Nachricht *f*, Bekanntmachung *f*; Anzeige *f*, Ankündigung *f*; Kündigung *f*; Be(ob)achtung *f*; △ *nicht* Notiz; *at short* ~ kurzfristig; *give* ~ *that* bekanntgeben, daß; *give (a week's)* ~ (acht Tage vorher) kündigen; *take* ~ *of* Notiz nehmen von; *without* ~ fristlos; **2.** bemerken; (besonders) beachten *od.* achten auf (*acc.*); △ *nicht* notieren; **~a-ble** □ [~əbl] wahrnehmbar; bemerkenswert; **~ board** *Brt.* Schwarzes Brett.

no-ti-fi-ca-tion [nəʊtɪfɪ'keɪ∫n] Anzeige f, Meldung f; Bekanntmachung f; **~·fy** ['nəʊtıfaı] *et.* anzeigen, melden; j-n benachrichtigen.

no·tion ['nəʊʃn] Begriff *m*, Vorstellung f; Absicht f; ~s *pl. Am.* Kurzwaren *pl.*

no·to·ri·ous □ [nəʊ'tɔːrıəs] notorisch; all-, weltbekannt; berüchtigt.

not·with·stand·ing *prp.* ['nɒtwıθ-'stændıŋ] ungeachtet, trotz (*gen.*).

nought [nɔːt] Null f; *poet. od. veraltet* Nichts *n.*

noun *gr.* [naʊn] Substantiv *n*, Hauptwort *n.*

nour·ish ['nʌrıʃ] (er)nähren; *fig.* hegen; **~ing** [~ıŋ] nahrhaft; **~ment** [~mənt] Ernährung f; Nahrung(s-mittel *n*) f.

nov·el ['nɒvl] 1. neu; ungewöhnlich; 2. Roman *m*; △ *nicht* Novelle; **~ist** [~ıst] Romanschriftsteller(in); **no-vel·la** [nəʊ'velə] (*pl. -las, -le* [-liː]) Novelle f; **~ty** ['nɒvltı] Neuheit f.

No·vem·ber [nəʊ'vembə] November *m.*

nov·ice ['nɒvıs] Neuling *m*, Anfänger(in) (*at auf e-m Gebiet*); *eccl.* Novize *m*, f.

now [naʊ] 1. nun, jetzt; eben; *just* ~ gerade eben; ~ *and again od. then* dann u. wann; 2. *cj. a.* ~ *that* nun da.

now·a·days ['naʊədeız] heutzutage.

no·where ['nəʊweə] nirgends.

nox·ious □ ['nɒkʃəs] schädlich.

noz·zle ⊕ ['nɒzl] Düse f; Tülle f.

nu·ance [njuː'ɑːns] Nuance f, Schattierung f.

nub [nʌb] Knötchen *n*; kleiner Klumpen; *the ~ fig.* der springende Punkt (*of* bei *e-r Sache*).

nu·cle·ar ['njuːklıə] nuklear, Nuklear..., atomar, Atom...; Kern...; **~-free** atomwaffenfrei; **~-pow·ered** atomgetrieben; **~ pow·er sta·tion** Kernkraftwerk *n*; **~ re·ac·tor** Kernreaktor *m*; **~ war·head** ✕ Atomsprengkopf *m*; **~ weap·ons** *pl.* Kernwaffen *pl.*; **~ waste** Atommüll *m.*

nu·cle·us ['njuːklıəs] (*pl. -clei* [-klıaı]) Kern *m.*

nude [njuːd] 1. nackt; 2. *paint.* Akt *m.*

nudge [nʌdʒ] 1. *j-n* anstoßen, (an-) stupsen; 2. Stups(er) *m.*

nug·get ['nʌgıt] (*bsd.* Gold)Klumpen *m.*

nui·sance ['njuːsns] Ärgernis *n*, Un-

fug *m*, Plage f; lästiger Mensch; Nervensäge f; *what a ~!* wie ärgerlich!; *be a ~ to s.o.* j-m lästig fallen; *make a ~ of o.s.* den Leuten auf die Nerven gehen *od.* fallen.

nuke *Am. sl.* [njuːk] Kernwaffe f.

null [nʌl] 1. nichtssagend; ~ *and void* null u. nichtig; 2. ⊕, ⚡ Null f; **null·li·fy** ['nʌlıfaı] zunichte machen; aufheben, ungültig machen; **null·li·ty** [~ətı] Nichtigkeit f, Ungültigkeit f.

numb [nʌm] 1. starr (*with* vor); taub (*empfindungslos*); 2. starr *od.* taub machen; **~ed** erstarrt.

num·ber ['nʌmbə] 1. ⚡ Zahl f; (*Auto-, Haus- etc.*) Nummer f; (An)Zahl f; Heft *n*, Ausgabe f, Nummer f (*e-r Zeitschrift etc.*); (*Autobus- etc.*)Linie f; *without* ~ zahllos; *in* ~ an der Zahl; 2. zählen; numerieren; **~less** [~lıs] zahllos; **~·plate** *bsd. Brt. mot.* Nummernschild *n.*

nu·me·ral ['njuːmərəl] 1. Zahl(en)...; 2. ⚡ Ziffer f; *ling.* Numerale *n*, Zahlwort *n*; **~·rous** □ [~əs] zahlreich.

nun [nʌn] Nonne f; **~·ne·ry** ['nʌnərı] Nonnenkloster *n.*

nup·tial ['nʌpʃl] 1. Hochzeits..., Ehe...; 2. **~s** *pl.* Hochzeit f.

nurse [nɜːs] 1. Kindermädchen *n*; *a. dry-~* Säuglingsschwester f; *a. wet-~* Amme f; (Kranken)Pflegerin f, (Kranken)Schwester f; *at* ~ in Pflege; *put out to* ~ in Pflege geben; 2. stillen, nähren; großziehen; pflegen; hätscheln; **~·ling** ['nɜːslıŋ] Säugling *m*; Pflegling *m*; **~·maid** Kindermädchen *n*; **nur·se·ry** [~sərı] Kinderzimmer *n*; ✿ Baum-, Pflanzschule f; **~ rhymes** *pl.* Kinderlieder *pl.*, -reime *pl.*; **~ school** Kindergarten *m*; **~ slope** *Ski:* Idiotenhügel *m.*

nurs·ing ['nɜːsıŋ] Stillen *n*; (Kranken)Pflege f; **~ bot·tle** (Säuglings-, Saug)Flasche f; **~ home** *Brt.* Privatklinik f.

nurs·ling ['nɜːslıŋ] = nurseling.

nur·ture ['nɜːtʃə] 1. Pflege f; Erziehung f; 2. aufziehen; (er)nähren.

nut [nʌt] ✿ Nuß f; ⊕ (Schrauben-) Mutter f; *sl.* verrückter Kerl; *be* ~*s sl.* verrückt sein; **~·crack·er** ['nʌt-krækə] *mst* ~*s pl.* Nußknacker *m*; **~·meg** ✿ ['nʌtmeg] Muskatnuß f.

nu·tri·ment ['njuːtrımənt] Nahrung f.

nu·tri·tion [nju:'trɪʃn] Ernährung f; Nahrung f; **~tious** □ [~ʃəs], **~tive** □ ['nju:trɪtɪv] nahrhaft.

nut·shell ['nʌtʃel] Nußschale f; in a ~ in aller Kürze; **~ty** ['nʌtɪ] (-ier, -iest) voller Nüsse; nußartig; sl. verrückt.

ny·lon ['naɪlɒn] Nylon n; **~s** pl. Nylonstrümpfe pl.

nymph [nɪmf] Nymphe f.

O

o [əʊ] 1. oh!; ach!; 2. in Telefonnummern: Null f.

oaf [əʊf] Dummkopf m; Tölpel m.

oak ♀ [əʊk] Eiche f.

oar [ɔː] 1. Ruder n; 2. rudern; **~s·man** ['ɔːzmən] (pl. -men) Ruderer m.

o·a·sis [əʊ'eɪsɪs] (pl. -ses [-si:z]) Oase f (a. fig.).

oat [əʊt] mst ~s pl. ♀ Hafer m; feel one's ~s F groß in Form sein; Am. sich wichtig vorkommen; sow one's wild ~s sich die Hörner abstoßen.

oath [əʊθ] (pl. oaths [əʊðz]) Eid m, Schwur m; Fluch m; be on ~ unter Eid stehen; take (make, swear) an ~ e-n Eid leisten, schwören.

oat·meal ['əʊtmiːl] Hafermehl n.

ob·du·rate □ ['ɒbdjʊrət] verstockt.

o·be·di·ence [ə'biːdjəns] Gehorsam m; **~ent** □ [~t] gehorsam.

o·bei·sance [əʊ'beɪsəns] Ehrerbietung f; Verbeugung f; do (make, pay) ~ to s.o. j-m huldigen.

o·bese [əʊ'biːs] fett(leibig); **o·bes·i·ty** [~tɪ] Fettleibigkeit f.

o·bey [ə'beɪ] gehorchen (dat.); Befehl etc. befolgen, Folge leisten (dat.).

o·bit·u·a·ry [ə'bɪtjʊərɪ] Todesanzeige f; Nachruf m; attr. Todes..., Toten...

ob·ject 1. ['ɒbdʒɪkt] Gegenstand m; Ziel n, Zweck m, Absicht f; Objekt n (a. gr.); 2. [əb'dʒekt] v/t. einwenden (to gegen); v/i. et. dagegen haben (to ger. daß).

ob·jec·tion [əb'dʒekʃn] Einwand m, -spruch m; **~tio·na·ble** □ [~əbl] nicht einwandfrei; unangenehm.

ob·jec·tive [əb'dʒektɪv] 1. □ objektiv, sachlich; 2. Ziel n; opt. phot. Objektiv n.

ob·li·ga·tion [ɒblɪ'geɪʃn] Verpflichtung f; econ. Schuldverschreibung f; be under an ~ to s.o. j-m (zu Dank)

verpflichtet sein; be under ~ to inf. die Verpflichtung haben, zu inf.; **ob·lig·a·to·ry** □ [ə'blɪgətərɪ] verpflichtend, (rechts)verbindlich.

o·blige [ə'blaɪdʒ] (zu Dank) verpflichten; nötigen, zwingen; ~ s.o. j-m e-n Gefallen tun; much ~d sehr verbunden, danke bestens; **o·blig·ing** □ [~ɪŋ] verbindlich, zuvor-, entgegenkommend, gefällig.

o·blique □ [ə'bliːk] schief, schräg.

o·blit·er·ate [ə'blɪtəreɪt] auslöschen, tilgen (a. fig.); Schrift ausstreichen; Briefmarken entwerten.

o·bliv·i·on [ə'blɪvɪən] Vergessen(heit f) n; **~ous** □ [~əs]: be ~ of s.th. et. vergessen haben; be ~ to s.th. blind sein gegen et., et. nicht beachten.

ob·long ['ɒblɒŋ] länglich; rechteckig.

ob·nox·ious □ [əb'nɒkʃəs] anstößig; widerwärtig, verhaßt.

ob·scene □ [əb'siːn] unanständig.

ob·scure □ [əb'skjʊə] 1. □ dunkel; fig. dunkel, unklar; unbekannt; 2. verdunkeln; **ob·scu·ri·ty** [~rətɪ] Dunkelheit f (a. fig.); Unbekanntheit f; Niedrigkeit f (der Herkunft).

ob·se·quies ['ɒbsɪkwɪz] pl. Trauerfeier(lichkeiten pl.) f.

ob·serv·a·ble □ [əb'zɜːvəbl] bemerkbar; bemerkenswert; **~vance** [~ns] Befolgung f; Brauch m; **~vant** □ [~t] beachtend; aufmerksam; **~va·tion** [ɒbzə'veɪʃn] Beobachtung f; Bemerkung f; attr. Beobachtungs...; Aussichts...; **~va·to·ry** [əb'zɜːvətrɪ] Observatorium n, Stern-, Wetterwarte f.

ob·serve [əb'zɜːv] v/t. be(ob)achten; sehen; Brauch etc. (ein)halten; Gesetz etc. befolgen; bemerken, äußern; v/i. sich äußern.

ob·sess [əbˈses] heimsuchen, quälen; ~ed by od. with besessen von; **ob·ses·sion** [~eʃn] Besessenheit f; **ob·ses·sive** □ psych. [~sɪv] zwanghaft, Zwangs...

ob·so·lete [ˈɒbsəliːt] veraltet.

ob·sta·cle [ˈɒbstəkl] Hindernis n.

ob·sti|na·cy [ˈɒbstɪnəsɪ] Hartnäckigkeit f; Eigensinn m; ~**nate** □ [~t] halsstarrig; eigensinnig; hartnäckig.

ob·struct [əbˈstrʌkt] verstopfen, -sperren; blockieren; (be)hindern; **ob·struc·tion** [~kʃn] Verstopfung f; Blockierung f; Behinderung f; Hindernis n; **ob·struc·tive** □ [~ktɪv] blockierend; hinderlich.

ob·tain [əbˈteɪn] erlangen, erhalten, erreichen, bekommen; **ob·tai·na·ble** econ. [~əbl] erhältlich.

ob·trude [əbˈtruːd] (sich) aufdrängen (on dat.); **ob·tru·sive** □ [~sɪv] aufdringlich.

ob·tuse □ [əbˈtjuːs] stumpf; dumpf; begriffsstutzig.

ob·vi·ate [ˈɒbvɪeɪt] beseitigen; vorbeugen (dat.).

ob·vi·ous □ [ˈɒbvɪəs] offensichtlich, augenfällig, klar, einleuchtend.

oc·ca·sion [əˈkeɪʒn] **1.** Gelegenheit f; Anlaß m; Veranlassung f; (festliches) Ereignis; on the ~ of anläßlich (gen.); **2.** veranlassen; ~**al** □ [~l] gelegentlich, Gelegenheits...

Oc·ci·dent [ˈɒksɪdənt] Westen m; Okzident m; Abendland n; 2·**den·tal** □ [ɒksɪˈdentl] abendländisch, westlich.

oc·cu|pant [ˈɒkjʊpənt] bsd. ⚖ Besitzergreifer(in); Besitzer(in); Bewohner(in); Insass|e m, -in f; ~**pa·tion** [ɒkjʊˈpeɪʃn] Besitz(nahme f) m; ✗ Besetzung f, Besatzung f, Okkupation f; Beruf m; Beschäftigung f; ~**py** [ˈɒkjʊpaɪ] einnehmen; in Besitz nehmen; ✗ besetzen; besitzen; innehaben; bewohnen; in Anspruch nehmen; beschäftigen.

oc·cur [əˈkɜː] (-rr-) vorkommen; sich ereignen; it ~red to me mir fiel ein; ~**rence** [əˈkʌrəns] Vorkommen n; Vorfall m, Ereignis n.

o·cean [ˈəʊʃn] Ozean m, Meer n.

o'clock [əˈklɒk] Uhr (bei Zeitangaben); (at) five ~ (um) fünf Uhr.

Oc·to·ber [ɒkˈtəʊbə] Oktober m.

oc·u|lar □ [ˈɒkjʊlə] Augen...; ~**list** [~ɪst] Augenarzt m.

odd □ [ɒd] ungerade (Zahl); einzeln;

nach Zahlen: und einige od. etwas darüber; überzählig; gelegentlich; sonderbar, merkwürdig; ~**i·ty** [ˈɒdətɪ] Seltsamkeit f; ~**s** [ɒdz] oft sg. (Gewinn)Chancen pl.; Vorteil m; Vorgabe f (im Spiel); Verschiedenheit f; Unterschied m; Uneinigkeit f; be at ~ with s.o. mit j-m im Streit sein, uneins sein mit j-m; the ~ are that es ist sehr wahrscheinlich, daß; ~ and ends Reste pl.; Krimskrams m.

ode [əʊd] Ode f (Gedicht).

o·di·ous □ [ˈəʊdjəs] verhaßt; ekelhaft.

o·do(u)r [ˈəʊdə] Geruch m; Duft m.

of prp. [ɒv, əv] von; Ort: bei (the battle ~ Quebec); um (cheat s.o. ~ s.th.); von, an (dat.) (die ~); aus (~ charity); vor (dat.) (afraid ~); auf (acc.) (proud ~); über (acc.) (ashamed ~); nach (smell ~ roses; desirous ~); von, über (acc.) (speak ~ s.th.); an (acc.) (think ~ s.th.); Herkunft: von, aus; Material: aus, von; nimble ~ foot leichtfüßig; the city ~ London die Stadt London; the works ~ Dickens Dickens' Werke; your letter ~ ... Ihr Schreiben vom ...; five minutes ~ twelve Am. fünf Minuten vor zwölf.

off [ɒf] **1.** adv. fort, weg; ab, herunter(...), los(...); entfernt; Zeit: bis hin (3 months ~); aus(-), ab(geschaltet) (Licht etc.), zu (Hahn etc.); ab(-), los(gegangen) (Knopf etc.); frei (von Arbeit); ganz, zu Ende; econ. flau; verdorben (Fleisch etc.); fig. aus, vorbei; be ~ fort od. weg sein; (weg)gehen; ~ and on ab u. an; ab u. zu; well (badly) ~ gut (schlecht) daran; **2.** prp. fort von, weg von (... ab, weg, herunter); abseits von, entfernt von; frei von (Arbeit); ⚓ auf der Höhe von; be ~ duty dienstfrei haben; be ~ smoking nicht mehr rauchen; **3.** adj. (weiter) entfernt; Seiten..., Neben...; (arbeits-, dienst)frei; econ. flau, still, tot; int. fort!, weg!; raus!

of·fal [ˈɒfl] Abfall m; ~**s** pl. bsd. Brt. Fleischerei: Innereien pl.

of·fence, Am. **-fense** [əˈfens] Angriff m; Beleidigung f; Kränkung f; Ärgernis n, Anstoß m; Vergehen n, Verstoß m; ⚖ Straftat f.

of·fend [əˈfend] beleidigen, verletzen, kränken; verstoßen (against gegen); **~er** [~ə] Übel-, Missetäter(in); ½ Straffällige(r m) f; first ~ ½ Vorbestrafte(r m) f, Ersttäter(in).

of·fen·sive [ə'fensiv] **1.** □ beleidigend; anstößig; ekelhaft; Offensiv..., Angriffs...; **2.** Offensive f.

of·fer ['ɔfə] **1.** Angebot n; Anerbieten n; ~ of marriage Heiratsantrag m; **2.** v/t. anbieten (a. econ.); Preis, Möglichkeit etc. bieten; Preis, Belohnung aussetzen; Gebet, Opfer darbringen; sich bereit erklären zu; Widerstand leisten; v/i. sich bieten; **~ing** [~rɪŋ] eccl. Opfer(n) n; Anerbieten n, Angebot n.

off·hand ['ɔf'hænd] aus dem Stegreif, auf Anhieb; Stegreif..., unvorbereitet; ungezwungen, frei.

of·fice ['ɔfɪs] Büro n; Geschäftsstelle f; Amt n; Pflicht f; Dienst m, Gefälligkeit f; eccl. Gottesdienst m; ♀ Ministerium n; ~ hours pl. Dienststunden pl., Geschäftszeit f; **of·fi·cer** [~ə] Beamt|e(r) m, -in f; Polizist m, Polizeibeamte(r) m; ✕ Offizier m.

of·fi·cial [ə'fɪʃl] **1.** □ offiziell, amtlich; Amts...; **2.** Beamt|e(r) m, -in f.

of·fi·ci·ate [ə'fɪʃɪeɪt] amtieren.

of·fi·cious □ [ə'fɪʃəs] aufdringlich, übereifrig; offiziös, halbamtlich.

off–licence Brt. ['ɔflaɪsəns] Schankkonzession f über die Straße; **~print** Sonderdruck m; **~set** ausgleichen; **~shoot** ♀ Sproß m, Ableger m; **~side** ['ɔf'saɪd] **1.** Sport: Abseits(stellung f, -position f) n; mot. Fahrerseite f; **~door** Fahrertür f; **2.** Sport: abseits; **~spring** ['ɔfsprɪŋ] Nachkomme(nschaft f) m; fig. Ergebnis n.

of·ten ['ɔfn] oft(mals); häufig.

o·gle ['əʊgl]: ~ (at) liebäugeln mit, schöne Augen machen (dat.).

o·gre ['əʊgə] (menschenfressender) Riese.

oh [əʊ] oh!; ach!

oil [ɔɪl] **1.** Öl n; **2.** ölen; schmieren (a. fig.); **~cloth** ['ɔɪlklɔθ] Wachstuch n; **~rig** (Öl)Bohrinsel f; **~skin** Ölleinwand f; **~s** pl. Ölzeug n; **~y** □ ['ɔɪlɪ] (-ier, -iest) ölig (a. fig.); fettig; schmierig (a. fig.).

oint·ment ['ɔɪntmənt] Salbe f.

O.K., o·kay Br. ['əʊ'keɪ] **1.** richtig, gut, in Ordnung; **2.** int. einverstanden!; gut!, in Ordnung!; **3.** genehmigen, zustimmen (dat.).

old [əʊld] (~er, ~est, a. elder, eldest) alt; altbekannt; erfahren; ~ age (das) Alter; ~ people's home Alters-, Altenheim n; **~fash·ioned** ['əʊld'fæʃnd] altmodisch; ♀ **Glo·ry** Sternenbanner n (Flagge der U.S.A.); **~ish** ['əʊldɪʃ] ältlich.

ol·fac·to·ry anat. [ɔl'fæktərɪ] Geruchs...

ol·ive ['ɔlɪv] ♀ Olive f; Olivgrün n.

O·lym·pic Games [ə'lɪmpɪk'geɪmz] pl. Olympische Spiele pl.; Summer (Winter) ~ pl. Olympische Sommer-(Winter)spiele pl.

om·i·nous □ ['ɔmɪnəs] unheilvoll.

o·mis·sion [əʊ'mɪʃn] Unterlassung f; Auslassung f.

o·mit [ə'mɪt] (-tt-) unterlassen; auslassen.

om·nip·o·tence [ɔm'nɪpətəns] Allmacht f; **~tent** □ [~t] allmächtig.

om·nis·ci·ent □ [ɔm'nɪsɪənt] allwissend.

on [ɔn] **1.** prp. mst auf (dat., acc.); an (dat.) (~ the wall, ~ the Thames); Richtung, Ziel: auf (acc.) ... (hin), an (acc.), nach (dat.) ... (hin) (march ~ London); fig. auf (acc.) ... (hin) (~ his authority); Zeitpunkt: an (dat.) (~ Sunday, ~ the 1st of April); (gleich) nach, bei (~ his arrival); gehörig zu, beschäftigt bei (~ a committee), ~ the "Daily Mail"); Zustand: in (dat.), auf (dat.), zu (~ duty, ~ fire, ~ leave); Thema: über (acc.) (talk ~ a subject); nach (dat.) (~ this model); von (dat.) (live ~ s.th.); ~ the street Am. auf der Straße; get ~ a train bsd. Am. in e-n Zug einsteigen; ~ hearing it als ich etc. es hörte; **2.** an(geschaltet) (Licht etc.), eingeschaltet, laufend, auf (Hahn etc.); (dar)auf(legen, -schrauben etc.); Kleidung: an(haben, -ziehen) (have a coat ~); auf(behalten) (keep one's hat ~); weiter(gehen, -sprechen etc.); and so ~ und so weiter; ~ and ~ immer weiter; ~ to ... auf (hinauf od. hinaus); be ~ im Gange sein, los sein; thea. gespielt werden; laufen (Film).

once [wʌns] **1.** adv. einmal; je(mals); einst; at ~ (so)gleich, sofort; zugleich; all at ~ plötzlich; for ~ diesmal, ausnahmsweise; ~ (and) for all ein für allemal; ~ again, ~ more noch einmal; ~ in a while dann und wann; **2.** cj. a. ~ that sobald.

NO

one [wʌn] ein(e); einzig; eine(r, -s); man; eins; ∼'s sein(e); ∼ day eines Tages; ∼ Smith ein gewisser Smith; ∼ another einander; ∼ by ∼, ∼ after another, ∼ after the other e-r nach dem andern; be at ∼ with s.o. mit j-m einig sein; I for ∼ ich für meinen Teil; the little ∼s pl. die Kleinen pl.

o·ner·ous □ ['ɒnərəs] schwer(wiegend).

one·self [wʌn'self] sich (selbst); (sich) selbst; ∼**-sid·ed** □ ['wʌn'saidid] einseitig; ∼**·way** ['wʌnweı]: ∼ street Einbahnstraße f; ∼ ticket Am. einfache Fahrkarte; ⚒ einfaches Ticket.

on·ion ♗ ['ʌnjən] Zwiebel f.

on·look·er ['ɒnlukə] Zuschauer(in).

on·ly ['əunlı] 1. adj. einzige(r, -s); 2. adv. nur, bloß; erst; ∼ yesterday erst gestern; 3. cj. ∼ (that) nur daß.

on·rush ['ɒnrʌʃ] Ansturm m.

on·set ['ɒnset], **on·slaught** ['ɒnslɔːt] Angriff m; Anfang m; 𝓈 Ausbruch m (e-r Krankheit).

on·ward ['ɒnwəd] 1. adj. fortschreitend; 2. a. ∼s adv. vorwärts, weiter.

ooze [uːz] 1. Schlamm m; 2. v/i. sickern; ∼ away fig. schwinden; v/t. ausströmen, -schwitzen.

o·paque □ [əu'peık] (∼r, ∼st) undurchsichtig.

o·pen ['əupən] 1. □ offen; geöffnet, auf; frei (Feld etc.); öffentlich; offen, unentschieden; offen, freimütig; freigebig; fig. zugänglich (to dat.), aufgeschlossen (to für); 2. in the ∼ (air) im Freien; come out into the ∼ fig. an die Öffentlichkeit treten; 3. v/t. öffnen; eröffnen (a. fig.); v/i. sich öffnen, aufgehen; sich öffnen, aufmachen; anfangen; ∼ into führen nach (Tür etc.); ∼ on to hinausgehen auf (acc.) (Fenster etc.); ∼ out sich ausbreiten; ∼**air** ['əupən'eə] im Freien (stattfindend), Freilicht..., Freiluft...; ∼**armed** ['əupən'ɑːmd] herzlich, warm; ∼**er** ['əupnə] (Büchsen- etc.)Öffner m; ∼**eyed** ['əupən-'aɪd] staunend; wach; mit offenen Augen; ∼**hand·ed** ['əupən'hændıd] freigebig, großzügig; ∼**heart·ed** ['əupənhɑːtıd] offen(herzig), aufrichtig; ∼**ing** ['əupnıŋ] (Er)Öffnung f; freie Stelle; Gelegenheit f; attr. Eröffnungs...; ∼**mind·ed** fig. ['əu-pən'maındıd] aufgeschlossen.

op·e·ra ['ɒpərə] Oper f; ∼**glass(·es** pl.) Opernglas n.

op·e·rate ['ɒpəreıt] v/t. bewirken, (mit sich) bringen; ⊕ Maschine bedienen, et. betätigen; Unternehmen betreiben; v/i. ⊕ arbeiten, funktionieren, laufen; wirksam werden od. sein; ✕ operieren; 𝓈 operieren (on od. upon s.o. j-n); operating room Am., operating-theatre Brt. Operationssaal m; ∼**ra·tion** [ɒpə'reıʃn] Wirkung f (on auf acc.); ⊕ Betrieb m, Tätigkeit f; 𝓈, ✕ Operation f; be in ∼ in Betrieb sein; come into ∼ ⚖ in Kraft treten; ∼**ra·tive** ['ɒpərətıv] 1. □ wirksam; tätig; praktisch; 𝓈 operativ; 2. Arbeiter m; ∼**ra·tor** [∼eıtə] ⊕ Bedienungsperson f; Telephonist(in).

o·pin·ion [ə'pınjən] Meinung f; Ansicht f; Stellungnahme f; Gutachten n; in my ∼ meines Erachtens.

op·po·nent [ə'pəunənt] Gegner m.

op·por·tune □ ['ɒpətjuːn] passend; rechtzeitig; günstig; ∼**tu·ni·ty** [ɒpə-'tjuːnətı] (günstige) Gelegenheit f.

op·pose [ə'pəuz] entgegen-, gegenüberstellen; sich widersetzen, bekämpfen; **op·posed** entgegengesetzt; be ∼ to gegen ... sein; **op·po·site** ['ɒpəzıt] 1. □ gegenüberliegend; entgegengesetzt; 2. prp. u. adv. gegenüber; 3. Gegenteil n, -satz m; **op·po·si·tion** [ɒpə'zıʃn] das Gegenüberstehen; Widerstand m; Gegensatz m; Widerspruch m; Opposition f (a. pol.).

op·press [ə'pres] be-, unterdrücken; **op·pres·sion** [∼ʃn] Unterdrückung f; Druck m, Bedrängnis f; Bedrücktheit f; **op·pres·sive** □ [∼sıv] (be-) drückend; hart, grausam; schwül (Wetter).

op·tic ['ɒptık] Augen..., Seh...; ∼ **op·ti·cal** □ [∼l] optisch; **op·ti·cian** [ɒp'tıʃn] Optiker m.

op·ti·mis·m ['ɒptımızəm] Optimismus m.

op·tion ['ɒpʃn] Wahl(freiheit) f; Alternative f; econ. Vorkaufsrecht n, Option f; ∼**al** □ [∼l] freigestellt, wahlfrei.

op·u·lence ['ɒpjuləns] (großer) Reichtum m, Überfluß m.

or [ɔː] oder; ∼ else sonst.

o·rac·u·lar □ [ɒ'rækjulə] orakelhaft.

o·ral □ ['ɔːrəl] mündlich; Mund...

or·ange ['ɒrındʒ] 1. Orange n (Farbe); ♗ Orange f, Apfelsine f; 2.

orange(farben); **~ade** [ˈɒrɪndʒˈeɪd] Orangenlimonade f.

o·ra·tion [ɔːˈreɪʃn] Rede f; **or·a·tor** [ˈɒrətə] Redner m; **or·a·to·ry** [~rɪ] Redekunst f, Rhetorik f; eccl. Kapelle f.

orb [ɔːb] Ball m; Himmelskörper m; poet. Augapfel m, Auge n.

or·bit [ˈɔːbɪt] **1.** Kreis-, Umlaufbahn f; get od. put into ~ in e-e Umlaufbahn gelangen od. bringen; **2.** v/t. die Erde etc. umkreisen; Satelliten etc. auf e-e Umlaufbahn bringen; v/i. die Erde etc. umkreisen, sich auf e-r Umlaufbahn bewegen.

or·chard [ˈɔːtʃəd] Obstgarten m.

or·ches·tra [ˈɔːkɪstrə] ♪ Orchester n; Am. thea. Parkett n.

or·chid ♀ [ˈɔːkɪd] Orchidee f.

or·dain [ɔːˈdeɪn] anordnen, verfügen; zum Priester weihen.

or·deal fig. [ɔːˈdiːl] schwere Prüfung; Qual f, Tortur f.

or·der [ˈɔːdə] **1.** Ordnung f, Anordnung f, Reihenfolge f; Befehl m; econ. Bestellung f, Auftrag m; econ. Zahlungsauftrag m; parl. etc. (Geschäfts)Ordnung f; Klasse f, Rang m; Orden m (a. eccl.); take (holy) ~s in den geistlichen Stand treten; in ~ to inf. um zu inf.; in ~ that damit; out of ~ nicht in Ordnung; defekt; nicht in Betrieb; make to ~ auf Bestellung anfertigen; **2.** (an-, ver)ordnen; befehlen; econ. bestellen; j-n schicken; **~ly** [ˈɔːdəlɪ] **1.** ordentlich; fig. ruhig; **2.** ✕ (Offiziers)Bursche m; ✕ Sanitätssoldat m; Krankenpfleger m.

or·di·nal [ˈɔːdɪnl] **1.** Ordnungs...; **2.** a. ~ number ♣ Ordnungszahl f.

or·di·nance [ˈɔːdɪnəns] Verordnung f.

or·di·nary □ [ˈɔːdnrɪ] üblich, gewöhnlich, normal; ⚠ nicht ordinär.

ord·nance ✕ [ˈɔːdnəns] Artillerie f, Geschütze pl.; Feldzeugwesen n.

ore [ɔː] Erz n.

or·gan [ˈɔːgən] ♪ Orgel f; Organ n; **~grind·er** [~graɪndə] Leierkastenmann m; **~ic** [ɔːˈgænɪk] (~ally) organisch; **~is·m** [ˈɔːgənɪzəm] Organismus m; **~i·za·tion** [ɔːgənaɪˈzeɪʃn] Organisation f; **~ize** [ˈɔːgənaɪz] organisieren; **~iz·er** [~ə] Organisator(in).

o·ri·ent [ˈɔːrɪənt] **1.** ♀ Osten m; Orient m, Morgenland n; **2.** orientieren;

~en·tal [ɔːrɪˈentl] **1.** □ orientalisch, östlich; **2.** ♀ Oriental|e m, -in f; **~en·tate** [ˈɔːrɪənteɪt] orientieren.

or·i·fice [ˈɒrɪfɪs] Mündung f; Öffnung f.

or·i·gin [ˈɒrɪdʒɪn] Ursprung m; Anfang m; Herkunft f.

o·rig·i·nal [əˈrɪdʒənl] **1.** □ ursprünglich; originell; Original...; **2.** Original n; **~i·ty** [ərɪdʒəˈnælətɪ] Originalität f; **~ly** [əˈrɪdʒnəlɪ] originell; ursprünglich, zuerst.

o·rig·i·nate [əˈrɪdʒneɪt] v/t. hervorbringen, schaffen; v/i. entstehen, v/i. entspringen; **~na·tor** [~ə] Urheber(in).

or·na|ment 1. [ˈɔːnəmənt] Verzierung f; fig. Zierde f; **2.** [~ment] verzieren, schmücken; **~men·tal** □ [ɔːnəˈmentl] schmückend, Zier...

or·nate □ [ɔːˈneɪt] reichverziert, reichgeschmückt; überladen.

or·phan [ˈɔːfn] **1.** Waise f; **2.** a. ~ed verwaist; **~age** [~ɪdʒ] Waisenhaus n.

or·tho·dox □ [ˈɔːθədɒks] orthodox; strenggläubig; üblich, anerkannt.

os·cil·late [ˈɒsɪleɪt] schwingen; fig. schwanken.

o·si·er ♀ [ˈəʊʒə] Korbweide f.

os·prey zo. [ˈɒsprɪ] Fischadler m.

os·ten·si·ble □ [ɒˈstensəbl] Zurschaulich.

os·ten·ta|tion [ɒstenˈteɪʃn] Zurschaustellung f; Protzerei f; **~tious** □ [~ʃəs] großtuerisch, prahlerisch.

os·tra·cize [ˈɒstrəsaɪz] verbannen; ächten.

os·trich zo. [ˈɒstrɪtʃ] Strauß m.

oth·er [ˈʌðə] andere(r, -s); the ~ day neulich; the ~ morning neulich morgens; every ~ day jeden zweiten Tag; **~wise** [~waɪz] anders; sonst.

ot·ter [ˈɒtə] zo. Otter m; Otterfell n.

ought v/aux. [ɔːt] (verneint: ~ not, oughtn't) ich, du etc. sollte(st) etc.; you ~ to have done it Sie hätten es tun sollen.

ounce [aʊns] Unze f (= 28,35 g).

our [ˈaʊə] unser; ~s [ˈaʊəz] der, die, das uns(e)re; unser; **~selves** [aʊəˈselvz] uns (selbst); wir selbst.

oust [aʊst] verdrängen, -treiben, hinauswerfen; e-s Amtes entheben.

out [aʊt] **1.** aus; hinaus(gehen, -werfen etc.); heraus(kommen etc.); aus(brechen etc.); außen, draußen; nicht zu Hause; Sport: aus, draußen; aus der Mode; vorbei; erloschen; aus(gegangen); verbraucht; (bis) zu Ende;

~ and about (wieder) auf den Beinen; way ~ Ausgang m; ~ of aus (... heraus); hinaus; außerhalb; außer Atem etc.; aus; Furcht etc.; von (in nine cases ~ of ten); be ~ of s.th. et. nicht mehr haben; 2. Ausweg m; the ~s pl. parl. die Opposition; 3. econ. übernormal, Über... (Größe); 4. int. hinaus!, raus!

out|bal·ance ['aʊt'bæləns] überwiegen, -treffen; ~**bid** [aʊt'bɪd] (-dd-; -bid) überbieten; ~**board** ['aʊtbɔːd] Außenbord...; ~**break** ['aʊtbreɪk] Ausbruch m; ~**build·ing** ['aʊtbɪldɪŋ] Nebengebäude n; ~**burst** ['aʊtbɜːst] Ausbruch m (a. fig.); ~**cast** ['aʊtkɑːst] 1. ausgestoßen; 2. Ausgestoßene(r m) f; ~**come** ['aʊtkʌm] Ergebnis n; △ nicht das Aus-kommen; ~**cry** ['aʊtkraɪ] Aufschrei m, Schrei m der Entrüstung; ~**dat·ed** ['aʊt'deɪtɪd] überholt, ver-altet; ~**dis·tance** ['aʊt'dɪstns] (weit) überholen; ~**do** [aʊt'duː] (-did, -done) übertreffen; ~**door** ['aʊtdɔː] Außen..., außerhalb des Hauses, im Freien, draußen; ~**doors** [aʊt'dɔːz] draußen, im Freien.

out·er ['aʊtə] äußere(r, -s) Außen...; ~**most** [~məʊst] äußerst.

out|fit ['aʊtfɪt] Ausrüstung f, Aus-stattung f; F Haufen m, Trupp m, (Arbeits)Gruppe f; Am.✕ Einheit f; ~**fit·ter** Brt. [~ə] Herrenausstat-ter m; ~**go·ing** ['aʊtgəʊɪŋ] 1. weg-, ab-gehend; 2. Ausgehen n; ~s pl. (Geld)Ausgaben pl.; ~**grow** ['aʊt'grəʊ] (-grew, -grown) herauswach-sen aus (Kleidern); größer werden als, hinauswachsen über (acc.); ~**house** ['aʊthaʊs] Nebengebäude n; Am. Außenabort m.

out·ing ['aʊtɪŋ] Ausflug m.

out|last ['aʊt'lɑːst] überdauern, -le-ben; ~**law** ['aʊtlɔː] Geächtete(r m) f; ~**lay** ['aʊtleɪ] (Geld)Auslage(n pl.) f, Ausgabe(n pl.) f; ~**let** ['aʊtlet] Aus-laß m, Abfluß m, Austritt m, Abzug m; econ. Absatzmarkt m; Am. ⚡ An-schluß m, Steckdose f; fig. Ventil n; ~**line** ['aʊtlaɪn] 1. Umriß m; Über-blick m; Skizze f; 2. umreißen, skiz-zieren; ~**live** [aʊt'lɪv] überleben; ~**look** ['aʊtlʊk] Ausblick m (a. fig.); Auffassung f; ~**ly·ing** ['aʊtlaɪɪŋ] entlegen; ~**match** ['aʊt'mætʃ] weit

übertreffen; ~**num·ber** [aʊt'nʌm-bə] an Zahl übertreffen; ~**pa·tient** ['aʊtpeɪʃnt] ambulanter Patient, am-bulante Patientin; ~**post** ['aʊtpəʊst] Vorposten m; ~**pour·ing** ['aʊtpɔː-rɪŋ] (bsd. Gefühls)Erguß m; ~**put** ['aʊtpʊt] Output m: econ. u. ⊕ Ar-beitsertrag m, -leistung f; econ. Pro-duktion f, Ausstoß m, Ertrag m; ⚡ Ausgangsleistung f; ≵ Ausgang m (an Geräten); Computer: (Daten-)Ausgabe f; ~**rage** ['aʊtreɪdʒ] 1. Aus-schreitung f; Gewalttat f; 2. gröblich verletzen od. beleidigen; Gewalt an-tun (dat.); ~**ra·geous** □ [aʊt'reɪ-dʒəs] abscheulich; empörend, uner-hört; ~**reach** ['aʊt'riːtʃ] weiter rei-chen als; ~**right** [adj. 'aʊtraɪt, adv. aʊt'raɪt] gerade heraus; völlig; direkt; ~**run** [aʊt'rʌn] (-nn-; -ran, -run) schneller laufen als; fig. über-treffen, hinausgehen über (acc.); ~**set** ['aʊtset] Anfang m; Aufbruch m; ~**shine** ['aʊt'ʃaɪn] (-shone) über-strahlen; fig. a. in den Schatten stellen; ~**side** [aʊt'saɪd] 1. Außen-seite f; das Äußere; Sport: Außen-stürmer m; at the (very) ~ (aller-)höchstens; attr.: ~ left (right) Sport: Links-(Rechts-)Außen m; 2. adj. äußere(r, -s), Außen...; außerhalb, draußen; äußerste(r, -s) (Preis); 3. adv. draußen, außerhalb; heraus, hinaus; 4. prp. außerhalb; ~**sid·er** [~ə] Außenseiter(in), -stehende(r m) f; ~**size** ['aʊtsaɪz] Übergröße f; ~**skirts** ['aʊtskɜːts] pl. Außenbezir-ke pl., (Stadt)Rand m; ~**smart** F ['aʊt'smɑːt] überlisten; ~**spo·ken** [aʊt'spəʊkən] offen, freimütig; △ nicht ausgesprochen; ~**spread** ['aʊt'spred] ausgestreckt, -breitet; ~**stand·ing** ['aʊt'stændɪŋ] hervor-ragend (a. fig.); ausstehend (Schuld); ungeklärt (Frage); unerledigt (Ar-beit); ~**stretched** ['aʊtstretʃt] = outspread; ~**strip** ['aʊt'strɪp] (-pp-) überholen (a. fig.).

out·ward ['aʊtwəd] 1. äußere(r, -s); äußerlich; nach (dr)außen gerichtet; 2. adv. mst ~s (nach) auswärts, nach (dr)außen; ~**ly** [~lɪ] äußerlich; an der Oberfläche.

out|weigh ['aʊt'weɪ] schwerer sein als; fig. überwiegen; ~**wit** [aʊt'wɪt] (-tt-) überlisten; ~**worn** ['aʊtwɔːn] erschöpft; fig. abgegriffen; über-holt.

o·val ['əʊvl] 1. □ oval; 2. Oval n.

ov·en ['ʌvn] Backofen m.

o·ver ['əʊvə] 1. über; hinüber; darüber; herüber; drüben; über ...darüber(...); et. über(geben etc.); über(kochen etc.); um(fallen, -werfen etc.); herum(drehen etc.); von Anfang bis Ende, durch(lesen etc.), ganz, über u. über; (gründlich) über(legen etc.); nochmals, wieder; übermäßig, über...; darüber, mehr; übrig; zu Ende, vorüber, vorbei, aus; (all) ~ again noch einmal, (ganz) von vorn; ~ against gegenüber (dat.); all ~ ganz vorbei; ~ and again immer wieder; 2. prp. über; über (acc.) ...hin(weg); ~ and above neben, zusätzlich zu.

o·ver|act ['əʊvər'ækt] e-e Rolle übertreiben; ~**all** ['əʊvərɔ:l] 1. Brt. (Arbeits)Kittel m; ~s pl. Arbeitsanzug m, Overall m; 2. gesamt, Gesamt...; ~**awe** ['əʊvər'ɔ:] einschüchtern; ~**bal·ance** [əʊvə'bæləns] 1. Übergewicht n; 2. das Gleichgewicht verlieren; umkippen; aus dem Gleichgewicht bringen; überwiegen (a. fig.); ~**bear·ing** □ [əʊvə'beərɪŋ] anmaßend; ~**board** ♜ ['əʊvəbɔ:d] über Bord; ~**cast** ['əʊvəka:st] bewölkt; ~**charge** [əʊvə'tʃɑ:dʒ] 1. ⚡, ⊕ überladen; e-n Betrag zuviel verlangen (for für); 2. Überpreis m; Aufschlag m; ~**coat** ['əʊvəkəʊt] Mantel m; ~**come** ['əʊvə'kʌm] (-came, -come) überwinden, -wältigen; ~**crowd** [əʊvə'kraʊd] überfüllen; ~**do** [əʊvə'du:] (-did, -done) zu viel tun; übertreiben; zu sehr kochen od. braten; überanstrengen; ~**draw** ['əʊvə'drɔ:] (-drew, -drawn) econ. Konto überziehen; fig. übertreiben; ~**dress** [əʊvə'dres] (sich) übertrieben anziehen; ~**due** [əʊvə'dju:] (über)fällig; ~**eat** [əʊvər'i:t] (-ate, -eaten): a. ~ o.s. sich überessen; ~**flow** 1. ['əʊvə'fləʊ] v/t. überfluten, -schwemmen; v/i. überfließen, -laufen; 2. ['əʊvəfləʊ] Überschwemmung f; Überschuß m; ⊕ Überlauf m; ~**grow** ['əʊvə'grəʊ] (-grew, -grown) v/t. überwuchern; v/i. zu groß werden; ~**grown** [~n] überwuchert; übergroß; ~**hang** 1. ['əʊvə'hæŋ] (-hung) v/t. über (dat.) hängen; v/i. überhängen; 2. ['əʊvəhæŋ] Überhang m; ~**haul** ['əʊvə'hɔ:l] Maschine überholen; ~**head** 1.

adv. [əʊvə'hed] (dr)oben; 2. adj. ['əʊvəhed] Hoch..., Ober...; econ. allgemein (Unkosten); 3. ~s pl. econ. allgemeine Unkosten pl.; ~**hear** [əʊvə'hɪə] (-heard) (zufällig) belauschen, (mit an)hören; △ nicht überhören; ~**joyed** [əʊvə'dʒɔɪd] ﬅ Overkill m; fig. Übermaß n, Zuviel n (of an dat.); ~**lap** [əʊvə'læp] (-pp-) übergreifen auf (acc.); sich überschneiden (mit); ⊕ überlappen; ~**lay** [əʊvə'leɪ] (-laid) belegen, überziehen; ~**leaf** [əʊvə'li:f] umseitig; ~**load** [əʊvə'ləʊd] überladen; ~**look** [əʊvə'lʊk] übersehen (a. fig.); ~ing the sea mit Blick auf das Meer; ~**much** [əʊvə'mʌtʃ] zu viel; ~**night** [əʊvə'naɪt] 1. über Nacht; stay ~ übernachten; 2. Nacht..., Übernachtungs...; ~**pass** bsd. Am. ['əʊvəpa:s] (Straßen-, Eisenbahn)Überführung f; ~**pay** [əʊvə'peɪ] (-paid) zu viel bezahlen; ~**peo·pled** [əʊvə'pi:pld] übervölkert; ~**plus** ['əʊvəplʌs] Überschuß m (of an dat.); ~**pow·er** ['əʊvə'paʊə] überwältigen; ~**rate** ['əʊvə'reɪt] überschätzen; ~**reach** [əʊvə'ri:tʃ] übervorteilen; ~ o.s. sich übernehmen; ~**ride** fig. [əʊvə'raɪd] (-rode, -ridden) sich hinwegsetzen über (acc.); umstoßen; ~**rule** [əʊvə'ru:l] überstimmen; 🏛 Urteil aufheben; ~**run** [əʊvə'rʌn] (-nn-; -ran, -run) Land überfluten; ✗ herfallen über (acc.); überwuchern; Signal überfahren; Zeit überziehen; be ~ with wimmeln von; ~**sea(s)** [əʊvə'si:(z)] 1. überseeisch, Übersee...; 2. in od. nach Übersee; ~**see** [əʊvə'si:] (-saw, -seen) beaufsichtigen; ~**seer** ['əʊvəsɪə] Aufseher m; Vorarbeiter m; ~**shad·ow** [əʊvə'ʃædəʊ] überschatten (a. fig.); fig. in den Schatten stellen; ~**sight** ['əʊvəsaɪt] Versehen n; ~**sleep** [əʊvə'sli:p] (-slept) verschlafen; ~**state** [əʊvə'steɪt] übertreiben; ~**state·ment** [~mənt] Übertreibung f; ~**strain** 1. [əʊvə'streɪn] überanstrengen; ~ o.s. sich übernehmen; 2. ['əʊvəstreɪn] Überanstrengung f.

o·vert □ ['əʊvə:t] offen(kundig).

o·ver|take ['əʊvə'teɪk] (-took, -taken) einholen; j-n überraschen; überholen; ~**tax** ['əʊvə'tæks] zu hoch besteuern; *fig.* überschätzen; überfordern); **~throw 1.** ['əʊvə'θrəʊ] (-threw, -thrown) (um)stürzen (*a. fig.*); besiegen; **2.** ['əʊvəθrəʊ] (Um-)Sturz *m*; Niederlage *f*; **~time** *econ.* ['əʊvətaɪm] Überstunden *pl.*; be on ~, *do* ~ Überstunden machen.

o·ver·ture ['əʊvətjʊə] ♪ Ouvertüre *f*; ♪ Vorspiel *n*; *mst* ~s *pl.* Vorschlag *m*, Antrag *m*.

o·ver|turn ['əʊvə'tɜːn] (um)stürzen (*a. fig.*); **~weight** ['əʊvəweɪt] Übergewicht *n*; **~whelm** ['əʊvə'welm] überschütten (*a. fig.*); überwältigen (*a. fig.*); **~work** ['əʊvə'wɜːk] **1.** Überarbeitung *f*; **2.** sich überarbeiten; überanstrengen; **~wrought** ['əʊvə'rɔːt] überarbeitet; überreizt.

owe [əʊ] *Geld*, *Dank etc.* schulden, schuldig sein; verdanken.

ow·ing ['əʊɪŋ]: be ~ zu zahlen sein; ~

to infolge (*gen.*); wegen (*gen.*); dank (*dat.*).

owl *zo.* [aʊl] Eule *f*.

own [əʊn] **1.** eigen; selbst; einzig, (innig) geliebt; **2.** my ~ mein Eigentum; *a house of one's* ~ ein eigenes Haus; *hold one'* s ~ standhalten; **3.** besitzen; zugeben; anerkennen; sich bekennen (*to* zu).

own·er ['əʊnə] Eigentümer(in); **~ship** ['əʊnəʃɪp] Eigentum(srecht) *n*.

ox *zo.* [ɒks] (*pl.* oxen ['ɒksn]) Ochse *m*; Rind *n*.

ox·i·da·tion 🔔 [ɒksɪ'deɪʃn] Oxydation *f*, Oxydierung *f*; **ox·ide** 🔔 ['ɒksaɪd] Oxyd *n*; **ox·i·dize** 🔔 ['ɒksɪdaɪz] oxydieren.

ox·y·gen 🔔 ['ɒksɪdʒən] Sauerstoff *m*.

oy·ster *zo.* ['ɔɪstə] Auster *f*.

o·zone 🔔 ['əʊzəʊn] Ozon *n*.

P

pace [peɪs] **1.** Schritt *m*; Gang *m*; Tempo *n*; **2.** *v/t.* abschreiten; durchschreiten; *v/i.* (einher)schreiten; ~ up and down auf u. ab gehen.

pa·cif·ic [pə'sɪfɪk] (~ally) friedlich.

pac·i|fi·ca·tion [pæsɪfɪ'keɪʃn] Beruhigung *f*, Besänftigung *f*; **~fy** ['pæsɪfaɪ] Schnuller *m*; **~fy** [~aɪ] beruhigen, besänftigen.

pack [pæk] **1.** Pack(en) *m*, Paket *n*, Ballen *m*, Bündel *n*; *Am.* Packung *f* (*Zigaretten*); Meute *f* (*Hunde*); Rudel *n* (*Wölfe*); Pack *n*, Bande *f*; ⚔, *Kosmetik*: Packung *f*; *a.* ~ of cards Spiel *n* Karten; *a.* ~ of films *phot.* Filmpack *m*; *a* ~ of lies ein Haufen Lügen; **2.** *v/t.* (voll)packen; bepacken; vollstopfen; zusammenpferchen; *econ.* eindosen; ⊕ (ab-) dichten; *Am.* ~ *Revolver etc.* (bei sich) tragen; *oft* ~ up zusammen-, ver-, ein-, abpacken; *mst* ~ off (rasch) fortschicken, -jagen; *v/i.* sich *gut etc.* verpacken *od.* konservieren lassen; *oft* ~ up (zusammen)packen; send s.o. ~ing j-n fortjagen; **~age** ['pækɪdʒ] Pack *m*, Ballen *m*; Paket *n*; Packung *f*; Frachtstück *n*; ~ tour

Pauschalreise *f*; **~er** [~ə] Packer(in); *Am.* Konservenhersteller *m*; **~et** [~ɪt] Päckchen *n*; Packung *f* (*Zigaretten*); *a.* **~boat** ⚓ Postschiff *n*; **~ing** [~ɪŋ] Packen *n*; Verpackung *f*; **~thread** Bindfaden *m*.

pact [pækt] Vertrag *m*, Pakt *m*.

pad [pæd] **1.** Polster *n*; *Sport*: Beinschutz *m*; Schreib-, Zeichenblock *m*; Abschußrampe *f* (*für Raketen*); a. ink-~ Stempelkissen *n*; **2.** (-dd-) (aus)polstern, wattieren; **~ding** ['pædɪŋ] Polsterung *f*, Wattierung *f*.

pad·dle ['pædl] **1.** Paddel *n*; ⚓ (Rad-) Schaufel *f*; **2.** paddeln; planschen; **~wheel** ⚓ Schaufelrad *n*.

pad·dock ['pædək] (Pferde)Koppel *f*; *Pferderennsport*: Sattelplatz *m*; *Motorsport*: Fahrerlager *n*.

pad·lock ['pædlɒk] Vorhängeschloß *n*.

pa·gan ['peɪgən] **1.** heidnisch; **2.** Heid|e *m*, -in *f*.

page[1] [peɪdʒ] **1.** Seite *f* (*e-s Buches*, *e-r Zeitung etc.*); **2.** paginieren.

page[2] [~] **1.** (Hotel)Page *m*; **2.** j-n ausrufen lassen.

pag·eant ['pædʒənt] historisches Festspiel; Festzug m.

paid [peɪd] pret. u. p.p. von pay 2.

pail [peɪl] Eimer m.

pain [peɪn] 1. Schmerz(en pl.) m; Kummer m; ~s Mühe f; on od. under ~ of death bei Todesstrafe; be in (great) ~ (große) Schmerzen haben; take ~s sich Mühe geben; 2. j-n schmerzen, j-m weh tun; ~ful □ ['peɪnfl] schmerzhaft; schmerzlich; peinlich; mühsam; ~less □ [~lɪs] schmerzlos; ~s·tak·ing □ [~zteɪkɪŋ] sorgfältig, gewissenhaft.

paint [peɪnt] 1. Farbe f; Schminke f; Anstrich m; 2. (an-, be)malen; (an-) streichen; (sich) schminken; ~box ['peɪntbɒks] Malkasten m; ~brush (Maler)Pinsel m; ~er [~ə] Maler(in); ~ing [~ɪŋ] Malen n; Malerei f; Gemälde n, Bild n.

pair [peə] 1. Paar n; a ~ of ... ein Paar ..., ein(e) ...; a ~ of scissors e-e Schere; 2. zo. sich paaren; zusammenpassen; ~ off Paare bilden; paarweise wegehen.

pa·ja·ma(s) Am. [pə'dʒɑːmə(z)] = pyjama(s).

pal [pæl] Kumpel m, Kamerad m.

pal·ace ['pælɪs] Palast m, Schloß n.

pal·a·ta·ble □ ['pælətəbl] wohlschmeckend, schmackhaft (a. fig.).

pal·ate ['pælɪt] anat. Gaumen m; fig. Geschmack m.

pale¹ [peɪl] Pfahl m; fig. Grenzen pl.

pale² [~] 1. □ (~r, ~st) blaß, bleich, fahl; ~ ale helles Bier; 2. blaß od. bleich werden; erbleichen lassen; ~ness ['peɪlnɪs] Blässe f.

pal·ings ['peɪlɪŋz] pl. Pfahlzaun m.

pal·i·sade [pælɪ'seɪd] Palisade f; ~s pl. Am. Steilufer n.

pal·let ['pælɪt] Strohsack m, -lager n.

pal·li·ate ['pælɪeɪt] ✍ lindern; fig. bemänteln; ~a·tive ['~ətɪv] Linderungsmittel n.

pal·lid ['pælɪd] blaß; ~lid·ness [~nɪs], ~lor [~ə] Blässe f.

palm [pɑːm] 1. Handfläche f; ✍ Palme f; 2. in die Hand verbergen; ~ s.th. off on od. upon s.o. j-m et. andrehen; ~tree ✍ ['pɑːmtriː] Palme f.

pal·pa·ble □ ['pælpəbl] fühlbar; fig. handgreiflich, klar, eindeutig.

pal·pi·tate ✍ ['pælpɪteɪt] klopfen (Herz); ~ta·tion ✍ [pælpɪ'teɪʃn] Herzklopfen n.

pal·sy ['pɔːlzɪ] 1. ✍ Lähmung f; fig. Ohnmacht f; 2. fig. lähmen.

pal·ter ['pɔːltə] sein Spiel treiben (with s.o. mit j-m).

pal·try □ ['pɔːltrɪ] (-ier, -iest) armselig; wertlos.

pam·per ['pæmpə] verzärteln.

pam·phlet ['pæmflɪt] Broschüre f; (kurze, kritische) Abhandlung; △ nicht Pamphlet.

pan [pæn] Pfanne f; Tiegel m.

pan- [~] all..., ganz..., gesamt..., pan..., Pan...

pan·a·ce·a [pænə'sɪə] Allheilmittel n.

pan·cake ['pænkeɪk] Pfann-, Eierkuchen m.

pan·da zo. ['pændə] Panda m; ~ car Brt. (Funk)Streifenwagen m; ~ cross·ing Brt. Fußgängerübergang m mit Druckampel.

pan·de·mo·ni·um fig. [pændɪ'məʊnjəm] Hölle(nlärm m) f.

pan·der ['pændə] 1. Vorschub leisten (to dat.); veraltet sich als Kuppler betätigen; 2. veraltet Kuppler m.

pane [peɪn] (Fenster)Scheibe f.

pan·e·gyr·ic [pænɪ'dʒɪrɪk] Lobrede f.

pan·el ['pænl] 1. arch. Fach n, (Tür-) Füllung f, (Wand)Täfelung f; ⚡, ⊕ Instrumentenbrett n, Schalttafel f; ⚖ Geschworenenliste f; ⚖ die Geschworenen pl.; die Diskussionsteilnehmer pl.; 2. (bsd. Brt. -ll-, Am. -l-) täfeln.

pang [pæŋ] plötzlicher Schmerz; fig. Angst f, Qual f.

pan·han·dle ['pænhændl] 1. Pfannenstiel m; Am. schmaler Fortsatz (e-s Staatsgebiets); 2. Am. F betteln.

pan·ic ['pænɪk] 1. panisch; 2. Panik f; 3. (-ck-) in Panik geraten.

pan·sy ✍ ['pænzɪ] Stiefmütterchen n.

pant [pænt] nach Luft schnappen, keuchen, schnaufen.

pan·ther zo. ['pænθə] Panther m; Am. Puma m.

pan·ties ['pæntɪz] pl. (Damen-) Schlüpfer m; Kinderhöschen n.

pan·ti·hose bsd. Am. ['pæntɪhəʊz] Strumpfhose f.

pan·try ['pæntrɪ] Speisekammer f.

pants [pænts] pl. bsd. Am. Hose f; bsd. Brt. Unterhose f; bsd. Brt. Schlüpfer m.

pap [pæp] Brei m; △ nicht Papp, Pappe.

pa·pa [pə'pɑː] Papa m.

P

pa·pal □ ['peɪpl] päpstlich.

pa·per ['peɪpə] **1.** Papier *n*; Zeitung *f*; schriftliche Prüfung; Prüfungsarbeit *f*; Vortrag *m*, Aufsatz *m*; ∼s *pl.* (Ausweis)Papiere *pl.*; **2.** tapezieren; **∼·back** Taschenbuch *n*, Paperback *n*; **∼·bag** (Papier)Tüte *f*; **∼·clip** Büroklammer *f*; **∼·hang·er** Tapezierer *m*; **∼·mill** Papierfabrik *f*; **∼·weight** Briefbeschwerer *m*.

pap·py ['pæpɪ] (-*ier*-, -*iest*) breiig.

par [pɑː] *econ.* Nennwert *m*, Pari *n*; *at* ∼ zum Nennwert; *be on a* ∼ *with* ebenbürtig sein (*dat.*).

par·a·ble ['pærəbl] Gleichnis *n*.

par·a·chute ['pærəʃuːt] Fallschirm *m*; **∼·chut·ist** [∼ɪst] Fallschirmspringer(in).

pa·rade [pəˈreɪd] **1.** ✕ (Truppen-) Parade *f*; Zurschaustellung *f*, Vorführung *f*; (Strand)Promenade *f*; (Um)Zug *m*; *make a* ∼ *of fig.* zur Schau stellen; **2.** ✕ antreten (lassen); ✕ vorbeimarschieren (lassen); zur Schau stellen; **∼·ground** ✕ Exerzier-, Paradeplatz *m*.

par·a·dise ['pærədaɪs] Paradies *n*.

par·a·gon ['pærəgɒn] Vorbild *n*, Muster *n*.

par·a·graph ['pærəgrɑːf] *print.* Absatz *m*, Abschnitt *m*; kurze Zeitungsnotiz; ✓ nicht ⚡ Paragraph.

par·al·lel ['pærəlel] **1.** parallel; **2.** ₳ Parallele *f* (*a. fig.*); Gegenstück *n*; Vergleich *m*; *without* (*a*) ∼ ohnegleichen; **3.** (-*l-*, *Brt. a.* -*ll*-) vergleichen; entsprechen; gleichen; parallel (ver)laufen zu.

par·a·lyse, *Am.* **-lyze** ['pærəlaɪz] ⚕ lähmen (*a. fig.*); *fig.* zunichte machen; **pa·ral·y·sis** ⚕ [pəˈrælɪsɪs] (*pl.* -*ses* [-siːz]) Paralyse *f*, Lähmung *f*.

par·a·mount ['pærəmaunt] höher stehend (*to als*), übergeordnet, oberste(r, -s); höchste(r, -s); *fig.* größte(r, -s).

par·a·pet ['pærəpɪt] ✕ Brustwehr *f*; Brüstung *f*; Geländer *n*.

par·a·pher·na·li·a [pærəfəˈneɪljə] *pl.* Ausrüstung *f*; Zubehör *n*, *m*.

par·a·site ['pærəsaɪt] Schmarotzer *m*.

par·a·sol ['pærəsɒl] Sonnenschirm *m*.

par·a·troop·er ✕ ['pærətruːpə] Fallschirmjäger *m*; **∼s** ✕ [∼s] *pl.* Fallschirmtruppen *pl.*

par·boil ['pɑːbɔɪl] ankochen.

par·cel ['pɑːsl] **1.** Paket *n*, Päckchen *n*; Bündel *n*; Parzelle *f*; **2.** (*bsd. Brt.* -*ll*-, *Am.* -*l*-) ∼ *out* aus-, aufteilen.

parch [pɑːtʃ] rösten, (aus)dörren.

parch·ment ['pɑːtʃmənt] Pergament *n*.

pard *Am. sl.* [pɑːd] Partner *m*.

par·don ['pɑːdn] **1.** Verzeihung *f*; ⚖ Begnadigung *f*; **2.** verzeihen; ⚖ begnadigen; ∼? wie bitte?; ∼ *me!* Entschuldigung!; **∼·a·ble** □ [∼əbl] verzeihlich.

pare [peə] (be)schneiden (*a. fig.*); schälen.

par·ent ['peərənt] Elternteil *m*, Vater *m*, Mutter *f*; *fig.* Ursache *f*; ∼*s pl.* Eltern *pl.*; **∼·teacher meeting** Schule: Elternabend *m*; **∼·age** [∼rɪdʒ] Abstammung *f*; **pa·ren·tal** [pəˈrentl] elterlich.

pa·ren·the·sis [pəˈrenθɪsɪs] (*pl.* -*ses* [-siːz]) Einschaltung *f*; *print.* (runde) Klammer.

par·ing ['peərɪŋ] Schälen *n*; (Be-) schneiden *n*; ∼*s pl.* Schalen *pl.*; Schnipsel *pl.*

par·ish ['pærɪʃ] **1.** Kirchspiel *n*, Gemeinde *f*; **2.** Pfarr..., Kirchen...; *pol.* Gemeinde...; ∼ *council* Gemeinderat *m*; **pa·rish·ion·er** [pəˈrɪʃənə] Gemeindemitglied *n*.

par·i·ty ['pærətɪ] Gleichheit *f*.

park [pɑːk] **1.** Park *m*, Anlagen *pl.*; Naturschutzgebiet *n*, Park *m*; *Am.* (Sport)Platz *m*; *the* ∼ *Brt.* F der Fußballplatz; *mst car-*∼ Parkplatz *m*; **2.** *mot.* parken.

par·ka ['pɑːkə] Parka *f*, *m*.

park·ing *mot.* ['pɑːkɪŋ] Parken *n*; *no* ∼ Parkverbot, Parken verboten; **∼ disc** Parkscheibe *f*; **∼ fee** Parkgebühr *f*; **∼ lot** *Am.* Parkplatz *m*; **∼ me·ter** Parkuhr *f*; **∼ or·bit** *Raumfahrt:* Parkbahn *f*; **∼ tick·et** Strafzettel *m* (*wegen falschen Parkens*).

par·lance ['pɑːləns] Ausdrucksweise *f*, Sprache *f*.

par·ley ['pɑːlɪ] **1.** *bsd.* ✕ Verhandlung *f*; **2.** *bsd.* ✕ verhandeln; sich besprechen.

par·lia·ment ['pɑːləmənt] Parlament *n*; **∼·men·tar·i·an** [pɑːləmənˈteərɪən] Parlamentarier(in); **∼·men·ta·ry** □ [pɑːləˈmentərɪ] parlamentarisch; Parlaments...

par·lo(u)r ['pɑːlə] *veraltet* Wohnzimmer *n*; Empfangs-, Sprechzimmer *n*; *beauty* ∼ *Am.* Schönheitssalon *m*; ~ **car** *Am.* 🚃 Salonwagen *m*; ~**maid** Stuben-, Hausmädchen *n*.

pa·ro·chi·al ☐ [pə'rəukjəl] Pfarr..., Kirchen..., Gemeinde...; *fig.* engstirnig, beschränkt.

pa·role [pə'rəul] **1.** ⚔ Parole *f*; ⚖ bedingte Haftentlassung; ⚖ Hafturlaub *m*; *he is out on* ~ ⚔ er wurde bedingt entlassen; er hat Hafturlaub; **2.** ~ *s.o.* ⚖ j-n bedingt entlassen; j-m Hafturlaub gewähren.

par·quet ['pɑ:kei] Parkett(fußboden *m*) *n*; *Am. thea.* Parkett *n*.

par·rot ['pærət] **1.** *zo.* Papagei *m* (*a. fig.*); **2.** nachplappern.

par·ry ['pæri] abwehren, parieren.

par·si·mo·ni·ous ☐ [pɑ:si'məunjəs] sparsam, geizig, knaus(e)rig.

pars·ley 🌿 ['pɑ:sli] Petersilie *f*.

par·son ['pɑ:sn] Pfarrer *m*; ~**age** [~idʒ] Pfarrei *f*, Pfarrhaus *n*.

part [pɑ:t] **1.** Teil *m*; Anteil *m*, Seite *f*; Partei *f*; *thea., fig.* Rolle *f*; Stimme *f*; Gegend *f*; *Am.* (*Haar*)Scheitel *m*; *a man of* (*many*) ~*s* ein fähiger Mensch; *take* ~ *in s.th.* an e-r Sache teilnehmen; *take s.th. in bad* (*good*) ~ *et.* (nicht) übelnehmen; *for my* ~ ich für mein(en) Teil; *for the most* ~ meistens; *in* ~ teilweise, zum Teil; *on the* ~ *of* von seiten, seitens (*gen.*); *on my* ~ meinerseits; **2.** *adj.* Teil...; **3.** *adv.* teils; **4.** *v/t.* (ab-, ein-, zer)teilen; trennen; *Haar* scheiteln; ~ *company* sich trennen (*with* von); *v/i.* sich trennen (*with* von).

par·take [pɑ:'teik] (*-took, -taken*) teilnehmen, -haben; ~ *of Mahlzeit* einnehmen.

par·tial ☐ ['pɑ:ʃl] Teil..., teilweise, partiell; parteiisch, eingenommen (*to für*); ~**i·al·i·ty** [pɑ:ʃi'æliti] Parteilichkeit *f*; Vorliebe *f* (*for* für).

par·tic·i·pant [pɑ:'tisipənt] Teilnehmer(in); ~**pate** [~eit] teilnehmen, sich beteiligen (*in* an *dat.*); ~**pa·tion** [pɑ:tisi'peiʃn] Teilnahme *f*, Beteiligung *f*.

par·ti·ci·ple *gr.* ['pɑ:tisipl] Partizip *n*, Mittelwort *n*.

par·ti·cle ['pɑ:tikl] Teilchen *n*. ☐

par·tic·u·lar [pə'tikjulə] **1.** ☐ besondere(r, -s), einzeln, Sonder...; genau, eigen; wählerisch; **2.** Einzelheit *f*; ~*s pl.* nähere Umstände *pl. od.* Angaben *pl.*; Personalien *pl.*; *in* ~ insbesondere; ~**i·ty** [pətikju'læriti] Besonderheit *f*; Ausführlichkeit *f*;

Eigenheit *f*; ~**ly** [pə'tikjuləli] besonders.

part·ing ['pɑ:tiŋ] **1.** Trennung *f*, Abschied *m*; (*Haar*)Scheitel *m*; ~ *of the ways bsd. fig.* Scheideweg *m*; **2.** Abschieds...

par·ti·san [pɑ:ti'zæn] Parteigänger(in); ⚔ Partisan *m*; *attr.* Partei-.

par·ti·tion [pɑ:'tiʃn] **1.** Teilung *f*; Scheidewand *f*; Verschlag *m*; Fach *n*; **2.** ~ *off* abteilen, abtrennen.

part·ly ['pɑ:tli] teilweise, zum Teil.

part·ner ['pɑ:tnə] **1.** Partner(in); **2.** zusammenbringen; sich zusammentun mit (*j-m*); ~**ship** [~ʃip] Teilhaber-, Partnerschaft *f*; *econ.* Handelsgesellschaft *f*.

part-own·er ['pɑ:təunə] Miteigentümer(in).

par·tridge *zo.* ['pɑ:tridʒ] Rebhuhn *n*.

part-time ['pɑ:ttaim] **1.** *adj.* Teilzeit..., Halbtags...; **2.** *adv.* halbtags.

par·ty ['pɑ:ti] Partei *f*; ⚔ Abteilung *f*; (Arbeits-, Reise)Gruppe *f*; (*Rettungs- etc.*)Mannschaft *f*; Party *f*, Gesellschaft *f*; Beteiligte(r *m*) *f*; *co.* Type *f*, Individuum *n*; △ *nicht Partie*; ~ **line** *pol.* Parteilinie *f*; ~**pol·i·tics** *sg. od. pl.* Parteipolitik *f*.

pass [pɑ:s] **1.** Passier-, Erlaubnisschein *m*; △ *nicht (Reise)Pass*; ⚔ Urlaubsschein *m*; Bestehen *n* (*e-s Examens*); *Brt. univ.* einfacher Grad; kritische Lage; *Sport:* Paß *m*, (Ball)Abgabe *f*, Vorlage *f*, Zuspiel *n*; (Gebirgs)Paß *m*; Durch-, Zugang *m*; *Karten:* Passen *n*; Handbewegung *f*, (Zauber)Trick *m*; ⸗ Annäherungsversuch *m*; *free* ~ Freikarte *f*; **2.** *v/i.* (vorbei)gehen, (-)fahren, (-)kommen, (-)ziehen *etc.*; *in andere Hände* übergehen, übertragen werden (*to* auf *acc.*); *von e-m Zustand* übergehen; herumgereicht werden, von Hand zu Hand gehen; *Sport:* (den Ball) abspielen *od.* abgeben *od.* passen (*to* zu); vergehen, vorübergehen (*Zeit, Schmerz etc.*); angenommen werden, gelten; durchkommen; die Prüfung) bestehen; *parl.* Rechtskraft erlangen; *Karten:* passen; *bsd. biblisch:* sich zutragen, passieren, geschehen (*it came to* ~ *that* es begab sich *od.* es geschah, daß); △ *nicht passen = fit*; ~ *away* sterben; ~ *by* vorüber- *od.* vorbeigehen an (*dat.*), passieren; ~ *for od.* as gelten für *od.*

als, gehalten werden für; ~ off vonstatten gehen; ~ out F ohnmächtig werden; v/t. vorbei-, vorübergehen, -fahren, -fließen, -kommen, -ziehen etc. an (dat.); et. passieren; vorbeifahren an (dat.), überholen (a. mot.); durch-, überschreiten, durchqueren, passieren; vorbeilassen; reichen, geben; streichen (mit der Hand); Sport: Ball abspielen, abgeben, passen (to zu); Examen bestehen; Prüfling bestehen od. durchkommen lassen; et. durchgehen lassen; Zeit ver-, zubringen; Geld in Umlauf bringen; Gesetz verabschieden; Vorschlag etc. durchbringen, annehmen; Urteil abgeben; Meinung äußern; Bemerkung machen; fig. (hinaus)gehen über (acc.), übersteigen; ~·a·ble □ ['pɑːsəbl] passierbar; gangbar; gültig (Geld); leidlich.

pas·sage ['pæsɪdʒ] Durchgang m; Durchfahrt f; Durchreise f; Korridor m, Gang m; Reise f, (Über)Fahrt f, Flug m; parl. Annahme f (e-s Gesetzes); ♪ Passage f; (Text)Stelle f; bird of ~ Zugvogel m.

pass·book econ. ['pɑːsbʊk] Bankbuch n; Sparbuch n.

pas·sen·ger ['pæsɪndʒə] Passagier m, Fahr-, Fluggast m, Reisende(r m) f, (Auto- etc.)Insasse m.

pass·er-by ['pɑːsə'baɪ] (pl. passersby) Vorbei-, Vorübergehende(r m) f, Passant(in).

pas·sion ['pæʃn] Leidenschaft f; (Gefühls)Ausbruch m; Wut f, Zorn m; ♀ eccl. Passion f; ♀ Week eccl. Karwoche f; ~·ate □ [~ət] leidenschaftlich.

pas·sive □ ['pæsɪv] passiv (a. gr.); teilnahmslos; untätig.

pass·port ['pɑːspɔːt] (Reise)Paß m.

pass·word ['pɑːswɜːd] Kennwort n.

past [pɑːst] 1. vergangen, pred. vorüber; gr. Vergangenheits...; frühere(r, -s); for some time ~ seit einiger Zeit; ~ tense gr. Vergangenheit f, Präteritum n; 2. adv. vorbei; 3. prp. Zeit: nach, über (acc.); über ... (acc.) hinaus; an ... (dat.) vorbei; half ~ two halb drei; ~ endurance unerträglich; ~ hope hoffnungslos; 4. Vergangenheit f (a. gr.).

paste [peɪst] 1. Teig m; Kleister m; Paste f; 2. (be)kleben; ~·board ['peɪstbɔːd] Pappe f; attr. Papp...

pas·tel [pæ'stel] Pastell(zeichnung f) n.

pas·teur·ize ['pæstəraɪz] pasteurisieren, keimfrei machen.

pas·time ['pɑːstaɪm] Zeitvertreib m, Freizeitbeschäftigung f.

pas·tor ['pɑːstə] Pastor m, Seelsorger m; ~·al □ [~rəl] Hirten...; idyllisch; eccl. pastoral.

pas·try ['peɪstrɪ] Kuchen m, Torte f; Konditorwaren pl., Feingebäck n; ~·cook Konditor m.

pas·ture ['pɑːstʃə] 1. Weide(land n) f; Grasfutter n; 2. (ab)weiden.

pat [pæt] 1. Klaps m; Portion f (Butter); 2. (-tt-) tätscheln; klopfen; 3. gerade recht; parat, bereit.

patch [pætʃ] 1. Fleck m; Flicken m; Stück n Land; ♣ Pflaster n; in ~es stellenweise; 2. flicken; ~·work ['pætʃwɜːk] Patchwork n; contp. Flickwerk n.

pate F [peɪt]: bald ~ Platte f (Glatze).

pa·tent ['peɪtənt, Am. 'pætənt] 1. offen(kundig); patentiert; Patent...; ~ agent, Am. ~ attorney Patentanwalt m; letters ~ ['pætənt] pl. Patenturkunde f; ~ leather Lackleder n; 2. Patent n; Privileg n, Freibrief m; Patenturkunde f; 3. patentieren (lassen); ~·ee [peɪtən'tiː] Patentinhaber(in).

pa·ter·nal □ [pə'tɜːnl] väterlich(erseits); ~·ni·ty [~tɪ] Vaterschaft f.

path [pɑːθ] (pl. paths [pɑːðz]) Pfad m; Weg m.

pa·thet·ic [pə'θetɪk] (~ally) kläglich, bemitleidenswert, mitleiderregend; △ nicht pathetisch.

pa·thos ['peɪθɒs] Mitleid n; das Mitleiderregende; △ nicht Pathos.

pa·tience ['peɪʃns] Geduld f; Ausdauer f; Brt. Patience f (Kartenspiel); **pa·tient** [~t] 1. □ geduldig; 2. Patient(in).

pat·i·o ['pætɪəʊ] (pl. -os) Terrasse f; Innenhof m, Patio m.

pat·ri·mo·ny ['pætrɪmənɪ] väterliches Erbteil.

pat·ri·ot ['peɪtrɪət] Patriot(in); ~·ic [pætrɪ'ɒtɪk] (~ally) patriotisch.

pa·trol [pə'trəʊl] 1. ✕ Patrouille f; (Polizei)Streife f; on ~ auf Patrouille, auf Streife; 2. (-ll-) (ab)patrouillieren, auf Streife sein (in dat.), s-e Runde machen (in dat.); ~ car (Funk)Streifenwagen m; ~·man [~mæn] (pl. -men) Am. Polizist m

P

(auf Streife); *Brt.* motorisierter Pannenhelfer (*e-s Automobilclubs*).

pa·tron ['peɪtrən] Schirmherr *m*; Gönner *m*; (Stamm)Kunde *m*; Stammgast *m*; ~ **saint** *eccl.* Schutzheilige(r) *m*; △ *nicht Patrone*;

pat·ron·age ['pætrənɪdʒ] Schirmherrschaft *f*; Gönnerschaft *f*; Kundschaft *f*; Schutz *m*; **pat·ron·ize** [~aɪz] fördern, unterstützen; (Stamm)Kunde *od.* Stammgast sein bei; gönnerhaft *od.* herablassend behandeln.

pat·ter ['pætə] plappern; prasseln (*Regen*); trappeln (*Füße*).

pat·tern ['pætən] **1.** Muster *n* (*a. fig.*); Modell *n*; **2.** (nach)bilden, formen (*after, on* nach).

paunch ['pɔːnʃ] (dicker) Bauch.

pau·per ['pɔːpə] Arme(r *m*) *f*.

pause [pɔːz] **1.** Pause *f*; △ *nicht thea., Schule: Pause*; **2.** e-e Pause machen.

pave [peɪv] pflastern; ~ *the way for fig.* den Weg ebnen für; **~·ment** ['peɪvmənt] *Brt.* Bürgersteig *m*; Pflaster *n*; *Am.* Fahrbahn *f*.

paw [pɔː] **1.** Pfote *f*, Tatze *f*; **2.** F betatschen; F derb *od.* ungeschickt anfassen; ~ (*the ground*) (mit den Hufen *etc.*) scharren.

pawn [pɔːn] **1.** *Schach:* Bauer *m*; Pfand *n*; *in od.* at ~ verpfändet; **2.** verpfänden; **~·bro·ker** ['pɔːnbrəʊkə] Pfandleiher *m*; **~·shop** Leihhaus *n*.

pay [peɪ] **1.** (Be)Zahlung *f*; Sold *m*; Lohn *m*; **2.** (*paid*) *v/t.* (be)zahlen; (be)lohnen; sich lohnen für; *Aufmerksamkeit* schenken; *Besuch* abstatten; *Ehre* erweisen; *Kompliment* machen; ~ *attention to* heed to achtgeben auf (*acc.*); ~ *down*, ~ *cash* bar bezahlen; ~ *in* einzahlen; ~ *into* einzahlen auf (*ein Konto*); ~ *off et.* ab(be)zahlen; *j-n* bezahlen u. entlassen; *j-n* voll auszahlen; *v/i.* zahlen; sich lohnen; ~ *for* (*fig.* für) *et.* bezahlen; **~·a·ble** ['peɪəbl] zahlbar, fällig; **~·day** Zahltag *m*; **~·ee** [peɪ'iː] Zahlungsempfänger(in) *f*; ~ **en·ve·lope** *Am.* Lohntüte *f*; **~·ing** ['peɪɪŋ] lohnend; **~·mas·ter** Zahlmeister *m*; **~·ment** [~mənt] (Be-, Ein-, Aus-) Zahlung *f*; Lohn *m*, Sold *m*; ~ **pack·et** *Brt.* Lohntüte *f*; ~ **phone** *Brt.* Münzfernsprecher *m*; **~·roll** Lohnliste *f*; ~ **slip** Lohn-, Gehalts-

streifen *m*; ~ **sta·tion** *Am.*, ~ **tel·e·phone** Münzfernsprecher *m*.

pea ♀ [piː] Erbse *f*.

peace [piːs] Frieden *m*; Ruhe *f*; at ~ in Frieden; **~·a·ble** □ ['piːsəbl] friedliebend, friedlich; **~·ful** □ [~fl] friedlich; **~·mak·er** Friedensstifter(in).

peach ♀ [piːtʃ] Pfirsich(baum) *m*.

pea·cock *zo.* ['piːkɒk] Pfau(hahn) *m*; **~·hen** *zo.* Pfauhenne *f*.

peak [piːk] Spitze *f*; Gipfel *m*; Mützenschild *n*, -schirm *m*; *attr.* Spitzen...; Höchst..., Haupt...; ~ *hours pl.* Hauptverkehrs-, Stoßzeit *f*; **~·ed** [~t] spitz.

peal [piːl] **1.** (Glocken)Läuten *n*; Glockenspiel *n*; Dröhnen *n*; ~s *of laughter* schallendes Gelächter; **2.** erschallen (lassen); dröhnen.

pea·nut ♀ ['piːnʌt] Erdnuß *f*.

pear ♀ [peə] Birne *f*; Birnbaum *m*.

pearl [pɜːl] **1.** Perle *f* (*a. fig.*); *attr.* Perl(en)...; **2.** tropfen, perlen; **~·y** ['pɜːlɪ] (*-ier, -iest*) perlenartig, Perl(en)...

peas·ant ['peznt] **1.** Kleinbauer *m*; **2.** kleinbäuerlich, Kleinbauern...; **~·ry** [~rɪ] Kleinbauernstand *m*; *die* Kleinbauern *pl.*

peat [piːt] Torf *m*.

peb·ble ['pebl] Kiesel(stein) *m*.

peck [pek] **1.** Viertelscheffel *m* (= *9,087 Liter*); *fig.* Menge *f*; **2.** picken, hacken (*at* nach); *Körner etc.* aufpicken.

pe·cu·li·ar □ [pɪ'kjuːljə] eigen(tümlich); besondere(r, -s); seltsam; **~·i·ty** [pɪkjuːlɪ'ærətɪ] Eigenheit *f*; Eigentümlichkeit *f*.

pe·cu·ni·a·ry [pɪ'kjuːnjərɪ] Geld...

ped·a·gog·ics [pedə'gɒdʒɪks] *mst sg.* Pädagogik *f*; **~·gogue**, *Am. a.* **~·gog** ['pedəgɒg] Pädagoge *m*; F Pedant *m*, Schulmeister *m*.

ped·al ['pedl] **1.** Pedal *n*; *attr.* Fuß...; **3.** (*bsd. Brt. -ll-, Am. -l-*) das Pedal treten; radfahren; *Rad* fahren, treten.

pe·dan·tic [pɪ'dæntɪk] (*~ally*) pedantisch.

ped·dle ['pedl] hausieren gehen (mit); ~ *drugs* mit Drogen handeln; **~·r** [~lə] *Am.* = pedlar; Drogenhändler *m*.

ped·es·tal ['pedɪstl] Sockel *m* (*a. fig.*).

pe·des·tri·an [pɪ'destrɪən] **1.** zu Fuß; *fig.* prosaisch, trocken; **2.** Fußgänger(in); ~ **cross·ing** Fußgängerübergang m; ~ **pre·cinct** Fußgängerzone f.

ped·i·gree ['pedɪgriː] Stammbaum m.

ped·lar ['pedlə] Hausierer m; Drogen-, Rauschgifthändler m.

peek [piːk] **1.** spähen, gucken, lugen; **2.** flüchtiger od. heimlicher Blick.

peel [piːl] **1.** Schale f, Rinde f, Haut f; **2.** v/t. schälen; a. ~ off abschälen, Folie etc. abziehen; Kleid abstreifen; v/i. a. ~ off sich (ab)schälen, abblättern.

peep [piːp] **1.** neugieriger od. verstohlener Blick; Piep(s)en n; **2.** gucken, neugierig od. verstohlen blicken; a. ~ out hervorschauen; fig. sich zeigen; piep(s)en; ~**hole** ['piːphəʊl] Guckloch n.

peer [pɪə] **1.** spähen, lugen; ~ at (sich) genau ansehen, anstarren; **2.** Gleiche(r m) f; Brt. Peer m; ~**·less** ☐ ['pɪəlɪs] unvergleichlich.

peev·ish ☐ ['piːvɪʃ] verdrießlich, gereizt.

peg [peg] **1.** (Holz)Stift m, Zapfen m, Dübel m, Pflock m; (Kleider)Haken m; Brt. (Wäsche)Klammer f; (Zelt-) Hering m; ♪ Wirbel m; fig. Aufhänger m; take s.o. down a ~ (or two) F j-m e-n Dämpfer aufsetzen; **2.** (-gg-) festpflocken; mst ~ out Grenze abstecken; ~ away, ~ along F dranbleiben (at an e-r Arbeit); ~**·top** ['pegtɒp] Kreisel m.

pel·i·can zo. ['pelɪkən] Pelikan m.

pel·let ['pelɪt] Kügelchen n; Pille f; Schrotkorn n.

pell-mell ['pel'mel] durcheinander.

pelt [pelt] **1.** Fell n, (rohe) Haut, (Tier)Pelz m; **2.** v/t. bewerfen; v/i. a. ~ down (nieder)prasseln (Regen etc.).

pel·vis anat. ['pelvɪs] (pl. -vises, -ves [-viːz]) Becken n.

pen [pen] **1.** (Schreib)Feder f; Federhalter m; Füller m; Pferch m, (Schaf)Hürde f; **2.** (-nn-) schreiben; ~ in, ~ up einpferchen, -sperren.

pe·nal ☐ ['piːnl] Straf...; strafbar; ~ code Strafgesetzbuch n; ~ servitude Zwangsarbeit f; ~**·ize** [~əlaɪz] bestrafen; **pen·al·ty** ['penltɪ] Strafe f; Sport: a. Strafpunkt m; Fußball: Elfmeter m; ~ area Fußball: Strafraum m; ~ goal Fußball: Elfmetertor n; ~ kick Fußball: Frei-, Strafstoß m.

pen·ance ['penəns] Buße f.

pence [pens] pl. von penny.

pen·cil ['pensl] **1.** (Blei-, Zeichen-, Farb)Stift m; **2.** (bsd. Brt. -ll-, Am. -l-) zeichnen; (mit Bleistift) aufschreiben od. anzeichnen od. anstreichen; Augenbrauen nachziehen; ~**·sharp·en·er** Bleistiftspitzer m.

pen|dant, ~**dent** ['pendənt] (Schmuck)Anhänger m.

pend·ing ['pendɪŋ] **1.** ⫶ schwebend; **2.** prp. während; bis zu.

pen·du·lum ['pendjʊləm] Pendel n.

pen·e·tra·ble ☐ ['penɪtrəbl] durchdringbar; ~**trate** [~eɪt] durchdringen; fig. ergründen (into an in acc.); vordringen (to bis zu); ~**trat·ing** ☐ [~ɪŋ] durchdringend, scharf (Verstand); scharfsinnig; ~**tra·tion** [penɪ'treɪʃn] Durch-, Eindringen n; Scharfsinn m; ~**tra·tive** ☐ ['penɪtrətɪv] s. penetrating.

pen-friend ['penfrend] Brieffreund (-in).

pen·guin zo. ['peŋgwɪn] Pinguin m.

pen·hold·er ['penhəʊldə] Federhalter m.

pe·nin·su·la [pə'nɪnsjʊlə] Halbinsel f.

pe·nis anat. ['piːnɪs] Penis m.

pen·i·tence ['penɪtəns] Buße f, Reue f; ~**tent** [~t] **1.** ☐ reuig, bußfertig; **2.** Büßer(in); ~**ten·tia·ry** Am. [penɪ'tenʃərɪ] (Staats)Gefängnis n.

pen|knife ['pennaɪf] (pl. -knives) Taschenmesser n; ~**name** Schriftstellername m, Pseudonym n.

pen·nant ⚓ ['penənt] Wimpel m.

pen·ni·less ☐ ['penɪlɪs] ohne e-n Pfennig (Geld), mittellos.

pen·ny ['penɪ] (pl. -nies, coll. pence [pens]) a. new ~ Brt. Penny m (= 1 p = £ 0.01); Am. Cent(stück n) m; fig. Pfennig m; ~**weight** englisches Pennygewicht (= 1,5 g).

pen·sion ['penʃn] **1.** Rente f, Pension f, Ruhegeld n; △ nicht Pension (Fremdenheim); **2.** oft ~ off pensionieren; ~**er** [~ə] Pensionär(in).

pen·sive ☐ ['pensɪv] nachdenklich.

pen·tath|lete [pen'tæθliːt] Sport: Fünfkämpfer(in); ~**lon** [~ɒn] Sport: Fünfkampf m.

Pen·te·cost ['pentɪkɒst] Pfingsten n.

pent·house ['penthaʊs] Penthouse n, -haus n, Dachterrassenwohnung f; Vor-, Schutzdach n.

permissive

pent-up ['pent'ʌp] an-, aufgestaut (*Ärger etc.*).

pe·nu·ri·ous □ [pɪ'njʊərɪəs] arm; geizig; **pen·u·ry** ['penjʊrɪ] Armut f, Not f; Mangel m.

peo·ple ['pi:pl] **1.** Volk n, Nation f; Leute pl.; Angehörige pl.; coll. die Leute pl.; man; **2.** besiedeln, bevölkern.

pep F [pep] **1.** Elan m, Schwung m, Pep m; ~ **pill** Aufputschpille f; **2.** (-pp-) mst ~ up j-n od. et. in Schwung bringen.

pep·per ['pepə] **1.** Pfeffer m; **2.** pfeffern; ~**mint** ♥ Pfefferminze f; Pfefferminzbonbon m, n; ~**y** [~rɪ] pfeffrig; fig. hitzig.

per [pɜː] per, durch; pro, für, je.

per·am·bu·la·tor bsd. Brt. ['præmbjʊleɪtə] = pram.

per·ceive [pə'siːv] (be)merken, wahrnehmen, empfinden; erkennen.

per cent, Am. **per·cent** [pə'sent] Prozent n.

per·cen·tage [pə'sentɪdʒ] Prozentsatz m; Prozente pl.; (An)Teil m.

per·cep·ti·ble □ [pə'septəbl] wahrnehmbar, merklich; ~**tion** [~pʃn] Wahrnehmung(svermögen n) f; Erkenntnis f; Auffassung(sgabe) f.

perch [pɜːtʃ] **1.** zo. Barsch m; Rute f (= 5,029 m); (Sitz)Stange f (für Vögel); **2.** sich setzen od. niederlassen, sitzen (Vögel); auf et. Hohes setzen.

per·co·late ['pɜːkəleɪt] Kaffee etc. filtern, durchsickern lassen; durchsickern (a. fig.); gefiltert werden; ~**la·tor** [~ə] Kaffeemaschine f, -automat m.

per·cus·sion [pə'kʌʃn] Schlag m, Erschütterung f; ♣ Abklopfen n; ♪ coll. Schlagzeug n; ~ **instrument** ♪ Schlaginstrument n.

per·e·gri·na·tion [perɪgrɪ'neɪʃn] Wanderschaft f; Wanderung f.

pe·remp·to·ry □ [pə'remptərɪ] bestimmt; zwingend; herrisch.

pe·ren·ni·al □ [pə'renjəl] immer wiederkehrend, beständig; immerwährend; ♥ perennierend.

per·fect 1. ['pɜːfɪkt] □ vollkommen; vollendet; virtuos; gänzlich, völlig; **2.** [~] a. ~ **tense** gr. Perfekt n; **3.** [pə'fekt] vervollkommnen; vollenden; ~**fec·tion** [~kʃn] Vollendung f; Vollkommenheit f; fig. Gipfel m.

per·fid·i·ous □ [pə'fɪdɪəs] treulos (to

gegen), verräterisch; ~**fi·dy** ['pɜːfɪdɪ] Treulosigkeit f, Verrat m.

per·fo·rate ['pɜːfəreɪt] durchlöchern.

per·force [pə'fɔːs] notgedrungen.

per·form [pə'fɔːm] verrichten, ausführen, tun; Pflicht etc. erfüllen; thea., ♪ aufführen, spielen, vortragen (a. v/i.); ~**ance** [~əns] Verrichtung f, Ausführung f; Leistung f; thea., ♪ Aufführung f, Vorstellung f; Vortrag m; ~**er** [~ə] Künstler(in).

per·fume 1. ['pɜːfjuːm] Duft m, Wohlgeruch m; Parfüm f; **2.** [pə'fjuːm] mit Duft erfüllen, parfümieren.

per·func·to·ry □ [pə'fʌŋktərɪ] mechanisch; oberflächlich.

per·haps [pə'hæps, præps] vielleicht.

per·il ['perəl] **1.** Gefahr f; **2.** gefährden; ~**ous** □ [~əs] gefährlich.

pe·rim·e·ter [pə'rɪmɪtə] ♣ Umkreis m; Umgrenzungslinie f, Grenze f.

pe·ri·od ['pɪərɪəd] Periode f; Zeitraum m; gr. bsd. Am. Punkt m; gr. Gliedsatz m, Satzgefüge n; (Unterrichts)Stunde f; physiol. Periode f (der Frau); ~**ic** [pɪərɪ'ɒdɪk] periodisch; ~**i·cal** [~ɪkl] **1.** □ periodisch; **2.** Zeitschrift f.

per·ish ['perɪʃ] umkommen, zugrunde gehen; ~**a·ble** □ [~əbl] leicht verderblich; ~**ing** □ [~ɪŋ] bsd. Brt. F sehr kalt; F verdammt, -flixt.

per·jure ['pɜːdʒə]: ~ o.s. e-n Meineid leisten; ~**ju·ry** [~rɪ] Meineid m; commit ~ e-n Meineid leisten.

perk [pɜːk]: ~ up v/i. sich wieder erholen, munter werden (Person); v/t. Kopf heben, Ohren spitzen; schmücken, verschönern; j-n aufmöbeln, munter machen.

perk·y □ ['pɜːkɪ] (-ier, -iest) munter; keck, dreist, flott.

perm F [pɜːm] **1.** Dauerwelle f; **2.** j-m e-e Dauerwelle machen.

per·ma·nence ['pɜːmənəns] Dauer f; ~**nent** □ [~t] dauernd, ständig; dauerhaft; Dauer...; ~ **wave** Dauerwelle f.

per·me·a·ble □ ['pɜːmjəbl] durchlässig; ~**ate** [~ɪeɪt] durchdringen; dringen (into in acc., through durch).

per·mis·si·ble □ [pə'mɪsəbl] zulässig; ~**sion** [~ʃn] Erlaubnis f; ~**sive** □ [~sɪv] zulässig, erlaubt; tolerant; (sexuell) freizügig; ~ **society** tabufreie Gesellschaft.

per·mit 1. [pə'mɪt] (*-tt-*) erlauben, gestatten; **2.** ['pɜːmɪt] Erlaubnis *f*, Genehmigung *f*; Passierschein *m*.

per·ni·cious □ [pə'nɪʃəs] verderblich, schädlich; *✗* bösartig.

per·pen·dic·u·lar □ [pɜːpən'dɪkjʊlə] senkrecht; aufrecht; steil.

per·pe·trate ['pɜːpɪtreɪt] verüben.

per·pet·u·al □ [pə'petʃʊəl] fortwährend, ständig, ewig; **~ate** [~eɪt] bewahren; verewigen.

per·plex [pə'pleks] verwirren; **~i·ty** [~ətɪ] Verwirrung *f*.

per·se·cute ['pɜːsɪkjuːt] verfolgen; **~cu·tion** [pɜːsɪ'kjuːʃn] Verfolgung *f*; **~cu·tor** ['pɜːsɪkjuːtə] Verfolger (-in).

per·se·ver·ance [pɜːsɪ'vɪərəns] Beharrlichkeit *f*, Ausdauer *f*; **~e** [pɜːsɪ'vɪə] beharren; aushalten.

per·sist [pə'sɪst] beharren, bestehen (*in auf dat.*); fortdauern, anhalten; **~sis·tence**, **~sis·ten·cy** [~əns, ~sɪ] Beharrlichkeit *f*; Hartnäckigkeit *f*, Ausdauer *f*; **~sis·tent** [~ənt] beharrlich, ausdauernd; anhaltend.

per·son ['pɜːsn] Person *f* (*a. gr.*, 𝄞); **~age** [~ɪdʒ] (hohe *od.* bedeutende) Persönlichkeit; **~al** □ [~l] persönlich (*a. gr.*); *attr.* Personal-; Privat...; **~ data** *pl.* Personalien *pl.*; **~al·i·ty** [pɜːsə'nælətɪ] Persönlichkeit *f*; *personalities pl.* anzügliche *od.* persönliche Bemerkungen *pl.*; **~i·fy** [pɜː'sɒnɪfaɪ] verkörpern; **~nel** [pɜːsə'nel] Personal *n*, Belegschaft *f*; *✗* Mannschaften *pl.*; *⚓, ✈* Besatzung *f*; **~ department** Personalabteilung *f*; **~ manager**, **~ officer** Personalchef *m*.

per·spec·tive [pə'spektɪv] Perspektive *f*; Ausblick *m*, Fernsicht *f*.

per·spic·u·ous □ [pə'spɪkjʊəs] klar.

per·spi·ra·tion [pɜːspə'reɪʃn] Schwitzen *n*; Schweiß *m*; **~spire** [pə'spaɪə] (aus)schwitzen.

per·suade [pə'sweɪd] überreden; überzeugen; **~sua·sion** [~ʒn] Überredung *f*; Überzeugung *f*, (feste) Meinung; Glaube *m*; **~sua·sive** □ [~sɪv] überredend; überzeugend.

pert □ [pɜːt] keck (*a. fig. Hut*), vorlaut, frech, naseweis.

per·tain [pɜː'teɪn] (*to*) gehören (*dat. od.* zu); betreffen (*acc.*).

per·ti·na·cious □ [pɜːtɪ'neɪʃəs] hartnäckig, zäh.

per·ti·nent □ ['pɜːtɪnənt] sachdienlich, relevant, zur Sache gehörig.

per·turb [pə'tɜːb] beunruhigen.

pe·rus·al [pə'ruːzl] sorgfältige Durchsicht; **~e** [~z] (sorgfältig) durchlesen; prüfen.

per·vade [pə'veɪd] durchdringen.

per·verse □ [pə'vɜːs] *psych.* pervers; eigensinnig, verstockt; vertrackt (*Sache*); **~ver·sion** [~ʃn] Verdrehung *f*; Abkehr *f*; *psych.* Perversion *f*; **~ver·si·ty** [~ətɪ] *psych.* Perversität *f*; Eigensinn *m*, Verstocktheit *f*.

per·vert 1. [pə'vɜːt] verdrehen; verführen; **2.** *psych.* ['pɜːvɜːt] perverser Mensch.

pes·si·mis·m ['pesɪmɪzəm] Pessimismus *m*.

pest [pest] lästiger Mensch, Nervensäge *f*; lästige Sache, Plage *f*; *zo.* Schädling *m*; △ *nicht* Pest (*Seuche*).

pes·ter ['pestə] belästigen.

pes·ti·lent □ ['pestɪlənt], **~len·tial** □ [pestɪ'lenʃl] *bsd. veraltet* schädlich; *mst co.* ekelhaft, abscheulich.

pet¹ [pet] **1.** (zahmes) (Haus)Tier; Liebling *m*; **2.** Lieblings...; Tier...; **~** *dog* Schoßhund *m*; **~** *name* Kosename *m*; **~** *shop* Tierhandlung *f*, Zoogeschäft *n*; **3.** (*-tt-*) (ver)hätscheln; streicheln, liebkosen; F Petting machen.

pet² [~]: *in a* **~** verärgert.

pet·al ⚘ ['petl] Blütenblatt *n*.

pe·ti·tion [pɪ'tɪʃn] **1.** Bittschrift *f*, Eingabe *f*, Gesuch *n*; **2.** bitten, ersuchen; ein Gesuch einreichen (*for* um), e-n Antrag stellen (*for* auf *acc.*).

pet·ri·fy ['petrɪfaɪ] versteinern.

pet·rol ['petrəl] Benzin *n*; △ *nicht Petroleum*; **~** *pump* Zapfsäule *f*; **~** *station* Tankstelle *f*.

pe·tro·le·um ⛏ [pɪ'trəʊljəm] Petroleum *n*, Erd-, Mineralöl *n*; **~** *refinery* Erdölraffinerie *f*.

pet·ti·coat ['petɪkəʊt] Unterrock *m*.

pet·ting F ['petɪŋ] Petting *n*.

pet·tish □ ['petɪʃ] launisch, reizbar.

pet·ty □ ['petɪ] (*-ier, -iest*) klein, geringfügig, Bagatell...; **~** *cash* Portokasse *f*; **~** *larceny* 𝄞 einfacher Diebstahl.

pet·u·lant □ ['petjʊlənt] gereizt.

pew [pjuː] Kirchenbank *f*.

pew·ter ['pjuːtə] Zinn *n*; Zinngeschirr *n*; Zinnkrug *m*.

phan·tom ['fæntəm] Phantom *n*, Trugbild *n*; Gespenst *n*.

piece

phar·ma·cy ['fɑːməsɪ] Pharmazie f; Apotheke f.

phase [feɪz] Phase f.

pheas·ant zo. ['feznt] Fasan m.

phe·nom·e·non [fɪ'nɒmɪnən] (pl. -na [-ə]) Phänomen n, Erscheinung f.

phi·al ['faɪəl] Phiole f, Fläschchen n.

phi·lan·thro·pist [fɪ'lænθrəpɪst] Philanthrop m, Menschenfreund m.

phi·lol·o·gist [fɪ'lɒlədʒɪst] Philologe m, -in f; **~·gy** [~ɪ] Philologie f.

phi·los·o·pher [fɪ'lɒsəfə] Philosoph m; **~·phize** [~aɪz] philosophieren; **~·phy** [~ɪ] Philosophie f.

phlegm [flem] Schleim m; Phlegma n.

phone F [fəʊn] = telephone.

pho·net·ics [fə'netɪks] sg. Phonetik f, Lautlehre f.

pho·n(e)y sl. ['fəʊnɪ] **1.** Fälschung f; Schwindler(in); **2.** (-ier, -iest) falsch, unecht.

phos·pho·rus 🜍 ['fɒsfərəs] Phosphor m.

pho·to F ['fəʊtəʊ] (pl. -tos) Foto n, Bild n.

pho·to- [~] Licht..., Photo..., Foto...; **~·cop·i·er** Fotokopiergerät n; **~·cop·y 1.** Fotokopie f; **2.** fotokopieren.

pho·to·graph ['fəʊtəgrɑːf] **1.** Fotografie f (Bild), △ nicht Fotograf; **2.** fotografieren; **~·tog·ra·pher** [fə'tɒgrəfə] Fotograf(in); **~·tog·ra·phy** [~ɪ] Fotografie f, △ nicht Fotografie (Bild).

phras·al ['freɪzl]: **~** verb Verb n mit Adverb (und Präposition); **phrase** [freɪz] **1.** (Rede)Wendung f, Redensart f, (idiomatischer) Ausdruck; △ nicht Phrase (leere Redensart); **~ book** Sprachführer m; **2.** ausdrücken.

phys·i·cal ['fɪzɪkl] physisch; körperlich; physikalisch; **~** education, **~** training Leibeserziehung f; **~** handicap Körperbehinderung f; **~·ly** handicapped körperbehindert; **phy·si·cian** [fɪ'zɪʃn] Arzt m; △ nicht Physiker; **~·i·cist** ['fɪzɪsɪst] Physiker m; **~·ics** [~ɪks] sg. Physik f.

phy·sique [fɪ'ziːk] Körper(bau) m, Statur f; △ nicht Physik.

pi·an·o ['pjænəʊ] (pl. -os) Klavier n.

pi·az·za [pɪ'ætsə] Piazza f, (Markt-) Platz m; Am. (große) Veranda.

pick [pɪk] **1.** = pickaxe; (Aus)Wahl f; take your **~** suchen Sie sich etwas

aus; **2.** (auf)hacken; (auf)picken (Vogel); entfernen; pflücken; Knochen abnagen; bohren od. stochern in (dat.); Schloß mit e-m Dietrich öffnen, F knacken; Streit vom Zaun brechen; (sorgfältig) (aus)wählen; Am. ♪ Saiten zupfen, Banjo spielen; **~** one's nose in der Nase bohren; **~** one's teeth in den Zähnen (herum-) stochern; **~** s.o.'s pocket j-n bestehlen; have a bone to **~** with s.o. mit j-m ein Hühnchen zu rupfen haben; **~** out et. auswählen; heraussuchen; **~** up aufhacken; aufheben, -lesen, -nehmen; aufpicken (Vogel); Spur aufnehmen; Täter aufgreifen; F et. aufschnappen; sich e-e Fremdsprache aneignen; (im Auto) mitnehmen od. abholen; F j-n zufällig kennenlernen, aufgabeln; sich erholen; a. **~** up speed mot. schneller werden; **~·a·back** ['pɪkəbæk] huckepack; **~·axe**, Am. **~·ax** Spitzhacke f.

pick·et ['pɪkɪt] **1.** Pfahl m; ✗ Feldwache f; Steikposten m; **~** line Steikpostenkette f; **2.** mit Steikposten besetzen, Steikposten aufstellen vor (dat.); Steikposten stehen.

pick·ings ['pɪkɪŋz] pl. Überbleibsel pl., Reste pl.; Ausbeute f; Profit m, (unehrlicher) Gewinn.

pick·le ['pɪkl] **1.** (Salz)Lake f; mst **~s** pl. Eingepökelte(s) n, Pickles pl.; F mißliche Lage; **2.** einlegen, (-)pökeln; **~d herring** Salzhering m.

pick·lock ['pɪklɒk] Einbrecher m; Dietrich m; **~·pock·et** Taschendieb m; **~·up** Ansteigen n; Tonabnehmer m; Kleinlieferwagen m; F Straßenbekanntschaft f.

pic·nic ['pɪknɪk] **1.** Picknick n; **2.** (-ck-) ein Picknick machen, picknicken.

pic·to·ri·al [pɪk'tɔːrɪəl] **1.** □ malerisch; illustriert; **2.** Illustrierte f.

pic·ture ['pɪktʃə] **1.** Bild n; Gemälde n; bildschöne Sache od. Person; Film m; attr. Bilder...; **~s** pl. bsd. Brt. Kino n; put s.o. in the **~** j-n ins Bild setzen, j-n informieren; **2.** abbilden; fig. schildern, beschreiben; fig. sich et. vorstellen; **~ post·card** Ansichtskarte f; **pic·tur·esque** [pɪktʃə'resk] malerisch.

pie [paɪ] Pastete f; gedeckter Obstkuchen.

pie·bald ['paɪbɔːld] (bunt)scheckig.

piece [piːs] **1.** Stück n; Teil m, n (e-r

P

Maschine etc., ~e-s Services); *Schach*: Figur f; *Brettspiel*: Stein m; *by the* ~ stückweise; im Akkord; *a* ~ *of advice* ein Rat; *a* ~ *of news* e-e Neuigkeit; *of a* ~ einheitlich; *give s.o. a* ~ *of one's mind* j-m gründlich die Meinung sagen; *take to* ~*s* zerlegen; 2. ~ *together* zusammensetzen, -stük-keln, -flicken; **~meal** ['pi:smi:l] stückweise; **~work** Akkordarbeit f; *do* ~ im Akkord arbeiten.

pier [pɪə] Pfeiler m; Pier m, Hafendamm m, Mole f, Landungsbrücke f.

pierce [pɪəs] durchbohren, -stechen, -stoßen; durchdringen; eindringen (*in acc.*).

pi·e·ty ['paɪətɪ] Frömmigkeit f; Pietät f.

pig [pɪg] *zo.* Schwein n (*a. fig.* F); *bsd. Am.* Ferkel n; *sl. contp.* Bulle m (*Polizist*).

pi·geon ['pɪdʒɪn] Taube f; **~hole** 1. Fach n; 2. in Fächer einordnen.

pig|head·ed ['pɪg'hedɪd] dickköpfig; **~i·ron** ['pɪgaɪən] Roheisen n; **~skin** Schweinsleder n; **~sty** Schweinestall m; **~tail** (Haar)Zopf m.

pike [paɪk] × *hist.* Pike f, Spieß m; *zo.* Hecht m; Schlagbaum m; Mautstraße f; Maut f.

pile [paɪl] 1. Haufen m; Stapel m, Stoß m; F Haufen m, Masse f; ⚡ Batterie f; Pfahl m; Flor m (*Stoff, Teppich*); ~*s pl.* ⚕ Hämorrhoiden pl.; (*atomic*) ~ Atommeiler m, (Kern)Reaktor m; 2. *oft* ~ *up*, ~ *on* (an-, auf)häufen, (auf)stapeln, aufschichten.

pil·fer ['pɪlfə] stehlen, F stibitzen.

pil·grim ['pɪlgrɪm] Pilger(in); **~age** [~ɪdʒ] Pilger-, Wallfahrt f.

pill [pɪl] Pille f (*a. fig.*); *the* ~ die (Antibaby)Pille.

pil·lage ['pɪlɪdʒ] 1. Plünderung f; 2. plündern.

pil·lar ['pɪlə] Pfeiler m, Ständer m; Säule f; **~box** *Brt.* Briefkasten m.

pil·li·on *mot.* ['pɪljən] Soziussitz m.

pil·lo·ry ['pɪlərɪ] 1. Pranger m; 2. an den Pranger stellen; *fig.* anprangern.

pil·low ['pɪləʊ] (Kopf)Kissen n; **~case**, **~slip** (Kopf)Kissenbezug m.

pi·lot ['paɪlət] 1. ✈ Pilot m; ⚓ Lotse m; *fig.* Führer m; 2. Versuchs..., Probe..., Pilot...; ~ *film* TV Pilotfilm m; ~ *scheme* Versuchsprojekt n; 3. lotsen; steuern.

pimp [pɪmp] 1. Kuppler m; Zuhälter m; 2. sich als Kuppler betätigen; Zuhälter sein.

pim·ple ['pɪmpl] Pickel m, Pustel f.

pin [pɪn] 1. (Steck-, Krawatten-, Hut- etc.)Nadel f; ⊕ Pflock m, Bolzen m, Stift m, Dorn m; ♪ Wirbel m; *Kegeln*: Kegel m; *Bowling*: Pin m; (*clothes*) ~ *bsd. Am.* Wäscheklammer f; (*drawing-*) ~ *Brt.* Reißzwecke f; 2. (-nn-) (an)heften, anstecken (*to an acc.*), befestigen (*to an dat.*); pressen, drücken (*against, to* gegen, an *acc.*).

pin·a·fore ['pɪnəfɔ:] Schürze f.

pin·cers ['pɪnsəz] *pl.* (*a pair of* ~ e-e) (Kneif)Zange.

pinch [pɪntʃ] 1. Kneifen n; Prise f (*Salz, Tabak etc.*); *fig.* Druck m, Not f; 2. *v/t.* kneifen, zwicken, (ein)klemmen; drücken (*Schuh etc.*); F klauen; *v/i.* drücken (*Schuh, Not etc.*); *a.* ~ *and scrape* sich einschränken, knausern.

pin·cush·ion ['pɪnkʊʃn] Nadelkissen n.

pine [paɪn] 1. ♀ Kiefer f, Föhre f; 2. sich abhärmen; sich sehnen (*for* nach); **~ap·ple** ♀ ['paɪnæpl] Ananas f; **~cone** ♀ Kiefernzapfen m.

pin·ion ['pɪnjən] 1. *zo.* Flügelspitze f; *zo.* Schwungfeder f; ⊕ Ritzel n (*Antriebsrad*); 2. die Flügel stutzen (*dat.*); fesseln (*to an acc.*).

pink [pɪŋk] 1. ♀ Nelke f; Rosa n; *be in the* ~ (*of condition od. health*) in Top- *od.* Hochform sein; 2. rosa(farben).

pin-mon·ey ['pɪnmʌnɪ] (selbstverdientes) Taschengeld (*der Hausfrau*).

pin·na·cle ['pɪnəkl] *arch.* Spitztürmchen n; (*Berg*)Spitze f; *fig.* Gipfel m, Höhepunkt m.

pint [paɪnt] Pint n (= 0,57 *od. Am.* 0,47 Liter); *Brt.* F Halbe f (*Bier*).

pi·o·neer [paɪə'nɪə] 1. Pionier m (*a.* ✕); 2. den Weg bahnen (*dat.*).

pi·ous □ ['paɪəs] fromm, religiös.

pip [pɪp] *vet.* Pips m; F miese Laune; (*Obst*)Kern m; Auge n (*auf Würfeln etc.*); ✕ *Brt.* F Stern m (*Rangabzeichen*); kurzer, hoher Ton.

pipe [paɪp] 1. Rohr n, Röhre f; Pfeife f (*a.* ♪); ♫ *nicht* (*Triller*)Pfeife; ♪ Flöte f; Pfeifen n, Lied n (*e-s Vogels*); Luftröhre f; Pipe f (*Weinfaß* = 477, 3 Liter); 2. (durch Rohre) leiten;

pfeifen; flöten; piep(s)en (*Vogel etc.*); **~line** ['paɪplaɪn] Rohrleitung *f*; *Erdöl, Erdgas etc.*: Pipeline *f*; **~r** [~ə] Pfeifer *m*.

pip·ing ['paɪpɪŋ] 1. pfeifend, schrill; **~ hot** siedend heiß; 2. Rohrleitung *f*, **-netz** *n*; *Schneiderei*: Paspel *f*, Biese *f*; Pfeifen *n*, Piep(s)en *n*.

pi·quant □ ['piːkənt] pikant.

pique [piːk] 1. Groll *m*; 2. kränken, reizen; **~ o.s. on** sich brüsten mit.

pi·ra·cy ['paɪərəsɪ] Piraterie *f*, Seeräuberei *f*; **pi·rate** [~ət] 1. Pirat *m*, Seeräuber *m*; Piratenschiff *n*; **~ radio station** Piratensender *m*.

piss V [pɪs] pissen; **~ off!** verpiß dich!, hau ab!

pis·tol ['pɪstl] Pistole *f*.

pis·ton ⊕ ['pɪstən] Kolben *m*; **~rod** Kolben-, Pleuelstange *f*; **~stroke** Kolbenhub *m*.

pit [pɪt] 1. Grube *f* (*a.* ⚒, *anat.*); ✗ Miete *f*; Fallgrube *f*; Falle *f*; *Motorsport*: Box *f*; *Sport*: Sprunggrube *f*; *thea. Brt.* Parterre *n*; *a.* orchestra ~ *thea.* Orchestergraben *m*; *Am.* (Obst)Stein *m*, Kern *m*; Pockennarbe *f*; 2. (-*tt*-) ✗ einmieten; mit Narben bedecken; *Am.* entsteinen, -kernen.

pitch [pɪtʃ] 1. *min.* Pech *n*; *Brt.* Stand(platz) *m* (*Straßenhändler etc.*); ♪ Tonhöhe *f*; Grad *m*, Stufe *f*, Höhe *f*; Gefälle *n*, Neigung *f*; Wurf *m* (*a. Sport*); *bsd. Brt. Sport*: Spielfeld *n*, Platz *m*; ⚓ Stampfen *n* (*Schiff*); 2. *v/t.* werfen; schleudern; Zelt, Lager aufschlagen, -stellen; ♪ (an)stimmen; **~ too high** *fig.* Erwartungen zu hoch stecken; *v/i.* ⚒ (sich) lagern; hinschlagen; ⚓ stampfen (*Schiff*); **~ into** F herfallen über (*acc.*); **~black** ['pɪtʃ'blæk], **~dark** pechschwarz; stockdunkel.

pitch·er ['pɪtʃə] Krug *m*; *Baseball*: Werfer *m*.

pitch·fork ['pɪtʃfɔːk] Heu-, Mistgabel *f*.

pit·e·ous □ ['pɪtɪəs] kläglich.

pit·fall ['pɪtfɔːl] Fallgrube *f*; *fig.* Falle *f*.

pith [pɪθ] Mark *n*; *fig.* Kern *m*; *fig.* Kraft *f*; **~y** □ ['pɪθɪ] (-*ier*, -*iest*) markig, kernig.

pit·i·a·ble □ ['pɪtɪəbl] bemitleidenswert; erbärmlich; **~ful** □ [~fl] bemitleidenswert; erbärmlich; jäm-

merlich (*a. contp.*); **~less** □ [~lɪs] unbarmherzig.

pit·tance ['pɪtəns] Hungerlohn *m*.

pit·y ['pɪtɪ] 1. Mitleid *n* (*on* mit); *it is a ~* es ist schade; 2. bemitleiden.

piv·ot ['pɪvət] 1. ⊕ (Dreh)Zapfen *m*; *fig.* Dreh-, Angelpunkt *m*; 2. sich drehen (*on, upon* um).

piz·za ['piːtsə] Pizza *f*.

pla·ca·ble □ ['plækəbl] versöhnlich.

plac·ard ['plækɑːd] 1. Plakat *n*; Transparent *n*; 2. anschlagen; mit e-m Plakat bekleben.

place [pleɪs] 1. Platz *m*; Ort *m*; Stelle *f*; Stätte *f*; (Arbeits)Stelle *f*, (An-)Stellung *f*; Wohnsitz *m*, Haus *n*, Wohnung *f*; Wohnort *m*; *soziale* Stellung *f*; **~ of delivery** *econ.* Erfüllungsort *m*; **give ~ to** j-m Platz machen; *in ~* an die Stelle (*gen.*); *out of ~* fehl am Platz; 2. stellen, legen, setzen; *j-n* ein-, anstellen; *Auftrag* erteilen (*with s.o.* j-m); **be ~d** *Sport*: sich placieren; *I can't ~ him* *fig.* ich weiß nicht, wo ich ihn hintun soll (*identifizieren*); **~name** ['pleɪsneɪm] Ortsname *m*.

plac·id □ ['plæsɪd] sanft; ruhig.

pla·gia|rism ['pleɪdʒjərɪzəm] Plagiat *n*; **~rize** [~raɪz] plagiieren.

plague [pleɪg] 1. Seuche *f*; Pest *f*; Plage *f*; 2. plagen, quälen.

plaice *zo.* [pleɪs] Scholle *f*.

plaid [plæd] Plaid *n*.

plain [pleɪn] 1. □ klar; deutlich; einfach, schlicht; unscheinbar, wenig anziehend; häßlich (*Frau*); offen (u. ehrlich); einfarbig; rein (*Wahrheit, Unsinn etc.*); 2. *adv.* klar, deutlich; 3. Ebene *f*, Flachland *n*; the Great ~s *pl. Am.* die Prärien *pl.* (*im Westen der USA*); **~ choc·olate** (zart)bittere Schokolade; **~clothes man** ['pleɪn'kləʊðmən] (*pl. -men*) Polizist *m od.* Kriminalbeamte(r) *m* in Zivil; **~ deal·ing** Redlichkeit *f*; **~s·man** (*pl. -men*) *Am.* Präriebewohner *m*.

plain·tiff ⚖ ['pleɪntɪf] Kläger(in); **~tive** □ [~v] traurig, klagend.

plait [plæt, *Am.* pleɪt] 1. (Haar-*etc.*)Flechte *f*; Zopf *m*; 2. flechten.

plan [plæn] 1. Plan *m*; 2. (-*nn*-) planen; entwerfen; ausarbeiten.

plane [pleɪn] 1. flach, eben; 2. Ebene *f*, (ebene) Fläche *f*; ✈ Tragfläche *f*; Flugzeug *n*; ⊕ Hobel *m*; *fig.* Stufe *f*, Niveau *n*; *by ~* mit dem Flugzeug, auf dem Luftweg; **3.** (ein)ebnen; ⊕ hobeln; ⚔ fliegen.

plan·et *ast.* ['plænɪt] Planet *m*.

plank [plæŋk] **1.** Planke *f*, Bohle *f*, Diele *f*; *pol.* Programmpunkt *m*; **2.** dielen; verschalen; ~ *down* F *et.* hinknallen; *Geld* auf den Tisch legen, blechen.

plant [plɑːnt] **1.** ♀ Pflanze *f*; ⊕ Anlage *f*; Fabrik *f*; **2.** (an-, ein)pflanzen (*a. fig.*); bepflanzen; besiedeln; anlegen; (auf)stellen; *Schlag* versetzen; **plan·ta·tion** [plæn'teɪʃn] Pflanzung *f*, Pflanzen *f*; Besied(e)lung *f*; ~**er** ['plɑːntə] Pflanzer *m*; Plantagenbesitzer *m*; ⚲ Pflanzmaschine *f*; Übertopf *m*.

plaque [plɑːk] (Schmuck)Platte *f*; Gedenktafel *f*; ⚕ Zahnbelag *m*.

plash [plæʃ] platschen.

plas·ter ['plɑːstə] **1.** ⚕ Pflaster *n*; *arch.* (Ver)Putz *m*; *a.* ~ *of Paris* Gips *m* (*a.* ⚕); Stuck *m*; **2.** verputzen; bekleben; ⚕ ein Pflaster legen auf (*acc.*); ~ *cast* Gipsabdruck *m*, -abguß *m*; ⚕ Gipsverband *m*.

plas·tic ['plæstɪk] **1.** (~*ally*) plastisch; Plastik...; **2.** *oft* ~*s sg.* Plastik(material) *n*, Kunststoff *m*.

plate [pleɪt] **1.** Platte *f*; Teller *m*; (Bild)Tafel *f*; Schild *n*; (Kupfer-, Stahl)Stich *m*; (Tafel)Besteck *n*; *Baseball:* Heimbase *n*; ⊕ Grobblech *n*; **2.** plattieren; panzern.

plat·form ['plætfɔːm] Plattform *f*; *geol.* Hochebene *f*; ⚒ Bahnsteig *m*; *Brt.* Plattform *f* (*bsd. am Busende*, *Am.* ⚒ *bsd. am Wagenende*); (Redner)Tribüne *f*, Podium *n*; ⊕ Rampe *f*, Bühne *f*; *pol.* Parteiprogramm *n*; *bsd. Am.* pol. Aktionsprogramm *n* (*im Wahlkampf*).

plat·i·num *min.* ['plætɪnəm] Platin *n*.

plat·i·tude *fig.* ['plætɪtjuːd] Plattheit *f*.

pla·toon ⚔ [plə'tuːn] Zug *m*.

plat·ter *Am. od. veraltet* ['plætə] (Servier)Platte *f*.

plau·dit ['plɔːdɪt] Beifall *m*.

plau·si·ble ☐ [plɔːzəbl] glaubhaft.

play [pleɪ] **1.** Spiel *n*; Schauspiel *n*, (Theater)Stück *n*; ⊕ Spiel *n*; *fig.* Spielraum *m*; **2.** spielen; ⊕ Spiel (-raum) haben; ⊕ sich bewegen (*Kolben etc.*); ~ *back Ball* zurückspielen (*to* zu); *Tonband* abspielen; ~ *off fig.* ausspielen (*against* gegen); ~ *on*, ~ *upon fig. j-s Schwächen* aus-

nutzen; ~*ed out fig.* erledigt, erschöpft; ~**back** ['pleɪbæk] Playback *n*, Wiedergabe *f*, Abspielen *n*; ~**bill** Theaterplakat *n*; *Am.* Programm (-heft) *n*; ~**boy** Playboy *m*; ~**er** [~ə] (Schau)Spieler(in); Plattenspieler *m*; ~**fel·low** Spielgefährt|e *m*, -in *f*; ~**ful** ☐ [~fl] verspielt; spielerisch, scherzhaft; ~**girl** Playgirl *n*; ~**go·er** [~ɡəʊə] (*bsd.* häufige[r]) Theaterbesucher(in); ~**ground** Spielplatz *m*; Schulhof *m*; ~**house** *thea.* Schauspielhaus *n*; Spielhaus *n* (*für Kinder*); ~**mate** = *playfellow*; Gespiel|e *m*, -in *f*; ~**thing** Spielzeug *n*; ~**wright** Dramatiker *m*.

plea [pliː] ⚖ Einspruch *m*; Ausrede *f*; Gesuch *n*; *on the* ~ *of od. that* unter dem Vorwand (*gen.*) *od.* daß.

plead [pliːd] (~*ed, bsd. schott., Am. pled*) *v/i.* ⚖ plädieren; ~ *for* für *j-n* sprechen; sich einsetzen für; ~ (*not*) *guilty* sich (nicht) schuldig bekennen; *v/t.* sich berufen auf (*acc.*), vorschützen; *Sache* vertreten; ⚖ (als Beweis) anführen; ~**ing** ⚖ ['pliːdɪŋ] Plädoyer *n*.

pleas·ant ☐ ['pleznt] angenehm, erfreulich; freundlich; sympathisch; ~**ry** [~rɪ] Scherz *m*, Spaß *m*.

please [pliːz] (*j-m*) gefallen, angenehm sein; befriedigen; belieben; ~ bitte; (*yes*), ~ (ja), bitte; (oh ja,) gerne; ~ *come in!* bitte, treten Sie ein!; ~ *yourself* (ganz) wie Sie wünschen; ~**d** erfreut, zufrieden; *be* ~ *at* erfreut sein über (*acc.*); *be* ~ *to do et.* gerne tun; ~ *to meet you!* angenehm!; *be* ~ *with* befriedigt sein von; Vergnügen haben an (*dat.*).

pleas·ing ☐ ['pliːzɪŋ] angenehm, gefällig.

plea·sure ['pleʒə] Vergnügen *n*, Freude *f*; Belieben *n*; *attr.* Vergnügungs...; *at* ~ nach Belieben; ~**boat** Vergnügungs-, Ausflugsdampfer *m*; ~**ground** (Park)Anlage(n *pl.*) *f*; Vergnügungspark *m*.

pleat [pliːt] **1.** (Plissee)Falte *f*; **2.** fälteln, plissieren.

pled [pled] *pret. u. p.p. von plead.*

pledge [pledʒ] **1.** Pfand *n*; Zutrinken *n*, Toast *m*; Versprechen *n*, Gelöbnis *n*; **2.** verpfänden; *j-m* zutrinken; *he* ~*d himself* er gelobte.

ple·na·ry ['pliːnərɪ] Voll..., Plenar...

plen·i·po·ten·tia·ry [plenɪpə'tenʃərɪ] (General)Bevollmächtigte(r *m*) *f*).

plen·ti·ful ☐ ['plentɪfl] reichlich.
plen·ty ['plentɪ] **1.** Fülle *f*, Überfluß *m*; ~ *of* reichlich; **2.** F reichlich.
pli·a·ble ☐ ['plaɪəbl] biegsam; *fig.* geschmeidig, nachgiebig.
pli·ers ['plaɪəz] *pl.* (*a pair of* ~ e-e) (Draht-, Kombi)Zange.
plight [plaɪt] (schlechter) Zustand, schwierige Lage, Notlage *f*.
plim·soll *Brt.* ['plɪmsəl] Turnschuh *m*.
plod [plɒd] (-*dd*-) *a.* ~ *along*, ~ *on* sich dahinschleppen; ~ *away* sich abplagen (*at* mit), schuften.
plop [plɒp] (-*pp*-) plumpsen *od.* (*bsd. ins Wasser*) platschen (lassen).
plot [plɒt] **1.** Stück *n* Land, Parzelle *f*, Grundstück *n*; (geheimer) Plan, Komplott *n*, Anschlag *m*, Intrige *f*; Handlung *f* (*e-s Dramas etc.*); **2.** (-*tt*-) *v/t.* auf-, einzeichnen; planen, anzetteln; *v/i.* sich verschwören (*against* gegen).
plough, *Am.* **plow** [plaʊ] **1.** Pflug *m*; **2.** (um)pflügen; **~·share** ['plaʊʃeə] Pflugschar *f*.
pluck [plʌk] **1.** Rupfen *n*, Zupfen *n*, Zerren *n*, Reißen *n*; Zug *m*, Ruck *m*; Innereien *pl.*; *fig.* Mut *m*, Schneid *m*; **2.** pflücken; *Vogel* rupfen (*a. fig.*); zupfen, ziehen, zerren, reißen (*at* an *dat.*); ♪ *Saiten* zupfen; ~ *up courage* Mut fassen; **~·y** F ☐ ['plʌkɪ] (-*ier*, -*iest*) mutig.
plug [plʌɡ] **1.** Pflock *m*, Dübel *m*, Stöpsel *m*; ⚡ Stecker *m*; ⚡ F Steckdose *f*; Hydrant *m*; *mot.* (Zünd-) Kerze *f*; (Zahn)Plombe *f*; Priem *m* (*Kautabak*); *Rundfunk, TV:* F Empfehlung *f*, Tip *m*, Werbung *f*; **2.** *v/t.* (-*gg*-) Zahn plombieren; F im *Rundfunk etc.* (ständig) Reklame machen für; *a.* ~ *up* zu-, verstopfen, zustöpseln; ~ *in* ⚡ *Gerät* einstecken.
plum [plʌm] ♀ Pflaume(nbaum *m*) *f*; Rosine *f* (*a. fig.*).
plum·age ['pluːmɪdʒ] Gefieder *n*.
plumb [plʌm] **1.** lot-, senkrecht; **2.** (Blei)Lot *n*; **3.** *v/t.* lotrecht machen; loten; sondieren (*a. fig.*); Wasser- *od.* Gasleitungen legen in; *v/i.* als Rohrleger arbeiten; **~·er** ['plʌmə] Klempner *m*, Installateur *m*; **~·ing** [~ɪŋ] Klempnerarbeit *f*; Rohrleitungen *pl.*; sanitäre Installation.
plume [pluːm] **1.** Feder *f*; Federbusch *m*; **2.** mit Federn schmücken;

das Gefieder putzen; ~ *o.s. on* sich brüsten mit.
plum·met ['plʌmɪt] Senkblei *n*.
plump [plʌmp] **1.** *adj.* drall, prall, mollig; ~ F glatt (*Absage etc.*); △ *nicht plump*; **2.** *a.* ~ *down* (hin-) plumpsen (lassen); **3.** Plumps *m*; **4.** *adv.* F unverblümt, geradeheraus.
plum **pud·ding** ['plʌm'pʊdɪŋ] Plumpudding *m*.
plun·der ['plʌndə] **1.** Plünderung *f*; Raub *m*, Beute *f*; △ *nicht Plunder*; **2.** plündern.
plunge [plʌndʒ] **1.** (Ein-, Unter-) Tauchen *n*; (Kopf)Sprung *m*; Sturz *m*; *take the* ~ *fig.* den entscheidenden Schritt wagen; **2.** (ein-, unter-) tauchen; (sich) stürzen (*into* in *acc.*); *e-e Waffe ins Herz etc.* stoßen; ♣ stampfen (*Schiff*).
plu·per·fect *gr.* ['pluːˈpɜːfɪkt] *a.* ~ *tense* Plusquamperfekt *n*, Vorvergangenheit *f*.
plu·ral *gr.* ['plʊərəl] Plural *m*, Mehrzahl *f*; **~·i·ty** [plʊəˈrælətɪ] Mehrheit *f*, Mehrzahl *f*; Vielzahl *f*.
plus [plʌs] **1.** *prp.* plus; **2.** *adj.* positiv; Plus...; **3.** Plus *n*; Mehr *n*.
plush [plʌʃ] Plüsch *n*.
ply [plaɪ] **1.** Lage *f*, Schicht *f* (*Stoff, Sperrholz etc.*); Strähne *f* (*Garn etc.*); *fig.* Neigung *f*; *three-*~ dreifach (*Garn etc.*); dreifach gewebt (*Teppich*); **2.** *v/t.* handhaben, umgehen mit; *fig. j-m* zusetzen, *j-n* überhäufen (*with* mit); *v/i. regelmäßig* fahren (*between* zwischen); **~·wood** ['plaɪwʊd] Sperrholz *n*.
pneu·mat·ic [njuːˈmætɪk] (~*ally*) Luft...; pneumatisch, ~ (*tyre*) ⊕ Luftreifen *m*.
pneu·mo·ni·a ♂ [njuːˈməʊnjə] Lungenentzündung *f*.
poach[1] [pəʊtʃ] wildern.
poach[2] [~] pochieren; ~*ed eggs* *pl.* verlorene Eier *pl.*
poach·er ['pəʊtʃə] Wilddieb *m*, Wilderer *m*.
pock ♂ [pɒk] Pocke *f*, Blatter *f*.
pock·et ['pɒkɪt] **1.** (Hosen- *etc.*)Tasche *f*; ✂ = *air pocket*; **2.** einstecken (*a. fig.*); *Am. pol. Gesetzesvorlage* nicht unterschreiben; *Gefühl* unterdrücken; **3.** Taschen...; **~·book** Notizbuch *n*; Brieftasche *f*; *Am.* Geldbeutel *m*; *Am.* Handtasche *f*; Taschenbuch *n*; ~ **cal·cu·la·tor**

Taschenrechner *m*; **~knife** (*pl. -knives*) Taschenmesser *n*.

pod ♐ [pɒd] Hülse *f*, Schale *f*, Schote *f*.

po·em [ˈpəʊɪm] Gedicht *n*.

po·et [ˈpəʊɪt] Dichter *m*; **~ess** [~ɪs] Dichterin *f*; **~·ic** [pəʊˈetɪk] (**~ally**), **~·i·cal** □ [~kl] dichterisch; **~·ics** [~ks] *sg.* Poetik *f*; **~·ry** [ˈpəʊɪtrɪ] Dichtkunst *f*; Dichtung *f*; *coll.* Dichtungen *pl.*, Gedichte *pl.*

poi·gnan|cy [ˈpɔɪnənsɪ] Schärfe *f*; **~t** [~t] scharf; *fig.* bitter; *fig.* ergreifend.

point [pɔɪnt] **1.** Spitze *f*; *geogr.* Landspitze *f*; *gr.*, Å, *phys. etc.* Punkt *m*; Å (Dezimal)Punkt *m*, Komma *n*; *phys.* Grad *m* (*e-r Skala*); ⚓ Kompaßstrich *m*; Auge *n* (*auf Spielkarten etc.*); Punkt *m*, Stelle *f*, Ort *m*; springender Punkt; Zweck *m*, Ziel *n*; Pointe *f*; *fig.* hervorstechende Eigenschaft; **~** *pl. Brt.* ⚓ Weiche *f*; **~** *of view* Stand-, Gesichtspunkt *m*; *the* **~** *is that* ... die Sache ist die, daß ...; *make a* **~** *of s.th.* auf e-r Sache bestehen; *there is no* **~** *in doing* es hat keinen Zweck, zu tun; *in* **~** *of* hinsichtlich (*gen.*); *to the* **~** zur Sache (gehörig); *off od. beside the* **~** nicht zur Sache (gehörig); *on the* **~** *of ger.* im Begriff zu *inf.*; *beat s.o. on* **~s** j-n nach Punkten schlagen; *win od. lose on* **~s** nach Punkten gewinnen *od.* verlieren; *winner on* **~s** Punktsieger *m*; **2.** *v/t.* (zu)spitzen; **~** *at Waffe etc.* richten auf (*acc.*); (*mit dem Finger*) zeigen auf (*acc.*); **~** *out* zeigen; *fig.* hinweisen auf (*acc.*); *v/i.* **~** *at* deuten, weisen auf (*acc.*); **~** *to* nach e-r Richtung weisen; hinweisen auf (*acc.*); **~·ed** □ [ˈpɔɪntɪd] spitz(ig); Spitz...; *fig.* scharf; **~·er** [~ə] Zeiger *m*; Zeigestock *m*; *zo.* Vorstehhund *m*; **~·less** [~lɪs] stumpf; witzlos; zwecklos.

poise [pɔɪz] **1.** Gleichgewicht *n*; (Körper-, Kopf)Haltung *f*; **2.** *v/t.* im Gleichgewicht halten; *Kopf etc.* tragen, halten; *v/i.* schweben.

poi·son [ˈpɔɪzn] **1.** Gift *n*; **2.** vergiften; **~·ous** □ [~əs] giftig (*a. fig.*).

poke [pəʊk] **1.** Stoß *m*, Puff *m*; F Faustschlag *m*; **2.** *v/t.* stoßen, puffen; *Feuer* schüren; **~** *fun at* sich über j-*n* lustig machen; **~** *one's nose into everything* F s-e Nase überall hineinstecken; *v/i.* stoßen, stochern.

pok·er [ˈpəʊkə] Feuerhaken *m*.

---

pok·y [ˈpəʊkɪ] (**-ier, -iest**) eng; schäbig.

po·lar [ˈpəʊlə] polar; **~** *bear zo.* Eisbär *m*.

Pole[1] [pəʊl] Pole *m*, Polin *f*.

pole[2] [~] Pol *m*; Stange *f*; Mast *m*; Deichsel *f*; *Sport:* (Sprung)Stab *m*.

pole·cat *zo.* [ˈpəʊlkæt] Iltis *m*; *Am.* Skunk *m*, Stinktier *n*.

po·lem|ic [pəˈlemɪk], *a.* **~·i·cal** □ [~kl] polemisch.

pole-star [ˈpəʊlstɑː] *ast.* Polarstern *m*; *fig.* Leitstern *m*.

pole-vault [ˈpəʊlvɔːlt] **1.** Stabhochsprung *m*; **2.** stabhochspringen; **~·er** [~ə] Stabhochspringer *m*; **~·ing** [~ɪŋ] Stabhochspringen *n*, -sprung *m*.

po·lice [pəˈliːs] **1.** Polizei *f*; △ *nicht Police*; **2.** überwachen; **~·man** (*pl. -men*) Polizist *m*; **~·of·fi·cer** Polizeibeamte(r) *m*, Polizist *m*; **~** *sta·tion* Polizeiwache *f*, -revier *n*; **~·wom·an** (*pl. -women*) Polizistin *f*.

pol·i·cy [ˈpɒlɪsɪ] Politik *f*; Taktik *f*; Klugheit *f*; (Versicherungs)Police *f*; *Am.* Zahlenlotto *n*.

po·li·o ✚ [ˈpəʊlɪəʊ] Polio *f*, Kinderlähmung *f*.

Pol·ish[1] [ˈpəʊlɪʃ] **1.** polnisch; **2.** *ling.* Polnisch *n*.

pol·ish[2] [ˈpɒlɪʃ] **1.** Politur *f*; Schuhcreme *f*; *fig.* Schliff *m*; **2.** polieren; *Schuhe* putzen; *fig.* verfeinern.

po·lite □ [pəˈlaɪt] (**~r, ~st**) artig, höflich; **~·ness** [~nɪs] Höflichkeit *f*.

pol·i|tic □ [ˈpɒlɪtɪk] diplomatisch; klug; **po·lit·i·cal** □ [pəˈlɪtɪkl] politisch; staatlich, Staats...; **~·ti·cian** [pɒlɪˈtɪʃn] Politiker *m*; **~·tics** [ˈpɒlɪtɪks] *oft sg.* Politik *f*.

pol·ka [ˈpɒlkə] Polka *f*; **~** *dot* Punktmuster *n* (*auf Stoff*).

poll [pəʊl] **1.** Wählerliste *f*; Stimmenzählung *f*; Wahl *f*; Stimmenzahl *f*; (Ergebnis *n* e-r) (Meinungs)Umfrage *f*; **2.** *v/t. Wahlstimmen* erhalten; *v/i.* wählen.

pol·len ♐ [ˈpɒlən] Blütenstaub *m*.

poll·ing [ˈpəʊlɪŋ] Wählen *n*, Wahl *f*; **~** *booth* Wahlkabine *f*, -zelle *f*; **~** *district* Wahlbezirk *m*; **~** *place Am.*, **~** *station bsd. Brt.* Wahllokal *n*.

poll-tax [ˈpəʊltæks] Kopfsteuer *f*.

pol|lut·ant [pəˈluːtənt] Schadstoff *m*; **~·lute** [~t] be-, verschmutzen; verunreinigen; *eccl.* entweihen; **~·lu·tion** [~ʃn] Verunreinigung *f*; (Luft-, Wasser-, Umwelt)Verschmutzung *f*.

po·lo ['pəʊləʊ] *Sport*: Polo *n*; **~neck** Rollkragen(pullover) *m*.

pol|yp zo., ♣ ['pɒlɪp], **~y·pus** ♣ [~əs] (*pl. -pi* [-paɪ], *-puses*) Polyp *m*.

pom·mel ['pʌml] **1.** (Degen-, Sattel)Knopf *m*; **2.** (*bsd. Brt. -ll-, Am. -l-*) = **pummel**.

pomp [pɒmp] Pomp *m*, Prunk *m*.

pom·pous □ ['pɒmpəs] pompös, prunkvoll; aufgeblasen; schwülstig.

pond [pɒnd] Teich *m*, Weiher *m*.

pon·der ['pɒndə] *v/t.* erwägen; *v/i.* nachdenken; **~a·ble** [~rəbl] wägbar; **~ous** □ [~rəs] schwer(fällig).

pon·tiff ['pɒntɪf] Hohepriester *m*; Papst *m*.

pon·toon [pɒn'tu:n] Ponton *m*; **~ bridge** Pontonbrücke *f*.

po·ny zo. ['pəʊnɪ] Pony *n*, kleines Pferd; *Am.* Mustang *m*, (halb)wildes Pferd.

poo·dle zo. ['pu:dl] Pudel *m*.

pool [pu:l] **1.** Teich *m*; Pfütze *f*, Lache *f*; (Schwimm)Becken *n*; Pool *m*; *Karten*: Gesamteinsatz *m*; *econ.* Ring *m*, Kartell *n*; *mst* ~s *pl.* (Fußball- *etc.*)Toto *n*, *m*; **~room** *Am.* Billardspielhalle *f*; Wettannahmestelle *f*; **2.** *econ.* ein Kartell bilden; *Geld, Unternehmen etc.* zusammenlegen.

poop ♣ [pu:p] Heck *n*; *a.* ~ **deck** (erhöhtes) Achterdeck.

poor □ [pʊə] arm(selig); dürftig; schlecht; **~ly** ['pʊəlɪ] **1.** *adj.* kränklich, unpäßlich; **2.** *adv.* arm(selig), dürftig; **~ness** [~nɪs] Armut *f*.

pop¹ [pɒp] **1.** Knall *m*; F Limo *f* (*Limonade*); **2.** (*-pp-*) *v/t.* knallen lassen; *Am.* Mais rösten; schnell *wohin* tun *od.* stecken; *v/i.* knallen; *mit adv.* huschen; ~ **in** hereinplatzen (*Besuch*).

pop² [~] **1.** *a.* ~ **music** Schlagermusik *f*; Pop(musik *f*) *m*; **2.** volkstümlich, beliebt; Schlager...; Pop...; ~ **concert** Popkonzert *n*; ~ **singer** Schlagersänger(in) (~s); ~ **song** Schlager *m*.

pop³ *Am.* F [~] Paps *m*, Papa *m*; Opa *m* (*alter Herr*).

pop·corn ['pɒpkɔ:n] Popcorn *n*, Puffmais *m*.

pope [pəʊp] *mst* ♀ Papst *m*.

pop-eyed F ['pɒpaɪd] glotzäugig.

pop·lar ♀ ['pɒplə] Pappel *f*.

pop·py ♀ ['pɒpɪ] Mohn *m*; **~cock** F Quatsch *m*, dummes Zeug.

pop·u|lace ['pɒpjʊləs] *die* breite Masse, *das* Volk; *contp.* Pöbel *m*; **~lar** □ [~ə] Volks...; volkstümlich, populär, beliebt; **~lar·i·ty** [pɒpjʊ'lærətɪ] Popularität *f*, Beliebtheit *f*.

pop·u|late ['pɒpjʊleɪt] bevölkern, besiedeln; *mst pass.* bewohnen; **~la·tion** [pɒpjʊ'leɪʃn] Bevölkerung *f*; **~lous** □ ['pɒpjʊləs] dichtbesiedelt, -bevölkert.

porce·lain ['pɔ:slɪn] Porzellan *n*.

porch [pɔ:tʃ] Vorhalle *f*, Portal *n*, Vorbau *m*; *Am.* Veranda *f*.

por·cu·pine zo. ['pɔ:kjʊpaɪn] Stachelschwein *n*.

pore [pɔ:] **1.** Pore *f*; **2.** ~ **over** *et.* eifrig studieren.

pork [pɔ:k] Schweinefleisch *n*; **~y** F ['pɔ:kɪ] **1.** (*-ier, -iest*) fett; dick; **2.** *Am.* = **porcupine**.

porn F [pɔ:n] = **porno**.

por|no F ['pɔ:nəʊ] **1.** (*pl. -nos*) Porno (*-film*) *m*; **2.** Porno...; **~nog·ra·phy** [pɔ:'nɒgrəfɪ] Pornographie *f*.

po·rous □ ['pɔ:rəs] porös.

por·poise zo. ['pɔ:pəs] Tümmler *m*.

por·ridge ['pɒrɪdʒ] Haferbrei *m*.

port¹ [~] Hafen(stadt *f*) *m*.

port² [~] ♣ (Lade)Luke *f*; ♣, ✈ Bullauge *n*.

port³ ♣, ✈ [~] Backbord *n*.

port⁴ [~] Portwein *m*.

por·ta·ble ['pɔ:təbl] tragbar.

por·tal ['pɔ:tl] Portal *n*, Tor *n*.

por|tent ['pɔ:tent] (Vor)Zeichen *n*, Omen *n*; Wunder *n*; **~ten·tous** □ [pɔ:'tentəs] unheilvoll; wunderbar.

por·ter ['pɔ:tə] (Gepäck)Träger *m*; *bsd. Brt.* Pförtner *m*, Portier *m*; *Am.* 🚋 Schlafwagenschaffner *m*; Porter (-bier *n*) *m*, *n*.

port·hole ♣, ✈ ['pɔ:thəʊl] Bullauge *n*.

por·tion ['pɔ:ʃn] **1.** (An)Teil *m*; Portion *f* (*Essen*); Erbteil *n*; Aussteuer *f*; *fig.* Los *n*; **2.** ~ **out** aus-, verteilen (*among* unter *acc.*).

port·ly ['pɔ:tlɪ] (*-ier, -iest*) korpulent.

por·trait ['pɔ:trɪt] Porträt *n*, Bild *n*.

por·tray [pɔ:'treɪ] (ab)malen, porträtieren; schildern; **~al** [~əl] Porträtieren *n*; Schilderung *f*.

pose [pəʊz] **1.** Pose *f*; Haltung *f*; **2.** aufstellen; *Problem, Frage* stellen; aufwerfen; posieren; Modell sitzen *od.* stehen; ~ **as** sich ausgeben als *od.* für.

posh F [pɒʃ] schick, piekfein.

po·si·tion [pə'zɪʃn] Position f, Lage f, Stellung f (a. fig.); Stand m; fig. Standpunkt m.

pos·i·tive ['pɒzətɪv] **1.** □ bestimmt, ausdrücklich; feststehend, sicher; unbedingt; positiv; bejahend; überzeugt; rechthaberisch; **2.** phot. Positiv n.

pos|sess [pə'zes] besitzen, haben; beherrschen; fig. erfüllen; ~ o.s. of et. in Besitz nehmen; ~**sessed** besessen; ~**ses·sion** [~ʃn] Besitz m; fig. Besessenheit f; ~**ses·sive** gr. [~sɪv] **1.** □ possessiv, besitzanzeigend; ~ case Genitiv m; **2.** Possessivpronomen n, besitzanzeigendes Fürwort; Genitiv m; ~**ses·sor** [~sə] Besitzer(in).

pos·si·bil·i·ty [pɒsə'bɪlətɪ] Möglichkeit f; ~**ble** ['pɒsəbl] möglich; ~**bly** [~lɪ] möglicherweise, vielleicht; if I ~ can wenn ich irgend kann.

post [pəʊst] **1.** Pfosten m; Posten m; Stelle f, Amt n; bsd. Brt. Post f; ~ exchange Am. Einkaufsstelle f; ~ Plakat etc. anschlagen; aufstellen, postieren; eintragen; bsd. Brt. Brief etc. einstecken, abschicken, aufgeben; ~ up j-n informieren.

post- ['pəʊst] nach…, Nach…

post·age ['pəʊstɪdʒ] Porto n; ~ stamp Briefmarke f.

post·al □ ['pəʊstl] **1.** postalisch, Post…; ~ order Brt. Postanweisung f; **2.** a. ~ card Am. Postkarte f.

post|-bag bsd. Brt. ['pəʊstbæg] Postsack m, -beutel m; ~**box** bsd. Brt. Briefkasten m; ~**card** Postkarte f; a. picture ~ Ansichtskarte f; ~**code** Brt. Postleitzahl f.

post·er ['pəʊstə] Plakat n; Poster n, m.

pos·te·ri·or [pɒ'stɪərɪə] **1.** □ später (to als); hinter; **2.** oft ~s pl. Hinterteil n.

pos·ter·i·ty [pɒ'sterətɪ] Nachwelt f; Nachkommen(schaft f) pl.

post-free bsd. Brt. ['pəʊst'friː] portofrei.

post-grad·u·ate ['pəʊst'grædʊət] **1.** nach dem ersten akademischen Grad; **2.** j., der nach dem ersten akademischen Grad weiterstudiert.

post-haste ['pəʊst'heɪst] schnellstens.

post·hu·mous □ ['pɒstjʊməs] nachgeboren; post(h)um.

post|man bsd. Brt. ['pəʊstmən] (pl. -men) Briefträger m; ~**mark 1.** Poststempel m; **2.** (ab)stempeln; ~**mas·ter** Postamtsvorsteher m; ~ **of·fice** Post(amt n) f; ~-**of·fice box** Post(schließ)fach n; ~-**paid** portofrei.

post·pone [pəʊst'pəʊn] ver-, aufschieben; ~**ment** [~mənt] Verschiebung f, Aufschub m.

post·script ['pəʊsskrɪpt] Postskriptum n.

pos·ture ['pɒstʃə] **1.** (Körper)Haltung f, Stellung f; **2.** posieren, sich in Positur werfen.

post-war ['pəʊst'wɔː] Nachkriegs…

po·sy ['pəʊzɪ] Sträußchen n.

pot [pɒt] **1.** Topf m; Kanne f; Tiegel m; F Sport: Pokal m; sl. Hasch n (Haschisch); sl. Grass n (Marihuana); **2.** (-tt-) in e-n Topf tun; einlegen.

po·ta·to [pə'teɪtəʊ] (pl. -toes) Kartoffel f; s. chip 1, crisp 3.

pot-bel·ly ['pɒtbelɪ] Schmerbauch m.

po·ten|cy ['pəʊtənsɪ] Macht f; Stärke f; physiol. Potenz f; ~t [~t] mächtig; stark; physiol. potent; ~**tial** [pə-'tenʃl] **1.** potentiell; möglich; **2.** potential n; Leistungsfähigkeit f.

poth·er ['pɒðə] Aufregung f.

pot-herb ['pɒthɜːb] Küchenkraut n.

po·tion ['pəʊʃn] (Arznei-, Gift-, Zauber)Trank m.

pot·ter¹ ['pɒtə]: ~ about herumwerkeln.

pot·ter² [~] Töpfer(in); ~**y** [~rɪ] Töpferei f; Töpferware(n pl.) f.

pouch [paʊtʃ] Tasche f; Beutel m (a. zo.); anat. Tränensack m.

poul·ter·er ['pəʊltərə] Geflügelhändler m.

poul·tice ✠ ['pəʊltɪs] Packung f.

poul·try ['pəʊltrɪ] Geflügel n.

pounce [paʊns] **1.** Satz m, Sprung m; Herabstoßen n (= es Raubvogels), **2.** sich stürzen, Raubvogel: herabstoßen (on, upon auf acc.).

pound¹ [paʊnd] Pfund n (Gewicht); ~ (sterling) Pfund n (Sterling) (abbr. £ = 100 pence).

pound² [~] Tierheim n; Abstellplatz m (für polizeilich abgeschleppte Fahrzeuge).

pound³ [~] (zer)stoßen; stampfen; hämmern, trommeln, schlagen.

-pound·er ['paʊndə] …pfünder m.

pour [pɔː] v/t. gießen, schütten; ~ out

Getränk eingießen; *v/i.* strömen, rinnen.

pout [paʊt] **1.** Schmollen *n*; **2.** *v/t.* Lippen aufwerfen; *v/i.* schmollen.

pov·er·ty [ˈpɒvətɪ] Armut *f*; Mangel *m*.

pow·der [ˈpaʊdə] **1.** Pulver *n*; Puder *m*; **2.** pulverisieren; (sich) pudern; bestreuen; **~·box** Puderdose *f*; **~·room** Damentoilette *f*.

pow·er [ˈpaʊə] **1.** Kraft *f*; Macht *f*; Gewalt *f*; ⚡ Vollmacht *f*; & Potenz *f*; *in* ~ an der Macht, im Amt; **2.** ⊕ antreiben; *rocket-~ed* raketengetrieben; **~·cur·rent** ⚡ Starkstrom *m*; **~ cut** ⚡ Stromsperre *f*; Strom-, Netzausfall *m*; **~·ful** □ [~fl] mächtig; kräftig; wirksam; **~·less** □ [~lɪs] macht-, kraftlos; **~·plant** = *power-station*; **~ pol·i·tics** *oft sg.* Machtpolitik *f*; **~·sta·tion** Elektrizitäts-, Kraftwerk *n*.

pow·wow *Am.* F [ˈpaʊwaʊ] Versammlung *f*.

prac·ti|ca·ble □ [ˈpræktɪkəbl] durchführbar; begeh-, befahrbar (*Weg*); brauchbar; **~·cal** □ [~l] praktisch; tatsächlich; sachlich; *~ joke* Streich *m*; **~·cal·ly** [~lɪ] so gut wie.

prac·tice, *Am. a.* **-tise** [ˈpræktɪs] **1.** Praxis *f*; Übung *f*; Gewohnheit *f*; Brauch *m*; Praktik *f*; *it is common* ~ es ist allgemein üblich; *put into* ~ in die Praxis umsetzen; **2.** *Am.* = *practise*.

prac·tise, *Am. a.* **-tice** [~] *v/t.* in die Praxis umsetzen; ausüben; betreiben; üben; *v/i.* (sich) üben; praktizieren; ~ *on,* ~ *upon j-s Schwäche* ausnutzen; **~d** geübt (*in* in *dat.*) (*Person*).

prac·ti·tion·er [prækˈtɪʃnə]: *general* ~ praktischer Arzt; *legal* ~ Rechtsanwalt *m*.

prai·rie [ˈpreərɪ] Grasebene *f*; Prärie *f*(*in Nordamerika*); **~ schoo·ner** *Am.* Planwagen *m*.

praise [preɪz] **1.** Lob *n*; **2.** loben, preisen; **~·wor·thy** [ˈpreɪzwɜːðɪ] lobenswert.

pram *bsd. Brt.* F [præm] Kinderwagen *m*.

prance [prɑːns] sich bäumen, steigen; tänzeln (*Pferd*); (einher)stolzieren.

prank [præŋk] Streich *m*.

prate [preɪt] **1.** Gefasel *n*, Geschwafel *n*; **2.** faseln, schwafeln.

prat·tle [ˈprætl] **1.** Geplapper *n*; **2.** (*et.* daher)plappern.

prawn *zo.* [prɔːn] Garnele *f*.

pray [preɪ] beten; inständig (er)bitten; bitte!

prayer [preə] Gebet *n*; inständige Bitte; *oft* ~*s pl.* Andacht *f*; *the Lord's* ♀ das Vaterunser; **~·book** [ˈpreəbʊk] Gebetbuch *n*.

pre- [priː-; prɪ] *zeitlich:* vor, vorher, früher als; *räumlich:* vor, davor.

preach [priːtʃ] predigen; **~·er** [ˈpriːtʃə] Prediger/in.

pre·am·ble [priːˈæmbl] Einleitung *f*.

pre·car·i·ous □ [prɪˈkeərɪəs] unsicher, bedenklich; gefährlich.

pre·cau·tion [prɪˈkɔːʃn] Vorkehrung *f*, Vorsicht(smaßregel, -smaßnahme) *f*; **~·a·ry** [~ʃnərɪ] vorbeugend.

pre|cede [priːˈsiːd] voraus-, vorangehen (*dat.*); **~·ce·dence,** **~·ce·den·cy** [~əns, ~sɪ] Vorrang *m*; **~·ce·dent** [ˈpresɪdənt] Präzedenzfall *m*.

pre·cept [ˈpriːsept] Grundsatz *m*.

pre·cinct [ˈpriːsɪŋkt] Bezirk *m*; *Am.* Wahlbezirk *m*, -kreis *m*; *Am.* (Polizei)Revier *n*; ~*s pl.* Umgebung *f*; Bereich *m*; Grenzen *pl.*; *pedestrian* ~ Fußgängerzone *f*.

pre·cious [ˈpreʃəs] **1.** □ kostbar; edel (*Steine etc.*); F schön, nett, fein; **2.** *adv.* F reichlich, herzlich.

pre·ci·pice [ˈpresɪpɪs] Abgrund *m*.

pre·cip·i·tate 1. [prɪˈsɪpɪteɪt] *v/t.* (hinab)stürzen; 🜆 (aus)fällen; *fig.* beschleunigen; *v/i.* 🜆 *meteor.* sich niederschlagen; **2.** □ [~tət] überstürzt, hastig; **3.** 🜆 [~] Niederschlag *m*; **~·ta·tion** [prɪsɪpɪˈteɪʃn] Sturz *m*; 🜆 Niederschlagen *n*; *meteor.* Niederschlag *m*; *fig.* Überstürzung *f*, Hast *f*; **~·tous** □ [prɪˈsɪpɪtəs] steil (abfallend), jäh.

pré·cis [ˈpreɪsiː] (*pl.* -*cis* [-siːz]) (gedrängte) Übersicht, Zusammenfassung *f*.

pre|cise □ [prɪˈsaɪs] genau; **~·ci·sion** [~ˈsɪʒn] Genauigkeit *f*; Präzision *f*.

pre·clude [prɪˈkluːd] ausschließen; *e-r Sache* vorbeugen; *j-n* hindern.

pre·co·cious □ [prɪˈkəʊʃəs] frühreif; altklug.

pre·con|ceived [ˈpriːkənˈsiːvd] vorgefaßt (*Meinung*); **~·cep·tion** [~ˈsepʃn] vorgefaßte Meinung.

pre·cur·sor [priːˈkɜːsə] Vorläufer(in).

pred·a·to·ry [ˈpredətərɪ] Raub...

pre·de·ces·sor ['priːdɪsesə] Vorgänger(in).

pre·des·ti·nate [priː'destɪneɪt] vorherbestimmen; **~tined** auserwählt, vorherbestimmt.

pre·de·ter·mine ['priːdɪ'tɜːmɪn] vorher festsetzen; vorherbestimmen.

pre·dic·a·ment [prɪ'dɪkəmənt] mißliche Lage, Zwangslage f.

pred·i·cate 1. ['predɪkeɪt] behaupten; gründen, basieren (on auf dat.); 2. gr. [~kət] Prädikat n, Satzaussage f.

pre·dict [prɪ'dɪkt] vorhersagen; **~dic·tion** [~kʃn] Prophezeiung f.

pre·di·lec·tion [priːdɪ'lekʃn] Vorliebe f.

pre·dis·pose ['priːdɪ'spəʊz] j-n (im voraus) geneigt od. empfänglich machen (to für); **~po·si·tion** [~pə-'zɪʃn]: ~ to Neigung f zu; bsd. 🇸 Anfälligkeit f für.

pre·dom·i·nance [prɪ'dɒmɪnəns] Vorherrschaft f; Vormacht(stellung) f; fig. Übergewicht n; **~nant** □ [~t] vorherrschend; **~nate** [~eɪt] die Oberhand haben; vorherrschen.

pre·em·i·nent □ [priː'emɪnənt] hervorragend.

pre·emp·tion [priː'empʃn] Vorkauf(srecht n) m; **~tive** [~tɪv] Vorkaufs...; 🇽 Präventiv...

pre-ex·ist ['priːɪg'zɪst] vorher dasein.

pre·fab ['priːfæb] Fertighaus n.

pre·fab·ri·cate ['priː'fæbrɪkeɪt] vorfabrizieren.

pref·ace ['prefɪs] 1. Vorrede f, Vorwort n, Einleitung f; 2. einleiten.

pre·fect ['priːfekt] Präfekt m; Schule: Brt. Aufsichts-, Vertrauensschüler(in).

pre·fer [prɪ'fɜː] (-rr-) vorziehen, bevorzugen, lieber haben od. mögen od. tun; 🇮 Klage einreichen; befördern.

pref·e·ra·ble □ ['prefərəbl] (to) vorzuziehen(d) (dat.), besser (als); **~ra·bly** [~lɪ] vorzugsweise, besser; **~rence** [~əns] Vorliebe f; Vorzug m; **~ren·tial** □ [prefə'renʃl] bevorzugt; Vorzugs...

pre·fer·ment [prɪ'fɜːmənt] Beförderung f.

pre·fix ['priːfɪks] Präfix n, Vorsilbe f.

preg·nan·cy ['pregnənsɪ] Schwangerschaft f; Trächtigkeit f (Tier); fig. Bedeutung(sgehalt m) f, Tragweite

f; **~t** □ [~t] schwanger; trächtig (Tier); fig. ideenreich; fig. bedeutungsvoll; △ nicht prägnant.

pre·judge ['priː'dʒʌdʒ] im voraus od. vorschnell be- od. verurteilen.

prej·u·dice ['predʒʊdɪs] 1. Voreingenommenheit f, Vorurteil n; Nachteil m, Schaden m; 2. j-n (günstig od. ungünstig) beeinflussen, einnehmen (in favour of für; against gegen); benachteiligen; e-r Sache Abbruch tun; ~d (vor)eingenommen; **~di·cial** □ [predʒʊ'dɪʃl] nachteilig.

pre·lim·i·na·ry [prɪ'lɪmɪnərɪ] 1. □ vorläufig; einleitend; Vor...; 2. Einleitung f; Vorbereitung f.

prel·ude ['prelju:d] Vorspiel n.

pre·ma·ture □ [premə'tjʊə] vorzeitig, verfrüht; fig. vorschnell.

pre·med·i·tate [priː'medɪteɪt] vorher überlegen; ~d vorsätzlich; **~ta·tion** [priːmedɪ'teɪʃn] Vorbedacht m.

prem·i·er ['premjə] 1. erste(r, -s); 2. Premierminister m.

prem·is·es ['premɪsɪz] pl. Grundstück n, Gebäude n od. pl., Anwesen n; Lokal n.

pre·mi·um ['priːmjəm] Prämie f; econ. Agio n; Versicherungsprämie f; at a ~ über pari; fig. sehr gefragt.

pre·mo·ni·tion [priːmə'nɪʃn] (Vor-)Warnung f; (Vor)Ahnung f.

pre·oc·cu·pied [priː'ɒkjʊpaɪd] gedankenverloren; **~py** [~aɪ] ausschließlich beschäftigen; j-n (völlig) in Anspruch nehmen.

prep F [prep] = preparation, preparatory school.

prep·a·ra·tion [prepə'reɪʃn] Vorbereitung f; Zubereitung f; **pre·par·a·to·ry** □ [prɪ'pærətərɪ] vorbereitend; ~ (school) Vor(bereitungs)schule f.

pre·pare [prɪ'peə] v/t. vorbereiten; zurechtmachen; (zu)bereiten; (aus-)rüsten; v/i. sich vorbereiten, (sich) anschicken; **~d** □ bereit.

pre·pay ['priː'peɪ] (-paid) vorausbezahlen; frankieren.

pre·pon·de·rance [prɪ'pɒndərəns] Übergewicht n; **~rant** [~t] überwiegend; **~rate** [~reɪt] überwiegen.

prep·o·si·tion gr. [prepə'zɪʃn] Präposition f, Verhältniswort n.

pre·pos·sess [priːpə'zes] einnehmen; **~ing** □ [~ɪŋ] einnehmend, anziehend.

pre·pos·ter·ous [prɪ'pɒstərəs] absurd; lächerlich, grotesk.

pre·req·ui·site ['priː'rekwɪzɪt] Vorbedingung f, (Grund)Voraussetzung f.

pre·rog·a·tive [prɪ'rɒgətɪv] Vorrecht n.

pres·age ['presɪdʒ] **1.** (böses) Vorzeichen; (Vor)Ahnung f; **2.** (vorher) ankündigen; prophezeien.

pre·scribe [prɪ'skraɪb] vorschreiben; ⚕ verschreiben.

pre·scrip·tion [prɪ'skrɪpʃn] Vorschrift f, Verordnung f; ⚕ Rezept n.

pres·ence ['prezns] Gegenwart f, Anwesenheit f; ~ of mind Geistesgegenwart f.

pres·ent[1] ['preznt] **1.** □ gegenwärtig; anwesend, vorhanden; jetzig; laufend (Jahr etc.); vorliegend (Fall etc.); ~ tense gr. Präsens n, Gegenwart f; **2.** Gegenwart f, gr. a. Präsens n; Geschenk n; at ~ jetzt; for the ~ vorläufig.

pre·sent[2] [prɪ'zent] (dar)bieten; thea., Film: bringen, zeigen; Rundfunk, TV: bringen, moderieren; vorlegen, (-)zeigen; j-n vorstellen; (über)reichen; (be)schenken.

pre·sen·ta·tion [prezən'teɪʃn] Schenkung f; Überreichung f; Geschenk n; Vorstellung f (Person); Schilderung f; thea., Film: Darbietung f; Rundfunk, TV: Moderation f; Einreichung f (Gesuch); Vorlage f.

pres·ent-day ['preznt'deɪ] heutig, gegenwärtig, modern.

pre·sen·ti·ment [prɪ'zentɪmənt] Vorgefühl n, (mst böse Vor)Ahnung f.

pres·ent·ly ['prezntlɪ] bald (darauf); Am. zur Zeit, jetzt.

pres·er·va·tion [prezə'veɪʃn] Bewahrung f, Schutz m, Erhaltung f (a. fig.); Konservierung f; Einmachen n, -kochen n; **pre·ser·va·tive** [prɪ'zɜːvətɪv] **1.** bewahrend; konservierend; **2.** Konservierungsmittel n.

pre·serve [prɪ'zɜːv] **1.** bewahren, behüten; erhalten; einmachen; Wild hegen; a. hunt. (Jagd)Revier n, (Jagd-, Fisch)Gehege n; fig. Reich n; mst ~s pl. das Eingemachte.

pre·side [prɪ'zaɪd] den Vorsitz führen (at, over bei).

pres·i·den·cy ['prezɪdənsɪ] Vorsitz m; Präsidentschaft f; **~dent** [~t] Präsident(in); Vorsitzende(r m) f; Rektor m; Am. econ. Direktor m.

press [pres] **1.** Druck m (a. fig.); (Wein- etc.)Presse f; Druckerei f; Verlag m; Druck(en n) m; a. printing-~ Druckerpresse f; die Presse (Zeitungswesen); bsd. (Wäsche-) Schrank m; Bügeln n; Andrang m, (Menschen)Menge f; **2.** v/t. (aus-) pressen; (zusammen)drücken; drücken auf (acc.); Kleider plätten, bügeln; (be)drängen; bestehen auf (dat.); aufdrängen (on dat.); be ~ed for time es eilig haben; v/i. pressen, drücken; plätten, bügeln; (sich) drängen; ~ for dringen od. drängen auf (acc.); fordern; ~ on (zügig) weitermachen; ~ **a·gen·cy** Nachrichtenbüro n, Presseagentur f; ~ **a·gent** Presseagent m; ~**but·ton** ⚡ ['presbʌtn] Druckknopf m; ~**ing** □ [~ɪŋ] dringend; ~**stud** Brt. Druckknopf m; **pres·sure** [~ʃə] Druck m (a. fig.); Bedrängnis f, Belastung f.

pres·tige [pre'stiːʒ] Prestige n.

pre·su·ma·ble □ [prɪ'zjuːməbl] vermutlich; ~**me** [~'zjuːm] v/t. annehmen, vermuten, voraussetzen; sich et. herausnehmen; v/i. sich erdreisten; anmaßend sein; ~ on, ~ upon ausnutzen od. mißbrauchen (acc.).

pre·sump·tion [prɪ'zʌmpʃn] Vermutung f; Wahrscheinlichkeit f; Anmaßung f; ~**tive** □ [~tɪv] mutmaßlich; ~**tu·ous** □ [~tjʊəs] überheblich; vermessen.

pre·sup·pose [priːsə'pəʊz] voraussetzen; ~**po·si·tion** ['priːsʌpə'zɪʃn] Voraussetzung f.

pre·tence, Am. **-tense** [prɪ'tens] Vortäuschung f; Vorwand m; Schein m, Verstellung f.

pre·tend [prɪ'tend] vorgeben; vortäuschen; heucheln; Anspruch erheben (to auf acc.); ~**ed** □ angeblich.

pre·ten·sion [prɪ'tenʃn] Anspruch m (to auf acc.); Anmaßung f.

pre·ter·it(e) gr. ['pretərɪt] Präteritum n, erste Vergangenheit.

pre·text ['priːtekst] Vorwand m.

pret·ty ['prɪtɪ] **1.** □ (-ier, -iest) hübsch; niedlich; nett; **2.** adv. ziemlich.

pre·vail [prɪ'veɪl] die Oberhand haben od. gewinnen; (vor)herrschen; maßgebend od. ausschlaggebend sein; ~ on od. upon s.o. to do s.th. j-n dazu bewegen, et. zu tun; ~**ing** □ [~ɪŋ] (vor)herrschend.

prev·a·lent ☐ ['prevələnt] (vor)herrschend, weitverbreitet.

pre·var·i·cate [prɪ'værɪkeɪt] Ausflüchte machen.

pre|vent [prɪ'vent] verhindern, -hüten, e-r Sache vorbeugen; j-n hindern; **~·ven·tion** [~ʃn] Verhinderung f, Verhütung f; **~·ven·tive** ☐ [~tɪv] bsd. ♣ vorbeugend.

pre·view ['priːvjuː] Vorschau f; Vorbesichtigung f.

pre·vi·ous ☐ ['priːvjəs] vorher-, vorausgehend, Vor...; voreilig; **~ to** bevor, vor (dat.); **~ knowledge** Vorkenntnisse pl.; **~·ly** [~lɪ] vorher, früher.

pre-war [priː'wɔː] Vorkriegs...

prey [preɪ] 1. Raub m, Beute f; beast of **~** Raubtier n; bird of **~** Raubvogel m; be od. fall a **~** to die Beute (gen.) werden; fig. geplagt werden von; 2. **~** on, **~** upon zo. Jagd machen auf (acc.), fressen (acc.); fig. berauben (acc.), ausplündern (acc); fig. ausbeuten (acc.); fig. nagen od. zehren an (dat.).

price [praɪs] 1. Preis m; Lohn m; 2. Waren auszeichnen; den Preis festsetzen für; fig. bewerten, schätzen; **~·less** ['praɪslɪs] von unschätzbarem Wert, unbezahlbar.

prick [prɪk] 1. Stich m; ∨ Schwanz m (Penis); **~s** of conscience Gewissensbisse pl.; 2. v/t. (durch)stechen; fig. peinigen; a. **~** out Muster ausstechen; **~** up one's ears die Ohren spitzen; v/i. stechen; **~·le** ['prɪkl] Stachel m, Dorn m; **~·ly** [~lɪ] (-ier, -iest) stach(e)lig.

pride [praɪd] 1. Stolz m; Hochmut m; take (a) **~** in stolz sein auf (acc.); 2. **~** o.s. on od. upon stolz sein auf (acc.).

priest [priːst] Priester m.

prig [prɪg] Tugendbold m, selbstgefälliger Mensch; Pedant m.

prim ☐ [prɪm] (-mm-) steif; prüde.

pri·ma|cy ['praɪməsɪ] Vorrang m; **~·ri·ly** [~rəlɪ] in erster Linie; **~·ry** ☐ [~rɪ] 1. ursprünglich; hauptsächlich; primär; elementar; höchst; Erst..., Ur..., Anfangs...; Haupt...; 2. a. **~** election Am. pol. Vorwahl f; **~·ry school** Brt. Grundschule f.

prime [praɪm] 1. ☐ erste(r, -s), wichtigste(r, -s), Haupt...; erstklassig, vorzüglich; **~** cost econ. Selbstkosten pl.; **~** minister Premierminister m, Ministerpräsident m; **~** number ♣ Primzahl f; **~** time TV Hauptsendezeit f, beste Sendezeit; 2. fig. Blüte(zeit) f; das Beste, höchste Vollkommenheit; 3. v/t. vorbereiten; Pumpe anlassen; instruieren; paint. grundieren.

prim·er ['praɪmə] Fibel f, Elementarbuch n.

pri·m(a)e·val [praɪ'miːvl] uranfänglich, Ur...

prim·i·tive ☐ ['prɪmɪtɪv] erste(r, -s), ursprünglich, Ur...; primitiv.

prim·rose ♣ ['prɪmrəʊz] Primel f.

prince [prɪns] Fürst m; Prinz m; **prin·cess** [prɪn'ses, attr. 'prɪnses] Fürstin f; Prinzessin f.

prin·ci·pal ['prɪnsəpl] 1. ☐ erste(r, -s), hauptsächlich, Haupt...; △ nicht prinzipiell; 2. Hauptperson f; Vorsteher m; (Schul)Direktor m, Rektor m; Chef(in); ♣♣ Haupttäter(in); econ. (Grund)Kapital n; **~·i·ty** [prɪnsɪ-'pælətɪ] Fürstentum n.

prin·ci·ple ['prɪnsəpl] Prinzip n, Grundsatz m; on **~** grundsätzlich, aus Prinzip.

print [prɪnt] 1. print. Druck m (a. Schriftart); Druckbuchstaben pl.; (Finger- etc.)Abdruck m; bedruckter Kattun, Druckstoff m; (Stahl-, Kupfer)Stich m; phot. Abzug m; Drucksache f, bsd. Am. Zeitung f; in **~** gedruckt; out of **~** vergriffen; 2. (ab-, auf-, be)drucken; in Druckbuchstaben schreiben; fig. einprägen (on dat.); **~** off od. out) phot. abziehen, kopieren; **~** out Computer: ausdrucken; **~-out** Computer: Ausdruck m; **~ed matter** ✆ Drucksache f; **~·er** ['prɪntə] (Buch- etc.)Drucker m.

print·ing ['prɪntɪŋ] Druck m; Drucken n; phot. Abziehen n, Kopieren n; **~·ink** Druckerschwärze f; **~-of·fice** (Buch)Druckerei f; **~-press** Druckerpresse f.

pri·or ['praɪə] 1. früher, älter (to als); 2. adv. **~ to** vor (dat.); 3. eccl. Prior m; **~·i·ty** [praɪ'ɒrɪtɪ] Priorität f; Vorrang m; mot. Vorfahrt(srecht n) f.

prise bsd. Brt. [praɪz] = prize².

pris·m ['prɪzəm] Prisma n.

pris·on ['prɪzn] Gefängnis n; **~·er** [~ə] Gefangene(r m) f; Häftling m; take s.o. **~** j-n gefangennehmen.

pri·va·cy ['prɪvəsɪ] Zurückgezogenheit f; Privatleben n; Intim-, Privatsphäre f; Geheimhaltung f.

pri·vate ['praɪvɪt] **1.** □ privat, Privat...; persönlich; vertraulich; geheim; ~ *parts pl.* Geschlechtsteile *pl.*; **2.** ⚔ gemeiner Soldat; *in* ~ privat, im Privatleben; unter vier Augen.

pri·va·tion [praɪ'veɪʃn] Not *f*, Entbehrung *f*.

priv·i·lege ['prɪvɪlɪdʒ] Privileg *n*; Vorrecht *n*; **~d** privilegiert.

priv·y □ ['prɪvɪ] (*-ier, -iest*): ~ *to* eingeweiht in (*acc.*); ♀ *Council* Staatsrat *m*; ♀ *Councillor* Geheimer Rat (*Person*); ♀ *Seal* Geheimsiegel *n*.

prize[1] [praɪz] **1.** (Sieges)Preis *m*, Prämie *f*, Auszeichnung *f*; (Lotterie-) Gewinn *m*; **2.** preisgekrönt; Preis...; ~*-winner* Preisträger(in); **3.** (hoch-) schätzen.

prize[2], *bsd. Brt.* **prise** [praɪz] (auf-) stemmen; ~ *open* aufbrechen.

pro[1] [prəʊ] für; ⚠ *nicht pro = per.*

pro[2] F [~] *Sport*: Profi *m*.

pro- [prəʊ] (eintretend) für, pro..., ...freundlich.

prob·a|bil·i·ty [prɒbə'bɪlətɪ] Wahrscheinlichkeit *f*; **~·ble** □ ['prɒbəbl] wahrscheinlich.

pro·ba·tion [prə'beɪʃn] Probe *f*, Probezeit *f*; ⚖ Bewährung(sfrist) *f*; ~ *officer* Bewährungshelfer(in).

probe [prəʊb] **1.** ⚕, ⊕ Sonde *f*; *fig.* Sondierung *f*; ⚠ *nicht Probe*; *lunar* ~ Mondsonde *f*; **2.** sondieren; untersuchen; ⚠ *nicht proben, probieren.*

prob·lem ['prɒbləm] Problem *n*; ⛢ Aufgabe *f*; **~·at·ic** [prɒblə'mætɪk] (*~ally*), **~·at·i·cal** □ [~kl] problematisch, zweifelhaft.

pro·ce·dure [prə'si:dʒə] Verfahren *n*; Handlungsweise *f*.

pro·ceed [prə'si:d] weitergehen (*a. fig.*); sich begeben (*to* nach); fortfahren; vor sich gehen; vorgehen; *Brt. univ.* promovieren; ~ *from* kommen *od.* ausgehen *od.* herrühren von; ~ *to* schreiten *od.* übergehen zu, sich machen an (*acc.*); **~·ing** [~ɪŋ] Vorgehen *n*; Handlung *f*; **~s** *pl.* ⚖ Verfahren *n*, (Gerichts)Verhandlung(en *pl.*) *f*; (Tätigkeits)Bericht *m*; **~s** ['prəʊsi:dz] *pl.* Erlös *m*, Ertrag *m*, Gewinn *m*.

pro|cess ['prəʊses] **1.** Fortschreiten *n*, Fortgang *m*; Vorgang *m*; Verlauf *m* (*der Zeit*); Prozeß *m*, Verfahren *n*; ⚠ *nicht* ⚖ *Prozeß*; *in* ~ im Gange; *in* ~ *of construction* im Bau (befindlich); **2.** ⊕ bearbeiten; ⚖ gerichtlich belangen; ⚠ *nicht prozessieren*; **~·ces·sion** [prə'seʃn] Prozession *f*; **~·ces·sor** ['prəʊsesə] Prozessor *m*.

pro·claim [prə'kleɪm] proklamieren, erklären, ausrufen.

proc·la·ma·tion [prɒklə'meɪʃn] Proklamation *f*, Bekanntmachung *f*; Erklärung *f*.

pro·cliv·i·ty *fig.* [prə'klɪvətɪ] Neigung *f*.

pro·cras·ti·nate [prəʊ'kræstɪneɪt] zaudern.

pro·cre·ate ['prəʊkrɪeɪt] (er)zeugen.

pro·cu·ra·tor ⚖ ['prɒkjʊəreɪtə] Bevollmächtigte(r) *m*.

pro·cure [prə'kjʊə] *v/t.* be-, verschaffen; *v/i.* Kuppelei betreiben.

prod [prɒd] **1.** Stich *m*, Stoß *m*; *fig.* Ansporn *m*; **2.** (*-dd-*) stechen, stoßen; *fig.* anstacheln, anspornen.

prod·i·gal ['prɒdɪgl] **1.** □ verschwenderisch; *the* ~ *son* der verlorene Sohn; **2.** Verschwender(in).

pro·di·gious □ [prə'dɪdʒəs] erstaunlich, ungeheuer; **prod·i·gy** ['prɒdɪdʒɪ] Wunder *n* (*Sache od. Person*); *child od. infant* ~ Wunderkind *n*.

prod·uce[1] ['prɒdju:s] (Natur)Erzeugnis(se *pl.*) *n*, (Landes)Produkte *pl.*; Ertrag *m*; ⊕ Leistung *f*, Ausstoß *m*.

pro|duce[2] [prə'dju:s] produzieren; erzeugen, herstellen; hervorbringen; *Zinsen etc.* (ein)bringen; heraus-, hervorziehen; (vor)zeigen; *Beweis etc.* beibringen; *Gründe* vorbringen; ⛢ *Linie* verlängern; *Film* produzieren; *fig.* hervorrufen, erzielen; **~·duc·er** [~ə] Erzeuger(in), Hersteller(in); *Film, TV*: Produzent(in); *thea., Rundfunk*: *Brt.* Regisseur(in).

prod·uct ['prɒdʌkt] Produkt *n*, Erzeugnis *n*.

pro·duc|tion [prə'dʌkʃn] Produktion *f*; Erzeugung *f*, Herstellung *f*; Erzeugnis *n*; Hervorbringen *n*; Vorlegung *f*, Beibringung *f*; *thea. etc.* Inszenierung *f*; **~·tive** □ [~tɪv] produktiv; ertragreich, fruchtbar; schöpferisch; **~·tive·ness** [~nɪs], **~·tiv·i·ty** [prɒdʌk'tɪvətɪ] Produktivität *f*.

prof F [prɒf] Professor *m*.

pro|fa·na·tion [prɒfə'neɪʃn] Entweihung *f*; **~·fane** [prə'feɪn] **1.** □ profan, weltlich; gottlos, lästerlich; **2.** entweihen; **~·fan·i·ty** [~'fænətɪ] Gottlosigkeit *f*; Fluchen *n*.

P

pro|fess [prə'fes] (sich) bekennen (zu); erklären; beteuern; *Reue etc.* bekunden; *Beruf* ausüben; lehren; **~fessed** □ erklärt; angeblich; Berufs...; **~fes·sion** [~ʃn] Bekenntnis *n*; Erklärung *f*; Beruf *m*; **~fes·sion·al** [~nl] **1.** □ Berufs...; Amts...; professionell; beruflich; fachmännisch; freiberuflich; **~** *man* Akademiker *m*; **2.** Fachmann *m*; *Sport:* Berufsspieler(in), -sportler(in), Profi *m*; Berufskünstler(in); **~fes·sor** [~sə] Professor(in); *Am.* Dozent(in).

prof·fer ['profə] **1.** anbieten; **2.** Anerbieten *n*.

pro·fi·cien|cy [prə'fıʃənsı] Tüchtigkeit *f*; **~t** [~t] □ tüchtig; bewandert.

pro·file ['prəʊfaıl] Profil *n*.

prof|it ['profıt] **1.** Gewinn *m*, Profit *m*; Vorteil *m*, Nutzen *m*; **2.** *v/t. j-m* nützen; *v/i.* **~** *from od.* by Nutzen ziehen aus; **~·i·ta·ble** □ [~bl] nützlich, vorteilhaft; gewinnbringend, einträglich; **~·i·teer** [profı'tıə] **1.** Schiebergeschäfte machen; **2.** Profitmacher *m*, Schieber *m*; **~·it-shar·ing** ['profıtʃeərıŋ] Gewinnbeteiligung *f*.

prof·li·gate ['proflıgət] lasterhaft; verschwenderisch.

pro·found □ [prə'faʊnd] tief; tiefgründig, gründlich, profund.

pro·fuse □ [prə'fju:s] verschwenderisch; (über)reich; **~fu·sion** *fig.* [~ʒn] Überfluß *m*, (Über)Fülle *f*.

pro·gen·i·tor [prəʊ'dʒenıtə] Vorfahr *m*, Ahn *m*; **prog·e·ny** ['prodʒənı] Nachkommen(schaft *f*) *pl.*; *zo.* Brut *f*.

prog·no·sis ⚕ [prog'nəʊsıs] (*pl.* -ses [~si:z]) Prognose *f*.

prog·nos·ti·ca·tion [prəgnostı'keıʃn] Vorhersage *f*.

pro·gram ['prəʊgræm] **1.** *Computer:* Programm *n*; *Am.* = *Brt.* programme 1; **2.** (-mm-) *Computer:* programmieren; *Am.* = *Brt.* programme 2; **~er** [~ə] = programmer.

pro|gramme, *Am.* **-gram** ['prəʊgræm] **1.** Programm *n*; *Rundfunk, TV:* a. Sendung *f*; **2.** (vor)programmieren; planen; **~gram·mer** [~ə] *Computer:* Programmierer(in).

pro·gress 1. ['prəʊgres] Fortschritt(e *pl.*) *m*; Vorrücken *n* (*a.* ⚔); Fortgang *m*; *in* **~** im Gange; **2.** [prə'gres] fortschreiten; **~gres·sion** [~ʃn] Fort-

schreiten *n*; Weiterentwicklung *f*; ⚔ Reihe *f*; **~gres·sive** [~sıv] **1.** □ fortschreitend; fortschrittlich; **2.** *pol.* Progressive(r *m*) *f*.

pro|hib·it [prə'hıbıt] verbieten; verhindern; **~hi·bi·tion** [prəʊı'bıʃn] Verbot *n*; Prohibition *f*; **~hi·bi·tion·ist** [~ʃənıst] Prohibitionist *m*; **~hib·i·tive** □ [prə'hıbıtıv] verbietend; Schutz...; unerschwinglich (*Preis*).

proj·ect¹ ['prodʒekt] Projekt *n*; Vorhaben *n*, Plan *m*.

pro|ject² [prə'dʒekt] *v/t.* planen, entwerfen; werfen, schleudern; projizieren; *v/i.* vorspringen, -ragen; **~jec·tile** [~aıl] Projektil *n*, Geschoß *n*; **~jec·tion** [~kʃn] Werfen *n*; Entwurf *m*; Vorsprung *m*, vorspringender Teil; ⚔, *phot.* Projektion *f*; **~jec·tor** *opt.* [~tə] Projektor *m*.

pro·le·tar·i·an [prəʊlı'teərıən] **1.** proletarisch; **2.** Proletarier(in).

pro·lif·ic [prə'lıfık] (**~**ally) fruchtbar.

pro·logue, *Am. a.* **-log** ['prəʊlɒg] Prolog *m*.

pro·long [prə'lɒŋ] verlängern.

prom·e·nade [prɒmə'nɑ:d] **1.** (Strand)Promenade *f*; **2.** promenieren.

prom·i·nent □ ['prɒmınənt] vorstehend, hervorragend (*a. fig.*); *fig.* prominent.

pro·mis·cu·ous □ [prə'mıskjʊəs] unordentlich, verworren; sexuell freizügig.

prom|ise ['prɒmıs] **1.** Versprechen *n*; *fig.* Aussicht *f*; **2.** versprechen; **~is·ing** □ [~ıŋ] vielversprechend; **~is·so·ry** [~ərı] versprechend; **~** *note econ.* Eigenwechsel *m*.

prom·on·to·ry ['prɒməntrı] Vorgebirge *n*.

pro|mote [prə'məʊt] *et.* fördern; *j-n* befördern; *Am. Schule:* versetzen; *parl.* unterstützen; *econ.* gründen; *Verkauf durch Werbung* steigern; *econ.* werben für; *Boxkampf etc.* veranstalten; **~mot·er** [~ə] Förderer *m*, Befürworter *m*; *Sport:* Veranstalter *m*; **~mo·tion** [~əʊʃn] Förderung *f*; Beförderung *f*; *econ.* Gründung *f*; *econ.* Verkaufsförderung *f*, Werbung *f*; △ *nicht* Promotion.

prompt [prɒmpt] **1.** □ umgehend, unverzüglich, sofortig; bereit(willig); pünktlich; **2.** *j-n* veranlassen; *Gedanken* eingeben; *j-m* vorsagen, soufflieren; **~er** ['prɒmptə] Souffleu|r *m*, -se *f*; **~ness** [~nɪs] Schnelligkeit *f*; Bereitschaft *f*.

prom·ul·gate ['prɒmʌlgeɪt] verkünden; verbreiten.

prone □ [prəʊn] (*~r*, *~st*) mit dem Gesicht nach unten (liegend); hingestreckt; *be ~ to fig.* neigen zu.

prong [prɒŋ] Zinke *f*; Spitze *f*.

pro·noun *gr.* ['prəʊnaʊn] Pronomen *n*, Fürwort *n*.

pro·nounce [prə'naʊns] aussprechen; verkünden; erklären für.

pron·to F ['prɒntəʊ] fix, schnell.

pro·nun·ci·a·tion [prənʌnsɪ'eɪʃn] Aussprache *f*.

proof [pruːf] **1.** Beweis *m*; Probe *f*; *print.* Korrekturfahne *f*, -bogen *m*; *print.*, *phot.* Probeabzug *m*; **2.** fest; *in Zssgn*: ...fest, ...beständig, ...dicht, ...sicher; **~read** ['pruːfriːd] (*-read* [-red]) Korrektur lesen; **~read·er** Korrektor *m*.

prop [prɒp] **1.** Stütze *f* (*a. fig.*); **2.** (*-pp-*) *a.* **~ up** stützen; *sich, et.* lehnen (*against* gegen).

prop·a·gate ['prɒpəgeɪt] (sich) fortpflanzen; verbreiten; **~ga·tion** [prɒpə'geɪʃn] Fortpflanzung *f*; Verbreitung *f*.

pro·pel [prə'pel] (*-ll-*) (vorwärts-, an)treiben; **~ler** [~ə] Propeller *m*, (Schiffs-, Luft)Schraube *f*; **~ling pen·cil** [~ɪŋ'pensl] Drehbleistift *m*.

pro·pen·si·ty *fig.* [prə'pensətɪ] Neigung *f*.

prop·er □ ['prɒpə] eigen(tümlich); passend; richtig; anständig, korrekt; zuständig; *bsd. Brt.* F ordentlich, tüchtig, gehörig; Eigen...; **~ name** Eigenname *m*; **~ty** [~tɪ] Eigentum *n*, Besitz *m*; Vermögen *n*; Eigenschaft *f*.

proph·e·cy ['prɒfɪsɪ] Prophezeiung *f*; **~sy** [~aɪ] prophezeien, weissagen.

proph·et ['prɒfɪt] Prophet *m*.

pro·pi·ti·ate [prə'pɪʃɪeɪt] günstig stimmen, versöhnen; **~tious** □ [~ʃəs] gnädig; günstig.

pro·por·tion [prə'pɔːʃn] **1.** Verhältnis *n*; Gleichmaß *n*; (An)Teil *m*; **~s** *pl.* (Aus)Maße *pl.*; **2.** in das richtige Verhältnis bringen; **~al** □ [~l] proportional; = **~ate** □ [~nət] im richtigen Verhältnis (*to* zu), angemessen.

pro·pos·al [prə'pəʊzl] Vorschlag *m*, (*a.* Heirats)Antrag *m*; Angebot *n*; **~e**

[~z] *v/t.* vorschlagen; beabsichtigen, vorhaben; e-n Toast ausbringen auf (*acc.*); **~** *s.o.'s health* auf j-s Gesundheit trinken; *v/i.* e-n Heiratsantrag machen (*to dat*); **prop·o·si·tion** [prɒpə'zɪʃn] Vorschlag *m*, Antrag *m*; *econ.* Angebot *n*; Behauptung *f*.

pro·pound [prə'paʊnd] *Frage etc.* vorlegen; vorschlagen.

pro·pri·e·ta·ry [prə'praɪətərɪ] Eigentümer..., Besitzer...; Eigentums...; *econ.* gesetzlich geschützt (*Arznei*, *Ware*); **~tor** [~ə] Eigentümer *m*, Geschäftsinhaber *m*; **~ty** [~ɪ] Richtigkeit *f*; Schicklichkeit *f*, Anstand *m*; *the proprieties pl.* die Anstandsformen *pl.*

pro·pul·sion ⊕ [prə'pʌlʃn] Antrieb *m*.

pro·rate *Am.* [prəʊ'reɪt] anteilmäßig auf- *od.* verteilen.

pro·sa·ic *fig.* [prəʊ'zeɪɪk] (*~ally*) prosaisch, nüchtern, trocken.

prose [prəʊz] Prosa *f*.

pros·e·cute ['prɒsɪkjuːt] (*a.* strafrechtlich) verfolgen; *Gewerbe etc.* betreiben; *z/z* anklagen (*for* wegen); **~cu·tion** [prɒsɪ'kjuːʃn] Durchführung *f* (*e-s Plans etc.*); Betreiben *n* (*e-s Gewerbes etc.*); *z/z* Strafverfolgung *f*, Anklage *f*; **~cu·tor** *z/z* ['prɒsɪkjuːtə] Ankläger *m*; *public ~* Staatsanwalt *m*.

pros·pect 1. ['prɒspekt] Aussicht *f* (*a. fig.*); *econ.* Interessent *m*; △ möglicher Prospekt; **2.** [prə'spekt]: **~** *for* ⚒ schürfen nach; bohren nach (*Öl*).

pro·spec·tive □ [prə'spektɪv] (zu-)künftig, voraussichtlich.

pro·spec·tus [prə'spektəs] (*pl. -tuses*) (Werbe)Prospekt *m*.

pros·per ['prɒspə] *v/i.* Erfolg haben; gedeihen, blühen; *v/t.* begünstigen; segnen; **~i·ty** [prɒ'sperətɪ] Gedeihen *n*, Wohlstand *m*, Glück *n*; *econ.* Wohlstand *m*, Konjunktur *f*, Blüte (-zeit) *f*; **~ous** □ ['prɒspərəs] erfolgreich, blühend; wohlhabend; günstig.

pros·ti·tute ['prɒstɪtjuːt] Prostituierte *f*, Dirne *f*; *male ~* Strichjunge *m*.

pros·trate 1. ['prɒstreɪt] hingestreckt; erschöpft; daniederliegend; demütig; gebrochen; **2.** [prɒ'streɪt] niederwerfen; erschöpfen; *fig.* niederschmettern; **~tra·tion** [~ʃn] Niederwerfen *n*, Fußfall *m*; Erschöpfung *f*.

P

pros·y *fig.* ['prəʊzɪ] (*-ier, -iest*) prosaisch; langweilig.

pro·tag·o·nist [prəʊ'tægənɪst] *thea.* Hauptfigur *f; fig.* Vorkämpfer(in).

pro|tect [prə'tekt] (be)schützen; **~tec·tion** [~k∫n] Schutz *m;* ₔₜ (Rechts)Schutz *m; econ.* Schutzzoll *m;* △ *nicht* Protektion; **~tec·tive** [~tɪv] (be)schützend; Schutz...; **~ duty** Schutzzoll *m;* **~tec·tor** [~ə] (Be)Schützer *m;* Schutz-, Schirmherr *m;* **~tec·tor·ate** [~ərət] Protektorat *n.*

pro·test ['prəʊtest] Protest *m;* Einspruch *m;* **2.** [prə'test] *v/i.* protestieren (*against* gegen); *v/t. Am.* protestieren gegen; beteuern.

Prot·es·tant ['prɒtɪstənt] **1.** protestantisch; **2.** Protestant(in).

prot·es·ta·tion [prɒtə'steɪ∫n] Beteuerung *f;* Protest *m* (*against* gegen).

pro·to·col ['prəʊtəkɒl] **1.** Protokoll *n;* **2.** (*-ll-*) protokollieren.

pro·to·type ['prəʊtətaɪp] Prototyp *m,* Urbild *n.*

pro|tract [prə'trækt] in die Länge ziehen, hinziehen.

pro|trude [prə'tru:d] heraus-, (her)vorstehen, -ragen, -treten; herausstrecken; **~tru·sion** [~ʒn] Herausragen *n,* (Her)Vorstehen *n,* Hervortreten *n.*

pro·tu·ber·ance [prə'tju:bərəns] Auswuchs *m,* Beule *f.*

proud □ [praʊd] stolz (*of* auf *acc.*).

prove [pru:v] (*proved, proved od. bsd. Am.* proven) *v/t.* be-, er-, nachweisen; prüfen; *v/i.* sich herausstellen *od.* erweisen (als); ausfallen; **prov·en** ['pru:vən] **1.** *Am. p.p. von* prove; **2.** be-, erwiesen; bewährt.

prov·e·nance ['prɒvənəns] Herkunft *f.*

prov·erb ['prɒvɜ:b] Sprichwort *n.*

pro·vide [prə'vaɪd] *v/t.* besorgen, beschaffen, liefern; bereitstellen; versorgen, ausstatten; ₔₜ vorsehen, festsetzen; *v/i.* (vor)sorgen; **~d** (*that*) vorausgesetzt, daß; sofern.

prov·i|dence ['prɒvɪdəns] Vorsehung *f;* Voraussicht *f,* Vorsorge *f;* **~dent** □ [~t] vorausblickend, vorsorglich; haushälterisch; **~den·tial** □ [prɒvɪ'den∫l] durch die (göttliche) Vorsehung bewirkt; glücklich, günstig.

pro·vid·er [prə'vaɪdə] Ernährer *m*

(*der Familie*); *econ.* Lieferant *m.*

prov·ince ['prɒvɪns] Provinz *f; fig.* Gebiet *n; fig.* Fach *n,* Aufgabenbereich *m;* **pro·vin·cial** [prə'vɪn∫l] **1.** □ Provinz..., provinziell; kleinstädtisch; **2.** Provinzbewohner(in).

pro·vi·sion [prə'vɪʒn] Beschaffung *f;* Vorsorge *f;* ₔₜ Bestimmung *f;* Vorkehrung *f,* Maßnahme *f;* **~s** *pl.* (Lebensmittel)Vorrat *m,* Proviant *m,* Lebensmittel *pl.;* △ *nicht* Provision; **~al** □ [~l] provisorisch.

pro·vi·so [prə'vaɪzəʊ] (*pl. -sos, Am. a. -soes*) Bedingung *f,* Vorbehalt *m.*

prov·o·ca·tion [prɒvə'keɪ∫n] Herausforderung *f;* **pro·voc·a·tive** [prə'vɒkətɪv] herausfordernd; aufreizend.

pro·voke [prə'vəʊk] reizen; herausfordern; provozieren.

prov·ost ['prɒvəst] Rektor *m* (*gewisser Colleges*); *schott.* Bürgermeister *m;* ✕ [prə'vəʊ]: **~ marshal** Kommandeur *m* der Militärpolizei.

prow ⚓ [praʊ] Bug *m.*

prow·ess ['praʊɪs] Tapferkeit *f.*

prowl [praʊl] **1.** *v/i. a.* **~ about, ~ around** herumstreichen; *v/t.* durchstreifen; **2.** Herumstreifen *n;* **~ car** *Am.* ['praʊlkɑ:] (Funk)Streifenwagen *m.*

prox·im·i·ty [prɒk'sɪmətɪ] Nähe *f.*

prox·y ['prɒksɪ] (Stell)Vertreter(in); (Stell)Vertretung *f,* Vollmacht *f;* **by ~** in Vertretung.

prude [pru:d] prüder Mensch; **be a ~** prüde sein.

pru|dence ['pru:dns] Klugheit *f,* Vernunft *f;* Vorsicht *f;* **~dent** □ [~t] klug, vernünftig; vorsichtig.

prud·er·y ['pru:dərɪ] Prüderie *f;* **~ish** □ [~ɪ∫] prüde, spröde.

prune [pru:n] **1.** Backpflaume *f;* **2.** ✄ beschneiden (*a. fig.*); *a.* **~ away, ~ off** wegschneiden.

pru·ri·ent □ ['prʊərɪənt] geil, lüstern.

pry[1] [praɪ] neugierig gucken *od.* sein; **~ about** herumschnüffeln; **~ into** s-e Nase stecken in (*acc.*).

pry[2] [~] = prize².

psalm [sɑ:m] Psalm *m.*

pseu·do- ['psju:dəʊ] Pseudo..., falsch.

pseu·do·nym ['psju:dənɪm] Pseudonym *n,* Deckname *m.*

psy·chi·a|trist [saɪ'kaɪətrɪst] Psychiater *m;* **~try** [~ɪ] Psychiatrie *f.*

psy|chic ['saɪkɪk] (~ally), **~·chi·cal** [~kl] psychisch, seelisch.

psy|cho·log·i·cal □ [saɪkə'lɒdʒɪkl] psychologisch; **~·chol·o·gist** [saɪ'kɒlədʒɪst] Psychologe m, -in f; **~·chol·o·gy** [~ɪ] Psychologie f.

pub Brt. F [pʌb] Pub n, Kneipe f.

pu·ber·ty ['pju:bətɪ] Pubertät f.

pu·bic anat. ['pju:bɪk] Scham...; ~ **bone** Schambein n; ~ **hair** Schamhaare pl.

pub·lic ['pʌblɪk] **1.** □ öffentlich; staatlich, Staats...; allgemein bekannt; ~ **spirit** Gemein-, Bürgersinn m; **2.** Öffentlichkeit f; die Öffentlichkeit, das Publikum, die Leute; △ *nicht* Publikum = audience.

pub·li·can bsd. Brt. ['pʌblɪkən] Gastwirt m.

pub·li·ca·tion [pʌblɪ'keɪʃn] Bekanntmachung f; Veröffentlichung f; Verlagswerk n; monthly ~ Monatsschrift f.

pub·lic| con·ve·ni·ence Brt. ['pʌblɪk kən'vi:njəns] öffentliche Bedürfnisanstalt; ~ **health** öffentliches Gesundheitswesen; ~ **hol·i·day** gesetzlicher Feiertag; ~ **house** Brt. s. pub.

pub·lic·i·ty [pʌb'lɪsətɪ] Öffentlichkeit f; Reklame f, Werbung f.

pub·lic| li·bra·ry ['pʌblɪk 'laɪbrərɪ] Leihbücherei f; ~ **re·la·tions** pl. Public Relations pl., Öffentlichkeitsarbeit f; ~ **school** Brt. Public School f (exklusives Internat); Am. staatliche Schule.

pub·lish ['pʌblɪʃ] bekanntmachen; veröffentlichen; Buch etc. herausgeben, verlegen; **~·ing house** Verlag m; **~·er** [~ə] Herausgeber m, Verleger m; **~s** pl. Verlag(sanstalt f) m.

puck·er ['pʌkə] **1.** kleine Falte; **2.** a. ~ **up** Lippen, Mund: (sich) verziehen od. spitzen; Stirn: (sich) runzeln; Falten bilden in (dat.) od. werfen.

pud·ding ['pʊdɪŋ] Pudding m; (feste) Süßspeise, Nachspeise f, -tisch m; (Art) Fleischpastete f; black ~ Blutwurst f; white ~ Preßsack m.

pud·dle ['pʌdl] Pfütze f.

pu·er·ile ['pjʊəraɪl] kindisch.

puff [pʌf] **1.** kurzer Atemzug, Schnaufer m; leichter Windstoß, Hauch m; Zug m (beim Rauchen); (Dampf-, Rauch)Wölkchen n; (Puder)Quaste f; **2.** (auf)blasen; pusten; paffen; schnauben, schnaufen, keuchen; ~ **out**, ~ **up** sich (auf)blähen;

~ed eyes geschwollene Augen; ~ed sleeve Puffärmel m; ~ **pas·try** ['pʌf 'peɪstrɪ] Blätterteiggebäck n; **~·y** [~ɪ] (-ier, -iest) böig; kurzatmig; geschwollen; aufgedunsen; bauschig.

pug zo. [pʌg] a. ~-dog Mops m.

pug·na·cious □ [pʌg'neɪʃəs] kampflustig; streitsüchtig.

pug-nose ['pʌgnəʊz] Stupsnase f.

puke sl. [pju:k] (aus)kotzen.

pull [pʊl] **1.** Ziehen n, Zerren n; Zug m; Ruck m; print. Fahne f, (Probe-) Abzug m; Ruderpartie f; Griff m; Zug m (at an e-r Zigarette etc.); Schluck m (at aus e-r Flasche); fig. Einfluß m, Beziehungen pl., Vorteil m; **2.** ziehen; zerren; reißen; zupfen; pflücken; rudern; ~ **about** herumzerren; ~ **ahead** of vorbeiziehen an (dat.), überholen (acc.) (Auto etc.); ~ **away** anfahren (Bus etc.); sich losreißen (from von); ~ **down** niederreißen; ~ **in** einfahren (Zug); anhalten (Fahrzeug, Boot); ~ **off** F zustande bringen, schaffen; ~ **out** herausfahren (of aus), abfahren (Zug etc.); ausscheren (Fahrzeug); fig. sich zurückziehen, aussteigen; ~ **over** (s-n Wagen) an die od. zur Seite fahren; ~ **round** Kranken durchbringen; durchkommen (Kranker); ~ **through** j-n durchbringen; ~ o.s. together sich zusammennehmen, sich zusammenreißen; ~ **up** Fahrzeug, Pferd anhalten; (an)halten; ~ **up with**, ~ **up to** j-n einholen.

pul·ley ⊕ ['pʊlɪ] Rolle f; Flaschenzug m; Riemenscheibe f.

pull-in Brt. ['pʊlɪn] Raststätte (bsd. a. für Fernfahrer); **~·o·ver** Pullover m; **~·up** Brt. = pull-in.

pulp [pʌlp] Brei m; Fruchtfleisch n; ⊕ Papierbrei m; ~ **magazine** Schundblatt n.

pul·pit ['pʊlpɪt] Kanzel f.

pulp·y □ ['pʌlpɪ] (-ier, -iest) breiig; fleischig.

pul·sate [pʌl'seɪt] pulsieren, schlagen; **pulse** [pʌls] Puls(schlag) m.

pul·ver·ize ['pʌlvəraɪz] v/t. pulverisieren; v/i. zu Staub werden.

pum·mel ['pʌml] (bsd. Brt. -ll-, Am. -l-) mit den Fäusten bearbeiten, verprügeln.

pump [pʌmp] **1.** Pumpe f; Pumps m; **2.** pumpen; F j-n aushorchen, -fragen; ~ **up** Reifen etc. aufpumpen; ~ **at·tend·ant** Tankwart m.

pumpkin

pump·kin ♀ [ˈpʌmpkɪn] Kürbis *m*.

pun [pʌn] **1.** Wortspiel *n*; **2.** (*-nn-*) ein Wortspiel machen.

Punch¹ [pʌntʃ] Kasperle *n*, *m*; ~*and-Judy show* Kasperletheater *n*.

punch² [~] **1.** Locheisen *n*; Locher *m*; Lochzange *f*; (Faust)Schlag *m*; Punsch *m*; **2.** (aus)stanzen; lochen; aufnehmen (*auf Lochkarten*); *bsd. Am. Kontrolluhr* stechen, *Karte* stempeln; schlagen (*mit der Faust*), boxen; (ein)hämmern auf (*acc.*); *Am. Rinder* treiben; ~(*ed*) *card* Lochkarte *f*; ~(*ed*) *tape* Lochstreifen *m*.

punc·til·i·ous □ [pʌŋkˈtɪlɪəs] peinlich genau; (übertrieben) förmlich.

punc·tu·al □ [ˈpʌŋktjʊəl] pünktlich; ~**i·ty** [pʌŋktjʊˈælɪtɪ] Pünktlichkeit *f*.

punc·tu·ate *gr.* [ˈpʌŋktjʊeɪt] interpunktieren; ~**a·tion** *gr.* [pʌŋktjʊˈeɪʃn] Interpunktion *f*, Zeichensetzung *f*; ~ *mark* Satzzeichen *n*.

punc·ture [ˈpʌŋktʃə] **1.** (Ein)Stich *m*, Loch *n*; Reifenpanne *f*; **2.** durchstechen; ein Loch machen in (*dat. od. acc.*); platzen (*Ballon*), *mot.* e-n Platten haben.

pun·gen·cy [ˈpʌndʒənsɪ] Schärfe *f*; ~**t** [~t] stechend, beißend, scharf.

pun·ish [ˈpʌnɪʃ] (be)strafen; ~**a·ble** □ [~əbl] strafbar; ~**ment** [~mənt] Strafe *f*; Bestrafung *f*.

punk [pʌŋk] *sl.* kleiner *od.* junger Ganove; Punk *m* (*a.* ♩); Punker *m*; ~ *rock*(*er*) ♩ Punkrock(er) *m*.

pu·ny □ [ˈpjuːnɪ] (*-ier, -iest*) winzig; schwächlich.

pup *zo.* [pʌp] Welpe *m*, junger Hund.

pu·pa *zo.* [ˈpjuːpə] (*pl. -pae* [-piː], *-pas*) Puppe *f*.

pu·pil [ˈpjuːpl] *anat.* Pupille *f*; Schüler(in); Mündel *m*, *n*.

pup·pet [ˈpʌpɪt] Marionette *f* (*a. fig.*); △ *nicht* Puppe = doll; ~**show** Puppenspiel *n*.

pup·py [ˈpʌpɪ] *zo.* Welpe *m*, junger Hund; *fig.* Schnösel *m*.

pur·chase [ˈpɜːtʃəs] **1.** (An-, Ein-) Kauf *m*; ⚖ Erwerb(ung *f*) *m*; Anschaffung *f*; ⊕ Hebevorrichtung *f*; Halt *m*; *make* ~*s* Einkäufe machen; **2.** (er)kaufen; ⚖ erwerben; ⊕ hochwinden; ~**chas·er** [~ə] Käufer(in).

pure □ [pjʊə] (~*r*, ~*st*) rein; pur; ~**bred** [ˈpjʊəbred] reinrassig.

pur·ga·tive ⚕ [ˈpɜːɡətɪv] **1.** abführ-

rend; **2.** Abführmittel *n*; ~**to·ry** [~ərɪ] Fegefeuer *n*.

purge [pɜːdʒ] **1.** ⚕ Abführmittel *n*; *pol.* Säuberung *f*; **2.** *mst fig.* reinigen; *pol.* säubern; ⚕ abführen.

pu·ri·fy [ˈpjʊərɪfaɪ] reinigen; läutern.

pu·ri·tan [ˈpjʊərɪtən] (*hist.* ♀) **1.** Puritaner(in); **2.** puritanisch.

pu·ri·ty [ˈpjʊərətɪ] Reinheit *f* (*a. fig.*).

purl [pɜːl] murmeln (*Bach*).

pur·lieus [ˈpɜːljuːz] *pl.* Umgebung *f*.

pur·loin [pɜːˈlɔɪn] entwenden.

pur·ple [ˈpɜːpl] **1.** purpurn, purpurrot; **2.** Purpur *m*; **3.** (sich) purpurn färben.

pur·port [ˈpɜːpət] **1.** Sinn *m*, Inhalt *m*; **2.** behaupten, vorgeben.

pur·pose [ˈpɜːpəs] **1.** Absicht *f*, Vorhaben *n*; Zweck *m*; Entschlußkraft *f*; *for the* ~ *of ger.* um zu *inf.*; *on* ~ absichtlich; *to the* ~ zweckdienlich; *to no* ~ vergebens; **2.** beabsichtigen, vorhaben; ~**ful** □ [~fl] zweckmäßig; absichtlich; zielbewußt; ~**less** □ [~lɪs] zwecklos; ziellos; ~**ly** [~lɪ] absichtlich.

purr [pɜː] schnurren (*Katze*); summen (*Motor*).

purse [pɜːs] **1.** Geldbeutel *m*, -börse *f*; *Am.* (Damen)Handtasche *f*; Geldgeschenk *n*; Siegprämie *f*; *Boxen:* Börse *f*; ~ *snatcher Am.* Handtaschenräuber *m*; **2.** ~ (*up*) *one's lips* die Lippen schürzen.

pur·su·ance [pəˈsjuːəns]: *in (the)* ~ *of* bei der Ausführung *od.* Ausübung (*gen.*); ~**ant** □ [~t]: ~ *to* gemäß *od.* entsprechend (*dat.*).

pur·sue [pəˈsjuː] verfolgen (*a. fig.*); streben nach; *Beruf* nachgehen; *Studium* betreiben; fortsetzen, -fahren in (*dat.*); ~**su·er** [~ə] Verfolger (-in); ~**suit** [~t] Verfolgung *f*; *mst* ~*s pl.* Beschäftigung *f*.

pur·vey [pəˈveɪ] *Lebensmittel* liefern; ~**or** [~ə] Lieferant *m*.

pus [pʌs] Eiter *m*.

push [pʊʃ] **1.** (An-, Vor)Stoß *m*; Schub *m*; Druck *m*; Notfall *m*; Anstrengung *f*, Bemühung *f*; F Schwung *m*, Energie *f*, Tatkraft *f*; **2.** stoßen; schieben; drängen; *Knopf* drücken; (an)treiben; *a.* ~ *through* durchführen; *Anspruch etc.* durchsetzen; F verkaufen, *Rauschgift* pushen; ~ *s.th. on s.o.* j-m et. aufdrängen; ~ *one's way* sich durch- *od.* vordrängen; ~ *along*, ~ *on*, ~ *forward*

weitermachen, -gehen, -fahren *etc.*;
~but·ton ⊕['pʊʃbʌtn] Druckknopf
m, -taste *f*; **~chair** *Brt.* (Falt)Sport-
wagen *m* (*für Kinder*); **~er** F [~ə]
Pusher *m* (*Rauschgifthändler*); **~
o·ver** Kinderspiel *n*, Kleinigkeit *f*;
be a ~ for auf *j-n* od. *et.* hereinfallen.
pu·sil·lan·i·mous □ [pju:sɪˈlænɪ-
məs] kleinmütig.
puss [pʊs] Mieze *f*, Kätzchen *n*, Katze *f* (*alle a. fig.* = *Mädchen*); **pus·sy**
['pʊsɪ], *a.* **~cat** Mieze *f*, Kätzchen *n*;
pus·sy·foot F leisetreten, sich nicht
festlegen.
put [pʊt] (*-tt-*; *put*) *v/t.* setzen, legen,
stellen, stecken, tun; bringen (*ins
Bett*); verwenden; *Frage* stellen,
vorlegen; *Sport: Kugel* stoßen; werfen; ausdrücken, sagen; ~ *to school*
zur Schule schicken; ~ *s.o. to work*
j-n an die Arbeit setzen; ~ *about
Gerüchte* verbreiten; ♣ den Kurs
(*e-s Schiffes*) ändern; ~ *across Idee
etc.* an den Mann bringen, verkaufen; ~ *back* zurückstellen (*a. Uhr*),
-tun; *fig.* aufhalten; ~ *by Geld* zurücklegen; ~ *down v/t.* hin-, niederlegen, -setzen, -stellen; *j-n* absetzen;
aussteigen lassen; (auf-, nieder-)
schreiben; eintragen; zuschreiben
(*to dat.*); *Aufstand* niederschlagen;
Mißstand unterdrücken; (*a. v/i.*) ∦
landen, aufsetzen; ~ *forth Kräfte*
aufbieten; *Knospen etc.* treiben; ~
forward Uhr vorstellen; *Meinung
etc.* vorbringen; ~ *o.s. forward* sich
bemerkbar machen; ~ *in v/t.* herein-,
hineinlegen, -setzen, -stellen, -stek-
ken; hineintun; *Anspruch* erheben;
Gesuch einreichen; *Urkunde* vorlegen; *Antrag* stellen; *j-n* einstellen;
Bemerkung einwerfen; *v/i.* einkehren
(*at* in *dat.*); ♣ einlaufen (*at* in *dat.*); ~
off v/t. Kleider ablegen (*a. fig.*); auf-,
verschieben; vertrösten; *j-n* abbringen; hindern; *Passagiere* aussteigen
lassen; *v/i.* ♣ auslaufen; ~ *on Kleider*
anziehen, *Hut, Brille* aufsetzen; *Uhr*
vorstellen; *Tempo* beschleunigen;
an-, einschalten; vortäuschen, -spie-

len; ~ *on airs* sich aufspielen; ~ *on
weight* zunehmen; ~ *out v/t.* ausmachen, (-)löschen; verrenken; (her-)
ausstrecken; verwirren; ärgern; *j-m*
Ungelegenheiten bereiten; *Kraft*
aufbieten; *Geld* ausleihen; *v/i.* ♣
auslaufen; ~ *right* in Ordnung bringen; ~ *through teleph.* verbinden (*to*
mit); ~ *together* zusammensetzen;
zusammenstellen; ~ *up v/t.* hinauf-
legen, -stellen; hochheben, -schie-
ben, -ziehen; *Bild etc.* aufhängen;
Haar hochstecken; *Schirm* aufspan-
nen; *Zelt etc.* aufstellen; errichten,
bauen; *Ware* anbieten; *Preis* erhöhen; *Widerstand* leisten; *Kampf* liefern; *Gäste* unterbringen, (bei sich)
aufnehmen; *Bekanntmachung* anschlagen; *v/i.* ~ *up* at einkehren *od.*
absteigen in (*dat.*); ~ *up for* kandidieren für, sich bewerben um; ~ *up
with* sich gefallen lassen, sich abfinden mit.
pu·tre·fy ['pju:trɪfaɪ] verwesen.
pu·trid □ ['pju:trɪd] faul, verfault,
-west; *sl.* scheußlich, saumäßig; **~i-
ty** [pju:'trɪdətɪ] Fäulnis *f*.
put·ty ['pʌtɪ] **1.** Kitt *m*; **2.** kitten.
put-you-up *Brt.* F ['pʊtju:ʌp]
Schlafcouch *f*, -sessel *m*.
puz·zle ['pʌzl] **1.** Rätsel *n*; schwierige
Aufgabe; Verwirrung *f*; Geduld(s)-
spiel *n*; **2.** *v/t.* verwirren; *j-m* Kopf-
zerbrechen machen; ~ *out* austüf-
teln; *v/i.* verwirrt sein; sich den
Kopf zerbrechen; **~head·ed** konfus.
pyg·my ['pɪgmɪ] Pygmäe *m*; Zwerg
m; *attr.* zwergenhaft.
py·ja·ma *Brt.* [pəˈdʒɑːmə] Schlafanzug..., Pyjama...; **~s** *Brt.* [~əz] *pl.*
Schlafanzug *m*, Pyjama *m*.
py·lon ['paɪlən] (Leitungs)Mast *m*.
pyr·a·mid ['pɪrəmɪd] Pyramide *f*.
pyre ['paɪə] Scheiterhaufen *m*.
Py·thag·o·re·an [paɪθægəˈrɪən] **1.**
pythagoreisch; **2.** Pythagoreer *m*.
py·thon *zo.* ['paɪθn] Pythonschlange
f.
pyx *eccl.* [pɪks] Hostienbehälter *m*.

Q

quack¹ [kwæk] **1.** Quaken n; **2.** quaken.

quack² [~] **1.** Scharlatan m; a. ~ *doctor* Quacksalber m, Kurpfuscher m; **2.** quacksalberisch; **3.** quacksalbern (an *dat.*); **~·er·y** ['kwækəri] Quacksalberei f.

quad·ran|gle ['kwɒdræŋgl] Viereck n; viereckiger Innenhof (*e-s College*); **~·gu·lar** □ [kwɒˈdræŋgjʊlə] viereckig.

quad·ren·nial □ [kwɒˈdrenɪəl] vierjährig; vierjährlich (wiederkehrend).

quad·ru|ped ['kwɒdrʊped] Vierfüß(l)er m; **~·ple** [~pl] **1.** □ vierfach; Vierer...; **2.** (sich) vervierfachen; **~·plets** [~plɪts] pl. Vierlinge pl.

quag·mire ['kwægmaɪə] Sumpf(land n) m, Moor n; Morast m.

quail¹ zo. [kweɪl] Wachtel f.

quail² [~] verzagen; (vor Angst) zittern (*before* vor *dat.*; *at* bei).

quaint □ [kweɪnt] anheimelnd, malerisch; wunderlich, drollig.

quake [kweɪk] **1.** zittern, beben (*with*, *for* vor *dat.*); **2.** F Erdbeben n.

Quak·er ['kweɪkə] Quäker m.

qual·i·fi·ca·tion [kwɒlɪfɪˈkeɪʃn] Qualifikation f, Eignung f, Befähigung f; Einschränkung f; gr. nähere Bestimmung; **~·fy** ['kwɒlɪfaɪ] (sich) qualifizieren; befähigen; bezeichnen; gr. näher bestimmen; einschränken; abschwächen, mildern; **~·ty** [~tɪ] Eigenschaft f; Beschaffenheit f; econ. Qualität f.

qualm [kwɑːm] Übelkeit f; oft ~s pl. Skrupel m, Bedenken n; △ *nicht* Qualm.

quan·da·ry ['kwɒndərɪ] verzwickte Lage, Verlegenheit f.

quan·ti·ty ['kwɒntɪtɪ] Quantität f, Menge f; große Menge.

quan·tum ['kwɒntəm] (pl. -ta [-tə]) Quantum n, Menge f; phys. Quant n.

quar·an·tine ['kwɒrəntiːn] **1.** Quarantäne f; **2.** unter Quarantäne stellen.

quar|rel ['kwɒrəl] **1.** Streit m; **2.** (*bsd. Brt. -ll-, Am. -l-*) (sich) streiten; **~·some** □ [~səm] zänkisch, streitsüchtig.

quar·ry ['kwɒrɪ] **1.** Steinbruch m; *hunt.* (Jagd)Beute f; *fig.* Fundgrube f; **2.** Steine brechen.

quart [kwɔːt] Quart n (= *1,136 l*).

quar·ter ['kwɔːtə] **1.** Viertel n, vierter Teil; Viertel(stunde f) n; Vierteljahr n, Quartal n; Viertelpfund n; Viertelzentner m; Am. Vierteldollar m (= *25 Cents*); Sport: (Spiel)Viertel n; (*bsd.* Hinter)Viertel n (*e-s Schlachttiers*); (Stadt)Viertel n; (Himmels-, Wind)Richtung f; Gegend f, Richtung f; ✕ Gnade f, Pardon m; ~s pl. Quartier n (a. ✕), Unterkunft f; a ~ (*of an hour*) e-e Viertelstunde; a ~ to (*Am. of*) od. a ~ past (*Am. after*) Uhrzeit: (ein) Viertel vor od. nach; at close ~s in od. aus nächster Nähe; *from official* ~s von amtlicher Seite; **2.** vierteln, in vier Teile teilen; beherbergen; ✕ einquartieren; **~·back** American Football: wichtigster Spieler der Angriffsformation; **~·day** Quartalstag m; **~·deck** ♨ Achterdeck n; **~·fi·nal** Sport: Viertelfinalspiel n; a pl. Viertelfinale n; **~·ly** [~lɪ] **1.** vierteljährlich; **2.** Vierteljahresschrift f; **~·mas·ter** ✕ Quartiermeister m.

quar·tet(te) ♪ [kwɔːˈtet] Quartett n.

quar·to [kwɔːˈtəʊ] (pl. -tos) Quart n (-format) n.

quartz min. [kwɔːts] Quarz m; ~ *clock* Quarzuhr f; ~ *watch* Quarzarmbanduhr f.

qua·si ['kwɑːzaɪ] gleichsam, sozusagen; Quasi..., Schein...

qua·ver ['kweɪvə] **1.** Zittern n; ♪ Triller m; **2.** mit zitternder Stimme sprechen od. singen; ♪ trillern.

quay [kiː] Kai m.

quea·sy □ ['kwiːzɪ] (-ier, -iest) empfindlich (*Magen, Gewissen*); *I feel* ~ mir ist übel od. schlecht.

queen [kwiːn] Königin f (a. zo.); *Karten, Schach*: Dame f; sl. Schwule(r) m, Homo m; ~ *bee* Bienenkönigin f; **~·like** ['kwiːnlaɪk], **~·ly** [~lɪ] wie e-e Königin, königlich.

queer [kwɪə] sonderbar, seltsam; wunderlich; komisch; F schwul (*homosexuell*).

quench [kwentʃ] *Flammen, Feuer* (aus)löschen; *Durst etc.* löschen, stillen; *Hoffnung* zunichte machen.

quer·u·lous □ ['kwerʊləs] quengelig, mürrisch, verdrossen.

que·ry ['kwɪərɪ] **1.** Frage(zeichen n) f;

Zweifel *m*; **2.** (be)fragen; (be-, an-)zweifeln.

quest [kwest] **1.** Suche *f*; **2.** suchen (*for* nach).

ques·tion [ˈkwestʃən] **1.** Frage *f*; Problem *n*; (Streit)Frage *f*, (Streit-)Punkt *m*; Zweifel *m*; Sache *f*, Angelegenheit *f*; *beyond (all)* ~ ohne Frage; *in* ~ fraglich; *call in* ~ *et.* anbezweifeln; *that is out of the* ~ das kommt nicht in Frage; **2.** (be)fragen; ↯↯ vernehmen, -hören; *et.* an-, bezweifeln; ~**·a·ble** □ [~əbl] fraglich; fragwürdig; ~**·er** [~ə] Fragesteller(-in); ~ **mark** Fragezeichen *n*; ~**mas·ter** *Brt.* Quizmaster *m*; ~**naire** [kwestiəˈneə] Fragebogen *m*.

queue [kju:] **1.** Reihe *f* (*von Personen etc.*), Schlange *f*; **2.** *mst* ~ *up* Schlange stehen; anstehen; sich anstellen.

quib·ble [ˈkwibl] **1.** Spitzfindigkeit *f*, Haarspalterei *f*; **2.** spitzfindig sein; ~ *with s.o. about od. over s.th.* sich mit j-m über *et.* herumstreiten.

quick [kwik] **1.** schnell, rasch; prompt; aufgeweckt, wach (*Verstand*); scharf (*Auge, Gehör*); lebhaft; hitzig, aufbrausend; *be* ~! mach schnell!; **2.** lebendes Fleisch; *cut s.o. to the* ~ j-n tief verletzen; ~**en** [ˈkwikən] anregen, beleben; (sich) beschleunigen; ~**freeze** (-*froze*, -*frozen*) einfrieren, tiefkühlen; ~**ie** F [~I] auf die schnelle gemachte Sache; kurze Sache; ~**ly** [~lı] schnell, rasch; ~**ness** [~nıs] Schnelligkeit *f*; rasche Auffassungsgabe; Schärfe *f* (*des Auges etc.*); Lebhaftigkeit *f*; Hitzigkeit *f*; ~**sand** Treibsand *m*; ~**set hedge** *bsd. Brt.* lebende Hecke; Weißdornhecke *f*; ~**sil·ver** Quecksilber *n*; ~**wit·ted** geistesgegenwärtig; schlagfertig.

quid[1] [kwid] Priem *m* (*Kautabak*).

quid[2] *Brt. sl.* [~] (*pl.* ~) Pfund *n* (*Sterling*).

qui·es|cence [kwaiˈesns] Ruhe *f*, Stille *f*; ~**cent** □ [~t] ruhend; *fig.* ruhig, still.

qui·et [ˈkwaiət] **1.** □ ruhig, still; *be* ~! sei still!; **2.** Ruhe *f*; *on the* ~ heimlich (, still u. leise); **3.** *bsd. Am.* = ~**en** *bsd. Brt.* [~tn] *v/t.* beruhigen; *v/i. mst* ~ *down* sich beruhigen; ~**ness** [~nıs], **qui·e·tude** [ˈkwaiitju:d] Ruhe *f*, Stille *f*.

quill [kwil] *a.* ~**-feather** *zo.* (Schwung-, Schwanz)Feder *f*; *a.*

~**pen** Federkiel *m*; *zo.* Stachel *m* (*des Stachelschweins*).

quilt [kwilt] **1.** Steppdecke *f*; **2.** steppen; wattieren.

quince ♀ [kwins] Quitte *f*.

quin·ine [kwiˈni:n, *Am.* ˈkwaınaın] Chinin *n*.

quin·quen·ni·al □ [[kwɪŋˈkwenıəl] fünfjährig; fünfjährlich.

quin·sy ✿ [ˈkwinzı] Mandelentzündung *f*.

quin·tal [ˈkwintl] Doppelzentner *m*.

quin·tes·sence [kwınˈtesns] Quintessenz *f*; Inbegriff *m*.

quin·tu|ple [ˈkwintjupl] **1.** □ fünffach; **2.** fünfffachen; ~**plets** [~lıts] *pl.* Fünflinge *pl.*

quip [kwip] **1.** geistreiche Bemerkung; Sticheleı *f*; **2.** (-*pp-*) witzeln, spötteln.

quirk [kwɜ:k] Eigenart *f*, seltsame Angewohnheit; Laune *f* (*des Schicksals etc.*); *arch.* Hohlkehle *f*.

quit [kwit] **1.** (-*tt-*; *Brt.* ~**ted** *od.* ~, *Am. mst* ~) *v/t.* verlassen; *Stellung* aufgeben; aufhören mit; *v/i.* aufhören; weggehen; ausziehen (*Mieter*); *give notice to* ~ j-m kündigen; **2.** *pred. adj.* frei, los.

quite [kwait] ganz, völlig, vollständig; ziemlich, recht; ganz, sehr, durchaus; ~ *nice* ganz *od.* recht nett; ~ (*so*)! ganz recht; ~ *the thing* F ganz große Mode; *she's* ~ *a beauty* sie ist e-e wirkliche Schönheit.

quits *pred. adj.* [kwits]: *be* ~ *with s.o.* mit j-m quitt sein.

quit·ter F [ˈkwitə] Drückeberger *m*.

quiv·er[1] [ˈkwivə] zittern, beben.

quiv·er[2] [~] Köcher *m*.

quiz [kwiz] **1.** (*pl. quizzes*) Prüfung *f*, Test *m*; Quiz *n*; **2.** (-*zz-*) ausfragen; j-n prüfen; ~**mas·ter** *bsd. Am.* [ˈkwizmɑ:stə] Quizmaster *m*; ~**zi·cal** □ [~ıkl] spöttisch; komisch.

quoit [kɔit] Wurfring *m*; ~*s sg.* Wurfringspiel *n*.

quo·rum [ˈkwɔ:rəm] beschlußfähige Anzahl *od.* Mitgliederzahl.

quo·ta [ˈkwəʊtə] Quote *f*, Anteil *m*, Kontingent *n*.

quo·ta·tion [kwəʊˈteıʃn] Anführung *f*, Zitat *n*; Beleg(stelle *f*) *m*; *econ.:* (Börsen-, Kurs)Notierung *f*; Preis (-angabe *f*) *m*; Kostenvoranschlag *m*; ~ **marks** *pl.* Anführungszeichen *pl.*

quote [kwəʊt] anführen, zitieren;

econ. Preis nennen, berechnen; *Börse:* notieren (*at* mit).

quoth *veraltet* [kwəʊθ]: ~ *I* sagte ich.

quo·tid·i·an [kwɒˈtɪdɪən] täglich.

quo·tient ⅄ [ˈkwəʊʃnt] Quotient *m.*

R

rab·bi [ˈræbaɪ] Rabbiner *m.*

rab·bit [ˈræbɪt] Kaninchen *n.*

rab·ble [ˈræbl] Pöbel *m*, Mob *m*; **~rous·er** [~ə] Aufrührer *m*, Demagoge *m*; **~rous·ing** □ [~ɪŋ] aufwieglerisch, demagogisch.

rab·id □ [ˈræbɪd] tollwütig (*Tier*); *fig.* wild, wütend.

ra·bies *vet.* [ˈreɪbiːz] Tollwut *f.*

rac·coon *zo.* [rəˈkuːn] Waschbär *m.*

race[1] [reɪs] Rasse *f*; Geschlecht *n*, Stamm *m*; Volk *n*, Nation *f*; (Menschen)Schlag *m.*

race[2] [~] **1.** Lauf *m* (*a. fig.*); (Wett-)Rennen *n*; Strömung *f*; ~s *pl.* Pferderennen *n*; **2.** rennen; rasen; um die Wette laufen *od.* fahren (mit); ⊕ durchdrehen; **~course** [ˈreɪskɔːs] Rennbahn *f*, -strecke *f*; **~horse** Rennpferd *n*; **rac·er** [ˈreɪsə] Läufer (-in); Rennpferd *n*; Rennboot *n*; Rennwagen *m*; Rennrad *n.*

ra·cial □ [ˈreɪʃl] rassisch; Rassen...

rac·ing [ˈreɪsɪŋ] (Wett)Rennen *n*; (Pferde)Rennsport *m*; *attr.* Renn...

rack [ræk] **1.** Gestell *n*; Kleiderständer *m*; Gepäcknetz *n*; Raufe *f*, Futtergestell *n*; Folter(bank) *f*; *go to ~ and ruin* verfallen (*Gebäude, Person*); dem Ruin entgegentreiben (*Land, Wirtschaft*); **2.** strecken; foltern, quälen (*a. fig.*); ~ *one's brains* sich den Kopf zermartern.

rack·et [ˈrækɪt] **1.** (*Tennis*)Schläger *m*; Lärm *m*; Trubel *m*; F Schwindel (-geschäft *n*) *m*, Gaunerei *f*; Strapaze *f*; **2.** lärmen; sich amüsieren.

rack·e·teer [rækəˈtɪə] Gauner *m*, Erpresser *m*; **~ing** [~ərɪŋ] Gaunereien *pl*, Gaunerei *f.*

ra·coon *Brt. zo.* [rəˈkuːn] = raccoon.

rac·y □ [ˈreɪsɪ] (*-ier, -iest*) kraftvoll, lebendig; stark; würzig; urwüchsig; gewagt.

ra·dar [ˈreɪdə] Radar(gerät) *n.*

ra·di·ance [ˈreɪdjəns] Strahlen *n*, strahlender Glanz (*a. fig.*); **~ant** □ [~t] strahlend, leuchtend (*a. fig. with* vor *dat.*).

ra·di·ate [ˈreɪdɪeɪt] (aus)strahlen; strahlenförmig ausgehen; **~·a·tion** [reɪdɪˈeɪʃn] (Aus)Strahlung *f*; **~a·tor** [ˈreɪdɪeɪtə] Heizkörper *m*; *mot.* Kühler *m.*

rad·i·cal [ˈrædɪkl] **1.** □ ♀, ⅄ Wurzel...; Grund...; radikal, drastisch; eingewurzelt; *pol.* radikal; **2.** *pol.* Radikale(r *m*) *f*; ⅄ Wurzel *f*; ♫ Radikal *n.*

ra·di·o [ˈreɪdɪəʊ] (*pl. -os*) **1.** Radio (-apparat *n*) *n*; Funk(spruch) *m*; Funk...; ~ *play* Hörspiel *n*; ~ *set* Radiogerät *n*; *by*~ über Funk; *on the* ~ im Radio; **2.** funken; **~ac·tive** radioaktiv; ~ *waste* Atommüll *m*; **~·ac·tiv·i·ty** Radioaktivität *f*; **~·ther·a·py** Strahlen-, Röntgentherapie *f.*

rad·ish ♀ [ˈrædɪʃ] Rettich *m*; (*red*) ~ Radieschen *n.*

ra·di·us [ˈreɪdjəs] (*pl. -dii* [-dɪaɪ], *-uses*) Radius *m.*

raf·fle [ˈræfl] **1.** Tombola *f*, Verlosung *f*; **2.** verlosen.

raft [rɑːft] **1.** Floß *n*; **2.** flößen; **~er** ⊕ [~ftə] (Dach)Sparren *m*; **~s·man** (*pl. -men*) Flößer *m.*

rag[1] [ræg] Lumpen *m*; Fetzen *m*; Lappen *m*; *in* ~*s* zerlumpt; ~*and-bone man bsd. Brt.* Lumpensammler *m.*

rag[2] *sl.* [~] **1.** Unfug *m*; Radau *m*; Schabernack *m*; **2.** (*-gg-*) *j-n* aufziehen; *j-n* anschnauzen; *j-m* e-n Schabernack spielen; herumtollen, Radau machen.

rag·a·muf·fin [ˈrægəmʌfɪn] zerlumpter Kerl; Gassenjunge *m.*

rage [reɪdʒ] **1.** Wut(anfall *m*) *f*, Zorn *m*, Raserei *f*; Wüten *n*, Toben *n* (*der Elemente etc.*); Sucht *f*, Gier *f* (*for* nach); Manie *f*; Ekstase *f*; *it is* (*all*) *the* ~ es ist jetzt die große Mode; **2.** wüten, rasen (*a. fig.*).

rag·ged □ ['rægɪd] rauh; zottig; zackig; zerlumpt; ausgefranst.

raid [reɪd] **1.** (feindlicher) Überfall, Streifzug *m*; (Luft)Angriff *m*; Razzia *f*; **2.** einbrechen in (*acc.*); überfallen; plündern.

rail¹ [reɪl] schimpfen.

rail² [~] **1.** Geländer *n*; Stange *f*; ⚓ Reling *f*; 🚂 Schiene *f*; (Eisen)Bahn *f*; *by* ~ mit der Bahn; *off the* ~*s fig.* aus dem Geleise, durcheinander; verrückt; *run off* (*leave, jump*) *the* ~*s* entgleisen; **2.** *a.* ~ *in* mit e-m Geländer umgeben; ~ *off* durch ein Geländer (ab)trennen.

rail·ing ['reɪlɪŋ], *a.* ~*s pl.* Geländer *n*.

rail·ler·y ['reɪlərɪ] Neckerei *f*, Stichelei *f*.

rail·road *Am.* ['reɪlrəʊd] Eisenbahn *f*.

rail·way *bsd. Brt.* ['reɪlweɪ] Eisenbahn *f*; ~**man** (*pl.* -men) Eisenbahner *m*.

rain [reɪn] **1.** Regen *m*; ~*s pl.* Regenfälle *pl.*; *the* ~*s pl.* die Regenzeit (*in den Tropen*); ~ *or shine* bei jedem Wetter; **2.** regnen; *it never* ~*s but it pours* es kommt immer gleich knüppeldick; im Unglück kommt selten allein; ~**bow** ['reɪnbəʊ] Regenbogen *m*; ~**coat** Regenmantel *m*; ~**fall** Regenmenge *f*; ~**proof** **1.** regen-, wasserundurchlässig; imprägniert (*Stoff*); **2.** Regenmantel *m*; ~**y** □ ['reɪnɪ] (-*ier*, -*iest*) regnerisch; Regen...; *a* ~ *day fig.* Notzeiten *pl.*

raise [reɪz] *oft* ~ *up* (auf-, hoch-) heben; (*oft fig.*) erheben; errichten; erhöhen (*a. fig.*); Geld etc. aufbringen; *Anleihe* aufnehmen; *Familie* gründen; *Kinder* aufziehen; (auf)erwecken; anstiften; züchten, ziehen; *Belagerung etc.* aufheben.

rai·sin ['reɪzn] Rosine *f*.

rake [reɪk] **1.** Rechen *m*, Harke *f*; Wüstling *m*; Lebemann *m*; **2.** *v/t.* (glatt)harken; (~)rechen; *fig.* durchstöbern; *v/i.* ~ *about* (herum)stöbern; ~**off** F ['reɪkɒf] (Gewinn)Anteil *m*.

rak·ish □ ['reɪkɪʃ] schnittig; liederlich, ausschweifend; verwegen, keck.

ral·ly ['rælɪ] **1.** Sammeln *n*; Treffen *n*; (Massen)Versammlung *f*; Kundgebung *f*; Erholung *f*; *mot.* Rallye *f*; **2.** (sich ver)sammeln; sich erholen

ram [ræm] **1.** *zo.* Widder *m*, Schafbock *m*; ☌ *ast.* Widder *m*; ⊕, ⚓ Ramme *f*; **2.** (-*mm*-) (fest)rammen; ⚓ rammen; ~ *s.th. down s.o.'s throat fig.* j-m et. eintrichtern.

ram·ble ['ræmbl] **1.** Streifzug *m*; Wanderung *f*; **2.** umherstreifen; abschweifen; ~**bler** [~ə] Wanderer *m*; *a.* ~ *rose* ♣ Kletterrose *f*; ~**bling** [~ɪŋ] abschweifend; weitschweifend; weitläufig.

ram·i·fy ['ræmɪfaɪ] (sich) verzweigen.

ramp [ræmp] Rampe *f*.

ram·pant □ ['ræmpənt] wuchernd; *fig.* zügellos.

ram·part ['ræmpɑːt] Wall *m*.

ram·shack·le ['ræmʃækl] baufällig; wack(e)lig; klapp(e)rig.

ran [ræn] *pret. von run 1.*

ranch [rɑːntʃ, *Am.* ræntʃ] Ranch *f*, Viehfarm *f*; ~**er** ['rɑːntʃə, *Am.* 'ræntʃə] Rancher *m*, Viehzüchter *m*; Farmer *m*.

ran·cid □ ['rænsɪd] ranzig.

ran·co(u)r ['ræŋkə] Groll *m*, Haß *m*.

ran·dom ['rændəm] **1.** *at* ~ aufs Geratewohl, blindlings; **2.** ziel-, wahllos; zufällig; willkürlich.

rang [ræŋ] *pret. von ring¹ 2.*

range [reɪndʒ] **1.** Reihe *f*; (Berg-) Kette *f*; *econ.* Kollektion *f*, Sortiment *n*; Herd *m*; Raum *m*; Umfang *m*, Bereich *m*; Reichweite *f*; Schußweite *f*; Entfernung *f*; (ausgedehnte) Fläche; Schießstand *m*; offenes Weidegebiet; *at close* ~ aus nächster Nähe; *within* ~ *of vision* in Sichtweite; *a wide* ~ *of* ... eine große Auswahl an ...; **2.** *v/t.* (ein)reihen, ordnen; *Gebiet etc.* durchstreifen; *v/i.* in e-r Reihe od. Linie stehen; (umher)streifen; sich erstrecken, reichen; zählen, gehören (*among, with zu*); ~ *from* ... *to* ..., ~ *between* ... *and* ... sich zwischen ... und ... bewegen (*von Preisen etc*); **rang·er** ['reɪndʒə] Förster *m*; Aufseher *m* e-s Forsts od. Parks; Angehörige(r) *m* e-r berittenen Schutztruppe.

rank [ræŋk] **1.** Reihe *f*, Linie *f*; ✕ Glied *n*; Klasse *f*; Rang *m*, Stand *m*; ~*s pl.*, *the* ~ *and file* die Mannschaften *pl.*; *fig.* die große Masse; **2.** *v/t.* einreihen, (ein)ordnen; einstufen; *v/i.* sich reihen, sich ordnen; gehören (*among, with zu*); e-n Rang od. e-e Stelle einnehmen (*above* über *dat.*); ~ *as* gelten als; **3.** üppig; ranzig; stinkend; scharf; kraß; △ *nicht rank* (= *slim, slender*).

ran·kle *fig.* ['ræŋkl] nagen, weh tun.

ran·sack ['rænsæk] durchwühlen, -stöbern, -suchen; ausrauben.

ran·som ['rænsəm] **1.** Lösegeld *n*; Auslösung *f*; **2.** loskaufen, auslösen.

rant [rænt] **1.** Schwulst *m*; **2.** Phrasen dreschen; mit Pathos vortragen.

rap¹ [ræp] **1.** Klaps *m*; Klopfen *n*; **2.** (-*pp*-) schlagen; pochen, klopfen.

rap² *fig.* [~] Heller *m*, Deut *m*.

ra·pa|cious □ [rə'peɪʃəs] habgierig; (raub)gierig; **~·ci·ty** [rə'pæsətɪ] Habgier *f*; (Raub)Gier *f*.

rape¹ [reɪp] **1.** Notzucht *f*, Vergewaltigung *f* (*a. fig.*); **2.** rauben; vergewaltigen.

rape² ♀ [~] Raps *m*.

rap·id ['ræpɪd] **1.** □ schnell, rasch, rapid(e); steil; **2.** ~*s pl.* Stromschnelle(n *pl.*) *f*; **ra·pid·i·ty** [rə'pɪdətɪ] Schnelligkeit *f*.

rap·proche·ment *pol.* [ræ'prɔʃ-mãːŋ] Wiederannäherung *f*.

rapt □ [ræpt] entzückt; versunken; **rap·ture** ['ræptʃə] Entzücken *n*; *go into* ~*s* in Entzücken geraten.

rare □ [reə] (~*r*, ~*st*) selten; *phys.* dünn (*Luft*); halbgar, nicht durchgebraten (*Fleisch*); F ausgezeichnet, köstlich.

rare·bit ['reəbɪt]: *Welsh* ~ überbackener Käsetoast.

rar·e·fy ['reərɪfaɪ] (sich) verdünnen.

rar·i·ty ['reərətɪ] Seltenheit *f*; Rarität *f*.

ras·cal ['rɑːskəl] Schuft *m*; *co.* Gauner *m*, Schlingel *m*; **~·ly** [~lɪ] schuftig; erbärmlich.

rash¹ □ [ræʃ] hastig, vorschnell; übereilt; unbesonnen; waghalsig; △ *nicht rasch*.

rash² ♂ [~] (Haut)Ausschlag *m*.

rash·er ['ræʃə] Speckscheibe *f*.

rasp [rɑːsp] **1.** Raspel *f*; **2.** raspeln; kratzen; krächzen.

rasp·ber·ry ♀ ['rɑːzbərɪ] Himbeere *f*.

rat [ræt] *zo.* Ratte *f*; *pol.* Überläufer *m*; *smell a* ~ Lunte *od.* den Braten riechen; ~*s! sl.* Quatsch!

rate [reɪt] **1.** (Verhältnis)Ziffer *f*; Rate *f*; Verhältnis *n*; (Aus)Maß *n*; Satz *m*; Preis *m*, Gebühr *f*; Taxe *f*; (Gemeinde)Abgabe *f*, (Kommunal-)Steuer *f*; Grad *m*, Rang *m*, Klasse *f*; Geschwindigkeit *f*; *at any* ~ auf

jeden Fall; ~ *of exchange* (Umrechnungs-, Wechsel)Kurs *m*; ~ *of interest* Zinssatz *m*, -fuß *m*; **2.** (ein-)schätzen; besteuern; △ *nicht raten*; ~ *among* rechnen, zählen zu (*dat.*).

ra·ther ['rɑːðə] eher, lieber; vielmehr; besser gesagt; ziemlich, fast; ~*!* F und ob!, allerdings!; *I had od. would* ~ (*not*) *go* ich möchte lieber (nicht) gehen.

rat·i·fy *pol.* ['rætɪfaɪ] ratifizieren.

rat·ing ['reɪtɪŋ] Schätzung *f*; Steuersatz *m*; ♣ Dienstgrad *m*; ♣ (Segel-) Klasse *f*; Matrose *m*; *TV* Einschaltquote *f*.

ra·tio ⅍ ['reɪʃɪəʊ] (*pl.* -os) Verhältnis *n*.

ra·tion ['ræʃn] **1.** Ration *f*, Zuteilung *f*; **2.** rationieren.

ra·tion·al □ ['ræʃənl] vernunftgemäß; vernünftig; (*a.* ⅍) rational; △ *nicht rationell*; **~·i·ty** [ræʃə'nælətɪ] Vernunft *f*; **~·ize** *econ.* ['ræʃnəlaɪz] rationalisieren.

rat race ['rætreɪs] harter (Konkurrenz)Kampf.

rat·tle ['rætl] **1.** Gerassel *n*; Geklapper *n*; Geplapper *n*; Klapper *f*; Röcheln *n*; **2.** rasseln (mit); klappern; rütteln; rattern; plappern; röcheln; ~ *off* herunterrasseln; **~·brain**, **~·pate** Hohl-, Wirrkopf *m*; Schwätzer(in) *f*; **~·snake** *zo.* Klapperschlange *f*; **~·trap** *fig.* Klapperkasten *m* (*Fahrzeug*).

rat·tling ['rætlɪŋ] **1.** *adj.* rasselnd; F schnell, flott; **2.** F *adv.* sehr, äußerst; ~ *good* prima.

rau·cous □ ['rɔːkəs] heiser, rauh.

rav·age ['rævɪdʒ] **1.** Verwüstung *f*; **2.** verwüsten; plündern.

rave [reɪv] rasen, toben; schwärmen (*about*, *of* von).

rav·el ['rævl] (*bsd. Brt.* -*ll*-, *Am.* -*l*-) *v/t.* verwickeln; ~ (*out*) auftrennen; *fig.* entwirren; *v/i. a.* ~ *out* ausfasern, aufgehen.

ra·ven *zo.* ['reɪvn] Rabe *m*.

rav·e·nous □ ['rævənəs] gefräßig; heißhungrig; gierig; raubgierig.

ra·vine [rə'viːn] Hohlweg *m*; Schlucht *f*; Klamm *f*.

rav·ings ['reɪvɪŋz] *pl.* irres Gerede; Delirien *pl.*

rav·ish ['rævɪʃ] entzücken; hinreißen; **~·ing** □ [~ɪŋ] hinreißend, entzückend; **~·ment** [~mənt] Entzücken *n*.

raw □ [rɔ:] roh; Roh...; wund; rauh (*Wetter*); ungeübt, unerfahren; **~boned** ['rɔ:bəund] knochig, hager; **~hide** Rohleder *n*.

ray [reɪ] Strahl *m*; *fig.* Schimmer *m*.

ray·on ['reɪɔn] Kunstseide *f*.

raze [reɪz] *Haus etc.* abreißen; *Festung* schleifen; *fig.* ausmerzen, tilgen; **~** *s.th.* **to the ground** et. dem Erdboden gleichmachen.

ra·zor ['reɪzə] Rasiermesser *n*; Rasierapparat *m*; **~blade** Rasierklinge *f*; **~edge** *fig.* kritische Lage; *be on a* **~** auf des Messers Schneide stehen.

re- [ri:] wieder, noch einmal, neu; zurück, wider.

reach [ri:tʃ] **1.** Griff *m*; Reichweite *f*; Fassungskraft *f*; *beyond* **~**, *out of* **~** unerreichbar; *within easy* **~** leicht erreichbar; **2.** *v/i.* reichen; langen; greifen; sich erstrecken; △ *nicht* (*aus*)*reichen*; *v/t.* (hin-, her)reichen, (hin-, her)langen; erreichen, erzielen; *a.* **~** *out* ausstrecken.

re·act [rɪ'ækt] reagieren (*to* auf *acc.*); (ein)wirken (*on, upon* auf *acc.*).

re·ac·tion [rɪ'ækʃn] Reaktion *f* (*a.* ⚛ *pol.*); Rückwirkung *f*; **~a·ry** [~nərɪ] **1.** reaktionär; **2.** Reaktionär(in).

re·ac·tor *phys.* [rɪ'æktə] (Kern-) Reaktor *m*.

read 1. [ri:d] (*read* [red]) lesen; deuten; (an)zeigen (*Thermometer*); studieren; sich *gut etc.* lesen (lassen); lauten; **~** *to s.o.* j-m vorlesen; **~** *medicine* Medizin studieren; **2.** [red] *pret. u. p. p. von 1*; **rea·da·ble** □ ['ri:dəbl] lesbar; leserlich; lesenswert; **read·er** [~ə] (Vor)Leser(in); *typ.* Korrektor *m*; Lektor *m*; *univ.* Dozent *m*; Lesebuch *n*.

read·i·ly ['redɪlɪ] *adv.* gleich; leicht; bereitwillig, gern; **~ness** [~nɪs] Bereitschaft *f*; Bereitwilligkeit *f*; Schnelligkeit *f*.

read·ing ['ri:dɪŋ] Lesen *n*; Lesung *f* (*a. parl.*); Stand *m* (*des Thermometers*); Belesenheit *f*; Lektüre *f*; Lesart *f*; Auslegung *f*; Auffassung *f*; *attr.* Lese.

re·ad·just ['ri:ə'dʒʌst] wieder in Ordnung bringen; wieder anpassen; ⊕ nachstellen; **~ment** [~mənt] Wiederanpassung *f*; Neuordnung *f*; ⊕ Korrektur.

read·y □ ['redɪ] (*-ier*, *-iest*) bereit, fertig; bereitwillig; im Begriff (*to do* zu tun); schnell; schlagfertig, ge-

wandt; leicht; *econ.* bar; **~** *for use* gebrauchsfertig; *get* **~** (sich) fertig machen; **~** *cash*, **~** *money* Bargeld *n*; **~made** fertig, Konfektions...

re·a·gent ⚗ [ri:'eɪdʒənt] Reagens *n*.

real □ [rɪəl] wirklich, tatsächlich, real, wahr, eigentlich; echt; △ *nicht reell*; **~ estate** Grundbesitz *m*, Immobilien *pl*.

re·al·is·m ['rɪəlɪzəm] Realismus *m*; **~t** [~ɪst] Realist *m*; **~tic** [rɪə'lɪstɪk] (*~ally*) realistisch; sachlich; wirklichkeitsnah.

re·al·i·ty [rɪ'ælətɪ] Wirklichkeit *f*.

re·al·i·za·tion [rɪəlaɪ'zeɪʃn] Realisierung *f* (*a. econ.*); Verwirklichung *f*; Erkenntnis *f*; **~ze** ['rɪəlaɪz] sich klarmachen; erkennen; begreifen, einsehen; verwirklichen; realisieren (*a. econ.*); zu Geld machen.

real·ly ['rɪəlɪ] wirklich, tatsächlich; **~!** ich muß schon sagen!

realm [relm] Königreich *n*; Reich *n*; Bereich *m*.

real·tor *Am.* ['rɪəltə] Grundstücksmakler *m*; **~ty** 🏠 [~ɪ] Grundeigentum *n*, -besitz *m*.

reap [ri:p] *Korn* schneiden; *Feld* mähen; *fig.* ernten; **~er** ['ri:pə] Schnitter(in); Mähmaschine *f*.

re·ap·pear ['ri:ə'pɪə] wieder erscheinen.

rear [rɪə] **1.** *v/t.* auf-, großziehen; züchten; (er)heben; *v/i. Pferd:* sich aufbäumen; **2.** Rück-, Hinterseite *f*; Hintergrund *m*; *mot.*, ⚓ Heck *n*; ✗ Nachhut *f*; *at* (*Am. in*) *the* **~** *of* hinter (*dat.*); **3.** Hinter..., Rück...; **~** *wheel drive* Hinterradantrieb *m*; **~ad·mi·ral** ✗ ['rɪə'ædmərəl] Konteradmiral *m*; **~guard** ✗ Nachhut *f*; **~lamp**, **~light** *mot.* Rücklicht *n*.

re·arm ✗ ['ri:'ɑ:m] (wieder)aufrüsten; **re·ar·ma·ment** ✗ [~mə-mənt] (Wieder)Aufrüstung *f*.

rear|most ['rɪəməust] hinterste(r, -s); **~view mir·ror** *mot.* Rückspiegel *m*; **~ward** [~wəd] **1.** *adj.* rückwärtig; **2.** *adv. a.* **~s** rückwärts.

rea·son ['ri:zn] **1.** Vernunft *f*; Verstand *m*; Recht *n*, Billigkeit *f*; Ursache *f*, Grund *m*; *by* **~** *of* wegen; *for this* **~** aus diesem Grund; *listen to* **~** Vernunft annehmen; *it stands to* **~** *that* es leuchtet ein, daß; **2.** *v/i.* vernünftig *od.* logisch denken; argumentieren; *v/t.* folgern, schließen (*from* aus); *a.* **~** *out* (logisch) durchdenken; ~ *away* wegdiskutieren; ~ *s.o. into (out of) s.th.* j-m et. ein-(aus)reden; **rea·so·na·ble** □ [~əbl] vernünftig; angemessen; berechtigt.

re·as·sure ['riːə'ʃuə] (nochmals) versichern; beteuern; beruhigen.

re·bate ['riːbeɪt] *econ.* Rabatt *m*, Abzug *m*; Rückzahlung *f*.

reb·el[1] ['rebl] **1.** Rebell *m*; Aufrührer *m*; Aufständische(r) *m*; **2.** rebellisch, aufrührerisch.

re·bel[2] [rɪ'bel] rebellieren, sich auflehnen; **~·lion** [~ljən] Empörung *f*; **~·lious** [~ljəs] = *rebel*[1] 2.

re·birth ['riː'bɜːθ] Wiedergeburt *f*.

re·bound [rɪ'baʊnd] **1.** zurückprallen; **2.** [*mst* 'riːbaʊnd] Rückprall *m*; *Sport:* Abpraller *m*.

re·buff [rɪ'bʌf] **1.** schroffe Abweisung, Abfuhr *f*; **2.** abblitzen lassen, abweisen.

re·build ['riː'bɪld] (*-built*) wieder aufbauen.

re·buke [rɪ'bjuːk] **1.** Tadel *m*; **2.** tadeln.

re·but [rɪ'bʌt] (*-tt-*) widerlegen, entkräften.

re·call [rɪ'kɔːl] **1.** Zurückrufung *f*; Abberufung *f*; Widerruf *m*; *beyond ~, past ~* unwiderruflich; **2.** zurückrufen; ab(be)rufen; sich erinnern an (*acc.*); j-n erinnern (*to an acc.*); widerrufen; *econ. Kapital* kündigen.

re·ca·pit·u·late [riːkə'pɪtjʊleɪt] kurz wiederholen, zusammenfassen.

re·cap·ture ['riː'kæptʃə] wieder ergreifen; ✕ zurückerobern; *fig.* wiedereinfangen.

re·cast ['riː'kɑːst] (*-cast*) ⊕ umgießen; umarbeiten, neu gestalten; *thea. Rolle* umbesetzen.

re·cede [rɪ'siːd] zurücktreten; *receding* fliehend (*Kinn, Stirn*).

re·ceipt [rɪ'siːt] **1.** Empfang *m*; Eingang *m* (*von Waren*); Quittung *f*; △ *nicht* 🍴, *Koch-Rezept*; *~s pl.* Einnahmen *pl.*; **2.** quittieren.

re·cei·va·ble [rɪ'siːvəbl] *econ.* ausstehend; **re·ceive** [~v] empfangen; erhalten; bekommen; aufnehmen; annehmen; anerkennen; **re·ceived** (allgemein) anerkannt; **re·ceiv·er** [~ə] Empfänger *m*; *teleph.* Hörer *m*; Hehler *m* (*Steuer- etc.*) Einnehmer *m*; *official ~* ⚖ Konkursverwalter *m*.

re·cent □ ['riːsnt] neu; frisch; modern; *~ events pl.* die jüngsten Ereignisse *pl.*; **~·ly** [~lɪ] kürzlich, vor kurzem, neulich.

re·cep·ta·cle [rɪ'septəkl] Behälter *m*.

re·cep·tion [rɪ'sepʃn] Aufnahme *f* (*a. fig.*); Empfang *m* (*a. Rundfunk, TV*); Annahme *f*; **~ desk** Rezeption *f* (*im Hotel*); **~·ist** [~ɪst] Empfangsdame *f*, -chef *m*; Sprechstundenhilfe *f*; **~ room** Empfangszimmer *n*.

re·cep·tive □ [rɪ'septɪv] empfänglich, aufnahmefähig (*of*, *to* für).

re·cess [rɪ'ses] Unterbrechung *f*, (*Am. a.* Schul)Pause *f*; *bsd. parl.* Ferien *pl.*; (entlegener) Winkel; Nische *f*; *~es pl. fig. das* Innere, Tiefe(n *pl.*) *f*; **re·ces·sion** [~ʃn] Zurückziehen *n*, Zurücktreten *n*; *econ.* Rezession *f*, Konjunkturrückgang *m*.

re·ci·pe ['resɪpɪ] (Koch)Rezept *n*.

re·cip·i·ent [rɪ'sɪpɪənt] Empfänger (-in).

re·cip·ro·cal [rɪ'sɪprəkl] wechselseitig, gegenseitig; **~·cate** [~eɪt] *v/i.* sich erkenntlich zeigen; sich hin- und herbewegen; *v/t. Glückwünsche etc.* erwidern; **~·ci·ty** [resɪ'prɒsətɪ] Gegenseitigkeit *f*.

re·cit·al [rɪ'saɪtl] Bericht *m*; Erzählung *f*; ♪ (Solo)Vortrag *m*, Konzert *n*; **rec·i·ta·tion** [resɪ'teɪʃn] Hersagen *n*; Vortrag *m*; **re·cite** [rɪ'saɪt] vortragen; aufsagen; berichten.

reck·less □ ['reklɪs] unbekümmert; rücksichtslos; leichtsinnig.

reck·on ['rekən] *v/t.* (er-, be)rechnen; *a.* ~ *for*, ~ *as* schätzen als, halten für; ~ *up* zusammenzählen; *v/i.* rechnen; denken, vermuten; ~ *on*, ~ *upon* sich verlassen auf (*acc.*); **~·ing** ['rek(n)ɪ] Rechnen *n*; (Ab-, Be-) Rechnung *f*; *be out in one's ~* sich verrechnet haben.

re·claim [rɪ'kleɪm] zurückfordern; *j-n* bekehren, bessern; zivilisieren; *urbar* machen; ⊕ (zurück)gewinnen.

re·cline [rɪ'klaɪn] (sich) (zurück)lehnen; liegen, ruhen; *~d* liegend.

re·cluse [rɪ'kluːs] Einsiedler(in).

rec·og·ni·tion [rekəg'nɪʃn] Anerkennung *f*; (Wieder)Erkennen *n*; **~·ze** ['rekəgnaɪz] anerkennen; (wieder-) erkennen; zugeben, einsehen.

re·coil 1. [rɪ'kɔɪl] zurückprallen; zurückschrecken; **2.** ['riːkɔɪl] Rückstoß *m*, -lauf *m*.

rec·ol·lect[1] [rekə'lekt] sich erinnern an (*acc.*).

re·col·lect[2] ['ri:kə'lekt] wieder sammeln; ~ *o.s.* sich fassen.

rec·ol·lec·tion [rekə'lekʃn] Erinnerung *f* (*of an acc.*); Gedächtnis *n*.

rec·om·mend [rekə'mend] empfehlen; **~·men·da·tion** [rekəmen'deɪʃn] Empfehlung *f*; Vorschlag *m*.

rec·om·pense ['rekəmpens] **1.** Belohnung *f*, Vergeltung *f*; Entschädigung *f*; Ersatz *m*; **2.** belohnen, vergelten; entschädigen; ersetzen.

rec·on·cile ['rekənsaɪl] aus-, versöhnen; in Einklang bringen; schlichten; **~·cil·i·a·tion** [rekənsɪlɪ'eɪʃn] Ver-, Aussöhnung *f*.

re·con·di·tion ['ri:kən'dɪʃn] wieder herrichten; ⊕ überholen.

re·con·nais·sance [rɪ'kɒnɪsəns] ✕ Aufklärung *f*, Erkundung *f*; *fig.* Übersicht *f*; **~·noi·tre**, *Am.* **~·noi·ter** [rekə'nɔɪtə] erkunden, auskundschaften.

re·con·sid·er ['ri:kən'sɪdə] wieder erwägen; nochmals überlegen.

re·con·sti·tute ['ri:'kɒnstɪtju:t] wiederherstellen.

re·con·struct ['ri:kən'strʌkt] wieder aufbauen; **~·struc·tion** [~kʃn] Wiederaufbau *m*, Wiederherstellung *f*.

re·con·vert ['ri:kən'vɜ:t] umstellen.

rec·ord[1] ['rekɔ:d] Aufzeichnung *f*; ✄ Protokoll *n*; (Gerichts)Akte *f*; Urkunde *f*; Register *n*, Verzeichnis *n*; (schriftlicher) Bericht; Ruf *m*, Leumund *m*; Schallplatte *f*; *Sport:* Rekord *m*; *place on* ~ schriftlich niederlegen; ~ *office* Archiv *n*; *off the* ~ inoffiziell.

re·cord[2] [rɪ'kɔ:d] aufzeichnen, schriftlich niederlegen; *auf Schallplatte etc.* aufnehmen; **~·er** [~ə] Aufnahmegerät *n*; *bsd.* Tonband-Gerät *n*, Kassetten-Recorder *m*; ♪ Blockflöte *f*; **~·ing** [~ɪŋ] Rundfunk, *TV:* Aufzeichnung *f*, -nahme *f*; **~ play·er** ['rekɔ:d-] Plattenspieler *m*.

re·count [rɪ'kaʊnt] erzählen.

re·coup [rɪ'ku:p] *j-n* entschädigen (*for* für); *et.* wiedereinbringen.

re·course [rɪ'kɔ:s] Zuflucht *f*; *have* ~ *to* (s-e) Zuflucht nehmen zu.

re·cov·er [rɪ'kʌvə] *v/t.* wiedererlangen, -bekommen, -finden; *Verluste* wiedereinbringen, wiedergutmachen; *Schulden etc.* eintreiben; *Fahrzeug, Schiff etc.* bergen; *be* ~*ed*

wiederhergestellt sein; *v/i.* sich erholen; genesen; **~·y** [~rɪ] Wiedererlangung *f*; Bergung *f*; Genesung *f*; Erholung *f*; *past* ~ unheilbar krank.

re·cre·ate ['rekrɪeɪt] *v/t.* erfrischen; *v/i. a.* ~ *o.s.* ausspannen, sich erholen; **~·a·tion** [rekrɪ'eɪʃn] Erholung *f*.

re·crim·i·na·tion [rɪkrɪmɪ'neɪʃn] Gegenbeschuldigung *f*.

re·cruit [rɪ'kru:t] **1.** Rekrut *m*; *fig.* Neuling *m*; **2.** ergänzen; *Truppe* rekrutieren; ✕ Rekruten ausheben.

rec·tan·gle A ['rektæŋgl] Rechteck *n*.

rec·ti·fy ['rektɪfaɪ] berichtigen; verbessern; ⚡ gleichrichten; **~·tude** [~tju:d] Geradheit *f*, Redlichkeit *f*.

rec·tor ['rektə] Pfarrer *m*; Rektor *m*; **~·to·ry** [~rɪ] Pfarre(i) *f*; Pfarrhaus *n*.

re·cum·bent [rɪ'kʌmbənt] liegend.

re·cu·pe·rate [rɪ'kju:pəreɪt] sich erholen; *Gesundheit* wiedererlangen.

re·cur [rɪ'kɜ:] (-rr-) wiederkehren (*to* zu), sich wiederholen; zurückkommen (*to auf acc.*); **~·rence** [rɪ'kʌrəns] Rückkehr *f*, Wiederauftreten *n*; **~·rent** □ [~nt] wiederkehrend.

re·cy·cle [rɪ'saɪkl] *Abfälle* wiederverwerten; **~·cling** [~ɪŋ] Wiederverwertung *f*.

red [red] **1.** rot; ~ *heat* Rotglut *f*; ~ *tape* Bürokratismus *m*; **2.** Rot *n*; *bsd. pol.* Rote(r *m*) *f*; *be in the* ~ in den roten Zahlen sein.

red| breast *zo.* ['redbrest] *a. robin* ~ Rotkehlchen *n*; **~·cap** Militärpolizist *m*; *Am.* Gepäckträger *m*; **~·den** ['redn] (sich) röten; erröten; **~·dish** [~ɪʃ] rötlich.

re·dec·o·rate ['ri:'dekəreɪt] *Zimmer* neu streichen *od.* tapezieren.

re·deem [rɪ'di:m] zurück-, loskaufen; ablösen; *Versprechen* einlösen; büßen; entschädigen für; erlösen; **2·er** *eccl.* [~ə] Erlöser *m*, Heiland *m*.

re·demp·tion [rɪ'dempʃn] Rückkauf *m*; Auslösung *f*; Erlösung *f*.

re·de·vel·op [ri:dɪ'veləp] *Gebäude, Stadtteil* sanieren.

red|-hand·ed ['red'hændɪd]: *catch s.o.* ~ *j-n* auf frischer Tat ertappen; **~·head** Rotschopf *m*; **~·head·ed** rothaarig; **~·hot** rotglühend; *fig.* hitzig; **2 In·di·an** Indianer(in); **~·let·ter day** Festtag *m*; *fig.* Freuden-, Glückstag *m*; denkwürdiger Tag; **~·ness** [~nɪs] Röte *f*; **~·nosed** rotnasig.

red·o·lent ['redələnt] duftend.

re·dou·ble ['riː'dʌbl] (sich) verdoppeln.

re·dress [rɪ'dres] **1.** Abhilfe f; Wiedergutmachung f; ⁂ Entschädigung f; **2.** abhelfen (dat.); abschaffen, beseitigen; wiedergutmachen.

red-tap·ism ['red'teɪpɪzm] Bürokratismus m.

re·duce [rɪ'djuːs] verringern, -mindern; einschränken; Preise herabsetzen; zurückführen, bringen (to auf, in acc., zu); verwandeln (to in acc.), machen zu; ♃, ♒ reduzieren; 🩸 einrenken; ⊗ writing schriftlich niederlegen; **re·duc·tion** [rɪ'dʌkʃn] Herabsetzung f, (Preis)Nachlaß m, Rabatt m; Verminderung f, Verkleinerung f; Reduktion f; Verwandlung f; 🩸 Einrenkung f.

re·dun·dant □ [rɪ'dʌndənt] überflüssig; übermäßig; weitschweifig.

reed [riːd] ♣ Schilfrohr n; Rohrflöte f.

re·ed·u·ca·tion ['riːedjuˈkeɪʃn] Umschulung f, Umerziehung f.

reef [riːf] (Felsen)Riff n; ⚓ Reff n.

ree·fer [riː'fə] Seemannsjacke f; sl. Marihuanazigarette f.

reek [riːk] **1.** Gestank m, unangenehmer Geruch; **2.** stinken, unangenehm riechen (of nach).

reel [riːl] **1.** Haspel f; (Garn-, Film-) Rolle f, Spule f; **2.** v/t. ~ (up) (auf-) wickeln, (-)spulen; v/i. wirbeln; schwanken; taumeln.

re·e·lect ['riːɪ'lekt] wiederwählen.

re·en·ter [riː'entə] wieder eintreten (in acc.).

re·es·tab·lish ['riːɪ'stæblɪʃ] wiederherstellen.

ref F [ref] = referee.

re·fer [rɪ'fɜː]: ~ to ver- od. überweisen an (acc.); sich beziehen auf (acc.); erwähnen (acc.); zuordnen (dat.); befragen (acc.), nachschlagen in (dat.); zurückführen auf (acc.), zuschreiben (dat.).

ref·er·ee [refə'riː] Schiedsrichter m; Boxen: Ringrichter m.

ref·er·ence ['refrəns] Referenz f, Empfehlung f, Zeugnis n; Verweis(ung f) m, Hinweis m; Erwähnung f, Anspielung f; Bezugnahme f; Beziehung f; Nachschlagen n, Befragen n; in od. with ~ to was ... betrifft, bezüglich (gen.); ~ book Nachschlagewerk n; ~ library Handbibliothek f; ~ number Aktenzei-

chen n; make ~ to et. erwähnen.

ref·er·en·dum [refə'rendəm] Volksentscheid m.

re·fill 1. ['riː'fɪl] Nachfüllung f; Ersatzpackung f; Ersatzmine f (Kugelschreiber etc.); **2.** ['riː'fɪl] (sich) wieder füllen, auffüllen.

re·fine [rɪ'faɪn] ⊕ raffinieren, veredeln; verfeinern, kultivieren; (sich) läutern; ~ on, ~ upon et. verfeinern, -bessern; ⚑ fein, vornehm; ~·ment [~mənt] Vered(e)lung f; Verfeinerung f; Läuterung f; Feinheit f, Vornehmheit f; **re·fin·e·ry** [~əri] ⊕ Raffinerie f; metall. (Eisen)Hütte f.

re·fit ⚓ ['riː'fɪt] (-tt-) v/t. ausbessern; neu ausrüsten; v/i. ausgebessert werden; neu ausgerüstet werden.

re·flect [rɪ'flekt] v/t. zurückwerfen, reflektieren; widerspiegeln (a. fig.); zum Ausdruck bringen; v/i. ~ on, ~ upon nachdenken über (acc.); sich abfällig äußern über (acc.); ein schlechtes Licht werfen auf (acc.); **re·flec·tion** [~kʃn] Reflexion f, Zurückstrahlung f; Widerspiegelung f (a. fig.); Reflex m; Spiegelbild n; Überlegung f; Gedanke m; abfällige Bemerkung; **re·flec·tive** □ [~tɪv] reflektierend, zurückstrahlend; nachdenklich.

re·flex ['riːfleks] **1.** Reflex...; **2.** Widerschein m, Reflex m (a. physiol.).

re·flex·ive □ gr. [rɪ'fleksɪv] reflexiv, rückbezüglich.

re·for·est ['riː'fɒrɪst] aufforsten.

re·form¹ [rɪ'fɔːm] **1.** Verbesserung f, Reform f; **2.** verbessern, reformieren; (sich) bessern.

re·form² ['riː'fɔːm] (sich) neu bilden; ⚔ (sich) neu formieren.

ref·or·ma·tion [refə'meɪʃn] Reformierung f; Besserung f; eccl. ♀ Reformation f; **re·for·ma·to·ry** [rɪ'fɔːmətəri] **1.** Besserungs-, Reform...; **2.** Brt. veraltet, Am. Besserungsanstalt f; **re·form·er** [~ə] eccl. Reformator m; bsd. pol. Reformer m.

re·fract [rɪ'frækt] Strahlen etc. brechen; **re·frac·tion** [~kʃn] (Strahlen-) Brechung f; **re·frac·to·ry** □ [~ktəri] widerspenstig; 🩸 hartnäckig; ⊕ feuerfest.

re·frain [rɪ'freɪn] **1.** sich enthalten (from gen.), unterlassen (from acc.); **2.** Kehrreim m, Refrain m.

re·fresh [rɪ'freʃ] (o.s. sich) erfrischen, stärken; Gedächtnis etc. auf-

re·fri·ge·rate [rɪ'frɪdʒəreɪt] kühlen; **~ra·tor** [~ə] Kühlschrank *m*, -raum *m*; ~ **van**, *Am.* ~ **car** 🚃 Kühlwagen *m*.

re·fu·el ['ri:'fjʊəl] (auf)tanken.

ref·uge ['refju:dʒ] Zuflucht(sstätte) *f*; Verkehrsinsel *f*; **~·u·gee** [refjʊ'dʒi:] Flüchtling *m*; ~ *camp* Flüchtlingslager *n*.

re·fund 1. [ri:'fʌnd] zurückzahlen; ersetzen; 2. ['ri:fʌnd] Rückzahlung *f*; Erstattung *f*.

re·fur·bish ['ri:'fɜ:bɪʃ] aufpolieren (*a. fig.*).

re·fus·al [rɪ'fju:zl] abschlägige Antwort; (Ver)Weigerung *f*; Vorkaufsrecht *n* (*of auf acc.*).

re·fuse¹ [rɪ'fju:z] *v/t.* verweigern; abweisen, ablehnen; ~ *to do s.th.* sich weigern, etwas zu tun; *v/i.* sich weigern; verweigern (*Pferd*).

ref·use² ['refju:s] Ausschuß *m*; Abfall *m*, Müll *m*.

re·fute [rɪ'fju:t] widerlegen.

re·gain [rɪ'geɪn] wiedergewinnen.

re·gal □ ['ri:gl] königlich, Königs...

re·gale [rɪ'geɪl] fürstlich bewirten; ~ *o.s. on* sich gütlich tun an (*dat.*), schwelgen in (*dat.*).

re·gard [rɪ'gɑ:d] 1. (Hoch)Achtung *f*; Rücksicht *f*; Hinblick *m*, -sicht *f*; *with ~ to* hinsichtlich (*gen.*); ~*s pl.* Grüße *pl.* (*bsd. in Briefen*); *kind* ~*s* herzliche Grüße; 2. ansehen; betrachten; (be)achten; betreffen; ~ *s.o. as* j-n halten für; *as* ~*s was ...* betrifft; **~·ing** [~ɪŋ] hinsichtlich (*gen.*); **~·less** □ [~lɪs]: ~ *of* ohne Rücksicht auf (*acc.*), ungeachtet (*gen.*).

re·gen·e·rate [rɪ'dʒenəreɪt] (sich) erneuern; (sich) regenerieren; (sich) neu bilden.

re·gent ['ri:dʒənt] Regent(in); *Prince* ♀ Prinzregent.

re·gi·ment ✕ ['redʒɪmənt] 1. Regiment *n*; 2. [~mənt] organisieren; reglementieren; **~als** ✕ [redʒɪ'mentlz] *pl.* Uniform *f*.

re·gion ['ri:dʒən] Gegend *f*, Gebiet *n*; *fig.* Bereich *m*; **~al** □ [~l] regional; örtlich; Regional..., Orts...

re·gis·ter ['redʒɪstə] 1. Register *n*, Verzeichnis *n*; ⊕ Schieber *m*, Ventil *n*; ♪ Register *n*; Zählwerk *n*; *cash* ~ Registrierkasse *f*; 2. registrieren; (sich) eintragen *od.* -schreiben (las-

sen); (sich) anmelden; (an)zeigen, auf-, verzeichnen; *Postsache* einschreiben (lassen); *Brt. Gepäck* aufgeben; sich *polizeilich* melden; **~ed** *letter* Einschreibebrief *m*.

re·gis·trar [redʒɪ'strɑ:] Standesbeamte(r) *m*; **~·tra·tion** [~eɪʃn] Eintragung *f*; Anmeldung *f*; *mot.* Zulassung *f*; ~ *fee* Anmeldegebühr *f*; **~·try** ['redʒɪstrɪ] Eintragung *f*; Registratur *f*; Register *n*; ~ *office* Standesamt *n*.

re·gress ['ri:gres], **re·gres·sion** [rɪ'greʃn] Rückwärtsbewegung *f*; rückläufige Entwicklung.

re·gret [rɪ'gret] 1. Bedauern *n*; Schmerz *m*; 2. (*-tt-*) bedauern; *Verlust* beklagen; **~·ful** □ [~fl] bedauernd; **~·ta·ble** □ [~əbl] bedauerlich.

reg·u·lar □ ['regjʊlə] regelmäßig; regulär, normal, gewohnt; geregelt, geordnet; genau, pünktlich; richtig, recht, ordentlich; F richtig(gehend); ✕ regulär; **~·i·ty** [regjʊ'lærɪtɪ] Regelmäßigkeit *f*; Richtigkeit *f*; Ordnung *f*.

reg·u·late ['regjʊleɪt] regeln, ordnen; regulieren; **~·la·tion** [regjʊ'leɪʃn] 1. Regulierung *f*; ~*s pl.* Vorschrift *f*, Bestimmung *f*; 2. vorschriftsmäßig.

re·hash *fig.* ['ri:'hæʃ] 1. wiederaufwärmen; 2. Aufguß *m*.

re·hears·al [rɪ'hɜ:sl] *thea.*, ♪ Probe *f*; Wiederholung *f*; **~e** [rɪ'hɜ:s] *thea.* proben; wiederholen; aufsagen.

reign [reɪn] 1. Regierung *f*; *a. fig.* Herrschaft *f*; 2. herrschen, regieren.

re·im·burse [ri:ɪm'bɜ:s] j-n entschädigen; *Kosten* erstatten.

rein [reɪn] 1. Zügel *m*; 2. zügeln.

rein·deer *zo.* ['reɪndɪə] Ren(tier) *n*.

re·in·force ['ri:ɪn'fɔ:s] verstärken; **~·ment** [~mənt] Verstärkung *f*.

re·in·state ['ri:ɪn'steɪt] wiedereinsetzen; wieder instand setzen.

re·in·sure ['ri:ɪn'ʃʊə] rückversichern.

re·it·e·rate [ri:'ɪtəreɪt] (dauernd) wiederholen.

re·ject [rɪ'dʒekt] ab-, zurückweisen; abschlagen; verwerfen; ablehnen; **re·jec·tion** [~kʃn] Verwerfung *f*; Ablehnung *f*; Zurückweisung *f*.

re·joice [rɪ'dʒɔɪs] *v/t.* erfreuen; *v/i.* sich freuen (*at, over über acc.*); **re·joic·ing** [~ɪŋ] 1. □ freudig; 2. Freude *f*; ~*s pl.* Freudenfest *n*.

re·join ['ri:'dʒɔɪn] sich wieder vereinigen; wieder zurückkehren zu; [rɪˈdʒɔːn] erwidern.

re·ju·ve·nate [rɪˈdʒuːvɪneɪt] verjüngen.

re·kin·dle [ˈriːˈkɪndl] (sich) wieder entzünden.

re·lapse [rɪˈlæps] **1.** Rückfall *m*; **2.** zurückfallen, rückfällig werden; e-n Rückfall haben.

re·late [rɪˈleɪt] *v/t.* erzählen; in Beziehung bringen; *v/i.* sich beziehen (*to* auf *acc.*); **re·lat·ed** verwandt (*to* mit).

re·la·tion [rɪˈleɪʃn] Bericht *m*, Erzählung *f*; Verhältnis *n*; Verwandtschaft *f*; Verwandte(r *m*) *f*; ~*s pl.* Beziehungen *pl.*; *in* ~ *to* in bezug auf (*acc.*); ~**ship** [~ʃɪp] Verwandtschaft *f*; Beziehung *f.*

rel·a·tive [ˈrelətɪv] **1.** ☐ relativ, verhältnismäßig; bezüglich (*to gen.*); *gr.* Relativ..., bezüglich; entsprechend; **2.** *gr.* Relativpronomen *n*, bezügliches Fürwort; Verwandte(r *m*) *f.*

re·lax [rɪˈlæks] (sich) lockern; nachlassen (in *dat.*); (sich) entspannen, ausspannen; ~**a·tion** [riːlækˈseɪʃn] Lockerung *f*; Nachlassen *n*; Entspannung *f*, Erholung *f.*

re·lay[1] [ˈriːleɪ] Ablösung *f*; ⚡ Relais *n*; *Rundfunk*: Übertragung *f*; *Sport*: Staffel *f*; **2.** [riːˈleɪ] *Rundfunk*: übertragen.

re·lay[2] [ˈriːˈleɪ] *Kabel etc.* neu verlegen.

re·lay race [ˈriːleɪreɪs] *Sport*: Staffellauf *m.*

re·lease [rɪˈliːs] **1.** Freilassung *f*; Befreiung *f*; Freigabe *f*; *Film*: oft first~ Uraufführung *f*; ⊕, *phot.* Auslöser *m*; **2.** freilassen; erlösen; freigeben; *Recht* entlasten; übertragen; *Film* uraufführen; ⊕ auslösen.

rel·e·gate [ˈrelɪgeɪt] verbannen; verweisen (*to* an *acc.*).

re·lent [rɪˈlent] sich erweichen lassen; ~**less** ☐ [~lɪs] unbarmherzig.

rel·e·vant ☐ [ˈreləvənt] sachdienlich; zutreffend; relevant, erheblich.

re·li·a·bil·i·ty [rɪlaɪəˈbɪlətɪ] Zuverlässigkeit *f*; ~**ble** ☐ [rɪˈlaɪəbl] zuverlässig.

re·li·ance [rɪˈlaɪəns] Vertrauen *n*; Verlaß *m.*

rel·ic [ˈrelɪk] (Über)Rest *m*; Reliquie *f.*

re·lief [rɪˈliːf] Erleichterung *f*; (angenehme) Unterbrechung *f*; Unter-

stützung *f*; ✕ Ablösung *f*; ✕ Entsatz *m*; Hilfe *f*; *arch. etc.* Relief *n.*

re·lieve [rɪˈliːv] erleichtern; mildern, lindern; *Arme etc.* unterstützen; ✕ ablösen; ✕ entsetzen; (ab)helfen (*dat.*); entlasten, befreien; (angenehm) unterbrechen, beleben; *to* ~ *o.s. od. nature* seine Notdurft verrichten.

re·li·gion [rɪˈlɪdʒən] Religion *f*; ~**gious** ☐ [~əs] Religions...; religiös; gewissenhaft.

re·lin·quish [rɪˈlɪŋkwɪʃ] aufgeben; verzichten auf (*acc.*); loslassen.

rel·ish [ˈrelɪʃ] **1.** (Wohl)Geschmack *m*; Würze *f*; Genuß *m*; *fig.* Reiz *m*; *with great* ~ mit großem Appetit; *fig.* mit großem Vergnügen, *bsd. iro.* mit Wonne; **2.** genießen; gern essen; Geschmack *od.* Gefallen finden an (*dat.*).

re·luc|tance [rɪˈlʌktəns] Widerstreben *n*, *bsd. phys.* Widerstand *m*; ~**tant** ☐ [~t] widerstrebend, widerwillig.

re·ly [rɪˈlaɪ]: ~ *on*, ~ *upon* sich verlassen auf (*acc.*), bauen auf (*acc.*).

re·main [rɪˈmeɪn] **1.** (ver)bleiben; übrigbleiben; **2.** ~*s pl.* Überbleibsel *pl.*, (Über)Reste *pl.*; *a.* mortal ~*s* sterblichen Überreste *pl.*; ~**der** [~də] Rest *m.*

re·mand 🕮 [rɪˈmɑːnd] **1.** ~ *s.o.* (*in custody*) j-n in die Untersuchungshaft zurückschicken; **2.** *a.* ~ *in custody* Zurücksendung *f* in die Untersuchungshaft; *prisoner on* ~ Untersuchungsgefangene(r *m*) *f*; ~ *home centre Brt.* Untersuchungsgefängnis *n* für Jugendliche.

re·mark [rɪˈmɑːk] **1.** Bemerkung *f*; Äußerung *f*; **2.** *v/t.* bemerken; äußern; *v/i.* sich äußern (*on, upon* über *acc.*, zu); **re·mar·ka·ble** ☐ [~əbl] bemerkenswert; außergewöhnlich.

rem·e·dy [ˈremədɪ] **1.** (Heil-, Hilfs-, Gegen-, Rechts)Mittel *n*; (Ab)Hilfe *f*; **2.** heilen; abhelfen (*dat.*).

re·mem|ber [rɪˈmembə] sich erinnern an (*acc.*); denken an (*acc.*); beherzigen; ~ *me to her* grüße sie von mir; ~**brance** [~rəns] Erinnerung *f*; Gedächtnis *n*; Andenken *n*; ~*s pl.* Empfehlungen *pl.*, Grüße *pl.*

re·mind [rɪˈmaɪnd] erinnern (*of* an *acc.*); ~**er** [~ə] Mahnung *f.*

rem·i·nis·cence [remɪˈnɪsns] Erin-

replace

nerung *f*; **~·cent** □ [~t] (sich) erinnern.

re·miss □ [rɪˈmɪs] (nach)lässig; **re·mis·sion** [rɪˈmɪʃn] Vergebung *f* (der Sünden); Erlaß *m* (*von Strafe etc.*); Nachlassen *n*.

re·mit [rɪˈmɪt] (*-tt-*) *Sünden* vergeben; *Schuld etc.* erlassen; nachlassen in (*dat.*); überweisen; **~·tance** *econ.* [~əns] (Geld)Sendung *f*, Überweisung *f*, Rimesse *f*.

rem·nant [ˈremnənt] (Über)Rest *m*.

re·mod·el [ˈriːˈmɒdl] umbilden.

re·mon·strance [rɪˈmɒnstrəns] Einspruch *m*; Protest *m*; **rem·on·strate** [ˈremənstreɪt] Vorhaltungen machen (*about* wegen; *with s.o.* j-m); protestieren.

re·morse [rɪˈmɔːs] Gewissensbisse *pl.*; Reue *f*; *without ~* unbarmherzig; **~·less** □ [~lɪs] unbarmherzig.

re·mote [rɪˈməʊt] (*~r, ~st*) entfernt, entlegen; *~ control* ⊕ Fernlenkung *f*, -steuerung *f*; Fernbedienung *f*; **~·ness** [~nɪs] Entfernung *f*.

re·mov·al [rɪˈmuːvl] Entfernen *n*; Beseitigung *f*; Umzug *m*; Entlassung *f*; *~ van* Möbelwagen *m*; **~·e** [~uːv] **1.** *v/t.* entfernen; wegräumen, wegschaffen; beseitigen; entlassen; *v/i.* (aus-, um-, ver)ziehen; **2.** Entfernung *f*; *fig.* Schritt *m*, Stufe *f*; (Verwandtschafts)Grad *m*; **~·er** [~ə] (Möbel)Spediteur *m*.

re·mu·ne·rate [rɪˈmjuːnəreɪt] entlohnen; belohnen; entschädigen; vergüten; **~·ra·tive** □ [~rətɪv] lohnend.

Re·nais·sance [rəˈneɪsəns] *die* Renaissance.

re·nas·cence [rɪˈnæsns] Wiedergeburt *f*; Erneuerung *f*; Renaissance *f*; **~·cent** [~nt] wiederauflebend, -erwachend.

ren·der [ˈrendə] berühmt, *schwierig*, möglich etc. machen; wiedergeben; *Dienst etc.* leisten; *Ehre etc.* erweisen; *Dank* abstatten; übersetzen; ♪ vortragen; *thea.* gestalten, interpretieren; *Grund* angeben; *econ. Rechnung* vorlegen; übergeben; machen zu; *Fett* auslassen; **~·ing** [~rɪŋ] Wiedergabe *f*; Vortrag *m*; Interpretation *f*; Übersetzung *f*; Übertragung *f*; *arch.* Rohbewurf *m*.

ren·di·tion [renˈdɪʃn] Wiedergabe *f*; Interpretation *f*; Vortrag *m*.

ren·e·gade [ˈrenɪgeɪd] Abtrünnige(r *m*) *f*.

re·new [rɪˈnjuː] erneuern; *Gespräch etc.* wiederaufnehmen; *Kraft etc.* wiedererlangen; *Vertrag, Paß* verlängern; **~·al** [~əl] Erneuerung *f*; Verlängerung *f*.

re·nounce [rɪˈnaʊns] entsagen (*dat.*); verzichten auf (*acc.*); verleugnen.

ren·o·vate [ˈrenəʊveɪt] renovieren; erneuern.

re·nown [rɪˈnaʊn] Ruhm *m*, Ansehen *n*; **re·nowned** berühmt, namhaft.

rent[1] [rent] Riß *m*; Spalte *f*.

rent[2] [~] **1.** Miete *f*; Pacht *f*; △ *nicht Rente*; *for ~* zu vermieten; **2.** (ver)mieten, (-)pachten; *Auto etc.* leihen; **~·al** [ˈrentl] Miete *f*; Pacht *f*; Leihgebühr *f*.

re·nun·ci·a·tion [rɪnʌnsɪˈeɪʃn] Entsagung *f*; Verzicht *m* (*of* auf *acc.*).

re·pair [rɪˈpeə] **1.** Ausbesserung *f*, Reparatur *f*; *~s pl.* Instandsetzungsarbeiten *pl.*; *~ shop* Reparaturwerkstatt *f*; *in good ~* in gutem Zustand, gut erhalten; *out of ~* baufällig; **2.** reparieren, ausbessern; wiedergutmachen.

rep·a·ra·tion [repəˈreɪʃn] Wiedergutmachung *f*; Entschädigung *f*; *~s pl. pol.* Reparationen *pl.*

rep·ar·tee [rɑːˈtiː] schlagfertige Antwort; Schlagfertigkeit *f*.

re·past *lit.* [rɪˈpɑːst] Mahl(zeit *f*) *n*.

re·pay [riːˈpeɪ] (*-paid*) *et.* zurückzahlen; *Besuch* erwidern; *et.* vergelten; *j-n* entschädigen; **~·ment** [~mənt] Rückzahlung *f*.

re·peal [rɪˈpiːl] **1.** Aufhebung *f* (*von Gesetzen*); **2.** aufheben; widerrufen.

re·peat [rɪˈpiːt] **1.** (sich) wiederholen; nachsprechen; aufsagen; nachliefern; aufstoßen (*on dat.*) (*Essen*); **2.** Wiederholung *f*; ♪ Wiederholungszeichen *n*; *oft ~ order econ.* Nachbestellung *f*.

re·pel [rɪˈpel] (*-ll-*) *Feind* zurückschlagen; *fig.* zurückweisen; *j-n* abstoßen; **~·lent** [~ənt] abstoßend (*a. fig.*).

re·pent [rɪˈpent] bereuen; **re·pentance** [~əns] Reue *f*; **re·pen·tant** [~t] reuig, reumütig.

re·per·cus·sion [riːpəˈkʌʃn] Rückprall *m*; *mst pl. ~s* Auswirkungen *pl*

re·per·to·ry [ˈrepətərɪ] *thea.* Repertoire *n*; *fig.* Fundgrube *f*.

rep·e·ti·tion [repɪˈtɪʃn] Wiederholung *f*; Aufsagen *n*; Nachbildung *f*.

re·place [rɪˈpleɪs] wieder hinstellen

od. -legen; ersetzen; an j-s Stelle treten; ablösen; **~ment** [~mənt] Ersatz *m.*

re·plant ['riːˈplɑːnt] umpflanzen.

re·plen·ish [rɪˈplenɪʃ] (wieder) auffüllen; ergänzen; **~ment** [~mənt] Auffüllung *f;* Ergänzung *f.*

re·plete [rɪˈpliːt] reich ausgestattet, voll(gepfropft) (*with* mit).

rep·li·ca ['replɪkə] *Kunst:* Originalkopie *f;* Nachbildung *f.*

re·ply [rɪˈplaɪ] **1.** antworten, erwidern (*to* auf *acc.*); **2.** Antwort *f,* Erwiderung *f; in ~ to your letter* in Beantwortung Ihres Schreibens; **~-paid** *envelope* Freiumschlag *m.*

re·port [rɪˈpɔːt] **1.** Bericht *m;* Meldung *f,* Nachricht *f;* Gerücht *n;* Ruf *m;* Knall *m; (school)* ~ (Schul)Zeugnis *n;* **2.** berichten (über *acc.*); (sich) melden; anzeigen; *it is* ~ed *that* es heißt (daß); ~ed *speech gr.* indirekte Rede; **~er** [~ə] Reporter(in), Berichterstatter(in).

re·pose [rɪˈpəʊz] **1.** Ruhe *f;* **2.** *v/t.* (*o.s.* sich) ausruhen; (aus)ruhen lassen; ~ *trust, etc. in* Vertrauen etc. setzen auf *od.* in (*acc.*); *v/i.* (sich) ausruhen; ruhen; beruhen (*on* auf *dat.*).

re·pos·i·to·ry [rɪˈpɒzɪtərɪ] (Waren-) Lager *n; fig.* Fundgrube *f,* Quelle *f.*

rep·re·hend [reprɪˈhend] tadeln.

rep·re·sent [reprɪˈzent] darstellen; verkörpern; *thea.* Rolle darstellen, *Stück* aufführen; (fälschlich) hinstellen, darstellen (*as, to be* als); vertreten; **~sen·ta·tion** [reprɪzen-ˈteɪʃn] Darstellung *f; thea.* Aufführung *f;* Vertretung *f;* **~sen·ta·tive** [reprɪˈzentətɪv] **1.** darstellend (*of acc.*); (stell)vertretend; *a. parl.* repräsentativ; typisch; **2.** Vertreter (-in); Bevollmächtigte(r *m) f;* Repräsentant(in), *parl.* Abgeordnete(r *m) f; House of ~s Am. parl.* Repräsentantenhaus *n.*

re·press [rɪˈpres] unterdrücken; *psych.* verdrängen; **re·pres·sion** [~ʃn] Unterdrückung *f; psych.* Verdrängung *f.*

re·prieve [rɪˈpriːv] **1.** Begnadigung *f;* (Straf)Aufschub *m; fig.* Gnadenfrist *f;* **2.** begnadigen; j-m Strafaufschub *od. fig.* e-e Gnadenfrist gewähren.

rep·ri·mand ['reprɪmɑːnd] **1.** Verweis *m;* **2.** j-m e-n Verweis erteilen.

re·print 1. [riːˈprɪnt] neu auflegen *od.*

drucken, nachdrucken; **2.** ['riːprɪnt] Neuauflage *f,* Nachdruck *m.*

re·pri·sal [rɪˈpraɪzl] Repressalie *f,* Vergeltungsmaßnahme *f.*

re·proach [rɪˈprəʊtʃ] **1.** Vorwurf *m;* Schande *f;* **2.** vorwerfen (*s.o. with s.th.* j-m et.); Vorwürfe machen; **~ful** □ [~fl] vorwurfsvoll.

rep·ro·bate ['reprəbeɪt] **1.** verkommen, verderbt; **2.** verkommenes Subjekt; **3.** mißbilligen; verdammen.

re·pro·cess [riːˈprəʊses] *Kernbrennstoffe* wiederaufbereiten; **~ing plant** Wiederaufbereitungsanlage *f.*

re·pro·duce [riːprəˈdjuːs] (wieder-) erzeugen; (sich) fortpflanzen; wiedergeben, reproduzieren; **~duc·tion** [~ˈdʌkʃn] Wiedererzeugung *f;* Fortpflanzung *f;* Reproduktion *f;* **~duc·tive** [~tɪv] Fortpflanzungs...

re·proof [rɪˈpruːf] Tadel *m,* Rüge *f.*

re·prove [rɪˈpruːv] tadeln, rügen.

rep·tile *zo.* ['reptaɪl] Reptil *n.*

re·pub·lic [rɪˈpʌblɪk] Republik *f;* **~li·can** [~ən] **1.** republikanisch; **2.** Republikaner(in).

re·pu·di·ate [rɪˈpjuːdɪeɪt] nicht anerkennen; ab-, zurückweisen; *j-n* verstoßen.

re·pug·nance [rɪˈpʌgnəns] Abneigung *f,* Widerwille *m;* **~nant** □ [~t] abstoßend; widerlich.

re·pulse [rɪˈpʌls] **1.** ⚔ Abwehr *f;* Zurück-, Abweisung *f;* **2.** ⚔ zurückschlagen, abwehren; zurück-, abweisen; **re·pul·sion** Abscheu *m,* Widerwille *m; phys.* Abstoßung *f;* **re·pul·sive** □ [~ɪv] abstoßend (*a. phys.*), widerwärtig.

rep·u·ta·ble □ ['repjʊtəbl] angesehen, achtbar; ehrbar, anständig; **~tion** [repjʊˈteɪʃn] Ruf *m,* Ansehen *n;* **re·pute** [rɪˈpjuːt] **1.** Ruf *m;* **2.** halten für; *be* ~d (*to be*) gelten als; **re·put·ed** vermeintlich; angeblich.

re·quest [rɪˈkwest] **1.** Bitte *f,* Gesuch *n;* Ersuchen *n; econ.* Nachfrage *f; by* ~, *on* ~ auf Wunsch; *in (great)* ~ (sehr) gesucht *od.* begehrt; ~ *stop* Bedarfshaltestelle *f;* **2.** *um et.* bitten *od.* ersuchen; *j-n* (höflich) bitten *od.*

re·quire [rɪˈkwaɪə] verlangen, fordern; brauchen, erfordern; *if* ~d falls notwendig; **~d** erforderlich; **~ment** [~mənt] (An)Forderung *f;* Erfordernis *n;* **~s** *pl.* Bedarf *m.*

req·ui·site ['rekwɪzɪt] **1.** erforderlich; **2.** Erfordernis *n*; (Bedarfs-, Gebrauchs)Artikel *m*; *toilet* ~s *pl.* Toilettenartikel *pl.*; △ *nicht* (Bühnen-) *Requisit*; ~**si·tion** [rekwɪ'zɪʃn] **1.** Anforderung *f*; ⚔ Requisition *f*; **2.** anfordern; ⚔ requirieren.

re·quite [rɪ'kwaɪt] *j-m et.* vergelten.

re·sale ['riːseɪl] Wieder-, Weiterverkauf *m*; ~ *price* Wiederverkaufspreis *m*.

re·scind [rɪ'sɪnd] *Urteil* aufheben; *Vertrag* annullieren; **re·scis·sion** [rɪ'sɪʒn] Aufhebung *f*; Annullierung *f*.

res·cue ['reskjuː] **1.** Rettung *f*; Hilfe *f*; Befreiung *f*; **2.** retten; befreien.

re·search [rɪ'sɜːtʃ] **1.** Forschung *f*; Untersuchung *f*; Nachforschung *f*; **2.** forschen, Forschungen anstellen; *et.* untersuchen, erforschen; ~**er** [~ə] Forscher(in).

re·sem·blance [rɪ'zembləns] Ähnlichkeit *f* (*to* mit); ~**ble** [rɪ'zembl] gleichen, ähnlich sein (*dat.*).

re·sent [rɪ'zent] übelnehmen; sich ärgern über (*acc.*); ~**ful** □ [~fl] übelnehmerisch; ärgerlich; ~**ment** [~mənt] Ärger *m*; Groll *m*; △ *nicht* Ressentiment.

res·er·va·tion [rezə'veɪʃn] Reservierung *f*, Vorbestellung *f* (*von Zimmern etc.*); Vorbehalt *m*; Reservat(ion *f*) *n*; *central* ~ *Brt.* Mittelstreifen *m* (*der Autobahn*).

re·serve [rɪ'zɜːv] **1.** Reserve *f* (*a.* ⚔); Vorrat *m*; *econ.* Rücklage *f*; Zurückhaltung *f*; Vorbehalt *m*; *Sport:* Ersatzmann *m*; **2.** aufbewahren, aufsparen; (sich) vorbehalten; (sich) zurückhalten mit; *Platz etc.* reservieren (lassen), belegen, vorbestellen; ~**d** □ *fig.* zurückhaltend, reserviert.

res·er·voir ['rezəvwɑː] Behälter *m* (*für Wasser etc.*); Sammel-, Staubecken *n*; *fig.* Reservoir *n*.

re·side [rɪ'zaɪd] wohnen, ansässig sein, s-n Wohnsitz haben; ~ *in fig.* innewohnen (*dat.*).

res·i·dence ['rezɪdəns] Wohnsitz *m*, -ort *m*; Aufenthalt *m*; (Amts)Sitz *m*; (herrschaftliches) Wohnhaus; Residenz *f*; ~ *permit* Aufenthaltsgenehmigung *f*; ~**dent** [~t] **1.** wohnhaft; ortsansässig; **2.** Ortsansässige(r *m*) *f*, Einwohner(in); Bewohner(in); Hotelgast *m*; *mot.* Anlieger *m*; ~**den-**

tial [rezɪ'denʃl] Wohn...; ~ *area* Wohngegend *f*.

re·sid·u·al [rɪ'zɪdjʊəl] übrig(geblieben); zurückbleibend; restlich; **res·i·due** ['rezɪdjuː] Rest *m*; Rückstand *m*.

re·sign [rɪ'zaɪn] *v/t.* aufgeben; *Amt* niederlegen; überlassen; verzichten auf (*acc.*); ~ *o.s. to* sich ergeben in (*acc.*); sich abfinden mit; *v/i.* zurücktreten; **res·ig·na·tion** [rezɪg-'neɪʃn] Rücktritt(sgesuch *n*) *m*; Resignation *f*; ~**ed** □ ergeben, resigniert.

re·sil·i·ence [rɪ'zɪlɪəns] Elastizität *f*; *fig.* Unverwüstlichkeit *f*; ~**ent** [~t] elastisch; *fig.* unverwüstlich.

res·in ['rezɪn] **1.** Harz *n*; **2.** harzen.

re·sist [rɪ'zɪst] widerstehen (*dat.*); Widerstand leisten; sich widersetzen (*dat.*); ~**ance** [~əns] Widerstand *m* (*a.* ⚡, *phys.*); *med.* Widerstandsfähigkeit *f*; *line of least* ~ Weg *m* des geringsten Widerstands; **re·sis·tant** [~nt] widerstandsfähig.

res·o·lute □ ['rezəluːt] entschlossen, energisch; ~**lu·tion** [rezə'luːʃn] Entschlossenheit *f*; Bestimmtheit *f*; Beschluß *m*; *pol.* Resolution *f*; Lösung *f*.

re·solve [rɪ'zɒlv] **1.** *v/t.* auflösen; *fig.* lösen; *Zweifel etc.* zerstreuen; beschließen, entscheiden; *v/i. a.* ~ *o.s.* sich auflösen; beschließen; ~ *on*, ~ *upon* sich entschließen zu; **2.** Entschluß *m*; Beschluß *m*; ~**d** □ entschlossen.

res·o·nance ['rezənəns] Resonanz *f*; ~**nant** □ [~t] nach-, widerhallend.

re·sort [rɪ'zɔːt] **1.** Zuflucht *f*; Ausweg *m*; Aufenthalt(sort) *m*; Erholungsort *m*; *health* ~ Kurort *m*; *seaside* ~ Seebad *n*; *summer* ~ Sommerfrische *f*; **2.** ~ *to* oft besuchen; seine Zuflucht nehmen zu.

re·sound [rɪ'zaʊnd] widerhallen (lassen).

re·source [rɪ'sɔːs] Hilfsquelle *f*, -mittel *n*; Zuflucht *f*; Findigkeit *f*; ~s *pl.* (*natürliche*) Reichtümer *pl.*, Mittel *pl.*, Bodenschätze *pl.*; ~**ful** □ [~fl] einfallsreich, findig.

re·spect [rɪ'spekt] **1.** Beziehung *f*, Hinsicht *f*; Achtung *f*, Respekt *m*; Rücksicht *f*; *with* ~ *to* ... was ... (an)betrifft; *in this* ~ in dieser Hinsicht; ~s *pl.* Empfehlungen *pl.*, Grüße *pl.*; *give my* ~s *to* ... grüßen Sie ...

von mir; **2.** v/t. achten, schätzen; respektieren; betreffen; as ~s ... was ... (an)betrifft; **re·spec·ta·ble** □ [~əbl] ehrbar; anständig; angesehen, geachtet (*Mensch*); ansehnlich, beachtlich (*Summe*); **~ful** □ [~fl] ehrerbietig; yours ~ly hochachtungsvoll; **~ing** [~ɪŋ] hinsichtlich (*gen.*).

re·spec·tive □ [rɪ'spektɪv] jeweilig; we went to our ~ places wir gingen jeder an seinen Platz; **~ly** [~lɪ] beziehungsweise.

res·pi·ra·tion [respə'reɪʃn] Atmung f; **~tor** ☞ [~] ['respəreɪtə] Atemgerät n.

re·spire [rɪ'spaɪə] atmen.

res·pite ['respaɪt] Frist f; Aufschub m; Stundung f; Ruhepause f (*from* von); without (a) ~ ohne Unterbrechung.

re·splen·dent □ [rɪ'splendənt] glänzend, strahlend.

re·spond [rɪ'spɒnd] antworten, erwidern; ~ to reagieren od. ansprechen auf (*acc.*).

re·sponse [rɪ'spɒns] Antwort f, Erwiderung f; fig. Reaktion f; meet with little ~ wenig Anklang finden.

re·spon·si·bil·i·ty [rɪspɒnsə'bɪlɪtɪ] Verantwortung f; on one's own ~ auf eigene Verantwortung; sense of ~ Verantwortungsgefühl n; take (accept, assume) the ~ for die Verantwortung übernehmen für; **~ble** □ [rɪ'spɒnsəbl] verantwortlich; verantwortungsvoll.

rest¹ [rest] **1.** Ruhe f; Rast f; Pause f; Unterbrechung f; Erholung f; ⊕ Stütze f; (*Telefon*)Gabel f; have od. take a ~ sich ausruhen; be at ~ ruhig sein; **2.** v/i. ruhen; rasten; schlafen (*auf acc.*); ~ on, ~ upon ruhen auf (*Blick, Last*); fig. beruhen auf (*dat.*); ~ with fig. liegen bei (*Fehler, Verantwortung*); v/t. (aus)ruhen lassen; stützen (on auf); lehnen (against gegen).

rest² [~]: the ~ der Rest; and all the ~ of it und so weiter und so fort; for the ~ im übrigen.

res·tau·rant ['restərɔ̃:ŋ, ~rɒnt] Restaurant n, Gaststätte f.

rest·ful □ ['restfl] ruhig, erholsam.

rest·ing-place ['restɪŋpleɪs] Ruheplatz m; (letzte) Ruhestätte f.

res·ti·tu·tion [restɪ'tjuːʃn] Wiederherstellung f; Rückerstattung f.

res·tive □ ['restɪv] widerspenstig.

rest·less □ ['restlɪs] ruhelos; rastlos;

unruhig; **~ness** [~nɪs] Ruhelosigkeit f; Rastlosigkeit f; Unruhe f.

res·to·ra·tion [restə'reɪʃn] Wiederherstellung f; Wiedereinsetzung f; Restaurierung f; Rekonstruktion f, Nachbildung f; (Rück)Erstattung f; **~tive** [rɪ'stɒrətɪv] **1.** stärkend; **2.** Stärkungsmittel n.

re·store [rɪ'stɔː] wiederherstellen; wiedereinsetzen (to in acc.); restaurieren; (rück)erstatten, zurückgeben; zurücklegen; ~ s.o. (to health) j-n wiederherstellen.

re·strain [rɪ'streɪn] zurückhalten (from von); in Schranken halten; bändigen, zügeln; Gefühle unterdrücken; **~t** [~t] Zurückhaltung f; Beschränkung f, Zwang m.

re·strict [rɪ'strɪkt] be-, einschränken; **re·stric·tion** [~kʃn] Be-, Einschränkung f; without ~s uneingeschränkt.

rest room Am. ['restruːm] Toilette f (e-s Hotels etc.).

re·sult [rɪ'zʌlt] **1.** Ergebnis n, Resultat n; Folge f; **2.** folgen, sich ergeben (from aus); ~ in hinauslaufen auf (acc.), zur Folge haben.

re·sume [rɪ'zjuːm] wiederaufnehmen; fortsetzen; Sitz wieder einnehmen; **re·sump·tion** [rɪ'zʌmpʃn] Wiederaufnahme f; Fortsetzung f.

re·sur·rec·tion [rezə'rekʃn] Wiederaufleben n; ♀ eccl. Auferstehung f.

re·sus·ci·tate [rɪ'sʌsɪteɪt] wiederbeleben; fig. wieder aufleben lassen.

re·tail 1. ['riːteɪl] Einzelhandel m; by ~, adv. ~ im Einzelhandel; **2.** [~] Einzelhandels...; **3.** [riː'teɪl] im Einzelhandel verkaufen; **~er** [~ə] Einzelhändler(in).

re·tain [rɪ'teɪn] behalten; zurück-(be)halten; beibehalten.

re·tal·i·ate [rɪ'tælɪeɪt] v/t. Unrecht vergelten; v/i. sich rächen; **~a·tion** [rɪtælɪ'eɪʃn] Vergeltung f.

re·tard [rɪ'tɑːd] verzögern, aufhalten, hemmen; (mentally) ~ed psych. (geistig) zurückgeblieben.

retch [retʃ] würgen (beim Erbrechen).

re·tell [riː'tel] (-told) nacherzählen; wiederholen.

re·ten·tion [rɪ'tenʃn] Zurückhalten n; Beibehaltung f; Bewahrung f.

re·think [riː'θɪŋk] (-thought) et. nochmals überdenken.

ret·i·cent □ ['retɪsənt] verschwiegen; schweigsam; zurückhaltend.

ret·i·nue ['retɪnjuː] Gefolge n.

re·tire [rɪ'taɪə] v/t. zurückziehen; pensionieren; v/i. sich zurückziehen; zurück-, abtreten; sich zur Ruhe setzen; in Pension od. Rente gehen, sich pensionieren lassen; **~d** □ zurückgezogen; pensioniert, im Ruhestand (lebend); ~ **pay** Ruhegeld n; **~ment** [~mənt] Sichzurückziehen n; Ausscheiden n, Aus-, Rücktritt m; Ruhestand m; Zurückgezogenheit f; **re·tir·ing** [~rɪŋ] zurückhaltend; ~ **pension** Ruhegeld n.

re·tort [rɪ'tɔːt] **1.** (scharfe od. treffende) Erwiderung; **2.** (scharf od. treffend) erwidern.

re·touch ['riː'tʌtʃ] et. überarbeiten; phot. retuschieren.

re·trace [rɪ'treɪs] zurückverfolgen; ~ one's steps zurückgehen.

re·tract [rɪ'trækt] v/t. Angebot zurückziehen; Behauptung zurücknehmen; Krallen, ✈ Fahrgestell einziehen; v/i. eingezogen werden (Krallen, ✈ Fahrgestell).

re·train [riː'treɪn] umschulen.

re·tread 1. [riː'tred] Reifen runderneuern; **2.** ['riː'tred] runderneuerter Reifen.

re·treat [rɪ'triːt] **1.** Rückzug m; Zuflucht(sort m) f; Schlupfwinkel m; sound the ~ ✕ zum Rückzug blasen; **2.** sich zurückziehen.

ret·ri·bu·tion [retrɪ'bjuːʃn] Vergeltung f.

re·trieve [rɪ'triːv] wiederfinden, -bekommen; wiedergewinnen, -erlangen; wiedergutmachen; hunt. apportieren.

ret·ro- ['retrəʊ] (zu)rück...; **~ac·tive** □ ✝ [retrəʊ'æktɪv] rückwirkend; **~grade** ['retrəʊgreɪd] rückläufig; rückschrittlich; **~spect** [~spekt] Rückblick m; **~spec·tive** □ [retrəʊ'spektɪv] (zu)rückblickend; ✝ rückwirkend.

re·try ✝ ['riː'traɪ] wiederaufnehmen, neu verhandeln.

re·turn [rɪ'tɜːn] **1.** Rück-, Wiederkehr f; Wiederauftreten n; Brt. Rückfahrkarte f, ✈ Rückflugticket n; econ. Rückzahlung f; Rückgabe f; Entgelt n, Gegenleistung f; (amtlicher) Bericht; (Steuer)Erklärung f; parl. Wahl f (e-s Abgeordneten); Sport: Rückspiel n; Tennis etc.: Rückschlag m, Return m; Erwiderung f; attr. Rück...; **~s** pl. econ. Umsatz m; Ertrag m, Gewinn m;

many happy ~s of the day herzliche Glückwünsche zum Geburtstag; in ~ for (als Gegenleistung) für; by ~ (of post), by ~ mail Am. postwendend; ~ match Sport: Rückspiel n; ~ ticket Brt. Rückfahrkarte f, ✈ Rückflugticket n; **2.** v/i. zurückkehren, -kommen; wiederkommen; v/t. zurückgeben; Geld zurückzahlen; zurückschicken, -senden; zurückstellen, -bringen, -tun; Gewinn abwerfen; (zur Steuerveranlagung) angeben; parl. Abgeordneten wählen; Tennis etc.: Ball zurückschlagen, -geben; erwidern; vergelten; ~ a verdict of guilty ✝ j-n schuldig sprechen.

re·u·ni·fi·ca·tion pol. ['riːjuːnɪfɪ'keɪʃn] Wiedervereinigung f.

re·un·ion ['riː'juːnjən] Wiedervereinigung f; Treffen n, Zusammenkunft f.

re·val·ue econ. [riː'væljuː] Währung aufwerten.

re·veal [rɪ'viːl] enthüllen; offenbaren; **~ing** [~ɪŋ] aufschlußreich.

rev·el ['revl] (bsd. Brt. -ll-, Am. -l-) ausgelassen sein; ~ in schwelgen in (dat.); sich weiden an (dat.).

rev·e·la·tion [revə'leɪʃn] Enthüllung f; Offenbarung f.

rev·el·ry ['revlrɪ] lärmende Festlichkeit.

re·venge [rɪ'vendʒ] **1.** Rache f; bsd. Sport, Spiel: Revanche f; in ~ for als Rache für; **2.** rächen; **~ful** □ [~fl] rachsüchtig; **re·veng·er** [~ə] Rächer(in).

rev·e·nue econ. ['revənjuː] Staatseinkünfte pl., -einnahmen pl.

re·ver·be·rate phys. [rɪ'vɜːbəreɪt] zurückwerfen; zurückstrahlen; widerhallen.

re·vere [rɪ'vɪə] (ver)ehren.

rev·e·rence ['revərəns] **1.** Verehrung f; Ehrfurcht f; **2.** (ver)ehren; **~rend** [~d] **1.** ehrwürdig; **2.** Geistliche(r) m.

rev·e·rent □ ['revərənt], **~ren·tial** □ [revə'renʃl] ehrerbietig, ehrfurchtsvoll.

rev·er·ie ['revərɪ] (Tag)Träumerei f.

re·ver·sal [rɪ'vɜːsl] Umkehrung f, Umschwung m; **~e** [~ɜːs] **1.** Gegenteil n; Rück-, Kehrseite f; mot. Rückwärtsgang m; Rückschlag m; **2.** □ umgekehrt; Rück(wärts)...; in ~ order in umgekehrter Reihenfolge; ~ gear mot. Rückwärtsgang m; ~ side linke (Stoff)Seite f; **3.** umkehren; Ur-

teil umstoßen; **~·i·ble** □ [~əbl] doppelseitig (tragbar).

re·vert [rɪ'vɜːt] (*to*) zurückkehren (zu *dat.*); zurückkommen (auf *acc.*); wieder zurückfallen (in *acc.*); ᵇⁱᵒ zurückfallen (an *j-n*).

re·view [rɪ'vjuː] **1.** Nachprüfung *f*, (Über)Prüfung *f*, Revision *f*; ✕ Parade *f*; Rückblick *m*; (Buch)Besprechung *f*, Kritik *f*, Rezension *f*; *pass s.th. in ~* et. Revue passieren lassen; **2.** (über-, nach)prüfen; ✕ besichtigen; *Buch etc.* besprechen, rezensieren; *fig.* überblicken, -schauen; **~er** [~ə] Rezensent(in).

re·vise [rɪ'vaɪz] überarbeiten, durchsehen, revidieren (*a.* den Stoff) wiederholen (*für e-e Prüfung*); *Brt.* (für e-e Prüfung); **re·vi·sion** [rɪ'vɪʒn] Revision *f*; Überarbeitung *f*; *Brt.* Wiederholung *f* (des Stoffs) (*für e-e Prüfung*).

re·viv·al [rɪ'vaɪvl] Wiederbelebung *f*; Wiederaufleben *n*, -blühen *n*; Erneuerung *f*; *fig.* Erweckung *f*; **re·vive** [~aɪv] wiederbeleben; wiederaufleben (lassen); wiederherstellen; sich erholen.

re·voke [rɪ'vəʊk] widerrufen, zurücknehmen, rückgängig machen.

re·volt [rɪ'vəʊlt] **1.** Revolte *f*, Aufstand *m*, -ruhr *m*; **2.** *v/i.* sich auflehnen, revoltieren (*against* gegen); *v/t. fig.* abstoßen; **~ing** □ [~ɪŋ] abstoßend; ekelhaft; scheußlich.

rev·o·lu·tion [revə'luːʃn] ⊕ Umdrehung *f*; *fig.* Revolution *f* (*a. pol.*), Umwälzung *f*, Umschwung *m*; **~·ar·y** [~ərɪ] **1.** revolutionär; Revolutions...; **2.** *pol. u. fig.* Revolutionär(in); **~·ize** [~ʃnaɪz] revolutionieren.

re·volve [rɪ'vɒlv] *v/i.* sich drehen (*about, round* um); *~ around fig.* sich um *j-n od. et.* drehen; *v/t.* drehen; **re·volv·ing** [~ɪŋ] sich drehend, Dreh...

re·vue *thea.* [rɪ'vjuː] Revue *f*; Kabarett *n*.

re·vul·sion *fig.* [rɪ'vʌlʃn] Abscheu *m*.

re·ward [rɪ'wɔːd] **1.** Belohnung *f*; Entgelt *n*; **2.** belohnen; **~·ing** □ [~ɪŋ] lohnend; dankbar (*Aufgabe*).

re·write [riː'raɪt] (*-wrote, -written*) neu (*od.* um)schreiben.

rhap·so·dy ['ræpsədɪ] ♪ Rhapsodie *f*; *fig.* Schwärmerei *f*, Wortschwall *m*.

rhe·to·ric ['retərɪk] Rhetorik *f*; *fig. contp.* leere Phrasen *pl.*

rheu·ma·tism ✗ ['ruːmətɪzəm] Rheumatismus *m*.

rhu·barb ♀ ['ruːbɑːb] Rhabarber *m*.

rhyme [raɪm] **1.** Reim *m*; Vers *m*; *without ~ or reason* ohne Sinn u. Verstand; **2.** (sich) reimen.

rhyth|m ['rɪðəm] Rhythmus *m*; **~·mic** [~mɪk] (*~ally*), **~·mi·cal** □ [~mɪkl] rhythmisch.

rib [rɪb] **1.** *anat.* Rippe *f*; **2.** (*-bb-*) F hänseln, aufziehen.

rib·ald ['rɪbəld] lästerlich, zotig.

rib·bon ['rɪbən] Band *n*; Ordensband *n*; Farbband *n*; Streifen *m*; **~s** *pl.* Fetzen *pl.*

rib cage *anat.* ['rɪbkeɪdʒ] Brustkorb *m*.

rice ♀ [raɪs] Reis *m*.

rich [rɪtʃ] **1.** □ reich (*in an dat.*); prächtig, kostbar; fruchtbar, fett (*Erde*); voll (*Ton*); schwer, nahrhaft (*Speise*); schwer (*Wein, Duft*); satt (*Farbe*); **2.** *the ~ pl.* die Reichen *pl.*; **~es** ['rɪtʃɪz] *pl.* Reichtum *m*, Reichtümer *pl.*

rick ✓ [rɪk] (Stroh-, Heu)Schober *m*.

rick·ets ✗ ['rɪkɪts] *sg. od. pl.* Rachitis *f*; **rick·et·y** [~ɪ] ✗ rachitisch; wack(e)lig (*Möbel*).

rid [rɪd] (*-dd-; rid*) befreien, frei machen (*of* von); *get ~ of* loswerden.

rid·dance F ['rɪdəns]: *Good ~!* Die (die, das) wären wir (Gott sei Dank) los!

rid·den ['rɪdn] **1.** *p.p. von ride 2*; **2.** *in Zssgn:* geplagt von ...

rid·dle[1] ['rɪdl] Rätsel *n*.

rid·dle[2] [~] **1.** grobes (Draht)Sieb; **2.** durchsieben; durchlöchern.

ride [raɪd] **1.** Ritt *m*; Fahrt *f*; Reitweg *m*; **2.** (*rode, ridden*) *v/i.* reiten; fahren (*on a bicycle* auf e-m Fahrrad; *in, Am. on a bus* im Bus); *v/t. Pferd etc.* reiten; *Fahr-, Motorrad* fahren, fahren auf (*dat.*); **rid·er** ['raɪdə] Reiter(in).

ridge [rɪdʒ] **1.** (Gebirgs)Kamm *m*, Grat *m*; *arch.* First *m*; ✓ Rain *m*.

rid·i·cule ['rɪdɪkjuːl] **1.** Spott *m*; **2.** lächerlich machen, verspotten; **ri·dic·u·lous** □ [rɪ'dɪkjʊləs] lächerlich.

rid·ing ['raɪdɪŋ] Reiten *n*; *attr.* Reit...

riff-raff ['rɪfræf] Gesindel *n*.

ri·fle[1] ['raɪfl] Gewehr *n*; Büchse *f*.

ri·fle[2] [~] (aus)plündern; durchwühlen.

rift [rɪft] Riß *m*, Sprung *m*; Spalte *f*.

rig[1] [rɪg] (*-gg-*) manipulieren.
rig[2] [~] 1. ⚓ Takelage *f*; ⊕ Bohranlage *f*, -turm *m*, Förderturm *m*; F Aufmachung *f*; 2. (*-gg-*) *Schiff* auftakeln; ~ up F (behelfsmäßig) herrichten, zusammenbauen; **~ging** ⚓ ['rɪgɪŋ] Takelage *f*.

right [raɪt] 1. □ recht; richtig; rechte(r, -s), Rechts...; *all* ~! in Ordnung!, gut!; *that's all* ~! das macht nichts!, schon gut!, bitte!; *I am perfectly all* ~ mir geht es ausgezeichnet; *that's* ~! richtig!, ganz recht!, stimmt!; *be* ~ recht haben; *put* ~, *set* ~ in Ordnung bringen; berichtigen, korrigieren; 2. *adv.* rechts; recht, richtig; gerade(wegs), direkt; ganz (und gar); genau, gerade; ~ *away* sofort; ~ *on* geradeaus; *turn* ~ (sich) nach rechts wenden, rechts abbiegen; 3. Recht *n*; Rechte *f* (*a. pol.*, *Boxen*), rechte Seite *od.* Hand; *by* ~ *of* auf Grund (*gen.*); *on od. to the* ~ rechts; 4. aufrichten; *et.* wiedergutmachen; in Ordnung bringen; **~·down** ['raɪtdaʊn] regelrecht; **~eous** □ ['raɪtʃəs] rechtschaffen; selbstgerecht; gerecht(fertigt), berechtigt; **~·ful** □ [~l] rechtmäßig; gerecht; **~·hand** rechtshändig; **~·ly** [~lɪ] richtig; mit Recht; **~ of way** Durchgangsrecht *n*; *mot.* Vorfahrt(srecht *n*) *f*; **~·wing** *pol.* rechte(r, -s), rechtsgerichtet.

rig·id □ ['rɪdʒɪd] starr, steif; *fig.* streng, hart; **~·i·ty** [rɪ'dʒɪdətɪ] Starrheit *f*; Strenge *f*, Härte *f*.

rig·ma·role ['rɪgmərəʊl] Geschwätz *n*.

rig·or·ous □ ['rɪgərəs] streng, rigoros; (peinlich) genau.

rig·o(u)r ['rɪgə] Strenge *f*, Härte *f*.

rile [raɪl] ärgern, reizen.

rim [rɪm] Rand *m*; Krempe *f*; Felge *f*; Radkranz *m*; **~·less** ['rɪmlɪs] randlos (*Brille*); **~·med** mit (e-m) Rand.

rime *lit.* [raɪm] Rauhreif *m*.

rind [raɪnd] Rinde *f*, Schale *f*; (*Speck*)Schwarte *f*.

ring[1] [rɪŋ] 1. Klang *m*; Geläut(e) *n*; Klingeln *n*, Läuten *m*; (*Telefon*)Anruf *m*; *give s.o. a* ~ j-n anrufen; 2. (*rang, rung*) läuten; klingeln; klingen; erschallen; *bsd. Brt. teleph.* anrufen; ~ *the bell* läuten, klingeln; *bsd. Brt. teleph.*: ~ *back* zurückrufen;

~ *off* (den Hörer) auflegen, Schluß machen; ~ *s.o. up* j-n *od.* bei j-m anrufen.

ring[2] [~] 1. Ring *m*; Kreis *m*; Manege *f*; (*Box*)Ring *m*; (Verbrecher-, Spionage- *etc.*)Ring *m*; 2. umringen; beringen; **~·bind·er** ['rɪŋbaɪndə] Ringbuch *n*; **~·lead·er** Rädelsführer *m*; **~·let** [~lɪt] (Ringel)Locke *f*; **~·master** Zirkusdirektor *m*; **~ road** *Brt.* Umgehungsstraße *f*; Ringstraße *f*; **~·side**: *at the* ~ *Boxen*: am Ring; ~ *seat* Ringplatz *m*; Manegenplatz *m*.

rink [rɪŋk] (*bsd. Kunst*)Eisbahn *f*; Rollschuhbahn *f*.

rinse [rɪns] *oft* ~ *out* (ab-, aus)spülen.

ri·ot ['raɪət] 1. Aufruhr *m*; Tumult *m*, Krawall *m*; *run* ~ randalieren; 2. Krawall machen, randalieren; e-n Aufstand machen; **~·er** [~ə] Aufrührer(in); Randalierer *m*; **~·ous** □ [~əs] aufrührerisch; lärmend; ausgelassen, wild.

rip [rɪp] 1. Riß *m*; 2. (*-pp-*) (auf-, zer)reißen, (-)schlitzen; F sausen, rasen.

ripe □ [raɪp] reif; **rip·en** ['raɪpən] reifen (lassen); reif werden; **~·ness** [~nɪs] Reife *f*.

rip·ple ['rɪpl] 1. kleine Welle; Kräuselung *f*; Rieseln *n*; 2. (sich) kräuseln; rieseln.

rise [raɪz] 1. (An-, Auf)Steigen *n*; (Preis-, Gehalts-, Lohn)Erhöhung *f*; Steigung *f*; Anhöhe *f*; Ursprung *m*; *fig.* Aufstieg *m*; *give* ~ *to* verursachen, führen zu; 2. (*rose, risen*) sich erheben, aufstehen; die Sitzung schließen; auf-, hoch-, emporsteigen; (an)steigen; sich erheben, emporragen; aufkommen (*Sturm etc.*); *eccl.* auferstehen; aufgehen (*Sonne, Samen*); entspringen (*Fluß*); (an)wachsen; sich steigern; sich erheben, revoltieren; *beruflich etc.* aufsteigen; ~ *to the occasion* sich der Lage gewachsen zeigen; **ris·en** ['rɪzn] *p.p. von rise* 2; **ris·er** ['raɪzə]: *early* ~ Frühaufsteher(in).

ris·ing ['raɪzɪŋ] (An-, Auf)Steigen *n*; *ast.* Aufgehen *n*, -gang *m*; Aufstand *m*.

risk [rɪsk] 1. Gefahr *f*, Wagnis *n*, Risiko *n* (*a. econ.*); *be at* ~ in Gefahr sein; *run the* ~ *of doing s.th.* Gefahr laufen, *et.* zu tun; *run od. take a* ~ ein Risiko eingehen; 2. wagen, riskieren; **~·y** □ ['rɪskɪ]

(-ier, -iest) riskant, gefährlich, gewagt.

rite [raɪt] Ritus m; Zeremonie f.

rit·u·al ['rɪtʃʊəl] **1.** ☐ rituell; Ritual...; **2.** Ritual n.

ri·val ['raɪvl] **1.** Rival|e m, -in f, Konkurrent(in); **2.** rivalisierend, Konkurrenz...; **3.** (bsd. Brt. -ll-, Am. -l-) rivalisieren od. konkurrieren mit; ~ry [~rɪ] Rivalität f; Konkurrenz (-kampf m) f.

riv·er ['rɪvə] Fluß m, Strom m (a. fig.); ~side **1.** Flußufer n; **2.** am Ufer (gelegen).

riv·et ['rɪvɪt] **1.** ⊕ Niet(e f) m, n; **2.** ⊕ (ver)nieten; fig. Blick etc. heften; fig. fesseln.

riv·u·let ['rɪvjʊlɪt] Flüßchen n.

road [rəʊd] (Auto-, Land)Straße f; fig. Weg m; on the ~ unterwegs; thea. auf Tournee; ~ ac·ci·dent Verkehrsunfall m; ~block ['rəʊdblɒk] Straßensperre f; ~ map Straßenkarte f; ~ safe·ty Verkehrssicherheit f; ~side **1.** Straßen-, Wegrand m; **2.** an der Landstraße (gelegen); ~way Fahrbahn f; ~ works pl. Straßenbauarbeiten pl.; ~wor·thy mot. verkehrssicher.

roam [rəʊm] v/i. (umher)streifen, (-)wandern; v/t. durchstreifen.

roar [rɔː] **1.** brüllen; brausen, tosen, donnern; **2.** Brüllen n, Gebrüll n; Brausen n; Krachen n, Getöse n; schallendes Gelächter.

roast [rəʊst] **1.** Braten m; **2.** braten, rösten; **3.** gebraten; ~ beef Rost- od. Rinderbraten m.

rob [rɒb] (-bb-) (be)rauben; ~ber ['rɒbə] Räuber m; ~ber·y [~rɪ] Raub m; ~ with violence 🏴 schwerer Raub.

robe [rəʊb] (Amts)Robe f, Talar m; Bade-, Hausmantel m, Morgenrock m.

rob·in zo. ['rɒbɪn] Rotkehlchen n.

ro·bot ['rəʊbɒt] Roboter m.

ro·bust ☐ [rə'bʌst] robust, kräftig.

rock [rɒk] **1.** Fels(en) m; Klippe f; Gestein n; Brt. Zuckerstange f; △ nicht Rock; on the ~s mit Eiswürfeln (Whisky etc.); kaputt, in die Brüche gegangen (Ehe); ~ crystal Bergkristall m; **2.** schaukeln, wiegen; erschüttern (a. fig.).

rock·er ['rɒkə] Kufe f; Am. Schaukelstuhl m; Brt. Rocker m; off one's ~ sl. übergeschnappt.

rock·et ['rɒkɪt] Rakete f; attr. Raketen...; ~-pro·pelled mit Raketenantrieb; ~ry [~rɪ] Raketentechnik f.

rock·ing-chair ['rɒkɪntʃeə] Schaukelstuhl m; ~-horse Schaukelpferd n.

rock·y ['rɒkɪ] (-ier, -iest) felsig, Felsen...

rod [rɒd] Rute f; Stab m; ⊕ Stange f.

rode [rəʊd] pret. von ride 2.

ro·dent zo. ['rəʊdənt] Nagetier n.

ro·de·o [rəʊ'deɪəʊ] (pl. -os) Rodeo m, n.

roe¹ zo. [rəʊ] Reh n.

roe² zo. [~] a. hard ~ Rogen m; a. soft ~ Milch f.

rogue [rəʊg] Schurke m, Gauner m; Schlingel m, Spitzbube m; **ro·guish** ☐ ['rəʊgɪʃ] spitzbübisch.

role, rôle thea. [rəʊl] Rolle f (a. fig.).

roll [rəʊl] **1.** Rolle f; Brötchen n, Semmel f; (bsd. Namens-, Anwesenheits)Liste f; Brausen n; (Donner-) Rollen n; (Trommel)Wirbel m; 🏴 Schlingern n; **2.** v/t. rollen; wälzen; walzen; Zigarette drehen; ~ up Ärmel hochkrempeln; mot. Fenster hochkurbeln; v/i. rollen; fahren; sich wälzen; (g)rollen (Donner); dröhnen; brausen; wirbeln (Trommel); 🏴 schlingern; ~-call ['rəʊlkɔːl] Namensaufruf m; ✕ Appell m.

roll·er ['rəʊlə] Rolle f, Walze f; (Locken)Wickler m; 🏴 Sturzwelle f, Brecher m; △ nicht Roller; ~ coast·er Achterbahn f; ~ skate Rollschuh m; ~-skate Rollschuh laufen; ~ skat·ing Rollschuhlaufen n; ~ tow·el Rollhandtuch n.

rol·lick·ing ['rɒlɪkɪŋ] übermütig.

roll·ing ['rəʊlɪŋ] rollend etc.; Roll..., Walz...; ~ mill ⊕ Walzwerk n; ~ pin Nudelholz n.

roll-neck ['rəʊlnek] **1.** Rollkragen (-pullover) m; **2.** Rollkragen...; ~ed [~t] Rollkragen...

Ro·man ['rəʊmən] **1.** römisch; **2.** Römer(in).

ro·mance¹ [rəʊ'mæns] **1.** (Ritter-, Vers)Roman m; Abenteuer-, Liebesroman m; Romanze f (a. fig.); Romantik f, Zauber m.

Ro·mance² ling. [~] a. ~ languages die romanischen Sprachen pl.

Ro·ma·ni·an [ruː'meɪnjən] **1.** rumänisch; **2.** Rumän|e m, -in f; ling. Rumänisch n.

ro·man|tic [rə'mæntɪk] **1.** (~ally)

romantisch (veranlagt); **2.** Romantiker(in); Schwärmer(in); **~ti·cis·m** [~sɪzəm] Romantik f.

romp [rɒmp] **1.** Tollen n, Toben n; Range f, Wildfang m; **2.** a. ~ about, ~ around herumtollen, -toben; **~ers** ['rɒmpəz] pl. einteiliger Spielanzug.

roof [ruːf] **1.** Dach n (a. fig.); ~ of the mouth anat. Gaumen m; **2.** mit e-m Dach versehen; ~ in, ~ over überdachen; **~ing** ['ruːfɪŋ] **1.** Material n zum Dachdecken; **2.** Dach...; ~ felt Dachpappe f; **~ rack** bsd. Brt. mot. Dachgepäckträger m.

rook [rʊk] **1.** Schach: Turm m; zo. Saatkrähe f; **2.** betrügen (of um).

room [ruːm] **1.** Raum m; Platz m; Zimmer n; fig. Spielraum m; ~s pl. (Miet)Wohnung f; **2.** Am. wohnen; **~er** ['ruːmə] bsd. Am. Untermieter(in); **~ing-house** [~ɪŋhaʊs] Fremdenheim n, Pension f; **~mate** Zimmergenosse m, -in f; **~y** □ [~ɪ] (-ier, -iest) geräumig.

roost [ruːst] **1.** Schlafplatz m (von Vögeln); Hühnerstange f; **2.** sich zum Schlaf niederhocken (Vögel); **~er** bsd. Am. zo. ['ruːstə] (Haus-) Hahn m.

root [ruːt] **1.** Wurzel f; **2.** v/i. Wurzeln schlagen; wühlen (for nach); ~ about, ~ around herumwühlen (among in dat.); v/t. tief einpflanzen; ~ out ausrotten; ~ up ausgraben; **~ed** ['ruːtɪd] eingewurzelt; deeply ~ fig. tief verwurzelt; stand ~ to the spot wie angewurzelt stehen(bleiben).

rope [rəʊp] **1.** Tau n; Seil n; Strick m; Schnur f (Perlen etc.); be at the end of one's ~ mit s-m Latein am Ende sein; know the ~s sich auskennen; **2.** verschnüren; festbinden; ~ off (durch ein Seil) absperren od. abgrenzen; **~ lad·der** Strickleiter f; **~tow** Schlepplift m; **~way** ['rəʊpweɪ] (Seil)Schwebebahn f.

ro·sa·ry eccl. ['rəʊzərɪ] Rosenkranz m.

rose¹ [rəʊz] ♦ Rose f; (Gießkannen-) Brause f; Rosa-, Rosenrot n.

rose² [~] pret. von rise 2.

ros·trum ['rɒstrəm] (pl. -tra [-trə], -trums) Rednertribüne f, -pult n.

ros·y □ ['rəʊzɪ] (-ier, -iest) rosig.

rot [rɒt] **1.** Fäulnis f; Brt. F Quatsch m; **2.** (-tt-) v/t. (ver)faulen lassen; v/i. (ver)faulen, (-)modern, verrotten.

ro·ta·ry ['rəʊtərɪ] rotierend, sich

drehend; Rotations...; **ro·tate** [rəʊ'teɪt] rotieren od. kreisen (lassen), (sich) drehen; ♪ die Frucht wechseln; **ro·ta·tion** [~ʃn] Rotation f, (Um)Drehung f, Umlauf m; Wechsel m, Abwechslung f.

ro·tor bsd. ⚙ ['rəʊtə] Rotor m.

rot·ten □ ['rɒtn] verfault, faul(ig); morsch; mies; gemein; feel ~ sl. sich beschissen fühlen.

ro·tund □ [rəʊ'tʌnd] rundlich.

rough [rʌf] **1.** adj. □ rauh; roh; grob; barsch; hart; holp(e)rig, uneben; grob, ungefähr (Schätzung); unfertig, Roh...; ~ draft Rohfassung f, Konzept n; ~ draft Rohfassung f; **2.** adv. roh, rauh, hart; **3.** Rauhe n, Grobe n; holp(e)riger Boden; Golf: Rough n; **4.** an-, aufrauhen; ~ it primitiv od. ungewohnt leben; **~age** ['rʌfɪdʒ] Ballaststoffe pl.; **~cast 1.** ⊕ Rohputz m; **2.** unfertig; **3.** (-cast) ⊕ roh verputzen; roh entwerfen; **~en** [~n] rauh werden; an-, aufrauhen; **~neck** Am. F Grobian m; Ölbohrarbeiter m; **~ness** [~nɪs] Rauheit f; rauhe Stelle; Roheit f; Grobheit f; rauhe Stelle; Roheit f; **~shod**: ride ~ over j-n rücksichtslos behandeln; rücksichtslos über et. hinweggehen.

round [raʊnd] **1.** adj. □ rund; voll (Stimme etc.); abgerundet (Stil); unverblümt; a ~ dozen ein rundes Dutzend; in ~ figures auf- od. abgerundet (Zahlen); **2.** adv. rund-, rings(her)um; überall, auf od. von od. nach allen Seiten; ask s.o. ~ j-n zu sich einladen; ~ about ungefähr; all the year ~ das ganze Jahr hindurch; the other way ~ umgekehrt; **3.** prp. (rund)um; um (... herum); in od. auf (dat.) ... herum; **4.** Rund n, Kreis m; Runde f; (Leiter)Sprosse f; Brt. Scheibe f (Brot etc.); (Dienst-) Runde f, Rundgang m; ✽ Visite f (in e-r Klinik); ♪ Kanon m; (Lach-etc.)Salve f; 100 ~s ✕ 100 Schuß (Munition); **5.** rund machen od. werden; (herum)gehen od. (-)fahren um, biegen um; ~ off abrunden; fig. krönen, beschließen; ~ up Zahl etc. aufrunden (to auf acc.); Vieh zusammentreiben; Leute etc. zusammentrommeln, auftreiben; **~a·bout** ['raʊndəbaʊt] **1.** ~ way od. route Umweg m; in a ~ way fig. auf Umwegen; **2.** Brt. Karussell n; Brt. Kreisverkehr m; **~ish** [~ɪʃ] rundlich;

~ trip Rundreise f; Am. Hin- u. Rückfahrt f, ✕ Hin- u. Rückflug m; **~trip:** ~ ticket Am. Rückfahrkarte, ✕ Rückflugticket n; **~up** Zusammentreiben n (von Vieh).

rouse [rauz] v/t. wecken; Wild aufjagen; j-n aufrütteln; j-n reizen, erzürnen; Zorn erregen; ~ o.s. sich aufraffen; v/i. aufwachen.

route [ru:t, ✕ a. raut] (Reise-, Fahrt)Route f, (-)Weg m; (Bahn-, Bus-, Flug)Strecke f; ✕ Marschroute f.

rou·tine [ru:'ti:n] **1.** Routine f; **2.** üblich, routinemäßig, Routine...

rove [rəʊv] umherstreifen, -wandern; durchstreifen, -wandern.

row[1] [rəʊ] Reihe f.

row[2] F [raʊ] **1.** Krach m, Lärm m; (lauter) Streit, Krach m; **2.** (sich) streiten.

row[3] [rəʊ] **1.** Rudern n; Ruderpartie f; **2.** rudern; **~boat** Am. ['rəʊbəʊt] Ruderboot n; **~er** [~ə] Ruder|er m, -in f; **~ing boat** Brt. [~ɪŋbəʊt] Ruderboot n.

roy·al □ ['rɔɪəl] königlich; **~ty** [~tɪ] Königtum n; Königswürde f; coll. das Königshaus, die königliche Familie; Tantieme f.

rub [rʌb] **1.** give s.th. a good ~ et. (ab)reiben; et. polieren; **2.** (-bb-) v/t. reiben; polieren; (wund) scheuern; ~ down abschmirgeln, abschleifen, trockenreiben, (ab)frottieren; ~ in einreiben; ~ it in fig. F darauf herumreiten; ~ off ab-, wegreiben, ab-, wegwischen; ~ out Brt. ausradieren; ~ up aufpolieren; ~ s.o. up the wrong way j-n verstimmen; v/i. reiben (against, on an dat., gegen).

rub·ber ['rʌbə] **1.** Gummi n, m; (Radier)Gummi m; Wischtuch n; ~s pl. Am. (Gummi)Überschuhe pl.; Brt. Turnschuhe pl.; **~ band** Gummiband n; ~ **cheque**, Am. ~ **check** geplatzter Scheck; **~neck** Am. F **1.** Gaffer(in); **2.** gaffen; **~y** [~rɪ] gummiartig; zäh, wie Gummi (Fleisch).

rub·bish ['rʌbɪʃ] Schutt m; Abfall m, Müll m, Kehricht m; fig. Schund m; Quatsch m, Blödsinn m; **~ bin** Brt. Mülleimer m; **~ chute** Müllschlucker m.

rub·ble ['rʌbl] Schutt m.

ru·by ['ru:bɪ] Rubin(rot n) m.

ruck·sack ['rʌksæk] Rucksack m.

rud·der ['rʌdə] ⚓ (Steuer)Ruder n; ✕ Seitenruder m.

rud·dy □ ['rʌdɪ] (-ier, -iest) rot, rötlich; frisch, gesund.

rude □ [ru:d] (~r, ~st) unhöflich, grob; unanständig; heftig, wild; ungebildet; einfach, kunstlos.

ru·di·men·ta·ry [ru:dɪ'mentərɪ] elementar, Anfangs...; **~ments** ['ru:dɪmənts] pl. Anfangsgründe pl.

rue·ful □ ['ru:fl] reuig.

ruff [rʌf] Halskrause f.

ruf·fle ['rʌfl] **1.** Krause f, Rüsche f; Kräuseln n; **2.** kräuseln; Haare, Federn sträuben; zerknüllen; fig. aus der Ruhe bringen; (ver)ärgern.

rug [rʌg] (Reise-, Woll)Decke f; Vorleger m, Brücke f, (kleiner) Teppich.

rug·ged □ ['rʌgɪd] rauh (a. fig.); wild, zerklüftet, schroff.

ru·in ['ru:ɪn] **1.** Ruin m, Verderben n, Untergang m; mst ~s pl. Ruine(n pl.) f, Trümmer pl.; **2.** ruinieren, zugrunde richten, zerstören, zunichte machen, zerrütten; **~ous** □ [~əs] verfallen, ruinös.

rule [ru:l] **1.** Regel f; Spielregel f; Vorschrift f; Satzung f; Herrschaft f, Regierung f; Lineal n; as a ~ in der Regel; work to ~ Dienst nach Vorschrift tun; ~s pl. (Geschäfts-, Gerichts- etc.)Ordnung f; ~(s) of the road Straßenverkehrsordnung f; **2.** v/t. beherrschen; herrschen über (acc.); lenken, leiten; anordnen, verfügen; liniieren; ~ out ausschließen; v/i. herrschen; **rul·er** ['ru:lə] Herrscher(in); Lineal n.

rum [rʌm] Rum m; Am. Alkohol m.

rum·ble ['rʌmbl] rumpeln, poltern, (g)rollen (Donner), knurren (Magen).

ru·mi·nant zo. ['ru:mɪnənt] **1.** wiederkäuend; **2.** Wiederkäuer m; **~nate** [~eɪt] zo. wiederkäuen; fig. grübeln (about, over über acc.).

rum·mage ['rʌmɪdʒ] **1.** gründliche Durchsuchung; Ramsch m; ~ sale Am. Ramschverkauf m; Wohltätigkeitsbasar m; **2.** a. ~ about herumstöbern, -wühlen (among, in in dat.).

ru·mo(u)r ['ru:mə] **1.** Gerücht n; 2. △ nicht rumoren; it is ~ed man sagt od. munkelt, es gebe das Gerücht.

rump [rʌmp] Steiß m, Hinterteil n, -keulen pl.

rum·ple [ˈrʌmpl] zerknittern, -knüllen, -wühlen; △ *nicht rumpeln.*

run [rʌn] **1.** (-nn-; *ran, run*) v/i. laufen, rennen, eilen; fahren; verkehren, fahren, gehen (*Zug, Bus*); fließen, strömen; verlaufen (*Straße*), führen (*Weg*); ⊕ laufen; in Betrieb *od.* Gang sein; gehen (*Uhr etc.*); schmelzen (*Butter etc.*); zer-, auslaufen (*Farbe*); lauten (*Text*) gehen (*Melodie*); laufen (*Theaterstück, Film*), gegeben werden; ⚖ gelten, laufen; *econ.* stehen *od.* (*dat.*) (*Preis etc.*); *bsd. Am. pol.* kandidieren (*for* für); ~ *across s.o.* j-n zufällig treffen, auf j-n stoßen; ~ *after* hinterher-, nachlaufen; ~ *along!* F ab mit dir!; ~ *away* davonlaufen; ~ *away with* durchbrennen mit; durchgehen mit (*Temperament etc.*); ~ *down* ablaufen (*Uhr etc.*); *fig.* herunterkommen; ~ *dry* austrocknen; ~ *into* (hinein)laufen *od.* (-)rennen in (*acc.*); fahren gegen; *j-n* zufällig treffen; geraten in (*Schulden etc.*); sich belaufen auf (*acc.*); ~ *low* knapp werden; ~ *off with* = ~ *away with*; ~ *out* ablaufen (*Zeit*); ausgehen, knapp werden; ~ *out of petrol* kein Benzin mehr haben; ~ *over* überlaufen, -fließen; überfliegen, durchgehen, -lesen; ~ *short* knapp werden; ~ *short of petrol* kein Benzin mehr haben; ~ *through* überfliegen, durchgehen, -lesen; ~ *up to* sich belaufen auf (*acc.*); v/t. *Strecke* durchlaufen, *Weg* einschlagen; fahren, laufen lassen; *Zug, Bus* fahren *od.* verkehren lassen; *Hand etc.* gleiten lassen; *Geschäft* betreiben; *Betrieb* führen, leiten; fließen lassen; *Temperatur, Fieber* haben; ~ *down* an-, überfahren; *fig.* schlechtmachen; herunterwirtschaften; ~ *errands* Besorgungen *od.* Botengänge machen; ~ *s.o. home* F j-n nach Hause bringen *od.* fahren; ~ *in Auto* einfahren; F *Verbrecher* einbuchten; ~ *over* überfahren; ~ *s.o. through* j-n durchbohren; ~ *up Preis etc.* in die Höhe treiben; *Rechnung etc.* auflaufen lassen; **2.** Laufen *n*, Rennen *n*, Lauf *m*; Verlauf *m*; Fahrt *f*; Spazierfahrt *f*; Reihe *f*, Folge *f*, Serie *f*; *econ.* Ansturm *m*, Run *m*, stürmische Nachfrage; *Am.* Bach *m*; *Am.* Laufmasche *f*; Gehege *n*; Auslauf *m*, (Hühner)Hof *m*; *Sport:* Bob-, Rodelbahn *f*; (Ski)Abfahrt(sstrecke) *f*; freie Benutzung; *thea., Film:* Laufzeit *f*; *have a ~ of 20 nights thea.* 20mal nacheinander gegeben werden; *in the long ~* auf die Dauer; *in the short ~* fürs nächste; *on the ~* auf der Flucht.

run·a·bout F *mot.* [ˈrʌnəbaut] kleiner leichter Wagen; **~·a·way** Ausreißer *m*.

rung[1] [rʌŋ] *p.p. von ring*[1] 2.

rung[2] [~] (Leiter)Sprosse *f* (*a. fig.*).

run·let [ˈrʌnlɪt] Rinnsal *m*; **~·nel** [~l] Rinnsal *n*; Rinnstein *m*.

run·ner [ˈrʌnə] Läufer(in); Bote *m*; (Schlitten-, Schlittschuh)Kufe *f*; Schieber *m* (*am Schirm*); Läufer *m*; Tischläufer *m*; *Am.* Laufmasche *f*; Ausläufer *m*; **~ bean** *Brt.* ♥ Stangenbohne; **~-up** [~r'ʌp] (*pl. runners-up*) *Sport:* Zweite(r *m*) *f*.

run·ning [ˈrʌnɪŋ] **1.** laufend; fließend; *two days* ~ zwei Tage hintereinander; **2.** Laufen *n*; Rennen *n*; **~board** Trittbrett *n*.

run·way ✈ [ˈrʌnweɪ] Start-, Lande-, Rollbahn *f*.

rup·ture [ˈrʌptʃə] **1.** Bruch *m*, Riß *m*; (Zer)Platzen *n*; **2.** brechen; bersten, (zer)platzen.

ru·ral □ [ˈruərəl] ländlich, Land...

ruse [ruːz] List *f*, Kniff *m*, Trick *m*.

rush[1] ♥ [rʌʃ] Binse *f*.

rush[2] [~] **1.** Jagen *n*, Hetzen *n*, Stürmen *n*; Eile *f*; (An)Sturm *m*; Andrang *m*; *econ.* stürmische Nachfrage; Hetze *f*, Hochbetrieb *m*; **2.** v/i. stürzen, jagen, hetzen, stürmen; ~ *at* sich stürzen auf (*acc.*); ~ *in* hereinstürzen, -stürmen; v/t. jagen, hetzen, drängen, (an)treiben; losstürmen auf (*acc.*), angreifen; schnell (*wohin*) bringen; **~ hour** [ˈrʌʃaʊə] Hauptverkehrszeit *f*, Stoßzeit *f*; **~-hour traf·fic** Stoßverkehr *m*.

Rus·sian [ˈrʌʃn] **1.** russisch; **2.** Russ|e *m*, -in *f*; *ling.* Russisch *n*.

rust [rʌst] **1.** Rost *m*; Rostbraun *n*; **2.** (ver-, ein)rosten lassen.

rus·tic [ˈrʌstɪk] **1.** (~*ally*) ländlich, rustikal; bäurisch; **2.** Bauer *m*.

rus·tle [ˈrʌsl] **1.** rascheln (mit *od.* in *dat.*); rauschen; *Am. Vieh* stehlen; **2.** Rascheln *n*.

rust|·less [ˈrʌstlɪs] rostfrei; **~·y** □ [~ɪ] (*-ier, -iest*) rostig; *fig.* eingerostet.

rut[1] [rʌt] Wagenspur *f*; *bsd. fig.* ausgefahrenes Geleise.

rut² *zo.* [~] Brunst *f*, Brunft *f*.
ruth·less □ ['ruːθlɪs] umbarmherzig; rücksichts-, skrupellos.

rut|ted ['rʌtɪd], **~ty** [~ɪ] (-ier, -iest) ausgefahren (*Weg*).
rye ♀ [raɪ] Roggen *m*.

S

sa·ble ['seɪbl] *zo.* Zobel *m*; Zobelpelz *m*; △ *nicht* Säbel.
sab·o·tage □ ['sæbətɑːʒ] **1.** Sabotage *f*; **2.** sabotieren.
sa·bre, *Am. mst* **~ber** ['seɪbə] Säbel *m*.
sack [sæk] **1.** Plünderung *f*; Sack *m*; *Am.* (Einkaufs)Tüte *f*; Sackkleid *n*; *get the* ~ F entlassen werden; *give s.o. the* ~ F j-n entlassen; F j-m den Laufpaß geben; **2.** plündern; einsacken; F rausschmeißen, entlassen; F j-m den Laufpaß geben; **~cloth** ['sækkløθ], **~ing** [~ɪŋ] Sackleinen *n*, -leinwand *f*.
sac·ra·ment *eccl.* ['sækrəmənt] Sakrament *n*.
sa·cred □ ['seɪkrɪd] heilig; geistlich.
sac·ri·fice ['sækrɪfaɪs] **1.** Opfer *n*; *at a* ~ *econ.* mit Verlust; **2.** opfern; *econ.* mit Verlust verkaufen.
sac·ri·lege ['sækrɪlɪdʒ] Sakrileg *n*; Entweihung *f*; Frevel *m*; **~·le·gious** □ [sækrɪ'lɪdʒəs] frevelhaft.
sad □ [sæd] traurig; jämmerlich, elend; schlimm; dunkel, matt.
sad·den ['sædn] traurig machen *od.* werden.
sad·dle ['sædl] **1.** Sattel *m*; **2.** satteln; *fig.* belasten; **~r** [~ə] Sattler *m*.
sad·is·m ['seɪdɪzəm] Sadismus *m*.
sad·ness ['sædnɪs] Traurigkeit *f*.
safe [seɪf] **1.** □ [~*r*, ~*st*] sicher; unversehrt; zuverlässig; **2.** Safe *m*, *n*, Geldschrank *m*; Fliegenschrank *m*; **~·con·duct** freies Geleit; Geleitbrief *m*; **~·guard** ['seɪfɡɑːd] **1.** Schutz *m* (*against* gegen, vor *dat.*); **2.** sichern, schützen (*against* gegen, vor *dat.*).
safe·ty ['seɪftɪ] Sicherheit *f*; Sicherheits...; **~·belt** Sicherheitsgurt *m*; **~is·land** *Am.* Verkehrsinsel *f*; **~·lock** Sicherheitsschloß *n*; **~·pin** Sicherheitsnadel *f*; **~·ra·zor** Rasierapparat *m*.
saf·fron ['sæfrən] Safran(gelb *n*) *m*.

sag [sæg] (-*gg*-) durchsacken; ⊕ durchhängen; abfallen, (herab)hängen; sinken, fallen, absacken.
sa·ga·cious □ [sə'ɡeɪʃəs] scharfsinnig; **~·ci·ty** [sə'ɡæsətɪ] Scharfsinn *m*.
sage¹ [seɪdʒ] **1.** □ [~*r*, ~*st*] klug, weise; **2.** Weise(r) *m*.
sage² ♀ [~] Salbei *m*, *f*.
said [sed] *pret. u. p.p. von* say 1.
sail [seɪl] **1.** Segel *n od. pl.*; (Segel-) Fahrt *f*; Windmühlenflügel *m*; (Segel)Schiff(e *pl.*) *n*; *set* ~ auslaufen (*for* nach); **2.** *v/i.* segeln, fahren; auslaufen (*Schiff*); absegeln; *fig.* schweben; *v/t.* ♣ befahren; *Schiff* steuern; *Segelboot* segeln; **~·boat** *Am.* ['seɪlbəʊt] Segelboot *n*; **~·er** [~ə] Segler *m* (*Schiff*); **~·ing-boat** *Brt.* [~ɪŋbəʊt] Segelboot *n*; **~·ing-ship** [~ɪŋʃɪp], **~·or** [~ə] Seemann *m*; Matrose *m*; *be a good* (*bad*) ~ (nicht) seefest sein; **~·plane** Segelflugzeug *n*.
saint [seɪnt] **1.** Heilige(r *m*) *f*; [*vor npr.* snt] Sankt ...; **2.** heiligsprechen; **~·ly** ['seɪntlɪ] heilig, fromm.
saith *veraltet od. poet.* [seθ] *3. sg. pres. von* say 1.
sake [seɪk]: *for the* ~ *of* um ... (*gen.*) willen; *for my* ~ meinetwegen; *for God's* ~ um Gottes willen.
sa·la·ble ['seɪləbl] = saleable.
sal·ad ['sæləd] Salat *m*.
sal·a·ried ['sælərɪd] (fest)angestellt, (-)bezahlt; ~ *employee* Angestellte(r *m*) *f*, Gehaltsempfänger(in).
sal·a·ry ['sælərɪ] Gehalt *n*; ~ **earn·er** [~ɜːnə] Angestellte(r *m*) *f*, Gehaltsempfänger(in).
sale [seɪl] Verkauf *m*; Ab-, Umsatz *m*; (Saison)Schlußverkauf *m*; Auktion *f*; *for* ~ zu verkaufen; *be on* ~ verkauft werden, erhältlich sein.
sale·a·ble *bsd. Brt.* ['seɪləbl] verkäuflich.

satin

sales|clerk *Am.* ['seɪlzklɑːk] (Laden)Verkäufer(in); **~man** [~mən] (*pl.* -men) Verkäufer *m*; (Handels)Vertreter *m*; **~wom·an** (*pl.* -women) Verkäuferin *f*; (Handels)Vertreterin *f*.

sa·li·ent □ ['seɪljənt] vorspringend; *fig.* ins Auge springend, hervorstechend.

sa·line ['seɪlaɪn] salzig, Salz...

sa·li·va [sə'laɪvə] Speichel *m*.

sal·low ['sæləʊ] blaß, bleich, fahl.

sal·ly ['sælɪ]: ~ *forth*, ~ *out* sich aufmachen.

salm·on *zo.* ['sæmən] Lachs *m*, Salm *m*.

sa·loon [sə'luːn] Salon *m*; (Gesellschafts)Saal *m*; erste Klasse (*auf Schiffen*); *Am.* Kneipe *f*, Wirtschaft *f*, Saloon *m*; ~ (*car*) *Brt. mot.* Limousine.

salt [sɔːlt] 1. Salz *n*; *fig.* Würze *f*; 2. salzig; gesalzen, gepökelt; Salz...; Pökel...; 3. (ein)salzen; pökeln; **~cel·lar** ['sɔːltselə] Salzfäßchen *n*, -streuer *m*; **~pe·tre**, *Am.* **~pe·ter** 🔥 [~piːtə] Salpeter *m*; **~wa·ter** Salzwasser...; **~y** [~ɪ] (-*ier*, -*iest*) salzig.

sa·lu·bri·ous □ [sə'luːbrɪəs], **sal·u·ta·ry** □ ['sæljʊtərɪ] heilsam, gesund.

sal·u·ta·tion [sælju:'teɪʃn] Gruß *m*, Begrüßung *f*; Anrede *f* (*im Brief*).

sa·lute [sə'luːt] 1. Gruß *m*; ⚔ Salut *m*; 2. (be)grüßen; ⚔ salutieren.

sal·vage ['sælvɪdʒ] 1. Bergung(sgut *n*) *f*; Bergegeld *n*; 2. bergen; retten.

sal·va·tion [sæl'veɪʃn] Erlösung *f*; (Seelen)Heil *n*; Rettung *f*; ♀ *Army* Heilsarmee *f*.

salve¹ [sælv] retten, bergen.

salve² [~] 1. Salbe *f*; *fig.* Balsam *m*, Trost *m*; △ *nicht* Salve; 2. *fig.* beschwichtigen, beruhigen.

same [seɪm]: *the* ~ der-, die-, dasselbe; *all the* ~ trotzdem; *it is all the* ~ *to me* es ist mir (ganz) gleich.

sam·ple ['sɑːmpl] 1. Probe *f*, Muster *n*; 2. probieren; kosten.

san·a·to·ri·um [sænə'tɔːrɪəm] (*pl.* -*ums*, -*a* [-ə]) Sanatorium *n*.

sanc·ti·fy ['sæŋktɪfaɪ] heiligen; weihen; **~ti·mo·ni·ous** □ [sæŋktɪ'məʊnjəs] scheinheilig; **~tion** ['sæŋkʃn] 1. Sanktion *f*; Billigung *f*, Zustimmung *f*; 2. billigen; **~ti·ty** [~tətɪ] Heiligkeit *f*; **~tu·a·ry** [~jʊərɪ] Heiligtum *n*; *das* Allerheiligste; Asyl

n; Schutzgebiet *n* (*für Tiere*); *seek* ~ *with* Zuflucht suchen bei.

sand [sænd] 1. Sand *m*; ~*s pl.* Sand(-fläche *f*) *m*; Sandbank *f*; 2. mit Sand bestreuen; schmirgeln.

san·dal ['sændl] Sandale *f*.

sand|-glass ['sændglɑːs] Sanduhr *f*, Stundenglass *n*; **~hill** Sanddüne *f*; **~pip·er** *zo.* Strandläufer *m*; *common* ~ Flußuferläufer *m*.

sand·wich ['sænwɪdʒ] 1. Sandwich *n*; 2. einklemmen, -zwängen; *a.* ~ *in fig.* ein-, dazwischenschieben.

sand·y ['sændɪ] (-*ier*, -*iest*) sandig; rotblond.

sane [seɪn] (~*r*, ~*st*) geistig gesund; ⚖ zurechnungsfähig; vernünftig.

sang [sæŋ] *pret. von* sing.

san·gui·na·ry □ ['sæŋgwɪnərɪ] blutdürstig; blutig; **~guine** □ [~wɪn] leichtblütig; zuversichtlich; rot, frisch, blühend (*Gesichtsfarbe*).

san·i·tar·i·um *Am.* [sænɪ'teərɪəm] (*pl.* -*ums*, -*a* [-ə]) = sanatorium.

san·i·ta·ry □ ['sænɪtərɪ] Gesundheits..., gesundheitlich, sanitär... (*a.* ⊕); ~ *napkin Am.*, ~ *towel* Damenbinde *f*.

san·i·ta·tion [sænɪ'teɪʃn] Hygiene *f*; sanitäre Einrichtungen *pl.*

san·i·ty ['sænətɪ] geistige Gesundheit; ⚖ Zurechnungsfähigkeit *f*; gesunder Verstand.

sank [sæŋk] *pret. von* sink 1.

San·ta Claus ['sæntə'klɔːz] der Weihnachtsmann, der Nikolaus.

sap [sæp] 1. Saft *m* (*in Pflanzen*); *fig.* Lebenskraft *f*; 2. (*-pp*-) untergraben (*a. fig.*); **~less** ['sæplɪs] saft-, kraftlos; **~ling** [~lɪŋ] junger Baum.

sap·phire ['sæfaɪə] Saphir *m*.

sap·py ['sæpɪ] (-*ier*, -*iest*) saftig; *fig.* kraftvoll.

sar·cas·m ['sɑːkæzəm] Sarkasmus *m*.

sar·dine *zo.* [sɑː'diːn] Sardine *f*.

sash [sæʃ] Schärpe *f*; (schiebbarer) Fensterrahmen; **~win·dow** ['sæʃwɪndəʊ] Schiebefenster *n*.

sat [sæt] *pret. u. p.p. von* sit.

Sa·tan ['seɪtən] Satan *m*.

satch·el ['sætʃəl] Schulmappe *f*, -tasche *f*, -ranzen *m*.

sate [seɪt] übersättigen.

sa·teen [sæ'tiːn] (Baum)Wollsatin *m*.

sat·el·lite ['sætəlaɪt] Satellit *m*; *a.* ~ *state* Satellit(enstaat *m*).

sa·ti·ate ['seɪʃɪeɪt] übersättigen.

sat·in ['sætɪn] (Seiden)Satin *m*.

S

satire

sat|ire ['sætaɪə] Satire *f*; **~ir·ist** [~ərɪst] Satiriker(in); **~ir·ize** [~raɪz] verspotten.

sat·is·fac|tion [sætɪs'fækʃn] Befriedigung *f*; Genugtuung *f*; Zufriedenheit *f*; *eccl.* Sühne *f*; Gewißheit *f*; **~to·ry** *f* [~'fæktərɪ] befriedigend, zufriedenstellend.

sat·is·fy ['sætɪsfaɪ] befriedigen, zufriedenstellen; überzeugen; *be satisfied* with zufrieden sein mit.

sat·u·rate 🔊 *u. fig.* ['sætʃəreɪt] sättigen.

Sat·ur·day ['sætədɪ] Sonnabend *m*, Samstag *m*.

sat·ur·nine □ ['sætənaɪn] düster, finster.

sauce [sɔːs] 1. Soße *f*; △ *nicht Bratensoße*; *Am.* Kompott *n*; *fig.* Würze *f*, Reiz *m*; F Frechheit *f*; *none of your ~!* werd bloß nicht frech!; F frech sein zu *j-m*; **~boat** ['sɔːsbəʊt] Soßenschüssel *f*; **~pan** Kochtopf *m*; Kasserolle *f*.

sau·cer ['sɔːsə] Untertasse *f*.

sauc·y □ ['sɔːsɪ] (*-ier, -iest*) frech; F flott, keß.

saun·ter ['sɔːntə] 1. Schlendern *n*, Bummel *m*; 2. schlendern, bummeln.

saus·age ['sɒsɪdʒ] Wurst *f*; *a. small~* Würstchen *n*.

sav|age ['sævɪdʒ] 1. □ wild; roh, grausam; 2. Wilde(r *m*) *f*; Rohling *m*, Barbar(in); **~ag·er·y** [~ərɪ] Wildheit *f*; Roheit *f*, Grausamkeit *f*.

sav·ant ['sævənt] Gelehrte(r) *m*.

save [seɪv] 1. retten; *eccl.* erlösen; bewahren; (auf-, er)sparen; schonen; 2. *rhet. prp. u. cj.* außer (*dat.*); *~ for* bis auf (*acc.*); *~ that* nur daß.

sav·er ['seɪvə] Retter(in); Sparer(in); *it is a time-~* es spart Zeit.

sav·ing ['seɪvɪŋ] 1. □ ...sparend; rettend, befreiend; 2. Rettung *f*; *~s pl.* Ersparnisse *pl.*

sav·ings| ac·count ['seɪvɪŋz'əˈkaʊnt] Sparkonto *n*; **~bank** Sparkasse *f*; **~de·pos·it** Spareinlage *f*.

sa·vio(u)r ['seɪvjə] Retter *m*; *the ℛ eccl.* der Erlöser, der Heiland.

sa·vo(u)r ['seɪvə] 1. (Wohl)Geschmack *m*; *fig.* Beigeschmack *m*; *fig.* Würze *f*, Reiz *m*; 2. *fig.* genießen; *fig.* schmecken, riechen (*of* nach); **~y** □ [~rɪ] schmackhaft; appetitlich; pikant.

saw¹ [sɔː] *pret. von see¹*.

saw² [~] Sprichwort *n*.

saw³ [~] 1. (*~ed od. ~n, ~ed*) sägen; 2. Säge *f*; **~dust** ['sɔːdʌst] Sägemehl *n*, -späne *pl.*; **~mill** Sägewerk *n*; **~n** [sɔːn] *p.p. von saw³* 1.

Sax·on ['sæksn] 1. sächsisch; *ling. oft* germanisch; 2. Sachse *m*, Sächsin *f*.

say [seɪ] 1. (*said*) sagen; auf-, hersagen; berichten; *~ grace* das Tischgebet sprechen; *what do you ~...?*, *oft what ~ you to ...?* was hältst du von ...?, wie wäre es mit ...?; *it ~s* es lautet (*Schreiben etc.*); *it ~s here* hier heißt es; *that is to ~* das heißt; (*and*) *that's ~ing s.th.* (und) das will was heißen; *you don't ~ (so)!* was Sie nicht sagen!; *I ~* sag(en Sie) mal!; ich muß schon sagen!; *he is said to be ...* er soll ... sein; *no sooner said than done* gesagt, getan; 2. Rede *f*, Wort *n*; Mitspracherecht *n*; *let him have his ~* laß(t) ihn (doch auch mal) reden *od.* s-e Meinung äußern; *have a od. some (no) ~ in s.th.* et. (nichts) zu sagen haben bei et.; **~ing** ['seɪŋ] Reden *n*; Sprichwort *n*, Redensart *f*; Ausspruch *m*; *it goes without ~* es versteht sich von selbst; *as the ~ goes* wie es so schön heißt.

scab [skæb] 🔊, 🐾 Schorf *m*; *vet.* Räude *f*; *sl.* Streikbrecher *m*.

scab·bard ['skæbəd] (Schwert-) Scheide *f*.

scaf·fold ['skæfəld] (Bau)Gerüst *n*; Schafott *n*; **~ing** [~ɪŋ] (Bau)Gerüst *n*.

scald [skɔːld] 1. Verbrühung *f*; 2. verbrühen; *Milch* abkochen; *~ing hot* kochendheiß; glühendheiß (*Tag etc.*).

scale¹ [skeɪl] 1. Schuppe *f*; Kesselstein *m*; 🦷 Zahnstein *m*; 2. (sich) (ab)schuppen, ablösen; ⊕ *Kesselstein* abklopfen; 🦷 *Zähne vom Zahnstein reinigen.

scale² [~] 1. Waagschale *f*; (*a pair of*) *~s pl.* (-e-) Waage *f*; 2. wiegen.

scale³ [~] 1. 🎵 Stufenleiter *f*; ♪ Tonleiter *f*; Skala *f*; Maßstab *m*; *fig.* Ausmaß *n*; 2. ersteigen; *~ up* (*down*) maßstab(s)getreu vergrößern (verkleinern).

scal·lop ['skɒləp] 1. *zo.* Kammuschel *f*; *Näherei*: Langette *f*; 2. ausbogen.

scalp [skælp] 1. Kopfhaut *f*; Skalp *m*; 2. skalpieren.

scal·y ['skeɪlɪ] (*-ier, -iest*) schuppig.

scamp [skæmp] **1.** Taugenichts *m*; **2.** pfuschen bei.

scam·per ['skæmpə] **1.** *a.* ~ *about*, ~ *around* (herum)tollen, herumhüpfen; hasten; **2.** (Herum)Tollen *n*, Herumhüpfen *n*.

scan [skæn] (*-nn-*) *Verse* skandieren; genau prüfen; forschend ansehen; *Horizont etc.* absuchen; *Computer*, *Radar*, *TV*: abtasten; *Überschriften etc.* überfliegen.

scan·dal ['skændl] Skandal *m*; Ärgernis *n*; Klatsch *m*; **~·ize** [∼dəlaɪz]: *be ∼d at s.th.* über et. empört *od.* entrüstet sein; **~·ous** □ [∼əs] skandalös, anstößig.

Scan·di·na·vi·an [skændɪˈneɪvjən] **1.** skandinavisch; **2.** Skandinavier(in); *ling.* Skandinavisch *n*.

scant □ [skænt] knapp, gering; **~·y** □ ['skæntɪ] (*-ier*, *-iest*) knapp, spärlich, kärglich, dürftig.

-scape [skeɪp] *in Zssgn*: ...landschaft, Bild.

scape|goat ['skeɪpgəʊt] Sündenbock *m*; **~·grace** [∼greɪs] Taugenichts *m*.

scar [skɑː] **1.** Narbe *f*; *fig.* (Schand-) Fleck *m*, Makel *m*; Klippe *f*; **2.** (*-rr-*) e-e Narbe *od.* Narben hinterlassen (auf *dat.*); ~ *over* vernarben.

scarce [skeəs] (~*r*, ~*st*) knapp; rar, selten; **~·ly** ['skeəslɪ] kaum; **scar·ci·ty** [∼ətɪ] Mangel *m*, Knappheit *f* (*of* an *dat.*).

scare [skeə] **1.** erschrecken; ~ *away*, ~ *off* verscheuchen; *be ∼d (of s.th.)* (vor et.) Angst haben; **2.** Schreck(en) *m*, Panik *f*; **~·crow** ['skeəkrəʊ] Vogelscheuche *f* (*a. fig.*).

scarf [skɑːf] (*pl. scarfs* [∼fs], *scarves* [∼vz]) Schal *m*, Hals-, Kopf-, Schultertuch *n*.

scar·let ['skɑːlət] **1.** Scharlach(rot *n*) *m*; **2.** scharlachrot; ~ *fever* ♣ Scharlach *m*; ~ *runner* ♣ Feuerbohne *f*.

scarred [skɑːd] narbig.

scarves [skɑːvz] *pl. von scarf*.

scath·ing *fig.* ['skeɪðɪŋ] vernichtend.

scat·ter ['skætə] (sich) zerstreuen; aus-, verstreuen; auseinanderstieben (*Vögel etc.*); **~·brain** F Schussel *m*; **~ed** verstreut; vereinzelt.

sce·na·ri·o [sɪˈnɑːrɪəʊ] (*pl. -os*) *Film:* Drehbuch *n*.

scene [siːn] Szene *f*; Schauplatz *m*; ~*s pl.* Kulissen *pl.*; **sce·ne·ry** ['siːnərɪ] Szenerie *f*; Bühnenbild *n*, Kulissen *pl.*, Dekoration *f*; Landschaft *f*.

scent [sent] **1.** (*bsd.* Wohl)Geruch *m*, Duft *m*; *bsd. Brt.* Parfüm *n*; *hunt.* Witterung *f*; *gute etc.* Nase; Fährte *f* (*a. fig.*); **2.** wittern; *bsd. Brt.* parfümieren; **~·less** ['sentlɪs] geruchlos.

scep|tic, *Am.* **skep-** ['skeptɪk] Skeptiker(in); **~·ti·cal**, *Am.* **skep-** □ [∼l] skeptisch.

scep·tre, *Am.* **-ter** ['septə] Zepter *n*.

sched·ule ['ʃedjuːl, *Am.* 'skedʒuːl] **1.** Verzeichnis *n*, Tabelle *f*; Plan *m*; *bsd. Am.* Fahr-, Flugplan *m*; *be ahead of* ~ dem Zeitplan voraus sein; *be behind* ~ Verspätung haben; im Rückstand sein; *be on* ~ (fahr)planmäßig *od.* pünktlich ankommen; **2.** (in e-e Liste *etc.*) eintragen; festlegen, -setzen, planen; **~d** planmäßig (*Abfahrt etc.*); ~ *flight* ✈ Linienflug *m*.

scheme [skiːm] **1.** Schema *n*; Plan *m*, Projekt *n*, Programm *n*; Intrige *f*; Pläne machen; intrigieren, Ränke schmieden.

schol·ar ['skɒlə] Gelehrte(r *m*) *f*; Gebildete(r *m* *f*); *univ.* Stipendiat(in); *veraltet:* Schüler(in); **~·ly** *adj.* [∼lɪ] gelehrt; **~·ship** [∼ʃɪp] Gelehrsamkeit *f*; *univ.* Stipendium *n*.

school [skuːl] **1.** *zo.* Schwarm *m*; Schule *f* (*a. fig.*); *univ.* Fakultät *f*; *Am.* Hochschule *f*; *at* ~ auf *od.* in der Schule; **2.** schulen, ausbilden; *Tier* dressieren; **~·boy** ['skuːlbɔɪ] Schüler *m*; **~·chil·dren** *pl.* Schulkinder *pl.*, Schüler *pl.*; **~·fel·low** Mitschüler(in); **~·girl** Schülerin *f*; **~·ing** [∼ɪŋ] (Schul)Ausbildung *f*; **~·mas·ter** Lehrer *m*; **~·mate** Mitschüler(in); **~·mis·tress** Lehrerin *f*; **~·teach·er** Lehrer(in).

schoo·ner ['skuːnə] ⚓ Schoner *m*; *Am.* großes Bierglas; *Brt.* großes Sherryglas; *Am.* = *prairie schooner*.

sci·ence ['saɪəns] Wissenschaft *f*; *a. natural* ~ die Naturwissenschaft(en *pl.*); Kunst(fertigkeit) *f*, Technik *f*; ~ **fic·tion** Science-fiction *f*.

sci·en·tif·ic [saɪənˈtɪfɪk] (∼*ally*) (natur)wissenschaftlich; exakt, systematisch; kunstgerecht.

sci·en·tist ['saɪəntɪst] (Natur)Wissenschaftler(in).

scin·til·late ['sɪntɪleɪt] funkeln.

sci·on ['saɪən] Sproß *m*, Sprößling *m*.

scis·sors ['sɪzəz] *pl.* (*a pair of* ~ e-e) Schere.

scoff [skɒf] **1.** Spott *m*; **2.** spotten.

S

scold

scold [skəʊld] **1.** zänkisches Weib; **2.** (aus)schelten; schimpfen.

scol·lop ['skɒləp] = *scallop*.

scone [skɒn] weiches Teegebäck.

scoop [skuːp] **1.** Schaufel *f*, Schippe *f*; Schöpfkelle *f*; F Coup *m*, gutes Geschäft; *Zeitung*: F Exklusivmeldung *f*, Knüller *m*; **2.** schöpfen, schaufeln; ~ *up* (auf)schaufeln; hochheben, -nehmen; zusammenraffen.

scoot·er ['skuːtə] (Kinder)Roller *m*; (Motor)Roller *m*.

scope [skəʊp] Bereich *m*; Gesichtskreis *m*, (geistiger) Horizont; Spielraum *m*.

scorch [skɔːtʃ] *v/t.* versengen, -brennen; *v/i.* ~s of (dahin)rasen.

score [skɔː] **1.** Kerbe *f*; Zeche *f*, Rechnung *f*; 20 Stück; *Sport*: (Spiel)Stand *m*, Punkt-, Trefferzahl *f*, (Spiel)Ergebnis *n*; große (An-)Zahl, Menge *f*; ♩ Partitur *f*; ~s of viele; *four* ~ achtzig; *run up a* ~ Schulden machen; *on the* ~ *of* wegen (*gen.*); **2.** einkerben; die Punkte anschreiben; *Sport*: *Punkte, Treffer* erzielen, *Tore* schießen; ♩ instrumentieren; *Am.* F scharf kritisieren.

scorn [skɔːn] **1.** Verachtung *f*; Spott *m*; **2.** verachten; verschmähen; **~·ful** □ ['skɔːnfl] verächtlich.

Scot [skɒt] Schotte *m*, -in *f*.

Scotch [skɒtʃ] **1.** schottisch; **2.** *ling.* Schottisch *n*; schottischer Whisky; *the* ~ die Schotten *pl.*; **~·man** ['skɒtʃmən], **~·wom·an** = *Scotsman, Scotswoman*.

scot-free ['skɒt'friː] ungestraft.

Scots [skɒts] = *Scotch*; *the* ~ *pl.* die Schotten *pl.*; **~·man** ['skɒtsmən] (*pl. -men*) Schotte *m*; **~·wom·an** (*pl. -women*) Schottin *f*.

Scot·tish ['skɒtɪʃ] schottisch.

scoun·drel ['skaʊndrəl] Schurke *m*.

scour¹ ['skaʊə] scheuern; reinigen.

scour² [~] durchsuchen, -stöbern.

scourge [skɜːdʒ] **1.** Geißel *f* (*a. fig.*); *fig.* Plage *f*; **2.** geißeln.

scout [skaʊt] **1.** *bsd.* ✕ Späher *m*, Kundschafter *m*; *Sport*: Spion *m*, Beobachter *m*; ♣ Aufklärungskreuzer *m*; ✈ Aufklärer *m*; *Brt. mot.* motorisierter Pannenhelfer; (*boy*) ~ Pfadfinder *m*; (*girl*) ~ *Am.* Pfadfinderin *f*; *talent* ~ Talentsucher *m*; **2.** auskundschaften; *bsd.* ✕ auf Erkundung sein; ~ *about,*

~ *around* sich umsehen (*for* nach).

scowl [skaʊl] **1.** finsteres Gesicht; **2.** finster blicken.

scrab·ble ['skræbl] (be)kritzeln; scharren; krabbeln.

scrag *fig.* [skræg] Gerippe *n* (*dürrer Mensch etc.*).

scram·ble ['skræmbl] **1.** klettern; sich balgen (*for* um); **~d eggs** *pl.* Rührei *n*; **2.** Kletterei *f*; Balgerei *f*; *fig.* Gerangel *n*.

scrap [skræp] **1.** Stückchen *n*, Fetzen *m*; (Zeitungs)Ausschnitt *m*, Bild *n* (*zum Einkleben*); Altmaterial *n*; Schrott *m*; ~s *pl.* Abfall *m*, (*bsd. Speise*)Reste *pl.*; **2.** (*-pp-*) ausrangieren; verschrotten; **~·book** ['skræpbʊk] Sammelalbum *n*.

scrape [skreɪp] **1.** Kratzen *n*, Scharren *n*; Kratzfuß *m*; Kratzer *m*, Schramme *f*; *fig.* Klemme *f*; **2.** schaben; kratzen; scharren; (*entlang-*)streifen.

scrap·heap ['skræphiːp] Abfall-, Schrotthaufen *m*; **~·i·ron**, **~·met·al** Alteisen *n*, Schrott *m*; **~·pa·per** Schmierpapier *n*; Altpapier *n*.

scratch [skrætʃ] **1.** Kratzer *m*, Schramme *f*; Kratzen *n*; *Sport*: Startlinie *f*; **2.** zusammengewürfelt; improvisiert; *Sport*: ohne Vorgabe; **3.** (*zer*)kratzen; (*zer*)schrammen; (sich) kratzen, *Tier* kraulen; ~ *out,* ~ *through,* ~ *off* aus-, durchstreichen; ~ *pad* *Am.* Notizblock *m*; ~ *pa·per* *Am.* Schmierpapier *n*.

scrawl [skrɔːl] **1.** kritzeln; **2.** Gekritzel *n*.

scraw·ny ['skrɔːnɪ] (*-ier, -iest*) dürr.

scream [skriːm] **1.** Schrei *m*; Gekreisch *n*; *he is a* ~ F er ist zum Schreien komisch; **2.** schreien, kreischen.

screech [skriːtʃ] = *scream*; **~·owl** *zo.* ['skriːtʃaʊl] Schleiereule *f*.

screen [skriːn] **1.** Wand-, Ofen-, Schutzschirm *m*; (Film)Leinwand *f*; *der Film, das Kino*; *Radar, TV, Computer*: Bildschirm *m*; Sandsieb *n*; Fliegengitter *n*; *fig.* Schutz *m*, Tarnung *f*; **2.** abschirmen (*a.* ~ *off*) (*from* gegen); (be)schützen (*from* vor *dat.*); ✕ tarnen; *Sand etc.* (durch)sieben; *Bild* projizieren; *TV* senden; *Film* vorführen, zeigen; verfilmen; *fig. j-n* decken; *fig. Personen* überprüfen; **~·play** ['skriːnpleɪ] Drehbuch *n*.

screw [skru:] 1. Schraube *f*; (Flugzeug-, Schiffs)Schraube *f*; Propeller *m*; 2. schrauben; ∨ bumsen, vögeln; ~ *up* zuschrauben; ~ *up one's courage* sich ein Herz fassen; **~·ball** *Am. sl.* ['skru:bɔ:l] komischer Kauz, Spinner *m*; **~·driv·er** Schraubenzieher *m*; **~·jack** Wagenheber *m*.

scrib·ble ['skrɪbl] 1. Gekritzel *n*; 2. kritzeln.

scrimp [skrɪmp], **~·y** ['skrɪmpɪ] (*-ier*, *-iest*) = skimp(y).

script [skrɪpt] Schrift *f*; Handschrift *f*; *print.* Schreibschrift *f*; Manuskript *n*; *Film*, *TV*: Drehbuch *n*.

Scrip·ture ['skrɪptʃə]: (*Holy*) ~, *The* (*Holy*) ~*s pl.* die Heilige Schrift.

scroll [skrəʊl] Schriftrolle *f*; *arch.* Volute *f*; Schnecke *f* (*am Geigenhals*); Schnörkel *m*.

scro·tum *anat.* ['skrəʊtəm] (*pl.* -ta [-tə], -tums) Hodensack *m*.

scrub[1] [skrʌb] Gestrüpp *n*, Buschwerk *n*; Knirps *m*; *contp.* Null *f* (*Person*); *Am. Sport:* zweite (Spieler)Garnitur.

scrub[2] [~] 1. Schrubben *n*, Scheuern *n*; 2. (*-bb-*) schrubben, scheuern.

scru·ple ['skru:pl] 1. Skrupel *m*, Zweifel *m*, Bedenken *n*; 2. Bedenken haben; **~·pu·lous** □ [~jʊləs] voller Skrupel; gewissenhaft; ängstlich.

scru·ti·nize ['skru:tɪnaɪz] (genau) prüfen; **~·ny** [~ɪ] forschender Blick; genaue (*bsd.* Wahl)Prüfung.

scud [skʌd] 1. (Dahin)Jagen *n*; (dahintreibende) Wolkenfetzen *pl.*; Bö *f*; 2. (*-dd-*) eilen, jagen.

scuff [skʌf] schlurfen.

scuf·fle ['skʌfl] 1. Balgerei *f*, Rauferei *f*; 2. sich balgen, raufen.

scull [skʌl] 1. Skull *n* (*kurzes Ruder*); Skullboot *n*; 2. rudern, skullen.

scul·le·ry ['skʌlərɪ] Spülküche *f*.

sculp·tor ['skʌlptə] Bildhauer *m*; **~·tress** [~trɪs] Bildhauerin *f*; **~·ture** [~tʃə] 1. Bildhauerei *f*; Skulptur *f*, Plastik *f*; 2. (heraus)meißeln, formen.

scum [skʌm] (Ab)Schaum *m*; *the ~ of the earth fig.* der Abschaum der Menschheit.

scurf [skɜ:f] (Haut-, *bsd.* Kopf-) Schuppen *pl.*

scur·ri·lous □ ['skʌrɪləs] gemein, unflätig; ⚠ *nicht* skurril.

scur·ry ['skʌrɪ] hasten, huschen.

scur·vy[1] 🏥 ['skɜ:vɪ] Skorbut *m*.

scur·vy[2] □ [~] (*-ier*, *-iest*) (hunds-) gemein.

scut·tle ['skʌtl] 1. Kohleneimer *m*; 2. = *scurry*; sich hastig zurückziehen.

scythe 🔗 [saɪð] Sense *f*.

sea [si:] See *f*, Meer *n* (*a. fig.*); hohe Welle; *at* ~ auf See; (*all*) *at* ~ *fig.* (völlig) ratlos; *by* ~ auf dem Seeweg, mit dem Schiff; **~·board** ['si:bɔ:d] Küste(ngebiet *n*) *f*; **~·coast** Meeresküste *f*; **~·far·ing** ['si:feərɪŋ] seefahrend; **~·food** Meeresfrüchte *pl.*; **~·go·ing** ⚓ (hoch)seetüchtig; (Hoch)See...; **~·gull** *zo.* (See)Möwe *f*.

seal[1] [si:l] 1. Siegel *n*; Stempel *m*; ⊕ Dichtung *f*; *fig.* Bestätigung *f*; 2. versiegeln; *fig.* besiegeln; ~ *off fig.* abriegeln; ~ *up* (fest) verschließen *od.* abdichten.

seal[2] *zo.* [~] Robbe *f*, Seehund *m*.

sea-lev·el ['si:levl] Meeresspiegel *m*, -höhe *f*.

seal·ing-wax ['si:lɪŋwæks] Siegellack *m*.

seam [si:m] 1. Naht *f*; ⚓ Fuge *f*; *geol.* Flöz *n*; Narbe *f*; ⚠ *nicht* Saum; 2. ~ *together* zusammennähen; ~*ed with Gesicht*: zerfurcht von.

sea·man ['si:mən] (*pl.* -men) Seemann *m*, Matrose *m*.

seam·stress ['semstrɪs] Näherin *f*.

sea·plane ['si:pleɪn] Wasserflugzeug *n*; **~·port** Seehafen *m*; Hafenstadt *f*; ~ **pow·er** Seemacht *f*.

sear [sɪə] versengen, -brennen; 🌿 ausbrennen; verdorren (lassen); *fig.* verhärten.

search [sɜ:tʃ] 1. Suche *f*, Suchen *n*, Forschen *n*; ⚖ Fahndung *f* (*for* nach); Unter-, Durchsuchung *f*; *in ~ of* auf der Suche nach; 2. *v/t.* durch-, untersuchen; 🌿 sondieren; *Gewissen* erforschen; prüfen; ~ *me!* F keine Ahnung!; *v/i.* suchen, forschen (*for* nach); ~ *into* untersuchen, ergründen; **~·ing** □ ['sɜ:tʃɪŋ] forschend, prüfend; eingehend (*Prüfung etc.*); **~·light** (Such)Scheinwerfer *m*; **~·par·ty** Suchmannschaft *f*; **~·war·rant** ⚖ Haussuchungs-, Durchsuchungsbefehl *m*.

sea-shore ['si:ʃɔ:] See-, Meeresküste *f*; **~·sick** seekrank; **~·side:** *at the* ~ am Meer; *go to the* ~ ans Meer fahren; ~ *place*, ~ *resort* Seebad *n*.

sea·son ['si:zn] 1. Jahreszeit *f*; (rechte) Zeit; Saison *f*; *Brt.* F = *season-*

S

ticket; cherries are now in ~ jetzt ist Kirschenzeit; *out of ~* nicht (auf dem Markt) zu haben; *fig.* zur Unzeit; *with the compliments of the ~* mit den besten Wünschen zum Fest; **2.** (aus)reifen (lassen); würzen; *Holz:* ablagern; abhärten (*to* gegen); **sea·so·na·ble** □ [~əbl] zeitgemäß; rechtzeitig; **~al** □ [~ənl] saisonbedingt, Saison...; **~ing** [~ɪŋ] Würze *f* (*a. fig.*); Gewürz *n*; **~tick·et** □ Zeitkarte *f*; *thea.* Abonnement *n*.

seat [si:t] **1.** Sitz *m*; Sessel *m*, Stuhl *m*, Bank *f*; (Sitz)Platz *m*; Platz *m*, Sitz *m* (*im Theater etc.*); Landsitz *m*; Gesäß *n*; Hosenboden *m*; Sitz *m* (*Mitgliedschaft*), *pol. a.* Mandat *m*; *fig.* Stätte *f*, Ort *m*, Schauplatz *m*; *s. take 1*; **2.** (hin)setzen; e-n (neuen) Hosenboden einsetzen in (*acc.*); fassen, Sitzplätze haben für; *be ~ed* einnehmen Sie Platz!; *remain ~ed* sitzen bleiben; **~belt** ✂, *mot.* ['si:tbelt] Sicherheitsgurt *m*.

sea·ur·chin *zo.* ['si:z:tʃn] Seeigel *m*; **~ward** ['si:wəd] **1.** *adj.* seewärts gerichtet; **2.** *adv. a.* **~s** seewärts; **~weed** ♣ (See)Tang *m*; **~wor·thy** seetüchtig.

se·cede [sɪ'si:d] sich trennen, abfallen (*from* von).

se·ces·sion [sɪ'seʃn] Abfall *m*, Abspaltung *f*, Sezession *f*; **~ist** [~ɪst] Abtrünnige(r *m*) *f*.

se·clude [sɪ'klu:d] abschließen, absondern; **se·clud·ed** einsam; zurückgezogen; abgelegen; **se·clu·sion** [~ʒn] Zurückgezogen-, Abgeschiedenheit *f*.

sec·ond ['sekənd] **1.** □ zweite(r, -s); *~ to none* unübertroffen; *on ~ thought* nach reiflicher Überlegung; **2.** als zweite(r, -s), an zweiter Stelle; **3.** *der, die, das Zweite*; Sekundant *m*; Beistand *m*; Sekunde *f*; **~s** *pl.* Ware(n *pl.*) *f* zweiter Wahl, zweite Wahl; **4.** sekundieren (*dat.*); unterstützen; **~·a·ry** □ [~əri] sekundär, untergeordnet; Neben...; Hilfs...; Sekundär..; *~ education* höhere Schulbildung; *~ modern (school)* Brt. (*etwa*) Kombination *f* aus Real- u. Hauptschule; *~ school* höhere Schule; **~hand** aus zweiter Hand; gebraucht; antiquarisch; **~·ly** [~lɪ] zweitens; **~·rate** zweitklassig.

se·cre·cy ['si:krɪsɪ] Heimlichkeit *f*;

Verschwiegenheit *f*; **~t** [~t] **1.** □ geheim; Geheim...; verschwiegen; verborgen; **2.** Geheimnis *n*; *in ~* heimlich, insgeheim; *be in the ~* eingeweiht sein; *keep s.th. a ~ from s.o.* j-m et. verheimlichen.

sec·re·ta·ry ['sekrətrɪ] Schriftführer *m*; Sekretär(in); ♀ *of State* Brt. Staatssekretär *m*; Brt. Minister *m*; Am. Außenminister *m*.

se·crete [sɪ'kri:t] verbergen; *biol.* absondern; **se·cre·tion** [~ʃn] Verbergen *n*; *biol.*, 𝔰 Absonderung *f*; **se·cre·tive** [~tɪv] verschlossen, geheimnistuerisch.

se·cret·ly ['si:krɪtlɪ] heimlich.

sec·tion ['sekʃn] 𝔰 Sektion *f*; Schnitt *m*; Teil *m*; Abschnitt *m*; ⅓ Paragraph *m*; *print.* Absatz *m*; Abteilung *f*; Gruppe *f*.

sec·u·lar □ ['sekjələ] weltlich.

se·cure [sɪ'kjʊə] **1.** □ sicher; fest; gesichert; **2.** (sich et.) sichern; schützen; garantieren; befestigen; fest (ver)schließen; **se·cu·ri·ty** [~rətɪ] Sicherheit *f*; Sicherheitsmaßnahmen *pl.*; Sorglosigkeit *f*; Garantie *f*; Bürge *m*; Kaution *f*; *securities pl.* Wertpapiere *pl.*; *~ check* Sicherheitskontrolle *f*.

se·dan [sɪ'dæn] Am. mot. Limousine *f*; **~(-chair)** Sänfte *f*.

se·date [sɪ'deɪt] gesetzt; ruhig.

sed·a·tive *mst* 𝔰 ['sedətɪv] **1.** beruhigend; **2.** Beruhigungsmittel *n*.

sed·en·ta·ry □ ['sedntrɪ] sitzend; seßhaft.

sed·i·ment ['sedɪmənt] Sediment *n*; (Boden)Satz *m*; *geol.* Ablagerung *f*.

se·di·tion [sɪ'dɪʃn] Aufruhr *m*; **~tious** □ [~əs] aufrührerisch.

se·duce [sɪ'dju:s] verführen; **se·duc·er** [~ə] Verführer *m*; **se·duc·tion** [sɪ'dʌkʃn] Verführung *f*; **se·duc·tive** □ [~tɪv] verführerisch.

sed·u·lous □ ['sedjələs] emsig.

see¹ [si:] (*saw, seen*) *v/t.* sehen; nachsehen; einsehen; sich überlegen; *I ~!* ich verstehe; ach so!; *~ about* sich kümmern um; *I'll ~ about it* ich will es mir überlegen; *~ into* untersuchen, nachgehen; *~ through* j-n od. et. durchschauen; *~ to* sich kümmern um; *v/t.* sehen; besuchen; dafür sorgen (, daß); j-n aufsuchen od. konsultieren; einsehen; *~ s.o. home* j-n nach Hause bringen od. begleiten; *~ you!* bis dann!, auf bald!; *~ off* j-n verabschieden (*at am Bahnhof etc.*); **~ out** *j-n* hinausbegleiten; *et.* zu Ende sehen *od.* erleben; **~ through** *et.* durchhalten; *j-m* durchhelfen; **live to ~** erleben.

see² [~] (erz)bischöflicher Stuhl.

seed [si:d] **1.** Same(n) *m*, Saat(gut *n*) *f*; (Obst)Kern *m*; *coll.* Samen *pl.*; *mst* **~s** *pl. fig.* Saat *f*, Keim *m*; **go od. run to ~** schießen (*Salat etc.*); *fig.* herunterkommen; **2.** *v/t.* (be)säen; entkernen; *v/i.* in Samen schießen; **~·less** ['si:dlɪs] kernlos (*Obst*); **~·ling** [~lɪŋ] Sämling *m*; **~·y** □ F [~ɪ] (*-ier, -iest*) schäbig; elend.

seek [si:k] (*sought*) suchen; begehren; trachten nach.

seem [si:m] (er)scheinen; **~·ing** □ ['si:mɪŋ] scheinbar; **~·ly** [~lɪ] (*-ier, -iest*) schicklich.

seen [si:n] *p.p. von* see¹.

seep [si:p] (durch)sickern.

seer ['si:ə] Seher(in), Prophet(in).

see-saw ['si:sɔ:] **1.** Wippen *n*; Wippe *f*, Wippschaukel *f*; **2.** wippen; *fig.* schwanken.

seethe [si:ð] sieden; schäumen (*a. fig.*); *fig.* kochen.

seg·ment ['segmənt] Abschnitt *m*; Segment *n*.

seg·re·gate ['segrɪgeɪt] absondern, (*a. nach Rassen, Geschlechtern etc.*); trennen; **~·ga·tion** [segrɪ'geɪʃn] Absonderung *f*; Rassentrennung *f*.

seize [si:z] ergreifen, packen, fassen; an sich reißen; ⚖ beschlagnahmen; *j-n* ergreifen, festnehmen; (ein)nehmen, erobern; *fig.* erfassen.

sei·zure ['si:ʒə] Ergreifung *f*; ⚖ Beschlagnahme *f*; 🏥 Anfall *m*.

sel·dom *adv.* ['seldəm] selten.

se·lect [sɪ'lekt] **1.** auswählen, -lesen, -suchen; **2.** ausgewählt; erlesen; exklusiv; **se·lec·tion** [~kʃn] Auswahl *f*; Auslese *f*; **~·man** (*pl. -men*) Stadtrat *m* (*in den Neuenglandstaaten*).

self [self] **1.** (*pl. selves* [selvz]) Selbst *n*, Ich *n*; **2.** *pron.* selbst; *econ. od.* F = myself, *etc.*; **~·as·sured** ['self'ʃʊəd] selbstbewußt; -sicher; **~·cen·t(e)red** egozentrisch; **~·col·o(u)red** einfarbig; gleichmäßig in der Farbe; einfarbig; **~·com·mand** Selbstbeherrschung *f*; **~·con·ceit** Eigendünkel *m*; **~·con·ceit·ed** eingebildet, überheblich; **~·con·fi·dence** Selbstvertrauen *n*, -bewußtsein *n*; **~·con·fi·dent** selbstsicher, -bewußt; **~-**

con·scious □ befangen, gehemmt, unsicher; △ *nicht* selbstbewußt; **~·con·tained** (in sich) geschlossen, selbständig; *fig.* verschlossen; *Brt.* abgeschlossene Wohnung; **~·con·trol** Selbstbeherrschung *f*; **~·de·fence**, *Am.* **~·de·fense** Selbstverteidigung *f*; **in ~** in Notwehr; **~·de·ni·al** Selbstverleugnung *f*; **~·de·ter·min·a·tion** *bsd. pol.* Selbstbestimmung *f*; **~·em·ployed** selbständig (*Handwerker etc.*); **~·ev·i·dent** selbstverständlich; **~·gov·ern·ment** *pol.* Selbstverwaltung *f*, Autonomie *f*; **~·help** Selbsthilfe *f*; **~·in·dul·gent** nachgiebig gegen sich selbst; zügellos; **~·in·struc·tion** Selbstunterricht *m*; **~·in·terest** Eigennutz *m*, eigenes Interesse; **~·ish** □ [~ɪʃ] selbstsüchtig; **~·made** selbstgemacht; **~ man** Selfmademan *m*; **~·pit·y** Selbstmitleid *n*; **~·pos·ses·sion** Selbstbeherrschung *f*; **~·re·li·ant** [~rɪ'laɪənt] selbstsicher, -bewußt; **~·re·spect** Selbstachtung *f*; **~·right·eous** □ selbstgerecht; **~·serv·ice 1.** mit Selbstbedienung, Selbstbedienungs...; **2.** Selbstbedienung *f*; **~·willed** eigenwillig, -sinnig.

sell [sel] (*sold*) *v/t.* verkaufen (*a. fig.*); *j-m et.* aufschwatzen; *v/i.* sich verkaufen (lassen), gehen (*Ware*); verkauft werden (*at, for* für); **~ off, ~ out** *econ.* ausverkaufen; **~·er** ['selə] Verkäufer(in); **good ~** *econ.* gutgehender Artikel.

selves [selvz] *pl. von* self 1.

sem·blance ['sembləns] Anschein *m*; Gestalt *f*.

se·men *biol.* ['si:men] Samen *m*, Sperma *n*.

sem·i· ['semɪ] halb..., Halb...; **~·co·lon** Semikolon *n*, Strichpunkt *m*; **~·de·tached (house)** Doppelhaushälfte *f*; **~·fi·nal** *Sport:* Halb-, Semifinalspiel *n*; **~s** *pl.* Halb-, Semifinale *n*, Vorschlußrunde *f*.

sem·i·nar·y ['semɪnərɪ] (Priester)Seminar *n*; *fig.* Schule *f*.

semp·stress ['sempstrɪs] Näherin *f*.

sen·ate ['senɪt] Senat *m*.

sen·a·tor ['senətə] Senator *m*.

send [send] (*sent*) senden, schicken; ⚡ senden; (*mit adj. od. p.pr.*) machen; **~ s.o. mad** *j-n* wahnsinnig machen; **~ for** nach *j-m* schicken, *j-n* kommen lassen, *j-n* holen *od.* rufen (lassen); ~ *forth* aussenden, -strahlen; hervorbringen; veröffentlichen; ~ *in* einsenden, -schicken, -reichen; ~ *up fig. Preise etc.* steigen lassen, in die Höhe treiben; ~ *word to s.o.* j-m Nachricht geben; **~er** ['sendə] Absender(in).

se·nile ['si:naɪl] greisenhaft, senil; **se·nil·i·ty** [sɪ'nɪlətɪ] Senilität *f.*

se·ni·or ['si:njə] **1.** *nachgestellt:* senior; älter; rang-, dienstälter; Ober...; ~ *citizens pl.* ältere Mitbürger *pl.*, Senioren *pl.*; ~ *partner econ.* Seniorpartner *m;* **2.** Ältere(r *m*) *f;* Rang-, Dienstältere(r *m*) *f;* Senior(in); *he is my ~ by a year* er ist ein Jahr älter als ich; **~·i·ty** [si:nɪ'ɒrətɪ] höheres Alter *od.* Dienstalter.

sen·sa·tion [sen'seɪʃn] (Sinnes)Empfindung *f;* Gefühl *n;* Eindruck *m;* Sensation *f;* **~·al** □ [~l] sensationell; aufsehenerregend.

sense [sens] **1.** Sinn *m (of* für*);* Empfindung *f,* Gefühl *n;* Verstand *m;* Bedeutung *f;* Ansicht *f; in (out of) one's ~s* bei (von) Sinnen; *bring s.o. to his od. her ~s* j-n zur Vernunft bringen; *make ~* Sinn haben; *talk ~* vernünftig reden; **2.** spüren, fühlen.

sense·less □ ['senslɪs] bewußtlos; unvernünftig, sinnlos; (Sinn); **~ness** [~nɪs] Bewußtlosigkeit *f;* Unvernunft *f;* Sinnlosigkeit *f.*

sen·si·bil·i·ty [sensɪ'bɪlətɪ] Sensibilität *f,* Empfindungsvermögen *n; phys. etc.* Empfindlichkeit *f; sensibilities pl.* Empfindsamkeit *f,* Zartgefühl *n.*

sen·si·ble □ ['sensəbl] vernünftig; spür-, fühlbar; ⚠ *nicht sensibel; be ~ of s.th.* sich e-r Sache bewußt sein; et. empfinden.

sen·si·tive □ ['sensɪtɪv] empfindlich (*to* gegen); Empfindungs...; sensibel, empfindsam, feinfühlig; **~tive·ness** [~nɪs], **~tiv·i·ty** [sensɪ'tɪvətɪ] Sensibilität *f;* Empfindlichkeit *f.*

sen·sor ⊕ ['sensə] Sensor *m.*

sen·su·al □ ['sensjʊəl] sinnlich.

sen·su·ous □ ['sensjʊəs] sinnlich; Sinnes...; sinnenfroh.

sent [sent] *pret. u. p.p. von* send.

sen·tence ['sentəns] **1.** ⚖ (Straf)Urteil *n; gr.* Satz *m; serve one's ~* s-e Strafe absitzen; **2.** verurteilen.

sen·ten·tious □ [sen'tenʃəs] aufgeblasen, salbungsvoll.

sen·tient □ ['senʃnt] empfindungsfähig.

sen·ti·ment ['sentɪmənt] (seelische) Empfindung, Gefühl *n;* Meinung *f;* = *sentimentality;* **~ment·al** □ [sentɪ'mentl] empfindsam; sentimental; **~men·tal·i·ty** [sentɪmen-'tælətɪ] Sentimentalität *f.*

sen·ti·nel ['sentɪnl], **~try** ✕ [~rɪ] Wache *f,* (Wach[t])Posten *m.*

sep·a·ra·ble □ ['sepərəbl] trennbar; **~rate 1.** □ ['seprət] (ab)getrennt, gesondert, separat; einzeln; **2.** ['sepəreɪt] (sich) trennen; (sich) absondern; (sich) scheiden; aufteilen (*into in acc.*); **~ra·tion** [sepə'reɪʃn] Trennung *f;* Scheidung *f.*

sep·sis 🏥 ['sepsɪs] (*pl. -ses* [-sɪːz]) Sepsis *f (Blutvergiftung).*

Sep·tem·ber [sep'tembə] September *m.*

sep·tic 🏥 ['septɪk] (*~ally*) septisch.

se·pul·chral □ [sɪ'pʌlkrəl] Grab...; *fig.* düster, Grabes...

sep·ul·chre, *Am.* **-cher** ['sepəlkə] Grab(stätte *f,* -mal *n*) *n.*

se·quel ['si:kwəl] Folge *f;* Nachspiel *n;* (Roman- *etc.*)Fortsetzung *f; a four-~ program(me) TV* ein Vierteiler *m,* e-e vierteilige Serie.

se·quence ['si:kwəns] (Aufeinander-, Reihen)Folge *f; Film:* Szene *f;* ~ *of tenses gr.* Zeitenfolge *f;* **se·quent** [~t] (aufeinander)folgend.

se·ques·trate ⚖ [sɪ'kwestreɪt] *Eigentum* einziehen; beschlagnahmen.

ser·e·nade ♪ [serə'neɪd] **1.** Serenade *f,* Ständchen *n;* **2.** j-m ein Ständchen bringen.

se·rene □ [sɪ'riːn] klar; heiter; ruhig; **se·ren·i·ty** [sɪ'renətɪ] Heiterkeit *f;* Ruhe *f.*

ser·geant ['sɑːdʒənt] ✕ Feldwebel *m;* (Polizei)Wachtmeister *m.*

se·ri·al □ ['sɪərɪəl] **1.** serienmäßig, Reihen..., Serien..., Fortsetzungs...; **2.** Fortsetzungsroman *m;* (Hörspiel-, Fernseh)Folge *f,* Serie *f.*

se·ries ['sɪərɪːz] (*pl. -ries*) Reihe *f;* Serie *f;* Folge *f.*

se·ri·ous □ ['sɪərɪəs] ernst; ernsthaft, ernstlich; ⚠ *nicht seriös; be ~* es ernst meinen (*about* mit); **~ness** [~nɪs] Ernst(haftigkeit *f*) *m.*

ser·mon ['sɜːmən] *eccl.* Predigt *f; iro.* (Moral-, Straf)Predigt *f.*

ser·pent *zo.* ['sɜːpənt] Schlange *f;* **~·pen·tine** [~aɪn] schlangenförmig;

gewunden, kurvenreich, Serpenti-
nen...

se·rum ['sɪərəm] (*pl.* *-rums*, *-ra*
[-rə]) Serum *n*.

ser·vant ['sɜːvənt] *a.* domestic ∼
Diener(in), Hausangestellte(r *m*) *f*;
Dienstbote *m*, -mädchen *n*, Bedien-
stete(r *m*) *f*; civil ∼ *s.* civil; public ∼
Staatsbeamt(er, -in); Angestellte(r *m*)
f im öffentlichen Dienst.

serve [sɜːv] **1.** *v/t.* dienen (*dat.*);
Dienstzeit (*a.* ✕) ableisten; *Lehre*
machen; *Strafe* verbüßen; genügen (*dat.*); *j-n*, *Kunden* bedienen;
Essen servieren, auftragen, reichen;
Getränk servieren, einschenken;
versorgen (*with* mit); *j-n schändlich*
behandeln; nützen, dienlich sein
(*dat.*); *Zweck* erfüllen; *Tennis etc.*:
Ball aufschlagen; *Volleyball*: *Ball*
aufgeben; (*it*) ∼*s him right* (das)
geschieht ihm ganz recht; ∼ *out et.*
aus-, verteilen; *v/i.* dienen (*a.* ✕; *as*,
for als); *econ.* bedienen; nützen; genügen; *Tennis etc.*: aufschlagen;
Volleyball: aufgeben; ∼ *at table* (bei
Tisch) servieren, bedienen; **2.** *Tennis etc.*: Aufschlag *m*.

ser·vice ['sɜːvɪs] **1.** Dienst *m*; *econ. etc.*
Bedienung *f*; Gefälligkeit *f*; Gottesdienst *m*; Versorgung(sdienst *m*,
-sbetrieb *m*) *f*; ✕ (Wehr-, Militär-)
Dienst *m*; ⊕ Wartung *f*, *mot. a.*
Inspektion *f*; Service *m*, Kunden-
dienst *m*; (Zug- *etc.*)Verkehr *m*; Service *n*; *Tennis etc.*: Aufschlag *m*;
Volleyball: Aufgabe *f*; *be at s.o.'s* ∼
j-m zur Verfügung stehen; **2.** ⊕
warten, pflegen; **∼·vi·cea·ble** □
[∼əbl] brauchbar, nützlich, praktisch; strapazierfähig; ∼ **ar·e·a** Brt.
(Autobahn)Raststätte *f*; ∼ **charge**
Bedienungszuschlag *m*; Bearbei-
tungsgebühr *f*; ∼ **sta·tion** Tankstelle
f; (Reparatur)Werkstatt *f*.

ser·vile □ ['sɜːvaɪl] sklavisch (*a. fig.*);
unterwürfig, kriecherisch; **∼·vil·i·ty**
[sɜː'vɪlətɪ] Unterwürfigkeit *f*, Krie-
cherei *f*.

serv·ing ['sɜːvɪŋ] Portion *f*.

serv·i·tude ['sɜːvɪtjuːd] Knechtschaft *f*; Sklaverei *f*.

ses·sion ['seʃn] Sitzung(speriode) *f*;
be in ∼ *parl.* tagen.

set [set] **1.** (*-tt-*; *set*) *v/t.* setzen;
stellen; legen; *in e-n Zustand* (ver-)
setzen, bringen; veranlassen zu;
ein-, herrichten, ordnen; ⊕ (ein-)

stellen; *Uhr*, *Wecker* stellen; *Edelstein* fassen; besetzen (*with* mit *Edel-
steinen*); *Flüssigkeit* erstarren lassen;
Haar legen; ✂ *Bruch*, *Knochen* einrenken, -richten; ♪ vertonen; *print.*
absetzen; *Aufgabe* stellen; *Zeitpunkt*, *Preis* festsetzen; *Rekord* aufstellen; ∼ *s.o. laughing* j-n zum
Lachen bringen; ∼ *an example* ein
Beispiel geben; ∼ *one's hopes on* s-e
Hoffnung setzen auf (*acc.*); ∼ *the
table* den Tisch decken; ∼ *one's
teeth* die Zähne zusammenbeißen; ∼
at ease beruhigen; ∼ *s.o.'s mind at
rest* j-n beruhigen; ∼ *great (little)
store by* großen (geringen) Wert
legen auf (*acc.*); ∼ *aside* beiseite
legen, weglegen; ✂ aufheben; verwerfen; ∼ *forth* darlegen; ∼ *off* hervorheben; ∼ *up* errichten; aufstellen;
einrichten, gründen; *Regierung* bilden; *j-n* etablieren; *v/i.* untergehen
(*Sonne etc.*); gerinnen, fest werden;
erstarren (*a. Gesicht*, *Muskel*); ✂ *sich*
einrenken; *hunt.* vorstehen (*Hund*);
∼ *about doing s.th.* sich daranma-
chen, et. zu tun; ∼ *about s.o.* F über
j-n herfallen; ∼ *forth* aufbrechen; ∼ *in*
einsetzen (beginnen); ∼ *off* aufbrechen; ∼ *on* angreifen; ∼ *out* aufbrechen; ∼ *to* sich daran machen (*to do*
zu tun); ∼ *up* sich niederlassen; ∼ *up
as* sich ausgeben für; **2.** fest; starr;
festgesetzt, bestimmt; bereit, entschlossen; vorgeschrieben; ∼ *fair*
Barometer: beständig; ∼ *phrase* fest-
stehender Ausdruck; ∼ *speech*
wohlüberlegte Rede; **3.** Satz *m*, Garnitur *f*; Service *n*; Set *n*, *m* (*Platz-
deckchen*); gesammelte Ausgabe (*e-s
Autors*); (Schriften)Reihe *f*, (Artikel)Serie *f*; *Radio*, *TV*: Gerät *n*,
Apparat *m*; *thea.* Bühnenausstat-
tung *f*; *Film*: Szenenaufbau *m*; *Tennis*: Satz *m*; *hunt.* Vorstehen *n*
(*Hund*); ✔ Setzling *m*; (Personen-)
Kreis *m*, *contp.* Clique *f*; Sitz *m*,
Schnitt *m* (*Kleidung*); *poet.* Untergang *m* (*Sonne*); *fig.* Richtung *f*, Tendenz *f*; *have a shampoo and* ∼ sich
die Haare waschen und legen lassen;
∼·back *fig.* ['setbæk] Rückschlag *m*.

set·tee [se'tiː] kleines Sofa.

set the·o·ry ♣ ['set 'θɪərɪ] Mengen-
lehre *f*.

set·ting ['setɪŋ] Setzen *n*; Einrichten
n; Fassung *f* (*Edelstein*); Gedeck *n*;
⊕ Einstellung *f*; *thea.* Bühnenbild *n*;

Film: Ausstattung *f;* ♪ Vertonung *f;* (*Sonnen-* etc.)Untergang *m;* Umgebung *f;* Schauplatz *m; fig.* Rahmen *m.*

set·tle ['setl] **1.** Sitzbank *f;* **2.** *v/t.* vereinbaren, abmachen, festsetzen; erledigen, in Ordnung bringen, regeln; *Frage* etc. klären, entscheiden; *Geschäft* abschließen; *Rechnung* begleichen; *econ. Konto* ausgleichen; *Streit* beilegen; *a. ~ down* beruhigen; *Kind* versorgen; *j-n* beruflich; *häuslich* unterbringen; vermachen (*on dat.*); *Rente* aussetzen (*on dat.*); ansiedeln; *Land* besiedeln; *~ o.s.* sich niederlassen; *~ one's affairs* s-e Angelegenheiten (*vor dem Tode*) in Ordnung bringen; *that ~s it* F damit ist der Fall erledigt; *that's ~d* then das ist also klar; *v/i.* sich niederlassen *od.* setzen; *a. ~ down* sich ansiedeln *od.* niederlassen; sich (*häuslich*) niederlassen; sich senken (*Grundmauern* etc.); beständig werden (*Wetter*); *a. ~ down fig.* sich beruhigen, sich legen; sich setzen (*Trübstoffe*); sich klären (*Flüssigkeit*); sich legen (*Staub*); *~ back* sich (gemütlich) zurücklehnen; *~ down to* sich widmen (*dat.*); *~ in* sich einrichten; sich einleben *od.* eingewöhnen; *~ upon* sich entschließen zu; *~d fest;* geregelt (*Leben*); beständig (*Wetter*); **~·ment** [~mǝnt] (Be)Siedlung *f;* Klärung *f,* Erledigung *f;* Übereinkunft *f,* Abmachung *f;* Bezahlung *f;* Schlichtung *f,* Beilegung *f;* ⚖ (*Eigentums*)Übertragung *f;* **~·r** [~ǝ] Siedler *m.*

sev·en ['sevn] **1.** sieben; **2.** Sieben *f;* **~·teen** [~'ti:n] **1.** siebzehn; **2.** Siebzehn *f;* **~·teenth** [~θ] siebzehnte(r, -s); **~·th** ['sevnθ] **1.** □ sieb(en)te(r, -s); **2.** Sieb(en)tel *n;* **~·th·ly** [~lI] sieb(en)tens; **~·ti·eth** [~tIIθ] siebzigste(r, -s); **~·ty** [~tI] **1.** siebzig; **2.** Siebzig *f.*

sev·er ['sevǝ] (sich) trennen; zerreißen; *fig.* (auf)lösen.

sev·e·ral □ ['sevrǝl] mehrere; verschieden; einige; einzeln; eigen; getrennt; **~·ly** [~lI] einzeln, gesondert, getrennt.

sev·er·ance ['sevǝrǝns] (Ab)Trennung *f; fig.* (Auf)Lösung *f,* Abbruch *m.*

se·vere □ [sI'vIǝ] (~r, ~st) streng; scharf; hart; rauh (*Wetter*); hart

(*Winter*); ernst, finster (*Ausdruck* etc.); heftig (*Schmerz* etc.); schlimm, schwer (*Krankheit* etc.); **se·ver·i·ty** [sI'verǝtI] Strenge *f,* Härte *f;* Heftigkeit *f,* Stärke *f;* Ernst *m.*

sew [sǝʊ] (*sewed, sewn od. sewed*) nähen; heften.

sew·age ['sju:tIdʒ] Abwasser *n.*

sew·er¹ ['sǝʊǝ] Näherin *f.*

sew·er² [sjʊǝ] Abwasserkanal *m;* **~·age** ['sjʊǝrIdʒ] Kanalisation *f.*

sew·ing ['sǝʊIŋ] Nähen *n;* Näharbeit *f; attr.* Näh...; **~n** [sǝʊn] *p.p. von* sew.

sex [seks] Geschlecht *n;* Sexualität *f;* Sex *m.*

sex·ton ['sekstǝn] Küster *m* (u. Totengräber *m*).

sex·u·al □ ['seksjʊǝl] geschlechtlich, Geschlechts..., sexuell, Sexual...; *~ intercourse* Geschlechtsverkehr *m;* **~·y** F [~I] (*-ier, -iest*) sexy, aufreizend.

shab·by □ ['ʃæbI] (*-ier, -iest*) schäbig; gemein.

shack [ʃæk] Hütte *f,* Bude *f.*

shack·le ['ʃækl] **1.** Fessel *f* (*fig. mst pl.*); **2.** fesseln.

shade [ʃeId] **1.** Schatten *m* (*a. fig.*); (*Lampen-* etc.)Schirm *m;* Schattierung *f; Am.* Rouleau *n; fig.* Nuance *f; fig.* F Spur *f;* **2.** beschatten; verdunkeln (*a. fig.*); abschirmen; schützen; schattieren; *~ off* allmählich übergehen (lassen) (*into in acc.*).

shad·ow ['ʃædǝʊ] **1.** Schatten *m* (*a. fig.*); Phantom *n; fig.* Spur *f;* **2.** *e-n* Schatten werfen auf (*acc.*); *fig. j-n* beschatten, überwachen; **~·y** [~I] (*-ier, -iest*) schattig, dunkel; unbestimmt, vage.

shad·y □ ['ʃeIdI] (*-ier, -iest*) schattenspendend; schattig, dunkel; F zweifelhaft.

shaft [ʃɑːft] Schaft *m;* Stiel *m; poet.* Pfeil *m* (*a. fig.*); *poet.* Strahl *m;* ⊕ Welle *f;* Deichsel *f;* ⚒ Schacht *m.*

shag·gy ['ʃægI] (*-ier, -iest*) zottig.

shake [ʃeIk] **1.** (*shook, shaken*) *v/t.* schütteln; rütteln an (*dat.*); erschüttern; *~ down* herunterschütteln; *~ hands* sich die Hand geben *od.* schütteln; *~ off* abschütteln (*a. fig.*); *~ up* Bett aufschütteln; *fig.* aufrütteln; *v/i.* zittern, beben, wackeln, (sch)wanken (*with vor dat.*); ♪ trillern; *~ down* kampieren; **2.** Schütteln *n;* Erschütterung *f;* Beben *n;* ♪

Triller m; (*Milch- etc.*)Shake m; **~down** ['ʃeɪkdaʊn] **1.** (Behelfs-) Lager n; *Am.* F Erpressung f; *Am.* F Durchsuchung f; **2.** *adj.*: ~ *flight* ✈ Testflug m; ~ *voyage* ⚓ Testfahrt f; **shak·en** [~ən] *p.p. von* shake 1; 2. *adj.* erschüttert.

shak·y □ ['ʃeɪkɪ] (*-ier, -iest*) wack(e)lig (*a. fig.*); (sch)wankend; zitternd; zitt(e)rig.

shall v/*aux.* [ʃæl] (*pret. should; verneint:* ~ *not,* shan't) ich, du *etc.* soll(st) *etc.*; *ich werde, wir werden.*

shal·low ['ʃæləʊ] **1.** □ seicht; flach; *fig.* oberflächlich; **2.** seichte Stelle, Untiefe f; **3.** (sich) verflachen.

sham [ʃæm] **1.** falsch; Schein...; **2.** (Vor)Täuschung f, Heuchelei f; Fälschung f; Schwindler(in); △ *nicht* Scham; **3.** (*-mm-*) v/*t.* vortäuschen; v/*i.* sich verstellen, simulieren; ~ *ill* sich krank stellen.

sham·ble ['ʃæmbl] watscheln; **~s** *sg.* Schlachtfeld n, wüstes Durcheinander, Chaos n.

shame [ʃeɪm] **1.** Scham f; Schande f; *for* ~!, ~ *on you!* pfui!, schäm dich!; *put to* ~ beschämen; **2.** beschämen; *j-m* Schande machen; **~faced** □ ['ʃeɪmfeɪst] schamhaft, schüchtern; **~ful** □ [~fl] schändlich, beschämend; **~less** □ [~lɪs] schamlos.

sham·poo [ʃæm'puː] **1.** Shampoo n, Schampon n, Schampun n; Kopf-, Haarwäsche f; *s. set* 3; **2.** Kopf, Haare waschen; *j-m* den Kopf *od.* die Haare waschen.

sham·rock ♣ ['ʃæmrɒk] Kleeblatt n.

shank [ʃæŋk] (Unter)Schenkel m, Schienbein n; △ *nicht* (Ober)Schenkel; ♣ Stiel m; (⚓ Anker)Schaft m.

shan·ty ['ʃæntɪ] Hütte f, Bude f; Seemannslied n.

shape [ʃeɪp] **1.** Gestalt f, Form f (*a. fig.*); *körperliche od. geistige* Verfassung; **2.** v/*t.* gestalten, formen, bilden; anpassen (*to dat.*); v/*i.* *a.* ~ *up* sich entwickeln; **~d** [~t] ...förmig; **~less** ['ʃeɪplɪs] formlos; **~ly** [~lɪ] (*-ier, -iest*) wohlgeformt.

share [ʃeə] **1.** (An)Teil m; Beitrag m; *econ.* Aktie f; ⚔ Kux m; ✒ Pflugschar f; *have a* ~ *in* Anteil haben an (*dat.*); *go* ~*s* teilen; **2.** v/*t.* teilen; v/*i.* teilhaben (*in an dat.*); **~·crop·per** ['ʃeəkrɒpə] *kleiner Farmpächter (in den USA)*; **~·hold·er** *econ.* Aktionär(in).

shark [ʃɑːk] *zo.* Hai(fisch) m; Gauner m, Betrüger m; (*Kredit- etc.*)Hai m; *Am. sl.* Kanone f (*Könner*).

sharp [ʃɑːp] **1.** □ scharf (*a. fig.*); spitz; steil, jäh; schneidend, stechend; heftig; hitzig; beißend, scharf; durchdringend, schrill; schnell; pfiffig, schlau, gerissen; ♪ (*um e-n Halbton*) erhöht; *C* ~ ♪ Cis n; **2.** *adv.* scharf; jäh, plötzlich; ♪ zu hoch; pünktlich, genau; *at eight o'clock* ~ Punkt 8 (Uhr); *look* ~! F paß auf!, gib acht!; F *mach fix od.* schnell!; **3.** ♪ Kreuz n; ♪ durch ein Kreuz erhöhte Note; F Gauner m; **~·en** ['ʃɑːpən] (ver)schärfen; spitzen; verstärken; **~·en·er** [~ə] (*Messer*)Schärfer m; (*Bleistift*)Spitzer m; **~·er** [~ə] Gauner m, Schwindler m; Falschspieler m; **~·eyed** [~'aɪd] scharfsichtig; *fig. a.* scharfsinnig; **~·ness** [~nɪs] Schärfe f (*a. fig.*); **~·shoot·er** Scharfschütze m; **~·sight·ed** [~'saɪtɪd] scharfsichtig; *fig. a.* scharfsinnig; **~·wit·ted** [~'wɪtɪd] scharfsinnig.

shat·ter ['ʃætə] zerschmettern, -schlagen; *Gesundheit, Nerven* zerstören, -rütten.

shave [ʃeɪv] **1.** (shaved, shaved *od. als adj.* shaven) (sich) rasieren; (ab-) schaben; (glatt)hobeln; streifen; *a.* knapp vorbeikommen an (*dat.*); **2.** Rasieren n, Rasur f; *have* (*od. get*) *a* ~ sich rasieren (lassen); *have a close od. narrow* ~ mit knapper Not davonkommen *od.* entkommen; *that was a close* ~ das ist gerade noch einmal gutgegangen!; **shav·en** ['ʃeɪvn] *p.p. von* shave 1; **shav·ing** [~ɪŋ] **1.** Rasieren n; **~s** *pl.* (*bsd.* Hobel)Späne *pl.*; **2.** Rasier...

shawl [ʃɔːl] Umhängetuch n; Kopftuch n.

she [ʃiː] **1.** sie; **2.** Sie f; *zo.* Weibchen n; **3.** *adj. in Zssgn, bsd. zo.*: weiblich, ...weiblich-, ...in; **~·dog** Hündin f; **~·goat** Geiß f.

sheaf [ʃiːf] (*pl.* sheaves) ✒ Garbe f; Bündel n.

shear [ʃɪə] **1.** (sheared, shorn *od.* sheared) scheren; **2.** (*a pair of*) ~*s pl.* (e-e) große Schere.

sheath [ʃiːθ] (*pl.* sheaths [~ðz]) Scheide f; Futteral n, Hülle f; **~e** [ʃiːð] in die Scheide *od.* in ein Futteral stecken; *bsd.* ⊕ umhüllen.

sheaves [ʃiːvz] *pl. von* sheaf.

she·bang *bsd. Am. sl.* [ʃəˈbæŋ]: *the whole* ~ der ganze Kram.

shed[1] [ʃed] (*-dd-*; *shed*) aus-, vergießen; verbreiten; *Blätter etc.* abwerfen.

shed[2] [⁓] Schuppen *m*; Stall *m*.

sheen [ʃiːn] Glanz *m* (*bsd. Stoff*).

sheep [ʃiːp] (*pl. sheep*) *zo.* Schaf *n*; Schafleder *n*; **~·dog** *zo.* [ˈʃiːpdɒg] Schäferhund *m*; **~·fold** Schafhürde *f*; **~·ish** □ [⁓ɪʃ] einfältig; verlegen; **~·man** (*pl. -men*) *Am.*, **~·mas·ter** *Brt.* Schafzüchter *m*; **~·skin** Schaffell *n*; Schafleder *n*; *Am.* F Diplom *n*.

sheer [ʃɪə] rein; bloß; glatt; hauchdünn; steil; senkrecht; direkt.

sheet [ʃiːt] Bett-, Leintuch *n*, Laken *n*; (*Glas- etc.*)Platte *f*; ⊕ ...blech *n*; Blatt *n*, Bogen *m* (*Papier*); weite Fläche (*Wasser etc.*); ⚓ Schot(e) *f*, Segelleine *f*; *the rain came down in* ~*s* es regnete in Strömen; **~ i·ron** ⊕ Eisenblech *n*; **~ light·ning** Wetterleuchten *n*.

shelf [ʃelf] (*pl. shelves*) (Bücher-, Wand- *etc.*)Brett *n*, Regal *n*, Fach *n*; Riff *n*; *on the* ~ *fig.* ausrangiert.

shell [ʃel] **1.** Schale *f*; ⚕ Hülse *f*, Schote *f*; Muschel *f*; Schneckenhaus *n*; *zo.* Panzer *m*; Gerüst *n*, Gerippe *n*, *arch. a.* Rohbau *m*; ⚔ Granate *f*; (Geschoß-, Patronen)Hülse *f*; *Am.* Patrone *f*; **2.** schälen; enthülsen; ⚔ (mit Granaten) beschießen; **~·fire** [ˈʃelfaɪə] Granatfeuer *n*; **~·fish** *zo.* Schal(en)tier *n*; ~ *pl.* Meeresfrüchte *pl.*; ⚠ *nicht Schellfisch*; **~·proof** bombensicher.

shel·ter [ˈʃeltə] **1.** Schutzhütte *f*, -raum *m*, -dach *n*; Zufluchtsort *m*; Obdach *n*; Schutz *m*, Zuflucht *f*; *take* ~ Schutz suchen; *bus* ~ Wartehäuschen *n*; **2.** *v/t.* (be)schützen; beschirmen; *j-m* Schutz *od.* Zuflucht gewähren; *v/i.* Schutz *od.* Zuflucht suchen.

shelve [ʃelv] *v/t.* in ein Regal stellen; *fig. et.* auf die lange Bank schieben; *fig. et.* zurückstellen; *v/i.* sanft abfallen (*Land*).

shelves [ʃelvz] *pl. von shelf.*

she·nan·i·gans F [ʃɪˈnænɪgəns] *pl.* Blödsinn *m*, Mumpitz *m*; übler Trick.

shep·herd [ˈʃepəd] **1.** Schäfer *m*, Hirt *m*; **2.** hüten; führen; leiten.

sher·iff *Am.* [ˈʃerɪf] Sheriff *m*.

shield [ʃiːld] **1.** (Schutz)Schild *m*;

Wappenschild *m*, *n*; *fig.* Schutz *m*; **2.** (be)schützen (*from vor dat.*); *j-n* decken.

shift [ʃɪft] **1.** Veränderung *f*, Verschiebung *f*, Wechsel *m*; Notbehelf *m*; List *f*, Kniff *m*, Ausflucht *f*; (Arbeits)Schicht *f*; *work in* ~*s* Schicht arbeiten; *make* ~ es fertigbringen (*to do zu tun*); sich behelfen; sich durchschlagen; **2.** *v/t.* (um-, aus)wechseln, verändern; *a. fig.* verlagern, -schieben, -legen; *Schuld etc.* (ab)schieben (*onto auf acc.*); ~ *gear(s) bsd. Am. mot.* schalten; *v/i.* wechseln; sich verlagern *od.* -schieben; *bsd. Am. mot.* schalten (*into, to in acc.*); ~ *from one foot to the other* von e-m Fuß auf den anderen treten; ~ *in one's chair* auf s-m Stuhl *ungeduldig etc.* hin u. her rutschen; ~ *for o.s.* sich selbst (weiter)helfen; **~·less** □ [ˈʃɪftlɪs] hilflos; faul; **~·y** □ [⁓ɪ] (*-ier, -iest*) *fig.* gerissen; verschlagen; unzuverlässig.

shil·ling [ˈʃɪlɪŋ] *altes englisches Währungssystem:* Schilling *m*.

shin [ʃɪn] **1.** *a.* **~·bone** Schienbein *n*; **2.** (*-nn-*) ~ *up* hinaufklettern.

shine [ʃaɪn] **1.** Schein *m*; Glanz *m*; **2.** *v/i.* (*shone*) scheinen; leuchten; *fig.* glänzen, strahlen; *v/t.* (*shined*) polieren, putzen.

shin·gle [ˈʃɪŋgl] Schindel *f*; *Am.* F (Firmen)Schild *n*; grober Strandkies; ~*s sg.* ⚕ Gürtelrose *f*.

shin·y [ˈʃaɪnɪ] (*-ier, -iest*) blank, glänzend.

ship [ʃɪp] Schiff *n*; F Flugzeug *n*; F Raumschiff *n*; **2.** (*-pp-*) ⚓ an Bord nehmen *od.* bringen; ⚓ verschiffen; *econ.* transportieren, versenden; ⚓ (an)heuern; ⚓ sich anheuern lassen; **~·board** ⚓ [ˈʃɪpbɔːd]: *on* ~ an Bord; **~·ment** [⁓mənt] Verschiffung *f*; Versand *m*; Schiffsladung *f*; **~·own·er** Reeder *m*; **~·ping** [⁓ɪŋ] Verschiffung *f*; Versand *m*; *coll.* Schiffe *pl.*, Flotte *f*; *attr.* Schiffs...; Versand...; **~·wreck** Schiffbruch *m*; **~·wrecked 1.** *be* ~ schiffbrüchig werden *od.* sein; **2.** schiffbrüchig, *fig. a.* gescheitert; **~·yard** (Schiffs-)Werft *f*.

shire [ʃaɪə, *in Zssgn:* ...ʃə] Grafschaft *f*.

shirk [ʃɜːk] sich drücken (*vor dat.*); **~·er** [ˈʃɜːkə] Drückeberger(in).

S

shirt [ʃɜːt] (Herren-, Ober)Hemd n; a. ~ blouse Hemdbluse f; ~sleeve ['ʃɜːtsliːv] 1. Hemdsärmel m; 2. hemdsärmelig; leger, ungezwungen; ~waist Am. Hemdbluse f.

shit ∨ [ʃɪt] 1. Scheiße f (a. fig.); Scheißen n; 2. (-tt-; shit) scheißen.

shiv·er ['ʃɪvə] 1. Splitter m; Schauer m, Zittern n, Frösteln n; 2. zersplittern; zittern, (er)schauern, frösteln; ~·y [~rɪ] fröstelnd.

shoal [ʃəʊl] 1. Schwarm m (bsd. von Fischen); Masse f; Untiefe f, seichte Stelle; Sandbank f; 2. flach(er) werden.

shock [ʃɒk] 1. Garbenhaufen m; (Haar)Schopf m; (heftiger) Stoß; (a. seelische) Erschütterung; Schock m; Schreck m, (plötzlicher) Schlag (to für); ⚡ (Nerven)Schock m; 2. erschüttern; fig. schockieren, empören; ~·ab·sorb·er ⊕ Stoßdämpfer m; ~·ing □ ['ʃɒkɪŋ] schockierend, empörend, anstößig; haarsträubend; F scheußlich.

shod [ʃɒd] pret. u. p.p. von shoe 2.

shod·dy ['ʃɒdɪ] 1. Reißwolle f; fig. Schund m; 2. (-ier, -iest) falsch; minderwertig, schäbig.

shoe [ʃuː] 1. Schuh m; Hufeisen n; 2. (shod) beschuhen; beschlagen; ~·black ['ʃuːblæk] Schuhputzer m; ~horn Schuhanzieher m; ~lace Schnürsenkel m; ~mak·er Schuhmacher m; ~shine bsd. Am. Schuhputzen n; ~ boy Am. Schuhputzer m; ~string Schnürsenkel m.

shone [ʃɒn, Am. ʃəʊn] pret. u. p.p. von shine 2.

shook [ʃʊk] pret. von shake 1.

shoot [ʃuːt] 1. Jagd f; Jagd(revier n) f; Jagdgesellschaft f; ♀ Schößling m, (Seiten)Trieb m; 2. (shot) v/t. (ab)schießen; erschießen; werfen, stoßen; fotografieren, aufnehmen, Film drehen; unter e-r Brücke etc. hindurchschießen; über et. hinwegschießen; ♀ treiben; ⚡ (ein)spritzen; ~ up sl. Heroin etc. drücken; v/i. schießen; jagen; stechen (Schmerz); (dahin-, vorbei- etc.)schießen; (-)jagen, (-)rasen; ♀ sprießen, keimen; fotografieren; filmen; ~ ahead of überholen (acc.); ~·er ['ʃuːtə] Schütze, -in; F Schießeisen n (Schußwaffe).

shoot·ing ['ʃuːtɪŋ] 1. Schießen n; Schießerei f; Erschießung f; Jagd f;

Film: Dreharbeiten pl.; 2. stechend (Schmerz); ~·gal·ler·y Schießstand m, -bude f; ~·range Schießplatz m; ~ star Sternschnuppe f.

shop [ʃɒp] 1. Laden m, Geschäft n; Werkstatt f; Betrieb m; talk ~ fachsimpeln; 2. (-pp-) mst go ~ping einkaufen gehen; ~ as·sis·tant Brt. ['ʃɒpəsɪstənt] Verkäufer(in); ~·keep·er Ladenbesitzer(in); ~·lift·er [~lɪftə] Ladendieb(in); ~·lift·ing [~lɪŋ] Ladendiebstahl m; ~·per [~ə] Käufer(in); ~·ping [~ɪŋ] 1. Einkauf m, Einkaufen n; Einkäufe pl. (Ware); do one's ~ (s-e) Einkäufe machen; 2. Laden..., Einkaufs...; ~ bag Am. Trag(e)tasche f; ~ centre (Am. center) Einkaufszentrum n; ~ street Geschäfts-, Ladenstraße f; ~·stew·ard [~'stjuːəd] gewerkschaftlicher Vertrauensmann; ~·walk·er Brt. [~wɔːkə] Aufsicht(sperson) f (im Kaufhaus); ~·win·dow Schaufenster n.

shore [ʃɔː] 1. Küste f, Ufer n, Strand m; Strebebalken m, Stütze f; on ~ an Land; 2. ~ up abstützen.

shorn [ʃɔːn] p.p. von shear 1.

short [ʃɔːt] 1. adj. kurz; klein; knapp; kurz angebunden, barsch (with gegen); mürbe (Gebäck); stark, unverdünnt (alkoholisches Getränk); in ~ kurz(um); ~ of knapp an (dat.); 2. adv. plötzlich, jäh, abrupt; ~ of abgesehen von, außer (dat.); come od. fall ~ of et. nicht erreichen; cut ~ plötzlich unterbrechen; stop ~ plötzlich innehalten, stutzen; stop ~ of zurückschrecken vor (dat.); s. run 1; ~·age ['ʃɔːtɪdʒ] Fehlbetrag m; Knappheit f, Mangel m (of an dat.); ~·com·ing [~'kʌmɪŋ] Unzulänglichkeit f; Fehler m, Mangel m; ~ cut Abkürzung(sweg m) f; take a ~ (den Weg) abkürzen; ~·dat·ed econ. kurzfristig; ~·dis·tance Nah...; ~·en ['ʃɔːtn] v/t. (ab-, ver)kürzen; v/i. kürzer werden; ~·en·ing [~ɪŋ] Backfett n; ~·hand ['ʃɔːthænd] Kurzschrift f; ~ typist Stenotypistin f; ~·ly [~lɪ] adv. kurz; bald; ~·ness [~nɪs] Kürze f; Mangel m; Schroffheit f; ~s pl. (a pair of ~s) Shorts pl.; bsd. Am. (e-e) (Herren)Unterhose; ~·sight·ed □ ['ʃɔːt'saɪtɪd] kurzsichtig (a. fig.); ~·term econ. ['ʃɔːtɜːm] kurzfristig; ~ wave ⚡ Kurzwelle f; ~·wind·ed □ ['ʃɔːt'wɪndɪd] kurzatmig.

S

shot [ʃɒt] **1.** *pret. u. p.p. von* shoot 2; **2.** Schuß *m*; Abschuß *m*; Geschoß *n*, Kugel *f*; *a.* small ~ Schrot(kugeln *pl.*) *m*, *n*; Schußweite *f*; *guter etc.* Schütze; *Fußball etc.*: Schuß *m*, *Basketball etc.*: Wurf *m*, *Tennis*, *Golf*: Schlag *m*; *phot.*, *Film*: Aufnahme *f*; 💉 F Spritze *f*, Injektion *f*; F Schuß *m* (*Drogeninjektion*); *fig.* Versuch *m*; *fig.* Vermutung *f*; have a ~ *at et.* versuchen; *not by a long* ~ F noch lange nicht; *big* ~ F großes Tier; ~**gun** [ˈʃɒtgʌn] Schrotflinte *f*; ~ *marriage etc.* wedding F Mußheirat *f*; ~ **put** *Sport*: Kugelstoßen *n*; Stoß *m* (*mit der Kugel*); ~**put·ter** [~pʊtə] *Sport*: Kugelstoßer(in).

should [ʃʊd, ʃəd] *pret. von* shall.

shoul·der [ˈʃəʊldə] **1.** Schulter *f* (*a. v. Tieren*; *fig.* Vorsprung); Achsel *f*; *Am.* Bankett *n* (*Straßenrand*); **2.** auf die Schulter *od.* fig. auf sich nehmen; ✕ schultern; drängen; ~**blade** *anat.* Schulterblatt *n*; ~**strap** Träger *m* (*am Kleid etc.*); ✕ Schulter-, Achselstück *n*.

shout [ʃaʊt] **1.** (lauter) Schrei *od.* Ruf; Geschrei *n*; **2.** (laut) rufen; schreien.

shove [ʃʌv] **1.** Schubs *m*, Stoß *m*; **2.** schieben, stoßen.

shov·el [ˈʃʌvl] **1.** Schaufel *f*; **2.** (*bsd. Brt. -ll-, Am. -l-*) schaufeln.

show [ʃəʊ] **1.** (showed, shown *od.* showed) *v/t.* zeigen; ausstellen; erweisen; beweisen; ~ *in* herein-, hineinführen; ~ *off* zur Geltung bringen; ~ *out* heraus-, hinausführen; -bringen; ~ *round* herumführen; ~ *up* herauf-, hinaufführen; *j-n* bloßstellen; *et.* aufdecken; *v/i. a.* ~ *up* sichtbar werden *od.* sein; sich zeigen; zu sehen sein; ~ *off* angeben, prahlen, sich aufspielen; ~ *up* F auftauchen, sich blicken lassen; **2.** (Her)Zeigen *n*; Zurschaustellung *f*; Ausstellung *f*; Vorführung *f*, -stellung *f*, Schau *f*; F (Theater-, Film-) Vorstellung *f*, (*Rundfunk-*, *Fernseh-*) Sendung *f*, Show *f*; *leerer* Schein; *on* ~ zu besichtigen; ~**biz** F [ˈʃəʊbɪz], ~ **busi·ness** Showbusineß *n*, Showgeschäft *n*, Vergnügungs-, Unterhaltungsbranche *f*; ~**case** Schaukasten *m*, Vitrine *f*; ~**down** Aufdecken *n* der Karten (*a. fig.*); *fig.* Kraftprobe *f*.

show·er [ˈʃaʊə] **1.** (Regen- *etc.*)

Schauer *m*; Dusche *f*; *fig.* Fülle *f*; **2.** *v/t.* überschütten, -häufen; *v/i.* gießen; (sich) brausen *od.* duschen; ~ *down* niederprasseln; ~**y** [~rɪ] (-*ier*, -*iest*) regnerisch.

show-jump·er [ˈʃəʊdʒʌmpə] *Sport*: Springreiter(in); ~**jump·ing** [~ɪŋ] *Sport*: Springreiten *n*; ~**n** [~n] *p.p. von* show 1; ~**room** Ausstellungsraum *m*; ~**win·dow** Schaufenster *n*; ~**y** [~ɪ] [~ɪ] (-*ier*, -*iest*) prächtig; protzig.

shrank [ʃræŋk] *pret. von* shrink.

shred [ʃred] **1.** Stückchen *n*, Fetzen *m* (*a. fig.*); *fig.* Spur *f*; **2.** (-*dd*-) zerfetzen; in Streifen schneiden.

shrew [ʃruː] zänkisches Weib.

shrewd ☐ [ʃruːd] scharfsinnig; schlau.

shriek [ʃriːk] **1.** schriller Schrei; Gekreisch *n*; **2.** kreischen, schreien.

shrill [ʃrɪl] **1.** ☐ schrill, gellend; **2.** schrillen, gellen; *et.* kreischen.

shrimp [ʃrɪmp] *zo.* Garnele *f*, Krabbe *f*; *fig. contp.* Knirps *m*.

shrine [ʃraɪn] Schrein *m*.

shrink [ʃrɪŋk] (*shrank, shrunk*) (ein-, zusammen)schrumpfen (lassen); einlaufen; zurückweichen (*from vor dat.*); zurückschrecken (*from, at vor dat.*); ~**age** [ˈʃrɪŋkɪdʒ] Einlaufen *n*; (Ein-, Zusammen)Schrumpfen *n*; Schrumpfung *f*; *fig.* Verminderung *f*.

shriv·el [ˈʃrɪvl] (*bsd. Brt. -ll-, Am. -l-*) (ein-, zusammen)schrumpfen (lassen), (ver)welken (lassen).

shroud [ʃraʊd] **1.** Leichentuch *n*; *fig.* Schleier *m*; **2.** in ein Leichentuch (ein)hüllen; *fig.* hüllen.

Shrove·tide [ˈʃrəʊvtaɪd] Fastnachts-, Faschingszeit *f*; ~ **Tues·day** Fastnachts-, Faschingsdienstag *m*.

shrub [ʃrʌb] Strauch *m*; Busch *m*; ~**be·ry** [ˈʃrʌbərɪ] Gebüsch *n*.

shrug [ʃrʌg] **1.** (-*gg*-) (die Achseln) zucken; **2.** Achselzucken *n*.

shrunk [ʃrʌŋk] *p.p. von* shrink; ~**en** [ˈʃrʌŋkən] *adj.* (ein-, zusammen)geschrumpft.

shuck *bsd. Am.* [ʃʌk] **1.** Hülse *f*, Schote *f*; ~*s!* F Quatsch!; **2.** enthülsen.

shud·der [ˈʃʌdə] **1.** schaudern; (er-) zittern, (er)beben; **2.** Schauder *m*.

shuf·fle [ˈʃʌfl] **1.** *Karten*: mischen; schlurfen (mit); Ausflüchte machen; △ *nicht schaufeln*; ~ *off Klei-*

dung abstreifen; *fig. Verantwortung etc.* abwälzen (*on, upon* auf *acc.*); **2.** (Karten)Mischen *n*; Schlurfen *n*; Umstellung *f*; (*Kabinetts*)Umbildung *f*; *fig.* Ausflucht *f*, Schwindel *m*.

shun [ʃʌn] (*-nn-*) (ver)meiden.

shunt [ʃʌnt] **1.** 🚂 Rangieren *n*; Weiche *f*; ⚡ Nebenschluß *m*; **2.** 🚂 rangieren; ⚡ nebenschließen; beiseite schieben; *fig. et.* aufschieben.

shut [ʃʌt] (*-tt-; shut*) (sich) schließen; zumachen; ~ *down Betrieb* schließen; ~ *off Wasser, Gas etc.* abstellen; ~ *up* einschließen; *Haus etc.* verschließen; einsperren; ~ *up!* F halt die Klappe!; ~**ter** [ˈʃʌtə] Fensterladen *m*; *phot.* Verschluß *m*; ~ **speed** *phot.* Belichtung(szeit) *f*.

shut·tle [ˈʃʌtl] **1.** ⊕ Schiffchen *n*; Pendelverkehr *m*; *s.* **space** ~; **2.** *etc.* pendeln; ~**cock** *Sport*: Federball *m*; ~ **di·plo·ma·cy** *pol.* Pendeldiplomatie *f*; ~ **ser·vice** Pendelverkehr *m*.

shy [ʃaɪ] **1.** □ (~*er od.* shier, ~*est od.* shiest) scheu; schüchtern; **2.** scheuen (*at vor dat.*); ~ *away from fig.* zurückschrecken vor (*dat.*); ~**ness** [ˈʃaɪnɪs] Schüchternheit *f*; Scheu *f*.

Si·be·ri·an [saɪˈbɪərɪən] **1.** sibirisch; **2.** Sibirier(in).

sick [sɪk] krank (*of an dat.*; *with vor dat.*); überdrüssig (*of gen.*); *fig.* krank (*of von dat.*; *for nach*); *be* ~ sich übergeben (müssen); *be* ~ *of s.th. et.* satt haben; *fall* ~ krank werden; *I feel* ~ mir ist schlecht *od.* übel; *go* ~, *report* ~ sich krank melden; ~**ben·e·fit** *Brt.* [ˈsɪkbenɪfɪt] Krankengeld *n*; ~**en** [~ən] *v/i.* krank werden; kränkeln; ~ *at* sich ekeln vor (*dat.*); *v/t.* krank machen; anekeln.

sick·le [ˈsɪkl] Sichel *f*.

sick-leave [ˈsɪkliːv] Fehlen *n* wegen Krankheit; *be on* ~ wegen Krankheit fehlen; ~**ly** [~lɪ] (*-ier, -iest*) kränklich; schwächlich; bleich, blaß; ungesund (*Klima*); ekelhaft; matt (*Lächeln*); ~**ness** [~nɪs] Krankheit *f*; Übelkeit *f*.

side [saɪd] **1.** Seite *f*; ~ *by* ~ Seite an Seite; *take* ~*s with* Partei ergreifen für; **2.** Seiten...; Neben...; **3.** Partei ergreifen (*with* für); ~**board** [ˈsaɪdbɔːd] Anrichte *f*, Sideboard *n*; ~**car** *mot.* Beiwagen *m*; **sid·ed** ...seitig; ~

dish Beilage *f* (*Essen*); ~**long 1.** *adv.* seitwärts; **2.** *adj.* seitlich; Seiten...; ~**road**, ~**street** Seitenstraße *f*; ~**stroke** *Sport*: Seitenschwimmen *n*; ~**track 1.** 🚂 Nebengleis *n*; **2.** 🚂 auf ein Nebengleis schieben; *fig.* ablenken; ~**walk** *Am.* Bürgersteig *m*; ~**ward(s)** [~wəd(z)], ~**ways** seitlich; seitwärts.

sid·ing [ˈsaɪdɪŋ] Nebengleis *n*.

si·dle [ˈsaɪdl]: ~ *up to s.o.* sich an j-n heranmachen.

siege [siːdʒ] Belagerung *f*; △ *nicht Sieg*; *lay* ~ *to* belagern; *fig. j-n* bestürmen.

sieve [sɪv] **1.** Sieb *n*; **2.** (durch)sieben.

sift [sɪft] sieben; *fig.* sichten, prüfen.

sigh [saɪ] **1.** Seufzer *m*; **2.** seufzen; sich sehnen (*for nach*).

sight [saɪt] **1.** Sehvermögen *n*, Sehkraft *f*, Auge(nlicht) *n*; Anblick *m*; Sicht *f* (*a. econ.*); Visier *n*; *fig.* Auge *n*; ~*s pl.* Sehenswürdigkeiten *pl.*; *at* ~, *on* ~ sofort; *at* ~ vom Blatt (*singen etc.*); *at the* ~ *of* beim Anblick (*gen.*); *at first* ~ auf den ersten Blick; *catch* ~ *of* erblicken; *know by* ~ vom Sehen kennen; *lose* ~ *of* aus den Augen verlieren; (*with*)*in* ~ in Sicht(weite); **2.** sichten, erblicken; (an)visieren; ~**ed** [ˈsaɪtɪd] ...sichtig; ~**ly** [~lɪ] (*-ier, -iest*) ansehnlich, stattlich; ~**see** (*-saw, -seen*): *go* ~*ing* e-e Besichtigungstour machen; ~**see·ing** [~ɪŋ] Besichtigung *f* von Sehenswürdigkeiten; ~ *tour* Besichtigungstour *f*, (Stadt)Rundfahrt *f*; ~**se·er** [~ə] Tourist(in).

sign [saɪn] **1.** Zeichen *n*; Wink *m*; Schild *n*; *in* ~ *of* zum Zeichen (*gen.*); **2.** winken, Zeichen geben; (unter-) zeichnen, unterschreiben.

sig·nal [ˈsɪɡnl] **1.** Signal *n* (*a. fig.*); Zeichen *n*; **2.** bemerkenswert; außerordentlich; **3.** (*bsd. Brt. -ll-, Am. -l-*) (ein) Zeichen geben; signalisieren; ~**ize** [~nəlaɪz] auszeichnen; hervorheben.

sig·na·to·ry [ˈsɪɡnətərɪ] **1.** Unterzeichner(in); **2.** unterzeichnend; ~ *powers pl. pol.* Signatarmächte *pl.*; ~**ture** [~tʃə] Signatur *f*; Unterschrift *f*; ~ *tune Rundfunk, TV:* Kennmelodie *f*.

sign·board [ˈsaɪnbɔːd] (Aushänge-) Schild *n*; ~**er** [~ə] Unterzeichner(in).

sig·net [ˈsɪɡnɪt] Siegel *n*.

S

sig·nif·i|cance [sɪgˈnɪfɪkəns] Bedeutung f; **~cant** □ [~t] bedeutsam; bezeichnend (*of* für); **~ca·tion** [sɪgnɪfɪˈkeɪʃn] Bedeutung f, Sinn m.

sig·ni·fy [ˈsɪgnɪfaɪ] andeuten; zu verstehen geben; bedeuten.

sign·post [ˈsaɪnpəʊst] Wegweiser m.

si·lence [ˈsaɪləns] **1.** (Still)Schweigen n; Stille f, Ruhe f; **~!** Ruhe!; *put od. reduce to* **~** = **2.** zum Schweigen bringen; **si·lenc·er** [~ə] ⊕ Schalldämpfer m; *mot.* Auspufftopf m.

si·lent □ [ˈsaɪlənt] still; schweigend; schweigsam; stumm; **~ partner** *Am. econ.* stiller Teilhaber.

silk [sɪlk] Seide f; *attr.* seiden; **~en** [ˈsɪlkən] seiden, Seiden...; **~stocking** *Am.* vornehm; **~worm** *zo.* Seidenraupe f; **~y** □ [~ɪ] (*-ier, -iest*) seidig, seidenartig.

sill [sɪl] Schwelle f; Fensterbrett n.

sil·ly □ [ˈsɪlɪ] (*-ier, -iest*) albern, töricht, dumm, verrückt.

silt [sɪlt] **1.** Schlamm m; **2.** *mst* **~ up** verschlammen.

sil·ver [ˈsɪlvə] **1.** Silber n; **2.** silbern, Silber...; **3.** versilbern; silb(e)rig *od.* silberweiß werden; **~ plate**, **~ware** Tafelsilber n; **~y** [~ɪ] silberglänzend; *fig.* silberhell.

sim·i·lar □ [ˈsɪmɪlə] ähnlich, gleich; **~i·ty** [sɪmɪˈlærətɪ] Ähnlichkeit f.

sim·i·le [ˈsɪmɪlɪ] Gleichnis n.

si·mil·i·tude [sɪˈmɪlɪtjuːd] Gestalt f, Ebenbild n; Gleichnis n.

sim·mer [ˈsɪmə] leicht kochen, *od.* sieden (lassen); *fig.* kochen (*with* vor *dat.*), gären (*Gefühl, Aufstand*); **~ down** sich beruhigen *od.* abregen.

sim·per [ˈsɪmpə] **1.** einfältiges Lächeln; **2.** einfältig lächeln.

sim·ple □ [ˈsɪmpl] (*~r, ~st*) einfach; schlicht; einfältig; arglos, naiv; **~hearted** arglos, **~minded** einfältig, arglos, naiv; **~ton** [~tən] Einfaltspinsel m.

sim·plic·i·ty [sɪmˈplɪsətɪ] Einfachheit f; Unkompliziertheit f; Schlichtheit f; Einfalt f; **~fi·ca·tion** [sɪmplɪfɪˈkeɪʃn] Vereinfachung f; **~fy** [ˈsɪmplɪfaɪ] vereinfachen.

sim·ply [ˈsɪmplɪ] einfach; bloß.

sim·u·late [ˈsɪmjʊleɪt] vortäuschen; simulieren; ✕, ⊕ *a.* Bedingungen, Vorgänge (wirklichkeitsgetreu) nachahmen.

sim·ul·ta·ne·ous □ [sɪmlˈteɪnjəs] gleichzeitig, simultan.

sin [sɪn] **1.** Sünde f; **2.** (-*nn*-) sündigen.

since [sɪns] **1.** *prp.* seit; **2.** *adv.* seitdem; **3.** *cj.* seit(dem); da (ja).

sin·cere □ [sɪnˈsɪə] aufrichtig, ehrlich, offen; *Yours* **~ly** *Briefschluß:* Mit freundlichen Grüßen; **sin·cer·i·ty** [~ˈserətɪ] Aufrichtigkeit f; Offenheit f.

sin·ew *anat.* [ˈsɪnjuː] Sehne f; **~y** [~juːɪ] sehnig; *fig.* kraftvoll.

sin·ful □ [ˈsɪnfl] sündig, sündhaft.

sing [sɪŋ] (*sang, sung*) singen; **~ to** *s.o.* j-m vorsingen.

singe [sɪndʒ] (ver-, ab)sengen.

sing·er [ˈsɪŋə] Sänger(in).

sing·ing [ˈsɪŋɪŋ] Gesang m, Singen n; **~ bird** Singvogel m.

sin·gle [ˈsɪŋgl] **1.** □ einzig; einzeln; Einzel...; einfach; ledig, unverheiratet; *bookkeeping by* **~ entry** einfache Buchführung; *in* **~ file** im Gänsemarsch; **2.** *Brt.* einfache Fahrkarte, ✓ einfaches Ticket; Single f (*Schallplatte*); Single m, Unverheiratete(r m) f; *Brt.* Einpfund-, Am. Eindollarschein m; **~s sg., pl.** *Tennis:* Einzel n; **3.** **~ out** auswählen, -suchen; **~breast·ed** knapp (*Jacke etc.*); **~en·gined** ✈ einmotorig; **~hand·ed** eigenhändig, allein; **~heart·ed** □, **~mind·ed** □ aufrichtig; zielstrebig.

sin·glet *Brt.* [ˈsɪŋglɪt] ärmelloses Unterhemd *od.* Trikot.

sin·gle-track 🚄 [ˈsɪŋgltræk] eingleisig; F *fig.* einseitig.

sin·gu·lar [ˈsɪŋgjʊlə] **1.** □ einzigartig; eigenartig; sonderbar; **2.** *a.* **~ number** *gr.* Singular m, Einzahl f; **~i·ty** [sɪŋgjʊˈlærətɪ] Einzigartigkeit f; Eigentümlich-, Seltsamkeit f.

sin·is·ter □ [ˈsɪnɪstə] unheilvoll; böse.

sink [sɪŋk] **1.** (*sank, sunk*) *v/i.* sinken; ein-, nieder-, unter-, versinken; sich senken; (ein)dringen, (-)sickern; *v/t.* (ver)senken; *Brunnen* bohren; *Geld* fest anlegen; **2.** Ausguß m, Spüle f; **~ing** [ˈsɪŋkɪŋ] (Ein-, Ver)Sinken n; Versenken n; 🕯 Schwäche(gefühl n) f; *econ.* Tilgung f; **~fund** (Schulden)Tilgungsfonds m.

sin·less □ [ˈsɪnlɪs] sünd(en)los, sündenfrei.

sin·ner [ˈsɪnə] Sünder(in).

sin·u·ous □ [ˈsɪnjʊəs] gewunden.

sip [sɪp] **1.** Schlückchen n; **2.** (-*pp*-)

v/t. nippen an (*dat.*) *od.* von; schlückchenweise trinken; *v/i.* nippen (*at* an *dat. od.* von).

sir [sɜː] Herr *m* (*Anrede*); ♀ [sə] Sir *m* (*Titel*).

sire ['saɪə] *mst poet.* Vater *m*; Vorfahr *m*; *zo.* Vater(tier *n*) *m*.

si·ren ['saɪərən] Sirene *f*.

sir·loin ['sɜːlɔɪn] Lendenstück *n*.

sis·sy F ['sɪsɪ] Weichling *m*.

sis·ter ['sɪstə] (*a.* Ordens-, Ober-, Kranken)Schwester *f*; **~hood** [~hʊd] Schwesternschaft *f*; **~-in-law** [~rɪnlɔ:] (*pl. sisters-in-law*) Schwägerin *f*; **~·ly** [~lɪ] schwesterlich.

sit [sɪt] (*-tt-*; *sat*) *v/i.* sitzen; e-e Sitzung halten, tagen; *fig.* liegen, stehen; **~ down** sich setzen; **~ in** ein Sit-in veranstalten; **~ in for** für j-n einspringen; **~ up** aufrecht sitzen; aufbleiben; *v/t.* sitzen; sitzen auf (*dat.*).

site [saɪt] Lage *f*; Stelle *f*; Stätte *f*; (Bau)Gelände *n*.

sit-in ['sɪtɪn] Sit-in *n*.

sit·ting ['sɪtɪŋ] Sitzung *f*; **~ room** Wohnzimmer *n*.

sit·u·at·ed ['sɪtjʊeɪtɪd] gelegen; *be* **~** liegen, gelegen sein; **~·a·tion** [sɪtjʊ'eɪʃn] Lage *f*; Stellung *f*, Stelle *f*.

six [sɪks] **1.** sechs; **2.** Sechs *f*; **~·teen** ['sɪks'ti:n] **1.** sechzehn; **2.** Sechzehn *f*; **~·teenth** [~θ] sechzehnte(r, -s); **~th** [sɪksθ] **1.** sechste(r, -s); **2.** Sechstel *n*; **~th·ly** ['sɪksθlɪ] sechstens; **~·ti·eth** [~tɪɪθ] sechzigste(r, -s); **~·ty** [~tɪ] **1.** sechzig; **2.** Sechzig *f*.

size [saɪz] **1.** Größe *f*; Format *n*; **2.** nach Größe(n) ordnen; **~ up** F abschätzen; **~d** von *od.* in ... Größe.

siz(e)·a·ble □ ['saɪzəbl] (ziemlich) groß.

siz·zle ['sɪzl] zischen; knistern; brutzeln; *sizzling* (*hot*) glühendheiß.

skate [skeɪt] **1.** Schlittschuh *m*; Rollschuh *m*; **2.** Schlittschuh laufen, eislaufen; Rollschuh laufen; **~·board** ['skeɪtbɔ:d] **1.** Skateboard *n*; **2.** Skateboard fahren; **skat·er** [~ə] Schlittschuhläufer(in); Rollschuhläufer(in); **skat·ing** [~ɪŋ] Schlittschuh-, Eislaufen *n*, Eislauf *m*; Rollschuhlauf(en *n*) *m*.

ske·dad·dle F ['skɪ'dædl] abhauen.

skein [skeɪn] Strang *m*, Docke *f*.

skel·e·ton ['skelɪtn] Skelett *n*; Gerippe *n*; Gestell *n*; *attr.* Skelett...; ✕

Stamm...; **~ key** Nachschlüssel *m*.

skep|tic ['skeptɪk], **~·ti·cal** [~l] *Am.* = *sceptic(al)*.

sketch [sketʃ] **1.** Skizze *f*; Entwurf *m*; *thea.* Sketch *m*; **2.** skizzieren; entwerfen.

ski [ski:] **1.** (*pl. skis, ski*) Schi *m*, Ski *m*; *attr.* Schi..., Ski...; **2.** Schi *od.* Ski laufen *od.* fahren.

skid [skɪd] **1.** Bremsklotz *m*; ✈ (Gleit)Kufe *f*; *mot.* Rutschen *n*, Schleudern *n*; **~ mark** *mot.* Bremsspur *f*; **2.** (*-dd-*) rutschen; schleudern.

skid·doo *Am. sl.* ['skɪ'du:] abhauen.

ski·er ['ski:ə] Schi-, Skiläufer(in); △ *nicht Skier*; **~·ing** [~ɪŋ] Schi-, Skilauf(en *n*) *m*, -fahren *n*, -sport *m*.

skil·ful □ ['skɪlfl] geschickt; geübt.

skill [skɪl] Geschicklichkeit *f*, Fertigkeit *f*; **~ed** geschickt; ausgebildet, Fach...; **~ worker** Facharbeiter *m*.

skill·ful *Am.* □ ['skɪlfl] = *skilful*.

skim [skɪm] **1.** (*-mm-*) abschöpfen; *Milch* entrahmen; (hin)gleiten über (*acc.*); *Buch* überfliegen; **~ through** durchblättern; **2.** **~ milk** Magermilch *f*.

skimp [skɪmp] *j-n* knapphalten, sparen an; knausern (*on* mit); **~·y** □ ['skɪmpɪ] (*-ier, -iest*) knapp; dürftig.

skin [skɪn] **1.** Haut *f*; Fell *n*; Schale *f*; **2.** (*-nn-*) *v/t.* (ent)häuten; abbalgen; schälen; *v/i. a.* **~ over** zuheilen; **~-deep** ['skɪn'di:p] (nur) oberflächlich; **~-diving** Sporttauchen *n*; **~·flint** Knicker *m*; **~·ny** [~ɪ] (*-ier, -iest*) mager; **~·ny-dip** F nackt baden.

skip [skɪp] **1.** Sprung *m*; **2.** (*-pp-*) *v/i.* hüpfen, springen; seilhüpfen; *v/t.* überspringen.

skip·per ['skɪpə] ♣ Schiffer *m*; ♣, ✕, *Sport:* Kapitän *m*.

skir·mish ['skɜ:mɪʃ] **1.** ✕ *u. fig.* Geplänkel *n*; **2.** plänkeln.

skirt [skɜ:t] **1.** (Damen)Rock *m*; (Rock)Schoß *m*; *oft* **~s** *pl.* Rand *m*, Saum *m*; **2.** (um)säumen; (sich) entlangziehen an (*dat.*); **~·ing-board** *Brt.* ['skɜ:tɪŋbɔ:d] Scheuerleiste *f*.

skit [skɪt] Stichelei *f*; Satire *f*; **~·tish** □ ['skɪtɪʃ] ausgelassen; scheu (*Pferd*).

skit·tle ['skɪtl] Kegel *m*; *play* (*at*) **~s** kegeln; **~·al·ley** Kegelbahn *f*.

skulk [skʌlk] (herum)schleichen; lauern; sich drücken.

S

skull [skʌl] Schädel *m*.
skul(l)·dug·ge·ry F [skʌl'dʌgərɪ] Gaunerei *f*.
skunk *zo.* [skʌŋk] Skunk *m*, Stinktier *n*.
sky [skaɪ] *oft* skies *pl.* Himmel *m*; **~·jack** F ['skaɪdʒæk] Flugzeug entführen; **~·jack·er** [~ə] Flugzeugentführer(in); **~·lab** *Am.* Raumlabor *n*; **~·lark** 1. *zo.* Feldlerche *f*; 2. F Blödsinn treiben; **~·light** Oberlicht *n*, Dachfenster *n*; **~·line** Horizont *m*; Silhouette *f*; **~·rock·et** F in die Höhe schießen (*Preise*), sprunghaft ansteigen; **~·scrap·er** Wolkenkratzer *m*; **~·ward(s)** [~wəd(z)] himmelwärts.
slab [slæb] Platte *f*, Fliese *f*; (dicke) Scheibe (*Käse etc.*).
slack [slæk] 1. ☐ schlaff; locker; (nach)lässig; flau (*a.* econ.); 2. ♪ Lose *f* (*schlaffes Taustück*); Flaute *f* (*a.* econ.); Kohlengrus *m*; **~·en** ['slækən] nachlassen; (sich) verringern; (sich) lockern; (sich) entspannen; (sich) verlangsamen; **~s** *pl.* Freizeithose *f*.
slag [slæg] Schlacke *f*.
slain [sleɪn] *p.p. von* slay.
slake [sleɪk] *Kalk* löschen; *Durst* löschen, stillen.
slam [slæm] 1. Zuschlagen *n*; Knall *m*; 2. (-mm-) *Tür etc.* zuschlagen, zuknallen; *et. auf den Tisch etc.* knallen.
slan·der ['slɑːndə] 1. Verleumdung *f*; 2. verleumden; **~·ous** ☐ [~rəs] verleumderisch.
slang [slæŋ] 1. Slang *m*; Berufssprache *f*; lässige Umgangssprache; 2. *j-n* wüst beschimpfen.
slant [slɑːnt] 1. schräge Fläche; Abhang *m*; Neigung *f*; Standpunkt *m*, Einstellung *f*; Tendenz *f*; 2. schräg legen *od.* liegen; sich neigen; **~·ing** *adj.* ☐ ['slɑːntɪŋ], **~·wise** *adv.* [~waɪz] schief, schräg.
slap [slæp] 1. Klaps *m*, Schlag *m*; 2. (-pp-) e-n Klaps geben (*dat.*); schlagen; klatschen; **~·jack** *Am.* ['slæpdʒæk] *Art* Pfannkuchen *m*; **~·stick** (Narren)Pritsche *f*; *a.* ~ comedy *thea.* Slapstickkomödie *f*.
slash [slæʃ] 1. Hieb *m*; Schnitt(wunde *f*) *m*; Schlitz *m*; 2. (auf)schlitzen, schlagen, hauen; *fig.* scharf kritisieren.
slate [sleɪt] 1. Schiefer *m*; Schiefertafel *f*; *bsd. Am. pol.* Kandidatenliste *f*;

2. mit Schiefer decken; *Brt.* F heftig kritisieren; *Am.* F *Kandidaten* aufstellen; **~·pen·cil** ['sleɪt'pensl] Griffel *m*.
slat·tern ['slætən] Schlampe *f*.
slaugh·ter ['slɔːtə] 1. Schlachten *n*; *fig.* Blutbad *n*, Gemetzel *n*; 2. schlachten; *fig.* niedermetzeln; **~·house** Schlachthaus *n*, -hof *m*.
Slav [slɑːv] 1. Slaw|e *m*, -in *f*; 2. slawisch.
slave [sleɪv] 1. Sklav|e *m*, -in *f* (*a.* fig.); 2. sich (ab)placken, schuften.
slav·er ['slævə] 1. Geifer *m*, Sabber *m*; 2. geifern, sabbern.
sla·ve·ry ['sleɪvərɪ] Sklaverei *f*; Plackerei *f*; **slav·ish** ☐ [~ɪʃ] sklavisch.
slay *rhet.* [sleɪ] (*slew, slain*) erschlagen; töten; △ *nicht* slagen.
sled [sled] 1. = sledge[1] 1; 2. (-dd-) = sledge[1] 2.
sledge[1] [sledʒ] 1. Schlitten *m*; 2. Schlitten fahren, rodeln.
sledge[2] [~] *a.* ~·hammer Schmiedehammer *m*.
sleek [sliːk] 1. ☐ glatt, glänzend (*Haar, Fell*); geschmeidig; 2. glätten.
sleep [sliːp] 1. (*slept*) *v/i.* schlafen; ~ (*up*)*on od. over et.* überschlafen; ~ *with* s.o. mit j-m schlafen (*Geschlechtsverkehr haben*); *v/t.* schlafen; *j-n* für die Nacht unterbringen; ~ *away Zeit* verschlafen; 2. Schlaf *m*; *get od. go to* ~ einschlafen; *put to* ~ *Tier* einschläfern; **~·er** ['sliːpə] Schlafende(r *m*) *f*; ♠ Schwelle *f*; ♠ Schlafwagen *m*; **~·ing** [~ɪŋ] schlafend; Schlaf...; Ձing Beau·ty Dornröschen *n*; **~·ing-car(·riage)** ♠ Schlafwagen *m*; **~·ing part·ner** *Brt. econ.* stiller Teilhaber; **~·less** ☐ [~lɪs] schlaflos; **~·walk·er** Schlafwandler(in); **~·y** ☐ [~ɪ] (-ier, -iest) schläfrig; müde; verschlafen.
sleet [sliːt] 1. Schneeregen *m*; Graupelschauer *m*; 2. *it was* ~*ing* es gab Schneeregen; es graupelte.
sleeve [sliːv] Ärmel *m*; ⊕ Muffe *f*; *Brt.* (Schall)Plattenhülle *f*; **~·link** ['sliːvlɪŋk] Manschettenknopf *m*.
sleigh [sleɪ] 1. (*bsd. Pferde*)Schlitten *m*; 2. (im) Schlitten fahren.
sleight [slaɪt]: ~ *of hand* (Taschenspieler)Trick *m*; Fingerfertigkeit *f*.
slen·der ☐ ['slendə] schlank; schmächtig; *fig.* schwach; dürftig.

slow-worm

slept [slept] *pret. u. p.p. von* sleep 1.
sleuth [slu:θ] *a.* ~**hound** Spürhund
m (a. fig. Detektiv).
slew [slu:] *pret. von* slay.
slice [slaıs] **1.** Schnitte *f*, Scheibe *f*,
Stück *n*; (An)Teil *m*; **2.** (in) Scheiben
schneiden; aufschneiden.
slick [slık] **1.** □ *adj.* glatt, glitschig; F
geschickt, raffiniert; **2.** *adv.* direkt;
3. Ölfleck *m*, -teppich *m*; ~**er** *Am.* F
['slıkə] Regenmantel *m*; gerissener
Kerl.
slid [slıd] *pret. u. p.p. von* slide 1.
slide [slaıd] **1.** *(slid)* gleiten (lassen);
rutschen; schlittern; ausgleiten; ~
into fig. in et. hineinschlittern; *let
things* ~ *fig.* die Dinge laufen lassen;
2. Gleiten *n*, Rutschen *n*, Schlittern
n; Rutschbahn *f*; Rutsche *f*; ⊕
Schieber *m*; *phot.* Dia(positiv) *n*;
Brt. (Haar)Spange *f*; *a. land*~ Erdrutsch *m*; ~**rule** ['slaıdru:l] Rechenschieber *m*.
slid·ing □ ['slaıdıŋ] gleitend, rut-
schend; Schiebe...; ~ *time Am. econ.*
Gleitzeit *f*.
slight [slaıt] **1.** □ leicht; schmächtig;
schwach; gering, unbedeutend; **2.**
Geringschätzung *f*; **3.** geringschätzig behandeln; beleidigen, kränken.
slim (-*mm*-) [slım] **1.** □ schlank,
dünn; *fig.* gering, dürftig; *2. e-e*
Schlankheitskur machen, abnehmen.
slime [slaım] Schlamm *m*; Schleim
m; **slim·y** ['slaımı] (-*ier*, -*iest*)
schlammig; schleimig; *fig.* schmierig; kriecherisch.
sling [slıŋ] **1.** (Stein)Schleuder *f*;
Schlinge *f* (*zum Tragen*); Tragrie-
men *m*; ✠ Schlinge *f*, Binde *f*; **2.**
(*slung*) schleudern; auf-, umhän-
gen; *a.* ~ *up* hochziehen; △ *nicht*
schlingen.
slink [slıŋk] (*slunk*) schleichen.
slip [slıp] **1.** (-*pp*-) gleiten (lassen);
rutschen; ausgleiten, -rutschen;
(ver)rutschen; loslassen; ~ *away*
wegschleichen, sich fortstehlen; ~ *in
Bemerkung* dazwischenwerfen; ~ *into* hineinstecken *od.* hineinschieben
in (*acc.*); ~ *off* (*on*) Ring, Kleid *etc.*
abstreifen (überstreifen); ~ *up* (e-n)
Fehler machen; *have* ~*ped s.o.'s
memory od. mind* j-m entfallen sein;
2. (Aus)Gleiten *n*, (-)Rutschen *n*;
Fehltritt *m* (*a. fig.*); (Flüchtigkeits-)
Fehler *m*; Fehler *m*, Panne *f*; Strei-

fen *m*, Zettel *m*; *econ.* (Kontroll)Ab-
schnitt *m*; (Kissen)Bezug *m*; Unter-
kleid *n*, -rock *m*; △ *nicht* Slip; *a* ~ *of a
boy (girl)* ein schmächtiges Bürsch-
chen (ein zartes Ding); ~ *of the
tongue* Versprecher *m*; *give s.o. the
~* j-m entwischen; ~**ped disc** ✠ [slıpt
'dısk] Bandscheibenvorfall *m*; ~**per**
['slıpə] Pantoffel *m*, Hausschuh *m*;
~**per·y** □ [~rı] (-*ier*, -*iest*) glatt,
schlüpfrig; ~**road** *Brt.* Autobahn-
auffahrt *f*, -ausfahrt *f*; ~**shod** [~ʃɒd]
schlampig, nachlässig.
slit [slıt] **1.** Schlitz *m*, Spalt *m*; **2.** (-*tt*-;
slit) (auf-, zer)schlitzen.
slith·er ['slıðə] gleiten, rutschen.
sliv·er ['slıvə] Splitter *m*.
slob·ber ['slɒbə] **1.** Sabber *m*, Geifer
m; **2.** (be)geifern, (be)sabbern.
slo·gan ['sləʊgən] Slogan *m*; Schlagwort *n*; Werbespruch *m*.
sloop ⚓ [slu:p] Schaluppe *f*.
slop [slɒp] **1.** Krankensüppchen *n*; ~*s
pl.* Spül-, Schmutzwasser *n*; **2.**
(-*pp*-) *v/t.* verschütten; *v/i.* ~ *over*
überschwappen.
slope [sləʊp] **1.** (Ab)Hang *m*; Neigung *f*, Gefälle *n*; **2.** ⊕ abschrägen;
abfallen; schräg verlaufen; (sich)
neigen.
slop·py □ ['slɒpı] (-*ier*, -*iest*) naß,
schmutzig; schlampig; labb(e)rig
(*Essen*); rührselig.
slot [slɒt] Schlitz *m*, (Münz)Einwurf
m.
sloth [sləʊθ] Faulheit *f*; *zo.* Faultier
n.
slot-ma·chine ['slɒtməʃi:n] (Wa-
ren-, Spiel)Automat *m*.
slouch [slaʊtʃ] **1.** krumm *od.* (nach-)
lässig dastehen *od.* dasitzen; F (herum)latschen; **2.** schlaffe, schlechte
Haltung *f*; ~ *hat* Schlapphut *m*.
slough¹ [slaʊ] Sumpf(loch *n*) *m*.
slough² [slʌf] Haut abwerfen.
slov·en ['slʌvn] unordentlicher
Mensch; Schlampe *f*; ~**ly** [~lı]
schlampig.
slow [sləʊ] **1.** □ langsam; schwerfällig; träge; *be* ~ nachgehen (*Uhr*); **2.**
adv. langsam; **3.** ~ *down*, ~ *up v/t.*
Geschwindigkeit verlangsamen, -rin-
gern; *v/i.* langsamer werden; ~**coach**
['sləʊkəʊtʃ] Langweiler *m*; ~**down**
(**strike**) *Am. econ.* Bummelstreik *m*;
~ **mo·tion** *phot.* Zeitlupe *f*; ~**poke**
Am. = slowcoach; ~**worm** *zo.*
Blindschleiche *f*.

S

sludge [slʌdʒ] Schlamm *m*; Matsch *m*.

slug [slʌg] **1.** *zo.* Wegschnecke *f*; Stück *n* Rohmetall; *bsd. Am.* (Pistolen)Kugel *f*; *Am.* (Faust)Schlag *m*; **2.** (*-gg-*) *Am.* F *j-m* e-n harten Schlag versetzen.

slug|gard ['slʌgəd] Faulpelz *m*; **~gish** □ [~ɪʃ] träge; *econ.* schleppend.

sluice ⊕ [slu:s] Schleuse *f*.

slums [slʌmz] *pl.* Slums *pl.*, Elendsviertel *n od. pl.*

slum·ber ['slʌmbə] **1.** *mst* ~*s pl.* Schlummer *m*; **2.** schlummern.

slump [slʌmp] **1.** plumpsen; (hin)fallen, stürzen (*Preise*); **2.** *econ.* (Kurs-, Preis)Sturz *m*; (starker) Konjunkturrückgang.

slung [slʌŋ] *pret. u. p.p. von* sling 2.

slunk [slʌŋk] *pret. u. p.p. von* slink.

slur [slɜ:] **1.** (*-rr-*) verunglimpfen, verleumden; undeutlich (aus)sprechen; ♪ *Töne* binden; **2.** Verunglimpfung *f*, Verleumdung *f*; undeutliche Aussprache; ♪ Bindebogen *m*.

slush [slʌʃ] Schlamm *m*, Matsch *m*; Schneematsch *m*; Kitsch *m*.

slut [slʌt] Schlampe *f*; Nutte *f*.

sly □ [slaɪ] (*~er*, *~est*) schlau, listig; hinterlistig; *on the* ~ heimlich.

smack [smæk] **1.** (Bei)Geschmack *m*; Schmatz *m* (*Kuß*); Schmatzen *n*; klatschender Schlag, Klatsch *m*; Klaps *m*; (Peitschen)Knall *m*; *fig.* Spur *f*, Andeutung *f*; **2.** schmecken (*of* nach); klatschend schlagen; knallen (mit); *j-m* e-n Klaps geben; ~ *one's lips* schmatzen.

small [smɔ:l] **1.** klein; gering; wenig; unbedeutend; bescheiden; (sozial) niedrig; kleinlich; △ *nicht schmal*; *feel* ~ sich schämen; sich ganz klein und häßlich vorkommen; *look* ~ beschämt *od.* schlecht dastehen; *the* ~ *hours* die frühen Morgenstunden *pl.*; *in a* ~ *way* bescheiden; **2.** ~ *of the back anat.* Kreuz *n*; ~*s pl. Brt.* F Unterwäsche *f*, Taschentücher *pl. etc.*; *wash one's* ~*s* kleine Wäsche waschen; ~ **arms** ['smɔ:lɑːmz] *pl.* Handfeuerwaffen *pl.*; ~ **change** Kleingeld *n*; ~**ish** [~ɪʃ] ziemlich klein; ~**pox** ⚕ [~pɒks] Pocken *pl.*; ~ **talk** oberflächliche Konversation *f*; ~**time** F unbedeutend.

smart [smɑːt] **1.** □ klug; gewandt, geschickt; gerissen; raffiniert; elegant, schick, fesch; forsch; flink; hart, scharf; heftig; schlagfertig; ~ *aleck* F Klugscheißer *m*; **2.** stechender Schmerz; **3.** schmerzen; leiden; ~**ness** ['smɑːtnɪs] Klugheit *f*; Gewandtheit *f*; Gerissenheit *f*; Eleganz *f*; Schärfe *f*.

smash [smæʃ] **1.** *v/t.* zerschlagen, -trümmern; (zer)schmettern; *fig.* vernichten; *v/i.* zersplittern; krachen; zusammenstoßen; *fig.* zusammenbrechen; **2.** heftiger Schlag; Zerschmettern *n*; Krach *m*; Zusammenbruch *m* (*a. econ.*); *Tennis etc.*: Schmetterball *m*; *a.* ~ *hit* F toller Erfolg; ~**ing** *bsd. Brt.* F ['smæʃɪŋ] toll, sagenhaft; ~**up** Zusammenstoß *m*; Zusammenbruch *m*.

smat·ter·ing ['smætərɪŋ] oberflächliche Kenntnis.

smear [smɪə] **1.** (be-, ein-, ver-)schmieren; *fig.* verleumden; **2.** Schmiere *f*; Fleck *m*.

smell [smel] **1.** Geruch(ssinn) *m*; Duft *m*; Gestank *m*; **2.** (*smelt od. smelled*) *v/t.* riechen (*an dat.*); *v/i.* riechen (*at an dat.*); duften; stinken; ~**y** ['smelɪ] (*-ier, -iest*) übelriechend, stinkend.

smelt[1] [smelt] *pret. u. p.p. von* smell 2.

smelt[2] *metall.* [~] *Erz* (ein)schmelzen, verhütten.

smile [smaɪl] **1.** Lächeln *n*; **2.** lächeln; ~ *at j-n* anlächeln.

smirch [smɜːtʃ] besudeln.

smirk [smɜːk] grinsen.

smith [smɪθ] Schmied *m*.

smith·e·reens ['smɪðə'riːnz] *pl.* Stücke *pl.*, Splitter *pl.*, Fetzen *pl.*

smith·y ['smɪðɪ] Schmiede *f*.

smit·ten ['smɪtn] betroffen, heimgesucht; *fig.* hingerissen (*with* von); *humor.* verliebt, -knallt (*with* in *acc.*).

smock [smɒk] Kittel *m*.

smog [smɒg] Smog *m*.

smoke [sməʊk] **1.** Rauch *m*; *have a* ~ (eine) rauchen; **2.** rauchen; qualmen; dampfen; räuchern; ~**dried** ['sməʊkdraɪd] geräuchert; **smok·er** [~ə] Raucher(in); ⚙ F Raucher(abteil *n*) *m*; ~**stack** 🚂, ⚓ Schornstein *m*.

smok·ing ['sməʊkɪŋ] Rauchen *n*; *attr.* Rauch(er)...; ~**com·part·ment** ⚙ Raucherabteil *n*.

smok·y □ ['sməʊkɪ] (-ier, -iest) rauchig; verräuchert.

smooth [smuːð] **1.** □ glatt; eben; ruhig (⊕, *Meer, Reise*); sanft (*Stimme*); flüssig (*Stil etc.*); mild (*Wein*); (aal)glatt, gewandt (*Benehmen*); **2.** glätten; *fig.* besänftigen; ~ **away** *fig.* wegräumen; ~ **down** sich glätten; glattstreichen; ~ *out Falte* glattstreichen; ~**ness** ['smuːðnɪs] Glätte *f.*

smoth·er ['smʌðə] ersticken.

smo(u)l·der ['sməʊldə] schwelen.

smudge [smʌdʒ] **1.** (ver-, be)schmieren; schmutzig werden; **2.** Schmutzfleck *m.*

smug [smʌg] (-gg-) selbstgefällig.

smug·gle ['smʌgl] schmuggeln; ~**r** [~ə] Schmuggler(in).

smut [smʌt] Ruß(fleck) *m*; Schmutzfleck *m*; *fig.* Zote(n *pl.*) *f*; △ *nicht* Schmutz; **2.** (-tt-) beschmutzen; ~**ty** □ ['smʌtɪ] (-ier, -iest) schmutzig.

snack [snæk] Imbiß *m*; *have a* ~ e-e Kleinigkeit essen; ~**bar** ['snækbɑː] Snackbar *f*, Imbißstube *f.*

snaf·fle ['snæfl] *a.* ~ *bit* Trense *f.*

snag [snæg] (Ast-, Zahn)Stumpf *m*; *bsd. Am.* Baumstumpf *m* (*bsd. unter Wasser*); *fig.* Haken *m.*

snail *zo.* [sneɪl] Schnecke *f.*

snake *zo.* [sneɪk] Schlange *f*; △ *nicht* Schnecke.

snap [snæp] **1.** (Zu)Schnappen *n*, Biß *m*; Knacken *n*, Krachen *n*; Knacks *m*; Knall *m*; Schnappschloß *n*; F *phot.* Schnappschuß *m*; *fig.* F Schwung *m*, Schmiß *m*; *cold* ~ Kälteeinbruch *m*; **2.** (-pp-) *v/i.* schnappen (*at* nach); zuschnappen (*Schloß*); krachen; knacken; knallen; (zer)brechen; zerkrachen; -springen, -reißen; schnauzen; ~ *at* s.o. j-n anschnauzen; ~ *to it!, Am.* ~ *it up! sl.* mach schnell!, Tempo!; ~ *out of it! sl.* hör auf (damit)!, komm, komm!; *v/t.* (er)schnappen, beißen; schnell greifen nach; knallen mit; (auf- *od.* zu)schnappen *od.* (-)knallen lassen; *phot.* knipsen; zerbrechen; j-n anschnauzen, anfahren; ~ *one's fingers* mit den Fingern schnalzen; ~ *one's fingers at fig.* j-n, et. nicht ernst nehmen; ~ *out Worte* hervorstoßen; ~ *up* wegschnappen; an sich reißen; ~**fas·ten·er** ['snæpfɑːsnə] Druckknopf *m*; ~**pish** □ [~ɪ] bissig; schnippisch; ~**py** [~ɪ] (-ier, -iest) bissig; F flott; F schnell; *make*

it ~*!, Brt. a.* look ~*!* F mach fix!; ~**shot** Schnappschuß *m*, Momentaufnahme *f.*

snare [sneə] **1.** Schlinge *f*, Falle *f* (*a. fig.*); **2.** fangen; *fig.* umgarnen.

snarl [snɑːl] **1.** wütend knurren; **2.** Knurren *n*, Zähnefletschen *n*; Knoten *m*; *fig.* Gewirr *n.*

snatch [snætʃ] **1.** schneller Griff; Ruck *m*; Stückchen *n*; **2.** schnappen; ergreifen; *et.* an sich reißen; nehmen; ~ *at* greifen nach.

sneak [sniːk] **1.** *v/i.* schleichen; *Brt. sl.* petzen; *v/t. sl.* stibitzen; **2.** F Leisetreter *m*, Kriecher *m*; *Brt. sl.* Petze *f*; ~**ers** *bsd. Am.* ['sniːkəz] *pl.* Turnschuhe *pl.*

sneer [snɪə] **1.** höhnisches Grinsen; höhnische Bemerkung; **2.** höhnisch grinsen; spotten; *et.* höhnen.

sneeze [sniːz] **1.** niesen; **2.** Niesen *n.*

snick·er ['snɪkə] *bsd. Am.* kichern; *bsd. Brt.* wiehern.

sniff [snɪf] schnüffeln, schnuppern; *fig.* die Nase rümpfen.

snig·ger *bsd. Brt.* ['snɪgə] kichern.

snip [snɪp] **1.** Schnitt *m*; Schnipsel *m*, *n*; **2.** (-pp-) schnippeln, schnipseln.

snipe [snaɪp] **1.** *zo.* Schnepfe *f*; **2.** aus dem Hinterhalt schießen; **snip·er** ['snaɪpə] Heckenschütze *m.*

sniv·el ['snɪvl] (*bsd. Brt.* -ll-, *Am.* -l-) schniefen; schluchzen; plärren.

snob [snɒb] Snob *m*; ~**bish** □ ['snɒbɪʃ] versnobt.

snoop F [snuːp] **1.** ~ *about,* ~ *around* F *fig.* herumschnüffeln; **2.** Schnüffler(in).

snooze F [snuːz] **1.** Nickerchen *n*; **2.** ein Nickerchen machen; dösen.

snore [snɔː] **1.** schnarchen; **2.** Schnarchen *n.*

snort [snɔːt] schnauben; prusten.

snout [snaʊt] Schnauze *f*; Rüssel *m.*

snow [snəʊ] **1.** Schnee *m*; *sl.* Snow *m*, Schnee *m* (*Kokain, Heroin*); **2.** schneien; ~*ed in* *od. up* eingeschneit; *be* ~*ed under fig.* erdrückt werden; ~**bound** ['snəʊbaʊnd] eingeschneit; ~**capped**, ~**clad**, ~**cov·ered** schneebedeckt; ~**drift** Schneewehe *f*; ~**drop** ♥ Schneeglöckchen *n*; ~**white** schneeweiß; 2 **White** Schneewittchen *n*; ~**y** □ [~ɪ] (-ier, -iest) schneeig; schneebedeckt, verschneit; schneeweiß.

snub [snʌb] **1.** (-bb-) j-n vor den Kopf stoßen, brüskieren; j-m über den Mund fahren; *j-n* schneiden; **2.** Brüskierung *f*; **~nosed** ['snʌb-nəʊzd] stupsnasig.

snuff [snʌf] **1.** Schnuppe *f* (*e-r Kerze*); Schnupftabak *m*; *take*~ schnupfen; **2.** *Kerze* putzen; schnuppen.

snuf·fle ['snʌfl] schnüffeln; näseln.

snug □ [snʌg] (*-gg-*) geborgen; behaglich; enganliegend; **~·gle** ['snʌgl] sich anschmiegen *od.* kuscheln (*up to s.o.* an j-n).

so [səʊ] so; also; deshalb; *I hope~* ich hoffe es; *I think ~* ich glaube *od.* denke schon; *are you tired? –~ I am* bist du müde? Ja; *you are tired, ~ am I* du bist müde, ich auch; *~ far* bisher.

soak [səʊk] *v/t.* einweichen; durchnässen; (durch)tränken; *~ in* einsaugen; *~ up* aufsaugen; *v/i.* sich vollsaugen; ein-, durchsickern.

soap [səʊp] **1.** Seife *f*; *soft~* Schmierseife *f*; *fig.* Schmeichelei *f*; **2.** ab-, einseifen; **~·box** ['səʊpbɒks] Seifenkiste *f*; improvisierte Rednerbühne; **~·y** □ [~ɪ] (*-ier, -iest*) seifig; *fig.* F schmeichlerisch.

soar [sɔː] (hoch) aufsteigen, sich erheben; in großer Höhe fliegen *od.* schweben; ⚡ segeln, gleiten.

sob [sɒb] **1.** Schluchzen *n*; **2.** (*-bb-*) schluchzen.

so·ber ['səʊbə] **1.** □ nüchtern; **2.** ernüchtern; *~ down, ~ up* nüchtern machen *od.* werden; **~·bri·e·ty** [səʊ'braɪətɪ] Nüchternheit *f*.

so-called ['səʊ'kɔːld] sogenannt.

soc·cer ['sɒkə] Fußball *m* (*Spiel*).

so·cia·ble ['səʊʃəbl] **1.** □ gesellig; gemütlich; **2.** geselliges Beisammensein.

so·cial ['səʊʃl] **1.** □ gesellig; gesellschaftlich; sozial; sozialistisch; Sozial...; **2.** geselliges Beisammensein; *~ in·sur·ance* Sozialversicherung *f*.

so·cial·is·m ['səʊʃəlɪzəm] Sozialismus *m*; **~·ist** [~ɪst] **1.** Sozialist(in); **2.** = **~·is·tic** [səʊʃə'lɪstɪk] (*~ally*) sozialistisch; **~·ize** ['səʊʃəlaɪz] sozialisieren; verstaatlichen; gesellschaftlich verkehren (*with* mit).

so·cial|· sci·ence ['səʊʃl'saɪəns] Sozialwissenschaft *f*; *~ se·cu·ri·ty* Sozialhilfe *f*; *be on ~* Sozialhilfe beziehen; *~ serv·ic·es pl.* staatliche Sozialleistungen *pl.*; *~ work* Sozialarbeit *f*; *~ work·er* Sozialarbeiter(in).

so·ci·e·ty [sə'saɪətɪ] Gesellschaft *f*; Verein *m*, Vereinigung *f*.

so·ci·ol·o·gy [səʊsɪ'ɒlədʒɪ] Soziologie *f*.

sock [sɒk] Socke *f*; Einlegesohle *f*.

sock·et ['sɒkɪt] *anat.* (Augen-, Zahn-) Höhle *f*; *anat.* (Gelenk)Pfanne *f*; ⊕ Muffe *f*; ⚡ Fassung *f*; ⚡ Steckdose *f*; ⚡ (Anschluß)Buchse *f*.

sod [sɒd] Grasnarbe *f*; Rasenstück *n*.

so·da ['səʊdə] 🜹 Soda *f, n*; Soda (-wasser) *n*; **~·foun·tain** Siphon *m*; *Am.* Erfrischungshalle *f*, Eisbar *f*.

sod·den ['sɒdn] durchweicht; teigig.

soft [sɒft] **1.** □ weich; mild; sanft; sacht, leise; gedämpft (*Licht etc.*); leicht, angenehm (*Arbeit*); weichlich; *a. ~ in the head* F einfältig, doof; alkoholfrei (*Getränk*); weich (*Drogen*); **2.** *adv.* sanft, leise; **~·en** ['sɒfn] *v/t.* weich machen; *Farbe, Stimme etc.* dämpfen; *Wasser* enthärten; *j-n* erweichen; *fig.* mildern; *v/i.* weich(er) *od.* sanft(er) *od.* mild(er) werden; **~·head·ed** doof; **~·heart·ed** weichherzig; **~·land** *Raumfahrt:* weich landen; *~ land·ing Raumfahrt:* weiche Landung; **~·ware** *Computer:* Software *f* (*Programme etc.*); *Sprachlabor:* Software *f*, Begleitmaterial *n*; **~·y** F [~ɪ] Trottel *m*; weichlicher Typ; Schwächling *m*.

sog·gy ['sɒgɪ] (*-ier, -iest*) durchnäßt; feucht.

soil [sɔɪl] **1.** Boden *m*, Erde *f*; Fleck *m*; Schmutz *m*; **2.** (be)schmutzen; schmutzig machen *od.* werden.

so·journ ['sɒdʒɜːn] **1.** Aufenthalt *m*; **2.** sich (vorübergehend) aufhalten.

sol·ace ['sɒləs] **1.** Trost *m*; **2.** trösten.

so·lar ['səʊlə] Sonnen...

sold [səʊld] *pret. u. p.p. von* sell.

sol·der ⊕ ['sɒldə] **1.** Lot *n*; **2.** löten.

sol·dier ['səʊldʒə] Soldat *m*; **~·like**, **~·ly** [~lɪ] soldatisch; **~·y** [~rɪ] Militär *n*, Soldaten *pl.*

sole¹ □ [səʊl] alleinig, einzig, Allein...; *~ agent* Alleinvertreter *m*.

sole² [~] **1.** (Fuß-, Schuh)Sohle *f*; △ *nicht Sole*; **2.** besohlen.

sole³ *zo.* [~] Seezunge *f*.

sol·emn □ ['sɒləm] feierlich; ernst; **so·lem·ni·ty** [sə'lemnətɪ] Feierlichkeit *f*; **~·em·nize** ['sɒləmnaɪz] feiern; *Trauung* feierlich vollziehen.

so·li·cit [sə'lɪsɪt] (dringend) bitten (um); sich anbieten (*Prostituierte*).

so·lic·i·ta·tion [səlɪsɪ'teɪʃn] dringen-

de Bitte; ~**tor** [sə'lisitə] *Brt.* 🎓
(*nicht plädierender*) Anwalt; *Am.*
Agent *m*, Werber *m*; ~**tous** □ [~əs]
besorgt (*about, for* um, wegen); ~ *of*
begierig nach; ~ *to do* bestrebt zu
tun; ~**tude** [~ju:d] Sorge *f*, Besorgnis *f*.

sol·id ['sɒlɪd] **1.** □ fest; derb, kräftig;
stabil; massiv; 🅰 körperlich, räum-
lich, Raum...; gewichtig, triftig; so-
lid(e), gründlich; solid(e), zuverlässig (*Person*); einmütig, solidarisch; *a*
~ *hour* e-e volle Stunde; **2.** fester
Stoff; *geom.* Körper *m*; ~*s pl.* feste
Nahrung; **sol·i·dar·i·ty** [sɒlɪ'dærətɪ]
Solidarität *f*.

so·lid·i·fy [sə'lɪdɪfaɪ] fest werden
(lassen); verdichten; ~**ty** [~tɪ] Soli-
dität *f*.

so·lil·o·quy [sə'lɪləkwɪ] Selbstge-
spräch *n*; *bsd. thea.* Monolog *m*.

sol·i·taire [sɒlɪ'teə] Solitär *m*; *Am.*
Karten: Patience *f*.

sol·i·ta·ry □ ['sɒlɪtərɪ] einsam; einzeln; einsiedlerisch; ~**tude** [~ju:d]
Einsamkeit *f*; Verlassenheit *f*; Öde *f*.

so·lo ['səʊləʊ] (*pl. -los*) Solo *n*; 🎵
Alleinflug *m*; ~**ist** ♪ [~ɪst] Solist *m*.

sol·u·ble ['sɒljʊbl] löslich; *fig.* lösbar.

so·lu·tion [sə'lu:ʃn] (Auf)Lösung *f*.

solve [sɒlv] lösen; **sol·vent** ['sɒlvənt]
1. 🜀 (auf)lösend; *econ.* zahlungsfä-
hig; **2.** 🜀 Lösungsmittel *n*.

som·bre, *Am.* **-ber** □ ['sɒmbə] düster, trüb(e); *fig.* trübsinnig.

some [sʌm, səm] (irgend)ein; *vor pl.*:
einige, ein paar, manche; etwas; etwa; ℱ beachtlich, vielleicht ein (*in
Ausrufen*); ~ *20 miles* etwa 20 Mei-
len; *to ~ extent* einigermaßen;
~**bod·y** [~'sʌmbədɪ] (irgend) jemand,
irgendeiner; ~**day** eines Tages;
~**how** irgendwie; ~ *or other* irgendwie; ~**one** (irgend) jemand, irgendeiner; ~**place** *Am.* = *somewhere.*

som·er·sault ['sʌməsɔ:lt] **1.** Salto *m*;
Purzelbaum *m*; *turn a* ~ = **2.** e-n
Salto machen; e-n Purzelbaum
schlagen.

some|**thing** ['sʌmθɪŋ] (irgend) et-
was; ~ *like* so etwas wie, so ungefähr;
~**time 1.** irgendwann; **2.** ehemali-
ge(r, -s); ~**times** manchmal;
~**what** etwas, ziemlich; ~**where**
irgendwo(hin).

son [sʌn] Sohn *m*.

sonde [sɒnd] *Raumfahrt:* Sonde *f*.

song [sɒŋ] Lied *n*; Gesang *m*; Ge-

dicht *n*; *for a* ~ für ein Butterbrot;
~**bird** [~'sɒŋbɜ:d] Singvogel *m*;
~**ster** [~stə] Singvogel *m*; Sänger *m*;
~**stress** [~rɪs] Sängerin *f*.

son·ic ['sɒnɪk] Schall...; ~**boom**, *Brt.*
a. ~ **bang** Überschallknall *m*.

son-in-law ['sʌnɪnlɔ:] (*pl. sons-in-
law*) Schwiegersohn *m*.

son·net ['sɒnɪt] Sonett *n*.

so·nor·ous □ [sə'nɔ:rəs] klangvoll.

soon [su:n] bald; früh; gern; *as od. so
~ as* sobald als *od.* wie; *as ~ as:* so
eher; früher; lieber; ~ *or later* früher
oder später; *the ~ the better* je eher,
desto besser; *no ~ ... than* kaum ...
als; *no ~ said than done* gesagt,
getan.

soot [sʊt] **1.** Ruß *m*; **2.** verrußen.

soothe [su:ð] beruhigen, besänftigen,
beschwichtigen; lindern, mildern;
sooth·ing □ ['su:ðɪŋ] besänftigend;
lindernd; **sooth·say·er** ['su:θseɪə]
Wahrsager(in).

soot·y □ ['sʊtɪ] (*-ier, -iest*) rußig.

sop [sɒp] **1.** eingetunkter *od.* -weich-
ter Bissen; **2.** (*-pp-*) eintunken.

so·phis·ti·cat·ed [sə'fɪstɪkeɪtɪd] anspruchsvoll, kultiviert; intellektuell;
blasiert; 🜨 hochentwickelt; 🜨 kompliziert; verfälscht; **soph·ist·ry**
['sɒfɪstrɪ] Spitzfindigkeit *f*.

soph·o·more *Am.* ['sɒfəmɔ:] Col-
lege-Student(in) *od.* Schüler(in) e-r
High-School im zweiten Jahr.

sop·o·rif·ic [sɒpə'rɪfɪk] **1.** (~*ally*) einschläfernd; **2.** Schlafmittel *n*.

sor·cer|er ['sɔ:sərə] Zauberer *m*, Hex-
enmeister *m*; ~**ess** [~ɪs] Zauberin *f*,
Hexe *f*; ~**y** [~ɪ] Zauberei *f*, Hexerei *f*.

sor·did □ ['sɔ:dɪd] schmutzig; schäbig, elend, miserabel.

sore [sɔ:] **1.** □ (~*r*, ~*st*) schlimm,
entzündet; wund, weh; gereizt; verärgert, böse; *a ~ throat* Halsschmer-
zen *pl.*; **2.** Wunde *f*, Entzündung *f*;
~**head** *Am.* ℱ ['sɔ:hed] mürrischer
Mensch.

sor·rel ['sɒrəl] **1.** rotbraun; **2.** *zo.*
Fuchs *m* (*Pferd*); ♣ Sauerampfer *m*.

sor·row ['sɒrəʊ] **1.** Kummer *m*, Leid
n; Schmerz *m*, Jammer *m*; **2.**
trauern; sich grämen; ~**ful** □ [~fl]
traurig, betrübt.

sor·ry □ ['sɒrɪ] (*-ier, -iest*) betrübt,
bekümmert; traurig, erbärmlich; *be
~ about s.th.* et. bereuen *od.* bedauern; *I am (so)* ~! es tut mir (sehr)
leid, Verzeihung!; ~! Verzeihung!,

S

Entschuldigung!; *I am ~ for him* er tut mir leid; *we are ~ to say* wir müssen leider sagen.

sort [sɔːt] **1.** Sorte *f*, Art *f*; *what ~ of* was für; *of a ~, of ~s* F so was wie; *~ of* F gewissermaßen; *out of ~s* F nicht auf der Höhe; **2.** sortieren; *~ out* (aus-) sortieren; *fig.* in Ordnung bringen.

sot [sɒt] Säufer *m*, Trunkenbold *m*.

sough [saʊ] **1.** Rauschen *n*; **2.** rauschen.

sought [sɔːt] *pret. u. p.p. von* seek.

soul [səʊl] Seele *f* (*a. fig.*); Inbegriff *m*; ♪ Soul *m*.

sound [saʊnd] **1.** □ gesund; intakt; *econ.* solid(e), stabil, sicher; vernünftig; ♕ gültig; zuverlässig; kräftig, tüchtig; fest, tief (*Schlaf*); **2.** Ton *m*, Schall *m*, Laut *m*, Klang *m*; ♪ Sound *m*; ♣ Sonde *f*; Sund *m*, Meerenge *f*; Fischblase *f*; **3.** (er)tönen, (-)klingen; erschallen (lassen); sich *gut etc.* anhören; sondieren; ♣ (aus-) loten; ♣ abhorchen; **~ bar·ri·er** Schallgrenze *f*, -mauer *f*; **~film** [ˈsaʊndfilm] Tonfilm *m*; **~ing** ♣ [~ɪŋ] Lotung *f*; *~s pl.* lotbare Wassertiefe *f*; **~less** □ [~lɪs] lautlos; **~ness** [~nɪs] Gesundheit *f* (*a. fig.*); **~pol·lu·tion** Lärmbelästigung *f*; **~proof** schalldicht; **~track** *Film:* Tonspur *f*; Filmmusik *f*; **~wave** Schallwelle *f*.

soup [suːp] **1.** Suppe *f*; (*some*) ~ e-e Suppe; **2.** ~ *up* F *Motor* frisieren.

sour [ˈsaʊə] **1.** □ sauer; *fig.* verbittert; **2.** *v/t.* säuern; *fig.* ver-, erbittern; *v/i.* sauer (*fig.* verbittert) werden.

source [sɔːs] Quelle *f*; Ursprung *m*.

sourish □ [ˈsaʊərɪʃ] säuerlich; **~ness** [~nɪs] Säure *f*; *fig.* Bitterkeit *f*.

souse [saʊs] eintauchen; (mit Wasser) begießen; *Fisch etc.* einlegen, -pökeln.

south [saʊθ] **1.** Süd(en *m*); **2.** südlich, Süd...; **~east** [ˈsaʊθˈiːst] **1.** Südosten *m*; **2.** südöstlich; **~east·er** Südostwind *m*; **~east·ern** südöstlich.

south·er·ly [ˈsʌðəlɪ], **~n** [~n] südlich, Süd...; **~n·most** südlichste(r, -s).

south·ward(s) *adv.* [ˈsaʊθwəd(z)] südwärts, nach Süden.

south|-west [ˈsaʊθˈwest] **1.** Südwesten *m*; **2.** südwestlich; **~west·er** [~ə] Südwestwind *m*; ♣ Südwester *m*; **~west·er·ly**, **~west·ern** südwestlich.

sou·ve·nir [suːvəˈnɪə] Souvenir *n*, Andenken *n*.

sove·reign [ˈsɒvrɪn] **1.** □ höchste(r, -s); unübertrefflich; unumschränkt, souverän; **2.** Herrscher(in); Monarch(in); Sovereign *m* (*alte brit. Goldmünze von 20 Shilling*); **~ty** [~ənti] höchste (Staats)Gewalt; Souveränität *f*, Landeshoheit *f*.

So·vi·et [ˈsəʊvɪət] Sowjet *m*; *attr.* sowjetisch, Sowjet...

sow¹ [saʊ] *zo.* Sau *f*, (Mutter-) Schwein *n*; ⊕ Sau *f*; ⊕ Massel *f*.

sow² [səʊ] (*sowed, sown od. sowed*) (aus)säen, ausstreuen; besäen; **~n** [~n] *p.p. von* sow².

spa [spɑː] Heilbad *n*; Kurort *m*.

space [speɪs] **1.** (Welt)Raum *m*; Raum *m*, Platz *m*; Zwischenraum *m*; Zeitraum *m*; **2.** *mst ~ out* *print.* sperren; **~ age** Weltraumzeitalter *m*; **~ cap·sule** [ˈspeɪskæpsjuːl] Raumkapsel *f*; **~craft** Raumfahrzeug *n*; **~ flight** (Welt)Raumflug *m*; **~lab** Raumlabor *n*; **~port** Raumfahrtzentrum *n*; **~ probe** (Welt-) Raumsonde *f*; **~ re·search** (Welt-) Raumforschung *f*; **~ship** Raumschiff *n*; **~ shut·tle** Raumfähre *f*; **~ sta·tion** (Welt)Raumstation *f*; **~suit** Raumanzug *m*; **~ walk** Weltraumspaziergang *m*; **~wom·an** (*pl. -women*) (Welt)Raumfahrerin *f*.

spa·cious □ [ˈspeɪʃəs] geräumig; weit; umfassend.

spade [speɪd] Spaten *m*; *Karten:* Pik *n*, Grün *n*; *king of ~s* Pik-König *m*; *call a ~ a ~* das Kind beim (rechten) Namen nennen.

span [spæn] **1.** Spanne *f*; *arch.* Spannweite *f*; △ *nicht* Span; **2.** (-nn-) um-, überspannen; (aus)messen.

span·gle [ˈspæŋgl] **1.** Flitter *m*, Paillette *f*; **2.** mit Flitter *od.* Pailletten besetzen; *fig.* übersäen.

Span·iard [ˈspænjəd] Spanier(in).

Span·ish [ˈspænɪʃ] **1.** spanisch; **2.** *ling.* Spanisch *n*; *the ~ pl. coll.* die Spanier *pl.*

spank F [spæŋk] verhauen; **2.** Klaps *m*, Schlag *m*; **~ing** [ˈspæŋkɪŋ] **1.** *adj.* □ schnell, flott; tüchtig, gehörig; **2.** *adv.:* ~ *clean* blitzsauber; ~ *new* funkelnagelneu; **3.** F Haue *f*, Tracht *f* Prügel.

span·ner ⊕ [ˈspænə] Schraubenschlüssel *m*.

spar [spɑː] **1.** ♣ Spiere *f*; ⚒ Holm *m*; **2.** (-rr-) *Boxen:* sparren; *fig.* sich streiten.

spare [speə] **1.** □ sparsam; kärglich, mager; überzählig; überschüssig; Ersatz...; Reserve...; ~ **part** Ersatzteil *n*, *a. m*; ~ **room** Gästezimmer *n*; ~ **time** *od.* **hours** Freizeit *f*, Mußestunden *pl.*; **2.** ⊕ Ersatzteil *n*, *a. m*; **3.** (ver)schonen; erübrigen; entbehren; (übrig)haben (für); ersparen; sparen mit; scheuen; △ *nicht* Geld *etc.* **sparen.**

spar·ing □ ['speərɪŋ] sparsam.

spark [spɑ:k] **1.** Funke(n) *m*; **2.** Funken sprühen; ~**ing-plug** *Brt. mot.* ['spɑ:kɪŋplʌg] Zündkerze *f*.

spar·kle ['spɑ:kl] **1.** Funke(n) *m*; Funkeln *n*; **2.** funkeln; blitzen; perlen (*Wein*); ~**kling** □ [~ɪŋ] funkelnd, sprühend; *fig.* geistsprühend; spritzig; ~ **wine** Schaumwein *m*.

spark-plug *Am. mot.* ['spɑ:kplʌg] Zündkerze *f*.

spar·row *zo.* ['spærəʊ] Sperling *m*, Spatz *m*; ~**hawk** *zo.* Sperber *m*.

sparse □ [spɑ:s] spärlich, dünn.

spasm ['spæzəm] 𝒮 Krampf *m*; Anfall *m*; **spas·mod·ic** [spæz'mɒdɪk] (~*ally*) □ krampfhaft, -artig; *fig.* sprunghaft.

spas·tic 𝒮 ['spæstɪk] **1.** (~*ally*) spastisch; **2.** Spastiker(in).

spat [spæt] *pret. u. p.p. von* spit².

spa·tial □ ['speɪʃl] räumlich.

spat·ter ['spætə] (be)spritzen.

spawn [spɔ:n] **1.** *zo.* Laich *m*; *fig. contp.* Brut *f*; **2.** *zo.* laichen; *fig.* hervorbringen.

speak [spi:k] (*spoke, spoken*) *v/i.* sprechen, reden (*to* mit; *about* über *acc.*); ~ **out**, ~ **up** laut u. deutlich sprechen; offen reden; ~ **to s.o.** 1 *in od.* mit j-m sprechen; *v/t.* (aus)sprechen; sagen; äußern; *Sprache* sprechen (können); ~**er** ['spi:kə] Sprecher(in), Redner(in); ♀ *parl.* Sprecher *m*, Präsident *m*; *Mr* ♀! Herr Vorsitzender!

spear [spɪə] **1.** Speer *m*; Spieß *m*, Lanze *f*; **2.** durchbohren, aufspießen.

spe·cial ['speʃl] **1.** □ besondere(r, -s); speziell; Sonder...; Spezial...; **2.** Hilfspolizist *m*; Sonderausgabe *f*; Sonderzug *m*; *Rundfunk, TV:* Sondersendung *f*; *Am.* Tagesgericht *n* (*im Restaurant*); *Am. econ.* Sonderangebot *n*; *on ~ Am. econ.* im Angebot; ~**ist** [~əlɪst] Spezialist(in), Fachmann *m*; 𝒮 Facharzt *m*, -ärztin

f; **spe·ci·al·i·ty** [speʃɪ'ælətɪ] Besonderheit *f*; Spezialfach *n*; *econ.* Spezialität *f*; ~**ize** ['speʃəlaɪz] besonders anführen; (sich) spezialisieren; ~**ty** *bsd. Am.* [~tɪ] = speciality.

spe·cies ['spi:ʃi:z] (*pl. -cies*) Art *f*, Spezies *f*.

spe|cif·ic [spɪ'sɪfɪk] (~*ally*) spezifisch; besondere(r, -s); bestimmt; ~**ci·fy** ['spesɪfaɪ] spezifizieren, einzeln angeben; ~**ci·men** [~mɪn] Probe *f*, Muster *n*; Exemplar *n*.

spe·cious □ ['spi:ʃəs] blendend, bestechend; trügerisch; Schein...

speck [spek] Fleck(en) *m*; Stückchen *n*; △ *nicht* Speck; ~**le** ['spekl] Fleck(en) *m*, Sprenkel *m*, Tupfen *m*; ~**led** gefleckt, gesprenkelt, getüpfelt.

spec·ta·cle ['spektəkl] Schauspiel *n*; Anblick *m*; △ *nicht der* Spektakel; (*a pair of*) ~**s** *pl.* (e-e) Brille.

spec·tac·u·lar [spek'tækjʊlə] **1.** □ spektakulär, sensationell, aufsehenerregend; **2.** große (Fernseh)Schau, Galavorstellung *f*.

spec·ta·tor [spek'teɪtə] Zuschauer (-in).

spec|tral □ ['spektrəl] gespenstisch; ~**tre**, *Am.* ~**ter** [~ə] Gespenst *n*.

spec·u|late ['spekjʊleɪt] grübeln, nachsinnen; *econ.* spekulieren; ~**lation** [spekjʊ'leɪʃn] theoretische Betrachtung; Nachdenken *n*; Grübeln *n*; *econ.* Spekulation *f*; ~**la·tive** □ ['spekjʊlətɪv] grüblerisch; theoretisch; *econ.* spekulativ; ~**la·tor** [~eɪtə] *econ.* Spekulant *m*.

sped [sped] *pret. u. p.p. von* speed 2.

speech [spi:tʃ] Sprache *f*; Reden *n*, Sprechen *n*; Rede *f*, Ansprache *f*; *make a ~* e-e Rede halten; ~**day** *Brt.* ['spi:tʃdeɪ] *Schule:* (Jahres-)Schlußfeier *f*; ~**less** □ [~lɪs] sprachlos.

speed [spi:d] **1.** Geschwindigkeit *f*, Tempo *n*, Schnelligkeit *f*, Eile *f*; ⊕ Drehzahl *f*; *mot.* Gang *m*; *phot.* Lichtempfindlichkeit *f*; *phot.* Belichtungszeit *f*; *sl.* Speed *n* (*Aufputschmittel*); **2.** (*sped*) *v/i.* (dahin-) eilen, schnell fahren, rasen; ~ **up** (*pret. u. p.p. speeded*) *od.* die Geschwindigkeit erhöhen; *v/t.* rasch befördern; ~ **up** (*pret. u. p.p. speeded*) beschleunigen; ~**boat** ['spi:dbəʊt] Rennboot *n*; ~**ing** *mot.* [~ɪŋ] zu schnelles Fahren, Geschwindig-

S

keitsüberschreitung f; **~ lim·it** Geschwindigkeitsbegrenzung f, Tempolimit n; **~·o** F mot. [~əʊ] (pl. -os) Tacho m; **~·om·e·ter** mot. [spɪˈdɒmɪtə] Tachometer m, n; **~·up** [ˈspiːdʌp] Beschleunigung f, Temposteigerung f; econ. Produktionserhöhung f; **~·way** Sport: Speedwayrennen n; Speedwaybahn f; Am. mot. Schnellstraße f; Am. Sport: mot. Rennstrecke f; **~·y** □ [~ɪ] (-ier, -iest) schnell, rasch.

spell [spel] **1.** Weile f, Weilchen n; Anfall m; Zauber(spruch) m; fig. Zauber m; a ~ of fine weather e-e Schönwetterperiode; hot ~ Hitzewelle f; **2.** ~ s.o. at s.th. j-n bei et. ablösen; (spelt od. Am. spelled) buchstabieren; richtig schreiben; bedeuten; geschrieben werden, sich schreiben; **~·bound** [ˈspelbaʊnd] (wie) gebannt, fasziniert, gefesselt; **~·er** [~ə]: be a good od. bad ~ in Rechtschreibung gut od. schlecht sein; **~·ing** [~ɪŋ] Buchstabieren n; Rechtschreibung f; **~·ing-book** Fibel f.

spelt [spelt] pret. u. p.p. von spell 2.

spend [spend] (spent) verwenden; Geld ausgeben; verbrauchen; verschwenden; Mühe aufwenden; Zeit zu-, verbringen; △ nicht spenden; ~ o.s. sich erschöpfen; **~·thrift** [ˈspendθrɪft] Verschwender(in).

spent [spent] **1.** pret. u. p.p. von spend; **2.** adj. erschöpft, matt.

sperm [spɜːm] Sperma n, Samen m.

sphere [sfɪə] Kugel f; Erd-, Himmelskugel f; fig. Sphäre f; (Wirkungs)Kreis m, Bereich m, Gebiet n; **spher·i·cal** □ [ˈsferɪkl] sphärisch; kugelförmig.

spice [spaɪs] **1.** Gewürz(e pl.) n; fig. Würze f; Anflug m; **2.** würzen.

spick and span [ˈspɪkənˈspæn] blitzsauber; wie aus dem Ei gepellt; funkelnagelneu.

spic·y □ [ˈspaɪsɪ] (-ier, -iest) würzig; gewürzt; fig. pikant.

spi·der zo. [ˈspaɪdə] Spinne f.

spig·ot [ˈspɪɡət] (Faß)Zapfen m; (Zapf-, Am. Leitungs)Hahn m.

spike [spaɪk] **1.** Stift m; Spitze f; Dorn m; Stachel m; ♀ Ähre f; Sport: Spike m; ~s pl. Rennschuhe, mot.: Spikes pl.; **2.** festnageln; mit (Eisen-) Spitzen etc. versehen; **~ heel** Pfennigabsatz m.

spill [spɪl] **1.** (spilt od. spilled) v/t. ver-, ausschütten; Blut vergießen; verstreuen; Reiter abwerfen; sl. ausplaudern; s. milk 1; v/i. überlaufen; sl. auspacken, singen; **2.** Sturz m (vom Pferd etc.).

spilt [spɪlt] pret. u. p.p. von spill 1.

spin [spɪn] **1.** (-nn-; spun) v/t. spinnen; schnell drehen, (herum)wirbeln; Wäsche schleudern; Münze hochwerfen; fig. sich et. ausdenken, erzählen; ~ s.th. out et. in die Länge ziehen, et. ausspinnen; v/i. spinnen; sich drehen; ✈ trudeln; mot. durchdrehen (Räder); ~ along dahinrasen; **2.** schnelle Drehung; Schleudern n (Wäsche); ✈ Trudeln n; go for a ~ e-e Spritztour machen.

spin·ach ♀ [ˈspɪnɪdʒ] Spinat m.

spin·al anat. [ˈspaɪnl] bot., zo. Rückgrat...; ~ column Wirbelsäule f, Rückgrat n; ~ cord, ~ marrow Rückenmark n.

spin·dle [ˈspɪndl] Spindel f.

spin·dri·er [ˈspɪndraɪə] (Wäsche-) Schleuder f; **~·dry** Wäsche schleudern; **~·dry·er** = spin-drier.

spine [spaɪn] anat. Wirbelsäule f, Rückgrat n; bot., zo. (Gebirgs)Grat m; (Buch)Rücken m.

spin·ning-mill [ˈspɪnɪŋmɪl] Spinnerei f; **~·top** Kreisel m; **~·wheel** Spinnrad n.

spin·ster [ˈspɪnstə] ⚖ unverheiratete Frau; alte Jungfer.

spin·y ♀, zo. [ˈspaɪnɪ] (-ier, -iest) stach(e)lig.

spi·ral [ˈspaɪərəl] **1.** □ spiralig; Spiral...; gewunden; ~ staircase Wendeltreppe f; **2.** Spirale f.

spire [ˈspaɪə] (Turm-, Berg- etc.)Spitze f; Kirchturm(spitze f) m.

spir·it [ˈspɪrɪt] **1.** Geist m; Schwung m; Elan m; Mut m; Gesinnung f; ⚗ Spiritus m; ~s pl. alkoholische od. geistige Getränke pl., Spirituosen pl.; high (low) ~s pl. gehobene (gedrückte) Stimmung; **2.** ~ away od. off wegschaffen, -zaubern; **~·ed** □ [~id] lebhaft; energisch; feurig (Pferd etc.); geistvoll; **~·less** □ [~lɪs] geistlos; temperamentlos; mutlos.

spir·i·tu·al [ˈspɪrɪtjʊəl] **1.** □ geistig; geistlich; geistreich; **2.** ♪ (Neger-) Spiritual m; **~·ism** [~ɪzəm] Spiritismus m.

spirt [spɜːt] = spurt².

spit¹ [spɪt] **1.** (Brat)Spieß m; geogr. Landzunge f; **2.** (-tt-) aufspießen.

spit² [~] **1.** Speichel *m*, Spucke *f*; Fauchen *n*; F Ebenbild *n*; **2.** (*-tt-*; *spat od. spit*) spucken; fauchen; sprühen (*fein regnen*); *a.* ~ **out** (aus-) spucken.

spite [spaɪt] **1.** Bosheit *f*; Groll *m*; *in* ~ *of trotz* (*gen.*); **2.** *j-n* ärgern; **~·ful** □ ['spaɪtfl] boshaft, gehässig.

spit-fire ['spɪtfaɪə] Hitzkopf *m*.

spit·tle ['spɪtl] Speichel *m*, Spucke *f*.

spit·toon [spɪ'tuːn] Spucknapf *m*.

splash [splæʃ] **1.** Spritzer *m*, (Spritz-) Fleck *m*; Klatschen *n*, Platschen *n*; **2.** (be)spritzen; platschen; planschen; (hin)klecksen; ~ *down* wassern (*Raumkapsel*); **~·down** Wasserung *f*.

splay [spleɪ] **1.** Ausschrägung *f*; **2.** *v/t.* spreizen; ausschrägen; *v/i.* ausgeschrägt sein; **~·foot** ['spleɪfʊt] Spreizfuß *m*.

spleen [spliːn] *anat.* Milz *f*; schlechte Laune.

splen|did □ ['splendɪd] glänzend, prächtig, herrlich; F großartig, hervorragend; **~·do(u)r** [~ə] Glanz *m*, Pracht *f*, Herrlichkeit *f*.

splice [splaɪs] spleißen; *Film* zusammenkleben.

splint ⚕ [splɪnt] **1.** Schiene *f*; **2.** schienen.

splin·ter ['splɪntə] **1.** Splitter *m*; **2.** (zer)splittern; ~ *off* (*fig.* sich) absplittern.

split [splɪt] **1.** Spalt *m*, Riß *m*, Sprung *m*; *fig.* Spaltung *f*; **2.** gespalten; **3.** (*-tt-*; *split*) *v/t.* (zer)spalten; zerreißen; sich in *et.* teilen; ~ *hairs* Haarspalterei treiben; ~ *one's sides laughing od. with laughter* sich totlachen; *v/i.* sich spalten; zerspringen, (-)platzen, (-)bersten; **~·ting** ['splɪtɪŋ] heftig, rasend (*Kopfschmerz*).

splut·ter ['splʌtə] (heraus)stottern; zischen; stottern (*Motor*).

spoil [spɔɪl] **1.** *mst* ~*s pl.* Beute *f*; *fig.* Ausbeute *f*, Gewinn *m*; **2.** (*spoilt od. spoiled*) verderben; ruinieren; *Kind* verwöhnen, -ziehen; **~·er** *mot.* ['spɔɪlə] Spoiler *m*; **~·sport** Spielverderber(in); **~·t** [~t] *pret. u. p.p. von spoil 2.*

spoke¹ [spəʊk] Speiche *f*; (Leiter-) Sprosse *f*.

spoke² [~] *pret. von speak*; **spok·en** ['spəʊkən] **1.** *p.p. von speak*; **2.** gesprochen (*Sprache*); **~s·man** [~smən] (*pl. -men*) Wortführer *m*,

Sprecher *m*; **~s·wom·an** (*pl. -women*) Wortführerin *f*, Sprecherin *f*.

sponge [spʌndʒ] **1.** Schwamm *m*; F *fig.* Schmarotzer(in); *Brt.* = sponge-cake; **2.** *v/t.* mit e-m Schwamm (ab)wischen; ~ *off* weg-, abwischen; ~ *up* aufsaugen, -wischen; *v/i. fig.* schmarotzen; **~·cake** F *fig.* [~ə] Biskuitkuchen *m*; **spong·er** F *fig.* [~ə] Schmarotzer(in); **spong·y** [~ɪ] (*-ier, -iest*) schwammig.

spon·sor ['spɒnsə] **1.** Bürg|e *m*, -in *f*; (Tauf)Pat|e *m*, -in *f*; Förderer *m*, Gönner(in); Schirmherr(in); Geldgeber(in), Sponsor(in); **2.** bürgen für; fördern; die Schirmherrschaft (*gen.*) übernehmen; *Rundfunk-, TV-Sendung, Sportler* sponsern; **~·ship** [~ʃɪp] Bürgschaft *f*; Patenschaft *f*; Schirmherrschaft *f*; Unterstützung *f*, Förderung *f*.

spon·ta·ne|i·ty [spɒntə'neɪətɪ] Spontaneität *f*, eigener Antrieb; Ungezwungenheit *f*; **~·ous** □ [spɒn'teɪnjəs] spontan; unvermittelt; ungezwungen, natürlich; von selbst (entstanden); Selbst...

spook [spuːk] Spuk *m*; **~·y** ['spuːkɪ] (*-ier, -iest*) gespenstisch, Spuk...

spool [spuːl] Spule *f*, Rolle *f*; *a.* ~ *of thread Am.* Garnrolle *f*.

spoon [spuːn] **1.** Löffel *m*; **2.** löffeln; **~·ful** ['spuːnfʊl] (*ein*) Löffel(voll) *m*.

spo·rad·ic [spə'rædɪk] (*~ally*) sporadisch, gelegentlich, vereinzelt.

spore ♜ [spɔː] Spore *f*, Keimkorn *n*.

sport [spɔːt] **1.** Sport(art *f*) *m*; Zeitvertreib *m*; Spaß *m*, Scherz *m*; F feiner Kerl; ~*s pl.* Sport *m*; *Brt. Schule:* Sportfest *n*; **2.** *v/i.* herumtollen; spielen; *v/t.* F stolz (*zur Schau*) tragen, protzen mit; **spor·tive** □ ['spɔːtɪv] verspielt; ~*s* [~s] Sport...; **~s·man** (*pl. -men*) Sportler *m*; **~s·wom·an** (*pl. -women*) Sportlerin *f*.

spot [spɒt] **1.** Fleck *m*; Tupfen *m*; Makel *m*; Stelle *f*, Ort *m*; ⚕ Leberfleck *m*; ⚕ Pickel *m*; *Rundfunk, TV:* (Werbe)Spot *m*; *Brt.* F Tropfen *m*, Schluck *m*; *a.* ~ *of Brt.* F etwas; *on the* ~ auf der Stelle, sofort; **2.** *econ.* sofort liefer- *od.* zahlbar; **3.** (*-tt-*) F beflecken; sprenkeln; entdecken, erspähen, erkennen; fleckig werden; **~·less** □ ['spɒtlɪs] fleckenlos; **~·light** *thea.*

Scheinwerfer(licht *n*) *m*; **~ter** [~ə] Beobachter *m*; ✕ Aufklärer *m*; **~ty** [~ɪ] (*-ier, -iest*) fleckig; pickelig.

spouse [spaʊz] Gatt|e *m*, -in *f*.

spout [spaʊt] **1.** Tülle *f*, Schnabel *m*; Strahlrohr *n*; (Wasser)Strahl *m*; **2.** (heraus)spritzen; hervorsprudeln.

sprain ⚕ [spreɪn] **1.** Verstauchung *f*; **2.** sich *et.* verstauchen.

sprang [spræŋ] *pret. von* spring 2.

sprat *zo.* [spræt] Sprotte *f*.

sprawl [sprɔːl] sich rekeln; ausgestreckt daliegen; ♀ wuchern.

spray [spreɪ] **1.** Sprühregen *m*, Gischt *m*, Schaum *m*; Spray *m*, *n*; ~sprayer; **2.** zerstäuben; (ver)sprühen; besprühen; *Haar* sprayen; **~er** ['spreɪə] Zerstäuber *m*, Sprüh-, Spraydose *f*.

spread [spred] **1.** (*spread*) *v/t.* a. ~ out ausbreiten; ausstrecken; spreizen; ausdehnen; verbreiten; belegen; *Butter etc.* (auf)streichen; *Brot etc.* streichen; *the table* den Tisch decken; *v/i.* sich aus- od. verbreiten; sich ausdehnen; **2.** Aus-, Verbreitung *f*; Ausdehnung *f*; Spannweite *f*; Fläche *f*; (*Bett*)Decke *f*; (*Brot*)Aufstrich *m*; F Festessen *n*.

spree F [spriː]: *go* (*out*) *on a* ~ e-e Sauftour machen; *go on a buying* (*shopping, spending*) ~ wie verrückt einkaufen.

sprig ♀ [sprɪg] kleiner Zweig.

spright·ly ['spraɪtlɪ] (*-ier, -iest*) lebhaft, munter.

spring [sprɪŋ] **1.** Sprung *m*, Satz *m*; ⊕ (Sprung)Feder *f*; Sprungkraft *f*, Elastizität *f*; Quelle *f*; *fig.* Triebfeder *f*; *fig.* Ursprung *m*; Frühling *m* (*a. fig.*), Frühjahr *n*; **2.** (*sprang* od. *Am.* *sprung, sprung*) *v/t.* springen lassen; (zer)sprengen; *Wild* aufjagen; ~ *a leak* ⚓ leck werden; ~ *a surprise on s.o.* j-n überraschen; *v/i.* springen; entspringen (*from dat.*), *fig.* herkommen, stammen (*from* von); ♀ sprießen; ~ *up* aufkommen (*Ideen etc.*); **~board** ['sprɪŋbɔːd] Sprungbrett *n*; **~tide** Springflut *f*; *poet.*, **~time** Frühling(szeit *f*) *m*, Frühjahr *n*; **~y** [~ɪ] (*-ier, -iest*) federnd.

sprin|kle ['sprɪŋkl] (be)streuen; (be)sprengen; *impers.* regnen (*fein regnen*); **~kler** [~ə] Berieselungsanlage *f*; Sprinkler *m*; Rasensprenger *m*; **~kling** [~ɪŋ] Sprühregen

m; *a* ~ *of fig.* ein wenig, ein paar.

sprint [sprɪnt] *Sport* **1.** sprinten; spurten; **2.** Sprint *m*; Spurt *m*; **~er** ['sprɪntə] *Sport:* Sprinter(in), Kurzstreckenläufer(in).

sprite [spraɪt] Kobold *m*.

sprout [spraʊt] **1.** sprießen; wachsen (lassen); **2.** ♀ Sproß *m*; (*Brussels*)~s *pl.* ♀ Rosenkohl *m*.

spruce[1] □ [spruːs] schmuck, adrett.

spruce[2] ♀ [~] *a.* ~ *fir* Fichte *f*, Rottanne *f*.

sprung [sprʌŋ] *pret. u. p.p. von* spring 2.

spry [spraɪ] munter, flink.

spun [spʌn] *pret. u. p.p. von* spin 1.

spur [spɜː] **1.** Sporn *m* (*a. zo.*, ♀); Vorsprung *m*, Ausläufer *m* (*e-s Berges*); *fig.* Ansporn *m*; △ *nicht* Spur; *on the* ~ *of the moment* dem Eingebung des Augenblicks folgend, spontan; **2.** (*-rr-*) *e-m Pferd* die Sporen geben; *oft* ~ *on fig.* anspornen.

spu·ri·ous □ ['spjʊərɪəs] unecht, gefälscht.

spurn [spɜːn] verschmähen, verächtlich zurückweisen.

spurt[1] [spɜːt] **1.** plötzlich aktiv werden; *Sport:* spurten, sprinten; **2.** plötzliche Aktivität *od.* Anspannung; *Sport:* Spurt *m*, Sprint *m*.

spurt[2] [~] **1.** (heraus)spritzen; **2.** (*Wasser- etc.*)Strahl *m*.

sput·ter ['spʌtə] = splutter.

spy [spaɪ] **1.** Spion(in); Spitzel *m*; **2.** erspähen, entdecken; (aus)spionieren; ~ *on,* ~ *upon* j-m nachspionieren; *j-n* bespitzeln; *Gespräch etc.* abhören; **~glass** ['spaɪglɑːs] Fernglas *n*; **~hole** Guckloch *n*, Spion *m*.

squab·ble ['skwɒbl] **1.** Zank *m*, Kabbelei *f*; **2.** sich zanken.

squad [skwɒd] Gruppe *f* (*a.* ✕); *Polizei:* (*Überfall- etc.*)Kommando *n*; Dezernat *n*; *i.e.* *car Am.* (Funk)Streifenwagen *m*; **~ron** ✕ ['skwɒdrən] Schwadron *f*; (*Panzer*)Bataillon *n*; ✠ Staffel *f*; ⚓ Geschwader *n*.

squal·id □ ['skwɒlɪd] schmutzig, verwahrlost, -kommen, armselig.

squall [skwɔːl] **1.** *meteor.* Bö *f*; Schrei *m*; ~s *pl.* Geschrei *n*; **2.** schreien.

squal·or ['skwɒlə] Schmutz *m*.

squan·der ['skwɒndə] verschwenden, -geuden.

square [skweə] **1.** □ (vier)eckig; quadratisch, Quadrat...; ... im Quadrat; rechtwink(e)lig; vierschrötig (*Per-*

stain

son); stimmend, in Ordnung; quitt, gleich; anständig, ehrlich, offen; F altmodisch, spießig; **2.** Quadrat *n*; Viereck *n*; Feld *n* (*e-s* Brettspiels); öffentlicher Platz; Winkel(maß *n*) *m*; *sl.* altmodischer Spießer; **3.** quadratisch *od.* rechtwink(e)lig machen; *Zahl* ins Quadrat erheben; *Schultern* straffen; *Sport: Kampf* unentschieden beenden; *econ. Konten* ausgleichen; *econ. Schuld* begleichen; *fig.* in Einklang bringen *od.* stehen (*with* mit); anpassen (*to an acc.*); passen (*with* zu); **~built** ['skweə'bɪlt] vierschrötig; **~** *dance bsd. Am.* Square dance *m*; **~** *mile* Quadratmeile *f*; **~toed** *fig.* altmodisch, steif.

squash[1] [skwɒʃ] **1.** Gedränge *n*; Brei *m*, Matsch *m*; *Brt.* (Orangen- *etc.*) Saft *m*; *Sport:* Squash *n*; **2.** (zer-, zusammen)quetschen; zusammendrücken.

squash[2] ♀ [~] Kürbis *m*.

squat [skwɒt] **1.** (*-tt-*) hocken, kauern; sich ohne Rechtstitel ansiedeln (auf *dat.*); *leerstehendes Haus* besetzen; **~** *down* sich hinhocken; **2.** in der Hocke; untersetzt, vierschrötig; **~ter** ['skwɒtə] Squatter *m*, illegaler Siedler; Schafzüchter *m* (*in Australien*); Hausbesetzer(in); **~** *movement* Hausbesetzerszene *f*.

squawk [skwɔːk] **1.** kreischen, schreien; **2.** Gekreisch *n*, Geschrei *n*.

squeak [skwiːk] quiek(s)en, piepen, piepsen; quietschen.

squeal [skwiːl] schreien, kreischen; quietschen, kreischen (*Bremsen etc.*); quiek(s)en, piep(s)en.

squeamish □ ['skwiːmɪʃ] empfindlich; mäkelig; heikel; penibel.

squeeze [skwiːz] **1.** (aus-, zusammen)drücken, (-)pressen, (aus)quetschen; sich zwängen *od.* quetschen; **2.** Druck *m*; Gedränge *n*; **squeez·er** ['skwiːzə] (Frucht)Presse *f*.

squelch *fig.* [skweltʃ] unterdrücken.

squid *zo.* [skwɪd] Tintenfisch *m*.

squint [skwɪnt] schielen; blinzeln.

squire ['skwaɪə] Großgrundbesitzer *m*, Gutsherr *m*.

squirm F [skwɜːm] sich winden.

squir·rel *zo.* ['skwɪrəl, *Am.* 'skwɜːrəl] Eichhörnchen *n*.

squirt [skwɜːt] **1.** Spritze *f*; Strahl *m*; F Wichtigtuer *m*; **2.** spritzen.

stab [stæb] **1.** Stich *m*, (Dolch- *etc.*)Stoß *m*; △ *nicht* Stab; **2.** (*-bb-*)

v/t. niederstechen; *et.* aufspießen; *v/i.* stechen (*at* nach).

sta·bil·i·ty [stə'bɪlətɪ] Stabilität *f*; Standfestig-, Beständigkeit *f*; **~ize** ['steɪbəlaɪz] stabilisieren.

sta·ble[1] □ ['steɪbl] stabil, fest.

sta·ble[2] [~] **1.** Stall *m*; **2.** in den Stall bringen; im Stall halten; im Stall stehen (*Pferd*).

stack [stæk] **1.** ✔ (Heu-, Stroh-, Getreide)Schober *m*; Stapel *m*; F Haufen *m*; Schornstein(reihe *f*) *m*; **~s** *pl.* (Haupt)Magazin *n* (*e-r Bibliothek*); **2.** *a.* **~** *up* (auf)stapeln.

sta·di·um ['steɪdjəm] (*pl. -diums, -dia* [-djə]) Sport: Stadion *n*.

staff [staːf] **1.** Stab *m* (*a.* ✗), Stock *m*; Stütze *f*; (*pl. staves* [steɪvz]) ♪ Notensystem *n*; (Mitarbeiter)Stab *m*; Personal *n*, Belegschaft *f*; Beamtenstab *m*; Lehrkörper *m*; **2.** (mit Personal, Beamten *od.* Lehrern) besetzen; **~** *member* Mitarbeiter(in); **~** *room* Lehrerzimmer *n*.

stag *zo.* [stæg] Hirsch *m*.

stage [steɪdʒ] **1.** *thea.* Bühne *f*; *das* Theater; *fig.* Schauplatz *m*; Stufe *f*, Stadium *n*, Phase *f*; Teilstrecke *f*, Fahrzone *f* (*Bus etc.*); Etappe *f*; ⊕ Bühne *f*, Gerüst *n*; ⊕ Stufe *f* (*e-r Rakete*); **2.** inszenieren; veranstalten; **~coach** *hist.* ['steɪdʒkəʊtʃ] Postkutsche *f*; **~craft** dramaturgisches *od.* schauspielerisches Können; **~** *de·sign* Bühnenbild *n*; **~** *de·sign·er* Bühnenbildner(in); **~** *di·rec·tion* Regieanweisung *f*; **~** *fright* Lampenfieber *n*; **~** *man·ag·er* Inspizient *m*; **~** *prop·er·ties* *pl.* Requisiten *pl.*

stag·ger ['stægə] **1.** *v/i.* (sch)wanken, taumeln, torkeln; *fig.* (sch)wanken(d werden); *v/t.* ins Wanken bringen; *Arbeitszeit etc.* staffeln; *fig.* überwältigen, sprachlos machen; **2.** (Sch)Wanken *n*, Taumeln *n*; ✗ Staffelung *f*.

stag·nant □ ['stægnənt] stehend (*Gewässer*); stagnierend; stockend; *econ.* still, flau; *fig.* träge; **~nate** ['stægneɪt] stagnieren, stillstehen, stocken.

staid □ [steɪd] gesetzt; ruhig.

stain [steɪn] **1.** Fleck *m*; Beize *f*; *fig.* Schandfleck *m*; **2.** *v/t.* beschmutzen, beflecken; färben, *Holz* beizen, *Glas* bemalen; *v/i.* Flecken verursachen; schmutzen; **~ed** *glass* Buntglas *n*;

~·less □ ['steɪnlɪs] rostfrei, nichtrostend; *bsd. fig.* fleckenlos.

stair [steə] Stufe *f*; *~s pl.* Treppe *f*, Stiege *f*; **~·case** ['steəkeɪs], **~·way** Treppe(nhaus *n*) *f*.

stake [steɪk] **1.** Pfahl *m*, Pfosten *m*; Marterpfahl *m*; (Wett-, Spiel)Einsatz *m (a. fig.)*; *~s pl.* Pferderennen: Dotierung *f*; Rennen *n*; *pull up ~s bsd. Am. fig.* F s-e Zelte abbrechen; *be at ~ fig.* auf dem Spiel stehen; **2.** wagen, aufs Spiel setzen; *~ off*, *~ out* abstecken.

stale □ [steɪl] *(~r, ~st)* alt *(nicht frisch)*; schal, abgestanden; verbraucht *(Luft)*; *fig.* fad.

stalk¹ [stɔːk] Stengel *m*, Stiel *m*, Halm *m*.

stalk² [~] *v/i. hunt.* (sich an)pirschen; *~ along* (einher)stolzieren; *v/t.* sich heranpirschen an *(acc.)*; verfolgen, hinter *j-m* herschleichen.

stall¹ [stɔːl] **1.** Box *f (im Stall)*; △ *nicht Stall*; (Verkaufs)Stand *m*, (Markt)Bude *f*; Chorstuhl *m*; *~s pl. Brt. thea.* Parkett *n*; **2.** *v/t.* Tier in Boxen unterbringen; *Motor* abwürgen; *v/i.* absterben *(Motor)*.

stall² [~] ausweichen; *a. ~ for time* Zeit schinden; *Sport*: auf Zeit spielen.

stal·li·on *zo.* ['stæljən] (Zucht-) Hengst *m*.

stal·wart □ ['stɔːlwət] stramm, kräftig; *bsd. pol.* treu.

stam·i·na ['stæmɪnə] Ausdauer *f*, Zähigkeit *f*; Durchhaltevermögen *n*, Kondition *f*.

stam·mer ['stæmə] **1.** stottern, stammeln; **2.** Stottern *n*.

stamp [stæmp] **1.** (Auf)Stampfen *n*; Stempel *m (a. fig.)*; △ *nicht Poststempel*; (Brief)Marke *f*; *fig.* Gepräge *n*; *fig.* Art *f*; **2.** (auf)stampfen; aufstampfen mit; (ab)stempeln *(a. fig.)*; frankieren; (auf)prägen; *~ out* (aus)stanzen.

stam·pede [stæm'piːd] **1.** Panik *f*, wilde, panische Flucht; (Massen-) Ansturm *m*; **2.** *v/i.* durchgehen; *v/t.* in Panik versetzen.

stanch [stɑːntʃ] *s.* staunch¹,².

stand [stænd] **1.** *(stood)* *v/i.* stehen; sich befinden; bleiben; *fig.* festbleiben; *mst ~ still* stillstehen, stehenbleiben; *v/t.* stellen; aushalten; (v)ertragen; sich *et.* gefallen lassen; ertragen; sich *e-r Sache* unterziehen;

Probe bestehen; *e-e Chance* haben; F spendieren; *~ a round* F e-e Runde schmeißen; *~ about* herumstehen; *~ aside* beiseite treten; *~ back* zurücktreten; *~ by* dabeisein, -stehen; bereitstehen; *fig. zu j-m* halten *od.* stehen, helfen; *~ for* kandidieren für; bedeuten; eintreten für; F sich *et.* gefallen lassen; *~ in* einspringen *(for s.o.* für *j-n)*; *~ in for Film: j-n* doubeln; *~ off* sich entfernt halten; *fig.* Abstand halten; *~ on (fig.* be)stehen auf *(dat.)*; *~ out* hervorstehen, -treten; sich abheben *(against* gegen); aus-, durchhalten; *fig.* herausragen; standhalten *(dat.)*; *~ over* liegenbleiben; (sich) vertagen *(to* auf *acc.)*; *~ to* stehen zu; ✗ in Bereitschaft stehen *od.* versetzen; *~ up* aufstehen, sich erheben; sich aufrichten *(Stacheln etc.)*; *~ up for* eintreten für; *~ up to* mutig gegenüberstehen *(dat.)*; standhalten *(dat.)*; *~ upon = ~ on*; **2.** Stand *m*; Stillstand *m*; (Stand)Platz *m*, Standort *m*; Stand(platz) *m (für Taxis)*; (Verkaufs-, Messe)Stand *m*; *fig.* Standpunkt *m*; Ständer *m*; Tribüne *f*; *bsd. Am.* Zeugenstand *m*; *make a ~ against* sich entgegenstellen *(dat.)*.

stan·dard ['stændəd] **1.** Standarte *f*, Fahne *f*, Flagge *f*; Standard *m*, Norm *f*; Maßstab *m*; Niveau *n*, Stand *m*, Grad *m*; Münzfuß *m*; *(Gold- etc.)*Währung *f*; Ständer *m*; **2.** maßgebend; normal; Normal...; **~·ize** [~aɪz] nach(ein),norm(ier)en, standardisieren, vereinheitlichen.

stand|-by ['stændbaɪ] **1.** *(pl. -bys)* Beistand *m*, Hilfe *f*; Bereitschaft *f*; Ersatz *m*; **2.** Not..., Ersatz..., Reserve...; Bereitschafts...; **~·in** *Film*: Double *n*; Ersatzmann *m*, Vertreter(in).

stand·ing ['stændɪŋ] **1.** stehend *(a. fig.)*; (fest)stehend; *econ.* laufend; ständig; **2.** Stellung *f*, Rang *m*; Ruf *m*, Ansehen *n*; Dauer *f*; *of long ~* alt; **~ or·der** *econ.* Dauerauftrag *m*; **~·room** Stehplatz *m*.

stand|-off·ish ['stænd'ɒfɪʃ] reserviert, (sehr) ablehnend, zurückhaltend; **~·point** Standpunkt *m*; **~·still** Stillstand *m*; *be at a ~* stocken, ruhen, an e-m toten Punkt angelangt sein; **~·up** stehend; im Stehen (eingenommen) *(Essen)*; *~ collar* Stehkragen *m*.

stank [stæŋk] *pret. von* stink 2.

stan·za ['stænzə] Stanze *f*; Strophe *f*.

sta·ple[1] ['steɪpl] Haupterzeugnis *n*; Hauptgegenstand *m*; *attr.* Haupt...

sta·ple[2] [~] **1.** Krampe *f*; Heftklammer *f*; **2.** heften; △ *nicht* stapeln; **~r** [~ə] Heftmaschine *f*.

star [stɑː] **1.** Stern *m*; *thea., Film, Sport:* Star *m*; △ *nicht zo.* Star; The ♀s and Stripes *pl.* das Sternenbanner (*der USA*); **2.** (*-rr-*) mit Sternen schmücken; die *od.* e-e Hauptrolle spielen; in der *od.* e-r Hauptrolle zeigen; *a film* ~*ring* ... ein Film mit ... in der Hauptrolle.

star·board ⚓ ['stɑːbəd] Steuerbord *n*.

starch [stɑːtʃ] **1.** (Wäsche)Stärke *f*; *fig.* Steifheit *f*; **2.** *Wäsche* stärken.

stare [steə] **1.** Starren *n*; starrer *od.* erstaunter Blick; **2.** (~ *at an*)starren; erstaunt blicken.

stark [stɑːk] **1.** *adj.* □ starr; rein, bar, völlig (*Unsinn*); △ *nicht* stark; **2.** *adv.* völlig.

star·light ['stɑːlaɪt] Sternenlicht *n*.

star·ling *zo.* ['stɑːlɪŋ] Star *m*.

star·lit ['stɑːlɪt] stern(en)klar.

star|ry ['stɑːrɪ] (*-ier, -iest*) Stern(en)...; **~ry-eyed** F naiv; romantisch; **~span·gled** [~spæŋgld] sternenbesät; *The* ♀ *Banner* das Sternenbanner (*Flagge u. Nationalhymne der USA*).

start [stɑːt] **1.** Auffahren *n*, -schrecken; Schreck *m*; Start *m*; Aufbruch *m*, Abreise *f*, Abfahrt *f*, ✈ Abflug *m*, Start *m*; Beginn *m*, Anfang *m*; *Sport:* Vorgabe *f*; *fig.* Vorsprung *m*; *get the* ~ *of j-m* j-m zuvorkommen; **2.** *v/i.* auffahren, hochschrecken; stutzen; sich auf den Weg machen, aufbrechen; abfahren (*Zug*), auslaufen (*Schiff*), ✈ abfliegen, starten; *Sport:* starten; anspringen (*Motor*), anlaufen (*Maschine*); anfangen, beginnen; ~ *from scratch* F ganz von vorne anfangen; *v/t.* in Gang setzen *od.* bringen, ⊕ *a.* anlassen; anfangen, beginnen; *Sport:* starten (*launɔ*), **~er** ['stɑːtə] *Sport:* Starter *m; mot.* Anlasser *m*, Starter *m*; **~s** *pl.* F Vorspeise *f*.

start|le ['stɑːtl] erschrecken; aufschrecken; **~ling** [~lɪŋ] erschreckend; überraschend, aufsehenerregend.

starv|a·tion [stɑːˈveɪʃn] Hungern *n*;

Verhungern *n*, Hungertod *m*; *attr.* Hunger...; **~e** [stɑːv] verhungern (lassen); *fig.* verkümmern (lassen).

state [steɪt] **1.** Zustand *m*; Stand *m*; Staat *m; mst* ♀ *pol.* Staat *m*; *attr.* Staats...; *lie in* ~ feierlich aufgebahrt liegen; **2.** angeben; erklären, darlegen; feststellen; festsetzen, -legen; ♀ **De·part·ment** *Am. pol.* Außenministerium *f*; **~·ly** ['steɪtlɪ] (*-ier, -iest*) stattlich; würdevoll; erhaben; **~ment** [~mənt] Angabe *f*; (Zeugenetc.)Aussage *f*; Darstellung *f*; Erklärung *f*, Verlautbarung *f*, Statement *n*; Aufstellung *f*, *bsd. econ.* (Geschäfts-, Monats- *etc.*)Bericht *m*; ~ *of account* Kontoauszug *m*; **~·room** Staatszimmer *n*; ⚓ (Einzel)Kabine *f*; **~·side**, ♀**·side** *Am.* **1.** *adj.* USA-..., Heimat...; **2.** *adv.* in den Staaten; nach den *od.* in die Staaten (zurück); **~s·man** *pol.* [~smən] (*pl.* -men) Staatsmann *m*.

stat·ic ['stætɪk] (*~ally*) statisch.

sta·tion ['steɪʃn] **1.** Platz *m*, Posten *m*; Station *f*; (*Polizei- etc.*)Wache *f*; (*Tank- etc.*)Stelle *f*; (Fernseh-, Rundfunk)Sender *m*; ⛟ Bahnhof *m*; ⚓, ✖ Stützpunkt *m*; Stellung *f*, Rang *m*; **2.** aufstellen, postieren, ⚓, ✖ stationieren; **~·a·ry** □ [~ərɪ] (still)stehend; fest(stehend); gleichbleibend; **~·er** [~ə] Schreibwarenhändler *m*; **~'s** (*shop*) Schreibwarenhandlung *f*; **~·er·y** [~rɪ] Schreibwaren *pl.*; Briefpapier *n*; **~·mas·ter** ⛟ Stationsvorsteher *m*; **~ wag·on** *Am. mot.* Kombiwagen *m*.

sta·tis·tics [stəˈtɪstɪks] *pl. u. sg.* Statistik *f*.

stat|u·a·ry ['stætjʊərɪ] Bildhauer (-kunst *f*) *m*; **~·ue** [~uː] Standbild *n*, Plastik *f*, Statue *f*.

stat·ure ['stætʃə] Statur *f*, Wuchs *m*.

sta·tus ['steɪtəs] Zustand *m*; (Familien)Stand *m*; Stellung *f*, Rang *m*; Status *m*.

stat·ute ['stætjuːt] Statut *n*, Satzung *f*; Gesetz *n*.

staunch[1] [stɔːntʃ] *Blut(ung)* stillen.

staunch[2] □ [~] treu, zuverlässig.

stave [steɪv] **1.** Faßdaube *f*; Strophe *f*; **2.** (staved *od.* stove) *mst* ~ *in* eindrücken; ein Loch schlagen in (*acc.*): ~ *off* abwehren.

stay [steɪ] **1.** ⊕ Strebe *f*, Stütze *f*; ⚖ Aufschub *m*; (vorübergehender) Aufenthalt *m*; ~s *pl.* Korsett *n*; **2.** blei-

S

ben (*with* s.o. bei j-m); sich (vor-übergehend) aufhalten, wohnen (*at*, *in* in dat.; *with* s.o. bei j-m); △ *nicht* *stehen*; ~ *away* (*from*) fernbleiben (dat.), wegbleiben (von); ~ *up* auf-bleiben, wach bleiben.

stead [sted]: *in his* ~ an s-r Stelle; **~·fast** □ ['stedfəst] fest, unerschüt-terlich; standhaft; unverwandt (*Blick*).

stead·y ['stedɪ] **1.** *adj.* □ (-*ier*, -*iest*) fest; gleichmäßig, stetig, (be)stän-dig; zuverlässig; ruhig, sicher; **2.** *adv.*: *go* ~ *with* s.o. F (fest) mit j-m gehen; **3.** festigen, fest *od.* sicher *od.* ruhig machen *od.* werden; sich be-ruhigen; **4.** F feste Freundin, fester Freund.

steak [steɪk] Steak *n.*

steal [stiːl] **1.** (*stole*, *stolen*) *v/t.* steh-len (*a. fig.*); *v/i.* stehlen; ~ *away* sich davonstehlen.

stealth [stelθ]: *by* ~ heimlich, ver-stohlen; **~·y** □ ['stelθɪ] (-*ier*, -*iest*) heimlich, verstohlen.

steam [stiːm] **1.** Dampf *m*; Dunst *m*; *attr.* Dampf...; **2.** *v/i.* dampfen; ~ *up* (sich) beschlagen (*Glas*); *v/t.* Speisen dünsten, dämpfen; **~·er** ♣ ['stiːmə] Dampfer *m*; **~·y** □ [~ɪ] (-*ier*, -*iest*) dampfig, dampfend; dunstig; be-schlagen (*Glas*).

steel [stiːl] **1.** Stahl *m*; **2.** stählern, Stahl...; **3.** *fig.* stählen, wappnen; **~·work·er** ['stiːlwɜːkə] Stahlarbeiter *m*; **~·works** *sg.* Stahlwerk *n*.

steep [stiːp] **1.** □ steil, jäh; F toll; **2.** einweichen; eintauchen; ziehen las-sen; *be* ~*ed in* s.th. *fig.* von et. durchdrungen sein.

stee·ple ['stiːpl] (spitzer) Kirchturm; **~·chase** Pferdesport: Hindernisren-nen *n*; *Leichtathletik*: Hindernislauf *m*.

steer[1] *zo.* [stɪə] junger Ochse; △ *nicht* *Stier*.

steer[2] [~] steuern, lenken; **~·age** ♣ ['stɪərɪdʒ] Steuerung *f*; Zwischen-deck *n*; **~·ing col·umn** *mot.* [~ɪŋ-kɒləm] Lenksäule *f*; **~·ing wheel** ♣ Steuerrad *n*; *mot. a.* Lenkrad *n*.

stem [stem] **1.** (Baum-, Wort)Stamm *m*; Stiel *m*; Stengel *m*; **2.** (-*mm*-) stammen (*from* von); eindämmen; *Blut(ung)* stillen; ankämpfen gegen.

stench [stentʃ] Gestank *m.*

sten·cil ['stensl] Schablone *f*; *print.* Matrize *f.*

ste·nog·ra·pher [ste'nɒgrəfə] Steno-graph(in); **~·phy** [~ɪ] Stenographie *f.*

step [step] **1.** Schritt *m*, Tritt *m*; kurze Strecke; (Treppen)Stufe *f*; Tritt-brett *n*; *fig.* Fußstapfe *f*; (*a pair of*) ~*s pl.* (e-e) Trittleiter; *mind the* ~*!* Vorsicht, Stufe!; *take* ~*s fig.* Schrit-te unternehmen; **2.** (-*pp*-) *v/i.* schrei-ten, treten; gehen; △ *nicht steppen*; ~ *out* forsch ausschreiten; *v/t.* ~ *off*, ~ *out* abschreiten; ~ *up* ankurbeln, steigern.

step- [~] *in Zssgn*: Stief...; **~·fa·ther** ['stepfɑːðə] Stiefvater *m*; **~·moth·er** Stiefmutter *f.*

steppe [step] Steppe *f.*

step·ping-stone *fig.* ['stepɪŋstəʊn] Sprungbrett *n.*

ster·e·o ['sterɪəʊ] (*pl.* -*os*) *Radio etc.*: Stereo *n*; Stereogerät *n*; *attr.* Ste-reo...

ster·ile ['steraɪl] unfruchtbar; steril; **ste·ril·i·ty** [ste'rɪlətɪ] Sterilität *f*; **~·il·ize** ['sterəlaɪz] sterilisieren.

ster·ling ['stɜːlɪŋ] **1.** lauter, echt, ge-diegen; **2.** *econ.* Sterling *m* (*Wäh-rung*).

stern [stɜːn] **1.** □ ernst; finster; streng, hart; **2.** ♣ Heck *n*; **~·ness** ['stɜːnnɪs] Ernst *m*; Strenge *f.*

stew [stjuː] **1.** schmoren, dämpfen; **2.** Eintopf *m*, Schmorgericht *n*; *be in a* ~ in heller Aufregung sein.

stew·ard [stjʊəd] Verwalter *m*; ♣, ✈ Steward *m*; (Fest)Ordner *m*; **~·ess** ♣, ✈ ['stjʊədɪs] Stewardeß *f.*

stick [stɪk] **1.** Stock *m*; Stecken *m*; trockener Zweig; Stengel *m*, Stiel *m*; (*Lippen- etc.*)Stift *m*; Stab *m*; Stange *f*; (*Besen- etc.*)Stiel *m*; ~*s pl.* Klein-holz *n*; **2.** (*stuck*) *v/i.* stecken(blei-ben); (fest)kleben (*to* an dat.); sich heften (*to* an *acc.*); ~ *at nothing* vor nichts zurückschrecken; ~ *out* ab-, hervor-, herausstehen; ~ *to* bleiben bei; *v/t.* (ab)stechen; stecken, heften (*to* an *acc.*); kleben; F *Messer* stoßen; F et., j-n (v)ertragen, ausstehen; ~ *out* heraus(r)ecken; ~ *it out* F durch-halten; **~·er** [~ə] F Aufkleber *m*; *antinuke* ~ *sl.* Anti-Kernwaffen-Aufkleber *m*; **~·ing plas·ter** [~ɪŋ-plɑːstə] Heftpflaster *n.*

stick·y □ ['stɪkɪ] (-*ier*, -*iest*) klebrig; schwierig, heikel.

stiff [stɪf] **1.** □ steif; starr; hart; fest; mühsam; stark (*alkoholisches Ge-tränk*); *be bored* ~ F zu Tode gelangweilt sein; *keep a* ~ *upper lip* Haltung bewahren; **2.** *sl.* Leiche *f*; **~en** [´stıfn] (sich) versteifen; steif werden, erstarren; **~-necked** [´~´nekt] halsstarrig.

sti·fle [´staıfl] ersticken; *fig.* unterdrücken.

stile [staıl] Zauntritt *m*.

sti·let·to [stı´letəʊ] (*pl. -tos, -toes*) Stilett *n*; ~ **heel** Pfennigabsatz *m*.

still [stıl] **1.** *adj.* □ still; ruhig; unbeweglich; **2.** *adv.* noch (immer), (immer) noch; **3.** *cj.* und doch, dennoch; **4.** still; beruhigen; **5.** Destillierapparat *m*; **~-born** [´stılbɔːn] totgeboren; **~ life** (*pl. still lifes od. lives*) *paint.* Stilleben *n*; **~-ness** [~nıs] Stille *f*, Ruhe *f*.

stilt [stılt] Stelze *f*; **~ed** □ [´stıltıd] gestelzt (*Stil*).

stim·u·lant [´stımjʊlənt] **1.** 🡒 stimulierend; **2.** 🡒 Reiz-, Aufputschmittel *n*; Genußmittel *n*; Anreiz *m*; **~late** [~eıt] 🡒 stimulieren (*a. fig.*), anregen, aufputschen; *fig. a.* anspornen; **~la·tion** [stımjʊ´leıʃn] 🡒 Reiz *m*, Reizung *f*; Anreiz *m*, Antrieb *m*, Anregung *f*; **~lus** [´stımjʊləs] (*pl. -li* [-laı:]) 🡒 Reiz *m*; (An)Reiz *m*, Antrieb *m*.

sting [stıŋ] **1.** Stachel *m*; Stich *m*, Biß *m*; **2.** (*stung*) stechen; brennen; schmerzen; *fig.* anstacheln, reizen.

stin·gi·ness [´stındʒınıs] Geiz *m*; **~gy** □ [~ı] (*-ier, -iest*) geizig, knaus(e)rig; dürftig.

stink [stıŋk] **1.** Gestank *m*; **2.** (*stank od. stunk, stunk*) stinken.

stint [stınt] **1.** Einschränkung *f*; Arbeit *f*; **2.** knausern mit; einschränken; *j-n* knapphalten.

stip·u·late [´stıpjʊleıt] *a.* ~ *for* ausbedingen, ausmachen, vereinbaren; **~la·tion** [stıpjʊ´leıʃn] Abmachung *f*; Klausel *f*, Bedingung *f*.

stir [stɜː] **1.** Rühren *n*; Bewegung *f*; Aufregung *f*, Aufruhr *m*; Aufsehen *n*; **2.** (*-rr-*) (sich) rühren; (sich) bewegen; erwachen; (um)rühren; *fig.* erregen; ~ *up* aufhetzen; *Streit etc.* entfachen.

stir·rup [´stırəp] Steigbügel *m*.

stitch [stıtʃ] **1.** Stich *m*; Masche *f*; Seitenstechen *n*; **2.** nähen; heften.

stock [stɒk] **1.** (Baum)Strunk *m*; Pfropfunterlage *f*; Griff *m*; (Gewehr)Schaft *m*; ⚠ *nicht Stock*; Stamm *m*, Familie *f*, Herkunft *f*,

Rohstoff *m*; (Fleisch-, Gemüse-) Brühe *f*; Vorrat *m*; *econ.* Waren(lager *n*) *pl.*; (Wissens)Schatz *m*; *a. live~* Vieh(bestand *m*) *n*; *econ.* Stammkapital *n*; *econ.* Anleihekapital *n*; ~*s pl. econ.* Effekten *pl.*; Aktien *pl.*; Staatspapiere *pl.*; *in (out of)* ~ *econ.* (nicht) vorrätig *od.* auf Lager; *take~* *econ.* Inventur machen; *take* ~ *of fig.* sich klarwerden über (*acc.*); **2.** vorrätig; Serien..., Standard...; *fig.* stehend, stereotyp; **3.** ausstatten, versorgen; *econ. Waren* führen, vorrätig haben.

stock·ade [stɒ´keıd] Palisade(nzaun *m*) *f*.

stock|breed·er [´stɒkbriːdə] Viehzüchter *m*; **~brok·er** *econ.* Börsenmakler *m*; **~ex·change** *econ.* Börse *f*; ~ **farm·er** Viehzüchter *m*; **~hold·er** *bsd. Am. econ.* Aktionär(in).

stock·ing [´stɒkıŋ] Strumpf *m*.

stock|job·ber *econ.* [´stɒkdʒɒbə] Börsenhändler *m*; *Am.* Börsenspekulant *m*; ~ **mar·ket** *econ.* Börse *f*; **~still** stockstill, unbeweglich; **~tak·ing** *econ.* Bestandsaufnahme *f* (*a. fig.*), Inventur *f*; **~y** [~ı] (*-ier, -iest*) stämmig, untersetzt.

stok·er [´stəʊkə] Heizer *m*.

stole [stəʊl] *pret. von steal 1*; **sto·len** [´stəʊlən] *p.p. von steal 1*.

stol·id □ [´stɒlıd] gleichmütig, stur.

stom·ach [´stʌmək] **1.** Magen *m*; Leib *m*, Bauch *m*; *fig.* Lust *f*; **2.** *fig.* (v)ertragen; **~ache** Magenschmerzen *pl.*, Bauchweh *n*; **~ up·set** Magenverstimmung *f*.

stone [stəʊn] **1.** Stein *m*; (Obst)Stein *m*, (-)Kern *m*; (*pl. stone*) *Brt.* Gewichtseinheit (*= 14 lb. = 6,35 kg*); **2.** steinern; Stein...; **3.** steinigen; entsteinen, -kernen; **~blind** [´stəʊn´blaınd] stockblind; **~dead** mausetot; **~deaf** stocktaub; **~ma·son** Steinmetz *m*; ~ **ware** [~weə] Steinzeug *n*.

ston·y □ [´stəʊnı] (*-ier, -iest*) steinig; *fig.* steinern, kalt.

stood [stʊd] *pret. u. p.p. von stand 1*.

stool [stuːl] Hocker *m*, Schemel *m*; ⚠ *nicht Stuhl*; ⚝ Stuhl(gang) *m*; **~-pigeon** [´stuːlpıdʒın] Lockvogel *m*; Spitzel *m*.

stoop [stuːp] **1.** *v/i.* sich bücken; gebeugt gehen; *fig.* sich erniedrigen *od.* herablassen; *v/t.* neigen, beugen; **2.** gebeugte Haltung.

S

stop [stɒp] **1.** (-pp-) v/t. aufhören (mit); stoppen; anhalten; aufhalten; hindern; *Zahlungen, Tätigkeit etc.* einstellen; *Zahn* plombieren; *Blut* stillen; *a.* ~ *up* ver-, zustopfen; v/i. (an)halten, stehenbleiben, stoppen; aufhören; bleiben; ~ *dead* plötzlich stehenbleiben *od.* aufhören; ~ *off* F kurz haltmachen; ~ *over* kurz haltmachen; Zwischenstation machen; ~ *short* plötzlich anhalten; **2.** Halt *m;* Stillstand *m;* Ende *n;* Pause *f;* ♪ *etc.* Aufenthalt *m;* ﹖ Station *f;* (Bus-) Haltestelle *f;* ♨ Anlegestelle *f; phot.* Blende *f; mst full* ~ *gr.* Punkt *m;* **~gap** ['stɒpgæp] Notbehelf *m;* **~light** *mot.* Brems-, Schlußlicht *n;* **~o·ver** *bsd. Am.* Zwischenstation *f;* ✈ Zwischenlandung *f;* **~page** [~ɪdʒ] Unterbrechung *f;* Stopp *m;* (Verkehrs)Stockung *f,* Stau *m;* Verstopfung *f;* (Gehalts-, Lohn)Abzug *m;* Sperrung *f (e-s Schecks);* (Arbeits-, Zahlungs- *etc.*)Einstellung *f;* **~per** [~ə] Stöpsel *m,* Pfropfen *m;* **~ping** ♬ [~ɪŋ] Plombe *f;* ~ **sign** *mot.* Stoppschild *n;* **~watch** Stoppuhr *f.*

stor·age ['stɔːrɪdʒ] Lagerung *f,* Speicherung *f; Computer:* Speicher *m;* Lagergeld *n; attr.* Speicher... (*a. Computer*).

store [stɔː] **1.** Vorrat *m;* Lagerhaus *n;* Brt. Kauf-, Warenhaus *n; bsd. Am.* Laden *m,* Geschäft *n; fig.* Fülle *f,* Reichtum *m;* △ *nicht Store; in* ~ vorrätig, auf Lager; **2.** versorgen; *a.* ~ *up,* ~ *away* (auf)speichern, (ein)lagern; ⚡, *Computer:* speichern; **~house** ['stɔːhaʊs] Lagerhaus *n; fig.* Fundgrube *f;* **~keep·er** Lagerverwalter *m; bsd. Am.* Ladenbesitzer (-in).

sto·rey, *bsd. Am.* **-ry** ['stɔːrɪ] Stock (-werk *n*) *m.*

-sto·reyed, *bsd. Am.* **-sto·ried** ['stɔːrɪd] mit ... Stockwerken, ...stöckig.

stork *zo.* [stɔːk] Storch *m.*

storm [stɔːm] **1.** Sturm *m;* Unwetter *n;* Gewitter *n;* **2.** stürmen; toben; **~y** □ [~ɪ] (-ier, -iest) stürmisch.

sto·ry¹ ['stɔːrɪ] Geschichte *f;* Erzählung *f; thea. etc.* Handlung *f;* F Lüge *f,* Märchen *n; short* ~ Kurzgeschichte *f;* Erzählung *f.*

sto·ry² *bsd. Am.* [~] = storey.

stout □ [staʊt] stark, kräftig; derb; dick; tapfer.

stove¹ [stəʊv] Ofen *m,* Herd *m.*

stove² [~] *pret. u. p.p. von* stave 2.

stow [stəʊ] (ver)stauen, packen; ~ *away* wegräumen; **~a·way** ♨, ✈ ['stəʊəweɪ] blinder Passagier.

strad·dle ['strædl] die Beine spreizen; rittlings sitzen auf (*dat.*).

strag·gle ['strægl] verstreut liegen *od.* stehen; herumstreifen; (hinterher-) bummeln; ♀ *etc.* wuchern; **~gly** [~ɪ] (-ier, -iest) verstreut (liegend); ♀ *etc.* wuchernd; unordentlich (*Haar*).

straight [streɪt] **1.** *adj.* □ gerade; glatt (*Haar*); pur (*Whisky etc.*); aufrichtig, offen, ehrlich; *put* ~ in Ordnung bringen; **2.** *adv.* gerade(aus); gerade(wegs); direkt; klar (*denken*); ehrlich, anständig; *a.* ~ *out* offen, rundheraus; ~ *away* sofort; **~en** ['streɪtn] v/t. gerademachen, (gerade)richten; ~ *out* in Ordnung bringen; v/i. gerade werden; ~ *up* sich aufrichten; **~·for·ward** □ [~'fɔːwəd] ehrlich, redlich, offen; einfach.

strain [streɪn] **1.** *biol.* Rasse *f,* Art *f;* (Erb)Anlage *f,* Hang *m,* Zug *m;* ⊕ Spannung *f;* (Über)Anstrengung *f;* Anspannung *f;* Belastung *f;* Druck *m;* ♫ Zerrung *f; fig.* Ton(art *f) m; mst* ~*s pl.* ♪ Weise *f,* Melodie *f;* **2.** v/t. (an)spannen; (über)anstrengen; ♫ sich *et.* zerren *od.* verstauchen; *fig et.* strapazieren, überfordern; durchseihen, filtern; v/i. sich spannen; sich anstrengen; sich abmühen (*after* um); zerren (*at* an *dat.*); **~ed** [~d] gezwungen, unnatürlich; **~er** ['streɪnə] Sieb *n,* Filter *m.*

strait [streɪt] (*in Eigennamen* ♀s *pl.*) Meerenge *f,* Straße *f;* ~*s pl.* Not (-lage) *f;* **~ened** ['streɪtnd]: *in* ~ *circumstances* in beschränkten Verhältnissen; **~jack·et** Zwangsjacke *f.*

strand [strænd] **1.** Strang *m;* (Haar-) Strähne *f; poet.* Gestade *n,* Ufer *n;* △ *nicht Strand;* **2.** auf den Strand setzen; *fig.* stranden (lassen).

strange □ [streɪndʒ] (~*r,* ~*st*) fremd; seltsam, sonderbar; **strang·er** ['streɪndʒə] Fremde(r *m) f.*

stran·gle ['stræŋgl] erwürgen.

strap [stræp] **1.** Riemen *m;* Gurt *m;* Band *n;* Träger *m* (*Kleid*); **2.** (-pp-) festschnallen; mit e-m Riemen schlagen.

strat·a·gem ['strætədʒəm] (Kriegs-) List *f.*

stra·te·gic [strə'tiːdʒɪk] (~*ally*) stra-

stroller

tegisch; **strat·e·gy** ['strætɪdʒɪ] Strategie f.

stra·tum geol. ['strɑːtəm] (pl. -ta [~tə]) Schicht f (a. fig.), Lage f.

straw [strɔː] 1. Stroh(halm m) n; 2. Stroh...; **~·ber·ry** ⚘ ['strɔːbərɪ] Erdbeere f.

stray [streɪ] 1. (herum)streunen; (herum)streifen; sich verirren; 2. verirrt, streunend; vereinzelt; 3. verirrtes od. streunendes Tier.

streak [striːk] 1. Strich m, Streifen m; fig. Spur f; fig. (Glücks- etc.)Strähne f; ~ of lightning Blitzstrahl m; 2. streifen; rasen, flitzen.

stream [striːm] 1. Bach m, Flüßchen n; Strom m, Strömung f; 2. strömen; tränen (Augen); triefen; flattern, wehen; **~er** ['striːmə] Wimpel m; (flatterndes) Band.

street [striːt] Straße f; attr. Straßen...; in (Am. on) the ~ auf der Straße; **~car** Am. ['striːtkɑː] Straßenbahn(wagen m) f.

strength [streŋθ] Stärke f, Kraft f; on the ~ of auf ... hin, auf Grund (gen.); **~en** ['streŋθən] v/t. (ver)stärken; fig. bestärken; v/i. stark werden.

stren·u·ous □ ['strenjʊəs] rührig, emsig; eifrig; anstrengend.

stress [stres] 1. Ton m, Akzent m, Betonung f; fig. Nachdruck m; fig. Belastung f, Anspannung f, Druck m; Stress m; 2. betonen.

stretch [stretʃ] 1. v/t. strecken; (aus)dehnen; (an)spannen; recken; fig. übertreiben; fig. es nicht allzu genau nehmen mit; ~ out ausstrecken; v/i. sich erstrecken; sich dehnen (lassen); 2. Strecken n; Dehnen n; Anspannung f; Übertreibung f; Zeit (-raum m, -spanne) f; Strecke f, Fläche f; **~er** ['stretʃə] (Kranken-)Trage f.

strew [struː] (strewed, strewn od. strewed) (be-, ver)streuen; **~n** [~n] p.p. von strew.

strick·en adj. ['strɪkən] heimgesucht, schwer betroffen; ergriffen.

strict [strɪkt] streng; genau; **~ly** speaking genaugenommen; **~ness** ['strɪktnɪs] Genauigkeit f; Strenge f.

strid·den ['strɪdn] p.p. von stride 1.

stride [straɪd] 1. (strode, stridden) (a. ~ out aus)schreiten; überschreiten; 2. großer Schritt.

strife [straɪf] Streit m, Hader m.

strike [straɪk] 1. econ. Streik m; (Öl-, Erz)Fund m; ✕ (Luft)Angriff m; ✕ Atomschlag m; be on ~ streiken; go on ~ in (den) Streik treten; a lucky ~ ein Glückstreffer; 2. (struck) v/t. schlagen; treffen; stoßen; schlagen od. stoßen gegen od. auf (acc.); stoßen od. treffen auf (acc.); Flagge, Segel streichen; ♩ Ton anschlagen; Streichholz anzünden; ein Feuer machen; Zelt abbrechen; einschlagen in (acc.) (Blitz); Wurzel schlagen; j-n beeindrucken; j-m auf- od. einfallen; ~ off, ~ out (aus)streichen; ~ up ♩ anstimmen; Freundschaft schließen; v/i. schlagen; ⚓ auflaufen (on auf acc.); econ. streiken; ~ home fig. ins Schwarze treffen; **strik·er** econ. ['straɪkə] Streikende(r m) f; **strik·ing** □ [~ɪŋ] Schlag...; auffallend; eindrucksvoll; treffend.

string [strɪŋ] 1. Schnur f; Bindfaden m; Band n; Faden m, Draht m; (Bogen)Sehne f; ⚘ Faser f; Reihe f, Kette f; ♩ Saite f; ~s pl. ♩ Streichinstrumente pl., die Streicher pl.; pull the ~s fig. der Drahtzieher sein; no ~s attached ohne Bedingungen; 2. (strung) spannen; Perlen etc. aufreihen; ♩ besaiten; bespannen; (ver-, zu)schnüren; Bohnen abziehen; be strung up angespannt od. erregt sein; **~band** ♩ ['strɪŋbænd] Streichorchester n.

strin·gent □ ['strɪndʒənt] streng, scharf; zwingend; knapp.

string·y ['strɪŋɪ] (-ier, -iest) faserig; sehnig; zäh.

strip [strɪp] 1. (-pp-) entkleiden (a. fig.); a. ~ off abziehen, abstreifen, (ab)schälen; (sich) ausziehen; a. ~ down ⊕ zerlegen, auseinandernehmen; fig. entblößen, berauben; 2. Streifen m.

stripe [straɪp] Streifen m; ✕ Tresse f.

strip·ling ['strɪplɪŋ] Bürschchen n.

strive [straɪv] (strove, striven) streben; sich bemühen; ringen (for um);

striv·en ['strɪvn] p.p. von strive.

strode [strəʊd] pret. von stride 1.

stroke [strəʊk] 1. Schlag m; Streich m, Stoß m; Strich m; ⚕ Schlag(anfall) m; ~ of (good) luck Glücksfall m; 2. streichen über; streicheln.

stroll [strəʊl] 1. schlendern, (herum)bummeln; herumziehen; 2. Bummel m, Spaziergang m; **~er** ['strəʊlə] Bummler(in), Spaziergänger(in); Am. (Falt)Sportwagen m.

S

strong □ [strɒŋ] stark; kräftig; energisch; überzeugt; fest; stark, schwer (*Getränk etc.*); **~box** [ˈstrɒŋbɒks] Geld-, Stahlkassette *f*; **~hold** Festung *f*; *fig.* Hochburg *f*; **~mind·ed** willensstark; **~room** Stahlkammer *f*, Tresor(raum) *m*.

strove [strəʊv] *pret. von* strive.

struck [strʌk] *pret. u. p.p. von* strike 2.

struc·ture [ˈstrʌktʃə] Bau(werk *n*) *m*; Struktur *f*, Gefüge *n*; Gebilde *n*.

strug·gle [ˈstrʌgl] **1.** sich (ab)mühen; kämpfen, ringen; sich winden, zappeln, sich sträuben; **2.** Kampf *m*, Ringen *n*; Anstrengung *f*.

strum [strʌm] (-*mm*-) klimpern (auf).

strung [strʌŋ] *pret. u. p.p. von* string 2.

strut [strʌt] **1.** (-*tt*-) *v/i.* stolzieren; *v/t.* ⊕ abstützen; **2.** Stolzieren *n*; ⊕ Strebe(balken *m*) *f*, Stütze *f*.

stub [stʌb] **1.** (Baum)Stumpf *m*; Stummel *m*; Kontrollabschnitt *m*; **2.** (-*bb*-) (aus)roden; sich *die Zehe* anstoßen; **~ out** *Zigarette etc.* ausdrücken.

stub·ble [ˈstʌbl] Stoppel(n *pl.*) *f*.

stub·born □ [ˈstʌbən] eigensinnig; widerspenstig; stur; hartnäckig.

stuck [stʌk] *pret. u. p.p. von* stick 2; **~up** F [ˈstʌkˈʌp] hochnäsig.

stud[1] [stʌd] **1.** Beschlagnagel *m*; Ziernagel *m*; Knauf *m*; Manschetten-, Kragenknopf *m*; **2.** (-*dd*-) mit Nägeln *etc.* beschlagen; übersäen.

stud[2] [~] Gestüt *n*; △ *nicht* Stute; **~horse** (Zucht)Hengst *m*; **~book** Gestütbuch *n*; **~farm** Gestüt *n*; **~mare** Zuchtstute *f*.

stu·dent [ˈstjuːdnt] Student(in); *Am.* Schüler(in).

stud·ied □ [ˈstʌdɪd] einstudiert; gesucht, gewollt; wohlüberlegt.

stu·di·o [ˈstjuːdɪəʊ] (*pl.* -os) Atelier *n*, Studio *n*; (Fernseh-, Rundfunk-) Studio *n*, Aufnahme-, Senderaum *m*.

stu·di·ous □ [ˈstjuːdjəs] fleißig; eifrig bemüht; sorgfältig, peinlich.

stud·y [ˈstʌdɪ] **1.** Studium *n*; Studier-, Arbeitszimmer *n*; *paint. etc.* Studie *f*; *studies pl.* Studium *n*, Studien *pl.*; *in a brown ~* in Gedanken versunken, geistesabwesend; **2.** (ein)studieren; lernen; studieren, erforschen; sich bemühen um.

stuff [stʌf] **1.** Stoff *m*; Zeug *n*; **2.** *v/t.* (voll-, aus)stopfen; füllen; △ *nicht* stopfen (*ausbessern*); *v/i.* sich vollstopfen; **~ing** [ˈstʌfɪŋ] Füllung *f*; **~·y** □ [~ɪ] (-*ier*, -*iest*) dumpf, muffig, stickig; langweilig, fad; F spießig; F prüde.

stum·ble [ˈstʌmbl] **1.** Stolpern *n*, Straucheln *n*; Fehltritt *m*; **2.** stolpern, straucheln; **~across**, **~on**, **~upon** zufällig stoßen auf (*acc.*).

stump [stʌmp] **1.** Stumpf *m*, Stummel *m*; **2.** *v/t.* F verblüffen; *v/i.* stampfen, stapfen; **~·y** □ [ˈstʌmpɪ] (-*ier*, -*iest*) gedrungen; plump.

stun [stʌn] (-*nn*-) betäuben (*a. fig.*).

stung [stʌŋ] *pret. u. p.p. von* sting 2.

stunk [stʌŋk] *pret. u. p.p. von* stink 2.

stun·ning □ F [ˈstʌnɪŋ] toll, phantastisch.

stunt[1] [stʌnt] Kunststück *n*; (Reklame)Trick *m*; Sensation *f*; **~man** *Film:* Stuntman *m*, Double *n*.

stunt[2] [~] (im Wachstum *etc.*) hemmen; **~ed** [ˈstʌntɪd] verkümmert.

stu·pe·fy [ˈstjuːpɪfaɪ] betäuben; *fig.* verblüffen.

stu·pen·dous □ [stjuːˈpendəs] verblüffend, erstaunlich.

stu·pid □ [ˈstjuːpɪd] dumm, einfältig; stumpfsinnig; blöd; **~·i·ty** [stjuːˈpɪdətɪ] Dummheit *f*; Stumpfsinn *m*.

stu·por [ˈstjuːpə] Erstarrung *f*, Betäubung *f*.

stur·dy □ [ˈstɜːdɪ] (-*ier*, -*iest*) robust, kräftig; *fig.* entschlossen.

stut·ter [ˈstʌtə] **1.** stottern; stammeln; **2.** Stottern *n*; Stammeln *n*.

sty[1] [staɪ] Schweinestall *m*.

sty[2], **stye** ✱ [~] Gerstenkorn *n*.

style [staɪl] **1.** Stil *m*; Mode *f*; (Mach)Art *f*; Titel *m*, Anrede *f*; **2.** nennen; entwerfen; gestalten.

styl·ish □ [ˈstaɪlɪʃ] stilvoll; elegant; **~ish·ness** [~nɪs] Eleganz *f*; **~·ist** [~ɪst] Stilist(in).

suave □ [swɑːv] verbindlich; mild.

sub- [sʌb] Unter..., unter...; Neben..., untergeordnet; Hilfs...; fast ...

sub·di·vi·sion [ˈsʌbdɪvɪʒn] Unterteilung *f*; Unterabteilung *f*.

sub·due [səbˈdjuː] unterwerfen; bezwingen; bändigen; dämpfen.

sub·ject 1. [ˈsʌbdʒɪkt] unterworfen; untergeben; abhängig; untertan; ausgesetzt (*to dat.*); *be ~ to* neigen zu; ~ *to* vorbehaltlich (*gen.*); **2.** [~] Untertan(in); Staatsbürger(in), -angehörige(r *m*) *f*; *gr.* Subjekt *n*, Satzgegenstand *m*; Thema *n*, Gegenstand *m*; (Lehr-, Schul-, Studien-)Fach *n*; **3.** [səb'dʒekt] unterwerfen; *fig.* unterwerfen, -ziehen, aussetzen (*to dat.*); **~·jec·tion** [~kʃn] Unterwerfung *f*; Abhängigkeit *f*.

sub·ju·gate ['sʌbdʒʊɡeɪt] unterjochen, -werfen.

sub·junc·tive *gr.* [səb'dʒʌŋktɪv] *a.* ~ *mood* Konjunktiv *m*.

sub·lease ['sʌb'liːs], **~·let** (-*tt*-; -*let*) untervermieten.

sub·lime □ [sə'blaɪm] erhaben.

sub·ma·chine gun ['sʌbmə'ʃiːn ɡʌn] Maschinenpistole *f*.

sub·ma·rine ['sʌbməriːn] **1.** unterseeisch, Untersee...; **2.** ⚓, ⚔ Unterseeboot *n*.

sub·merge [səb'mɜːdʒ] (unter)tauchen; überschwemmen.

sub·mis·sion [səb'mɪʃn] Unterwerfung *f*; Unterbreitung *f*; **~·sive** □ [~sɪv] unterwürfig; ergeben.

sub·mit [səb'mɪt] (-*tt*-) (sich) unterwerfen *od.* -ziehen; unterbreiten, vorlegen; sich fügen *od.* ergeben (*to dat. od. in acc.*).

sub·or·di·nate 1. □ [sə'bɔːdɪnət] untergeordnet; nebensächlich; ~ *clause gr.* Nebensatz *m*; **2.** [~] Untergebene(r *m*) *f*; **3.** [~eɪt] unterordnen.

sub·scribe [səb'skraɪb] *v/t.* Geld stiften, spenden (*to* für); *Summe* zeichnen; mit *s-m Namen* unterzeichnen, unterschreiben mit; *v/i.* ~ *to Zeitung etc.* abonnieren; **~·scrib·er** [~ə] (Unter)Zeichner(in); Spender(in); Abonnent(in); *teleph.* Teilnehmer(in), Anschluß *m*.

sub·scrip·tion [səb'skrɪpʃn] Vorbestellung *f*, Subskription *f*; (Mitglieds)Beitrag *m*; Spende *f*.

sub·se·quent ['sʌbsɪkwənt] (nach-)folgend; **~·ly** nachher; später.

sub·ser·vi·ent □ [səb'sɜːvjənt] dienlich; unterwürfig.

sub·side [səb'saɪd] sinken *od.* sich senken; sich setzen; sich legen (*Wind etc.*); ~ *into* versinken in (*acc.*); **~·sid·i·a·ry** [~'sɪdjərɪ] **1.** □ Hilfs...; Neben..., untergeordnet; **2.** *econ.* Tochter(gesellschaft) *f*; **~·si·dize** ['sʌbsɪdaɪz] subventionieren; **~·si·dy** [~ɪ] Beihilfe *f*; Subvention *f*.

sub·sist [səb'sɪst] leben, sich ernähren (*on* von); **~·sis·tence** [~əns] Dasein *n*, Existenz *f*; (Lebens)Unterhalt *m*.

sub·stance ['sʌbstəns] Substanz *f*; *das* Wesentliche, Kern *m*, Gehalt *m*; Vermögen *n*.

sub·stan·dard ['sʌb'stændəd] unter der Norm; ~ *film* Schmalfilm *m*.

sub·stan·tial □ [səb'stænʃl] wesentlich; wirklich (vorhanden); beträchtlich; reichlich; kräftig; stark; solid; vermögend; namhaft (*Summe*).

sub·stan·ti·ate [səb'stænʃɪeɪt] beweisen, begründen.

sub·stan·tive *gr.* ['sʌbstəntɪv] Substantiv *n*, Hauptwort *n*.

sub·sti·tute ['sʌbstɪtjuːt] **1.** an die Stelle setzen *od.* treten (*for* von); ~ *s.th. for s.th.* et. durch et. ersetzen, et. gegen et. austauschen *od.* -wechseln; **2.** Stellvertreter(in), Vertretung *f*; Ersatz *m*; **~·tu·tion** [sʌbstɪ'tjuːʃn] Stellvertretung *f*; Ersatz *m*; *Sport:* Auswechslung *f*.

sub·ter·fuge ['sʌbtəfjuːdʒ] Vorwand *m*, Ausflucht *f*; List *f*.

sub·ter·ra·ne·an □ ['sʌbtə'reɪnjən] unterirdisch.

sub·ti·tle ['sʌbtaɪtl] Untertitel *m*.

sub·tle □ ['sʌtl] (~*r*, ~*st*) fein(sinnig); subtil; scharf(sinnig).

sub·tract ⅍ [səb'trækt] abziehen, subtrahieren.

sub·trop·i·cal ['sʌb'trɒpɪkl] subtropisch.

sub·urb ['sʌbɜːb] Vorstadt *f*, -ort *m*; **~·ur·ban** [sə'bɜːbən] vorstädtisch.

sub·ven·tion [səb'venʃn] Subvention *f*.

sub·ver·sion [səb'vɜːʃn] Umsturz *m*; **~·sive** □ [~sɪv] umstürzlerisch, subversiv; **~t** [~t] stürzen.

sub·way ['sʌbweɪ] (Straßen-, Fußgänger)Unterführung *f*; *Am.* Untergrundbahn *f*, U-Bahn *f*.

suc·ceed [sək'siːd] *v/i.* Erfolg haben; glücken, gelingen; ~ *to* folgen (*dat.*) *od.* auf (*acc.*), nachfolgen (*dat.*); *v/t.* (nach)folgen (*dat.*), *j-s* Nachfolger werden.

suc·cess [sək'ses] Erfolg *m*; **~·ful** □ [~fl] erfolgreich.

suc·ces·sion [sək'seʃn] (Nach-, Erb-, Reihen)Folge *f*; *in* ~ nacheinander; **~·sive** □ [~sɪv] aufeinanderfolgend; **~·sor** [~ə] Nachfolger(in).

S

suc·co(u)r [ˈsʌkə] 1. Hilfe f; 2. helfen.
suc·cu·lent □ [ˈsʌkjʊlənt] saftig.
suc·cumb [səˈkʌm] unter-, erliegen.
such [sʌtʃ] solche(r, -s); derartige(r, -s); so; ~ a man ein solcher Mann; ~ as diejenigen, welche; wie.
suck [sʌk] 1. saugen (an dat.); aussaugen; lutschen (an dat.); 2. Saugen n; ~er [ˈsʌkə] Saugorgan n; ♀ Wurzelschößling m; F Trottel m, Simpel m; ~le [˞l] säugen, stillen; ~ling [˞lɪŋ] Säugling m.
suc·tion [ˈsʌkʃn] (An)Saugen n; Sog m; attr. (An)Saug...
sud·den □ [ˈsʌdn] plötzlich; (all) of a ~ (ganz) plötzlich.
suds [sʌdz] pl. Seifenlauge f; Seifenschaum m; ~y [ˈsʌdzɪ] (-ier, -iest) schaumig.
sue [sjuː] v/t. verklagen (for auf acc., wegen); a. ~ out erwirken; v/i. nachsuchen (for um); klagen.
suede, suède [sweɪd] Wildleder n.
su·et [ˈsjʊɪt] Nierenfett n, Talg m.
suf·fer [ˈsʌfə] v/i. leiden (from an, unter dat.); büßen; v/t. erleiden, erdulden; (zu)lassen; ~ance [˞rəns] Duldung f; ~er [˞ə] Leidende(r m) f; Dulder(in); ~ing [˞ɪŋ] Leiden n.
suf·fice [səˈfaɪs] genügen; ~ it to say es genügt wohl, wenn ich sage.
suf·fi·cien|cy [səˈfɪʃnsɪ] genügende Menge; Auskommen n; ~t [˞t] genügend, genug, ausreichend; be ~ genügen, (aus)reichen.
suf·fix [ˈsʌfɪks] Suffix n, Nachsilbe f.
suf·fo·cate [ˈsʌfəkeɪt] ersticken.
suf·frage [ˈsʌfrɪdʒ] (Wahl)Stimme f; Wahl-, Stimmrecht n.
suf·fuse [səˈfjuːz] übergießen; überziehen.
sug·ar [ˈʃʊgə] 1. Zucker m; 2. zuckern; ~ba·sin, bsd. Am. ~ bowl Zuckerdose f; ~cane ♀ Zuckerrohr n; ~coat überzuckern; fig. versüßen; ~y [˞rɪ] zuckerig; fig. zuckersüß.
sug|gest [səˈdʒest, Am. a. səgˈdʒest] vorschlagen, anregen; nahelegen; hinweisen auf (acc.); Gedanken eingeben; andeuten; denken lassen an (acc.); ~ges·tion [˞tʃən] Anregung f, Vorschlag m; psych. Suggestion f; Eingebung f; Andeutung f; ~ges·tive □ [˞tɪv] anregend; vielsagend; zweideutig; be ~ of s.th. auf et. hindeuten; an et. denken lassen; den Eindruck von et. erwecken.

su·i·cide [ˈsjʊɪsaɪd] 1. Selbstmord m; Selbstmörder(in); commit ~ Selbstmord begehen; 2. Am. Selbstmord begehen.
suit [sjuːt] 1. (Herren)Anzug m; (Damen)Kostüm n; Anliegen n; Werben n (um e-e Frau); Karten: Farbe f; ⅌ Prozeß m; follow ~ fig. dem Beispiel folgen, dasselbe tun; 2. v/t. j-m passen, zusagen, bekommen; j-n kleiden, j-m stehen, passen zu; ~ oneself tun, was e-m beliebt; ~ yourself mach, was du willst; ~ s.th. to et. anpassen (dat.) od. an (acc.); be ~ed geeignet sein (for, to für, zu); v/i. passen; **sui·ta·ble** □ [ˈsjuːtəbl] passend, geeignet (for, to für, zu); ~case (Hand)Koffer m.
suite [swiːt] Gefolge n; ♪ Suite f; Zimmerflucht f, Suite f; (Möbel-, Sitz)Garnitur f, (Zimmer)Einrichtung f.
sui·tor [ˈsjuːtə] Freier m; ⅌ Kläger(in).
sul·fur, etc. Am. [ˈsʌlfə] s. sulphur, etc.
sulk [sʌlk] schmollen, eingeschnappt sein; ~i·ness [ˈsʌlkɪnɪs], ~s pl. Schmollen n; ~y [˞ɪ] 1. □ (-ier, -iest) verdrießlich; schmollend; 2. Sport: Sulky n, Traberwagen m.
sul·len □ [ˈsʌlən] verdrossen, mürrisch; düster, trübe.
sul·ly mst fig. [ˈsʌlɪ] beflecken.
sul|phur ⚗ [ˈsʌlfə] Schwefel m; ~phu·ric** ⚗ [sʌlˈfjʊərɪk] Schwefel...
sul·tri·ness [ˈsʌltrɪnɪs] Schwüle f.
sul·try □ [ˈsʌltrɪ] (-ier, -iest) schwül; fig. heftig, hitzig.
sum [sʌm] 1. Summe f; Betrag m; Rechenaufgabe f; fig. Inbegriff m; do ~s rechnen; 2. (-mm-) ~ up zusammenzählen, addieren; j-n kurz einschätzen; Situation erfassen; zusammenfassen.
sum|ma·rize [ˈsʌməraɪz] zusammenfassen; ~ma·ry** [˞rɪ] 1. □ kurz (zusammengefaßt); ⅌ Schnell...; 2. (kurze) Inhaltsangabe, Zusammenfassung f.
sum·mer [ˈsʌmə] Sommer m; ~ school Ferienkurs m; ~ly [˞lɪ], ~y [˞rɪ] sommerlich.
sum·mit [ˈsʌmɪt] Gipfel m (a. fig.).
sum·mon [ˈsʌmən] auffordern; (einbe)rufen; ⅌ vorladen; ~ up Mut etc. zusammennehmen, auf-

bieten; **~s** Aufforderung *f*; ⚖ Vorladung *f*.

sump·tu·ous □ ['sʌmptjʊəs] kostspielig; üppig, aufwendig.

sun [sʌn] 1. Sonne *f*; *attr.* Sonnen...; 2. (-nn-) der Sonne aussetzen; **~** (o.s.) sich sonnen; **~** sich sonnen; **~bath** ['sʌnbɑːθ] Sonnenbad *n*; **~beam** Sonnenstrahl *m*; **~burn** Sonnenbräune *f*; Sonnenbrand *m*.

sun·dae ['sʌndeɪ] Eisbecher *m* mit Früchten.

Sun|day ['sʌndɪ] Sonntag *m*; *on* **~** (am) Sonntag; *on* **~s** sonntags.

sun|di·al ['sʌndaɪəl] Sonnenuhr *f*; **~down** = sunset.

sun|dries ['sʌndrɪz] *pl.* Diverse(s) *n*, Verschiedene(s) *n*; **~dry** [ʌɪ] verschiedene.

sung [sʌŋ] *p.p.* von sing.

sun·glass·es ['sʌnglɑːsɪz] *pl.* (a pair of **~** e-e) Sonnenbrille.

sunk [sʌŋk] *pret. u. p.p.* von sink 1.

sunk·en *adj.* ['sʌŋkən] versunken; tiefliegend; *fig.* eingefallen.

sun|ny □ ['sʌnɪ] (-ier, -iest) sonnig; **~rise** Sonnenaufgang *m*; **~set** Sonnenuntergang *m*; **~shade** Sonnenschirm *m*; Markise *f*; **~shine** Sonnenschein *m*; **~stroke** ♒ Sonnenstich *m*; **~tan** (Sonnen)Bräune *f*.

su·per F ['suːpə] super, toll, prima, Spitze, Klasse.

su·per- ['sjuːpə] Über..., über...; Ober..., ober...; Super..., Groß...; **~a·bun·dant** □ [ʌrə'bʌndənt] überreichlich; überschwenglich; **~an·nu·ate** [sjuːpə'rænjʊeɪt] pensionieren; **~d** pensioniert; veraltet.

su·perb □ [sjuː'pɜːb] prächtig, herrlich, großartig; ausgezeichnet.

su·per|charg·er *mot.* ['sjuːpətʃɑːdʒə] Kompressor *m*; **~cil·i·ous** □ [ʌ'sɪlɪəs] hochmütig; **~fi·cial** □ [ʌ'fɪʃl] oberflächlich; **~fine** [ʌ'faɪn] extrafein; **~flu·i·ty** [ʌ'fluːətɪ] Überfluß *m*; **~flu·ous** □ [sjuː'pɜːflʊəs] überflüssig; überreichlich; **~heat** ⊕ ['sjuːpə'hiːt] überhitzen; **~hu·man** □ [ʌ'hjuːmən] übermenschlich; **~im·pose** [ʌrɪm'pəʊz] darauf-, darüberlegen; überlagern; **~in·tend** [ʌrɪn'tend] die (Ober)Aufsicht haben über (*acc.*), überwachen; leiten; **~in·tend·ent** [ʌənt] 1. Leiter *m*, Direktor *m*; (Ober)Aufseher *m*, Inspektor *m*; *Brt.* Kommissar (-in); *Am.* Polizeichef *m*; *Am.*

Hausverwalter *m*; 2. aufsichtführend.

su·pe·ri·or [sjuːˈpɪərɪə] 1. □ höhere(r, -s), höherstehend, vorgesetzt; besser, hochwertiger; überlegen (*to dat.*); hervorragend; 2. Höherstehende(r) (*m f*) *f*, *bsd.* Vorgesetzte(r *m*) *f*; *mst* Father ♀ *eccl.* Superior *m*; *mst* Lady ♀, Mother ♀ *eccl.* Oberin *f*; **~i·ty** [sjuːpɪərɪˈɒrətɪ] Überlegenheit *f*.

su·per·la·tive [sjuːˈpɜːlətɪv] 1. □ höchste(r, -s); überragend; 2. *a.* **~ degree** *gr.* Superlativ *m*.

su·per|mar·ket ['sjuːpəmɑːkɪt] Supermarkt *m*; **~nat·u·ral** □ [ʌ'nætʃrəl] übernatürlich; **~nu·me·ra·ry** [ʌ'njuːmərərɪ] 1. überzählig; zusätzlich; 2. Zusatzperson *f*, -sache *f*; *thea.*, *Film:* Statist(in); **~scrip·tion** [ʌ'skrɪpʃn] Über-, Aufschrift *f*; **~sede** [ʌ'siːd] ersetzen; verdrängen; absetzen; ablösen; **~son·ic** *phys.* [ʌ'sɒnɪk] Überschall...; **~sti·tion** [ʌ'stɪʃn] Aberglaube *m*; **~sti·tious** □ [ʌəs] abergläubisch; **~vene** [ʌ'viːn] (noch) hinzukommen; dazwischenkommen; **~vise** [ʌvaɪz] beaufsichtigen, überwachen; **~vi·sion** [ʌ'vɪʒn] (Ober)Aufsicht *f*; Beaufsichtigung *f*, Überwachung *f*; **~vi·sor** [ʌvaɪzə] Aufseher(in); Leiter(in).

sup·per ['sʌpə] Abendessen *n*; *the (Lord's)* ♀ das heilige Abendmahl.

sup·plant [sə'plɑːnt] verdrängen.

sup·ple ['sʌpl] 1. □ (**~r**, **~st**) geschmeidig; 2. geschmeidig machen.

sup·ple|ment 1. ['sʌplɪmənt] Ergänzung *f*; Nachtrag *m*; (Zeitungs-*etc.*)Beilage *f*; 2. [ʌment] ergänzen; **~men·tal** [ʌ'mentl], **~men·ta·ry** [ʌərɪ] Ergänzungs...; nachträglich; Nachtrags...

sup·pli·ant ['sʌplɪənt] 1. □ demütig bittend, flehend; 2. Bittsteller(in).

sup·pli·cate ['sʌplɪkeɪt] demütig bitten; (an)flehen; **~ca·tion** [sʌplɪ'keɪʃn] demütige Bitte.

sup·pli·er [sə'plaɪə] Lieferant(in); *a.* **~s** *pl.* Lieferfirma *f*.

sup·ply [sə'plaɪ] 1. liefern; *e-m Mangel* abhelfen; *e-e Stelle* ausfüllen; beliefern, ausstatten, versorgen; ergänzen; 2. Lieferung *f*; Versorgung *f*; Zufuhr *f*; *econ.* Angebot *n*; (Stell)Vertretung *f*; *mst* supplies *pl.* Vorrat *m*; *econ.* Artikel *m*, Bedarf *m*;

parl. bewilligter Etat; ~ *and demand econ.* Angebot u. Nachfrage.

sup·port [sə'pɔ:t] **1.** Stütze *f*; Hilfe *f*; ⊕ Träger *m*; Unterstützung *f*; (Lebens)Unterhalt *m*; **2.** tragen, (ab)stützen; unterstützen; unterhalten, sorgen für (*Familie etc.*); ertragen; ~**er** [~ə] Anhänger(in) (*a. Sport*), Befürworter(in).

sup·pose [sə'pəuz] annehmen; voraussetzen; vermuten; *he is* ~*d to do* er soll tun; ~ *we go* gehen wir!; wie wär's, wenn wir gingen?; *what is that* ~*d to mean?* was soll denn das?; *I* ~ *so* ich nehme es an, vermutlich. **sup·posed** □ [sə'pəuzd] vermeintlich; ~**pos·ed·ly** [~dlɪ] angeblich.

sup·po·si·tion [sʌpə'zɪʃn] Voraussetzung *f*; Annahme *f*, Vermutung *f*.

sup|press [sə'pres] unterdrücken; ~**pres·sion** [~ʃn] Unterdrückung *f*.

sup·pu·rate 🔊 ['sʌpjuəreɪt] eitern.

su·prem·a·cy [sju'preməsɪ] Oberhoheit *f*; Vorherrschaft *f*; Überlegenheit *f*; Vorrang *m*; ~**e** □ [sju:'pri:m] höchste(r, -s); oberste(r, -s); Ober ..; größte(r, -s).

sur·charge 1. [sɜ:'tʃɑ:dʒ] e-n Zuschlag *od.* ein Nachporto *etc.* erheben auf (*acc.*); **2.** ['sɜ:tʃɑ:dʒ] Zuschlag *m*; Nach-, Strafporto *n*; Über-, Aufdruck *m* (*auf Briefmarken*).

sure [ʃuə] **1.** *adj.* □ (~*r*, ~*st*): ~ (*of*) sicher, gewiß (*gen.*), überzeugt (von); *make* ~ *that* sich (davon) überzeugen, daß; **2.** *adv. Am.* F wirklich; *it* ~ *was cold Am.* F es war vielleicht kalt!; ~*!* klar!, aber sicher!; ~ *enough* ganz bestimmt; tatsächlich; ~**ly** ['ʃuəlɪ] sicher(lich); **sure·ty** [~tɪ] Kaution *f*; Bürge *m*.

surf [sɜ:f] **1.** Brandung *f*; **2.** *Sport:* surfen.

sur·face ['sɜ:fɪs] **1.** (Ober)Fläche *f*; ⚓ Tragfläche *f*; **2.** ⚓ auftauchen (*U-Boot*).

surf|board ['sɜ:fbɔ:d] Surfbrett *n*; ~**boat** Brandungsboot *n*.

sur·feit ['sɜ:fɪt] **1.** Übersättigung *f*; Überdruß *m*; **2.** (sich) übersättigen *od.* -füttern.

surf·er ['sɜ:fə] *Sport:* Surfer(in), Wellenreiter(in); ~**ing** [~ɪŋ], ~**rid·ing** [~raɪdɪŋ] *Sport:* Surfen *n*, Wellenreiten *n*.

surge [sɜ:dʒ] **1.** Woge *f*; **2.** wogen; (vorwärts)drängen; *a.* ~ *up* (auf)wallen (*Gefühle*).

sur·geon ['sɜ:dʒən] Chirurg *m*; ~**ge·ry** [~rɪ] Chirurgie *f*; operativer Eingriff, Operation *f*; *Brt.* Sprechzimmer *n*; ~ *hours pl. Brt.* Sprechstunde(n *pl.*) *f*.

sur·gi·cal □ ['sɜ:dʒɪkl] chirurgisch.

sur·ly □ ['sɜ:lɪ] (*-ier, -iest*) mürrisch; grob.

sur·mise 1. ['sɜ:maɪz] Vermutung *f*; **2.** [sɜ:'maɪz] vermuten.

sur·mount [sɜ:'maunt] überwinden.

sur·name ['sɜ:neɪm] Familien-, Nach-, Zuname *m*.

sur·pass *fig.* [sə'pɑ:s] übersteigen, -treffen; ~**ing** [~ɪŋ] unvergleichlich.

sur·plus ['sɜ:pləs] **1.** Überschuß *m*, Mehr *n*; **2.** überschüssig; Über(schuß)...

sur·prise [sə'praɪz] **1.** Überraschung *f*; ⚔ Überrump(e)lung *f*; **2.** überraschen; ⚔ überrumpeln.

sur·ren·der [sə'rendə] **1.** Übergabe *f*; Kapitulation *f*; Aufgabe *f*, Verzicht *m*; Hingabe *f*; **2.** *v/t. et.* übergeben; aufgeben; *v/i.* sich ergeben (*to dat.*), kapitulieren; sich hingeben *od.* überlassen (*to dat.*).

sur·ro·gate ['sʌrəgɪt] Ersatz *m*; ~ *mother* Leihmutter *f*.

sur·round [sə'raund] umgeben; ⚔ umzingeln, -stellen; ~**ing** [~ɪŋ] umliegend; ~**ings** *pl.* Umgebung *f*.

sur·tax ['sɜ:tæks] Steuerzuschlag *m*.

sur·vey 1. [sə'veɪ] überblicken; sorgfältig prüfen; begutachten; *Land* vermessen; **2.** ['sɜ:veɪ] Überblick *m* (*a. fig.*); sorgfältige Prüfung; Inspektion *f*, Besichtigung *f*; Gutachten *n*; (Land)Vermessung *f*; (Lage-) Karte *f*, (-)Plan *m*; ~**or** [sə'veɪə] Landmesser *m*; (amtlicher) Inspektor.

sur·viv·al [sə'vaɪvl] Überleben *n*; Fortleben *n*; Überbleibsel *n*; ~ *kit* Überlebensausrüstung *f*; ~**vive** [~aɪv] überleben, am Leben bleiben; noch leben; fortleben; bestehen bleiben; ~**vi·vor** [~ə] Überlebende(r *m*) *f*.

sus·cep·ti·ble □ [sə'septəbl] empfänglich (*to für*); empfindlich (*to gegen*); *be* ~ *of et.* zulassen.

sus·pect 1. [sə'spekt] (be)argwöhnen; in Verdacht haben, verdächtigen; vermuten, befürchten; **2.** ['sʌspekt] Verdächtige(r *m*) *f*; **3.** [~] = ~**ed** [sə'spektɪd] verdächtig.

sus·pend [sə'spend] (auf)hängen;

aufschieben; in der Schwebe lassen; *Zahlung* einstellen; *Verfahren etc.* aussetzen; suspendieren; *Sport:* j-n sperren; **~ed** [~ɪd] schwebend; hängend; *a.* zur Bewährung ausgesetzt; suspendiert; **~er** [~ə] *Brt.* Strumpf-, Sockenhalter *m*; (*a pair of*) ~s *pl. Am.* Hosenträger *pl.*

sus|pic·ion [sə'spɪʃn] Verdacht *m*; Mißtrauen *n*; *fig.* Spur *f*; **~·cious** ☐ [~əs] verdächtig; mißtrauisch.

sus·tain [sə'steɪn] stützen, tragen; *u. fig.*); erleiden; *Familie* ernähren; j-m Kraft geben; *xtx e-m Einspruch* stattgeben.

sus·te·nance ['sʌstɪnəns] (Lebens-) Unterhalt *m*; Nahrung *f*.

swab [swɔb] **1.** Scheuerlappen *m*, Mop *m*; *⚕* Tupfer *m*; *⚕* Abstrich *m*; **2.** (*-bb-*) ~ *up* aufwischen.

swad·dle ['swɔdl] *Baby* wickeln; **~·dling-clothes** [~ɪŋkləʊðz] *pl.* Windeln *pl.*

swag·ger ['swægə] stolzieren; prahlen, großtun.

swal·low[1] *zo.* ['swɔləʊ] Schwalbe *f*.

swal·low[2] [~] **1.** Schlund *m*; Schluck *m*; **2.** (hinunter-, ver)schlucken; *Beleidigung* einstecken, schlucken; F für bare Münze nehmen.

swam [swæm] *pret. von* swim 1.

swamp [swɔmp] **1.** Sumpf *m*; **2.** überschwemmen (*a. fig.*); *Boot* volllaufen lassen; **~y** ['swɔmpɪ] (*-ier, -iest*) sumpfig.

swan *zo.* [swɔn] Schwan *m*.

swank F [swæŋk] **1.** Angabe *f*, Protzerei *f*; **2.** angeben, protzen; **~y** ☐ ['swæŋkɪ] (*-ier, -iest*) protzig, angeberisch.

swap F [swɔp] **1.** Tausch *m*; **2.** (*-pp-*) (ein-, aus)tauschen.

swarm [swɔːm] **1.** (Bienen- *etc.*) Schwarm *m*; Haufen *m*, Schar *f*, Horde *f*; **2.** schwärmen (*Bienen*); wimmeln (*with* von).

swar·thy ☐ ['swɔːðɪ] (*-ier, -iest*) dunkel(häutig).

swash [swɔʃ] plan(t)schen.

swat [swɔt] (*-tt-*) *Fliege etc.* totschlagen.

sway [sweɪ] **1.** Schwanken *n*; Einfluß *m*; Herrschaft *f*; **2.** schwanken; (sich) wiegen; schwingen; beeinflussen; beherrschen.

swear [sweə] (*swore, sworn*) schwören; fluchen; ~ *s.o. in* j-n vereidigen.

sweat [swet] **1.** Schweiß *m*; Schwitzen *n*; *by the* ~ *of one's brow* im Schweiße seines Angesichts; *in a* ~, F *all of a* ~ in Schweiß gebadet (*a. fig.*); **2.** (*sweated, Am. mst sweat*) *v/i.* schwitzen; *v/t.* (aus)schwitzen; in Schweiß bringen; *econ.* schuften lassen, ausbeuten; **~er** ['swetə] Sweater *m*, Pullover *m*; *econ.* Ausbeuter *m*; **~·shirt** Sweatshirt *n*; ~ *suit Sport: bsd. Am.* Trainingsanzug *m*; **~y** ☐ [~ɪ] (*-ier, -iest*) schweißig; verschwitzt.

Swede [swiːd] Schwed|e *m*, -in *f*.

Swed·ish ['swiːdɪʃ] **1.** schwedisch; **2.** *ling.* Schwedisch *n*.

sweep [swiːp] **1.** (*swept*) fegen (*a. fig.*), kehren; gleiten *od.* schweifen über (*acc.*) (*Blick*); (majestätisch) einherschreiten *od.* (dahin)rauschen; **2.** (*fig. Dahin*)Fegen *n*; Kehren *n*; schwungvolle Bewegung; Schwung *m*; Spielraum *m*, Bereich *m*; *bsd. Brt.* Schornsteinfeger *m*; *make a clean* ~ gründlich aufräumen (*of* mit); *Sport:* überlegen siegen; **~er** ['swiːpə] (Straßen)Kehrer(in); Kehrmaschine *f*; **~·ing** ☐ [~ɪŋ] schwungvoll; umfassend; **~·ings** *pl.* Kehricht *m*, Müll *m*.

sweet [swiːt] **1.** ☐ süß; lieblich; freundlich; frisch; duftend; *have a* ~ *tooth* gern Süßes essen; **2.** *Brt.* Süßigkeit *f*, Bonbon *m*, *n*; *Brt.* Nachtisch *m*; Süße(r *m*) *f*; Schatz *m* (*als Anrede*); **~·en** ['swiːtn] (ver)süßen; **~·heart** Schatz *m*, Liebste(r *m*) *f*; **~·ish** [~ɪʃ] süßlich; **~·meat** Bonbon *m*, *n*; kandierte Frucht; **~·ness** [~nɪs] Süße *f*, Süßigkeit *f*; ~ *pea* ♀ Gartenwicke *f*; ~ *shop Brt.* Süßwarenladen *m*.

swell [swel] **1.** (*swelled, swollen od. swelled*) *v/i.* (an)schwellen; sich (auf)blähen; sich bauschen; *v/t.* (an)schwellen lassen; aufblähen; **2.** *Am.* F prima; **3.** Anschwellen *n*; Schwellung *f*; ⚓ Dünung *f*; **~·ing** ['swelɪŋ] Schwellung *f*, Geschwulst *f*.

S

swelter

swel·ter ['sweltə] vor Hitze umkommen.

swept [swept] *pret. u. p.p. von* sweep 1.

swerve [swɜːv] **1.** ausbrechen (*Auto, Pferd*); *mot.* das Steuer *od.* den Wagen herumreißen; schwenken (*Straße*); **2.** *mot.* Schlenker *m*; Ausweichbewegung *f*; Schwenk *m* (*e-r Straße*).

swift □ [swift] schnell, eilig, flink; **~ness** ['swiftnɪs] Schnelligkeit *f*.

swill [swil] **1.** (Ab)Spülen *n*; Spülicht *n*; **2.** (ab)spülen; F saufen.

swim [swim] **1.** (*-mm-*; *swam, swum*) (durch)schwimmen; schweben; *my head ~s* mir ist schwind(e)lig; **2.** Schwimmen *n*; *go for a ~* schwimmen gehen; *have od. take a ~* baden, schwimmen; *be in the ~* auf dem laufenden sein; **~mer** ['swimə] Schwimmer(in); **~ming** [~ɪŋ] **1.** Schwimmen *n*; **2.** Schwimm...; **~bath(s** *pl.*) Brt. *bsd.* Hallenbad *n*; **~pool** Schwimmbecken *n*, Swimmingpool *m*; Schwimmbad *n*; (*a pair of*) *~trunks pl.* (e-e) Badehose; **~suit** Badeanzug *m*.

swin·dle ['swɪndl] **1.** beschwindeln; betrügen; △ *nicht* schwindeln; **2.** Schwindel *m*, Betrug *m*.

swine [swaɪn] Schwein *n*.

swing [swɪŋ] **1.** (*swung*) schwingen; schwenken; schlenkern; baumeln (lassen); (sich) schaukeln; sich (*in den Angeln*) drehen (*Tür*); F baumeln, hängen; **2.** Schwingen *n*; Schwung *m*; Schaukel *f*; Spielraum *m*; *in full ~* in vollem Gange; **~door** ['swɪŋdɔː] Drehtür *f*.

swin·ish ['swaɪnɪʃ] schweinisch.

swipe [swaɪp] **1.** schlagen (*at* nach); F klauen; **2.** harter Schlag.

swirl [swɜːl] **1.** (herum)wirbeln, strudeln; **2.** Wirbel *m*, Strudel *m*.

Swiss [swɪs] **1.** schweizerisch, Schweizer...; **2.** Schweizer(in); *the ~ pl.* die Schweizer *pl.*

switch [swɪtʃ] **1.** Gerte *f*; *Am.* 🚂 Weiche *f*; ⚡ Schalter *m*; falscher Zopf; **2.** peitschen; *bsd. Am.* 🚂 rangieren; ⚡ (um)schalten; *fig.* wechseln, überleiten; *~ off* ⚡ ab-, ausschalten; *~ on* ⚡ an-, einschalten; **~board** ⚡ ['swɪtʃbɔːd] Schaltbrett *n*, -tafel *f*.

swiv·el ['swɪvl] **1.** ⊕ Drehring *m*;

attr. Dreh...; **2.** (*bsd. Brt.* -ll-, *Am.* -l-) (sich) drehen; schwenken.

swol·len ['swəʊlən] *p.p. von* swell 1.

swoon [swuːn] *veraltet* **1.** Ohnmacht *f*; **2.** in Ohnmacht fallen.

swoop [swuːp] **1.** *~ down on od. upon* herabstoßen auf (*acc.*) (*Raubvogel*); *fig.* herfallen über (*acc.*); **2.** Herabstoßen *n*; Razzia *f.*

swop F [swɒp] = swap.

sword [sɔːd] Schwert *n*; **~s·man** ['sɔːdzmən] (*pl.* -men) Fechter *m.*

swore [swɔː] *pret. von* swear.

sworn [swɔːn] *p.p. von* swear.

swum [swʌm] *p.p. von* swim 1.

swung [swʌŋ] *pret. u. p.p. von* swing 1.

syc·a·more ♌ ['sɪkəmɔː] Bergahorn *m*; *Am.* Platane *f.*

syl·la·ble ['sɪləbl] Silbe *f.*

syl·la·bus ['sɪləbəs] (*pl.* -buses, -bi [-baɪ]) (*bsd. Vorlesungs*)Verzeichnis *n*; *bsd.* Lehrplan *m.*

sym·bol ['sɪmbl] Symbol *n*, Sinnbild *n*; **~·ic, ~·i·cal** □ [sɪm'bɒlɪk], [~kl] sinnbildlich; **~·is·m** ['sɪmbəlɪzəm] Symbolik *f*; **~·ize** [~aɪz] symbolisieren.

sym|met·ric, ~·met·ri·cal □ [sɪ'metrɪk], [~kl] symmetrisch, ebenmäßig; **~·me·try** ['sɪmɪtrɪ] Symmetrie *f*; Ebenmaß *n.*

sym·pa|thet·ic [sɪmpə'θetɪk] (*~ally*) mitfühlend; △ *nicht* sympathisch; *~ strike* Sympathiestreik *m*; **~·thize** ['sɪmpəθaɪz] sympathisieren, mitfühlen; **~·thy** [~ɪ] Anteilnahme *f*, Mitgefühl *n*; △ *nicht* Sympathie.

sym·pho·ny ♪ ['sɪmfənɪ] Symphonie *f.*

symp·tom ['sɪmptəm] Symptom *n.*

syn·chro|nize ['sɪŋkrənaɪz] *v/i.* gleichzeitig sein; synchron gehen (*Uhr*) *od.* laufen (*Maschine*); *v/t.* Uhren abstimmen; Film, TV synchronisieren; *Geschehen* aufeinander abstimmen; **~·nous** □ [~əs] gleichzeitig; synchron.

syn·di·cate ['sɪndɪkət] Syndikat *n.*

syn·o·nym ['sɪnənɪm] Synonym *n*; **sy·non·y·mous** □ [sɪ'nɒnɪməs] synonym; gleichbedeutend.

sy·nop·sis [sɪ'nɒpsɪs] (*pl.* -ses [-siːz]) Übersicht *f*, Zusammenfassung *f.*

syn·tax *gr.* ['sɪntæks] Syntax *f.*

syn·the·sis ['sɪnθəsɪs] (*pl.* -ses [-siːz]) Synthese *f*; **~·thet·ic** [sɪn'θetɪk], **~·thet·i·cal** □ [~kl] synthetisch.

sy·ringe ['sırındʒ] **1.** Spritze *f*; **2.** (be-, ein-, aus)spritzen.

syr·up ['sırəp] Sirup *m*.

sys|tem ['sıstəm] System *n*;

physiol. Organismus *m*, Körper *m*; Plan *m*, Ordnung *f*; **~te·mat·ic** [sıstı'mætık] (**~ally**) systematisch.

T

ta *Brt. int.* F ['tɑː] danke.

tab [tæb] Streifen *m*; Etikett *n*, Schildchen *n*, Anhänger *m*; Schlaufe *f*, (Mantel)Aufhänger *m*; F Rechnung *f*.

ta·ble ['teɪbl] **1.** Tisch *m*; Tafel *f*; Tisch-, Tafelrunde *f*; Tabelle *f*, Verzeichnis *n*; = *tableland*; *at* ~ bei Tisch; *turn the* ~s den Spieß umdrehen (*on* s.o. j-m gegenüber); **2.** auf den Tisch legen; tabellarisch anordnen; **~cloth** Tischtuch *n*, -decke *f*; **~land** Tafelland *n*, Plateau *n*, Hochebene *f*; **~lin·en** Tischwäsche *f*; **~mat** Set *n*; **~ set** *Rundfunk, TV*: Tischgerät *n*; **~spoon** Eßlöffel *m*.

tab·let ['tæblıt] Täfelchen *n*; (Gedenk)Tafel *f*; (Schreib- *etc.*)Block *m*; Stück *n* (*Seife*); Tafel *f* (*Schokolade*); Tablette *f*; △ *nicht Tablett*.

table|top ['teɪbltɒp] Tischplatte *f*; **~ware** Geschirr *n* u. Besteck *n*.

ta·boo [tə'buː] **1.** tabu, unantastbar; verboten; verpönt; **2.** Tabu *n*; **3.** *et.* für tabu erklären.

tab·u|lar □ ['tæbjʊlə] tabellarisch; **~late** [~eɪt] tabellarisch (an)ordnen.

ta·cit □ ['tæsıt] stillschweigend; **ta·ci·turn** □ [~ɜːn] schweigsam.

tack [tæk] **1.** Stift *m*, Reißnagel *m*, Zwecke *f*; Heftstich *m*; ♣ Halse *f*; ♣ Gang *m* (*beim Lavieren*); *fig.* Weg *m*; **2.** *v/t.* heften (*to* an *acc.*); *v/i.* ♣ wenden; *fig.* lavieren.

tack·le ['tækl] **1.** Gerät *n*; ♣ Takel-, Tauwerk *n*; ⊕ Flaschenzug *m*; *Fußball*: Angreifen *n*; **2.** (an)packen; *Fußball*: angreifen; in Angriff nehmen; lösen, fertig werden mit.

tack·y ['tækı] (*-ier, -iest*) klebrig; *Am.* F schäbig.

tact [tækt] Takt *m*, Feingefühl *n*; **~ful** □ ['tæktfl] taktvoll.

tac·tics ['tæktıks] *pl. u. sg.* Taktik *f*.

tact·less □ ['tæktlıs] taktlos.

tad·pole *zo.* ['tædpəʊl] Kaulquappe *f*.

taf·fe·ta ['tæfıtə] Taft *m*.

taf·fy *Am.* ['tæfı] = *toffee*; F Schmus *m*, Schmeichelei *f*.

tag [tæg] **1.** (Schnürsenkel)Stift *m*; Schildchen *n*, Etikett *n*; loses Ende, Fetzen *m*, Lappen *m*; Redensart *f*, Zitat *n*; *a. question* ~ *gr.* Frageanhängsel *n*; Fangen *n* (*Kinderspiel*); **2.** (*-gg-*) etikettieren, auszeichnen; anhängen (*to, on* to an *acc.*); ~ *along* F mitkommen; ~ *along behind* s.o. hinter j-m hertrotten *od.* -zockeln.

tail [teɪl] **1.** Schwanz *m*; Schweif *m*; hinteres Ende, Schluß *m*; ~s *pl.* Rückseite *f* (*e-r Münze*); F Frack *m*; *turn* ~ davonlaufen; ~s *up* in Hochstimmung, fidel; **2.** ~ *after* s.o. j-m hinterherlaufen; ~ s.o. F j-n beschatten; ~ *away*, ~ *off* abflauen, sich verlieren; nachlassen; **~back** *mot.* ['teɪlbæk] Rückstau *m*; **~coat** [~'kəʊt] Frack *m*; **~light** *mot. etc.* [~laıt] Rück-, Schlußlicht *n*.

tai·lor ['teɪlə] **1.** Schneider *m*; **2.** schneidern; **~made** Schneider..., Maß...

taint [teɪnt] **1.** (Schand)Fleck *m*, Makel *m*; (verborgene) Anlage (*zu e-r Krankheit*); **2.** beflecken; verderben; ♂ anstecken; verderben, schlecht werden (*Fleisch etc.*).

take [teɪk] **1.** (*took, taken*) *v/t.* nehmen; (an-, ein-, entgegen-, heraus-, hin-, mit-, weg)nehmen; fassen, packen, ergreifen; fangen; ♘ gefangennehmen; sich aneignen, Besitz ergreifen von; (hin-, weg)bringen; △ *nicht herbringen*; *et. gut etc.* aufnehmen; *Beleidigung* hinnehmen; *et.* ertragen, aushalten; halten (*for* für); auffassen; *fig.* fesseln; *phot. et.* aufnehmen, *Aufnahme* machen; *Temperatur* messen; *Notiz* machen, niederschreiben; *Prüfung* machen, ablegen; *Rast, Ferien etc.* machen; *Urlaub, ein Bad* nehmen; sich *e-e Krankheit* holen; *Speisen* zu sich nehmen, *Mahlzeit* einnehmen; *Zeitung* beziehen; *Zug, Bus etc.* nehmen; *Weg* wählen; *j-n wohin* führen; *Preis* gewinnen; *Gelegenheit, Maßnahmen* ergreifen; *Vorsitz etc.* übernehmen; *Eid* ablegen; *Zeit, Geduld* erfordern, brauchen; *Zeit* dauern; *Mut* fassen; *Anstoß* nehmen; *I* ~ *it that* ich nehme an, daß; ~ *it or leave it* F mach, was du willst; ~*n all in all* im großen (u.) ganzen; *be* ~*n* besetzt sein; *be* ~*n ill* od. F *bad* krank werden; *be* ~*n with* begeistert od. entzückt sein von; ~ *breath* verschnaufen; ~ *comfort* sich trösten; ~ *compassion on* Mitleid mit *j-m* haben; sich erbarmen (*gen.*); ~ *counsel* beraten; ~ *a drive* e-e Fahrt machen; ~ *fire* Feuer fangen; ~ *in hand* unternehmen; ~ *hold of* ergreifen; ~ *a look* e-n Blick tun od. werfen (*at auf acc.*); *Can I* ~ *a message?* Kann ich et. ausrichten?; ~ *to pieces* auseinandernehmen, zerlegen; ~ *pity on* Mitleid haben mit; ~ *place* stattfinden; spielen (*Handlung*); △ *nicht* Platz nehmen; ~ *a risk* ein Risiko eingehen od. auf sich nehmen; ~ *a seat* Platz nehmen; ~ *a walk* e-n Spaziergang machen; ~ *my word for it* verlaß dich drauf; ~ *along* mitnehmen; ~ *apart* auseinandernehmen, zerlegen; ~ *around j-n* herumführen; ~ *away* wegnehmen; ... *to* ~ *away* Brt. *Schild:* ... zum Mitnehmen; ~ *down* herunternehmen; *Gebäude* abreißen; notieren; ~ *from j-m* wegnehmen; *A* abziehen von; ~ *in* kürzer od. enger machen; *Zeitung* halten; aufnehmen (*als Gast etc.*); *Lage* überschauen; *fig.* einschließen; verstehen; erfassen; F *j-n* reinlegen; *be* ~*n in* reingefallen sein; ~ *in lodgers* (*Zimmer*) vermieten; ~ *off ab-*, wegnehmen; *Kleidungsstück* ablegen, ausziehen; *Hut* abnehmen; *e-n Tag etc.* Urlaub machen; ~ *on* an-, übernehmen; *Arbeiter etc.* einstellen; *Fahrgäste* zusteigen lassen; ~ *out* heraus-, entnehmen; *Fleck* entfernen; *j-n* ausführen; *Versicherung* abschließen; ~ *over Amt, Aufgabe, Idee etc.* übernehmen; ~ *up* aufheben, -nehmen; sich befassen

mit; *Fall, Idee etc.* aufgreifen; *Raum, Zeit* in Anspruch nehmen; *v/i.* ♣ wirken, anschlagen (*Medikament*); F gefallen, ankommen, ziehen; ~ *after j-m* nachschlagen; ~ *off* abspringen; ⚙, *Raumfahrt:* starten; ~ *on* Anklang finden; ~ *over* die Amtsgewalt *etc.* übernehmen; ~ *to* sich hingezogen fühlen zu, Gefallen finden an; ~ *to doing s.th.* anfangen et. zu tun; ~ *up with* sich anfreunden mit; **2.** *Fischerei:* Fang *m*; (*Geld*)Einnahme(n *pl.*) *f*; *hunt.* Beute *f*; Anteil *m* (*of an dat.*); *Film:* Szene(naufnahme) *f*; ~**a·way** ['teɪkəweɪ] **1.** zum Mitnehmen; **2.** Restaurant *n* mit Straßenverkauf; ~**in** F [~ɪn] Schwindel *m*, Betrug *m*; **tak·en** [~ən] *p.p. von* take 1; ~**off** [~ɒf] Absprung *m*, ⚙, *Raumfahrt:* Start *m*, Abflug *m*; Abheben *n*; F Nachahmung *f*.

tak·ing ['teɪkɪŋ] **1.** □ F anziehend, fesselnd, einnehmend; ansteckend; **2.** (An-, Ab-, Auf-, Ein-, Ent-, Hin-, Weg- *etc.*)Nehmen *n*; Inbesitznahme *f*; ✗ Einnahme *f*; F Aufregung *f*; ~**s** *pl. econ.* Einnahme(n *pl.*) *f*.

tale [teɪl] Erzählung *f*; Geschichte *f*; Märchen *n*, Sage *f*; *tell* ~**s** klatschen; *it tells its own* ~ es spricht für sich selbst; ~**bear·er** ['teɪlbeərə] Zuträger(in), Klatschmaul *n*.

tal·ent ['tælənt] Talent *n*, Begabung *f*, Anlage *f*; ~**ed** talentiert, begabt.

talk [tɔːk] **1.** Gespräch *n*; Unterhaltung *f*; Unterredung *f*; Plauderei *f*; Vortrag *m*; Geschwätz *n*; Sprache *f*, Art *f* zu reden; **2.** sprechen; reden; plaudern; ~ *to s.o.* mit *j-m* sprechen od. reden; ~**a·tive** □ ['tɔːkətɪv] gesprächig, geschwätzig; ~**er** [~ə] Schwätzer(in); Sprechende(r *m*) *f*; ~**show** *TV* Talk-Show *f*; ~**show host** *TV* Talkmaster *m*.

tall [tɔːl] groß; lang; hoch; F übertrieben, unglaublich; *that's a* ~ *order* F das ist ein bißchen viel verlangt.

tal·low ['tæləʊ] Talg *m*.

tal·ly ['tælɪ] **1.** *econ.* (Ab-, Gegen-) Rechnung *f*; Kontogegenbuch *n*; Etikett *n*, Kennzeichen *n*; *Sport:* Punkt(zahl *f*) *m*; **2.** in Übereinstimmung bringen; übereinstimmen.

tal·on ['tælən] Kralle *f*, Klaue *f*.

tame [teɪm] **1.** □ (~*r*, ~*st*) zahm; folgsam; harmlos; lahm, fad(e); **2.** zähmen, bändigen.

tam·per ['tæmpə]: ~ *with* sich (unbefugt) zu schaffen machen an (*dat.*); *j-n* zu bestechen suchen; *Urkunde* fälschen.

tam·pon ⚕ ['tæmpɔn] Tampon *m*.

tan [tæn] **1.** Lohe *f*; Lohfarbe *f*; (Sonnen)Bräune *f*; **2.** lohfarben; **3.** (-*nn*-) gerben; bräunen; braun werden.

tang [tæŋ] scharfer Geruch *od.* Geschmack; (scharfer) Klang; ♆ Seetang *m*.

tan·gent ['tændʒənt] Å Tangente *f*; *fly od.* go off at a ~ plötzlich (vom *Thema*) abschweifen.

tan·ge·rine ♆ [tændʒə'ri:n] Mandarine *f*.

tan·gi·ble □ ['tændʒəbl] fühl-, greifbar; klar.

tan·gle ['tæŋgl] **1.** Gewirr *n*; *fig.* Verwirrung *f*, -wicklung *f*; **2.** (sich) verwirren, -wickeln.

tank [tæŋk] **1.** *mot.*, ✕ *etc.* Tank *m*; (Wasser)Becken *n*, Zisterne *f*; **2.** ~ (*up*) auf-, volltanken.

tank·ard ['tæŋkəd] Humpen *m*, *bsd.* (Bier)Seidel *n*.

tank·er ['tæŋkə] ♆ Tanker *m*; ✈ Tankflugzeug *n*; *mot.* Tankwagen *m*.

tan|ner ['tænə] Gerber *m*; **~·ne·ry** [ˌrɪ] Gerberei *f*.

tan·ta·lize ['tæntəlaɪz] quälen.

tan·ta·mount ['tæntəmaʊnt] gleichbedeutend (*to* mit).

tan·trum ['tæntrəm] Wutanfall *m*.

tap [tæp] **1.** leichtes Klopfen; (Wasser-, Gas-, Zapf)Hahn *m*; Zapfen *m*; Schankstube *f*; *on* ~ vom Faß (*Bier*); ~*s pl. Am.* ✕ Zapfenstreich *m*; **2.** (-*pp*-) leicht pochen, klopfen, tippen (*on, at* auf, an, gegen *acc.*); anzapfen (*a.* Telefonleitung); abzapfen; **~·dance** ['tæpdɑːns] Steptanz *m*.

tape [teɪp] **1.** schmales Band, Streifen *m*; *Sport:* Zielband *n*; *tel.* Papierstreifen *m*; *Computer, Fernschreiber:* Lochstreifen *m*; (Magnet-, Video-, Ton)Band *n*; *s.* red tape; **2.** mit e-m Band befestigen; mit Klebestreifen verkleben; auf (Ton)Band aufnehmen; *TV* aufzeichnen; **~ cas·sette** Tonbandkassette *f*; **~ deck** Tapedeck *n*; **~·li·bra·ry** Bandarchiv *n*; **~·meas·ure** Bandmaß *n*.

ta·per ['teɪpə] **1.** dünne Wachskerze; **2.** *adj.* spitz (zulaufend); **3.** *v/i.* *oft* ~ off spitz zulaufen; *v/t.* zuspitzen.

tape|-re·cord ['teɪprɪkɔːd] auf (Ton)Band aufnehmen; **~ re·cord·er**

(Ton)Bandgerät *n*; **~ re·cord·ing** (Ton)Bandaufnahme *f*; **~ speed** Bandgeschwindigkeit *f*.

ta·pes·try ['tæpɪstrɪ] Gobelin *m*; ⚠ *nicht* Tapete.

tape·worm *zo.* ['teɪpwɜːm] Bandwurm *m*.

tap·room ['tæprʊm] Schankstube *f*.

tar [tɑː] **1.** Teer *m*; **2.** (-*rr*-) teeren.

tar·dy □ ['tɑːdɪ] (-*ier*, -*iest*) langsam; *Am.* spät.

tare *econ.* [teə] Tara *f*.

tar·get ['tɑːgɪt] (Schieß-, Ziel)Scheibe *f*; ✕, *Radar:* Ziel *n*; *fig.* (Leistungs- *etc.*)Ziel *n*, (-)Soll *n*; *fig.* Zielscheibe *f* (*des Spottes etc.*); **~ area** ✕ Zielbereich *m*; **~ group** *econ.* Werbung: Zielgruppe *f*; **~ language** *ling.* Zielsprache *f*; **~ practice** Scheiben-, Übungsschießen *n*.

tar·iff ['tærɪf] (*bsd.* Zoll)Tarif *m*.

tar·nish ['tɑːnɪʃ] **1.** *v/t.* ⊕ matt *od.* blind machen; *fig.* trüben; ⚠ *nicht* tarnen; *v/i.* matt *od.* trüb werden, anlaufen; **2.** Trübung *f*; Belag *m*.

tar·ry ['tɑːrɪ] (-*ier*, -*iest*) teerig.

tart [tɑːt] **1.** □ sauer, herb; *fig.* scharf, beißend; **2.** *bsd. Brt.* Obstkuchen *m*, (Obst)Torte *f*; *sl.* Flittchen *n*.

tar·tan ['tɑːtn] Tartan *m*: Schottentuch *n*; Schottenmuster *n*.

task [tɑːsk] **1.** Aufgabe *f*; Arbeit *f*; *take to* ~ zur Rede stellen; **2.** beschäftigen; in Anspruch nehmen; **~ force** ⚓, ✕ Sonder-, Spezialeinheit *f*; Sonderdezernat *n* (*der Polizei*).

tas·sel ['tæsl] Troddel *f*, Quaste *f*.

taste [teɪst] **1.** Geschmack *m*; (Kost-) Probe *f*; Neigung *f*, Vorliebe *f* (*for* für, zu); **2.** kosten; (ab)schmecken; *Essen* anrühren; schmecken (*of* nach); versuchen; **~·ful** □ ['teɪstfl] schmackhaft; *fig.* geschmackvoll; **~·less** □ [ˌlɪs] fad(e); *fig.* geschmacklos.

tast·y □ ['teɪstɪ] (-*ier*, -*iest*) schmackhaft.

ta-ta *int.* F ['tæ'tɑː] auf Wiedersehen!

tat·ter ['tætə] Fetzen *m*.

tat·tle ['tætl] **1.** klatschen, tratschen; **2.** Klatsch *m*, Tratsch *m*.

tat·too [tə'tuː] **1.** (*pl.* -*toos*) ✕ Zapfenstreich *m*; Tätowierung *f*; **2.** *fig.* trommeln; tätowieren.

taught [tɔːt] *pret. u. p.p. von* teach.

taunt [tɔːnt] **1.** Stichelei *f*, Spott *m*; **2.** verhöhnen, -spotten.

taut □ [tɔːt] straff; angespannt.

tav·ern *veraltet* ['tævn] Wirtshaus *n*, Schenke *f*.

taw·dry □ ['tɔːdrɪ] (*-ier, -iest*) billig, geschmacklos; knallig.

taw·ny ['tɔːnɪ] (*-ier, -iest*) lohfarben.

tax [tæks] **1.** Steuer *f*, Abgabe *f*; *fig.* Inanspruchnahme *f* (*on*, *upon gen.*); **2.** besteuern; *z̄t̄z̄* Kosten schätzen; *fig.* stark in Anspruch nehmen; auf e-e harte Probe stellen; *j-n* zur Rede stellen; ~ *s.o. with s.th.* j-n e-r Sache beschuldigen; **~·a·tion** [tæk'seɪʃn] Besteuerung *f*; Steuer(n *pl.*) *f*; *bsd. z̄t̄z̄* Schätzung *f*.

tax·i F ['tæksɪ] **1.** *a.* ~*-cab* Taxi *n*, Taxe *f*; **2.** (*~ing, taxying*) mit e-m Taxi fahren; *✈* rollen; ~ **driv·er** Taxifahrer(in); ~ **rank**, *bsd. Am.* ~ **stand** Taxistand *m*.

tax·pay·er ['tæ͜kspeɪə] Steuerzahler(in); ~ **re·turn** Steuererklärung *f*.

tea [tiː] Tee *m*; *s.* high tea; ~**bag** ['tiːbæɡ] Tee-, Aufgußbeutel *m*.

teach [tiːtʃ] (*taught*) lehren, unterrichten, *j-m et.* beibringen; ~**·a·ble** ['tiːtʃəbl] gelehrig; lehrbar; ~**·er** [~ə] Lehrer(in); ~**·in** [~ɪn] Teach-in *n*.

tea|**·co·sy** ['tiːkəʊzɪ] Teewärmer *m*; ~**·cup** Teetasse *f*; *storm in a* ~ *fig.* Sturm *m* im Wasserglas; ~**·ket·tle** Tee-, Wasserkessel *m*.

team [tiːm] Team *n*, Arbeitsgruppe *f*; Gespann *n*; *Sport u. fig.*: Mannschaft *f*, Team *n*; ~**·ster** *Am.* ['tiːmstə] LKW-Fahrer *m*; ~**·work** Zusammenarbeit *f*, Teamwork *n*, Zusammenspiel *n*.

tea·pot ['tiːpɒt] Teekanne *f*.

tear[1] [teə] **1.** (*tore, torn*) zerren; (zer-) reißen; rasen, stürmen; **2.** Riß *m*.

tear[2] [tɪə] Träne *f*; *in* ~*s* weinend, in Tränen (aufgelöst); ~**·ful** □ ['tɪəfl] tränenreich; weinend.

tea·room ['tiːrʊm] Teestube *f*.

tease [tiːz] necken, hänseln; ärgern.

teat [tiːt] *zo.* Zitze *f*; *anat.* Brustwarze *f* (*der Frau*); (Gummi)Sauger *m*.

tech·ni·cal □ ['teknɪkl] technisch; *fig.* rein formal; Fach...; ~**·i·ty** [teknɪ'kælətɪ] technische Besonderheit *od.* Einzelheit; Fachausdruck *m*; reine Formsache.

tech·ni·cian [tek'nɪʃn] Techniker(in); Facharbeiter(in).

tech·nique [tek'niːk] Technik *f*, Verfahren *n*, Methode *f*; ⚠ *nicht Technik* (*Technologie*).

tech·nol·o·gy [tek'nɒlədʒɪ] Technologie *f*.

ted·dy| **bear** ['tedɪbeə] Teddybär *m*; ♀ **boy** Halbstarke(r) *m*.

te·di·ous □ ['tiːdjəs] langweilig, ermüdend; weitschweifig.

teem [tiːm] wimmeln, strotzen (*with* von).

teen|**·age(d)** ['tiːneɪdʒ(d)] im Teenageralter; für Teenager; ~**·ag·er** [~ə] Teenager *m*.

teens [tiːnz] *pl.* Teenageralter *n*; Teenager *pl.*; *be in one's* ~ ein Teenager sein.

tee·ny[1] F ['tiːnɪ] Teeny *m* (*Teenager*); ~**·bopper** F *junger Teenager* (*bsd. Mädchen*)*, der alles mitmacht, was gerade 'in' ist*.

tee·ny[2] F [~], *a.* ~*-wee·ny* F [~'wiːnɪ] (*-ier, -iest*) klitzeklein, winzig.

tee shirt ['tiːʃɜːt] = T-shirt.

teeth [tiːθ] *pl. von* tooth; ~**·e** [tiːð] zahnen, (die) Zähne bekommen.

tee·to·tal·(l)er [tiː'təʊtlə] Abstinenzler(in).

tel·e·cast ['telɪkɑːst] **1.** Fernsehsendung *f*; **2.** (*-cast*) im Fernsehen übertragen *od.* bringen.

tel·e·course ['telɪkɔːs] Fernsehlehrgang *m*, -kurs *m*.

tel·e·gram ['telɪɡræm] Telegramm *n*.

tel·e·graph ['telɪɡrɑːf] **1.** Telegraf *m*; **2.** telegrafieren; ~**·ic** [telɪ'ɡræfɪk] (*~ally*) telegrafisch; im Telegrammstil.

te·leg·ra·phy [tɪ'leɡrəfɪ] Telegrafie *f*.

tel·e·phone ['telɪfəʊn] **1.** Telefon *n*, Fernsprecher *m*; **2.** telefonieren; anrufen; ~**·booth**, ~ **box** *Brit.* Telefon-, Fernsprechzelle *f*; **tel·e·phon·ic** [telɪ'fɒnɪk] (*~ally*) telefonisch; ~ **ki·osk** *Brit.* = telephone booth; **te·leph·o·ny** [tɪ'lefənɪ] Fernsprechwesen *n*.

tel·e·pho·to lens *phot.* ['telɪ'fəʊtəʊ 'lenz] Teleobjektiv *n*.

tel·e·print·er ['telɪprɪntə] Fernschreiber *m*.

tel·e·scope ['telɪskəʊp] **1.** Fernrohr *n*; **2.** (sich) ineinanderschieben.

tel·e·type·writ·er *Am.* ['telɪ'taɪpraɪtə] Fernschreiber *m*.

tel·e·vise ['telɪvaɪz] im Fernsehen übertragen *od.* bringen.

tel·e·vi·sion ['telɪvɪʒn] Fernsehen *n*; *on* ~ im Fernsehen; *watch* ~ fernsehen; *a.* ~ *set* Fernsehapparat *m*, -gerät *n*.

terminal

tel·ex ['teleks] **1.** Telex *n*, Fernschreiben *n*; **2.** *j-m et.* telexen *od.* per Fernschreiben mitteilen.

tell [tel] (*told*) *v/t.* sagen, erzählen; erkennen; nennen; unterscheiden; zählen; ~ *s.o. to do s.th.* j-m sagen, er solle et. tun; ~ *off* abzählen; F abkanzeln; *v/i.* erzählen (*of* von; *about* über *acc.*); sich auswirken (*on* auf *acc.*); sitzen (*Hieb etc.*); ~ *on s.o.* j-n verpetzen; *you never can* ~ man kann nie wissen; **~·er** *bsd. Am.* ['telə] (Bank)Kassierer *m*; **~·ing** □ [~ɪŋ] wirkungsvoll; aufschlußreich, vielsagend; **~·tale** ['telteɪl] **1.** Klatschbase *f*, Petze *f*; **2.** *fig.* verräterisch.

tel·ly *Brt.* F ['telɪ] Fernseher *m*.

te·mer·i·ty [tɪ'merətɪ] Verwegenheit *f*; Frechheit *f*.

tem·per ['tempə] **1.** mäßigen, mildern; ⊕ tempern; *Stahl* härten; **2.** ⊕ Härte(grad *m*) *f*; Temperament *n*, Charakter *m*; Laune *f*, Stimmung *f*; Wut *f*; *keep one's* ~ sich beherrschen; *lose one's* ~ in Wut geraten.

tem·pe·ra·ment ['tempərəmənt] Temperament *n*; **~·ra·men·tal** □ [tempərə'mentl] von Natur aus; launisch; **~·rance** ['tempərəns] Mäßigkeit *f*; Enthaltsamkeit *f*; **~·rate** □ [~rət] gemäßigt; zurückhaltend; maßvoll; mäßig; **~·ra·ture** [~prətʃə] Temperatur *f*.

tem·pest ['tempɪst] Sturm *m*; Gewitter *n*; **~·pes·tu·ous** □ [tem'pestjəs] stürmisch; ungestüm.

tem·ple ['templ] Tempel *m*; *anat.* Schläfe *f*.

tem·po·ral □ ['tempərəl] zeitlich; weltlich; **~·ra·ry** □ [~rɪ] zeitweilig; vorläufig; vorübergehend; Not...; (Aus)Hilfs..., Behelfs...; **~·rize** [~raɪz] Zeit zu gewinnen suchen.

tempt [tempt] *j-n* versuchen; verleiten; (ver)locken; **temp·ta·tion** [temp'teɪʃn] Versuchung *f*; Reiz *m*; **~·ing** □ ['temptɪŋ] verführerisch.

ten [ten] **1.** zehn; **2.** Zehn *f*.

ten·a·ble ['tenəbl] haltbar (*Argument etc.*); verliehen (*Amt*).

te·na·cious □ [tɪ'neɪʃəs] zäh; gut (*Gedächtnis*); *be* ~ *of s.th.* zäh an et. festhalten; **~·ci·ty** [tɪ'næsɪtɪ] Zähigkeit *f*; Festhalten *n*; Verläßlichkeit *f* (*des Gedächtnisses*).

ten·ant ['tenənt] Pächter *m*; Mieter *m*.

tend [tend] *v/i.* sich bewegen, streben (*to* nach, auf ... zu); *fig.* tendieren, neigen (*to* zu); *v/t.* pflegen; hüten; ⊕ bedienen; **ten·den·cy** ['tendənsɪ] Tendenz *f*; Richtung *f*; Neigung *f*; Zweck *m*.

ten·der ['tendə] **1.** □ zart; weich; empfindlich; heikel (*Thema*); sanft, zart, zärtlich; **2.** Angebot *n*; *econ.* Kostenanschlag *m*; 🚅, ⚓ Tender *m*; *legal* ~ gesetzliches Zahlungsmittel; **3.** anbieten; *Entlassung* einreichen; **~·foot** (*pl.* **-foots**, **-feet**) *Am.* F Neuling *m*, Anfänger *m*, Greenhorn *n*; **~·loin** Filet *n*; **~·ness** [~nɪs] Zartheit *f*; Zärtlichkeit *f*.

ten·don *anat.* ['tendən] Sehne *f*.

ten·dril ♀ ['tendrɪl] Ranke *f*.

ten·e·ment ['tenɪmənt] Wohnhaus *n*; Mietwohnung *f*; *a.* ~ *house* Miethaus *n*.

ten·nis ['tenɪs] Tennis *n*; ~ *court* Tennisplatz *m*.

ten·or ['tenə] Fortgang *m*, Verlauf *m*; Inhalt *m*; ♪ Tenor *m*.

tense [tens] **1.** *gr.* Zeit(form) *f*, Tempus *n*; **2.** □ (~*r*, ~*st*) gespannt (*a. fig.*); straff; (über)nervös, verkrampft; **ten·sion** ['tenʃn] Spannung *f*.

tent [tent] **1.** Zelt *n*; **2.** zelten.

ten·ta·cle *zo.* ['tentəkl] Fühler *m*; Fangarm *m* (*e-s Polypen*).

ten·ta·tive □ ['tentətɪv] versuchend; Versuchs...; vorsichtig, zögernd, zaghaft; ~*ly* versuchsweise.

ten·ter·hooks *fig.* ['tentəhʊks]: *be on* ~ wie auf (glühenden) Kohlen sitzen.

tenth [tenθ] **1.** zehnte(r, -s); **2.** Zehntel *n*; **~·ly** ['tenθlɪ] zehntens.

ten·u·ous □ ['tenjʊəs] dünn; zart, fein; *fig.* dürftig.

ten·ure ['tenjʊə] Besitz(art *f*, -dauer *f*) *m*; ~ *of office* Amtsdauer *f*.

tep·id □ ['tepɪd] lau(warm).

term [tɜːm] **1.** (bestimmte) Zeit, Dauer *f*; Frist *f*; Termin *m*; Zahltag *m*; Amtszeit *f*; ⚖ Sitzungsperiode *f*; Semester *n*, Quartal *n*, Trimester *n*; (Fach)Ausdruck *m*, Wort *n*, Bezeichnung *f*; Begriff *m*; ~*s pl.* (Vertrags)Bedingungen *pl.*; Beziehungen *pl.*; *be on good* (*bad*) ~*s with* gut (schlecht) stehen mit; *they are not on speaking* ~*s* sie sprechen nicht (mehr) miteinander; *come to* ~*s* sich einigen (*f*; **2.** (be)nennen; bezeichnen als.

ter·mi·nal ['tɜːmɪnl] **1.** □ End...;

letzte(r, -s); 🕮 unheilbar; **~ly** zum
Schluß; 2. Endstück n; 🜲 Pol m; 🜲
etc. Endstation f; Terminal m, n:
Flughafenabfertigungsgebäude n;
Brt. Endstation der Zubringerlinie
zum u. vom Flughafen; Zielbahnhof
für Containerzüge; Computer: Terminal n, Datenendstation f, Abfra-
gestation f; **~nate** [~neɪt] begrenzen; beend(ig)en; Vertrag lösen,
kündigen; **~na·tion** [tɜːmɪˈneɪʃn]
Beendigung f; Ende n; gr. Endung f.
ter·mi·nus ['tɜːmɪnəs] (pl. -ni [-naɪ],
-nuses) Endstation f.

ter·race ['terəs] Terrasse f; Häuser-
reihe f (an erhöht gelegener Straße);
~d terrassenförmig (angelegt); **~d
house** Brt. = **~ house** Brt. Reihen-
haus n.

ter·res·tri·al □ [tɪˈrestrɪəl] irdisch;
Erd...; bsd. zo., 🜲 Land...

ter·ri·ble □ ['terəbl] schrecklich.

ter·rif·ic F [təˈrɪfɪk] (~ally) toll, phantastisch; irre (Geschwindigkeit, Hitze
etc.).

ter·ri·fy ['terɪfaɪ] j-m Angst u.
Schrecken einjagen.

ter·ri·to·ri·al □ [terɪˈtɔːrɪəl] territorial, Land...; **~ry** ['terɪtərɪ] Territorium n, (Hoheits-, Staats)Gebiet n.

ter·ror ['terə] (tödlicher) Schrecken,
Entsetzen n; Terror m; **~ism**
[~rɪzm] Terrorismus m; **~ist** [~rɪst]
Terrorist(in); **~ize** [~raɪz] terrorisie-
ren.

terse □ [tɜːs] (~r, ~st) knapp; kurz u.
bündig.

test [test] 1. Probe f; Versuch m; Test
m; Untersuchung f; (Eignungs)Prü-
fung f; 🜲 Reagens n; 2. probieren;
prüfen; testen; 3. Probe..., Versuchs..., Test...

tes·ta·ment ['testəmənt] Testament
n; last will and **~** 🜲 Testament n.

tes·ti·cle anat. ['testɪkl] Hode(n m)
m, f.

tes·ti·fy ['testɪfaɪ] bezeugen; (als
Zeuge) aussagen.

tes·ti·mo·ni·al [testɪˈməʊnjəl] (Füh-
rungs)Zeugnis n; Zeichen n der Anerkennung; **~ny** ['testɪmənɪ] 🜲
Zeugenaussage f; Beweis m.

test tube ['testtjuːb] 1. 🜲 Reagenz-
glas n; 2. 🜲 Retorten...

tes·ty □ ['testɪ] (-ier, -iest) gereizt,
reizbar, kribbelig.

teth·er ['teðə] 1. Haltestrick m; fig.
Spielraum m; at the end of one's **~**

fig. am Ende s-r Kräfte; 2. anbinden.

text [tekst] Text m; Bibelstelle f;
~book ['tekstbʊk] Lehrbuch n.

tex·tile ['tekstaɪl] 1. Textil..., Gewebe...; 2. **~s** pl. Webwaren pl., Textilien pl.

tex·ture ['tekstʃə] Gewebe n; Gefüge
n; Struktur f.

than [ðæn, ðən] als; △ nicht dann.

thank [θæŋk] 1. danken (dat.); **~ you**
danke; no, **~** you nein, danke; (yes),
~ you ja, bitte; 2. **~s** pl. Dank m; **~s**
danke (schön); no, **~s** nein, danke;
~s to dank (dat. od. gen.); **~ful**
['θæŋkfl] dankbar; **~less** □ [~lɪs]
undankbar; **~s·giv·ing** [~sgɪvɪŋ] bsd.
Dankgebet n; ♀ (Day) Am. (Ernte-)
Dankfest n.

that [ðæt, ðət] 1. pron. u. adj. (pl.
those [ðəʊz]) jene(r, -s), der, die,
das, der-, die-, dasjenige; solche(r,
-s); ohne pl.: das; 2. adv. F so, derma-
ßen; **~** much so viel; 3. relative pron.
(pl. that) der, die, das, welche(r, -s)
4. cj. daß; damit; weil; da, als.

thatch [θætʃ] 1. Dachstroh n; Stroh-
dach n; 2. mit Stroh decken.

thaw [θɔː] 1. Tauwetter n; (Auf-)
Tauen n; 2. (auf)tauen.

the [ðiː; vor Vokalen: ðɪ; vor Konso-
nanten: ðə] 1. bestimmter art. der, die,
das, pl. die; 2. adv. desto, um so; **~** ...
~ je ... desto; s. sooner.

the·a·tre, Am. **-ter** ['θɪətə] Theater
n; fig. (Kriegs)Schauplatz m; **the·at-
ri·cal** □ [θɪˈætrɪkl] Theater...; fig.
theatralisch.

thee Bibel od. poet. [ðiː] dich;

theft [θeft] Diebstahl m.

their [ðeə] pl. ihr(e); **~s** [~z] der (die,
das) ihrige od. ihre.

them [ðem, ðəm] sie (acc. pl.); ihnen.

theme [θiːm] Thema n.

them·selves [ðəmˈselvz] sie (acc. pl.)
selbst; sich (selbst).

then [ðen] 1. adv. dann; damals; da;
denn; also, folglich; by **~** bis dahin;
inzwischen; every now and **~** ab u.
zu, gelegentlich; there and **~** sofort;
now **~** also (nun); 2. attr. adj. damalig.

thence lit. [ðens] daher; von da.

the·o·lo·gian [θɪəˈləʊdʒən] Theolo-
ge m; **the·ol·o·gy** [θɪˈɒlədʒɪ] Theologie f.

the·o·ret·ic [θɪəˈretɪk] (~ally), **~ret·i-
cal** □ [~kl] theoretisch; **~ry** ['θɪərɪ]
Theorie f.

threadbare

ther·a·peu·tic [θerə'pju:tɪk] **1.** (~ally) therapeutisch; **2.** ~s *mst sg.* Therapeutik *f*; ~**py** ['θerəpɪ] Therapie *f*.

there [ðeə] da, dort; darin; (da-, dort)hin; *int.* da!, na!; ~s, *pl.* ~ are es gibt, es ist, es sind; ~**a·bout(s)** ['ðeərəbaʊt(s)] da herum; so ungefähr; ~**af·ter** ['ðeə'ɑːftə] danach; ~**by** ['ðeə'baɪ] dadurch; ~**fore** ['ðeəfɔː] darum, deswegen, deshalb, daher; ~**up·on** [ðeərə'pɒn] darauf (-hin); ~**with** [ðeə'wɪð] damit.

ther·mal ['θɜːml] **1.** □ Thermal...; *phys.* thermisch, Wärme..., Hitze...; **2.** Thermik *f*.

ther·mom·e·ter [θə'mɒmɪtə] Thermometer *n*.

these [ðiːz] *pl. von this.*

the·sis ['θiːsɪs] (*pl. -ses* [-siːz]) These *f*; Dissertation *f*.

they [ðeɪ] *pl.* sie; man.

thick [θɪk] **1.** □ dick; dicht; trüb; legiert (*Suppe*); heiser; dumm; F dick befreundet; ~ **with** über u. über bedeckt von; voll von, voller; *that's a bit* ~! *sl.* das ist ein starkes Stück!; **2.** dickster Teil; *fig.* Brennpunkt *m*; *in the* ~ *of* mitten in (*dat.*); ~**en** ['θɪkən] (sich) verdicken; (sich) verstärken; legieren; (sich) verdichten; dick(er) werden; ~**et** [~ɪt] Dickicht *n*; ~**head·ed** dumm; ~**ness** [~nɪs] Dicke *f*, Stärke *f*, Dichte *f*; ~**set** dicht(gepflanzt); untersetzt; ~**skinned** *fig.* dickfellig.

thief [θiːf] (*pl. thieves* [θiːvz]) Dieb(in); **thieve** [θiːv] stehlen.

thigh *anat.* [θaɪ] (Ober)Schenkel *m*.

thim·ble ['θɪmbl] Fingerhut *m*.

thin [θɪn] **1.** □ (-*nn*-) dünn; licht; mager; spärlich, dürftig; schwach; fadenscheinig (*bsd. fig.*); **2.** (-*nn*-) verdünnen; (sich) lichten; abnehmen.

thine *Bibel od. poet.* [ðaɪn] dein(e); der (die, das) deinige *od.* deine.

thing [θɪŋ] Ding *n*; Sache *f*; Gegenstand *m*; Geschöpf *n*; ~s *pl.* Sachen *pl.*; die Dinge *pl.* (*Umstände*); *the* ~ das Richtige.

think [θɪŋk] (*thought*) *v/i.* denken (*of* an *acc.*); überlegen, nachdenken (*about* über *acc.*); meinen, glauben; ~ *of* sich erinnern an (*acc.*); sich *et.* ausdenken; daran denken, beabsichtigen; *v/t. et.* denken; meinen, glauben; sich vorstellen; halten für; *et.* halten (*of* von); beabsichtigen, vor-

haben; ~ *s.th.* over sich et. überlegen, über et. nachdenken.

third [θɜːd] **1.** □ dritte(r, -s); **2.** Drittel *n*; ~**ly** ['θɜːdlɪ] drittens; ~**rate** [~'reɪt] drittklassig.

thirst [θɜːst] Durst *m*; ~**y** □ ['θɜːstɪ] (*-ier, -iest*) durstig; dürr (*Boden*); *be* ~ Durst haben, durstig sein.

thir·teen ['θɜː'tiːn] **1.** dreizehn; **2.** Dreizehn *f*; ~**teenth** [~iːnθ] dreizehnte(r, -s); ~**tieth** ['θɜːtɪɪθ] dreißigste(r, -s); ~**ty** ['θɜːtɪ] **1.** dreißig; **2.** Dreißig *f*.

this [ðɪs] (*pl. these* [ðiːz]) diese(r, -s); ~ *morning* heute morgen; ~ *is John speaking teleph.* hier (spricht) John.

this·tle ♦ ['θɪsl] Distel *f*.

thong [θɒŋ] (Leder)Riemen *m*.

thorn [θɔːn] Dorn *m*; ~**y** ['θɔːnɪ] (*-ier, -iest*) dornig; *fig.* schwierig; heikel.

thor·ough □ ['θʌrə] gründlich, genau; vollkommen; vollständig, völlig; vollendet; ~**bred** Vollblut (-pferd) *n*; *attr.* Vollblut...; ~**fare** Durchgangsstraße *f*, Hauptverkehrsstraße *f*; *no* ~! Durchfahrt verboten!; ~**go·ing** gründlich; kompromißlos; durch u. durch.

those [ðəʊz] *pl. von that 1.*

thou *Bibel od. poet.* [ðaʊ] du.

though [ðəʊ] obgleich, obwohl, wenn auch; zwar; jedoch, doch; *as* ~ als ob.

thought [θɔːt] **1.** *pret. u. p.p. von think*; **2.** Gedanke *m*, Einfall *m*; (Nach)Denken *n*; *on second* ~s nach reiflicher Überlegung; ~**ful** □ ['θɔːtfl] gedankenvoll, nachdenklich; rücksichtsvoll (*of* gegen); ~**less** □ [~lɪs] gedankenlos, unbesonnen; rücksichtslos (*of* gegen).

thou·sand ['θaʊzənd] **1.** tausend; **2.** (*pl.* ~s) Tausend *n*; ~**th** [~ntθ] **1.** tausendste(r, -s); **2.** Tausendstel *n*.

thrash [θræʃ] verdreschen, -prügeln; *Sport:* j-m e-e Abfuhr erteilen; ~ *about*, ~ *around* sich *im Bett etc.* hin u. her werfen; um sich schlagen; zappeln (*Fisch*); ~ *out fig.* gründlich erörtern; ~**ing** ['θræʃɪŋ] Dresche *f*, Tracht *f* Prügel.

thread [θred] **1.** Faden *m* (*a. fig.*); Zwirn *m*, Garn *n*; ⊕ (Schrauben-) Gewinde *n*; **2.** einfädeln; aufreihen; *fig.* sich durchwinden (durch); ~**bare** ['θredbeə] fadenscheinig (*a. fig.*); *fig.* abgedroschen.

threat [θret] (Be)Drohung f; **~en** ['θretn] (be-, an)drohen; **~en·ing** [⁓ɪŋ] drohend; bedrohlich.

three [θriː] **1.** drei; **2.** Drei f; **~fold** ['θriːfəʊld] dreifach; **~pence** ['θrepəns] altes englisches Währungssystem: Dreipencestück n; **~score** ['θriː'skɔː] sechzig.

thresh ✔ [θreʃ] dreschen; **~er** ['θreʃə] Drescher m; Dreschmaschine f; **~ing** [⁓ɪŋ] Dreschen n; **~ing-ma·chine** Dreschmaschine f.

thresh·old od. lit. ['θreʃhəʊld] Schwelle f.

threw [θruː] pret. von throw 1.

thrice veraltet od. lit. [θraɪs] dreimal.

thrift [θrɪft] Sparsamkeit f; Wirtschaftlichkeit f; **~less** □ ['θrɪftlɪs] verschwenderisch; **~y** □ [⁓ɪ] (-ier, -iest) sparsam; poet. gedeihend.

thrill [θrɪl] **1.** v/t. erschauern lassen, erregen, packen; v/i. (er)beben, erschauern, zittern; **2.** Zittern n, Erregung f; (Nerven)Kitzel m, Sensation f; Beben n; **~er** ['θrɪlə] Reißer m, Thriller m (Kriminalfilm, -roman etc.); **~ing** [⁓ɪŋ] spannend, aufregend.

thrive [θraɪv] (thrived od. throve, thrived od. thriven) gedeihen; fig. blühen; Erfolg haben; **~n** ['θrɪvn] p.p. von thrive.

throat [θrəʊt] Kehle f, Gurgel f, Schlund m; Hals m; clear one's ~ sich räuspern.

throb [θrɒb] **1.** (-bb-) (heftig) pochen, klopfen, schlagen; pulsieren; **2.** Pochen n; Schlagen n; Pulsschlag m.

throm·bo·sis ✼ [θrɒmˈbəʊsɪs] (pl. -ses [-siːz]) Thrombose f.

throne [θrəʊn] Thron m.

throng [θrɒŋ] **1.** Gedränge n; (Menschen)Menge f; **2.** sich drängen (in dat.).

thros·tle zo. ['θrɒsl] Drossel f.

throt·tle ['θrɒtl] **1.** erdrosseln; ~ back, ~ down mot. ⊕ drosseln, Gas wegnehmen; **2.** a. ~-valve mot. ⊕ Drosselklappe f.

through [θruː] **1.** prp. durch; hindurch; Am. (von ...) bis; Monday ~ Friday Am. von Montag bis Freitag; **2.** adj. Durchgangs...; durchgehend; ~ car Am., ~ carriage, ~ coach Brt. ⦻ Kurswagen m; ~ flight ✈ Direktflug m; ~ travel(l)er Transitreisende(r m) f; **~out** [θruːˈaʊt] **1.** prp. überall in (dat.); während; **2.** adv.

durch und durch, ganz und gar, durchweg; **~put** econ. Computer: Durchsatz m.

throve [θrəʊv] pret. von thrive.

throw [θrəʊ] **1.** (threw, thrown) (ab)werfen, schleudern; Am. Wettkampf etc. absichtlich verlieren; Würfel werfen; Zahl werfen; ⊕ ein-, ausschalten; ~ over fig. aufgeben; ~ up hochwerfen; erbrechen, sich übergeben; fig. et. aufgeben, hinwerfen; **2.** Wurf m; **~·a·way** ['θrəʊəweɪ] **1.** et. zum Wegwerfen, z. B. Reklamezettel m; **2.** Wegwerf...; Einweg...; **~n** [θrəʊn] p.p. von throw 1.

thru Am. [θruː] = through.

thrum [θrʌm] (-mm-) klimpern auf (od. on auf) (dat.).

thrush zo. [θrʌʃ] Drossel f.

thrust [θrʌst] **1.** Stoß m; Vorstoß m; ⊕ Druck m, Schub m; **2.** (thrust) stoßen; stecken, schieben; ~ o.s. into sich drängen in (acc.); ~ upon s.o. j-m aufdrängen.

thud [θʌd] **1.** (-dd-) dumpf (auf-) schlagen, F bumsen; **2.** dumpfer (Auf)Schlag, F Bums m.

thug [θʌg] (Gewalt)Verbrecher m, Schläger m.

thumb [θʌm] **1.** Daumen m; **2.** ~ a lift od. ride per Anhalter fahren; ~ through a book ein Buch durchblättern; well-~ed Buch etc.: abgegriffen; **~·tack** Am. ['θʌmtæk] Reißzwecke f, -nagel m, Heftzwecke f.

thump [θʌmp] **1.** dumpfer Schlag; **2.** v/t. heftig schlagen od. hämmern od. pochen gegen od. auf (acc.); v/i. (auf)schlagen; (laut) pochen (Herz).

thun·der ['θʌndə] **1.** Donner m; **2.** donnern; **~·bolt** Blitz m (u. Donner m); **~·clap** Donnerschlag m; **~·ous** □ [⁓rəs] donnernd; **~·storm** Gewitter n; **~·struck** fig. wie vom Donner gerührt.

Thurs·day ['θɜːzdɪ] Donnerstag m.

thus [ðʌs] so; also, somit.

thwart [θwɔːt] **1.** durchkreuzen, vereiteln; **2.** Ruderbank f.

thy veraltet od. poet. [ðaɪ] dein(e).

tick¹ zo. [tɪk] Zecke f.

tick² [⁓] **1.** Ticken n; (Vermerk)Häkchen n, Haken m; **2.** v/i. ticken; v/t. anhaken; ~ off abhaken.

tick³ [⁓] Inlett n; Matratzenbezug m.

tick·er tape ['tɪkəteɪp] Lochstreifen

T

m; ~ parade bsd. Am. Konfettiparade f.

tick·et ['tıkıt] **1.** Fahrkarte f, -schein m; Flugkarte f, Ticket n; (Eintritts-, Theater- etc.)Karte f; mot. Strafzettel m, gebührenpflichtige Verwarnung; Etikett n, (Kenn)Zeichen n, (Preis- etc.)Zettel m; bsd. Am. pol. (Wahl-, Kandidaten)Liste f; **2.** etikettieren, Ware auszeichnen; ~ can·cel·(l)ing ma·chine (Fahrschein)Entwerter m; ~ col·lec·tor 🚮 (Bahnsteig)Schaffner m; (au·to·mat·ic) ~ ma·chine Fahrkartenautomat m; ~ of·fice 🚮 Fahrkartenschalter m; thea. Kasse f.

tick|le ['tıkl] kitzeln (a. fig.); ~·lish □ [~lıʃ] kitz(e)lig; fig. heikel.

tid·al ['taıdl]: ~ wave Flutwelle f.

tid·bit Am. ['tıdbıt] = titbit.

tide [taıd] **1.** Gezeiten pl.; Ebbe f u. Flut f; fig. Strom m, Strömung f; in Zssgn: Zeit f; high ~ Flut f; low ~ Ebbe f; **2.** ~ over fig. hinwegkommen od. j-m hinweghelfen über (acc.).

ti·dy ['taıdı] **1.** □ (-ier, -iest) ordentlich, sauber, reinlich, aufgeräumt; F ganz schön, beträchtlich (Summe); **2.** Behälter m; Abfallkorb m; **3.** a. ~ up zurechtmachen; in Ordnung bringen; aufräumen.

tie [taı] **1.** (Schnür)Band n; Schleife f, Krawatte f, Schlips m; fig. Band n, Bindung f; fig. (lästige) Fessel, Last f; Sport: Punkt-, parl. Stimmengleichheit f; Sport: (Ausscheidungs)Spiel n; Am. 🚮 Schwelle f; **2.** v/t. (an-, fest-, zu)binden; v/i. Sport: punktgleich sein; mit Adverbien: ~ down fig. binden (to an acc.); ~ in with passen zu; verbinden od. koppeln mit; ~ up zu-, an-, verzusammenbinden; ~-in econ. ['taıın] Kopplungsgeschäft n, -verkauf m; a book movie ~ Am. etwa: das Buch zum Film.

tier [tıə] Reihe f; Rang m.

tie-up ['taıʌp] (Ver)Bindung f; econ. Fusion f; Stockung f; bsd. Am. Streik m.

ti·ger zo. ['taıgə] Tiger m.

tight [taıt] **1.** □ dicht; fest; eng; knapp (sitzend); straff, (an)gespannt; econ. knapp; F blau, besoffen; F knick(e)rig, geizig; be in a ~ corner od. place od. F spot fig. in der Klemme sein; **2.** adv. fest; hold ~ festhalten; ~·en ['taıtn] fest-, anzie-

hen; Gürtel enger schnallen; a. ~ up (sich) zusammenziehen; ~-fist·ed knick(e)rig, geizig; ~·ness Festigkeit f; Dichte f; Straffheit f; Knappheit f; Enge f; Geiz m; ~s [taıts] pl. (Tänzer-, Artisten)Trikot n; bsd. Brt. Strumpfhose f.

ti·gress zo. ['taıgrıs] Tigerin f.

tile [taıl] **1.** (Dach)Ziegel m; Kachel f; Platte f; Fliese f; **2.** (mit Ziegeln etc.) decken; kacheln; fliesen.

till¹ [tıl] (Laden)Kasse f.

till² [~] **1.** prp. bis (zu); **2.** cj. bis.

till³ ⸤ [~] bestellen, bebauen; ~·age ['tılıdʒ] (Land)Bestellung f; Ackerbau m; Ackerland n.

tilt [tılt] **1.** (Wagen)Plane f; Kippen n; Neigung f; Stoß m; **2.** (um)kippen.

tim·ber ['tımbə] **1.** (Bau-, Nutz)Holz n; 🚢 Spant m; Baumbestand m, Bäume pl.; **2.** zimmern.

time [taım] **1.** Zeit f; Uhrzeit f; Frist f; Mal n; ♪ Takt m; Tempo n; ~s pl. mal, ...mal; ~ is up die Zeit ist um od. abgelaufen; for the ~ being vorläufig; have a good ~ sich gut unterhalten od. amüsieren; what's the ~?, what ~ is it? wieviel Uhr ist es?, wie spät ist es?; ~ and again immer wieder; all the ~ ständig, immer; at a ~ auf einmal, zusammen; at any ~, at all ~s jederzeit; at the same ~ gleichzeitig, zur selben Zeit; in ~ rechtzeitig; in no ~ im Nu, im Handumdrehen; on ~ pünktlich; **2.** messen, (ab)stoppen; zeitlich abstimmen; timen (a. Sport), den richtigen Zeitpunkt wählen od. bestimmen für; ~ card Stechkarte f; ~ clock Stechuhr f; ~·hon·o(u)red ['taımbnəd] altehrwürdig; ~·ly [~lı] (-ier, -iest) (recht)zeitig; ~·piece Uhr f; ~ sheet Stechkarte f; ~ sig·nal Rundfunk, TV: Zeitzeichen n; ~·ta·ble Terminkalender m; Fahr-, Flug-, Stundenplan m.

tim|id □ ['tımıd], ~·or·ous ['~ərəs] ängstlich; schüchtern.

tin [tın] **1.** Zinn n; Weißblech n; bsd. Brt. (Konserven)Dose f, (-)Büchse f; **2.** (-nn-) verzinnen; bsd. Brt. (in Büchsen) einmachen, eindosen.

tinc·ture ['tıŋktʃə] **1.** Farbe f; Tinktur f; fig. Anstrich m; **2.** färben.

tin·foil ['tın'fɔıl] Stanniol(papier) n.

tinge [tındʒ] **1.** Tönung f; fig. An-

tingle

flug *m*, Spur *f*; **2.** tönen, färben; *fig.* e-n Anstrich geben (*dat.*).

tin·gle ['tɪŋgl] klingen; prickeln.

tink·er ['tɪŋkə] herumpfuschen, -basteln (*at an dat.*).

tin·kle ['tɪŋkl] klingeln (mit).

tin| o·pen·er *bsd. Brt.* ['tɪnəʊpnə] Dosenöffner *m*; **~ plate** Weißblech *n*.

tin·sel ['tɪnsl] Flitter *m*; Lametta *n*.

tint [tɪnt] **1.** (zarte) Farbe; (Farb)Ton *m*, Tönung *f*, Schattierung *f*; **2.** (leicht) färben; tönen.

ti·ny □ ['taɪnɪ] (*-ier*, *-iest*) winzig, sehr klein.

tip [tɪp] **1.** Spitze *f*; Filter *m* (*e-r Zigarette*); Trinkgeld *n*; Tip *m*, Wink *m*; leichter Stoß; *Brt.* Schuttabladeplatz *m*; **2.** (*-pp-*) mit e-r Spitze versehen; (um)kippen; *j-m* ein Trinkgeld geben; *a.* **~ off** *j-m* e-n Tip *od.* Wink geben.

tip·sy □ ['tɪpsɪ] (*-ier*, *-iest*) angeheitert.

tip·toe ['tɪptəʊ] **1.** auf Zehenspitzen gehen; **2.** on ~ auf Zehenspitzen.

tire¹ *Am.* ['taɪə] = tyre.

tire² *zo.* [~] ermüden, müde machen *od.* werden; **~d** □ müde; **~less** □ ['taɪəlɪs] unermüdlich; **~some** □ [~səm] ermüdend; lästig.

tis·sue ['tɪʃu:] Gewebe *n*; Papiertaschentuch *n*; = ~ **pa·per** Seidenpapier *n*.

tit¹ [tɪt] = teat.

tit² *zo.* [~] Meise *f*.

tit·bit *bsd. Brt.* ['tɪtbɪt] Leckerbissen *m*.

tit·il·late ['tɪtɪleɪt] kitzeln.

ti·tle ['taɪtl] (Buch-, Ehren- *etc.*)Titel *m*; Überschrift *f*; ⚖ Rechtsanspruch *m*; **~d** ad(e)lig.

tit·mouse *zo.* ['tɪtmaʊs] (*pl. -mice*) Meise *f*.

tit·ter ['tɪtə] **1.** kichern; **2.** Kichern *n*.

tit·tle ['tɪtl]: not one od. a ~ of it kein od. nicht ein Jota (davon); **~tat·tle** [~tætl] Schnickschnack *m*.

to [tu:, tʊ, tə] **1.** *prp.* zu; gegen, nach, an, in, auf; bis zu, bis an (*acc.*); um zu; für; *a quarter* ~ *one* (ein) Viertel vor eins; *from Monday* ~ *Friday Brt.* von Montag bis Freitag; ~ *me etc.* mir *etc.*; *I weep* ~ *think of* it ich weine, wenn ich daran denke; *here's* ~ *you!* auf Ihr Wohl!, prosit!; **2.** *adv.* zu, geschlossen; *pull* ~ Tür zuziehen; *come* ~ (wieder) zu

sich kommen; ~ *and fro* hin u. her, auf u. ab.

toad [təʊd] Kröte *f*; **~stool** ⚕ ['təʊdstu:l] (größerer Blätter)Pilz; Giftpilz *m*; **~y** [~ɪ] **1.** Speichellecker(in); *b.* **2.** *fig.* vor *j-m* kriechen.

toast [təʊst] **1.** Toast *m*; Toast *m*, Trinkspruch *m*; **2.** toasten; rösten; *fig.* wärmen; trinken auf (*acc.*).

to·bac·co [tə'bækəʊ] (*pl. -cos*) Tabak *m*; **~nist** [~ənɪst] Tabakhändler *m*.

to·bog·gan [tə'bɒgən] **1.** Rodelschlitten *m*; **2.** rodeln.

to·day [tə'deɪ] heute.

tod·dle ['tɒdl] auf wack(e)ligen Beinen gehen (*bsd. Kleinkind*); F (dahin)zotteln.

tod·dy ['tɒdɪ] Toddy *m* (*Art Grog*).

to-do F [tə'du:] Lärm *m*; Getue *n*, Aufheben *n*.

toe [təʊ] **1.** *anat.* Zehe *f*; Spitze *f* (*von Schuhen etc.*); **2.** mit den Zehen berühren.

tof·fee, *a.* **~·fy** ['tɒfɪ] Sahnebonbon *m*, *n*, Toffee *n*.

to·geth·er [tə'geðə] zusammen; zugleich; *Tage etc.* nacheinander.

toil [tɔɪl] **1.** mühselige Arbeit, Mühe *f*, Plackerei *f*; **2.** sich plagen.

toi·let ['tɔɪlɪt] Toilette *f*; **~·pa·per** Toilettenpapier *n*.

toils *fig.* [tɔɪlz] *pl.* Schlingen *pl.*, Netz *n*.

to·ken ['təʊkən] Zeichen *n*; Andenken *n*, Geschenk *n*; *as a* ~, *in* ~ *of* als *od.* zum Zeichen (*gen.*).

told [təʊld] *pret. u. p.p. von* tell.

tol·e·ra·ble □ ['tɒlərəbl] erträglich; **~rance** [~ns] Toleranz *f*; Nachsicht *f*; **~rant** □ [~t] tolerant (*of gegen*); **~rate** [~eɪt] dulden; ertragen; **~ra·tion** [tɒlə'reɪʃn] Duldung *f*.

toll [təʊl] **1.** Straßenbenutzungsgebühr *f*, Maut *f*; Standgeld *n* (*auf e-m Markt etc.*); *fig.* Tribut *m*, (Zahl *f* der) Todesopfer *pl.*; *the* ~ *of the road* die Verkehrsopfer *pl.*; **2.** läuten; **~bar** ['təʊlbɑ:]; **~gate** Schlagbaum *m*.

to·ma·to ⚕ [tə'mɑ:təʊ, *Am.* tə'meɪtəʊ] (*pl. -toes*) Tomate *f*.

tomb [tu:m] Grab(mal) *n*.

tom·boy ['tɒmbɔɪ] Wildfang *m*.

tomb·stone ['tu:mstəʊn] Grabstein *m*.

tom·cat *zo.* ['tɒm'kæt] Kater *m*.

tom·fool·e·ry [tɒm'fu:lərɪ] Unsinn *m*.

to·mor·row [təˈmɒrəʊ] morgen.

ton [tʌn] Tonne f (*Gewichtseinheit*); △ *nicht* Ton.

tone [təʊn] **1.** Ton m, Klang m, Laut m; (Farb)Ton m; **2.** (ab)tönen; ~ **down** (sich) abschwächen *od.* mildern.

tongs [tɒŋz] pl. (a pair of ~ e-e) Zange.

tongue [tʌŋ] *anat.* Zunge f; Sprache f; (Schuh)Lasche f; *hold one's* ~ den Mund halten; ~**tied** *fig.* [ˈtʌŋtaɪd] stumm, sprachlos.

ton·ic [ˈtɒnɪk] **1.** (~ally) tonisch; stärkend, belebend; **2.** ♪ Grundton m; Stärkungsmittel n, Tonikum n.

to·night [təˈnaɪt] heute abend *od.* nacht.

ton·nage ♫ [ˈtʌnɪdʒ] Tonnage f.

ton·sil *anat.* [ˈtɒnsl] Mandel f; ~**li·tis** ♫ [tɒnsɪˈlaɪtɪs] Mandelentzündung f.

too [tuː] zu, allzu; auch, ebenfalls.

took [tʊk] pret. von take 1.

tool [tuːl] Werkzeug n, Gerät n; ~**bag** [ˈtuːlbæg] Werkzeugtasche f; ~**box** Werkzeugkasten m; ~**kit** Werkzeugtasche f.

toot [tuːt] **1.** blasen, tuten; hupen; **2.** Tuten n.

tooth [tuːθ] (pl. teeth [tiːθ]) Zahn m; ~**ache** [ˈtuːθeɪk] Zahnschmerzen pl.; ~**brush** Zahnbürste f; ~**less** □ [~lɪs] zahnlos; ~**paste** Zahnpasta f, -creme f; ~**pick** Zahnstocher m.

top¹ [tɒp] **1.** ober(st)es Ende; Oberteil n; Spitze f (a. fig.); Gipfel m (a. fig.); Wipfel m; Kopf(ende n) m; (Topf- etc.)Deckel m; *mot.* Verdeck n; Stulpe f (am Stiefel); *at the* ~ *of one's voice* aus vollem Halse; *on* ~ oben(auf); obendrein; *on* ~ *of* (oben) auf (dat.); **2.** oberste(r, -s), höchste(r, -s) Höchst..., Spitzen...; **3.** (-pp-) oben bedecken; überragen (a. fig.); an der Spitze e-r Liste etc. stehen; ~ *up Tank etc.* auf-, nachfüllen; ~ *s.o. up* j-m nachschenken.

top² [~] Kreisel m.

top|boots [ˈtɒpˈbuːts] pl. Stulpenstiefel pl.; ~ **hat** Zylinder(hut) m.

top·ic [ˈtɒpɪk] Gegenstand m, Thema n; ~**al** □ [~l] lokal; aktuell.

top|less [ˈtɒplɪs] oben ohne, Obenohne-...; ~**most** höchste(r, -s), oberste(r, -s).

top·ple [ˈtɒpl] (~*down*, ~ *over* um-)kippen.

top·sy-tur·vy □ [ˈtɒpsɪˈtɜːvɪ] auf den Kopf (gestellt), das Oberste zuunterst; drunter u. drüber.

torch [tɔːtʃ] Fackel f; *a. electric* ~ *bsd.* Brt. Taschenlampe f; ~**light** [ˈtɔːtʃlaɪt] Fackelschein m; ~ *procession* Fackelzug m.

tore [tɔː] pret. von tear¹ 1.

tor·ment 1. [ˈtɔːment] Qual f, Marter f; **2.** [tɔːˈment] quälen, peinigen, plagen.

torn [tɔːn] p.p. von tear¹ 1.

tor·na·do [tɔːˈneɪdəʊ] (pl. -does, -dos) Wirbelsturm m, Tornado m.

tor·pe·do [tɔːˈpiːdəʊ] (pl. -does) **1.** Torpedo m; **2.** ♨ torpedieren (a. fig.).

tor·pid □ [ˈtɔːpɪd] starr; apathisch; träge; ~**i·ty** [tɔːˈpɪdətɪ], ~**ness** [~nɪs], **tor·por** [~ə] Apathie f, Stumpfheit f; Erstarrung f, Betäubung f.

tor|rent [ˈtɒrənt] Sturz-, Wildbach m; reißender Strom; fig. Strom m, Schwall m; ~**ren·tial** [təˈrenʃl]: ~ *rain(s)* sintflutartige Regenfälle.

tor·toise zo. [ˈtɔːtəs] Schildkröte f.

tor·tu·ous □ [ˈtɔːtjʊəs] gewunden.

tor·ture [ˈtɔːtʃə] **1.** Folter(ung) f; Tortur f; **2.** foltern.

toss [tɒs] **1.** (Hoch)Werfen n, Wurf m; Zurückwerfen n (Kopf); **2.** werfen, schleudern; a. ~ *about* (sich) hin- u. herwerfen; schütteln; ~ *off* *Getränk* hinunterstürzen; *Arbeit* hinhauen; a. ~ *up* hochwerfen; losen (*for* um) (*durch Münzwurf*).

tot F [tɒt] Knirps m (*kleines Kind*).

to·tal [ˈtəʊtl] **1.** □ ganz, gänzlich; total; gesamt; **2.** Gesamtbetrag m, -menge f; **3.** (bsd. Brt. -ll-, Am. -l-) sich belaufen auf (acc.); ~**i·tar·i·an** [təʊtælɪˈteərɪən] totalitär; ~**i·ty** [təʊˈtælətɪ] Gesamtheit f.

tot·ter [ˈtɒtə] torkeln, (sch)wanken, wackeln.

touch [tʌtʃ] **1.** (sich) berühren; anrühren; anfassen; grenzen *od.* stoßen an (acc.); fig. rühren; erreichen; ♪ anschlagen; *a bit* ~*ed fig.* ein bißchen verrückt; ~ *at* ♨ anlegen in (dat.); ~ *down* ✈ aufsetzen; ~ *up* auffrischen; retuschieren; **2.** Berührung f; Tastsinn m, -gefühl n; Verbindung f, Kontakt m; leichter Anfall; Anflug m; besondere Note; ♪ Anschlag m; (Pinsel)Strich m; ~**and-go** [ˈtʌtʃənˈgəʊ] gewagte Sache; *it is* ~ es steht auf des Messers Schneide; **~ing** □ [~ɪŋ] rührend; **~stone** Prüfstein *m*; **~y** □ [~ɪ] (*-ier, -iest*) empfindlich; heikel.

tough □ [tʌf] zäh (*a. fig.*); robust, stark; hart, grob, brutal, übel; **~en** ['tʌfn] zäh machen *od.* werden; **~ness** [~nɪs] Zähigkeit *f.*

tour [tʊə] 1. (Rund)Reise *f*, Tour *f*; Rundgang *m*, -fahrt *f*; *thea.* Tournee *f* (*a. Sport*); *s. conduct* 2; 2. (be)reisen; **~ist** ['tʊərɪst] Tourist(in); ~ *agency*, ~ *bureau*, ~ *office* Reisebüro *n*; Fremdenverein *m*; ~ *season* Reisesaison *f*, -zeit *f.*

tour·na·ment ['tʊənəmənt] Turnier *n.*

tou·sle ['taʊzl] (zer)zausen.

tow [təʊ] 1. Schleppen *n*; *take in* ~ ins Schlepptau nehmen; 2. (ab)schleppen; treideln; ziehen.

to·ward(s) [tə'wɔːd(z)] gegen; nach ... zu, auf (*acc.*) ... zu; (*als Beitrag*) zu.

tow·el ['taʊəl] 1. Handtuch *n*; 2. (*bsd. Brt. -ll-, Am. -l-*) (ab)trocknen; (ab)reiben.

tow·er ['taʊə] 1. Turm *m*; *fig.* Stütze *f*, Bollwerk *n*; *a.* ~ *block* (Büro-, Wohn)Hochhaus *n*; 2. (hoch)ragen, sich erheben; **~ing** □ ['taʊərɪŋ] (turm)hoch; rasend (*Wut*).

town [taʊn] 1. Stadt *f*; 2. Stadt...; städtisch; **~ cen·tre**, *Am.* **~ cen·ter** Innenstadt *f*, City *f*; ~ *clerk Brt.* städtischer Verwaltungsbeamter; ~ *coun·cil Brt.* Stadtrat *m* (*Versammlung*); ~ **coun·ci(l)·lor** *Brt.* Stadtrat *m*, -rätin *f*; ~ **hall** Rathaus *n*; **~s·folk** ['taʊnzfəʊk] Städter *pl.*; **~ship** Stadtgemeinde *f*; Stadtgebiet *n*; **~s·man** (*pl. -men*) Städter *m*; (Mit-)Bürger *m*; **~s·peo·ple** *pl.* = *townsfolk*; **~s·wom·an** (*pl. -women*) Städterin *f*; (Mit)Bürgerin *f.*

tox·ic ['tɒksɪk] (*~ally*) giftig; Gift...; **~in** [~ɪn] Giftstoff *m.*

toy [tɔɪ] 1. Spielzeug *n*; Tand *m*; **~s** *pl.* Spielsachen *pl.*, -waren *pl.*; 2. Spielzeug...; Miniatur...; Zwerg...; 3. spielen.

trace [treɪs] 1. Spur *f* (*a. fig.*); 2. nachspüren (*dat.*), *j-s* Spur folgen; verfolgen; herausfinden; (auf)zeichnen; (durch)pausen.

trac·ing ['treɪsɪŋ] Pauszeichnung *f.*

track [træk] 1. Spur *f*, Fährte *f*; 🚆 Gleis *n*, Geleise *n u. pl.*; Pfad *m*;

Computer, Tonband: Spur *f*; (Raupen)Kette *f*; *Sport*: (Renn-, Aschen-) Bahn *f*; ~*-and-field Sport*: Leichtathletik...; ~ *events pl. Sport*: Laufdisziplinen *pl.*; ~ *suit* Trainingsanzug *m*; 2. nachgehen, -spüren (*dat.*), verfolgen; ~ *down*, ~ *out* aufspüren; ~*ing station Raumfahrt*: Bodenstation *f.*

tract [trækt] Fläche *f*, Strecke *f*, Gegend *f*; Traktat *n*, Abhandlung *f.*

trac·ta·ble □ ['træktəbl] lenk-, fügsam.

trac·tion ['trækʃn] Ziehen *n*, Zug *m*; ~ *engine* Zugmaschine *f*; **~·tor** ⊕ [~tə] Trecker *m*, Traktor *m.*

trade [treɪd] 1. Handel *m*; Gewerbe *n*, Beruf *m*, Handwerk *n*; 2. Handel treiben, handeln; ~ *on* ausnutzen; ~ **mark** Warenzeichen *n*; ~ **price** Großhandelspreis *m*; **trad·er** ['treɪdə] Händler *m*; **~s·man** [~zmən] (*pl. -men*) (Einzel)Händler *m*; **~(s) un·i·on** Gewerkschaft *f*; **~(s) un·i·on·ist** Gewerkschaftler(in); **~ wind** Passat(wind) *m.*

tra·di·tion [trə'dɪʃn] Tradition *f*; Überlieferung *f*; **~·al** □ [~l] traditionell.

traf·fic ['træfɪk] 1. Verkehr *m*; Handel *m*; 2. (*-ck-*) (*a. illegal*) handeln (*in* mit).

traf·fi·ca·tor *Brt. mot.* ['træfɪkeɪtə] (Fahrt)Richtungsanzeiger *m*, Blinker *m.*

traf·fic| cir·cle *Am.* ['træfɪk'sɜːkl] Kreisverkehr *m*; ~ **jam** (Verkehrs-) Stau *m*, Verkehrsstockung *f*; ~ **light(s** *pl.*) Verkehrsampel *f*; ~ **sign** Verkehrszeichen *n*, -schild *n*; ~ **sig·nal** = *traffic light(s)*; ~ **war·den** *Brt.* Politesse *f.*

trag·e·dy ['trædʒɪdɪ] Tragödie *f*; **~·gic** [~ɪk] (*~ally*), **trag·i·cal** □ [~kl] tragisch.

trail [treɪl] 1. Schleppe *f*; Spur *f*; Pfad *m*, Weg *m*; *fig.* Schweif *m*; 2. *v/t.* hinter sich herziehen; verfolgen; beschatten; *v/i.* schleifen; sich schleppen; ♥ sich ranken; **~er** ['treɪlə] ♥ Kriechpflanze *f*; *mot.* Anhänger *m*; *Am. mot.* Wohnwagen *m*, Wohnanhänger *m*, Caravan *m*; *Film, TV*: (Programm)Vorschau *f.*

train [treɪn] 1. (Eisenbahn)Zug *m*; *allg.* Zug *m*; Gefolge *n*; Reihe *f*, Folge *f*, Kette *f*; Schleppe *f* (*am Kleid*); 2. erziehen; (sich) schulen;

abrichten; (sich) ausbilden; *Sport:* trainieren; sich üben; **~ee** [treɪ'niː] in der Ausbildung Stehende(r *m*) *f*; Auszubildende(r *m*) *f*; **~er** [''] Ausbilder *m*; *Sport:* Trainer *m*; **~ing** [-ɪŋ] Ausbildung *f*; Üben *n*; *bsd. Sport:* Training *n*.

trait [treɪ] (Charakter)Zug *m*.

trai·tor [ˈtreɪtə] Verräter *m*.

tram(·car) *Brt.* [ˈtræm(kaː)] Straßenbahn(wagen *m*) *f*.

tramp [træmp] **1.** Getrampel *n*; Wanderung *f*; Tramp *m*, Landstreicher *m*; **2.** trampeln, treten; (durch)wandern; **tram·ple** [ˈtræmpl] (herum-, zer)trampeln.

trance [traːns] Trance *f*.

tran·quil □ [ˈtræŋkwɪl] ruhig; gelassen; **~(l)i·ty** [træŋˈkwɪlətɪ] Ruhe *f*; Gelassenheit *f*; **~(l)ize** [ˈtræŋkwɪlaɪz] beruhigen; **~(l)iz·er** [-aɪzə] Beruhigungsmittel *n*.

trans- [trænz] jenseits; durch; über.

trans·act [trænˈzækt] abwickeln, abmachen; **~ac·tion** [-kʃn] Erledigung *f*; Geschäft *n*, Transaktion *f*.

trans·al·pine [ˈtrænzˈælpaɪn] transalpin(isch).

trans·at·lan·tic [ˈtrænzətˈlæntɪk] transatlantisch, Übersee...

tran·scend [trænˈsend] überschreiten, hinausgehen über (*acc.*); übertreffen; **~scen·dence**, **~scen·den·cy** [-əns, -ənsɪ] Überlegenheit *f*; *phls.* Transzendenz *f*.

tran·scribe [trænˈskraɪb] abschreiben; *Kurzschrift* übertragen.

tran·script [ˈtrænskrɪpt], **~scrip·tion** [trænˈskrɪpʃn] Abschrift *f*; Umschrift *f*.

trans·fer 1. [trænsˈfɜː] (-*rr*-) *v/t.* übertragen; versetzen, -legen; *Geld* überweisen; *Sport: Spieler* transferieren (*to* zu), abgeben (*to* an *acc.*); *v/i.* übertreten; *Sport:* wechseln (*Spieler*); 🚎 *etc.* umsteigen; **2.** [ˈtrænsfɜː] Übertragung *f*; Versetzung *f*, -legung *f*; *econ.* (Geld)Überweisung *f*; *Sport:* Transfer *m*, Wechsel *m*; 🚎 *etc.* Umsteigefahrschein *m*; **~a·ble** [trænsˈfɜːrəbl] übertragbar.

trans·fig·ure [trænsˈfɪgə] umgestalten; verklären.

trans·fix [trænsˈfɪks] durchstechen; **~ed** *fig.* versteinert, starr (*with* vor *dat.*).

trans|form [trænsˈfɔːm] umformen;

um-, verwandeln; **~for·ma·tion** [trænsfəˈmeɪʃn] Umformung *f*; Um-, Verwandlung *f*.

trans|fuse 🖊 [trænsˈfjuːz] *Blut* übertragen; **~fu·sion** 🖊 [-ʒn] (Blut-) Übertragung *f*, (-)Transfusion *f*.

trans|gress [trænsˈgres] *v/t.* überschreiten; *Gesetze etc.* übertreten, verletzen; *v/i.* sich vergehen; **~gres·sion** [-ʃn] Überschreitung *f*; Übertretung *f*; Vergehen *n*; **~gres·sor** [-sə] Übeltäter(in); Rechtsbrecher(in).

tran·sient [ˈtrænzɪənt] **1.** □ = *transitory*; **2.** *Am.* Durchreisende(r *m*) *f*.

tran·sis·tor [trænˈsɪstə] Transistor *m*.

tran·sit [ˈtrænsɪt] Durchgang *m*; Transit-, Durchgangsverkehr *m*; *econ.* Transport *m* (*von Waren*).

tran·si·tion [trænˈsɪʒn] Übergang *m*.

tran·si·tive □ *gr.* [ˈtrænsɪtɪv] transitiv.

tran·si·to·ry □ [ˈtrænsɪtərɪ] vorübergehend; vergänglich, flüchtig.

trans|late [trænsˈleɪt] übersetzen, -tragen; *fig.* umsetzen; **~la·tion** [-ʃn] Übersetzung *f*, -tragung *f*; **~la·tor** [-ə] Übersetzer(in).

trans·lu·cent □ [trænzˈluːsnt] lichtdurchlässig.

trans·mi·gra·tion [ˈtrænzmaɪˈgreɪʃn] Seelenwanderung *f*.

trans·mis·sion [trænzˈmɪʃn] Übermittlung *f*; Übertragung *f*; *biol.* Vererbung *f*; *phys.* Fortpflanzung *f*; *mot.* Getriebe *n*; *Rundfunk, TV:* Sendung *f*.

trans·mit [trænzˈmɪt] (-*tt*-) übermitteln, -senden; übertragen; *Rundfunk, TV:* senden; *biol.* vererben; *phys.* (weiter)leiten; **~ter** [-ə] Übermittler(in); *tel. etc.* Sender *m*.

trans·mute [trænzˈmjuːt] um-, verwandeln.

trans·par·ent □ [trænsˈpærənt] durchsichtig (*a. fig.*).

tran·spire [trænˈspaɪə] ausdünsten, -schwitzen; *fig.* durchsickern.

trans|plant [trænsˈplɑːnt] umpflanzen; verpflanzen (*a.* 🖊); **~plan·ta·tion** [ˈtrænsplɑːnˈteɪʃn] Verpflanzung *f* (*a.* 🖊).

trans|port 1. [trænsˈpɔːt] transportieren, befördern, fortschaffen; *fig. j-n* hinreißen; **2.** [ˈtrænspɔːt] Transport *m*, Beförderung *f*; Versand *m*; Verkehr *m*; Beförderungsmittel *n*;

T

Transportschiff n, -flugzeug n; *in a* ~ *of rage* außer sich vor Wut; *be in* ~*s of* außer sich sein vor (*Freude etc.*); ~**por·ta·tion** ['trænspɔːˈteɪʃn] Transport m, Beförderung f.

trans·pose [trænsˈpəʊz] versetzen, umstellen; ♪ transponieren.

trans·verse □ ['trænzvɜːs] querlaufend; Quer...

trap [træp] **1.** Falle f (a. fig.); ⊕ Klappe f; sl. Schnauze f (Mund); *keep one's* ~ *shut* sl. die Schnauze halten; *set a* ~ *for s.o.* j-m e-e Falle stellen; **2.** (-pp-) (in e-r Falle) fangen; fig. in e-e Falle locken; ~**door** ['træpdɔː] Falltür f; thea. Versenkung f.

tra·peze [trəˈpiːz] Trapez n.

trap·per ['træpə] Trapper m, Fallensteller m, Pelztierjäger m.

trap·pings fig. ['træpɪŋz] pl. Schmuck m, Putz m, Drum u. Dran n.

trash [træʃ] bsd. Am. Abfall m, Abfälle pl., Müll m; Unsinn m, F Blech n; Gesindel n; Kitsch m; ~ **can** Am. Abfall-, Mülleimer m; Am. Abfall-, Mülltonne f; ~**y** □ ['træʃɪ] (-ier, -iest) wertlos, kitschig.

trav·el ['trævl] **1.** (bsd. Brt. -ll-, Am. -l-) v/i. reisen; sich bewegen; bsd. fig. schweifen, wandern; v/t. bereisen; **2.** das Reisen; ⊕ (Kolben)Hub m; ~*s* pl. Reisen pl.; ~ **a·gen·cy, ~ bu·reau** Reisebüro n; ~(**l)er** [~ə] Reisende(r m) f; ~'s *cheque* (Am. check) Reisescheck m.

tra·verse ['trævəs] durch-, überqueren; durchziehen; führen über (acc.).

trav·es·ty ['trævɪstɪ] **1.** Travestie f; Karikatur f, Zerrbild n; **2.** travestieren; ins Lächerliche ziehen.

trawl ⚓ [trɔːl] **1.** (Grund)Schleppnetz n; **2.** mit dem Schleppnetz fischen; ~**er** ⚓ ['trɔːlə] Trawler m.

tray [treɪ] (Servier)Brett n, Tablett n; Ablagekorb m.

treach·er·ous □ ['tretʃərəs] verräterisch, treulos; (heim)tückisch; trügerisch; ~**y** [~ɪ] (*to*) Verrat m (an dat.), Treulosigkeit f (gegen).

trea·cle ['triːkl] Sirup m.

tread [tred] **1.** (*trod, trodden od. trod*) treten; (be)schreiten; trampeln; **2.** Tritt m, Schritt m; ⊕ Lauffläche f; mot. Profil n; **trea·dle** ['tredl] Pedal

n; Tritt m; ~**mill** Tretmühle f (a. fig.).

trea·son ['triːzn] Verrat m; ~**so·na·ble** □ [~əbl] verräterisch.

treas·ure ['treʒə] **1.** Schatz m, Reichtum m; ~ *trove* Schatzfund m; **2.** sehr schätzen; ~ *up Schätze* sammeln, anhäufen; ~**ur·er** [~rə] Schatzmeister m; Kassenwart m.

treas·ur·y ['treʒərɪ] Schatzkammer f; ♀ Finanzministerium n; ♀ **Bench** Brt. parl. Regierungsbank f; ♀ **De·part·ment** Am. Finanzministerium n.

treat [triːt] **1.** v/t. behandeln, umgehen mit; betrachten; ~ *s.o. to s.th.* j-m et. spendieren; ~ *with* verhandeln mit; **2.** Vergnügen n; school ~ Schulausflug m, -fest n; *it is my* ~ es geht auf meine Rechnung.

trea·tise ['triːtɪz] Abhandlung f.

treat·ment ['triːtmənt] Behandlung f.

treat·y ['triːtɪ] Vertrag m.

tre·ble ['trebl] **1.** □ dreifach; **2.** ♪ Diskant m, Sopran m; *Radio*: Höhen pl.; **3.** (sich) verdreifachen.

tree [triː] Baum m.

tre·foil ⚘ ['trefɔɪl] Klee m.

trel·lis ['trelɪs] **1.** ⚘ Spalier n; **2.** vergittern; ⚘ am Spalier ziehen.

trem·ble ['trembl] zittern.

tre·men·dous □ [trɪˈmendəs] schrecklich, ungeheuer, gewaltig; F enorm.

trem·or ['tremə] Zittern n; Beben n.

trem·u·lous □ ['tremjʊləs] zitternd, bebend.

trench [trentʃ] **1.** ✕ Schützen)Graben m; Furche f; **2.** v/t. mit Gräben durchziehen; v/i. ✕ Schützen)Graben ausheben.

tren·chant □ ['trentʃənt] scharf.

trend [trend] **1.** Richtung f; fig. (Ver)Lauf m; fig. Trend m, Entwicklung f, Tendenz f; **2.** tendieren, neigen; ~**y** bsd. Brt. F ['trendɪ] (-ier, -iest) modern.

trep·i·da·tion [trepɪˈdeɪʃn] Zittern n; Angst f, Beklommenheit f.

tres·pass ['trespəs] **1.** ⚖ unbefugtes Betreten; Vergehen n; **2.** ~ (*up)on* ⚖ widerrechtlich betreten; über Gebühr in Anspruch nehmen; *no* ~*ing* Betreten verboten; ~**er** ⚖ [~ə] Rechtsverletzer m; Unbefugte(r m) f.

tres·tle ['tresl] Gestell *n*, Bock *m*.
tri·al ['traɪəl] **1.** Versuch *m*; Probe *f*, Prüfung *f* (*a. fig.*); ⅋ Prozeß *m*, Verhandlung *f*; *fig.* Plage *f*; *on* ~ auf *od.* zur Probe; *give s.th. od. s.o. a* ~ e-n Versuch mit et. *od.* j-m machen; *be on* ~ ⅋ angeklagt sein; *put s.o. on* ~ ⅋ j-n vor Gericht bringen; **2.** Versuchs..., Probe...
tri·an·gle ['traɪæŋgl] Dreieck *n*; **~gu·lar** □ [traɪ'æŋjʊlə] dreieckig.
tribe [traɪb] (Volks)Stamm *m*; *contp.* Sippe *f*; ♀, *zo.* Klasse *f*.
tri·bu·nal ⅋ [traɪ'bjuːnl] Gericht(s-hof) *n*; **trib·une** ['trɪbjuːn] Tribun *m*; Tribüne *f*.
trib·u·ta·ry ['trɪbjʊtərɪ] **1.** □ zins-pflichtig; *fig.* helfend; *geogr.* Neben...; **2.** Nebenfluß *m*; **~ute** [~juːt] Tribut *m* (*a. fig.*), Zins *m*; Anerken-nung *f*.
trice [traɪs]: *in a* ~ im Nu.
trick [trɪk] **1.** Kniff *m*, List *f*, Trick *m*; Kunststück *n*; Streich *m*; (schlechte) Angewohnheit; *play a* ~ *on s.o.* j-m e-n Streich spielen; **2.** überlisten, F hereinlegen; **~e·ry** ['trɪkərɪ] Betrü-gerei *f*.
trick·le ['trɪkl] tröpfeln, rieseln.
trick·ster ['trɪkstə] Gauner(in); **~y** □ [~ɪ] (*-ier, -iest*) verschlagen; F heikel; verzwickt, verwickelt, schwierig.
tri·cy·cle ['traɪsɪkl] Dreirad *n*.
tri·dent ['traɪdənt] Dreizack *m*.
tri·fle ['traɪfl] **1.** Kleinigkeit *f*; Lappa-lie *f*; *a* ~ ein bißchen, ein wenig, etwas; **2.** *v/i.* spielen; spaßen; *v/t.* ~ *away* verschwenden; **~fling** □ [~ɪŋ] geringfügig; unbedeutend.
trig·ger ['trɪgə] Abzug *m* (*am Ge-wehr*); *phot.* Auslöser *m*.
trill [trɪl] **1.** Triller *m*; gerolltes r; **2.** trillern; *bsd.* das r rollen.
tril·lion ['trɪljən] *Brt.* Trillion *f*; *Am.* Billion *f*.
trim [trɪm] **1.** □ (*-mm-*) ordentlich; schmuck; gepflegt; **2.** (guter) Zu-stand; Ordnung *f*; *in good* ~ in Form; **3.** (*-mm-*) zurechtmachen, in Ordnung bringen; (*a.* ~ *up* heraus-)putzen, schmücken; *Kleider etc.* be-setzen; stutzen, trimmen, (be-)schneiden; ⚓, ⚙ trimmen; **~ming** ['trɪmɪŋ]: ~*s pl.* Besatz *m*; Zutaten *pl.*, Beilagen *f.* (*e-r Speise*).
Trin·i·ty *eccl.* ['trɪnɪtɪ] Dreieinigkeit *f*.

trin·ket ['trɪŋkɪt] wertloses Schmuck-stück.
trip [trɪp] **1.** (kurze) Reise, Fahrt *f*; Ausflug *m*, Spritztour *f*; Stolpern *n*, Fallen *n*; Fehltritt *m* (*a. fig.*); *fig.* Versehen *n*, Fehler *m*; F Trip *m* (*Drogenrausch*); **2.** (*-pp-*) *v/i.* trip-peln; stolpern; *fig.* (e-n) Fehler ma-chen; *v/t. a.* ~ *up* j-m ein Bein stellen (*a. fig.*).
tri·par·tite [traɪ'pɑːtaɪt] dreiteilig.
tripe [traɪp] Kaldaunen *pl.*, Kutteln *pl.*
tri·ple □ ['trɪpl] dreifach; ~ *jump* Sport: Dreisprung *m*; **~lets** [~ɪts] *pl.* Drillinge *pl.*
trip·li·cate **1.** ['trɪplɪkɪt] dreifach; **2.** [~keɪt] verdreifachen.
tri·pod ['traɪpɒd] Dreifuß *m*; *phot.* Stativ *n*.
trip·per *bsd. Brt.* ['trɪpə] Ausflüg-ler(in).
trite □ [traɪt] abgedroschen, banal.
tri·umph ['traɪəmf] **1.** Triumph *m*, Sieg *m*; **2.** triumphieren; **~um·phal** [traɪ'ʌmfl] Sieges..., Triumph...; **~um·phant** □ [~ənt] triumphie-rend.
triv·i·al □ [~'trɪvɪəl] bedeutungslos; unbedeutend, trivial; alltäglich.
trod [trɒd] *pret. u. p.p. von tread 1*; **~den** ['trɒdn] *p.p. von tread 1*.
trol·le·y ['trɒlɪ] *Brt.* Handwagen *m*, Gepäckwagen *m*, Kofferkuli *m*, Ein-kaufswagen *m*, Sackkarre(n *m*) *f*, Golf: Caddie *m*; *Brt.* ☶ Draisine *f*; *Brt.* Tee-, Servierwagen *m*; ⚡ Kon-taktrolle *f* (*e-s Oberleitungsfahr-zeugs*); *Am.* Straßenbahn(wagen *m*) *f*; **~bus** O(berleitungs)bus *m*.
trol·lop ['trɒləp] F Schlampe *f*; leich-tes Mädchen, Hure *f*.
trom·bone ♪ [trɒm'bəʊn] Posaune *f*.
troop [truːp] **1.** Trupp *m*, Haufe(n) *m*; ~*s pl.* ⚔ Truppen *pl.*; **2.** sich scharen; (*herein- etc.*)strömen, mar-schieren; ~ *away,* ~ *off* F abziehen; ~ *the colours Brt.* ⚔ e-e Fahnenpa-rade abhalten; **~er** ⚔ ['truːpə] Ka-vallerist *m*.
tro·phy ['trəʊfɪ] Trophäe *f*.
trop·ic ['trɒpɪk] **1.** Wendekreis *m*; ~*s pl.* Tropen *pl.*; **2.** (~*ally*), **~i·cal** □ [~kl] tropisch.
trot [trɒt] **1.** Trott *m*, Trab *m*; **2.** (*-tt-*) trotten; traben (lassen).
trou·ble ['trʌbl] **1.** Mühe *f*, Plage *f*, Last *f*, Belästigung *f*, Störung *f*;

Unannehmlichkeiten *pl.*, Schwierigkeiten *pl.*, Schereien *pl.*, Ärger *m*; *ask od.* look for ~ unbedingt Ärger haben wollen; *take (the)* ~ sich (die) Mühe machen; **2.** stören, beunruhigen, belästigen; quälen, plagen; *j-m* Mühe machen; *(sich)* bemühen; bitten *(for* um); *don't* ~ *yourself* bemühen Sie sich nicht; *what's the* ~? was ist los?; **~·mak·er** Unruhestifter(in); **~·some** □ [~səm] beschwerlich; lästig.

trough [trɔf] Trog *m*; Rinne *f*; Wellental *n*.

trounce [traʊns] verprügeln.

troupe *thea.* [truːp] Truppe *f*.

trou·ser ['traʊzə]: *(a pair of)* ~*s pl.* (e-e) (lange) Hose; Hosen *pl.*; *attr.* Hosen...; ~ **suit** Hosenanzug *m*.

trous·seau ['truːsəʊ] Aussteuer *f*.

trout *zo.* [traʊt] Forelle(n *pl.*) *f*.

trow·el ['traʊəl] Maurerkelle *f*.

tru·ant ['truːənt] Schulschwänzer(in); *play* ~ (die Schule) schwänzen.

truce ⚔ [truːs] Waffenstillstand *m*.

truck [trʌk] **1.** ⚙ offener Güterwagen; *bsd. Am.* Last(kraft)wagen *m*, Lkw *m*; Transportkarren *m*; Tausch(handel) *m*; *Am.* Gemüse *n*; **2.** (ver)tauschen; **~·er** *Am.* ['trʌkə] Lastwagen-, Fernfahrer *m*; **~ farm** *Am.* Gemüsegärtnerei *f*.

truc·u·lent □ ['trʌkjʊlənt] wild, roh, grausam; gehässig.

trudge [trʌdʒ] sich (mühsam dahin-)schleppen; (mühsam) stapfen.

true □ [truː]: *(~r, ~st)* wahr; echt, wirklich; treu; genau; richtig; *(it is)* ~ gewiß, freilich, zwar; *come* ~ in Erfüllung gehen; wahr werden; ~ *to nature* naturgetreu.

tru·ly ['truːlɪ] wirklich; wahrhaft; aufrichtig; genau; treu; *Yours* ~ *Briefschluß:* Hochachtungsvoll.

trump [trʌmp] **1.** Trumpf(karte *f*) *m*; **2.** (über)trumpfen; ~ *up* erfinden.

trum·pet ['trʌmpɪt] **1.** ♩ Trompete *f*; **2.** trompeten; *fig.* ausposaunen.

trun·cheon ['trʌntʃən] (Gummi-)Knüppel *m*, Schlagstock *m*.

trun·dle ['trʌndl] rollen.

trunk [trʌŋk] (Baum)Stamm *m*; Rumpf *m*; Rüssel *m*; (Schrank)Koffer *m*, Truhe *f*; *Am. mot.* Kofferraum *m*; **~·call** *Brt. teleph.* ['trʌŋkkɔːl] Ferngespräch *n*; **~·line** ⚙ Hauptlinie *f*; *teleph.* Fernleitung *f*; **~s**

[trʌŋks] *pl.* Turnhose *f*; Badehose *f*; *Sport:* Shorts *pl.*; *bsd. Brt.* (Herren-)Unterhose *f*.

truss [trʌs] **1.** Bündel *n*, Bund *n*; ⚕ Bruchband *n*; *arch.* Träger *m*, Fachwerk *n*; **2.** (zs.-)binden; *arch.* stützen.

trust [trʌst] **1.** Vertrauen *n*; Glaube *m*; Kredit *m*; Pfand *n*; Verwahrung *f*; ⚖ Treuhand *f*; ⚖ Treuhandvermögen *n*; *econ.* Trust *m*; *econ.* Kartell *n*; ~ *company* ✝ Treuhandgesellschaft *f*; *in* ~ zu treuen Händen; **2.** *v/t.* (ver)trauen *(dat.)*; anvertrauen, übergeben *(s.o. with s.th., s.th. to s.o.* j-m et.); zuversichtlich hoffen; *v/i.* vertrauen *(in, to auf acc.)*; **~·ee** ⚖ [trʌs'tiː] Sach-, Verwalter *m*; Treuhänder *m*; **~·ful** □ ['trʌstfl], **~·ing** □ [~ɪŋ] vertrauensvoll; **~·wor·thy** □ [~wɜːðɪ] vertrauenswürdig, zuverlässig.

truth [truːθ] *(pl.* ~*s* [truːðz, truːθs]) Wahrheit *f*; Wirklichkeit *f*; Genauigkeit *f*; **~·ful** □ ['truːθfl] wahr(-heitsliebend).

try [traɪ] **1.** versuchen; probieren; prüfen; ⚖ verhandeln über *et. od.* gegen *j-n*; vor Gericht stellen; *die Augen etc.* angreifen; sich bemühen *od.* bewerben *(for* um); ~ *on Kleid* anprobieren; ~ *out* ausprobieren; **2.** Versuch *m*; **~·ing** □ ['traɪɪŋ] anstrengend; kritisch.

tsar *hist.* [zɑː] Zar *m*.

T-shirt ['tiːʃɜːt] T-Shirt *n*.

tub [tʌb] **1.** Faß *n*; Zuber *m*, Kübel *m*; *Brt.* F (Bade)Wanne *f*; *Brt.* F (Wannen)Bad *n*.

tube [tjuːb] Rohr *n*; ⚡ Röhre *f*; Tube *f*; *(inner* ~ Luft)Schlauch *m*; Tunnel *m*; *die* (Londoner) U-Bahn; *the* ~ *Am.* F die Röhre, die Glotze *(Fernseher)*; **~·less** ['tjuːblɪs] schlauchlos.

tu·ber ♀ ['tjuːbə] Knolle *f*.

tu·ber·cu·lo·sis ⚕ [tjuːbɜːkjʊ'ləʊsɪs] Tuberkulose *f*.

tu·bu·lar □ ['tjuːbjʊlə] röhrenförmig.

tuck [tʌk] **1.** Biese *f*; Abnäher *m*; **2.** stecken; ~ *away* weg-, verstecken; ~ *in*, ~ *up* (warm) zudecken; ~ *s.o. up in bed* j-n ins Bett packen; ~ *up Rock* schürzen; *Ärmel* hochkrempeln.

Tues·day ['tjuːzdɪ] Dienstag *m*.

tuft [tʌft] Büschel *n*; (Haar)Schopf *m*.

tug [tʌg] **1.** Zerren, heftiger Ruck *m*; *a.*

~boat ⚓ Schlepper *m*; *fig.* Anstrengung *f*; **2.** (*-gg-*) ziehen, zerren; ⚓ schleppen; sich mühen; ~ **of war** Tauziehen *n*.

tu·i·tion [tjuːˈɪʃn] Unterricht *m*; Schulgeld *n*.

tu·lip ♀ [ˈtjuːlɪp] Tulpe *f*.

tum·ble [ˈtʌmbl] **1.** fallen; stürzen; purzeln; taumeln; sich wälzen; **2.** Sturz *m*; Wirrwarr *m*; ~**down** baufällig; ~**r** [~ə] Becher *m*; *zo.* Tümmler *m*.

tu·mid □ [ˈtjuːmɪd] geschwollen.

tum·my F [ˈtʌmɪ] Bäuchlein *n*.

tu·mo(u)r ✴ [ˈtjuːmə] Tumor *m*.

tu·mult [ˈtjuːmʌlt] Tumult *m*; **tu·mul·tu·ous** □ [tjuːˈmʌltjʊəs] lärmend; stürmisch.

tun [tʌn] Faß *m*.

tu·na *zo.* [ˈtuːnə] Thunfisch *m*.

tune [tjuːn] **1.** Melodie *f*; ♪ (Ein-)Stimmung *f*; *fig.* Harmonie *f*; *in* ~ (gut)gestimmt; *out of* ~ verstimmt; **2.** ♪ stimmen; ~ *in v/i.* (das Radio *etc.*) einschalten; *v/t.* das Radio *etc.* einstellen (*to auf acc.*); ~ *up* die Instrumente stimmen; *Motor* tunen; ~**ful** □ [ˈtjuːnfl] melodisch; ~**less** □ [~lɪs] unmelodisch.

tun·er [ˈtjuːnə] *Radio, TV:* Tuner *m*.

tun·nel [ˈtʌnl] **1.** Tunnel *m*; ⚒ Stollen *m*; **2.** (*bsd. Brt. -ll-, Am. -l-*) e-n Tunnel bohren (durch).

tun·ny *zo.* [ˈtʌnɪ] Thunfisch *m*.

tur·bid □ [ˈtɜːbɪd] trüb; dick(flüssig); *fig.* verworren, wirr.

tur·bine ⚙ [ˈtɜːbaɪn] Turbine *f*.

tur·bot *zo.* [ˈtɜːbət] Steinbutt *m*.

tur·bu·lent □ [ˈtɜːbjʊlənt] unruhig; ungestüm; stürmisch, turbulent.

tu·reen [təˈriːn] Terrine *f*.

turf [tɜːf] **1.** (*pl.* ~*s, turves*) Rasen *m*; Torf *m*; *the* ~ die (Pferde)Rennbahn; der Pferderennsport *m*; **2.** mit Rasen bedecken.

tur·gid □ [ˈtɜːdʒɪd] geschwollen.

Turk [tɜːk] Türk|e *m*, -in *f*.

tur·key [ˈtɜːkɪ] *zo.* Truthahn *m*, -henne *f*, Pute(r *m*) *f*; *talk* ~ *bsd. Am.* F offen *od.* sachlich reden.

Turk·ish [ˈtɜːkɪʃ] **1.** türkisch; **2.** *ling.* Türkisch *n*.

tur·moil [ˈtɜːmɔɪl] Aufruhr *m*, Unruhe *f*; Durcheinander *n*.

turn [tɜːn] **1.** *v/t.* (um-, herum)drehen; (um)wenden; *Seite* umdrehen; -blättern; lenken, richten; verwandeln; *j-n* abbringen (*from* von); ab-

wenden; *Text* übertragen, -setzen; bilden, formen; ⊕ drechseln; *Laub* verfärben; ~ *a corner* um eine Ecke biegen; ~ *loose* los-, freilassen; ~ *s.o. sick j-n* krank machen; ~ *sour Milch* sauer werden lassen; *s. somersault*; ~ *s.o. against j-n* aufhetzen gegen; ~ *aside* abwenden; ~ *away* abwenden; abweisen; ~ *down* umbiegen; *Kragen* umschlagen; *Bett* aufdecken; *Decke* zurückschlagen; *Gas etc.* klein(er) stellen; *Radio etc.* leiser stellen; *j-n, et.* ablehnen; ~ *in bsd. Am.* einreichen, -senden; ~ *off Gas, Wasser etc.* abdrehen; *Licht, Radio etc.* ausschalten, -machen; ~ *on Gas, Wasser etc.* aufdrehen; *Gerät* anstellen; *Licht, Radio etc.* anmachen, einschalten; F antörnen; F anmachen (*a. sexuell*); ~ *out econ. Waren* produzieren; hinauswerfen; = *turn off*; ~ *over econ. Waren* umsetzen; umdrehen; *Seite* umblättern; umwerfen; übergeben (*to dat.*); überlegen; ~ *up* nach oben drehen *od.* biegen; *Kragen* hochschlagen; *Ärmel* hochkrempeln; *Hose etc.* auf-, umschlagen; *Gas etc.* aufdrehen; *Radio etc.* lauter stellen; *v/i.* sich drehen (lassen); sich (um-, herum)drehen; *mot.* wenden; sich (ab-, hin-, zu)wenden; (ab-, ein)biegen; e-e Biegung machen (*Straße etc.*); sich (ver)wandeln; umschlagen (*Wetter etc.*); *Christ, grau etc.* werden; ~ (*sour*) sauer werden (*Milch*); ~ *about* sich umdrehen; ⚔ kehrtmachen; ~ *aside*, ~ *away* sich abwenden; ~ *back* zurückkehren; ~ *in* F ins Bett gehen; ~ *off abbiegen*; ~ *out gut etc.* ausfallen, -gehen; sich herausstellen (als); ~ *over* sich umdrehen; ~ *to* nach *rechts etc.* abbiegen; sich zuwenden (*dat.*); sich an *j-n* wenden; werden zu; ~ *up fig.* auftauchen; **2.** (Um)Drehung *f*; Biegung *f*, Kurve *f*, Kehre *f*; (einzelne) Windung (*e-s Kabels etc.*); Wendung *f*; Wendepunkt *m* (*a. fig.*); Wende *f*; Wechsel *m*; Gestalt *f*, Form *f*; (kurzer) Spaziergang; (kurze) Fahrt; Reihe(nfolge) *f*; Dienst *m*, Gefallen *m*, Zweck *m*; Neigung *f*, Talent *n*; F Schrecken *m*; ~ (*of mind*) Denkart *f*, -weise *f*; *at every* ~ auf Schritt und Tritt; *by* ~*s* abwechselnd; *in* ~ der Reihe nach; *it is my* ~ ich bin an der Reihe; *take* ~*s* (mit)einander *od.* sich (gegenseitig) ab-

wechseln (*at* in *dat.*, bei); *does it
serve your* ~? ist Ihnen damit gedient?; ~**coat** ['tɜ:nkəʊt] Abtrünnige(r) *m*, Überläufer(in) *m*; ~**er** [~ə]
Drechsler *m*; Dreher *m*.

turn·ing ['tɜ:nɪŋ] ⊕ Drehen *n*, Drechseln *n*; Biegung *f*; Straßenecke *f*;
(Weg)Abzweigung *f*; Querstraße *f*;
~**point** *fig.* Wendepunkt *m*.

tur·nip ⚘ ['tɜ:nɪp] (*bsd.* Weiße) Rübe.

turn·out ['tɜ:naʊt] Aufmachung *f*,
bsd. Kleidung *f*; Teilnahme *f*, Besucher(zahl *f*) *pl.*, Beteiligung *f*;
econ. Gesamtproduktion *f*; ~**over**
['tɜ:nəʊvə] *econ.* Umsatz *m*; Personalwechsel *m*, Fluktuation *f*; ~**pike**
a. ~ *road Am.* gebührenpflichtige
Schnellstraße *f*; ~**stile** Drehkreuz *n*;
~**table** ♣ Drehscheibe *f*; Plattenteller *m*; ~**up** *Brt.* Hosenaufschlag
m.

tur·pen·tine ♫ ['tɜ:pəntaɪn] Terpentin *n*.

tur·pi·tude ['tɜ:pɪtju:d] Verworfenheit *f*.

tur·ret ['tʌrɪt] Türmchen *n*; ✕, ⚓
Geschützturm *m*.

tur·tle *zo.* ['tɜ:tl] (See)Schildkröte *f*;
~**dove** *zo.* Turteltaube *f*; ~**neck**
Rollkragen *m*; *a.* ~ *sweater* Rollkragenpullover *m*.

tusk [tʌsk] Fangzahn *m*; Stoßzahn *m*;
Hauer *m*.

tus·sle ['tʌsl] 1. Rauferei *f*, Balgerei *f*;
2. raufen, sich balgen.

tus·sock ['tʌsək] (Gras)Büschel *n*.

tut *int.* [tʌt] ach was!; Unsinn!

tu·te·lage ['tju:tɪlɪdʒ] ♟ Vormundschaft *f*; (An)Leitung *f*.

tu·tor ['tju:tə] 1. Privat-, Hauslehrer
m; *Brt. univ.* Tutor *m*; *Am. univ.*
Assistent *m* (*mit Lehrauftrag*); 2. unterrichten; schulen, erziehen; **tu·to·ri·al** [tju:'tɔ:rɪəl] 1. *Brt. univ.* Tutorenkurs *m*; 2. Tutor(en)...

tux·e·do *Am.* [tʌk'si:dəʊ] (*pl.* -dos,
-does) Smoking *m*.

TV F ['ti:vi:] 1. TV *n*, Fernsehen *n*;
Fernseher *m*, Fernsehapparat *m*; *on*
~ im Fernsehen; 2. Fernseh...

twang [twæŋ] 1. Schwirren *n*; *mst
nasal* ~ näselnde Aussprache; 2.
schwirren (lassen); näseln; klimpern
od. kratzen auf (*dat.*), zupfen.

tweak [twi:k] zwicken, kneifen.

tweet [twi:t] zwitschern.

tweez·ers ['twi:zəz] *pl.* (*a pair of* ~
e-e) Pinzette.

twelfth [twelfθ] 1. zwölfte(r, -s); 2.
Zwölftel *n*; 2-**night** ['twelfˈnaɪt]
Dreikönigsabend *m*.

twelve [twelv] 1. zwölf; 2. Zwölf *f*.

twen·ti·eth ['twentɪɪθ] zwanzigste(r,
-s); ~**ty** [~ɪ] 1. zwanzig; 2. Zwanzig
f.

twice [twaɪs] zweimal.

twid·dle ['twɪdl] herumdrehen (an
dat.); (herum)spielen mit (*od.* with
mit).

twig [twɪg] dünner Zweig, Ästchen *n*.

twi·light ['twaɪlaɪt] Zwielicht *n*; (*bsd.*
Abend)Dämmerung *f*; *fig.* Verfall *m*.

twin [twɪn] 1. Zwillings...; doppelt; 2.
Zwilling *m*; ~*s pl.* Zwillinge *pl.*; *attr.*
Zwillings...; ~**bedded room**, ~**bedded**
bettzimmer *n*; ~ **brother** Zwillingsbruder *m*; ~**engined** ✈ zweimotorig; ~**jet** ✈ zwei-, doppelstrahlig; ~**lens reflex camera** *phot.*
Spiegelreflexkamera *f*; ~ **sister** Zwillingsschwester *f*; ~ **town** Partnerstadt *f*; ~ **track** Doppelspur *f* (*e-s
Tonbands*).

twine [twaɪn] 1. Bindfaden *m*,
Schnur *f*; Zwirn *m*; 2. sich drehen;
verflechten; (sich) schlingen *od.*
winden; umschlingen, -ranken.

twinge [twɪndʒ] stechender
Schmerz, Zwicken *n*, Stich *m*.

twin·kle ['twɪŋkl] 1. funkeln, blitzen;
huschen, zwinkern; 2. Funkeln *n*,
Blitzen *n*; (Augen)Zwinkern *n*, Blinzeln *n*.

twirl [twɜ:l] 1. Wirbel *m*; 2. wirbeln.

twist [twɪst] 1. Drehung *f*; Windung
f; Biegung *f*; (Gesichts)Verzerrung
f; Twist *m*, Garn *n*; Kringel *m*, Zopf
m (*Backwaren*); ♪ Twist *m*; *fig.* Entstellung *f*; *fig.* (ausgeprägte) Neigung *od.* Veranlagung; 2. (sich) drehen *od.* winden; zs.-drehen; verdrehen; (sich) verziehen *od.* -zerren;
♪ twisten, Twist tanzen.

twit *fig.* [twɪt] (-*tt*-) j-n aufziehen.

twitch [twɪtʃ] 1. zupfen (an *dat.*);
zucken mit (*od.* with vor); 2.
Zuckung *f*.

twit·ter ['twɪtə] 1. zwitschern; 2. Gezwitscher *n*; *in a* ~, *all of a* ~ aufgeregt.

two [tu:] 1. zwei; *in* ~*s* zu zweit, zu
zweien; *in* ~ entzwei; *put* ~ *and* ~
together sich einen Vers darauf machen; 2. Zwei *f*; ~**bit** *Am.* F ['tu:bɪt]
25-Cent-...; *fig.* unbedeutend, klein;
~**cy·cle** *Am.* ⊕ Zweitakt...; ~

edged ['tu:'edʒd] zweischneidig; **~fold** ['tu:'fəʊld] zweifach; **~ pence** Brt. ['tʌpəns] zwei Pence pl.; **~pen·ny** Brt. ['tʌpnɪ] zwei Pence wert; **~piece** ['tu:'pi:s] **1.** zweiteilig; **2.** a. ~ dress Jackenkleid; a. ~ swimming-costume Zweiteiler m; **~seat·er** mot., ✈ ['tu:'si:tə] Zweisitzer m; **~stroke** bsd. Brt. ⊕ ['tu:'strəʊk] Zweitakt...; **~way** Doppel...; ~ adapter ⚡ Doppelstecker m; ~ traffic Gegenverkehr m.

ty·coon Am. F [taɪ'ku:n] Industriemagnat m; oil ~ Ölmagnat m.

type [taɪp] **1.** Typ m; Urbild n; Vorbild n; Muster n; Art f, Sorte f; print. Type f, Buchstabe m; true to ~ artgemäß, typisch; set in ~ setzen; **2.** v/t. et. mit der Maschine (ab)schreiben, (ab)tippen; v/i. maschineschreiben, tippen; **~writ·er**

[taɪpraɪtə] Schreibmaschine f; ~ ribbon Farbband n.

ty·phoid 🕮 ['taɪfɔɪd] **1.** typhös; ~ fever = **2.** (Unterleibs)Typhus m.

ty·phoon [taɪ'fu:n] Taifun m.

ty·phus 🕮 ['taɪfəs] Flecktyphus m, -fieber m; △ nicht Typhus.

typ·i·cal □ ['tɪpɪkl] typisch; bezeichnend, kennzeichnend (of für); **~fy** [~faɪ] typisch sein für; versinnbildlichen.

typ·ist ['taɪpɪst] Maschinenschreiber(in); Schreibkraft f.

ty·ran·nic [tɪ'rænɪk] (~ally), **~ni·cal** □ [~kl] tyrannisch.

tyr·an·nize ['tɪrənaɪz] tyrannisieren; **~ny** [~ɪ] Tyrannei f.

ty·rant ['taɪərənt] Tyrann(in).

tyre Brt. ['taɪə] (Rad-, Auto)Reifen m.

Tyr·o·lese [tɪrə'li:z] **1.** Tiroler(in); **2.** tirolisch, Tiroler...

tzar hist. [zɑ:] Zar m.

U

u·biq·ui·tous □ [ju:'bɪkwɪtəs] allgegenwärtig, überall zu finden(d).

ud·der ['ʌdə] Euter n.

ug·ly □ ['ʌglɪ] (-ier, -iest) häßlich; schlimm; gemein; widerwärtig, übel.

ul·cer 🕮 ['ʌlsə] Geschwür n; **~ate** [~reɪt] eitern (lassen); **~ous** 🕮 [~rəs] eiternd.

ul·te·ri·or □ [ʌl'tɪərɪə] jenseitig; weiter; später(liegend), versteckt.

ul·ti·mate □ ['ʌltɪmət] äußerste(r, -s), letzte(r, -s); End...; **~ly** [~lɪ] letztlich; schließlich.

ul·ti·ma·tum [ʌltɪ'meɪtəm] (pl. -tums, -ta [-tə]) Ultimatum n.

ul·tra ['ʌltrə] übermäßig; extrem; super...; Ultra..., ultra...; **~fash·ion·a·ble** [~'fæʃənəbl] hypermodern; **~mod·ern** hypermodern.

um·bil·i·cal cord anat. [ʌm'bɪlɪkl kɔ:d] Nabelschnur f.

um·brel·la [ʌm'brelə] Regenschirm m; ✕, ✈ Abschirmung f; fig. Schutz m.

um·pire ['ʌmpaɪə] **1.** Schiedsrichter m; **2.** als Schiedsrichter fungieren

(bei); schlichten; Sport: a. Spiel leiten.

un- [ʌn] un..., Un...; ent...; nicht...

un·a·bashed ['ʌnə'bæʃt] unverfroren; unerschrocken.

un·a·bat·ed ['ʌnə'beɪtɪd] unvermindert.

un·a·ble ['ʌn'eɪbl] unfähig, außerstande, nicht in der Lage.

un·ac·com·mo·dat·ing ['ʌnə'kɒmədeɪtɪŋ] unnachgiebig; ungefällig.

un·ac·coun·ta·ble □ ['ʌnə'kaʊntəbl] unerklärlich, seltsam.

un·ac·cus·tomed ['ʌnə'kʌstəmd] ungewohnt; ungewöhnlich.

un·ac·quaint·ed ['ʌnə'kweɪntɪd]: be ~ with s.th. et. nicht kennen, mit e-r Sache nicht vertraut sein.

un·ad·vised □ ['ʌnəd'vaɪzd] unbesonnen, unüberlegt; unberaten.

un·af·fect·ed □ ['ʌnə'fektɪd] unberührt; ungerührt; ungekünstelt.

un·aid·ed ['ʌn'eɪdɪd] ohne Unterstützung, (ganz) allein; bloß (Auge).

un·al·ter·a·ble □ [ʌn'ɔ:ltərəbl] unveränderlich; **un·al·tered** ['ʌn'ɔ:ltəd] unverändert.

u·na·nim·i·ty [juːnəˈnɪmətɪ] Einmütigkeit *f*; **u·nan·i·mous** □ [juːˈnænɪməs] einmütig, -stimmig.

un·an·swe·ra·ble □ [ʌnˈɑːnsərəbl] unwiderleglich; **un·an·swered** [ˈʌnˈɑːnsəd] unbeantwortet.

un·ap·proa·cha·ble □ [ˈʌnəˈprəʊtʃəbl] unzugänglich, unnahbar.

un·apt □ [ʌnˈæpt] ungeeignet.

un·a·shamed □ [ˈʌnəˈʃeɪmd] schamlos.

un·asked [ʌnˈɑːskt] ungefragt; ungebeten; uneingeladen.

un·as·sist·ed □ [ˈʌnəˈsɪstɪd] ohne Hilfe *od.* Unterstützung.

un·as·sum·ing □ [ˈʌnəˈsjuːmɪŋ] anspruchslos, bescheiden.

un·at·tached [ˈʌnəˈtætʃt] nicht gebunden; ungebunden, ledig, frei.

un·at·trac·tive □ [ˈʌnəˈtræktɪv] wenig anziehend, reizlos, unattraktiv.

un·au·thor·ized [ʌnˈɔːθəraɪzd] unberechtigt; unbefugt.

un·a·vai·la·ble □ [ˈʌnəˈveɪləbl] nicht verfügbar; **un·a·vail·ing** [⁓ɪŋ] vergeblich.

un·a·void·a·ble □ [ˈʌnəˈvɔɪdəbl] unvermeidlich.

un·a·ware [ˈʌnəˈweə]: *be* ~ *of et.* nicht bemerken; ~**s** [⁓z] unversehens, unvermutet; versehentlich.

un·backed [ˈʌnˈbækt] ohne Unterstützung; ungedeckt (*Scheck*).

un·bal·anced [ʌnˈbælənst] unausgeglichen; *of* ~ *mind* geistesgestört.

un·bear·a·ble □ [ʌnˈbeərəbl] unerträglich.

un·beat·en [ʌnˈbiːtn] ungeschlagen, unbesiegt; unübertroffen.

un·be·com·ing □ [ˈʌnbɪˈkʌmɪŋ] unkleidsam; unpassend, unschicklich.

un·be·known(st) [ˈʌnbɪˈnəʊn(st)] (*to*) ohne (*j-s*) Wissen; unbekannt (*to dat.*).

un·be·lief *eccl.* [ˈʌnbɪˈliːf] Unglaube *m*.

un·be·lie·va·ble □ [ˈʌnbɪˈliːvəbl] unglaublich; **un·be·liev·ing** □ [ˈʌnbɪˈliːvɪŋ] ungläubig.

un·bend [ˈʌnˈbend] (*-bent*) (sich) entspannen; aus sich herausgehen, auftauen; ~**ing** □ [⁓ɪŋ] unbiegsam; *fig.* unbeugsam.

un·bi·as(s)ed □ [ˈʌnˈbaɪəst] unvoreingenommen; *tz* unbefangen.

un·bid·(den) [ˈʌnˈbɪd(n)] unaufgefordert; ungebeten; ungeladen.

un·bind [ˈʌnˈbaɪnd] (*-bound*) losbinden, befreien; lösen; den Verband abnehmen von.

un·blush·ing □ [ʌnˈblʌʃɪŋ] schamlos.

un·born [ˈʌnˈbɔːn] (noch) ungeboren; (zu)künftig, kommend.

un·bos·om [ʌnˈbʊzəm] offenbaren.

un·bound·ed □ [ˈʌnˈbaʊndɪd] unbegrenzt; *fig.* grenzen-, schrankenlos.

un·bri·dled *fig.* [ʌnˈbraɪdld] ungezügelt; ~ *tongue* lose Zunge.

un·bro·ken □ [ˈʌnˈbrəʊkən] ungebrochen; unversehrt; ununterbrochen; nicht zugeritten (*Pferd*).

un·bur·den [ʌnˈbɜːdn]: ~ *o.s.* (*to s.o.*) (j-m) sein Herz ausschütten.

un·but·ton [ˈʌnˈbʌtn] aufknöpfen.

un·called-for [ʌnˈkɔːldfɔː] unerwünscht; unverlangt; unpassend.

un·can·ny □ [ʌnˈkænɪ] (*-ier, -iest*) unheimlich.

un·cared-for [ʌnˈkeədfɔː] unbeachtet; vernachlässigt; ungepflegt.

un·ceas·ing □ [ʌnˈsiːsɪŋ] unaufhörlich.

un·ce·re·mo·ni·ous □ [ˈʌnserɪˈməʊnjəs] ungezwungen; grob; unhöflich.

un·cer·tain □ [ʌnˈsɜːtn] unsicher; ungewiß; unbestimmt; unzuverlässig; ~**ty** [⁓tɪ] Unsicherheit *f*.

un·chal·lenged [ʌnˈtʃæləndʒd] unangefochten.

un·change·a·ble □ [ʌnˈtʃeɪndʒəbl] unveränderlich, unwandelbar; **un·changed** [ʌnˈtʃeɪndʒd] unverändert; **un·chang·ing** □ [ʌnˈtʃeɪndʒɪŋ] unveränderlich.

un·char·i·ta·ble □ [ʌnˈtʃærɪtəbl] lieblos; unbarmherzig; unfreundlich.

un·checked [ˈʌnˈtʃekt] ungehindert; unkontrolliert.

un·civ·il □ [ˈʌnˈsɪvl] unhöflich; **un·civ·i·lized** [⁓vəlaɪzd] unzivilisiert.

un·claimed [ˈʌnˈkleɪmd] nicht beansprucht; unzustellbar (*bsd. Brief*).

un·clasp [ˈʌnˈklɑːsp] auf-, loshaken, auf-, losschnallen; aufmachen.

un·cle [ˈʌŋkl] Onkel *m*.

un·clean □ [ˈʌnˈkliːn] unrein.

un·close [ˈʌnˈkləʊz] (sich) öffnen.

un·come·ly [ˈʌnˈkʌmlɪ] (*-ier, -iest*) unattraktiv, unschön; reizlos; unpassend.

un·com·for·ta·ble □ [ʌnˈkʌmfətəbl]

unbehaglich, ungemütlich; unangenehm.

un·com·mon □ [ˈʌnˈkɒmən] ungewöhnlich.

un·com·mu·ni·ca·tive □ [ˈʌnkə-
ˈmjuːnɪkətɪv] wortkarg, verschlossen.

un·com·plain·ing □ [ˈʌnkəmˈpleɪ-
nɪŋ] klaglos, ohne Murren, geduldig.

un·com·pro·mis·ing □ [ʌnˈkɒm-
prəmaɪzɪŋ] kompromißlos.

un·con·cern [ˈʌnkənˈsɜːn] Unbe-
kümmertheit f; Gleichgültigkeit f;
~**ed** □ unbekümmert; unbeteiligt;
gleichgültig; uninteressiert (with an
dat.).

un·con·di·tion·al □ [ˈʌnkənˈdɪʃənl]
bedingungs-, vorbehaltlos.

un·con·firmed [ˈʌnkənˈfɜːmd] un-
bestätigt; eccl. nicht konfirmiert.

un·con·nect·ed □ [ˈʌnkəˈnektɪd] un-
verbunden; unzusammenhängend.

un·con·quer·a·ble □ [ʌnˈkɒŋkərəbl]
unüberwindlich, unbesiegbar; **un-
con·quered** [ʌnˈkɒŋkəd] unbesiegt.

un·con·scio·na·ble □ [ʌnˈkɒnʃnəbl]
gewissen-, skrupellos; F unverschämt, unmäßig, übermäßig.

un·con·scious □ [ʌnˈkɒnʃəs] unbewußt; ⚕ bewußtlos; ~**ness** ⚕ [~nɪs]
Bewußtlosigkeit f.

un·con·sti·tu·tion·al □ [ˈʌnkɒnstɪ-
ˈtjuːʃənl] verfassungswidrig.

un·con·trol·la·ble □ [ˈʌnkənˈtrəʊ-
ləbl] unkontrollierbar; unbe-
herrscht; **un·con·trolled** □ [ˈʌn-
kənˈtrəʊld] unbeaufsichtigt; unbe-
herrscht.

un·con·ven·tion·al □ [ˈʌnkən-
ˈvenʃənl] unkonventionell; unüb-
lich; ungezwungen.

un·con·vinced [ˈʌnkənˈvɪnst] nicht
überzeugt (of von); **un·con·vinc-
ing** [~ɪŋ] nicht überzeugend.

un·cork [ʌnˈkɔːk] entkorken.

un·count·a·ble [ʌnˈkaʊntəbl] un-
zählbar; ~**ed** ungezählt.

un·coup·le [ʌnˈkʌpl] ab-, aus-, los-
koppeln.

un·couth □ [ʌnˈkuːθ] ungehobelt.

un·cov·er [ʌnˈkʌvə] aufdecken, frei-
legen; entblößen.

unc·tion [ˈʌŋkʃn] Salbung f (a. fig.);
Salbe f; ~**tu·ous** □ [~tjʊəs] fettig,
ölig; fig. salbungsvoll.

un·cul·ti·vat·ed □ [ˈʌnˈkʌltɪveɪtɪd],
un·cul·tured [~tʃəd] unkultiviert.

un·dam·aged [ˈʌnˈdæmɪdʒd] unbeschädigt, unversehrt, heil.

un·daunt·ed □ [ˈʌnˈdɔːntɪd] unerschrocken, furchtlos.

un·de·ceive [ˈʌndɪˈsiːv] j-m die Augen öffnen; j-n aufklären.

un·de·cid·ed □ [ˈʌndɪˈsaɪdɪd] unentschieden, offen; unentschlossen.

un·de·fined □ [ˈʌndɪˈfaɪnd] unbestimmt; unbegrenzt.

un·de·mon·stra·tive □ [ˈʌndɪˈmɒn-
strətɪv] zurückhaltend, reserviert.

un·de·ni·a·ble □ [ˈʌndɪˈnaɪəbl] un-
leugbar; unbestreitbar.

un·der [ˈʌndə] **1.** adv. unten; darunter; **2.** prp. unter; **3.** adj. untere(r, -s);
in Zssgn: unter..., Unter...; ungenügend, zu gering; ~**bid** [ʌndəˈbɪd]
(-dd-; -bid) unterbieten; ~**brush**
[ˈʌndəbrʌʃ] Unterholz n; ~**carriage** [ˈʌndəkærɪdʒ] 𝕵 Fahrwerk n,
-gestell n; mot. Fahrgestell n;
~**clothes** [ˈʌndəkləʊðz] pl., ~**clothing** [~ðɪŋ] Unterkleidung f, -wäsche
f; ~**cut** [ʌndəˈkʌt] (-tt-; -cut) Preise
unterbieten; ~**dog** [ˈʌndədɒg] Ver-
lierer m, Unterlegene(r m) f; der
sozial Schwächere od. Benachteilig-
te; ~**done** [ʌndəˈdʌn] nicht gar,
nicht durchgebraten; ~**es·ti·mate**
[ʌndərˈestɪmeɪt] unterschätzen;
~**fed** [ʌndəˈfed] unterernährt; ~**go**
[ʌndəˈgəʊ] (-went, -gone) durchmachen; erdulden; sich unterziehen
(dat.); ~**grad·u·ate** [ʌndəˈgrædʒu·
ʊət] Student(in); ~**ground** [ˈʌndə-
graʊnd] **1.** unterirdisch; Untergrund...; **2.** bsd. Brt. Untergrundbahn f, U-Bahn f; ~**growth** [ˈʌndə-
grəʊθ] Unterholz n; ~**hand** [ʌndə-
ˈhænd] unter der Hand; heimlich;
~**lie** [ˈʌndəˈlaɪ] (-lay, -lain) zugrunde liegen (dat.); ~**line** [ʌndəˈlaɪn]
unterstreichen; ~**ling** contp. [ˈʌn-
dəlɪŋ] Untergebene(r m) f; ~**mine**
[ˈʌndəˈmaɪn] unterminieren; fig. untergraben; schwächen; ~**most** [ˈʌn-
dəməʊst] unterste(r, -s); ~**neath**
[ʌndəˈniːθ] **1.** prp. unter(halb); **2.**
adv. unten; darunter; ~**pass** [ˈʌn-
dəpɑːs] Unterführung f; ~**pin** [ʌn-
dəˈpɪn] (-nn-) untermauern (a. fig.);
~**plot** [ˈʌndəplɒt] Nebenhandlung
f; ~**priv·i·leged** [ʌndəˈprɪvɪlɪdʒd]
benachteiligt; ~**rate** [ˈʌndəˈreɪt] unterschätzen; ~**sec·re·ta·ry** [ˈʌndə-
ˈsekrətərɪ] Staatssekretär m; ~**sell**
econ. [ʌndəˈsel] (-sold) j-n unter-

bieten; *Ware* verschleudern; **~shirt** *Am.* ['ʌndəʃɜːt] Unterhemd *n*; **~signed** ['ʌndəsaɪnd]: *the* ~ der, die Unterzeichnete; **~size(d)** [ʌndə'saɪz(d)] zu klein; **~skirt** ['ʌndəskɜːt] Unterrock *m*; **~staffed** ['ʌndə'stɑːft] (personell) unterbesetzt; **~stand** [ʌndə'stænd] (*-stood*) verstehen; sich verstehen auf (*acc.*); (als sicher) annehmen, erfahren, hören; (sinngemäß) ergänzen; *make o.s. understood* sich verständlich machen; *an understood thing* e-e abgemachte Sache; **~stand·a·ble** [~əbl] verständlich; **~stand·ing** [~ɪŋ] Verstand *m*; Einvernehmen *n*; Verständigung *f*, Abmachung *f*, Einigung *f*; Voraussetzung *f*; **~state** [ʌndə'steɪt] zu gering angeben; abschwächen; **~state·ment** [~mənt] Understatement *n*, Untertreibung *f*; **~take** [ʌndə'teɪk] (*-took*, *-taken*) unternehmen; übernehmen; sich verpflichten; **~tak·er** ['ʌndəteɪkə] Leichenbestatter *m*; Beerdigungs-, Bestattungsinstitut *n*; △ *nicht Unternehmer*; **~tak·ing** [ʌndə'teɪkɪŋ] Unternehmen *n*; Zusicherung *f*; ['ʌndəteɪkɪŋ] Leichenbestattung *f*; **~tone** ['ʌndətəʊn] leiser Ton; *fig.* Unterton *m*; **~val·ue** [ʌndə'væljuː] unterschätzen; **~wear** ['ʌndəweə] Unterkleidung *f*, -wäsche *f*; **~wood** ['ʌndəwʊd] Unterholz *n*.

un·de·served □ ['ʌndɪ'zɜːvd] unverdient; **un·de·serv·ing** □ [~ɪŋ] unwürdig.

un·de·signed □ ['ʌndɪ'zaɪnd] unbeabsichtigt, unabsichtlich.

un·de·si·ra·ble □ ['ʌndɪ'zaɪərəbl] **1.** □ unerwünscht; **2.** unerwünschte Person.

un·de·vel·oped [ʌndɪ'veləpt] unerschlossen (*Gelände*); unentwickelt.

un·de·vi·at·ing □ ['ʌn'diːvɪeɪtɪŋ] unentwegt.

un·dies F ['ʌndɪz] *pl.* (Damen)Unterwäsche *f*.

un·dig·ni·fied □ [ʌn'dɪgnɪfaɪd] unwürdig, würdelos.

un·dis·ci·plined [ʌn'dɪsɪplɪnd] undiszipliniert; ungeschult.

un·dis·guised □ ['ʌndɪs'gaɪzd] nicht verkleidet; *fig.* unverhohlen.

un·dis·put·ed □ ['ʌndɪs'spjuːtɪd] unbestritten.

un·do [ʌn'duː] (*-did*, *-done*) aufmachen; (auf)lösen; ungeschehen machen, aufheben; vernichten; **~ing** [~ɪŋ] Aufmachen *n*; Ungeschehenmachen *n*; Vernichtung *f*; Verderben *n*; **un·done** ['ʌn'dʌn] zugrunde gerichtet, ruiniert, erledigt.

un·doubt·ed □ [ʌn'daʊtɪd] unzweifelhaft, zweifellos.

un·dreamed [ʌn'driːmd], **un·dreamt** [ʌn'dremt]: ~*-of* ungeahnt.

un·dress [ʌn'dres] (sich) entkleiden *od.* ausziehen; **~ed** unbekleidet.

un·due □ ['ʌn'djuː] unpassend; übermäßig; *econ.* noch nicht fällig.

un·du·late ['ʌndjʊleɪt] wogen; wallen; wellenförmig verlaufen; **~la·tion** [ʌndjʊ'leɪʃn] wellenförmige Bewegung.

un·du·ti·ful □ ['ʌn'djuːtɪfl] ungehorsam; pflichtvergessen.

un·earth ['ʌn'ɜːθ] ausgraben; *fig.* aufstöbern; **~ly** [ʌn'ɜːθlɪ] überirdisch; unheimlich; *at an* ~ *hour* F zu e-r unchristlichen Zeit.

un·eas·i·ness [ʌn'iːzɪnɪs] Unruhe *f*; Unbehagen *n*; **~y** □ [ʌn'iːzɪ] (*-ier*, *-iest*) unbehaglich; unruhig; unsicher.

un·ed·u·cat·ed □ [ʌn'edjʊkeɪtɪd] ungebildet.

un·e·mo·tion·al □ ['ʌnɪ'məʊʃənl] leidenschaftslos; passiv; nüchtern.

un·em·ployed ['ʌnɪm'plɔɪd] **1.** arbeitslos; ungenützt; **2.** *the* ~ *pl.* die Arbeitslosen *pl.*; **~ploy·ment** [~mənt] Arbeitslosigkeit *f*.

un·end·ing □ [ʌn'endɪŋ] endlos.

un·en·dur·a·ble □ ['ʌnɪn'djʊərəbl] unerträglich.

un·en·gaged ['ʌnɪn'geɪdʒd] frei.

un·e·qual □ ['ʌn'iːkwəl] ungleich; nicht gewachsen (*to dat.*); **~(l)ed** unerreicht, unübertroffen.

un·err·ing □ ['ʌn'ɜːrɪŋ] unfehlbar.

un·es·sen·tial ['ʌnɪ'senʃl] unwesentlich, unwichtig.

un·e·ven □ ['ʌn'iːvn] uneben; ungleich(mäßig); ungerade (*Zahl*).

un·e·vent·ful □ ['ʌnɪ'ventfl] ereignislos; ohne Zwischenfälle.

un·ex·am·pled ['ʌnɪg'zɑːmpld] beispiellos.

un·ex·cep·tio·na·ble □ ['ʌnɪk'sepʃnəbl] einwandfrei; einwandfrei.

un·ex·pec·ted □ ['ʌnɪk'spektɪd] unerwartet.

un·ex·plained ['ʌnɪk'spleɪnd] unerklärt.

un·fad·ing [ʌn'feɪdɪŋ] nicht welkend; unvergänglich; echt (*Farbe*).

un·fail·ing □ [ʌnˈfeɪlɪŋ] unfehlbar, nie versagend; unerschöpflich; *fig.* treu.

un·fair □ [ʌnˈfeə] unfair; ungerecht; unehrlich.

un·faith·ful □ [ʌnˈfeɪθfl] un(ge)treu, treulos; nicht wortgetreu.

un·fa·mil·i·ar [ʌnfəˈmɪljə] ungewohnt; unbekannt; nicht vertraut (*with* mit).

un·fas·ten [ʌnˈfɑːsn] aufmachen; lösen; **~ed** unbefestigt, lose.

un·fath·o·ma·ble □ [ʌnˈfæðəməbl] unergründlich.

un·fa·vo(u)·ra·ble □ [ʌnˈfeɪvərəbl] ungünstig; unvorteilhaft.

un·feel·ing □ [ʌnˈfiːlɪŋ] gefühllos.

un·fil·i·al □ [ʌnˈfɪljəl] respektlos, pflichtvergessen (*Kind*).

un·fin·ished [ʌnˈfɪnɪʃt] unvollendet; unfertig; unerledigt.

un·fit [ʌnˈfɪt] **1.** □ ungeeignet, untauglich; *Sport*: nicht fit, nicht in (guter) Form; **2.** (-*tt*-) ungeeignet *od.* untauglich machen.

un·fix [ʌnˈfɪks] losmachen, lösen.

un·fledged [ʌnˈfledʒd] ungefiedert, (noch) nicht flügge; *fig.* unreif.

un·flinch·ing □ [ʌnˈflɪntʃɪŋ] entschlossen, unnachgiebig; unerschrocken.

un·fold [ʌnˈfəʊld] (sich) entfalten *od.* öffnen; [ʌnˈfəʊld] darlegen, enthüllen.

un·forced [ʌnˈfɔːst] ungezwungen.

un·fore·seen [ʌnfɔːˈsiːn] unvorhergesehen, unerwartet.

un·for·get·ta·ble □ [ʌnfəˈgetəbl] unvergeßlich.

un·for·giv·ing [ʌnfəˈgɪvɪŋ] unversöhnlich, nachtragend.

un·for·got·ten [ʌnfəˈgɒtn] unvergessen.

un·for·tu·nate [ʌnˈfɔːtʃnət] **1.** □ unglücklich; **2.** Unglückliche(r *m*) *f*; **~ly** [~lɪ] unglücklicherweise, leider.

un·found·ed □ [ʌnˈfaʊndɪd] unbegründet, grundlos.

un·friend·ly [ʌnˈfrendlɪ] (-*ier*, -*iest*) unfreundlich; ungünstig.

un·furl [ʌnˈfɜːl] entfalten, aufrollen.

un·fur·nished [ʌnˈfɜːnɪʃt] unmöbliert.

un·gain·ly [ʌnˈgeɪnlɪ] unbeholfen, plump, linkisch.

un·gen·er·ous □ [ʌnˈdʒenərəs] nicht freigebig; kleinlich; unfair.

un·god·ly □ [ʌnˈgɒdlɪ] gottlos; F scheußlich; *at an* ~ *hour* F zu e-r unchristlichen Zeit.

un·gov·er·na·ble □ [ʌnˈgʌvənəbl] unlenksam; zügellos, wild.

un·grace·ful □ [ʌnˈgreɪsfl] ungraziös, ohne Anmut; unbeholfen.

un·gra·cious □ [ʌnˈgreɪʃəs] ungnädig; unfreundlich.

un·grate·ful □ [ʌnˈgreɪtfl] undankbar.

un·guard·ed □ [ʌnˈgɑːdɪd] unbewacht; ungeschützt; unvorsichtig.

un·guent *pharm.* [ˈʌŋgwənt] Salbe *f*.

un·ham·pered [ʌnˈhæmpəd] ungehindert.

un·hand·some □ [ʌnˈhænsəm] unschön.

un·han·dy □ [ʌnˈhændɪ] (-*ier*, -*iest*) unhandlich; ungeschickt; unbeholfen.

un·hap·py □ [ʌnˈhæpɪ] (-*ier*, -*iest*) unglücklich.

un·harmed [ʌnˈhɑːmd] unversehrt.

un·health·y □ [ʌnˈhelθɪ] (-*ier*, -*iest*) ungesund.

un·heard-of [ʌnˈhɜːdɒv] unerhört; beispiellos.

un·heed·ed □ [ʌnˈhiːdɪd] unbeachtet; **~ing** □ sorglos.

un·hes·i·tat·ing □ [ʌnˈhezɪteɪtɪŋ] ohne Zögern; anstandslos.

un·ho·ly □ [ʌnˈhəʊlɪ] (-*ier*, -*iest*) unheilig; gottlos; F *s. ungodly*.

un·hook [ʌnˈhʊk] auf-, loshaken.

un·hoped-for [ʌnˈhəʊptfɔː] unverhofft, unerwartet.

un·hurt [ʌnˈhɜːt] unverletzt.

u·ni- [ˈjuːnɪ] uni..., ein..., einzig.

u·ni·corn [ˈjuːnɪkɔːn] Einhorn *n*.

u·ni·fi·ca·tion [juːnɪfɪˈkeɪʃn] Vereinigung *f*; Vereinheitlichung *f*.

u·ni·form [ˈjuːnɪfɔːm] **1.** □ gleichförmig, -mäßig, gleich; einheitlich; **2.** Uniform *f*, Dienstkleidung *f*; **3.** uniformieren; **~·i·ty** [juːnɪˈfɔːmətɪ] Gleichförmigkeit *f*; Einheitlichkeit *f*, Übereinstimmung *f*.

u·ni·fy [ˈjuːnɪfaɪ] verein(ig)en; vereinheitlichen.

u·ni·lat·er·al □ [juːnɪˈlætərəl] einseitig.

un·i·ma·gi·na·ble □ [ʌnɪˈmædʒɪnəbl] unvorstellbar; **~tive** □ [ʌnɪˈmædʒɪnətɪv] phantasie-, einfallslos.

un·im·por·tant □ [ʌnɪmˈpɔːtənt] unwichtig, unbedeutend.

U
V

un·im·proved [ˈʌnɪmˈpruːvd] nicht kultiviert, unbebaut (*Land*); unverbessert.

un·in·formed [ˈʌnɪnˈfɔːmd] nicht unterrichtet *od.* eingeweiht.

un·in·hab·i·ta·ble [ˈʌnɪnˈhæbɪtəbl] unbewohnbar; **~it·ed** [~tɪd] unbewohnt.

un·in·jured [ˈʌnˈɪndʒəd] unbeschädigt, unverletzt.

un·in·tel·li·gi·ble □ [ˈʌnɪnˈtelɪdʒəbl] unverständlich.

un·in·ten·tion·al □ [ˈʌnɪnˈtenʃənl] unabsichtlich, unbeabsichtigt.

un·in·te·rest·ing □ [ˈʌnˈɪntrɪstɪŋ] uninteressant.

un·in·ter·rupt·ed □ [ˈʌnɪntəˈrʌptɪd] ununterbrochen.

u·ni·on [ˈjuːnjən] Vereinigung *f*; Verbindung *f*; Union *f*; Verband *m*, Verein *m*, Bund *m*; *pol.* Vereinigung *f*, Zusammenschluß *m*; Gewerkschaft *f*; **~ist** [~ɪst] Gewerkschaftler(in); **≳ Jack** Union Jack *m* (*britische Nationalflagge*); **~ suit** *Am.* Hemdhose *f* (mit langem Bein).

u·nique □ [juːˈniːk] einzigartig, einmalig.

u·ni·son ♪ *u. fig.* [ˈjuːnɪzn] Einklang *m*.

u·nit [ˈjuːnɪt] Einheit *f*; ⊕ (Bau)Einheit *f*; ⊁ Einer *m*.

u·nite [juːˈnaɪt] (sich) vereinigen, (sich) verbinden; **u·nit·ed** vereinigt, vereint; **u·ni·ty** [ˈjuːnətɪ] Einheit *f*; Einigkeit *f*, Eintracht *f*.

u·ni·ver·sal □ [juːnɪˈvɜːsl] allgemein; allumfassend; Universal...; Welt...; **~i·ty** [ˈjuːnɪvɜːˈsælətɪ] Allgemeinheit *f*; umfassende Bildung; Vielseitigkeit *f*.

u·ni·verse [ˈjuːnɪvɜːs] Weltall *n*, Universum *n*.

u·ni·ver·si·ty [juːnɪˈvɜːsətɪ] Universität *f*; **~ graduate** Akademiker *m*.

un·just □ [ˈʌnˈdʒʌst] ungerecht; **un·jus·ti·fi·a·ble** □ [ʌnˈdʒʌstɪfaɪəbl] nicht zu rechtfertigen(d), unentschuldbar.

un·kempt [ˈʌnˈkempt] ungekämmt, zerzaust; ungepflegt.

un·kind □ [ʌnˈkaɪnd] unfreundlich.

un·know·ing □ [ˈʌnˈnəʊɪŋ] unwissend; unbewußt; **un·known** [~n] **1.** unbekannt; **~ to me** ohne mein Wissen; **2.** der, die, das Unbekannte.

un·lace [ʌnˈleɪs] aufschnüren.

un·latch [ˈʌnˈlætʃ] *Tür* aufklinken.

un·law·ful □ [ˈʌnˈlɔːfl] ungesetzlich, widerrechtlich, illegal.

un·lead·ed [ˈʌnledɪd] bleifrei.

un·learn [ˈʌnˈlɜːn] (-ed *od.* -learnt) verlernen.

un·less [ənˈles] wenn ... nicht, außer wenn ..., es sei denn, daß ...

un·like [ˈʌnˈlaɪk] **1.** *adj.* □ ungleich; **2.** *prp.* unähnlich (s.o. j-m); anders als; im Gegensatz zu; **~ly** [ʌnˈlaɪklɪ] unwahrscheinlich.

un·lim·it·ed [ʌnˈlɪmɪtɪd] unbegrenzt.

un·load [ˈʌnˈləʊd] ent-, ab-, ausladen; ♣ *Ladung* löschen.

un·lock [ˈʌnˈlɒk] aufschließen; **~ed** unverschlossen.

un·looked-for [ʌnˈlʊktˈfɔː] unerwartet, überraschend.

un·loose, un·loos·en [ʌnˈluːs, ʌnˈluːsn] lösen; lockern; losmachen.

un·love·ly [ˈʌnˈlʌvlɪ] reizlos, unschön; **un·lov·ing** □ [~ɪŋ] lieblos.

un·luck·y □ [ʌnˈlʌkɪ] (-ier, -iest) unglücklich; unheilvoll; **be ~** Pech haben.

un·make [ˈʌnˈmeɪk] (-made) aufheben, widerrufen, rückgängig machen; umbilden; j-n absetzen.

un·man [ˈʌnˈmæn] (-nn-) entmannen; entmutigen; **~ned** *Raumflug*: unbemannt.

un·man·age·a·ble □ [ʌnˈmænɪdʒəbl] unkontrollierbar.

un·mar·ried [ˈʌnˈmærɪd] unverheiratet, ledig.

un·mask [ˈʌnˈmɑːsk] (sich) demaskieren; *fig.* entlarven.

un·matched [ˈʌnˈmætʃt] unerreicht, unübertroffen, unvergleichlich.

un·mean·ing □ [ʌnˈmiːnɪŋ] nichtssagend.

un·mea·sured [ʌnˈmeʒəd] ungemessen; unermeßlich.

un·mer·it·ed [ˈʌnˈmerɪtɪd] unverdient.

un·mind·ful □ [ʌnˈmaɪndfl]: *be ~ of* nicht achten auf (*acc.*); nicht denken an (*acc.*).

un·mis·ta·ka·ble □ [ˈʌnmɪˈsteɪkəbl] unverkennbar; unmißverständlich.

un·mit·i·gat·ed [ʌnˈmɪtɪgeɪtɪd] ungemildert; *an ~ scoundrel* ein Erzhalunke.

un·mo·lest·ed [ˈʌnməˈlestɪd] unbelästigt.

un·mount·ed [ˈʌnˈmaʊntɪd] unberitten; ungefaßt (*Schmuckstein*); nicht aufgezogen (*Bild*).

un·moved □ [ʌnˈmuːvd] unbewegt, ungerührt.

un·named [ʌnˈneɪmd] ungenannt.

un·nat·u·ral □ [ʌnˈnætʃrəl] unnatürlich.

un·ne·ces·sa·ry □ [ʌnˈnesəsərɪ] unnötig; überflüssig.

un·neigh·bo(u)r·ly [ʌnˈneɪbəlɪ] nicht gutnachbarlich; unfreundlich.

un·nerve [ʌnˈnɜːv] entnerven.

un·no·ticed [ʌnˈnəʊtɪst] unbemerkt.

un·ob·jec·tio·na·ble □ [ˈʌnəbˈdʒekʃnəbl] einwandfrei.

un·ob·serv·ant □ [ˈʌnəbˈzɜːvənt] unachtsam; **un·ob·served** □ [~d] unbemerkt.

un·ob·tai·na·ble [ˈʌnəbˈteɪnəbl] unerreichbar.

un·ob·tru·sive □ [ˈʌnəbˈtruːsɪv] unaufdringlich, bescheiden.

un·oc·cu·pied [ʌnˈɒkjʊpaɪd] unbesetzt; unbewohnt; unbeschäftigt.

un·of·fend·ing [ʌnəˈfendɪŋ] harmlos.

un·of·fi·cial □ [ʌnəˈfɪʃl] nichtamtlich, inoffiziell.

un·op·posed [ʌnəˈpəʊzd] ungehindert.

un·os·ten·ta·tious □ [ˈʌnɒstənˈteɪʃəs] anspruchslos; unauffällig; schlicht.

un·owned [ʌnˈəʊnd] herrenlos.

un·pack [ʌnˈpæk] auspacken.

un·paid [ʌnˈpeɪd] unbezahlt.

un·par·al·leled [ʌnˈpærəleld] einmalig, beispiellos, ohnegleichen.

un·par·don·a·ble □ [ʌnˈpɑːdnəbl] unverzeihlich.

un·per·ceived □ [ʌnpəˈsiːvd] unbemerkt.

un·per·turbed [ʌnpəˈtɜːbd] ruhig, gelassen.

un·pick [ʌnˈpɪk] *Naht etc.* auftrennen.

un·placed [ʌnˈpleɪst]: *be* ~ *Sport:* sich nicht placieren können.

un·pleas·ant □ [ʌnˈpleznt] unangenehm, unerfreulich; unfreundlich; **~ness** [~nɪs] Unannehmlichkeit *f*; Unstimmigkeit *f*.

un·pol·ished [ʌnˈpɒlɪʃt] unpoliert; *fig.* ungehobelt, ungebildet.

un·pol·lut·ed [ʌnpəˈluːtɪd] unverschmutzt, unverseucht, sauber (*Umwelt*).

un·pop·u·lar □ [ʌnˈpɒpjʊlə] un-

populär, unbeliebt; **~·i·ty** [ʌnˌpɒpjʊˈlærətɪ] Unbeliebtheit *f*.

un·prac·ti·cal □ [ʌnˈpræktɪkl] unpraktisch; **~·ticed**, *Am.* **~·ticed** [ʌnˈpræktɪst] ungeübt.

un·pre·ce·dent·ed □ [ʌnˈpresɪdəntɪd] beispiellos; noch nie dagewesen.

un·prej·u·diced □ [ʌnˈpredʒʊdɪst] unbefangen, unvoreingenommen.

un·pre·med·i·tat·ed □ [ˈʌnprɪˈmedɪteɪtɪd] unüberlegt; nicht vorsätzlich.

un·pre·pared □ [ˈʌnprɪˈpeəd] unvorbereitet.

un·pre·ten·tious □ [ˈʌnprɪˈtenʃəs] bescheiden, schlicht.

un·prin·ci·pled [ʌnˈprɪnsəpld] ohne Grundsätze; gewissenlos.

un·prof·i·ta·ble □ [ʌnˈprɒfɪtəbl] unrentabel.

un·proved, un·prov·en [ʌnˈpruːvd, ʌnˈpruːvn] unbewiesen.

un·pro·vid·ed [ˈʌnprəˈvaɪdɪd]: ~ *with* nicht versehen mit, ohne; ~ *for* unversorgt, mittellos.

un·pro·voked □ [ˈʌnprəˈvəʊkt] ohne Anlaß, grundlos.

un·qual·i·fied [ʌnˈkwɒlɪfaɪd] unqualifiziert, ungeeignet; uneingeschränkt.

un·ques·tio·na·ble □ [ʌnˈkwestʃənəbl] unzweifelhaft, fraglos; **~·tion·ing** □ [~ɪŋ] bedingungslos, blind.

un·quote [ʌnˈkwəʊt]: ~! Ende des Zitats!

un·rav·el [ʌnˈrævl] (*bsd. Brt. -ll-*, *Am. -l-*) auftrennen; (sich) entwirren.

un·re·al □ [ʌnˈrɪəl] unwirklich, irreal; **un·re·a·lis·tic** [ˈʌnrɪəˈlɪstɪk] (~*ally*) wirklichkeitsfremd, unrealistisch.

un·rea·so·na·ble □ [ʌnˈriːznəbl] unvernünftig; unsinnig; unmäßig.

un·rec·og·niz·a·ble □ [ʌnˈrekəgnaɪzəbl] nicht wiederzuerkennen(d).

un·re·deemed □ [ˈʌnrɪˈdiːmd] *eccl.* unerlöst; nicht eingelöst (*Rechnung*, *Pfand*); ungetilgt (*Schuld*).

un·re·fined [ˈʌnrɪˈfaɪnd] nicht raffiniert, roh, Roh...; *fig.* unkultiviert.

un·re·flect·ing □ [ˈʌnrɪˈflektɪŋ] gedankenlos, unüberlegt.

un·re·gard·ed □ [ˈʌnrɪˈgɑːdɪd] unbeachtet; unberücksichtigt.

un·re·lat·ed □ [ˈʌnrɪˈleɪtɪd] ohne Beziehung (*to* zu).

un·re·lent·ing □ [ˈʌnrɪˈlentɪŋ] erbarmungslos; unvermindert.

un·rel·i·a·ble □ [ˈʌnrɪˈlaɪəbl] unzuverlässig.

un·re·lieved □ [ˈʌnrɪˈliːvd] ungemildert; ununterbrochen.

un·re·mit·ting □ [ˈʌnrɪˈmɪtɪŋ] unablässig, unaufhörlich; unermüdlich.

un·re·quit·ed □ [ˈʌnrɪˈkwaɪtɪd]: ~ *love* unerwiderte Liebe.

un·re·served □ [ˈʌnrɪˈzɜːvd] rückhaltlos; frei, offen; nicht reserviert.

un·re·sist·ing □ [ˈʌnrɪˈzɪstɪŋ] widerstandslos.

un·re·spon·sive □ [ˈʌnrɪˈspɒnsɪv] unempfänglich (*to* für); teilnahmslos.

un·rest [ˈʌnˈrest] Unruhe *f*, *pol.* a. Unruhen *pl*.

un·re·strained □ [ˈʌnrɪˈstreɪnd] ungehemmt; uneingeschränkt.

un·re·strict·ed □ [ˈʌnrɪˈstrɪktɪd] uneingeschränkt.

un·right·eous □ [ˈʌnˈraɪtʃəs] ungerecht; unredlich.

un·ripe [ˈʌnˈraɪp] unreif.

un·ri·val(l)ed [ʌnˈraɪvld] unvergleichlich, unerreicht, einzigartig.

un·roll [ˈʌnˈrəʊl] ent-, aufrollen; sich entfalten.

un·ruf·fled [ˈʌnˈrʌfld] glatt; *fig.* gelassen, ruhig.

un·ru·ly [ʌnˈruːlɪ] (*-ier, -iest*) ungebärdig, widerspenstig.

un·safe □ [ʌnˈseɪf] unsicher.

un·said [ʌnˈsed] unausgesprochen.

un·sal(e)·a·ble [ʌnˈseɪləbl] unverkäuflich.

un·san·i·tar·y [ʌnˈsænɪtərɪ] unhygienisch.

un·sat·is·fac·to·ry □ [ˈʌnsætɪsˈfæktərɪ] unbefriedigend, unzulänglich; **~fied** [ˈʌnˈsætɪsfaɪd] unbefriedigt; **~fy·ing** □ [~ɪŋ] = *unsatisfactory*.

un·sa·vo(u)r·y □ [ˈʌnˈseɪvərɪ] unappetitlich (*a. fig.*), widerwärtig.

un·say [ˈʌnˈseɪ] (*-said*) zurücknehmen, widerrufen.

un·scathed [ˈʌnˈskeɪðd] unversehrt, unverletzt.

un·schooled [ˈʌnˈskuːld] ungeschult, nicht ausgebildet; unverbildet.

un·screw [ˈʌnˈskruː] *v/t.* ab-, los-, aufschrauben; *v/i.* sich abschrauben lassen.

un·scru·pu·lous □ [ʌnˈskruːpjʊləs] bedenken-, gewissen-, skrupellos.

un·sea·soned [ˈʌnˈsiːznd] nicht abgelagert (*Holz*); ungewürzt; *fig.* nicht abgehärtet.

un·seat [ˈʌnˈsiːt] *Reiter* abwerfen; *j-n* s-s Postens entheben; *j-m* s-n Sitz (im Parlament) nehmen.

un·see·ing □ [ʌnˈsiːɪŋ] *fig.* blind; *with ~ eyes* mit leerem Blick.

un·seem·ly [ʌnˈsiːmlɪ] ungehörig.

un·self·ish □ [ʌnˈselfɪʃ] selbstlos, uneigennützig; **~ness** [~nɪs] Selbstlosigkeit *f*.

un·set·tle [ˈʌnˈsetl] durcheinanderbringen; beunruhigen; aufregen; erschüttern; **~d** unbeständig, veränderlich (*Wetter*).

un·shak·en [ˈʌnˈʃeɪkən] unerschüttert; unerschütterlich.

un·shaved, un·shav·en [ˈʌnˈʃeɪvd, ~n] unrasiert.

un·ship [ˈʌnˈʃɪp] ausschiffen.

un·shrink·a·ble [ˈʌnˈʃrɪŋkəbl] nicht einlaufend (*Stoff*); **~ing** □ [ʌnˈʃrɪŋkɪŋ] unverzagt, furchtlos.

un·sight·ly [ʌnˈsaɪtlɪ] häßlich.

un·skil(l)·ful □ [ˈʌnˈskɪlfl] ungeschickt; **un·skilled** ungelernt.

un·so·ci·a·ble □ [ʌnˈsəʊʃəbl] ungesellig; **un·so·cial** [~l] unsozial; asozial; *work ~ hours Brt.* außerhalb der normalen Arbeitszeit arbeiten.

un·sol·der [ˈʌnˈsɒldə] los-, ablöten.

un·so·lic·it·ed [ˈʌnsəˈlɪsɪtɪd] unaufgefordert; *~ goods econ.* unbestellte Ware(n).

un·solv·a·ble [ʌnˈsɒlvəbl] ⚗ unlöslich; *fig.* unlösbar; **un·solved** [~d] ungelöst.

un·so·phis·ti·cat·ed [ˈʌnsəˈfɪstɪkeɪtɪd] ungekünstelt, natürlich, naiv.

un·sound □ [ˈʌnˈsaʊnd] ungesund; verdorben; wurmstichig, morsch; nicht stichhaltig (*Beweis*); verkehrt; *of ~ mind* ⚖ unzurechnungsfähig.

un·spar·ing □ [ʌnˈspeərɪŋ] freigebig; schonungslos, unbarmherzig.

un·spea·ka·ble □ [ʌnˈspiːkəbl] unsagbar, unbeschreiblich, entsetzlich.

un·spoiled, un·spoilt [ˈʌnˈspɔɪld, ~t] unverdorben; nicht verzogen (*Kind*).

un·spo·ken [ˈʌnˈspəʊkən] ungesagt; *~of* unerwähnt.

un·stead·y □ [ˈʌnˈstedɪ] (*-ier, -iest*) unsicher; schwankend, unbeständig; unregelmäßig; *fig.* unsolide.

un·strained [ˈʌnˈstreɪnd] unfiltriert; *fig.* ungezwungen.

un·strap ['ʌn'stræp] (-pp-) ab-, auf-, losschnallen.

un·stressed *ling.* ['ʌn'strest] unbetont.

un·strung ['ʌn'strʌŋ] ♪ saitenlos; ♪ entspannt (*Saite*); *fig.* zerrüttet, entnervt (*Person*).

un·stuck ['ʌn'stʌk]: *come ~* sich lösen, abgehen; *fig.* scheitern (*Person, Plan*).

un·stud·ied ['ʌn'stʌdɪd] ungekünstelt, natürlich.

un·suc·cess·ful □ ['ʌnsək'sesfl] erfolglos, ohne Erfolg.

un·suit·a·ble □ ['ʌn'sju:təbl] unpassend; unangemessen.

un·sure ['ʌn'ʃɔ:] (*~r, ~st*) unsicher.

un·sur·passed ['ʌnsə'pɑ:st] unübertroffen.

un·sus·pect|ed □ ['ʌnsə'spektɪd] unverdächtig; unvermutet; **~·ing** □ [*~ɪŋ*] nichts ahnend; arglos.

un·sus·pi·cious □ ['ʌnsə'spɪʃəs] nicht argwöhnisch, arglos; unverdächtig.

un·swerv·ing □ [ʌn'swɜ:vɪŋ] unbeirrbar.

un·tan·gle [ʌn'tæŋgl] entwirren.

un·tapped ['ʌn'tæpt] ungenutzt (*Reserven, Energie*).

un·teach·a·ble □ ['ʌn'ti:tʃəbl] unbelehrbar (*Person*); nicht lehrbar (*Sache*).

un·ten·a·ble ['ʌn'tenəbl] unhaltbar (*Theorie etc.*).

un·ten·ant·ed ['ʌn'tenəntɪd] unbewohnt.

un·thank·ful □ ['ʌn'θæŋkfl] undankbar.

un·think|a·ble [ʌn'θɪŋkəbl] undenkbar; **~·ing** □ [ʌn'θɪŋkɪŋ] gedankenlos.

un·thought ['ʌn'θɔ:t] unüberlegt; *~-of* unvorstellbar; unerwartet.

un·ti·dy □ [ʌn'taɪdɪ] (*-ier, -iest*) unordentlich.

un·tie ['ʌn'taɪ] aufknoten, *Knoten etc.* lösen; losbinden.

un·til [ən'tɪl] **1.** *prp.* bis; **2.** *cj.* bis (daß); *not ~* erst als *od.* wenn.

un·time·ly [ʌn'taɪmlɪ] vorzeitig; ungelegen.

un·tir·ing □ [ʌn'taɪərɪŋ] unermüdlich.

un·to ['ʌntu] = *to*.

un·told ['ʌn'təʊld] unerzählt; ungesagt; unermeßlich; unsäglich.

un·touched ['ʌn'tʌtʃt] unberührt (*Essen etc.*); *fig.* ungerührt.

un·trou·bled ['ʌn'trʌbld] ungestört; ruhig.

un·true □ ['ʌn'tru:] unwahr, falsch.

un·trust·wor·thy ['ʌn'trʌstwɜ:ðɪ] unzuverlässig, nicht vertrauenswürdig.

un·truth·ful □ ['ʌn'tru:θfl] unwahr; unaufrichtig; falsch.

un·used¹ ['ʌn'ju:zd] unbenutzt, ungebraucht.

un·used² ['ʌn'ju:st] nicht gewöhnt (*to* an *acc.*); nicht gewohnt (*to doing* zu tun).

un·u·su·al □ [ʌn'ju:ʒʊəl] ungewöhnlich.

un·ut·ter·a·ble □ [ʌn'ʌtərəbl] unaussprechlich.

un·var·nished *fig.* ['ʌn'vɑ:nɪʃt] ungeschminkt.

un·var·y·ing □ [ʌn'veərɪŋ] unveränderlich.

un·veil [ʌn'veɪl] entschleiern; *Denkmal etc.* enthüllen.

un·versed ['ʌn'vɜ:st] unbewandert, unerfahren (*in* in *dat.*).

un·want·ed ['ʌn'wɒntɪd] unerwünscht.

un·war·rant·ed [ʌn'wɒrəntɪd] ungerechtfertigt, unberechtigt.

un·wel·come [ʌn'welkəm] unwillkommen.

un·well [ʌn'wel]: *she is od. feels ~* sie fühlt sich unwohl *od.* unpäßlich, sie ist unpäßlich.

un·whole·some ['ʌn'həʊlsəm] ungesund (*a. fig.*).

un·wiel·dy □ [ʌn'wi:ldɪ] unhandlich, sperrig; unbeholfen.

un·will·ing □ ['ʌn'wɪlɪŋ] widerwillig; ungern; *be ~ to do* et. nicht wollen.

un·wind ['ʌn'waɪnd] (-*wound*) auf-, loswickeln; (sich) abwickeln; F sich entspannen, abschalten.

un·wise □ ['ʌn'waɪz] unklug.

un·wit·ting □ [ʌn'wɪtɪŋ] unwissentlich, unabsichtlich.

un·wor·thy □ [ʌn'wɜ:ðɪ] unwürdig; *he is ~ of it* er verdient es nicht, er ist es nicht wert.

un·wrap ['ʌn'ræp] auswickeln, auspacken, aufwickeln.

un·writ·ten □ ['ʌnrɪtn]: *~ law* ungeschriebenes Gesetz.

un·yield·ing □ [ʌn'ji:ldɪŋ] starr, fest; *fig.* unnachgiebig.

un·zip [ʌn'zɪp] (-pp-) den Reißverschluß öffnen (*gen.*).

up [ʌp] **1.** *adv.* nach oben, hoch, (her-, hin)auf, in die Höhe, empor, aufwärts; oben; von ... an; flußaufwärts; in der *od.* in die (*bsd.* Haupt-) Stadt; *Brt. bsd.* in *od.* nach London; in (*dat.*) (*up North*); aufrecht, gerade; *Baseball*: am Schlag; ~ *to* hinauf nach *od.* zu; bis (zu); **2.** *adj.* aufwärts..., nach oben; oben; hoch; aufgegangen (*Sonne*); gestiegen (*Preise*); abgelaufen, um (*Zeit*); auf (-gestanden); ~ *and about* wieder auf den Beinen; *it is* ~ *to him* es liegt an ihm; *es hängt von ihm ab; what are you* ~ *to?* was machst du (*there* da)?; *what's* ~? was ist los?; ~ *train* Zug *m* nach der Stadt; **3.** *prp.* hinauf; ~ *(the) country* landeinwärts; **4.** (*-pp-*) *v/i.* aufstehen, sich erheben; (an)treiben; *Preise etc.* erhöhen; **5.** *the* ~*s and downs* Auf u. Ab, die Höhen u. Tiefen (*of life* des Lebens).

up-and-com·ing [ˈʌpənˈkʌmɪŋ] aufstrebend, vielversprechend.

up·bring·ing [ˈʌpbrɪŋɪŋ] Erziehung *f*.

up·com·ing *Am.* [ˈʌpkʌmɪŋ] bevorstehend.

up·coun·try [ˈʌpˈkʌntrɪ] landeinwärts; im Inneren des Landes (gelegen).

up·date [ʌpˈdeɪt] auf den neuesten Stand bringen.

up·end [ʌpˈend] hochkant stellen; *Gefäß* umstülpen.

up·grade [ʌpˈgreɪd] *j-n* (im Rang) befördern.

up·heav·al *fig.* [ʌpˈhiːvl] Umwälzung *f*.

up·hill [ˈʌpˈhɪl] bergauf; *fig.* mühsam.

up·hold [ʌpˈhəʊld] (*-held*) aufrechterhalten, unterstützen; ⚖ bestätigen.

up·hol·ster [ʌpˈhəʊlstə] *Möbel* polstern; ~**hol·ster·er** [~rə] Polsterer *m*; ~**hol·ster·y** [~ɪ] Polsterung *f*; (Möbel)Bezugsstoff *m*; Polstern *n*; Polsterei *f*.

up·keep [ˈʌpkiːp] Instandhaltung(skosten *pl.*) *f*; Unterhalt(ungskosten *pl.*) *m*.

up·land [ˈʌplənd] *mst* ~*s pl.* Hochland *n*.

up·lift *fig.* [ʌpˈlɪft] aufrichten, erbauen.

up·on [əˈpɒn] = *on*; *once* ~ *a time there was* es war einmal.

up·per [ˈʌpə] obere(r, -s), höhere(r, -s), Ober...; ~**most** **1.** *adj.* oberste(r, -s), höchste(r, -s); **2.** *adv.* obenan, ganz oben.

up·raise [ʌpˈreɪz] er-, hochheben.

up·right [ˈʌpraɪt] **1.** ☐ aufrecht; *fig.* rechtschaffen; **2.** (senkrechte) Stütze, Träger *m*.

up·ris·ing [ˈʌpraɪzɪŋ] Erhebung *f*, Aufstand *m*.

up·roar [ˈʌprɔː] Aufruhr *m*; ~**i·ous** ☐ [ʌpˈrɔːrɪəs] lärmend, laut, tosend (*Beifall*), schallend (*Gelächter*).

up·root [ʌpˈruːt] entwurzeln; (her-)ausreißen.

up·set [ʌpˈset] (*-set*) umwerfen, (um)stürzen, umkippen, umstoßen; durcheinanderbringen (*a. fig.*); *Magen* verderben; *fig. j-n* aus der Fassung bringen; *be* ~ aufgeregt sein, aus der Fassung sein, durcheinander sein.

up·shot [ˈʌpʃɒt] Ergebnis *n*.

up·side down [ˈʌpsaɪdˈdaʊn] das Oberste zuunterst; verkehrt (herum).

up·stairs [ˈʌpˈsteəz] die Treppe hinauf, (nach) oben.

up·start [ˈʌpstɑːt] Emporkömmling *m*.

up·state *Am.* [ˈʌpsteɪt] im Norden (des Bundesstaates).

up·stream [ˈʌpˈstriːm] fluß-, stromaufwärts.

up·tight F [ˈʌptaɪt] nervös.

up·to·date [ˈʌptəˈdeɪt] modern; auf dem neuesten Stand.

up·town *Am.* [ˈʌpˈtaʊn] im *od.* in das Wohn- *od.* Villenviertel.

up·turn [ˈʌptɜːn] Aufschwung *m*.

up·ward(s) [ˈʌpwəd(z)] aufwärts (gerichtet).

u·ra·ni·um ⚛ [jʊəˈreɪnjəm] Uran *n*.

ur·ban [ˈɜːbən] städtisch, Stadt...; ~**e** ☐ [ɜːˈbeɪn] höflich; gebildet.

ur·chin [ˈɜːtʃɪn] Bengel *m*.

urge [ɜːdʒ] **1.** *j-n* (be)drängen (*to do* zu tun); dringen auf *etc.*; *Recht* geltend machen; *oft* ~ *on j-n* drängen, (an)treiben; **2.** Drang *m*; ~**gen·cy** [ˈɜːdʒənsɪ] Dringlichkeit *f*; Drängen *n*; ~**gent** ☐ [~t] dringend; dringlich; eilig.

u·ri·nal [ˈjʊərɪnl] Harnglas *n*; (Männer)Toilette *f*, Pissoir *n*; ~**nate** [~eɪt] urinieren; **u·rine** [~ɪn] Urin *m*, Harn *m*.

U
V

urn [ɜːn] Urne *f*; Tee-, Kaffeemaschine *f*.

us [ʌs, əs] uns; *all of* ～ wir alle; *both of* ～ wir beide.

us·age ['juːzɪdʒ] Brauch *m*, Gepflogenheit *f*; Sprachgebrauch *m*; Behandlung *f*; Verwendung *f*, Gebrauch *m*.

use 1. [juːs] Gebrauch *m*, Benutzung *f*, Verwendung *f*; Gewohnheit *f*, Übung *f*, Brauch *m*; Nutzen *m*; *(of)* *no* ～ nutz-, zwecklos; *have no* ～ *for* keine Verwendung haben für; *Am.* F nicht mögen; **2.** [juːz] gebrauchen, benutzen, ver-, anwenden; handhaben; ～ *up* ver-, aufbrauchen; *I* ～*d to do* ich pflegte zu tun, früher tat ich; **～d** [juːzd] ge-, verbraucht; [juːst] gewöhnt *(to an acc.)*, gewohnt *(to zu od. acc.)*; **～·ful** □ ['juːsfl] brauchbar, nützlich; Nutz...; **～·less** □ ['juːslɪs] nutz-, zwecklos, unnütz.

ush·er ['ʌʃə] **1.** □ Türhüter *m*, Pförtner *m*; *fig.* geistige Leere; Platzanweiser *m*; **2.** *mst.* ～ *in* herein-, hineinführen; **～·ette** ['ʌʃə'ret] Platzanweiserin *f*.

u·su·al □ ['juːʒʊəl] gewöhnlich, üblich, gebräuchlich.

u·sur·er ['juːʒərə] Wucherer *m*.

u·surp [juːˈzɜːp] sich *et.* widerrechtlich aneignen, an sich reißen; **～·er** [～ə] Usurpator *m*.

u·su·ry ['juːʒʊrɪ] Wucher(zinsen *pl.*) *m*.

u·ten·sil [juːˈtensl] Gerät *n*.

u·te·rus *anat.* ['juːtərəs] *(pl.* ～*ri* [-raɪ]) Gebärmutter *f*.

u·til·i·ty [juːˈtɪlətɪ] **1.** Nützlichkeit *f*, Nutzen *m*; *utilities pl.* Leistungen *pl.* der öffentlichen Versorgungsbetriebe; **2.** Gebrauchs... **u·ti·li·za·tion** [juːtɪlaɪ'zeɪʃn] *(Aus-)* Nutzung *f*, Verwertung *f*, -wendung *f*; **～·lize** ['juːtɪlaɪz] *(aus)*nutzen, verwerten, -wenden.

ut·most ['ʌtməʊst] äußerste(r, -s).

U·to·pi·an [juːˈtəʊpjən] **1.** utopisch; **2.** Utopist *m*.

ut·ter ['ʌtə] **1.** □ *fig.* äußerste(r, -s), völlig; **2.** äußern; *Seufzer etc.* ausstoßen, von sich geben; *Falschgeld etc.* in Umlauf setzen; **～·ance** ['ʌtərəns] Äußerung *f*, Ausdruck *m*; Aussprache *f*; **～·most** ['ʌtəməʊst] äußerste(r, -s).

U-turn ['juːtɜːn] *mot.* Wende *f*; *fig.* Kehrtwendung *f*.

u·vu·la *anat.* ['juːvjʊlə] *(pl.* -*lae* [-liː], -*las)* (Gaumen)Zäpfchen *n*.

V

va·can·cy ['veɪkənsɪ] Leere *f*; freies Zimmer *(Hotel)*; offene *od.* freie Stelle; **～·cant** □ [～t] leer *(a. fig.)*; frei *(Zimmer, Sitzplatz)*; leer(stehend), unbewohnt *(Haus)*; offen, frei *(Stelle)*; unbesetzt, vakant *(Amt)*; *fig.* geistesabwesend.

va·cate [vəˈkeɪt, *Am.* ˈveɪkeɪt] räumen, *Stelle* aufgeben, aus *e-m Amt* scheiden; *Amt* niederlegen; **va·ca·tion** [vəˈkeɪʃn, *Am.* verˈkeɪʃn] **1.** *bsd. Am.* Schulferien *pl.*; *univ.* Semesterferien *pl.*; ✝✝ Gerichtsferien *pl.*; *bsd. Am.* Urlaub *m*, Ferien *pl.*; *be on* ～ *bsd. Am.* im Urlaub sein, Urlaub machen; *take a* ～ *bsd. Am.* sich Urlaub nehmen, Urlaub machen; **2.** *bsd. Am.* Urlaub machen;

va·ca·tion·ist *bsd. Am.* [～ʃənɪst] Urlauber(in).

vac·cin·ate ['væksɪneɪt] impfen; **～·cin·a·tion** [væksɪ'neɪʃn] *(Schutz-)* Impfung *f*; **～·cine** ✖ ['væksiːn] Impfstoff *m*.

vac·il·late *mst fig.* ['væsɪleɪt] schwanken.

vac·u·ous □ *fig.* ['vækjʊəs] leer, geistlos.

vac·u·um ['vækjʊəm] **1.** *(pl.* -*uums*, -*ua* [-jʊə]) *phys.* Vakuum *n*; ～ *bottle* Thermosflasche *f*; ～ *cleaner* Staubsauger *m*; ～ *flask* Thermosflasche *f*; **～·packed** vakuumverpackt; **2.** *v/t.* *(mit dem Staubsauger)* saugen; *v/i.* (staub)saugen.

vag·a·bond ['væɡəbɒnd] Landstreicher(in).

va·ga·ry ['veɪgərɪ] wunderlicher Einfall; Laune *f*, Schrulle *f*.

va·gi|na *anat.* [və'dʒaɪnə] Vagina *f*, Scheide *f*; **~nal** *anat.* [⸴nl] vaginal, Vaginal..., Scheiden...

va|grant ['veɪgrənt] **1.** □ wandernd, vagabundierend; *fig.* unstet; **2.** Landstreicher(in).

vague □ [veɪg] (**~r**, **~st**) vage, verschwommen; unbestimmt; unklar.

vain □ [veɪn] eitel, eingebildet; nutzlos, vergeblich; **in** ~ vergebens, vergeblich, umsonst.

vale □ [veɪl] *poet. od. in Namen*: Tal *n*.

val·e·dic·tion [vælɪ'dɪkʃn] Abschied(sworte *pl.*) *m*.

val·en·tine ['væləntaɪn] Valentinsgruß *m* (*am Valentinstag, 14. Februar, gesandt*); am Valentinstag erwählte(r) Liebste(r).

va·le·ri·an ♥ [və'lɪərɪən] Baldrian *m*.

val·et ['vælɪt] (Kammer)Diener *m*; Hoteldiener *m*.

val·e·tu·di·nar·i·an [vælɪtjuːdɪ'neərɪən] **1.** kränklich; hypochondrisch; **2.** kränklicher Mensch; Hypochonder *m*.

val·i·ant □ ['væljənt] tapfer, mutig.

val|id □ ['vælɪd] triftig, stichhaltig; berechtigt; gültig; *be* ~ gelten; *become* ~ Rechtskraft erlangen; **~i·date** ⊞ [⸴eɪt] für gültig erklären, bestätigen; **~id·i·ty** [və'lɪdətɪ] (⊞ *Rechts*)Gültigkeit *f*; Stichhaltigkeit *f*; Richtigkeit *f*.

va·lise [və'liːz] Reisetasche *f*.

val·ley ['vælɪ] Tal *n*.

val·o(u)r ['vælə] Mut *m*, Tapferkeit *f*.

val·u·a·ble ['væljʊəbl] **1.** □ wertvoll; **2.** **~s** *pl.* Wertsachen *pl.*

val·u·a·tion [væljʊ'eɪʃn] Bewertung *f*, Schätzung *f*; Schätz-, Taxwert *m*.

val·ue ['væljuː] **1.** Wert *m*; *econ.* Währung *f*; *mst* **~s** *pl. fig.* (*kulturelle od. sittliche*) Werte *pl.*; **at** ~ *econ.* zum Tageskurs; *give* (*get*) *good* ~ *for money econ.* reell bedienen (bedient werden); **2.** (ab)schätzen, veranschlagen; *fig.* schätzen, bewerten; **~-ad·ded tax** *econ.* (*abbr. VAT*) Mehrwertsteuer *f*; **~d** veranschlagt; geschätzt; **~·less** [⸴jʊlɪs] wertlos.

valve [vælv] ⊕ Ventil *n*; (*Herz- etc.*) Klappe *f*; *Brt.* ⚡ (Radio-, Fernseh-) Röhre *f*.

vam·pire ['væmpaɪə] Vampir *m*.

van¹ [væn] Lieferwagen *m*; *bsd. Brt.*

🚃 Güter-, Gepäckwagen *m*; F Wohnwagen *m*.

van² ✗ [⸴] = *vanguard*.

van·dal·ize ['vændəlaɪz] wie die Vandalen hausen in (*dat.*), mutwillig zerstören, verwüsten.

vane [veɪn] Wetterfahne *f*; (Propeller)Flügel *m*; ⊕ Schaufel *f*.

van·guard ✗ ['vænɡɑːd] Vorhut *f*.

va·nil·la [və'nɪlə] Vanille *f*.

van·ish ['vænɪʃ] verschwinden.

van·i·ty ['vænətɪ] Eitelkeit *f*; Nichtigkeit *f*; ~ *bag* Kosmetiktäschchen *n*; ~ *case* Kosmetikkoffer *m*.

van·quish ['væŋkwɪʃ] besiegen.

van·tage ['vɑːntɪdʒ] *Tennis*: Vorteil *m*; **~-ground** günstige Stellung.

vap·id □ ['væpɪd] schal; fad(e).

va·por·ize ['veɪpəraɪz] verdampfen, verdunsten (lassen).

va·po(u)r ['veɪpə] Dampf *m*, Dunst *m*; ~ *trail* ✈ Kondensstreifen *m*.

var·i·a·ble ['veərɪəbl] **1.** □ veränderlich, wechselnd, unbeständig; ⊕ ver-, einstellbar; **2.** veränderliche Größe; **~ance** [⸴ns]: *be at* ~ (*with*) uneinig sein (mit *j-m*), anderer Meinung sein (als *j-d*); im Widerspruch stehen (zu); **~ant** [⸴nt] **1.** abweichend, verschieden; **2.** Variante *f*; **~a·tion** [veərɪ'eɪʃn] Schwankung *f*, Abweichung *f*; Variation *f*.

var·i·cose veins ['værɪkəʊs veɪnz] *pl.* Krampfadern *pl.*

var·ied □ ['veərɪd] verschieden, mannigfaltig; verändert.

va·ri·e·ty [və'raɪətɪ] Mannigfaltigkeit *f*, Vielzahl *f*, Abwechslung *f*; *econ.* Auswahl *f*; Sorte *f*, Art *f*; Spielart *f*, Variante *f*; *for a* ~ *of reasons* aus den verschiedensten Gründen; ~ *show* Varietévorstellung *f*; ~ *theatre* Varieté(theater) *n*.

var·i·ous □ ['veərɪəs] verschiedene, mehrere; verschiedenartig.

var·mint F ['vɑːmɪnt] *zo.* Schädling *m*; Halunke *m*.

var·nish ['vɑːnɪʃ] **1.** Firnis *m*; Lack *m*; Politur *f*; *fig.* Tünche *f*; **2.** firnissen; lackieren; *Möbel* (auf)polieren; *fig.* beschönigen.

var·si·ty ['vɑːsətɪ] *Brt.* F Uni *f* (*Universität*); *a.* ~ *team Am.* Universitäts-, College-, Schulmannschaft *f*.

var·y ['veərɪ] (sich) (ver)ändern; variieren; wechseln (mit *etc.*); abweichen *od.* verschieden sein (*from* von); **~ing** □ [⸴ɪŋ] unterschiedlich.

vase [vɑːz, *Am.* veɪs, veɪz] Vase *f*.

vast □ [vɑːst] ungeheuer, gewaltig, riesig, umfassend, weit.

vat [væt] Faß *n*, Bottich *m*.

vau·de·ville *Am.* [ˈvəʊdəvɪl] Varieté *n*.

vault¹ [vɔːlt] **1.** (Keller)Gewölbe *n*; Wölbung *f*; Stahlkammer *f*, Tresorraum *m*; Gruft *f*; **2.** (über)wölben.

vault² [~] **1.** *bsd. Sport:* Sprung *m*; **2.** *v/i.* springen (*over* über *acc.*); *v/t.* überspringen, springen über (*acc.*); **~·ing-horse** [ˈvɔːltɪŋhɔːs] *Turnen:* Pferd *n*; **~·ing-pole** *Stabhochsprung:* Sprungstab *m*.

've *abbr.* [v] = have.

veal [viːl] Kalbfleisch *n*; ~ *chop* Kalbskotelett *n*; ~ *cutlet* Kalbsschnitzel *n*; *roast* ~ Kalbsbraten *m*.

veer [vɪə] (sich) drehen; *Auto:* a. plötzlich die Richtung ändern, ausscheren.

vege·ta·ble [ˈvedʒtəbl] **1.** Gemüse...; pflanzlich; **2.** Pflanze *f*; *mst* ~s *pl.* Gemüse *n*.

veg·e·tar·i·an [vedʒɪˈteərɪən] **1.** Vegetarier(in); **2.** vegetarisch; **~·tate** *fig.* [ˈvedʒɪteɪt] (dahin)vegetieren; **~·ta·tive** □ [~tətɪv] vegetativ; wachstumfördernd.

ve·he·mence [ˈviːɪməns] Heftigkeit *f*, Gewalt *f*; **~·ment** □ [~t] heftig; ungestüm.

ve·hi·cle [ˈviːɪkl] Fahrzeug *n*, Beförderungsmittel *n*; *fig.* Vermittler *m*, Träger *m*; *fig.* Ausdrucksmittel *n*.

veil [veɪl] **1.** Schleier *m*; **2.** (sich) verschleiern; *fig.* verbergen.

vein [veɪn] *anat.* Vene *f*; Ader *f* (*a. fig.*); *fig.* Veranlagung *f*, Neigung *f*; *fig.* Stimmung *f*.

ve·loc·i·pede *Am.* [vɪˈlɒsɪpiːd] (Kinder)Dreirad *n*.

ve·loc·i·ty ⊕ [vɪˈlɒsətɪ] Geschwindigkeit *f*.

vel·vet [ˈvelvɪt] **1.** Samt *m*; **2.** aus Samt, Samt...; **~·y** [~ɪ] samtig.

ve·nal [ˈviːnl] käuflich; bestechlich, korrupt.

vend [vend] verkaufen; **~·er** [ˈvendə] (*Straßen*)Händler *m*, (-)Verkäufer *m*; **~·ing-ma·chine** [ˈvendɪŋməˈʃiːn] (Verkaufs)Automat *m*; **~·or** [~ɔː] *bsd.* ⚖ Verkäufer(in); (Verkaufs)Automat *m*.

ve·neer [vəˈnɪə] **1.** Furnier *n*; *fig.* äußerer Anstrich, Tünche *f*; **2.** furnieren.

ven·e·ra·ble □ [ˈvenərəbl] ehrwürdig; **~·rate** [~eɪt] (ver)ehren; **~·ra·tion** [venəˈreɪʃn] Verehrung *f*.

ve·ne·re·al [vɪˈnɪərɪəl] Geschlechts...; ~ *disease* ⚕ Geschlechtskrankheit *f*.

Ve·ne·tian [vɪˈniːʃn] **1.** venezianisch; ♀ *blind* (Stab)Jalousie *f*; **2.** Venezianer(in).

ven·geance [ˈvendʒəns] Rache *f*; *with a* ~ F wie verrückt, ganz gehörig.

ve·ni·al □ [ˈviːnjəl] verzeihlich; *eccl.* läßlich (*Sünde*).

ven·i·son [ˈvenɪzn] Wildbret *n*.

ven·om [ˈvenəm] (*bsd.* Schlangen-) Gift *n*; *fig.* Gift *n*, Gehässigkeit *f*; **~·ous** □ [~əs] giftig (*a. fig.*).

ve·nous [ˈviːnəs] Venen...; venös.

vent [vent] **1.** (Abzugs)Öffnung *f*; Luft-, Spundloch *n*; Schlitz *m*; *give* ~ *to* = 2. *v/t. fig. s-m Zorn etc.* Luft machen, *s-e Wut etc.* auslassen, abreagieren (*on* an *dat.*).

ven·ti·late [ˈventɪleɪt] ventilieren, (be-, ent-, durch)lüften; *fig.* erörtern; **~·la·tion** [ventɪˈleɪʃn] Ventilation *f*, Lüftung *f*; *fig.* Erörterung *f*; **~·la·tor** [ˈventɪleɪtə] Ventilator *m*.

ven·tril·o·quist [venˈtrɪləkwɪst] Bauchredner *m*.

ven·ture [ˈventʃə] **1.** Wagnis *n*, Risiko *n*; Abenteuer *n*; *econ.* Unternehmen *n*; *econ.* Spekulation *f*; *at a* ~ auf gut Glück; **2.** (sich) wagen; riskieren.

ve·ra·cious □ [vəˈreɪʃəs] wahrhaftig; wahrheitsgemäß.

verb *gr.* [vɜːb] Verb *n*, Zeitwort *n*; **~·al** □ [ˈvɜːbl] wörtlich; mündlich; **ver·bi·age** [ˈvɜːbɪɪdʒ] Wortschwall *m*; **ver·bose** □ [vɜːˈbəʊs] wortreich, langatmig.

ver·dant □ [ˈvɜːdənt] grün; *fig.* unreif.

ver·dict [ˈvɜːdɪkt] ⚖ (Urteils)Spruch *m* (*der Geschworenen*); *fig.* Urteil *n*; *bring in* od. *return a* ~ *of guilty* auf schuldig erkennen.

ver·di·gris [ˈvɜːdɪgrɪs] Grünspan *m*.

ver·dure [ˈvɜːdʒə] (frisches) Grün.

verge [vɜːdʒ] **1.** Rand *m*, Grenze *f*; Bankett *n* (*Straße*); *on the* ~ *of am* Rande (*gen.*), dicht vor (*dat.*); *on the* ~ *of despair* (*tears*) der Verzweiflung (den Tränen) nahe; **2.** ~ (*up*)*on* grenzen an (*acc.*) (*a. fig.*).

ver·i·fy [ˈverɪfaɪ] (nach)prüfen; beweisen; bestätigen.

ver·i·si·mil·i·tude [verısı'mılıtju:d] Wahrscheinlichkeit f.

ver·i·ta·ble □ ['verıtəbl] wahr, wirklich.

ver·mi·cel·li [vɜ:mı'selı] Fadennudeln pl.

ver·mic·u·lar [vɜ:'mıkjʊlə] wurmartig.

ver·mi·form ap·pen·dix anat. ['vɜ:mıfɔ:m ə'pendıks] Wurmfortsatz m.

ver·mil·i·on [və'mıljən] 1. Zinnoberrot n; 2. zinnoberrot.

ver·min ['vɜ:mın] Ungeziefer n; Schädling(e pl.) m; fig. Gesindel n, Pack n; **~ous** [~əs] voller Ungeziefer.

ver·nac·u·lar [və'nækjʊlə] 1. □ einheimisch; Volks...; 2. Landes-, Volkssprache f; Jargon m.

ver·sa·tile □ ['vɜ:sətaıl] vielseitig; flexibel.

verse [vɜ:s] Vers(e pl.) m; Strophe f; Dichtung f; **~d** [~t] bewandert; be (well) ~ in sich (gut) auskennen in (dat.).

ver·si·fy ['vɜ:sıfaı] v/t. in Verse bringen; v/i. Verse machen.

ver·sion ['vɜ:ʃn] Übersetzung f; Fassung f, Darstellung f; Lesart f; ⊕ Ausführung f, Modell n (Auto etc.).

ver·sus ['vɜ:səs] ⚖, Sport: gegen.

ver·te|bra anat. ['vɜ:tıbrə] (pl. -brae [~ri:]) Wirbel m; **~brate** zo. [~rət] Wirbeltier n.

ver·ti·cal □ ['vɜ:tıkl] vertikal, senkrecht.

ver·tig·i·nous □ [vɜ:'tıdʒınəs] schwindlig; schwindelnd (Höhe).

ver·ti·go ['vɜ:tıgəʊ] (pl. -gos) Schwindel(anfall) m.

verve [vɜ:v] Schwung m, Begeisterung f.

ver·y ['verı] 1. adv. sehr; vor sup.: aller...; the ~ best das allerbeste; 2. adj. gerade, genau; bloß; rein; der-, die-, dasselbe; the ~ same ebenderselbe; in the ~ act auf frischer Tat; gerade dabei; the ~ thing genau das (richtige); the ~ thought der bloße Gedanke (of an acc.).

ves·i·cle ['vesıkl] Bläschen n.

ves·sel ['vesl] Gefäß n (a. anat., ⚓, fig.); ⚓ Fahrzeug n, Schiff n.

vest [vest] Brt. Unterhemd n; Am. Weste f.

ves·ti·bule ['vestıbju:l] anat. Vorhof m; (Vor)Halle f; Am. 🚋 (Harmonika)Verbindungsgang m; ~ train Am.

🚋 Zug m mit (Harmonika)Verbindungsgängen.

ves·tige fig. ['vestıdʒ] Spur f.

vest·ment ['vestmənt] Amtstracht f, Robe f.

ves·try eccl. ['vestrı] Sakristei f; Gemeindesaal m.

vet F [vet] 1. Tierarzt m; Am. ✗ Veteran m; 2. (-tt-) co. verarzten; gründlich prüfen.

vet·e·ran ['vetərən] 1. altgedient; erfahren; 2. Veteran m.

vet·e·ri·nar·i·an Am. [vetərı'neərıən] Tierarzt m.

vet·e·ri·na·ry ['vetərınərı] 1. tierärztlich; 2. a. ~ surgeon Brt. Tierarzt m.

ve·to ['vi:təʊ] 1. (pl. -toes) Veto n; 2. sein Veto einlegen gegen.

vex [veks] ärgern; schikanieren; **~a·tion** [vek'seıʃn] Verdruß m; Ärger(nis n) m; **~a·tious** [~ʃəs] ärgerlich.

vi·a ['vaıə] über, via.

vi·a·duct ['vaıədʌkt] Viadukt m, n.

vi·al ['vaıəl] Phiole f, Fläschchen n.

vi·brate [vaı'breıt] vibrieren; zittern; **vi·bra·tion** [~n] Schwingung f; Zittern n, Vibrieren n.

vic·ar eccl. ['vıkə] Vikar m; **~age** [~rıdʒ] Pfarrhaus n.

vice¹ [vaıs] Laster n; Untugend f; Fehler m; ~ squad Sittenpolizei f, -dezernat n.

vice² Brt. ⊕ [~] Schraubstock m.

vi·ce³ prp. ['vaısı] an Stelle von.

vice⁴ F [vaıs] Vize m; attr. stellvertretend, Vize...; **~roy** ['vaısrɔı] Vizekönig m.

vi·ce ver·sa ['vaısı'vɜ:sə] umgekehrt.

vi·cin·i·ty [vı'sınətı] Nachbarschaft f; Nähe f.

vi·cious □ ['vıʃəs] lasterhaft; bösartig; boshaft; fehlerhaft.

vi·cis·si·tude [vı'sısıtju:d] Wandel m, Wechsel m; **~s** pl. Wechselfälle pl., das Auf u. Ab.

vic·tim ['vıktım] Opfer n; **~ize** [~aız] (auf)opfern; schikanieren; (ungerechterweise) bestrafen.

vic|tor ['vıktə] Sieger(in); **Ɐto·ri·an** hist. [vık'tɔ:rıən] Viktorianisch; **~to·ri·ous** □ [~ıəs] siegreich; Sieges...; **~to·ry** ['vıktərı] Sieg m.

vict·ual ['vıtl] 1. (bsd. Brt. -ll-, Am. -l-) (sich) verpflegen od. verproviantieren; 2. mst **~s** pl. Lebensmittel pl.,

Proviant *m*; ~(l)er [~ə] Lebensmittellieferant *m*.

vid·e·o ['vɪdɪəʊ] **1.** (*pl.* -os) Video(gerät *n*, -recorder *m*) *n*; *Computer*: Bildschirm-, Bildsicht-, Datensichtgerät *n*; *Am.* Fernsehen *n*; **2.** Video...; *Am.* Fernseh...; ~ **cas·sette** Videokassette *f*; ~ **disc** Bildplatte *f*; ~ **game** Videospiel *n*; ~ **phone** Bildtelefon *n*; ~ **tape 1.** Videoband *n*; **2.** auf Videoband aufnehmen; ~ **tape re·cord·er** Videorecorder *m*.

vie [vaɪ] wetteifern (*with* mit; *for* um).

Vi·en·nese [vɪə'niːz] **1.** Wiener(in); **2.** wienerisch, Wiener...

view [vjuː] **1.** Sicht *f*, Blick *m*; Besichtigung *f*; Aussicht *f* (*of* auf *acc.*); Anblick *m*; Ansicht *f* (*a. fig.*); Absicht *f*; *in* ~ sichtbar, zu sehen; *in* ~ *of* im Hinblick auf (*acc.*); angesichts (*gen.*); *on* ~ zu besichtigen; *with a* ~ *to* im *od.* in der Absicht zu *inf.*; *have* (*keep*) *in* ~ im Auge haben (behalten); **2.** *v/t.* ansehen, besichtigen; *fig.* betrachten; *v/i.* fernsehen; ~ **da·ta** *pl.* Bildschirmtext *m*; ~ **er** ['vjuːə] Fernsehzuschauer(in), Fernseher(in); ⊕ Diabetrachter *m*; ~ **find·er** *phot.* [~faɪndə] (Bild)Sucher *m*; ~ **less** [~lɪs] ohne eigene Meinung; *poet.* unsichtbar; ~ **point** Gesichts-, Standpunkt *m*.

vig·il ['vɪdʒɪl] Nachtwache *f*; ~ **i·lance** [~əns] Wachsamkeit *f*; ~ **i·lant** [~t] wachsam.

vig·or·ous ['vɪgərəs] kräftig; energisch; nachdrücklich; ~ **o(u)r** ['vɪgə] Kraft *f*; Vitalität *f*; Energie *f*; Nachdruck *m*.

Vi·king ['vaɪkɪŋ] **1.** Wiking(er) *m*; **2.** wikingisch, Wikinger...

vile [vaɪl] gemein; abscheulich.

vil·lage ['vɪlɪdʒ] Dorf *n*; ~ **green** Dorfanger *m*, -wiese *f*; ~ **lag·er** [~ə] Dorfbewohner(in).

vil·lain ['vɪlən] Schurke *m*, Schuft *m*, Bösewicht *m*; ~ **ous** [~əs] schurkisch; F scheußlich; ~ **y** [~ɪ] Schurkerei *f*.

vim F [vɪm] Schwung *m*, Schmiß *m*.

vin·di·cate ['vɪndɪkeɪt] rechtfertigen; rehabilitieren; ~ **ca·tion** [vɪndɪ'keɪʃn] Rechtfertigung *f*.

vin·dic·tive [vɪn'dɪktɪv] rachsüchtig, nachtragend.

vine ❦ [vaɪn] Wein(stock) *m*, (Wein-)Rebe *f*; △ *nicht* Wein (*Getränk*).

vin·e·gar ['vɪnɪgə] (Wein)Essig *m*.

vine|-grow·ing ['vaɪngrəʊɪŋ] Weinbau *m*; ~ **yard** ['vɪnjəd] Weinberg *m*.

vin·tage ['vɪntɪdʒ] **1.** Weinlese *f*; (Wein)Jahrgang *m*; **2.** klassisch; erlesen; altmodisch; ~ *car mot.* Oldtimer *m*; ~ **tag·er** [~ə] Weinleser(in).

vi·o·la ♪ [vɪ'əʊlə] Bratsche *f*.

vi·o·late ['vaɪəleɪt] verletzen; *Eid etc.* brechen; vergewaltigen; ~ **la·tion** [vaɪə'leɪʃn] Verletzung *f*; (Eid- *etc.*) Bruch *m*; Vergewaltigung *f*.

vi·o·lence ['vaɪələns] Gewalt(tätigkeit) *f*; Heftigkeit *f*; ~ **lent** [~t] gewaltsam, -tätig; heftig.

vi·o·let ❦ ['vaɪələt] Veilchen *n*.

vi·o·lin ♪ [vaɪə'lɪn] Violine *f*, Geige *f*.

VIP F ['viː'aɪ'piː] prominente Persönlichkeit.

vi·per *zo.* ['vaɪpə] Viper *f*, Natter *f*.

vi·ra·go [vɪ'rɑːgəʊ] (*pl.* -gos, -goes) Zankteufel *m*, Drachen *m*.

vir·gin ['vɜːdʒɪn] **1.** Jungfrau *f*; ~ **al** [~l] jungfräulich; Jungfern...; ~ **i·ty** [və'dʒɪnətɪ] Jungfräulichkeit *f*.

vir·ile ['vɪraɪl] männlich; Mannes...; **vi·ril·i·ty** [vɪ'rɪlətɪ] Männlichkeit *f*; *physiol.* Mannes-, Zeugungskraft *f*.

vir·tu·al ☐ ['vɜːtʃʊəl] eigentlich; ~ **ly** [~ɪ] praktisch.

vir·tue ['vɜːtʃuː] Tugend *f*; Vorzug *m*; *in od. by* ~ *of* kraft, vermöge (*beide gen.*); *make a* ~ *of necessity* aus der Not e-e Tugend machen; ~ **tu·os·i·ty** [vɜːtjʊ'ɒsətɪ] Virtuosität *f*; ~ **tu·ous** ☐ ['vɜːtʃʊəs] tugendhaft; rechtschaffen; △ *nicht* virtuos.

vir·u·lent ☐ ['vɪrʊlənt] ✿ (sehr) giftig, bösartig (*a. fig.*).

vi·rus ✿ ['vaɪərəs] Virus *n*, *m*; *fig.* Gift *n*.

vi·sa ['viːzə] Visum *n*, Sichtvermerk *m*; ~ **ed**, ~ **'d** [~d] mit e-m Sichtvermerk *od.* Visum versehen.

vis·cose ['vɪskəʊs] Viskose *f*; ~ *silk* Zellstoffseide *f*.

vis·count ['vaɪkaʊnt] Vicomte *m*; ~ **ess** [~ɪs] Vicomtesse *f*.

vis·cous ☐ ['vɪskəs] zähflüssig.

vise *Am.* ⊕ [vaɪs] Schraubstock *m*.

vis·i·bil·i·ty [vɪzɪ'bɪlətɪ] Sichtbarkeit *f*; Sichtweite *f*; ~ **ble** ☐ ['vɪzəbl] sichtbar; *fig.* (er)sichtlich; *pred.* zu sehen (*Sache*); zu sprechen (*Person*).

vi·sion ['vɪʒn] Sehvermögen *n*, -kraft *f*; *fig.* Seherblick *m*; Vision *f*; ~ **a·ry** [~ərɪ] **1.** phantastisch; **2.** Hellseher(in); Phantast(in).

vis·it ['vɪzɪt] **1.** *v/t.* besuchen; aufsu-

U V

chen; besichtigen; *fig.* heimsuchen; ~ *s.th.* on *s.o. eccl.* j-n für et. (be)strafen; *v/i.* e-n Besuch *od.* Besuche machen; *Am.* plaudern (*with* mit); **2.** Besuch *m*; △ *nicht* 🎯 *Visite* (*im Krankenhaus*); **~i·ta·tion** [vɪzɪˈteɪʃn] Besuch *m*; Besichtigung *f*; *fig.* Heimsuchung *f*; **~·it·or** [ˈvɪzɪtə] Besucher(in), Gast *m*.

vi·sor [ˈvaɪzə] Visier *n*; (Mützen-) Schirm *m*; *mot.* Sonnenblende *f*.

vis·ta [ˈvɪstə] (Aus-, Durch)Blick *m*.

vis·u·al □ [ˈvɪzjʊəl] Seh..., Gesichts...; visuell; ~ *aids pl. Schule:* Anschauungsmaterial *n*; ~ *display unit Computer:* Bildschirm-, Bildsicht-, Datensichtgerät *n*; ~ *instruction Schule:* Anschauungsunterricht *m*; **~·ize** [~aɪz] sich vorstellen, sich im Bild machen von

vi·tal □ [ˈvaɪtl] **1.** Lebens...; lebenswichtig; wesentlich; (hoch)wichtig; vital; ~ *parts pl.* = **2.** ~*s pl.* lebenswichtige Organe *pl.*, edle Teile *pl.*; **~·i·ty** [vaɪˈtæləti] Lebenskraft *f*, Vitalität *f*; **~·ize** [ˈvaɪtəlaɪz] beleben.

vit·a·min [ˈvɪtəmɪn] Vitamin *n*; ~ *deficiency* Vitaminmangel *m*.

vi·ti·ate [ˈvɪʃɪeɪt] verderben; beeinträchtigen.

vit·re·ous □ [ˈvɪtrɪəs] Glas..., gläsern.

vi·va·cious □ [vɪˈveɪʃəs] lebhaft; **vi·vac·i·ty** [vɪˈvæsətɪ] Lebhaftigkeit *f*.

viv·id □ [ˈvɪvɪd] lebhaft, lebendig.

vix·en [ˈvɪksn] Füchsin *f*; zänkisches Weib, Drachen *m*.

V-neck [ˈviːnek] V-Ausschnitt *m*; **V-necked** [~t] mit V-Ausschnitt.

vo·cab·u·la·ry [vəˈkæbjʊlərɪ] Wörterverzeichnis *n*; Wortschatz *m*.

vo·cal □ [ˈvəʊkl] stimmlich, Stimm...; laut; ♪ Vokal..., Gesang...; klingend; *ling.* stimmhaft; **~·ist** [~əlɪst] Sänger(in); **~·ize** [~aɪz] (*ling.* stimmhaft) aussprechen.

vo·ca·tion [vəʊˈkeɪʃn] Berufung *f*; Beruf *m*; **~·al** [~ənl] beruflich, Berufs...; ~ *adviser* Berufsberater *m*; ~ *education* Berufsausbildung *f*; ~ *guidance* Berufsberatung *f*; ~ *school Am.* (*etwa*) Berufsschule *f*; ~ *training* Berufsausbildung *f*.

vo·cif·er·ate [vəˈsɪfəreɪt] schreien; **~·ous** □ [~əs] schreiend; lautstark.

vogue [vəʊg] Mode *f*; *be in* ~ (in) Mode sein.

voice [vɔɪs] **1.** Stimme *f*; *active (passive)* ~ *gr.* Aktiv *n* (Passiv *n*); *give* ~ *to* Ausdruck geben *od.* verleihen (*dat.*); **2.** äußern, ausdrücken; *ling.* (stimmhaft) (aus)sprechen.

void [vɔɪd] **1.** leer; ✝ (rechts)unwirksam, ungültig; ~ *of* frei von, arm an (*dat.*), ohne; **2.** Leere *f*; *fig.* Lücke *f*.

vol·a·tile [ˈvɒlətaɪl] 🜍 flüchtig (*a. fig.*); flatterhaft.

vol·ca·no [vɒlˈkeɪnəʊ] (*pl.* -noes, -nos) Vulkan *m*.

vo·li·tion [vəˈlɪʃn] Wollen *n*, Wille(nskraft *f*) *m*; *of one's own* ~ aus eigenem Entschluß.

vol·ley [ˈvɒlɪ] **1.** Salve *f*; (*Geschoß- etc.*)Hagel *m*; *fig.* Schwall *m*; *Tennis:* Flugball *m*; **2.** *mst* ~ *out* e-n Schwall von *Worten etc.* von sich geben; *e-e* Salve *od.* Salven (ab)feuern; *fig.* hageln; (dröhnen; **~·ball** *Sport:* Volleyball(spiel *n*) *m*.

volt ⚡ [vəʊlt] Volt *n*; **~·age** ⚡ [ˈvəʊltɪdʒ] Spannung *f*; **~·me·ter** ⚡ Volt-, Spannungsmesser *m*.

vol·u·bil·i·ty [vɒljʊˈbɪlətɪ] Redegewandtheit *f*; **~·ble** □ [ˈvɒljʊbl] (rede)gewandt.

vol·ume [ˈvɒljuːm] Band *m* (*e-s Buches*); Volumen *n*; *fig.* Masse *f*, große Menge; (*bsd.* Stimm)Umfang *m*; ⚡ Lautstärke *f*; **vo·lu·mi·nous** □ [vəˈljuːmɪnəs] vielbändig; umfangreich, voluminös.

vol·un·ta·ry □ [ˈvɒləntərɪ] freiwillig; **~·teer** [vɒlənˈtɪə] **1.** Freiwillige(r *m*) *f*; **2.** *v/i.* freiwillig dienen; sich freiwillig melden; sich erbieten; *v/t.* *Dienste etc.* freiwillig anbieten; *sich e-e Bemerkung* erlauben.

vo·lup·tu·a·ry [vəˈlʌptjʊərɪ] Lüstling *m*; **~·ous** □ [~əs] wollüstig; üppig; sinnlich.

vom·it [ˈvɒmɪt] **1.** *v/t.* (er)brechen; *v/i.* (sich er)brechen; **2.** Erbrochene(s) *n*; Erbrechen *n*.

vo·ra·cious □ [vəˈreɪʃəs] gefräßig, gierig, unersättlich; **vo·rac·i·ty** [vɒˈræsətɪ] Gefräßigkeit *f*, Gier *f*.

vor·tex [ˈvɔːteks] (*pl.* -texes, -tices [-tɪsiːz]) Wirbel *m*, Strudel *m* (*mst fig.*).

vote [vəʊt] **1.** (Wahl)Stimme *f*; Abstimmung *f*; Stimm-, Wahlrecht *n*; Beschluß *m*, Votum *n*; ~ *of no confidence* Mißtrauensvotum *n*; *take a* ~ *on s.th.* über et. abstimmen; **2.** *v/t.* wählen; bewilligen; *v/i.* abstimmen;

wählen; ~ *for* stimmen für; F für *et.* sein; **vot·er** ['vəʊtə] Wähler(in).

vot·ing ['vəʊtɪŋ] Abstimmung *f*, Stimmabgabe *f*; *attr.* Wahl...; ~ **pa·per** Stimmzettel *m.*

vouch [vaʊtʃ]: ~ *for* (sich ver)bürgen für; **~·er** ['vaʊtʃə] Beleg *m*, Unterlage *f*; Gutschein *m*; **~·safe** [vaʊtʃ'seɪf] gewähren; geruhen (*to do* zu tun).

vow [vaʊ] **1.** Gelübde *n*; (Treu-) Schwur *m*; *take a* ~, *make a* ~ ein Gelübde ablegen; **2.** geloben.

vow·el *ling.* ['vaʊəl] Vokal *m*, Selbstlaut *m.*

voy·age ['vɔɪɪdʒ] **1.** *längere* (See-,

Flug)Reise; **2.** *lit.* reisen; **~·ag·er** ['vɔɪədʒə] (See)Reisende(r *m*) *f.*

vul·gar □ ['vʌlgə] gewöhnlich, unfein, ordinär; vulgär; pöbelhaft; geschmacklos; ~ *tongue* Volkssprache *f*; **~·i·ty** [vʌl'gærətɪ] ungehobeltes Wesen; Ungezogenheit *f*; Geschmacklosigkeit *f.*

vul·ne·ra·ble □ ['vʌlnərəbl] verwundbar (*a. fig.*); ✕, *Sport:* ungeschützt, offen; *fig.* angreifbar.

vul·pine ['vʌlpaɪn] Fuchs..., fuchsartig; schlau, listig.

vul·ture *zo.* ['vʌltʃə] Geier *m.*

vy·ing ['vaɪɪŋ] wetteifernd.

W

wad [wɒd] **1.** (*Watte*)Bausch *m*; Pfropf(en) *m*; Banknotenbündel *n*; **2.** (-*dd*-) wattieren, auspolstern; zu e-m Bausch zusammenpressen; **~·ding** ['wɒdɪŋ] Einlage *f*, Füllmaterial (*zum Verpacken etc.*); Wattierung *f*; Watte *f.*

wad·dle ['wɒdl] **1.** watscheln; **2.** watschelnder Gang, Watscheln *n.*

wade [weɪd] *v/i.* waten; ~ *through fig.* F sich (hin)durcharbeiten; *v/t.* durchwaten.

wa·fer ['weɪfə] Waffel *f*; Oblate *f*; *eccl.* Hostie *f.*

waf·fle¹ ['wɒfl] Waffel *f.*

waf·fle² *Brt.* F [~] schwafeln.

waft [wɑːft] **1.** wehen; **2.** Hauch *m.*

wag [wæg] **1.** (-*gg*-) wackeln *od.* wedeln (mit); **2.** Schütteln *n*; Wedeln *n*; Spaßvogel *m.*

wage¹ [weɪdʒ] *Krieg* führen, *Feldzug* unternehmen (*on, against* gegen).

wage² [~] *mst* ~*s pl.* (Arbeits)Lohn *m*; **~·earn·er** *econ.* ['weɪdʒɜːnə] Lohnempfänger(in); ~ **freeze** *econ.* Lohnstopp *m*; ~ **pack·et** *econ.* Lohntüte *f.*

wa·ger ['weɪdʒə] **1.** Wette *f*; **2.** wetten.

wag·gish □ ['wægɪʃ] schelmisch.

wag·gle ['wægl] wackeln (mit).

wag·(g)on ['wægən] (Last-, Roll-) Wagen *m*; *Brt.* 🚂 (offener) Güterwagen; **~·er** [~nə] Fuhrmann *m.*

wag·tail *zo.* ['wægteɪl] Bachstelze *f.*

waif *lit.* [weɪf] verlassenes *od.* verwahrlostes Kind.

wail [weɪl] **1.** (Weh)Klagen *n*; **2.** (weh)klagen; schreien, wimmern, heulen (*a.* Wind).

wain·scot ['weɪnskət] (Wand)Täfelung *f.*

waist [weɪst] Taille *f*; schmalste Stelle; ⚓ Mitteldeck *n*; **~·coat** ['weɪskəʊt] Weste *f*; **~·line** ['weɪstlaɪn] *Schneiderei:* Taille *f.*

wait [weɪt] **1.** *v/i.* warten (*for* auf *acc.*); *a.* ~ *at* (*Am.* on) *table* bedienen, servieren; ~ *on, upon* j-n bedienen; *v/t.* abwarten; **2.** Warten *n*; *lie in* ~ *for s.o.* j-m auflauern; **~·er** ['weɪtə] Kellner *m*; ~, *the bill* (*Am.* check), *please!* (Herr) Ober, bitte zahlen!

wait·ing ['weɪtɪŋ] Warten *n*; Dienst *m*; *in* ~ diensttuend; **~·room** Wartezimmer *n*; 🚂 *etc.* Wartesaal *m.*

wait·ress ['weɪtrɪs] Kellnerin *f*, Bedienung *f*; ~, *the bill* (*Am.* check), *please!* Fräulein, bitte zahlen!

waive [weɪv] verzichten auf (*acc.*).

wake [weɪk] **1.** ⚓ Kielwasser *n* (*a. fig.*); *in the* ~ *of* im Kielwasser (*e-s* Schiffes); *fig.* im Gefolge (*gen.*); **2.** (woke *od.* waked, woken *od.* waked) *v/i. a.* ~ *up* aufwachen; *v/t. a.* ~ *up* (auf) ['weɪkfl] wachsam; schlaflos; **wak·en** [~ən] = wake 2.

wale [weɪl] Strieme(n *m*) *f*.

walk [wɔːk] **1.** *v/i.* gehen (*a.* Sport), zu Fuß gehen, laufen; spazierengehen; wandern; im Schritt gehen; ~ **out** *econ.* streiken; ~ *out on* F im Stich lassen; *v/t.* (zu Fuß) gehen; führen; *Pferd* im Schritt gehen lassen; begleiten; durchwandern; *auf u. ab* gehen *in od. auf* (*dat.*); **2.** (Spazier-) Gang *m*; Spazierweg *m*; ~ *of life* (soziale) Schicht; Beruf *m*; ~**er** [ˈwɔːkə] Spaziergänger(in); Sport: Geher *m*; *be a good* ~ gut zu Fuß sein.

walk·ie-talk·ie [ˈwɔːkɪˈtɔːkɪ] Walkie-talkie *n*, tragbares Funksprechgerät.

walk·ing [ˈwɔːkɪŋ] (Zufuß)Gehen *n*; Spazierengehen *n*, Wandern *n*; *attr.* Spazier...; Wander...; ~ **pa·pers** *pl. Am.* F Laufpaß *m* (*Entlassung*); ~**stick** Spazierstock *m*; ~**tour** Wanderung *f*.

walk|-out *econ.* [ˈwɔːkaʊt] Ausstand *m*, Streik *m*; ~**over** Spaziergang *m*, leichter Sieg; ~**up** *Am.* (Miets-) Haus *n* ohne Fahrstuhl; Wohnung *f* in e-m Haus ohne Fahrstuhl.

wall [wɔːl] **1.** Wand *f*; Mauer *f*; **2.** *a.* ~ *in* mit e-r Mauer umgeben; ~ *up* zumauern.

wal·let [ˈwɒlɪt] Brieftasche *f*.

wall·flow·er *fig.* [ˈwɔːlflaʊə] Mauerblümchen *n*.

wal·lop F [ˈwɒləp] *j-n* verdreschen.

wal·low [ˈwɒləʊ] sich wälzen.

wall|-pa·per [ˈwɔːlpeɪpə] **1.** Tapete *f*; **2.** tapezieren; ~**sock·et** ⚡ (Wand-) Steckdose *f*; ~**to-**~ ~ *carpet* Spannteppich *m*; ~ *carpeting* Teppichboden *m*.

wal·nut ♀ [ˈwɔːlnʌt] Walnuß(baum *m*) *f*.

wal·rus *zo.* [ˈwɔːlrəs] Walroß *n*.

waltz [wɔːls] **1.** Walzer *m*; **2.** Walzer tanzen.

wan □ [wɒn] (-*nn*-) blaß, bleich, fahl.

wand [wɒnd] Zauberstab *m*.

wan·der [ˈwɒndə] herumwandern, -laufen; umherstreifen; △ *nicht in e-m Gebiet wandern = hike*; *fig.* abschweifen; irregehen; phantasieren.

wane [weɪn] **1.** abnehmen (*Mond*); *fig.* schwinden; **2.** Abnehmen *n*.

wan·gle F [ˈwæŋgl] *v/t.* deichseln, hinkriegen; *v/i.* mogeln.

want [wɒnt] **1.** Mangel *m* (*of an dat.*);

Bedürfnis *n*; Not *f*; **2.** *v/i.* ermangeln (*for gen.*); *he* ~*s for nothing* es fehlt ihm an nichts; *v/t.* wünschen, (haben) wollen; bedürfen (*gen.*), brauchen; nicht (genug) haben; *it* ~*s s.th.* es fehlt an et. (*dat.*); *he* ~*s energy* es fehlt ihm an Energie; ~*ed money*, gesucht; ~*ing* [~ɪŋ]: *be* ~ es fehlen lassen (*in an dat.*); unzulänglich sein.

wan·ton [ˈwɒntən] **1.** □ mutwillig; ausgelassen; **2.** herumtollen.

war [wɔː] **1.** Krieg *m*; *attr.* Kriegs...; *make od. wage* ~ Krieg führen (*on, against gegen*); **2.** (-*rr*-) streiten, kämpfen.

war·ble [ˈwɔːbl] trillern; trällern.

ward [wɔːd] **1.** (Krankenhaus)Station *f*, Abteilung *f*; Krankenzimmer *n*; (Gefängnis)Trakt *m*; Zelle *f*; (Stadt-, Wahl)Bezirk *m*; ⚖ Mündel *n*; *in* ~ ⚖ unter Vormundschaft (stehend); **2.** ~ *off* abwehren; **war·den** [ˈwɔːdn] Aufseher *m*; *univ.* Rektor *m*; *Am.* (Gefängnis)Direktor *m*; ~**er** [ˈwɔːdə] *Brt.* Aufsichtsbeamte(r) *m* (*im Gefängnis*).

war·drobe [ˈwɔːdrəʊb] Garderobe *f*; Kleiderschrank *m*; ~ *trunk* Schrankkoffer *m*.

ware [weə] *in Zssgn:* Ware(n *pl.*) *f*, Artikel *m od. pl.*; △ *nicht* (Einkaufs-) Ware.

ware·house **1.** [ˈweəhaʊs] (Waren-) Lager *n*; Lagerhaus *n*, Speicher *m*; △ *nicht Warenhaus*; **2.** [~z] auf Lager bringen; (ein)lagern.

war|fare [ˈwɔːfeə] Krieg(führung *f*) *m*; ~**head** ✕ Spreng-, Gefechtskopf *m* (*e-r Rakete etc.*).

war·i·ness [ˈweərɪnɪs] Vorsicht *f*.

war·like [ˈwɔːlaɪk] kriegerisch.

warm [wɔːm] **1.** □ warm (*a. fig.*); heiß; *fig.* hitzig; **2.** *et.* Warmes; (Auf-, An)Wärmen *n*; **3.** *v/t. a.* ~ *up* (auf-, an-, er)wärmen; *v/i. a.* ~ *up* warm werden, sich erwärmen; warmlaufen (*Motor etc.*); ~**th** [~θ] Wärme *f*.

warn [wɔːn] warnen (*of, against* vor *dat.*); verwarnen; ermahnen; verständigen; ~**ing** [ˈwɔːnɪŋ] (Ver-) Warnung *f*; Mahnung *f*; Kündigung *f*; *attr.* warnend, Warn...

warp [wɔːp] *v/i.* sich verziehen (*Holz*); *v/t. fig.* verdrehen, -zerren; beeinflussen; *j-n* abbringen (*from* von).

war|rant [ˈwɒrənt] **1.** Vollmacht *f*; Rechtfertigung *f*; Berechtigung *f*; ⚖ (Vollziehungs-, Haft- *etc.*)Befehl *m*; Berechtigungsschein *m*; ~ *of arrest* ⚖ Haftbefehl *m*; **2.** bevollmächtigen; rechtfertigen; verbürgen, garantieren; ~**ran·ty** *econ.* [~tɪ]: *it's still under* ~ darauf ist noch Garantie.

war·ri·or [ˈwɒrɪə] Krieger *m*.

wart [wɔːt] Warze *f*; Auswuchs *m*.

war·y □ [ˈweərɪ] (*-ier*, *-iest*) wachsam, vorsichtig.

was [wɒz, wəs] *1. und 3. sg. pret. von* be: war; *pret. pass. von* be: wurde.

wash [wɒʃ] **1.** *v/t.* waschen; (ab)spülen; ~ *up* abwaschen, abspülen; *v/i.* sich waschen (lassen); *vom Wasser* gespült *od.* geschwemmt werden; ~ *up Brt.* Geschirr spülen; **2.** Waschen *n*; Wäsche *f*; Wellenschlag *m*; Spülwasser *n*; *mouth*~ Mundwasser *f*; **3.** Wasch...; ~**a·ble** [ˈwɒʃəbl] waschbar; ~**and-wear** bügelfrei; pflegeleicht; ~**ba·sin** Waschbecken *n*; ~**cloth** *Am.* Waschlappen *m*; ~**er** [ˈwɒʃə] Wäscherin *f*; Waschmaschine *f*; = *dishwasher*; ⊕ Unterlegscheibe *f*; ~**er·wom·an** (*pl. -women*) Waschfrau *f*; ~**ing** [ˈwɒʃɪŋ] **1.** Waschen *n*; Wäsche *f*; ~*s pl.* Spülwasser *n*. **2.** Wasch...; ~**ing ma·chine** Waschmaschine *f*; ~**ing pow·der** Waschpulver *n*, -mittel *n*; ~**ing-up** *Brt.* Abwasch *m*; ~**rag** *Am.* Waschlappen *m*; ~**y** [ˈwɒʃɪ] (*-ier*, *-iest*) wässerig, wäßrig.

wasp *zo.* [wɒsp] Wespe *f*.

wast·age [ˈweɪstɪdʒ] Verlust *m*; Vergeudung *f*.

waste [weɪst] **1.** wüst, öde; unbebaut; überflüssig; Abfall...; *lay* ~ verwüsten; **2.** Verschwendung *f*, -geudung *f*; Abfall *m*; Ödland *n*, Wüste *f*; **3.** *v/t.* verwüsten; verschwenden; verzehren; *v/i.* verschwendet werden; ~**ful** □ [ˈweɪstfl] verschwenderisch; ~ **paper** Abfallpapier *n*; Altpapier *n*; ~**pa·per bas·ket** [weɪstˈpeɪpəbɑːskɪt] Papierkorb *m*; ~ **pipe** [ˈweɪstpaɪp] Abflußrohr *n*.

watch [wɒtʃ] **1.** Wache *f*; (Taschen-, Armband)Uhr *f*; **2.** *v/i.* zusehen, zuschauen; wachen; ~ *for* warten auf (*acc.*); ~ *out* (*for*) aufpassen, achtgeben (auf *acc.*); sich hüten (vor *dat.*); ~ *out!* Achtung!, Vorsicht!; *v/t.* bewachen; beobachten; achtgeben auf

(*acc.*); *Gelegenheit* abwarten; ~**dog** [ˈwɒtʃdɒg] Wachhund *m*; *fig.* Überwacher(in); ~**ful** □ [~fl] wachsam; ~**mak·er** Uhrmacher *m*; ~**man** [~mən] (*pl. -men*) (Nacht)Wächter *m*; ~**word** Kennwort *n*, Parole *f*.

wa·ter [ˈwɔːtə] **1.** Wasser *n*; Gewässer *n*; *drink the* ~*s* Brunnen trinken; **2.** *v/t.* bewässern; (be)sprengen; (be)gießen; mit Wasser versorgen; tränken; verwässern (*a. fig.*); *v/i.* wässern (*Mund*); tränen (*Augen*); ~**clos·et** (Wasser)Klosett *n*; ~**col·o·u(r** Wasser-, Aquarellfarbe *f*; Aquarell(malerei *f*); ~**course** Wasserlauf *m*; Fluß-, Strombett *n*; Kanal *m*; ~**cress** ♣ Brunnenkresse *f*; ~**fall** Wasserfall *m*; ~**front** an ein Gewässer grenzender Stadtbezirk, Hafengebiet *n*, -viertel *n*; ~**ga(u)ge** ⊕ Wasserstand(s)anzeiger *m*; Pegel *m*; ~**hole** Wasserloch *n*.

wa·ter·ing [ˈwɔːtərɪŋ] Bewässern *n*; (Be)Gießen *n*; Tränken (*von Vieh*); ~**can** Gießkanne *f*; ~**place** Wasserstelle *f*; Tränke *f*; Bad(eort *m*) *n*; ~**pot** Gießkanne *f*.

wa·ter| lev·el [ˈwɔːtəlevl] Wasserspiegel *m*; Wasserstand(slinie *f*) *m*; ⊕ Wasserwaage *f*; ~**logged** [~lɒgd] ⚓ voll Wasser (*Boot*); vollgesogen (*Erdreich*); ~**main** ⊕ Hauptwasserrohr *n*; ~**mark** Wasserzeichen *n* (*Papier*); ~**mel·on** ♣ Wassermelone *f*; ~**pol·lu·tion** Wasserverschmutzung *f*; ~ **po·lo** *Sport:* Wasserball(spiel *n*) *m*; ~**proof** **1.** wasserdicht; **2.** Regenmantel *m*; **3.** imprägnieren; wasserdicht machen; ~**shed** *geogr.* Wasserscheide *f*; *fig.* Wendepunkt *m*; ~**side** Fluß-, Seeufer *n*; ~**ski·ing** *Sport:* Wasserski(laufen) *n*; ~**tight** wasserdicht; *fig.* unanfechtbar; stichhaltig (*Argument*); ~**way** Wasserstraße *f*; ~**works** *oft sg.* Wasserwerk *n*; *turn on the* ~ *fig.* F losheulen; ~**y** [~rɪ] wässerig, wäßrig.

watt ⚡ [wɒt] Watt *n*.

wave [weɪv] **1.** Welle *f* (*a. phys.*); Woge *f*; Winken *n*; **2.** *v/t.* wellen; schwingen; schwenken; ~ *s.o. aside* j-n beiseite winken; *v/i.* wogen, wehen, flattern; ~ *at od. to s.o.* j-m (zu)winken, j-m ein Zeichen geben; ~**length** [ˈweɪvlenθ] *phys.* Wellenlänge *f* (*a. fig.*).

wa·ver [ˈweɪvə] (sch)wanken; flakkern.

wav·y □ ['weɪvɪ] (*-ier, -iest*) wellig; wogend.

wax¹ [wæks] **1.** Wachs *n*; Siegellack *m*; Ohrenschmalz *n*; **2.** wachsen; bohnern.

wax² [~] zunehmen (*Mond*).

wax|en *fig.* ['wæksən] wächsern; **~·works** *sg.* Wachsfigurenkabinett *n*; **~·y** [~ɪ] (*-ier, -iest*) wachsartig; weich.

way [weɪ] **1.** Weg *m*; Straße *f*; Art *f u.* Weise *f*; (Eigen)Art; Strecke *f*; Richtung *f*; *fig.* Hinsicht *f*; **~ in** Eingang *m*; **~ out** Ausgang *m*; *fig.* Ausweg *m*; *right of* **~ ₂** Wegerecht *n*; *bsd. mot.* Vorfahrt(srecht *n*) *f*; *this* **~** hierher, hier entlang; *by the* **~** übrigens; *by* **~** *of* durch; *on the* **~**, *on one's* **~** unterwegs; *out of the* **~** ungewöhnlich; *under* **~** in Fahrt; *give* **~** zurückweichen; *mot.* die Vorfahrt lassen (*to dat.*); nachgeben; abgelöst werden (*to* von); sich hingeben (*to dat.*); *have one's* **~** s-n Willen haben; *lead the* **~** vorangehen; **2.** *adv.* weit; **~·bill** Frachtbrief *m*; **~·far·er** *veraltet od. lit.* [~feərə] Wanderer *m*; **~·lay** [weɪ'leɪ] (*-laid*) *j-m* auflauern; *j-n* abfangen, abpassen; **~·out** F äußerst ungewöhnlich; toll, super; **~·side** ['weɪsaɪd] **1.** Wegrand *m*; **2.** am Wege; **~ sta·tion** *Am.* Zwischenstation *f*; **~ train** *Am.* Bummelzug *m*; **~·ward** □ [~wəd] launisch; eigensinnig.

we [wiː, wɪ] wir.

weak □ [wiːk] schwach; schwächlich; dünn (*Getränk*); **~·en** ['wiːkən] *v/t.* schwächen; *v/i.* schwach werden; **~·ling** [~lɪŋ] Schwächling *m*; **~·ly** [~lɪ] (*-ier, -iest*) schwächlich; **~·mind·ed** [wiːk'maɪndɪd] schwachsinnig; **~·ness** [~knɪs] Schwäche *f*.

weal [wiːl] Strieme(n *m*) *f*.

wealth [welθ] Reichtum *m*; *econ.* Besitz *m*, Vermögen *n*; *fig.* Fülle *f*; **~·y** □ ['welθɪ] (*-ier, -iest*) reich; wohlhabend.

wean [wiːn] entwöhnen; **~** *s.o. from s.th.* *j-m et.* abgewöhnen.

weap·on ['wepən] Waffe *f*.

wear [weə] **1.** (*wore, worn*) *v/t.* am *Körper* tragen; zur Schau tragen; *a.* **~** *away,* **~** *down,* **~** *off,* **~** *out Kleidung etc.* abnutzen, abtragen, verschleißen, *Reifen* abfahren; *a.* **~** *out* ermüden; *j-s Geduld* erschöpfen; *a.* **~**

away, **~** *down* zermürben; entkräften; *v/i.* sich *gut etc.* tragen *od.* halten; *a.* **~** *away,* **~** *down,* **~** *off,* **~** *out* sich abnutzen *od.* abtragen, verschleißen; sich abfahren (*Reifen*); **~** *off fig.* sich verlieren; **~** *on* sich dahinschleppen (*Zeit etc.*); **~** *out fig.* sich erschöpfen; **2.** Tragen *n*; (Be-) Kleidung *f*; Abnutzung *f*; *for hard* **~** strapazierfähig; *the worse for* **~** abgetragen; **~ and tear** Verschleiß *m*; **~·er** ['weərə] Träger *m*.

wear|i·ness ['wɪərɪnɪs] Müdigkeit *f*; Überdruß *m*; **~·i·some** □ [~səm] ermüdend; langweilig; **~·y** ['wɪərɪ] **1.** □ (*-ier, -iest*) müde; überdrüssig; ermüdend; anstrengend; **2.** ermüden; überdrüssig werden (*of gen.*).

wea·sel *zo.* ['wiːzl] Wiesel *n*.

weath·er ['weðə] **1.** Wetter *n*, Witterung *f*; **2.** *v/t.* dem Wetter aussetzen; *♪ Sturm* abwettern; *fig.* überstehen; *v/i.* verwittern; **~·beat·en** vom Wetter mitgenommen; **~ bu·reau** Wetteramt *n*; **~ chart** Wetterkarte *f*; **~ fore·cast** Wetterbericht *m*, -vorhersage *f*; **~·worn** verwittert.

weave [wiːv] (*wove, woven*) weben; flechten; *fig.* ersinnen, erfinden; **weav·er** ['wiːvə] Weber *m*.

web [web] Gewebe *n*, Netz *n*; *zo.* Schwimm-, Flughaut *f*; **~·bing** ['webɪŋ] Gurtband *n*.

wed [wed] (*-dd-; wedded od. selten: wed*) heiraten; *fig.* verbinden (*to* mit); **~·ding** ['wedɪŋ] **1.** Hochzeit *f*; **2.** Hochzeits..., Braut..., Trau...; **~** *ring* Ehe-, Trauring *m*.

wedge [wedʒ] **1.** Keil *m*; **2.** (ver)keilen; (ein)keilen, (-)zwängen (*in* in *acc.*).

wed·lock ['wedlɒk] *born in (out of)* **~** ehelich (unehelich) geboren.

Wednes·day ['wenzdɪ] Mittwoch *m*.

wee [wiː] klein, winzig; *a* **~** *bit* ein klein wenig.

weed [wiːd] **1.** Unkraut *n*; **2.** jäten; säubern (*of* von); **~** *out fig.* ausson-dern, -sieben; **~·kill·er** ['wiːdkɪlə] Unkrautvertilgungsmittel *n*; **~s** [wiːdz] *pl. mst widow's* **~** Witwenkleidung *f*; **~·y** ['wiːdɪ] (*-ier, -iest*) voll Unkraut, verunkrautet; F schmächtig.

week [wiːk] Woche *f*; *this day* **~** heute in *od.* vor e-r Woche; **~·day** ['wiːkdeɪ] Wochentag *m*; **~·end** [wiːk'end] Wochenende *n*; **~·end·er** [~ə] Wo-

chenendausflügler(in); **~·ly** ['wiːklɪ]
1. wöchentlich; Wochen...; **2.** ~
paper Wochenblatt *n*, Wochen-
(zeit)schrift *f*.

weep [wiːp] (*wept*) weinen; tropfen;
~ing ['wiːpɪŋ] □ *willow* ♀ Trauer-
weide *f*; **~·y** F [\ɪ] (*-ier*, *-iest*) weiner-
lich; rührselig, sentimental.

weigh [weɪ] *v/t.* (ab)wiegen; *fig.* ab-,
erwägen; ~ *anchor* ♣ den Anker
lichten; **~ed down** niedergedrückt;
v/i. wiegen (*a. fig.*); ~ *on*, ~ *upon* lasten auf
(*dat.*).

weight [weɪt] **1.** Gewicht *n* (*a. fig.*);
Last *f*; *fig.* Bedeutung *f*; *fig.* Last *f*,
Bürde *f*; *put on* ~, *gain* ~ zunehmen;
lose ~ abnehmen; **2.** beschweren;
belasten; **~·less** [\lɪs] ge wichtsch wch-
relos; **~·less·ness** [\nɪs] Schwerelosig-
keit *f* (*a. Raumfahrt*); **~ lift·ing**
[\lɪftɪŋ] *Sport*: Gewichtheben *n*; **~·y**
□ [\ɪ] (*-ier*, *-iest*) (ge)wichtig,
wuchtig.

weir [wɪə] Wehr *n*; Fischreuse *f*.

weird □ [wɪəd] Schicksals...; unheimlich; F sonderbar, seltsam.

wel·come ['welkəm] **1.** willkommen;
you are ~ *to inf.* es steht Ihnen frei,
zu *inf.*; (*you are*) ~! nichts zu danken!, bitte sehr!; **2.** Willkomm(en *n*)
m; **3.** willkommen heißen; *fig.* begrüßen.

weld ⊕ [weld] (ver-, zusammen-)
schweißen.

wel·fare ['welfeə] Wohl(ergehen) *n*;
Sozialhilfe *f*; Wohlfahrt *f*; **~ state**
pol. Wohlfahrtsstaat *m*; **~ work** So-
zialarbeit *f*; **~ work·er** Sozialarbei-
ter(in).

well[1] [wel] **1.** Brunnen *m*; Quelle *f*; ⊕
Bohrloch *n*; Fahrstuhl-, Licht-,
Luftschacht *m*; **2.** quellen.

well[2] [\] **1.** (*better*, *best*) wohl; gut;
ordentlich, gründlich; gesund; *be* ~,
feel ~ sich wohl fühlen; *be* ~ *off* in
guten Verhältnissen leben, wohlhabend sein; **2.** *int.* nun!, na!; **~·**
bal·anced [wel'bælənst] ausgewo-
gen (*Diät*); (innerlich) ausgeglichen;
~·be·ing Wohl(befinden) *n*; **~·born**
aus guter Familie; **~·bred** wohlerzo-
gen; **~·de·fined** deutlich; klar um-
rissen; **~·done** gutgemacht; (gut)
durchgebraten (*Fleisch*); **~·in·ten·**
tioned [\ɪn'tenʃnd] wohlmeinend;
gutgemeint; **~·known** bekannt; **~·**
man·nered mit guten Manieren;

~·nigh ['welnaɪ] beinahe; **~·off**
[wel'ɒf] wohlhabend; **~·read** bele-
sen; **~·timed** (zeitlich) günstig, im
richtigen Augenblick; *Sport*: gutge-
timed (*Paß etc.*); **~·to-do** wohlhabend; **~·worn** abgetragen; *fig.* abgedroschen.

Welsh [welʃ] **1.** walisisch; **2.** *ling.*
Walisisch *n*; *the* ~ *pl.* die Waliser *pl.*;
~ rab·bit, **~ rare·bit** überbackener
Käsetoast.

welt [welt] Strieme *m*.

wel·ter ['weltə] Wirrwarr *m*, Durcheinander *n*.

wench *veraltet* [wentʃ] (*bsd.* Bauern-)
Mädchen *n*.

went [went] *pret. von* go 1.

wept [wept] *pret. u. p.p. von* weep.

were [wɜː, wə] **1.** *pret. von* be: *du
warst*, *Sie waren*, *wir waren*, *ihr
wart*; **2.** *pret. pass. von* be: wurde(n);
3. *subj. pret. von* be: wäre(n).

west [west] **1.** West(en *m*); *a.* Westen
m, westlicher Landesteil; *the* 2 der
Westen, die Weststaaten *pl.* (*der
USA*); *pol.* der Westen; **2.** West...,
westlich; **3.** westwärts, nach Westen; **~·er·ly** ['westəlɪ] westlich;
~·ern [\ən] **1.** westlich; **2.** Western
m, Wildwestfilm *m*; **~·ward(s)**
[\wəd(z)] westwärts.

wet [wet] **1.** naß, feucht; **2.** Nässe *f*,
Feuchtigkeit *f*; **3.** (*-tt-*; *wet od wet-
ted*) naß machen, anfeuchten.

weth·er *zo.* ['weðə] Hammel *m*.

wet-nurse ['wetnɜːs] Amme *f*.

whack [wæk] (knallender) Schlag; F
(An)Teil *m*; **~ed** [\t] fertig, erledigt
(*erschöpft*); **~ing** ['wækɪŋ] **1.** F
Mords...; **2.** (*Tracht f*) Prügel *pl.*

whale *zo.* [weɪl] Wal *m*; **~·bone**
['weɪlbəʊn] Fischbein *n*; **~ oil** Tran
m.

whal·er ['weɪlə] Walfänger *m* (*a.
Schiff*); **~·ing** [\ɪŋ] Walfang *m*.

wharf [wɔːf] (*pl.* wharfs, wharves
[\vz]) Kai *m*.

what [wɒt] **1.** was; wie; was für ein(e),
welche(r, -s), *vor pl.*: was für; (*das*)
was; *know* ~'s ~ Bescheid wissen; ~
about ...? wie steht's mit ...?; ~ *for*?
wozu?; ~ *of it*?, *so* ~? na und?; ~
next? was sonst noch?; *iro.* noch
was?, das fehlte noch!; ~ *a
blessing*! was für ein Segen!; ~ *with
...*, *with ...* teils durch ..., teils
durch ...; **2.** *int.* was!, wie!;
fragend: was?, wie?; **~·(so·)ev·er**

wheat ⚭ [wi:t] Weizen *m*.

whee·dle ['wi:dl] beschwatzen; ~ *s.th. out of s.o.* j-m et. abschwatzen.

wheel [wi:l] 1. Rad *n*; Steuer(rad) *n*; Lenkrad *n*; *bsd. Am.* F (Fahr)Rad *n*; Töpferscheibe *f*; Drehung *f*; ✗ Schwenkung *f*; 2. rollen, fahren, schieben; sich drehen; ✗ schwenken; *bsd. Am.* F radeln; ~**bar·row** ['wi:lbærəʊ] Schubkarre(n *m*) *f*; ~**chair** Rollstuhl *m*; ~**ed** mit Rädern; fahrbar; *in Zssgn:* ...räd(e)rig.

-wheel·er ['wi:lə] *in Zssgn* Wagen *od.* Fahrzeug mit ... Rädern.

wheeze [wi:z] schnaufen, keuchen.

whelp [welp] 1. *zo.* Welpe *m*; Junge(s) *n*; F Balg *m*, *n* (*ungezogenes Kind*); 2. (Junge) werfen.

when [wen] 1. wann; 2. wenn; als; während, obwohl, wo ... (doch).

whence [wens] woher, von wo.

when·(so·)ev·er [wen(səʊ)'evə] (im-mer) wenn, sooft (als); *fragend:* wann denn.

where [weə] wo; wohin; ~ ... *from?* woher?; ~ ... *to?* wohin?; ~**a·bouts** 1. [weərə'baʊts] wo etwa; 2. ['weərə-baʊts] Aufenthalt(sort) *m*, Verbleib *m*; ~**as** [weər'æz] wohingegen, während (doch); ~**at** [~r'æt] woran, wobei, worauf; ~**by** [weə'baɪ] wodurch; ~**fore** ['weəfɔ:] weshalb; ~**in** [weər'ɪn] worin; ~**of** [~r'ɒv] wovon; ~**u·pon** [~rə'pɒn] worauf(hin); **wher·ev·er** [~r'evə] wo(hin) (auch) immer; ~**with·al** ['weəwɪðɔ:l] *die* (nötigen) Mittel *pl.*, *das* nötige (Klein)Geld.

whet [wet] (-tt-) wetzen, schärfen; *fig.* anstacheln.

wheth·er ['weðə] ob; ~ *or no* so oder so.

whet·stone ['wetstəʊn] Schleifstein *m*.

whey [weɪ] Molke *f*.

which [wɪtʃ] 1. welche(r, -s); 2. der, die, das; was; ~**ev·er** [~'evə] welche(r, -s) (auch) immer.

whiff [wɪf] 1. Hauch *m*; Duftwolke *f*, Geruch *m*; F Zigarillo *m*, *n*; Zug *m* (*beim Rauchen*); *have a few* ~ s ein paar Züge machen; 2. paffen; F duften (*unangenehm riechen*).

while [waɪl] 1. Weile *f*, Zeit *f*; *for a* ~ e-e Zeitlang; 2. *mst* ~ *away* sich *die* Zeit vertreiben; verbrin-

gen; 3. *a. whilst* [waɪlst] während.

whim [wɪm] Laune *f*, Grille *f*.

whim·per ['wɪmpə] 1. wimmern, winseln; 2. Wimmern *n*, Winseln *f*; △ *nicht* Wimper.

whim·si·cal □ ['wɪmzɪkl] wunder-lich; launisch (*a. Wetter etc.*); ~**sy** ['wɪmzɪ] Grille *f*, Laune *f*.

whine [waɪn] winseln; wimmern.

whin·ny ['wɪnɪ] wiehern.

whip [wɪp] 1. (-pp-) *v/t.* peitschen; geißeln (*a. fig.*); j-n verprügeln; schlagen; *a.* Eier, Sahne schlagen; ~*ped cream* Schlagsahne *f*, -rahm *m*; ~*ped eggs pl.* Eischnee *f*; *v/i.* sausen, flitzen; 2. Peitsche *f*; (Reit-) Gerte *f*.

whip·ping ['wɪpɪŋ] (Tracht *f*) Prügel *pl.*; ~**top** Kreisel *m*.

whip·poor·will *zo.* ['wɪppʊəwɪl] Ziegenmelker *m*.

whirl [wɜ:l] 1. wirbeln; (sich) dre-hen; 2. Wirbel *m*, Strudel *m*; ~**pool** ['wɜ:lpu:l] Strudel *m*, ~**wind** [~wɪnd] Wirbelwind *m*, -sturm *m*.

whir(r) [wɜ:] (-rr-) schwirren.

whisk [wɪsk] 1. schnelle *od.* heftige Bewegung; Wisch *m*; Staubwedel *m*; *Küche:* Schneebesen *m*; 2. *v/t.* (ab-, weg)wischen, (ab-, weg)fegen; *mit dem Schwanz schlagen; Eier* schlagen; ~ *away* schnell verschwin-den lassen, wegnehmen; *v/i.* hu-schen, flitzen. **whis·ker** ['wɪskə] Barthaar *n*; ~*s pl.* Backenbart *m*.

whis·per ['wɪspə] 1. flüstern; 2. Flü-stern *n*, Geflüster *n*; *in a* ~, *in* ~*s* flüsternd, im Flüsterton.

whis·tle ['wɪsl] 1. pfeifen; 2. Pfeife *f*; Pfiff *m*; F Kehle *f*; ~ *stop Am.* ⚭ Bedarfshaltestelle *f*; Kleinstadt *f*; *pol.* kurzes Auftreten (*e-s Kandida-ten im Wahlkampf*).

Whit [wɪt] *in Zssgn:* Pfingst...

white [waɪt] 1. (~*r*, ~*st*) weiß; rein; F anständig; Weiß...; 2. Weiß(e) *n*; Weiße(r *m*) *f* (*Rasse*); ~**col·lar** [waɪt'kɒlə] Büro..., ~ *worker* (Büro-) Angestellte(r *m*) *f*; ~ **heat** Weißglut *f*; ~ **lie** Notlüge *f*, fromme Lüge; **whit·en** ['waɪtn] weiß machen *od.* werden; bleichen; ~**ness** [~nɪs] Weiße *f*; Blässe *f*; ~**wash** 1. Tünche *f*; 2. weißen, tünchen; *fig.* reinwa-schen.

whit·ish ['waɪtɪʃ] weißlich.

Whit·sun ['wɪtsn] Pfingst...; ~**tide** Pfingsten *n od. pl.*

whit·tle ['wɪtl] schnitze(l)n; ~ away schwächen, beschneiden, herabsetzen, kürzen.

whiz(z) [wɪz] (-zz-) zischen, sausen.

who [hu:, hʊ] wer; welche(r, -s), der, die, das.

who·dun(n)·it F [hu:'dʌnɪt] Krimi m (Kriminalroman, -stück, -film).

who·ev·er [hu:'evə] wer (auch) immer.

whole [həʊl] **1.** ☐ ganz; voll(ständig); heil, unversehrt; **2.** Ganze(s) n; the ~ of London ganz London; on the ~ im großen (u.) ganzen; im allgemeinen; ~**heart·ed** ☐ [həʊl'hɑ:tɪd] aufrichtig; ~**meal** ['həʊlmi:l] Vollkorn...; ~ bread Vollkornbrot n; ~**sale 1.** econ. Großhandel m; **2.** econ. Großhandels...; **3.** fig. Massen...; ~ dealer = ~**sal·er** [~ə] econ. Großhändler m; ~**some** ☐ [~səm] gesund; ~ wheat bsd. Am. = wholemeal.

whol·ly adv. ['həʊllɪ] ganz, gänzlich.

whom [hu:m, hʊm] Objektkasus von who.

whoop [hu:p] **1.** (bsd. Freuden)Schrei m; ✽ Keuchen n (bei Keuchhusten); **2.** schreien, a. ~ with joy jauchzen; ~ it up F auf den Putz hauen (ausgelassen feiern); ~**ee** F ['wʊpi:]: make ~ auf den Putz hauen (ausgelassen feiern); ~**ing-cough** ✽ ['hu:pɪŋkɒf] Keuchhusten m.

whore [hɔ:] Hure f.

whose [hu:z] gen. sg. u. pl. von who.

why [waɪ] **1.** warum, weshalb; ~ so? wieso?; **2.** int. nun (gut); ja doch.

wick [wɪk] Docht m.

wick·ed ☐ ['wɪkɪd] böse, schlecht, schlimm; ~**ness** [~nɪs] Bosheit f.

wick·er ['wɪkə] aus Weiden geflochten, Weiden..., Korb...; ~ basket Weidenkorb m; ~ bottle Korbflasche f; ~**chair** Korbstuhl m; ~**work** Korbwaren pl.; Flechtwerk n.

wick·et ['wɪkɪt] Pförtchen n; Kricket: Dreistab m, Tor n.

wide [waɪd] adj. ☐ u. adv. weit; ausgedehnt; großzügig; breit; weitab; ~ awake völlig (od. hell)wach; aufgeweckt, wach; 3 feet ~ 3 Fuß breit; **wid·en** ['waɪdn] (sich) verbreitern; (sich) erweitern (Wissen etc.); ~**o·pen** ['waɪd'əʊpən] weitgeöffnet; Am. äußerst großzügig (in der Gesetzesdurchführung); ~**spread** weitverbreitet; ausgedehnt.

wid·ow ['wɪdəʊ] Witwe f; attr. Witwen...; ~**ed** verwitwet; ~**er** [~ə] Witwer m.

width [wɪdθ] Breite f, Weite f.

wield [wi:ld] Einfluß etc. ausüben.

wife [waɪf] (pl. wives [~vz]) (Ehe-)Frau f, Gattin f.

wig [wɪg] Perücke f.

wild [waɪld] **1.** adj. ☐ wild; toll; rasend; wütend; ausgelassen; planlos; ~ about (ganz) verrückt nach; **2.** adv.: run ~ verwildern (Garten etc.; a. fig. Kinder etc.); talk ~ (wild) drauflosreden; dummes Zeug reden; **3.** a. ~**s** pl. Wildnis f; ~**cat** ['waɪldkæt] **1.** zo. Wildkatze f; econ. Am. Schwindelunternehmen n; **2.** wild (Streik); econ. Am. Schwindel...; **wil·der·ness** ['wɪldənɪs] Wildnis f, Wüste f; ~**fire** ['waɪldfaɪə]: like ~ wie ein Lauffeuer; ~**life** coll. wildlebende Tiere (u. wildwachsende Pflanzen).

wile [waɪl] List f; ~**s** pl. a. Schliche pl.

will [wɪl] **1.** Wille m; Wunsch m; Testament n; of one's own free ~ aus freien Stücken; **2.** v/aux. (pret. would; verneint: ~ not, won't) ich, du etc. will(st) etc.; ich werde, wir werden; wollen; werden; **3.** wollen; durch Willenskraft zwingen; entscheiden; ⚖ vermachen.

wil(l)·ful ☐ ['wɪlfl] eigensinnig; absichtlich, bsd. ⚖ vorsätzlich.

will·ing ☐ ['wɪlɪŋ] pred. gewillt, willens, bereit; (bereit)willig.

will-o'-the-wisp ['wɪlədə'wɪsp] Irrlicht n.

wil·low ♀ ['wɪləʊ] Weide f; ~**y** fig. [~ɪ] geschmeidig; gertenschlank.

will·pow·er ['wɪlpaʊə] Willenskraft f.

wil·ly-nil·ly ['wɪlɪ'nɪlɪ] wohl oder übel.

wilt [wɪlt] (ver)welken.

wi·ly ☐ ['waɪlɪ] (-ier, -iest) listig, gerissen.

win [wɪn] **1.** (-nn-; won) v/t. gewinnen; erringen; erlangen; erreichen; j-n dazu bringen (to do zu tun); ~ s.o. over od. round j-n für sich gewinnen; v/i. gewinnen, siegen; **2.** Sport: Sieg m.

wince [wɪns] (zusammen)zucken.

winch [wɪntʃ] Winde f; Kurbel f.

wind[1] [wɪnd] **1.** Wind m; Atem m, Luft f; ✽ Blähung(en pl.) f; the ~ sg. od. pl. ♪ die Bläser; **2.** hunt. wittern;

außer Atem bringen; verschnaufen lassen.

wind² [waɪnd] (**wound**) v/t. winden, wickeln, schlingen; kurbeln; (**winded** od. **wound**) *Horn* blasen; ∼ **up** *Uhr* aufziehen; *Rede etc.* beschließen; v/i. sich winden; sich schlängeln; ∼ **up** (*bsd.* s-e *Rede*) schließen (*by saying* mit den Worten); F enden, landen.

wind|bag F [ˈwɪndbæg] Schwätzer *m*; ∼**fall** Fallobst *n*; Glücksfall *m*.

wind·ing [ˈwaɪndɪŋ] **1.** Windung *f*; **2.** sich windend; ∼ *stairs pl.* Wendeltreppe *f*; ∼ **sheet** Leichentuch *n*.

wind-in-stru·ment ♪ [ˈwɪndɪnstrʊmənt] Blasinstrument *n*.

wind·lass ⊕ [ˈwɪndləs] Winde *f*.

wind·mill [ˈwɪnmɪl] Windmühle *f*.

win·dow [ˈwɪndəʊ] Fenster *n*; Schaufenster *n*; Schalter *m*; ∼**dress·ing** Schaufensterdekoration *f*; *fig.* Aufmachung *f*, Mache *f*; ∼**shade** *Am.* Rouleau *n*; ∼ **shop·ping** Schaufensterbummel *m*; *go* ∼ e-n Schaufensterbummel machen.

wind|pipe *anat.* [ˈwɪndpaɪp] Luftröhre *f*; ∼**screen**, *Am.* ∼**shield** *mot.* Windschutzscheibe *f*; ∼ **wiper** Scheibenwischer *m*; ∼**surf·ing** *Sport:* Windsurfing *n*, -surfen *n*.

wind·y □ [ˈwɪndɪ] (*-ier, -iest*) windig (*a. fig. inhaltlos*); geschwätzig.

wine [waɪn] Wein *m*; ∼**press** [ˈwaɪnpres] (Wein)Kelter *f*.

wing [wɪŋ] **1.** Flügel *m* (*a.* ✗ *u. arch.*, *Sport, pol.*); Schwinge *f*; *Brt. mot.* Kotflügel *m*; ✈ Tragfläche *f*; ✈, ✗ Geschwader *n*; ∼*s pl. thea.* Seitenkulisse *f*; *take* ∼ weg-, auffliegen; *on the* ∼ im Flug; **2.** fliegen; *fig.* beflügeln.

wink [wɪŋk] **1.** Blinzeln *n*, Zwinkern *n*; *not get a* ∼ *of sleep* kein Auge zutun; *s.* forty; **2.** blinzeln od. zwinkern (mit); blinken (*Licht*); △ *nicht winken*; ∼ *at j-m* zublinzeln; *fig.* ein Auge zudrücken bei *et.*

win|ner [ˈwɪnə] Gewinner(in); Sieger(in); ∼**ning** [ˈwɪnɪŋ] **1.** □ einnehmend, gewinnend; **2.** ∼*s pl.* Gewinn *m*.

win|ter [ˈwɪntə] **1.** Winter *m*; **2.** überwintern; den Winter verbringen; ∼**ter** *sports pl.* Wintersport *m*; ∼**try** [∼trɪ] winterlich; *fig.* frostig.

wipe [waɪp] (ab-, auf)wischen; reinigen; (ab)trocknen; ∼ *out* auswischen; wegwischen, (aus)löschen;

fig. vernichten; ∼ *up* aufwischen; *Geschirr* abtrocknen; **wip·er** *mot.* [ˈwaɪpə] Scheibenwischer *m*.

wire [ˈwaɪə] **1.** Draht *m*; ∉ Leitung *f*; F Telegramm *n*; *pull the* ∼*s der Drahtzieher sein*; *s-e Beziehungen spielen lassen*; **2.** (ver)drahten; telegrafieren; ∼**drawn** spitzfindig; ∼**less** [∼lɪs] □ drahtlos, Funk...; **2.** *Brt.* Radio(apparat *m*) *n*; *on the* ∼ im Radio *od.* Rundfunk; **3.** funken; ∼**net·ting** [waɪəˈnetɪŋ] Maschendraht *m*; ∼**tap** [ˈwaɪətæp] (*-pp-*) Telefongespräche abhören, die Telefonleitung anzapfen.

wir·y □ [ˈwaɪərɪ] (*-ier, -iest*) drahtig, sehnig.

wis·dom [ˈwɪzdəm] Weisheit *f*, Klugheit *f*; ∼**tooth** Weisheitszahn *m*.

wise¹ □ [waɪz] (∼*r*, ∼*st*) weise, klug; verständig; erfahren; ∼ *guy* F Klugscheißer *m*.

wise² *veraltet* [∼] Weise *f*, Art *f*.

wise·crack F [ˈwaɪzkræk] **1.** witzige Bemerkung; **2.** witzeln.

wish [wɪʃ] **1.** wünschen; wollen; ∼ *for* (sich) *et.* wünschen; ∼ *s.o. well* (*ill*) j-m Gutes (Böses) wünschen; **2.** Wunsch *m*; ∼**ful** □ [ˈwɪʃfl] sehnsüchtig; ∼ *thinking* Wunschdenken *n*.

wish·y-wash·y [ˈwɪʃɪwɒʃɪ] wäßrig, dünn; *fig.* seicht, saft- u. kraftlos.

wisp [wɪsp] Bündel *n*; Strähne *f*.

wist·ful □ [ˈwɪstfl] sehnsüchtig.

wit¹ [wɪt] Geist *m*, Intelligenz *f*, Witz *m*; *a.* ∼*s pl.* Verstand *m*; geistreicher Mensch; △ *nicht Witz = joke*; *be at one's* ∼*'s od.* ∼*s' end* mit s-r Weisheit am Ende sein; *keep one's* ∼*s about one* e-n klaren Kopf behalten.

wit² [∼]: *to* ∼ *bsd.* ⚖ nämlich, das heißt.

witch [wɪtʃ] Hexe *f*, Zauberin *f*; ∼**craft** [ˈwɪtʃkrɑːft], ∼**e·ry** [∼ərɪ] Hexerei *f*; ∼**hunt** *pol.* Hexenjagd *f* (*for*, *against* auf *acc.*).

with [wɪð] mit; nebst; bei; von; durch; vor (*dat.*); ∼ *it* F up to date, modern.

with·draw [wɪðˈdrɔː] (*-drew*, *-drawn*) v/t. ab-, ent-, zurückziehen; zurücknehmen; *Geld* abheben; v/i. sich zurückziehen; zurücktreten; *Sport:* auf den Start verzichten; ∼**al** [∼əl] Zurückziehung *f*, -nahme *f*; Rücktritt *m*; *bsd.* ✗ Ab-, Rückzug *m*; *econ.* Abheben *n* (*von Geld*); *Sport:*

Startverzicht *m*; ✻ Entziehung *f*; ~ *cure* ✻ Entziehungskur *f*; ~ *symptoms pl.* ✻ Entzugserscheinungen *pl.*

with·er ['wɪðə] *v/i.* (ver)welken, verdorren, austrocknen; *v/t.* welken lassen.

with·hold [wɪð'həʊld] (*-held*) zurückhalten; ~ *s.th. from s.o.* j-m et. vorenthalten.

with·in [wɪ'ðɪn] **1.** *adv.* im Innern, drin(nen); zu Hause; **2.** *prp.* in(nerhalb); ~ *doors* im Hause; ~ *call* in Rufweite; **~·out** [wɪ'ðaʊt] **1.** *adv.* (dr)außen; äußerlich; **2.** *prp.* ohne.

with·stand [wɪð'stænd] (*-stood*) widerstehen (*dat.*).

wit·ness ['wɪtnɪs] **1.** Zeug|e *m*, -in *f*; *bear* ~ *to* Zeugnis ablegen von, et. bestätigen; ~ *to* bezeugen; Zeuge sein von et.; beglaubigen; ~ *box*, *Am.* ~ *stand* Zeugenstand *m*.

wit·ti·cis·m ['wɪtɪsɪzəm] witzige Bemerkung; **~·ty** □ [~ɪ] (*-ier, -iest*) witzig; geistreich.

wives [waɪvz] *pl. von* **wife**.

wiz·ard ['wɪzəd] Zauberer *m*; Genie *n*, Leuchte *f*.

wiz·en(ed) ['wɪzn(d)] schrump(e)lig.

wob·ble ['wɒbl] schwanken, wackeln.

woe [wəʊ] Weh *n*, Leid *n*; ~ *is me!* wehe mir!; **~·be·gone** ['wəʊbɪgɒn] jammervoll; **~·ful** □ ['wəʊfl] jammervoll, traurig, elend.

woke [wəʊk] *pret. u. p.p. von* **wake** 2; **wok·en** ['wəʊkən] *p.p. von* **wake** 2.

wold [wəʊld] hügeliges Land.

wolf [wʊlf] **1.** (*pl.* **wolves** [~vz]) *zo.* Wolf *m*; **2.** *a.* ~ *down* (gierig) ver- *od.* hinunterschlingen; **~·ish** □ ['wʊlfɪʃ] wölfisch, Wolfs...

wom·an ['wʊmən] **1.** (*pl.* **women** ['wɪmɪn]) Frau *f*; F (Ehe)Frau *f*; F Freundin *f*; F Geliebte *f*; **2.** weiblich; ~ *doctor* Ärztin *f*; ~ *student* Studentin *f*; **~·hood** [~hʊd] die Frauen *pl.*; Weiblichkeit *f*; **~·ish** □ [~ɪʃ] weibisch; **~·kind** [~'kaɪnd] die Frauen (-welt *f*) *pl.*; **~·like** [~laɪk] fraulich; **~·ly** [~lɪ] weiblich.

womb [wuːm] Gebärmutter *f*; Mutterleib *m*; *fig.* Schoß *m*.

wom·en ['wɪmɪn] *pl. von* **woman**; ♀'s *Liberation (Movement)*, F ♀'s *Lib* [lɪb] Frauenemanzipationsbewegung *f*; **~·folk, ~·kind** die Frauen *pl.*; F Weibervolk *n*.

won [wʌn] *pret. u. p.p. von* **win** 1.

won·der ['wʌndə] **1.** Wunder *n*; Verwunderung *f*, Erstaunen *n*; *work* ~s Wunder wirken; **2.** sich wundern; gern wissen mögen, sich fragen; *I* ~ *if you could help me* vielleicht können Sie mir helfen; **~·ful** □ [~fl] wunderbar, -voll; **~·ing** □ [~rɪŋ] staunend, verwundert.

wont [wəʊnt] **1.** gewohnt; *be* ~ *to do* gewohnt sein zu tun, zu tun pflegen; **2.** Gewohnheit *f*; *as was his* ~ wie es s-e Gewohnheit war.

won't [~] = **will not**.

wont·ed ['wəʊntɪd] gewohnt.

woo [wuː] werben um; locken.

wood [wʊd] Holz *n*; *oft* ~*s pl.* Wald *m*, Gehölz *n*; Holzfaß *n*; ~ *pl.* Wald *m*, *touch* ~! unberufen!, toi, toi, toi!; *he cannot see the* ~ *for the trees* er sieht den Wald vor lauter Bäumen nicht; **~·cut** ['wʊdkʌt] Holzschnitt *m*; **~·cut·ter** Holzfäller *m*; *Kunst*: Holzschnitzer *m*; **~·ed** [~ɪd] bewaldet; **~·en** □ [~n] hölzern, aus Holz, Holz...; *fig.* ausdruckslos; **~·man** [~mən] (*pl.* -men) Förster *m*; Holzfäller *m*; **~·peck·er** *zo.* [~pekə] Specht *m*; **~·s·man** [~zmən] (*pl.* -men) Waldbewohner *m*; **~·wind** ♪ [~wɪnd] Holzblasinstrument *n*; *the* ~ *sg. od. pl.* die Holzbläser *pl.*; **~·work** Holzwerk *n*; **~·y** [~ɪ] (*-ier, -iest*) waldig; holzig.

wool [wʊl] Wolle *f*; **~·gath·er·ing** ['wʊlgæðərɪŋ] Verträumtheit *f*; **~·(l)en** ['wʊlən] **1.** wollen, Woll...; ~*s pl.* Wollsachen *pl.*; **~·ly** ['wʊlɪ] **1.** (*-ier, -iest*) wollig; Woll...; verschwommen (*Ideen*); **2.** woollies *pl.* F Wollsachen *pl.*

word [wɜːd] **1.** Wort *n*; Vokabel *f*; Nachricht *f*; ✕ Losung(swort *n*) *f*; Versprechen *n*; Befehl *m*; Spruch *m*; ~*s pl.* Wörter *pl.*; Worte *pl.*; *fig.* Wortwechsel *m*, Streit *m*; Text *m* (*e-s Liedes*); *have a* ~ *with* mit j-m sprechen; **2.** (*in Worten*) ausdrücken, (ab)fassen; **~·ing** ['wɜːdɪŋ] Wortlaut *m*, Fassung *f*; **~·or·der** *gr.* Wortstellung *f* (*im Satz*); **~·pro·cess·ing** *Computer*: Textverarbeitung *f*; **~·pro·ces·sor** *Computer*: Textverarbeitungsanlage *f*, -system *n*; **~·split·ting** Wortklauberei *f*.

word·y □ ['wɜːdɪ] (*-ier, -iest*) wortreich; Wort...

wore [wɔː] *pret. von* **wear** 1.

work [wɜːk] **1.** Arbeit *f*; Werk *n*; *attr.*

Arbeits...; ~s pl. ⊕ (Uhr-, Feder-)Werk n; ⚔ Befestigungen pl.; ~s sg. Werk n, Fabrik f; ~ of art Kunstwerk n; at ~ bei der Arbeit; be in ~ Arbeit haben; be out of ~ arbeitslos sein; set to ~, set od. go about one's ~ an die Arbeit gehen; ~s council Betriebsrat m; **2.** v/i. arbeiten (at, on an dat.); ⊕ funktionieren, gehen; wirken; fig. gelingen, klappen; ~ to rule econ. Dienst nach Vorschrift tun; v/t. ver-, bearbeiten; Maschine etc. bedienen; betreiben; fig. bewirken; ~ one's way sich durcharbeiten; ~ off ab-, aufarbeiten; Gefühl abreagieren; econ. Ware abstoßen; ~ out Plan ausarbeiten; Aufgabe lösen; ausrechnen; ~ up verarbeiten (into zu); Interesse wecken; ~ o.s. up sich aufregen.

wor·ka·ble □ ['wɜːkəbl] bearbeitungs-, betriebsfähig; ausführbar.

work|a·day ['wɜːkədeɪ] Alltags...; ~bench ⊕ Werkbank f; ~book Schule: Arbeitsheft n; ~day Werktag m; on ~s werktags; ~er [~ə] Arbeiter(in).

work·ing ['wɜːkɪŋ] **1.** ~s pl. Arbeitsweise f, Funktionieren n; **2.** arbeitend; Arbeits...; Betriebs...; ~class Arbeiter...; ~day Werk-, Arbeitstag m; ~hours pl. Arbeitszeit f.

work·man ['wɜːkmən] (pl. -men) Arbeiter m; Handwerker m; ~like [~laɪk] kunstgerecht, fachmännisch; ~ship [~ʃɪp] Kunstfertigkeit f.

work|out ['wɜːkaʊt] F Sport: (Konditions)Training n; Erprobung f; ~shop Werkstatt f; Werkraum m; ~shy arbeitsscheu, faul; ~to-rule econ. Dienst m nach Vorschrift; ~woman (pl. -women) Arbeiterin f.

world [wɜːld] Welt f; a ~ of e-e Unmenge (von); bring (come) into the ~ zur Welt bringen (kommen); think the ~ of große Stücke halten auf (acc.); ~class (von) Weltklasse, von internationalem Format (Sportler, etc.); ♀ Cup Fußballweltmeisterschaft f; Skisport: Weltcup m.

word·ly ['wɜːldlɪ] (-ier, -iest) weltlich; Welt...; ~wise weltklug.

world| pow·er pol. ['wɜːldpaʊə] Weltmacht f; ~wide weltweit, weltumspannend; Welt...

worm [wɜːm] **1.** zo. Wurm m (a. fig.); **2.** ein Geheimnis entlocken (out of dat.); ~ o.s. sich schlängeln; fig. sich

einschleichen (into in acc.); ~eat·en ['wɜːmiːtn] wurmstichig; fig. veraltet, altmodisch.

worn [wɔːn] p.p. von wear 1; ~out ['wɔːnˈaʊt] abgenutzt; abgetragen; verbraucht (a. fig.); müde, erschöpft; abgezehrt; verhärmt.

wor·ried □ ['wʌrɪd] besorgt, beunruhigt.

wor·ry ['wʌrɪ] **1.** (sich) beunruhigen, (sich) ängstigen, sich sorgen; (sich) aufregen; ärgern; zerren an (dat.), (ab)würgen; plagen, quälen; don't ~! keine Angst od. Sorge!; **2.** Unruhe f; Sorge f; Ärger m.

worse [wɜːs] (comp. von bad) schlechter, schlimmer, ärger; ~ luck! leider!; um so schlimmer!; **wors·en** ['wɜːsn] (sich) verschlechtern.

wor·ship ['wɜːʃɪp] **1.** Verehrung f; Gottesdienst m; Kult m; **2.** (bsd. Brt. -pp-, Am. -p-) v/t. verehren; anbeten; v/i. den Gottesdienst besuchen; ~(p)er [~ə] Verehrer(in); Kirchgänger(in).

worst [wɜːst] **1.** adj. (sup. von bad) schlechteste(r, -s), schlimmste(r, -s), ärgste(r, -s); **2.** adv. (sup. von badly) am schlechtesten, am schlimmsten, am ärgsten; **3.** der, die, das Schlechteste od. Schlimmste od. Ärgste; at (the) ~ schlimmstenfalls.

wor·sted ['wʊstɪd] Kammgarn n.

worth [wɜːθ] **1.** wert; ~ reading lesenswert; **2.** Wert m; ~less ['wɜːθlɪs] wertlos; unwürdig; ~while [~ˈwaɪl] der Mühe wert; ~y □ ['wɜːðɪ] (-ier, -iest) würdig; wert.

would [wʊd] pret. von will 2; I ~ like ich hätte gern; ~be ['wʊdbiː] Möchtegern...; angehend, zukünftig.

wound¹ [wuːnd] **1.** Wunde f, Verletzung f (beide a. fig.), Verwundung f; fig. Kränkung f; **2.** verwunden, verletzen (beide a. fig.).

wound² [waʊnd] pret. u. p.p. von wind².

wove [wəʊv] pret. von weave; **wov·en** ['wəʊvn] p.p. von weave.

wow int. F [waʊ] Mensch!, toll!

wran·gle ['ræŋgl] **1.** sich streiten od. zanken; **2.** Streit m, Zank m.

wrap [ræp] **1.** (-pp-) v/t. oft ~ up (ein)wickeln; fig. (ein)hüllen; be ~ped up in gehüllt sein in (acc.); ganz aufgehen in (dat.); v/i. ~ up sich einhüllen od. -packen; **2.** Hülle f;

Decke *f*; Schal *m*; Mantel *m*; ~**per**
['ræpə] Hülle *f*, Umschlag *m*; *a.*
postal ~ Streifband *n*; ~**ping** [~ɪŋ]
Verpackung *f*; ~*paper* Einwickel-,
Pack-, Geschenkpapier *n*.

wrath *lit.* [rɔːθ] Zorn *m*, Wut *f*.

wreak *lit.* [riːk] *Rache* üben, *Wut etc.*
auslassen (*on, upon* an *j-m*).

wreath [riːθ] (*pl.* **wreaths** [~ðz])
(Blumen)Gewinde *n*, Kranz *m*, Girlande *f*; Ring *m*, Kreis *m*; ~**e** [riːð]
v/t. (um)winden; *v/i.* sich ringeln *od.*
kräuseln.

wreck [rek] **1.** Wrack *n*; Trümmer
pl.; Schiffbruch *m*; *fig.* Untergang
m; **2.** zertrümmern, -stören; zugrunde richten, ruinieren; *be* ~*ed* ♣
scheitern, Schiffbruch erleiden; *in*
Trümmer gehen; 🚃 entgleisen; ~
age ['rekɪdʒ] Trümmer *pl.*; Wrack-
teile *pl.*; ~**ed** [rekt] schiffbrüchig;
ruiniert; ~**er** ['rekə] ♣ Bergungs-
schiff *n*, -arbeiter *m*; *bsd. hist.*
Strandräuber *m*; Abbrucharbeiter
m; *Am. mot.* Abschleppwagen *m*;
~**ing** [~ɪŋ] *bsd. hist.* Strandraub *m*; ~
company Am. Abbruchfirma *f*; ~
service Am. mot. Abschleppdienst
m.

wren *zo.* [ren] Zaunkönig *m*.

wrench [rentʃ] **1.** reißen, zerren, ziehen; entwinden (*from s.o.* *j-m*); *☆*
verrenken, -stauchen; ~ *open* aufreißen; **2.** Ruck *m*; *☆* Verrenkung *f*,
-stauchung *f*; Schmerz *m*; ⊕
Schraubenschlüssel *m*.

wrest [rest] reißen; ~ *s.th. from s.o.*
j-m et. entreißen.

wres·tle ['resl] ringen (mit); ~**tler**
[~ə] *bsd. Sport:* Ringer *m*; ~**tling**
[~ɪŋ] *bsd. Sport:* Ringen *n*.

wretch [retʃ] Elende(r *m*) *f*; Kerl
m.

wretch·ed □ ['retʃɪd] elend.

wrig·gle ['rɪgl] sich winden *od.*
schlängeln; ~ *out of s.th.* sich aus e-r
Sache herauswinden.

-wright [raɪt] *in Zssgn:* ...macher *m*,
...bauer *m*.

wring [rɪŋ] (*wrung*) *Hände* ringen;
(aus)wringen; pressen; *Hals* umdrehen; abringen (*from s.o.* *j-m*); ~
s.o.'s heart j-m zu Herzen gehen.

wrin·kle ['rɪŋkl] **1.** Runzel *f*, Falte *f*;
2. (sich) runzeln.

wrist [rɪst] Handgelenk *n*; ~*watch*
Armbanduhr *f*; ~**band** ['rɪstbænd]
Bündchen *n*, (Hemd)Manschette *f*;
Armband *n*.

writ [rɪt] Erlaß *m*; gerichtlicher Befehl; *Holy* ♀ *die* Heilige Schrift.

write [raɪt] (*wrote, written*) schreiben; ~ *down* auf-, niederschreiben;
writ·er ['raɪtə] Schreiber(in); Ver-
fasser(in); Schriftsteller(in).

writhe [raɪð] sich krümmen.

writ·ing ['raɪtɪŋ] Schreiben *n* (*Tätigkeit*); Aufsatz *m*; Werk *n*; (Hand-)
Schrift *f*; Schriftstück *n*; Urkunde
f; Stil *m*; *attr.* Schreib...; *in* ~
schriftlich; ~**case** Schreibmappe *f*;
~ **desk** Schreibtisch *m*; ~ **pad**
Schreibblock *m*; ~ **pa·per** Schreib-
papier *n*.

writ·ten ['rɪtn] **1.** *p.p. von* write; **2.**
adj. schriftlich.

wrong [rɒŋ] **1.** □ unrecht; verkehrt,
falsch; *be* ~ unrecht haben; nicht in
Ordnung sein; falsch gehen (*Uhr*);
go ~ schiefgehen; *be on the* ~ *side of*
sixty über 60 (Jahre alt) sein; **2.**
Unrecht *n*; Beleidigung *f*; Irrtum *m*,
Unrecht *n*; *be in the* ~ unrecht
haben; **3.** unrecht tun (*dat.*); ungerecht behandeln; ~**do·er** ['rɒŋduːə]
Übeltäter(in); ~**ful** □ [~fl] ungerecht; unrechtmäßig.

wrote [rəʊt] *pret. von* write.

wrought i·ron [rɔːt'aɪən] Schmiede-
eisen *n*; ~**-i·ron** ['rɔːt'aɪən] schmie-
deeisern.

wrung [rʌŋ] *pret. u. p.p. von* wring.

wry □ [raɪ] (*-ier, -iest*) schief,
krumm, verzerrt.

X

X·mas F ['krɪsməs] = *Christmas.*

X-ray [eks'reɪ] **1.** ~*s pl.* Röntgen-
strahlen *pl.*; **2.** Röntgen...; **3.** durch-

leuchten, röntgen.

xy·lo·phone ♪ ['zaɪləfəʊn] Xylophon
n.

Z

Y

yacht ⚓ [jɒt] 1. (Segel-, Motor)Jacht *f*; (Renn)Segler *m*; 2. auf e-r Jacht fahren; segeln; **~club** ['jɒtklʌb] Segel-, Jachtklub *m*; **~ing** [~ɪŋ] Segelsport *m*; *attr.* Segel...

Yan·kee F ['jæŋkɪ] Yankee *m* (*Spitzname für Nordamerikaner*).

yap [jæp] (-pp-) kläffen; F quasseln; F meckern.

yard [jɑːd] Yard *n* (= 0,914 *m*); ⚓ Rah(e) *f*; Hof *m*; (Bau-, Stapel)Platz *m*; *Am.* Garten *m*; **~ measure** ['jɑːdmeʒə], **~stick** Yardstock *m*, -maß *n*.

yarn [jɑːn] Garn *n*; F Seemannsgarn *n*; abenteuerliche Geschichte.

yawl ⚓ [jɔːl] Jolle *f*.

yawn [jɔːn] 1. gähnen; 2. Gähnen *n*.

yea F [jeɪ] ja.

year [jɜː] Jahr *n*; **~ly** ['jɜːlɪ] jährlich.

yearn [jɜːn] sich sehnen (*for* nach); **~ing** ['jɜːnɪŋ] 1. Sehnen *n*, Sehnsucht *f*; 2. □ sehnsüchtig.

yeast [jiːst] Hefe *f*; Schaum *m*.

yell [jel] 1. (gellend) schreien; aufschreien; 2. (gellender) Schrei; Anfeuerungs-, Schlachtruf *m*.

yel·low ['jeləʊ] 1. gelb; F hasenfüßig (*feig*); Sensations...; 2. Gelb *n*; 3. (sich) gelb färben; **~ed** vergilbt; **~ fe·ver** 🩺 Gelbfieber *n*; **~ish** [~ɪʃ] gelblich; **~ pag·es** *pl. teleph.* die gelben Seiten, Branchenverzeichnis *n*.

yelp [jelp] 1. (auf)jaulen (*Hund etc.*); aufschreien; 2. (Auf)Jaulen *n*; Aufschrei *m*.

yeo·man ['jəʊmən] (*pl.* -men) freier Bauer.

yep F [jep] ja.

yes [jes] 1. ja; doch; 2. Ja *n*.

yes·ter·day ['jestədɪ] gestern.

yet [jet] 1. *adv.* noch; schon (*in Fragen*); sogar; *as ~* bis jetzt; *not ~* noch nicht; 2. *cj.* aber (dennoch), doch.

yew 🌿 [juː] Eibe *f*.

yield [jiːld] 1. *v/t.* (ein-, hervor)bringen; *Gewinn* abwerfen; *v/i.* ♪ tragen; sich fügen, nachgeben; 2. Ertrag *m*; **~ing** □ ['jiːldɪŋ] nachgebend; *fig.* nachgiebig.

yip·pee *int.* F [jɪ'piː] hurra!

yo·del ['jəʊdl] 1. Jodler *m*; 2. (*bsd. Brt.* -ll-, *Am.* -l-) jodeln.

yoke [jəʊk] 1. Joch *n* (*a. fig.*); Paar *n* (*Ochsen*); Schultertrage *f*; 2. an-, zusammenspannen; *fig.* paaren (*to* mit).

yolk [jəʊk] (Ei)Dotter *m*, *n*, Eigelb *n*.

yon [jɒn], **~der** *lit.* ['jɒndə] da *od.* dort drüben.

yore [jɔː]: *of ~* ehemals, ehedem.

you [juː; jʊ] du, ihr, Sie; man.

young [jʌŋ] 1. □ jung; jung, klein; 2. (Tier)Junge *pl.*; *the ~* die jungen Leute, die Jugend; *with ~* trächtig; **~ster** ['jʌŋstə] Junge *m*.

your [jɔː] dein(e), euer(e), Ihr(e); **~s** [jɔːz] deine(r, -s), euer, euere(s), Ihre(r, -s); ♀, *Bill Briefschluß:* Dein Bill; **~self** [jɔː'self] (*pl.* **yourselves** [~vz]) du, ihr, Sie selbst; dir, dich, euch, sich; *by ~* allein.

youth [juːθ] (*pl.* **~s** [~ðz]) Jugend *f*; junger Mann, Jüngling *m*; *~ hostel* Jugendherberge *f*; **~ful** □ ['juːθfl] jugendlich.

Yu·go·slav ['juːgəʊslɑːv] 1. jugoslawisch; 2. Jugoslaw|e *m*, -in *f*.

yule·tide *bsd. poet.* ['juːltaɪd] Weihnachten *n*, Weihnachtszeit *f*.

Z

zeal [ziːl] Eifer *m*; **~ot** ['zelət] Eiferer *m*; **~ous** □ ['zeləs] eifrig; eifrig bedacht (*for auf acc.*); innig, heiß.

ze·bra *zo.* ['ziːbrə] Zebra *n*; **~ cross·ing** ['zebrə-] Zebrastreifen *m* (*Fußgängerübergang*).

zen·ith ['zenɪθ] Zenit *m*; *fig.* Höhepunkt *m*.

ze·ro ['zɪərəʊ] 1. (*pl.* -ros, -roes) Null *f*; Nullpunkt *m*; 2. Null...; ~ (*economic*) *growth* Nullwachstum *n*; ~ *option pol.* Nullösung *f*; *have* ~

interest in s.th. F null Bock auf et.
haben.

zest [zest] **1.** Würze *f* (*a. fig.*); Lust *f*,
Freude *f*; Genuß *m*; **2.** würzen.

zig·zag ['zɪgzæg] **1.** Zickzack *m*;
Zickzacklinie *f*, -kurs *m*, -weg *m*; **2.**
im Zickzack laufen *od.* fahren *etc.*

zinc [zɪŋk] **1.** *min.* Zink *n*; **2.** verzin-
ken.

zip [zɪp] **1.** Schwirren *n*; F Schwung
m; = *zip-fastener*; **2.** (*-pp-*): ~ *s.th.*
open den Reißverschluß von et.öff-
nen; ~ *s.o. up* j-m den Reißverschluß zumachen; ~ **code** *Am.* Post-
leitzahl *f*; ~**·fas·ten·er** *bsd. Brt.*

['zɪpfɑːsnə], ~**·per** *Am.* [~ə] Reißverschluß *m.*

zo·di·ac *ast.* ['zəʊdɪæk] Tierkreis *m.*

zone [zəʊn] Zone *f*; *fig.* Gebiet *n.*

zoo [zuː] (*pl.* ~s) Zoo *m.*

zo·o·log·i·cal □ [zəʊə'lɒdʒɪkl] zoolo-
gisch; ~ *garden*(s) zoologischer Garten.

zo·ol·o·gy [zəʊ'ɒlədʒɪ] Zoologie *f.*

zoom [zuːm] **1.** surren; ✈ steil
hochziehen; F sausen; *phot.* Film:
zoomen; ~ *in on s.th. phot.* Film:
et. heranholen; ~ *past* F vorbei-
sausen; **2.** Surren *n*; ✈ Steilflug
m.

Z

APPENDIX

German Proper Names

Aachen ['ɑ:xən] *n* Aachen, Aix-la-Chapelle.

Adenauer ['ɑ:dənaʊər] *first chancellor of the German Federal Republic.*

Adler ['ɑ:dlər] *Austrian psychologist.*

Adria ['ɑ:dria] *f* Adriatic Sea.

Afrika ['ɑ:frika] *n* Africa.

Ägypten [ɛ'gyptən] *n* Egypt.

Albanien [al'bɑ:njən] *n* Albania.

Algerien [al'ge:rjən] *n* Algeria.

Algier ['alʒi:r] *n* Algiers.

Allgäu ['algɔʏ] *n* Al(l)gäu (*region of Bavaria*).

Alpen ['alpən] *pl.* Alps *pl.*

Amerika [a'me:rika] *n* America.

Anden ['andən] *pl.* the Andes *pl.*

Antillen [an'tilən] *f/pl.* Antilles *pl.*

Antwerpen [ant'verpən] *n* Antwerp.

Apenninen [ape'ni:nən] *m/pl.* Apennines *pl.*

Argentinien [argen'ti:njən] *n* Argentina, the Argentine.

Ärmelkanal ['ɛrməlkanɑ:l] *m* English Channel.

Asien ['ɑ:zjən] *n* Asia.

Athen [a'te:n] *n* Athens.

Äthiopien [eti'o:pjən] Ethiopia.

Atlantik [at'lantik] *m* Atlantic.

Australien [aʊ'strɑ:ljən] *n* Australia.

Bach [bax] *German composer.*

Baden-Württemberg ['bɑ:dən-'vyrtəmberk] *n* Land of the German Federal Republic.

Barlach ['barlax] *German sculptor.*

Basel ['bɑ:zəl] *n* Bâle, Basle.

Bayern ['baɪərn] *n* Bavaria (*Land of the German Federal Republic*).

Becher ['beçər] *German poet.*

Beckmann ['bɛkman] *German painter.*

Beethoven ['be:tho:fən] *German composer.*

Belgien ['bɛlgjən] *n* Belgium.

Belgrad ['bɛlgrɑ:t] *n* Belgrade.

Berg [berk] *Austrian composer.*

Berlin [ber'li:n] *n* Berlin.

Bermuda-Inseln [ber'mu:daⁱnzəln] *f/pl.* Bermudas *pl.*

Bern [bern] *n* Bern(e).

Bismarck ['bismark] *German statesman.*

Bloch [blɔx] *German philosopher.*

Böcklin ['bœkli:n] *German painter.*

Bodensee ['bo:dənze:] *m* Lake of Constance.

Böhm [bø:m] *Austrian conductor.*

Böhmen ['bø:mən] *n* Bohemia.

Böll [bœl] *German author.*

Bonn [bɔn] *n capital of the German Federal Republic.*

Brahms [brɑ:ms] *German composer.*

Brandt [brant] *German politician.*

Brasilien [bra'zi:ljən] *n* Brazil.

Braunschweig ['braʊnʃvaık] *n* Brunswick.

Brecht [brɛçt] *German dramatist.*

Bremen ['bre:mən] *n* Land of the German Federal Republic.

Bruckner ['bruknər] *Austrian composer.*

Brüssel ['brysəl] *n* Brussels.

Budapest ['bu:dapɛst] *n* Budapest.

Bukarest ['bu:karɛst] *n* Bucharest.

Bulgarien [bul'gɑ:rjən] *n* Bulgaria.

Calais [ka'lɛ] *n*: Straße von ∼ Straits of Dover.

Calvin [kal'vi:n] *Swiss religious reformer.*

Chile ['tʃi:lə] *n* Chile.

China ['çi:na] *n* China.

Christus ['kristus] *m* Christ.

Daimler ['daımlər] *German inventor.*

Dänemark ['dɛ:nəmark] *n* Denmark.

Deutschland ['dɔʏtʃlant] *n* Germany.

Diesel ['di:zəl] *German inventor.*

Döblin [dø'bli:n] *German author.*

Dolomiten [dolo'mi:tən] *pl.* the Dolomites *pl.*

Donau ['do:naʊ] *f* Danube.

Dortmund ['dɔrtmunt] *n industrial city in West Germany.*

Dresden ['dre:sdən] *n capital of Saxony.*

Dublin ['dʌblin] *n Dublin.*

Dünkirchen ['dy:nkirçən] *n Dunkirk.*

Dürer ['dy:rər] *German painter.*

Dürrenmatt ['dyrənmat] *Swiss dramatist.*

Düsseldorf ['dysəldɔrf] *n capital of North Rhine-Westphalia.*

Ebert ['e:bərt] *first president of the Weimar Republic.*

Egk [ɛk] *German composer.*

Eichendorff ['aiçəndɔrf] *German poet.*

Eiger ['aigər] *Swiss mountain.*

Einstein ['ainʃtain] *German physicist.*

Elbe ['ɛlbə] *f German river.*

Elsaß ['ɛlzas] *n Alsace.*

Engels ['ɛŋəls] *German philosopher.*

England ['ɛŋlant] *n England.*

Essen ['ɛsən] *n industrial city in West Germany.*

Europa [ɔʏ'ro:pa] *n Europe.*

Feldberg ['fɛltbɛrk] *German mountain.*

Finnland ['finlant] *n Finland.*

Florenz [flo'rɛnts] *n Florence.*

Fontane [fɔn'ta:nə] *German author.*

Franken ['fraŋkən] *n Franconia.*

Frankfurt ['fraŋkfurt] *n Frankfort.*

Frankreich ['fraŋkraiç] *n France.*

Freud [frɔʏt] *Austrian psychologist.*

Frisch [friʃ] *Swiss author.*

Garmisch ['garmiʃ] *n health resort in Bavaria.*

Genf [gɛnf] *n Geneva; ~er See m Lake of Geneva.*

Genua ['ge:nua] *n Genoa.*

Gibraltar [gi'braltar] *n Gibraltar.*

Goethe ['gøːtə] *German poet.*

Grass [gras] *German author.*

Graubünden [grau'byndən] *n the Grisons.*

Griechenland ['griːçənlant] *n Greece.*

Grillparzer ['grilpartsər] *Austrian dramatist.*

Grönland ['grøːnlant] *n Greenland.*

Gropius ['groːpjus] *German architect.* [Great Britain.\]

Großbritannien [groːsbri'tanjən] *n*

Großglockner [groːs'glɔknər] *Austrian mountain.*

Grünewald ['gryːnəvalt] *German painter.*

Haag [haːk]: *Den ~ The Hague.*

Habsburg *hist.* ['haːpsburk] *n Hapsburg (German dynasty).*

Hahn [haːn] *German chemist.*

Hamburg ['hamburk] *n Land of the German Federal Republic.*

Händel ['hɛndəl] *Handel (German composer).*

Hannover [ha'noːfər] *n Hanover (capital of Lower Saxony).*

Hartmann ['hartman] *German composer.*

Harz [haːrts] *m Harz Mountains pl.*

Hauptmann ['hauptman] *German dramatist.*

Haydn ['haidən] *Austrian composer.*

Hegel ['heːgəl] *German philosopher.*

Heidegger ['haidegər] *German philosopher.*

Heidelberg ['haidəlbɛrk] *n university town in West Germany.*

Heine ['hainə] *German poet.*

Heinemann ['hainəman] *president of the German Federal Republic.*

Heisenberg ['haizənbɛrk] *German physicist.*

Heißenbüttel ['haisənbytəl] *German poet.*

Helgoland ['hɛlgolant] *n Heligoland.*

Helsinki ['hɛlziŋki] *n Helsinki.*

Henze ['hɛntsə] *German composer.*

Hesse ['hɛsə] *German poet.*

Hessen ['hɛsən] *n Hesse (Land of the German Federal Republic).*

Heuß [hɔʏs] *first president of the German Federal Republic.*

Hindemith ['hindəmit] *German composer.*

Hohenzollern *hist.* [hoːən'tsɔlərn] *n German dynasty.*

Hölderlin ['hœldərliːn] *German poet.*

Holland ['hɔlant] *n Holland.*

Indien ['indjən] *n India.*

Inn [in] *m affluent of the Danube.*

Innsbruck ['insbruk] *n capital of the Tyrol.*

Irak [i'raːk] *m Iraq, a. Irak.*

Irland ['irlant] *n Ireland.*

Island ['iːslant] *n Iceland.*

Israel ['israɛl] *n Israel.*

Italien [i'taːljən] *n Italy.*

Japan ['ja:pan] *n* Japan.

Jaspers ['jaspərs] *German philosopher*.

Jesus ['je:zus] *m* Jesus.

Jordanien [jɔr'da:njən] *n* Jordan.

Jugoslawien [jugo'sla:vjən] *n* Yugoslavia.

Jung [juŋ] *Swiss psychologist*.

Jungfrau ['juŋfrau] *f Swiss mountain*.

Kafka ['kafka] *Czech author*.

Kanada ['kanada] *n* Canada.

Kant [kant] *German philosopher*.

Karajan ['ka:rajan] *Austrian conductor*.

Karlsruhe [karls'ru:ə] *n city in South-Western Germany*.

Kärnten ['kɛrntən] *n* Carinthia.

Kassel ['kasəl] *n* Cassel.

Kästner ['kɛstnər] *German author*.

Kiel [ki:l] *n capital of Schleswig-Holstein*.

Kiesinger ['ki:ziŋər] *German politician*.

Klee [kle:] *Swiss-born painter*.

Kleist [klaist] *German poet*.

Klemperer ['klɛmpərər] *German conductor*.

Koblenz ['ko:blɛnts] *n* Coblenz, Koblenz.

Kokoschka [ko'kɔʃka] *Austrian painter*.

Köln [kœln] *n* Cologne.

Kolumbien [ko'lumbjən] *n* Columbia.

Kolumbus [ko'lumbus] *m* Columbus.

Königsberg ['kø:niçsbɛrk] *n capital of East Prussia*.

Konstanz ['kɔnstants] *n* Constance.

Kopenhagen [kopən'ha:gən] *n* Copenhagen.

Kordilleren [kɔrdil'je:rən] *f/pl. the* Cordilleras *pl*.

Kreml ['kre:məl] *m the* Kremlin.

Leibniz ['laibnits] *German philosopher*.

Leipzig ['laiptsiç] *n* Leipsic.

Lessing ['lesiŋ] *German poet*.

Libanon ['li:banɔn] *m* Lebanon.

Liebig ['li:biç] *German chemist*.

Lissabon ['lisabɔn] *n* Lisbon.

London ['lɔndɔn] *n* London.

Lothringen ['lo:triŋən] *n* Lorraine.

Lübeck ['ly:bɛk] *n city in West Germany*.

Luther ['lutər] *German religious reformer*.

Luxemburg ['luksəmburk] *n* Luxemb(o)urg.

Luzern [lu'tsɛrn] *n* Lucerne.

Maas [ma:s] *f* Meuse.

Madrid [ma'drit] *n* Madrid.

Mahler ['ma:lər] *Austrian composer*.

Mailand ['mailant] *n* Milan.

Main [main] *m German river*.

Mainz [maints] *n* Mayence (*capital of Rhineland-Palatinate*).

Mann [man] *name of three German authors*.

Marokko [ma'rɔko] *n* Morocco.

Marx [marks] *German philosopher*.

Matterhorn ['matərhɔrn] *Swiss mountain*.

Meißen ['maisən] *n* Meissen.

Meitner ['maitnər] *Austrian-born female physicist*.

Memel ['me:məl] *f frontier river in East Prussia*.

Menzel ['mɛntsəl] *German painter*.

Mexiko ['mɛksiko] *n* Mexico.

Mies van der Rohe ['mi:sfandər-'ro:ə] *German architect*.

Mittelamerika ['mitəlʔa'me:rika] *n* Central America.

Mitteleuropa ['mitəlʔɔʏ'ro:pa] *n* Central Europe.

Mittelmeer ['mitəlme:r] *n* Mediterranean (Sea).

Moldau ['mɔldau] *f Bohemian river*.

Mörike ['mø:rikə] *German poet*.

Mosel ['mo:zəl] *f* Moselle.

Mössbauer ['mœsbauər] *German physicist*.

Moskau ['mɔskau] *n* Moscow.

Mozart ['mo:tsart] *Austrian composer*.

München ['mynçən] *n* Munich (*capital of Bavaria*).

Neapel [ne'a:pəl] *n* Naples.

Neisse ['naisə] *f German river*.

Neufundland [nɔʏ'funtlant] *n* Newfoundland.

Neuseeland [nɔʏ'ze:lant] *n* New Zealand.

Niederlande ['ni:dərlandə] *n/pl. the* Netherlands *pl*.

Niedersachsen ['ni:dərzaksən] *n* Lower Saxony (*Land of the German Federal Republic*).

Nietzsche ['ni:tʃə] *German philosopher*.

Nil [ni:l] *m* Nile.
Nordamerika ['nɔrtªaˈmeːrika] *n* North America.
Nordrhein-Westfalen ['nɔrtraɪnvestˈfaːlən] *n* North Rhine-Westphalia (*Land of the German Federal Republic*).
Nordsee ['nɔrtzeː] *f* German Ocean, North Sea.
Norwegen ['nɔrveːgən] *n* Norway.
Nürnberg ['nyrnberk] *n* Nuremberg.

Oder ['oːdər] *f* German river.
Orff [ɔrf] *German composer*.
Oslo ['ɔslo] *n* Oslo.
Ostasien ['ɔstˈaːzjən] *n* Eastern Asia.
Ostende [ɔstˈendə] *n* Ostend.
Österreich ['øːstəraɪç] *n* Austria.
Ostsee ['ɔstzeː] *f* Baltic.

Palästina [paleˈstiːna] *n* Palestine.
Paris [paˈriːs] *n* Paris.
Persien ['perzjən] *n* Persia.
Pfalz [pfalts] *f* Palatinate.
Philippinen [filiˈpiːnən] *f/pl.* Philippine Islands *pl.*
Planck [plaŋk] *German physicist.*
Polen ['poːlən] *n* Poland.
Pommern ['pɔmərn] *n* Pomerania.
Porsche ['pɔrʃə] *German inventor.*
Portugal ['pɔrtugal] *n* Portugal.
Prag [praːg] *n* Prague.
Preußen *hist.* ['prɔysən] *n* Prussia.
Pyrenäen [pyreˈnɛːən] *pl.* Pyrenees *pl.*

Regensburg ['reːgənsburk] *n* Ratisbon.
Reykjavik ['raɪkjaviːk] *n* Reykjavik.
Rhein [raɪn] *m* Rhine.
Rheinland-Pfalz ['raɪnlantˈpfalts] *n* Rhineland-Palatinate (*Land of the German Federal Republic*).
Rilke ['rilkə] *Austrian poet.*
Rom [roːm] *n* Rome.
Röntgen ['rœntgən] *German physicist.*
Ruhr [ruːr] *f* German river; **Ruhrgebiet** ['ruːrgəbiːt] *n* industrial centre of West Germany.
Rumänien [ruˈmɛːnjən] *n* Ro(u)mania.
Rußland ['ruslant] *n* Russia.

Saale ['zaːlə] *f* German river.
Saar [zaːr] *f affluent of the Moselle;* **Saarbrücken** [zaːrˈbrykən] *n*

capital of the Saar; **Saarland** ['zaːrlant] *n* Saar (*Land of the German Federal Republic*).
Sachsen ['zaksən] *n* Saxony.
Scherchen ['ʃerçən] *German conductor.*
Schiller ['ʃilər] *German poet.*
Schlesien ['ʃleːzjən] *n* Silesia.
Schleswig-Holstein ['ʃleːsviçˈhɔlʃtaɪn] *n Land of the German Federal Republic.*
Schönberg ['ʃøːnberk] *Austrian composer.*
Schottland ['ʃɔtlant] *n* Scotland.
Schubert ['ʃuːbərt] *Austrian composer.* [*poser.*]
Schumann ['ʃuːman] *German com-*
Schwaben ['ʃvaːbən] *n* Swabia.
Schwarzwald ['ʃvartsvalt] *m* Black Forest.
Schweden ['ʃveːdən] *n* Sweden.
Schweiz [ʃvaɪts] *f:* die ~ Switzerland.
Sibirien [ziˈbiːrjən] *n* Siberia.
Siemens ['ziːməns] *German inventor.*
Sizilien [ziˈtsiːljən] *n* Sicily.
Skandinavien [skandiˈnaːvjən] *n* Scandinavia.
Sofia ['zɔfja] *n* Sofia.
Sowjetunion [zɔˈvjetⁱunjoːn] *f* the Soviet Union.
Spanien ['ʃpaːnjən] *n* Spain.
Spitzweg ['ʃpitsveːk] *German painter.* [*losopher.*]
Spranger ['ʃpraŋər] *German phi-*
Steiermark ['ʃtaɪərmark] *f* Styria.
Stifter ['ʃtiftər] *Austrian author.*
Stockholm ['ʃtɔkhɔlm] *n* Stockholm.
Storm [ʃtɔrm] *German poet.*
Strauß [ʃtraus] *Austrian composer.*
Strauss [ʃtraus] *German composer.*
Stresemann ['ʃtreːzəman] *German statesman.*
Stuttgart ['ʃtutgart] *n capital of Baden-Württemberg.*
Südamerika ['zyːtˈaˈmeːrika] *n* South America.
Sudan [zuˈdaːn] *m* S(o)udan.
Syrien ['zyːrjən] *n* Syria.

Themse ['tɛmzə] *f* Thames.
Thoma ['toːma] *German author.*
Thüringen ['tyːriŋən] *n* Thuringia.
Tirana [tiˈraːna] *n* Tirana.
Tirol [tiˈroːl] *n* the Tyrol.
Trakl ['traːkəl] *Austrian poet.*

Tschechoslowakei [tʃɛçoslovaˈkaɪ]
 f: die ~ Czechoslovakia.
Türkei [tyrˈkaɪ] *f*: die ~ Turkey.

Ungarn [ˈuŋgarn] *n* Hungary.
Ural [uˈraːl] *m* Ural (Mountains *pl.*).

Vatikan [vatiˈkaːn] *m the* Vatican.
Venedig [veˈneːdiç] *n* Venice.
Vereinigte Staaten [vərˈaɪniçtə ˈʃtaːtən] *m/pl. the* United States *pl.*
Vierwaldstätter See [fiːrˈvaltʃtɛtər ˈzeː] *m* Lake of Lucerne.

Wagner [ˈvaːgnər] *German composer.*
Wankel [ˈvaŋkəl] *German inventor.*
Warschau [ˈvarʃau] *n* Warsaw.

Weichsel [ˈvaɪksəl] *f* Vistula.
Weiß [vaɪs] *German dramatist.*
Weizsäcker [ˈvaɪtszɛkər] *German physicist.*
Werfel [ˈverfəl] *Austrian author.*
Weser [ˈveːzər] *f German river.*
Westdeutschland *pol.* [ˈvestdɔytʃlant] *n* West Germany.
Wien [viːn] *n* Vienna.
Wiesbaden [ˈviːsbaːdən] *n capital of Hesse.*

Zeppelin [ˈtsɛpəliːn] *German inventor.*
Zuckmayer [ˈtsukmaɪər] *German dramatist.*
Zweig [tsvaɪg] *Austrian author.*
Zürich [ˈtsyːriç] *n* Zurich.
Zypern [ˈtsyːpərn] *n* Cyprus.

German Abbreviations

a. a. O. *am angeführten Ort* in the place cited, *abbr.* loc. cit.; l. c.

Abb. *Abbildung* illustration.

Abf. *Abfahrt* departure, *abbr.* dep.

Abg. *Abgeordnete* Member of Parliament, *etc.*

Abk. *Abkürzung* abbreviation.

Abs. *Absatz* paragraph; *Absender* sender.

Abschn. *Abschnitt* paragraph, chapter. [dept.]

Abt. *Abteilung* department, *abbr.*

a. D. *außer Dienst* retired.

Adr. *Adresse* address.

AG *Aktiengesellschaft* joint-stock company, *Am.* (stock) corporation.

allg. *allgemein* general.

a. M. *am Main* on the Main.

Ank. *Ankunft* arrival.

Anm. *Anmerkung* note.

a. O. *an der Oder* on the Oder.

a. Rh. *am Rhein* on the Rhine.

Art. *Artikel* article.

atü *Atmosphärenüberdruck* atmospheric excess pressure.

Aufl. *Auflage* edition.

b. *bei* at; with; *with place names:* near, *abbr.* nr; care of, *abbr.* c/o.

Bd. *Band* volume, *abbr.* vol.; **Bde.** *Bände* volumes, *abbr.* vols.

beil. *beiliegend* enclosed.

Bem. *Bemerkung* note, comment, observation.

bes. *besonders* especially.

betr. *betreffend, betrifft, betreffs* concerning, respecting, regarding.

Betr. *Betreff, betrifft letter:* subject, re. [reference to.]

bez. *bezahlt* paid; *bezüglich* with

Bez. *Bezirk* district.

Bhf. *Bahnhof* station. [sionally.]

bisw. *bisweilen* sometimes, occa-

BIZ *Bank für Internationalen Zahlungsausgleich* Bank for International Settlements.

Bln. *Berlin* Berlin.

BRD *Bundesrepublik Deutschland* Federal Republic of Germany.

BRT *Bruttoregistertonnen* gross register tons.

b. w. *bitte wenden* please turn over, *abbr.* P.T.O.

bzw. *beziehungsweise* respectively.

C *Celsius* Celsius, *abbr.* C.

ca. *circa, ungefähr, etwa* about, approximately, *abbr.* c.

cbm *Kubikmeter* cubic met|re, *Am.* -er.

ccm *Kubikzentimeter* cubic centimet|re, *Am.* -er, *abbr.* c.c.

CDU *Christlich-Demokratische Union* Christian Democratic Union.

cm *Zentimeter* centimet|re, *Am.* -er.

Co. *Kompagnon* partner; *Kompanie* Company.

CSU *Christlich-Soziale Union* Christian Social Union.

d. Ä. *der Ältere* senior, *abbr.* sen.

DB *Deutsche Bundesbahn* German Federal Railway.

DDR *Deutsche Demokratische Republik* German Democratic Republic.

DGB *Deutscher Gewerkschaftsbund* Federation of German Trade Unions.

dgl. *dergleichen, desgleichen* the like.

d. Gr. *der Große* the Great.

d. h. *das heißt* that is, *abbr.* i. e.

d. i. *das ist* that is, *abbr.* i. e.

DIN, Din *Deutsche Industrie-Norm* (-en) German Industrial Standards.

Dipl. *Diplom* diploma.

d. J. *dieses Jahres* of this year; *der Jüngere* junior, *abbr.* jr, jun.

DM *Deutsche Mark* German Mark.

d. M. *dieses Monats* instant, *abbr.* inst.

do. *dito* ditto, *abbr.* do.

d. O. *der (die, das) Obige* the above-mentioned.

dpa, DPA *Deutsche Presse-Agentur* German Press Agency.

Dr. *Doktor* Doctor, *abbr.* Dr; ~ **jur.** *Doktor der Rechte* Doctor of Laws (LL.D.); ~ **med.** *Doktor der Me-*

dizin Doctor of Medicine (M.D.); ~ **phil.** *Doktor der Philosophie* Doctor of Philosophy (D. ph[il]., Ph. D.); ~ **theol.** *Doktor der Theologie* Doctor of Divinity (D. D.).

DRK *Deutsches Rotes Kreuz* German Red Cross.

dt(sch). *deutsch* German.

Dtz., Dtzd. *Dutzend* dozen.

d. Verf. *der Verfasser* the author.

ebd. *ebenda* in the same place.

ed. *edidit = hat (es) herausgegeben.*

eig., eigtl. *eigentlich* properly.

einschl. *einschließlich* including, inclusive, *abbr.* incl.

entspr. *entsprechend* corresponding.

Erl. *Erläuterung* explanation, (explanatory) note.

ev. *evangelisch* Protestant.

e. V. *eingetragener Verein* registered association, incorporated, *abbr.* inc.

evtl. *eventuell* perhaps, possibly.

EWG *Europäische Wirtschaftsgemeinschaft* European Economic Community, *abbr.* EEC.

exkl. *exklusive* except(ed), not included.

Expl. *Exemplar* copy.

Fa. *Firma* firm; *letter:* Messrs.

FDGB *Freier Deutscher Gewerkschaftsbund* Free Federation of German Trade Unions.

FDP *Freie Demokratische Partei* Liberal Democratic Party.

FD(-Zug) *Fernschnellzug* long-distance express.

ff. *sehr fein* extra fine; *folgende Seiten* following pages.

Forts. *Fortsetzung* continuation.

Fr. *Frau* Mrs.

frdl. *freundlich* kind.

Frl. *Fräulein* Miss.

g *Gramm* gram(me).

geb. *geboren* born; *geborene ...* née; *gebunden* bound.

Gebr. *Gebrüder* Brothers.

gef. *gefällig(st)* kind(ly).

gegr. *gegründet* founded.

geh. *geheftet* stitched.

gek. *gekürzt* abbreviated.

Ges. *Gesellschaft* association, company; society. [registered.]

ges. gesch. *gesetzlich geschützt*

gest. *gestorben* deceased.

gez. *gezeichnet* signed, *abbr.* sgd.

GmbH *Gesellschaft mit beschränkter Haftung* limited liability company, *abbr.* Ltd., *Am.* closed corporation under German law.

ha *Hektar* hectare.

Hbf. *Hauptbahnhof* central *or* main station.

Hbg. *Hamburg* Hamburg.

h. c. *honoris causa* = ehrenhalber *academic title:* honorary.

Hr., Hrn. *Herr(n)* Mr.

hrsg. *herausgegeben* edited, *abbr.* ed.

Hrsg. *Herausgeber* editor, *abbr.* ed.

i. *im, in* in.

i. A. *im Auftrage* for, by order, under instruction.

i. allg. *im allgemeinen* in general, generally speaking.

i. Durchschn. *im Durchschnitt* on an average. [sive.]

inkl. *inklusive, einschließlich* inclu-

i. J. *im Jahre* in the year.

Ing. *Ingenieur* engineer.

Inh. *Inhaber* proprietor.

'Interpol *Internationale Kriminalpolizei-Kommission* International Criminal Police Commission, *abbr.* ICPC. [substitute.]

i. V. *in Vertretung* by proxy, as a

Jb. *Jahrbuch* annual.

jr., jun. *junior, der Jüngere* junior *abbr.* jr, jun.

Kap. *Kapitel* chapter.

kath. *katholisch* Catholic.

Kfm. *Kaufmann* merchant.

kfm. *kaufmännisch* commercial.

Kfz. *Kraftfahrzeug* motor vehicle.

kg *Kilogramm* kilogram(me).

KG *Kommanditgesellschaft* limited partnership.

Kl. *Klasse* class; *school:* form.

km *Kilometer* kilomet|re, *Am.* -er.

'Kripo *Kriminalpolizei* Criminal Investigation Department, *abbr.* CID.

Kto. *Konto* account, *abbr.* a/c.

kW *Kilowatt* kilowatt, *abbr.* kw.

kWh *Kilowattstunde* kilowatt hour.

l *Liter* lit|re, *Am.* -er.

LDP *Liberal-Demokratische Partei* Liberal Democratic Party.

lfd. *laufend* current, running.

lfde. Nr. *laufende Nummer* consecutive number.

Lfg., Lfrg. *Lieferung* delivery; instalment, part.

Lit. *Literatur* literature.

Lkw. *Lastkraftwagen* lorry, truck.

lt. *laut* according to.

m *Meter* met|re, *Am*, -er.

m. A. n. *meiner Ansicht nach* in my opinion.

M. d. B. *Mitglied des Bundestages* Member of the Bundestag.

m. E. *meines Erachtens* in my opinion.

MEZ *mitteleuropäische Zeit* Central European Time.

mg *Milligramm* milligram(me[s]), *abbr.* mg.

Mill. *Million(en)* million(s).

mm *Millimeter* millimet|re, *Am*. -er.

möbl. *möbliert* furnished.

MP *Militärpolizei* Military Police.

mtl. *monatlich* monthly.

m. W. *meines Wissens* as far as I know.

N *Nord(en)* north.

nachm. *nachmittags* in the afternoon, *abbr.* p. m.

n. Chr. *nach Christus* after Christ, *abbr.* A. D.

n. J. *nächsten Jahres* of next year.

n. M. *nächsten Monats* of next month.

No., Nr. *Numero, Nummer* number, *abbr.* Nº.

NS *Nachschrift* postscript, *abbr.* P. S.

O *Ost(en)* east.

o. B. *ohne Befund* ✂ without findings.

od. *oder* or.

OEZ *osteuropäische Zeit* time of the East European zone.

OHG *Offene Handelsgesellschaft* ordinary partnership.

o. J. *ohne Jahr* no date.

p. Adr. *per Adresse* care of, *abbr.* c/o.

Pf *Pfennig German coin*: pfennig.

Pfd. *Pfund German weight*: pound.

PKW, Pkw. *Personenkraftwagen* (motor) car.

P. P. *praemissis praemittendis* omitting titles, to whom it may concern.

p.p., p.pa., ppa. *per procura* by proxy, *abbr.* per pro.

Prof. *Professor* professor.

PS *Pferdestärke(n)* horse-power, *abbr.* H.P., h.p.; *postscriptum, Nachschrift* postscript, *abbr.* P. S.

qkm *Quadratkilometer* square kilomet|re, *Am*. -er. [*Am*. -er.]

qm *Quadratmeter* square met|re,]

Reg. Bez. *Regierungsbezirk* administrative district.

Rel. *Religion* religion.

resp. *respektive* respectively.

S *Süd(en)* south.

S. *Seite* page.

s. *siehe* see, *abbr.* v., vid. (= *vide*).

s. a. *siehe auch* see also.

Sa. *Summa, Summe* sum, total.

s. d. *siehe dies* see this.

SED *Sozialistische Einheitspartei Deutschlands* United Socialist Party of Germany.

sen. *senior, der Ältere* senior.

sm *Seemeile* nautical mile.

s. o. *siehe oben* see above.

sog. *sogenannt* so-called.

SPD *Sozialdemokratische Partei Deutschlands* Social Democratic Party of Germany.

St. *Stück* piece; *Sankt* Saint.

St(d)., Stde. *Stunde* hour, *abbr.* h.

Str. *Straße* street, *abbr.* St.

s. u. *siehe unten* see below.

s. Z. *seinerzeit* at that time.

t *Tonne* ton.

tägl. *täglich* daily, per day.

Tel. *Telephon* telephone; *Telegramm* wire, cable.

TH *Technische Hochschule* technical university *or* college.

u. *und* and.

u. a. *und andere(s)* and others; *unter anderem or anderen* among other things, inter alia.

u. ä. *und ähnliche(s)* and the like.

U.A.w.g. *Um Antwort wird gebeten* an answer is requested, *répondez s'il vous plaît, abbr.* R.S.V.P.

u. dgl. (m.) *und dergleichen (mehr)* and the like.

u. d. M. *unter dem Meeresspiegel* below sea level; **ü. d. M.** *über dem Meeresspiegel* above sea level.

UdSSR *Union der Sozialistischen Sowjetrepubliken* Union of Soviet Socialist Republics.

u. E. *unseres Erachtens* in our opinion. [following.]

u. f., u. ff. *und folgende* and the]

UKW *Ultrakurzwelle* ultra-short wave, very high frequency, *abbr.* VHF.

U/min. *Umdrehungen in der Minute* revolutions per minute, *abbr.* r.p.m.

urspr. *ursprünglich* original(ly).

US(A) *Vereinigte Staaten (von Amerika)* United States (of America).

usw. *und so weiter* and so on, *abbr.* etc. [stances permitting.]

u. U. *unter Umständen* circum-]

v. *von, vom* of; from; by.

V *Volt* volt; *Volumen* volume.

V. *Vers* line, verse.

v. Chr. *vor Christus* before Christ, *abbr.* B. C.

VEB *Volkseigener Betrieb* People's Own Undertaking.

Verf., Vf. *Verfasser* author.

Verl. *Verlag* publishing firm; *Verleger* publisher.

vgl. *vergleiche* confer, *abbr.* cf.

v.g.u. *vorgelesen, genehmigt, unterschrieben* read, confirmed, signed.

v. H. *vom Hundert* per cent.

v. J. *vorigen Jahres* of last year.

v. M. *vorigen Monats* of last month.

vorm. *vormittags* in the morning, *abbr.* a. m.; *vormals* formerly.

Vors. *Vorsitzender* chairman.

v. T. *vom Tausend* per thousand.

VW *Volkswagen* Volkswagen, People's Car.

W *West(en)* west; *Watt* watt(s).

WE *Wärmeeinheit* thermal unit.

WEZ *westeuropäische Zeit* Western European time (Greenwich time).

WGB *Weltgewerkschaftsbund* World Federation of Trade Unions, *abbr.* WFTU.

Wwe. *Witwe* widow.

Z. *Zahl* number; *Zeile* line.

z. *zu, zum, zur* at; to.

z. B. *zum Beispiel* for instance, *abbr.* e. g.

z. H(d). *zu Händen* attention of, to be delivered to, care of, *abbr.* c/o.

z. S. *zur See* of the navy.

z. T. *zum Teil* partly.

Ztg. *Zeitung* newspaper.

Ztr. *Zentner* centner.

Ztschr. *Zeitschrift* periodical.

zus. *zusammen* together.

zw. *zwischen* between; among.

z. Z(t). *zur Zeit* at the time, at present, for the time being.

American and British Proper Names

Aberdeen [æbə'di:n] *Stadt in Schottland.*
Adam ['ædəm] *Adam m.*
Adelaide ['ædəleɪd] *Stadt in Australien.*
Aden ['eɪdn] *Hauptstadt des Südjemen.*
Africa ['æfrɪkə] *Afrika n.*
Aix-la-Chapelle ['eɪksla:ʃæ'pel] *Aachen n.*
Alabama [ælə'bæmə] *Staat der USA.*
Alaska [ə'læskə] *Staat der USA.*
Alberta [æl'bɜːtə] *Provinz in Kanada.*
Alderney ['ɔːldənɪ] *e-e der Kanalinseln.*
Alleghany ['ælɪgeɪnɪ] *Fluß u. Gebirge in USA.*
Alsace [æl'sæs] *Elsaß n.*
America [ə'merɪkə] *Amerika n.*
Andes ['ændiːz] *die Anden.*
Andrew ['ændruː] *Andreas m.*
Ann(e) [æn] *Anna f.*
Anthony ['æntənɪ, 'ænθənɪ] *Anton m.*
Antilles [æn'tɪliːz] *die Antillen.*
Appalachians [æpə'leɪtʃjənz] *die Appalachen (Gebirge in USA).*
Arizona [ærɪ'zəʊnə] *Staat der USA.*
Arkansas ['ɑːkənsɔː] *Fluß u. Staat der USA.*
Arlington ['ɑːlɪŋtən] *Nationalfriedhof bei Washington.*
Ascot ['æskət] *Stadt in England mit berühmter Rennbahn.*
Asia ['eɪʃə] *Asien n.*
Athens ['æθɪnz] *Athen n.*
Atlantic [ət'læntɪk] *der Atlantik.*
Auckland ['ɔːklənd] *Hafenstadt in Neuseeland.*
Austen ['ɒstɪn] *engl. Autorin.*
Australia [ɒ'streɪljə] *Australien n.*
Austria ['ɒstrɪə] *Österreich n.*
Avon ['eɪvən] *Fluß u. Grafschaft in England.*
Azores [ə'zɔːz] *die Azoren.*

Bahamas [bə'hɑːməz] *die Bahamainseln.*

Balkans ['bɔːlkənz] *der Balkan.*
Balmoral [bæl'mɒrəl] *Königsschloß in Schottland.*
Basle [bɑːl] *Basel n.*
Baltimore ['bɔːltɪmɔː] *Hafenstadt in USA.*
Bath [bɑːθ] *Badeort in England.*
Bavaria [bə'veərɪə] *Bayern n.*
Bedfordshire ['bedfədʃə] *Grafschaft in England.*
Belfast [bel'fɑːst] *Hauptstadt von Nordirland.*
Belgium ['beldʒəm] *Belgien n.*
Ben Nevis [ben'nevɪs] *höchster Berg in Großbritannien.*
Berkshire ['bɑːkʃə] *Grafschaft in England.*
Berlin [bɜː'lɪn] *Berlin n.*
Bermudas [bə'mjuːdəz] *die Bermudainseln.*
Bern(e) [bɜːn] *Bern n.*
Bess(ie) ['bes(ɪ)] *Kurzform von Elizabeth.*
Bill(y) ['bɪl(ɪ)] *Kurzform von William.*
Birmingham ['bɜːmɪŋəm] *Industriestadt in England.*
Bob [bɒb] *Kurzform von Robert.*
Boston ['bɒstən] *Stadt in USA.*
Bournemouth ['bɔːnməθ] *Seebad in England.*
Bridget ['brɪdʒɪt] *Brigitte f.*
Brighton ['braɪtn] *Seebad in England.*
Bristol ['brɪstl] *Hafenstadt in England.*
British Columbia ['brɪtɪʃ kə'lʌmbɪə] *Provinz in Kanada.*
Britten ['brɪtn] *engl. Komponist.*
Brontë ['brɒntɪ] *Name dreier engl. Autorinnen.*
Brooklyn ['brʊklɪn] *Stadtteil von New York.*
Brussels ['brʌslz] *Brüssel n.*
Buckingham Palace ['bʌkɪŋəm 'pælɪs] *Königsschloß in London.*
Buckinghamshire ['bʌkɪŋəm[ʃə] *Grafschaft in England.*
Buddha ['bʊdə] *Buddha m.*
Burma ['bɜːmə] *Birma n.*
Burns [bɜːnz] *schott. Dichter.*
Byron ['baɪərən] *engl. Dichter.*

Calcutta [kælˈkʌtə] Kalkutta *n.*

California [kæliˈfɔːnjə] Kalifornien *n* (*Staat der USA*).

Cambridge [ˈkeimbridʒ] **1.** *engl. Universitätsstadt*; **2.** *Stadt in USA, Sitz der Harvard-Universität*; **3.** *a.* ~**shire** [~ʃə] *Grafschaft in England.*

Canada [ˈkænədə] Kanada *n.*

Canary Islands [kəˈnɛəri ˈailəndz] *die* Kanarischen Inseln.

Canberra [ˈkænbərə] *Hauptstadt von Australien.*

Canterbury [ˈkæntəbəri] *Stadt in England, Erzbischofssitz.*

Capetown [ˈkeiptaun] Kapstadt *n.*

Cardiff [ˈkɑːdif] *Hauptstadt von Wales.*

Carinthia [kəˈrinθiə] Kärnten *n.*

Carlyle [kɑːˈlail] *schott. Autor.*

Carnegie [kɑːˈnegi] *amer. Industrieller.*

Caroline [ˈkærəlain] Karoline *f.*

Carrie [ˈkæri] *Kurzform von Caroline.*

Carter [ˈkɑːtə] *Präsident der USA.*

Catherine [ˈkæθərin] Katharina *f.*

Cecil [ˈsesl, ˈsisl] *männlicher Vorname.*

Cecilia [siˈsiljə], **Cecily** [ˈsisili, ˈsesili] Cäcilie *f.*

Ceylon [siˈlɒn] Ceylon *n.*

Chamberlain [ˈtʃeimbəlin] *Name mehrerer brit. Staatsmänner.*

Charlemagne [ˈʃɑːləmein] Karl der Große.

Charles [tʃɑːlz] Karl *m.*

Chaucer [ˈtʃɔːsə] *engl. Dichter.*

Cheshire [ˈtʃeʃə] *Grafschaft in England.*

Chesterfield [ˈtʃestəfiːld] *Industriestadt in England.*

Cheviot Hills [ˈtʃeviət ˈhilz] *Grenzgebirge zwischen England u. Schottland.*

Chicago [ʃiˈkɑːgəu] *Industriestadt in USA.*

China [ˈtʃainə] China *n.*

Churchill [ˈtʃɜːtʃil] *brit. Staatsmann.*

Cincinatti [sinsiˈnæti] *Stadt in USA.*

Cissie [ˈsisi] Cilli *f.*

Cleveland [ˈkliːvlənd] **1.** *Grafschaft in England*; **2.** *Industrie- u. Hafenstadt in USA.*

Clyde [klaid] *Fluß in Schottland.*

Coleridge [ˈkəuləridʒ] *engl. Dichter.*

Cologne [kəˈləun] Köln *n.*

Colorado [kɒləˈrɑːdəu] *Name zweier Flüsse u. Staat der USA.*

Columbia [kəˈlʌmbiə] *Fluß in USA.*

Connecticut [kəˈnetikət] *Fluß u. Staat der USA.*

Constance [ˈkɒnstəns] **1.** Konstanze *f*; **2.** Konstanz *n*; Lake ~ Bodensee *m.*

Cooper [ˈkuːpə] *amer. Autor.*

Copenhagen [kəupnˈheigən] Kopenhagen *n.*

Cordilleras [kɔːdiˈljeərəz] *die* Kordilleren (*amer. Gebirge*).

Cornwall [ˈkɔːnwəl] *Grafschaft in England.*

Coventry [ˈkɒvəntri] *Industriestadt in England.*

Cromwell [ˈkrɒmwəl] *engl. Staatsmann.*

Cumbria [ˈkʌmbriə] *Grafschaft in England.*

Cyprus [ˈsaiprəs] Zypern *n.*

Czechoslovakia [ˈtʃekəusləuˈvækiə] *die* Tschechoslowakei.

Dallas [ˈdæləs] *Stadt in USA.*

Daniel [ˈdænjəl] Daniel *m.*

Danube [ˈdænjuːb] Donau *f.*

Darwin [ˈdɑːwin] *engl. Naturforscher.*

David [ˈdeivid] David *m.*

Defoe [diˈfəu] *engl. Autor.*

Delaware [ˈdeləweə] *Fluß u. Staat der USA.*

Denmark [ˈdenmɑːk] Dänemark *n.*

Denver [ˈdenvə] *Stadt in USA.*

Derbyshire [ˈdɑːbiʃə] *Grafschaft in England.*

Detroit [dəˈtrɔit] *Industriestadt in USA.*

Devon(shire) [ˈdevn(ʃə)] *Grafschaft in England.*

Diana [daiˈænə] Diana *f.*

Dick [dik] *Kurzform von Richard.*

Dickens [ˈdikinz] *engl. Autor.*

Disraeli [disˈreili] *engl. Staatsmann.*

District of Columbia [ˈdistrikt əv kəˈlʌmbiə] *Bezirk um Washington, Bundesdistrikt der USA.*

Dorset(shire) [ˈdɔːsit(ʃə)] *Grafschaft in England.*

Dover [ˈdəuvə] *Hafenstadt in England.*

Downing Street [ˈdauniŋ striːt] *Straße in London mit der Amtswohnung des Prime Minister.*

Doyle [dɔil] *schott. Autor.*

Dublin [ˈdʌblin] *Hauptstadt der Republik Irland.*

Dunkirk [dʌnˈkɜːk] Dünkirchen *n.*

Durham ['dʌrəm] *Grafschaft in England.*

East Sussex ['iːst 'sʌsɪks] *Grafschaft in England.*
Edinburgh ['edɪnbərə] Edinburg *n.*
Edison ['edɪsn] *amer. Erfinder.*
Egypt ['iːdʒɪpt] Ägypten *n.*
Eire ['eərə] *irischer Name der Republik Irland.*
Eisenhower ['aɪznhaʊə] *Präsident der USA.*
Eliot ['eljət] **1.** *engl. Autorin;* **2.** *engl. Dichter, geboren in USA.*
Elizabeth [ɪ'lɪzəbəθ] Elisabeth *f.*
Emerson ['eməsn] *amer. Philosoph.*
England ['ɪŋglənd] England *n.*
Epsom ['epsəm] *Stadt in England mit Pferderennplatz.*
Erie ['ɪərɪ]: *Lake* ~ Eriesee *m (e-r der fünf Großen Seen Nordamerikas).*
Essex ['esɪks] *Grafschaft in England.*
Ethel ['eθl] *weiblicher Vorname.*
Ethiopia [iːθɪ'əʊpjə] Äthiopien *n.*
Eton ['iːtn] *berühmte Public School.*
Europe ['jʊərəp] Europa *n.*
Eve [iːv] Eva *f.*

Falkland Islands ['fɔːlklənd 'aɪləndz] *die Falklandinseln.*
Faulkner ['fɔːknə] *amer. Autor.*
Fawkes [fɔːks] *Haupt der Pulververschwörung (1605).*
Finland ['fɪnlənd] Finnland *n.*
Florida ['flɒrɪdə] *Staat der USA.*
Folkestone ['fəʊkstən] *Hafenstadt in England.*
Ford [fɔːd] **1.** *amer. Industrieller;* **2.** *Präsident der USA.*
France [frɑːns] Frankreich *n.*
Frances ['frɑːnsɪs] Franziska *f.*
Francis ['frɑːnsɪs] Franz *m.*
Franklin ['fræŋklɪn] *amer. Staatsmann u. Physiker.*

Gainsborough ['geɪnzbərə] *engl. Maler.*
Galveston(e) ['gælvɪstən] *Hafenstadt in USA.*
Geneva [dʒɪ'niːvə] Genf *n; Lake* ~ Genfer See *m.*
Geoffrey ['dʒefrɪ] Gottfried *m.*
George [dʒɔːdʒ] Georg *m.*
Georgia ['dʒɔːdʒjə] *Staat der USA.*
Germany ['dʒɜːmənɪ] Deutschland *n.*
Gershwin ['gɜːʃwɪn] *amer. Komponist.*

Gettysburg ['getɪzbɜːg] *Stadt in USA.*
Gibraltar [dʒɪ'brɔːltə] Gibraltar *n.*
Giles [dʒaɪlz] Julius *m.*
Gill [gɪl] *weiblicher Vorname.*
Gladstone ['glædstən] *brit. Staatsmann.*
Glasgow ['glɑːsgəʊ] *Hafenstadt in Schottland.*
Gloucester ['glɒstə] *Stadt in England; a.* ~**shire** [~ʃə] *Grafschaft in England.*
Great Britain ['greɪt 'brɪtn] Großbritannien *n.*
Greece [griːs] Griechenland *n.*
Greene [griːn] *engl. Autor.*
Greenland ['griːnlənd] Grönland *n.*
Greenwich ['grɪnɪdʒ] *Vorort von London.*
Guernsey ['gɜːnzɪ] *e-e der Kanalinseln.*
Guy [gaɪ] Guido *m,* Veit *m.*

Hague [heɪg]: *The* ~ Den Haag.
Halifax ['hælɪfæks] *Name zweier Städte in England u. Kanada.*
Hampshire ['hæmpʃə] *Grafschaft in England.*
Hanover ['hænəʊvə] Hannover *n.*
Harlem ['hɑːləm] *Stadtteil von New York.*
Harrow ['hærəʊ] *Nordwestl. Stadtbezirk Groß-Londons mit berühmter Public School.*
Harvard University ['hɑːvəd juːnɪ'vɜːsətɪ] *amer. Universität.*
Harwich ['hærɪdʒ] *Hafenstadt in England.*
Hawaii [hə'waɪiː] *Staat der USA.*
Hebrides ['hebrɪdiːz] *die Hebriden.*
Heligoland [he'lɪgəʊlænd] Helgoland *n.*
Helsinki ['helsɪŋkɪ] Helsinki *n.*
Hemingway ['hemɪŋweɪ] *amer. Autor.*
Henry ['henrɪ] Heinrich *m.*
Hereford and Worcester ['herɪfədən'wʊstə] *Grafschaft in England.*
Hertfordshire ['hɑːfədʃə] *Grafschaft in England.*
Hogarth ['həʊgɑːθ] *engl. Maler.*
Hollywood ['hɒlɪwʊd] *Filmstadt in Kalifornien, USA.*
Houston ['hjuːstən] *Stadt in USA.*
Hudson ['hʌdsn] *Fluß in USA.*
Hugh [hjuː] Hugo *m.*
Hull [hʌl] *Hafenstadt in England.*

Humberside [ˈhʌmbəsaɪd] *Grafschaft in England.*

Hungary [ˈhʌŋɡərɪ] *Ungarn n.*

Huron [ˈhjuːərən]: *Lake* ~ *Huronsee m (e-r der fünf Großen Seen Nordamerikas).*

Huxley [ˈhʌkslɪ] *engl. Autor.*

Iceland [ˈaɪslənd] *Island n.*

Idaho [ˈaɪdəhəʊ] *Staat der USA.*

Illinois [ɪlɪˈnɔɪ] *Fluß u. Staat der USA.*

India [ˈɪndjə] *Indien n.*

Indiana [ɪndɪˈænə] *Staat der USA.*

Indies [ˈɪndɪz]: *East* ~ *Ostindien n; West* ~ *Westindien n.*

Iowa [ˈaɪəʊə] *Staat der USA.*

Iran [ɪˈrɑːn] *Iran m.*

Iraq [ɪˈrɑːk] *Irak m.*

Ireland [ˈaɪələnd] *Irland n.*

Isle of Man [ˈaɪləvˈmæn] *Insel in der Irischen See.*

Isle of Wight [ˈaɪləvˈwaɪt] *Insel u. Grafschaft vor der Südküste Englands.*

Israel [ˈɪzreɪəl] *Israel n.*

Italy [ˈɪtəlɪ] *Italien n.*

Jack [dʒæk] *Kurzform von James.*

James [dʒeɪmz] *Jakob m.*

Jane [dʒeɪn] *Johanna f.*

Japan [dʒəˈpæn] *Japan n.*

Jefferson [ˈdʒefəsn] *Präsident der USA, Verfasser der Unabhängigkeitserklärung von 1776.*

Jeremy [ˈdʒerɪmɪ] *männlicher Vorname.*

Jersey [ˈdʒɜːzɪ] *e-e der Kanalinseln; ~ City Staat in USA.*

Jesus (Christ) [ˈdʒiːzəs (ˈkraɪst)] *Jesus (Christus) m.*

Jim [dʒɪm] *Kurzform von James.*

Joan [dʒəʊn] *Johanna f.*

Job [dʒəʊb] *Hiob m.*

Joe [dʒəʊ] *Kurzform von Joseph.*

John [dʒɒn] *Johann(es) m, Hans m.*

Johnson [ˈdʒɒnsn] 1. *engl. Autor;* 2. *Präsident der USA.*

Joseph [ˈdʒəʊzɪf] *Joseph m.*

Joule [dʒuːl] *engl. Physiker.*

Joyce [dʒɔɪs] *irischer Autor.*

Kansas [ˈkænzəs] *Fluß u. Staat der USA.*

Karachi [kəˈrɑːtʃɪ] *Hafenstadt in Pakistan.*

Kashmir [kæʃˈmɪə] *Kaschmir n.*

Kate [keɪt] *Käthe f.*

Keats [kiːts] *engl. Dichter.*

Kennedy [ˈkenɪdɪ] *Präsident der USA; ~ Airport Flughafen von New York.*

Kent [kent] *Grafschaft in England.*

Kentucky [kenˈtʌkɪ] *Fluß u. Staat der USA.*

King [kɪŋ] *amer. Bürgerrechtskämpfer.*

Kipling [ˈkɪplɪŋ] *engl. Dichter.*

Klondike [ˈklɒndaɪk] *Fluß u. Landschaft in Kanada u. Alaska.*

Kremlin [ˈkremlɪn] *der Kreml.*

Labrador [ˈlæbrədɔː] *Halbinsel Nordamerikas.*

Lancashire [ˈlæŋkəʃə] *Grafschaft in England.*

Lancaster [ˈlæŋkəstə] *Name zweier Städte in England u. USA; s. Lancashire.*

Lawrence [ˈlɒrəns] *engl. Autor.*

Lebanon [ˈlebənən] *der Libanon.*

Leeds [liːdz] *Industriestadt in England.*

Leicester [ˈlestə] *Stadt in England; a. ~shire* [~ʃə] *Grafschaft in England.*

Leslie [ˈlezlɪ] *männlicher u. weiblicher Vorname.*

Lewis [ˈluːɪs] *Ludwig m.*

Libya [ˈlɪbɪə] *Libyen n.*

Lincoln [ˈlɪŋkən] 1. *Präsident der USA;* 2. *Stadt in USA;* 3. *Stadt in England;* 4. *a. ~shire* [~ʃə] *Grafschaft in England.*

Lisbon [ˈlɪzbən] *Lissabon n.*

Liverpool [ˈlɪvəpuːl] *Hafen- u. Industriestadt in England.*

London [ˈlʌndən] 1. *London n;* 2. *amer. Autor.*

Los Angeles [lɒsˈændʒɪliːz] *Stadt in USA.*

Louisiana [luːiːzɪˈænə] *Staat der USA.*

Lucerne [luːˈsɜːn] *Luzern n; Lake of* ~ *Vierwaldstätter See m.*

Luxembourg [ˈlʌksəmbɜːɡ] *Luxemburg n.*

Mabel [ˈmeɪbl] *weiblicher Vorname.*

Mackenzie [məˈkenzɪ] *Strom in Nordamerika.*

Madge [mædʒ] *weiblicher Vorname.*

Madrid [məˈdrɪd] *Madrid n.*

Maine [meɪn] *Staat der USA.*

Malta [ˈmɔːltə] *Malta n.*

Manchester [ˈmæntʃɪstə] *Industriestadt u. Grafschaft in England.*

Manhattan [mæn'hætn] *Stadtteil von New York.*

Manitoba [mænɪ'təʊbə] *Provinz in Kanada.*

Margaret ['mɑːgərɪt] Margarete *f.*

Mark [mɑːk] Markus *m.*

Mary ['meərɪ] Maria *f.*

Maryland ['meərɪlænd] *Staat der USA.*

Massachusetts [mæsə'tʃuːsɪts] *Staat der USA.*

Mat(h)ilda [mə'tɪldə] Mathilde *f.*

Ma(t)thew ['mæθjuː] Matthäus *m.*

Maud [mɔːd] *Kurzform von Mat(h)ilda.*

Maugham [mɔːm] *engl. Autor.*

Maurice ['mɒrɪs] Moritz *m.*

May [meɪ] *Kurzform von Mary.*

Melbourne ['melbən] *Stadt in Australien.*

Merseyside ['mɜːzɪsaɪd] *Grafschaft in England.*

Miami [maɪ'æmɪ] *Badeort in Florida, USA.*

Michigan ['mɪʃɪgən] *Staat der USA;* **Lake ~** Michigansee *m (e-r der fünf Großen Seen Nordamerikas).*

Miller ['mɪlə] *amer. Dramatiker.*

Millicent ['mɪlɪsnt] *weiblicher Vorname.*

Milton ['mɪltən] *engl. Dichter.*

Milwaukee [mɪl'wɔːkiː] *Stadt in USA.*

Minneapolis [mɪnɪ'æpəlɪs] *Stadt in USA.*

Minnesota [mɪnɪ'səʊtə] *Staat der USA.*

Mississippi [mɪsɪ'sɪpɪ] *Strom u. Staat der USA.*

Missouri [mɪ'zʊərɪ] *Fluß u. Staat der USA.*

Mohammed [məʊ'hæmed] Mohammed *m.*

Monroe [mən'rəʊ] **1.** *Präsident der USA;* **2.** *amer. Filmschauspielerin.*

Montana [mɒn'tænə] *Staat der USA.*

Montgomery [mənt'gʌmərɪ] *brit. Feldmarschall.*

Montreal [mɒntrɪ'ɔːl] *Stadt in Kanada.*

Moore [mʊə] *engl. Bildhauer.*

Morocco [mə'rɒkəʊ] Marokko *n.*

Moscow ['mɒskəʊ] Moskau *n.*

Moselle [məʊ'zel] Mosel *f.*

Munich ['mjuːnɪk] München *n.*

Nancy ['nænsɪ] *weiblicher Vorname.*

Nebraska [nɪ'bræskə] *Staat der USA.*

Nelson ['nelsn] *engl. Admiral.*

Netherlands ['neðələndz] *die Niederlande.*

Nevada [ne'vɑːdə] *Staat der USA.*

New Brunswick [njuː'brʌnzwɪk] *Provinz in Kanada.*

Newcastle ['njuːkɑːsl] *Hafenstadt in England.*

New Delhi [njuː'delɪ] *Hauptstadt von Indien.*

New England [njuː'ɪŋglənd] Neuengland *n.*

Newfoundland ['njuːfəndlənd] Neufundland *n.*

New Hampshire [njuː'hæmpʃə] *Staat der USA.*

New Jersey [njuː'dʒɜːzɪ] *Staat der USA.*

New Mexico [njuː'meksɪkəʊ] Neumexiko *n (Staat der USA).*

New Orleans [njuː'ɔːlɪəns] *Hafenstadt in USA.*

Newton ['njuːtn] *engl. Physiker.*

New York [njuː'jɔːk] *Stadt u. Staat der USA.*

New Zealand [njuː'ziːlənd] Neuseeland *n.*

Niagara [naɪ'ægərə] Niagara *m (Fluß zwischen Erie- u. Ontariosee).*

Nicholas ['nɪkələs] Nikolaus *m.*

Nixon ['nɪksən] *Präsident der USA.*

Norfolk ['nɔːfək] *Grafschaft in England.*

Northampton [nɔː'θæmptən] *Stadt in England; a.* **~shire** [~ʃə] *Grafschaft in England.*

North Carolina ['nɔːθ kærə'laɪnə] Nordkarolina *n (Staat der USA).*

North Dakota ['nɔːθ də'kəʊtə] Norddakota *n (Staat der USA).*

Northumberland [nɔː'θʌmbələnd] *Grafschaft in England.*

Northwest Territories [nɔː'θwest 'terɪtərɪz] Nordwestterritorien *pl. (Kanada).*

North Yorkshire ['nɔːθ 'jɔːkʃə] *Grafschaft in England.*

Norway ['nɔːweɪ] Norwegen *n.*

Norwich ['nɒrɪdʒ] *Stadt in England.*

Nottingham ['nɒtɪŋəm] *Stadt in England; a.* **~shire** [~ʃə] *Grafschaft in England.*

Nova Scotia ['nəʊvə'skəʊʃə] *Provinz in Kanada.*

Oceania [əʊʃɪ'eɪnjə] Ozeanien *n.*

Ohio [əʊˈhaɪəʊ] *Fluß u. Staat der USA.*

Oklahoma [əʊkləˈhəʊmə] *Staat der USA.*

Oliver [ˈɒlɪvə] *männlicher Vorname.*

Omaha [ˈəʊməhɑː] *Stadt in USA.*

O'Neill [əʊˈniːl] *amer. Dramatiker.*

Ontario [ɒnˈteərɪəʊ] *Provinz in Kanada;* Lake ~ *Ontariosee m (e-r der fünf Großen Seen Nordamerikas).*

Oregon [ˈɒrɪɡən] *Staat der USA.*

Orkney Islands [ˈɔːknɪ ˈaɪləndz] *die Orkneyinseln.*

Orwell [ˈɔːwəl] *engl. Autor.*

Osborne [ˈɒzbən] *engl. Dramatiker.*

Ostend [ɒˈstend] *Ostende n.*

Ottawa [ˈɒtəwə] *Hauptstadt von Kanada.*

Oxford [ˈɒksfəd] *engl. Universitätsstadt; a.* ~shire [~ʃə] *Grafschaft in England.*

Pacific [pəˈsɪfɪk] *der Pazifik.*

Pakistan [pɑːkɪˈstɑːn] *Pakistan n.*

Paris [ˈpærɪs] *Paris n.*

Patricia [pəˈtrɪʃə] *weiblicher Vorname.*

Patrick [ˈpætrɪk] *männlicher Vorname.*

Paul [pɔːl] *Paul m.*

Pearl Harbor [ˈpɜːl ˈhɑːbə] *Hafenstadt auf Hawaii.*

Peg(gy) [ˈpeɡ(ɪ)] *Kurzform von Margaret.*

Pennsylvania [pensɪlˈveɪnjə] *Pennsylvanien n (Staat der USA).*

Peter [ˈpiːtə] *Peter m.*

Philadelphia [fɪləˈdelfjə] *Stadt in USA.*

Philippines [ˈfɪlɪpiːnz] *die Philippinen.*

Pittsburgh [ˈpɪtsbɜːɡ] *Stadt in USA.*

Plymouth [ˈplɪməθ] *Hafenstadt in England.*

Poe [pəʊ] *amer. Autor.*

Poland [ˈpəʊlənd] *Polen n.*

Portsmouth [ˈpɔːtsməθ] *Hafenstadt in England.*

Portugal [ˈpɔːtjʊɡl] *Portugal n.*

Potomac [pəˈtəʊmək] *Fluß in USA.*

Prague [prɑːɡ] *Prag n.*

Prince Edward Island [prɪnsˈedwəd ˈaɪlənd] *Provinz in Kanada.*

Pulitzer [ˈpʊlɪtsə] *amer. Journalist.*

Purcell [ˈpɜːsl] *engl. Komponist.*

Quebec [kwɪˈbek] *Provinz u. Stadt in Kanada.*

Reagan [ˈreɪɡən] *Präsident der USA.*

Reynolds [ˈrenldz] *engl. Maler.*

Rhine [raɪn] *Rhein m.*

Rhode Island [rəʊdˈaɪlənd] *Staat der USA.*

Rhodesia [rəʊˈdiːzjə] *Rhodesien n.*

Richard [ˈrɪtʃəd] *Richard m.*

Robert [ˈrɒbət] *Robert m.*

Rockefeller [ˈrɒkɪfelə] *amer. Industrieller.*

Rocky Mountains [ˈrɒkɪˈmaʊntɪnz] *Gebirge in USA.*

Roger [ˈrɒdʒə] *männlicher Vorname.*

Romania [ruːˈmeɪnjə] *Rumänien n.*

Rome [rəʊm] *Rom n.*

Roosevelt [ˈrəʊzəvelt] *Name zweier Präsidenten der USA.*

Rugby [ˈrʌɡbɪ] *berühmte Public School.*

Russell [ˈrʌsl] *engl. Philosoph.*

Russia [ˈrʌʃə] *Rußland n.*

Salinger [ˈsælɪndʒə] *amer. Autor.*

Salop [ˈsæləp] *Grafschaft in England.*

Sam [sæm] *Kurzform von Samuel.*

Samuel [ˈsæmjʊəl] *Samuel m.*

San Francisco [sænfrənˈsɪskəʊ] *Hafenstadt in USA.*

Saskatchewan [səsˈkætʃɪwən] *Provinz in Kanada.*

Scandinavia [skændɪˈneɪvjə] *Skandinavien n.*

Scotland [ˈskɒtlənd] *Schottland n;* ~ Yard *Polizeipräsidium in London.*

Seattle [sɪˈætl] *Hafenstadt in USA.*

Shakespeare [ˈʃeɪkspɪə] *engl. Dichter.*

Shaw [ʃɔː] *engl. Dramatiker.*

Shelley [ˈʃelɪ] *engl. Dichter.*

Shetland Islands [ˈʃetlənd ˈaɪləndz] *die Shetlandinseln.*

Sillitoe [ˈsɪlɪtəʊ] *engl. Autor.*

Singapore [sɪŋɡəˈpɔː] *Singapur n.*

Snowdon [ˈsnəʊdn] *Berg in Wales.*

Somerset(shire) [ˈsʌməsɪt(ʃə)] *Grafschaft in England.*

South Carolina [ˈsaʊθ kærəˈlaɪnə] *Südkarolina n (Staat der USA).*

South Dakota [ˈsaʊθ dəˈkəʊtə] *Süddakota n (Staat der USA).*

South Yorkshire [ˈsaʊθ ˈjɔːkʃə] *Grafschaft in England.*

Spain [speɪn] *Spanien n.*

Staffordshire [ˈstæfədʃə] *Grafschaft in England.*

Stevenson [ˈstiːvnsn] *schott. Autor.*

St. Lawrence [snt ˈlɒrəns] *der St.-Lorenz-Strom.*

St. Louis [snt'lʊɪs] *Industriestadt in USA.*

Stratford ['strætfəd]: ⁓-on-Avon *Geburtsort Shakespeares.*

Styria ['stɪrɪə] *Steiermark f.*

Suffolk ['sʌfək] *Grafschaft in England.*

Superior [su:'pɪərɪə]: *Lake* ⁓ *Oberer See m (e-r der fünf Großen Seen Nordamerikas).*

Surrey ['sʌrɪ] *Grafschaft in England.*

Susan ['su:zn] *Susanne f.*

Sweden ['swi:dn] *Schweden n.*

Swift [swɪft] *engl. Autor.*

Switzerland ['swɪtsələnd] *die Schweiz.*

Sydney ['sɪdnɪ] *Hafen- u. Industriestadt in Australien.*

Tennessee [tenə'si:] *Fluß u. Staat der USA.*

Tennyson ['tenɪsn] *engl. Dichter.*

Texas ['teksəs] *Staat der USA.*

Thackeray ['θækərɪ] *engl. Autor.*

Thames [temz] *Themse f.*

Thatcher ['θætʃə] *engl. Politikerin.*

Thomas ['tɒməs] *Thomas m.*

Tokyo ['təʊkɪəʊ] *Tokio n.*

Tom(my) ['tɒm(ɪ)] *Kurzform von Thomas.*

Toronto [tə'rɒntəʊ] *Stadt in Kanada.*

Trafalgar [trə'fælgə] *Vorgebirge bei Gibraltar (Seesieg Nelsons 1805).*

Truman ['tru:mən] *Präsident der USA.*

Turkey ['tɜ:kɪ] *die Türkei.*

Turner ['tɜ:nə] *engl. Maler.*

Twain [tweɪn] *amer. Autor.*

Tyne and Wear ['taɪnən'wɪə] *Grafschaft in England.*

Tyrol ['tɪrəl] *Tirol n.*

Ulster ['ʌlstə] *Ulster n (Nordirland).*

United States of America [ju:'naɪtɪd 'steɪtsəvə'merɪkə] *die Vereinigten Staaten von Amerika.*

Utah ['ju:tɑ:] *Staat der USA.*

Vancouver [væn'ku:və] *Stadt in Kanada.*

Vatican ['vætɪkən] *Vatikan m.*

Venice ['venɪs] *Venedig n.*

Vermont [vɜ:'mɒnt] *Staat der USA.*

Vienna [vɪ'enə] *Wien n.*

Virginia [və'dʒɪnjə] *Staat der USA.*

Vivian ['vɪvɪən] *männlicher u. weiblicher Vorname.*

Wales [weɪlz] *Wales n.*

Wallace ['wɒlɪs] *engl. Autor.*

Wall Street ['wɔ:l stri:t] *Straße u. Finanzzentrum in New York.*

Warsaw ['wɔ:sɔ:] *Warschau n.*

Warwickshire ['wɒrɪkʃə] *Grafschaft in England.*

Washington ['wɒʃɪŋtən] **1.** *Präsident der USA;* **2.** *Staat der USA;* **3.** *Bundeshauptstadt der USA.*

Waterloo [wɔ:tə'lu:] *Dorf in Belgien (Niederlage Napoleons 1815).*

Watt [wɒt] *schott. Erfinder.*

Wellington ['welɪŋtən] **1.** *engl. Feldherr u. Staatsmann;* **2.** *Hauptstadt von Neuseeland.*

West Midlands ['west 'mɪdləndz] *Grafschaft in England.*

West Sussex ['west 'sʌsɪks] *Grafschaft in England.*

West Virginia ['west və'dʒɪnjə] *Staat der USA.*

West Yorkshire ['west 'jɔ:kʃə] *Grafschaft in England.*

White House ['waɪt haʊs] *das Weiße Haus (Amtssitz des Präsidenten der USA).*

Whitman ['wɪtmən] *amer. Dichter.*

Wilde [waɪld] *engl. Autor u. Dramatiker.*

Wilder ['waɪldə] *amer. Dramatiker.*

Will [wɪl] *Kurzform von William.*

William ['wɪljəm] *Wilhelm m.*

Wilson ['wɪlsn] **1.** *Präsident der USA;* **2.** *brit. Politiker.*

Wiltshire ['wɪltʃə] *Grafschaft in England.*

Wimbledon ['wɪmbldən] *Vorort von London (Tennisturniere).*

Winnipeg ['wɪnɪpeg] *See u. Stadt in Kanada.*

Wisconsin [wɪs'kɒnsɪn] *Fluß u. Staat der USA.*

Wolfe [wʊlf] *amer. Autor.*

Woolf [wʊlf] *engl. Autorin.*

Worcester ['wʊstə] *Industriestadt in England.*

Wordsworth ['wɜ:dzwəθ] *engl. Dichter.*

Wyoming [waɪ'əʊmɪŋ] *Staat der USA.*

Yale University ['jeɪl ju:nɪ'vɜ:sətɪ] *amer. Universität.*

Yellowstone ['jeləʊstəʊn] *Fluß u. Nationalpark der USA.*

York [jɔ:k] *Stadt in England;* ⁓**shire** [⁓ʃə] *Grafschaft in England.*

Yosemite [jəʊˈsemɪtɪ] *Nationalpark der USA.*

Yugoslavia [juːgəʊˈslɑːvjə] *Jugoslawien n.*

Yukon [ˈjuːkɒn] *Fluß und Territorium in Kanada.*

Zimbabwe [zɪmˈbɑːbwɪ] *Simbabwe n.*

American and British Abbreviations

abbr. *abbreviated* abgekürzt; *abbreviation* Abk., Abkürzung *f.*

ABC *American Broadcasting Company* (*amer. Rundfunkgesellschaft*).

AC *alternating current* Wechselstrom *m.*

A/C *account* (Bank)Konto *n.*

acc(t). *account* Konto *n*, Rechnung *f.*

AEC *Atomic Energy Commission* Atomenergie-Kommission *f.*

AFL–CIO *American Federation of Labor & Congress of Industrial Organizations* (*größter amer. Gewerkschaftsverband*).

AFN *American Forces Network* (*Rundfunkanstalt der amer. Streitkräfte*).

AI *Amnesty International.*

AL *Alabama.*

Alta *Alberta.*

AK *Alaska.*

AM *amplitude modulation* MW, Mittelwelle *f.*

a.m. *ante meridiem* (*lateinisch = before noon*) vormittags.

AP *Associated Press* (*amer. Nachrichtenbüro*).

AR *Arkansas.*

ARC *American Red Cross* Amer. Rotes Kreuz.

arr. *arrival* Ank., Ankunft *f.*

ASA *American Standards Association* Amer. Normungs-Organisation *f.*

AZ *Arizona.*

BA *Bachelor of Arts* Bakkalaureus *m* der Philosophie; *British Airways* (*brit. Fluggesellschaft*).

BBC *British Broadcasting Corporation* (*brit. Rundfunkgesellschaft*).

BC *British Columbia.*

B/E *bill of exchange* Wechsel *m.*

Beds. *Bedfordshire.*

Benelux *Belgium, Netherlands, Luxembourg* (*Zollunion*).

Berks. *Berkshire.*

BFN *British Forces Network* (*Sender der brit. Streitkräfte in Deutschland*).

BL *Bachelor of Law* Bakkalaureus *m* des Rechts.

bldg *building* Gebäude *n.*

BM *Bachelor of Medicine* Bakkalaureus *m* der Medizin.

BO *body odour* Körpergeruch *m.*

BOT *Board of Trade* Handelsministerium *n* (*in Großbritannien*).

BR *British Rail* (*Eisenbahn in Großbritannien*).

Brit. *Britain* Großbritannien *n*; *British* britisch.

Bros. *brothers* Gebrüder *pl.* (*in Firmenbezeichnungen*).

BS *Bachelor of Science* Bakkalaureus *m* der Naturwissenschaften; *British Standard* Brit. Norm *f.*

BSI *British Standards Institution* Brit. Normungs-Organisation *f.*

Bucks. *Buckinghamshire.*

C *Celsius, centigrade* (*Thermometereinteilung*).

c. *cent(s)* Cent *m od. pl.*; *circa* ca., ungefähr, zirka; *cubic* Kubik...

CA *California.*

C/A *current account* Girokonto *n.*

Cambs. *Cambridgeshire.*

Can. *Canada* Kanada *n*; *Canadian* kanadisch.

CBS *Columbia Broadcasting System* (*amer. Rundfunkgesellschaft*).

CD *compact disc* CD-Platte *f*, Kompaktschallplatte *f.*

cf. *confer* vgl., vergleiche.

Ches. *Cheshire.*

CIA *Central Intelligence Agency* (*amer. Geheimdienst*).

CID *Criminal Investigation Department* (*brit. Kriminalpolizei*).

c.i.f. *cost, insurance, freight* Kosten, Versicherung und Fracht einbegriffen.

CO *Colorado.*

Co. *Company* Gesellschaft *f*; *County* Grafschaft *f*, Kreis *m.*

c/o *care of* p.A., per Adresse, bei.

COD *cash* (*Am. collect*) *on delivery* Zahlung bei Empfang, gegen Nachnahme.

C of E Church of England (englische Staatskirche).
Corn. Cornwall.
cp. compare vgl., vergleiche.
CT Connecticut.
Cumb. Cumberland.
cwt. hundredweight (etwa 1) Zentner m.

DC direct current Gleichstrom m.
D.C. District of Columbia (mit der amer. Hauptstadt Washington).
DE Delaware.
dep. departure Abf., Abfahrt f.
Dept. Department Abt., Abteilung f.
Derby. Derbyshire.
Devon. Devonshire.
disc. discount Diskont m, Abzug m.
div. dividend Dividende f.
DJ disc jockey Diskjockey m.
Dors. Dorsetshire.
doz. dozen Dutzend n od. pl.
Dpt. Department Abt., Abteilung f.
Dur(h). Durham.
dz. dozen Dutzend n od. pl.

E east Ost(en m); eastern östlich; English englisch.
ea. each jeder.
ECU European Currency Unit europäische Währungseinheit.
Ed., ed. edition Auflage f; edited hrsg., herausgegeben; editor Hrsg., Herausgeber m.
EDP electronic data processing EDV, elektronische Datenverarbeitung.
EEC European Economic Community EWG, Europäische Wirtschaftsgemeinschaft.
EFTA European Free Trade Association EFTA, Europäische Freihandelsgemeinschaft od. -zone.
e.g. exempli gratia (lateinisch = for instance) z. B., zum Beispiel.
Enc. enclosure(s) Anlage(n pl.) f.
Ess. Essex.

F Fahrenheit (Thermometereinteilung).
f. feminine weiblich; foot, pl. feet Fuß m od. pl.; following folgend.
FAO Food and Agricultural Organization Organisation f für Ernährung und Landwirtschaft (der UN).
FBI Federal Bureau of Investigation (Bundeskriminalamt der USA).

fig. figure(s) Abb., Abbildung(en pl.) f.
FL Florida.
FM frequency modulation UKW, Ultrakurzwelle f.
FO Foreign Office Brt. Auswärtiges Amt.
f.o.b. free on board frei Schiff.
fol. folio Folio n, Seite f.
fr. franc(s) Franc(s pl.) m.
ft foot, pl. feet Fuß m od. pl.

g gramme g, Gramm n.
GA Georgia.
gal. gallon Gallone f.
GATT General Agreement on Tariffs and Trade Allgemeines Zoll- und Handelsabkommen.
GB Great Britain Großbritannien n.
GI government issue von der Regierung ausgegeben; Staatseigentum n; fig. amer. Soldat.
Glos. Gloucestershire.
GMT Greenwich Mean Time WEZ, Westeuropäische Zeit.
GP general practitioner Arzt m (Ärztin f) für Allgemeinmedizin.
GPO General Post Office Hauptpostamt n.
gr. gross brutto.

h. hour(s) Std., Stunde(n pl.) f.
Hants. Hampshire.
HBM His (Her) Britannic Majesty Seine (Ihre) britannische Majestät.
H.C. House of Commons Unterhaus n.
Herts. Hertfordshire.
hf. half halb.
HI Hawaii.
H.L. House of Lords Oberhaus n.
H.M. His (Her) Majesty Seine (Ihre) Majestät.
H.M.S. His (Her) Majesty's Ship (Steamer) Seiner (Ihrer) Majestät Schiff n (Dampfschiff n).
H.O. Home Office Brt. Innenministerium n.
H.P., hp horsepower PS, Pferdestärke f.
H.Q., Hq. Headquarters Stab(squartier n) m, Hauptquartier n.
H.R. House of Representatives Repräsentantenhaus n (der USA).
H.R.H. His (Her) Royal Highness Seine (Ihre) Königliche Hoheit.

IA *Iowa.*

ICBM *intercontinental ballistic missile* interkontinentaler ballistischer Flugkörper.

ID *Idaho.*

I.D. *Intelligence Department* Nachrichtenamt *n.*

i.e. *id est* (*lateinisch* = *that is to say*) d. h., das heißt.

IL *Illinois.*

IMF *International Monetary Fund* Internationaler Währungsfonds.

IN *Indiana.*

in. *inch(es)* Zoll *m od. pl.*

Inc. *Incorporated* (amtlich) eingetragen.

inst. *instant* d. M., dieses Monats.

IOC *International Olympic Committee* Internationales Olympisches Komitee.

I of W *Isle of Wight.*

IOU *I owe you* Schuldschein *m.*

Ir. *Ireland* Irland *n*; *Irish* irisch.

IRC *International Red Cross* Internationales Rotes Kreuz.

JP *Justice of the Peace* Friedensrichter *m.*

Jr *junior* jr., jun., der Jüngere.

k.o. *knock(ed) out* Boxen: k.o. (ge)schlagen; *fig.* erledigt.

KS *Kansas.*

l. *litre(s)* Liter *n, m od. pl.*

£ *pound sterling* Pfund *n* Sterling (*Währung*).

LA *Louisiana.*

Lab *Labrador.*

Lancs. *Lancashire.*

lb. *pound(s)* Pfund *n od. pl.* (*Gewicht*).

L/C *letter of credit* Kreditbrief *m.*

Leics. *Leicestershire.*

Lincs. *Lincolnshire.*

LP *long playing record* LP, Langspielplatte *f.*

Ltd. *limited* mit beschränkter Haftung.

m. *male* männlich; *metre* m, Meter *n, m*; *mile* Meile *f*; *minute* Min., Minute *f.*

MA *Massachusetts.*

M.A. *Master of Arts* Magister *m* der Philosophie.

Man *Manitoba.*

MD *Maryland.*

M.D. *Medicinae Doctor* (*lateinisch* =

Doctor of Medicine) Dr. med., Doktor *m* der Medizin.

ME *Maine.*

MI *Michigan.*

MN *Minnesota.*

MO *Missouri.*

M.O. *money order* Postanweisung *f.*

Mon. *Monmouthshire.*

MP, M.P. *Member of Parliament* Parlamentsabgeordnete(r *m*) *f*; *Military Police* Militärpolizei *f.*

m.p.h. *miles per hour* Stundenmeilen *pl.*

Mr *Mister* Herr *m.*

MRP *manufacturer's recommended price* unverbindliche Preisempfehlung.

Mrs *Mistress* Frau *f.*

MS *Mississippi*; *manuscript* Manuskript *n.*

Ms *Anrede für Frauen ohne Berücksichtigung des Familienstandes.*

Mt *Mount* Berg *m.*

N *north* Nord(en *m*); *northern* nördlich.

n. *noon* Mittag *m.*

NASA *National Aeronautics and Space Administration* NASA *f* (*amer. Luftfahrt- und Raumforschungsbehörde*).

NATO *North Atlantic Treaty Organization* NATO *f*, Nordatlantikpakt-Organisation *f.*

NB *New Brunswick.*

N.B. *nota bene* (*lateinisch* = *note well*) NB, notabene.

NBC *National Broadcasting Company* (*amer. Rundfunkgesellschaft*).

NC *North Carolina.*

ND *North Dakota*; *Newfoundland.*

NE *north-east* Nordost(en *m*); *north-eastern* nordöstlich; *Nebraska.*

NH *New Hampshire.*

N.H.S. *National Health Service* Nationaler Gesundheitsdienst (*in Großbritannien*).

NJ *New Jersey.*

NM *New Mexico.*

Norf. *Norfolk.*

Northants. *Northamptonshire.*

Northumb. *Northumberland.*

Notts. *Nottinghamshire.*

NS *Nova Scotia.*

NV *Nevada.*

NW *north-west* Nordwest(en *m*); *north-western* nordwestlich.

NY *New York.*
N.Y.C. *New York City* Stadt *f* New York.

o/a *on account of* für Rechnung von.
OAS *Organization of American States* Organisation *f* amerikanischer Staaten.
O.E.C.D. *Organization for Economic Cooperation and Development* Organisation *f* für wirtschaftliche Zusammenarbeit und Entwicklung.
OH *Ohio.*
O.H.M.S. *On His (Her) Majesty's Service* im Dienste Seiner (Ihrer) Majestät; Dienstsache *f.*
OK *Oklahoma.*
O.K. o.k., in Ordnung.
Ont *Ontario.*
OPEC *Organization of Petroleum-Exporting Countries* Organisation *f* erdölexportierender Staaten.
OR *Oregon.*
Oxon. *Oxfordshire.*
oz. *ounce* Unze.

p (new) *penny od.* pence Penny *m.*
PA *Pennsylvania.*
p.a. *per annum* (*lateinisch* = *yearly*) jährlich.
Pan Am *Pan American World Airways* (*amer. Fluggesellschaft*).
PC *Personal Computer* PC, Personalcomputer *m.*
P.C. *police constable* Schutzmann *m.*
p.c. *per cent* %, Prozent *n od. pl.*
pd. *paid* bezahlt.
P.E.N., *mst* **PEN Club** *Poets, Playwrights, Editors, Essayists, and Novelists* Pen-Club *m* (*Internationale Vereinigung von Dichtern, Dramatikern, Redakteuren, Essayisten und Romanschriftstellern*).
Ph.D. *Philosophiae Doctor* (*lateinisch* = *Doctor of Philosophy*) Dr. phil., Doktor *m* der Philosophie.
PM *Prime Minister* Premierminister(in).
p.m. *post meridiem* (*lateinisch* = *after noon*) nachmittags, abends.
P.O. *Post Office* Postamt *n*; *postal order* Postanweisung *f.*
POD *pay on delivery* Nachnahme *f.*
P.S. *postscript* PS, Nachschrift *f.*
pt *pint* Pinte *f* (*etwa* $^1/_2$ *l*).

P.T.O., p.t.o. *please turn over* b.w., bitte wenden.
PX *Post Exchange* Verkaufsläden *pl* (*der amer. Streitkräfte*).

Que *Quebec.*
qt *quart* Quart *n* (*etwa 1 l*).

R.A.F. *Royal Air Force* Königlich-Brit. Luftwaffe *f.*
RC *Roman Catholic* rk, r.-k., römisch-katholisch.
Rd. *Road* Str., Straße *f.*
ref. (*in*) *reference* (*to*) (mit) Bezug *m* (auf); Empfehlung *f.*
regd. *registered* eingetragen; eingeschrieben.
reg.tn. *register ton* RT, Registertonne *f.*
resp. *respective(ly)* bzw., beziehungsweise.
ret. *retired* i.R., im Ruhestand.
Rev. *Reverend* Pfarrer *m.*
rev *revolution* Umdrehung *f.*
RI *Rhode Island.*
R.N. *Royal Navy* Königlich-Brit. Marine *f.*
R.R. *Railroad Am.* Eisenbahn *f.*
RSVP *répondez s'il vous plaît* (*französisch* = *please reply*) u.A.w.g., um Antwort wird gebeten.

S *south* Süd(en *m*); *southern* südlich.
s. *second(s)* Sek., Sekunde(n *pl.*) *f.*
$ *dollar* Dollar *m.*
S.A. *South Africa* Südafrika *n*; *South America* Südamerika *n*; *Salvation Army* Heilsarmee *f.*
Salop. *Shropshire.*
Sask *Saskatchewan.*
SC *South Carolina*; *Security Council* Sicherheitsrat *m* (*der UN*).
SD *South Dakota.*
SE *south-east* Südost(en *m*); *south-eastern* südöstlich; *Stock Exchange* Börse *f.*
SEATO *South East Asia Treaty Organization* Südostasienpakt-Organisation *f.*
Soc. *society* Gesellschaft *f*; Verein *m.*
Som. *Somersetshire.*
Sq. *Square* Platz *m.*
sq. *square* ... Quadrat...
Sr *senior* sen., der Ältere.
S.S. *steamship* Dampfer *m.*
St(.) *Saint* ... Sankt ...; *Station* Bahnhof *m*; *Street* Straße *f.*
Staffs. *Staffordshire.*

St.Ex. *Stock Exchange* Börse *f.*
stg. *sterling* Sterling *m* (*brit. Währungseinheit*).
Suff. *Suffolk.*
SW *south-west* Südwest(en *m*); *south-western* südwestlich.
Sx *Sussex.*
Sy *Surrey.*

t *ton(s)* Tonne(n *pl.*) *f.*
TM *trademark* Warenzeichen *n.*
TMO *telegraph money order* telegraphische Geldanweisung.
TN *Tennessee.*
TO *Telegraph (Telephone) Office* Telegraphen-(Fernsprech)amt *n.*
TU *Trade(s) Union(s)* Gewerkschaft(en *pl.*) *f.*
TUC *Trade(s) Union Congress* brit. Gewerkschaftsverband *m.*
TV *television* Fernsehen *n.*
TWA *Trans World Airlines* (*amer. Fluggesellschaft*).
TX *Texas.*

UK *United Kingdom* Vereinigtes Königreich (*England, Schottland, Wales und Nordirland*).
UN(O) *United Nations (Organization)* UN(O) *f*, (Organisation *f* der) Vereinte(n) Nationen *pl.*
UNESCO *United Nations Educational, Scientific, and Cultural Organization* Organisation *f* der Vereinten Nationen für Erziehung, Wissenschaft und Kultur.
UNICEF *United Nations International Children's Emergency Fund* Weltkinderhilfswerk *n* der UNO.
UPI *United Press International* (*amer. Nachrichtenagentur*).
US(A) *United States (of America)*

US(A) *pl.*, Vereinigte Staaten *pl.* (von Amerika).
UT *Utah.*

v. *verse* Vers *m*; *versus* (*lateinisch = against*) gegen; *vide* (*lateinisch = see*) s., siehe.
VA *Virginia.*
VF *video frequency* Videofrequenz *f.*
viz. *videlicet* (*lateinisch = namely*) nämlich.
vol(s). *volume(s)* Band *m* (Bände *pl.*).
VT *Vermont.*

W *west* West(en *m*); *western* westlich.
WA *Washington.*
Warks. *Warwickshire.*
WC *water closet* WC *n*, Wasserklosett *n.*
W.F.T.U. *World Federation of Trade Unions* Weltgewerkschaftsbund *m.*
W.H.O. *World Health Organization* Weltgesundheitsorganisation *f* (*der UN*).
WI *Wisconsin.*
W.I. *West Indies* Westindien *n.*
Wilts. *Wiltshire.*
Worcs. *Worcestershire.*
wt. *weight* Gewicht *n.*
W.V. *West Virginia.*
WY *Wyoming.*

Xmas *Christmas* Weihnachten *n.*

yd(s). *yard(s)* Elle(n *pl.*) *f.*
Y.M.C.A. *Young Men's Christian Association* CVJM, Christlicher Verein Junger Männer.
Yorks. *Yorkshire.*
Y.W.C.A. *Young Women's Christian Association* Christlicher Verein Junger Mädchen.

Alphabetical List of the German Irregular Verbs

Infinitive – Preterite – Past Participle

backen - backte (buk) - gebacken
bedingen - bedang (bedingte) - bedungen (*conditional*: bedingt)
befehlen - befahl - befohlen
beginnen - begann - begonnen
beißen - biß - gebissen
bergen - barg - geborgen
bersten - barst - geborsten
bewegen - bewog - bewogen
biegen - bog - gebogen
bieten - bot - geboten
binden - band - gebunden
bitten - bat - gebeten
blasen - blies - geblasen
bleiben - blieb - geblieben
bleichen - blich - geblichen
braten - briet - gebraten
brauchen - brauchte - gebraucht (*v/aux.* brauchen)
brechen - brach - gebrochen
brennen - brannte - gebrannt
bringen - brachte - gebracht
denken - dachte - gedacht
dreschen - drosch - gedroschen
dringen - drang - gedrungen
dürfen - durfte - gedurft (*v/aux.* dürfen)
empfehlen - empfahl - empfohlen
erlöschen - erlosch - erloschen
erschrecken - erschrak - erschrocken
essen - aß - gegessen
fahren - fuhr - gefahren
fallen - fiel - gefallen
fangen - fing - gefangen
fechten - focht - gefochten
finden - fand - gefunden
flechten - flocht - geflochten
fliegen - flog - geflogen
fliehen - floh - geflohen
fließen - floß - geflossen
fressen - fraß - gefressen
frieren - fror - gefroren
gären - gor (*esp. fig.* gärte) - gegoren (*esp. fig.* gegärt)
gebären - gebar - geboren

geben - gab - gegeben
gedeihen - gedieh - gediehen
gehen - ging - gegangen
gelingen - gelang - gelungen
gelten - galt - gegolten
genesen - genas - genesen
genießen - genoß - genossen
geschehen - geschah - geschehen
gewinnen - gewann - gewonnen
gießen - goß - gegossen
gleichen - glich - geglichen
gleiten - glitt - geglitten
glimmen - glomm - geglommen
graben - grub - gegraben
greifen - griff - gegriffen
haben - hatte - gehabt
halten - hielt - gehalten
hängen - hing - gehangen
hauen - haute (hieb) - gehauen
heben - hob - gehoben
heißen - hieß - geheißen
helfen - half - geholfen
kennen - kannte - gekannt
klingen - klang - geklungen
kneifen - kniff - gekniffen
kommen - kam - gekommen
können - konnte - gekonnt (*v/aux.* können)
kriechen - kroch - gekrochen
laden - lud - geladen
lassen - ließ - gelassen (*v/aux.* lassen)
laufen - lief - gelaufen
leiden - litt - gelitten
leihen - lieh - geliehen
lesen - las - gelesen
liegen - lag - gelegen
lügen - log - gelogen
mahlen - mahlte - gemahlen
meiden - mied - gemieden
melken - melkte (molk) - gemolken (gemelkt)
messen - maß - gemessen
mißlingen - mißlang - mißlungen
mögen - mochte - gemocht (*v/aux.* mögen)

müssen - mußte - gemußt (v/aux. müssen)
nehmen - nahm - genommen
nennen - nannte - genannt
pfeifen - pfiff - gepfiffen
preisen - pries - gepriesen
quellen - quoll - gequollen
raten - riet - geraten
reiben - rieb - gerieben
reißen - riß - gerissen
reiten - ritt - geritten
rennen - rannte - gerannt
riechen - roch - gerochen
ringen - rang - gerungen
rinnen - rann - geronnen
rufen - rief - gerufen
salzen - salzte - gesalzen (gesalzt)
saufen - soff - gesoffen
saugen - sog - gesogen
schaffen - schuf - geschaffen
schallen - schallte (scholl) - geschallt (for erschallen a. erschollen)
scheiden - schied - geschieden
scheinen - schien - geschienen
schelten - schalt - gescholten
scheren - schor - geschoren
schieben - schob - geschoben
schießen - schoß - geschossen
schinden - schund - geschunden
schlafen - schlief - geschlafen
schlagen - schlug - geschlagen
schleichen - schlich - geschlichen
schleifen - schliff - geschliffen
schließen - schloß - geschlossen
schlingen - schlang - geschlungen
schmeißen - schmiß - geschmissen
schmelzen - schmolz - geschmolzen
schneiden - schnitt - geschnitten
schrecken - schrak - † geschrocken
schreiben - schrieb - geschrieben
schreien - schrie - geschrie(e)n
schreiten - schritt - geschritten
schweigen - schwieg - geschwiegen
schwellen - schwoll - geschwollen
schwimmen - schwamm - geschwommen
schwinden - schwand - geschwunden [gen]
schwingen - schwang - geschwun-gen)
schwören - schwor - geschworen
sehen - sah - gesehen
sein - war - gewesen
senden - sandte - gesandt
sieden - sott - gesotten
singen - sang - gesungen

sinken - sank - gesunken
sinnen - sann - gesonnen
sitzen - saß - gesessen
sollen - sollte - gesollt (v/aux. sollen)
spalten - spaltete - gespalten (ge-spaltet)
speien - spie - gespie(e)n
spinnen - spann - gesponnen
sprechen - sprach - gesprochen
sprießen - sproß - gesprossen
springen - sprang - gesprungen
stechen - stach - gestochen
stecken - steckte (stak) - gesteckt
stehen - stand - gestanden
stehlen - stahl - gestohlen
steigen - stieg - gestiegen
sterben - starb - gestorben
stieben - stob - gestoben
stinken - stank - gestunken
stoßen - stieß - gestoßen
streichen - strich - gestrichen
streiten - stritt - gestritten
tragen - trug - getragen
treffen - traf - getroffen
treiben - trieb - getrieben
treten - trat - getreten
triefen - triefte (troff) - getrieft
trinken - trank - getrunken
trügen - trog - getrogen
tun - tat - getan
verderben - verdarb - verdorben
verdrießen - verdroß - verdrossen
vergessen - vergaß - vergessen
verlieren - verlor - verloren
verschleißen - verschliß - ver-schlissen
verzeihen - verzieh - verziehen
wachsen - wuchs - gewachsen
wägen - wog (wägte) - gewogen (gewägt)
waschen - wusch - gewaschen
weben - wob - gewoben
weichen - wich - gewichen
weisen - wies - gewiesen
wenden - wandte - gewandt
werben - warb - geworben [den*))
werden - wurde - geworden (wor-)
werfen - warf - geworfen
wiegen - wog - gewogen
winden - wand - gewunden
wissen - wußte - gewußt [wollen))
wollen - wollte - gewollt (v/aux.)
wringen - wrang - gewrungen
ziehen - zog - gezogen
zwingen - zwang - gezwungen

---

* only in connexion with the past participles of other verbs, *e.g.* er ist *gesehen worden* he has been seen.

Alphabetical List of the English Irregular Verbs

Infinitive – Preterite – Past Participle

Irregular forms marked with asterisks (*)
can be exchanged for the regular forms.

arise (*sich erheben*) – arose - arisen
awake (*erwachen*) - awoke - awoke*
be (*sein*) - was - been
bear (*tragen; gebären*) - bore - getragen: borne - *geboren*: born
beat (*schlagen*) - beat - beat(en)
become (*werden*) - became - become
beget (*zeugen*) - begot - begotten
begin (*anfangen*) - began - begun
bend (*beugen*) - bent - bent
bereave (*berauben*) - bereft* - bereft*
beseech (*dringend bitten*) - besought -
besought
bet (*wetten*) - bet* - bet*
bid ([*ge*]*bieten*) - bade, bid - bid(den)
bide (*abwarten*) - bode* - bided
bind (*binden*) - bound - bound
bite (*beißen*) - bit - bitten
bleed (*bluten*) - bled - bled
bless (*segnen; preisen*) - blest* - blest*
blow (*blasen*) - blew - blown
break (*brechen*) - broke - broken
breed (*aufziehen*) - bred - bred
bring (*bringen*) - brought - brought
build (*bauen*) - built - built
burn (*brennen*) - burnt* - burnt*
burst (*bersten*) - burst - burst
buy (*kaufen*) - bought - bought
cast (*werfen*) - cast - cast
catch (*fangen*) - caught - caught
choose (*wählen*) - chose - chosen
cleave ([*sich*] *spalten*) - cleft, clove* -
cleft, cloven*
cling (*sich* [*an*]*klammern*) - clung -
clung
clothe ([*an-, be*]*kleiden*) - clad* -
clad*
come (*kommen*) - came - come
cost (*kosten*) - cost - cost
creep (*kriechen*) - crept - crept
crow (*krähen*) - crew* - crowed
cut (*schneiden*) - cut - cut
deal (*handeln*) - dealt - dealt
dig (*graben*) - dug - dug
dive ([*unter*]*tauchen*) - dived, *Am. a.*

dove - dived
do (*tun*) - did - done
draw (*ziehen*) - drew - drawn
dream (*träumen*) - dreamt* -
dreamt*
drink (*trinken*) - drank - drunk
drive (*treiben; fahren*) - drove -
driven
dwell (*wohnen*) - dwelt* - dwelt*
eat (*essen*) -ate - eaten
fall (*fallen*) - fell - fallen
feed (*füttern*) - fed - fed
feel (*fühlen*) - felt - felt
fight (*kämpfen*) - fought - fought
find (*finden*) - found - found
fit ([*an*]*passen*) - fitted, *Am. a.* fit-
fitted, *Am. a.* fit
flee (*fliehen*) - fled - fled
fling (*schleudern*) - flung - flung
fly (*fliegen*) - flew - flown
forbid (*verbieten*) - forbade - forbidden
forget (*vergessen*) - forgot - for-
gotten
forsake (*aufgeben; verlassen*) - for-
sook - forsaken
freeze ([*ge*]*frieren*) - froze - frozen
get (*bekommen*) - got - got, *Am.* gotten
gild (*vergolden*) - gilt* - gilt*
give (*geben*) - gave - given
go (*gehen*) - went - gone
grind (*mahlen*) - ground - ground
grow (*wachsen*) - grew - grown
hang (*hängen*) - hung - hung
have (*haben*) - had - had
hear (*hören*) - heard - heard
heave (*heben*) - hove* - hove*
hew (*hauen, hacken*) - hewed - hewn*
hide (*verbergen*) - hid - hidden
hit (*treffen*) - hit - hit
hold (*halten*) - held - held
hurt (*verletzen*) - hurt - hurt
keep (*halten*) - kept - kept
kneel (*knien*) - knelt* - knelt*
knit (*stricken*) - knit* - knit*

know (*wissen*) - knew - known
lay (*legen*) - laid - laid
lead (*führen*) - led - led
lean ([*sich*] [*an*]*lehnen*) - leant* - leant*
leap ([*über*]*springen*) - leapt* - leapt*
learn (*lernen*) - learnt* - learnt*
leave (*verlassen*) - left - left
lend (*leihen*) - lent -lent
let (*lassen*) - let - let
lie (*liegen*) - lay - lain
light (*anzünden*) - lit* - lit*
lose (*verlieren*) - lost - lost
make (*machen*) - made - made
mean (*meinen*) -meant - meant
meet (*begegnen*) - met - met
mow (*mähen*) - mowed - mown*
pay (*zahlen*) - paid - paid
plead (*plädieren*) - pleaded, *bsd. schott., Am.* pled - pleaded, *bsd. schott., Am.* pled
put (*setzen, stellen*) - put - put
read (*lesen*) - read - read
rid (*befreien*) - rid - rid
ride (*reiten*) - rode - ridden
ring (*läuten*) - rang - rung
rise (*aufstehen*) - rose - risen
run (*laufen*) - ran - run
saw (*sägen*) - sawed - sawn*
say (*sagen*) - said - said
see (*sehen*) - saw - seen
seek (*suchen*) - sought - sought
sell (*verkaufen*) - sold - sold
send (*senden*) - sent - sent
set (*setzen*) - set - set
sew (*nähen*) - sewed - sewn*
shake (*schütteln*) - shook - shaken
shave ([*sich*] *rasieren*) - shaved - shaven*
shear (*scheren*) - sheared - shorn
shed (*ausgießen*) - shed - shed
shine (*scheinen*) - shone - shone
shit (*scheißen*) - shit - shit
shoe (*beschuhen*) - shod - shod
shoot (*schießen*) - shot - shot
show (*zeigen*) - showed - shown*
shrink ([*ein*]*schrumpfen*) - shrank - shrunk
shut (*schließen*) - shut - shut
sing (*singen*) - sang - sung
sink (*sinken*) - sank - sunk
sit (*sitzen*) - sat - sat
slay (*erschlagen*) - slew - slain
sleep (*schlafen*) - slept - slept
slide (*gleiten*) - slid - slid
sling (*schleudern*) - slung - slung
slink (*schleichen*) - slunk - slunk

slit (*schlitzen*) - slit - slit
smell (*riechen*) - smelt* - smelt*
sow ([*aus*]*säen*) - sowed - sown*
speak (*sprechen*) - spoke - spoken
speed (*eilen*) - sped* - sped*
spell (*buchstabieren*) - spelt* - spelt*
spend (*ausgeben*) - spent - spent
spill (*verschütten*) - spilt* - spilt*
spin (*spinnen*) - spun - spun
spit ([*aus*]*spucken*) - spat - spat
split (*spalten*) - split - split
spoil (*verderben*) - spoilt* - spoilt*
spread (*verbreiten*) - spread - spread
spring (*springen*) - sprang, *Am.* sprung - sprung
stand (*stehen*) - stood - stood
stave (*den Boden einschlagen*) - stove* - stove*
steal (*stehlen*) - stole - stolen
stick (*stecken*) - stuck - stuck
sting (*stechen*) - stung - stung
stink (*stinken*) - stank, stunk - stunk
strew ([*be*]*streuen*) - strewed - strewn*
stride (*über-, durchschreiten*) - strode - stridden
strike (*schlagen*) - struck - struck
string (*spannen*) - strung - strung
strive (*streben*) - strove - striven
swear (*schwören*) - swore - sworn
sweat (*schwitzen*) - sweat* - sweat*
sweep (*fegen*) - swept - swept
swell ([*an*]*schwellen*) - swelled - swollen
swim (*schwimmen*) - swam - swum
swing (*schwingen*) - swung - swung
take (*nehmen*) - took - taken
teach (*lehren*) - taught - taught
tear (*ziehen*) - tore - torn
tell (*sagen*) - told - told
think (*denken*) - thought - thought
thrive (*gedeihen*) - throve* - thriven*
throw (*werfen*) - threw - thrown
thrust (*stoßen*) - thrust - thrust
tread (*treten*) - trod - trodden, trod
wake (*wachen*) - woke* - woke(n)*
wear ([*Kleider*] *tragen*) - wore - worn
weave (*weben*) - wove - woven
wed (*heiraten*) - wedded, *selten* wed - wedded, *selten* wed
weep (*weinen*) - wept - wept
wet (*nässen*) - wet* - wet*
win (*gewinnen*) - won - won
wind (*winden*) - wound - wound
wring ([*aus*]*wringen*) - wrung - wrung
write (*schreiben*) - wrote - written

Numerals

Cardinal Numbers

0 null *nought, zero, cipher*	51 einundfünfzig *fifty-one*
1 eins *one*	60 sechzig *sixty*
2 zwei *two*	61 einundsechzig *sixty-one*
3 drei *three*	70 siebzig *seventy*
4 vier *four*	71 einundsiebzig *seventy-one*
5 fünf *five*	80 achtzig *eighty*
6 sechs *six*	81 einundachtzig *eighty-one*
7 sieben *seven*	90 neunzig *ninety*
8 acht *eight*	91 einundneunzig *ninety-one*
9 neun *nine*	100 hundert *a or one hundred*
10 zehn *ten*	101 hundert(und)eins *a hundred*
11 elf *eleven*	*and one*
12 zwölf *twelve*	200 zweihundert *two hundred*
13 dreizehn *thirteen*	300 dreihundert *three hundred*
14 vierzehn *fourteen*	572 fünfhundert(und)zweiund-
15 fünfzehn *fifteen*	siebzig *five hundred and*
16 sechzehn *sixteen*	*seventy-two*
17 siebzehn *seventeen*	1000 tausend *a or one thousand*
18 achtzehn *eighteen*	1972 neunzehnhundertzweiund-
19 neunzehn *nineteen*	siebzig *nineteen hundred and*
20 zwanzig *twenty*	*seventy-two*
21 einundzwanzig *twenty-one*	500 000 fünfhunderttausend *five*
22 zweiundzwanzig *twenty-two*	*hundred thousand*
23 dreiundzwanzig *twenty-three*	1 000 000 eine Million *a or one*
30 dreißig *thirty*	*million*
31 einunddreißig *thirty-one*	2 000 000 zwei Millionen *two*
40 vierzig *forty*	*million*
41 einundvierzig *forty-one*	1 000 000 000 eine Milliarde *a or*
50 fünfzig *fifty*	*one milliard (Am. billion)*

Ordinal Numbers

1. erste *first (1st)*	**11.** elfte *eleventh*
2. zweite *second (2nd)*	**12.** zwölfte *twelfth*
3. dritte *third (3rd)*	**13.** dreizehnte *thirteenth*
4. vierte *fourth (4th)*	**14.** vierzehnte *fourteenth*
5. fünfte *fifth (5th), etc.*	**15.** fünfzehnte *fifteenth*
6. sechste *sixth*	**16.** sechzehnte *sixteenth*
7. siebente *seventh*	**17.** siebzehnte *seventeenth*
8. achte *eighth*	**18.** achtzehnte *eighteenth*
9. neunte *ninth*	**19.** neunzehnte *nineteenth*
10. zehnte *tenth*	**20.** zwanzigste *twentieth*

21. einundzwanzigste *twenty-first*
22. zweiundzwanzigste *twenty-second*
23. dreiundzwanzigste *twenty-third*
30. dreißigste *thirtieth*
31. einunddreißigste *thirty-first*
40. vierzigste *fortieth*
41. einundvierzigste *forty-first*
50. fünfzigste *fiftieth*
51. einundfünfzigste *fifty-first*
60. sechzigste *sixtieth*
61. einundsechzigste *sixty-first*
70. siebzigste *seventieth*
71. einundsiebzigste *seventy-first*
80. achtzigste *eightieth*
81. einundachtzigste *eighty-first*

90. neunzigste *ninetieth*
100. hundertste (*one*) *hundredth*
101. hundert(und)erste (*one*) *hundred and first*
200. zweihundertste *two hundredth*
300. dreihundertste *three hundredth*
572. fünfhundert(und)zweiundsiebzigste *five hundred and seventy-second*
1000. tausendste (*one*) *thousandth*
1970. neunzehnhundert(und)siebzigste *nineteen hundred and seventieth*
500000. fünfhunderttausendste *five hundred thousandth*
1000000. millionste (*one*) *millionth*
2000000. zweimillionste *two millionth*

Fractional Numbers and other Numerical Values

$^1/_2$ halb *one* or *a half*
$^1/_2$ eine halbe Meile *half a mile*
$1^1/_2$ anderthalb or eineinhalb *one and a half*
$2^1/_2$ zweieinhalb *two and a half*
$^1/_3$ ein Drittel *one* or *a third*
$^2/_3$ zwei Drittel *two thirds*
$^1/_4$ ein Viertel *one fourth, one* or *a quarter*
$^3/_4$ drei Viertel *three fourths, three quarters*
$1^1/_4$ ein und eine viertel Stunde *one hour and a quarter*
$^1/_5$ ein Fünftel *one* or *a fifth*
$3^4/_5$ drei vier Fünftel *three and four fifths*
0,4 null Komma vier *point four* (*.4*)
2,5 zwei Komma fünf *two point five* (*2.5*)

einfach *single*
    zweifach *double, twofold*
    dreifach *threefold, treble, triple*
    vierfach *fourfold, quadruple*
    fünffach *fivefold, quintuple*

einmal *once*
    zweimal *twice*
    drei-, vier-, fünfmal *three* or *four* or *five times*
    zweimal soviel(e) *twice as much* or *many*

erstens, zweitens, drittens *first(ly), secondly, thirdly; in the first* or *second* or *third place*

$2 \times 3 = 6$ zwei mal drei ist sechs, zwei multipliziert mit drei ist sechs *twice three are* or *make six, two multiplied by three are* or *make six*

$7 + 8 = 15$ sieben plus acht ist fünfzehn *seven plus eight are fifteen*

$10 - 3 = 7$ zehn minus drei ist sieben *ten minus three are seven*

$20 : 5 = 4$ zwanzig (dividiert) durch fünf ist vier *twenty divided by five make four*

German Weights and Measures

I. Linear Measure

1 mm   *Millimeter* millimet|re, *Am.* -er = 0.039 inch

1 cm   *Zentimeter* centimet|re, *Am.* -er = 10 mm = 0.394 inch

1 m   *Meter* met|re, *Am.* -er = 100 cm = 1.094 yards = 3.281 feet

1 km   *Kilometer* kilomet|re, *Am.* -er = 1000 m = 0.621 mile

1 sm   *Seemeile* nautical mile = 1852 m

II. Square Measure

1 mm²   *Quadratmillimeter* square millimet|re, *Am.* -er = 0.002 square inch

1 cm²   *Quadratzentimeter* square centimet|re, *Am.* -er = 100 mm² = 0.155 square inch

1 m²   *Quadratmeter* square met|re, *Am.* -er = 10000 cm² = 1.196 square yards = 10.764 square feet

1 a   *Ar* are = 100 m² = 119.599 square yards

1 ha   *Hektar* hectare = 100 a = 2.471 acres

1 km²   *Quadratkilometer* square kilomet|re, *Am.* -er = 100 ha = 247.11 acres = 0.386 square mile

III. Cubic Measure

1 cm³   *Kubikzentimeter* cubic centimet|re, *Am.* -er = 1000 mm³ = 0.061 cubic inch

1 m³   *Kubikmeter* cubic met|re, *Am.* -er = 1000000 cm³ = 35.315 cubic feet = 1.308 cubic yards

1 RT   *Registertonne* register ton = 2,832 m³ = 100 cubic feet

IV. Measure of Capacity

1 l   *Liter* lit|re, *Am.* -er = 1.760 pints = *U.S.* 1.057 liquid quarts *or* 0.906 dry quart

1 hl   *Hektoliter* hectolit|re, *Am.* -er = 100 l = 2.75 bushels = *U.S.* 26.418 gallons

V. Weight

1 g   *Gramm* gram(me) = 15.432 grains

1 Pfd.   *Pfund* pound (German) = 500 g = 1.102 pounds avdp.

1 kg   *Kilogramm* kilogram(me) = 1000 g = 2.205 pounds avdp. = 2.679 pounds troy

1 Ztr.   *Zentner* centner = 100 Pfd. = 0.984 hundredweight = 1.102 *U.S.* hundredweights

1 dz   *Doppelzentner* = 100 kg = 1.968 hundredweights = 2.204 *U.S.* hundredweights

1 t   *Tonne* ton = 1000 kg = 0.984 long ton = *U.S.* 1.102 short tons

American and British Weights and Measures

1. Linear Measure
1 inch (in.) = 2,54 cm
1 foot (ft)
   = 12 inches = 30,48 cm
1 yard (yd)
   = 3 feet = 91,439 cm
1 perch (p.)
   = 5¹/₂ yards = 5,029 m
1 mile (m.)
   = 1,760 yards = 1,609 km

2. Nautical Measure
1 fathom (f., fm)
   = 6 feet = 1,829 m
1 nautical mile
   = 6,080 feet = 1853,18 m

3. Square Measure
1 square inch (sq. in.)
   = 6,452 cm²
1 square foot (sq. ft)
   = 144 square inches
   = 929,029 cm²
1 square yard (sq. yd)
   = 9 square feet = 8361,26 cm²
1 square perch (sq. p.)
   = 30¹/₄ square yards = 25,293 m²
1 rood
   = 40 square perches = 10,117 a
1 acre (a.) = 4 roods = 40,47 a
1 square mile
   = 640 acres = 258,998 ha

4. Cubic Measure
1 cubic inch (cu. in.)
   = 16,387 cm³
1 cubic foot (cu. ft)
   = 1,728 cubic inches = 0,028 m³
1 cubic yard (cu. yd)
   = 27 cubic feet = 0,765 m³
1 register ton (reg. ton)
   = 100 cubic feet = 2,832 m³

5. Measure of Capacity
Dry and Liquid Measure
1 British or imperial gill (gl, gi.)
   = 0,142 l
1 British or imperial pint (pt)
   = 4 gills = 0,568 l
1 British or imperial quart (qt)
   = 2 pints = 1,136 l
1 British or imp. gallon (imp. gal.)
   = 4 imperial quarts = 4,546 l

Dry Measure
1 British or imperial peck (pk)
   = 2 imperial gallons = 9,092 l
1 Brit. or imp. bushel (bu., bus.)
   = 8 imperial gallons = 36,366 l
1 Brit. or imp. quarter (qr)
   = 8 imperial bushels = 290,935 l

Liquid Measure
1 Brit. or imp. barrel (bbl, bl)
   = 36 imperial gallons = 163,656 l

*

1 U.S. dry pint = 0,551 l
1 U.S. dry quart
   = 2 dry pints = 1,101 l
1 U.S. dry gallon
   = 4 dry quarts = 4,405 l
1 U.S. peck
   = 2 dry gallons = 8,809 l
1 U.S. bushel
   = 8 dry gallons = 35,238 l
1 U.S. gill = 0,118 l
1 U.S. liquid pint
   = 4 gills = 0,473 l
1 U.S. liquid quart
   = 2 liquid pints = 0,946 l
1 U.S. liquid gallon
   = 8 liquid pints = 3,785 l
1 U.S. barrel
   = 31½ liquid gallons = 119,228 l

1 U.S. barrel petroleum
= 42 liquid gallons = 158,97 l

6. Avoirdupois Weight

1 grain (gr.) = 0,065 g
1 dram (dr.)
= 27.344 grains = 1,772 g
1 ounce (oz.)
= 16 drams = 28,35 g
1 pound (lb.)
= 16 ounces = 453,592 g
1 quarter (qr)
= 28 pounds = 12,701 kg
(*U.S.A.* 25 pounds
= 11,339 kg)
1 hundredweight (cwt.)
= 112 pounds

= 50,802 kg (*U.S.A.* 100 pounds
= 45,359 kg)

1 ton (t.)
(*a.* long ton) = 20 hundredweights = 1016,05 kg (*U.S.A.*,
a. short ton, = 907,185 kg)
1 stone (st.) = 14 pounds = 6,35 kg

7. Troy Weight

1 grain = 0,065 g
1 pennyweight (dwt.)
= 24 grains = 1,555 g
1 ounce
= 20 pennyweights = 31,103 g
1 pound = 12 ounces = 373,242 g